PARKER'S WINE BUYER'S GUIDE Sixth Edition

The Complete, Easy-to-Use Reference on
Recent Vintages, Prices, and Ratings for More Than
8,000 Wines from All the Major Wine Regions

ROBERT M. PARKER, JR.,
WITH
PIERRE-ANTOINE ROVANI

SIMON & SCHUSTER
New York   London   Toronto   Sydney   Singapore

SIMON & SCHUSTER
Rockefeller Center
1230 Avenue of the Americas
New York, NY 10020

For information about special discounts for bulk purchases,
please contact Simon & Schuster Special Sales:
1-800-456-6798 or business@simonandschuster.com

Manufactured in the United States of America

3   5   7   9   10   8   6   4   2

Library of Congress Cataloging-in-Publication Data
Parker, Robert M.
[Wine buyer's guide]
Parker's wine buyer's guide—6th ed. / Robert M. Parker, Jr.
with Pierre-Antoine Rovani.
p.   cm.
"Complete, easy-to-use reference on recent vintages, prices, and ratings
for more than 8,000 wines from all the major wine regions."
Includes index.
1. Wine and wine making.   I. Title: Wine buyer's guide.
II. Rovani, Pierre-Antoine.   III. Title.
TP548 .P287 2002
641.2'2—dc21   2002070562

ISBN 0-7432-2931-2

Portions of this book were previously published in the author's
bimonthly newsletter, *The Wine Advocate*.

ACKNOWLEDGMENTS

To the following people, thanks for your support: Hanna, Johanna, and Eric Agostini; the late Jean-Michel Arcaute; Jim Arseneault; Ruth and the late Bruce Bassin; Jean-Claude Berrouet; Bill Blatch; Jean-Marc Blum; Thomas B. Böhrer; Monique and the late Jean-Eugène Borie; Christopher Cannan; Dick Carretta; Corinne Cesano; Bob Cline; Jean Delmas; Dr. Albert H. Dudley III; Alain Dutournier; Barbara Edelman; Jonathan Edelman; Michael Etzel; Paul Evans; Terry Faughey; Joel Fleischman; Han Cheng Fong; Maryse Fragnaud; Laurence and Bernard Godec; Dan Green; Philippe Guyonnet-Duperat; Josué Harari; Alexandra Harding; Kenichi Hori; Dr. David Hutcheon; Barbara G. and Steve R. R. Jacoby; Jean-Paul Jauffret; Nathaniel, Archie, and Denis Johnston; Ed Jonna; Allen Krasner; Françoise Laboute; Susan and Bob Lescher; Dr. Jay Miller; Christian, Jean-François, and Jean-Pierre Moueix; Jerry Murphy; Bernard Nicolas; Jill Norman; Les Oenarchs (Bordeaux); Les Oenarchs (Baltimore); Daniel Oliveros; Bob Orenstein; Frank Polk; Bruno Prats; Dr. Alain Raynaud; Martha Reddington; Dominique Renard; Huey Robertson; Helga and Hardy Rodenstock; Dany and Michel Rolland; Yves Rovani; Carlo Russo; Ed Sands; Erik Samazeuilh; Bob Schindler; Ernie Singer; Park B. Smith; Betsy Sobolewski; Jeff Sokolin; Elliott Staren; Daniel Tastet-Lawton; Steven "Ho" Verlin; Peter Vezan; Robert Vifian; Larry Wiggins; Jeanyee Wong; Dominique and Gérard Yvernault; Murray Zeligman.

A very special thanks is in order for the people who have done a splendid job in bringing this mass of information to book form: Amanda Murray, my editor at Simon & Schuster, and her assistant, Nancy Fann; my copy editors, Suzanne Anderson, Lynn Anderson, Anne Cherry, Virginia Clark, and Kate Lapin; Hanna Agostini, my assistant and translator in France; and Joan Passman and Annette Piatek, my assistants stateside. All were immensely helpful, and I am indebted to them. I also wish to acknowledge the superb contributions of my assistant and colleague, Pierre-Antoine Rovani.

In memory of a great woman and terrific mother,
Ruth "Siddy" Parker
May 14, 1924–April 8, 2002

and

In memory of a dear friend and wine lover,
Carol "Ma" Smith
September 9, 1950–May 16, 2002

CONTENTS

What Constitutes a Great Wine?　29

THE WINES OF WESTERN EUROPE　*41*

Chapter 1: France　43

Chapter 2: Italy　909

Chapter 3: Germany and Austria　1114

Chapter 4: Spain and Portugal　1136

THE WINES OF NORTH AMERICA　*1177*

Chapter 5: California　1179

Chapter 6: Oregon　1452

Chapter 7: Washington State　1478

Chapter 8: The Mid-Atlantic States　1499

THE BEST OF THE REST　*1501*

Chapter 9: Australia and New Zealand　1503

Chapter 10: Argentina and Chile　1594

Chapter 11: South Africa　1597

Index　1599

INTRODUCTION

HOW TO USE THIS GUIDE

This book is both an educational manual and a buying guide; it is not an encyclopedic listing of wine producers and growers. It is intended to make you a more formidable, more confident wine buyer by providing you with sufficient insider's information to permit the wisest possible choice when you make a wine-buying decision. The finest producers as well as the best known (not necessarily a guarantee of quality) from the world's greatest viticultural regions are evaluated, as well as many of the current and upcoming releases available in the marketplace. If readers cannot find a specific vintage of a highly regarded wine, they still have at their fingertips a wealth of information and evaluations concerning the best producers for each viticultural area. Readers should be confident in knowing that they will rarely make a mistake (unless, of course, the vintage is absolutely dreadful) with a producer rated "outstanding" or "excellent" in this buying manual. These producers are the finest and most consistent in the world. Taste is obviously subjective, but I have done my best to provide an impartial and comprehensive consumer's guide, whose heart, soul, and value are the evaluations (star ratings) of the world's finest producers.

Note: Readers should recognize that my assistant, Pierre-Antoine Rovani, has written the tasting notes and numerical scores for chapters on Burgundy, Washington, Alsace, Oregon, the Loire, Germany, New Zealand, and South Africa.

ORGANIZATION

Each section on a specific viticultural region covered in this manual is generally organized as follows:

1. An overview of the viticultural region
2. A buying strategy
3. A summary of the quality of recent vintages for the area
4. A quick reference chart to that area's best producers/growers
5. Tasting commentaries, a specific numerical rating for the wine, and a general retail price range for a 750-ml bottle of wine. The Wine Price Guide on page 5 explains the coding system.

VITICULTURAL AREAS COVERED

This guide covers the world's major viticultural regions. In Western Europe, France and Italy receive the most detailed coverage, followed by Spain, Portugal, and Germany. In North America, California receives significant coverage, reflecting its dominance in the marketplace. The wine regions represented most significantly in wine shops are given much more detailed coverage than minor areas whose wines are rarely seen in or exported to the United States. Consequently, the sections dealing with Bordeaux, Burgundy, Champagne, Alsace, and the Rhône Valley in France; Piedmont and Tuscany in Italy; and California receive priority in terms of amount of coverage because those regions produce the world's greatest wines. In each section there is a thorough analysis of the region's producers, its overachievers and underachievers, as well as the region's greatest wine values.

RATING THE PRODUCERS AND GROWERS

Who's who in the world of wine becomes readily apparent after years of tasting the wines and visiting the vineyards and wine cellars of the world's producers and growers. Great producers are, unfortunately, still quite rare, but certainly more growers and producers today are making better wine, with better technology and more knowledge. The charts that follow rate the best producers on a five-star system, awarding five stars and an "outstanding" to those producers deemed to be the very best, four stars to those producers who are "excellent," three stars to "good" producers, and two stars to those producers rated "average." Since the aim of this book is to provide you with the names of the very best producers, its overall content is dominated by the top producers rather than the less successful ones.

Those few growers/producers who have received five-star ratings are those who make the world's finest wines, and they have been selected for this rating because of the following two reasons: First, they make the greatest wine of their particular viticultural region, and second, they are remarkably consistent and reliable even in mediocre and poor vintages. Ratings, whether numerical ratings of individual wines or classifications of growers, are always likely to create controversy among not only the growers but wine tasters themselves. But if done impartially, with a global viewpoint and firsthand, on-the-premises (*sur place*) knowledge of the wines, the producers, and the type and quality of the winemaking, such ratings can be reliable and powerfully informative. The important thing for readers to remember is that those growers/producers who received either a four-star or five-star rating are producers to search out; I suspect few consumers will ever be disappointed with one of their wines. The three-star growers/producers are less consistent but can be expected to make average to above-average wines in the very good to excellent vintages. Their weaknesses can be either from the fact that their vineyards are not as strategically placed, or because for financial or other reasons they are unable to make the severe selections necessary to create only the finest-quality wine.

The rating of the growers/producers of the world's major viticultural regions is perhaps the most important point of this book. Years of wine tasting have taught me many things, but the more one tastes and assimilates the knowledge of the world's regions, the more one begins to isolate the handful of truly world-class growers and producers who seem to rise above the crowd in great as well as mediocre vintages. I always admonish consumers against blind faith in one grower or producer, or in one specific vintage. But the producers and growers rated "outstanding" and "excellent" are as close to a guarantee of high quality as you are likely to find.

VINTAGE SUMMARIES

Although wine advertisements proclaiming "a great vintage" abound, I have never known more than several viticultural areas of the world to have a great vintage in the same year. The chances of a uniformly great vintage are extremely remote, simply because of significantly different microclimates, soils, and so on in every wine-producing region. It is easy to fall into the trap of thinking that because Bordeaux had great vintages in 1982, 1990, and 2000, every place else in Europe did too. Certainly in both 1982 and 2000, nothing could have been further from the truth. Nevertheless, a Bordeaux vintage's reputation unfortunately seems to dictate what the world thinks about many other wine-producing areas. This obviously creates many problems, since in poor Bordeaux vintages, the Rhône or Alsace or Champagne could have an excellent vintage, and in great Bordeaux vintages those same areas could have bad years because of poor climate conditions. For California, many casual observers seem to think every year is a top year, and this image is, of course, promoted by that state's publicity-conscious Wine Institute. It may be true that California rarely has a disastrous vintage, but tasting certainly proves that 1988, 1989, and 1998 are different in style and more irregular in quality than either 1994 or 1995. Yet no other viticultural area in the world has enjoyed as many consecutive great vintages as California has in the 1990s; with the exception of 1998, all have been terrific years for California. In this guide, there are vintage summaries for each viticultural area because the vintages are so very different in both quantity and quality. Never make the mistake of assuming that one particular year is great everywhere or poor everywhere.

TASTING NOTES AND RATINGS

When possible, most of my tastings are done in peer-group, single-blind conditions; in other words, the same type of wines are tasted against each other, and the producers' names are not known. The ratings reflect an independent, critical look at the wines. Neither price nor the reputation of the grower/producer affects the rating in any manner. I spend three months every year tasting in vineyards. During the other nine months of the year, I devote six- and sometimes seven-day workweeks to tasting and writing. I do not participate in wine judgings or trade tastings for many reasons, but principal among these are: 1) I prefer to taste from an entire bottle of wine, 2) I find it essential to have properly sized and cleaned professional tasting glasses, 3) the temperatures of the wine must be correct, and 4) I prefer to determine the amount of time allocated for the number of wines I will critique.

The numerical rating given is a guide to what I think of the wine vis-à-vis its peer group. Certainly, wines rated above 85 are good to excellent, and any wine rated 90 or above is outstanding for its particular type. While some would suggest that scoring is not well suited to a beverage that has been romantically extolled for centuries, wine is no different from any other consumer product. There are specific standards of quality that full-time wine professionals recognize, and there are benchmark wines against which all others can be judged. I know of no one with three or four different glasses of wine in front of him or her, regardless of how good or bad the wines might be, who cannot say, "I prefer this one to that one." Scoring wines is simply taking a professional's opinion and applying a numerical system to it on a consistent basis. Moreover, scoring permits rapid communication of information to expert and novice alike. The score given for a specific wine reflects the quality of the wine at its best. I often tell people that evaluating a wine and assigning a score to a beverage that may change and evolve for up to 10 or more years is analogous to taking a photograph of a marathon runner. Much can be ascertained, but, as with a picture of a moving object, the wine will also evolve and change. I try to retaste wines from obviously badly corked or defective bottles, since a wine from such a single bad bottle does not indicate an entirely spoiled batch. If retasting is not possible, I reserve judgment on that wine. Many of the wines reviewed have been tasted several times, and the score represents a cumulative average of the wine's performance in tastings to date. Scores do not reveal the most important facts about a wine. The written commentary (tasting notes) that accompanies the ratings is a better source of information than any score regarding the wine's style and personality, its quality level relative to its peers, and its relative value and aging potential.

Here, then, is a general guide to interpreting the numerical ratings:

90–100: Equivalent to an A and given for an outstanding or a special effort. Wines in this category are the very best produced for their type. There is a big difference between a 90 and a 99, yet both are top marks. Few wines actually make it into this top category, simply because there are not that many truly profound wines.

80–89: Equivalent to a B in school; such a wine, particularly in the 85–89 range, is very good. Many of the wines that fall into this range are often great values as well. I have many of these wines in my personal cellar.

70–79: Represents a C, or an average mark, but obviously 79 is a much more desirable rating than 70. Wines that receive scores of 75–79 are generally pleasant, straightforward wines that lack complexity, character, or depth. If inexpensive, they may be ideal for uncritical quaffing.

Below 70: A D or an F, depending on where you went to school. It is a sign of an unbalanced, flawed, or terribly dull or diluted wine of little interest to the discriminating consumer.

Note: A point score in parentheses (75–80) signifies an evaluation made before the wine was bottled.

In terms of awarding points, my scoring system starts with a potential of 50 points. The wine's general color and appearance merit up to 5 points. Since most wines today are well made, thanks to modern technology and the increased use of professional oenologists, most tend to receive at least 4, and often 5, points. The aroma and bouquet merit up to 15 points, depending on the intensity level and dimension of the aroma and bouquet, as well as the wine's cleanliness. The flavor and finish merit up to 20 points, and again, intensity of flavor, balance, cleanliness, and depth and length on the palate are all important considerations when giving out points. Finally, the overall quality level or potential for further evolution and improvement—aging—merits up to 10 points.

Scores are important for the reader to gauge a professional critic's overall qualitative placement of a wine among its peers. However, it is also vital to consider the description of the wine's style, personality, and potential. No scoring system is perfect, but a system that provides for flexibility in scores, if applied by the same experienced taster without prejudice, can quantify different levels of wine quality and can be a responsible, reliable, uncensored, and highly informative account that provides the reader with one professional's judgment. However, there can never be any substitute for your own palate nor any better education than tasting the wine yourself.

QUOTED PRICES

For a number of reasons, no one suggested retail price for a particular wine is valid throughout the country. Take Bordeaux as an example. Bordeaux is often sold as "wine futures" two full years before the wine is bottled and shipped to America. This opening or base price can often be the lowest price one will encounter for a Bordeaux wine, particularly if there is a great demand for the wines because the vintage is reputed to be excellent or outstanding. As for other imported wines, prices will always vary for Bordeaux according to the quality of the vintage, the exchange rate of the dollar against foreign currencies, and the time of purchase by the retailer, wholesaler, or importer—was the wine purchased at a low futures price in the spring following the vintage, or when it had peaked in price and was very expensive?

Another consideration in pricing is that in many states wine retailers can directly import the wines they sell and can thereby bypass middlemen, such as wholesalers, who usually tack on their own 25% markup. The bottom line in all of this is that in any given vintage for Bordeaux, or for any imported wine, there is no standard suggested retail price. Prices can differ by as much as 50% for the same wine in the same city. However, in cities where there is tremendous competition among wine shops, the markup for wines can be as low as 10% or even 5%, significantly less than the normal 50–55% markup for full retail price in cities where there is little competition. I always recommend that consumers pay close attention to wine shop advertisements in major newspapers and wine publications. For example, *The New York Times*'s Living Section and *The Wine Spectator* are filled with wine advertisements that are a barometer for the market price of a given wine. Readers should remember, however, that prices differ considerably, not only within the same state but within the same city. The approximate price range reflects the suggested retail price that includes a 40–60% markup by the retailer in most major metropolitan areas. Therefore, in many states in the Midwest and in other less populated areas where there is little competition among wine merchants, the price may be higher. In major competitive marketplaces where there are frequent discount wars, such as Washington, D.C., New York, San Francisco, Boston, Los Angeles, Chicago, and Dallas, prices are often lower. The key for you as a reader and consumer is to follow the advertisements in major newspapers and to shop around. Most major wine retailers feature sales in the fall and spring; summer is the slow season and generally the most expensive time to buy wine.

Following is the price guide I have used throughout the book.

WINE PRICE GUIDE CODES
A: Inexpensive/less than $10
B: Moderate/$10–15
C: Expensive/$15–25
D: Very expensive/$25–50
E: Luxury/$50–75
EE: Super luxury/$75–125
EEE: More than $125

THE ROLE OF A WINE CRITIC
"A man must serve his time to every trade save censure—critics all are ready made." Thus wrote Lord Byron. It has been said often enough that anyone with a pen, notebook, and a few bottles of wine can become a wine critic. And that is exactly the way I started when, in late summer 1978, I sent out a complimentary issue of what was then called the *Baltimore/Washington Wine Advocate*.

Two principal forces shaped my view of a wine critic's responsibilities. I was then, and remain today, significantly influenced by the independent philosophy of consumer advocate Ralph Nader. Moreover, I was marked by the indelible impression left by my law school professors, who in the post-Watergate era pounded into their students' heads a broad definition of conflict of interest. These two forces have governed the purpose and soul of my newsletter, *The Wine Advocate*, and of my books.

In short, the role of the critic is to render judgments that are reliable. They should be based on extensive experience and on a trained sensibility for whatever is being reviewed. In practical terms, this means the critic should be blessed with the following attributes:

Independence: It is imperative for a wine critic to pay his own way. Gratuitous hospitality in the form of airline tickets, hotel rooms, guest houses, etc., should never be accepted either abroad or in this country. What about wine samples? I purchase more than 75% of the wines I taste, and though I have never requested samples, I do not feel it is unethical to accept unsolicited samples that are shipped to my office. Many wine writers claim that these favors do not influence their opinions. Yet how many people in any profession are prepared to bite the hand that feeds them? Irrefutably, the target audience is the wine consumer, not the wine trade. While it is important to maintain a professional relationship with the trade, I believe the independent stance required of a consumer advocate often, not surprisingly, results in an adversarial relationship with the wine trade. It can be no other way. In order to pursue this independence effectively, it is imperative to keep one's distance from the trade. This may be misinterpreted as aloofness, but such independence guarantees hard-hitting, candid, and uninfluenced commentary.

Courage: Courage manifests itself in what I call the "democratic tasting." Judgments ought to be made solely on the basis of the product in the bottle, not the pedigree, the price, the rarity, or one's like or dislike of the producer. The wine critic who is totally candid may be considered dangerous by the trade, but an uncensored, independent point of view is of paramount importance to the consumer. A judgment of wine quality must be based on what is in the bottle. This is wine criticism at its purest, most meaningful. In a tasting, a $10 bottle of petit château Pauillac should have as much of a chance as a $200 bottle of Lafite-Rothschild or Latour. Overachievers should be spotted, praised, and their names highlighted and shared with the consuming public. Underachievers should be singled out for criticism and called to account for their mediocrities. Outspoken and irreverent commentary is unlikely to win many friends from the wine commerce, but wine buyers are entitled to such information. When a critic bases his or her judgment on what others think, or on the wine's pedigree, price, or perceived potential, wine criticism is nothing more than a sham.

Experience: It is essential to taste extensively across the field of play to identify the benchmark reference points and to learn winemaking standards throughout the world. This is the most time-consuming and expensive aspect of wine criticism, as well as the most fulfilling for the critic, yet it is rarely practiced. Lamentably, what often transpires is that a tasting of 10 or 12 wines from a specific region or vintage will be held, and the writer then issues a definitive judgment on the vintage based on a microscopic proportion of the wines. This is irresponsible—indeed, and appalling. It is essential for a wine critic to taste as comprehensively as is physically possible, which means tasting every significant wine produced in a region or vintage before reaching qualitative conclusions. Wine criticism, if it is ever to be regarded as a serious profession, must be a full-time endeavor, not the habitat of part-timers dabbling in a field that is so complex and requires such time commitment. Wine and vintages, like everything in life, cannot be reduced to black-and-white answers.

It is also essential to establish memory reference points for the world's greatest wines. There is such a diversity of wine and multitude of styles that this may seem impossible. But tasting as many wines as one possibly can in each vintage, and from all of the classic wine regions, helps one memorize benchmark characteristics that form the basis for making comparative judgments between vintages, wine producers, and wine regions.

Individual Accountability: While I have never found anyone's wine-tasting notes compelling reading, notes issued by consensus of a committee are the most insipid and often the most misleading. Judgments by committees tend to sum up a group's personal preferences. But how do they take into consideration the possibility that each individual may have reached his or her decision using totally different criteria? Did one judge adore the wine because of its typicity while another decried it for the same reason, or was the wine's individuality given greater merit? It is impossible to know. That is never in doubt when an individual authors a tasting critique. Committees rarely recognize wines of great individuality. Sadly, a look at the results of tasting competitions reveals that well-made mediocrities garner the top prizes, and thus blandness is elevated to the status of a virtue. Wines with great individuality and character never win a committee tasting because at least one taster will find something objectionable about the wine.

I have always sensed that individual tasters, because they are unable to hide behind the collective voice of a committee, hold themselves to a greater degree of accountability. The opinion of a reasonably informed and comprehensive individual taster, despite the taster's prejudices and predilections, is always a far better guide to the ultimate quality of the wine than the consensus of a committee. At least the reader knows where the individual stands, whereas with a committee, one is never quite sure.

Emphasis on Pleasure and Value: Too much wine writing focuses on glamorous French wine regions such as Burgundy and Bordeaux, and on California Cabernet Sauvignon and Chardonnay. These are important, and they make up the backbone of most serious wine enthusiasts' cellars. But value and diversity in wine types must always be stressed. The unhealthy legacy of the English wine-writing establishment that a wine has to taste bad young to be great old should be thrown out. Wines that taste great young, such as Chenin Blanc,

Dolcetto, Beaujolais, Côtes du Rhône, Merlot, and Zinfandel, are no less serious or compelling because they must be drunk within a few years rather than cellared for a decade or more before consumption. Wine is, in the final analysis, a beverage of pleasure, and intelligent wine criticism should be a blend of both hedonistic and analytical schools of thought—to the exclusion of neither.

The Focus on Qualitative Issues: It is an inescapable fact that too many of the world's renowned growers/producers have intentionally permitted production levels to soar to such extraordinary heights that many wines' personalities, concentrations, and characters are in jeopardy. While there remain a handful of fanatics who continue, at some financial sacrifice, to reject significant proportions of their harvest to ensure that only the finest-quality wine is sold under their name, they are dwindling in number. For much of the last decade production yields throughout the world have broken records with almost every new vintage. The results are wines that increasingly lack character, concentration, and staying power. The argument that more carefully and competently managed vineyards inevitably result in larger crops is nonsense.

In addition to high yields, advances in technology have provided the savoir faire to produce more correct wines, but the abuse of practices such as acidification and excessive fining and filtration have compromised the final product. These problems are rarely and inadequately addressed by the wine-writing community. Wine prices have never been higher, but is the consumer always getting a better wine? The wine writer has the responsibility to give broad qualitative issues high priority.

Candor: No one argues with the incontestable fact that tasting is a subjective endeavor. The measure of an effective wine critic should be his or her timely and useful rendering of an intelligent laundry list of good examples of different styles of winemaking in various price categories. Articulating in an understandable fashion why the critic finds the wines enthralling or objectionable is manifestly important both to the reader and to the producer. The critic must always seek to educate and to provide meaningful guidelines, never failing to emphasize that there is no substitute for the consumer's palate, nor any better education than the reader's own tasting of the wine. The critic has the advantage of having access to the world's wine production and must try to minimize bias. Yet the critic should always share with readers the reasoning behind bad reviews. For example, I will never be able to overcome my dislike for vegetal-tasting New World Cabernets, overtly herbaceous red Loire Valley wines, or excessively acidified New World whites.

My ultimate goal in writing about wines is to seek out the world's greatest wines and greatest wine values. In the process of ferreting out those wines, the critic should never shy away from criticizing those producers whose wines are found lacking. Given the fact that the consumer is the true taster of record, the "taste no evil" approach to wine writing serves no one but the wine trade. Constructive and competent criticism has proven that it can benefit producers as well as consumers, since it forces underachievers to improve the quality of their fare, and, by lauding overachievers, it encourages them to maintain high standards to the benefit of all who enjoy and appreciate good wine.

About Wine

HOW TO BUY WINE

If you have made your choices in advance, buying wine seems simple enough—you go to your favorite wine merchant and purchase a few bottles. However, there are some subtleties to buying wine that one must be aware of in order to ensure that the wine is in healthy condition and is unspoiled.

To begin with, take a look at the bottle of wine you are about to buy. Wine abuse is revealed by the condition of the bottle in your hand. First of all, if the cork has popped above the rim of the bottle and is pushed out on the lead or plastic capsule that covers the top of the bottle, look for another bottle to buy. Wines that have been exposed to very high temperatures expand in the bottle, putting pressure on the cork and pushing it upward against the capsule. And the highest-quality wines, those that have not been overly filtered or pasteurized, are the most vulnerable to the ill effects of abusive transportation or storage. A wine that has been frozen in transit or storage will likewise push the cork out, and though freezing a wine is less damaging than heating it, both are hazardous to its health. Any cork that is protruding above the rim of the bottle is a bad sign. The bottle should be returned to the shelf and never, ever purchased.

Finally, there is a sign indicating poor storage conditions that can generally be determined only after the wine has been decanted, though sometimes it can be spotted in the neck of the bottle. Wines that have been exposed to very high temperatures, particularly deep, rich, intense red wines, often form a heavy coat or film of coloring material on the inside of the glass. With a Bordeaux less than 3 years old, a coating such as this generally indicates that the wine has been subjected to very high temperatures and has undoubtedly been damaged. However, one must be careful here, because this type of sediment does not always indicate a poor bottle of wine; vintage port regularly throws it, and so do the huge, rich Rhône and Piedmontese wines.

On the other hand, there are two conditions consumers frequently think are signs of a flawed wine when nothing could be further from the truth. Some uninformed consumers return bottles of wine for the very worst reason—because of a small deposit of sediment in the bottom of the bottle. In fact, this is the healthiest sign one could find in most bottles of wine. The tiny particles of sandlike sediment that precipitate to the bottom of a bottle simply indicate that the wine has been naturally made and has not been subjected to a traumatic flavor- and character-eviscerating filtration. Such wine is truly alive and is usually full of all its natural flavors. However, keep in mind that white wines rarely throw a deposit, and it is rare to see a deposit in young wines under 2–3 years of age.

Another reason that wine consumers erroneously return bottles to retailers is the presence of small crystals called tartrate precipitates. These crystals are found in all types of wines but appear most commonly in white wines from Germany and Alsace. They often shine and resemble little slivers of cut glass. They simply mean that somewhere along its journey a wine was exposed to temperatures below 40°F. in shipment, and the cold has caused some tartaric crystals to precipitate. These are harmless, tasteless, and totally natural in many bottles of wine. They have no effect on the quality and normally signify that the wine has not been subjected to an abusive, sometimes damaging, cold stabilization treatment by the winery for cosmetic purposes only.

Fortunately, most of the better wine merchants, wholesalers, and importers are more cognizant today of the damage that can be done by shipping wine in unrefrigerated containers, especially in the middle of summer. However, far too many wines are still tragically damaged by poor transportation and storage, and it is the consumer who suffers. A general rule is that heat is much more damaging to fine wines than cold. Remember, there are still plenty of wine merchants, wholesalers, and importers who treat wine no differently than they treat beer or liquor, and the wine buyer must therefore be armed with a bit of knowledge before he or she buys a bottle of wine.

HOW TO STORE WINE

Wine has to be stored properly if it is to be served in a healthy condition. All wine enthusiasts know that subterranean wine cellars which are vibration free, dark, damp, and kept at a constant 55° F. are considered perfect for wine. However, few of us have such perfect accommodations for our beloved wines. While these conditions are ideal, most wines will thrive and develop well under other circumstances. I have tasted many old Bordeaux wines from closets and basements that have reached 65–70° F. in summer, and the wines have been perfect. In cellaring wine, keep the following rules in mind and you will not be disappointed with a wine that has gone over the hill prematurely.

First of all, in order to cellar wines safely for 10 years or more, keep them at 65° F., perhaps 68°, but no higher. If the temperature rises to 70° F., be prepared to drink your red wines within 10 years. Under no circumstances should you store and cellar white wines more than 1–2 years at temperatures above 70° F. Wines kept at temperatures above 65° will age faster, but unless the temperature exceeds 70°, will not age badly. If you can somehow keep the temperature at 65° or below, you will never have to worry about the condition of your wines. At 55° F., the ideal temperature according to the textbooks, the wines actually evolve so slowly that your grandchildren are likely to benefit from the wines more than you. Constancy in temperature is most essential, and any changes in temperature should occur slowly. White wines are much more fragile and much more sensitive to temperature changes and higher temperatures than red wines. Therefore, if you do not have ideal storage conditions, buy only enough white wine to drink over a 1–2-year period.

Second, be sure that your storage area is odor free, vibration free, and dark. A humidity level above 50% is essential; 70–75% is ideal. The problem with a humidity level over 75% is that the labels become moldy and deteriorate. A humidity level below 40% will keep the labels in great shape but will cause the corks to become very dry, possibly shortening the potential life expectancy of your wine. Low humidity is believed to be nearly as great a threat to a wine's health as high temperature. There has been no research to prove this, and limited studies I have done are far from conclusive.

Third, always bear in mind that wines from vintages which produce powerful, rich, concentrated, full-bodied wines travel and age significantly better than wines from vintages that produce lighter-weight wines. Transatlantic or cross-country transport is often traumatic for a fragile, lighter-styled wine from either Europe or California, whereas the richer, more intense, bigger wines from the better vintages seem much less travel-worn after their journey.

Fourth, I always recommend buying a wine as soon as it appears on the market, assuming of course that you have tasted the wine and like it. The reason for this is that there are still too many American wine merchants, importers, wholesalers, and distributors who are indifferent to the way wine is stored. This attitude still persists, though things have improved dramatically over the last decade. The important thing for you as a consumer to remember, after inspecting the bottle to make sure it appears healthy, is to stock up on wines as quickly as they come on the market and to approach older vintages with a great deal of caution and hesitation unless you have absolute faith in the merchant from whom you bought the wine. Furthermore, you should be confident that your merchant will stand behind the wine if it is flawed from poor storage.

THE QUESTION OF HOW MUCH AGING

The majority of wines taste best when they are just released or consumed within 1–2 years of the vintage. Many wines are drinkable at 5, 10, or even 15 years of age, but based on my experience only a small percentage are more interesting and more enjoyable after extended cellaring than they were when originally released.

It is important to have a working definition of what the aging of wine actually means. I define the process as nothing more than the ability of a wine, over time, 1) to develop more pleasurable nuances, 2) to expand and soften in texture and, for red wines, to exhibit an additional melting away of tannins, and 3) to reveal a more compelling aromatic and flavor profile. In short, the wine must deliver additional complexity, increased pleasure, and more interest as an older wine than it did when released. Only such a performance can justify the

purchase of a wine in its youth for the purpose of cellaring it for future drinking. Unfortunately, only a tiny percentage of the world's wines falls within this definition of aging.

It is fundamentally false to believe that a wine cannot be serious or profound if it is
drunk young. In France, the finest Bordeaux, the northern Rhône Valley wines (particularly
l'Hermitage and Côte Rôtie), a few red Burgundies, some Châteauneuf-du-Papes, and, surprisingly, many of the sweet white Alsace wines and sweet Loire Valley wines do indeed age
well and are frequently much more enjoyable and complex when drunk 5, 10, or even 15
years after the vintage. But virtually all other French wines—from Champagne to Côtes du
Rhône, from Beaujolais to the petits châteaux of Bordeaux, and the vast majority of red and
white Burgundies—are better in their youth.

The French have long adhered to the wine-drinking strategy that younger is better. Centuries of wine consumption, not to mention gastronomic indulgences, have taught the French
something that Americans and Englishmen have failed to grasp: Most wines are more pleasurable and friendly when young.

The French know that the aging and cellaring of wines, even those of high pedigree, are
often fraught with more disappointments than successes. Nowhere is this more in evidence
than in French restaurants, especially in Bordeaux, the region that boasts what the world
considers the longest-lived dry red wines. A top vintage of Bordeaux can last for 20–30
years, sometimes 40 or more, but look at the wine lists of Bordeaux's best restaurants. The
great 1990s have long disappeared down the throats of Frenchmen and -women. Even the
tannic, young, yet potentially very promising 1996s, which Americans have squirreled away
for drinking later this century, are now hard to find. Why? Because they have already been
consumed. Many of the deluxe restaurants, particularly in Paris, have wine lists of historic
vintages, but these are largely for rich tourists.

This phenomenon is not limited to France. Similar drinking habits prevail in the restaurants of Florence, Rome, Madrid, and Barcelona. Italians and Spaniards also enjoy their
wines young. This is not to suggest that Italy does not make some wines that improve in the
bottle. In Tuscany, for example, a handful of Chiantis and some of the finest new-breed Tuscan red wines (e.g., the famed Cabernet Sauvignon called Sassicaia) will handsomely repay
extended cellaring, but most never get the opportunity. In the Piedmont section of northern
Italy, no one will deny that a fine Barbaresco or Barolo improves after a decade in the bottle.
But by and large, all of Italy's other wines are meant to be drunk young, a fact that Italians
have long known and that you should observe as well.

With respect to Spain, it is the same story, although a Spaniard's tastes differ considerably
from the average Italian's or Frenchman's. In Spain, the intense smoky vanilla aroma of new
oak (particularly American) is prized. As a result, the top Spanish wine producers from the
most renowned wine region, Rioja, and other viticultural regions as well tend to age their
wines in oak barrels so that they can develop this particular aroma. Additionally, unlike
French and Italian wine producers, or even their New World counterparts, Spanish wineries
are reluctant to release their wines until they are fully mature. As a result, most Spanish
wines are smooth and mellow when they arrive on the market. While they may keep for 5–10
years, they generally do not improve. This is especially true with Spain's most expensive
wines, the Reservas and Gran Reservas from Rioja, which are usually not released until 5–8
years after the vintage. The one exception may be the wine long considered Spain's greatest
red, the Vega Sicilia Unico. This powerful wine, frequently released when it is already 10 or
20 years old (the immortal 1970 was released in 1995), does appear capable of lasting for
20–35 years after its release. Yet I wonder how much it improves.

What does all this mean to you? Unlike any other wine consumers in the world, most
American and many English wine enthusiasts fret over the perfect moment to drink a wine.
There is none. Almost all modern-day vintages, even ageworthy Bordeaux or Rhône Valley
wines, can be drunk when released. Some will improve, but many will not. If you enjoy drink-

ing a 1989 Bordeaux now, who would be so foolish as to suggest that you are making an error because the wine will be appreciably better in 5–10 years?

In America and Australia, winemaking is much more dominated by technology. Though a handful of producers still adhere to the artisanal, traditional way of making wine as done in Europe, most treat the vineyard as a factory and the winemaking as a manufacturing process. As a result, such techniques as excessive acidification, brutally traumatic centrifugation, and eviscerating sterile filtration are routinely utilized to produce squeaky-clean, simplistic, sediment-free, spit-polished, totally stable yet innocuous wines with statistical profiles that fit neatly within strict technical parameters. Yet it is these same techniques that denude wines of their flavors, aromas, and pleasure-giving qualities. Moreover, they reveal a profound lack of respect for the vineyard, the varietal, the vintage, and the wine consumer, who, after all, is seeking pleasure, not blandness.

In both Australia and California, the alarming tendency of most Sauvignon Blancs and Chardonnays to collapse in the bottle and to drop their fruit within 2–3 years of the vintage has been well documented. Yet some of California's and Australia's most vocal advocates continue to advise wine consumers to cellar and invest (a deplorable word when it comes to wine) in Chardonnays and Sauvignon Blancs. It is a stupid policy. If the aging of wine is indeed the ability of a wine to become more interesting and pleasurable with time, then the rule of thumb to be applied to American and Australian Sauvignon Blancs and Chardonnays is that they must be drunk within 12 months of their release unless the consumer has an eccentric fetish for fruitless wines with blistering acidity and scorching alcohol levels. Examples of producers whose Chardonnays and Sauvignon Blancs can last for 5–10 years and improve during that period can be found, but they are distressingly few.

With respect to red wines, a slightly different picture emerges. Take, for example, the increasingly fashionable wines made from the Pinot Noir grape. No one doubts the immense progress made in both California and Oregon in turning out fragrant, supple Pinot Noirs that are delicious upon release. But I do not know of any American producer who is making Pinot Noir that can actually improve beyond 10–12 years in the bottle. And this is not in any way a criticism.

Even in Burgundy there are probably no more than a dozen producers who make their wines in such a manner that they improve and last for more than a decade. Many of these wines can withstand the test of time in the sense of being survivors, but they are far less interesting and pleasurable at age 10 than when they were 2 or 3 years old. Of course, producers and retailers who specialize in these wines will argue otherwise, but they are in the business of selling. Do not be bamboozled by the public relations arm of the wine industry or the fallacious notion that red wines all improve with age. If you enjoy them young, and most likely you will, then buy only the quantities needed for near-term consumption.

America's most famous dry red wine, however, is not Pinot Noir but Cabernet Sauvignon, particularly from California and to a lesser extent from Washington State. The idea that most California Cabernet Sauvignons improve in the bottle is a myth. Nonetheless, the belief that all California Cabernet Sauvignons are incapable of lasting in the bottle is equally unfounded. Today no one would be foolish enough to argue that the best California Cabernets cannot tolerate 15 or 20, even 25 or 30 years of cellaring.

I frequently have the opportunity to taste 20- to 30-year-old California Cabernet Sauvignons, and they are delicious. But have they significantly improved because of the aging process? A few of them have, though most still tend to be relatively grapy, somewhat monolithic, earthy, and tannic at age 20. Has the consumer's patience in cellaring these wines for all those years justified the expense and the wait? Lamentably, the answer will usually be no. Most of these wines are no more complex or mellow than they were when young.

Because these wines will not crack up and fall apart, there is little risk associated with stashing the best of them away, but I am afraid the consumer who patiently waits for the proverbial "miracle in the bottle" will find that wine cellaring can all too frequently be an expensive exercise in futility.

If you think it over, the most important issue is why so many of today's wines exhibit scant improvement in the aging process. While most have always been meant to be drunk when young, I am convinced that much of the current winemaking philosophy has led to numerous compromises in the winemaking process. The advent of micropore sterile filters, so much in evidence at every modern winery, may admirably stabilize a wine, but, regrettably, these filters also destroy the potential of a wine to develop a complex aromatic profile. When they are utilized by wine producers who routinely fertilize their vineyards excessively, thus overcropping, the results are wines with an appalling lack of bouquet and flavor.

The prevailing winemaking obsession is to stabilize wine so it can be shipped to the far corners of the world 12 months a year, stand upright in overheated stores indefinitely, and never change or spoil if exposed to extremes of heat and cold, or unfriendly storage conditions. For all intents and purposes, the wine is no longer alive. This is fine, even essential, for inexpensive jug wines, but for the fine-wine market, where consumers are asked to pay $20 or more per bottle, it is a winemaking tragedy. These stabilization and production techniques thus affect the aging of wine because they preclude the development of the wine's ability to evolve and to become a more complex, tasty, profound, and enjoyable beverage.

HOW TO SERVE WINE

There are really no secrets for proper wine service—all one needs is a good corkscrew; clean, odor-free glasses; and a sense of how wines should be served and whether a wine needs to be aired or allowed to breathe. The major mistakes that most Americans, as well as most restaurants, make are 1) fine white wines are served entirely too cold, 2) fine red wines are served entirely too warm, and 3) too little attention is given to the glass into which the wine is poured. (It might contain a soapy residue or stale aromas picked up from a closed china closet or cardboard box.) All of these things can do much more to damage the impact of a fine wine and its subtle aromas than you might imagine. Most people tend to think that the wine must be opened and allowed to "breathe" well in advance of serving. Some even think a wine must be decanted, a rather elaborate procedure, but not essential unless sediment is present in the bottle and the wine has to be poured carefully off. With respect to breathing or airing wine, I am not sure anyone has all the answers. Certainly, no white wine requires any advance opening and pouring. Red wines can be enjoyed within 15–30 minutes of being opened and poured into a clean, odor- and soap-free wine decanter. There are of course examples that can always be cited where the wine improves for 7–8 hours, but these are quite rare. Although these topics seem to dominate much of the discussion in wine circles, a much more critical aspect for me is the appropriate temperature of the wine and of the glass in which it is to be served. The temperature of red wines is very important, and in America's generously heated dining rooms, temperatures are often 75–80° F., higher than is good for fine red wine. A red wine served at such a temperature will taste flat and flabby, with its bouquet diffuse and unfocused. The alcohol content will also seem higher than it should be. The ideal temperature for most red wines is 62–67° F.; light red wine such as Beaujolais should be chilled to 55° F. For white wines, 55–60° F. is perfect, since most will show all their complexity and intensity at this temperature, whereas if they are chilled to below 45° F., it will be difficult to tell, for instance, whether the wine is a Riesling or a Chardonnay.

In addition, there is the important issue of the glasses in which the wine is to be served. An all-purpose, tulip-shaped glass of 8–12 ounces is a good start for just about any type of wine, but think the subject over carefully. If you go to the trouble and expense of finding and storing wine properly, shouldn't you treat the wine to a good glass? The finest glasses for both technical and hedonistic purposes are those made by the Riedel Company of Austria. I have to admit that I was at first skeptical about these glasses. George Riedel, the head of his family's crystal business, claims to have created these glasses specifically to guide (by specially designed rims) the wine to a designated section of the palate. The rims, combined with the general shape of the glass, emphasize and promote the different flavors and aromas of a given varietal.

I have tasted an assortment of wines in his glasses, including a Riesling glass, Chardonnay glass, Pinot Noir glass, and Cabernet Sauvignon glass, all part of his Sommelier Series. For comparative purposes, I then tasted the same wines in the Impitoyables glass, the INAO tasting glass, and the conventional tulip-shaped glass. The results were consistently in favor of the Riedel glasses. American Pinot Noirs and red Burgundies performed far better in his huge 37-ounce, 9½-inch-high Burgundy goblet (model number 400/16) than in the other stemware. Nor could any of the other glassware compete when I was drinking Cabernet- and Merlot-based wines from his Bordeaux goblet (model number 400/00), a 32-ounce, 10½-inch-high, magnificently shaped glass. His Chardonnay glass was a less convincing performer, but I was astounded by how well the Riesling glass (model number 400/1), an 8-ounce glass that is 7¾ inches high, seemed to highlight the personality characteristics of Riesling.

George Riedel realizes that wine enthusiasts go to great lengths to buy wine in sound condition, store it properly, and serve it at the correct temperature. But how many connoisseurs invest enough time exploring the perfect glasses for their Pichon-Lalande, Méo-Camuzet, Clos de Vougeot, or Maximin-Grunhaus Riesling Kabinett? His mission, he says, is to provide the "finest tools," enabling the taster to capture the full potential of a particular varietal. His glasses have convincingly proved his case time and time again in my tastings. I know of no finer tasting or drinking glasses than the Sommelier Series glasses from Riedel.

I have always found it amazing that most of my wine-loving friends tend to ignore the fact that stemware is just as important as making the right choice in wine. When using the Riedel glasses, one must keep in mind that every one of these glasses has been engineered to enhance the best characteristic of a particular grape varietal. Riedel believes that regardless of the size of the glass, they work best when they are filled to no more than one-quarter of their capacity. If I were going to buy these glasses (the Sommelier Series tends to run $40–70 a glass), I would unhesitatingly purchase both the Bordeaux and Burgundy glasses. They outperformed every other glass by a wide margin. The magnificent 37-ounce Burgundy glass, with a slightly flared lip, directs the flow of a Burgundy to the tip and the center of the tongue so that it avoids contact with the sides of the tongue, which deemphasizes the acidity and makes the Burgundy taste rounder and more supple. This is not just trade puffery on Riedel's part. I have experienced the effect enough times to realize that these glasses do indeed control the flow and, by doing so, enhance the character of the wine. The 32-ounce Bordeaux glass, which is nearly the same size as the Burgundy glass, is more conical, and the lip serves to direct the wine toward the tip of the tongue, where the taste sensors are more acutely aware of sweetness. This enhances the rich fruit in a Cabernet/Merlot-based wine before the wine spreads out to the sides and back of the palate, where it picks up the more acidic, tannic elements.

All of this may sound absurdly highbrow or esoteric, but the effect of these glasses on fine wine is profound. I cannot emphasize enough what a difference they make. If the Sommelier Series sounds too expensive, Riedel does make less expensive lines that are machine-made rather than hand-blown. The most popular are the Vinum glasses, which sell for about $20 per glass. The Bordeaux Vinum glass is a personal favorite as well as a spectacular glass not only for Bordeaux but for Rhône wines and white Burgundies. There are also numerous other glasses designed for Nebbiolo-based wines, rosé wines, old white wines, and port wines, as well as a specially designed glass for sweet Sauternes-type wines.

For more complete information about prices and models, readers can get in touch with Riedel Crystal of America, PO Box 446, 24 Aero Road, Bohemia, NY 11716; telephone number (631) 567-7575. For residents of or visitors to New York City, Riedel has a showroom at 41 Madison Avenue (at Twenty-sixth Street).

Two other good sources for fine wineglasses include St. George Crystal in Jeannette, Pennsylvania, at (724) 523-6501, and the all-purpose Cristal d'Arques Oenologist glass. I have found that the latter works exceptionally well with white wines such as Sauvignon Blanc, Chardonnay, Riesling, and Marsanne, and red wines such as Cabernet Sauvignon, Merlot, Malbec, Syrah, Zinfandel, Gamay, Mourvèdre, and Sangiovese. For very fragrant red wines such as those produced from Pinot Noir, Nebbiolo, and Grenache, this glass is acceptable, but I prefer other stemware. Designed by Dany Rolland, the gifted oenologist, wife, and partner of Libourne's Michel Rolland, the dimensions are: height 8 inches (4½ inches of which for the stem); circumference 10 inches at the base of the tulip-shaped bowl, narrowing to 8 inches at the rim; capacity 12 ounces, or a half bottle of wine. Another fine glassware source is Spiegelau from Germany. For information on where their glasses are sold, readers should visit their Web site, www.Spiegelau.com.

And, last but not least, remember: No matter how clean the glass appears to be, be sure to rinse the glass or decanter with unchlorinated well or mineral water just before it is used. A decanter or wineglass left sitting for any time is a wonderful trap for room and kitchen odors that are undetectable until the wine is poured and they yield their off-putting smells. That and soapy residues left in the glasses have ruined more wines than any defective cork or, I suspect, poor storage from an importer, wholesaler, or retailer. I myself put considerable stress on one friendship simply because I continued to complain at every dinner party about the soapy glasses that interfered with the enjoyment of the wonderful Bordeaux wines being served.

FOOD AND WINE MATCHUPS

The art of serving the right bottle of wine with a specific course or type of food has become terribly overlegislated, to the detriment of the enjoyment of both wine and food. Newspaper and magazine columns, even books, are filled with precise rules that seemingly make it a sin not to have chosen the perfect wine to accompany the meal. The results have been predictable. Instead of enjoying a dining experience, most hosts and hostesses fret, usually needlessly, over their choice of which wine to serve with the meal.

The basic rules of the wine/food matchup game are not difficult to master. These are the tried-and-true, allegedly cardinal principles, such as young wines before old wines, dry wines before sweet wines, white wines before red wines, red wines with meat and white wines with fish. However, these general principles are riddled with exceptions, and your choices are a great deal broader than you have been led to expect. One of France's greatest restaurant proprietors once told me that if people would simply pick their favorite wines to go along with their favorite dishes, they would be a great deal happier. Furthermore, he would be pleased not to have to witness so much nervous anxiety and apprehension on their faces. I'm not sure I can go that far, but since my gut feeling is that there are more combinations of wine and food that work reasonably well than do not, let me share some of my basic observations about this whole field. There are several important questions you should consider:

Does the food offer simple or complex flavors? America's—and I suppose the wine world's—two favorite grapes, Chardonnay and Cabernet Sauvignon, can produce majestic wines of exceptional complexity and flavor depth. However, as food wines, they are remarkably one-dimensional and work well only with dishes that have relatively straightforward and simple flavors. Cabernet Sauvignon marries beautifully with basic meat-and-potato dishes, filet mignon, lamb fillets, steaks, etc. Furthermore, as Cabernet Sauvignon– and Merlot-based wines get older and more complex, they require simpler and simpler dishes to complement their complex flavors. Chardonnay goes beautifully with most fish courses, but when one adds different aromas and scents to a straightforward fish dish—by grilling, or by adding ingredients in an accompanying sauce—Chardonnays are often competitive rather than complementary wines to serve. The basic rule, then, is simple, uncomplex wines with complex dishes, and complex wines with simple dishes.

What are the primary flavors in both the wine and food? A complementary wine choice can often be made if one knows what to expect from the primary flavors in the food to be eaten. The reason creamy and buttery sauces with fish, lobster, even chicken or veal work well with Chardonnay or white Burgundies is because of the buttery, vanilla aromas in the fuller, richer, lustier styles of Chardonnay. On the other hand, a mixed salad with an herb dressing and pieces of grilled fish or shellfish beg for an herbaceous, smoky Sauvignon Blanc or French Sancerre or Pouilly-Fumé from the Loire Valley. For the same reason, a steak au poivre in a creamy brown sauce with its intense, pungent aromas and complex flavors requires a big, rich, peppery Rhône wine such as a Châteauneuf-du-Pape or Gigondas.

Are the texture and flavor intensity of the wine proportional to the texture and flavor intensity of the food? Did you ever wonder why fresh, briny, sea-scented oysters that are light and zesty taste so good with a Muscadet from France or a lighter-styled California Sauvignon Blanc or Italian Pinot Grigio? It is because these wines have the same weight and light texture as the oysters. Why is it that the smoky, sweet, oaky, tangy flavors of a grilled steak or loin of lamb work best with a Zinfandel or Rhône Valley red wine? The full-bodied, supple, chewy flavors of these wines complement a steak or loin of lamb cooked over a wood fire. Sauté the same steak or lamb in butter or bake it in the oven, and the flavors are less complex; then a well-aged Cabernet Sauvignon– or Merlot-based wine from California, Bordeaux, or Australia is called for.

Another telling example of the importance of matching the texture and flavor intensity of the wine with the food is the type of fish you have chosen to eat. Salmon, lobster, shad, and bluefish have intense flavors and a fatty texture, and therefore require a similarly styled, lusty, oaky, buttery Chardonnay to complement them. On the other hand, trout, sole, turbot, and shrimp are leaner, more delicately flavored fish and therefore mandate lighter, less intense wines such as nonoaked examples of Chardonnay from France's Mâconnais region or Italy's Friuli–Venezia Giulia area. In addition, a lighter-styled Champagne or German Riesling (a dry Kabinett works ideally) goes extremely well with trout, sole, or turbot, but falls on its face when matched against salmon, shad, or lobster. One further example of texture and flavor matchups is the classic example of a heavy, unctuous, rich, sweet Sauternes with foie gras. The extravagantly rich and flavorful foie gras cannot be served with any other type of wine, as it would overpower a dry red or white wine. The fact that both the Sauternes and the foie gras have intense, concentrated flavors and similar textures is the exact reason why this combination is so decadently delicious.

What is the style of wine produced in the vintage that you have chosen? Several of France's greatest chefs have told me they prefer off years of Bordeaux and Burgundy to great years, and have instructed their sommeliers to buy the wines for the restaurant accordingly. How can this be? From the chef's perspective, the food, not the wine, should be the focal point of the meal. They fear that a great vintage of Burgundy or Bordeaux with wines that are exceptionally rich, powerful, and concentrated not only takes attention away from their cuisine but makes matching a wine with the food much more troublesome. Thus, chefs prefer a 1987 Bordeaux on the table with their food as opposed to a super-concentrated 1982 or 1990, or a 1989 red Burgundy over a 1990. The great vintages, though marvelous wines, are not always the best vintages to choose for the ultimate matchup with food. Lighter-weight yet tasty wines from so-so years complement delicate and understated cuisine considerably better than the great vintages, which should be reserved for very simple food courses.

Is the food served in a sauce? Years ago, at Michel Guerard's restaurant in Eugénie-les-Bains, I ordered fish served in a red wine sauce. Guerard recommended a red Graves wine from Bordeaux, because the sauce was made from a reduction of fish stock and a red Graves.

The combination was successful and opened my eyes for the first time to the possibilities of fish with red wine. Since then I have had tuna in a green peppercorn sauce accompanied by a California Cabernet Sauvignon (a great match), and salmon sautéed in a red wine sauce happily married to a young vintage of red Bordeaux. A white wine with any of these courses would not have worked. Another great match was veal in a creamy morel sauce with a Tokay from Alsace.

A corollary to this principle of letting the sauce dictate the type of wine you order is when the actual food is prepared with a specific type of wine. For example, coq au vin, an exquisite peasant dish, can be cooked and served in either a white wine or red wine sauce. I have found when I had coq au vin au Riesling, a dry Alsace Riesling with it is simply extraordinary. In Burgundy I have often had coq au vin in a red wine sauce consisting of a reduced Burgundy wine, and the choice of a red Burgundy makes the dish even more special.

When you travel, do you drink locally produced wines with the local cuisine? It is no coincidence that the regional cuisines of Bordeaux, Burgundy, Provence, and Alsace in France, and Tuscany and Piedmont in Italy, seem to enhance and complement the local wines. In fact, most restaurants in these areas rarely offer wines from outside the local region, thus mandating the drinking of the locally produced wines. One always wonders what came first, the cuisine or the wine? Certainly, America is beginning to develop its own regional cuisine, but except for California and the Pacific Northwest, few areas promote the local wines as appropriate matchups with the local cuisine. For example, in my backyard a number of small wineries make an excellent white wine called Seyval Blanc, which is the perfect foil for both the oysters and blue channel crabs from the Chesapeake Bay. Yet few restaurants in the Baltimore-Washington area promote these local wines, which is a shame. Regional wines with regional foods should be a top priority not only when traveling in Europe but also in America's viticultural areas.

Have you learned the best and worst wine and food matchups? If this entire area of wine and food combinations still seems too cumbersome, then your best strategy is simply to learn some of the greatest combinations as well as some of the worst. I can also add a few pointers I have learned through my own experiences, usually bad ones. Certain wine and food relationships of contrasting flavors can be sublime. Perhaps the best example is a sweet, creamy-textured Sauternes wine with a salty aged Stilton or Roquefort cheese. The combination of two opposite sets of flavors and textures is sensational in this particular instance. Another great combination is Alsatian Gewurztraminers and Rieslings with ethnic cuisine such as Indian and Chinese. The juxtaposition of sweet and sour combinations and the spiciness of both cuisines seem to work beautifully with these two wines from Alsace.

One of the great myths about wine and food matchups is that red wines work well with cheese. The truth of the matter is that they hardly ever work well with cheese. Most cheeses, especially favorite wine cheeses such as Brie and double and triple creams have a very high fat content, and most red wines suffer incredibly when drunk with them. If you want to shock your guests but also enjoy wine with cheese, serve a white wine made from the Sauvignon Blanc grape such as a Sancerre or Pouilly-Fumé from France. The dynamic personalities of these two wines and their tangy, zesty acidity stand up well to virtually all types of cheese, but they go especially well with fresh goat cheeses.

Another myth is that dessert wines go best with desserts. Most people seem to like Champagne or a sweet Riesling, sweet Chenin Blanc, or a Sauternes with dessert. Putting aside that chocolate-based desserts are always in conflict with any type of wine, I find that dessert wines are best served as the dessert or after the dessert. Whether it be cake, fruit tarts, ice cream, or candy, I've always enjoyed dessert wines more when they are the centerpiece of attention than when they are accompanying a sweet dessert.

If wine and food matchups still seem too complicated for you, remember that in the final analysis, a good wine served with a good dish to good company is always in good taste. *À votre santé!*

WHAT'S BEEN ADDED TO YOUR WINE?

Over the last decade people have become much more sensitive to what they put in their bodies. The hazards of excessive smoking, fat consumption, and high blood pressure are taken seriously by increasing numbers of people, not just in America but in Europe as well. While this movement is to be applauded, an extremist group, labeled by observers as "neoprohibitionists" or "new drys," has tried to exploit the individual's interest in good health by promoting the image that the consumption of any alcoholic beverage is an inherently dangerous abuse that undermines society and family. These extremist groups do not care about moderation; they want the total elimination of wine (one of alcohol's evil spirits) from the marketplace. In the process, they have misrepresented wine and consistently ignored specific data that demonstrates that moderate wine drinking is more beneficial than harmful to individuals. Unfortunately, the law prohibits the wine industry from promoting the proven health benefits of wine.

Wine is the most natural of all beverages, but it is true that additives can be included in a wine (the neoprohibitionists are taking aim at these as being potentially lethal). Following are those items that can be added to wine.

Acids Most cool-climate vineyards never need to add acidity to wine, but in California and Australia, acidity is often added to give balance to the wines, as grapes from these hot climate areas often lack sufficient natural acidity. Most serious wineries add tartaric acidity, the same type of acidity found naturally in wine. Less quality-oriented wineries dump in pure citric acid, which results in the wine tasting like a lemon/lime sorbet.

Clarification agents A list of items that are dumped into wine to cause suspended particles to coagulate includes morbid names such as dried ox blood, isinglass, casein (milk powder), kaolin (clay), bentonite (powdered clay), and the traditional egg whites. These fining agents are designed to make the wine brilliant and particle free; they are harmless, and top wineries either don't use them or use them minimally.

Oak Many top-quality red and white wines spend most of their lives aging in oak barrels. It is expected that wine stored in wood will take on some of the toasty, smoky, vanilla flavors of wood. These aromas and flavors, if not overdone, add flavor complexity to a wine. Cheap wine can also be marginally enhanced by the addition of oak chips, which provide a more aggressive, raw flavor of wood. But remember, oak only works with certain types of wine, and its usage is analogous to a chef's use of salt, pepper, or garlic. In excessive amounts or with the wrong dish, the results are ghastly.

Sugar In most of the viticultural regions of Europe except for southern France, Portugal, and Spain, the law permits the addition of sugar to the fermenting grape juice in order to raise alcohol levels. This practice, called chaptalization, is performed in cool years when the grapes do not attain sufficient ripeness. It is never done in the hot climate of California or in most of Australia, where low natural acidity, not low sugars, is the problem. Judicious chaptalization raises the alcohol level by 1–2%.

Sulfites All wines must now carry a label indicating that the wine contains sulfites. Sulfite (also referred to as SO_2 or sulfur dioxide) is a preservative used to kill bacteria and microorganisms. It is sprayed on virtually all fresh vegetables and fruits, but a tiny percentage of the population, especially asthmatics, are allergic to SO_2. The fermentation of wine produces some sulfur dioxide naturally, but it is also added to oak barrels by burning a sulfur stick inside the barrel in order to kill any bacteria; it is added again at bottling to prevent the wine from oxidizing. Quality wines should never smell of sulfur (a burning-match smell) because serious wine-makers keep the sulfur level very low. Some wineries do not employ sulfites.

When used properly, sulfites impart no smell or taste to the wine and, except for those who have a known allergy to them, are harmless to the general population. Used excessively, sulfites impart the aforementioned unpleasant smell and a prickly taste sensation. Obviously, people who are allergic to sulfites should not drink wine, just as people who are allergic to fish roe should not eat caviar.

Tannin   Tannin occurs naturally in the skins and stems of grapes, and the content from the crushing of the grape skins and subsequent maceration of the skins and juice is usually more than adequate to provide sufficient natural tannin. Tannin gives a red wine grip and backbone, while also acting as a preservative. However, on rare occasions tannin is added to a spineless wine.

Yeasts   While many wine-makers rely on the indigenous wild yeasts in the vineyard to start the fermentation, it is becoming more common to employ cultured yeasts for this procedure. There is no health hazard here, but the increasing reliance on the same type of yeast for wines from all over the world leads to wines with similar bouquets and flavors.

ORGANIC WINES

Organic wines, produced without fungicides, pesticides, or chemical fertilizers, with no additives or preservatives, continue to gain considerable consumer support. In principle, organic wines should be as excellent as nonorganic. Because most organic wine producers tend to do less manipulation and processing of their wines, the consumer receives a product that is far more natural than those wines which have been manufactured and processed to death.

There is tremendous potential for huge quantities of organic wines, particularly from viticultural areas that enjoy copious quantities of sunshine and wind, the so-called Mediterranean climate. In France, the Languedoc-Roussillon region, Provence, and the Rhône Valley have the potential to produce organic wines if their proprietors desire. Much of California could do so as well. Parts of Australia and Italy also have weather conditions that encourage the possibility of developing organic vineyards.

THE DARK SIDE OF WINE

The Growing International Standardization of Wine Styles

Although technology allows wine-makers to produce wines of better and better quality, the continuing obsession with technically perfect wines is unfortunately stripping wines of their identifiable and distinctive character. Whether it is excessive filtration of wines or insufficiently critical emulation of winemaking styles, the downside of modern winemaking is that it is now increasingly difficult to tell an Italian Chardonnay from one made in France or California or Australia. When the corporate wine-makers of the world begin to make wines all in the same way, designing them to offend the least number of people, wine will no doubt lose its fascinating appeal and individualism to become no better than most brands of whiskey, gin, Scotch, or vodka. One must not forget that the great appeal of wine is that it is a unique, distinctive, fascinating beverage and different every time one drinks it. Wine-makers and the owners of wineries, particularly in America, must learn to take more risks so as to preserve the individual character of their wines, even though some consumers may find them bizarre or unusual. It is this distinctive quality of wine that will ensure its future.

Destroying the Joy of Wine by Excessive Acidification,
Overzealous Fining, and Abrasive Filtration

Since the beginning of my career as a professional wine critic, I have tried to present a strong case against the excessive manipulation of wine. One look at the producers of the world's greatest wines will irrefutably reveal that the following characteristics are shared by all of them—whether they be from California, France, Italy, Spain, or Germany: 1) They are driven to preserve the integrity of the vineyard's character, the varietal's identity, and the vintage's personality. 2) They believe in low crop yields. 3) Weather permitting, they harvest only physiologically mature (versus analytically ripe) fruit. 4) They use simplistic winemaking and cellar techniques, in the sense that they are minimal interventionists, preferring to permit the wine to make itself. 5) Though they are not opposed to fining or filtration if the wine is unstable or unclear, if the wine is made from healthy, ripe grapes and is stable and clear, they will absolutely refuse to strip it by excessive fining and filtration at bottling.

Producers who care only about making wine as fast as possible and collecting their accounts receivable quickly also have many things in common. They turn out neutral, vapid, mediocre wines, and they are believers in huge crop yields, with considerable fertilization to promote massive crops, as large as the vineyard can render (six or more tons per acre, compared to modest yields of three tons per acre). Their philosophy is that the vineyard is a manufacturing plant and cost efficiency dictates that production be maximized. They rush their wine into bottle as quickly as possible in order to get paid. They believe in processing wine, such as centrifuging it initially, then practicing multiple fining and filtration procedures, particularly a denuding sterile filtration. This guarantees that the wine is lifeless but stable, so the wine's being able to withstand temperature extremes and stand upright on a grocery store's shelf has priority over giving the consumer a beverage of pleasure. These wineries harvest earlier than anybody else because they are unwilling to take any risk, delegating all questions to their oenologists, who, they know, have as their objectives security and stability, which is in conflict with the consumer's goal of finding joy in wine.

The effect of excessive manipulation of wine, particularly overly aggressive fining and filtration, is dramatic. It destroys a wine's bouquet as well as its ability to express its *terroir* and varietal character. It also mutes the vintage's character. Fining and filtration can be done lightly, causing only minor damage, but most wines produced in the New World (California, Australia, and South America in particular) and most bulk wines produced in Europe are sterile-filtered. This procedure requires numerous prefiltrations to get the wines clean enough to pass through a micropore membrane filter. This system of wine stability and clarification strips, eviscerates, and denudes a wine of much of its character.

Some wines can suffer such abuse with less damage. Thick, tannic, concentrated Syrah- and Cabernet Sauvignon–based wines may even survive these wine lobotomies, diminished in aromatic and flavor dimension, but still alive. Wines such as Pinot Noir and Chardonnay are destroyed in the process.

Thanks to a new generation of producers, particularly in France, aided by a number of specialist importers from America, there has been a movement against unnecessary fining and filtration. One only has to look at the extraordinary success enjoyed by such American importers as Kermit Lynch, Weygandt-Metzler, North Berkeley Imports, and Robert Kacher to realize how much consumer demand exists for a natural, unfiltered, uncompromised wine that is a faithful representation of its vineyard and vintage. Most serious wine consumers do not mind not being able to drink the last half ounce of a wine because of sediment. They know this sediment means they are getting a flavorful, authentic, unprocessed wine that is much more representative than one that has been stripped at bottling.

Other small importers who have followed the leads of Lynch, Weygandt-Metzler, North Berkeley, and Kacher include Neal Rosenthal Select Vineyards (New York, New York); Eric Solomon of European Cellars (New York, New York); Don Quattlebaum of New Castle Imports (Myrtle Beach, South Carolina); Fran Kysela of Kysela Père et Fils (Winchester, Virginia); Martine Saunier of Martine's Wines (San Rafael, California); Jorgé Ordonnez (Dedham, Massachusetts); Leonardo Lo Cascio (Hohokus, New Jersey); Dan Philips (Oxnard, California); Ted Schrauth (West Australia); John Larchet (Australia); Jeffrey Davies (West Nyack, New York); and Alain Junguenet (Watchung, New Jersey), to name some of the best known. They often insist that their producers not filter those wines shipped to the United States, resulting in a richer, more ageworthy wine being sold in America than elsewhere in the world. Even some of our country's largest importers, most notably Kobrand, Inc., in New York City, are encouraging producers to move toward more gentle and natural bottling techniques.

I am certain there would have been an even more powerful movement to bottle wines naturally with minimal clarification if the world's wine press were to examine the effect of excessive fining and filtration. It is difficult to criticize many American wine writers, because the vast majority of them are part-timers. Few have the time or resources to taste the same wines before and after bottling. Yet I am disappointed that many of our most influential writers and publications have remained strangely silent, particularly in view of the profound negative impact filtration can have on the quality of fine wine. The English wine-writing corps, which includes many veteran, full-time wine writers, has an appalling record on this issue, especially in view of the fact that many of them make it a practice to taste before and after bottling. For those who care about the quality of wine, and the preservation of the character of the vineyard, vintage, and varietal, the reluctance of so many writers to criticize the wine industry undermines the entire notion of wine appreciation.

Even a wine writer of the stature of Hugh Johnson comes out strongly on the side of processed, neutral wines that can be safely shipped 12 months of the year. Readers may want to consider Johnson's, and his coauthor, James Halliday's, comments in their book *The Vintner's Art—How Great Wines Are Made.* Halliday is an Australian wine writer and winery owner, and Hugh Johnson may be this century's most widely read wine author. In their book they chastise the American importer Kermit Lynch for his "romantic ideals," which they describe as "increasingly impractical." Johnson and Halliday assert, "The truth is that a good fifty percent of those artisan Burgundies and Rhônes are bacterial time bombs." Their plea for compromised and standardized wines is supported by the following observation: "The hard reality is that many restaurants and many consumers simply will not accept sediment." This may have been partially true in America 20 years ago, but today the consumer not only wants but demands a natural wine. Moreover, the wine consumer understands that sediment in a bottle of fine wine is a healthy sign. The position, which both writers take, that modern-day winemaking and commercial necessity require that wines be shipped 12 months a year and be durable enough to withstand months on retailers' shelves in both cold and hot temperature conditions is highly debatable. America now has increasing numbers of responsible merchants, importers, and restaurant sommeliers who go to great lengths to guarantee the client a healthy bottle of wine that has not been abused. Astonishingly, Johnson and Halliday conclude that consumers cannot tell the difference between a filtered and an unfiltered wine! In summarizing their position, they state, "but leave the wine for 1, 2, or 3 months (one cannot tell how long the recovery process will take), and it is usually impossible to tell the filtered from the non-filtered wine, provided the filtration at bottling was skillfully carried out." After 14 years of conducting such tastings, I find this statement not only unbelievable but insupportable! Am I to conclude that all of the wonderful wines I have tasted from cask that were subsequently damaged by vigorous fining and filtration were bottled by incompetent people who did not know how to filter? Am I to think that the results of the extensive comparative tastings (usually blind) that I have done of the same wine, filtered versus unfiltered, were bogus? Are the enormous aromatic, flavor, textural, and qualitative differences that are the result of vigorous clarification techniques figments of my imagination? Astoundingly, the wine industry's reluctance to accept responsibility for preserving all that the best vineyards and vintages can achieve is excused rather than condemned.

If excessive fining and filtration are not bad enough, consider the overzealous additions of citric and tartaric acids employed by Australian and California oenologists to perk up their wines. You know the feeling—you open a bottle of Australian or California Chardonnay and not only is there no bouquet (because it was sterile-filtered), but tasting the wine is like biting into a fresh lemon or lime. It is not enjoyable. What you are experiencing is the result of the misguided philosophy among New World wine-makers to add too much acidity as a cheap life insurance policy for their wines. This "life insurance" is in fact a death certificate. Because these producers are unwilling to reduce their yields and unwilling to assume any risk, and because they see winemaking as nothing more than a processing technique, they generously add acidity. It does serve as an antibacterial, antioxidant agent, thus helping to keep the wine fresh. But those who acidify the most are usually those who harvest appallingly high crop yields, so there is little flavor to protect! After 6–12 months of bottle age, what little fruit is present fades, and the consumer is left with a skeleton of sharp, shrill acid levels, alcohol, and wood (if utilized), but no fruit—an utterly reprehensible way of making wine.

I do not object to the use of these techniques for bulk and jug wines that the consumer is buying for value, or because of brand-name recognition. But for any producer to sell a wine as a handcrafted, artisanal product at $20 or more a bottle, these practices are shameful. Anyone who tells you that excessive acidification, fining, and filtration do not damage a wine is either a fool or a liar.

The Inflated Wine Pricing of Restaurants

Given the vast sums of discretionary income that Americans spend eating at restaurants, a strong argument could be made that the cornerstone of increased wine consumption and awareness would be wine drinking in restaurants. However, most restaurants treat wine as a luxury item, marking it up an exorbitant 200–500%, thereby effectively discouraging the consumption of wine. This practice of offering wines at huge markups also serves to reinforce the mistaken notion that wine is only for the elite and the superrich.

The wine industry does little about this practice, being content merely to see its wines placed on a restaurant's list. But the consumer should revolt and avoid those restaurants that charge exorbitant wine prices, no matter how sublime the cuisine. This is nothing more than legitimized mugging of the consumer.

Fortunately, things are slightly better today than they were a decade ago, as some restaurant owners are now regarding wine as an integral part of the meal, and not merely as a device to increase the bill.

Collectors versus Consumers

I have reluctantly come to believe that many of France's greatest wine treasures—the first growths of Bordeaux, including the famous sweet nectar made at Château d'Yquem, Burgundy's most profound red wines from the Domaine de la Romanée-Conti, and virtually all of the wines from the tiny white wine appellation of Montrachet—are never drunk or, should I say, swallowed. Most of us who purchase or cellar wine do so on the theory that eventually every one of our splendid bottles will be swirled, sloshed, sniffed, sipped, and, yes, guzzled, with friends. That, of course, is one of the joys of wine, and those of you who partake of this pleasure are true wine lovers. There are, however, other types of wine collectors—the collector-investor, the collector-spitter, and even the nondrinking collector.

Several years ago I remember being deluged with telephone calls from a man wanting me to have dinner with him and tour his private cellar. After several months of resisting, I finally succumbed. A very prominent businessman, he had constructed an impressive cellar beneath his sprawling home. It was enormous and immaculately kept, with state-of-the-art humidity and temperature controls. I suspect it contained in excess of 10,000 bottles. There were cases of such thoroughbreds as Pétrus, Lafite-Rothschild, Mouton-Rothschild, and rare vintages of the great red Burgundies such as Romanée-Conti and La Tache, and to my astonishment there were also hundreds of cases of 10- and 15-year-old Beaujolais, Pouilly-Fuissé, Dolcetto, and California Chardonnays—all wines that should have been drunk during their first 4 or 5 years of life. I diplomatically suggested that he should inventory his cellar, as there seemed to be a number of wines that mandated immediate consumption.

About the time I spotted the fifth or sixth case of what was undoubtedly 10-year-old Beaujolais vinegar, I began to doubt the sincerity of my host's enthusiasm for wine. These unthinkable doubts (I was much more naive then than I am now) were amplified at dinner. As we entered the sprawling kitchen and dining room complex, he proudly announced that neither he nor his wife actually drank wine, and then asked if I would care for a glass of mineral water, iced tea—or, if I preferred, a bottle of wine. During my sorrowful drive home that evening, I lamented the fact that I had not opted for the mineral water. For when I made the mistake of requesting wine with the meal, my host proceeded to grab a bottle of wine that one of his friends suggested should be consumed immediately. It was a brown-colored, utterly repugnant, senile Bordeaux from 1969, perhaps the worst vintage in the last 25 years. Furthermore, the château was a notorious underachiever from the famous commune of Pauillac. The wine he chose does not normally merit buying in a good vintage, much less a pathetic one. I shall never forget my host opening the bottle and saying, "Well, Bob, this wine sure smells good."

Regrettably, this nondrinking collector continues to buy large quantities of wine, not for investment, and obviously not for drinking. The local wine merchants tell me his type is not rare. To him, a collection of wine is like a collection of crystal, art, sculpture, or china—something to be admired, to be shown off, but never, ever to be consumed.

More ostentatious by far is the collector-spitter, who thrives on gigantic tastings where 50, 60, sometimes even 70 or 80 vintages of great wines, often from the same château, can be "tasted." Important members of the wine press are invited (at no charge, of course) in the hope that this wine happening will receive a major article in the *The New York* or *Los Angeles Times,* and the collector's name will become recognized and revered in the land of winedom. These collector-spitters relish rubbing elbows with famous proprietors and telling their friends, "Oh, I'll be at Château Lafite-Rothschild next week to taste all of the château's wines between 1870 and 1987. Sorry you can't be there." I have, I confess, participated in several of these events and have learned from the exercise of trying to understand them that their primary purpose is to feed the sponsor's enormous ego, and often the château's ego as well.

I am not against academic tastings where a limited number of serious wine enthusiasts sit down to taste 20 or 30 different wines (usually young ones), because that is a manageable number that both neophytes and connoisseurs can generally grasp. But to taste 60 or more rare and monumental vintages at an eight- or twelve-hour tasting marathon is excessive. To put it simply, what happens at these tastings is that much of the world's greatest, rarest, and most expensive wines are spit out. No wine taster I have ever met could conceivably remain sober, even if only the greatest wines were swallowed. I can assure you, there is only remorse in spitting out a 1929 or 1945 Mouton-Rothschild.

Recollections of these events have long troubled me. I vividly remember one tasting held at a very famous restaurant in Los Angeles where a number of compelling bottles from one of France's greatest estates were opened. Many of them were exhilarating. Yet, whether it was the otherworldly 1961 or the opulent 1947, the reactions I saw on the faces of those 40 or so people, each of whom had paid several thousand dollars to attend, made me wonder whether we were tasting 50 different vintages of France's greatest wines or 50 bottles of Pepto-Bismol. Fortunately, the organizer did appear to enjoy the gathering and appreciate the wines, but among the guests I never once saw a smile or any enthusiasm or happiness in the course of this extraordinary 12-hour tasting.

I remember another marathon tasting held in France by one of Europe's leading collector-spitters, which lasted all day and much of the night. There were over 90 legendary wines served, and midway through the afternoon I was reasonably certain there was not a sober individual remaining except for the chef and his staff. By the time the magnum of 1929 Mouton-Rothschild was served (one of the century's greatest wines), I do not think there was a guest left, myself included, who was competent enough to know whether he was drinking claret or Beaujolais.

I have also noticed at these tastings that many collector-spitters did not even know when a bottle was corked (had the smell of moldy cardboard and was defective), or when a bottle was oxidized and undrinkable, proving the old saying that money does not always buy good taste. Of course, most of these tastings are media happenings designed to stroke the host's vanity. All too frequently they undermine the principle that wine is a beverage of pleasure, and that is my basic regret.

The third type of collector, the investor, is motivated by the possibility of reselling the wines for profit. Eventually, most or all of these wines return to the marketplace, and much of it wends its way into the hands of serious consumers who share it with their spouses or good friends. Of course, they often must pay dearly for the privilege, but wine is not the only product that falls prey to such manipulation. I hate to think of wine being thought of primarily as an investment, but the world's finest wines do appreciate significantly in value, and it would be foolish to ignore the fact that more and more shrewd investors are looking at wine as a way of making money.

Unspeakable Practices

It is a frightening thought, but I have no doubt that a sizeable percentage (10–25%) of the wines sold in America have been damaged because of exposure to extremes of heat. Smart consumers have long been aware of the signs of poor storage. They have only to look at the bottle. As discussed earlier in the How to Buy Wine section (page 7), the first sign that a bottle has been poorly stored is when a cork is popped above the rim and is pushed out against the lead or plastic capsule that covers the top of the bottle.

Another sign that the wine has been poorly stored is seepage, or legs, down the rim of the bottle. This is the sometimes sticky, dry residue of a wine that has expanded, seeped around the cork, and dripped onto the rim, almost always due to excessively high temperatures in transit or storage. Few merchants take the trouble to wipe the legs off, and they can often be spotted on wines shipped during the heat of the summer or brought into the United States through the Panama Canal in un-air-conditioned containers. Consumers should avoid buying wines that show dried seepage legs originating under the capsule and trickling down the side of the bottle.

You should also be alert for young wines (those less than four years old) that have more than one-half inch of air space, or ullage, between the cork and the liquid level in the bottle. Modern bottling operations generally fill bottles within one-eighth inch of the cork, and more than one-half inch of air space should arouse your suspicion.

The problem, of course, is that too few people in the wine trade take the necessary steps to ensure that the wine is not ruined in shipment or storage. The wine business has become so commercial that wines, whether from California, Italy, or France, are shipped year-round, regardless of weather conditions. Traditionally, wines from Europe were shipped only in the spring or fall, when temperatures encountered in shipment would be moderate, assuming they were not shipped by way of the Panama Canal. The cost of renting an air-conditioned or heated container for shipping wines adds anywhere from 20 to 40 cents to the wholesale cost of the bottle, but when buying wines that cost over $200 a case, I doubt the purchaser would mind paying the extra premium knowing that the wine will not smell or taste cooked when opened.

Many importers claim to ship in reefers (the trade jargon for temperature-controlled containers), but only a handful actually do. America's largest importer of high-quality Bordeaux wine rarely, if ever, uses reefers and claims to have had no problems with its shipments. Perhaps they would change their minds if they had witnessed the cases of 1986 Rausan-

Ségla, 1986 Talbot, 1986 Gruaud-Larose, and 1986 Château Margaux that arrived in the Maryland-Washington, D.C., market with stained labels and pushed-out corks. Somewhere between Bordeaux and Washington, D.C., these wines had been exposed to torridly high temperatures. It may not have been the fault of the importer, as the wine passed through a number of intermediaries before reaching its final destination. But pity the poor consumers who buy these wines, put them in their cellars, and open them 10 or 15 years in the future. Who will grieve for them?

The problem with temperature extremes is that the naturally made, minimally processed, hand-produced wines are the most vulnerable to this kind of abuse. Therefore, many importers, not wanting to assume any risks, have gone back to their suppliers and demanded "more stable" wines. Translated into real terms this means the wine trade prefers to ship vapid, denuded wines that have been "stabilized," subjected to a manufacturing process, and either pasteurized or sterile-filtered so they can be shipped 12 months a year. While their corks may still pop out if subjected to enough heat, their taste will not change, because for all intents and purposes these wines are already dead when they are put in the bottle. Unfortunately, only a small segment of the wine trade seems to care.

While there are some wine merchants, wholesalers, and importers who are cognizant of the damage that can be done when wines are not protected, and who take great pride in representing hand-made, quality products, the majority of the wine trade continues to ignore the risks. They would prefer that the wine be denuded by pasteurization, cold stabilization, or a sterile filtration. Only then can they be shipped safely under any weather conditions.

Wine Producers' Greed

Are today's wine consumers being hoodwinked by the world's wine producers? Most growers and/or producers have intentionally permitted production yields to soar to such extraordinary levels that the concentration and character of their wines are in jeopardy. There remain a handful of fanatics who continue, at some financial sacrifice, to reject a significant proportion of their harvest in order to ensure that only the finest-quality wine is sold under their name. However, they are dwindling in number. Fewer producers are prepared to go into the vineyard and cut bunches of grapes to reduce the yields. Fewer still are willing to cut back prudently on fertilizers. For much of the last decade, production yields throughout the world continued to break records with each new vintage. The results are wines that increasingly lack character, concentration, and staying power. In Europe, the most flagrant abuses of overproduction occur in Germany and Burgundy, where yields today are three to almost five times what they were in the 1950s. The argument that the vineyards are more carefully and competently managed, and that this results in larger crops, is misleading. Off the record, many a seriously committed wine producer will tell you that "the smaller the yield, the better the wine."

If one wonders why the Domaine Leroy's Burgundies taste richer than those from other domaines, it is due not only to quality winemaking but to the fact that their yields are one-third those of other Burgundy producers. If one asks why the best Châteauneuf-du-Papes are generally Rayas, Pégaü, Bonneau, and Beaucastel, it is because their yields are one-half those of other producers of the appellation. The same assertion applies to J. J. Prüm and Müller-Catoir in Germany. Not surprisingly, they have conservative crop yields that produce one-third the amount of wine of their neighbors.

While I do not want to suggest there are no longer any great wines, and that most of the wines now produced are no better than the plonk peasants drank in the 19th century, the point is that overfertilization, modern sprays that prevent rot, the development of highly prolific clonal selections, and the failure to keep production levels modest have all resulted in yields that may well be combining to destroy the reputations of many of the most famous wine regions of the world. Trying to find a flavorful Chardonnay from California today is not much easier than finding a concentrated red Burgundy that can age gracefully beyond 10 years. The production yields of Chardonnay in California have often resulted in wines that have only a faint character of the grape and seem almost entirely dominated by acidity and/or the smell of oak barrels. What is appalling is that there is so little intrinsic flavor. Yet Chardonnays remain the most popular white wine in this country, so what incentive is there to lower yields?

Of course, if the public, encouraged by a noncritical, indifferent wine media, is willing to pay top dollar for mediocrity, then little is likely to change. However, if consumers start insisting that $15 or $20 should at the very minimum fetch a wine that provides far more pleasure, perhaps that message will gradually work its way back to the producers.

Wine Writers' Ethics and Competence

The problems just described have only occasionally been acknowledged by the wine media, which generally has a collective mind-set of never having met a wine it doesn't like.

Wine writing in America has rarely been a profitable or promising full-time occupation. Historically, the most interesting work was always done by those people who sold wine. There's no doubting the influence or importance of the books written by Alexis Lichine and Frank Schoonmaker. But both men made their fortunes by selling rather than writing about wine, and both managed to write about wine objectively, despite their ties to the trade.

There are probably not more than a dozen or so independent wine experts in this country who support themselves entirely by writing. Great Britain has long championed the cause of wine writers and looked upon them as true professionals. But even there, with all their experience and access to the finest European vineyards, most of the successful wine writers have been involved in the sale and distribution of wine. Can anyone name an English wine writer who criticized the performance of Lafite-Rothschild between 1961 and 1974, or Château Margaux between 1964 and 1977? Meanwhile, the consumer was getting screwed.

It is probably unrealistic to expect writers to develop a professional expertise with wine without access and support from the trade, but such support can compromise their findings. If they are beholden to wine producers for the wines they taste, they are not likely to fault them. If their trips to vineyards are the result of the wine-maker's largesse, they are unlikely to criticize what they have seen. If they are lodged at the châteaux and their trunks are filled with cases of wine (as, sadly, is often the case), can a consumer expect them to be critical, or even objective?

Putting aside the foolish notion that a wine writer is going to bite the hand that feeds him, there is the problem that many wine writers are lacking the global experience essential to evaluate wine properly. What has emerged from such inexperience is a school of wine writing that is primarily trained to look at the wine's structure and acid levels, and this philosophy is too frequently in evidence when judging wines. The level of pleasure that a wine provides, or is capable of providing in the future, would appear to be irrelevant. The results are wine evaluations that read as though one were measuring the industrial strength of different grades of cardboard rather than a beverage that many consider nature's greatest gift to mankind. Balance is everything in wine, and wines that taste too tart or tannic rarely ever age into flavorful, distinctive, charming beverages. While winemaking and wine technology are indeed better, and some of the most compelling wines ever made are being produced today, there are far too many mediocre wines sitting on the shelves that hardly deserve their high praise.

There are, however, some interesting trends. The growth of *The Wine Spectator*, with its staff of full-time writers obligated to follow a strict code of non–conflict of interest, has resulted in better and more professional journalism. It also cannot be discounted that this flashy magazine appears twice a month. This is good news for the wine industry, frequently under siege by the antialcohol extremists. Finally, to *The Wine Spectator*'s credit, more of their tasting reports are authored by one or two people, not an anonymous, secretive committee. I have already aired my criticism of wine magazines and tastings whose evaluations are the result of a committee's vote.

Given the vitality of our nation's best wine guides, it is unlikely that wine writers will have less influence in the future. The thousands and thousands of wines that come on the market, many of them overpriced and vapid, require consumer-oriented reviews from the wine-writing community. But until a greater degree of professionalism is attained, until more experience is evidenced by wine writers, until their misinformed emphasis on a wine's high acidity and structure is forever discredited, until most of the English wine media begin to understand and adhere to the basic rules of conflict of interest, until we all remember that this is only a beverage of pleasure, to be seriously consumed but not taken too seriously, then and only then will the quality of wine writing and the wines we drink improve. Will all of this happen, or will we be reminded of these words of Marcel Proust: "We do not succeed in changing things according to our desire, but gradually our desire changes. The situation that we hope to change because it was intolerable becomes unimportant. We have not managed to surmount the obstacle as we are absolutely determined to do, but life has taken us round to it, let us pass it, and then if we turn round to gaze at the road past, we can barely catch sight of it, so imperceptible has it become."

IN VINO VERITAS?

I have no doubt that the overwhelming majority of rare and fine wine that is sold today, either at retail or through one of the numerous wine auctions, involves legitimate bottles. Yet over the last six months I have accumulated enough evidence to suggest that some warning flags need to be raised before this insidious disease becomes a vinous ebola. Shrewd buyers, reputable merchants, and auction companies that specialize in top vintages take measures to authenticate bottles of wine that may cost thousands of dollars. The top auction houses, aware of the growing evidence of phony bottles, are going to great lengths to authenticate the legitimacy of each wine they sell. Nevertheless, a con artist can easily reproduce a bottle (the finest Bordeaux châteaux use glass bottles that are among the cheapest and easiest to obtain in the world), a label, a cork, and a capsule, deceiving even the most astute purchaser. Think it over—high-quality, limited-production, rare wine may be the only luxury-priced commodity in the world that does not come with a guarantee of authenticity, save for the label and cork, and the former can be easily duplicated with one of today's high-tech scanners.

The wine marketplace has witnessed obscene speculation for such modern-day vintages as 1990, certain 1989s, and, of course, 1982. The existence of dishonest segments of society with only one objective, to take full advantage of the enormous opportunity that exists to make a quick buck by selling bogus wines, is not that shocking. It has always been a problem, but based on the number of letters and telephone calls I have received from victims who have been the recipients of suspiciously labeled wines, with even more doubtful contents, it is a subject that needs to be addressed.

It was nearly 20 years ago that I saw my first fraudulent bottles of fine wine. Cases of 1975 Mouton-Rothschild were being sold in New York for below their market value. The wine was packed in shabby cardboard cases with washed-out labels. In addition to those warning signs, the bottles had the words "Made in Canada" on the bottom, and the capsules did not have the characteristic Mouton embossed printing. Blatant recklessness and the slipshod work of the criminal made the fraud easy to detect.

Many producers of these limited-production, rare wines are aware of the frauds perpetuated with their products, but they have largely chosen to maintain a low profile for fear that widespread dissemination of potentially inflammatory information will unsettle (to put it mildly) the fine-wine marketplace. No doubt the news that a hundred or so phony cases of Château ABC are floating around in the world marketplace would suppress the value of the wine. The estates that make the world's most cherished wines (and we all know who they are) need to develop a better system for guaranteeing the authenticity of their product, but, lamentably, few to date have been so inclined. Four of the elite Bordeaux châteaux do make it more difficult for counterfeiting pirates. Pétrus has, since the 1988 vintage, utilized a special label that when viewed under a specific type of light reveals a code not apparent under normal lighting conditions. In 1996, Pétrus went further, instituting an engraved bottle with the word *Pétrus* etched in the glass. Château d'Yquem incorporates a watermark in their label. Haut-Brion was among the first to utilize a custom-embossed bottle in 1957. In 1996, Lafite-Rothschild also launched an antifraud engraved bottle. More recently, Château Margaux has inserted a special code in the print of each bottle. Whether creating more sophisticated labels that are not as easy to reproduce (with serial numbers, watermarks, etc.), or employing a fraud squad devoted to tracking down the provenance of these phony bottles—something must be done.

Space does not permit me to discuss all the shocking frauds I have learned of or have been called in to help prove. I myself have seen phony bottles of Domaine Leflaive Montrachet, Château Rayas, Cheval Blanc, Vieux Château Certan, and Le Pin. Reports of phony bottles come in with surprising frequency and have been confirmed in conversations with retailers, both in this country and in England. They have told me of fraudulent cases of 1989 and 1982 Le Pin, 1982 Pétrus, 1982 and 1975 Lafleur, 1947 Cheval Blanc, 1928 Latour, and 1900 Margaux, with nonbranded blank corks and photocopied labels! With respect to the 1928 Latour, the merchant, suspecting he had been duped, opened it and told me he was sure it was a young California Pinot Noir. One major American merchant, outraged at being sold phony wine, attempted to contact the European seller, only to find out he had moved, with no forwarding address, from his office in Paris. The seller has never been found.

A wine buyer from one of this country's most prominent restaurants recently told me about problems he had encountered when opening expensive bottles for his clients. All of these wines had been purchased from a reputable merchant who had bought the wine from a gray marketeer selling private cellars in Europe. Corks of 1961 Haut-Brion and 1970 Latour were either illegible or intentionally had the vintage scratched off. Since this buyer had vast tasting experience with these wines, detection of the fraud was relatively easy. He was convinced that the 1961 Haut-Brion was fraudulent, as it tasted like a much lighter vintage of Haut-Brion (he suspected it to be the 1967). In the case of the 1970 Latour, the cork had been badly altered to resemble the 1970, but closer inspection revealed it to be the 1978 Latour.

What is so surprising is that most fraudulent efforts to date appear to be the work of kindergarten criminals, indicated by washed-out, photocopied labels, unconvincing corks, and lack of distinguishing château/domaine signs on labels, bottles, corks, or capsules. However, with the technology available today, authentic-looking bottles, capsules, corks, and labels can be easily duplicated, and for these counterfeits, only a person who knows the taste of the wine could tell if the contents were bogus.

SAFETY GUIDELINES

1. *Dealing with the gray market:* To date, almost all the fraudulent bottles have come from wines purchased in the so-called gray market. This means the wines have not gone through the normal distribution channel, where a contractual relationship exists between the producer and the vendor. Bottles of French wines with the green French tax stamps on the top of the capsule have obviously been purchased in France and then resold to gray market operators. I do not want to denigrate the best of the gray market operators, because I am a frequent purchaser from these sources, and those I know are legitimate, serious, and professional about what they buy. Nevertheless, it is irrefutable that most of the suspicious wine showing up is from rogue gray market operators.

2. *Label awareness:* Wine bottles that have easily removable neck labels to indicate the vintage are especially prone to tampering. It is easy to transfer a neck label from a poor vin-

tage to one with a great reputation. Sadly, almost all Burgundies fall into this category, as well as some Rhône Valley wines. Many of the top Burgundy producers have begun to brand the cork with the appropriate vintage and vineyard, particularly if it is a premier or grand cru. However, this is a relatively recent practice, largely implemented in the late 1980s by top estates and *négociants*. The only way a buyer can make sure the cork matches the neck and bottle labels is to remove the capsule. Any purchaser who is the least bit uneasy about the provenance of a wine should not hesitate to pull off the capsule. Irregular, asymmetrical labels with tears and smears of glue are a sign that someone may have tampered with the bottle. Perhaps the trend (now widely employed by California wineries such as Robert Mondavi and Kendall-Jackson) to discontinue the use of capsules should be considered by top estates in France, Italy, and Spain. An alternative would be to design a capsule with a window slot, permitting the purchaser to have a view of the cork's vintage and vineyard name. A more practical as well as inexpensive alternative would be to print the name of the vineyard and vintage on the capsule, in addition to the cork.

Badly faded, washed-out labels (or photocopied labels) should be viewed with sheer horror! However, readers should realize that moldy or deteriorated labels from a damp, cold cellar are not signs of fraudulent wines but, rather, of superb cellaring conditions. I have had great success at auctions buying old vintages that have moldy, tattered labels. Most speculators shy away from such wines because their priority is investing, not consumption.

3. *Know the market value:* Most purchasers of expensive rare wines are extremely knowledgeable about the market value of these wines. If the wine is being offered at a price significantly lower than fair market value, it would seem incumbent on the purchaser to ask why he or she is the beneficiary of such a great deal. Remember, if it sounds too good to be true, it probably is.

4. *Origin verification:* For both rare old vintages and young wines, demanding a guarantee as to the provenance of the wine being purchased is prudent. As a corollary, it is imperative that readers deal with reputable merchants who will stand behind the products they sell. If a merchant refuses to provide details of the origin of where the wine was purchased, take your business elsewhere, even if it means laying out more money for the same wine.

5. *Lot numbers:* Because of some tainted Perrier water a few years ago, the European community now requires most potable beverages to carry a lot number (but only those sold to member nations, thus excluding the United States). This is usually a tiny number located somewhere on the label that begins with the letter *L*, followed by a serial number, which can range from several digits to eight or more. Most producers use the vintage as part of the lot number. In the case of Domaine Leflaive, the vintage year is indicated by the last two digits of the lot number. However, in some instances (i.e., Comtes des Lafon), the first two numbers provide the vintage year. For Lynch-Bages or Pichon-Longueville Baron, the vintage appears in the middle of the number. But be advised, many tiny growers do not use lot numbers on those wines sold to non-ECC countries (the United States, for example). Virtually all the Bordeaux châteaux have used lot numbers since the 1989 vintage.

6. *No sediment in older wines:* Wines more than 10–15 years old, with no sediment and/or with fill levels that reach the bottom of the cork should always be viewed with suspicion. Several Burgundian *négociants* sell "reconditioned" bottles of ancient vintages that have fills to the cork and lack sediment. I have always been skeptical of this practice, but those *négociants* claim they have a special process for siphoning off the sediment. Certainly no Bordeaux château utilizes such an unusual and debatable method. Wines that have been recorked at a Bordeaux château will indicate that, either on the cork or on both the label and the cork. The year in which the wine was recorked will usually be indicated. Among the most illustrious estates of Bordeaux, only Pétrus refuses to recork bottles because so many suspicious bottles have been brought to them for recorking. Both Cheval Blanc and Latour indi-

cate both on the cork and the label the date and year of recorking. In these cases, the authentic bottles will have very good fills as the wine has been topped off, but older vintages still display considerable sediment.

7. *Unmarked cardboard cases:* Wines that have been packaged in unlabeled cardboard boxes are always suspicious, because every Burgundy domaine uses its own customized cardboard box with the name of the estate as well as the importer's name printed on the box, and almost all the prominent Bordeaux châteaux use wooden boxes with the name of the château as well as the vintage branded into the wood. However, to complicate matters, readers should realize that wines from private cellars consigned to auction houses usually must be repackaged in unmarked cardboard boxes since they had been stored in bins in a private cellar.

8. *Rare, mature vintages in large formats:* Great wines from ancient rare vintages such as 1900, 1921, 1926, 1928, 1929, 1945, 1947, 1949, and 1950 (especially the Pomerols) that are offered in large formats, particularly double magnums, jeroboams, imperials, and the extremely rare Marie-Jeanne (a three-bottle size), should be scrutinized with the utmost care. Christian Moueix told me that a European vendor had offered rare vintages of Pétrus in Marie-Jeanne formats. To the best of Moueix's knowledge, Pétrus never used Marie-Jeanne bottles! Large formats of rare old vintages were used very sparingly at most top châteaux, so if you contemplate purchasing an imperial of 1900 Margaux, be sure to verify the wine's authenticity.

9. *Common sense:* The need to develop a relationship with experienced and reputable merchants is obvious, but too often consumers are seduced by the lowest price. If it is an $8 Corbières, that's fine, but a prized vintage of a first growth Bordeaux is not likely to be sold cheaply.

I hope the industry will address these issues in a more forthright manner and begin to take more action designed to protect its members as well as consumers. Additionally, I urge those renowned estates that benefit from glowing reviews to recognize that it is only in their long-term interest to relentlessly seek a solution to this problem, and combine their efforts and resources to track down those responsible for fabricating fraudulent bottles of expensive wine. Surely the time has come for more sophisticated labels (with serial numbers and watermarks), designer bottles that are less easy to replicate, and capsules with vintages and vineyard names. An open avenue of communication with the wine buyer, where these frauds can be identified and confirmed, and the commercial and consumer marketplace fully apprised of the problem, is essential to preserve the authenticity of the world's finest wines, as well as the integrity and security of purchasing fine wine.

What Constitutes a Great Wine?

What is a great wine? One of the most controversial subjects of the vinous world, isn't greatness in wine, much like a profound expression of art or music, something very personal and subjective? Much as I agree that the appreciation and enjoyment of art, music, or wine is indeed personal, high quality in wine, as in art and music, does tend to be subject to widespread agreement. Except for the occasional contrarian, greatness in art, music, or wine, if difficult to define precisely, enjoys a broad consensus.

Many of the most legendary wines of this century—1945 Mouton-Rothschild, 1945 Haut-Brion, 1947 Cheval Blanc, 1947 Pétrus, 1961 Latour, 1982 Mouton-Rothschild, 1982 Le Pin, 1982 Léoville-Las Cases, 1989 Haut-Brion, 1990 Château Margaux, and 1990 Pétrus, to name some of the most renowned red Bordeaux—are profound and riveting wines, even though an occasional discordant view about them may surface. Tasting is indeed subjective, but like most of the finest things in life, though there is considerable agreement as to what represents high quality, no one should feel forced to feign fondness for a work of Picasso or Beethoven, much less a bottle of 1961 Latour.

One issue about the world's finest wines that is subject to little controversy relates to how such wines originate. Frankly, there are no secrets to the origin and production of the world's finest wines. Great wines emanate from well-placed vineyards with microclimates favorable to the specific types of grapes grown. Profound wines, whether from France, Italy, Spain, California, or Australia, are also the product of conservative viticultural practices that emphasize low yields and physiologically rather than analytically ripe fruit. After 19 years spent tasting over 200,000 wines, I have never tasted a superb wine made from underripe fruit. Does anyone enjoy the flavors present when biting into an underripe orange, peach, apricot, or cherry? Low yields and ripe fruit are essential for the production of extraordinary wines, yet it is amazing how many wineries never seem to understand this fundamental principle.

In addition to the commonsense approach of harvesting mature (ripe) fruit, and discouraging, in a viticultural sense, the vine from overproducing, the philosophy employed by a winery in making wine is of paramount importance. Exceptional wines (whether red, white, or sparkling) emerge from a similar philosophy, which includes the following: 1) permit the vineyard's *terroir* (soil, microclimate, distinctiveness) to express itself; 2) allow the purity and characteristics of the grape varietal or blend of varietals to be represented faithfully in the wine; 3) follow an uncompromising, noninterventionalistic winemaking philosophy that eschews the food-processing, industrial mind-set of high-tech winemaking—in short, give the wine a chance to make itself naturally without the human element attempting to sculpture or alter the wine's intrinsic character, so that what is placed in the bottle represents as natural an expression of the vineyard, varietal, and vintage as is possible. In keeping with this overall philosophy, wine-makers who attempt to reduce traumatic clarification procedures such as fining and filtration, while also lowering sulfur levels (which can dry out a wine's fruit, bleach color from a wine, and exacerbate the tannin's sharpness) produce wines with far more aromatics and flavors, as well as more enthralling textures. These are wines that offer consumers their most compelling and rewarding drinking experiences.

Assuming there is a relatively broad consensus as to how the world's finest wines originate, what follows is my working definition of an exceptional wine. In short, what are the characteristics of a great wine?

The Ability to Please Both the Palate and the Intellect
Great wines offer satisfaction on a hedonistic level and also challenge and satiate the intellect. The world offers many delicious wines that appeal to the senses but are not complex. The ability to satisfy the intellect is a more subjective issue. Wines that experts call "complex" are those that offer multiple dimensions in both their aromatic and flavor profiles, and have more going for them than simply ripe fruit and a satisfying, pleasurable, yet one-dimensional quality.

CLASSIC EXAMPLES
1990 Dom Perignon Champagne
1994 Philip Togni Cabernet Sauvignon Napa
1999 Guigal Côte Rôtie La Mouline
1995 Müller-Catoir Mussbacher Eselhart Rieslaner
1999 Turley Cellars Zinfandel Hayne Vineyard
2001 Clarendon Hills Old Vine Grenache Blewitt Vineyard

The Ability to Hold the Taster's Interest

I have often remarked that the greatest wines I've ever tasted could easily be recognized by bouquet alone. These profound wines could never be called monochromatic or simple. They hold the taster's interest, not only providing the initial tantalizing tease but possessing a magnetic attraction in their aromatic intensity and nuanced layers of flavors.

CLASSIC EXAMPLES

1999 Chapoutier Hermitage Pavillon
1998 l'Evangile (Pomerol)
1995 Soldera Brunello di Montalcino
1999 Peter Michael Chardonnay Point Rouge
1997 Baumard Savennières Cuvée Spéciale
1997 Bryant Family Vineyard Cabernet Sauvignon Napa

The Ability to Offer Intense Aromas and Flavors Without Heaviness

An analogy can be made to eating in the finest restaurants. Extraordinary cooking is characterized by purity, intensity, balance, texture, and compelling aromas and flavors. What separates exceptional cuisine from merely good cooking, and great wines from good wines, is their ability to deliver extraordinary intensity of flavor without heaviness. It has been easy in the New World (especially in Australia and California) to produce wines that are oversized, bold, big, rich, but heavy. Europe's finest wineries, with many centuries more experience, have mastered the ability to obtain intense flavors without heaviness. However, New World viticultural areas (particularly in California) are quickly catching up, as evidenced by the succession of remarkable wines produced in Napa, Sonoma, and elsewhere in the Golden State during the 1990s. Many of California's greatest wines of the 1990s have sacrificed none of their power and richness, but no longer possess the rustic tannin and oafish feel on the palate that characterized so many of their predecessors of 10 and 20 years ago.

CLASSIC EXAMPLES

1995 Coche-Dury Corton Charlemagne
1997 Claude Dugat Griottes-Chambertin
1990 Bruno Giacosa Barbaresco Santo Stefano
2001 Yves Cuilleron Condrieu Vieilles Vignes
1995 Leflaive Chevalier-Montrachet
2000 Paul Cotat Sancerre Les Monts Damnes

The Ability of a Wine to Taste Better with Each Sip

Most of the finest wines I have ever drunk were better with the last sip than the first, revealing more nuances and more complex aromas and flavors as the wine unfolded in the glass. Do readers ever wonder why the most interesting and satisfying glass of wine is often the last one in the bottle?

CLASSIC EXAMPLES

1996 Marcassin Chardonnay Marcassin Vineyard
1996 Mouton-Rothschild (Pauillac)
1994 Fonseca Vintage Port
1996 Léoville-Las Cases (St.-Julien)
1994 Taylor Vintage Port
1999 Montiano Umbria
1998 l'Eglise-Clinet (Pomerol)
1994 Screaming Eagle Cabernet Sauvignon Napa

The Ability of a Wine to Improve with Age

This is, for better or worse, an indisputable characteristic of great wines. One of the unhealthy legacies of the European wine writers (who dominated wine writing until the last decade) is the belief that in order for a wine to be exceptional when mature, it had to be nasty when young. My experience has revealed just the opposite—wines that are acidic, astringent, and generally fruitless and charmless when young become even nastier and less drinkable when old. That being said, it is true that new vintages of top wines are often unformed and in need of 10–12 years of cellaring (in the case of top California Cabernets, Bordeaux, and Rhône wines), but those wines should always possess a certain accessibility so that even inexperienced wine tasters can tell the wine is—at the minimum—made from very ripe fruit. If a wine does not exhibit ripeness and richness of fruit when young, it will not develop nuances with aging. Great wines unquestionably improve with age. I define "improvement" as the ability of a wine to become significantly more enjoyable and interesting in the bottle, offering more pleasure old than when it was young. Many wineries (especially in the New World) produce wines they claim "will age," but this is nothing more than a public relations ploy. What they should really say is that they "will survive." They can endure 10–20 years of bottle age, but they were more enjoyable in their exuberant youthfulness.

CLASSIC EXAMPLES
1982 Latour (Pauillac)
1971 G. Conterno Barolo Monfortino
1989 Haut-Brion (Graves)
1998 Beaucastel Châteauneuf-du-Pape
1985 Sassicaia (Tuscany)
1990 Climens (Barsac/Sauternes)
1994 Laville-Haut-Brion (Graves)

The Ability of a Wine to Offer a Singular Personality

Their singular personalities set the greatest wines produced apart from all others. It is the same with the greatest vintages. The abused usage of a description such as "classic vintage" has become nothing more than a reference to what a viticultural region does in a typical (normal) year. Exceptional wines from exceptional vintages stand far above the norm, and they can always be defined by their singular qualities—both aromatically and in their flavors and textures. The opulent, sumptuous qualities of the 1982 and 1990 red Bordeaux; the rugged tannin and immense ageability of the 1986 red Bordeaux; the seamless, perfectly balanced 1994 Napa and Sonoma Cabernet Sauvignons and proprietary blends; and the plush, sweet fruit, high alcohol, and glycerin of the 1990 Barolos and Barbarescos are all examples of vintage individuality.

CLASSIC EXAMPLES
1990 Tertre-Rôteboeuf (St.-Emilion)
1990 Sandrone Barolo Boschis
1989 Clinet (Pomerol)
1991 Dominus Proprietary Red Wine Napa
1994 Colgin Cabernet Sauvignon Napa
1992 Beringer Cabernet Sauvignon Private Reserve Napa
1982 Mouton-Rothschild (Pauillac)
1986 Château Margaux (Margaux)
1996 Lafite-Rothschild (Pauillac)

MAKING SENSE OF *TERROIR*

> "Knowing in part may make a fine tale,
> but wisdom comes from seeing the whole."—An Asian proverb

And so it is with the concept of *"terroir,"* that hazy, intellectually appealing notion that a plot of soil plays the determining factor in a wine's character. The French are the world's most obsessed people regarding the issue of *terroir*. And why not? Many of that country's most renowned vineyards are part of an elaborate hierarchy of quality based on their soil and exposition. And the French would have everyone believe that no one on planet Earth can equal the quality of their Pinot Noir, Chardonnay, Cabernet, Syrah, etc., because their privileged *terroir* is unequaled. One of France's most celebrated wine regions, Burgundy, is often cited as the best place to search for the fullest expression of *terroir*. Proponents of *terroir* (the terroirists) argue that a particular piece of ground and its contribution to what is grown there give its product a character distinctive and apart from that same product grown on different soils and slopes. Burgundy, with its classifications of grand cru and premier cru vineyards, village vineyards, and generic viticultural areas, is the terroirists' "raison d'être."

Lamentably, *terroir* has become such a politically correct buzzword that in some circles it is an egregious error not to utter some profound comments about finding "a sense of somewhereness" when tasting a Vosne-Romanée Les Malconsorts or a Latricières-Chambertin. Leading terroirists such as wine producer Lalou Bize-Leroy, Burgundy wine broker Becky Wasserman, and author Matt Kramer make a persuasive and often eloquent case about the necessity of finding, as Kramer puts it, "the true voice of the land" in order for a wine to be legitimized.

Yet like so many things about wine, especially tasting it, there is no scientific basis for anything Bize, Wasserman, or Kramer propose. What they argue is what most Burgundians and owners of France's finest vineyards give lip service to—that for a wine to be authentic and noble it must speak of its *terroir*.

On the other side of this issue are the "realists," or should I call them modernists. They suggest that *terroir* is merely one of many factors that influence the style of a wine. The realists argue that a multitude of factors determine a wine's style, quality, and character. Soil, exposition, and microclimate *(terroir)* most certainly impart an influence, but so do the following:

1. Rootstock—Is it designed to produce prolific or small crop levels?

2. Yeasts—Does the wine-maker use the vineyard's wild yeasts or are commercial yeasts employed? Every yeast, wild or commercial, will give a wine a different set of aromatics, flavor, and texture.

3. Yields and vine age—High yields from perennial overcroppers result in diluted wine. Low yields, usually less than two tons per acre or 35–40 hectoliters per hectare, result in wines with much more concentration and personality. Additionally, young vines have a tendency to overproduce, whereas old vines produce small berries and less wine. Crop thinning is often employed with younger vineyards to increase the level of concentration.

4. Harvest philosophy—Is the fruit picked underripe to preserve more acidity, or fully ripe to emphasize the lushness and opulence of a given varietal?

5. Vinification techniques and equipment—There are an amazing number of techniques that can change the wine's aromas and flavors. Moreover, equipment choice (different presses, destemmers, etc.) can have a profound influence on the final wine.

6. *Élevage* (or the wine's upbringing)—Is the wine brought up in oak barrels, concrete vats, stainless steel, or large oak vats (which the French call *foudres*)? What is the percentage of new oak? What is the type of oak (French, Russian, American, etc.)? All of these elements exert a strong influence on the wine's character. Additionally, transferring wine

(racking) from one container to another has an immense impact on a wine's bouquet and flavor. Is the wine allowed to remain in long contact with its lees (believed to give the wine more aromatic complexity and fullness)? Or is it racked frequently for fear of picking up an undesirable lees smell?

7. Fining and filtration—Even the most concentrated and profound wines that terroirists consider quintessential examples of the soil can be eviscerated and stripped of their personality and richness by excessive fining and filtering. Does the wine-maker treat the wine with kid gloves, or is the wine-maker a manufacturer/processor bent on sculpturing the wine?

8. Bottling date—Does the wine-maker bottle early to preserve as much fruit as possible, or does he bottle later to give the wine a more mellow, aged character? Undoubtedly, the philosophy of when to bottle can radically alter the character of a wine.

9. Cellar temperature and sanitary conditions—Some wine cellars are cold and others are warm. Different wines emerge from cold cellars (development is slower and the wines are less prone to oxidation) than from warm cellars (the maturation of aromas and flavors is more rapid and the wines are quicker to oxidize). Additionally, are the wine cellars clean or dirty?

These are just a handful of factors that can have extraordinary impact on the style, quality, and personality of a wine. As the modernists claim, the choices that man himself makes, even when they are unquestionably in pursuit of the highest quality, can contribute far more to a wine's character than the vineyard's *terroir*.

If one listens to Robert Kacher, a realist, or to Matt Kramer, a terroirist, it is easy to conclude that they inhabit different worlds. But the irony is that in most cases, they tend to agree as to the producers making the finest wines.

If you are wondering where I stand on *terroir*, I do believe it is an important component in the production of fine wine. If one is going to argue *terroir*, the wine has to be made from exceptionally low yields, fermented with only the wild yeasts that inhabit the vineyard, brought up in a neutral medium such as old barrels, cement tanks, or stainless steel, given minimal cellar treatment, and bottled with little or no fining or filtration. However, I would argue that the most persuasive examples of *terroir* arise not from Burgundy but, rather, from Alsace or Austria.

If I were to take up the cause of the terroirists, I would use one of Alsace's greatest domaines, that of Leonard and Olivier Humbrecht, to make a modest case for *terroir*. The Humbrechts do everything to emphasize the differences in their vineyard holdings. Yet, why is it so easy to identify the wines of Zind-Humbrecht in a blind tasting? Certainly their Hengst-Riesling tastes different from their Riesling from Clos St.-Urbain. The question is, is one tasting the *terroir* or the wine-maker's signature? Zind-Humbrecht's wines, when matched against other Alsatian wines, are more powerful, rich, and intense. Zind-Humbrecht's yields are lower and they do not filter the wine at bottling. These wines possess not only an identifiable wine-maker's signature but also a distinctive vineyard character.

Terroir, as used by many of its proponents, is often a convenient excuse for upholding the status quo. If one accepts that *terroir* is everything, and is essential to legitimize a wine, how should consumers evaluate the wines from Burgundy's most famous grand cru vineyard, Chambertin? This 32-acre vineyard boasts 23 different proprietors. But only a handful of them appear committed to producing an extraordinary wine. Everyone agrees this is a hallowed piece of ground, but I can think of only a few—Domaine Leroy, Domaine Ponsot, Domaine Rousseau, and Trapet—producing wines that merit the stratospheric reputation of this vineyard. Yet the Chambertins of these producers are completely different in style. The Trapet wine is the most elegant, supple, and round, Leroy's is the most tannic, backward, concentrated, and meaty, and Rousseau's is the darkest-colored, most dominated by new oak, and most modern in style, taste, and texture. Among the other 18 or 20 producers (and I am not even thinking about the various *négociant* offerings), what Burgundy wine enthusiasts are likely to encounter on retailers' shelves ranges from mediocre to appallingly thin and insipid.

What wine, may I ask, speaks for the soil of Chambertin? Is it the wine of Leroy, the wine of Trapet, or the wine of Rousseau? Arguments such as this can be made with virtually any significant Bordeaux or Burgundy vineyard. Which has that notion of "somewhereness" that is raised by the terroirists to validate the quality of a vineyard?

Are terroirists kindergarten intellectuals who should be doing more tasting and less talking? Of course not. But they can be accused of naively swallowing the tallest tale in Burgundy. On the other hand, the realists should recognize that no matter how intense and concentrated a wine can be from a modest vineyard in Givry, it will never have the sheer complexity and class of a Vosne-Romanée grand cru from a conscientious producer.

In conclusion, think of *terroir* as you do salt, pepper, and garlic. In many dishes they can represent an invaluable component, imparting wonderful aromas and flavors, yet alone, they do not make the dish. Moreover, all the hyperventilation over *terroir* obscures the most important issue of all—identifying and discovering those producers who make wines worth drinking and savoring!

RECOMMENDED READING

Following is a personal list of publications and books I have found to offer authoritative information and reliable opinion on the world's wines.

JOURNALS AND MAGAZINES

La Revue du Vin de France, 38–48 Rue Victor-Hugo, 92532 Levallios-Perret, France; fax 011 33 1 41 40 23 09. France's leading wine magazine is available only in French, but if you are bilingual and a French wine enthusiast, this is a must-read. Europe's finest taster, Michel Bettane, has left the teaching profession to write full-time for this magazine, only enhancing its value. In addition to Bettane, a group of highly respected tasters contribute extremely well written articles on French vineyards and producers. The magazine does accept advertising.

International Wine Cellar, PO Box 20021, Cherokee Station, New York, NY 10021; telephone 1-800-WINE-505. $54 for six bimonthly issues, written by Stephen Tanzer and others. For over a decade Stephen Tanzer has published *International Wine Cellar*. Tanzer is a fine taster and a good writer, and his publication, which accepts no advertising, is extremely reliable for both European and American wines. If you are seriously interested in the upscale wine market, this is an essential publication.

The Wine Advocate, PO Box 311, Monkton, MD 21111; telephone (410) 329-6477. $50 for six bimonthly issues, written by a guy named Robert M. Parker, Jr. Much of this book is based on articles and tasting notes that have appeared in my journal aimed at the serious wine enthusiast. The publication accepts no advertising.

Decanter, Broadway House, 1st Floor, 2-6 Fulham Broadway, London SW6 5UE, UK; fax 011 44 20 7381 5282. England's dominant wine publication, *Decanter* gives readers a British point of view. The wine tastings and notes are well behind the state-of-the-art tastings that emerge from American publications, but some of the feature pieces are very good if you like the conservative British point of view.

The Wine Spectator, (subscriptions) PO Box 37367, Boone, IA 50037-0367; telephone 1-800-752-7799. $50 per year. The world's most widely read wine magazine. Publisher Marvin Shanken continues to fine-tune and improve an already strong magazine devoted to covering the wines of the world. No one does a better job in keeping its readers abreast of current events in the wine world. Mixing restaurant pieces with extensive wine ratings, as well as highly laudable articles on traveling in various wine regions, food and wine matchups, interesting recipes, and profiles of leading wine personalities, publisher Shanken has built this onetime obscure newsletter into a serious publication read around the world. This magazine is required reading for wine enthusiasts. It does accept advertising.

BOOKS

Burton Anderson, *Vino* (New York: Alfred Knopf) and *The Wine Atlas of Italy* (New York: Simon & Schuster). *Vino* was a breakthrough on the importance and potential of Italian wine. *The Wine Atlas of Italy* is a very good reference book for the wine regions of that beautiful country.

Alexis Bespaloff, *Frank Schoonmaker's Encyclopedia* (New York: William Morrow). This dry but well-researched reference should be a part of all wine enthusiasts' libraries.

Thierry Bettane and Michel Desseauve, *Le Classement 2001* (Luxembourg: Wine and Food Data International). This is a Michelin Guide–styled book that rates those French wine producers Bettane and Desseauve consider the finest. It is based on a one- to three-star system and includes a short synopsis on each estate. Tasting notes are nonexistent, which is a flaw.

Michael Broadbent, *The Great Vintage Wine Book, editions I and II* (London: Mitchell Beazley). Broadbent was the first to make an art out of exceptionally descriptive and meaningful tasting notes. Moreover, he is a gifted taster whose experience in classic, older Bordeaux vintages is unmatched.

Stephen Brook, *Bordeaux, The People, Power, and Politics* (London: Mitchell Beazley), and *Wine People* (New York: Vendange Press). An excellent look at the world of Bordeaux through the eyes of one of the most talented British wine writers. Brook's candid analysis of Bordeaux is topflight. *Wine People* consists of mini profiles and biographies of people whom Stephen Brook considers the who's who of wine. It is a stylish, handsome book, but there are major omissions, as well as some dubious entries. Nevertheless, this beautifully done book is a worthy addition to wine literature.

Oz Clarke, *Essential Wine Book, Annual Wine Guide*, and *Regional Wine Guides* (New York: Simon & Schuster). These lively, informative, well-written books from this multitalented English wine writer offer a candor and lively prose more typical of the American wine-writing style than the English. The witty Oz Clarke is also a terrific taster.

James M. Gabler, *Wine Into Words—A History and Bibliography of Wine Books in the English Language* (Baltimore: Bacchus Press). This superbly organized, comprehensive book needs to be updated, but it is an essential contribution to the history of wine writing, as well as a much-needed reference work.

Rosemary George, *The Wines of the South of France* (London: Faber & Faber). The first book dedicated to extensive coverage of France's Languedoc-Roussillon region. It is an exceptionally well written book from one of Britain's least known but most professional as well as respected Masters of Wine.

James Halliday, *The Wine Atlas of Australia and New Zealand* and *The Wine Atlas of California* (New York: Viking Press). These two extraordinary classic guides on two important wine regions are unequaled in their scope and quality. While the atlas on Australia and New Zealand is impressive, Halliday's tome on California is a tour de force, offering the finest perspective of California wine yet authored. It is destined to be a reference for years to come.

Hugh Johnson, *Modern Encyclopedia of Wine, The History of Wine*, and *The World Atlas of Wine* (New York: Simon & Schuster). These classic reference books written by the world's best-selling wine writer should be part of every wine lover's library. In 2001, the *Atlas* was brilliantly updated and enlarged with significant contributions by English prima donna Jancis Robinson.

Matt Kramer, *Making Sense of Wine, Making Sense of California*, and *Making Sense of Burgundy* (New York: William Morrow). Whether you agree or disagree with winedom's most articulate terroirist, Kramer's provocative books offer aggravating as well as controversial insights and perspectives that are required reading. It is of little importance to Kramer that he is incapable of proving much of what he postulates, but the ride he gives readers is well worth the price of admission.

John Livingstone-Learmonth, *The Wines of the Rhône Valley* (London: Faber & Faber). One of the finest books on the great wines of the Rhône Valley, this reliable guide is a must-purchase for partisans of the wines from this great winemaking region.

Jay McInerney, *Bacchus and Me: Adventures in the Wine Cellar* (New York: The Lyons Press). The famous novelist known for *Bright Lights, Big City* turns his irreverent pen and palate to wine. The result is a splendid wine adventure that showcases his immense writing skills and surprisingly gifted palate.

Robert M. Parker, Jr., *Bordeaux, Burgundy,* and *The Wines of the Rhône Valley and Provence* (New York: Simon & Schuster). All three books are comprehensive consumer guides offering passionate but critical, independent, and uncensored views of three important winemaking regions.

Edmund Penning-Rowsell, *The Wines of Bordeaux* (London: Penguin Books). A classic reference for the history of Bordeaux, and its most renowned proprietors and their châteaux.

Jancis Robinson, *Vines, Grapes, and Wines* (New York: Alfred Knopf); *Vintage Time Charts* (London: Weidenfeld & Nicholson); and *The Oxford Companion to Wine* (New York: Oxford University Press). A gifted wine writer, Robinson's three classics are authoritative evidence of this woman's seemingly infinite ability to fashion informative, accurate books that are essential reading.

Norman S. Roby and Charles E. Olken, *The New Connoisseurs' Handbook of California Wines* (New York: Alfred A. Knopf). This mini A-to-Z reference on West Coast wines reads as if it were written by a government accountant, but it does provide valuable thumbnail sketches of virtually all Oregon, Washington, and California wineries.

Andrew Sharp, *Wine Taster's Secrets—A Step by Step Guide to the Art of Wine Tasting* (Toronto: Warwick). An extremely well written book with the most informative and perceptive chapters on wine tasting I have read. This is the finest book for both beginners and serious wine collectors about the actual tasting process—lively, definitive, and candid.

Steven Spurrier and Michel Dovaz, *Académie du Vin Introductory Course to Wine* (London: Willow Books). Along with Kevin Zraley's classic, this is one of the finest guides to winedom for beginners.

Tom Stevenson, *The Wines of Alsace* (London: Faber & Faber). The definitive work on the underrated wines of Alsace. Extremely thorough, accurate, and erudite, this is a must-purchase for enthusiasts of these wines.

James Suckling, *Vintage Port* (New York: The Wine Spectator Press). This is the only reliable, comprehensive consumer's guide to vintage port. Suckling's exceptionally well done book merits considerable attention from port enthusiasts.

Harry Waugh, *Harry Waugh's Diaries* (publisher unknown). In late November 2001, at age 97, Harry Waugh died. One of the greatest gentlemen ever to inhabit the wine world, Waugh was an extraordinary ambassador for the joys of wine connoisseurship. I recall fondly his lectures stateside when he toured on behalf of Les Amis du Vin. I remember even better a blind tasting of 1975 Bordeaux in London in the mid-1980s. Waugh, who had lost his sense of smell because of an automobile accident, correctly identified more of the 1975s than any of the distinguished group of participants, which included Michael Broadbent, Edmund Penning-Rowsell, Clive Coates, and me. About one wine he said, "I'm sad I can't smell it because the weight and texture suggest it must be the 1975 Latour." Of course he was right. His multiple-volume series *Harry Waugh's Diaries* were written records of his tastings—candid, refreshing, and always informative. I'm sure they can still be found on Internet Web sites dedicated to purchasing books.

Alan Young, *Making Sense of Wine Tasting* (Sydney: Lennard). An underrated book from an Australian who has clearly given an exceptional amount of thought to the process of tasting wine, this classic has remained undiscovered by much of the world's wine press.

Kevin Zraley, *Windows on the World Wine Course* (New York: Sterling Press). This is the finest introductory guide to wine. I highly recommend it to readers who are trying to get a handle on the complicated world of vino. A fun and very informed read. Even connoisseurs who think they already know it all will learn something from Zraley's classic.

THE WINE WORLD'S BIGGEST LIES

15. The reason the price is so high is because the wine is rare and great.
14. You probably had a "corked" bottle.
13. It is going through a dumb period.
12. We ship and store all our wines in temperature-controlled containers.
11. You didn't let it breathe long enough.
10. You let it breathe too long.
9. Sediment is a sign of a badly made wine.
8. Boy, are you lucky—this is my last bottle (case).
7. Just give it a few years.
6. We picked before the rains.
5. The rain was highly localized; we were lucky it missed our vineyard.
4. There's a lot more to the wine business than just moving boxes.
3. Parker (or *The Wine Spectator*) is going to give it a 94 in the next issue.
2. This is the greatest wine we have ever made and, coincidentally, it is the only wine we now have to sell.
1. It's supposed to smell and taste like that.

A TONGUE-IN-CHEEK GUIDE TO UNDERSTANDING
THE LANGUAGE OF THE WINE-MAKER

What They Say in the Vineyard/Winery	*What They Really Mean in Plain English*
1. This is a classic vintage for cellaring!	The wine is excessively tannic, and it will undoubtedly lose most of its fruit long before the tannin melts away.
2. This is a supple, fruity wine that is very commercial.	This is a thin, diluted, watery wine made from a vineyard that was atrociously overcropped. It should have a shelf life of 1–4 years.
3. One can sense the nobility of *terroir* in the aromas and taste of this wine.	The weather during the growing season and harvest was so cold and wet that the grapes never matured, some even rotted, and the wine tastes only of acidity, tannin, wood, alcohol, and copious quantities of damp earth—*terroir* triumphs again.
4. We were fortunate enough to harvest before the rain.	We harvested before the last deluge (and we forgot to inform you that prior to the last inundation it had rained heavily for the previous 5–10 days).
5. This is a classic vintage in the style of the great traditional years of the region.	Once again we did not have enough sunshine and heat to ripen the grapes, thus we produced wines that are hard, acidic, angular, compact, and tannic from underripe fruit. Only a fool would buy this.
6. Do you want to taste my wines?	I actually have one or two barrels of exquisite *cuvée vieilles vignes* made from exceptionally ripe fruit that I set aside for

7. Those people who follow organic or biodynamic farming in the vineyard are phony, pseudoviticulturists.

all my importers, clients, and those nosy, obtrusive wine writers in order to give them an impression of what I am capable of achieving.

We use every chemical treatment known to man—insecticides, herbicides, tons of nitrogen and other fertilizers, including Miracle-Gro, in an effort to kill everything in the vineyard, except of course, the vine!

8. Mr. Parker knows nothing.

We cannot influence him, nor can we bribe him. A shameful man, he doesn't even write in his publication what we tell him to. Why can't we go back to the old days when we could stuff a trunkful of samples into a wine critic's car and get the reviews we desired?

9. This is the greatest wine I have ever made in my life.

This is the only wine we have to sell.

10. This wine is closed and needs time because it has just been recently bottled.

The malady of the bottling is a myth because anybody who bottles naturally, with very low SO_2 and no fining or filtering, knows perfectly well that the wine tastes just as good in the bottle as it did in the cask. However, we are modern-day industrialists or, as we say, "wine processors." We utilize large quantities of sulfur, and, in addition, we eviscerate our wines by abusive fining and filtering. Thus we use the *"maladie à la mise"* excuse to justify the poor performance of our wines. If the truth be known, our wines have been stripped, nuked, and denuded, and they are incapable of improvement in the future. (Amazingly, writers and buyers have been swallowing this B.S. for at least the last four decades!)

11. Parker (or any other wine critic/writer) never tasted my wine!

I did not get a 90-point score.

12. Parker (or any other wine critic/writer) likes only heavily oaked, internationally styled fruit bombs.

I did not get a 90-point score.

WINE ON THE INTERNET

While the Internet has not proven to be as valuable for wine consumers as I had anticipated, there are some sites with strong followings that offer important consumer feedback. The problem with these sites is that participants have to be careful of misinformation being spread by cyberterrorists who represent competing wines or have malicious hidden agendas and do not reveal their connections to the wine trade or personal bias. Nevertheless, there are numerous fine sources for wine-buying information as well as travel tips. Following is a list of the best of these.

www.wineloverspage.com: A popular and comprehensive Internet site run by Robin Garr. It has a strong following and dynamic, active message board with good postings by an enthusiastic membership.

www.marksquires'E-Zineonwine.com: The most civilized wine discussion board on the Internet. Lawyer Mark Squires keeps the rantings, whinings, and misinformation levels at a minimum, and thus the discussions tend to be well focused, intense, and informative. For me, this is the most serious of the wine discussion boards.

www.winespectator.com: This popular site offers subscription-only access to the *Spectator*'s database, along with free daily news articles that are of considerable interest. Aesthetically, it is one of the most attractive wine sites. The discussion forums have never captured much interest.

www.decanter.com: This site should be better than it is, but it is often worth checking out for news items and that quirky British point of view.

www.magnumvinum.fr: This French site actually sells wine but also incorporates a message board for members of *The Revue du Vin de France* magazine. It is in French, but for those who read this language, it is worthwhile.

www.westcoastwine.net: Brad Harrington runs this excellent site, which, along with Mark Squires's, is one of the purist sites for wine-tasting notes and interesting thoughts from the membership. Like the Squires site, there is rarely much whining, and the tasting notes are candid, honest, and for the most part reliable. A lot of top palates inhabit this site and generously share their thoughts on the world's wines. This is one of my favorite sites to surf.

www.communities.msn@at/bordeauxwineenthusiast/messageboard.msnw: Another terrific place to find well-reasoned tasting notes, this site leans toward the great wines of Bordeaux. Neither extreme egos nor taste bashers are tolerated, thus the name-calling and rants common on many sites are not found on this serious, highly informative site. It is available in many languages.

www.wine-pages.com: This superb site focuses on the UK wine scene. It is an all-inclusive site with excellent postings as well as a British perspective. It is a friendly, easily navigated site with plenty of bells and whistles.

www.jancisrobinson.com: Jancis Robinson is one of Britain's leading ladies of wine. Her Web site is basic, but she charges a subscription fee for access to her "purple pages." It seems overpriced for the material offered, but no one should ignore the musings of the chatty Jancis.

www.wineanorak.com: This excellent site, run by Jamie Goode, is very British/Euro focused, and thus may be of less interest to North Americans. Nevertheless, it offers considerable value. The attention to wine novices is a particularly useful attraction.

www.wine-people.com: A user-friendly site, with excellent tasting notes and commentary from one of the most reliable but underrated sources for wine information, Arthur Johnson.

www.eRobertParker.com: This site is by subscription only (at the lofty price of $100 per year), but readers have access to over a decade's worth of *Wine Advocate* tasting notes, as well as never-released tasting and dining commentaries by two very serious eaters and imbibers—Pierre Rovani and Robert Parker. In addition to the enormous amount of resource material available, it is an extremely fast site operationally.

THE WINES OF WESTERN EUROPE

France
Alsace
Bordeaux
Burgundy and Beaujolais
Champagne
The Loire Valley
The Languedoc-Roussillon
Provence
The Rhône Valley
Bergerac and the Southwest

Italy
Piedmont
Tuscany
Other Significant Red Wines of Italy

Germany and Austria

Spain and Portugal

1. FRANCE

ALSACE

Which viticultural area produces the most versatile white wines to match with food? What region continues to be an underutilized source of amazing values? Where do top wine professionals and true connoisseurs turn for whites of extraordinary aging potential, immediate hedonistic appeal, and affordable daily drinking?

The answer to all these questions is Alsace, a fairy-tale viticultural area in northeastern France and one of the most beautiful wine-producing regions on earth.

True connoisseurs of wine must find it appalling that so many importers trip over each other trying to find yet another excessively priced, overcropped, generally insipid Italian white or overacidified Australian Chardonnay that provides little joy, while ignoring the treasures of Alsace. Why have these wines failed to earn the popularity they so richly deserve?

For consumers who love wine with food, Alsace produces many dry, surprisingly flavorful, personality-filled wines that generally offer superb value for the dollar. Alsace also makes it easy for the consumer to understand its wines. As in California, the wines are named after the grape varietal used to make them and, in addition, one of Alsace's 51 grand cru vineyards can be annexed to the name of the varietal. When that occurs, it usually means the wine sells at a price two to three times higher than wines that do not come from grand cru vineyards.

Another remarkable aspect of Alsace wines is how long-lived a top Riesling, Gewurztraminer, and Tokay-Pinot Gris can be. Ten to twenty years of longevity is not out of the question for the totally dry, regular *cuvées* and grands crus, while the rich, opulent Vendange Tardive and the supersweet, luxuriously priced dessert wines called Sélection de Grains Nobles can survive and benefit from even longer bottle age.

However, uninitiated consumers are typically reluctant to try wines from Alsace. Alsatian bottles are shaped like those from Germany, and many consumers refuse even to taste them because they dislike the stylistically different German wines, or still have bad memories of the torrents of insipid Liebfraumilchs and Piesporters sold in the U.S. in the 1960s and 1970s. In European markets, the sales of quality producers are negatively affected by the massive quantities of industrially crafted, tasteless wines made from high-yielding vineyards on the Alsatian plain (fields that are better suited to growing cabbages for sauerkraut, the main ingredient of Alsace's most famous dish: choucroute garni). Thankfully, these wines do not reach American shores. Also, Alsatian wines (even those that are completely dry) tend to be fruity and personality-filled, something that shocks consumers accustomed to tasteless or oak-dominated whites. Finally, and this is a problem Alsatian producers need to resolve (for their own benefit), many wines whose labels would lead a consumer to believe they were

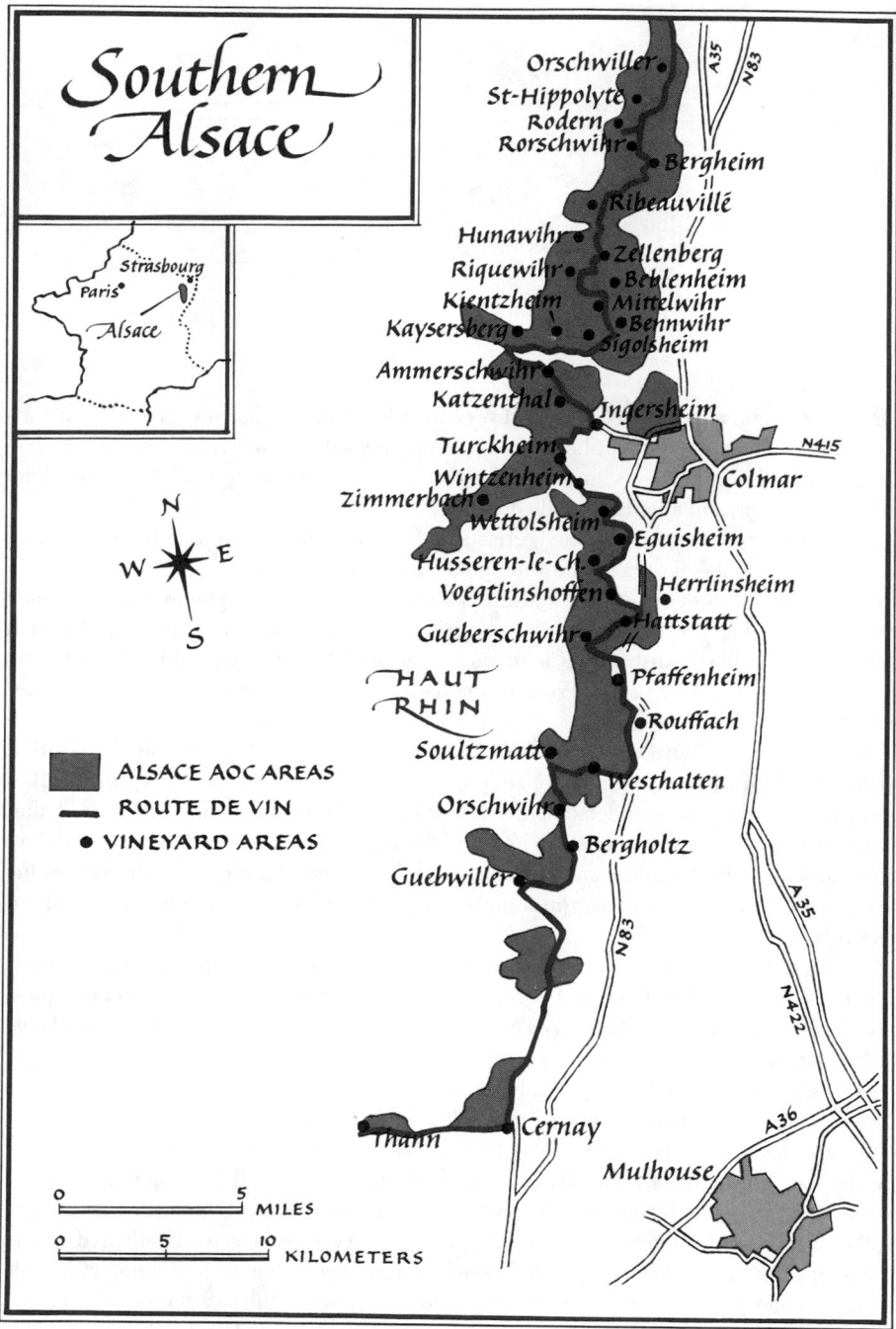

Southern Alsace

Orschwiller
St-Hippolyte
Rodern
Rorschwihr
Bergheim
Ribeauvillé
Hunawihr
Zellenberg
Riquewihr
Beblenheim
Kientzheim
Mitelwihr
Kaysersberg
Bennwihr
Sigolsheim
Ammerschwihr
Katzenthal
Ingersheim
Turckheim
Wintzenheim
Colmar
Zimmerbach
Wettolsheim
Eguisheim
Husseren-le-Ch.
Herrlinsheim
Voegtlinshoffen
Hattstatt
Gueberschwihr

HAUT
RHIN
Pfaffenheim
Rouffach
Soultzmatt
Orschwihr
Westhalten
Bergholtz
Guebwiller

Thann
Cernay
Mulhouse

Strasbourg
Paris
Alsace

N
W E
S

ALSACE AOC AREAS
ROUTE DE VIN
VINEYARD AREAS

0   5 MILES
0   5   10 KILOMETERS

N83
A35
N415
N83
A35
N422
A36

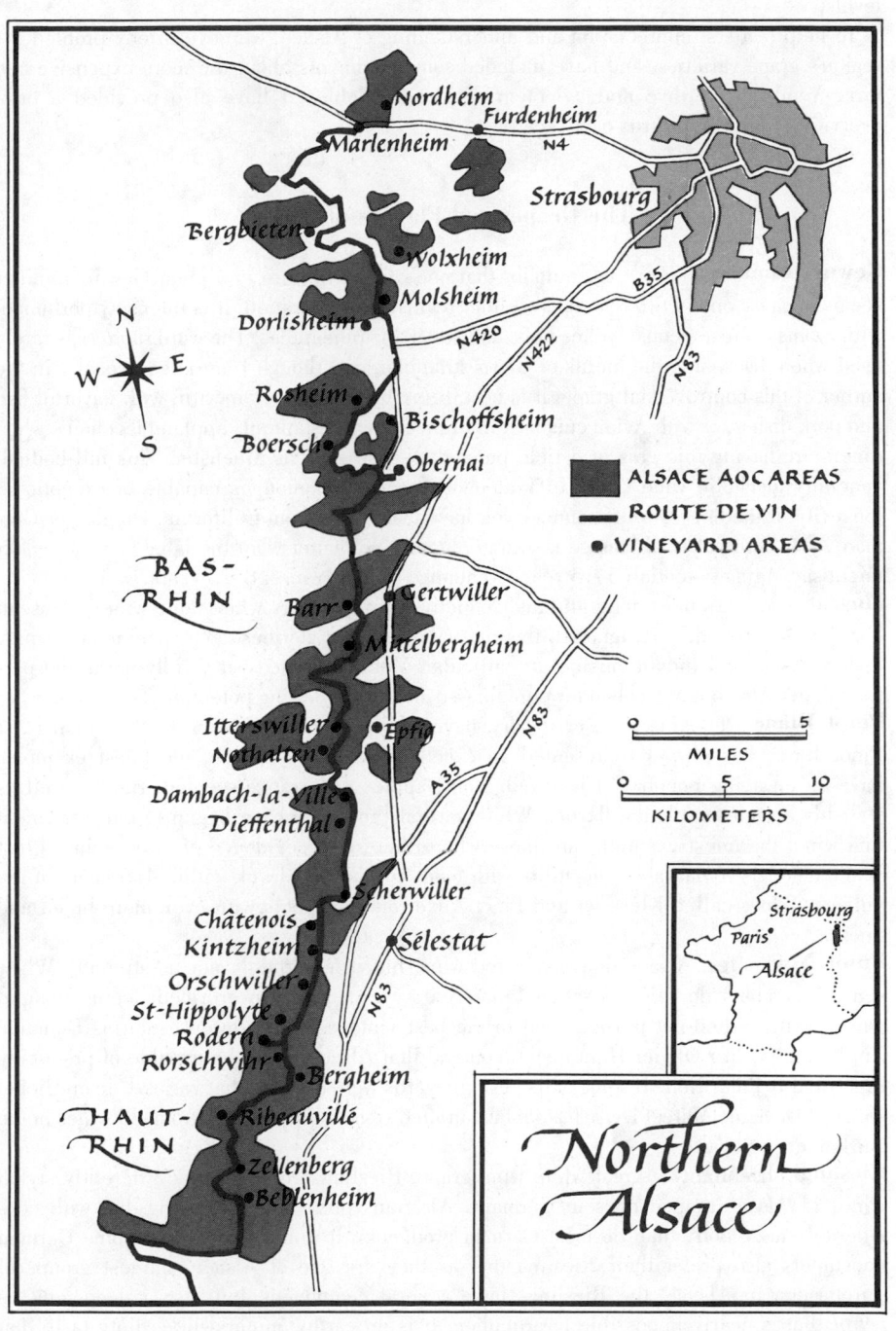

Northern Alsace

Nordheim
Furdenheim
Marlenheim
Strasbourg
Bergbieten
Wolxheim
Molsheim
Dorlisheim
N420
N422
B35
N83
Rosheim
Bischoffsheim
Boersch
Obernai

BAS-RHIN

Barr
Gertwiller
Mittelbergheim

Itterswiller
Nothalten
Epfig
Dambach-la-Ville
Dieffenthal

N83

A35

Scherwiller
Châtenois
Sélestat
Kintzheim
Orschwiller
St-Hippolyte
Rodern
Rorschwihr
Bergheim
HAUT-RHIN
Ribeauvillé
Zellenberg
Beblenheim

N4

N83

ALSACE AOC AREAS
ROUTE DE VIN
VINEYARD AREAS

0   5
MILES

0   5   10
KILOMETERS

N W E S

Paris
Strasbourg
Alsace

dry actually contain significant levels of residual sugar. To reduce consumer confusion and render the buying process easier, the labels on these wines should indicate their sugar levels.

To help readers' appreciation and understanding of Alsace, we have briefly profiled the region's grape varieties, and have included some comments about the more expensive and rarer Vendange Tardive and Sélection de Grains Nobles. I have also provided a brief overview of the grands crus of Alsace.

The Grapes and Flavors of Alsace

Gewurztraminer   There is no doubt that one's first exposure to a great Gewurztraminer seems to cause one of two reactions—either revulsion or adoration. It is intensely perfumed, with aromas of rose petals, lychee nuts, and superripe pineapples. The word *subtlety* is rarely used when discussing the merits of Gewurztraminer, and though I am unequivocally in the corner of this controversial grape, it is best drunk by itself as an apéritif, with flavorful fish and pork dishes, or with Asian cuisines. In France, great restaurants applaud its choice when diners are having foie gras or a rich, pungent cheese such as Muenster. This full-bodied, generally alcoholic wine (13.5–14% alcohol is not uncommon) is capable of exceptional longevity. If the only Gewurztraminer you have tasted was from California, Oregon, or Germany, you have not really tasted Gewurztraminer—no matter what the label or wine-maker might say. Aging potential: 5–15 years; Vendange Tardive wines: 8–25 years.

Muscat   Alsace's most delightful and seductively fragrant dry white table wine is Muscat. Terribly underrated, even ignored, this dry wine makes a glorious accompaniment to spicy dishes, Asian and Indian cuisine, in particular. Medium-bodied yet vividly floral and perfumed, dry Alsatian Muscats offer pure finesse and charm. Aging potential: 3–5 years.

Pinot Blanc   Looking for a crisp, dry, flavorful, complex white wine for less than $20? Pinot Blanc has always represented an excellent value. In Alsace, the finest examples have an engaging bouquet of honeyed, stony, apple- and orange-scented fruit, as well as stylishly elegant, applelike flavors. While several producers have begun to barrel-ferment this wine, the finest examples are those where there is no evidence of wood aging. Pinot Blanc also has remarkable versatility with food, and is best drunk within 4–5 years of the vintage. Wines called Klevener and Pinot Auxerrois are Pinots with even more breed and finesse.

Pinot Noir   Yes, Alsace does make red wine, but it is certainly not its strength. While some exceptions do exist, Alsatian Pinot Noirs are generally overpriced, feeble, insipid wines, with washed-out flavors, even in the best vintages. Top growers, such as Domaine Zind-Humbrecht's Olivier Humbrecht, contend that Alsace would be capable of producing high-quality Pinot Noirs if some of its best vineyards were used for that varietal. Jean-Michel Deiss of Domaine Marcel Deiss has, in fact, crafted some delicious reds from old wines in the Burlenberg vineyard.

Riesling   Irrefutably a great white wine grape, Riesling produces very differently styled wines in Alsace than it does in Germany. Alsatians prefer their Riesling dry, with considerably more body than do most German producers. It would appear that some German consumers also prefer their Riesling dry, as they are one of Alsace's largest groups of purchasers. In Alsace, the Rieslings have a floral component, but also a deep *goût de pétrol* that is nearly impossible to articulate. It is an earthy, mineral-like, flinty taste that differs considerably from the slatelike, steely character found in many Rieslings from Germany's Mosel vineyards. Less floral than their German counterparts, with more of a pineapple, honeyed, orange-peel character, Alsace Rieslings are medium- to full-bodied wines that can also age remarkably well. Aging potential: 3–15 years; Vendange Tardive wines: 5–25 years.

Sylvaner   This is the least appealing grape of Alsace. The wines often lack an interesting bouquet, tending to be neutral, even vegetal to smell. Because of its high acidity, Sylvaner should frequently be employed as a blending grape rather than be permitted to stand by itself. Aging potential: 1–5 years.

Tokay-Pinot Gris   Capable of producing wines as compelling as the greatest Chardonnays, Tokay-Pinot Gris reaches its height as a dry, full-bodied wine in Alsace. It is a super grape that, when picked late and fermented nearly dry or completely dry, offers a huge perfume of buttery, creamy, smoky fruit, unctuous, intense flavors, and considerable power and palate presence. Its style mandates the same types of food (rich fish dishes, etc.) with which one would normally serve a grand cru white Burgundy. The Vendange Tardive Tokay-Pinot Gris wines from Alsace can contain 14–15% alcohol naturally, and they can age well. Aging potential: 4–10 years; Vendange Tardive wines: 5–20 years.

A NOTE ABOUT VENDANGE TARDIVE AND SÉLECTION DE GRAINS NOBLES WINES
The late-harvested Vendange Tardive wines of Alsace are made from fully ripened (not overripe) fruit, and are powerful, rich, large-scaled wines that range in alcohol content from 14.3 to 16%. The levels of concentration and extract can be majestic. Depending on the producer, a Vendange Tardive wine can be fermented completely dry or left with a slight degree of residual sugar. The best of these offerings are superlative expressions of winemaking and can provide thrilling as well as provocative drinking. They also age extremely well. A little-known fact is that they frequently age longer and more gracefully than France's premier and grand cru white Burgundies. Any late-harvested wine will have the designation "Vendange Tardive" on the label. The wines called Sélection de Grains Nobles represent the sweet, nectarlike, rare, and luxury-priced segment of the Alsatian wine hierarchy. They are often riveting because their sumptuous levels of fruit extract are unencumbered by aromas of new oak. Alsatian wine-makers, as a general rule, eschew new wood casks. In effect, these wines are essences of their varietals. A Sélection de Grains Nobles can easily last 15–30 years. Many of these wines now cost over $100—for a half bottle!

RECENT VINTAGES

2000—Few 2000s from Alsace's finest producers were tasted prior to this book going to press, yet it is clear that this vintage's potential is outstanding. Where yields were controlled, grapes sorted, and gray rot or acid rot–infested bunches disposed of, 2000 was capable of delivering pure, densely packed wines of immense depth and balance. However, this is not a great vintage that elevates the quality of poor or average producers, as enormous vineyard work was necessary to guarantee success.

1999—Alsace's 1999 vintage is the least attractive this region has produced since the 1992 and 1991, yet top estates miraculously produced superb wines. Mired in rain and rot-inducing humidity, it was saved from disaster by good weather in late August and early September. By mid-September the rains returned, rendering harvesting a game of "picking between the storms," as one grower put it. Early-ripening varietals such as Pinot Blanc, Sylvaner, and Muscat could be harvested during the dry, sunny period, but those that require a longer hang time, heat, or loads of sunshine fared poorly. Riesling appears to be the vintage's weakness, and the majority lack depth, focus, and ripeness. Gewurztraminer, a varietal that craves heat and sun, is better, yet most 1999s lack the ostentatious, fruit-driven personalities its admirers crave.

1998—The 1998 vintage in Alsace, as with the rest northern France, was a difficult one. However, because Alsatian producers have the luxury of enormous versatility in their selection of harvest dates and the styles of wines they will fashion, the results (at least from the top 20–25 estates) are excellent or outstanding. May and June were warm months, leading to a precocious yet even flowering. Cool temperatures and rains swept in during the last days of June and lasted until the middle of July, at which point, hot, droughtlike conditions settled over Alsace until mid- to late August. During this period, the searing sun and abnormally high temperatures led to grapes being burned (as also in Burgundy).

The weather did another about-face in late August, shifting from heat and drought to cold and plentiful quantities of rain. This continued until the third week of September, when two weeks of gorgeous weather graced the region. It was in this window that many growers began harvesting Pinot Blanc, Muscat, and Gewurztraminer (primarily from valley floor vineyards as well as those on the lower slopes). On September 30 the skies opened again, inundating the region with rain until October 12, when ideal weather returned.

Many producers compared their top 1998s with wines produced in 1990 and 1994, the two finest years of the decade. For the Vendange Tardive, Sélection de Grains Nobles, and most grands crus, this comparison is not without merit. The best examples exhibit superb ripeness, loads of complexity-inducing botrytis, and wonderful balancing acidity. From the best estates, these wines were all harvested in the second harvesting window in October.

1997—The 1997 vintage is wonderful for Gewurztraminer, and less so for Tokay-Pinot Gris and Riesling. The warmth of the summer led to a drop in natural acidities, which accentuates Gewurztraminer's flamboyance but renders Rieslings and other varietals less complex and ageworthy. This is an early-drinking vintage, displaying Mother Nature's perfect timing after the superstructured and tightly wound 1996s.

1996—This vintage is uneven in quality. It produced some extraordinary wines as well as many high-acid scorchers. What made the difference? Yields. Cool temperatures and dry winds from the north dominated the weather in August and September, resulting in grapes with abnormally high acidity levels. Those producers who cultivate high yields (in Alsace vignerons have been known to harvest up to 100 hectoliters per hectare) do not have the fruit to counterbalance the acidity. However, conscientious producers like Olivier Humbrecht (he averaged 31 h/h in 1996) crafted wines of extraordinary balance, with loads of concentration and the ability to age remarkably well. This is a vintage where many of the Tokay-Pinot Gris, as well as the majority of Gewurztraminers, lack the opulence and hedonistic appeal generally associated with these varietals because of their high acid profiles. Riesling performed best in this vintage, with powerful petrol qualities and extraordinary delineation plainly in evidence. The finest Rieslings of 1996 will be extremely ageworthy. Few sweet wines were crafted in 1996 because there was very little botrytis.

1995—The 1995 vintage is uneven in quality. The best producers crafted magnificent Rieslings, Muscats, and Tokay-Pinot Gris while others crafted wines lacking in character, fruit, and concentration. A cold, rainy September was followed by a spectacular October and November. Producers who picked early out of fear harvested unripe grapes with high levels of acidity. Those with the courage and professionalism to wait were rewarded by a long late season with ideal weather conditions. However, 1995 is not a vintage for Gewurztraminer, as this varietal requires warm temperatures to express its flamboyant personality.

1994—The 1994s produced from the finest hillside vineyards, as well as those controlled by growers who crop-thinned and kept yields small, produced massive, extremely concentrated wines. Though September's weather was fitful, those producers who harvested late were rewarded with an extraordinarily sunny and warm October. Unlike 1993, 1992, and 1991, there are abundant quantities of high-octane, rich, full-bodied Vendange Tardive wines, particularly from the finest vineyards and producers. At the top level, this is a great year.

1993—The 1993s have turned out well, as Alsace escaped the bad weather that battered much of France. The wines are lighter than the 1992s, with better acidity and more structure, as well as clean, ripe fruit. They will not be long-lived. Most 1993s will require consumption in their youth. Very little Vendange Tardive or the sweet nectar Sélection de Grains Nobles was produced in this vintage.

1992—Alsace fared far better than most of southern France in this vintage. The harvest was the earliest since 1976, and the producers reported very high yields, with a lot of ripeness and richness, but wines that are extremely low in acidity. There are a lot of near-term drinking wines that are forward, juicy, and user-friendly.

1991—This is Alsace's toughest vintage since 1987. Nevertheless, some producers, such as Domaine Weinbach and Zind-Humbrecht, made wines that it is hard to believe came from a mediocre to below-average-quality year. Most wines are relatively light, overly acidic, and slightly green, in complete contrast to the soft, fruity 1992s.

1990—Amazingly, this vintage is even more consistent in quality than 1989. There were fewer Vendange Tardive and Sélection de Grains Nobles wines produced, which should be good news for consumers looking for the drier Alsatian wines. I was impressed with the quality of all the varietals, but top marks must go to the glorious Rieslings, which are superior even to the 1989s. The Gewurztraminers, which were so stunningly perfumed and rich in 1989, are slightly less intense in 1990, but perhaps better balanced and less overwhelming. All things considered, this is a top-notch vintage that looks to be every bit as good as such previous great vintages as 1989, 1985, and 1983.

1989—This vintage most resembles 1983 in that the wines are superripe, strong, forceful, and heady, with exceptional perfume, and, at times, mind-boggling richness. The vintage produced amazing quantities of Vendange Tardive and Sélection de Grains Nobles wines. In fact, at the sweeter end of the spectrum, 1989 is probably unequaled by any recent Alsace vintage. Even the totally dry wines tend to be massive. There is plenty of great wine from which to pick, although most wines' aging potential will have to be monitored, given the relatively low acidity.

1988—A very good vintage that suffers only when compared with 1989 and 1990. The very dry, stylish wines may lack the concentration and sheer drama of the 1989s and 1990s; they are, nevertheless, elegant, suave, and graceful. Most of the top Rieslings, Gewurztraminers, and grands crus will easily last for a decade or more.

OLDER VINTAGES

1987 is surprisingly good, particularly in view of its so-so reputation. Some producers, such as Domaine Zind-Humbrecht, made superb wines in 1987. Overall, the quality is at least good, and in many cases excellent. Hardly any Vendange Tardive or Sélection de Grains Nobles were made in this vintage because of fall rains. 1986 was a patchy vintage, but, as is expected from the finest producers, Domaines Zind-Humbrecht and Weinbach made many glorious wines even in this difficult year. To the extent one can still find any 1985s, it is one of the four or five best vintages for Alsace in the last 15 years. The wines are rich, with decent acidity, and are evolving gracefully in the bottle. They should provide delicious drinking and, in the case of the better Tokay-Pinot Gris, Rieslings, and Gewurztraminers, are capable of lasting for at least another decade. The 1984 and 1982 vintages get my vote as the two worst of the decade, and are of no interest. However, 1983 was another great vintage for Alsace. I bought nearly 20 cases of the 1983s and have drunk them with immense pleasure since their release. Despite their low acidity and relatively intense, concentrated style, they have displayed no signs of cracking up. Many of the bigger-styled Rieslings and Gewurztraminers are still improving. If anyone is lucky enough to find well-stored bottles of 1976s, 1971s, or 1967s, these wines can provide remarkable evidence of the aging potential of

Alsace's top wines. I suspect the only places they may appear are at auctions, and probably at alluring prices.

THE SIGNIFICANCE OF ALSACE'S GRAND CRU SYSTEM

Alsace, like Burgundy, has developed a complicated grand cru system that is still the subject of considerable controversy. Many of the best hillside vineyards in Alsace have been included in the grand cru classification. However, there is no qualitative justification for excluding the *monopole* (single-proprietor) vineyards from being considered grands crus. For this reason, irrefutably superb sites such as the Clos Ste.-Hune, Clos Windsbuhl, and Clos des Capucins are deprived of such status (Clos Ste.-Hune is part of a grand cru that the Trimbachs are entitled to list on the label; however, if they were to do so, they would be prevented from listing the famous Clos name). Moreover, some of the region's top producers—Hugel, Beyer, and Trimbach—have refused to indicate any grand cru designation on their top *cuvées*, despite the fact that the bulk of their *réserve* wines are made from grand cru vineyards. Add to these problems the fact that the politicians of each wine village in Alsace have effectively persuaded authorities to give them their "own" grand cru. The political concessions have already resulted in over 50 grands crus, nearly 20 more than what is permitted in Burgundy's Côte d'Or. Moreover, some of these vineyards have not yet had their boundaries defined by the authorities. In spite of its weaknesses, the grand cru system is an incentive for producers to achieve the best from the most privileged hillside vineyards.

To help readers understand the grands crus, which will, for better or worse, become of increasing significance, we have listed the major grands crus in alphabetical order, along with the best producers from each grand cru. Additionally, we have attempted to summarize some of the more relevant characteristics of each vineyard from information provided by the Alsace Wine Information Bureau.

The Principal Grands Crus of Alsace

Altenberg de Bergbieten   SIZE: 67.3 acres; RELEVANT FACTS: Hillside vineyard with a full southeast exposure and gypsum, clay, and gravelly soil; PRIVILEGED VARIETALS: Riesling and Gewurztraminer are considered superb, and Tokay-Pinot Gris and Muscat are also grown on these slopes.

Altenberg de Bergheim   SIZE: 80.6 acres; RELEVANT FACTS: Limestone and marl dominate the soil of this hillside vineyard, which is renowned for its superb Riesling and, to a lesser extent, for its Gewurztraminer; PRIVILEGED VARIETALS: Riesling and Gewurztraminer; BEST PRODUCERS: Marcel Deiss, Charles Koehly, Gustave Lorentz, Sylvie Spielman.

Brand   SIZE: 140 acres; RELEVANT FACTS: This gorgeous hillside vineyard behind the village of Turckheim has a south-southeast exposure. The soil is deep granite, laced with black mica. PRIVILEGED VARIETALS: Riesling, Tokay-Pinot Gris, and Gewurztraminer; BEST PRODUCERS: Zind-Humbrecht, Pierre Sparr, Albert Boxler.

Eichberg   SIZE: 142.3 acres; RELEVANT FACTS: Not far from Colmar, Eichberg is renowned for its Gewurztraminers, followed by Tokay-Pinot Gris and Riesling. With its limestone/marl soil and gentle southeast slope, this area can produce powerful wines in hot, sunny years. PRIVILEGED VARIETALS: Gewurztraminer, Riesling, and Tokay-Pinot Gris; BEST PRODUCERS: Leon Beyer's Comtes d'Eguisheim (100% from the Eichberg vineyard), Kuentz-Bas Gewurztraminer, Gérard Schueller, Scherer.

Engelberg   SIZE: 27 acres; RELEVANT FACTS: A limestone/marl soil that drains exceptionally well; PRIVILEGED VARIETALS: Gewurztraminer and Riesling.

Florimont   SIZE: 27 acres; RELEVANT FACTS: This steep, south- and east-facing limestone vineyard is located outside the village of Ingersheim. PRIVILEGED VARIETAL: Gewurztraminer.

Frankstein   SIZE: 131 acres; RELEVANT FACTS: Actually four separate parcels, this is a steep, southeast-facing vineyard with superb drainage. PRIVILEGED VARIETALS: Riesling and Gewurztraminer.

Froehn   SIZE: 32 acres; RELEVANT FACTS: Located outside the village of Zellenberg, this small grand cru has a reputation for long-lived wines. PRIVILEGED VARIETALS: Gewurztraminer, Tokay-Pinot Gris, and Muscat.

Furstentum   SIZE: 68 acres; RELEVANT FACTS: This superbly situated, steep, hillside vineyard not far from Kaysersberg has a warm microclimate, producing full-bodied, rich wines. PRIVILEGED VARIETALS: Gewurztraminer, Riesling, and Tokay-Pinot Gris; BEST PRODUCERS: Domaine Wienbach, Domaine Bott-Geyl, Domaine Albert Mann, Domaine Marc Tempé, Paul Blanck.

Geisberg   SIZE: 21 acres; RELEVANT FACTS: A steep, terraced vineyard overlooking the charming village of Ribeauvillé, Geisberg is known for its very gravelly and limestone-mixed soils, and its powerful, elegant wines. PRIVILEGED VARIETAL: Riesling; BEST PRODUCER: Trimbach (Cuvée Frédéric Emile).

Gloeckelberg   SIZE: 57.8 acres; RELEVANT FACTS: Located near the villages of St.-Hippolyte and Rodern, this moderate-sized vineyard has a south and southeast exposure with round, relatively acidic soil composed of sand, gypsum, and gravel. PRIVILEGED VARIETALS: Tokay-Pinot Gris, followed by Gewurztraminer; BEST PRODUCER: Charles Koehly.

Goldert   SIZE: 111.9 acres; RELEVANT FACTS: One of the more stricking vineyards in Alsace, located north of the village of Gueberschwihr, Goldert is situated at a relatively high altitude with deep calcareous soil and an east-southeasterly exposure. It is particularly renowned for its well-drained soils that produce superb Gewurztraminer and Muscat. PRIVILEGED VARIETALS: Gewurztraminer, followed by Muscat; BEST PRODUCERS: Ernest Burn, Zind-Humbrecht.

Hatschbourg   SIZE: 116.8 acres; RELEVANT FACTS: Located south of Colmar, near the village of Voegtlinshoffen, this hillside vineyard has a calcareous, marllike soil that provides excellent drainage, and a south-southeast exposure. PRIVILEGED VARIETALS: Gewurztraminer, followed by Tokay-Pinot Gris and Riesling.

Hengst   SIZE: 187.2 acres; RELEVANT FACTS: This relatively large vineyard, south of the village of Wintzenheim, has a south-southeast exposure. The combined calcareous and marl soils tend to produce rich, full-bodied wines. PRIVILEGED VARIETALS: Gewurztraminer, followed by Tokay-Pinot Gris and Riesling; BEST PRODUCERS: Josmeyer, Zind-Humbrecht, Albert Mann, Barmès-Buecher.

Kanzlerberg   SIZE: 8.1 acres; RELEVANT FACTS: This tiny vineyard near the village of Bergheim, just west of the grand cru Altenberg, has a very heavy clay/limestone soil intermixed with gypsum and marl. Powerful wines emerge from this gem of a vineyard. PRIVILEGED VARIETALS: Tokay-Pinot Gris and Gewurztraminer; BEST PRODUCER: Gustave Lorentz.

Kastelberg   SIZE: 14.3 acres; RELEVANT FACTS: This steeply terraced vineyard in the very northern part of Alsace's viticultural region, near Andlau, is composed of deep layers of schist and quartz, the perfect soil base for Riesling. PRIVILEGED VARIETAL: Riesling; BEST PRODUCERS: Marc Kreydenweiss.

Kessler   SIZE: 70.4 acres; RELEVANT FACTS: Steep, terraced vineyards composed of red sandstone, clay, and sand are situated in the very southern part of Alsace's viticultural region, with a stunning southeast exposure. PRIVILEGED VARIETALS: Gewurztraminer and Tokay-Pinot Gris, followed by Riesling; BEST PRODUCERS: Dirler.

Kirchberg de Barr   SIZE: 92 acres; RELEVANT FACTS: Located in the northern section of Alsace's viticultural region, behind the village of Barr, this vineyard has a southeast exposure and a soil base of calcareous marl with underlying beds of limestone and gravel. PRIVILEGED VARIETALS: Gewurztraminer, Riesling, and Tokay-Pinot Gris; BEST PRODUCER: Domaine M. & V. Stoeffler.

Kirchberg de Ribeauvillé SIZE: 28.2 acres; RELEVANT FACTS: The stony, claylike soil, with a south-southwest exposure, produces relatively full-bodied wines that require some time in the bottle to develop their bouquets. PRIVILEGED VARIETALS: Riesling and Muscat, followed by Gewurztraminer; BEST PRODUCER: Trimbach, Jean Sipp.

Kitterlé SIZE: 63.7 acres; RELEVANT FACTS: Perhaps the most striking terraced vineyard in Alsace, Kitterlé, which sits on the photogenic, steep slopes overlooking the town of Gueb-willer, has three different exposures: south, southeast, and southwest. The soils consist of red sandstone, with plenty of quartz intermixed with lighter, sandier, gravelly soil that produces wines of extraordinary richness and aging potential. PRIVILEGED VARIETALS: Gewurztraminer, Riesling, and Tokay-Pinot Gris; BEST PRODUCER: Schlumberger (astonishing wines from this vineyard).

Mambourg SIZE: 161 acres; RELEVANT FACTS: Mambourg, a hillside vineyard overlooking the village of Sigolsheim, has a calcareous and marl-like soil that produces very low yields and is ideal for Gewurztraminer. PRIVILEGED VARIETALS: Gewurztraminer, followed by Tokay-Pinot Gris, Muscat, and Riesling; BEST PRODUCER: Sparr.

Mandelberg SIZE: 29.7 acres; RELEVANT FACTS: Located near the village of Mittelwihr, this hillside vineyard has a marl and limestone soil base. PRIVILEGED VARIETALS: Gewurz-traminer, followed by Riesling; BEST PRODUCER: Domaine Bott-Geyl.

Marckrain SIZE: 111.7 acres; RELEVANT FACTS: Calcareous marl soil with clay makes up this vineyard, located just south of the village of Bennwihr. The heavy soil produces rela-tively rich, fragrant, full-bodied wines. PRIVILEGED VARIETALS: Gewurztraminer and Tokay-Pinot Gris.

Moenchberg SIZE: 29.5 acres; RELEVANT FACTS: Light, red sandstone intermixed with limestone makes up the soil of this hillside vineyard in northern Alsace, between the villages of Andlau and Eichhoffen. PRIVILEGED VARIETAL: Riesling; BEST PRODUCERS: Ostertag, Krey-denweiss.

Muenchberg SIZE: 62 acres; RELEVANT FACTS: Light gravelly, sandy, nutrient-poor soil is ideal for producing closed but highly concentrated wines. PRIVILEGED VARIETAL: Riesling.

Ollwiller SIZE: 86.5 acres; RELEVANT FACTS: Located in the southernmost sector of Alsace's viticultural region, near the village of Wuenheim (situated midway between Gueb-willer and Thann), this hillside vineyard with a southeast exposure has soils made up of red sandstone and clay. PRIVILEGED VARIETALS: Riesling and Gewurztraminer.

Osterberg SIZE: 59.3 acres; RELEVANT FACTS: With stony, claylike soils, the Osterberg vineyard is located near the village of Ribeauvillé. PRIVILEGED VARIETALS: Riesling, Gewurz-traminer, and Tokay-Pinot Gris; BEST PRODUCER: Trimbach.

Pfersigberg SIZE: 138 acres; RELEVANT FACTS: Gravelly soils with rich deposits of magne-sium make up this vineyard, located near the village of Eguisheim within view of the three ruined towers that dominate the hillside above Husseren-les-Châteaux. PRIVILEGED VARI-ETALS: Gewurztraminer, Tokay-Pinot Gris, Riesling, and Muscat; BEST PRODUCERS: Barmès-Buecher, Kuentz-Bas, Scherer, Domaine Gérard Schueller.

Pfingstberg SIZE: 69 acres; RELEVANT FACTS: With its southeast exposure and location in the southern part of Alsace's viticultural region, just to the north of Guebwiller, the red sand-stone and mica-based soils produce classic, long-lived wines. PRIVILEGED VARIETALS: Gewurztraminer, Tokay-Pinot Gris, and Riesling; BEST PRODUCER: Albrecht.

Praelatenberg SIZE: 29.6 acres; RELEVANT FACTS: This hillside vineyard, located beneath the formidable mountaintop château of Haut-Koenigsbourg, possesses a heavy but well-drained soil consisting of gravel and quartz. PRIVILEGED VARIETALS: Riesling, followed by Gewurztraminer and Muscat.

Rangen SIZE: 46.4 acres; RELEVANT FACTS: One of the greatest of the grands crus, this vineyard, located at the very southern end of the viticultural region of Alsace, on steeply terraced hillsides with a full southerly exposure, has a soil base composed of volcanic rocks, schist, and numerous outcroppings of rocks. PRIVILEGED VARIETALS: Tokay-Pinot Gris, Gewurztraminer, and Riesling; BEST PRODUCERS: Zind-Humbrecht, Bernard Schoffit Schaetzel.

Rosacker   SIZE: 67.2 acres; RELEVANT FACTS: Located north of the village of Hunawihr, near the Clos Windsbuhl (one of the finest enclosed vineyards, called "clos"), this hillside vineyard with its east-southeast exposure is planted on calcareous, magnesium-enriched, heavy soil, with some sandstone. The greatest enclosed vineyard of Alsace, Trimbach's Clos Ste.-Hune is located within Rosacker but is not labeled as such (by law, Trimbach must choose whether to label it by its grand cru or by its significantly more famous name). PRIVILEGED VARIETALS: Riesling, followed by Gewurztraminer; BEST PRODUCER: Mittnacht-Klack.

Saering   SIZE: 66 acres; RELEVANT FACTS: The Saering vineyards, with their east-southeasterly exposure, form part of the same striking hillside that contains the famous Kitterlé vineyard. Both overlook the bustling town of Guebwiller. The soil at Saering is heavy, sandy, mixed gravel and chalk, perfect for Riesling. PRIVILEGED VARIETAL: Riesling; BEST PRODUCERS: Jean-Pierre Dirler.

Schlossberg   SIZE: 197 acres; RELEVANT FACTS: Steep, terraced, sandy, gravelly, mineral-rich soils dominate this vineyard, located behind the charming village of Kaysersberg in the direction of Kientzheim. This is one of the largest grands crus, so quality varies enormously. PRIVILEGED VARIETAL: Riesling; BEST PRODUCERS: Domaine Weinbach, Pierre Sparr, Albert Mann.

Schoenenbourg   SIZE: 99 acres; RELEVANT FACTS: This outstanding, as well as scenically beautiful, steep vineyard behind the walled village of Riquewihr is rich in marl, gypsum, sandstone, and fine gravelly soil. PRIVILEGED VARIETALS: Riesling, followed by Muscat and some Tokay-Pinot Gris; BEST PRODUCERS: Hugel (their top *cuvées* usually contain high percentages of Riesling from the Schoenenbourg vineyard), Deiss, Beyer, Mittnacht-Klack, Marc Tempé.

Sommerberg   SIZE: 66.7 acres; RELEVANT FACTS: One of the steepest hillside vineyards in Alsace, Sommerberg is composed of hard granite and black mica, and has a full southerly orientation. The vineyard is located behind the village of Niedermorschwihr. PRIVILEGED VARIETAL: Riesling; BEST PRODUCERS: Albert Boxler, Bernard Schoffit.

Sonnenglanz   SIZE: 81.5 acres; RELEVANT FACTS: The southeasterly exposure and sloping hillside location, with vines planted on relatively heavy soil in a particularly dry microclimate, make Sonnenglanz one of the most favorable vineyard sites for Tokay-Pinot Gris and Gewurztraminer. PRIVILEGED VARIETALS: Tokay-Pinot Gris and Gewurztraminer; BEST PRODUCER: Bott-Geyl.

Spiegel   SIZE: 45.2 acres; RELEVANT FACTS: Located between Guebwiller and Bergholtz in the southern area of Alsace, the Spiegel vineyards are on sandy soils with a full easterly exposure. PRIVILEGED VARIETALS: Tokay-Pinot Gris and Gewurztraminer; BEST PRODUCER: Dirler.

Sporen   SIZE: 54.3 acres; RELEVANT FACTS: This great vineyard for Gewurztraminer, planted on deep, rich soils with a great deal of phosphoric acid, overlooks the splendid, pretty-as-a-postcard village of Riquewihr. The wines that emerge are among the richest and longest-lived in the region, although they need time in the bottle to develop. PRIVILEGED VARIETALS: Gewurztraminer, followed by Tokay-Pinot Gris; BEST PRODUCERS: Hugel (their top *cuvées* of Gewurztraminer are almost entirely made from the Sporen vineyard), Mittnacht-Klack.

Steinert   SIZE: 93.8 acres; RELEVANT FACTS: The stony limestone soils of this vineyard, located on a sloping hillside in a particularly dry area of Alsace, produce very aromatic wines. PRIVILEGED VARIETALS: Gewurztraminer, followed by Tokay-Pinot Gris and Riesling.

Steingrubler   SIZE: 47 acres; RELEVANT FACTS: Another hillside vineyard with a sandy soil at the top slopes, and richer, less-well-drained soils at the bottom of the slopes, Steingrubler has a reputation for producing wines of great longevity. PRIVILEGED VARIETALS: Riesling and Gewurztraminer.

Steinklotz   SIZE: 59.3 acres; RELEVANT FACTS: This most northerly grand cru Alsace vineyard, located near the village of Marlenheim, has a south-southeasterly orientation and very gravelly calcareous soils. PRIVILEGED VARIETALS: Tokay-Pinot Gris, followed by Riesling and Gewurztraminer.

Vorbourg   SIZE: 178 acres; RELEVANT FACTS: This vineyard, located near the village of Rouffach in the southern sector of Alsace's viticultural region, is composed of limestone- and marl-enriched soils spread over the hillside, with a south-southeast exposure. Ideal ripening conditions exist in this relatively hot, dry microclimate. PRIVILEGED VARIETALS: Riesling, Gewurztraminer, Tokay-Pinot Gris, and Muscat; BEST PRODUCER: Domaine du Clos St.-Landelin (Muré).

Wiebelsberg   SIZE: 25.5 acres; RELEVANT FACTS: This spectacularly situated hillside vineyard, overlooking the village of Andlau, is planted on well-drained sandstone, sandy soils. PRIVILEGED VARIETAL: Riesling; BEST PRODUCERS: Marc Kreydenweiss.

Wineck-Schlossberg   SIZE: 59.2 acres; RELEVANT FACTS: Located west of the city of Colmar in the foothills of the Vosges Mountains, near the village of Katzenthal, this relatively obscure grand cru vineyard is planted on deep granite soils, producing very long-lived, subtle wines. PRIVILEGED VARIETALS: Riesling, followed by Gewurztraminer.

Winzenberg   SIZE: 123 acres; RELEVANT FACTS: Located in the northern Bas-Rhin sector of Alsace, with a south-southeast exposure, and a granite, mica-infused soil base, this is one of the least-known grands crus. PRIVILEGED VARIETALS: Riesling, followed by Gewurztraminer.

Zinnkoepflé   SIZE: 153 acres; RELEVANT FACTS: This stunningly beautiful, steep hillside vineyard, oriented toward the south-southeast and planted on deep beds of sandstone in the southern part of Alsace's viticultural region near Soultzmatt, produces powerful, spicy, rich wines. PRIVILEGED VARIETALS: Gewurztraminer, followed by Riesling and Tokay-Pinot Gris.

Zotzenberg   SIZE: 84 acres; RELEVANT FACTS: This vineyard, located north of Epfig just south of Barr, has an easterly and southerly exposure, and is planted on marl- and limestone-based soils. The gradual sloping hillside is best known for its Gewurztraminer and Riesling. PRIVILEGED VARIETALS: Gewurztraminer and Riesling.

THE MOST FAMOUS CLOS OF ALSACE

Some of Alsace's greatest wines come not from grand cru vineyards, but from vineyards entitled to be called "clos" (meaning enclosed or walled vineyards). The most famous of these clos include the spectacular Clos des Capucins (12.6 acres), just outside the village of Kaysersberg, owned by the remarkable Madame Faller of Domaine Weinbach. Extraordinary Riesling, Gewurztraminer, and Tokay-Pinot Gris that are often far superior to most grands crus emerge from this vineyard. The Clos Gaensbroennel (14.8 acres), located near the northerly village of Barr, has provided me with some of the most remarkable and long-lived Gewurztraminers I have had the pleasure to taste. Clos Gaensbroennel is owned by Willm. Perhaps the best-known clos in all of Alsace is Clos Ste.-Hune (3.08 acres), owned by the famous firm of Trimbach in Ribeauvillé. It is planted entirely with Riesling. Rieslings from this vineyard, often referred to as the Romanée-Conti of Alsace, generally require 5 years of cellaring to attain their peak and can easily last and evolve in a graceful manner for 15–20 or more years.

Other exceptional clos include the Clos St.-Imer (12.5 acres), owned by Ernest Burn. As the tasting notes evidence, the Riesling, Gewurztraminer, and Tokay-Pinot Gris from this spectacularly placed clos near the village of Gueberschwihr rank among the very finest in all of Alsace. Near Rouffach is one of the largest enclosed Alsace vineyards, the Clos St.-Landelin (39.5 acres), owned by the Domaine du Clos St.-Landelin (René Muré). Rich, full-bodied, opulent Gewurztraminer, Riesling, Tokay-Pinot Gris, and even a splendid dry Muscat are made from this enclosed hillside vineyard's grapes.

The Domaine Zind-Humbrecht also owns two well-known vineyards entitled to the clos designation. Their most famous is the Clos St.-Urbain (12.5 acres). This sensationally located, steeply terraced vineyard, planted on granite soils, with a full southeasterly exposure near the village of Thann, makes astonishingly rich, long-lived Gewurztraminer, Riesling, and Tokay-Pinot Gris. The latter wine, for my money, is the Montrachet of Alsace. The other great clos owned by Zind-Humbrecht is the Clos Windsbuhl (11.1 acres). Located on a steep hillside behind the magnificent church of Hunawihr and near the renowned Trimbach vineyard of Clos Ste.-Hune, Clos Windsbuhl is planted on a limestone and stony soil, with an east-southeast exposure. Majestic Gewurztraminer is produced, as well as small quantities of Tokay-Pinot Gris and Riesling.

Though I am less familiar with the following vineyards, I have been impressed with the Clos Zisser (12.5 acres), owned by the Domaine Klipfel and planted entirely with Gewurztraminer. Other well-known clos with which I have less experience include proprietor Jean Sipp's Clos du Schlossberg (3 acres) outside the village of Ribeauvillé. Finally, Marc Kreydenweiss has consistently made some of the finest dry Muscat from the Clos Rebgarten (0.5 acre), which is planted on sandy, gravely soil just outside the village of Andlau.

The wines from these clos are every bit as sensational as, and in many cases greatly superior to, many of the grands crus. *In vino politiques?*

BUYING STRATEGY

Readers searching out wines for immediate consumption will tremendously enjoy the 1997s, and the finest 1998s. The 1999s from the region's best producers are well worth searching out, particularly those of Domaines Weinbach and Zind-Humbrecht, and preliminary tastings of the 2000s indicate that they appear to be excellent.

IN SEARCH OF THE BEST
(Alsace's Greatest Wines, on Par with the World's Finest)

Bott-Geyl Gewurztraminer Furstentum
Bott-Geyl Gewurztraminer Sonnenglanz
    Vieilles Vignes
Bott-Geyl Muscat Schoenenbourg
Bott-Geyl Tokay-Pinot Gris Sonnenglanz
Albert Boxler Riesling Brand
Albert Boxler Riesling Sommerberg
Ernest or J. et F. Burn Gewurztraminer
    Clos St.-Imer Goldert
Ernest or J. et F. Burn Gewurztraminer
    Clos St.-Imer Goldert Cuvée La Chapelle
Ernest or J. et F. Burn Riesling Clos St.-
    Imer Goldert
Ernest or J. et F. Burn Tokay-Pinot Gris
    Clos St.-Imer Goldert
Ernest or J. et F. Burn Tokay-Pinot Gris
    Clos St.-Imer Goldert Cuvée La Chapelle
Marcel Deiss Gewurztraminer Altenberg
Marcel Deiss Riesling Altenberg
Marcel Deiss Riesling Engelgarten Vieilles
    Vignes

Marcel Deiss Riesling Grasberg
Marcel Deiss Riesling Schoenenbourg
Albert Mann Gewurztraminer Furstentum
Albert Mann Gewurztraminer Hengst
Albert Mann Gewurztraminer Steingrubler
Albert Mann Riesling Schlossberg
Albert Mann Tokay-Pinot Gris Hengst
Domaine Schoffit Gewurztraminer Rangen
    Clos St.-Théobald
Domaine Schoffit Riesling Rangen Clos
    St.-Théobald
Domaine Schoffit Tokay-Pinot Gris Rangen
    Clos St.-Théobald
Domaine Trimbach Gewurztraminer
    Seigneurs de Ribeaupierre
Domaine Trimbach Riesling Clos Ste.-
    Hune
Domaine Trimbach Riesling Cuvée
    Frédéric Emile
Domaine Weinbach Gewurztraminer Cuvée
    Laurence Altenbourg

Domaine Weinbach Gewurztraminer Cuvée
   Laurence Furstentum
Domaine Weinbach Riesling Schlossberg
Domaine Weinbach Tokay-Pinot Gris Ste.-
   Catherine
Zind-Humbrecht Gewurztraminer Clos
   Windsbuhl
Zind-Humbrecht Gewurztraminer Goldert
Zind-Humbrecht Gewurztraminer
   Heimbourg
Zind-Humbrecht Gewurztraminer Hengst
Zind-Humbrecht Gewurztraminer Rangen
   Clos St.-Urbain
Zind-Humbrecht Gewurztraminer
   Wintzenheim
Zind-Humbrecht Riesling Brand

Zind-Humbrecht Riesling Clos Hauserer
Zind-Humbrecht Riesling Clos Windsbuhl
Zind-Humbrecht Riesling Gueberschwihr
Zind-Humbrecht Riesling Herrenweg
Zind-Humbrecht Riesling Rangen Clos St.-
   Urbain
Zind-Humbrecht Riesling Herrenweg de
   Turckheim
Zind-Humbrecht Riesling Wintzenheim
Zind-Humbrecht Tokay-Pinot Gris Clos
   Jebsal
Zind-Humbrecht Tokay-Pinot Gris
   Heimbourg
Zind-Humbrecht Tokay-Pinot Gris Vieilles
   Vignes

RATING ALSACE'S BEST PRODUCERS

Where a producer has been assigned a range of stars (***/****), the lower rating has been used for placement in this hierarchy.

* * * * * (OUTSTANDING)

Albert Boxler
Ernest Burn
Marcel Deiss
Marc Kreydenweiss
Albert Mann

Domaine du Clos St.-Landelin
Bernard and Robert Schoffit
Domaine Trimbach (top *cuvées*)
Domaine Weinbach
Zind-Humbrecht

* * * * (EXCELLENT)

Bott-Gey (****/*****)
Barmès-Buecher
Jean-Pierre Dirler
Hugel (Cuvées Jubilee and Tradition)
Josmeyer (single-vineyard *cuvées*)
Domaine Ostertag (****/*****)

Mittnacht-Klack
René Muré
Charles Schleret (****/*****)
M. & V. Stoeffler
Marc Tempé

* * * (GOOD)

J. B. Adam (***/****)
Lucien Albrecht (***/****)
Léon Beyer
L. Kirman
Charles Koehly et Fils (***/****)
Kuentz-Bas
Josmeyer (regular *cuvées*)
Gustave Lorentz
Château d'Orschwihr (***/****)

Scherer
J.-P. Schmitt
Gérard Schueller et Fils (***/****)
Jean Sipp (***/****)
Pierre Sparr (***/****)
Sylvie Spielman (***/****)
Domaine Trimbach (regular *cuvées*)
Gérard Weinzorn

* * (AVERAGE)

Domaine Josephet Christian Binner (**/***)
Paul Blanck
Jean-Marie Haag (**/***)

Bruno Hunold
Schlumberger (**/***)
Wolfberger

J. B. ADAM (AMMERSCHWIHR)

1997	Gewurztraminer Sélection de Grains Nobles		
	Collection Privée JBA	E/500ml	93
1997	Gewurztraminer Vendanges Tardives	D	90
1998	Riesling Kaefferkopf Cuvée Jean-Baptiste	C	88+
1998	Riesling Kaefferkopf Vieilles Vignes	D	89+
1997	Riesling Vendanges Tardives	D	88
1998	Tokay-Pinot Gris Letzenberg Cuvée Jean-Baptiste	D	89
1997	Tokay-Pinot Gris Sélection de Grains Nobles		
	Collection Privée JBA	E/500ml	89

This good-quality *négociant* firm produces wines that are sold at reasonable prices. Wines marked "Cuvée Jean-Baptiste" or "JBA" are produced entirely from estate-grown vineyards.

The spice- and mineral-scented 1998 Riesling Kaefferkopf Cuvée Jean-Baptiste is a medium- to full-bodied wine with a lovely, oily texture. Intense liquid minerals are found throughout this well-made and concentrated effort's flavor profile, as well as throughout its long finish. The more powerful 1998 Riesling Kaefferkopf Vieilles Vignes very closely resembles the Cuvée Jean-Baptiste, yet it is even more intense, expressive, and persistent. Both of these wines should be consumed between now–2009.

The floral, talcum, and white fruit–scented 1997 Riesling Vendanges Tardives is medium-bodied and extremely well balanced. Its silky-textured core of fruit reveals candied liquid mineral flavors. Anticipated maturity: now–2008.

Aromatically, the 1998 Tokay-Pinot Gris Letzenberg Cuvée Jean-Baptiste displays ginger-bread-like aromas. Velvety-textured and medium- to full-bodied, it is a flavorful, yellow fruit–packed wine. Well concentrated and fat, it will be at its peak of maturity between now–2009. The 1997 Tokay-Pinot Gris Sélection de Grains Nobles Collection Privée JBA has an explosive, ripe peach and apricot-laden nose. Medium- to full-bodied and viscous, this spicy, red and yellow fruit–flavored offering is sweet, plump, and intensely flavorful. Anticipated maturity: 2003–2012.

The smoke- and spice-scented 1997 Gewurztraminer Vendanges Tardives is medium- to full-bodied, and layered with yellow fruits and rose petals. This flavorful, thick wine's fruit dominates its flavor profile, as well as its admirably long, lush finish. Drink this beauty over the course of the next 10 years. Spiced pears, superripe peaches, and botrytis can be discerned in the complex aromatics of the 1997 Gewurztraminer Sélection de Grains Nobles Collection Privée JBA. This full-bodied, viscously textured, highly expressive wine is packed with concentrated, oily layers of red, yellow, and white fruits. Spectacular to drink today, it will certainly last for a dozen years or more.

DOMAINE BARMÈS-BUECHER (WETTOLSHEIM)

1998	Gewurztraminer Hengst Vendanges Tardives	E	93+
1998	Gewurztraminer Pfersigberg	D	90+
1997	Gewurztraminer Pfersigberg	D	93
1998	Gewurztraminer Rosenberg	C	90
1997	Gewurztraminer Rosenberg	C	89
1998	Gewurztraminer Steingrübler	D	92
1999	Gewurztraminer Wintzenheim	D	88
1998	Gewurztraminer Wintzenheim	D	90+
1997	Gewurztraminer Wintzenheim	C	90
1998	Pinot Auxerrois Rosenberg	C	88
1998	Pinot d'Alsace	C	89
1997	Pinot d'Alsace	B	88
1998	Pinot Blanc Rosenberg	C	89

1997	Pinot Blanc Rosenberg	C	89
1997	Pinot Noir Vieilles Vignes	D	89
1999	Riesling Hengst	D	88+
1998	Riesling Hengst	D	92
1997	Riesling Hengst	D	93+
1998	Riesling Herrenweg	C	88
1998	Riesling Kruett	D	89+
1998	Riesling Leimenthal	D	93
1997	Riesling Leimenthal	D	92+
2000	Riesling Leimenthal de Wettolsheim	D	91
1998	Riesling Rosenberg	C	89
1997	Riesling Rosenberg	C	91
2000	Riesling Rosenberg de Wettolsheim	D	89+
1998	Riesling Tradition	C	88
1997	Tokay-Pinot Gris Herrenweg	C	90+
1997	Tokay-Pinot Gris Rosenberg	C	91
1998	Tokay-Pinot Gris Rosenberg "B"	D	89
1998	Tokay-Pinot Gris Rosenberg "H"	D	89+
1998	Tokay-Pinot Gris Rosenberg Vendanges Tardives	E	94+
1998	Tokay-Pinot Gris Rosenberg Vieilles Vignes	D	90+
1999	Tokay-Pinot Gris Wintzenheim Sélection de Grains Nobles	EE/500ml	88+

Some overripe Chardonnay was blended with Auxerrois to fashion the 1997 Pinot d'Alsace. It reveals sweet white peach and mineral aromas followed by a medium- to full-bodied, luscious, and vibrant personality. This lovely wine is thirst-quenching, plump, flavorful, delineated, and filled with lemony minerals, peaches, and apple-like flavors. It should be consumed over the next 3–4 years.

Barmès-Buecher's 1997 Pinot Blanc Rosenberg is a fabulous effort. Its chalk and gun flint–scented nose leads to a silky-textured, medium-bodied, powerful core of white fruits, flowers, stones, and minerals. It is an excellent Pinot Blanc, extremely well focused, flavorful, and long. Anticipated maturity: now–2003. The 1997 Riesling Rosenberg is a significantly more serious, powerful, tight wine. It bursts with liquid chalk aromas as well as an assertive flavor profile composed of clay, minerals, lemons. Medium- to full-bodied and satin-textured, it reveals toasted almond flavors in its exceptionally long finish. It is complex, concentrated, and backward. Anticipated maturity: now–2010+.

François Barmès's 1997 Riesling Hengst is a superb wine. Aromas of candied lemons, quartz, and minerals are found in this medium-bodied, racy effort. It has admirable richness, vibrancy, and balance, as well as extraordinary purity. Lemon zest, pears, and steely minerals compose its profound flavor profile. This first-rate wine should hit its stride in 2002 and will easily hold through 2012. The 1997 Riesling Leimenthal offers aromas of pink grapefruits, talcum powder, and pears. It is a medium-bodied, tangy, extremely well focused wine with such density of fruit and exceptional balance that its 34 grams of residual sugar (per liter) are barely noticeable. Candied raspberries and honeyed melons are found in its powerful, velvety-textured character. Anticipated maturity: now–2012.

The 1997 Tokay-Pinot Gris Rosenberg was crafted from vines located in the upper portion of the Barmès's parcel. It reveals Meursault-like toasted hazelnut aromas and a lacy, impeccably detailed personality. It is less powerful than the previous wine yet more tightly wound, precise, refined, and feminine. This medium-bodied, concentrated, nut-flavored effort will require patience. Anticipated maturity: 2003–2010. Produced from 28 hectoliter per hectare yields (extremely low by Alsatian standards), the 1997 Tokay-Pinot Gris Herrenweg offers inviting aromas of honeysuckle-laced yellow fruits. It is medium-bodied, crammed with layers of *mirabelles* (yellow plums), dried white raisins, and candied lemons. This forward, focused, expressive effort is concentrated and powerful. With a year or two of cellaring my score may prove to have been too conservative. Drink it between now–2008.

The 1997 Gewurztraminer Rosenberg reveals dazzling aromas of lychee nuts bathing in rose water. This plump, concentrated, pure, spicy wine is well balanced, focused, and verging on flashy. It is rich, layered, and extremely flavorful. Anticipated maturity: now–2004.

Barmès's 1997 Gewurztraminer Wintzenheim displays smoky, earthy, perfumed scents. Poached pears, cloves, raspberries, flowers, juniper berries, and loads of spices can be discerned in this elegant Gewurz. Medium-bodied, delineated, and well proportioned, this complex wine should be consumed between now–2006.

I am guilty of passionately loving ostentatious Gewurztraminers and am generally unmoved by attempts to restrain this varietal's characteristic gaudiness. However, Barmès-Buecher floored me with the 1997 Gewurztraminer Pfersigberg, which combines refinement with power. Beguiling aromas of perfume, bergamot, roses, and honeysuckle lead to a flavorful yet elegant core of cherries, minerals, sweetened Earl Grey tea, and well-ripened white fruits. This medium- to full-bodied wine has admirable breadth, concentration, and length. While it will last significantly longer because of its laudable equilibrium, I suggest drinking it over the next 5 years.

"White wine is my work, red wine is my passion," said François Barmès. With this he poured me the finest Alsatian red I have had to date. The 1997 Pinot Noir Vieilles Vignes was produced from 36-year-old vines in the grand cru Hengst vineyard at yields only Lalou Bize-Leroy could fathom—20 hectoliters per hectare! Readers who cannot believe that Alsace is capable of producing first-rate reds need to taste this impressive wine. After a five-day cold maceration and a three-week-long fermentation, Barmès placed the wines in 100% new oak and performed *bâtonnage* until the malolactic fermentation. In an attempt to promote richness, Barmès topped off the barrels with lees throughout the wine's 13-month *élevage*. The resulting wine is medium to dark ruby-colored and exhibits blackberry, plum, spicy oak, as well as smoked bacon aromas. Waxy cherries, coffee, and black fruits are found in this medium- to full-bodied, intensely flavored, chewy-textured, concentrated, dense wine. Impressive! Anticipated maturity: now–2005.

To François Barmès, "1998 was a great vintage, much better than 1997, which was a year that displayed fruit, not minerals." He feels that 1998 is "noble and crystalline, close to 1990 in its concentration and balance." Loads of minerals can be found in the aromatics of the 1998 Pinot Auxerrois Rosenberg. Medium-bodied and expansive, this mineral, herbal tea, verbena, jasmine, gravel, and spice-flavored wine is expansive and satin-textured. Anticipated maturity: now–2004. Produced predominantly from Auxerrois, the 1998 Pinot d'Alsace displays an apricot-scented nose. Medium-bodied and well-ripened, this blood orange, pear, mineral, spiced apple, and cinnamon-flavored offering is silky-textured and quite fruit-forward. Concentrated and lush, it should be at its best over the next 3–4 years. The 1998 Pinot Blanc Rosenberg has a nose reminiscent of apples, spices, and powerful mineral notes. Fresh, floral, and refined, it is packed with gravel, candied berries, white flowers, and potpourri-like flavors. Medium-bodied, extroverted, and expansive, it is a wonderful example of this varietal. Anticipated maturity: now–2005.

Produced from younger vines, the 1998 Riesling Tradition displays gorgeous aromas of minerals, herbal tea, and bergamot (the exotic orange used to flavor Earl Grey tea). Light- to medium-bodied, pure, and lemony, it is a wine to drink over the next 4–5 years. The creamy tea-scented 1998 Riesling Herrenweg (from the driest microclimate in France, according to François Barmès) is an expansive, medium-bodied wine. This dry, gravel, stone, and mineral-flavored wine has a broad, fresh personality. Anticipated maturity: now–2005. The precise, almost searing nose of the 1998 Riesling Kruett leads to a detailed, highly focused and defined lemon, white berry, flower, and mineral-flavored character. This light- to medium-bodied wine will appeal enormously to those readers searching for delineation and refinement. Drink it over the next 7–9 years.

The crystalline 1998 Riesling Rosenberg has medium body and a broad-shouldered character, crammed with minerals, earth, quartz, and hints of spring onions. This concentrated deep, delineated, and exceptionally long wine should be consumed over the next 10 years.

The 1998 Riesling Hengst offers rich, pure, powerful mineral aromas. Satin-textured and medium-bodied, this broad, gorgeously balanced wine is packed with creamed white fruits, minerals, and lemons. It is beautifully detailed, elegant, and has a long, clean, well-delineated finish. Anticipated maturity: now–2012.

Sweetened tea, verbena, and minerals are found in the aromas of the 1998 Riesling Leimenthal. This medium-bodied, rich, silky-textured wine is highly concentrated, profound, and intense. Its suave character displays herbal tea, jasmine, and mineral flavors that last throughout its awesomely long and elegant finish. Anticipated maturity: now–2009.

In 1998 François Barmès produced two Tokay-Pinot Gris Rosenbergs, one from the lower part of the hillside, which sports a "B" at the upper left of the label (for *bas* in French, meaning low) and one from the upper section of his parcel that shows the letter "H" for *haut* in French. The 1998 Tokay-Pinot Gris Rosenberg "B" reveals intense aromas of minerals, smoke, and buttery spices. This creamy-textured, medium-bodied wine is powerful, elegant, and extremely well balanced. Its easygoing, thick core of apricots and peaches is fresh and immensely flavorful. Drink it over the next seven years. The 1998 Tokay-Pinot Gris Rosenberg "H" offers expressive herbal tea and floral aromas. This broad, medium-bodied, mineral-dominated offering is more focused and possibly longer in the finish than its "B" counterpart. Anticipated maturity: now–2011. From the very top of Barmès's Rosenberg parcel, he has crafted the 1998 Tokay-Pinot Gris Rosenberg Vieilles Vignes. It reveals smoky, buttery, white fruit, and flower aromas. On the palate, it is deep, concentrated, and fresh. Medium-bodied, this dry, white fruit–packed wine has the potential to reach even greater heights as it develops with age. Anticipated maturity: now–2012.

The 1998 Gewurztraminer Rosenberg has a subdued floral nose. This feminine, concentrated, and flavorful wine is medium-bodied and intense, yet lacelike in its structure. Violets, roses, and copious quantities of spices are found throughout its personality and exceptionally long finish. Anticipated maturity: now–2005. The 1998 Gewurztraminer Wintzenheim offers a deep, spiced apple, pear, and juniper berry–scented nose. Medium-bodied, broad, and expressive, it is crammed with spices, almond cookies, raspberries, and potpourri. This highly expressive, intense wine is silky-textured and enormously appealing. Drink it over the next 5 years. The delightfully fresh 1998 Gewurztraminer Pfersigberg at first revealed aromas reminiscent of spring onions. With air, lychee nuts and apples came to the fore. On the palate, this medium-bodied wine reveals refined layers of creamy white fruit and berries. It is not quite as expressive as the Wintzenheim, but more graceful in its demeanor. Anticipated maturity: now–2006.

The 1998 Gewurztraminer Steingrübler reveals floral, spicy scents. This intense, deep, rose, white currant, cherry, and raspberry-flavored wine is powerful, concentrated, and medium- to full-bodied. It is refined, harmonious, and graceful, yet muscular and full-blown. Drink it over the next 6–7 years. The youthful 1998 Gewurztraminer Hengst Vendanges Tardives has yet to develop its aromatic profile. It remains tightly wound and has magnificent potential. This profound, medium-bodied wine has an extraordinary breadth of white and red berries in its intense, precise, and rich personality. Anticipated maturity: now–2012.

The 1998 Tokay-Pinot Gris Rosenberg Vendanges Tardives offers an extraordinary aromatic profile of spiced apples, poached pears, and potpourri. Medium- to full-bodied and oily-textured, it is opulent, complex, and detailed. With huge underlying richness, this highly botrytised, intense offering coats the palate with sweet minerals and huge quantities of white fruits. This beautifully balanced wine should be at its peak of maturity between 2004–2015.

The 1999 Riesling Hengst reveals spiced pear scents and a ripe pear, apple, and spice-flavored character. This is a successful 1999 Riesling, a vintage that was quite tough on this varietal. This wine has excellent depth of fruit and a light- to medium-bodied personality. Drink it over the next 6–7 years. The 1999 Gewurztraminer Wintzenheim offers lychee nut and rosewater aromas as well as flavors. On the palate, this medium-bodied wine is boisterous with loads of in-your-face, exotic flavors. It is delicious, yet lacks the concentration or complexity to merit a higher rating. Drink it over the next 5 years.

The 1999 Tokay-Pinot Gris Wintzenheim Sélection de Grains Nobles exhibits spicy, yellow/white fruit aromas. This is a plump, well-made wine with sweet red berry, cinnamon, and assorted spice flavors. It lacks the depth and concentration generally found in Alsatian Sélections de Grains Nobles, yet is an excellent, sweet wine made for relatively near-term drinking (for a late harvest wine). Anticipated maturity: now–2010.

The 2000 Riesling Rosenberg de Wettolsheim offers gorgeous, sweet verbena aromas. This light- to medium-bodied wine has outstanding focus, delineation, and breadth. It is juicy, filled with minerals, quartz, and hints of bergamot. Anticipated maturity: now–2008. The outstanding 2000 Riesling Leimenthal de Wettolsheim is medium-bodied, concentrated, and ample. This plump yet extremely well focused wine offers loads of minerals and flowers in its exceedingly ripe and delineated character. Drink this beauty over the next 8–9 years.

MAISON LÉON BEYER (EGUISHEIM)

1990	Gewurztraminer Cuvée des Comtes d'Eguisheim	D	89
1983	Gewurztraminer Sélection de Grains Nobles	EEE	91
1997	Riesling Cuvée des Comtes d'Eguisheim	E	89+
1995	Riesling Cuvée des Comtes d'Eguisheim	D	92
1997	Riesling Les Ecaillers	D	88
1995	Riesling Les Ecaillers	D	89
1997	Tokay-Pinot Gris Cuvée des Comtes d'Eguisheim	D	89

Each year the Léon Beyer *négociant* firm produces a Riesling from grand cru vineyards named Les Ecaillers (the French term for people who shuck oysters) in a bone-dry style. The 1997 Riesling Les Ecaillers reveals floral aromas intermingled with hints of petrol. It is a rich wine, with chalky, anise-laden fruit, white raisins, and hints of Cynar (an Italian artichoke liqueur), and should be consumed over the next 6–7 years. The excellent 1995 Riesling Les Ecaillers offers intense minerally aromatics as well as a powerful personality crammed with creamed/spiced minerals, clay, earth, rubber, toasted almonds, and flowers. It is medium-bodied, dense, concentrated, and possesses an admirably long, pure finish. It should be consumed over the next 6 years.

The 1997 Riesling Cuvée des Comtes d'Eguisheim is extremely backward and unevolved. Its muted aromatics were unyielding, even with coaxing, and its tight character appeared to provide me with only a glimpse of its potential. That being said, it has impressive underlying richness, exceptional balance, and medium to full body. With considerable effort, sweet white fruits, anise, assorted spices, minerals, and chalklike flavors begin to emerge from its tightly wound personality. Anticipated maturity: 2004–2012+. The fabulous 1995 Riesling Cuvée des Comtes d'Eguisheim offers petrol scents and a massively ripe yet dry character. Layers of candied lemons, quartz, and honeysuckle blossoms are evident in this wine's crystalline flavor profile. It is medium- to full-bodied, superbly focused, and in need of cellaring. Anticipated maturity: now–2012. Lemon-imbued peach aromas can be found in the medium-bodied 1997 Tokay-Pinot Gris Cuvée des Comtes d'Eguisheim. It is a rich, plump, smoky, flavorful, silky-textured wine. Virtually dry, yet redolent with sweet peaches and apricots, it has exceptional balance and focus. Anticipated maturity: now–2008.

Marc Beyer, this firm's director, is maintaining Léon Beyer's tradition of marketing a portion of its wines when they are ready to drink, a particularly expensive proposition given France's inventory tax laws. The 1990 Gewurztraminer Cuvée des Comtes d'Eguisheim has an evolved goldish color and enthralling aromas of toasted apricots, caramelized ginger, bergamot, and spice cake. It is a dry, well-crafted, fully mature wine with roasted peach, mineral, and gingerbread flavors. I would have elected to drink this wine earlier in its life (I prefer Gewurz and Zinfandel to be flamboyant and ostentatious), yet it is still well proportioned, medium- to full-bodied, silky-textured, flavorful, and a delight. It should be consumed over the next 2–3 years. The 1983 Gewurztraminer Sélection de Grains Nobles, recently re-released in honor of the new millennium, has a gold color and aromas of candied peaches, apricots, and roasted coffee. It is a refined wine with outstanding precision and definition. Medium-bodied and mouthcoating, it offers flavors reminiscent of toasted red cherries, nuts, and assorted yellow fruits. Its slightly alcoholic finish prevented it from obtaining a more exalted review. This wine needs to be consumed over the next 4–5 years.

DOMAINE JOSEPH ET CHRISTIAN BINNER (AMMERSCHWIHR)

1997 Gewurztraminer Kaefferkopf Vendanges Tardives	D	88

The 1997 Gewurztraminer Kaefferkopf Vendanges Tardives reveals aromas of roses and a medley of spices. This medium-bodied and supple wine has an oily-textured core of well-ripened peaches. Well balanced and harmonious, it is neither a cloying nor markedly sweet VT. It will be at its best if drunk over the next 6–7 years.

PAUL BLANCK (KAYSERSBERG)

1995 Riesling Furstentum Sélection de Grains Nobles	E	88
1998 Riesling Furstentum Vieilles Vignes	D	89+
1998 Riesling Sommerberg	D	88

The 1995 Riesling Furstentum Sélection de Grains Nobles reveals delightful aromatics of honeyed minerals. This is a well-made, medium-bodied wine that is somewhat pasty, yet proposes an excellent depth of sweet minerals, dried honey, and raspberry flavors. Drink this sweet late-harvest wine over the next 8–9 years. The 1998 Riesling Sommerberg bursts from the glass with intense mineral, honey, and spice aromas. Medium-bodied and broad, this is a tasty gingerbread- and spice-flavored wine, satin-textured, expressive, and possessing excellent concentration. Drink it over the next 6–7 years. The 1998 Riesling Furstentum Vieilles Vignes exhibits mineral and pear aromas. This is a rich, fat, lush, and sexy wine. Medium- to full-bodied and plump, it coats the palate with loads of white fruit flavors. It is the only 1998 I tasted from Blanck with the depth of fruit that could potentially earn an outstanding rating. Anticipated maturity: now–2010.

DOMAINE BOTT-GEYL (BÉBLENHEIM)

1999 Gewurztraminer Béblenheim	C	88
1998 Gewurztraminer Béblenheim	C	89
1997 Gewurztraminer Béblenheim	C	89+
1999 Gewurztraminer Furstentum	D	91
1998 Gewurztraminer Furstentum	D	92+
1997 Gewurztraminer Furstentum Vendanges Tardives	D/500ml	95
1998 Gewurztraminer Schlosselreben de Béblenheim	C	91
1999 Gewurztraminer Sonnenglanz	D	90+
1998 Gewurztraminer Sonnenglanz Sélection de Grains Nobles	E/500ml	96+
1998 Gewurztraminer Sonnenglanz Vendanges Tardives	D/500ml	94+
1997 Gewurztraminer Sonnenglanz Vendanges Tardives	D/500ml	94+

1998	Gewurztraminer Sonnenglanz Vieilles Vignes	D	94+
1997	Gewurztraminer Sonnenglanz Vieilles Vignes	D	92
1998	Muscat Riquewihr	B	88
1999	Muscat d'Alsace Riquewihr	B	88
1998	Pinot d'Alsace Béblenheim	B	88
1997	Pinot d'Alsace Béblenheim	B	88
1999	Pinot Gris Furstentum	D	88+
1999	Pinot Gris Sélection de Grains Nobles	E	92
1999	Pinot Gris Sonnenglanz	D	90
1999	Pinot Gris Sonnenglanz Vendanges Tardives	D	91
1999	Riesling Burgreben de Zellenberg	B	88
1998	Riesling Burgreben de Zellenberg	B	88
1997	Riesling Burgreben de Zellenberg	B	88
1998	Riesling Grafenreben de Zellenberg	C	89+
1997	Riesling Grafenreben de Zellenberg	C	89
1999	Riesling Mandelberg	D	90+
1998	Riesling Mandelberg	D	91
1997	Riesling Mandelberg	D	90+
1999	Riesling Schoenenbourg	D	90
1998	Riesling Schoenenbourg	D	90+
1997	Riesling Schoenenbourg	D	91
1999	Sonnenglanz	D	90
1998	Tokay-Pinot Gris Béblenheim	C	88
1998	Tokay-Pinot Gris Sonnenglanz	D	93+
1997	Tokay-Pinot Gris Sonnenglanz	D	91
1997	Tokay-Pinot Gris Sonnenglanz Vendanges Tardives	D/500ml	92+
1997	Tokay-Pinot Gris Sonnenglanz Sélection de Grains Nobles	E/500ml	97

The youthful Jean-Christophe Bott has caused the reputation of this estate to skyrocket to the forefront of Alsatian quality producers. Even though he is based in the small village of Béblenheim, Bott has a broad vinous horizon. He tastes wines from the world over, honing his palate and building the gustatory experience and knowledge required of the finest winemakers.

Revealing floral, mineral-infused aromas, the 1997 Pinot d'Alsace Béblenheim is a medium-bodied, rich, broad wine. Its flavor profile, composed of honeysuckle blossoms and melony fruit, is expressive, soft, and silky-textured. Drink it over the next 3–4 years.

Minerals intermingled with almonds are found in the 1997 Riesling Burgreben de Zellenberg's nose. At present it is tightly wound, crisp, and backward, yet excellent underlying richness can be detected with aeration. Crystalline quartzlike flavors combined with a powerful punch of citrus fruit in the mid-palate promise a bright future for this light- to medium-bodied wine. Anticipated maturity: now–2008. The 1997 Riesling Grafenreben de Zellenberg exhibits a crisp nut, earth, and stone-laden nose followed by a vibrant, light- to medium bodied character. This unevolved, apple, clay, and chalk-flavored dry wine is assertive, delineated, and possesses excellent grip. Anticipated maturity: now–2009.

The 1997 Gewurztraminer Béblenheim boasts enthralling scents of rose water and plump yellow fruits. On the palate it reveals admirable richness, depth, as well as opulent layers of candied red berries, marzipan, spices, and lychee nuts. It is medium-bodied, fat, and off-dry. Anticipated maturity: now–2005. The 1997 Riesling Mandelberg displays a nose composed of smoky liquid minerals, white flowers, and nuts. It is an extremely concentrated, pure wine, with mouthcoating richness, a medium body, admirable breadth of minerally pears, and superb balance. This flavorful yet unevolved offering possesses a core of tightly wound fruit that should be a sight to behold when it blossoms with bottle age. Anticipated maturity: now–2010+.

White peaches awash in minerals and fresh earth are found in the 1997 Riesling Schoenenbourg's aromatics. The wine offers massive richness, plump petrol-infused pears, melons, and apples, as well as a deep minerality that is discernable in its exceptionally long finish. It is medium-bodied, concentrated, and impeccably balanced. Drink it between now–2010+. The 1997 Tokay-Pinot Gris Sonnenglanz has a muted nose that revealed pears and honeyed apples with aeration. It is medium- to full-bodied, expansive, luxurious, and crammed with overripe peaches, yellow plums, and loads of honey. I could not help but grin as I tasted this expressive, powerful, opulent, satin-textured, and forward wine. Drink it over the next 8 years. My grin turned into a broad smile as I lifted the 1997 Gewurztraminer Sonnenglanz Vieilles Vignes to my nose. Its mouthwatering aromas of spice-laced lychee nuts, rose water, and cherries lead to a decadent core of tropical fruits, raspberries, and perfume. This ostentatious (yet not obnoxiously so) wine is oily-textured, fat, thick, and immensely flavorful. It should be consumed over the next 7 years.

Sweet peach and apricot aromas are found in the 1997 Tokay-Pinot Gris Sonnenglanz Vendanges Tardives' nose. On the palate, a powerful punch of dried honey, bergamot, pillow-plums, and honey-dripping grapefruits greets the taster. This medium- to full-bodied, viscously textured yet pure and well-balanced wine is concentrated, intense, and showy. It is approachable now but will easily hold through 2014. Readers who crave gaudy Gewurz will flip for the 1997 Gewurztraminer Furstentum Vendanges Tardives. Peony, rosewater, and honeysuckle aromatics are followed by an immense mouthful of apricots, cherries, mangoes, mint, red currants, honey, and perfume. This full-bodied, hugely powerful wine is thickly textured yet fresh and well proportioned. It is a mind-bogglingly expressive effort, crafted in a take-no-prisoners style. Drink it over the next decade. The 1997 Gewurztraminer Sonnenglanz Vendanges Tardives is less evolved and at present more civilized. Crafted from a separate parcel than the Vieilles Vignes *cuvée*, this wine has refined aromas dominated by flowers, chalk, and minerals. It is more feminine, precise, focused, and detail-oriented than the previous offering yet remains extremely flavorful. Red fruits, roses, pink grapefruits, and pineapples vie with underlying minerals for the taster's attention in this medium- to-full-bodied, velvety-textured wine. Anticipated maturity: now–2010+.

The 800 (500ml) bottles of 1997 Tokay-Pinot Gris Sonnenglanz Sélection de Grains Nobles are the result of a painstaking sorting of the same parcel of vines used to craft the Vendanges Tardives. Even after considerable coaxing its muted nose only displayed massive sweetness and hints of botrytis-laced fruit. On the palate, this show-stopper is pure, dense, opulent, elegant, full-bodied, and immensely concentrated. Layer upon layer of plums, flowers, anise, red fruits, apricots, peaches, passion fruit, and spices are found in its viscous personality and throughout its unending, syrupy finish. It is splendid to sip now and will age effortlessly for 30–40 years.

Produced from a blend of four varietals, including Pinot Blanc, Auxerrois, and Tokay-Pinot Gris, the smoky, mineral, and spice-scented 1998 Pinot d'Alsace Béblenheim is a delightful, medium-bodied wine. Silky-textured and suave, this creamy, flavorful, rich offering is packed with lemons, flowers, and honeysuckle. Drink it over the next 4 years.

The aromatically floral 1998 Riesling Burgreben de Zellenberg has excellent purity to its medium-bodied character. Lemons, limes, and a creamy minerality can be discerned in this fresh, well-delineated, and long wine. Anticipated maturity: now–2007. The 1998 Riesling Grafenreben de Zellenberg has subdued chalk, mineral, and floral aromas. On the palate, however, it is highly expressive, with lots of depth to its lemon, white fruit, and mineral-flavored character. Broad and concentrated, this offering should be drunk between now–2010.

The outstanding 1998 Riesling Schoenenbourg reveals gorgeous purity to its fresh herbal tea aromatic profile. Medium-bodied, lively, and crystalline, this quartz, lemon, lime, and candied grapefruit–flavored wine is well detailed, refined, and harmonious. Anticipated maturity: 2004–2012. Complex, botrytised aromas of yellow fruits can be discerned in the nose of the 1998 Riesling Mandelberg. Medium- to full-bodied, it exhibits tea, spice, cedar, and pear flavors. Well focused and delineated, this intricate wine should be at its best between 2003–2012. Demure orange blossom aromas can be discerned in the nose of the 1998 Muscat Riquewihr. Rich, broad, and plum, this medium-bodied wine has deliciously expressive orangelike flavors. Drink it over the next 3–4 years.

The medium- to full-bodied 1998 Tokay-Pinot Gris Béblenheim has a buttery, creamy, sexy opulence to its white fruit and lemon-infused character. Thick and rich, yet ripe and vivacious, it will provide succulent drinking over the next 7 years. The 1998 Gewurztraminer Béblenheim offers fresh floral and spice aromas. Soft, suave, and supple, this oily-textured, medium- to full-bodied wine is packed with opulent layers of raspberries, cherries, and white flowers. This extravagant, lush, sexy offering should be consumed over the next 4–5 years.

Limestone, flowers, and minerals can be discerned in the aromatics of the 1998 Gewurztraminer Schlosselreben de Béblenheim. Medium- to full-bodied and hedonistically textured, it is packed with jammy white and red fruits. This is a complex, immensely flavorful, extroverted Gewurz for those who enjoy the ostentatiousness that can be found in this sometimes full-blown varietal. Drink it over the next 5–6 years. The 1998 Tokay-Pinot Gris Sonnenglanz is a rich, velvety-textured, apricot, peach, and honeyed lemon–flavored wine. Quite youthful and undeveloped (it has yet to fully develop its nose), this is a mouthcoatingly rich, powerful, and highly concentrated Pinot Gris. Well balanced and exceptionally long in the finish, it is a wine that will require patience. Anticipated maturity: 2004–2012+.

The 1998 Gewurztraminer Furstentum has subdued floral aromas. This medium- to full-bodied, hedonistically textured, plump wine displays spiced apples, poached pears, and cherries in its profound character. Drink it over the next 8–9 years. Loads of flowers and candied pink grapefruits are found in the aromatic profile of the 1998 Gewurztraminer Sonnenglanz Vieilles Vignes. This well-focused, fresh, rose water and raspberry-flavored wine has a broad, powerful personality. Layers upon layers of thick fruits coat the palate, yet this outstanding offering is able to remain vibrant and bright. Its extraordinarily long finish reveals its varietal's trademark lychee and rose characteristics. Drink this beauty over the next 8–9 years.

The superrich 1998 Gewurztraminer Sonnenglanz Vendanges Tardives is packed with apricots and hyperripe peaches. Massively deep and hedonistically decadent, this is an in-your-face Gewurz, not meant for the weak at heart. Anticipated maturity: now–2012. Roses and red berries can be discerned in the as yet unformed nose of the 1998 Gewurztraminer Sonnenglanz Sélection de Grains Nobles. This full-bodied, unbelievably dense wine is unctuously textured and packed to the gills with jammy apricots, red berry syrup, and creamed lychees. As with most topflight SGNs, it is thrilling to drink young, but will undoubtedly benefit from the harmonizing effects of cellaring. Anticipated maturity: 2004–2015.

The 1999 Muscat d'Alsace Riquewihr offers delightful orange blossom and mineral aromas. Medium-bodied and plump, this is a rich, raspberry and candied orange–flavored offering. It is satin-textured, fat, and enormously appealing. Drink this lovely apéritif wine within the next 2 years. The 1999 Riesling Burgreben de Zellenberg has a lemon zest, white flower, and mineral-scented nose. It is creamy-textured, medium-bodied, and offers raspberry, mango, and apricot flavors in its thick character. Drink this sexy wine over the next 5–6 years.

The aromatically rich, mineral-scented 1999 Riesling Schoenenbourg is medium- to full-bodied and silky-textured. It is a complex, plump, raspberry, stone, flint, and mineral-flavored wine. This broad, big, and expressive offering also possesses a long, fruit-filled finish. It is an outstanding offering that should be drunk over the next 7–8 years. The 1999 Riesling Mandelberg exhibits liquid mineral aromas and a rich, fat, yet focused character. Loads of detail can be found in its herbal tea, bergamot, flint, and verbena-flavored personality, as well as in its exceedingly long finish. This is a medium- to full-bodied wine with a satin texture and a highly expressive character. Drink it over the next 8–9 years.

The rose-scented 1999 Gewurztraminer Béblenheim is an easygoing, medium-bodied offering. Pears and apples can be found in its superripe, soft, supple character. Drink this straightforward yet delicious Gewurz over the next 4–5 years.

It appears to be fashionable in Alsace to produce multivarietal single-vineyard wines, and Jean-Christophe Bott has thrown his hat into the ring as well. The 1999 Sonnenglanz has a floral, red berry–scented nose and a light- to medium-bodied character. Copious quantities of raspberries and cherries can be found in its well-fashioned, silky-textured personality. Its flavors are beautifully detailed, wrapped in a lush, glycerin-filled character, and last throughout its seamless finish. Anticipated maturity: now–2009. The smoky pear-scented 1999 Pinot Gris Furstentum offers loads of yellow plums in its plump, expressive character. It is velvety-textured, expressive, and loaded with fruit whose flavors last throughout its supple finish. Drink it over the next 8 years.

The 1999 Pinot Gris Sonnenglanz has delectable apricot, peach, pear, and white flower aromas. It is gorgeously ripe with fat waves of yellow/white fruits, minerals, and smoke that can be discerned in its complex and thick character. This is a persistent wine with outstanding depth of fruit and a harmonious personality. Anticipated maturity: now–2009.

The white pepper and lychee nut–scented 1999 Gewurztraminer Sonnenglanz is medium-bodied and satin-textured. Though not boisterous, this wine has enormous amounts of fruit, mostly white berries, currants, pears, and apples, in its well-balanced character. It is soft, expressive, and juicy. Drink it over the next 6–7 years. The 1999 Gewurztraminer Furstentum is a floral, yellow fruit–scented wine. Raspberries, red currants, apples, pears, and spices are found in its rich, sumptuous character. This luscious wine will be at its best if consumed over the next 7 years.

Loads of yellow fruits can be discerned in the aromatics of the 1999 Pinot Gris Sonnenglanz Vendanges Tardives. This broad, candied berry, pear, peach, apricot, and spice-flavored wine is medium-bodied, plump, and easy to love. It is fruit-driven, dense, creamy-textured, and has an admirably long, sweet, luscious finish. Drink it over the next 12–14 years. The spice-scented 1999 Pinot Gris Sélection de Grains Nobles is a fat, rich, and opulent wine. Peaches, apricots, and candied quince can be found in its highly expressive character. Drink this glycerin-filled, boisterous wine over the next 15–18 years.

DOMAINE ERNEST BURN (GUEBERSCHWIHR)

1999	Gewurztraminer Clos St. Imer La Chapelle Goldert	D	88
1998	Gewurztraminer Clos St. Imer La Chapelle Goldert	D	92
1997	Gewurztraminer Clos St. Imer La Chapelle Goldert	D	93
1994	Gewurztraminer Clos St. Imer Goldert Sélection de Grains Nobles	EE	97
1998	Gewurztraminer Clos St. Imer Goldert Vendanges Tardives	E	92
1995	Gewurztraminer Clos St. Imer Goldert Vendanges Tardives	E	93
1998	Muscat Clos St. Imer La Chapelle Goldert	D	93
1997	Muscat Clos St. Imer La Chapelle Goldert	D	91
2000	Pinot Blanc	C	(88–89)
1998	Riesling Clos St. Imer La Chapelle Goldert	D	91
1997	Riesling Clos St. Imer La Chapelle Goldert	D	92+

1998 Tokay-Pinot Gris	D	88
1994 Tokay-Pinot Gris Clos St. Imer Goldert Sélection de Grains Nobles	E	97
1995 Tokay-Pinot Gris Clos St. Imer Goldert Vendanges Tardives	E	93
2000 Tokay-Pinot Gris Clos St. Imer La Chapelle Goldert	D	(92–94+)
1998 Tokay-Pinot Gris Clos St. Imer La Chapelle Goldert	D	92
1997 Tokay-Pinot Gris Clos St. Imer La Chapelle Goldert	D	91+

The grand cru Goldert vineyard lies just north of the picturesque village of Gueberschwihr. Within its *terroir* is the Clos St. Imer, a *monopole* (or solely-owned) parcel belonging to Domaine Ernest Burn. Some of the finest Alsatian wines I have tasted hailed from this parcel. The 1997 Riesling Clos St. Imer La Chapelle Goldert displays smoky wood and mineral aromas. It is a magnificent, medium-bodied wine that expands on the palate to reveal broad layers of sweet poached pears, red berries, minerals, and spices. It is elegant, powerful, pure, impressively concentrated, as well as admirably long and flavorful in the finish. This wine will evolve gracefully for 12+ years if the lucky few who acquire it can keep their hands off it.

Is it a coincidence that in most years my two favorite Muscats come from the Goldert vineyard? Domaine Zind-Humbrecht and Domaine Burn both craft extraordinarily aromatic and flavorful wines from this east-facing vineyard. The 1997 Muscat Clos St. Imer La Chapelle Goldert has beguiling orange blossom, rose, and raspberry aromas. Its flavor profile fabulously follows through on its nose's promise, delivering loads of red fruits, spices, and orange soda. It is medium- to full-bodied, well delineated, vibrant, and has impeccable balance. This first-rate Muscat should be drunk over the next 6–7 years. The 1997 Tokay-Pinot Gris Clos St. Imer La Chapelle Goldert is an outstanding, smoky yellow fruit–scented wine. It is thickly textured, lush, dense, medium- to full-bodied, and displays copious quantities of plump juicy peaches, yellow plums, and honeyed apples. Additionally, this compelling offering is complex, concentrated, and well proportioned. Anticipated maturity: now–2009.

Magnificently refined scents of rose water can be found in the aromatics of the 1997 Gewurztraminer Clos St. Imer La Chapelle Goldert. Readers who crave flamboyant yet not boisterous Gewurz will love this gem. It is rich, opulent, velvety-textured, medium- to full-bodied, and loaded with sweet white fruits, lychee nuts, and cherries. It is extremely well focused and elegant yet powerful and flavorful. Drink it over the next 7–8 years. The slightly gold-colored 1995 Gewurztraminer Clos St. Imer Goldert Vendanges Tardives has enthralling spice, botrytis, and pineapple aromas. This is a luxuriously textured, lush, complex, concentrated wine with tangy candied grapefruit, honeyed peach, raspberry, and mineral flavors. It is massively rich and dense while maintaining impeccable balance. Furthermore, it possesses a mind-numbingly long, pure, flavorful finish. Anticipated maturity: now–2008.

Honeyed minerals, peaches, and hickory smoke can be found in the aromatics of the 1995 Tokay-Pinot Gris Clos St. Imer Goldert Vendanges Tardives. This wine has admirable grip, focus, and balance in its medium- to full-bodied personality. Its flavor profile, filled with raspberries, cherries, apricots, peaches, and yellow plums, is concentrated and powerful. It should be consumed over the next 12+ years. The 1994 Tokay-Pinot Gris Clos St. Imer Sélection de Grains Nobles is a show-stopper! Expressive, botrytis-laced apricot jam aromas are followed by a caramelized peach, spice, white raisin, and roasted red fruit–flavored personality. This sweet, full-bodied, viscous, and velvety-textured wine boggles the mind with its never-ending layers of pure, syrupy fruits. Anticipated maturity: now–2020.

The 1994 Gewurztraminer Clos St. Imer Goldert Sélection de Grains Nobles is liquid dessert. Scents of roses, candied oranges, pineapples, and cherries are followed by a concentrated core of red fruits, lychee nuts, spices, and tangerines. This luxurious, well-balanced, powerful, hugely expressive, full-bodied wine boasts an amazingly long and flavorful finish. Drink it over the next 10 years.

To Francis Burn, "1998 is a great vintage, even though it was difficult because of the rains. However, 1999 is even more difficult, we'll see what happens." He went on to explain that while "maturation levels in 1990 and 1997 rose on a continual, steady pace, in 1998 it was stagnant before shooting up in an extremely short time span. This October concentration reduced the water in the grapes and left sugar, tannin, and acid."

The smoky, plum-scented 1998 Tokay-Pinot Gris is medium-bodied, rich, and packed with superripe yellow fruits, tangy lemons, herbs, and flowers. This vivacious, silky wine will be at its best if consumed over the next 5–6 years. The 1998 Riesling Clos St. Imer La Chapelle Goldert offers a delightful nose of candied lemons and minerals. This beautifully focused, rich, intense, elegant wine is reminiscent of a hypothetical blend of 1996 (due to its vibrancy) with a 1997 (because of its depth of fruit). Its flavor profile is packed with quinine, pears, flowers, and stonelike elements. Anticipated maturity: now–2010+.

Burn's 1998 Muscat Clos St. Imer La Chapelle Goldert may well be the world's finest apéritif wine. Produced from 30-year-old vines, its aromas burst from the glass, revealing red cherries, raspberries, and mandarin oranges. This opulent, medium- to full-bodied wine has excellent breadth to its floral, potpourri, red berry, and orange blossom–flavored character. This immensely flavorful wine has outstanding balance and is sure to be a show-stopper if consumed over the next 6 years.

Tobacco smoke-infused peaches can be discerned in the aromatics of the 1998 Tokay-Pinot Gris Clos St. Imer La Chapelle Goldert. Medium- to full-bodied, dense, plump, and rich, it reveals layers of botrytis-infused peaches, apricots, cloves, and fresh herbs. This outstanding Pinot Gris should be at its best between 2003–2012. Pure, fresh lychee aromas are found in the nose of the 1998 Gewurztraminer Clos St. Imer La Chapelle Goldert. This extravagant, medium- to full-bodied, and intense wine offers rich, oily-textured red fruits, blood oranges, lychee nuts, and roses in its exuberant personality. Readers searching for an extroverted, luscious Gewurztraminer that is reminiscent of those produced in the 1997 vintage need look no further. This wine will be at its best if consumed over the next 5–6 years.

From the outstanding 1998 vintage hails the 1998 Gewurztraminer Clos St. Imer Goldert Vendanges Tardives. Poached peaches, raspberries, currants, and flowers are found in its beautifully nuanced aromatics. Medium-bodied and opulent, this velvety-textured wine coats the palate with rich layers of apricots, lychee nut, and peaches. It is a fresh, floral wine loaded with flavor and beautifully balanced. Drink it over the next 10 years. The 1999 Gewurztraminer Clos St. Imer La Chapelle Goldert is a plump, oily-textured wine. Peaches, roses, and violets can be found in its aromatics. Medium-bodied and fat, it reveals a hint of warmth (from alcohol), yet delivers loads of yellow fruit and spices. Drink it over the next 6 years.

Burn's 2000 Pinot Blanc is a superb example of what this varietal can achieve. Aromatically, it displays rich scents of honeyed nuts, poached pears, and candied apples. Medium-bodied and fleshy, this is a delightful, fruit-filled, plump, zesty wine. Assorted white fruits are intermingled with spices in its lush character. Drink it over the next 3–4 years. The smoky peach-scented 2000 Tokay-Pinot Gris Clos St. Imer La Chapelle Goldert is a magnificently harmonious, boisterous wine. Awesome layers of apricots, peaches, smoky minerals, and spices coat the palate in this seamless and exceedingly well balanced offering. It is powerful, dense, and concentrated. This outstanding wine looks to be one of the stars of Alsace's 2000 vintage. Anticipated maturity: 2004–2012+.

DOMAINE MARCEL DEISS ET FILS (BERGHEIM)

1997	Altenberg Grand Vin Bergheim	EE	94
1996	Altenberg Grand Vin Bergheim	EE	90
1995	Altenberg Grand Vin Bergheim	EE	92+
1998	Altenberg Grand Vin de Bergheim	EE	94

1998 Gentil du Burg	D	89
1997 Gentil du Burg	D	89
1996 Gentil du Burg	D	90
1998 Gewurztraminer Altenberg de Bergheim	E	91
1997 Gewurztraminer Altenberg de Bergheim Sélection de Grains Nobles	E	93+
1996 Gewurztraminer Altenberg de Bergheim Sélection de Grains Nobles	E	93
1997 Gewurztraminer Bergheim	D	90
1998 Gewurztraminer Burg	D	89+
1997 Gewurztraminer Burg	D	89
1997 Muscat d'Alsace Bergheim	C	88
1998 Pinot Blanc Bergheim	C	90
1998 Pinot Gris Altenberg de Bergheim	E	94
1997 Pinot Gris Bergheim	E	88
1997 Pinot Noir Burlenberg Vieilles Vignes	E	88
1998 Riesling Altenberg de Bergheim	E	91
1997 Riesling Altenberg de Bergheim	E	93
1996 Riesling Altenberg de Bergheim	E	92
1998 Riesling Béblenheim	C	88
1997 Riesling Burg	E	91
1998 Riesling Englegarten	D	89
1997 Riesling Englegarten	D	90
1998 Riesling Grasberg	D	89
1997 Riesling Grasberg	D	89+
1998 Riesling Schoenenbourg	E	92+
1997 Riesling Schoenenbourg	E	93+

It is an accepted fact that Jean-Michel Deiss crafts some of Alsace's finest whites, yet his reds remain relatively unknown. Produced from moderate yields and a purist's philosophy that would be revolutionary in Burgundy (never any chaptalization, acidification, deacidification, artificial yeasts, fining, or filtering), these are well worth consumer attention. Deiss's passionate dedication to terroirs and quality winemaking is unimpeachable. He is also an irascible, impatient man, with a firmly held "my way or the highway" mentality that can lead to problems with his less conscientious neighbors. While many vignerons complain about his tactics, all of them respect his intentions and wines. Deiss has built a brand-new winery across the street from his home in picturesque Bergheim. A large, well-equipped facility, it will permit him to extend his wines' *élevage*, a necessary step to attain his goal of abandoning filtration on his whites.

Deiss, who enjoys being controversial, has bottled his 1997 Pinot Noir Burlenberg Vieilles Vignes in the Burgundy-shaped bottle rather than the normal Alsatian flute. It reveals sweet red cherry, plum, and smoked bacon aromas. It is a broad, concentrated, medium- to full-bodied wine with excellent structure and length. Red/black fruits bathed in creamy mocha are found in this soft, expressive offering. Drink it over the next 4–5 years.

The 1997 Muscat d'Alsace Bergheim (50% Muscat Ottonel and 50% Muscat d'Alsace) bursts with enthralling orange blossom aromas. It is refined, light- to medium-bodied, refreshing, and detailed. Loads of candied tangerines and raspberries are found in its silky-textured character. Anticipated maturity: now–2003. The 1997 Riesling Englegarten displays well-ripened pears, bergamot, and smoke aromas. It is richly layered, dense, lush, broad, and focused. This is a plump, powerful wine with superb balance, as well as honey, mineral, and Earl Grey tea flavors. Medium- to full-bodied and expressive, it is delicious now, yet it will easily hold through 2006. The apple- and mineral-scented 1997 Riesling

Grasberg offers a concentrated, medium- to full-bodied core of yellow plums, sweet pears, and lees. This satin-textured, deep wine appears to be holding most of its fruit in reserve, suggesting an outstanding future. Anticipated maturity: now–2009.

I was astounded by the power, complexity, concentration, and magnificent length of the 1997 Riesling Schoenenbourg. Medium- to full-bodied, it has the texture and depth of fruit of a first-rate red wine. This cherry, raspberry, cassis, chalk, and baked peach–flavored offering is well balanced, lively, yet fat and deeply ripe. Anticipated maturity: now–2010. The 1997 Riesling Altenberg de Bergheim exhibits crisp aromas of minerals, chalk, and assorted citrus fruits. Medium- to full-bodied and forward, it possesses a magnificent breadth of steel, candied lemons, white flowers, acacia blossoms, and oranges. This well-focused, expressive, and velvety-textured wine has an exceptionally long, pure, and classy finish. Drink it between now–2012.

In the past, Alsatians would often make "field blends"—assemblages of the different types of vines from a given *terroir*. Presently, there appears to be a revival of this practice. One of the two field blends produced by Jean-Michel Deiss is the Gentil du Burg. The 1997 is an enchanting wine that displays candied orange rind, honeysuckle, and perfumed aromas. It is medium-bodied, wonderfully expressive, floral, and filled with red berries, pears, as well as chalk flavors. This silky-textured offering will be at its best if consumed before 2005.

The chalk- and mineral-scented 1997 Pinot Gris Bergheim is medium-bodied, tightly wound, and backward. Its concentrated core displays excellent richness as well as smoky pears, apples, and honeysuckle. This austere wine should blossom with a year or two of cellaring to reveal its full potential. Anticipated maturity: now–2006.

The 1997 vintage produced luxuriously fruity, expressive, ripe Gewurztraminers and Deiss's effort from the vineyard surrounding his native village of Bergheim is textbook. It offers tangerine, rose bud, lychee, honeysuckle, and chalk aromas as well as a magnificently balanced medium to full body. This embracing, layered, broad wine is crammed with captivating spiced/poached fruits, perfume, and minerals that last throughout its pure, extensive finish. Drink it over the next 6 years.

Revealing aromas of crushed wild red berries and flowers, the 1997 Riesling Burg is a deeply flavorful, powerful, fresh, delineated wine. Its soft texture and medium to full body is crammed with well-ripened raspberries, cherries, and limes. Anticipated maturity: now–2007. The 1996 Gentil du Burg reveals intensely ripe scents reminiscent of assorted herbal liqueurs topped off with cinnamon cream. Its nose is more evolved than I would have imagined for such a young wine. On the palate it is medium-bodied, focused, immensely expressive, velvety-textured, and densely packed with superripe, spicy white fruits. Anticipated maturity: now–2004. Profound mineral-dominated aromatics are found in the 1996 Riesling Altenberg de Bergheim. This gorgeously silky-textured, medium-bodied, and deeply concentrated wine has outstanding richness and ripeness. Candied lemons awash in spicy cream can be discerned in its opulent yet structured core as well as in its long finish. Drink this beauty over the next decade.

The 1997 Gewurztraminer Burg satisfies Deiss's desire that *terroir* should dominate the varietal. Lacking the varietal's ostentatiousness, it is an excellent effort, with rosebud, floral, and assorted spice aromas. On the palate it is well defined, focused, and medium-bodied. Offering subdued floral flavors intermingled with chalk and minerals, this softly textured wine should be consumed over the next 4–5 years. It will last for at least a decade, pleasing those who enjoy earth- and mineral-dominated Gewurztraminers. Produced from 28 hectoliter per hectare yields, the 1997 Gewurztraminer Altenberg de Bergheim Sélection de Grains Nobles offers intense aromas of rose water and lychee nuts. It has an extremely tight core of fruit. After considerable coaxing it reveals complex layers of liquid minerals awash in apricot and mango jam. This wine is exceptionally concentrated, complex, and dense. Anticipated maturity: now–2010+. The slightly gold-colored 1996 Gewurztraminer Altenberg de Bergheim

Sélection de Grains Nobles exhibits sweet, honeyed, herbal, and caramelized aromas. On the palate, candied red currants, poached pears, baked apples, and minerals can be found in this powerful, explosive wine. It is luxuriously textured, medium- to full-bodied, profound, complex, and thick. Anticipated maturity: now–2007+.

Beginning with the 1995 vintage, Deiss has been producing a "field blend" in his parcel of the grand cru Altenberg de Bergheim vineyard. It was crafted from every varietal he perceives as "noble" and indigenous to Alsace (primarily Tokay-Pinot Gris, Gewurztraminer, and Riesling with smaller amounts of Chasselas, Muscat, Pinot Auxerrois, and Pinot Blanc). I tasted the three vintages that have been bottled, as well as the 1998 still in barrel (stunning!), and was immensely impressed with the results of Deiss's work.

The 1997 Altenberg Grand Vin Bergheim is stupendous. It offers pure aromas of smoky minerals followed by a medium- to full-bodied, fat, dense core of concentrated fruit. Multiple layers of expansive, powerful, and rich red berries, minerals, poached pears, spices, and smoked bacon can be discerned in this deep wine. It is a regal, opulently textured, and admirably long wine. I suggest drinking it now and over the next decade. The 1996 Altenberg Grand Vin Bergheim reveals evolved, honeyed malt scents. It is immensely rich, thickly-textured, plump, and medium- to full-bodied. Creamy bergamot, mocha, and sugarcoated minerals are found in this wine's flavorful personality. Drink it over the next 4–5 years. Fresh, crisp, pure, tangy minerals and lemons are found in the 1995 Altenberg Grand Vin Bergheim's aromatics. This highly focused, powerful, and extracted wine reveals a crystalline character filled with citrus juice–covered quartz. It is still tight yet has substantial underlying richness and concentration. Anticipated maturity: now–2010+.

"The 1998 vintage is a good one, better than 1999, but certainly not great. The vines simply had too much trouble coping with nature's mood swings," said straight-talking Jean-Michel Deiss. The 1998 Pinot Blanc Bergheim is fashioned from four different varietals, with Auxerrois (60%) dominating. It was vinified and aged half in *cuves* and half in *barriques*. Its expressive white flower aromas lead to a beautifully rich, medium-bodied character. Apples, pears, and fresh hazelnuts can be found in this silky-textured, pure, and precise wine. Its long, appealing finish displays a superb mineral component.

Rich aromas of tea and flowers are found in the nose of the 1998 Riesling Béblenheim. Medium-bodied, broad, and silky-textured, this fresh, well-balanced, lemony wine is concentrated, structured, and firm. Anticipated maturity: now–2006. The 1998 Riesling Englegarten reveals lovely sweetened herbal tea and peach aromas. Medium-bodied, elegant, tight, and harmonious, this extremely well balanced yet plump wine is crammed with white flowers, slate, and blood oranges. It should be at its peak of maturity between now–2010. Onions, honeyed yellow fruits, and fresh herbs can be discerned in the nose of the 1998 Riesling Grasberg. Its flavor profile, a compote of white fruits, verbena, jasmine, and minerals, is well structured and possesses excellent richness. Drink it between now–2010+.

The 1998 Gentil du Burg is a field blend, produced from an assortment of varietals harvested and vinified together. Fresh herbs and candied oranges can be found in its delightful aromatics. This medium- to full-bodied, rich, broad, yet elegant wine is packed with mineral slate, spiced pear, roses, red berries, and juniper berries. Complex and intense, this multi-faceted wine will be at its best if drunk over the next 8–9 years. Hints of gold can be discerned in the color of the 1998 Riesling Altenberg de Bergheim. Yellow and white fruits, raisins, and nutmeg are found in its aromatic profile. Medium- to full-bodied, it displays jammy apricot and peach flavors, intermingled with verbena, cloves, and sweet yellow plums. This well-focused, satin-textured wine has a long, warm (alcoholic) finish. Drink it over the next 8–9 years.

Readers who are lucky enough to acquire Deiss's 1998 Riesling Schoenenbourg are advised that it will require decanting (for near-term drinking) because it is in a reductive state. (Deiss says that this is the "sickness of the Schoenenbourg," and is typical for wines from this *terroir*.) With air, it displays pure, searing, mineral, and fresh herb aromas. Its medium-to full-bodied, soft, silky palate is precise, tightly wound, and crammed with herbal tea, sweet yellow and white fruits, as well as copious quantities of spices whose flavors last throughout its exceptionally long finish. Anticipated maturity: 2003–2012+. The 1998 Pinot Gris Altenberg de Bergheim was produced from low (23 h/h) yields. It displays boisterous, rich, smoky apricot aromas. This full-bodied, oily-textured wine is packed with compotes of apricots, pears, and spices. It has huge depth, massive richness, and density. Concentrated and well structured, it also has a long, honeyed lemon-packed finish. Drink it over the next 12 years.

Loads of cinnamon, juniper, ginger, and other assorted spices can be discerned in the aromatics of the 1998 Gewurztraminer Burg. Medium- to full-bodied, broad, and sultry, this fresh, yellow fruit and spice-laden wine is well structured and masculine. Drink this concentrated and extroverted offering over the next 6 years. Warm cumin and lively apricot aromas are found in the nose of the 1998 Gewurztraminer Altenberg de Bergheim. Medium- to full-bodied and opulently textured, this supple, sexy, intense wine is packed with raisins, yellow plum compote, and spices. Anticipated maturity: now–2007.

Produced as a field blend (primarily Pinot Gris, Gewurztraminer, and Riesling, with smaller amounts of Chasselas, Muscat, Auxerrois, and Pinot Blanc) the 1998 Altenberg Grand Vin de Bergheim displays caramel and grilled nut aromas. This medium- to full-bodied wine has a magnificent personality filled with fresh herbs, licorice, resin, spices, minerals, cherries, and raspberries. This complex, highly concentrated, extroverted wine is harmonious, fresh, and youthful. Its extraordinarily long finish is pure and highly defined. Anticipated maturity: now–2010+.

DOMAINE JEAN-MARIE HAAG (SOULTZMATT)

2000 Pinot Gris Vignes Blanches	C	88
1999 Pinot Gris Zinnkoepflé Cuvée Théo	D	88
1997 Riesling Zinnkoepflé Cuvée Marion Vendange Tardive	D/500ml	88

The bergamot-scented 1997 Riesling Zinnkoepflé Cuvée Marion Vendange Tardive is plump, well made, silky-textured, and rich. Its thickly-textured flavor profile is filled with sweet Earl Grey tea and citrus fruits. This well-balanced and concentrated wine should be consumed over the next decade. White flowers and berries are intermingled with apple aromas in the nose of the 1999 Pinot Gris Zinnkoepflé Cuvée Théo. Light- to medium-bodied and possessing an expressive honeyed pear, apricot, and white peach–flavored character, this well-made wine is highly expressive and flavorful. Drink it over the next 6–7 years. The 2000 Pinot Gris Vignes Blanches has lovely fresh white fruit and honey aromas. It is denser and richer than the previous wine and possesses a medium-bodied, anise- and honeysuckle-flavored personality. Produced from its vineyard's first fruit (planted in 1996), it is a lovely wine for drinking over the next 3 years.

MAISON HUGEL (RIQUEWIHR)

1998 Gewurztraminer "Hugel" Hommage à Jean Hugel	E	89+
1997 Gewurztraminer "Hugel" Hommage à Jean Hugel	E	92
1998 Gewurztraminer "Hugel" Jubilee	D	89
1997 Gewurztraminer "Hugel" Jubilee	D	90
1998 Gewurztraminer "Hugel" Sélection de Grains Nobles	EEE	94
1997 Gewurztraminer "Hugel" Sélection de Grains Nobles "R"	EEE	94
1997 Gewurztraminer "Hugel" Sélection de Grains Nobles "S"	EEE	94+
1998 Gewurztraminer "Hugel" Tradition	C	88
1998 Gewurztraminer "Hugel" Vendange Tardive	E	93
2000 Pinot Gris "Hugel" Jubilee	D	(89–90)

1998 Pinot Gris "Hugel" Jubilee	D	88
1998 Riesling "Hugel" Hommage à Jean Hugel	E	89+
1997 Riesling "Hugel" Hommage à Jean Hugel	E	89+
2000 Riesling "Hugel" Jubilee	D	(88–89)
1998 Riesling "Hugel" Jubilee	D	88+
1997 Riesling "Hugel" Jubilee	D	90
1998 Riesling "Hugel" Sélection de Grains Nobles	EEE	96+
1998 Riesling "Hugel" Vendange Tardive	D	92+
1995 Riesling "Hugel" Vendange Tardive	E	95
1998 Tokay-Pinot Gris "Hugel" Hommage à Jean Hugel	E	90
1997 Tokay-Pinot Gris "Hugel" Hommage à Jean Hugel	E	91
1998 Tokay-Pinot Gris "Hugel" Sélection de Grains Nobles	EEE	94
1989 Tokay-Pinot Gris "Hugel" Sélection de Grains Nobles	EEE	93+

The outstanding 1997 Riesling "Hugel" Jubilee is crafted entirely from grand cru vineyards yet this firm refuses to acknowledge it on their labels due to their long-held belief that the process used to determine and define the grand crus was flawed. It displays powerful aromas of sweet minerals and honeysuckle blossoms. This light- to medium-bodied, silky-textured offering is complex, flavorful, deep, and focused. Additionally, its Earl Grey tea–dominated flavor profile is extremely well proportioned and admirably long. Anticipated maturity: now–2007. Produced exclusively from the grand cru Sporen vineyard, the 1997 Gewurztraminer "Hugel" Jubilee exhibits wonderful aromas of smoke-laden minerals and lychee nuts. This is a large, broad, opulent wine packed with expressive tropical fruits, sweet rose water, lychees, and spices. It is medium- to full-bodied, powerful, as well as dense, yet maintains outstanding purity, elegance, and balance. Drink it over the next decade.

To celebrate his 50th vintage with the firm, this family-owned *négociant* chose to create a new *cuvée* to honor Jean "Johnny" Hugel. The Hommage à Jean Hugel is from grapes harvested at the Vendange Tardive (Jean Hugel is the author of the legislation governing VTs) level yet does not indicate it as such on the label. The 1997 Riesling "Hugel" Hommage à Jean Hugel reveals intense aromas of minerals followed by a sweet tea, candied lemon, and pear-flavored core. This potentially outstanding offering has broad, rich layers of fruit, a tightly wound inner core, and superb delineation. It is medium-bodied, extremely well balanced, and built for extended cellaring. Anticipated maturity: now–2012+.

Demure scents of smoke-imbued flowers are found in the medium-bodied 1997 Tokay-Pinot Gris "Hugel" Hommage à Jean Hugel. This honeyed wine is silky-textured, concentrated, and was such a delight to taste that I was seriously tempted to swallow. Its toasty apricot- and peach-filled flavor profile is significantly more forward than the numerous VTs I've had in the past from this firm. Drink it over the next 12–15 years. The 1997 Gewurztraminer "Hugel" Hommage à Jean Hugel is a winner! Its mouthwatering nose is an amalgamation of perfumes, flowers, rose water, and lychee nuts. This satiny wine coats the mouth with viscous layers of candied tropical fruits and loads of spices. It is powerfully flavored, well structured, and surprisingly refined. Anticipated maturity: now–2008.

White peaches, spices, and smoke can be discerned in the aromatics of the 1998 Pinot Gris "Hugel" Jubilee. This medium-bodied, rich wine possesses lovely balance and loads of pear and apricot-like flavors. Its long, supple finish exhibits additional waves of spiced fruits. Drink it over the next 6 years.

Jean Hugel, who officially retired in 1997, firmly believed that Vendange Tardive wines should be made only in the greatest vintages. The superb 1995 Riesling "Hugel" Vendange Tardive possesses that all too rare marriage of power and elegance. Harvested at 15.2% natural potential alcohol, this is an extremely complex wine with loads of quinine, yellow fruit, sweet tea, and liquid mineral aromas. It has huge depth to its botrytis-laced core of fruit. This rich, opulent, and highly detailed wine is loaded with exotic fruits, spiced pears, minerals, and tea. It is styled in a luxurious manner, yet retains enormous refinement. This exceptional wine can be consumed over the next 15–20 years.

This firm has just released a superb 1989 Tokay-Pinot Gris "Hugel" Sélection de Grains Nobles. Copious quantities of smoky/spicy peaches, apricots, and poached pears can be found in this medium- to full-bodied wine. It is highly focused, velvety-textured, fresh, and youthful, even after 10 years of bottle age. Caramelized orange rinds, apricot jam, loads of botrytis, and yellow plums are discernible in this elegant offering's personality. It is magnificent to drink now, yet should improve over the next dozen years.

The youthful-looking (he appears to be 24, but is actually 44!) Marc Hugel has been solely responsible for this firm's wine-making and equipment since 1983, inheriting the duties from his uncle Jean (known as "Johnny"). Each wine-maker I spoke with had a different take on what varietals did best in the 1998 vintage. Marc Hugel's opinion was that Riesling is the star of the show. They are "splendid, with exceptional vibrance and perfect acidity. The Gewurztraminers are successful, with nice balance and a good, spicy character. It seems to me that the Pinot Gris are the least successful." Produced from vines located in the heart of the grand cru Schoenenbourg Vineyard, the 1998 Riesling "Hugel" Jubilee displays sweet herbal tea and citrus aromas. This bright, intense, concentrated, and focused wine is pure, crystalline, and complex. Deep layers of minerals, fresh herbs, and quartzlike flavors are found in this bright, wonderful wine. Anticipated maturity: 2003–2012.

The 1998 Gewurztraminer "Hugel" Tradition offers a nose of smoky minerals and roses. It has appealing richness to its broad yet well-detailed character. Red berries, stones, white flowers, and spices are found in its easygoing, almost dry flavor profile. Drink it over the next 4–5 years. Produced entirely from vines located in the grand cru Sporen Vineyard, the 1998 Gewurztraminer "Hugel" Jubilee is a rich, supple, opulent wine. Its spice and lychee nut–dominated nose gives way to a personality crammed with spices and raspberries. This well-made if somewhat warm (alcoholic) wine will be at its best if consumed over the next 4 years.

Minerals, quinine, and hints of lemons are discerned in the aromatics of the 1998 Riesling "Hugel" Hommage à Jean Hugel. This medium-bodied, well-focused wine offers loads of dry minerals, chalk, white flowers, and spices. While it undoubtedly has more residual sugar than the regular Rieslings, most tasters would have trouble discerning it in this off-dry wine. Within a few short years, the sugar should have been absorbed, and the wine should be married to dishes as if it were dry. Anticipated maturity: now–2010+.

The ripe, apple-scented 1998 Tokay-Pinot Gris "Hugel" Hommage à Jean Hugel is opulently rich, crammed with smoky yellow fruits, and possesses a long, well-delineated finish. This off-dry wine is still in an extremely youthful state, and will benefit enormously from cellaring. Anticipated maturity: 2004–2012+. The sweet, yellow fruit–scented 1998 Gewurztraminer "Hugel" Hommage à Jean Hugel is a plump, opulent wine. Its superripe apple-flavored character is warm (slightly alcoholic) and will require some cellaring to harmonize. It is thick-textured, medium- to full-bodied, and has a mineral, stony quality in its long, somewhat alcoholic finish. Drink between now–2008.

The tonic and fresh lemon rind–scented 1998 Riesling "Hugel" Vendange Tardive has gorgeous depth to its personality. Layers of mineral-tinged white fruits, quinine, and dried honey can be found in this well-focused and balanced wine. It is magnificent to drink now as a sweet wine (however, this is not a massively sweet or unctuous offering). With 10 years or so of cellaring, this offering will act as an off-dry to dry wine. Anticipated maturity: now–2016+.

The 1998 Gewurztraminer "Hugel" Vendange Tardive displays a beautiful nose of spices, rose water, apricots, and hints of candied citrus rinds. This medium- to full-bodied, rich and opulent, yet fresh wine exhibits superb balance and focus, while covering the palate with lusciously flavorful fruit. Silky textured and dense, it is a hedonist's delight. Drink it over the next 10–12 years. Hugely intense mineral and floral aromas burst from the glass of 1998

Riesling "Hugel" Sélection de Grains Nobles. This magnificently complex wine coats the palate with unending layers of sweetened Earl Grey tea, white fruits, flowers, raspberries, and other assorted red berries. This magnificently concentrated and powerful wine is well balanced, elegant, and refined. Anticipated maturity: 2005–2020.

The sweet peach-scented 1998 Tokay-Pinot Gris "Hugel" Sélection de Grains Nobles is crammed with unctuous layers of smoky yellow fruits. This botrytis-laden wine is full-bodied, complex (everything from porcini mushrooms to bananas can be found in its character), and extremely long in the finish. Anticipated maturity: 2005–2015.

Aromatically, the 1998 Gewurztraminer "Hugel" Sélection de Grains Nobles is unbelievably spicy. This youthful wine is intensely rich and thick. Oily layers of raspberries and creamy yellow fruits (mostly apricots) are found in its dense personality. Intricate, yet forward, complex, and generous, this opulent wine should be at its finest between 2005–2015.

Hugel's U.S. importer informed me that they would not be offering many 1999s on the American market and were, for all intents and purposes, skipping the vintage by proposing wines from the outstanding 1998 vintage until the 2000s are released in 2002.

The 2000 Riesling "Hugel" Jubilee reveals sweet herbal tea and minerals in its boisterous aromatics. This is a fresh, lively, plump wine with excellent palate presence. It is medium-bodied, bright, loaded with candied lemons, and has a delightfully flavorful and long finish. Drink it over the next 7–8 years. The 2000 Pinot Gris "Hugel" Jubilee has extremely smokey aromatics. This rich, fat, peach, mineral, apricot, and smoke-flavored wine is silky-textured and medium-bodied. Layer upon layer of sultry fruit conquers the taster's palate. Its forward, almost opulent personality is surprising given Hugel's track record of making wines that are normally reserved in their youth. Drink it over the next 9 years.

The Hugels fashioned two 1997 Gewurztraminer "Hugel" Sélection de Grains Nobles wines, both produced from the same parcel yet harvested on different dates. The 1997 Gewurztraminer "Hugel" Sélection de Grains Nobles "R" (this letter can only be seen on the lot number that appears in small print on the front label) was picked on October 30 at 19.6 natural potential alcohol and retains 103 grams of residual sugar. It has an explosive rose, white flower, and lychee nut–scented nose as well as a rich and oily-textured personality. This full-bodied, opulent wine is surprisingly accessible for such a young SGN. It is crammed with spices, jammy apricots, peaches, and minerals whose flavors last throughout its stunningly long finish. Drink it over the next 20–25 years. The 1997 Gewurztraminer "Hugel" Sélection de Grains Nobles "S" was harvested on October 28, two days prior to the previous wine, with a natural potential alcohol of 21.7, and retains 142 grams of residual sugar. It has an intensely jammy nose composed of a myriad of fruits. On the palate, this is a wine of huge depth and richness. Massive layers of yellow fruits can be found in its jammy, oily personality. This is an SGN with exemplary equilibrium that requires some cellaring to civilize it. Anticipated maturity: 2005–2030+.

DOMAINE BRUNO HUNOLD (ROUFFACH)

1997 Gewurztraminer Sélection de Grains Nobles	D/375ml	89

Readers wishing to discover the glories of Alsatian Sélection de Grains Nobles without spending an arm and a leg should try Hunold's 1999 Gewurztraminer Sélection de Grains Nobles. It boasts hugely sweet red berry and floral aromas that lead to a rich, plump, and sultry personality. Medium-bodied and satin-textured, it is crammed with assorted yellow fruits, candied peaches, and apricot jam–like flavors. This wine has excellent balance and a long, fruit-filled finish. Drink it over the next 10 years.

MAISON JOSMEYER ET FILS (WINTZENHEIM)

2000 Riesling Les Pierrets	D	88
2000 Tokay-Pinot Gris Brand	E	89+

The 2000 Riesling Les Pierrets offers wet gravel aromas as well as an ample, satin-textured, and medium-bodied personality. It has nice depth to its pear- and apple-laden core of fruit. This wine has excellent grip and the necessary density to cope with its 8.9 grams of residual sugar (per liter). Anticipated maturity: now–2006.

The 2000 Tokay-Pinot Gris Brand offers smoked-pear aromas and a well-balanced, persistent medium-bodied personality. Focused and possessing excellent grip, this wine also exhibits a fat, ripe, and densely layered core. Pears, apples, spices, and stones can be discerned in its expressive flavor profile. Anticipated maturity: now–2010.

DOMAINE L. KIRMAN (EPFIG)

1997 Gewurztraminer Cuvée Prestige	C	88
1996 Gewurztraminer Vendange Tardive	D/500ml	89+

Surprisingly for a 1997 produced from this varietal (most are flamboyant), the 1997 Gewurztraminer Cuvée Prestige has subdued aromatics that reveal hints of lychee fruit and roses. On the palate, this oily-textured, medium- to full-bodied, highly expressive wine is packed with spices, mangoes, lychee nuts, and other assorted tropical fruits. It is refined for a Gewurztraminer and appears to have more residual sugar than the 6–8 grams per liter I was told, yet it is full-flavored and delicious. Drink it over the next 4 years with spicy dishes or pungent cheeses. The 1996 Gewurztraminer Vendange Tardive offers superripe aromas of tropical fruits, Cynar (an Italian artichoke liqueur), and a myriad of spices. Mangoes, papaya, white raisins, rosebuds, and minerals can be found in this medium- to full-bodied wine. It is impeccably balanced, concentrated, complex, and offers a long, sweetness-dominated finish. Anticipated maturity: now–2005.

DOMAINE CHARLES KOEHLY ET FILS (RODERN)

1998 Gewurztraminer Ste.-Hippolyte	C	88
1997 Pinot Gris Ste.-Hippolyte	C	88

The ripe apricot and peach-scented 1997 Pinot Gris Ste.-Hippolyte is medium-bodied and oily-textured. This ample, opulent wine exhibits a lush, fat personality filled with yellow fruits and spices. It has excellent balance and breadth. This fruit-forward offering should be consumed over the next 4 years. The 1998 Gewurztraminer Ste.-Hippolyte bursts from the glass with lovely lychee nut and rosewater aromas. Medium-bodied and luscious, it regales the palate with a myriad of floral flavors (mostly roses and violets). This satin-textured wine has excellent depth and a long, supple finish. Drink it over the next 5–6 years.

DOMAINE MARC KREYDENWEISS (ANDLAU)

1998 Gewurztraminer Kritt	C	89
1997 Gewurztraminer Kritt	C	89
1997 Gewurztraminer Kritt Vendange Tardive	D	91
1996 Gewurztraminer Kritt Vendange Tardive	D	91
1997 Klevner Kritt	C	89
1997 Muscat Clos Rebgarten	C	88
1998 Pinot Gris Lerchenberg	C	88
1997 Pinot Gris Lerchenberg	C	88+
1998 Pinot Gris Moenchberg	D	91
1997 Pinot Gris Moenchberg	D	92
1997 Pinot Gris Moenchberg Vendange Tardive	D	92
1998 Pinot Gris Clos Rebberg	D	89+
1997 Pinot Gris Clos Rebberg	D	90+
1997 Pinot Gris Clos Rebberg Vendange Tardive	D	94
1997 Riesling Andlau	C	89

1998 Riesling Kastelberg	D	92+
1997 Riesling Kastelberg	D	93+
1998 Riesling Wiebelsberg	D	89+
1997 Riesling Wiebelsberg	D	89
1997 Riesling Wiebelsberg Vendange Tardive	D	92+

The intelligent, inquisitive, and highly talented Marc Kreydenweiss has recently purchased an estate (the Domaine des Perrières) in the Costières de Nîmes, joining the large number of wine-makers, wineries, and *négociants* from Bordeaux, Burgundy, and the Rhône who are rushing to the south of France to purchase acreage and produce wines. Unlike most of the others, however, Kreydenweiss has found a way to be present in Alsace the vast majority of the time. He has hired a person in the south of France to take care of the vines. Kreydenweiss appears to oversee the harvest and vinification, then trucks up the barrels to Andlau, where they undergo their *élevage* under his watchful eye. Kreydenweiss was the first Alsatian to adopt biodynamic viticultural methods. The list of vignerons who have followed his philosophy reads like a veritable *Who's Who* of Alsatian producers: François Barmès (Domaine Barmès-Buecher), Jean-Michel Deiss (Domaine Marcel Deiss), Olivier Humbrecht (Domaine Zind-Humbrecht), André Ostertag (Domaine Ostertag), Marc Tempé (Domaine Marc Tempé), and others.

Like Château Mouton-Rothschild, Kreydenweiss commissions a different artist (who is paid in wine) to design the artwork for each new vintage's label.

The following two wines are absolutely bone-dry (0–2 grams of residual sugar per liter) yet crammed with flavor and character. Produced from an enclosed vineyard whose Alsatian name means "garden of vines," the 1997 Muscat Clos Rebgarten displays an elegant nose of stones, minerals, orange blossoms, and raspberry coulis. It is light- to medium-bodied, precise, satin-textured, and laced with floral, perfumed flavors. This well-proportioned wine should be consumed over the next 5 years. Crafted from vines planted in the granite-dominated soils around Kreydenweiss's native village, the 1997 Riesling Andlau exhibits fabulous honeysuckle, white flower, and rose aromatics. It is an extremely well-focused, pure, and crystalline wine with powerful mineral, quinine, and quartz flavors. This medium-bodied and softly textured wine's exceptionally long finish reveals traces of candied lemons and gravel. Anticipated maturity: now–2005.

The steel, iron, and crystalline nose of the 1997 Riesling Wiebelsberg is followed by a rich, plump, silky-textured core of minerals. This medium-bodied, concentrated wine is dense and powerful, with an impressively long and pure finish. Anticipated maturity: now–2010.

The 1997 Pinot Gris Lerchenberg offers sweet, smoky pear and apple-infused aromatics. This is a rich wine, with excellent balance, medium body, and assertive smoke, mineral, and tangy lemon flavors. It appears to be holding most of its concentrated personality in reserve. Anticipated maturity: now–2008. Kreydenweiss's parcel of Pinot Gris Clos Rebberg is planted on 24 terraces across this steep vineyard's slope. The 1997 exhibits aromas reminiscent of spiced vegetables sautéed in sweet butter. It is light- to medium-bodied, immensely complex, well focused, and packed with rich layers of stones, flint, and pears. Intensely flavored and unbelievably long in the finish, this elegant wine should be drunk over the next decade.

Produced from 15-year-old vines, the bergamot, sweetened tea leaf, and mineral-scented 1997 Pinot Gris Moenchberg has 16 grams of residual sugar (per liter) yet tastes totally dry. Its expressive, medium-bodied personality is exceptionally broad, deep, and velvety-textured. Loads of smoky pears, apples, rock dust, minerals, and hickory can be discerned. This layered, outstanding Pinot Gris should be consumed over the next dozen years.

Crafted from 55-year-old vines that yielded only 30 h/h in 1997, the show-stopping Riesling Kastelberg offers profound aromas of white peaches, stones, and minerals. This super-serious yet generous wine is packed with concentrated layers of seashells, flint, and chalk in its gorgeously delineated personality. It is medium-bodied, rich, highly structured, and powerful. This magnificent effort should be at its peak between 2003–2015. The sweetened Earl Grey tea and mineral-scented 1997 Riesling Wiebelsberg Vendange Tardive exhibits a stone/chalk-flavored character. It is an extraordinarily refined yet hugely flavorful medium-bodied wine with 25 grams of residual sugar that are virtually unnoticeable. This impeccably balanced offering's precision, delineation, and length stand as testimony to Kreydenweiss's brilliant winemaking. Anticipated maturity: now–2017.

The 1997 Klevner Kritt (late-harvest Pinot Blanc) has awesome aromas of sweet/spicy minerals awash in red and white currants. It is elegant, complex, and concentrated with a delightful flavor profile composed of multiple layers of creamed white peaches and pears. This wine has excellent balance, freshness, and focus. Why not drink it in its youth while the fruit dominates its personality? Anticipated maturity: now–2005. The creamed mineral and rose water–scented 1997 Gewurztraminer Kritt has a subtle style, atypical for most ostentatious Gewurztraminers. It is refined, pure, and beautifully wrought. Medium-bodied, satin-textured, well balanced, and filled with perfumed minerals, this offering will be an ideal accompaniment to delicately spiced dishes. Drink it over the next 7 years.

Produced from a sorting of the ripest grapes in the Kritt vineyard, the 1997 Gewurztraminer Kritt Vendange Tardive reveals perfumed and floral aromas. Its medium- to full-bodied flavor profile, reminiscent of creamy white peaches, is powerful, explosive, and highly concentrated. This wine has superb equilibrium, intensity, and elegance to its satin-textured character. Anticipated maturity: now–2007. The 1996 Gewurztraminer Kritt Vendange Tardive is equally outstanding yet different. Hugely expressive aromatics of deeply spiced kumquats are followed by a superripe core of herbal liqueurs, raspberries, cherries, and chalk. It is medium-bodied, refined, delineated, and immensely flavorful. Drink it over the next 6–7 years.

The 1997 Pinot Gris Clos Rebberg Vendange Tardive combines Kreydenweiss's ethereal, elegant, well-proportioned style of winemaking with opulence and immense power. Smoky pear, apple, and mineral aromas lead to a huge explosion of apricots, peaches, bergamot, sweet herbs, and flowers. This magnificent wine is medium-bodied, velvety-textured, and possesses a mind-numbingly long, pure finish. Anticipated maturity: now–2015. The 1997 Pinot Gris Moenchberg Vendange Tardive is sweeter (55 grams of residual sugar per liter as compared to 40 for the Clos Rebberg VT), yet more subdued aromatically. Its spiced flower scents give way to a powerful punch of roasted and creamed white/yellow fruits whose expressive flavors last throughout the wine's mid-palate and extended finish. It is medium-bodied, focused, well balanced, concentrated, and plump. Anticipated maturity: now–2012.

White flowers and bergamot are found in the aromatics of the 1998 Riesling Wiebelsberg. This light- to medium-bodied, feminine, detail-oriented wine is packed with loads of white fruits, minerals, and flowers. Well made and exhibiting excellent grip, this potentially outstanding Riesling should be at its peak of maturity between now–2010+.

The 1998 Riesling Kastelberg, produced from 27 h/h yields, displays chalk, limestone, white berries, and slight hints of botrytis in its aromatics. Medium-bodied, broad, graceful, yet powerful, this concentrated, sweet herbal tea, spice cake, and pear-flavored wine has a sumptuous mouth-feel. Magnificent to drink today, it should become even better with cellaring. Anticipated maturity: 2003–2012+.

The 1998 Pinot Gris Lerchenberg reveals buttery, smoky, floral, and chalk aromas. Light- to medium-bodied, it has a white fruit and grilled nut character. This well-balanced and focused wine should be consumed over the next 5–6 years. The white flower and crisp apple–scented 1998 Pinot Gris Clos Rebberg is medium-bodied, velvety-textured, and supple. This broad, mineral, candied lemon, white berry, honeysuckle, and raspberry-flavored wine is complex and luscious. Anticipated maturity: now–2010.

The 1998 Pinot Gris Moenchberg offers chalk, white fruits, and talcum powder aromas.

This medium-bodied, highly expressive, focused wine is crammed with peaches, spiced apples, minerals, and hints of cumin. Feminine and satin-textured, it has lovely detail to its forward, flavorful personality. Drink it between now–2010+. The rose water, lychee nut, and perfume-scented 1998 Gewurztraminer Kritt is a rich, supple, medium-bodied wine. This expressive offering has a long, flavor-packed, supple finish. Drink it over the next 5–6 years.

MAISON KUENTZ-BAS (HUSSEREN-LES-CHÂTEAUX)

1997 Gewurztraminer Eichberg	D	89
1997 Gewurztraminer Eichberg Vendange Tardive	D	89+
1997 Gewurztraminer Pfersigberg Vendange Tardive	D	88
1997 Gewurztraminer Réserve Personnelle	D	88
1998 Riesling Cuvée Jérémy Sélection de Grains Nobles	D	92
1998 Riesling Pfersigberg Cuvée Caroline Vendange Tardive	D	91
1998 Riesling Rangen de Thann	D	91
1998 Tokay-Pinot Gris Cuvée Caroline Vendange Tardive	D	90
1997 Tokay-Pinot Gris Cuvée Caroline Vendange Tardive	D	90+
1998 Tokay-Pinot Gris Eichberg	D	88

Note: Wines labeled "Tradition" are Kuentz-Bas's *négociant* bottlings, and those marked "Réserve Personnelle" are from estate-owned vineyards.

Kuentz-Bas has produced the first-rate 1998 Riesling Rangen de Thann from purchased grapes (in fact, the firm's contract stipulated that they would harvest the grape equivalent of 1,000 liters of wine). It displays lovely aromatics of white fruits, spices, and liquid minerals and a medium- to full-bodied personality. Structurally, it is more reminiscent of a 1996 because of its lemon juice tanginess, purity, and crystalline precision, yet it possesses 1997's richness. Citrus fruits, loads of minerals, chalk, and sweetened tea can be found in its satin-textured flavor profile and throughout its exceptional finish. Anticipated maturity: now–2008+. The 1998 Riesling Pfersigberg Cuvée Caroline Vendange Tardive's nose displays smoky honeysuckle blossoms and assorted sugarcoated white flowers. It is a mouth-coating, medium- to full-bodied, expressive wine with forward bergamot, red cherry, candied peach, and honeyed apple flavors. This powerful, well-balanced, silky-textured offering will be at its peak between now–2010+. Kuentz-Bas's 1998 Riesling Cuvée Jérémy Sélection de Grains Nobles exhibits leesy, floral, spiced apple, poached pear, and bergamot aromas. It is an explosive wine with massive breadth, power, and sweetness. This concentrated, backward, medium- to full-bodied, compelling offering is crammed with candied yellow fruits, sugar-filled tea, and minerals. Anticipated maturity: 2003–2015.

Aromatically, the 1998 Tokay-Pinot Gris Eichberg reveals lemony peaches and flower blossoms. This opulent, expressive, velvety-textured, medium- to full-bodied wine is filled with spicy bergamot, white fruits, and smoky flavors. It is off-dry, yet tangy and vibrant. Drink it over the next 7 years. The 1997 Tokay-Pinot Gris Cuvée Caroline Vendange Tardive has spicy apricot aromas followed by a medium- to full-bodied, opulent, expressive character. This peach, pineapple, and yellow plum–flavored wine is silky-textured, concentrated, impeccably balanced, and possesses an impressively long finish. Anticipated maturity: now–2010+. Peaches, talc, flowers, and perfume are found in the 1998 Tokay-Pinot Gris Cuvée Caroline Vendange Tardive's nose. This is a huge, plump, medium- to full-bodied, viscous wine crammed with apricot jam. It is denser, thicker, and sweeter than the 1997 yet does not possess that wine's impressive equilibrium. This VT appears to have SGN levels of residual sugar yet I would opt for drinking it sooner rather than later. Anticipated maturity: now–2006.

Readers who are not fans of boisterous, flamboyant Gewurztraminers will admire Kuentz-Bas's 1997s. The warm-harvest weather tended to exacerbate this varietal's assertive characteristics, yet this firm crafted more subdued Gewurztraminers than most of its peers. The

1997 Gewurztraminer Réserve Personnelle reveals floral, delicate rosewater scents. On the palate, it is medium-bodied, focused, and has refined layers of lychee nut, raspberry, and spice flavors. It is flavorful and expressive, but not gaudy or ostentatious. Drink it over the next 4–5 years. The floral nose of the 1997 Gewurztraminer Eichberg is followed by a well-proportioned, medium-bodied, elegant personality. This rose-filled wine is feminine, detailed, and satin-textured. Though not particularly concentrated or powerful, it has both an expressive and refined palate. Anticipated maturity: now–2004.

The 1997 Gewurztraminer Eichberg Vendange Tardive reveals a rose water–scented nose reminiscent of the aromas encountered in many Arab desserts. It has brilliant definition and structure as well as loads of delicate lychee, mineral, and raspberry flavors. This medium- to full-bodied Vendange Tardive is not overly sweet and will make an excellent accompaniment to pungent cheeses (such as Alsace's famous Muenster). If it gathers more weight in the bottle it may ultimately merit an outstanding rating. Drink it over the next 6–8 years.

The stylish 1997 Gewurztraminer Pfersigberg Vendange Tardive has demure aromatics, revealing only slight floral notes. Light- to medium-bodied, bright, it offers lemon-infused minerals, peaches, and apricots. This offering is for those who do not particularly care for this exuberant varietal yet are searching for an excellent off-dry, well-focused wine to go with moderately spicy foods. Anticipated maturity: now–2005.

DOMAINE GUSTAVE LORENTZ (BERGHEIM)

1995 Gewurztraminer Altenberg de Bergheim	D	88
1995 Riesling Altenberg de Bergheim	D	89

The 1995 Riesling Altenberg de Bergheim offers a nose of white flowers and minerals. This is a tangy, lemon, lime, earth, petrol, and stone-flavored wine. Light- to medium-bodied, it is satin-textured, vivacious, and exceedingly well focused. It is presently at its peak and will easily hold another 6 years. The 1995 Gewurztraminer Altenberg de Bergheim has dense earth, mineral, and yellow fruit aromas. Readers who are turned off by the more ostentatious examples of this varietal will particularly enjoy this wine's discreet flavor profile. Medium-bodied and lively, it offers stone, citrus fruit, poached pear, and floral elements in its silky core. Drink it over the next 3–4 years.

DOMAINE ALBERT MANN (WETTOLSHEIM)

1998 Gewurztraminer	C	88
1997 Gewurztraminer Altenbourg Vendange Tardive	D/500ml	94
1999 Gewurztraminer Furstentum	C	92
1998 Gewurztraminer Furstentum	C	92
1998 Gewurztraminer Furstentum Sélection de Grains Nobles	D/375ml	96
1997 Gewurztraminer Furstentum Sélection de Grains Nobles	E/500ml	95+
1999 Gewurztraminer Furstentum Vendanges Tardives	D/500ml	91
1999 Gewurztraminer Steingrubler	C	90
1998 Gewurztraminer Steingrubler	C	91
1999 Pinot Auxerrois Vieilles Vignes	B	88
1998 Pinot Auxerrois Vieilles Vignes	B	88
1999 Pinot Noir Vieilles Vignes	D	88
1997 Riesling Altenbourg Vendange Tardive	D/500ml	90
1995 Riesling Cuvée Antoine	E	96
1998 Riesling Fleck Vendange Tardive	D	92+
1999 Riesling Furstentum	C	91
1998 Riesling Furstentum Vendange Tardive	D	95

1999	Riesling Schlossberg	C	89
1999	Tokay-Pinot Gris Altenbourg Sélection de Grains Nobles	D/375ml	94
1998	Tokay-Pinot Gris Altenbourg Sélection de Grains Nobles	E/375ml	95
1998	Tokay-Pinot Gris Altenbourg Sélection de Grains Nobles "Le Tri"	EE/375ml	97
1999	Tokay-Pinot Gris Altenbourg Vendange Tardive	D/500ml	92+
1997	Tokay-Pinot Gris Altenbourg Vendange Tardive	D/500ml	93
1999	Tokay-Pinot Gris Furstentum	C	92
1998	Tokay-Pinot Gris Furstentum	D	89+
1999	Tokay-Pinot Gris Hengst	C	90
1998	Tokay-Pinot Gris Hengst	C	89
1997	Tokay-Pinot Gris Hengst	C	89
1999	Tokay-Pinot Gris Pfersigberg	C	90
1999	Tokay-Pinot Gris Vieilles Vignes	C	89
1998	Tokay-Pinot Gris Vieilles Vignes	C	88

Maurice and Jacky Barthelmé's Domaine Albert Mann may be one of Alsace's finest estates, yet they continue to charge consumer-friendly prices. The honeydew melon, apricot, and pear-scented 1999 Pinot Auxerrois Vieilles Vignes is rich, plump, and medium-bodied. Excellent, deep, layered flavors of apples, poached pears, and honeysuckle last throughout its appealingly long finish. Drink this lovely offering over the next 4 years. The scrumptious 1998 Pinot Auxerrois Vieilles Vignes exhibits smoky yellow fruit scents and a thick, silky-textured, medium- to full-bodied personality. Well balanced, with excellent grip and focus, this superb value has a pear, apple, peach, honeysuckle, and mineral-flavored character. Drink it over the next 4 years.

The 1997 Tokay-Pinot Gris Hengst has 13.1% alcohol and 49 grams of residual sugar per liter (g/l rs). It reveals peach, apricot, and mineral aromas that are followed by an exceedingly rich, broad, medium- to full-bodied character. This Early Grey tea and yellow fruit–flavored wine has excellent depth, balance, and length. Anticipated maturity: now–2009.

Botrytis and bergamot scents are found in the gorgeously focused, profound, powerful 1997 Riesling Altenbourg Vendange Tardive. As VTs go, this wine is relatively dry and will absorb most of its 28 g/l rs with cellaring. It is medium- to full-bodied, deep, extremely well proportioned, and offers layers of white/yellow fruits and minerals in its velvety-textured personality. Drink it over the next 15 years. The significantly sweeter (64 g/l rs) 1997 Tokay-Pinot Gris Altenbourg Vendange Tardive bursts from the glass with powerful mineral and peach aromas. This roasted peanut, pineapple, mango, peach, and stone-flavored wine is medium- to full-bodied, highly expressive, and extremely persistent. Anticipated maturity: now–2012+.

Aromatically, the 1997 Gewurztraminer Altenbourg Vendange Tardive boasts assertive lychee, rose blossom, spice, and botrytis aromas. It is a medium- to full-bodied, sweet, captivating, layered wine. Loads of red cherries, raspberries, and tropical fruits can be found in this boisterous, satin-textured offering. Drink it over the next 7–8 years. The extraordinary 1997 Gewurztraminer Furstentum Sélection de Grains Nobles has a superb nose reminiscent of spices immersed in rose water. This massive, botrytis-infected, hugely concentrated wine has gorgeous balance to its tropical fruit and cherry-flavored personality. Hugely sweet yet elegant, it possesses an amazingly long and complex finish. While it will certainly last for 30+ years, I would suggest drinking it before 2009 to fully enjoy its flamboyant nature.

This estate crafted first-rate Rieslings in 1995, including the recently released Cuvée Antoine. It offers complex aromatics reminiscent of toasted minerals, lemons, bergamot, and dried honey. This full-bodied, massively layered wine is luscious, super-concentrated, and crammed with candied orange rinds, quince, rocks, earth, pineapples, and botrytis-dusted apples. It is amazingly intricate, impeccably balanced, and should age gracefully for another 15+ years. Sadly, only a minuscule quantity of this mind-blowing gem was produced.

Maurice Barthelmé, who, with his wine-maker brother and their wives, administers this estate, feels that 1998 does not have the power of 1997, yet it is "a great vintage, ranking along with 1994 and 1989, for Alsace's best producers." He went on to say that "Gewurztraminer is unequivocally and incontestably the varietal that performed the best in the 1998 vintage, and is maybe the greatest vintage ever for this grape."

Produced from the Altenbourg and Rosenberg vineyards, the 1998 Tokay-Pinot Gris Vieilles Vignes has a deeply smoky, yellow plum–filled nose. This pure, satin-textured, medium-bodied offering is plump, has a lovely depth of fruit, and is well balanced. This exuberant wine can be drunk over the next 5–6 years. The 1998 Tokay-Pinot Gris Hengst reveals wonderfully ripe apricot aromas and flavors. Medium-bodied and lush, red currants, raspberries, and hints of dried acacia blossom honey are found in its extroverted personality. Anticipated maturity: now–2006. The 1998 Tokay-Pinot Gris Furstentum has a complex, botrytised nose, smoke, anise, and plump gooseberries. This medium-bodied, silky textured wine is packed with spices, peaches, and yellow plums. Its long finish reveals hints of warmth due to this wine's relatively elevated alcohol. Anticipated maturity: now–2008.

The highly extroverted, nearly ostentatious aromas of the 1998 Gewurztraminer reveal rose water, lychee nuts, and spices. This satin-textured, fresh, feminine, elegant wine is packed with flowers, spices, lilacs, and candied raspberries. Medium-bodied and well balanced, it can be drunk over the course of the next 4–5 years. The 1998 Gewurztraminer Furstentum exhibits an elegant floral nose reminiscent of Moroccan spices (dried chiles, ginger, cinnamon, curry, and a myriad of others) as well as a compelling note reminiscent of freshly chopped spring onions. This lush, rich, opulent wine is crammed with botrytis, red cherries, raspberries, and flowers. Medium- to full-bodied, and possessing a long, flavorful finish, it should be at its best if consumed between now–2007. The sautéed porcini, yellow plum, and honeydew melon–scented 1998 Gewurztraminer Steingrubler is rich and complex. Red berries, loads of flowers, English breakfast tea, minerals, blood oranges, and dandelions are found in this intricate offering. While it does not possess the luxurious personality of the Furstentum, the Steingrubler wows with its myriad of flavors. Drink it over the next 5–6 years.

Candied lemon and herbal teas are found in the aromatic profile of the 1998 Riesling Fleck Vendange Tardive. Medium-bodied, silky textured, and tangy, this wine offers outstanding focus and delineation to its lemony, mineral-dominated personality. Anticipated maturity: now–2012+. The spectacular 1998 Riesling Furstentum Vendange Tardive offers gorgeous aromas of peaches, apricots, and spices. This broad, flavorful, creamy wine is elegant and powerful. It possesses beautiful purity to its botrytis and mineral-flavored core. This wine offers that compelling juxtaposition of muscle and refinement found only in the greatest of vinous treasures. Anticipated maturity: 2003–2015+.

The 1998 Gewurztraminer Furstentum Sélection Grains Nobles was harvested on October 28. It projects a mouthwatering rose water and flower-filled nose. Medium- to full-bodied and oily-textured, it has extraordinary purity to its jammy apricot, peach, red berry, and spice-flavored character. This supple, elegant, and powerful wine is sure to wow tasters over the next 12–15 years. Dense, smoky, yellow plum jam aromas can be discerned in the 1998 Tokay-Pinot Gris Altenbourg Sélection Grains Nobles. Medium- to full-bodied and refined, this viscous wine is crammed with candied cherry, botrytis, crammed with apricot jelly and tangy peaches. It has admirable equilibrium, complexity of flavors, and an awesome length. Anticipated maturity: 2005–2018+. The 1998 Tokay-Pinot Gris Altenbourg Sélection Grains Nobles "Le Tri" was harvested one week before the previous wine (on October 21) from the same parcel of vines. The fermentation and *élevage* occurred in new Allier *barriques*. Aromatically, it offers hints of oak spice amidst a yellow fruit–dominated nose. On the palate, crushed raspberries, cherries, and other assorted red berries are found in this magnificent, complex, broad, medium- to full-bodied wine. It is deep, intense, elegant, and immensely flavorful. While difficult to resist, it should be at its peak of maturity between 2006–2020.

Lovers of Pinot Noir who have never had an excellent one from Alsace should try Albert Mann's ruby-colored 1999 Pinot Noir Vieilles Vignes. Most of this wine emerges from Pinot Noir planted in two grand cru vineyards (Hengst and Pfersigberg) and harvested at 40 hectoliters per hectare, far lower than most Burgundies from the same vintage. It exhibits a sweet red and black cherry–scented nose that leads to a medium-bodied, softly-textured character. Juicy blackberries and cherries can be found in this delightfully sweet, pure, supple wine. Its finish is long, filled with fruit, and reveals extremely well ripened tannin. Drink this beauty over the next 4 years. The sweet tea–scented 1999 Riesling Schlossberg is medium-bodied and has excellent depth of fruit. Fresh herb, mineral, and hot gravel characteristics can be found in its complex, silky-textured personality. Drink it over the next 6–7 years. The intense 1999 Riesling Furstentum is medium-bodied. This wine explodes on the palate with layer after layer of pear, apple, spice, mineral, and verbena, whose flavors linger for up to 40 seconds. It is extremely well balanced, rich, and elegant. Drink it over the next 8–9 years.

The 1999 Tokay-Pinot Gris Vieilles Vignes exhibits smoky apricot and floral aromas. Medium-bodied, broad, and forward, it is filled with potpourri, sweet pear, and fresh floral flavors. Well balanced and expressive, this is a wine to drink over the next 6 years. The dried honey, caramel, apricot, and pear-scented 1999 Tokay-Pinot Gris Pfersigberg is medium-bodied, rich, and packed with fruit. Loads of *sur-maturité*-laced apricots, peaches, apples, and pears emerge from its extravagant character. While most Pinot Gris ameliorate with cellaring, this is a wine to drink over the next 5–6 years. The 1999 Tokay-Pinot Gris Furstentum has beguiling floral, pear, and apricot aromas. Medium-bodied, broad, and expansive, this is a well-balanced wine that should stand the test of time. Assorted yellow fruits, spices, and anise can be found in its lush, satin-textured personality, as well as in its persistent and supple finish. Drink this outstanding wine between 2004–2012. The smoke, mineral, and spice-scented 1999 Tokay-Pinot Gris Hengst is medium- to full-bodied and luscious. It has huge breadth to its pear, apple, and apricot-filled flavor profile. It is a sumptuous wine with an extremely long finish revealing a hint of alcoholic warmth. Drink it over the next 10–12 years.

The outstanding 1999 Gewurztraminer Steingrubler explodes from the glass with raspberries, strawberries, and apricots. Medium-bodied and plump, it has a delightful palate presence loaded with mango, lychee nut, and roselike flavors. Though this is an expressive wine, it is not from the over-the-top school of Gewurztraminer. Drink it over the next 5–7 years.

The 1999 Gewurztraminer Furstentum has marvelously refined floral, pear, and apple aromas. Medium-bodied and oily-textured, it possesses a delightful character packed with cherries, raspberries, spices, and apricots, whose flavors linger in its impressively long, smooth finish. Anticipated maturity: now–2009. The 1999 Gewurztraminer Furstentum Vendanges Tardives explodes in the nose and on the palate with copious quantities of pears, apple, raspberries, and strawberries. This medium-bodied wine was produced from vines over 50 years of age and retains 63 grams of residual sugar per liter. It is extremely well balanced and possesses a long, sultry finish. Anticipated maturity: now–2018.

The smoke and candied pear–scented 1999 Tokay-Pinot Gris Altenbourg Vendange Tardive has superb balance and focus to its sweet white/yellow fruit–filled personality. This is an intense peach, apricot, poached pear, and spice-flavored wine that is powerful and muscular, yet remarkably feminine and elegant. In spite of 56 grams of residual sugar, it tastes relatively dry thanks to its vivid acidity. Anticipated maturity: 2005–2020. The 1999 Tokay-Pinot Gris Altenbourg Sélection de Grains Nobles sports 132 grams of residual sugar per liter. It explodes from the glass with honeyed apricots and peaches. On the palate, this wine has extraordinary depth to its spice, apricot jam, and peach Melba–like flavors. It is a sumptuous, sweet, sexy wine that will offer a magnificent marriage with foie gras. Drink it between 2006–2025.

JULIAN MEYER (NOTHALTEN)

1997 Muscat Petite Fleur	C	89

The 1997 Muscat Petite Fleur exhibits a fruit cocktail, floral, and lavender-scented nose. Medium-bodied, fresh, and dry, this seductively styled wine is meant to be drunk as an apéritif or with light dishes. Given the bouquet's fragility, drink it within the next year.

MAISON RENÉ MURÉ (ROUFFACH)

1998 Gewurztraminer Côte de Rouffach	C	88
1999 Tokay-Pinot Gris Côte de Rouffach	B	88

Note: This firm is the *négociant* arm of Domaine du Clos St.-Landelin and bears the name of its owner.

The René Muré *négociant* firm produces wines from grapes purchased on approximately 25 hectares of vines primarily located in the Côte de Rouffach. (This is a large, 150+-hectare appellation that covers the areas of a number of communes south of Colmar.) Virtually all of the grapes it purchases are from limestone-based soils, and in an effort to ensure ripeness and quality, the firm pays the growers double the going rate on potential alcohol.

The 1998 Gewurztraminer Côte de Rouffach reveals aromas of fresh lychee nuts. Medium-bodied and creamy-textured, this flavorful wine has a personality dominated by roses and exotic fruits. This exuberant yet not ostentatious Gewurztraminer will be best if consumed over the next 4 years. The smoky, apricot-scented 1999 Tokay-Pinot Gris Côte de Rouffach is packed with rich, fat, glycerin-imbued, smoky yellow fruits. Plump, flavorful, and opulent, it will drink well for 3–4 years.

CHÂTEAU D'ORSCHWIHR (ORSCHWIHR)

1999 Gewurztraminer Bollenberg	B	88
1998 Gewurztraminer Bollenberg	B	88
1999 Pinot Blanc Cuvée Drachenfels	B	88
1997 Riesling Enchenberg Vieux Thann	B	88
1997 Riesling Rangen	D	88
1996 Riesling Rangen	D	88
1995 Tokay-Pinot Gris Vendange Tardive	D/500ml	92
1994 Tokay-Pinot Gris Sélection de Grains Nobles	D/375ml	93+

Hubert Hartmann, the proprietor of this estate, adorns his labels with the words *"vin non chaptalise"* (nonchaptalized wine), which sets him apart from the region's lesser growers who depend on added sugar to provide the illusion of ripeness. None of Alsace's finest producers ever add sugar to their fermenting wines, yet sadly most of their colleagues depend on it.

The 1999 Pinot Blanc Cuvée Drachenfels is a superb value. Its mineral-dominated aromas are penetrating, and it offers a light- to medium-bodied, rich character with excellent depth of fruit. Loads of juicy citrus fruits, pears, and tangy minerals can be found in this plump yet refreshingly zesty wine. It is silky-textured, well ripened, and extremely flavorful. Drink it over the next 3–4 years.

The apricot-scented 1996 Riesling Rangen is light- to medium-bodied and plump. It offers overripe, cookie dough, and candied lemon flavors in its rich, velvety-textured personality. Drink it over the next 3–4 years. The graham cracker and gingerbread-scented 1997 Riesling Rangen is light- to medium-bodied and has a baked white fruit, stone, and somewhat chemical flavor. This lush, pure, and flavorful wine also possesses a long, fruit-packed finish. Drink it over the next 5 years.

The 1999 Gewurztraminer Bollenberg bursts from the glass with lychee nuts and roses galore. Fresh red fruits, including cherries and raspberries, are intermingled with white flowers, lychee, and poached pears in this well-delineated and balanced offering. It is light- to medium-bodied, extroverted, yet exhibits more restraint than many Gewurztraminers. It should be consumed over the next 4–5 years. Rich aromas of yellow fruits and spices are found in the nose of the 1998 Gewurztraminer Bollenberg. Medium-bodied and ample, it is thick, floral, spicy, and loaded with apples and pears. Its well-structured finish reveals the warmth (alcohol) often found in the aftertastes of the 1998s. Anticipated maturity: now–2007.

The 1995 Tokay-Pinot Gris Vendange Tardive displays loads of smoky white fruits in its aromatic profile. This medium-bodied wine is rich, broad, and beautifully precise. Loads of tangy red berries, apricots, and white peaches are intermingled with hints of smoke-infused minerals in this deep, well-ripened wine. It is at its peak of maturity, yet will hold for another 10 years.

The 1997 Riesling Enchenberg Vieux Thann has shy, floral flavors that give way to a chalk, mineral, quinine, and citrus fruit–dominated character. This medium-bodied wine is harmonious, nuanced, and silky-textured. Anticipated maturity: now–2005.

The gold/amber-colored 1994 Tokay-Pinot Gris Sélection de Grains Nobles exudes extraordinary aromatics reminiscent of baked peaches, candied lemon zests, fruitcake, butterscotch, caramel, plum pie, and diverse spices. It bursts on the palate with cherry, raspberry, apricot, and sugarcoated orange flavors. This graceful, medium-bodied, and beautifully proportioned wine behaves as if it were at its peak of maturity, yet it has the balance and stuffing required for extended cellaring. Anticipated maturity: now–2012+.

DOMAINE OSTERTAG (EPFIG)

1998	Gewurztraminer Fronholz Sélection de Grains Nobles	EE	93+
1998	Gewurztraminer Fronholz Vendange Tardive	E	93
1997	Gewurztraminer Fronholz Vendange Tardive	D	90+
2000	Gewurztraminer Vignobles d'Epfig	C	88
1998	Gewurztraminer Vignobles d'Epfig	C	88
1997	Gewurztraminer Vignobles d'Epfig	C	89
1998	Muscat Fronholz	D	89
1997	Muscat Fronholz Vendange Tardive	D	90
1998	Pinot Blanc Barriques	C	88
1997	Pinot Blanc Barriques	C	88
1998	Pinot Gris Barriques	C	89
1998	Pinot Gris Fronholz	D	88
1997	Pinot Gris Fronholz	D	88
1996	Pinot Gris Fronholz	D	89
1999	Pinot Gris Muenchberg	D	91+
1998	Pinot Gris Muenchberg	D	90
1996	Pinot Gris Muenchberg	D	91+
1997	Pinot Gris Muenchberg Vendange Tardive	E	90
1999	Pinot Gris Zellberg	D	91
1998	Pinot Gris Zellberg	D	88
1997	Pinot Gris Zellberg	D	90
1996	Pinot Gris Zellberg	D	89+
1999	Riesling Fronholz	D	89
1998	Riesling Fronholz	D	89+
1997	Riesling Fronholz	D	88
1999	Riesling Heissenberg	D	88
1998	Riesling Heissenberg	D	91

1997 Riesling Heissenberg	D	88
1996 Riesling Heissenberg	D	89+
1999 Riesling Muenchberg	D	92
1998 Riesling Muenchberg	D	94
1997 Riesling Muenchberg	D	90+
1996 Riesling Muenchberg	D	91
1997 Riesling Muenchberg Vendange Tardive	D	92+
2000 Riesling Vignoble d'Epfig	C	88
1998 Riesling Vignoble d'Epfig	C	88

The 1997 Pinot Blanc Barriques was vinified entirely in oak, spending eight months in 227-liter Burgundian barrels (10% of which were new). It has excellent aromatic depth, revealing white flowers with a deft touch of oak spices. This wine boasts admirable richness, concentration, and depth to its well-focused mineral- and chalk-packed character. Drink it over the next 4–5 years.

Even though André Ostertag did not use any oak in the vinification of his 1997 Riesling Fronholz, it displays wood-laced white fruit aromas. It has a layered, creamy-textured personality filled with complex mineral and citrus fruit flavors. A medium-bodied wine, it has excellent grip, concentration, and balance. Anticipated maturity: now–2004. The 1997 Riesling Heissenberg exhibits fabulous aromatics composed of honeysuckle, earth, acacia blossoms, minerals, and toasted almonds. It bursts on the palate with an aggressive punch of cream soda and anise flavors. This richly textured wine is flavorful, medium-bodied, and would have merited a higher score if the finish had been longer. Drink it over the next 5–6 years.

After considerable coaxing, the outstanding 1997 Riesling Muenchberg's muted nose revealed only talcum powder scents. This is a powerful wine, with exceptional focus, precision, and crystalline purity to its lemony character. It is light- to medium-bodied, admirably balanced, tightly wound, and capable of extended cellaring. Anticipated maturity: now–2010+.

The 1996 Riesling Heissenberg reveals brilliant mineral and spicy lemon aromas. Medium-bodied, it has excellent purity, delineation, and focus to its personality. This fresh, silky-textured wine is mineral-packed and offers a long, lime-laced finish. Anticipated maturity: now–2009. Mouthwatering aromas of crème brûlée and spices are found in the 1996 Riesling Muenchberg's nose. On the palate, this medium-bodied, vibrant wine is crammed with spice cake flavors that are intermingled with hints of candied lemons. Even though its aromatics and flavor profile exhibit some evolution this gem should last for at least 7 years.

The 1997 Pinot Gris Fronholz, vinified and aged in oak barrels (30% new), was bottled without fining or filtration. It offers a spicy nose with bourbon-like aromas followed by a toasty, smoky, salty, tangy personality. This admirably rich yet focused offering is medium-bodied, satin-textured, and impressively long. Drink it over the next 6 years. Aromatically, the medium-bodied 1997 Pinot Gris Zellberg displays sun-baked gravel. This wine, also bottled unfined and unfiltered, has outstanding breadth and richness. It is extremely spicy, loaded with smoky white fruits, concentrated, and boasts a velvety texture. Anticipated maturity: now–2007.

All three of Ostertag's Pinot Gris from the 1996 vintage had extraordinarily long finishes, a testimony to moderate yields and superb ripeness. The 1996 Pinot Gris Fronholz reveals sweet aromas of spicy malt balls that give way to its medium-bodied and silky-textured personality. It possesses a creamed spice bread, mineral, and poached pear–filled flavor profile. Drink it over the next 6 years. Displaying roasted white fruit aromas, the 1996 Pinot Gris Zellberg bursts forth with a superspicy, candied lemon–filled character. This is a medium-bodied, etched, deeply flavorful wine. Tightly wound, it reveals hints of oak in its exceptionally long finish. Anticipated maturity: now–2007. The 1996 Pinot Gris Muenchberg offers smoked bacon, spicy oak, candied, and floral scents. This is an extremely well made, medium-bodied wine densely packed with copious quantities of peaches, apricots, pears, and baked apples spiced with new oak. Luxuriously textured, rich, and concentrated, it offers a superb, candied lemon–flavored finish. Anticipated maturity: now–2012.

André Ostertag believes his wines (save the VTs and SGNs) should be dry—with the notable exception of Gewurztraminer. "This varietal requires some residual sugar to express itself. I used to make them in a dry style but I was never happy with the way they came out." The 1997 Gewurztraminer Vignobles d'Epfig displays refined, sweet aromas of honeysuckle blossoms and rose water. This medium-bodied wine is silky-textured, plump, feminine, rich, and filled with well-delineated lychee and pineapple fruit. Drink it over the next 5 years.

The 1997 Muscat Fronholz Vendange Tardive has fabulously refined orange blossom, candied tangerine zest, and acacia aromas. This hedonistic offering is fat, medium- to full-bodied, and packed with smile-inducing fruit. Luscious layers of raspberries, cherries, and flowers are found amidst juicy orange flavors. I do not believe it has the balance required for aging, but who cares? This delivers pleasure! Drink it over the next 4–5 years.

Readers who have tasted many Alsatian Vendanges Tardives and have found them to be too expressive, heavy-handed, or sweet to accompany meals may want to taste Ostertag's 1997s. While they have high levels of residual sugar (the following three wines have, in order, 81, 73, and 130 grams per liter), they are not ponderous, heavy-handed, or excessively assertive as some VTs can be. In fact, they are so well balanced, elegant, and easy to drink that I did a double take when I heard the sugar levels that they supported. The 1997 Riesling Muenchberg Vendange Tardive exhibits demure mineral aromas that lead to a superbly focused, refined core of bergamot and candied citrus fruits that seemingly last forever. It has lovely density and power, yet is graceful and complex. Anticipated maturity: now–2015+. Peaches imbued with new oak spices are found in the medium-bodied 1997 Pinot Gris Muenchberg's aromatics. This concentrated, proportioned, and extremely well crafted wine boasts an apricot, yellow plum, and spice-laden character. This flavorful yet highly drinkable VT will be at its best if consumed over the next 15 years. The 1997 Gewurztraminer Fronholz Vendange Tardive displays a nose of creamed sweet spices. This yellow plum, cherry, pineapple, and lychee-flavored wine is expressive, well defined, and feminine. It has loads of concentration, power, and depth of fruit yet maintains surprising elegance. Drink it over the next 7–8 years.

The 1998 Riesling Vignoble d'Epfig has a milky, mocha, and creamed lemon–scented nose. On the palate it is gorgeously focused, packed with lemons, white berries, and cherries. This precise, elegant, well-delineated, medium-bodied wine will offer excellent drinking over the next 6 years. Produced entirely in Burgundian barrels, as opposed to the traditional Alsatian *foudres*, Ostertag's 1998 Pinot Blanc Barriques displays a buttered toast–scented nose. Light- to medium-bodied and crystalline, it offers lemon, mineral, chalk, and quartz flavors. This well-delineated and pure wine should be consumed over the next 4–5 years.

The lively 1998 Pinot Gris Barriques exhibits crème brûlée– and lemon-scented aromas. This rich, layered, medium-bodied wine is broad, pure, and precise. Its flavorful core of lemons and minerals leads to a long, clean finish. Drink this beauty over the next 6–7 years.

The 1998 Gewurztraminer Vignoble d'Epfig reveals a floral, perfumed nose of potpourri and assorted spices. Light- to medium-bodied, delicate, and elegant, it has good breadth to its creamy-textured, white fruit–flavored core. Drink it over the next 4 years. The 1998 Muscat Fronholz has super aromas of tangerines and dried honey. On the palate, herbal tea flavors dominate in this beautifully concentrated, medium-bodied wine. Satin-textured and extremely flavorful, it is well delineated and pure. Drink it over the next 3–4 years.

Flowers and loads of red and white berries can be found in the aromatics of the 1998 Riesling Fronholz. This expressive mineral, tea, and verbena-flavored wine has lovely depth and detail to its personality. Delightfully fresh and focused, it should be consumed over the next 7–9 years. The 1998 Riesling Heissenberg was fermented and raised for six months in Burgundian barrels (20% new). Hints of toast can be discerned in its mineral-dominated aromas. Medium-bodied, broad, and rich, it has outstanding depth and concentration to its spiced fruit–flavored character. This intense and powerful wine should be drunk between now–2012. The intensely aromatic 1998 Riesling Muenchberg reveals fresh herbs, stones, and spices. Medium-bodied and masculine, this broad-shouldered, muscular wine will require cellaring. It is broad, deep, focused, and packed with lemony minerals and copious quantities of spices. Anticipated maturity: 2004–2014.

The next three wines had been bottled a few hours before my visit to the estate and appeared to suffer both aromatically and gustatorially. In short, they may be better than these tasting notes suggest. Oak and buttered toast can be discerned in the aromatics of the 1998 Pinot Gris Fronholz. Light- to medium-bodied, and revealing lemony quartz and woody crystalline flavors, this is a well-made, focused, detail-oriented Pinot Gris to be consumed over the next 4 years. The toast-scented 1998 Pinot Gris Zellberg offers candied lemon, minerals, and limes in its delineated, light- to medium-bodied character. Tangy citrus fruits can be found throughout its flavor profile, as well as in its long, defined finish. Anticipated maturity: now–2007. Spicy buttered brioche and white flowers are found in the 1998 Pinot Gris Muenchberg's nose. Medium-bodied, complex, and concentrated, this intense wine coats the palate with layers of anise, spices, and butterscotch. Anticipated maturity: now–2009.

The enthralling aromatics of the 1998 Gewurztraminer Fronholz Vendange Tardive are filled with rich red cherries and apricots. Medium- to full-bodied, broad, elegant, and highly concentrated, this candied raspberry, peach, and jammy yellow plum–flavored wine is fresh and enormously pure. Moreover, it has a long, graceful, harmonious finish. Drink this beauty over the next dozen years.

Potentially better, the 1998 Gewurztraminer Fronholz Sélection de Grains Nobles exhibits botrytised white berries and red berries, as well as spices in its intense aromatics. Medium- to full-bodied, plump, and crammed with a myriad of spices, this cherry juice–flavored wine has admirable concentration and power. An extremely classy wine, it is superb to drink today, but potentially will be even better with cellaring. Anticipated maturity: 2003–2012.

The 2000 Riesling Vignoble d'Epfig has enormously appealing white flower aromas. Light- to medium-bodied, zesty, and pure, it offers delightful candied lemon and mineral flavors in its focused, well-delineated character. Drink this wine over the next 4–5 years.

The spice- and apricot-scented 2000 Gewurztraminer Vignoble d'Epfig is medium-bodied and satin-textured. This is a rich, fat, rose, candied apple, and spice-flavored wine that has excellent grip to its refined yet opulent character. An elegantly styled Gewurztraminer, it avoids the over-the-top exoticism this varietal can possess. Drink it over the next 4–5 years.

The 1999 Riesling Fronholz has a quinine-scented nose. Light- to medium-bodied and extremely well focused, this is a linear, somewhat lean, yet concentrated wine. It is bright, dry, and loaded with fresh mineral flavors. Drink it over the next 6 years. The tightly wound 1999 Riesling Heissenberg has a light- to medium-bodied character. Plump white fruits and flowers can be discerned in its fresh yet focused and lacelike personality. Drink this delicious wine over the next 6 years. The outstanding 1999 Riesling Muenchberg displays liquid minerals and herbal teas in its aromatics. Medium-bodied and satin-textured, this is a wine of huge complexity. Earth, stones, minerals, pear, and apple can be found throughout its elegant personality as well as in its extraordinarily long finish. This fascinating wine will be at its best if consumed between 2003–2010.

The ripe apple and smoke-scented 1999 Pinot Gris Zellberg is medium- to full-bodied. Rich layers of smoky apples, spices, and poached pears emerge from this refined, nuanced, and detailed wine. It is hugely concentrated yet pure and wonderfully delineated. Anticipated maturity: now–2008. The 1999 Pinot Gris Muenchberg bursts from the glass with spices, ripe peaches, and pears. Medium-bodied, fat, and rich, this is a pure, satin-textured wine with extraordinary layers of white and yellow fruits whose flavors last throughout its exemplary finish. Purity, power, and elegance are its hallmarks. Drink it between 2003–2012.

DOMAINE DU CLOS ST.-LANDELIN (ROUFFACH)

1999 Clos St.-Landelin	D	90
1999 Gewurztraminer Schultzengass	D	89
1998 Gewurztraminer Schultzengass	D	89
1999 Gewurztraminer Vorbourg	D	90
1999 Gewurztraminer Vorbourg Clos St.-Landelin	D	90+
1998 Gewurztraminer Vorbourg Clos St.-Landelin Vendange Tardive	D	92
1999 Muscat Vorbourg Clos St.-Landelin Vendanges Tardives	E	92
1999 Riesling Vorbourg	D	89+
1998 Riesling Vorbourg	C	89
1999 Riesling Vorbourg Clos St.-Landelin	D	92
1998 Riesling Vorbourg Clos St.-Landelin	D	91
1999 Riesling Zinnkoepflé	D	89
1998 Sylvaner Cuvée Oscar Clos St.-Landelin	C	88
1998 Terroir	D	90
1999 Tokay-Pinot Gris Clos St.-Landelin Vorbourg	D	90
1999 Tokay-Pinot Gris Lutzental	C	90
1998 Tokay-Pinot Gris Lutzental	D	90

Note: This estate's owner, René Muré, also owns a *négociant* firm that bears his name.

Four-fifths of this 20-hectare estate are located in the *monopole* Clos St.-Landelin, a south-facing parcel of the grand cru Vorbourg. Organically farmed, the domaine produces an average of 40 hectoliters per hectare. While the estate's oldest vines (pre–World War II) are maintained, new plantings are tightly spaced, with 1.3 meters between rows, and 80 centimeters between each vine (resulting in 9,600–10,000 vines per hectare). Five presses are employed at each harvest to permit long, low-pressure pressings (some last 12–15 hours). This is one of the only estates in Alsace to employ the Burgundian *bâtonnage* (stirring of the lees) technique, performing it for the first 13 months of the 18-month *élevage*. Every attempt is made not to filter the wines. However, if it is deemed required, a three-micron filter is used. René Muré, this estate's owner, feels that 1998 is a more charming vintage than 1997, pointing out that it has the same maturity, yet slightly more acidity and structure.

The 1998 Riesling Vorbourg's rich aromatic profile is composed of sweetened herbal tea and bergamot. Medium- to full-bodied and broad, it exhibits lovely mineral and pineapple flavors. This precise, well-focused, and long-finishing wine can be consumed over the next 7–9 years. Named after René Muré's father, the 1998 Sylvaner Cuvée Oscar Clos St.-Landelin is a rich, medium- to full-bodied, broad-shouldered wine. Possessing excellent grip, this well-balanced offering is crammed with almonds and well-ripened yellow fruits. Anticipated maturity: now–2004.

The 1998 Tokay-Pinot Gris Lutzental (a small valley-like area on the plateau above the Clos St.-Landelin) reveals smoky yellow fruit scents. This expansive apricot, peach, and yellow plum–flavored wine is complex and medium- to full-bodied. Raspberries, citrus fruits, plump pears, and minerals can also be found in this harmonious, embracing offering. Anticipated maturity: now–2008. Produced from a vineyard located at the base of the Clos St.-Landelin, the 1998 Gewurztraminer Schultzengass (this name in Alsatian means "the little road that soldiers walk on," from the Roman legions once using it as a passage to Colmar) offers subtle yellow fruit aromas. On the palate, it is wonderfully ripe, opulent, and sexy. Red cherries, raspberries, and fresh herbs are found in this medium- to full-bodied, satin-textured offering. Drink it over the next 4–5 years.

The 1998 Terroir is produced from a blend of five varietals, including Gewurztraminer, Riesling, Pinot Blanc, and Tokay-Pinot Gris. Its *élevage* was performed in first- and second-year oak barrels purchased from a producer in Meursault. It is extremely Burgundian in character, which may explain why Muré opted for a Burgundy-style bottle instead of the traditional Alsatian flute. Spicy minerals and acacia blossoms can be discerned in its aromatics. On the palate, it reveals a delicious breadth of flavors, including touches of vanilla, spice cake, apricots, pears, and candied lemons. This highly expressive wine is the most successful of the Burgundian-styled Alsatian wines I have tasted. It is powerful, flavorful, expressive, well structured, and balanced. Anticipated maturity: now–2005.

The 1998 Riesling Vorbourg Clos St.-Landelin offers mineral and white flower aromas. This candied lemon and mineral-flavored wine has outstanding focus, richness, definition, and breadth. Medium-bodied and wonderfully pure, with air it exhibits touches of smoke, almond, white peaches, and even hints of grapefruit. Anticipated maturity: 2003–2012.

The youthful 1998 Gewurztraminer Vorbourg Clos St.-Landelin Vendange Tardive has not yet developed its aromatics. On the palate, however, it is a superrich, oily-textured, and ample offering. Readers searching for a refined, well-detailed, elegant, and powerful Gewurztraminer will love its yellow plum, lychee, and rose-flavored character. While it is not the most opulent and concentrated Gewurztraminer, it admirably combines elegance with exuberance. Anticipated maturity: 2003–2008.

The petrol, smoke, and white peach–scented 1999 Tokay-Pinot Gris Lutzenthal is a plump, fat, medium-bodied wine. Opulent layers of yellow fruits can be found in its lush, oily-textured personality. This rich wine is crammed with sultry peaches and apricots whose flavors last throughout its long finish. Drink it over the next 7 years. Lychee nuts immersed in rose water can be discerned in the aromatics of the 1999 Gewurztraminer Schultzengass. This sexy, curvaceous wine is rich yet detail-oriented. Waves of exotic fruits and spices characterize its highly expressive character. This wine should please those who search out boisterous Gewurz, as well as those seeking more restrained examples. Drink it over the next 6 years.

The talcum powder and mineral-scented 1999 Riesling Zinnkoepflé is a rich, fat, medium-bodied wine. Toasted pear, mineral, and smoke flavors can be discerned in this satin-textured and youthfully tight wine. It has outstanding depth and excellent balance. Drink it between 2004–2010. The pear and white peach–scented 1999 Riesling Vorbourg is juicy and medium-bodied. Hints of candied citrus fruits are intermingled with white peaches, pears, and apples in this silky-textured, zesty wine. It is concentrated, seamless, loaded with fruit, and offers a harmonious, long finish. Anticipated maturity: 2004–2012.

The opulent 1999 Riesling Clos St.-Landelin Vorbourg has a nose of white flowers, talcum powder, and superripe pears. This medium- to full-bodied wine is deeper, more concentrated, and longer in the finish than the Vorbourg. Copious amounts of white fruits intermingled with spices, baby powder, and white pepper can be found in its intense character. Drink it between 2004–2012. The chalk, flower, and cream-scented 1999 Clos St.-Landelin is milky, silky-textured, and medium-bodied. Superripe apples, minerals, toasted pears, and hints of apricots can be found in its core fruit. This dense, complex wine also reveals traces of pepper in its long, supple finish. Drink it over the next 9 years.

The smoky, pear-scented 1999 Tokay-Pinot Gris Clos St.-Landelin Vorbourg is a soft, silky-textured, medium-bodied wine. Yellow fruits are intermingled with smoke in this rich, plump offering. This luscious, concentrated wine should be consumed between 2003–2009.

The rosebush and potpourri-scented 1999 Gewurztraminer Vorbourg is fat, spicy, and extroverted. Medium-bodied and satin-textured, it is loaded with spiced poached pears, ripe apricots, red flowers, and hints of cardamom. Drink this beauty over the next 6 years.

The fat, medium- to full-bodied 1999 Gewurztraminer Clos St.-Landelin Vorbourg displays rose and talc aromas. Juicy minerals, white peaches, assorted pit fruits, smoke, and red flowers can be discerned in this dense, softly textured wine's personality. Relatively refined, it is concentrated and loaded with fruit. Drink it over the next 7–8 years. The juicy, candied orange and pound cake–scented 1999 Muscat Vorbourg Clos St.-Landelin Vendanges Tardives is a beautifully balanced, medium- to full-bodied wine. This off-dry gem coats the palate with flavors reminiscent of tangerine candies and orange blossoms. It is fresh, zesty, yet rich and plump, with a long, supple, fruit-filled finish. Drink it over the next 6–8 years.

DOMAINE SCHERER (HUSSEREN-LES-CHÂTEAUX)

1997 Gewurztraminer	B	88
1997 Gewurztraminer Eichberg	C	89+

Readers searching for an expressive, flamboyant wine to purchase by the case should seriously consider Scherer's 1997 Gewurztraminer. This exceptional value boasts gaudy aromas of lychee nuts, rose water, and honeyed peaches. It is medium-bodied, mouthcoating, extremely flavorful, and loaded with superripe white/red fruits. Drink it over the next 3–4 years.

Aromatically more subdued, the 1997 Gewurztraminer Eichberg displays rose petals and sweet spices. It is a medium- to full-bodied, elegant (yet assertive), velvety-textured offering packed with layers of pears, Earl Grey tea, tropical fruits, and minerals. As this wine's nose sorts itself out in the bottle it may ultimately merit a 90-point score. Anticipated maturity: now–2004.

DOMAINE CHARLES SCHLERET (TURCKHEIM)

1997 Gewurztraminer Herrenweg Cuvée Exceptionelle Sélection de Grains Nobles	E	94
1998 Gewurztraminer Herrenweg Cuvée Réserve	C	89
1997 Gewurztraminer Cuvée du 3ème Millénaire Réserve Vendange Tardive	D/500ml	95
1997 Pinot Blanc Herrenweg	B	88
1998 Pinot Gris Herrenweg	C	90
1998 Riesling Herrenweg	C	88
1997 Riesling Herrenweg	C	88+
1997 Riesling Herrenweg Cuvée Exceptionelle Sélection de Grains Nobles	E	93
1995 Riesling Herrenweg Cuvée Spéciale Vendange Tardive	D	92+
1997 Tokay-Pinot Gris Herrenweg	C	89
1997 Tokay-Pinot Gris Herrenweg Cuvée Spéciale Vendange Tardive	D	95

I loved the talcum powder and flower-filled nose of the 1997 Pinot Blanc Herrenweg. It has a fabulous oily texture, medium body, and a delicate yet flavorful core of minerals and honeysuckle blossoms. This vibrant and elegant wine begs to be quaffed, but its complex, nuanced character demands some degree of introspection. Drink this exceptional value over the next 5 years. The earth- and clay-scented 1997 Riesling Herrenweg reveals excellent depth of fruit, medium body, and an oily texture. It is extremely expressive, packed with stonelike flavors, and lingers on the palate for an exceptionally long time. If this wine comes to terms with some alcoholic heat in the finish it will merit a higher score. Anticipated maturity: now–2006.

Charles Schleret fashions Vendange Tardives and Sélection de Grains Nobles with significantly less residual sugar than the majority of his peers, "I want subtlety, not sugar," he says. The 1995 Riesling Herrenweg Cuvée Spéciale Vendange Tardive is an outstanding wine. It offers beguiling aromas of dried honey, flowers, and sweetened Earl Grey tea. This etched, glycerin-packed, gorgeously rendered, medium-bodied offering is highly detailed, well balanced, and complex. It is filled with liquid minerals and flowers that last throughout its impressive finish. Drink it over the next dozen years. The riveting 1997 Riesling Herrenweg Cuvée Exceptionelle Sélection de Grains Nobles exhibits feminine raspberry and floral aromas. It is a subtle wine, with precise perfumed, lacelike flavors of cherries, red currants, and hints of minerals. This concentrated, velvety-textured wine is amazingly complex, nuanced, and light on its feet for an SGN. Anticipated maturity: now–2015.

The lush, medium-bodied 1997 Tokay-Pinot Gris Herrenweg displays smoky yellow fruit aromas and an opulent, expressive personality. This satin-textured wine boasts hickory smoke–imbued apricots and·peaches in its flavor profile. It is thick, powerful, and luxurious, yet gorgeously detailed. Anticipated maturity: now–2007.

The almost dry 1997 Tokay-Pinot Gris Herrenweg Cuvée Spéciale Vendange Tardive is a head-turning, magnificent wine. In a few years, when its relatively low levels of residual sugar have been absorbed, it will be a great dry wine. Mouthwatering aromas of perfumed flowers lead to an extraordinarily balanced Tokay. Etched with apricots, peaches, wild strawberries, and raspberries, this feminine beauty lingers on the palate for up to a minute. It is intense, massively complex, and brilliantly defined. Anticipated maturity: 2003–2015.

The 1997 Gewurztraminer Herrenweg Cuvée Exceptionelle Sélection de Grains Nobles offers an undeveloped nose of flowers and minerals. This oily-textured (nearly viscous) wine is expansive, and elegant. With sublime definition to the lychee, flower, and rose water flavors, this is a classy, lacelike, highly delineated offering. For a 1997 Gewurztraminer it is not gaudy, opulent, or flamboyant. It should be consumed over the next decade.

Charles Schleret announced upon my arrival that he had won four gold medals for his 1998s (the Sylvaner, the Riesling Herrenweg, the Pinot Noir, and the Pinot Gris Herrenweg) at the Concours Générale de Paris, and was "the most honored independent grower of France. I search for finesse. It makes it easier to consume the wine. It should be avoided to be too rich. Sure, it can be impressive if you taste a few drops, but wines are made to be drunk." Schleret fashions highly detailed, elegant wines that consistently get excellent reviews in this publication, as well as at the medal ceremonies in Paris, Brussels, and elsewhere. Almonds and white flowers are found in the aromatics of the 1998 Riesling Herrenweg. This detail-oriented, light-bodied, extremely subtle wine displays lovely apple, mineral, floral, and stonelike flavors. This well-made, lacelike offering should be consumed over the next 5–6 years.

The goldish, straw-colored 1998 Pinot Gris Herrenweg exhibits smoky, botrytis-laced aromas. Light- to medium-bodied, feminine, and exquisitely elegant, this complex wine is filled with well-delineated peach, spice, anise, and fresh herb flavors. It is admirably balanced and possesses a long, supple, flavorful finish. Anticipated maturity: now–2010.

The fresh lychee nut–scented 1998 Gewurztraminer Herrenweg Cuvée Réserve is a rose-infused, highly defined, spicy, and floral wine. It is an exquisitely graceful Gewurztraminer without any of the exuberance or ostentatiousness that some readers (though I am certainly not one of them) dislike in this varietal. Drink it over the next 4–5 years.

Schleret did not produce any Vendange Tardive or Sélection de Grains Nobles wines in the 1998 vintage. However, he is now releasing the 1997 Gewurztraminer Cuvée du 3ème Millénaire Réserve Vendange Tardive in honor of the millennium. It displays tropical fruit aromas reminiscent of bananas, pineapples, and mangoes. On the palate, it combines superb detail and elegance with great underlying power. Roses and violets are intermingled with loads of red berries in this medium-bodied, pure, highly defined, harmonious wine. Its supple, textured character lasts for an unbelievable amount of time in its flavor-packed, yet graceful finish. This magnificent Gewurztraminer can be consumed over the next 10–12 years.

DOMAINE J.-P. SCHMITT (SCHERWILLER)

1999 Riesling Rittersberg Réserve Personnelle	C	89

The 1999 Riesling Rittersberg Réserve Personnelle bursts from the glass with aromas reminiscent of white flowers and red currants. This light-bodied, focused Riesling is dominated by red fruit, mostly raspberry, and floral notes. It has loads of underlying minerals, and a fresh, immensely appealing character. Drink this lacelike yet flavorful offering over the next 5–6 years.

DOMAINE SCHOFFIT (COLMAR)

1999 Gewurztraminer Harth Cuvée Alexandre	C	89
1998 Gewurztraminer Harth Cuvée Alexandre	C	89
1997 Gewurztraminer Harth Cuvée Alexandre Vieilles Vignes	D	88
1998 Gewurztraminer Harth Vieilles Vignes Sigillé de Qualité	E	90
1999 Gewurztraminer Rangen de Thann Clos St.-Théobald	D	93
1997 Gewurztraminer Rangen de Thann Clos St.-Théobald	D	92
1998 Gewurztraminer Rangen de Thann Clos St.-Théobald Sélection de Grains Nobles	E/500ml	95
1997 Muscat Cuvée Alexandre	C	89+
1999 Muscat Cuvée Tradition	C	88
1999 Muscat Rangen de Thann Clos St.-Théobald	D/500ml	90
1998 Muscat Rangen de Thann Clos St.-Théobald Sélection de Grains Nobles	E/500ml	92
1998 Pinot Blanc Auxerrois Cuvée Caroline	C	88
1997 Pinot Blanc Harth	C	90
1998 Riesling Harth Cuvée Alexandre	D	90
1997 Riesling Harth Cuvée Alexandre	C	89+
1999 Riesling Harth Cuvée Caroline	C	89
1998 Riesling Harth Cuvée Tradition	C	88
1999 Riesling Rangen de Thann Clos St.-Théobald	D	93+
1997 Riesling Rangen de Thann Clos St.-Théobald	D	93
1997 Riesling Rangen de Thann Clos St.-Théobald #10	D	95+
1998 Riesling Rangen de Thann Clos St.-Théobald Sélection de Grains Nobles	E/500ml	96+
1998 Riesling Rangen de Thann Clos St.-Théobald Vendanges Tardives	D	94+
1999 Riesling Sommerberg	D	89+
1997 Riesling Sommerberg	D	90
1999 Tokay-Pinot Gris Rangen de Thann Clos St.-Théobald	D	94+
1997 Tokay-Pinot Gris Rangen de Thann Clos St.-Théobald	D	92
1999 Tokay-Pinot Gris Rangen de Thann Clos St.-Théobald Sélection de Grains Nobles	E/375ml	96
1997 Tokay-Pinot Gris Rangen de Thann Clos St.-Théobald Sélection de Grains Nobles	EE/500ml	98
1998 Tokay-Pinot Gris Rangen de Thann Clos St.-Théobald Sélection de Grains Nobles Lot #1	EE/500ml	97+
1998 Tokay-Pinot Gris Rangen de Thann Clos St.-Théobald Sélection de Grains Nobles Lot #2	E/500ml	98+
1999 Tokay-Pinot Gris Rangen de Thann Clos St.-Théobald Vendange Tardive	E	94
1998 Tokay-Pinot Gris Rangen de Thann Clos St.-Théobald Vendange Tardive	E/500ml	95

1997 Tokay-Pinot Gris Vendange Tardive	E	89+
1999 Tokay-Pinot Gris Vieilles Vignes Cuvée Alexandre	D	89
1998 Tokay-Pinot Gris Vieilles Vignes Cuvée Alexandre	D	89
1998 Tokay-Pinot Gris Vieilles Vignes Sigillé de Qualité	E	92

Almost half of Schoffit's total production of the prodigious 1997 Pinot Blanc Harth was sold to North America. It displays gorgeous aromatics composed of white flowers intermingled with candied almonds. On the palate, this medium- to full-bodied, broad, fresh, tangy, deeply rich wine has superb balance, a silky texture, and layers of smoky yellow fruits with hints of lemon. It tastes more like a first-rate Tokay-Pinot Gris than a Pinot Blanc! Anticipated maturity: now–2004. Schoffit's 1997 Muscat Cuvée Alexandre boasts a mouthwatering nose of orange blossoms, raspberry coulis, and candied tangerine zests. Unlike many Muscats that deliver fabulous aromatics but relatively boring flavors, this one satisfies both the nose and the palate. Red and orange fruits are intermingled with spices in this fat, broad, mouth-coating wine. An ideal apéritif or accompaniment to Asian cuisine, this wine is low in acid yet fresh and lively. Anticipated maturity: now–2004.

Revealing a nose of minerals, chalk, flowers, and citrus fruits, the 1997 Riesling Harth Cuvée Alexandre is a wonderfully expressive wine. It has superb richness, width, complexity, concentration, and a flavorful core of honeysuckle blossoms and liquid minerals. Anticipated maturity: now–2006. Produced from 31-year-old vines, the 1997 Riesling Sommerberg has perfumed aromas of acacia flowers and chalk. It is a medium-bodied, tightly wound wine with powerful stone and mineral flavors. Concentrated, intense, and exceptionally long in the finish, this offering will require patience. Drink it between now–2007.

In 1997, Bernard Schoffit crafted two Rieslings from his parcel on the steep Rangen vineyard. The vines located on the upper portion of the slope, farthest from the Thur river, were not affected by botrytis and fashioned a superb wine that bears Schoffit's normal Riesling Rangen de Thann Clos St.-Théobald label. It reveals a fresh nose of lemon drops and minerals. This dry wine is bright, highly concentrated, complex, and medium- to full-bodied. Powerful and expansive minerals, stones, assorted citrus fruits, and smokelike flavors inundate the taster's palate. Not surprisingly, it has a formidably long finish. It is an expressive and precise Riesling that will evolve gorgeously. Anticipated maturity: now–2010. The spectacular 1997 Riesling Rangen de Thann Clos St.-Théobald #10 was produced from grapes affected by botrytis. This wine was produced from Schoffit's parcel closest to the river. It displays a super-concentrated nose of liquid minerals, smoke, botrytis, and roasted peanuts. This extraordinarily ripe wine is broad, opulent, and crammed with apricots, peaches, quince, caramelized minerals, and candied lemons. Tighter and more backward than its sibling, its medium- to full-bodied core exhibits compelling concentration, complexity, intensity, and length. Drink this gem between 2003–2014.

The 1997 Tokay-Pinot Gris Vendange Tardive, which fermented for nearly 11 months, is made from equal parts of the Rangen and vineyards bordering the city of Colmar. Its nose is extremely tight, revealing only sweet, smoky aromas. On the palate, this wine reveals thick layers of yellow and red fruits. It is well balanced, yet at present awkward, requiring a year or two of cellaring to sort itself out. Anticipated maturity: now–2009.

The outstanding 1997 Tokay-Pinot Gris Rangen de Thann Clos St.-Théobald has a massively expressive nose of botrytis-laced apricot jam. This fat, honeyed, medium-bodied wine is densely packed with sweet yellow fruits, candied lemons, and red currants. It is well proportioned, fresh, elegant, and boasts a long, flavorful finish. Drink it between now–2012.

Only 360 500ml bottles of the 1997 Tokay-Pinot Gris Rangen de Thann Clos St.-Théobald Sélection de Grains Nobles were produced. This extraordinary nectar has lively aromas reminiscent of smoky minerals awash in sweet peach juice. Its medium- to full-bodied core is penetrating, expansive, and layered with abundant apricots, peaches, raspberries, stones, chalk, pineapples, candied limes, and cherries. Well balanced, it is the essence of Pinot Gris. Moreover, this wine has the capacity to age for 30+ years.

Produced from 45- to 50-year-old vines, the 1997 Gewurztraminer Harth Cuvée Alexandre Vieilles Vignes bursts with aggressive, blatantly obvious aromas of concentrated rose water and perfume. A quintessential hedonistic fruit bomb, it is plump, low in acid, expansive, an immensely flavorful wine. Through not particularly complex or structured, it is amazingly forward and luscious, with copious flavors suggestive of sweet mangoes, peaches, ginger, and jasmine. Drink it over the next 4 years.

The opulent, hedonistic, sexy 1997 Gewurztraminer Rangen de Thann Clos St.-Théobald manages to maintain an appealing level of refinement and class. Its lychee, red fruit, and floral nose leads to a tropical fruit, spiced pear, fruitcake, spicy, tangy flavor profile. This huge, mouthcoating offering is massively ripe, intense, and complex. It will hold for many years, so I suggest drinking it over the next 5–6 years to profit from its exuberance and decadence.

The dedicated and highly talented Bernard Schoffit described 1998 as "a nice year, particularly in the top wines." Also, he views it as "the greatest year ever in the Rangen for sweet wines. The acidity is higher than 1990, and they have better balance. In short, the early part of the growing season was excellent, the middle bad, and the end superb. For owners of parcels in the Rangen, it was this year or never for making great wines."

Botrytised, ripe peach aromas are found in the 1998 Pinot Blanc Auxerrois Cuvée Caroline. This plump, medium-bodied, satin-textured, lush wine is opulent and reveals sexy layers of apricot. Drink this seductive offering over the next 3–4 years.

Bernard Schoffit, starting with the 1998 vintage, has changed what used to be known as his "Cuvée Prestige" to "Cuvée Tradition." The 1998 Riesling Harth Cuvée Tradition offers fresh mineral and earth aromas. This is a full-flavored, entry-level Riesling, crammed with lemons, candied citrus fruits, and hints of clay. It has lovely delineation and focus, and a pure, long finish. This medium-bodied wine should be consumed over the next 5 years.

Schoffit's Cuvée Alexandre offerings are fashioned from extremely rich grapes that have attained Vendange Tardive levels of ripeness. The 1998 Riesling Harth Cuvée Alexandre offers complex mineral and botrytis aromas. This deep, expansive, and medium-bodied wine is plump, rich, and youthful. Pears, apricots, and plums can be found in its layered, luscious, yet fresh character. Anticipated maturity: now–2012. The 1998 Tokay-Pinot Gris Vieilles Vignes Cuvée Alexandre offers delightful aromatics of smoke and ripe apples. It possesses huge richness in its tropical, yellow fruit–flavored character. This fat yet well-balanced wine is medium- to full-bodied and should be consumed over the next 7–9 years.

The 1998 Tokay-Pinot Gris Vieilles Vignes Sigillé de Qualité has intense aromas of peaches, minerals, and smoke. This precise, yet massively rich and oily-textured wine coats the palate with apricots, tropical fruits, and hints of lemon. Full-bodied and concentrated, it also possesses a long, pure, drawn-out finish. Anticipated maturity: 2003–2012. Rich, smoky aromas can be discerned in the nose of the 1998 Gewurztraminer Harth Cuvée Alexandre. This broad, concentrated, deep wine is packed with apricots, peaches, hints of rose water, and appealing potpourri flavors. Anticipated maturity: now–2005.

Apricots, roses, violets, and tobacco can be discerned in the aromatics of the 1998 Gewurztraminer Harth Vieilles Vignes Sigillé de Qualité. Medium-bodied and well concentrated, this floral, rose, candied raspberry, and apricot-flavored wine is well balanced and seductive. Its velvety texture and exuberant personality last throughout its long, supple, finish. Drink it over the next 5–6 years.

Schoffit's 1998 Muscat Rangen de Thann Clos St.-Théobald Sélection de Grains Nobles displays aromas of white fruits intermingled with herbal teas. None of this varietal's trademark orange rind and orange blossom characteristics can be discerned. This intensely deep, oily-textured, hugely concentrated wine's flavor profile is dominated by red fruits and apricots. Its long, sweet, pure, and refined finish reveals some of this wine's high levels of alcohol (14.4%). Anticipated maturity: 2004–2012+. The 1998 Tokay-Pinot Gris Rangen de Thann Clos St.-Théobald Vendange Tardive offers a massively rich nose reminiscent of peach and apricot jam. This full-bodied, silky-textured "oil of Tokay" coats the palate with untold layers of dense yellow fruit nectars. It has outstanding balance, precision, and a wonderful citrus tanginess that appears in its extraordinarily long finish. Anticipated maturity: 2005–2015+.

The spectacular 1998 Riesling Rangen de Thann Clos St.-Théobald Sélection de Grains Nobles exhibits gorgeous, spicy, fresh herb, and white fruit aromas. This oily-textured, full-bodied, apricot jelly–flavored wine is extremely youthful and densely concentrated. It is seamless, with its copious layers of jammy fruit lasting from its attack through an unbelievably long finish. This wine has the potential, as it develops and evolves, to merit an even more exalted review. Anticipated maturity: 2007–2019. Produced from grapes harvested the fourth week of October, the 1998 Gewurztraminer Rangen de Thann Clos St.-Théobald Sélection de Grains Nobles has an intensely ripe, fruit-packed nose. On the palate it displays outstanding balance, loads of smoky, earthy white and yellow fruits, as well as huge concentration, sweetness, and length. Anticipated maturity: 2005–2020+.

Bernard Schoffit fashioned two SGNs from his Tokay-Pinot Gris parcels in the Rangen de Thann. Harvested on October 20, with yields of 20 h/h, the 1998 Tokay-Pinot Gris Rangen de Thann Clos St.-Théobald Sélection de Grains Nobles Lot #2 has a hugely sweet, yellow fruit–dominated nose. Full-bodied, broad, and expansive, it is jam-packed with yellow plums, quince, and peach cobbler flavors. It is a wine of untold power, elegance, and depth. It possesses gorgeous balance, and a character that may ultimately merit a perfect score as this gem of a wine evolves and opens in time. Anticipated maturity: 2005–2020+. Schoffit's favorite of the two, according to his U.S. importer, Peter Weygandt, is the Lot #1, harvested on October 10, with yields of only 12 h/h. Aromatically, it exhibits sweet yellow fruits and spices. It is a wine of extraordinary focus, delineation, and concentration. It appears to be even better balanced and to possess even more grip than Lot #2, but lacks that wine's unbelievable density and expression of fruit. That being said, readers would be hard-pressed to find wines with this offering's level of concentration. It would be fascinating, 10–15 years from now, to see how these two wines have progressed. Qualitatively, one would expect them both to be scratching at the door of perfection. Anticipated maturity: 2005–2020+.

The orange blossom–scented 1999 Muscat Cuvée Tradition has gorgeous balance to its light- to medium-bodied personality. Appealing raspberries, orange zest, and spices can be found in its expressive, concentrated character. Drink it over the next 2 years. There are only 550 centiliter bottles of the 1999 Muscat Rangen de Thann Clos St.-Théobald. It has a super-ripe nose of raspberries, strawberries, and orange blossoms. On the palate, it is rich, broad, and expansive. This medium-bodied, orange peel, lemon, and raspberry jam–flavored wine has a velvety texture and an admirably long, persistent finish. Drink it over the next 4 years.

From vines averaging 40 years of age, the 1999 Riesling Harth Cuvée Caroline has ripe pear and apple aromas. This is an intense, medium-bodied wine with excellent grip. Its concentrated, white fruit–filled character is broad, lush, and has an admirably long finish. Drink it over the next 10 years. Only 60 cases of the 1999 Riesling Sommerberg were produced. This is a bone-dry wine with mineral aromas and a rich yet tightly wound personality. Loads of pears and minerals can be discerned in its character, yet it appears shy, disclosing only a portion of its ultimate potential. Anticipated maturity: 2004–2010.

The outstanding 1999 Riesling Rangen de Thann Clos St.-Théobald has explosive smoky mineral aromas. Medium- to full-bodied and superrich, this is a muscular, powerful wine with a velvety-textured character. Poached pears immersed in minerals and liquid smoke can be found in its highly concentrated, backward character. It is a magnificent Riesling that will require cellaring. Anticipated maturity: 2006–2015. The 1998 Riesling Rangen de Thann Clos St.-Théobald Vendanges Tardives reveals sweet herbal tea and mineral aromas in its amazingly focused personality. Loads of pears, peaches, apricots, and zesty minerals can be detected in this extraordinarily fresh yet rich and luscious wine. Its flavors are intense, well defined, and linger in an impressively long, sweet, supple finish. Anticipated maturity: 2004–2020.

The 1999 Gewurztraminer Harth Cuvée Alexandre has a rose water and violet-scented nose. Oily-textured and medium-bodied, it is an expansive, highly detailed, yet powerful and rich wine. Roses, lychee nuts, and a myriad of spices characterize this highly expressive offering. Drink this luscious, sexy wine over the next 7 years.

The hugely concentrated 1999 Gewurztraminer Rangen de Thann Clos St.-Théobald has roses and potpourri in its aromatics. This is a massively expressive wine crammed with red fruits, lychee nuts, and roses. Medium- to full-bodied and boisterous, it has great balance, freshness, and a spectacularly long finish. Drink it over the next 10 years.

The 1999 Tokay-Pinot Gris Vieilles Vignes Cuvée Alexandre, from vines averaging 45 years of age, has smoky pear aromas and a medium-bodied personality. This ample wine is loaded with pears, smoke, apricots, and hints of botrytis. It is pure, well delineated as well as balanced, and has a long, detailed finish. Anticipated maturity: 2003–2010.

The stunning 1999 Tokay-Pinot Gris Rangen de Thann Clos St.-Théobald resonates with loads of yellow fruits. This hugely intense, medium- to full-bodied wine has extraordinary power and depth. It is opulently structured, exhibiting countless layers of apricots, white peaches, and spices in addition to an exquisite finish. This luxurious wine can be consumed young, yet should be even more compelling with cellaring. Projected maturity: now–2018.

The botrytis- and apricot-scented 1999 Tokay-Pinot Gris Rangen de Thann Clos St.-Théobald Vendange Tardive has gorgeous definition to its apricot, peach, pear, smoke, and candied apple–flavored character. Medium- to full-bodied and muscular, it is an extravagant wine that marvelously marries power with definition. Anticipated maturity: 2005–2020.

The 1999 Tokay-Pinot Gris Rangen de Thann Clos St.-Théobald Selection de Grains Nobles was harvested at 15 hectoliters per hectare at a natural potential alcohol of 20%. A wine of magnificent purity, balance, and power, it exhibits jammy apricot, peach compote, and spice aromas as well as flavors. It is hugely concentrated, unctuously sweet, yet has outstanding equilibrium. It stuns the taster with its unbridled fruit, yet retains exquisite delineation. Drink this marvelous nectar over the next 35 years.

DOMAINE GÉRARD SCHUELLER ET FILS (HUSSEREN-LES-CHÂTEAUX)

1998 Gewurztraminer Bildstoeckle	D	89
1997 Gewurztraminer Bildstoeckle	D	90
1997 Gewurztraminer Bildstoeckle Sélection de Grains Nobles	D	89+
1997 Gewurztraminer Bildstoeckle Vendanges Tardives	D	88+
1989 Gewurztraminer Sélection de Grains Nobles	EE/500ml	94
1997 Gewurztraminer Vendanges Tardives	D	92+
1996 Riesling Eichberg Vendanges Tardives	E	88+
1998 Riesling Pfersigberg	C	89+
1995 Riesling Pfersigberg	C	90
1996 Tokay-Pinot Gris Réserve	D	91
1994 Tokay-Pinot Gris Sélection de Grains Nobles	E/500ml	91+
1989 Tokay Pinot Gris Sélection de Grains Nobles	E/500ml	92

The honey-dusted citrus- and mineral-scented 1996 Riesling Eichberg Vendanges Tardives is a medium-bodied, stony, tightly wound, and brilliantly focused wine. Though it is a VT, it appears dry on the palate. Like many Alsatian Rieslings from this high-acid vintage, this admirably long wine will require patience. Anticipated maturity: 2003–2012+.

Botrytis and smoky apricots can be discerned in the aromatics of the 1989 Tokay-Pinot

Gris Sélection de Grains Nobles. Medium-bodied, satin-textured, and elegant, it offers peaches and other assorted yellow fruits in its powerful, sweet personality, as well as in its extensive finish. Anticipated maturity: now–2012+.

The 1997 Gewurztraminer Bildstoeckle reveals rosewater, ginger, and lemongrass aromas. This extroverted wine is packed with fresh lychee nuts, spices, and candied lemons. While it sports 9 grams of residual sugar per liter, it comes across as dry. Drink this well-crafted and long-finishing offering over the course of the next 3–4 years.

The 1997 Gewurztraminer Bildstoeckle Vendanges Tardives exhibits smoky, apricot, white peach, spice, and rose petal aromas. Medium-bodied and oily-textured, this peach, lychee nut, and spice-flavored wine has excellent balance and concentration. This offering has considerable residual sugar, but it is barely noticeable. Anticipated maturity: now–2007. Botrytis, honeyed minerals, and yellow fruits are found in the nose of the 1997 Gewurztraminer Bildstoeckle Sélection de Grains Nobles. While its impressively concentrated character is tight and ungiving at present, it is loaded with spicy yellow fruits that last throughout its persistent finish. Medium-bodied and focused, it is a wine to consume between 2004–2012+.

The 1995 Riesling Pfersigberg displays earthy, immensely ripe yellow fruit aromas. It is a concentrated powerhouse (1995 was a spectacular vintage for Riesling in Alsace) with citrus, rubber, liquid mineral, white peach, and botrytis flavors. This medium- to full-bodied wine has a satiny-texture, impeccable balance, and loads of depth. Anticipated maturity: now–2009. Produced from 30 h/h yields (extremely low for Alsace), the 1996 Tokay-Pinot Gris Réserve exhibits smoky apricot and clay aromas. Medium- to full-bodied and superbly balanced, this wine is extracted, has admirable depth of yellow/white fruits, salt, and reveals hints of Cynar liqueur (an attribute I often find in extremely ripe Rieslings, Chenin Blancs, and Tokays). Drink it over the next 8 years.

The 1994 Tokay-Pinot Gris Sélection de Grains Nobles offers expressive, botrytis-laced sweet peach aromas. This well-balanced, medium- to full-bodied wine has a luscious texture and a long, sweet finish. Smoky minerals, tropical fruits, apricots, and flower blossoms can be found in its assertive flavor profile. Anticipated maturity: now–2010. Intense aromas of tropical fruits, lychee nuts, raspberries, and peanut oil can be found in the 1989 Gewurztraminer Sélection de Grains Nobles. This luxurious wine is opulent, velvety-textured, and massively powerful. Unlike some SGNs, however, this wine is eminently drinkable. Neither too heavy nor too sweet, it is complex, well proportioned, balanced, and represents the essence of Gewurztraminer—lychee nuts, rose water, assorted red fruits, mangoes, papaya, and a myriad of spices. Drink this gem over the next 8–10 years.

The herbal tea and mineral-scented 1998 Riesling Pfersigberg is medium-bodied and complex. Loads of minerals, toasted nuts, and pears can be found in this satin-textured, highly detailed wine. It possesses a long and extremely expressive finish. Drink it over the next 6–7 years. Loads of spices and cherry juice can be found in the aromas and flavors of the 1998 Gewurztraminer Bildstoeckle. This lush, medium-bodied wine is oily-textured, plump, and has excellent density and depth. Drink this ostentatious, sexy, luscious Gewurztraminer over the next 6 years. The nose of the 1997 Gewurztraminer Vendanges Tardives is like standing right next to a large rosebush covered with blooms. Medium-bodied and revealing outstanding focus and breadth, this potpourri, violet, and rose water–flavored wine is absolutely gorgeous. It has outstanding depth of fruit, beautiful balance, and an exceptionally long, fresh finish. Anticipated maturity: now–2014.

DOMAINE JEAN SIPP (RIBEAUVILLÉ)

1998 Gewurztraminer Cuvée Particulière	C	88
1998 Gewurztraminer Vieilles Vignes	C	88
1998 Riesling Kirchberg de Ribeauvillé	D	91
1998 Riesling Vieilles Vignes	C	88+

The mineral-scented 1998 Riesling Vieilles Vignes has the richness often indicative of wines from this vintage. On the palate, dense citrus and mineral flavors dominate this medium-bodied, satin-textured wine. It is extremely well focused, yet packed with flavor. Drink it over the next 4–5 years. The 1998 Riesling Kirchberg de Ribeauvillé is a more concentrated, powerful, and stone-infused version of the preceding wine. Intense mineral, gravel, and candied grapefruit flavors are found in this muscular offering. Its finish is extremely long and filled with fruit. Drink it over the next 8–9 years.

The fat and sexy 1998 Gewurztraminer Cuvée Particulière boasts rosewater, violet, and lychee nut aromas. It is medium- to full-bodied, plump, loaded with fruit, spices, and English candies. Drink this expressive beauty over the next 5–6 years. The spice, floral, and rose-scented 1998 Gewurztraminer Vieilles Vignes is medium-bodied and beautifully detailed. On the palate, it expresses raspberry, poached pears, spice, and delicate touches of mango in its delineated yet fruit-forward character. Anticipated maturity: now–2011.

PIERRE SPARR (SIGOLSHEIM)

1999 Gewurztraminer Mambourg Sélection de Grains Nobles	EE	92+
1998 Gewurztraminer Mambourg Vendanges Tardives	D	89
1998 Pinot Gris Prestige	C	88
1996 Pinot Gris Sélection de Grains Nobles	EE	91
1998 Riesling Brand	D	88
1996 Riesling Schoenenberg Vendanges Tardives	C/500ml	89

The 1998 Riesling Brand, harvested on October 21 at 53 hectoliters per hectare, exhibits an expressive mineral, pear, and apple-scented nose. Light- to medium-bodied, rich, and packed with quince, apples, and anise, this excellent wine has admirable depth of fruit and an impressively long finish. Anticipated maturity: now–2006.

The 1998 Pinot Gris Prestige has deep, rich aromas of superripe pears and honey. Medium-bodied, fat, and plump, this is an opulent, almond, yellow fruit, and spice-flavored wine. It has excellent depth as well as a long, lush finish. Anticipated maturity: now–2010+.

The 1996 Riesling Schoenenberg Vendanges Tardives displays spicy baked fruit, orange blossom, and candied berry aromas. It is concentrated, opulent, and broad. Loads of sweet, sugarcoated lemon, lime, and mineral flavors can be found in its fresh, deep, admirably long personality. Drink it over the next 10 years.

The 1998 Gewurztraminer Mambourg Vendanges Tardives has fresh, floral, and red berry aromas. It is lush, lively, and packed with copious quantities of spices and white fruits. This medium-bodied, elegant, delineated wine has excellent concentration and depth. Drink it over the next 6–8 years.

Only 180 cases of the 1999 Gewurztraminer Mambourg Sélection de Grains Nobles were produced. (Sparr dedicated his oldest parcel of vines in the Mambourg Vineyard for this wine, harvesting at a paltry 19 h/h.) Botrytis, baked cherries, quince, and spices can be found in its intricate aromatic profile. Medium-bodied, intense, and mouthcoating, this wine is crammed with candied cherry, botrytis, rose water, and jellied lychee flavors. It is powerful, extremely long in the finish, and quite refined. Drink it over the next 10 years.

The exceptionally well delineated 1996 Pinot Gris Sélection de Grains Nobles has a floral, honeyed nose. This light- to medium-bodied wine has superb red berry fruit characteristics. White flowers, raspberries, and currants can be found throughout its pristine, elegant flavor profile, as in the long, pure finish. Anticipated maturity: now–2015.

DOMAINE SYLVIE SPIELMAN (BERGHEIM)

1998 Gewurztraminer Altenberg de Bergheim	D	93
1998 Gewurztraminer Blosenberg Bergheim	C	90
1998 Gewurztraminer Kanzlerberg	C	91

1997 Gewurztraminer Kanzlerberg Sélection de Grains Nobles	E/500ml	94
1999 Pinot Blanc Réserve Bergheim	B	88
1998 Tokay-Pinot Gris Blosenberg Bergheim	C	88+

Produced from 80% Auxerrois Gros and 20% Pinot Blanc, the 1999 Pinot Blanc Réserve Bergheim is an excellent value. The superspicy nose leads to a soft, light- to medium-bodied character. This is a juicy, well-balanced wine with luscious mineral and spice flavors. Drink it over the next 3–4 years. The demure, apricot-scented 1998 Tokay-Pinot Gris Blosenberg Bergheim is soft, luscious, and medium-bodied. Its plump, satin-textured personality reveals excellent depth and good structure. Lovely yellow fruit and spice flavors can be found in its expressive core. Anticipated maturity: now–2007.

The rich, hugely expressive lychee nut and rose-scented 1998 Gewurztraminer Blosenberg Bergheim has outstanding depth and breadth. Medium-bodied, spicy, and ample, this cherry- and raspberry-flavored wine is deep and super spicy. Drink this boisterous Gewurztraminer over the next 7–8 years. Flowers, smoke, and spices can be discerned in the aromatics of the 1998 Gewurztraminer Kanzlerberg. Medium-bodied and oily-textured, this is an opulent yet detailed wine with gorgeous layers of lychee nuts, quince, and rose water, whose flavors last throughout its persistent finish. Drink it over the next 8 years.

The 1998 Gewurztraminer Altenberg de Bergheim has an extraordinarily spicy nose. This chewy, meaty, medium- to full-bodied wine coats the palate with poached pears, candied apples, apricots, peaches, and copious quantities of assorted spices. It is powerful, opulent, and has an admirably long and supple finish. Anticipated maturity: now–2010. The 1997 Gewurztraminer Kanzlerberg Sélection de Grains Nobles displays roses, spices, and hints of mocha in its aromatics. Full-bodied and oily, this is a sumptuous wine that offers wave upon wave of roses, violets, raspberries, and white peaches. It is gorgeously detailed, thick, and possesses an exceptionally long, pure, and nuanced finish. Anticipated maturity: now–2015.

DOMAINE M. & V. STOEFFLER (BARR)

2000 Gewurztraminer Cuvée Prestige	C	89
2000 Gewurztraminer Kirchberg de Barr	D	90
1998 Gewurztraminer Vendanges Tardives	D	91
1999 Riesling Kirchberg de Barr	C	86
1998 Riesling Kirchberg de Barr	C	88
1998 Riesling Muhlforst	B	88
1998 Riesling Muhlforst Vendanges Tardives	D	92
2000 Tokay-Pinot Gris Cuvée Prestige	C	88+
2000 Tokay-Pinot Gris Kirchberg de Barr	C	92

Martine and Vincent Stoeffler are both oenologists and run this 13-hectare estate in the town of Barr. I was ecstatic to see the quality of wines emanating from this biodynamic estate. The 1998 Riesling Muhlforst exhibits an expressive nose of liquid mineral. It is vibrant, tangy, loaded with bright lemon and mineral flavors, and possesses a vibrant, superfocused personality. Drink it over the next 5–6 years.

The 1998 Riesling Kirchberg de Barr clearly shows the fact that this vintage, in contrast to 1999, favored Riesling. Loads of minerals and pears can be discerned in its aromatics. This wine has loads of depth to its medium-bodied, pure, liquid mineral-filled character. It is concentrated and possesses a long, supple finish. Anticipated maturity: now–2010.

Baked apples and poached pears can be detected in the aromatics of the 2000 Tokay-Pinot Gris Cuvée Prestige. This well-balanced wine is highly detailed, expressive, and loaded with apricot and white peach–like flavors. Anticipated maturity: now–2008. The pear- and peach-scented 2000 Tokay-Pinot Gris Kirchberg de Barr has loads of purity and concentration in its medium-bodied personality. Gorgeous layers of cherry, sweet herbal tea, poached pear, and hints of apricot can be found throughout its character and its satin-textured, long finish. This outstanding Alsatian white can be drunk now or cellared for a decade.

The 2000 Gewurztraminer Cuvée Prestige bursts from the glass with rose water and lychee fruit–like aromas. This well-balanced wine is highly expressive yet elegant, revealing precise floral, lychee nut, and spice flavors. It is medium-bodied, satin-textured, and has considerable palate presence. Drink it over the next 7 years. The cherry juice and apple-scented 2000 Gewurztraminer Kirchberg de Barr is light- to medium-bodied and balanced. This refined, delineated effort is crammed with assorted red fruits, pears, apples, and spices. It is a feminine, wonderfully expressive wine to drink over the next 7 years.

The 1998 Riesling Muhlforst Vendanges Tardives reveals mineral, dried honey, and quinine aromas. This powerful wine is medium-bodied, and has outstanding depth and focus and a marvelously linear character. Stones, liquid minerals, and spiced pears can be found throughout its highly defined yet rich personality as well as in its long, satiny finish. Drink it over the next 12–14 years. The 1998 Gewurztraminer Vendanges Tardives exhibits cherry, raspberry, and spice aromas. This delightful, red fruit–filled wine is sweet, detailed, elegant, and pure. Medium-bodied and loaded with flavor, yet retaining high levels of refinement, this is a lush, exuberant 1998 for drinking over the next dozen years.

DOMAINE MARC TEMPÉ (ZELLENBERG)

1998 Gewurztraminer Furstentum	D	93
1997 Gewurztraminer Mambourg Sélection de Grains Nobles	EE	97
1997 Gewurztraminer Mambourg Vendange Tardive	E	90+
1998 Gewurztraminer Rodelsberg	D	92
1997 Gewurztraminer Schoenenbourg	D	93
1998 Gewurztraminer Zellenberg	D	88
1997 Gewurztraminer Zellenberg	D	88
1997 Pinot Blanc Priegel	C	89+
1999 Pinot Blanc Zellenberg	C	88
1997 Pinot Blanc Zellenberg	C	88
1998 Riesling Burgreben	D	90
1997 Riesling Mambourg Vendange Tardive	E	93+
1998 Riesling St.-Hippolyte	C	88
1997 Riesling Zellenberg	C	89+
1998 Tokay-Pinot Gris Furstentum	D	89+
1997 Tokay-Pinot Gris Schoenenbourg Vendange Tardive	E	92+
1998 Tokay-Pinot Gris Vieilles Vignes	D	88
1997 Tokay-Pinot Gris Zellenberg	D	88
1997 Tokay-Pinot Gris Zellenberg Vendange Tardive	E	91

Note: Readers who are considering traveling to Alsace should know that Marc Tempé's wife, Anne Marie, has a wonderful wine shop (La Sommelière) in Colmar, next to the Eglise St.-Martin. I was amazed to see loads of superb Burgundies and Rhônes in this shop at a fraction of the prices they sell for in the United States.

I am ecstatic to see the quality of the wines produced at this new estate (1995 was the debut vintage). Subscribers need to be aware that Marc Tempé vinifies and bottles his wines with high levels of CO_2 (a natural by-product of extensive lees contact). Because it is a natural preservative, he uses little SO_2. The following wines improved significantly with aeration, so decanting them may be beneficial. I tasted most of them twice, the first time immediately after they had been uncorked, and then again 48 hours later without any protection other than their cork. In every instance the contact with air had a positive effect.

Produced from a blend of 60% Pinot Blanc and 40% Pinot Auxerrois, the 1997 Pinot Blanc

Zellenberg reveals fresh honeyed pear aromas and a delightful, medium-bodied personality. Crisp apples, candied almonds, and flowers can be found in this lively, elegant wine. This exciting, flavorful, vibrant offering will be at its best if consumed over the next 4 years. The 1997 Pinot Blanc Priegel (100% Pinot Blanc) displays a nose of perfume, acacia blossoms, and hints of honey. It is a medium-bodied, beautifully expressive, rich, rather broad wine. Honeysuckle, marzipan, and pear flavors dominate its silky-textured, well-focused character. It is hard to resist drinking, but it will certainly evolve beautifully for 6 years or more.

Powerful aromas of minerals are found in the 1997 Riesling Zellenberg's nose. This wine sports a big, strong character filled with stone and quartzlike flavors. It is satiny-textured, light- to medium-bodied, intense, pure, with a crystalline precision. As its tightly wound core of concentrated fruit unfolds, it may merit even more praise. Drink it between now–2006+.

The 1997 Tokay-Pinot Gris Zellenberg displays malt ball and smoke-laced aromas. This medium-bodied wine was partially vinified in third- and fourth-year barrels. It is filled with mocha-covered apricot flavors and is rich and creamy, yet fresh and focused. Anticipated maturity: now–2006. The flavorful yet subtle 1997 Gewurztraminer Zellenberg reveals delicate floral aromas in addition to a medium-bodied personality. It is well crafted, offers excellent richness, and displays rosewater and perfumed flavors. This elegantly styled Gewurztraminer will be at its best if drunk over the next 4–5 years.

The 1997 Tokay-Pinot Gris Zellenberg Vendange Tardive exhibits fresh, floral, oak spice–laden aromatics. Medium-bodied, concentrated, and well defined, this wine is densely packed with peach, apricot, honeysuckle, and smoke flavors. Silky-textured, with outstanding depth, it is beautifully wrought. Anticipated maturity: now–2010.

The backward 1997 Tokay-Pinot Gris Schoenenbourg Vendange Tardive will require patience. Beguiling aromas of minerals, sweetened tea, smoke, and stones are found in this medium-bodied, oily-textured wine. Its tight, highly concentrated core expands with aeration to reveal plump layers of peach-imbued chalk flavors that lasted for up to 45 seconds on the palate. In the near term this wine's demure and delicious personality will deliver pleasure, yet with bottle age it will sing! Anticipated maturity: now–2012+.

I adored Tempé's 1997 Riesling Mambourg Vendange Tardive. It displays honey-covered bergamot aromas as well as an opulent, medium- to full-bodied, and velvety-textured personality. This complete wine has breathtaking breadth, precision, concentration, and delineation. Loads of white peaches, spices, minerals, and flowers are found in its focused flavor profile. Anticipated maturity: now–2015.

The 1997 Gewurztraminer Schoenenbourg is a delight. Its mouthwatering almond cookie drenched in rosewater aromatics are followed by a palate-coating personality crammed with raspberries, cherries, lychee nuts, candied pineapples, and flowers. Full-flavored, feminine, and expressive, this wine is gorgeously detailed yet powerful. Its oily-textured waves of fruit and long finish are admirable. Drink it over the next decade.

The aromatically muted 1997 Gewurztraminer Mambourg Vendange Tardive was difficult to evaluate. While it has the components of an outstanding wine—concentration, power, balance, richness, complexity, and length—it is foursquare, highly structured, and largely impossible to penetrate. With coaxing, its oily-textured, medium- to full-bodied, dense character offers glimpses of sweet lychees, rose water, and mangoes. Two or three years of patience appears warranted. Anticipated maturity: now–2010+.

Flowers, pears, and apples can be found in the aromatics of the 1998 Riesling St.-Hippolyte. This bright, rich, deep, medium-bodied wine displays pure, fresh, mineral and herbal flavors. It is presently tight and therefore will require some cellaring. Anticipated maturity: 2003–2010. Bright lemons, minerals, and spiced apples are found in the aromatics of the 1998 Riesling Burgreben. This powerful, zesty, concentrated wine has a focused, light- to medium-bodied, elegant character. It admirably combines muscle with crystalline grace. Anticipated maturity: 2003–2012.

Produced from vines over 40 years old, the 1998 Tokay-Pinot Gris Vieilles Vignes has honeyed anise and spice cake aromas. Fashioned entirely in third- and fourth-year oak barrels, this rich, creamy, crème brûlée–flavored offering is fresh and well focused. The 1998 Tokay-Pinot Gris Furstentum reveals almond cookie aromas. Medium-bodied and wonderfully rich, it is a broad, flavorful, yet elegant wine. Almond paste, lemon, and fresh orange zest can be found in this flavorful, expressive wine. Anticipated maturity: 2004–2014.

Produced from yields under 30 hectoliters per hectare (a rarity in Alsace), the 1998 Gewurztraminer Zellenberg has a rose- and potpourri-scented nose. Light- to medium-bodied, focused, and tangy, this floral, spicy, satin-textured wine is highly expressive. Its long, structured finish reveals some of the warmth (alcohol) that is found in a large number of wines in the 1998 vintage. Drink it over the next 5 years.

Loads of spices, candied nuts, and smoke can be found in the 1998 Gewurztraminer Rodelsberg. Medium-bodied and hugely expressive, this silky-textured wine juxtaposes purity and femininity with untold quantities of yellow fruits, minerals, roses, herbal tea, jasmine, and raspberries, all lasting throughout its unbelievably long finish. This outstanding Gewurztraminer should be drunk over the next 5–6 years. The 1998 Gewurztraminer Furstentum offers mouthwatering aromas of raspberries, cherries, and abundant spices. Hugely intense, broad, and deep, this cherry juice, currant, and lemon-flavored gem harmoniously marries muscle with grace and elegance. Anticipated maturity: now–2006.

The recently released 1997 Gewurztraminer Mambourg Sélection de Grains Nobles was produced from vines over 60 years old. Bottled without fining or filtration (extremely rare in Alsace) after having spent two years on its lees, this is unquestionably a spectacular wine. White and yellow peaches, apricots, and sweet red berries vie for the taster's aromatic attention. On the palate, apricot compote, raspberries, cherries, potpourri, and loads of spices can be found in this refined, oily-textured, medium-bodied wine. It offers a mouthful of creamy layers of hugely concentrated fruit that last throughout its exceptionally long finish. Anticipated maturity: now–2020. The 1999 Pinot Blanc Zellenberg (40% of which is Auxerrois) has highly expressive mineral, spice, white flower, and pear aromas. It has excellent breadth to its honeydew melon, anise, spice, and flower-filled personality. Medium-bodied and with a lovely panoply of flavors, this is a fruit-forward, distinctive, and persistent wine for drinking over the next 2–3 years.

MAISON TRIMBACH (RIBEAUVILLÉ)

2000	Clos Ste.-Hune	EEE	94+
1998	Gewurztraminer	C	88
1997	Gewurztraminer	C	89
2000	Gewurztraminer Cuvée des Seigneurs Ribeaupierre	D	92
1999	Gewurztraminer Cuvée des Seigneurs Ribeaupierre	D	88
1998	Gewurztraminer Cuvée des Seigneurs Ribeaupierre	D	90
1997	Gewurztraminer Cuvée des Seigneurs Ribeaupierre	D	91+
1996	Gewurztraminer Cuvée des Seigneurs Ribeaupierre	D	88
1998	Gewurztraminer Réserve	C	88+
2000	Gewurztraminer Sélection de Grains Nobles Hors Choix	EE	97
2000	Gewurztraminer Vendange Tardive	D	93
1999	Gewurztraminer Vendange Tardive	D	89
1998	Gewurztraminer Vendange Tardive	D	93
1997	Gewurztraminer Vendange Tardive	D	93
1996	Pinot Gris Hommage à Georgette Trimbach	D	92+
2000	Pinot Gris Hommage à Jeanne	D	93
2000	Pinot Gris Réserve	C	89
2000	Pinot Gris Réserve Personnelle	D	90

1998 Pinot Gris Réserve Personnelle	D	88
1997 Pinot Gris Réserve Personnelle	D	88
2000 Pinot Gris Sélection de Grains Nobles Hors Choix	EEE	96
2000 Pinot Gris Vendanges Tardives	E	92+
1998 Riesling Clos Ste.-Hune	E	95+
1997 Riesling Clos Ste.-Hune	E	91+
1996 Riesling Clos Ste.-Hune	E	93+
1995 Riesling Clos Ste.-Hune	E	94+
2000 Riesling Frédéric-Emile	D	91
1999 Riesling Frédéric-Emile	D	88+
1998 Riesling Frédéric-Emile	D	91+
1997 Riesling Frédéric-Emile	D	90+
1995 Riesling Frédéric-Emile	D	92+
2000 Riesling Frédéric-Emile Sélection de Grains Nobles	EE	94+
2000 Riesling Frédéric-Emile Vendange Tardive	E	92
1998 Riesling Frédéric-Emile Vendange Tardive	E	95+
2000 Riesling Réserve	C	88+
1998 Riesling Réserve	C	90

The Trimbach *négociant* house is well known throughout the world for the stunning Rieslings it crafts under the Frédéric-Emile and Clos Ste.-Hune labels. The Frédéric-Emile bottlings (prior to 1967 they were labeled as "Grande Réserve") are fashioned from 40-year-old vines in an estate-owned parcel that overlaps on two grands crus, Geisberg and Osterberg.

The tightly wound, aromatically floral, medium-bodied 1997 Riesling Frédéric-Emile reveals superb complexity, purity, and admirable length. This is a rich, backward, silky-textured, chalk/mineral-dominated wine with extraordinary balance and focus. Anticipated maturity: now–2012+. The beguiling 1995 Riesling Frédéric-Emile exhibits a profound nose of minerals, chalk, granite, and citrus fruits that leads to a highly nuanced, medium- to full-bodied character. Massively powerful layers of rocks, pears, candied limes, and minerals are found in this rich, fabulously dense offering. Additionally, it is focused, hugely concentrated, and possesses an exceptionally long finish. Anticipated maturity: now–2012.

The world-renowned Riesling Clos Ste.-Hune is produced from 40-year-old vines in a 1.38-hectare parcel (3.4 acres) located within the Rosacker grand cru. Some of the finest Rieslings I have ever tasted have hailed from this tiny plot. The 1997 Riesling Clos Ste.-Hune displays strong floral aromas interlaced with ripe apricots. Reminiscent of a restrained Viognier, it reveals flavors of peaches, perfume, chalk, and honeysuckle blossoms in its opulently textured personality. This medium- to full-bodied, extraordinarily rich wine possesses a superbly focused, mineral-dominated finish. As it sorts itself out in Trimbach's cold cellars, it should come together to become one of the finest Clos Ste.-Hunes of the decade. Anticipated maturity: 2005–2012+. Crisp, youthful aromas of lemons are found in the medium-bodied, dense, and highly focused 1996 Riesling Clos Ste.-Hune. On the palate it offers extraordinarily powerful layers of lime-drenched minerals, a vibrant satiny texture, and huge richness. This unbelievably long wine is massively structured, concentrated, and backward. It will require patience. Drink this gem between 2005–2015. The 1995 Riesling Clos Ste.-Hune remains unevolved and tight but is certainly one the greatest wines to have been crafted from this tiny *monopole* (solely-owned vineyard). As always, my score reflects what I was able to perceive in the wine, yet I am convinced its mind-numbing richness and concentration are holding back enormous reserves. A profound nose of creamed herbs, minerals, candied limes, and poached pears leads to a superrich, dry, viscous core of fruit. Layer upon layer of stones, gravel, spiced apples, and liquid minerals captivate the palate for well over a minute. This is a riveting wine, with untold complexity, power, and precision. Anticipated maturity: 2005–2015+.

The floral, smoky, pear-scented 1997 Pinot Gris Réserve Personnelle has lovely apple, peach, and spice flavors in its plump, medium-bodied character. This wine has excellent grip, balance, and a soft texture. It is lush, flavorful, and immensely pleasing. Drink it over the next 7 years.

The outstanding 1996 Pinot Gris Hommage à Georgette Trimbach is a magnificent wine with huge potential. Its sublime aromatics reveal poached pears dripping with honey and a myriad of spices. On the palate it is broad, crammed with candied white fruits, and medium- to full-bodied. It is wonderfully ripe, impeccably balanced, and satisfies both the hedonistic desire for opulence as well as the intellectual requirement for nuance. The Trimbachs are planning to release this superb Pinot Gris in 2000, when they believe it will have begun to absorb its 14 grams of residual sugar per liter. Anticipated maturity: now–2010+.

Pierre and Jean Trimbach seemed almost apologetic as they served the 1997 Gewurztraminer, explaining that it was in a completely atypical style for their firm. I loved it. Pure, fresh, almost gaudy aromas of rose water and lychee nuts burst from its opulent, medium- to full-bodied core. It is a flamboyant, oily-textured, well-balanced wine with loads of pineapple, candied orange rind, and honeysuckle flavors. Drink it over the next 7 years.

The aromatically muted 1997 Gewurztraminer Cuvée des Seigneurs de Ribeaupierre has wonderful elegance, complexity, balance, and hedonistic appeal in its medium- to full-bodied personality. This backward wine will undoubtedly be a sublime Gewurztraminer once its exotic red berry and mango-filled core sorts itself out. It offers velvety layers of fruit in a flashy yet refined manner. Anticipated maturity: now–2009. Creamed herbal aromas are found in the medium- to full-bodied 1996 Gewurztraminer Cuvée des Seigneurs de Ribeaupierre. This subdued-styled Gewurz has excellent focus, freshness, and balance, yet lacks the opulence encountered in this firm's 1997s. Grapefruit, flowers, and hints of roses are found in this beautifully etched, elegant offering. Drink it over the next 5 years.

The 1997 Gewurztraminer Vendange Tardive is a sexy, luxurious, exotic wine. Lovers of full-throttle, in-your-face Gewurztraminers will find all they can handle in this highly expressive, flamboyant offering. Extravagant aromas of fresh lychee nuts and spices immersed in rose water explode from the glass. This full-bodied, sweet (50 grams residual sugar per liter), hedonistic wine is oily-textured and densely packed with tropical fruits and juicy over-ripe peaches. It is surprisingly pure and well balanced for such a flashy wine. Anticipated maturity: now–2012.

The expressive nose of the 1998 Riesling Réserve offers powerful mineral and gravel scents. Candied lemons, crisp pears, and quartz can be discerned in this medium-bodied, delineated, well-focused wine. Its velvety texture, pure, bone-dry character has a gorgeous mouth-feel. In addition, this wine has an impressively long and supple finish. Anticipated maturity: now–2008. Flowers, tropical fruits, smoke, stones, and wet gravel can be discerned in the aromatics of the 1998 Riesling Frédéric-Emile. This intensely rich, concentrated, deep wine is drenched in lemons, minerals, and stones. Its impressive finish reveals tangy lime notes. Anticipated maturity: 2004–2012+. The 1998 Riesling Clos Ste.-Hune is a spectacular wine. It displays a magnificent aromatic purity, with complex herbal, mineral, and crisp pear scents. Medium- to full-bodied, and awesomely broad, powerful, and harmonious, this tightly wound, slate, chalk, lemon-lime, quartz, and cocoa powder–flavored wine is silky-textured and breathtakingly intense. It should be at its peak of maturity between 2006–2015+.

The 1998 Pinot Gris Réserve Personnelle displays smoky pear, spice cake, and butter scents. Light- to medium-bodied and spicy, this silky-textured wine offers apple, apricot, and white peach flavors. Well made and balanced, it should be drunk over the course of the next 6 years. The 1998 Gewurztraminer has well-etched floral and rose aromas. Juniper berries, perfume, potpourri, and violets can be found in this absolutely lovely, light- to medium-bodied wine. Satin-textured and fresh, it is feminine and bone-dry. Drink it over the next 4 years.

Aromatically restrained, the 1998 Gewurztraminer Réserve reveals smoky flower and rose water aromas. This broad, white flower, pear, spice, and potpourri-flavored wine is expressive, and has an appealing intensity to its character. Anticipated maturity: now–2005.

The 1998 Gewurztraminer Cuvée des Seigneurs Ribeaupierre has a similar nose with a more intense, concentrated, and complex character. Raspberries, flowers, and roses can be found in this pure, deep, and silky-textured wine. Anticipated maturity: 2003–2008.

The magnificent 1998 Riesling Frédéric-Emile Vendange Tardive (only 2,000 bottles were produced) was fashioned from a parcel in the uppermost reaches of the Frédéric-Emile sector of the Osterberg Grand Cru. Botrytis, quince, candied lemons, and bergamot are found in its complex aromas. Sugarcoated lemons, spices, ginger, stones, and dried honey can be discerned in this minerally, silky-textured beauty. Medium-bodied and concentrated, it has spectacular balance and focus. Anticipated maturity: 2006–2016+.

The 1998 Gewurztraminer Vendange Tardive reveals botrytized yellow plum aromas. This sweet peach, tangy mango, stone, yellow plum, and pineapple-flavored wine is opulent, oily-textured, and medium- to full-bodied. Even though it is thick and lush, it somehow retains admirable freshness and zestiness. Anticipated maturity: 2003–2012.

The 1999 Riesling Frédéric-Emile reveals a racy, liquid mineral and lime-scented nose. It is light-bodied, highly delineated, and displays good depth of stone, lemon, and quartzlike flavors. This highly focused, tightly wound, laserlike wine will require 4–5 years of cellaring. Anticipated maturity: 2003–2010.

The 1999 Gewurztraminer Cuvée des Seigneurs de Ribeaupierre has a delightful spice, fresh lychee nut, and rose-scented nose. It is light- to medium-bodied and exhibits delightful rose, violet, and assorted spice flavors. Well balanced, fresh, and flavorful (yet not boisterous), this is a delightful Gewurz to drink over the next 7 years. The medium-bodied 1999 Gewurztraminer Vendange Tardive reveals a myriad of flowers and spices in its aromas. This is a medium-bodied, satin-textured, late-harvest wine that is neither cloying, unctuous, nor heavy. It is elegantly strewn with beautifully detailed floral and lychee flavors. This is not a concentrated monster but a VT that can easily be paired with foods even in the near term. Anticipated maturity: now–2011.

The excellent 2000 Riesling Réserve has wonderfully ripe varietal-specific mineral and citrus aromas. It is medium-bodied, concentrated, harmonious, and extremely well focused. Assorted stone, gravel, and mineral flavors can be discerned in its expressive, driven character. Drink it over the next 10–12 years. According to Jean Trimbach, the 2000 Riesling Frédéric-Emile has the highest level of dry extract (23 grams per liter) of any Frédéric-Emile ever made. (The same is true for the 2000 Clos Ste.-Hune.) This Riesling reveals demure mineral aromas and a concentrated, tightly wound character. Layers of minerals and gravel can be found intertwined with candied citrus fruits in its juicy, yet structured personality. It is intense, yet immensely youthful, and demands cellaring. Anticipated maturity: 2005–2015.

According to Trimbach, the 2000 Clos Ste.-Hune equals the 1990. "However, in the long term, the 2000s may even be better. We shall wait and see." The wine has intense mineral and herbal tea aromas that give way to a powerful, yet backward flavor profile, densely packed with liquid minerals, spices, smoke, quinine, and candied lime. For those willing to wait, this medium- to full-bodied Riesling should rival some of the greatest Clos Ste.-Hunes produced (1981, 1983, 1989, 1990, 1995, 1996, and 1998).

The 2000 Pinot Gris Réserve Personnelle is a richer, riper, denser, and more powerful version of the Réserve model. Medium- to full-bodied and sporting a smoky mineral-scented nose, it coats the palate with velvety-textured layers of white peaches, smoke, minerals, and spices. This is an extremely well made wine for consuming between 2005–2014.

The 2000 Pinot Gris Hommage à Jeanne was produced from a selection of Trimbach's best Pinot Gris parcels (all harvested at over 15% natural potential alcohol). It sports 25 grams per liter of dry extract and 20 grams per liter of residual sugar. While at most firms this wine would merit a Vendanges Tardives bottling, the Trimbachs chose to pay homage to Jeanne

Trimbach, the mother of Bernard and Hubert, who turned 100 in May 2000 and continues to drink Alsace's lovely nectars to this day. This gorgeous wine has mineral- and smoke-imbued white peach aromas. On the palate it is medium- to full-bodied, dense, and rich. Layer after layer of apricot, poached pear, white peach, and spices can be found in its highly expressive, velvety-textured personality. It is an intensely concentrated, wonderfully balanced, fresh, structured wine. Drink it between 2005–2018.

To Jean Trimbach, 2000 is better than 1990 for both Pinot Gris and Gewurztraminer. The 2000 Gewurztraminer Cuvée des Seigneurs Ribeaupierre has lovely rose, lychee nut aromas that lead to a medium- to full-bodied, refined, expressive character. Peaches, apricots, rose water, lychee nuts, and violets can be found in its elegant yet expressive personality. It is concentrated, gorgeously balanced, and intense. Anticipated maturity: 2004–2012.

The 2000 Riesling Frédéric-Emile Vendange Tardive has mouthwatering liquid mineral aromas. Light- to medium-bodied, full, and precise, this is a gorgeous, highly nuanced wine with herbal tea, mineral, and quince flavors that last throughout its admirably long finish. Anticipated maturity: 2004–2015.

The botrytis- and apricot-scented 2000 Pinot Gris Vendanges Tardives has an elegant, medium-bodied character crammed with white peaches. This focused, extremely well balanced, and silky-textured wine is powerful, yet delicate. Anticipated maturity: 2006–2015.

The rose- and violet-scented 2000 Gewurztraminer Vendange Tardive is a plump, rich, medium-bodied wine. Yellow fruits, raspberries, strawberries, and apricots can be found in its sultry character. This highly expressive wine also possesses a long, pure finish. Anticipated maturity: now–2012.

The superconcentrated 2000 Riesling Frédéric-Emile Sélection de Grains Nobles has lemon candy, herbal tea, mineral, and slate aromas and flavors. This is a bright, highly delineated, yet rich wine with loads of sweet, luscious flavors. Drink it over the next 20+ years.

The 2000 Pinot Gris Sélection de Grains Nobles Hors Choix explodes from the glass with apricots, white peaches, and boisterous notes of botrytis. Medium- to full-bodied, intense, and broad, this is a lush and layered wine. Copious quantities of yellow fruits are intermingled with smoke, spices, and botrytis in this huge yet highly focused and persistent wine. Absolutely stunning, it should easily last for 30 years or more.

The apricot-scented 2000 Gewurztraminer Sélection de Grains Nobles Hors Choix is massive, a white peach, assorted yellow fruit, and zesty lemon-flavored wine. It has unreal depth to its super-concentrated character. While possessing immense power and a sumptuous core of syrupy fruit, this wine also boasts lively, tangy acidity that renders it brilliantly balanced. It may well be the finest sweet Gewurztraminer I have ever tasted from Trimbach. Anticipated maturity: now–2025.

DOMAINE WEINBACH (KAYSERSBERG)

1999 Gewurztraminer Altenbourg Cuvée Laurence	E	92
1998 Gewurztraminer Altenbourg Cuvée Laurence	E	93
1997 Gewurztraminer Altenbourg Cuvée Laurence	E	93
1999 Gewurztraminer Altenbourg Quintessence de Grains Nobles	EEE	97
1998 Gewurztraminer Altenbourg Quintessence de Grains Nobles	EEE	97
1997 Gewurztraminer Altenbourg Quintessence de Grains Nobles	EEE	99
1999 Gewurztraminer Altenbourg Vendange Tardive	E	94
1998 Gewurztraminer Altenbourg Vendange Tardive	EE	93
1999 Gewurztraminer Furstentum Cuvée Laurence	D	90+
1998 Gewurztraminer Furstentum Sélection de Grains Nobles	EEE	94
1997 Gewurztraminer Furstentum Vendange Tardive	EE	94+
1999 Gewurztraminer Cuvée Laurence	E	90+
1998 Gewurztraminer Cuvée Laurence	E	91+

Year	Wine		
1997	Gewurztraminer Cuvée Laurence	E	92
1999	Gewurztraminer Cuvée Théo	D	90
1998	Gewurztraminer Cuvée Théo	D	90
1997	Gewurztraminer Cuvée Théo	D	89
1999	Gewurztraminer Réserve Personnelle	C	88
1998	Gewurztraminer Réserve Personnelle	D	88
1997	Gewurztraminer Réserve Personnelle	D	88
1997	Muscat Réserve	D	88
1999	Pinot Blanc Réserve	C	89
1999	Riesling Cuvée Ste.-Catherine	D	90
1998	Riesling Cuvée Ste.-Catherine	D	91+
1997	Riesling Cuvée Ste.-Catherine	E	92
1999	Riesling Cuvée Théo	D	88+
1998	Riesling Cuvée Théo	D	89+
1997	Riesling Cuvée Théo	D	88+
1999	Riesling Réserve Personnelle	C	88
1999	Riesling Schlossberg	D	89
1998	Riesling Schlossberg	D	89+
1997	Riesling Schlossberg	D	90+
1999	Riesling Schlossberg Cuvée Ste.-Catherine	D	91
1998	Riesling Schlossberg Cuvée Ste.-Catherine	E	92
1997	Riesling Schlossberg Cuvée Ste.-Catherine Cuvée du Centenaire	E	93+
1999	Riesling Schlossberg Cuvée Ste.-Catherine l'Inédit!	E	93
1998	Riesling Schlossberg Cuvée Ste.-Catherine l'Inédit!	E	93+
1998	Riesling Schlossberg Sélection de Grains Nobles	EEE	95
1994	Riesling Schlossberg Sélection de Grains Nobles	EEE	98
1998	Riesling Schlossberg Vendange Tardive	EE	93+
1997	Riesling Schlossberg Vendange Tardive	EE	95
1999	Riesling Vendanges Tardives	EE	90
1998	Riesling Vendanges Tardives	EE	90
1999	Sylvaner Réserve	B	88
1999	Tokay-Pinot Gris Altenbourg Cuvée Laurence	E	92+
1998	Tokay-Pinot Gris Altenbourg Cuvée Laurence	E	94
1997	Tokay-Pinot Gris Altenbourg Cuvée Laurence	E	93+
1998	Tokay-Pinot Gris Altenbourg Sélection de Grains Nobles	EEE	99
1999	Tokay-Pinot Gris Altenbourg Vendange Tardive	E	94
1999	Tokay-Pinot Gris Cuvée Laurence	D	91
1998	Tokay-Pinot Gris Cuvée Laurence	E	92
1997	Tokay-Pinot Gris Cuvée Laurence	E	92
1999	Tokay-Pinot Gris Cuvée Ste.-Catherine	D	89
1998	Tokay-Pinot Gris Cuvée Ste.-Catherine	D	89
1997	Tokay-Pinot Gris Cuvée Ste.-Catherine	E	90
1999	Tokay-Pinot Gris Sélection de Grains Nobles	EEE	95
1998	Tokay-Pinot Gris Sélection de Grains Nobles	EEE	95
1997	Tokay-Pinot Gris Quintessence de Grains Nobles	EEE	96+
1995	Tokay-Pinot Gris Quintessence de Grains Nobles Cuvée du Centenaire	EEE	99
1997	Tokay-Pinot Gris Vendange Tardive	EE	93+
1996	Tokay-Pinot Gris Vendange Tardive	EE	94

Since Laurence Faller took over the winemaking duties at Domaine Weinbach (1993–94) there have been marked stylistic changes in the wines. They remain extremely well made, rich, and concentrated but are less generous in their youth than under the former wine-maker's régime. I am, however, convinced that the wines presently being produced at this famed estate will be longer-lived than those from the past.

Restrained aromas of creamed oranges are found in the 1997 Muscat Réserve. As Mme Collette Faller, this domaine's charming matriarch, said, "this is a Muscat whose mouth holds the promises made by the nose." Powerful layers of tangerine-imbued minerals coat the palate in this full-throttle wine. It is medium- to full-bodied, intensely expressive, and silky-textured. Drink it over the next 4–5 years. The 1997 Riesling Cuvée Théo has a muted, un-evolved nose yet a strong, concentrated character. This light- to medium-bodied, crisp wine has broad lemon-drenched mineral flavors. It is tightly wound at present but will blossom into a rich and expressive offering with cellaring. Anticipated maturity: now–2008.

The Fallers crafted four Rieslings from their 9-hectare (22.2 acres) parcel in the tenderloin of the Schlossberg grand cru (the Vendange Tardive is reviewed later in this entry). The 1997 Riesling Schlossberg reveals earth and mineral scents that give way to a medium-bodied, su-perprecise personality. This backward wine is exceptionally pure, focused, and vibrant. It is densely packed with chalk, clay, mineral, and citrus fruit flavors that last throughout its im-pressively long finish. Drink it between now–2010. Over 90% of the grapes used to craft the 1997 Riesling Cuvée Ste.-Catherine are from the 25- to 45-year-old vines in the lower por-tion of the Faller's Schlossberg parcel. Aromatically displaying sweetened tea–laced miner-als, this is a boldly expressive, medium- to full-bodied, and refined wine. It boasts exquisite purity, power, breadth, and length in its chalky lemon juice flavors. Anticipated maturity: now–2010+. The 1997 Riesling Schlossberg Cuvée Ste.-Catherine Cuvée du Centenaire is a magnificent wine whose flavors remain on the palate even longer than it takes to pronounce its name. Its stony aromas are followed by an unbelievable explosion of crystalline minerals, spices, and citrus fruits. This medium- to full-bodied massively rich and concentrated wine is bracing, crisp, and tightly wound. I would not be surprised if my score appears conserva-tive after it has had a few years of bottle age. Anticipated maturity: 2003–2012.

Produced from grapes harvested in both the Clos des Capucins and the Schlossberg vine-yards, the 1997 Tokay-Pinot Gris Cuvée Ste.-Catherine exhibits buttered and jammy apricot aromas. This is an opulent, velvety-textured wine with exotic white raisin and peach flavors. Medium- to full-bodied and lush, it is concentrated and well balanced. Drink it over the next 8 years. The 1997 Tokay-Pinot Gris Cuvée Laurence is an even more hedonistic, complex, focused, concentrated, and intense version of the previous wine. Produced from vines located in the lower section of the Altenbourg vineyard, it displays honeysuckle and smoke-covered peach aromas. This superb wine has extraordinary balance, grip, and precision combined with lovely opulence. Anticipated maturity: now–2010.

Smoky minerals are found in the 1997 Tokay-Pinot Gris Altenbourg Cuvée Laurence's nose. This luxurious, lush, medium- to full-bodied, velvety-textured wine is densely packed with yellow plums, apricots, and raisins. It is highly structured, in desperate need of cellar-ing, and offers an exceptionally long, delineated finish. Drink it between now–2010+.

The 1997 Gewurztraminer Réserve Personnelle offers rosewater scents that lead to a medium-bodied, focused personality filled with luscious layers of perfumed and spiced ly-chee nuts. This oily-textured, flashy wine will require near-term consumption. Drink it over the next 4–5 years. The medium-bodied 1997 Gewurztraminer Cuvée Théo offers refined flo-ral aromas, a luscious texture, and loads of spicy cherries, lychees, and pink grapefruits. This opulent yet elegant wine is beautifully rendered, and an absolute delight to drink. Antici-pated maturity: now–2005.

Produced from a vineyard located below the Altenbourg grand cru, the 1997 Gewurztraminer Cuvée Laurence displays gorgeous plump lychee and rosewater aromatics. It is medium- to full-bodied, satin-textured, and crammed with copious quantities of pineapples, red currants, raspberries, candied grapefruits, and flowers. This tangy, concentrated, and highly expressive wine will be at its best if drunk over the next 7 years. The floral 1997 Gewurztraminer Altenbourg Cuvée Laurence is an embracing, flamboyant, luxurious, and medium- to full-bodied wine. Waves of clove-spiked lychees, cherries, mangoes, and pineapples are found in its sexy personality. This powerful, expressive offering is bold enough to put tasters used to insipid wines into catatonic shock. Anticipated maturity: now–2006.

Due to the rarity and astronomical prices of the following Vendange Tardive and Sélection de Grains Nobles wines, I have decided to provide only abbreviated tasting notes.

The 1997 Gewurztraminer Furstentum Vendange Tardive has an unyielding, muted nose and a magnificently spicy, full-bodied personality. Its highly expressive flavor profile is hedonistic, velvety-textured, and loaded with raspberry coulis, perfume, and lychees. This powerfully concentrated wine will require a year or two of cellaring for its aromas to develop and should be consumed over the following decade.

The 1997 Tokay-Pinot Gris Vendange Tardive displays enthralling aromas of apricots and pears dripping with honey. This medium- to full-bodied, thickly textured wine has admirable focus, balance, and powerful superripe peach flavors intermingled with white raisins. It is intensely concentrated and complex. Anticipated maturity: now–2012+.

The sweet tea and raspberry-scented 1997 Riesling Schlossberg Vendange Tardive is an extraordinarily focused, pure, and precise wine. It coats the palate with intense white/red berry fruit whose flavors seemingly linger for minutes. Anticipated maturity: now–2015+.

The recently released 1994 Riesling Schlossberg Sélection de Grains Nobles has unbelievably profound aromas of almonds and minerals, as well as an ethereal character crammed with mentholated exotic fruits and honey. This stunner exhibits show-stopping balance, purity, concentration, and length. Drink it over the next 25+ years.

The gold-colored 1996 Tokay-Pinot Gris Vendange Tardive combines the bright acidity of its vintage with copious quantities of candied oranges, tangy apricots, and creamed herbs. This magnificently bold wine should be at its peak between now–2014.

As though its wines at the Sélection de Grains Nobles level were not concentrated and powerful enough to knock tasters off their feet, Domaine Weinbach crafts some of the most intense wines on earth under the Quintessence de Grains Nobles moniker. These jammy, syrupy nectars combine massive sugar levels with bracing acidity. Readers should be aware that these wines are meant for sipping in lieu of dessert. They are simply too intense and dominating to be matched with most foods.

The sugarcoated peach and apricot-scented 1997 Tokay-Pinot Gris Quintessence de Grains Nobles has superb elegance. It has the requisite acidity to balance its extraordinary thick and juicy core of overripe yellow fruit, candied cherry, and raspberry jam–like flavors. Anticipated maturity: now–2030+. The gold-colored 1997 Gewurztraminer Altenbourg Quintessence de Grains Nobles boasts unprecedented quantities of red fruits, golden peaches, candied tangerines, quince jam, raisins, and spices in its full-bodied, massively powerful personality. Drink this standard setter over the next 15–30 years. I could almost smell the huge acidity levels in the 1995 Tokay-Pinot Gris Quintessence de Grains Nobles Cuvée du Centenaire. Aromatically reminiscent of Chave's or Chapoutier's Hermitage Vin de Pailles, it offers sugarcoated raisin scents that lead to a perfect balancing act between jammy fruit and bracing acid. This wine may well outlive everyone reading these words. Anticipated maturity: now–Doomsday.

The Faller home, located just outside the picturesque village of Kaysersberg, was, prior to the French Revolution, a Capuchin (a branch of the Franciscan Order) monastery. The vine- and rosebush-covered land enclosed by the estate's walls is named the Clos des Capucins, and all of Domaine Weinbach's wines list its name on the vintage tag and bear a sketch of a Capuchin monk. (For those readers who enjoy trivia, the Italian word for Capuchin is *cappuccino*, or little hat, the same name used for the coffee drink with the "little hat" of foamed milk.) The old monastery, with its magnificent woodwork and marvelously large kitchen, is where the disarming Collette Faller and her two daughters, Laurence and Catherine, reside and manage the estate (the Domaine's winery occupies a more modern building attached to the house). While Mme Faller and Catherine are responsible for the business aspects of this important estate, Laurence handles the winemaking duties. Are there three lovelier ladies to be found in one house?

Collette Faller "adores the 1998 vintage," while her generally subdued daughter Laurence referred to it as "interesting, very pretty, and underappreciated by Alsatians." The younger Faller went on to say that the growing season had been a study in contrasts. "In May and early June it was hot so we had an early flowering, then it turned cold and wet. This lasted through August when we experienced massive heat, to the point where we even had some burnt grapes. We then had a cold and rainy early September that was followed by two weeks of gorgeous weather. Harvest began in this period for the varieties that ripen early, like Muscat. We then had two weeks of rain, until October 13, before great weather set in for our second batch of harvesting." According to Laurence Faller, concentration levels were good for every varietal, which she attributes to botrytis. "We had some parcels that were picking up a degree of potential alcohol each day, and our Rieslings were all harvested with at least 15% natural potential alcohol, something we've never witnessed. The botrytis provided richness while maintaining good acidity, though the acid levels are not as high as 1995 or 1996. We had some gray rot on the Pinot Gris but simply sorted that out."

Lush lime scents are found in the delightful aromatics of the 1998 Riesling Cuvée Théo. This is a well-structured, pure, suave, concentrated, dense, yet elegant wine. Loads of spices, minerals, and fresh, crisp white fruits can be found in this chewy textured, medium-bodied offering. Anticipated maturity: now–2008. The 1998 Riesling Schlossberg reveals aromas of pink grapefruits and tropical fruits. Medium-bodied, this liquid mineral, fresh slate, and grapefruit-flavored wine has a long, firm finish. Anticipated maturity: 2004–2012.

The herbal tea and lemon-scented refined 1998 Riesling Cuvée Ste.-Catherine is a gorgeously focused, medium-bodied wine. Rich layers of citrus fruits can be found in this powerful yet lacelike offering. This pure, precise wine has an extremely long, graceful finish. Anticipated maturity: 2003–2012. The medium-bodied 1998 Riesling Schlossberg Cuvée Ste.-Catherine was produced from over 60-year-old vines, and displays subdued fresh herbs, tea, and white fruits in its complex and defined aromatic profile. On the palate, this wine is also well delineated, muscular, detailed, and elegant. Anticipated maturity: 2003–2012+. The 1998 Riesling Schlossberg Cuvée Ste.-Catherine l'Inédit! was produced from similarly old vines as the previous wine, but from a neighboring parcel, harvested at 15.2% natural potential alcohol. Its sweet, mineral, spice, and pear-scented nose leads to a wine of huge richness and breadth. This medium- to full-bodied, dense, and deep effort has extraordinary flavors of herb-tinged minerals and candied lemons. This exceptionally long and pure Riesling should be at its best between 2003–2015.

Botrytis and ripe white fruits are evident in the nose of the 1998 Tokay-Pinot Gris Cuvée Ste.-Catherine. This rich, botrytised, pear, and apple-flavored wine has excellent focus, and a long, smoky, mineral-laden finish. Anticipated maturity: now–2009. Sweet spice and botrytis aromas are found in the nose of the medium- to full-bodied 1998 Tokay-Pinot Gris Cuvée Laurence. Fresh mint and poached pears are present in this broad, complex, intense, concentrated wine. Harvested at 16.6% potential alcohol, it admirably hides its 14% finished alcohol in thick, luscious fruit. Drink this beauty between 2003–2012+. The 1998 Tokay-Pinot Gris Altenbourg Cuvée Laurence, harvested at a whopping 17% natural potential alcohol, offers delectable smoky yellow fruit aromas. This medium- to full-bodied wine has magnificent richness to its creamed tea, apricot compote–flavored character. Broad, thick, yet fresh and nuanced, it is a show-stopper. Anticipated maturity: 2003–2015+.

The 1998 Gewurztraminer Réserve Personnelle has a flower- and botrytis-scented nose. On the palate, roses, assorted flowers, and red fruits can be discerned in this well-delineated and -focused, medium-bodied wine. Its long, mineral-laden finish does reveal the alcoholic heat evidenced in many 1998s. Anticipated maturity: now–2005.

Sea salt and spicy fruits are found in the aromatics of the 1998 Gewurztraminer Cuvée Théo. Medium-bodied and opulently textured, this delightful rose, red fruit (in particular, currants)–filled wine is complex, rich, yet elegant. Drink it over the next 5–6 years.

The 1998 Gewurztraminer Cuvée Laurence has a nose reminiscent of acacia blossoms, dried honey, and assorted spices. Yellow plums, raspberries, creamed sweet fruits, violets, and botrytis can be found its fresh, hedonistic character. This concentrated, powerful wine should be drunk over the next 9–10 years.

A plethora of spices and plump yellow fruits can be discerned in the nose of the 1998 Gewurztraminer Altenbourg Cuvée Laurence. Medium-bodied, velvety-textured, and decadently styled, this thick, honeyed wine is packed with a compote of yellow fruits, cloves, and juniper berries. This extroverted, sexy wine should be consumed over the next 10 years.

Domaine Weinbach's 1998 Riesling Vendanges Tardives' nose displays fresh lemony minerals. Medium-bodied, rich, and creamy-textured, this is a soft, supple wine that exhibits plump candied citrus fruits and hints of minerals. While it lacks the focus and penetrating qualities of this estate's best VTs, it is opulent and immensely pleasurable. Drink it over the next 10 years. Gorgeous flower and white fruit scents are found in the pure aromatics of the 1998 Riesling Schlossberg Vendange Tardive. Velvety-textured and medium- to full-bodied, it has outstanding focus, definition, and elegance. Raspberries and blood oranges make up this superb sweet wine's personality. Anticipated maturity: 2004–2016+.

The 1998 Riesling Schlossberg Sélection de Grains Nobles has penetrating citrus-infused mineral and sweet herbal tea aromatics. Dense, concentrated, and full-bodied, it has a viscous, quince-packed character. Thick yet surprisingly fresh and well balanced, this superb wine should be at its peak between 2005–2020+. The 1998 Gewurztraminer Altenbourg Vendange Tardive reveals aromas reminiscent of rose petals and fresh lychee nuts. It is full-bodied and lush, with a well-delineated, broad, elegant character. Sweet red fruits are found in its rich yet focused flavor profile. Anticipated maturity: now–2012+. A subtle spicy mélange and perfumelike aromas make up the nose of the 1998 Gewurztraminer Furstentum Sélection de Grains Nobles. Massively concentrated and thick, this luxuriant wine has an oily texture and full body. Its layers of spicy red fruits coat the palate and linger throughout its impressively long, flavor-packed finish. Anticipated maturity: 2003–2020.

The stunning 1998 Tokay-Pinot Gris Altenbourg Sélection de Grains Nobles was produced from an entire parcel of vines, without sorting, so there is a reasonable quantity of this earth-shattering nectar (1,867 bottles). Its hyperspicy nose displays loads of botrytis-infused smoky yellow fruits. On the palate, this full-bodied wine surges forth with a panoply of apricots, peaches, and sweetened herbal tea–like flavors. Intense and massively rich, it somehow maintains an unreal precision. This impeccably balanced offering is magnificently concentrated and extravagantly textured, yet impressively elegant and graceful. Anticipated maturity: 2006–2025+. The 1998 Tokay-Pinot Gris Sélection de Grains Nobles has flowers, creamed yellow fruits, almond cookies, and oaklike spices (yet no new or young wood was employed) in its aromatics. Reminiscent of a hugely rich vanilla-infused crème brûlée, this full-bodied wine is as sweet as molasses (170 grams of residual sugar per liter) yet has the requisite acidity for outstanding balance. Drink it between 2003–2014+.

Intensely expressive roses and minerals are found in the nose of the 1998 Gewurztraminer Altenbourg Quintessence de Grains Nobles. This voluminous wine is unctuously textured and possesses an almost impenetrably dense core. Cherry jam, raspberry jelly, and copious quantities of spices can be discerned within its personality. Sporting 205 grams of residual sugar per liter, this backward, ultrarich wine will require cellaring. Sip it between 2006–2020+.

According to Laurence Faller, producing quality wine in 1999 was possible if yields were kept at moderate levels and the grapes were harvested late in order to obtain full physiological ripeness. This estate harvested between October 9 and November 16, circumventing two large periods of rain. "I like this vintage a great deal, because we did what we needed to do to make beautiful wines," said Mlle Faller. Interestingly, the estate's two least expensive wines are considerable successes, as these varietals appear to have done particularly well in 1999. Exhibiting smoky, ripe white fruit and dried honey–like aromas, the 1999 Sylvaner Réserve is a rich, tangy, medium-bodied wine. This well-focused offering is highly expressive, bursting with quinine, mineral, and pear flavors. This excellent value is a first-rate example of its varietal and should be consumed over the next 2–3 years.

The 1999 Pinot Blanc Réserve has demure stone and floral scents. It is opulently textured, medium-bodied, and crammed with plump apples and pears. This wonderfully ripe wine reveals hints of minerals in its long, supple finish. Anticipated maturity: now–2004.

The mineral-scented 1999 Riesling Réserve Personnelle has a plump, silky personality. This is a rich, mouthcoating wine that displays gorgeously tangy mineral flavors in its soft, persistent character. Drink it over the next 4–5 years.

The 1999 Riesling Cuvée Théo exhibits mineral, pear, and apple aromas. Quinine, citrus fruits, and minerals are found in this well-focused, medium-bodied wine. It is well balanced, fresh, pure, and flavorful. The mineral-scented 1999 Riesling Schlossberg displays zesty pear, white flower, and stonelike flavors. It has excellent focus, purity, and balance to its tightly wound, youthful character. This wine reveals lovely concentration, yet will require cellaring to blossom. Anticipated maturity: 2004–2010.

Loads of minerals, stones, and herbal tea can be found in the delightful aromatics of the 1999 Riesling Cuvée Ste.-Catherine. This wine has lovely breadth to its rich, plump, and deep personality. It is lush, rich, and loaded with liquid mineral–like flavors. This well-delineated wine is medium- to full-bodied, and has an admirably persistent finish. Anticipated maturity: 2004–2010. The 1999 Riesling Schlossberg Cuvée Ste.-Catherine has vivid aromatic intensity to its mineral- and quinine-scented nose. Loads of toasty minerals, sun-dried gravel, pears, and bergamot can be found in its precise flavor profile. This wine has laserlike focus, yet with a silky-textured, fruit-forward character. Drink it between 2004–2012. The 1999 Riesling Schlossberg Cuvée Ste.-Catherine l'Inédit! has a sumptuous, liquid mineral–laced nose. This wine has superb concentration, richness, depth, and length. Layers of candied apples, poached pears, spices, and bergamot are found throughout this gem's character. Its sultry quinine-infused finish appears dry, yet conceals 21 grams of residual sugar. Anticipated maturity: 2005–2015.

Loads of smoky yellow fruits are found in the aromatics of the 1999 Tokay-Pinot Gris Cuvée Ste.-Catherine. This opulently textured, medium-bodied wine exhibits sexy white peach and apricot flavors in its plump, seamless character. Drink this over the next 6 years. The 1999 Tokay-Pinot Gris Cuvée Laurence has fresh, crisp, apricot, and peach aromas. It is an intense, rich, medium- to full-bodied wine. Smoky yellow fruits are found in its deep, sexy, broad personality and throughout its soft, long finish. There are no jagged edges in this well-balanced and highly expressive wine. Anticipated maturity: 2004–2010.

The 1999 Tokay-Pinot Gris Altenbourg Cuvée Laurence has demure, tangy, smoky fruit aromas. This medium- to full-bodied wine has gorgeous depth to its yellow fruit, toast, and smoke-crammed character. It is luxuriously textured, with admirable ripeness and a lush, fruit-filled finish. This outstanding Pinot Gris should be consumed between 2005–2015.

The 1999 Gewurztraminer Réserve Personnelle bursts from the glass with sensual rose water and lychee nut aromas. It is a feminine, light- to medium-bodied wine with rose petal and spice flavors. This fresh, delightfully expressive offering should be consumed over the next 5 years. The lychee- and rose-scented 1999 Gewurztraminer Cuvée Théo is a rich, expansive, medium-bodied offering. At this stage, this supple, lush, and fruit-packed (mostly white peaches and apricots) wine tastes more like a Pinot Gris than a Gewurztraminer. However, hints of mango and other exotic fruits come to the fore in its sumptuously textured finish. Drink it between 2003–2007.

The smoky, yellow fruit–scented 1999 Gewurztraminer Cuvée Laurence has a medium- to full-bodied, fruit-packed character. Lushly textured, balanced, and elegant, this wine has outstanding depth to its peach, apricot, and spice-flavored character; it will require 2 years of cellaring to expand and blossom. Anticipated maturity: 2004–2009. The white flower, peach, and smoke-scented 1999 Gewurztraminer Altenbourg Cuvée Laurence is a plump, well-focused, medium- to full-bodied wine. Roses, spices, white peaches, and honeysuckle characterize its fat, deep personality. Additionally, this wine possesses an admirably long and pure finish. It is not an exotically styled or flavored Gewurztraminer, but it delivers loads of highly nuanced flavors in its rich yet delineated character. Anticipated maturity: 2005–2012. Candied and jammy white peaches burst from the glass of the 1999 Gewurztraminer Furstentum Cuvée Laurence. This full-bodied, opulent, lush wine is hugely rich and possesses impressive depth. Layers of sweet white fruits, spices, and mango are intermingled with hints of red berries throughout its sultry character and its exceptionally long, pure finish. This is a boisterous, full-flavored Gewurz for drinking over the next 10–12 years.

The sweet, white flower–scented 1999 Riesling Vendanges Tardives has loads of berries, violets, and white flowers in its well-balanced, medium-bodied personality. Unlike many Vendanges Tardives, this wine is ready to drink. It is fruit-forward and extremely well made. Anticipated maturity: now–2012+. The 1999 Tokay-Pinot Gris Altenbourg Vendange Tardive has fresh white flower, peach, and poached pear aromas. Medium-bodied and spicy, this refined, richly layered wine has excellent balance to its bergamot, sweet herbal tea, pear, and anise-flavored character. It is gorgeously defined, highly concentrated, and possesses a luxuriously long and flavorful finish. Drink this superb wine between 2005–2016.

The 1999 Gewurztraminer Altenbourg Vendange Tardive explodes from the glass with roses, lychee nuts, and spices. Full-bodied, rich, and opulent, this is a compellingly huge yet elegant offering. Its exuberant personality possesses candied berries, rose water, violets, mangoes, poached pears, and clove notes. Anticipated maturity: now–2014.

Intense aromas of smoke-laden pears, quinine, bergamot, and peaches dominate the superb 1999 Tokay-Pinot Gris Sélection de Grains Nobles. Full-bodied, lush, and refined, this is an opulently rich, luscious wine, crammed with copious quantities of white and yellow fruits. It is harmonious, exceptionally well balanced, and bursting with flavor. Many SGNs are too jellied and intense to drink in their youth, but Mlle Faller has crafted one with impeccable equilibrium. Anticipated maturity: now–2030. The 1999 Gewurztraminer Altenbourg Quintessence de Grains Nobles is a stunning spice and orange zest–scented wine. Medium- to full-bodied and luxurious, it is satin-textured and feminine. This extraordinarily rich wine is reminiscent of syrup-drenched white peaches, lychee nuts, roses, and candy, yet it retains an admirably elegant touch. This magnificent wine has exceptional concentration and depth as well as a distinctive personality. Anticipated maturity: now–2025.

DOMAINE GÉRARD WEINZORN (NIEDERMORSCHWIHR)

1998 Riesling Brand	D	88
1999 Riesling Sommerberg	D	88

The 1999 Riesling Sommerberg has rich, fresh, mineral aromas. This broad yet light-bodied wine has excellent purity and focus to its mineral and white berry–flavored character. It is concentrated, rich, and expressive. Drink it over the next 6–7 years.

Gorgeous lemon and mineral aromas are found in the nose of the 1998 Riesling Brand.

This wine has excellent depth of minerals, flowers, pears, and apples in its precise yet fat personality. Anticipated maturity: now–2006.

WOLFBERGER (EGUISHEIM)

1998 Tokay-Pinot Gris Rangen	E	88

The massive Wolfberger firm produces 10 million liters of wine per year (almost 13.5 million bottles), accounting for close to 10% of Alsace's total production. Wolfberger owns a number of cooperatives as well as estates (including Alsace's second-largest estate, the Domaine Jux). All told, Wolfberger owns over 1,300 hectares (over 3,200 acres) of vineyards in Alsace, including parcels in 13 grands crus. Additionally, Wolfberger purchases 5% of its production as part of its *négociant* business. Wolfberger bottles wines under its own name (labels can be either yellow or black, depending on what its distributors want, but the wine remains the same; for example, Wolfberger's American importer prefers yellow labels) and also markets wines bearing labels of estates or cooperatives it has purchased (Domaine Jux, Alsace-Willm, Dambach-la-Ville, and Vieille Armand, for example).

The 1998 Tokay-Pinot Gris Rangen has grilled hazelnut aromas. It is a medium-bodied, velvety-textured, rich, suave, broad wine crammed with jammy, almost pasty yellow fruits. Its long finish suffers a little bit from the warmth (alcohol) found in a number of wines in the 1998 vintage. Anticipated maturity: now–2006.

DOMAINE ZIND-HUMBRECHT (TURCKHEIM)

1999 Gewurztraminer Goldert	D	91
1997 Gewurztraminer Goldert	D	96
1998 Gewurztraminer Goldert Vendanges Tardives	D	94+
1999 Gewurztraminer Gueberschwihr	D	88
1998 Gewurztraminer Gueberschwihr	D	88
1999 Gewurztraminer Heimbourg	D	91
1998 Gewurztraminer Heimbourg	D	90+
1997 Gewurztraminer Heimbourg	D	96
1999 Gewurztraminer Heimbourg Vendanges Tardives	EE	92
1998 Gewurztraminer Heimbourg Vendanges Tardives	EE	93
1999 Gewurztraminer Hengst	D	92
1998 Gewurztraminer Hengst	D	94
1997 Gewurztraminer Hengst	D	95
1999 Gewurztraminer Herrenweg de Turckheim	D	90
1998 Gewurztraminer Herrenweg de Turckheim	D	89
1997 Gewurztraminer Herrenweg de Turckheim	D	94
1999 Gewurztraminer Rangen de Thann Clos St.-Urbain	E	91
1997 Gewurztraminer Rangen de Thann Clos St.-Urbain	E	98+
1998 Gewurztraminer Rangen de Thann Clos St.-Urbain Vendange Tardive	E	97+
1998 Gewurztraminer Turckheim	C	88
1999 Gewurztraminer Clos Windsbuhl	D	91
1998 Gewurztraminer Clos Windsbuhl	D	92
1997 Gewurztraminer Clos Windsbuhl	D	94+
1999 Gewurztraminer Wintzenheim	C	88
1998 Gewurztraminer Wintzenheim	C	88
1997 Gewurztraminer Wintzenheim	D	92
1999 Gewurztraminer Wintzenheim Vieilles Vignes	D	89
1999 Muscat Goldert	D	88
1998 Muscat Goldert	D	89

1997	Muscat Goldert	D	90
1998	Muscat Herrenweg de Turckheim	C	88
1997	Muscat Herrenweg de Turckheim	C	89
1999	Pinot d'Alsace	C	88
1998	Pinot d'Alsace	C	89
1997	Pinot d'Alsace	C	90
1999	Riesling Brand	E	92
1998	Riesling Brand	E	93+
1997	Riesling Brand	E	96+
1998	Riesling Gueberschwir	C	88
1997	Riesling Gueberschwir	C	90
1999	Riesling Clos Hauserer	D	90+
1998	Riesling Clos Hauserer	D	90
1997	Riesling Clos Hauserer	D	92
1999	Riesling Heimbourg	D	91
1998	Riesling Heimbourg	D	90+
1997	Riesling Heimbourg	D	90
1999	Riesling Herrenweg de Turckheim	D	90
1998	Riesling Herrenweg de Turckheim	D	89
1997	Riesling Herrenweg de Turckheim	D	92
1999	Riesling Rangen de Thann Clos St.-Urbain	E	91+
1998	Riesling Rangen de Thann Clos St.-Urbain	E	94+
1997	Riesling Rangen de Thann Clos St.-Urbain	E	96+
1998	Riesling Rangen de Thann Clos St.-Urbain Sélection de Grains Nobles	EEE	96
1999	Riesling Turckheim	D	88+
1998	Riesling Turckheim	D	89+
1997	Riesling Turckheim L14B	D	91+
1997	Riesling Turckheim L240	D	93
1997	Riesling Clos Windsbuhl	D	95
1998	Riesling Clos Windsbuhl Vendanges Tardives	EE	94+
1997	Riesling Wintzenheim	C	89
1999	Tokay-Pinot Gris Heimbourg	D	91+
1998	Tokay-Pinot Gris Heimbourg	D	92
1997	Tokay-Pinot Gris Heimbourg	D	91
1999	Tokay-Pinot Gris Herrenweg	D	89+
1997	Tokay-Pinot Gris Herrenweg de Turckheim	D	90
1997	Tokay-Pinot Gris Clos Jebsal	D	95+
1998	Tokay-Pinot Gris Clos Jebsal Sélection de Grains Nobles	EEE	98
1997	Tokay-Pinot Gris Clos Jebsal Sélection de Grains Nobles	EEE	97
1996	Tokay-Pinot Gris Clos Jebsal Sélection de Grains Nobles	EEE	99
1994	Tokay-Pinot Gris Clos Jebsal Sélection de Grains Nobles Trie Spéciale	EEE	99
1999	Tokay-Pinot Gris Clos Jebsal Vendanges Tardives	E	92+
1998	Tokay-Pinot Gris Clos Jebsal Vendanges Tardives	EE	93+
1997	Tokay-Pinot Gris Rangen de Thann Clos St.-Urbain	E	95+
1998	Tokay-Pinot Gris Rangen de Thann Clos St.-Urbain Sélection de Grains Nobles	EEE	98
1998	Tokay-Pinot Gris Rangen de Thann Clos St.-Urbain Vendanges Tardives	EE	96+
1997	Tokay-Pinot Gris Rotenberg	D	92+

1998 Tokay-Pinot Gris Rotenberg Vendanges Tardives	EE	92
1999 Tokay-Pinot Gris Rotenberg Vieilles Vignes	D	94
1999 Tokay-Pinot Gris Vieilles Vignes	D	91
1998 Tokay-Pinot Gris Vieilles Vignes	D	90
1997 Tokay-Pinot Gris Vieilles Vignes	D	92
1999 Tokay-Pinot Gris Clos Windsbuhl	D	93
1998 Tokay-Pinot Gris Clos Windsbuhl	D	93
1997 Tokay-Pinot Gris Clos Windsbuhl	D	94

I do not know what is more mind-boggling, the quality of Domaine Zind-Humbrecht's wines or Olivier Humbrecht's complete dedication to quality. This tall, powerful, and intellectual man may well be the finest wine-maker in the world. Who else faces the same number of vastly different varietals and extremely varying weather conditions yet consistently crafts superlative wines? The day I spent tasting his 1997s and visiting the estate's vineyards will remain with me my entire life. Olivier Humbrecht is an inspiration.

It was by pure chance that I learned that Humbrecht had converted his vineyard parcels to biodynamic farming. "I do not believe in publicizing such actions because it is not the method that makes great wines, it is just an investment in the future of the vineyards." A very analytical person, Humbrecht was the first vigneron I have spoken with who was able to describe certain strange biodynamic practices (like burying a cow's horn in compost) in logical, scientific ways. From his vineyard work to his moderate yields to the long and late harvests (the 1997s were harvested over a 20-day period at optimum ripeness) to the extended and soft pressings (lasting between 20 and 48 hours per wine—each one of his three pneumatic presses is used but once a day), Olivier Humbrecht has no peers.

Léonard Humbrecht, Olivier's father, who created this estate in 1959 when he married Geneviève Zind, was Alsace's first—and remains the foremost—proponent of low yields and the importance of high-quality *terroir*. He had the vision to see that moderate yields and *terroir* played a major part in a wine's ultimate quality while his neighbors produced as much as they could. When his peers wished to sell or exchange hillside vineyards for high-producing ones on flatlands, they always knew they had a willing listener in Léonard Humbrecht. When the Montrachet of Alsace, the Rangen de Thann, was so difficult and expensive to work that some of its slopes had literally been abandoned, in came Léonard Humbrecht with his commitment and dedication to quality. The *terroirs* on which Olivier Humbrecht crafts his magic were acquired and nurtured by his father for years. It is only fitting that the younger Humbrecht's winemaking would be at the level of his father's vision.

In a region where yields often surpass 100 hectoliters per hectare (h/h), where only a half dozen or so vignerons keep their estate's average yields below 60 h/h, not one single parcel owned by Domaine Zind-Humbrecht surpassed 45 h/h, and the estate averaged 40 h/h overall. Furthermore, not a single vat was chaptalized (none has ever been acidified). The richness in Zind-Humbrecht's wines comes from grapes, not sugar bags.

The 1997 Pinot d'Alsace offers tropical fruit, candied orange, and floral aromas. It is a medium- to full-bodied, silky-textured wine with exceptional density, richness, and broad red currant, poached pear, and chalk flavors. This wine has the generosity of fruit to be drunk immediately upon release as well as the backbone for aging. Drink it over the next 5–6 years.

Phenomenal aromas of tangerines, acacia blossoms, and sweet cherries explode from the 1997 Muscat Herrenweg de Turckheim. Since older vines produce lower yields and Muscat generally sells for a pittance compared to other varieties, Alsatians tend to replace their vines that are older than 25 years. This wine, crafted from 50-year-old vines, has an intensely assertive character crammed with candied orange zests and spices. It is concentrated, massively flavorful, and exceptionally long in the finish. One of the few wines to work with asparagus, it can also be matched with spicy foods or served as an apéritif. Drink it over the next 3–4 years. Surprisingly for this aromatic varietal, the bone-dry 1997 Muscat Goldert had a totally muted, unformed nose. On the palate it is luscious, extremely elegant, and offers mineral, stone, honeysuckle blossoms, and red currants. This fresh, stylish, and complex offering should be consumed over the next 4–5 years.

Minerals and chalk can be discerned in the 1997 Riesling Wintzenheim's tightly wound aromas. This wine's explosion of steely minerals and lemons conquers the taster's palate. According to Olivier Humbrecht, it has low acidity yet appears vibrant. This medium-bodied, powerful, fresh, rich, flavorful offering delivers loads of pleasure. It is the last vintage of Riesling Wintzenheim as the Humbrechts ripped out the vines immediately after the harvest to plant other varietals they feel are better suited to its *terroir.* "The vines seemed to know it was their last chance, so they made the best wine they've ever produced," said Humbrecht. Drink it over the next 4–5 years. The closed nose of the 1997 Riesling Gueberschwihr was reluctant. More revealing on the palate, it offers superb chalk, petrol, pineapple, earth, apricot, and mineral flavors in its mouthcoating, velvety-textured personality. It has outstanding balance, concentration, power, and precision. Anticipated maturity: now–2006.

Humbrecht crafted two separate Riesling Turckheims in 1997. There are two visual clues to differentiate between them: One is marked with lot number L14B and is in Domaine Zind-Humbrecht's typical nongrand cru bottle, and the other (lot number L240) was bottled in the heavier, taller bottle generally reserved for the estate's grands crus. The 1997 Riesling Turckheim L14B has a superexpressive nose of chalk, flowers, and granite. It is thick, massively rich, dense, and possesses a citrus fruit and flower-filled flavor profile. It is a well-balanced and focused wine, yet my instincts would suggest drinking it in its youth. Anticipated maturity: now–2006. The 1997 Riesling Turckheim L240 was produced from a parcel of vines located in the grand cru Brand vineyard. It displays profound aromas of flowers, red berries, bergamot, minerals, and chalk. This medium- to full-bodied wine has exceptional ripeness, richness, and length. Its mouthcoating yet penetrating flavor profile is composed of pineapple, granite, quartz, and candied orange zests. Anticipated maturity: now–2012.

Assorted candied citrus and white fruits are found in the 1997 Riesling Herrenweg de Turckheim's aromatics. This is a big, masculine bruiser of a wine, with loads of concentration, fabulous balance, and a personality crammed with cherries, raspberries, and flowers. It is broad, velvety-textured, and offers an admirably long, citrus-flavored finish. Anticipated maturity: now–2010. Produced from 25-year-old vines, the 1997 Riesling Clos Hauserer reveals a nose of bergamot, roses, and minerals. It is extremely complex, fresh, elegant, and feminine. This pure, tangy wine offers loads of floral minerals, a silky texture, and a medium to full body. Drink it between now–2010+.

The steep slopes of the Clos Windsbuhl, a *monopole* (solely owned vineyard), are impossible to farm with a tractor, so the Humbrechts employ horses. Its 1997 Riesling has profound aromas of chalk and minerals that lead to a full-bodied, ethereal (*aérien* in French) core. This magnificent dry wine is amazingly pure, powerful, concentrated, deep, balanced, and long. According to the Humbrechts, there was not a single sign of rot, noble or otherwise, on this offering's grapes. It is satin-textured and exhibits flavors reminiscent of fresh herbs, flowers, stones, Cynar, minerals, and tangy citrus fruits. Anticipated maturity: now–2015.

Aromatically, the 1997 Riesling Heimbourg offers new oak spices (though it never saw any oak) intermingled with white flowers and almonds. Produced from young vines on steep slopes near the Clos Jebsal, it is creamy-textured, medium- to full-bodied, and fresh. Its lovely hazelnut, white/red currant, and yellow fruit flavors are reminiscent of a first rate Meursault Narvaux. It is markedly less complex as well as shorter than the otherworldly Clos Windsbuhl. Drink it over the next 7 years.

Analytically, the 1997 Riesling Rangen de Thann Clos St.-Urbain is identical to the stunning 1994. Produced from the steep southern exposure slopes of the vineyard that is Alsace's Montrachet, it offers mind-blowing aromatic complexity, with well-defined flowers, stones, earth, and minerals competing with bergamot, pears, and white peaches for the taster's attention. On the palate it displays magnificent purity, delineation, elegance, power, richness, and focus. This medium- to full-bodied, silky-textured wine is massively dense, concentrated, and intense without being heavy. Anticipated maturity: now–2015.

Years ago, a dear friend set out to demonstrate to me that the Brand (which means "burn") vineyard was every bit the equal of the more renowned Rangen de Thann when it came to producing superlative Rieslings. He was right. Ten to 20% of its vines are 25 years old, and the remaining 80–90% are well over 40. The 1997 Brand joins the long list of stunning Rieslings crafted by Humbrecht from this southerly-exposed hillside vineyard. An embracing, superrich nose of spices, poached pears, and cherries gives way to a thickly textured, highly expressive, full-bodied core. This velvety bombshell is crammed with bergamot, acacia blossoms, honeyed white peaches, and clay, whose flavors last throughout its mind-boggling finish.

The father and son Humbrecht team stated that in 1997 Tokay-Pinot Gris was the only varietal affected by noble rot (*Botrytis cinerea*). The 1997 Tokay-Pinot Gris Herrenweg de Turckheim reveals evidence of botrytis (30% of its grapes were affected) in its mineral and sautéed mushroom–scented nose. This broad, immensely appealing, medium- to full-bodied wine is crammed with apricots, peaches, and honeysuckle blossoms. It is forward, satin-textured, generous, and powerful. Drink it over the next 7–8 years. The gold-colored 1997 Tokay-Pinot Gris Vieilles Vignes (60–70% botrytis affected) was harvested at Grains Nobles levels of maturity, yet Humbrecht chose to forgo labeling it as such (or even as a Vendange Tardive) because he does not believe it will age as well as wines with those monikers should. It offers a rich, botrytis-laced nose and a dense, oily-textured, medium- to full-bodied character. This layered wine offers super peach, apricot, bergamot, earth, smoke, and mineral flavors in its hugely pleasurable core of fruit. Anticipated maturity: now–2008.

None of the grapes that fashioned the remaining five Tokay-Pinot Gris had any evidence of noble rot. According to Humbrecht, in his 40 years as a vigneron he has never seen Tokays achieve such high levels of maturity without the influence of botrytis. Surprisingly, Zind-Humbrecht's 1997 Tokays from the Heimbourg, Rotenberg, and Rangen vineyards tasted more like first-rate Chablis than Alsatian Pinot Gris. The pale-colored (almost clear), bone-dry 1997 Tokay-Pinot Gris Heimbourg displays a tightly wound nose of white flowers with hints of yellow fruit in the background. On the palate, this gorgeously focused, precise, medium- to full-bodied offering reveals powerful mineral, stone, and gun flint flavors. Tangy lemons are discernible in its admirably long and pure finish. Anticipated maturity: now–2015+.

Produced from 30 h/h yields, the 1997 Tokay-Pinot Gris Rotenberg offers a crystalline nose of steel, chalk, and minerals. It is sublimely precise, balanced, and focused. This medium- to full-bodied wine's gun flint–dominated flavor profile has the stuffing, equilibrium, and concentration to enable it to age gracefully for 20 years or more. According to Olivier Humbrecht, the 1997 Tokay-Pinot Gris Rangen de Thann Clos St.-Urbain fermented violently for three months. Toasted almonds and minerals are discernable in this full-bodied offering's aromatics. It has stellar focus, precision, complexity, power, and purity in its hyper-concentrated character. This bone-dry, fresh, hugely flavorful (yet lacelike), unbelievably long wine exhibits finely detailed mineral flavors reminiscent of a show-stopping Chablis. Anticipated maturity: now–2020.

Candied apricots and exotic fruits emanate from a glass of the 1997 Tokay-Pinot Gris Clos Windsbuhl. This hugely powerful, intense wine is full-bodied, dense, explosive, and fresh. While it lacks the delicate nuances of the previous offering, it regales the palate with untold quantities of yellow fruits and minerals. It is velvety-textured, complex, and its extensive finish offers loads of apricot and chalk flavors. Drink it between now–2015+.

The 1997 Tokay-Pinot Gris Clos Jebsal attained 15.3% alcohol while retaining 25 grams of residual sugar. This wine reveals a fresh bergamot- and rose-scented nose. Thick, velvety-textured, full-bodied, and explosive, it possesses world-class power. Extremely floral, it has hints of stones in the background. Youthfully angular and undeveloped, it will require 4–5 years of cellaring. Anticipated maturity: 2004–2020.

The Humbrechts believe 1997 is the greatest Gewurz vintage since 1990, with the possible exception of 1994. Readers who crave ostentatious Gewurztraminers will flip for Zind-Humbrecht's flamboyant 1997s. The 1997 Gewurztraminer Wintzenheim, harvested at Vendange Tardive levels of maturity, offers explosive, almost obnoxious aromas of lychee nuts and jasmine bathed in rose water. This massively expressive, gaudy, full-bodied wine bursts on the palate with untold layers of spicy pineapples, flowers, and candied pink grape-fruits. Drink it with assertively spiced Asian dishes or pungent cheeses over the next 7 years.

Offering significantly more elegant, detailed aromas of minerals and flowers, the medium- to full-bodied 1997 Gewurztraminer Herrenweg de Turckheim is a highly expressive yet re-fined wine. It offers copious quantities of red berries, juicy apricots, roses, and papaya in its lovely, concentrated personality. Enthrallingly, this silky-textured wine combines purity with power. Anticipated maturity: now–2006. Amazingly, the 1997 Gewurztraminer Clos Winds-buhl supports 16.4% alcohol with only a barely noticeable warm kiss in its unbelievably long finish. This bone-dry stunner blows away the theory that Gewurztraminer has to contain residual sugar to be expressive and powerful. It is full-bodied, satin-textured, and crammed with minerals/stones awash in pineapple juice. Anticipated maturity: now–2006. The ex-traordinarily floral and honeyed aromatics of the medium- to full-bodied 1997 Gewurz-traminer Hengst lead to an impeccably balanced character. Broad waves of minerals, pears, and candied apples drenched in lychee juice are found in its superexpressive core. This velvety-textured wine should be consumed between now–2006.

The 1997 Gewurztraminer Goldert exhibits mouthwatering aromas reminiscent of fruit cake, candied orange rinds, spices, minerals, and chalk. It is thick, hugely flavorful, full-bodied, and densely packed with cherries, peaches, orange blossoms, and a myriad of spices that linger throughout its impressive finish. This stupendous wine would have been labeled as an SGN at the majority of estates. Drink it over the next decade.

Produced from vines planted in 1949, the botrytis, apricot, peach, and bergamot-scented 1997 Gewurztraminer Heimbourg supports 16.3% alcohol and 40 grams of residual sugar per liter. This magnificently delineated wine conquers the palate with jasmine, rose water, poached/spiced pears, and baked apples. It is refined yet hugely powerful, complex yet for-ward. Its intensely long finish reveals a trace of heat from its high alcohol that prevented its score from reaching the stratosphere. Drink it over the next 7–8 years. Regrettably, only 500 bottles of the stunning, gold-colored 1997 Gewurztraminer Rangen de Thann Clos St.-Urbain exist. The result of microscopic yields (12–15 h/h), this nectar's aromas and flavors are presently dominated by fresh mangoes. When all is said and done, this full-bodied, detailed, magnificently refined, hugely flavorful wine may merit a perfect score. The manner in which Humbrecht combines astronomical richness and power with impeccable precision and purity is pure genius. Stones, chalk, minerals, Asian teas, flint, roses, and innumerable tropical fruits are found in this blockbuster. Minutes after having been emptied, my glass continued to present awesome mineral and honeyed fruit scents. Readers fortunate enough to acquire this benchmark setter should consume it between now–2010.

Since the Sélection de Grains Nobles offerings from Domaine Zind-Humbrecht, each an essence of the Tokay-Pinot Gris varietal, are extraordinarily rare and expensive I will spare readers detailed descriptions and only include abbreviated notes. The 1997 Tokay-Pinot Gris Clos Jebsal Sélection de Grains Nobles is slightly gold-colored, offers jammy apricot, cherry, and strawberry scents, as well as hyperdense, supersweet character. It is full-bodied, intense, and packed with jellied yellow fruits and minerals. Anticipated maturity: now–2040. The

1996 Tokay-Pinot Gris Clos Jebsal Sélection de Grains Nobles has the potential to live for 50 or more years. Quince, smoke, and honey aromas lead to a bracing, cranberry, candied orange zest, red currant, sweet tea, rose, and jammy apricot–crammed personality. It has perfect balance, a full body, and unbelievable length. Anticipated maturity: now–2050+. The 1994 Tokay-Pinot Gris Clos Jebsal Sélection de Grains Nobles Trie Spéciale is the sweetest, densest wine Olivier Humbrecht has ever fashioned. It has 540 grams of residual sugar per liter and 12 grams of acid. As Humbrecht noted, "it makes no noise when poured into a glass, it is completely silent!" Needless to say, this purée of fruit-flavored syrup sets new standards in power, concentration, and length.

Humbrecht fashioned an impressive line-up of 1998s from what he described as "an extreme vintage, from beginning to end . . . too hot and too dry (causing vine stress and sun burned grapes), and weather that was both humid and rainy." However, he feels that quality growers could produce excellent wines because, in the end, they had sufficient ripeness and good, balanced acidity levels. "It was a great year for botrytis. It came in a three-day onslaught, which is perfect if your grapes are ripe. However, those vignerons whose vines carry high yields may have had problems," he added. Stylistically, Humbrecht feels 1998 can best be compared to either 1985 or 1986, respectively good and excellent vintages that were huge qualitative successes for Domaine Zind-Humbrecht. "I am more proud of my 1998s than I am of my 1997s because of all the difficulties I had to surmount," said Humbrecht. Like the other top estates of Alsace, Zind-Humbrecht divided their harvesting dates between the early period of good weather and the later one. "The wines produced from the first group are characterized by a healthy crop of fruity wines, the second by impressive ripeness levels and a high percentage of noble rot," he stated. "Qualitatively, I can't think of better trios of vintages than 1988, 1989, 1990, and 1996, 1997, and 1998."

Produced from a blend of three varietals (including Auxerrois and Pinot Blanc) in the Clos Windsbuhl, Herrenweg, and Rotenberg vineyards, the 1998 Pinot d'Alsace reveals rich, honeyed white fruit aromas. Medium-bodied, broad, and supple, it is a silky-textured wine loaded with ripe pears and grapefruits. An opulent offering, its long finish displays appealing tangy lemon attributes. Drink it over the next 5 years.

Orange blossoms and earth tones can be found in the 1998 Muscat Herrenweg de Turckheim's nose. Light- to medium-bodied and bone-dry, this satin-textured wine exhibits flavors reminiscent of mandarin oranges and minerals. Drink up.

Also completely dry, the 1998 Muscat Goldert displays subdued floral aromas as well as a medium-bodied personality. Rich yet well detailed, it is an elegant wine dominated by white flower and mineral elements. Anticipated maturity: now–2003.

The 1998 Riesling Gueberschwihr's aromatics reveal herbal tea, earth, and loads of minerals. Pineapples, pink grapefruits, and other citrus fruits are found in its well-focused character. Light- to medium-bodied and bone-dry, it is a flavorful, velvety-textured wine to drink over the next 6–7 years. Produced from the estate's youngest vines in the Brand vineyard (17 years old on average), the 1998 Riesling Turckheim reveals tropical fruit aromas. Medium-bodied and fresh, it is packed with expressive mineral flavors. This refined, concentrated, vibrant wine will be at its peak between now–2007.

Aromatically, the old-vine (50 years on average) 1998 Riesling Herrenweg de Turckheim reveals honeyed minerals and herbal tea–like scents. Medium-bodied, broad, and dry, it offers flavors reminiscent of stones and passion fruit. It is forward and almost lacelike in structure. Drink it over the next 7 years. Produced from grapes harvested at 14.2% natural potential alcohol, the 1998 Riesling Clos Hauserer is dominated by minerals both in its aromas and flavor profile. This rich medium-bodied wine has a fresh, expansive mouth that displays hints of ripe apples as well as stones to go with its expressive minerality. It is precise, completely dry, and has a long, clean-cutting finish. Anticipated maturity: now–2010.

The flower blossom and sweetened herbal tea–scented 1998 Riesling Heimbourg has a suave, feminine, medium-bodied personality. Creamy pears and loads of yellow fruits are found in this fruit-forward yet focused offering. It should be at its best between now–2012.

As is invariably the case with Rieslings from the Brand vineyard, Humbrecht's 1998 was one of my favorite wines of the visit. Powerful mineral scents are intermingled with lively pears and apples in its rich aromas. Medium- to full-bodied and revealing gorgeous definition as well as purity, it is an elegant, awesomely focused offering. Loads of minerals, stones, and white fruit flavors are found in its expressive personality as well as throughout its huge finish. Anticipated maturity: 2003–2014+. The botrytis-laden 1998 Riesling Rangen de Thann Clos St.-Urbain fermented for over a year. Hints of gold can be discerned in its color, and it displays a smoky, apricot, peach, and tropical fruit-filled nose reminiscent of a Pinot Gris. On the palate, this opulent, medium- to full-bodied wine is crammed with spiced apples, super-ripe yellow fruits, and layers of minerals, earth, and stones. Broad and intense, it is both sublimely rich and fresh. This impeccably balanced wine has the potential to become even grander with cellaring. Anticipated maturity: 2005–2014+.

The 1998 Riesling Clos Windsbuhl Vendanges Tardives was fashioned from the grapes Olivier Humbrecht harvested last (on October 24). Its toasted nut and flower-scented nose leads to a nuanced, beautifully precise personality. Creamy pears, candied lemons, and sweet apricots are found in this plump, yet graceful wine. Concentrated and complex, it admirably combines delicacy and power. Drink it between 2003–2015.

Virtually all of Domaine Zind-Humbrecht's 1998 Pinot Gris were harvested at Vendanges Tardives levels of ripeness, yet only the most complex, botrytised, and sweetest were labeled as VTs. Thick, creamed mocha is found in the aromatics of the 1998 Pinot Gris Vieilles Vignes. This hedonistic wine is seductively layered with sweet apricot and marzipan flavors. This medium- to full-bodied, sexy, fruit-forward offering should be consumed over the next 8 years. The 1998 Pinot Gris Heimbourg displays jammy pear, botrytis, and peach aromas. Medium- to full-bodied and opulent, it is a lush, pure wine that conquers the palate with wave after wave of sweet peaches. This extroverted, fruity offering should be consumed over the next 12 years.

Unlike Humbrecht's other 1998s from this varietal, the 1998 Pinot Gris Clos Windsbuhl does not reveal any influence of botrytis in its smoky apricot-scented aromatics. Minerals, cherries, raspberries, and other assorted red fruits dominate this medium- to full-bodied wine's personality. It is pure, intricate, and wonderfully rich. Its extravagant character is satin-textured, luxurious, and elegant. Anticipated maturity: 2004–2012+.

Produced from vines planted in 1946, the 1998 Gewurztraminer Wintzenheim exhibits delectable rosewater aromas. Light- to medium-bodied and expressive, this is an elegant yet flavorful wine. Red berries, lychee nuts, and powerful floral notes are found in its precise personality. Drink it over the next 4 years. Violets are found in the 1998 Gewurztraminer Turckheim's aromatics. This rich, medium-bodied wine is lacelike in its makeup. Refined spicy floral notes and minerals can be discerned it its detailed character. Anticipated maturity: now–2004. The 1998 Gewurztraminer Gueberschwihr, fashioned from the estate's oldest vines, reveals cherry, spice, and roselike aromas. Medium- to full-bodied and opulent, this oily-textured wine's character is filled with abundant fresh spices. Ginger, juniper berries, and clove are found in its pure, graceful flavors. Drink it over the next 6–7 years.

Roses and spices (mostly cloves) make up the nose of the 1998 Gewurztraminer Herrenweg de Turckheim. Almost dry, its medium-bodied character is broad, floral, massively spicy, and reveals some of the warmth (alcohol) often found in this vintage's wines. Its long, silky finish displays the citrus rind bitterness generally associated with this varietal. Anticipated maturity: now–2007. Aromatically, the 1998 Gewurztraminer Heimbourg boasts sweet white fruits and spices. Medium-bodied and elegant, this clear-cut wine is filled with red berry, candied white fruit, and powerful floral elements. It is broad, fat, and graceful. Its impressive finish displays lovely lemony touches. Drink it over the next 8–9 years.

The 1998 Gewurztraminer Clos Windsbuhl offers a nose of red berries, pears, and spices. This medium- to full-bodied wine's velvety-textured character is crammed with flavors reminiscent of almond cookie dough, sweet red cherries, creamed raspberries, and roses. Highly detailed and precise, it is boisterously expressive yet elegant and graceful. Anticipated maturity: now–2012. The magnificent rose- and lychee-scented 1998 Gewurztraminer Hengst is full-bodied and oily-textured. Thick, yet fresh, detailed, and polished, it is packed with lychee nuts. The wine's high level of alcohol (15.9%) slightly shows through the dense fruit, but its extroverted, focused, and fruit-dominated personality more than makes up for it. Anticipated maturity: now–2012.

Produced from Humbrecht's oldest parcel of vines in the Rotenberg vineyard, the 1998 Tokay-Pinot Gris Rotenberg Vendanges Tardives reveals deep, smoky apricot aromas. Harvested at a penurious 10 h/h, this medium-to-full-bodied wine is round, ample, with remarkable opulence. Jammy apricots and red cherries are found in its supple, sexy character. Drink it over the next 12 years. The caramel-scented 1998 Tokay-Pinot Gris Clos Jebsal Vendanges Tardives offers candied orange zests, a strong minerality, and jammy (almost syrupy) yellow fruit flavors. Even though this is a thick, oily-textured wine, it is also racy because of its tangy underlying acidity. Medium- to full-bodied and harmonious, it is still in a tight, youthful state. Anticipated maturity: 2004–2015. The extraordinary 1998 Tokay-Pinot Gris Rangen de Thann Clos St.-Urbain Vendanges Tardives has a mouthwatering nose of candied blood oranges lightly dusted with botrytis-caused spiciness. Creamed red, yellow, and white fruits are interspersed with earth, minerals, and gravel in this complex, concentrated, full-bodied behemoth. Its massive personality is well buttressed by its superb acidity, and this muscular yet graceful wine has an unbelievably long finish. Anticipated maturity: 2005–2025.

Rich floral aromas burst from the 1998 Gewurztraminer Heimbourg Vendanges Tardives. Loads of spices, roses, pears, candied apples, violets, and red berries are found in this medium- to full-bodied offering. It is a lush, exuberant wine with a velvety-textured, explosive personality. Drink it between now–2012. Aromatically, the 1998 Gewurztraminer Goldert Vendanges Tardives appeared to be in a reductive state, displaying leathery scents. Humbrecht maintains that these aromas are nothing more than this wine's expression of its deep minerality. On the palate, it is mind-boggling. Oily layers of intense mineral, floral (roses and violets), and red fruit flavors can be discerned in its hugely concentrated and powerful character. It is full-bodied, gorgeously detailed, and balanced. Anticipated maturity: 2003–2014+.

The superlative 1998 Gewurztraminer Rangen de Thann Clos St.-Urbain Vendange Tardive has the amber/gold color of a Sélection de Grains Nobles. In the nose, candied oranges, botrytis, red berries, and earth compete for the taster's olfactory attention. A hedonist's delight, this full-bodied, decadently viscous offering is also refreshing to taste. The mouth-feel is tantamount to millions of tiny puffy pillows filled with caramel, cocoa, minerals, candied citrus fruit zests, and lemony stones. Seductive, intricate, and profound, it does not reflect any of its varietal's trademark lychee, rosewater, floral scents and flavors. It represents, according to Olivier Humbrecht, "the pure essence of the Rangen *terroir*." Anticipated maturity: 2004–2018+.

"In 1999 we started harvesting early, and we finished late. In between we dodged the rains and waited for optimal ripeness. There were huge differences in maturity from parcel to parcel and varietal to varietal. It was a vintage where it paid to be patient." Humbrecht began our tasting of his estate's 1999s with those words. In a typical vintage, Humbrecht employs his staff and an additional 30 part-time harvesters for the picking. In 1999, due to all the starts and stops involved in the month-long harvest, Humbrecht had to hire 130 people. He echoed Laurence Faller's feelings, however, by stating that "if people were willing to incur the expenses required and to be as thorough as was necessary, 1999 could produce great wines."

The gorgeously rich, ripe aromas of the 1999 Pinot d'Alsace reveal apricot, peach, smoke, and spice scents. This candied citrus, verbena, and apricot-flavored wine has excellent grip as well as focus. According to Olivier Humbrecht, it is analytically the same as the 1998, but with slightly more tartaric acid and, therefore, the sensation is of less richness, yet this wine offers loads of fresh, zesty fruits in its medium-bodied personality. Drink it over the next 4–5 years.

The mineral-scented 1999 Muscat Goldert is light- to medium-bodied and reveals a rich, fruit-filled attack that leads to a firm, tangy finish. Pears, apples, and oranges are found in this vivacious offering. Drink it over the next 2 years.

Produced from the young vines of the Brand vineyard blend (planted in 1976 and 1977), the 1999 Riesling Turckheim has a spicy, liquid mineral, and chalk-scented nose. Light- to medium-bodied and possessing excellent depth of fruit, this crystalline wine offers pear, red berry, and gravel flavors. Drink it over the next 4–5 years. The 1999 Riesling Herrenweg de Turckheim has demure spice and herbal tea aromas. This ripe, rich, satin-textured wine is medium-bodied and displays outstanding amplitude. White and red berries are intermingled with quinine, bergamot, and spices in this complex, highly detailed wine. It is intense, youthfully tight, and has the concentration and depth for cellaring. Anticipated maturity: now–2010.

The talcum powder and mineral-scented 1999 Riesling Clos Hauserer is light-bodied, detailed, and delineated. This beautifully ripe, mineral and citrus fruit–flavored wine is bright, has outstanding grip, and possesses a long, herbal tea-laden finish. This beautifully nuanced wine may very well improve with age. Anticipated maturity: 2003–2012. The spice- and verbena-scented 1999 Riesling Heimbourg is light- to medium-bodied, plump, and satin-textured. Minerals and spices can be found in its expressive, soft, sexy character. It is complex, detailed-oriented, and exhibits outstanding concentration. Anticipated maturity: 2003–2012.

The 1999 Riesling Rangen de Thann Clos St.-Urbain bursts from the glass with flint, smoke, and spice aromas. Light- to medium-bodied and silky-textured, this is a juicy, delineated wine with an extensive personality crammed with minerals, talcum powder, smoke, and copious quantities of spices. Drink it over the next 12–14 years. The liquid mineral–scented 1999 Riesling Brand, harvested at 25 h/h, is a velvety-textured, medium-bodied wine. The richest of Humbrecht's 1999 Rieslings, it has a sexy, lush, feminine character filled with ripe pears, fruit pulp, herbal tea, and spices. It has outstanding depth and a long finish that reveals berrylike fruits. Drink it over the next dozen years.

According to Humbrecht, all of his 1999 Tokay-Pinot Gris contain some residual sugar because "it was impossible to make a totally dry Pinot Gris in 1999 if you wanted the fruit to be ripe." Smoky apricots and botrytis are discerned in the nose of the 1999 Tokay-Pinot Gris Herrenweg. Light- to medium-bodied and revealing excellent breadth, this is a beautifully detailed, intense pear, mineral, and white berry–flavored wine. It has outstanding depth to its intense personality. Drink it between 2003–2009. Liquid smoke and poached pears can be found in the aromatics of the 1999 Tokay-Pinot Gris Vieilles Vignes. This medium-bodied, silky-textured wine has gorgeous detail to its floral character. It is pure, highly focused, and displays pears, apples, and spices in its soft, lush personality. Drink it between 2004–2012. The sexy 1999 Tokay-Pinot Gris Heimbourg has aromas that are surprisingly reminiscent of buttery crawfish. Ripe apples, pears, and loads of botrytis can be discerned in its opulent yet zesty personality. Anticipated maturity: 2003–2012.

The 1999 Tokay-Pinot Gris Clos Windsbuhl has smoky mineral aromas. Medium-bodied, this silky-textured wine offers layers of apples, peaches, and white berries in its rich, lush, yet highly detailed, lacelike character. It has outstanding fat and depth, yet its fruit is, at present, youthfully restrained. This wine has immense complexity and an intense, powerful character. Drink it between 2005–2015. The 1999 Tokay-Pinot Gris Rotenberg Vieilles Vignes has, according to Humbrecht, the highest acidity of all of his 1999 Tokays and performed its malolactic fermentation. Citrus fruits can be found in its aromas and flavors. Medium- to full-bodied and exuberant, it explodes on the palate with powerful waves of red berries, white currants, candied lemons, and a myriad of spices. This is an opulent yet zesty wine, with immense power and depth. While it is not made for those requiring immediate gratification, it will repay those with patience. Drink it between 2006–2017.

The spice- and mineral-scented 1999 Gewurztraminer Gueberschwihr is light- to medium-bodied and demure. Minerals and spices can be found throughout its persistent personality. It is a well-made wine for those who shy away from boisterous Gewurztraminers. Drink it over the next 2–3 years. As with the previous Humbrecht Gewurztraminers, the 1999 Gewurztraminer Wintzenheim is completely dry. It offers minerals and flowers in its aromas and flavors. Light- to medium-bodied and well structured, this steely, focused wine has excellent grip and beautifully nuanced flavors. Drink it over the next 2–3 years.

The 1999 Gewurztraminer Wintzenheim Vieilles Vignes (from 55-year-old vines) offers spicy rosewater aromas. Medium-bodied and velvety-textured, it is soft, silky, and feminine. This plump, floral, white fruit–flavored wine has delightful detail in its personality. Drink it over the next 5–6 years. The lychee nut and rose-scented 1999 Gewurztraminer Herrenweg de Turckheim is a soft, rich, spicy wine. White peaches, sweet berries, and assorted flowers can be found in this plump yet detailed wine. Drink this concentrated and expressive Gewurz over the next 6–7 years.

Loads of spices and a scent reminiscent of Louisiana steamed crawdads can be found in the nose of the 1999 Gewurztraminer Clos Windsbuhl. Medium-bodied and dense, this is a roasted, smoky wine, loaded with dense layers of spices. An elegant, highly nuanced, and detailed wine for drinking over the next 7 years.

The 1999 Gewurztraminer Goldert has a smoky, spice-laden nose. It is more reminiscent of a Tokay-Pinot Gris than a Gewurztraminer due to its spicy, smoky, petrol, and citrus fruit–packed personality. It is broad, intense, and lively. This wine has outstanding amplitude, lively acidity, and loads of flavor. Drink it over the next 7–8 years. The talcum powder, flower, and spice-scented 1999 Gewurztraminer Hengst has a delightful satin-textured character. Medium-bodied and fresh, it regales the taster's palate with roses, violets, and hints of white fruits. This delineated and detailed wine should be consumed over the next 7–8 years.

The mineral-scented 1999 Gewurztraminer Rangen de Thann Clos St.-Urbain, like the Goldert, is more reminiscent of a Tokay-Pinot Gris than a Gewurztraminer. Copious quantities of smoke and spice can be discerned in its lush yet detailed character. Minerals, metallic shavings, cinnamon, and cardamom can be found in its flavor profile. While it will not satisfy consumers yearning for an archetypal Gewurztraminer, those yearning for a highly focused, spicy Tokay will be delighted with this offering. Drink it over the next 7–8 years.

The Riesling-like 1999 Gewurztraminer Heimbourg bursts from the glass with bold, petrol-like aromas. On the palate, this wine again acts more like a Riesling than a Gewurztraminer. Smoky, pear, white peach, mineral, and petrol characteristics come out in its highly focused character. It also has outstanding breadth, delineation, and concentration. Drink it over the next 7–8 years. The floral, smoke, and mineral-scented 1999 Tokay-Pinot Gris Clos Jebsal Vendanges Tardives smells and tastes almost like a Riesling Vendanges Tardives. Loads of liquid minerals are found in its layered, velvety personality. It has outstanding depth, a fresh character, and a long, flavorful finish. Drink it over the next 12–14 years.

The quince, tarragon, and fresh fennel-scented 1999 Gewurztraminer Heimbourg Vendanges Tardives has a well-defined, broad, medium-bodied personality. Spices, minerals, and smoky fennel come across in its feminine character. This is a complex and delineated wine for drinking over the next 12 years.

The 1998 Riesling Rangen de Thann Clos St.-Urbain Sélection de Grains Nobles sports 11.5% alcohol and 130 grams of residual sugar. It bursts from the glass with magnificent mineral and lemony caramel aromas. It is medium- to full-bodied, admirably focused, and possesses a laserlike, syrupy personality. Its candied, jellied apricot flavors are rendered lively by its stupendous acidity. This incredibly long wine is powerful, highly expressive, and intense. It has the potential to last 25 or more years.

The 1998 Tokay-Pinot Gris Rangen de Thann Clos St.-Urbain Sélection de Grains Nobles has 13.5% alcohol and 160 grams of residual sugar. Even though no new oak was employed, its aromatics reveal vanilla, powerful smoke, and spice scents. This is a raspberry, apricot, peach, spice, and toast-flavored wine with magnificent breadth and an unbelievably long finish. Even though its flavor profile is unctuous, almost jellied in character, it possesses brilliant focus. This is an extraordinary wine with an enormous upside. Drink it over the course of the next 25–30+ years. The exotic fruit–scented 1998 Tokay-Pinot Gris Clos Jebsal Sélection de Grains Nobles conquers the taster's palate with wave upon wave of thick apricots and peaches. This superdense, fat, almost compotelike wine has exemplary balance due to its vivacious acidity. It is full-bodied, intensely sweet, hugely concentrated, and immensely powerful. Drink it over the next 30+ years.

BORDEAUX

The Basics

TYPES OF WINE

Bordeaux is the world's largest supplier of high-quality, ageworthy table wine, from properties usually called châteaux. The production in the 1980s and 1990s has varied between 25 and 60 million cases of wine a year, of which 75% is red.

Red Wine   Much of Bordeaux's fame rests on its production of dry red table wine, yet only a tiny percentage of Bordeaux's most prestigious wine comes from famous appellations such as Margaux, St.-Julien, Pauillac, and St.-Estèphe, all located in an area called the Médoc, and Graves, Pomerol, and St.-Emilion. From these areas the wine is expensive yet consistently high in quality.

White Wine   Bordeaux produces sweet, rich, honeyed wines from two famous areas called Sauternes and Barsac. An ocean of dry white wine is made, most of it insipid and neutral in character, except for the excellent dry white wines made in the Graves area, and its subappellation, Pessac-Léognan.

GRAPE VARIETIES

Following are the most important types of grapes used in the red and white wines of Bordeaux.

RED WINE VARIETIES

For red wines, three major grape varieties are planted in Bordeaux, as well as two minor varieties, one of which—Petit Verdot—is discussed below. The type of grape used has a profound influence on the style of wine that is ultimately produced.

Cabernet Sauvignon   The grape is highly pigmented, very astringent, and tannic, and provides the framework, strength, dark color, character, and longevity for the wines in a majority of the vineyards in the Médoc. It ripens late, is resistant to rot because of its thick skin, and has a pronounced black currant aroma, which is sometimes intermingled with subtle herbaceous scents that take on the smell of cedarwood and tobacco with aging. Virtually all Bordeaux châteaux blend Cabernet Sauvignon with other red grape varieties. In the Médoc, the average percentage of Cabernet Sauvignon in the blend ranges from 40% to 85%; in Graves, 40% to 60%; in St.-Emilion, 10% to 50%; and in Pomerol, 0% to 20%. Furthermore, the blends change according to the vintage. For example, when climatic conditions favor Cabernet Sauvignon (1996 and 1986 are the most obvious), a higher percentage of Cabernet will be utilized in the final blend.

Merlot   Utilized by virtually every wine château in Bordeaux because of its ability to provide a round, generous, fleshy, supple, alcoholic wine, Merlot ripens, on an average, one to two weeks earlier than Cabernet Sauvignon. In the Médoc this grape reaches its zenith, and several Médoc châteaux use high percentages of it (Palmer, Cos d'Estournel, Haut-Marbuzet, and Pichon-Lalande), but its fame is in the wines it renders in Pomerol, where it is used profusely. In the Médoc the average percentage of Merlot in the blend ranges from 5% to 45%; in Graves, from 20% to 40%; in St.-Emilion, 25% to 95%; and in Pomerol, 35% to 100%. Merlot produces wines with less color saturation as well as lower acidity and tannin than Cabernet Sauvignon. As a general rule, wines with a high percentage of Merlot are drinkable much earlier than wines with a high percentage of Cabernet Sauvignon, but frequently age just as well. However, some Merlot-based wines can be even more backward than a Médoc (Pétrus, for example). In years where growing conditions favor Merlot, a higher percentage is often used in the blend (1998, 1995, and 1994, for example).

Cabernet Franc   A relative of Cabernet Sauvignon that ripens slightly earlier, Cabernet Franc (called Bouchet in St.-Emilion and Pomerol) is used in small to modest proportions in order to add complexity and bouquet to a wine. Cabernet Franc has a pungent, often very spicy, sometimes weedy, olivelike aroma. It does not have the fleshy, supple character of Merlot, nor the astringence, power, and color of Cabernet Sauvignon. In the Médoc the average percentage of Cabernet Franc used in the blend is 0% to 30%; in Graves, 5% to 25%; in St.-Emilion, 25% to 66%; in Pomerol, 5% to 50%.

Petit Verdot   A useful but generally difficult red grape because of its very late ripening characteristics, Petit Verdot provides intense color, mouth-gripping tannins, and high sugar and thus high alcohol when it ripens fully, as it did in 1982, 1996, and 2000 in Bordeaux. When unripe it has a nasty, sharp, acidic character. In the Médoc, few châteaux use more than 5% in the blend, and those that do are generally properties like Palmer and Pichon-Lalande, which use high percentages of Merlot. Petit Verdot is virtually nonexistent in Pomerol and St.-Emilion.

WHITE WINE VARIETIES

Bordeaux produces both dry and sweet white wine. There are only three grape varieties used: Sauvignon Blanc and Sémillon, for dry and sweet wine, and Muscadelle, which is used sparingly.

Sauvignon Blanc   Used for making both the dry white wines of Graves and the sweet white wines of the Barsac/Sauternes region, Sauvignon Blanc renders a very distinctive wine

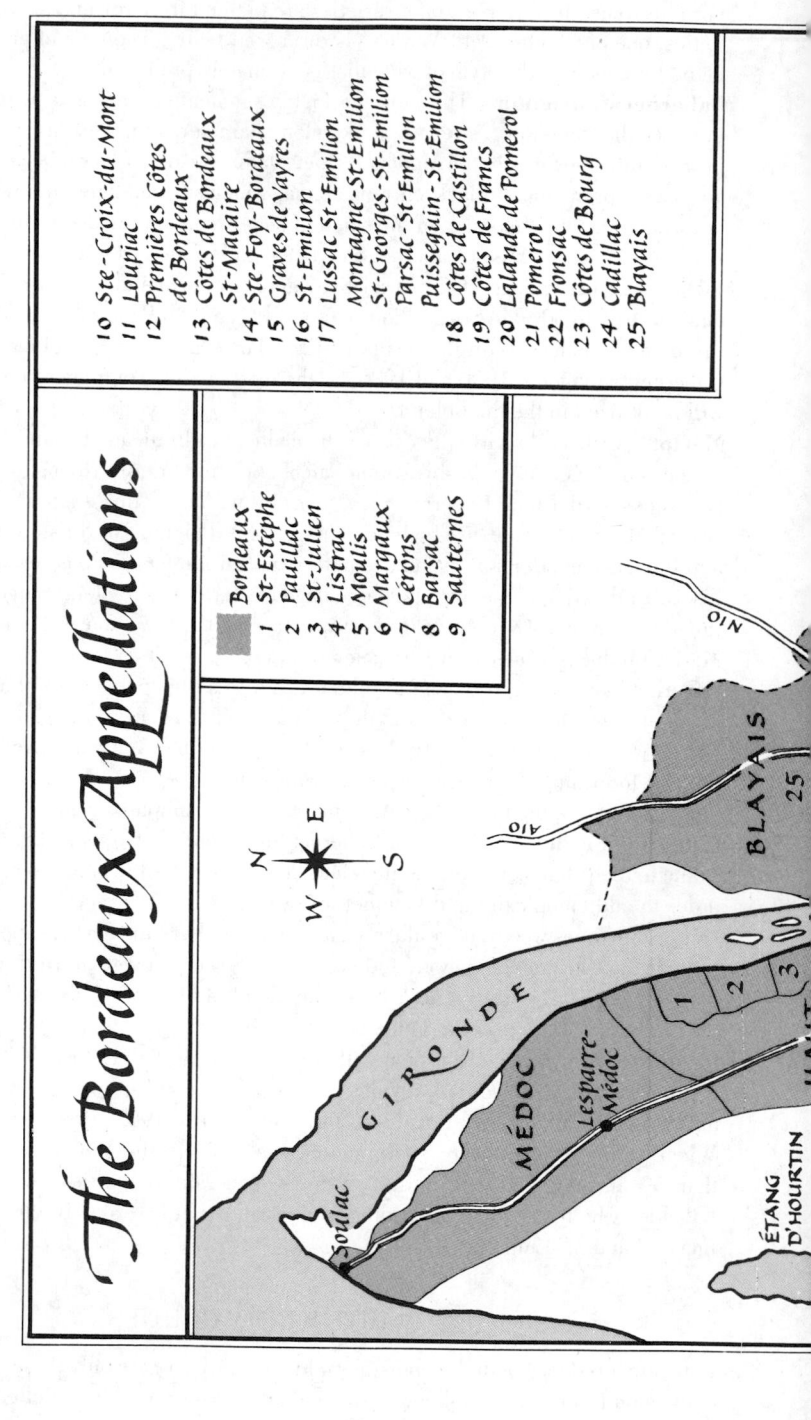

The Bordeaux Appellations

Bordeaux
1 St-Estèphe
2 Pauillac
3 St-Julien
4 Listrac
5 Moulis
6 Margaux
7 Cérons
8 Barsac
9 Sauternes

10 Ste-Croix-du-Mont
11 Loupiac
12 Premières Côtes
    de Bordeaux
13 Côtes de Bordeaux
14 St-Macaire
15 Ste-Foy-Bordeaux
16 Graves de Vayres
17 St-Emilion
   Lussac St-Emilion
   Montagne-St-Emilion
   St-Georges-St-Emilion
   Parsac-St-Emilion
   Puisseguin-St-Emilion
18 Côtes de Castillon
19 Côtes de Francs
20 Lalande de Pomerol
21 Pomerol
22 Fronsac
23 Côtes de Bourg
24 Cadillac
25 Blayais

with a pungent, somewhat herbaceous aroma, and crisp, austere, mineral-laced flavors. Among the dry white Graves, a few châteaux employ 100% Sauvignon Blanc, but most blend it with Semillon. Less Sauvignon Blanc is used in the winemaking blends in the Sauternes region than in Graves.

Sémillon   Very susceptible to the famous "noble rot" called *Botrytis cinerea*, which is essential to the production of excellent, sweet wines, Sémillon imparts a fat, rich, creamy, intense texture to both the dry wines of Graves and the rich, sweet wines of Sauternes. Sémillon is quite fruity when young, and wines with a high percentage of Sémillon seem to take on weight and viscosity as they age. For these reasons, higher percentages of Sémillon are used in making the sweet wines of the Barsac/Sauternes region than in the white wines of Graves.

Muscadelle   The rarest of the white wine grapes planted in Bordeaux, Muscadelle is a fragile grape susceptible to disease, but when healthy and mature, it produces a wine with an intense flowery, perfumed character. It is used only in tiny proportions by châteaux in the Barsac/Sauternes region, and is increasingly being utilized by some white wine producers of Graves to add exotic, tropical fruit nuances.

Major Appellations

Following are the general flavor characteristics of Bordeaux's most notable types of wines.

St.-Estèphe   While the wines of St.-Estèphe are known for their hardness because of the heavier, thicker soil in this area, the châteaux have more Merlot planted in their vineyards than elsewhere in the Médoc. Although generalizations can be dangerous, most St.-Estèphe wines possess less expressive and flattering bouquets, have a tougher character, and are more stern, tannic wines than those found elsewhere in the Médoc. They are usually full-bodied, with considerable aging potential.

Pauillac   A classic Pauillac seems to define what most people think of as Bordeaux—a rich black currant, cedary bouquet, followed by medium- to full-bodied flavors with a great deal of richness and tannin. The fame of this area corresponds with high prices.

St.-Julien   St.-Julien is frequently indistinguishable from a Pauillac. The wines of St.-Julien are filled with rich curranty fruit, and smell of cedar and spices. The overall quality of this appellation's winemaking is superb—consumers, take note!

Margaux   Margaux are the lightest wines of the Médoc, but in great vintages they are perhaps the most seductive. Until the late 1990s, the overall quality of the winemaking in this appellation was appallingly lower than that of any other appellation in the Médoc, but yesterday's underperformers have largely disappeared. A great Margaux in a top vintage has an undeniable floral, berry-scented bouquet backed up by the smell of new oak, licorice, and earth. In body and tannin, Margaux wines, despite elevated percentages of Cabernet Sauvignon, tend to mature more quickly than the St.-Juliens, Pauillacs, or St.-Estèphes. For bouquet lovers, the best wines of Margaux can be compelling.

Graves and Pessac-Léognan Red   These are the easiest of all Bordeaux wines to pick out in blind tastings, as they have a distinctive mineral smell, along with the scent and taste of tobacco, cedar, and hot rocks. Graves are generally the lightest wines made in Bordeaux, but they are intensely flavorful and savory.

St.-Emilion   It is difficult to generalize about the taste of St.-Emilions, given the divergent styles, but most St.-Emilions tend to be softer and fleshier wines than Médocs. Increasingly, the top wines are as succulent and lush as Pomerols. Because of the elevated percentages of Cabernet Franc planted in this appellation, St.-Emilions can have a distinctive herbaceous, cedary bouquet, but Merlot continues to take a bigger and bigger share of the final blend. Since the early 1990s, this appellation has exploded with new producers and with wines of higher and higher quality. Moreover, the so-called "garage wine" movement started in St.-

Emilion in the early 1990s and continues to flourish as young, highly motivated people compete for attention with distinctive wines made from tiny yields and ripe fruit. For quality and diversity, this is the most exciting appellation of Bordeaux.

Pomerol   Pomerols are often called the Burgundies of Bordeaux because of their rich, supple, more monolithic personalities, but they age extremely well and are undeniable choices for hedonists, as they provide oodles of rich black currant, black cherry, and sometimes blackberry fruit. In the great vintages one can find an exquisite opulence in these wines, but once past the top two dozen estates, quality is irregular.

Graves and Pessac-Léognan White   The top-notch whites are aged in oak and made from the Sauvignon Blanc and Sémillon grapes. They often start off life excessively oaky, but fill out beautifully with age and develop creamy, rich flavors that marry beautifully with the oak. The finest examples easily last 20–25 years.

Barsac/Sauternes   Depending on the vintage and the degree of the noble rot (botrytis) that affects the grapes, the wines can either taste fat, ripe, and characterless in those years when there is little botrytis, or wonderfully exotic with a bouquet of honeyed tropical fruits, buttered nuts, and crème brûlée in those great vintages where there has been plenty of the noble rot.

Satellite Appellations   There are very large quantities of wine produced in a bevy of other, lesser-known, appellations of Bordeaux. Most of these wines are widely commercialized in France, but have met with little success in America because of this country's obsession with luxury names and prestigious appellations. For the true connoisseur, the wines of Bordeaux's satellite appellations can in fact represent outstanding bargains, particularly in top vintages such as 1982, 1990, and 2000, where excellent climatic conditions and the improved use of modern technology by many of these estates resulted in a vast selection of fine wines at modest prices. Following are the most important satellite appellations.

Fronsac and Canon-Fronsac—In the 18th and 19th centuries the vineyards sprinkled over the hillsides and hollows of Fronsac and Canon-Fronsac—just a few miles west of Libourne—were better known than the wines of Pomerol and sold for higher prices than the wines of St.-Emilion. But because access to Pomerol was easier and because most of the brokers had their offices in Libourne, the vineyards of Pomerol and St.-Emilion were exploited more than those of Fronsac and Canon-Fronsac. Consequently, this area fell into a long period of obscurity from which it has just recently begun to rebound.

Lalande-de-Pomerol—Lalande-de-Pomerol is a satellite commune of nearly 2,250 acres of vineyards located just north of Pomerol and Néac. The vineyards, which produce only red wine, are planted on relatively light, gravelly, sandy soils with the meandering river Barbanne as the appellation's northern boundary. The top level of good Lalande-de-Pomerol is easily the equivalent of a mid-level Pomerol. The only downside to the wines of Lalande-de-Pomerol is that they generally need to be consumed within 5–6 years of the vintage.

Côtes de Bourg—The Côtes de Bourg, a surprisingly vast appellation of nearly 10,000 acres, is located on the right bank of the Gironde River, just a five-minute boat ride from the more famous appellation of Margaux. The vineyards here are actually older than those in the Médoc, as this attractively hilly area was once the center of the strategic forts built during the Plantagenet period of France's history. The views from the hillside vineyards adjacent to the river are magnificent. The local chamber of commerce has attempted to draw the public's attention to this area by calling Bourg "the Switzerland of the Gironde." They should instead stress the appeal of the best wines from the Côtes de Bourg, which display an uncomplicated but fruity, round, appealing style, and talk up the lovely port village of the area, the ancient hillside town of Bourg-Sur-Gironde.

Blaye—There are just over 6,700 acres of vines in the Blaye region, located directly north of Bourg. The best vineyard areas are entitled to the appellation Premières Côtes de Blaye. While there are quantities of white wine produced in the Blaye region, most of the Premières

Côtes de Blaye are dedicated to the production of red wine, which is very similar to the red wine of Bourg. At its best, it is forward, round, richly fruity, soft, and immensely satisfying in a low-key manner.

Loupiac and Ste.-Croix-de-Mont—With the wine prices of Barsac and Sauternes soaring, I predict a more important role for the producers of the sweet white wines of Loupiac and Ste.-Croix-du-Mont. These two appellations, 24 miles south of Bordeaux on the right bank of the Garonne, facing Barsac and Sauternes across the river, have an ideal southern exposure. These areas received appellation status in 1930, and many observers believe the excellent exposure of the top vineyards and the clay/limestone soil base is favorable for producing sweet wines, particularly in view of the fact that the morning mists—so essential for the formation of the noble rot *Botrytis cinerea*—are a common occurrence in this area. The entire appellation of Loupiac consists of 1,359 acres. Although the sweet wines are receiving increasing attention from wine lovers, dry white wines, as well as a moderate quantity of dry red wines, are also produced.

AGING POTENTIAL OF RECENT TOP VINTAGES FOR THE FINEST WINES
St.-Estèphe: 8–35 years; 2000, 1996, 1995, 1990, 1986, 1982
Pauillac: 8–40 years; 2000, 1996, 1995, 1990, 1986, 1982
St.-Julien: 8–35 years; 2000, 1996, 1995, 1990, 1986, 1982
Margaux: 8–30 years; 2000, 1999, 1996, 1995, 1990, 1986, 1983
Pessac-Léognan Red: 8–30 years; 2000, 1998, 1995, 1990, 1989, 1988, 1982
St.-Emilion: 8–25 years; 2000, 1998, 1995, 1990, 1989, 1988, 1982
Pomerol: 5–30 years; 2000, 1998, 1995, 1990, 1989, 1988, 1982
Pessac-Léognan White: 5–20 years; 2000, 1998, 1997, 1995, 1994, 1989, 1988, 1983
Barsac/Sauternes: 10–50 years; 1998, 1990, 1989, 1988, 1986, 1983, 1976, 1975
Fronsac/Canon-Fronsac: 5–20 years; 2000, 1998
Lalande-de-Pomerol: 3–6 years; 2000, 1998
Bourg: 3–10 years; 2000, 1998
Blaye: 2–4 years; 2000
Loupiac: 5–15 years; 1998, 1997, 1996, 1990, 1989, 1988
Ste.-Croix-de Mont: 4–12 years; 1998, 1997, 1996, 1990, 1989, 1988

OVERALL QUALITY LEVEL
Of all the great viticultural regions of the world, Bordeaux consistently produces wine of the highest level of quality. Although there is an ocean of one-dimensional, innocuous wines, bad wine is rare. For the world's top producers of Cabernet Sauvignon, Merlot, and Cabernet Franc, Bordeaux remains the point of reference.

MOST IMPORTANT INFORMATION TO KNOW
For the wine consumer trying to develop a degree of expertise when buying the wines of Bordeaux, the most important information to learn is which wine-producing estates (châteaux) are producing the best wines today. A review of the top categories of châteaux in Bordeaux is a quick way to learn of those producers with high commitments to quality. However, consumers should also familiarize themselves generally with the styles of the wines from the different appellations. Some tasters will prefer the austere, sterner style of Bordeaux represented by St.-Estèphe or Pauillac, whereas others will love the lavish lushness and opulence of a Pomerol. It has been my experience that the Graves wines, with their distinctive mineral scent and tobacco bouquet, are often the least-favored wines for neophytes, but with more experience this character becomes one that is admired by connoisseurs. As far as the famous official classifications of wine quality in Bordeaux, they are all out of date and should be of only academic interest to the consumer. These historic classifications were employed both to

promote more wines and to establish well-delineated benchmarks of quality. But because of negligence, incompetence, or just plain greed, some of these châteaux produce mediocre and poor wines that hardly reflect their placement in these classifications. A more valid guideline to the quality of Bordeaux wines is the rating of producers starting on page 192; these ratings reflect the overall quality of the wines produced rather than their historical pedigree.

BORDEAUX VINTAGE SUMMARIES: 1945–2000

This is a general assessment and profile of the Bordeaux vintages 1945 through 2000. While the top wines for each acceptable vintage are itemized, the perception of a vintage is a general view of that particular viticultural region. In mediocre and poor vintages, good wines can often be made by skillful vintners willing to make a careful selection of only the best grapes and *cuvées* of finished wine. In good or even great years, thin, diluted, characterless wines can be made by incompetent and greedy producers. For wine consumers, a vintage summary is important as a general guide to the level of potential excellence that can be attained in a particular year by a conscientious grower or producer of wine.

2000—A Quick Study (9-12-00)

St.-Estèphe*****   Pessac-Léognan/Graves Red*****
Pauillac*****   Pessac-Léognan/Graves White***
St.-Julien*****   Pomerol*****
Margaux*****   St.-Emilion*****
Médoc/Haut-Médoc Crus Bourgeois****   Barsac/Sauternes***

Size: A very large crop.
Important information: The millennium vintage is the finest overall Bordeaux ever. It is also absurdly expensive.
Maturity status: A year for the patient connoisseur, the top 2000s are powerful, oversized, dense, concentrated, and tannic. The big wines will not begin to drink well until 2007–2010, possibly later.
Price: For the first growth, super second, and limited-production wines, preposterous opening prices reflected the insatiable worldwide demand for these wines. The international market manipulation by many châteaux was reprehensible.

The undoubtedly fabled millennium vintage for the history books certainly did not begin that way. Since I am in Bordeaux in January and March each year, my diaries suggest that while January seemed reasonably cold for midwinter, March was very mild and warm. As *négociant* Bill Blatch, of Vintex, points out in his meticulously thorough summary of the weather conditions leading to the 2000 harvest, the major problem in spring 2000 was one of the worst outbreaks of mildew Bordeaux had experienced in many decades. Vignerons expended considerable effort to control it. It also dampened their early enthusiasm for what was shaping up as a very difficult beginning to the 2000 growing season. Flowering came later than in 1999, but despite concerns about the schizophrenic weather in June, alternating heat and cold, the result was a relatively large, uniform crop of Cabernet Sauvignon, Merlot, and Cabernet Franc. Despite frazzled nerves, there were only small outbreaks of the dreaded vine diseases, surprising in view of the patchy weather throughout May, June, and July. In short, no one expected the flowering or the vintage to turn out so well. As anyone who spent time in western Europe during the summer of 2000 knows, June was an unusually damp, overcast, cool month. However, Bordeaux's actual rainfall came in two large storms in early June, and the remainder of the month was dry. The threat of rain, always apparent, remained more a menace than a reality. July was an even more difficult month of cool, overcast conditions and rain. The average temperatures for the month, however, fell within the normal range for Bordeaux. Moreover, despite the general impression among vignerons that July was deficient in terms of sunshine, final statistics proved otherwise. The break in what seemed an uninspiring weather pattern that began in March finally broke on July 29, when a huge high pressure area stalled over France. This dry and hot stationary system remained over Bordeaux (and much of southern France) for most of the next two months. Despite what had appeared to have been sufficient rainfall in early summer, droughtlike conditions began to emerge. As the grapes began to size up, they also developed thick skins from a lack of moisture, particularly in August. As is always the case, those vineyards planted on the most gravelly, thin soils were far more affected by hydric stress than those with moisture-retentive, clay-based soils.

To quote Bill Blatch, "For the first time in ten years, it did not rain—or almost didn't, during the harvest." Bordeaux's average amount of rainfall in September is 75 mm (about 3 inches). In 2000, it was a meager 43 mm (under 2 inches), most of it from a September 19 thunderstorm. September also experienced some exceptional heat waves, particularly early in the month, which helped to thicken the already dense skins. This only served to further concentrate the wines. The harvest began on September 14 for the precocious *terroirs* of Merlot in Pomerol and St.-Emilion. It continued for the next 2–3 weeks, with virtually all of the right bank Merlot fermenting in the vat by September 28. The earlier harvesters began the Cabernet Sauvignon harvest in late September. Essentially, the entire harvest was finished by October 10. The weekend of September 29–October 1 was rainy, but it did not cause concern, given the fact that the Merlot harvest was finished, and the thick-skinned Cabernet Sauvignon had no problem withstanding the rain. Nor was the Cabernet Franc affected, with most producers picking "exceptional" Cabernet Franc during the end of September and the first few days of October.

In summary, what began as a mixed, uninspiring, unusual early growing season from March through July turned around completely in August and September. French wine producers often say that June makes the quantity, August makes the style, and September makes the quality. That was never more true than in 2000, when August left its stylistic imprint on the wines' enormous tannic content and richness, and the nearly flawless month of September (the finest since 1990) produced many wines of exhilarating quality—at all levels of the Bordeaux hierarchy.

THE WINES

While official yields have not yet been released, it is clear that the 2000 crop is slightly smaller than the 1999. At the top level, yields of 35–55 hectoliters per hectare were modest by modern-day standards. Most producers experienced textbook vinifications (because of higher acidities), with very few difficulties despite grapes with high sugars. Many Merlots hit 14% and Cabernets pushed 13%. However, for reasons that are not totally clear, many wines had relatively high acidity levels, in addition to robust but ripe tannin, as well as surprising fatness. While technical measurements of tannin and dry extract can be misleading, especially when compared to taste performances, there is no doubt that many wines possess record levels of tannin as well as extract.

My tastings confirm that the 2000 vintage has produced some of the most immense, black-colored, concentrated, powerful, and tannic wines of the last 30 years. For that reason, the vintage is difficult to compare with any of its predecessors that qualify as superstar years. The wines are generally less accessible than the 1982s, 1989s, and 1990s, but are possibly more concentrated, blacker-colored, heavier, and thicker than the 1986s, 1995s, or 1996s were at a similar age. Moreover, the finest 2000s possess the most impressive length, structure, concentration, and delineation that I have experienced in 23 years of tasting new Bordeaux vintages. Additionally, the vintage appears to be remarkably consistent throughout all appellations, although the sweetest spots in 2000 are St.-Julien, Pauillac, and the sector straddling the Pomerol/St.-Emilion border (precisely where Cheval Blanc faces l'Evangile and La Conseillante). But don't get obsessed by this analysis, as there are superb wines in all appellations! In 1998, Merlot was the undeniably favored varietal, with Pomerol, St.-Emilion, and Graves turning in more consistent as well as higher-level qualitative perform-ances than the Médoc. In 1999, it was difficult to pick a favorite varietal, as it came down to yields, selection, and overall winemaking. In 2000, there are fabulous Merlots and profound Cabernet Sauvignons, as well as compelling wines made with high percentages of Cabernet Franc, a varietal that excelled. While some feel this vintage is a modern-day clone of 1955 or 1970, it seems to me that the 2000s are far superior. Why? Better winemaking (look at the renaissance occurring in Margaux and Graves as well as the explosion of sumptuous wines in St.-Emilion), improved viticulture, fully equipped cellars, riper fruit, and a more rigorous se-lection process in putting only the finest vats under the grand vin label are the easy answers. Worldwide competition, educated consumers, and relentless critical scrutiny from the wine press are more complicated reasons. In short, it is a phenomenal year that might turn out to be one of the greatest vintages Bordeaux has ever produced, particularly in view of the num-ber of outstanding (90 points or higher) wines. However, the striking paradox for 2000 is the shortage of monumental wines, which seems unusual given the splendid overall quality level.

For the first time since 1990, the smaller wineries of Bordeaux, from the crus bourgeois to the petits châteaux, have often produced wines well above their modest pedigrees. Readers will notice the wines' saturated black/purple colors (which have more in common with a young Napa Cabernet or New World Syrah than with Bordeaux). At the same time, the wines are extraordinarily powerful, concentrated, and dense, with dazzling levels of extract, high tannin, good acidity levels, and formidable concentration as well as length. The finest 2000s appear to possess a staggering 30–40 years of longevity. Are they a hypothetical blend of 1990 and 1996?

The only questions at present are:

1. *Will these wines firm up in cask and concentrate even more, and will the tannin become sweeter?* It is too early to know, but one possible reason to be wary of some 2000s is the ex-tremely high tannin levels, combined with higher than normal acidity. For some Pomerols, twenty years of cellaring may reveal wines that have more in common with the austere 1975s than with fleshy years such as 1990 and 1982.

2. *Are the finest St.-Emilions and Pomerols superior to the great wines made in 1998 and 1990?* Overall, I believe 1998 is undeniably a superior vintage in Pomerol. For St.-Emilion, it depends on the performance of each château. Some St.-Emilions are obviously very tannic, but others (particularly Ausone and Cheval Blanc) are prodigious.

3. *Are the finest Cabernet Sauvignon–based Médocs better than the classic, long-lived 1996s?* Overall, the 2000 Médocs are consistently superior to 1995 and 1996, if only be-cause in the Margaux appellation virtually all of its classified growths were performing up to their pedigrees. Also, several 2000 St.-Juliens outdistance their 1996 counterparts (espe-cially Léoville-Barton, Talbot, Gruaud-Larose, Branaire, and Beychevelle). Elsewhere, the majority of 1996 Pauillacs and St.-Estèphes would seem to be slightly more dense, complex, balanced, and concentrated than their 2000 equivalents, with the exception of Calon-Ségur. As for the performance of the Médoc's four first growths, both Latour and Mouton-Rothschild made 2000s that surpass their 1996s. Lafite-Rothschild and Margaux have produced com-pelling wines equivalent to their 1996s.

THE BEST WINES

St.-Estèphe: Lafon-Rochet, Montrose, Calon-Ségur
Pauillac: d'Armailhac, Clerc-Milon, Forts de Latour, Grand-Puy-Lacoste, Lafite-Rothschild, Latour, Lynch-Bages, Mouton-Rothschild, Pichon-Longueville Baron, Pichon-Longueville Comtesse de Lalande, Pontet-Canet

St.-Julien: Beychevelle, Branaire, Ducru-Beaucaillou, Gruaud-Larose, Léoville-Barton, Léoville-Las Cases, Léoville-Poyferré, Talbot

Margaux: Brane-Cantenac, Cantenac-Brown, Clos du Jaugueyron, Giscours, Kirwan, Lascombes, Malescot-St.-Exupéry, Château Margaux, Palmer, Pavillon Rouge de Margaux

Médoc/Haut-Médoc/Moulis/Listrac and Right Bank Cru Bourgeois: Domaine de l'A, d'Aiguilhe, Belle Vue, Cap de Faugères, de Chambrun, Clos Chaumont, Clos l'Eglise (Côtes de Castillon), Dubois-Grimon, Fougas-Maldorer, Marsau, Reignac, Roc de Cambes, Sociando-Mallet, Tour de Mirambeau Passion

Pessac-Léognan/Graves Red: Branon, Les Carmes-Haut-Brion, La Chapelle de la Mission, de Fieuzal, Haut-Bailly, Haut-Bergey, Haut-Brion, Larrivet-Haut-Brion, La Louvière, Malartic-Lagravière, La Mission-Haut-Brion, Pape-Clément, Smith-Haut-Lafitte, La Tour-Haut-Brion

Pomerol: Bon Pasteur, Certan de May, Certan-Marzelle, Clinet, Clos l'Eglise, La Conseillante, La Croix St.-Georges, l'Eglise-Clinet, l'Evangile, La Fleur de Gay, Hosanna, Lafleur, Le Moulin, Nénin, Pensées de Lafleur, Petit-Village, Pétrus, Le Pin, Rouget, Trotanoy, Vieux Château Certan

Fronsac and Canon-Fronsac: Fontenil, Haut Carles

St.-Emilion: Angélus, Ausone, Barde-Haut, Beau-Séjour Bécot, Beauséjour-Duffau, Bellefont-Belcier, Berliquet, Canon-La-Gaffelière, Chapelle d'Ausone, Chauvin, Cheval Blanc, Clos Dubreuil, Clos Fourtet, Clos de l'Oratoire, Clos St.-Martin, Clos de Sarpe, La Clusière, Côte de Baleau, La Couspaude, Croix de Labrie, La Dominique, Faugères, Figeac, La Fleur de Jaugue, La Fleur Morange, La Gaffelière, La Gomerie, Gracia, Grand Corbin Despagne, Grand Mayne, Grand Pontet, Grandes Murailles, l'Hermitage, Laplagnotte, Lusseau, Lynsolence, Magdelaine, Magrez-Fombrauge, Milens, Monbousquet, La Mondotte, Pavie, Pavie Decesse, Pavie Macquin, Péby-Faugères, Le Petit Cheval, Pipeau, Quinault l'Enclos, Rocher-Bellevue d'Angélique, Rol Valentin, du Tertre, Le Tertre-Rôteboeuf, La Tour-Figeac, Troplong Mondot, Trottevieille, Valandraud, Yon-Figeac

1999—A Quick Study (9-12-99)

St.-Estèphe**	Pessac-Léognan/Graves Red***
Pauillac***	Pessac-Léognan/Graves White***
St.-Julien***	Pomerol****
Margaux****	St.-Emilion****
Médoc/Haut-Médoc/Crus Bourgeois/ Moulis/Listrac**	Barsac/Sauternes***

Size: A gigantic crop, even more abundant than 1998.

Important information: A virulent hailstorm devastated some of the top St.-Emilion vineyards on September 5.

Maturity status: Low acidity yet superb balance, ripe tannin, and medium weight suggest early drinkability but the finest wines' impeccable balance and elegance recall 1962.

Price: Sold at the same prices as 1998s, the 1999s appear to represent the finest bargains of all the vintages of the late 1990s.

It is hard to believe, but in the decade of the 1990s only 1990 and 1997 have given Bordeaux relatively dry Septembers. As much as it rained in September, 1999 (over 150 mm, or 6 inches), this year will be remembered for several other weather extremes. The tempest (in reality a hurricane) that slashed across the Bordeaux region the night of December 27 was the singular weather event of the year. The violence of this storm devastated huge forests and destroyed 100- to 200-year-old trees with the undiscriminating fury of a barbarian army razing the countryside. Anyone who has visited the Médoc or the forest of Les Landes to the south of the city can attest to the unprecedented damage caused by this hurricane, which hit wind speeds of over 120 miles an hour. Heightening the tragedy of Bordeaux's furious storm was that two days before, an equally powerful storm of hurricane force winds ripped apart northern France, causing major destruction in Paris's beautiful Bois de Boulogne and the nearby Palace of Versailles. The other extreme weather event, which had a more direct effect on the harvest, was the freak hailstorm that punched its way through a small zone of St.-Emilion's most famous vineyards on September 5. All the vineyards that were touched, which included such premiers grands crus as Canon, Angélus, Beau-Séjour-Bécot, Beauséjour-Duffau, and Clos Fourtet, as well as the grands crus Côte de Baleau, Patris, Laniote, Grand-Pontet, Franc Mayne, Grand Mayne, Grandes Murailles, Clos St.-Martin, Dassault, Larmande, Berliquet, and La Gomerie, were forced to harvest immediately to save whatever they could. Surprisingly, many of these wines are much better than early forecasters predicted.

Aside from these extreme and unusual weather events, 1999 can be summed up as an excessively wet and abnormally hot year that has produced few compelling wines.

The climatic circumstances and grape maturation in the summer of 1999 were not unusual. The flowering occured quickly under fine conditions in late May and early June. On average, June and July were dry and hot, but August was extremely hot as well as stormy. In early August, major storms dumped more than 2–3 inches of water across the region on August 3, 6, and 7. With the lunar eclipse on August 11, the storms stopped, and Bordeaux was virtually rain and storm free until the heavens reopened prior to the harvest on September 12. The one exception was the aforementioned hailstorm on September 5. Virtually everyone in Bordeaux harvested between September 12 and October 5. The success of such châteaux as Lafleur in Pomerol and Haut-Brion in Graves can be attributed to the fact that much of their harvest was finished before the *grosses pluies* (big rains) fell on September 20. There was only one totally dry day after September 20, and by the time the Médoc châteaux had brought in their last Cabernet Sauvignon, a beautiful high pressure system settled over Bordeaux on October 5 and continued uninterrupted for nearly two weeks, a pattern that had occurred in 1998 as well but seemed doubly cruel in 1999. The heavy rainfall, which would have devastated Bordeaux harvests in the early 1980s, 1970s, and before, is now addressed with greater care. Lower crop yields, meticulous leaf pulling, and antirot spraying are effective up to a point, but many of the most renowned châteaux have invested significantly in the concentration machines that eliminate water from the grape must, either through osmosis or entropy. In the mid-eighties, there were only a few of these machines in operation (Léoville-Las Cases was one of the first to use reverse osmosis to try to concentrate diluted grape must). Now, just about every wealthy estate has such a machine, save for a handful of traditionalists (Haut-Brion, Pétrus, Château Margaux) who still believe concentration is best achieved in the vineyard, not by high technology in the cellar. However, though there is no doubt that these machines work, only 10–20 years of bottle aging will reveal whether or not they alter or mute important *terroir* nuances at the expense of concentration.

The 1999 crop size was large, about 5% bigger than 1998. There is no shortage of wine, but once again, virtually all of the châteaux that received high scores made severe selections, declassifying 25–70% of their production in order to put the finest wine possible into the bottle. Contrast this to the situation 10–15 years ago, when an extreme declassification represented no more than 10–15% of the crop.

THE STYLE OF THE WINES

In many vintages it is easy to say that this or that grape, or this or that particular appellation appeared to have fared better than another. With the exception of St.-Estèphe, a total disappointment, every other appellation has its share of excellent, good, mediocre, and diluted wines. If one appellation appears more consistent in quality, it is Margaux. For decades the region's most notable underachiever, the resurrection of this once moribund appellation is a reality. It is good to see so many Margaux châteaux getting their act together. Many very good 1999s were produced in Margaux.

Because of the extremely warm August and September, there is a hot-year character to the wines—low acidity, generally sweet, silky tannin, and an absence of herbaceousness and austerity. However, even with concentration machines, the effect of more than 6 inches of rain cannot be totally eliminated. In my tasting notes, I frequently used the words "not much middle," meaning that the wine smelled and tasted good initially, but had a huge hole in the middle as well as a tannic, alcoholic finish. I wrote these words so often that I began abbreviating them as "nmm." In many ways, that abbreviation symbolizes the problem many châteaux experienced when trying to harvest under the drenching rain and extract as much flavor as possible from ripe but diluted grapes. The wines have good color, aromas, and tannin, but there is an absence of fat, succulence, charm, and pleasure in their middle. Nevertheless, there are some excellent wines. In particular, the first growths appear to have risen above the trials and tribulations of this frustrating harvest to produce wines significantly better than the super seconds and other classified growths. In that sense, it is a year where the first growths shine, justifying their prestigious pedigrees and their internet.com-like prices.

In addition to the proliferation of reverse osmosis and entropy concentration machines, increasing numbers of "garage" wines are being produced, particularly in St.-Emilion. There is no stopping this new phenomenon in spite of the hostility it has received from *négociants*, the Médoc's aristocracy, and those reactionaries in favor of preserving Bordeaux's status quo. These wines are not the destabilizing influence many old-timers would have consumers believe. What's wrong with an energetic person taking a small piece of property and trying to turn out something sensational? Admittedly, the prices for many of these wines are ridiculous, and no one knows how they will evolve or taste ten years from now, but the present level of quality can be thrilling. If they are overpriced, it is because too many consumers can't say no, and continue to drive up prices for these limited-quantity gems. Nevertheless they are here to stay, and there now appears to be movement to produce garage wines in the Médoc, an extremely unsettling idea for many of the big landed estates who, frankly, are jealous of the high prices these wines fetch.

THE BEST WINES

St.-Estèphe: none
Pauillac: d'Armailhac, Lafite-Rothschild, Latour, Lynch-Bages, Mouton-Rothschild
St.-Julien: Ducru-Beaucaillou, Léoville-Las Cases, Pichon-Longueville Baron
Margaux: Brane-Cantenac, Clos du Jaugueyron, d'Issan, Kirwan, Château Margaux, Marojallia Philippe Porcheron, Palmer
Médoc/Haut-Médoc/Moulis/Listrac and Right Bank Cru Bourgeois: d'Aiguilhe, Belle Vue
Pessac-Léognan/Graves Red: Haut-Brion
Pessac-Léognan/Graves White: Haut-Brion-Blanc, Laville-Haut-Brion, Pape-Clément, Plantiers-Haut-Brion
Pomerol: Bon Pasteur, l'Eglise-Clinet, La Fleur de Gay, Gazin, Hosanna, Lafleur, Pétrus
St.-Emilion: Angélus, Ausone, Barde-Haut, Canon-La-Gaffelière, Cheval Blanc, Clos Dubreuil, Clos de l'Oratoire, La Clusière, Croix de Labrie, Figeac, La Gomerie, Gracia, Grand Mayne, Pierre de Lune, Monbousquet, La Mondotte, Pavie, Pavie Decesse, Pavie Macquin, Péby-Faugères, Quinault l'Enclos, Tertre-Rôteboeuf, Valandraud

1998—A Quick Study (9-15-98)

St.-Estèphe**

Pauillac***

St.-Julien***

Margaux***

Médoc/Haut-Médoc Crus Bourgeois**

Graves Red****

Graves White****

Pomerol*****

St.-Emilion*****

Barsac/Sauternes****

Size: A slightly smaller crop than in 2000, 1999, 1996, and 1995.

Important information: A year that favored the Merlot grape, hence a superb vintage in Pomerol and St.-Emilion, where the wines are powerful and tannic. In the Médoc, quality is good but variable.

Maturity status: Most wines will require considerable cellaring as they possess elevated tannin.

Price: The Médoc prices fell 20–25% below the 1997 prices. Elsewhere the prices are very high, especially for the top-flight Pomerols and St.-Emilions.

In 20 years of tasting young Bordeaux, there have always been vintages where one appellation, or a certain sector, produces more complete and interesting wines. Never before have I tasted a vintage where the differences between regions have been so extreme. There may be some historical references among ancient vintages, but so much has changed today that I question the legitimacy of such analogies. Certainly 1975 turned out a bevy of exceptionally powerful, tannic Pomerols and a handful of stunning wines from Graves, but elsewhere, relatively hard, charmless wines were produced. In Bordeaux, it is not uncommon to hear 1964 being compared to 1998, especially by successful producers. The former French Minister of Agriculture declared 1964 "the vintage of the century" before any grapes were picked. Early harvesters, particularly those in the precocious *terroirs* of Pomerol and, to a lesser extent, St.-Emilion and Graves, turned in very good to superlative performances (i.e., Cheval Blanc, Pétrus, Lafleur, La Mission-Haut-Brion, Trotanoy, Figeac), but the Médoc's Cabernet Sauvignon had not been harvested by the time the deluge arrived. The result was a dreadful vintage for the Médoc, with only a handful of surprising exceptions (i.e., Latour and Montrose).

1998 is different. Viticulture is better, vineyards are healthier, the serious châteaux practice strict selections for their grand vin, and modern-day technology offers temperature-controlled fermentation tanks and, for the wealthiest, concentration machines that incorporate reverse osmosis and the removal of water by vacuum. For those reasons alone, 1998 is superior to both 1975 and 1964.

March 1998 was an exceptionally hot month in Bordeaux, which propelled the vineyards to a roaring and precocious start. However, April was generally cold and wet. May also began unseasonably cold and damp, but by the second week a high pressure system settled over much of southwestern France, and the remainder of the month was warm and dry. The number crunchers predicted that the harvest would begin in mid-September if the summer turned out to be normal. In spite of erratic weather in June, the flowering in most regions took place with none of the dreaded problems such as *coulure*. The end of June was spectacularly warm and sunny, causing optimism to rise throughout Bordeaux.

Is any weather normal today? July was a bizarre month by Bordeaux standards. High temperatures with occasional thunderstorms serving to irrigate the vineyards traditionally define this month in the Aquitaine. Yet July 1998 was unseasonably cool, overcast, and, as Bill Blatch said in his *Vintage Report,* "drab." The hours of sunshine during the month were particularly deficient, even though the average temperatures fell within normal parameters. In short, there had been only three days of extremely hot weather. One weather phenomenon that might explain some of the superconcentrated, massive Pomerols was a hailstorm that damaged some of the vineyards in Pomerol's tenderloin district—the so-called plateau—

which forced the vignerons to do an early *vendange verte* (green harvest and/or crop thin-ning). Unquestionably, this accounts for the fact that yields in Pomerol were extremely low by modern-day standards (30–35 hectoliters per hectare on average).

French vignerons believe "June makes the quantity, August makes the style, and Septem-ber makes the quality." August was destined to put its imprint on the 1998 Bordeaux. The boring, overcast conditions of July were replaced by an intense high pressure system that produced one of the most torrid heat waves Bordeaux has ever had to suffer. For more than half the month, temperatures exceeded 95 degrees Fahrenheit, and between August 7–11, the mercury soared over 100 degrees (not unusual in northern Napa Valley but rare in Bor-deaux). Because of qualitative advances in viticulture such as leaf pulling and culling out ex-cess bunches, this intense heat wave had the effect of roasting/sunburning many grapes, a common problem in hotter climates, such as southern France and California, but rarely en-countered in Bordeaux. In addition to the punishing heat, August brought on drought condi-tions. By the end of the month, the vines had begun to exhibit extraordinary stress. Leaves turned yellow, and the malnourished vines began to curtail photosynthesis (blockage of ma-turity). As many producers have said, this huge heat wave, accompanied by the excessive drought, largely determined the style of many 1998s. The grapes shriveled up and their skins became extremely thick, resulting in the powerful, tannic constitution of the 1998s.

By the beginning of September, growers were hoping for rain to reignite the maturity process. Their wishes came true. On September 2, 3, and 4, the area received a series of light showers, which were beneficial for the rain-starved vineyards. The weather cleared on Sep-tember 5, and ideal conditions ensued through September 11. During this period, much of the white wine crop, not only in the high-rent district of Pessac-Léognan but also in the generic Bordeaux appellations as well as Entre-Deux-Mers, was harvested under textbook conditions. Beginning on September 11, much of Bordeaux experienced three days of rela-tively heavy rainfall. If August had been wet, this would undoubtedly have been deleterious, but the water-depleted soil and vines thrived with the additional rainfall. To the surprise of most observers, the analyses of the vineyards after these rains showed little difference in sug-ars, acids, and dry extract. In short, the heavy rains of September and lighter showers of the following days had no serious effect on quality. September 15 to 27 was a period of excep-tional weather. It was during this period that most of the Merlot in Pomerol, the Médoc, and St.-Emilion was harvested—under superb conditions. By the time the weather began to dis-integrate, during the weekend of September 26 and 27, Pomerol had virtually finished the harvest, and much of the Merlot in St.-Emilion and the Médoc had been picked. It takes no genius to realize that this beneficial period of weather undoubtedly explains why Pomerol is 1998's most favored appellation. Between September 26 and October 1, a whopping 70 mm of rain (nearly 3 inches) fell throughout Bordeaux. The late Jean-Eugène Borie, the propri-etor of Ducru-Beaucaillou, was buried on October 1, and more than a dozen people told me that driving to his funeral was nearly impossible because the Médoc's Route du Vin was in-undated by the soaking rains. The Médoc's Cabernet Sauvignon was not yet ripe, but how much water could it take? By the end of September, the amount of rainfall in the Médoc was virtually the same as 1994, an interesting statistic to remember as readers peruse my tasting notes. The Cabernet Franc harvest was completed after the heavy rainfall of late September and October 1. In the Médoc, the Cabernet Sauvignon harvest continued until mid-October. Another important statistic to remember is that except for October 3, 6, and 7, rain, some-times heavy, fell every day between October 1 and October 12. By the time the weather cleared on October 13, there was little unharvested Cabernet Sauvignon left in the Médoc.

Yields in Pomerol were relatively small (between 25–40 hectoliters per hectare), and in the Médoc, around 50 h/h. All things considered, this would appear to be a year in which the top appellations have produced less wine than 1997, 1996, 1995, or, for that matter, 1994.

The northern Médoc (St.-Julien, Pauillac, and St.-Estèphe) has so many superstar estates that it is usually the source for a bevy of terrific wines, even in difficult vintages. Certainly there are good Médocs in 1998, but these areas represent the most uninspiring appellations of the vintage. If readers were to buy on color alone, they would invest huge sums in the 1998 northern Médocs, because they are all well-colored wines (the influence of modern technology and the grapes' thick skins). However, the wines lack fat, charm, and are often exceedingly tannic, with pinched/compressed personalities. They possess plenty of grip and a boatload of tannin, but are irrefutably inferior to the Médocs of 1995 and 1996. Moreover, most of them lack the charm of the finest 1997s. This is not to say that some fine wines won't emerge, but the Médoc is the least impressive region of 1998. However, several qualitative titans did emerge, i.e., Lafite-Rothschild and Mouton-Rothschild.

In the southern Médoc, particularly the appellation of Margaux (usually the most disappointing area for high-quality wines), the wines are more complete, with sweeter tannin and riper fruit. There are few great wines, but there are many good ones. Many châteaux that have been beaten up by my critical prose in recent years have turned in competent performances. Overall, it appears that the area's finer drainage served these vineyards well.

South of Bordeaux, in Pessac-Léognan, 1998 is a very good vintage. Some of the most elegant, complete wines of the vintage were produced in Pessac-Léognan, and the appellation's most precocious *terroirs* (Haut-Brion, La Mission-Haut-Brion, Pape-Clément) were favored by the early-ripening Merlot and the excellent weather during the first three weeks of September. The dry white wines of Graves and Pessac-Léognan are also very good, but, paradoxically, only a handful have proven to be exceptional.

The excitement in this vintage is primarily focused in St.-Emilion and Pomerol. It does not take a great palate to recognize wines that are often black in color, extremely ripe, thick, and rich, yet also tannic. In St.-Emilion, Bordeaux's most exciting appellation given the extraordinary number of sexy wines being produced, there are few disappointments and many superb wines, though a shortage of true superstars. One of the silver linings of this vintage is how many tasty "little" wines I found in Bordeaux's generic and satellite appellations. In addition to the excitement in St.-Emilion, the fever of quality and competition has spread to the surrounding satellites, and a number of delicious Merlot-based wines are being produced from these lesser appellations. Additionally, because of the high concentration of Merlot (which was ripe and succulent in 1998) in many of these vineyards, numerous attractive wines have been produced. Retailers, restaurants, and consumers looking for values will be pleased to learn that there will be some tasty, early-to-drink Merlot-based wines from the least prestigious (and least expensive) Bordeaux vineyards.

THE BEST WINES

St.-Estèphe: Montrose
Pauillac: Carruades de Lafite, Clerc-Milon, Grand-Puy-Lacoste, Lafite-Rothschild, Latour, Mouton-Rothschild, Pichon-Longueville Baron
St.-Julien: Clos du Marquis, Ducru Beaucaillou, Léoville-Barton, Léoville-Las Cases
Margaux: Kirwan, Malescot-St.-Exupéry, Château Margaux, Palmer
Pessac-Léognan/Graves Red: Les Carmes-Haut-Brion, Haut-Brion, Larrivet-Haut-Brion, La Mission-Haut-Brion, Pape Clément, Smith-Haut-Lafitte
Pessac-Léognan/Graves White: Carbonnieux, Haut-Brion-Blanc, Laville-Haut-Brion, La Louvière, Pape Clément, Plantiers-Haut-Brion, Smith-Haut-Lafitte
Pomerol: Bon Pasteur, Clinet, Clos l'Eglise, La Conseillante, La Croix du Casse, L'Eglise-Clinet, L'Evangile, La Fleur de Gay, La Fleur-Pétrus, Gazin, La Grave à Pomerol, Lafleur, Latour à Pomerol, Le Moulin, Nénin, Pétrus, Trotanoy, Vieux Château Certan

St.-Emilion: Angélus, Ausone, Barde-Haut, Beau-Séjour Bécot, Canon-La-Gaffelière, Cheval Blanc, Clos Badon, Clos Dubreuil, Clos Fourtet, Clos de l'Oratoire, Clos St.-Martin, Clos de Sarpe, La Clusière, La Couspaude, Croix de Labrie, La Dominique, Faugères, Ferrand-Lartigue, Figeac, La Fleur de Jaugue, La Gomerie, Gracia, Grand-Mayne, Grand-Murailles, Magdelaine, Monbousquet, La Mondotte, Pavie, Pavie Decesse, Pavie Macquin, Péby-Faugères, Quinault l'Enclos, Rol Valentin, Le Tertre-Rôteboeuf, La Tour-Figeac, Troplong Mondot, Valandraud, Vieux-Château-Chauvin

1997—A Quick Study (9-5-97)

St.-Estèphe***	Graves Red***
Pauillac***	Graves White**
St.-Julien***	Pomerol****
Margaux***	St.-Emilion****
Médoc/Haut-Médoc Crus Bourgeois**	Barsac/Sauternes***

Size: An exceptionally abundant vintage, but slightly less than in 1996 and 1995.

Important information: A seductive, user-friendly, soft (low acidity/high pHs) vintage that will have exceptionally broad appeal because of the wines' precociousness and evolved personalities. Most wines will have to be drunk during their first decade of life.

Maturity status: A quickly evolving vintage that, except for the most concentrated wines, will be over the hill in 10–12 years.

Price: Despite talk of dropping prices in view of the fact that 1997 was less successful than the very high-priced 1996 and 1995 vintages, most producers increased prices, largely because of the unprecedentedly ruthless selections they made in order to put good wine in the bottle, resulting in a marketplace that remains clogged with 1997s. When sold at distress prices, essential if these wines are to move, many represent very good values.

The wine trade has continued to unload their stocks of 1997s, so excellent values exist! Stylistically, the wines, whether Merlot- or Cabernet Sauvignon–based, are characterized by very good ripeness (often an element of overripeness is present), extremely low acidity, high pHs, and juicy, succulent personalities with sweet tannin and an easily appreciated, friendly style. While exceptions exist, and some profoundly concentrated, long-lived wines were produced, this is a vintage that will require consumption at a relatively early age. Almost all the best petits châteaux, cru bourgeois, and lesser cru classé wines already offer delicious drinking. I fully expect these wines to be best drunk within their first 2–6 years of life. The top classified growths, particularly those estates that produced bigger, more dense wines, will be capable of lasting 10–15 years, but all of them will have appeal and charm when released.

In contrast with 1996, where the Cabernet Sauvignon–dominated wines were clearly superior to the Merlot-based wines, no appellation stands out in 1997 as being superior to any other. The Pomerols are superior to their 1996 counterparts, and there is a bevy of exciting 1997 St.-Emilions, but soft, open-knit, supple-textured, somewhat diffuse wines are commonplace in every appellation. After considerable reflection over which vintage 1997 could be compared with, I found it impossible to find a similar vintage in my 20 years of tasting Bordeaux. Other vintages (1985) were easy to taste from barrel and possessed a similar smoothness and tenderness, but 1997 differs considerably from 1985. Most 1997s are not "big," muscular wines; rather, they are graceful and seductive, full of charm and elegance, yet somewhat fragile. I believe this vintage will be ideal for restaurants and consumers looking for immediate gratification. Because of that, there is no intelligent reason for speculators to "invest" in this vintage and drive the prices up. However, the market has become increasingly complicated, and the demand for top-quality Bordeaux remains insatiable.

I think everyone who enjoys a good glass of wine will find the 1997s attractive. Consumers are unlikely to be knocked out by their depth or flavor intensity, but they are well-made, soft, user-friendly wines that are highly complementary to such vintages as 2000, 1998, 1996, 1995, and 1994, all tannic years that require significant bottle age.

The 1997 vintage began auspiciously. I spend the final 2 weeks of March in Bordeaux each year and March 1997 was the hottest I have ever experienced. Temperatures were in the mid-80s, and even hit 90 degrees on occasion, making me think it was late June rather than March. This hot weather jump-started the vineyards, causing a roaring vegetative cycle. The flowering occured at the earliest dates on record, leading many châteaux to conclude that the harvest would be well under way by mid-August. The flowering hit a few glitches and tended to drag on for nearly a month. The irregular flowering, which led to uneven ripening of the grapes, was exacerbated by the unusual pattern of summer weather. The weather was hot at the beginning of June, but it cooled off and became very wet later in the month. July was abnormal. Usually a torridly hot month in Bordeaux, in 1997 it was cool yet humid. By the end of July high pressure had settled in and the weather became sultry. July was followed by unusual tropical-like weather in August, with record-breaking levels of humidity as well as high temperatures. Despite extensive crop-thinning and leaf-pulling efforts by well-run châteaux, the prolonged flowering, unusual end of June, and tropical August (growers said it felt more like Bangkok than Bordeaux) created severely uneven ripening within each grape bunch. The complaint heard most often was that within each bunch of grapes there were red grapes, green grapes, and rose-colored grapes—a nightmare scenario for growers.

The incredibly early spring, bud break, and flowering did prompt some Pessac-Léognan properties to harvest (in full view of the nation's television cameras) their white wine grapes as early as August 18. This made 1997 an "earlier" vintage than the legendary year of 1893. Just after the beginning harvest for the whites, the hot tropical weather deteriorated, and a succession of weather depressions buffeted Bordeaux. From August 25 through September 1, sizable quantities of rain fell throughout the region. The fact that so many 1997s are soft, with low acidity, but without the great concentration and density found in the finest 1996s and 1995s, is no doubt attributable to these heavy rains. One need not be a nuclear physicist to understand the taste of wines made from bloated grapes. Producers who panicked and began picking in early September, fearing the onset of rot and further weather deterioration, made the vintage's least successful wines. However, those who had the intestinal fortitude and discipline to wait were rewarded with a fabulous September. Aside from a few scattered rain showers on the 12th and 13th, it was one of the driest, sunniest Septembers this century. The later a producer was able to wait, the more the vines, and subsequently the wine, benefited.

Virtually all of the Merlot was picked between September 2 and 23. The Cabernet Franc was harvested between mid-September and early October. The Cabernet Sauvignon harvest began slowly in mid-September but lasted even longer, with some producers waiting until mid-October to harvest their last Cabernet Sauvignon parcels.

One of the more intriguing statistics about this unusual weather pattern is the extraordinary "hang time" the grapes enjoyed between the date of flowering and the harvest date. In Bordeaux, the general rule is that if producers can get 110 days between flowering and harvest, they will harvest mature grapes. In 1997 it was not bizarre for the Merlot vineyards to be harvested 115–125 days after flowering. For the Cabernet Sauvignon, a whopping 140 days was not an unusual hang time. Normally this would be a sign of extraordinary flavor concentration, but the weather at the end of August destroyed all hopes for a great vintage.

Yields were relatively modest, and when the overall production for Bordeaux was tabulated, the region's harvest was slightly smaller than either 1996 or 1995. More important, and the obvious explanation for the quality at the classified growth level, is the unprecedented selection that took place. It was not unusual to learn that 50–30% of a château's total crop was all that was deemed acceptable for the estate's grand vin.

THE BEST WINES

St.-Estèphe: Cos d'Estournel, Montrose

Pauillac: Lafite-Rothschild, Latour, Lynch Bages, Mouton-Rothschild, Pichon-Longueville Baron

St.-Julien: Branaire, Gloria, Gruaud-Larose, Lagrange, Léoville-Barton, Léoville-Las Cases, Léoville-Poyferré, Talbot

Margaux: D'Angludet, Château Margaux

Médoc/Haut-Médoc Crus Bourgeois: Sociando-Mallet

Graves Red: Les Carmes-Haut-Brion, Domaine de Chevalier, Haut-Brion, Pape-Clément, Smith-Haut-Lafitte

Graves White: Domaine de Chevalier, Fieuzal, Haut-Brion, Laville-Haut-Brion, Smith-Haut-Lafitte

Pomerol: Clinet, Clos l'Eglise, l'Eglise-Clinet, l'Evangile, Lafleur, Lafleur-Pétrus, Pétrus, Le Pin, Trotanoy

St.-Emilion: Angélus, Ausone, Cheval Blanc, Clos de l'Oratoire, Fougère, Gracia, Grandes Murailles, l'Hermitage, Monbousquet, La Mondotte, Moulin St.-Georges, Pavie Decesse, Pavie Macquin, Troplong Mondot, Valandraud

1996—A Quick Study (9-16-96)

St.-Estèphe*****	Graves Red****
Pauillac*****	Graves White***
St.-Julien*****	Pomerol***
Margaux****	St.-Emilion****
Médoc/Haut-Médoc Crus Bourgeois***	Barsac/Sauternes****

Size: An exceptionally large crop, just behind the superabundant 1995 and 1986 vintages.

Important information: In addition to being the most expensive young Bordeaux vintage in history, with opening prices 50–100% above the opening future prices of the 1995s, this is a great vintage for the Médoc and Cabernet Sauvignon–based wines.

Maturity status: The powerful Cabernet Sauvignon–based wines of the Médoc will be more accessible than the vintage 1996 most closely resembles, 1986, but in general, the wines will require 10–15 years of cellaring following bottling. The wines from Graves and the right bank will be more accessible at a younger age, and should be drinkable by 7–10 years of age.

Price: This is a very expensive vintage with record-breaking prices. However, prices have remained largely unchanged over the last 6 years. Today the great 1996 northern Médocs look attractively priced vis à vis 2000!

For more than 20 years I have followed (in considerable detail) the weather patterns during Bordeaux's spring, summer, and early fall. I have also studied available information on the weather patterns for virtually every significant Bordeaux vintage this century. Several conclusions can be readily gleaned from such weather statistics. Most of Bordeaux's greatest years have been the product of exceptionally hot, dry summers, with below-average rainfall and above-average temperatures. While a number of this century's celebrated vintages have had moderate amounts of rain in September, unless a significant quantity falls the effect on quality has usually been minor. Given the number of high-quality wines produced in 1996, Bordeaux's weather from March through mid-October was decidedly unusual. The winter of 1996 was wet and mild. When I arrived in Bordeaux on March 19, 1996, I thought it was mid-June rather than March, thanks to the blast of heat the region was experiencing. This heat wave lasted the entire 12 days I was there. Many growers predicted an early flowering and, consequently, an early harvest. The heat wave broke in early April, with a cold period followed by another burst of surprisingly high temperatures in mid-April. Atypically, the month of May was relatively cool. When I returned to France for 17 days in mid-June, the country was experiencing blazingly torrid temperatures in the 90+ degree range. This made for a quick and generally uniform flowering. In Bordeaux most estates were thrilled with the flowering, which took only 3–4 days rather than the usual 7–10. The cold spell that hit during the end of May and beginning of June caused severe *millerandange* (the failure of a vine to set its entire bunch fully, thus reducing yields) for the warmer *terroirs* on the plateau of Pomerol. By the end of June a large, precocious crop was anticipated. Except for the reduced crop size in Pomerol, viticulturally speaking, things could not have looked better. But then the weather turned truly bizarre.

While the period between July 11 and August 19 was relatively normal (statistically it was slightly cooler and wetter than usual), the first 11 days of July and the period between August 25 and 30 received abnormally huge quantities of rainfall, in addition to below-normal temperatures. Statistics can be misleading, as evidenced by the fact that while the normal amount of rainfall for Bordeaux during the month of August is just over 2 inches (53 mm), in 1996 the quantity of rainfall was a whopping 6 inches (144 mm). Yet the heaviest rainfall was localized, with over 4 inches falling on Entre-deux-Mers and St.-Emilion, 2 inches on Margaux, 1.75 inches on St.-Julien, 1.5 inches on Pauillac, and under an inch in St.-Estèphe and the northern Médoc. I remember telephoning several friends in Bordeaux around America's Labor Day weekend and receiving conflicting viewpoints about the prospects for the 1996 vintage. Those in the southern Graves and on the right bank were obviously distressed, expressing concern that the vintage was going to be a disaster along the lines of 1974. They hoped that a miraculous September would turn it into a 1988 or 1978. In contrast, those in the Médoc, especially from St.-Julien north, were optimistic, sensing that a good September would result in a terrific vintage. The large quantities of rain that had bloated the grapes to the south and east had largely missed the Médoc. The below-average quantity of rain the Médoc did receive kept the vines flourishing, as opposed to shutting down photosynthesis as a result of excessive heat and drought, which occurred in 1995 and 1989.

Large quantities of early-September rain had been a pernicious problem in 1991, 1992, 1993, 1994, and to a lesser extent 1995, but this climatic pattern would not repeat itself in 1996. Between August 31 and September 18 was a remarkable string of 18 sunny days, followed by light showers throughout the region on September 18–19. There was drizzle on September 21, then several days of clear weather, and, finally, the arrival of heavy rains the evening of September 24 that lasted through the 25th. Another important characteristic of this period between August 31 and September 24 was the omnipresent gusty, dry easterly and northeasterly winds that played a paramount role in drying the vineyards after the late August rains. Moreover, these winds were consistently cited by producers as the reason sugar accumulated at rates that seemed impossible at the end of August. Another beneficial aspect to this windy period was that any potential for rot was minimalized by Mother Nature's antibiotic.

The Merlot harvest took place during the last 2 weeks of September. The Cabernet Franc was harvested during late September and the first 4–5 days of October. The later-ripening, thicker-skinned Cabernet Sauvignon grapes were harvested between the end of September and October 12. Except for a good-size rainfall throughout the region on October 4, the weather in October was sunny and dry, offering textbook conditions for harvesting Cabernet Sauvignon. In fact, most Médoc producers saw a distinct parallel between the Cabernet Sauvignon harvest in 1996 and that of 1986. While rain had marred the 1986 harvest for the early-ripening varietals (such as Merlot and Cabernet Franc), it stopped, to be followed by a nearly perfect 4 weeks of dry, windy, sunny weather, during which the Cabernet Sauvignon harvest took place under ideal conditions. Given this weather pattern, it is not surprising that most of 1996's finest wines emerged from the Médoc, which harvested Cabernet 10–18 days later than vineyards having high proportions of Merlot.

As was expected from the highly successful flowering during the torrid month of June, the 1996 Bordeaux harvest produced an abundant crop (6.5 million hectoliters), which is marginally below the 1995 crop size (6.89 million hectoliters). However, readers should recognize that the production of some of the top Pomerol estates, especially those on the plateau, was off by 30–50%. In St.-Emilion many estates produced 10–15% less wine than normal. Most of the top Médoc estates produced between 45 and 55 hectoliters per hectare, about 20–30% less than their 1986 yields.

In conclusion, there are eight things to know about the 1996 vintage:

1. Until 2000, this was the most expensive young Bordeaux vintage in the history of the region, with opening prices 50–100% above the opening prices for the 1995s.

2. In contrast with 1995, which had a fabulous summer marred by a rainy September, 1996's weather pattern was most unusual. 1996 started off as one of the earliest vintages of the century, with blazingly hot weather in early spring, followed by a cold period, and then torrid temperatures in June. The summer was relatively normal, except for several abnormally cold periods. Late August, usually hot and dry, witnessed freakish quantities of rain, in addition to below normal temperatures. September was a relatively dry and, most important, windy month. The gusty northern winds played a paramount role in drying out the vineyards after the late August rains. In addition, these winds (along with the dry, sunny days) were the primary reason for the extraordinary accumulation of sugar in the grapes, particularly the Cabernet Sauvignon, which was harvested very late.

3. A giant crop was produced, with quantities slightly below the 1995 crop.

4. This is an irregular vintage without the quality consistency of 1995. The great strength of 1996 is the Cabernet Sauvignon–dominated wines of the Médoc.

5. I spent several weeks in November 1997 tasting through all the wines again, and in the 20 years I have been visiting the area and tasting young Bordeaux vintages, I have never experienced Cabernet Sauvignon as rich, ripe, pure, and intense as the finest 1996 Médocs exhibit. I believe some Cabernet Sauvignon–based wines of the Médoc may turn out to be among the greatest red wines Bordeaux has produced in the last 50 years.

6. The 1996 vintage is most comparable to the 1986 because of the weather pattern and the fact that the late-picked Cabernet Sauvignon was so successful for both vintages. When I first tasted the 1996s it was easy to see the comparison, as it was in November 1997. However, the finest 1996 Cabernet-based wines of the Médoc have a sweetness, completeness, and aromatic and flavor dimensions that exceed the greatest 1986s.

7. The lofty prices fetched by the 1996s in the overheated Bordeaux marketplace of 1997 ensured that many 1996s, particularly wines below the first growth and super second levels, have not sold through to the consumer.

8. It is no secret that Pomerol, St.-Emilion, and Graves (including the northern tier with the appellation of Pessac-Léognan) were less successful, but there were still some extraordinary wines produced in these appellations. However, readers should be aware that none of these appellations is as consistent in quality as 1995.

THE BEST WINES

St.-Estèphe: Calon-Ségur, Cos d'Estournel, Haut-Marbuzet, Lafon-Rochet, Montrose
Pauillac: d'Armailhac, Batailley, Clerc-Milon, Duhart-Milon, Grand-Puy-Lacoste, Haut-Batailley, Lafite-Rothschild, Latour, Lynch-Bages, Lynch-Moussas, Mouton-Rothschild, Pichon-Longueville Baron, Pichon-Longueville Comtesse de Lalande, Pontet-Canet
St.-Julien: Branaire (Duluc Ducru), Ducru Beaucaillou, Gloria, Gruaud-Larose, Hortevie, Lagrange, Léoville-Barton, Léoville-Las Cases, Léoville-Poyferré, Talbot
Margaux: d'Angludet, d'Issan, Kirwan, Malescot-St.-Exupéry, Château Margaux, Palmer, Rausan-Ségla, du Tertre

Médoc/Haut-Médoc and Right Bank Crus Bourgeois: Cantemerle, Charmail, Domaine
de Chiroulet Réserve, Les Grandes Chênes Cuvée Prestige, La Lagune, Lanessan,
Reignac Cuvée Spéciale, Roc de Cambes, Sociando-Mallet
Graves Red: Les Carmes-Haut-Brion, Haut-Bailly, Haut-Brion, La Mission-Haut-Brion,
Pape-Clément, Smith-Haut-Lafitte, La Tour-Haut-Brion
Graves White: de Fieuzal, Haut-Brion, Laville-Haut-Brion, Pape-Clément, Smith-Haut-
Lafitte
Pomerol: Beau-Soleil, Bon Pasteur, Clinet, La Conseillante, La Croix-du-Casse, l'Eglise-
Clinet, l'Evangile, La Fleur de Gay, Lafleur-Pétrus, Gazin, Grand-Puy-Lacoste, Lafleur,
Latour à Pomerol, Pétrus, Le Pin, Trotanoy, Vieux Château Certan
St.-Emilion: Angélus, l'Arrosée, Ausone, Beau-Séjour-Bécot, Beauséjour-Duffau, Canon-
La-Gaffelière, Cheval Blanc, Clos Fourtet, Clos de l'Oratoire, La Couspaude, La
Dominique, Ferrand-Lartigue, La Gaffelière, La Gomerie, Grand Mayne, Grand-Pontet,
Larmande, Monbousquet, La Mondotte, Moulin St.-Georges, Pavie Macquin, Rol
Valentin, Tertre-Rôteboeuf, Troplong Mondot, Trotte Vieille, Valandraud

1995—A Quick Study (9-20-96)

St.-Estèphe****	Graves Red****/*****
Pauillac****	Graves White***
St.-Julien****	Pomerol*****
Margaux****	St.-Emilion****
Médoc/Haut-Médoc Crus Bourgeois***	Barsac/Sauternes**

Size: Another huge harvest, just short of the record-setting crop of 1986. However, most
major châteaux crop-thinned, and yields were more modest. In addition to crop thinning, the
selection process of the top first growths, super seconds, and quality-oriented châteaux was
severe, resulting in far less wine being produced under their grand vin label than in such
abundant vintages as 1989 and 1990.

Important information: A consistent, top-notch vintage. Almost all the major appellations
turned in exceptional wines of uniform quality.

Maturity status: While it has been reported that the highly successful 1995 Merlot crop resulted in precocious wines meant to be consumed immediately, all of my tastings have revealed that while the Merlot is undoubtedly successful, the Merlot, Cabernet Sauvignon, and
Cabernet Franc produced wines with considerable weight, tannin, and structure. Although
there are obvious exceptions, most of the finest 1995 Bordeaux are classic *vin de garde* wines
with considerable tannin and, while accessible, they require bottle age. I do not see the big
wines being close to full maturity before 2005.

Price: An extremely expensive Bordeaux vintage, both as futures and in the bottle.

June, July, and August made the 1995 vintage, as they were among the driest and hottest
months in the last 40 years. However, like most vintages since 1991, the Bordelais could not
get past the first week of September without the deterioration of weather conditions. The
showery weather lasted only between September 7 and 19, rather than the entire month, as it
had in 1992, 1993, and 1994, and, to a lesser extent, 1991. Unlike the record rainfall of 275
mm in September 1992, and 175 mm in September 1994, the rainfall in September 1995 was
only 145 mm. In the northern Médoc communes of St.-Julien, Pauillac, and Pomerol, the
amount of rain ranged from 91–134 mm. While it was a huge harvest, the key to the most successful 1995s appears to have been a severe selection once the wines had finished alcoholic
and malolactic fermentations. The Merlot was certainly ripe, but this was the first vintage
since 1990 where the Cabernet Sauvignon (at least the late-harvested Cabernet) was extremely ripe. Most châteaux that delayed their harvest until late September were rewarded
with physiologically mature Cabernet Sauvignon.

In short, there are four things to remember about the 1995 vintage, a year that should be considered both exceptional and uniform:

1. In spite of a rainy September, the outstanding success enjoyed by many châteaux in the 1995 vintage was the result of splendid weather in June, July, and August, a period that was among the driest and hottest in the last 40 years.

2. A huge crop of wine was produced, but the ruthless selection process employed by many top châteaux has resulted in more modest quantities of top classified-growths than in abundant vintages such as 1989 and 1990.

3. This vintage has turned out to be consistently uniform throughout all appellations. From cask, the vintage looked particularly strong in St.-Julien, Pauillac, and Pomerol, but since bottling, it does not appear to have any regional weaknesses except for the dry whites of Graves and the sweet whites of Barsac/Sauternes, which are pleasant but generally of average quality.

4. It is hard to generalize about the overall style of a vintage, but readers should not assume that the highly successful 1995 Merlot crop resulted in precocious wines meant to be consumed immediately. My tastings revealed that while the Merlot and Cabernet Sauvignon had taken on flesh, weight, and fat during their time in barrel (*élevage*), they had also taken on more delineation and tannin. While there are obviously exceptions, most of the finest 1995 Bordeaux are classic *vin de garde* wines with considerable tannin and, while accessible, they require bottle age.

THE BEST WINES

St.-Estèphe: Calon-Ségur, Cos d'Estournel, Cos Labory, Lafon-Rochet, Montrose

Pauillac: d'Armailhac, Clerc-Milon, Grand-Puy-Lacoste, Haut-Batailley, Lafite-Rothschild, Latour, Lynch-Bages, Mouton-Rothschild, Pichon-Longueville Baron, Pichon-Longueville Comtesse de Lalande, Pontet-Canet

St.-Julien: Branaire (Duluc Ducru), Ducru Beaucaillou, Gloria, Gruaud-Larose, Lagrange, Léoville-Barton, Léoville-Las Cases, Léoville-Poyferré, Talbot

Margaux: d'Angludet, Malescot-St.-Exupéry, Château Margaux, Palmer, Rausan-Ségla

Médoc/Haut-Médoc Crus Bourgeois: Charmail, La Lagune, Roc de Cambes, Sociando-Mallet

Graves Red: de Fieuzal, Haut-Bailly, Haut-Brion, La Mission-Haut-Brion, Pape-Clément, Smith-Haut-Lafitte, La Tour-Haut-Brion

Graves White: de Fieuzal, Haut-Brion, Laville-Haut-Brion, Pape-Clément, Smith-Haut-Lafitte

Pomerol: Bon Pasteur, Bourgneuf, Certan de May, Clinet, La Conseillante, La Croix-du-Casse, l'Eglise-Clinet, l'Evangile, Lafleur de Gay, Gazin, Grand-Puy-Lacoste, La Grave à Pomerol, Lafleur, Lafleur-Pétrus, Latour à Pomerol, Pétrus, Le Pin, Trotanoy, Vieux Château Certan

St.-Emilion: Angélus, l'Arrosée, Ausone, Beau-Séjour-Bécot, Canon-La-Gaffelière, Cheval Blanc, Clos Fourtet, Clos de l'Oratoire, Corbin-Michotte, La Couspaude, La Dominique, Ferrand-Lartigue, Figeac, La Fleur-de-Jaugue, La Gomerie, Grand Mayne, Grand Pontet, Larmande, Magdelaine, Monbousquet, Moulin St.-Georges, Pavie-Macquin, Tertre-Rôteboeuf, Troplong Mondot, Valandraud

1994—A Quick Study (9-24-94)

St.-Estèphe***	Graves Red****
Pauillac***	Graves White*****
St.-Julien***	Pomerol****
Margaux***	St.-Emilion***
Médoc/Haut-Médoc Crus Bourgeois**	Barsac/Sauternes*

Size: Another exceptionally large Bordeaux crop; however, the top properties had to be exceptionally severe in their selection process in order to bottle only the finest *cuvées* under the grand vin label. Consequently production of the top estates is relatively modest.

Important information: A hot, dry summer provided the potential for a great vintage, but the weather deteriorated in September, and a whopping 175 mm of rain fell between September 7 and September 29. Producers who were unwilling to declassify 30–50% of their harvest were incapable of making top-quality wines. Merlot was the most successful grape in this inconsistent vintage. Even the most successful Médocs employed a higher percentage of Merlot than Cabernet Sauvignon, which had a tendency to be austere and herbaceous, with very high tannin. Another key to understanding 1994 is that the best-drained vineyards (those lying next to the Gironde in the Médoc and Graves) tended to produce good wines, assuming they made a strict selection.

Maturity status: Most 1994s will be slow to evolve, given their relatively high tannin levels. This is a classic *vin de garde* vintage, with the top wines well colored and quite structured and powerful. They require additional bottle age.

Price: Initially reasonably priced, the 1994s have benefited from the international interest and, at times, speculation in all good-quality Bordeaux vintages. Prices appear to be high for the vintage's potential.

At the top level, 1994 has produced some excellent, even outstanding, wines, with far higher peaks of quality than 1993. However, too many have not fared well since bottling, with the fragile fruit stripped out by excessive fining and filtration. As a result, the wines' more negative characteristics, a hollowness and high levels of harsh tannin, are well displayed. The 1994 could have been an exceptional vintage had it not rained, at times heavily, for 13 days between September 7–29. As is so often the case with a vintage that enjoyed 3 months of superb weather during the summer, only to be negatively affected by excessive rain before and during the harvest, the willingness of the producer to declassify 30–50% of the harvest was often the difference between producing a high-quality wine and one that is out of balance.

The overall characteristic of the 1994s is a backwardness, caused in large part by the high tannin levels. Yet the vintage's great successes possess the fruit and extract necessary to balance out the tannin. Those who failed to make a strict selection, or had too little Merlot to flesh out and counterbalance the more austere Cabernet Sauvignon, have turned out dry, hard, lean, and attenuated wines. The 1994 is unquestionably an irregular vintage and is more frustrating to taste through than 1993, but some outstanding wines were produced. Shrewd buyers will find a number of smashing wines, but this is a vintage where cautious selection is mandatory. In 1994, much like 1993, the most favored appellations were those that either had a high percentage of Merlot planted or had exceptionally well-drained soils. As in 1993, Pomerol appears once again to have been the most favored region. However, that is not a blanket endorsement of all Pomerols, as there are disappointments. The Graves and Médoc estates close to the Gironde, with gravelly, deep, stony, exceptionally well-drained soils, also had the potential to produce rich, well-balanced wines. However, it was essential in 1994, particularly in the Médoc, to eliminate a considerable quantity of the crop (the top estates eliminated 30–50% or more) and to utilize a higher percentage of Merlot in the final blend. Moreover, the wines had to be bottled "softly," without excessive fining and filtering, which will eviscerate flavors and body.

THE BEST WINES

St.-Estèphe: Cos d'Estournel, Lafon-Rochet, Montrose

Pauillac: Clerc-Milon, Grand-Puy-Lacoste, Lafite-Rothschild, Latour, Lynch-Bages, Mouton-Rothschild, Pichon-Longueville Baron, Pichon-Longueville Comtesse de Lalande, Pontet-Canet

St.-Julien: Brainaire-Ducru, Clos du Marquis, Ducru-Beaucaillou, Hortevie, Lagrange, Léoville-Barton, Léoville Las Cases, Léoville-Poyferré
Margaux: Malescot-St.-Exupéry, Château Margaux
Médoc/Haut-Médoc and Right Bank Crus Bourgeois: Roc de Cambes, Sociando-Mallet
Graves Red: Bahans-Haut-Brion, Haut-Bailly, Haut-Brion, La Mission-Haut-Brion, Pape-Clément, Smith-Haut-Lafitte
Graves White: Domaine de Chevalier, de Fieuzal, Haut-Brion, Laville-Haut-Brion, Pape-Clément, Smith-Haut-Lafitte, La Tour-Martillac
Pomerol: Beauregard, Bon Pasteur, Certan de May, Clinet, La Conseillante, La Croix du Casse, La Croix de Gay, l'Eglise-Clinet, l'Evangile, La Fleur de Gay, Gazin, Lafleur, Lafleur-Pétrus, Latour à Pomerol, Pétrus, Le Pin
St.-Emilion: Angélus, l'Arrosée, Beau-Séjour-Bécot, Beauséjour-Duffau, Canon-La-Gaffelière, Cheval Blanc, Clos Fourtet, La Dominique, Ferrand-Lartigue, Forts de Latour, Grand-Pontet, Larcis-Ducasse, Magdelaine, Monbousquet, Pavie Macquin, Tertre-Rôteboeuf, Troplong Mondot, Valandraud
Barsac/Sauternes: none

1993—A Quick Study (9-26-93)

St.-Estèphe**	Graves Red***
Pauillac**	Graves White***
St.-Julien**	Pomerol***
Margaux*	St.-Emilion**
Médoc/Haut-Médoc Crus Bourgeois*	Barsac/Sauternes*

Size: A very large crop.
Important information: Another vintage conceived under deplorable weather conditions. However, this one offers a number of pleasant surprises. It has produced more attractive clarets than either 1992 or 1991.
Maturity status: The finest wines should continue to drink well through 2005–2006.
Price: The last reasonably priced vintage of the nineties still available in the marketplace, the 1993s came out at low prices and have remained essentially reasonably priced.

In some quarters 1993 was written off as a terrible vintage due to the enormous amount of rainfall in September. The amount of rainfall that fell in 1991 and 1992 was frightfully high, but what fell in and around Bordeaux in September 1993 broke a 30-year average rainfall record by an astonishing 303%! For this reason it was easy to conclude that no one could possibly have made good wine. Moreover, the spring weather was equally atrocious, with significant rainfall in both April and June. However, July was warmer than normal, and August was exceptionally hot and sunny. In fact, before the weather deteriorated on September 6, the proprietors were beginning to think that an exceptional vintage was attainable. The September rain destroyed this optimism, but because of exceptionally cold, dry weather between the deluges, the rot that growers feared the most did not occur. Most châteaux harvested when they could, finishing around mid-October.

The better wines of 1993 suggest it is a deeply colored and richer, potentially better vintage than either 1991 or 1992. The wines have an unripe Cabernet Sauvignon character, good structure, more depth and length than expected, and some evidence of dilution.

THE BEST WINES

St.-Estèphe: Cos d'Estournel, Montrose
Pauillac: Clerc-Milon, Grand-Puy-Ducasse, Grand-Puy-Lacoste, Latour, Mouton-Rothschild

St.-Julien: Clos du Marquis, Hortevie, Lagrange, Léoville-Barton, Léoville-Las Cases,
    Léoville-Poyferré
Margaux: Château Margaux
Médoc/Haut-Médoc Crus Bourgeois: Sociando-Mallet
Graves Red: Bahans-Haut-Brion, de Fieuzal, Haut-Bailly, Haut-Brion, La Mission-Haut-
    Brion, Smith-Haut-Lafitte, La Tour-Haut-Brion
Graves White: Haut-Brion, Laville-Haut-Brion, Smith-Haut-Lafitte
Pomerol: Beaurégard, Bon Pasteur, Clinet, La Conseillante, La Croix de Gay, l'Eglise-
    Clinet, l'Evangile, La Fleur de Gay, Gazin, Lafleur, Latour à Pomerol, Pétrus, Le Pin,
    Trotanoy
St.-Emilion: Angélus, l'Arrosée, Beau-Séjour-Bécot, Beauséjour-Duffau, Canon-La-
    Gaffelière, Cheval Blanc, La Dominique, Ferrand-Lartigue, Grand Pontet, Magdelaine,
    Monbousquet, Pavie Macquin, Tertre-Rôteboeuf, Troplong Mondot, Valandraud
Barsac/Sauternes: none

1992—A Quick Study (9-29-92)

St.-Estèphe**	Graves Red**
Pauillac**	Graves White***
St.-Julien**	Pomerol***
Margaux*	St.-Emilion**
Médoc/Haut-Médoc Crus Bourgeois*	Barsac/Sauternes*

Size: A large crop was harvested, but the top properties implemented a ruthless selection. Consequently, quantities of the top wines were modest.

Important information: At the top level, the 1992s are pleasantly soft, yet even the finest wines had trouble avoiding the taste of dilution and herbaceousness from the excessive amounts of rain that fell before and during the harvest.

Maturity status: Most 1992s should be drunk during their first 10–12 years of life.

Price: Because of the vintage's poor to mediocre reputation, prices are very low. The real value of this vintage is that many of the first growths could be purchased for $35–40, and the second through fifth growths for $15–25 . . . remarkably low prices in the overheated Bordeaux wine market.

The 1992 vintage was not marked by a tragic frost, as in 1991, but, rather, by excessive rainfall at the worst possible time. Following a precocious spring, with an abundance of humidity and warm weather, the flowering of the vines occurred 8 days earlier than the 30-year average, raising hopes of an early harvest. The summer was exceptionally hot, with June wet and warm, July slightly above normal in temperature, and August well above normal. However, unlike such classic hot, dry years as 1982, 1989, and 1990, there was significant rainfall (more than 3 times the normal amount) in August. For example, 193 mm of rain were reported in the Bordeaux area in August 1992 (most of it falling during several violent storms the last 2 days of the month), compared to 22 mm in 1990 and 63 mm in 1989.

By mid-August, it was evident that the harvest would be enormous. For the serious estates, it was imperative that crop thinning be employed to reduce the crop size. Properties that crop-thinned produced wines with more richness than the light, diluted offerings of those that did not. The first two weeks of September were dry, though abnormally cool. During this period the Sauvignon and Sémillon were harvested under ideal conditions, which explains the excellent and sometimes outstanding success (despite high yields) of the 1992 white Graves.

From September 20 through most of October the weather was unfavorable, with considerable rain interspersed with short periods of clear weather. The harvest for the majority of estates took place over a long period of time, although most of the Merlot crop from both sides of the Gironde was harvested during 3 days of clear, dry weather on September 29, 30, and October 1. Between October 2 and October 6, more violent rainstorms lashed the region, and the châteaux, realizing that nothing could be gained from waiting, harvested under miserable weather conditions. To make good wine it was essential to hand-pick the grapes, leaving the damaged, diseased fruit on the vine. An even stricter selection was necessary in the cellars.

Overall, 1992 is a more successful vintage than 1991 because no appellation produced a high percentage of poor wines, such as happened in Pomerol and St.-Emilion in 1991. The 1992s are the modern-day equivalents of the 1973s. But with better vinification techniques, stricter selection, better equipment, and more attention to yields, the top properties produced 1992s that are more concentrated, richer, and overall better wines than the best 1973s, or, for that matter, the 1987s. All the 1992s tend to be soft, fruity, and low in acidity, with light to moderate tannin levels and moderate to good concentration.

The appellation that appears to have fared best is Pomerol. Certainly the top properties of the firm of Jean-Pierre Moueix crop-thinned severely. In the case of their two flagship estates, Trotanoy and Pétrus, Christian Moueix boldly employed an innovative technique, covering these two vineyards with black plastic at the beginning of September. The heavy rains that subsequently fell accumulated on the plastic and ran off instead of saturating the soil. I have seen photographs of this elaborate, costly endeavor and, after tasting the wines, I can say that Moueix's daring and brilliance paid off. Trotanoy and Pétrus are two of the three most concentrated wines of the vintage, confirming that the incredible amount of labor required to cover the 21-acre Trotanoy vineyard and 28-acre Pétrus vineyard with black plastic was well worth the effort. Elsewhere there are successes and failures in every appellation, with no real consistency to be found. Those properties that were attentive to the enormous crop size and crop-thinned, were lucky enough to complete part of their harvest before the deluge of October 2–6, and discarded any questionable grapes have turned out fruity, soft, charming wines that, like the 1991s, will have to be drunk in their first 10–12 years of life.

THE BEST WINES

St.-Estèphe: Haut-Marbuzet, Montrose
Pauillac: Lafite-Rothschild, Latour, Pichon-Longueville Baron
St.-Julien: Ducru-Beaucaillou, Gruaud-Larose, Léoville-Barton, Léoville-Las Cases
Margaux: Giscours, Château Margaux, Palmer, Rausan-Ségla
Graves Red: Carbonnieux, Haut-Bailly, Haut-Brion, La Louvière, La Mission-Haut-Brion, Smith-Haut-Lafitte
Graves White: Domaine de Chevalier, de Fieuzal, Haut-Brion, Laville-Haut-Brion, Smith-Haut-Lafitte
Pomerol: Bon Pasteur, Certan de May, Clinet, La Conseillante, l'Eglise-Clinet, l'Evangile, La Fleur de Gay, Gazin, Lafleur, Lafleur-Pétrus, Pétrus
St.-Emilion: l'Angélus, l'Arrosée, Beauséjour-Duffau, Canon, Fonroque, Magdelaine, Troplong Mondot, Valandraud
Barsac/Sauternes: none

1991—A Quick Study (9-30-91)

St.-Estèphe**	Graves Red**
Pauillac**	Graves White 0
St.-Julien**	Pomerol 0
Margaux*	St.-Emilion 0
Médoc/Haut-Médoc Crus Bourgeois 0	Barsac/Sauternes**

Size: A very small crop, largely because the killer freeze during the weekend of April 20–21 destroyed most of the crop in Pomerol and St.-Emilion.

Important information: A disaster in the right bank appellations of Pomerol and St.-Emilion, but as one proceeds north in the Médoc, the quality improves. Some surprisingly pleasant, even good, wines were produced in Pauillac and St.-Estèphe.

Maturity status: The wines are maturing quickly and should be drunk by 2003.

Price: Because of its terrible reputation, this has always been an easily affordable vintage.

The year 1991 is remembered for the big freeze in April. Temperatures dropped as low as –9 degrees centigrade, destroying most vineyards' first-generation buds. The worst destruction occurred in Pomerol and St.-Emilion, east of the Gironde. Less damage occurred in the northern Médoc, especially in the northeastern sector of Pauillac and the southern half of St.-Estèphe. The spring that followed the devastating freeze did see the development of new buds, called "second-generation fruit" by viticulturists. Because the crop size was expected to be small, optimists began to suggest that 1991 could resemble 1961 (a great year shaped by a spring killer frost that reduced crop size). Of course, this hope was based on the assumption that the weather would remain sunny and dry during the growing season. By the time September arrived, most estates realized that the Merlot harvest could not begin until late September and the Cabernet Sauvignon harvest until mid-October. The second-generation fruit had retarded most vineyards' harvest schedules, yet sunny skies in late September gave hope for another 1978-ish "miracle year." Then, on September 25, an Atlantic storm dumped 116 mm of rain, precisely twice the average rainfall for the entire month! In Pomerol and St.-Emilion there was significant dilution, some rot, and unripe grapes. In the Médoc much of the Cabernet Sauvignon was not yet fully ripe, but many estates recognized that it was too risky to wait any longer. Those estates that harvested between October 13–19, before the outbreak of 6 consecutive days of heavy rain (another 120 mm), picked unripe but surprisingly healthy and low-acid Cabernet Sauvignon. Those properties that had not harvested by the time the second deluge arrived were unable to make quality wine. The 1991 vintage is a poor, frequently disastrous year for most estates in Pomerol and St.-Emilion. I find it inferior to 1984, making it the worst vintage for these two appellations since the appalling 1969s. Many well-known estates in Pomerol and St.-Emilion completely declassified their wines, including such renowned St.-Emilion estates as l'Arrosée, Ausone, Canon, Cheval Blanc, La Dominique, and Magdelaine. In Pomerol several good wines were somehow made, but overall it was a catastrophe for this tiny appellation. Among the better-known Pomerol châteaux that declassified their entire crop are Beauregard, Bon Pasteur, l'Evangile, Le Gay, La Grave à Pomerol, Lafleur, Latour à Pomerol, Pétrus, Trotanoy, and Vieux Château Certain.

Despite all this bad news, some soft, pleasant, light- to medium-bodied wines did emerge from Graves and those Médoc vineyards adjacent to the Gironde. Consumers will be surprised by the quality of many of these wines, particularly from St.-Julien, Pauillac, and St.-Estèphe. In these northern Médoc appellations, much of the first-generation fruit was not destroyed by the frost, resulting in diluted but physiologically riper fruit than the second-generation products. However, the good wines must be priced low or no consumer interest will be justified. The appellations that stand out for consistently good wines in 1991 are St.-Julien, Pauillac, and St.-Estèphe. These areas suffered less frost damage to the first-generation grapes. Virtually all of the better-run estates in these appellations made above average, sometimes excellent, wine. Because the intelligent properties in the Médoc utilized more Merlot in the blend rather than the unripe Cabernet Sauvignon, the 1991s are soft, forward wines that need to be drunk by 2005.

THE BEST WINES

St.-Estèphe: Cos d'Estournel, Lafon-Rochet, Montrose

Pauillac: Forts de Latour, Grand-Puy-Lacoste, Lafite-Rothschild, Latour, Lynch-Bages, Mouton-Rothschild, Pichon-Longueville Baron, Pichon-Longueville Comtesse de Lalande, Réserve de la Comtesse

St.-Julien: Beychevelle, Branaire-Ducru, Clos du Marquis, Ducru-Beaucaillou, Langoa-Barton, Léoville-Barton, Léoville-Las Cases

Margaux: Giscours, Château Margaux, Palmer, Rausan-Ségla

Medoc/Haut-Médoc Crus Bourgeois: Citran

Graves Red: Carbonnieux, Domaine de Chevalier, Haut-Brion, La Mission-Haut-Brion, Pape-Clément, Smith-Haut-Lafitte, La Tour-Haut-Brion

Graves White: none

Pomerol: Clinet

St.-Emilion: l'Angélus, Troplong Mondot

Barsac/Sauternes: none

1990—A Quick Study (9-12-90)

St.-Estèphe*****	Graves Red****
Pauillac*****	Graves White***
St.-Julien*****	Pomerol*****
Margaux****	St.-Emilion*****
Médoc/Haut-Médoc Crus Bourgeois****	Barsac/Sauternes***

Size: Enormous; one of the largest crops ever harvested in Bordeaux.

Important information: The hottest year since 1947 and the sunniest year since 1949 caused extraordinary stress in some of the best vineyards in the Graves and Médoc. Consequently, the heavier soils from such appellations as St.-Estèphe, the limestone hillsides and plateau areas of St.-Emilion, and the Fronsacs excelled, as did those top châteaux that made a severe selection.

Maturity status: Exceptionally low-acid wines, but high tannins have consistently suggested early accessibility. The most complete wines have another 20–25 years of longevity, but there is not a wine from this vintage that cannot be drunk with a great deal of pleasure.

Price: Opening future prices were down 15–20% below 1989, but no modern-day Bordeaux vintage, with the exception of 1982, has appreciated more in price than 1990.

Most of the great Bordeaux vintages of this century are the result of relatively hot, dry years. For that reason alone, 1990 should elicit considerable attention. The most revealing fact about the 1990 vintage is that it is the second-hottest vintage of the century, barely surpassed by 1947. It is also the second-sunniest vintage, eclipsed only by 1949.

The weather of 1990 was auspicious because of its potential to produce great wines, but weather is only one part of the equation. The summer months of July and August were the driest since 1961, and August was the hottest since 1928, the first year records were kept. September was not a particularly exceptional month weather-wise and 1990 was the second-wettest year among the great hot-year vintages, surpassed only by 1989. As in 1989, the rain fell at periods that were cause for concern. Most producers have been quick to state that the rain in September was beneficial. They argue that the Cabernet Sauvignon grapes were still too small and their skins too thick. Many Cabernet vines had shut down, and the grapes refused to mature because of the excessive heat and drought. The rain, the producers suggest, promoted further ripening and alleviated the blocked state of maturity. This is an appealing argument that has merit. While some panicked and harvested too soon after these rainstorms, the majority of the top estates got the harvest dates covered.

When tasting the wines from 1990, the most striking characteristic is their roasted quality, no doubt the result of the extremely hot summer. The September rains may have partially alleviated the stress from which those vineyards planted with Cabernet in the lighter, better-drained soils were suffering, but they also swelled many of the grape bunches and no doubt contributed to another prolifically abundant crop size.

There is no doubt that the great vintages have all been relatively hot, dry years. But was 1990 too torrid? Were the yields so high that in spite of the exceptional weather there were just too many grapes to make profound wines? The weather in 1990 put even more stress on the Bordeaux vineyards than the heat and drought of 1989. One of the keys to understanding this vintage is that the finest wines of 1990 have emerged from 1) those vineyards planted on the heavier, less well drained, less desirable vineyard soil, and 2) those top châteaux that employed a particularly ruthless selection process. For example, heavier soils from such appellations as St.-Estèphe, Fronsac, and the hillside and plateau vineyards of St.-Emilion produced richer, more concentrated, and more complete wines than many of the top vineyards planted on the fine, well-drained, gravel-based soils of Margaux and the Graves.

The crop size was enormous in 1990, approximately equivalent to the quantity of wine produced in 1989. In reality, more wine was actually made, but because the French authorities intervened and required significant declassifications, the actual declared limit matches 1989, which means that for both vintages the production is 30% more than in 1982. Officially, however, many châteaux (especially the first growths and super seconds) made even stricter selections in 1990 than in 1989, and the actual quantity of wine declared by many producers under the grand vin label is less than in 1989. The second consecutive year of great heat, sunshine, and drought apparently caused even more stress for those vineyards planted in light, gravelly soil than in 1989. Many proprietors in the Graves and Margaux regions suggested that they were almost forced to harvest their Cabernet too soon because it was drying up on the vine. This, combined with extremely high yields, no doubt explains why the Graves and Margaux appellations, much as in 1989 and 1982 (also hot, dry years), were less successful. Yet each appellation produced some brilliant wines.

Across almost every appellation, the overall impression one gets of the dry red wines is that of extremely low acidity (as low as and in some cases even lower than in 1989), high tannins (in most cases higher than in 1989), but an overall impression of softness and forward, precocious, extremely ripe, sometimes roasted flavors. Because the tannins are so soft (as in 1982, 1985, and 1989), these wines will provide considerable enjoyment when they are young, yet they possess decades or more of longevity.

Some surprising strengths in this vintage include most of the Médoc first growths (Mouton-Rothschild being the exception). It can be said that they have made richer, fuller, more complete wines in 1990 than in 1989. Elsewhere in the Médoc, particularly in St.-Julien and Pauillac, a bevy of relatively soft, round, forward, fruity wines with high alcohol, high, soft tannin, and extremely low acidity have been made. For me, the most intriguing aspect of the 1990 vintage is that as the wines aged in cask and continued their evolution in bottle, the vintage took on additional weight and structure, much like 1982 (but not 1989). I clearly underestimated some of the St.-Juliens and Pauillacs early on, as it was apparent at the time of bottling that these appellations had generally produced many profoundly rich, concentrated wines that were to be the greatest young Bordeaux since 1982. The fly in the ointment when attempting to comprehend this vintage early on was that two of Bordeaux's superstars, Mouton-Rothschild and Pichon-Lalande, produced wines that were far less complete than their 1989s. Their wines were somewhat disappointing for the vintage and well below the quality of their peers. The puzzling performances of these two châteaux continue to be confirmed in all my tastings through 2000. However, the other top wines in the Médoc have gained considerable stature and richness. They are the most exciting wines produced in Bordeaux between 1982 and 2000.

On the right bank, it first appeared that Pomerol enjoyed a less successful vintage than 1989, with the exception of those estates situated on the St.-Emilion border—l'Evangile, La Conseillante, and Bon Pasteur—which from the beginning had obviously produced wines richer than their 1989 counterparts. However, as the Pomerols evolved in cask, the vintage, while never quite approaching 1989 in terms of greatness, did seem to strengthen from an overall perspective, with the wines gaining weight, definition, and complexity. The 1990 vintage produced some profoundly great Pomerols, but overall, the vintage is less harmonious than 1989. St.-Emilion, never a consistent appellation, has produced perhaps its most homogeneous and greatest vintage of the last 50 years for all three sectors of the appellation—the plateau, the vineyards at the foot of the hillsides, and the vineyards on sandy, gravelly soil. It is interesting to note that Cheval Blanc, Figeac, Pavie, l'Arrosée, Ausone, and Beauséjour-Duffau produced far greater 1990s than 1989s. In particular, both Cheval Blanc and Beauséjour-Duffau look to be wines of legendary quality. Figeac is not far behind, with the 1990 being the finest wine made at this estate since its 1982 and 1964.

The dry white wines of Graves, as well as generic white Bordeaux, have enjoyed a very good vintage that is largely superior to 1989, with two principal exceptions, Haut-Brion-Blanc and Laville-Haut-Brion. There is no doubt that the 1989 Haut-Brion-Blanc and 1989 Laville-Haut-Brion are two of the greatest white Graves ever produced. Both are far richer and more complete than their 1990s. Poor judgment in picking the 1989s too soon was not repeated with the 1990s, which have more richness and depth than most 1989s.

As for the sweet white wines of the Barsac/Sauternes region, this vintage was historic in the sense that most of the sweet white wine producers finished their harvest before the red wine producers, something that had not happened since 1949. Powerful, sweet, and sugary in cask and early in bottling, the wines have slowly begun to take on more complexity and focus. It really comes down to personal preference as to whether readers prefer 1990, 1989, or 1988 Barsacs and Sauternes, but there is no question this is the third and last vintage of a glorious trilogy, with the most powerful and concentrated Barsacs and Sauternes produced in many years. The wines, which boast some of the most impressive statistical credentials I have ever seen, are monster-sized in their richness and intensity. They possess 30–40 years of longevity. Will they turn out to be more complex and elegant than the 1988s? My instincts suggest they will not, but they are immensely impressive, blockbuster wines.

In summary, readers should consider the following points with respect to the 1990 vintage:

1. I have consistently written that 1990 is a greater vintage overall than 1989. I have also stated that, in my opinion, 1990 is an even greater vintage than 1982, particularly in view of the fact that a number of estates making superb wine today were not especially well managed or motivated in 1982. For examples of this, readers need look no further than such châteaux as Angélus, Beauséjour-Duffau, Canon La Gaffelière, Clinet, Clos Fourtet, l'Eglise-Clinet, La Fleur de Gay, Gazin, Lafon-Rochet, Lagrange (St.-Julien), Monbousquet, Pape-Clément, Phélan-Ségur, Pichon-Longueville Baron, Smith-Haut-Lafitte, Tertre-Rôteboeuf, Troplong Mondot, and Valandraud, all estates that were trying to produce superlative wine in the nineties and were indifferently administered (or nonexistent, in the case of Valandraud) in 1982. It is undoubtedly one of the greatest young Bordeaux vintages of modern times, with a style not dissimilar from 1982, but with more consistency from top to bottom. Yet the extraordinary concentration and opulence of the most profound 1982s still exceed that of the best 1990s.

2. With the exception of Pomerol, and the two splendid performances by La Mission-Haut-Brion and Haut-Brion in 1989, 1990 usually triumphs in side-by-side tastings of the two vintages. There are several other exceptions, but in general the 1990s are more concentrated, complex, and rich than their 1989 counterparts, excepting, of course, the Pomerols and 1989 La Mission-Haut-Brion and Haut-Brion, undoubtedly legendary wines.

3. Prices for the 1990s are high, and, sadly, I do not see any direction but upward. There are too many wealthy people in the world who insist on having the best of the best at any cost.

The wine market today is considerably more diversified and broad than it was 5 or 10 years ago. Furthermore, a depressed economy in one country is not likely to cause a decline in prices for the greatest wines from the greatest vintages—a sad but inescapable conclusion based on today's international wine market.

4. In looking at the finest Bordeaux vintages this century, it seems apparent that there are two types of great vintages. There are torridly hot, dry years that produce low-acid wines with explosive levels of fruit and what the French call *sur-maturité* (overripeness). Wines from these type of vintages tend to be delicious young because of their ripe tannin and low acidity. It is easy to think that such vintages will not keep, but based on some ancient vintages that possessed these characteristics, the wines have proved ageworthy for a remarkably long time. Great vintages that fall in this category include 1900, 1921, 1929, 1947, 1949, 1959, 1961, 1982, 1989, 1990, and 2000.

The other type of great Bordeaux vintage produces extremely concentrated but formidably tannic wines that taste more dominated by Cabernet Sauvignon. These wines are almost impenetrable when young and, as a result test their purchasers' patience for decades. This type of great vintage is often a more questionable purchase, since 10–20 years of cellaring is often required in order for the wine to shed sufficient tannin to be enjoyable. The greatest recent vintages for wines of this style include 1926, 1928, 1945, 1948, 1955 (for the Médoc and Graves), 1975 (for the Pomerols and a selected handful of other estates), 1986, 1996 (but only for the Médoc), and probably 2000, which tends to be a synthesis of both styles.

THE BEST WINES

St.-Estèphe: Calon-Ségur, Cos d'Estournel, Cos Labory, Haut-Marbuzet, Montrose, Phélan-Ségur

Pauillac: Les Forts-de-Latour, Grand-Puy-Lacoste, Lafite-Rothschild, Latour, Lynch-Bages, Pichon-Longueville Baron

St.-Julien: Branaire-Ducru, Gloria, Gruaud-Larose, Lagrange, Léoville-Barton, Léoville-Las Cases, Léoville-Poyferré

Margaux: Malescot-St.-Exupèry, Château Margaux, Palmer, Rausan-Ségla

Médoc/Haut-Médoc/Moulis/Listrac/Crus Bourgeois: Lanessan, La Tour St.-Bonnet, Moulin-Rouge, Sociando-Mallet, Tour Haut-Caussan, Tour du Haut-Moulin

Graves Red: Haut-Bailly, Haut-Brion, La Louvière, La Mission-Haut-Brion, Pape-Clément

Graves White: Domaine de Chevalier, Clos Floridene, de Fieuzal, La Tour-Martillac

Pomerol: Bon Pasteur, Certan de May, Clinet, La Conseillante, l'Eglise-Clinet, l'Evangile, La Fleur de Gay, Gazin, Lafleur, Petit-Village, Pétrus, Le Pin, Trotanoy, Vieux Château Certan

Fronsac/Canon Fronsac: Canon-de-Brem, de Carles, Cassagne-Haut-Canon-La-Truffière, Fontenil, Pez-Labrie, La Vieille-Cure

St.-Emilion: l'Angélus, l'Arrosée, Ausone, Beauséjour-Duffau, Canon, Canon-La-Gaffelière, Cheval Blanc, La Dominique, Figeac, Grand Mayne, Pavie, Pavie Macquin, Tertre-Rôteboeuf, Troplong Mondot

Barsac/Sauternes: Climens, Coutet, Coutet Cuvée Madame, Doisy-Daëne, Lafaurie-Peyraguey, Rabaud-Promis, Raymond-Lafon, Rieussec, Sigalas-Rabaud, Suduiraut, La Tour Blanche, d'Yquem

1989—A Quick Study (8-31-89)

St.-Estèphe****   Graves Red***
Pauillac*****   Graves White**
St.-Julien****   Pomerol*****
Margaux***   St.-Emilion****
Médoc/Haut-Médoc Crus Bourgeois****   Barsac/Sauternes****

Size: Mammoth; along with 1990 and 1986, the largest declared crop in the history of Bordeaux.

Important information: Excessively hyped vintage by virtually everyone but the Bordeaux proprietors. American, French, and even English writers were all set to declare it the vintage of the century until serious tasters began to question the extract levels, phenomenally low acid levels, and the puzzling quality of some wines. However, plenty of rich, dramatic, fleshy wines have been produced that should age reasonably well.

Maturity status: High tannins and extremely low acidity, much like 1990, suggest early drinkability, with only the most concentrated wines capable of lasting 20–30 or more years. In 2002 the right bank and Graves wines are approaching maturity. The Médocs remain perplexingly disjointed and awkward.

Price: The most expensive opening prices of any vintage, until 1995, 1996, and the most costly vintage ever until 2000.

The general news media, primarily ABC television and *The New York Times,* first carried the news that several châteaux began their harvest during the last days of August, making 1989 the earliest vintage since 1893. An early harvest generally signifies a torrid growing season and below-average rainfall—almost always evidence that a top-notch vintage is achievable. In his annual *Vintage and Market Report,* Peter Sichel reported that between 1893 and 1989, only 1947, 1949, 1970, and 1982 were years with a similar weather pattern, but none of these was as hot as 1989.

Perhaps the most revealing and critical decision (at least from a qualitative perspective) was the choice of picking dates. Never has Bordeaux enjoyed such a vast span of time (August 28 to October 15) over which to complete the harvest. Some châteaux, most notably Haut-Brion and the properties managed by Christian Moueix in Pomerol and St.-Emilion, harvested during the first week of September. Other estates waited and did not finish their harvesting until mid-October. During the second week of September, one major problem developed. Much of the Cabernet Sauvignon, while analytically mature and having enough sugar potentially to produce wines with 13% alcohol, was actually not ripe physiologically. Many châteaux, never having experienced such growing conditions, became indecisive. Far too many deferred to their oenologists, who saw technically mature grapes that were quickly losing acidity. The oenologists, never ones to take risks, advised immediate picking. As more than one proprietor and *négociant* said, by harvesting the Cabernet too early, a number of châteaux lost their chance to produce some of the greatest wines of a lifetime. This, plus the enormously large crop size, probably explains the good yet uninspired performance of so many wines from the Graves and Margaux appellations. There was clearly no problem with the early-picked Merlot, much of which came in between 13.5% and a whopping 15% alcohol level—unprecedented in Bordeaux. Those properties who crop-thinned—Pétrus and Haut-Brion—had yields of 45–55 hectoliters per hectare and super concentration. Those who did not crop-thin had yields as preposterously high as 80 h/h.

Contrary to reports of a totally "dry harvest," there were rain showers on September 10, 13, 18, and 22 that did little damage except for those who panicked and harvested the day after the rain. Some of the lighter-style wines may very well be the result of jittery châteaux owners who unwisely picked after the showers. The overall production was, once again, staggeringly high.

In general, the wines are the most alcoholic Bordeaux I have ever tasted, ranging from 12.8% to over 14.5% for some Pomerols. Acidities are extremely low and tannin levels surprisingly high. Consequently, in looking at the structural profile of the 1989s, one sees wines 1–2% higher in alcohol than the 1982s or 1961s, with much lower acidity levels than the 1982s, 1961s, and 1959s, yet high tannin levels. Fortunately the tannins are generally ripe and soft, à la 1982, rather than dry and astringent as in 1988. This gives the wines a big, rich, fleshy feel in the mouth, similar to the 1982s. The top 1989s have very high glycerin levels, but are they as concentrated as the finest 1982s, 1990s, 1995s, and 1996s? In Margaux the answer is a resounding "No," as this is clearly the least-favored appellation, much as it was in 1982. In Graves, except for Haut-Brion, La Mission-Haut-Brion, Haut-Bailly, and de Fieuzal, the wines are relatively light and undistinguished. In St.-Emilion, the 1982s and 1990s are more consistent and more deeply concentrated. Some marvelously rich, enormously fruity, fat wines were made in St.-Emilion in 1989, but there is wide irregularity in quality. However, in the northern Médoc, primarily St.-Julien, Pauillac, and St.-Estèphe, as well as in Pomerol, many exciting, full-bodied, very alcoholic, and tannic wines have been made. The best of these seem to combine the splendidly rich, opulent, fleshy texture of the finest 1982s with the power and tannin of the 1990s yet, curiously, taste less concentrated than these two vintages. As with the 1982s, this is a vintage that will probably be enjoyable to drink over a broad span of years. Despite the high tannin levels, the low acidities combined with the high glycerin and alcohol levels give the wines a fascinatingly fleshy, full-bodied texture. While there is considerable variation in quality, the finest 1989s from Pomerol, St.-Julien, Pauillac, and St.-Estèphe will, in specific cases, rival some of the greatest wines of the last 20 years.

THE BEST WINES

St.-Estèphe: Cos d'Estournel, Haut-Marbuzet, Meyney, Montrose, Phélan-Ségur

Pauillac: Clerc-Milon, Grand-Puy-Lacoste, Lafite-Rothschild, Lynch-Bages, Mouton-Rothschild, Pichon-Longueville Baron, Pichon-Longueville Comtesse de Lalande

St.-Julien: Beychevelle, Branaire-Ducru, Ducru-Beaucaillou, Gruaud-Larose, Lagrange, Léoville-Barton, Léoville-Las Cases, Talbot

Margaux: Cantemerle, Château Margaux, Palmer, Rausan-Ségla

Médoc/Haut-Médoc/Moulis/Listrac/Crus Bourgeois: Beaumont, Le Boscq, Chasse-Spleen, Gressier Grand-Poujeaux, Lanessan, Maucaillou, Moulin-Rouge, Potensac, Poujeaux, Sociando-Mallet, La Tour de By, Tour Haut-Caussan, Tour du Haut-Moulin, La Tour St.-Bonnet, Vieux-Robin

Graves Red: Bahans-Haut-Brion, Haut-Bailly, Haut-Brion, La Louvière, La Mission-Haut-Brion

Graves White: Clos Floridene, Haut-Brion, Laville-Haut-Brion

Pomerol: Bon Pasteur, Clinet, La Conseillante, Domaine de l'Eglise, l'Eglise-Clinet, l'Evangile, Lafleur, Lafleur de Gay, Lafleur-Pétrus, Le Gay, Les Pensées de Lafleur, Pétrus, Le Pin, Trotanoy, Vieux Château Certan

Fronsac/Canon Fronsac: Canon, Canon-de-Brem, Canon-Moueix, Cassagne-Haut-Canon-La-Truffière, Dalem, La Dauphine, Fontenil, Mazeris, Moulin-Haut-Laroque, Moulin-Pey-Labrie

St.-Emilion: Angélus, Ausone, Cheval Blanc, La Dominique, La Gaffelière, Grand Mayne, Magdelaine, Pavie, Pavie Macquin, Soutard, Tertre-Rôteboeuf, Troplong Mondot, Trottevieille

Barsac/Sauternes: Climens, Coutet, Coutet-Cuvée Madame, Doisy-Védrines, Guiraud, Lafaurie-Peyraguey, Rabaud-Promis, Raymond-Lafon, Rieussec, Suduiraut, Suduiraut-Cuvée Madame, La Tour Blanche, d'Yquem

1988—A Quick Study (9-20-88)

St.-Estèphe***   Graves Red*****
Pauillac****   Graves White***
St.-Julien****   Pomerol****
Margaux***   St.-Emilion***
Médoc/Haut-Médoc Crus Bourgeois**   Barsac/Sauternes*****

Size: A large crop equivalent in size to 1982, meaning 30% less wine than was produced in 1989 and 1990.

Important information: Fearing a repeat of the rains that destroyed 1987's great potential, many producers once again pulled the trigger too soon on their harvesting teams. Unfortunately, copious quantities of Médoc Cabernet Sauvignon were picked too early.

Maturity status: Because of good acid levels and relatively high, more astringent tannins, there is no denying the potential of the 1988s to last for 20 or 30 years. How many of these wines will retain enough fruit to stand up to the tannin remains to be seen. In 2002, most 1988s are drinking well, yet have retained considerable vigor and freshness.

Price: Ranging 20–50% below more glamorous vintages, so the best wines offer considerable value.

The year 1988 is a good though rarely thrilling vintage of red wines, but it is one of the greatest vintages of this century for the sweet wines of Barsac and Sauternes.

The problem with the red wines is a lack of superstar performances on the part of the top châteaux. This will no doubt ensure that 1988 will always be regarded as a very good rather than excellent year. While the 1988 crop size was large, it was exceeded in size by the two vintages that followed it, 1989 and 1990. The average yield in 1988 was between 45 and 50 hectoliters per hectare, approximately equivalent to the quantity of wine produced in 1982. The wines tend to be well colored, tannic, and firmly structured. The less successful wines exhibit a slight lack of depth and finish short, with noticeably green, astringent tannins. Yet Graves and the northern Médoc enjoyed a fine, rather deliciously styled vintage.

These characteristics are especially evident in the Médoc, where it was all too apparent that many châteaux, apprehensive about the onset of rot and further rain (as in 1987), panicked and harvested their Cabernet Sauvignon too early. Consequently they brought in Cabernet that often achieved only 8–9% sugar readings. Those properties that waited, or made a severe selection, produced the best wines.

In Pomerol and St.-Emilion the Merlot was harvested under ripe conditions, but, because of the severe drought in 1988, the skins of the grapes were thicker and the resulting wines were surprisingly tannic and hard. In St.-Emilion many properties reported bringing in Cabernet Franc at full maturity and obtaining sugar levels higher than ever before. However, despite such optimistic reports, much of the Cabernet Franc tasted fluid and diluted in quality. Therefore, St.-Emilion, contrary to anecdotal claims, exhibits great irregularity in quality.

The appellation of Graves probably produced the best red wines of Bordeaux in 1988.

While there is no doubt that the richer, more dramatic, fleshier 1989s have taken much of the public's attention away from the 1988s, an objective look at the 1988 vintage reveals some surprisingly strong performances in appellations such as Margaux, Pomerol, Graves and in properties in the northern Médoc that eliminated their early-picked Cabernet Sauvignon or harvested much later. 1988 is not a particularly good year for the crus bourgeois because many harvested too soon. The lower prices they receive for their wines do not permit the crus bourgeois producers to make the strict selection necessary in years like 1988.

On the other hand, Barsac and Sauternes had a superstar vintage. With a harvest that lasted until the end of November and textbook weather conditions for the formation of *Botrytis cinerea,* 1988 is considered by some authorities to be one of the finest vintages since 1937. Almost across the board, including the smaller estates, the wines have an intense smell of honey, coconut, oranges, and other tropical fruits. It is a remarkably rich vintage, with wines that display extraordinary levels of botrytis and great concentration of flavor, yet the rich, unctuous, opulent textures are balanced beautifully by zesty, crisp acidity. It is this latter component that makes these wines so special.

THE BEST WINES

St.-Estèphe: Calon-Ségur, Haut-Marbuzet, Meyney, Phélan-Ségur
Pauillac: Clerc-Milon, Lafite-Rothschild, Latour, Lynch-Bages, Mouton-Rothschild,
 Pichon-Longueville Baron, Pichon-Longueville Comtesse de Lalande
St.-Julien: Gruaud-Larose, Léoville-Barton, Léoville-Las Cases, Talbot
Margaux: Monbrison, Rausan-Ségla
Médoc/Haut-Médoc/Moulis/Listrac/Crus Bourgeois: Fourcas-Loubaney, Gressier Grand-
 Poujeaux, Poujeaux, Sociando-Mallet, Tour du Haut-Moulin
Graves Red: Les Carmes Haut-Brion, Domaine de Chevalier, Haut-Bailly, Haut-Brion,
 La Louvière, La Mission-Haut-Brion, Pape-Clément
Graves White: Domaine de Chevalier, Clos Floridene, Couhins-Lurton, de Fieuzal,
 Laville-Haut-Brion, La Louvière, La Tour-Martillac
Pomerol: Bon Pasteur, Certan de May, Clinet, l'Eglise-Clinet, La Fleur de Gay, Gombaude-
 Guillot Cuvée Speciale, Lafleur, Petit-Village, Pétrus, Le Pin, Vieux Château Certan
St.-Emilion: Angélus, Ausone, Canon-la-Gaffelière, Clos des Jacobins, Larmande,
 Tertre-Rôteboeuf, Troplong Mondot
Barsac/Sauternes: d'Arche, Broustet, Climens, Coutet, Coutet-Cuvée Madame, Doisy-
 Daëne, Doisy-Dubroca, Guiraud, Lafaurie-Peyraguey, Lamothe-Guignard, Rabaud-
 Promis, Rayne-Vigneau, Rieussec, Sigalas-Rabaud, Suduiraut, La Tour Blanche

1987—A Quick Study (10-3-87)

St.-Estèphe**	Graves Red***
Pauillac**	Graves White****
St.-Julien**	Pomerol***
Margaux**	St.-Emilion**
Médoc/Haut-Médoc Crus Bourgeois*	Barsac/Sauternes*

Size: A moderately sized crop that looks almost tiny in the scheme of the gigantic yields during the rest of the 1980s.

Important information: The most underrated vintage of the 1980s, producing a surprising number of ripe, round, tasty wines, particularly from Pomerol, Graves, and the most seriously run estates in the northern Médoc.

Maturity status: The best examples were delicious and should have been consumed by 2000.

Price: Low prices are the rule rather than the exception for this sometimes attractive, low-priced vintage.

More than one Bordelais has said that if the rain had not arrived during the first two weeks of October 1987, ravaging the quality of the unharvested Cabernet Sauvignon and Petit Verdot, then 1987—not 1989 or 1982—would be the most extraordinary vintage of the 1980s. Wasn't it true that August and September had been the hottest two months in Bordeaux since 1976? But the rain did fall, plenty of it, and it dashed hopes for a top vintage. Yet much of the Merlot was primarily harvested before the rain. The early-picked Cabernet Sauvignon was adequate, but that picked after the rains began was in very poor condition. Thanks in part to the two gigantic crops of 1985 and 1986, both record years at the time, most Bordeaux châteaux had full cellars and were mentally prepared to eliminate the vats of watery Cabernet Sauvignon harvested in the rains that fell for 14 straight days in October. The results for the top estates are wines that are light- to medium-bodied, ripe, fruity, round, even fat, with low tannins, low acidity, and lush, captivating, charming personalities.

Though there is a tendency to look at 1987 as a poor year and to compare it with such other recent uninspiring vintages as 1977, 1980, and 1984, the truth is that the wines could not be more different. In the 1977, 1980, and 1984 vintages the problem was immaturity because of cold, wet weather leading up to the harvest. In 1987 the problem was not a lack of maturity, as the Merlot and Cabernet were ripe, but rather that the rains diluted fully mature, ripe grapes. 1987 is the most underrated vintage of the decade for those estates where a strict selection was made and/or the Merlot was harvested in sound condition. The wines are deliciously fruity, forward, clean, fat, and soft, without any degree of rot. Prices remain a bargain, even though the quantities produced were relatively small. This is a vintage that I search out on restaurant wine lists. I have bought a number of the wines for my cellar because I regard 1987, much like 1976, as a very soft, forward vintage that produced wines for drinking in their first decade of life. Most of them are now in decline.

THE BEST WINES

St.-Estèphe: Cos d'Estournel

Pauillac: Lafite-Rothschild, Latour, Mouton-Rothschild, Pichon-Longueville Baron, Pichon-Longueville Comtesse de Lalande

St.-Julien: Gruaud-Larose, Léoville-Barton, Léoville-Las Cases, Talbot

Margaux: d'Angludet, Château Margaux, Palmer

Médoc/Haut-Médoc/Moulis/Listrac/Crus Bourgeois: none

Graves Red: Bahans-Haut-Brion, Domaine de Chevalier, Haut-Brion, La Mission-Haut-Brion, Pape-Clément

Graves White: Domaine de Chevalier, Couhins-Lurton, de Fieuzal, Laville-Haut-Brion, La Tour-Martillac

Pomerol: Certan de May, Clinet, La Conseillante, l'Evangile, La Fleur de Gay, Petit-Village, Pétrus, Le Pin

St.-Emilion: Ausone, Cheval Blanc, Clos des Jacobins, Clos St.-Martin, Grand Mayne, Magdelaine, Tertre-Rôteboeuf, Trottevieille

Barsac/Sauternes: Coutet, Lafaurie-Peyraguey

1986—A Quick Study (9-23-86)

St.-Estèphe****	Graves Red***
Pauillac*****	Graves White**
St.-Julien*****	Pomerol***
Margaux****	St.-Emilion***
Médoc/Haut-Médoc/Crus Bourgeois***	Barsac/Sauternes*****

Size: Colossal; one of the largest crops ever produced in Bordeaux.

Important information: An irrefutably great year for the Cabernet Sauvignon grape in the northern Médoc, St.-Julien, Pauillac, and St.-Estèphe. The top 1986s beg for more cellaring, and one wonders how many purchasers of these wines will lose their patience before the wines have reached full maturity.

Maturity status: The wines from the crus bourgeois, Graves, and the right bank can be drunk now, but the impeccably structured Médocs will not become accessible until 2005.

Price: Still realistic except for a handful of the superstar wines.

The year 1986 is without doubt a great vintage for the northern Médoc, particularly for St.-Julien, Pauillac, and St.-Estèphe, where many châteaux produced wines that are their deepest and most concentrated since 1982, and with 20–30 plus years of longevity. Yet it should be made very clear to readers that unlike the great vintage of 1982, or very good vintages of 1983 and 1985, the 1986s are not flattering wines to drink young. Most of the top wines of the Médoc will require a minimum of a decade of cellaring to shed their tannins, which are the highest ever measured for a Bordeaux vintage. If you are not prepared to wait for the 1986s to mature, this is not a vintage that makes sense to buy. If you can defer your gratification, then many wines will prove to be the most exhilarating Bordeaux wines produced since 1982.

Why did 1986 turn out to be such an exceptional year for many Médocs as well as Graves wines and produce Cabernet Sauvignon grapes of uncommon richness and power? The weather during the summer of 1986 was very dry and hot. In fact, by the beginning of September Bordeaux was in the midst of a severe drought that began to threaten the final maturity process of the grapes. Rain did come, first on September 14 and 15, which enhanced the maturity process and mitigated the drought conditions. This rain was welcome, but on September 23 a ferocious, quick-moving storm thrashed the city of Bordeaux, the Graves region, and the major right bank appellations of Pomerol and St.-Emilion.

The curious aspect of this major storm, which caused widespread flooding in Bordeaux, was that it barely sideswiped the northern Médoc appellations of St.-Julien, Pauillac, and St.-Estéphe. Those pickers who started their harvest around the end of September found bloated Merlot grapes and unripe Cabernets. Consequently, the top wines of 1986 came from those châteaux that 1) did most of their harvesting after October 5, or 2) eliminated from their final blend the early-picked Merlot, as well as the Cabernet Franc and Cabernet Sauvignon harvested between September 23 and October 4. After September 23 there were an extraordinary 23 days of hot, windy, sunny weather that turned the vintage into an exceptional one for those who delayed picking. It is, therefore, no surprise that the late-harvested Cabernet Sauvignon in the northern Médoc—picked after October 6 but primarily between October 9 and 16—produced wines of extraordinary intensity and depth. To no one's surprise, Château Margaux and Château Mouton-Rothschild, which produced the vintage's two greatest wines, took in the great majority of their Cabernet Sauvignon between October 11–16.

In Pomerol and St.-Emilion, those châteaux that harvested soon after the September 23 deluge got, predictably, much less intense wines. Those that waited (i.e., Vieux Château Certan, Lafleur, Le Pin) made much more concentrated, complete wines. As in most vintages, the harvest date in 1986 was critical, and without question the late pickers made the finest wines. Perhaps the most perplexing paradox to emerge from the 1986 vintage is the generally high quality of the Graves wines, particularly in spite of the fact that this area was ravaged by the September 23 rainstorm. The answer in part may be that the top Graves châteaux eliminated more Merlot from the final blend than usual, therefore producing wines with a much higher percentage of Cabernet Sauvignon.

Finally, the size of the 1986 crop established another record, as the harvest exceeded the bumper crop of 1985 by 15% and was 30% larger than the 1982 harvest. This overall production figure, equaled in both 1989 and 1990, is somewhat deceiving, as most of the classified Médoc châteaux made significantly less wine in 1986 than in 1985. It is for that reason, as well as the super maturity and tannin levels of the Cabernet Sauvignon grape, that most Médocs are noticeably more concentrated, more powerful, and more tannic in 1986 than they were in 1985. All things considered, 1986 offers numerous exciting, as well as exhilarating wines of profound depth and exceptional potential for longevity. Yet I continue to ask myself, How many readers are willing to defer their gratification until the turn of the century, when these wines will be ready to drink?

THE BEST WINES

St.-Estèphe: Cos d'Estournel, Montrose
Pauillac: Clerc-Milon, Grand-Puy-Lacoste, Haut-Bages-Libéral, Lafite-Rothschild, Latour, Lynch-Bages, Mouton-Rothschild, Pichon-Longueville Baron, Pichon-Longueville-Comtesse de Lalande
St.-Julien: Beychevelle, Ducru-Beaucaillou, Gruaud-Larose, Lagrange, Léoville-Barton, Léoville-Las Cases, Talbot

Margaux: Margaux, Palmer, Rausan-Ségla

Médoc/Haut Médoc/Moulis/Listrac/Crus Bourgeois: Chasse-Spleen, Fourcas-Loubaney, Gressier-Grand Poujeaux, Lanessan, Maucaillou, Poujeaux, Sociando-Mallet

Graves Red: Domaine de Chevalier, Haut-Brion, La Mission-Haut-Brion, Pape-Clément

Graves White: none

Pomerol: Certan de May, Clinet, l'Eglise-Clinet, La Fleur de Gay, Lafleur, Pétrus, Le Pin, Vieux Château Certan

St.-Emilion: l'Arrosée, Canon, Cheval Blanc, Figeac, Pavie, Le Tertre-Rôteboeuf

Barsac/Sauternes: Climens, Coutet-Cuvée Madame, de Fargues, Guiraud, Lafaurie-Peyraguey, Raymond-Lafon, Rieussec, d'Yquem

1985—A Quick Study (9-29-85)

St.-Estèphe***	Graves Red****
Pauillac****	Graves White****
St.-Julien****	Pomerol****
Margaux***	St.-Emilion***
Médoc/Haut-Médoc Crus Bourgeois***	Barsac/Sauternes**

Size: A very large crop (a record at the time) that was subsequently surpassed by harvest sizes in 1986, 1989, 1990, and most of the large harvests of 1995, 1996, 1999, and 2000.

Important information: The top Médocs may turn out to represent clones of the gorgeously seductive, charming 1953 vintage. Most of the top wines are surprisingly well developed, displaying fine richness, a round, feminine character, and exceptional aromatic purity and complexity. It is a fully mature, delicious vintage.

Maturity status: Seemingly drinkable from their release, the 1985s continue to develop quickly, yet should last in the top cases for another 10–15 years. The top crus bourgeois were delicious, but should have been consumed before 2000.

Price: Released at outrageously high prices, the 1985s have not appreciated in value to the extent of other top vintages.

Any vintage, whether in Bordeaux or elsewhere, is shaped by the weather pattern. The 1985 Bordeaux vintage was conceived in a period of apprehension. January 1985 was the coldest since 1956. (I was there on January 16 when the temperature hit a record low, –14.5 degrees C.) However, fear of damage to the vineyard was greatly exaggerated by the Bordelais. One wonders about the sincerity of such fears and whether they were designed to push up prices for the 1983s and create some demand for the overpriced 1984s. In any event, the spring and early summer were normal, if somewhat more rainy and cool than usual in April, May, and June. July was slightly hotter and wetter than normal, August was colder than normal but extremely dry. The September weather set a meteorological record—the sunniest, hottest, and driest September ever measured. The three most recent top vintages—1961, 1982, and 1989—could not claim such phenomenal weather conditions in September.

The harvest commenced at the end of September, and three things became very apparent in the period between September 23 and September 30. 1) The Merlot was fully mature and excellent in quality. 2) The Cabernet Sauvignon grapes were not as ripe as expected and barely reached 11% natural alcohol. 3) The enormous size of the crop caught everyone off guard. The drought of August and September had overly stressed the many Cabernet vineyards planted in gravelly soil and actually retarded the ripening process. The smart growers stopped picking Cabernet, risking foul weather but hoping for higher sugar levels. The less adventurous settled for good rather than very good Cabernet Sauvignon. The pickers who waited and picked their Cabernet Sauvignon in mid-October clearly made the best wines, as the weather held up throughout the month of October. Because of the drought, there was little botrytis in the Barsac and Sauternes regions. Those wines have turned out to be mono-lithic, straightforward, and fruity though lacking complexity and depth.

In general, 1985 is an immensely seductive and attractive vintage that has produced nu-merous well-balanced, rich, very perfumed yet tender wines. The 1985s are destined to be consumed over the next 15 years while waiting for the tannins of the 1986s to melt away and for richer, fuller, more massive wines from vintages such as 1982, 1989, 1990, and 1996 to reach full maturity. The year 1985 was a year of great sunshine, heat, and drought, so much so that many of the vineyards planted on lighter, more gravelly soil were stressed.

In the Médoc, 1985 produced an enormous crop. Where the châteaux made a strict selec-tion, the results are undeniably charming, round, precocious, opulent wines with low acidity and an overall elegant, almost feminine quality. The tannins are soft and mellow. Interest-ingly, in the Médoc it is one of those years, much like 1989, where the so-called super seconds, such as Cos d'Estournel, Lynch-Bages, Léoville-Las Cases, Ducru-Beaucaillou, Pichon-Longueville Comtesse de Lalande, and Léoville-Barton, made wines that rival and in some cases even surpass the more illustrious first growths. In many vintages (1986, for ex-ample) the first growths soar qualitatively above the rest. That is not the case for 1985.

In the best-case scenario, the top 1985s may well evolve along the lines of the beautiful, charming 1953 vintage.

Most of the Médoc growers, who were glowing in their opinion of 1985, called the vintage a blend in style between 1982 and 1983. Others compared 1985 to 1976. Both of these posi-tions seem far off the mark. The 1985s are certainly lighter, without nearly the texture, weight, or concentration of the finest 1982s or 1986s, but at the same time most 1985s are far richer and fuller than the 1976s. On Bordeaux's right bank, in Pomerol and St.-Emilion, the Merlot was brought in at excellent maturity levels, although many châteaux had a tendency to pick too soon (such as Pétrus and Trotanoy). While the vintage is not another 1982 or 1989, it certainly is a fine year in Pomerol. It is less consistent in St.-Emilion because too many producers harvested their Cabernet before it was physiologically fully mature. Interest-ingly, many of the Libournais producers compared 1985 stylistically to 1971.

The vintage, which is one of seductive appeal, was priced almost too high when first re-leased. The wines have not appreciated to the extent that many deserve and now look more reasonably priced than at any time in the past.

THE BEST WINES

St.-Estèphe: Cos d'Estournel, Haut-Marbuzet
Pauillac: Lafite-Rothschild, Lynch-Bages, Mouton-Rothschild, Pichon-Longueville
  Comtesse de Lalande
St.-Julien: Ducru-Beaucaillou, Gruaud-Larose, Léoville-Barton, Léoville-Las Cases, Talbot
Margaux: d'Angludet, Lascombes, Château Margaux, Palmer, Rausan-Ségla
Graves Red: Haut-Brion, La Mission-Haut-Brion
Grayes White: Domaine de Chevalier, Haut-Brion, Laville-Haut-Brion
Pomerol: Certan de May, La Conseillante, l'Eglise-Clinet, l'Evangile, Lafleur, Le Pin, Pétrus
St.-Emilion: Canon, Cheval Blanc, de Ferrand, Soutard, Tertre-Rôteboeuf
Barsac/Sauternes: d'Yquem

1984—A Quick Study (10-5-84)

St.-Estèphe*	Graves Red**
Pauillac*	Graves White*
St.-Julien*	Pomerol*
Margaux*	St.-Emilion**
Médoc/Haut-Médoc Crus Bourgeois*	Barsac/Sauternes*

Size: A small- to medium-sized crop of primarily Cabernet-based wine.

Important information: The least attractive current vintage for drinking today, the 1984s, because of the failure of the Merlot crop, are essentially Cabernet-based wines that remain well colored but are compact, stern, and forbiddingly backward and tannic.

Maturity status: These wines need to be consumed; most of them are angular and excessively tannic. Their acidity and tannin will make them hard to "kill," but they will never be very pleasurable.

Price: Virtually any 1984 can be had for a song, as most retailers who bought this vintage are stuck with the wines.

The problem that existed early on with the 1984s and that continues to present difficulties today is that the wines lack an important percentage of Merlot to counterbalance their narrow, compact, high-acid, austere, and tannic character. Consequently there is a lack of fat and charm, but these herbaceous wines are deep in color, as they were made from Cabernet.

Unquestionably the late pickers made the best wines, and most of the more interesting wines have emerged from the Médoc and Graves. They will be longer-lived but probably less enjoyable than the wines from the other two difficult vintages of that decade, 1980 and 1987.

In St.-Emilion and Pomerol, the vintage, if not quite an unqualified disaster, is disappointing. Many top properties—Ausone, Canon, Magdelaine, Belair, La Dominique, Couvent-des-Jacobins, and Tertre-Daugay—declassified their entire crop. It was the first vintage since 1968 or 1972 in which many of these estates made no wine under their label. Even at Pétrus only 800 cases were made, as opposed to the 4,500 cases produced in both 1985 and 1986.

THE BEST WINES

St.-Estèphe: Cos d'Estournel
Pauillac: Latour, Lynch-Bages, Mouton-Rothschild, Pichon-Longueville Comtesse de Lalande
St.-Julien: Gruaud-Larose, Léoville-Las Cases
Margaux: Margaux
Graves Red: Domaine de Chevalier, Haut-Brion, La Mission-Haut-Brion
Graves White: none
Pomerol: Pétrus, Trotanoy
St.-Emilion: Figeac
Barsac/Sauternes: d'Yquem

1983—A Quick Study (9-26-83)

St.-Estèphe**	Graves Red****
Pauillac***	Graves White****
St.-Julien***	Pomerol***
Margaux*****	St.-Emilion****
Médoc/Haut-Médoc Crus Bourgeois**	Barsac/Sauternes****

Size: A large crop, with overall production slightly inferior to 1982, but in the Médoc most properties produced more wine than they did in 1982.

Important information: Bordeaux, as well as all of France, suffered from an atypically tropical heat and humidity attack during the month of August. This caused considerable over-ripening as well as the advent of rot in certain *terroirs*, particularly in St.-Estèphe, Pauillac, Pomerol, and the sandier plateau sections of St.-Emilion.

Maturity status: At first the vintage was called more classic (or typical) than 1982, with greater aging potential. Two decades later the 1983s are far more evolved and, in most cases, fully mature—unlike the 1982s. In fact, this is a vintage that attained full maturity at an accelerated pace.

Price: Prices for the best 1983s remain fair.

The successes that have emerged from 1983 are first and foremost from the appellation of Margaux, which enjoyed its greatest vintage of the decade. In fact, this perennial underachieving appellation produced many top wines, with magnificent efforts from Château Margaux, Palmer, and Rausan-Ségla (the vintage of resurrection for this famous name), as well as d'Issan and Brane-Cantenac. These wines remain some of the best-kept secrets of the decade. The other appellations had numerous difficulties, and the wines have not matured as evenly or as gracefully as some prognosticators had suggested. The northern Médoc, particularly the St.-Estèphes, are disappointing. The Pauillacs range from relatively light, overly oaky, roasted wines that are hollow in the middle, to some exceptional successes, most notably from Pichon-Longueville Comtesse de Lalande, Mouton-Rothschild, and Lafite-Rothschild.

The St.-Juliens will not be remembered for their greatness, with the exception of a superb Léoville-Poyferré. In 1983 Léoville-Poyferré is, amazingly, as good as the other two Léovilles, Léoville-Las Cases and Léoville-Barton. During the eighties there is not another vintage where such a statement could be made. The Cordier siblings, Gruaud-Larose and Talbot, made good wines, but overall 1983 is not a memorable year for St.-Julien.

In Graves, the irregularity continues, with wonderful wines from those Graves châteaux in the Pessac-Léognan area (Haut-Brion, La Mission-Haut-Brion, Haut-Bailly, Domaine de Chevalier, and de Fieuzal), but with disappointments elsewhere. On the right bank, in Pomerol and St.-Emilion, inconsistency is again the rule of thumb. Most of the hillside vineyards in St.-Emilion performed well, but the vintage was mixed on the plateau and in the sandier soils, although Cheval Blanc made one of its greatest wines of the decade. In Pomerol, it is hard to say who made the best wine, but the house of Jean-Pierre Moueix did not fare well in this vintage. Other top properties, such as La Conseillante, l'Evangile, Lafleur, Certan de May, and Le Pin, all made wines that are not far off the quality of their great 1982s.

THE BEST WINES

St.-Estèphe: none

Pauillac: Lafite-Rothschild, Mouton-Rothschild, Pichon-Longueville Comtesse de Lalande

St.-Julien: Gruaud-Larose, Léoville-Las Cases, Léoville-Poyferré, Talbot

Margaux: d'Angludet, Brane-Cantenac, Cantemerle (southern Médoc), d'Issan, Margaux, Palmer, Prieuré-Lichine, Rausan-Ségla

Médoc/Haut Médoc/Moulis/Listrac/Crus Bourgeois: none

Graves Red: Domaine de Chevalier, Haut-Bailly, Haut-Brion, La Louvière, La Mission-Haut-Brion

Graves White: Domaine de Chevalier, Laville-Haut-Brion

Pomerol: Certan de May, l'Evangile, Lafleur, Pétrus, Le Pin

St.-Emilion: l'Arrosée, Ausone, Belair, Canon, Cheval Blanc, Figeac, Larmande

Barsac/Sauternes: Climens, Doisy-Daëne, de Fargues, Guiraud, Lafaurie-Peyraguey, Raymond-Lafon, Rieussec, d'Yquem

1982—A Quick Study (9-13-82)

St.-Estèphe*****	Graves Red***
Pauillac*****	Graves White**
St.-Julien*****	Pomerol*****
Margaux***	St.-Emilion*****
Médoc/Haut-Médoc Crus Bourgeois****	Barsac/Sauternes***

Size: An extremely abundant crop, which at the time was a record year but has been equaled and surpassed in volume by other top vintages such as 1989, 1990, 1995, 1996, and 2000.

Important information: The most concentrated and potentially complex and profound wines between 1961 and 1990 were produced in virtually every appellation except for Graves and Margaux.

Maturity status: Most crus bourgeois should have been drunk by the late 1990s. The lesser wines in St.-Emilion, Pomerol, Graves, and Margaux are fully mature. For the bigger-styled Pomerols, St.-Emilions, and the northern Médocs—St.-Julien, Pauillac, and St.-Estèphe— the wines are evolving at a glacial pace. They have lost much of their baby fat and have gone into a much more tightly knit, massive yet much more structured, tannic state. The biggest wines look set for at least another 20 years of life based on tastings done in 2000 and 2001.

Price: With the exception of 1990, no modern-day Bordeaux vintage since 1961 has accelerated as much in price, and yet it continues to appreciate in value. Prices are now so frightfully high, consumers who did not purchase these wines as futures can only look back with envy at those who bought the 1982s when they were first offered as futures at what now appear to be bargain basement prices. Who can remember a great vintage being sold at such enticing opening case prices for châteaux like Pichon-Lalande ($110), Léoville-Las Cases ($160), Ducru-Beaucaillou ($150), Pétrus ($600), Cheval Blanc ($550), Château Margaux ($550), Certan de May ($180), La Lagune ($75), Grand-Puy-Lacoste ($85), Cos d'Estournel ($145), and Canon ($105)? These were the average prices for which the 1982s were sold during the spring, summer, and fall of 1983! Yet potential buyers should be careful, as many fraudulent 1982s have shown up in the marketplace, particularly Pétrus, Lafleur, Le Pin, Cheval Blanc, and the Médoc first growths.

When I issued my report on the 1982 vintage in the April 1983 *Wine Advocate,* I remember feeling that I had never tasted richer, more concentrated, more promising wines than the 1982s. Two decades later, despite some wonderfully successful years such as 1985, 1986, 1989, 1990, 1995, 1996, and 2000, 1982 remains the modern-day point of reference for the greatness Bordeaux can achieve.

The finest wines of the vintage have emerged from the northern Médoc appellations of St.-Julien, Pauillac, and St.-Estèphe, as well as from Pomerol and St.-Emilion. They have hardly changed since their early days in barrel, and while displaying a degree of richness, opulence, and intensity I have rarely seen, as they approach their 20th birthdays, the vintage's top wines remain relatively unevolved and backward. The wines from other appellations have matured much more quickly, particularly those from Graves and Margaux and the lighter, lesser wines from Pomerol, St.-Emilion, and the crus bourgeois.

Today, no one could intelligently deny the greatness of the 1982 vintage. However, in 1983 this vintage was received among America's wine press with a great deal of skepticism. There was no shortage of outcries about these wines' lack of acidity and "California" style after the vintage's conception. It was suggested by some writers that 1981 and 1979 were "finer vintages," and that the 1982s, "fully mature," should have been "consumed by 1990." Curiously, these writers fail to include specific tasting notes. Of course, wine tasting is subjective, but such statements are nonsense, and it is impossible to justify such criticism of this vintage, particularly in view of how fine the top 1982s taste in 1998, and how richly as well as slowly the first growths, super seconds, and great wines of the northern Médoc, Pomerol and St.-Emilion are evolving. Even in Bordeaux the 1982s are now placed on a pedestal and spoken of in the same terms as 1961, 1949, 1945, and 1929. Moreover, the marketplace and auction rooms, perhaps the only true measure of a vintage's value, continue to push prices for the top 1982s to stratospheric levels. Recent tastings of the 1982s continue to suggest that the top wines of the northern Médoc need another 5 or so years of cellaring. Most of the best wines seem largely unevolved since their early days in cask. They have fully recovered from the bottling and display the extraordinary expansive, rich, glycerin- and extract-laden palates that should serve these wines well over the next 10–20 years. If the 1982 vintage remains sensational for the majority of St.-Emilions, Pomerols, St.-Juliens, Pauillacs, and St.-Estèphes, the weakness of the vintage becomes increasingly more apparent with the Margaux and Graves wines. Only Château Margaux seems to have survived the problems of over-production, the loosely knit, flabby Cabernet Sauvignon wines from which so many other Margaux properties suffered. The same can be said for the Graves, which are light and disjointed when compared to the lovely 1983s Graves produced. Only La Mission-Haut-Brion and Haut-Brion produced better 1982s than 1983s.

On the negative side are the prices one must now pay for a top wine from 1982. Is this why the vintage still receives cheap shots from a handful of American writers? Those who bought them as futures made the wine buys of the century. For today's generation of wine enthusiasts, 1982 is what 1945, 1947, 1949, 1959, and 1961 were for an earlier generation.

Finally, the sweet wines of Barsac and Sauternes in 1982, while maligned originally for their lack of botrytis and richness, are not that bad. In fact, d'Yquem and the Cuvée Madame of Château Suduiraut are two remarkably powerful, rich wines that can stand up to the best of the 1983s, 1986s, and 1988s.

THE BEST WINES

St.-Estèphe: Calon-Ségur, Cos d'Estournel, Haut-Marbuzet, Montrose
Pauillac: Les Forts de Latour, Grand-Puy-Lacoste, Haut-Batailley, Lafite-Rothschild, Latour, Lynch-Bages, Mouton-Rothschild, Pichon-Longueville Baron, Pichon-Longeville Comtesse de Lalande
St.-Julien: Beychevelle, Branaire-Ducru, Ducru-Beaucaillou, Gruaud-Larose, Léoville-Barton, Léoville-Las Cases, Léoville-Poyferré, Talbot
Margaux: Margaux, La Lagune (southern Médoc)
Médoc/Haut Médoc/Moulis/Listrac/Crus Bourgeois: Tour Haut-Caussan, Maucaillou, Potensac, Poujeaux, Sociando-Mallet, La Tour St.-Bonnet
Graves Red: Haut-Brion, La Mission-Haut-Brion, La Tour-Haut-Brion
Graves White: none
Pomerol: Bon Pasteur, Certan de May, La Conseillante, l'Enclos, l'Evangile, Le Gay, Lafleur, Latour à Pomerol, Petit-Village, Pétrus, Le Pin, Trotanoy, Vieux Château Certan
St.-Emilion: l'Arrosée, Ausone, Canon, Cheval Blanc, La Dominique, Figeac, Pavie
Barsac/Sauternes: Raymond-Lafon, Suduiraut-Cuvée Madame, d'Yquem

1981—A Quick Study (9-28-81)

St.-Estèphe**	Graves Red**
Pauillac***	Graves White**
St.-Julien***	Pomerol***
Margaux**	St.-Emilion**
Médoc/Haut-Médoc Crus Bourgeois*	Barsac/Sauternes*

Size: A moderately large crop that in retrospect now looks modest.
Important information: The first vintage in a succession of hot, dry years that would continue nearly uninterrupted through 1990. The year 1981 would have been a top vintage had the rain not fallen immediately prior to the harvest.
Maturity status: Most 1981s are close to full maturity, yet the best examples are capable of lasting another 5 or so years.
Price: A largely ignored and overlooked vintage, 1981 remains a reasonably good value.

This vintage has been labeled more "classic" than either 1983 or 1982. What classic means to those who call 1981 a classic vintage is that this year is a typically good Bordeaux vintage of medium-weight, well-balanced, graceful wines. Despite a dozen or so excellent wines, 1981 is in reality only a good vintage, surpassed in quality by both 1982 and 1983 and also by 1978 and 1979.

The year 1981 could have been an outstanding vintage had it not been for the heavy rains that fell just as the harvest was about to start. There was a dilution of the intensity of flavor in the grapes as heavy rains drenched the vineyards between October 1–5 and again between October 9–15. Until then the summer had been perfect. The flowering occurred under excellent conditions; July was cool, but August and September hot and dry. One can only speculate that had it not rained, 1981 might well have turned out to be one of the greatest vintages in the post–World War II era. The year did produce a large crop of generally well colored wines of medium weight and moderate tannin. The dry white wines have turned out well but should have been consumed by now. Both Barsacs and Sauternes suffered as a result of the rains, and no truly compelling wines have emerged from these appellations.

There are a number of successful wines in 1981, particularly from Pomerol, St.-Julien, and Pauillac. Twenty years later, the 1981s have generally reached their plateau of maturity, and only the best will keep for another 5–7 years. The wines' shortcomings are their lack of richness, flesh, and intensity, qualities that more recent vintages have possessed. Most red wine producers had to chaptalize (add sugars) significantly because the Cabernets were harvested under 11% natural alcohol and the Merlot under 12%, no doubt because of the rain.

THE BEST WINES

St.-Estèphe: none
Pauillac: Lafite-Rothschild, Latour, Pichon-Longueville Comtesse de Lalande
St.-Julien: Ducru-Beaucaillou, Gruaud-Larose, Léoville-Las Cases, St.-Pierre
Margaux: Giscours, Margaux
Médoc/Haut-Médoc Crus Bourgeois: none
Graves Red: La Mission-Haut-Brion
Graves White: none
Pomerol: Certan de May, La Conseillante, Pétrus, Le Pin, Vieux Château Certan
St.-Emilion: Cheval Blanc
Barsac/Sauternes: Climens, de Fargues, d'Yquem

1980—A Quick Study (10-14-80)

St.-Estèphe*	Graves Red**
Pauillac**	Graves White*
St.-Julien**	Pomerol**
Margaux**	St.-Emilion*
Médoc/Haut-Médoc Crus Bourgeois*	Barsac/Sauternes****

Size: A moderate-sized crop was harvested.
Important information: Nothing very noteworthy can be said about this mediocre vintage.
Maturity status: With the exception of Château Margaux and Pétrus, virtually every 1980 should have been consumed.
Price: Low.

This vintage resulted largely in light, diluted, frequently disappointing wines that have an unmistakable vegetal and herbaceous taste and are often marred by excessive acidity as well as tannin. Those producers who made a strict selection and who picked exceptionally late, such as the Mentzelopoulos family at Château Margaux (the wine of the vintage), made softer, rounder, more interesting wines that began to drink well in the late 1990s and should continue to drink well until the turn of the century. However, the number of properties that could be said to have made wines of good quality are few.

As always in wet, cool years, those vineyards planted on lighter, gravelly, well-drained soils, such as some of the Margaux and Graves properties, tend to get better maturity and ripeness. Not surprisingly, the top successes generally come from these areas, although several Pauillacs, because of a very strict selection, also have turned out well. As disappointing as the 1980 vintage was for the red wine producers, it was an excellent year for the producers of Barsac and Sauternes. The ripening and harvesting continued into late November, generally under ideal conditions. This permitted some rich, intense, high-class Barsac and Sauternes to be produced. Unfortunately, their commercial viability suffered from the reputation of the red wine vintage. Anyone who comes across a bottle of 1980 Climens, d'Yquem, or Raymond-Lafon will immediately realize that this is an astonishingly good year.

THE BEST WINES

St.-Estèphe: none
Pauillac: Latour, Pichon-Longueville Comtesse de Lalande
St.-Julien: Talbot
Margaux: Margaux
Médoc/Haut-Médoc/Moulis/Listrac/Crus Bourgeois: none
Graves Red: Domaine de Chevalier, La Mission-Haut-Brion
Graves White: none
Pomerol: Certan de May, Pétrus
St.-Emilion: Cheval Blanc
Barsac/Sauternes: Climens, de Fargues, Raymond-Lafon, d'Yquem

1979—A Quick Study (10-3-79)

St.-Estèphe**	Graves Red****
Pauillac***	Graves White**
St.-Julien***	Pomerol***
Margaux****	St.-Emilion**
Médoc/Haut-Médoc Crus Bourgeois**	Barsac/Sauternes*

Size: A huge crop that established a record at that time.
Important information: In the last two decades this is one of the only cool years that turned out to be a reasonably good vintage.
Maturity status: Contrary to earlier reports, the 1979s have matured very slowly, largely because the wines have relatively hard tannins and good acidity, two characteristics that most of the top vintages during the decade of the eighties have not possessed.
Price: Because of the lack of demand, and the vintage's average-to-good reputation, prices remain low except for a handful of the limited-production, glamour wines of Pomerol.

1979 has become the forgotten vintage in Bordeaux. A record-setting crop that produced relatively healthy, medium-bodied wines that displayed firm tannins and good acidity closed out the 1970s. Considered inferior to 1978 when conceived, the 1979 vintage will prove superior—at least in terms of aging potential. Yet aging potential alone is hardly sufficient to evaluate a vintage, and many 1979s remain relatively skinny, malnourished, lean, compact wines that naive commentators have called classic rather than thin. Despite the inconsistency from appellation to appellation, a number of strikingly good, surprisingly flavorful, rich wines have emerged from appellations such as Margaux, Graves, and Pomerol.

With few exceptions, there is no hurry to drink the top 1979s, since their relatively high acid levels (compared to more recent hot-year vintages), good tannin levels, and sturdy framework should ensure that the top 1979s age well for at least another 10–15 years.

This was not a good vintage for the dry white wines of Graves or the sweet white wines of Barsac and Sauternes. The dry whites did not achieve full maturity, and there was never enough botrytis for the Barsac and Sauternes to give the wines the honeyed complexity that is fundamental to their success.

Prices for 1979s, where they can still be found, are the lowest of any good recent Bordeaux vintage, reflecting the general lack of excitement for most 1979s.

THE BEST WINES

St.-Estèphe: Cos d'Estournel
Pauillac: Lafite-Rothschild, Latour, Pichon-Longueville Comtesse de Lalande
St.-Julien: Gruaud-Larose, Léoville-Las Cases
Margaux: Giscours, Margaux, Palmer, du Tertre
Graves Red: Les Carmes Haut-Brion, Domaine de Chevalier, Haut-Bailly, Haut-Brion, La Mission-Haut-Brion
Pomerol: Certan de May, l'Enclos, l'Evangile, Lafleur, Pétrus
St.-Emilion: Ausone
Barsac/Sauternes: none

1978—A Quick Study (10-7-78)

St.-Estèphe**	Graves Red****
Pauillac***	Graves White****
St.-Julien***	Pomerol**
Margaux***	St.-Emilion***
Médoc/Haut-Médoc Crus Bourgeois**	Barsac/Sauternes**

Size: A moderate-sized crop was harvested.
Important information: The year Harry Waugh, England's gentlemanly wine commentator, dubbed "the miracle year."
Maturity status: Most wines are fully mature.
Price: Overpriced for years, the 1978s are fairly priced 24 years after the vintage.

The year 1978 turned out to be an outstanding vintage for the red wines of Graves and a good vintage for the red wines from the Médoc, Pomerol, and St.-Emilion. There was a lack of botrytis for the sweet white wines of Barsac and Sauternes, and the results were monolithic, straightforward wines of no great character. The dry white Graves, much like the red wines of that appellation, turned out exceedingly well. The general view of this vintage is that it is a very good to excellent year. The two best appellations are Graves and Margaux, which have the lighter, better-drained soils that support cooler-weather years. In fact, Graves (except for the disappointing Pape-Clément) probably enjoyed its greatest vintage after 1961. The wines, which at first appeared intensely fruity, deeply colored, moderately tannic, and medium-bodied, have aged much faster than the higher-acid, more firmly tannic 1979. Most 1978s had reached full maturity 12 years after the vintage, and some commentators were expressing their disappointment that the wines were not better than they had believed.

The problem is that, much like in 1979, 1981, and 1988, there is a shortage of truly superstar wines. There are a number of good wines, but the lack of excitement in the majority of wines has tempered the postvintage enthusiasm. Moreover, the lesser wines in 1978 have an annoyingly vegetal, herbaceous taste because those vineyards not planted on the best soils never fully ripened despite the impressively hot, dry *fin de saison*. Another important consideration is that the selection process, so much a fundamental principle in the 1980s, was employed less during the 1970s, as many properties simply bottled everything under the grand vin label. Many proprietors today feel that 1978 could have lived up to its early promise had a stricter selection been in effect when the wines were made.

This was a very difficult vintage for properties in the Barsac/Sauternes region because very little botrytis formed owing to the hot, dry autumn. The wines, much like the 1979s, are chunky and full of glycerin and sugar, but they lack grip, focus, and complexity.

THE BEST WINES

St.-Estèphe: none

Pauillac: Les Forts de Latour, Grand-Puy-Lacoste, Latour, Pichon-Longueville Comtesse de Lalande

St.-Julien: Ducru-Beaucaillou, Gruaud-Larose, Léoville-Las Cases, Talbot

Margaux: Giscours, La Lagune (southern Médoc), Margaux, Palmer, Prieuré-Lichine, du Tertre

Médoc/Haut-Médoc/Moulis/Listrac/Crus Bourgeois: none

Graves Red: Les Carmes Haut-Brion, Domaine de Chevalier, Haut-Bailly, Haut-Brion, La Mission-Haut-Brion, La Tour-Haut-Brion

Graves White: Domaine de Chevalier, Haut-Brion, Laville-Haut-Brion

Pomerol: Lafleur

St.-Emilion: l'Arrosée, Cheval Blanc

Barsac/Sauternes: none

1977—A Quick Study (10-3-77)

St.-Estèphe 0	Graves Red*
Pauillac 0	Graves White*
St.-Julien 0	Pomerol 0
Margaux 0	St.-Emilion 0
Médoc/Haut-Médoc Crus Bourgeois 0	Barsac/Sauternes*

Size: A small crop was produced.

Important information: A dreadful vintage, clearly the worst since 1972; it remains, in a pejorative sense, unequaled since.

Maturity status: The wines, even the handful that were drinkable, should have been consumed by the mid-1980s.

Price: Despite distress sale prices, there are no values to be found.

1976—A Quick Study (9-13-76)

St.-Estèphe***	Graves Red*
Pauillac***	Graves White***
St.-Julien***	Pomerol***
Margaux**	St.-Emilion***
Médoc/Haut-Médoc Crus Bourgeois*	Barsac/Sauternes****

Size: A huge crop, the second largest of the decade, was harvested.

Important information: This hot, droughtlike vintage could have proved to be the vintage of the decade had it not been for preharvest rains.

Maturity status: The 1976s tasted fully mature and delicious when released in 1979. Yet the best examples continue to offer delightful, sometimes delicious drinking. It is one of a handful of vintages where the wines have never closed up and been unappealing. Yet virtually every 1976 (with the exception of Ausone) should have been consumed by 2000.

Price: The 1976s have always been reasonably priced because they have never received accolades from the wine pundits.

I had fully expected that these wines would have to be consumed before the end of the decade of the 1980s. However, the top 1976s appear to have stayed at their peak of maturity without fading or losing their fruit. I wish I had bought more of this vintage given how delicious the best wines have been over such an extended period of time. They will not make old bones, and one must be very careful with the weaker 1976s, which have lacked intensity and depth from the beginning. These wines were extremely fragile and have increasingly taken on a brown cast to their color as well as losing their fruit. Nevertheless, the top wines continue to offer delicious drinking and persuasive evidence that even in a relatively diluted, extremely soft-style vintage, with dangerously low acid levels, Bordeaux wines, where well stored, can last 15 or more years.

The 1976 vintage was at its strongest in the northern Médoc appellations of St.-Julien, Pauillac, and St.-Estèphe, weakest in Graves and Margaux, and mixed in the Libournais appellations of Pomerol and St.-Emilion. The wine of the vintage is Ausone.

For those who admire decadently rich, honeyed, sweet wines, this is one of the two best vintages of the 1970s, given the abundant quantities of botrytis that formed in the vineyards and the lavish richness and opulent style of the wines of Barsac/Sauternes.

THE BEST WINES

St.-Estèphe: Cos d'Estournel, Montrose
Pauillac: Haut-Bages-Libéral, Lafite-Rothschild, Pichon-Longueville Comtesse de Lalande
St.-Julien: Beychevelle, Branaire-Ducru, Ducru-Beaucaillou, Léoville-Las Cases, Talbot
Margaux: Giscours, La Lagune (southern Médoc)
Médoc/Haut Médoc/Moulis/Listrac/Crus Bourgeois: Sociando-Mallet
Graves Red: Haut-Brion
Graves White: Domaine de Chevalier, Laville-Haut-Brion
Pomerol: Pétrus
St.-Emilion: Ausone, Cheval Blanc, Figeac
Barsac/Sauternes: Climens, Coutet, de Fargues, Guiraud, Rieussec, Suduiraut, d'Yquem

1975—A Quick Study (9-22-75)

St.-Estèphe**	Graves Red**
Pauillac***	Graves White***
St.-Julien***	Pomerol*****
Margaux**	St.-Emilion***
Médoc/Haut-Médoc Crus Bourgeois***	Barsac/Sauternes****

Size: After the abundant vintages of 1973 and 1974, 1975 was a moderate-sized crop.

Important information: After three consecutive poor to mediocre years, the Bordelais were ready to praise to the heavens the 1975 vintage.

Maturity status: The slowest-evolving vintage in the last 30 years.

Price: Trade and consumer uneasiness concerning the falling reputation of this vintage, as well as the style of even the top wines (which remain hard, closed, and nearly impenetrable), make this an attractively priced year for those with the knowledge to select the gems, and the patience to wait for them to mature.

Is this the year of the great deception, or the year where some irrefutably classic wines were produced? There are some undeniably great wines in the 1975 vintage, but the overall quality level is distressingly uneven, and the number of failures is too numerous to ignore. I have always been struck by the tremendous difference in the quality of wines in this vintage. To this day the wide swings in quality remain far greater than in any other recent year. For example, how could La Mission-Haut-Brion, Pétrus, l'Evangile, and Lafleur produce such profoundly great wines yet many of their neighbors fail completely? This remains one of the vintage's mysteries. This is a vintage for true Bordeaux connoisseurs who have the patience to wait the wines out. The top examples, which usually come from Pomerol, St.-Julien, and Pauillac (the extraordinary success of La Mission-Haut-Brion and La Tour-Haut-Brion and, to a lesser extent, Haut-Brion, is an exception to the sad level of quality in Graves), are wines that have still not reached their apogees. Could the great 1975s turn out to resemble wines from a vintage such as 1928, which took 30-plus years to reach full maturity? The great successes of this vintage are capable of lasting and lasting because they have the richness and concentration of ripe fruit to balance out their tannins. However, many wines are too dry, too astringent, or too tannic to develop gracefully.

THE BEST WINES

St.-Estèphe: Haut-Marbuzet, Meyney, Montrose
Pauillac: Lafite-Rothschild, Latour, Mouton-Rothschild, Pichon-Longueville Comtesse de Lalande
St.-Julien: Branaire-Ducru, Gloria, Gruaud-Larose, Léoville-Barton, Léoville-Las Cases
Margaux: Giscours, Palmer
Médoc/Haut-Médoc/Moulis/Listrac/Crus Bourgeois: Greysac, Sociando-Mallet, La Tour St.-Bonnet
Graves Red: Haut-Brion, La Mission-Haut-Brion, Pape-Clément, La Tour-Haut-Brion
Pomerol: l'Eglise-Clinet, l'Enclos, l'Evangile, Le Gay, Lafleur, Lafleur-Pétrus, Nénin, Pétrus, Trotanoy, Vieux Château Certan
St.-Emilion: Cheval Blanc, Figeac, Magdelaine, Soutard
Barsac/Sauternes: Climens, Coutet, de Fargues, Raymond-Lafon, Rieussec, d'Yquem

1974—A Quick Study (9-20-74)

St.-Estèphe*	Graves Red**
Pauillac*	Graves White*
St.-Julien*	Pomerol*
Margaux*	St.-Emilion*
Médoc/Haut-Médoc Crus Bourgeois*	Barsac/Sauternes*

Size: An enormous crop was harvested.
Important information: Should you still have stocks of the 1974s, it is best to consume them over the next several years, or donate them.
Maturity status: A handful of the top wines of the vintage are still alive and well, but aging them any further will prove fruitless.
Price: These wines were always inexpensive, and I can never imagine them fetching a decent price unless you find someone in need of this year to celebrate a birthday.

The appellation of choice in 1974 turned out to be Graves. While most 1974s remain hard, tannic, hollow wines lacking ripeness, flesh, and character, a number of the Graves estates did produce surprisingly spicy, interesting wines. Though somewhat compact and attenuated, they are still enjoyable to drink. The two stars are La Mission-Haut-Brion and Domaine de Chevalier, followed by Latour in Pauillac and Trotanoy in Pomerol. Should you have remaining stocks of these wines in your cellar, it would be foolish to push your luck. In spite of their well-preserved status, my instincts suggest drinking them now. The vintage was equally bad in the Barsac/Sauternes region. I have never seen a bottle to taste.

It is debatable as to which was the worst vintage during the decade of the seventies—1972, 1974, or 1977.

1973—A Quick Study (9-20-73)

St.-Estèphe**	Graves Red*
Pauillac*	Graves White**
St.-Julien**	Pomerol**
Margaux*	St.-Emilion*
Médoc/Haut-Médoc Crus Bourgeois*	Barsac/Sauternes*

Size: Enormous; one of the largest crops of the seventies.
Important information: A sadly rain-bloated, swollen crop of grapes in poor to mediocre condition was harvested.
Maturity status: The odds are stacked against finding a 1973 that is still in good condition, at least from a regular-size bottle.
Price: Distressed sale prices, even for those born in this year.

The wines were totally drinkable when released in 1976. By the beginning of the 1980s, they were in complete decline, save Pétrus.

THE BEST WINES

St.-Estèphe: de Pez
Pauillac: Latour
St.-Julien: Ducru-Beaucaillou
Margaux: none
Médoc/Haut-Médoc/Moulis/Listrac/Crus Bourgeois: none
Graves Red: Domaine de Chevalier, La Tour-Haut-Brion
Graves White: none
Pomerol: Pétrus
St.-Emilion: none
Barsac/Sauternes: d'Yquem

1972—A Quick Study (10-7-72)

St.-Estèphe 0	Graves Red*
Pauillac 0	Graves White 0
St.-Julien 0	Pomerol 0
Margaux*	St.-Emilion*
Médoc/Haut-Médoc Crus Bourgeois 0	Barsac/Sauternes 0

Size: A moderate-sized crop was harvested.
Important information: Rivals 1977 as the worst vintage of the decade.
Maturity status: Most wines have long been over the hill.
Price: Extremely low.

There are no longer any wines from 1972 that would be of any interest to consumers.

THE BEST WINES†

St.-Estèphe: none
Pauillac: Latour
St.-Julien: Branaire-Ducru, Léoville Las Cases
Margaux: Giscours, Rausan-Ségla
Médoc/Haut-Médoc/Moulis/Listrac/Crus Bourgeois: none
Graves Red: La Mission-Haut-Brion, La Tour-Haut-Brion
Graves White: none
Pomerol: Trotanoy
St.-Emilion: Cheval Blanc, Figeac
Barsac/Sauternes: Climens

1971—A Quick Study (9-25-71)

St.-Estèphe**	Graves Red***
Pauillac***	Graves White**
St.-Julien***	Pomerol****
Margaux***	St.-Emilion***
Médoc/Haut-Médoc Crus Bourgeois**	Barsac/Sauternes****

Size: Small to moderate crop size.

Important information: A good to very good, stylish vintage, with the strongest efforts emerging from Pomerol and the sweet wines of Barsac/Sauternes.

Maturity status: Every 1971 has been fully mature for nearly a decade, with only the best *cuvées* capable of lasting another decade.

Price: The small crop size kept prices high, but most 1971s, compared with other good vintages of the last 30 years, are slightly undervalued.

Buying 1971s now could prove dangerous unless the wines have been exceptionally well stored. There are a handful of wines that have just reached full maturity—Pétrus, Latour, Trotanoy, La Mission-Haut-Brion. Well-stored examples of these wines will continue to drink well for at least another 5–10 years. Elsewhere, storage is everything. This could be a vintage at which to take a serious look provided one can find reasonably priced, well-preserved bottles. The sweet wines of Barsac and Sauternes were successful and are in full maturity. The best of them have at least 1–2 decades of aging potential and will certainly outlive all of the red wines produced in 1971.

THE BEST WINES

St.-Estèphe: Montrose
Pauillac: Latour, Mouton-Rothschild
St.-Julien: Beychevelle, Gloria, Gruaud-Larose, Talbot
Margaux: Palmer
Médoc/Haut-Médoc/Moulis/Listrac/Crus Bourgeois: none
Graves Red: Haut-Brion, La Mission-Haut-Brion, La Tour-Haut-Brion
Graves White: none
Pomerol: Petit-Village, Pétrus, Trotanoy
St.-Emilion: Cheval Blanc, La Dominique, Magdelaine
Barsac/Sauternes: Climens, Coutet, de Fargues, d'Yquem

† This list is for informational purposes only as I suspect all of the above wines, with the possible exception of Pétrus, are in serious decline unless found in larger-format bottlings that have been perfectly stored.

1970—A Quick Study (9-27-70)

St.-Estèphe***   Graves Red****
Pauillac***   Graves White***
St.-Julien***   Pomerol****
Margaux***   St.-Emilion***
Médoc/Haut-Médoc Crus Bourgeois***   Barsac/Sauternes***

Size: An enormous crop that was a record setter at the time.

Important information: The first modern-day abundant crop that combined high quality with large quantity.

Maturity status: Initially, the 1970s were called precocious and early maturing. Most of the big 1970s have aged very slowly and are now in full maturity, with only a handful of exceptions. The smaller wines, crus bourgeois, and lighter-weight Pomerols and St.-Emilions should have been drunk by 1980.

Price: Expensive, no doubt because this is the most popular vintage between 1961 and 1982.

Between the two great vintages 1961 and 1982, 1970 has proved to be the best year, producing wines that were attractively rich and full of charm and complexity. They have aged more gracefully than many of the austere 1966s and seem fuller, richer, more evenly balanced, and more consistent than the hard, tannic, large-framed but often hollow and tough 1975s. The year 1970 proved to be the first modern-day vintage that combined high production with good quality. Moreover, it was a uniform and consistent vintage throughout Bordeaux, with every appellation able to claim its share of top-quality wines.

The weather conditions during the summer and early fall were perfect. There was no hail, no weeks of drenching downpours, no frost, and no spirit-crushing inundation at harvesttime. It was one of those rare vintages where everything went well, and the Bordelais harvested one of the largest and healthiest crops they had ever seen.

1970 was the first vintage that I tasted out of cask, visiting a number of châteaux with my wife as a tourist on my way to the cheap beaches of Spain and north Africa during summer vacations in 1971 and 1972. Even from their early days I remember the wines exhibiting dark color, an intense richness of fruit, fragrant, ripe perfume, full body, and high tannin. Yet when compared with the finest vintages of the eighties and nineties, 1970 seems to suffer. Undoubtedly, the number of top wines from vintages such as 1982, 1985, 1986, 1988, 1989, 1990, 1994, 1995, and 1996 exceed those produced in 1970. As for the sweet wines, they have had to take a backseat to the 1971s because there was less botrytis. Although impressively big and full, they lack the complexity, delicacy, and finesse of the best 1971s.

The 1970s will no doubt continue to sell at high prices for decades to come, because this is the most consistent, and in some cases outstanding, vintage between 1961 and 1982.

THE BEST WINES

St.-Estèphe: Cos d'Estournel, Haut-Marbuzet, Lafon-Rochet, Montrose, Les Ormes-de-Pez, de Pez

Pauillac: Grand-Puy-Lacoste, Haut-Batailley, Latour, Lynch-Bages, Mouton-Rothschild, Pichon-Longueville Comtesse de Lalande

St.-Julien: Ducru-Beaucaillou, Gloria, Gruaud-Larose, Léoville-Barton, St.-Pierre

Margaux: Giscours, Lascombes, Palmer

Médoc/Haut-Médoc/Moulis/Listrac/Crus Bourgeois: Sociando-Mallet

Graves Red: Domaine de Chevalier, de Fieuzal, Haut-Bailly, La Mission-Haut-Brion, La Tour-Haut-Brion

Graves White: Domaine de Chevalier, Laville-Haut-Brion

Pomerol: La Conseillante, Lafleur, Lafleur-Pétrus, Latour à Pomerol, Pétrus, Trotanoy

St.-Emilion: l'Arrosée, Cheval Blanc, La Dominique, Figeac, Magdelaine
Barsac/Sauternes: d'Yquem

1969—A Quick Study (10-6-69)

St.-Estèphe 0	Graves Red*
Pauillac 0	Graves White 0
St.-Julien 0	Pomerol*
Margaux 0	St.-Emilion 0
Médoc/Haut-Médoc Crus Bourgeois 0	Barsac/Sauternes*

Size: Small.
Important information: My candidate for the most undesirable wines produced in Bordeaux in the last 30 years.
Maturity status: I never tasted a 1969, except for Pétrus, that could have been said to have had any richness or fruit. I have not seen any of these wines except for Pétrus for a number of years, but they must be unpalatable.
Price: Amazingly, the vintage was offered at a relatively high price, but almost all the wines except for a handful of the big names are totally worthless.

In the Barsac and Sauternes region, a few proprietors managed to produce acceptable wines, particularly d'Arche.

1968—A Quick Study (9-20-68)

St.-Estèphe 0	Graves Red*
Pauillac 0	Graves White 0
St.-Julien 0	Pomerol 0
Margaux 0	St.-Emilion 0
Médoc/Haut-Médoc Crus Bourgeois 0	Barsac/Sauternes 0

Size: A small, disastrous crop in terms of both quality and quantity.
Important information: A great year for California Cabernet Sauvignon, but not for Bordeaux.
Maturity status: All of these wines must be passé.
Price: Another worthless vintage.

At one time wines such as Figeac, Gruaud-Larose, Cantemerle, La Mission-Haut-Brion, Haut-Brion, and Latour were palatable. Should anyone run across these wines today, the rule of caveat emptor would seemingly be applicable, as I doubt that any of them would have much left to enjoy.

1967—A Quick Study (9-25-67)

St.-Estèphe**	Graves Red***
Pauillac**	Graves White**
St.-Julien**	Pomerol***
Margaux**	St.-Emilion***
Médoc/Haut-Médoc Crus Bourgeois*	Barsac/Sauternes****

Size: An abundant crop was harvested.
Important information: A Graves, Pomerol, St.-Emilion year that favored the early-harvested Merlot.
Maturity status: Most 1967s were drinkable when released in 1970 and should have been consumed by 1980. Only a handful of wines (Pétrus and Latour, for example), where well stored, will keep for another few years but are unlikely to improve.
Price: Moderate.

This is a vintage that clearly favored Pomerol and, to a lesser extent, Graves. Holding on to these wines any longer seems foolish, but I have no doubt that some of the biggest wines, such as Latour, Pétrus, Trotanoy, and perhaps even Palmer, will last for another 5–10 years. Should one find any of the top wines listed below in a large-format bottle (magnums, double magnums, and so forth) at a reasonable price, my advice would be to take the gamble. As unexciting as most red wines turned out in 1967, the sweet wines of Barsac and Sauternes were rich and honeyed, with gobs of botrytis present. However, readers must remember that only a handful of estates were truly up to the challenge of making great wines during this very depressed period for the wine production of Barsac/Sauternes.

THE BEST WINES

St.-Estèphe: Calon-Ségur, Montrose
Pauillac: Latour
St.-Julien: none
Margaux: Giscours, La Lagune (southern Médoc), Palmer
Médoc/Haut-Médoc/Moulis/Listrac/Crus Bourgeois: none
Graves Red: Haut-Brion, La Mission-Haut-Brion
Graves White: none
Pomerol: Pétrus, Trotanoy, La Violette
St.-Emilion: Cheval Blanc, Magdelaine, Pavie
Barsac/Sauternes: Suduiraut, d'Yquem

1966—A Quick Study (9-26-66)

St.-Estèphe***	Graves Red****
Pauillac***	Graves White***
St.-Julien***	Pomerol***
Margaux***	St.-Emilion**
Médoc/Haut-Médoc Crus Bourgeois**	Barsac/Sauternes**

Size: An abundant crop was harvested.
Important information: The most overrated "top" vintage of the last 37 years.
Maturity status: The best wines are in their prime, but most wines are losing their fruit before their tannins.
Price: Expensive and overpriced.

Conceived in somewhat the same spirit as 1975 (overhyped after several unexciting years, particularly in the Médoc), 1966 never developed as well as many of its proponents would have liked. The wines, now 37 years of age, for the most part have remained austere, lean, unyielding, and tannic, losing their fruit before their tannin melts away. Some notable exceptions do exist. Who could deny the exceptional wine made at Latour (the wine of the vintage) or the great Palmer? The sweet wines of Barsac and Sauternes are also mediocre. Favorable conditions for the development of *Botrytis cinerea* never occurred. I would be skeptical about buying most 1966s except for one of the unqualified successes of the vintage.

THE BEST WINES

St.-Estèphe: none
Pauillac: Grand-Puy-Lacoste, Latour, Mouton-Rothschild, Pichon-Longueville Comtesse de Lalande
St.-Julien: Branaire-Ducru, Ducru-Beaucaillou, Gruaud-Larose, Léoville-Las Cases
Margaux: Lascombes, Palmer

Médoc/Haut-Médoc/Moulis/Listrac/Crus Bourgeois: none
Graves Red: Haut-Brion, La Mission-Haut-Brion, Pape-Clément
Pomerol: Lafleur, Trotanoy
St.-Emilion: Canon
Barsac/Sauternes: none

1965—A Quick Study (10-2-65)

St.-Estèphe 0	Graves Red 0
Pauillac 0	Graves White 0
St.-Julien 0	Pomerol 0
Margaux 0	St.-Emilion 0
Médoc/Haut-Médoc Crus Bourgeois 0	Barsac/Sauternes 0

Size: A tiny vintage.
Important information: The quintessential vintage of rot and rain.
Maturity status: Tasted terrible from the start and must be totally reprehensible today.
Price: Worthless.

1964—A Quick Study (9-22-64)

St.-Estèphe***	Graves Red*****
Pauillac*	Graves White***
St.-Julien*	Pomerol*****
Margaux**	St.-Emilion****
Médoc/Haut-Médoc Crus Bourgeois*	Barsac/Sauternes*

Size: A large crop was harvested.
Important information: The classic example of a vintage where the early-picked Merlot and Cabernet Franc produced great wine, and the late-harvested Cabernet Sauvignon, particularly in the Médoc, was inundated, resulting in numerous big-name failures in the Médoc.
Maturity status: The Médocs are past their prime, but the larger-scaled wines of Graves, Pomerol, and St.-Emilion can last another 5–10 years.
Price: Smart Bordeaux enthusiasts have always recognized the greatness of this vintage in Graves, Pomerol, and St.-Emilion, and consequently prices have remained high. Nevertheless, compared to glamour years such as 1959 and 1961, the top right bank and Graves 1964s are not only underrated but in some cases underpriced as well.

Pity the buyer who purchased Lafite-Rothschild, Mouton-Rothschild, Lynch-Bages, Calon-Ségur, or Château Margaux! Yet not everyone made disappointing wine. Montrose in St.-Estèphe and Latour in Pauillac made the two greatest wines of the Médoc.

The top wines from Graves, St.-Emilion, and Pomerol are exceptionally rich, full-bodied, opulent, and concentrated wines, with high alcohol, an opaque color, super length, and unbridled power. Amazingly, they are far richer, more interesting, and more complete wines than the 1966s and, in many cases, compete with the finest wines of the 1961 vintage. Because of low acidity, all of the wines reached full maturity by the mid-eighties. The best examples exhibit no sign of decline and can easily last for another 5–10 or more years.

THE BEST WINES

St.-Estèphe: Montrose
Pauillac: Latour
St.-Julien: Gruaud-Larose
Margaux: none

Médoc/Haut-Médoc/Moulis/Listrac/Crus Bourgeois: none
Graves Red: Domaine de Chevalier, Haut-Bailly, Haut-Brion, La Mission-Haut-Brion
Pomerol: La Conseillante, Lafleur, Lafleur-Pétrus, Pétrus, Trotanoy, Vieux Château Certan
St.-Emilion: l'Arrosée, Cheval Blanc, Figeac, Soutard
Barsac/Sauternes: none

1963—A Quick Study (10-7-63)

St.-Estèphe 0	Graves Red 0
Pauillac 0	Graves White 0
St.-Julien 0	Pomerol 0
Margaux 0	St.-Emilion 0
Médoc/Haut-Médoc Crus Bourgeois 0	Barsac/Sauternes 0

Size: A small- to moderate-size crop was harvested.
Important information: A dreadfully poor year that rivals 1965 for the feebleness of its wines.
Maturity status: The wines must now be awful.
Price: Worthless.

1962—A Quick Study (10-1-62)

St.-Estèphe****	Graves Red***
Pauillac****	Graves White****
St.-Julien****	Pomerol***
Margaux***	St.-Emilion***
Médoc/Haut-Médoc Crus Bourgeois***	Barsac/Sauternes****

Size: An abundant crop size—in fact, one of the largest of the sixties.
Important information: A terribly underrated vintage that had the misfortune of following one of the greatest vintages of the century.
Maturity status: The Bordeaux old-timers claim the 1962s drank beautifully by the late 1960s and continued to fill out and display considerable character, fruit, and charm in the seventies. The top 1962s are still lovely, rich, round wines full of finesse and elegance.
Price: Undervalued, particularly when one considers the prices of its predecessor, 1961, and the overpriced 1966s.

Coming after the great vintage of 1961, this vintage appears to be the most undervalued year for Bordeaux in the post–World War II era. Elegant, supple, very fruity, round, and charming wines that were neither too tannic nor too massive were produced in virtually every appellation. Not only was the vintage very successful in most appellations, but it was a top year for the dry white wines of Graves and the sweet nectars from Barsac/Sauternes.

THE BEST WINES

St.-Estèphe: Cos d'Estournel, Montrose
Pauillac: Batailley, Lafite-Rothschild, Latour, Lynch-Bages, Mouton-Rothschild,
    Pichon-Longueville Comtesse de Lalande
St.-Julien: Ducru-Beaucaillou, Gruaud-Larose
Margaux: Margaux, Palmer
Médoc/Haut-Médoc/Moulis/Listrac/Crus Bourgeois: none
Graves Red: Haut-Brion, Pape-Clément
Graves White: Domaine de Chevalier, Laville-Haut-Brion

Pomerol: Lafleur, Pétrus, Trotanoy, La Violette
St.-Emilion: Magdelaine
Barsac/Sauternes: d'Yquem

1961—A Quick Study (9-22-61)

St.-Estèphe*****	Graves Red*****
Pauillac*****	Graves White***
St.-Julien*****	Pomerol*****
Margaux*****	St.-Emilion***
Médoc/Haut-Médoc Crus Bourgeois***	Barsac/Sauternes**

Size: An exceptionally tiny crop was produced; in fact, this is the last vintage where a minuscule crop resulted in high quality.

Important information: One of the legendary vintages of the century.

Maturity status: The wines, drinkable young, have, with only a handful of exceptions, reached maturity and were all at their apogee by 1990. Most of the prestige examples will keep for at least another 5–10 years, but many 1961s have begun to fade.

Price: The tiny quantities plus exceptional quality have made the 1961s the most dearly priced mature vintage of great Bordeaux in the marketplace. Moreover, prices will only increase, given the microscopic quantities that remain—an auctioneer's dream vintage. But buyers beware—many 1961s have been poorly stored or traded frequently. Moreover, there are some fraudulent 1961s that show up in the marketplace.

The year 1961 is one of ten great vintages produced in the post–World War II era. The wines have always been prized for their sensational concentration and magnificent penetrating bouquets of superripe fruit and rich, deep, sumptuous flavors. Delicious when young, these wines, which have all reached full maturity except for a handful of the most intensely concentrated examples, are marvelous to drink. However, I see no problem in holding the best-stored bottles for at least another 10 years.

THE BEST WINES

St.-Estèphe: Cos d'Estournel, Haut-Marbuzet, Montrose
Pauillac: Grand-Puy-Lacoste, Latour, Lynch-Bages, Mouton-Rothschild, Pichon-
    Longueville Comtesse de Lalande, Pontet-Canet
St.-Julien: Beychevelle, Ducru-Beaucaillou, Gruaud-Larose, Léoville-Barton
Margaux: Malescot St.-Exupéry, Margaux, Palmer
Médoc/Haut-Médoc/Moulis/Listrac/Crus Bourgeois: none
Graves Red: Haut-Bailly, Haut-Brion, La Mission-Haut-Brion, La Tour-Haut-Brion,
    Pape-Clément
Graves White: Domaine de Chevalier, Laville-Haut-Brion
Pomerol: l'Eglise-Clinet, l'Evangile, Lafleur, Latour à Pomerol, Pétrus, Trotanoy
St.-Emilion: l'Arrosée, Canon, Cheval Blanc, Figeac, Magdelaine
Barsac/Sauternes: none

1960—A Quick Study (9-9-60)

St.-Estèphe**	Graves Red**
Pauillac**	Graves White*
St.-Julien**	Pomerol*
Margaux*	St.-Emilion*
Médoc/Haut-Médoc Crus Bourgeois 0	Barsac/Sauternes*

Size: A copious crop was harvested.

Important information: The two rainy months of August and September were 1960's undoing.

Maturity status: Most 1960s should have been consumed within their first 10–15 years of life.

Price: Low.

I would guess that even Latour wine, which was the most concentrated wine of the vintage according to the Bordeaux cognoscenti, is now in decline.

1959—A Quick Study (9-20-59)

St.-Estèphe*****   Graves Red*****
Pauillac*****   Graves White****
St.-Julien****   Pomerol***
Margaux****   St.-Emilion**
Médoc/Haut-Médoc Crus Bourgeois***   Barsac/Sauternes*****

Size: Average.

Important information: The first of the modern-day years to be designated "vintage of the century."

Maturity status: The wines, maligned in their early years for having low acidity and lacking backbone (reminiscent of the 1982s), have aged more slowly than the more highly touted 1961s. In fact, comparisons between the top wines of the two vintages often reveal the 1959s to be less evolved, with deeper color and more richness and aging potential.

Price: Never inexpensive, the 1959s have become increasingly more expensive as serious connoisseurs have begun to realize that this vintage not only rivals 1961 but in specific cases surpasses it.

This is an irrefutably great vintage. The wines, which are especially strong in the northern Médoc and Graves and less so on the right bank (Pomerol and St.-Emilion were still recovering from the devastating deep freeze of 1956), are among the most massive and rich wines ever made in Bordeaux. In fact, the two modern-day vintages that are frequently compared to 1959 are the 1982 and 1989. Those comparisons may have merit.

The 1959s have evolved at a glacial pace and are often in better condition (especially the first growths Lafite-Rothschild and Mouton-Rothschild) than their 1961 counterparts, which are even more highly touted. The wines do display the effects of having been made in a classic, hot, dry year, with just enough rain to keep the vineyards from being stressed. They are full-bodied, extremely alcoholic and opulent, with high degrees of tannin and extract. Their colors have remained impressively opaque and dark and display less brown and orange than the 1961s. If there is one nagging doubt about many of the 1959s, it is whether they will ever develop the sensational perfume and fragrance that is so much a part of the greatest Bordeaux vintages. Perhaps the great heat during the summer of 1959 did compromise this aspect of the wines, but it is still too soon to know.

THE BEST WINES

St.-Estèphe: Cos d'Estournel, Montrose, Les Ormes-de-Pez

Pauillac: Lafite-Rothschild, Latour, Lynch-Bages, Mouton-Rothschild, Pichon-Longueville Baron

St.-Julien: Ducru-Beaucaillou, Langoa-Barton, Léoville-Barton, Léoville-Las Cases

Margaux: Lascombes, Malescot St.-Exupéry, Margaux, Palmer

Graves Red: Haut-Brion, La Mission-Haut-Brion, Pape-Clément, La Tour-Haut-Brion

Pomerol: l'Evangile, Lafleur, Latour à Pomerol, Pétrus, Trotanoy, Vieux Château Certan

St.-Emilion: Cheval Blanc, Figeac

Barsac/Sauternes: Climens, Suduiraut, d'Yquem

1958—A Quick Study (10-7-58)

St.-Estèphe*	Graves Red***
Pauillac*	Graves White**
St.-Julien*	Pomerol*
Margaux*	St.-Emilion**
Médoc/Haut-Médoc Crus Bourgeois*	Barsac/Sauternes*

Size: A small crop was harvested.

Important information: An unfairly maligned vintage.

Maturity status: The wines are now fading badly. The best examples almost always emerge from the Graves appellation.

Price: Inexpensive.

I have fewer than two dozen tasting notes of 1958s, but several that do stand out are all from the Graves appellation. I most recently had the 1958 Haut-Brion in January 1996. It was still a relatively tasty, round, soft, fleshy, tobacco- and mineral-scented and -flavored wine, but one could see that it would have been much better if it had been consumed 10–15 years earlier. Even richer was the 1958 La Mission-Haut-Brion, which should still be excellent if well-preserved bottles can be found.

1957—A Quick Study (10-4-57)

St.-Estèphe**	Graves Red***
Pauillac***	Graves White**
St.-Julien**	Pomerol*
Margaux*	St.-Emilion*
Médoc/Haut-Médoc Crus Bourgeois*	Barsac/Sauternes***

Size: A small crop.

Important information: A brutally cold, wet summer.

Maturity status: Because the summer was so cool, the red wines were extremely high in acidity, which has helped them stand the test of time. Where well-kept examples of 1957 can be found, this could be a vintage to purchase, provided the price is right.

Price: The wines should be realistically and inexpensively priced given the fact that 1957 does not enjoy a good reputation.

For a vintage that has never been received very favorably, I have been surprised by how many respectable and enjoyable wines I have tasted, particularly from Pauillac and Graves. In fact, I would serve my most finicky friends the 1957 La Mission-Haut-Brion or 1957 Haut-Brion. And I would certainly be pleased to drink the 1957 Lafite-Rothschild. I had two excellent bottles of Lafite in the early 1990s but have not seen the wine since.

1956—A Quick Study (10-14-56)

St.-Estèphe 0	Graves Red 0
Pauillac 0	Graves White 0
St.-Julien 0	Pomerol 0
Margaux 0	St.-Emilion 0
Médoc/Haut-Médoc Crus Bourgeois 0	Barsac/Sauternes 0

Size: Minuscule quantities of pathetically weak wine were produced.

Important information: The coldest winter in Bordeaux since 1709 did unprecedented damage to the vineyards, particularly those in Pomerol and St.-Emilion.

Maturity status: I have not seen a 1956 in more than 18 years and have a total of only five notes on wines from this vintage.

Price: A worthless vintage produced worthless wines.

1955—A Quick Study (9-21-55)

St.-Estèphe****   Graves Red****
Pauillac****   Graves White***
St.-Julien****   Pomerol***
Margaux***   St.-Emilion****
Médoc/Haut-Médoc Crus Bourgeois**   Barsac/Sauternes****

Size: A large, healthy crop was harvested.

Important information: For a vintage that is now more than 45 years old, this tends to be an underrated, undervalued year, although it is not comparable to 1953 or 1959. Yet the wines have generally held up and are firmer and more solidly made than the once glorious 1953s.

Maturity status: After a long period of sleep, the top wines appear to finally be fully mature. They exhibit no signs of decline.

Price: Undervalued, except for La Mission-Haut-Brion, the wine of the vintage, if not the decade.

For the most part, the 1955s have always come across as relatively stern, slightly tough-textured, yet impressively deep, full wines with fine color and excellent aging potential. What they lack, as a general rule, is fat, charm, and opulence.

THE BEST WINES

St.-Estèphe: Calon-Ségur, Cos d'Estournel, Montrose, Les Ormes-de-Pez
Pauillac: Latour, Lynch-Bages, Mouton-Rothschild
St.-Julien: Léoville-Las Cases, Talbot
Margaux: Palmer
Graves Red: Haut-Brion, La Mission-Haut-Brion, Pape-Clément
Pomerol: l'Evangile, Lafleur, Latour à Pomerol, Pétrus, Vieux Château Certan
St.-Emilion: Cheval Blanc, La Dominique, Soutard
Barsac/Sauternes: d'Yquem

1954—A Quick Study (10-10-54)

St.-Estèphe 0   Graves Red*
Pauillac*   Graves White 0
St.-Julien*   Pomerol 0
Margaux 0   St.-Emilion 0
Médoc/Haut-Médoc Crus Bourgeois 0   Barsac/Sauternes 0

Size: A small crop was harvested.

Important information: A terrible late-harvest vintage conducted under appalling weather conditions.

Maturity status: It is hard to believe anything from this vintage would still be worth drinking.

Price: The wines have no value.

1953—A Quick Study (9-28-53)

St.-Estèphe*****   Graves Red****
Pauillac*****   Graves White***
St.-Julien*****   Pomerol***
Margaux****   St.-Emilion***
Médoc/Haut-Médoc Crus Bourgeois***   Barsac/Sauternes***

Size: An average-size crop was harvested.

Important information: One of the most seductive and hedonistic Bordeaux vintages ever produced.

Maturity status: According to Bordeaux old-timers, the wines were absolutely delicious during the 1950s, even more glorious in the 1960s, and sublime during the 1970s. Charm, roundness, fragrance, and a velvety texture were the hallmarks of this vintage, which now must be approached with some degree of caution unless the wines have been impeccably stored and/or are available in larger-format bottlings.

Price: No vintage with such appeal will ever sell at a reasonable price. Consequently, the 1953s remain luxury-priced wines.

1953 must be the only Bordeaux vintage where it is impossible to find a dissenting voice about the quality of the wines. Bordeaux old-timers and some of our senior wine commentators (particularly Edmund Penning-Rowsell and Michael Broadbent) talk of 1953 with adulation. Apparently the vintage never went through an unflattering stage. In Bordeaux, when a château pulls out a 1953 it is usually in mint condition, and these are some of the most beautifully sumptuous, rich, charming clarets anyone could ever desire. A more modern-day reference point for 1953 may be the very best 1985s, perhaps even some of the lighter 1982s, although my instincts tell me the 1982s are more alcoholic, richer, fuller, heavier wines. If you have the discretionary income necessary to buy this highly prized vintage, prudence should dictate that the wines be from cold cellars and/or in larger-format bottles.

THE BEST WINES

St.-Estèphe: Calon-Ségur, Cos d'Estournel, Montrose

Pauillac: Grand-Puy-Lacoste, Lafite-Rothschild, Lynch-Bages, Mouton-Rothschild

St.-Julien: Beychevelle, Ducru-Beaucaillou, Gruaud-Larose, Langoa-Barton, Léoville-Barton, Léoville-Las Cases, Talbot

Margaux: Cantemerle (southern Médoc), Margaux, Palmer

Graves Red: Haut-Brion, La Mission-Haut-Brion

Pomerol: La Conseillante

St.-Emilion: Cheval Blanc, Figeac, Magdelaine, Pavie

Barsac/Sauternes: Climens, d'Yquem

1952—A Quick Study (9-17-52)

St.-Estèphe**	Graves Red***
Pauillac***	Graves White***
St.-Julien***	Pomerol****
Margaux**	St.-Emilion***
Médoc/Haut-Médoc Crus Bourgeois**	Barsac/Sauternes**

Size: A small crop was harvested.

Important information: The 1952 vintage was at its best in Pomerol, which largely completed its harvest prior to the rains.

Maturity status: Most wines have always tasted hard and too astringent, lacking fat, charm, and ripeness. The best bottles could provide surprises.

Price: Expensive, but well-chosen Pomerols may represent relative values.

THE BEST WINES

St.-Estèphe: Calon-Ségur, Montrose

Pauillac: Latour, Lynch-Bages

St.-Julien: none
Margaux: Château Margaux, Palmer
Graves Red: Haut-Brion, La Mission-Haut-Brion, Pape-Clément
Pomerol: Lafleur, Lafleur-Pétrus, Pétrus, Trotanoy
St.-Emilion: Cheval Blanc, Magdelaine
Barsac/Sauternes: none

1951—A Quick Study (10-9-51)

St.-Estèphe 0	Graves Red 0
Pauillac 0	Graves White 0
St.-Julien 0	Pomerol 0
Margaux 0	St.-Emilion 0
Médoc/Haut-Médoc Crus Bourgeois 0	Barsac/Sauternes 0

Size: A tiny crop was harvested.
Important information: Even today 1951 is considered one of the all-time worst vintages for dry white, dry red, and sweet wines from Bordeaux.
Maturity status: Undrinkable young, undrinkable old.
Price: A worthless vintage.

1950—A Quick Study (9-17-50)

St.-Estèphe**	Graves Red***
Pauillac***	Graves White***
St.-Julien***	Pomerol*****
Margaux***	St.-Emilion****
Médoc/Haut-Médoc Crus Bourgeois*	Barsac/Sauternes****

Size: An abundant crop was harvested.
Important information: Many of the Pomerols are great, yet they have been totally ignored by the chroniclers of the Bordeaux region.
Maturity status: Most Médocs and Graves are now in decline. The top heavyweight Pomerols can be splendid, with years of life still left.
Price: The quality of the Pomerols is no longer a secret.

The two best appellations were St.-Emilion, which produced a number of rich, full, intense wines that aged quickly, and Pomerol, which had its fourth superb vintage in succession—unprecedented in the history of that area. The wines are unbelievably rich, unctuous, and concentrated and in many cases are capable of rivaling the greatest Pomerols of such more highly renowned vintages as 1947 and 1949. The other appellation that prospered in 1950 was Barsac/Sauternes. Fanciers of these wines still claim 1950 is one of the greatest of the post–World War II vintages for sweet wines.

THE BEST WINES

St.-Estèphe: none
Pauillac: Latour
St.-Julien: none
Margaux: Margaux
Médoc/Haut-Médoc/Moulis/Listrac/Crus Bourgeois: none
Graves Red: Haut-Brion, La Mission-Haut-Brion
Pomerol: l'Eglise-Clinet, l'Evangile, Lafleur, Lafleur-Pétrus, Le Gay, Latour à Pomerol, Pétrus, Vieux Château Certan

St.-Emilion: Cheval Blanc, Figeac, Soutard
Barsac/Sauternes: Climens, Coutet, Suduiraut, d'Yquem

1949—A Quick Study (9-27-49)

St.-Estèphe*****	Graves Red*****
Pauillac*****	Graves White***
St.-Julien*****	Pomerol****
Margaux****	St.-Emilion****
Médoc/Haut-Médoc Crus Bourgeois***	Barsac/Sauternes*****

Size: A small crop was harvested.
Important information: The driest and sunniest vintage since 1893 and rivaled (weather-wise, not qualitatively) in more recent years only by 1990.
Maturity status: The finest wines are still in full blossom, displaying remarkable richness and concentration, but their provenance and history of storage are critical factors when contemplating a purchase.
Price: Frightfully expensive.

Among the four extraordinary vintages of the late forties—1945, 1947, 1948, and 1949—this has always been my favorite. The wines, slightly less massive and alcoholic than the 1947s, also appear to possess greater balance, harmony, and fruit than the 1945s and more complexity than the 1948s. In short, the top wines are magnificent. 1949 is certainly one of the most exceptional vintages of this century. Only the right bank wines (except for Cheval Blanc) appear inferior to the quality of their 1947s. In the Médoc and Graves it is a terrific vintage, with nearly everyone making wines of astounding ripeness, richness, opulence, power, and length. Even the sweet wines of Barsac and Sauternes were exciting. Buying 1949s today will cost an arm and a leg as these are among the most expensive and sought-after wines of the 20th century.

THE BEST WINES

St.-Estèphe: Calon-Ségur, Cos d'Estournel, Montrose
Pauillac: Grand-Puy-Lacoste, Latour, Mouton-Rothschild
St.-Julien: Gruaud-Larose, Léoville-Barton, Talbot
Margaux: Palmer
Graves Red: Haut-Brion, La Mission-Haut-Brion, Pape-Clément
Pomerol: La Conseillante, l'Eglise-Clinet, l'Evangile, Lafleur, Latour à Pomerol, Pétrus, Trotanoy, Vieux Château Certan
St.-Emilion: Cheval Blanc
Barsac/Sauterness: Climens, Coutet, d'Yquem

1948—A Quick Study (9-22-48)

St.-Estèphe***	Graves Red****
Pauillac****	Graves White***
St.-Julien****	Pomerol***
Margaux****	St.-Emilion***
Médoc/Haut-Médoc Crus Bourgeois***	Barsac/Sauterness**

Size: An average to below-average crop size was harvested.
Important information: A largely ignored but good to excellent vintage overshadowed by both its predecessor and successor.

Maturity status: The hard and backward characteristics of these wines have served them well during their evolution. Most of the larger, more concentrated 1948s are still attractive wines. *Price:* Undervalued given their age and quality.

Despite the high quality of the wines, they never caught on with claret enthusiasts. And who can fault the wine buyers? The 1947s were more flashy, opulent, alcoholic, and full-bodied, and the 1949s more precocious and rich than the harder, tougher, more tannic and unforthcoming 1948s. This is a vintage that in many cases has matured more gracefully than the massive 1947s. The top wines tend still to be in excellent condition. Prices remain reasonable, if only in comparison to what one has to pay for 1947 and 1949.

THE BEST WINES

St.-Estèphe: Cos d'Estournel
Pauillac: Grand-Puy-Lacoste, Latour, Lynch-Bages, Mouton-Rothschild
St.-Julien: Langoa-Barton, Léoville-Barton (the wine of the Médoc)
Margaux: Cantemerle (southern Médoc), Château Margaux, Palmer
Graves Red: La Mission-Haut-Brion, Pape-Clément
Pomerol: l'Eglise-Clinet, Lafleur, Latour à Pomerol, Petit-Village, Pétrus, Vieux Château
  Certan
St.-Emilion: Cheval Blanc
Barsac/Sauternes: none

1947—A Quick Study (9-15-47)

St.-Estèphe***	Graves Red****
Pauillac***	Graves White***
St.-Julien***	Pomerol*****
Margaux**	St.-Emilion*****
Médoc/Haut-Médoc Crus Bourgeois*	Barsac/Sauternes***

Size: An abundant crop was harvested.
Important information: A year of extraordinary extremes in quality, with some of the most portlike, concentrated wines ever produced in Bordeaux. This is also a vintage of unexpected failures (such as the Lafite-Rothschild).
Maturity status: Except for the most concentrated and powerful Pomerols and St.-Emilions, this is a vintage that requires immediate consumption because many wines have gone over the top and are now exhibiting excessive volatile acidity and dried-out fruit.
Price: Preposterously high because this was another "vintage of the century."

This quintessentially hot-year vintage produced many wines that are among the most enormously concentrated, portlike, intense wines I have ever tasted. Most of the real heavyweights in this vintage have emerged from Pomerol and St.-Emilion.

The top wines are something to behold if only because of their excessively rich, sweet style, which comes closest in modern-day terms to 1982. Yet I know of no 1982 that has the level of extract and intensity of the greatest 1947s.

THE BEST WINES

St.-Estèphe: Calon-Ségur
Pauillac: Grand-Puy-Lacoste, Mouton-Rothschild
St.-Julien: Ducru-Beaucaillou, Léoville Las Cases
Margaux: Château Margaux

Graves Red: Haut-Brion, La Mission-Haut-Brion, La Tour-Haut-Brion
Pomerol: Clinet, La Conseillante, l'Eglise-Clinet, l'Enclos, l'Evangile, Lafleur, Lafleur-
   Pétrus, Latour à Pomerol, Nenin, Pétrus, Rouget, Vieux Château Certan
St.-Emilion: Canon, Cheval Blanc, Figeac, La Gaffelière-Naudes
Barsac/Sauternes: Climens, Suduiraut

1946—A Quick Study (9-30-46)

St.-Estèphe**	Graves Red*
Pauillac**	Graves White 0
St.-Julien**	Pomerol 0
Margaux*	St.-Emilion 0
Médoc/Haut-Médoc Crus Bourgeois 0	Barsac/Sauternes 0

Size: A small crop was harvested.
Important information: The only year in the post–World War II era where the Bordeaux vine-
yards were invaded by locusts.
Maturity status: The wines must certainly be over the hill.
Price: Except for the rare bottle of Mouton-Rothschild needed by billionaires to complete
their collections, most of these wines have little value.

1945—A Quick Study (9-13-45)

St.-Estèphe****	Graves Red*****
Pauillac*****	Graves White*****
St.-Julien*****	Pomerol*****
Margaux****	St.-Emilion*****
Médoc/Haut-Médoc Crus Bourgeois****	Barsac/Sauternes*****

Size: A tiny crop was harvested.
Important information: The most acclaimed vintage of the century.
Maturity status: Certain wines from this vintage (only those that have been stored impecca-
bly) are still not fully mature.
Price: The most expensive clarets of the century.

   No vintage in the post–World War II era enjoys the reputation of the 1945. The great wines,
and they are numerous, could well last for another 20–30 years, making a mockery of most of
the more recent great vintages that must be consumed within 25–30 years of the vintage.

THE BEST WINES

St.-Estèphe: Calon-Ségur, Montrose, Les Ormes-de-Pez
Pauillac: Latour, Mouton-Rothschild, Pichon-Longueville Comtesse de Lalande, Pontet-
   Canet
St.-Julien: Gruaud-Larose, Léoville-Barton, Talbot
Margaux: Château Margaux, Palmer
Graves Red: Haut-Brion, La Mission-Haut-Brion, La Tour-Haut-Brion
Graves White: Laville-Haut-Brion
Pomerol: l'Eglise-Clinet, Gazin, Lafleur, Lafleur-Pétrus, Latour à Pomerol, Pétrus, Rouget,
   Trotanoy, Vieux Château Certan
St.-Emilion: Canon, Cheval Blanc, Figeac, La Gaffelière-Naudes, Larcis-Ducasse,
   Magdelaine
Barsac/Sauternes: Suduiraut, d'Yquem

RATING BORDEAUX'S BEST PRODUCERS OF DRY RED WINES

Where a producer has been assigned a range of stars (***/****), the lower rating has been used for placement in this hierarchy.

* * * * * *(OUTSTANDING)*

Angélus (St.-Emilion)
Ausone (St.-Emilion)
Canon-La-Gaffelière (St.-Emilion)
Cheval Blanc (St.-Emilion)
Clos l'Eglise (Pomerol) (since 1998)
La Conseillante (Pomerol)
Ducru-Beaucaillou (St.-Julien)
l'Eglise-Clinet (Pomerol)
l'Evangile (Pomerol)
La Gomerie (St.-Emilion)
Grand-Puy-Lacoste (Pauillac)
Gruaud-Larose (St.-Julien)
Haut-Brion (Graves)
Lafite-Rothschild (Pauillac)
Lafleur (Pomerol)
Lafleur-Pétrus (Pomerol) (since 1995)
Latour (Pauillac)
Léoville-Barton (St.-Julien)
Léoville-Las Cases (St.-Julien)
Léoville-Poyferré (St.-Julien)
Lynch-Bages (Pauillac)

Magrez-Fombrauge (St.-Emilion)
Château Margaux (Margaux)
La Mission-Haut-Brion (Graves)
Monbousquet (St.-Emilion)
La Mondotte (St.-Emilion)
Montrose (St.-Estèphe)
Mouton-Rothschild (Pauillac)
Palmer (Margaux)
Pape-Clément (Graves)
Pavie (St.-Emilion)
Pavie Macquin (St.-Emilion)
Péby-Faugères (St.-Emilion)
Pétrus (Pomerol)
Pichon-Longueville Baron (Pauillac)
Pichon-Longueville-Comtesse de Lalande
   (Pauillac)
Le Pin (Pomerol)
Tertre-Rôteboeuf (St.-Emilion)
Troplong-Mondot (St.-Emilion)
Trotanoy (Pomerol)
Valandraud (St.-Emilion)

* * * * *(EXCELLENT)*

l'Arrosée (St.-Emilion)
Barde-Haut (St.-Emilion)
Beau Séjour-Bécot (St.-Emilion)
Beauséjour-Duffau (St.-Emilion)
Belle Vue (St.-Emilion)
Bon Pasteur (Pomerol)
Branon (Pessac-Léognan)
Calon-Ségur (St.-Estèphe)
Les Carmes-Haut-Brion (Graves)
Certan de May (Pomerol)
De Chambrun (Lalande-de-Pomerol)
Domaine de Chevalier (Graves)
Clerc-Milon (Pauillac)
Clinet (Pomerol)
Clos Dubreuil (St.-Emilion)
Clos de l'Oratoire (St.-Emilion)
Clos St.-Martin (St.-Emilion)
La Clusière (St.-Emilion)
Cos d'Estournel (St.-Estèphe)
Côte de Baleau (St.-Emilion)
La Couspaude (St.-Emilion)
La Croix de Labrie (St.-Emilion)

La Dominique (St.-Emilion)
Duhart-Milon-Rothschild (Pauillac)
Faugères (St.-Emilion)
Ferrand-Lartique (St.-Emilion)
Figeac (St.-Emilion)
La Fleur de Gay (Pomerol)
La Fleur de Jaugue (St.-Emilion)
Les Forts de Latour (Pauillac)
Gazin (Pomerol)
Gracia (St.-Emilion)
Grand Mayne (St.-Emilion)
Grandes-Murailles (St.-Emilion)
Haut-Bailly (Graves)
Haut-Bergey (Graves) (since 1998)
Haut-Marbuzet (St.-Estèphe)
Hosanna (Pomerol)
d'Issan (Margaux)
Lafon-Rochet (St.-Estèphe)
Lagrange (St.-Julien)
Larmande (St.-Emilion)
Latour à Pomerol (Pomerol)
La Louvière (Graves)

Malescot-St.-Exupéry (Margaux)
Marojallia (Margaux)
Le Moulin (Pomerol)
Moulin St.-Georges (St.-Emilion)
Nénin (Pomerol) (since 1998)
Pavie Decesse (St.-Emilion)
Le Plus de La Fleur Bouard (Lalande-de-
    Pomerol)
Pontet-Canet (Pauillac)

Quinault l'Enclos (St.-Emilion)
Rausan-Ségla (Margaux)
Rol Valentin (St.-Emilion)
St.-Pierre (St.-Julien)
Smith-Haut-Lafitte (Graves)
Sociando-Mallet (Haut-Médoc)
Talbot (St.-Julien)
Vieux Château Certan (Pomerol)

* * * *(GOOD)*

d'Angludet (Margaux)
d'Armailhac (Pauillac)
Bahans-Haut-Brion (Graves)
Balestard-La-Tonnelle (St.-Emilion)
Batailley (Pauillac)
Beauregard (Pomerol)
Bel-Air (Lalande-de-Pomerol)
Bellegrave (Pomerol)
Belles-Graves (Lalande-de-Pomerol)
Bertineau St.-Vincent (Lalande-de-
    Pomerol)
Beychevelle (St.-Julien)
Bonalgue (Pomerol)
Le Boscq (Médoc)
Bourgneuf (Pomerol)
Branaire-Ducru (St.-Julien)
Brane-Cantenac (Margaux) (since 1998)
Cadet-Piola (St.-Emilion)
Canon (Canon-Fronsac)
Canon (St.-Emilion)
Canon de Brem (Canon-Fronsac)
Canon-Moueix (Canon-Fronsac)
Cantemerle (Macau)
Cantenac-Brown (Margaux)
Cap de Mourlin (St.-Emilion)
Carbonnieux (Graves)
de Carles (Fronsac)
Carruades de Lafite (Pauillac)
Cassagne-Haut-Canon-La Truffière (Canon-
    Fronsac)
Certan-Giraud (Pomerol)
Chantegrive (Graves)
La Chapelle de la Mission (Graves)
Chasse-Spleen (Moulis)***/****
Chauvin (St.-Emilion)
Citran (Haut-Médoc)
Clos du Clocher (Pomerol)
Clos Fourtet (St.-Emilion)
Clos des Jacobins (St.-Emilion)
Clos du Marquis (St.-Julien)

Clos René (Pomerol)
La Clotte (St.-Emilion)
Corbin (St.-Emilion)
Corbin-Michotte (St.-Emilion)
Cormeil-Figeac (St.-Emilion)
Cos Labory (St.-Estèphe)
Coufran (Haut-Médoc)
Château Courrière Rongieras (Lussac-St.-
    Émilion)
Coutelin-Merville (St.-Estèphe)
Couvent des Jacobins (St.-Emilion)
La Croix du Casse (Pomerol)
La Croix de Gay (Pomerol)
La Croix de Cabrie (St.-Emilion)
Croizet-Bages (Pauillac)
Croque Michotte (St.-Emilion)
Dalem (Fronsac)
La Dame de Montrose (St.-Estèphe)
Dassault (St.-Emilion)
Daugay (St.-Emilion)
La Dauphine (Fronsac)
Dauzac (Margaux)
Destieux (St.-Emilion)
Domaine de l'Eglise (Pomerol)
l'Enclos (Pomerol)
de Ferrand (St.-Emilion)
de Fieuzal (Graves)
Lafleur (St.-Emilion)
Fongaban (Puisseguin-St.-Emilion)
Fonplégade (St.-Emilion)
Fontenil (Fronsac)
Fourcas-Loubaney (Listrac)
Franc-Mayne (St.-Emilion)
La Gaffelière (St.-Emilion)
La Garde Réserve du Château (Graves)
Le Gay (Pomerol)
Giscours (Margaux)
Gloria (St.-Julien)
Gombaude-Guillot (Pomerol)
Grand-Corbin (St.-Emilion)

Grand-Pontet (St.-Emilion)
Grand-Puy-Ducasse (Pauillac)
Les Grandes Chênes (Médoc)
La Grave à Pomerol (Trigant de Boisset)
   (Pomerol)
Guillot-Clauzel (Pomerol)
La Gurgue (Margaux)
Haut-Bages-Libéral (Pauillac)
Haut-Batailley (Pauillac)
Haut-Corbin (St.-Emilion)
Haut-Faugères (St.-Emilion)
Haut-Sociondo (Blaye)
l'Hermitage (St.-Emilion)
Hortevie (St.-Julien)
Château Hostens-Picant (Sainte-Foy)
Jonqueyrès (Bordeaux Supérieur)
Kirwan (Margaux)
Labégorce-Zédé (Margaux)
Lalande-Borie (St.-Julien)
Lanessan (Haut-Médoc)
Langoa-Barton (St.-Julien)
Laplagnotte-Bellevue (St.-Emilion)
Larrivet-Haut-Brion (Graves)
Lascombes (Margaux)
Lucie (St.-Emilion)
Lusseau (St.-Emilion)
Lynch-Moussas (Pauillac)
Magdelaine (St.-Emilion)
Magneau (Graves)
Malartic-Lagravière (Graves)
Marjosse (Bordeaux)
Marquis de Terme (Margaux)
Maucaillou (Moulis)
Mazeris (Canon-Fronsac)
Meyney (St.-Estèphe)
Monbrison (Margaux)
Moulin-Haut-Laroque (Fronsac)
Moulin-Pey-Labrie (Canon-Fronsac)
Moulin Rouge (Haut-Médoc)
Olivier (Graves)
Les Ormes-de-Pez (St.-Estèphe)
Les Ormes-Sorbet (Médoc)
Parenchère (Bordeaux Supérieur)
Patache d'Aux (Medoc)

du Pavillon (Canon-Fronsac)
Pavillon Rouge de Margaux (Margaux)
Les Pensées de Lafleur (Pomerol)
Petit-Village (Pomerol)
Pey Labrie (Canon-Fronsac)
Peyredon-Lagravette (Listrac)
de Pez (St.-Estèphe)
Phélan-Ségur (St.-Estèphe)
Pibran (Pauillac)
Picque-Caillou (Graves)
de Pitray (Côtes de Castignon)
Plaisance (Premières Côtes de Bordeaux)
Potensac (Médoc)
Poujeaux (Moulis)
Prieuré-Lichine (Margaux)
Réserve de la Comtesse (Pauillac)
Roc des Cambes (Côtes de Bourg)
Rochebelle (St.-Emilion)
Rouet (Fronsac)
St.-Pierre (St.-Julien)
de Sales (Pomerol)
La Serre (St.-Emilion)
Siran (Margaux)
Soudars (Haut-Médoc)
Soutard (St.-Emilion)
Tayac (Côtes de Bourg)
Tertre-Daugay (St.-Emilion)
La Tonnelle (Blaye)
La Tour de By (Médoc)
La Tour Figeac (St.-Emilion)
La Tour-Haut-Brion (Graves)
Tour Haut-Caussan (Médoc)
Tour du Haut-Moulin (Haut-Médoc)
La Tour du Pin Figeac Moueix (St.-
   Emilion)
La Tour-St. Bonnet (Médoc)
La Tour Seguy (Bourg)
La Tourelles de Longueville (Pauillac)
Trotte Vieille (St.-Emilion)
Veyry (Côtes de Castillon)
La Vieille-Cure (Fronsac)
Vieux Fortin (St.-Emilion)
La Violette (Pomerol)

* * (AVERAGE)

Beaumont (Haut-Médoc)
Belair (St.-Emilion)
Belgrave (Haut-Médoc)
La Cabanne (Pomerol)
Chambert-Marbuzet (St.-Estèphe)

Clarke (Listrac)
Clos la Madeleine (St.-Emilion)
Cordeillan-Bages (Pauillac)
La Croix (Pomerol)
Durfort-Vivens (Margaux)

Faurie de Souchard (St.-Emilion)

Ferrière (Margaux)

Feytit-Clinet (Pomerol)

La Fleur Gazin (Pomerol)

La Fleur Pourret (St.-Emilion)

Fonbadet (Pauillac)

Fonréaud (Listrac)

Fonroque (St.-Emilion)

Fourcas-Dupré (Listrac)

Fourcas-Hosten (Listrac)

de France (Graves)

Château Gassies (Premières Côtes de
    Bordeaux)

Gressier Grand Poujeaux (Moulis)

Haut-Bages-Averous (Pauillac)

Haut-Sarpe (St.-Emilion)

Le Jurat (St.-Emilion)

Lagrange (Pomerol)

La Lagune (Ludon)

Lamarque (Haut-Médoc)

Larcis-Ducasse (St.-Emilion)

Larose-Trintaudon (Haut-Médoc)

Laroze (St.-Emilion)

Larruau (Margaux)

Liversan (Haut-Médoc)

Malescasse (Haut-Médoc)

Marbuzet (St.-Estèphe)

Martinens (Margaux)

Mazeyres (Pomerol)

Montviel (Pomerol)

Moulin du Cadet (St.-Emilion)

Pedesclaux (Pauillac)

Petit-Faurie-Soutard (St.-Emilion)

Petit-Figeac (St.-Emilion)

Plince (Pomerol)

Pouget (Margaux)

Puy-Blanquet (St.-Emilion)

Rahoul (Graves)

Rauzan-Gassies (Margaux)

Rocher-Bellevue-Figeac (St.-Emilion)

Rolland-Maillet (St.-Emilion)

Taillefer (Pomerol)

La Tour-Martillac (Graves)

La Tour de Mons (Margaux)

Vieux Clos St.-Emilion (St.-Emilion)

Villemaurine (St.-Emilion)

RATING BORDEAUX'S BEST PRODUCERS OF DRY WHITE WINES

* * * * * *(OUTSTANDING)*

Domaine de Chevalier (Pessac-Léognan)

de Fieuzal (Pessac-Léognan)

Haut-Brion (Pessac-Léognan)

Laville-Haut-Brion (Pessac-Léognan)

La Louvière (Pessac-Léognan)

* * * * *(EXCELLENT)*

Aile d'Argent (Bordeaux)

Carbonnieux (Pessac-Léognan)

Clos Floridene (Pessac-Léognan)

Couhins-Lurton (Pessac-Léognan)

Larrivet-Haut-Brion (Pessac-Léognan)

Malartic-Lagravière (Pessac-Léognan)

Pape-Clément (Pessac-Léognan)

Pavillon Blanc de Château Margaux
    (Bordeaux)

Smith-Haut-Lafitte (Pessac-Léognan)

La Tour-Martillac (Pessac-Léognan)

* * * *(GOOD)*

d'Archambeau (Graves)

Bauduc Les Trois Hectares (Bordeaux)

Blanc de Lynch-Bages (Pauillac)

Bouscaut (Pessac-Léognan)

Caillou Blanc de Talbot (Bordeaux)

Carsin (Bordeaux)

Domaine Challon (Bordeaux)

Chantegrive (Graves)

La Closière (Bordeaux)

Château Coucheroy (Pessac-Léognan)

Doisy-Daëne (Bordeaux)

Château Ferbos (Graves)

Ferrande (Graves)

G de Château Guiraud (Bordeaux)

La Garde-Réserve du Château (Graves)

Château Graville-Lacoste (Graves)

Haut-Gardère (Graves)

Loudenne (Bordeaux)

Château de Malle (Graves)

Château Millet (Graves)

Numéro 1 (Bordeaux)

Pirou (Graves)

Plaisance (Bordeaux)   Reynon (Bordeaux)
Pontac Monplaisir (Graves)   Château de Rochemorin (Pessac-
R de Rieussec (Bordeaux)   Léognan)
Rahoul (Graves)   Roquefort (Bordeaux)
Respide (Graves)   Thieuley (Bordeaux)

* *(AVERAGE)

de France (Graves)   Olivier (Graves)

RATING BORDEAUX'S BEST PRODUCERS OF BARSACS/SAUTERNES

* * * * *(OUTSTANDING)

Climens (Barsac)   Lafaurie-Peyraguey (Sauternes)
Coutet-Cuvée Madame (Barsac)   Rieussec (Sauternes)
Doisy-Daëne l'Extravagance (Barsac)   d'Yquem (Sauternes)

* * * *(EXCELLENT)

d'Arche-Pugneau (Sauternes)   Guiraud (Sauternes)
Coutet (regular *cuvée*) (Barsac)   Rabaud-Promis (Sauternes)
Doisy-Dubroca (Barsac)   Raymond-Lafon (Sauternes)
de Fargues (Sauternes)   Suduiraut (Sauternes)****/*****
Gilette (Sauternes)   La Tour Blanche (Sauternes)

* * *(GOOD)

d'Arche (Sauternes)   Lamothe-Despujols (Sauternes)
Bastor-Lamontagne (Sauternes)   Lamothe-Guignard (Sauternes)***/****
Broustet (Barsac)   Liot (Sauternes)
Caillou (Barsac)   de Malle (Sauternes)
Clos Haut-Peyraguey (Sauternes)   Nairac (Barsac)
Doisy-Daëne (Barsac)   Piada (Barsac)
Doisy-Dubroca (Barsac)   Rabaud-Promis (Sauternes)
Doisy-Védrines (Barsac)   Rayne-Vigneau (Sauternes)
Filhot (Sauternes)   Romer du Hayot (Sauternes)
Haut-Claverie (Sauternes)   Roumieu-Lacoste (Barsac)
Les Justices (Sauternes)   Sigalas-Rabaud (Sauternes)
Lamothe (Sauternes)

* *(AVERAGE)

Myrat (Sauternes)   Suau (Barsac)

GETTING A HANDLE ON SECONDARY LABELS

Secondary wines with secondary labels are not a recent development. Léoville-Las Cases
first made a second wine (Clos du Marquis) in 1904, and in 1908 Château Margaux produced
its first Le Pavillon Rouge du Château Margaux.

Yet two decades ago, about the only second labels most Bordeaux wine enthusiasts encountered were those from Latour (Les Forts de Latour), Margaux (Le Pavillon Rouge du
Château Margaux), and perhaps that of Lafite-Rothschild (Moulin des Carruades). Today, virtually every classified growth, as well as many crus bourgeois and numerous estates in
Pomerol and St.-Emilion, has second labels for those batches of wine deemed not sufficiently
rich, concentrated, or complete to go into their top wine, or grand vin. This has been one of

the major developments of the eighties, fostered no doubt by the enormous crop sizes in most of the vintages. A handful of cynics have claimed it is largely done to keep prices high, but such charges are nonsense. The result has generally been far higher quality for a château's best wine. It allows a château to declassify the production from young vines, from vines that overproduce, and from parcels harvested too soon or too late, into a second or perhaps even a third wine that still has some of the quality and character of the château's grand vin.

The gentleman who encouraged most châteaux to develop second wines was the famed oenologist Professor Emile Peynaud. Over the last decade, the number of second wines has increased more than tenfold. Some properties, such as Léoville-Las Cases, have even begun to utilize a third label for wines deemed not good enough for the second label.

Of course, all this complicates buying decisions for consumers. The wine trade has exacerbated matters by seizing on the opportunity to advertise wine that "tastes like the grand vin" for one-half to one-third the price. In most cases, there is little truth to such proclamations. I find that most second wines have only a vague resemblance to their more esteemed siblings. Most are the product of throwing everything that would normally have been discarded into another label for commercial purposes. Some second wines, such as those of the first growths, particularly Les Forts de Latour and Bahans-Haut-Brion, are indeed excellent, occasionally outstanding (taste the 1982 Les Forts de Latour or 1989 Bahans-Haut-Brion), and can even resemble the style and character of the grand vin. But the words *caveat emptor* should be etched strongly in the minds of consumers who routinely purchase the second labels of Bordeaux châteaux thinking they are getting something reminiscent of the property's top wine.

In an effort to clarify the situation of second labels, the following chart rates the secondary wines on a 1- to 5-star basis. While I think it is important to underscore the significance that the stricter the selection, the better the top wine, it is also important to remember that most second wines are rarely worth the price asked.

Note: Where a second wine merits purchasing, the vintage is listed.

EXPLANATION OF THE STARS
*****The finest second wines
****Very good second wines
***Pleasant second wines
**Average-quality second wines
*Of little interest

SECONDARY LABELS

GRAND VIN	SECOND VIN
Andron-Blanquet	St.-Roch**
Angélus	Carillon de l'Angélus**
d'Angludet	Domaine Baury**
d'Arche	d'Arche-Lafaurie**
l'Arrosée	Les Côteaux du Château l'Arrosée**
Balestard-La-Tonnelle	Les Tourelles de Balestard**
Bastor-Lamontagne	Les Remparts du Bastor**
Beau Séjour-Bécot	Tournelle des Moines**
Beaumont	Moulin-d'Arvigny*
Beauséjour-Duffau	La Croix de Mazerat**
Belair	Roc-Blanquant*
Beychevelle	Amiral de Beychevelle***
	Réserve de l'Amiral***

Bonalgue	Burgrave*
Bouscaut	Valoux**
Branaire-Ducru	Duluc**
Brane-Cantenac	Château Notton**
	Domaine de Fontarney**
Broustet	Château de Ségur**
La Cabanne	Compostelle**
Cadet-Piola	Chevaliers de Malta**
Caillou	Petit-Mayne*
Calon-Ségur	Marquis de Ségur**
Canon	Clos J. Kanon**
Canon-La-Gaffelière	Côte Migon-La-Gaffelière**
Cantemerle	Villeneuve de Cantemerle**
Cantenac-Brown	Canuet**
	Lamartine**
Carbonnieux	La Tour-Léognan**
Certan-Giraud	Clos du Roy**
Chambert-Marbuzet	MacCarthy**
Chasse-Spleen	l'Ermitage de Chasse-Spleen**
Chauvin	Chauvin Variation*
Cheval Blanc	Le Petit Cheval***
Climens	Les Cyprès de Climens**
Clos Fourtet	Domaine de Martialis**
Clos Haut-Peyraguey	Haut-Bommes**
Clos René	Moulinet-Lasserre**
Columbier-Monpelou	Grand Canyon**
Corbin-Michotte	Les Abeilles**
Cos d'Estournel	Pagodes de Cos***
Couvent-des-Jacobins	Beau-Mayne***
La Croix	Le Gabachot**
Croizet-Bages	Enclos de Moncabon*
Dauzac	Laborde**
Doisy-Védrines	La Tour-Védrines**
La Dominique	Saint-Paul de la Dominique**
Ducru-Beaucaillou	La Croix**
Duhart-Milon-Rothschild	Moulin de Duhart**
Durfort-Vivens	Domaine de Curé-Bourse*
l'Eglise-Clinet	La Petite l'Eglise***
de Fieuzal	l'Abeille de Fieuzal**
Figeac	Grangeneuve**
Fonplégade	Château Côtes Trois Moulins**
La Gaffelière	Clos la Gaffelière**
	Château de Roquefort**
Giscours	Cantelaude**
Gloria	Haut-Beychevelle Gloria**
	Peymartin**
Grand Mayne	Les Plantes du Mayne**
Grand-Puy-Ducasse	Artigues-Arnaud**
Grand-Puy-Lacoste	Lacoste-Borie**
Gruaud-Larose	Sarget de Gruaud-Larose***

Guiraud	Le Dauphin**
Haut-Bailly	La Parde de Haut-Bailly***
Haut-Batailley	La Tour d'Aspic**
Haut-Brion	Bahans-Haut-Brion***** (2000, 1998, 1995, 1990, 1989, 1988, 1987)
Haut-Marbuzet	Tour de Marbuzet**
d'Issan	Candel**
Labegorcé-Zédé	Château de l'Amiral**
Lafite-Rothschild	Carruades de Lafite**** (2000, 1998, 1996, 1995, 1990, 1989)
Lafleur	Les Pensées de Lafleur***** (2000, 1990, 1989, 1988)
Lafon-Rochet	Le Numéro 2 de Lafon-Rochet***
Lagrange	Les Fiefs de Lagrange***
La Lagune	Ludon-Pomiès-Agassac**
Lanessan	Domaine de Sainte-Gemme**
Larmande	Château des Templiers**
Lascombes	Segonnes**
	La Gombaude**
Latour	Les Forts de Latour***** (2000, 1999, 1996, 1995, 1990, 1989, 1982, 1978)
Léoville-Barton	Lady Langoa**** (1989)
Léoville-Las Cases	Clos du Marquis***** (1996, 1995, 1994, 1990, 1989, 1988, 1986, 1982)
	Grand Parc***
Léoville-Poyferré	Moulin-Riche**
La Louvière	L de Louvière****
	Coucheray**
	Clos du Roi**
Lynch-Bages	Haut-Bages-Averous****
Malescot St.-Exupéry	de Loyac*
	Domaine du Balardin*
de Malle	Château de Sainte-Hélène**
Château Margaux	Pavillon Rouge du Château Margaux**** (2000, 1999, 1996, 1995, 1990)
Marquis de Terme	Domaine des Gondats**
Maucaillou	Cap de Haut**
	Franc-Caillou**
Meyney	Prieuré de Meyney***
Monbrison	Cordat***
Montrose	La Dame de Montrose**** (2000, 1999, 1996, 1991, 1990)
Mouton-Rothschild	Le Petit-Mouton*** (2000, 1999)
Palmer	Alter Ego de Palmer*** (2000, 1999)
Pape-Clément	Le Clémentin du Pape-Clément***
Phélan-Ségur	Franck Phélan***
Pichon-Longueville Baron	Les Tourelles de Pichon***
Pichon-Longueville Comtesse de Lalande	Réserve de la Comtesse**** (2000, 1997, 1996, 1995)

Pontet-Canet	Les Hauts de Pontet**
Potensac	Gallais-Bellevue**
	Lassalle**
	Goudy-la-Cardonne**
Poujeaux	La Salle de Poujeaux**
Le Prieuré	Château L'Olivier**
Prieuré-Lichine	Clairefont**
Rabaud-Promis	Domaine de L'Estremade**
Rahoul	Petit Rahoul**
Rausan-Ségla	Lamouroux**
Rieussec	Clos Labère***
St.-Pierre	Clos de Uza**
	St.-Louis-le-Bosq**
de Sales	Chantalouette**
Siran	Bellegarde**
	St.-Jacques**
Smith-Haut-Lafitte	Les Hauts de Smith-Haut-Lafitte*
Sociando-Mallet	Lartigue de Brochon**
Soutard	Clos de la Tonnelle**
Talbot	Connétable de Talbot***
Tertre-Daugay	Château de Roquefort***
La Tour-Blanche	Mademoiselle de Saint-Marc***
La Tour de By	Moulin de la Roque*
	La Roque de By*
Tour Haut-Caussan	La Landotte**
La Tour-Martillac	La Grave-Martillac**
Troplong Mondot	Mondot***
Valandraud	Virginie de Valandraud***
Vieux Château Certan	Clos de la Gravette***

THE BEST WINE VALUES IN BORDEAUX
(High-quality estates for under $20 a bottle)

St.-Estèphe none

Pauillac none

St.-Julien none

Margaux and the Southern Médoc none

Pessac-Léognan/Graves none

Moulis and Listrac none

Médoc and Haut-Médoc none

Pomerol none

St.-Émilion none

Lalande-de-Pomerol Bertineau St.-Vincent, De Chambrun, La Fleur-Bouard, Grand-Ormeau, Jean de Gué Cuvée Prestige, Haut-Chaigneau, Le Sergue

Côtes de Bourg Fougas-Maldoror, Roc de Cambes

Côtes de Blaye Bel-Air La Royère, Clos Lascombes, Garreau, Gigault Cuvée Viva, Grands Maréchaux, Peyraud, Roland La Garde, Ségonzac Vieilles Vignes

Côtes de Francs Marsau, La Prade

Bordeaux Generic, Premières Côtes, and Supèrieur Bonnet, Caris, Carsin Black Label, Clos Chaumont, La Cour d'Argent, Domaine de Courtelliac, La Doyenne, de la Garde,

Marjosse, Parenchère Cuvée Raphaël, Le Pin Beausoleil, Plaisance Tradition, Reignac, Thébot, Thieuley

Côtes de Castillon d'Aiguilhe, Brisson, Cap de Faugères, Dubois-Grimon, Le Pin de Belcier, Veyry, Vieux-Champ-de-Mars

Fronsac/Canon-Fronsac Fontenil, Haut-Carles, Sainte-Colombe, Les Trois-Croix, La Vieille-Cure

Barsac/Sauternes none

St.-Georges St.-Emilion La Griffe de Cap d'Or

Puisseguin-St.-Emilion Branda, La Mauriane

Entre-Deux-Mers (dry white wines) none

Bordeaux Premières Côtes and Generic Bordeaux (dry white wines) none

Buying Bordeaux Wine Futures

THE PITFALLS AND PLEASURES

The purchase of wine, already fraught with plenty of pitfalls for consumers, becomes immensely more complex and risky when one enters the wine futures sweepstakes.

On the surface, buying wine futures is nothing more than investing money in a case or cases of wine at a predetermined "future price" long before the wine is bottled and shipped to this country. You invest your money in wine futures on the assumption that the wine will appreciate significantly in price between the time you purchase the future and the time the wine has been bottled and imported to America. Purchasing the right wine, from the right vintage, in the right international financial climate, can represent significant savings. On the other hand, it can be quite disappointing to invest heavily in a wine future only to witness the wine's arrival 12 to 18 months later at a price equal to or below the future price and to discover that the wine is inferior in quality as well.

For years, future offerings have been largely limited to Bordeaux wines, although they are seen occasionally from other regions. In Bordeaux, during the spring following the harvest, the estates or châteaux offer for sale a portion of their crops. The first offering, or *première tranche*, usually offers a good indication of the trade's enthusiasm for the new wine, the prevailing market conditions, and the ultimate price the public will have to spend.

Those brokers and *négociants* who take an early position on a vintage frequently offer portions of their purchases to importers/wholesalers/retailers to make available publicly as a wine "future." These offerings are usually made to the retail shopper during the first spring after the vintage. For example, the 2000 Bordeaux vintage was being offered for sale as a wine future in April/May 2001. Purchasing wine at this time is not without numerous risks. While 90% of the quality of the wine and the style of the vintage can be ascertained by professionals tasting the wine in its infancy, the increased interest in buying Bordeaux wine futures has led to a soaring number of journalists, some qualified, some not, to judge young Bordeaux wines. The results have been predictable. Many writers serve no purpose other than to hype the vintage as great, and have written more glowing accounts of a vintage than the publicity firms doing promotion for the Bordeaux wine industry.

Consumers should read numerous points of view from trusted professionals and ask the following questions: 1) Is the professional taster experienced in tasting young as well as old Bordeaux vintages? 2) How much time does the taster actually spend tasting Bordeaux during the year, visiting the properties, and thinking about the vintage? 3) Does the professional taster express his or her viewpoint in an independent, unbiased form, free of trade advertising? 4) Has the professional looked deeply at the weather conditions, harvesting conditions, grape variety ripening profiles, and soil types that respond differently depending on the weather scenario? And, most important, 5) does the taster/critic follow up the barrel tasting by purchasing most of the finest wines in bottle from retailers in the United States?

Writers must be prepared to invest in the bottled wine to guarantee that what they taste from barrel is the same as what has been bottled. For 23 years I have heard rumors of "writers' *cuvées*," special juiced-up samples that are designed to impress tasters and are not representative of the true blend at the château. This is largely a myth as evidenced by the tastings I have done from bottled vintages. In most cases, the bottled wines are better than when tasted from cask, at least in the case of classified-growth Bordeaux. Nevertheless, the professional critic must always be on guard against being set up.

When wine futures are offered for sale there is generally a great deal of enthusiasm for the newest vintage from both the proprietors and the wine trade. The saying in France that "the greatest wines ever made are the ones that are available for sale" are words many wine producers and merchants live by. The business of the wine trade is to sell wine, and consumers should be aware that they will no doubt be inundated with claims of "great wines from a great vintage at great prices." The hard sell has been used time and time again for good vintages and, in essence, has undermined the credibility of many otherwise responsible retailers, as well as a number of journalists. In contrast, those writers who fail to admit or to recognize greatness where warranted are no less inept and irresponsible.

In short, there are only four valid reasons to buy Bordeaux wine futures.

1. Are you buying top-quality, preferably superb, wine from an excellent or, better yet, a great vintage?

No vintage can be reviewed in black-and-white terms. Even in the greatest vintages there are disappointing appellations and mediocre wines. At the same time, vintages that are merely good to very good can produce some superb wines. Knowing who the underachievers and overachievers are is paramount in making a good buying decision. There is no reason to buy wines as futures except for the top performers in a given vintage, because prices generally will not appreciate in the period between the release of the future prices and when the wines are bottled. The exceptions are always the same—top wines and great vintages. If the financial climate is such that the wine will not be at least 25–30% more expensive when it arrives in the marketplace, most purchasers are better off investing their money elsewhere.

2. Do the prices you must pay look good enough that you will ultimately save money by paying less for the wine as a future than for the wine when it is released in 2–3 years?

Many factors must be taken into consideration to make this determination. In certain years, Bordeaux may release its wines at lower prices than it did the previous year (the most recent examples are 1986 and 1990). There is also the question of the international marketplace. In 2002 the American dollar is still relatively strong, but the unsettling events of the September 2001 terrorist attacks on America are certain to have long-term repercussions. The international marketplace conditions, the perceived reputation of a given vintage, and the rarity of a particular estate all must be considered in determining whether the wine will become much more expensive when released than when offered as a wine future.

3. Do you want to be guaranteed of getting top, hard-to-find wine from a producer with a great reputation who makes only small quantities of wine?

Even if the vintage is not irrefutably great, or you cannot be assured that prices will increase, there are always a handful of small estates, particularly in Pomerol and St.-Emilion, that produce such limited quantities of wine and who have such loyal worldwide followers that their wines warrant buying as a future, if only to reserve your case from an estate whose wines have pleased you in the past. In Pomerol, limited-production wines such as Le Pin, Clinet, La Conseillante, l'Evangile, La Fleur de Gay, Lafleur, and Bon Pasteur have produced many popular wines during the decades of the eighties and nineties, yet are very hard to find in the marketplace. In St.-Emilion, some of the less-renowned yet modestly sized estates such as l'Angélus, l'Arrosée, Grand Mayne, Pavie-Macquin, La Dominique, Tertre-Rôteboeuf, and Troplong Mondot produce wines that are not easy to find after bottling. In addition, there is a burgeoning number of St.-Emilion "garage wines" that are high in quality but made in limited quantities of 500–1,000 cases. Consequently, their admirers throughout the world frequently reserve and pay for these wines as futures. Limited-production wines from high-quality estates merit buying futures even in good to very good years.

4. Do you want to buy wine in half bottles, magnums, double magnums, jeroboams, or imperials? Frequently overlooked as one of the advantages of buying wine futures is the fact that you can request that your merchant have the wines bottled to your specifications. There is always a surcharge for such bottlings, but if you have children born in a certain year, or you want the luxury of buying half bottles (a size that makes sense for daily drinking), the only time to do this is when buying the wine as a future.

Finally, should you decide to enter the futures market, be sure you know the other risks involved. The merchant you deal with could go bankrupt, and your unsecured sales slip would make you one of probably hundreds of unsecured creditors of the bankrupt wine merchant hoping for a few cents on your investment. Another risk is that the merchant's supplier could go bankrupt or be fraudulent. You may get a refund from the wine merchant, but you will not get your wine. Therefore, be sure to deal only with a wine merchant who has dealt in selling wine futures before and is financially solvent. In addition, make sure you buy wine futures only from a merchant who has received confirmed commitments as to the quantities of wine he or she will receive. Some merchants sell Bordeaux futures to consumers before they have received commitments from suppliers. Be sure to ask for proof of the merchant's allocations. If you do not, the words *caveat emptor* could have special significance for you.

For many Bordeaux enthusiasts, buying wine futures of the right wine, in the right vintage, at the right time guarantees that they have liquid gems worth 4 or 5 times the price they paid for the wine. However, history has proven that only a handful of vintages over the last 20 years have appreciated to that extent in their first two or three years (e.g., 1982 and 1990).

DOMAINE DE L'A (CÔTES DE CASTILLON)

2000	C	(90–92)
1999	C	(87–88)

This is an amazing effort from the up-and-coming Côtes de Castillon appellation, which, by the way, is a good source for numerous bargain-priced sleepers from 2000. Proprietor Stéphane Derencourt is one of Bordeaux's most talented wine-makers.
2000: This astonishing blend of 60% Merlot, 25% Cabernet Franc, and 15% Cabernet Sauvignon offers an explosive bouquet of wood smoke, black raspberries, and dry portlike intensity. Full-bodied and unctuously textured, with an ostentatious personality, this remarkable wine is moderately priced given its appellation. It will drink well during its first 10 years of life. It is a major sleeper of the vintage.
1999: Another sleeper of the vintage, this excellent, dark-purple, medium-bodied Côtes de Castillon exhibits sweet black cherry and blackberry fruit in its supple, rich, fleshy personality. It is best drunk over the next 5–6 years.

D'AIGUILHE (CÔTES DE CASTILLON)

2000	D	(90–92)
1999	C	90
1998	C	87

This is the newest property acquired by Stephan von Neipperg, the owner of Canon La-Gaffelière, Clos de l'Oratoire, and La Mondotte. 2000 is the first vintage in which he controlled the viticulture as well as the vinification and, as one can well imagine, the result was simply exceptional. Let's just hope the price remains reasonable. Smart Bordeaux enthusiasts should be purchasing this wine at the earliest opportunity.

2000: The saturated black/purple of the 2000 is followed by aromas of licorice, incense, blackberries, chocolate, and coffee. Full-bodied, with tremendous layers of fruit and concentration, this offering possesses the mass, richness, and complexity of a serious classified growth. I would opt for drinking it during its first 8–10 years of life. Wow! A sleeper of the vintage.

1999: Also a sleeper of the vintage, this dazzling blend of 80% Merlot and 20% Cabernet Franc exhibits a black/purple color, followed by an exotic nose of spice box, licorice, coffee, and Asian spices. Full-throttle fruit flavors, an unctuous texture, and a seamless personality can be found in this outstanding example of a Côtes de Castillon. Moreover, it will drink well young, yet age nicely for a decade. Don't miss it!

1998: This elegantly styled effort offers sweet licorice, fruitcake, and jammy cherry/black currant aromas as well as flavors. This juicy, medium-bodied, soft 1998 possesses a nice texture in addition to a delicious, long finish. Anticipated maturity: now–2008.

ANDREAS (ST.-EMILION)

2000	D	(85–86)
1999	D	87
1998	D	86

A wine produced under the consultation of Jean-Luc Thunevin, Andreas is a solidly made effort.

2000: This medium-weight, moderately extracted, 100% Merlot possesses a monolithic character but good purity, fine ripeness, and a layered mouth feel. Anticipated maturity: now–2006.

1999: A better balanced effort than the 1998, with lower acidity and sweeter fruit, but not as much depth, the 1999 Andreas is an attractive, up-front St.-Emilion for uncritical quaffing.

1998: Abundant quantities of creamy oak, smoke, espresso, and black fruits emerge from this dark ruby-colored, tannic 1998. It possesses power and guts but appears slightly disjointed. Drink it over the next 4–5 years.

ANGÉLUS (ST.-EMILION)

2000	EEE	(96–98)
1999	EE	88
1998	EE	93
1997	E	89
1996	EE	91+
1995	EE	95

Angélus may have been the first mediocre St.-Emilion estate to resurrect its image and become the catalyst for the qualitative revolution in this appellation. Since 1988, there has not been a hiccup. Hubert de Boüard, the manager of Angélus, has had enormous influence on the higher overall quality level of many St.-Emilions. It is only justice to his talent that Angélus was elevated to premier grand cru status in 1996's reclassification.

2000: The finest Angélus since the 1990 and 1989, in terms of pure classicism and potential longevity, the 2000 may ultimately surpass those two vintages. Unmistakably, this is a *vin de garde*, a huge, massive, firm, extraordinarily well delineated Angélus with terrific purity and freshness. The color is a saturated portlike purple/black. With airing, the reluctant aromatics reveal scents of licorice, truffles, blackberries, plums, crème de cassis, smoke, and incense. The wine is excruciatingly tannic but also phenomenally concentrated, full-bodied, and rich. Paradoxically, it is viscous yet has good acidity, one of the unusual characteristics of the 2000 vintage. This gives the wine freshness and delineation in spite of surreal levels of extract and richness. This looks to be one of the wines of the vintage. Anticipated maturity: 2008–2035.

1999: Angélus was among the vineyards forced to harvest early because of a damaging hail-storm that swept through a small sector of St.-Emilion on September 5. Amazingly, this wine has turned out brilliantly, having put on weight, flesh, and dimension during its *élevage*. The finest of the hail-damaged vineyard wines in 1999, this full-bodied offering should turn out to be outstanding. The color is a dense purple. The bouquet offers up aromas of roasted meats, black fruits, toast, and spice. Lush and opulent, it is a credit to the quality-conscious propri-etor. Anticipated maturity: now–2015.

1998: A dazzling effort, the 1998 boasts an opaque purple color in addition to an exceptional bouquet of smoke, licorice, plums, black raspberries, and blackberries. As the wine sits in the glass, coffee and chocolate also emerge. Full-bodied, flamboyant, well delineated, and beautifully balanced as well as layered, with well-integrated tannin in the powerful, rich fin-ish, this 1998 will be at its best between 2003–2020.

1997: The saturated, deep ruby/purple 1997 is a big, rich, smoky St.-Emilion exhibiting this estate's telltale characteristics of Provençal olives, black cherry liqueur, prunes, and toasty new oak. The biggest of St.-Emilion's premiers grands crus classés in 1997, it is soft, supple, and ideal for consuming over the next 10 years.

1996: A massive, powerful Angélus, this wine exhibits a saturated black/ruby/purple color as well as an impressively endowed nose of dried herbs, roasted meats, new saddle leather, plum liqueur, and cassis. In the mouth, olive notes make an impression. This sweet, full-bodied, exceptionally concentrated wine is atypically backward and ferociously tannic. It was revealing more sweetness and forwardness immediately prior to bottling, but I would now recommend another 7–8 years of cellaring. Anticipated maturity: 2007–2025.

1995: A superb effort in this vintage, Angélus's opaque purple-colored 1995 is a massive, powerful, rich offering with plenty of ripe, sweet tannin. The wine's aromatics include scents of Provençal olives, jammy black cherries, blackberries, truffles, and toast. A very full-bodied wine, it is layered, thick, and pure. This is the most concentrated of the 1995 St.-Emilion premiers grands crus. Anticipated maturity: now–2025.

Past Glories: 1994 (92), 1993 (92), 1990 (96), 1989 (96), 1988 (91)

D'ANGLUDET (MARGAUX)

2000	D	(88–90)
1999	D	88
1998	D	86
1997	C	(87–89)
1996	C	88
1995	C	88

Through hard work and talent, the late Peter Sichel took this château from virtual post–World War II obscurity to international prominence. Year after year, the wines qualify as sleepers of the vintage, but prices remain modest.

2000: The 2000 d'Angludet possesses a dense ruby/purple color as well as a sweet perfume of blackberry and cassis fruit, smoke, and underbrush. Ripe, deep, and medium-bodied, with admirable fruit concentration and well-balanced glycerin, tannin, and alcohol, this is a sleeper of the vintage. Anticipated maturity: now–2016.

1999: Another sleeper of the vintage, this juicy, mid-weight 1999 reveals copious quantities of fruit and extract, low acidity, a dense ruby/purple color, and noteworthy flavors of cassis, blueberries, and minerals. Drink it during its first decade of life.

1998: Dark ruby-colored, with a peppery cassis, plum, and subtle herb-scented bouquet, the 1998 d'Angludet is round, straightforward, and monolithic. Consume it over the next 5–6 years.

1997: The 1997—a sleeper of the vintage—performed freakishly well in my tastings. It reveals a deep purple color and gobs of chewy, fat, blackberry and mocha-tinged cherry fruit. Opulent, with superb fruit purity and medium to full body, it has low acidity and a seductive, fleshy personality. Anticipated maturity: now–2012.

1996: Another sleeper, this wine is as fine from bottle as it was from cask. Deeply colored, with a ripe cassis and blackberry-scented nose and subtle notions of licorice and melted road tar, it shows excellent richness, medium body, and moderate tannin in its jammy, rich finish. It should age nicely. Anticipated maturity: now–2015

1995: In contrast to the powerful, tannic 1996, the 1995 is a silky, supple, charming, forthcoming wine. The color is a healthy saturated deep ruby/purple, and the wine offers up gobs of jammy black fruits intermixed with subtle herbs, spice, and toast. In the mouth, the wine displays excellent richness, a layered, medium-bodied personality, well-disguised tannin and acidity, and a hedonistic mouth-feel. Anticipated maturity: now–2010. A sleeper.

L'ARCHANGE (ST.-EMILION)

2000		D	(88–90)

This new entry into the St.-Emilion portfolio is produced by highly respected oenologist Pascal Chatonnet.

2000: This wine exhibits a deep saturated purple color along with a sweet nose of jammy black cherries, raspberries, and currants. Ripe and full-bodied, with outstanding flavor extraction and decent acidity, the 2000 l'Archange possesses high tannin (like many wines of this vintage) but impressive ripeness as well as a sense of fullness. Anticipated maturity: 2005–2016.

D'ARMAILHAC (PAUILLAC)

2000	E	(90–93)
1999	D	90
1998	D	89
1997	D	87
1996	D	87
1995	D	89

D'Armailhac, another up-and-coming Pauillac estate, remains, to the consuming public, the least well known of the three Pauillac properties of the late Baron Philippe de Rothschild (the others are Mouton-Rothschild and Clerc-Milon). The 1989 and 1995 are excellent, the 1999 and 2000 is extremely promising, and the 2000 is the finest d'Armailhac produced to date. Moreover, prices remain realistic.

2000: The 2000 is the finest d'Armailhac I have ever tasted. An exotic, spicy, gorgeously rich blend of 58% Cabernet Sauvignon and 42% Merlot, it exhibits a dense garnet/plum/purple color in addition to a big, smoky nose of espresso, nuts, Asian spices, black plums, currants, and leather. Superbly concentrated, with sweet tannin, and a thick, juicy texture. Anticipated maturity: 2005–2020.

1999: Though it is surpassed by the 2000, the 1999 is potentially one of the finest d'Armailhacs yet produced, along with the 1995. This blend of 42% Merlot, 35% Cabernet Sauvignon, and 23% Cabernet Franc reveals a roasted coffee, black currant, cedary, toasty bouquet, fleshy, fat, succulent flavors, medium to full body, abundant glycerin, ripe tannin, and low acidity. It is a hedonistic Pauillac fruit bomb that should become more delineated before bottling. Anticipated maturity: now–2017.

1998: This is another Médoc 1998 that is revealing more mid-palate, flesh, concentration, and sweeter tannin in bottle than during its *élevage*. A blend of 42% Cabernet Sauvignon, 20% Cabernet Franc, and 38% Merlot, this black/purple-colored claret exhibits sweet aromas of licorice, incense, Asian spices, cedar, plums, and black currants. Full-bodied and sweet on the entry, with good acidity, definition, and ripe tannin, it will be drinkable young yet last for 12–15 years.

1997: Dark plum/garnet, with an evolved, mature, cedary, spicebox, fruitcake, coffee, smoky, fruit-scented bouquet, this seductive, medium-bodied, fruit-driven 1997 offers plenty of appeal. Drink this spicy Pauillac over the next 5–6 years.

1996: This wine is just as successful as the seductive 1995. The 1996's saturated ruby color is followed by sweet, roasted herb, and black currant aromas with lush toasty oak notes. A blend of 45% Cabernet Sauvignon, 30% Merlot, and 25% Cabernet Franc, this medium-weight, elegant yet richly fruity wine possesses enough tannin to last 2 decades, but it will be one 1996 Médoc that will be drinkable at an early age. Anticipated maturity: 2004–2018.

1995: The 1995 blend was 50% Cabernet Sauvignon, 18% Cabernet Franc, and 32% Merlot. This deep ruby/purple-colored wine possesses low acidity, plenty of sweet tannin, and, in both its aromatics and flavors, gobs of ripe cassis fruit are nicely framed by the judicious use of toasty oak. Flavorful, round, generous, and hedonistic, this is a crowd-pleaser! Anticipated maturity: now–2012.

ARMENS (ST.-EMILION)

2000	**D**	**(87–88)**

Comte Léo de Malet, proprietor of La Gaffelière, is also the owner of this up-and-coming estate of St.-Emilion. His son, Alexandre de Malet, is responsible for the vinifications.

2000: This structured, muscular, backward 2000 offers notes of minerals, red cherries, earth, and wood. Medium-bodied and well concentrated, it will be very good to excellent when released. Anticipated maturity: 2004–2016.

L'ARROSÉE (ST.-EMILION)

2000	**E**	**(89–90)**
1999	**E**	**87**
1998	**E**	**86**
1997	**D**	**86**
1996	**E**	**87+?**
1995	**E**	**90**

L'Arrosée is usually a high-quality and traditional wine. Unique in style, it is fleshy but firm and powerful, as well as rich and fragrant.

2000: Such a traditional style is somewhat passé in St.-Emilion, but there is much to like in this graceful, delicate 2000. Moderately intense notes of brambleberries, earth, hickory smoke, and sweet cherries emerge from this dark ruby-colored wine. In the mouth, it offers Burgundy-like flavors of raspberries and minerals as well as fresh, lively acidity. Drink this medium-bodied, stylish, graceful l'Arrosée between 2004–2016.

1999: A deep ruby color is followed by notes of plums, toasty new oak, and berry fruit. This medium-bodied wine hits the palate with a bit of compression and tastes pinched and insubstantial. Anticipated maturity: now–2012.

1998: Scents of overripe red cherries, along with a boatload of toasty new oak are present in this delicate, lacy, medium-bodied St.-Emilion. A 90-point nose is followed by 82-point flavors, hence the score. This 1998 should drink well for 10 years, but it does not attain the quality level of many of its St.-Emilion peers.

1997: A wine of finesse and elegance, this tasty, soft, medium-bodied effort exhibits light tannin, ripe cherry fruit, and an expressive bouquet consisting of damp soil, red fruit, and flower scents. Consume it over the next 2–3 years.

1996: A tightly knit, closed wine, the 1996 l'Arrosée has not yet begun to put on weight or re-

veal its true character. It possesses a medium-dark ruby color and muted aromatics that, with
airing, offer notes of dusty minerals mixed with black cherries and raspberries. Subtle high
quality toasty oak makes an appearance along with black raspberry and cherry fruit. This
firmly knit, sinewy, austere, elegant wine displays some positive potential, but I would appear to have overrated it based on cask tastings. Anticipated maturity: 2004–2016.

1995: With a medium-dark ruby color, and a complex, kirsch, toasty, smoky, deliciously
complex and fruity nose, this fragrant wine offers a wealth of raspberry, currant, and cherry-
like fruit. It is not a blockbuster but rather an elegant, multidimensional, round, velvety-
textured wine with a lushness and sweetness of fruit that make it irresistible. This is one of
the more seductive wines of the vintage. Anticipated maturity: now–2012.

Past Glories: 1990 (93), 1986 (92), 1985 (93), 1982 (93), 1961 (94)

AURÉLIUS (ST.-EMILION)

2000	D (87–88)

This 4,000-case *cuvée* of 85% Merlot and 15% Cabernet Franc is the product of the large St.-
Emilion cooperative.

2000: Contrary to most of the wines produced by the co-op, which are relatively straightforward and commercially styled, the 2000 Aurelius offers impressive density and ripeness,
some new oak, and a medium-bodied, moderately tannic finish. It will drink well for the next
8 years.

AUSONE (ST.-EMILION)

2000	EEE	(96–100)
1999	EEE	95
1998	EEE	94+
1997	EEE	91
1996	EEE	93+
1995	EEE	93

Alain Vauthier, who now has sole control of this estate, is taking its quality to a higher level.
Under his inspired ownership, Ausone continues to make benchmark St.-Emilions designed
to last 50–100 years. A stricter selection process at the estate has resulted in the production
of a small quantity of second wine. Readers should not hesitate to check out La Chapelle
d'Ausone. The 2000 (rated 90–91) possesses some of its bigger sibling's character but is
more supple, with black fruit and mineral notes presented in a fresh, lively style. This
medium-bodied, classy effort will drink well for 10–12 years.

2000: The spellbinding 2000 is nearly perfect. Its deep ruby/purple color is followed by an
ethereal nose of earth, mineral, blueberry, raspberry, and other assorted black fruit aromas.
There is no evidence of wood, even though 100% new oak is utilized, and malolactic fermentation occurred in barrel. Approachable for an infant Ausone, this perfectly balanced effort
represents the quintessential model of power, elegance, and harmony. The finish lasts nearly
a minute. This wine is almost transparent, with layers of concentrated, authoritatively intense
black fruits. There is plenty of tannin lurking on the back of the palate. This prodigious Ausone is both large scale and delicate. Most Ausones require 15–20 years of cellaring (some
fans say 40–50), but I, optimistically, feel it will be accessible by 2010. It is a candidate for
50–60 years of aging.

1999: The 1999 nearly equals the spectacular 1998. Whether it will ultimately have the immortal aging potential of its older sibling remains to be seen. It boasts gorgeous aromas of
black fruits, flowers, smoke, licorice, and subtle wood. Fabulously concentrated, with sensational persistence on the palate, sweet tannin, and admirable balance as well as stature, this
is a medium-bodied wine of exceptional pedigree and aging potential. Anticipated maturity:
2008–2040. I suspect it will be the longest-lived wine of the vintage.

1998: A dense opaque purple color offers up restrained but pure aromas of liquid minerals, blackberries, black raspberries, and flowers. Medium- to full-bodied, with high tannin but a long, superpure, symmetrical mouth-feel, this dazzling, extremely complex Ausone requires 6–10 years of cellaring. Anticipated maturity: 2010–2050.

1997: One of the finest wines of the vintage, this dark purple-colored effort reveals black raspberry, blackberry, mineral, and floral aromas in its complex, multidimensional bouquet. In the mouth, it is medium-bodied, with sweet, ripe fruit, firm tannin, good acidity for the vintage, and a long, impressively endowed, moderately tannic finish. Moreover, it will be one of the vintage's longest-lived wines. Anticipated maturity: 2007–2020.

1996: As I suspected, the 1996 is beginning to shut down. I left it in the glass for nearly 30 minutes and was impressed with the nuances that developed. The color is a dense ruby/black/purple. Reluctant aromas of blueberries, blackberries, minerals, flowers, truffles, and subtle new oak eventually emerge. Elegant on the attack, with sweet ripeness, and a delicate, concentrated richness, the hallmark of this wine is subtlety rather than flamboyance. A sweet mid-palate sets it apart from many of the uninspiring Ausones of the 1980s and 1970s. The wine is stylish and, at present, understated, with tremendous aging potential. Anticipated maturity: 2008–2040.

1995: Ausone's extraordinary minerality is present in the 1995, yet there are more aromatics, a richer, more multidimensional palate impression, and a fuller texture—all with the *terroir* brilliantly expressed. The wine boasts a dense ruby/purple color, and an emerging but tightly knit nose of spring flowers, minerals, earth, and black fruits. Rich, with an opulent texture and surprising sexiness for a young vintage of Ausone, the medium-bodied 1995 displays exquisite balance between its acid, tannin, alcohol, and fruit. Although it is not yet seamless, all the elements are present for an extraordinary evolution in the bottle. Given its backward style, this wine will require 4–5 years of cellaring and will age at a glacial pace for 30–40 years. Anticipated maturity: 2004–2045.

Past Glories: 1990 (92+), 1988 (91), 1983 (94), 1982 (95+), 1929 (96), 1921 (92), 1900 (94), 1874 (96)

BAHANS-HAUT-BRION (PESSAC-LÉOGNAN)

2000	D	(88–90)
1999	D	87
1998	D	88
1997	D	(86–87)
1996	D	88
1995	D	89

Bahans-Haut-Brion—the second wine of the famous Château Haut-Brion—is consistently one of the best second wines produced in Bordeaux and also one of my favorites.

2000: The 2000 offers a tangy, ripe, red and black currant–scented perfume with notes of earth and lead pencil in the background. With elegance, purity, a round, medium-bodied, sweet attack, fine balance, and a nicely knit finish, it possesses some of the character of its bigger sibling, but not the depth, structure, or mass. This wine should drink well for 10 years, possibly longer.

1999: The 1999 is another strong effort. It possesses good density, a sweet entry, a supple texture, as well as excellent purity and ripeness. 35% of the estate's total production was included in Bahans-Haut-Brion. Drink before 2010.

1998: Readers looking for the taste of Haut-Brion for about one-third the price should check out the 1998 Bahans-Haut-Brion. It possesses a scorched-earth, mineral, smoky, red and black currant–scented bouquet, terrific complexity, purity and elegance, and a harmonious palate. Tannin in the finish suggests that 1–2 years of cellaring may be required, but this is a serious effort that should age well for 15+ years.

1997: The 1997 Bahans-Haut-Brion exhibits a dark ruby color and a subtle mineral, tobacco, earthy, black plum and currant–scented nose. Light tannin is present in the finish, but this is an up-front hedonistic wine to drink during its first 5–6 years of life.

1996: The 1996 Bahans-Haut-Brion showed every bit as well in bottle as it did during its *élevage*. This atypically powerful, tobacco and black fruit–scented wine is much less forward than normal, but it shows much richness, exhibiting a nose that is unmistakably Haut-Brion-like. It reveals roasted herbs, scorched earth, and sweet black fruits in both its aromas and flavors. This tannic, structured Bahans will be at its finest between until 2012.

1995: The 1995 is an aromatic, round, complex, elegant wine that possesses all the characteristics of its bigger, richer sibling, but with less depth and more immediate appeal. Very "Graves" in style, with its smoky, roasted nose and sweet, smoke-infused black cherry and currant fruit, it should drink well for 5–7 years.

Past Glories: 1989 (90)

BALESTARD (BORDEAUX)

2000	D	(88–89)
1999	D	88
1998	D	87
1997	C	87

Vinified under the auspices of Jean-Luc Thunevin, of Valandraud fame, Jean-Charles Castex's Balestard is one of the finest generic Bordeaux that money can buy. This wine, which can compete with many classified growths, represents a very good value as prices remain reasonable.

2000: Smoky notes of roasted herbs, blackberry and cherry fruit, supple tannin, and a silky, long, sexy finish suggest consumption over the next 4–5 years.

1999: Though this wine can compete with some of the "big boys," it is best drunk during its first 5–6 years of life to take advantage of its exuberant, richly fruity style. It is a serious effort, revealing complex aromas of coffee-infused black cherry and berry fruit.

1998: A sleeper of the vintage, the 1998 offers up aromas and flavors of coffee, prunes, figs, chocolate, and berry fruit. This medium-bodied, plush, richly fruity effort can be enjoyed over the next 3–5 years.

1997: This smoky, surprisingly rich, creamy-textured wine displays intense notes of cherry jam, plumlike fruit, and spicy new oak. A tasty Bordeaux to drink now.

BALESTARD-LA-TONNELLE (ST.-EMILION)

2000	D	(86–88)
1999	D	85
1998	D	86
1997	C	78
1996	D	83
1995	D	86

2000: This wine comes across like a 1982, with its fat, chewy, ripe, nearly over-the-top style. There are gobs of black cherry fruit as well as copious glycerin, but not a great deal of complexity has emerged. The finish is lush. Anticipated maturity: now–2010.

1999: Low acidity gives the dark ruby/purple 1999 an up-front appeal. It possesses copious quantities of attractive cassis and cherry fruit, medium body, and an alluring, fleshy style. Give it 1–2 years to shed its rugged tannin, and enjoy it over the next 8 years.

1998: A medium-bodied, spicy, earthy effort, the 1998 exhibits notions of cured olives, ripe cherries, cassis, and spice box. Although not complex, it is a solid, muscular wine that gives a mouthful of tasty St.-Emilion. Anticipated maturity: now–2010.

1997: This wine reveals tannin, in addition to a compressed, one-dimensional personality, without enough sweetness, glycerin, or fruit to stand up to the wine's structure.

1996: The 1996 exhibits an evolved ruby/garnet color, a spicy, earthy, dried herb–scented nose, medium body, and a nearly mature personality with sweet cherry fruit in the finish. Drink it over the next 3–4 years.

1995: This 1995 reveals the low acidity and the ripeness of the vintage, as well as medium to full body. However, it was disjointed on the three occasions I tasted it. It is the type of wine that may pick up more definition and personality with age. My judgment may be conservative, as this wine has plenty of guts.

BARDE-HAUT (ST.-EMILION)

2000	D	(91–93)
1999	D	90
1998	D	90
1997	C	90

The omnipresent Michel Rolland is in charge of Barde-Haut's winemaking.

2000: The easy-to-understand 2000 is full-bodied, concentrated, and obviously produced from extremely ripe fruit. Along with all the fruit comes more tannin than in previous vintages. The structured, masculine 2000 displays impeccable purity as well as abundant quantities of dense, smoky black fruit, new saddle leather, toast, and mineral scents and flavors. It is a closed and backward Barde-Haut, so patience will be needed. Anticipated maturity: 2005–2020.

1999: A successful effort, the black/ruby/purple 1999 Barde-Haut displays low acidity in its plump, opulently textured personality. Luscious, rich, and expansive, this medium- to full-bodied 1999 is already difficult to resist. Anticipated maturity: now–2014.

1998: A deep ruby/purple is accompanied by pure, sweet aromas of blackberry and blueberry jam, revealing nicely integrated oak. This wine exhibits medium to full body, a fat, concentrated mid-palate with structure as well as definition, admirable length and richness, low acidity, and abundant fruit and extract. Anticipated maturity: now–2018.

1997: From the first tasting, this wine has possessed all of the earmarks of one of the vintage's stars, and is a sleeper of the vintage. A saturated blue/purple color is followed by sumptuous aromas of blackberry/blueberry jam. This medium-bodied St.-Emilion offers rich, multi-layered flavors in an elegant yet authoritatively rich style. Its tannin is now nicely melted, and there is gorgeous purity, a sweet mid-palate, and fine length in this stunning offering. One of the vintage's richest, best-balanced efforts, it can be drunk now and over the next 10 years.

BARET (PESSAC-LÉOGNAN)

1999	C	86
1998	C	86

The Ballande family, who recently bought Prieuré-Lichine, are slowly improving the quality of the wines from this estate and Denis Durbourdieu has been brought in to assist. The vineyards are planted with 60% Cabernet Sauvignon and 40% Merlot.

1999: There is more concentration as well as riper fruit in the 1999 than in the 1998. Sweet berry fruit, spice box, herbs, smoke, and earth are present in this attractive, medium-bodied, pure, ripe, luscious effort. Drink it over the next 8 years.

1998: Soft, ripe, and made in a Graves style, the 1998 reveals notes of tobacco, scorched earth, and soft cherry/currant fruit. The wine is elegant, with sweet tannin, attractive ripe fruit, and medium body. Enjoy it over the next 5–6 years.

Other vintage tasted: 2000 (82–84)

BATAILLEY (PAUILLAC)

2000	D	(87–88+)
1999	D	86
1998	D	87
1997	C	84
1996	C	87
1995	C	87

Batailley, a traditionally styled Pauillac, is often difficult to assess in its youth. It never performs as well young as it does at 10–12 years of age. Shrewd buyers should know that the quality of Batailley's wines have improved greatly and that the prices remain reasonable.

2000: The deep ruby/purple, restrained 2000 Batailley offers scents of minerals, underbrush, and black currants, and a structured, medium-bodied, moderately long finish. Anticipated maturity: 2007–2018. The French would say this wine is intended for the *"goût anglais"* ("English taste").

1999: Lacking the weight of the 1998, the dark ruby-colored, medium-bodied 1999 is surprisingly soft, with sweet black cherry and cassis fruit intermixed with minerals, smoke, and earth. Drink it over the next 10–12 years.

1998: An excellent dark plum color is followed by scents of tobacco, cedar, black currant, and earth. There is good ripeness, medium to full body, smoky, herb-tinged flavors, and fine length. The tannin is firm but not excessive. This 1998 is tasting significantly better from bottle than it did during its *élevage*. Anticipated maturity: 2004–2017.

1997: Notes of herbs, tobacco, and currant fruit mixed with damp soil aromas can be found in this traditionally made Pauillac. With medium body, grip, and tannin, it is more evolved and softer than expected for this generally ageworthy wine. Give it 1–2 years of cellaring, and consume it over the next decade.

1996: Batailley's 1996 is a well-structured, old-style Pauillac with a dense ruby/purple color, earthy, cedar-tinged, black currant fruit in the aromatics and flavors, medium body, an excellent mid-palate, good depth, and a moderately tannic, firm, but pure finish. This very good to excellent Batailley will keep for 2 decades. Anticipated maturity: 2003–2020.

1995: The 1995 has turned out well, displaying a dark ruby/purple color and aromas of minerals, black currants, and smoky new oak. In the mouth, it is a medium-weight, backward, well-delineated Pauillac with plenty of tannin and a true *vin de garde* style. Anticipated maturity: now–2015.

BEAU-SÉJOUR BÉCOT (ST.-EMILION)

2000	E	(91–94)
1999	D	87
1998	D	91
1997	D	89
1996	D	89
1995	D	89

Since Beau-Séjour Bécot regained its premier grand cru classé status in the 1996 St.-Emilion classification, the wines have been generally top rank, with the 1998 and 2000 the finest yet tasted. Brothers Gérard and Dominique Bécot have accomplished admirable work.

2000: This modern-style St.-Emilion displays abundant wood, although the 2000 is better integrated than some past vintages. Deep and full-bodied, it reveals an excellent saturated purple color, sweet black cherry and currant fruit intermixed with smoke and toast, outstanding purity, and considerable fat, but the vintage's hard, earthy tannin makes an appearance in the finish. This is an example of a wine where the fat is underneath the tannin rather than on top. Anticipated maturity: 2006–2018.

1999: Despite the hailstorm that forced this estate to harvest early, the 1999 has turned out surprisingly well. It reveals an opaque ruby color as well as an excellent bouquet of smoke, licorice, new oak, and black fruits. The wine is medium- to full-bodied, with a sweet entry, but the finish is short, and exhibits less volume than the 1998. Nevertheless, this is a very good to excellent effort for the vintage. Anticipated maturity: now–2014.

1998: As most recent vintages have, the 1998 exhibits flamboyant, obvious new oak, but unlike other years, there is more concentration, power, and depth behind the vanilla/toast notes. Full-bodied, dense, and chewy, with copious peppery, herb-tinged, red currant, black currant, and blackberry fruit, this is a lush, generously endowed offering with a lightly tannic finish. Anticipated maturity: now–2016.

1997: One of the stars of the vintage, this sexy St.-Emilion offers a big, smoky, toasty new oak–scented nose with jammy strawberry and cherry fruit. Low acidity gives the wine a plump, fleshy feel. Medium- to full-bodied, gorgeously pure, and attractive, it can be enjoyed over the next 4–5 years.

1996: The lavishly oaked, hedonistically styled 1996 exhibits a dark plum/purple color. The nose offers up sweet jammy fruit (primarily black currants and cherries) intermixed with toasty new oak. Medium-bodied, with excellent, nearly outstanding richness, a nicely layered mid-palate, and sweet tannin in the long finish, it should last 15+ years.

1995: Beau-Séjour Bécot's sexy 1995 offers a dark plum color, followed by a sweet, vanilla, spicy, black cherry, and curranty nose that jumps from the glass. In the mouth, this is a supple, round, hedonistically styled claret with copious quantities of palate-pleasing plushness, no hard edges, and an impressively endowed, rich finish. Anticipated maturity: now–2014.

BEAULIEU COMTES DE TASTES (BORDEAUX SUPÉRIEUR)

2000	B	(87–88)

2000: This is an eye-opening offering that should be bottled unfined and unfiltered. The 2000 was made from 70% Merlot and 30% Cabernet Sauvignon and aged in 50% new oak casks. This dense, chewy, fleshy Bordeaux Supérieur offers scents of cassis, fudge, and espresso. Deep, superpure, ripe, and mouth-filling, this high-quality offering is a terrific value. Drink it during its first 4–5 years of life. Case purchases should be mandatory with this one.

BEAUREGARD (POMEROL)

2000	D	(88–90)
1999	D	87
1998	D	88
1997	C	87
1996	C	87
1995	C	87

Though the Beauregard wines remain precocious, they are more seductive and more consistent lately, with more flesh and power than before. They are fairly priced for their appellation.

2000: A heavy, flamboyant display of smoky oak, plums, and overripe black cherries provides an exotic introduction to this full-bodied, soft, round, international-style Pomerol. This hedonistic wine is already delicious. Anticipated maturity: now–2012.

1999: A fruit bomb filled with savory black cherries, berries, and plums, as well as smoke, coffee, and dried herbs, this fleshy, medium- to full-bodied, low-acid 1999 has some tannin lurking under the surface. Anticipated maturity: now–2014.

1998: The deep ruby/purple-colored 1998 Beauregard exhibits a perfume of smoke, black cherry, cough syrup, chocolate, and smoky wood. Thick, tannic, and medium- to full-bodied, it will benefit from some cellaring, and keep for 12 years.

1997: Another sexy, open-knit, elegant, sweet, round, short-lived, but pleasurable Pomerol, the 1997 Beauregard offers abundant grilled herbs, toasty oak, and black cherry fruit aromas and flavors. Medium-bodied and supple, it is ideal for drinking over the next 5–6 years.

1996: Beauregard's deep ruby-colored 1996 reveals a sweet, jammy cherry-scented nose with noticeable strawberry notes. The wine is medium-bodied, soft, elegant, and moderately weighty with hints of toasty new oak. It should drink well for 4–5 years.

1995: An excellent wine, this 1995 offers an alluring deep ruby color with a smoky, vanilla, berry, chocolate-scented nose. Medium-bodied and ripe, with sweet fruit, moderate tannin, and low acidity, this is a fine example of Beauregard. Anticipated maturity: now–2010.

BEAUSÉJOUR-DUFFAU-LAGAROSSE (ST.-EMILION)

2000	E	(91–95)
1999	E	88
1998	E	89
1997	D	85
1996	E	87?
1995	E	?

Beauséjour-Duffau is known for its very high-quality wines, especially since the mid-1980s. They remain some of the most complex, ethereal St.-Emilions, generally dense and powerful but reserved and austere, with a mineral character. They are not for those unable to defer gratification as they usually require a decade of cellaring before their tannins begin to melt.

2000: Undoubtedly the finest Beauséjour-Duffau produced since the perfect 1990, the 2000 boasts an opaque black/purple color. What follows is a tannic, tight, structured, dense personality offering predominant characteristics of blackberry liqueur and minerals. The sweet attack gives way to a structured, serious, ageworthy wine with an abundance of tannin as well as very good acidity. Marvelous purity, high extraction, and laserlike clarity characterize this well-endowed 2000. Once again, patience will be a virtue. Anticipated maturity: 2008–2030.

1999: A complex nose of black- and blueberries, flowers, and an omnipresent note of liquid stones/minerals is followed by a pure, sweet, ripe, medium-bodied wine. It does not follow through with a great deal of depth on the palate, and exhibits firmness and leanness in the finish. Will those characteristics age out in 2–3 years? Anticipated maturity: 2004–2018.

1998: This dark ruby/purple-colored, mid-weight, restrained, graceful effort reveals aromas and flavors of minerals, blueberries, and flowers, not dissimilar from some of Burgundy's grand cru Vosne-Romanées. Nicely textured and soft, with adequate tannin to frame its medium-bodied style, it is approachable yet should age nicely for 12 years.

1997: This 1997 has turned out to be significantly lighter than expected. Smoky new oak, minerals, and a plum/cherry fruit concoction provide a pretty, elegant, lighter-styled St.-Emilion exhibiting moderate tannin in the finish. There is good complexity but little density or depth. Anticipated maturity: now–2008.

1996: It appears that I overestimated the quality of this wine. Out of bottle it seems to have very little of the multidimensional concentration and intensity it showed during its *élevage*. Dark ruby-colored, with the attractive telltale black raspberry and pronounced mineral characteristics of this small vineyard's products, it seems lighter and more angular in bottle than in cask tastings. Its moderately long finish is filled with dry, astringent tannin. This wine is very good, but it is not outstanding, as I had expected it to be. Moreover, the 1996 Beauséjour-Duffau will have a tendency to dry out given the way the tannin is behaving. Anticipated maturity: 2005–2015.

1995: On numerous occasions this wine was gorgeous from cask, exhibiting a saturated dark purple color, and a sweet kirsch, black cherry, mineral, and truffle-like character not dissimilar from the old-vine intensity found in Lafleur, the great Pomerol. However, the wine was totally closed when I tasted it after bottling, with earth, minerals, and black fruits emerging after extended airing. In the mouth, it was completely shut down, with extremely high levels of tannin. I am reserving judgment.

Past Glories: 1990 (100)

BEAUSOLEIL (POMEROL)

2000	D	(86–87?)
1999	D	87
1998	D	87
1997	C	85
1996	C	(86–88)
1995	C	87

2000: A deep dark ruby/purple color is followed by reticent but promising aromas of earth, minerals, black cherries, and raspberries. A firm tannic underpinning dominates this cleanly made but gritty, austerely styled 2000. Whether or not it will evolve gracefully is open to speculation. Anticipated maturity: 2005–2015?

1999: Good extraction, low acidity, full body, and abundant quantities of smoky, berry, and caramel-infused fruit provide an attractive, hedonistic mouthful of jammy Pomerol. Enjoy it over the next 8 years.

1998: This dark ruby-colored offering reveals mocha, caramel, jammy black plums, cherries, and smoke characteristics, a soft, up-front, medium- to full-bodied personality, and an open-knit, creamy texture. Drink this sexy 1998 over the next 8 years.

1997: A touch of gritty tannin in the finish is the only negative of this medium-bodied, solidly made, unpretentious 1997. It offers sweet cherry fruit, spicy wood, and a direct personality. Drink it over the next 2–3 years.

1996: This wine has put on considerable flesh and weight during its *élevage*. Beausoleil has produced a dense ruby/purple-colored 1996 with plenty of spicy new oak and vanilla in its aromatic profile. There are copious quantities of sweet blueberry and cassis fruit, low acidity, dense, ripe, sweet fruit on the attack, medium body, and a round, lush finish. The wine possesses some tannin, but it is a forward-style Pomerol. Anticipated maturity: now–2008.

1995: A deep ruby/purple-colored wine with a cassis nose that soars from the glass, this deep, medium to full-bodied, richly fruity, dense, concentrated Pomerol is a sleeper of the vintage. Anticipated maturity: now–2007.

BEL-AIR (LALANDE-DE-POMEROL)

1999	B	(76–79)
1998	B	87

1999: The 1999 Bel-Air is thin, tart, hard, and unexpressive.

1998: A very good value, this delicious, dark plum/ruby-colored offering reveals copious quantities of sweet, nearly overripe black cherry fruit, low acidity, a succulent texture, medium body, and a clean, lush finish. Drink it over the next 7–8 years.

Other vintage tasted: 2000 (84–86)

BEL-AIR GRANDE CUVÉE (BORDEAUX SUPÉRIEUR)

2000	B	(87–88)

2000: Another impressively made Bordeaux Supérieur, Bel-Air Grande Cuvée possesses a deep ruby/purple color, a soft, plush, consumer-friendly personality, copious quantities of fruit as well as glycerin, and light to moderate tannin. Meant to be consumed during its first 4–5 years of life, it should be a good value as well as a sleeper of the vintage.

BEL-AIR LA ROYÈRE (PREMIÈRES CÔTES DE BLAYE)
1997   **B   (85–86)**

1997: A serious "little" wine made with the consulting assistance of Valandraud's Jean-Luc Thunevin, this 1997 boasts an opaque ruby/purple color, excellent ripeness, a straightforward character, good fruit, and fine length. Drink it over the next 2–3 years.
Other vintages tasted: 2000 (85–86), 1999 (82–85)

BELAIR (ST.-EMILION)
1997   **D   86**
1996   **D   86**

1997: Wine-maker Pascal Delbeck appears to have produced an atypically soft, forward, appealing 1997. A dark ruby color is followed by aromas of sweet, mineral-infused, black cherry fruit, medium body, and light tannin in the round, attractive finish. Anticipated maturity: now–2010.
1996: An angular, light-bodied, mineral-scented wine came across as austere and spartan, lacking fruit glycerin, and flesh. Anticipated maturity: 2003–2012.
Other vintage tasted: 1998 (74–76)

BELGRAVE (HAUT-MÉDOC)
1999   **D   88**
1998   **D   87**

After a long period in the qualitative doldrums, Belgrave is producing much better wines.
1999: Sweet, concentrated, jammy blackberry and cassis fruit emerge from this dark purple-colored offering. The 1999 is the finest Belgrave I have ever tasted over the last 30 years. The texture is fleshy, and the wine is medium- to full-bodied, low in acidity, and long in the finish. Let's hope it gets into the bottle in the same condition. Anticipated maturity: now–2015.
1998: The 1998's dark purple color is accompanied by classy smoky, black currant, wet stone, and new oak aromas. Medium-bodied and elegant, with fine depth as well as a nicely textured, moderately tannic finish, it will be at its best between 2004–2015.
Other vintage tasted: 2000 (87–88+)

BELLE-VUE (HAUT-MÉDOC)
2000   **C   (88–90)**
1999   **C   (90–91)**
1998   **C   87**

Belle-Vue is an impressive operation that is producing high-quality efforts from low yields of 35–45 hectoliters per hectare (comparable with the finest classified growths). The vineyards are planted with 50% Cabernet Sauvignon, 40% Merlot, and 10% Petit Verdot, but the blend varies slightly with each vintage. The wines are aged 16 months in 80% new French oak and are never filtered prior to bottling. Annual production averages 2,500 cases.
2000: A sleeper of the vintage, this blend of 54% Cabernet Sauvignon, 34% Merlot, and 12% Petit Verdot is an amazing Haut-Médoc. It exhibits a saturated black/purple color as well as a sweet nose of tobacco, blackberry, and cassis fruit, medium to full body, an excellent texture, and superb purity. There are 2,500 cases of this offering, which tipped the scales at 12.8% natural alcohol.
1999: A spectacular effort, the opaque ruby/purple-colored 1999 (a blend of 48% Cabernet Sauvignon, 37% Merlot, and 15% Petit Verdot) boasts a terrific bouquet of crème de cassis, licorice, toasty oak, and cedar. Fat, chewy, and rich, with superb concentration as well as a sweet mid-palate, it should drink well when released and last for 12–15 years.

1998: An excellent wine of classified growth quality, the 1998 offers deep black currant, spicy new oak, tobacco, and spice box aromas. Medium-bodied, with soft tannin (particularly for this vintage), it can be drunk now and over the next 5–6 years.

BELLEFONT-BELCIER (ST.-EMILION)

2000	D	(90–92)
1999	D	87
1998	D	87
1997	C	84
1996	C	87
1995	C	85

Bellefont-Belcier has improved greatly over recent years, with the 1999 and 2000 being the finest wines I have ever tasted from this estate. Since 1999, Marc Dworkin, formerly in charge of Larmande, controls the vinification at the estate. Shrewd buyers are advised to keep an eye on this former underachiever, as prices remain reasonable.

2000: Undoubtedly the finest Bellefont-Belcier yet produced, the deep plum/purple-colored 2000 reveals a sweet, smoky, spicy, cedary, jammy cherry/currant-scented bouquet. The wine is deep, rich, and fleshy, with terrific fruit purity, abundant glycerin, full body, and impressive ripe tannin. It will drink well early, and keep for 15+ years.

1999: Marc Dworkin seems to have extracted more character and flesh than normally expected from Bellefont-Belcier. A sleeper of the vintage, this opaque ruby/purple-colored effort exhibits bountiful fruit, abundant glycerin, and a fleshy, blackberry/cherry in-your-face style. The wood is nicely integrated and the acidity is low in this creamy-textured 1999, which will have mass appeal. Anticipated maturity: now–2012.

1998: A very good effort from Bellefont-Belcier, the 1998 reveals abundant quantities of spice box, smoky new oak, cedar, black cherries, leather, and herbs, presented in a medium-bodied, fleshy style with sweet tannin as well as good definition. Anticipated maturity: now–2010.

1997: The 1997 has turned out far better than expected from barrel tastings. Open-knit, easy to taste and understand, it possesses adequate acidity, some tannin, and a medium-bodied, spicy, cherry-scented nose, adequate flavor concentration, and a touch of toasty new oak. Lightweight yet pleasant, it can be enjoyed over the next 3 years.

1996: The excellent 1996 is a potential sleeper of the vintage. The wine offers a dark ruby color and sweet black cherry fruit intermixed with smoke, dried herbs, and toast. This round, generous, medium- to full-bodied wine is already delicious; enjoy it over the next 5 years.

1995: The 1995 is somewhat of a sleeper, exhibiting a dense color and rich, jammy black fruits intermingled with scents of herb, licorice, and toast. Thick, chewy flavors reveal fine extraction and glycerin. This is a soft, low-acid, opulent wine for drinking before 2003.

BELLEGRAVE (POMEROL)

1998	D	(85–86)
1997	D	87
1996	D	84

Jean-Marie Bouldy's wines are generally soft, easy to drink and to understand, with seductive fruit. They are meant to be consumed in their youth. Prices are reasonable for the appellation.

1998: Surprisingly soft and open-knit, without the power and tannin often present in this vintage, this dark ruby-colored 1998 displays round, fruity flavors (primarily spice and cherries), good weight, but not the overall charm found in the 1997. It will require consumption during its first 7–8 years of life.

1997: Bellegrave's 1997 appears to be better than its 1998, atypical for these two vintages in Pomerol. Dark ruby-colored, with a sexy, open-knit, plum, cherry, currant, and spicy wood-scented bouquet, abundant fruit, low acidity, lush ripeness, and an evolved personality, it will offer delicious drinking now and over the next 3–4 years. It is an appealing, medium-weight Pomerol that is loaded with fruit.

1996: An open-knit, soft, smoky, black cherry–scented wine with spicy oak in the background, this pure, pleasant, light-bodied 1996 is ideal for drinking over the next 3 years.

BELLEVUE (ST.-EMILION)

2000	E	(92–95)

Nicolas Thienpont of Pavie Macquin, along with wine consultant guru Stephen Derencourt (La Mondotte, Canon-La-Gaffelière, Clos de l'Oratoire), are responsible for this blockbuster debut release, made from tiny yields of 30 hectoliters per hectare and a blend of 80% Merlot and 20% Cabernet Franc.

2000: The opaque purple color of this wine is accompanied by spectacular aromatics of sweet, rich, mineral-infused blackberry, crème de cassis, smoke, licorice, and vanilla. The wine displays extraordinary opulence, a sexy, lush, low-acid, well-delineated personality, layers of flavor, massive extract, and a 45-second, sweetly tannic finish. For a debut effort, this is a remarkable wine, but I would not expect less from this proprietor, and the fact that this well-placed vineyard has vines that average 40 years of age. Anticipated maturity: 2003–2020.

BELLISLE MONDOT (ST.-EMILION)

2000	D	(88–90)

This well-placed property is to be taken seriously. The wine's vinification is supervised by St.-Emilion's leading revolutionary, Jean-Luc Thunevin.

2000: The 2000 is the finest wine I have tasted from Bellisle Mondot. It exhibits a saturated blue/plum/purple color as well as a big smoky, ripe nose of black fruits intermixed with mocha, toast, earth, and exhilarating levels of black cherry and cassis fruit. Full-bodied and intense, with an impressively thick mid-palate and long finish, this sleeper of the vintage may merit an even higher score once it has been bottled. Anticipated maturity: 2005–2016.

BELREGARD-FIGEAC (ST.-EMILION)

2000	C	(84–86?)

2000: Belregard-Figeac's internationally styled 2000 is uninspiring. A heavy overlay of new oak obliterates much of the fruit. Although the wine possesses depth and intensity, it could have come from anywhere. Anticipated maturity: 2004–2009.

BERLIQUET (ST.-EMILION)

2000	D	(90–91)
1999	D	88
1998	D	89
1997	C	88

This is another up-and-coming St.-Emilion estate that has improved greatly over recent years under the inspired leadership of Patrick de Lesquen, who has brought in the talented Patrick Valette to oversee the vinifications. The 1998, 1999 and 2000 are sleepers, the 2000 clearly their best wine yet. Unfortunately, prices here have followed the qualitative trend.

2000: The finest Berliquet yet made. A dense ruby/purple wine with impressive aromatics (primarily jammy currants, black cherries, earth, licorice, and vanilla), this classically structured, pure St.-Emilion possesses nearly perfect equilibrium, power married to elegance, and enough vibrant acidity to provide focus. Anticipated maturity: 2005–2020.

1999: An opaque purple-colored, full-bodied, thick effort with low acid, jammy blackberry and cherry flavors, excellent purity, and an opulent personality, this 1999 will be drinkable before its 1998 counterpart. Anticipated maturity: now–2015.

1998: One of the finest Berliquets I have tasted to date, this dark ruby/purple-colored offering exhibits dense, saturated, flavorful black cherry notes intermixed with licorice, spice box, tobacco, and earth. Full-bodied, ripe, and concentrated, with moderate tannin and a closed but impressively built personality, this wine needs several years to resolve all of its tannin. Anticipated maturity: 2004–2016.

1997: An excellent example of the vintage, the 1997 Berliquet exhibits abundant amounts of sweet black currant fruit, along with cedar, spice box, and toasty aromas. Medium- to full-bodied, thick, and rich, with moderate tannin, fine sweetness, an open-knit texture, and admirable length, it will be at its best between now and 2012.

BERNADOTTE (HAUT-MÉDOC)

2000	C	(88–90)
1999	C	87
1998	C	87
1997	C	(85–87)
1996	C	85?

Acquired in 1997 by Mme de Lencquesaing, the owner of Pichon-Lalande, 1999 was the first vintage over which the Pichon-Lalande staff had total control of the viticulture and winemaking. The 2000 is clearly the best young wine I have ever tasted from this estate.

2000: A succulent, concentrated, deep ruby/purple-colored wine, it exhibits considerable finesse as well as copious black currant fruit intermixed with spice box, chocolate, and cedar. Sweet tannin and good acidity provide delineation. It is a blend of 60% Cabernet Sauvignon and 40% Merlot. Anticipated maturity: now–2012.

1999: A blend of 53% Cabernet Sauvignon and 47% Merlot, this dark ruby/purple-colored 1999 exhibits a lovely, open-knit texture, smoky chocolate and cassis flavors, medium body, excellent ripeness, and the delicacy of its more famous sibling, Pichon-Lalande. Drink it over the next 5–6 years.

1998: This dark ruby-colored blend of 40% Cabernet Sauvignon, 45% Merlot, 14% Cabernet Franc, and 1% Petit Verdot reveals a cedary, red and black currant–scented bouquet, medium body, burly tannin, and very good to excellent texture, ripeness, and overall harmony. Consume it over the next 8 years.

1997: The interesting 1997 (a blend of 60% Cabernet Sauvignon and 40% Merlot) exhibits a Pauillac-like cedary, leafy tobacco, black currant fruitiness. Soft and round, with low acidity, elegance, and fine length, it should be consumed over the next 4–5 years.

1996: The blend of the 1996 is identical to that of the 1997, being composed of 60% Cabernet Sauvignon and 40% Merlot. The staff of Pichon-Lalande bottled but did not vinify this wine. It possesses a medium ruby color, plum, black currant, and dried herb scents and flavors, with dry tannin in the finish. Nevertheless, this is a well-made, delicate Bordeaux that should drink well for 3–4 years.

BERTINEAU ST.-VINCENT (LALANDE-DE-POMEROL)

1999	C	87
1998	C	87
1997	C	85

This property owned by Dany and Michel Rolland consistently produces one of the finest values in Lalande-de-Pomerol.

1999: Black cherries, leather, spice box, and earthlike notes are abundant in both the aromatics and flavors of this medium-bodied, velvety-textured, forward effort. Drink it over the next 3–4 years.

1998: Sweet strawberry and cherry jam aromas are offered in this medium dark ruby-colored wine. Additionally, it reveals soft, sweet tannin, a plush texture, and an easygoing finish. Consume it over the next 3 years. It is a sleeper of the vintage.

1997: A good effort, this deep ruby-colored wine exhibits spicy, cherry fruit, earth, and herbs. Medium-bodied and tasty, with low acidity, it should be drunk now.

Other vintage tasted: 2000 (85–86)

BEYCHEVELLE (ST.-JULIEN)

2000	D	(90–91)
1999	D	86
1998	D	87
1997	C	78
1996	D	86
1995	D	85

The wines of Beychevelle are generally soft and smooth, and accessible in their youth. Recent vintages have shown some improvement and, while they are fully mature by 10 years of age, they have the requisite stuffing to withstand 15 or more years of cellaring. Shrewd consumers should note that Beychevelle is not one of St.-Julien's most expensive crus classés.

2000: The finest Beychevelle since 1989, this floral-scented wine offers notes of blueberries, red currants, minerals, and spice. Restrained, subtle, measured, but beautifully rich, delicate, and fruity, it needs 2–3 years of cellaring, and should evolve gracefully for two decades. How reassuring it is to see Beychevelle produce a wine of such stature!

1999: A soft, plump, savory offering, the mid-weight 1999 offers attractive levels of black raspberries, cherries, and currants. Some new oak is present, but it remains in the background. Graceful and symmetrical, but without much delineation, it should drink well for 10 years.

1998: This elegant, stylish, well-delineated Beychevelle offers finesse and beauty in a medium-bodied, firmly structured, flavorful format. Red and black currants, licorice, minerals, spice, and tar notes are subtle but persuasive. While it does not cut an enormous swath across the palate, the wine's acidity, alcohol, and tannin are well balanced. Anticipated maturity: now–2016.

1997: Sinewy, medium-bodied, with firm tannin as well as a soft, evolved style, this diluted effort is pleasant but lacking concentration and length. Drink it over the next 2–3 years.

1996: Beychevelle's 1996 reveals an evolved dark plum color. The nose offers toasty new oak in an open, charming style, and berry fruit intermixed with spice. It is an uninspiring example, particularly for such a top-notch *terroir,* but the wine is medium-bodied and cleanly made, with moderate longevity. Anticipated maturity: now–2012.

1995: This wine performed better from cask. Out of bottle it displays a medium ruby color and a distinctive nose of underbrush, damp earth, and loamy-tinged black currant fruit. Moderately tannic, with medium body and some angularity, the 1995 possesses good extract but not much soul or character. Anticipated maturity: now–2012.

Past Glories: 1986 (92), 1982 (91), 1953 (92), 1928 (97)

BON PASTEUR (POMEROL)

2000	E	(91–93+)
1999	E	90
1998	E	91
1997	D	88
1996	E	88
1995	E	89

Bon Pasteur is the home estate of Dany and Michel Rolland, both brilliant oenologists. Rolland's wonderful 1982, 1988, 1989, 1990, 1995, 1996, 1998 and 2000 stand as testimony to his talent.

2000: A bigger, more muscular effort than the superb 1998, Bon Pasteur 2000 will be quite long-lived. A deep, saturated purple color is accompanied by sumptuous aromas of mocha, truffles, prunes, blackberries, and cassis with toast added for extra complexity. Medium- to full-bodied and more structured, powerful, and tannic than the exceptional 1998, it will require 2–3 years of cellaring. Made in a *vin de garde* style, it will keep for two decades.

1999: The opaque ruby/purple-colored 1999 has put on weight during its *élevage*. Revealing a concentrated, rich plum, blackberry, cola, and smoky bouquet, this chewy, rich, low-acid, fat Pomerol is less delineated than the 1998, and thus will be best drunk upon its release as well as over the following 8–10 years. It is an impressive wine for the vintage.

1998: Undoubtedly one of the finest Bon Pasteurs since 1982, the dense purple-colored 1998 boasts a beautifully rich, complex perfume of blackberries, plums, lead pencil, cherries, mocha, and caramel. Powerful and rich, with a multilayered texture and an opulent, viscous finish revealing enough sweet tannin for definition, this is a terrific, full-bodied, seamless effort. Anticipated maturity: now–2016.

1997: Readers looking for a delicious wine with scents and flavors of chocolate, smoke, cherry, black currant, and plum will admire the fleshy, open-knit, medium-bodied 1997 Bon Pasteur. Seamless and smooth, with surprisingly fine concentration, it is reminiscent of a 1987, but has more muscle and richness. Drink it over the next 8 years.

1996: The 1996 is lighter in bottle than it was in cask. The wine reveals dry, slightly gritty tannin in the finish, which kept my score on the conservative side. It exhibits spicy new oak, medium body, abundant smoky black cherry and mocha–tinged fruit, good weight, excellent purity, and a firm, structured, muscular finish and it should evolve nicely for 8–10 years.

1995: The outstanding 1995 offers a dark plum color and high-quality aromatics consisting of toast, lead pencil, smoke, and black cherry and currant fruit. In the mouth it is sweet, medium-bodied, round, spicy, and succulently textured, with a plump, fleshy finish. Anticipated maturity: now–2012.

Past Glories: 1990 (91), 1989 (90), 1982 (96)

BONALGUE (POMEROL)

2000	D	(87–89)
1999	D	87
1998	D	87
1997	C	86
1996	C	86
1995	C	86

Bonalgue is consistently one of the better values from Pomerol, an appellation that has become frightfully expensive.

2000: The 2000 Bonalgue is a dense, powerful, concentrated effort exhibiting scents of black raspberries, underbrush, creosote, and wood. In the mouth it is sweet and dense, with moderate tannin. There is a certain robustness to the wine's finish that comes across as slightly rustic, but this 2000 is definitely a sleeper of the vintage. Anticipated maturity: 2003–2016.

1999: An impressive effort that has fattened considerably over the last year, this dark ruby/plum-colored wine displays notes of prunes, blackberries, tar, and chocolate. Rich, fleshy, and full-bodied, with low acidity, excellent purity, and a long, lusty finish, it is meant to be drunk during its first 8 years of life.

1998: Deep ruby/purple-colored, with a ripe nose of black cherries, earth, underbrush, smoke, and mocha, the 1998 is dense, chewy, and succulent, with oodles of fruit as well as glycerin. A fleshy, up-front character will provide appeal over the next 8 years.

1997: A jammy prune, raisin, sweet cherry–scented bouquet jumps from the glass of this medium ruby-colored wine. Attractive, soft, and diffuse, this medium-bodied effort requires consumption over the next 1–2 years.

1996: The 1996 is another example of this consistently well made wine. It offers up a sweet nose of plum fruit intertwined with cherries. Sweet fruit, good fat, and a touch of oak give the wine a plump, savory mouth-feel. This is a charming, bistro-styled red with more depth and ripeness than many wines costing twice as much. Drink it over the next 2–3 years.

1995: A dark ruby-colored wine with sweet, spicy, berry fruit and a roasted peanut–scented nose, the 1995 Bonalgue is soft, round, and velvety-textured, with low acidity and moderate weight. It is an attractive wine for near-term drinking. Anticipated maturity: now–2004.

LE BOSCQ (MÉDOC)

1996 Vieilles Vignes	B	86
1995 Vieilles Vignes	B	85

1996: A delicious, richly fruity wine, this 1996 offers a deep color, a good mid-palate, and a moderately long, medium-bodied, spicy, rich finish. Anticipated maturity: now–2008

1995: This attractive, medium-bodied, cleanly made wine offers good value and immediate drinkability, with spicy black currant flavor and scent and fine depth. It will keep for 3–4 years.

Other vintage tasted: 1999 (83–85)

BOURGNEUF-VAYRON (POMEROL)

2000	D	(86–87?)
1999	D	88?
1998	D	89+?
1997	D	87?
1996	D	87+?
1995	D	89

Bourgneuf-Vayron seems to be exploiting the full potential of its vineyard, so consumers better watch out. They should know, however, that certain vintages show a green pepper character that may not appeal to everyone.

2000: The 2000 does not possess the concentration levels of the 1998 or 1999, but is typically big-boned and burly, revealing notes of tar, earthy black fruits, and oak. The 2000 is very 1975-ish—concentrated as well as tannic. If it does not dry out, it may deserve a higher score.

1999: Another rustic, powerful, concentrated, dense, full-bodied, masculine-styled effort, the 1999 reveals mouth-searing levels of tannin in addition to abundant licorice, plum, prune, blackberry, and cherry fruit. It is atypically backward, especially for a 1999 right bank offering. Anticipated maturity: 2005–2020.

1998: A dense saturated ruby/purple color is followed by aromas of green peppercorns, plums, roasted meat, leather, tobacco, and black fruits. The wine is chunky, full-bodied, concentrated, and chewy, with tough tannin in the finish. If the green pepper component becomes better integrated and the tannin melts away, this 1998 will merit an outstanding rating, but patience will be required. Is this a wine for those with 19th-century tastes? Anticipated maturity: 2006–2020.

1997: A strong albeit rustic effort, this opaque dark ruby/purple-colored 1997 reveals herbaceous black cherry, earthy, and licorice aromas, a tannic, medium- to full-bodied, chewy constitution, less charm than most 1997s, but more weight, intensity, and volume. If the tannin becomes better integrated, this wine may merit an even higher score. Anticipated maturity: 2003–2012.

1996: The 1996 has turned out well, although it is somewhat monolithic. The color is saturated ruby/plum. The wine has an earthy, black cherry, licorice, and dried herb–scented nose, medium to full body, and muscular, concentrated flavors with moderately high tannin. If more complexity emerges with aging, this Bourgneuf will score in the high eighties. It is a mouth-filling, robust Pomerol to drink before 2012.

1995: A sleeper of the vintage, Bourgneuf's 1995 is one of the finest wines I have tasted from this estate. The color is an opaque purple, and the wine offers a closed but promising nose of black cherries, raspberries, and coffee-tinged fruit. Packed and stacked, as they say in the vernacular, this medium- to full-bodied, powerful, mouth-filling Pomerol is big, bold, and boisterous. If additional complexity develops in this excellent, decadently rich wine, it will merit an outstanding rating. Anticipated maturity: now–2014.

BOUSCAUT (PESSAC-LÉOGNAN)

2000	D	(84–86)
1999	D	83
1998	C	75

2000: Finally, a reasonably good effort from this underachiever, Bouscaut's 2000 possesses a dark ruby/purple color in addition to aromas of spicy new oak and red and black currant fruit. While superficial, there is more to it than most previous vintages have contained. Medium-bodied, with sweet tannin, and a nicely textured, moderately endowed finish, it will drink well until 2015.

1999: Sweet ripe currants, cherries, and berries intermixed with minerals, smoke, and new oak compete in this soft, straightforward, pleasant offering. Drink it over the next 10 years.

1998: Although the color is an attractive dark ruby, this light- to medium-bodied effort reveals considerable hollowness in the mid-palate. While some of Pessac-Léognan aromas of scorched earth, red currant, and gravel emerge, there is little depth or length. Anticipated maturity: now–2012.

BOYD-CANTENAC (MARGAUX)

2000	D	(88–89+)
1999	D	88
1998	D	86
1997	C	(82–85)

2000: A sleeper of the vintage, this opaque purple-colored Margaux offers a sweet perfume of acacia flowers, smoke, black currants, and foresty notes. Medium- to full-bodied, concentrated, and pure, with outstanding equilibrium as well as noticeable but well-integrated sweet tannin, it will drink well between 2006–2018.

1999: An excellent effort, this deep ruby/purple-colored 1999 offers abundant black fruits intermixed with mineral and floral scents. Rich, with low acidity, medium body, and a nicely textured finish, this pure claret will be at its best between 2003–2015.

1998: Elegant and sweet but relatively light, this medium-bodied, attenuated Margaux reveals dusty, earthy, black currant, and cedar notes as well as moderate length and depth. It is meant to be drunk over the next 8 years.

1997: Although there is some density in this wine, it comes across as somewhat savage and rustic, with an excessive amount of tannin for its delicate fruit. The color is a healthy dark ruby, and the wine reveals attractive aromatics, but there is a ferocious tannin level, and none of the charm or opulence found in the top 1997s.

BRANAIRE-DUCRU (ST.-JULIEN)

2000	D	(91–93)
1999	D	89
1998	D	89

1997	D	87
1996	D	89
1995	D	90

2000: The 2000 is a sweet, medium- to full-bodied, pure offering with terrific balance, ripe fruit, excellent delineation, and a sense of freshness. It should ultimately rival the 1996, 1995, 1989, and 1982 as one of the finest Branaires of the last 25 years. Moderate tannin in the finish suggests that some cellaring is required. Anticipated maturity: 2003–2025.

1999: I underrated this wine when I tasted it from cask. The dark ruby/purple 1999 exhibits medium to full body, a fat, supple-textured personality, excellent flavor ripeness, and an opulent mouth-feel. This successful effort will drink well upon release and last 15 years. Anticipated maturity: now–2016.

1998: A dense ruby/purple is accompanied by an attractive bouquet of lead pencil, graphite, black currants, raspberries, and spice. Medium-bodied, with beautifully knit flavors revealing excellent definition, this subtle, restrained yet persuasive 1998 displays a distinctive style. Anticipated maturity: 2003–2016.

1997: This is a delicious, attractive, dark ruby/plum-colored offering with complex notes of lead pencil, minerals, black raspberries, currants, and new oak. Medium-bodied, with light tannin, this elegant wine is on a fast evolutionary track. Drink this delicious claret over the next 3–4 years.

1996: I had concerns about the 1996 Branaire turning too tannic when I tasted it during its *élevage*. However, 3 tastings out of bottle revealed a textbook Branaire, with a telltale floral, raspberry, and black currant–scented nose intermixed with minerals and floral nuances. Elegant and pure, with surprising lushness and sweet, well-integrated tannin, this medium-bodied, finesse-styled wine should be at its finest between 2005–2018.

1995: A beauty in the elegant, restrained, finesse school of winemaking, the dark ruby/purple-colored 1995 Branaire exhibits a floral, cranberry, cherry, and black currant–scented nose intermixed with high-quality toasty new oak. Medium-bodied, with excellent definition, supple tannin, and an attractive, alluring personality, this pleasant, measured yet complex wine should drink well young and keep for two decades.

Past Glories: 1989 (92), 1982 (90), 1975 (91)

BRANDA (PUISSÉGUIN ST.-EMILION)

1999	C	87
1998	C	88

Branda, an emerging star from this satellite appellation, is made with the assistance of St.-Emilion's superstar winemaking guru Jean-Luc Thunevin. This wine usually represents a good value.

1999: Also seductive, but with less volume and slightly shorter than the 1998, the dark ruby-colored, richly fruity 1999 is a charming candidate for near-term consumption. It is luscious, medium-bodied, and silky, but does not possess the power of the 1998. Drink it over the next 2–3 years.

1998: A dark ruby/purple color is followed by an attractive, sexy nose of cedar, black fruits, earth, and oak. This ripe, soft, round 1998 offers appealing levels of concentrated fruit, a silky texture, and immediate accessibility. Enjoy it over the next 3–4 years. A sleeper of the vintage.

BRANE-CANTENAC (MARGAUX)

2000	D	(91–93)
1999	D	88
1998	D	88
1997	C	84

Henri Lurton has resurrected this estate over recent vintages, particularly since 1998, with the 2000 being its greatest success since the 1961.

2000: The dense ruby/purple-colored 2000 offers complex, elegant floral notes intermixed with black currant, cherry, smoke, and earth. Rich and velvety-textured, with a long, impressive, seamless finish, this pure, concentrated, mouth-filling Brane-Cantenac is a tribute to the talent of its author. Anticipated maturity: 2004–2020.

1999: An evolved, soft, dark ruby/garnet-colored wine, the 1999 Brane-Cantenac exhibits a cedary, spice box, herbaceous, leathery, cherry-scented nose, medium body, low acidity, and an elegant, complex, lush finish. Already drinkable, it appears to be evolving at an accelerated pace. Anticipated maturity: now–2012.

1998: Along with the 2000, the 1998 is the finest Brane-Cantenac produced in many years. This dark ruby-colored, elegant, savory effort offers abundant quantities of herb-tinged, smoky, earthy, black currant fruit intermixed with licorice and toast. Fleshy, medium-bodied, and ripe, with moderate tannin, this is a well-made, classic Margaux that should be at its best between 2005–2017.

1997: A medium plum/ruby color is accompanied by aromas of cedar, balsam wood, and red/black currants. Elegant, light- to medium-bodied, and round, with no hard edges but little concentration, this wine should be consumed over the next 2–3 years.

BRANON (PESSAC-LÉOGNAN)

2000	E	(92–95)

Perhaps the first garage wine from the Graves region, Branon is made under the auspices of Jean-Luc Thunevin. The production of this 60% Merlot and 40% Cabernet Franc blend averages 200 cases.

2000: The spectacular dense opaque purple-colored 2000 Branon boasts a phenomenally intense bouquet of smoky earth, melted road tar, blackberry, and cherry scents. Full-bodied, with notes of coffee, black fruits, earth, and fudge, the wine is sweet, round, and rich. Underlying all the fat and depth is considerable tannin. This is a marvel! Anticipated maturity: 2003–2018.

BRISSON (CÔTES DE CASTILLON)

2000	C	(89–90)
1999	C	86
1998	C	88

Brisson is consistently one of my favorite sleepers of the vintage, and a candidate for the best value in terms of pennies for points.

2000: This sexy, richly fruity, medium- to full-bodied, charming, seductive wine is impossible to ignore. It exhibits glorious levels of black cherry and berry fruit intermixed with smoke, minerals, and oak. Luscious and opulent, it is a thrill to drink. It will perform beautifully for 4–5 years and will probably last even longer.

1999: A dark ruby/purple color is accompanied by aromas of black fruits, vanilla, and smoke. This lighter-styled but excellent, pure, mid-weight claret is best consumed during its first 5–6 years of life.

1998: This wine provides excellent, hedonistic, smoky, coffee-infused, black cherry and berry aromas and flavors. Medium- to full-bodied and lush, it is reminiscent of a high-class St.-Emilion. Enjoy this super value over the next 4–5 years.

BROWN (PESSAC-LÉOGNAN)

2000	C	(88–90)
1999	C	87
1998	C	87

2000: Earthy, dried herb, ketchup, black currant, and barbecue spices result in a complex aromatic profile. Elegant, medium-bodied, rich, and flavorful, with supple tannin as well as a surprisingly long, authoritative finish, this is a sleeper of the vintage and Brown's finest offering to date. Anticipated maturity: now–2015.

1999: Dark ruby-colored, with smoky, spicy, earth, mineral, black cherry and currant aromas, the seamless 1999 reveals excellent concentration, low acidity, and considerable character. Anticipated maturity: now–2009.

1998: Soft scorched-earth, currant, cherry, and graphite-like flavors characterize this spicy, sweet, medium-bodied, elegant, supple offering. A delicious textbook Graves made in a medium-weight style, it will drink well for 4–5 years.

LA CABANNE (POMEROL)

2000		C	(83–86?)

2000: Highly extracted, hard, tough tannins obliterate this wine's fruit. Though cleanly made, with good plum and black cherry fruit and notes of balsam wood and new oak, the mouth-searing tannin levels will undoubtedly be problematic. Drink it between now–2011.

CALON-SÉGUR (ST.-ESTÈPHE)

2000	EE	(93–95)
1999	E	(88–89+)
1998	E	89+
1997	D	80
1996	E	92
1995	E	92+

This estate, which possesses one of the greatest *terroirs* of Bordeaux, is faring particularly well under the administration of Madame Gasqueton, whose 1995s and 1996s are two unqualified back-to-back successes. Prices at Calon-Ségur are extremely reasonable. However, consumers should be warned that the wines are very slow to evolve and blossom and that they are never ready to drink earlier than 5–10 years of age.

2000: A profound wine, possibly the greatest since 1982. Calon-Ségur has made a powerful dark purple wine with abundant fruit, massive depth, and a 40-second finish. Anticipated maturity: 2010–2040.

1999: I was entirely too harsh on this wine when tasted during the first year of its *élevage*. Having put on weight and filled out in the mid-palate, it is, atypically, one 1999 that will require 4–5 years of cellaring. It exhibits a dense ruby/purple color, smoky, earthy aromas of dried herbs, roasted meats, and black fruits. Well made, with considerable tannin, a good mid-palate, and a moderately long finish, it will be at its best between 2006–2025.

1998: Although austere tannin kept this wine from obtaining an outstanding score, it exhibits plenty of complexity in its earthy truffle, black cherry, currant, plum, and herb-scented bouquet as well as flavors. Moderately tannic, with good weight, it is a classically styled 1998. Despite the fact that Calon-Ségur tends to utilize about 35% Merlot in the final blend, it is not one of the more precocious efforts of the vintage. Anticipated maturity: 2008–2030.

1997: A soft, weedy Calon-Ségur, with a washed-out ruby color, herb, pepper, and earthy aromas, light to medium body, and low tannin, this 1997 should be consumed over the next 2 years.

1996: Prior to bottling, I thought the 1996 Calon-Ségur would be a match for the spectacular 1995, but the two vintages tasted blind, side by side, on two occasions convinced me that the 1995 has the edge because of its element of *sur-maturité* and more accessible, richer mid-palate. The 1996 may not be as profound as I had predicted from cask, but it is an exceptional wine. Dark ruby-colored, with a complex nose of dried herbs, Asian spices, and black cherry jam intermixed with cassis, it possesses outstanding purity, and considerable tannin

in the finish. This classic, medium- to full-bodied, traditionally made wine improves dramatically with airing, suggesting it will have a very long life. Anticipated maturity: 2009–2028.
1995: As I have said many times since I first tasted this wine, the 1995 is one of the great sleepers of the vintage. The wine has closed down completely since bottling, but this sensational effort may ultimately merit an even higher score. The wine is opaque purple. With coaxing, the tight aromatics reveal some weedy cassis intertwined with truffles, chocolate, and beef blood–like aromas. On the palate, there is an element of *sur-maturité*, fabulous density and purity, and a boatload of tannin. This deep, broodingly backward, classic Bordeaux will require a decade of cellaring. Anticipated maturity: 2005–2035.
Past Glories: 1990 (90), 1988 (91), 1982 (94)

CAMBON LA PELOUSE (HAUT-MÉDOC)

2000	B	(87–88)

2000: A sleeper of the vintage, the 2000 Cambon La Pelouse is a blend of 50% Merlot, 35% Cabernet Sauvignon, and 15% Cabernet Franc. Sweet, ripe, and medium-bodied, it displays sumptuous layers of black cherry and currant fruit with subtle oak in the background. Fleshy, open-knit, and expansive, it will provide joyous drinking over its first 4–6 years of life.

CANON (ST.-EMILION)

2000	D	(88–89)
1999	D	87
1998	D	88
1997	C	82
1996	C	80
1995	C	74

This famous cru on the hillsides outside medieval St.-Emilion has rebounded after a series of miserable performances. Though the wines are not of the quality one would expect from a premier cru of St.-Emilion, they have started to improve, especially since 1998.
2000: Canon's 2000 is a dark ruby-colored, elegant, medium-bodied effort displaying notions of flowers, minerals, earth, black cherries, and currants. It possesses excellent concentration, purity, and balance. Moderate tannin in the finish suggests that some cellaring is required. Anticipated maturity: 2005–2020.
1999: Despite the hail that forced this property to harvest early, the 1999 has turned out reasonably well. Slightly more austere than its older sibling, with more noticeable earthy, mineral overtones, it exhibits black fruit characteristics as well as an attenuated finish. Anticipated maturity: 2004–2015.
1998: Made in an elegant, restrained, subtle but interesting style, the dark ruby-colored 1998 Canon offers a sweet nose of crushed stones intertwined with flowers, red and black fruits, and moderate tannin. An attractive, charming, mid-weight effort, it will be at its finest before 2015.
1997: This is a pleasant, delicate, medium ruby-colored wine with emaciated, underwhelming dried herb and sweet cherry fruit notes. Drink this medium-bodied effort over the next 2–3 years.
1996: The 1996 Canon is a lean, austere, delicate wine with a dark ruby color and medium body but little intensity or length. Angular and compressed, it is likely to dry out over the next decade. Anticipated maturity: now–2015.
1995: I could not find any redeeming qualities in this sinewy, thin, austere, high-acid, ferociously tannic wine. As hard as I tried, I could not see any positive outcome for this wine's development. Anticipated maturity: now–2008.
Past Glories: 1989 (92), 1982 (94), 1959 (95)

CANON DE BREM (CANON-FRONSAC)

1999	C	86
1998	C	88
1997	C	86
1996	C	78
1995	C	86

1999: New oak as well as herb-tinged black cherry fruit are found in this moderately endowed, well-made, elegant, finesse-styled 1999. Anticipated maturity: now–2007.

1998: A sleeper of the vintage, the 1998 Canon de Brem exhibits aromas of minerals, scorched earth, black cherries, and raspberries. This dense, concentrated, classic effort possesses firm tannin as well as excellent potential for longevity. Pure and balanced, it is reminiscent of a top-class St.-Emilion. Anticipated maturity: 2003–2015.

1997: An elegant, tasty, fruity, medium ruby-colored effort, the 1997 possesses low acidity, sweet tannin, and obvious cherry fruit. Drink in 2–3 years.

1996: This is a dark ruby-colored, stylish, medium-bodied, structured, elegant wine without much depth or fruit. Drink it over the next 3–4 years.

1995: A dark plum/ruby color is followed by a wine with plenty of spice, and a distinctive mineral *terroir* characteristic intermingled with sweet plum and cherry fruit. Medium-bodied and dense, this muscular claret will be approachable young but should also age nicely for 7–8 years.

Other vintage tasted: 2000 (85–86?)

CANON-LA-GAFFELIÈRE (ST.-EMILION)

2000	E	(94–96)
1999	D	91
1998	E	93
1997	D	90
1996	E	90
1995	E	91+

Another superb St.-Emilion estate run with passion, vision, and commitment to quality by Comte Stephan von Neipperg. Since 1988, it has been one of St.-Emilion's star performers. Though it is difficult to pick a favorite, the 2000 is unquestionably one of the greatest Canon-La-Gaffelières yet produced.

2000: The opaque blue/purple-colored 2000 Canon-La-Gaffelière offers a fabulous perfume of roasted espresso, chocolate fudge, jammy blackberry and cassis fruit, smoke, vanilla, licorice, and Asian spices. It possesses terrific viscosity, an enormously concentrated mouthfeel, yet good freshness as well as delineation, multiple layers of flavor, and a spectacular blockbuster finish. This is a profoundly great wine! Anticipated maturity: now–2020.

1999: Another terrific effort, this opaque blue/purple-colored 1999 offers notes of melted asphalt, espresso, chocolate, blackberries, prunes, Asian spices, and new oak. Sexy, with slightly less complexity than the 1998, but lower acidity, and a plumper, fatter, more hedonistic style, it can be drunk upon its release and over the following 12–14 years.

1998: This saturated purple-colored 1998 offers sumptuous aromas of prunes, blueberries, overripe black cherries, chocolate, coffee, and spicy new oak. Full-bodied, opulent, and expressive, this flamboyant effort is crammed with glycerin and extract. The tannin is sweet in this accessible, multilayered 1998. Anticipated maturity: 2004–2022.

1997: One of the most exotic, thick, rich wines of the vintage (as well as one of its few stars), the 1997 reveals a dense plum/purple color in addition to sumptuous aromatics of vanilla, licorice, Asian spices, roasted coffee, and jammy black cherry and berry fruit. Medium- to full-bodied, with silky tannin and low acidity, this thick, seamless, exotic St.-Emilion should drink well for 12 years. One of the vintage's most impressive efforts.

1996: One of St.-Emilion's most impressively constituted and expressive wines. From its saturated purple color to its soaring aromatics (toast, jammy black fruits, chocolate, roasted coffee, and smoke), this full-bodied, meaty, chewy, powerful wine is loaded with extract and sweet tannin and possesses a layered, multidimensional finish. It should continue to improve for a decade and drink well for 15–20 years. Anticipated maturity: 2007–2020

1995: A massive wine with a chocolaty, thick, cigar box, black currant, and cherry-scented nose, this full-bodied wine is crammed with layers of fruit, extract, glycerin, and alcohol. Spicy yet rich, with high tannin, the 1995 Canon-La-Gaffelière will need a minimum of 2–3 years of cellaring. The finish is long and rich, the tannin sweet rather than astringent. Anticipated maturity: 2004–2020.

Past Glories: 1994 (90), 1990 (92)

CANON-MOUEIX (CANON-FRONSAC)

1999	C	86
1998	C	87
1997	B	86
1996	C	86

1999: Light- to medium-bodied, pleasant, straightforward, and soft, this is a pretty but insubstantial cherry/mineral-scented and -flavored wine. Drink it over the next 3–5 years.

1998: A dark ruby color accompanies scents of earth, black cherries, kirsch, and spice. Another fleshy, nicely textured, concentrated effort, the 1998 Canon-Moueix possesses enough tannin to warrant 1–2 more years of cellaring. Anticipated maturity: now–2012.

1997: Aromas and flavors of plums and cherries are evident in this open-knit, spicy, delicious, elegant, soft wine. Savory, round, and medium-bodied, it is ideal for drinking over the next 2–3 years.

1996: This dark ruby-colored wine possesses fine depth, a spicy, sweet nose of berry fruit, pepper, and dried herbs, medium body, and fine ripeness. Though well made, it is slightly short in the finish. Drink this sound Canon-Fronsac over the next 3–4 years.

Other vintage tasted: 2000 (84–86)

CANTEMERLE (HAUT-MÉDOC)

1999	D	86
1998	D	84
1997	C	84
1996	D	87
1995	D	86

This property deserves a higher ranking than its 1855 classification. The style of Cantemerle is rich, supple fruitiness, and an intensely fragrant bouquet.

1999: Sweet currant/plum fruit intermixed with herbs, earth, licorice, and leather are nicely meshed in this medium-bodied, well-textured, subtle yet savory effort. The wine's low acidity and ripe tannin suggest early drinkability. Enjoy it during its first decade of life.

1998: Dark ruby-colored with a purple edge, this slightly herbaceous, medium-bodied, lighter-styled 1998 offers attractive aromas and flavors, but it lacks depth and length. Drink it over the next 7–8 years.

1997: The tasty 1997 is a light- to medium-bodied, round, richly fruity wine with lower acidity and less structure and tannin than its more muscular older sibling. Offering an attractive display of red fruits, minerals, and spice, it should drink well during its first decade of life.

1996: Judging by the cask tastings, I had hoped this wine would turn out closer to outstanding, but it is excellent, if not quite as stunning as I had expected. It is more forward and light in bottle than during its *élevage*, but it is a stylish example of Cantemerle. The 1996 offers a dark ruby color and a sweet nose of black raspberries, subtle new oak, and acacia. There is fine sweetness and solid tannin in this elegant, symmetrical effort. Anticipated maturity: 2003–2015.

1995: The 1995 does not possess the depth of the 1996, and reveals a more evolved medium ruby color that is already lightening at the edge. Peppery, herb-tinged red currant fruit aromas are pleasant but uninspiring. This medium-bodied, straightforward wine lacks the depth, dimension, and power of a top-flight classified growth. It will be at its best before 2010.

Other vintage tasted: 2000 (87–88)

Past Glories: 1989 (91), 1983 (91), 1961 (92), 1953 (94)

CANTENAC (ST.-EMILION)

2000		
	C	(87–88)

Cantenac is a reasonably priced St.-Emilion, a commodity that is increasingly difficult to find.

2000: While not complex, this 2000 is a fruit-driven, fat, ripe, in-your-face effort that will provide tasty drinking over the next 4–5 years.

CANTENAC-BROWN (MARGAUX)

2000	D	(89–91)
1999	D	89
1998	D	88
1997	C	85
1996	C	86
1995	C	78

2000: The finest Cantenac-Brown I have ever tasted, this full-bodied, layered, concentrated, saturated purple-colored 2000 offers pure aromas and flavors of black currants, minerals, and flowers. Moderately high but sweet tannin is found in the 25- to 30-second finish. Patience, however, is required because of the structured nature of this offering. Anticipated maturity: 2006–2025.

1999: Along with the 2000, the 1999 is potentially one of the very best Cantenac-Browns produced in 2–3 decades. This dense ruby/purple-colored wine exhibits a sweet bouquet of black fruits intertwined with licorice, spice box, fennel, and graphite. Full-bodied and rich, with sweet tannin, low acidity, excellent delineation as well as length, and an impressive, expansive, pure mid-palate, it will be drinkable between 2004–2018.

1998: Elegant, sweet, floral-infused, black currant and blackberry fruit, along with licorice, earth, and even a note of truffles are present in this medium-bodied wine's aromas and flavors. Moreover, there is excellent concentration, good purity, and sweet tannin. Not a blockbuster, but a well-made, symmetrical 1998 to drink between 2003–2016.

1997: The softness of the 1997 vintage has given this effort plenty of charm and precociousness. The color is dark ruby purple, and the wine offers up sweet black raspberry/cassis fruit intermixed with licorice, underbrush, and oaky aromas. The wine is medium-bodied, with a supple texture, good purity, and a low-acid, plump finish. Anticipated maturity: now–2014.

1996: While tannic, the 1996 looks to be one of the better efforts produced under the AXA administration. The color is a deep ruby purple. The wine offers simple but pleasing aromas of black currants, licorice, and vanilla. In the mouth it is medium- to full-bodied, powerful, muscular, somewhat foursquare, but mouth-filling and rich. Anticipated maturity: 2004–2015.

1995: Although the 1995 reveals a good color, it has been consistently angular, austere, and too tannic. This is a lean, spartan style of claret that is likely to dry out before enough tannin melts away to reach a balance with the wine's fruit. Anticipated maturity: now–2010.

CAP DE FAUGÈRES (CÔTES DE CASTILLON)

2000	C	(89–91)
1999	C	89
1998	C	88

This excellent sleeper is owned by Corinne Guisez. Michel Rolland is the consulting oenologist.

2000: Another top-notch Côtes de Castillon that hit the bull's eye in 2000, the saturated ruby purple Cap de Faugères offers a black currant, meaty-scented bouquet as well as rich, full-bodied flavors with outstanding concentration, purity, and overall balance.

1999: Sharing most of the 1998's characteristics, the 1999 possesses sweeter tannin, lower acidity, and a chocolate character. It may turn out to be even more sexy and hedonistic than its older sibling. Anticipated maturity: now–2010.

1998: This dense ruby/purple-colored effort offers rich, concentrated blackberry and cassis fruit intermixed with smoke, licorice, and toast. High extraction and dense, supple tannin provide a full impact on the palate. Although not complex, it is a beautifully made, substantially sized 1998 with no hard edges. Drink it over the next 7–8 years.

CAP DE MOURLIN (ST.-EMILION)

2000	C	(85–86)

2000: This monolithic wine does not lack for concentration, but it seems somewhat muted, foursquare, and dull. Drink it over the next 6–7 years.

CARBONNIEUX (PESSAC-LÉOGNAN)

2000	C	(88–90)
1999	C	87
1998	C	87
1997	C	81
1996	C	86
1995	C	87

Carbonnieux is never big, but it is complex, medium-weight, and drinkable at a young age, preferably within 7 to 8 years following the vintage.

2000: The 2000 offers aromas and flavors of black cherries, vanilla, spice, and camphor. Soft and smooth, it is well balanced, harmonious, and pure. Drink it over the next 12–15 years.

1999: While good, the 1999 Carbonnieux lacks stuffing. Moderately intense aromas of toasty oak, black cherry jam, and minerals are followed by a straightforward, medium-bodied, pleasant wine with some tannin in the finish. Drink it over the next 7–8 years.

1998: Very Burgundy-like in its vivid black cherry/smoky nose, this medium-bodied, somewhat light but racy, tasty wine is graceful in a low-keyed manner. It will not make old bones, but it is well-knit and charming. Enjoy it over the next 10 years.

1997: This is a light-bodied, picnic-styled claret with evidence of dilution as well as soft cherry/raspberry fruit flavors reminiscent of a lighter-styled Burgundy. Drink it over the next 2–3 years.

1996: A stylish, medium-bodied, dark ruby-colored wine with attractive cherry and raspberry fruit intermixed with toasty notes in both the aromatics and flavors. This elegant wine reveals a Volnay-like personality. It should keep for a 6–7 years.

1995: An attractive, sexy effort from Carbonnieux, this medium-bodied, deep ruby-colored wine reveals subtle aromas of smoky oak intertwined with tobacco, kirsch, and black currant fruit. In the mouth, elegance, balance, suppleness, finesse, and an overall allure characterize this round, lightly tannic, lush, and captivating claret. Anticipated maturity: now–2011.

LES CARMES-HAUT-BRION (PESSAC-LÉOGNAN)

2000	E	(91–95)
1999	D	88
1998	D	90
1997	D	87
1996	D	87
1995	D	87

This tiny treasure, located in a beautiful park in the suburbs of Pessac, is a must-visit for travelers to Bordeaux. I have been praising this estate's wines for a number of years. The quality is superb, and they remain an excellent bargain even though the minuscule production makes them hard to find. They are a blend of 55% Merlot, 40% Cabernet Franc, and 5% Cabernet Sauvignon.

2000: The spectacular 2000 is a great achievement. A sleeper of the vintage, this dense ruby/purple offering exhibits a gorgeously sweet nose of smoke, damp earth, coffee, black currants, and cigar tobacco. Opulently textured (due to malolactics in barrel), with stunning purity, richness, and a long, concentrated finish, this may be a modern-day clone of the profound 1959, which first attracted me to this estate's wines. Anticipated maturity: 2003–2025.

1999: A supple, soft, medium-weight, deep ruby/purple-colored Les Carmes-Haut-Brion, the 1999 reveals a sexy bouquet of roasted nuts, pepper, incense, hickory smoke, and black currants. Medium-bodied, with low acidity and a fleshy, up-front personality, it will be delicious upon release, and drink well for 12–15 years thereafter.

1998: A stunning wine, as well as one of the sleepers of the vintage, the dense purple 1998 offers up classic Graves aromas of tar, roasted meats, scorched earth, black currants, and barbecue spices. It is beautifully elegant, yet rich, concentrated, and deep, with medium to full body, laudable sweetness on the entry, and ripe tannin in the finish. A bottle kept open for 24 hours was significantly better than it was upon opening, suggesting that this wine will have terrific longevity. Haut-Brion enthusiasts are advised to check out this beautifully made offering. Anticipated maturity: 2004–2020.

1997: Smells reminiscent of hippie incense jump from the glass of this complex wine fragrant with herb, tobacco, smoke, and pepper. Medium ruby-colored, with light to medium body, it is full of finesse, fruit, charm, and suppleness. This is a sexy offering to enjoy over the next 2–3 years. Though it has neither great depth nor length, it is beautifully complex and supple.

1996: A medium ruby-colored, sexy, seductive Graves, with loads of tobacco-tinged jammy cherry fruit intermixed with smoke and earth, this spicy, round, generous 1996 reveals no hard edges and continues to be one of the most stylish, underrated wines from the Pessac-Léognan region. Although it will not be long-lived, this wine offers plenty of appeal for drinking over the next 7–8 years.

1995: A classic example of the Graves smoky, tobacco-tinged, berry fruit, this small jewel of an estate has produced a medium-bodied, sweet, round, berry, complex, elegant, savory 1995 with no hard edges. Low acidity and a luscious, ripe Merlot component dominate the wine, giving it immediate appeal. This is a plump, delicious wine for consuming over the next 6–7 years.

Past Glories: 1959 (93)

CARRUADES DE LAFITE (PAUILLAC)

2000	D	(90–92)
1999	D	89
1998	D	90
1997	D	88
1996	D	89
1995	D	87

This has become one of the finest second wines produced.

2000: The 2000 Carruades de Lafite, a blend of 51.4% Cabernet Sauvignon, 42.3% Merlot, and the rest Petit Verdot, reveals an elegant, finesse-like character as well as notes of minerals, pencil shavings, cherries, wet stones, and subtle oak. Medium-bodied, stylish, and streamlined, it will be drinkable between 2003–2016.

1999: This wine could turn out to be as stunning as the 1998. Made from 69% Cabernet Sauvignon and 31% Merlot, it is more seductive and sweeter, with lower acidity as well as a riper style. Full and rich, this classic wine is made in the Lafite-Rothschild style. Drink it over the next 10 years.

1998: The 1998 (a blend of 61% Cabernet Sauvignon, 33% Merlot, 4.5% Cabernet Franc, and 1.5% Petit Verdot) is an outstanding effort. Very Lafite-like but more supple and forward, it exhibits a dense ruby/purple color in addition to an excellent bouquet of black fruits, smoke, earth, and minerals, supple tannin, an excellent texture, and a long, fine finish. Anticipated maturity: now–2015.

1997: The 1997 (a blend of 32% Merlot, with the rest mainly Cabernet Sauvignon and a small portion of Cabernet Franc) is dark ruby with purple nuances. The wine is soft, fleshy, and round, with more up-front fat than Lafite, but not nearly the length nor perfume. Supple, with low acidity, and an easygoing, silky finish, it will drink well until 2006.

1996: The 1996, a blend of 63% Cabernet Sauvignon and 37% Merlot, possesses as much power, ripeness, and fleshy fruit (because of the high percentage of Merlot) as I have ever detected in this offering. While it does not quite have the characteristics of Lafite, being fleshier and more accessible, it is a beautifully made wine with a subtle dosage of toasty new oak, an appealing texture, and excellent length. Given its power, this second wine will need 1–2 years of cellaring and keep for 15+ years (I would not be surprised to see it last two decades).

1995: The 1995 is a 40% Merlot/60% Cabernet Sauvignon blend. It exhibits more of the trademark characteristics of its bigger sibling. Elegant, with spicy new oak, lead pencil, and creamy black currant fruit, this is a medium-bodied, finesse-styled wine with excellent purity and overall equilibrium. It is much more accessible than the 1996, and should drink well between now–2010.

CERTAN DE MAY (POMEROL)

2000	EE	(90–93)
1999	EE	87
1998	EE	86?
1997	EE	87
1996	EE	87?
1995	EE	90+

One of my favorite Pomerols of the late 1970s and 1980s (1982, 1985, 1986, and 1988 are terrific), Certan de May has rebounded powerfully after several undistinguished performances in the late 1990s. The 2000 is their finest effort since the 1988 and 1990.

2000: A deep ruby/purple is followed by scents of overripe tomatoes, blackberries, plums, underbrush, a Rhône-like character, and Provençal herbs. This successful but surprisingly atypical 2000 is fat, fleshy, and soft, with low acidity and a corpulent personality. Flavors of new saddle leather, ketchup, and roasted meats intermingle in an exotic, spicy style. Anticipated maturity: 2003–2018.

1999: This dark ruby/garnet, evolved, mid-weight Pomerol displays lightness and a lack of concentration. You will find attractive sweet berry, strawberry, mocha, and herb-tinged fruit in addition to a short finish. Anticipated maturity: now–2010.

1998: This wine, which I tasted on three separate occasions after bottling, performed significantly below the potential it revealed from barrel. One sample was extremely vegetal as well as diluted. Essentially, this is a medium ruby/garnet-colored, lean effort lacking concentration. It reveals notes of herbs, saddle leather, spice box, red currants and cherries, but readers used to the superb Certan de May from 1979, 1981, 1982, 1985, and 1988 will find it disappointing. Anticipated maturity: now–2010.

1997: Toasty oak and earthlike overtones compete for the taster's attention in this tannic, medium-bodied effort. With herb-tinged black cherry fruit and a spicy personality, this 1997 can be drunk over the next 4–5 years.

1996: This wine reveals an intensely aromatic cedar, dried herb, and black cherry–scented nose, but its abrasive tannin level is troublesome. Although well made, it displays a gritty texture, medium body, and an angular, rustic character to the tannin. If that softens (which I doubt), this wine will merit its 87 point score. Anticipated maturity: 2004–2015.

1995: The impressive 1995 exhibits a dense ruby/purple color and a moderately intense nose of black olives, cedar, raspberries, and cherry fruit intermixed with toasty new oak. In the mouth, the new oak is noticeable, as is an elevated level of tannin. Notwithstanding the aggressive vanilla flavors and powerful tannin, this wine has outstanding depth, and a layered, concentrated style with considerable muscle and power. It is a big, backward, formidably endowed Certan de May—clearly the finest wine made at this estate since the 1988 and 1990—but patience is most definitely required. Anticipated maturity: 2006–2020.

Past Glories: 1990 (91), 1988 (92+), 1986 (90), 1985 (94), 1982 (96+), 1981 (90), 1979 (93), 1945 (96)

CERTAN-GIRAUD (POMEROL)

1998	E	85
1997	E	86
1996	E	84
1995	E	87

This 10-acre property, planted with 71% Merlot and 29% Cabernet Franc, well situated on the plateau of Pomerol, was acquired by the Jean-Pierre Moueix firm in 1999 and renamed Hosanna. I suggest that Bordeaux insiders keep an eye on this up-and-coming estate.

1998: The 1998 tastes much more diffuse than it did prior to bottling, with tasty black cherry fruit but little weight or depth. It is attractive in a low-key, superficial way. Drink it over the next 7–8 years.

1997: A soft, earthy, ripe, jammy wine with low acidity, plum and cherry fruit, and considerable near-term appeal, the 1997 should be drunk over the next 4–5 years.

1996: I suspect a far richer, more complex wine could have emerged from this outstanding Pomerol *terroir*. The 1996 possesses a medium ruby color, and an evolved, complex nose of cedar, kirsch, roasted herbs, and spice. Good fruit combines with moderate levels of glycerin in this medium-bodied, richly fruity yet essentially one-dimensional, straightforward Pomerol. Drink it before 2005.

1995: Sweet, jammy flavors border on overripeness. The wine displays a deep ruby color with a flamboyant nose of smoke and black fruits. There is noticeable glycerin on the palate, medium to full body, low acidity, and plenty of power, intensity, and richness in this big, fleshy, mouth-filling, savory, hedonistic Pomerol. Anticipated maturity: now–2009.

CERTAN-MARZELLE (POMEROL)

2000	E	(89–91)

A new wine being launched by Christian Moueix, Certan-Marzelle comes from a parcel of the original Certan-Giraud vineyard. Sadly, the production is only 1,000 cases.

2000: This sexy, lush, soft, supple, disarming wine exhibits a deep ruby/purple followed by a sweet, expressive Pomerol that is a total hedonistic turn-on. This may be Christian Moueix's answer to the famed Le Pin. Anticipated maturity: now–2014.

DE CHAMBRUN (LALANDE-DE-POMEROL)

2000	D	(91–93)
1999	D	89
1998	D	90
1997	C	88
1996	C	88

Along with La Fleur de Bouard, de Chambrun is the most impressive wine currently being produced in Lalande-de-Pomerol. However, unlike La Fleur de Bouard, Chambrun's production is minuscule—only 3.5 acres of vines. Under the inspired leadership of Jean-Philippe Janoueix, this estate is emerging as one of the superstars of this bucolic appellation, a source of up-front, delicious Pomerol-styled wines that sell for reasonable prices.

2000: A stunning sleeper of the vintage, this wine takes concentration and intensity to extremely high levels. De Chambrun has been one of the finest Lalande-de-Pomerols made over recent vintages, but the 2000 is extra-special. An explosive bouquet of roasted meat, blackberries, coffee, and chocolate soars from the glass. Unctuously-textured, with terrific concentration, great purity, and nicely integrated new oak, this full-bodied, blockbuster effort should be consumed during its first 7–8 years of life to take advantage of its fat, fruit, and exuberant style.

1999: Believe it or not, the 1999 may turn out even better than the brilliant 1998. It is a fatter, broader, more expansive effort, with a creamier texture, lower acidity, and an overripe character. Notes of black fruits, prunes, cassis, vanilla, and chocolate are prominent in both the aromas and flavors. Unctuously textured, thick, and hedonistic, it should be delicious upon release and last a decade.

1998: An impressive, opaque ruby/purple-colored effort, the 1998 exhibits sweet aromatics of black fruits intermixed with spice box, vanilla, and jam. Opulent, muscular, thick, and full-bodied, with moderate tannin, and outstanding purity as well as symmetry, it will be at its finest until 2012.

1997: A deep ruby/purple color is accompanied by a thick, juicy nose of black fruits, truffles, dried herbs, earth, and grilled meat aromas. Surprisingly dense and concentrated, with moderate tannin, this is an atypically big, muscular 1997. Anticipated maturity: now–2010.

1996: The excellent 1996 exhibits a deep ruby/purple color, and sweet, blackberry and jammy cherry aromas and flavors. Medium-bodied, with impressive glycerin, sweet tannin, and a long, lush, concentrated finish, it may be the finest Lalande-de-Pomerol from this vintage. Anticipated maturity: now–2010.

CHANTEGRIVE (GRAVES)

2000	B	(87–88)

Among the lower-priced Graves, Chantegrive usually represents a very good value.

2000: The excellent 2000 displays aromas of scorched earth, ripe black cherry and currant fruit, tobacco, and cigar smoke. Ripe, medium-bodied, soft, and attractive, it will be drinkable upon release and age well for a decade.

CHAPELLE-HAUT-BRION (PESSAC-LÉOGNAN)

2000	D	(90–91)
1998	C	89
1997	C	83
1996	C	86
1995	C	90

Readers looking for an excellent value should seek out this limited-production second wine of La Mission-Haut-Brion.

2000: The top-notch 2000 offers a sweet, jammy nose of caramel, blackberries, cassis, and smoke. High levels of glycerin coat the mouth like melting marrow. Sweet, deep, full-bodied, and hedonistic, revealing much of La Mission-Haut-Brion's style, it is best consumed during its first 10–12 years of life.

1998: The 1998 Chapelle is a gorgeously complex, rich, Graves-styled wine with a smoky, tobacco, black currant, earth-scented nose, fat, luscious, concentrated, seamless flavors, and beautifully integrated acidity and tannin. This fleshy, complex offering is already delicious yet will last a decade. Thirty thousand bottles were produced.

1997: The soft, round, herb-tinged 1997 is up-front, easy to understand, fruity, straightforward, and simple. Drink now.

1996: The 1996 is a soft, round, lovely, cedary, smoky, complex wine with medium body and luscious sweet fruit. It will not make old bones, but for a textbook Graves to drink over the next 5–7 years, this wine has considerable merit.

1995: The 1995 is a sleeper, and one of the better second wines of this vintage. It comes across as more extracted than the 1996, but offers a lovely, rich, medium-bodied, well-endowed personality. The wine reveals much of the character of La Mission-Haut-Brion in its sweet berry fruit intertwined with smoke, tobacco, and roasted herbs. Round, spicy, and generous, with no hard edges, it will provide ideal drinking over the next 5–7 years.

CHARMAIL (HAUT-MÉDOC)

2000	C	(88–90)
1999	C	89
1998	C	88
1997	C	87
1996	C	88
1995	C	88

One of the finest crus bourgeois in Haut-Médoc, Charmail is made in an interesting manner. It may be the only property to employ a 2-week cold prefermentation under liquid nitrogen. This brilliantly made blend of 55% Merlot, 25% Cabernet Sauvignon, and 20% Cabernet Franc unquestionably competes with some Médoc classified growths.

2000: A star among the Médoc's crus bourgeois, Charmail's 2000 boasts a black/purple color as well as a sweet, seductive bouquet of licorice, blackberries, and cassis. Pure, medium-bodied, and loaded at the front end, with moderate tannin in the finish, this full, concentrated Haut-Médoc will hit its peak in 1–2 years and evolve nicely for 10–15.

1999: This impressive, dark purple Charmail exhibits smoky crème de cassis aromas, sweet, ripe, low acid, plump flavors, medium to full body, and an exceptional finish with no hard edges. This seamless wine should drink well for 10 years.

1998: Revealing more structure and tannin than normal, the deep ruby/purple-colored 1998 exhibits abundant black fruits on the attack, but a pinched although impressive structured mid-palate and finish. This medium-bodied wine will keep for 10 years.

1997: An excellent effort, the 1997 exhibits a dark ruby/purple color in addition to sweet, blackberry/cassis and high-quality toasty oak aromas. Medium-bodied and supple, with fine ripeness, a chewy mid-palate, and a low-acid, plush finish, it should be consumed over the next 3–4 years.

1996: This wine exhibits an opaque black/purple color, sweet blackberry, raspberry, and cassis fruit, medium to full body, luxuriant, hedonistic, smoky, jammy fruit flavors, and copious quantities of sweet tannin. A severe selection has resulted in a Merlot-dominated wine that includes 30% Cabernet Sauvignon and 20% Cabernet Franc. Anticipated maturity: now–2010.

1995: The opaque purple-colored 1995 offers a moderately intense nose of jammy blackberries and currants, terrific fruit on the attack, medium to full body, outstanding purity, low acidity, and a fleshy texture. It can be drunk now as well as over the next 6–7 years.

CHASSE-SPLEEN (MOULIS)

2000	C	(88–89)
1997	C	86
1996	C	86?
1995	C	86

Chasse-Spleen has consistently produced fine wine that for the last three decades has often been as good as a third growth. Unfortunately, prices have jumped as consumers have started to realize that the wine was undervalued.

2000: A classic, muscular, rich yet elegant effort made in a medium- to full-bodied, concentrated style, the 2000 Chasse-Spleen possesses abundant quantities of minerals, earth, black cherry, and cassis fruit. It will need 4–5 years of cellaring and will keep for two decades.

1997: Dark ruby-purple colored, with aromas of spice, black currants, vanilla, and berries, this medium-bodied wine reveals very good to excellent depth, fine overall balance, ripe tannin, and not a great deal of acidity. It should drink well for 6–7 years.

1996: Although this wine possesses impressive structure and enough depth of fruit, it is disjointed and exhibits an astringent finish—largely because of the high tannin level. Deep purple in color, with medium body and strong tannins both in the flavor and finish, it is made in a style that will not provide much charm or pleasure for 4–5 years, but it should keep 15 years.

1995: This wine has everything in its aromatics and attack, and very little at the back of the mouth—not a good sign for long-term aging. It possesses a dark ruby/purple color, and black currant fruit intermixed with smoke and weediness. Drink it over the next 5–7 years.

Other vintages tasted: 1999 (81-84), 1998 (?)

Past Glories: 1989 (91), 1986 (90), 1985 (90), 1975 (90), 1975 (90), 1970 (90), 1949 (94)

CHAUVIN (ST.-EMILION)

2000	E	(90–92+)
1999	D	89
1998	D	89+
1997	D	88
1996	D	88
1995	D	87

Under the inspired leadership of Béatrice Ondet and Marie-France Février, this property is fashioning better and better wines. Moreover, prices remain reasonable. Until 1999, the estate produced a luxury micro *cuvée* called Vieux-Château-Chauvin. This truly spectacular St.-Emilion came from a small vineyard that is now included in the standard Château Chauvin.

2000: A great effort, the blockbuster, opaque blue/purple 2000 boasts tannic but powerful, superconcentrated flavors. Dense and chewy, this *vin de garde* displays all the hallmarks of a classic claret. Although one of the finest Chauvins ever made, patience will be necessary. Anticipated maturity: 2007–2025.

1999: The 1999 offers a deep ruby/purple color and jammy blackberry/cassis fruit intermixed with smoke and new wood. This low-acid, opulently textured, hedonistic St.-Emilion fruit bomb will be drinkable upon release and over the following decade.

1998: A deep, saturated ruby/purple color is followed by aromas of blackberry and cherry fruit intertwined with licorice, spice box, underbrush, and cedar. This thick, full-bodied, concentrated 1998 exhibits sweet tannin as well as excellent purity. Low acidity in addition to gorgeous up-front fruit suggest early drinkability. Anticipated maturity: 2003–2015.

1997: The 1997 Chauvin is a seductive, silky-textured effort with a dark ruby/purple color as well as abundant fat, juicy, jammy black cherry/currant fruit and toasty oak. A supple, low-acid wine with good depth and no hard edges, it should be consumed over the next 4–5 years.

1996: The 1996 exhibits a dark ruby color and an excellent bouquet of toast intermixed with jammy cherry fruit. There is good glycerin, medium body, an overall sense of elegance, fine equilibrium, and a tasty, richly fruity finish. Some tannin is present, but this is a stylish, finesse-driven wine that should drink nicely for 8 years.

1995: Deep ruby-purple colored, with a sweet, nearly overripe, jammy nose of black fruits, oak, and spice, this lush, attractively textured, plump St.-Emilion will need to be drunk over the next 5–7 years because of its extremely low acidity.

CHEVAL BLANC (ST.-EMILION)

2000	**EEE**	**(99–100)**
2000 Le Petit Cheval	**E**	**(90–92)**
1999	**EEE**	**94**
1998	**EEE**	**95+**
1997	**EEE**	**88**
1996	**EEE**	**90**
1995	**EEE**	**90+**

Under the auspices of Pierre Lurton, Cheval Blanc is on a roll, with its 2000 qualifying as the wine of the vintage and the 1998 and 1999 representing its finest back-to-back vintages since 1982 and 1983. In particular, the 1999 seems to gain in stature and volume every time I taste it.

2000: Readers can put money on this one . . . it's a no-brainer, Cheval Blanc 2000 is the wine of the vintage! Approximately 50% of the harvest made the grand vin. This wine offers an explosion of berry fruits, a texture akin to cashmere, and layers of melted tannin infused with awesome levels of extract and fruit. Seamless, extraordinarily pure, and perhaps a modern-day clone of the 1949, the 2000 Cheval Blanc has everything one would ever want in a wine. It is not as enormous as some 2000s, but it has a level of intensity and concentration without any sense of heaviness that sets it apart from most wines. Moreover, the tannins are melted and totally unobtrusive in a wine that, analytically, is high in tannin. The glorious nose of blueberries, blackberries, coconut, new saddle leather, and flowers is to die for. The texture is so plush that the palate gets lost in a dizzying smorgasbord of flavors and aromas. This is the greatest young Cheval Blanc I have ever tasted, and, yes, it even surpasses, at this stage in its development, the 1990 and 1982! If there is one wine worth killing for in 2000, it is Cheval Blanc. As a postscript, this wine is a blend of 50% Cabernet Franc and 50% Merlot.

2000 Le Petit Cheval: For those not lucky or rich enough to purchase the 2000 Cheval Blanc, there is an alternative . . . the 2000 Le Petit Cheval, which possesses some of its bigger sibling's character. A blend of equal parts Merlot and Cabernet Franc (40% of the production made it into this wine), it does not have the mass or depth of the Cheval, but this exceptional effort offers sweet, concentrated, plush flavors, wonderful opulence, and super density. This beauty will be drinkable upon release, and will last 12–15 years. Believe it or not, the 2000 Le Petit Cheval is better than some vintages of Cheval Blanc have been over the last two decades.

1999: The immensely sexy, totally disarming 1999 (a blend of 55% Merlot and 45% Cabernet Franc) boasts a deep purple color in addition to gorgeous aromas of jammy black fruits, coffee, cedar, and minerals. As the wine sits in the glass, additional nuances of kirsch and orange marmalade become apparent. A seamless classic, with an unctuous texture, gorgeous levels of fruit, and no hard edges, this compelling Cheval Blanc will be gorgeous to drink young, yet will last two decades. Anticipated maturity: now–2020.

1998: This blend of 55% Cabernet Franc and 45% Merlot exhibits a dark ruby/purple color as well as classic aromas of menthol, plums, mulberries, and assorted black fruits. The oak, texture, acidity, and tannin are all beautifully integrated. While full-bodied, elegant, concentrated, and impeccably balanced, it requires several years of cellaring. As I suspected it has put on considerable weight since bottling. Anticipated maturity: 2007–2030.

1997: A seductive, fragrant style of Cheval Blanc, with moderate density and weight, this immediately appealing 1997 exhibits an exotic nose of coconut, plums, cherry liqueur, and sweet, toasty oak. The wine's alluring personality is accompanied by fine suppleness, low acidity, medium body, and current drinkability. Consume it over the next 5–6 years.

1996: The elegant, moderately weighted 1996 Cheval Blanc reveals a deep garnet/plum, evolved color. Quintessentially elegant, with a complex nose of black fruits, coconut, smoke, and toast, this medium-bodied wine exhibits sweet fruit on the attack, substantial complexity, and a lush, velvety-textured finish. It is very soft and evolved for a 1996. Anticipated maturity: now–2015.

1995: A pretty, attractive Cheval Blanc, the 1995 contains a higher percentage of Merlot in the final blend than usual (50% Merlot/50% Cabernet Franc). This wine has not developed as much fat or weight as its younger sibling the 1996, but it appears to be an outstanding Cheval Blanc, with an enthralling and exotic bouquet of smoke, black currant, and coffee. Complex, rich, medium- to full-bodied flavors are well endowed and pure, with surprisingly firm tannin in the finish. Unlike the sweeter, riper 1996, the 1995 may be more structured and potentially longer-lived. Anticipated maturity: now–2020.

Past Glories: 1990 (100), 1986 (92), 1985 (93), 1983 (95), 1982 (100), 1981 (90), 1975 (90), 1964 (95), 1961 (93), 1959 (92), 1955 (90), 1953 (95), 1949 (96), 1948 (96), 1947 (100), 1921 (98)

DOMAINE DE CHEVALIER (PESSAC-LÉOGNAN)

2000	**E**	**(88–90)**
1999	**E**	**89**
1998	**E**	**87**
1997	**D**	**85**
1996	**E**	**88**
1995	**E**	**80?**

The red wines of Domaine de Chevalier do not resemble the intense, rich, earthy style of Graves best exemplified by Haut-Brion or La Mission Haut-Brion. They do possess a subtle mineral, earthy aspect, but tend to be much lighter bodied and more Médoc in style. Since 1983, there has been an intentional effort to produce bigger and more structured wines, but the excessive oakiness of some vintages has been a concern. However, this trait was more restrained over recent years, particularly since 1998, and the 1999 and 2000 are the finest wines produced at the estate in the last 10–15 years.

2000: One of the finest Domaine de Chevaliers produced in the last decade, the 2000 is made in an elegant style, with the oak more restrained than in previous examples. This deep ruby/purple-colored offering exhibits notes of roasted herbs, vanilla, red and black currants, wet stones, and tobacco. It will undoubtedly develop more complexity as it ages. Medium-bodied, beautifully concentrated, it reveals moderate tannin in the finish. Anticipated maturity: 2003–2020.

1999: The dark ruby/purple-colored 1999 offers aromas of melted asphalt intertwined with tobacco, cedar, spice box, and black currants. Revealing better-integrated oak than recent vintages have exhibited, as well as sweet tannin, a lusty, plush mid-palate and finish, and beautifully sweet fruit that unfolds on the palate in a graceful manner, it will be drinkable upon release and over the following 10 years.

1998: This dark ruby-colored Domaine de Chevalier reveals aggressive spicy new oak in the nose, along with notions of tobacco, smoke, and black cherries. While medium-bodied and stylish, it lacks the necessary depth to qualify as one of the stars of the vintage. Anticipated maturity: now–2015.

1997: Medium light ruby-colored, with sweet, smoky, herb-tinged, toasty, cherry, and berry flavors, this is an attractive, light- to medium-bodied wine with soft tannin, low acidity, and little depth or finish. Drink it over the next 4–5 years.

1996: The 1996 has turned out beautifully from the bottle. It is an exceptionally elegant wine, with well-integrated oak, and tobacco-tinged cherry and cassis fruit. It appears to be a return to the style of the 1970s and early 1980s. Lush, with excellent concentration, a beautiful texture, and a flattering, potentially complex aromatic profile, this medium-bodied wine should be at its finest between 2003–2016.

1995: A shockingly high oak component obliterates any attempt to discern the level of fruit that might be present. Yes, the wine is backward; yes, it is light-bodied; yes, it hints at having some minerality: but where are the weight, ripeness, and fruit intensity? Drink it from 2007–2015.

CIEUX SUR TERRE (ST.-EMILION)

1998	C 87

The 1998 is my first experience with this estate, located just outside the St.-Emilion satellite village of St.-Hippolyte.

1998: Made from a blend of 70% Merlot, 20% Cabernet Franc, and 10% Cabernet Sauvignon, with a five-day cold maceration, and 45 days of maceration total, it was bottled without filtration after spending its entire *élevage* in new French oak. The wine possesses a dark ruby/purple color as well as a sweet bouquet of black cherries, blackberries, currants, spice box, tobacco, minerals, and subtle new oak. Well defined and pure, this looks to be a very good effort. Anticipated maturity: 2003–2016.

CITRAN (HAUT-MÉDOC)

1999	C 86
1998	C 86
1996	C 87
1995	C 86

The wines of Citran have been glorious over past years. If there is any criticism, it would be that the use of new oak gives them a dramatic, even charred, character that may not please those who prefer delicate and subtle clarets. They usually can keep for at least a decade. Prices have gone up slightly over recent years.

1999: A deep ruby/purple color is accompanied by a moderately endowed bouquet of smoke, licorice, and blackberry/currant fruit. Soft and round, this 1999 is best drunk in its first decade of life. Anticipated maturity: now–2010.

1998: The dark ruby-colored 1998 Citran exhibits sweet blackberry and toasty new oak aromas, medium weight, an attractive fleshiness, soft tannin, and good elegance. Drink it over the next 5–6 years.

1996: Opaque ruby/purple, with plenty of intensity, fruit, body, glycerin, and tannin, the 1996 is a forceful, muscular, broad-shouldered claret for drinking between 2003–2015.

1995: Softer than the 1996, the deep ruby/purple-colored 1995 reveals licorice, vanilla, and ripe black currant fruit presented in a straightforward but savory, mouth-filling style. Drink it over the next 4–5 years.

Other vintage tasted: 1997 (86)

CLARKE (LISTRAC)

1999	C 86
1998	C 87

1999: The 1999 is a nicely textured, dark plum/ruby-colored offering with cassis fruit inter-mixed with earth, licorice, and spice. Medium-bodied, with low acidity, ripe tannin, and an attractive finish with no hardness, it should be consumed during its first decade of life.

1998: A serious effort, the 1998 reveals complex aromatics of lead pencil, red and black cur-rants, minerals, and spice box. Graceful and medium-bodied, it possesses good ripeness and abundant quantities of well-integrated, sweet tannin. Anticipated maturity: 2003–2015. *Other vintage tasted:* 2000 (87–88)

CLERC-MILON (PAUILLAC)

2000	D	(90–92+)
1999	D	89
1998	D	91
1997	C	89
1996	D	90
1995	D	89

Until 1985, the wines of Clerc-Milon were frequently light and undistinguished, but recent vintages display a lush fruity quality, greater depth and flavor dimension, and lavish quanti-ties of toasty new oak. Given their quality, these wines are currently undervalued.

2000: A massive Pauillac, the 2000 Clerc-Milon (a blend of 67% Cabernet Sauvignon and 33% Merlot) displays zesty acidity, high tannin, and impressive levels of extract as well as richness. Its dense plum/purple color is followed by sweet aromas of smoke, coffee, black-berries, barbecue spices, and licorice. The attack is sweet, but then the tannin kicks in, as does the wine's surprising acidity. Full, powerful, and long, it will require patience, atypical for Clerc-Milon. Anticipated maturity: 2008–2025.

1999: A sweet nose of cassis, cedar, chocolate, and smoked herbs is followed by a round, rich, delicious, medium- to full-bodied wine. It is a perfect foil to the gargantuan 1998. The seductive, complex, low-acid, plump 1999 has fleshed out during its *élevage*. Anticipated maturity: now–2016.

1998: A superb effort, the 1998 is, along with the 2000, one of the finest Clerc-Milons I have tasted. A blend of 50% Cabernet Sauvignon, 33% Merlot, 14% Cabernet Franc, and 3% Petit Verdot, this is a blockbuster, oversized offering for this estate. Full-bodied and super-extracted, with power to burn, this rich, concentrated wine demands 6–7 years of cellaring. It is not dissimilar from the enormously constituted, majestic yet backward 1998 Mouton-Rothschild. Anticipated maturity: 2008–2025.

1997: Because of its low acidity and evolved style, the 1997 Clerc-Milon deserves con-sumers' attention. Readers will enjoy its lush, concentrated, cassis/blackberry notes inter-twined with coffee, smoke, spice, and chocolate. Drink this lush, hedonistic offering over the next 8–10 years.

1996: The 1996 is among the finest wines I have ever tasted from this estate. Lavishly oaked, with gobs of toast and rich fruit, it is more massive and concentrated than previous vintages. The color is dense ruby/purple. The bouquet offers notes of roasted coffee, tobacco, and jammy cassis. Though surprisingly soft and opulent on the attack, the midsection and finish reveal the wine's full body, high flavor extraction, and moderate tannin. This complete, large-scaled Clerc-Milon will be at its finest between 2005–2018.

1995: The 1995 Clerc-Milon, a 56% Cabernet Sauvignon, 30% Merlot, 14% Cabernet Franc blend, reveals more tannin and grip than the 1996 (ironically, the 1995 has more of a 1996 vintage character, and vice-versa for the 1996). This attractive dark ruby/purple-colored wine has impressive credentials, and may merit an outstanding score with another year or two in the bottle. It offers a gorgeous nose of roasted herbs, meats, cedar, cassis, spice, and vanillin. This dense, medium- to full-bodied wine possesses outstanding levels of extract, plenty of glycerin, and a plush, layered, hedonistic finish. A luscious, complex wine, it reveals enough tannin and depth to warrant 15 or more years of cellaring. Anticipated maturity: now–2015.

CLINET (POMEROL)

2000	EE	(90–92)
1999	EE	88
1998	EE	90?
1997	E	89
1996	EE	91+?
1995	EE	96

This property hit its apogee in 1989 and 1990. Because of its tannic character, it usually requires a few years' cellaring before it is ready to drink.

2000: The 2000 Clinet possesses a saturated ruby/purple color, a masculine, muscular, medium- to full-bodied style, hard tannin, sweet, concentrated fruit, good purity, and a disjointed, jagged personality. It will require patience. Anticipated maturity: 2004–2020.

1999: The 1999 exhibits an impressive deep purple color as well as superb, pure, smoky, coffee, licorice-infused black cherry and berry aromas and flavors. The wine is dense, rich, and medium- to full-bodied but again disjointed. Chalky tannin in the finish needs to become better integrated. Anticipated maturity: 2006–2020.

1998: I had high hopes for this wine prior to bottling, but Clinet often goes through a reduced, awkward stage following bottling. The 1998 reveals a dense, thick-looking purple color, as well as a closed bouquet. With coaxing, notes of damp earth, spicy new oak, truffles, blackberry, and plum fruit emerge. Dense, with jagged tannin, considerable power, and a roasted, chocolatey character, this wine has not yet meshed together. I had hoped it would be less disjointed, but I still feel there is a strong likelihood that it will deserve an outstanding score. However, patience will be required. Anticipated maturity: 2008–2020.

1997: The 1997 Clinet has turned out better than expected from barrel. Its exotic nose of truffles, vanilla, plum liqueur, black fruits, and Asian spices leads to a plump, fat wine with notes of coffee, coconut cream, and blackberries. Surprisingly dense, and revealing more tannin than most 1997s, it should drink well for 10 years. Although a top success, it is one of the less pleasurable 1997s for current consumption. Anticipated maturity: 2003–2012+.

1996: This is a backward, muscular, highly extracted wine with a boatload of tannin, thus the question mark. The saturated plum/purple color is followed by an aggressively oaky nose with scents of roasted coffee, blackberries, and prunes. It is somewhat of a freak for a 1996 Pomerol given its richness, intensity, and overripe style. Medium-bodied and powerful but extremely closed and in need of 5–6 years of cellaring, it will be interesting to follow this wine's evolution to determine if the tannin fully integrates itself into the wine's concentrated style. If not, it will have a slight rusticity to its tannin and structure. I sense this wine will be much more controversial than I had anticipated. Anticipated maturity: 2007–2020.

1995: Another extraordinary wine made in a backward *vin de garde* style, the 1995 Clinet represents the essence of Pomerol. The blackberry, cassis-like fruit of this wine is awesome. The color is saturated black/purple, and the wine extremely full-bodied and powerful, with layers of glycerin-imbued fruit, massive richness, plenty of licorice, blackberry, and cassis flavors, full body, and a thick, unctuous texture. This is a dense, impressive offering that should continue to improve for another 10–25 years. Anticipated maturity: 2006–2025.

Past Glories: 1990 (92), 1989 (99), 1988 (90)

CLOS BADON (ST.-EMILION)

2000	C	(87–89)
1999	C	88
1998	C	90

This small (just under 20 acres) vineyard situated near La Gaffelière has always held great promise. It is owned by St.-Emilion's omnipresent Jean-Luc Thunevin. The wines are generally rich, opulently textured, and made from extremely ripe fruit. The debut vintage was 1998.

2000: The soft 2000 Clos Badon is lighter than expected, given Thunevin's talent. This superficial albeit pretty wine offers abundant quantities of cherry as well as red and black currant fruit, medium body, and an easygoing finish. Consume it over the next 5–6 years.

1999: Although less complete than the 1998, the luscious 1999 reveals overripe notes of black cherries, figs, chocolate, and smoky new oak. Consume this hedonistic, richly fruity St.-Emilion before 2010.

1998: A sexy, ripe, opulently styled effort, the 1998 offers abundant quantities of chocolate, coffee, fruitcake, and berry aromas and flavors. This lush, expansive, juicy, full-bodied wine will not make old bones, but will provide impressive drinking over the next 6–7 years. It is a sleeper of the vintage.

CLOS CHAUMONT (PREMIERES CÔTES DE BORDEAUX)

2000	B	(89–91)
1999	B	88
1998	B	88

These three are sleepers of their respective vintages. Proprietor Pieter Verbeek's wines are a blend of 60% Merlot, 35% Cabernet Sauvignon, and 5% Cabernet Franc and have become one of the smartest choices for consumers looking for great bargains

2000: The sensational Clos Chaumont 2000 is a seriously endowed offering with a deep ruby/ purple as well as notes of melted fudge, espresso, blackberries, and cherries. In the mouth, it is layered, unctuous, thick, and juicy, with gobs of fruit and abundant glycerin. There are no hard edges to this velvety-textured, knockout effort. Enjoy it over the next 5–6 years.

1999: While the 1999 may turn out to be as excellent as the 1998, it does not appear to have the weight of its older sibling. However, it does have the charm as well as gorgeously ripe black cherry and cassis fruit presented in a medium- to full-bodied, velvety-textured style. Anticipated maturity: now–2006.

1998: The delicious 1998 Clos Chaumont exhibits a dark ruby/purple color as well as a gorgeous nose of black fruits intermixed with spice box, lead pencil, and cedar. Rich, medium- to full-bodied, and fat, this nicely textured, fleshy wine can be drunk now and over the next 7–8 years. Smart readers will be purchasing this by the case.

CLOS DU CLOCHER (POMEROL)

2000	D	(88–90)
1999	D	88
1998	D	88
1997	C	85
1996	C	86
1995	C	86

In the best vintages, the wines of Clos du Clocher are generously flavored, full-bodied, and attractive despite their lack of polish and finesse. Unfortunately, prices are rather high because of the small production that is gobbled up by fans from the Benelux countries.

2000: A sweet, soft, surprisingly seductive Pomerol, the 2000 Clos du Clocher is atypical of many wines from this appellation. Hedonistic and fleshy, with copious quantities of mocha and blackberry/cherry fruit in addition to a hint of caramel and coffee, this full, rich, supple wine will be delicious over its first 10–14 years of life.

1999: Potentially outstanding, the dense black/ruby/purple-colored 1999 exhibits super extraction and a deep, smoky, mocha, plum, and cherry-scented and -flavored personality. Full-bodied, rich, and multilayered, with an excellent texture as well as impressive overall symmetry, it may turn out to be one of the finest Clos du Clochers made in the last 20 years. Anticipated maturity: now–2018.

1998: A serious, structured, moderately tannic effort, the dense ruby/purple-colored 1998 offers aromas and flavors of black raspberries, cherries, plums, Asian spices, earth, and new oak. Although it possesses a fat, succulent mid-palate as well as excellent sweetness from glycerin and ripeness, it requires an additional 1–2 years of aging. Anticipated maturity: 2003–2015.

1997: The 1997 has a touch of prunes and raisiny fruit with an element of overripeness. The wine is dark ruby-colored, medium-bodied, spicy, and medium-weight. Its low acidity and forward, fragile style suggest drinking it over the next 3–4 years.

1996: The 1996 displays a distinctive note of Chinese tea, cherry jam, and dried herbs. Open-knit, with low acidity and a plump, savory, seductive style, this medium-bodied wine should drink well for 3–4 years.

1995: A soft, well-made, attractive Pomerol, the 1995 offers smoky, dried herb, black cherry aromas intermixed with earth and spicy oak. Round and fruity, with moderate tannin in the finish, this is a medium-bodied, straightforward, yet pleasing Pomerol. Anticipated maturity: now–2010.

CLOS DUBREUIL (ST.-EMILION)

2000	E	(91–94)
1999	E	91
1998	E	92
1997	E	89

A quintessential St.-Emilion *vin de garage*, this 3-acre, 300-case winery is managed by Louis Mitjavile, the son of François Mitjavile (of Tertre-Rôteboeuf fame), who fashions wines in the same ripe and sensual style favored by his father.

2000: This superb wine offers complexity and finesse married to power and density. A saturated blue/purple color is accompanied by scents of licorice, crème de cassis, cherry liqueur, smoke, and liquefied minerals. Full-bodied, with an expansive palate, moderate but sweet tannin, and a glycerin-imbued, supple finish, it will be at its finest between 2003–2016.

1999: Similarly styled but lower in acidity, plump, and fat, with overripe blackberries as well as cherries intermingled with smoke, licorice, fruitcake, chocolate, and espresso, the unctuously textured, full-bodied 1999 boasts superb purity, low acidity, and a blockbuster finish. Anticipated maturity: now–2016.

1998: A spectacular offering, this massive, full-bodied 1998 boasts huge, concentrated, chocolate, cedar, coffee, blackberry, and cherry aromas as well as flavors. This low-acid, multidimensional effort possesses oodles of glycerin, extract, and richness. It is a fabulously exotic, full-flavored, mouth-staining wine to drink over the next 12–15 years.

1997: One of the stars of the vintage, this creamy-textured 1997 exhibits a sweet cedar, chocolate, and fruitcake-scented nose. Additionally, copious quantities of black raspberries and cherries emerge with airing. Ripe and sensual (the style favored by Louis Mitjavile's father), with low acidity, this gorgeous, user-friendly wine will have huge appeal. Drink it over the next 4–5 years.

CLOS L'EGLISE (CÔTES DE CASTILLON)

2000	D	(89–91)
1999	D	88

This estate, one of Côtes de Castillon's up-and-coming stars, is owned by St.-Emilion movers and shakers Gérard Perse (Monbousquet, Pavie, and Pavie Decesse) and Dr. Alain Raynaud (Quinault l'Enclos). Their debut vintage was 1999.

2000: This highly extracted, rich, pure, black/purple-colored, dense, medium-bodied wine reveals beautifully etched black currant and blackberry fruit intermixed with earth and toast. Stylish, concentrated, and rich, it is a worthy addition to the ever-increasing portfolio of high-quality wines from this St.-Emilion's satellite appellation. Anticipated maturity: now–2012.

1999: Aged in 100% new oak, the 1999 exhibits a dense ruby/purple color as well as a sweet nose of plum liqueur intermixed with creamy new oak, black cherry jam, and spice. Dense, medium- to full-bodied, and opulent, it is a rich, fruity effort that should drink well for 5–6 years, perhaps longer. It is a sleeper of the vintage.

CLOS L'EGLISE (POMEROL)

2000	EE	(95–97)
1999	EE	92
1998	EE	95
1997	E	90

Since its acquisition in 1997 by the Cathiard-Garcin family, Clos l'Eglise has become one of the finest Pomerols. Michel Rolland has been brought in as a consultant, and the wines have gone from being appallingly mediocre to fabulous, and since 2000, a superb garage wine called Branon is being produced there. Consumers should know that the Garcin-Cathiards also own Haut-Bergey in Graves.

2000: A prodigious effort from a very good to excellent rather than outstanding vintage for Pomerol, Clos l'Eglise, is one of the candidates for the Pomerol of the vintage. The complex, concentrated 2000 should equal the fabulous 1998. This forward effort offers sumptuous aromas of mocha, cigar tobacco, leather, blueberries, plums, and kirsch. Opulent, concentrated, full-bodied, savory, and thick, it possesses a voluptuous texture as well as a stunningly pure finish. While it will not live as long as Lafleur or Pétrus, it represents a terrific choice for drinking over the next 10–15 years. Anticipated maturity: now–2020.

1999: I tasted this wine on three different occasions in Bordeaux. From two of the tastings, I thought it might ultimately turn out to be as good as the 1998. It offers a dark plum/garnet color, smoky, complex aromatics of caramel, black fruits, and cherry liqueur, medium to full body, admirable richness and purity, and a supple texture. The question is, will it ultimately reveal the grace and depth of the 1998? Anticipated maturity: now–2015.

1998: A classic Pomerol, the 1998 boasts a superb, complex bouquet of mocha fudge, vanilla, black cherries, roasted coffee, smoke, and berries. The dazzlingly explosive aromatic display is followed by a creamy-textured, medium- to full-bodied, beautifully layered wine with no hard edges. A supple texture leads to a finish with notes of caramel and spice that lingers for 40+ seconds. This is a gorgeous, complex Pomerol. Anticipated maturity: now–2018.

1997: One of the few stars of this soft, consumer-friendly vintage, Clos l'Eglise has fashioned a dark ruby/purple-colored, sexy wine with ostentatious aromas of mocha, fudge, coffee, and sweet berry fruit intermixed with toasty new oak. Medium- to full-bodied, opulently textured, with low acidity, abundant glycerin, and lovely fruit, this is a triumph for the vintage. Drink this gorgeous Pomerol over the next 12 years.

CLOS FOURTET (ST.-EMILION)

2000	E	(90–92)
1999	D	87
1998	D	90
1997	D	87
1996	D	89
1995	D	88

This estate was sold in February 2001 by the Lurton family to Paris businessman Philippe Cuvelier. Clos Fourtet is an estate to follow—and buy.

2000: A strong effort from this premier grand cru classé, the 2000 exhibits a black/purple color as well as an exotic, flamboyant bouquet of jammy black cherries and blackberries intertwined with licorice, smoke, and new oak. Deep, opulent, and sexy, with low acidity, abundant glycerin, and concentrated fruit, it will be hard to resist after bottling. Anticipated maturity: now–2020.

1999: Soft and hedonistic, the low-acid, plump, corpulent 1999 exhibits a dense ruby/purple color, good flesh, abundant quantities of jammy black fruit, and a medium- to full-bodied, lush finish. It will drink well during its first 12–15 years of life.

1998: A strong effort, the dark ruby/purple 1998 offers pure blackberry and cherry aromas with subtle wood and licorice in the background. Medium-bodied, exceptionally pure, with low acidity as well as silky tannin, this sexy offering is ideal for drinking now and over the next 14–15 years.

1997: This easygoing, delicious, creamy-textured 1997 exhibits abundant toasty new oak along with jammy black fruits. There is not much grip or tannin in this supple, richly fruity, charming, tasty St.-Emilion. Enjoy it over the next 7–8 years.

1996: On one of the three occasions I tasted the 1996 from bottle I rated it outstanding (90 points). The color is a saturated dark ruby. The nose offers up sweet black raspberry and blackberry fruit intermixed with toasty oak and floral scents. It is fleshy, surprisingly expansive and forward for a 1996, with low acidity, and a long, multilayered, fruit-driven finish. The tannin is ripe, and thus the fruit comes forward and the wine is seductive and charming. This 1996 possesses the weight, richness, and extract to last 15–20 years, but it should be drinkable early. I would not be surprised if readers feel my score is too conservative based on how well this wine is showing. Anticipated maturity: 2003–2018.

1995: A very fine effort, the 1995 exhibits a medium dark plum color, followed by sweet black cherry and kirsch fruit intertwined with minerals and toasty oak. Tightly wound on the palate, with medium body, excellent delineation and purity, and a spicy finish with plenty of grip, this example has closed down considerably since bottling, but it does possess excellent sweetness and depth. However, the tannin is more elevated, so this 1995 will require patience. Anticipated maturity: 2004–2018.

CLOS GRAND FAURIE (ST.-EMILION)

2000	C	(84–86)

A pinched, compressed texture kept my score low in this otherwise well-made wine. While it possesses high tannin, there is good, ripe cherry fruit on the attack as well as medium body. Anticipated maturity: 2004–2012.

CLOS DES JACOBINS (ST.-EMILION)

1997	C	85
1996	C	82

Despite reasonably good wines, Clos des Jacobins receives little publicity and is probably the least well known of all Cordier estates. It has been consistent over the last decade.

1997: The 1997 reveals more cassis in its sweet, jammy nose, lower acidity, a riper, plusher texture, and more volume and length. Drink now.

1996: The straightforward, pleasant, soft, fruity 1996 exhibits a licorice and Provençal herb-scented nose, and medium-bodied, open-knit, cherrylike flavors. It should be drunk now.

Other vintage tasted: 1999 (82–84)

CLOS DU JAUGUEYRON (MARGAUX/HAUT-MÉDOC)

2000 Margaux	D	(91–93)
1999 Margaux	D	91

1998 Margaux	D	89
1999 Haut-Médoc	C	87
1998 Haut-Médoc	C	87

I hesitated to review these wines because production is microscopic. The ancient vines are believed to be prephylloxeric. However, the total production (100 cases) qualifies this as an ultimate garage wine from proprietor Michel Theron.

2000 Margaux: The opaque purple 2000 boasts a glorious nose of violets, blackberries, cassis, minerals, and smoke. Deep, expansive, rich, and exciting, this full-bodied, sensational Margaux challenges the finest 2000s of the appellation. Anticipated maturity: 2005–2020.

1999 Margaux: This sensational 1999 is at the same quality level as the Marojallia (the other garage wine from this appellation). A dense purple color is followed by scents of jammy black fruits intermixed with smoke, licorice, and truffles. Deep, full-bodied, textured, and super-pure as well as harmonious, this terrific offering should drink well for 10–15 years.

1999 Haut-Médoc: An excellent, dark ruby-colored effort, the 1999 Haut-Médoc exhibits spicy oak, black currants, licorice, and spice box aromas. With low acidity, it is best drunk during its first 4–5 years of life.

1998 Margaux: A dense dark ruby/purple color is accompanied by an elegant, seductive, fleshy mid-palate, copious glycerin, and gorgeous floral-infused black currant fruit with a touch of licorice and toast. This outstanding 1998 should be consumed over the next decade.

1998 Haut-Médoc: A solidly made effort, with sweet black currant fruit, medium body and tannin, and spicy new oak, the 1998 Haut-Médoc should be consumed over the next 4–5 years.

CLOS DU MARQUIS (ST.-JULIEN)

2000	D	(88–90)
1999	D	88
1998	D	90
1997	C	86
1996	D	90
1995	D	90

Clos du Marquis, the second wine of Léoville-Las Cases, is frequently as good as or better than many Médoc classified growths.

2000: The 2000 is a blend of 68% Cabernet Sauvignon, 25% Merlot, and the rest Cabernet Franc and Petit Verdot. Its opaque ruby/purple color is followed by a sweet nose of earthy black cherries and currants intermixed with minerals, spice box, and vanilla. There is good underlying acidity, medium to full body, excellent to outstanding concentration, and a structured, moderately tannic finish. It will require 2–3 years of cellaring and should age nicely for 15+ years.

1999: An opaque ruby/purple color is followed by sweet black currant, lead pencil, mineral, and spicy oak aromatics. This medium-bodied 1999 should be delicious upon release. Anticipated maturity: now–2015.

1998: A superb effort, the 1998 exhibits abundant quantities of black currant and cherry fruit subtly dosed with toasty oak. A medium- to full-bodied, nicely textured, pure effort, with a moderately tannic finish, it resembles Léoville-Las Cases, but without the weight, overall length, and power. Anticipated maturity: now–2014.

1997: The dark ruby/purple-colored 1997 is an attractive, elegant, medium-bodied effort with low acidity and abundant tasty, lush fruit.

1996: Terrific and clearly of second or third growth quality, this dark purple-colored wine reveals much of its bigger sibling's structure, brooding backwardness, and rich, expansive character. The wine is less massive than Léoville-Las Cases, but exhibits plenty of sweet kirsch black currant fruit intermixed with high quality, subtle new oak, and steely, mineral characteristics. Rich and medium- to full-bodied, with ripe tannin, a dazzling Clos du Marquis. Anticipated maturity: now–2018.

1995: The 1995 is the quintessentially elegant style of Léoville-Las Cases, with copious quantities of sweet fruit, outstanding depth, ripeness, and overall equilibrium, but no sense of heaviness. Like so many of this estate's great wines, everything is in proper proportion, with the acidity, alcohol, and tannin well integrated. The 1995, which is slightly more up front and precocious than the 1996, can be drunk now as well as over the next 12 years.

CLOS DE L'ORATOIRE (ST.-EMILION)

2000	E	(91–94)
1999	D	92
1998	D	92
1997	C	89
1996	D	90
1995	D	89

Stephan von Neipperg (also the proprietor of Canon-La-Gaffelière and La Mondotte) has completely resurrected this property, now one of the finest in St.-Emilion. Clos de l'Oratoire remains fairly priced for its quality.

2000: A terrific effort, the thick, blue/black/purple 2000 exhibits soaring aromas of coffee, blackberry liqueur, cedar, licorice, and Asian spices. In the mouth, the wine is compellingly concentrated, with sweet glycerin and highly extracted flavors on the attack. There is noticeable tannin, but it never overwhelms this full-bodied, large-scaled, concentrated yet impeccably balanced wine. It is a classic offering meant for long-term aging. Anticipated maturity: 2004–2020.

1999: Another outstanding effort, the forward, plump, dark purple 1999 possesses terrific concentration of black fruits intermixed with smoke, earth, truffles, and new wood. The wine is dense, full-bodied, low in acidity, extremely ripe, and hedonistic. The tannin is largely concealed by the wine's glycerin and fat. Anticipated maturity: now–2015.

1998: An opaque blue/purple color is accompanied by a sensational bouquet of melted fudge, plums, Asian spices, blackberries, and prunes. Smoky, barbecue-like spices also emerge with airing. Full-bodied, superextracted, rich, pure, and mouth-saturating, this large-scaled effort can be consumed with pleasure, but it will age for 20 years. Anticipated maturity: now–2020.

1997: One of the stars of the vintage, this opaque ruby/purple-colored wine offers copious quantities of jammy black cherries and lavish, smoky new oak. Fat, fleshy, and rich, with sweet tannin, medium to full body, and gorgeous concentration and fruit, it can be drunk now and will last 10–12 years.

1996: The 1996 is even better out of bottle than it was from cask. The wine boasts an opaque plum/purple color. Intense aromas of Asian spices, espresso, roasted meats, and sweet, exotic cedar and blackberry fruit soar from the glass of this exotic, ostentatiously styled St.-Emilion. It is medium- to full-bodied, with moderate tannin, a sweet mid-palate (always a good sign), and a dense, concentrated, long, powerful finish. This muscular, impressively endowed offering should drink well until 2017.

1995: An impressive, possibly outstanding, wine, the 1995 Clos de l'Oratoire is a sleeper of the vintage. This dense ruby/purple-colored offering possesses attractive, meaty, sweet cherry fruit in the nose, intertwined with smoky, toasty oak. Medium- to full-bodied, spicy, and layered on the palate, the wine reveals fine delineation, grip, and tannin in the long, heady, impressively endowed finish. Anticipated maturity: now–2015.

CLOS DES PRINCES (ST.-EMILION)

2000	C	(88–90)

2000: The 2000 Clos des Princes is stunning. Notes of coffee, blackberries, cassis, and cola jump from the glass of this full-bodied, fat, chewy, ripe, dense, highly extracted effort. With excellent balance, sweet tannin, and enough acidity for delineation, it is best consumed during its first 10–15 years of life. Unquestionably a sleeper of the vintage.

CLOS PUY-ARNAUD (CÔTES DE CASTILLON)

2000	B	(86–87)

2000: Made from 70% Merlot, 20% Cabernet Franc, and 10% Cabernet Sauvignon, this Côtes de Castillon possesses good sweetness, a velvety texture, and a pure, fruity style. If more complexity develops, its score will move up. Anticipated maturity: now–2007.

CLOS RENÉ (POMEROL)

2000	C	(88–89)
1999	C	87
1998	C	86

2000: A user-friendly Pomerol, Clos René's 2000 possesses a deep plum/purple color in addition to a sweet perfume of kirsch, smoke, espresso, and caramel. Well made and supple, with medium body, a sweet attack, a plush mid-palate, and light to moderate tannin in its easygoing finish, it will drink well during its first 10 years of life. A sleeper of the vintage.
1999: Cut from the same cloth as the 1998, this medium-bodied effort exhibits smoky, spicy, black cherry fruit aromas with a touch of new oak in the background. Drink this soft offering over the near term, 5–6 years.
1998: Soft, round, and medium-bodied, the 1998 possesses copious quantities of black cherry fruit, toasty new oak, low acidity, and an up-front, savory style. Drink it over the next 5–7 years.
Past Glories: 1947 (95)

CLOS ST.-JULIEN (ST.-EMILION)

2000	C	(88–89)

2000: This intriguing blend of equal parts Merlot and Cabernet Franc reveals a creamy texture, considerable flavor authority, rich, up-front, black cherry and toast notes, low acid, high glycerin, and ripe tannin. A sleeper of the vintage, it should drink well for 10 years.

CLOS ST.-MARTIN (ST.-EMILION)

2000	D	(91–94)
1999	D	87
1998	D	90
1997	C	86

This tiny gem of a vineyard is another of the emerging high-quality St.-Emilion estates. Readers should note that the proprietors of this estate are the Reiffers family, who own Les Grandes Murailles and Côte de Baleau.
2000: Dominated by minerals, the Clos St.-Martin 2000 exhibits an opaque purple color followed by scents of wet stones, black fruits, earth, underbrush, and new oak. Powerful, dense, and chewy, with high tannin and crisp acidity, it will age well for 20 years. Anticipated maturity: 2005–2022.
1999: This wine, which may turn out to be outstanding, is quite an achievement for Clos St.-Martin, which was forced to harvest earlier than desired because of the freak hailstorm in early September. The dense ruby/purple is accompanied by sweet aromas of blueberries,

cherries, crushed stones, vanilla, and licorice. Deep, long, medium- to full-bodied, and ripe, with well-integrated tannin and acidity, it is an impressive effort. Anticipated maturity: 2004–2015.

1998: A classic *vin de garde,* the dense, dark ruby/purple-colored 1998 reveals subtle notes of minerals, black raspberries, cherries, and smoky oak. Medium- to full-bodied, extremely well delineated, and moderately tannic, it requires 2–3 years of cellaring. Patience here will be a virtue unusual for many 1998 St.-Emilions. Anticipated maturity: 2004–2018.

1997: Burgundy-styled, with abundant black cherry aromas and flavors, this medium-bodied 1997 exhibits notions of dried herbs, earth, and spice. Pure, with an underlying minerality, it can be drunk now and over the next 5–7 years.

CLOS DE SARPE (ST.-EMILION)

2000	E	(91–95)
1999	E	90
1998	E	91+

This limited-production (1,000 cases) offering from Jean-Guy Beyney qualifies as a garage wine. It is a muscular, full-throttle blend of 85% Merlot and 15% Cabernet Franc aged in 100% new oak, with malolactic in barrel, bottled without fining or filtration.

2000: This wine displays an opaque plum/purple color as well as a gorgeous, earthy bouquet revealing scents of new saddle leather, roasted meats, underbrush, plum liqueur, black cherries, caramel, and beef blood. There is an aggressive overlay of oak, enormous body, powerful tannin, and a mouth-staining finish, impressive as well as aggressive. This offering may be a throwback to another era, but it has 30–40 years of longevity. A serious *vin de garde,* this 2000 should be purchased only by those with both patience and youth on their sides. Anticipated maturity: 2008–2030.

1999: This wine possesses extremely sweet tannin as well as flamboyant levels of toasty new oak, powerful, concentrated, blackberry and cherry flavors, considerable glycerin, and a structured, dense, mouth-filling style. It is not a shy wine by any means. Anticipated maturity: 2005–2020.

1998: The 1998 is a structured, closed but enormously concentrated, rich, full-bodied effort that should turn out to be a sleeper of the vintage. My only reservation is the high tannin level, but it seems ripe and reasonably well integrated. There are dazzling levels of black fruits intermixed with mineral, crushed stone, licorice, and vanilla. Anticipated maturity: 2005–2015.

CLOS DE LA VIEILLE EGLISE (POMEROL)

2000	C	(86–87?)

2000: There is a lot going on in this wine in terms of a velvety texture, excellent concentration, and a saturated ruby/purple color. However, the overlay of new oak is excessive, and the wine has an international style rather than one that could be quickly identified as Pomerol. Nevertheless, it is cleanly made and very good, if somewhat oaky. Anticipated maturity: 2003–2012.

LA CLOTTE (ST-EMILION)

2000	D	(90–91)
1999	D	88
1998	C	89

These offerings are intensely fruity, fleshy, savory, opulent St.-Emilions that will not make old bones but deliver immense gratification. Moreover, La Clotte is normally a very good value.

2000: One of the numerous 2000 sleepers of the vintage, this is the finest La Clotte I have tasted. Just over 1,000 cases are produced from a blend of 70% Merlot and 30% Cabernet

Franc. An opaque purple color is accompanied by aromas of fudge, black cherries, coffee, caramel, and minerals. Elegant and rich, with sweet fruit, supple tannin, and a loaded personality, it will provide gorgeous drinking during its first 10 years of life.

1999: Identical to the 1998, except for slightly lower acidity and more spice, the 1999 offers black cherry and plum fruit as well as spice box, cedar, and earth. Anticipated maturity: now–2012.

1998: A seductive, dark ruby/plum-colored effort, the 1998 exhibits a viscous texture, rich, spicy, berry fruit, and abundant quantities of plums as well as cherries. Medium- to full-bodied, it is best drunk over the next 8 years.

LA CLUSIÈRE (ST.-EMILION)

2000	EE	(94–96)
1999	EE	91
1998	E	90+

Based on the three vintages fashioned by the new owner, it appears that this estate is attempting to become the Le Pin of St.-Emilion.

2000: A sensational blockbuster, this 100% Merlot possesses both class and sophistication. The opaque black/purple is followed by aromas of vanilla, blackberry liqueur, minerals, overripe cherries, chocolate, and espresso. Remarkably seamless in the mouth, with abundant tannin lurking beneath the surface, the 2000 outperforms the famous Le Pin in terms of depth, exoticism, and longevity. A masterpiece! Anticipated maturity: 2006–2025.

1999: A complementary vintage to the more tannic, structured 1998, the dark ruby/purple 1999 is a sexy, open-knit, flamboyant, flashy wine with gorgeous levels of black cherry and raspberry fruit intermixed with notes of minerals, licorice, earth, and smoky oak. It possesses high levels of glycerin, low acidity, and outstanding depth as well as persistence. Anticipated maturity: 2003–2018.

1998: The 1998 possesses an opaque purple color as well as a firm but promising bouquet of black fruits, crushed stones, and smoky new oak. There is plenty of depth and purity as well as a well-delineated style in this backward, tannic, muscular effort. While it is the finest La Clusière yet produced, it requires 4–5 years of cellaring. Anticipated maturity: 2005–2020.

LA CONSEILLANTE (POMEROL)

2000	EEE	(96–98)
1999	EEE	88
1998	EEE	90
1997	EE	88
1996	EE	88
1995	EE	89

If there is any criticism to address to this property (I love the wine, as evidenced by my reviews over the last two decades), it would be a slight lack of concentration in certain vintages, which prevents it from competing with its neighbors, Cheval Blanc and Pétrus. Highly prized, La Conseillante is generally expensive.

2000: The 2000 is a profound wine, revealing more concentration than usual. Undoubtedly the finest effort produced here since their glorious duo of 1990 and 1989, it boasts a dense ruby/purple color in addition to a spectacular nose of smoke-infused black raspberries and kirsch. As the wine sits in the glass, the nose builds, offering explosive aromas of new wood, Asian spice, and an exotic hint of incense. Velvety-textured and gorgeously pure, with extraordinary levels of glycerin, low acidity, moderately high tannin, and a multitiered palate presence, this fabulous *terroir* has produced one of the vintage's legends. Anticipated maturity: now–2025.

1999: Having put on weight since last year, the 1999 is a candidate for an outstanding score.

The acidity is low, and the ruby-garnet color is relatively evolved, revealing a touch of pink at the edge. Knockout aromatics of licorice, tobacco, spice box, black raspberries, cherries, and dried herbs are exceptional. The wine possesses weight similar to the 1998, but it is fleshier and fatter because of lower acidity. Drink this lush, compelling Pomerol during its first 12–15 years of life.

1998: An evolved dark plum/garnet color is followed by captivating, sexy raspberry, soy, Asian spice, kirsch, and toasty vanilla aromas. While not a blockbuster, this opulently textured, medium-bodied effort is a model of elegance, harmony, finesse, and complexity. Why can't Burgundy grands crus be this balanced and seductive? This wine's low acidity as well as wonderfully ripe fruit invite immediate consumption, and it should last 12–15 years.

1997: Dark ruby-colored, with lavish, high-quality toasty new oak intermixed with black raspberry fruit, this open-knit, medium-bodied, complex wine changes quickly in the glass, revealing smoky, mocha-infused notes. Although not massive, it is sexy, charming, and fruity—in short, a typical La Conseillante. Consume it over the next 10 years.

1996: La Conseillante has turned out an open-knit, seductive wine in the generally tough-textured, tannic year of 1996. The color is a deep ruby. The wine possesses medium body and a sweet, open-knit nose of black raspberries intermixed with toast, licorice, and smoke. Soft, round, and charming, this *terroir*'s raspberry fruit is well displayed. This 1996 can be drunk now but should keep nicely for 12 years. Anticipated maturity: now–2014.

1995: It is tempting to give this wine an outstanding score because of its seductiveness. However, I do not think it possesses quite the level of extract and concentration to merit an exceptional rating. Nevertheless, it is an extremely pleasing style of claret. The deep ruby color is followed by an open-knit black cherry, raspberry, and smoky, roasted herb–scented nose. There is round, lush, ripe fruit, medium body, exceptional elegance and purity, and a soft, velvety-textured finish. Think of it as liquid charm and silk. Anticipated maturity: now–2014.

Past Glories: 1990 (98), 1989 (97), 1986 (89), 1985 (94), 1983 (88), 1982 (95), 1981 (91), 1970 (92), 1959 (95), 1953 (90), 1949 (97), 1947 (91)

CORBIN (ST.-EMILION)

2000	C	(88–89)
1999	C	87
1998	C	88

2000: This sexy, explosively fruity effort may not have as much body and depth as previous Corbins, but it is opulent, precocious for a 2000, and flattering to taste. The deep ruby/purple color is followed by an array of black fruits in the up-front aromatics and flavor profile. This user-friendly, delicious, hedonistic St.-Emilion will provide abundant pleasure for a decade or more.

1999: Another open-knit, expansive, slightly less defined effort, the deep ruby-colored 1999 possesses plenty of jammy black cherry fruit, low acidity, smoke, Asian spices, and wood. Enjoy it during its first decade of life.

1998: A fine effort, Corbin's 1998 is a fat, fleshy, dense, richly fruity offering with aromas and flavors of black cherries, spice box, earth, and licorice. There is good glycerin, a chewy entry and mid-palate, ripe tannin, and a soft, succulent finish. Anticipated maturity: now–2012.

CORBIN-MICHOTTE (ST.-EMILION)

1998	C	(86–87)
1997	C	86
1996	C	86
1995	C	89

1998: This fruit-driven, succulent, juicy, easygoing St.-Emilion offers an intriguing nose of dried herbs, seaweed, and black cherries. Soft, medium-bodied, and velvety-textured, it is a candidate for early consumption—over the next 4–5 years.

1997: The 1997 is a jammier-styled wine than the 1996, with elements of *sur-maturité*, and good fat, cherry/berry fruit intermixed with smoke, earth, and spice scents. It is a medium-bodied, potentially excellent wine for the vintage with low acidity, and a seductive, hedonistic appeal. Drink it over the next 3–4 years

1996: The 1996 follows in the style of most Corbin-Michottes, even though the vintage had a tendency to produce tannic, hard wines. However, Corbin-Michotte seems always to aim for ripeness, and a seductive, forward, fruity style with no hard edges. The dark ruby-colored 1996 is round and soft, with plenty of herb-tinged berry fruit intermixed with smoke and earth. Ripe and medium-bodied, it is ideal for drinking over the next 5–7 years.

1995: A hedonistic effort from Corbin-Michotte, the 1995 reveals a deep ruby color, a jammy plum, cherry, and spice box–scented nose, and medium-bodied, lush, low-acid, juicy, opulently textured, fruity flavors. This is an exuberantly fruity, tasty St.-Emilion. On a pure scale of pleasure, it merits even higher marks. Anticipated maturity: now–2007.

CORMEIL-FIGEAC (ST.-EMILION)

1998	C	86
1997	C	85

1998: A thicker, juicier, jammier wine than the 1997, the full-bodied 1998 displays plenty of power and concentration. This dense, saturated ruby/purple-colored, opulently textured 1998 should drink well for 10 years.

1997: An easygoing, attractive, fruit-driven effort with little density or weight, this is a tasty herb- and currant-tinged wine to consume over the next 1–2 years. If wines such as this were inexpensive, they would be ideal choices for restaurants.

COS D'ESTOURNEL (ST.-ESTÈPHE)

2000	EE	(90–92)
1999	EE	88
1998	E	88
1997	E	87
1996	EE	93+
1995	EE	95

Despite changes in ownership, the winemaking philosophy has remained the same, as Jean-Guillaume Prats continues to oversee the estate.

2000: Jean-Guillaume Prats was not sure whether a small lot of Cabernet Franc would ultimately be added to the blend I tasted. However, whatever his final decision, the 2000 will clearly surpass both the 1998 and 1999, but I do not see it ever attaining the level of quality of the 1996, 1995, or 1990. Made from yields of 40–42 hectoliters per hectare, it presently is a blend of 60% Cabernet Sauvignon and 40% Merlot. A dense ruby/purple color is accompanied by scents of green peppers, spice, cedar, and minerals. The aromatics suggest considerable complexity as this wine ages, but the austere, earthy, tannic, compressed style is not for everybody. Medium-bodied and beautifully pure, this 2000 may always remain somewhat on the tough side because of an austere, abundantly tannic finish. Anticipated maturity: 2007–2020.

1999: The 1999 has fleshed out during its *élevage*. A very good, deep ruby/purple effort with sweeter tannin than the 1998, it offers classic aromas of cigar box, black currants, cherries, and plums. Medium-weight and elegant, with more of a mid-palate than it exhibited when I tasted it *en primeur*, this stylish, silky wine will be delicious upon release. Anticipated maturity: now–2015.

1998: This elegant, stylish, graceful wine is an attractive, dark ruby/purple-colored effort with subtle notes of sweet oak, licorice, herbs, and black fruits. While not massive, it is medium-bodied and ripe, with sweet tannin. A selection of 48% was utilized in this blend of 60% Cabernet Sauvignon and 40% Merlot. Anticipated maturity: 2004–2018.

1997: Forty percent of the harvest made it into this flattering, delicious wine with abundant charm and herb-tinged blackberry and cherry fruit. A dark ruby color in this medium-bodied, appealing St.-Estèphe. A blend of 55% Cabernet Sauvignon and 45% Merlot, it should drink well for 5–7 years.

1996: Made from 65% Cabernet Sauvignon and 35% Merlot, this is a huge, backward wine reminiscent of the 1986. The 1996 possesses an opaque purple color as well as pure aromatics consisting of cassis, grilled herbs, coffee, and toasty new oak. Massive in the mouth and one of the most structured and concentrated young Cos d'Estournels I have ever tasted, this thick, structured, tannic wine has closed down significantly since bottling. It requires 5–6 years of cellaring and should last 30–35 years. It is fabulous, but patience is required. Anticipated maturity: 2006–2030.

1995: A wine of extraordinary intensity and accessibility, the 1995 is a sexier, more hedonistic offering than the muscular, backward 1996. Opulent, with forward aromatics (gobs of black fruits intermixed with toasty scents and a boatload of spice), this terrific Cos possesses remarkable intensity, full body, and layers of jammy fruit nicely framed by the wine's new oak. Because of low acidity and sweet tannin, the 1995 will be difficult to resist young, although it will age 2–3 decades. Anticipated maturity: now–2025.

Past Glories: 1994 (91), 1990 (95), 1986 (95), 1985 (93), 1982 (96), 1961 (92), 1959 (92), 1953 (93)

COS LABORY (ST.-ESTÈPHE)

2000	D	(87–88+)
1999	D	85
1998	D	86
1997	C	86
1996	D	88
1995	D	88+?

For decades one of the most disappointing of all classified growths, Cos Labory has emerged over the last 15 years as a wine well worth buying. Moreover, prices remain reasonable.

2000: A fat, opulently styled effort with tannin lurking under the surface, this dark purple-colored St.-Estèphe exhibits aromas of earth, blackberry and cassis fruit, licorice, dried herbs, and leather. The wine is rich on the entry but narrows slightly, finishing with plenty of glycerin, extract, and tannin. Anticipated maturity: 2003–2018.

1999: There is some charm apparent in this lightweight, soft, fruity but insubstantial effort. Consume it over the next 5–7 years.

1998: This medium-bodied, peppery, herbaceous offering lacks depth. The color is a dark ruby, and the wine reveals nice berry and cassis fruit but little else. Drink it over the next 6–7 years.

1997: I was in error with respect to my severe judgment of this wine during its *élevage*. The truth is always in the bottle, and the 1997 is far better from bottle than it was from cask. A medium plum/ruby color is followed by a charming raspberry/cherry, Burgundy-like fruitiness, excellent ripeness, and a superficial attack and finish. This is a tasty, accessible, user-friendly wine to drink over the next 5–6 years.

1996: My concerns about the 1996's tannic ferocity were alleviated by its performance out of bottle. It has turned out to be a classic, dark ruby/purple-colored St.-Estèphe with earthy black currant fruit, medium to full body, moderate tannin, and excellent purity. As the wine sits in the glass, blackberry jam and mineral notes emerge. This well-made, reasonably priced wine should drink well between 2005–2018.

1995: Although this dark ruby/purple-colored Cos Labory is more charming since bottling, aromatically it is closed, with red and black fruits just beginning to emerge. In the mouth, dusty tannin appears elevated, giving the wine a hard, dry, rough-textured finish. However, there is medium to full body, plenty of sweet, ripe fruit on the attack, and my instincts suggest that there is good extract behind the wall of tannin. Not a wine for readers seeking immediate gratification. Anticipated maturity: 2003–2015.

CÔTE DE BALEAU (ST.-EMILION)

2000	D	(89–91)
1999	D	87
1998	D	89+?

An up-and-coming St.-Emilion estate owned by the Reiffers family, also the proprietors of Clos St.-Martin and Les Grandes Murailles. Production is just under 3,000 cases. This wine's upbringing is overseen by the omnipresent Michel Rolland.

2000: Of the three wines made by the Reiffers family, the 2000 Côte de Baleau is the tightest and most sinewy. Its dense opaque ruby/purple color is followed by a sweet nose of black cherries and cassis, medium to full body, moderately high tannin, and a long, concentrated finish with excellent precision as well as clarity. Anticipated maturity: 2005–2016.

1999: A deep ruby/purple color is followed by aromas of earth, black cherries, raspberries, plums, and spice. This medium-bodied, elegant, finely delineated 1999 needs 1–2 years of cellaring. Anticipated maturity: 2004–2015.

1998: A serious, tight-fisted St.-Emilion, this dense ruby/purple effort reveals impressive thickness as well as notes of minerals, flowers, cherries, and spice box that are reminiscent of the aromas found in hillside St.-Emilions such as Canon and Ausone. Well delineated and elegant, with a terrific mid-palate and finish, it requires 3–4 years of cellaring, and could turn out to be outstanding if it fleshes out and the tannin becomes sweeter and better integrated. Anticipated maturity: 2005–2020.

Other vintage tasted: 1997 (85)

COUCY-MAURÈZE (BORDEAUX)

2000	B	(87–88)

2000: A sleeper of the vintage that should be priced reasonably, this 12,000-case blend of 70% Merlot, 20% Cabernet Franc, and 10% Cabernet Sauvignon should be widely available. Made under the supervision of Jean-Luc Thunevin, it exhibits plenty of plum and black cherry fruit intermixed with spicy aromas. Deep, medium- to full-bodied, and ripe, with a savory, supple finish, it is meant to be consumed during its first 4 years of life.

COUFRAN (HAUT-MÉDOC)

1997	C	84
1996	C	86
1995	C	85

This estate owned by the Miailhe family generally produces well-made and pleasant wines that also represent fairly good values. As a general rule, they must be drunk within 6–8 years after the vintage.

1997: A fine effort from this reliable cru bourgeois, Coufran's 1997 exhibits a saturated dark purple color, attractive jammy cranberry and cassis fruit, moderate tannin, medium body, and low acidity. It should last 4–5 years.

1996: This well-made, succulently textured 1996 exhibits a deep ruby color, spicy oak, black cherry/mocha-tinged fruit, and a moderately long finish. It should drink well for 3–4 years.
1995: A soft, easygoing, medium-bodied Coufran, the elegant 1995 displays attractive ripe red currant fruit intermixed with cherry, weedy, spicy scents. It should drink well for 4–5 years.
Other vintages tasted: 1999 (82–85), 1998 (86–87)

LA COUR D'ARGENT (BORDEAUX)

2000	B	(86–87)

2000: This attractive wine is very fairly priced. Made from 95% Merlot and 5% Cabernet Franc, this deep ruby/purple-colored generic Bordeaux possesses straightforward aromas and flavors of cherry jam. It is cleanly made, nicely textured, and soft, with supple tannin and a fresh, lively, vibrant finish. Drink it over the next 2–3 years. Why can't California produce wines such as this?

DOMAINE DE COURTEILLAC (BORDEAUX SUPÉRIEUR)

2000	B	(87–88)

2000: Another intelligent choice for readers seeking value rather than prestige, this structured, juicy, ripe, medium-bodied effort possesses abundant quantities of mocha, black cherry, and currant flavors, light tannin, and a fine finish. It should drink well for 3–4 years.

LA COUSPAUDE (ST.-EMILION)

2000	EE	(90–92)
1999	E	87
1998	E	92
1997	D	88
1996	E	89
1995	E	90

Another garage operation, this St.-Emilion micro *cuvée* is generally a blend of 70% Merlot, with the rest Cabernet Franc and sometimes some Cabernet Sauvignon. There are about 3,000 cases, a relatively large amount for a *vin de garage*. This is another in the exotic Le Pin school of St.-Emilions, made from extremely ripe fruit and bottled without filtration. The upbringing at La Couspaude is far from traditional, as the wines enjoy the so-called 200% new oak *élevage* after having completed their malolactics in 100% new oak. The talented Michel Rolland oversees the vinifications at the estate.
2000: Dense ruby/purple-colored, with lavish quantities of toasty new oak as well as blueberry, kirsch, and currant scents, this medium- to full-bodied 2000 possesses outstanding concentration and noticeable but sweet tannin. Because of a stronger tannic backbone in addition to slightly elevated acidity, this wine may ultimately turn out to be more classic as well as longer-lived than previous efforts. Anticipated maturity: 2004–2018.
1999: If my memory is correct, this vineyard suffered hail damage during the freak storm that hit some of the St.-Emilion villages in early September 1999. Perhaps that is why the wine tastes a bit short, but it is no wimpy claret. An opaque purple color is accompanied by sweet black cherry and raspberry aromas, good density, and admirable ripeness, but it appears undernourished. Anticipated maturity: 2003–2012.
1998: Possibly the finest La Couspaude to date, the 1998 displays flamboyant notes of toasty new oak as well as an exotic personality. Unctuous, thick, full-bodied, seamless flavors redolent of plums, cherry liqueur, and vanilla cascade over the palate. Low acidity and plush, concentrated, jammy fruit add to the impressive, hedonistic qualities of this explosively rich wine. Anticipated maturity: now–2015.
1997: The 1997 is an exotic, rich, thick, jammy wine with abundant black cherry aromas mixed with scents of roasted coffee, smoke, and toasty new oak. With low acidity and a deli-

cious, medium-bodied, ostentatious personality, this seductive offering can be drunk now and over the next 8 years.

1996: La Couspaude's 1996 has turned out well. This is a richly fruity, sexy, medium-bodied, surprisingly soft and fragrant 1996. Its open-knit aromatics consisting of toast, cherry liqueur, smoke, and black currants are followed by a luscious, soft, lightly tannic wine. It is destined to be drunk during its first 10–12 years of life.

1995: The 1995 La Couspaude exhibits a ripe, jammy kirsch, black currant, and licorice-scented nose with plenty of smoky, toasty notes. Full-bodied, with low acidity and a flamboyant personality, this wine will unquestionably cause heads to turn. Traditionalists may argue that it is too obvious and sexy, but it is fun wine to taste, and no one can argue that it does not provide pleasure—and isn't that the ultimate objective of drinking this stuff? Moreover, it will age well and become even more civilized with cellaring. Anticipated maturity: now–2015.

COUVENT-DES-JACOBINS (ST.-EMILION)

2000	C	(88–89)
1999	C	86
1998	C	86

2000: The finest wine produced at this beautiful estate since the mid-1980s, the 2000 reveals a deep ruby/purple color as well as a sweet, up-front bouquet of black cherry jam. Deep, medium- to full-bodied, ripe, low in acidity, and hedonistic, it is meant to be consumed now and over the next 12–15 years.

1999: A sweet, ripe, black fruit, smoky new oak, and Asian spice–scented bouquet is followed by a deep, fleshy, chewy, medium- to full-bodied wine. The 1999 is an attractive, easy-going, consumer-friendly claret to enjoy during its first decade of life.

1998: This is a medium-bodied, straightforward effort offering up scents of earth, ripe black cherries, dried Provençal herbs, and new wood. A lean, austere finish kept my score low. Anticipated maturity: 2003–2012.

LA CROIX-CANON (CANON-FRONSAC)

1999	C	86
1998	C	88
1997	C	87
1996	C	86

1999: A light- to medium-bodied, well-balanced effort with notions of minerals, tar, and herb-tinged black cherry fruit. It will be easy to drink when released next year. Anticipated maturity: now–2007.

1998: Sweet, ripe raspberry and cherry fruit, good flesh, medium body, and an excellent texture result in a delicious Canon-Fronsac to enjoy over the next 10 years. Although this wine is clearly excellent, I had high hopes that it would turn out to be outstanding. It does not appear to be as rich and complex after bottling. Nevertheless, it remains a sleeper of the vintage. Anticipated maturity: now–2012.

1997: A beautiful wine for the vintage, the 1997 exhibits a Burgundy-like style not dissimilar from a Corton. Earthy/mineral aromas intermixed with black cherries are powerful and rich. A successful effort for both the vintage and appellation, this medium-bodied wine should be consumed over the next 5–6 years.

1996: The splendid *terroir* has produced a deep ruby-colored 1996 with a stylish, complex, elegant nose of sweet cherry jam meshed with floral scents and spice. It presents light fruit on the attack, medium body, light to moderate tannin, and a fine texture and finish. Drink it over the next 4–5 years.

Other vintage tasted: 2000 (84–86)

LA CROIX DU CASSE (POMEROL)

2000	D	(88–90?)
1999	D	89
1998	D	90
1997	D	88
1996	D	88
1995	D	90

La Croix du Casse is producing better wines with each new vintage. This up-and-coming estate remains an unheralded but high-class source of rich, concentrated Pomerols.

2000: This wine displays some of the problems encountered in certain 2000s. Highly extracted but extremely dry, austere tannins are ferocious and unrelenting. The wine exhibits impressive color saturation and plenty of black fruit, earth, and spicy new oak characteristics, but the tannin level is bothersome. Certainly the 2000 is concentrated, pure, and well made, but in the war between fruit and tannin, history usually favors the tannin. Anticipated maturity: 2008–2018?

1999: A potential sleeper, the opaque ruby/purple 1999 displays superripe *(sur-maturité)* flavors of jammy black fruits intermixed with minerals, smoke, spice box, and new oak. Layered, with low acidity as well as a thick, expansive texture, this top-flight Pomerol should evolve more quickly than the 1998 yet age well. Anticipated maturity: 2003–2015.

1998: An outstanding effort, as well as one of the sleepers of the vintage, this dense ruby/purple-colored 1998 exhibits ripe, jammy notes of blackberries and cherries intermixed with licorice, smoke, and new wood. Full-bodied, with terrific fruit extraction, considerable muscle, and moderate tannin levels, it is not a wine to gulp down over the near term. Anticipated maturity: 2005–2016.

1997: A sleeper of the vintage, which enjoys essentially the same winemaking team as Clinet, this wine exhibits a dark plum color in addition to open-knit aromas of black cherries, plums, cedar, herbs, coffee, and vanilla. Round, delicious, and easy to understand and consume, this sexy, medium-bodied 1997 should drink well for 4–5 years.

1996: An impressive Pomerol from proprietor Jean-Michel Arcaute, the 1996 possesses a saturated plum/purple color and a pure nose of spicy, sweet oak, minerals, black fruits, and prunes. The wine is surprisingly open-knit for a 1996, with an expansive, medium- to full-bodied, succulent texture. There is tannin in the finish, but it is nearly obscured by the wine's glycerin, fruit extraction, and ripeness. Drink this attractive, silky Pomerol now and over the next 10 years.

1995: An outstanding wine, the dense ruby/purple 1995 offers up a knockout nose of blackberries, cassis, minerals, and spicy new oak. Medium- to full-bodied, with plenty of toastlike flavors and abundantly sweet fruit imbued with glycerin and tannin, this wine possesses a long mid-palate as well as a finish that builds in the mouth. An impressively built, pure, rich Pomerol that merits considerable attention. Anticipated maturity: now–2015.

LA CROIX DE GAY (POMEROL)

2000	E	(88–89)
1999	E	87
1998	E	87
1997	E	86
1996	E	85
1995	E	87

2000: La Croix de Gay's Burgundy-styled Pomerols are never heavyweights. The 2000 offers sweet strawberry and cherry fruit presented in a medium-bodied, judiciously oaked format. The acidity is low, the tannin is ripe, and the wine is fleshy and succulent. Enjoy it over the next decade.

1999: It would appear that the level of richness as well as extract is slightly better in the 1999 than the 1998, characteristics I also noticed in the estate's luxury *cuvée*, La Fleur de Gay. The dark ruby/purple-colored 1999 La Croix de Gay exhibits a sweet nose of blackberries and cherries as well as a structured, extracted, medium- to full-bodied personality with moderate tannin in the finish. This creamy-textured effort will be delicious upon its release next year. Anticipated maturity: now–2014.

1998: Moderately intense aromas of sweet black cherry fruit intermixed with minerals, smoke, and spice box are followed by a well-balanced, harmonious wine with excellent richness, sweetness (from glycerin), and a spicy, soft finish. Drink it over the next 10 years.

1997: Readers seeking a Bordeaux that imitates a premier cru Beaune will enjoy this sweet, elegant, cherry-scented and -flavored, medium-bodied effort. Revealing Burgundy-like characteristics, it is low in acidity and not terribly concentrated, but elegant, alluring, and ideal for drinking over the next 3–4 years.

1996: The medium ruby-colored 1996 displays a moderately intense nose of roasted herbs intermixed with cherry jam. Seductive, easygoing, open-knit, and light, its low acidity and accessible style suggest consumption over the next 3–4 years.

1995: This is a seductive, elegant, attractive Pomerol with a deep ruby color and plenty of sweet plum, cherry, and berry fruit intermixed with subtle toasty new oak. The wine is round and lush, with copious fruit and enough glycerin to provide a nicely layered texture in a stylish format. Anticipated maturity: now–2006.

Past Glories: 1964 (90), 1947 (92)

CROIX DE LABRIE (ST.-EMILION)

2000	EE	(91–94+)
1999	EE	92
1998	EE	93

Owner Michel Puzio has expanded production to a whopping 750 cases—great news, as this has been one of St.-Emilion's most dazzling garage wines over the last three vintages (made with the consultation of Jean-Luc Thunevin of Valandraud fame).

2000: An extraordinarily pure expression of fruit and *terroir*. An opaque purple color is followed by a full-bodied, layered wine offering intriguing notions of fire embers, truffles, black cherries, and cassis fruit. Thick and highly extracted, but not heavy, it possesses more tannin than the 1998, as well as sufficient fruit and glycerin for balance. This exceptional effort will evolve beautifully for 15+ years. It is not to be missed!

1999: The deep, rich, thick, dense purple-colored, unctuously textured 1999 offers explosive espresso notes intermingled with blackberry, cassis, and appealing chocolaty fruit characteristics. A full-bodied, lavishly rich wine. Anticipated maturity: now–2012.

1998: An opaque purple color is accompanied by aromas of roasted meat, black fruits, spicy oak, and coffee. The wine displays supple tannin, explosive richness, immense body, and beautifully integrated acidity as well as tannin. What a shame there are not 5,000 cases of this blockbuster effort. Anticipated maturity: now–2014.

LA CROIX DE ROCHE (BORDEAUX SUPÉRIEUR)

2000	B	(86–87)

2000: This sweet, fruity, luscious, bargain-priced wine exhibits a dark ruby color, excellent purity, and a sexy style. Drink it over the next 1–2 years.

LA CROIX ST.-GEORGES (POMEROL)

2000	D	(91–94)
1999	D	91

This estate belongs to Jean-Philippe Janoueix, who also owns de Chambrun, another superb up-and-coming Lalande-de-Pomerol. This 100% Merlot comes from clay and gravel soils and is vinified in open-top vats, with regular punching-downs. Malolactics occur in new oak barrels and the wines are bottled without fining or filtration. Yields are kept around 42 hectoliters per hectare. The debut vintage of this new operation was 1999.

2000: This sleeper of the vintage is a large-scaled effort. It is a powerful, dense, concentrated, muscular, opaque ruby/purple-colored wine with plenty of cassis fruit. Aromatically it remains tight yet provocative, revealing earthy, leathery black fruits. Give it 2–3 years of cellaring, and consume it over the following 15 years. Very impressive!

1999: The 1999 is deep, rich, and smoky, with copious quantities of jammy black cherry and kirschlike fruit as well as caramel notes. Very full-bodied, with superb concentration and purity, this sleeper of the vintage will provide a generous mouthful of succulent, low-acid Merlot. Anticipated maturity: 2004–2015.

CROIZET-BAGES (PAUILLAC)

2000	D	(86–88)
1999	D	85
1998	C	81
1997	C	(78–83)
1996	C	87
1995	C	85

2000: Though Croizet-Bages is never a blockbuster Pauillac, the 2000 possesses more concentration and charm than many. Its deep ruby/purple color is accompanied by creamy black currant, cedar, and toast aromas, excellent purity, a rich, medium-bodied style, and sweet tannin in the moderately long finish. It will be early-maturing. Anticipated maturity: now–2014.

1999: Supple tannin, a fleshy entry on the palate, and a medium-bodied finish give the 1999 Croizet-Bages limited appeal. This above-average offering will require consumption within its first decade of life.

1998: Soft, herbal, superficial characteristics as well as notes of cedar, licorice, and red currants describe this medium-bodied, straightforward effort. Drink it over the next 5–6 years.

1997: This soft, round, elegant wine is not concentrated, but it does possess moderately sweet jammy cassis and red currant fruit intermixed with spicy, smoky oak. Already soft, it is ideal for consuming during its first decade of life. Anticipated maturity: now–2010.

1996: This wine has turned out even better than I had expected, continuing the estate's progression in quality that began several years ago. The dark ruby color is followed by sweet, elegant notes of black currants, cherries, spicy oak, and cedar. The wine is medium-bodied, with sweet tannin and a moderately long finish. Purely made, with good depth, it represents one of the more forward Pauillacs of the vintage. Anticipated maturity: 2003-2014

1995: Based on its performance from cask, I had hoped the 1995 would be slightly better. Nevertheless, it has turned out to be a good claret, made in a lighter style. The medium ruby color is followed by straightforward, soft berry and black currant–scented aromatics. In the mouth, the wine reveals an attractive, spicy, fleshy feel, not much weight or depth, but a superficial charm and fruitiness. Anticipated maturity: now–2009.

CROQUE MICHOTTE (ST.-EMILION)

1999	C	86
1998	C	87

1999: Soft and slightly diffuse, this dark plum/ruby-colored effort offers tasty, herb-tinged black fruits in the nose, but in the mouth it is flabby, with only a moderately endowed personality. It will be ready to drink upon release and will evolve for a decade.

1998: A moderately intense, sweet nose of cherry jam, dried herbs, cedar, and spice box is followed by a fleshy, medium-bodied wine with good balance and a savory, soft finish. Drink it over the next decade.

CROS FIGEAC (ST.-EMILION)

1999	C	87
1998	C	87

1999: Another fruity, consumer-friendly, lush, medium-bodied, dark plum/purple-colored offering, the 1999 exhibits sweet, smoky, black cherry fruit, new oak, and copious glycerin as well as fat. Anticipated maturity: now–2008.

1998: This sexy, jammy St.-Emilion is meant to be consumed during its first 7–10 years of life. A dark plum/ruby color is followed by appealing aromas of sweet oak and chocolaty, herb-tinged black currant fruit. The wine is fleshy, expansive, low in acidity, and supple.

LES CRUZELLES (LALANDE-DE-POMEROL)

2000	C	(87–89)

This estate was recently purchased by the proprietor of l'Eglise-Clinet, Denis Durantou. The first vintage he has vinified is 2000, and the result is impressive.

2000: The dense purple color is followed by a sweet bouquet of black fruits. In the mouth it is medium-bodied, with excellent concentration, low acidity, and a layered, creamy finish. Drink it over the next decade.

DALEM (FRONSAC)

1999	C	86
1998	C	86
1997	C	85
1995	C	85

A consistently well-made, attractive Fronsac, Dalem's offerings remain bargain-priced.

1999: Fruity, with excellent ripeness, purity, and overall balance, this spicy, soft, medium-bodied 1999 should drink well for 5–7 years.

1998: The 1998 is a medium-bodied, fruit-driven wine with excellent purity, no hard edges, and plenty of spice, black cherry, and currant fruit presented in an attractive, supple format. Drink it over the next 6–7 years.

1997: Moderately intense, elegant, dried cherry, earth, and spice box scents and flavors can be found in this medium-bodied, soft, lightly tannic Fronsac. Enjoy it over the next 4–5 years.

1995: A good, solid wine, the ruby-colored 1995 Dalem displays minerals, berry fruit, and weediness in the scents and flavors, as well as a soft underbelly and mild tannin in the moderately long finish. It should drink well for 5 years.

Other vintage tasted: 2000 (85–86)

DASSAULT (ST.-EMILION)

2000	C	(85–87)
1999	C	86
1998	C	87
1997	C	86
1996	C	76?
1995	C	85

Dassault is another St.-Emilion estate that is producing better wines. These are soft, fruit-driven offerings meant to be consumed during their first decade of life, although I suspect they may last longer.

2000: Though superficial and one-dimensional, Dassault's 2000 is appealing for its direct, candid display of uncomplicated black currant and cherry fruit mixed with oak, earth, and spice. Round, fleshy, and delicious, but neither complex nor long-lived, it will be drinkable between now–2010.

1999: Made in a similar style, the deep ruby-colored 1999 offers up jammy black cherry and spice box notes as well as a lush texture, low acidity, and a fleshy finish. Drink it over the next 7–8 years.

1998: A dark ruby color is accompanied by a sweet bouquet of blueberry and black currant fruit. This medium-bodied, low-acid, fleshy, richly fruity, smooth 1998 will provide delicious drinking over the next 7–8 years.

1997: Medium plum-colored, with an attractive, easygoing attack, this richly fruity 1997 reveals aromas and flavors of plums, black cherries, licorice, dried herbs, and tar. Medium-bodied, with no hard edges, it should be drunk over the next 3–4 years.

1996: This wine was suspicious in cask samples because of a distinctive mustiness. Dassault has corrected this problem with the 1997, but the 1996 is one-dimensional and sterile, nowhere near the quality of some of Dassault's older vintages, nor the delicious, fruit-driven 1997.

1995: This wine offers a purple saturated color, a sweet fleshy character, and plenty of guts and appeal. Drink before 2006.

DAUGAY (ST.-EMILION)

1998	C	87
1997	C	84
1996	C	85
1995	C	85

1998: Jammy, juicy strawberry and black cherry aromas intermix with herb, spice box, and earth notes in Daugay's fragrant bouquet. Rich, intense, and powerful, with plenty of fruit, glycerin, and body, this substantial yet monolithic wine should drink well during its first 10 years of life.

1997: This is a lighter-styled, medium-bodied, ripe, pleasant but superficial St.-Emilion. There is good sweet fruit, but little density and length. It will provide uncritical quaffing over the next 2–3 years.

1996: Daugay's 1996 is a spicy, medium-bodied, Cabernet Franc–dominated wine with weedy red and black currant and tobacco notes, good depth, and more softness than many wines from this sector of St.-Emilion. Drink it over the next 4–5 years.

1995: The 1995 is meaty and ripe, with a deep ruby color, a sense of elegance, herb-tinged black fruit, good ripeness, and a lush palate feel. Drink before 2005.

Other vintage tasted: 1999 (78–81)

LA DAUPHINE (FRONSAC)

1999	C	85
1998	C	87
1997	C	86
1996	C	86
1995	C	87

1999: Lighter-bodied than the 1998, the 1999 exhibits a moderate ruby color, along with aromas and flavors of caramel, cherries, cola, and earth. Drink it over the next 4–5 years.

1998: A captivating, big, sweet, spicy, cinnamony, earthy currant, and cherry-scented nose is followed by a medium-bodied, plump wine with attractive fruit, good volume, a plush texture, and an up-front, delicious style. Consume it over the next 6–7 years.

1997: Abundant notes of iron, minerals, and jammy cherries emerge from this round, supple-textured, light- to medium-bodied 1997. Drink it over the next 3–4 years.

1996: This wine possesses a dark ruby color and soft, pleasant, straightforward flavors of cherries, ripe plums, dried herbs, and minerals. Smoothly textured and light- to medium-bodied, it is a fruity, cleanly made wine to enjoy over the next 2–3 years.

1995: A fine effort, the 1995 reveals more fat, fruit, and lushness than its 1996 sibling. The color is a healthy dark ruby, and the nose offers aromas of cinnamon, black cherries, currants, and spice. Revealing a lovely combination of fruit and spice, this round, medium-bodied wine possesses excellent concentration, low acidity, and a precocious appeal. Anticipated maturity: now–2003.

Other vintage tasted: 2000 (83–85)

DAUZAC (MARGAUX)

2000	D	(88–90)
1999	D	88
1998	D	87
1997	C	78
1996	C	86
1995	C	86+

Under the excellent administration of André Lurton, Dauzac is clearly on the rebound.

2000: Aromas of roasted fruit, herbs, toast, and blackberries jump from the glass of this sweet, soft, opulent Margaux. Disarming and sexy, this ripe, round, mouth-filling wine reveals no hard edges. Anticipated maturity: now–2016.

1999: This opaque purple-colored wine is one of the finest Dauzacs yet produced. A touch of toasty new oak nicely complements the Asian spice, black currant, blueberry, and smoky/mineral aromas and flavors. With low acidity and a forward personality, this highly extracted as well as surprisingly powerful 1999 cuts a large swath across the palate. Anticipated maturity: 2003–2016.

1998: A saturated dark ruby/purple color is followed by elegant floral and red and black currant aromas. The wine is well structured, medium-bodied, and ripe, with fine length as well as a deep mid-palate. Anticipated maturity: now–2017.

1997: The 1997 possesses a hollow middle and a washed-out, clipped/compressed finish. It lacks fruit concentration and comes across as diluted. Anticipated maturity: now–2007.

1996: This wine offers sweet black currant fruit intertwined with smoke, herbs, and new oak. Medium-bodied, with good extract, moderate depth and tannin, and a ripe finish, it will drink well between now–2015. It is a good middle-weight Margaux.

1995: A broodingly backward, tannic, dark ruby-colored wine, Dauzac's 1995 borders on being too austere, but there is enough sweet black currant fruit, as well as medium body and a fleshy mid-palate to elicit enthusiasm. While this will never be a great claret, it is a well-made, competent Margaux that will age nicely. Anticipated maturity: 2003–2015.

DESTIEUX (ST.-EMILION)

2000	C	(88–90)
1999	C	87
1998	C	87
1997	C	86
1996	C	86+
1995	C	85

These are earthy, powerful, slightly rustic but personality-filled wines capable of lasting 10–12 years. Moreover, they generally represent very good values.

2000: The 2000 offers a dense opaque purple color and a sweet nose of blackberry fruit intermixed with cherry liqueur and cassis. Smoke, earth, and oak are also apparent. In the mouth, the wine is full-bodied and rich, with moderately high, manageable tannin, and the structure is not intimidating. This offering requires 2–3 years of cellaring; it should age well for 16–17 years. A sleeper of the vintage.

1999: The first vintage to be vinified in a new *cuvière* built by Christian Dauriac, the dense purple-colored 1999 possesses sweeter, friendlier tannin, as well as a medium- to full-bodied, thick, juicy, concentrated personality. Anticipated maturity: now–2014.

1998: Dense ruby/purple-colored, with earthy licorice, beef, blackberry, plum, and subtle underbrush aromas, this powerful, moderately tannic, rich, chewy, robust wine will be at its best between 2003–2014.

1997: In an earthy, muscular, aggressive St.-Emilion style, the dark ruby-colored 1997 Destieux exhibits fine depth, rustic tannin, and a robust personality. Displaying power over finesse, it should drink well for 8 years.

1996: The dark ruby/purple 1996 displays sweet blackberry and cherry fruit, medium body, aggressive tannin, and a savory character. It will keep for a decade or more. Anticipated maturity: now–2012.

1995: Well made, with a deep ruby/purple color and sweet, earthy black currant aromas, this medium-bodied, moderately tannic wine reveals good fruit on the attack, spice, leather, and iron in the flavors, and good depth, but some hardness in the finish. Anticipated maturity: now–2010.

LA DOMINIQUE (ST.-EMILION)

2000	D	(90–92)
1999	D	88
1998	D	90
1997	C	87
1996	D	88
1995	D	89

La Dominique, owned by the Fayat family, has been one of my favorite St.-Emilions since the late 1970s. Despite the high quality of its wines (overseen by Michel Rolland), La Dominique remains a very fairly priced St.-Emilion.

2000: This soft, easy-to-drink 2000 is similar to the 1990 but more diffuse. Dense purple-colored, with a candied orange, prune, raisin, blackberry, and cherry-scented bouquet revealing noticeable new oak, this medium- to full-bodied St.-Emilion possesses a certain overripeness as well as excellent purity and a lush finish. If it takes on more delineation and structure, it will merit an outstanding rating. Anticipated maturity: now–2015.

1999: Fat, but without the weight and definition of the 1998, the dark ruby/purple-colored 1999 exhibits blackberry jam, asphalt, licorice, herb, and earth aromas. Juicy and succulent, it is best consumed during its first decade of life.

1998: The 1998 is a soft, fat, voluptuously textured, opulent effort with a dense ruby/purple color, and gorgeous aromas of olives, black cherry jam, blackberries, chocolate, and espresso. This full-bodied wine is hedonistic, flashy, and nearly decadent in its display of luxurious fruit, high glycerin, and spice. Anticipated maturity: now–2015.

1997: This attractive, open-knit, delicious wine offers abundant quantities of sweet, toasty oak as well as jammy black cherries and raspberries in its moderately intense aromatics. Medium body, low acidity, and admirable flesh and fruit result in a delightful St.-Emilion. A savory offering for drinking over the next 4–5 years.

1996: This smoky, lavishly oaked wine reveals an impressive dark ruby/purple color. The nose offers up plenty of toast along with black cherries, raspberries, and dried herbs and smoke. The wine provides sweet fruit on the attack, low acidity, medium body, and a nicely textured finish with fat/glycerin in evidence. Anticipated maturity: now–2012.

1995: While 1995 is also a tannic vintage for La Dominique, there is sweeter fruit than in the 1996, as well as more ripeness and intensity (at least at present) in the wine's moderately intense nose of vanilla, blackberry, and raspberry fruit. In the mouth there is good sweetness, medium to full body, moderate tannin, and a layered, rich, classic tasting profile. Anticipated maturity: 2003–2016.

LA DOYENNE (PREMIÈRES CÔTES DE BORDEAUX)

2000	C	(87–88)
1999	C	87
1998	C	89

Value hunters should check out this wine, a sleeper pick in several vintages. From modest yields of 45 hectoliters per hectare, this blend of 70% Merlot, 20% Cabernet Sauvignon, and 10% Cabernet Franc is bottled unfiltered by La Doyenne's conscientious producer. It can compete with wines costing five times as much!

2000: The 2000 La Doyenne reveals a dark ruby color, abundant quantities of black jammy fruit, good glycerin and fat, medium body, and a low-acid, lush finish. It will require consumption during its first 2–3 years of life to take advantage of its exuberance and fruity style.

1999: The medium-bodied, richly fruity 1999 is well made, though not as dense or weighty as the 1998. Nevertheless, it is a good value to be consumed over the next 2–3 years.

1998: A terrific value for the vintage, the dense ruby/purple 1998 reveals notes of coffee, mocha, black cherries, and smoke. Fleshy, with a fine texture as well as full body, this is a delicious, hedonistic wine to drink over the next 2–4 years.

DUBOIS-GRIMON (CÔTES DE CASTILLON)

2000	C	(90–91)
1999	C	88
1998	C	89+

This is one of the little-known, new-wave, luxury Côtes de Castillons that offers stunningly high quality.

2000: A spectacular effort, this massively concentrated yet beautifully balanced 2000 has both power and freshness. Deep black fruit flavors intermixed with licorice and smoke dominate this seamless, velvety-textured offering. Delicious now, it will be even better in 2–3 years and should age well for a decade.

1999: More oak, lower acidity, and similar lavish quantities of blackberry and cassis fight for the taster's attention in this impressive, opulently textured, big, thick, juicy, succulent, flashy 1999. Anticipated maturity: now–2010.

1998: Wow! A saturated black/ruby/purple color is accompanied by sweet aromas of blackberry liqueur intermixed with cherry, smoke, licorice, and earth. This top-notch effort may ultimately merit a 90-point score given its superb concentration, purity, and palate-saturating flesh and extract. There are no hard edges in this substantial wine, which will benefit from 6–12 months cellaring. Anticipated maturity: now–2012.

DUCRU-BEAUCAILLOU (ST.-JULIEN)

2000	EE	(93–95)
1999	E	91
1998	E	91+
1997	D	87
1996	EE	96
1995	EE	94

I affectionately call Ducru-Beaucaillou the "Lafite-Rothschild of St.-Julien."

2000: Another prodigious Ducru-Beaucaillou, the 2000 may ultimately be as compelling as the 1996 and 1995, two fabulous efforts. It offers a terrific nose of red and black currants, blueberries, minerals, and spice. Sweet, with multiple dimensions, medium to full body, fabulous purity, and a long finish with unobtrusive oak and moderately high tannin, it may not have the density of the 1996, but is more accessible at the same age. A blend of 78% Cabernet Sauvignon, 20% Merlot, and 2% Cabernet Franc, it will be at its finest between 2006–2030.

1999: Superb raspberry/blueberry aromas combine with floral/mineral notes to create a nuanced bouquet in this classic, measured, subtle, graceful effort. Medium-bodied as well as beautifully rich and textured, this is Bordeaux at its finest and most delicate. Anticipated maturity: 2004–2020.

1998: A supremely elegant, dense purple-colored effort, the 1998 reveals aromas of cassis, black raspberries, minerals, and currants. Precise, well delineated, and medium- to full-bodied, with magnificent purity and understated elegance, this noble, restrained wine reveals a tannic finish, suggesting that 4–5 more years of cellaring is warranted. Anticipated maturity: 2005–2025.

1997: A classy, complex bouquet of lead pencil, mineral, earth, cassis, and flowers jumps from the glass of this dark ruby/purple-colored 1997. Evolved and elegant, with noticeable tannin, it exhibits both breed and class as well as moderate weight, excellent depth, purity, and symmetry. Enjoy it now and over the next 10 years—at the minimum.

1996: I tasted the 1996 Ducru-Beaucaillou on four separate occasions from bottle, and was twice able to taste it blind against the fabulous 1995. It is a marginal call, but the 1996 appears slightly longer, with a deeper mid-palate. It also reveals more tannin in the finish. Many readers may see these two remarkable wines as identical twins, but I suspect the 1996 is more muscular, concentrated, and classic. It exhibits a saturated ruby/purple color, as well as a knockout nose of minerals, licorice, cassis, and an unmistakable lead pencil smell that I often associate with top vintages of Lafite-Rothschild. It is sweet and full-bodied, yet unbelievably rich, with no sense of heaviness or flabbiness. The wine possesses high tannin, but it is extremely ripe, and the sweetness of the black currant– and spice-tinged Cabernet Sauvignon fruit is pronounced. This profound, backward Ducru-Beaucaillou is a must-purchase if you can still find it. It will be fascinating for readers who own both the 1995 and 1996 to follow the evolution of these two exceptional vintages. Anticipated maturity: 2008–2035.

1995: Once again, this wine is of first growth quality, not only from an intellectual perspective but in its hedonistic characteristics. More open-knit and accessible than the 1996, Ducru's 1995 exhibits a saturated ruby/purple color, followed by a knockout nose of blueberry and black raspberry/cassis fruit intertwined with minerals, flowers, and subtle toasty new oak. Like its younger sibling, the wine possesses a sweet, rich mid-palate (from extract and ripeness, not sugar), layers of flavor, good delineation and grip, but generally unobtrusive tannin and acidity. A classic, compelling example of Ducru-Beaucaillou that should not be missed. Anticipated maturity: 2003–2025.

Past Glories: 1994 (90), 1986 (92), 1985 (92), 1982 (94), 1978 (90), 1970 (92), 1961 (96), 1959 (90), 1953 (93), 1947 (93)

DUHART-MILON (PAUILLAC)

2000		D	(88–90)
1999		D	88
1998		D	89+
1997		C	87
1996		D	90
1995		D	87

Now under the management of Charles Chevalier (also responsible for a bevy of spectacular Lafite-Rothschilds over recent years), this wine is taking on more weight, richness, and complexity. Duhart-Milon is an estate to watch, as prices remain fairly reasonable in view of the quality.

2000: The 2000 is slightly austere but made in a light, elegant, refreshing style. It may lack fat and exuberance, but there is no doubting its purity as well as transparent expression of Duhart-Milon's *terroir*. A blend of 80.5% Cabernet Sauvignon and 19.5% Merlot, it will benefit from 2–3 years of cellaring and age nicely for 15+ years.

1999: Made from a blend of 90% Cabernet Sauvignon and 10% Merlot, the 1999 possesses sweet berry fruit, supple tannin, an open-knit, fleshy style, and excellent equilibrium/harmony. It will be drinkable young and will last 15 years.

1998: This dense ruby/purple blend of 67% Cabernet Sauvignon and 23% Merlot has filled out nicely during its upbringing in wood. It exhibits a fruitcake, cedar, spice box, plum, black raspberry, and currant-scented bouquet, excellent richness, moderate levels of sweet tannin, fine purity, and a complex style. Anticipated maturity: 2005–2020.

1997: This impressively saturated dark ruby/purple-colored wine offers up copious quantities of sweet black currant fruit, vanilla, and minerals. Suave, with sweet fruit on the attack, medium body, ripe tannin, and a lush finish, it will drink well for a decade.

1996: A strong case can be made that this is the finest Duhart-Milon produced since the 1982. The color is a saturated dark ruby/purple. The bouquet offers aromas of blackberry fruit intermixed with licorice, minerals, and dried herbs. Rich and intense, with considerable finesse and medium to full body, it displays outstanding concentration and purity. Anticipated maturity: 2005–2020.

1995: Made from a blend of 80% Cabernet Sauvignon/20% Merlot, the 1995 is slightly sweeter, more supple, and slender than the broader-shouldered 1996. The wine's bouquet offers aromas of ripe berry fruit intermixed with minerals, toasty oak, and spice. Medium-bodied, with fine extract, it is a finesse-styled Pauillac (in the best sense of the word). Anticipated maturity: now–2014.

Past Glories: 1982 (93)

DOMAINE DE L'EGLISE (POMEROL)

2000	D	(88–90)
1999	D	87
1998	D	87
1997	C	85

2000: Potentially one of the finest wines this estate has produced, the 2000 possesses more texture, sweet fruit, and concentration than previous vintages. Moreover, the oak has been tamed. A firm, muscular, structured effort (as many 2000 Pomerols tend to be), it reveals good depth, intensity, and ageability. Anticipated maturity: 2006–2020.

1999: The deep ruby/purple 1999 exhibits scents of ripe black cherry liqueur, chocolate, smoke, and toasty oak. Low-acid, plump, and corpulent, it is approachable but should age for 15–20 years. Anticipated maturity: now–2015.

1998: Soft, plump, forward, and deep ruby-colored, the 1998 offers abundant quantities of toffee, black cherry, mocha, chocolate, and toasty new oak aromas as well as flavors. Drink this medium-bodied, user-friendly wine over the next 10 years.

1997: Intriguing roasted coffee, berry, chocolate, and toast aromas emerge from this medium dark ruby-colored wine. Round, plump, and succulent, with moderately good concentration, and a short finish, this is a cleanly made, competent Pomerol to drink now.

Past Glories: 1989 (90)

L'EGLISE-CLINET (POMEROL)

2000	EEE	(94–96)
1999	EEE	92

1998	EEE	94+
1997	EEE	91
1996	EEE	93
1995	EEE	96

Under the inspired leadership of Denis Durantou, this wine is frequently one of Bordeaux's superstars, particularly when Pomerol experiences a ripe, excellent vintage—rivaling Pétrus! 2000: While the 2000 is not as exceptional as the property's 1998, Durantou has fashioned a deep ruby/purple-colored Pomerol with pure black raspberry and cherry aromas and flavors, medium to full body, sweet but noticeable tannin, and good acidity. Not as massive as the 1998, but it is impeccably made, well balanced, and impressive. Anticipated maturity: 2010–2035.

1999: I mistakenly underestimated this wine when I tasted it *en primeur*. The deep ruby/purple-colored 1999 has filled out during its *élevage*, although it does appear to possess less structure than the 1998. The wine is fleshy with soft tannin as well as notes of blackberries, black raspberries, chocolate, earth, and leather. The diffuseness evident last year has disappeared, and the wine is delineated as well as focused. This full-bodied, beautifully concentrated, rich, creamy-textured 1999 is outstanding. Anticipated maturity: 2003–2025.

1998: This effort should turn out to be one of the longest-lived Pomerols of the vintage. It is backward, and has closed down since bottling, but make no mistake about it, this is a dazzling, serious *vin de garde*. An opaque purple color is followed by a restrained but promising bouquet of sweet black raspberries intermixed with vanilla, caramel, and minerals. The wine is full-bodied, powerfully tannic, beautifully textured, and crammed with extract (an assortment of black fruits). While it is bursting at the seams, purchasers will need to wait a minimum of 6–7 years. Anticipated maturity: 2008–2035.

1997: One of the vintage's most concentrated, seductive, and ageworthy offerings, this dark ruby/purple-colored 1997 possesses gorgeous symmetry, abundant quantities of seductive black raspberry and cherry fruit, full body, a fat, chewy mid-palate, and roasted blackberries, coffee, and toasty oak in the finish. A superb effort for the vintage, it can be drunk now (because of its low acidity and sweet tannin) or cellared for 15+ years. Bravo!

1996: One of the few profound Pomerols in 1996, l'Eglise-Clinet turned out an uncommonly rich, concentrated wine that is performing well from bottle, even though it is displaying a more tightly knit structure than it did from cask. The dark ruby/purple color is followed by notes of charcoal, jammy cassis, raspberries, and a touch of *sur-maturité*. Spicy oak emerges as the wine sits in the glass. It is fat, concentrated, and medium- to full-bodied, with a layered, multidimensional, highly nuanced personality. This muscular Pomerol will require 2–3 years of bottle age. Anticipated maturity: 2004–2020.

1995: One of the vintage's most awesome wines, l'Eglise-Clinet's 1995 has been fabulous from both cask and bottle. The color is opaque purple. The wine is closed aromatically, but it does offer a concoction of black raspberries, kirsch, smoke, cherries, and truffles. Full-bodied and rich, with high tannin, but profound levels of fruit and richness, this dense, exceptionally well delineated, layered, multidimensional l'Eglise-Clinet only hints at its ultimate potential. This looks to be a legend in the making. I could not get over the extraordinary texture of this wine in the mouth. Intensity and richness without heaviness—a tour de force in winemaking! Anticipated maturity: 2008–2030.

Past Glories: 1994 (90), 1990 (92), 1989 (90?), 1986 (92), 1985 (95), 1975 (92), 1971 (92), 1961 (92), 1959 (96), 1950 (95), 1949 (99), 1947 (100), 1945 (98), 1921 (100)

L'ENCLOS (POMEROL)

2000	C	(84–86)
1997	C	86
1995	C	86

2000: The 2000, like other recent examples of l'Enclos, is light and lacks density and concentration. Notes of caramel, mocha, and cherries are present in this medium-bodied, soft Pomerol. It requires consumption during its first 4–5 years of life.

1997: An easygoing, low-acid, plump claret, the 1997 displays moderately rich, chocolate, and mocha-tinged black cherry fruit, medium body, a supple texture, and a short finish. Ideal for drinking over the next 2–4 years.

1995: The dark ruby/purple color is followed by a satiny-textured, mocha, coffee, and cherry-scented and -flavored wine. Low acidity gives this wine a forward, plump personality. Drink over the next 3–4 years.

Other vintages tasted: 1999 (80–82), 1998 (85–86)

EPICUREA (CÔTES DE BOURG)

2000		B	(87–88)

2000: A special *cuvée* produced from low yields and old vines at Château Martinens in the Côtes de Bourg, this blend of 90% Merlot and 10% Malbec exhibits a dense opaque purple color, a sweet blue- and blackberry-scented bouquet, excellent ripeness, moderate tannin, and medium body. A sleeper of the vintage, it should age nicely for 4–5 years.

D'ESCURAC (MÉDOC)

2000		B	(87–88)

2000: A sleeper of the vintage, this meticulously made cru bourgeois offers a deep ruby/purple color as well as attractive, intense notes of minerals and black currants, medium- to full-bodied flavors, excellent purity and balance, and light to moderate tannin. It should drink well for 6–7 years.

L'EVANGILE (POMEROL)

2000	EEE	(96–99)
1999	EEE	89
1998	EEE	94+
1997	E	89
1996	EE	90?
1995	EE	92+

The Rothschild family, the major shareholders in l'Evangile, intend to push this wine's quality to Pétrus-like levels, which should not be difficult, given the spectacular *terroir* and the impeccable high quality that already exists.

2000: Is the 2000 a clone of the spectacular 1975? A deep ruby/purple-colored effort, it offers a gorgeous perfume of black raspberries, licorice, truffles, and crème de cassis. In the mouth a firm, tannic structure is followed by considerable fat as well as well-displayed blackberry and raspberry liqueur characteristics. There is more new oak than usual, but it is well integrated. Backward, dense, and full-bodied, patience will be required. A classic! Anticipated maturity: 2008–2030.

1999: One hundred percent new oak was employed for this blend of 75% Merlot and 25% Cabernet Franc. Though almost identical to the 1998, the 1999 comes across as sweeter, with lower acidity, riper tannin, and a more seamless, hedonistic personality. A dense ruby/purple color is followed by thick, rich, fleshy flavors. This is a candidate to be one of the most precocious l'Evangiles of the last decade. Anticipated maturity: now–2016.

1998: A blend of 80% Merlot and 20% Cabernet Franc aged in 45% new oak, this terrific l'Evangile is stuffed with concentrated blackberry and raspberry fruit. There is also an acacialike floral character that gives the wine even more complexity. Notes of toffee, licorice, and truffles add to the aromatic fireworks. The wine is full-bodied, with superb purity as well as moderate tannin in the finish. The 1998 should be the finest l'Evangile since the superb 1995 and 1990. Anticipated maturity: 2003–2020+.

1997: A pure truffle and black raspberry–scented nose with oak in the background defines the classic style of l'Evangile. Nearly outstanding, this sexy, ripe, medium-bodied wine offers gorgeous levels of fruit, not a great deal of density, length, or tannin, but plenty of near-term appeal. Many consumers will probably score this offering higher on the pleasure meter than score I gave it—it is very seductive. Anticipated maturity: now–2012.

1996: Much like its neighbor Clinet, the 1996 l'Evangile will undoubtedly be a controversial wine. The wine gives the impression of being overextracted in its dark ruby/purple color and notes of prunes, raisins, Chinese black tea, blackberries, and cherry liqueur. It is rich and powerful, as well as tannic and disjointed, medium- to full-bodied, with excellent richness and a long, overripe finish. It may take 1–2 years to round into shape, but this could turn out to be an outstanding wine. Anticipated maturity: 2003–2016.

1995: Tasted three times, this wine is closed, backward, and marginally less impressive after bottling than it was from cask. It is still an outstanding l'Evangile that may prove to be longer-lived than the sumptuous 1990, but perhaps not as opulently styled. It remains one of the year's top efforts. The dense ruby/purple color is accompanied by aromas of minerals, black raspberries, earth, and spice. The bottled wine seems toned down (too much fining and filtration?), compared with the prebottling samples, which had multiple layers of flesh and flavor. High tannin in the finish and plenty of sweet fruit on the palate suggest that this wine will turn out to be extra-special. Could it have been even better if the filters had been junked in favor of a natural bottling? I think so, yet, that being said, the wine's ferocious tannin level cannot conceal its outstanding ripeness, purity, and depth. However, do not expect this Pomerol to be drinkable for another 3–4 years, which is longer than I initially expected. Anticipated maturity: 2005–2020.

Past Glories: 1994 (92), 1990 (96), 1989 (90), 1985 (95), 1983 (90), 1982 (96), 1975 (96), 1961 (99), 1947 (97)

FAIZEAU VIEILLES VIGNES (MONTAGNE-ST.-EMILION)

1999	**B**	**87**
1998	**B**	**86**

If these sold for a lower price, they would be decent values.

1999: The dark ruby/purple-colored 1999 possesses a sweet aromatic profile of jammy black fruits, vanilla, and underbrush. Medium-weight, with low acidity, this fleshy, attractive wine should be delicious young. Anticipated maturity: now–2012.

1998: A dark ruby color accompanies earthy, black cherry, and chocolate aromas and flavors revealing hints of oak. The wine is medium-bodied and ripe, with some earthiness and burly tannin. Anticipated maturity: now–2010.

Other vintage tasted: 2000 (87–88)

FAUGÈRES (ST.-EMILION)

2000	**D**	**(90–91)**
1999	**D**	**90**
1998	**D**	**90**
1997	**C**	**87**
1996	**C**	**87**
1995	**C**	**87**

Corinne Guisez fashions a standard *cuvée* as well as a superb garage wine from a special parcel called Péby-Faugères (an homage to her late husband). She also produces a topflight Côtes de Castillon called Cap de Faugères. All three wines are reasonably priced. Not surprisingly, Corinne Guisez has hired Michel Rolland as consulting oenologist.

2000: The 2000 Faugères rivals the wine produced in 1998. The color is a dense blue/purple, and the aromatics offer abundant quantities of sweet oak, smoke, black currants, and cherries. There is structure and tannin married with a ripe finish in this classy effort. With outstanding purity and moderate weight in the mouth, this is an intensely flavorful St.-Emilion. Anticipated maturity: 2006–2017.

1999: A strong effort in a challenging vintage, this dense ruby/purple-colored effort offers aromas of black fruits, smoke, licorice, minerals, and acacia flowers. Rich and full, with low acidity, wonderful chewiness, and a soft, approachable, user-friendly style, it can be drunk now or over the next 10 years.

1998: A wine of beautiful purity, symmetry, and grace, this complex, dark purple 1998 reveals abundant quantities of black fruits infused with notions of new oak and graphite, medium to full body, sweet tannin, admirable elegance, and beautiful richness. Anticipated maturity: now–2015.

1997: This fine wine exhibits a dark plum/ruby color, copious quantities of spicy oak, earth, black cherry and berry fruit aromas and flavors, dry tannin, good ripeness, moderate oak, and a medium-bodied, structured finish. It should drink nicely for 7–8 years.

1996: Faugères has turned out a dense ruby/purple-colored 1996, offering aromas of toasty new oak, black fruits, and spice. Rich and medium- to full-bodied, with moderate tannin, it is a sleeper of the vintage. Anticipated maturity: now–2012.

1995: Dark ruby/purple-colored with a smoky, sexy nose of black cherry fruit, licorice, vanilla, and spice, this medium-bodied, elegant yet flavorful, mouth-filling St.-Emilion possesses excellent depth and fine overall balance. The long finish exhibits some tannin, but overall this is an accessible, up-front claret to consume over the next 5–7 years. A sleeper.

FAURIE DE SOUCHARD (ST.-EMILION)

1999	C	86
1998	C	87

1999: Dark ruby/purple-colored, with a spice box, mineral, and black fruit–scented nose, the medium-weight 1999 reveals moderate tannin as well as low acidity. Anticipated maturity: now–2015.

1998: A plum/ruby color is followed by soft, round, attractive aromas of spice box, cherry, smoke, and earth. The medium-bodied wine is elegant and stylish, with a supple finish. Drink it over the next 8 years.

Other vintage tasted: 2000 (87–88)

FERRAND-LARTIGUE (ST.-EMILION)

2000	E	(89–90)
1999	E	89
1998	E	90
1997	D	88
1996	E	90
1995	E	89

Though not a premier grand cru or even a grand cru classé, Ferrand-Lartigue is superior to many wines with those higher pedigrees. Quantities produced are very small, and consumers generally rush to buy the wines *en primeur*. The debut vintage was 1993.

2000: The 2000 is an elegant, streamlined, more tannic version of Ferrand-Lartigue. It shows beautiful notes of sweet red cherries intermixed with black currants, earth, and copious quantities of toasty new oak. Initially, the wine appears somewhat internationally styled, but a classic Bordeaux flavor profile emerges, along with finesse as well as abundant quantities of sweet red and black fruit. Moderately tannic, it is best cellared for 1–2 years (atypical for this estate) and drunk over the following 10 years.

1999: A soft, medium-weight, dark ruby/purple-colored offering, the sexy 1999 offers a sweet, jammy nose of black fruits intermixed with licorice, smoke, and toasty new oak. It possesses a lovely attack as well as a plush, fleshy mid-palate, and a velvety finish. Anticipated maturity: now–2010.

1998: Ferrand-Lartigue's 1998 exhibits a dark ruby/purple color as well as a tight but promising, internationally styled bouquet of new oak, black fruits, and saddle leather. The wine is medium- to full-bodied, with excellent purity, and clean, rich, concentrated flavors. Critics might argue that it is too "international," but it is an outstanding effort. Anticipated maturity: now–2015.

1997: A sleeper of the vintage, the 1997 Ferrand-Lartigue reveals more tannin and grip/structure than many of its St.-Emilion peers, but there is plenty of vanilla-infused, ripe black cherry and currant fruit, medium body, and a long, spicy finish. It should age well for 5–7 years.

1996: The 1996 is one of St.-Emilion's stars. The dense purple-colored 1996 reveals lavish toasty new oak in the nose intermixed with framboise, kirsch, and black currant fruit. In the mouth, it displays a sweet mid-palate, gorgeous purity, moderate tannin, and a round, impressively long finish. It will be atypically long-lived for a wine from this estate. Anticipated maturity: now–2013.

1995: A sexy, open-knit wine, the 1995 Ferrand-Lartigue exhibits a dark ruby/purple color, a jammy, candied fruit and toasty-scented nose, ripe, velvety-textured, complex, generous black cherry and cassis flavors, and low acidity. This medium-bodied, already delicious wine is ideal for drinking now and over the next 8 years. A sleeper of the vintage.

FERRIÈRE (MARGAUX)

1998	**D**	**86**
1997	**D**	**84**
1996	**D**	**86**
1995	**D**	**86+**

The wines of Ferrière have considerably improved, particularly since 1995.

1998: This medium-weight 1998 gained in density during its *élevage*. It possesses moderately intense, sweet black currant and spice box aromas, medium body, excellent ripeness on the attack, and a narrow mid-palate and finish. Anticipated maturity: 2003–2012.

1997: A solidly made, competent effort, the 1997 Ferrière is easy to drink and understand. While it lacks concentration, it offers pleasant red and black fruits, some earthy, spicy notes, and a quick finish. Enjoy it over the next 2–3 years.

1996: This 1996 exhibits a dark ruby color, and a stern, unevolved, backward personality with hard tannin in the finish. Nevertheless, there is fine ripeness, good purity, and a medium-bodied, traditional style. Anticipated maturity: 2004–2014.

1995: The 1995 is probably the best Ferrière I have ever tasted. The wine exhibits an impressively saturated ruby/purple color, and an attractive nose of sweet toasty oak, licorice, and jammy black fruits. In the mouth, the attack begins well, with good ripeness, purity, and fruit, but it narrows out with an uninspiring mid-palate and gobs of tannin in an astringent, tough-textured finish. The tannin should become better integrated with another 2 years of bottle age. This is a well-made Ferrière, with a firm, angular personality, and plenty of aging potential. Anticipated maturity: 2004–2015.

FEYTIT-CLINET (POMEROL)

1998	**D**	**(87–89)**

1998: If memory serves, this is the finest Feytit-Clinet I have tasted. Dark purple-colored, with a deep, intense, extracted feel, the 1998 is a moderately closed yet promising medium-to full-bodied wine with excellent richness and earthy, licorice, and black cherry/cranberry-like fruit flavors. There is plenty of glycerin, moderately high tannin, and a mouth-filling personality to this large-scaled effort from one of Pomerol's perennial underachievers. Anticipated maturity: now–2016.

Other vintage tasted: 2000 (86–88)

DE FIEUZAL (PESSAC-LÉOGNAN)

2000	D	(89–91)
1999	D	87
1998	D	86
1997	C	85
1996	D	88+
1995	D	90

These wines are among some of the more dazzling Graves, with the 2000 being the strongest success in nearly a decade.

2000: The earthy, dense purple-colored 2000 is more narrowly constructed than many of the top Pessac-Léognans, but it exhibits pure, smoky, black currant and cherry fruit, mineral, and new oak aromas. Medium-bodied, with sweet tannin, and a well-defined, structured personality and finish, it will be at its peak between 2003–2015.

1999: This soft-styled, light- to medium-bodied 1999 exhibits aromas of red currants, smoke, earth, and new oak. While it possesses more fat and density than its 1998 sibling, it lacks the concentration expected of a top estate. Anticipated maturity: 2003–2015.

1998: The medium dark ruby 1998 Fieuzal offers aromas of grilled herbs, tobacco smoke, and red currants. This austere, light- to medium-bodied effort lacks the concentration found in top de Fieuzals. Anticipated maturity: now–2015.

1997: The dark ruby/purple-colored 1997 offers jammy black fruit aromas intermixed with lavish quantities of toasty new oak. The wine is low in acidity, without the volume and power of the 1996, but it is a well-made, forward effort. Anticipated maturity: now–2012.

1996: Fieuzal's 1996 exhibits a saturated purple color, in addition to an intense charcoal, smoky, mineral, and black fruit–scented nose. Highly extracted and rich, with a sweet, concentrated mid-palate, and plenty of muscle and tannin in the moderately long finish, this backward yet promising Fieuzal should last for two decades. Anticipated maturity: 2006–2020.

1995: This quintessentially elegant wine reveals a deep ruby/purple color and an attractive smoky, black currant, mineral, and floral-scented nose. There are sweet, ripe, lush flavors, medium body, ripe tannin, and a velvety texture that borders on opulence. There is no heaviness to the wine. Moreover, tannin, acidity, and alcohol are all under good control. This seamless, extremely well made claret is a candidate for early drinking, yet it possesses excellent aging potential. Anticipated maturity: 2003–2020.

FIGEAC (ST.-EMILION)

2000	E	(92–94)
1999	E	90
1998	E	90
1997	D	76
1996	D	82
1995	E	89

I know the proprietors of this estate think I have been unduly tough on their wines, but I am in fact a huge fan of Figeac. Always a wine of finesse, it can sometimes underwhelm tasters because of a sense of dilution, but this is not the case for 1998, 1999, and 2000, an impressive trilogy for the estate. This property appears finally to be living up to the responsibilities of its splendid *terroir*.

2000: The gorgeous 2000 boasts tobacco-tinged black currant fruit intertwined with Asian spices, new oak, and earth, fabulous purity, medium to full body, gorgeous freshness, and a long, concentrated, classy style. A wine of grace, purity, harmony, and complexity, it is a sensational Figeac. Anticipated maturity: now–2020.

1999: Potentially even better than the 1998, Figeac's deep ruby/purple-colored 1999 boasts a gorgeous nose of black fruits intermixed with incense, spice box, and cigar smoke. A beautiful texture, full body, low acidity, and abundant quantities of glycerin and fat add to this complex wine's immense appeal. It will undoubtedly firm up, but will be destined for early consumption, although it has the depth and overall equilibrium to last for two decades. Anticipated maturity: now–2018.

1998: As befitting a wine with considerable Cabernet Sauvignon and Cabernet Franc in the blend, this is a stylish, mid-weight effort with an opulent, complex bouquet of licorice, Asian spices, tobacco, and fruit cake. Obvious black currants, smoke, vanilla, and new saddle leather are prominent in the wine's beautifully knit flavors. This opulent, rich, concentrated, layered, pure, complex 1998 reveals low acidity as well as ripe tannin, suggesting it will be impossible to resist young. Anticipated maturity: now–2016.

1997: This wine, which was light but charming prior to bottling, appears to have lost what little flesh and allure it once possessed. Light ruby-colored, with insignificant body, a cedary, washed-out, vegetal nose, and short finish, it is a thin, disappointing St.-Emilion. Drink it over the next 3–4 years.

1996: Medium ruby-colored, with a mature nose of cedar, tobacco, fruitcake, and cherry fruit, it is a light, medium-bodied wine with evidence of dilution. The finish is abrupt with light tannin. Drink it over the next 4–5 years.

1995: The 50th-anniversary release of the proprietors, the Manoncourt family, the 1995 Figeac is a gorgeously complex, dark ruby-colored wine that is all delicacy and complexity. The multidimensional, alluring, smoky, toasty, Asian spice, menthol, and cherry-scented nose is followed by soft, round, rich, kirschlike flavors intermixed with black currants, herbs, and weedy tobacco. While it is less impressive in the mouth, the nose is outstanding. This is a soft, forward style of Figeac that can be drunk young or cellared. Anticipated maturity: now–2010.

Past Glories: 1990 (94), 1982 (93), 1970 (90), 1964 (94), 1961 (94?), 1959 (91), 1955 (95), 1953 (93), 1949 (94)

LA FLEUR (ST.-EMILION)

1999	D	86
1998	D	89
1997	C	84
1996	C	86
1995	C	87

Readers looking for in-your-face, deliciously fruity, seductive St.-Emilion should check out this value-priced wine.

1999: Similar in style to the 1998, but lighter, this medium-bodied, fruit-driven 1999 will provide disarming/captivating drinking when released. It will not be long-lived, but should evolve easily for 4–5 years.

1998: A sleeper of the vintage, this offering has turned out to be the best La Fleur I have ever tasted. Deep ruby-colored, with an opulent, sexy nose of jammy black cherries and berries, its fresh, lively flavors reveal terrific fruit, a chewy texture, and good balance. This medium-bodied St.-Emilion fruit bomb should drink well for 6–7 years.

1997: Although it is close in style to the 1996, the 1997 possesses more body and structure.

It has a deep ruby color in addition to a rich, jammy nose, low acidity, good volume and weight in the mouth, and an attractive, clean finish. Anticipated maturity: now–2009.

1996: The excellent 1996 La Fleur is a good choice for restaurants and consumers looking for a wine with immediate drinkability. The medium ruby-colored 1996 reveals a gorgeous nose of overripe cherries intermixed with framboise and currants. In the mouth, the wine is medium-bodied, with a velvety texture, fine purity, and gobs of fruit. This satiny-textured claret will continue to drink well for 3–5 years.

1995: This seductive, medium- to full-bodied, round, velvety-textured St.-Emilion is medium deep ruby-colored, with an evolved, lovely nose of jammy black cherries, strawberries, and spice. The supple palate is all finesse, fruit, and succulence. Drink this delicious 1995 La Fleur now and over the next 4–5 years.

LA FLEUR DE BOÜARD (LALANDE-DE-POMEROL)

2000	D	(89–90+)
2000 Le Plus de la Fleur de Boüard	E	(90–93+)
1999	D	90
1998	D	89

This is a new acquisition of Hubert de Boüard, the proprietor of Angélus. That estate's practices of low yields, harvesting very ripe fruit, and minimal clarification/manipulation of the wine have been implemented here. While Hubert de Boüard did not control the viticulture and vinification for the 1998, he did oversee all aspects of the 1999. Beginning with the 2000 vintage, he is fashioning, alongside his traditional *cuvée,* a micro *cuvée* of 4,500 bottles called Le Plus de La Fleur de Boüard that is a candidate for the undisputed superstar of Lalande-de-Pomerol. Both wines merit considerable interest and should be purchased before the world marketplace catches on—and the price soars.

2000: This black/purple-colored wine offers a perfumed nose of black fruits, coffee, smoke, and flowers. Fat, with low acidity as well as a viscous texture with considerable fruit and glycerin, it should drink well for 8–10 years.

2000 Le Plus de La Fleur de Boüard: This wine is extremely concentrated, with huge levels of glycerin, powerful, thick, highly extracted flavors with no hard edges, and roasted coffee, blackberry liqueur, crème de cassis, and vanilla characteristics in its massive, full-bodied, super-endowed style. Think of it this way . . . if La Mondotte were a Lalande-de-Pomerol, it might taste like this. Anticipated maturity: now–2012+.

1999: The first vintage to be totally controlled by Hubert de Boüard, this is an exotic, flamboyant, explosive offering boasting an opaque blue/purple color as well as a gorgeously sweet nose of blueberries, blackberries, licorice, and Asian spices. Dense, full-bodied, and undeniably superb, it is an amazing accomplishment for Lalande-de-Pomerol. Consume it over the following 12–15 years.

1998: A dense black/plum/purple color is followed by a smoky, licorice, blackberry, and cassis-scented bouquet. Rich and long, with medium to full body, sweet tannin, and abundant glycerin, this 1998 can be drunk now and over the next 10 years.

LA FLEUR DU CHÂTEAU BOUQUEYRAN (LISTRAC)

2000	D	(88–90)

From a vineyard owned by Philippe Porcheron, the proprietor of Marojallia, there are 600+ cases of this 50% Cabernet Sauvignon, 40% Merlot, and 10% Petit Verdot blend.

2000: An undeniable sleeper of the vintage, this wine exhibits an opaque blue/purple color in addition to aromas of sweet black raspberry, cherry, and currant fruit, new oak, creosote, and spice box. This impressively layered, concentrated, ripe, medium- to full-bodied 2000 requires 1–2 years of cellaring and should age well for 12–15 years.

LA FLEUR DU CHÂTEAU ROSE ST.-CROIX (LISTRAC)

2000   **D   (88–89)**

This limited-production *cuvée* (600+ cases) is a blend of equal parts Cabernet Sauvignon and Merlot from another vineyard owned by Philippe Porcheron, the proprietor of Marojallia.

2000: A legitimate sleeper of the vintage, this 2000 is firmly structured and earthy. It offers notes of soy, barbecue spices, minerals, and black cherry/currant fruit. Deep and chewy, with impressive length, this serious effort should age well. Anticipated maturity: 2003–2015.

LA FLEUR DE GAY (POMEROL)

2000	**EE**	**(92–94)**
1999	**EE**	**91**
1998	**E**	**90**
1997	**E**	**87**
1996	**EE**	**85**
1995	**EE**	**90+**

This is a 100% Merlot luxury *cuvée* produced from La Croix de Gay's finest vineyard parcel. Some brilliant wines have been produced, and the 2000 seems to be the estate's finest success since 1989 and 1990.

2000: The serious, ageworthy 2000 La Fleur de Gay exhibits high tannin but equally impressive levels of black raspberry fruit as well as subtle notes of oak. There is brilliant balance and delineation in addition to a medium- to full-bodied, elegant, pure style. However, patience is warranted. Anticipated maturity: 2006–2020.

1999: I grossly underestimated this wine when I tasted it *en primeur*. After a few supplementary months of *élevage*, it now looks to be outstanding, perhaps even better than the 1998. The dense ruby/purple-colored 1999 offers a gorgeously sweet bouquet of licorice, coffee, toast, and black raspberry/cherry fruit. Voluptuously textured, rich, beautifully concentrated, pure, powerful, elegant as well as ageworthy, with an expansive mid-palate, it will drink well between 2003–2018.

1998: Along with the 2000, the 1998 may be one of the finest La Fleur de Gays produced since 1990. This elegant, dark ruby/purple wine exhibits aromas of lead pencil, blackberries, black raspberries, licorice, and vanilla. Deep, rich, and full-bodied, with excellent ripeness, beautiful symmetry as well as harmony, and moderate tannin in the finish, it will be at its best until 2016.

1997: An evolved medium ruby color offers cranberry, dried herb, cherry, and subtle spicy oak aromas. Medium-bodied and supple-textured, the wine exhibits a certain sexiness but little depth or density. This pretty, elegant, precocious Pomerol reveals some fat, but is best drunk over the next 3–4 years.

1996: Given this vineyard's *terroir*, the 1996 is a light, disappointing effort. Its nose of new oak, dried herbs, and red fruits is followed by an elegant, compressed wine that is correctly made though uninspiring. There is dry, astringent tannin in the finish. I do not believe this wine will soften and fatten up, so consume it over the next 5–6 years.

1995: The 1995 has shut down following bottling. The color is a healthy dense ruby/purple. The nose displays aromas of minerals, toast, a touch of prunes, and gobs of black cherries and cassis intertwined with vanilla from new oak casks. This medium-bodied wine exhibits fennel-like black currant flavors, high tannin, and impressive purity, depth, and length. Anticipated maturity: 2003–2018.

Past Glories: 1990 (92), 1989 (94+), 1988 (93), 1987 (90)

LA FLEUR DE JAUGUE (ST.-EMILION)

2000	**D**	**(90–91)**
2000 Jaugue Blanc	**C**	**(87–88)**

1999	D	87
1998	D	90
1997	C	87
1996	C	87
1995	C	89

This impeccably run estate deserves more attention. This consistently well made, delicious St.-Emilion, capable of lasting a decade or more, still sells for a song (under $20). What is so impressive about La Fleur de Jaugue is its purity, symmetry, and elegance. The second wine, Jaugue Blanc, is also worthy of attention.

2000: The 2000 exhibits a deep purple color followed by sumptuous aromas of minerals, black cherries, cassis, and subtle new oak. Medium- to full-bodied, pure, and natural-tasting, with a long finish, it will be drinkable upon release and will age nicely for 10–14 years. It is a sleeper of the vintage and the finest wine yet produced at this estate.

2000 Jaugue Blanc: A sexy, open-knit, richly fruity, charming 2000 with considerable appeal, this medium-bodied, pure, honest wine should be drunk during its first 7–8 years of life. It is an excellent value.

1999: This wine, which has put on weight during its *élevage*, looks to be another sleeper of the vintage. The color is a dense garnet/ruby/purple. There is terrific fruit, copious glycerin, medium to full body, low acidity, and an overripe black cherry/berry character. It is a beautifully pure, symmetrical, seamless effort. Anticipated maturity: now–2008.

1998: A sleeper of the vintage, this concentrated, powerful yet elegant 1998's bouquet is reminiscent of an overripe Griottes-Chambertin. Blackberry, earth, mineral, and jammy cherry aromas jump from the glass. Deep, fleshy, and full-bodied, with supple tannin, low acidity, and a sexy, hedonistic style, this succulent St.-Emilion will be drinkable early. Anticipated maturity: now–2012.

1997: A sleeper of the vintage, this excellent wine reveals copious quantities of herb-tinged black cherry fruit, smoke, and earthy aromas. Nicely concentrated, low in acidity, with superb fruit and overall harmony, this is a serious effort from a relatively maligned vintage. Sweet, with neither vegetal characteristics nor sharpness, it can be drunk over the next 3–5 years.

1996: The wine is deep ruby-colored, with plenty of sweet cherry and plum-like fruit intermixed with dried herbs, smoke, and a touch of earth and new oak. Fleshy, with excellent texture, and ripe fruit, it is a very fine, tasty St.-Emilion to enjoy over the next 3–5 years.

1995: Unquestionably a sleeper of the vintage, this delicious, dark plum/purple-colored offering reveals fleshy, jammy red and black fruits (primarily cherries and cassis) in the nose, sweet vanilla, medium to full body, excellent, nearly outstanding ripeness and depth, and a low-acid, sumptuous, opulent personality. This is a delicious, plump, juicy St.-Emilion to consume over the next 7–8 years.

LA FLEUR MONGIRON (BORDEAUX)

2000	B	(87–88)

2000: A sleeper of the vintage, this generic Bordeaux possesses aromas and flavors of strawberry jam intermixed with black currants, wood, and minerals. With surprising concentration and fat, a sweet attack, and a long finish, it will drink well for 2–3 years. Shrewd value hunters should be aware that the 2000 vintage offers abundant wines priced under $20 that offer high quality.

LA FLEUR MORANGE (ST.-EMILION)

2000	C	(88–91+)

A new discovery, this 70% Merlot and 30% Cabernet Franc garage wine, made from a 5-acre parcel of 60-year old vines, has been aged in 100% new oak and subjected to such creative qualitative treatments as extensive crop thinning, *microbullage, pigeage*, and aging on its lees. The result is impressive. Readers should pay close attention to La Fleur Morange.

2000: This sumptuous wine is medium- to full-bodied, layered, concentrated, unevolved, and grapy. There is admirable depth, sweetness, glycerin, and concentration in this opaque purple-colored effort. I would not be surprised to see it burst forth with an extra 6–12 months' *élevage*. Anticipated maturity: 2005–2020.

LA FLEUR-PÉTRUS (POMEROL)

2000	EE	(92–95)
1999	E	89
1998	EE	93
1997	E	89
1996	E	89+
1995	E	90

Christian Moueix is trying to push this estate's quality level to greater heights, as evidenced by recent vintages. He has acquired the finest section of old vines from Château Le Gay, and has instituted a more rigorous selection in both the vineyard and cellars. The winery itself is also being renovated. Some of La Fleur-Pétrus's finest wines are now being produced, and that means prices can only escalate.

2000: This delicate, graceful, dark ruby-colored Pomerol reveals scents of sweet cherries and kirsch. Made in an elegant style, it lacks the depth and exceptional richness found in such great vintages as 1998. Moderate tannin in the finish suggests it will age well for 18–20 years.

1999: An interesting bouquet of caramel, truffles, cherry liqueur, and spice is evolved and seductive. This medium-bodied, deliciously fruity 1999 reveals no hard edges in its low-acid, well-balanced, concentrated finish. Anticipated maturity: now–2014.

1998: Along with the 1995, the 1998 La Fleur-Pétrus is one of the finest I have tasted. Dense ruby/purple-colored, the wine exhibits aromas and flavors of Chinese black tea, raspberries, kirsch, and flowers. Elegant yet crammed with concentrated fruit, it is symmetrical, harmonious, and long, with tremendous persistence on the palate. While not a blockbuster/heavyweight, it is a wine of finesse and richness that admirably balances power with elegance. A great success! Anticipated maturity: 2003–2020.

1997: This 1997 is sexy, opulently textured, and full-flavored, with low acidity as well as delicious, up-front appeal. Lavish cherry fruit intermixes with mocha, dried herbs, spice box, and toasty oak in this medium- to full-bodied, fruit-driven wine. Already evolved, complex, and tasty, it will age well for 10 years.

1996: The 1996 boasts an impressively saturated ruby/purple color, as well as a pure, sweet nose of cherries, plum liqueur, spicy oak, and floral scents. The wine possesses excellent depth, medium body, superb purity, and an overall elegant personality offering a combination of power and finesse. Anticipated maturity: now–2015.

1995: Dazzling since birth, the 1995 has not lost a thing since bottling. A saturated dark purple color suggests a wine of considerable depth and concentration. The nose offers up gorgeous aromas of sweet kirsch intermixed with black raspberry, mineral, and smoky notes. Full-bodied, with superb richness and purity, loads of tannin, and a layered, multidimensional personality, this terrific La Fleur-Pétrus is the finest wine I have tasted at this property in the 20 years I have been visiting Bordeaux. A splendid effort! Anticipated maturity: 2005–2025.

Past Glories: 1989 (91), 1982 (90?), 1975 (90), 1961 (92), 1952 (91), 1950 (95), 1947 (90)

FOMBRAUGE (ST.-EMILION)

2000	D	(90–91)
2000 Magrez-Fombrauge	EEE	(96–100)

1999	D	89
1998	D	86

Fombrauge, the largest vineyard in St.-Emilion, was acquired in 1999 by Bernard Magrez, who also owns, among several other properties, Pape-Clément and La Tour-Carnet. Production has been lowered, and a serious selection process introduced, so that only the finest lots make it into the grand vin. The new ownership's efforts are already noticeable in the 1999 vintage. Beginning with the 2000, the new proprietor has started producing a super garage wine called Magrez-Fombrauge, the vinification of which is overseen by Michel Rolland, the brilliant Libourne oenologist. This micro *cuvée* of 420 cases emerges from the finest parcel of the estate. Produced from 20- to 25-year-old vines, the blend is 70% Merlot and 30% Cabernet Franc. However, the standard *cuvée* in 2000 is also a great success; in fact, it is the finest Fombrauge ever made.

2000: A sleeper and a superstar of the vintage, the deep purple color is followed by sweet, jammy cherry and black currant fruit intertwined with subtle smoke and mineral characteristics. Medium- to full-bodied and fleshy, with refreshing acidity, superb ripeness, and a long finish, this supple effort should drink well for 12–15 years.

2000 Magrez-Fombrauge: A spectacular, unctuously textured blockbuster with a saturated blue/purple color as well as a striking bouquet of black fruits, minerals, and vanilla. In the mouth, the wine exhibits terrific purity, a lively style in spite of the remarkable viscosity and intensity, full body, and perfect balance. Great stuff, it should age exceptionally well because of the vintage's higher-than-normal acidity, at least for such ripe fruit. Anticipated maturity: 2005–2020.

1999: A deep ruby purple color is followed by chocolate, coffee, cherry syrup, and toasty new oak aromas as well as flavors. This wine is ripe, rich, structured, and dense. A sleeper of the vintage. Anticipated maturity: 2003–2015.

1998: Soft, ripe berry fruit presented un a straightforward, medium-bodied style is attractive in a low-keyed, restrained way. Anticipated maturity: now–2007.

FONPLEGADE (ST.-EMILION)

2000	C	(88–90)

This estate has underperformed for many years despite its privileged *terroir*. However, things have greatly improved since Christian Moueix has taken over the viticulture and winemaking, so much so that the 2000 is the finest Fonplegade in nearly two decades. Thankfully, there are 4,000 cases of this wine.

2000: This structured, deep, concentrated wine exhibits high levels of tannin but equally impressive levels of extract and richness. Medium- to full-bodied, with plum, black currant, and cherry fruit intermixed with mineral and earth, this pure, rich St.-Emilion is an admirable achievement. It is a blend of 70% Merlot, 25% Cabernet Franc, and 5% Cabernet Sauvignon. Anticipated maturity: 2005–2018.

FONROQUE (ST.-EMILION)

2000	C	(85–86)
1997	C	78
1996	C	76
1995	C	87

2000: Spicy aromas of new saddle leather, cherry and currant fruit, as well as liquid minerals compete for the taster's attention. This ripe, medium-bodied offering displays more depth than many recent vintages, but earth and tannin dominate the finish. Over time, the battle between the fruit and tannin will undoubtedly favor the latter. Anticipated maturity: 2003–2009.

1997: This dark ruby-colored wine reveals earthy, mineral characteristics, medium body, and an austere personality. It is likely to dry out over the next 3–4 years.

1996: A lean, hard, rustic wine, the 1996 Fonroque reveals animal scents, gritty tannin, and a lack of fruit and intensity.

1995: This dark ruby-colored, spicy, medium- to full-bodied wine exhibits a firm but promising nose of iron, earth, jammy kirsch, and currant fruit, excellent richness, a distinctive earth/truffle component throughout its flavors, and moderate tannin in the solid finish. Muscular but fleshy, this is a fine effort from Fonroque. Anticipated maturity: now–2012.

FONTENIL (FRONSAC)

NV	Le Défi Fontenil	C	(89–91)
2000		C	(90–91)
1999		C	88
1998		C	88
1997		C	86
1996		C	84
1995		C	87

Fontenil, the home estate of Dany and Michel Rolland, is currently the finest estate in Fronsac, producing wines that are consistently excellent values.

Nonvintage Le Défi de Fontenil: This 100% Merlot blend is an exciting, exotic, exuberant, lush, opulently styled wine for drinking over the next 7–8 years. It is loaded with smoke-infused, coffee, berry, and chocolaty fruit, low acidity, glycerin, and fat. A sleeper of the vintage. The appellation authorities should be embarrassed that this wine is not considered legitimate.

2000: The exquisite purity of the black raspberry fruit intermixed with licorice and vanilla is impressive. Moreover, this saturated purple-colored effort is full, rich, and precise. Look for it to drink well for 10–15 years. There are 3,000 cases of this wine. A sleeper.

1999: Sweet blackberry fruit, vanilla, and smoky barbecue spice–like aromas emerge from this dense ruby/purple-colored 1999. Supple-textured, round, and delicious, it is best consumed during its first 7–8 years of life.

1998: A serious *vin de garde*, the dense ruby/purple-colored 1998 offers abundant quantities of blackberries intermixed with licorice and coffee. Structured, dense, and concentrated, it can be drunk now–2014.

1997: Ripe raspberry and cherry fruit are lovingly presented in an easygoing, medium-bodied, supple format. Enjoy this 1997 over the next 5–6 years. It will have many admirers because of its directness and elegance.

1996: Fontenil's 1996 is very good for the vintage, with cigar box, cedar, and berry fruit, medium body, moderate tannin, and good structure. It is more austere than the plump 1995.

1995: The 1995 is a delicious, soft, sweet, plum, black cherry, mineral, licorice, and vanilla-scented example with medium body, good to excellent depth, and well-integrated tannin, acidity, and alcohol. It should drink well for 6–7 years.

LES FORTS DE LATOUR (PAUILLAC)

2000	D	(90–92)
1999	D	88
1998	D	88
1997	D	87
1996	D	90
1995	D	89+

2000: The 2000 Les Forts de Latour, a blend of 65% Cabernet Sauvignon and 35% Merlot, is topflight, and probably as good as the excellent 1996. It boasts a dense ruby/purple color as well as aromas of chocolate, minerals, earth, cedar, and black fruits. The wine possesses refreshing underlying acidity, sweet tannin, and a full-bodied, long finish. It will be delicious young but keep for two decades.

1999: The 1999, a blend of 61% Cabernet Sauvignon and 39% Merlot, represents 35% of the crop. A sexy, soft, low-acid, fleshy wine, it offers aromas and flavors of prunes, blackberries, and smoke. It will be luscious to drink during its first 10–12 years of life.

1998: This wine exhibits a dark ruby/purple color as well as a nose of black fruits, ketchup, earth, and minerals. Moderately tannic and closed, it is reminiscent of its bigger brother. Give it 2–3 years of cellaring and enjoy it over the next two decades.

1997: The 1997 is an elegant, ripe, supple-textured, easy-to-drink effort. It reveals a rich, blackberry, jammy nose nicely intermingled with spice and earth. Soft, with low acidity, medium body and good length, this precocious wine should drink well during the next 6–7 years.

1996: The dense ruby/purple-colored 1996 Les Forts de Latour is exceedingly tannic, with cassis and mushroom-like notes in the aromatics. This full-bodied wine is impressively constituted and one of the finest of the last 20 years from this estate. Anticipated maturity: 2005–2018.

1995: The terrific, dark ruby/purple-colored 1995 Les Forts de Latour possesses a sweet, jammy black fruit–scented nose intertwined with smoky minerals, earth, and spicy oak. The wine is surprisingly thick and rich in the mouth, with its glycerin and concentration of fruit largely concealing the moderate tannin. This excellent, sweet wine is less powerful but more accessible than the 1996. Anticipated maturity: now–2015.

Past Glories: 1990 (90), 1982 (92)

FOUGAS-MALDOROR (CÔTES DE BOURG)

2000	C	**(90–93)**
1999	C	**88**
1998	C	**90**

This terrific Côtes de Bourg, along with the famed Roc des Cambes, represents the benchmark for this appellation's greatest wines. Jean-Yves Béchet, the proprietor, spares no expense and makes no compromise to turn out this sumptuous blend of 50% Merlot, 25% Cabernet Sauvignon, and 25% Cabernet Franc. Thrifty readers should squirrel these wines away by the case.

2000: A spectacular sleeper of the vintage, this exquisite offering possesses a deep blue/purple color, and a striking nose of fudge, cocoa, plums, blackberries, and currants. Ripe, supple-textured, medium- to full-bodied, and mouthcoating, this luscious, hedonistic Côtes de Bourg is a thrill to drink. It should be consumed over the next 7–8 years.

1999: The 1999 may turn out to be as stunning as the 1998. The dense ruby/purple color is followed by aromas and flavors of fudge, coffee, smoke, licorice, and jammy blackberry fruit. Consume this superb, fleshy, opulently textured wine over the next 6–7 years. Wow!

1998: A dense black/purple color is accompanied by smoky, roasted aromas with elements of chocolate, blackberries, and cassis. Explosively rich and superconcentrated, with no hard edges, this is an amazing Côtes de Bourg that must be tasted to be believed. Drink it over the next 8 years.

FOURCAS-DUPRÉ (LISTRAC)

1997	B	**85**
1996	B	**85**
1995	B	**84**

1997: An attractive wine with plenty of black currant fruit, this 1997 provides a ripe entry on the palate, good purity, medium body, and nice length. It should drink well for 2–3 years.

1996: The 1996 reveals spicy, berry fruit intermixed with minerals, herbs, and earth. This attractive, soft claret is ideal for drinking now.

1995: The 1995 is more elegant and less deep than the 1996, but cleanly made and spicy, with berry/cherry fruit. Drink it now.

Other vintages tasted: 2000 (87–88), 1999 (83–85)

FOURCAS-LOUBANEY (LISTRAC)

1997	C	85

1997: Fourcas-Loubaney is consistently one of the finest examples from Listrac. The 1997 is forward, with excellent, smoky, toasty, black currant fruit. On the palate, the wine is round, low in acidity, with easy to understand and appreciate fruit, glycerin, and sweet tannins. This velvety-textured wine will drink well for 3–4 years.

Other vintages tasted: 2000 (86–87), 1999 (83–85), 1998 (85–87)

FRANC-MAILLET (POMEROL)

2000	C	(87–88)
2000 Cuvée Jean-Baptiste	D	(88–89+)
1999 Cuvée Jean-Baptiste	D	(88–90)
1998 Cuvée Jean-Baptiste	D	87

St.-Emilion's "bad boy," Jean-Luc Thunevin, is behind the vinification and upbringing of this small Pomerol estate.

2000: This wine offers up notes of caramel, plums, cherries, and sweet kirsch. Softer than the Cuvée Jean-Baptiste, it should drink well between 2003–2014.

2000 Cuvée Jean-Baptiste: Although very close in style to the regular *cuvée* (exhibiting the same aromas of caramel, plums, cherries, and sweet kirsch), this wine exhibits more color saturation, volume, extract, glycerin, and a longer finish. It is also more structured and muscular. It may turn out to be outstanding with 2–3 years of cellaring. Anticipated maturity: 2005–2016.

1999 Cuvée Jean-Baptiste: A significantly more concentrated, layered, and impressive wine than the 1998, the 1999 Cuvée Jean-Baptiste exhibits a dense ruby/purple color as well as a gorgeous nose of blackberries, blueberries, smoke, espresso, and cherry liqueur. Deep, layered, and voluptuously textured, it is undoubtedly a sleeper of the vintage. If it is bottled without much clarification, look for an outstanding rating. Anticipated maturity: now–2014.

1998 Cuvée Jean-Baptiste: A good effort, this 1998 offers sweet berry, mocha, and fruit intermixed with coffee and caramel. Medium-bodied, ripe, supple, and moderately weighty, its low acidity and plump fruit suggest it should be drunk over the next 5–7 years.

FRANC-MAYNE (ST.-EMILION)

2000	C	(88–90)
1999	C	87
1998	C	88
1997	C	76

2000: An elegant as well as concentrated 2000, this dense ruby/purple-colored wine reveals sweet, jammy red and black fruit, and aromas of underbrush and spicy new wood. Deep, chiseled, and well delineated, with good acidity, sweetness from glycerin, and moderately high tannin, this looks to be one of the best Franc-Maynes ever made. It is a sleeper of the vintage. Anticipated maturity: 2006–2018.

1999: The deep purple 1999 is an impressive effort from Franc Mayne. It possesses sweet tannin a luscious, concentrated, multilayered mid-palate, and abundant quantities of black fruits intermixed with smoke, licorice, and earth. Dense, opulent, and full-bodied, with admirable sweetness, it will be delicious upon release and last 15–16 years.

1998: A very good effort, this medium-bodied 1998 reveals plenty of toasty new oak along with jammy black cherry and cassis fruit, excellent purity, sweet tannin, and fine overall symmetry. It will be at its prime between 2003–2015.

1997: Dark ruby-colored, with an earthy, herbaceous, black cherry–scented bouquet, this lean, medium-bodied 1997 lacks depth and length. Drink it over the next 5–6 years.

DE FRANCE (PESSAC-LÉOGNAN)

2000	C	(84–86)
1996	C	80
1995	C	78

2000: A competent offering from the Graves region, this smoky, earthy 2000 comes across as one-dimensional, but it displays ripe, pure, black and red currants, minerals, and vanilla. Drink this medium-bodied claret over its first decade of life.

1996: De France's 1996 displays an herbal, smoky, weedy, red fruit–scented nose and flavors. There is good spice, medium body, ripeness, and moderate tannin, but overall, this is a linear, lighter-styled effort. Drink it over the next 5–6 years.

1995: This wine is clean, soft, pleasant, elegant and fruity, but one-dimensional.

Other vintages tasted: 1999 (83–84), 1998 (74–76)

DE FRANCS LES CERISIERS (CÔTES DE FRANCS)

2000	B	(88–89)

This wine is the result of a partnership between the Boüard and Hébrard families. The 2000 is the finest example I have tasted since they began producing it over a decade ago.

2000: The 2000 boasts explosive sweet black cherry fruit, smoke, and new oak aromas. Medium-bodied, intense, supple, and stunning, it should drink well for 6–7 years.

LA GAFFELIÈRE (ST.-EMILION)

2000	D	(89–91)
1999	D	87
1998	D	89
1997	C	85
1996	D	87
1995	D	87

Always one of the more elegant, restrained, graceful St.-Emilions, the wines of La Gaffelière have been showing more stuffing in their mid-palate, as well as greater sweetness and concentration over the recent vintages.

2000: La Gaffelière's 2000 exhibits a deep ruby/purple color along with a sweet bouquet of black cherries, currants, minerals, and subtle new oak. Medium-bodied, stylish, and graceful, with considerable finesse as well as moderate tannin in the finish, the balance and overall harmony suggest this wine is a keeper. Anticipated maturity: 2006–2020.

1999: This deep ruby/purple effort reveals new oak, medium body, excellent raspberry and cherry fruit, and a spicy, clean finish. It should turn out to be very good, possibly excellent with 2–5 years of bottle age. Anticipated maturity: 2003–2016.

1998: Elegant and soft, with admirable restraint as well as subtlety, yet surprising richness and seductiveness, the 1998 offers pure notes of strawberries and black cherries gently infused with high-quality toasty oak. Round, medium-bodied, and well balanced, it can be drunk now and over the next 10–12 years.

1997: This wine has turned out to be lighter than I initially thought. Nevertheless, it is a pleasant cranberry and cherry-scented and -flavored effort with considerable finesse, medium body, and undeniable elegance. Drink it over the next 5–7 years.

1996: This is a quintessentially elegant wine, with charm, sweet fruit, and a velvety texture.

Tannin in the finish suggests that it will last longer than expected. The color is a deep ruby, and the nose offers up sweet black cherries intermixed with a peppery, mineral character, subtle new oak, and well-integrated acidity and tannin. The finish is long and pure. Anticipated maturity: now–2012.

1995: This dark ruby-colored wine offers spicy, smoky oak and soft, ripe cherry and red currant flavors presented in a compressed but alluring, medium-bodied, finesse-filled format. Some tannin is present, but the overall impression is one of pretty fruit and a dry, crisp finish. Anticipated maturity: now–2010.

LA GARDE (PESSAC-LÉOGNAN)

1999	C	87
1998	C	87

1999: Deep ruby-colored with a smoky, earthy bouquet, medium body, and a smooth finish, this 1999 can be drunk over the next 5–6 years.

1998: An excellent red currant, smoky, gravelly, red fruit–scented bouquet is accompanied by a medium-bodied, plush, attractively fruity wine. The oak is restrained, and the acidity and tannin are well integrated in this supple effort. Enjoy it over the next 6–7 years.

Other vintage tasted: 2000 (87–88)

GARREAU (CÔTES DE BLAYE)

2000	B	(86–88)
2000 Cuvée Armande	C	(88–89)
1998	B	87

This excellent estate, one of the Côtes de Blaye's qualitative leaders, fashions very fine wines that value-conscious readers should seek out. The blend is generally 75% Cabernet Sauvignon and 25% Merlot.

2000: The 2000 Garreau displays a surprisingly full-bodied personality for a wine from this appellation. New oak and black fruit characteristics are followed by a supple-textured, round, generously endowed wine that should be bottled with neither fining nor filtration. It should drink well for 3–4 years, perhaps longer.

2000 Cuvée Armande: This micro *cuvée* of super-concentrated Cabernet Sauvignon and Merlot is aged in 100% new oak, and is also scheduled to be bottled without clarification. This wine may merit an outstanding score when released. It is a dense, full-bodied, complex 2000 comparable to wines costing 3–5 times as much. Flavors of cassis, minerals, cedar, and smoky new oak are intense as well as persuasive. This sleeper of the vintage will be at its peak between 2003–2008.

1998: This wine was bottled unfined and unfiltered. It offers a dense dark ruby/purple color as well as a gorgeously sweet bouquet of black fruits, earth, and wood. Drink it over the next 4–5 years.

LE GAY (POMEROL)

2000	D	(88–90?)
1999	D	87
1998	D	89
1997	C	86
1996	D	74
1995	D	82

In January 1999 I had the pleasure of tasting the 1945, 1947, 1948, and 1950 Le Gays from magnum. All of them remain superlative wines, the 1950, 1947, and 1945 flirting with perfection. However, recent vintages of this wine have proved disappointing, and this can probably be explained by the sale in 1995 of the tenderloin section of Le Gay vineyard (a parcel of old-vine Merlot) to Lafleur-Pétrus with a view to propelling this latter estate to a higher quality level. However, Le Gay seems to have come around lately, fashioning better wines, with the 1998 being its finest success in the last 10–15 years.

2000: A confusing wine to comprehend, the deep plum/ruby 2000 exhibits aromas suggesting excellent ripeness, but in the mouth, the wine reveals earth and austere tannin. Less tannic than some of the excessively hard vintages of the nineties, this old-style, sinewy, muscular effort possesses notes of saddle leather, truffles, and black cherries. I concur with the Frenchman who described this wine as *"pour le goût anglais."* Anticipated maturity: 2006–2017.

1999: Dark ruby-colored with supple tannin, this medium-weight, forward Le Gay lacks the weight and substance found in the 1998. Nevertheless, it is a solidly made, rustic Pomerol to drink during its first 10–15 years of life.

1998: One of the finest Le Gays of the last decade, this dark plum/purple-colored 1998 exhibits an earthy, truffle, smoke, iron, graphite, black cherry, and plum-scented bouquet. It is less rustic, with sweeter tannin than normal, fleshier, riper, more concentrated fruit, medium to full body, and a long, spicy finish. Anticipated maturity: 2004–2016.

1997: Medium ruby-colored, with an up-front, lush, earthy, spice box, and cherry-scented nose, this attractive, medium-bodied effort reveals moderate intensity, good sweetness on the attack, and light tannin in the easygoing finish. Drink it over the next 3–4 years.

1996: There is no mid-palate in the dark ruby-colored, hollow, tannic 1996, nor does it exhibit much depth, charm, or fat. Anticipated maturity: now–2008.

1995: Lacking the depth, flesh, fruit, and charm that one expects in most Pomerols, this dark ruby-colored wine exhibits an excess of tannin, body, and structure for the amount of fruit it possesses. It will not provide near-term consumption given its severe personality. Anticipated maturity: 2005–2015.

Past Glories: 1989 (90), 1950 (98), 1949 (96), 1947 (100), 1945 (94)

GAZIN (POMEROL)

2000	E	(89–90+?)
1999	E	89
1998	E	90
1997	D	87?
1996	E	89
1995	E	90+

This superbly situated vineyard, adjacent to Pétrus and just down the road from l'Evangile and La Conseillante, has made an impressive rebound and has been producing wines of higher and higher quality for over a decade, good news for consumers, as it has the potential to produce 10,000 cases. The wines are full-bodied and exhibit abundant depth and power, as well as noticeable toasty new oak—sometimes too much new oak, cause for concern in certain vintages like 1997, 1998, and 2000.

2000: Gazin's 2000 is a sterner, harder style than either the 1999 or 1998. Notes of new oak, saddle leather, plums, black cherries, and cassis are noticeable underneath the heavy overlay of wood and structure. This is a muscular, concentrated, powerful wine with fine purity and richness. If everything comes together, it will merit an outstanding score, but it is no sure thing. Anticipated maturity: 2007–2020.

1999: An excellent Gazin, the 1999 has put on weight during its *élevage*. Its opaque black/ruby/purple color is even more saturated than 1998's. The ostentatious new oak (often a prominent characteristic of a young Gazin) is better integrated than usual. Notes of licorice, plums, roasted espresso, and blackberries leap from the glass of this aromatic, full-bodied, powerful, muscular, oversized Pomerol. It reveals generous depth in addition to a textured, long, moderately tannic finish. Anticipated maturity: 2004–2020.

1998: A dense ruby/purple color is followed by aromas of charred wood, coffee, blackberry, and cherry fruit, and new saddle leather. Full-bodied, dense, chewy, and intense, this muscular as well as backward *vin de garde* requires cellaring. Anticipated maturity: 2005–2020.

1997: A dark plum color is accompanied by an exotic nose of roasted espresso beans, sweet cherry jam, and lavish toasty oak. Soft, round, and medium-bodied, with attractive fruit, this wine pushes the oak to its limit, but there is no doubting its luscious fruit and seductive, open-knit style. Drink it over the next 6–7 years.

1996: The 1996 is an atypically tannic, serious Gazin with a dense ruby/purple color, and lavish quantities of toasty new oak in the nose intermixed with licorice, black cherries, and mocha/coffee notes. The wine displays excellent concentration but is backward, with medium to full body and moderately high tannin. Give it 3–4 years of cellaring as it is potentially long-lived, and unquestionably an impressive effort for a 1996 Pomerol. Anticipated maturity: 2005–2018.

1995: This deep ruby/purple-colored wine has shut down following bottling, and while it hints at some of its exotic grilled herb and meat–like character, the reluctant nose reveals primarily new oak, smoke, spice, and background jammy fruit. On the palate, the wine is deep, medium- to full-bodied, refined, and, except for some noticeably hard tannin in the finish, relatively seamless. This expansively flavored wine offers plenty of spice, new oak, fruit, and depth. Anticipated maturity: now–2018.

Past Glories: 1994 (90), 1990 (93), 1961 (93)

GIGAULT CUVÉE VIVA (PREMIÈRES CÔTES DE BLAYE)

2000	C	(88–89)
1999	C	88
1998	C	89

Gigault is one of the most impressive wines I have tasted from the Côtes de Blaye.

2000: The deep ruby/purple-colored 2000 displays uncomplicated but gorgeous levels of black cherry and berry fruit nicely touched by subtle wood. Sweet, rich, and fleshy, with low acidity and well-integrated tannin, it should drink well for 4–5 years. Don't miss it!

1999: This excellent dark ruby/purple-colored 1999 offers notes of wild blueberries, smoke, and minerals, medium to full body, sweet fruit flavors buttressed by low acidity, and ripe tannin. It is a beautiful, fruit-driven effort that should drink well for 5–7 years.

1998: A sleeper of the vintage, this lovely Côtes de Blaye is produced from low yields of 38 hectoliters per hectare. A dense ruby/purple color is followed by gorgeous aromas of chocolate, blackberry and cherry fruit, and smoky oak. Sweet, rich, and concentrated, with excellent harmony and low acidity, this wine can compete with many selling for 2–3 times the price. Enjoy it over the next 4–5 years.

GISCOURS (MARGAUX)

2000	D	(90–92)
1999	D	89
1998	D	87
1997	C	85
1996	C	84
1995	C	85

Giscours had a mixed record in the 1980s, producing wines that were perhaps too supple and commercial in style, but it has rebounded nicely, and the 2000 seems to be its best wine in decades.

2000: It has been a long time since Giscours has produced a wine of such majesty. Readers would have to go back to 1978, 1975, or 1970 to find a Giscours of such complexity, richness, and ageability. An opaque blue/purple is followed by a terrific bouquet of sweet earth intermixed with crème de cassis and smoke. Abundant quantities of ripe, concentrated fruit are well displayed in this medium- to full-bodied, pure, layered, multidimensional wine. Given the fact that Giscours has not been producing wines of such pedigree for so long, this is undoubtedly a sleeper of the vintage, and well worth latching on to, as it is going to be accessible young. Moreover, given this estate's recent history, the price should be low. Anticipated maturity: 2003–2020.

1999: A deep ruby/purple color is followed by sweet, jammy plum, earth, licorice, herb, and blackberry aromas. While fat, fleshy, and concentrated, this 1999 has retained some of its Margaux-like elegance. It will be delicious when released. Anticipated maturity: now–2012.

1998: The 1998 Giscours is a supple, consumer-friendly, commercially styled offering with considerable appeal. Jammy black fruits intermingle with spicy oak in this medium-bodied, straightforward yet plump, cedary, tasty, savory effort. Enjoy it over the next 10–12 years.

1997: Spicy wood and ripe but diluted dried herb and smoky red and black currant aromas and flavors comprise this pleasant, straightforward, supple-textured 1997. Drink it during its first 6–8 years of life.

1996: Giscours's 1996 is atypical for the vintage, being soft, forward, and open-knit, with an absence of tannin. The wine exhibits a dark ruby color and attractive berry fruit, but it is straightforward and easygoing. Drink it during its first decade of life.

1995: An easygoing claret with plenty of crowd appeal, this dark ruby-colored 1995 exhibits roasted herb and meaty, black currant, and cherry fruit scents. Underbrush and herbaceousness are intertwined with ripe fruit on the palate of this medium-bodied, spicy, pleasant, soft wine with some tannin in the finish. Anticipated maturity: now–2010.

Past Glories: 1978 (90), 1975 (92)

GLORIA (ST.-JULIEN)

1998	C	86
1996	C	88
1997	C	86
1996	C	87
1995	C	88

Gloria, which remains very much an insider's wine, has pushed the level of quality higher over the last years. Value-conscious consumers should check out this estate, as prices remain reasonable.

1998: This is an attractively fat, commercially styled, surprisingly soft 1998. It displays herb-tinged berry fruit, notes of saddle leather, and a medium-bodied, round finish. It should drink well for 7–8 years.

1997: This cunningly made wine offers mouth-filling levels of herb-tinged black cherry and cassis fruit. There is plenty of glycerin in this velvety-textured, medium-bodied Gloria. Pure plump, and succulent, it is all a claret should be. Drink within its first decade of life.

1996: Hedonistic, plump, and precocious, the 1996 is low in acidity and rich in cedary black currant fruit. Medium-bodied and lush, it will provide delicious drinking young yet will age for 10–12 years.

1995: As charming and as precocious as the 1996, the 1995 is lower in acidity and may not possess quite its density and power, but readers looking for high-class claret with immediate appeal would be foolish to pass it by. Drink before 2005.

GOMBAUDE-GUILLOT (POMEROL)

2000	C	(75–79?)

2000: The worst characteristics of the 1975 vintage came to mind when I tasted this hard, lean, tannic, attenuated, sinewy 2000. If it does not fill out, it will not even merit the estimated score.

LA GOMERIE (ST.-EMILION)

2000	EE	(92–94)
1999	EE	89
1998	EE	94
1997	EE	89
1996	EE	92
1995	EE	93

This small St.-Emilion operation is run by Gérard and Dominique Bécot, the owners of Beau-Séjour Bécot and Grand Pontet. A Le Pin look-alike from St.-Emilion, this garage wine is a 100% Merlot *cuvée* produced from a 38-year-old, 6.5-acre vineyard, made from extremely ripe fruit and low yields, with malolactic fermentation in barrel. It usually spends 18 months in 100% new oak before being bottled with neither fining nor filtration. Approximately 9,000 bottles are produced in an abundant vintage. Not surprisingly, Michel Rolland is the estate's consulting oenologist.

2000: Potentially as superb as the spectacular 1998, the 2000 possesses more structure, tannin, and delineation than previous vintages, but there is no shortage of explosive concentration. The opaque purple color is followed by aromas of sweet, creamy black raspberries, kirsch, and blackberries. It is full-bodied and dense, with superb concentration, surprisingly vibrant acidity for such a ripe wine, and a long, moderately tannic yet voluptuous finish. It will be accessible upon release, and will evolve well for 15–18 years. This is Merlot at its most exotic, concentrated, hedonistic, and powerful.

1999: This dense ruby/purple-colored Merlot fruit bomb displays the essence of black fruits in its huge aromatics and plush, low-acid, corpulent mid-palate and flavor profile. Superrich and easy to drink it should firm up a bit with age and be a flamboyant wine to enjoy during its first 10–12 years of life. Anticipated maturity: now–2012.

1998: A spectacular effort, this blockbuster, in-your-face St.-Emilion boasts a saturated purple color as well as a gorgeous bouquet of framboise, blackberries, and smoky oak, an unctuous texture, full body, and a seamless finish with low acidity and ripe tannin. This 1998 scores high on both pleasure and cerebral meters. Anticipated maturity: now–2014.

1997: This wine could have deserved an outstanding rating, yet the lavish oak and international style are controversial. Nevertheless, it is a hedonistic, dark ruby/purple-colored, exotic, ostentatious 1997 with superb fruit and concentration. Enjoy it over the next decade.

1996: The spectacular 1996 La Gomerie exhibits a dark ruby color, and explosive aromatics of toast, roasted nuts, kirsch, and assorted black fruits. It is full-bodied, with sweet tannin and a ripe, intensely concentrated finish with high levels of glycerin and extract. This flamboyant wine should be at its finest until 2018.

1995: The debut vintage for La Gomerie, the 1995 is dense ruby/purple, and the nose offers up exotic aromas of Asian spices, soy, coffee, and ripe berry/cherry fruit. This full-bodied, thick, unctuously textured wine is marvelously concentrated, with plenty of sweet, well-integrated tannin. The acidity is low, which only adds to the voluptuous personality of this strikingly rich, head-turning effort. Anticipated maturity: now–2012.

GRACIA (ST.-EMILION)

2000	EE	(92–94)
1999	EE	92
1998	EE	92
1997	EE	89

This is one of the infamous garage wines that has many Médoc aristocrats unsettled as well as jealous of the prices these small gems are fetching. Gracia is produced from a 4.4-acre vineyard with microscopic yields of 22 hectoliters per hectare. It is made with the assistance of

Ausone's famed proprietor, Alain Vauthier. Like many garage wines, it is aged in 100% new oak. The blend is essentially Merlot with some Cabernet Franc and sometimes a dollop of Cabernet Sauvignon.

2000: Even better than the 1998 and 1999, the 2000 (a blend of 79% Merlot, 16% Cabernet Franc, and 5% Cabernet Sauvignon) is a thick, unctuously textured St.-Emilion with a dense purple color and gorgeous aromas of black cherry jam intermixed with graphite, earth, Asian spices, and vanillin. Full-bodied and sweet (because of fruit ripeness), it finishes with an explosive, voluptuous texture. Anticipated maturity: 2004–2016.

1999: Produced from yields of 20 hectoliters per hectare, the superb 1999 has fleshed out during its *élevage*. It reveals a saturated purple color, and a juicy nose of blackberry jam, minerals, smoke, and licorice. Full-bodied, with a more velvety texture than the 1998, this stunning effort should offer a thrill a sip when released. Anticipated maturity: now–2015.

1998: A spectacular effort, the 1998 exhibits an opaque purple color as well as a gorgeous bouquet of overripe black cherries intermixed with blackberries, blueberries, licorice, and smoky oak. Full-bodied, low in acidity, opulent, fleshy, and undeniably disarming, it offers layers of fruit in addition to sweet tannin in the finish. Anticipated maturity: now–2016.

1997: This wine is powerfully extracted, rich, full-bodied, and concentrated, with abundant quantities of smoky oak intertwined with liqueur-like, intense black cherry and berry fruit. Low acidity, supple tannin, and a rich, long finish are authoritative and impressive. Drink it over the next 10 years.

GRAND CORBIN-DESPAGNE (ST.-EMILION)

2000	D	(90–92)
1999	D	89
1998	D	88+
1997	D	85

Grand Corbin-Despagne is an up-and-coming St.-Emilion estate fashioning muscular, powerful wines that require cellaring. 1998 is the breakthrough vintage for this property, which is located on the gravelly plateau of St.-Emilion, not far from Cheval Blanc and La Conseillante. As the following tasting notes indicate, the 1999s and 2000s are topflight.

2000: A serious, muscular 2000 built to keep, this St.-Emilion, which has been producing far better wines over the last few years, has turned out a deep plum/purple-colored wine revealing aromas and flavors of damp earth, black currants, plums, licorice, and minerals. Chewy, pure, full-bodied, and tannic, with decent acidity, patience will be required. Anticipated maturity: 2004–2020. It is a sleeper of the vintage.

1999: A deep ruby/purple color is followed by closed but promising, impressive aromas of jammy black fruits, earth, leather, and roasted herbs. The wine is sweet, medium- to full-bodied, and thick, with surprising tannin and density in the finish. Although not as backward as the 1998, it is made in a *vin de garde*, traditional style. Anticipated maturity: 2004–2016.

1998: With a dense ruby/purple color, this closed yet promising, large-scaled, muscular 1998 offers earthy black currant and cherry aromas intertwined with scents of minerals and smoke. Powerful, dense, thick, and tannic, it is an uncompromising *vin de garde* requiring 4–5 years of cellaring. Anticipated maturity: 2006–2016.

1997: This competent, dark ruby-colored effort reveals soft berry fruit, a touch of herbaceousness, and a medium-bodied finish. Drink it over the next 2 years.

GRAND MAYNE (ST.-EMILION)

2000	D	(91–93+)
1999	D	91
1998	D	94

1997	D	87
1996	D	88
1995	D	90

Grand Mayne is one of St.-Emilion's best-run properties. Aside from a couple of hiccups in the early 1990s, the quality has been consistently excellent, often outstanding. Proprietor Jean-Pierre Nony, who died in June 2001, had done an exemplary job at this estate since 1989. It will be interesting to compare his 2000—a wonderful testimony to his talent—with his spectacular 1998.

2000: The opaque purple, full-bodied wine reveals sweet, mineral-infused, blackberry and cassis aromas and flavors, superb ripeness, a fresh, lively acidity that provides uplift as well as delineation, and a long, chewy, ripe, tannic finish. Although it will not be as approachable young as the 1998 is, the 2000 should mature gracefully. It may have even greater longevity because of the higher acid profile and more elevated tannin level. Anticipated maturity: 2006–2025.

1999: Like Grand Mayne's 1998, the 1999 is putting on weight at an accelerated pace. Exhibiting low acidity as well as a smoky blackberry, coffee, and chocolate-scented bouquet, it is full-bodied, opulent, and rich. Anticipated maturity: now–2016.

1998: The 1998, which has continued to gain weight, richness, and volume after bottling, may be, along with the 2000, the most concentrated and powerful Grand Mayne yet produced. A saturated purple color is accompanied by a phenomenal nose of licorice, smoke, graphite, and cassis aromas (reminiscent of dry vintage port). This huge, massive effort is low in acidity, highly extracted, with an unctuous texture, gobs of glycerin, and a multidimensional, chewy, long finish. A dazzling wine, and undoubtedly a sleeper of the vintage. Anticipated maturity: 2003–2020.

1997: The telltale dark ruby color, pronounced minerality, and pure black raspberry fruit are the hallmarks of most Grand Mayne vintages. The 1997 possesses some tannin, but the overall impression is of an elegant, medium-bodied, slightly lighter than usual wine with sweet fruit and the potential to drink well for 5–7 years.

1996: I had this wine three times from bottle, rating it 88 once and 89 twice. I decided to go with the more conservative rating given the wine's backward style. The 1996 Grand Mayne exhibits a dense purple color and an attractive nose of white flowers, sweet blackberries, cherries, minerals, and toast. It is medium- to full-bodied, with excellent depth, an elegant personality, and a clean, mineral-like finish with moderate tannin. New oak is noticeable in the flavors. Anticipated maturity: 2003–2014.

1995: An unqualified sleeper of the vintage, the opaque purple-colored 1995 Grand Mayne displays a sweet, creamy, black raspberry–scented nose with subtle notes of smoky, toasty oak. Both powerful and elegant, this wine exhibits layers of richness, nicely integrated acidity and tannin, and an impressive full-bodied, long finish. This offering should be drinkable in its youth and keep for over a decade. Anticipated maturity: now–2013.

Past Glories: 1990 (90), 1989 (92)

GRAND ORMEAU (LALANDE-DE-POMEROL)

1998	C	(88–89)
1998 Cuvée de Madelaine	C	89
1997	C	86

Run by J. C. Beton, this property, one of the finest in Lalande-de-Pomerol, is very consistent in good vintages.

1998: A potential sleeper of the vintage, thick, jammy, black raspberry/cherry notions emerge from this saturated dark purple-colored wine. Low acidity, full body, and good concentration further characterize this excellent, possibly outstanding effort. Anticipated maturity: now–2008.

1998 Cuvée de Madelaine: This impressive *cuvée* exhibits a dark ruby/purple color in addition to aromas of blackberries, cassis, earth, truffles, and spicy oak. Lush and voluptuously textured, it reveals low acidity, excellent depth, and a long, fleshy finish. Enjoy it over the next 5–7 years.

1997: Dark ruby-colored, with cherry, smoke, cola, and tan aromas, this lovely, fruity, nicely developed, in-your-face 1997 should be consumed over the next 2–3 years.

Other vintages tasted: 2000 (86–88), 1999 (86–87+)

GRAND PONTET (ST.-EMILION)

2000	E	(90–92)
1998	E	90
1997	D	87
1996	D	89
1995	D	88

This up-and-coming St.-Emilion estate has been quite good over the last few vintages, but the quality has exploded in 2000, offering an extra dimension in both aromas and flavors. Grand Pontet is undervalued in today's wine market, a rarity for Bordeaux. Value-conscious consumers take note.

2000: A blend of 75% Merlot, 15% Cabernet Franc, and 10% Cabernet Sauvignon produced from modest yields of 30 hectoliters per hectare, this opaque purple-colored, fat, ripe, exotic, flamboyant effort is a St.-Emilion fruit bomb made in a modern style. With loads of character, glycerin, fruit, and concentration, it will be adored by consumers. Anticipated maturity: now–2015.

1998: One of the finest Grand Pontets yet tasted, the saturated black/purple-colored 1998 offers a knockout nose of nearly overripe blackberry fruit, kirsch, licorice, smoke, and toasty new oak. Full-bodied, powerful, and rich, with impressive equilibrium, this concentrated, rich, deep wine will be even better after another 1–2-years of bottle age. It will last 15–16 years. Impressive!

1997: Another St.-Emilion at the top of its game, Grand Pontet's delicious 1997 exhibits the vintage's finest characteristics—fleshy, succulent, low-acid, plump spice, and cherry fruit nicely infused with toasty new oak. This lush, hedonistic effort should continue to drink well for 5–7 years.

1996: The 1996 is a flamboyant, dark ruby/purple-colored wine with a soaring bouquet of plum liqueur, toasty new oak, black cherries, smoke, and dried herbs. In the mouth, evidence of *sur-maturité* jamminess and richness emerge from this rich, spicy, impressively endowed wine. There is tannin in the medium- to full-bodied finish. Anticipated maturity: 2003–2014.

1995: Dark ruby/purple with a forward, evolved nose of spice, black cherries, and toast, this supple, round, generous, medium- to full-bodied wine possesses low acidity and some tannin in the finish. There is good delineation to this plump, succulently styled wine that can be drunk now as well as over the next 10 years.

Other vintage tasted: 1999 (82–83)

GRAND-PUY-DUCASSE (PAUILLAC)

2000	D	(85–86)
1999	C	87
1998	C	87
1997	C	78
1996	C	87
1995	C	87

The current prices for Grand-Puy-Ducasse are below those of most other Pauillacs, making it a notable value for the fine quality that this estate now routinely achieves.

2000: A perfumed nose of spice box, cedar, and black fruits is followed by an austere, moderately tannic, lean, light Pauillac. The wine narrows in the mouth, and reveals austerity in the finish. Anticipated maturity: now–2012.

1999: This ruby/purple-colored, low-acid offering displays a sweet, cassis-scented nose, a seductive, fleshy entry on the palate, a succulent texture, and a ripe finish. Already flattering to drink, it will be delicious when released and will last a decade.

1998: Black fruits dominate the moderately intense nose of this saturated ruby/purple 1998. Medium-bodied, savory, and user-friendly, it suffers only from a lack of complexity. Drink it over the next 10 years.

1997: The 1997 Grand-Puy-Ducasse is dark ruby-colored, with a sweet black fruit–scented nose intermixed with weedy scents, vanilla, and earth. The mid-palate is plump and round, but the wine displays an abrupt finish with a certain austerity and angularity. This offering requires more flesh and concentration to merit a higher score. Anticipated maturity: now–2010.

1996: This estate, which tends to turn out forward, soft Pauillacs, has made a firmer, more structured wine in 1996. The color is a healthy dark ruby with purple nuances. The nose offers up aromas of cassis, dusty, earthy notes, tobacco leaf, cedar, and spice. Medium-bodied, with excellent depth and ripeness and the Cabernet Sauvignon component dominating its personality, this is a fine Grand-Puy-Ducasse. Anticipated maturity: now–2015.

1995: Dark ruby with purple nuances, this supple, lush, fruity Pauillac possesses medium body, light-intensity new oak, soft tannin, and low acidity. Made in a clean, medium-bodied, user-friendly, accessible style, this wine will have many fans. Anticipated maturity: now–2010.

GRAND-PUY-LACOSTE (PAUILLAC)

2000	E	(90–93)
1999	E	89+
1998	E	90
1997	D	87
1996	E	93+
1995	E	95

A classic, workmanlike effort that turns out outstanding wines seems to be the motto of Xavier Borie's Grand-Puy-Lacoste. Even in less than thrilling vintages, this estate produces a chewy, robust Pauillac offering sumptuous cassis fruit. Grand-Puy-Lacoste has become one of the most popular wines in Bordeaux, largely because of its unabashed, exuberant, blackberry/cassis fruit character, and full-bodied, hedonistic appeal.

2000: Grand-Puy-Lacoste's trademark characteristic in the top vintages, its crème de cassis fruit character, is abundantly displayed in the 2000, a blend of 78% Cabernet Sauvignon, 20% Merlot, and 2% Cabernet Franc. The wine exhibits a deep purple color, sweet cassis notes, superb ripeness, and full-bodied, concentrated, rich flavors. The 2000 will admirably compete with the finest Grand-Puy-Lacostes to date—the 1982, 1990, 1995 and 1996. Anticipated maturity: 2003–2025.

1999: Aromas of cassis, minerals, spice, and vanilla are found in the 1999. Although similar to the 1998, the 1999 possesses softer tannin as well as a more evolved, sweeter entry and finish. Potentially outstanding, it is reminiscent of the 1985. Anticipated maturity: 2003–2016.

1998: The 1998 reveals a classic crème de cassis–scented nose along with powerful, tight, firmly structured flavors. While moderate tannin is present, there is more than enough extract and depth behind the tannin to support the enthusiastic rating. However, this wine needs 1–2 more years of cellaring and should keep for 16–18 years. No, it's not the 1990 or 1982, but it is a topflight claret.

1997: The telltale blackberry/cassis character is well displayed in this dark ruby/purple wine. There is excellent ripe fruit, soft tannin, low acidity, and a delicious, easygoing personality. Although it will not make old bones, it is a ripe, soft, attractive, evolved Bordeaux for consuming over the next 6–7 years.

1996: This is unquestionably a profound Grand-Puy-Lacoste, but it is excruciatingly backward. It reveals an essence of crème de cassis character that sets it apart from other Pauillacs. The wine is displaying plenty of tannin, huge body, and sweet black currant fruit intermixed with minerals and subtle oak. Massive, extremely structured, and with 25–30 or more years of longevity, this immensely styled wine will require 7–8 years of patience, perhaps longer. A superb, classic Pauillac. Anticipated maturity: 2007–2030.

1995: Another unbelievably rich, multidimensional, broad-shouldered wine, with slightly more elegance and less weight than the powerhouse 1996, this gorgeously proportioned, medium- to full-bodied, fabulously ripe, rich, cassis-scented and -flavored Grand-Puy-Lacoste is another beauty. It is already drinkable and should keep 25 years. This classic Pauillac is a worthy rival to the otherworldly 1996. Anticipated maturity: now–2025.

Past Glories: 1994 (90), 1990 (95), 1986 (91), 1982 (95), 1970 (91), 1959 (92), 1949 (96), 1947 (94)

GRANDES-MURAILLES (ST.-EMILION)

2000	D	(91–93)
1999	D	87
1998	D	90
1997	D	87

The Reiffers family owns three small, very impressive (since the late 1990s) St.-Emilion estates. In addition to Grandes-Murailles, they own the small estate of Côte de Baleau and Clos St. Martin. Since 1998, this trio has been extremely close in quality, but in 2000, I have a marginal preference for Grandes-Murailles. It is the blackest in color of the three Reiffers offerings, with the sweetest fruit and tannin. The wines have greatly improved since Michel Rolland has been brought in as a consultant. Annual production averages 700 cases and the blend is generally 90% Merlot and 10% Cabernet Franc.

2000: The 2000 exhibits an opaque purple color followed by aromas and flavors of blueberry and blackberry ice cream intermixed with iron, coffee, and minerals. Exceptionally pure, expressive, and seductive, this full-bodied wine offers admirable richness, expansiveness, and seamlessness, the latter component particularly admirable given the vintage's high tannin. Grandes-Murailles should be a reasonably priced sleeper. Anticipated maturity: 2004–2020.

1999: A lighter version of the 1998, the deep ruby/purple, fat, richly fruity 1999 displays attractive levels of plum, cherry, and raspberry fruit intermixed with crushed stones and spicy new oak. It should drink well for 10 years.

1998: A sleeper of the vintage, as well as one of the finest Grandes-Murailles I have ever tasted, this deep, saturated ruby/purple-colored 1998 offers up blueberry, plum, raspberry, and black cherry fruit intertwined with toast and minerals. Supple, complex, and medium- to full-bodied, with a boatload of fruit and richness, there are no hard edges in this seamless, classic St.-Emilion. Anticipated maturity: now–2016.

1997: The dark plum-colored 1997 displays considerable density as well as a sweet, open-knit, cherry/blueberry jam, mineral, and spicy, smoky oak-scented bouquet. The wine is medium-bodied, silky-textured, with low acidity and a spicy, richly fruity, nicely layered finish. Moderate tannin suggests it may improve beyond a decade, but I would opt to drink it over the near term.

GRANDS CHAMPS (ST.-EMILION)

2000 Cuvée Christophe	C	(87–88)

2000 Cuvée Christophe: A perfumed nose of raspberries, blueberries, and blackberries highlights this elegant, medium-bodied effort. It possesses good depth, freshness, vibrancy, and a moderately tannic finish. Enjoy it over its first 5–7 years of life.

LES GRANDS MARÉCHAUX (PREMIÈRES CÔTES DE BLAYE)

2000	B	(87–88)
1998	B	86

Another overachieving estate from the Côtes de Blaye, this 50-acre vineyard, planted with 70% Merlot, 15% Cabernet Sauvignon, and 15% Cabernet Franc, produces value-priced wines usually meant to be consumed during their first 2–3 years of life.

2000: The 2000 is a structured, brawny offering, with tannin and muscle as well as ripe berry fruit presented in a full-bodied, powerful format. It should be drunk during its first 4–6 years of life to take advantage of its exuberance and rustic personality.

1998: The soft, charming, berry-scented and -flavored 1998 is uncomplicated but savory and delicious. It is a well-made wine for its class.

LA GRANGÈRE (ST.-EMILION)

2000	D	(88–90)

The debut release from Nadia and Pierre Durand (horse buffs may remember him as France's gold-medal winner in the equestrian championships held in South Korea), the 2000 La Grangère was made with the assistance of oenologist Denis Dubourdieu.

2000: An excellent, classic claret, it offers a smoky, blackberry, licorice, and cherry-scented and -flavored personality, sweet tannin, medium to full body, excellent concentration, and good freshness as well as overall harmony. Give it 1–2 years of cellaring and enjoy it over the following 15–16 years. It is a sleeper of the vintage.

LA GRAVE À POMEROL (POMEROL)

2000	C	(88–90)
1999	C	88
1998	C	90
1997	C	87
1996	C	(86–87)
1995	C	88

This estate, previously called La Grave Trigant de Boisset, has been owned by Christian Moueix since 1971, and there is no question he has been upgrading the quality over recent years. While it is not among the most expensive Pomerols, neither is it among the finest values of the appellation. However, the high quality of recent vintages (the gorgeous 1998 being the finest wine produced to date) makes this estate's wines worthy of attention.

2000: The medium-weight, soft 2000 lacks the substance of the 1998 but, paradoxically, has underlying hard tannin. It offers deep berry and cherry fruit intertwined with hints of spice box, dried herbs, and cedar. This delicate effort is best consumed during its first decade of life.

1999: A lighter-weight version of the 1998, this deep ruby-colored 1999 exhibits elegant, sweet black cherry and mocha fruit, toasty subtle oak in the background, a soft, low-acid attack, and medium-bodied, stylish, seamless flavors. Drink it over the next decade.

1998: Is this a *petit* Pétrus? While it does not have the weight, power, or volume of Pétrus, the 1998 displays character similar to that of its more majestic sibling. The finest La Grave à Pomerol I have ever tasted, it boasts a deep ruby color as well as a gorgeously elegant, sweet, graceful perfume of jammy blackberries and cherries intermixed with toasty oak and mocha.

Refined and sweet, with a savory mid-palate, medium body, ripe fruit, and admirable succulence as well as grace, its tannin is beautifully integrated, and the wine is hedonistic and complex. Drink it over the next 12 years. A sleeper of the vintage!

1997: A sexy, open-knit wine, this 1997 reveals toffee/caramel notes intermixed with herb-infused cherry fruit, vanilla, and toasty oak. Medium-bodied, moderately intense, sweet, harmonious, jammy, and velvety-textured, this delicious offering can be consumed over the next 3–4 years.

1996: A well-made, smoky, coffee- and cherry-scented wine, the 1996 La Grave à Pomerol exhibits good concentration, nicely integrated acidity and tannin, and a round, attractive softness that makes it an ideal candidate for consumption in its youth. Anticipated maturity: now–2007.

1995: One of the strongest efforts from this property over recent years, this lovely, charming 1995 reveals a deep ruby color and plenty of sweet cherry fruit intertwined with high-quality, spicy new oak. Medium-bodied, with excellent concentration and a nicely layered, sexy personality, this is a textbook mid-weight Pomerol for drinking over the next 7–8 years.

LA GRAVIÈRE (ST.-EMILION)

2000	D	(88–89)
1999	D	87
1998	D	88

2000: Although not complex, this impressive sleeper of the vintage contains a high percentage of Merlot. Medium- to full-bodied, with ostentatious levels of fruit and intensity, this opaque purple St.-Emilion exhibits good purity, ripeness, and a chunky, robust finish. Drink it over the next 10–12 years.

1999: A lower-acid, more seductive version of the 1998, with less definition and a more evolved style, the 1999 will drink well for 5–6 years.

1998: The 1998 is an open-knit, sexy, dark ruby wine with plenty of sweet spice, jammy black cherry fruit, cigar box, and vanilla in the aromatics as well as flavors. Displaying excellent texture, supple tannin, and low acidity, it will drink well for a decade.

GRIFFE DE CAP D'OR (ST.-GEORGES-ST.-EMILION)

2000	C	(87–88)
1999	C	87
1998	C	89+?

This special *cuvée* from Château Cap d'Or in St.-Georges-St.-Emilion is made under the auspices of Jean-Luc Thunevin. The wines are pleasant, and prices remain reasonable. Value-conscious consumers take note.

2000: This attractive, supple-textured, dark ruby/purple 2000 offers pure raspberry and cherry fruit, medium body, and low acidity. Enjoy it over the next 3–4 years.

1999: The 1999 displays less intensity, definition, and volume. Made in a soft, silky style, it possesses earthy black cherry fruit with a touch of smoke and espresso. Medium-bodied and well made, it is best drunk during its first 5–6 years of life.

1998: Undeniably a sleeper of the vintage, this dense ruby/purple, big, full-bodied, muscular 1998 may possess too much tannin and rusticity, but there is no denying the tremendous quantities of fruit, glycerin, and palate presence. If the tannin mellows and becomes better integrated, it will merit a 90-point score. If not, think of it as a substantial, corpulent, albeit rustic mouthful of concentrated wine. Drink it over the next 6–7 years.

GRUAUD-LAROSE (ST.-JULIEN)

2000	E	(93–95)
1999	E	89+

1998	E	88
1997	D	87
1996	E	89
1995	E	89

For decades, Gruaud-Larose produced St.-Julien's most massive and backward wine. The estate was purchased in 1997 by Jacques Merlaut, the well-known proprietor of many other châteaux, including Chasse-Spleen. Under the new ownership, there has been a trend toward a more refined, less rustic style, and I expect this winemaking direction to continue. The production is large and the quality consistently high, some vintages, like 1979, 1982, 1985, 1986, 1996, 1999, and 2000, of first growth quality.

2000: The finest effort from this estate since 1990, Gruaud-Larose has turned out a less animalistic, opaque purple classic displaying notes of smoke, ripe black currants, minerals, earth, pepper, and barbecue spices. The wine has a firm tannic underpinning, full body, and a thick, rich style with noticeable creamy new oak. This is a true *vin de garde* that will require considerable patience given its structure and tannin levels. Anticipated maturity: 2010–2035.

1999: One of the stars of the vintage, this impressive effort is totally different from the old, blockbuster, animalistic Gruaud-Laroses of the 1960s, 1970s, and 1980s. An opaque purple color is accompanied by copious quantities of jammy cassis, blackberries, and spicy new oak. Medium- to full-bodied, with soft tannin, low acidity, and a nicely layered texture, it will be at its best between 2003–2020.

1998: Gruaud-Larose has fashioned an elegant, less rustic wine than previous vintages. The color is a healthy dark ruby/purple. The bouquet offers aromas of plums, black raspberries, and cassis. Stylish, with medium to full body, sweet tannin, and excellent purity as well as overall symmetry, it will drink well between 2004–2016.

1997: The 1997 Gruaud-Larose is a soft, fleshy effort loaded with olive- and licorice-tinged black cherry and cassis fruit. Smoky new saddle leather notes also emerges as the wine sits in the glass. Offering excellent richness, medium body, moderate weight, low acidity, and soft tannin, it will provide delicious, surprisingly complex, savory drinking for 7–8 years.

1996: In bottle, Gruaud-Larose appears to have returned to the form it possessed when I first tasted it from cask—a stylish, surprisingly civilized wine without the muscle and power expected from both this *terroir* and vintage. It still possesses excellent density, as well as roasted herb, licorice, and black currant flavors intermixed with incense-like smells. The wine is medium- to full-bodied, pure, rich, and forward, especially for the vintage. Anticipated maturity: 2004–2018.

1995: Revealing more grip and tannin since bottling, the 1995 Gruaud-Larose exhibits a dark ruby color and a nose of sweet black cherries, licorice, earth, and spice. Rich, with medium to full body, high tannin, and subtle oak in the background, it is nearly as structured and tannic as the 1996. The two vintages are more similar than dissimilar. Anticipated maturity: 2005–2020.

Past Glories: 1990 (95), 1986 (94+), 1985 (90), 1983 (90), 1982 (96), 1961 (96), 1953 (93), 1945 (96+), 1928 (97)

JEAN DE GUE CUVÉE PRESTIGE (LALANDE-DE-POMEROL)

2000	C	(88–90)
1999	C	88
1998	C	88

An up-and-coming Lalande-de-Pomerol estate owned by the Aubert family, readers should seek out this wine for its lavish richness and flamboyant personality.

2000: A lusty yet delineated Lalande-de-Pomerol, this flattering, in-your-face effort reveals copious amounts of new oak in addition to sweet, jammy, nearly overripe black cherries, raspberries, and plums. There is sweet glycerin on the attack, wonderful purity, and a plump, fleshy mouth-feel. Drink it over the next 5–6 years.

1999: Sweet, jammy fruit, low acidity, and plump, ostentatious notes of smoky new oak intermixed with blackberry and crème de cassis characterize this full-bodied, ripe, opulent 1999. Drink it over the next 6–7 years.

1998: Deep ruby/purple, with jammy black fruit, cherry liqueur, and smoky oak aromas, this opulently textured, fleshy wine is meant to be consumed during its first 5–6 years of life.

GUIBOT LA FOURVIEILLE (PUISSÉGUIN-ST.-EMILION)

2000	B	(87–88)

2000: A 100% Merlot *cuvée* from this satellite appellation, the 2000 Guibot La Fourvieille exhibits dense notes of cherry liqueur, coffee, and chocolate. Long, ripe, and fruit-driven with good punch and length, it will drink well for 7–8 years. This sleeper of the vintage should be reasonably priced.

HAUT-BAGES-LIBÉRAL (PAUILLAC)

1998	C	86
1997	C	87
1996	C	87+
1995	C	85

This estate belongs to the Merlaut family, who also own, among other properties, the famed St. Gruaud-Larose. Since the mid-1970s, the wines have been well made, characterized by power and richness and by cassis-dominated aromas (no doubt due to the high percentage of Cabernet Sauvignon in the blend). Undervalued in view of their quality, these wines may still be purchased at reasonable prices.

1998: Weedy, with moderately high tannin in the finish, this dark ruby/purple Pauillac offers sweet cassis, dried herbs, and earth aromas. After good ripeness on the attack, the wine becomes more compressed, typical of many 1998 Médocs. Anticipated maturity: 2003–2012.

1997: A delicious wine for the vintage, this 1997 reveals plenty of herb, cedar, and black currant fruit, medium body, fine concentration and stuffing, low acidity, and a soft, attractive, velvety-textured finish. Neither dense nor long-lived, it is an ideal selection for restaurants as well as consumers looking for a wine to drink over the next 4–5 years.

1996: This very good 1996 reveals an element of jammy black currant fruit intermixed with dried roasted herbs, sweet earthy smells, and new oak. It offers excellent definition, moderate tannin, medium to full body, and a long finish. As the wine sits in the glass, elements of the Cabernet Sauvignon's *sur-maturité* become noticeable. It is a sleeper of the vintage, and possibly a realistic value because Haut-Bages Libéral rarely sells for an excessive price. Anticipated maturity: 2004–2017.

1995: The 1995 possesses a bit more depth and intensity than its younger sibling, but it is also lean and austere. The attractive saturated ruby/purple color suggests plenty of intensity, which is evident on the attack, but, again, the mid-palate is deficient in fruit, glycerin, and concentration, and the finish is dry, with a high level of tannin. This wine may soften with more bottle age and become better than my rating suggests. Let's hope so. Anticipated maturity: 2003–2012.

Past Glories: 1986 (90), 1982 (91)

HAUT-BAILLY (PESSAC-LÉOGNAN)

2000	D	(89–91)
1999	D	83
1998	D	87

1997	C	86
1996	D	87
1995	D	90

Never an easy wine to evaluate young, Haut-Bailly, which I have a tendency to underesti-mate, is a wine of undeniable finesse, elegance, and restraint, and often tastes weak and in-substantial when 5–6 months old. However, I was surprised by the strong performance of the 2000. The new American owners are obviously making a stricter selection, and I was told that they are now doing malolactic in barrel, which undoubtedly gives the wine more charm at this early age.

2000: Only 45% of the production made it into this blend of 53% Merlot and 47% Cabernet Sauvignon. The 2000 Haut-Bailly exhibits the finesse, elegance, and restraint for which this cru is known, as well as deeper fruit with more body and density. Gorgeous notes of black raspberries, crushed cherries, and black currants intermixed with balsam wood, vanilla, and earth are hard to ignore. This may be the finest Haut-Bailly produced in the last 20 years. Anticipated maturity: 2006–2025.

1999: The disappointing 1999 is thin and lean, with tough tannin and no depth or concentra-tion.

1998: Haut-Bailly's 1998 is a fruit-driven, soft, black currant and cherry-scented and -flavored wine with undeniable elegance, but not much volume, depth, or length. Anticipated maturity: now–2010.

1997: Light- to medium-bodied, with pleasant spicy tobacco and sweet black cherry/berry fruit, this low-acid, delicate wine can be drunk now and over the next 4–5 years.

1996: Haut-Bailly's 1996 displays less charm than previous vintages, but it does offer mod-erately intense red currant/cherry fruit combined with earth, smoke, and new oak. An ele-gant, medium-bodied wine with dry tannin in the finish, it will never be a heavyweight, but it possesses considerable personality and potential complexity. Anticipated maturity: 2003–2015.

1995: A beauty, this deep ruby-colored wine offers a classic smoky cherry, red and black currant–scented nose, sweet, lush, forward fruit, medium body, true delicacy and elegance (as opposed to thinness and dilution), perfect balance, and a lovely, long, supple, velvety-textured finish. This is a ballerina of a claret, with beautiful aromatics, lovely flavors, and im-peccable equilibrium. Anticipated maturity: now–2018.

Past Glories: 1990 (92), 1961 (93), 1928 (90)

HAUT-BATAILLEY (PAUILLAC)

2000	C	(89–91)
1999	C	86
1998	C	86
1997	C	86
1996	C	89
1995	C	89

Readers need to take a serious look at this estate, which has always produced good but rarely inspiring wines. Proprietor Xavier Borie is attempting to upgrade the quality of Haut-Batailley, which often has more in common with a mid-weight St.-Julien than a Pauillac.

2000: The 2000 displays considerable charm, finesse, and sweetness in its soft, fleshy, medium-bodied personality. There are copious quantities of black fruits with dried herbs in the background, a touch of toasty oak, and moderate, sweet tannin. Anticipated maturity: now–2015.

1999: Made in a light, straightforward, medium-bodied style, with no hard edges but not a great deal of concentration, length, or volume, this 1999 should be consumed during its first decade of life.

1998: A touch of austerity recalls some of the less desirable characteristics of this vintage in the Médoc. The 1998 exhibits firmness along with good, sweet, berry fruit intermixed with mineral, cassis, and spice notes. Medium-bodied and elegant, this effort is best drunk earlier rather than later. Anticipated maturity: now–2014.

1997: Made in a lighter, finesse style, this fluid, charming, ripe, medium-bodied 1997 exhibits smoky black currant fruit, pleasing ripeness, and attractive levels of fruit. It should be drunk over the next 5–6 years for its undeniably easygoing personality.

1996: The wine exhibits a dense purple color, as well as a wonderfully sweet, classic Pauillac nose of black currants and cigar box notes. Powerful for Haut-Batailley (normally a light, elegant, supple Pauillac), the 1996 possesses intense fruit, medium to full body, ripe tannin, and a surprisingly long, layered finish. This appears to be a classic. Anticipated maturity: 2003–2015.

1995: Silky, sexy, supple, and altogether a gorgeous effort from Haut-Batailley, the 1995 is a medium-bodied, seamless, beautifully pure Pauillac with gobs of black currant fruit intermixed with smoke, vanilla, and lead pencil. Already approachable, it promises to become even better over the next 4–5 years. A very hedonistic wine.

HAUT-BERGEY (PESSAC-LÉOGNAN)

2000	E	**(92–94)**
1999	D	89
1998	D	87

Haut-Bergey's new owner, the Cathiard-Garcin family, had the foresight to bring in both Michel Rolland and Jean-Luc Thunevin to provide consultation. Given the undeniable talent of this brain trust, there is no doubt this property has, in one vintage (2000), emerged as a star of Pessac-Léognan.

2000: This is a profound sleeper of the vintage. One of the most complex wines of the vintage, at least aromatically, it boasts a soaring bouquet of smoke, scorched earth, coffee, black fruits, and tobacco. The palate is also compelling. It is a wine of considerable finesse rather than power, with its hallmark gorgeous layers of fruit that cascade over the taste buds without any sense of weight. This ripe, long, silky-textured, complex 2000 is a textbook Graves, satisfying both the hedonist and the intellectual in us. Not to be missed! Anticipated maturity: now–2015.

1999: The 1999 has turned out slightly better than the 1998. It offers a complex, smoky, mineral, spice box, tobacco, and black cherry–scented bouquet, medium to full body, and a soft, plush, appealing personality. Anticipated maturity: now–2010.

1998: Elegant, spicy, tobacco, cranberry, and red cherry characteristics emerge from this finesse-styled, sweet, flavorful, medium-bodied wine. Already delicious as well as complex, it is best consumed over the next decade.

HAUT-BRION (PESSAC-LÉOGNAN)

2000	EEE	**(96–98)**
1999	EEE	93
1998	EEE	96+
1997	EEE	89
1996	EEE	92+
1995	EEE	96

All things considered—viticultural management, winemaking, *élevage*, and overall attention to detail—there is probably no more experienced and talented Bordeaux wine deity than Jean-Bernard Delmas of Haut-Brion. Think about it . . . his résumé begins with the 1961 Haut-Brion! As an American who has witnessed some of the brilliant efforts by other Bordelais wine-makers who have given their expertise to projects in California, I lament the fact that Jean Delmas has not had the opportunity to provide consultation for the production of California Cabernet Sauvignon.

Haut-Brion is situated essentially within the city of Bordeaux, although it is officially in a suburb. This gives it one of the area's warmest and most precocious *terroirs*, a fact that has favored it in numerous vintages. The estate is undoubtedly making wine that merits its first growth status. In fact, the vintages from 1978 onward have always proved to be among the finest wines produced in Bordeaux, as well as personal favorites.

2000: The 2000 Haut-Brion possesses tremendous richness, and a highly nuanced, complex personality with abundant quantities of black fruits, minerals, vanilla, and subtle earth. While less exuberant and powerful when compared to its neighbor and sibling, La Mission, it is more delicate yet thick, juicy, succulent, and clearly cut from the same mold as the famed 1989 and 1990. However, the 2000 seems to possess more of an obvious overlay of tannin as well as a degree of precision and freshness, largely attributed to slightly higher acidity. A superlative effort, it will be fascinating to compare it with the bevy of exceptional efforts produced at this estate over the last decade (1998, 1996, 1995, 1990, and 1989). Anticipated maturity: 2007–2035.

1999: A modern-day version of the 1979 or 1962, but with sweeter fruit as well as better selection and winemaking, this dark ruby/purple, elegant effort reveals the scorched earth, black fruit, and mineral characteristics that so distinctively speak of Haut-Brion's famed *terroir*. The wine is beautifully balanced, with abundant quantities of sweet fruit, low acidity, and a more forward, less muscular stature than its older sibling, the 1998. It should be drinkable at a relatively early age. Anticipated maturity: 2006–2020.

1998: A prodigious Haut-Brion. It exhibits a dense ruby/purple color in addition to a tight but incredibly promising nose of smoke, earth, minerals, lead pencil, black currants, cherries, and spice. This full-bodied wine unfolds slowly but convincingly on the palate, revealing a rich, multitiered, stunningly pure, symmetrical style with wonderful sweetness, ripe tannin, and a finish that lasts nearly 45 seconds. It tastes like liquid nobility. There is really no other way of describing it. It is unquestionably the finest Haut-Brion since the fabulous 1989 and 1990. However, patience is warranted as it is not as flashy and forward as those two vintages. Anticipated maturity: 2008–2035.

1997: This light- to middle-weight Haut-Brion exhibits an evolved, sweet red and black currant nose with notions of scorched earth, minerals, and tobacco. Although not big, it exhibits fine ripeness, harmony, and elegance, velvety tannin, and sweet fruit presented in a charming, open-knit, evolved format. The wine is comparable to the fine Haut-Brions produced in such difficult rain-plagued vintages as 1993 and 1994. Anticipated maturity: 2001–2014.

1996: The backward 1996 Haut-Brion was closed when I tasted it after bottling. Out of barrel, this wine exhibited far more forthcoming aromatics as well as a sweeter mid-palate. I had expected it to be more forward, and thus slightly downgraded the wine, although I am thrilled to own it and follow what appears to be a slow evolution. It will be a potentially long-lived wine, but I suspect it is slightly less successful than the extraordinary 1995. The 1996 exhibits a deep ruby/purple color and a surprisingly tight bouquet. With aeration, notes of fresh tobacco, dried herbs, smoke, asphalt, and black fruits emerge—but reluctantly. It is tannic and medium-bodied, with outstanding purity and a layered, multidimensional style. However, the finish contains abundant tannin, suggesting that this wine needs 5–6 years of cellaring. Anticipated maturity: 2008–2030.

1995: This wine has been brilliant on every occasion I have tasted it. More accessible and forward than the 1996, it possesses a saturated ruby/purple color, as well as a beautiful, knockout set of aromatics, consisting of black fruits, vanilla, spice, and wood-fire smoke. Multidimensional and rich, with layers of ripe fruit, and beautifully integrated tannin and acidity, this medium- to full-bodied wine is a graceful, seamless, exceptional Haut-Brion that should drink surprisingly well young. Anticipated maturity: now–2030.

Past Glories: 1994 (93), 1993 (92), 1992 (90), 1990 (96), 1989 (100), 1988 (91), 1986 (96), 1985 (94), 1982 (94), 1979 (93), 1978 (90?), 1975 (93+), 1964 (90), 1961 (100), 1959 (100), 1957 (90), 1955 (97), 1953 (95), 1949 (91), 1945 (100), 1928 (97), 1926 (97)

HAUT-BRISSON (ST.-EMILION)

2000		C	89

2000: Another sleeper of the vintage, this excellent St.-Emilion estate has fashioned a beautifully pure, medium- to full-bodied, opaque purple wine offering a moderately intense bouquet of melted licorice, graphite, blackberries, and cassis with a hint of new oak in the background. Deep, chewy, full-bodied, and elegant, with vibrant acidity as well as moderate tannin in the long finish, it will be at its finest between 2003–2015.

HAUT-CARLES (FRONSAC)

NV	La Preuve par Carles	C	(90–92)
2000		C	(90–92)
1999		C	88
1998		C	88
1997		C	87

Another consistently high-quality Fronsac producer, Haut-Carles is one of the three best wines from this bucolic appellation and is well worth buying given its quality/price rapport. This top-notch Fronsac estate utilized plastic sheets to cover part of its vineyard in 2000. Consequently, under French law, that part of the production had to be declassified as a *vin de table.* However, the two 2000 *cuvées* are essentially similar and both superb.

Nonvintage La Preuve par Carles: This wine is as long, concentrated, and intense as the standard 2000 *cuvée,* but it may ultimately have more fat, less definition, and less aging potential. It exhibits a saturated purple color followed by sweet notes of black fruits, minerals, truffles, licorice, and graphite. It will be drinkable upon release and will last 15 years.

2000: The 2000 Haut-Carles is essentially identical to the nonvintage *vin de table,* with its saturated purple robe, as well as sweet aromas of black fruits, minerals, truffles, licorice, and graphite. Long, concentrated, and intense, it can be drunk now and within the next 15–18 years.

1999: This dark purple 1999 offers an elegant, sweet, black fruit, liquid stone, and mineral-scented bouquet. There is superb ripe fruit on the attack, and the medium-weight, elegant finish reveals low acidity. With beautiful harmony as well as purity and a sweet mid-palate, it will drink well until 2014.

1998: An excellent dark purple color accompanies aromas of minerals, blackberries and blueberries, licorice, and spice box. Medium-bodied, beautifully pure, well delineated, and moderately tannic, it will be at its apogee between now–2012+.

1997: A dense dark ruby/purple color is followed by sumptuous aromas of blackberries, raspberries, and minerals. This gorgeously ripe, fat, supple-textured, medium-bodied Fronsac is seductive and alluring. Drink it over the next 5–7 years. Bravo!

HAUT-CHAIGNEAU (LALANDE-DE-POMEROL)

2000		C	(88–89)
1999		C	(85–87)
1998		C	86

Oenologist Pascal Chatonnet, the man responsible for discovering the causes behind the choranisol contamination that plagued a bevy of Bordeaux properties in the early 1990s, produces fine Lalande-de-Pomerols at Haut-Chaigneau.

2000: A sleeper of the vintage, the deep, concentrated, pure, elegant 2000 Haut-Chaigneau possesses abundant amounts of black fruits intermixed with notes of caramel. Succulent, pure, and fleshy, it is best drunk over the next 6–7 years.

1999: The 1999's excellent dark ruby/purple color is accompanied by scents of sweet, jammy blackberries, spicy oak, licorice, and earth. This low-acid, plush wine is best drunk during its first 5 years of life.

1998: A dark plum color is followed by scents of cherries, spice box, and new oak. This medium-bodied, attractively supple 1998 should be consumed during its first 4–5 years of life.

HAUT-CONDISSAS PRESTIGE (HAUT-MÉDOC)

2000	**C**	**(88–90)**
1999	**C**	**(87–88)**
1998	**C**	**88**

Haut-Condissas is the luxury *cuvée* from Rollan de By, a well-run Médoc estate owned by Jean and Catherine Guyon.

2000: This serious, ripe wine possesses considerable depth, power, and concentration. A saturated purple color is followed by aromas of toast, black currants, cherries, smoke, and earth. Full-bodied, moderately tannic, and impressive, it will be at its peak until 2014.

1999: A deep dark ruby/purple color is accompanied by a low-acid, fat, ripe wine with concentrated blackberry and cassis fruit, excellent texture, and a sweet, flattering, luscious finish. Anticipated maturity: now–2010.

1998: An excellent, dense ruby/purple wine, the 1998 offers up a sweet nose of lead pencil, minerals, black currants, cedar, and licorice. Medium- to full-bodied, with sweet tannin, rich, concentrated fruit, and exceptional elegance as well as balance, this classy, graceful claret should age handsomely. Anticipated maturity: 2003–2014.

HAUT-GRAVET (ST.-EMILION)

2000	**D**	**(90–92)**
1998	**D**	**88**

The owners of Haut-Gravet also produce La Couspaude and Jean de Gué, of St.-Emilion and Lalande-de-Pomerol respectively.

2000: The 2000 seems to be the finest wine this estate has yet produced. The saturated purple-colored 2000 Haut-Gravet offers a sweet nose of blackberry, cherry, and cassis fruit intermixed with smoke and toast. Full-bodied, opulent, rich, and concentrated, with superb purity as well as melted tannin, it will be at its best between 2006–2020. A sleeper of the vintage.

1998: This appears to be a potential sleeper of the vintage. It is an abundantly fruity, glycerin-imbued, medium-bodied wine with surprising elegance for its fruit-driven personality. There is plenty of black raspberry and jammy cherry fruit intermixed with subtle new oak. The wine possesses low acidity, well-integrated moderate tannin, a seamless personality, and a surprisingly fine, concentrated finish. This effort performed well in my tastings. Anticipated maturity: now–2010.

Other vintage tasted: 1999 (86–87+?)

HAUT-MAILLET (POMEROL)

1997	**C**	**77**
1996	**C**	**80**

1997: The 1997 exhibits more tannin than the 1996, in addition to an austere, tight personality. I don't believe the fruit comes forward while the tannin melts away, so look for this offering to be attenuated and compressed. Anticipated maturity: now–2007.

1996: This light- to medium-bodied, pleasant, straightforward, simple Pomerol displays an evolved plum/garnet color, moderate levels of cranberry and cherry fruit, a sweet attack, and a soft, straightforward personality. Drink it over the next 1–2 years.

HAUT-MARBUZET (ST.-ESTÈPHE)

1997	C	85
1996	C	88
1995	C	87

1997: While good, the aggressively woody Haut-Marbuzet reveals a hollow midsection, but it offers soft, ripe, earthy coffee and black cherry fruit in a pleasant, medium-bodied format. A bit more concentration, extract, and length would have been preferable. Drink it now.

1996: Telltale lavish, toasty new oak aromas jump from the glass of the dark ruby/purple 1996. Well made, attractive, and boldly wooded, the wine's rich fruit easily compensates for all the oak. The 1996 does not possess the depth found in the 1990, 1989, and 1982, but they are excellent wines. This medium-bodied, spicy, lush, open-knit wine will keep for 10 years.

1995: The 1995 reveals gobs of kirsch and coffee in its nose, along with smoky, toasty, oaky notes. Medium-bodied, with smoky black currant fruit, low acidity, good lushness, and a layered palate, this is a hedonistic, accessible 1995 to drink over the next 6–7 years.

Other vintages tasted: 1999 (83–85), 1998 (85–87)

Past Glories: 1990 (93), 1986 (90), 1982 (94), 1975 (90), 1970 (90), 1961 (90)

HAUT-VILLET (ST.-EMILION)

2000	C	(87–88?)
2000 Cuvée Pomone	D	(87–89+?)
1999	C	89
1999 Cuvée Pomone	D	89
1998	C	87
1998 Cuvée Pomone	D	89+?

I often have difficulty assessing these wines, largely because I have never tasted a mature Haut-Villet, so I do not know if they are capable of absorbing all their tannin and wood. They are muscular, concentrated, full-bodied, aggressive St.-Emilions. The Cuvée Pomone is Haut-Villet's luxury garage *cuvée*. It is extremely muscular, with heavy, almost excessive new oak, and a tannic, powerful style that suggests that two decades of cellaring are possible. It is a far bigger wine than the regular *cuvée*, but will it age as gracefully? Although I have some reservations, there is no question it is worth a gamble given its impressive extract level.

2000: The impressively saturated color of the 2000 Haut-Villet is followed by a dense, muscular wine that is somewhat intimidating from a tannin and structural perspective. If everything comes together, this wine will merit a score in the upper 80s.

2000 Cuvée Pomone: The 2000 Haut-Villet Cuvée Pomone possesses better ripeness, volume, and richness than the standard *cuvée*, but also more new oak and tannin. It could turn out to be special, but it will have to become more seamless and less disjointed. Anticipated maturity: 2006–2020.

1999: A smaller-sized version of the luxury *cuvée*, this opaque ruby/purple offering reveals abundant ripe fruit, low acidity, a sweeter, more expansive, friendlier style than the 1998, with lower acidity but less aging potential. An excellent wine, it is potentially as good, if not as big, as the luxury *cuvée*, Pomone. Anticipated maturity: 2003–2014.

1999 Cuvée Pomone: Slightly friendlier than the 1998 standard *cuvée*, this sweet, black/purple effort reveals plenty of jammy cherry notes intermixed with lavish quantities of new oak, low acidity, plump, glycerin-imbued, highly extracted flavors, and a velvety-textured finish. Anticipated maturity: 2004–2016.

1998: A serious, deep ruby/purple effort, the regular *cuvée* reveals tannin levels similar to the more oaky, luxury *cuvée*, as well as excellent concentration, a firm *vin de garde* style, and a spicy, long finish. Anticipated maturity: 2005–2016.

1998 Cuvée Pomone: A saturated ruby/purple color is followed by flamboyant aromas of toasty, smoky new oak as well as jammy blackberries and cherries. The wine is thick, powerful, tannic, full-bodied, and in need of 5–7 years of cellaring. If the tannin becomes fully integrated, this offering will merit an outstanding score. Anticipated maturity: 2007–2020.

LES HAUTS-CONSEILLANTS (LALANDE-DE-POMEROL)

1998	B	82

1998: Jammy black fruits reveal little complexity, but they hit the palate with good lushness, sweet glycerin, medium body, and a pure, nicely concentrated finish. Drink it over the next 5–6 years.

Other vintages tasted: 2000 (87–88), 1997 (84)

L'HERMITAGE (ST.-EMILION)

2000	E	(90–91)
1999	E	88
1998	E	89+
1997	E	88

This 10-acre vineyard planted with 65% Merlot and 35% Cabernet Franc is another micro estate producing several hundred cases from a blend of 70% Merlot and 30% Cabernet Franc. Production averages 800 cases annually.

2000: The 2000 is an impressive effort from l'Hermitage. A savory, sweet, fruit-driven wine (800 cases produced), with copious ripeness, glycerin, and flavor, this hedonistic St.-Emilion exhibits black fruit, earth, and new oak flavors in its full-bodied character. Drink it over the next 10–12 years.

1999: The deep ruby/purple 1999 reveals a jammy bouquet, low acidity, opulently textured, chewy flavors, little complexity, but plenty of fruit and glycerin. If more delineation and refinement emerge, this wine will merit a higher score. Anticipated maturity: 2003–2012.

1998: Dense ruby/purple, with blackberry, licorice, cherry, and toasty new-oak aromas as well as flavors, this deep, medium- to full-bodied St.-Emilion is chewy, dense, concentrated, and well made. The pure, concentrated, moderately tannic finish suggests that 1–2 years of cellaring is warranted. Anticipated maturity: 2003–2016.

1997: Deep saturated ruby, with copious quantities of sweet, jammy cherry and black currant fruit complemented by high-quality, toasty oak, this medium-bodied 1997 displays excellent richness, a soft, velvety texture, light tannin, and low acidity. Drink it over the next 4–5 years.

HORTEVIE (ST.-JULIEN)

1996	D	88
1995	D	87

Proprietor Henri Pradère makes fine wine from this estate, which consists essentially of old-vine parcels that are vinified and aged separately from Pradère's other St.-Julien estate, Terrey-Gros-Cailloux. Hortevie is consistently an attractive, plump, juicy, succulent effort, made in an very approachable style.

1996: Performing well, the deep opaque purple-colored 1996 offers sweet, ripe, jammy cassis and cherry fruit, and fleshy, full-bodied flavors with moderate tannin in the finish. The tannin is sweet, ripe, and mature, so this wine will not require an inordinate amount of patience. It is a potential sleeper of the vintage. Anticipated maturity: now–2012.

1995: This dense purple wine displays a delicious personality, from its no-holds-barred, un-complicated but intense, creamy, black currant, cedar, and smoky-scented nose to its deep, chewy, spicy, fleshy flavors. Fruit, glycerin, body, and tannin are the major components of this St.-Julien, which can be drunk young or cellared. Anticipated maturity: now–2012. It is another sleeper of the vintage.
Other vintage tasted: 1998 (84–86)

HOSANNA (POMEROL)

2000	**D**	**(92–94)**
1999	**D**	**90**

This estate, superbly situated on the plateau of Pomerol, was formerly known as Château Certan-Giraud and renamed Hosanna in 1999 after its acquisition by the Moueix family. Christian Moueix merits praise for bringing it to a splendid new level of quality. The property has been reduced to the tenderloin section of what was Certan-Giraud and is now a 10-acre vineyard planted with 70% Merlot and 30% Cabernet Franc. Readers should think of this wine as Pomerol's version of Cheval Blanc, as that seems to be the intention of the new own-ers. Hosanna is on the upswing, so prices will only increase. About 1,500 cases are now pro-duced annually.
2000: The 2000 Hosanna, a blend of 70% Merlot and 30% Cabernet Franc, comes closest in aroma, taste, and texture to the famed Cheval Blanc, less than a mile away. Deep ruby/pur-ple, with a gorgeous bouquet of exotic spices, black and blue fruits, and hints of truffles, this lush, concentrated, medium-bodied 2000 offers exquisite elegance, charm, and finesse. Seamless as well as beautifully knit, it is the antithesis of a vintage known for producing tan-nic, powerful wines. This effort is all fruit, glycerin, complexity, and seduction. Anticipated maturity: 2003–2016.
1999: This is the first vintage where Christian Moueix controlled the entire viticulture and vinification. The 1999 Hosanna reveals the silky, complex, black fruit, menthol, exotic spice, and new saddle leather notes in addition to medium to full body, aromas and flavors of blue-berries and black fruits, low acidity, and beautiful texture as well as ripeness. Anticipated maturity: now–2015.

D'ISSAN (MARGAUX)

2000	**E**	**(91–93)**
1999	**E**	**90**
1998	**C**	**87**
1997	**D**	**86**
1996	**D**	**88**
1995	**D**	**87**

This property continues to reassert itself, with a renewed commitment to quality. Readers need to pay attention to the efforts of young Emmanuel Cruse, who has racheted up the level of d'Issan, producing wines over recent years that surpass by far the previous vintages. In particular, the 1999 and 2000 are the best back-to-back vintages I have tasted from this property.
2000: The finest d'Issan I have tasted, the 2000, a blend of 70% Cabernet Sauvignon and 30% Merlot (60% of the crop made it into the grand vin), exhibits a saturated purple color, and an intense bouquet of licorice, black currants, and acacia flowers. This structured, rich, medium-bodied wine has superb purity, harmony, and length. More tannic and muscular than the seductive 1999, this wine looks set to have a brilliant future. Anticipated maturity: 2007–2025.
1999: One of the finest d'Issans of the last 25–30 years, this dense ruby-purple wine offers an intense bouquet of smoke, flowers, black currants, and licorice. Elegant yet powerful, deli-

cate and rich, this should turn out to be a quintessential example of Margaux's gracefulness and purity. The tannin is also very sweet. A sleeper of the vintage. Anticipated maturity: 2003–2020.

1998: The dark ruby, elegant, finesse-filled 1998 d'Issan reveals a floral, licorice, herb, and blackberry/currant-scented bouquet. Medium-bodied, with sweet tannin, a soft entry on the palate, fine concentration, a pure finish, and moderate tannin, it will be at its best between now–2014.

1997: An elegant, dark plum-colored effort, this 1997 reveals sweet cranberry, black cherry, licorice, and floral aromas. Medium-bodied, ripe, and round, with low acidity, it is a lovely, stylish, soft wine to consume over the next 5–7 years.

1996: The 1996 d'Issan has turned out beautifully in bottle. It exhibits a dark ruby/purple color and an elegant, floral, blackberry, and smoky-scented nose. The wine is medium-bodied and complex in the mouth, with subtle new oak, gorgeously ripe, sweet black currant fruit, and well-integrated tannin and acidity. This quintessential Margaux-styled wine is elegant and rich. Anticipated maturity: 2004–2020.

1995: An excellent d'Issan, with more noticeable tannin than the 1996, the 1995 possesses a deep ruby color, an excellent spicy, weedy, licorice, and black currant–scented nose, sweet fruit on the attack, and very good purity, ripeness, and overall balance. The wine is well made and more backward than the 1996, even though I suspect the latter wine has more tannin. Anticipated maturity: 2003–2014.

KIRWAN (MARGAUX)

2000	D	(91–92+)
1999	D	91
1998	D	90
1997	C	87
1996	D	88
1995	D	85

This once moribund estate has totally reversed itself after a long period of mediocrity. Under the inspired leadership of Nathalie Schyler, over the last 6–7 years it has produced wines that generally qualify as sleepers of their respective vintages. In particular, the 1998, 1999, and 2000 are a trio of unprecedented successes for Kirwan, 2000 probably being its finest wine to date. This is another Margaux property that has begun producing better wines at appealing prices.

2000: An opaque purple color is accompanied by an explosive bouquet of smoky black fruits, minerals, earth, and new oak. As the wine sits in the glass, notions of licorice emerge. This is a powerful, concentrated *vin de garde* with enormous depth, extract, and richness. If everything comes into total harmony, my score may turn out to be low. Made in a blockbuster, superconcentrated style, it will age for 30 years. Anticipated maturity: 2008–2030.

1999: The most glorious Kirwan ever made, this saturated purple offering reveals a gorgeous nose of Asian spice, licorice, blueberries, blackberries, and cassis. Moreover, there is extraordinary purity, multiple dimensions, a sensational mid-palate, and a finish that lasts 40–45 seconds. This classic qualifies as another sleeper of the vintage. Anticipated maturity: 2005–2025.

1998: A sleeper of the vintage, the opaque purple 1998 boasts a smoky, licorice, cassis, and mineral-scented bouquet. Full-bodied, powerful, yet elegant, it successfully balances complexity with an unbridled richness and power. Very impressive, particularly in view of its exceptional concentration, it will handsomely repay cellaring of 20 years or more. Anticipated maturity: 2006–2025.

1997: An attractive, dark ruby/purple effort, the 1997 Kirwan offers sweet cassis fruit, copious new oak, a fleshy, succulent texture, and an attractive, well-balanced finish with nicely integrated acidity and tannin. Consume this sexy Margaux over the next 7–8 years.

1996: The 1996 Kirwan is a highly extracted, rich, medium-bodied wine with a deep ruby/purple color and ripe cassis fruit intermixed with a touch of new oak, prunes, and spice. The wine has come together nicely since I first tasted it from cask. It appears to be an excellent, nearly outstanding effort. There is moderate tannin in the finish, so give this beefy, rich, muscular wine 4–5 years of cellaring. Anticipated maturity: 2006–2025.

1995: Aggressive new oak and vanilla dominate this wine's personality. This dark ruby/purple 1995 displays sweet cranberry and jammy black currant fruit on the attack, but narrows in the mouth with a compressed quality. Nevertheless, there is fine purity, medium body, and plenty of tannin. This effort would have been given a higher score if its fruit had been deep enough to absorb the wood. Anticipated maturity: now–2018.

LABEGORCE-ZÉDÉ (MARGAUX)

2000	C	(86–87)
1998	C	85
1997	C	85
1996	C	86
1995	C	85

2000: Notes of creamy vanilla (from American oak) are present in this plump, medium-bodied, nearly rustic 2000. While it displays a pleasant directness, it needs to shed some rough edges in order to merit a higher score. Anticipated maturity: now–2012.

1998: Round, attractive, sweet tannin gives this 1998 an up-front, expansive appeal. The fruit is ripe and redolent with black cherries and berries. The wine is velvety-textured, medium-bodied, and ideal for drinking over the next 5–7 years.

1997: A lovely well-made cru bourgeois Margaux, the 1997 Labegorce-Zédé possesses good ripeness, sweet licorice, Asian spice, cherry, and black currant fruit, medium body, and light tannin in the supple finish. Drink over the next 4–5 years.

1996: The 1996 is dense, peppery, and smoky, with some austerity but rich, medium-bodied flavors, as well as fine power, depth, and ripeness. The wine will keep for 8–10 years.

1995: The dark ruby-colored 1995 exhibits a tarry, licorice, plum, and earthy-scented nose, medium-bodied, soft, round flavors, and immediate appeal. It should drink well for 1–2 years.

Other vintage tasted: 1999 (85–86)

LAFITE-ROTHSCHILD (PAUILLAC)

2000	EEE	(96–100)
1999	EEE	95
1998	EEE	98
1997	EEE	92
1996	EEE	100
1995	EEE	95

Administrator Charles Chevalier has accomplished brilliant work since he took charge in 1994 of Lafite-Rothschild's winemaking. This estate is now unquestionably the star among the Médoc's first growths, producing riveting wines in every vintage since Chevalier's ascension to power. The 1996 was the wine of the vintage, and the 1997 was unquestionably the finest first growth of the year. Furthermore, even though 1998 favored the Merlot-based wines of St.-Emilion, Pomerol, and, to a lesser extent, Graves, Lafite-Rothschild is again a strong candidate for the wine of the vintage. The 1999 and 2000 are also fine successes. It is no secret that when only a tiny percentage of the harvest is included in the final blend, there is little room for compromise. Since 1998, the winery uses a new engraved bottle designed to prevent imitations.

2000: The 2000 Lafite-Rothschild contains an extremely high percentage of Cabernet Sauvignon (93.3%), with the balance Merlot. A mere 36% of the crop made it into the grand vin. This is a noble, elegant Lafite, without the density and thickness of the 1998 or 1996. It reveals a transparency and might be considered the archetypal Lafite that was made during several of the estate's finest vintages of the 1950s. Lighter in style, and elegant, its compelling aromatics (black fruits, minerals, lead pencil as well as cedar) draw the taster's attention. In the mouth, this medium-bodied wine exhibits excellent concentration, a certain lightness, and beautifully pure, well-delineated, laserlike clarity to its component parts. It is a monument to finesse and elegance, a style that Lafite-Rothschild can do better than any other Bordeaux château. Interestingly, the château's analysis boasts that the tannin levels in 2000 are higher than in 1996! Anticipated maturity: 2009–2050.

1999: A great effort for the vintage, the 1999 possesses a more open-knit, slightly friendlier style than the 1998, with sweet tannin, lower acidity, and plump, corpulent, earthy, black fruit notes intertwined with a touch of toast and berries. The wine is opulent and pure, with a sensational mid-palate (much like the 1998), and a 35+-second finish. This wine will be approachable upon release, yet will last 25 or more years. In the best-case scenario, could the 1999 Médocs, much like this effort, be modern-day clones of their 1962 counterparts? Anticipated maturity: 2004–2025.

1998: A blend of 81% Cabernet Sauvignon and 19% Merlot, this wine represents only 34% of Lafite's total harvest. In a less than perfect Médoc vintage, it has been spectacular since birth, putting on more weight and flesh over the last year. This opaque purple 1998 is close to perfection. The spectacular nose of lead pencil, smokey, mineral, and black currant fruit soars majestically from the glass. The wine is elegant yet profoundly rich, revealing the essence of Lafite's character. The tannin is sweet, and the wine is spectacularly layered yet never heavy. The finish is sweet, superrich, yet impeccably balanced and long (50+ seconds). Anticipated maturity: 2007–2035.

1997: Only 26% of the crop made it into the final blend, resulting in only 15,000 cases of the 1997 Lafite-Rothschild. Readers should not ignore this wine because of the negative press surrounding the 1997 vintage. It boasts an opaque dense purple color in addition to a gorgeously sweet, expansive perfume of cedar wood, black currants, lead pencil, and minerals, a fat mid-palate, medium body, explosive fruit and richness, soft tannin, and a velvety texture. It is a beautiful, compelling Lafite-Rothschild that can be drunk young, yet promises to evolve for 15+ years. Although one of the most forward Lafites ever tasted, it is all the more captivating because of this characteristic. Don't miss it!

1996: Tasted three times since bottling, the 1996 Lafite-Rothschild is unquestionably this renowned estate's greatest wine since the 1986 and 1982. Only 38% of the crop was deemed grand enough to be put into the final blend, which is atypically high in Cabernet Sauvignon (83% Cabernet Sauvignon, 7% Cabernet Franc, 7% Merlot, and 3% Petit Verdot). This massive wine may be the biggest, largest-scaled Lafite I have ever tasted. It will require many years to come around, so I suspect all of us past the age of 50 might want to think twice about laying away multiple cases of this wine. The wine exhibits a thick-looking, ruby/purple color and a knockout nose of lead pencil, minerals, flowers, and black currant scents. Extremely powerful and full-bodied, with remarkable complexity for such a young wine, this huge Lafite is oozing with extract and richness, yet has managed to preserve its quintessentially elegant personality. This wine is even richer than it was prior to bottling. It should unquestionably last 40–50 years. Anticipated maturity: 2012–2050.

1995: The 1995 Lafite-Rothschild (only one-third of the harvest made it into the final blend) is composed of 75% Cabernet Sauvignon, 17% Merlot, and 8% Cabernet Franc. It exhibits a dark ruby/purple color and a sweet, powdered mineral, smoky, weedy, cassis-scented nose. Beautiful sweetness of fruit is present in this medium-bodied, tightly knit but gloriously pure, well-delineated Lafite. The 1995 is not as powerful or as massive as the 1996, but it is beautifully made with outstanding credentials, in addition to remarkable promise. Anticipated maturity: 2008–2028.

Past Glories: 1994 (90+?), 1990 (92+), 1989 (90+), 1988 (94), 1986 (100), 1983 (93), 1982 (100), 1976 (93), 1975 (92?), 1959 (99), 1934 (90), 1921 (93), 1870 (96), 1864 (92), 1848 (96)

LAFLEUR (POMEROL)

2000	**EEE**	**(96–98+)**
2000 Pensées de Lafleur	**E**	**(90–91)**
1999	**EEE**	**93+**
1998	**EEE**	**92+?**
1997	**EEE**	**88?**
1996	**EEE**	**90+?**
1995	**EEE**	**93+**

Lafleur is one of my all-time favorite Bordeaux wines, and while recent vintages have been excellent to outstanding, they have lacked the extra dimension necessary to rank them among Pomerol's highest echelon, and one could wonder whether Lafleur had been bypassed by some of its rivals, such as Trotanoy, Clos l'Eglise, Lafleur-Pétrus, and l'Evangile. The 1999 and 2000 came at the right time, when I had started to think that this wine had shifted from its powerful, massive, full-throttle, and broodingly backward style.

2000: Though most 2000 Pomerols, particularly from the plateau, tend to be less impressive than their 1998 counterparts, Lafleur is an exception, largely because of the high percentage of Cabernet Franc in the final blend. The opaque purple 2000 Lafleur represents a return to the powerful yet prodigiously concentrated style that made this estate so famous. It is not a wine for neophytes or those unwilling to defer their gratification for more than a decade. Dense and sweet, it possesses a complex bouquet of liquid minerals, black raspberry liqueur, kirsch, truffles, currants, and incense. Extremely long as well as excruciatingly tannic, but well balanced by its wealth of fruit and extract, this monster full-bodied Lafleur may resemble the 1975 when it becomes fully mature. Anticipated maturity: 2015–2040. Sadly, there are only about 1,000 cases produced from Lafleur's minuscule vineyard.

2000 Pensées de Lafleur: I rarely get excited by second wines, but the terrific 2000 Pensées de Lafleur is a sleeper of the vintage. It offers glorious levels of black cherry fruit intermixed with liquid minerals presented in a medium to full-bodied, dense, supple style. While it displays some tannin, it does not possess the enormous weight, power, or structure of its more famous sibling.

1999: The 1999 appears to be a sure bet. Readers may recall that Lafleur was one of the few Bordeaux vineyards to harvest before the heavy rains. The result is a dense purple-colored wine with terrific cherry cough syrup, licorice, truffle, and mineral aromas. Although tannic, it is full-bodied, dense, opulent, super-concentrated, and extremely long and well balanced. It may turn out to be the finest Pomerol of the vintage. Anticipated maturity: 2007–2025.

1998: If the fruit holds, and this wine does not dry out, it will merit an outstanding score. However, readers need to be cautioned that this is an austere, frightfully tannic Lafleur that is somewhat atypical for this property. The wine is loaded as well as concentrated (dusty black cherry fruit dominates), but from both barrel and bottle it has consistently revealed a hard, astringent edge. It comes across more like a Médoc than a right bank offering. If the fruit holds up, it could turn out like the spectacular 1979, but the ragged tannin and leathery, dusty components are worrisome. Anticipated maturity: 2010–2035?

1997: The dark ruby-colored 1997 is impossibly tannic, with a tough texture and lean constitution. Paradoxically, the wine has weight, ripeness, and richness, but its dry, astringent finish is reminiscent of a 1998 Médoc. This wine's development is questionable, but I have serious reservations about its ratio of tannin to fruit. It may turn out to be excellent, but patience will be required. Anticipated maturity: 2006–2015.

1996: As I suspected, the 1996 Lafleur is a painfully backward, austere wine that represents a modern-day clone of this estate's 1966. It possesses a backward, tannic, Médoc-like character, with none of Pomerol's hallmark generosity. The wine exhibits a saturated dark purple color as well as a distinctive mineral, black raspberry, and berry-scented nose with the steely, mineral Lafleur character well displayed. Powerful, long, and rich but excruciatingly tannic, this wine may or may not resolve all of its tannin. In short, it is an impressively constituted wine that is no sure thing. Anticipated maturity: 2012–2025.

1995: Another awesome Lafleur, but it is also an amazingly backward, tannic monster that will need more cellaring than any Médoc in this vintage. The wine boasts an opaque black/purple color, as well as a closed but promising nose that represents the essence of blackberry, raspberry, and cherry fruit. Intertwined with those aromas is the telltale mineral *terroir* of Lafleur, full body, blistering dry, astringent tannin, and a layered, weighty feel on the palate. This is the kind of young claret that I couldn't wait to rush out and buy two decades ago, but now I have to be content to admire it and wish I were 20 years younger. It is formidable, prodigious, and oh, so promising, but I cannot see it being ready to drink before the end of the second decade of this century. Anticipated maturity: 2020–2050.

Past Glories: 1994 (93+), 1993 (90), 1992 (88), 1990 (97), 1989 (95+), 1988 (94), 1986 (91+), 1985 (96), 1983 (93), 1982 (100), 1979 (98+), 1978 (93), 1975 (100), 1966 (96), 1962 (91), 1961 (98), 1955 (92), 1950 (100), 1949 (96+), 1947 (100), 1945 (100)

LAFLEUR-GAZIN (POMEROL)

2000	D	(86–88?)
1999	D	86
1998	D	89
1997	C	85
1996	C	86

The wines of Lafleur-Gazin are produced by the firm of Jean-Pierre Moueix, which farms this estate under a lease arrangement. They are supple, round, and straightforward in style, and I am surprised that they are so simple and light, given the location of the vineyards, between those of Gazin and Lafleur.

2000: A sweet, superficial, but attractive effort, the 2000 Lafleur-Gazin reveals chalky tannin in the finish. A dark ruby/purple color is accompanied by ripe plum, prune, and berry fruit, medium body, and plenty of structure and tough tannin. Anticipated maturity: 2003–2014.

1999: Dark ruby-colored, with notes of berries, currants, tar, earth, and herbs, this medium-bodied, lightweight Pomerol is best drunk during its first 4–5 years of life.

1998: One of the sleepers of the vintage, this is the finest Lafleur-Gazin I have tasted in many years. The wine is deep ruby/plum/purple with a sweet, sexy bouquet of overripe black cherries, kirsch, smoke, and spice box. The seductive, fat, concentrated palate is open-knit and loaded with fruit, glycerin, and character. The acidity is low, the tannin ripe, and the finish succulent as well as velvety. Drink it over the next 12 years.

1997: A distinctive, herbaceous, earthy/cherry nose precedes a structured, tannic, medium-bodied, leathery, old-style wine. Its exuberance and directness are attractive. Drink it over the next 3–5 years.

1996: This medium-bodied, well-made, elegant 1996 offers attractive coffee- and tobacco-tinged berry fruit, surprising softness for the vintage, and good overall equilibrium. Drink it over the next 8–10 years.

LAFLEUR DE PLINCE (POMEROL)

2000	C	(87–89)

2000: A sleeper of the vintage, 2000 is the first Lafleur de Plince I have tasted. It reveals a deep purple color in addition to sweet aromas of black raspberries, kirsch, licorice, and truffles. Medium- to full-bodied and deep, with well-integrated tannin, outstanding purity, and a sense of *terroir* as well as nobility, it impressively marries power with finesse. Anticipated maturity: 2003–2015.

LAFON-ROCHET (ST.-ESTÈPHE)

2000	D	(90–91)
1999	D	87
1998	D	88
1997	C	87
1996	C	90
1995	C	89+

The Tesseron family, who has done so much to propel Pontet-Canet into the limelight, continues to upgrade the quality of Lafon-Rochet. This is another Bordeaux estate performing well above its classification. To date, prices have not caught up with the quality that has emerged over recent years.

2000: A saturated black/purple color is followed by broodingly backward yet intense aromas of jammy blackberries, earth, vitamins, licorice, and new oak. There is good fat, a concentrated, full-bodied, multilayered palate, and a sweet mid-palate as well as finish—always a good sign. This should be a long-lived 2000, despite what appears to be considerable accessibility. It is a sleeper of the vintage. Anticipated maturity: 2004–2020.

1999: A lighter-weight effort from Lafon-Rochet, the softer 1999 comes close to being diffuse. Berry and currant flavors are presented in a medium-weight style. Anticipated maturity: now–2012.

1998: A dense purple color is accompanied by a tannic, smoky, concentrated, earthy wine with abundant blackberry and cassis fruit, underbrush, minerals, and a steely character, and a powerful, tannic finish. Anticipated maturity: 2003–2016.

1997: This dark plum-colored, sexy, soft, medium-bodied, low-acid Lafon Rochet reveals chewy black fruits intermixed with new wood and minerals. Exhibiting good density and ripeness, it is a very good effort in this accessible, drinker-friendly vintage. Anticipated maturity: now–2008.

1996: One of the sleepers of the 1996 vintage, Lafon-Rochet has turned out an atypically powerful, rich, concentrated wine bursting with black currant fruit. The opaque purple color gives way to a medium- to full-bodied, tannic, backward wine with terrific purity, a sweet, concentrated mid-palate, and a long, blockbuster finish. This wine remains one of the finest values from the luxury-priced 1996 vintage and is well worth purchasing by readers who are willing to invest 3–4 years of patience; it should keep for two decades. Anticipated maturity: 2005–2020.

1995: This wine will definitely improve after a few more years in bottle. Although it has closed down since bottling, it is an impressively endowed, rich, sweet cassis-smelling and -tasting Lafon-Rochet. The wine's impressively saturated deep ruby/purple is accompanied by vanilla, earth, and spicy scents, medium to full body, excellent to outstanding richness, and moderate tannin in the powerful, well-delineated finish. Anticipated maturity: 2003–2018.

LAGRANCE (POMEROL)

2000	D	(84–86)
1998	D	87
1997	D	85
1996	C	76

2000: Notes of green pepper, dried herbs, and red fruits emerge from this elegant, lean, austerely styled Pomerol. Lacking flesh and charm, it will become increasingly hard as it ages.

1998: A dense ruby/purple color and sweet blackberry and cherry fruit can be found in this medium- to full-bodied, nicely concentrated wine. With power, moderate tannin, and good intensity, it should age well. Anticipated maturity: 2004–2015.

1997: Medium ruby-colored, with evolved, mature notes of melted road tar, sweet underbrush, red currants, and cherries, this soft, easy-to-drink 1997 should have plenty of appeal. Drink it over the next 2 years.

1996: The average-quality 1996 displays an herbaceous, saddle leather–scented nose that lacks fruit. It is medium-bodied, with decent concentration and a rustic, earthy finish. This wine also possesses entirely too much tannin for the amount of fruit. Anticipated maturity: now–2007.

Other vintage tasted: 1999 (82–84)

LAGRANGE (ST.-JULIEN)

2000	D	(88–96?)
1999	D	88
1998	D	88
1997	C	85
1996	D	90
1995	D	90

No expense has been spared here, and the wines have gone from distressingly irregular to stunning in an amazingly short period of time. Vintages from 1985 onward have shown impressive depth of flavor welded to plenty of tannin and toasty new oak and a savory and lush style. Moreover, Lagrange currently remains underpriced given its present level of quality.

2000: While 2000 is unquestionably a great vintage for St.-Julien, on the two occasions I tasted Lagrange, it was dominated by its wood, and was a bit disjointed. It possesses a saturated ruby/purple color as well as plenty of earth and new oak in the aromatics, a touch of chocolate on the attack, medium body, high tannin, and a jagged finish. This wine is undoubtedly excellent, but will it come together in a more symmetrical manner? Anticipated maturity: 2004–2016.

1999: An expansive perfume of black fruits intermixed with smoke, Asian spices, and licorice jumps from this dark, dense ruby/purple wine. The tannin is sweet, the acidity low, the finish persistent, and the overall impression one of fatness and opulence. It will be ready to drink upon release. Anticipated maturity: now–2015.

1998: This dark ruby-colored, elegant, attractive effort offers spicy new oak, medium body, excellent concentration as well as depth, surprising softness, and early appeal. As with many Médocs, Lagrange's tannins are much friendlier since bottling. Anticipated maturity: now–2015.

1997: Light- to medium-bodied, with spicy oak, red currant, and cherry fruit, this well-made, lightly tannic effort will provide uncritical drinking over the next 4–5 years.

1996: Opaque purple, with a backward yet promising nose of classically pure cassis intermixed with toast and spice, this medium- to full-bodied, powerful yet stylish wine possesses superb purity, a nicely layered feel in the mouth, and plenty of structure. It will not be an early-drinking St.-Julien but one to lay away for 3–4 years more and enjoy over the next 2–3 decades. Anticipated maturity: 2006–2022.

1995: The 1995 Lagrange is similar to the 1996, but the fruit is sweeter, the acidity lower, and the wine less marked by Cabernet Sauvignon. The color is a deep ruby/purple. The wine boasts a roasted herb, charcoal, black currant, mineral, and new oak–scented nose. Medium- to full-bodied and ripe, with copious quantities of jammy black cherry and cassis flavors presented in a low-acid, moderately tannic style, this well-endowed, purely made wine requires cellaring. Anticipated maturity: 2003–2020.

Past Glories: 1990 (93), 1989 (90), 1986 (92)

LA LAGUNE (HAUT-MÉDOC)

1999	C	(81–84)
1998	C	78
1997	C	86
1996	C	86
1995	C	88

Since 1976, La Lagune has emerged as one of the great—and surprisingly reasonably priced—crus classés of the Médoc. The estate has had a very good track record since that date, except for the 1998s and 1999s, which have proven quite disappointing.

1999: Light-bodied but decently balanced, this pleasant, picnic-styled claret exhibits a medium ruby color in addition to herbaceous, earthy, red fruit flavors, toasty new oak, and a short but unobtrusive finish. Drink it over the next 3–4 years.

1998: The good news is that this is an elegant, friendly wine. The bad news is that there is not much to it, and the finish is short and compressed. The wine reveals toasty new oak, moderately ripe cherry fruit, and sweet tannin, but there is little concentration or mid-palate in this good, middle-weight Bordeaux. Consume it over the next 5–6 years.

1997: Spicy notes of saddle leather, kirsch, vanilla, and roasted nuts emerge from the moderately intense bouquet of this fruity, medium-bodied, soft, accessible 1997. While it lacks density, aging potential, and concentration, it is a charming wine to drink over the next 3–4 years.

1996: This is another tannic, austere 1996, but it is well endowed. Copious aromas of spicy new oak are present in the moderately intense bouquet, as well as cherry notes intertwined with dried herbs. The wine is medium-bodied and well made, with good spice, a slight austerity, and moderate tannin in the long finish. In many vintages La Lagune can be drunk at an early age, but this effort will require another 3–4 years of patience. Anticipated maturity: 2006–2018.

1995: La Lagune's seductively styled 1995 displays a dark ruby color as well as copious amounts of black cherry, kirsch, and plumlike fruit nicely dosed with high-quality smoky, toasty oak. This medium-bodied, elegant, round, generous, charming wine can be drunk young, or cellared for a decade or more. Anticipated maturity: now–2012.

Past Glories: 1990 (90), 1989 (90), 1982 (92), 1978 (88), 1976 (89), 1970 (89)

LANESSAN (HAUT-MÉDOC)

2000	C	(88–90)
1998	C	87
1997	C	87
1996	C	88

This underrated Médoc consistently produces wines of fifth growth quality.

2000: The sleeper 2000 is tannic yet juicy, structured, and intense, with copious quantities of black currant fruit tinged with cedar and damp earth notes. Medium- to full-bodied, pure, and classic, it will be at its peak between 2006–2016.

1998: This wine is dark ruby-colored, with spicy black currant and cherry fruit, medium body, high tannin, and good thickness, but the tannin may never fully dissipate. Anticipated maturity: 2004–2015.

1997: An excellent wine for the vintage, the evolved, complex aromatics exhibit cedar, dried herbs, tobacco, and copious quantities of red and black fruits. Medium-bodied and supple-textured, it is ideal for drinking now and over the next 8–10 years.

1996: A sleeper of the vintage, Lanessan's 1996 boasts an impressively saturated dark ruby/purple color and knockout aromatics of melted chocolate, asphalt, and cassis. Deep, rich, and medium-bodied, with excellent concentration and purity, this impressively endowed, flavorful, well-structured wine should be at its finest between 2004–2016.

1995: The 1995 reveals less power and muscle than the 1996, but more elegance and fleshy, weedy, tobacco-tinged red and black currant fruit presented in a soft, supple, alluring, medium-bodied format. Anticipated maturity: now–2008.

Other vintage tasted: 1999 (86–87)

LANGOA-BARTON (ST.-JULIEN)

2000	D	(88–90)
1999	D	88+?
1998	E	89+
1997	D	84
1996	E	86+?
1995	E	86+?

Proprietor Anthony Barton, whose other estate is the well-known Léoville-Barton, deserves credit for keeping Langoa-Barton's prices realistic and at the same time producing some of St.-Julien's finest wines. This property does not always receive the respect it merits, but its wines, especially the most recent vintages, are extremely strong.

2000: Compared to its prodigious sibling, Léoville-Barton, Langoa-Barton's 2000 is a more sinewy, less noble wine with a deep ruby/purple color, plenty of muscle, wood, earth, and black fruits, and more aggressive tannin. While it should age well, it does not possess the majestic richness and flavor dimension of the 1999. Anticipated maturity: 2006–2035.

1999: In contrast to its burly older sibling, the 1999 is a soft, luscious, yet concentrated effort with low acidity, sweet tannin, and excellent, possibly outstanding concentration as well as complexity. It, too, will require 4–5 years of cellaring (unusual for a 1999), but it will keep for 20 years. Anticipated maturity: 2005–2020.

1998: A dense ruby/purple color as well as a muscular, ageworthy personality are found in this "no BS" sort of wine. It possesses loads of body, impressive concentration, and firm tannin in the finish. However, it is a wine for those who are able to defer their gratification, as it requires another 4–5 years of cellaring. Anticipated maturity: 2006–2025.

1997: Not a top-notch effort, Langoa Barton's medium ruby-colored 1997 exhibits sweet herb-tinged, berry, and currant aromas, spicy, cedary, medium-bodied flavors, low acidity, and a pleasant but undistinguished finish. Drink it over the next 4–5 years.

1996: I consistently found this 1996 to be a hard wine. Despite its deep ruby/purple color, it is monolithic, with notes of earth and black currant fruit submerged beneath a tannic structure. Although medium-bodied, with some weight and extract, the wine is ferociously hard and backward. Give it 3–5 years of cellaring and hope for the best. Anticipated maturity: 2008–2020.

1995: The 1995 Langoa-Barton has been perplexing to evaluate. It is woody, monolithic, and exceptionally tannic, without the fruit and flesh necessary to provide equilibrium. There are some positive components—a saturated dark ruby/purple color, hints of ripe fruit, and pure, clean flavors—but the wine's angularity/austerity is troublesome. It will probably be a good but old-style claret that will never resolve all of its tannic bite. Anticipated maturity: 2003–2016.

Past Glories: 1959 (90), 1953 (90), 1948 (93)

LAPLAGNOTTE-BELLEVUE (ST.-EMILION)

2000 Laplagnotte	E	(90–91)
2000	D	(85–86)

1998	D	86
1997	D	84
1996	D	86
1995	D	86

This estate is owned by Claude de Labarre, one of the former coproprietors of Cheval Blanc. The vineyard is planted with 70% Cabernet Sauvignon, 20% Cabernet Franc, and 10% Merlot. The wines of Laplagnotte-Bellevue are generally elegant, fruity, straightforward, and savory, and are reasonably priced. Since 2000, the estate has started producing a micro *cuvée* called Laplagnotte.

2000 Laplagnotte: The debut release of this garage wine, the 2000 Laplagnotte, is impressive. This opaque purple-colored wine offers sweet, rich blackberry and cherry fruit intermixed with smoke, minerals, and vanilla. Opulent and full-bodied, with enough acidity and structure for vibrancy and definition, it will require patience. Anticipated maturity: 2005–2016.

2000: The 2000 Laplagnotte-Bellevue is a straightforward, fruity, elegant offering with notes of raspberries and cherries. Medium-bodied and tannic, it is best consumed over the next 5–8 years.

1998: A beguiling, dark ruby-colored wine with black cherry fruit, undeniable elegance, a feminine style, and sweet raspberry fruit in the mouth. It is medium-bodied, soft, succulent, and ideal for drinking over the next 7–8 years.

1997: The charming, open-knit, richly fruity 1997 is light- to medium-bodied and soft, with no hard edges. Drink it over the next 2–4 years.

1996: A soft, richly fruity wine, the 1996 exhibits medium dark ruby color, an elegant, sweet nose of black cherry fruit mixed with floral scents, earth, and spice, and dry tannin in the finish. This is an elegant, finesse-styled, fruit-driven wine for enjoying over the next 2–4 years.

1995: A pretty wine, with sweet cherry fruit and vanilla in the nose, this ruby/purple effort possesses good ripeness on the attack, soft tannin, low acidity, and a round, easygoing finish. Anticipated maturity: now–2006.

Other vintage tasted: 1999 (84–86)

LARCIS-DUCASSE (ST.-EMILION)

2000	D	(87–89)
1999	D	81
1998	D	86
1996	D	81
1995	D	87

Although it benefits from one of St.-Emilion's finest *terroirs*, this underachiever continues to turn out good but uninspiring wines.

2000: This great *terroir* never quite lives up to its potential, but the 2000 is one of the finest efforts in recent years. It reveals a classy nose of wet stones, cherry liqueur, dried herbs, and earth, beautiful purity, medium body, and a sense of elegance, style, and overall balance. It should drink well for 10–15 years.

1999: Insubstantial, with narrow characteristics of tobacco and weediness dominating its personality, this wine possesses hard tannin as well as an austere finish. My rating may be generous. Anticipated maturity: 2003–2009.

1998: The 1998 exhibits a dark ruby color, a herbaceous, sweet, black cherry, mineral, olive, cedar, and spice box–scented bouquet, medium body, light tannin, and a short finish. It is a wine to consume over the next 7–10 years.

1996: The 1996 Larcis-Ducasse possesses a medium ruby color followed by a forward, soft, commercially pleasing cherry, herb, and earth-scented nose. The wine is medium-bodied, straightforward, and simple. Drink it over the next 3–4 years.

1995: The 1995 exhibits a dark ruby/purple color with moderate saturation. A spicy, ripe, richly fruity nose with hints of earth and new oak is moderately intense. Some tannin, good purity, medium body, and a firm, measured, elegant style suggest this wine can last 8 more years.

Other vintage tasted: 1997 (84)

Past Glories: 1945 (90)

LARMANDE (ST.-EMILION)

2000	D	(87–88)
1999	D	87
1998	D	87
1997	D	86
1996	D	88
1995	D	88

This estate has produced very good to excellent wines since the mid-1970s. The key to their quality is late harvesting, a strict selection, and relatively low yields. Few premiers grands crus classés have such a track record, and not many of them can boast such consistently fine efforts.

2000: The 2000 Larmande was tasted on three separate occasions. My tasting notes were somewhat variable, but it never performed as well as I had hoped. It reveals a more compressed, less open-knit style than in the past, with noticeable structure, tight, hard tannin, and a certain austerity. Nevertheless, there is excellent purity, with notes of wet stones, crème de cassis, and toast and good weight. The finish is pinched, dry, and austere. Anticipated maturity: 2006–2016.

1999: Medium body, soft tannin, and olive-tinged black cherry and smoky oak aromas as well as flavors are found in the 1999 Larmande. It also possesses good flesh, a sweet attack, and a velvety finish. Anticipated maturity: now–2010.

1998: This wine is initially tight, but with airing, aromas of licorice, spice box, berries, herbs, and leather emerge. It is a medium- to full-bodied, well-made, attractive, well-structured effort. Anticipated maturity: 2003–2015.

1997: Abundant, moderately intense aromas of toasty new oak intermingled with scents of plum liqueur, licorice, and Provençal herbs are followed by a muscular, ripe wine with a distinctive cherry jam–like flavor profile. This solidly made, lightly tannic effort should be at its finest before 2008.

1996: Larmande's 1996 is a big, toasty, rich, licorice, Asian spice, fruitcake, and smoky black cherry–scented and –flavored wine. It reveals medium body, good richness, moderate tannin, and a long, concentrated finish. It will keep for 10 or more years.

1995: The 1995 is cut from the same mold as the 1996, except the 1995 possesses more accessible glycerin and fruit, as well as lower acidity. It offers a dense ruby/purple color, and an intense herb, toasty, jammy blackberry, and cassis-scented nose intertwined with wood fire–like aromas. The wine is soft, round, and medium- to full-bodied, with a sexy combination of glycerin, fruit, sweet tannin, and heady alcohol. It should drink well for 7–8 years.

Past Glories: 1988 (90)

LAROSE-TRINTAUDON (HAUT-MÉDOC)

1996 Larose-Trintaudon	C	86
1996 Larose-Perganson	C	86

1996 Larose-Trintaudon: This deep ruby-colored wine offers sweet jammy black cherry and currant fruit, spicy oak, surprising depth and richness, and a convincing mid-palate and length. This seriously made, fruit-driven 1996 will drink well for 3–4 years.

1996 Larose-Perganson: This wine exhibits more new oak than the 1996 Larose-Trintaudon in its aromatics and flavors, with excellent fleshy fruit, medium body, and good purity. It, too, should drink well for 3–4 years.

Other vintages tasted: Larose-Perganson: 2000 (85–86), 1999 (85–86), 1998 (85–87), 1997 (86). Larose-Trintaudon: 2000 (85–86), 1998 (83–85+?), 1997 (85)

LAROZE (ST.-EMILION)

2000	**C**	**(87–88)**
1999	**C**	**87**
1998	**C**	**87**
1997	**C**	**84**

This property has rebounded nicely, producing over recent years a succession of overtly fruity, soft, open-knit, user-friendly wines.

2000: In a tannic year, Laroze has fashioned a deep ruby-colored, ripe 2000 with excellent definition, sweet fruit, but a superficial character. It will require consumption during its first 6–7 years of life.

1999: A deep ruby/purple color is followed by black cherry and berry fruit, earth, and smoke aromas. Sweet on the attack, with medium to full body, low acidity, and excellent length, the 1999 Laroze may turn out to be a sleeper of the vintage if it holds its weight and fruit. Anticipated maturity: now–2012.

1998: The 1998 Laroze is a graceful, medium-bodied, richly fruity St.-Emilion that will provide delicious drinking during its first decade of life. The color is a dark ruby, and the wine offers plenty of black cherry, kirsch, and spicy notes. Fleshy and already delicious, it can be drunk now and over the next 8 years.

1997: Medium-bodied, lighter, and less evolved than the 1996, the ruby-colored 1997 offers good purity, and a spicy, well-delineated finish. Anticipated maturity: now–2006.

LARRIVET-HAUT-BRION (PESSAC-LÉOGNAN)

2000	**D**	**(90–92)**
1999	**D**	**89**
1998	**D**	**88**
1997	**C**	**86**

Christine and Philippe Gervoson have greatly increased the quality of the wine from this splendidly situated estate in Pessac-Léognan. Improvements began in 1996, and the estate has hit peaks in both 1998 and 2000, although 1999 and 1997 are also fine wines. Michel Rolland is the consulting oenologist.

2000: The 2000 Larrivet-Haut-Brion, a blend of equal parts Merlot and Cabernet Sauvignon, is an impressive sleeper of the vintage. A dense opaque purple color is followed by aromas of minerals, spices, black cherries, and currants. Complex notes of incense and licorice also emerge. On the palate, the wine is opulent, full-bodied, and earthy, with sweet tannin, low acidity, and superb concentration as well as purity. A beauty! Anticipated maturity: 2003–2020.

1999: The 1999 may turn out to be as good as the 1998. Although slightly softer as well as lighter, it is a seductive effort offering aromas and flavors of tar, scorched earth, tobacco, and red and black currant fruit. Medium-bodied, soft, spicy, and already delicious, it will provide seductive drinking upon its release. Anticipated maturity: now–2014.

1998: Classic scents of smoky tobacco, cigar box, scorched earth, black currants, and cherries are vividly displayed in this wine's intense aromas. In the mouth, it is medium-bodied, spicy, and soft, as well as expressive. This elegant beauty may eventually merit an even higher score. Anticipated maturity: now–2015.

1997: Spicy, peppery, Provençal *garrigue*, smoky aromas, sweet fruit, attractive ripeness, low acidity, and fine concentration characterize this easygoing, dark ruby-colored wine. Consume it over the next 4 years.

LASCOMBES (MARGAUX)

2000	D	(90–92)
1998	D	83
1997	C	77
1996	C	80
1995	C	79?

Since its acquisition by an American consortium in 1999, this estate is in the capable hands of Yves Vatelot, one of the partners of Lascombes as well as the proprietor of the overachieving generic Bordeaux, Reignac. Alain Raynaud (of Quinault l'Enclos and La Fleur de Gay) has been brought in as a consultant. It is clearly an estate to watch closely, given the immense investment being made in the vineyard and winery, the very strict selection process now employed, and the immense talent of the two men who now oversee the winemaking.

2000: Only 30% of the crop went into the 2000 Lascombes, and the final blend of 58% Cabernet Sauvignon, 35% Merlot, 7% Petit Verdot has produced the finest Lascombes in over 35 years. Lascombes's 2000, a sleeper of the vintage, exhibits a deep ruby purple color as well as sweet, concentrated, jammy black currant fruit intermixed with dried herbs, earth, cedar, and spice. This deep, velvety-textured, charming, sexy wine has such low acidity and ripe tannin that it will be hard to resist young. Anticipated maturity: now–2016.

1998: The light-styled 1998 Lascombes offers sweet cherry fruit intermixed with cedar, spice box, and dried herbs. Although it lacks depth, this offering is symmetrical, well balanced, and elegant. Enjoy it over the next 10 years.

1997: The 1997 Lascombes is made in an up-front, light- to medium-bodied, soft style, but at present the oak seems excessive for the moderate quantities of fruit. It will need to be drunk during its first 7–8 years of life.

1996: This is a mainstream, oaky, soft, fruity wine without much depth or length. It is open-knit, with dried herb and black currant fruit in its moderately intense aromatics. The short finish reveals no hard edges. Drink it over the next 4–5 years.

1995: Far less impressive after bottling than it was from cask, this wine is now a candidate for drying out, given its hollow middle and hard, austere, angular finish. The color is medium ruby, and the wine has moderate weight and sweet fruit in the nose and on the attack, but it closes down to reveal a tart, spartan personality. Anticipated maturity: now–2008.

Other vintages tasted: 1999 (77–79)

Past Glories: 1959 (90)

LATOUR (PAUILLAC)

2000	EEE	(96–100)
1999	EEE	94
1998	EEE	90
1997	EEE	89
1996	EEE	97
1995	EEE	96+

The wine of Latour is an impeccable and classic model of excellence in both great and mediocre vintages. For that reason, many have long considered this estate's wine to be Médoc's finest. All in all, Latour remains one of the most concentrated, rich, tannic, and full-bodied wines in the world. When mature, it has a compelling bouquet of fresh walnuts and leather, black currants, and gravelly, mineral scents. On the palate it is never heavy, and exhibits an extraordinary freshness. The estate was bought several years ago by Paris businessman François Pinault. Under the new ownership, the winery and cellars have undergone a major renovation, with enormous improvements in both the *cuverie* and aging cellars. Recent vintages continue the trend and remain faithful to the style that has made Latour famous worldwide.

2000: The 2000 Latour is one of the vintage's most compelling efforts. Yields from the old vines from which most of this *cuvée* is produced were 37 hectoliters per hectare. Forty-eight percent of the crop was utilized in the grand vin. It is a blend of 77% Cabernet Sauvignon, 16% Merlot, 4% Cabernet Franc, and 3% Petit Verdot. A prodigious effort, it appears to be the star of the Médoc first growths. Despite its thick, viscous appeal, the total acid is 3.7 grams per liter, quite high considering that most great vintages of Latour possess 3.2–3.3. This wine possesses sweet tannin, amazing presence and concentration, extraordinary purity, and phenomenally ripe, pristine, unctuous but not heavy notes of black fruits. It is a model of power, symmetry, and grace, with a finish that lasts for over 45 seconds. This Latour is an early candidate to surpass the 1996, 1995, and 1990! Anticipated maturity: 2008–2050.

1999: A terrific effort, this sexy, open-knit, opulent effort possesses plenty of tannin, but it is largely concealed by the wine's wealth of fruit, high extraction level, and noticeable glycerin as well as unctuosity. Dense ruby/purple, with a sweet, evolved nose of black fruits (cassis and blackberries), cedar, spice box, and liquid minerals, this powerful yet seamless Latour will be surprisingly accessible at an unusually young age. Long and full-bodied, with the acidity, tannin, alcohol, and wood all beautifully integrated, it will be at its finest between 2007–2030. A classic!

1998: Not a blockbuster, super-concentrated classic such as the 1996, 1995, 1990, or 1982, the 1998 possesses a dark garnet/purple color in addition to a complex bouquet of under-brush, cedar, walnuts, and licorice-tinged black currants. Although medium- to full-bodied and moderately tannic, it lacks the expansiveness in the mid-palate necessary to be truly great. Moreover, the tannin is slightly aggressive, although that is hardly unusual in such a young Latour. Anticipated maturity: 2009–2030.

1997: A flavorful, savory Latour, without a great deal of density or power, the 1997 exhibits sweet, walnut-tinged, black currant fruit intertwined with minerals and subtle wood. Nicely textured, with adequate acidity, ripe tannin, and a medium-bodied finish, this smooth effort should drink well for 10–12 years.

1996: Fifty-six percent of the 1996 production made it into the grand vin, a blend of 78% Cabernet Sauvignon, 17% Merlot, 4% Cabernet Franc, and 1% Petit Verdot. It is a massive, backward wine that comes close to being a monster. The 1996 appears to be a modern-day version of the 1966 or 1970, rather than the sweeter, more sumptuous, fatter styles of the 1982 or 1990. The wine reveals an opaque ruby/purple color and reticent but emerging aromas of roasted nuts, blackberry fruit, tobacco, and coffee, with hints of toast in the background. Massive and full-bodied in the mouth, it possesses extremely high tannin, fabulous concentration and purity, and an impeccably long finish. This wine will require at least 10 years of cellaring. Anticipated maturity: 2012–2040.

1995: I have been blown away by this wine on recent occasions, and all of my hopes for its being a prodigious example of Latour after bottling have proven to be correct. The wine is a more unctuously textured, sweet, accessible Latour than the 1996. Wow! What a fabulous, profound wine this has turned out to be. It is unquestionably one of the great wines of the vintage and will probably need 10 years of cellaring before it can be approached. The wine reveals an opaque purple color and a knockout nose of chocolate, walnuts, minerals, spice, and blackberry and cassis fruit. Exceptionally full-bodied, with exhilarating levels of glycerin, richness, and personality, this wine, despite its low acidity, possesses extremely high levels of tannin to go along with its equally gargantuan proportions of fruit. It is a fabulous Latour that should age effortlessly for 40–50 years.

Past Glories: 1994 (92?), 1993 (89), 1990 (98+), 1986 (90), 1982 (100), 1978 (94), 1975 (93+), 1971 (93), 1970 (98+), 1966 (96), 1964 (90), 1962 (94), 1961 (100), 1959 (98+), 1949 (100), 1948 (94), 1945 (96), 1928 (100), 1926 (93), 1924 (94), 1921 (90)

LATOUR À POMEROL (POMEROL)

2000	E	(90–92)
1999	E	89
1998	E	90
1997	D	88
1996	E	88
1995	E	89+

This vineyard controlled by the Libourne firm of Jean-Pierre Moueix produces a powerful, fleshy, opulent, and dark-colored style of Pomerol; often majestic and sometimes among the two or three greatest of their appellation (1947, 1948, 1950, 1959, 1961 and 1970). Except for the 1982, and perhaps the 1998, nothing in the last 30+ years has rivaled those legends, but for a limited-production Pomerol of such quality, this wine remains a relative bargain.

2000: Notes of caramel, balsam wood, and mineral-infused black cherries and plums emerge from this dark ruby-colored 2000. In the mouth, firm tannin compresses the texture. Early in its life, this medium-bodied effort lacked concentration and power but has improved significantly. While sweet, expansive, and much richer than I expected, this 2000 should rival the 1998. Anticipated maturity: 2003–2018.

1999: This forward, evolved, dark ruby/plum 1999 exhibits a bouquet of sweet new oak, caramel, and cherry fruit. Excellent on the palate, open-knit, and delicious, it will be ready to drink upon release. Anticipated maturity: now–2012.

1998: A beautiful effort, the 1998 is one of the finest wines produced at this estate in the last 30 years. However, it is unlikely to turn out better than the 1970 or 1982. Revealing characteristics of vanilla, leather, highly extracted black cherry fruit, and caramel, this deep, rich, full-bodied, powerful, layered, sweetly tannic 1998 is not as profound as I originally thought, but it is still an outstanding wine. Anticipated maturity: 2004–2020.

1997: This type of wine will please many consumers, so readers should give it a try, assuming it is not priced out of reach. A dark ruby color is followed by a deep, rich, excellent display of roasted nuts, jammy berry fruit, dried herbs, and tomato skins. It is seductive, lush, and medium- to full-bodied, with impressive levels of glycerin, fruit, and intensity. Low acidity and a forward style suggest it is best consumed over the next 4–5 years, although it will undoubtedly last longer.

1996: This wine has turned out well after bottling, revealing a saturated dark ruby color and excellent blackberry and cherry aromas intermixed with toast, roasted nuts, and vanilla. Medium-bodied, with admirable concentration, moderate levels of spicy oak, and sweet tannin, this dense wine is already delicious. Anticipated maturity: now–2014.

1995: The 1995 Latour à Pomerol should develop into an outstanding wine, but it was revealing considerable grip and structure following bottling. It possesses a dark ruby/purple color, as well as a distinctive nose of smoked herbs, black fruits, iron, mulberries, and spice. The wine is generous, ripe, and mouth-filling, with medium to full body and excellent richness and purity, but the wine's tannic clout and slight bitterness kept it from receiving an outstanding score. One or two more years in the bottle could result in an excellent, perhaps outstanding Latour à Pomerol. Anticipated maturity: 2004–2020.

Past Glories: 1982 (93), 1970 (94), 1961 (100), 1959 (98), 1950 (99), 1948 (98), 1947 (100), 1945 (100)

DES LAUVES (ST.-EMILION)

2000	C	(86–88)

2000: An opaque ruby/purple is accompanied by aromas of new oak and black fruits. This straightforward, substantial, internationally styled St.-Emilion exhibits rustic tannin but good texture in the mouth as well as plenty of weight and depth. Anticipated maturity: 2003–2015.

LÉOVILLE-BARTON (ST.-JULIEN)

2000	EEE	(96–98)
1999	E	88+
1998	E	91
1997	D	86
1996	E	92
1995	E	91

After a period of inconsistency in the 1970s, Léoville-Barton has produced a string of brilliant wines in the 1980s and 1990s under the auspices of Anthony Barton. While this estate does not enjoy as flattering a reputation as Léoville-Las Cases or Ducru-Beaucaillou, it does produce one of the topflight St.-Juliens. Readers seeking classic, muscular, extremely long-lived Bordeaux should always keep this outstanding classified growth in mind. It continues to sell for a price well below its intrinsic value.

2000: One of the vintage's undeniable superstars, the 2000 Léoville-Barton transcends anything made at this property in the last 50 years. An opaque purple color is accompanied by reluctant aromas of cassis, earth, oak, and licorice. The spectacular quality becomes even more evident in the mouth. The wine is enormous but symmetrical, with thrilling levels of concentration, beautifully integrated acidity, tannin, and wood, and a finish that lasts nearly a minute. This is a massive, complex effort with uncanny balance for a wine of such size and magnitude. It is one of the wines of the vintage and a modern-day classic! Anticipated maturity: 2008–2040.

1999: The vintage's lower acids give the 1999 Léoville-Barton a more forward character than normal. The color is a dense ruby/purple. The wine reveals fine body and a softer, friendlier, mainstream style than the 1998, in addition to abundant weight and richness. Cedar, cassis, minerals, underbrush, and earth dominate both the aromatics and flavors. I suspect it will firm up after bottling. Anticipated maturity: 2004–2025.

1998: This opaque purple, muscular, full-bodied, classically made St.-Julien displays impressive concentration, chewy, highly extracted flavors of black fruits, iron, earth, and spicy wood, a powerful mouth-feel, and three decades of longevity. A pure, uncompromising, traditionally styled wine, it is to be admired for its authenticity, class, and quality. Anticipated maturity: 2007–2035.

1997: The elegant spice box, cedar, oak, and red and black currant–scented and –flavored 1997 Léoville-Barton reveals surprising softness, medium body, low acidity, and ripe tannin. Drink it over the next 8 years.

1996: The impressive 1996 is a classic for the vintage. Though backward, it exhibits a dense ruby/purple color in addition to abundant black currant fruit intertwined with spicy oak and truffle-like scents. The wine is brilliantly made, full-bodied, and tightly structured with plenty of muscle and outstanding concentration and purity. It should turn out to be a long-lived Léoville-Barton and somewhat of a sleeper of the vintage. However, patience will be required. Anticipated maturity: 2007–2030.

1995: Somewhat closed and reticent after bottling but still impressive, the 1995 possesses a dark ruby/purple color and an oaky nose with classic scents of cassis, vanilla, cedar, and spice. Dense and medium- to full-bodied, with softer tannin and more accessibility than the 1996 but not quite the packed and stacked effect on the palate, the 1995 is an outstanding textbook St.-Julien that will handsomely repay extended cellaring. Anticipated maturity: 2004–2025.

Past Glories: 1994 (90+), 1990 (94+), 1989 (90), 1986 (92), 1985 (92), 1982 (93+), 1975 (90), 1961 (92), 1959 (94), 1953 (95), 1949 (95), 1948 (96), 1945 (98)

LÉOVILLE-LAS CASES (ST.-JULIEN)

Year		
2000	EEE	(94–96)
1999	EEE	91
1998	EEE	93
1997	EEE	90
1996	EEE	98+
1995	EEE	95

My visit to Léoville-Las Cases in January 2001 was not an easy one, because it was the first time in 22 years that Michel Delon, the "Lion of Saint-Julien," was not present to lead the tasting. His death in July 2000 is profoundly lamented. The estate is in the capable hands of his son, Jean-Hubert.

Léoville-Las Cases is unquestionably one of the great names and wines of Bordeaux. Since 1982, it has consistently been of first growth quality, with some vintages superior to several first growths. The wines are generally deeply colored, tannic, big, and concentrated, and potentially long-lived. Over recent years, they have also exhibited both power and elegance in a harmonious style. These traditional St.-Juliens require patience, as they are ready to drink only after 10–15 years' aging. If the 1855 classification were revised, Léoville-Las Cases would surely receive serious support for first growth status.

2000: A sleek, super-concentrated, pure Léoville-Las Cases has once again been produced. Yields were approximately 47 hectoliters per hectare, and only 35% of the crop was utilized in the grand vin. This wine is dominated by its high proportion of Cabernet Sauvignon (76.14%, with the balance being 14.4% Cabernet Franc and the rest Merlot). Opaque black/purple, with a reticent but promising bouquet of crème de cassis, blackberry and cherry liqueur, vanilla, minerals, and spice box, this medium- to full-bodied, rich 2000 explodes on the back of the palate with high tannin as well as zesty acidity. A backward *vin de garde*, it will require 8–10 years of cellaring. Jean-Hubert Delon thinks his 2000 will match the prodigious wines produced in 1996, 1990, 1986, and 1982, although the style is different. As great as it is, I am not convinced it will achieve the majestic stature of those wines, but time will tell. Anticipated maturity: 2010–2040.

1999: A seductive, dark ruby/purple offering, the 1999 exhibits aromas of sweet black fruits intertwined with cedar, lead pencil, and vanilla. Medium- to full-bodied, with low acidity, it is forward, precocious, and already delicious. This seductive effort will drink well, atypically, at a young age. Anticipated maturity: 2003–2015.

1998: The 1998 has turned out to be one of the vintage's superb Médocs. It boasts an opaque black/purple color as well as a classic Léoville-Las Cases display of lead pencil, gorgeously pure black raspberries and cherries, smoke, and graphite. A classic entry on the palate reveals firm tannin, medium to full body, superb concentration and purity, and a totally symmetrical mouth-feel. This wine is a worthy successor to such classic Las Cases vintages as 1988, 1995, and 1996. Anticipated maturity: 2006–2025.

1997: A star of the vintage, this classy, cedary, black currant and sweet cherry–scented, dense ruby-colored Las Cases exhibits a beautiful dosage of new oak, medium body, expansive, sweet, concentrated flavors, plenty of glycerin, and exceptional purity. For a Léoville-Las Cases it is low in acidity and already delicious. Anticipated maturity: now–2016.

1996: Having previously rated it nearly perfect in the *en primeur* tastings, I was apprehensive of a letdown about tasting the 1996 Léoville-Las Cases once it had been bottled, but that concern was quickly dismissed once I put my nose in the glass. A profound Léoville-Las Cases, it is one of the great modern-day wines of Bordeaux, rivaling what the estate has done in vintages such as 1990, 1986, and 1982. The 1996's hallmark remains a *sur-maturité* (over-ripeness) of the Cabernet Sauvignon grape. Yet the wine has retained its intrinsic classicism, symmetry, and profound potential for complexity and elegance. The black/purple color is followed by a spectacular nose of cassis, cherry liqueur, toast, and minerals. It is powerful and rich on the attack, with beautifully integrated tannin and massive concentration yet no hint of heaviness or disjointedness. As this wine sits in the glass it grows in stature and richness. It is a remarkable, seamless, palate-staining, and extraordinarily elegant wine—the quintessential St.-Julien made in the shadow of its next-door neighbor, Latour. Despite the sweetness of the tannin, I would recommend cellaring this wine for 7–8 years. Anticipated maturity: 2007–2035.

1995: If it were not for the prodigious 1996, everyone would be concentrating on getting their hands on a few bottles of the fabulous 1995 Léoville-Las Cases, which is one of the vintage's great success stories. The wine boasts an opaque ruby/purple color and exceptionally pure, beautifully knit aromas of black fruits, minerals, vanilla, and spice. On the attack it is staggeringly rich, yet displays more noticeable tannin than its younger sibling. Exceptionally ripe cassis fruit, the judicious use of toasty new oak, and a thrilling mineral character intertwined with the high quality of fruit routinely obtained by Las Cases make this a compelling effort. There is probably nearly as much tannin as in the 1996, but it is not as perfectly sweet as in the 1996. The finish is incredibly long in this classic. Only 35% of the harvest was of sufficient quality for the 1995 Léoville-Las Cases. Anticipated maturity: 2005–2025.

Past Glories: 1994 (93), 1993 (90), 1992 (90), 1990 (96), 1989 (91), 1988 (92), 1986 (98+), 1985 (93), 1983 (91), 1982 (100), 1978 (90), 1975 (92+)

LÉOVILLE-POYFERRÉ (ST.-JULIEN)

2000	EEE	(92–95)
1999	E	89
1998	E	88
1997	D	87
1996	E	93
1995	E	90+

Of the three Léovilles of St.-Julien, Poyferré is the least well known and the most undervalued, most certainly because of its irregular track record since 1961. However, things have changed over recent years, with the modernization of the cellars, the making of a second wine, the use of more new oak for the *élevage*, and the increasingly watchful eyes of coproprietor Didier Cuvelier, who brought in Michel Rolland as a consultant. It is now a wine well worth consumers' attention.

2000: Made in the style of the 1990, with more freshness and less of a roasted character, this fabulous effort boasts a saturated blue/purple color as well as thick-tasting blackberry and black currant fruit intermixed with licorice. There is true opulence in addition to gorgeous levels of fruit, glycerin, and extract. The tannin is more elevated than in the 1990, but the 2000 is a sensational Poyferré. Anticipated maturity: 2005–2030.

1999: Dark ruby/purple, with an overripe nose of black fruits intermixed with minerals, smoke, and toasty new oak, this deep, voluptuously textured wine possesses low acidity, a fat, fleshy mid-palate, and a surprisingly long finish. It could easily develop into an outstanding St.-Julien with early accessibility. Anticipated maturity: 2003–2016.

1998: The dark ruby-colored, medium-bodied 1998 offers aromas of underbrush, black currants, cherries, minerals, and vanilla. While sweet, rich, and stylish, it lacks the depth necessary to merit an outstanding score. Drink it over the next 12–14 years.

1997: Medium ruby-colored with purple nuances, this ripe St.-Julien exhibits delicious, sweet cassis fruit mixed with high-quality toasty oak. The wine possesses fat, accessible fruit flavors, attractive glycerin, and no hardness. Neither big nor muscular, it is a medium-bodied, elegant, savory, charming, and delicious effort to be enjoyed over the next 4–5 years.

1996: This fabulous 1996 was tasted three times from bottle, and it is, along with the 2000, the finest wine produced by this estate since their blockbuster 1990. Medium- to full-bodied, with a saturated black/purple color, the nose offers notes of cedar, jammy black fruits, smoke, truffles, and subtle new oak. In the mouth there is impressive fruit extraction, a tannic structure, and a classic display of power and finesse. The longer it sat in the glass, the more impressive the wine became. Backward and massive in terms of its extract and richness, this should prove to be a sensational Léoville-Poyferré for drinking over the next 30 years. Anticipated maturity: 2007–2028.

1995: While not as backward as the 1996, the opaque purple 1995 is a tannic, unevolved, dense, concentrated wine that will require 4–5 more years of cellaring. The 1995 exhibits toast, black currant, mineral, and subtle tobacco in its complex yet youthful aromatics. Powerful, dense, concentrated cassis and blueberry flavors might be marginally softer than in the 1996, but there is still plenty of grip and structure to this big wine. Anticipated maturity: 2005–2030.

Past Glories: 1990 (96), 1983 (90), 1982 (94), 1900 (93)

LEZONGARS (PREMIÈRES CÔTES DE BORDEAUX)

2000	**B**	**(87–88)**

2000: Another Thunevin project, this dense ruby/purple 2000 displays a velvety texture, layers of red and black currant fruit, power, richness, harmony, and depth but little complexity. An excellent value as well as a sleeper of the vintage, it should drink well for 4–5 years. The French would call it *un vin de plaisir.*

LILIAN-LADOUYS (ST.-ESTÈPHE)

1997	**C**	**?**
1996	**C**	**86**
1995	**C**	**81**

1997: Tasted three times with similar notes, this wine reveals a musty, damp cardboard smell that is off-putting.

1996: Performing better than the 1995, Lilian Ladouys's 1996 reveals a deep ruby color and earthy, mineral, cherry, and black currant aromas with oaky notes in the background. This medium-bodied, tannic wine comes across as well balanced, monolithic, and generally well made and ageworthy. Anticipated maturity: now–2012.

1995: Austere, tightly knit, and excessively tannic and structured for the amount of fruit, this dark ruby-colored wine is muted aromatically. It appears to be all structure and grip in the mouth. Additional fruit and charm may be there, but neither was poking its head through the wine's hardness when I last tasted it.

LA LOUVIÈRE (PESSAC-LÉOGNAN)

2000	**C**	**(89–91)**
1999	**C**	**87**
1998	**C**	**88**
1997	**C**	**83**
1996	**C**	**87**
1995	**C**	**87**

This estate owned by André Lurton produces one of the most consistently well made wines of Pessac-Léognan, as well as one of the better values of this appellation, in both red and white. While unclassified, La Louvière is superior to many of the crus classés. In particular, recent vintages have been on a quality level equivalent to a Médoc fourth growth.

2000: The 2000 is the finest La Louvière since the 1990 and 1988. A complex, smoky tobacco, earth, black currant, and cherry jam–scented nose is followed by a medium- to full-bodied, supple-textured, voluptuous, fat, fleshy, low-acid wine. It will no doubt firm up and age nicely. Anticipated maturity: 2003–2016.

1999: Exhibiting aromas of fruitcake, spice box, tobacco, and red currants, the more herbaceous, medium-bodied, soft, easygoing 1999 does not possess the stuffing of the 1998. Nevertheless, it is delicious and complex. Anticipated maturity: now–2010.

1998: An excellent dark ruby/purple effort, the 1998 offers a classic scorched earth, smoky, black cherry, and currant-scented bouquet. Medium-bodied, with sweet tannin, well-integrated acidity, and excellent flavor as well as richness, it is a complex, textbook Graves. Anticipated maturity: now–2014.

1997: The 1997 is more evolved than the 1996, with low acidity and intense black cherry and cassis fruit intertwined with smoky, toasty, new oak scents. Fleshy and forward, with medium body and rich fruitiness, it should drink well for 7–8 years.

1996: The dark ruby/purple, ripe 1996 exhibits an excellent combination of sweet black currant fruit meshed with notes of Provençal olives, licorice, smoke, and toasty new oak. With medium to full body, excellent sweetness, and a layered, concentrated finish, this wine should be at its finest between 2003–2015.

1995: An exceptionally seductive, open-knit 1995, La Louvière's telltale tobacco, smoky, leafy, herb-tinged red and black currant fruit jumps from the glass of this aromatic wine. Exhibiting excellent ripeness, a supple texture, medium body, and a delicious, roasted fruitiness, this textbook Graves can be drunk now or over the next 7–8 years.

Past Glories: 1990 (red) (90)

LUSSEAU (ST.-EMILION)

2000	C	(90–91)
1998	C	88
1997	C	87
1996	C	86
1995	C	86

Laurent Lusseau, the cellar manager for Château Monbousquet, produces this underrated, very fine limited-production wine.

2000: The finest Lusseau to date, the 2000 is a joyous, fat, succulent, in-your-face St.-Emilion with abundant quantities of fruit and glycerin. However, it does not possess substantial structure or tannin, so consumption during its first 7–8 years of life is warranted.

1998: The 1998 Lusseau is a sexy, smoky, hedonistically styled wine with jammy black cherry fruit infused with toasty notes. Medium-bodied and soft, with copious quantities of fruit, this low-acid, lusty St.-Emilion will be admired for its open-knit, consumer-friendly style. Anticipated maturity: now–2010.

1997: Superior to the 1996, the 1997 exhibits a denser, more saturated color, along with a jammy, black raspberry and berry-scented nose intertwined with earth and spice aromas. With copious quantities of fruit, medium to full body, and excellent purity, it is a sexy, low-acid St.-Emilion to drink now and over the next 6–7 years.

1996: The medium-bodied 1996 offers black cherry fruit and currants in both the aromatics and flavors. Attractive and soft, with a plump richness, this friendly wine should drink well for 2–3 years.

1995: This Merlot-dominated wine offers an attractive cranberry, cherry, smoky nose, and a medium-bodied, lush, richly fruity, succulent style with plenty of hedonistic appeal. It should be drunk over the next 1–2 years.

Other vintage tasted: 1999 (85–87)

LYNCH-BAGES (PAUILLAC)

2000	EE	(94–96)
1999	E	90
1998	E	89
1997	D	86

1996	E	91+
1995	E	90

After a slump between 1971 and 1979, Lynch-Bages has produced an uninterrupted series of fine wines, largely because of the immense accomplishment of Jean-Michel Cazes. Today nobody would argue that this wine's present quality is akin to second growth. Lynch-Bages is generally a robust, rich, opulent Pauillac, combining the character and class of the top efforts of this appellation.

2000: A prodigious Lynch-Bages, the finest wine to emerge from this popular château since the 1989 and 1990, the 2000 exhibits a saturated purple color as well as exploding aromatics of new saddle leather, crème de cassis, creosote, truffles, and oak. A sweet entry reveals a full-bodied, concentrated, succulent style with tremendous class and charm. This mouth-filling, lush, super-concentrated, gorgeously pure Lynch-Bages stains the palate. It will undoubtedly firm up during its barrel aging, or after bottling, but it offers a hedonistic mouthful of massive Pauillac at present. Anticipated maturity: 2004–2025. For statisticians, it is a blend of 71% Cabernet Sauvignon, 16% Merlot, 11% Cabernet Franc, and 2% Petit Verdot, aged in 70% new French oak.

1999: This wine is reminiscent of the low-acid, up-front, fleshy 1985 Lynch-Bages. A deep ruby/purple color is accompanied by sweet, fat, crème de cassis aromas and flavors intermixed with leather, underbrush, and cedar. Displaying a gorgeous texture, full body, and a precocious, sexy, low-acid personality, it will drink well upon release and over the following 15 years.

1998: Made somewhat in the style of the 1988, this austere, medium-weight Lynch-Bages reveals notes of new saddle leather, tobacco, olives, and black fruits. Although not a big, concentrated Pauillac, it is graceful, elegant, with character and style. Anticipated maturity: 2003–2016.

1997: The good news is that this tastes like Lynch-Bages, with jammy black currant fruit intermixed with cedar wood, herbs, spice, and pepper. However, it is a lighter-styled yet friendly Lynch-Bages with creamy new oak, low acidity, and a medium-bodied, attractive albeit superficial appeal. Drink it over the next 3–4 years.

1996: Lynch-Bages has turned out an outstanding 1996 that is less forward than the 1990 or 1995, and built along the lines of the tannic, blockbuster 1989. It offers an opaque purple color and outstanding aromatics consisting of dried herbs, tobacco, cassis, and smoky oak. Full-bodied and classic in its proportions, this dense, chewy, pure Lynch-Bages will have considerable longevity. Anticipated maturity: 2005–2025.

1995: On the three occasions I tasted the 1995 out of bottle it came across in an elegant, restrained, 1985/1953 Lynch-Bages style. While attractive and soft, with obvious tannin in the background, the 1995 is not made in the blockbuster style of the 1996, 1990, 1989, or 1986. Deep ruby-colored, with an evolved nose of sweet, smoky, earthy, black currant fruit, this fleshy, round, seductive, fat and fruity Lynch-Bages should drink well young, yet age for 15 years. Anticipated maturity: now–2015.

Past Glories: 1990 (93), 1989 (95+), 1988 (90), 1986 (90), 1985 (91), 1982 (94), 1970 (91), 1961 (94), 1959 (94), 1955 (92), 1953 (90), 1952 (91), 1945 (92)

LYNCH-MOUSSAS (PAUILLAC)

2000	C	(86–88)
1999	C	87
1998	C	87
1997	C	81
1996	C	86
1995	C	86

Lynch-Moussas is owned and controlled by the Castéja family, who operate the well-known Bordeaux *négociant* business Borie-Manoux. The wines of this estate were generally light and simple; but vintages from 1995 onward have been very well made, with the 1998 and 2000 being the finest yet produced by this traditional underperformer.

2000: One of the finest offerings from Lynch-Moussas, the 2000 offers a deep purple color as well as a classic nose of crème de cassis, spice box, and cedar. Like many of its peers, it possesses abundant sweetness and opulence, low acidity, and a long, moderately tannic finish. Anticipated maturity: now–2016.

1999: While this dark ruby/purple, medium-weight Lynch-Moussas is supple, straightforward, and charming, it does not possess much weight or substance. Enjoy it over its first 10–12 years of life.

1998: One of the finest Lynch-Moussas yet produced, along with the 2000, the 1998 exhibits a deep ruby/purple color in addition to a sweet nose of cassis (not dissimilar from their nearby neighbor Grand-Puy-Lacoste), medium body, fine purity, and admirable harmony. Not a blockbuster, it will provide delicious drinking now and last for 12–15 years.

1997: The 1997 is a lean, elegant, light-bodied, short wine with some sweet fruit. It appears it will always remain a foursquare, monolithic wine with barely sufficient depth. Anticipated maturity: now–2007.

1996: A very good example of Lynch-Moussas, the 1996's saturated dark ruby/plum color is accompanied by textbook aromas of black currants, smoky new oak, minerals, and tobacco. Well made, with moderate tannin, excellent purity, and a medium-bodied, ripe, melted asphalt–flavored finish, this seductive wine should drink well at a young age. Anticipated maturity: 2004–2012.

1995: After bottling, the 1995 Lynch-Moussas is a very good wine, with a dark ruby color, spicy, cedary, cassis fruit in its moderately endowed nose, good ripeness and flesh on the attack, and a dry, clean, moderately tannic finish with grip and delineation. Anticipated maturity: now–2016.

LYNSOLENCE (ST.-EMILION)

2000	E	(90–91)
1999	E	88
1998	E	89

This St.-Emilion garage wine is made from a five-acre parcel of 35-year-old Merlot vines planted on sandy, gravelly soils (shared by neighboring Monbousquet and Valandraud) and tiny yields of less than 30 hectoliters per hectare. The wines undergo over a month of *cuvaison*, and age in 100% new oak. The annual production averages 650 cases. The debut vintage was 1998.

2000: A deep ruby/purple color is accompanied by sweet scents of black cherries, blackberries, vanillin, minerals, and a touch of scorched earth. This medium- to full-bodied, plump, opulently styled St.-Emilion initially comes across as a fruit bomb, then settles down to reveal surprising structure, definition, and length. With outstanding purity and a long mouthfeel, it will be at its finest between 2003–2015.

1999: Dark ruby/purple, with an excellent nose of black and red fruits (cherries and raspberries), this deep, rich, low-acid, concentrated wine is foursquare, but it possesses plenty of depth, concentration, and texture. If it develops more complexity, the score should rise. Anticipated maturity: now–2010.

1998: A dark ruby/purple color is followed by a jammy bouquet of black fruits, and a medium- to full-bodied, straightforward, juicy, succulent, fleshy wine. There is good structure under all the fat and fruit, but it does not possess the complexity and nobility often found in these micro *cuvées*. Drink it over the next 10 years.

MAGDELAINE (ST.-EMILION)

2000	E	(90–91)
1999	E	88
1998	E	92
1997	D	87
1996	E	88
1995	E	91

2000: A lacy, graceful, restrained offering, the 2000 Magdelaine is the epitome of elegance and delicacy. The deep ruby color is accompanied by sweet cherry/plum aromas, a ripe attack, medium body, and poised, exceptionally well delineated flavors. The tannin is moderate but ripe. Anticipated maturity: 2003–2016.

1999: A success for the vintage, this dark ruby-colored 1999 exhibits toasty new oak along with fleshy, elegant black cherry scents intermixed with toast and minerals. Spicy, medium-bodied, soft, and lightly tannic, it will be at its best before 2014.

1998: Undoubtedly the finest effort from Magdelaine in many years, the deep saturated ruby-colored 1998 offers up concentrated, jammy black cherry as well as subtle vanilla aromas. On the palate, it is full-bodied, opulent, and ripe, with outstanding concentration, purity, and moderate tannin in the finish. This Merlot-based St.-Emilion displays considerable intensity and structure. Anticipated maturity: 2005–2020.

1997: This well-made, dark ruby-colored effort exhibits good body and a roasted herb/fruit characteristic intermixed with minerals, coffee, and strawberry/cherry fruit—hallmarks of this Merlot-based St.-Emilion. The wine's low acidity, medium body, and precociousness suggest it should be consumed over the next 5–6 years.

1996: I am pleased with how the 1996 Magdelaine has turned out after bottling, as the wine appears to have more to it than I suspected. Its dark ruby color is accompanied by a telltale nose of kirsch and cherry jam, intermixed with spicy new oak. Medium-bodied, elegant, and harmonious, this wine will undoubtedly close down, but should open nicely, offering a stylish, classic St.-Emilion for drinking between 2003–2015.

1995: A terrific effort from Magdelaine, the 1995 possesses a saturated ruby/purple color and a sweet, kirsch, and black cherry–scented nose with notes of sexy toast and vanilla. The wine is ripe, rich, and full-bodied, with outstanding intensity, purity, and equilibrium. It is a beautiful, harmonious, long, surprisingly seductive and accessible Magdelaine that will have many admirers. Anticipated maturity: now–2020.

Past Glories: 1990 (92), 1989 (90), 1961 (92), 1959 (90)

MALARTIC-LAGRAVIÈRE (PESSAC-LÉOGNAN)

2000	D	(90–92)
1999	D	89
1998	D	89
1997	C	88
1996	C	76
1995	C	76

Under the inspired leadership of Alfred-Alexandre Bonnie and his wife, Michelle, who bought Malartic in 1997, this estate is now making some of the finest wines of Pessac-Léognan. A complete makeover of the château, *cuvérie*, and aging cellars have resulted in a space-age winemaking facility, and after strong efforts in 1997 and 1998, Malartic-Lagravière has turned in elegant, concentrated, rich wines in 1999 and 2000, the latter its finest success to date.

2000: The finest Malartic-Lagravière produced in 40 years, this exquisite wine boasts classic aromas of tobacco, black currants, smoke, and earth, medium- to full-bodied, pure, seductive flavors, a velvety texture, terrific definition, and a real palate presence without a great deal of weight. This is a sexy, complex, superb wine to drink young, but it is capable of lasting 15+ years. Anticipated maturity: 2003–2018.

1999: Another excellent effort from this property, the dark ruby/purple, medium-weight 1999 offers earthy root vegetable aromas intermixed with cassis and cherries. Stylish and re-strained, revealing good weight, as well as the region's renowned scorched earth/melted as-phalt notes, it will drink well during its first 10–12 years of life.

1998: The 1998 represents a breakthrough effort for this property. The color is a dense, dark ruby/purple, and the nose reveals stylish, sweet black currant fruit intermixed with earth, minerals, licorice, and spice box. The wine is medium-bodied, with ripe tannin, no hard edges, and a beautifully knit, concentrated finish that lasts over 30 seconds. Anticipated ma-turity: now–2015.

1997: Undoubtedly a sleeper of the vintage, this exceptionally charming, complex, elegant 1997 is not big, weighty, or powerful, yet it offers cedar, roasted herb, and sweet plum/cherry fruit in its aromas and flavors. The taster is seduced by the wine's silky, seamless texture, gor-geous aromatics, low acidity, and lovely levels of fruit. It will not make old bones, but who can resist it now? Enjoy it over the next 4–5 years.

1996: The unsubstantial 1996 reveals a feeble light ruby color. It offers plenty of new oak and moderate cherry fruit in the nose, medium body, and a pleasant, straightforward, one-dimensional finish. The wine possesses tannin and structure, but not much extract or rich-ness. Anticipated maturity: now–2010.

1995: There is excessive toasty new oak in this medium-bodied, straightforward, monolithic example. Soft plum and cherry fruit are present, but the wine is too woody and tannic.

MALESCOT ST.-EXUPÉRY (MARGAUX)

2000	E	(92–94)
1999	E	90
1998	E	90
1997	D	82
1996	D	90
1995	D	90

This is a another Margaux property that has returned to form after a largely disappointing pe-riod during the 1960s, 1970s, and 1980s. Since the beginning of the 1990s, the wines of Malescot are much richer and more intense than previously, with the recent vintages being very good to excellent. In particular, the 2000 looks to be a great success.

2000: This is the most concentrated and complete Malescot St.-Exupéry since their fabulous 1961. It is the quintessential model of elegance, finesse, and lightness, but the flavors are in-tense—a difficult combination to achieve. This dense/opaque purple wine offers a perfumed, floral, blackberry, cassis nose with mineral and new oak subtlety displayed in the back-ground. In the mouth, it is authoritatively flavorful and intense but does not appear to have a great deal of weight. Yet there is depth, length, and compelling harmony. This brilliant wine is a terrific model for why Bordeaux produces the world's greatest wines, combining intensity of flavor and power without heaviness, something virtually impossible to duplicate anywhere else in the world. Anticipated maturity: 2003–2020.

1999: Dense ruby/purple, with a friendly, open-knit perfume of red and black fruits, smoke, minerals, and vanilla, this 1999 offers a velvety texture, medium body, and lovely fruit as well as purity. It will have many friends when released next year. Anticipated maturity: now–2014.

1998: A classic, this 1998 combines elegance with lovely textured, rich flavors of black cher-ries and currants, resulting in a quintessential Bordeaux unlike any other wine produced in the world. The wine possesses an ethereal lightness, layers of fruit, and a diaphanous frame-work. More nuances appear with each sip. Tasters will find notes of blackberries, plums, currants, tar, spice box, and minerals. A beautifully etched wine, it will be at its finest between 2003–2017.

1997: Straightforward, soft, diluted, elegant but undernourished, this medium-bodied 1997 should be consumed over the next 4–5 years.

1996: This impressively constructed wine offers a saturated deep ruby/purple color, followed by elegant aromas of berry fruit intermixed with tobacco, flowers, and vanilla. It is layered and medium- to full-bodied, with outstanding purity and fruit extraction. Although deep, rich, and powerful for a wine from this estate, it has not lost any of its elegance or potential complexity. Anticipated maturity: 2006–2025.

1995: This wine may merit an outstanding rating. It offers a classic Margaux combination of elegance and richness. Medium-bodied, with delicate, beautifully ripe black currant and floral aromas that compete with subtle new oak, the 1995 Malescot hits the palate with a lovely concoction of fruit, nicely integrated tannin and acidity, and a stylish, graceful feel. This quintessentially elegant Bordeaux should continue to improve in bottle. A beauty! Anticipated maturity: now–2018.

Past Glories: 1990 (90), 1961 (92), 1959 (90)

CHÂTEAU MARGAUX (MARGAUX)

2000	EEE	(96–98)
1999	EEE	94
1998	EEE	91+
1997	EE	90
1996	EEE	99
1995	EEE	95

The Mentzelopoulos family, who bought this property in 1977, needed only one vintage to produce a wine worthy of this estate's premier grand cru status. Today, Margaux is consistently topflight. The style is one of opulent richness, with a deep, complex bouquet of ripe black currants, spicy vanilla, and violets. Today the estate is owned jointly by the Mentzelopoulos and Agnelli families, and managed by Paul Pontallier.

2000: For Paul Pontallier, the 2000 is the most tannic and concentrated in polyphenols of any Château Margaux in the last 40 years. A blend of 80% Cabernet Sauvignon, 10% Merlot, 7% Petit Verdot, and 3% Cabernet Franc (nearly identical to the 1996), this wine represents only 40% of the production. There is remarkable ripeness to the tannin, giving it a contradictory feel. It is a traditionally styled Bordeaux with plenty of structure, tannin, and weight, but the sweetness of the tannin brings it into the modern-day school of winemaking. Notes of blueberries, crème de cassis, and flowers are present in this medium- to full-bodied Margaux. A touch of licorice, subtle new oak, and a savory, expansive, full-bodied palate are brilliantly displayed in this pure, symmetrical effort. Surprisingly refreshing acidity gives the wine a zesty delineation that the very ripe years (i.e., 1982, 1983, 1989, and 1990) lack. Pontallier thinks this may be the greatest Margaux yet made under the Mentzelopoulus administration, "a new reference." A fabulous wine, to be sure, I will defer judgment given the enviable record of superlative wines made over the last 20 years. Could it really be superior to the 1996, 1990, 1986, 1985, 1983, and 1982?

1999: Approximately 38% of the production made it into the 1999 Château Margaux. A dense ruby/purple offering, it possesses extraordinary balance as well as a classic, seductive bouquet of blackberries, truffles, licorice, and smoke. A quintessential Margaux, this seductive, sexy, yet beautifully balanced effort displays impeccably integrated acidity, tannin, and alcohol. It will be atypically delicious young, yet will age for 2–3 decades. Readers should think of the 1999 as a lighter version of the 1990. Anticipated maturity: 2004–2025.

1998: The 1998 Margaux is taking on a character reminiscent of the 1988 vintage. The color is a dense ruby/purple. The wine is tannic and austere but elegant, with notes of asphalt, blackberries, acacia flowers, and sweet, toasty oak. Subtle, rich, nicely textured, and medium-bodied, it is built for the long haul. Anticipated maturity: 2006–2030.

1997: Undoubtedly a success for the vintage, this immensely charming, dark ruby/purple wine exhibits floral, black currant, and smoky, toasty oak aromas. There is admirable richness, excellent ripeness, not a great deal of density, or the superb concentration found in such renowned vintages as 1996, 1995, and 1990, but plenty of finesse, suppleness, and character. It can be drunk young or cellared for 12 years.

1996: The 1996 Château Margaux is undoubtedly one of the great classics produced under the Mentzelopoulos regime. In many respects, it is the quintessential Château Margaux, as well as the paradigm for this estate, combining measured power, extraordinary elegance, and admirable complexity. The color is opaque purple. The wine offers extraordinarily pure notes of blackberries, cassis, toast, and flowers, gorgeous sweetness, a seamless personality, and full body, with nothing out of place. The final blend (85% Cabernet Sauvignon, 10% Merlot, and the rest Petit Verdot and Cabernet Franc) contains the highest percentage of Cabernet Sauvignon since the 1986. Both Corinne Mentzelopoulos and administrator Paul Pontallier claim they prefer it to the 1995, which is saying something, given how fabulous that wine has turned out. When tasted side by side, the 1996 does taste more complete and longer, though just as backward. My instincts suggest this wine will shut down, but at present it is open-knit, tasting like a recently bottled wine. The fruit is exceptionally sweet and pure, and there are layers of flavor in the mouth. Is it capable of surpassing the quality of the 1995, 1990, 1986, 1983, and 1982? Time will tell. Personally, I prefer the opulence and viscosity of the 1990 from a purely hedonistic standpoint, but I do believe the 1996 will develop an extraordinary perfume, and possess the same level of richness as the most concentrated vintages Margaux has produced. It is one of the strongest candidates for the wine of the vintage. Anticipated maturity: 2005–2040.

1995: The 1995 has continued to flesh out after bottling, developing into a great classic. The color is opaque ruby/purple. The nose offers aromas of licorice and sweet, smoky new oak intermixed with jammy black fruits, licorice, and minerals. The wine is medium- to full-bodied, with extraordinary richness, fabulous equilibrium, and hefty tannin in the finish. In spite of its large size and youthfulness, this wine is user-friendly and accessible. This is a thrilling Margaux that will always be softer and more evolved than its broader-shouldered sibling, the 1996. How fascinating it will be to follow the evolution of both of these vintages over the next half century. Anticipated maturity: 2005–2040.

Past Glories: 1994 (92), 1990 (100), 1986 (96+), 1985 (94), 1983 (96), 1982 (98+), 1981 (91), 1979 (93), 1978 (92), 1961 (93), 1953 (98), 1947 (92), 1928 (98), 1900 (100)

MARJOSSE (BORDEAUX)

2000	B	88

This estate is owned by Pierre Lurton, the manager of Cheval Blanc. The wines—whether red or white—are always a reliable value. The 2000 is the finest Marjosse yet produced.

2000: A blend of 60% Merlot, 30% Cabernet Sauvignon, and 10% Cabernet Franc, the 2000 Marjosse's gorgeous deep ruby/purple is followed by a perfumed, sweet, smoky bouquet revealing overripe cherries, plums, and currants. Deep, velvety-textured, and low in acidity, this plump, hedonistic generic Bordeaux will drink beautifully for 3–4 years. There are nearly 10,000 cases of this sleeper of the vintage.

Other vintages tasted: 1999 (81–83), 1998 (85–86)

MAROJALLIA (MARGAUX)

2000	EE	91–93
1999	EE	92

This wine is a creation of Murielle Thunevin, the wife of St.-Emilion's revolutionary and highly influential wine-maker Jean-Luc Thunevin, produced in Margaux's Arsac commune from a 7.5-acre vineyard. Consumers should also keep an eye on Marojallia's second wine, Clos Margalène, a very good value.

2000: A classy, elegant, intensely flavored effort. There are approximately 420 cases of this 50% Merlot/50% Cabernet Sauvignon blend. Medium-bodied, moderately tannic, and stylish, it offers aromas and flavors of black raspberries, graphite, licorice, and currants. In the mouth, it is precise, with a sense of nobility to its delicate, refreshing, vibrant personality. Anticipated maturity: 2005–2018.

1999: The debut release (a blend of 75% Cabernet Sauvignon and 25% Merlot) has fleshed out beautifully during its *élevage* and is unquestionably of second or third growth quality. It easily merits an outstanding rating. There are 600 cases of this Margaux *vin de garage*. Rich, with pure black currant fruit mixed with vanilla, licorice, and mineral notes, this medium- to full-bodied 1999 possesses low acidity, stunning concentration, and a seamless, multilayered personality. Anticipated maturity: 2005–2025.

Other wines tasted: Clos Margalène 2000 (87–88), 1999 (85–87)

MARQUIS DE TERME (MARGAUX)

2000	D	(87–88)
1999	D	(78–80?)

2000: An opaque purple color is accompanied by a burly, medium- to full-bodied Margaux with attractive notions of smoky oak, flowers, and black fruits, fine ripeness as well as purity, and a compressed but powerful finish. Anticipated maturity: 2004–2018.

1999: Two samples tasted revealed thin, diluted fruit, medium body, good color, and a firm finish. It will be interesting to retaste this wine.

MARSAU (CÔTES-DE-FRANCS)

2000	C	(90–91)
1999	C	88
1998	C	87

From his estate in Côtes-de-Francs proprietor Jean-Marie Chadronnier produces 100% Merlot wines that consistently qualify as sleepers of their respective vintage. These Pomerol look-alikes sell for reasonable prices. Unfortunately, availabilities are small.

2000: A dead ringer for a Pomerol, this wine boasts a saturated ruby/purple color as well as sweet crème de cassis, black cherry, smoke, and oak aromas. Is it the Pétrus of the Côtes-de-Francs? Lush, medium- to full-bodied, and opulent, this sleeper of the vintage should be drunk during its first 7–8 years of life.

1999: With plenty of glycerin as well as low acidity, this lusty, deep ruby/purple-colored 1999 offers gorgeous levels of fruit presented in a medium-bodied, pure, impeccably well-made style. It will drink well for a decade.

1998: A deep ruby/purple color is accompanied by sweet aromas of caramel, mocha, and black cherry liqueur. This medium-bodied, supple offering is reminiscent of a high-class Pomerol or St.-Emilion. Its abundant quantities of Merlot give it its lush, hedonistic appeal. Drink it over the next decade.

LA MAURIANE (PUISSEGUIN-ST.-EMILION)

1999	C	87
1998	C	87

This wine is made with the consulting assistance of St.-Emilion's ubiquitous Jean-Luc Thunevin.

1999: Fat, lush, fleshy, herb-tinged black cherry flavors mixed with smoke and spice result in an easygoing, mouth-filling St.-Emilion meant for early consumption. Enjoy it over the next 1–2 years.

1998: A soft, attractive spice box, cedar, herb, black cherry, and vanilla-scented bouquet is accompanied by lush, ripe, up-front flavors. This well-made 1998 represents good value. It is meant to be consumed over the next 3–4 years.

Other vintage tasted: 2000 (86–87)

MAZERIS (CANON-FRONSAC)

1998	**C**	**87**
1997	**C**	**85**
1996	**C**	**84**

The wines of Mazeris usually present aromas of black raspberry and mineral, are backward with considerable structure, and are meant for long-term aging.

1998: This 1998 reveals the distinctive black raspberry, earthy, *terroir*-driven character typical of Mazeris. Loaded with gritty tannin, it displays a dusty, rich, backward personality, an opaque purple color, and admirable structure and power. Give it 1–2 years of bottle age, and drink it over the following decade.

1997: The 1997 is significantly better than the 1996, offering excellent fruit, medium body, good ripeness, and a dark ruby/purple color. It should drink well for 8 years.

1996: The 1996 exhibits the distinctive raspberry/black fruit character typical of this estate along with considerable minerality. Also, Mazeris's unevolved style and structure give this 1996 more leanness and aggressive tannin than usual. Potentially, the wine could dry out, but it is above average and well made in a medium-bodied, muscular, tannic style. Anticipated maturity: now–2007.

Other vintage tasted: 1999 (83–85)

MAZEYRES (POMEROL)

1999	**C**	**85**
1998	**C**	**88**
1997	**C**	**72**
1996	**C**	**74**

1999: A straightforward, competent effort, the dark ruby-colored 1999 exhibits notes of herbs, strawberry and berry fruit, a soft texture, and spicy oak. Consume it over the next 7–8 years.

1998: One of the finest efforts Mazeyres has yet produced, the deep ruby/purple 1998 offers attractive, intense aromas of mocha, black cherries, and coffee. Plush, dense, and medium- to full-bodied, with no hard edges, it is an excellent candidate for 8–12 years of drinkability.

1997: Light-bodied but surprisingly tannic, this herbaceous, vegetal-tasting wine is short and uninteresting.

1996: Overt aromas of green pepper combined with herbaceousness in the mouth are the undoing of this lean, diluted, medium ruby-colored wine. Drink it over the next 4–5 years.

MEYNEY (ST.-ESTÈPHE)

1997	**C**	**(78–80)**
1996	**C**	**85**

1997: I tasted the 1997 Meyney only once, but it was extremely diluted, light, and soft, with little character or depth. It appears to be a commercial, one-dimensional effort designed to be consumed in its first 5–7 years of life.

1996: A soft, easygoing, ripe, dried herb and red currant–scented wine, this 1996 is surpris-

ingly open and evolved. It is made in a mainstream, consumer-friendly style that will have wide appeal, although it is neither concentrated nor complex. Drink it over the next 6 years.
Other vintage tasted: 1998 (82–84)
Past Glories: 1989 (90), 1986 (90), 1982 (90), 1975 (90)

MILENS (ST.-EMILION)

2000		C	(88–91)
1999		C	88
1998		C	88

St.-Emilion's well-known revolutionary Jean-Luc Thunevin oversees the vinification of Milens, a wine well worth checking out.

2000: A sleeper of the vintage, this soft, supple, low-acid 2000 possesses medium to full body, gorgeously plump black cherry and plum notes intermixed with soy and graphite, and moderate but well-integrated tannin. Drink this luscious offering over the next decade.

1999: This low-acid, expressive, smoky, black cherry and espresso-infused, medium- to full-bodied, supple St.-Emilion is already delicious. It will not make old bones, but will provide immense enjoyment over the next 6–7 years.

1998: An attractive, lush, open-knit, expansive St.-Emilion, Milens's 1998 will please both the masses and connoisseurs. It possesses a dense ruby color, full body, and attractive black cherry fruit intermixed with smoke, earth, and spice box. This lusty effort reveals consultant Jean-Luc Thunevin's style. A spicy, low-acid, corpulent finish adds to the hedonistic pleasure. Anticipated maturity: now–2008.

MILLE ROSES (HAUT-MÉDOC)

2000		C	(87–88)

From the southern Médoc, not far from Giscours, this estate has fashioned a classy, feminine, soft, richly fruity, supple-textured wine with notes of black fruits, flowers, and truffles. Medium-bodied and graceful, it should drink well for 4–5 years. It is a sleeper of the vintage.

LA MISSION-HAUT-BRION (PESSAC-LÉOGNAN)

2000		EEE	(98–100)
1999		EEE	91
1998		EEE	93+
1997		E	87
1996		EEE	89+?
1995		EEE	91

Like its neighbor Haut-Brion, La Mission-Haut-Brion is owned since 1983 by the Dillon family and managed by the articulate Jean Delmas. Until 1986, the estate went through a period of transition, but starting with 1987, it has produced a string of consistently fine wines that rank among the top Bordeaux.

2000: This is the most extraordinary La Mission made since the 1989, as well as one of the wines of the vintage. Given its structure and overall mass, it may even surpass the 1989. Analytically, it possesses more tannin than 1989, but that is not always a determining factor in a wine's enjoyment. A blend of 58% Merlot, 32% Cabernet Sauvignon, and 10% Cabernet Franc, the 2000 La Mission boasts a striking nose of black fruits, scorched earth, and minerals. It possesses an unctuous texture yet comes across as fresh in spite of its massive, full-bodied, thick, dense, profoundly deep personality. Long and rich, with high levels of melted tannin, this prodigious effort is a bigger, chewier wine than Haut-Brion, but will it develop the same surreal aromatics? I say yes—a legend in the making! Anticipated maturity: 2005–2030.

1999: Elegant, smoky, black currant and blueberry-like aromas reveal complexity, finesse, and purity. On the palate, the wine is harmonious, medium-bodied, concentrated, and stylish. In weight, style, and overall personality, this appears to be a modern-day clone of the 1962. Anticipated maturity: 2003–2020.

1998: Complex aromas of scorched earth, minerals, black fruits, lead pencil, and subtle wood accompany this classic, full-bodied La Mission. It boasts superb purity, an expansive, concentrated mid-palate, and sweet tannin in the long, muscular, yet refined finish. This superb La Mission Haut-Brion, which requires 5–6 years of cellaring, gets my nod as the finest La Mission since the super duo produced in 1989 and 1990. Anticipated maturity: 2007–2030.

1997: This dark ruby/plum wine offers a big, spicy tobacco leaf and black fruit–scented nose, more structure and tannin than its famous sibling (Haut-Brion), good depth, medium body, and enough accessibility to be consumed now (although it will improve for 4–5 years and last for a dozen or more).

1996: Much like its sibling, Haut-Brion, the 1996 La Mission-Haut-Brion was closed and backward when I last tasted it six months after bottling. It should have had sufficient time to overcome any suppression from going from wood to glass. It possesses considerable potential, and I would not be surprised to see it improve. The color is a healthy plum/purple, and the wine exhibits some of the black fruit, smoky mineral character of La Mission, but it is medium-bodied and moderately high in tannin, with notes of cedar. The finish was totally closed, with the tannin in danger of dominating the wine's fruit. This muscular, structured La Mission will take longer to come around than I originally predicted. Anticipated maturity: 2007–2020.

1995: The 1995 La Mission-Haut-Brion was tight and closed when I tasted it after bottling, not revealing as much fragrance or forwardness as it did on the multiple occasions I tasted it from cask. However, the wine is obviously high-class, exhibiting a dense ruby/purple color, and a reticent but promising nose of roasted herbs, sweet, peppery, spicy fruit, medium to full body, and admirable power, depth, and richness. As outstanding as it is, readers should not expect the 1995 to tower qualitatively over vintages such as 1994. Anticipated maturity: 2003–2020.

Past Glories: 1994 (91), 1993 (90), 1990 (95), 1989 (100), 1988 (90), 1986 (91), 1985 (92), 1982 (100), 1981 (90), 1979 (91), 1978 (96), 1975 (98), 1964 (91), 1961 (100), 1959 (100), 1955 (100), 1953 (93), 1952 (93), 1950 (95), 1949 (100), 1948 (93), 1947 (95), 1945 (94), 1929 (97)

MONBOUSQUET (ST.-EMILION)

2000	EEE	(95–98)
1999	EE	94
1998	EE	94
1997	E	90
1996	EE	90
1995	E	92

Gérard Perse, the proprietor, deserves congratulations and accolades for the immense work he has accomplished. This estate, formerly known for producing soft, Beaujolais-styled efforts best consumed during their first 7–8 years of life, was turned around in 1994, and has produced since then a string of phenomenal efforts. With his acquisition of Pavie, Pavie Decesse, and La Clusière, Perse has quickly become one of the most powerful players of the appellation, fashioning some of the most flamboyant and seductive clarets in St.-Emilion, if not in all Bordeaux. This is good news for consumers, since Perse is obsessed with quality. He maintains yields under 30 hectoliters per hectare, and does everything to ensure a natural expression of his vineyards' *terroirs*. Perse's secret also lies in the oxygenation of the wine's lees, aging on the lees, little racking, and no fining or filtering before bottling.

Monbousquet is a show-stopper in any tasting, blind or otherwise. At a blind tasting in

New York City, Monbousquet was inserted as one of the sleeper picks in a tasting of the top 1995s and was selected as the finest wine by a majority of the more than 125 people in attendance!

2000: Perse feels the 2000 Monbousquet is his finest to date, though it is hard to see how this wine could be better than the 1999, 1998, or 1995. Less exotic but more powerful, concentrated, and classic than previous vintages, the 2000 (7,500 cases) is a blend of 70% Merlot, 20% Cabernet Franc, and 10% Cabernet Sauvignon. It boasts an opaque purple color reminiscent of dry vintage port. The toasty new oak, so much a controversial component of previous vintages, is better integrated in 2000. The wine is sweet (abundant cherry, black currant, and blackberry notes) and full-bodied, with remarkable delineation, enormous concentration, and virtually perfect balance, symmetry, and purity. This spectacular wine clearly transcends its *terroir*. Anticipated maturity: 2004–2020.

1999: Made in a nearly over-the-top style, the saturated purple 1999 exhibits overripe blackberry, blueberry, cassis, chocolate, espresso, and toasty oak notes. This exotic, lush effort possesses immense chewy texture, low acidity, gorgeous purity, and a viscous finish. A thrilling effort, this full-bodied, creamy-textured wine is neither heavy nor disjointed. While it will be ready to drink upon release, it may not have the aging potential of the 1998. Anticipated maturity: now–2016.

1998: This wine's explosive richness is undoubtedly due to its small yields. The final blend, 60% Merlot, 30% Cabernet Sauvignon, and 10% Cabernet Franc, boasts a saturated plum/purple color in addition to an exotic bouquet of Asian spices, plum liqueur, prunes, and blackberries. Extremely full-bodied, unctuously textured, structured, and well defined, this spectacular achievement will drink well young, yet last for two decades. Anticipated maturity: 2003–2020.

1997: One of the vintage's superstars, this dark plum/purple-colored 1997 offers flamboyant, explosive aromas of vanilla, cherry jam, licorice, and new oak. Deep, concentrated, rich, and surprisingly chewy (especially for a 1997), this full-bodied, gorgeously concentrated and proportioned St.-Emilion will be hard to resist young. There is some tannin to be shed, but the wine is so ostentatious, it is impossible to ignore. Anticipated maturity: now–2014.

1996: The 1996 Monbousquet is another outstanding effort. The wine is more tannic than the 1995, but it exhibits an exotic nose of kirsch, cassis, roasted herbs, espresso, and mocha. It possesses excellent texture, impressive depth and richness, and sweet toasty oak. The saturated dark ruby/purple color suggests a dense wine. The finish is both long and well delineated, with moderate tannin. This beautifully etched Monbousquet will take several years longer to come around than the flamboyant, open-knit 1995. Anticipated maturity: now–2017.

1995: Although similar to the 1996, the 1995's fruit is more accessible, and the tannin is elevated, but it is buffered by lower acidity as well as more glycerin and fat. The 1995 offers an opaque purple color and a glorious nose of new oak, spice, and abundant black fruits. This full-bodied, superextracted, multilayered wine must be tasted to be believed—especially for readers who remember Monbousquet as the soft, innocuous, commercially styled St.-Emilion it was for many decades. The 1995 has more accessibility than the blockbuster 1996, but it still requires 1–2 years of cellaring. Anticipated maturity: 2003–2022.

Past Glories: 1994 (90)

MONBRISON (MARGAUX)

2000	C	(88–89)
1999	C	87
1998	C	87
1996	C	85
1995	C	86

It is good to see Monbrison return to form after a period of irregularity. The 1995, 1996, 1998, 1999, and 2000 are worthy of attention. Consumers take note.

2000: Unquestionably the finest Monbrison since some of the excellent efforts produced in the early and mid-1980s, the deep ruby/purple 2000 exhibits a sweet nose of minerals, black currants, fennel, charcoal, licorice, toasty oak, and acacia flowers. Rich and medium- to full-bodied, it shows moderate tannin as well as an overall sense of elegance and balance. A sleeper of the vintage. Anticipated maturity: 2003–2016.

1999: As in many 1999 Margaux, the fruit is sweet and pure and the wine is well balanced, with low acidity, excellent ripeness, and a full-bodied, well-balanced flavor profile. The tannin, acidity, wood, and alcohol are all nicely integrated. While not a powerhouse, this is a graceful, well-made Monbrison to drink over the next 10 years.

1998: An excellent ripe black currant, cherry, and spicy new oak–scented bouquet is followed by a medium-bodied, soft yet structured wine with plenty of ripe fruit as well as an earthy, dusty finish. This complex, pure offering is best drunk during its first decade of life.

1996: The 1996 appears to be a good effort, although certain samples revealed a slight cardboard character in the nose that could have been attributed to defective corks. Assuming this is not an intrinsic problem, the wine offers a deep ruby purple color, medium body, ripe fruit, and an elegant, restrained, noteworthy format. Anticipated maturity: 2003–2015.

1995: The 1995 Monbrison is a correct, medium-bodied, elegant, dark ruby-colored wine with sweet fruit but a measured, polite style. Drink before 2006.

LA MONDOTTE (ST.-EMILION)

2000	EEE	(96–98)
1999	EEE	95
1998	EEE	96+
1997	EEE	94
1996	EEE	97+

The ultimate garage wine, La Mondotte is ultraconcentrated, frightfully expensive, and worth every cent. Since its debut in 1996, its consistently qualifies as a sleeper of the vintage. Though Bordeaux's most concentrated effort, readers should not think it is all muscle, flesh, extract, and new wood. This wine possesses elegance, complexity, and, with time, a distinctive *terroir* character will emerge. This amazing micro *cuvée* emerges from a 30-year-old parcel of Merlot near Tertre-Rôteboeuf and Canon-La-Gaffelière. Annual production averages 800 cases.

2000: This wine undoubtedly has its critics, as it is almost portlike in style, but it is a totally dry, amazing effort that in 2000 needs to be consumed with a spoon. Essentially a syrup of St.-Emilion, it boasts an opaque purple color and an extraordinary perfume of smoke, coffee, mocha, chocolate, and blackberry/cassis liqueur. What keeps it from being an over-the-top, overly extracted wine is the extraordinary purity, symmetry, and balance that accompany its powerful, massive personality. It has less weight than most super-duper California Cabernet Sauvignons, but for a Bordeaux, it is an enormously endowed offering. There is a boatload of tannin in the viscous, thick 2000, as well as beautifully integrated oak. Like the 1999, 1998, 1997, and 1996, this is one of the wines of the vintage. The final blend was 75% Merlot and 25% Cabernet Franc. Anticipated maturity: 2008–2035.

1999: An opaque purple color is followed by an exotic, sweet bouquet of jammy black raspberries, cherries, and blackberries, smoke, barbecue spice (hickory?), licorice, and coffee. Thick, sweet flavors reveal abundant glycerin, low acidity, and an enormous wealth of concentrated fruit as well as ripeness. Will this amazing effort possess the definition or tannic structure of the 1998? A 1997 La Mondotte on steroids? Anticipated maturity: now–2025.

1998: An amazing tour de force in winemaking, this massive, opaque black/purple offering boasts an extraordinarily pure nose of black fruits intermixed with cedar, vanilla, fudge, and espresso. It is unctuously textured, with exhilarating levels of blackberry/cassis fruit and ex-tract, as well as multiple dimensions that unfold on the palate. The 50-second finish reveals moderately high tannin. Despite its similarity to dry vintage port, it is not a wine to drink early. It is a colossal wine! Anticipated maturity: 2008–2035.

1997: An amazing effort, and unquestionably one of the wines of the vintage, La Mondotte's 1997 boasts a saturated purple color as well as an explosive nose of blackberries, violets, minerals, and sweet toasty oak. Huge and massive, yet gorgeously proportioned, it possesses an unctuous texture with no hard edges. More seductive and easier to drink than the behe-moth 1996, it should be consumed between now–2015.

1996: An amazing wine, the 1996 La Mondotte is amazing for both its appellation and the vin-tage, revealing a remarkable level of richness, profound concentration, and integrated tannin. The thick purple color suggests a wine of extraordinary extract and richness. This super-concentrated wine offers a spectacular nose of roasted coffee, licorice, blueberries, and black currants intermixed with smoky new oak. It possesses full body, a multidimensional, layered personality with extraordinary depth of fruit, a seamless texture, amazing viscosity, and a long, 45-second finish. The tannin is sweet and well integrated. This blockbuster St.-Emilion should be at its best between 2006–2025. A dry, vintage port Fonseca!

MONTROSE (ST.-ESTÈPHE)

2000	EE	(94–96)
1999	EE	89
1998	E	90+
1997	D	87
1996	E	91+
1995	E	93

Since 1989, this property has consistently produced the finest wine in St.-Estèphe. In partic-ular, its 1989, 1990, 1996 and 2000 are noteworthy efforts.

2000: A sensational Montrose, the 2000 may be the finest produced since the 1996 and 1990. A blend of 63% Cabernet Sauvignon, 31% Merlot, 4% Cabernet Franc, and 2% Petit Verdot (56% of the crop was utilized in the final wine), this sensational, opaque purple-colored 2000 offers a terrific nose of melted licorice, crème de cassis, blackberries, minerals, and smoke. The wine is full-bodied, unctuously textured, fleshy, and pure, with high but sweet tannin levels. The finish lasts over 40 seconds. Like most Montrose, the blockbuster 2000 will undoubtedly reveal more tannin as it ages. Anticipated maturity: 2008–2035.

1999: I seriously underestimated the quality of this wine during the *en primeur* tastings. Like a half dozen or so other Médocs that I underscored at that time, my concerns about a lack of a mid-palate have evaporated, as these wines have fleshed out beautifully. We always need to remember that the purpose of barrel aging is to sweeten the tannin, develop more complexity, and concentrate the wines. That is exactly what has happened. The dense ruby/purple-colored 1999 Montrose exhibits a sweet nose of black fruits, iron, graphite, and smoke. Medium-bodied, with a supple, open-knit personality, low acidity, excellent concentration, and well-integrated tannin, it is not as burly or classic as the 1998, but it is a beautifully made, forward style of Montrose that should be ready to drink in 1–2 years and last for 15–18. If it keeps developing in this manner, it will merit an outstanding score. Anticipated maturity: 2004–2018.

1998: A classic effort, the 1998 Montrose exhibits a dense purple color in addition to a sweet nose of jammy cassis, licorice, earth, and smoke. It is a powerful and full-bodied wine with well-integrated tannin. Given Montrose's tendency to shut down, it is performing better out of bottle than I expected. Anticipated maturity: 2005–2030.

1997: The 1997 Montrose has turned even better than expected. Although lighter and less concentrated than usual, fragrant aromas of plum liqueur, soil, cedar, and leather are attractive. Round and tasty, with good fruit, low acidity, and fine ripeness, it will drink well for 3–4 years.

1996: The 1996 Montrose reveals outstanding potential. It boasts a saturated dark ruby/purple color, and aromas of new oak, jammy black currants, smoke, minerals, and new saddle leather. This multilayered wine is rich and medium- to full-bodied, with sweet tannin, a nicely textured, concentrated mid-palate, and an impressively long finish. Anticipated maturity: 2009–2025.

1995: An explosively rich, exotic, fruity Montrose, the 1995 displays even more fat and extract than the 1996. There is less Cabernet Sauvignon in the 1995 blend, resulting in a fuller-bodied, more accessible, and friendlier style. The wine exhibits an opaque black/ruby/purple color, as well as a ripe nose of black fruits, vanilla, and licorice. Powerful yet surprisingly accessible (the tannin is velvety and the acidity low), this terrific example of Montrose should be drinkable at a young age. Anticipated maturity: 2003–2028.

Past Glories: 1994 (91), 1990 (100), 1989 (96), 1986 (91), 1982 (91), 1970 (92+), 1964 (92), 1961 (95), 1959 (95), 1955 (94), 1953 (96)

MONTVIEL (POMEROL)

1998		C	85

1998: Dark ruby-colored, with more ripe fruit and lower acidity than its older sibling, the 1998 Montviel is a foursquare, monolithic effort that should drink well for 7 years.
Other vintage tasted: 1999 (82–84)

LE MOULIN (POMEROL)

2000	E	(90–93)
1999	E	89
1998	E	90
1997	D	86

This tiny estate, which burst on the scene with a sumptuous 1998, continues to offer wines that have more in common with Le Pin in flavor and exoticism than price. Made in a similar style, with extravagant, toasty new oak and ripe Merlot fruit, they display flamboyant notes of caramel, mocha, and jammy berry/cherry fruit. Readers should take note.

2000: The opulent 2000 Le Moulin offers a deep plum/ruby color and a gorgeously sweet nose of black raspberry jam intermixed with flowers, coffee, and caramel. Voluptuous and fleshy, it is both hedonistically and intellectually satisfying. Drink it over the next 5–15 years.

1999: Low acidity gives this plump, garnet-colored wine an open-knit, expansive texture. Beautifully fruity (abundant quantities of jammy red and black fruits) with notions of smoke, this evolved, full-bodied, long, potentially outstanding 1999 will require consumption during its first 8–10 years of life.

1998: A hedonistic, exotic, creamy-textured effort, the 1998 exhibits gorgeous espresso, plum, raspberry, and cherry liqueur aromas as well as flavors. Medium- to full-bodied and lush, it is best consumed over the next 10 years.

1997: A solid effort for the vintage, the 1997 Le Moulin possesses cherry/raspberry fruit, medium body, fine ripeness, no herbaceousness or sharpness, but a pinched finish. Its personality invites consumption over the next 4–5 years.

MOULIN DU CADET (ST.-EMILION)

2000		C	(79–82?)

2000: A narrowly focused effort, with a dark ruby color, sweet cherry fruit on the attack, and hard tannin, this 2000 quickly dries out, becoming pinched as well as compressed. Drink it over its first 7–8 years of life.

MOULIN-PEY-LABRIE (CANON-FRONSAC)

1998	**C**	**88**
1997	**C**	**87**
1995	**C**	**85+**

This has always been a serious Canon-Fronsac estate, and recent vintages continue to support its position as one of the stars of that bucolic yet potentially promising appellation.

1998: Dense ruby/purple-colored, with sweet, black cherry and cassis aromas supported by wood and mineral notions, this fat, ripe, opulently textured Moulin-Pey-Labrie possesses admirable fruit and ripeness. A sleeper of the vintage, it can be drunk young or cellared for 10–12 years.

1997: Excellent aromas of smoked duck, roasted coffee, Asian spices, and black cherry fruit jump from the glass of this complex, evolved, well-made 1997. Medium-bodied and ripe, with an outstanding mid-palate and texture, this delicious, forward wine can be consumed over the next 4–5 years.

1995: A well-made, nicely structured, cleanly etched wine, this 1995 offers a deep ruby color, sweet cherry and mineral fruit, some spicy, loamy, earthy notes, and moderate tannin in the long finish. This wine will easily evolve for 5–6 years more.

Other vintages tasted: 2000 (86–87), 1999 (85–86)

MOULIN ST.-GEORGES (ST.-EMILION)

2000	**C**	**(90–92)**
1999	**C**	**90**
1998	**C**	**89**
1997	**C**	**87**
1996	**C**	**89**
1995	**C**	**90**

This estate is owned by Alain Vauthier, best known for having resurrected the quality of Ausone over the last 5–6 years. Readers should think of Moulin St.-Georges as a more forward, earlier drinking, inexpensive alternative to Ausone. Those who can neither afford nor invest the requisite patience in Ausone should seek out its smaller sibling.

2000: Vinified in the style of its more famous sibling, this 2000 emphasizes pure, authentic blackberry, black raspberry, and currant fruit with a touch of minerals and wood. The wine is deep, structured, moderately tannic, and impressive. More backward than previous vintages, it is a high-class, elegant offering to drink between 2003–2014.

1999: A softer version of the 1998, the 1999 may turn out to be slightly better because of its lower acidity, fatter, fleshier texture, and seductive personality. A dense ruby/purple color is accompanied by blackberry, cassis, subtle wood, and licorice aromas and flavors. Anticipated maturity: now–2012.

1998: Elegant blackberry, licorice, and mineral notes jump from the glass of this medium-weight, stylish, exceptionally pure offering. It reveals impressive levels of black fruits as well as nicely integrated acidity, tannin, and wood. With decanting, this 1998 can be drunk now, but it promises to age well for 12 years.

1997: The 1997 exhibits a fruit-driven nose of raspberries and cherries, followed by sweet jammy flavors, medium body, low acidity, and a soft, plump finish. It should drink well for 2–3 years.

1996: This dark ruby/purple-colored 1996 offers a complex nose of plums and other black fruits, steely mineral notes, and subtle new oak. A classic, elegant, rich, medium-bodied wine with outstanding purity, to be drunk before 2015.

1995: A gorgeous wine, and another sleeper of the vintage, the 1995 Moulin St. Georges exhibits a dense purple color, and a sweet, black raspberry and currant nose intertwined with high-quality toasty oak and minerals. Deep, rich, impressively pure, ripe, elegant, and harmonious, this gorgeous, persuasive St.-Emilion has a bright future. Anticipated maturity: now–2016.

MOULINET (POMEROL)

2000		C (82–84?)

Starting with 2000, Christian Moueix has assumed control over the viticulture and winemaking at this estate, which has had an undistinguished history.

2000: The 2000 looks to be a decent beginning, as it possesses more color, grip, and depth than in the past. However, it still comes across as monolithic and foursquare as well as tannic. Anticipated maturity: 2005–2012.

MOUTON-ROTHSCHILD (PAUILLAC)

2000	EEE	(96–98+?)
1999	EEE	93
1998	EEE	96
1997	EEE	90
1996	EEE	94
1995	EEE	95+

Mouton-Rothschild is the place and wine that the late Baron Philippe de Rothschild singularly created. Through the production of an opulently rich and remarkably deep and exotic style of Pauillac, he was the only person able to effectuate a change in the 1855 Médoc classification. In 1973, Mouton was classified as a "first growth," and there is no question that several vintages of this wine qualify as some of the best Bordeaux I have ever tasted (1929, 1945, 1947, 1953, 1955, 1959, 1982), though, I have also encountered numerous mediocre bottles. Recent vintages have been topflight, especially from 1995 onward, and are evidence that Mouton remains faithful to its classification and reputation under the auspices of Philippine de Rothschild.

2000: Is this another 1986 in the making? The 2000 is a blend of 86% Cabernet Sauvignon and 14% Merlot (80% of the production, which averaged 35 hectoliters per hectare). A potentially immortal wonder, Mouton's 2000 is so thick, it almost needs to be drunk with a spoon. At the same time, it has brutally high tannin. There is a lot going on in this backward effort, including phenomenal concentration and extract and a huge nose of smoke, crème de cassis, truffles, and new saddle leather. A wine of enormous constitution and awesome power, but neophytes and readers unwilling to invest 20 years of cellaring should look elsewhere. If the tannin becomes more integrated, and the wine increasingly seamless, it will merit its lofty rating. However, if the tannin becomes more abrasive, or the wine totally shuts down, the score will drop. This is a long-term prospect for prospective purchasers, given the fact that most Moutons made with this level of extract and tannin need 15–20 years of cellaring (look at the still-infant 1982 and 1986). Nevertheless, this is a fabulously pure, brilliant achievement, perhaps destined for your children's children. Anticipated maturity: 2020–2060.

1999: Made in a softer style than the 1998, many readers will prefer this "friendlier" blend of 78% Cabernet Sauvignon, 18% Merlot, and 4% Cabernet Franc. It exhibits a dense ruby/purple color as well as a less complex bouquet than its older sibling, but more sweet cassis fruit, coffee, and smoke. Long and lush, with low acidity, ripe tannin, and medium to full body, it should be reasonably approachable upon release, yet evolve nicely for 20–25 years. Could this be a modern-day clone of the 1962?

1998: Surprise, surprise! The 1998 Mouton has emerged as the greatest wine produced at this estate since the perfect 1986, of which the 1998 is somewhat reminiscent. Like many of its peers, it has filled out spectacularly during its *élevage*. Now in bottle, this opaque black/purple offering has increased in stature, richness, and size. A blend of 86% Cabernet Sauvignon, 12% Merlot, and 2% Cabernet Franc (57% of the production was utilized), it is an extremely powerful, super-concentrated wine offering notes of roasted espresso, crème de cassis, smoke, new saddle leather, graphite, and licorice. It is massive in the mouth, with awesome concentration, mouth-searing tannin levels, and a saturated flavor profile that grips the mouth with considerable intensity. This is another 50-year Mouton, but patience will be required, as it will not be close to drinkability for at least a decade. This wine rivals the 1986, 1995, and 1990! Anticipated maturity: 2012–2050.

1997: Only 55% of the harvest was utilized for the 1997 Mouton-Rothschild. One of the most forward and developed Moutons of recent years, it possesses all the charm and fleshiness this vintage can provide. A blend of 82% Cabernet Sauvignon, 13% Merlot, 3% Cabernet Franc, and 2% Petit Verdot, the wine exhibits a dense ruby/purple color, and an open-knit nose of cedar wood, blackberry liqueur, cassis, and coffee. Fleshy, ripe, and mouth-filling, with low acidity, soft tannin, and admirable concentration and length, this delicious Pauillac is already drinkable and should age for 12+ years. An impressive effort for this vintage.

1996: This estate's staff believes that the 1996 Mouton-Rothschild is far more complex than the 1995 but less massive. I agree that among the first growths, this wine is showing surprising forwardness and complexity in its aromatics. It possesses an exuberant, flamboyant bouquet of roasted coffee, cassis, smoky oak, and soy sauce. The impressive 1996 Mouton-Rothschild offers impressive aromas of black currants, framboise, coffee, and new saddle leather. This full-bodied, ripe, rich, concentrated, superbly balanced wine is paradoxical in the sense that the aromatics suggest a far more evolved wine than the flavors reveal. Anticipated maturity: 2007–2030. By the way, the 1996 blend was identical to the 1995–72% Cabernet Sauvignon, 20% Merlot, and 8% Cabernet Franc.

1995: This profound Mouton is more accessible than the more muscular 1996. A blend of 72% Cabernet Sauvignon, 9% Cabernet Franc, and 19% Merlot, it reveals an opaque purple color and reluctant aromas of cassis, truffles, coffee, licorice, and spice. In the mouth, the wine is "great stuff," with superb density, a full-bodied personality, rich mid-palate, and a layered, profound finish that lasts 40+ seconds. There is outstanding purity and high tannin, but my instincts suggest this wine is lower in acidity and slightly fleshier than the brawnier, bigger 1996. However, both are great efforts from Mouton-Rothschild. Anticipated maturity: 2004–2030.

Past Glories: 1994 (91+), 1989 (90), 1986 (100), 1985 (90), 1983 (90), 1982 (100), 1970 (93?), 1966 (90), 1962 (92), 1961 (98?), 1959 (100), 1955 (97), 1953 (95), 1949 (94), 1947 (97), 1945 (100)

NÉNIN (POMEROL)

Year		
2000	E	(91–93)
1999	E	88
1998	E	90
1997	D	87
1996	D	85
1995	D	86

Since this property was acquired in 1997 by the Delon family (proprietors of Léoville-Las Cases), and under the auspices of Jean-Hubert Delon, Nénin is quickly surging to the forefront of Pomerols.

2000: One of the few 2000 Pomerols that is superior to its 1998 counterpart. A blend of 73% Merlot and 27% Cabernet Franc, from yields of 30 hectoliters per hectare, it is powerful as well as complex. Opaque purple, with a full-bodied, opulent style backed up by high tannin and decent acidity, it reveals more cedar and floral notes (because of the high percentage of Cabernet Franc) in its chocolate, blackberry, and cherry-scented bouquet. Gorgeously pure, thick, and rich, it is a candidate for a long life. Anticipated maturity: 2005–2025.

1999: Dark ruby/purple, with a subdued nose of earthy black fruits, minerals, and mocha, the medium-bodied, elegant 1999 Nénin reveals light to moderate tannin in the finish. It will be drinkable upon release and will evolve nicely for 10–15 years.

1998: Along with the 2000, this is the finest Nénin in many decades. The dense ruby/purple 1998 exhibits aromas of coffee, melted caramel, vanilla, plums, and black cherry jam. It is full-bodied, with an unctuous texture, superb purity, and a silky, seamless finish. There is abundant tannin submerged beneath the wine's fatness and richness. Anticipated maturity: 2004–2025.

1997: The Delons did not have control over the vineyard and entire vinification for this vintage, but they instituted a strict selection, resulting in an attractive, elegant, richly fruity wine with copious quantities of cherries and black currants presented in a lush, supple style. It should drink well for 7–8 years.

1996: This was not an easy vintage in Pomerol. Although the 1996 Nénin exhibits lean, rustic tannin in the finish, it offers pleasant plum and chocolaty fruit, medium body, and clean winemaking. Given the balance between fruit and tannin, I would recommend consuming it over the next 3–4 years.

1995: The 1995 exhibits a healthy, medium dark ruby color, plenty of sweet, jammy cherry/plumlike fruit in the nose, medium body, low acidity, and a loosely knit but attractively smooth texture and finish. Drink within 1–2 years.

OLIVIER (PESSAC-LÉOGNAN)

2000	D	(88–89)
1999	D	87
1998	D	89
1997	C	86
1996	C	86
1995	C	84

After years of uninspiring performances, Olivier's vineyards, crowned by a gorgeous medieval moated château, is beginning to fashion elegant, stylish, richly fruity wines. The full potential of the vineyards is beginning to be exploited, and recent vintages have been the finest tasted from this onetime underachiever. As the tasting notes suggest, the 1998 and 2000 seem to be its finest efforts yet produced.

2000: A sexy, lush effort, this deep ruby/purple, medium-bodied 2000 exhibits plenty of grapy black currant fruit, smoke, tobacco, and spice box aromas. Rich, with excellent purity as well as low acidity and ripe tannin in the finish, it will drink well upon release and over the following decade. It is the finest Olivier in more than 25 years.

1999: Aromas of ripe currants, tar, smoke, strawberry jam, and tobacco emerge from this medium-bodied, supple-textured, lush Graves. It should drink well for 8–10 years.

1998: A dark plum/ruby color is accompanied by a sexy bouquet of cigar tobacco, red and black currants, earth, and vanilla. This medium-bodied, seamless, lush, savory 1998 is difficult to resist. How long it will age is debatable, but it will certainly drink well for 10–15 years.

1997: Deep ruby/purple, with a straightforward, sweet, black cherry/berry character complemented by tobacco leaf and toasty new oak, Olivier's medium-bodied, low-acid, fruit-driven 1997 should be consumed over the next 7–8 years.

1996: The 1996 is a soft, medium-bodied wine with a moderate display of red and black currants, adequate acidity, and sweet tannin. Though not a big wine, it is well constructed and harmonious. Anticipated maturity: now–2012.

1995: Compact, lean, tannic, and more austere than the 1996, the 1995 is a light- to medium-bodied, competent but inspiring effort. Anticipated maturity: now–2008.

LES ORMES-DE-PEZ (ST. ESTÈPHE)

2000	C	(88–90)
1999	C	86
1998	C	87
1997	C	80
1996	C	86
1995	C	86

Les Ormes-de-Pez is a popular wine, in large part because of its generously flavored, plump, sometimes sweet and fat personality, and also thanks to the promotional efforts of the owner, Jean-Michel Cazes. This is a cru bourgeois to which consumers looking for high quality at modest prices should always give serious consideration.

2000: A sleeper of the vintage, this cru bourgeois has fashioned a fleshy, opulent, deep purple 2000 with low acidity, admirable thickness and juiciness, and abundant quantities of licorice-infused cassis and blackberry fruit. Pure and accessible, it will be delicious young yet will also age nicely for 10–12 years. This is the finest effort from this château in more than a decade.

1999: With good fatness as well as chewy raspberry and cherry fruit, this straightforward, seamless effort does not possess much weight or length. It will provide competent drinking over the next 5–6 years.

1998: A successful effort, as well as a reasonably good value, this dark ruby/purple 1998 exhibits copious quantities of cassis fruit along with earthy underbrush notes. Medium- to full-bodied, with fine concentration, excellent texture, and a soft, spicy, peppery finish, it will drink well for 10 years.

1997: The 1997 is round and easygoing, with low acidity and a nose of vanilla, dried herbs, and red currant fruit. Much lighter than the 1996, it is best drunk over the next 2–3 years.

1996: A potential sleeper of the vintage, this wine exhibits a saturated dark ruby color, and an excellent blackberry- and cassis-scented nose with smoky oak in the background. It is sweet, opulently textured, surprisingly accessible and round, with an excellent finish. This is one of the finest wines from Les Ormes-de-Pez. Anticipated maturity: now–2014.

1995: I am tempted to say that this wine is too obviously commercial, but it is still an attractive, soft, round, medium to dark ruby-colored claret with herb, black cherry, and currant fruit notes. Lush, with some elegance, medium body, soft tannin, and an easygoing finish, this wine should be drunk during its first 7–8 years of life.

LES ORMES-SORBET (MÉDOC)

1996	C	86
1995	C	85

A perennial overachiever, this well-run property turns out stylish, attractive, medium-weight wines that represent good value.

1996: This excellent wine offers an elegant, moderately scented nose of black fruits, spicy oak, and minerals. Rich in flavor, harmonious, and with sweet tannin in the finish, it should be drunk over the next 2–3 years.

1995: The 1995 is medium-bodied and attractive, with red and black fruits intermixed with minerals and subtle new oak. It is more angular and possesses less weight and ripeness than the 1996, but it is a worthy choice for value-conscious readers.

Other vintages tasted: 2000 (86–87), 1999 (81–83)

PALMER (MARGAUX)

2000	EEE	(92–94+)
1999	EE	95
1998	EE	91

1997	E	87
1996	EE	91+
1995	EE	90

Palmer can be as profound as many first growths, and in vintages such as 1961, 1966, 1967, 1970, 1975, 1983, 1989, and 1995, it is better than many. The style of Palmer is one of sensational fragrance and bouquet, so much so that great vintages can be identified in blind tastings by their smell alone. The wine's texture is rich, often supple and lush, and it is always deeply fruity and concentrated. Recent vintages have been formidable efforts. Recently co-proprietor Frank Mahler-Besse and manager Bertrand Bouteiller have also started producing a very good second wine called Alter Ego de Palmer, which will, no doubt, help to further increase the quality of the grand vin.

2000: The 2000 is a blend of 52% Cabernet Sauvignon and 48% Merlot and represents a selection of 45% of the total production. This Palmer is a massive *vin de garde* exhibiting abundant amounts of the vintage's high tannin. However, readers should not worry about it turning out like the austere 1975. It possesses a dense purple color, powerful yet ripe, provocative notes of plums, black cherries, coffee, and new saddle leather, and huge fruit concentration. One of the most backward Palmers I have tasted, it exhibits a sweet mid-palate as well as well-integrated, ripe tannin. The 2000 is a perfect contrast to Palmer's sexy, supple 1999. Potential purchasers will need patience, but it should be one of the longest-lived Palmers made in the last three decades. Anticipated maturity: 2009–2040.

1999: A brilliant success, Palmer's 1999 is even better than their 1998 or 2000. A blend of 46% Merlot, 48% Cabernet Sauvignon, and 6% Petit Verdot (only 58% of the harvest made it into the final wine), it boasts an opaque blue/purple color as well as sweet aromas of licorice, jammy cassis, smoke, lead pencil, and minerals. Surprisingly tannic for the vintage, this muscular, gorgeously proportioned, classic effort should be one of the wines of the vintage, at least in the Médoc. Anticipated maturity: 2006–2025.

1998: A classic Margaux, the 1998 Palmer has put on weight and fleshed out during its *élevage* in barrel. It displays a dense purple color as well as a sumptuous bouquet of black fruits, licorice, melted asphalt, toast, and a touch of acacia flowers. Full-bodied, with brilliant definition, this blend of equal parts Merlot and Cabernet Sauvignon, with a dollop of Petit Verdot, will age well for 20–30 years. It is one of the Médoc's, as well as the Margaux appellation's, finest wines of the vintage. Anticipated maturity: 2005–2028.

1997: A seductive style of Palmer, the 1997 will have many admirers (assuming they can afford it). It boasts a dark ruby/plum/purple color in addition to a seductive bouquet of sweet berry fruit and an elegant, medium-bodied, fruit-driven, easygoing, fleshy personality. While there is little weight and density, the wine's harmony is excellent. Drink it over the next 6–7 years.

1996: This wine, a blend of 55% Cabernet Sauvignon, 40% Merlot, and 5% Petit Verdot, is performing well. It boasts an impressively saturated purple color, in addition to a backward yet intense nose of black plums, currants, licorice, and smoke. Following terrific fruit on the attack, the wine's structure and tannin take over. This impressively endowed, surprisingly backward Palmer may develop into a modern-day version of the 1966. There is plenty of sweet fruit, and the tannin is well integrated, but the wine requires another 4–5 years of cellaring. Anticipated maturity: 2007–2028.

1995: This wine includes an extremely high percentage of Merlot (about 43%). It is a gloriously opulent, low-acid, fleshy Palmer that will be attractive in its youth and yet keep well. Dark ruby/purple, with smoky, toasty new oak intertwined with gobs of jammy cherry fruit and floral and chocolate nuances, this medium- to full-bodied, plump yet elegant wine is impressive. Anticipated maturity: now–2020.

Past Glories: 1989 (95), 1983 (97), 1978 (90), 1975 (90), 1970 (95+), 1966 (96), 1962 (91), 1961 (99), 1945 (97), 1928 (96), 1900 (96)

PAPE-CLÉMENT (PESSAC-LÉOGNAN)

2000	EE	(92–95)
1999	EE	91
1998	EE	93
1997	E	87
1996	E	90
1995	E	90

In the last half of the 1980s, Pape-Clément became one of the stars of Bordeaux, producing profound efforts in 1986, 1988, 1990, 1996, and 1998. At its best, this wine is characterized by a fascinating and compelling bouquet that offers up gobs of black fruits intermingled with strong smells of tobacco and minerals. Because of the relatively high percentage of Merlot in the blend, it can be drunk extremely young, yet can age easily for several decades in the best vintages. In 1999, the estate was bought by Bernard Magrez, who is also the proprietor of Fombrauge and La Tour Carnet. Given the new owner's commitment to quality, one can imagine that Pape-Clément will continue improving, a trend already noticeable in the 2000, which surpasses anything yet made at the estate.

2000: An awesome offering, the 2000 should surpass the great Pape-Cléments made in 1998, 1996, 1995, 1990, 1988, and 1986, and perhaps even the wonderful duo made in 1959 and 1961. I had this wine on three separate occasions, and at each tasting it was riveting, with phenomenal extract and richness as well as elegance and overall balance. Yields were a modest 47 hectoliters per hectare. This blend of equal parts Cabernet Sauvignon and Merlot (approximately 55% of the production made it into the final wine) possesses staggeringly concentrated coffee, earthy, tobacco, mineral, black currant, and cherry scents in the complex aromatics. In the mouth, notes of soy also make an appearance. Full-bodied, rich yet elegant, with fabulous purity, great palate presence, and terrific concentration as well as complexity, this dazzling effort may be the finest Pape-Clément ever made! Anticipated maturity: 2005–2025. Wow!

1999: Stylish lead pencil, plum, raspberry, currant, and spice box aromas emerge from this dark ruby/purple 1999. It offers an excellent entry on the palate, good structure, sweet tannin, and fine depth as well as texture. While it may not turn out to be as majestic as the 1998, it is a high-class effort. Anticipated maturity: 2003–2018.

1998: A prodigious effort from Pape-Clément, this wine is smoking. It boasts a dense ruby/purple color in addition to a terrific nose of charcoal, blackberries, cassis, tobacco, minerals, and spice. This brilliantly focused, medium- to full-bodied 1998 already reveals a boatload of complexity as well as a remarkably long finish. A large-sized effort for this estate, it exhibits a sweet mid-palate and ripe tannin. Anticipated maturity: 2003–2025. Bravo!

1997: An attractive, complex wine, the 1997 Pape-Clément exhibits a dark, saturated ruby color in addition to a gorgeous, smoky, herb, red currant, and cherry liqueur–scented bouquet, a silky texture, spicy oak, and a round, complex, low-acid, fleshy finish. As the wine sat in the glass, notes of hot bricks/scorched earth also emerged. This is a complex, supple, delicious wine to drink over the next 8–10 years.

1996: This is another elegant, complex, distinctive wine that depends on its aromatic complexity and harmonious display of fruit and structure for appeal. It will not knock tasters down with a display of power or muscle. The color is a healthy dark ruby. The wine offers up roasted herb, tobacco, sweet cranberry, and black currant fruit aromas. It is medium-bodied, with a rich, layered, silky impression, excellent purity, and soft tannin in the finish. Surprisingly forward for a 1996, it appears to be on a rapid evolutionary track, although it will keep for 12 or more years.

1995: A softer, more accessible version of the more tannic 1996, Pape-Clément's 1995 exhibits a deep ruby/purple color and a lovely nose of spice, lead pencil, minerals, smoke, and tobacco-tinged black currants. Rich and ripe, with medium body, sweet fruit on the attack, and an overall sense of elegance and impeccable equilibrium, this beautifully knit, complex wine is already enjoyable. Anticipated maturity: now–2015.

Past Glories: 1990 (93), 1988 (92), 1986 (92), 1961 (92)

PAS DE L'ANE (ST.-EMILION)

1999	C	(88–90)

1999: A sleeper of the vintage, this debut effort under the omnipresent management of Jean-Luc Thunevin boasts a dense ruby/purple color in addition to a sweet chocolaty, blackberry, and currant-scented nose, low acidity, a fat, luscious texture, and a heady finish. It is a hedonistic St.-Emilion fruit bomb to drink over the next 5–6 years.

PAVIE (ST.-EMILION)

2000	EEE	(96–99)
1999	EEE	95
1998	EEE	95+
1997	D	85
1996	E	(84–86)
1995	D	78

Proprietor Gérard Perse has fashioned three of the greatest Pavies of the 20th century (1998, 1999, and 2000) in the first three vintages he has had total control over the viticulture, vinification, and *élevage*. Working with the renowned Michel Rolland, his oenologist, and Dr. Alain Raynaud of Château Quinault l'Enclos, Perse has done significant vineyard replanting, reduced yields to a lowly 30 hectoliters per hectare, built a new *cuverie* and cellar, and instituted a draconian selection process to produce the finest wine money can provide. If wine is to be judged by what is in the bottle, Pavie has become a fabulous first growth–quality estate, offering extraordinary elegance married to awesome levels of richness.

2000: It is too soon to proclaim that the 2000 is better than the 1999 or 1998, but it is unquestionably a more backward effort with additional structure and tannin. At the same time, the concentration is fabulous. Structured, with an opaque ruby/purple color, Pavie's 2000 exhibits aromas of liquid minerals, black cherry liqueur, cassis, and flowers. The wine is full-bodied yet extraordinarily precise, with uncanny elegance, fabulous purity, and astonishing length. Although elevated, the tannin is sweet as well as nicely integrated. However, this 2000 will require considerable patience, unlike the more supple, fleshier 1999, or classic 1998. Except for some of Bordeaux's provincial knuckleheads (who resent outsiders), this is widely acclaimed as one of the region's most singular and greatest wines. Anticipated maturity: 2010–2040.

1999: This is a more hedonistic, sweet, expansive, and unctuous rendition of the 1998. The acidity is lower, and the color an even more saturated purple/black. The bouquet offers fabulous minerality along with copious quantities of thick, succulent, black raspberry, cassis, and cherry liqueur fruit, all nicely dosed with subtle smoky new oak. It is a wine of immense richness, layers of concentration, and a viscous, long finish that should ensure 30–40 years of drinkability. It may ultimately surpass the 1998. Anticipated maturity: 2005–2040.

1998: A 50-year wine, this opaque purple offering exhibits a strong, precise nose of black fruits, liquid minerals, smoke, and graphite. Extremely full-bodied yet brilliantly delineated, powerful, and awesomely concentrated, it boasts a fabulous mid-palate as well as a finish that lasts for nearly a minute. This *vin de garde* requires 4–5 years of cellaring. A tour de force in winemaking, it has the potential to be the most profound Pavie ever produced, except for its two successors. Anticipated maturity: 2006–2045.

1997: Perse did not make this wine, but he did insist upon a strict selection, resulting in an elegant, medium-bodied, soft, cherry- and spice-scented, pleasant, picnic-styled Bordeaux. It should drink well for 4–5 years.

1996: The dark ruby-colored 1996 Pavie exhibits a pinched, tart personality with moderate quantities of red currant fruit in the nose, along with earth and spice. Although it exhibits good, clean winemaking, this understated, lean, angular wine does not possess much stuffing, flesh, or length. It should keep for 10 years. Anticipated maturity: now–2012.

1995: Medium plum/ruby in color, with a distinctive peppery, leafy, spicy nose and vague hints of red cherry and currant fruit, this is a rigid, austere wine with an angular personality and severe tannin. There is some ripe fruit on the attack, but that is quickly dominated by the wine's structural components. This may turn out to be a pleasant wine, but my best guess is that it will dry out. Anticipated maturity: now–2010.

Past Glories: 1990 (92), 1986 (90), 1961 (90)

PAVIE DECESSE (ST.-EMILION)

2000	EEE	(93–96)
1999	EEE	94
1998	EE	91+
1997	D	86
1996	C	(84–86)
1995	C	78

This is another estate that has been resurrected under the inspired leadership of Gérard Perse, who has done so much at Monbousquet as well as at Pavie and its neighboring vineyard, La Clusière. Pavie Decesse has never produced better wines than those fashioned under the helmsmanship of Perse and his consultants, oenologist Michel Rolland and Dr. Alain Raynaud, from Quinault l'Enclos. The vineyard, which benefits from a noble *terroir,* produces sweeter, more approachable wines than its bigger, more famous sibling, Pavie.

2000: The fabulous 2000 Pavie Decesse is more approachable than its prestigious sibling, Pavie. The color is an opaque black/ruby. The nose offers up aromas of melted licorice, incense, smoke, and jammy blackberry and cherry fruit. Unctuously textured, with lower acidity and less structure than Pavie, this super-concentrated offering should be drinkable within 3–4 years and keep for 20–25. It is a better bet for earlier consumption than the more structured, backward, formidable Pavie. This is a magical elixir that satiates both the hedonistic and intellectual senses. Anticipated maturity: 2005–2025.

1999: The greatest Pavie Decesse I have ever tasted, this opaque blue/purple 1999 boasts fabulous intensity, compelling opulence, and a prodigious, explosive finish. Super-extracted yet neither heavy nor unbalanced, this multidimensional wine reveals layers of concentrated fruit, gorgeous purity, and fabulous black fruit flavors intermixed with cold steel, minerals, licorice, and subtle smoky new oak. A dazzling winemaking tour de force, it should turn out to be one of the vintage's superstars and longest-lived efforts. Anticipated maturity: 2004–2024.

1998: Wet stones, minerals, vanilla, black cherries, and smoke aromas as well as flavors are present in this powerful, muscular, medium- to full-bodied 1998. Crammed with fruit and built for the long haul, it is not as accessible as many of this vintage's offerings. Anticipated maturity: 2005–2025.

1997: The first vintage where the vinification was controlled by Perse, Raynaud, and Rolland. Dense ruby/purple, with copious quantities of black raspberry and cherry fruit intermixed with spicy oak, this deep, rich, medium- to full-bodied 1997 possesses sweet tannin, low acidity, excellent length, and admirable concentration. Already delicious, it promises to keep for 12–14 years—atypically long for a 1997.

1996: Perse has the unenviable task of trying to sell the 1996 Pavie Decesse, the last vintage made under the old regime. The wine is pleasant, but there is very little to it. Moreover, the dry tannin in the finish suggests that graceful aging will be almost impossible. The overall impression is one of leanness, high tannin, and not enough fruit or concentration. This wine has no place to go but down. Anticipated maturity: now–2007.

1995: Now that it is in bottle, the 1995 Pavie Decesse is extraordinarily austere, with elevated tannin levels, some sweet black currant, cranberry, and cherry fruit, but a hollow mid-palate, and a dry, sharp finish with noticeable astringent tannin. I liked this wine much better from three separate cask tastings, but two tastings from bottle have made me question my earlier reviews. Anticipated maturity: now–2010.

Past Glories: 1990 (90)

PAVIE-MACQUIN (ST.-EMILION)

2000	E	(92–94)
1999	E	90
1998	E	95
1997	D	90
1996	D	89+?
1995	D	89+?

This property, which is farmed biodynamically, has a high percentage of extremely old vines and is run by one of the Thienpont family members. It has been producing brilliant wines for most of the last decade. Pavie-Macquin continues to behave as if it were the Lafleur of St.-Emilion. The old-vine intensity, backstrapping, super-concentrated, highly extracted style with an abundance of fruit, body, and tannin, combine to produce a noteworthy candidate for extended cellaring. Production from the estate's 36 acres (planted with 70% Merlot, 25% Cabernet Franc, and 5% Cabernet Sauvignon) averages 4,000 cases.

2000: Not a wine for hedonists seeking immediate gratification, the 2000 Pavie-Macquin requires 8–10 years of cellaring. Is it better than the 1998? I do not think so, but it is an extremely close competition. A black/purple color is followed by gorgeously pure aromas of black raspberries, blackberries, cherries, liquid minerals, truffles, and Asian spices. Fleshy, ripe, glycerin-imbued flavors hit the palate with a crescendo, but the tannin kicks in the 40+-second finish. The wine is full-bodied and high in tannin but balanced by sumptuous levels of fruit, glycerin, and extract. Anticipated maturity: 2007–2030.

1999: The 1999, which has continued to flesh out during its upbringing, is one of the most concentrated and potentially long-lived wines of the vintage. An opaque ruby/purple color is followed by jammy kirsch, blackberry, and smoky graphite aromas. The essence of this vineyard's *terroir* is apparent in this huge yet supple-textured, super-concentrated as well as layered effort. Like the 1998, it is a prodigious offering. Anticipated maturity: 2004–2025.

1998: Nearly exaggerated levels of intensity, extract, and richness are apparent in this opaque blue/purple wine. Sumptuous aromas of blueberries, blackberries, and cherries combine with smoke, licorice, vanilla, and truffles to create a compelling aromatic explosion. The wine is fabulously dense, full-bodied, and layered, with multiple dimensions, gorgeous purity, and superbly integrated acidity as well as tannin. One of the most concentrated wines of the vintage, it possesses immense potential, but patience is required. Anticipated maturity: 2006–2030.

1997: Exhibiting a saturated black/purple color, the 1997 requires 2–3 more years' cellaring (atypical of the vintage). It boasts superb flavors of cassis, blackberries, minerals, licorice, and new oak. Intense, powerful, and backward, this is a classic, long-lived Bordeaux made in an uncompromising fashion. Although a blockbuster effort for the vintage, it is not as seductive as some of its peers. Anticipated maturity: 2006–2015+.

1996: The 1996 Pavie-Macquin could be served next to the 1996 Lafleur. They appear to be cut from the same uncompromising old-vine, superconcentrated yet backward, ferociously tannic style. Some of the *terroir*'s telltale mineral and blueberry fruit comes through in the nose and flavors, but this medium-bodied, structured, muscular wine will require 8 years of cellaring. Anticipated maturity: 2010–2020.

1995: Made in a style similar to the 1996, the 1995 reveals copious quantities of black fruits, obvious old-vine intensity (note the minerals and deep mid-palate), but mouth-searing levels of tannin will be enjoyed only by masochists. There are many good things about this wine, but the elevated tannin level is cause for concern. If the tannin melts away and the fruit holds, this will be an outstanding effort. Anticipated maturity: 2008–2025.

Past Glories: 1990 (91), 1989 (90)

LE PAVILLON DE BOYREIN (GRAVES)

2000	**C**	**(86–87)**

2000: A lighter-styled 2000, this soft effort exhibits aromas of earth, tobacco, smoke, and red cherries. Easygoing yet complex, it requires consumption during its first 2–3 years of life.

PEBY-FAUGÈRES (ST.-EMILION)

2000	**EEE**	**(95–98)**
1999	**E**	**93**
1998	**E**	**95**

1998 is the debut vintage of this luxury *cuvée* carved out of the Faugères vineyard, from a parcel of primarily Merlot with small quantities of Cabernet Franc. Judging by the first three vintages, Peby-Faugères is unquestionably worthy of attention. If you can find any, don't hesitate—it's that good.

2000: I had this wine on three occasions and rated it between 95 and 98+. Like the 1998 (one of the wines of the vintage), the 2000 appears to be another prodigious effort. This awesome St.-Emilion represents the essence of flavor, with an elegance, complexity, and overall symmetry that sets it apart from many of the so-called garage wines. A saturated black/blue/purple color is accompanied by spectacular aromas of blackberries, blueberries, cassis, and acacia flowers. Toasty oak can be discerned, but it is totally absorbed by the wine's wealth of fruit. In the mouth, this seamless classic is full-bodied, layered, and intense, but neither heavy nor portlike, with multiple dimensions, moderately high tannin, and a 50+-second finish. How does it compare to the 1998? The two wines are essentially equivalent in quality, but the 2000 may be both riper and higher in tannin—a paradoxical combination. Anticipated maturity: 2006–2020+.

1999: There are humongous quantities of jammy blueberry and blackberry aromas as well as flavors in this less delineated (than the 1998), sweet, full-bodied, opulently textured, rich, hedonistic 1999. If it develops a bit more definition, it could rival its older sibling. Extremely showy when I last tasted it, I see no reason why it would close down. Anticipated maturity: now–2016.

1998: A terrific effort, and one of the stars of the vintage, the 1998 boasts an opaque, thick-looking, black/purple color in addition to gorgeous aromatics consisting of blackberries, blueberries, smoke, minerals, and vanilla. Extremely full-bodied and rich yet harmonious, with a seamless personality as well as beautifully integrated acidity and tannin, this blockbuster effort is one of the great surprises of the vintage. Anticipated maturity: 2003–2018+.

PÉDÉSCLAUX (PAUILLAC)

2000	**C**	**(84–86)**

In a time when it is virtually impossible to find a classified-growth Bordeaux not living up to its pedigree, Pédésclaux continues to meander along, making indifferent albeit solid, cleanly made wines that lack distinction.

2000: The 2000 Pédésclaux possesses a dark ruby color and moderate levels of currant fruit, earth, spice box, and cedar. Its character reveals hints of Pauillac, but the wine lacks stuffing as well as length. Drink it over the next decade.

PETIT-BOCQ (ST.-ESTÈPHE)

1996	B	(86–87)
1995	B	86

This is a seriously run, small estate of 17+ acres planted with 70% Merlot, 25% Cabernet Sauvignon, and 5% Cabernet Franc. Its wines generally merit interest, particularly for those seeking value in Bordeaux.

1996: A potential sleeper of the vintage, this reasonably priced, well-made St.-Estèphe displays a dense ruby/purple color, as well as plenty of cassis and fruit in its straightforward but satisfying nose. Ripe, with dense, sweet flavors on the attack, and chewy levels of glycerin, this foursquare yet plump, attractive wine should drink well for 5–6 years.

1995: The 1995 Petit-Bocq exhibits a deep ruby color, attractive sweet, rich fruit, nice spice, good purity, and a medium-bodied, seamless personality. This is a stylish, supple St.-Estèphe to consume over the next 3–4 years.

PETIT-VILLAGE (POMEROL)

2000	E	(90–92)
1999	E	88
1998	E	89+
1997	D	81
1996	D	86
1995	D	86

Another Pomerol estate that has improved in quality over recent years.

2000: A striking bouquet of candied black fruits, allspice, cinnamon, and herbs jumps from the glass of this dense purple-colored Pomerol. The intriguing fragrance reveals notes of mincemeat as it sits in the glass, an exotic element. The wine is rich, ripe, and full-bodied, with outstanding purity, concentration, and thickness. Drink this in-your-face Pomerol now and over the next 15–16 years.

1999: Having filled out during its *élevage*, the 1999 is a soft, sexy, creamy-textured wine with a dense ruby/purple color as well as a big, sweet nose of fudge, mocha, blackberries, and cherries. Ripe, succulent, and hedonistic, this low-acid wine will provide gorgeous drinking young, but it possesses enough depth to age for 12 years.

1998: A strong candidate for an outstanding rating, this dark ruby/purple wine offers a sweet nose of plums, prunes, blackberries, chocolate, and mocha. Soft on the entry, revealing notes of smoke, licorice, and coffee, this fleshy, multilayered effort finishes with abundant glycerin, tannin, and extract. Another 1–2 years of cellaring is warranted. Anticipated maturity: 2003–2016.

1997: A light, pleasant wine with a cherry candy–like character intermixed with obvious toasty new oak, this diluted but easygoing Pomerol can be drunk over the next 1–2 years.

1996: The 1996 Petit-Village exhibits an intriguing, intense bouquet of smoked herbs, grilled meats, and cherry jam. In the mouth, black currants make an appearance, along with lavish quantities of wood. Medium-bodied with low acidity, this sexy, accessible, luscious, hedonistic Pomerol will drink well between now and 2007.

1995: The wine has an evolved dark garnet/ruby color, sweet, smoky, herb, and cherry perfume, and fat, round, generously endowed, straightforward but satisfying flavors. This is a seductive, hedonistic, plump style of Pomerol that will offer uncritical drinking prior to 2007.

Past Glories: 1990 (90), 1988 (92), 1982 (93)

PÉTRUS (POMEROL)

2000	**EEE**	**(96–100)**
1999	**EEE**	**94**
1998	**EEE**	**100**
1997	**EEE**	**91**
1996	**EEE**	**92**
1995	**EEE**	**96+**

Pétrus, the undisputed king of Pomerol and probably the most famous red wine in the world, was inconsistent between 1976 and 1988, but since 1989 there have been few Bordeaux wines that match this property for its extraordinary combination of power, richness, complexity, and elegance. The following wines are all noteworthy efforts.

2000: The 2000 Pétrus (only 2,600 cases produced) is a brilliant effort from this noble *terroir*. The dense plum/ruby/purple color is accompanied by sweet aromas of cranberry and cherry liqueur intermixed with plums and black currants. As always, the wood is kept in the background so the fruit can come forward. The wine is full-bodied, with plenty of well-integrated, sweet tannin. Long and rich, this offering will no doubt close down as most vintages of Pétrus do. Is this a hypothetical blend of the 1998 and 1975? Anticipated maturity: 2010–2035.

1999: The 2,400 cases of 1999 Pétrus will provide gorgeous drinking for the multimillionaires who can afford it. Opaque ruby/purple-colored, with sweet black cherry, mulberry, and smoky, truffle-infused fruit, this full-bodied, opulent effort will be drinkable at an earlier age than the more brawny 1998. It is less dense than its neighbor, Lafleur, but beautifully knit, with great purity, and superb concentration and overall symmetry. Anticipated maturity: 2005–2025.

1998: Christian Moueix feels the 1998 is even better than his 1989 or 1990, and he may ultimately be proven right. However, it will be a decade or more before it can be known which of these profound efforts might turn out to be the most compelling. The 1998 Pétrus is unquestionably a fabulous effort, boasting a dense plum/purple color as well as an extraordinary nose of black fruits intermixed with caramel, mocha, and vanilla. Exceptionally pure, super-concentrated, and extremely full-bodied, with admirable underlying acidity as well as sweet tannin, it reveals a superb mid-palate in addition to the luxurious richness for which this great property is known. The finish lasts for 40–45 seconds. Patience will definitely be required. Production was 2,400 cases. Anticipated maturity: 2008–2040. Quite an awesome wine!

1997: The backward 1997 (2,300 cases produced) needs 2–3 years of cellaring. The dense plum/ruby/purple color is accompanied by a closed bouquet of mocha, dried tomato skin, and black fruits. In the mouth it is one of the most muscular 1997s, exhibiting outstanding concentration, length, intensity, and depth, copious tannin, and a fine mouth-feel. Consider the 1997 Pétrus a modern-day version of their superb 1967. Anticipated maturity: 2006–2025.

1996: The 1996 Pétrus is a big, monolithic, foursquare wine with an impressively opaque purple color and sweet berry fruit intermixed with earth, toast, and coffee scents. Full-bodied and muscular, with high levels of tannin, and a backward style, this wine (less than 50% of the production was bottled as Pétrus) will require patience. It is a mammoth example, but without the sweetness of the 1997 or the pure, exceptional richness and layers of the multidimensional 1995. Anticipated maturity: 2010–2035.

1995: It is interesting how this wine continues to evolve. Unquestionably one of the vintage's superstars, the 1995 Pétrus is taking on a personality similar to the extraordinarily backward, muscular 1975. This is not a Pétrus that can be approached in its youth (in contrast to the perfect duo of 1989 and 1990). The wine exhibits an opaque ruby/purple color, followed by a knockout nose of toast, jammy black fruits, and roasted coffee. On the palate, it possesses teeth-staining extract levels, massive body, and rich, sweet black fruits buttressed by powerful, noticeable tannin. A formidably endowed wine with layers of extract, this is a huge, tannic, monstrous-sized Pétrus that will require a minimum of 5 years' cellaring. Forget all the nonsense about Merlot producing sweet, soft, ready-to-drink wines, because low-yielding, old Merlot vines made in the way of Pétrus and other top Pomerols frequently possess as much aging potential as any great Cabernet Sauvignon–based wine in the world. Look for the 1995 Pétrus to last for 50+ years. Anticipated maturity: 2007–2050.

Past Glories: 1994 (93+), 1993 (92+), 1992 (90+), 1990 (100), 1989 (100), 1988 (91), 1982 (98?), 1975 (98+), 1971 (95), 1970 (98+), 1967 (92), 1964 (97), 1962 (91), 1961 (100), 1959 (93), 1950 (99), 1949 (95), 1948 (95), 1947 (100), 1945 (98+), 1929 (100), 1921 (100), 1900 (89)

PEYROU (CÔTES DE CASTILLON)

2000	B (87–88)

2000: Another delicious offering from Côtes de Castillon, this blend of 80% Merlot, 10% Cabernet Sauvignon, and 10% Cabernet Franc displays an excellent dark ruby/purple color, and sweet, jammy black fruit aromas intermixed with spicy oak and underbrush. Ripe and soft, with a sweet attack, it finishes with delicious levels of glycerin and tannin. Drink it over the next 4–5 years.

DE PEZ (ST.-ESTÈPHE)

2000	C (87–88)

This estate has greatly improved under the auspices of the new proprietor, the Roederer house, a firm that has worked miracles with the Rhône Valley *négociant* Delas. Major investments in the château, cellars, and vineyard have resulted in a superb 2000. Judging by what Roederer is doing in the Rhône Valley, one can imagine that this vintage is the first of a series of very fine wines.

2000: The impressive 2000 exhibits the vintage's deep ruby/purple color, high tannin levels, a muscular structure, and medium- to full-bodied, dense cassis flavors with a hint of minerals/wet stones. Anticipated maturity: 2007–2020.

PHÉLAN-SÉGUR (ST.-ESTÈPHE)

2000	C	(86–88)
1999	C	81
1998	C	85
1997	C	83
1996	C	86
1995	C	84

Despite the efforts of the Gardiniers, who bought this estate in the 1980s, most vintages of the 1990s have been rather disappointing. However, the 2000 is a fine effort. Prices are fairly high in view of the quality.

2000: The wine exhibits a dense ruby/purple color, a soft, smooth entry on the palate, medium body, low acidity, ripe tannin, and copious quantities of black fruits, licorice, and spice. Anticipated maturity: now–2012.

1999: Because it possesses less tannin, the 1999 is more charming than the 1998. It exhibits strawberry, cherry, and black currant fruit, a touch of minerals, earth, and underbrush. Although round and pleasant, it lacks depth. Drink it over the next 6–7 years.

1998: Soft, peppery, and herbaceous, with some spice, this lightweight, medium-bodied 1998 requires consumption over the next 6–7 years.

1997: The 1997 is a light-bodied, slightly herbaceous, and diluted wine with a straightforward, pleasant feel, but not much depth or length. It should drink well for 1–2 years.

1996: This well-made cru bourgeois exhibits a dark ruby color and a round, attractive nose of black currants, raspberries, and earth. Medium-bodied, with sweet tannin and good purity, this wine should drink well for 6–7 years.

1995: Consistently open-knit, soft, and pleasant, but essentially one-dimensional and monochromatic, the 1995 Phélan-Ségur offers enjoyable fruit in the nose, but it lacks the depth and richness of other top vintages of this well-placed St.-Estèphe cru bourgeois. Anticipated maturity: now–2005.

PIBRAN (PAUILLAC)

2000	C	(87–88)
1999	C	87
1998	C	87
1997	C	73
1996	C	89

2000: Readers looking for a generous, full-flavored, uncomplicated, supple-textured, reasonably priced 2000 Pauillac should check out this wine. A deep ruby/purple color is accompanied by copious amounts of black currant fruit, low acidity, and some viscosity. This is a hedonistic, full-throttle Pauillac that should drink well for 10–12 years. If it develops more complexity, it will merit an even higher score.

1999: The 1999 Pibran exhibits a dense ruby color in addition to a classic Pauillac nose of cedarwood, black currants, underbrush, and new oak. A dense, plush, forward, precocious offering, it is meant to be drunk upon release and should age nicely for a decade or more. Anticipated maturity: now–2015.

1998: A fine effort from Pibran, the 1998 exhibits austere tannin as well as copious quantities of ripe cassis fruit, a straightforward, medium- to full-bodied style, plenty of spice, and a user-friendly personality. Anticipated maturity: now–2015.

1997: In contrast to the 1996, the 1997 is a disappointment. It displays distinctive herbaceous aromas, a short, compressed personality, and no depth or intensity. I was surprised to see such a mediocre wine following the strong performance in 1996.

1996: The 1996 Pibran has turned out to be a sleeper of the vintage. A big, muscular wine, it boasts a saturated purple color and sweet cassis fruit intermeshed with cedar and spice. In the mouth it is medium- to full-bodied, with ripe, well-integrated tannin, adequate acidity, and a long, well-delineated finish. It is a blend of 70% Cabernet Sauvignon and the balance mostly Merlot, with a dollop of Cabernet Franc. This large-scaled Pauillac should drink well between 2004–2016.

PICHON-LONGUEVILLE BARON (PAUILLAC)

2000	E	(94–96)
1999	E	90
1998	E	90
1997	D	86
1996	E	91
1995	E	90

2000: The finest effort from this estate since their terrific back-to-back vintages of 1989 and 1990, the perfumed, opaque purple 2000 exhibits classy, complex aromas of incense, black fruits, vanilla, and spice box with a touch of charcoal in the background. On the attack, this full-bodied, impeccably balanced wine is powerful and sweet, with high levels of glycerin, superb concentration, beautifully integrated acidity and tannin, and a spectacularly long, layered finish. It is a profound effort from this second growth Pauillac. Anticipated maturity: 2005–2030.

1999: A sexier, more opulent and hedonistic Pichon-Baron than the 1998, the 1999's dense ruby/purple color is the introduction to a low-acid wine with a silky texture and good fleshiness. It offers jammy black fruits intermixed with licorice, incense, leather, and toast. Opulent and fat, it will be drinkable upon release and last 16 years.

1998: A definitive Pauillac, the dense purple 1998 Pichon-Baron offers up a sweet bouquet of licorice, smoke, asphalt, blackberries, and crème de cassis. In the mouth the wine is elegant rather than full-blown, with medium body, sweet fruit, nice texture on the attack and mid-palate, and moderate tannin in the long finish. No, not as profound as the 1996, 1990, or 1989, but an outstanding effort. Anticipated maturity: 2006–2020.

1997: Complex, evolved, mature, cedar, spice box, and black currant aromas emerge from this ruby/garnet-colored offering. Soft, with sweet tannin, spicy oak, and ripe fruit but no significant depth, this is an open-knit, attractive Pauillac to enjoy now and over the next 4–5 years.

1996: Pichon-Longueville Baron's 1996 has turned out to be even better than I thought from cask. The high percentage of Cabernet Sauvignon in the blend (about 80%) resulted in a wine that has put on weight in bottle. An opaque purple color is accompanied by beautiful aromas of tobacco, new saddle leather, roasted coffee, and cassis. It is dense, medium- to full-bodied, and backward, with moderately high tannin but plenty of sweet fruit, glycerin, and extract to balance out the wine's structure. This well-endowed, classic Pauillac should be at its finest between 2006–2022.

1995: A stylish, elegant, more restrained style of Pichon-Longueville Baron, with less obvious new oak than usual, this deep ruby/purple wine offers a pure black currant–scented nose with subtle aromas of coffee and smoky toasty oak. In the mouth, the wine displays less weight and muscle than the 1996, but it offers suave, elegant, rich fruit presented in a medium- to full-bodied, surprisingly lush style. Anticipated maturity: now–2016.

Past Glories: 1990 (96), 1989 (95+), 1988 (90), 1982 (92)

PICHON-LONGUEVILLE-COMTESSE DE LALANDE (PAUILLAC)

2000	EE	(95–97)
1999	E	88
1998	E	87
1997	E	88
1996	EE	96
1995	EE	96

After producing in 1995 and 1996 its two best back-to-back vintages since the 1982 and 1983, Pichon-Lalande went through a slump in 1997 and 1998, but nicely rebounded with a good 1999 and a sumptuous 2000 that is one of the stars of the vintage.

2000: A formidable effort, Pichon-Lalande is one of the superstars of the vintage. The blend of 50% Cabernet Sauvignon, 34% Merlot, 10% Petit Verdot (from vines planted in 1932), and 6% Cabernet Franc has resulted in a spectacularly complex, rich wine that will easily rival the last great Pichon-Lalande produced, the 1996. The 2000 offers an intensely spicy blackberry, cassis, and smoky-scented perfume with hints of espresso, barbecue spice, and cedar. Enormously rich on the attack, with some smokiness, superb purity, high but sweet, ripe tannin, its style is similar to the 1996, but there is an element of aromatic complexity that may transcend that superb vintage. Powerful for this estate, yet with perfect harmony and purity, it will be drinkable between 2004–2030. Bravo!

1999: A blend of 47% Merlot, 37% Cabernet Sauvignon, 9% Cabernet Franc, and 7% Petit Verdot, the 1999 Pichon-Lalande is putting on weight as it evolves in cask. The color is a deep ruby with purple nuances. Medium- to full-bodied, with a sexy nose of caramel, tobacco, sweet black currants, and spice, it is a silky-textured, seductive effort that may merit an outstanding rating if it develops more length and mid-palate. It has evolved well over the last year, and is now displaying more of Pichon-Lalande's class and nobility. Anticipated maturity: now–2018.

1998: Aromas of tobacco smoke, cedar, cherries, and black currants emerge from the moderately intense, complex bouquet. This wine has evolved nicely, revealing some austerity in its medium-weight, delicate, slightly herbaceous personality. Drink it over the next 12–15 years.

1997: One of the vintage's stars in the Médoc, this hedonistic, luscious, sexy, opulently textured Pichon-Lalande is a blend of 55% Cabernet Sauvignon, 30% Merlot, 10% Petit Verdot, and 5% Cabernet Franc. Exhibiting a dark ruby color with purple nuances, it is open-knit, with plentiful quantities of roasted herbs, smoky oak, vanilla, and creamy black currant fruit. A lush texture, low acidity, and an accessible, velvety-textured style will have many admirers. Consume it over the next 6–7 years.

1996: The 1996 Pichon-Lalande is just as awesome from bottle as it was from multiple cask tastings. For Pichon-Lalande, the percentage of Cabernet Sauvignon is atypically high. This wine normally contains 35–50% Merlot in the blend, but the 1996 is a blend of 75% Cabernet Sauvignon, 15% Merlot, 5% Cabernet Franc, and 5% Petit Verdot. Only 50% of the estate's production made it into the grand vin. The color is a saturated ruby/purple. The nose suggests sweet, nearly overripe Cabernet Sauvignon, with its blueberry/blackberry/cassis scents intermixed with high-quality, subtle, toasty new oak. Deep and full-bodied, it exhibits fabulous concentration and a sweet, opulent texture. Given its abnormally high percentage of Cabernet Sauvignon, I would suspect it will close down. It possesses plenty of tannin, but the wine's overwhelming fruit richness dominates its personality. Could the 1996 turn out to be as extraordinary as the 1982? Anticipated maturity: 2004–2025.

1995: What sumptuous pleasures await those who purchase either the 1996 or 1995 Pichon-Lalande. It is hard to choose a favorite, although the 1995 is a smoother, more immediately sexy and accessible wine. It is an exquisite example of Pichon-Lalande, with the Merlot component giving the wine a coffee/chocolate/cherry component to go along with the Cabernet Sauvignon's and Cabernet Franc's complex blackberry/cassis fruit. The wine possesses an opaque black/ruby/purple color and sexy, flamboyant aromatics of toast, black fruits, and cedar. Exquisite on the palate, this full-bodied, layered, multidimensional wine should prove to be one of the vintage's most extraordinary success stories. Anticipated maturity: now–2020.

Past Glories: 1994 (91), 1989 (92), 1988 (90), 1986 (94), 1985 (90), 1983 (94), 1982 (99), 1979 (90), 1978 (92), 1975 (90), 1961 (95), 1945 (96)

PICQUE-CAILLOU (PESSAC-LÉOGNAN)

2000	**C**	**(87–88)**
1999	**C**	**86**
1998	**C**	**85**

2000: This classy, complex Pessac-Léognan is as good as its 1998 counterpart. In this sleeper of the vintage, notes of scorched earth, cranberry jam, black cherries, and spice are followed by a sweet, medium-bodied, impeccably balanced, restrained, yet flavorful wine. Enjoy it over the next 6–7 years.

1999: The 1999 is the most concentrated, finest Picque-Caillou I have tasted in many years. It possesses the classic elegance one expects from this vineyard, as well as more richness and volume on the palate. A deep ruby color reveals purple nuances. The wine exhibits abundant quantities of black fruits intermixed with minerals, spice box, gravel, and earth. Low acidity gives it an evolved, up-front, precocious appeal. Drink it over the next 10 years.

1998: This elegant, medium-bodied 1998 is a classic Graves with its tobacco, smoke, tar, and earthiness. It offers good fruit, medium body, and a straightforward, pleasant style. Drink it over the next 5–6 years.

PIERRE DE LUNE (ST.-EMILION)

2000	D	(88–90)
1999	D	90

2000: Another of an unprecedented number of sleepers of the vintage, Pierre de Lune is an open-knit, expansive, ripe, chewy, fruit-driven effort with copious levels of glycerin, no hard edges, and a seamless, full-bodied, flattering personality. I suspect there is some tannin lurking beneath the fruit and glycerin. Anticipated maturity: now–2014.

1999: This is a 200-case garage wine from the manager of Clos Fourtet. If you can find it, buy it! The opaque purple-colored 1999 offers up notes of blueberry liqueur intermixed with cassis, licorice, and toasty new oak. Dense and full-bodied, with low acidity, sweet tannin, and an ostentatious personality, this effort will surprise many tasters. Anticipated maturity: now–2018.

LE PIN (POMEROL)

2000	EEE	(96–98)
1998	EEE	93
1997	EEE	86?
1996	EEE	91
1995	EEE	93+

When the Thienpont family bought this tiny vineyard situated in the very heart of the plateau of Pomerol, it was, by their own admission, to fashion a Pétrus-like wine of great richness and majesty. The first vintages were simply superb, and Le Pin quickly got to be not only one of the greatest Pomerols but also Bordeaux's most exotic and luxurious, not to mention most expensive, wine. However, the estate now has to face considerable competition from all the new St.-Emilion upstarts, the wines of which often match Le Pin and sell for more reasonable prices.

2000: A sweet, jammy, soft, fleshy, round, delicious offering, the 2000 Le Pin exhibits scents of coconut, aggressive but toasty new oak, caramel, and vanilla. Somehow, the proprietor has managed to subdue some of the vintage's high levels of tannin. This wine comes across as ripe, with low acidity, astonishing concentration, and a beautifully sweet, rich, sexy personality. A seamless wine, it will be drinkable upon release. Anticipated maturity: now–2015. The finest Le Pin since the 1990 and 1982!

1998: A beautifully made, dark ruby/garnet/plum-colored wine, the 1998 Le Pin offers an exotic bouquet of coconut, kirsch, and jammy blackberries, all flamboyantly dosed with smoky new oak. It is dense, rich, and plush, with a good tannic framework. While this remains an outstanding and compelling Pomerol, it is matched by many far less expensive, equally prodigious alternatives that have emerged recently. Anticipated maturity: 2003–2018.

1997: While not the strongest effort from this small estate, Le Pin's 1997 reveals an excessive amount of oak for the concentration of fruit. However, even richer vintages have tended to reveal abundant oak early in life, only to have it absorbed as the wine ages. The 1997 possesses sweet currant and cherry fruit, abundant toasty oak, and a seductive style, but the oak is elevated. The wine will probably not last long enough for the wood to become fully integrated. Or am I wrong about that? Anticipated maturity: now–2008.

1996: The 1996 Le Pin has softened and is now extremely open-knit, with a dark ruby color and evolved notes of roasted coffee, melted chocolate, exotic coconut scents, and jammy black cherry fruit. Round, soft, supple-textured, and medium-bodied, this is one of the most flamboyant yet evolved wines of the vintage. There is very little production of the 1996 Le Pin since only one-third of the harvest made it into the final blend. Anticipated maturity: now–2012.

1995: A dense ruby-colored Le Pin, the 1995 offers up aromas of lead pencil, roasted nuts, smoke, spice, fruitcake, and black cherries intermixed with white chocolate. Luscious and full-bodied, with low acidity but plenty of grip and tannin in the finish, this wine, with its abundant cola, kirsch, and black raspberry flavors, appears to be every bit as structured and tannic as the 1996. Anticipated maturity: now–2018.

Past Glories: 1994 (91+), 1993 (90), 1990 (98), 1989 (96), 1988 (92), 1986 (91), 1985 (93), 1983 (98), 1982 (100)

LE PIN BEAU SOLEIL (BORDEAUX SUPÉRIEUR)

2000	C	(87–89)

2000: An amazing effort for a Bordeaux Supérieur, this opaque purple 2000 is unquestionably a sleeper of the vintage. Made from 60% Merlot, 20% Cabernet Franc, and the rest Cabernet Sauvignon plus a tiny dose of Malbec, it tastes like a classified growth. Complex aromatics of black currants, cherries, and earth are abundantly present in this pure, layered, nuanced wine. Don't let this one get by you! It will drink well for 3–4 years.

LE PIN DE BELCIER (CÔTES DE CASTILLON)

1999	C	86
1998	C	86

1999: Soft, round, and hedonistic, with plenty of smoky wood and jammy black currant/cherry fruit, this 1999 displays low acidity as well as a fleshy, plump personality. It is best drunk during its first 3–4 years of life.

1998: Big, spicy new oak aromas border on exaggeration. In the mouth, however, the wine exhibits good elegance, sweet cherry and black currant fruit, and a nicely knit, medium-bodied, well-balanced personality. If the oak fades, this wine will be even better. Drink it over the next 4–5 years.

PIPEAU (ST.-EMILION)

2000	C	(90–91)
1999	C	89
1998	C	88

A new discovery, Pipeau is undoubtedly a sleeper in all three of the following vintages, as well as one of the best values to emerge from St.-Emilion in many years.

2000: A fruit bomb deluxe, it offers a sexy combination of blackberry, black raspberry, and cherry fruit, with subtle oak in the background. Though thicker and more tannic than the 1998, this medium-bodied wine displays silky tannin and a layered, fat, rich personality. It must be drunk during its first decade of life. It is a sleeper of the vintage and a super value.

1999: The 1999 may turn out to be even better than the 1998. Smoky, black cherry liqueur aromas jump from the glass of this lush, hedonistic, fruit-filled wine. Dense, fat, flattering, and chewy, it is best consumed during its first 7–8 years of life.

1998: The dark ruby/purple 1998 offers lush, gorgeous, cherry and blackberry flavors and reveals little evidence of oak. The wine is smoky, lush, unbelievably flattering to drink, a complete *vin de plaisir,* as the French say. Because of its low acidity, this fruit bomb should be drunk over the next 6–7 years.

PLAISANCE (ST.-EMILION)

2000	C	(87–89+)
1998	C	87

2000: An attractive, complex bouquet of minerals, black currants, blueberries, and smoke is followed by a well-extracted, pure, ripe, sizable wine with moderate levels of tannin as well as enough acidity for definition. It possesses class and style, as well as the potential for 15 or more years of longevity. This is a sleeper of the vintage.

1998: A supple, rich St.-Emilion, the 1998 Plaisance exhibits aromas and flavors of spicy cherry and new oak. Fleshy, with admirable depth, and a style not dissimilar from some of the better St.-Emilions. Drink it over the next 8 years.

PLINCE (POMEROL)

1999	C	86
1998	C	85

1999: Sweet jammy cherry fruit, smoke, coffee, and dried herb notes emerge from this dark ruby-colored 1999. Made in a lighter style, this well-balanced, soft effort should be drunk during its first 5–6 years of life.

1998: Spicy new oak along with moderate levels of cherries, plums, coffee, and caramel make a gentle but attractive appearance in this wine's aromas and flavors. It is best consumed over the next 4–5 years.

LA POINTE (POMEROL)

2000	C	(86–87)
1999	C	87
1998	C	84

2000: This is an elegant, soft, medium-bodied, straightforward wine with a superficial appeal of black cherry fruit intermixed with earth, oak, and spice. Although slightly compressed, it is well made and clean. Drink it over the next decade.

1999: If this wine is put in the bottle without excessive clarification, it could turn out to be a sleeper of the vintage. Its deep ruby/purple color is accompanied by an excellent, multi-layered personality, a chewy texture, abundant quantities of plum, cherry, cola, and mocha flavors, excellent concentration, sweet tannin, and low acidity. Anticipated maturity: now–2012.

1998: Soft, fruity, and diffuse, this elegant, lightweight effort is pleasant but lacks substance as well as follow-through on the palate. Drink it over the next 2–3 years.

PONT-CLOQUET (POMEROL)

2000	C	(88–89)

2000: A sleeper of the vintage, this little-known Pomerol is a dense black/purple, chewy, voluptuous offering exhibiting licorice, plum, blackberry, and cherry flavors, superb purity, and a long finish. It may merit an outstanding score if more complexity develops. Anticipated maturity: now–2014.

PONTET-CANET (PAUILLAC)

2000	D	(92–95)
1999	D	88
1998	D	86
1997	D	85?
1996	D	92+
1995	D	92

This estate was propelled among the top-flight Pauillacs with its sleeper offering in 1994 and brilliant wines produced in 1995, 1996 and 2000. However, the 1997s, 1998s, and 1999s are definitely inferior in quality to the aforementioned vintages. Despite current market prices, Pontet-Canet remains a fairly good value.

2000: A spectacular effort from Pontet-Canet, the 2000 rivals its 1996, 1995, and their stunning 1994. The opaque ruby/purple-colored 2000 offers a gorgeously pure, intense bouquet of blackberry liqueur, cassis, smoke, and Asian spices. In that respect, it is similar to Mouton-Rothschild. The Pontet-Canet displays a firm, classic feel in the mouth, high tannin, medium to full body, exceptional concentration as well as purity, and a long finish. Bravo! Anticipated maturity: 2007–2030.

1999: Ripe, sweet black currant, underbrush, and earth scents emerge from this dark ruby/purple wine. With low acidity, a seductive, fleshy, chewy texture, and very good to excellent concentration, this charming, precocious Pontet-Canet is best drunk during its first 10–14 years of life.

1998: A pleasant, dark ruby-colored, elegant Pauillac, the 1998 displays hollowness on the mid-palate along with notes of red and black currants, tobacco, dried herbs, and earth. Though solidly made, there is not much depth. Anticipated maturity: 2004–2012.

1997: This wine was severe, tannic, gritty, and attenuated on two of the three occasions I had it from bottle. I have lowered the score and added a question mark because the wine lacks the color saturation of the barrel samples and exhibits more herbaceousness, and the tannin is astringent. Perhaps it is going through an awkward stage of development, but right now I am less enthusiastic. Anticipated maturity: now–2010.

1996: I was shocked by how backward the 1996 Pontet-Canet was on the three occasions I tasted it. This wine possesses superb potential, but it appears it will require a few years of patience. The color is a saturated dark purple. With coaxing, the wine offers aromas of black currant jam intertwined with minerals, sweet oak, and spice. A full-bodied wine, it possesses layered, concentrated, sweet fruit, with an elevated level of ripe tannin. Anticipated maturity: 2010–2035.

1995: An old-style Pauillac, yet made with far more purity and richness than the estate's ancient vintages, this broad-shouldered, muscular, classic wine exhibits a saturated purple color and sensationally dense, rich, concentrated, cassis flavors that roll over the palate with impressive purity and depth. The wine is tannic and closed but powerful and rich. It appears to possess length and intensity similar to the 1996. This is a great young Pauillac. Anticipated maturity: 2005–2025.

Past Glories: 1994 (93), 1961 (94?), 1945 (93), 1929 (90)

POTENSAC (MÉDOC)

2000	C	(87–88)
1999	C	86
1998	C	87
1997	C	85
1996	C	89
1995	C	87

Owned by the Delon family of Léoville-Las Cases, Potensac has been a noteworthy offering for more than two decades.

2000: With yields of 35 hectoliters per hectare, and a selection process that allowed only 60% of the crop in this cru bourgeois, Potensac sets the standard for its peers. The elegant, fresh, deep ruby/purple 2000 reveals a grapy, red currant, black cherry, mineral, earth, and wood-scented bouquet. It will be long-lived for a wine of its class. Anticipated maturity: now–2015.

1999: Dark ruby-colored, with jammy cherry and raspberry fruit, a straightforward personality, and an easygoing, medium-bodied finish, the 1999 should drink well for 4–5 years.

1998: A solidly made Potensac, with spice box and black currant fruit, this medium-bodied effort reveals sweet fruit, moderate weight, and excellent purity. Drink it over the next 4–6 years.

1997: A soft, cedary, herbaceous but pleasant, round, elegant style of wine, with berry and red currant fruit and a smooth finish, the 1997 Potensac can be enjoyed over the next 1–2 years.

1996: One of the most amazing wines this estate has ever produced. It rivals the 1982, being even richer and potentially longer-lived. It boasts a dark purple color, as well as a sweet, earthy black currant and cherry liqueur–scented nose. There is terrific fruit intensity and purity, as well as moderate tannin in the medium-bodied, impressively rich finish. This wine, which is already drinking well, should last until 2014. A sleeper of the vintage.

1995: Elegant, complex, and evolved, the saturated dark ruby-colored 1995 exhibits herb-tinged, black currant/weedy cassis–like flavors that are supple, round, generous, and appealing. This wine does not possess the power and density of fruit found in the 1996, but it is a delicious, reasonably priced claret that should have broad crowd appeal for 6–7 years or more. A sleeper.

POUJEAUX (MOULIS)

1999	C	89
1998	C	88
1997	C	89
1996	C	86
1995	C	87

The star of Moulis, as well as a perennial sleeper/best buy qualitative pick in the Médoc, this estate continues to turn out excellent wines. Readers skeptical of the 1997 vintage should try Poujeaux, one of the stars of that year—it is totally delicious and gives a good idea of the immense potential of this estate.

1999: A lower-acid, more supple version of the 1998, and though the 1998 displays riper, jammier fruit, I am not convinced it is a better effort. Seductive and fleshy, it is best consumed during its first 10–15 years of life.

1998: The 1998's dark ruby/purple color is accompanied by a sweet nose of cranberries, blackberries, minerals, and toasty oak. The wine is medium- to full-bodied, with excellent texture, fine depth, and sweet tannin in the finish. As always, it is a wine of class and length. Anticipated maturity: now–2016.

1997: Undoubtedly a sleeper of the vintage, and probably the finest 1997 cru bourgeois, Poujeaux's 1997 exhibits a dense purple color as well as a sweet nose of black fruits complemented by toasty oak and loamy soil scents. Textured, layered, and rich, with low acidity and an excellent ripe finish, it can be drunk now and over the next 10–12 years. Bravo!

1996: Opaque purple, with moderately high tannin yet excellent sweet black currant fruit, this medium-bodied, well-structured, muscular, densely packed Poujeaux will require 4–5 years of cellaring. Anticipated maturity: 2006–2015.

1995: A very good wine, with grip, tannin, medium to full body, and excellent ripeness, this unevolved, backward yet promising Poujeaux needs cellaring. There is some mineral-tinged, sweet black currant fruit in both the aromatics and flavors. Anticipated maturity: 2003–2015.

Other vintage tasted: 2000 (87–88)

PRIEURÉ-LICHINE (MARGAUX)

2000	D	(88–89)
1999	D	87
1998	C	87
1996	C	86
1995	C	85

Readers are advised to take a closer look at this property. Prieuré-Lichine has been bought recently by the Ballande family, who also own Château Baret, in the Graves region. The cellars have undergone a major renovation, the vineyards have been restructured, and the property is doing malolactic fermentation in barrel as well as *microbullage* (oxygenation of the lees, as practiced in some Burgundy and St.-Emilion cellars). All this has translated into a superb 1999, and a 2000 that is unquestionably Prieuré-Lichine's finest success to date.

2000: The finest offering from this estate in three decades, this medium-bodied, elegant, dense ruby/purple 2000 exhibits copious amounts of black fruits intermixed with mineral, licorice, spice box, dried herb, and floral characteristics. Sweet and rich, with no hard edges, lush tannin, low acidity, and a moderately long finish, it is not a huge wine built for the long haul, but should be at its prime between 2004–2016.

1999: The 1999 displays the same characteristics of the 1998 in addition to more fruit, texture, glycerin, and volume. The result is a nearly outstanding, seductive, multidimensional Prieuré-Lichine with more fat and ripe fruit than I have seen in many years. Drink it over the next 10–12 years.

1998: Finesse, elegance, as well as admirable flavors are characteristics of this dark ruby-colored, lighter-styled 1998. Offering abundant quantities of berry fruit, cassis, and spice box aromas and flavors, and an excellent texture, this evolved, delicious Margaux is best consumed during its first decade of life.

1996: Medium ruby-colored with a leafy dried tobacco, red currant, and berry-scented nose, this 1996 displays good ripeness, spicy new oak, and a forward, juicy style. It is not a powerful, backward 1996, but rather, a stylish, open-knit claret for consuming over the next 5–6 years.

1995: I expected this wine to turn out better than it has. Hard tannin in the finish, and a slight hollowness in the mid-palate kept my score down. The wine reveals a dark ruby color, light to medium body, good aromatics (earth, underbrush, sweet cherries, and vanilla), and pleasing ripe fruit on the attack. The severe finish is dry and austere. Anticipated maturity: now–2008.

PRIEURÉ-MALESAN (PREMIÈRES CÔTES DE BLAYE)

2000	B	(86–87)

2000: This large Blaye estate, owned by Bernard Magrez (the proprietor of Pape-Clément), has fashioned a fine value. Fat, soft, and lush, the 2000 is made in a fruity, up-front style with plenty of currant/cherry aromas and flavors. Drink it over the next 1–2 years.

PRIEURS DE LA COMMANDÉRIE (POMEROL)

2000	C	(83–85?)

2000: High levels of wood in addition to dry, astringent tannin, and an austere personality are cause for concern about this wine's future potential, which otherwise has very good concentration.

QUINAULT L'ENCLOS (ST.-EMILION)

2000	E	(92–94)
1999	E	93
1998	E	94
1997	D	88

This is an emerging St.-Emilion superstar run by Dr. Alain and Françoise Raynaud. Situated within the Libourne city limits on gravelly soils, Quinault could be called the Haut-Brion of St.-Emilion given the fact that it 1) is totally surrounded by a *clos* (wall enclosure), 2) is within the city limits, and 3) posseses stony topsoils. Since their first vintage in 1997, the Raynauds have taken this 37-acre walled vineyard to new heights. They continue to experiment with concentration techniques, but the wine that ultimately results from a blend of 80% Merlot, 10% Cabernet Sauvignon, and 10% Cabernet Franc is beautifully pure and elegant, with considerable aging potential. The last three vintages have been profound.

2000: The 2000 offers an opaque purple color as well as a beautiful floral nose with scents of blueberries, black raspberries, minerals, and subtle spicy oak. It displays a character akin to a Burgundy grand cru in its aromatics and finesse. In the mouth there is great fruit, length, opulence, and elegance. While it may not be as dense as the 1998, it is a rich, concentrated, medium- to full-bodied, brilliantly crafted, and impressively well delineated 2000. Anticipated maturity: 2005–2018.

1999: Not dissimilar from the 1998, the 1999 offers a dense purple color as well as superrich aromas and flavors of blueberries, blackberries, prunes, and smoky oak. A silkier, thicker character is undoubtedly due to lower acidity and more glycerin. If the 1999 has more texture, the 1998 is more complex, at least at this time. Anticipated maturity: now–2017.

1998: An elegant as well as powerful effort, this dense ruby/purple-colored 1998 reveals notes of plums, black raspberries, vanilla, minerals, licorice, and spice. Exceptionally rich, with an outstanding texture, this medium- to full-bodied wine possesses a distinctive, individualistic style, largely because of its floral, blueberry fruit flavors. Though accessible, it will age for 20 years. Anticipated maturity: now–2020.

1997: If the 1997 lacks density and length, it still reveals an unmistakable similarity to Lafleur, the famed Pomerol. Kirsch, spice, and mineral notes are the hallmarks of this wine, which combines breed, power, and elegance. Supple tannin, a medium-bodied, plush texture, and fine purity characterize this delicious, complex, stylish St.-Emilion. Drink it now as well as over the next 10+ years.

RAHOUL (GRAVES)

2000	C	(86–88)
1996	C	78

2000: Dark ruby-colored with an elegant, medium-bodied personality, soft tannin, and notes of herbs, smoke, tobacco, and cherry fruit, this stylish Graves should be at its best before 2012.

1996: Medium dark ruby, with an earthy, smoky nose intermixed with weedy tobacco, this lean, austere wine's personality is dominated by tannin. Perhaps more flesh and charm will emerge with aging. Anticipated maturity: now–2007.

RAUSAN-SÉGLA (MARGAUX)

2000	E	(90–92)
1999	E	88
1998	E	89
1997	D	79
1996	D	88
1995	D	88+

Under new ownership, the cellars and winemaking facilities have undergone a major renovation, and the vineyards have been entirely restructured. Despite these investments, I am still waiting for the new proprietors to hit the bull's eye with this renowned estate. However, I must admit that the 1998s and 1999s are very good efforts and it seems that the 2000 continues the trend favorably. The omnipresent Michel Rolland has been brought in as a consultant, no doubt to try to tame some of this wine's formidable tannins.

2000: This wine reveals notes of green pepper in the otherwise enticing bouquet of black fruits, minerals, and vanillin, medium to full body, an austere, structured personality, and copious tannin. While I initially thought it would taste better, there is a lot going on in this 2000, so perhaps my score is unduly conservative. There is no question that this wine has considerable upside potential. Anticipated maturity: 2008–2020.

1999: Only 35% of the crop made it into the 1999's final blend (58% Cabernet Sauvignon, 40% Merlot, and 2% Petit Verdot). Softer than the 1998, it possesses a deep ruby/purple color, sweet blackberry and cherry aromas, a seductive entry on the palate, medium body, and a lush, consumer-friendly personality revealing neither austerity nor tannic astringency. Anticipated maturity: 2003–2015.

1998: A blend of 65% Cabernet Sauvignon and 35% Merlot, this classic, austerely styled Médoc exhibits medium to full body, true breed as well as class, and excellent aromas of subtle herbs, cedar, cassis, and new wood. Rich, sweet on the attack, and moderately tannic, it will benefit from 4–5 more years of cellaring. Anticipated maturity: 2006–2018.

1997: This herbaceous, medium-bodied, lighter effort possesses a dark ruby color, attractive berry fruit, and a pleasant earthy, floral bouquet. However, there is little length and a compressed feeling to the wine's personality.

1996: The dense, ruby/purple, unfriendly 1996 is tannic, backward, and in need of 8 years of cellaring. The wine does seem to possess the requisite fruit and extract, however, to stand up to its powerful structure. Though pure and rich, this wine should not be touched for at least a decade. The sweet cassis aromas of this Cabernet Sauvignon–dominated wine are combined with floral and mineral notes. Anticipated maturity: 2010–2025.

1995: Unfortunately, this was one of the few wines of that vintage that I was able to taste only once after bottling. Nevertheless, it is a classic *vin de garde*, with a saturated ruby/purple color and a tight but promising nose of sweet plum and cassis fruit intertwined with underbrush, vanilla, and licorice scents. The wine is ripe, medium- to full-bodied, and rich, as well as unyielding, ferociously tannic, pure, and layered. The finish is extremely dry, with a brooding angularity and toughness. In spite of this, my instincts suggest the requisite depth is present to balance out the structure. This effort will also require a decade of cellaring. Anticipated maturity: 2007–2025.

RAUZAN-DESPAGNET (BORDEAUX SUPÉRIEUR)

2000 Cuvée Passion	C	(88–90)

2000: A sleeper of the vintage, this blend of 70% Merlot and 30% Cabernet Sauvignon exhibits a deep ruby/purple color in addition to a knockout nose of jammy cassis, licorice, and spice box, medium to full body, ripe tannin, and a long finish. It is hard to predict how these offerings from lower-rated *terroirs* will age, but this offering will drink beautifully for at least 5–6 years.

RAUZAN-GASSIES (MARGAUX)

2000	C	(87–88)
1999	C	87
1998	C	85
1996	C	75

Rauzan-Gassies tends toward heaviness for a Margaux. It can be fairly concentrated, but it does not display the fragrance normally associated with the best efforts of the appellation and, in most vintages, it reaches maturity surprisingly early for a classified growth. Reports emanate that this estate is on the upswing. While it is too early to judge whether this information is well founded, the 1999s and 2000s seem to be very good efforts from this perennial underperformer.

2000: One of the finest wines made at this estate in many years, the dark ruby/purple 2000 offers up scents of damp earth, underbrush, creosote, camphor, and black cherries. Ripe, long, deep, and medium- to full-bodied, with moderately high tannin as well as fine sweetness to balance the structure, this earthy effort will be at it best between 2003–2020.

1999: Much better than the 1998, the 1999 is, along with the 2000, one of the finest Rauzan-Gassies I have tasted. Cassis intermixed with earth, asphalt, prunes, black tea, and spice box aromas jump from the glass of this dark ruby/purple effort. The acidity is low, the concentration level impressive, and the wine beautifully textured, with all of its elements nicely integrated. Anticipated maturity: 2003–2017.

1998: This elegant, soft, fresh, light- to medium-bodied, pleasant wine lacks substance as well as depth. It will provide superficial charm over the next 3–4 years.

1996: The shallow, medium ruby-colored 1996 reveals earthy overtones, little depth, an attenuated, compressed personality, and an herbaceous finish. It will not improve. Anticipated maturity: now–2006.

REIGNAC (BORDEAUX)

2000	**D**	**(90–91)**

Reignac is the reference point for what can be achieved in Bordeaux's less prestigious appellations. Proprietor Yves Vatelot (also co-proprietor and manager of Lascombes) has hit the bull's eye in 2000—and that's saying something, given how good Reignac has been over the last 5–6 years. The 1998 and 1999 Reignac are selections from the finest lots of late-harvested fruit from the vineyard's best parcels. Yields do not exceed 35 hectoliters per hectare. They are aged 18 months in 100% new oak. The blend is generally 75% Merlot and 25% Cabernet Sauvignon.

2000: This awesome generic Bordeaux boasts a dense purple color as well as a sweet nose of crème de cassis intermixed with mineral, toast, and spice box aromas. Amazingly concentrated, rich, and full-bodied, with sweet tannin and a long finish, this 2000—believe it or not—is of classified-growth quality. If you don't believe me, insert it in a blind tasting against some of the best classified growths and see for yourself. It is a sleeper of the vintage. Anticipated maturity: now–2015.

1999: The 1999 exhibits a supple, lush texture as well as a sweet, velvety style. Its quality level is well above its official pedigree. Enjoy it during its first 5–7 years of life.

1998: The 1998 is a terrific effort for this appellation. The wine is medium- to full-bodied, with a Burgundy-like floral characteristic intermixed with black cherries, spicy oak, cigar box, and cedar.

RIOU DE THAILLAS (ST.-EMILION)

2000	**D**	**(88–89+)**

This small, quasi-garage wine is made by Jean-Yves Béchet, the owner of the stunning Côtes de Bourg estate Fougas-Maldoror. Unfortunately, there is not much of it, as the vineyard is just over 6 acres.

2000: Another sleeper of the vintage, this 2000 possesses considerable depth, purity, and ripeness. Full-bodied, with smoky, licorice, black cherry, and currant aromas and flavors, this well-balanced, moderately tannic wine will drink well between 2005–2016.

RIPEAU (ST.-EMILION)

2000	**C**	**(87–89)**
1999	**C**	**87**
1998	**C**	**85?**

Ripeau is an estate that consumers should keep an eye on, as the vinifications are now supervised by Dr. Alain Raynaud, of Quinault l'Enclos. The 1999 marks an improvement over previous vintages and the 2000 is the finest wine this underachieving estate has ever made. Because of this property's relatively short history, prices are still reasonable.

2000: Plum, cherry, and earthy aromas jump from the glass of this dense, chewy, supple 2000. Loaded with fruit and glycerin, this medium-bodied, moderately structured offering is best consumed during its first 8–10 years of life.

1999: A much improved Ripeau, the 1999 offers spicy new oak, black raspberry and cherry fruit, medium to full body, a sweet mid-palate, a harmonious personality, and a nicely textured finish. It should drink well for 10 years.

1998: A dark ruby/plum color accompanies a sweet nose of prunes and black fruits. This wine is somewhat of a paradox in that the entry on the palate is soft and jammy, but hard, harsh, rustic tannin takes over, and the wine becomes compressed as well as attenuated.

ROC DE CAMBES (CÔTES DE BOURG)

2000	D	(90–93)
1999	D	89
1998	D	91
1997	C	86
1996	C	88
1995	C	89

The undisputed leader from the Côtes de Bourg appellation, this estate owned by François Mitjavile, the proprietor of Tertre-Rôteboeuf, continues to turn out delicious, chocolate-scented and -flavored wines. If wine is a beverage of pleasure, Roc de Cambes satisfies that requirement impeccably. Lately, I had a magnum of 1989 and it continues to sing.

2000: A sensational offering, this may be the finest Roc des Cambes yet made. The 1989 and 1990 were close in quality, but the superripe, voluptuous, concentrated style, unctuous texture, and notes of chocolate, coffee, truffles, caramel, and black cherry/currant fruit are impossible to resist. Succulent and hedonistic, this Côtes de Bourg is a thrill to drink. Anticipated maturity: now–2010.

1999: The 1999, which may turn out to be outstanding, has put on weight during its *élevage* and now reveals a greater, fleshier mid-palate. Thick, juicy, and nearly as good as the compelling 1998, it will require consumption during its first 5–7 years of life. Bravo!

1998: One of the finest Roc des Cambes I have tasted, this exotic, flamboyant, explosively rich 1998 boasts dazzling aromatics of coffee, jammy berry fruit, incense, fudge, and spice. This hedonistic effort reveals no hard edges, a seamless texture, and plenty of juicy, succulent fruit. It is impossible to resist. Drink it over the next 6–7 years.

1997: Though less concentrated than expected, this is an attractive, light-bodied Roc des Cambes with pleasant characteristics of roasted coffee, chocolate, and sweet cherry fruit. Drink it before 2003.

1996: The dark ruby 1996 offers up a sweet, mocha, chocolaty nose with ripe berry fruit in the background. Though not complex, it is soft, velvety-textured, medium- to full-bodied, and a delicious, hedonistically styled wine that should continue to drink well for 2–3 years.

1995: The 1995 offers up a telltale Merlot nose of smoky, roasted coffee, sweet chocolate, mocha, and berry scents. Amazingly deep and rich, this is among the finest wines I have ever tasted from the Côtes de Bourg. There is low acidity, good fat, glycerin, and extract, and a layered, chunky, fleshy finish. It should drink well for 3–4 years.

Past Glories: 1990 (90)

ROCHEBELLE (ST.-EMILION)

1999	D	(85–86)
1998	D	88
1997	C	87
1996	C	87

1999: This well-placed property situated next to Troplong Mondot and close to La Mondotte, produces fine wines that remain reasonably priced for their quality level. The dark ruby/purple 1999 Rochebelle offers a foursquare, straightforward appeal in addition to sweet tannin, low acidity, and medium body. This fleshy effort should drink well upon release and last for a decade.

1998: Potentially a sleeper of the vintage, the 1998 exhibits a dense ruby/purple color in addition to a spicy blackberry- and cherry-scented bouquet with noticeable new oak. Fat, dense, and full-bodied, with excellent purity and length, it will be a savory, fleshy, mouth-filling St.-Emilion with a few more years of bottle age. Anticipated maturity: 2004–2016.

1997: The dark purple 1997 reveals aromas of black raspberry jam and toasty new oak. Medium-bodied and richly fruity, with excellent purity and low acidity, it should drink well during its first 10–12 years of life.

1996: The impressive 1996 Rochebelle displays a deep, saturated, ruby/purple color and a sweet nose of black currants, cherries, incense, and smoky oak. The wine possesses a sweet, fleshy texture, elements of *sur-maturité*, surprisingly low acidity for a 1996, and an expansive, nicely layered finish. If this wine were slightly more complex, it would have merited an even higher score. Anticipated maturity: now–2010.

ROCHER BELLEVUE CAPRICE D'ANGELIQUE (CÔTES DE CASTILLON)

2000	C	(90–92)

2000: An astonishing 100% Merlot is the first French wine made by Umbria's well-known winemaking guru Riccardo Cotarella. He has succeeded in pulling everything possible from this lower-level appellation. Notes of espresso, chocolate, blackberries, and jammy cherries soar from the glass of this opulently textured, fat, fleshy, opaque purple-colored effort. With low acidity, purity, and sweetness, it will provide beautiful drinking now and over the next 7–8 years. This is unquestionably a sleeper of the vintage. What will the Bordelais think of an Italian wine-maker fashioning a garage wine from a satellite appellation?

ROCHER-BELLEVUE-FIGEAC (ST.-EMILION)

2000	C	(86–88)
1999	C	86
1998	C	88
1997	C	84
1996	C	85
1995	C	85

2000: This dark plum-colored, soft, fruit-driven 2000 offers up notes of earth, underbrush, jammy black cherries, and iron. In the mouth it reveals excellent definition, medium body, very good concentration, and low to moderate levels of acidity as well as tannin. Consume it during its first 10–12 years of life.

1999: The dark plum/ruby 1999 reveals medium body and plenty of juicy, concentrated fruit in its mainstream, easy to understand, and delicious personality. Consume it during its first decade of life.

1998: A consumer-friendly effort with an attractive quality-price rapport, the dark plum-colored 1998 offers up cassis, kirsch, licorice, smoke, spice box, and leather aromas. The wine is medium- to full-bodied, with excellent richness, supple tannin, and a velvety finish. Drink it over the next 8 years. A sleeper of the vintage.

1997: The 1997 could pass for its older sibling, although it is slightly fatter with lower acidity than the 1996, with an element of jammy fruit.

1996: The 1996 is soft, open-knit, dark ruby-colored, evolved, fruity, and easy to understand and drink. It should be consumed over the next 5–6 years.

1995: A deep ruby color and attractive spicy, ripe fruit are up front and precocious in this mid-weight St.-Emilion. Drink it over the next 1–2 years.

ROL VALENTIN (ST.-EMILION)

2000	D	(91–94)
1999	D	89

1998	D	90
1997	C	88
1996	D	90

Young proprietor Eric Prissette is attempting to produce a Valandraud-style St.-Emilion at this estate. Rol Valentin emerges from a vineyard of 10.6 acres situated near Cheval Blanc and La Dominique and is generally a blend of 85% Merlot, 10% Cabernet Sauvignon, and 5% Cabernet Franc. It enjoys malolactic fermentation in barrel, aging on its lees, and, though unfined, does receive a light filtration. Among the fashionable micro *cuvées* of St.-Emilion, it is not one of the least expensive.

2000: Rol Valentin's finest wine to date. The opaque purple 2000 exhibits better integrated acidity than in past vintages as well as a velvety texture, succulent style, and gorgeous bouquet of sweet cherry liqueur intermixed with blackberry and black currant fruit. Opulently textured and full-bodied, with tannin lurking beneath the wealth of fruit and glycerin, this is an undeniably seductive, full-flavored wine that cuts a broad swath across the palate. Anticipated maturity: 2003–2016.

1999: A soft, jammy offering without the weight of the 1998. Nevertheless, it is very good. It exhibits a dark ruby/garnet color in addition to a sweet nose of black cherries intermixed with dried herbs, smoke, and earth. Spicy, medium-bodied, and soft, it requires consumption over the next decade.

1998: A superb effort, the dark ruby/purple-colored 1998 offers gorgeous aromas of flowers, blackberries, cherries, smoke, licorice, and spice box. It is deep, succulent, medium- to full-bodied, with decent acidity, superb purity, and a creamy texture. Tannin is present, but it is well integrated and balanced by the wine's depth. Anticipated maturity: now–2014.

1997: From barrel, this wine exhibited the potential to be outstanding. Now that it is in bottle, it is lighter, without sufficient aromatic or flavor dimension to merit an outstanding score. Nevertheless, there remains plenty to admire. The wine possesses a deep ruby color in addition to a sweet plum/cherry, woodsy bouquet with copious quantities of toasty new oak. A spicy St.-Emilion, with low acidity, medium body, and excellent richness and glycerin, it should drink well for 4–5 years.

1996: Rol Valentin has turned in an exemplary performance in 1996. A blend of 90% Merlot, 7% Cabernet Franc, and 3% Cabernet Sauvignon, this wine boasts a dark ruby/purple color, as well as a sweet nose of black currants intermixed with licorice, toasty new barrel aromas, and smoked herbs. Medium-bodied, rich, ripe, and hedonistically styled, it can be consumed now–2014.

ROLLAN DE BY (HAUT-MÉDOC)

2000	C	(87–88)
1999	C	(86–87)
1998	C	86

Rollan de By has become one of the finest Haut-Médoc cru bourgeois estates under the auspices of Jean and Catherine Guyon.

2000: A sleeper of the vintage, this fat, concentrated wine exhibits a deep ruby/purple color, attractive, mineral-infused, black currant fruit flavors, medium body, moderate tannin, and excellent ripeness as well as length. It should drink well for a decade.

1999: Dark ruby-colored, with a Médoc-like, black currant, tobacco, and spice-scented bouquet, this medium-bodied 1999 displays good depth, low acidity, and a forward appeal. Drink it over the next 7–8 years.

1998: Delicious currant, earth, underbrush, and tobacco characteristics make for a rich, medium-bodied yet elegant wine to drink over the next 7–8 years.

ROUET (FRONSAC)

2000	**B**	**(84–85)**

2000: Aromas and flavors of cranberries, strawberries, and tart red cherries characterize this medium-bodied, unsubstantial, elegant, refreshing, lighter-styled Fronsac. Drink it over the next 5 years.

ROUGET (POMEROL)

2000	**D**	**(90–92)**
1999	**D**	**89**
1998	**D**	**89**
1997	**C**	**86**
1996	**C**	**85**

Rouget's story is typical in modern-day Bordeaux—new money, a new owner, more attention to detail, and a stricter selection process result in a vastly superior wine. This property has clearly rebounded from a prolonged period of mediocrity, as evidenced by what they have achieved over recent vintages (in particular from 1997 on), producing the finest Rouget since their glory years of the 1940s, 1950s, and early 1960s.

2000: While the 2000 Rouget may not be better than the 1998, it is as good, with more burly tannin. Its dense opaque ruby color is followed by a powerful nose of earthy black fruits, pepper, and spice box. A muscular Pomerol styled à la 1975 (a topflight vintage for the appellation), with abundant fruit to back up its structure, it will be at its finest between 2004–2020.

1999: Made in a soft, low-acid, plump style, this dark plum/purple-colored, corpulent Pomerol exhibits abundant quantities of fudge-infused black cherry fruit aromas displaying a touch of toffee/caramel. Medium-bodied with low acidity, this is a hedonistic mouthful of nicely textured, fruit-driven wine. Anticipated maturity: now–2011.

1998: Dark ruby/purple-colored, with a ripe nose of chocolate, black fruits, brandy-macerated cherries, figs, and prunes, this medium- to full-bodied, plush Rouget reveals a chewy, concentrated texture as well as a ripe, fat finish. With a bit more definition and complexity, it would merit an outstanding score. Anticipated maturity: now–2015.

1997: A dark ruby color is followed by sweet, spicy, black cherry, dried herbs, and wood aromas. Elegant and round, with lush fruit, low acidity, and a seamless texture, this medium-bodied wine should be consumed over the next 4–5 years.

1996: The 1996 reveals a deceptively light ruby color, along with ripe fruit (cherries) and toasty new oak in the nose. It is a pretty, elegant wine with medium body and an unmistakable cherry flavor component. Readers should think of this as a Pomerol modeled along the lines of de Sales. Drink it over the next 2–3 years.

ROUILLAC (PESSAC-LÉOGNAN)

2000	**C**	**(87–88)**

2000: From a property with which I have had no prior experience, this sleeper of the vintage exhibits fine ripeness in its noteworthy bouquet of scorched earth, smoke, and red and black currants. Medium-weight, with soft tannin, and excellent symmetry as well as overall character, it will drink well over the next 5–7 years.

ROYLLAND (ST.-EMILION)

1999	**C**	**86**
1998	**C**	**87**
1997	**C**	**83**
1996	**C**	**86**

1999: Very close in style to the 1998, but with lower acidity and less concentration, this is a charming, fleshy, richly fruity wine to consume during its first 7–8 years of life.

1998: An attractive, supple, richly fruity offering, the 1998 Roylland exhibits good sweetness, medium body, low acidity, and a forward, up-front appeal. The aromas and flavors reveal black fruits, spice box, cedar, and licorice. Enjoy it over the next 5–6 years.

1997: The dark ruby-colored 1997 displays sweet fruit on the attack, but it narrows in the mouth. It should drink well for 2–3 years.

1996: The 1996 Roylland exhibits a dark ruby color and sweet berry fruit, dried herb, leafy tobacco, and sweet oak aromas. The wine's ripeness and lushness make it a successful effort for the vintage. It should drink well young yet age for 5–6 years.

Other vintage tasted: 2000 (86–87)

ST.-COLOMBE (CÔTES DE CASTILLON)

2000	**C**	**(86–87)**

2000: Another offering from Dr. Alain Raynaud and Gérard Perse, the 2000 St.-Colombe does not possess as much depth or richness as their Clos l'Eglise. Nevertheless, there is a lot to like in this soft, straightforward, richly fruity, berry-scented and -flavored effort. It possesses low acidity, ripe tannin, and a pure, elegant style. Drink it over the next 5–6 years.

ST.-DOMINGUE (ST.-EMILION)

2000	**D**	**(90–92)**
1999	**D**	**88?**
1998	**D**	**88**

When Clément Fayat was denied the right to include a neighboring parcel of vines in the vineyard of La Dominique, he decided it would produce a micro-cuvée or so-called *vin de garage*. St.-Domingue is vinified in the style of the new, fashionable St.-Emilions; the wines are generally exotic, opulent, and ripe, with aromas of toasty new oak. The debut vintage of this operation was 1998.

2000: This 2000 is made in an extravagantly rich, oaky, ripe style that many tasters will consider over-the-top. Soaring aromatics of new saddle leather, chocolate fudge, roasted espresso, prunes, blackberries, and cherries are followed by surprisingly good acidity, delineation, and richness. It is made in a late-harvest style. Anticipated maturity: 2003–2017.

1999: A similar exotic, smoky, coffee, prune, blackberry, and cherry jam–scented perfume is noticeable in this low-acid, fleshy, succulent wine. It is meant for consumers seeking a blast of high-quality fruit and plenty of toasty oak. Drink it during its first 10–12 years.

1998: The 1998 is made in an exotic, over-the-top style with portlike, ripe notes of prunes, blackberry jam, coffee, and toasty new oak. The flamboyant bouquet characteristics are also apparent in this medium- to full-bodied, oaky, low-acid, almost flabby wine. Although it will be controversial, it is undeniably delicious. Anticipated maturity: now–2010.

DE SALES (POMEROL)

2000	**C**	**(88–90)**
1999	**C**	**88**
1998	**C**	**88**
1997	**C**	**85**
1996	**C**	**79**
1995	**C**	**87**

After a period of mediocrity, de Sales is on the comeback trail, which is good news for readers looking for a more reasonably priced Pomerol. This large Pomerol estate has begun to reassert its position as one of the better values in high-quality wine from this tiny, bucolic appellation.

2000: The 2000 exhibits how excellent de Sales can be. This consumer-friendly wine displays copious levels of black cherry fruit, leather, balsam, spice box, and caramel. This soft, lush, pure offering is a sleeper of the vintage. Anticipated maturity: now–2014.

1999: Another excellent effort, this open-knit, jammy cherry, caramel-scented and -flavored, soft, elegant, fleshy wine offers abundant quantities of glycerin-imbued fruit. This sexy 1999 will provide delicious drinking upon release and last for a decade.

1998: The finest de Sales produced since the early 1980s, the medium ruby/garnet 1998 is forward and soft, revealing notions of white chocolate, mocha, and kirsch. Made in a seductive, luscious style, it possesses sweet tannin, a supple mid-palate as well as finish, and excellent concentration. Purchasers will have no need to defer their gratification. Anticipated maturity: now–2010.

1997: The 1997 has much more to it than the 1996, with sweeter fruit, lower acidity, and a clean, pure, black cherry, fruit-driven style. It should drink well for 4–6 years.

1996: Although it is a pleasant, medium ruby-colored wine, the 1996 de Sales is dry in the finish. It reveals ripe cherry fruit intermixed with dusty earthy elements as well as a suggestion of roasted nuts. Drink it over the next 1–2 years.

1995: This may turn out to be the best de Sales since the 1982. The wine displays a deep ruby color and a seductive nose of jammy cherries, earth, kirsch, and an intriguing note of balsam wood. In the mouth, this supple wine possesses very good concentration, a round, velvety texture, plenty of crowd appeal, and a clean, lush, berry-infused finish. Already drinking well, this 1995 Pomerol should keep for 2–4 years.

SANCTUS (ST.-EMILION)

1999	D	84
1998	D	80?

If this property is attempting to be a garage wine, it misses badly with its overoaked, underfruited style.

1999: Slightly better than 1998, with a more subtle but still dramatic wood treatment, this opaque ruby/purple 1999 exhibits light to medium body, low acidity, and a straightforward, one-dimensional style.

1998: New oak obliterates the character of this medium ruby-colored, modestly endowed effort. Drink it over the next 7–8 years.

Other vintage tasted: 2000 (86–87?)

SANSONNET (ST.-EMILION)

2000	D	(88–90)

Because of a series of poor performances, this estate was relegated to grand cru status at the 1996 St.-Emilion reclassification. Since then, its has been bought by the d'Aulan family, and under the auspices of the young and talented Patrick d'Aulan, it has rebounded nicely over recent vintages. The wine has turned around in 1999, and 2000 seems to be its finest success to date. This latter vintage was made under the supervision of the late Jean-Michel Arcaute, which probably explains its resemblance to Clinet.

2000: This opaque purple wine exhibits sweet, smoky aromas of prunes, black raspberries, cassis, and cherries. Firmly structured, medium- to full-bodied, and ripe, it is reminiscent of Clinet vintages of the late 1980s. If everything comes together, the 2000 Sansonnet will merit an outstanding score. There is plenty of concentration, potential complexity, and depth. Anticipated maturity: 2007–2018.

SÉNÉJAC (MÉDOC)

2000	B	(87–88)

Since this estate was acquired by Thierry Rustmann, manager of the St.-Julien classified-growth Talbot, the quality of Sénéjac has soared.

2000: A blend of 60% Cabernet Sauvignon, 30% Cabernet Franc, and 10% Merlot, this deep purple 2000 offers aromas of black currants, cedar, tobacco, and spice box, excellent concentration, fine purity, medium to full body, and ripe tannin. It should drink well for a decade. It is a sleeper of the vintage.

LE SERGUE (LALANDE-DE-POMEROL)

2000	C	(88–90)
1999	C	87
1998	C	87
1997	C	86

One of Bordeaux's most respected oenologists, Pascal Chatonnet, owns this small gem in Lalande-de-Pomerol.

2000: The 2000 le Sergue is a sleeper of the vintage. It offers an abundance of sweet, concentrated, glycerin-imbued fruit, thick kirsch and berry notes intermixed with a touch of mocha, cola, and caramel, terrific fruit purity, medium to full body, exceptional ripeness, and a low-acid, plush finish. It should be drunk over the next 5–6 years.

1999: Overripe black cherries and berries intermixed with earth and spice are symbolic of this beautifully made, pure, well-knit, low-acid wine. It should be consumed during its first 5–6 years of life.

1998: Rich, sweet berry fruit and spicy oak, admirable purity, and excellent balance characterize this mouth-filling, savory offering. Enjoy it over the next 6–7 years.

1997: A delicious, dark ruby, fruit-driven, unpretentious offering, this 1997 offers jammy black cherry/berry fruit and dried herbs. Ripe, fleshy, straightforward, and delicious, with low acidity, this unmanipulated wine should be drunk over the next 2–3 years.

SIRAN (MARGAUX)

2000	D	(87–88)
1999	D	87
1998	D	87
1997	C	79
1996	C	83
1995	C	87

2000: A chunky, robust, muscular offering with plenty of spicy new oak, a deep ruby/purple color, notes of licorice, incense, black currants, and dried herbs, excellent definition, medium body, and moderate tannin. Anticipated maturity: now–2018.

1999: The opaque ruby/purple 1999 Siran is impressive (not surprising, given how well the Margaux appellation performed in this vintage). It boasts a sweet nose of blackberries as well as earthy currants, medium to full body, copious tannin, low acidity, and a chewy, lush, concentrated, layered finish. A sleeper of the vintage, it will be drinkable between 2004–2016.

1998: A powerful, structured, dark ruby/purple effort, the muscular, dense, ageworthy 1998 is one of the finest Médoc cru bourgeois (black currants, earth, and oak dominate). Made in a closed but classic style, it will be at its finest between 2005–2020.

1997: The 1997 lacks fruit and richness in the mid-palate but does exhibit attractive cherry/currant aromas intermixed with minerals and smoky oak. The finish is attenuated. Anticipated maturity: now–2007.

1996: Siran's 1996 is a compressed, hard-textured, lean, austere wine with a medium ruby color and an angular personality. Anticipated maturity: 2003–2012.

1995: A very good effort from Siran, this dark ruby-colored wine offers attractive aromas of vanillin, spicy new oak, and sweet, creamy cassis fruit interspersed with subtle fennel and spice box notes. Medium-bodied and ripe, with savory richness, sweet tannin, and low acidity, this excellent, elegant Margaux is already accessible but will keep until 2014.

SMITH-HAUT-LAFITTE (PESSAC-LÉOGNAN)

2000	E	(92–94)
1999	E	90
1998	E	90
1997	D	87
1996	E	90
1995	E	90

Since the acquisition of this estate by the Cathiard family in 1990, this property has become one of Bordeaux's success stories, producing elegant, flavorful, complex, very complete wines.

2000: 2000 is the finest vintage yet produced during the nearly 10-year regime of the Cathiard family. As always, the wine displays considerable class, with an intense flavor profile as well as nobility, given its emphasis on balance and complexity with no heaviness. An opaque purple-colored effort, the 2000 exhibits beautifully knit notes of black fruits intermixed with smoke, lead pencil, minerals, and charcoal. Deep and medium-bodied, with laser clarity, superb purity, sweet tannin, low acidity, and an intense, concentrated finish, this is a brilliant wine! Anticipated maturity: 2005–2025.

1999: A dark ruby/purple color is accompanied by a sweet perfume of red and black currants, minerals, and smoke. The wine is medium-bodied and beautifully concentrated, with low acidity and a spicy, soft, supple finish. An impressive 1999! Anticipated maturity: now–2014.

1998: A beautiful wine of symmetry, finesse, and elegance, this deep ruby/purple offering reveals classic aromas of black currants, new wood, and scorched earth. This pure, medium-bodied, restrained, measured, graceful 1998 offers impressive overall symmetry as well as well-integrated tannin. Anticipated maturity: 2003–2018.

1997: Splendid aromatics of tobacco, ripe black currant fruit, minerals, and toasty oak emerge from this dark ruby-colored effort. Quintessentially elegant, with sweet fruit on the attack, medium body, and no hard edges, this smoothly textured wine can be drunk now as well as over the next 10 years.

1996: The quintessentially elegant Bordeaux. With a dark ruby/purple color, it displays a beautiful presentation of blackberry and cassis fruit nicely dosed with subtle new oak. On the attack, the wine is sweet and pure, with striking symmetry and a compellingly balanced mid-palate and finish. Although not as big as some blockbusters from this vintage, it is extremely complex (both aromatically and flavor-wise) and impressive for its restraint, subtlety, and impeccable balance. Anticipated maturity: 2003–2016

1995: The deep ruby/purple of this 1995 is followed by scents of roasted herbs intermixed with sweet black currant fruit, truffles, vanilla, and minerals. Lush, with ripe cassis fruit on the attack, outstanding balance, medium body, and layers of intensity, this is an elegant, graceful, smoothly textured, beautifully made Bordeaux. Anticipated maturity: now–2018.

SOCIANDO-MALLET (HAUT-MÉDOC)

2000	D	(90–91)
1999	D	87
1998	D	88+
1997	C	87
1996	D	90
1995	D	90

This great estate, with a subsoil nearly identical to that of Pauillac, fashions structured and massive wines that are often of classified-growth quality and require 8 to 10 years of aging. I have a number of older vintages in my cellar, and even years such as 1982 are still young and vibrant.

2000: The 2000 exhibits a classic bouquet of cedar, black currants, and minerals, high tannin, gorgeous concentration, and a structured, tannic yet concentrated, powerful finish. Is it a replay of the 1986? Anticipated maturity: 2010–2025.

1999: An elegant, stylish effort, the 1999 reveals red currant, mineral, and spicy aromas. In the mouth it is initially lean, but it builds in the mouth, revealing abundant quantities of black currant and mineral flavors, sweet tannin, and good concentration. It should drink well upon release and over the following 10–12 years.

1998: A deep ruby/purple combines with a sweet nose of minerals, blackberries, and cassis in this nicely textured, medium-bodied 1998. It possesses excellent concentration, firm tannin, and admirable purity as well as balance. Like many wines from this estate, it requires patience but will ultimately behave like a blue-chip classified growth. Anticipated maturity: 2004–2018.

1997: This excellent effort displays a dark ruby color as well as sweet, jammy fruit, moderate elegance, copious cassis flavors, and a medium-bodied, soft, low-acid finish. It is one of the few Sociando-Mallets that could be drunk upon release, but it will hold nicely until 2010.

1996: A classic Sociando-Mallet, with a style not dissimilar from the 1986, this wine boasts a saturated purple color, as well as an intense nose of cassis, chocolate, and minerals. Dense and medium-bodied, with outstanding purity, and high tannin, this beautifully made wine is better than many classified growths. Anticipated maturity: 2007–2020.

1995: This accessible yet tannic example of Sociando-Mallet possesses a deep ruby/purple, and excellent aromatics consisting of jammy black cherries, blackberries, and cassis, as well as subtle notes of minerals, earth, and new oak. This is a deep, long, muscular, tannic wine that is structurally similar to the 1996. It is not yet ready to drink. I suggest that readers wait 3–4 more years if they want to consume it at maturity. Anticipated maturity: 2006–2025.

Past Glories: 1990 (92), 1989 (90), 1986 (90), 1985 (90), 1982 (92)

TAILLEFER (POMEROL)

2000	D	(87–89)
1999	D	86
1998	D	85

2000: The finest Taillefer I have ever tasted from this longtime underachiever, the 2000 offers a deep purple color as well as a sweet bouquet of cassis, licorice, and melted caramel. Deep, medium- to full-bodied, with fat, well-integrated tannin, this is a sleeper of the vintage. Kudos to this estate! Anticipated maturity: 2003–2016.

1999: The dark ruby/plum/garnet 1999 exhibits more fat and glycerin than most Taillefers, medium body, and a sweet, supple finish. Consume it during its first 7–8 years of life.

1998: A dark ruby color is accompanied by aromas of sweet and sour cherries intermixed with earth and spice. The wine reveals copious tannin for a 1998, medium body, and an undistinguished finish. Anticipated maturity: 2003–2010.

TALBOT (ST.-JULIEN)

2000	D	(90–92)
1999	D	88
1998	D	88
1997	D	86
1996	D	90
1995	D	89

2000: This wine is sexy, seductive, and undeniably difficult to resist, even at such a young age. The deep ruby/purple color is followed by a wine with low acidity, sweet tannin, and copious quantities of blackberry and currant fruit intermixed with new oak and spice. Initially superficial, it seems to grow in the glass. While not a blockbuster, it is velvety textured, succulent, and delicious. It appears to be Talbot's finest effort since their prodigious 1986. Anticipated maturity: now–2018.

1999: An impressive effort for the vintage, this is an opulent, velvety textured 1999 that comes across as a hypothetical blend of a Pomerol and Burgundy. Notes of earth, black fruits (blackberries), spice box, and herbs compete for the taster's attention. Dense, nearly unctuous, and extremely ripe, with low acidity that adds to the textural fatness and richness, it will be delicious upon release, and last for 15–16+ years. Is it a modern-day clone of the 1962?

1998: The 1998 has greatly improved during its *élevage* and is performing better out of bottle than it did from cask. With age, the midsection has filled out and the wine has put on weight. A deep plum/garnet color is accompanied by an up-front, seductive nose of melted licorice, cedar, plums, black cherries, and cassis. This attractive Talbot is nicely textured and medium- to full-bodied, with sweet tannin. It is pleasing to see how this wine has matured. Anticipated maturity: 2003–2016.

1997: A light-bodied, pleasant, straightforward Talbot, the 1997 exhibits attractive cherry, black cherry, herb-tinged flavors. Consume this picnic-styled claret over the next 2–3 years.

1996: I tasted this wine three times after bottling, rating it 88, 89, and 90 with similar tasting notes. The wine is close to being outstanding, exhibiting a saturated dark ruby color, and excellent aromatics, consisting of black fruits intermixed with licorice, dried herbs, and roasted meat smells. It is full, with impressive extract, a fleshy texture, low acidity, excellent purity, and a long, deep, chewy finish. This 1996 will be drinkable at a young age, yet keep for 15–18 years. Anticipated maturity: 2003–2017.

1995: This wine has turned out to be more impressive from bottle than it was in cask. It is a charming, intensely scented wine with a telltale olive, earth, grilled beef, and black currant–scented bouquet soaring from the glass. Medium- to full-bodied, with low acidity, and round, luscious, richly fruity flavors, this is a meaty, fleshy, delicious Talbot that can be drunk now. Anticipated maturity: now–2012.

Past Glories: 1986 (96), 1983 (91), 1982 (96), 1953 (90), 1945 (94)

DU TERTRE (MARGAUX)

2000	**D**	**(90–92)**
1998	**D**	**87**
1997	**C**	**85**
1996	**C**	**88**
1995	**C**	**86**

This estate was sold in 1996 by Mme Gasqueton, of Calon-Ségur, to Eric Albada-Jelgersma, who also took out a lease on Château Giscours several years ago. The new owner has made a huge investment in the vineyards as well as in the winemaking facility, and this has paid handsome dividends, as evidenced by the beautifully knit, elegant yet concentrated 2000, the finest wine made at this estate since the surprisingly good 1979. This once perennial underachiever is a property that shrewd consumers would be well advised to keep an eye on.

2000: The opaque purple 2000 offers a sweet nose of black fruits intermixed with flowers, truffles, and new-barrel scents. This full-bodied effort possesses wonderful density, sweet tannin, and a long, concentrated, persuasive finish. Anticipated maturity: 2005–2020. Bravo!

1998: A sleeper of the vintage, this excellent du Tertre is reminiscent of this estate's fine 1979. Sweet aromas of black cherry jam infused with creosote and grilled notes emerge from this dark plum/ruby/purple 1998. Fragrant, with an expansive, rich personality, medium body, excellent concentration, and fine purity and harmony, this is a wine to drink during its first 12–15 years of life. To the estate's credit, they avoided the hard tannin that plagues some 1998 Médocs.

1997: This pleasant, soft, moderately endowed effort displays sweet berry fruit, Provençal herbs, and earth in its aromas and flavors. The wine lacks density, but it does not try to be more than it is. Medium-bodied, soft, and not excessively extracted, this delicate Margaux can be drunk over the next 2–3 years.

1996: A sleeper, du Tertre's 1996 exhibits a black ruby/purple color, a sweet black fruit–scented nose, medium to full body, well-integrated tannin, and fine purity and depth. This wine should age nicely yet have a degree of accessibility young. Anticipated maturity: 2004–2018.

1995: A chocolaty, berry-scented nose with weedy cassis, licorice, and earth aromas is followed by a medium-bodied wine with fine concentration. Although monolithic, the 1995 is well made, mouth-filling, and moderately tannic. Anticipated maturity: 2003–2015.

Other vintage tasted: 1999 (85–86)

TERTRE-DAUGAY (ST.-EMILION)

1999	C	87
1998	C	87

Readers should note that this estate has made significant qualitative improvements over the last decade.

1999: A strong effort from Tertre-Daugay, the 1999 exhibits a dense ruby/purple color as well as a stylish perfume of ripe berry fruit, tobacco, cedar, and spicy wood. Medium- to full-bodied and dense, yet soft, this is a candidate for delicious drinking upon release next year as well as over the following decade.

1998: Dark ruby/garnet-colored, with an elegant berry nose displaying scents of cedar, earth, and spice, this medium-bodied, nicely delineated 1998 is long, rich, and graceful. In an age of bold, flamboyant offerings, particularly from St.-Emilion, this wine's measured restraint and attractive ripeness as well as richness are to be applauded. Drink it over the next 10–12 years.

TERTRE-RÔTEBOEUF (ST.-EMILION)

2000	EE	(93–95)
1999	EE	91
1998	EE	94
1997	E	87
1996	EE	90
1995	EE	95

Tertre-Rôteboeuf (the "hill of the belching beef") is a 14.7-acre vineyard planted with 85% Merlot and 15% Cabernet Franc. Since the early 1980s, under the auspices of the talented François Mitjavile, this has been one of the most distinctive, exotic, compelling wines made in St.-Emilion. It is gorgeous to drink young, yet promises to age well for 15+ years in the finest vintages.

2000: An explosive, hedonistic, seductive, sexy fruit bomb, with complexity to spare, Tertre-Rôteboeuf's 2000 is one of the most exotic and singular wines of the vintage. Whether or not this wine turns out to be better than some recent classics (i.e., 1998, 1995, 1990, 1989), there is no question that it is a stunning effort. A dramatic, flamboyant, head-spinning nose of melted fudge, coffee, tobacco, kirsch, and cassis backed by smoke and scorched earth soars from the glass. In the mouth, this is the essence of Tertre-Rôteboeuf, full-bodied, superconcentrated, seamless, exotic, and hedonistic, as well as immensely satisfying on an intellectual level. This is great stuff! Anticipated maturity: 2003–2020.

1999: The 1999 has turned out exceptionally well, offering notes of melted fudge, coffee, overripe berry fruit, and smoky wood. Although it possesses less density and longevity than the 1998, it has put on weight during its *élevage,* and looks to be a terrific, forward, precocious Tertre-Rôteboeuf, Bordeaux at its most hedonistic and glitzy. Anticipated maturity: now–2014.

1998: A dramatic, flamboyant nose of roasted espresso intermixed with chocolate fudge, blackberries, Asian spices, and kirsch jumps from the glass of this ostentatious effort. Full-bodied and layered, with an unctuous texture, gorgeous purity, and an undeniable hedonistic explosion of fruit and glycerin, it can be drunk now or cellared for 15+ years. To my taste, it is (with perhaps the 2000) the finest Tertre-Rôteboeuf since 1990.

1997: This is a delicious wine with aromas and flavors of mocha, coffee, chocolate, cedar, and jammy red and black fruits. Medium- to full-bodied, with low acidity and little density but excellent fruit and a soft underbelly, it requires consumption over the next 3–4 years.

1996: The 1996 Tertre-Rôteboeuf is less sumptuous out of bottle than it was from cask. Nevertheless, this is an outstanding wine produced in the telltale style of this well-placed hillside vineyard. The color is a deep ruby, and the nose offers up hedonistic notes of smoke, crème brûlée, roasted coffee, and chocolate-covered cherries. This medium-bodied wine is exhibiting more structure, muscle, and tannin than I remember from cask. In fact, after the sweet aromatics and initial blast of fruit on the attack, the wine seems to close down, revealing moderate tannin in the very good finish. It should keep for 15 years.

1995: This is one vintage (1989 and 1990 were others) where Tertre-Rôteboeuf exhibits a Le Pin–like exotic richness and opulence. The wine exhibits a dense ruby/purple color and a compelling set of aromatics consisting of toast, ripe black cherry, and cassis fruit, intermixed with truffles, mocha, and toffee. Dense and full-bodied, with layers of intensely ripe fruit, this plump, gorgeously pure, expansively flavored, multidimensional wine will hold until 2018.

Past Glories: 1994 (90), 1990 (98), 1989 (95), 1988 (91), 1986 (91), 1985 (90)

LA TOUR-CARNET (HAUT-MÉDOC)

2000	C	(88–90)

This estate was recently purchased by Pape-Clément's proprietor, Bernard Magrez, who brought in famed oenologist Michel Rolland to oversee the vinification. Under the new ownership, the wines have improved dramatically, as evidenced by the 2000, a sleeper of the vintage and the finest La Tour-Carnet I have ever tasted.

2000: The opaque purple 2000 is a blend of 58% Merlot and the rest Cabernet Sauvignon with a touch of Cabernet Franc. The dense, powerful, concentrated wine displays superb ripeness, purity, and texture. A tannic, full-throttle effort, the likes of which I have never tasted from La Tour-Carnet, it requires 4–5 years of cellaring and should keep for 16–18 years.

LA TOUR-FIGEAC (ST.-EMILION)

2000	D	(89–91)
1998	D	90

After a series of mediocre performances, La Tour-Figeac has followed their exemplary 1998 (their first outstanding vintage since 1982) with a potentially superb 2000.

2000: Deep purple-colored, with notes of ripe plums, cherries, vanilla, and underbrush, this sweet, full-bodied, layered wine displays exceptional potential. The moderate tannin is accompanied by more than sufficient fruit, glycerin, and extract. This 2000 will be drinkable young but keep for two decades. It is a sleeper of the vintage. Anticipated maturity: 2003–2018.

1998: Dark ruby/purple with a sensational bouquet of smoke-infused blackberries, jammy cherries, and coffee, this thick, unctuously textured, rich, full-bodied, structured, moderately tannic wine is already gorgeous to drink. A sleeper of the vintage. Anticipated maturity: now–2015.

Other vintage tasted: 1999 (86–87)

LA TOUR-HAUT-BRION (PESSAC-LÉOGNAN)

2000	D	(90–92)
1999	D	90
1998	D	89
1997	C	86
1996	D	87
1995	D	89+

2000: This is the finest La Tour-Haut-Brion produced since the estate was acquired by the Dillon family in 1983. A blend of 52% Merlot, 43% Cabernet Sauvignon, and 5% Cabernet Franc, it reveals an opaque purple color as well as gorgeously sweet aromas of cassis fruit and smoke. Medium- to full-bodied and deep, with ripe tannin, excellent definition, and admirable freshness in its long, convincingly rich finish, it will be at its finest between 2006–2023.

1999: The dense ruby/purple 1999 reveals notes of lead pencil, smoke, earth, and black fruits in its spicy, medium-bodied personality. With excellent purity in addition to fine overall balance and length, it is already delicious. Anticipated maturity: now–2015.

1998: My rating may be too conservative, as the 1998 is showing as well as any La Tour-Haut-Brion from the 1990s. A dense ruby/purple color is followed by sweet aromas of black currants intermixed with tobacco, cedar, and spice box. The wine is beautifully pure, rich, and medium-bodied, with sweet tannin and well-integrated acidity as well as wood. It should drink well after several years of aging and last 15–18 years.

1997: An elegant, harmonious, spicy, aromatic offering without a great deal of body, the 1997 reveals sweet black currant and smoky tobacco-like flavors. Drink this soft wine over the next 4–5 years.

1996: La Tour-Haut-Brion's 1996 is an aromatic, surprisingly evolved wine for the vintage with a dark plum color and a pronounced, smoky, cassis, weedy, dried herb–scented bouquet. A medium-bodied, classic, mid-weight Bordeaux, with plenty of spice, sweet fruit, elegance, and complexity, it is a blend of 50% Cabernet Sauvignon and 50% Cabernet Franc. It should provide delicious drinking for 6–7 years.

1995: One of the finest La Tour-Haut-Brions of the last 15 years, the 1995 offers a heady perfume of coffee beans, tobacco, spice, smoke, grilled herbs, and sweet red and black fruits. It is long and round, with copious quantities of red currants as well as good underlying acid, which gives the wine definition, and a spicy, lush, sweet finish with light but noticeable tannin. Anticipated maturity: now–2015.

Past Glories: 1982 (98), 1978 (95), 1975 (96), 1961 (95), 1959 (92), 1955 (94), 1947 (95)

TOUR MAILLET (POMEROL)

2000	C	(87–88?)

2000: High tannin and aggressive new oak may be troublesome in this otherwise spicy, dense, muscular, concentrated 2000. While there are abundant quantities of earthy, smoky, black cherry, and mocha notes (characteristic of ripe Merlot) as well as serious substance, this wine's future is not a sure bet. Anticipated maturity: 2005–2016.

LA TOUR-MARTILLAC (PESSAC-LÉOGNAN)

2000	D	(87–88)
1998	D	87
1997	C	87
1996	C	83
1995	C	86

While the white wines of this estate have considerably improved since 1987 and have become profound Graves, the reds remain rather plain and straightforward, with an aging potential of 8–10 years.

2000: Scents of new oak, damp earth, tobacco, and red and black fruits emerge from this medium- to full-bodied, spicy, concentrated wine. With low acidity, ripe tannin, and fine potential, it will be drinkable between 2004–2016.

1998: A concentrated effort for this estate, the 1998 La Tour-Martillac exhibits sweet, toasty, black currant fruit intertwined with tar and earth scents. With ripe tannin, medium body, and fine balance, this excellent wine should drink well between 2003–2016.

1997: The 1997 is a richer, sweeter wine than the 1996 with more color, extract, and length. It offers smoky, toasty oak in the nose, attractive black currant fruit, and notes of licorice. It should drink well for 8 years.

1996: La Tour-Martillac's 1996 is a medium-bodied, straightforward wine with good spice, moderate fruit, and a simple personality. There is some tannin, but the wine is light. Anticipated maturity: now–2008.

1995: An olive, tobacco, smoky, red currant, and cherry-scented nose is followed by an elegant, medium-bodied, soft, smoothly textured wine that can be drunk now or over the next 5–6 years.

Other vintage tasted: 1999 (85–87)

TOUR DE MIRAMBEAU (BORDEAUX SUPÉRIEUR)

2000 Cuvée Passion	B	(90–91)

Along with Reignac and Balestard, this is one of the finest Bordeaux Supérieurs produced.

2000: A blend of 70% Merlot and 30% Cabernet Sauvignon, it offers a saturated ruby/purple color as well as a gorgeous bouquet of crème de cassis, licorice, spice box, and cedar. Full-bodied, ripe, dense, and thick, with well-integrated tannin, good acidity, and a long finish, it is an amazing accomplishment and a sleeper of the vintage. Kudos to the proprietor! Anticipated maturity: now–2010.

TOURANS TERRE BLANCHE (ST.-EMILION)

2000	C	(88–89)

Another wine fashioned by Umbria's famed wine-maker Riccardo Cotarella, this St.-Emilion is a more dense, thick, structured wine than his Côtes de Castillon. The estate's second wine, Paradis Tourans, is also quite good, rating (86–88) in 2000. It is reasonably priced and represents an interesting selection.

2000: Made in an opulent style, with a dense ruby/purple color, aromas and flavors of blackberries, cassis, and minerals, medium to full body, and significant tannin, this wine requires 2–3 years of cellaring and should keep for 12–15. It is another sleeper of the vintage.

LES TROIS CANONS (FRONSAC)

2000	C	(87–88)

This property is owned by Patrick Léon, who has done so much work at Mouton-Rothschild and Napa Valley's Opus One.

2000: This is the finest effort yet from Les Trois Canons. The 2000 displays good richness, a sweet, mineral-infused, cherry and black currant–scented nose, medium body, admirable tannin, and a clean, pure finish. It should drink well for a decade.

TROPLONG MONDOT (ST.-EMILION)

2000	E	(94–96)
1999	E	88

1998	E	93
1997	D	89
1996	E	89
1995	E	92

I am a huge fan of this property run by Christine Valette, who has been producing great St.-Emilions since the late 1980s, and have been an avid purchaser of many of her wines, particularly the 1988, 1989, and 1990. I tasted all three of these vintages in a mini-vertical recently, and they were sensationally good. Her fabulous 2000s and 1998s continue this trend.

2000: The 2000 is a fabulous offering, boasting a thick, opaque blue/purple color as well as highly extracted notes of blackberry and cassis fruit, minerals, espresso beans, and vanilla. It is dense and full-bodied, with high tannin, good acidity, and laser definition. The immense mid-palate and huge finish are formidably constructed and muscular. While this wine will age gracefully, patience is required. Anticipated maturity: 2008–2025. This is a classic, old-style *vin de garde* with modern-style tannin.

1999: This dense blue/purple 1999 reveals notes of licorice, blueberries, vanilla, and smoke, as well as a rich, medium-bodied, concentrated mid-palate. While the tannin is moderately high, it is sweet and balanced by the wine's concentrated, highly extracted style. The wine is atypical for a 1999 in its backwardness and obvious structure. Anticipated maturity: 2005–2020.

1998: A fabulous effort, this sleeper of the vintage may turn out to be, along with the 2000, one of the finest Troplong Mondots since the 1990. The black/purple 1998 exhibits floral, blueberry, blackberry, licorice, vanilla, and truffle-like aromas (or is it charcoal/graphite?). Dense, full-bodied, and pure, yet extremely fresh and elegant, this beautifully focused wine needs 3–4 years of cellaring. Anticipated maturity: 2005–2025.

1997: The gorgeously elegant, concentrated 1997 exhibits a dark ruby/purple color, and a beautifully knit, blackberry- and cherry-scented nose with toasty oak in the background. Not a massive effort, it offers beautifully supple fruit flavors, an attractive fragrance, a ripe, sweet mid-palate, and soft tannin. Drink this seductive, lush Troplong Mondot over the next 8 years.

1996: I am pleased with the way this wine has turned out. The ferocious tannin has been slightly tamed now that the wine is in bottle. Still a backward style of Troplong Mondot, it will require 5–6 years of cellaring. The wine exhibits a deep ruby/purple color and a powerful nose of licorice, black currants, and spicy new oak. There is sweet fruit on the attack and medium body, but the firm tannin gives the wine grip and delineation as well as a certain austerity. This wine does possess the requisite depth to support its tannic clout, but patience is required. Anticipated maturity: 2007–2019.

1995: Closed but immensely promising, this dark purple wine exhibits a reticent but intriguing nose of underbrush, jammy black fruits, minerals, and vanilla. Deep, rich, and medium-to full-bodied, with outstanding extract and purity, the wine possesses a seamless personality with sweeter, more integrated tannin than in the 1996. This is a *vin de garde* to cellar for another 3–4 years. It is not far off the splendid level of quality achieved in both 1989 and 1990. Anticipated maturity: 2005–2020.

Past Glories: 1994 (90), 1990 (98), 1989 (96)

TROTANOY (POMEROL)

2000	EEE	(92–95)
1999	EEE	89
1998	EEE	98
1997	EEE	89+?
1996	EEE	89+
1995	EEE	93+

After continuously expressing my disappointment with the wines produced at Trotanoy between 1983 and 1989, I am thrilled with what has been taking place since the 1990 vintage.
One of my favorite estates has returned to the form displayed during their glory years in the
1960s and early 1970s. Recent vintages, especially 1998 and 2000, are profound.

2000: Only time will tell whether or not this vintage of Trotanoy recalls the 1962 or 1975
when it reaches full maturity. At present, it is a muscular offering with elegant, deep, concentrated flavors. An earthy concoction of truffles, caramel, mocha, cherries, currants, and
plums is followed by a big, deep, masculine wine with moderately high tannin, abundant
power, and exceptional concentration. There is enough sweetness to balance the tannin, but
this 2000 needs cellaring. Anticipated maturity: 2007–2022.

1999: This medium- to full-bodied Trotanoy has turned out reasonably well. It reveals some
of this estate's masculine/muscular stature, but nowhere near the weight, concentration, or
extract of the 1998. It will be ready to drink at a much earlier age given its low acidity and
ripe, open-knit, expansive personality. Anticipated maturity: 2003–2016.

1998: Potentially the finest Trotanoy since the 1961, this structured, formidably endowed,
deep ruby/purple, full-bodied, superrich wine exhibits notes of toffee, truffles, and abundant
blackberry, cherry, and currant fruit. It cuts a large swath across the palate, and possesses
copious but sweet tannin as well as a chewy, muscular mid-palate and finish. This is a compelling effort from one of the great vineyards of Pomerol. Anticipated maturity: 2006–2030.

1997: The 1997 is an atypically structured, rich, powerful wine for the vintage, with hard
tannin in the finish. Ripe and medium-bodied, it has surprising depth as well as copious
quantities of plum, cherry, currant, truffle, herb, and earth aromas and flavors. This effort
should age for 12+ years. Could this be a modern-day version of the underrated 1967?

1996: I would not be surprised to see the 1996 Trotanoy improve with aging. When I saw it
about six months after bottling, it had begun to tighten up and close down. The wine possesses a dense, medium plum color, tight but promising aromatics, a sweet, pure core of
mineral-tinged blackberry and cherry fruit, plenty of power and richness, a chewy texture,
and muscle and firm tannin in the finish. Anticipated maturity: 2006–2017.

1995: A fabulous success for Trotanoy, this wine has considerable potential. The 1995 boasts
a saturated deep purple color, followed by a knockout nose of black truffles, cherries, raspberries, and kirsch fruit intermixed with spicy oak and beef blood–like scents. Full-bodied,
dense, and as powerful and backward as its rival, Lafleur, this broad-shouldered, superextracted Trotanoy is superb, but don't make the mistake of thinking it will provide easygoing
drinking over the near term. While splendid, this wine possesses extremely high tannin and
needs at least 2–3 more years of cellaring. Anticipated maturity: 2005–2025. Bravo!

Past Glories: 1990 (91), 1982 (94), 1975 (95), 1971 (93), 1970 (96), 1967 (91), 1964 (90),
1961 (98)

TROTTEVIEILLE (ST.-EMILION)

2000	D	(89–91)
1999	D	89
1998	D	86
1997	D	86
1996	D	87
1995	D	?

Over the last few years, proprietor Philippe Castéja has been making strong efforts to im-
prove the quality of not only Trottevieille but also his other estates, particularly Batailley in
Pauillac and Domaine l'Eglise in Pomerol. These wines are well worth seeking, particularly
Trottevieille, in view of its reasonable price and now high level of quality.

2000: This is the finest Trottevieille Philippe Castéja has yet produced. The elegant, concentrated 2000 (a blend of 50% Cabernet Franc, 47% Merlot, and 3% Cabernet Sauvignon) dis-

plays a dense ruby/purple color in addition to subtle notions of sweet new oak intermixed with cassis, black cherry liqueur, and licorice. In the mouth, the wine is medium- to full-bodied, with beautifully integrated acidity and tannin. Undoubtedly, the superlative quality of Cabernet Franc in 2000 has given this offering more complexity. Kudos to Monsieur Castéja. Anticipated maturity: 2004–2020.

1999: Deep ruby/purple-colored, with more depth than recent vintages have revealed, the 1999 offers aromas of toasty new oak, smoky blackberry and cassis fruit, licorice, and toast. This medium-bodied effort reveals no hard edges. It will be delicious young, but possesses good aging potential. Anticipated maturity: 2003–2010.

1998: A wine of finesse and elegance, without the weight and power of some of the newer, more fashionable St.-Emilions, Trottevieille's 1998 exhibits a dark ruby color as well as aromas of sweet blackberry and cherry fruit with smoky oak and mineral notes in the background. Round and elegant, it is a wine of finesse rather than power. Drink it over the next 10–12 years.

1997: Abundant quantities of toasty oak give this wine an international style. In the mouth, supple, sweet, plum/cherry fruit mixed with herbs, earth, and smoke are both user-friendly and delicious. While not big, dense, or ageworthy, for drinking over the next 2–4 years it is a pleasant, ripe, fruity, well-balanced offering.

1996: The 1996 Trottevieille is a step up over previous vintages. Soft and elegant, it possesses nicely integrated smoky new oak along with blackberry and cherry fruit. It is medium-bodied, with excellent purity, and a nicely textured, stylish finish. This will be a 1996 to enjoy now–2012.

1995: I had very good tasting notes of this wine before bottling, but in two tastings after bottling, the wine reveals an evolved medium ruby color already displaying amber at the edge. Additionally, it came across as austere, hard, tannic, and out of balance. This is completely at odds with prebottling samples, so I prefer to reserve my judgment.

Past Glories: 1989 (90)

VALANDRAUD (ST.-EMILION)

NV	L'Interdit de Valandraud	EE	(85–87?)
2000		EEE	(92–94)
1999		EEE	90
1998		EEE	93
1997		EEE	89

Proprietor Jean-Luc Thunevin and his wife, Murielle, are the de facto leaders of the St.-Emilion *vin de garage* effort. If that is not unsettling enough to the Médoc aristocracy, they are now starting up garage operations in Margaux (Marojallia) and in the Graves (Branon). There has been an explosion of interest in these micro *cuvées*, most of which offer impressive quality. Jean-Luc and Murielle's aim at Valandraud is to produce an enormously rich, concentrated, and beautifully delineated St.-Emilion with minimal handling and to bottle it without fining or filtration. They have succeeded in positioning their wine as a micro treasure that is sought by billionaire collectors throughout the world. However, even though I am a great admirer of Valandraud, I still cannot comprehend the extremely high price it fetches.

Nonvintage l'Interdit de Valandraud: There are 4,000 bottles of the nonvintage l'Interdit de Valandraud, which Thunevin was not allowed to vintage-date (it's a 2000) or designate as a St.-Emilion. Just as at Fontenil and Haut-Carles, the controversial laying of plastic on part of the vineyard to avoid possible rainfall (which did not occur) was rejected by appellation authorities as a legitimate viticulture technique. For whatever reasons, I thought this wine was far inferior to its sibling. A dark color and good attack are followed by a pinched, lean midsection, and an austere, acidic finish. Perhaps I had a bad sample, but I did not find this wine exciting.

2000: I tasted the 2000 on three separate occasions. While there were subtle differences, this is unquestionably a top wine. Proprietor Jean-Luc Thunevin appears to be aiming for a more elegant, measured style. A deep plum/purple color is accompanied by a sweet nose of black fruits, charcoal, earth, and smoke. Aromatically, it has the potential to be one of the most complex Valandrauds yet made, though it may not possess the fat and flesh of vintages such as 1998 and 1995. This medium- to full-bodied, pure, harmonious Valandraud exhibits well-integrated, moderately high tannin in the finish. Anticipated maturity: 2003–2016. There are 1,000 cases of 2000, and the final blend is 70% Merlot and 30% Cabernet Franc.

1999: Highly extracted, with more noticeable new oak, Valandraud's 1999 is a typical blend of 75% Merlot and 25% Cabernet Franc. It offers impressive overall symmetry, fabulous purity, and telltale notes of smoke, espresso, chocolate, currants, blackberries, and cherries. Full-bodied, with sweet tannin and a creamy texture, it will be delicious upon its release and until 2017.

1998: A classic St.-Emilion, the 1998 exhibits a dark plum/purple color as well as an elegant nose of mocha, coffee, cherries, blackberries, and chocolate. It has turned out to be more finesse-styled and less exotic than past vintages. This medium- to full-bodied, beautifully concentrated wine reveals chocolate overtones in the aromas and flavors. With exceptional purity, balance, and length, it should turn out to be one of the most elegant Valandrauds yet produced. Anticipated maturity: now–2020.

1997: One of the finest 1997s, Valandraud exhibits a dense ruby/purple color in addition to moderately intense aromas of spice box, licorice, plums, cherries, and toasty oak. Lush, full-bodied, and round, with excellent fruit richness, low acidity, and sweet tannin, it can be drunk now as well as over the next 7 years.

1996: This 1996 has firmed up significantly since bottling. Unfined and unfiltered, this viscous wine displays a telltale thickness of color (saturated dark ruby/plum/purple). The wine's exotic bouquet is just beginning to form, offering up notes of iodine, roasted coffee, jammy black fruits, and toast. In the mouth, it is medium- to full-bodied, with sweet tannin, terrific texture, and outstanding purity and length. Anticipated maturity: 2003–2018.

1995: This wine exhibits an opaque purple color and a sensational nose of roasted herbs, black fruits (cherries, currants, and blackberries), and high-class toasty oak (the latter more a nuance than a dominant characteristic). Very concentrated, with layers of fruit, glycerin, and extract, yet seamlessly constructed, this wine contains the stuff of greatness, and appears to be one the finest Valandrauds yet produced. The finish lasts over 30 seconds. The wine's high tannin is barely noticeable because of the ripeness and richness of fruit. Anticipated maturity: 2003–2020.

Past Glories: 1994 (94+), 1993 (93)

VALMENGAUX (BORDEAUX)

2000		B	(87–88)

2000: This tiny generic Bordeaux, owned by the children of Pierre Ferrand (of St.-Emilion's Ferrand-Lartigue garage winery), is made primarily from Merlot. The big, sweet nose of cola, berry fruit, and smoke is followed by a soft, lush wine meant to be consumed during its first 3–4 years of life. This wine is sold for a song.

VEYRY (CÔTES DE CASTILLON)

2000		B	(87–88)
1999		B	87
1998		B	87

This is another star from the up-and-coming appellation of Côtes de Castillon, situated adjacent to St.-Emilion. The wines, made under the auspices of Jean-Luc Thunevin, usually qualify as sleepers of the vintage and are very fairly priced.

2000: Veyry's 2000 is slightly tougher-textured and more firmly knit than previous vintages. Nevertheless, it offers admirably concentrated black cherry and cassis fruit, a sweet attack, and a narrow finish. This is an excellent offering. Anticipated maturity: now–2008.

1999: A Côtes de Castillon fruit bomb, this dense ruby/plum 1999 offers copious quantities of black fruits intermixed with smoke and vanilla. Rich, low in acidity, chewy, and disarming, this is a wine to consume during its first 6–7 years of life.

1998: An excellent wine and a reasonably good value, this 1998 possesses sweet black currant and cherry fruit, abundant quantities of smoky, spicy characteristics, low acidity, a plump, fleshy entry on the palate, and a long, seamless finish. Drink it over the next 4–5 years.

LA VIEILLE-CURE (FRONSAC)

1999	C	88
1998	C	87
1997	C	86
1996	C	86
1995	C	87

One of the finest Fronsac estates, La Vieille Cure is producing wines of Pomerol-like lushness and savory fruit that generally qualify as sleepers and represent good values.

1999: The 1999 is typically seductive, fleshy, and soft, with luscious, jammy black fruits and toasty oak evident in the aromas and flavors. Medium- to full-bodied, round, and disarming, with less structure and lower acidity than the 1998, it will be drinkable upon release and over the following 8–9 years.

1998: A dark ruby/purple color accompanies sweet aromatics of pure black cherries as well as currants intertwined with smoky oak. This medium- to full-bodied, fleshy, fruit-driven, velvety-textured effort will offer considerable appeal over the next 6–7 years.

1997: A surprisingly fine 1997, this wine exhibits jammy plum/currant notes, subtle oak, medium body, velvety tannin, and a lush, fruit-driven personality. It will have considerable appeal if drunk now and over the next 3–4 years.

1996: A sleeper of the vintage. The 1996 performed admirably in what is a more mixed Fronsac vintage. Deep ruby-colored, with plenty of sweet blackberry and cherry fruit in both its aromatics and flavors, this medium-bodied wine reveals toasty notes, moderate tannin, and 5–7 years of aging potential. It is quite well made.

1995: A delicious, attractive, Merlot-dominated wine, the 1995 presents a deep ruby color, attractively sweet, ripe, black cherry, kirsch, and cedar-tinged aromatics, round, ripe, medium-bodied flavors with some grip and tannin, excellent purity, and a nicely layered finish. This wine can be drunk now as well as over the next 3–4 years.

VIEUX CHAMPS DE MARS (CÔTES DE CASTILLON)

2000	C	(87–89)
2000 Cuvée Johanna	C	(88–90)
1999	C	(86–87)
1999 Cuvée Johanna	C	(87–88)
1998	C	87

This is another up-and-coming estate from the Côtes de Castillon. Its 42-acre vineyard produces blends of 80% Merlot, 10% Cabernet Sauvignon, and 10% Cabernet Franc. In 1999, Vieux Champ de Mars introduced a special old-vine Merlot (planted in 1904, and about 80% of the blend) and 20% Cabernet Franc *cuvée*. Both wines are put through a cold premaceration before fermentation, and then punched down in small oak fermenters, à la red Burgundy. They experience malolactic in barrel and represent the more creative side of St.-Emilion winemaking. To their credit, neither is fined nor filtered. These are great picks for consumers seeking high-quality wines to drink over the next decade that won't break the bank.

2000 Vieux Champs de Mars and 2000 Cuvée Johanna: Two more marvelous efforts from the Côtes de Castillon, these sleepers of the vintage both exhibit dense ruby/purple colors, viscous, concentrated flavors, and remarkable purity, ripeness, and fruit for wines of such pedigrees. The 2000 Vieux Champ de Mars is a blend of 80% Merlot, 10% Cabernet Sauvignon, and 10% Cabernet Franc from yields of 40 hectoliters per hectare. The 2000 Cuvée Johanna exhibits even greater ripeness, expansiveness, and intensity.

1999 Vieux Champ de Mars: Overripe black cherries intermixed with toasty oak and spice box aromas are captivating in this lush, medium-weight, delicious 1999. It is destined to be drunk during its first 3–4 years of life.

1999 Cuvée Johanna: The Cuvée Johanna possesses deeper, denser, more concentrated fruit than the regular bottling. Although nicely perfumed (blackberry and cherry fruit), it also exhibits more new oak. Plush, chewy, and Pomerol-like, it should drink well for 4–5 more years.

1998 Vieux Champ de Mars: A soft, dark ruby-colored effort, with abundant quantities of berry fruit intermixed with earth, herbs, and spice, this 1998 is supple and hedonistic, with plenty of fruit as well as glycerin. Enjoy it over the next 2 years.

VIEUX CHÂTEAU CERTAN (POMEROL)

2000	EEE	(92–95)
1999	EEE	92
1998	EEE	95
1997	E	85
1996	EE	87
1995	EE	88?

2000: The outstanding 2000 Vieux Château Certan has turned out to be superb and now approaches the quality of the majestic 1998. The deep plum/purple 2000 offers a complex nose of menthol, underbrush, black currants, cherries, mocha, and new wood. It hits the palate with beautiful purity as well as symmetry, medium to full body, and moderate tannin in the finish. It is one of the vintage's superstars, and a classic. Anticipated maturity: 2006–2025.

1999: A strong effort for the vintage, this elegant, medium- to full-bodied, dark ruby/purple wine exhibits aromas and flavors of blackberries, cherries, minerals, herbs, and earth. While it does not possess the weight of either the 1998 or 2000, there is plenty of tannin and muscle in the finish. It comes across more like a plush Médoc than a typical Pomerol. Anticipated maturity: 2007–2025.

1998: Undoubtedly the finest offering from this estate since 1990, the 1998 has closed down, but there is no doubting its fabulous potential. The color is a dense purple. The wine reveals high tannin, huge body, and classy black fruits intermixed with minerals, spice box, cedar, and tobacco. A long, persistent, tannic finish gives this majestic effort a closed but formidable personality. Patience will be required. It is a sensational Vieux Château Certan. Anticipated maturity: 2008–2030.

1997: Tobacco, cedar, herbs, cherry and plum notes are light in intensity but elegant and pleasant. Although it lacks depth, the wine possesses medium body, sweet tannin, and weediness. Drink it over the next 2–3 years.

1996: Tasted three times from bottle, the 1996 merited a slightly higher score on one occasion, but my policy is to go with the more conservative rating. The wine exhibits a dark plum color and a complex nose of roasted herbs, Asian spices, earth, and sweet black cherry fruit. A refined claret, with excellent concentration, a sweet mid-palate, and moderate tannin in the finish, it is a finesse-styled Pomerol. Anticipated maturity: 2003–2016.

1995: Frightful bottle variation left me perplexed about just where this wine fits in Bordeaux's qualitative hierarchy. I tasted the wine three times since bottling, all within a 14-day period. Twice the wine was extremely closed and firm, with an evolved plum/garnet color, high levels of tannin, sweet black currant, prune, and olive-tinged fruit, and astringent tannin in the medium-bodied finish. Those two bottles suggested the wine was in need of at least 4–5 years of cellaring and would keep for 20 years. The third bottle was atypically evolved, with a similar color, but it was far more open-knit, displaying Provençal herbs, black cherry, and cassis fruit in a medium-bodied, jammy, lush style. I expect marginal bottle variation, but while the quality was relatively the same in all three bottles, the forward, open-knit example left me puzzled.

Past Glories: 1990 (93), 1988 (91), 1986 (90), 1975 (90), 1964 (90), 1952 (94), 1950 (97), 1948 (98), 1947 (97), 1945 (98–100), 1928 (96)

VIEUX FORTIN (ST.-EMILION)

1998	C	(87–89)
1997	C	84
1996	C	86
1995	C	86

This consistently well-made St.-Emilion emerges from a vineyard not far from Figeac and Cheval Blanc. It usually represents a very good value.

1998: A sleeper of the vintage. This 1998's heady, intoxicating combination of black fruits, earth, and toast, and easy, open-knit, ebulliently fruity style make for a hedonistic drinking experience. There is more tannin than usual, but it is soft and well integrated. Drink this fleshy, well-made wine over the next 5–6 years.

1997: Not as successful as either the 1995 or the 1996, the medium-bodied 1997 is slightly austere, with hard tannin. It does reveal attractive black cherry fruit as well as good clean winemaking.

1996: Impressive for a wine in this price category, this deep ruby-colored St.-Emilion reveals a tobacco-tinged, black cherry–scented nose, and spicy, medium-bodied flavors with excellent purity and ripeness. Forward and soft for a 1996, without much structure or tannin, I would opt for drinking it over the next 2–3 years.

1995: The medium deep ruby-colored 1995 Vieux Fortin offers a moderately intense, herb-tinged berry, spice, and chocolate-scented nose, and a creamy texture. There is a tannic overlay, but the wine's primary appeal is its up-front fruit, plumpness, and easygoing, open-knit character. Anticipated maturity: now–2006.

VILLA BEL-AIR (GRAVES)

2000	C	(88–89)

2000: A sleeper of the vintage and the finest wine yet made at this estate, this textbook Graves exhibits sweet black cherry and mocha notes with tobacco and scorched earth characteristics in the background. A gorgeously supple, plush texture possesses wonderful up-front appeal. Layered, rich, and precocious, this is one 2000 that will not require extended cellaring. Anticipated maturity: now–2012.

VRAY CROIX DE GAY (POMEROL)

2000	C	(87–88+)
1998	C	86

2000: This dark ruby/purple Pomerol exhibits abundant quantities of sweet black cherry and plumlike fruit with a touch of mocha, caramel, earth, and balsam wood. It possesses excellent purity, good size, and plenty of substance, but the finish reveals extremely elevated tannin. If the wine does not dry out as it ages, it will merit a score in the upper 80s. Otherwise, it could become attenuated and out of balance after 7–8 years. This is a hard call to make at present. Anticipated maturity: 2004–2016?

1998: A pumped-up version of the 1997, with a dark ruby color and a jammy black cherry, earth, and wood-scented bouquet, this elegant, concentrated, pure, finely etched, stylish 1998 possesses enough tannin to warrant cellaring for 1–2 years. Anticipated maturity: 2004–2017.

YON-FIGEAC (ST.-EMILION)

2000   **C   (89–92)**

One of the most favored sectors in the 2000 vintage included the vineyards between Figeac and Cheval Blanc, as well as those on the Pomerol border (i.e., La Conseillante and L'Evangile). The 2000 Yon-Figeac, which emerges from this area, is the finest effort yet produced by this estate and a sleeper of the vintage. It should be released at a reasonable price and availability should be assured as the vineyard is relatively large (62 acres, planted with 80% Merlot and 20% Cabernet Franc).

2000: A big wine for this cru, despite some substantial tannin, it offers deep layers of smoky cassis and blackberry fruit. A blend of 90% Merlot and 10% Cabernet Franc, it boasts superb purity, a multilayered personality, gorgeous aromas, and a long, structured, powerful, concentrated finish with admirable purity. Anticipated maturity: 2004–2016. This is a very serious wine.

BURGUNDY AND BEAUJOLAIS

Burgundy is cherished by wine lovers because it produces the most majestic, glorious, and hedonistic Pinot Noir and Chardonnay on earth. Its wines can be the world's most complex, elegant, and harmonious. Furthermore, Burgundies, whether white or red, are some of the easiest wines to match with food.

AT FIRST GLANCE COMPLEX, BUT IN REALITY EASY TO GRASP

Typically, as people learn about wine, they gravitate first to California or Bordeaux, then tackle other regions, saving Burgundy for last because they view it as difficult to grasp. With Bordeaux a consumer only really needs to know the names of a few estates and a handful of the best vintages to be relatively certain of obtaining an appealing wine. With California, the same holds true, while vintage differences tend to be less marked. Burgundy, on the other hand, has producers that offer a wide range of wines with names that appear complicated, and its vintages vary vastly in quality. Yet Burgundy is actually easy to understand for the novice armed with some basic information. As with Bordeaux, California, and all the other wine regions of the world, knowing who the good producers are is paramount. Burgundy labels, which at first may seem daunting, in fact do display all the relevant information clearly

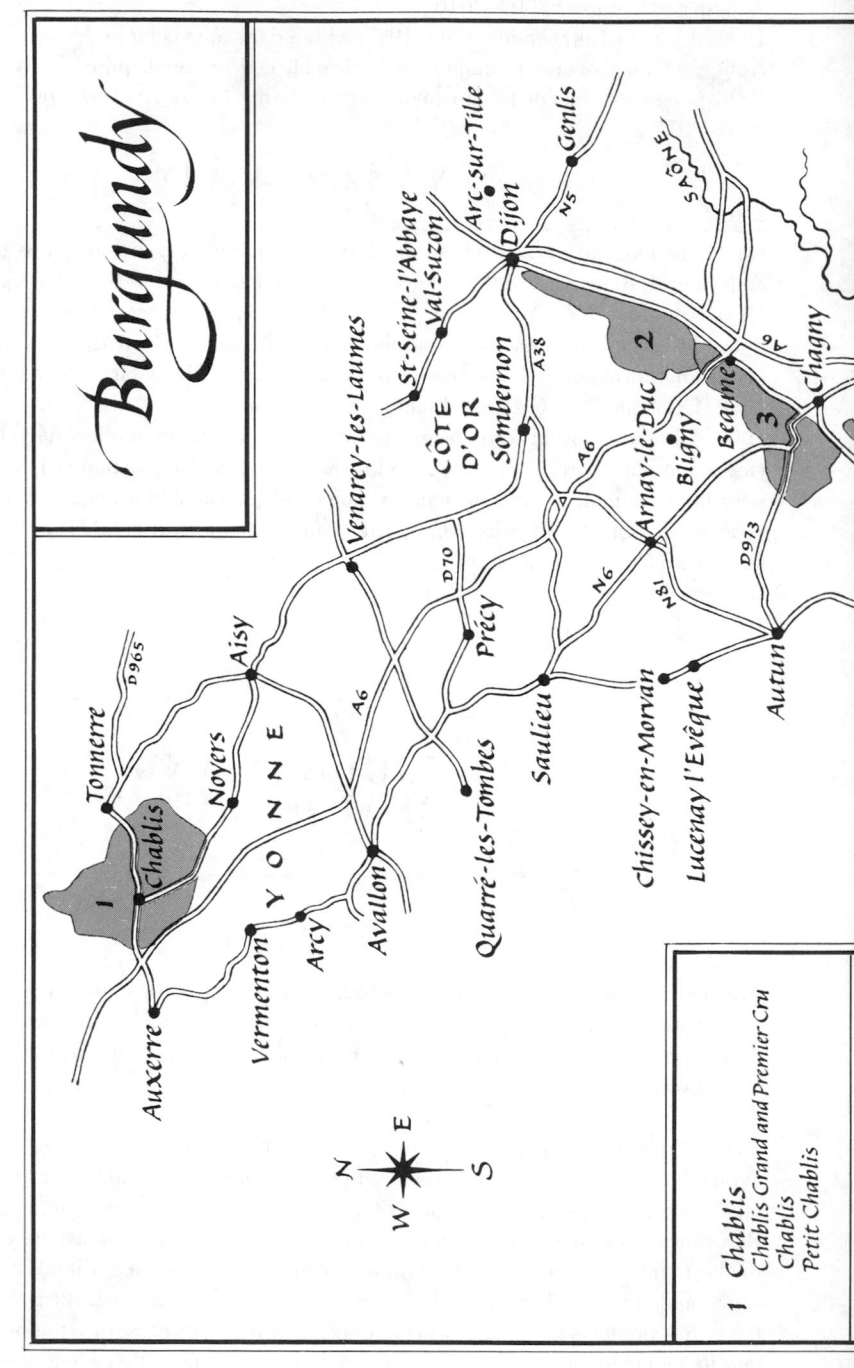

Burgundy

Chablis
Chablis Grand and Premier Cru
Chablis
Petit Chablis

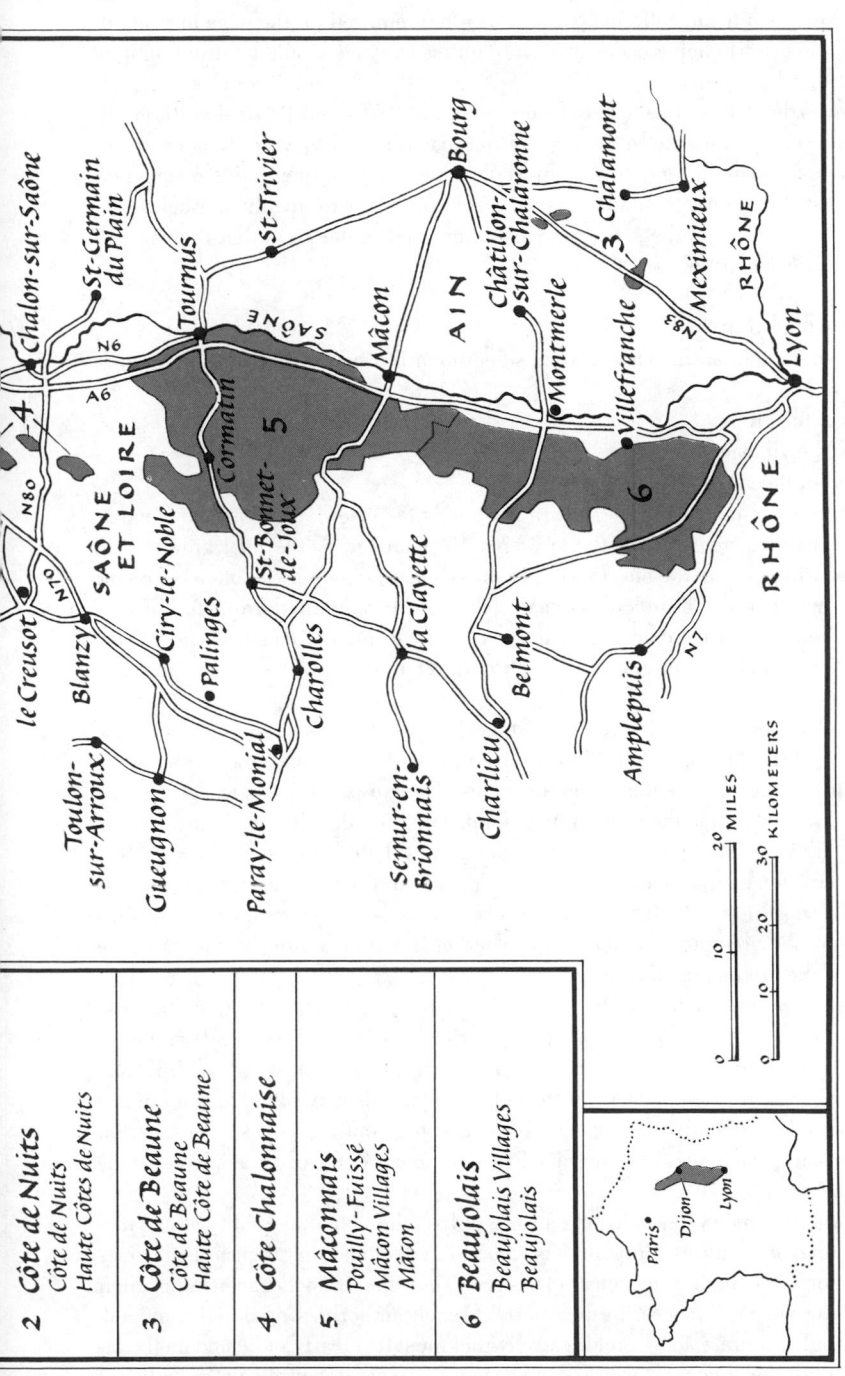

in a simple format. Also, there are only a few vintages of Burgundy that consumers should concentrate on purchasing. Additionally, unlike some other regions, like Italy's Piedmont and Bordeaux, where significant cellaring patience is often required for the wine to reach its peak of maturity, the overwhelming majority of Burgundies can and should be drunk in their first 5–8 years of life.

While Burgundy's detractors cling to beliefs formed in the 1970s and 1980s that Burgundy is overpriced, exceedingly variable in quality, and too complicated to waste time or money on, over the past dozen years Burgundy has enjoyed an unparalleled qualitative resurgence. Whereas in the past Burgundy's top-end wines were sold primarily to wealthy masochists, at present the quantities of outstanding Burgundy has increased to the point that they are enjoyed by a wide range of consumers.

THE SIMPLICITY OF BURGUNDY

There are three factors that are important when selecting a Burgundy. They are, in order of importance:

1. the quality of the grower
2. the merit of the vintage
3. the potential of the vineyard

Nothing is of more paramount significance in Burgundy (as elsewhere) than the commitment to quality and the competence of the grower/wine producer. While poor growers will produce mediocre wine even in the finest years, an outstanding vigneron can often overcome the negative characteristics of a difficult vintage. Also, an uncommitted grower's Musigny will often be outshone by a great domaine's village wine. Learning the names of the few top producers is therefore vital (consult the guide to Burgundy's best-known producers on pages 395–400).

Next in order of importance is the quality of the vintages. Because Burgundy is at the northern extremity of the zone in which Pinot Noir and Chardonnay can grow, variations in the weather can have an enormous impact on the wines. The growing season, wedged tightly between the cool, wet spring and the cold, rainy fall, must provide the vines with enough sun, water, and heat to flower, develop fruit, and ripen the grapes. Late frosts, hail, diseases bolstered by muggy weather, excessive rain, droughts, and early freezes all have great impact on the character of the resulting wine. It seems as if every year, a month before the harvest, Burgundy stands before the precipice. No one knows whether it will be a millennium vintage or one best suited for the production of vinegar.

Every growing region has vintage differences caused by its weather. However, because Burgundians work with the world's most fickle grape variety (Pinot Noir) and reside at the extremity of the growing region where this varietal can be successfully cultivated, variations in the weather have a larger impact on its wines than elsewhere. This may sound as if it renders the purchasing of good Burgundy difficult, yet, in reality, the contrary is true. Because few vintages are successful, consumers need learn only a small number of good years (consult the vintage guide on pages 400–410).

Last in order of importance when selecting a Burgundy is the potential quality of its vineyard. Over the course of centuries, Burgundians came to understand that their hillside vineyards varied in potential quality and characteristics. They therefore began naming their wines using specific vineyard names. In the 1930s, French authorities rendered it official, creating an amazingly accurate, four-level hierarchy that must be clearly indicated on the labels of all Burgundies: the "regional" wines (Appellation Bourgogne Contrôlée); the "village" wines, which indicate the name of their hometown (Appellation Vosne-Romanée Contrôlée, for example); the premier cru or first-growth wines (Appellation Premier Cru Contrôlée); and, at the top of the hierarchy, the grand cru or great growth wines (Appellation Grand Cru Contrôlée). Therefore, a consumer armed with information of Burgundy's finest estates and best vintages can clearly see where a wine falls within the hierarchy.

The greatest mistake a consumer can make when buying a Burgundy is to select it based on the appellation. Uninformed consumers are playing right into the hands of the plonk pushers if they seek a grand cru (Chambertin, Clos de Vougeot, Bâtard-Montrachet, etc.) or a premier cru without paying attention to the name of the producer. All buying decisions must be based first and foremost on the quality of the producer, then on the vintage, and last on the potential quality of the vineyard. Following this simple rule virtually assures success in the selection of Burgundies.

THE COMPLEXITY OF BURGUNDY

Consumers who wish to learn the intricacies of Burgundy are faced with an unending supply of information that renders the whole process extremely complicated (which may find to be another of this region's endearing traits). Burgundy's vineyards are extremely fragmented, a result of Napoléon's having abolished primogeniture laws. Consumers who believe that lofty appellations are indicative of quality will most often find themselves in possession of poor, expensive wines.

The nature of the Burgundy problem is perhaps best shown in the analogy between several famous Bordeaux vineyards and a handful of renowned Burgundy vineyards. Take the famous St.-Julien vineyard of Ducru-Beaucaillou in the heart of the Médoc. It is 124 acres in size. Compare it with its famous neighbor about 10 miles to the south, Château Palmer in Margaux, a vineyard of 111 acres in size. Any consumer who buys a bottle of a specific vintage of Ducru-Beaucaillou or Palmer will be getting exactly the same wine. Of course, it may have been handled differently or subjected to abuse in transportation or storage, but the wine that left the property was made by one winemaking team, from one blend, and the taste, texture, and aromatic profile of a specific vintage should not be any different whether drunk in Paris, Vienna, Tokyo, New York, or Los Angeles.

Compare that situation with the famous grand cru from Burgundy's Côte de Nuits, Clos de Vougeot. Clos de Vougeot has 124 acres, the same size as Ducru-Beaucaillou. Yet there is only one proprietor of the Bordeaux estate, while Clos de Vougeot is divided among more than 80 different proprietors. Many of these growers sell their production to *négociants*, but in any given vintage there are at least three dozen or more Clos de Vougeots in the marketplace. All of them are entitled to grand cru status, they vary in price from $70 to $600+ a bottle, but less than a half dozen are likely to be compelling wines. The remainder range in quality from very good to poor. Clos de Vougeot is most often cited as a microcosm of Burgundy—infinitely confusing, distressingly frustrating. Yet majestic wines do indeed come out of Clos de Vougeot from a few top producers.

Also consider the most renowned Burgundy vineyard—Chambertin. This 32-acre vineyard is 3 acres larger than Château Pétrus, maker of one of Bordeaux's most expensive red wines. Pétrus has only one producer, and there is only one wine from a given vintage, all of which has been blended prior to bottling, all of it equal in quality. But among Chambertin's 32 acres, there are more than 24 different proprietors, with only a handful of them committed to producing extraordinary wine. Most Chambertins sell for well in excess of $150 a bottle, yet most of them are mediocre.

The situation is the same among the rest of the greatest Burgundy vineyards. The 24-acre Musigny vineyard is split among 17 proprietors. The famed Richebourg vineyard of just under 20 acres is divided among *only* 12 proprietors (a low number by Burgundy standards). Even Burgundy's greatest white wine vineyard, Le Montrachet (20 acres), is divided among 15 producers. Only five or six of these proprietors consistently produce outstanding wines, yet all of them fetch $200–800+ a bottle.

The Basics—Burgundy

TYPES OF WINE

This modestly sized viticultural area in France's heartland, four hours by car southeast of Paris, produces on the average 22 million cases of dry red and white wine as well as tiny quantities of rosé. This represents 3% of France's total wine production.

Red Wine   Burgundy's dry red wines come from the Côte d'Or, which is divided into two distinct areas: the northern half, called the Côte de Nuits, and the southern portion, the Côte de Beaune. A bit farther south, red wines are made in the Côte Chalonnaise and even farther south in Beaujolais and Mâconnais.

White Wine   Dry white wine is made everywhere in Burgundy, but most of the production is centered in the Côte de Beaune, in the Côte Chalonnaise, in Mâconnais, and in Burgundy's most northern area, Chablis.

GRAPE VARIETIES

There are three major grapes used in Burgundy. Red Burgundies are made from Pinot Noir, the world's most fickle and troublesome grape. Although it is an extremely difficult grape to make into wine, when handled with care it produces the great, sumptuous, velvety reds of the Côte d'Or. The Gamay, another widely planted grape, offers up the succulent, spicy, effusively fruity, easy to drink and easy to understand wines of Beaujolais, and, when bended with Pinot Noir, Passetoutgrains. Chardonnay, the other major grape, produces the great white wines of Chablis, the Côte de Beaune, and the Mâconnais, as well as those from the Côte Chalonnaise. White grape varietals grown in smaller quantities in Burgundy include the Aligoté grape—planted mostly in less hospitable sites—and the Pinot Blanc and Pinot Beurrot, also called Pinot Gris (planted in minute quantities).

FLAVORS

When it is great, Pinot Noir produces the most complex, hedonistic, and remarkably thrilling red wine in the world, but the problem is that only a small percentage of Burgundy's wines attain this level. At its best, the bouquet is one filled with red fruits and exotic spices, and the taste is broad, expansive, round, lush, and soft. Great Burgundy always tastes sweeter than Bordeaux and has a significantly ligher color. Gamay is not drunk for its complexity but rather for its heady, direct, ripe, soft, fleshy, exuberant fruitiness and easygoing texture. Chardonnay can range from stony and mineral-scented with high acidity in Chablis, to buttery, smoky, creamy, decadently rich and tasting of sautéed almonds and hazelnuts in a great Côte de Beaune white Burgundy, to the beautifully rich, chalk-infused and lemony gems of the top Mâconnais producers.

AGING POTENTIAL

Seemingly nowhere in the wine world is ageworthiness as much an issue as it is in Burgundy. Each individual vintage, producer, and vineyard of origin have an enormous effect on a wine's capacity for aging. Furthermore, adequate transportation and storage conditions (important for all wines) are vital if one wishes to age a red or white Burgundy.

RED WINES

Côte de Nuits: 2–18+ years
Côte de Beaune: 2–15+ years
Beaujolais: 1–5+ years

WHITE WINES
Chablis: 1–10+ years
Côte de Beaune: 4–10+ years
Mâconnais: 1–8+ years

OVERALL QUALITY LEVEL
There are more great wines being crafted by more top-flight producers in Burgundy than ever before. However, this region continues to be filled with precarious pitfalls for the uninformed consumer. No matter which appellation one looks at in Burgundy, the range in quality from watery, poorly made, incompetent wines to majestic wines of great flavor and dimension is enormous.

BURGUNDY'S RENAISSANCE
The 1990s have witnessed a renaissance in Burgundy. The wines emanating from this region are, on the whole, far better than they were in the past. Today there are more high-quality producers crafting first-rate wines than ever before. Why? Consider the following:

1. *Négociant*-suppliers to estates: Even though this is an extremely old winemaking region, estate-bottled wines are a relatively new phenomenon. In fact, some of the first Burgundians to have begun this practice are still working today (Gevrey-Chambertin's Charles Rousseau and Volnay's Marquis d'Angerville, for example). In the past, Burgundian vignerons would harvest their grapes, ferment them, and then sell the wine to *négociants* who would take them through their *élevage* and bottle them. Over the past 50+ years, however, hundreds of vignerons—both good and bad—have switched from being *négociant*-suppliers to bottling their own wines.

While in some cases this trend has been a real positive for consumers (the great vignerons' wines were no longer being mixed with lesser ones to fashion *négociant cuvées*) it has also led to large quantities of expensive yet poor quality wines being made by producers with little to no training or knowledge about *élevage* and bottling techniques.

Furthermore, the amount of money a *négociant* pays for a wine is determined by its appellation, not its quality. A bad Chambertin sells for the same price as a great one. This system benefits growers whose vineyard practices produce high yields, not those who are quality conscious. This lesson was one that took many years to be unlearned by producers who switched from being *négociant*-suppliers to estate bottlers.

2. Appellation buying: For years uninformed or ill-informed consumers based their buying decisions on the appellation instead of the quality of the wine. This practice, perpetuated by the Burgundian obsession of ascribing all positive wine traits to *terroir*, provided ready markets for mediocre offerings from heralded vineyards or villages.

3. Insularity: In the past, Burgundy was extremely parochial. Growers only drank wines they themselves had made, so they had nothing to compare their work against. Some of the more adventurous might have tasted those wines produced in the same village. A famous producer from Chablis once told me that he had never tasted a wine that was not from Burgundy. Another well-known vigneron, this one from Gevrey-Chambertin, admitted that Chambolle-Musigny (only a few miles away) was like a foreign country to him; he knew none of the growers there and had never tasted their wines. Vineyard and cellar work was passed from father to son, so deficiencies in winemaking were carried over from generation to generation under the guise of tradition. The few new techniques that were adopted over the years generally tended to lower the quality of the wines (excessive fertilization, fining, and filtration, etc.) instead of improving them.

Because of this insularity, Burgundy has not experienced the revolutionizing and modernizing effects of high quality–oriented consultants who have encouraged and served as a catalyst for better and better wines. Bordeaux's Professor Emile Peynaud and Michel Roland and, in California, Tony Soter and Helen Turley, are but a few. Starting in the mid to late seventies, Guy Accad attempted to fulfill that role. His techniques (which included tight spacing of the vines, harvesting very ripe fruit, extended preformentation macerations with extremely high doses of sulfur), though controversial, were adopted by a number of domaines. Yet the results were mixed, Accad was buried by a barrage of criticism that his wines were not "typical" or "traditional," and today Accad has few clients and his influence is insignificant—at least when it comes to winemaking.

Renaissance: A younger generation has taken over the estates of their parents and have brought much-needed change to Burgundy. These vignerons, led by the likes of Christophe Roumier, Dominique Lafon, Jean-François Coche, and others, are well traveled, have tasted the finest wines produced throughout the world, exchange winemaking ideas, and competitively strive to produce the best wines they can. Throughout Burgundy new viticultural and vinification techniques are being tested, fining and filtering is being eschewed, and the fertilizers once used to produce huge yields are being abandoned. This generation, educated in winemaking schools and trained in the finest wineries the world over, is taking Burgundy to a level of quality never before achieved.

American consumers should be especially proud of the activist role that small specialty burgundy importers in this country have played in Burgundy's renaissance. Special recognition should be given to David Hinkle (North Berkeley Wines), Robert Kacher Selections, Patrick Lesec (a Paris broker), Louis/Dressner, Kermit Lynch Wine Merchant, Peter Vezan Selections (a Paris broker), Vineyard Brands (Robert Haas), and Weygandt-Metzler (Peter Weygandt). All of these importers have aggressively persuaded their growers to halt unnecessary fining and filtration if the wines are otherwise stable and clear. For many wines, Americans are getting far better Burgundy *cuvées* than any other consumers in the world because some growers bottle unfined and unfiltered wines only for sale in America. These American specialists have seen what damage can be done to wines by excessive crop yields, overmanipulation, and aggressive fining and filtration.

RATING BURGUNDY GROWERS, PRODUCERS, AND *NÉGOCIANTS*

No one will ever have a great deal of success selecting a Burgundy without a thorough knowledge of the finest growers and *négociants*. The most meticulous producers often make better wine in mediocre vintages than many less dedicated growers and producers make in great vintages. Knowing the finest producers in Burgundy is unquestionably the most important factor in your success in finding the best wines.

The following is a guide to the best red Burgundy producers. Consistency from year to year and among the producers' total range of wines were the most important considerations. One should be cognizant of the fact that many lower-rated producers may make specific wines that are qualitatively above their placement.

Note: The rankings provided for estates indicated by a † are based on their special *cuvées* crafted for North Berkeley Wine Imports. Many other Burgundy estates have special bottlings for their U.S. importers yet the differences between the "house *cuvées*" and the U.S. bottlings is not as marked as those crafted for North Berkeley. They are therefore not indicated.

Where a producer has been assigned a range of stars, ***/**** for example, the lower rating has been used for placement in this hierarchy. Where a producer is marked by a "since [date]," this means that its indicated ranking is only for those wines made since and including the marked vintage.

RATING BURGUNDY'S RED WINE PRODUCERS

***** *(OUTSTANDING)*

Domaine Marquis d'Angerville (Volnay)
Domaine d'Auvenay (St. Romain)
Domaine Jean Boillot (Volnay) (since 1997)
Domaine Claude Dugat (Gevrey-Chambertin)§
Domaine Dugat-Py (Gevrey-Chambertin)§
Domaine Robert Groffier (Morey-St.-Denis) (since 1995)§
Domaine Joblot (Givry)
Domaine Michel Lafarge (Volnay)
Domaine des Comtes Lafon (Meursault)

Domaine Leroy (Vosne-Romanée)§
Domaine Hubert Lignier (Morey-St.-Denis)
Domaine Denis Mortet (Gevrey-Chambertin) (since 1995)
Domaine de la Romanée-Conti (Vosne-Romanée)
Domaine Christian Serafin (Gevrey-Chambertin)
Domaine du Comte de Vogüé (Chambolle-Musigny)

**** *(EXCELLENT)*

Bertrand Ambroise (Prémeaux-Prissey)****/*****
Domaine de l'Arlot (Prémeaux-Prissey)
Domaine Robert Arnoux (Vosne-Romanée)****/*****
Domaine Ghislaine Barthod-Noellat (Chambolle-Musigny)
Bouchard Père et Fils (Beaune) (since 1995)
Philippe Charlopin (Gevrey-Chambertin)
Domaine Robert Chevillon (Nuits-St.-Georges)
Domaine Bruno Clair (Marsannay)
Domaine Jean-Jacques Confuron (Prémeaux-Prissey)****/*****
Domaine Dujac (Morey-St.-Denis)
Domaine Maurice Ecard et Fils (Savigny-les-Beaune)****/*****
Domaine René Engel (Vosne-Romanée)
Domaine Geantet-Pansiot (Gevrey-Chambertin)
Vincent Girardin (Santenay)
Domaine Henri Gouges (Nuits-St.-Georges) (since 1995)
Domaine Jean Grivot (Vosne-Romanée) (since 1993)****/*****
Domaine Anne Gros (Vosne-Romanée)****/*****
Louis Jadot (Beaune)****/*****

Domaine Jayer-Gilles (Magny-les-Villers)****/*****
Domaine Lécheneaut (Nuits-St.-Georges)****/*****
Frédéric Magnien (Morey-St.-Denis)****/*****
Domaine Michel Magnien (Morey-St.-Denis)****/*****
Domaine Méo-Camuzet (Vosne-Romanée)****/*****
Lucien Le Moine (Beaune)
Domaine Mugneret-Gibourg/Georges Mugneret (Vosne-Romanée) (since 1995)****/*****
Domaine Jacques-Frédéric Mugnier (Chambolle-Musigny)
Domaine des Perdrix (Prémeaux-Prissey) (since 1995)
Domaine Henri Perrot-Minot (Morey-St.-Denis) (since 1995)
Domaine Jacques Prieur (Meursault) (since 1995)
Domaine Jean Raphet (Morey-St.-Denis)
Antonin Rodet (Mercurey) (since 1995 on Cave Privée wines)
Domaine Joseph Roty (Gevrey-Chambertin)
Domaine Emmanuel Rouget (Flagey-Echézeaux)****/*****

§ These four superstar estates deserve special recognition for the spectacular wines they have crafted in the 1996, 1997, 1998, and 1999 vintages. Even when faced with the difficulties of the 1998 vintage, these estates produced lovely, recommendable wines that are a testimony to their brilliant vineyard and cellar work.

Domaine Georges et Christophe Roumier (Chambolle-Musigny)****/*****

Domaine Armand Rousseau (Gevrey-Chambertin)

Domaine du Clos de Tart (Morey-St.-Denis)

Domaine Tollot-Beaut et Fils (Chorey-les-Beaune)

*** (GOOD)

Domaine Pierre Amiot et Fils (Morey-St.-Denis)

Domaine Amiot-Servelle (Chambolle-Musigny)***/****

Domaine Arlaud Père et Fils (Nuits-St.-Georges)***/****†

Domaine Charles Audoin (Marsannay)

Domaine Xavier Besson (Givry)†

Domaine Bitouzet-Prieur (Volnay)

Domaine Simon Bize et Fils (Savigny-les-Beaune)

Domaine Jean-Yves Bizot (Vosne-Romanée)

Domaine Daniel Bocquenet (Nuits-St.-Georges)***/****

Domaine Jean-Marc Boillot (Pommard)***/****

Domaine Reyanne et Pascal Bouley (Volnay)

Domaine Alain Burguet (Gevrey-Chambertin)***/****

Domaine Jacques Cacheux et Fils (Vosne-Romanée)

Domaine Carré-Courbin (Beaune)

Domaine du Château de Chamirey (Mercurey)

Champy (Beaune)

Domaine Chandon de Briailles (Savigny-les-Beaune)

Domaine Jean Chauvenet (Nuits-St.-Georges)

Domaine Chauvenet-Chopin (Nuits-St.-Georges)***/****

Domaine Pascal Chevigny (Nuits-St.-Georges)***/****

Colin-Deléger (Chassagne-Montrachet)

Domaine Confuron/Cotétidot (Vosne-Romanée)

Domaine Edmond Cornu (Ladoix-Serrigny)

Domaine de Courcel (Pommard)

Domaine Pierre Damoy (Gevrey-Chambertin) (since 1997)***/****

Domaine Vincent Dancer (Chassagne-Montrachet)

Domaine Marius Delarche (Pernand-Vergelesses)***/****†

Joseph Drouhin (Beaune)

Domaine Jean-Luc Dubois (Chorey-les-Beaune)†

Domaine Dureuil-Janthial (Rully)***/****

Domaine Arnauld Ente (Meursault)

Domaine des Epeneaux (Pommard)***/****

Domaine Didier Erker (Givry)

Fery-Meunier (Nuits-St.-Georges)

Domaine Fontaine-Gagnard (Chassagne-Montrachet)

Domaine Jean-Noël Gagnard (Chassagne-Montrachet)

Alex Gambal (Beaune)***/****

Domaine Jean Garaudet (Pommard)***/****

Domaine Pierre Guillemot (Savigny-les-Beaune)

Domaine Antonin Guyon (Savigny-les-Beaune)

Domaine Guyon (Vosne-Romanée)

Domaine Henri Jouan (Morey-St.-Denis)

Domaine des Lambrays (Morey-St.-Denis) (since 1995)

Domaine Latour-Giraud (Meursault)

Domaine Philippe Leclerc (Gevrey-Chambertin)***/****

Domaine René Leclerc (Gevrey-Chambertin)***/****

Olivier Leflaive (Puligny-Montrachet)

Domaine Philippe Livera/Domaine des Tilleuils (Gevrey-Chambertin)†

Domaine du Château de la Maltroye (Chassagne-Montrachet)

Domaine Joseph Matrot (Meursault)

Domaine Maume (Gevrey-Chambertin)

Domaine du Château de Mercey (Mercurey)

Domaine François Mikulski (Meursault)

Domaine Jean-Marc Millot (Comblanchien)

Domaine Moissenet-Bonnard (Pommard)

Domaine Mongeard-Mugneret (Vosne-Romanée)***/****

Domaine Monthélie-Douhairet (Monthélie) (since 1995)

Bernard Morey et Fils (Chassagne-Montrachet)***/****

Domaine Albert Morot (Beaune)***/****

Domaine Lucien Muzard et Fils (Santenay)

Domaine Philippe Naddef (Couchey)***/****

Domaine Ponsot (Morey-St.-Denis)

Nicolas Potel (Nuits-St.-Georges)***/****

Domaine de la Pousse d'Or (Volnay) (since 1997)

Domaine Ramonet (Chassagne-Montrachet)

Domaine Henri Remoriquet (Nuits-St.-Georges)

Domaine Armelle et Bernard Rion (Vosne-Romanée)

Domaine Daniel Rion (Nuits-St.-Georges)***/****

Domaine Rossignol (Rossignol-Jenniard) (Volnay)

Domaine du Château de Rully (Rully)

Domaine Jean Tardy (Vosne-Romanée)

Domaine Jean et J. L. Trapet (Gevrey-Chambertin) (since 1995)***/****

Domaine A. & P. de Villaine (Bouzeron)

Domaine Christophe Violot-Guillemard (Pommard)

Domaine Thierry Violot-Guillemard (Pommard)

Domaine Joseph Voillot (Volnay)***/****

* * (AVERAGE)

Domaine Guy Amiot et Fils (Chassagne-Montrachet)**/***

Domaine Jean-Claude Belland (Santenay)**/***

Domaine Bertagna (Vougeot)**/***

Domaine Lucien Boillot et Fils (Gevrey-Chambertin)

Domaine Bonneau du Martray (Pernand-Vergelesses)**/***

Domaine Borgeot (Remigny)**/***

Domaine Jean-Marc Bouley (Volnay)**/***

Bourée Père et Fils (Gevrey-Chambertin)

Domaine Philippe Brenot (Santenay)**/***

Domaine du Manoir de la Bressandière (Pommard)

Domaine Lucien Camus-Brochon (Savigny-les-Beaune)**/***†

Chartron et Trébuchet (Puligny-Montrachet)

Domaine Marc Colin (St.-Aubin/Gamay)**/***

Alain Corcia Selections (Savigny-les-Beaune)

Domaine du Château de Cray

Domaine Henri Delagrange et Fils (Volnay)

Domaine Bruno Desaunay-Bissey (Flagey-Echézeaux)**/***

Domaine de la Ferté (Givry)**/***

Domaine Jean-Philippe Fichet (Meursault)**/***

Domaine Forey Père et Fils (Vosne-Romanée)

Domaine Génot-Boulanger (Meursault)**/***

Machard de Gramont (Nuits-St.-Georges)**/***

Domaine Rémi Jobard (Meursault)**/***

Labouré-Roi (Nuits-St.-Georges)

Domaine René Lamy-Pillot (Chassagne-Montrachet)

Louis Latour (Beaune)**/***

Domaine Aleth Leroyer-Girardin (Pommard)

Domaine Georges Lignier (Morey-St.-Denis)**/***

Domaine Prince Florent de Mérode (Ladoix-Serrigny)

Domaine du Château de Monthélie (Monthélie)

Domaine Jean-Marc Morey (Chassagne-Montrachet)

Domaine Pierre Morey (Meursault)

Domaine Denis Mugneret (Vosne-Romanée)

Domaine Fernand et Laurent Pillot (Chassagne-Montrachet)

Jean Pillot (Chassagne-Montrachet)

Domaine de la Poulette (Corgoloin)

Domaine du Château de Prémeaux (Prémeaux-Prissey)

Domaine Roland Rapet (Pernand-Vergelesses)**/***

Domaine Jean-Claude Rateau
(Beaune)**/***
Domaine Henri Rebourseau (Gevrey-
Chambertin)
Domaine Philippe Rossignol (Gevrey-
Chambertin)
Domaine Rossignol-Trapet (Gevrey-
Chambertin)**/***

Domaine Laurent Roumier (Chambolle-
Musigny)**/***
Domaine Saint Martin**/***
Domaine Jacky Truchot (Morey-St.-
Denis)**/***
Domaine des Varoilles (Gevrey-
Chambertin)**/***
Domaine Virot (Mercurey)*/**

RATING BURGUNDY'S WHITE WINE PRODUCERS

(including Côte de Beaune, Mâconnais, and Chablis wine producers)

* * * * * (OUTSTANDING)

Domaine d'Auvenay (St. Romain)
Domaine Daniel Barraud (Vergisson)
Domaine Jean Boillot (Volnay)
Henri Boillot (Meursault)
Domaine Bongran/Jean Thevenet
(Quintaine)
Domaine Jean-François Coche-Dury
(Meursault)
Domaine Cordier et Fils (Fuissé)
Domaine René et Vincent Dauvissat
(Chablis)
Domaine Guffens-Heynen (Vergisson)

Domaine des Comtes Lafon (Meursault)
Domaine Leflaive (Puligny-Montrachet)
Domaine Leroy (Vosne-Romanée)
Bernard Morey (Chassagne-Montrachet)
Domaine Michel Niellon (Chassagne-
Montrachet)
Domaine François et Jean-Marie Raveneau
(Chablis)
Domaine de la Romanée-Conti (Vosne-
Romanée)
Etienne Sauzet (Puligny-Montrachet)
Verget (Sologny)

* * * * (EXCELLENT)

Bertrand Ambroise (Prémeaux-
Prissey)****/*****
Domaine Guy Amiot et Fils (Chassagne-
Montrachet)
Domaine Billaud-Simon (Chablis)
Domaine Blain-Gagnard (Chassagne-
Montrachet)
Jean-Marc Boillot (Pommard)
Bouchard Père et Fils (Beaune) (since
1995)
Domaine Louis Carillon (Puligny-
Montrachet)****/*****
Domaine Bruno Clair (Marsannay)
Domaine Marc Colin (Gamay-St. Aubin)
Colin-Deléger (Chassagne-
Montrachet)****/*****
Domaine Marius Delarche (Pernand-
Vergelesses)
Domaine Jean-Paul Droin (Chablis)
Joseph Drouhin (Beaune)
Domaine Vincent Dureuil-Janthial (Rully)
Domaine Arnauld Ente (Meursault)

Domaine Fontaine-Gagnard (Chassagne-
Montrachet)
Domaine Jean-Noël Gagnard (Chassagne-
Montrachet)
Vincent Girardin (Santenay)
Domaine Guillemot-Michel
(Quintaine)****/*****
Louis Jadot (Beaune)
Domaine Patrick Javillier
(Meursault)****/*****
Domaine François Jobard (Meursault)
Domaine Rémi Jobard
(Meursault)****/*****
Domaine Roger Lassarat (Vergisson)
Louis Latour (Beaune)
Domaine du Duc de Magenta (Louis Jadot)
(Chassagne-Montrachet)
Domaine Louis Michel et Fils (Chablis)
Domaine François Mikulski (Meursault)
Marc Morey (Chassagne-Montrachet)
Domaine Jacques Prieur (Meursault) (since
1995)

Domaine du Château de Puligny-
Montrachet (Puligny-
Montrachet)****/*****
Domaine Ramonet (Chassagne-
Montrachet)
Jean Rijckaert (Leynes)
Domaine Robert-Denogent (Fuissé)

Antonin Rodet (Mercurey) (since 1995 on
Cave Privée wines)
Domaine Guy Roulot (Meursault)
Domaine Georges et Christophe Roumier
(Chambolle-Musigny)
Domaine Tollot-Beaut (Chorey-Beaune)
Domaine Valette (Vinzelles)****/*****

* * * *(GOOD)*

Domaine de l'Arlot (Prémeaux-
Prissey)***/****
Domaine Comte Armand (Pommard)
Domaine Barat (Chablis)
Domaine Jean-Claude Belland (Santenay)
Domaine Bitouzet-Prieur (Volnay)
Domaine Simon Bize (Savigny-les-
Beaune)
Domaine Etienne Boileau/Domaine du
Chardonnay (Chablis)***/****
Domaine Bonneau du Martray (Pernand-
Vergelesses)
Domaine Boyer-Martenot
(Meursault)***/****
Domaine Brintet (Mercurey)
Domaine Caillot (Meursault)
Domaine du Château de Chamirey
(Mercurey)
Domaine Chandon de Briailles (Savigny-
les-Beaune)
Chartron et Trébuchet (Puligny-
Montrachet)***/****
Domaine Alain Coche-Bizouard
(Meursault)***/****
Domaine Bernard Defaix (Milly-Chablis)
Domaine des Deux Roches (St. Véran)
Druid (Morey-St.-Denis)
Georges Dubœuf (Romanèche-Thorins)
Domaine Maurice Ecard (Savigny-les-
Beaune)
Domaine Jean-Philippe Fichet
(Meursault)***/****
Domaine du Château Génot-Boulanger
(Meursault)***/****
Domaine des Gerbeaux (Solutré)
Domaine Emilian Gillet/Jean Thevenet
(Quintaine)***/****
Domaine Henri Gouges (Nuits-St.-
Georges)***/****
Domaine Antonin Guyon (Savigny-les-
Beaune)

Domaine Thierry Hamelin (Lignorelles-
Chablis)
Domaine Jayer-Gilles (Magny-les-
Villers)***/****
Domaine Joblot (Givry)***/****
Laroche (Chablis)***/****
Domaine Latour-Giraud
(Meursault)***/****
Olivier Leflaive (Puligny-
Montrachet)***/****
Domaine du Château de la Maltroye
(Chassagne-Montrachet)
Domaine Manciat-Poncet (Charnay-les-
Mâcon)
Domaines Joseph/Pierre/Thierry Matrot
(Meursault)***/****
Domaine du Château de Mercey
(Mercurey)
Olivier Merlin (La Roche
Vineuse)***/****
Domaine de Montille (Meursault)***/****
Domaine Alice et Olivier de Moor
(Chablis)***/****
Bernard Moreau (Chassagne-Montrachet)
Jean-Marc Morey (Chassagne-
Montrachet)
Domaine Pierre Morey
(Meursault)***/****
Morey-Blanc (Meursault)
Domaine du Clos Noly (Mâconnais)
Domaine de Perraud (St. Véran)***/****
Jean Pillot (Chassagne-Montrachet)
Paul Pillot (Chassagne-Montrachet)
Domaine Denis Pommier (Poinchy-
Chablis)
Domaine Rapet Père et Fils (Pernand-
Vergelesses)
Domaine de Château de Rully (Rully)
Domaine Francine et Olivier Savary
(Maligny-Chablis)
Domaine de Vauroux (Chablis)

Domaine des Vieilles Pierres (St.
  Véran)

Domaine A. P. de Villaine (Bouzeron)
Domaine Robert Vocoret et Fils (Chablis)

** *(AVERAGE)*

Domaine Bachelet-Ramonet (Chassagne-
  Montrachet)
Domaine Bertagna**/***
Domaine Borgeot (Remigny)**/***
Domaine Philippe Brenot
  (Santenay)**/***
Domaine Sylvain Bzikot (Puligny-
  Montrachet)**/***
Domaine Pascal Chevigny (Nuits-St.-
  Georges)**/***
Domaine Condemine (Mâconnais)**/***
Alain Corcia Selections (Savigny-les-
  Beaune)**/***
Domaine Jean-Luc Dubois (Chorey-les-
  Beaune)**/***
Domaine Michel Dupont-Fahn (Meursault)
Domaine René Fleurot-Larose (Santenay)
Domaine Ghislaine et Jean-Hughes Goisot
  (St.-Bris-Le-Vineux)**/***

Labouré-Roi (Nuits-St.-Georges)
Lamy-Pillot (Santenay)
Domaine de Legères (Mâconnais)**/***
Méo-Camuzet (Vosne-Romanée)**/***
Domaine Mestre Père et Fils
  (Santenay)**/***
Château de Meursault (Meursault)
Domaine Michelot (Meursault)
Domaine Ponsot (Morey-St.-Denis)**/***
Domaine Jean-Claude Rateau
  (Beaune)**/***
Domaine du Château de Rontets
  (Fuissé)**/***
Domaine Philippe Rossignol (Nuits-St.-
  Georges)**/***
Domaine Thomas (Prissé)**/***
Domaine Christophe Viollot-Guillemard
  (Pommard)**/***

RECENT VINTAGES

2000—Reporting on the overall quality of the 2000 white Burgundies is a particularly difficult task, as they can be divided into two distinct groups. At the worst, part of the harvest
produced wines that are unpleasantly tart and lemony. On the positive side of the ledger,
there are many lush, floral wines filled with white-fruit flavors. The first group ranges in quality from poor to above average, and the second from excellent to outstanding. If 1999 offers
many good, very good, and excellent wines, yet few blockbusters, the 2000s are frustratingly
irregular. As is often the case in the wine world, the vintage offered growers the opportunity
to produce first-rate efforts. In short, success or failure was primarily determined by the dates
vignerons chose to harvest. From the perfect (copious and lightning-fast) flowering to a growing season that alternated between rain and sun, 2000 was the perfect vintage for producing
large quantities of wine. Some of Burgundy's finest vignerons, including such illustrious
names as Dominique Lafon and Jean-François Coche, maintained that they had never
worked so hard to control yields, to no avail.

Statistically, the record-setting 1999 harvest produced more wine than 2000, yet, as the
saying goes, there are "lies, damn lies, and statistics." Most growers readily admitted that
their vines produced as much as in 1999. Yet, because of intransigence on the part of the Institut National des Appellations d'Origines (INAO, the governing body of French appellations), they either left grapes on the vine at harvest or sent excess wine to France's
government-run distilleries as dictated by the law. Unlike 1999, the INAO rejected the Burgundians' plea for a 40% PLC (Plafond Limite de Classement, the percentage by which the
appellation's maximum allowable yield can be surpassed in a specific vintage), limiting them
to a 20% PLC.

Monday, September 11, 2000, was the official date growers could begin harvesting (the *ban
de vendange*), yet, as conscientious growers told me, "the grapes were not ripe." On the

evening of the 12th and morning of the 13th a freak storm struck the Côte Chalonnaise and Côte de Beaune, dumping huge amounts of rain (particularly on Santenay and Pommard). To exacerbate the growers' tension, some hail struck Rully, Meursault, Volnay, and Savigny-les-Beaune. The storm was highly localized, however. Lafon, for example, slept through the tempest, as it didn't hit the sector of Meursault in which he lives. He didn't know his Volnay Santenots vineyard had been struck until a colleague called with the news. A few miles away, the Muzards in Santenay had 770 cubic meters of mud in their cellars. To no one's surprise, the vast majority of growers stated that the storm had "no effect" on the quality of their wines. Amusingly, those who do not produce reds alleged that the Pinot Noir had been "severely compromised." Some white Burgundy producers did voice the opinion that their wines would have been more concentrated were it not for the large amounts of rain.

Either way, the storm's biggest impact on the 2000 white Burgundies is the fact that it propelled many growers to harvest earlier than they should have. As soon as the skies cleared on September 13 and 14, the race was on to pick as fast as possible. Growers who produce red wine started with their Pinot Noir, as rot was spreading like wildfire in those vineyards. Whites produced from grapes harvested immediately after the storm tasted unripe. They have shrill, tart, lemony acidities, no charm, and little fruit. Those that were harvested later, either because the growers had the courage to wait or because they were busy harvesting reds, have flesh, balance, and appealing white fruit–filled personalities. What often lacks in this vintage is that sense of completeness—depth, concentration, and that rich, vinous characteristic that can make white Burgundies so sublime. The finest 2000s will deliver considerable pleasure over the next 5–10 years, but only in rare instances will they age well because they lack the density of fruit essential for extended cellaring.

The top Côte de Beaune whites in 2000 are unquestionably better than the finest 1999s, yet the bottom of the barrel is worse than their counterparts in 1999. The finest 2000 white Burgundies can best be described as 1992s with less density; the worst resemble 1991s with an additional shot of lemon juice. In the Mâconnais, 1999 has the upper hand qualitatively, yet some spectacular, benchmark wines were fashioned in 2000. Consumers are well advised to search out the wines of Mâconnais's finest producers (Barraud, Bongran/Gillet, Cordier, Guffens, Guillemot-Michel, Lassarat, Merlin, Rijckaert, Valette, Verget, etc.), as they deliver loads of bang for the buck.

As this book went to press, only small numbers of 2000 red Burgundies had been tasted. It is clear, however, that 2000 is not a good vintage for the Côte de Beaune. The Côte de Nuits appears to have enjoyed more success.

1999—Burgundy's 1999 vintage, one of the largest on record, produced many good, very good, and excellent white wines, yet lacks show-stoppers. For the most part, they are harmonious, soft, easy to appreciate, and made for near-term drinking. While the weather in 1998 conspired to fashion low yields and wines of average quality (see *The Wine Advocate's* issue #128), in 1999 the Burgundian cellars were overflowing with wine.

A quick, early, and highly productive flowering was followed by ideal weather conditions for plant growth. Warmth, with alternating bright sun and rain, led to an explosion of growth that began with the first shoots the plant formed and continued until a dry phase in the month of August. The semi-drought of August led to hydric stress for vines located in soil-deficient hillside vineyards. At the end of the first week of September the skies brought just enough rain to restart photosynthesis, which had become dormant during the semi-drought. Ideal weather followed, leading to an early harvest (Côte de Beaune growers were allowed to pick on September 15). Cloudy skies and evening showers (mostly continual sprinkles, with the exception of a significant storm on the 19th) rendered the harvest wet yet endurable. However, for those courageous vignerons who wished to push physiological maturity, there were major rainstorms that began on the 23rd and returned intermittently over the next few days and weeks. Nonetheless, virtually every vigneron visited claimed that the grapes were exceedingly healthy.

The hugely successful flowering in 1999 guaranteed prolific yields. French legislation dictates that each appellation has a maximum allowable yield, the *Rendement de Base*. However, at the request of grower syndicates, a PLC (*Plafond Limite de Classement*, the percentage of increased production permitted in an appellation for a specific vintage) can be granted by the INAO (the Institut National des Appellations d' Origine, the governing body of French appellations). Generally these PLCs are in the 10–20% range, but in 1999 the INAO decided to permit a 40% PLC two months *after* the vintage.

As they approached the harvest, growers knew that their yields would be enormous, and were well aware that they would later be provided with a massive PLC. The vintage production statistics the French authorities maintains are based on the quantity of wine acknowledged by vignerons as having been produced, not the amount of grapes in the vineyards. Therefore, grapes that are sorted out or never harvested are not counted. In 1999 yields were still often way above the allowable range, leading to a proliferation of wine in the black market and resulting in wines that are either hidden from the authorities to be sold for cash to consumers or simply blended into the next short crop. Alternatively, many parcels were simply not harvested or grapes were dumped (one broker told me there were lines of grape-filled carts at the village dumps). Growers who admitted to overproduction had to send to the state-run distilleries whatever wines they had that exceeded authorized limits.

Obviously, 1999 generated significant quantities of wine, but is it any good? Yes, the 1999 white Burgundies are often good and sometimes excellent, but very few will be exceptional. Overall, the 1999s can be characterized as soft, supple wines without any angles to their lush personalities. *Harmonious* is a word that appears in my notebook many times. After the angularity of all too many of the 1998s, it was indeed a joy to encounter the 1999s. Another term that appears often in my notes is *pillowy*. I coined this term to describe the soft, round, "fluffy" wines that lacked the structure and depth for greatness yet were immensely appealing because of their comforting cushioned textures.

Wines with loads of concentration, structure, and/or depth are a rarity in 1999. The finest growers were able to flesh out excellent to outstanding levels of these characteristics in a few wines, particularly those from rich soils that offset August's drought with their water reserves (Meursault Charmes stood out in many tastings). This lack of depth of fruit means that "outside" influences such as oak and sulfur could leave substantial marks on the wines. In fact, many oenologists, fearful that the wines lacked sufficient acidity, increased their recommended doses of sulfur, to the detriment of the wines.

The 1999s were rarely chaptalized (had sugars added during fementation to raise potential alcohol) as they generally had high natural potential alcohols. Yet sugar is only one measure of ripeness. In order to obtain full phenolic ripeness a grape must have ripe skins, flesh, and seeds. A large number of 1999s give the impression that they lack true ripeness, most likely due to the excessive loads the vines were carrying as well as the hydric stress many vines suffered in August. This could be felt in the high percentage of wines that offered appealing attacks and mid-palates but lacked expressive noses and possessed dry, chalky finishes.

The overwhelming majority of 1999 white Burgundies taste fresh, lively, and well balanced. They are in general pleasant, fun, soft wines without overpowering aromas, flavors, or complexity. Two vineyards stood out as the sources of particularly good 1999s, the aforementioned Meursault Charmes and Montrachet. The 1999 white Burgundies do not have (with very few exceptions) the depth, concentration, or stuffing for long-term cellaring. Almost all of them can be drunk immediately upon release and over the next few years. Were it not for the absurd prices being charged for these wines in the United States (they are much more reasonable in Canada, France, and the rest of Europe), they could be heartily recommended for restaurants as well as consumers searching out pleasing, near-term drinking wines.

1998—In general, 1998 is an average to poor vintage for white Burgundies. Qualitatively, it suffers in comparison with 1995, 1996, and 1997. The region was successively blasted with cold, frost, hail, searing heat, and rain. While a few talented winemakers struggled to produce good to excellent wines (some even defied the odds by crafting outstanding ones), they were the exception. In short, consumers are advised to tread with enormous caution when contemplating the purchase of 1998 white Burgundies.

For the first time in recent memory (some say it also occurred in 1945), frost damaged the hillside premier cru and grand cru vineyards while sparing the less-heralded sites. Many of the Côte de Beaune, Côte Chalonnaise, and Mâconnais's finest vineyards suffered significant frost damage, with Meursault being the hardest hit (some growers there reported yields 70% below average in certain sites). Many Chardonnay vines responded by sprouting second-generation, less-yielding buds. Other incidents of frost were reported (most notably in May), but none wreaked as much havoc as the one in mid-April.

The flowering was long and uneven. Some vignerons said it lasted 16 days or more. As the grapes that result from the pollination of the flowers tend to form and ripen at the same rate (conventional wisdom says harvests should be a minimum of 100 days after flowering), long flowerings are never a good sign. In 1998, the fruits formed from the first flowers could ripen 16 days before those from the last flowers, resulting in uneven ripeness even within one parcel. Hail in late April, May (particularly in the Mâconnais and Chablisien), and July caused further damage to the vines and grapes.

Oïdium was a constant problem in 1998. This fungal disease, also known as powdery mildew, attacks the green parts of a vine and can lead to lower yields as well as off aromas and flavors if infected bunches are not sorted out at harvest. It is a fungus native to North America that was first detected in France in 1847, 20 years before phylloxera, another American export, devastated Europe's vineyards. Generally controllable with sulfur treatments, oïdium is typically less of a threat to Pinot Noir than to Chardonnay (yet, in 1998, both varietals were susceptible to attack). Constant vigilance was required, with sulfur treatments sometimes having to be applied every seven or eight days. While the oïdium in 1992 (the last vintage with significant outbreaks of this disease) was easily controllable and cured with sulfur treatments, it kept returning in 1998, according to Matrot. Grapes damaged by oïdium are easily spotted at harvest and can be sorted out by conscientious growers. However, if all the grapes from a parcel are infected, or if yields have been hugely dropped, say by frosts and hail, the incentive for throwing out large quantities of fruit at the sorting table is less. Interestingly, the vines hardest hit by the frosts and hail (i.e., the better hillside premiers and grands crus) suffered the most from oïdium outbreaks. Many vignerons postulated that those stressed vines had their defenses down, rendering them vulnerable to diseases.

As though frosts, hailstorms, and rampant oïdium were not enough, it was the hottest and driest August since 1947. Many vines, particularly those in young or unplowed parcels (and therefore without deep roots), went into a self-preserving dormant stage. A large number of south- and east-facing grapes were literally burned by the sun (conscientious growers sorted these out either in the vineyards—or on sorting tables). Scorched grapes can result in off aromas and flavors if they are not removed prior to fermentation.

But nature had not finished its punishment of the Burgundians. Two to three weeks of rain fell in late August and early September. While many vines required some precipitation to restart the maturation process, none needed the downpours that inundated the region. Honest vignerons admitted the presence of rot on the grapes. Some mentioned that they had been infected with *Botrytis cinerea* (also known as "noble rot"), while others conceded to less noteworthy fungi ("Let's just call it *bourgeois* rot" said Jean-Marie Guffens of Maison Verget and Domaine Guffens-Heynen). The rains stopped on September 17 and returned with a vengeance as a result of massive thunderstorms on the 26th. This sunny, dry, and windy nine-day period was described by vignerons as *"la fenêtre de beau temps"* (the window of good weather) that saved the vintage. During this period the harvest took place in the Mâconnais, Côte Chalonnaise, and Côte de Beaune. Chablis, a more northern region, harvested under the rainstorms that followed this "window."

The most successful 1998 white Burgundies are those that do not reflect the vintage's characteristics. It is a hard vintage to love, as the vast majority of its wines are neither rich, pure, harmonious, fruity, nor elegant. Furthermore, as was mentioned earlier, they do not reflect the characteristics of their *terroirs*. Shrill acidity, short dry finishes, hollow/dilute cores, oxidation, excessive sulfur, and/or off aromas as well as flavors are found in numerous 1998s. In this "upside-down vintage," as Lafon dubbed it, the finest wines produced were often from lesser sites, and many were crafted from high yields. The strip of hillside premier cru and grand cru vineyards that incurred huge frost damage was also highly susceptible to oïdium outbreaks. These same sites appear to have suffered more from the August heat/drought (the water table is deeper as the hill rises) and from the diluting effects of the preharvest rains than those on flatter land. Furthermore, many vignerons harvested their most prestigious vineyard holdings before their less-renowned ones out of fear that the rains would return. Often this resulted in an estate's premiers and grands crus being less ripe than its regional or village appellation wines.

Wines fashioned from the most stressed vines (because of frost, hail, oïdium, and sunburns) were often disjointed, angular, and exhibited a shrill acidity. According to the laboratory analyses cited by many vignerons, the overall acid levels in the 1998 white Burgundies is not high (in fact it is slightly below average in some wines), yet the lack of buttressing fruit makes it stand out in numerous premiers and grands crus.

The white wine–producing vineyards most affected by the frost, oïdium, drought, and sunburn appear to be the strip located 240 meters above sea level, including all or parts of virtually every premier cru in Meursault (the hardest-hit village), as well as many of its most renowned village appellation sites (including Narvaux, Tillets, Tessons, and Vireuils, among others). Puligny-Montrachet was not spared, with the damage primarily centered on the premiers crus les Folatières, Champs-Gain, Garenne, Combettes, Truffière, and Champs-Canet. Even sectors of Chevalier-Montrachet (a grand cru) were affected. Chassagne-Montrachet was mostly spared (and consequently made some of the finest 1998s from the Côte de Beaune), yet some premiers crus (including Vergers, Chaumées, and Virondots) evidenced some damage. The Côte de Beaune vineyards that were the most successful in 1998 are those that 1) are on flat or almost flat ground, and 2) have a deep (water-retaining) layer of earth. Wines from Montrachet, Bienvenue-Bâtard-Montrachet, Puligny-Montrachet Enseignères, and Chassagne-Montrachet Morgeot generally stood out in tastings. When all is said and done, the fact remains that the grapes never had the opportunity to ripen physiologically, and the wines, in general, lack fruit.

The prices being fetched for the 1998 white Burgundies is based on the increased worldwide demand that was created by the high quality of the 1995s, 1996s, and many 1997s— and they are simply not worth it.

Overall, the 1998 vintage for red Burgundies is of average to poor quality. There were recommendable Burgundies fashioned in 1998, the results of superhuman efforts on the part of their producers, yet the overwhelming majority are dominated by rough, unripe tannins. Colors range from light brown (evidence of rot), to saturated black. Aromatically, many offerings reveal dark plums, blackberries, and cracked black pepper, characteristics generally encountered in Argentinian Malbecs. A large number display delightful scents of exotic woods like balsam and sweet cedar that can easily entice the uninitiated yet in fact are the early signs of rot. In the mouth, 1998 red Burgundies initially offer baked dark fruit flavors but then finish abruptly with hard, astringent tannins (sometimes to the point where the taster's palate feels as though a rope has been dragged across it). Acidities are relatively low (most producers admitted that even more acidification was performed in 1998 than 1997) but grape sugars were high.

The April frost that principally struck Meursault and Puligny-Montrachet played a significant and nefarious role in the fashioning of 1998's whites, but it was less a factor with reds. The growing season was not propitious for making great wine. A long, uneven flowering (yet shorter than for the whites) was followed by cool, rainy weather. Oïdium (powdery mildew) was a significant problem for vignerons unaccustomed to seeing this disease attack Pinot Noir vines. The numerous sulfur treatments required to avoid oïdium and the onset of rot thickened the skins of the grapes, and some hypothesized that constant antirot spraying leads to rot forming on the inside of grape skins, rendering the sorting process useless.

This cool and wet period was followed by the scorching effects of Burgundy's hottest and driest August since 1947. Virtually every grower visited stated that south-facing grapes were deeply scorched by the sun. Equally important, a large number of Burgundians believe that vines on the slopes (particularly those dependent on roots close to the surface) went into a self-protective dormancy period to cope with both the heat and water deficiency.

Three weeks prior to harvest, Burgundy had yet to enjoy ideal growing and ripening conditions, and then the rains fell. Two to three weeks of rain brought the vines back to life, prompting excessive water intakes (and hence the resulting dilution) by the vines and the onset of rot. The rains stopped on September 17 and ideal conditions prevailed until the early part of the 26th, when the skies served up numerous thunderous downpours. If these nine days of clear, windy, and sunny weather had been followed by a harvest under equally good conditions, the story of the 1998s would have been quite different. Instead, those nine days were when the harvest took place. The vast majority of vignerons began harvesting on September 21 and were finished before the rains returned on the 26th.

What was the condition of the grapes at harvest? Many producers acknowledge the following problems—uneven ripeness, green "fluorescent" stems (the stems on optimally ripe grapes are brown and dried), rot, botrytis (a form of rot searched out by sweet white wine producers but loathed by red winemakers), as well as oïdium.

Immediately after fermentation, wine-makers were ecstatic. The season had posed so many problems that they were surprised to find fruit-dominated wines. Sure, they had firm, structured finishes, but the fruit was expressive and dominated the hard tannins. As *élevage* (the barrel aging process) progressed, and malolactic fermentations took place, the fruit diminished and the tannins remained. By the time the wines were ready to be bottled (and many will not even be bottled until this coming September) the tannins completely dominated the majority of wines. "The fruit evaporated as though it were a puddle in the Sahara desert," said one high-quality grower.

Consumers should beware. Terms like *classically structured, vin de garde* (cellaring wine), and *beautifully expressive of terroir* are being used by the trade for the 1998s as they were for the 1988s and 1993s. Is there a chance that the hard tannins in some of the 1998s will actually melt away? Possibly, but don't bet on it. At today's prices, gambling on a Pinot Noir's tannins is foolhardy.

1997—The 1997 white Burgundies are, in general, fat, ripe wines, yet sometimes perplexingly oxidative and alcoholic. In addition, excessive oak and sulfur aromas and flavors are not uncommon, and many wines had relatively abrupt finishes. Collectors searching for long-lived wines will be disappointed with the 1997 whites, yet readers who wish to purchase wines for near-term consumption will be quite pleased with what this vintage offers.

There is no doubt that 1997 is a very good vintage for whites from the Côte d'Or. The finest 1997s are from sites high on Burgundy's slopes (Corton-Charlemagne, Chevalier-Montrachet, etc.) as their lean soils offset the sometimes over-the-top richness of the vintage. The 1997 vintage does not compete with such outstanding years as 1992 or 1989, but is certainly better than 1994, 1993, and 1991. The Mâconnais, however, enjoyed an outstanding vintage and is responsible for many of 1997's most successful wines. Estates such as Daniel Barraud, Bongran, Guffens-Heynen, and Robert-Denogent crafted stellar Pouilly-Fuissés and Mâcons. In Chablis no one attained the level of quality achieved in 1995 or 1996 but, like the Côte d'Or, this region had a very good 1997. For reds, as the 1997 vintage approached harvest-time, reports out of Burgundy glowed with optimism. Grapes were healthy, as the late summer had been hot and dry, and vignerons were ecstatic.

Excessive heat in September brought an end to the growers' general ebullience. When the Côte de Beaune's *ban de vendange* (the first day the harvest can legally begin) was set for September 13, many vignerons came to the realization that grape sugars were high, yet full physiological ripeness had not been attained. More than one grower suggested that the stressed vines had stopped the maturation process because of the high temperatures and lack of rain. The vast majority of vignerons I spoke with said they waited at least a week after the *ban de vendange* to begin harvesting. This strategy worked wonders in the cooler 1996 vintage because the north wind and sunny days accelerated maturity without causing a loss of natural acidity in the grapes. In 1997, however, the days and evenings were warm, occasionally hot. Vignerons watched as phenolic ripeness inched its way forward and acidity levels dropped (many growers picked their reds *before* their whites).

At harvest, the high temperatures were troublesome. Some producers acknowledged that they were unable to prevent fermentations from starting earlier than desired. Flash alcoholic fermentations, immediately followed by rapid malolactic fermentations, which many growers believe decreases complexity, were reported throughout the Côte d'Or. Across the board, acidity levels were lower than average but not dangerously so.

The 1997 vintage for reds is outstanding only for the few top producers who understood how to harness the year's qualities. The majority of 1997 red Burgundies are beautifully ripe, dense, and fruit-driven wines. Many lack the complexity, depth, structure, and concentration for greatness but will provide delicious drinking for the first six years. Were it not for their frightfully high prices, these would have been ideal wines for restaurants and consumers searching out delicious near-term drinking. Stylistically reminiscent of the 1989s, the 1997 red Burgundies generally exhibit loads of ripe fruit characteristics in an easygoing, low-acid, and simple manner. Like most of the 1989s, the 1997s will be ready to drink upon release and should, for the most part, be drunk within the next seven years. However a few 1997s, notably wines produced by Domaine Leroy, Bertrand Ambroise, the Marquis d'Angerville, and the *domaine* wines from Maison Louis Jadot (to name but a few), should age remarkably well as they appear to have extraordinary structure.

1996—This is an excellent to outstanding vintage for white Burgundies. The best examples offer a combination of magnificent structure, ripeness, and aging potential. The vintage's finest wines have high acidity, total purity of flavors (rot and mildew were not a problem), excellent fruit ripeness (without any overripe or stewed-fruit problems), and impressive extract.

In the Côte d'Or, an exceedingly dry spring led to a late bud break for the vines' leaves in April. Rain in May (from then on the vintage qualifies as a drought year) provided the vines with necessary nourishment prior to June's dry, sunny warmth. During this ideal period, the flowering occurred rapidly and evenly. Numerous healthy grape bunches formed on each vine. Cool, sunny days (as in the Loire, Burgundians noted the "*luminosite*," or brightness, of the vintage) and cold nights combined with minimal precipitation and a persistent dry wind from the north throughout the summer and into the first days of November. This combination of good light for photosynthesis and cool evening temperatures promoted the ripening of the grapes without a significant loss of acidity (heat is blamed for reducing acid in grapes), while the gusty, unusually persistent north winds dehydrated (concentrated) the grapes. Chablis had a small harvest, caused largely by hail prior to flowering in May, a violent storm on June 8, and the dehydrating effects of wind.

Qualitatively, the top whites from 1996 are on a par with 1989, but stylistically they are completely different. These are fresher and livelier wines that can be cellared longer than the 1989s, however, they do not exhibit the thick textures and extraordinary ripeness of the latter vintage. This is not a vintage for those who love fat, unctuous, tropical, hedonistic, luscious white Burgundies.

1996 is an excellent to outstanding vintage for red Burgundies, certainly better than 1995, particularly in the Côte de Beaune. As with Chardonnay, the Pinot Noir vines had a rapid and even flowering, which led to numerous grape bunches on each vine. Many vignerons were concerned that the grapes would not fully ripen because each vine was so heavily loaded. By late August an extremely bright sun emerged, and a persistent cool and dry wind blew from the north, maintaining acidity levels and preventing the onset of any rot or mildew. The resulting harvest was copious, ripe, and healthy.

Stylistically, this vintage can best be characterized as "juicy." The wines appear to burst in the mouth like a juicy, ripe berry. These are lively, fresh, pleasure-giving wines that are fruit-driven and, to their credit, remarkably pure. In addition to the cherry, raspberry, and blackberry flavors common in top Burgundy vintages, 1996 offered copious amounts of blueberries and juicy black currants. The vintage's tannins are soft (I very rarely encountered wines with problematic tannins), which helped appellations such as Chassagne-Montrachet, Santenay, Nuits-St.-Georges, Fixin, and others that sometimes have difficulty coping with tannins.

I have one nagging reservation about all the accolades bestowed on 1996—the level of acidity. Wines produced by growers who harvested excessive yields do not have enough fruit to handle the vintage's acidity levels. Some of these wines have dried out and become unpleasant to drink relatively quickly. However, in 1996, quality-conscious producers crafted extraordinary wines capable of aging for a decade or more.

1995—This is the finest vintage for white Burgundies since 1989. From this hallowed region's most conscientious producers, the 1995 vintage frequently combines the ripeness, richness, and concentration of 1989 with the delineation, complexity, and volume of 1986. I do believe it will provide fabulous wines for both near- and long-term cellaring, depending on selection. Thick, oily textures and flavors of superripe fruits (in some instances reminiscent of red berries) are characteristics of many top 1995s. Several highly respected producers shared the view that their 1995s lacked the balancing acidity for long-term cellaring, but that deficiency only adds to their flattering, up-front appeal. Depending on what stage of the growing cycle the wines were in, snow in May severely damaged the flowering (*coulure*) and/or stunted the development of the fruit embryos (*millerandage*). With *coulure*, fewer grape bunches are formed because damaged flowers fall off the vine. In the case of *millerandage*, the undeveloped grape clusters remain on the vine but with tiny, undersized berries. At harvest, these berries (known in French as "*millerands*") contain small quantities of hugely concentrated juice. In both instances the result is the same—nature forces the hand of the vignerons by imposing lower yields, thus producing concentrated and oily-textured wines. A long, hot, dry summer further concentrated the juice in the grapes. Warm, sunny days provided the vine with the necessary sunshine to ripen the grapes. Moreover, a deficiency of rain in 1995 prevented the absorption of juice-diluting rainwater, which could have been a problem as rain did fall at harvest (though much too late to seriously dilute the wine). Additionally, much as in 1986, botrytis did affect certain producer's vineyards. However, I did not find any wines that exhibited negative botrytis flavors such as existed in a few 1986s, in particular, the extremely botrytised style of Comtes Lafon's 1986s. The ageworthiness of the 1995 white Burgundies is dependent on the presence of botrytis. Those wines that were affected with this noble rot will need to be drunk over the next 5–7 years, and the others should prove to be extremely ageworthy.

The 1995 vintage is very good to excellent for red Burgundies from the Côte de Nuits (the Côte de Beaune did not fair as well due to problems with rot), certainly the finest since the great 1990s set modern-day standards for lush, ageworthy Pinot Noirs. Going back, it is a finer vintage than 1988, 1987, and 1986, and will be more ageworthy than 1985. It is a year where certain producers produced stellar, mind-blowing wines, others crafted excellent and outstanding offerings, and some fashioned tannic wines that will never be pleasant to drink.

As with the whites, *coulure* and *millerandage* in the spring assured low yields, and a long, hot, dry summer concentrated the fruit flavors in the grapes. Some rainfall at harvesttime did cause some rot, particularly in the Côte de Beaune, but elimination of these grapes on the sorting tables mostly prevented the potential problem of stale mushroom flavors in the wines. Few wines I have tasted had any off aromas or flavors.

Overall, the 1995 red Burgundies are dark, thick, dense wines packed with concentrated fruit flavors and the necessary structure for aging. Some wines in this vintage are tannic (though less severe than 1988 and 1993). These wines will require extended cellaring.

1994—This was the fourth consecutive vintage where rain fell immediately before and during the harvest. Much of the Chardonnay crop was brought in with minimal dilution, and produced relatively low-acid, rich, high-alcohol, ripe wines that lack the charm and hedonistic pleasures associated with the 1992s. The vast majority of 1994 white Burgundies will need to be consumed by 2004. As for the red wines, the Pinot Noir vineyards were hit hard by heavy rains during September. The wines do not have the color, body, or intensity of the very good 1993s. The majority have the plummy fruit characteristics of the 1992s but tend to finish on dry, dusty tannins.

1993—The 1993 Chardonnay crop was abundant and sadly diluted by heavy rain immediately prior to the harvest. Many of the white wines are monolithic, lack interior flavor, and are simply shells of acidity and alcohol with light fruit and concentration. Those growers/producers who crop-thinned and had very low yields produced wines with more depth and concentration, but overall this is an average-quality year for white Burgundy. The 1993 vintage will have to be carried by the reputation of the very good reds. The red wines are unbelievably dark-colored, rich, and tannic, rather astonishing given the heavy rainstorms that pummeled the Côte d'Or in early September. The crop size was not large, and the Pinot skins were surprisingly resistant to the formation of rot though temperatures remained cool during the harvest. While there is impressive color (as deep in most cases as the 1990s), the wines do not reveal the fat and richness possessed by the finest 1990s. There is plenty of tannin and the wines have fine structure. The 1993 Burgundies will be more appreciated by readers with a Bordeaux mind-set than by those who prefer the traditional style of succulent, expansively rich, velvety-textured red Burgundies. The 1993s will require patience, but the top wines should turn out to be very good, and some exceptional, because of tiny yields and highly concentrated and extracted flavors. The 1993 vintage is unlikely to be one of precocious wines but, rather, one where some aging will be required. However, *caveat emptor!* The majority of 1993 red Burgundies do not have enough fruit to outlast the tannins. All too many 1993s will dry out like their 1988 counterparts.

1992—A glorious year of big, ripe, juicy, succulent white Burgundies and, at the top quality level, remarkably charming, round, delicious, low-acid, moderately concentrated reds. The white wines have moved through to the marketplace with considerable speed, not withstanding frightfully high prices. For the most part, 1992 white Burgundies will need to be consumed over the next 5 years. The red wines have been bashed by many wine-writing professionals, but the fact remains that there are plenty of top-quality, supple red wines from both the Côte de Beaune and Côte de Nuits that were offered at the lowest prices consumers had seen in more than a decade. Careful selection of the best wines is imperative, but treasures can be found in this vintage. The 1992s need to be consumed sooner rather than later.

1991—The stars of this vintage are usually from the Côte de Nuits. Because of abnormally low yields (15–35 hectoliters per hectare) the top wines display excellent concentration and richness. The finest 1991s are close in quality to the 1990s, and are richer, fuller, more complete wines than the finest 1988s, 1987s, and 1986s. These wines, which are often priced 25–40% below the 1990s, are worthy additions to any Burgundy connoisseur's cellar. Because the yields were so low, quantities of the top wines are small. Many producers made 50% less wine than they turned out in 1990. If the vintage has a dark side, it is the tannin level in many wines. Consumers must be careful, because balance is everything. Many 1991s possess tannin levels that may never melt away.

In the Côte de Beaune the vintage is much more difficult to peg, but there are numerous disappointments—wines that are excessively light and/or frightfully tannic and out of balance. This being said, the best producers (notably Volnay's Michel Lafarge) crafted gorgeous 1991s that will age remarkably well.

1990— This is a very good vintage for white Burgundies, but only a handful of producers achieved greatness, because the yields were entirely too high to obtain the requisite concentration. Those growers who meticulously pruned back to restrict their yields and who picked physiologically mature fruit have made stunning wines. There are some high-class wines in Chablis, above-average-quality wines in Meursault, and good to excellent wines in Puligny-Montrachet and Chassagne-Montrachet. One appellation that enjoyed considerable success is Corton-Charlemagne, where the wines are superior to the 1989s! At the top levels, the red wines are the finest red Burgundies of the last 50 years. They are darkly colored, with sumptuous, rich, thick fruit. Moreover, many of the wines possess excellent structure and moderate levels of sweet tannins. The 1990 vintage is one of those rare red Burgundy vintages that will offer an exceptionally broad window of drinkability. Qualitatively, it towers above such vintages as 1988 and 1985.

1989— It is a spectacular vintage for white burgundy, unquestionably the finest for the Côte de Beaune in more than 20 years. In their youth the 1989 red burgundies were delicious, forward, ripe, and flattering wines. At present, most 1989s should have been consumed as the vintage's high yields prevented long-term cellaring. There are exceptions, however. Many Volnays (this commune had the region's lowest yields due to a spring frost) and wines from Burgundy's top producers (Louis Jadot's for example) are coming into their own in 2002. The longest lived 1989s, though a small fraction of the total produced, will hold their plateau of maturity for another 5–7 years.

1988— The question about this vintage is why so many wine writers, above all the English press (who judge Burgundy as if it were Bordeaux), rated this vintage so highly. A handful of great wines were produced yet most reflect the high yields and astringent level of tannin. Over the past dozen years a horse race has taken place between the 1988s' tannin and their fruit. In Pinot Noir, highly tannic wines usually age poorly, and the 1988s have not been an exception. Burgundy enthusiasts who have stashed away quantities of 1988s are likely to be more disappointed than pleased by what they are finding. Most Burgundy growers are now in agreement that the 1988s are drying out on their tannin, leaving behind austere, hard shells. The lean, acidic 1988 white burgundies should have been consumed by now.

1987— From the top estates, delicious, supple red wines were made, which is amazing given the fact that most producers had to harvest under heavy rain. Recent tastings of 1987 red Burgundies indicate that the vast majority of them are past their plateau of maturity. Only the very finest wines from the top estates will have survived cellaring past 2000. A mediocre year for white wines.

1986— A great year for white Burgundy and an unexciting one for red Burgundy. Most of the red wines possess structure and tannin but are hollow on the mid-palate. Their lack of succulence and chewiness found in top years such as 1985 and 1990 makes them dubious choices. With very few exceptions, 1986 red Burgundies should have been consumed by 1996. 1986 white Burgundies were either reaching their peaks or were at full maturity by 2000. Having recently had the opportunity to taste the 1986s from Domaine Niellon, Louis

Jadot, Domaine Ramonet, and Domaine Coche-Dury, I can unequivocally state that these wines demonstrate the extraordinary heights Burgundian Chardonnays can attain.

1985—Initially proclaimed as Burgundy's vintage of the century, the white wines continue to merit the accolades they received, providing rich, sumptuous drinking. The top whites should last for another 5–7 years. Presently, the reds present a mixed bag of impressions. Some of the larger-scaled red wines appear muted, monolithic, and one-dimensional. The best of them continue to exhibit a healthy deep ruby color and good depth and weight. The lighter reds have taken on some amber at the edge and are soft and fruity but have not developed the aromatic complexity initially expected. The 1985 vintage has produced some outstanding wines, but as the 1985s have matured, the overall quality is mixed. Drink up.

1984—This is a poor vintage for Burgundy, in both red and white wines. The vintage was late, yields were low because of a poor flowering, and rains incessant. Because natural potential alcohols were in the 8–10% range, growers invariably over-chaptalized, making wines that could be appealing in their youth yet have dried out to reveal unripe, lean tannic shells. The 1984s should already have been consumed, as they were never long-lived wines, and are dubious choices today.

1983—The 1983 red burgundies were plagued by rampant rot. While natural sugar levels were abnormally high, far too many wines smell and taste of rot and/or are unbelievably tannic and astringent. Even the finest 1983s, from producers such as Roumier, the Domaine de la Romanée-Conti, Henri Jayer, Hubert Lignier, Mongeard-Mugneret, and Ponsot, are drying out at present. This is a poor vintage that should be approached with the greatest of caution.

Where Are Burgundy's Red Wine Values?

The glamour appellations of the Côte de Nuits and the Côte de Beaune offer high prices as well as irregular quality. As in the world's other best-known wine-growing regions, values are few and far between in Burgundy. However, if values are to be found, consumers must look beyond the most prestigious names and most renowned appellations, searching out some of the less highly acclaimed appellations. Following are some wines to check out in the Côte de Nuits, Côte de Beaune, and possibly the best source of red and white Burgundies, the Côte Chalonnaise, located just south of the Côte d'Or.

Aloxe-Corton Appellation (Côte de Beaune)   The highly sought after red and white grands crus from the famed Corton hillside lie mostly within Aloxe-Corton's appellation, yet this village's premier cru and village wines attract little consumer attention. While the majority of Aloxe-Cortons tend to be hard and lacking in charm, there are some excellent wines produced in this appellation.

The best wines include Jean-Claude Belland (Aloxe-Corton); Simon Bize (Aloxe-Corton Le-Suchots); Edmond et Pierre Cornu (Aloxe-Corton Les Moutottes, Aloxe-Corton Les Valozières, Aloxe-Corton Vieilles Vignes); Jean-Luc Dubois (Aloxe-Corton Les Brunettes Réserve); Génot-Boulanger (Aloxe-Corton Clos du Chapître); Antonin Guyon (Aloxe-Corton Les Vercots); Tollot-Beaut (Aloxe-Corton, Aloxe-Corton Les Fournières, Aloxe-Corton Les Vercots).

Auxey-Duresses Appellation (Côte de Beaune)   Auxey-Duresses has often been described as the poor person's Volnay. Such comments are pejorative and tend to irritate the local vignerons, who are proud of their spicy, robust, black cherry–scented and –flavored wine, which often possesses surprising aging potential. The key is ripe fruit. If the fruit is not ripe when picked, the tannins tend to be green and the acids can reach shrill levels.

The best wines include Comte Armand (Auxey-Duresses, Auxey-Duresses Premier Cru).

Bourgogne Appellation   Wines bearing this "regional" appellation can emanate from poor vineyard sites or can be the result of a "declassification" from a more acclaimed appellation. Many Bourgognes produced by *négociants* contain wines from Beaujolais and the Mâconnais. While most wines from this appellation are insipid, tart, and not worthy of consumer's attention, those produced by Burgundy's most conscientious producers are often, in the best vintages, excellent values for near-term drinking.

The best wines include Ghislaine Barthod-Noellat (Bourgogne); Alain Burguet (Bourgogne); Dugat-Py (Bourgogne); Robert Groffier (Bourgogne); Anne Gros (Bourgogne Pinot Noir); Michel Lafarge (Bourgogne); Philippe Leclerc (Bourgogne Les Bons Batons); Hubert Lignier (Bourgogne); Denis Mortet (Bourgogne); Georges Mugneret (Bourgogne); Emmanuel Rouget (Bourgogne).

Bourgogne Passetoutgrains Appellation   These wines, crafted from an assemblage of Pinot Noir and Gamay, are very rarely good. More often than not, even the finest producers treat their Passetoutgrains with disdain, bringing in extremely high yields and paying little attention to their vinification and *élevage*. However, the following two growers occasionally produce Bourgogne Passetoutgrains meriting consumer attention. These include Michel Lafarge (Bourgogne Passetoutgrain); Emmanuel Rouget (Bourgogne Passetoutgrain).

Chassagne-Montrachet (Côte de Beaune) Appellation   The downside to Chassagne-Montrachet's fame as one of Burgundy's great white wine villages is that few people pay attention to the tasty red wines with their Bing cherry, almond, earthy fruitiness. There are premiers crus that can be bought for $25–30 a bottle, making this an interesting market. Most red Chassagnes also have the virtue of lasting 10 years in a top vintage.

The best wines include Guy Amiot et Fils (Chassagne-Montrachet Clos St.-Jean, Chassagne-Montrachet La Maltroie); Borgeot (Chassagne-Montrachet Clos St.-Jean); Colin-Deléger (Chassagne-Montrachet Morgeot, Chassagne-Montrachet Vieilles Vignes); Jean-Noël Gagnard (Chassagne-Montrachet, Chassagne-Montrachet Morgeot, Chassagne-Montrachet Clos St.-Jean); Vincent Girardin (Chassagne-Montrachet Clos de la Boudriotte Vielles Vignes); Chassagne-Montrachet Morgeot Duc de Magenta (Louis Jadot) (Chassagne-Montrachet Morgeot); Château de la Maltroye (Chassagne-Montrachet Clos du Château de la Maltroye, Chassagne-Montrachet Clos St.-Jean); Bernard Morey (Chassagne-Montrachet Vieilles Vignes); Domaine Ramonet (Chassagne-Montrachet Clos de la Boudriotte).

Chorey-les-Beaune Appellation (Côte de Beaune)   From its best producers, this relatively unknown appellation just north of Beaune can make lovely early-drinking wines. The flat vineyards of Chorey are responsible for a multitude of poorly made, insipid, hollow, watery wines crafted from huge yields. However, conscientious growers produce wines in the $16–25 range that merit consumer attention.

The best wines include Jean-Luc Dubois (Chorey-Les-Beaune Clos du Margot Vieilles Vignes Réserve); Tollot-Beaut (Chorey-Les-Beaune).

Côte de Nuits-Villages Appellation (Côte de Nuits)   Wines bearing this appellation are produced from vineyards located in Corgoloin, Comblanchien, and Prissey (all three located south of Nuits-St.-Georges) as well as from Brochon and Fixin (two villages north of Gevrey-Chambertin). From the finest producers these wines reflect the dark fruit characteristics of the Côte de Nuits and can often be complex and ageworthy wines.

The best wines include Chauvenet-Chopin (Côte de Nuits-Villages); Chopin-Groffier (Côte de Nuits-Villages); Jean-Jacques Confuron (Côte de Nuits-Villages Les Vignottes); Edmond et Pierre Cornu (Côte de Nuits-Villages); Philippe Gavignet (Côte de Nuits-Villages Les Vignottes Réserve); Louis Jadot (Côte de Nuits-Villages); Robert Jayer-Gilles (Côte de Nuits-Villages).

Fixin Appellation (Côte de Nuits)   It may be situated next to the famed appellation Gevrey-Chambertin, but Fixin has never overcome its reputation of producing exceptionally robust, sturdy, muscular wines that are short on finesse. However, some producers excel in producing wines with serious flavor and balance.

The best wines include Philippe Livera (Fixin en Olivier Vieilles Vignes Réserve); Mongeard-Mugneret (Fixin); Philippe Naddef (Fixin); St. Martin (Fixin Hervelets).

Givry Appellation (Côte Chalonnaise)   Givry has one of the finest wine-makers in all of Burgundy, Jean-Marc Joblot, who crafts wines that compete with some of the finest of the Côte d'Or.

The best wines include: Xavier Besson (Givry Le Petit Pretan Réserve); Domaine de la Ferté (Givry); Joblot (Givry Clos du Bois Chevaux, Givry Clos du Cellier aux Moines, Givry Clos de la Servoisine).

Ladoix Appellation (Côte de Beaune)   Ladoix is Burgundy's least-known appellation, making it one of the more attractive places to shop, if you know the right addresses. Amazingly, the best Pinot Noirs here cost less than Pinot Noirs from California and Oregon. This is not an appellation to buy blindly, as the wines can be dusty and earthy, with too little fruit.

The best wines include Edmond Cornu (Ladoix, Ladoix Les Carrières, Ladoix Les Corvées, Ladoix Vieilles Vignes).

Marsannay Appellation (Côte de Nuits)   You are not likely to find great wines from this appellation, but good producers can make wines that are far above the normal quality level, which means something better than the compact, straightforward, hard, charmless Pinot Noirs that often emanate from Marsannay.

The best wines include Bruno Clair (Marsannay Les Grasses Têtes, Marsannay Les Longeroies, Marsannay Vaudenelles); Louis Jadot (Marsannay); Denis Mortet (Marsannay Les Longeroies); Philippe Naddef (Marsannay); Joseph Roty (Marsannay, Marsannay Champs St.-Etiennes, Marsannay Ouzeloy, Marsannay Sampagny).

Mercurey Appellation (Côte Chalonnaise)   Mercurey prices have risen to $25 a bottle as the world has begun to discover the progress Mercurey producers have made. This is an up-and-coming source of good wines.

The best producers include: Château de Chamirey (Mercurey); Vincent Dureuil-Janthial (Mercurey Le Bois de Lalier Réserve); Génot-Boulanger (Mercurey Les Sazenay); Château de Mercey (Mercurey en Sazenay); Domaine de Suremain (Mercurey Clos l'Eveque, Mercurey Clos Voyen); A. & P. de Villaine (Mercurey Les Montots).

Monthélie Appellation (Côte de Beaune)   The vineyards of Monthélie are adjacent to Volnay, yet the wines could not be more different. The old-style Monthélies are plagued by excessive tannin and body, but a younger generation of winemakers is bringing out the wines' fruit and character, hoping that consumers will make the one to two-minute trek from the neighboring villages of Volnay and Pommard to take a look at this hilltop village where most red Burgundies can still be bought for under $20–30 a bottle.

The best wines include: Bouchard Père et Fils (Monthélie Les Champs Fulliots); J. F. Coche-Dury (Monthélie); Jean Garaudet (Monthélie); Paul Garaudet (Monthélie, Monthélie Les Duresses, Monthélie Clos Gauthey); Comtes Lafon (Monthélie Les Duresses); Monthélie-Douhairet (Monthélie Duresses, Monthélie Le Meix Bataille); Eric de Suremain/Château de Monthélie (Monthélie Château de Monthélie, Monthélie sur la Velle).

Pernand-Vergelesses Appellation (Côte de Beaune)   This small village, nestled on the western side of the Corton hill, is little known and yet can produce—particularly in warm, dry years—high-quality wines. In the best vintages, Pernand's finest producers craft muscular, full-bodied, dark, fruit-packed, ageworthy wines.

The best wines include Chandon de Briailles (Pernand-Vergelesses Île de Vergelesses, Pernand-Vergelesses Les Vergelesses); Marius Delarche (Pernand-Vergelesses les Boutières Vieilles Vignes Réserve, Pernand-Vergelesses Île de Vergelesses Réserve, Pernand-Vergelesses Les Vergelesses Réserve); Antonin Guyon (Pernand-Vergelesses Les Vergelesses); Louis Jadot (Pernand-Vergelesses Clos de la Croix de Pierre); Roland Rapet (Pernand-Vergelesses Île de Vergelesses).

Rully Appellation (Côte Chalonnaise)   As with any appellation, one has to be well informed, but the spicy, cherry, strawberry, dusty aromas and flavors of a good Rully can be purchased for prices in the mid-teens to mid-twenties.

The best wines include Vincent Dureuil-Janthial (Rully en Guesnes Réserve, Rully Rosey Réserve); Château de Rully (Rully).

Santenay Appellation (Côte de Beaune)   It is amazing that Santenay continues to have problems overcoming its image as the last of the Côte d'Or appellations. Over 99% of its wine is red, all of it made from the Pinot Noir grape. The wine trade still bristles when reminded of a quotation from one of Britain's leading wine merchants, who said, "Life is too short to drink Santenay." Thanks largely to the efforts of Vincent Girardin, this village's top producer and one of the Côte d'Or's finest *négociants,* Santenay has become more fashionable. Thrifty consumers looking for a solid, frequently delicious bottle of Pinot Noir for $18–30 should search out this village's top wines. While many Santenays can be excessively tannic, hollow, and pleasureless, the good producers make a wine that is medium-weight by Burgundy standards, with a pronounced bouquet of strawberry and cherry fruit allied to a mineral, almost almond-like smell.

The best wines include: Jean-Claude Belland (Santenay Les Gravières); Borgeot (Santenay Beauregard); Bouchard Père et Fils (Santenay); Colin-Deléger (Santenay Les Gravières); Jean-Noël Gagnard (Santenay Clos de Tavannes); Vincent Girardin (Santenay Clos de la Confrerie, Santenay Les Gravières, Santenay La Maladière); Louis Jadot (Santenay Clos de Malte); Bernard Morey (Santenay Grand Clos Rousseau, Santenay Passetemps, Santenay Vieilles Vignes); Jean-Marc Morey (Santenay Grand Clos Rousseau).

Savigny-les-Beaune Appellation (Côte de Beaune)   Savigny-les-Beaune has a good reputation for light, fruit-scented (primarily cherry) wines that at their worst can have an overwhelming rusty, earthy undertone. The vineyards on the northern hillsides overlooking the Rhoin River, which cuts this appellation in half, produce the finest wine. Most sell for $18–$30 a bottle. They are not as inexpensive as Marsannay or Ladoix, but at their best they exhibit considerably more complexity as well as a compelling Pinot Noir perfume.

The best wines include Simon Bize (Savigny-les-Beaune les Bourgeots, Savigny-les-Beaune les Fourneaux, Savigny-les-Beaune Les Grands Liards, Savigny-les-Beaune Les Guettes, Savigny-les-Beaune Les Marconnets, Savigny-les-Beaune Les Serpentières, Savigny-les-Beaune Les Vergelesses); Jean Boillot (Savigny-les-Beaune Les Lavières); Bouchard Père et Fils (Savigny-les-Beaune, Savigny-les-Beaune Les Lavières); Lucien Camus-Brochon (Savigny-les-Beaune Les Grands Liards, Savigny-les-Beaune Les Lavières, Savigny-les-Beaune Les Narbantons, Savigny-les-Beaune Vieilles Vignes); Chandon de Briailles (Savigny-les-Beaune Les Lavières); Edmond et Pierre Cornu (Savigny-les-Beaune); Jean-Luc Dubois (Savigny-les-Beaune Les Picotins Vieilles Vignes Réserve); Maurice Ecard (Savigny-les-Beaune Les Jarrons, Savigny-les-Beaune Les Narbantons, Savigny-les-Beaune Les Peuillets, Savigny-les-Beaune Les Serpentières); Pierre Guillemot (Savigny-les-Beaune Les Jarrons, Savigny-les-Beaune Les Serpentières); Louis Jadot (Savigny-les-Beaune La Dominode, Savigny-les-Beaune Clos des Guettes, Savigny-les-Beaune Les Lavières, Savigny-les-Beaune Les Vergelesses); Albert Morot (Savigny-les-Beaune Les Vergelesses Clos la Bataillière); Tollot-Beaut (Savigny-les-Beaune Champs Chevreys, Savigny-les-Beaune Les Lavières).

The Basics—Beaujolais

Beaujolais wine is made from vineyards strung across a number of enchanted mountainsides that mark the beginning of what is known as France's Massif Central. The region of Beaujolais is 34 miles long from north to south, and 7 to 9 miles wide. The granite mountainsides range in height from 2,300 feet to more than 3,400 feet, and provide a backdrop for one of France's three most beautiful viticultural regions (the others being Alsace and the neighboring Mâconnais). There are nearly 4,000 growers making a living in this idyllic area. Some of them sell tiny portions of their crops locally, but most prefer to sell to one of the large firms that dominate the business.

The only grape permitted by law to be used in making Beaujolais is the Gamay, or Gamay Noir à jus blanc, its official name. It seems to thrive in the stony, schistous soils of the region. Most red wine grapes have trouble producing high-quality crops in granite-based soils, but Gamay seems to be a natural. The compelling characteristic of Gamay is its youthful, fresh, exuberant, crunchy fruit, which the vignerons of Beaujolais have learned to maximize by producing it in an unusual method called carbonic maceration. In this style of vinification, the grapes are not pressed but simply dumped in full bunches into a vat. Grapes at the very bottom of the vat burst because of the weight on top of them. That juice begins to ferment, warming up the vat and causing fermentation in the unbroken grapes to begin inside their skins. The advantage of this technique is that a wine's perfume and fruity intensity is related to what is inside the grape skin, and the acid and tannin are largely extracted from the breaking and pressing of the skins.

This interesting fermentation method results in fruity, exuberant, intensely perfumed wines that are ideal when chilled and drunk in the so-called nouveau style. Today this nouveau style is a phenomenon in the export markets, but it only started in the late 1970s. Nouveau Beaujolais, which can only be released on the third Thursday in November, accounts for nearly half of the enormous production of this region. It is one of France's most successful export items, and the insatiable thirst for this wine results in hundreds of thousands of cases being air-freighted to such far-flung locations as Sydney, Tokyo, Hong Kong, Seoul, San Francisco, New York, Stockholm, London, and, of course, Paris.

The Nouveau hysteria and incredible profits taken by the wine trade from the sales of Nouveau have resulted in a school of thought that has attempted to disparage not only the wine but those who consume it. This is all nonsense, because there is no doubting that in vintages such as 2000, delicious, zesty, exuberant, fresh, vibrantly fruity Beaujolais Nouveau is made. The only limitation is that it should be drunk within 3–4 months of its release. Beaujolais Nouveau has become a useful wine for introducing people to the glories of red wine. It has also weaned people off some of the sugary white Zinfandels and cloying Liebfraumilchs that dominated the marketplace not too long ago. A few arrogant wine snobs would have you believe it is not fashionable, but that is ludicrous.

However, to think of Beaujolais only in terms of Beaujolais Nouveau is to do this fascinating region a great injustice. In addition to Beaujolais Nouveau, there is Beaujolais Supérieur, which generally comes on the market about a month after Beaujolais Nouveau. There is also Beaujolais-Villages, which is an appellation unto itself, spread out over most of the entire Beaujolais appellation, where 39 communes have been selected by the legislature for producing some of the better wines of the region. Many of the top producers produce a Beaujolais-Villages Nouveau because it has a firmer, more robust character and can last three to four months longer than the straight Beaujolais Nouveau. If you are drinking Nouveau for its up-front, exuberant, fresh, unabashed fruitiness, then a good Beaujolais Nouveau will often be more pleasing than a Beaujolais-Villages Nouveau.

The glories of Beaujolais, aside from its narrow, winding roads, sleepy valleys, photogenic hillsides, and quaint, old villages, are the 10 Beaujolais crus. These wines all come from a village or group of villages in the northern end of the Beaujolais region; each cru is believed to have its own individual style.

A NOTE ON RECENT VINTAGES AND GENERAL CHARACTERISTICS OF THE TEN BEAUJOLAIS CRUS
Though examples of old bottles of Beaujolais that have retained their fruit can be found (in 1991 Robert Parker shared a bottle of 1929 Moulin-à-Vent at New York's superb restaurant Montrachet with its sommelier, Daniel Johnnes, and it was marvelously intact), most Beaujolais should be consumed within several years of the vintage. If you are going to take a gamble

on aging Beaujolais, it should be Moulin-à-Vent. It comes down to a matter of personal taste, but if you are buying these wines for their vibrant, up-front, exuberant, unabashed fruitiness, then drink them young!

With respect to a quick overview of the different crus and what you might expect, the top Beaujolais crus, from north to south, begin with St. Amour. St. Amour is a wine known for its good color, but it is often lacking in body and length, as the vineyards often fail to achieve maximum ripeness except in exceptionally hot, dry years such as 1989. When good, the wines exhibit a blackberry, raspberry fruitiness, medium body, and soft textures.

Juliénas is one of the larger appellations for top Beaujolais. There are many fine producers from Juliénas, so the competition for top-quality wine is intense. The finest examples display the exuberant, rich, fresh fruitiness of Beaujolais, backed up by plenty of body, intensity, and relatively high alcohol.

The smallest Beaujolais cru, Chénas, produces wines with a kinship to the full-bodied wines of its neighbor, Moulin-à-Vent. A top Chénas displays a deep, robust, intense color and a muscular, rich, concentrated style. It is a fuller, chunkier style of Beaujolais that occasionally lacks perfume and elegance. Given its rusticity, many Chénas can age for 4–5 years.

Moulin-à-Vent is often referred to as the King of Beaujolais, and it is certainly the most expensive. Moulin-à-Vent costs $3–5 more than other Beaujolais. Moulin-à-Vent produces the most powerful, concentrated, and ageworthy Beaujolais. While it is highly prized, in many ways it is atypical, resembling a medium-weight red burgundy from the Côte d'Or rather than an effusively fruity Beaujolais. The wines can easily last more than 10 years, particularly those from the best producers.

The same people who call Moulin-à-Vent King of Beaujolais refer to Fleurie as its Queen. With one of the bigger vineyard acreages, Fleurie may be the quintessential example of Beaujolais—heady, perfumed, and rich, without the weight, body, or tannin of the bigger wines from Moulin-à-Vent or Chénas. At its best it is a pure, lush, silky, fruity wine that is undeniably seductive and disarming.

Chiroubles's vineyards sit at the highest altitude of Beaujolais. The wines are considered the most ethereal and fragrant of all the Beaujolais cru. Chiroubles derives much of its character from its penetrating, pervasive aroma. However, it can lack body, can mature very quickly, and almost always must be drunk within 1–2 years for its freshness.

Morgon, the home of Beaujolais's resurgence of quality independent estates, has a reputation of being among the more robust and ageworthy of the Beaujolais crus. There is considerable variation in style, given the large size of this cru. Many wines are quite full and rich, while others are dull and hollow. A great Morgon will have exotic flavors of overripe cherries, peaches, and apricots as well as a taste of kirsch.

The newest of the Beaujolais crus, Régnié, offers many different styles. Most of the local cognoscenti claim a classic Régnié possesses an intense smell of cassis and raspberries. Relatively light- to medium-bodied, it needs to be drunk within 3 years of the vintage.

Brouilly, another large Beaujolais cru, produces relatively light, aromatic, fruity wines that are often no better than a Beaujolais-Villages. However, in the hands of the best producers, the wines have an additional degree of charm and fruit, making them ideal Beaujolais.

In contrast, the Côte de Brouilly is composed of vineyards on better-drained and -exposed slopes. The wines tend to be more alcoholic than those from Brouilly, with more body and glycerin. As for the generic Beaujolais and Beaujolais-Villages, again, the producer is most important. One of the best values in the marketplace is a top-quality Beaujolais or Beaujolais-Villages.

With respect to vintages, 1997 offers fat, round, wines filled with lush sweet fruit. An extremely hot August was followed by a September of warm days and cool nights ("It was the finest September of my career," said Georges Dubœuf, this region's most famous *négociant*) fashioning fruit-driven wines that have relatively low acidity levels—particularly when compared to the 1996s. The 1997s are wines that will be at their best early, and the majority will need to be consumed by 2003.

As elsewhere in central and northern France, rain was a concern in Beaujolais during the 1998 harvest. After an extremely hot and sunny month of August, harvesting began in the first days of September and was interrupted by showers every three days or so. Preliminary tastings reveal that conscientious growers were able to avoid the diluting effects of rain by harvesting each parcel at the optimal time. Those who crop-thin and have reasonable yields saw their grapes attain full maturity while their neighbors had to wait through the rains. Overall, 1998 appears to be a good vintage for Beaujolais, with appealingly forward fruit (yet not as lush as the 1997s) and nice balance. Most of them should be consumed by 2004.

The 1999 vintage produced excellent to outstanding wines in certain early-maturing appellations such as Régnié, Morgon, Fleurie, and Moulin-à-Vent yet was disappointing in Chiroubles, St. Amour, Chénas, and Juliénas, whose grapes never achieved physiological maturity. "We had enormous luck," said Georges Dubœuf when recounting the weather that fashioned the 1999 vintage in France's breathtakingly beautiful Beaujolais region. After a poor summer of cool temperatures and interminable rain, "we had two weeks of superb weather in September."

According to Dubœuf, the warmth, sun, and dry wind (blowing from the north) elevated sugar levels and concentrated the acidities. Dubœuf stated that a high percentage of his wines were barely chaptalized, a rarity in the Beaujolais. He feels 1999 "is not the vintage of the century for Beaujolais, yet is excellent."

A number of 1999s appear to suffer from the rapid ripening of their sugars. The natural potential alcohols rose faster than the actual physiological ripeness of the grapes. Therefore, some wines had difficulty assimilating the alcohol in their fruit (some finishes were quite warm and other wines showed some disjointedness), and others revealed hard tannins.

Georges Dubœuf believes 2000 is a "glorious" vintage for Beaujolais. As is always the case, certain appellations outperformed others. Chiroubles, Régnié, Morgon, Fleurie, Moulin-à-Vent, and Brouilly all had banner years, but the vineyards of Chénas, Juliénas, and St. Amour were damaged by successive hailstorms at the end of July. The best 2000s have magnificent colors, with deep ruby and purples hues. They are also supremely aromatic, bursting with raspberry and cherry scents. The 2000 Beaujolais vintage, from the most successful appellations have highly impressive depth of fruit, virtually perfect acidity for balance, and ripe tannins. Some of the wines are firmly structured and reveal loads of tannins, but they are generally ripe, sweet, and supple. The communes that did not fair too well, due to the hailstorms, have astringent finishes.

THE MÂCONNAIS: A CONSUMER'S PARADISE

The Mâconnais, a picturesque region south of the Côte d'Or and Côte Chalonnaise (on the northern border of Beaujolais, an hour south of Beaune), is responsible for producing the finest values in white Burgundy. Made entirely from Chardonnay, the finest Mâcons, Pouilly-Fuissés, and St.-Vérans can qualitatively compete with the best of the Côte de Beaune.

While many Côte de Beaune white Burgundies are priced in such a way that only billionaires can regularly drink them, the Mâconnais wines remain reasonable. The vast majority of this region's wines are insipid, underripe products of cooperatives, but the great wines of the Mâconnais can compete with any Chardonnays on earth.

THE "REAL" REALITIES OF BURGUNDY

Terroir—Facts and Myths: Consumers who have had the opportunity to visit Burgundy, meet with one of its vignerons, or talk with someone enthralled by this hallowed region's wines has certainly heard that *terroir* is the be-all and end-all of Burgundy's wines. Burgundians will tell you that their wines are good because of *terroir*, that their primary duty as vignerons is to allow *terroir* to express itself, and, from time to time, they will comment on a wine's *"goût de terroir"* (taste of *terroir*). So what does it all mean, and what is *terroir* anyway?

Terroir is a French word that encompasses all of the nonhuman effects on a wine's character. Geology, subsoil, topsoil, drainage, exposure to the sun, climate, microclimate, slope, and so on are all considered to be components of *terroir*. Using this definition it is plain to see that any parcel of vines—whether in France, Chile, Australia, the United States, etc.—has a *terroir*. The quality of the *terroir* and the characteristics it will impart on a wine will be different, but *terroirs* are everywhere. In fact, California winemakers, once the first to claim that all notions of *terroir* were bunk, have embraced the notion for their own wines. Over the course of the last decade, a multitude of single-vineyard wines have come out of California, and the Bureau of Alcohol, Tobacco and Firearms (ATF) has overseen the creation and enforcement of American Viticultural Areas (AVAs) since the early 1980s. Australia, seemingly the last bastion of anti-*terroir* winemakers is now the source of numerous single vineyard wines.

The fact, and it is undoubtedly a fact, that *terroir* plays a role in a given wine's aromatic and flavor profile is a given. Pinot Noir vines grown in clay-based soils are different from those grown in solid limestone. However, what Burgundian vignerons and the pseudo-intelligensia (so-called *terroirists*) will have you believe is that *terroir* is the most important factor governing a wine's quality and character. Simply put, this is nonsense.

Soil, exposition, and microclimate (all components of *terroir*) most certainly impart an influence on a wine's character, but the men and women who select which rootstocks to plant and who make all the key viticultural, harvesting, vinification, and *élevage* decisions also impart a huge influence. Consider the following:

1. Rootstock: Is it designed to produce prolific or small crop levels?

2. Yeasts: Does the winemaker use the vineyard's and winery's wild yeasts or are commercial yeasts employed? Every yeast, wild or commercial, will give a wine a different set of aromatics, flavor, and texture.

3. Yields and vine age: High yields from perennial overcroppers result in diluted wine. Low yields, usually less than 2 tons per acre, or 35–40 hectoliters per hectare, result in wines with much more concentration and personality. Additionally, young vines have a tendency to overproduce, whereas old vines produce small berries and less wine. Crop thinning is often employed with younger vineyards to increase the level of concentration.

4. Harvest philosophy: Is the fruit picked underripe to preserve more acidity, or fully ripe to emphasize the lushness and opulence of a given varietal?

5. Vinification techniques and equipment: There are an amazing number of techniques that can change the wine's aromas and flavors. Moreover, equipment choice (different presses, destemmers, etc.) can have a profound influence on the final wine.

6. *Élevage* (the wine's upbringing): Is the wine brought up in oak barrels, concrete vats, stainless steel, or large wood vats (*foudres*)? What is the percentage of new oak? All of these elements exert a strong influence on the wine's character. Additionally, transferring wine from one container to another (racking) has an immense impact on a wine's bouquet and flavor. Is the wine allowed to remain in long contact with its lees (believed to give the wine more aromatic complexity and fullness)? Or is it racked frequently for fear of picking up an undesirable lees smell?

7. Fining and filtration: Even the most concentrated and profound wines that *terroirists* consider quintessential examples of the soil can be eviscerated and stripped of their personality and richness by excessive fining and filtering. Does the winemaker treat the wine with kid gloves, or is the winemaker a manufacturer/processor bent on sculpturing the wine?

8. Bottling date: Does the winemaker bottle early to preserve as much fruit as possible, or later to give the wine a more mellow, aged character? Undoubtedly, the philosophy of when to bottle can radically alter the character of a wine.

9. Cellar temperature and sanitary conditions: Some wine cellars are cold and others are warm. Different wines emerge from cold cellars (development is slower and the wines are less prone to oxidation) than from warm cellars (where the maturation of aromas and flavors is more rapid and the wines are quicker to oxidize). Are the wine cellars clean or dirty?

These are just a handful of factors that can have extraordinary impact on the style, quality, and personality of a wine. The choices that people make, even when they are unquestionably in pursuit of the highest quality, can contribute far more to a wine's character than the vineyard's *terroir*.

Terroir provides a potential, and winemakers either tap that potential or they don't. The world's greatest winemaker, faced with Pinot Noir vines planted in Washington, D.C., would be incapable of fashioning a great wine because the *terroir* is simply not suited to grape production. Yet the qualitative potential of Burgundy's *terroirs* is huge, in good years. The problem is that few winemakers fulfill their vineyard's potential.

Terroir also has the potential to impart certain characteristics on wines. Just as certain flowering plants prefer acidic soils and sunny expositions, each varietal has its preferences that are reflected in the quality and makeup of its grapes and the resulting wines. Many *terroirists* claim that well-made Burgundies scream out their *terroir* in their aromas, textures, and flavors. Unquestionably, the *terroir* does impart certain characteristics and nuances, but it is always the hand of the winemaker that dominates.

For example, let's say one serves the five premier cru Beaunes of Domaine Albert Morot and one of Louis Jadot's and another from Tollot-Beaut in a blind tasting. The Jadot and Tollot-Beaut wines will stand out as being completely different from the Morots. This same exercise can be attempted with any appellation of Burgundy and the results will be the same: the winemaker's hand dominates.

However, for those looking for a fascinating tasting that truly delineates *terroir* differences, Bruno Clair has two neighboring Gevrey-Chambertins (Cazetiers and Clos St.-Jacques) that were planted the same year with the same rootstock, and are handled identically in the vineyard and winery. Yet there are profound differences between the two wines: the Cazetiers is generally more polished, elegant, and crisp, whereas the Clos St.-Jacques tends to be an in-your-face, powerful, explosive wine.

In conclusion, consumers should understand that a vineyard's *terroir* is a factor in a wine's character, but the preeminent factor is the quality of the producer who crafted it. All too often, the hyperventilation and hyperbole over *terroir* obscures the most important issue of all— identifying and discovering those producers who make wines worth drinking and savoring.

Are the wines of Burgundy as good today as they were 20 or 40 years ago? The wines of Burgundy are better today than they were in the past. First, there is no longer any evidence of adulterating red Burgundies. The illegal practice of blending inferior, more alcoholic, and more deeply colored wine from southern France and northern Africa, a wide practice until the early 1970s, appears to have been discontinued.

Second, many producers recognized the folly of planting clones of Pinot Noir (such as the Pinot Droit, which enabled prolific yields rather than quality) and, with the encouragement and support of the oenology departments of the leading universities, have begun to replant with lower-yielding Pinot Noir clones, such as the Pinot Fin called 115.

A third, and possibly even more important, quality factor has been the strong movement, started in the mid-1980s, to move away from the excessive fining and filtration of Pinot Noir and Chardonnay for fear of eviscerating the wine and removing its flavor. With the advent of modern technology, many growers learned how to bottle their wines as quickly as possible, aided immeasurably by German micropore filters and centrifuges that could clarify (and eviscerate) a wine with a push of a button. This eliminated the need for the cumbersome and labor-intensive racking. It also allowed the growers to be paid for their wines more quickly, since the wines could be rushed into the bottle. The results, all too often, were wonderfully brilliant, polished, attractive-looking wines that had little character or flavor. The excessive fining and filtration of wines continues to be a major problem in Burgundy. Yet more and more producers are assessing the need to fine on a vintage-by-vintage basis and have stopped filtering in response to increasing demands from some of America's finest Burgundy importers for natural, unprocessed, and unmanipulated wines. However, too many of those brokers and importers responsible for purchasing Burgundy have encouraged their producers to excessively fine and filter, rather than to assume responsibility for shipping the wine in temperature-controlled containers, and guaranteeing that the wine be distributed in a healthy condition. The growing number of American Burgundy importers who not only insist that their wines be minimally fined and filtered, but who also ship their wines in temperature-controlled containers, is to be applauded.

These factors, combined with lower yields, the use of higher-quality barrels, and improved sanitary conditions in the cellars, have resulted in more complete and aromatically complex as well as more flavorful wines. In addition, there is a new generation of highly motivated winemakers who are taking quality more seriously than ever. Such people as Lalou Bize-Leroy, Jean-Nicolas Méo, Christophe Roumier, Dominique Lafon, Jean-François Coche-Dury, Jacques Lardière, and Jean-Pierre de Smet are pushing themselves as well as their peers to produce the highest-quality Burgundies possible.

What are the significant differences in the wines of the Côte de Beaune and Côte de Nuits? The Côte d'Or, or Burgundy's Golden Slope, as it is sometimes called, is where the most profound wines from all of Burgundy are produced. However, there are significant differences between the two hillsides that make up the Côte d'Or. The Côte de Nuits, which starts just south of Dijon and runs south of Nuits St.-Georges, produces essentially all red wine, while the Côte de Beaune, which starts just north of Beaune and extends to Santenay south of Beaune, produces both superlative red and white wines.

The red wines of the Côte de Nuits tend to be fuller and slightly more tannic, and are characterized by a more earthy, black fruit (black currants, black cherries, and plums) and exotic character than those from the Côte de Beaune. Of course, these are generalizations, but the red wines from the Côte de Beaune tend to offer slightly less body as well as less tannin (Pommards being a notable exception), and seem to be filled with aromas and flavors of red fruits (strawberries, cherries, and red currants). In addition, they seem less earthy, less exotic, and in most cases less ageworthy, although there are exceptions. For example, one might argue that a big, rich, generous, virile Pommard from the Côte de Beaune is a larger-scaled, fuller wine than anything produced from Chambolle-Musigny in the Côte de Nuits.

While the Côte de Nuits produces only a handful of white wines, of which a few are superlative, the Côte de Beaune produces the world's greatest white wines from the Chardonnay grape. Whether it is the extraordinary long-lived, rich, precisely defined white wines of Corton-Charlemagne; the nutty, luscious, lusty, easy-to-drink Meursaults; the elegant, steely Puligny-Montrachets; or the opulent, fleshy Chassagne-Montrachets, the Côte de Beaune is known for both elegant, stylish reds and extraordinary whites.

Does Burgundy have to be handled or served differently from Bordeaux? The most striking thing to anyone who has eaten in a restaurant in Burgundy, or in the home of a Burgundy producer, is the revelation that rarely does a Burgundian decant a bottle of red Burgundy, even an old one with a great deal of sediment. In contrast to Bordeaux, where even young vintages are routinely decanted, the practice in Burgundy is simply to pull the cork and serve the wine directly from the bottle. Why is there was such a dramatic difference in wine service between these two regions? Is it based on the fact that Bordeaux actually improves with decantation and Burgundy does not? Or are there other reasons, based more on history?

Some Burgundians have suggested that Burgundy, being principally a land of farmers and small growers, never tolerated the sort of haute service and rigidity experienced in Bordeaux, which for centuries was dominated by the British, long known for their emphasis on formality. This is apparent in the way of life of both these regions today. It is quite unusual to find anyone in the wine trade or any professional taster traveling around Bordeaux without a suit and tie, but growers in Burgundy are never seen in a suit and tie. Casual dress is not only tolerated but accepted form when visiting the growers. Does this extend also to the table where a decanter clearly seems to imply a more pompous sort of service? Certainly the large English glassworks built in the 18th and 19th centuries promoted the use of decanters for claret, which has always seemed to have a heavier sediment than the lighter, finer sediment often found in Burgundies. Is this why it became routine to decant Bordeaux and not Burgundy? Perhaps, but many growers in Burgundy have said that decanters were looked upon as an extravagance and were therefore to be eschewed.

Much of a great Burgundy's character comes from its immense aromatic complexity. Bottle bouquet, particularly a highly nuanced one, can be very ephemeral and begin to break apart if exposed to air. Decanting a tight, young, austere Bordeaux can often make it seem more open after 20 or 30 minutes in a decanter. However, with only a handful of exceptions, excessive airing of Burgundy by decanting often causes it to lose its bouquet and become flaccid and formless. No doubt there are exceptions. Many of the *négociants* who have old stocks claim that certain ancient wines require a good one to two hours of breathing as well as decantation prior to being consumed. Also, as Burgundians have modernized their winemaking, including taking steps to reduce the wine's contact with air, many wines are in a reductive (lacking oxygen) state when bottled and therefore benefit from aeration.

White Burgundies (particularly when young) improve significantly with 20–25 minutes of airing. Superrich Montrachets from producers such as Ramonet or the Domaine de la Romanée-Conti are best served at room temperature (cool, not cold) and decanted, as aeration of 20–25 minutes tends to enhance these particular wines.

Another major difference between Burgundy and Bordeaux is the stemware in which Burgundy is often served. In Bordeaux, the standard tulip-shaped glass or the famous Institut National des Appellations d'Origine (INAO) glass is preferred. In Burgundy, a balloon-shaped, Cognac-styled, fat, squat glass with a short stem is found in the growers' cellars and *négociants* offices, and also in Burgundy's restaurants. It is believed that these broader glasses tend to accentuate the intense, heady Burgundian perfume. Some restaurants carry this to an extreme and offer their clients an oversized, 24-ounce glass. This glass is so large that the wine can actually get lost, and the bouquet disappears so quickly, the patron never has a chance to smell it. The small balloon-shaped, Cognac-styled glasses are excellent for Burgundy, but the INAO and tulip-shaped glasses should be used only for Bordeaux. It is extremely important that red Burgundy be served cooler than Bordeaux, preferably at 58–62 degrees Fahrenheit, no warmer. Red Burgundy, given its perfume, is best served at a slightly chilled temperature where the precision of its flavors and the purity and delineation of all the complex nuances in its bouquet can be deciphered. To prove the point, all you have to do is serve the same wine at 65–70 degrees and see how soupy, muddled, and alcoholic the wine tastes. Beaujolais should be served even colder, 53–56 degrees Fahrenheit, and good white Burgundy at 58–60 degrees Fahrenheit. A great Montrachet or Meursault should be served slightly warmer, at 60–65 degrees Fahrenheit, or at room temperature, assuming it is not over 68 degrees. It is foolish to spend the money for a compelling, complex white Burgundy and then overchill it, ushering its bouquet and flavors into hibernation.

In conclusion, there are two things to remember when serving and handling Burgundy as opposed to Bordeaux. First, Burgundy can be severely damaged by excessive aeration, whereas Bordeaux is rarely hurt, although it is debatable as to how much it improves with decanting. Second, Burgundy must be served slightly chilled to be at its very best, but Bordeaux can be served at 64–66 degrees Fahrenheit, a good 4 to 6 degrees warmer than for Burgundy.

What is the optimum age at which to drink red and white Burgundy? Trying to predict when most Burgundies will reach maturity is a particularly dangerous game to play, given the variation in winemaking techniques and philosophies employed by the growers and *négociants* in Burgundy. However, the majority of the wines of Chablis should be consumed in their first five or six years of life, as only a handful of Chablis producers (Raveneau, for example) make wines that last or improve after 6 years in the bottle.

In terms of the wines of Beaujolais and Mâconnais, while one can always point to a 10-year-old Beaujolais or an extraordinary Pouilly-Fuissé that lasted 10 or 20 years, these are indeed rare wines. Ninety-five percent of the wines of Beaujolais and Mâconnais should be drunk before they attain three years of age. Once past three years the odds are stacked against the consumer.

As for the big red and white wines of Burgundy's Côte d'Or, while it is a matter of taste, if readers are buying Burgundy and not drinking it within its first 10 years of life, I am convinced that they will be disappointed by most bottles opened after that time. Even the most rugged, concentrated, intense red and white Burgundies seem to shed their tannins surprisingly fast and reach a plateau of maturity 5–6 years after the vintage. At that point they begin to lose their freshness, and decay sets in after 10–12 years. Obviously the vintage itself can make a great deal of difference. Those who purchased 1982 red Burgundies should have consumed them well before 1992. Those who purchased 1983s and felt that time would only make these brawny, tannic, often rot-afflicted, controversial wines better are going to be disappointed. The once sensational 1985 red Burgundies were fully mature and excellent wines in 1995, but most have lost their fruit and pleasurable qualities by now. A good rule of thumb is to drink your red Burgundy within 10 years of the vintage, realizing there are certain vintages, such as 1997, 1996, 1995, 1993, 1990, 1988, 1978, 1976, and 1972 for red Burgundy, which may, for a handful of the finest examples, take more than 10 years to reach full maturity. But these are the exceptions, even for wines from those vintages.

The window of opportunity for drinking red and white Burgundy is one of the smallest of any great wine in the world. One of the great attributes of Bordeaux, and a reason, no doubt, why it commands the prices and international following it does, is the broad span of years over which it can be drunk. When a bottle of Bordeaux reaches its plateau of maturity, it can frequently remain there for 10, 15, sometimes 20 years before it begins a very slow process of decline. Burgundies can reach their plateau of maturity in five years and unceremoniously begin to fade after another six or seven months. The optimum drinking window for most red and white Burgundies is small and closes quickly. While Bordeaux has a broad, generous period over which it can be consumed, connoisseurs of Burgundy should pay fastidious attention to the development of their wines, or suffer the unsavory consequences. A tasting note on a top Burgundy may have meaning and reliability for only six months or less. Consequently, readers should attach significantly less importance to Burgundy tasting notes and devote more attention to the producer, the quality of his or her wines, and the producer's finest vineyards or offerings.

What should a great red Burgundy taste like when fully mature? It is easier to agree on those key factors that frequently result in great red Burgundy. In order of importance they are 1) the soil and exposition of the vineyard, 2) low yields, 3) physiologically ripe grapes, and 4) superior winemaking, which includes exacting sanitary conditions as well as vigilant concern over the wine's upbringing, with minimal intervention save for the occasional racking (transfer of the wine from one barrel to another barrel). All the greatest red Burgundies, at the very least, are the product of these factors. But red Burgundy at its most sublime is the most difficult wine to describe, as it matures quickly, goes through numerous stages of evolution, and can fade at an alarming pace. Truly profound red Burgundy is rare because the Pinot Noir grape possesses an unfathomable mystery that yields no telltale, discernible signature such as Cabernet Sauvignon or Chardonnay.

The greatest examples of mature red Burgundy all share the following characteristics.

First, they have penetrating and compelling bouquets that exhibit a decadent, even raunchy, almost decaying or aged-beef sort of smell, combined with an intense and exhilarating aroma of Asian spices, caramelized leaves, and dried herbs. Second, they have layers and layers of black and red fruits that virtually explode on the palate with a cascade of increasingly expanding textural sensations. They are relatively high in alcohol, possess adequate acidity rather than tannin for structural delineation, and textural finish, with a lusciousness and a silky quality that lasts several minutes. Drinking the finest mature red Burgundies is an experience akin to eating candy because of the extraordinary sweetness they convey.

What constitutes the aromatic and flavor profiles of great white Burgundy? Everyone who drinks wine no doubt has a strong idea of what the finest Chardonnays, particularly those from the New World, offer in terms of smell and taste. But how many of you have drunk truly profound white Burgundy? Certainly the frightfully high prices of $100–800 a bottle for grands crus limits their market to less than 1% of the wine-consuming public. Actually, comparing a great white Burgundy with a New World Chardonnay is almost unfair. The preponderant number of New World Chardonnays must be consumed within 2–3 years after the vintage. As enjoyable as they are, they often have all their components playing against one another rather than in complete harmony. Perhaps because most New World Chardonnays must be acidified, when one tastes them, the overall perception is one of separate but equal building blocks of acid, structure, fruit, and wood. On the other hand, great white Burgundies incorporate all these components, resulting in a blend where no one element has the upper hand. The greatest examples combine an extraordinary perfume of apples, honey, vanilla, wet stones, and sometimes oranges, lemons, and tangerines, with flavors that range from a smoky, buttery, and nutty taste, occasionally to peaches and, in the more opulent, ripe examples, to tropical fruits such as bananas, mangoes, and pineapples. Of course, what makes them so compelling is their precision and balance, with all of these marvelously complex components unfolding in the glass and on the palate. It should also be noted that some white Burgundies have the added advantage that in certain vintages a small percentage can last for as many as 10–20 years in the bottle, improving and developing more nuances as they age, but the number of them that truly improve beyond 7–8 years is minuscule. The greatest producers of white Burgundy all seem to share these characteristics in various proportions, depending on the quality of the vintage.

Is Burgundy as good a candidate for cellaring and aging as a top Bordeaux, Hermitage, California Cabernet, or Italian Barolo or Barbaresco? The answer to this question is a resounding "no." While some old-timers lament that Burgundy is not made the way it once was, they seem to have forgotten that most Burgundy has never aged extremely well. It is an incontestable truism that anyone who advises readers to lay away most Burgundies for a decade clearly does not have the consumer's best interests at heart. To reiterate once more, most modern-day red Burgundies, even from the finest vintages (e.g., 1990), should be consumed within 10–12 years of the vintage. This rule is even more restrictive for white Burgundies. The window of drinking opportunity is normally within 7–8 years of the vintage for white Burgundies. The reasons for this are simple. Red Burgundies, made from the Pinot Noir grape, simply do not have the tannin level or extraction of flavor to sustain them for more than 10–12 years. Additionally, the Pinot Noir grape's most distinct pleasures are its bouquet and its sweet, ripe, velvety fruitiness, both of which tend to be the first characteristics of a Pinot Noir to crack up and dissipate. Even the finest red Burgundies, while they may last two or more decades, are generally more enjoyable to drink in their first decade of life. Even the rare, long-lived, powerful vintages, such as 1959, 1964, 1969, and 1978, were best drunk during their first 10–15 years of life, although the finest examples of the top producers can still be wondrous today. Anyone who loves great red Burgundy should buy only enough to drink within the immediate future. Red Burgundy's suspect aging capabilities have always been a problem and are not due to any modern-day winemaking techniques, although high yields and addictive reliance on chemical fertilizers as well as fungicides, herbicides, and pesticides have further exacerbated red Burgundy's ability to age gracefully beyond a decade.

If you are buying Burgundy for drinking in 15 or 20 years, you should be restricting your purchases to the wines from no more than a half dozen or so producers. In particular, Domaine Leroy, Domaine du Comte de Vogüé, and small producers such as Comtes Lafon still produce wines that are compelling and sumptuous at 10 years of age and, in some cases, 20 years. Even Burgundy's most expensive and frequently greatest wines, those of such superlative producers as the Domaine de la Romanée-Conti, Domaine Méo-Camuzet, Domaine Dujac, and Philippe Leclerc, are usually at their best between 8–15 years of age, rarely improving or holding well beyond that.

Are the best wines of Burgundy viable candidates for investment? While investment in wine has become more popular given the luxury prices demanded for the top châteaux of Bordeaux, Burgundy has never represented as good an investment as Bordeaux. The practice of investing in wine for financial profit is abhorrent. It is done regularly, at least with the first growths and super second châteaux of Bordeaux, as well as a handful of the limited-production Pomerols and St.-Emilions. But there is a great deal of difference between buying Bordeaux and buying Burgundy. For starters, in the spring following the vintage, Bordeaux is offered as a wine future at what is called an "opening" or entry-level price. If the vintage is widely acclaimed and of great quality, the price is propelled in only one direction—upward. Burgundy is not sold as a wine future, although specialist merchants regrettably offer to sell Burgundy to their customers on a "prearrival" basis. This often requires the consumer to put up considerable monetary sums 6-12 months prior to arrival. In essence, consumers are financing the merchant's Burgundy purchases.

Today, most Burgundies from current vintages sell at prices higher than do the older vintages of the same wine. A review of any of the auction results from Christie's, Sotheby's, the Chicago Wine Company, or the numerous New York and California auctions illustrates this. Some of the greatest Burgundies from vintages from the 1940s, 1950s, and 1960s sell at prices significantly less than those from 1990, 1993, and 1995, three of the most recent highly regarded vintages. The reasons for this are 1) consumers lack confidence in Burgundy, 2) smart buyers recognize Burgundy's fragility and dubious aging potential, and 3) unlike Bordeaux, due to scarcity, there is virtually no information available to potential auction buyers on the evolution of older Burgundies. Rarely do these same wines appreciate in value after release. In fact, in most cases their value collapses. There are exceptions, such as some limited-production Montrachets and Romanée-Conti and La Tâche of the Domaine de la Romanée-Conti, as well as Comte de Vogüé's Musigny. All in all, Burgundy is a notoriously bad investment.

Why are the best Burgundies so expensive? The pricing of Burgundy can be explained entirely by the rules of supply and demand. Historically, Burgundy has had the unique and enviable situation of having far more admirers and prospective purchasers than available wine. This is particularly true at the premier cru and grand cru levels, which are usually the only Burgundies that merit purchasing, given the feeble qualities of most village and generic Burgundies. In addition, great Burgundy alone among the finest French wines has no competition from within the borders of France, or in most of the wine world. The problem at the premier cru and grand cru levels is exacerbated by the truly microscopic quantities of wine offered by the best producers, sometimes as few as 25, 100, or 300 cases—or 36 *bottles*, as for Vincent Leflaive's stupendous 1997 Montrachet. Some specific case production figures demonstrate the point dramatically. For example, the most expensive red Burgundies are those of the Domaine de la Romanée-Conti. In an abundant year, the production of their Romanée-Conti ranges from 300 to 500 cases. Their exclusively owned *monopole* vineyard, La Tâche, produces between 900 and 1,800 cases a year. One of Burgundy's most sought-after wine-makers, Claude Dugat, usually produces, in a prolific year, 50 cases of Griotte-

Chambertin and 100 cases of Charmes-Chambertin. Lalou Bize-Leroy, whose Domaine Leroy in Vosne-Romanée since 1988 has consistently produced Burgundy's most sublime and age-worthy wines, usually makes only 25 cases of her two grands crus of Musigny and Chambertin. The Domaine Roumier is one of the most revered names in Burgundy, and their Bonnes Mares is considered to be a heroic wine, but only 100 cases were made in the plentiful vintage of 1988. Everyone who loves great Burgundy considers Hubert Lignier's Clos de la Roche to be one of the top dozen or so red wines made in Burgundy, yet he rarely makes more than 300 cases.

By no means are these isolated examples. Louis Jadot's production of the excellent Beaune-Clos des Ursules is considered massive by Burgundy standards, but only 1,100 cases are made in a hugely abundant year, about one-fourth the amount of a very-limited-production Pomerol such as Pétrus! Jadot sells his wines to every civilized country in the world. How much of this lovely wine will make it to the shelves of the finest wine merchants in Omaha, Nebraska, or Edinborough, Scotland? Perhaps a case or two? In Bordeaux a production of 1,000 cases is considered minuscule. A favorite Bordeaux of wine consumers is the muscular and flavorful Lynch-Bages, and a popular California Cabernet Sauvignon is Robert Mondavi's exquisite Réserve. There are 35,000–45,000 cases of Lynch-Bages and 15,000–20,000 cases of Mondavi Réserve Cabernet produced.

This frustrating situation (at least for buyers) is similar for white Burgundies. There are usually no more than 50 cases made of J.F. Coche-Dury's ethereal Corton-Charlemagne. Louis Jadot, who makes sublime Corton-Charlemagne, can, in an abundant year, produce 1,200 cases, but that must be spread around not only to the restaurants of France but to Jadot's clients throughout the world. Even worse is the situation with the Domaine Ramonet's celestial Montrachet. A whopping 50 cases are made in an abundant vintage.

To exacerbate this already tenuous situation, Burgundies sold in the United States undergo significantly higher markups than wines from Bordeaux. Typically, a Burgundian estate has one U.S. importer. If the demand for the estate's wines is high, that importer will slap egregious margins on them. Bordeaux, on the other hand, is a competitive market, with many importers vying for consumers for the same wines.

Most of the finest grand cru and premier cru red and white Burgundies could be sold exclusively to a few of Europe's top restaurants, should the producers so desire. Of course, that is not their intention, and they try to ensure an equitable distribution to their suppliers throughout the world. But it is because of these tiny quantities that the prices for Burgundy are so astronomically high. As more and more wine connoisseurs from a growing number of countries demand fine wine, the pressure on suppliers will only create more and more exorbitant prices for the new vintages.

Why are the finest Burgundies so difficult to find in the American marketplace? The answer again relates to the tiny quantities of top wines that are produced. America is an extremely important purchaser of top-quality Burgundies, both red and white. In fact, consumers in other countries continually complain that the United States gets more than its fair share of Burgundies finest wines. So, how does the system work?

Each estate in Burgundy allocates wines to the importers that represent them around the world. The U.S. importers then allocate small quantities to the 10 or 12 best wine markets in the United States. Therefore, a top merchant may only end up with a case or two of Leflaive Chevalier-Montrachet, and six bottles of a Domaine de la Romanée-Conti Montrachet. However, since demand in the United States for the finest wines from the best vintages is huge, secondary channels (known as the "gray market") provide additional supply by selling to U.S. merchants allocations meant for other nation's markets. Nevertheless, overall production of the most highly sought after Burgundies is so small that supply will never match demand. These are the realities when dealing with Burgundy, and seemingly only add to its mystique.

Are estate-bottled Burgundies superior to those from the négociants? *Négociants* is the French word for a wine broker. *Négociants* include firms that do not own any vineyards. They rely totally on purchases of finished wines from growers, which they then sell under their own names. *Négociants* can also be firms that own vineyards. Several—for example, Faiveley and Bouchard Père et Fils—are among the largest vineyard owners in Burgundy. *Négociants* have long controlled the Burgundy wine business, as the movement of growers to estate-bottle their wines has been a relatively recent phenomenon. The fact that many of the most insipid and vapid Burgundies have consistently been produced by several of the largest and most prominent *négociants* has been the principal reason for the negative image many consumers have of a Burgundy *négociant*. *Négociants* have also been maligned by growers and importers, who argue that the most authentic and individualistic Burgundies can emerge only from individual domaines. The better *négociants* have responded in a positive manner to this criticism. Since the mid-eighties, Louis Jadot has been a reference point for high-quality *négociants*, as has Louis Latour for white wines. Other firms, particularly Bouchard Père et Fils, have significantly upgraded the quality of their wines.

The trend of estate-bottled Burgundies, started by the late founder of the *Revue du Vin de France*, Raymond Baudoin, and subsequently encouraged by the American importer, the late Frank Schoonmaker, has still not reached its zenith. The *négociants*, faced with losing many of their sources for wine, thanks to growers who decided to become freelancers and to estate-bottle their own production, not only tried to sign up certain growers to exclusivity contracts but recognized the need to improve the quality of their wines.

There are, however, *négociants* that continue to lag behind in quality. Among the most notable of these is the huge firm of Jean-Claude Boisset, the firms of Patriarche, Albert Bichot, and the highly promoted wines of La Reine-Pédauque. Today you are not likely to get a bad wine from these firms, but rather a sound, commercial one with no soul or personality. Admittedly, there must be a vast market for such wines, as these firms are among the wealthiest and most successful in France.

One argument frequently offered is that the wines of the *négociants* have the same taste. To me that seems irrelevant. The top *négociants*, while they respect the individual vineyard's *terroir* (Jadot's winemaker, Jacques Lardière, is one of Burgundy's most fervent *terroirists*), obviously employ the same philosophy in making all of their wines, and try to keep the identity of the vineyard and appellation unto itself. The wines of Louis Jadot all share a similar signature, but then so do the wines of domaines such as Roumier, Ponsot, Roty, Claude Dugat, or the Domaine de la Romanée-Conti. At the most meticulously run estate-bottled operation the same philosophy is employed for making each wine. The signature is just as prominent in a grower's cellar as it is in a *négociant*'s.

How is great red Burgundy made? Most Burgundy growers will only tell you so much, but the three most important components that contribute to great red burgundy are 1) the excellence of the vineyard, 2) low yields, and 3) the competence of the winemaker. If all three of these exist, the end result is likely to be quite compelling and exciting.

How all the different growers and *négociants* vinify and handle their wines differs far more in Burgundy than it does in Bordeaux. In Bordeaux, the basic winemaking and upbringing of the wine are essentially the same at all the major properties. In Burgundy, there are many different ways of making top-class red wine. Burgundy's finest winemakers may well be the best in the world as they have to surmount the fickle nature of Pinot Noir and the variable Burgundian climate. It would be fascinating to see what Bordeaux could produce if a top Burgundian vigneron were to move there. A top Burgundian's conscientiousness, backbreaking labor, and attention to detail both in the vineyard and in cellar can be awe-inspiring. Winemaking techniques that became routine over a decade ago in Burgundy are presently considered "cutting edge" in Bordeaux.

One of the most popular techniques today at the top level is partial or total destemming of the grapes. Destemming is the process whereby the stems are removed from the grape bunches. Many producers feel the stems impart a vegetal flavor to the wine and decrease the color, as well as add astringent tannin. For these reasons, many producers routinely destem 100% of the grapes. Other producers believe a certain percentage of stems adds structure and more character to the wine. Most of the finest producers tend to use between 50% and 100% new oak for their top premiers and grands crus. Many Burgundies taste excessively woody, but new oak is ideal for Pinot Noir and is the most sanitary vessel in which to make wine. However, high yields combined with the lavish use of new oak is a formula for thin, woody wines. As the controversial Jean-Marie Guffens (of Domaine Guffens-Heynen and Maison Verget fame) says, "No wine is overoaked, merely underwined."

Today many Burgundy producers follow the methods of Burgundy's most influential wine-maker, the recently retired Henri Jayer, who employs a five- to seven-day cold prefermenta-tion maceration of his Pinot Noir. Proponents of this practice believe this "cold soak" adds color, richness, aromatics, and fat to a wine.

But even these talented winemakers disagree on certain principles. Henri Jayer, the Do-maine de la Romanée-Conti, and the Domaine Ponsot believe that 90% of the wine is made in the vineyard and that "winemaking" in the cellars can destroy, but cannot contribute more than another 10% to, the final quality. They feel the search for high quality obligates the grower to prune back the vineyard, if conditions warrant, by cutting off grape bunches—in essence doing a "green harvest" in summer to reduce yields. To these producers, high yields are the undoing of the wine, regardless of how talented the winemaker is, or what wizardry can be accomplished within the cellar. On the other hand, some producers, most notably Jacques Seysses, argue that large yields are acceptable, and that concentration can still be obtained by the process of bleeding off the excess juice (which the French call *saigner*). This technique increases the proportion of skins and stems to the remaining juice and therefore, according to its proponents, increases the concentration. Henri Jayer claims this is nothing but a gimmick whose shortcomings become apparent after the wine spends five or six years in the bottle. Another area where these irrefutably great winemakers disagree concerns the per-centage of new oak used. Henri Jayer believes in 100% new oak, the firms of Bourée and Jadot significantly less, and the Domaine Ponsot abhors it altogether. However, it should be noted that the trend for premiers and grands crus in Burgundy is toward increased percent-ages of new oak. More great wines have emerged from an elevated use of new oak than from the absence of it.

Another school of winemaking embraces an extremely long period of cold maceration (with loads of sulfur) prior to fermentation, a technique that lasts well beyond the five to seven days employed by the Jayer-ists. It is practiced by a group of winemakers who have employed the controversial Nuits-St.-Georges oenologist Guy Accad to look after their winemaking. This practice has been condemned by many in Burgundy for producing wines that have more in common with Côte Rôtie than Pinot Noir. Accad does not believe in destemming, and allows the grape bunches to macerate chilled for 10 days or more before any fermentation starts. The other schools of thought for making top-quality red Burgundy basically eschew any of the cold maceration prior to fermentation. They believe in crushing and fermenting at warm temperatures in order to extract color, body, and tannin via a more traditional method. They disagree with those who argue that great aromatic Pinot Noir can be obtained only by a cool fermentation or cold maceration prior to fermentation. Some of the best examples of this school of thought include the Maison Louis Jadot, whose red wines are macerated for a long time, fermented at extremely high temperatures, yet still retain their aromatic purity and last and last in the bottle.

The big question is, what does the Domaine Leroy do, because these are unquestionably the most consistently brilliant, as well as among the most expensive, wines of Burgundy. Leroy's yields are half, sometimes one-third, that of the other domaines. That in itself is probably the reason why these wines attain such great concentration. The Domaine Leroy averages 20–25 hectoliters per hectare as opposed to the 40–50 obtained elsewhere. There is usually no destemming. A cold maceration of five to six days prior to fermentation, a long fermentation, and maceration using only wild yeasts are employed. The wines spend 15–18 months in 100% new oak casks and are bottled unfined and unfiltered.

As all of this indicates, there are a multitude of methods employed that can result in great wines. All of the producers I have mentioned are capable of producing some of the finest wines in Burgundy. Those people who tend to turn out neutral, vapid, mediocre red Burgundies seem also to possess the following things in common: 1) Their crop sizes are excessive; 2) they bottle either too early or too late; 3) they are processors and manufacturers of wine, practicing traumatic fining and filtering; and 4) they take no risks, as their goal is complete stability and/or sterility of the product. As a result, most of the wines are pale imitations of what red Burgundy should be.

How is great white Burgundy made? As with red Burgundy, there are a myriad of decisions a winemaker must make when crafting a white Burgundy. Reasonably low Chardonnay yields, while important, are not as vital as with Pinot Noir. Many of the best estates of the Côte de Beaune, producers of the some of the most sought-after white Burgundies, are known to harvest relatively high yields and yet are able to craft superlative wines.

Compared to red Burgundy producers, this region's white wine vignerons are extremely tight-lipped concerning pressing, vinification, and *élevage* techniques. Trying to obtain specific information generally results in a shrugging of the shoulders, a smile, and a statement such as "the wines make themselves."

There are a multitude of winemaking philosophies concerning white Burgundies. Producers such as François Jobard in Meursault never decant the must off its gross lees (*débourbage*), never stir the fine lees (*bâtonnage*) while the wines were in the barrel, and allow the *élevage* to last up to 18 months. Conversely, his nephew Rémi Jobard (who recently took over the estate from his father, Charles) generally performs a *débourbage*, employs regular *bâtonnages*, and bottles the wines within 11 months. Most Côte de Beaune winemakers ferment their whites in oak barrels, yet Colin-Deléger (a top Chassagne-Montrachet producer) begins the process in stainless steel tanks. At Puligny-Montrachet's famed Domaine Leflaive, the reverse is true. Leflaive ferments its whites and begins their *élevage* in barrel, then transfers them to large stainless steel vats for an extended upbringing period.

Countless conversations with top white Burgundy producers has shown, however, that the most important factors in crafting a superlative wine are 1) harvesting late in order to obtain full physiological ripeness (rot is less significant a concern with Chardonnay than with Pinot Noir), 2) sorting out unripe or unhealthy grapes, 3) a long and soft pressing, 4) quality clean barrels, 5) as few rackings as possible, 6) allowing the wines to "nourish" themselves on their fine lees, and 7) not stripping the wine of its richness and fruit by excessive fining and filtration prior to bottling. Furthermore, most high-quality white Burgundies at the premier cru and grand cru levels see about 50% to 100% new oak casks, but it can be a blend of different oaks.

Will the prices for Burgundy wines ever moderate? Unfortunately, the answer to this question is no. There is always the chance that an international financial crisis could precipitate a worldwide depression that would affect a luxury item such as fine wine. For example, prices for 1991 and 1992 red Burgundies dropped by 35–50% compared with the prices of 1989s and 1990s. But prices for 1993s, 1994s, 1995s, 1996s, and 1997s soared even higher. Prices for the 1999s and 2000s have dropped in France, but importers have raised their profits for American consumers. Given growing international demand for the top-quality wines of this region, the general trend for prices in Burgundy can only be upward. While the huge quantities of wines produced in Mâconnais, Beaujolais, and Chablis may show more variation in prices, the economic prognosis for the premiers and grands crus from Burgundy's famed Côte d'Or is for frighteningly higher prices. When one considers the fact that there are only 30 grands crus, producing barely 1% of the total wine of Burgundy, the unmistakable message conveyed is that prices can only escalate. Presently, there are more purchasers of fine wine throughout the world than ever before.

The wine market has become even more competitive in the last five years with aggressive purchasing by the Japanese, Swiss, Germans, and Pacific Rim countries, especially Singapore. Japan, a relative newcomer to the world of fine wine, overtook Switzerland in 1998 as the world's largest consumer of red Burgundies in both volume *and* value. In 1998's first quarter, Japan increased its purchases of red and white Burgundies by 100% (they have tripled their share of the market since early 1997). By 2001, Japan had slowed its purchases, but remains in the top three export markets for Burgundy.

The traditional markets of England and America will have to adjust to higher and higher prices or be isolated from the Burgundy marketplace. Eastern Europe, now that the walls of communism have been torn down, offers an entirely new market. The picture is changing in France itself as well. While France has traditionally consumed oceans of wine, it has lagged behind in appreciation for its own great wines. Increasing interest from Switzerland, Germany, Belgium, Sweden, and Denmark, all with strong economies and a thirst for fine wine, has further strained the supplies of good Burgundies.

As for the generic appellation wines, they certainly will not appreciate to the extent that the premiers crus and grands crus will. However, Burgundy, much like Bordeaux, has become somewhat of a caste system for wine producers. The greatest wines from the greatest producers are able to fetch astronomical prices because there is no shortage of wealthy clients prepared to buy them. While the prices exclude most consumers and students of wine, it does encourage them to look for values in the more obscure appellations, such as Santenay, Savigny-les-Beaune, and, of course, the up-and-coming appellations of the Côte Chalonnaise. While none of these wines will ever approach the magnificent qualities of a grand cru such as Musigny or Chambertin Clos de Bèze, they still have enough Burgundy character to satisfy a great majority of even the most demanding palates.

As for the great white Burgundies, when one considers that such great grands crus as Montrachet and Chevalier-Montrachet consist of only 19.7 and 18.1 acres respectively, it seems inevitable that prices will double or even triple over the next decade. Today's connoisseur of Burgundy must be prepared either to pay a high price, or to search elsewhere for great Pinot Noir and Chardonnay.

The growth of estate-bottled Burgundies is a relatively recent phenomenon. Who was responsible for that development? Raymond Baudoin, who died in 1953, was the man responsible for encouraging some of Burgundy's best small growers, such as Ponsot in Morey St.-Denis, Rousseau in Gevrey-Chambertin, Roumier in Chambolle-Musigny, Gouges in Nuits-St.-Georges, and d'Angerville in Volnay, to estate-bottle their wines. In the 1920s Baudoin founded *Revue du Vin de France,* which to this day remains the leading French wine publication. Baudoin had lamented the fact that the great Burgundies of the Côte d'Or were sold to *négociants,* and then lost their individual identities by being blended with a large quantity of inferior wine. He began to purchase barrels of wine directly from the growers, who would estate-bottle them for him. In turn, he sold them privately to clients and restaurants in Paris.

However, it was Frank Schoonmaker, the American importer, who deserves recognition for being the first to see the potential and quality of these estate-bottled Burgundies, and to expose the American market to them. Frank Schoonmaker died in 1976, and most wine neophytes, unfortunately, are probably not familiar with the significance of his contributions. For these wine consumers, *The Frank Schoonmaker Encyclopedia of Wine,* a classic that was first published in 1964 and most recently updated by the well-known New York wine writer Alex Bespaloff in 1988, is highly recommended. This encyclopedia is only one of the legacies Frank Schoonmaker left wine enthusiasts.

In 1935 Schoonmaker and some other investors formed the importing firm of Bates and Schoonmaker (at the same time men like Frederick Wildman and Julian Street were starting merchant businesses dedicated to the sale of fine French wine and estate-bottled Burgundies).

Schoonmaker's heir apparents include Robert Haas, who founded one of America's leading companies dedicated to estate-bottled Burgundies, and the late Alexis Lichine, who in the 1960s developed the idea of purchasing wine directly from the growers, commercializing it under his own name, but also indicating the name of the grower on the label.

These gentlemen were the cornerstones of the estate-bottled Burgundy movement. The Schoonmaker selections are represented today by Château and Estate. Frederick Wildman and Company is still an import firm in New York City, as is Vineyard Brands, the company started by Robert Haas in Chester, Vermont (now located in Birmingham, Alabama). Alexis Lichine sold his wine company to the English firm of Bass-Charrington and concentrated on his beloved Château Prieuré-Lichine, which he purchased in 1951.

As more and more growers begin to domaine-bottle their wines, the recognition and promotion of estate-bottled Burgundies has never been stronger. In addition to those mentioned, the American importers of estate-bottled Burgundy include the idiosyncratic, outspoken Berkeley importer Kermit Lynch; Robert Kacher Selections in Washington, D.C.; Martine Saunier Selections in San Rafael, California; Kysela Père et Fils in Winchester, Virginia; North Berkeley Wines in Berkeley, California; Louis/Dressner Selection in New York, New York; Weygandt-Metzler in Uniontown, Pennsylvania; Kobrand, Inc., a leading importer that also owns the excellent house of Louis Jadot; and a handful of American and French specialists living and working in France, who include the Paris-based Peter Vezan, a transplanted American who is one of the world's most knowledgeable people on the subject of Burgundy. Patrick Lesec is another broker in search of handcrafted great Burgundies. He has ferreted out many top growers, whose wine he sells to importers in America, the U.K., and Europe.

Red and White Burgundy

DOMAINE BERTRAND AMBROISE (PRÉMEAUX-PRISSEY)

1997	Clos de Vougeot	EE	(90–93)
2000	Corton-Charlemagne	EE	(92–94)
1999	Corton-Charlemagne	EE	(90–91)
1998	Corton-Charlemagne	EE	(89–91+)
1997	Corton-Charlemagne	EE	(90–92)
1999	Corton Le Rognet	EE	(94–97)
1997	Corton Le Rognet	EE	(92–94+)
1997	Corton-Vergennes Cuvée Paul Chanson (Hospices de Beaune)	EE	(90–92)
2000	Ladoix Les Gréchons	D	(90–91)
1997	Nuits-St.-Georges Rue de Chaux	D	(89–91)
1999	Nuits-St.-Georges Les Vaucrains	E	(91–93)
1997	Nuits-St.-Georges Les Vaucrains	E	(91–93)
1999	Vougeot Les Cras	E	(90–93)

Bertrand Ambroise is the straight-shooting owner and wine-maker of the estate that bears his name. His wines reflect his physique and personality. They are big, muscular, boisterous, powerful, intense, yet friendly as well as immensely pleasant. Ambroise was justifiably proud of his 1997 white Burgundies. Buttered toast, vanilla beans, anise, and honeysuckle blossoms are found in the 1997 Corton-Charlemagne's nose. It is a huge, dense, oak-laden, concentrated, and extremely dense wine. Its super-spicy flavor profile is loaded with poached

pears, caramelized apples, and minerals whose flavors last throughout its exceedingly persistent finish. Projected maturity: now–2006. The 1997 Corton-Vergennes Cuvée Paul Chanson is one of those extremely rare white Burgundies crafted primarily from Pinot Blanc (20%
is Chardonnay). It reveals white and red berries, spices, and honeysuckle aromas. Sweet
white peaches, minerals, creamed nuts, and oak spices are found in this velvety, concentrated, and profound wine. Its medium to full body is concentrated, dense, and displays impeccable ripeness of fruit. Readers who are used to Alsatian Pinot Blancs will find absolutely
no similarity to this offering. In fact, I doubt most tasters would be able to discern that it is
not a typical, Chardonnay-based white Burgundy. Drink it over the next 10 years.

Domaine Ambroise's 1997 reds are intense, packed with fruit, and powerful. The 1997
Nuits-St.-Georges Rue de Chaux is medium to dark ruby-colored, and boasts an exuberant,
black fruit-dominated nose. In its youthful state, it is more reminiscent of a top-flight Syrah
from the Northern Rhône than the Côte d'Or. Tar, cassis, and spices coat the taster's mouth in
this dense, medium- to full-bodied, powerful, masculine wine. Its thick-textured, intense
personality abandons any pretense of subtlety in favor of exuberance and power. Drink it over
the next 6–7 years. The dark-colored and superripe 1997 Nuits-St.-Georges Les Vaucrains
possesses a fresh nose of suave black fruits. This satin-textured, broad, structured wine is
reminiscent of blackberries, prunes, and figs, pureed in a blender. Medium- to full-bodied,
thick, and extremely ripe, it is a dense, in-your-face Pinot. Anticipated maturity:
now–2005+. The medium to dark ruby-colored 1997 Clos de Vougeot's nose is composed of
overripe red fruit aromas. This fat, verging on flabby, hyperdense, thick, and medium- to full-
bodied wine is not one to lay away in the cellar. Jellied cherries, blackberries, and cumin-
like spices are found in this *sur-maturité*-laced, slightly warm offering. It is hedonism
incarnate, opulent, sensual, and a wine that will require drinking in the short term. Anticipated maturity: now–2004. The dark, verging on black 1997 Corton Le Rognet reveals
roasted, stone, earth, licorice, blackberry, and road tar aromas. Superripe, yet not overripe
like the Clos de Vougeot, it saturates the palate with its powerful, dark flavors. This massive
Pinot Noir nectar is full-bodied, oily-textured, and possesses immensely sweet and ripe tannins. Anticipated maturity: now–2010.

Bertrand Ambroise's 1998 Corton-Charlemagne is a big success for the vintage. Harvested
at 13% natural potential alcohol, it displays a floral, spice-laden nose. This broad, concentrated, expressive, and intense wine is medium- to full-bodied and has an extremely long,
well-focused finish. Liquid minerals, anise, and ripe pears can be discerned throughout its
extensive personality. Anticipated maturity: now–2009.

Hints of toast can be detected in the deep, rich, white fruit–dominated aromas of the 1999
Corton-Charlemagne. This concentrated, broad, juicy, medium-bodied wine has outstanding
depth and a powerful, mineral-dominated flavor profile. It is pure, detailed, well-delineated,
and finishes with a long, lemon-flavored finish. Drink it over the next 6–7 years.

The outstanding 1999 Nuits-St.-Georges Les Vaucrains is a medium to dark ruby-colored
wine with intense black cherry and blackberry aromas. It is hugely dense, expansive, and
medium- to full-bodied. Massive layers of black fruits, cookie dough, and Asian spices can
be found in its satin-textured, pure, and delineated personality, as well as throughout its impressively long finish. Anticipated maturity: 2003–2010. The medium to dark ruby-colored
1999 Vougeot Les Cras may be the finest Vougeot tasted to date. It has an immensely appealing, deep nose of blackberries, spices, and currants. On the palate, this outstanding wine regales the taster with candied plums, sweet cherries, and notes of pomegranate. It is
satin-textured, lush, and forward, yet has the requisite structure for cellaring. Drink it over
the next 10 years. The intense, black-colored 1999 Corton Le Rognet reveals black fruit,
fresh herb, and Asian spice aromas. In 1999, however, Ambroise harvested 40 hectoliters per
hectare at 14.5% natural potential alcohol. This is a monster of a wine, crammed with blackberries, road tar, cherries, kirsch, and a myriad of spices. Its loads of exquisitely ripened tan-

nins are soaked in sweet, candied fruits. This powerful, chewy offering coats the taster's palate and lasts for almost a minute. It is, at present, unformed, yet will become civilized with cellaring. Anticipated maturity: 2006–2014+.

Ambroise's premier cru Ladoix Les Gréchons is consistently one of the finest values to be found in white Burgundies. The 2000 displays loads of spicy minerals intermingled with fresh thyme in its aromatics. It is medium to full-bodied, chewy, and velvety-textured. This concentrated, deep wine is broad and exhibits copious amounts of gravel, toasted nuts, butter, stones, and poached pears. It is a big wine, particularly for the vintage, yet reveals excellent balance and a harmonious character. Drink it over the next 8 years. Harvested at over 14% natural potential alcohol, the 2000 Corton-Charlemagne is unquestionably an outstanding wine. It bursts from the glass with loads of apples, spices, and toast scents. This intense, medium- to full-bodied, chewy-textured wine is crammed with apple pulp, pears, lemons, and copious quantities of spices. It is an opulent wine with a zesty personality. Anticipated maturity: 2004–2012.

Other recommended wines: 2000 Bourgogne Chardonnay (87–89), 2000 Bourgogne Hautes Côtes de Nuits (87–89), 1997 Chassagne-Montrachet La Maltroie (white) (88–90), 1997 Côte de Nuits-Villages (88–89), 1999 Côte de Nuits-Villages (88+), 1998 Ladoix Les Gréchons (88), 1999 Ladoix Les Gréchons (88–90), 1997 Meursault Charmes Cuvée Albert Grivault (Hospices de Beaune) (88–90), 2000 Meursault Poruzots (88–90), 1997 Nuits-St.-Georges (88–89), 1999 Nuits-St.-Georges Clos des Argillières (88–90), 1999 Nuits-St.-Georges en Rue de Chaux (88–90), 1999 Nuits-St.-Georges Vieilles Vignes (88–90), 2000 St.-Aubin Murgers des Dents de Chiens (88–89), 1998 St.-Romain (88), 1997 Vougeot Les Cras (89–90).

DOMAINE GUY AMIOT ET FILS (CHASSAGNE–MONTRACHET)

2000	Chassagne-Montrachet Les Caillerets	E	(89–91)
1999	Chassagne-Montrachet Les Caillerets	E	91+
1997	Chassagne-Montrachet Les Caillerets	E	90
2000	Chassagne-Montrachet Clos St.-Jean	E	(89–91)
1999	Chassagne-Montrachet Les Vergers	E	90
2000	Montrachet	EEE	(90–92+)
1999	Montrachet	EEE	94+
1998	Montrachet	EEE	90+
1997	Montrachet	EEE	95
1997	Puligny–Montrachet Les Demoiselles	EE	93

Guy Amiot, one of Chassagne-Montrachet's most talented producers, is an honest, straightforward man. When I asked him about acidification practices, he replied that he was against the procedure but had been compelled to acidify one-third of his *cuves* (vats). "I was criticized for the 1989s that did not age," he said. I heard this same complaint in a number of cellars—"Consumers want fully ripe fruit, they want ageworthy wines, yet they complain if we acidify to provide the necessary balance for cellaring," went the refrain. I cannot blame Burgundy producers who hear their customers complaints while noting that acidified Californian and Australian Chardonnays sell without similar concerns about their "artificial" equilibriums being expressed. However, experience suggests that acidified whites do not age gracefully. White Burgundies from near-term drinking vintages have their place. The 1989s, 1992s, 1994s, and the 1997s were fabulous wines to consume immediately upon their release. Is it not better to drink a wine when it is at its most pleasurable than to drink a tightly wound white or a tannic red years before it is ready?

Amiot says that the vines in his parcel of Chassagne-Montrachet Les Caillerets produce the "old-style" tiny berries whose juice is more concentrated and intense than what comes from the "newer-styled" vines. His 1997 has a gorgeous nose of flowers, minerals, stones, and peaches. This wine is medium- to full-bodied, silky, and austere (yet rich, broad, and thick). Chalk, flint, and minerals dominate its well-focused personality. Anticipated maturity: now–2007. The 1997 Puligny-Montrachet Les Demoiselles has floral, red berry, and mineral aromas that give way to an extracted, concentrated, and layered character. This rich, deep, well-balanced, and medium- to full-bodied wine has magnificent flavors of nuts, stones, and chalk. It is an intricate offering, combining power with detail and opulence with elegance. Anticipated maturity: now–2008. The profound nose of the 1997 Montrachet displays peaches, apricots, minerals, and buttered toast. This grand vin is full-bodied, admirably dense, intensely expressive, and conquers the palate with massive, oily waves of dried honey, hazelnut paste, chestnut cream, toasty minerals, grilled oak, and superripe white fruits. It is liquid decadence, a hedonistic fruit bomb, and as awesome a near-term drinking Montrachet as I can imagine. Drink it over the next 8–9 years.

The 1998 Montrachet was difficult to assess. Its aromas, composed of expressive buttered toast and creamy minerals, are outstanding. On the palate, it exhibits intensity, power, concentration, and focus. Lemons, minerals, and crisp green apples can be found throughout its flavor profile and exceedingly long finish. As this wine harmonizes and gains richness in the bottle, it will merit an even more exalted review. Anticipated maturity: 2003–2010.

The 1999 Chassagne-Montrachet Les Vergers (from 55- to 60-year old vines) reveals pear and flower aromas. Its medium-bodied personality displays gorgeous purity to its focused, crystalline, precise, and crisp character. It possesses powerful mineral flavors that last throughout its personality as well as its admirably long, pure finish. Anticipated maturity: now–2009. The 1999 Chassagne-Montrachet Les Caillerets has intense mineral and stone aromatics. Medium-bodied, masculine, and concentrated, this is a satin-textured, chewy wine. It coats the palate with layer upon layer of minerals, pears, and gravel. It is a stunning 1999 in that it combines the vintage's supple, pleasing mouth feel with depth, power, and length. Anticipated maturity: now–2010. The stupendous 1999 Montrachet has powerful spice, nut, and pear aromas. Medium- to full-bodied, intense, fat, and rich, this is a broad, lush, powerful wine. Its juicy flavor profile, composed of almond liqueur, quartz, minerals, and fresh pears as well as apples, lasts an exceedingly long time. This is a crystalline yet plump wine with excellent balance, focus, and muscle. Unquestionably one of the finest wines of the vintage, it should be at its peak between 2003–2012.

Other recommended wines: 1997 Chassagne-Montrachet Clos St.-Jean (89), 1999 Chassagne-Montrachet Clos St.-Jean (88), 1997 Chassagne-Montrachet Les Vergers (88+), 1998 Chassagne-Montrachet Les Vergers (89), 2000 Chassagne-Montrachet Les Vergers (89), 1998 Puligny-Montrachet Les Demoiselles (89), 1999 Puligny-Montrachet Les Demoiselles (89)

DOMAINE DU MARQUIS D'ANGERVILLE (VOLNAY)

1999	Volnay Clos des Ducs	D	(91–94)
1997	Volnay Clos des Ducs	E	(90–93+)
1999	Volnay Taillepieds	D	(91–93+)
1997	Volnay Taillepieds	E	(90–92)

The Marquis d'Angerville is one of Burgundy's deans, having witnessed numerous vintages throughout his career. When asked to rate the red wine vintages of the 1990s, he placed 1990 first, followed by a tie between 1999 and 1996, then 1997, 1995, 1992, 1991, 1993, and 1994. When I pointed out that 1998 was missing from the list, he hunched his shoulders and said, "We do not yet know 1998's fate, will it dry out or will it be good?" He says that 1999 "will age well, even though we did not think so early on; I now believe they will act like the 1989s." D'Angerville's 1989s, like many Volnays from the top producers (I've recently tasted some from Pousse d'Or, Comte Lafon, and Lafarge) are surprisingly youthful, fruit-packed, and fresh. "In 1989," he continued, "the best wines came from the lowest yields and the oldest vineyards. The same will be true in 1999."

This famed estate crafted wines in the difficult 1997 vintage that should age remarkably well. Aromatically, the medium to dark ruby-colored 1997 Volnay Taillepieds offers dark plums, violets, and candied black cherries. It is an expansive, medium- to full-bodied wine with great concentration, breadth, and richness and is thick, satin-textured, muscular, and well-structured. Stones, black fruits, and fresh herbs can be found in its fresh yet plump flavor profile. Drink it over the next 7+ years. The slightly darker colored 1997 Volnay Clos des Ducs displays super aromas of soy sauce, hoisin, and spices. This powerful yet elegant wine is jam-packed with sweet black fruits, flowers, stones, and herbs. A powerful, complex, and complete wine, it should be drunk over the next dozen years.

The outstanding 1999 Volnay Taillepieds has zesty dark fruit aromas. It is medium- to full-bodied, ample, broad, and packed with copious amounts of jammy and juicy plums, black currants, Asian spices, and black cherries. This is a powerful yet refined, seamless wine with prodigiously ripened tannin. Its finish is long, silky, and pure. Drink it over the next 10 years.

Produced from the Marquis d'Angerville's 2-hectare parcel, the 1999 Volnay Clos Des Ducs has a marvelous nose of Bing cherries, kirsch, worello cherries, and violets. This wine is medium- to full-bodied, gorgeously balanced, and possesses outstanding depth of velvety-textured fruit. It coats the taster's palate with cherries and blackberries, blueberries, flowers, and spices whose flavors last throughout its extraordinarily long, pure, and silky finish. This harmonious, refined beauty has copious amounts of superripe tannin that can be discerned under its waves of fruit. It has the density, balance, and structure for mid- to long-term cellaring. Anticipated maturity: 2005–2012+.

Other recommended wines: 1997 Volnay Champans (88–90), 1999 Volnay Champans (88–90), 1997 Volnay Premier Cru (labeled as Fremiets outside the U.S.) (88–89)

DOMAINE HERVÉ ARLAUD PÈRE ET FILS (NUITS-ST.-GEORGES)

1999 Bonnes Mares Cuvée Unique	EEE	91
1997 Bonnes Mares Réserve	EEE	93
1997 Charmes-Chambertin Réserve	EE	92
1998 Clos St.-Denis Réserve	EEE	91
1997 Clos St.-Denis Réserve	EEE	92
1997 Gevrey-Chambertin Les Combottes Réserve	E	90+

Note: These special "Cuvée Unique" and "Réserve" cuvées are prepared by the estate in collaboration with Peter Vezan and David Hinkle exclusively for the U.S. market.

The 1997 Gevrey-Chambertin Les Combottes Réserve reveals some cloudiness in its otherwise ruby-colored robe (a natural occurrence in some unfined/unfiltered wines). Aromatic of sweet cherries, white pepper, and red berries, this powerful, intense wine saturates the palate with copious quantities of *sur-maturité*-laced red and black fruit compotes as well as spices. It has outstanding structure, a velvety texture, and an opulent mouth-feel. It will merit an even higher score if it absorbs some of its lofty alcohol with cellaring. Anticipated maturity: now–2007. According to Peter Vezan, the estate's broker, Arlaud bottled his 1997 Charmes-Chambertin Réserve only 10 months after the vintage in order to preserve all of its lush fruit. Fresh herbs and blackberry aromas are discernible in the nose of this medium to dark ruby-colored wine. It is concentrated, medium- to full-bodied, luscious, and crammed with decadent layers of licorice, asphalt, and blackberry jam. Drink this soft, enormously pleasing wine over the next 5–6 years.

The ruby/purple 1997 Clos St.-Denis Réserve boasts deeply sweet cassis, cinnamon, and oak aromas. This spicy, huge, satin-textured, and luxuriant wine is packed with jellied strawberry and cherry flavors. Medium- to full-bodied, with good structure and length, it is a sexy, sensual, and luscious mouthful. Drink it over the next 6–7 years. The ruby/purple 1997 Bonnes Mares reveals juniper berry, clove, and red fruit scents. It is sultry, luscious, expansive, complex, and a more masculine wine than the Clos St.-Denis. Baked red fruits, stones, tar, and grilled oak flavors are found throughout its oily-textured core and impressively long finish. This medium- to full-bodied beauty delivers both hedonistic pleasure as well as intellectual gratification. Drink it over the next 7 years.

The ruby-colored 1998 Clos St.-Denis Réserve reveals an oaky, smoked bacon–scented nose. Medium- to full-bodied and opulently textured, this is a dense, well-focused, spicy, sweet cherry syrup–flavored wine. Fresh and exceptionally long in the finish, it does not display any of the vintage's characteristic hardness. It is well constituted and concentrated, and a delight to drink. Anticipated maturity: now–2006.

The outstanding medium to dark ruby-colored 1999 Bonnes Mares Cuvée Unique has sweet raspberry and cherry aromas. Medium-bodied and lush, it is the freshest and most harmonious of Arlaud's 1999s. Its flavor profile is crammed with gorgeous layers of dark cherries and candied raspberries. This well-made, satin-textured wine possesses a long, supple, sweet finish. Drink it over the next 8–9 years.

Other recommended wines: 1997 Chambolle-Musigny Vieilles Vignes Réserve (88), 1999 Charmes-Chambertin Cuvée Unique (88?), 1997 Clos de la Roche Réserve (89), 1999 Clos de la Roche Cuvée Unique (88?), 1999 Clos St.-Denis Cuvée Unique (88+), 1997 Morey-St.-Denis Les Chézeaux Réserve (88), 1997 Morey-St.-Denis Les Ruchots Réserve (89+), 1998 Morey-St.-Denis Les Ruchots Réserve (89), 1999 Morey-St.-Denis Les Ruchots Cuvée Unique (88+)

DOMAINE DE L'ARLOT (PRÉMEAUX-PRISSEY)

1999 Nuits-St.-Georges Clos des Forêts St.-Georges	E	(89–92)
1997 Nuits-St.-Georges Clos des Forêts St.-Georges	D	90+
1999 Romanée-St.-Vivant	EEE	(89–91)
1997 Romanée-St.-Vivant	EE	90

Jean-Pierre de Smet, the engaging director and wine-maker of this estate, described the 1997 vintage as "more pleasant and immediately gratifying than 1996, but it is not a great year, like the exceptional 1996 vintage will prove to be." Kudos to de Smet for putting his money where his mouth is. Upon sharing with me his opinion of the 1997s, he informed me that he had lowered the estate's prices to reflect the quality of its wines.

The medium to dark ruby-colored 1997 Nuits-St.-Georges Clos des Forêts St.-Georges displays gorgeous aromas of creamed dark cherries and talcum powder. It boasts a rich mouthful of suave black fruits, hints of tar, and grilled oak. This refined, medium- to full-bodied, juicy, and well-structured offering will be at its best if consumed over the next 7 years. The ruby-colored 1997 Romanée-St.-Vivant reveals aromas reminiscent of roses, violets, earth, and red berries. It is a seductive, broad, rich, and supple wine, with delicious, well-delineated red and dark fruit flavors. Crafted in an extremely detail-oriented, lacy style, this is a feminine offering. Anticipated maturity: now–2007.

Domaine de l'Arlot has averaged 34 hectoliters per hectare over the past 12 years, yet it produced 52 hectoliters (under 50 for the reds) in 1999, "and that's a real number, as we didn't bleed tanks, we had nothing to sort out, and we didn't leave any grapes behind in the vineyard," he added. Like many vignerons, de Smet felt his 1999s had immensely improved with *élevage*. "A year ago I found them heavy, but they have become focused and refined with time," he said.

The aromatically expressive, medium ruby-colored 1999 Nuits-St.-Georges Clos des Forêts St.-Georges has a nose of black currants and licorice. It is medium-bodied, dense, and has an outstanding depth of fruit to its blackberry, cherry, and oak-laced personality. This wine is satin-textured, rich, and persistent in the finish. Drink it over the next 9 years. The ruby-colored 1999 Romanée-St.-Vivant has a beguiling nose of violets, perfume, and sweet cherries. This elegant, feminine, highly detailed wine is light- to medium-bodied and displays red berry and floral flavors. Its firm finish does not detract from this classy offering's beautifully delineated and flavorful core. Drink it over the next 10 years.

Other recommended wines: 1999 Côte de Nuits-Villages Clos du Chapeau (88), 1997 Nuits-St.-Georges Clos de l'Arlot (88), 1997 Nuits-St.-Georges Clos de l'Arlot (white) (89), 1999 Nuits-St.-Georges Clos de l'Arlot (87–89), 1999 Nuits-St.-Georges Premier Cru (88–89), 1997 Vosne-Romanée Les Suchots (89), 1999 Vosne-Romanée Les Suchots (87–88)

DOMAINE ROBERT ARNOUX (VOSNE-ROMANÉE)

1999	Clos de Vougeot	EE	94
1998	Clos de Vougeot	EE	91
1999	Echézeaux	EE	91
1999	Romanée-St.-Vivant	EEE	91
1998	Romanée-St.-Vivant	EEE	93
1999	Vosne-Romanée Les Chaumes	E	90
1999	Vosne-Romanée aux Reignots	EE	92
1998	Vosne-Romanée aux Reignots	EE	90
1999	Vosne-Romanée Les Suchots	EE	93
1998	Vosne-Romanée Les Suchots	EE	93

This estate, which has been run by Pascal Laschaux since the death of his father-in-law, Robert Arnoux, is on fire. Its vineyard work and winemaking has never been better, a testimony to Laschaux's dedication and attention to detail. Formerly a pharmacist, Laschaux is young, dynamic, and extremely conscientious.

This estate fashioned some of the finest 1998s. Ripe red fruits jump from the glass of the 1998 Vosne-Romanée Aux Reignots. This medium-bodied, complex, palate-coating wine is concentrated, deep, and luscious. Sweet candied cherries are found throughout its supple character and long finish. Aged in 80% new oak barrels, the 1998 Clos de Vougeot has floral and raspberry/cherry fruit scents. Medium-bodied and satin-textured, it is a well-made, expressive, and concentrated wine. Fresh red fruits vie with oak spices for the taster's attention. Anticipated maturity: now–2008.

The medium to dark ruby-colored 1998 Vosne-Romanée Les Suchots has gorgeous oak-covered cherry aromas. Medium- to full-bodied and broad, this hedonistic wine coats the palate with creamed cherries. It has excellent structure (with its tannins buried in deep layers of fruit) and a long, silky, pure finish. Anticipated maturity: now–2008. The 1998 Romanée-St.-Vivant has a nose reminiscent of perfume, red flowers, spices, and white pepper. Medium- to full-bodied, and possessing outstanding depth, concentration, and elegance to its chewy-textured character, this is a jammy, red fruit–packed wine. Anticipated maturity: now–2010.

The medium to dark ruby-colored 1999 Vosne-Romanée Les Chaumes has cherry, raspberry, and fresh herb aromas. Medium-bodied and dense, this is a chewy, silky-textured wine with sweet, fresh red cherry flavors. It possesses loads of supple tannin, discernible in its long finish. Drink it over the next 7–8 years. The 1999 Vosne-Romanée aux Reignots is medium to dark ruby-colored and has a beguiling violet and perfume-scented nose. Medium-bodied, broad, and ample, this is a rich, opulent, cherry-flavored wine. It is thick, concentrated, harmonious, and seamless. Anticipated maturity: 2003–2010.

The ruby-colored and herbal, berry-scented 1999 Echézeaux has a lush, medium-bodied personality, outstanding harmony, and gorgeously defined flavors of flowers, red berries, and blueberries, whose flavors last throughout its long, pure finish. Anticipated maturity: now–2010. The medium to dark ruby-colored 1999 Clos de Vougeot, produced from 35–40 hectoliters per hectare yields, has a superb nose of superripe cherries, Asian spices, violets, and perfume. It is medium-bodied, sexy, and opulent. Copious quantities of *sur-maturité*-laced cherries, raspberries, and strawberries can be found throughout this sweet, penetrating, and lively wine. It has no hard edges to its seamless, full-flavored character. Anticipated maturity: 2004–2012.

The smoked bacon, violet, and blackberry-scented 1999 Vosne-Romanée Les Suchots has a medium to dark ruby color. It is medium-bodied, crammed with dense layers of blackberries, cherries, spices, and candied raspberries. This rich, concentrated, intense, chewy wine offers an admirably long, lush, fruit-filled finish. Drink it over the next decade. The medium to dark ruby-colored 1999 Romanée-St.-Vivant exhibits violet and blackberry aromas. This medium- to full-bodied wine is rich and flavorful, loaded with cherries, raspberries, blueberries, and juicy, superripe blackberries. It appeared to lack the exquisite harmony of this estate's finest 1999s, but it had been bottled only 72 hours prior to being tasted, which may well account for an ever-so-slight disjointedness. Anticipated maturity: 2004–2011.

Other recommended wines: 1999 Nuits-St.-Georges Corvées Pagets (89), 1999 Nuits-St.-Georges Les Procès (88), 1999 Nuits-St.-Georges Les Poisets (89), 1999 Vosne-Romanée Les Hautes Maizières (89)

DOMAINE D'AUVENAY (ST.-ROMAIN)

1999 Auxey-Duresses Les Boutonniers (white)	E	90
1997 Auxey-Duresses Les Boutonniers (white)	E	92
1999 Bonnes Mares	EEE	93+
1997 Bonnes Mares	EEE	94
2000 Chevalier-Montrachet	EEE	(91–92)
1999 Chevalier-Montrachet	EEE	93
1997 Chevalier-Montrachet	EEE	96
2000 Criots-Bâtard-Montrachet	EEE	(92–94)
1999 Criots-Bâtard-Montrachet	EEE	93
1997 Criots-Bâtard-Montrachet	EEE	93?
1999 Mazis-Chambertin	EEE	95
1997 Mazis-Chambertin	EEE	95+
2000 Meursault La Goutte d'Or	EEE	(92–93)
1999 Meursault La Goutte d'Or	EEE	91+
1997 Meursault La Goutte d'Or	EEE	93
2000 Meursault Narvaux	EE	(90–92)
1999 Meursault Narvaux	EE	90
1997 Meursault Narvaux	EE	92+
2000 Puligny-Montrachet Les Folatières	EEE	(90–91)
1999 Puligny-Montrachet Les Folatières	EEE	90
1997 Puligny-Montrachet Les Folatières	EEE	91
2000 Puligny-Montrachet La Richarde	EEE	(90–92)

Madame Lalou Bize-Leroy's privately owned estate Domaine d'Auvenay is not only one of Burgundy's most beautiful addresses, it also the source of many of its top wines. To nobody's surprise, Mme Bize-Leroy crafted extraordinary wines in 1997. She loves the 1997 vintage for both red and white wines. "These are distinguished and intellectual wines," she insisted. In fact, she feels her reds are *more* complex than her 1996s. Her 1997 whites are magnificent wines (as are her reds), impeccably balanced (she ferociously maintains that she does not acidify her wines—rumors to the contrary are omnipresent) and immensely rich. Their colors reflect traces of straw and gold, unlike the pale, virtually crystal clear 1996s.

Produced from a parcel planted in 1922, the powerful 1997 Auxey-Duresses Les Boutonniers has a chalk and rock dust–scented nose. Its explodes on the palate with intense liquid mineral flavors intermingled with juicy squirts of lemon juice. This medium- to full-bodied, dense, and magnificently defined wine has huge concentration, depth, and complexity. Drink it between now–2008. The 1997 Meursault Narvaux displays an oak-imbued and rich white fruit–laden nose. This massive, thick, chewy, and medium- to full-bodied offering is crammed with expansive metal, mineral, and hazelnut flavors. This beauty should be at its peak between now–2008.

Revealing fresh aromas of superripe fruits, the 1997 Meursault La Goutte d'Or is oily-textured and exuberant yet focused. This powerful, muscular, and full-bodied wine coats the palate with sweet pears, caramelized apples, candied oranges, minerals, hazelnut cream, and hints of quince. Anticipated maturity: now–2008. The 1997 Puligny-Montrachet Les Folatières's nose is less boisterous than those of the previous wines. It expresses sweet floral and earthy aromas followed by a fat, almost unctuously textured personality. This superb wine is redolent with layers of earth, acacia blossom, white truffles, and peaches. It does not appear to be as extraordinarily well balanced as her other offerings. It should be consumed between now–2005.

Mme Bize-Leroy's 1997 Criots-Bâtard-Montrachet, produced from a parcel on the vineyard's eastern extremity, has baked pear and apple aromas intermingled with spices. This is a profound, well-focused, and deeply ripe wine with flavors of marzipan, minerals, peanuts, and white flowers. It is medium- to full-bodied, forward, superexpressive, yet possibly revealing faint traces of oxidation. Nonetheless, it is so extraordinarily flavorful and muscular that I highly recommend it. Try it soon to see how it is evolving. The 1997 Chevalier-Montrachet is certainly one of the stars of the vintage. Aromatically, it reveals rocks, stones, and salty seashells. This magnificent masterpiece has unheard-of intensity, ripeness, and focus. Its overpowering minerality is gorgeously precise, revealing traces of anise, pears, and oak spices that last throughout the stupendous finish. Drink it between 2004–2012.

The dark ruby/purple 1997 Bonnes Mares exhibits deep aromas of baked plums, blackberries, and sealing wax. It is a thick, full-bodied, jammy wine with plump layers of roasted dark fruits and hints of leather and stones. While opulent, intense, and powerful, this wine is also somehow tightly wound and well structured. Its almost overripe character expresses itself in a thick, verging on waxy, texture. It is super to drink now, yet should hold for a dozen or more years. Surprisingly, given past experiences with Domaine d'Auvenay's Mazis-Chambertin, the 1997 is more forward, opulent, and luxuriant than the Bonnes Mares. Furthermore, this dark, almost black-colored effort it is more red fruit–dominated. It displays jammy and waxy cherry fruit scents. Its concentrated, rich, deep, and intensely sweet character is crammed with red fruits galore. This velvety-textured wine's amazingly long finish reveals superbly ripe, supple tannins. An extraordinary effort in any vintage, in this irregular one, it stands as a testimony to Leroy's immense talents and dedication. Anticipated maturity: now–2014+.

Produced from vines planted in 1923, the 1999 Auxey-Duresses Les Boutonniers exhibits limestone aromas. It is expressive, has outstanding purity and precision to its well-focused and deep personality, and is packed with lemon-infused minerals whose flavors last throughout its extensive finish. Anticipated maturity: now–2007. The mineral- and stone-scented 1999 Meursault Narvaux is light- to medium-bodied, concentrated, and refined. It has outstanding depth to its stone, pear, and mineral flavored personality, as well as an extremely long, pure finish. Anticipated maturity: now–2008.

The rich 1999 Meursault La Goutte d'Or displays aromas of fresh butter, ripe apples, and cream. It is plump, satin-textured, and offers thick layers of white fruits and spices. This is a powerful, medium-bodied wine with an impressively long finish. Anticipated maturity: now–2010. The 1999 Puligny-Montrachet Les Folatières is more demure aromatically yet richer and deeper on the palate. Medium-bodied and plump, it coats the palate with minerals, flowers, and spices that lead seamlessly to its admirably long finish. Anticipated maturity: now–2009.

The 1999 Criots-Bâtard-Montrachet has powerful mineral aromas. This oily-textured wine is thick, fat, and dense yet remains elegant and focused. It is harmonious, muscular, and has an intense mineral-laden core whose flavors are maintained throughout its extraordinarily long finish. Anticipated maturity: now–2014. The highly expressive nose of the 1999 Chevalier-Montrachet displays limestone and mineral aromas. Medium-bodied and satin-textured, it is crammed with stones, gravel, metal, pear, and candied citrus flavors. This intense, concentrated wine possesses superb purity, delineation, and richness. Anticipated maturity: now–2014.

The medium to dark ruby-colored 1999 Bonnes Mares reveals toasted almond, blackberry, and floral aromas. This plum, licorice, and cherry-flavored wine is medium- to full-bodied, highly structured, fresh, and precise. It coats the palate with compelling layers of sweet, dark flavors, as well as loads of ripe yet firm tannins. It also possesses an extraordinarily long finish. Anticipated maturity: 2004–2015+. The slightly darker-colored 1999 Mazis-Chambertin has an awesome nose that reveals violets, intense blackberries, and sweet cherries. This deep, profound wine has admirable focus, great purity, harmony, and a mind-bogglingly long finish. Loads of tangy morello cherries can be found throughout this exceptional wine's character. It is powerful, elegant, and extroverted. Anticipated maturity: 2006–2018+.

To Lalou Bize-Leroy, 2000 is "a special vintage. It reminds me of 1996, but with lower acidity. I like them particularly when estates did the necessary work to keep yields in the moderate range." Bize-Leroy did not have to chaptalize any of her 2000 whites (whereas she did the reds), even though she harvested extremely early, having obtained permission to pick her grapes before the official starting date (*ban de vendange*). When the massive storm of September 12, 2000, blanketed the region, Mme Bize-Leroy had just ended harvesting.

Intense spice and mineral aromas can be found in the aromatics of the 2000 Meursault Narvaux. Medium-bodied and intense, this is a zesty yet lush wine, crammed with fresh pear, lemon, and spice flavors. It has outstanding depth and a bright acid streak that runs uninhibited from the attack through this wine's persistent finish. Anticipated maturity: now–2012.

The stunning 2000 Meursault La Goutte d'Or detonates from the glass with hyperripe spicy pear and white peach aromas. Rich, plush, and fat, this is a medium- to full-bodied wine that exhibits pear, oak, and minerals galore. It is opulent and sports an extraordinarily long, pure, fruit-laden finish. Drink it over the next 12 years. The pear and white flower–scented 2000 Puligny-Montrachet Les Folatières has a medium-bodied personality crammed with toasted minerals. This silky-textured wine is concentrated, well balanced, and exuberantly flavored. Drink it over the next 9–10 years.

The 2000 Puligny-Montrachet La Richarde (from a parcel that used to be part of the premier cru Les Folatières but was recently declassified, as it was learned that the previous owner had added topsoil to it) is a mineral, earth, and white flower–scented wine. Richly opulent, this medium-bodied, lush offering presents minerals and buttered toast–like flavors in its velvety yet zesty character. Drink it over the next 10 years.

Creamy minerals and vanilla yogurt can be found in the aromatics of the 2000 Chevalier-Montrachet. Medium-bodied, it has a sultry, silky texture, a mineral-laden personality, and a broad yet vivacious character. Additionally, this wine reveals a long and pure finish. Anticipated maturity: now–2014. The 2000 Criots-Bâtard-Montrachet bursts from the glass with intense toast, mineral, and smoke aromas. This plush, medium-bodied wine offers layers of spicy minerals, buttered toast, and creamy pears in its deep, satin-textured, and persistent flavor profile. Anticipated maturity: now–2014.

Other recommended wines: 1997 Auxey-Duresses (91), 1999 Auxey-Duresses (89), 2000 Auxey-Duresses (89–90), 2000 Auxey-Duresses Les Boutonniers (89–90), 1997 Auxey-Duresses Les Clous (91), 1999 Auxey-Duresses Les Clous (88), 2000 Auxey-Duresses Les Clous (88–89), 1997 Bourgogne Aligoté Sous Chatelet (88), 1999 Bourgogne Aligoté Sous Chatelet (88), 2000 Bourgogne Aligoté Sous Chatelet (88–90), 1999 Meursault Chaumes de

Perrières (89), 2000 Meursault Chaumes de Perrières (89–90), 2000 Meursault Pré de Manche (89–90), 1999 Puligny-Montrachet La Richarde (89)

DOMAINE DANIEL ET MARTINE BARRAUD (VERGISSON)

1997	Pouilly-Fuissé Cuvée Vieilles Vignes	D	90
2000	Pouilly-Fuissé En Bulands Vieilles Vignes	D	(92–94)
1999	Pouilly-Fuissé En Bulands Vieilles Vignes	D	90
1998	Pouilly-Fuissé En Bulands Vieilles Vignes	D	90
1997	Pouilly-Fuissé En Bulands Vieilles Vignes Réserve	D	94+
2000	Pouilly-Fuissé Les Crays Vieilles Vignes	D	92
1999	Pouilly-Fuissé Les Crays Vieilles Vignes	D	91
1998	Pouilly-Fuissé Les Crays Vieilles Vignes	D	90
1997	Pouilly-Fuissé Les Crays Vieilles Vignes Réserve	D	94
2000	Pouilly-Fuissé La Roche	D	90
1997	Pouilly-Fuissé La Roche	D	91+
1997	Pouilly-Fuissé La Verchère Réserve	D	91
2000	Pouilly-Fuissé La Verchère Vieilles Vignes	D	90
1999	St.-Véran Les Pommards Réserve	D	90+
1997	St.-Véran Les Pommards Réserve	D	91

Note: In the 1997 vintage, wines marked "Réserve" are special unfined and unfiltered cuvées crafted with and for David Hinkle and Peter Vezan for the U.S. market.

Daniel Barraud can step out of his home each day, look at the neighboring hill, and see the residence of his good friend and fellow winemaking genius Jean-Marie Guffens. Both these men—with the crucial assistance of their wives—are crafting superlative wines that equal or surpass the finest offerings of the Côte de Beaune's grand cru vineyards. Barraud feels 1997 was his greatest harvest to date. The huge heat of August actually slowed maturation as the vines shut down in self-defense. Malic acid levels dropped, yet overall acidity levels were maintained. "Certain wines actually have the same acidity levels as the 1996s," said Barraud. He stretched the harvest for almost three weeks, starting on September 12 and ending on the 30th. "The heat was intense, but we were not worried because we studied the parcels. We took our time and I believe we harvested each parcel at the optimal moment. It was a wonderful Indian summer!"

The 1997 Pouilly-Fuissé La Roche reveals stone, quinine, flint, and toasted oak aromas. On the palate, this medium- to full-bodied, oily-textured, impeccably focused, and hugely expressive wine is filled with crisp peach, pear, and liquid mineral flavors. This boldly ripe yet superbly balanced wine has the capacity to age marvelously. Anticipated maturity: now–2007. Produced from 45- to 65-year-old vines located in the En Bulands, Les Crays, and Les Vignes Dessus vineyards, the 1997 Pouilly-Fuissé Cuvée Vieilles Vignes has a creamy, salty nose and an intensely ripe, concentrated candied lemon and chalk-flavored character. This medium- to full-bodied wine was aged in 50–60% new oak barrels, yet the wood is barely noticeable. Anticipated maturity: now–2005.

The 1997 St. Véran Les Pommards Réserve is certainly one of the finest wines I have tasted from this picturesque village. Its fresh nose of minerals and earth leads to an awesomely ripe character replete with peaches, pears, quince, and stones. This medium- to full-bodied offering's opulently thick texture and *sur-maturité* flavors do not prevent this wine from being bone dry, as evidenced by the long and mineral-laden finish. It should be at its peak between now–2006. Displaying aromas reminiscent of buttered toast, smoke, and chalk, the 1997 Pouilly-Fuissé La Verchère Réserve is an elegant, precise, yet dense wine. It is velvety-textured, medium- to full-bodied, with a concentrated core of white fruits and flint. Offering admirable balance, purity, and structure, it doesn't possess the previous wine's density or power, but rather has refinement and crystalline flavors. Anticipated maturity: now–2006.

Pouilly-Fuissé enjoyed a tremendous 1997. The 1997 Pouilly-Fuissé Les Crays Vieilles Vignes Réserve, crafted from a vineyard with a southern exposure, has a pineapple, mango, kumquat, and candied orange rind–infused nose. This immensely powerful yet impeccably balanced wine is full-bodied, oily-textured, and exceedingly expressive. While its 1996 counterpart was somewhat austere, this expansive offering saturates the palate with white peaches, spiced pears, red and white currants, stones, and an almost overpowering minerality that lingers in its stunningly long finish. Anticipated maturity: now–2007. The equally stellar (and potentially better) 1997 Pouilly-Fuissé En Bulands Vieilles Vignes Réserve has a more restrained yet no less beguiling nose. It reveals pure aromas of chalk, smoky flint, fruit pits, and rock dust followed by a superconcentrated and tightly wound personality. This velvety-textured, vibrant wine is crammed with mouth-coating layers of liquid minerals, melted stones, and earth. While Les Crays conquered with fruit, En Bulands does so with flavors of the earth and rocks. It is impeccably well made, mind-numbingly precise and possesses an amazingly long (40 seconds!) finish. I would not be surprised to see this wine gain more complexity. Anticipated maturity: now–2009.

Readers should note that the "floaters" that can be seen in bottles of the 1998 Pouilly-Fuissé En Bulands Vieilles Vignes are not detrimental to this wine's quality. In fact, they are evidence of Daniel Barraud's dedication to noninterventionist winemaking. Stones, pear, apples, and buttered toast can be discerned in this outstanding wine's aromatic profile. Thick, concentrated, and medium- to full-bodied, it is a powerful, flavorful, and intense wine. White fruits, minerals, and gravel are found throughout its expressive character, as well as in its long, delineated, and pure finish. Anticipated maturity: now–2006.

Aromatically, the 1998 Pouilly-Fuissé Les Crays Vieilles Vignes displays a myriad of spices and minerals. Medium- to full-bodied and tightly wound, it is a more elegant wine in this vintage than the En Buland, yet lacks that offering's flesh and flashy personality. It exhibits layers of anise, cardamon, and hints of cinnamon that come roaring back in an explosive manner in its long finish. Drink it over the next 7 years.

Mineral-imbued fresh oak can be discerned in the aromatics of the 1999 Pouilly-Fuissé Les Crays Vieilles Vignes. This medium-bodied, fat, focused, and deep wine is packed with minerals, apples, pears, and spices. It has outstanding concentration and depth of fruit, as well as an admirable, pure, and supple finish. This is a gorgeous 1999 with all of its qualities and none of its flaws. The nut and mineral-scented 1999 Pouilly-Fuissé En Bulands Vieilles Vignes is broad, ample, and medium-bodied. Beautifully detailed tropical fruits can be found in its well-made and -balanced character. Drink both of these wines over the next 7 years. The 1999 St.-Véran Les Pommards is certainly one of the finest St.-Vérans I have tasted. Flint, spice, and minerals are found in its detailed aromas. Medium-bodied, concentrated, and rich, this is a gorgeous wine filled with currants, pears, and candied apples. It is supple, velvety-textured, and possesses a long, pure finish. Anticipated maturity: now–2006.

As of the 2000 vintage, Barraud's parcel of Pouilly-Fuissé La Verchére averages over 40 years of age, satisfying the estate's standard for a Vieilles Vignes (old vines) designation. The 2000 has buttered mineral aromas and a satin-textured, medium-bodied character. It is flavorful, loaded with pears, and reveals outstanding depth as well as length. This pure, complex wine should be consumed between 2003–2010. Produced from 22-year-old vines, the 2000 Pouilly-Fuissé La Roche exhibits stony pear and spice aromas. This streamlined, gravel, stone, mineral, and white fruit–flavored offering is elegant, rich, and delineated. It is harmonious, bright, and exhibits a long, penetrating finish. Anticipated maturity: 2003–2012. The quinine- and verbena-scented 2000 Pouilly-Fuissé Les Crays Vieilles Vignes is velvety-textured and medium-bodied. Creamy stones, pears, and apples are found in this powerful and concentrated wine. It is harmonious, intense, deep, and reveals an exquisitely long finish. Anticipated maturity: 2003–2012.

Intense earth and mineral aromas can be discerned in the 2000 Pouilly-Fuissé En Bulands

Vieilles Vignes. It is medium-bodied, satin-textured, and displays enormous density to its sweet pear, apple, mineral, stone, earth, quinine, gravel, and lemon-flavored character. This is an extravagant Pouilly-Fuissé, crammed with copious quantities of fruit, and revealing exceptional grip as well as length. Anticipated maturity: 2004–2014.

Other recommended wines: 1998 Mâcon-Vergisson La Roche (88), 1999 Mâcon-Vergisson La Roche (89+), 2000 Mâcon-Vergisson La Roche (89), 1999 Pouilly-Fuissé En France (88), 2000 Pouilly-Fuissé En France (89), 1998 Pouilly-Fuissé La Roche (88), 1999 Pouilly-Fuissé La Roche (89), 1999 Pouilly-Fuissé La Vercherre (89), 1997 St.-Véran En Crêches (89+), 1999 St.-Véran En Crêches (89+), 2000 St.-Véran En Crêches (89), 2000 St.-Véran Les Pommards (89–90)

DOMAINE GHISLAINE BARTHOD (CHAMBOLLE-MUSIGNY)

1999 Chambolle-Musigny Les Beaux Bruns	E	(90–92)
1999 Chambolle-Musigny Les Charmes	E	(93–95)
1999 Chambolle-Musigny Les Châtelots	E	(89–90+)
1999 Chambolle-Musigny Les Cras	E	(89–90+)

This estate, nestled between the vines and the village of Chambolle-Musigny, crafts a wide range of wines from the appellation vineyards. A tasting at Barthod is always a fascinating study of this village's often lauded and rarely understood *terroirs*. To Barthod, 1999 is "an enchanting vintage." She described its wines as having "great aromas, richness, purity, a lovely balance, and very ripe fruit." She planned on bottling the 1999s earlier than usual, "while it's still on the fruit." The estate's yields were 42–46 hectoliters per hectare after a 5–10% bleeding of the tanks.

The medium to dark ruby-colored 1999 Chambolle-Musigny Les Châtelots has deep black cherry aromas. Medium-bodied and silky, it is packed with gorgeous layers of violets, raspberries, cherries, and strawberries. This is a lush, candied wine with a soft, suave, seamless finish. Drink it over the next 6–7 years. The similarly colored 1999 Chambolle-Musigny Les Beaux Bruns has compelling blackberry aromas. This gorgeously refined, medium-bodied wine has outstanding blackberry, juicy blueberry, and black cherry flavors in its well-structured, pure, juicy, and exceptionally long-finishing character. Anticipated maturity: 2003–2009.

The medium to dark ruby-colored 1999 Chambolle-Musigny Les Cras has mouthwatering plum and blackberry aromas. It is a medium-bodied wine with an ample blackberry and cassis-flavored character. Its firm finish will require cellaring. Anticipated maturity: 2005–2010. The stunning 1999 Chambolle-Musigny Les Charmes is medium to dark ruby-colored and has an explosive blackberry, raspberry, and superripe cherry-scented nose. Medium- to full-bodied, broad, and satin-textured, this is a superb wine that coats the palate with loads of cherries, violets, and candied black raspberries. Its perfumed, harmonious personality is feminine, expansive, and concentrated. Additionally, it reveals an exceptionally long, juicy, and delineated finish. It is the finest wine I have ever tasted from Mme Barthod. Anticipated maturity: 2005–2014.

Other recommended wines: 1999 Chambolle-Musigny Les Baudes (89–90), 1998 Chambolle-Musigny Les Beaux Bruns (88–90+), 1999 Chambolle-Musigny Les Véroilles (88–90?)

DOMAINE JEAN-CLAUDE BELLAND (SANTENAY)

1997 Chambertin	EE	90

Formerly known as Domaine Adrian Belland, this estate has a rich treasure trove of vineyards. In warm, ripe years, it can be an excellent source of red Burgundy. The medium to dark ruby-colored 1997 Chambertin offers aromas reminiscent of porcini mushrooms, cinnamon, and black cherries. This well-structured, medium- to full-bodied, jammy wine offers loads of earth, stone, plum, and black fruit compote flavors. It successfully marries the vintage's characteristic *sur-maturité* fruit with a beautifully ripened tannic backbone. Anticipated maturity: now–2007.

Other recommended wines: 1997 Chassagne-Montrachet Morgeot (88), 1997 Corton-Charlemagne (89+?), 1997 Corton-Grèves (89), 1997 Corton-Perrières (88), 1997 Corton Vigne au Saint (89)

DOMAINE JEAN-CLAUDE BESSIN (CHABLIS)

1997 Chablis Fourchaume	C	90
1999 Chablis Fourchaume (LF199)	C	90
1997 Chablis Valmur	D	90

I have been increasingly impressed by the Chablis from Bessin's 30-acre vineyard. A relatively recent estate bottler, Bessin sold in bulk until 1992. All of these offerings are tank-fermented and aged as well as put through full malolactic fermentation. Given their purity and concentration, these are excellent choices for readers seeking nonoaked examples of flinty, ripe, rich, Chardonnay-based wines.

The outstanding, medium-bodied 1997 Chablis Fourchaume displays copious quantities of crushed stones, seashells, and buttery lemonlike fruit in its aromatic and flavor profiles. In the mouth, the wine is dense, with terrific precision, purity, and overall depth. Because of the precociousness of the vintage, this 1997 Chablis should be consumed over the next 4–5 years. The most expensive as well as viscous and fat wine of this trio is the 1997 Chablis Valmur. It reveals more opulent, tropical fruit notes, and has been shaped more by the vintage than by *terroir*. Chewy and fruity, the lack of oak aging gives it even more fruit presence than many cask-aged efforts. Enjoy it over the next 4–5 years.

The outstanding 1999 Chablis Fourchaume (lot number LF199 on the label) was produced from a block of the estate's oldest vines in their parcel of Fourchaume. Though it was produced without any new oak, its nose has distinctive toast aromas intermingled with spices and minerals. Its medium-bodied flavor profile is crammed with anise, minerals, and pears. This satin-textured beauty has loads of power, and a long, detailed finish. Anticipated maturity: now–2007.

Other recommended wines: 1997 Chablis (88), 1997 Chablis Montmains (88)

DOMAINE BILLAUD-SIMON (CHABLIS)

1997 Chablis Les Clos	D	(92–94)
1997 Chablis Mont de Milieu Vieilles Vignes	D	90
1997 Chablis Preuses	D	(91–93)
1997 Chablis Vaudésir	D	(90–92)

This estate has been passed from father to son since 1815. The young, talented, intelligent, and energetic Samuel Billaud is presently at the reins. Throughout the Côte de Beaune, in the cellars of that region's established and rising stars, Billaud's name is constantly mentioned as Chablis's hope for the future. My tastings of his 1997s, as well as the consumption of numerous bottles of 1995s and 1996s stateside and in Beaune's restaurants, confirm the excellence of Billaud's work. If he were to abandon machine harvesting (only the grands crus and old-vine premiers crus are harvested by hand) and excessive manipulations (a cold stabilization, 2–4 rackings, three finings, and a filtration), there is no telling what heights this man could achieve. Billaud likes the 1997 vintage, describing it as "well-balanced and from an extremely healthy harvest." He is not as enthusiastic about the 1998 vintage, however. Some parcels were struck by devastating hailstorms (his Mont de Milieu vines produced only 50–60% of their normal loads), and the three weeks of rain prior to harvest brought rot and less than ideal maturity levels. "The 1998s will be reminiscent of the 1991s," said Billaud. Readers who can still find a few bottles of Billaud-Simon's 1996s on the market are well advised to consider them, particularly the upper-end cuvées. As Billaud said, "They are extremely rich and complex, well-balanced, and ageworthy, as their high acidity is covered by richness of fruit." Billaud is experimenting with the use of oak (the vast majority of modern-day Chablis are made in massive stainless steel tanks hooked up to computer systems that regulate temperature), with an *élevage* on the wines' fine lees (the Petit Chablis and Chablis are left on their lees two months, the other cuvées up to six months).

Billaud vinified and aged his 1997 Chablis Mont de Milieu Vieilles Vignes (55-year-old vines) half in stainless steel, and half in oak barrels ranging from 1–5 years old. The end result is an outstanding effort that displays a nose of minerals, toast, flowers, and faint hints of crème brûlée and vanilla bean. It has a steely, medium- to full-bodied core filled with white berries, flint, and pit fruits. This wine has superb ripeness, concentration, grip, and length. Anticipated maturity: now–2006.

The following wines were tasted directly from their tanks where they were awaiting fining, filtration, and bottling. Produced from 25-year-old vines, the 1997 Chablis Vaudésir has smoky mineral aromas and a magnificent medium to full body crammed with lemony white fruits, hazelnut cream, and minerals. It is opulent, extremely rich, broad, and has an impressively long and defined finish. This intense and flavorful wine should be consumed between now–2006. The 1997 Chablis Preuses (crafted from 55-year-old vines) reveals poached pear and toasty scents (an attribute of the Preuses vineyard, even if the wine was never aged in wood). It is oily ("glycerin heaven" was the description in my notes), packed with flinty minerals, and luxurious. This tangy and balanced yet opulent-textured and full-bodied wine is magnificently concentrated, deep, and powerful. Anticipated maturity: now–2007. I adored Billaud-Simon's 1997 Chablis Les Clos. Its complex and tight aromatics reveal loads of minerals, flint, clay, and sea shells. It is masculine, hugely dense, offers superripe apple flavors (reminiscent of applesauce), yet is as dry as the Sahara. This spectacularly rich, thick, fresh, yet brooding wine is velvety-textured, full-bodied, and possesses an exceedingly long finish that exhibits flint, stone, and chalk flavors. Anticipated maturity: 2003–2010.

Other recommended wines: 1996 Chablis Blanchots Vieilles Vignes (92+), 1997 Chablis Fourchaume (88+), 1996 Chablis Mont de Milieu (89), 1997 Chablis Mont de Milieu (88+), 1997 Chablis Montée de Tonnerre (89), 1998 Chablis Preuses (89+), 1997 Chablis Vaillons (88)

DOMAINE SIMON BIZE ET FILS (SAVIGNY-LES-BEAUNE)

1997 Corton-Charlemagne	EE	92
1997 Latricières-Chambertin	EE	(92–94)
1997 Savigny-les-Beaune Les Vergelesses	D	90

Patrick Bize credits his good friend Jean-Marie Raveneau (of Chablis fame) for having helped him learn some of the tricks to making first-rate whites. "The most important thing with whites is ripeness," he said. "We don't have the same fears of rot with Chardonnay that we have with Pinot Noir. And on Corton-Charlemagne it is almost impossible for rot to settle in so we wait a long time before harvesting."

Produced from 40- to 50-year-old vines, the 1997 Corton-Charlemagne has great aromatic depth. It offers scents of toasty minerals that give way to its medium- to full-bodied, broad, rich character. Its satiny flavor profile, composed of sweet white fruits, minerals, and bacon, is massively dense, well balanced, and extremely long in the finish. Bize, who believes he may have been the last to harvest his Corton parcel, has fashioned a truly wonderful wine in 1997, his first vintage with this newly acquired cru. Anticipated maturity: now–2007.

Patrick Bize echoed the sentiments expressed elsewhere in Burgundy when he said that for the first few months after the harvest, he did not like the reds from the 1997 vintage. "I loved the yields. They were a third less than 1996, ranging from 18 hectoliters per hectare to

30 hectoliters per hectare. The harvest was great, the grapes were healthy, yet from the moment we brought them in to approximately the following April, I just didn't like the way the vintage expressed itself in my wines. However, starting in April, May, then June, they gained weight in the barrels."

Bize, a producer who neither fines nor filters his reds, was in the process of bottling his wines when they were tasted for this report. The 1997 Savigny-les-Beaune Les Vergelesses is ruby-colored and has stony, roasted, dark fruit aromas. This medium- to full-bodied, broad, masculine, and structured wine offers a mouth full of blackberries, cassis, cedar, and tobaccolike flavors. It has outstanding grip, flavor intensity, and length. Anticipated maturity: now–2006. The superb, medium to dark ruby-colored 1997 Latricières-Chambertin has superripe black and red fruit aromas, intermingled with traces of game, earth, and fresh herbs. It is a dense, expansive, medium- to full-bodied wine with superripe (verging on overripe) flavors of blackberries, cassis, stone, earth, tar, and licorice. This is a highly concentrated, deep, thick, and velvety-textured wine that must be chewed to be believed. Anticipated maturity: now–2012.

Other recommended wines: 1997 Bourgogne Blanc Les Champlains Pinot Beurot (88), 1997 Savigny-les-Beaune Les Fourneaux (87–89), 1997 Savigny-les-Beaune Les Guettes (87–88+), 1997 Savigny-les-Beaune (white) (89), 1997 Savigny-les-Beaune Les Serpentières (88+)

DOMAINE JEAN-YVES BIZOT (VOSNE-ROMANÉE)

1997 Echézeaux	EE	(90–94+?)

There is no doubting the exemplary vineyard and cellar work performed by the young and conscientious Jean-Yves Bizot. His organic farming and noninterventionist winemaking techniques have been described and praised in *The Wine Advocate* (most recently in issue #118). There is no doubt that Bizot is a vigneron whose name consumers need to commit to memory. That being said, however, the 1997s tasted for this report were so hard, stemmy, oaky, and tannic as to raise serious concerns. "If it tastes too tannic, it is too tannic," said the brilliant Henri Jayer, Bizot's mentor. In the off-chance that they shed their tannins and soften with considerable cellaring, Bizot's will be stunning wines. Aromatically they are as intriguing and complex as any wines produced in the 1997 vintage. Their attacks reveal stupendous fruit, and then they shut down on a hardness that is rough and astringent.

Jean-Yves Bizot's 1997 Echézeaux has the greatest chance of outliving its tannic shell. The first words in my tasting book are, "1990 Montrose!" This wine, which is the result of paltry 16 hectoliter per hectare yields, displays the same monstrous levels of ripeness, density, concentration, and structure as that St.-Estèphe benchmark setter. Its magnificent aromatics are reminiscent of spices awash in perfume and blackberry liqueur. On the palate, licorice, asphalt, crème de cassis, and herbal notes burst forth before being conquered by the formidable tannins. This may be one of those rare Burgundies that will necessitate 20+ years of cellaring. If so it could ultimately merit a score in the mid- to upper 90s. However, Pinot Noir rarely copes well with tannins, unlike Cabernet Sauvignon–based wines, and experience suggest it will probably dry out before its substantial backbone softens. Anticipated maturity: 2007–2020?

DOMAINE BLAIN-GAGNARD (CHASSAGNE-MONTRACHET)

1999 Bâtard-Montrachet	EE	90
1997 Bâtard-Montrachet	EE	90
1999 Criots-Bâtard-Montrachet	EE	90
1997 Criots-Bâtard-Montrachet	EE	92+

Jean-Marc Blain, originally from a family of vignerons in the Sancerrois, is the director and wine-maker of this estate. His goal is to have his Chardonnay vines yield between 45 and 50 hectoliters per hectare (30–35 for his reds). He performs a light pressing with a pneumatic press to reduce the quantity of *bourbes* (gross lees), then drops the temperature of the musts to 12–14 degrees Celsius before transferring them to barrels (25–30% new) for fermentation and aging. All of the estate's wines are fined, filtered, and bottled at the domaine. Jean-Marc Blain told me that he is against the acidification of wines but was compelled to do it to his 1998 reds as they had dangerously high pHs.

Blain describes his 1997 whites as "pleasurable and delicate wines; they are refined, elegant, and have excellent ripeness. They should be drunk over the next ten years." I found them to be extremely well made, with the vintage's telltale ripeness and density yet with better structure than in most of the 1997s I tasted from the Côte de Beaune.

Blain harvested the 1997 Criots-Bâtard-Montrachet at 14.1% natural potential alcohol (the bottled wine has 13.9% alcohol because the "angel's share" evaporates). This wine has a sublime nose that combines elegance with *sur-maturité*. Scents of sweet pineapples are intertwined with tea leaves and sun-baked stones. It has an oily texture, medium to full body, and an intense flavor profile composed of chalk, white fruits, minerals, and toasty oak. Its impressive finish is extremely long, if a touch warm. This super wine should be at its best between now–2008. The 1997 Bâtard-Montrachet's nose was rather muted, only revealing deep richness and ripeness. On the palate, this broad, thick, and concentrated offering is medium-to full-bodied. It is crammed with mineral, chalk, slate, and ripe white fruits. Its finish, while correct, was considerably shorter than the Criots'. Anticipated maturity: now–2005+.

Blain performed more *bâtonnage* (stirring of the lees) than normal to try to give some richness to his 1999s. He feels this was successful in building some fat but also some aromas. "The 1999s were extremely muted at first but now they have beautiful noses." He also stated that he had not chaptalized any 1999s and had bottled them with more SO$_2$ than usual.

Harvested at 14.2% natural potential alcohol, the 1999 Criots-Bâtard-Montrachet has pure aromas of minerals, yellow fruits, and hints of almond. Produced from vines that are 23, 45, and more than 60 years old (in equal proportions), this medium-bodied wine has outstanding breadth and richness to its plump mineral and white fruit–flavored character. Its finish is at present marked by sulfur, but appears to be devoid of the tartness and dryness that characterize many 1999s. Anticipated maturity: now–2009. Buttered toast and spices can be found in the nose of the 1999 Bâtard-Montrachet. Medium- to full-bodied, rich, and ample, it is packed with lovely white fruit and nut flavors, as well as a deep minerality. Well-made, possessing a long, supple finish, this satin-textured wine should have the ability to withstand 10 years of cellaring.

Other recommended wines: 1997 Chassagne-Montrachet Boudriottes (89), 1997 Chassagne-Montrachet Caillerets (89+), 1999 Chassagne-Montrachet Caillerets (88), 1997 Chassagne-Montrachet Morgeot (89+)

DOMAINE DANIEL BOCQUENET (NUITS-ST.-GEORGES)

1997 Echézeaux   **EE   (90–93)**

"All of my 1997s taste more like wines from the Côtes du Rhône. I didn't acidify them, but certainly wish I had," said Daniel Bocquenet. He went on to say that malolactic fermentations were significantly later than usual, the opposite of what was said at virtually every other domaine in Burgundy. The wines were left on their lees throughout *élevage*, and were subjected to only one racking at the time of the final prebottling *assemblage*.

The dark ruby-colored 1997 Echézeaux is more reminiscent of a Châteauneuf-du-Pape than a wine from the Côte d'Or. Harvested at a whopping 13.7% natural potential alcohol, it exhibits a blackberry, pepper, Provençal herbs, and Asian spice–laden nose. This superripe, expansive, broad, deep, and powerful wine has the *sur-maturité* tar, licorice, cassis, and warmth one encounters in the southern Rhône, and ever so rarely in the northern climates of Burgundy. This opulent, intense wine should be drunk over the next 7 years.

Other recommended wines: 1997 Nuits-St.-Georges Aux St.-Juliens (88–90), 1999 Nuits-St.-Georges Aux St.-Juliens (88–90), 1997 Vosne-Romanée La Croix Blanche (87–89)

MAISON HENRI BOILLOT (MEURSAULT)

2000	Bâtard-Montrachet	EEE	(93–95)
2000	Chassagne-Montrachet Les Chaumées	E	90
2000	Chevalier-Montrachet	EEE	(95–97+)
1999	Chevalier-Montrachet	EEE	93
1998	Chevalier-Montrachet	EEE	92
1997	Chevalier-Montrachet	EEE	91
2000	Corton-Charlemagne	EEE	(91–93)
1999	Corton-Charlemagne	EEE	91
2000	Meursault Charmes	E	92
2000	Meursault Les Cras	E	93
1999	Meursault Genevrières	EE	90
2000	Meursault Perrières	EE	(90–92)
1997	Meursault Perrières	EE	91
2000	Montrachet	EEE	(92–93)
1999	Montrachet	EEE	95
2000	Puligny-Montrachet Les Folatières	EE	(91–93)
1999	Puligny-Montrachet Les Folatières	EE	91

This relatively new *négociant* firm has skyrocketed to the top echelon of Burgundy producers due to the uncompromising work of its owner and wine-maker, Henri Boillot (also the director and wine-maker of Domaine Jean Boillot).

The flower- and mineral-imbued nose of the 1997 Meursault Perriéres is quite elegantly defined. This is an extremely classy wine, with fresh and pure flavors of nuts, stones, as well as a traces of oak spices. Its medium to full body is silky-textured, delineated, and concentrated. Anticipated maturity: now–2006. Aromatically dominated by a powerful minerality, the 1997 Chevalier-Montrachet is medium- to full-bodied, dense, and massively ripe. Its character displays spiced/poached pears, marzipan, as well as candied hazelnuts and almonds. This thick wine's opulence and complexity would have merited an even higher score if its finish had not revealed some alcoholic warmth. Drink it over the next 5–6 years.

The flower and white fruit–scented 1998 Chevalier-Montrachet was harvested at 13.5% natural potential alcohol. This medium-bodied wine is surprisingly intense, powerful, and concentrated, given the generally weak nature of the 1998 white Burgundies. It has superb focus to its pure, elegant, and crystalline, mineral-dominated personality. Complex, harmonious, and long, Boillot's Chevalier appears to be one of the stars of the 1998 vintage. Drink it over the next 8 years.

Boillot's 1999s, both here at Maison Henri Boillot and at Domaine Jean Boillot, are some of Burgundies most refined, harmonious, and flavorful wines. Boillot vinified and aged his 1999 Meursault Genevrières entirely in new 350-liter oak barrels. It reveals fresh perfume, acacia blossom, and ripe pear aromas. This medium-bodied, buttery, rich, and well-balanced wine has gorgeous mineral, white fruit, and floral flavors. It is harmonious, balanced, and also possesses an outstanding, supple, and long finish. Drink it over the next 7–8 years.

The mineral, freshly cut flower, and sweet, toasted oak–scented 1999 Puligny-Montrachet Les Folatières is an outstanding light- to medium-bodied wine. Gorgeously focused, with outstanding depth, richness, and breadth, this pear, crisp apple, white flower, and nutmeg-flavored wine is one of the rare 1999 white Burgundies that should withstand cellaring. Anticipated maturity: now–2011. Sweet oak and spice aromas can be found in the nose of the 1999 Corton-Charlemagne. It has an enormously appealing velvety texture, medium body, and sexy buttery and spicy flavors. In 1999, many Corton-Charlemagnes were austere, tight, and ungenerous; the exceptions were those of Jean-François Coche and Henri Boillot. This opulent wine's flavorful character is seamless and admirably long. Anticipated maturity: now–2010.

The light- to medium-bodied 1999 Chevalier-Montrachet has one of the longest, purest finishes I have encountered in a young wine. Minerals and limestone scents are revealed in its aromatics. This is a crystalline Chevalier, with unbelievably precise quartz, stone, and floral flavors that penetrate the taster's palate and don't relinquish their grip for over two minutes. If it had been denser and deeper this wine would undoubtedly have merited an even higher score. Anticipated maturity: now–2012. The 1999 Montrachet displays stone, flower, spice, and mineral aromas. This superb wine has a medium-bodied, satin-textured character that is broad, elegant, and intense. Powerful candied lemon, pear, ripe apple, spice, and acacia blossom flavors are found in its harmonious, balanced personality as well as throughout its exceedingly long finish. Drink this beauty between 2004–2014.

The gravel- and mineral-scented 2000 Chassagne-Montrachet Les Chaumées has quartz-like purity to its medium-bodied character. It possesses outstanding grip, concentration, and length. Drink it over the next 7–8 years. An exquisite wine, the 2000 Meursault Les Cras explodes from the glass with rich apple and pear aromas. Medium- to full-bodied and super-ripe, this is an immensely rich, layered offering, with loads of minerals, white fruits, and spices. It is fresh, refined, and reveals enormous breadth as well as concentration. Anticipated maturity: now–2010.

The mineral- and chalk-scented 2000 Meursault Charmes is a powerful, deep wine. Intense and loaded with concentration, this refined beauty coats the taster's palate with poached pear and mineral flavors. It is highly expressive yet will generously repay cellaring. Anticipated maturity: 2004–2012. The aromatically demure 2000 Meursault Perrières is a hugely concentrated wine. It coats the taster's palate with tangy white fruits, minerals, buttered popcorn, and spices. Satin-textured and lively, this deep offering should be at its peak of maturity between 2004–2012.

The spice-scented 2000 Puligny-Montrachet Les Folatières is plump yet focused. Apples, spiced pears, and ripe yellow plums can be found in its intense, highly concentrated core. This is an elegant wine that seduces the palate with layers of pure, thick fruit flavors whose effects last throughout its admirably long finish. Drink it between 2004–2012. Scents of vanilla yogurt and spice unfold in the ripe, opulent, sexy 2000 Bâtard-Montrachet. Characterized by Boillot as "a vinous whore," this unctuous, intense, angle-free, medium- to full-bodied wine will please any hedonist. Its oily-textured character is buttered with tropical fruits, poached pears, spiced apples, and creamy anise. While it would never dawn on me to refer to a wine as a prostitute, I will admit to looking over my shoulder for vice cops. Drink it over the next 7–8 years.

Boillot's 2000 Chevalier-Montrachet is unquestionably one of the vintage's finest wines. Its aromatic profile, composed of smoky pears and juicy bacon, leads to an enormously elegant, crystalline personality. This rich, medium- to full-bodied wine is powerful, intense, and loaded with depth. Layers of spiced apples and poached pears can be found intermingled with minerals throughout this stunner's character as well as in its unbelievably long finish. It is pure, full-flavored, and prodigiously balanced. Anticipated maturity: now–2016. The spice-scented 2000 Montrachet is a juicy, medium-bodied wine. It displays a beautifully dense core of pears, apples, lemons, and minerals. While it does not have the same level of concentration and ripeness as the Chevalier, the Montrachet is fresh, deep, and gorgeously delineated. Drink it over the next 12 years. The rosemary, ripe pear, and spice-scented 2000 Corton-Charlemagne explodes on the palate with chewy, spicy white fruits. It is layered, deep, highly expressive, and enormously spicy. Anticipated maturity: 2004–2012.

Other recommended wines: 2000 Bourgogne Blanc (88), 2000 Chassagne-Montrachet (89), 1999 Meursault (88), 1997 Meursault Charmes (89), 1999 Meursault Charmes (88+), 1999 Meursault Les Cras (88), 2000 Meursault Genevrières (88–89), 1999 Meursault Perrières (89), 2000 Meursault Poruzots (89), 2000 Puligny-Montrachet (89)

DOMAINE JEAN BOILLOT ET FILS (VOLNAY)

1999 Beaune Les Epenottes	E	91
1997 Meursault Genevrières	EE	90
2000 Puligny-Montrachet Clos de la Mouchère	E	94
1999 Puligny-Montrachet Clos de la Mouchère	E	91
1997 Puligny-Montrachet Clos de la Mouchère	E	90
2000 Puligny-Montrachet Les Perrières	EE	93
1999 Puligny-Montrachet Les Perrières	EE	92+
1997 Puligny-Montrachet Les Perrières	EE	90
2000 Puligny-Montrachet Les Pucelles	EE	(92–95)
1999 Puligny-Montrachet Les Pucelles	EE	91
1997 Puligny-Montrachet Les Pucelles	EE	92
1999 Volnay Les Caillerets	EE	92+
1999 Volnay Les Chevrets	E	90
1999 Volnay Les Fremiets	E	93

Henri Boillot, this estate's director and wine-maker (it carries his father's name), is on fire. His attention to detail and dedication have raised the domaine to the level of the Côte de Beaune's finest producers. Boillot is dapper, extremely organized, precise, and orderly. I have never seen a cellar and tasting room as neat and tidy as Boillot's. Everything has its place. The barrels are in perfect alignment, the bottles arranged in a semicircle on the tasting room table each have exactly the same space between them, and their corks are stood dead center behind each bottle.

Boillot says he finds 1997 a "nice" vintage. He did not acidify, yet was concerned about the vintage's predisposition to produce "fat and dense wines," so he eschewed all *bâtonnage.* "White Burgundies need to have purity. Stirring the lees of the '97s would have added even more fat to wines that were already rich, losing any semblance of purity." It is this search for "purity" that led Boillot to use 350-liter barrels (the norm in Burgundy is 225 liters). He says the idea came from bottle sizes. He had been hearing for years that wines aged better in magnums, so he conducted blind tastings using halves, regular-sized bottles (750ml), and magnums to verify and ultimately prove the theory. Then, concerned with his belief that new 225-liter barrels masked his wines' "purity," he conducted tests using *fillettes* (112 liters), regular Burgundian-sized, and new 350-liter barrels crafted by the François Frères *tonnelerie.* While he was not surprised to find that the wine in the larger vessels were less marked by oak, he was surprised by another discovery: the 350-liter barrels needed significantly less topping off—they were losing less wine to evaporation. Boillot then surmised that there was a correlation with his aging tests with different bottle sizes. The larger vessels (all with the same-sized openings) better protected the wines from air and the harmful effects of oxygen.

The 1997 Meursault Genevrières, aged in equal portions new and first-year 350-liter barrels, displays superripe aromas of creamed hazelnuts and poached pears. It offers candied apples, apricots, mangoes, earth, allspice, and dried honey flavors. This medium- to full-bodied and lavishly textured wine is surprisingly polished and stylish given its *sur-maturité* characteristics. Anticipated maturity: now–2004. A combination of new and first-year traditional Burgundian barrels as well as new and first-year 350-liter barrels were used to fashion the 1997 Puligny-Montrachet Les Perrières. This hugely ripe wine exhibits butterscotch and mineral aromas. It is medium- to full-bodied, fat, yet has surprising precision and freshness for such a dense offering. This 1997 is dominated by sugarcoated nut and tropical fruit flavors. It should be consumed over the next 6 years.

The 1997 Puligny-Montrachet Clos de la Mouchère (a *monopole*, or solely-owned vineyard) was crafted using the same combination of cooperage that was used for the preceding wine. It exhibits candied apple, earth, and white flower scents. Complex flavors of cardamom, cinnamon, spiced pears, and minerals are found in this vibrant, medium- to full-bodied, elegant offering's broad character. Anticipated maturity: now–2006+. The superb 1997 Puligny-Montrachet Les Pucelles (aged entirely in 350-liter barrels, half new and the others one year old) boasts a myriad of spices and poached pears in its fabulous aromatics. Its flavor profile is strikingly spicy and loaded with white fruits, apricots, and honeyed flavors. This medium- to full-bodied and broad wine possesses an impressively long and toasty finish. Anticipated maturity: now–2007.

Both his reds and whites seem to go from strength to strength as Boillot adapts his techniques to nature. An extremely bright and meticulous man, Boillot has challenged himself to make the best wines he can, at any price. For example, he installed tables in the vineyards to sort out over 50% of his 2000 reds, leaving huge mounds containing tons of fruit. The next day the hill of harvested (yet rejected) grapes had disappeared, and others realized that Boillot was throwing out bunches better than what they had produced!

The fresh, floral and talcum powder–scented 1999 Puligny-Montrachet Les Perrières is medium- to full-bodied, and has superripe white fruit and floral flavors. This outstanding wine has superb depth, concentration, and focus. It is elegant, lush, and pure, and possesses a long finish. Anticipated maturity: now–2012. The 1999 Puligny-Montrachet Clos de la Mouchère offers detailed mineral aromas. Light- to medium-bodied and delineated, this satin-textured wine has good concentration to its metal, mineral, gravel, and pear-flavored character. Well focused and possessing an excellent finish, it is a very successful 1999. Anticipated maturity: now–2010. The perfumed floral- and nut-scented 1999 Puligny-Montrachet Les Pucelles was vinified and aged entirely in new 350-liter barrels. Light- to medium-bodied, floral, and mineral-flavored, it possesses outstanding focus, delineation, and concentration. Berries, both white and red, can be discerned in its refreshingly bright and pure finish. Drink it over the course of the next 9 years.

The outstanding medium to dark ruby-colored 1999 Beaune Les Epenottes is crammed with sweet raspberries, cherries, and candied strawberries. Medium- to full-bodied and satin-textured, this is a spicy wine filled with copious quantities of candied cherries and jammy blackberries. It is pure, seamless, powerful, and possesses an admirably long, silky finish. Drink this first-rate Beaune between now–2009. The medium to dark ruby-colored 1999 Volnay Les Chevrets, tasted both in Boillot's cellars and in the United States, has an appealingly dense nose of violets and black cherries. Medium- to full-bodied and powerful, it coats the palate with blackberries, graphite, licorice, and dark cherry flavors. This masculine, chewy, seamless wine is the result of moderate yields and impeccable winemaking. Its extremely long finish is completely fruit-dominated, yet reveals copious, well-ripened tannins. Anticipated maturity: 2003–2012.

The outstanding 1999 Volnay Les Fremiets, produced from 20-year-old vines, was also tasted twice. Violets, red cherries, and candied raspberries can be discerned in its aromatics. On the palate, this is a powerful wine with flavors of red and black cherry as well as blackberry. It is refined, intense, muscular, and utterly harmonious. This well-focused and balanced wine has a dazzling finish and an elegant, fruit-packed personality. Drink it over the next 10 years. The slightly darker-colored 1999 Volnay Les Caillerets has a stone- and blackberry-scented nose. This dense, backward dark fruit– and mineral-crammed wine may ultimately surpass the Fremiets as it evolves with age. At present, it has mind-boggling depth of fruit and loads of exquisitely ripened tannin. Anticipated maturity: 2005–2012+.

The 2000 Puligny-Montrachet Les Perrières offers anise, toast, white berry, and floral aromas. Chewy-textured and medium-bodied, it coats the taster's palate with liquid minerals, gravel, and white fruits. It reveals huge depth, a velvety texture, and highly expressive flavors that last throughout its impressive finish. Anticipated maturity: 2004–2012. The 2000 Puligny-Montrachet Clos de la Mouchère, from a *monopole* located within Puligny's Perrières vineyard, reveals spicy mineral aromas. This wine has huge concentration and power, loads of focus, and a chewy, satin-textured personality. Candied limes, gravel, minerals, pears, and anise can be found throughout its gorgeous, medium- to full-bodied core of fruit. It is highly expressive, beautifully rendered, and elegant. Anticipated maturity: 2005–2014.

When I tasted the 2000 Puligny-Montrachet Les Pucelles on September 10, 2001, it had just finished its malolactic fermentation. It explodes from the glass with assorted white fruits, spices, flowers, anise, and toast. On the palate, this medium- to full-bodied wine offers roasted pear, buttered popcorn, toast, copious spices, and candied apples. Like the Clos de la Mouchère, it is deep, immensely ripe, intense, and concentrated. This is a sumptuous, refined wine with an exquisitely long and supple finish. Drink it over the next 15 years.

Other recommended wines: 1997 Beaune Epenottes (89), 1997 Beaune Clos du Roi (88), 1999 Beaune Clos du Roi (88), 1998 Puligny-Montrachet (88), 2000 Puligny-Montrachet (89), 1998 Puligny-Montrachet Clos de la Mouchère (89), 1998 Puligny-Montrachet Les Perrières (88), 1998 Puligny-Montrachet Les Pucelles (89), 2000 Savigny-les-Beaune Les Vergelesses (88), 1997 Volnay Caillerets (89), 1998 Volnay Chevrets (88), 1997 Volnay Fremiets (88), 1998 Volnay Fremiets (89+)

MAISON JEAN-MARC BOILLOT (POMMARD)

1999 Pommard Jarollières	E	(89–91)
1999 Pommard Rugiens	EE	(93–95)
2000 Puligny-Montrachet Les Combettes	EE	91
1999 Puligny-Montrachet Les Combettes	EE	90
1999 Puligny-Montrachet La Garenne	E	91
2000 Puligny-Montrachet Les Pucelles	EE	91

"The 1999 vintage is exceptional for vignerons," said the intelligent, hardworking Jean-Marc Boillot. He feels the wines will be "good and pleasant young. Some may also age well; we could not have asked for more." He feels the 1999s can best be compared to the 1982: "They have great balance, with fat fruit and a crunchy (*croquant*) acidity." When asked why so many of his colleagues had acidified the 1999s since he felt they naturally possessed good acidity, Boillot said that "too many of them blindly listen to the oenologist, who are also acid salesmen. Each time they consult with an estate they make money, and then, if they recommend the addition of sulfur, acid, or other products they make more money. Artificial adjustments of acidity in whites never harmonize. This is an easy and obvious lesson to learn, yet many trust oenologists too much. In fact, in 1999, many who acidified were later told to deacidify! The only vignerons who truly had to acidify this vintage were those whose yields were astronomical." As is his normal practice, Boillot performed continuous weekly *bâtonnage* (stirring of the lees) until bottling. "Even though some vines suffered from heat and hydric stress in August, the year turned out wonderfully. The vintage shows through in the wines but the *terroir* characteristics are respected as well."

Pears and apples are intermingled with fresh earth notes in the aromatics of the 1999 Puligny-Montrachet La Garenne. This wine has gorgeous breadth, richness, focus, and precision to its medium-bodied personality. Lovely white berry fruit, stones, and minerals can be found throughout its character, as well as in its detailed and long finish. While generally not one of Boillot's finest premiers crus, it stood out in 1999. Anticipated maturity: now–2008. Marzipan, white flowers, and refined pear aromas can be found in the nose of the 1999 Puligny-Montrachet Les Combettes. This medium-bodied and elegant wine has some power in the attack, revealing layers of minerals and apples. It is well balanced, feminine, and beautifully detailed, but does not possess the grip or length of the La Garenne. Anticipated maturity: now–2009.

The 1999 Pommard Jarollières has a tar, blackberry, and cassis-scented nose. This in-your-face, powerful, asphalt, tar, blackberry, and licorice-flavored wine has outstanding depth, ripeness, and length. It is extremely ripe and has an impressive density of fruit. Anticipated maturity: 2004–2011. Produced from 80-year-old vines, the dark-colored 1999 Pommard Rugiens is extraordinary! Its backward, black fruit–laden nose leads to a full-bodied, chewy-textured syrup of wine. It is extremely thick, dense, packed with blackberry jam, spices, tar, and licorice. This fresh, muscular, intense wine has abundant superripe tannins immersed in jellied fruit flavors. Its exceedingly long finish reveals hints of toasty new oak. Anticipated maturity: 2005–2012+.

The exotic fruit-scented 2000 Puligny-Montrachet Les Combettes has an explosive, medium-bodied personality. Vinous, lush, and fat, this is a broad, highly expressive wine with poached pear and spiced apple flavors. Anticipated maturity: now–2011. The mineral- and spice-scented 2000 Puligny-Montrachet Les Pucelles is an ample truffle, spice, and clay-flavored wine. Plump and fruit-forward, it is silky-textured and plush. Anticipated maturity: now–2010.

Other recommended wines: 1999 Puligny-Montrachet (88+), 2000 Puligny-Montrachet (88), 1999 Puligny-Montrachet Les Champs-Canet (89), 2000 Puligny-Montrachet Les Champs-Canet (89), 1998 Puligny-Montrachet Les Combettes (89+), 2000 Puligny-Montrachet La Garenne (89), 1998 Puligny-Montrachet Les Referts (88), 1999 Puligny-Montrachet Les Referts (89), 1998 Puligny-Montrachet La Truffière (89+), 1999 Puligny-Montrachet La Truffière (89), 2000 Puligny-Montrachet La Truffière (89), 1999 Volnay (87–89), 1999 Volnay La Carrelle sous la Chapelle (87–89), 1999 Volnay Pitures (88–91), 1999 Volnay Roncerets (88–90)

DOMAINE DE LA BONGRAN/DOMAINE EMILIAN GILLET (QUINTAINE)

1997 Mâcon-Clessé Quintaine (Bongran)	D	93+
2000 Mâcon-Villages Cuvée Botrytis (Bongran)	E	94
1999 Mâcon-Villages Cuvée Levroutée (Bongran)	D	(91–93)
2000 Mâcon-Villages Quintaine (Bongran)	D	(90–92)
1999 Mâcon-Villages Quintaine (Bongran)	D	91
1997 Mâcon-Viré (Gillet)	C	91

There are legal crimes that people can be tried and convicted for, and moral crimes that often go unpunished. The creation of a new appellation (Viré-Clessé) that for all intents and purposes bans Jean Thevenet, Domaine Guillemot-Michel, and other top-quality producers is a moral crime. For years, Thevenet sold his wines under the now defunct Mâcon-Clessé Quintaine appellation. The new Viré-Clessé appellation, created by the syndicates of growers and the powerful *négociants* of the Côte de Beaune, has rules drafted specifically to ensure that Thevenet and his conscientious brethren are excluded. Thevenet, whose Domaine de la Bongran has been relegated to the lesser "Mâcon-Villages" appellation starting with the 1999, will nevertheless continue to make the same awe-inspiring wines he has produced for decades. Thevenet describes 1999 as "a great vintage, without excessive yields, slightly below 1989 in quality."

The 1997 Mâcon-Viré, sold under the Domaine Emilian Gillet label, reveals superb ripeness in its aromatics. Ripe pears, intermingled with cold steel, lemon, and stones make up this beauty's nose. On the palate, this medium- to full-bodied, soft, and superbly focused offering is crammed with liquid minerals, chalk, and traces of lime juice. It is concentrated, lively, and possesses an admirably long and precise finish. Anticipated maturity: now–2004.

The Domaine de la Bongran's 1997 Mâcon-Clessé Quintaine is a stunner. Its fresh, pure aromatics are composed of ripe apples, honeysuckle blossoms, and touches of spicy anise.

This massively intense wine is medium- to full-bodied, is hugely ripe, and possesses a sweet minerally backbone to its layered chalk and spiced pear flavor profile. Its personality has an awe-inspiring precision of flavors, enormous complexity, a mouthwatering oily texture, and an unbelievably long finish. This is an amazing Mâcon, one that should set a benchmark for others to emulate for decades to come. Anticipated maturity: now–2010.

The 1999 Mâcon-Villages Quintaine (Domaine de la Bongran) has a beautifully ripe, white flower– and talcum powder–scented nose. Hugely concentrated, this apple, pear, mineral, and verbena-flavored wine is medium-bodied, powerful, and highly expressive. Drink it over the next 9 years. Quince, orange blossoms, and apricots can be found in the aromas of Bongran's late harvest 1999 Mâcon-Villages Cuvée Levroutée. Medium- to full-bodied, lush, and satin-textured, this is a rich, feminine, extremely well-made wine. Minerals, assorted white fruits, and berries can be found throughout its spicy and opulently textured character, as well as in its long, detailed finish. Anticipated maturity: now–2012.

To Thevenet, "The 2000s remind me of 1990. They have that vintage's depth, concentration, focus, and brightness. It is a great vintage, with high maturity, some botrytis, and loads of fruit. The wines are ample, rich, and perfumed and may, in the long run, be even better than the 90s. The 1999 vintage, on the other hand, was more like 1989 or 1995, richer and also great, but in another style." The 2000 Mâcon-Villages Quintaine (Domaine de la Bongran) has a floral, ripe pear, and apple-scented nose. Medium-bodied, it coats the palate with minerals, white fruits, and gravel. This focused, rich yet crisp wine has exquisite balance, depth, and delineation. Anticipated maturity: now–2010. The pear, mango, and botrytis-scented 2000 Mâcon-Villages Cuvée Botrytis (Domaine de la Bongran) is an extraordinary wine. Candied lemons, minerals, and tropical fruits are found in its exceptionally well focused and persistent, medium-bodied character. This is late-harvest Chardonnay at its best, loaded with fruit, yet bright, zesty, and vivacious. Drink it over the next 15–18 years.

Other recommended wines and past glories: 1994 Mâcon Cuvée Botrytis (95), 1999 Mâcon-Villages Quintaine (Emilian Gillet) (89)

DOMAINE BONNEAU DU MARTRAY (PERNAND-VERGELESSES)

1999 Corton-Charlemagne	EE	(91–92+)
1998 Corton-Charlemagne	EE	91+

Unlike his colleagues in Meursault and Puligny-Montrachet, Jean-Charles de la Morinière did not have any frost or hail damage (and only traces of oïdium) in 1998. However, the famed Corton hill, on which is located Corton-Charlemagne, was not spared nature's wrath. The searing sun and heat of August burned a significant percentage of the grapes, so de la Morinière was compelled "to sort like crazy." While Jean-Charles de la Morinière wishes he could have harvested earlier, my impression is that the 1998 Corton-Charlemagne benefited from the extra hang time by gaining richness, breadth, opulence, and riper acidities. Its delightful tropical fruit (pineapple and passion fruit) and spiced apple aromas lead to its velvety-textured, medium-bodied personality. This is a harmonious 1998, without any of the angular acid and tart aspects that typify so many of this difficult vintage's efforts. Its long, seamless finish and dense, fruit-packed character are outstanding. Anticipated maturity: now–2010.

While most of his neighbors were harvesting the maximum allowable yields of 63 h/h or more, de la Morinière harvested his Corton-Charlemagne at 47 h/h, yet he still complained that this was 20% over his objective. The 1999 Corton-Charlemagne reveals lovely aromatic depth of minerals and spices. Medium-bodied, rich, and precise, this is a defined, pure, detailed wine filled with lemons, nuts, and pears. It is harmonious, elegant, and complete. Anticipated maturity: 2003–2012.

Other recommended wines: 1999 Corton (87–89), 1996 Corton-Charlemagne (92+), 1997 Corton-Charlemagne (89+), 2000 Corton-Charlemagne (88–90)

MAISON BOUCHARD PÈRE ET FILS (BEAUNE)

1998	Bâtard-Montrachet	EEE	(88–91)
1997	Bonnes Mares	EEE	(90–93)
1997	Chambertin	EEE	(92–95)
1999	Chambertin Clos de Bèze	EEE	92+
1997	Chambertin Clos de Bèze	EEE	(93–95+)
1999	Chevalier-Montrachet	EEE	(90–92)
1997	Chevalier-Montrachet	EEE	(90–92+)
2000	Chevalier-Montrachet La Cabotte	EEE	(91–93)
1999	Chevalier-Montrachet La Cabotte	EEE	(91–94)
1998	Chevalier-Montrachet La Cabotte	EEE	(90–93)
1997	Chevalier-Montrachet La Cabotte	EEE	(93–95)
1997	Clos Vougeot	EE	(91–94)
1997	Corton	E	(89–91+)
1997	Corton-Charlemagne	EEE	(89–91)
1997	Echézeaux	EE	(90–93)
1999	Gevrey-Chambertin Les Cazetiers	EE	90
1997	Gevrey-Chambertin Les Cazetiers	EE	(89–92)
1997	Meursault La Goutte d'Or	EE	(89–91)
1997	Meursault Les Perrières	EE	(91–92+)
2000	Montrachet	EEE	(91–92)
1999	Montrachet	EEE	(91–93)
1998	Montrachet	EEE	(90–93)
1997	Montrachet	EEE	(94–96+)
1997	Nuits-St.-Georges Les Cailles	E	(89–90+)
1997	Nuits-St.-Georges Clos des Argillières	E	(89–92)
1997	Nuits-St.-Georges Clos St.-Marc	E	(90–92)
1999	La Romanée	EEE	92
1997	La Romanée	EEE	(94–96)
1997	Volnay Taillepieds	D	(89–92)
1997	Vosne-Romanée Aux Reignots	EE	(90–93)

Bernard Hervet and Philippe Prost, the director and chief wine-maker respectively of Maison Bouchard, produced a large and delicious line up of 1997 white Burgundies. According to the pair, none of these wines was acidified, as they believe that process harms white wines (a few 1997 reds had their acidity "adjusted"). Prost and Hervet believe that well-ripened fruit is the key to crafting first-rate Chardonnays, and they claim to have been the last to harvest in many villages. Since they found the lees less than ideal (the opposite of 1996), the 1997s were racked soon after fermentation to maintain purity of fruit. Interestingly, Jean-Marie Guffens (Maison Verget) and Laurence Jobard (Maison Drouhin) echoed this sentiment, yet virtually all the other vignerons I spoke with claimed to have had perfectly healthy lees.

The Meursault Goutte d'Or exhibits a floral, perfumed, hazelnut, and anise-infused nose. It is deeply ripe, dense, very concentrated, and offers rich layers of candied pears and apple compote. This hedonistic offering is expansive and mouth-filling and has an admirably long palate-coating finish. Anticipated maturity: now–2005. The Meursault Les Perrières satisfies my cravings for both corporeal and intellectual gratification. It has a somewhat austere nose of roasted nuts, rocks, and wet stones that leads to a magnificently rich yet superbly focused character. This medium- to full-bodied beauty is profoundly ripe and complex, enormously concentrated, yet possesses lacelike precision in its mineral, earth, and crisp pear flavors. Its combination of superb balance and depth of fruit guarantee that it will be one of the more ageworthy 1997 white Burgundies. Anticipated maturity: now–2008. To ensure optimum ripeness, the Bouchard team harvested its parcel of Corton-Charlemagne three different times. It reveals a sweet baby powder (talcum) and toasted oak nose as well as an intensely ripe yet beautifully balanced character. Apples, metals, minerals, and flowerlike flavors can be found in this serious and tightly wound wine. Anticipated maturity: now–2007.

Beginning with the 1997 vintage, Maison Bouchard is offering two separate Chevalier-Montrachets, both from parcels owned and farmed by the firm. The first, which will have Bouchard's traditional Chevalier-Montrachet label, has a profound nose of minerals, chalk, and flowers. It is an outstanding wine, with magnificent richness of fruit, ripeness, and balance. Thick layers of stones and crisp white peaches can be found in its bright, vibrant, floral flavor profile. With an admirably long and precise finish, it should be at its peak between now–2007. The second, the 1997 Chevalier-Montrachet La Cabotte, was crafted from a tiny parcel of less than half an acre that the Bouchard team contends merits the Montrachet appellation. It is an absolutely stunning wine, with profound aromas of baked white fruits and stones. On the palate, this awesome offering combines 1997's telltale richness of fruit with impeccable balance and focus. Rich waves of deeply ripe pears, apples, nuts, and traces of peach pits are found in this dense, complex, and velvety-textured gem. Lucky tasters will also find that the blockbuster finish reveals layers of minerals. Anticipated maturity: now–2009+.

One of the finest wines of the vintage, Bouchard's Montrachet has an unbelievably refined and penetrating nose of candied nuts, flowers, and liquid minerals. This extraordinarily elegant offering has awesome balance, richness, and a profound depth to its tightly wound personality. Vibrant minerals, crisp pears, and stones are intermingled with flavors reminiscent of pineapple Life-Savers in this medium- to full-bodied and velvety beauty. It is spiritual, superbly focused, and magnificently precise. The vast majority of 1997 white Burgundies will have long passed into oblivion when this great wine reaches its peak of maturity. Anticipated maturity: 2005–2012+.

The most decadent and fruit-driven of Bouchard's impressive 1997 Volnays is the purple-colored Taillepieds. Its meaty, superripe, cherry-scented nose lead to a broad, medium- to full-bodied mouthful of licorice, blackberries, and road tar. This highly expressive, in-your-face offering is expansive, intense, and admirably concentrated. It may not be ageworthy, but its decadent, fruit-packed character is sure to please. Anticipated maturity: now–2005.

Baked cherries, violets, and stones are found in the aromatics of the medium to dark ruby-colored 1997 Corton. This is a chewy, extracted, masculine wine armed with loads of black fruits to combat its firm structure. Its highly impressive intensity of flavor, concentration, and exuberance are enough to dominate its gobs of sweet tannins. Anticipated maturity: now–2009. The 1997 Nuits-St.-Georges Les Cailles's reticent nose reluctantly reveals black fruit aromas. It explodes on the palate, however, with waves of licorice, eucalyptus, freshly laid road tar, blackberries, and sweet oak spices. This is a well-balanced, structured, medium- to full-bodied, and persistent wine that has the capacity for mid-term cellaring. Anticipated maturity: now–2008.

The medium to dark ruby-colored 1997 Nuits-St.-Georges Clos des Argillières displays aromas reminiscent of a compote of dark fruits. On the palate, this superripe (verging on overripe), medium- to full-bodied wine offers a mouthful of baked blackberries and black cherries. An opulent, luscious, velvety-textured wine, it will require drinking over the next 4–5 years. Quite unlike the typically structured, foursquare offerings from Nuits-St.-Georges, this wine is pure fruit and pleasure. The similarly colored 1997 Nuits-St.-Georges Clos St.-Marc exhibits sweet cassis and toasty oak aromas. It is not as lush as the Argillières, yet it is immensely concentrated and well structured. Tar, licorice, blackberry liqueur, and notes of earth can be discerned in this powerful, medium- to full-bodied wine. Anticipated maturity: now–2006. Aromatically, the medium to dark ruby-colored 1997 Gevrey-Chambertin Les Cazetiers reveals earth, stone, and saddle leather. This dense, powerful, thick, chewy wine is crammed with superripe dark fruits, shoe wax, and spices. It is an intense, medium- to full-bodied wine that will provide optimal drinking over the next 7+ years.

As with many Burgundian estates and *négociant* houses that used to filter as a matter of course, Maison Bouchard now is in the process of abandoning this detrimental process. I was informed that the outstanding 1997 Vosne-Romanée Aux Reignots would be one of a number of wines from this vintage that would not be filtered. Its sweet, floral, cinnamon, talcum powder, and cumin-scented nose leads to a profound, feminine, and complex personality. This is a wine that offers layers of candied red fruit, cherries, and spices in an immensely pleasurable and supple manner. Medium- to full-bodied, lush, and softly textured, its immensely long finish reveals exquisitely ripe tannins. Drink this beauty over the next 7 years. The medium to dark ruby-colored 1997 Echézeaux is one of the successes from a grand cru vineyard that generally underachieved in this vintage. It displays smoked bacon and candied red berry aromas, as well as a sweet cherry jam–filled, silky-textured, and opulent character. There are no hard edges in this flattering, forward, hedonistic wine. Anticipated maturity: now–2006.

The 1997 Clos de Vougeot is medium to dark ruby-colored and reveals a spicy nose filled with iodine, cinnamon, cardamon, and dark berry aromas. This extraordinarily ripe, dense, powerful, thick offering presents a mouth full of jammy red and black fruits. It is aggressive, verging on overripe, immensely flavorful, and will merit drinking over the next 6–7 years. The slightly darker-colored 1997 Bonnes Mares is crafted in a radically different style than the Clos de Vougeot. This floral-scented wine's personality is well delineated, elegant, fresh, and less showy than the previous wine. It is powerful yet harmonious, and reveals primarily dark fruit flavors. This refined, precise, medium- to full-bodied wine should be consumed over the next 8–9 years.

When compared to their lofty reputation, the Chambertin/Chambertin Clos de Bèze grands crus are generally underachievers. However, in the 1997 vintage, both of these vineyards attained levels of maturity that demonstrate their extraordinary potential. The dark-colored 1997 Chambertin exhibits profound aromas of wax and superripe chocolate-covered blackberries. Its powerful and expansive personality explodes on the palate, coating the taster's mouth with road tar, licorice, spiced oak, and cassis. This thick, full-bodied, muscular, and structured wine is intense and complex. It possesses the vintage's characteristics of *surmaturité* in the fruit, yet is crafted in such a way as to be well structured and capable of mid-term cellaring. Anticipated maturity: now–2010+. Similar in color, the 1997 Chambertin Clos de Bèze's nose offers peppery, cassis, and leather scents reminiscent of Châteauneuf-du-Pape. It is firm, structured, yet silky-textured, and layered with road tar, cigar box, kirsch, and plum flavors. This broad-shouldered, muscular, and highly expressive offering also possesses an extraordinarily long and flavor-packed finish. It is dense, sweet, full-bodied, and harmonious. Anticipated maturity: now–2010+.

The medium to dark ruby-colored 1997 La Romanée reveals a gorgeous, mouthwatering nose of smoked bacon intermingled with talcum powder and red berries. It has a creamy texture, great elegance, and a sublime character filled with well-delineated yet jammy red cherries, violets, and spices. This feminine, graceful, complete wine has awe-inspiring grace and length. Having tasted so many La Romanées that were undeserving of their grand cru status, it is immensely gratifying to encounter one with such power, harmony, refinement, and profundity. Anticipated maturity: now–2010+.

Philippe Prost, Maison Bouchard's wine-maker, stated that the flowering in 1998 had been so uneven that within one parcel there would be 8–15 days' difference in ripeness between vines separated by merely a few feet. This firm harvested its domaine-owned parcels in two successive passes over a 12-day period, with the intent of picking only those grapes that had attained maturity. Even so, Prost found many overripe bunches that produced oxidative *bourbes* (gross lees) after pressing. He therefore felt compelled to perform two *débourbages* (decanting off the gross less) to ensure the health of the remaining lees.

The sexy 1998 Bâtard-Montrachet displays intensely ripe yellow-fruit aromas. Medium- to full-bodied, concentrated, and dense, its layered core of poached pears and apricots coats the taster's palate. This long, flavorful, opulent wine may not stand the test of time, yet it is enormously pleasurable to drink. Anticipated maturity: now–2005. The highly impressive 1998 Chevalier-Montrachet La Cabotte exhibits dense, ripe fruits in its expressive aromatics. This medium- to full-bodied, plump, compelling wine is layered with pears, apples, hazelnuts, and minerals. Highly focused yet thick and rich, it is a profound 1998. Anticipated maturity: now–2010.

Bouchard's 1998 Montrachet is one of the finest wines fashioned in this vintage. Its mineral, hazelnut, and floral aromas give way to a rich, velvety, medium- to full-bodied personality. This exciting wine has buttered popcorn, creamed mineral, spice, and pear flavors in its vibrant yet plump core of fruit. Exceedingly well balanced and concentrated, it also possesses an intensely long and well-focused finish. Anticipated maturity: 2003–2010+.

In 1999, the Bouchard firm performed green harvests on 15 hectares (37 acres) of vines at a cost of $1,200 per hectare (a total of $18,000), yet still had high yields. Bernard Hervet, this *négociant*'s director, said that 1999 had provided them with both the highest natural potential alcohols and highest yields they had witnessed to date. "The 2000 vintage also has massive yields, but because the 40% PLC [the permissible overproduction beyond the maximum allowable yields] was rejected by the INAO [the French body that governs appellations], there will be a huge black market in wines [these are wines that are unreported and hidden from the authorities and then generally sold for cash to consumers, or blended into the next "short" vintage]." Philippe Prost, the firm's winemaker, commented on the fact that the 1999 whites had relatively low malic acids so the perception of acidity didn't diminish after malolactic fermentations. He added that in years when there isn't a great deal of density of fruit, the sediment drops out very quickly after *bâtonnage* (the stirring of the lees). "I like this vintage," he said. "It reflects the *terroirs* if the yields were not deliriously high."

Toast, minerals, and hazelnuts are found in the nose of the 1999 Chevalier-Montrachet. This medium-bodied wine has outstanding depth, breadth, density, and ripeness. White fruits, minerals, lemons, quartz, and spices characterize its elegant, crystalline personality. It is well balanced and pure and possesses a long, smooth, refined finish. Anticipated maturity: now–2010. The 1999 Chevalier-Montrachet La Cabotte has extraordinary aromatic depth to its nutcake, floral, and superripe pear-laden nose. Medium-bodied, powerful, and intense, this is a concentrated, refined, and focused wine, with outstanding depth, precision, and muscle. Its mineral, spice, and candied apple flavors last throughout its extraordinarily long, crystalline finish. Anticipated maturity: now–2012. Loads of spices, flowers, smoke, and toast can be found in the deep aromatics of the 1999 Montrachet. Medium-bodied and possessing outstanding concentration, definition, and depth of fruit, this citrus, lemon-lime, mineral, quartz, gravel, and earth-flavored wine has loads of power to its personality. It is complex, focused, pure, and crystalline. It is a harmonious, balanced, and complete wine. Drink it over the next 10–12 years.

The medium to dark ruby-colored 1999 Gevrey-Chambertin Les Cazetiers has a lush spice- and cherry-scented nose. Tobacco, blackberries, and sweet, ripe cassis can be found in this lovely, medium-bodied wine. It is concentrated, flavorful, and possesses loads of exquisitely ripened tannin. Drink it over the next 8 years. The medium to dark ruby-colored 1999 Chambertin Clos de Bèze has a beautiful nose of perfumed red and black fruits. This lively, gorgeously ripened wine is packed with cherries, blackberries, violets, and assorted freshly cut flowers. It is sweet, pure, supple, and has a long, seamless finish. Anticipated maturity: 2004–2012. The saturated, medium to dark ruby-colored 1999 La Romanée has a delectable talcum powder, superripe cherry, and perfume-scented nose. It has admirable amplitude and breadth in its medium- to full-bodied, softly textured personality. Cherry syrup and chocolate chip cookie dough–like flavors can be found in this sweet, beautifully structured wine. It possesses loads of tannins, yet they are ripe and supple. Anticipated maturity: 2004–2012.

To Bernard Hervet, Bouchard's director, 2000 is the finest vintage for white Burgundies in the last 10 years. (He classifies the other nine years in his order of preference as being 1992, 1996, 1997 and 1995 equally, 1999, 1992, 1994, and then a tie for last place with 1993 and 1998.) Philippe Prost, Bouchard's winemaker, also believes that 2000 is the finest vintage of the last decade, followed by 1992, 1997, 1996, 1995, 1999, 1998, 1991, 1994, and last, 1993. Said Hervet, "I've never tasted a range of wines as extraordinary in their youth. They have had harmony and balance since they were mere must [the prefermentation juice]. Not one rotten grape could be found in a bunch." Prost agreed, adding that in 1992 it was easy to make good wines, yet in 2000, one had to do some work, "particularly in maintaining acidity." He pointed out that the wines had "lower acid than the 1999s at harvest," yet while malolactic fermentations had little to no effect on the 1999s, they "made a big difference on the 2000s, whose pHs generally were .15 higher than the '99s."

The medium-bodied 2000 Chevalier-Montrachet La Cabotte boasts minerals, spices, and creamed nuts in its aromatics as well as its flavor profile. It is fresh, broad, layered, and concentrated. This densely packed wine is ample, harmonious, and displays an admirably long, delineated finish. Anticipated maturity: 2004–2012. The spice-scented 2000 Montrachet is a plump, toasted pear, nut, and mineral-flavored wine. Satin-textured and juicy, this medium-bodied offering has outstanding concentration, grip, and depth. Anticipated maturity: 2004–2012.

Other recommended wines: 1997 Bâtard-Montrachet (88–90+), 1999 Bâtard-Montrachet (88), 1997 Beaune Clos de la Mousse (87–88+), 1997 Beaune Grèves Vignes de l'Enfant Jésus (88–90+), 1999 Beaune Les Grèves Vignes de l'Enfant Jésus (87–89), 1997 Beaune Theurons (88–89), 1997 Chablis Bougros (88–90), 1999 Chambolle-Musigny (domaine) (89), 1998 Chevalier-Montrachet (88–90), 2000 Chevalier-Montrachet (87–89), 1999 Corton-Charlemagne (88–89), 1997 Meursault Charmes (87–89), 1997 Meursault Domaine Bouchard (87–89), 1997 Meursault Genevrières (88–90), 1999 Meursault Genevrières (domaine) (87–89), 1999 Meursault Goutte d'Or (domaine) (88–90), 2000 Meursault Poruzots (87–89), 1997 Nuits-St.-Georges Clos des Porrets St. Georges (88–89), 1997 Pommard Rugiens (88–90), 1997 Puligny-Montrachet Les Folatières (88–90+), 1997 Puligny-Montrachet Les Pucelles (88–90), 2000 Puligny-Montrachet Les Pucelles (87–89), 1997 Volnay Caillerets Ancienne Cuvée Carnot (88–90), 1997 Volnay Fremiets Clos de la Rougeotte (88–90)

DOMAINE REYANNE ET PASCAL BOULEY (VOLNAY)

1999	Volnay Champans	E	(89–92)
1997	Volnay Champans	E	(90–92)
1999	Volnay Clos des Chênes	E	(88–92)
1997	Volnay Clos des Chênes	E	(90–91)
1999	Volnay Roncerets	E	(89–92)
1999	Volnay Santenots	E	(89–91)

The 1997 vintage was particularly successful in Volnay, and this unheralded yet reliable estate succeeded in harnessing the vintage's best qualities. Pascal Bouley described 1997 as a very heterogeneous vintage, stating that the ripeness was irregular, and one had to pay close attention to each parcel's maturity. Early in the winemaking process, he felt this would not be a successful year. However, he later changed his mind as he saw the wines gain weight.

The medium to dark ruby-colored 1997 Volnay Clos des Chênes reveals sweet black raspberries intermingled with cassis aromas. This is a concentrated, extracted, medium- to full-bodied, chewy wine with powerful black cherry and black currant flavors. It is thick, presently rather backward, and tightly wound, yet filled with admirable layers of fruit. Anticipated maturity: now–2008. The similarly colored 1997 Volnay Champans offers ripe black fruit, leather, and earth scents. A foursquare, firm, medium- to full-bodied wine, its highly concentrated and structured personality offers a mouth full of blackberries and stones, as well as a rich, satin-textured, and admirably long character. Anticipated maturity: now–2009.

The 1999 Volnay Roncerets is medium to dark ruby-colored and offers an aromatic profile packed with red and black cherries. Candied red fruits, stones, assorted berries, and minerals can be found in this sweet, light- to medium-bodied, elegant wine. It has excellent to outstanding depth of fruit, a superripe character, and loads of fine tannins. Anticipated maturity: now–2008. Spices, blackberries, and hints of licorice characterize the aromas of the medium to dark ruby-colored 1999 Volnay Santenots. This masculine, tangy, and firm wine offers blackberry, cassis liqueur, and brambleberry flavors. It will benefit from cellaring. Anticipated maturity: 2003–2009. The slightly darker-colored 1999 Volnay Champans has a gorgeous nose of sweet blueberries, perfume, and cherries. Medium- to full-bodied and juicy, it has superb balance and loads of ripe tannin. Anticipated maturity: 2004–2009. Violets, perfume, and blackberries can be found in the nose of the 1999 Volnay Clos des Chênes. This medium to dark ruby-colored wine has abundant depth to its medium-bodied, rose, cassis, and blackberry-flavored personality. This spicy, silky-textured wine is fresh, plump, yet reveals some dry tannin in its finish. If the tannin softens with cellaring, it will merit a score on the high end of the range. If not, it will be at its best in the early years, and will merit a score at the lower end of the range. Anticipated maturity: now–2009.

Other recommended wine: 1997 Volnay Santenots (88–90)

DOMAINE BOYER-MARTENOT (MEURSAULT)

1997 **Meursault Charmes Réserve**	E	90
1997 **Meursault Les Narvaux Réserve**	E	90
1999 **Meursault Perrières Cuvée Unique**	EE	90+
1997 **Meursault Perrières Réserve**	EE	92
1997 **Meursault Les Tillets Réserve**	E	90+
1999 **Puligny-Montrachet Les Caillerets**	EE	90
1997 **Puligny-Montrachet Les Caillerets**	EE	91+

Note: The "Cuvée Unique" and "Réserve" cuvées are special North Berkeley Imports bottlings that are neither fined nor filtered.

Domaine Boyer-Martenot continues to produce first-rate Meursaults, and in 1997 Yves Boyer and his wife added an outstanding Puligny-Montrachet Les Caillerets to their impressive portfolio. All of the estate's special North Berkeley *cuvées* were bottled between September 10 and 18, 1998, one year after the harvest. Boyer-Martenot's 1997s are livelier than the norm for the vintage. Both Yves Boyer and Peter Vezan (the broker who oversees these selections) assured me that none of the wines had been acidified, and appeared perplexed as to why they were so vibrant and well delineated (an anomaly for 1997s). They informed me that unlike the majority of 1997s produced in Burgundian cellars, Boyer's had undergone their mallactic fermentations rather late because their natural acidity levels had been normal.

Displaying a mineral- and stone-laden nose, the 1997 Meursault Les Narvaux Réserve has superb richness in its medium- to full-bodied personality. This delicious wine coats the palate with delectable hazelnut cream, mineral, and golden fruit flavors that linger for nearly 30 seconds. While it appears to have the required balance for aging, my inclination would be to consume this wine over the next 5 years. Potentially better, the 1997 Meursault Les Tillets Réserve appears to combine the qualities of the 1996 and 1997 vintages. From 1996 it draws a dried mineral and rock dust–dominated nose, as well as a highly structured, super-elegant, delineated character. From 1997 it acquired a fat richness, velvety texture, and superb ripeness of fruit. Anticipated maturity: now–2006. The 1997 Meursault Charmes Réserve reveals toasty mineral and lemon-infused spice scents. It is a medium to full-bodied, thickly textured, broad, complex wine crammed with smoked nuts and grilled oak flavors. I was highly impressed by its concentration, depth of well-ripened fruit, and persistence. Readers should be aware that the oak is very dominant. It is nonetheless an outstanding effort. Drink it between now–2006.

Crafted from a parcel near the summit of Meursault Perrières, Boyer-Martenot's 1997 Réserve bottling is first-rate. A stone- and gravel-packed nose is followed by a tangy, highly focused, and extremely rich flavor profile. Layer upon layer of minerals, rocks, and crisp pears can be found in this medium- to full-bodied, silky-textured, extremely persistent wine. It should age remarkably well, particularly considering that it was made in a vintage that generally produced wines that warrant early consumption. Anticipated maturity: now–2007.

Yves Boyer and his wife purchased a small parcel of 25- to 30-year-old vines in Puligny-Montrachet Les Caillerets. The 1997, their first vintage, is superb, suggesting that consumers have another first-rate source from this heralded *terroir*. It displays dusty rock and mineral aromas as well as a medium- to full-bodied, dense core of pears, apples, stones, earth, spices, and white pepper. Similar to the Meursault Tillets described earlier, this wine also appears to be a synthesis of 1996's telltale focus and liveliness with 1997's characteristic richness and forward fruit. Anticipated maturity: now–2007.

The 1999 Meursault Perrières Cuvée Unique, produced from a parcel at the very highest point in the Perrières vineyard, offers smoky oak, stone, and mineral aromas. This wine has outstanding depth, focus, and length. It is rich, layered with white fruits and stones, and reveals a silky-textured, medium-bodied, and harmonious personality. It should be consumed over the next 5–6 years. The 1999 Puligny-Montrachet Les Caillerets, produced from a recently purchased parcel in the middle of the Clos du Caillerets, reveals white flower, spice, and saffron aromas. Light-to medium-bodied, and filled with minerals and gravel, it is a well-concentrated, fresh, crystalline wine. Its elegant flavor profile is complete, yet lacks the depth of fruit required for greatness. Drink it over the next 5–6 years.

Other recommended wines: 2000 Meursault Charmes Cuvée Unique (88), 1999 Meursault Genevrières (89), 2000 Meursault Genevrières (89), 1999 Meursault Narvaux Cuvée Unique (89), 2000 Meursault Narvaux Cuvée Unique (88), 1997 Meursault l'Ormeau Réserve (88), 1999 Meursault l'Ormeau Cuvée Unique (88), 2000 Meursault l'Ormeau Cuvée Unique (88), 2000 Meursault Perrières (88+), 1999 Meursault Les Tillets Cuvée Unique (88), 2000 Meursault Les Tillets Cuvée Unique (88), 1998 Puligny-Montrachet Les Caillerets (88), 2000 Puligny-Montrachet Les Caillerets (89)

DOMAINE PHILIPPE BRENOT (SANTENAY)

1998 Bâtard-Montrachet	EEE	90+
1997 Bâtard-Montrachet	EEE	90
1997 Chassagne-Montrachet En Remilly	E	90

Philippe Brenot, who impressed me with his 1996s, crafted opulent, verging on decadent 1997 white Burgundies. This dedicated vigneron's Chardonnay yields averaged between 20 and 30 hectoliters per hectare in 1997, with the Chassagne-Montrachet En Remilly yielding less than 15 hectoliters per hectare, an amazingly low, Leroy-like figure. Brenot states he neither chaptalized, acidified, or filtered any of his wines. According to Brenot, potential alcohol levels soared in his parcels in September. He tested his Bâtard parcel on September 10 and recorded 10.59% potential alcohol, yet when he returned four days later for a second round of tests, he was blown away to find that it had soared to 13.7% in the heat! By the time he had gathered his harvesters to pick the Bâtard parcel, it had risen to 14.1%, a figure rarely seen in Burgundy.

Philippe Brenot produced one barrel (25 cases) of 1997 Chassagne-Montrachet En Remilly from the 17 ares (0.4 acres) he owns. Its intensely ripe nose exhibits pears, apples, and stonelike aromas. The wine is extremely well crafted, with a broad flavor profile composed of acacia blossoms, white fruits, and a distinctive mineral characteristic that reveals itself in its long finish. This is a dense, deeply ripe, medium- to full-bodied wine that should be consumed over the next 5–6 years.

Brenot's 1997 Bâtard-Montrachet is a freak of nature. Like many of the 1997 wines I tasted from this vineyard, it verges on being overripe and flabby, and has a warm, almost alcoholic finish. In short, many 1997 Bâtards have more in common with some examples of slightly unbalanced New World Chardonnays than they do with white Burgundies. That said, Brenot's Bâtard is outstanding. Its nose is somewhat muted (it had just been bottled), yet its flavor profile is immensely impressive. This is a huge, opulently viscous, rich, dense wine. Oily layers of spicy overripe pears and apples can be found in its luscious personality. This is a wine for hedonists, not those looking for intellectual gratification. Drink it over the next 5 years.

Two-thirds of Philippe Brenot's large parcel of Bâtard-Montrachet was planted before 1936. (The remaining third is 12 years old.) His medium- to full-bodied 1998 exhibits gorgeously ripe fruit and toasted oak aromas. This thick, deep, yet structured wine is ample and possesses loads of lemon-tinged white fruits. This well-made and persistent offering should be consumed over the next 6–8 years.

Other recommended wines: 1999 Bâtard-Montrachet (88–90), 1998 Chassagne-Montrachet En Remilly (89–90), 1997 Puligny-Montrachet Les Enseignères (89), 1998 Puligny-Montrachet Les Enseignères (88)

DOMAINE ALAIN BURGUET (GEVREY-CHAMBERTIN)

1999 Gevrey-Chambertin Les Champeaux	E	(89–90+)
1999 Gevrey-Chambertin Mes Favorites	D	(89–90+)

The 51-year-old Alain Burguet, one of Burgundy's rare self-starters, has been making wines for 25 years. Over that time he has been able to piece together his 6.3-hectare estate (1 hectare of Bourgogne, 5 hectares of "villages" Gevrey-Chambertin, and 0.3 hectares of the premier cru Gevrey-Chambertin Les Champeaux) parcel by parcel. His yields in 1999 were high, as with the vast majority of estates, averaging 55–58 hectoliters per hectare on the Bourgogne and 47–48 hectoliters on the Gevrey-Chambertins. He bled out approximately 10–15% of the juice.

Formerly known as Burguet's Vieilles Vignes cuvée, the ruby-colored 1999 Gevrey-Chambertin Mes Favorites has a gorgeous nose of superripe plums and black cherries. It is an intense, juicy, medium- to full-bodied wine, crammed with blueberries, cherries, and blackberries. This tangy, satin-textured offering has an impressively long, focused, and silky finish. Drink it between 2005–2010. Violets, roses, and dark fruits are found in the aromatics of the 1999 Gevrey-Chambertin Les Champeaux. Medium-bodied and zesty, it is jam-packed with juicy blueberries as well as red and black cherries. This plush, densely packed wine has admirable length, concentration, and balance. Anticipated maturity: 2005–2012.

DOMAINE JACQUES CACHEUX (VOSNE-ROMANÉE)

1997 Vosne-Romanée La Croix Rameau	E	(89–91+)
1997 Vosne-Romanée Les Suchots	E	(89–91)

In 1997, extremely early and rapid malolactic fermentations were the story at this little-known estate. Patrice Cacheux, its director and wine-maker, appeared perplexed by how some of his wines had performed. For example, following the advice of his oenologist, he applied large quantities of SO_2 to his low-acid Nuits-St.-Georges to protect it from potential problems. It instantly went from being the darkest wine in the cellar, one packed with fruit according to Cacheux, to a light-colored and hard, dry effort.

"Twice a decade my Vosne-Romanée Les Suchots performs better than my Echézeaux, and 1997 is simply one of those years," said the forthright Cacheux. Medium to dark ruby-colored, it reveals elegant aromas of sweet blackberries and cassis. A medium- to full-bodied wine, it offers concentrated layers of fresh and tangy cherry fruit flavors. Elegant, well-balanced, and delineated, this effort will ultimately merit an outstanding score if its finish fleshes out. Drink it between now–2006. Crafted from 10-year-old vines, the bright ruby-colored 1997 Vosne-Romanée La Croix Rameau offers candied black cherry scents. It is an immensely appealing wine that regales the palate with mocha cream–covered red fruit, cassis, and sweet oak flavors. This refined, velvety-textured wine also possesses a long, focused, and silky finish. Anticipated maturity: now–2006.

Other recommended wine: 1997 Echézeaux (87–89+)

DOMAINE CAILLOT (MEURSAULT)

2000 Bâtard-Montrachet	EEE	(91–93)
1997 Bâtard-Montrachet	EEE	(89–92)
2000 Puligny-Montrachet Les Pucelles		(90–91)

Michel Caillot, a shy yet determined 37-year-old has recently modernized his winery, ensuring that he will be able to perform all his rackings and assemblages using gravity instead of pumps. Caillot's finest wine is Bâtard-Montrachet, crafted from 40- to 50-year-old vines located in the very middle of the vineyard. The 1997 has a resplendent nose filled with rich and ripe white fruits, minerals, and fresh earth. This medium- to full-bodied, extremely thick, chewy offering is surprisingly well balanced. It possesses overripe pear and apple compote flavors, an intense minerality, and mind-boggling focus for such an opulent wine. Anticipated maturity: now–2006.

The French toast–scented 2000 Puligny-Montrachet Les Pucelles has outstanding breadth and amplitude in its medium-bodied character. Velvety-textured and juicy, this is a broad, poached pear, spiced apple, and mineral-flavored wine. It is intense, fresh, and reveals a long, pure finish. Anticipated maturity: now–2009. The spiced apple and poached pear–scented 2000 Bâtard-Montrachet is medium- to full-bodied and displays outstanding depth in its chewy-textured character. It is fat yet fresh, and reveals numerous layers of sweet white fruits, vanilla, and cinnamon throughout its flavor profile and extensive finish. Anticipated maturity: now–2011.

Other recommended wines: 1997 Meursault La Barre (87–89), 2000 Meursault La Barre (88–89), 2000 Meursault Clos du Cromin (87–89), 2000 Meursault Le Limozin (88–89), 1997 Meursault Les Tessons (87–89), 2000 Meursault Les Tessons (88–90), 1997 Puligny-Montrachet Les Pucelles (88–89)

DOMAINE LOUIS CARILLON ET FILS (PULIGNY-MONTRACHET)

2000 Bienvenue-Bâtard-Montrachet	EEE	(91–93)
1999 Bienvenue-Bâtard-Montrachet	EEE	(90–92)
1998 Bienvenue-Bâtard-Montrachet	EEE	(90–93)
1997 Bienvenue-Bâtard-Montrachet	EEE	(92–94+)
2000 Puligny-Montrachet Les Perrières	E	(90–92)
1997 Puligny-Montrachet Les Perrières	E	(89–91)
1999 Puligny-Montrachet Les Referts	EE	(89–91)
1997 Puligny-Montrachet Les Referts	E	(89–91)

The congenial Jacques Carillon has been responsible for winemaking at this old family estate since 1985. Carillon hopes consumers will drink their 1997s while waiting for the 1996s to age. "1996 is a great vintage, one that will return the investment of patience. The 1997s won't age as well as the 1989s have, but they will be delicious young." The Carillons harvested their 1997s at an average of 13% natural alcohol, a high figure for Burgundy. Moreover, no wines were artificially acidified. Jacques Carillon noted that acid levels were low but that the relative percentage of tartaric to malic acid was high. He was correct in assuming that the malolactic fermentations would have no significant effect on his wines. Carillon pointed out an interesting fact concerning the 1997s—while wines from the 1996 vintage *began* their painstakingly slow malolactic fermentations in March following their harvest, the 1997s had *finished* malolactics by March 1998!

The gravel- and perfume-scented 1997 Puligny-Montrachet Les Perrières delivers an extremely flavorful mouthful of minerals and hazelnuts. This medium- to full-bodied, dense, oily, rich wine is better focused and balanced yet boisterous. Anticipated maturity: now–2005. The 1997 Puligny-Montrachet Les Referts exhibits chalk and ripe white fruit aromas. It is a thickly textured wine with huge density, admirable palate presence, and an excellent structure for the vintage. Its expressive and persistent flavor profile is composed of stones, earth, and white flowers. Drink it over the next 5–6 years.

The Carillons consistently craft one of the finest Bienvenue-Bâtard-Montrachets. Only 580 bottles of the outstanding 1997 were produced (average production is usually 600–750 bottles). This beauty, with scents of talcum powder, tropical fruit, stone, and chalk, has admirable richness and balance. It is tightly wound and austere, yet powerful and packed with dense layers of minerals and faint hints of candied lemons that linger throughout its extensive finish. I was blown away by its combination of precision and superripe qualities. Anticipated maturity: now–2006+. The 1998 Bienvenue-Bâtard-Montrachet exhibits awesome aromas of pears, peaches, roasted stones, buttered toast, and anise. Medium- to full-bodied and thick, it coats the palate with layers and layers of velvety, sweet white fruits, and hints of coffee and grilled oak. Lush and immensely flavorful, this wine would have bowled me over if it had possessed a more substantial finish. Drink it over the next 8–10 years.

The fresh earth- and flower-scented 1999 Puligny-Montrachet Les Referts is plump, rich, harmonious, and sexy. It is loaded with ripe apples, pears, and peaches. This satin-textured wine also possesses an extremely long, smooth finish. Drink it over the next 7 years. I was surprised by the Riesling-like aromatics of the 1999 Bienvenue-Bâtard-Montrachet. Rich, dried honey–laced minerals make up this outstanding wine's nose. It is well focused, deep, concentrated, and offers a long, nuanced, smooth finish. Drink it over the next 7–8 years.

When discussing the 2000s, Jacques Carillon stated something that was echoed in many of Burgundy's cellars during my visits. "When I saw the cold and rain of July, I never thought the 2000s would be this good." To him, the 2000s are "really pleasing wines but have less acidity and are, therefore, more standard than the '99s, which offered more subtlety, minerals, and were more Burgundian in their character." The toasted mineral–scented 2000 Puligny-Montrachet Les Perrières is rich, vinous, and medium-bodied. Buttered toast, earth, and minerals can be found in its intense, highly flavorful character. It is rich, beautifully ripe, and boasts a persistent, delineated finish. Anticipated maturity: now–2009. The 2000 Bienvenue-Bâtard-Montrachet has an explosive mineral, pear, and apple-scented nose. Medium-bodied and profound, it reveals pear, toast, stone, gravel, and fresh earth flavors in its highly expressive and persistent character. Anticipated maturity: 2005–2012.

Other recommended wines: 1997 Puligny-Montrachet Champs Canet (88–89+), 1999 Puligny-Montrachet Champs Canet (87–89), 2000 Puligny-Montrachet Champs Canet (87–89), 1997 Puligny-Montrachet Combettes (87–89), 2000 Puligny-Montrachet Combettes (88–89), 1999 Puligny-Montrachet Perrières (88–89), 1998 Puligny-Montrachet Les Referts (87–89), 2000 Puligny-Montrachet Les Referts (89–90)

Past Glories: 1986 Bienvenue-Bâtard-Montrachet (96), 1996 Bienvenue-Bâtard-Montrachet (97)

DOMAINE CARRÉ-COURBIN (BEAUNE)

1999 Volnay Clos de la Cave des Ducs	E	91
1999 Volnay Robardelles	E	90+

This little known Beaune estate is quietly producing excellent to outstanding wines, which seem to get better with each passing vintage. The dark ruby-colored 1999 Volnay Robardelles has austere blackberry aromas. This juicy, medium- to full-bodied wine is crammed with cherries, superripe blackberries, and hints of licorice. It is dense, has outstanding depth of fruit, and supple tannins discernible in its admirably long finish. Drink it between 2003–2011. The saturated dark ruby-colored 1999 Volnay Clos de la Cave des Ducs has a mouthwatering cookie dough and overripe plum-scented nose. Medium- to full-bodied and chewy-textured, this is an intense, powerful, layered wine with rich blackberry, cassis, and licorice flavors. It is dense, thick, and muscular. Anticipated maturity: 2004–2012.

Other recommended wines: 1999 Pommard Les Grands Epenots (89), 1997 Volnay Réserve (88), 1999 Volnay Vieilles Vignes (88)

DOMAINE CHANDON DE BRIAILLES (SAVIGNY-LES-BEAUNE)

1999 Corton-Charlemagne	EE	(89–91)
1997 Corton-Charlemagne	EE	91+
1999 Corton Clos du Roi	E	(89–90+)
1997 Corton Clos du Roi	E	(89–91)

Madame de Nicolay harvested her Chardonnay a week earlier than the Pinot Noir, a relatively common occurrence in the 1997 vintage yet a rarity in Burgundy. While her red wines were acidified, the whites were not adjusted. She was quite pleased with the sanitary conditions of the harvest, describing them as "perfect," adding that the lees were first-rate. The 1997 Corton-Charlemagne was harvested at 13.5% natural alcohol. It has intense aromatics of pears, candied apples, and buttered toast. This wine exhibits great richness, a broad, enveloping opulent personality, and layers of oily minerals and white fruits. It is refined, well balanced, and extremely well defined. Anticipated maturity: now–2006.

The Countess de Nicolay, the estate's owner and director, compares the red 1997 vintage to 1985, adding, "We could have made wines this good in 1985 if we had worked well in those days." She attributes her success to listening only partially to her oenologist ("He wanted us to add 200 grams of acid per barrel; we only used 80 grams"), and to her use of long-lived barrels (some are over 20 years old). "Old wood is significantly less porous than new oak, so we retained CO_2 extremely well. This protected us from problems like volatile acidity." Alcoholic and malolactic fermentations were quite rapid, both completed within 90 days of the harvest. The 1997 reds are lush, forward wines that will require relatively early drinking. The medium to dark ruby-colored 1997 Corton Clos du Roi reveals mouthwatering raspberry, plum, and sugarcoated cherry scents. Its satin-textured, medium- to full-bodied, soft, layered character displays stone as well as blackberry jam flavors. Drink it over the next 6–7 years.

The black cherry–scented, medium to dark ruby-colored 1999 Corton Clos du Roi has a masculine, rugged personality. Tar, licorice, blackberries, and spices can be found in its superripe yet firm personality. It possesses an extremely long, focused finish. Anticipated maturity: 2005–2011. The 1999 Corton-Charlemagne reveals a myriad of spices, flowers, and anise in its aromatics. Medium-bodied and harmonious, this is a pure, well-focused, pear- and apple-flavored wine. It is extremely well balanced and has a long, flavor-packed finish. Drink it over the next 7–8 years.

Other recommended wines: 1997 Corton (white) (89), 1997 Corton Bressandes (89–90), 1997 Corton Maréchaudes (88–89), 1997 Pernand-Vergelesses Ile de Vergelesses (88–89)

DOMAINE PHILIPPE CHARLOPIN (GEVREY-CHAMBERTIN)

1999 Chambertin	EE	(93–95)
1999 Charmes-Chambertin	E	(92–94)
1999 Clos St.-Denis	E	(92–94?)
1999 Echézeaux	E	(91–92+)
1999 Mazis-Chambertin	E	(93–95)

Philippe Charlopin prides himself on being one of Gevrey-Chambertin's last vignerons to harvest. In 1999 he started on September 23, after some of the rains, and he was subjected to many more storms over the 14 days it takes him to pick his 14 hectares (spread out through 18 appellations). In order to guarantee grape health, Charlopin sprays "lots of sulfur and copper" in his vineyards in mid-August. He also performs copious amounts of sorting. In 1999 he harvested 60 hectoliters per hectare in his village and premier cru vineyards, but threw out 15 hectoliters per hectare. His grands crus were harvested at 50 hectoliter per hectare yields, but only 35 hectoliters made it into the fermentation vats.

Charlopin's 1999 Echézeaux has a red fruit and oak spice–dominated nose. On the palate, it is filled with spices, violets, candied blackberries, and abundant cherries. It is tightly wound, tannic (yet ripe), and immensely flavorful. Additionally, this wine possesses an exceptionally long and pure finish. Anticipated maturity: 2005–2012+. Produced from 45-year-old vines, the blackberry jam and potpourri-scented 1999 Charmes-Chambertin has a chewy, medium-bodied personality. This wine has a lively mocha, cherry, rose, and toasted oak–flavored character whose flavors last throughout its exceptionally long finish. It is precise and delineated, yet dense and well focused. It is one of the most masculine Charmes-Chambertins I tasted from this vintage. Its admirable concentration and structure foretell a bright future. Anticipated maturity: 2004–2012.

The medium- to full-bodied 1999 Clos St.-Denis has unbelievable intensity to its sweet, plummy, black fruit, asphalt, and licorice aromas and flavors. This is a dense, powerful, thick wine that has a foursquare, firm, sturdy, tannic backbone. If the fruit ultimately overcomes its tannins, this wine will be outstanding and potentially exceptional, yet there is cause for concern that it may remain hard and rugged. Anticipated maturity: 2006–2015? The dark ruby-colored 1999 Mazis-Chambertin is exceptional. Its extroverted, sweet black cherry aromas lead to an overripe licorice, plum, blackberry syrup, and road tar–flavored personality. Medium- to full-bodied, big, dense, and chewy, this is a massively thick, profound offering. Anticipated maturity: 2006–2015. The dark ruby-colored 1999 Chambertin has licorice and blackberry syrup aromas. It is thick, medium- to full-bodied and loaded with asphalt, cassis, tangy currants, and assorted black fruits. Its fresh yet unctuously packed personality is boisterously flavored and intense. Anticipated maturity: 2005–2014.

Other recommended wines: 1999 Fixin (white) (88), 1999 Gevrey-Chambertin Vieilles Vignes (88–90), 1999 Marsannay En Montchenevoy (88–89)

CHARTRON ET TRÉBUCHET (PULIGNY-MONTRACHET)

2000 Bâtard-Montrachet	EEE	90
1999 Bâtard-Montrachet	EEE	91
1999 Bienvenue-Bâtard-Montrachet	EEE	90
2000 Chevalier-Montrachet Clos des Chevaliers	EEE	90
1999 Chevalier-Montrachet Clos des Chevaliers	EEE	90
1998 Chevalier-Montrachet Clos des Chevaliers	EEE	91
1997 Chevalier-Montrachet Clos des Chevaliers	EEE	92
1998 Corton-Charlemagne	EE	90
1999 Montrachet	EEE	94
1997 Montrachet	EEE	92
1999 Puligny-Montrachet Clos du Cailleret	EE	90+
1998 Puligny-Montrachet Clos du Cailleret	EE	90
1997 Puligny-Montrachet Clos du Cailleret	EE	91+

The 1997 Puligny-Montrachet Clos du Cailleret has dusty chalk and mineral aromas. This fat, intense, deep wine is more concentrated, refined, and elegant than the Clos de la Pucelle. It explodes on the palate with flavors reminiscent of pears, white peaches, apples, and toasty minerals. Drink it between now–2005. The impressive 1997 Chevalier-Montrachet Clos des

Chevaliers has an elegant nose made up of minerals, lemons, and stones. This well-focused, delineated, structured wine is rich, thick, and ripe. Its gravel, pear, and apple-laced flavor profile is medium- to full-bodied, concentrated, and undeniably persistent. Anticipated maturity: now–2005. A show-stopper, the crème brûlée, vanilla, and mineral-scented 1997 Montrachet is immensely ripe, extremely elegant, and well structured. This medium- to full-bodied wine offers powerful mineral and spiced pear flavors as well as an oily texture, and a long finish. It is rich, deeply flavorful, and forward. Anticipated maturity: now–2006.

The 1998 Puligny-Montrachet Clos du Cailleret exhibits mineral, pear, and acacia blossom aromas. Medium- to full-bodied, fat, and intense, this forward, flavorful wine also possesses an impressively long finish. Anticipated maturity: now–2006. The medium- to full-bodied 1998 Corton-Charlemagne reveals lactic, butter, and mocha scents. On the palate, flavors reminiscent of milk, minerals, and buttered popcorn can be found in this lush, persistent, and seemingly mature white Burgundy. Drink it over the next 3–4 years. The outstanding 1998 Chevalier-Montrachet Clos des Chevaliers displays toasty, mineral, and white flower aromas. This plump, superbly focused, medium-bodied wine is powerful and elegant, with awesome grip. Soft and supple, it is filled with spiced minerals, roasted white fruits, and anise. Anticipated maturity: now–2008.

Louis Trébuchet and Jean-Michel Chartron, this firm's directors, consider 1999 a "very good vintage." They appreciate its soft and forward fruit and believe that consumers will enjoy its wines right out of the gate. The shy nose of the 1999 Puligny-Montrachet Clos du Cailleret displays only hints of minerals and flowers. Medium-bodied, with impressive concentration and depth, this white fruit and mineral-flavored wine is dense, crystalline, and impressively long in the finish. Anticipated maturity: now–2008+.

The toasted oak–scented 1999 Bâtard-Montrachet is medium-bodied, oily-textured, rich, and concentrated. It offers layers of spices, pears, apples, and oak nuances in its powerful personality. This well-balanced, plump, and flavorful wine will be at its best consumed between 2003–2010. The 1999 Bienvenue-Bâtard-Montrachet offers minerals, stones, and hints of new oak in its nose. Medium-bodied, intense, broad, and delineated, it displays fresh white fruit, stones, and spiced oak flavors. This wine also reveals a long, flavor-packed, supple finish. Anticipated maturity: now–2008.

The 1999 Chevalier-Montrachet Clos des Chevaliers exhibits floral and spice aromas. Medium-bodied, well focused, and silky-textured, this wine has a mineral, salt, and talcum powder–flavored character that leads to a somewhat dry, yet appealing finish. It is an outstanding, feminine, lacelike wine. Anticipated maturity: now–2008. Flowers, white fruits, spices, and oak can be found in the aromatic profile of the 1999 Montrachet. This is a dense, concentrated, chewy-textured wine offering toast, spices, minerals, cinnamon, anise, and poached pears in its highly impressive personality. With a great finish, this superb, extremely long, soft, pure wine is packed with flavors. Anticipated maturity: 2003–2012.

To Jean-Michel Chartron, 2000 is a good year. The firm put the wines through a cold stabilization that precipitated much of the tartaric acid that gives many 2000s a shrill, lemony bite. This process resulted in wines that are softly pleasant, yet the majority lack the depth or fruit for excellent or outstanding reviews. Loads of spices and buttered toast aromas can be detected in the nose of the 2000 Bâtard-Montrachet. This medium-bodied offering is intense, well concentrated, and loaded with white fruit. An outstanding wine with impressive depth and length, it should be consumed over the next 8 years. The 2000 Chevalier-Montrachet Clos des Chevaliers exhibits mineral and charred oak aromas. Nicely balanced and soft textured, it is a silky, medium-bodied wine. Toasted minerals and gravel can be discerned in its beautifully nuanced character. Anticipated maturity: now–2011.

Other recommended wines: 1997 Bâtard-Montrachet (88), 1998 Bâtard-Montrachet (88), 1998 Bienvenue-Bâtard-Montrachet (89), 1999 Chablis Beauroy (88), 1997 Chassagne-Montrachet Les Morgeots (88), 1998 Chassagne-Montrachet Les Morgeots (89), 1999 Corton-

Charlemagne (88+), 2000 Corton-Charlemagne (89), 1998 Meursault Charmes (88), 1998 Puligny-Montrachet (88), 2000 Puligny-Montrachet Clos du Cailleret (88), 1997 Puligny-Montrachet Clos de la Pucelle (89+), 1998 Puligny-Montrachet Clos de la Pucelle (89), 1999 Puligny-Montrachet Clos de la Pucelle (89), 2000 Puligny-Montrachet Clos de la Pucelle (88), 1997 Puligny-Montrachet Les Folatières (88), 1999 Puligny-Montrachet Les Folatières (88), 1999 Puligny-Montrachet Les Referts (88), 1997 St.-Aubin Les Murgers des Dents de Chiens (88), 1999 St.-Aubin Les Murgers des Dents de Chiens (88)

DOMAINE CHAUVENET-CHOPIN (NUITS-ST.-GEORGES)

1999 Clos de Vougeot	EE	(89–91)
1997 Clos de Vougeot	EE	90+
1997 Nuits-St.-Georges Aux Argillats	E	90
1997 Nuits-St.-Georges Les Chaignots	E	90
1997 Nuits-St.-Georges Aux Thorey	E	(89–91)

Upon his retirement, Daniel Chopin (Domaine Chopin-Groffier) transferred his vines to his son-in-law, Hubert Chauvenet. The 1997 vintage is the first in which Domaine Chauvenet-Chopin controls all of the holdings of the former Domaine Chopin-Groffier. In a year where most Côte d'Or producers admitted to having been compelled to acidify their wines, Hubert Chauvenet informed me that he was philosophically against that practice, "because it abandons the typicity of the vintage and denatures the wines."

Aromatically, the just-bottled 1997 Nuits-St.-Georges Aux Argillats was unwilling to express its bouquet. It is, however, a wine that provides enormous pleasure on the palate. Oily-textured, opulent, and seductive, this medium- to full-bodied fruit bomb is crammed with loads of sweet (from ripeness, not sugar) blackberries. This sultry mouthful should be consumed over the next 5–6 years. The 1997 Nuits-St.-Georges Les Chaignots is medium to dark ruby-colored, and offers aromas of perfumed black fruits and violets. This medium- to full-bodied, structured, chewy, thick wine is crammed with blackberries and stone-laden fruit. A textbook Nuits-St.-Georges because of its foursquare and firm personality, yet the wine possesses sweet, supple tannins. Anticipated maturity: now–2007.

Five barrels of a similarly colored 1997 Clos de Vougeot were produced. Three were aged in new oak, two in first-year wood. It reveals a fresh, vibrant, red cherry, Asian spice–scented nose, as well as an explosive, medium- to full-bodied personality. This expressive, chewy, mouthcoating wine is jam-packed with candied blackberries, licorice, spices, and toasty oak. As with a number of 1997s from the famed Clos de Vougeot vineyard, this wine verges on being overripe. It is opulent, hedonistic, and quite sensual. Drink it over the next 8 years.

The potentially outstanding 1999 Nuits-St.-Georges Aux Thorey, from a new parcel purchased by Chauvenet, is medium to dark ruby-colored and has a sweet cherry, raspberry, and currant-scented nose. This is an expansive, medium-bodied wine with excellent depth of sweet cherry, raspberry, and strawberry fruit. It is pretty, elegant, and has a long, seamless finish. Drink it over the next 7–8 years. The similarly colored 1999 Clos de Vougeot has a red fruit–laced nose. This deep, sweet, spicy wine has excellent to outstanding ripeness. It is medium- to full-bodied and has deep red and black fruit flavors. It is harmonious, seamless, and should be at its peak of maturity between 2004–2010.

Other recommended wines: 1999 Côte de Nuits-Villages (88), 1997 Nuits-St.-Georges Les Murgers (88–90), 1997 Nuits-St.-Georges Vieilles Vignes (87–89), 1997 Vougeot (88)

DOMAINE PASCAL CHEVIGNY (VOSNE-ROMANÉE)

1997 Nuits-St.-Georges Les Hauts Pruliers Réserve	E	92
1998 Vosne-Romanée Champs-Perdrix Vieilles Vignes Réserve	E	90

1997	Vosne-Romanée Champs-Perdrix Vieilles Vignes Réserve	E	91+
1997	Vosne-Romanée Les Petits Monts	E	90
1998	Vosne-Romanée La Combe-Brûlée Réserve	E	92

Note: These are special "Réserve" *cuvées* prepared by the estate, Peter Vezan, and David Hinkle exclusively for the U.S. market.

Readers who tend to prefer Bordeaux or Rhône wines to those of Burgundy because of their dark fruit intensity should taste some of Pascal Chevigny's 1997 blockbusters. From one of the most intense Hautes Côtes de Nuits Vieilles Vignes Réserve ever crafted, to his inklike Vosne-Romanée Petits Monts Réserve, each of Chevigny's wines demonstrates the power and flavor intensity that can be achieved with physiologically ripe, well-extracted Pinot Noir fruit.

The dark ruby, almost black 1997 Nuits-St.-Georges Les Hauts Pruliers Réserve reveals powerful aromas of dark chocolate–covered blueberries and cassis. This is an immensely ripe, massive wine, with a fabulous, silky texture, medium to full body, and a gorgeous flavor profile composed of blackberries, dark cherries, and licorice. While it is supple and sensual, it also possesses an outstanding structure, and should be capable of mid-term aging. Anticipated maturity: now–2007+. The lightest-colored (yet still medium to dark ruby) wine produced by Chevigny in 1997, the Vosne-Romanée Champs-Perdrix Vieilles Vignes Réserve displays sweet black fruit scents. This is a huge, chewy, masculine, medium- to full-bodied wine densely packed with tar, cassis, chocolate, and supersweet tannins. Structured with the potential for long-term aging, this muscle-bound, thickly textured effort should be drunk between now–2012+. Aromatically, the virtually black 1997 Vosne-Romanée Les Petits Monts Réserve is reminiscent of blackberry liqueur, fresh herbs, and road tar. It has exquisite intensity to its chewy, highly structured, yet refined and elegant character. Black currants and blackberries are intermingled with licorice and charred flavors in this medium- to full-bodied and beautifully pure wine. A powerhouse, it is not meant for the weak at heart. Anticipated maturity: now–2009+.

The spice- and mocha-scented 1998 Vosne-Romanée Champs-Perdrix Réserve is medium- to full-bodied, superconcentrated, and has loads of intensity to its blackberry and cherry liqueur–flavored core. Fresh, extroverted, and mouth-filling, it is a powerful, highly expressive, and long-finishing wine. Anticipated maturity: now–2010. The saturated, dark ruby-colored 1998 Vosne-Romanée La Combe Brûlée Réserve has loads of boisterous, sweet, red fruit scents. Muscular, medium- to full-bodied, and lively, its red and black cherry fruit–dominated personality is deep and persistent. Anticipated maturity: now–2010.

Other recommended wines: 1997 Hautes Côtes de Nuits Réserve (89), 1997 Vosne-Romanée La Combe Brûlée Réserve (89)

DOMAINE ROBERT CHEVILLON (NUITS-ST.-GEORGES)

1999	Nuits-St.-Georges Les Cailles	E	(92–95)
1997	Nuits-St.-Georges Les Cailles	E	(88–91)
1999	Nuits-St.-Georges Les Chaignots	E	(89–91)
1999	Nuits-St.-Georges Les Perrières	E	(91–94)
1999	Nuits-St.-Georges Les Pruliers	E	(90–93+)
1997	Nuits-St.-Georges Les Pruliers	E	(88–91)
1999	Nuits-St.-Georges Les St.-Georges	E	(90–92)
1997	Nuits-St.-Georges Les St.-Georges	E	(89–92)
1999	Nuits-St.-Georges Les Vaucrains	E	(91–93+)
1997	Nuits-St.-Georges Les Vaucrains	E	(89–92)

Bertrand Chevillon, Robert Chevillon's son, described the 1997 growing season as extremely dry and hot. Yields on the estate's top three Nuits-St.-Georges vineyards, Les Cailles, Vaucrains, and St.-Georges, were one-third less than in 1996. Generally, lower yields translate to higher quality; however, there are exceptions to that rule, as 1990 and 1996 demonstrate. Domaine Robert Chevillon's extraordinary 1996s possessed significantly more depth, focus, concentration, complexity, and intensity than his well-made, yet rarely inspiring 1997s.

The ruby-colored 1997 Nuits-St.-Georges Les Pruliers displays stony dark fruit aromas. This medium- to full-bodied, well-concentrated, silky-textured wine is replete with black cherries, tar, licorice, and earthlike flavors. What score it ultimately merits within the provided range will be determined by how well the talented Robert Chevillon copes with its slightly dry finish. Anticipated maturity: now–2005. Crafted from 75-year-old vines (as are the two following wines), the 1997 Nuits-St.-Georges Les Cailles expresses mouthwatering tobacco, smoked bacon, and spice aromas. It is medium-bodied, creamy, and delightfully rich. Well structured and deeply ripe, displaying red cherries, stones, and cedar flavors galore, this is a seductive, smile-inducing offering. Drink it over the next 6–7 years.

The medium to dark ruby-colored 1997 Nuits-St.-Georges Les St.-Georges reveals boisterous red fruit aromas. Its personality is broad, expansive, and supple, displaying layer upon layer of silky cherry fruit and a beguiling underlying stonelike flavor. It is medium- to full-bodied, chewy, has excellent palate presence, and offers an admirably long finish filled with soft tannins. Anticipated maturity: now–2005. Similarly colored, the 1997 Nuits-St.-Georges Les Vaucrains exhibits an earth, fresh herb, cedar, spice, and blackberry-scented nose. This is a concentrated, well-extracted, masculine wine, crammed with sweet, softly textured fruits. It is significantly more structured than the previous wine. Verging on foursquare, it will require moderate patience. Anticipated maturity: now–2007.

The Chevillons feel that 1999 is "a great vintage, one of the best in years." A family known for their immense work in the vineyards, they performed what Bertrand Chevillon described as "unbelievable amounts of green harvesting in July." Their highest-yielding parcels, the ones that produce the village Nuits-St.-Georges, were harvested at 45 hectoliters per hectare, and none of the estate's wines was subjected to a bleeding of the tanks. These are top-notch Nuits-St.-Georges! The medium to dark ruby-colored 1999 Nuits-St.-Georges Les Chaignots has roasted blackberry, cassis, and stonelike scents. It is dense, velvety-textured, and packed with blueberries and blackberries. This charming, sweet, supple wine also possesses an incredibly pure and soft finish. It will be at its best if drunk over the next 7 years.

The medium to dark ruby-colored 1999 Nuits-St.-Georges Les Perrières has mouthwatering smoked bacon, juniper berry, and cherry aromas. Medium- to full-bodied, lush, and fat, it is packed with satiny layers of cherries, bacon, minerals, and candied blackberries. It has outstanding focus, balance, and precision. This superb wine should be consumed between 2003–2012. The slightly darker-colored 1999 Nuits-St.-Georges Les Pruliers exhibits blackberry and licorice aromas. Medium- to full-bodied and chewy, it exhibits jammy blackberry, cassis, and freshly laid road tar flavors. It is thick and dense, yet zesty and fresh. It possesses copious quantities of ripe, structure-giving tannin. Anticipated maturity: 2004–2012.

The dark ruby-colored 1999 Nuits-St.-Georges Les Cailles is magnificent. Its licorice, blackberry jelly, and plum aromas lead to a full-bodied personality. This massive, powerful, and penetrating wine has massive quantities of licorice-laced dark fruits that are intermingled with rocks and cassis. It is hugely dense yet bright. This Darth Vader of a wine also possesses an exceptionally long, pure finish. Anticipated maturity: 2005–2014. The medium to dark ruby-colored 1999 Nuits-St.-Georges Les St.-Georges has delicate blackberry aromas. It explodes on the palate with dense, chewy cherry fruits. It is a feminine, lush, medium-bodied wine without the power or intensity of the Cailles. Drink it over the next 10 years. The similarly colored 1999 Nuits-St.-Georges Les Vaucrains has blackberry and toasted oak aromas. This intense, thick-textured, medium- to full-bodied wine is packed with black currants, blackberries, licorice, and road tar. It is tight and foursquare yet reveals outstanding depth and density of fruit. Its firm finish lasts at least 45 seconds on the palate. This offering will require patience but may well merit an even greater score as its fruit unfolds with age. Anticipated maturity: 2005–2015.

Other recommended wines: 1999 Nuits-St.-Georges (87–89), 1999 Nuits-St.-Georges Les Bousselots (89–90), 1997 Nuits-St.-Georges Les Cailles (88–91), 1997 Nuits-St.-Georges Les Perrières (86–89), 1997 Nuits-St.-Georges Les Roncières (87–89), 1999 Nuits-St.-Georges Les Roncières (88–90)

DOMAINE BRUNO CLAIR (MARSANNAY-LA-CÔTE)

1997	Chambertin Clos de Bèze	EEE	(90–93)
1999	Corton-Charlemagne	EEE	90
1997	Corton-Charlemagne	EEE	(91–93)
1997	Gevrey-Chambertin Les Cazetiers	EE	(88–90+)
1997	Gevrey-Chambertin Clos St.-Jacques	EE	(90–92)
1999	Gevrey-Chambertin La Petite Chapelle	EE	(89–91)
1999	Savigny-les-Beaune La Dominode	E	(89–91)

Bruno Clair believes that the key to crafting first-rate whites on the hill of Corton is patience. "I realized in 1993 that the more I waited to harvest, the better the potential wine. It is always windy on the hill's south-facing slope, which prevents the onset of rot. On this *terroir* we can maintain good acidity levels while increasing maturity without any fear of rot." The 1997 Corton-Charlemagne displays mouthwatering aromas of marzipan, lees, and candied hazelnuts. It is a profound wine densely packed with honeysuckle blossoms, spiced pears, nuts, and caramel. This fat, medium- to full-bodied and velvety-textured offering is intensely flavorful, powerful, and possesses a long, palate-coating finish. Drink it over the next 7+ years.

Domaine Bruno Clair's Pinot Noir yields averaged an abnormally low 25 hectoliters per hectare in 1997 because of a hailstorm that struck Marsannay's vineyards on the morning of July 14 (France's Bastille Day as well as Clair's birthday). Both Clair and his winemaking partner, Philippe Le Brun, claim the 1997 reds will provide physical pleasure but not intellectual satisfaction. Both the medium- to dark ruby-colored 1997 Gevrey-Chambertin Les Cazetiers and the Clos St.-Jacques are crafted from vines planted in 1958. This Cazetiers has a reticent nose yet a lush, fruit-forward personality that boasts sweet red fruits and spiced creamy cherries. It has excellent grip and length to its medium- to full-bodied character. Drink it over the next 6 years. The medium- to dark ruby-colored 1997 Gevrey-Chambertin Clos St.-Jacques displays scents reminiscent of blackberries, toasty bread, and smoked bacon. It is a round, ample, sweet, feminine-styled offering, with nice grip and complexity to its baked fruit–filled flavor profile. Anticipated maturity: now–2006.

The 1997 Chambertin Clos de Bèze exhibits wonderful aromatics of sweet, overripe cherry fruit, talcum powder, flowers, and stones. This velvety-textured, medium- to full-bodied, expressive wine is packed with jammy red and black fruits and licorice. Drink it over the next 7–8 years.

It took 10 months for Clair's 1999 Corton-Charlemagne to complete its alcoholic fermentation. Its nose reveals huge ripeness and sweet apricot aromas intermingled with toasted oak. Medium- to full-bodied, ample, and rich, it is packed with cookie dough, buttery white fruits, spices, and subtle hints of anise. This outstanding wine shows the austerity common in many wines from this vineyard in 1999, yet it regales the taster with its exquisite ripeness and depth. Anticipated maturity: now–2009.

To Bruno Clair, 1999 is a "magnificent" vintage for Burgundy's reds—"It is very homogenous from Santenay to Marsannay." While I disagree, and believe the Côte de Beaune fared better than the Côte de Nuits, there is no doubting that Clair has fashioned some attractive wines. The 1999 Savigny-les-Beaune La Dominode offers a profound nose of blackberries and spices. This medium-bodied wine is crammed with dark fruits, hints of licorice, and flavors reminiscent of freshly laid asphalt. It is powerful, foursquare, austere, yet has a long, ripe tannin-filled finish. Anticipated maturity: 2004–2010. The ruby-colored 1999 Gevrey-Chambertin La Petite Chapelle exhibits fresh herb and red fruit aromas. This extremely soft wine has a satin-textured, medium body. Blackberries, cherries, and raspberries can be found throughout its supple personality as well as in its sweet, silky finish. Drink this beauty between 2003–2008.

Other recommended wines: 1996 Corton-Charlemagne (93+), 1998 Corton Charlemagne (88+), 1997 Gevrey-Chambertin Clos des Fontenys (88–90), 1999 Gevrey-Chambertin Clos St.-Jacques (87–89), 1997 Gevrey-Chambertin La Petite Chapelle (87–89), 1997 Morey-St.-Denis en la Rue Vergy (white) (89), 1997 Savigny-les-Beaune La Dominode (88–90)

DOMAINE JEAN-FRANÇOIS COCHE-DURY (MEURSAULT)

2000	Corton-Charlemagne	EEE	(94–95)
1999	Corton-Charlemagne	EEE	(92–93)
1998	Corton-Charlemagne	EEE	(88–91)
1997	Corton-Charlemagne	EEE	(91–93+)
2000	Meursault Caillerets	EE	(91–93)
1997	Meursault Caillerets	EE	(90–92)
2000	Meursault Chevalières	EE	(92–93+)
2000	Meursault Narvaux	E	(90–92)
1997	Meursault Narvaux	E	(89–90+)
2000	Meursault Perrières	EEE	(95–97)
1999	Meursault Perrières	EEE	(90–91+)
1997	Meursault Perrières	EEE	(91–93)
2000	Meursault Rougeots	EE	(93–94)
1999	Meursault Rougeots	EE	(90–91+)
1997	Meursault Rougeots	EE	(89–90+)
2000	Puligny-Montrachet Les Enseignères	EE	(90–92)

Domaine Coche-Dury's 1997s are candidly described by the forthright Jean-François Coche: "The white 1997s are easy wines, we will not have to wait for them. They have very good ripeness but they lack complexity and depth for greatness." He's right, with the exception of the Corton-Charlemagne and Meursault Perrières, both outstanding efforts. For comparison, he served me a glass of his 1996 Meursault Perrières (rated 99 points). It is a monumental work of art and one of the finest wines I have ever put to my lips.

I was pleasantly surprised to learn that Coche, certainly one of the finest producers of white Burgundies, "adores" California Chardonnays. Asked to list some he had recently tasted, he quickly replied that Kistler, Marcassin, and Newton Unfiltered were his favorites because they are *"très, très mûr mais avec une belle structure. Ce sont des vins de plaisir."* ("They are very, very ripe but with a good structure. They are wines of pleasure.")

My favorite of Coche's "Merusault" bottlings is the 1997 Meursault Narvaux. Fashioned from a parcel that touches Genevrières, this offering exhibits aromas reminiscent of golden fruits, red berries, and sweet oak spices. It is an ample, broad, spicy wine filled with flavors suggesting roasted pears, apples, and nuts. This medium- to full-bodied, well-balanced, velvety, sexy wine also possesses a beautifully long finish. Anticipated maturity: now–2004+. Revealing leesy and sweet vanilla bean scents, the 1997 Meursault Rougeots is silky-textured and thick. This sultry, ample, medium- to full-bodied wine is both extraordinarily spicy and filled with candied nuts and acacia blossoms. If its oak-dominated finish is absorbed by its copious fruit, this complex and concentrated wine may merit a higher score. Anticipated maturity: now–2007. I was enthralled by the 1997 Meursault Caillerets's sweet butter- and cinnamon-infused nose. Its flavor profile, crammed with apples, peach pits, minerals, and stones, also reveals traces of citrus fruits. This medium- to full-bodied and velvety wine has admirable breadth of flavors, superb focus, and a fine finish. Anticipated maturity: now–2006+. The 1997 Meursault Perrières displays lovely aromas of candied limes, lemons, minerals, rocks, and smoke. This is a hugely rich, medium- to full-bodied, viscously textured wine. It has great class and enormous elegance to its peach, stone, earth, clay, and red berry–filled flavor profile. Were it not for an austere and lightly dusty finish, I would have been even more enamored of this offering's rich panoply of flavors and exquisite texture. Anticipated maturity: now–2007+.

The 1997 Corton-Charlemagne exhibits superripe buttery pears, apples, and traces of tropical fruits in its nose. This is a huge wine, packed with layers of grilled nuts, peaches, almonds, and sweet white fruits that saturate the palate. It is full-bodied, expansive, and immensely opulent. Like many wines from the 1997 vintage, however, it appears to have trouble fully integrating its alcohol and finishes on a warm and slightly austere note. Drink it between now–2008.

"The 1999 vintage is much like 1982 in style, flavors, and character," said Coche. This extraordinary winemaker is respected throughout the Côte for his vineyard work, yet he too found himself with absurdly high yields. *Wine Advocate* subscribers who have dreamt of one day tasting some of his hard-to-find wines will be shocked to hear that he was forced to send full barrels to the state-run distillery to be converted into rubbing alcohol. "It drove me crazy! We worked hard in the vineyards, pruning tightly, removing any double shoots or buds we found, and yet the perfect flowering followed by ideal weather for prolific growth—sun, rain, sun, rain—all season had the grapes growing at unbelievable rates. I just couldn't keep up. And 2000 was the same. For the first time I was compelled to perform a green harvest but it had no effect because the bunches I left on the vines doubled in size, they just sucked up water! It is sad to see my wine hauled off to the distillery, but those are the rules. . . . For example, I worked like a dog in my 48-year old Bourgogne Aligoté vineyard, doing things no one would ever do to Aligoté, yet fully half of my production was distilled. The only other time we had yields like this was in 1959." He went on to tell me that "the old-timers say that good weather in June guarantees a large harvest the following year [science has proven this, as the shoot embryos are formed a year early] and June 2000 was superb, so we should expect to be deluged with grapes in 2001. I don't know if this is because of the greenhouse effect, but in recent years our winters have been mild and our growing seasons have been warm and sunny. Our flowers come earlier than ever and the weather is so good that our vines, that need to suffer to make great wine, are too happy. In May you can actually see them growing at extraordinary speed. With 1998, 1999, and 2000, nature has shown us three times that she is much stronger than we are, so 2001 will certainly be interesting."

Readers will be interested to hear that Coche has changed his labels for the Meursault Caillerets, Meursault Perrières, Corton-Charlemagne, and Volnay Premier Cru starting with the 1998 vintage. They are replicas of those used by his grandfather, with actual gold leaf in the borders. These beautiful labels cost Coche over a dollar per label, "but I thought they were gorgeous, so why not?" Like the old ones, the new labels state, *"Ce vin n'a pas subi de filtration"* ("This wine was not subjected to filtration"). Another piece of important news for the Coche-o-philes among the readership, Coche's 19-year-old son Raphaël is now working full-time with his father, hopefully learning the magic touches that have brought worldwide fame to his supertalented yet modest father.

The 1999 Meursault Rougeots exhibits crisp pear, spice, and mineral aromas. This hugely expressive, medium-bodied wine has outstanding amplitude to its imposing, chewy-textured, and velvety personality. Toast, liquid minerals, and spices can be found throughout its impressive, powerful character and finish. Drink it over the next 7 years. The 1999 Meursault

Perrières has a shy yet deep smoke, mineral, and spice-laden nose. This highly refined, gorgeously detailed wine is packed with minerals, toast, spices, and crisp pears. Medium-bodied, concentrated, and harmonious, this beautiful offering also possesses an extremely long and pure finish. Anticipated maturity: now–2010.

The 1999 Corton-Charlemagne reveals ripe white fruits and a powerful spice component in its aromatics. On the palate, this medium- to full-bodied wine is fresh, superripe, and expansive. Sweet apples, pears, and a myriad of spices coat the taster's palate and take it hostage for about a minute after it has been spit out. It is an extraordinarily long-finishing wine that is a tribute to Coche's talents, skills, and hard work. Anticipated maturity: now–2012.

The incomparable Jean-François Coche believes that 2000 "is a charmer. It produced exceptionally well balanced wines. The vintage it can most be compared to would be 1992." With the exception of Coche's Meursault Vireuils du Dessus, I agree with his assessment of his own estate's wines. The apple compote–scented 2000 Meursault Narvaux is medium- to full-bodied and oily-textured. Plump and rich, it coats the palate with superripe Red Delicious apples, yet retains admirable freshness. Its expressive flavors last throughout its extended finish. Anticipated maturity: now–2006. The spice- and flower-scented 2000 Puligny-Montrachet Les Enseignères is velvety-textured and medium- to full-bodied. This sexy wine is stacked in all the right places. Poached pears, buttered apples, cinnamon, and vanilla can be found in this spicy, extroverted beauty's core fruit. Anticipated maturity: now–2008.

The spiced white fruit–scented 2000 Meursault Chevalières combines power and elegance in its medium- to full-bodied personality. This broad, refined wine exhibits creamed anise, liquid mineral, and touches of vanilla in its elegant, harmonious character. Additionally, this wine has an exceptionally long and expressive finish. Drink it over the next 10 years. The smoky, mineral-scented 2000 Meursault Rougeots is intense, concentrated, and medium- to full-bodied. Muscular and dense, it is the finest Rougeots Coche has produced in years. Loads of white fruits are intermingled with butter and spices in this seamless offering. This offering has tremendous complexity, depth, and length. Anticipated maturity: now–2012.

The demure 2000 Meursault Caillerets is a plump, medium- to full-bodied, and broad wine. Highly detailed spices, minerals, pears, and apples can be found in its full-flavored, ample personality. It should be drunk over the next 10 years. The 2000 Meursault Perrières reveals spices, cinnamon, and vanilla in its deep, concentrated character. Medium- to full-bodied, it explodes on the palate with pears, apples, butter, gravel, stones, and minerals. It is velvety-textured and lush, and exhibits massive depth and an intensely pure, powerful, deep character. This is a Perrières that will give Coche's 1996 a run for its money. Drink it over the next 12–14 years. The toasted oak–scented 2000 Corton-Charlemagne has the austerity found in many of this vineyard's 2000 wines. However, it is vinous, rich, and broad. Pure flavors of minerals, toast, and spices can be found in its highly delineated, profound offering. Anticipated maturity: 2004–2015.

Other recommended wines: 1997 Bourgogne Chardonnay (88), 1999 Meursault Caillerets (88–89), 1997 Meursault Les Chevalières (89–90), 1999 Meursault Les Chevalières (88–90), 1999 Meursault Narvaux (88–90), 1997 Meursault Vireuils du Dessous (88–89), 1999 Meursault Vireuils du Dessous (88–89), 2000 Meursault Vireuils du Dessous (89–90), 1997 Meursault Vireuils du Dessus (88–90), 1999 Meursault Vireuils du Dessus (88–89), 1997 Puligny-Montrachet Les Enseignères (89–90), 1998 Puligny-Montrachet Les Enseignères (87–90), 1999 Puligny-Montrachet Les Enseignères (89–90)

DOMAINE MARC COLIN ET FILS (GAMAY-ST.-AUBIN)

1997	Bâtard-Montrachet (Domaine Pierre Colin)	EEE	91
2000	Chassagne-Montrachet Les Caillerets	E	90+
1999	Chassagne-Montrachet Les Caillerets	E	90
1999	Chassagne-Montrachet Les Vides Bourses	E	90

2000 Montrachet	EEE	92+
1999 Montrachet	EEE	92
1998 Montrachet	EEE	93+
1997 Montrachet	EEE	93+
2000 St.-Aubin Chatenière	D	90
2000 St.-Aubin En Remilly	D	91

"In 1996 we strived for richness, in 1997 we searched for finesse," says Pierre-Yves Colin, Marc Colin's elder son and this famed estate's wine-maker. He explained that they did significantly less *bâtonnage* (stirring of the lees) in 1997 than in 1996—once a week as opposed to two to three times a week. He pointed out that 1997's "lees were not great, so we performed more *débourbage* [the process of decanting the must off its gross lees] than normal, fearing the vintage's fragility could lead to easily oxidized wines." The alcoholic and malolactic fermentations were not a problem for Colin in 1997, the first dragging out over a three-week period, and the latter taking place between January and March following the harvest. Colin used very little SO$_2$ in 1997. After malolactic fermentations, Pierre-Yves Colin kept as much CO$_2$ as possible in the barrels to "promote freshness and finesse, the two attributes the vintage lacks." Colin stressed that he had not acidified any of his wines and performed minimal chaptalization because of the vintage's ripeness. I asked Colin to rate the vintages of the 1990s for white Burgundies from best to worst, a question I posed to many vignerons. He ranked 1996 as the finest, stressing that it is an aging vintage with extraordinary structure. Behind 1996 he listed 1997, 1995, 1992, 1990, 1993, 1991, and 1994.

The entire production of 1997 Bâtard-Montrachet (this parcel belongs to Pierre Colin, Pierre-Yves's uncle, and is sold under his name) is exported to Japan and the United States. Passion fruit, mangoes, and sweet butter aromas can be found in this immensely ripe, thick, heavy, concentrated wine. It is full-bodied, opulent, hedonistic, and layered with oily apricots, tropical fruits, and honeysuckle. While it will not make old bones, it delivers loads of decadent pleasure. Drink it over the next 4–5 years.

Readers who have had the rare opportunity to taste this estate's extraordinary Montrachets will be ecstatic to learn that Marc Colin and his two sons have postponed a previous decision to uproot and replant their 75- to 80-year-old parcel of vines. Each year they consider it, knowing that the replanting is inevitable, but, as Pierre-Yves said, "We realize we will have to do it, yet these old vines produce magnificent fruit." The parcel, located in a *clos* (walled-in area) in the Dents de Chiens sector of this most famous vineyard, is sandwiched between parcels owned by Domaine Jacques Prieur and Domaine Guy Amiot et Fils. As a tractor cannot access the 0.11 hectares (or 11 ares) of vines they own, the Colins are obliged to do all the vineyard work by hand, and soon they will have to replant without the assistance of any machinery. According to Colin, the parcel's old vines are extremely stressed, producing *coulure* (damaged flowering, which reduces yields) and *millerands* (stunted fruit embryos that produce tiny, blueberry-sized berries containing highly concentrated juice). The 1997 Montrachet displays a complex set of mineral, floral, and honeysuckle-laden aromatics. It is medium- to full-bodied and offers intense minerals and spicy white fruits. Extremely concentrated as well as refined, this 1997 avoids the heaviness of many of its peers. It is detailed, intricate, flavorful, and well balanced, with an unbelievably long finish. Drink it over the next 12–15 years.

Pierre-Yves Colin stated that in 1998, "The oïdium [powdery mildew] was infernal." His solution was to have his pickers sort the grape bunches as they were being picked. He defines the vintage as one of "full of promise, not a spontaneous one." He is convinced that they will age remarkably well, citing as evidence his experience that bottles opened for consumers who visited the estate tasted better two days after having been opened. The 1998 Montrachet (produced from 75- to 80-year-old vines) was harvested at 13.8% natural potential alcohol, and took seven months to ferment. Its nut-laden aromas give way to an intense, medium- to full-bodied personality. Thickly textured, massively ripe, concentrated, and powerful, this roasted almond– and mineral-flavored wine has extraordinary elegance and precision. The bottle tasted for this report had been opened and decanted for a few hours, yet appeared, fresh, youthful, and vibrant. Anticipated maturity: 2005–2012+.

Pierre-Yves Colin beautifully expressed something I heard throughout Burgundy: "Now that we have the 1999s in our cellar, we Burgundians are able to taste the 1998s for what they truly are." He pointed out that August, 1999's dryness had led to some hydric stress in vines located on very rocky soils "so they come across as better balanced than some others but are in fact less ripe." He said that the 1999s "are from perfectly healthy grapes, many were so ripe that their skins showed golden or pink colors." The oak-scented 1999 Chassagne-Montrachet Les Vides Bourses is medium-bodied and impressively concentrated. Lemons, minerals, and pears can be found throughout this broad, pure, deep wine. It is complex, powerful, and flavorful. Drink it over the next 8 years. The 1999 Chassagne-Montrachet Les Caillerets has a rich lemon, earth, and mineral-scented nose. Medium-bodied and silky-textured, it is extremely elegant, fresh, and deep. This well-concentrated wine also reveals a long, soft, yet intense and focused finish. Drink it over the next 8 years.

Flowers and minerals can be found in the nose of the 1999 Bâtard-Montrachet. This medium-bodied wine is intense, well focused, and rich. Silky-textured and pure, it offers nut, pear, and spice flavors in its long, crystalline finish. Anticipated maturity: now–2010. The demure aromas of the 1999 Montrachet reveal only hints of minerals and flowers. It is medium-bodied, concentrated, and fresh. On the palate, pears, white flowers, spices, and apple can be discerned in its gorgeously refined personality. Anticipated maturity: now–2011.

Pierre-Yves Colin states that his maturity levels were higher in 2000 than in 1999. "These are beautiful wines, with lots of minerality and finesse," he said. The Colin family are in the running for the title of King of St.-Aubin as they continually add new wines to their portfolio. In 2000, a vintage that appears to have favored the underrated St.-Aubin commune, the Colins produced nine St.-Aubins, all of which are recommended.

The 2000 St.-Aubin En Remilly is outstanding. Fresh herbs, candied apples, and ripe pears can be found in its rich aromatics. This wine possesses tremendous amplitude, medium body, and a velvety texture. Sweet pears are intermingled with lovely minerals in this gorgeous and persistent wine. Drink it over the next 6 years. Minerals and ripe white fruits can be found in the nose of the 2000 St.-Aubin Chatenière. Stones, lemons, apples, and pears can be found in this ample, layered wine. It is juicy, medium-bodied, and silky-textured. This offering has outstanding concentration and exquisite balance. Drink it over the next 6 years.

The 2000 Chassagne-Montrachet Les Caillerets exhibits mineral and stone aromatics. This broad wine has outstanding grip, focus, and freshness. Loads of gravel, stones, and minerals can be found in its lush character as well as in its long, supple finish. Drink it over the next 7–8 years. Colin's 2000 Montrachet has an immensely appealing nose with buttery minerals, spices, and anise. Rich, generous, and medium-bodied, it coats the palate with concentrated waves of honeyed minerals. This lush, deep offering will be at its best consumed between 2005–2012.

Other recommended wines: 1998 Bâtard-Montrachet (Domaine Pierre Colin) (89+), 1999 Bâtard-Montrachet (89+), 2000 Bâtard-Montrachet (89), 1997 Chassagne-Montrachet Les Caillerets (88+), 1997 Chassagne-Montrachet Champs-Gain (89), 1997 Puligny-Montrachet La Garenne (88), 1997 Puligny-Montrachet La Garenne (88), 2000 Puligny-Montrachet Le Trézin (89), 1997 St.-Aubin Le Charmois (89), 1999 St.-Aubin Le Charmois (89), 1997 St.-Aubin Les Combes (88), 1999 St.-Aubin Les Combes (88), 2000 St.-Aubin Corton (88), 2000 St.-Aubin Montceau (89), 1999 St.-Aubin Murgers des Dents de Chiens (88), 1999 St.-Aubin En Remilly (88), 2000 St.-Aubin Sentier du Clous (88)

DOMAINE COLIN-DELÉGER (CHASSAGNE-MONTRACHET)

1999	Bâtard-Montrachet	EEE	90
1997	Chassagne-Montrachet Les Vergers	E	90
1999	Chevalier-Montrachet	EEE	91
1998	Chevalier-Montrachet	EEE	90
1997	Chevalier-Montrachet	EEE	91
1999	Puligny-Montrachet Les Demoiselles	EE	91
1997	Puligny-Montrachet Les Demoiselles	EE	92
1997	Puligny-Montrachet La Truffière	EE	90+

Michel Colin, a gifted wine-maker, performed less *bâtonnage* than usual on his 1997 white Burgundies. While he felt compelled to "rectify" the acid levels of his reds, Colin did not touch the whites. These are fat, slightly flabby wines, yet they are expressive, full of fruit, delicious, and will require near- to mid-term consumption. Unlike most of his Burgundian colleagues, Colin begins the vinifications of his white wines in stainless steel tanks before transferring them to oak barrels. He believes this technique provides his wines with more elegance, freshness, and purity of fruit. The vast majority of high-quality producers perform the entire vinification and *élevage* of their wines in barrel. Another notable exception to this is Puligny's famous Domaine Leflaive, where the wines are transferred from barrels to tanks to finish the aging process.

I loved the tangy mineral and stone aromatics of the 1997 Chassagne-Montrachet Les Vergers. This is a well-focused wine. It offers medium to full body, citrus juice–covered minerals, and an oily texture. Its admirable finish is long, precise, and devoid of the pastiness and the alcoholic warmth I found in some of Colin-Deléger 1997s. Anticipated maturity: now–2004. Revealing aromas of freshly sauteed wild mushrooms and lemons, the layered 1997 Puligny-Montrachet La Truffière is a dense, medium- to full-bodied wine. I tremendously enjoyed its well-focused, fat, flavorful character (filled with powerful earth, marzipan, and floral tones), yet was less enthralled by its pasty mouth-feel. If time changes that characteristic, my score will appear to have been conservative. Nonetheless, this is an outstanding wine. It is powerful and possesses an admirably long finish. Anticipated maturity: now–2005.

Colin's 1997 Puligny-Montrachet Les Demoiselles is his most complete 1997. It exhibits floral, perfumed mineral scents, as well as a medium- to full-bodied and beautifully focused personality. Layers of earth, tangy white fruits, stones, and oak spices can be found in its complex and silky flavor profile. This elegant, well-delineated wine also boasts the longest and purest finish of any of Colin's 1997s. Drink it between now–2007+. The 1997 Chevalier-Montrachet reveals a nose of fresh minerals and buttered toast and a richly textured core of powerful peach pit, stone, and petrol flavors (reminiscent of a dry Alsatian Riesling). This medium- to full-bodied, fat, broad wine has beautiful focus and elegance. It would have merited an even more enthusiastic review were it not for a slight pastiness in its otherwise long and complex finish. Drink it between now–2007.

The 1998 Chevalier-Montrachet offers subtle mineral aromas. It is a tangy, broad, crystalline wine with lemon-lime, stone, and spicelike flavors. Fresh, pure, and focused, its long and delineated personality surprisingly finishes on a note reminiscent of a margarita. Drink it over the next 6 years.

Michel Colin's son Philippe feels that 1999 is a "good to very good year, however, it is better for reds than whites." He went on to add, "in 2000 we have the same yields and sugar levels yet we have more fruit in our wines." Freshly cut flowers can be found in the nose of the 1999 Puligny-Montrachet Les Demoiselles. Medium- to full-bodied, deep, complex, and rich, this wine has admirable purity and precision to its white fruit and mineral-flavored personality. It is extremely well made and possesses an extensive, crystalline finish. Anticipated maturity: now–2009.

Toast, pears, white peaches, and apples are intermingled with spices in the aromatics of the 1999 Bâtard-Montrachet. Medium- to full-bodied and possessing outstanding depth, this wine is rich, robust, and flavorful. Assorted white/yellow fruits, minerals, and spices can be found in this plump wine's character. It would have merited a more exalted review if it had a longer finish. Anticipated maturity: now–2010. The 1999 Chevalier-Montrachet reveals an outstanding nose. Complex nuances of spices, flowers, and white fruits can be discerned in its aromatics. Light- to medium-bodied, finely detailed, focused, and pure, this is a precise floral- and mineral-dominated wine. It is extremely well delineated, feminine, and flavorful. Anticipated maturity: 2003–2011.

Other recommended wines: 1997 Bâtard-Montrachet (88), 1998 Bâtard-Montrachet (89), 1997 Chassagne-Montrachet Les Chenevottes (88), 1997 Chassagne-Montrachet La Maltroie (white) (88+), 1997 Chassagne-Montrachet Morgeot (white) (89+), 1997 Chassagne-Montrachet Morgeot (white) (88), 1997 Chassagne-Montrachet En Remilly (88), 1999 Chassagne-Montrachet Les Vergers (89), 1999 Puligny-Montrachet La Truffière (89+)

DOMAINE JEAN-JACQUES CONFURON (PRÉMEAUX-PRISSEY)

1999 Chambolle-Musigny Premier Cru	E	(90–92)
1999 Clos de Vougeot	EE	(88–91)
1997 Clos de Vougeot	EE	90
1999 Nuits-St.-Georges Les Boudots	E	(89–91)
1999 Nuits-St.-Georges Les Chaboeufs	E	(92–93)
1999 Romanée-St.-Vivant	EEE	(89–92)
1998 Romanée-St.-Vivant	EEE	91+
1997 Romanée-St.-Vivant	EEE	91
1999 Vosne-Romanée Les Beauxmonts	E	(90–92)

Alain Meunier, this estate's highly talented wine-maker and director, is his own harshest critic. "I made mediocre wines in 1997. With this raw material I should have been capable of greatness. The grapes were immensely ripe and had virtually perfect health. I acidified nothing, maybe that was my problem." Readers who are fans of this domaine's elegant, harmonious style of wine need not be demoralized by Meunier's comments. His 1997s, though not up to the standards one expects from a grower of his talent, are excellent to outstanding. They have the lush, fruit-forward, and slightly warm (alcoholic) characteristics found in California's top Pinot Noirs. Furthermore, judging from the sparkle in his eye when discussing the 1998s, a vintage he is "extremely proud of," greatness will soon return to this estate.

The 1997 Clos de Vougeot is dark ruby-colored and reveals spicy, black fruit aromas. On the palate it is superripe (verging on overripe), dense, fat, candied, jellied, and crammed with a compote of cherry fruit. Its oily-textured, medium- to full-bodied personality ends on a grilled, oak-laden finish. Anticipated maturity: now–2004. The least New World–like of Meunier's offerings from the 1997 vintage is the Romanée-St.-Vivant. It offers fresh, sweet red cherry scents, and a character suggesting cookie dough and red fruit syrup. Medium- to full-bodied, rich, dense, and mouthcoating, this is a powerful, velvety, and persistent wine that finishes with loads of sweet tannins. Drink it over the next 6+ years.

Produced from vines planted in 1922 (the same parcel as that of Domaine Leroy), the medium to dark ruby-colored 1998 Romanée-St.-Vivant has floral, red fruit aromas. Blackberries and cherries can be found in this highly expressive, well-balanced, elegant offering. While it possesses a firm, tannic backbone, it is covered in loads of lush fruit. Drink it over the next 8 years.

The medium to dark ruby-colored 1999 Chambolle-Musigny Premier Cru has a gorgeous nose of black cherries, raspberries, and cookie dough. This superripe, plump, satin-textured wine is powerful yet feminine and elegant. It has outstanding depth of fruit and a long, supple, cherry-filled finish. Anticipated maturity: now–2009. The cherry syrup, cookie dough, floral, and blackberry compote–scented 1999 Vosne-Romanée Les Beauxmonts is a beautifully de-fined and refined, medium-bodied wine. This outstanding, tangy, fresh, and harmonious wine has outstanding grip to its red and blackberry-flavored core. Drink it between 2004–2010.

The 1999 Nuits-St.-Georges Les Boudots is medium to dark ruby-colored and has beguil-ing red fruit, spice, and violet aromas. This lovely cherry, raspberry, and strawberry-flavored wine has a soft attack and mid-palate that leads to a firm yet beautifully ripened finish. Drink it between 2004–2011. The dark-colored 1999 Nuits-St.-Georges Les Chaboeufs has dense, rich, cookie dough aromas. This huge, medium- to full-bodied wine coats the palate with lay-ers of dense red and black cherries, cedar, and Asian spices. It is extremely long, impres-sively powerful, and has outstanding depth of fruit. Anticipated maturity: 2003–2012.

The medium to dark ruby-colored 1999 Clos de Vougeot has demure blackberry aromas. This delicate, feminine wine offers floral (mostly violets) and spice flavors in its otherwise cassis-oriented character. It is firm, foursquare, and has loads of tannin. Drink it between 2005–2010. The dark ruby-colored 1999 Romanée-St.-Vivant displays raspberry, cherry, and blackberry aromas intermingled with freshly cut flowers. Medium- to full-bodied and ex-tremely spicy, this wine is packed with blackberries and black cherries. It is refined yet firm and highly structured. Its oak-laden finish reveals some alcoholic warmth. Anticipated matu-rity: 2004–2010.

Other recommended wines: 1997 Chambolle-Musigny (87–89), 1997 Chambolle-Musigny Premier Cru (88), 1999 Nuits-St.-Georges Les Fleurières (88), 1997 Vosne-Romanée Les Beauxmonts (88)

DOMAINE CONFURON-COTÉTIDOT (VOSNE-ROMANÉE)

1999 Mazis-Chambertin	EE	(90–92)

This old-vine (65 years old on average) 11-hectare estate had moderate 35 h/h yields in 1999. The reason, according to Yves Confuron, is the advanced age of the vines. The Con-furons are traditionalists in the sense they do their own vine selections, growing them in a greenhouse for later in-house grafting. Their vineyards are plowed regularly ("We were the first in the area to do so," said Confuron), they continue to do whole-cluster fermentations, and have never fined or filtered their wines. The estate's wines are aged in 25–30% new oak, 25–30% one-year-old barrels, and the remaining 40–50% in 2- to 4-year-old vessels.

The ruby-colored 1999 Mazis-Chambertin has a sweet, plummy, almost Amarone-like nose. Medium- to full-bodied and chewy-textured, this is a deep, fresh, jammy wine. Loads of superripe blackberries can be found intermingled with spices and licorice in this admirably long and supple, tannin-filled wine. Anticipated maturity: 2004–2009.

Other recommended wine: 1999 Echézeaux (88–90)

DOMAINE CORDIER PÈRE ET FILS (FUISSÉ)

1997 Pouilly-Fuissé Champs-Murgers	D	(89–91)
1998 Pouilly-Fuissé Juliette La Grande	E	94
1997 Pouilly-Fuissé Juliette La Grande	E	92
2000 Pouilly-Fuissé Au Metertière	D	90
1999 Pouilly-Fuissé Au Metertière	D	91
1998 Pouilly-Fuissé Au Metertière	D	92
1997 Pouilly-Fuissé Au Metertière	D	(90–92)
2000 Pouilly-Fuissé Vers Cras	D	(92–94)
1999 Pouilly-Fuissé Vers Cras	D	94
1998 Pouilly-Fuissé Vers Cras	D	94
1997 Pouilly-Fuissé Vers Cras	D	(91–93)
2000 Pouilly-Fuissé Vers Pouilly	D	(92–94)
1999 Pouilly-Fuissé Vers Pouilly	D	93+

1998 Pouilly-Fuissé Vers Pouilly	D	93
2000 Pouilly-Fuissé Vieilles Vignes	D	(92–93)
1999 Pouilly-Fuissé Vieilles Vignes	D	90
1998 Pouilly-Fuissé Vieilles Vignes	D	93
1997 Pouilly-Fuissé Vieilles Vignes	D	(89–91)
2000 Pouilly-Fuissé Vignes Blanches	D	(90–91)
1999 Pouilly-Fuissé Vignes Blanches (1st bottling)	D	92
1999 Pouilly-Fuissé Vignes Blanches (2nd bottling)	D	(92–93)
1998 Pouilly-Fuissé Vignes Blanches	D	91
1997 Pouilly-Fuissé Vignes Blanches	D	(90–92)
1998 Pouilly-Loché	D	90
2000 St.-Véran Clos la Côte	D	90
1999 St.-Véran Clos la Côte	D	90+
2000 St.-Véran Les Crais	D	90+

Christophe Cordier, the intense, thoughtful, bright, and cheery young man who runs this estate, is dedicated to producing high-quality wines. I was tremendously impressed with his 1996s, was ecstatic to see that his 1997s confirmed this future star's potential, and was blown away by his 1998s, 1999s, and 2000s. Cordier is undoubtedly one of the very best vignerons in Burgundy. His top Pouilly-Fuissés are as good or better than most premiers crus or grands crus from the Côte de Beaune costing many times more. Readers should ignore any bias they may have against wines from the Mâconnais and discover the greatness of which they are capable. Twenty to twenty-five percent of Christophe Cordier's 80,000-bottle production is exported to the United States.

The 1997 Pouilly-Fuissé Champs-Murgers (a blend of recently purchased 15-year-old parcels in the Champs and Murgers vineyards) was harvested at 14% natural alcohol. It displays a rich, creamy nose of white flowers, nuts, and stones. On the palate, this medium- to full-bodied, gorgeously ripe, velvety wine is crammed with sweet pears, marzipan, and anise flavors. While I suspect that it has a very modest amount of residual sweetness, it would certainly qualify as a dry wine. Anticipated maturity: now–2005. The 1997 Pouilly-Fuissé Vieilles Vignes, harvested at the same ripeness level as the previous wine, offers a dramatically different character. Spiced pear and earthy scents lead to an intense, tangy, almost Chablis-like personality. It offers great concentration, flavors reminiscent of two chalk-caked erasers slammed against each other, and an excellent hold. Drink it between now–2005. The impressive 1997 Pouilly-Fuissé Au Metertière reveals a deep nose crammed with earth and minerals. Wave upon wave of white chocolate–covered minerals coat the palate in this powerful and well-delineated wine. It is medium- to full-bodied, expansive, boldly flavored, yet still unevolved. Anticipated maturity: now–2006.

Cordier's most complete wine in 1997 is his super 1997 Pouilly-Fuissé Vers Cras. It displays a wet wool, sweat, and liquid mineral–scented nose as well as a gorgeously elegant, medium- to full-bodied, impeccably balanced character. Almond extract, acacia blossoms, and a myriad of spices can be found in this beautifully harmonious, silky-textured, tightly wound offering. Anticipated maturity: now–2007. The 1997 Pouilly-Fuissé Vignes Blanches was harvested at a huge 14.7% natural alcohol. It is Cordier's most intense 1997, exhibiting aromas verging on tropical notes, and a bracing personality. A mouthful, this full-bodied, dense wine assaults the palate with successive waves of powerful flavors of spiced pears, baked apples, honeysuckle, minerals, and flint. If it develops more harmony and elegance, it may merit a higher rating. Anticipated maturity: now–2007.

Produced from late-harvested fruit, the 1997 Pouilly-Fuissé Juliette La Grande displays pineapple and assorted tropical fruits laden with loads of botrytis. This full-bodied, muscular, yet fresh and opulent wine is reminiscent of a bourbon pound cake dusted with minerals and tons of spices. It is not, in any way, a typical Pouilly-Fuissé, Mâconnais, or Burgundy, given its late-harvest character. This wine would be best paired with spicy Asian cuisine. Drink it over the next 6–8 years.

When I visited Cordier in late October, 1998, I learned he had finished his 1998 harvest just a week earlier. Constantly tinkering with new approaches and techniques, Cordier had decided to cut the number of harvesters by half, employing 15 skilled hands instead of the normal 30. "I thought it would be easier to explain to 15 people exactly what I wanted them to do instead of to 30. I was able to do a better job of supervising the quality of their work." His 1998 harvest, spread out over a month, resulted in extremely low yields due to frost and hail damage. Some of his vineyards, such as Pouilly-Loché and Mâcon-Fuissé, had yields of 10 hectoliters per hectare. In his St.-Véran parcels, he produced one-third of what he was legally entitled. For example, Cordier is permitted to make, 12 barrels of St. Véran, yet he only produced 4 in 1998 and 5 in 1997.

Christophe Cordier crafted some of the 1998's very finest white Burgundies. Oak spices are intermingled with white fruits in the aromatics of his 1998 Pouilly-Loché. Medium- to full-bodied, velvety-textured, and expressive, it is concentrated, ample, and full-flavored. Pears, apples, spices, and minerals are found in this impressive and persistent wine. Drink it over the next 5 years.

The pear- and flint-scented 1998 Pouilly-Fuissé Au Metertière is medium- to full-bodied and reveals an astonishing breadth of complex mineral, flint, and tangy white fruit flavors. This superbly focused, balanced, classy wine has an intense and exceptionally long character. Anticipated maturity: now 2008. Loads of spices, stones, and hints of citrus fruits are found in the nose of the 1998 Pouilly-Fuissé Vieilles Vignes. This satin-textured, medium- to full-bodied wine shows magnificent ripeness in its mineral, stone, spice, and fruit-packed personality. It is exquisitely focused and delineated, while being rich, ample, and highly expressive. Anticipated maturity: now–2009.

The 1998 Pouilly-Fuissé Vignes Blanches is the tightest of these five Pouilly-Fuissés. Lemon and apple aromas lead to a citrus, mineral, spice, and earth-flavored personality. This concentrated and intense wine is quite flavorful, but appears to be holding much of its quality in reserve. Drink it between 2003–2009. The 1998 Pouilly-Fuissé Vers Pouilly reveals a nose of spices and creamed anise. Medium- to full-bodied, broad, and oily-textured, this is a rich, powerful, yet exquisitely detailed wine. Gun flint, flowers, and pears can be found in its superbly focused and defined personality. Anticipated maturity: now–2010.

Given a choice between the vast majority of the Côte de Beaune's grand crus and Cordier's Pouilly-Fuissé Vers Cras from the 1998 vintage, I would opt for young Christophe Cordier's wine. Toasted nuts and minerals can be discerned in its intricate aromatics. On the palate, it is medium- to full-bodied, silky-textured, and offers a magnificent breadth of ripe white fruits, intermingled with tangy, lively lemons and limes. This pure, exceptionally well balanced, and expressive wine has immense palate presence, nobility, and staying power. Drink it between now–2010+. The 1998 Pouilly-Fuissé Juliette La Grande has aromatics that bring to mind the nose of a great Vouvray. Quince, nuts, candied lemons, and white flowers burst from the glass. Full-bodied and full-flavored, this wine detonates on the palate with sweetened herbal tea, mineral, and spiced pear flavors. It is deep, rich, fat, yet crisp and exquisitely balanced. While this boisterous wine is atypical of its appellation, it is immensely impressive. Readers should note that this wine will be at its best accompanying highly expressive dishes. My inclination would be to suggest drinking this beauty in the near term; however, its copious quantities of concentrated fruit and zesty acidity may well allow it to age gracefully. Drink it over the next 5+ years.

While the vignerons of the Côte de Beaune obtained a ridiculously high PLC (the amount of overproduction allowed by law) of 40% in 1999, raising the maximum yields to 63 hectoliters per hectare for whites, those of Pouilly-Fuissé asked for, and received, a 20% PLC. Since they are normally entitled to produce 50 (h/h) this PLC raised their maximum production levels to 60 h/h, virtually the same as in the Côte de Beaune. What is interesting about this is that the Pouilly-Fuissé producers were guaranteed the maximum 40% PLC had they asked for it like their Côte de Beaune brethren, but they chose to be reasonable. Christophe Cordier's yields in his Pouilly-Fuissé parcels were 35 h/h, with natural potential alcohol levels of 13.6% across all the estate's vineyards.

The 1999 St.-Véran Clos la Côte has a demure, mineral-scented nose. This flint, stone, flower, and pear-flavored wine is medium-bodied. It is elegant, wonderfully expressive, and has an impressive core of fruit. Drink this beauty over the next 6 years. In a vintage that produced countless good, very good, and sometimes even excellent wines, it was rare to find a producer who could fashion a goodly number of outstanding offerings with the required depth, concentration, and length necessary for lofty scores. Cordier should be praised for his efforts. Harvested at 14% natural potential alcohol, the 1999 Pouilly-Fuissé Vieilles Vignes displays smoky flint and mineral aromas. This deep, precise, pure wine is densely packed, with chalk, stone, and quartzlike flavors that last throughout its admirably long finish. Drink it over the next 6 years.

Beautifully etched flowers and minerals can be found in the gorgeous aromatics of the 1999 Pouilly-Fuissé Au Metertière. This wide, rich, yet beautifully detailed wine is packed with lively stones, acacia blossoms, and minerals. It is deep, concentrated, and possesses an extremely long finish. This outstanding wine should be consumed over the next 7–8 years. The 1999 Pouilly-Fuissé Vers Pouilly has an outstanding nose of spices, fresh cream, and almond pastries. Wonderfully concentrated, this medium- to full-bodied wine coats the palate with rich and silky layers of minerals, flowers, and superripe fruit. It is well balanced, precise, and powerful, yet remains elegant and refined. Drink this gem over the next 9–10 years.

Cordier chose to do two bottlings from his Pouilly-Fuissé Vignes Blanches parcel, but there will be no differences marked on the labels. The 1999 Pouilly-Fuissé Vignes Blanches (first bottling) offers stone and white fruit aromas. This ample, broad, pure, muscular, rich, yet crystalline wine is medium- to full-bodied and satin-textured. Flint, stones, overripe pears, and apples can be found throughout this wine's personality. Anticipated maturity: now–2010. The 1999 Pouilly-Fuissé Vignes Blanches (second bottling) reveals dried white raisin, apple, and mineral aromas. On the palate, it is a slightly denser, fatter, richer, and longer mirror image of the first bottling. Drink both of these wines over the next 10 years.

The biggest and most powerful white Burgundy I tasted from the 1999 vintage may well be Cordier's Pouilly-Fuissé Vers Cras. Harvested at slightly over 14% natural potential alcohol, this wine's aromas burst from the glass with superripe fruits, flint, and minerals. On the attack, it is hugely powerful, yet continues to build to a muscular crescendo in the mid-palate. It is chewy, medium- to full-bodied, and loaded with massive spice and overripe white fruit flavors. While immensely appealing through its power and loads of persistent flavors, what is even more impressive is that it remains refined and well balanced. Anticipated maturity: now–2010.

According to Cordier, the 2000 vintage would "produce massive yields if you didn't constantly work hard in the vineyard. I was concerned, as the weather in July was awful. However, the last three weeks of August were super, which allowed us to harvest early [he started on September 10] and to bring in wines of exceptional maturity."

Fresh pears can be found in the aromatics of the 2000 St.-Veran Clos de la Côte. It explodes on the palate with minerals, zesty lemons, and tangy limes. It is rich and has outstanding grip as well as a medium-bodied, silky-textured character. Anticipated maturity: now–2008. The concentrated, powerful 2000 St.-Véran Les Crais has a citrus- and stone-scented nose. Medium-bodied and defined, this wine's flavor profile is dominated by minerals, limes, candied lemons, and crisp pears. Anticipated maturity: now–2008.

The 2000 Pouilly-Fuissé Vieilles Vignes aromatically reveals huge ripeness as well as toasted mineral scents. It is massively powerful, intense, zesty, and concentrated. This medium-bodied wine offers quinine-immersed minerals as well as poached pear flavors. Silky-textured, it is an in-your-face offering that should become more civilized with cellaring. Anticipated maturity: 2004–2012. The 2000 Pouilly-Fuissé Au Metertière was harvested at the end of October because of the rains that blanketed the region in late September and early October. It offers a smoky, mineral-scented nose and a superripe, focused, and tangy personality. While it is outstanding, coating the palate with copious quantities of minerals and citrus fruits, this wine lacks the concentration and depth of Cordier's finest Metertières. Drink it over the next 8–9 years. Lively, with scents of mineral and smoke, the 2000 Pouilly-Fuissé Vignes Blanches is fresh and highly expressive. Figs, lemons, and stone can be found in its medium-bodied character. Anticipated maturity: now–2011.

The stunning 2000 Pouilly-Fuissé Vers Pouilly is loaded. It bursts from the glass with citrus and mineral aromas and possesses an awesomely focused, medium-bodied personality. This crystalline, highly focused wine coats the palate with quartz, citrus fruits, minerals, and hints of quinine whose flavors linger throughout its extensive finish. Powerful, concentrated, complex, it is also highly detailed. Anticipated maturity: 2004–2012. The 2000 Pouilly-Fuissé Vers Cras was vinified and aged in 90% new oak barrels, yet the wine is in no way marked by wood. It reveals earthy mineral aromas and a tangy, zesty, medium-bodied personality. Hugely concentrated, this is a muscular, fresh, boisterous wine with an admirably persistent finish. Anticipated maturity: 2004–2012+.

Other recommended wines: 2000 Bourgogne Blanc Jean de la Vigne (89), 1999 Mâcon (1st bottling) (88), 1999 Mâcon (2nd bottling) (88–89), 2000 Mâcon Au Bois d'Allier (88), 1997 Mâcon-Fuissé (88), 1999 Mâcon-Fuissé (88–89), 2000 Mâcon-Fuissé (89), 2000 Pouilly-Fuissé (89), 1997 Pouilly-Loché (88), 1999 Pouilly-Loché (89), 2000 Pouilly-Loché (89), 1997 St.-Véran (88–90), 1999 St.-Véran Les Crays (89+)

DOMAINE DE COURCEL (POMMARD)

1999 Pommard Rugiens	E	(89–90+)

Yves Confuron, who also works at his family's estate in Vosne-Romanée (Confuron-Cotétidot), has been responsible for the administration and winemaking at the Domaine de Courcel since 1996. Over the past few years, this agronomist/oenologist has instituted significant changes to this estate's viticulture, including having the vineyards regularly plowed, and striving for lower yields. The estate produced 39 hectoliters per hectare in 1999 and 27 in 2000. "In these vintages, you could get moderate yields if you made the effort," he said. At harvest, the grapes are sorted twice, once in the vineyard, then again on sorting tables at the cuverie. Only the Bourgogne Rouge is destemmed, no wines are ever acidified, and the grapes are put through a 5- to 6-day cold maceration.

Yves Confuron makes classic, old-style Burgundies with rugged, somewhat rustic personalities, loaded with fruit, yet firm and foursquare. Produced from over 50-year-old vines from a one-hectare parcel, the medium- to dark ruby-colored 1999 Pommard Rugiens reveals sweet cherry and jammy raspberry aromas. This deep, gorgeously broad wine is crammed with sweet candied red fruits. It has a firm, stemmy, tannin-filled character that will require patience. Anticipated maturity: 2005–2012.

Other recommended wines: 1999 Pommard Fremiers (87–89), 1999 Pommard Grand Clos Des Epenots (87–89+?)

MAISON MICHEL COUTOUX (CHASSAGNE-MONTRACHET)

2000 Chassagne-Montrachet La Maltroie	E	91
2000 Chassagne-Montrachet Morgeot	E	90
2000 Meursault Genevrières	E	92
2000 Montrachet	EEE	93+
2000 Puligny-Montrachet Referts	EE	90

Michel Coutoux, who has been working for Michel Niellon, his renowned father-in-law, for ten years, has recently started a *négociant* business. Originally from Touraine, Coutoux continues to work full-time for Niellon and uses the techniques he learns there for his *négoce* wines. When asked what the main winemaking difference was between his style and his father-in-law's, he responded that he vinified and aged his wines almost entirely in barrel while Niellon uses stainless steel tanks for a percentage of his wines. Furthermore, Coutoux uses a slightly larger percentage of new oak. All of Maison Michel Coutoux's wines are produced from purchased juice.

Coutoux is among those Burgundians who believe that 2000 is a significantly better vintage than 1999. "It provided us with excellent maturity. It rained when the vines were thirsty and right before harvest. We benefited from northerly winds that dried the grapes from the storm of the 12th of September. Whereas the reds in the Côte de Beaune had significant levels of rot, the whites were healthy." Coutoux, who benefited early on from the wine world's attention because of his father-in-law's star status, is living up to expectations with an outstanding lineup of 2000s. The mineral- and clay-scented 2000 Chassagne-Montrachet Morgeot is a plump, pear, apple, and spice-flavored wine. It is broad, powerful, loaded with fruit, and possesses an admirably long, lush finish. Drink it over the next 9 years.

The 2000 Chassagne-Montrachet La Maltroie reveals sweet, smoky apricots and white peaches in its otherwise spice-laden nose. This sultry, expansive offering has outstanding depth, balance, and freshness. It is crammed with spiced white/yellow fruits that coat the taster's palate. Drink this highly expressive, sexy offering over the next 8 years. The almond, mineral, spice, and apricot-scented 2000 Puligny-Montrachet Les Referts is a plump, medium-bodied wine. Full of character and exquisitely balanced, it is juicy, supple, fruit-driven, and complex. It butters the mouth with spices, exotic fruits, and minerals. Drink it over the next 8–9 years.

The 2000 Meursault Genevrières displays toasted hazelnut and poached pear aromas. Medium- to full-bodied, velvety-textured, and chewy, it is an extravagant Meursault. Loaded with minerals, candied apples, white peaches, and toast, this fat, hugely concentrated wine is both intense and exquisitely long. Anticipated maturity: now–2011. Coutoux's 2000 Montrachet boasts smoky minerals, pears, and apples in its expressive aromatics. Medium-bodied and plump, this is a dense, deep, and gorgeously balanced wine. Loads of white fruits, minerals, and hints of quinine can be found throughout its concentrated, seamless personality, as well as in its exceptionally pure and long finish. It is unquestionably the finest wine this new *négociant* firm has ever crafted. Anticipated maturity: 2005–2015.

Other recommended wines: 1999 Meursault Genevrières (89), 2000 Meursault Narvaux (88), 1999 Meursault Perrières (89), 2000 Meursault Perrières (89+)

DOMAINE PIERRE DAMOY (GEVREY-CHAMBERTIN)

1999 Chambertin	EE	(92–93)
1999 Chambertin Clos de Bèze	EE	(92–94)

This estate, which for years produced wines far below their qualitative pedigrees, is back on track. Pierre Damoy (the domaine is named after his great-great-grandfather), who has run this estate since 1992, has significantly lowered yields (its grand cru parcels averaged between 24 and 35 hectoliters per hectare in 1999), has adopted noninterventionist winemaking, and now eschews fining and filtration.

Readers who are familiar with the history of Burgundy know that Napoleon ended the monarchy's laws of primogeniture (whereby the eldest son was the sole inheritor) and instituted laws forcing the equal partition of a family's assets among all its children. This has caused the fragmented parcelization of vineyards and estates. A prime example of this is the fact that Domaine Pierre Damoy is owned by a multitude of family members, with the present-day administrator, Pierre Damoy, owning less than 1%.

Blackberries, black cherries, and candied black raspberries can be found in the nose of the medium to dark ruby-colored 1999 Chambertin Clos de Bèze. This wine has outstanding depth and concentration. Loads of lively red cherries, strawberries, and blueberries can be found in its velvety-textured personality. Additionally, this wine possesses an exceptionally long, pure, and superripe tannin-filled finish. Anticipated maturity: 2004–2012. Pierre Damoy's 1999 Chambertin was harvested at 32 hectoliters per hectare. It is medium to dark ruby-colored and reveals licorice, sweet cherry, blackberry, toasted oak, and spice flavors. This full-bodied wine has huge concentration to its rich and intense character. It is highly structured and youthfully austere, yet loaded with powerful black fruits and a strong oak influence. Anticipated maturity: 2005–2013+.

Other recommended wine: 1999 Chapelle-Chambertin (89–90)

DOMAINE VINCENT DANCER (CHASSAGNE-MONTRACHET)

2000 Chassagne-Montrachet La Romanée	D	(90–92)
1997 Chassagne-Montrachet La Romanée	D	90
2000 Chevalier-Montrachet	EE	(92–93)
2000 Meursault Perrières	D	(90–92)
1999 Pommard Pézerolles	E	90

Burgundy is replete with old estates, passed on from father to son over the course of centuries. It is rare to find a "start-up," and even rarer to find a successful one. Yet, the young, talented, and inquisitive Vincent Dancer has in a few short years achieved what many have attempted and failed. By taking possession of vineyards owned by his family that had been locked into long-term sharecropping arrangements, Dancer has fashioned a small but well-furnished estate. In only his second vintage as a winemaker and estate owner, Dancer produced an outstanding 1997 Chassagne-Montrachet La Romanée. Its refined, sweet pear and floral aromas lead to an expressive, medium- to full-bodied character. This rich, creamy wine is packed with loads of white fruits and spices that last throughout its admirably long finish. Readers should note that Dancer owns one acre of this first-rate premier cru. Anticipated maturity: now–2005.

The delicious 1999 Pommard Pézerolles is medium to dark ruby-colored and has an intense nose of sweet candied cherries and violets. On the palate, this medium- to full-bodied wine offers opulent layers of blackberries, cherries, cassis, blueberries, jammy raspberries, and a myriad of spices. It is satin-textured, has outstanding palate presence, and a long, supple, sweet, tannin-filled finish. Drink this beautiful Pommard over the next 8–9 years.

Dancer who has a wonderful sense of humor, had just returned from a vacation in the United States when I visited the estate to taste his 2000s. "I loved the natural beauty of your national parks," he said, "as well as the unnatural beauty of the silicon stuffed sunbathers of Venice Beach." He believes that 2000 is an excellent vintage. "The 1999s may have been more elegant, but the 2000s have more fruit and are richer."

Loads of spices and minerals can be discerned in the 2000 Meursault Perrières. Medium- to full-bodied, broad, and velvety-textured, this is a forward, spice-driven wine with a long, thick finish. This early-drinking beauty should be consumed over the next 7 years. The superripe pear- and apple-scented 2000 Chassagne-Montrachet La Romanée has excellent depth to its vinous, medium- to full-bodied character. It is rich, layered, and coats the palate with copious quantities of white fruits and spices. Drink it over the next 9 years.

Dancer produces one barrel of Chevalier-Montrachet from a parcel planted in 1952. His 2000 reveals intense liquid mineral and spice aromas. It is medium- to full-bodied, oily-textured, plump, thick, and chewy. Loaded with viscous layers of pear and apple compote, this spicy wine combines freshness with fat exceptionally well. Drink between now–2013.

Other recommended wines: 1999 Chassagne-Montrachet La Romanée (89), 1999 Meursault Perrières (88–89)

DOMAINE RENÉ ET VINCENT DAUVISSAT (CHABLIS)

1997	Chablis Les Clos	E	(91–93)
1997	Chablis Forest	D	(88–91)
1997	Chablis Preuses	E	(90–92)
1997	Chablis Vaillons	D	(88–90+)

"The 1997 vintage produced very good wines. At harvest the grapes were gold-colored, showed no signs of rot, and had huge physiological ripeness," said Vincent Dauvissat, the energetic and bright director of this renowned estate. "They are the absolute opposites of the 1996s. The 1997s are wines of pleasure that can be drunk early but that will age longer than most people think. They are not overripe monsters because their was little loss of acidity after the malolactic fermentations." Dauvissat informed me that his yields were high in 1997, "but not massive" (they ranged from 60 hectoliters per hectare on the premiers crus to 50 h/h on the grands crus). None of Dauvissat's 1997s was chapitalized as they were harvested between 12.5% and 13.2% natural potential alcohol. Dauvissat was surprised that some of his 1996s finished their malolactic fermentations after the 1997s (most Chablis producers artificially force these secondary fermentations to occur quickly. In contrast, Dauvissat lets nature take its course).

The few readers who have extensive knowledge of Chablis's historical vintages may be interested to know that Dauvissat believes his 1997s most resemble the 1962s, another warm year that produced very ripe and healthy grapes. Qualitatively, Dauvissat ranks 1996 as the finest vintage of the 1990s, "it has the greatest combination of perfectly sanitary grapes, acid, and richness of fruit I have ever witnessed," he said. In his ranking of vintages, 1996 is followed by 1990, 1995, 1997, and 1992.

The following wines were tasted from barrel. The 1997 Chablis Vaillons has a nose composed of pineapple, wood spice, and anise. Expressive, feminine, and medium-bodied, it possesses a flavorful core of spicy white peaches, minerals, and almonds. This wine, which merited a "super good!" in my notebook, will be delicious to drink through 2005. Fresh gun flint–like aromas are found in the medium-bodied 1997 Chablis Forest. It has impressive richness, breadth, and freshness in its highly expressive, almond- and mineral-flavored character. This thick, chewy wine is expansive, powerful, and admirably well balanced. Anticipated maturity: now–2005. The foursquare, austere 1997 Chablis Les Preuses has a nose reminiscent of citrus fruits, minerals, and toasty spices. This is a structured, medium-bodied, flavorful, and impeccably proportioned wine. The offering's rich and broad personality is filled with pears, acacia blossoms, and flintlike flavors that linger throughout its long and focused finish. Anticipated maturity: now–2007. Dauvissat has fashioned a superb 1997 Chablis Les Clos. Its cold, brooding, tight, mineral-scented nose gives way to a hugely expansive and muscular character. Pears, apples, gooseberries, earth, and minerals are found in this broad-shouldered, medium- to full-bodied, and thick wine. It is masculine, concentrated, dense, and possesses admirable length. Drink it between now–2008.

Other recommended wines: 1996 Chablis (88), 1997 Chablis Séchet (88+)

DOMAINE MARIUS DELARCHE (PERNAND-VERGELESSES)

1998	Corton-Charlemagne Réserve	EE	91
1997	Corton-Charlemagne Réserve	EE	93
1997	Corton Le Corton Réserve	E	91
1997	Corton Renardes Réserve	E	90+

Note: These "Réserve" bottlings are special *cuvées* fashioned for David Hinkle and Peter Vezan for the U.S. market.

The spectacular 1997 Corton-Charlemagne Réserve will rival the wondrous 1996. Delarche's 1997 is more reminiscent of a first-rate Meursault Perrières than the typical Corton-Charlemagne because of its intense minerality, found in abundance both aromatically and in its flavor profile. Elegant, powerful, highly concentrated, this great wine reveals superb ripeness of fruit (mostly pears and apples), and is medium- to full-bodied, thick, yet extremely fresh and delineated. It presently displays loads of charred oak scents and flavors that should easily be integrated into its dense core of fruit with cellaring. Drink it between now–2008. The medium to dark ruby-colored 1997 Corton Renardes Réserve offers overripe peach and sweet cherry aromas. Medium- to full-bodied, powerful, as well as expansive, this complex cherry, apricot, earth, cedar, and herb-flavored wine displays admirable purity to its components. It is well structured, balanced, harmonious, and quite persistent. Drink it over the next 7–8 years. Were it not for some alcoholic warmth in the finish, the score for Delarche's 1997 Corton Le Corton Réserve would have been even higher. This medium to dark ruby/purple wine has embracing wax and coffee-laden aromas. On the palate, blackberries, red cherries, mocha, rosemary, and stones vie for the taster's attention in this seductive, complex, medium- to full-bodied wine. It has admirable depth, flavor, precision, and a long, if somewhat alcoholic, drawn-out finish. Anticipated maturity: now–2009.

The sweet, vanilla- and anise-scented 1998 Corton-Charlemagne Réserve is a medium- to full-bodied, velvety-textured wine. Fat, well-ripened white and yellow fruits can be found in this rich, overripe yet well-balanced wine. Its harmony, texture, and richness are unlike the overwhelming majority of 1998s. Lovers of oak will be enamored of this effort's grilled, wood-infused, fruity character. Anticipated maturity: now–2008.

Other recommended wines: 1999 Corton-Charlemagne Réserve (89), 2000 Corton-Charlemagne Réserve (89), 1997 Pernand-Vergelesses Île de Vergelesses Réserve (89), 1997 Pernand-Vergelesses Les Quartiers Réserve (white) (89), 1997 Pernand-Vergelesses Les Quartiers Réserve (white) (88)

MAISON JOSEPH DROUHIN (BEAUNE)

2000	Bâtard-Montrachet	EEE	(89–91)
1998	Bâtard-Montrachet	EEE	90
1998	Beaune Clos des Mouches (white)	EE	90
1999	Bonnes Mares	EE	(90–91)
2000	Chablis Les Clos	E	90+
1999	Chambertin	EE	(89–91)
1998	Clos de Vougeot	EE	90
1999	Corton	E	(91–93)
1999	Griotte-Chambertin	EE	(90–92)
2000	Montrachet Marquis de Laguiche	EEE	(90–92)
1999	Montrachet Marquis de Laguiche	EEE	(89–91)
1998	Montrachet Marquis de Laguiche	EEE	90
1997	Montrachet Marquis de Laguiche	EEE	(90–92+)

The 1997 Montrachet Marquis de Laguiche has splendid aromatics. Profound scents of minerals, earth, flowers, pears, and toasty oak lead to a broad, ample, concentrated, and rich character. This medium- to full-bodied wine has layers of minerals, stones, and white fruits in its core as well as its persistent finish. Anticipated maturity: now–2012.

Maison Drouhin's flagship wine, the Beaune Clos des Mouches was particularly successful in the 1998 vintage. Its spice, stone, and honeysuckle aromas are followed by a character of outstanding flavor intensity. Dried honey and lemon drop candies dominate the personality of this expansive, well-balanced, and extremely persistent wine. Anticipated maturity: now–2007. The expressive 1998 Bâtard-Montrachet expresses attractive aromas of nuts, flowers, and well-ripened white fruits. This lovely, plump, broad, and ample wine is medium- to full-bodied, thick, crammed with sweet pear flavors, and its long, tangy finish reveals notes of lemony fruits. Anticipated maturity: now–2007.

Drouhin's 1998 Montrachet Marquis de Laguiche offers flowers, nuts, and spices in its aromatics. This medium-bodied, spice cake and dried honey–laden, mineral-flavored wine is more harmonious than the majority of its 1998 brethren. It is expansive, well balanced, and possesses a long, smooth, and crystalline finish. Anticipated maturity: now–2009. Produced from Maison Joseph Drouhin's estate-owned vineyards, the medium to dark ruby-colored 1998 Clos de Vougeot has a sweet red cherry and vanilla-scented nose. Medium-bodied, intense, and creamy, this opulently textured, rich, jammy red fruit–flavored wine is softly styled and delicious. Drink it over the next 6–7 years.

According to Laurence Jobard, the wine-maker, 1999 was not a year for excessive *bâtonnage* for the whites—"you cannot extract what is simply not there." She went on to add that both natural potential alcohols and malic acid levels were elevated, so freshness was easy to maintain after malolactic fermentations. Since the wines had little protein, she only did minor fining before bottling. Mme Jobard informed me that this firm's vineyards are completely organically farmed, with tests being conducted on certain parcels to determine whether they should adopt biodynamic viticulture. The 1999 Montrachet Marquis de Laguiche bursts from the glass with toasted oak, mineral, and smoked bacon aromas. This broad, rich, and expansive wine has loads of apple, pear, and white peach flavors. It also proposes a long, pure finish that surprisingly seems to reveal some tannin (not a common characteristic of white Burgundies). Anticipated maturity: 2003–2010.

Robert Drouhin says that the 1999 red Burgundy vintage reminds him of 1961. "It has extremely ripe tannins, not quite like those of 1985, but still exquisite. This is one of the greatest vintages I've ever known." He went on to add that the region between Volnay and Aloxe-Corton "made wines of great concentration." Mme Laurence Jobard explained that they had "extended the time of *élevage* to build more richness in the wines."

The candied Bing cherry–scented 1999 Griotte-Chambertin has a zesty, lively nose as well as a medium to dark ruby-colored character. It is packed with layers of raspberries, blueberries, and jammy cherries whose seamless flavors last from the attack through its supple finish. Anticipated maturity: now–2010. The similarly colored 1999 Chambertin has an impressive floral and berry-laced nose. This well-made, medium-bodied wine has an impressive amount of blackberry and cherry fruits that covers its noticeable yet ripe tannin. Stones, fresh herbs, and a distinctive note of oak appear in its long finish. Anticipated maturity: now–2009. The 1999 Bonnes Mares reveals a saturated medium to dark ruby color, and a spicy, black cherry–imbued nose. This is a masculine, muscular, broad-shouldered wine with a medium-bodied personality crammed with coffee beans, blackberries, and cassis. It has outstanding density of fruit and the structure and depth required for moderate aging. Drink it between 2003–2012.

To Frédéric Drouhin, who is taking over day-to-day operations of this Beaune *négociant* firm from his father, Robert, Chablis fared better than the Côte d'Or in 2000 because there was no rain before harvest. He went on to inform me that the bulk prices that *négociants* paid for 2000s had dropped across the board, with the exception of the grands crus, which remained stable.

The floral 2000 Chablis Les Clos is medium- to full-bodied, and loaded with gun flint, mineral, and spice flavors. This wine has outstanding depth, balance, concentration, and length. It is seamless, highly expressive, and built to last. Anticipated maturity: now–2012. The 2000 Bâtard-Montrachet has creamy mineral and spicy aromas. It is medium-bodied, fat, and sports copious quantities of pears, spiced apples, as well as toasted minerals in its flavor profile and extensive finish. It has outstanding depth of fruit, intensity, and balance. Anticipated maturity: 2003–2012. Candied apples, poached pears, and hints of tangerine can be discerned in the tangy, medium-bodied 2000 Montrachet Marquis de Laguiche's personality. This well-made wine exhibits exceptional harmony in its fat yet vivacious personality. Citrus fruits are interspersed with minerals, flowers, and apples in its outstanding character. Anticipated maturity: 2005–2014.

Other recommended wines: 1997 Bâtard-Montrachet (88+), 1999 Bâtard-Montrachet (88), 1999 Beaune Clos des Mouches (white) (88), 1999 Beaune Clos des Mouches (red) (87–89), 1997 Bonnes Mares (88), 1999 Chablis Les Clos (88), 1997 Chablis Vaudésir (89+), 2000 Chablis Vaudésir (89), 1997 Chambertin (89), 1999 Chambolle-Musigny (87–89), 1997 Chambolle-Musigny Les Amoureuses (88), 1998 Chassagne-Montrachet Marquis de Laguiche (white) (89), 1998 Corton-Charlemagne (88+), 2000 Corton-Charlemagne (87–89), 1997 Grands-Echézeaux (89), 1999 Grands-Echézeaux (88–90), 1997 Griotte-Chambertin (88), 1999 Meursault Charmes (88), 1997 Meursault Perrières (88), 2000 Meursault Perrières (88), 1997 Musigny (88), 1999 Nuits-St.-Georges Les Procès (87–89), 1999 Puligny-Montrachet Les Folatières (88), 2000 Puligny-Montrachet Les Pucelles (88–89), 1997 Romanée-St.-Vivant (88+), 1999 Volnay Clos des Chênes (88–90), 1999 Vosne-Romanée Les Petits Monts (88–90)

DOMAINE DROUHIN-LAROZE (GEVREY-CHAMBERTIN)

| 1997 Clos de Vougeot | EE | 91+ |

The medium to dark ruby-colored 1997 Clos de Vougeot reveals ripe fruit and highly expressive spice aromas. This opulently textured, medium- to full-bodied, dense offering has outstanding grip, structure, and persistence. Layers of jammy blackberries, cherries, road tar, and loads of sweet oak are found in this powerful wine. Anticipated maturity: now–2009.

DOMAINE CLAUDE DUGAT (GEVREY-CHAMBERTIN)

1999 Charmes-Chambertin	EEE	96
1998 Charmes-Chambertin	EE	93
1997 Charmes-Chambertin	EE	(93–95)
1999 Gevrey-Chambertin	E	90
1999 Gevrey-Chambertin Lavaux St.-Jacques	EE	90+
1997 Gevrey-Chambertin Lavaux St.-Jacques	E	(92–93+)
1999 Gevrey-Chambertin Premier Cru	EE	(90–92)
1998 Gevrey-Chambertin Premier Cru	EE	90
1997 Gevrey-Chambertin Premier Cru	E	(90–92)
1999 Griotte-Chambertin	EEE	(93–96)
1998 Griotte-Chambertin	EEE	93
1997 Griotte-Chambertin	EEE	(93–95)

Claude Dugat, one of Burgundy's and the world's finest vignerons, works the vines that his grandfather, a noted horticulturist, had selected for their small bunches and berries, as well as for their concentrated juice. "My work in the vineyard is really to maintain the vines at 10 to 12 tiny clusters, and to make sure they are working hard for their food. I don't like to say that I make my vines suffer, because I love them. I prefer to say that I make them work hard for me. The only food I provide is a little manure from organically raised cattle when the vines' leaves show they need it, which is generally every four years," he said.

Dugat feels that, qualitatively, 1997 is not a great vintage (he places it between 1994 and 1995). "It is better than the 1989s. That may be because my yields were too high that year. I was disappointed at first, because seeing the grapes, I thought I had a great year on my hands. But in time, as they gathered strength, I ended up loving the wines." Consumers lucky enough to acquire Dugat's wines will find that once again he achieved magnificent ripeness, fashioning opulently textured wines that will be superb to drink upon release. However, while Dugat's 1995s and 1996s are wines that will age well, his 1997s, like most offerings from the Côte d'Or, will require drinking over the next 10 years.

Claude Dugat's 1997 Gevrey-Chambertin Premier Cru is medium to dark ruby-colored, and exhibits a profound nose of spice-laden, sweet, dark fruits. It is medium- to full-bodied, has superb balance and grip as well as a silky texture, and loads of jammy cherry fruit mingled with Asian spices. This fresh, supple, seductive wine should be consumed over the next 6–7 years. The slightly darker-colored 1997 Gevrey-Chambertin Lavaux St.-Jacques displays a nose reminiscent of a compote of black fruits and fresh herbs. It explodes on the palate with plummy fruit, a satin texture, and ample body. Luscious and rich, it verges on being overripe, yet has a flattering streak of freshness. Anticipated maturity: now–2006.

Both of Claude Dugat's grands crus are spectacular. Crafted from yields below 30 hectoliters per hectare, the medium to dark ruby-colored 1997 Charmes-Chambertin displays candied red cherry and spicy aromas. On the palate, it is opulent, sexy, refined, and gorgeously velvety. Flavors reminiscent of cinnamon-laced red cherry jam coat the palate, and linger for up to 30 seconds or more. This hedonistic wine will offer superb drinking over the next 6–10 years. The 1997 Griotte-Chambertin verges on being dark ruby-colored. At first glance, this wine appeared to be reticent, yet with aeration, it revealed sweet black fruits, fresh herbs, perfume, and spices. On the palate, pruny fruits, nutmeg, cinnamon, brown sugar, licorice, and superripe blackberries are found in this broad, plump wine. Neither as structured nor as expressive, forward, or opulent as the Charmes, however, in the Dugat style, it is quite expansive, medium- to full-bodied, and eminently drinkable. Its complex flavors seemingly last forever. It has power, grace, magnificent depth, and a beguiling satin texture. Anticipated maturity: now–2010.

The medium to dark ruby-colored 1998 Gevrey-Chambertin Premier Cru reveals sweet red cherry and spice aromas. Medium-bodied, broad, and packed with loads of black cherry and blackberry fruit, this wine is well concentrated and admirably persistent in the finish. While it certainly possesses the vintage's characteristic tannic structure, it is impressively buried in Dugat's trademark sweet, lush fruit. Drink it over the next 5–6 years. The medium to dark ruby-colored 1998 Charmes-Chambertin displays massive amounts of red and black fruit aromas. Medium- to full-bodied and chewy-textured, it coats the palate with blackberries, black cherries, and cassis. This intense, concentrated, and velvety-textured wine has firm tannins that are immersed in sweet, well-ripened fruit. Drink it over the next 8 years. Medium to dark ruby-colored and boasting black cherry aromas, the velvety-textured 1998 Griotte-Chambertin is perhaps less concentrated than the previous one, yet more elegant, intense, and persistent. Copious quantities of candied raspberries and cherries are found in its elegant, layered character. Drink it over the next 8 years.

The medium to dark ruby-colored 1999 Gevrey-Chambertin reveals lovely red cherry and sweet oak aromas. This pure, lush, medium-bodied wine is velvety-textured and filled with violets and candied cherries. It is plush and opulent and reveals sweet, supple tannins in its fresh, long finish. Drink it over the next 5–6 years. The slightly darker-colored 1999 Gevrey-Chambertin Premier Cru has a toasted oak and candied berry–scented nose. This medium-bodied wine's flavor profile is reminiscent of chocolate chip cookie dough immersed in cherry syrup, with just an infusion of vanilla-flavored oak. It is extroverted, opulent, and possesses a sexy, satiny texture. This concentrated, seamless wine should be consumed between 2003–2009.

Roasted oak and candied blackberries are found in the aromatics of the 1999 Gevrey-Chambertin Lavaux St.-Jacques. Stones, currants, and black cherries are found in this highly structured, tightly wound wine. It is austere for a Dugat offering, yet possesses tremendous underlying fruit. It will require some cellaring. Anticipated maturity: 2005–2010+. The medium to dark ruby-colored 1999 Charmes-Chambertin has a mouthwatering nose of Asian spices, blackberries, and black cherries. This luscious, opulent, medium- to full-bodied wine is creamy-textured and refined. Loads of red cherries, spices, candied raspberries, and touches of sweet oak can be found in this luxurious offering. It has an awesome depth of fruit as well as loads of exquisitely ripened, supple tannins. Additionally, this wine has an exceptionally long, pure finish. Drink it between 2005–2012. The tangy cherry, Asian spice, and hoisin-scented 1999 Griotte-Chambertin is medium to dark ruby-colored. This silky-textured beauty is loaded with creamed cherries, blackberry syrup, spices, and vanilla. It is fresh, focused, and sexy, yet well structured. Its immensely appealing fruit flavors last throughout its exceptional finish. Drink it between 2005–2012.

Other recommended wine: 1997 Gevrey-Chambertin (88–90)

DOMAINE BERNARD DUGAT-PY (GEVREY-CHAMBERTIN)

1999	Chambertin	EEE	(96–98+)
1997	Chambertin	EEE	(95–97+)
1999	Charmes-Chambertin	EEE	(92–94)
1998	Charmes-Chambertin	EEE	(93–95)
1997	Charmes-Chambertin	EEE	(92–95)
1998	Gevrey-Chambertin Coeur du Roi	EE	(88–90+)
1997	Gevrey-Chambertin Coeur du Roi	EE	(89–91)
1998	Gevrey-Chambertin Les Evocelles	EE	(89–92)
1999	Gevrey-Chambertin Lavaux St.-Jacques	EEE	(91–92)
1998	Gevrey-Chambertin Lavaux St.-Jacques	EE	(91–93)
1997	Gevrey-Chambertin Lavaux St.-Jacques	EE	(90–93)
1998	Gevrey-Chambertin Premier Cru	EE	(92–94)
1997	Gevrey-Chambertin Premier Cru	EE	(89–92)
1999	Mazis-Chambertin Vieilles Vignes	EEE	(94–95+)
1998	Mazis-Chambertin Vieilles Vignes	EEE	(92–95)
1997	Mazis-Chambertin Vieilles Vignes	EEE	(93–95)

Bernard Dugat is one of Burgundy's finest vignerons. Moreover, the progress at this estate since the 1992 vintage is nothing short of remarkable. For example, the 1993s were some of the finest wines made in that difficult year. Since then, Dugat has seemingly improved with each new vintage, a fact well documented in the pages of *The Wine Advocate*.

In the 1997 vintage, a year that brought moderate yields throughout the Côte, Dugat's averaged 20 h/h, including his Bourgogne Rouge. Some of his vineyards were harvested at 13 h/h. Consumers and wine-makers may often wonder what are the secrets to being an extraordinary producer. Dugat, his cousin Claude Dugat, Lalou Bize-Leroy, and other stars of Burgundy stress that the key is to do as much work as possible in the vineyard, and as little as possible in the winery. To this, the two Dugats add their good fortune at having inherited vines from their grandfather that produce tiny berries with superconcentrated juice. The estate's 1997s combine extraordinary ripeness with black colors and harmonious personalities.

Crafted from 50- to 88-year-old vines that yielded a paltry 16 h/h, the medium to dark ruby/purple 1997 Gevrey-Chambertin Coeur du Roi ("Heart of the King") displays cinnamon-infused creamy cherry scents. Untold quantities of cassis, black raspberries, and spices are found in its velvety-textured, medium- to full bodied personality. It has outstanding richness, fat, and exquisite ripeness. Drink it over the next 8 years. The medium to dark ruby-colored 1997 Gevrey-Chambertin Premier Cru was produced from parcels in the Corbeaux, Fonteny, and La Petite Chapelle vineyards, at less than half the yields achieved in 1996. Its black cherry and Asian spice aromatics are followed by a thick, oily-textured, and medium- to full-bodied character jam-packed with candied blackberries. This chewy, concentrated, persistent, and impeccably balanced wine should be at its peak of drinkability between now–2009.

The dark ruby-colored 1997 Gevrey-Chambertin Lavaux St.-Jacques offers aromas reminiscent of cherry pie, white truffles, chocolate, cinnamon, and blackberry syrup. This is an intense, concentrated, expansive, full-bodied, masculine wine. Powerful, brooding black fruits, mocha, and toasty oak flavors can be found in this broad-shouldered, muscular offering. Drink it between now–2010. One hundred cases of the dark ruby-colored 1997 Charmes-Chambertin were produced. Its magnificently sweet nose is crammed with cherries and creamy vanilla aromas. It is almost as charming and sexy as the out-of-this-world 1996.

Medium- to full-bodied, it offers loads of syrupy blackberries and cherries in addition to possessing the required structure for cellaring. Anticipated maturity: now–2009. Crafted from 53- and 56-year-old vines, the dark ruby-colored 1997 Mazis-Chambertin exhibits sweet black fruits, Asian spices, and hints of saddle leather in its austere and brooding aromatics. This full-bodied, broad-shouldered, muscular wine has flavors reminiscent of soy sauce, hoisin, earth, leather, and cassis. At present somewhat foursquare, this wine will require patience. Anticipated maturity: 2003–2012.

Only 152 bottles of the virtually black 1997 Chambertin were made. Those looking for nuance and delicacy in a young Burgundy should shy away from this wine—it is truly a hedonistic fruit bomb. Aromatically, it reveals creamy wild red berries, cherry pie filling, fruitcake, blueberry jam, milk chocolate, and hints of white pepper. This is a chewy, almost syrupy-textured monster with candied and jellied red fruit flavors that saturate the palate and seemingly linger forever. Anticipated maturity: 2004–2015. Burgundy's weather in 1997 was decidedly more New World–ish than is typical in this northerly region. Bernard Dugat's Chambertin reflects this in its massively ripe flavor profile and texture, yet he was able to masterfully maintain enough of the structure that has made Burgundy's Pinots famous throughout the world for this wine to be balanced and have some cellaring potential. Drink this extraordinary offering over the next 8–10 years. Bravo!

This is the only estate where all of the 1998s tasted merited recommending (the Bourgogne was not tasted). While they were still in barrel in March 2000, Bernard Dugat was preparing for bottling. After sorting, yields at this estate were minuscule (9 h/h for the Gevrey-Chambertin Les Evocelles and 18 h/h for the Gevrey-Chambertin Coeur du Roi, for example). Produced from 30- to 50-year-old vines, the 1998 Gevrey-Chambertin Vieilles Vignes reveals aromas of sweet cherries and plums. Medium-bodied and velvety-textured, it has a jammy, dark cherry, fruit-filled character. The vintage's firm tannins can be discerned under this wine's impressive layers of fruit, so it should be consumed sooner rather than later. Anticipated maturity: now–2004. The medium to dark ruby-colored 1998 Gevrey-Chambertin Coeur de Roi (50- to 80-year-old vines) has a licorice- and blackberry-scented nose. This medium- to full-bodied, intense, and structured wine has a firm, tannic backbone buried under loads of lively black fruits. While some would opt to cellar this wine in the hope that the fruit would outlast the tannin, I would suggest drinking it over the next 5 years.

Produced from 70+-year-old vines, the medium to dark ruby-colored 1998 Gevrey-Chambertin Les Evocelles exhibits sweet cherry, blackberry, and blueberry aromas. Medium- to full-bodied, thick, and inky, this extremely dense, super-concentrated, and intense wine is crammed with powerful black fruit flavors, intermingled with toasted oak. While it does possess the vintage's characteristic tannic backbone, it is, at present, covered in fruit. Anticipated maturity: now–2006. The 1998 Gevrey-Chambertin Premier Cru is fashioned from vines located (in equal proportions) in La Petite Chapelle, Fonteny, and Corbeaux. It is medium to dark ruby-colored, and reveals an intense blackberry, kirsch, and cookie dough–scented nose. Medium- to full-bodied, and offering magnificent concentration and power, this blueberry, black cherry, and toasted oak–flavored wine has huge depth and elegance. Fresh, expressive, and well delineated, it does not appear to suffer from any of the vintage's negative attributes. Anticipated maturity: now–2010. The saturated, dark ruby/purple 1998 Gevrey-Chambertin Lavaux St.-Jacques has toasted oak and overripe black fruit aromas. On the palate, flavors reminiscent of Welch's grape jelly, hoisin, and licorice can be found in this medium- to full-bodied wine. Fresh, bright, and intense, its profound layers of fruit cover a firm, tannic edge. Drink this wine over the next 4–5 years.

Bernard Dugat's 1998 Charmes-Chambertin is dark ruby-colored and offers a hugely spicy, candied cherry–scented nose. Loads of black fruits and sweet cherries, as well as asphalt and oak, can be found in this broad, medium- to full-bodied wine. Sweet, almost jammy fruit coats the taster's palate throughout this offering's well-ripened personality and long, focused finish. Anticipated maturity: now–2007. Produced from 60-year-old vines, the 1998 Mazis-Chambertin Vieilles Vignes has a tar- and blackberry-scented nose. This muscular, masculine, and highly expressive wine is full-bodied, inky, and firmly structured. Massively concentrated and intense, this may be one of the rare tannic Pinot Noirs whose fruit can sustain cellaring. Anticipated maturity: now–2008+?

Bernard Dugat crafted marvelous 1999s, including a Chambertin that is certainly one of the vintage's two or three finest wines. Waxy red cherries can be discerned in the deep aromatics of the 1999 Gevrey-Chambertin Lavaux St.-Jacques. This dense, candied wine is exquisitely ripe, offering a compote of black cherries, blackberries, licorice, and hints of oak in its flavor profile. Its exceptionally long and pure finish reveals massive quantities of marvelously ripened tannin. Drink it between 2004–2011. The 1999 Charmes-Chambertin is medium to dark ruby-colored and offers a knockout nose of sweet cherries, smoked bacon, and mint. This is a huge, medium- to full-bodied wine that is highly concentrated and expansive. Untold quantities of blackberries, cherries, and spices and hints of new toasty oak can be discerned in its layered character. This powerful yet feminine wine is loaded with ripe tannin. Anticipated maturity: 2005–2012+. Produced from 55- to 60-year-old vines, the dark-colored 1999 Mazis-Chambertin is profound. Its licorice, black cherry syrup, and chocolate chip cookie dough–scented nose leads to a hugely powerful, medium- to full-bodied character. This road tar, blackberry, cassis, and spice-flavored wine has the density, structure, and balance for moderate to long-term aging. Anticipated maturity: 2006–2015+.

Bernard Dugat's parcel of Chambertin is planted at 1,400 vines per acre and averages 80 years of age. No tractor can penetrate this densely planted parcel, so Bernard Dugat, his wife, daughter, and son are forced to do all the work by hand. The 1999 Chambertin is a magnificent, show-stopping wine. It is black-colored and bursts from the glass with licorice, cookie dough, blackberry, and cassis aromas. This is a massive, full-bodied wine with loads of sweet candied black fruits, licorice, freshly laid asphalt, spice, fresh herbs, and toasty oak flavors. It is mind-numbingly powerful, conquering the taster with wave upon wave of supple, syruplike fruit whose flavors last throughout its seemingly unending finish. This blockbuster Burgundy should be cellared for a minimum of 10 years and may last up to 20 or more years after that. It is one of the rare wines from this region that I would have no qualms about cellaring for 30 years.

Other recommended wines: 1999 Gevrey-Chambertin Coeur du Roi (87–89), 1999 Gevrey-Chambertin Les Evocelles (89–90), 1999 Gevrey-Chambertin Premier Cru (89–90), 1997 Gevrey-Chambertin Vieilles Vignes (87–89), 1998 Gevrey-Chambertin Vieilles Vignes (88), 1999 Vosne-Romanée Vieilles Vignes (88–90)

DOMAINE DUJAC (MOREY-ST.-DENIS)

1999	Bonnes Mares	EEE	(92–94)
1997	Bonnes Mares	EEE	94
1999	Charmes-Chambertin	EE	(90–91)
1997	Charmes-Chambertin	EE	90
1999	Clos de la Roche	EEE	(90–92+)
1997	Clos de la Roche	EEE	93+
1999	Clos St.-Denis	EEE	(89–91)
1997	Clos St.-Denis	EEE	92
1999	Echézeaux	EEE	(91–92)
1997	Echézeaux	EEE	90
1999	Gevrey-Chambertin Les Combottes	EE	(89–91)
1997	Gevrey-Chambertin Les Combottes	EE	90

Domaine Dujac's 1997s were seductive and enthralling. "This vintage corresponds perfectly to my taste in wine," said Jacques Seysses, the domaine's owner and wine-maker. "I want sen-

suality, charm, complexity, and harmony in my Burgundies. If a wine-maker goes out searching for power or color, harmony will automatically be lost," he went on to say. Low yields (in
the 29–30 h/h range), and what Seysses describes as "the richest year in natural sugars of my
life," helped Seysses make some of the finest wines ever crafted at this famed estate.

The 1997 Gevrey-Chambertin Les Combottes is ruby-colored and reveals aromas of sweet
red/black fruits dusted with talcum powder. Medium-bodied, this tangy, fresh, yet expansive
wine displays briary blackberry and cassis flavors. It is silky-textured, elegant, and tightly
wound. Anticipated maturity: now–2009. Spicy/earthy cherries can be discerned in the ruby-
colored 1997 Charmes-Chambertin's delightful aromatics. While not Seysses' most complex
wine, it is elegant, lush, and lively. Concentrated layers of black fruits are intermingled with
red berries, stones, and Asian spices in its character as well as in its 30+-second finish. Anticipated maturity: now–2008.

The ruby-colored 1997 Clos St.-Denis reveals sweet candied cherry aromas intermingled
with violets, roses, and spices. It possesses outstanding breadth, precision, and lacelike finesse, yet also reveals an impressive underlying power. This expressive, red berry–flavored,
and admirably persistent wine is already a delight to drink, yet has the capacity to mature and
evolve over the next 8–10 years. The beautifully ripe and ruby-colored 1997 Echézeaux displays delightful aromatics reminiscent of flowers, red cherries, and strawberry candy. It is
firmer, more structured, and less expressive than the Clos St.-Denis, yet offers a hugely pleasing and powerful burst of black fruits that saturate the taster's palate. This is a medium-
bodied, delineated, and refined wine that will be at its best if consumed over the next 7+ years.

The first-rate 1997 Clos de la Roche has exuberant aromas of red fruits and licorice. This
is a wine that combines Dujac's trademark elegance with power, density, and jammy, superripe flavors. Candied berries, chocolate-covered cherries, and red currant liqueur are found
in this medium- to full-bodied, complex, and mouthcoating offering. Anticipated maturity:
now–2009. This estate's 1997 Bonnes Mares is one of the most seductive wines fashioned in
this generally opulent and forward vintage. Ruby-colored and revealing a gorgeously feminine nose of salty, iodine-laced, sweet, red fruits, this is a fat, superripe, concentrated powerhouse. It regales the palate with dense layers of jammy black and red fruits interspersed
with earth and stones. This complex, extremely long-finishing, complete wine should offer
wonderful drinking over the next decade. Bravo!

"For the wines from my estate, the finest vintages of the 1990s have been '93, '95, and '99.
Only time will tell which is the best," said Jacques Seysses. He went on to add, "There is not
much to dislike about the 1999s. It is certainly a great vintage, there is quality as well as
quantity. They are easy to drink, and very ripe. There was no need to chaptalize."

The ruby-colored 1999 Gevrey-Chambertin Les Combottes exhibits a sweet, perfumed, red
fruit–scented nose. It has an excellent depth of red and black cherries in its medium-bodied,
supple-textured personality. This wine has excellent to outstanding grip, density of fruit, and
balance. Its long finish reveals copious amounts of ripe tannins that should melt away with
cellaring. Anticipated maturity: 2005–2012. The 1999 Charmes-Chambertin displays sweet
red and black berries as well as violets in its aromas. It is lush, ripe, concentrated, and has
excellent focus in its medium-bodied personality. This cherry-dominated wine also displays
hints of tangy raspberries and hints of new oak. It is pure, elegant, seamless, and has a long,
well-delineated finish. Anticipated maturity: now–2009.

Ruby-colored, the 1999 Clos St.-Denis exhibits earthy, blackberry aromas. Medium-bodied
and satin-textured, this is a firm, stony, black fruit and oak-influenced wine. It has outstanding concentration, balance, and harmony. Drink it over the next 10 years. Earth, stones, blackberries, and cassis can be discerned in the nose of the 1999 Clos de la Roche. On the palate,
this dark fruit, mineral, and spice-flavored wine is medium-bodied, firmly structured, and
tightly wound. It has outstanding depth of fruit as well as copious quantities of ripe tannins.
Anticipated maturity: 2004–2012. The 1999 Echézeaux reveals fresh herb, raspberry, and

cherry aromas. This sweet, lush, softly textured, medium-bodied wine offers blackberries, cherries, and spices in its flavor profile. It has outstanding structure, copious amounts of fruit, and a long, pure finish. Anticipated maturity: 2005–2010. Fresh herbs and spices can be found in the aromas of the 1999 Bonnes Mares. This wine is the brawniest of Dujac's 1999s, revealing a medium- to full-bodied character packed with superripe cherries, cassis, and blackberries. It is concentrated, deep, and admirably harmonious. In addition, this wine possesses an exceptionally long, pure, and delineated finish. Anticipated maturity: 2005–2012. *Other recommended wines:* 1997 Chambolle-Musigny Les Gruenchers (89), 1999 Chambolle-Musigny Les Gruenchers (87–89), 1997 Morey-St.-Denis Premier Cru (89), 1999 Morey-St.-Denis Premier Cru (88–89)

DOMAINE VINCENT DUREUIL-JANTHIAL (RULLY)

1999 Nuits-St.-Georges Clos des Argillières Cuvée Unique	E	90
2000 Rully La Margotée Cuvée Unique (white)	D	90
1999 Rully La Margotée Cuvée Unique (white)	D	90
1998 Rully La Margotée Réserve (white)	D	91
2000 Rully Le Meix Cadot Cuvée Unique (white)	D	91
1999 Rully Le Meix Cadot Cuvée Unique (white)	D	90
1998 Rully Le Meix Cadot Réserve (white)	D	90

Note: The "Cuvée Unique" and "Réserve" bottlings are special *cuvées* produced with and for David Hinkle and Peter Vezan for the U.S. market.

Produced from 70- to 80-year-old vines, the 1998 Rully Le Meix Cadot Réserve displays powerful pear, spice, and apple aromas. This medium- to full-bodied wine has excellent expansiveness, a velvety texture, and as a complex, flavorful personality. Minerals and stones are intermingled with red and white fruits in this wine's flavor profile and exceptionally long finish. Anticipated maturity: now–2007. The 1998 Rully La Margotée Réserve reveals soaring mineral aromas. This brilliantly focused, medium- to full-bodied wine is crammed with red berries, minerals, and hints of candied lemon. Obviously the result of *sur-maturité*-laced fruit, it is harmonious, possesses gorgeous depth, and is bright, vivacious, and intense. Anticipated maturity: now–2010.

The 1999 Rully La Margotée Cuvée Unique has oak-imbued, mineral aromas. Medium-bodied, refined, and beautifully defined, this rich, concentrated, and focused wine has a powerful streak of minerals and white fruits in its core. Additionally, it possesses a long, supple, and pure finish. Drink it over the next 6 years. The more masculine 1999 Rully Le Meix Cadot Cuvée Unique offers white fruit and oak aromas. It is deep, broad, medium-bodied, and packed with pears and fresh citrus fruits, as well as a myriad of spices. It may be more powerful than the Margotée, yet lacks that wine's length. It is beautifully concentrated and coats the palate with its nuanced and muscular flavors. Drink it over the next 6 years. The outstanding medium to dark ruby-colored 1999 Nuits-St.-Georges Clos des Argillières Cuvée Unique offers cherry, blackberry, and stone aromas. It is medium-bodied, expansive, opulent, and velvety-textured. Loads of blackberries and dark cherries can be found in its plummy, fat, plump personality as well as throughout its impressive, seamless finish. Drink it over the next 6–7 years.

Vincent Dureuil believes that 2000 is "between good and great as a vintage. It has unquestionably more depth than 1999." He reported that he experienced his highest yields since taking over the estate from his father (between 55 and 60 hectoliters per hectare), which he attributes to his vineyards compensating for the frost damage they experienced in both 1998 and 1999. In 2001, however, Dureuil's yields will be substantially lower, as he lost approximately 40% of his production in the massive hailstorm of August 2. "We are going to have to sort, resort, and sort again," said the young, hardworking Dureuil.

The 2000 Rully Le Meix Cadot Cuvée Unique bursts from the glass with almonds and white fruits. Produced from vines planted in 1920, this wine is medium- to full-bodied, dense, and layered. Minerals, apples, and pears can be found in its concentrated, intense personality. Drink it over the next 7–8 years. The spice and liquid mineral–scented 2000 Rully La Margotée Cuvée Unique offers smoky bacon, candied lemon, and mineral flavors. It is focused and has outstanding underlying richness as well as gorgeous delineation. This is a persistent wine that may well improve with cellaring. Anticipated maturity: 2003–2010.

Other recommended wines: 1997 Mercurey Le Bois de Lalier Réserve (red) (89), 1999 Mercury Le Bois de Lalier Cuvée Unique (red) (89), 1997 Nuits-St.-Georges Clos des Argilliéres Réserve (89+), 1997 Rully La Bergerie Réserve (white) (87–89), 1999 Rully La Bergerie Cuvée Unique (white) (88), 2000 Rully La Bergerie Cuvée Unique (white) (89), 1997 Rully La Crée Réserve (red) (89), 1997 Rully La Crée Réserve (white) (89+), 1999 Rully La Crée Cuvée Unique (white) (89), 2000 Rully La Crée Cuvée Unique (white) (88), 1997 Rully En Guesnes Réserve (red) (89), 1999 Rully Margotée Cuvée Unique (red) (88+), 1997 Rully La Martelle Réserve (white) (88-89+), 1997 Rully La Martelle Réserve (white) (89), 1997 Rully Le Meix-Cadot Réserve (white) (88–90+), 1999 Rully Plante-Moraine Cuvée Unique (red) (88+)

DOMAINE MAURICE ECARD ET FILS (SAVIGNY-LES-BEAUNE)

1999	Savigny-les-Beaune Les Jarrons	D	90
1997	Savigny-les-Beaune Les Jarrons	D	90
1999	Savigny-les-Beaune Les Narbantons	D	90+
1997	Savigny-les-Beaune Les Narbantons	D	90+
1999	Savigny-les-Beaune Les Peuillets	D	91
1997	Savigny-les-Beaune Les Peuillets	D	90
1999	Savigny-les-Beaune Les Serpentières	D	90

Maurice Ecard, the finest producer of Savigny-les-Beaune, produced delightful 1997s and 1999s. "What can I say about the 1998s?" he asked, "They never fully ripened. Vintages like 1997 and 1999 are dream years for me." Ecard, whose love of wine isn't blinded by his need to sell even the toughest vintages, said, "If all we ever made were 1997s and 1999s, we'd be quite happy. They have lots of fruit, and are fat and round."

The ruby-colored, dark fruit–scented 1997 Savigny-les-Beaune Les Peuillets is oily-textured and medium-bodied. Stones, metallic shavings, and jammy blackberries are found in this flavorful, concentrated wine. It has outstanding grip, and fruit density. Anticipated maturity: now–2007. The darker-colored 1997 Savigny-les-Beaune Les Narbantons has superb black fruit aromas. This broad, medium-bodied wine is loaded with plums, red cherries, and spices. It is lush, well structured, complex, and persistent. Drink it over the next 5–6 years.

The 1999 Savigny-les-Beaune Les Jarrons is medium to dark ruby-colored and boasts waxy black fruit scents. Medium- to full-bodied, rich, and firm, this is a silk-textured wine crammed with a compote of black cherries, spices, metallic shavings, grapes, and raspberries. Anticipated maturity: now–2009.

"I believe these 1999s will age just as well as my 1990s have." Ecard's yields in 1999 were low (45 h/h, without bleeding the tanks) when compared to his peers, but high for the estate. In 2000, another highly productive vintage, his yields averaged 45.6 h/h, still far below his colleagues ("the authorities were right to reject our request for a 40% PLC. If vignerons do their job, they'd never need one that high," he said).

The medium to dark ruby-colored 1999 Savigny-les-Beaune Les Serpentières reveals plum and superripe grape aromas intermingled with scents reminiscent of candle wax. This medium-bodied wine is rich, fat, and sexy. Loads of waxy plums, cherries, and blackberries are intermingled with hints of licorice in its personality. It has excellent structure and the capacity for aging. Anticipated maturity: 2003–2010. The dark cherry–scented 1999 Savigny-les-Beaune Les Peuillets is medium to dark ruby-colored. Medium-bodied and lush, it has outstanding stuffing in its velvety-textured character. Red cherries, assorted berries, and spices can be found in this satin-textured, harmonious, and seamless wine. In addition, it reveals copious amounts of ripe tannins in its admirably long finish. Anticipated maturity: 2003–2010+. Blackberries, grapes, and violets can be discerned in the aromatics of the 1999 Savigny-les-Beaune Les Narbantons. This is a more masculine wine than the previous one, revealing blackberry and dark cherry fruits. It is somewhat rustic, with a firm, foursquare character, yet this wine has the density and depth of fruit to sustain its tannin. Anticipated maturity: 2005–2011. The medium to dark ruby-colored 1999 Savigny-les-Beaune Les Jarrons offers black cherry, rose, and violet aromas. Dark berries are found in this well-balanced, juicy, firm, medium-bodied wine. It has outstanding depth and a silky texture that leads to a firm yet fruit-drenched finish. Anticipated maturity: 2004–2011.

Other recommended wines: 1999 Savigny-les-Beaune Les Clous (88), 1997 Savigny-les-Beaune Les Pimentiers (88), 1997 Savigny-les-Beaune Les Serpentières (89)

DOMAINE RENÉ ENGEL (VOSNE-ROMANÉE)

1998 Echézeaux	E	90
1998 Grands-Echézeaux	EE	91

The ruby-colored, floral, and red fruit–scented 1998 Echézeaux is rich, thick, and medium- to full-bodied. Plump, fat cherries can be found in this well-crafted, concentrated, fresh wine. Drink it over the next 6–8 years. The ruby-colored 1998 Grands-Echézeaux reveals plums and wild red berries in its aromatics. Medium- to full-bodied, dense, and concentrated, this wine has a chewy, asphalt, licorice, and jammy blackberry-flavored core. While it is firmly structured, it should have the requisite depth of fruit to survive its tannins—at least in the short to medium term. Anticipated maturity: now–2006.

DOMAINE ARNAUD ENTE (MEURSAULT)

1997 Meursault la Goutte d'Or	E	(90–93)
1997 Meursault En l'Ormeau	D	(88–90+)
2000 Meursault Vieilles Vignes	E	(88–91)
1997 Puligny-Montrachet Les Referts	E	(91–94)

Ente's first vintage as a wine-maker was 1992, the entire production of which was sold to *négociants*. He began bottling his wines with the 1994 vintage, and today Domaine Ente is well on its way to becoming a household name.

The 1997 Meursault En l'Ormeau is produced from vines that are more than 45 years old. Exhibiting dense white fruit aromas, this wine has medium to full body and a stunning flavor profile of yellow plums, candied hazelnuts, acacia, and sea salt. Most important, it is well balanced, with a thick texture yet a fresh personality. Anticipated maturity: now–2005. The 1997 Meursault Goutte d'Or can best be described as En l'Ormeau on steroids. Earth, minerals, and white fruits bordering on *sur-maturité* explode from the glass. Quite powerful, this glycerin-inbued, oily, satin-textured, medium- to full-bodied wine is crammed with sweet plums, toasted hazelnuts, and the same salty quality I noticed in the preceding offering. It should be succulent to drink from its release through at least 2005.

The 1997 Puligny-Montrachet Les Referts is also an extraordinary wine. Grilled almonds dominate the nose, yet, with coaxing, aromas of honeysuckle, anise, and acacia blossoms made their appearance. On the palate, this intense, white truffle oil, mocha, and mineral-packed wine is opulent and supersexy. It is full-bodied, dense, plump, immensely flavorful, and assertive. I do not believe it will make old bones, but doubt that readers will be able to resist its joys. What more can one ask for? Drink it over the next 5 years.

"The 1999 vintage is not bad, but 2000 will be great," said Arnaud Ente. His wines took a long time to ferment. For example, he still had barrels completing both their alcoholic and malolactic fermentations (I only tasted barrels that had completed their fermentations) on

November 6, 2000. "These late fermentations don't bother me, people that go crazy adding things to their barrels to speed up the process always screw up their wines, I'd rather let things proceed naturally. The longer it takes, the more complex the wine." Ente informed me that his wines averaged 14% natural potential alcohol in 1999. Ente produced five barrels of outstanding 1999 Meursault Vieilles Vignes (from vines more than 100 years old). Its nose is rich, plump, and packed with sweet yellow fruits and spiced apples. Medium- to full-bodied, ample, and concentrated, this gorgeous wine is harmonious, deep, and crammed with smoke-infused pears, apples, white peaches, and hints of apricots. Its extraordinary long finish displays a tangy freshness as well as copious quantities of spices. Drink this superb 1999 over the course of the next 8–9 years.

To Arnaud Ente, "The 2000 vintage is completely different from 1999. It has more acid and more fruit." In reference to the devastating storm of September 12, Ente stated, "It had little effect on our white wines, whose grapes remained healthy. However, we had big problems with our reds." Aromatically, the 2000 Meursault Vieilles Vignes reveals an intensely spicy nose. Concentrated and deep, this plump wine has excellent grip to its tangy apple, citrus, and pear-flavored character. Drink this fresh, expressive wine over the course of the next 8–9 years.

Other recommended wines: 1997 Bourgogne Blanc (87–89), 1999 Meursault (87–89), 1999 Meursault Goutte d'Or (88–90), 2000 Meursault Goutte d'Or (88–90), 1999 Puligny-Montrachet Les Referts (88–90), 2000 Puligny-Montrachet Les Referts (87–89), 1999 Volnay Santenots (88–89)

DOMAINE DES EPENEAUX/COMTE ARMAND (POMMARD)

1999 Pommard Clos des Epeneaux	D	(89–91+)

Wine-maker Pascal Marchand has left the Domaine des Epeneaux and been replaced by Benjamin Leroux, a bright young man with many of the same philosophies as his predecessor. The famed Pommard Clos des Epeneaux in 1999 was harvested and vinified in successive waves by age group. The assemblage is a medium to dark ruby-colored wine with blackberry, earth, and fresh herb notes. Some new oak shows through in its aromatics. This is a big, bold, foursquare, masculine wine with a chewy, rugged, powerful personality. It is loaded with gorgeously ripened tannin and has immense concentration as well as a long, focused finish. Anticipated maturity: 2005–2012.

Other recommended wines: 1997 Meursault Les Meix Chavaux (88–89), 1997 Pommard Clos des Epeneaux (88–91)

DOMAINE JEAN-PHILIPPE FICHET (MEURSAULT)

1997 Puligny-Montrachet Les Referts	E	(90–92)

I loved Fichet's sole premier cru, the 1997 Puligny-Montrachet Les Referts. Its aromas are imbued with white flowers, minerals, and a distinctly Riesling-like petrol quality. This extremely well-made 1997 has great definition, focus, and balance. It is a medium-bodied wine, crammed with ripe pears, stones, and earth flavors. Anticipated maturity: now–2006.

Other recommended wines: 1997 Meursault Les Chevalières (88–90), 1997 Meursault Le Tesson (88–90)

DOMAINE FONTAINE-GAGNARD (CHASSAGNE-MONTRACHET)

1997 Bâtard-Montrachet	EEE	91
1999 Chassagne-Montrachet La Romanée	E	90
1997 Chassagne-Montrachet Les Vergers	E	90
1999 Criots-Bâtard-Montrachet	EEE	91
1997 Criots-Bâtard-Montrachet	EEE	93

Richard Fontaine, a former jet engine engineer for the French air force, became the director and wine-maker for this estate after marrying Jacques Gagnard's (Domaine Gagnard Delagrange) daughter Laurence. His brother-in-law and next-door neighbor, Jean-Marc Blain (Domaine Blain-Gagnard), is married to Jacques Gagnard's other daughter, Claudine. For those readers who are still with me in this attempt to trace the roots of one of Chassagne's dominant families, Jean-Noël Gagnard (whose domaine bears his name), is Jacques Gagnard's brother. Each year, Jacques Gagnard gives a small plot of vines to each of his sons-in-law in an attempt to minimize France's estate tax ramifications. Unlike many Burgundian families that treat each other as rivals, Blain and Fontaine work hand in hand, sharing equipment, ideas, and harvesters.

Richard Fontaine is a tall, quiet, forthright, and dedicated man. Unhappy with some barrels he purchased from reputable *tonneliers,* Fontaine set out to become a cooperage expert. Presently, he travels each year to France's finest oak forests, picks out trees that are to his liking, and then ages the wood himself. Subsequently, he hires an artisan to build and toast the barrels to his exacting specifications. Unlike many of his tight-lipped colleagues, Fontaine was straightforward and honest about adding acid to his wines. The Morgeot was "rectified" as he felt its pH was dangerously high.

The potentially outstanding 1997 Chassagne-Montrachet Les Vergers is dense, rich, fat, yet extremely well balanced and medium-bodied. This stone- and mineral-scented offering is oily-textured as well as crammed with iron, steel flavors that segue into a magnificent minerality. Anticipated maturity: now–2007. The 1997 Bâtard-Montrachet has clay, earth, and mineral scents. It is medium- to full-bodied, immensely rich, dense, fat, and mouthcoating. This wine's *sur-maturité,* flavor-packed character (minerals, spiced pears, apples), luxurious texture, and admirable length guarantee it an outstanding score. However, like many Bâtards in this vintage, it borders on being flabby and heavy. It will make great drinking over the next 5 years. The 1997 Criots-Bâtard-Montrachet is magnificent. Flint, sea salt, chalk, and sun-baked stones can be discerned in its compelling aromatics. This is a complex, gorgeously focused, satin-textured, rather thick wine. Dense layers of toasty minerals, dried honey, roasted pears, anise, flower blossoms, spices, and an extremely appealing earthy quality coat the taster's palate. This superb Criots is medium- to full-bodied, impeccably balanced, and extremely long in the finish. Wow! Anticipated maturity: now–2008+.

"Without a natural disaster," exclaimed Richard Fontaine, "we no longer can be below the maximum allowable yields. Our weather and excellent viticultural techniques simply won't allow it. Anyone who says they were at or below 45 hectoliters per hectare [the permissible yields for white Burgundies] in 1999 or 2000 is a damn liar, it was completely impossible." To prove his point, he offered to provide me with a parcel of vines that I could prune, train, and work to my heart's content. He guaranteed that my parcel would be over the legal yields no matter how much work I put into them. Were it not for the commute between Washington and Chassagne-Montrachet, I would have accepted the challenge.

Fontaine felt compelled to acidify his 1999s, like many of his colleagues. He informed me that he had not acidified his 1991s, "and that taught me a lesson I have never forgotten. I got numerous letters from customers telling me how much they loved my 1991s, but I hated them. I knew they would not age!" The 1999 Chassagne-Montrachet La Romanée displays fresh talcum powder and floral aromas. Medium-bodied, dense, and deep, it is a harmonious, rich, plump, extroverted offering. Layers of red and white berries as well as pears dominate this lovely wine's personality. Minerals and stones can be found in the aromatics of the 1999 Criots-Bâtard-Montrachet. Herbal tea, minerals, and crisp pears are intermingled in this well-focused, plump, rich, medium-bodied wine. It has superb purity to its flavor profile and a long, smooth finish. Anticipated maturity: 2003–2011.

Other recommended wines: 1999 Bâtard-Montrachet (88+), 1997 Chassagne-Montrachet La Boudriotte (red) (89), 1997 Chassagne-Montrachet Les Caillerets (89), 1999 Chassagne-

Montrachet Les Caillerets (89), 1997 Chassagne-Montrachet Morgeot (red) (88), 1997 Chassagne-Montrachet Morgeot (white) (88), 1999 Chassagne-Montrachet Les Vergers (89), 1997 Pommard Rugiens (88), 1997 Volnay Clos des Chênes (89), 1999 Volnay Clos des Chênes (87–89)

DOMAINE FOUGERAY DE BEAUCLAIR (MARSANNAY)

1997 Bonnes Mares	EE	90+?

The ultimate quality of this estate's 1997 Bonnes Mares will be determined by its ability (or inability) to cope with its alcoholic, warm character, as well as with the hard tannins found throughout its personality. The wine's powerful and admirably concentrated core of jammy fruit is immensely impressive, certainly worthy of a score in the low to mid-90s. However, experience shows that Pinot Noirs often have the ability to "absorb" high levels of alcohol into their fruit, but it has considerably more difficulty coping with tannins. Anticipated maturity: 2004–2010?

DOMAINE DU CHÂTEAU DE FUISSÉ (FUISSÉ)

1997 Château Fuissé Pouilly-Fuissé	D	91+
1997 Château Fuissé Pouilly-Fuissé Les Brûlées	D	90
1997 Château Fuissé Pouilly-Fuissé Le Clos	D	91+
1997 Château Fuissé Pouilly-Fuissé Vieilles Vignes	E	(91–92+)

Readers need to be on the lookout for this domaine's special bottlings, recognizable by the moniker "Château Fuissé" in large bold letters across the label. They are delicious, complex, and concentrated wines that tend to be a significant step up in quality from the other offerings. The "Château Fuissé" wines, known at the domaine as the "crus," are made in 3,500- to 5,000-bottle lots. There are three single-vineyard offerings, and two assemblages.

Interestingly, because no new barrels are ever used at this domaine, the 1997 Château Fuissé Pouilly-Fuissé Les Brûlées exhibits oak-infused honeysuckle and white flower aromas. This massive, medium- to full-bodied, broad-shouldered, and mouthcoating wine has a thick and masculine personality. Stylistically more reminiscent of a Chassagne-Montrachet Morgeot than a wine from Fuissé, it has powerful earth and mineral flavors that last throughout its extended finish. Anticipated maturity: now–2005. The 1997 Château Fuissé Pouilly-Fuissé Le Clos combines the best qualities of the two previous crus. Its piney, mineral-laced nose leads to a stony, nutty, smoky, and floral character filled with orchard fruits and dried white raisins. It has the focus, freshness, and precision of Les Combettes and nearly as much power, density, and length as Les Brûlées. This complex, well-extracted wine should age well. Drink it between now–2007.

The 1997 Château Fuissé Pouilly-Fuissé (consumers should not confuse it with the regular Pouilly-Fuissé offering) is an assemblage crafted from 13 parcels. It displays wood, mineral, and floral aromas as well as a vibrant, superbly focused, medium- to full-bodied personality. This wine is exceedingly refined, with flavors of fruit pit, stone, flint, citrus, and cold steel. Anticipated maturity: now–2007+. With Elvis Presley singing in the background, I tasted from the two tanks containing the assembled final blend of the 1997 Château Fuissé Pouilly-Fuissé Vieilles Vignes. To my surprise, and to the consternation of the owners, each tank contained a distinctly different wine. The wines were qualitative equals, but had different textures and flavors profiles. The first revealed a somewhat muted stony nose and a magnificently focused, vibrant, intense core of salty minerals. The second, significantly oilier, offered flavors reminiscent of a hazelnut cream cake brushed with touches of lime juice. The owners were not sure if they should reblend the two, fine or filter them again, or bottle them as is. Anticipated maturity: now–2008.

Other recommended wines: 1997 Château Fuissé Pouilly-Fuissé Les Combettes (88+), 1997 St.-Véran (88)

DOMAINE JEAN-NOËL GAGNARD (CHASSAGNE-MONTRACHET)

2000	Bâtard-Montrachet	EEE	(89–92)
1999	Bâtard-Montrachet	EEE	(91–92)
1997	Bâtard-Montrachet	EEE	(89–91+)
2000	Chassagne-Montrachet Blanchots-Dessus	E	(90–92)
2000	Chassagne-Montrachet Les Caillerets	E	(90–92)
1999	Chassagne-Montrachet Les Caillerets	E	(89–91)
1997	Chassagne-Montrachet Les Caillerets	E	(89–91)
1997	Chassagne-Montrachet Clos de la Maltroie	E	(89–90+)
1997	Chassagne-Montrachet Morgeot (white)	E	(89–91)

Caroline Lestimé, Jean-Noël Gagnard's charming daughter, has taken on more of the responsibilities of running this estate. I'm a big fan of the generally rich and well-focused wines that emerge from these cellars. In 1997, a vintage that Lestimé claimed to be "extremely happy" with, Domaine Jean-Noël Gagnard crafted opulent, seductive, and luscious offerings for near-term drinking. In contrast to the 1996s, which require patience (the Les Caillerets and Bâtard are awesome wines!), the 1997s will deliver enormous pleasure during the first 5–8 years of their lives.

I adored the boisterousness of the 1997 Chassagne-Montrachet Clos de la Maltroie's pear and toasted nut–filled aromatics. This superexpressive wine displays huge ripeness, is medium- to full-bodied, and is filled with creamed hazelnuts. It is bold, satin-textured, and immensely pleasurable to drink right out of the barrel. Anticipated maturity: now–2004. Readers looking for luscious whites that are ready to drink the day they are purchased are well advised to search out this estate's 1997 Chassagne-Montrachet Morgeot. Its lip-smacking aromas of creamy pears and apples, with subtle hints of earth, are followed by an intensely expressive, fat, rather decadent personality. Ripe peaches, clay, hazelnut cream, and salty butter are all intertwined in this medium- to full-bodied, and plump offering. Anticipated maturity: now–2004.

The 1997 Chassagne-Montrachet Les Caillerets's more subdued and austere nose reluctantly displays mineral and toast aromas. An unyielding 1997, with airing, gorgeously pure chalk, mineral, flint, and toast flavors began to emerge. This is one of the rare 1997s to combine the vintage's richness with tangy natural acidity. Anticipated maturity: now–2008+. Lestimé uses 80% new oak barrels on the estate's Bâtard-Montrachet. The 1997 reveals impressive ripeness, spiced pears, and grilled oak aromas. It is a lovely wine, densely packed with buttery hazelnuts, creamed almonds, toasty apples, and tangy currants. This plump, fat, broad, medium- to full-bodied wine has good balance and an admirably long, nut-flavored finish. Drink it between now–2006.

Caroline Lestimé, Domaine Jean-Noël Gagnard's winemaker, finds the 1999s "fatter than the 1998s, I like them a lot." The 1999 Chassagne-Montrachet Les Caillerets has a refined, ripe, mineral- and quartz-laden nose. Medium-bodied and with outstanding amplitude, it is precise yet rich, broad, plump, and well balanced. Lemons, minerals, rocks, and pears can be found throughout its delicious character. It has outstanding grip and a long, pure finish. Anticipated maturity: now–2009. The 1999 Bâtard-Montrachet exhibits a deep nose of white fruits, toast, and minerals. Medium- to full-bodied, big, rich, and plump, this is an impressively layered and thick wine. It is one of the most robust and fat 1999s I tasted. Layers of yellow fruits coat the taster's palate and last throughout its exceptionally long finish. Anticipated maturity: 2003–2011.

An outstanding wine, the 2000 Chassagne-Montrachet Blanchots-Dessus boasts spiced lemon, toast, and mineral aromas. It is intense, concentrated, rich, and beautifully focused. Layers of minerals, spices, and pears can be found in its silky-textured, lush character. In addition, this wine possesses an admirably long finish. Anticipated maturity: now–2010. The creamed mineral, spice, and vanilla-scented 2000 Chassagne-Montrachet Les Caillerets is outstanding. It boasts huge concentration, intense flavors of minerals, spices, and pears, as well as a bright, lively character. It is loaded with fruit, highly expressive, and delightful. Drink it over the next 10 years. The 2000 Bâtard-Montrachet has a cardamom, toast, and mineral-scented nose. It boasts gorgeous concentration, loads of depth, and a medium-bodied personality. Candied lemons, minerals, and spices are discerned in its velvety-textured character. This layered wine should be at its best between 2003–2012.

Other recommended wines: 1998 Bâtard-Montrachet (87–89), 1997 Chassagne-Montrachet Blanchots-Dessus (88–90), 1997 Chassagne-Montrachet Champs-Gain (88–90), 2000 Chassagne-Montrachet Champs-Gain (87–89), 1999 Chassagne-Montrachet Les Chaumées (87–89), 2000 Chassagne-Montrachet Les Chaumées (87–89), 1997 Chassagne-Montrachet Chenevottes (87–88+), 2000 Chassagne-Montrachet Chenevottes (88–89), 1999 Chassagne-Montrachet La Maltroie (88–89), 2000 Chassagne-Montrachet La Maltroie (88–89), 1999 Chassagne-Montrachet Clos de la Maltroie (88–90), 2000 Chassagne-Montrachet Clos de la Maltroie (87–89), 1997 Chassagne-Montrachet Les Mazures (87–88), 1999 Chassagne-Montrachet Morgeot (red) (88–90), 1999 Chassagne-Montrachet Morgeot (white) (87–89), 2000 Chassagne-Montrachet Morgeot (white) (88–89), 1999 Chassagne-Montrachet Clos St.-Jean (red) (88–90), 1997 Santenay Clos des Tavannes (88–90)

MAISON ALEX GAMBAL (BEAUNE)

1999 Chapelle-Chambertin	EE	(88–91)
1999 Charmes-Chambertin	EE	(90–92)
1999 Clos de Vougeot	EE	(91–93)
1999 Echézeaux	EE	(90–93)
1999 Mazis-Chambertin	EE	(90–93)
1999 Nuits-St.-Georges Les Pruliers	E	(91–93+)
1999 Vosne-Romanée Vieilles Vignes	D	(90–91+)

Alex Gambal, who divides his time between Beaune and Boston, has fashioned numerous gorgeous 1999 red Burgundies. "Is it a great vintage?" he asked in anticipation of my question, "Pretty darn close. We would have set the world on fire if yields had been just a little smaller." The outstanding medium to dark ruby-colored 1999 Nuits-St.-Georges Les Pruliers has a sexy nose packed with waxy plums and blackberry jam. Medium- to full-bodied, broad-shouldered, and dense, it exhibits chewy licorice, roasted blackberry, plum jam, and blueberry syrup–like flavors. It has huge depth as well as an admirably long, harmonious, and sweet finish. Drink it over the next 6–7 years.

Produced from vines dating back to 1945, the dark ruby-colored 1999 Vosne-Romanée Vieilles Vignes has a nose of massive aromatic depth. Loads of black cherries and black-berries can be found in its spicy scents. Cookie dough, cherries, blueberries, and candied raspberries are found in its plush, opulent, yet elegant personality. This medium-bodied wine is a hedonist's delight. It has no hard edges and sports an impressively long, supple finish. Drink it over the next 8–9 years. From 55-year-old vines, the medium to dark ruby-colored 1999 Echézeaux has profound sweet cherry aromas. Medium-bodied and opulent, this is a complex, intense, perfumed offering. Loads of flowers, candied cherries, and blueberries can be found throughout its concentrated flavor profile as well as throughout its impressively long and supple finish. Anticipated maturity: 2004–2010.

The outstanding medium to dark ruby-colored 1999 Charmes-Chambertin has mouth-watering cookie dough, candle wax, and cherry syrup aromas. This is a lush, sexy, feminine wine with oily cherries, raspberries, and blueberries in its expressive personality. Though it lacks the density of the vintage's finest wines, it delivers loads of pleasure with its in-your-face, sweet fruit. Anticipated maturity: now–2007. The ruby-colored 1999 Chapelle-Chambertin has spicy blackberry aromas. Medium-bodied with excellent density of fruit, it coats the palate with satin-textured red and black cherries. Its finish is somewhat austere and structured, but it has excellent to outstanding quantities of fresh, well-ripened fruit flavors. Drink it over the next 8 years.

The smoked bacon–scented, medium to dark ruby-colored 1999 Clos de Vougeot is an outstanding, medium- to full-bodied wine. Silky-textured, pure, and sultry, it is a well-focused, decadently styled, spicy blackberry, candied blueberry, and cherry-flavored offering. Its thick yet juicy layers of dense fruits coat the palate. While it is packed with superripe flavors, they are well delineated. Its impressively long finish reveals loads of supple, cherry-coated tannin. This wonderful Clos de Vougeot should be consumed between 2005–2012. The slightly darker-colored, black cherry and Asian spice-scented 1999 Mazis-Chambertin has a gorgeous depth of tangy black fruit flavors. This sweet, plush, broad wine is reminiscent of thick black cherry juice loaded with juniper berries, cinnamon, and Asian spices. It is medium-bodied, harmonious, and seamless. Drink it over the next 10–12 years.

"I really love the 2000s because of the gorgeous fruit they have. Each time I taste them I'm enthralled by the white peaches they all show," says Alex Gambal. "Look, we're a new outfit and we're making progress in both our winemaking and the quality of our fruit sources. We're putting enormous work into our wines and I'm excited by the results," he added. Gambal is right on the money. This small *négociant* firm, located near Beaune's train is not only producing increasingly good wines, but their prices remain reasonable. Where else can wine lovers find three delicious Bourgogne blancs for under $20? Gambal's 2000s, while not reaching the 90-point cutoff for inclusion of their detailed notes, merit considerable attention due to their high quality and fair pricing.

Other recommended wines: 1999 Bonnes Mares (88–90), 1999 Bourgogne Chardonnay Cuvée Prestige (88), 2000 Bourgogne Chardonnay Cuvée Prestige (88), 1999 Chassagne-Montrachet (white) (89), 2000 Chassagne-Montrachet Champs-Gain (87–89), 2000 Chassagne-Montrachet Maltroie (89–90), 2000 Chassagne-Montrachet Morgeot (88–90), 1999 Fixin (white) (89), 1999 Gevrey-Chambertin Lavaux St.-Jacques (88–90), 1999 Meursault (88+), 2000 Meursault Cromin (88), 2000 Pouilly-Fuissé (87–89), 2000 St.-Aubin Sur Gamay (87–89), 2000 St.-Véran (88–89), 1999 Savigny-les-Beaune (87–89), 1999 Vosne-Romanée Beaux Monts (88–89+), 1999 Vosne-Romanée Malconsorts (88–90)

DOMAINE JEAN GARAUDET (POMMARD)

1999 Pommard Charmots	E	91+
1997 Pommard Charmots	E	92
1997 Pommard Noizons	D	90

The highly talented, if little known, Jean Garaudet commented on the fact that the grapes were harvested at extremely high temperatures in 1997. He attributes his being able to perform his usual 4- to 5-day cold maceration to the fact that he works with such small quantities of wine. The wines were aged on their lees for the duration of the *élevage*, and were bottled earlier than any other vintage in the history of this estate.

Crafted from vines averaging 45–50 years of age, the medium to dark ruby-colored 1997 Pommard Noizons has ripe raspberry, black cherry, and perfume aromas. It is a firm, masculine, dense, concentrated, and medium- to full-bodied wine, with flavors reminiscent of root beer, tar, licorice, and blackberries. It is broad-shouldered, powerful, and immensely flavorful. Drink this wonderful Pommard over the next 8 years. Garaudet's Pommard Charmots parcel has a full southerly exposure, and is composed of vines over 100 years old. The 1997 has an extremely demure nose, yet with air, it reveals gorgeously ripe black fruits amidst a talcum powder, perfume-like scent. It is extremely broad, full-bodied, dense, powerful, foursquare, and deeply ripe. Roasted blackberries and cassis are found in this delicious, tight wine. Its admirably long finish displays magnificent ripeness to its copious tannins. Anticipated maturity: now–2010+.

Fresh cherries, stones, and blackberries can be found in the aromas of the 1999 Pommard

Charmots. Medium to dark ruby-colored, this wine has excellent to outstanding intensity, density, depth, and length. It is loaded with fresh and jammy cherries whose flavors are intermingled with spices and mineral components. Its tannins, particularly for Pommard, an appellation known for its muscular, rustic wines, are ripe and supple. I sense that this wine, which is produced from extremely old vines, would have been otherworldly if its yields had been lower. Anticipated maturity: 2004–2010.

Other recommended wines: 1997 Beaune Clos des Mouches (88), 1999 Beaune Clos des Mouches (88), 1997 Monthélie (red) (88), 1999 Monthélie (red) (89), 1999 Pommard Noizons (89+)

DOMAINE GEANTET-PANSIOT (GEVREY-CHAMBERTIN)

1999 Chambolle-Musigny Premier Cru	E	92
1999 Charmes-Chambertin	EE	93
1998 Charmes-Chambertin	EE	91
1997 Charmes-Chambertin	E	92
1999 Gevrey-Chambertin Le Poissenot	E	90+
1998 Gevrey-Chambertin Le Poissenot	E	90
1997 Gevrey-Chambertin Le Poissenot	D	90

Wine is a beverage of pleasure, and those who subscribe to this philosophy will adore the luscious, seductive, opulent wines of Domaine Geantet-Pansiot. While they may not be the most complex, intellectually satisfying, or structured wines made in the Côte d'Or, they certainly merit inclusion in any list of that region's most hedonistic and pleasing offerings. Vincent Geantet, one of Gevrey-Chambertin's volunteer firemen as well as one of its top producers, performs *bâtonnage* once a week on his red wines prior to their malolactic fermentation. "While it might speed up the *élevage* process, I firmly believe it softens my tannins," he said.

The medium to dark ruby-colored 1997 Gevrey-Chambertin Le Poissenot displays perfumed, floral, ripe berry aromas. This dense, medium- to full-bodied, broad, gorgeously ripe wine is powerful and immensely flavorful. Creamed mocha, oak spices, compotes of red and black fruits, minerals, and stones can be found in its luscious personality. Its finish reveals copious quantities of tannins, yet they are supple and already in the process of melting away. Drink this beauty over the course of the next 7 years. The similarly colored 1997 Charmes-Chambertin is a hedonism addict's dream wine. Its blackberry and Asian spice–laden nose leads to a mouth full of palate-saturating black cherries, coffee, ice cream, and loads of sweet spices. This suave, rich, immensely dense, thick, and intense wine is broad and full-bodied. Anticipated maturity: now–2006+.

The medium to dark ruby-colored 1998 Gevrey-Chambertin Le Poissenot has floral, blackberry, violet, and licorice aromas. Medium- to full-bodied, oily-textured, and dense, this wine has outstanding richness as well as layer after layer of dark fruits. The vintage's characteristic hardness is discernible underneath this offering's luscious black raspberries and cherries. Drink it over the next 5 years. The ruby-colored 1998 Charmes-Chambertin has blackberry and black cherry aromas. Medium-bodied, pure, and luxuriously textured, this sweet and sexy wine will be at its best if consumed over the near term. At present, its copious layers of jammy red fruits coat its tannins. Drink it over the next 5 years.

Vincent Geantet crafts succulent red Burgundies that beg to be drunk. They are lush, sweet, crammed with fruit, and rarely have any hard edges. His obsession is to make wines that bring smiles to drinkers' faces, and he succeeds. Geantet is a firm believer in stirring the lees of red wines. "It envelops the tannin in fruit," he says, "and fruit is what gives joy."

The 1999 Chambolle-Musigny Premier Cru reveals sweet red berry and rose aromas. Plums, black cherries, and blackberries are found in this sexy, rich, deep, and concentrated wine. It is medium- to full-bodied, extroverted, forward, and boisterous. Copious quantities of fruit persist through its gorgeously pure and long finish. Anticipated maturity: now–2007.

Offering blackberry, currant, and fresh herb aromas, the medium-bodied 1999 Gevrey-Chambertin Le Poissenot is more closed than any of the previous wines. It is a concentrated, pure, masculine, powerful wine. It possesses outstanding depth of fruit at its black cherry and cassis-flavored core. Anticipated maturity: 2003–2010. Vincent Geantet's 1999 Charmes-Chambertin is a hedonist's dream. Plums, cherries, and raspberries can be found in its sweet, floral aromatics. Medium-bodied, concentrated, and beautifully defined, this outstanding wine is crammed with cherries and assorted red fruits whose flavors last throughout its seamless, harmonious, and long finish. Drink it over the next 12 years.

Other recommended wines: 1997 Chambolle-Musigny Vieilles Vignes (88), 1999 Chambolle-Musigny Vieilles Vignes (89+), 1997 Gevrey-Chambertin Les Jeunes Rois (88), 1999 Gevrey-Chambertin Les Jeunes Rois (89), 1997 Gevrey-Chambertin Vieilles Vignes (89+), 1999 Gevrey-Chambertin Vieilles Vignes (89), 1999 Marsannay Les Champs Perdrix (88)

DOMAINE GÉNOT-BOULANGER (MEURSAULT)

1997	Chassagne-Montrachet Les Chenevottes	D	(88–91)
1997	Corton-Charlemagne	E	(90–93)

The deep, earthy, red berry and spice-filled nose of the 1997 Chassagne-Montrachet Les Chenevottes is enthralling. This wine is medium- to full-bodied, rich, and gorgeously layered with pears, apples, flowers, as well as hints of lemon drops and cake batter. It is concentrated, oily-textured, and should ultimately merit an outstanding score postbottling. Anticipated maturity: now–2005. Harvested at a whopping 14% natural potential alcohol, the 1997 Corton-Charlemagne is a terrific wine. Mouthwatering aromas of toasted hazelnut–covered crème brûlée are interspersed with honeysuckle blossoms and loads of spices. This superrich (Chardonnay essence), dense, thickly textured wine will appeal to hedonists the world over. Its oily layers reveal toasty minerals, tropical white and yellow fruits, all awash in delightfully sweet new oak flavors. While the high level of alcohol is apparent in its long finish, it appears counterbalanced by this offering's massive fruit. Readers who appreciate top-flight California Chardonnays will adore this Corton-Charlemagne. Moreover, if it develops some elegance and finesse as it completes its *élevage*, my score will appear conservative. Anticipated maturity: now–2006.

Other recommended wines: 1997 Meursault Clos du Cromin (88), 1997 Meursault Les Vireuils (89)

MAISON VINCENT GIRARDIN (SANTENAY)

2000	Bâtard-Montrachet	EEE	(90–92)*
1998	Bâtard-Montrachet	EEE	92*
1997	Bâtard-Montrachet	EEE	92+*
1999	Bonnes Mares	EEE	(89–91)*
1999	Chambertin Clos de Bèze	EEE	(90–92)*
1997	Chambolle-Musigny Les Amoureuses	EE	90*
1999	Charmes-Chambertin	EE	(93–95)*
2000	Chassagne-Montrachet Le Cailleret	E	90*
1999	Chassagne-Montrachet Clos de la Truffière	E	90
1999	Chassagne-Montrachet Les Embrazées	E	90
1999	Chassagne-Montrachet Morgeot (white)	E	91+*
1997	Chassagne-Montrachet Morgeot (white)	E	90*
2000	Chevalier-Montrachet	EEE	90*
1999	Clos de la Roche	EE	(90–91)*
1999	Clos St.-Denis	EE	(89–90+)*
1999	Clos de Vougeot	EE	(91–92)*
1999	Corton Perrières	E	(92–94)*

1999	Corton Renardes	EE	(93–95)*
1997	Corton Renardes	EE	90*
1997	Echézeaux	EE	90+*
1999	Meursault Charmes	E	92*
1997	Meursault Perrières	E	91*
2000	Montrachet	EEE	(91–93)*
1999	Montrachet	EEE	(89–91)*
1999	Pommard Grands Epenots	E	(92–93+)*
1997	Pommard Grands Epenots Vieilles Vignes	EE	91*
1999	Pommard Rugiens	EE	(90–92)*
1997	Pommard Rugiens	EE	91*
1997	Puligny-Montrachet Les Combettes	EE	91*
2000	Puligny-Montrachet Les Folatières	EE	90*
1997	Puligny-Montrachet Les Perrières	E	90*
2000	Puligny-Montrachet Les Referts	EE	91
1999	Volnay Clos des Chênes	E	(90–92)*
1999	Volnay Santenots	E	(89–91)*
1997	Volnay Santenots	E	90+*

* These same wines are also available everywhere under the Baron de la Charrière label.

Vincent Girardin, the extremely talented owner and wine-maker of this *négociant* house, used a new, state-of-the-art pneumatic press for his 1997s. This new machine permitted Girardin to have a lighter touch during the pressing stage, and resulted in less gross lees than in the past. Therefore, Girardin's *débourbage* was shorter than usual. He informed me that he cold-stabilizes his whites at 8 degrees Celsius prior to alcoholic fermentation. For those with moderate yields, Girardin felt the key to crafting successful wines in 1997 was an early harvest. "That way we maintained good natural acidity."

Girardin's top whites, the grands and premiers crus, are at the same quality level as those crafted at Burgundy's other excellent domaines and *négociants*. What sets this firm apart are the bevy of delicious, eminently drinkable wines it produces from lesser known appellations, including its home village of Santenay. While their prices have increased in recent years, so has their quality. The superimpressive 1997 Meursault Perrières exhibits powerful mineral, nut, and stonelike aromas. Its rich, medium- to full-bodied, and expansive personality has delightfully spicy buttered toast flavors. It is well balanced (particularly for the vintage), dense, and should age gracefully. Drink it between now–2008.

According to Vincent Girardin, he crafted his 50 barrels of 1997 Chassagne-Montrachet Morgeot from both grapes and must acquired from five different proprietors. The finished wine has a floral and tea leaf–scented nose as well as a boldly assertive personality. This earth- and mineral-filled offering has exquisite richness, medium body, and tangy mineral components in its finish. Drink it over the next 6 years. Girardin's impressive 1997 Puligny-Montrachet Les Perrières has a gorgeous nose filled with perfume, flower blossoms, stones, and minerals. On the palate it offers sun-baked rocks, chalk, and red berry fruit. This is a dense, medium- to full-bodied, broad yet well-focused wine. Anticipated maturity: now–2007. The 1997 Puligny-Montrachet Les Combettes has mineral-dominated aromas that give way to its medium- to full-bodied, complex, and expressive character. It is a flavorful wine crammed with almond cakes, white flowers, minerals, stones, and a tangy citrus element. This super effort should be drunk between now–2008.

The 1997 Bâtard-Montrachet, crafted from 40- to 50-year-old vines located in the very middle of this famed grand cru vineyard, is one of the most successful Bâtards of the vintage. It reveals superb ripeness in its earthy, sweet marzipan-laced, white fruit–filled nose. This medium- to full-bodied wine is mouthcoating, dense, extremely thick, and opulent yet marvelously well focused. Its compotelike flavors include pears, apples, vanilla crème brûlée, stones, and herbs. This Bâtard has a long, buttered toast–filled finish. Drink from now–2010.

To Girardin, the key to producing successful 1997 reds was to harvest early in order to preserve acidity. He stated that the wines vinified at the estate were neither chaptalized nor acidified, and that all are bottled unfined and unfiltered. However, some of Girardin's offerings would have been better if they had remained on the vine slightly longer, as evidenced by their firm tannins. This *négoce* firm, located in the southern extremity of the Côte de Beaune, is expanding, adding selections from the Côte de Nuits. As he establishes contacts as well as long-term contracts with conscientious vineyard owners, Girardin's considerable winemaking talents will certainly lead to this firm's becoming a top source of northern Côte d'Or wines.

Crafted from purchased grapes, the ruby-colored 1997 Volnay Santenots displays fresh, blackberry-scented aromas. This refined, medium-bodied, mouth-filling wine is packed with flowers, licorice, and blueberry flavors. It reveals lovely depth of fruit, breadth, and a long, supple finish. Drink it over the next 7 years. Girardin acquired both grapes and wine to produce his ruby-colored 1997 Corton Renardes. Superripe jammy blackberries are found in the aromatics of this medium- to full-bodied, satin-textured, broad offering. It is chewy, loaded with black fruits, and reveals copious quantities of supple tannins in its extensive finish. Anticipated maturity: now–2008. The slightly darker-colored 1997 Pommard Grands Epenots Vieilles Vignes's nose exhibits mocha cream–covered cherry aromatics. The wine is medium- to full-bodied, dense, boisterous, and crammed with *sur-maturité*-laced blackberry compote and mint flavors. It won't make old bones, but guarantees to deliver loads of hedonistic pleasure over the next 5 years. The more structured, ruby-colored 1997 Pommard Rugiens reveals gamy, spicy red fruit scents. This is a broad, expressive, firm wine with flavors reminiscent of cedar, tobacco, and sweet red cherries. It is medium- to full-bodied, powerful, and possesses a backbone loaded with well-ripened tannins. Anticipated maturity: now–2007.

The medium to dark ruby-colored 1997 Chambolle-Musigny Les Amoureuses has beguiling violet-laced cassis aromas. Layers of sweet black currants and Asian spices are found in this medium- to full-bodied wine's character as well as throughout its impressively long, pure finish. Drink it over the next 7 years. Produced from purchased grapes and wine, the medium to dark ruby-colored 1997 Echézeaux has a nose composed of smoked bacon and blackberries. Tightly wound, it is a backward, structured offering with outstanding breadth and flavor intensity. Stones, black cherries, and cassis dominate its focused as well as persistent personality. Drink it over the next 7+ years.

The 1998 Bâtard-Montrachet offers delightful aromas of rich, buttery pears and a myriad of spices. Velvety-textured, thick, and plump, this powerful, well-made wine is full-bodied and crammed with layers of luscious fruits. Opulent yet focused, it is an extremely successful 1998, as well as a reflection of Girardin's innumerable talents as a winemaker and purchaser of some of the Côte de Beaune's finest fruit. Anticipated maturity: now–2007+.

Vincent Girardin describes 1999 as a "great but not spectacular year" for whites and feels it was even better for reds. "It was a perfectly healthy harvest," he said, "its grapes showed exemplary ripeness, with golden hues to their colors, and the acidities were perfect." When asked to list his favorite vintages of the 1990s for white Burgundies, Girardin placed 1992 first, followed by 1999, 1990, 1996, 1997, 1995, 1998, 1994, 1991, and 1993.

The outstanding 1999 Meursault Charmes displays floral aromas and a lusciously rich personality. This fat, concentrated, satin-textured wine is medium-bodied and possesses a deep flavor profile packed with spiced pears, stones, and minerals whose flavors last throughout its decadently supple and long finish. This gorgeously sensual wine should be consumed over the next 7–8 years. The rich 1999 Chassagne-Montrachet Les Embrazées reveals sweet pear scents. Medium-bodied, lush, and sexy, it is a fat, satin-textured wine with loads of spiced apple, anise, and juniper berry flavors. It is an outstanding wine that would have been even better if it had been more delineated and complex. Anticipated maturity: now–2007. The impressive 1999 Chassagne-Montrachet Clos de la Truffière has the qualities the Embrazées lacks, yet does not have that wine's decadently appealing personality. This is an earth- and oak-scented offering with a gorgeously intricate, medium-bodied character. Subtle apples, minerals, and pears emerge in the attack and grow in strength through the mid-palate, becoming powerful in the long, focused finish. Anticipated maturity: now–2009. In total disrespect for their *terroirs* (according to Burgundian wine-speak), I blended equal proportions of the Embrazées and Clos de la Truffière in my glass and found that the sum was greater than the parts.

The opulent 1999 Chassagne-Montrachet Morgeot has a shy, mineral-dominated nose. This medium- to full-bodied, velvety-textured wine is deep, balanced, and has a hugely plump, chewy personality. Layers of spiced pears, candied apples, and anise can be found throughout this sexy offering's personality as well as in its admirable long and pure finish. Drink it over the next 8–9 years. If Girardin's 1999 Montrachet had more depth of fruit it would be a show-stopper, as it has exceptional purity, focus, balance, and a stunning finish. This medium-bodied wine reveals a beguiling white flower and gravel-laden nose as well as a delicate flavor profile of fresh acacia blossoms and minerals that linger on the palate for an eternity. While it has all the hallmarks of a well-vinified and brilliantly raised wine, it falls short of being prodigious because of excessive yields. Drink it over the next 8–9 years.

Girardin has crafted an impressive line-up of 1999 reds. Stones, spices, and blackberries can be found in the nuanced aromas of the 1999 Volnay Santenots. On the palate, this gorgeous wine reveals violets, sweet black cherries, and cassis, in addition to a beguiling freshness. A concentrated wine, it also boasts an extremely long, supple, fruit-filled finish. Drink it over the next 8 years. The dark ruby-colored 1999 Volnay Clos des Chênes offers a mouthwatering nose of blackberry jam infused with new oak. Medium- to full-bodied, rich, and juicy, this powerful wine is packed with black cherries, cassis, and vanilla-laden oak. Anticipated maturity: 2003–2010.

The virtually black-colored 1999 Pommard Grands Epenots has an exuberant blackberry- and cassis-scented nose. This is a massive, full-bodied, powerful, pure wine. Concentrated layers of blackberries, licorice, and cassis can be found in this compelling Pommard. It also has magnificently ripe tannins in its long and supple finish. Anticipated maturity: 2003–2010. The slightly lighter-colored 1999 Pommard Les Rugiens has a gorgeous nose of flowers intermingled with red and black cherries. Fresh herbs, raspberries, blackberries, and cherries can be found in this medium- to full-bodied, spicy wine. It is broad-shouldered, structured, muscular, and packed with fruit. Drink it over the next 10 years.

Produced from 60-year-old vines, the dark ruby-colored 1999 Corton Perrières offers a magnificent nose of blackberries, black currants, and toasty new oak. This medium- to full-bodied, chunky, velvety-textured wine is highly concentrated and has outstanding depth of fruit. Layer upon layer of blackberries, currants, candied grapes, and flowers conquer one's palate in this powerful yet elegant wine. The tannins discernible in its long finish are amazingly supple and sweet. Anticipated maturity: 2003–2012. The similarly colored 1999 Corton Renardes has a mouthwatering nose of jammy plums, violets, cookie dough, and sweet blackberries. This wine has magnificent depth, richness, and concentration. Syrupy red and black fruits are intermingled with candied cherries in this oily-textured, seamless wine's personality. This is a majestic Corton. Anticipated maturity: 2004–2014.

The medium to dark ruby-colored 1999 Clos St.-Denis was muted aromatically when it was tasted. This is a highly extracted, medium-bodied, wine with flavors of blackberry, licorice, and freshly laid asphalt. It is powerful yet has a firm, foursquare structure. As it receives its final aeration prior to bottling, I believe this wine will soften and its fruit will become more expansive. Anticipated maturity: 2004–2010+. Sweet oak, spices, and fresh blackberries as well as cherries can be found in the aromatics of the 1999 Clos de la Roche. This muscular wine is highly extracted, tannic, and loaded with black cherries, licorice, and blackberries. It is extroverted, powerful, and possesses a long, tannin-filled finish. Anticipated maturity: 2004–2010+. The medium to dark ruby-colored 1999 Clos Vougeot has a spicy cherry and oak-filled nose. Loads of vanilla, raspberries, blackberries, and cherries can be found in this fruit-dominated wine. It possesses loads of ripe tannin, discernible in its admirably long finish, yet the overall personality is one of sweet, lush fruit. Anticipated maturity: 2003–2012.

The magnificent, dark ruby-colored 1999 Charmes-Chambertin has a fresh cherry, rose, and violet-scented nose. This medium- to full-bodied wine has exquisite breadth to its sweet oak-infused, cherry syrup, and perfume-flavored character. Harmonious as well as densely packed with superripe flavors, it possesses an impressively long, supple, and pure finish. This outstanding wine should be drunk over the next 10–12 years. The medium to dark ruby-colored 1999 Bonnes Mares reveals aromas of coffee, mocha cream, and blackberries. Medium-bodied and exhibiting sweet cherry, coffee bean, and fresh herb flavors, this is a lively wine for near-term drinking. It has good structure and loads of ripe tannin, yet the forward nature of its fruit signifies it should be drunk over the next 5–6 years. Fresh herbs, stones, and blackberries can be found in the aromatics of the medium to dark ruby-colored 1999 Chambertin Clos de Bèze. Medium-bodied and loaded with spices, sweet chocolate, blackberries, and currants, this is a firm wine whose copious tannins are encased in ripe fruit. Anticipated maturity: 2003–2010.

The 2000 Chassagne-Montrachet Le Cailleret boasts a gorgeous nose of liquid minerals, anise, and acacia blossoms. Juicy, velvety-textured, and medium-bodied, it possesses a flavor profile crammed with lemon-infused minerals. It is vivacious and zesty. Anticipated maturity: now–2008. The 2000 Puligny-Montrachet Les Referts reveals earthy mineral aromas and a rich, medium-bodied core of fruit. Concentrated and vinous, it reveals loads of spices, toast, butter, and smoke flavors. Drink it over the next 9 years. Freshly cut flowers can be discerned in the nose of the 2000 Puligny-Montrachet Les Folatières. Light- to medium-bodied, softly textured, and well delineated, this is an earthy, spicy, pear-flavored wine with a lacelike character. Anticipated maturity: now–2009.

Salted butter and a myriad of spices can be found in the aromatics of the 2000 Chevalier-Montrachet. This highly delineated, light- to medium-bodied wine is fresh, bright, and tangy. Minerals, limes, and lemons can be found throughout its flavor profile and its long, lacelike finish. Drink it over the next 10 years. The 2000 Bâtard-Montrachet reveals creamy white fruit and toast aromas. Medium-bodied and broad, this wine has outstanding depth to its roasted, toasted, pear, apple, and mineral-flavored character. It is dense yet highly focused and exhibits an admirably long and flavorful finish. Anticipated maturity: now–2011. The 2000 Montrachet reveals a mouthwatering sweet butter and candied pear–laced nose. Toasted minerals, crisp pears, and apples can be found in this outstanding wine's dense, silky-textured, medium body. Beautifully fashioned, it is loaded with depth and possesses a long, expressive finish. Anticipated maturity: now–2013.

Other recommended wines: 1997 Aloxe-Corton Clos du Chapître (88+)*, 1999 Bâtard-Montrachet (87–89)*, 1999 Chambolle-Musigny Les Charmes (87–89)*, 1997 Chassagne-Montrachet Les Caillerets (89+)*, 1998 Chassagne-Montrachet Les Caillerets (88+)*, 1999 Chassagne-Montrachet Les Caillerets (88)*, 1999 Chassagne-Montrachet Clos de la Boudriotte (88–90), 1998 Chassagne-Montrachet Les Morgeots (white) (88)*, 2000 Chassagne-Montrachet Les Morgeots (white) (89)*, 1999 Chassagne-Montrachet La Romanée (88)*, 2000 Chassagne-Montrachet Clos de la Truffière (89), 1997 Corton-Charlemagne (89+)*, 1998 Corton-Charlemagne (89+)*, 1999 Chevalier-Montrachet (88–90)*, 1997 Corton-Perrières (88+)*, 1997 Corton Clos du Roi (89)*, 1999 Maranges Clos des Loyères (87–89)*, 1997 Meursault Charmes (89+)*, 1998 Meursault Charmes (88)*, 2000 Meursault Charmes (89)*, 1999 Meursault Genevrières (89)*, 2000 Meursault Genevrières (89)*, 1999 Meursault Narvaux (88)*, 2000 Meursault Narvaux (89)*, 1998 Meursault Perrières (89)*, 2000

Meursault Poruzots (88), 1999 Morey-St.-Denis Les Millandes (88–89)*, 1997 Pommard Les Argillières (88+)*, 1997 Pommard Clos des Lambots Vieilles Vignes (88)*, 1999 Pommard Clos des Lambots Vieilles Vignes (88–90)*, 1999 Pommard Les Vignots (88–90)*, 1999 Puligny-Montrachet Champs-Gain (88), 1999 Puligny-Montrachet Enseignères (89)*, 1999 Puligny-Montrachet Perrières (88)*, 2000 Puligny-Montrachet Les Pucelles (89)*, 1997 Puligny-Montrachet Les Referts (89+), 1998 Puligny-Montrachet Les Referts (88), 1999 Romanée-St.-Vivant (89–90), 1997 St.-Aubin Les Murgers des Dents de Chiens (88)*, 1997 Santenay Les Gravières Vieilles Vignes (red) (88–89)*, 1997 Santenay Clos du Beauregard (white) (88+), 1999 Santenay Clos du Beauregard (white) (88), 1997 Santenay Beaurepaire (white) (88), 1999 Santenay Beaurepaire (white) (88), 1997 Santenay Les Gravières (white) (88)*, 1999 Santenay Les Gravières (red) (88–89)*, 1999 Savigny-les-Beaune Les Peuillets (88–89), 1997 Volnay Champans (89+)*, 1997 Volnay Clos des Chênes (89)*

DOMAINE HENRI GOUGES (NUITS-ST.-GEORGES)

1997	Nuits-St.-Georges Clos des Porets St.-Georges	E	(89–90+)
1999	Nuits-St.-Georges La Perrière (white)	EE	92
1999	Nuits-St.-Georges Les Pruliers	E	(89–92)
1997	Nuits-St.-Georges Les Pruliers	E	(90–92)
1999	Nuits-St.-Georges Les St.-Georges	EE	(89–91+)
1997	Nuits-St.-Georges Les St.-Georges	E	(91–93+)
1999	Nuits-St.-Georges Les Vaucrains	EE	(89–92)
1997	Nuits-St.-Georges Les Vaucrains	E	(91–93+)

From cask, the 1997s from Domaine Henri Gouges, an estate undergoing a noteworthy (and long overdue) qualitative resurgence, were some of the finest crafted in the Côte d'Or. Christian Gouges, responsible for the domaine's winemaking, described 1997 as "exceptional by its originality, its extreme maturity of Pinot Noir. The harvest conditions were perfectly sanitary, and the grapes were tiny, with very little juice. Our yields averaged 29.5 hectoliters per hectare." Unlike the vast majority of other estates, Domaine Gouges chose to "let nature express itself" by allowing the fermentations to start early. Whereas Christian Gouges's counterparts were rushing to refrigerate their grapes and must, he left everything alone. After two days, fermentation started and temperatures rose at what he described as normal. Since there was no chaptalization, the alcoholic fermentation process was completed within 12 days.

Gouges informed me that he experimented with acidification on one *cuve*, and found that it rendered the wine "severe, dry, and tannic." Beginning with the 1995 vintage, Christian Gouges has been working with his wines' lees, putting 8–10 liters of them into each barrel, as he believes that it augments the wines' density and richness. To illustrate this point, he indicated that the 1997 Nuits-St.-Georges Village had 10 liters of lees put into each barrel as the malolactic fermentation ended in March, yet when it was racked for bottling, just prior to our tasting, each barrel only contained 4–5 liters of lees. All of the estate's wines are now bottled unfined and unfiltered. "I do this because the wines are bright and have soft, ripe tannins, so why not act in as natural a way as possible?" said Gouges.

Aromatically, the medium to dark ruby-colored 1997 Nuits-St.-Georges Clos des Porets St.-Georges offers *garrigues* (the sun-baked herbs of Provence) aromas intermingled with spices and blackberries. Medium- to full-bodied and satin-textured, it offers concentrated layers of cassis, cedar, coffee, road tar, as well as blackberries. This flavorful, spicy, complex, and ample wine should be consumed over the next 7 years. The medium to dark ruby-colored 1997 Nuits-St.-Georges Les Pruliers reveals spicy, rosemary, and black fruit–laden aromas. This is a fat, dense, velvety-textured, and concentrated wine, with a medium to full body as well as Nuits-St.-Georges's trademark foursquare personality. Chocolate-covered blackberries and stones can be found in this highly expressive and well-extracted, persistent wine. Anticipated maturity: now–2008+. Juniper berries, clove, bittersweet chocolate, and Asian spices are found in the nose of the medium to dark ruby-colored 1997 Nuits-St.-Georges Les Vaucrains. A broad, dense, chewy, layered wine, its fresh flavor profile is crammed with sweet blueberries, plums, and spices. It is admirably balanced, possessing the requisite fruit and backbone to evolve magnificently well with cellaring. Anticipated maturity: now–2010. With aeration, the tightly wound 1997 Nuits-St.-Georges Les St.-Georges reluctantly revealed licorice, chocolate-covered black cherries, and fresh herbs. This expansive, rich, medium- to full-bodied, muscular wine is jam-packed with chocolate, mocha, and coffee flavors. It has extraordinary palate presence, a plump, satin-textured mouth feel, and a long, spicy, ripe, tannin-filled finish. Anticipated maturity: now–2010+.

The 1999 Nuits-St.-Georges Les Pruliers has a nose of fresh herbs, black cherries, and licorice. Medium- to full-bodied, satin-textured, and intense, it explodes on the palate with blackberries and road tar. Loads of supersweet tannin can be found in this highly expressive and persistent wine. Anticipated maturity: now–2012. The medium to dark ruby-colored 1999 Nuits-St.-Georges Les Vaucrains has beautifully pure, dark berry aromas. Medium-bodied and powerful, this stone, blackberry, currant, and licorice-flavored offering has outstanding depth of fruit as well as an admirably long, delineated finish. Its foursquare personality will require cellaring. Drink it between 2005–2012. The similarly colored 1999 Nuits-St.-Georges Les St.-Georges has blackberry, currant, and rosemary aromas. Rich, ample, and firm, it is a cherry, blackberry, and raspberry-flavored wine. This medium-bodied offering has loads of fruit that envelop its firmly tannic structure. Drink it between 2006–2012+.

Poached pears and spiced apples can be found in the superb aromatics of the 1999 Nuits-St.-Georges La Perrière. Medium- to full-bodied, plump and fat, this is an exceedingly ripe wine, crammed with loads of pears, anise, and toast flavors. It is harmonious, seamless, and reveals an admirably long, pure, and delineated finish. Drink it over the next 10 years.

Other recommended wines: 1997 Nuits-St.-Georges Les Chaignots (87–89+), 1997 Nuits-St.-Georges Chaines Carteaux (87–89), 1999 Nuits-St.-Georges Chaines Carteaux (88–90), 1999 Nuits-St.-Georges Clos des Porets (87–89), 1997 Nuits-St.-Georges La Perrière (white) (89)

DOMAINE ALBERT GRIVAULT (MEURSAULT)

1999 Meursault Perrières Clos des Perrières	EE	91

Completely replanted in 1985, the 0.95-hectare (2.38-acre) *monopole* (single-owner) Meursault Perrières Clos des Perrières is beginning to produce compelling wines as its vines reach maturity. A vertical tasting (from 1989 to 1999) of this vineyard's wines, conducted in Washington, D.C., in December 2000 clearly indicated that the estate is capable of crafting harmonious, silky-textured wines with considerable aging potential, even in some "difficult" vintages. Though I was unimpressed with the 1998, 1993, and the over-the-hill 1989, I was shocked by the quality of the 1990, 1991, and 1994. The 1999 Meursault Perrières Clos des Perrières reveals fresh aromas of spices and minerals in the nose. Medium-bodied and rich, this is a sea-salt, verbena, spice, and creamed pear–flavored wine. It has a marvelously silky texture, outstanding balance, and admirable length. Drink it over the next 10 years.

Past Glories: 1996 Meursault Perrières Clos des Perrières (89), 1995 Meursault Perrières Clos des Perrières (90), 1994 Meursault Perrières Clos des Perrières (89), 1992 Meursault Perrières Clos des Perrières (92), 1991 Meursault Perrières Clos des Perrières (89), 1990 Meursault Perrières Clos des Perrières (90), 1929 Clos de Vougeot (93)

DOMAINE JEAN GRIVOT (VOSNE-ROMANÉE)

1999	Clos de Vougeot	E	(89–91+)
1997	Clos de Vougeot	E	(91–93+)
1999	Echézeaux	EE	(92–94)
1997	Echézeaux	E	(89–91)
1999	Nuits-St.-Georges Les Boudots	E	(89–91)

1997 Nuits-St.-Georges Les Boudots	D	(89–91)
1997 Nuits-St.-Georges Les Pruliers	D	(89–91+)
1999 Richebourg	EEE	(95–97)
1997 Richebourg	EEE	(92–95)
1999 Vosne-Romanée Les Beaumonts	E	(90–92)
1999 Vosne-Romanée Les Suchots	E	(89–91)
1997 Vosne-Romanée Les Suchots	D	(88–91)

Note: Readers should know that Domaine Grivot's prices are lagging behind its qualitative resurgence.

According to Etienne Grivot, this estate's director and wine-maker, their grapes from the 1997 harvest were picked at 12–13.8% natural potential alcohol, with no traces of rot. "Vinification was relatively easy. However, the results were disappointing. By spring, the wines took on power and richness. One or two months after the malolactics were done, I realized it was going to be a very good vintage." Grivot went on to state that he did not believe that 1997 would be a "great cellaring vintage, yet they stay quite fresh when left open to breathe." He compares the vintage to 1964, yet believes that it has some of the qualities of 1959. It is "a vintage of seduction and charm. Consumers will be happy with what we've achieved," said Etienne Grivot. Whereas most wine-makers of the Côte d'Or rushed to cool the warm grapes as they came into the wineries, Grivot allowed them to sit. He said that fermentation began naturally after four days, and he proceeded to cool the juice as the cap was forming, to put the wines in a reductive state in order to use less SO_2.

The medium to dark ruby-colored 1997 Vosne-Romanée Les Suchots reveals rose, violet, and cherry aromas. This is an oily-textured, thick, dense wine with excellent grip. Loads of tangy currants and assorted red berries are found in its medium-bodied, smile-inducing personality. Drink it over the next 6 years. Harvested at 13.8% natural potential alcohol, the ruby-colored 1997 Nuits-St.-Georges Les Pruliers displays overripe grapy aromas interspersed with earth and spices. It is massive, expressive, powerful, and bold. Meaty black fruits, stones, and briary flavors saturate the palate and linger for 30+ seconds. My score will appear overly conservative if this boisterous offering gains complexity and focus with cellaring. Anticipated maturity: now–2006+. The more backward, foursquare, and structured 1997 Nuits-St.-Georges Les Boudots has a medium to dark ruby color. Medium- to full-bodied, it displays earth, flowers, and black fruits in its aromatics. On the palate, precise metal, brambleberry, game, stone, and blackberry flavors can be discerned in this firm offering. Anticipated maturity: now–2007+.

The 1997 Clos de Vougeot is medium to dark ruby-colored, and reveals an extremely ripe nose of dark berries, spices, and perfume. This magnificent offering bursts on the palate with black fruits, Asian spices, cherries, and hints of licorice. Medium- to full-bodied, powerful, expansive, broad, and yet elegant, this is a first-rate wine from a generally underachieving grand cru vineyard. Its forward, *sur-maturité*-laced fruit lead to a somewhat austere and structured yet supple, tannin-packed, long finish. Anticipated maturity: now–2008. Grivot's 1997 Echézaux is medium to dark ruby-colored and reveals black raspberry and cherry aromas. It offers admirable ripeness and breadth, a medium to full body, as well as loads of flowers, spices, black/red berries, and toasted oak flavors. This refined wine will require moderate patience due to its somewhat firm structure. Anticipated maturity: 2003–2008. The spectacular 1997 Richebourg offers an enthralling talcum powder, perfume, and red cherry–scented nose. This bold, expressive, powerful wine possesses the breed and intensity associated with its heralded vineyard. Immensely complex and muscular, this complete offering is masculine, refined, ample, and crammed with superripe cherries immersed in spices and black pepper. Drink this beauty over the next dozen years.

Produced from an average of 50 hectoliter per hectare yields, Etienne Grivot's 1999s were green harvested in two successive waves, dropping approximately 15% of the fruit (later he bled up to 8% of the juice). His wines finished their malolactic fermentations during the first days of January 2001. Grivot describes 1999 as "a vintage of harmony, one that gives both physical and spiritual pleasure. It is my dream Pinot Noir, with both power and charm." As is the tradition at this estate, none of its wines will be subjected to fining or filtering.

The floral and perfumed aromas of the ruby-colored 1999 Nuits-St.-Georges Les Boudots lead to an ample, satin-textured, medium-bodied personality. This lush, broad, rich wine has excellent to outstanding depth of candied cherries in its delightfully velvety personality. Drink it over the next 8 years. The similarly colored 1999 Vosne-Romanée Les Beaumonts has dramatic red fruit aromas. An intense wine, it has a plush, juicy, highly detailed, sweet, black cherry–filled flavor profile. Its character is tangy, lively, and reveals an extremely long, focused, soft finish. Anticipated maturity: 2003–2008. Sweet raspberries, red currants, and fresh herbs can be found in the aromatics of the 1999 Vosne-Romanée Les Suchots. Medium-bodied and silky-textured, it is firmer and more masculine than the previous wines. Cherries, strawberries, and raspberries dominate its expressive, structured character. Anticipated maturity: 2003–2008.

The ruby-colored 1999 Clos de Vougeot has gorgeously spicy, pure, raspberry aromas. Medium-bodied and refined, it is a harmonious, gorgeously ripened, satin-textured offering. Asian spices are intermingled with currants, raspberries, and cherries in this sweet, tannin-packed wine. It is a feminine, precise, and pure Clos de Vougeot to be drunk over the next 9 years. The medium to dark ruby-colored 1999 Echézeaux offers a nose of intense blackberry and fresh herb aromas. Medium- to full-bodied, rich, and ample, it is crammed with lush layers of cherries, blackberries, and spices. This sexy, extroverted wine has loads of sweet tannin in its personality. It is seamless, fruit-packed, and exciting. Drink it over the next 12 years. The similarly colored 1999 Richebourg is compelling. Its aromatics display great ripeness in their roasted dark berry, fresh herb, talcum, and plum scents. It is medium- to full-bodied, broad, and full-flavored. This is an elegant wine with loads of spicy, in-your-face fruit whose flavors last throughout its unbelievably long finish. It magnificently balances extroverted sweet fruit with refinement, precision, and delineation. This is not a dense, chewy wine, but one that is extraordinarily detailed and profound. Anticipated maturity: 2004–2012+.

Other recommended wines: 1999 Nuits-St.-Georges Les Roncières (88–89), 1997 Vosne-Romanée Les Beaumonts (86–89)

DOMAINE ROBERT GROFFIER (MOREY-ST.-DENIS)

1999 Bonnes Mares	EEE	93
1998 Bonnes Mares	EEE	91
1997 Bonnes Mares	EEE	94+
1999 Chambertin Clos de Bèze	EEE	95
1998 Chambertin Clos de Bèze	EEE	93
1997 Chambertin Clos de Bèze	EEE	95+
1999 Chambolle-Musigny Les Amoureuses	EE	92
1997 Chambolle-Musigny Les Amoureuses	EE	92
1997 Chambolle-Musigny Les Hauts Doix	E	90+
1998 Chambolle-Musigny Les Sentiers	EE	90
1997 Chambolle-Musigny Les Sentiers	EE	92

Robert Groffier and his son Serge crafted some of the most marvelous red Burgundies of the 1997 vintage. Readers should note that this estate has made extraordinary strides in recent years, and is presently in the top echelon of Burgundy producers. All of its 1997s can be highly recommended, due to the fact they were all treated with the same care and respect, including their Bourgogne Passe-Touts-Grains. The Groffiers employed a one-week-long cold maceration (at 10°C) prior to fermentation, and then dropped the temperature of the cellars to 10° before transferring the wines into barrel. They were left on their lees throughout their *élevage*, with SO$_2$ being injected directly into those lees using long syringes. The wines were bottled early in November to maintain fruit and freshness. The estate's highest yields in 1997 were 38 hectoliter per hectare for their Bourgogne. It is one of the finest regional appellation wines this taster has encountered.

The scrumptious 1997 Chambolle-Musigny Les Hauts Doix is medium to dark ruby-colored and exhibits licorice, violet, as well as candied blackberry aromas. This highly concentrated, expressive, and sultry wine is oily-textured, medium- to full-bodied, and dense. Moreover, wave after wave of soft, plump black fruits and herbs are found in its chewy, yet refined personality. Anticipated maturity: now–2005. The medium to dark ruby-colored 1997 Chambolle-Musigny Les Sentiers reveals a nose of sweet red berries, fresh herbs, and toasty oak. It is a gorgeous wine, with a soft, supple personality, crammed with red cherries, and dense layers of chocolate-covered blackberries. This elegant yet powerful and structured wine displays loads of silky tannins in its long and complex finish. A wine of opulence as well as nuance, it will bring enormous pleasure if drunk over the next 7 years. The slightly darker-colored 1997 Chambolle-Musigny Les Amoureuses has a nose reminiscent of sweet cookie dough immersed in cherry syrup. This is a broader, thicker, denser, and more structured wine than the Les Sentiers. Its muscular personality exhibits flavors of stones, black fruits, cassis, and red meat. Its slightly warm finish and jammy flavors suggest a hypothetical blend of a top-flight California Pinot Noir with a Burgundy. Anticipated maturity: now–2009.

Both of Domaine Robert Groffier's grand cru offerings are stars of the 1997 vintage. The dark ruby-colored 1997 Bonnes Mares offers beguiling aromas of waxy black and red fruits, fresh herbs, spicy oak, and roasted coffee. Its full-bodied, velvety textured personality explodes on the palate with copious quantities of jammy yet well-delineated fruit flavors. This is an awesome wine, thick, dense, well structured, balanced, harmonious, and enormously complex. While it is super to drink, it has the potential to evolve and gain in complexity over the next decade. The similarly colored 1997 Chambertin Clos de Bèze has a nose of immense ripeness and depth. This expansive, broad, powerful wine has exemplary purity and delineation to its mouthcoating candied cherry and cookie dough flavors. Full-bodied and satin-textured, this harmonious, complete wine reveals floral and earthlike tones in its extraordinarily long and supple finish. Anticipated maturity: now–2010+. Bravo!

The ruby-colored 1998 Chambolle-Musigny Les Sentiers displays red cherry, raspberry, and spice aromas. Medium-bodied and suave, this wine has opulence, depth, and excellent structure as well as length. Layers of red fruits can be found in its silky-textured character. Drink it over the next 5–6 years. The similarly colored, wild red berry–scented 1998 Bonnes Mares has a stone, red/black cherry, and brambleberry-flavored personality. It has wonderful breadth and concentration to its firm, masculine, muscular character. Drink it over the next 7–8 years. Medium to dark ruby-colored, and sporting a dark cherry, spice, and fresh herb–scented nose, the 1998 Chambertin Clos de Bèze is unquestionably one of the vintage's successes. Medium- to full-bodied, broad, and powerful, it is a pure, well-balanced, and ripened wine. Its copious yet supple tannins are, at present, buried in layers of red and black fruits. This well-structured and admirably persistent wine should be at its best over the next 8–9 years.

The Groffiers produced another set of magnificent wines in 1999. The medium-bodied 1999 Chambolle-Musigny Les Amoureuses is medium to dark ruby-colored. Jammy black-berries and earth can be discerned in its aromatics. This wine has outstanding density to its black cherry, licorice, and blackberry-filled character. It is concentrated, powerful, yet remains refined and well defined. Anticipated maturity: 2004–2010. Loads of raspberries, metal shavings, and leather can be discerned in the intense aromatics of the focused 1999 Bonnes Mares. This medium to dark ruby-colored wine has an explosive, powerful, and medium-bodied personality. It is finely etched, yet lush and superripe. Anticipated maturity:

2004–2012. The exceptional, medium to dark ruby-colored 1999 Chambertin Clos de Bèze has boisterous Asian spice and candied cherry aromas. Cookie dough, blackberry syrup, violets, candied cherries, and hints of licorice can be found in this muscular, opulent wine. Its liquid velvetlike personality screams of *sur-maturité*, yet it is fresh and delineated. It displays a prodigiously long, candied, supple finish. Anticipated maturity: 2004–2014.

Other recommended wines: 1997 Bourgogne (89), 1999 Bourgogne (88), 1999 Chambolle-Musigny Les Hauts Doix (89+), 1999 Chambolle-Musigny Les Sentiers (89–90), 1997 Gevrey-Chambertin (88+), 1999 Gevrey-Chambertin (89)

DOMAINE ANNE GROS (VOSNE-ROMANÉE)

1999 Clos de Vougeot Le Grand Maupertui	EEE	(92–94)
1998 Clos de Vougeot Le Grand Maupertui	EE	91
1997 Clos de Vougeot Le Grand Maupertui	EE	92
1999 Richebourg	EEE	(94–97)
1998 Richebourg	EEE	93
1997 Richebourg	EEE	94

Anne Gros, one of the success stories of the 1997 vintage, attributes the qualities found in her wines to low yields and the fact that her berries were so small. Across the board, her wines were harvested at 13–13.5% natural potential alcohol, extremely high for Burgundy. The pHs postmalolactics were at 3.5 without any acidification. Mme Gros's 1997s are not as dark or as highly extracted as her 1995s and 1996s. However, they appear to be more harmonious, generous, and hedonistic. The medium to dark ruby-colored 1997 Clos de Vougeot Le Grand Maupertui has an almost Rhône-like nose of black fruits and cracked black pepper. On the palate, a compote of superripe blackberries and cassis can be found in this elegant, medium- to full-bodied, spicy, herbal, and cumin-laced wine. It is thick, flavorful, well focused, and has a lovely, supple finish. Drink it over the next 9 years. The slightly darker colored 1997 Richebourg is a super wine. Its violet, herbal, spicy, and toasty nose leads to a silky-textured core of amazing depth, ripeness, and harmony. It is expansive and crammed with jellied black fruits that seemingly linger forever on the oak spice–infused finish. This is certainly not the biggest Richebourg Anne Gros has crafted in recent years, yet it will be the most pleasurable in its youth. Drink over the next 10+ years.

Dark fruits and oak spices can be discerned in the aromatics of the 1998 Clos de Vougeot Le Grand Maupertui. Medium- to full-bodied, dense, and concentrated, it is a fat, fruit-dominated wine. Blackberries, cherries, and loads of spices cover up this wine's structured character. Drink it over the next 7 years. The medium to dark ruby-colored 1998 Richebourg has a spice- and red fruit–scented nose. Full-bodied, sweet, and supple, this satin-textured wine has outstanding depth to its red fruit–flavored character. This feminine, well-defined, elegant Richebourg has loads of well-ripened tannins, providing it with a firm backbone. Anticipated maturity: now–2010.

Of 1999, Mme Gros says, "I love this vintage. It fits perfectly with my personal taste and it made itself. I had nothing to add to it. It has superb maturity, both in its sugar and in its phenolics, yet has excellent acidity." Mme Gros's yields ranged from a high of 53 h/h for her Vosne-Romanée Les Barreaux to 43 h/h for her Richebourg. She did not bleed off any juice.

Smoked bacon, juniper berries, candle wax, and cherries can be found in the nose of the medium to dark ruby-colored 1999 Clos de Vougeot Le Grand Maupertui. This full-bodied, chewy-textured, highly extracted wine is crammed with toast, blackberry syrup, Asian spices, and bacon. It is intense, plush, delineated, and has outstanding depth. Anticipated maturity: 2005–2015. The similarly colored 1999 Richebourg has a show-stopping, awesome nose of raspberries, strawberries, roses, red currants, candied cherries, and violets. It is a penetrating, feminine, elegant, precise, medium- to full-bodied wine. Though intensely refined and highly delineated, it sacrifices nothing in power and concentration. This exceptional offering possesses all the components for greatness. Its structure is formed by loads of superripe tannin, and its personality is dominated by hugely dense layers of fruit. Anticipated maturity: 2006–2017.

Other recommended wines: 1999 Bourgogne (88), 1999 Bourgogne Chardonnay (88), 1997 Chambolle-Musigny La Combe d'Orveaux (89), 1997 Vosne-Romanée Les Barreaux (89+), 1999 Vosne-Romanée Les Barreaux (88–89)

DOMAINE GUFFENS-HEYNEN (VERGISSON)

2000 Mâcon-Pierreclos	D	(89–91)
2000 Mâcon-Pierreclos En Chavigne	D	(94–96)
1997 Mâcon-Pierreclos En Chavigne	D	(90–92)
1997 Pouilly-Fuissé Clos des Petits Croux	EE	(92–93+)
2000 Pouilly-Fuissé Les Croux	EE	(91–93)
2000 Pouilly-Fuissé Les Hauts de Vignes	EE	(94–96)
1998 Pouilly-Fuissé Premier Jus	E	(89–92)
1997 Pouilly-Fuissé La Roche	E	(93–95)

Guffens-Heynen is the private estate of Jean-Marie Guffens (of Maison Verget fame) and his wife. Whereas at Verget, Guffens strives to fashion the finest wines he can from purchased grapes and must (unfermented juice), often resorting to tricks and technology, at Guffens-Heynen only the most simple and natural processes are employed. The results can be awe-inspiring. The outstanding 1997 Mâcon-Pierreclos En Chavigne offers vibrant aromas of acacia and honeysuckle blossoms. This velvety-textured, highly focused, and gorgeously ripe wine is broad, powerful, and structured. Its intense minerality is seemingly coated with candied nuts and a myriad of citrus fruits that last throughout its prolonged finish. It is a stunning Mâcon! Drink it between now–2006.

Domaine Guffens-Heynen's 1997 Pouilly-Fuissé La Roche is unbelievably great! Readers who have yet to taste a wine from the Mâconnais that can compete with the finest grands crus of the Côte de Beaune should experience this masterpiece. Its deeply ripe nose offers liquid mineral, rock, gravel, and almond paste aromas. It possesses a spiritual quality (the French call it *aérien*) that can sometimes be found in the finest Chevalier-Montrachets and Montrachets. It has magnificent focus, bold and deep flint and white fruit flavors, impeccable balance, and intense concentration. This medium- to full-bodied, oily-textured (yet bright and vivacious) offering also has a mind-bogglingly long, crisp, and pure finish. Wow! Anticipated maturity: now–2008+. Exhibiting an earthy, stone-laden nose, the 1997 Pouilly-Fuissé Les Crays, an even larger wine, is extraordinarily impressive because of its size, density, and beguiling—almost superripe—flavors. This full-bodied monster is viscous yet not ponderous or flabby. Its waves of poached/spiced pears, minerals, and earth flavors coat the palate in successive layers. Anticipated maturity: now–2008.

The impressive 1998 Pouilly-Fuissé Premier Jus exhibits lacelike, stone, and flint aromas. This crystalline wine is medium-bodied and packed with highly nuanced quartz, gravel, and citrus fruits. Its tangy personality displays awesome precision, grip, and cut. Its exceedingly long finish ends on salty, lime notes. Anticipated maturity: now–2008.

"I took huge risks in 1999 to make good wines and failed," said Guffens. "In 2000, my gambling paid off, big time." The 2000 Mâcon-Pierreclos is a rich, huge, velvety-textured, medium- to full-bodied wine. Liquid minerals, spices, and hints of smoke can be discerned in its aromas and flavors. It is lush, concentrated, and opulent. Drink it over the next 8–10 years.

Peter Vezan, this estate's broker, is an extremely honest man who has never led Robert Parker or me astray. If he has nothing good to say about a wine he represents, he says nothing. As I walked out of the Guffens-Heynen estate he said, "We've just tasted the greatest Mâcon ever produced." And he was right. The magnificent 2000 Mâcon-Pierreclos En Chavigne explodes from the glass with toasted mineral aromas. Medium- to full-bodied and viscous, this is a muscular, powerful, and intensely concentrated wine. It has unbelievable depth and length. Loads of smoky minerals and white fruits are found in this stunning wine's core. I would call this the Montrachet of the Mâconnais, yet it is finer than the majority of Montrachets I have tasted over the years. Anticipated maturity: 2003–2012.

The 2000 Pouilly-Fuissé Les Croux has mouthwatering mineral and spice aromas. On the palate, it is broad, juicy, concentrated, and medium-bodied. Spices, white berries, flint, and pears can be discerned in its highly expressive, well-balanced, and defined personality. Anticipated maturity: now–2012. The chewy 2000 Pouilly-Fuissé Les Hauts de Vignes is an awesome wine. Minerals, toast, stones, and smoke are found in its aromatics. It detonates on the palate with intense red and white currants, minerals, and pears. It is massive, has great breadth, purity, and definition. This extraordinarily complex wine should be at its peak of maturity between 2005–2015.

Other recommended wines: 1997 Mâcon-Pierreclos (88–90), 1999 Mâcon-Pierreclos (89), 1999 Mâcon-Pierreclos En Chavigne (88–90), 1997 Pouilly-Fuissé Les Croux (89–90)

DOMAINE GUILLEMOT-MICHEL (QUINTAINE)

1999 Mâcon-Villages Quintaine Sélection de Grains Cendrés	D/375ml	90

This estate is a first-rate source of outstanding, reasonably priced wines. Marc and Pierrette Guillemot are avid practitioners of biodynamic viticulture, taking organic farming to its extreme. Late harvesters, they are known to tour the region's vineyards on their tandem bicycle while others are picking—only weeks later will the Guillemots begin that yearly endeavor.

The 1999 Mâcon-Villages Quintaine Sélection de Grains Cendrés has gorgeous aromatics that burst from the glass with sweet botrytised yellow fruits and loads of minerals. Medium- to full-bodied, rich, creamy, and lush, this is an admirably deep and opulent late-harvest Chardonnay. Layers of candied apricots, quince, and sweet peaches are intermingled with loads of spices. It is thickly textured and possesses a long, soft, sweet, orange-infused finish. Drink it over the next 10 years.

Other recommended wines: 1997 Mâcon-Clessé Quintaine (89), 1998 Mâcon-Villages Quintaine (89), 1999 Mâcon-Villages Quintaine (88), 2000 Mâcon-Villages Quintaine (89)

DOMAINE GUYON (VOSNE-ROMANÉE)

1999 Aloxe-Corton Les Guerets	E	90
1997 Aloxe-Corton Les Guerets	D	90
1999 Echézeaux	EE	(91–93)
1997 Savigny-les-Beaune Les Peuillets	D	90
1999 Vosne-Romanée Les Orveaux	E	(90–92)

Out of nowhere this estate burst on the scene with delicious 1997s. The medium to dark ruby-colored 1997 Savigny-les-Beaune Les Peuillets offers scrumptious aromas of smoke-imbued sweet cherries. It is a lush, forward, opulently styled wine with outstanding intensity and density. This velvety-textured, blackberry and cassis-flavored beauty should be drunk over the next 5 years. The similarly colored 1997 Aloxe-Corton Les Guérets displays smoked bacon, blackberries, and Asian spice–like scents. This fruit-driven (yes, it's a "hedonistic fruit bomb"), soft, juicy, medium-bodied wine is jam-packed with candied black cherries. It won't make old bones, but who cares? This winner will deliver pleasure, what more can be asked? Drink it over the next 5+ years.

The outstanding 1999 Aloxe-Corton Les Guerets is medium to dark ruby-colored, and bursts from the glass with loads of sweet black cherries. On the palate, this gorgeously ripe, velvety-textured wine is rich, broad, and filled with blackberries, blueberries, and jammy red cherries. It is dense, plush, and possesses an admirably long, fruit-filled, supple finish. Drink it over the next 7 years.

Guyon's 1999 Vosne-Romanée Les Orveaux was harvested at under 35 hectoliters per hectare. It reveals a black cherry– and blackberry-scented nose. This is a harmonious, dense, dark fruit and licorice-flavored wine with outstanding concentration and an impressively long, sweet finish. It is highly structured, yet its tannins are admirably ripe and enveloped in cherry fruit. This wine will require patience. Drink it between 2005–2012. The dark ruby-colored 1999 Echézeaux has a highly expressive nose of black cherries and blackberries. It bursts on the palate with spices, candied plums, jammy black cherries, and notes reminiscent of freshly laid road tar. It is medium-bodied, reveals superb balance, and has a powerful yet refined, layered personality. It is loaded with massive quantities of prodigiously ripened tannin. Anticipated maturity: 2005–2012+.

Other recommended wine: 1999 Vosne-Romanée Les Brûlées (88–89)

DOMAINE ANTONIN GUYON (SAVIGNY-LES-BEAUNE)

1997 Corton-Charlemagne	EE	(89–91)

The 1997 Corton-Charlemagne, while not up to the level of this domaine's stellar 1995, is an outstanding wine. Sweet perfume, apples, pears, and flowers are found in its aromatics. On the palate, it displays a velvety texture, lovely grip, and breadth, and flavors reminiscent of nuts, dried honey, and acacia blossoms. Rather full-bodied, it has outstanding density and richness. Anticipated maturity: now–2006.

Other recommended wines: 1999 Aloxe-Corton Les Fournières (87–89), 1997 Meursault Charmes du Dessus (88–90), 1999 Pernand-Vergelesses Les Vergelesses (87–88+)

MAISON LOUIS JADOT (BEAUNE)

2000 Bâtard-Montrachet	EEE	(90–91)
1999 Bâtard-Montrachet	EEE	(89–91)
1998 Bâtard-Montrachet	EEE	(88–91)
1997 Bâtard-Montrachet	EEE	(91–93)
1997 Beaune Clos des Ursules	D	(89–91)
1997 Bonnes Mares	EE	(93–95+)
1997 Chambertin	EEE	(90–92+)
1999 Chambertin Clos de Bèze	EEE	(88–91)
1997 Chambertin Clos de Bèze	EEE	(94–96+)
1997 Chambolle-Musigny Les Amoureuses	EE	(90–93)
1999 Chambolle-Musigny Les Fuées	E	(90–92)
1999 Chapelle-Chambertin	EE	(92–95)
1997 Chapelle-Chambertin	EE	(91–93)
1997 Charmes-Chambertin	EE	(88–91)
1999 Chassagne-Montrachet Les Caillerets	E	(89–90+)
1997 Chassagne-Montrachet Morgeot (white)	E	(90–91)
1997 Chassagne-Montrachet Morgeot Duc de Magenta (white)	E	(89–90+)
1997 Chassagne-Montrachet La Romanée (white)	E	(89–91)
1999 Chevalier-Montrachet	EEE	(90–92)
1997 Chevalier-Montrachet	EEE	(91–93)
1999 Chevalier-Montrachet Les Demoiselles	EEE	(91–92+)
1998 Chevalier-Montrachet Les Demoiselles	EEE	(89–92)
1997 Chevalier-Montrachet Les Demoiselles	EEE	(93–94+)
1999 Clos de la Roche	EE	(89–91)
1997 Clos de la Roche	EE	(89–92)
1999 Clos St.-Denis	EE	(89–91)
1997 Clos St.-Denis	EE	(90–93)

1999	Clos de Vougeot	EE	(92–95)
1997	Clos de Vougeot	EE	(90–94)
2000	Corton-Charlemagne	EE	(90–92)
1999	Corton-Grèves	E	(88–91+)
1999	Corton-Pougets	E	(89–92+)
1997	Corton-Pougets	E	(89–91+)
1999	Criots-Bâtard-Montrachet	EEE	(89–91+)
1997	Criots-Bâtard-Montrachet	EEE	(90–91)
1999	Echézeaux	EE	(90–93)
1997	Echézeaux	EE	(89–92+)
1999	Gevrey-Chambertin Clos St.-Jacques	EE	(91–93)
1997	Gevrey-Chambertin Clos St.-Jacques	EE	(92–94+)
1997	Gevrey-Chambertin Estournelles St.-Jacques	E	(89–92)
1997	Grands-Echézeaux	EEE	(90–93)
1997	Mazis-Chambertin	EE	(90–93)
1999	Meursault Charmes	E	(89–91)
2000	Meursault Perrières	E	(90–91)
2000	Montrachet	EEE	(91–92)
1999	Montrachet	EEE	(93–95)
1998	Montrachet	EEE	(91–94)
1999	Musigny	EEE	(90–92)
1997	Musigny	EEE	(93–95+)
1999	Nuits-St.-Georges Les Boudots	E	(90–91)
1997	Nuits-St.-Georges Les Boudots	E	(90–92)
1999	Pommard Rugiens	E	(89–90+)
2000	Puligny-Montrachet Clos de la Garenne Duc de Magenta	E	(91–92+)
1998	Puligny-Montrachet Clos de la Garenne Duc de Magenta	E	(88–91+)
1997	Puligny-Montrachet Clos de la Garenne Duc de Magenta	E	(91–92+)
2000	Puligny-Montrachet Les Folatières	E	(89–91)
1999	Puligny-Montrachet Les Folatières	E	(89–91)
1997	Puligny-Montrachet Les Folatières	E	(89–91)
2000	Puligny-Montrachet Les Perrières	E	(91–92)
2000	Puligny-Montrachet Les Referts	E	(89–91)
1997	Puligny-Montrachet Les Referts	E	(91–92)
1997	Richebourg	EEE	(91–93+)
1997	Romanée-St.-Vivant	EEE	(90–93)
1997	Ruchottes-Chambertin	EE	(90–93)
1997	Volnay Clos de la Barre	D	(89–92)
1997	Volnay Santenots	D	(88–91)
1999	Vosne-Romanée Les Beaumonts	E	(91–93)
1997	Vosne-Romanée Les Malconsorts	E	(90–92)

Jacques Lardière, Maison Louis Jadot's wine-maker, in 2000 celebrated thirty years with the firm. Over that span Jadot has become the most respected of Beaune's large *négociant* houses. Lardière and the firm's director, Pierre-Henry Gagey, share the responsibility for the Jadot name's being synonymous with quality.

Everywhere I went throughout Burgundy in October and November 1998, vignerons chanted the same song—the 1997 whites are forward low acid wines that had rapid malolactic fermentations. The exception—Maison Jadot. I thought I was getting used to Lardière going against the grain, but he still surprises me. The fact that some of his white Burgundies were still in full malolactic was baffling, but what truly shocked me was a statement he made at the end of our white wine tasting: "The whites are delicious," Lardière said, "but the reds may be the greatest wines of my life. They are my 1947s or 1959s. I will probably never see anything like this vintage again." I looked at him with such disbelief that he walked me over to a few barrels and had me taste some profound wines. Stay tuned, as I will taste the entire range on my scheduled mid-January visit to Maison Jadot.

How does he do it? Why are things so different for Lardière than others? As I've mentioned before, asking the right questions does not guarantee an understandable answer. For example, on my last visit I asked Lardière if he had blocked the malolactic fermentations on some of his 1997 white Burgundies, a practice this firm frequently does in low-acid vintages (1983 and 1989 are two prominent examples). His response? "At Maison Jadot we do not block malos. We perturb the bacterias that cause it. They are much easier to perturb than humans, you know." I got no further, no matter how much I pressed for information.

Jadot's 1997 white Burgundies are super, among the finest of the vintage. Lardière's magic touch (he firmly stated that he does not acidify white wines) allowed these wines to have the vintage's telltale fat and richness, yet for the most part they retained focus, balance, and structure. I loved Jadot's wines from Chassagne-Montrachet's Morgeot vineyard. The 1997 Duc de Magenta offering has a mineral- and earth-laden nose and a superripe, medium- to full-bodied, dense character. Its flavor profile is packed with clay, poached pears, and baked apples. A concentrated, thick wine, it will be at its best if drunk over the next 5–6 years. The 1997 Chassagne-Montrachet Morgeot (domaine bottling) displays aromas of fresh earth, rocks, and grilled oak. It is a powerful, complex, profound wine with a gorgeous array of clay, pear, baked apple, and spicy wood flavors that last throughout its long finish. This medium- to full-bodied and fabulously expressive wine has excellent structure. Anticipated maturity: now–2006. Revealing a bold, mineral-dominated nose, the lovely 1997 Chassagne-Montrachet La Romanée is powerful and concentrated. Its broad, thickly textured, well-extracted flavor profile is loaded with red fruits, earth, and oak spices. In a vintage that fashioned heavy wines verging on flabbiness, it is amazing how fresh and focused this offering is. Anticipated maturity: now–2006.

The 1997 Puligny-Montrachet Les Referts has a mouthwatering nose of superripe pears and apples. This dense, oily-textured, and fat wine has traces of *sur-maturité* in its otherwise bright, spicy, and almond cookie–flavored character. It is medium- to full-bodied, thick, surprisingly well balanced, and offers an impressive finish. Anticipated maturity: now–2004. Displaying floral and anise aromas, the 1997 Puligny-Montrachet Les Folatières is broad and powerful, yet feminine. A medium-bodied, velvety-textured, forward wine, it is filled with flavors reminiscent of pears, minerals, apples, and honeysuckle. Drink it over the next 6 years. The outstanding 1997 Puligny-Montrachet Clos de la Garenne Duc de Magenta has a fresh earth- and stone-scented nose. This full-bodied, mouth-filling, explosive wine is dense yet refined. Candle wax, white peaches, and clay can be found in its powerful, harmonious, and concentrated flavor profile. It may ultimately merit a more glowing review if it resolves the slight warmth (alcohol) I detected in its finish. Drink it between now–2006.

Produced from purchased grape must, the 1997 Criots-Bâtard-Montrachet reveals a spicy anise- and mineral-infused nose. This expressive and forward offering is deep, intense, focused, and crammed with nutty pear flavors. It is extremely well crafted, medium- to full-bodied, and has outstanding extraction, density, and power. It will be at its best between now–2006. Jadot's 1997 Bâtard-Montrachet may be this vineyard's finest wine in 1997, as it aptly reflects the vintage's huge richness and density yet has remained in balance. It offers overripe aromas of tropical fruits intermingled with scents of clay and tangerines. On the palate it is massively broad and thickly textured yet has superb delineation to its candied pear and apple flavors. Concentrated and powerful, it appears to have the ability to age. Anticipated maturity: now–2008.

The 1997 Chevalier-Montrachet has an enthralling nose of minerals, gravel, and crisp white pears. This impeccably delineated and focused wine has outstanding depth, medium- to full-body, and a richly layered personality. Its flavor profile offers an intense minerality that coats the palate throughout its long finish. Anticipated maturity: now–2008. Jadot's 1997 Chevalier-Montrachet Les Demoiselles is a fabulous wine. Its nose was slightly reticent the day of my tasting, reluctantly revealing nuts, minerals, and stones. However, its spectacular presence on the palate more than demonstrated its greatness. This is an offering of outstanding richness and density. It is crammed with candied hazelnuts, almonds, and spicy minerals. It also has an ethereal quality that I sometimes find in the best Chevaliers. This is one of the rare 1997s from the Côte de Beaune that will age for at least a decade. Drink it between 2003–2012.

Those wine consumers who look with disdain at *négociant* wines, believing that only domaine-bottled offerings can be exceptional, will miss out on some of 1997's finest offerings. Maison Louis Jadot has produced some of the finest reds of the 1997 vintage. That being said, however, Jadot's most successful 1997s were crafted from vineyards owned by Domaine Jadot, Domaine Gagey, Domaine des Héritiers Jadot, and the assortment of estates that permit Jadot to farm their vineyards. Winemaker Jacques Lardière credits the high quality of his wines from this heterogeneous vintage to a number of factors. Yields were low, 30–40% less than in 1996. In fact, 1997 produced the lowest yields that Maison Jadot experienced in the past decade. For reds, yields ranging from 15–24 h/h within certain grand crus were the norm, not the exception. Whereas Jadot is used to producing 110 barrels of its Santenay Clos de Malte, in 1997 only 61 casks of that exceptional offering were crafted. Lardière also believes that it was imperative to harvest late. He describes the weather conditions from September 10 to October 10 as "exceptional and amazing." He went on to say, "Most vignerons harvested early because they were concerned about acidity. We harvested late, because our goal was full physiological maturity." The results speak for themselves. Jadot's natural potential alcohols ranged from 13.2–13.8% for their reds.

As opposed to their counterparts throughout the Côte d'Or, neither director Gagey nor Lardière is obsessed by the question of acidity. "Great vintages never have high acid levels," said Lardière. "1996 was special. It is an exception, because it has extremely high maturity. The combination of high levels of acidity and high ripeness are exceptionally rare." Asked to compare 1997 to prior vintages, Lardière focused on 1947 and 1959. "The 1997s, like the 1959s, are low in acid, yet have magnificent maturity. I expect them to behave over the coming years like those spectacular wines of 40 years ago." When confronted with the fact that 1997 is an irregular vintage for red Burgundies, Lardière scoffed and said, "People were afraid of the risks. They vinified Burgundies as though they were simply Pinot Noir. Not many people had the courage to macerate the wines enough. The 1997s required at least a 25- to 26-day maceration and fermentation."

Jadot's domaine holdings and purchased grapes were immediately cooled to 16°C upon arriving at the firm's new winery complex. Due to the high levels of natural potential alcohol, only a very few *cuves* were chaptalized. Whereas virtually every other Burgundian domaine described extremely rapid malolactic fermentations as one of the characteristics of the 1997 vintage, here the story was of long, drawn-out, secondary fermentations. In fact, Lardière credits the freshness of his wines to the lateness and length of their malolactics. As we were about to begin the tasting, Lardière smiled and said, "It would have been a crime for me to mess up this vintage. I will only see this level of ripeness maybe twice in my entire lifetime."

Astute readers of *The Wine Advocate* know that Maison Louis Jadot is a first-rate source of wines from the hillside overlooking the picturesque town of Beaune. Crafted to be delicious young, yet having repeatedly demonstrated their ageworthiness, these are wines to purchase by the case. Jadot's most famous Beaune is the Clos des Ursules. Out of my cold cellar the 1990 is just reaching its plateau of maturity and the 1997 promises to be its qualitative rival. It is medium to dark ruby-colored and offers black cherry, metal, and spice aromas. This intense, black cherry–dominated wine is medium- to full-bodied, powerful, well structured, and possesses outstanding richness as well as length. Like its sibling from the 1990 vintage, it will require (and merit) cellaring. Anticipated maturity: 2003–2009.

The medium to dark ruby-colored 1997 Volnay Santenots was a challenge to taste, yet it revealed enough to justify a first-rate write-up. Presently its aromatics are dominated by sweet, toasty oak, and its tightly wound flavor profile offers only hints of cedar, meat, and blackberries. However, there can be no doubt about this offering's outstanding depth, density, richness, or concentration. It is thick, velvety-textured, powerful, and intense. Anticipated maturity: now–2007+. Sixteen months after the harvest, the medium to dark ruby-colored 1997 Volnay Clos de la Barre was just finishing its malolactic fermentations. Fresh red and black fruits and toasty oak scents are discernible in its beguiling aromatics. This gorgeously dense, concentrated, sweet, medium- to full-bodied wine is crammed with fresh yet baked blackberry flavors. Its persistent finish reveals supple tannins, immersed in layer after layer of fruit. Drink it over the next 8 years.

The medium to dark ruby-colored and scrumptious 1997 Nuits-St.-Georges Les Boudots reveals exuberant blackberry and toasty oak aromas. This rich, softly textured, powerful, and pure wine is medium- to full-bodied, and exceptionally ripe. Freshly laid road tar, blackberries, stones, figs, and prunes can be discerned in its well-delineated, balanced, and highly expressive character. Anticipated maturity: now–2010. Embracing blackberry and toasty oak aromas can be discerned in the nose of the medium to dark ruby-colored 1997 Chambolle-Musigny Les Amoureuses. This velvety-textured, full-bodied fruit bomb is expansive, immensely rich, and profound. Complex, well structured, and jam-packed with blueberry liqueur, stone, meat, and violetlike flavors, it is a highly impressive and beguiling offering. Anticipated maturity: now–2010.

The stunning, dark purple-colored 1997 Bonnes Mares enthralls the nose with its extraordinary baked blackberry aromas. This is a wine of unbelievable power and concentration and exceptional extraction. Deep layers of cocoa powder–dusted figs and prunes vie for the taster's attention with a compote of red cherries, stones, and creamed mocha flavors. This full-bodied, velvety-textured, *sur-maturité*-laced wine lingers on the palate for at least 40 seconds. It is one of the wines of the vintage, a breathtaking Burgundy. Anticipated maturity: now–2012+. Equally awesome, but more structured and masculine, the dark ruby-colored 1997 Musigny regales with its blueberry and spiced toast aromas. This firm, muscular, and verging on foursquare wine displays black cherry, blackberry, rock, and mineral flavors. Presently tightly wound and backward, this powerhouse is immensely complex and persistent. Anticipated maturity: now–2012+.

The medium to dark ruby-colored, feminine 1997 Vosne-Romanée Les Malconsorts offers an expressive nose of roses, violets, and red currants. This is an expansive, medium- to full-bodied, satin-textured, highly detailed wine. Red currant compote, cherries, raspberries, and a multitude of flowers can be detected in its gorgeously ripe and pure flavor profile. Drink this beauty over the next 8 years. The medium to dark ruby-colored 1997 Echézeaux offers aromas that suggest sweet black fruits covering a slice of cinnamon- and vanilla-dusted French toast. Full-bodied, concentrated, and complex, this is a powerful wine crammed with Chinese black tea, licorice, blackberry jam, stone, earth, and baconlike flavors. Its admirably long finish boasts copious quantities of sweet tannins drowning in waves of fruit. Anticipated maturity: now–2010+.

Profound red cherry and rose aromas are found in the aromatics of the medium to dark ruby-colored 1997 Grands-Echézeaux. Baked mixed berries and Asian spices are found in this velvety-textured, wide, superrich, rather thick wine. Medium- to full-bodied, highly concentrated, and judiciously extracted, it is hugely flavorful and opulent yet well structured. This exceptional wine should be at its peak of maturity between now–2012. The slightly darker-colored 1997 Clos de Vougeot, a vineyard that was particularly successful in this vintage, reveals candied red fruit and myriad spices in its aromatics. This overripe, massively dense, yet fresh and exceptionally well-structured wine is crammed with layer after layer of red and black compotelike fruit. Loads of supple yet present tannins provide this blockbuster with the backbone for moderate to long-term aging. Anticipated maturity: now–2012+.

Jadot's 1997 Clos St.-Denis reveals a medium to dark ruby color, as well as a nose presently dominated by grilled oak scents. This is a hugely powerful, expansive, thick, medium- to full-bodied wine. Its baked blackberry, earth, and game-laden core leads to an exceptionally long, pure, and fresh finish. Anticipated maturity: now–2010+. The black/purple 1997 Clos de la Roche bursts from the glass with mocha and baked berry fruit aromas. This is a huge, thick, muscular wine with cocoa powder and blackberry jam flavors. Deep, intense, and chewy, this powerful offering also has an impressively long, fresh finish. Drink it between now–2012.

From a vintage where the overwhelming majority of estates complained about abnormally early and rapid malolactic fermentations, Lardière's 1997 Corton-Pougets was just finishing that secondary fermentation at the time of my visit, 16 months after the harvest. It is medium to dark ruby-colored and tight both in its aromas and flavor profile. With aeration, scents of black fruits and tar could be detected. On the palate, this dense, medium- to full-bodied, highly concentrated, austere wine reluctantly revealed brambleberries, stones, and licorice. It is backward, replete with loads of well-ripened tannins, and demands cellaring. Anticipated maturity: 2004–2012.

As has come to be expected from Jacques Lardière, he has crafted two outstanding premiers crus from Gevrey-Chambertin in the 1997 vintage. The Estournelles St.-Jacques reveals sweet cherry and black currant aromas, immersed in vanilla-infused oak. This is a wine of huge concentration and extract, with powerful cherry, stone, and mineral flavors. Medium- to full-bodied, persistent, and quite elegant, it should be at its peak of drinkability between now–2010. Readers fortunate enough to have encountered the 1990 Gevrey-Chambertin Clos St.-Jacques will be ecstatic to learn that Lardière hit another home run with the 1997. Harvested at a whopping 13.8% natural potential alcohol, this stunning, dark ruby-colored wine displays mouthwatering blackberry, smoked bacon, and stonelike aromas. This full-bodied, hugely dense, powerful, highly expressive offering is jam-packed with licorice, mint, eucalyptus, and cherry syrup. Impeccably balanced, opulent, forward, yet restrained and very well structured, this massive, refined wine will provide exceptional drinking over the course of the next 12+ years.

The medium to dark ruby-colored 1997 Charmes-Chambertin offers delightful red cherry aromas as well as an easygoing, medium- to full-bodied character. Sweet blackberries, cherries, and mocha flavors are found in this supple, seductive offering. It lacks the power, concentration, and density of Jadot's top 1997s, yet its fruit-driven character provides enormous sensory gratification. Anticipated maturity: now–2006+. The similarly colored 1997 Chapelle-Chambertin reveals cherry, blackberry, and stonelike aromas. This is a complex, well-extracted, masculine, concentrated wine filled with superripe cherry and earthlike flavors. Powerful, well structured, and harmonious, it will be at its best between now–2009+.

If the otherwise highly impressive 1997 Mazis-Chambertin had not revealed some alcoholic warmth in its finish, it would have merited a higher score. Medium to dark ruby-colored, and displaying beguiling and profound red cherry and violet scents, this soft, expansive, medium- to full-bodied, hugely concentrated wine offers exceptional drinking. Complex, hugely powerful, and amazingly persistent, it is a masculine, muscular, yet refined offering. Anticipated maturity: now–2010+.

Without doubt, one of the true stars of the vintage is Maison Louis Jadot's 1997 Chambertin Clos de Bèze. Harvested at an unheard of (for Burgundy) 14.2% natural potential alcohol, this black/purple benchmark setter displays saliva-inducing cookie dough and cherry syrup aromas. Immensely ripe and concentrated, yet pure, fresh, and noble, it conquers the taster with unending layers of jammy compotelike fruit flavors. Awesomely dense, deep, fresh, and refined, this stunner has the potential ultimately to merit a score in the high 90s. It seamlessly combines New World overripeness and fruit-forward characteristics with Burgundy's trademark balance, elegance, and structure. For the lucky few who secure bottles of this nectar, note that it should be at its peak of maturity between 2003–2015. Bravo!

Jacques Lardière, a quasi-mythical figure, is justifiably proud of his 1998 white Burgundies. "It was a year where one had to think," he said. "Nothing came easily." The grapes from the different estates that make up this firm's core of holdings (Domaine Jadot, Domaine des Héritiers de Louis Jadot, Domaine Gagey, etc.) were put through a severe sorting. "It was imperative that we get rid of any bunches that showed traces of oïdium or burnt berries," said Lardière. "I am convinced that the strange aromas, flavors, and textures you must have found in other estates' wines comes from the oïdium that literally covered Burgundy." Because a substantial percentage of Jadot's production is made from purchased musts (unfermented grape juice), Lardière was "extremely worried" that his must suppliers had not sorted out infected grapes before selling juice. "We did a more intense *débourbage* (decanting off the gross less) than usual and then in January we carefully tasted each lot to see if there was a trace of aromatic or flavor distortion. Only then did we start with our twice a week *bâtonnages*. We had no intention of stirring a wine if it had poor lees," Lardière explained.

Even though the vintage had exceedingly little malic acid ("it was eaten by the heat of August," said Lardière), he blocked (perturbed or interrupted as he would say) the malolactic fermentations because "that is how you allow Burgundies to be great and ageworthy." Maison Jadot's 1998 grand crus "will easily age for 30 or more years," Lardière boasted. In general, Jadot's wines (particularly the domaine bottlings and those from the estate of the Duc de Magenta) were more harmonious than the majority of 1998s.

The 1998 Puligny-Montrachet Clos de la Garenne Duc de Magenta is crafted from 75- to 100-year-old vines that were harvested at 13.8% natural potential alcohol. Its intensely rich aromas of mocha and spices lead to a fresh, medium- to full-bodied personality. This wine is loaded with ripe fruits, stones, minerals, chalk, fresh earth, and hints of red berries. This tense, expressive wine should be at its peak of drinkability between now–2008. Maison Louis Jadot purchases must from three different growers to fashion its Bâtard-Montrachet. The poached pear–scented 1998 reveals a medium-bodied, broad, silky-textured character. White fruits, minerals, and anise can be discerned throughout its long, lemon-infused character. Anticipated maturity: 2003–2010+.

Typically one of Jadot's longest-lived whites, the 1998 Chevalier-Montrachet Les Demoiselles will live up to its reputation. Flowers, stones, and minerals are found in its aromatics. This wine has admirable breadth, delineation, richness, and freshness in its medium-bodied character. Minerals and candied lemons can be found throughout its flavor profile and persistent finish. Anticipated maturity: 2004–2012. In 1998, Maison Louis Jadot purchased its Montrachet from two growers, producing a total of eight barrels (200 cases). Its acacia, spice, stone, and mineral nose gives way to a lively, broad-shouldered, medium- to full-bodied personality. This magnificent wine offers layers and layers of white ripe fruits, hints of toasted nuts, gravel, and poached pears. It wonderfully unites muscle with grace, and explosive, expressive fruit with refinement. Anticipated maturity: 2005–2012+.

Pierre-Henri Gagey describes 1999 as "a vintage of great purity and elegance." To Jacques Lardière it "provides us with a beautiful definition of Pinot Noir." According to Gagey and Lardière, the 1999 vintage, despite its plethoric yields, was saved by the three weeks of sunny weather that preceded the harvest. This firm conducted severe green harvests on its domaine-owned vineyards, "but even those of us who are serious about vineyard work had high yields in 1999," said Gagey. He added, "We defended those that asked for the 40% PLC (the permissible amount over the stated maximum yield) in 1999 because even the 25 estates of the Côte d'Or with the lowest yields in 1997 and 1998 were over the threshold in 1999. Yet, the authorities were absolutely right to restrict the PLC to 20% in 2000. Your readers need to know, however, that even with the 40% PLC, the permissible yields for grands crus in the Côte were 49 hectoliters per hectare, still the lowest in the world." According to Lardière, extensive lees work was required to give the white 1999s depth. He also stated that his grapes had normal levels of malic acidity, yet low levels of tartaric acidity. Both Lardière and Gagey like the 1999s white Burgundies, and they believe their wines will be delicious young and that many people will be surprised by their ability to age well. "My favorite 1999s? The Chassagne-Montrachets from deep, rich soils. They have exquisite depth," said Gagey.

The medium- to full-bodied 1999 Meursault Charmes reveals a rich nose filled with nuts, freshly cut flowers, and spices. This is a feminine wine with outstanding balance, richness, and lushness. Its gorgeous flavor profile is packed with spices, poached pears, and hints of vanilla that last throughout its long, smooth finish. Anticipated maturity: 2003–2010. The flower- and nut-scented 1999 Puligny-Montrachet Les Folatières is medium- to full-bodied, deep, and broad. Ripe pears, candied apples, and hints of mint can be discerned in this well-ripened, rich, yet focused offering. It is beautifully rendered, has excellent to outstanding concentration, as well as an exemplary finish. Anticipated maturity: 2004–2011. The 1999 Chassagne-Montrachet Les Caillerets has a mouthwatering, cookie dough–scented nose. Medium- to full-bodied, deep, and rich, this is a plump, poached pear, candied apple, and red berry–flavored offering. Its layers of fruit coat the taster's palate and linger throughout its smooth, long finish. Anticipated maturity: 2004–2010.

The 1999 Criots-Bâtard-Montrachet has a demure yet rich pear-dominated nose. Medium- to full-bodied, lush, and sexy, this broad, plump wine is packed with minerals and assorted white fruits, whose flavors last throughout its impressively long finish. Anticipated maturity: 2004–2010. Spices and minerals can be found in the nose of the 1999 Bâtard-Montrachet. Medium- to full-bodied, rich, deep, and powerful, this opulent wine is crammed with pears, minerals, spices, and anise. It is velvety-textured and well balanced. Anticipated maturity: 2003–2010. The 1999 Chevalier-Montrachet boasts a mineral, spice, and toast-laden nose. Medium-bodied, luxuriously rich, and layered, this is a focused, mineral, lemon, and pear-flavored wine. It is deep, complex, and possesses an admirably long, soft finish. Anticipated maturity: 2004–2012. The 1999 Chevalier-Montrachet Les Demoiselles has gorgeous, mouthwatering aromas of almonds and flowers. Medium- to full-bodied, sexy, broad, and opulent, this wine is also well delineated and refined. Flowers, crisp pears, and candied apples are found throughout its pure, fresh, and impressively long finish. Anticipated maturity: 2008–2018.

Harvested at 13.6% natural potential alcohol, the 1999 Montrachet has a magnificent spice cake, almond paste, and hazelnut-laden nose. Medium- to full-bodied and suggestive of liquid velvet, this is a big, deep, broad, well-focused wine. Pears, apples, stones, and a myriad of spices can be found throughout its highly expressive and flavorful character. It is a huge success for the vintage, and an exceptional wine in its own right. It should stand the test of time. Anticipated maturity: 2005–2014.

Toasty oak, sweet red cherries, and candied raspberries are found in the nose of the medium to dark ruby-colored 1999 Pommard Rugiens. Loads of red fruits and oak are intermingled with freshly cracked black pepper in this chewy-textured offering. Its velvety layers of fruit coat the palate and lead to a soft, supple finish unusual for a Pommard. Anticipated maturity: now–2009. The medium to dark ruby-colored 1999 Corton-Pougets has a magnificent nose of intensely sweet cherries. Medium-bodied and dense, it is crammed with blackberries, cassis, cherries, and firm yet ripe tannin. This wine will require cellaring. Anticipated maturity: 2006–2012+. The similarly colored, licorice-scented 1999 Corton-Grèves is a firm, stony and fresh, blackberry-packed, light- to medium-bodied wine. It is tightly wound, backward, and unyielding but appears to have the density of fruit and structure for cellaring. It is concentrated, deep, and possesses a long, pure finish. Drink it between 2006–2012.

The dark cherry and Asian spice–scented, medium to dark ruby-colored 1999 Nuits-St.-Georges Les Boudots is an outstanding, medium-bodied wine. Lush layers of candied raspberries, sweet cherries, and Asian spices can be found in its soft, velvety, pure, and juicy character, as well as in its long, satiny finish. Drink it over the next 8–9 years. The perfumed, candied cherry–scented 1999 Chambolle-Musigny Les Fuées is medium to dark ruby-colored. This soft, pure, and perfumed wine is lush, opulent, and sexy. Medium-bodied and filled with cherries, candied raspberries, talcum powder, and perfume, this supple wine possesses a long, superripe, tannin-filled finish. Drink it over the next 10 years.

The oak-scented, medium to dark ruby-colored 1999 Musigny offers a medium-bodied, tangy character. This floral, feminine, well-made, elegant wine displays sweet red cherry and raspberry flavors in its long, satin-textured character. It lacks the depth and power of Jadot's finest Musignys, yet is an outstanding, highly detailed, and delicious wine. Drink it between 2004–2012. The medium to dark ruby-colored 1999 Vosne-Romanée Les Beaumonts has an Asian spice and baked plum–scented nose. This fat, medium-bodied wine is crammed with cherries, raspberries, and jellied strawberries. It has outstanding depth of fruit and an impressively long, sweet finish. Drink it between 2004–2012. The sweet cherry syrup and cookie dough–scented 1999 Echézeaux is medium to dark ruby-colored. Medium-bodied and highly expressive, this is a fresh, pure, and delineated wine. Tangy cherries and raspberries are found throughout its boisterous personality as well as in its admirably long, sweet, and supple finish. It is concentrated, deep, and gorgeously ripe. Drink it over the next 12 years.

The sweet perfume, talcum powder, freshly cut flower, and candied cherry–scented 1999 Clos de Vougeot is a chewy-textured, medium- to full-bodied wine. This dense ("the densest wine we produced in 1999," said Pierre-Henri Gagey), powerful, and intense wine has loads of blackberry and cassis-like fruit intermingled with magnificently sweet tannin. Its impressively long finish reveals additional layers of candied fruits. Drink it between 2005–2012+. The medium to dark ruby-colored 1999 Clos St.-Denis has a gorgeous nose of flowers, talc, red currants, and cherries. This juicy, medium-bodied wine is filled with raspberries, strawberries, red cherries, and flowers. It is pure, zesty, and impeccably balanced. Drink it over the next 10 years. The 1999 Clos de La Roche has an earth, stone, and dark fruit–scented nose. Blackberries, licorice, and currants can be found in this medium-bodied wine's satiny character. It is loaded with gorgeously ripe tannin yet lacks the density and length that would earn it status as a great wine. Drink it over the next 10 years.

The medium to dark ruby-colored 1999 Gevrey-Chambertin Clos St.-Jacques has a roasted black fruit–scented nose. Medium-bodied, lush, and delicious, this is a pure, sweet red cherry and blackberry-flavored offering. While it does not have the power or concentration of Jadot's finest vintages of Clos St.-Jacques, this wine relies on elegance, purity, and definition. This is a gorgeous, flavorful, highly delineated effort that possesses copious quantities of supple tannin. Anticipated maturity: 2003–2012. The 1999 Chapelle-Chambertin is medium to dark ruby-colored and has an intense, penetrating, currant and blackberry-scented nose. Baked cherries, plums, spices, and hints of coffee can be found in this medium- to full-bodied, chewy wine. It is rich, pure, powerful, and has great length. Drink this dense, concentrated offering between 2005–2014. The medium to dark ruby-colored 1999 Chambertin Clos de Bèze, generally one of my very favorite wines from the Jadot portfolio, reveals subtle dark fruit aromas. It is medium-bodied, fresh, and tangy, revealing blackberries, zesty currants, and fresh black raspberries. Hints of tar can be discerned in its firm, foursquare finish. Anticipated maturity: 2005–2012.

The aromatics of the 2000 Meursault Perrières reflect this wine's intense ripeness. Poached pears and spiced apples emanate from the glass. It is medium-bodied, syrupy-textured, and has a lovely, broad, supple, lush character. This wine is plump yet exhibits outstanding balance. Anticipated maturity: 2004–2012.

Rich spices can be discerned in the aromatics of the 2000 Puligny-Montrachet Les Perrières. Medium-bodied, broad, and elegant, this is an intense wine loaded with spices, minerals, and pears. Well concentrated and powerful, it boasts the explosive power of a sprinter and the grace of a ballerina. Drink it between 2004–2012. The earth, mineral, and candied citrus–scented 2000 Puligny-Montrachet Les Referts is a zesty, medium-bodied wine. Satin-textured and vinous, it has outstanding intensity, depth, and concentration. This mineral- and stone-flavored offering also reveals margarita-like lime notes in its extensive finish. Anticipated maturity: 2004–2012. The smoky white fruit–scented 2000 Puligny-Montrachet Les Folatières has outstanding depth, power, and a rich, medium-bodied character. Satin-textured, it sports a vinous character, something often lacking in this vintage. Minerals, crisp apples, and pears are found throughout its well-defined personality and in its persistent finish. Drink it between 2005–2012. The rich and ample 2000 Puligny-Montrachet Clos de la Garenne Duc de Magenta detonates from the glass with spice cake aromas. This gorgeous wine has huge depth to its caramelized mineral and toasted hazelnut–flavored personality. It is seamless, harmonious, concentrated, and has an extensive finish. Anticipated maturity: 2004–2012.

The buttered mineral–scented 2000 Bâtard-Montrachet is rich, opulent, and medium-bodied. Loads of butter-dripping popcorn can be found in this zesty, concentrated wine's personality. Lemons and limes pop up in its finish, giving it a tangy, zesty component to offset its otherwise lush character. Anticipated maturity: 2004–2012. The mineral- and spice-scented 2000 Montrachet is light- to medium-bodied, yet rich and satin-textured. Highly focused, this wine exhibits outstanding depth and concentration. Waves of minerals intermingled with citrus fruits and pears can be discerned throughout its expressive character as well as in its lengthy finish. Anticipated maturity: 2004–2012. The 2000 Corton-Charlemagne has a creamy, talcum powder, and mocha-scented nose. Medium- to full-bodied, supple, and velvety-textured, it is an intensely flavored offering. It bastes the palate with creamed fruit and mineral flavors. Drink this harmonious, lush wine between 2004–2012.

Other recommended wines: 1997 Beaune Boucherottes (88–90), 1997 Beaune Les Bressandes (87–89), 1997 Beaune Les Chouacheux (88–90), 1997 Beaune Clos des Couchereaux (88–90+), 1999 Beaune Clos des Ursules (88–90+), 1999 Beaune Grèves (white) (87–89), 1997 Beaune Les Theurons (87–89+), 1997 Bienvenue-Bâtard-Montrachet (88–89?), 1998 Bienvenue-Bâtard-Montrachet (87–90), 1999 Bienvenue-Bâtard-Montrachet (88–90), 1999 Chambolle-Musigny (87–89), 1999 Chambolle-Musigny Les Amoureuses (87–89), 1999 Chambolle-Musigny Les Baudes (88–90), 1997 Chambolle-Musigny Les Fuées (88–90), 1997 Chassagne-Montrachet Les Grandes Ruchottes (white) (89–90), 1999 Chassagne-Montrachet Morgeot (white) (88–90), 1997 Chassagne-Montrachet Morgeot Duc de Magenta (red) (87–89), 1999 Chassagne-Montrachet Morgeot Duc de Magenta (white) (88–90), 2000 Chassagne-Montrachet Morgeot Duc de Magenta (white) (88–90), 1997 Corton (88–90), 1997 Corton-Charlemagne (89–90), 1998 Corton-Charlemagne (87–89+), 1999 Corton-Charlemagne (88–89), 1997 Corton-Grèves (88–89+), 1997 Corton-Vergennes (88–89), 1997 Côtes de Nuits-Villages (87–89), 1998 Criots-Bâtard-Montrachet (87–90), 1997 Meursault Bouchères (87–89), 1997 Meursault Charmes (89–90), 2000 Meursault Charmes (87–89), 1999 Meursault Les Genevrières (87–89), 2000 Meursault Les Genevrières (88–89), 1997 Meursault La Goutte d'Or (88–89), 1999 Meursault La Goutte d'Or (88–89), 1997 Nuits-St.-Georges Les Porrets (87–90), 1999 Nuits-St.-Georges Les Porrets (88–89), 1997 Pernand-Vergelesses Clos de la Croix de Pierre (87–89+), 1999 Pommard Clos de la Pouture (87–89), 1997 Puligny-Montrachet Les Champs-Gains (88–89+), 1999 Puligny-Montrachet Les Champs-Gains (88–90), 2000 Puligny-Montrachet Les Combettes (88–89), 1997 Puligny-

Montrachet Les Folatières (87–90), 1999 Puligny-Montrachet Clos de la Garenne Duc de Magenta (88–90), 1999 Puligny-Montrachet Les Perrières (88–90), 1997 Santenay Clos de Malte (red) (88–90), 1999 Santenay Clos de Malte (red) (87–89), 1999 Santenay Clos de Malte (white) (87–89), 1997 Savigny-les-Beaune La Dominode (88–90), 1997 Savigny-les-Beaune Clos des Guettes (red) (88–90), 1997 Savigny-les-Beaune Clos des Guettes (white) (87–89), 1999 Savigny-les-Beaune Clos des Guettes (red) (87–89), 1997 Savigny-les-Beaune Les Narbantons (88–90), 1997 Savigny-les-Beaune Les Vergelesses (87–89), 1999 Volnay Clos de la Barre (88–90), 1997 Vosne-Romanée Les Beaumonts (88–90+), 1997 Vosne-Romanée Les Petits Monts (87–89), 1999 Vosne-Romanée Les Suchots (88–90)

DOMAINE PATRICK JAVILLIER (MEURSAULT)

2000 Meursault Charmes "Mise Spéciale"	E	(88–91)
1997 Meursault Cuvée Tête de Murger	E	90+
2000 Meursault Cuvée Tête de Murger "Mise Spéciale"	E	(88–91)
1997 Meursault Les Narvaux "Mise Spéciale"	E	(89–91+)

Note: Javillier often fashions two bottlings: a "Mise Spéciale" (indicated on the label; it means special bottling) and the other a regular bottling (no special marking on the label). The "Mise Spéciale," a complex, broader, and fuller-bodied wine than the standard *cuvées,* is bottled 18 months after the harvest while the regular bottling, primarily destined for the European market (which supposedly prefers "leaner" wines), is done only after 11–14 months. The "Mise Spéciale" is bottled unfiltered whenever possible. Prior to 1996, the "Mise Spéciale" wines were labeled "Cuvée Spéciale."

The "house blend" of Meursault Casse Tête and Meursault Murgers is outstanding. Javillier decided to bottle his entire production of 1997 Meursault Tête de Murger in September, forgoing the production of a "Mise Spéciale." It displays intense ripe pear and lees aromas, as well as a rich, oily-textured, medium- to full-bodied character. Its flavor profile offers dense layers of sweet white fruits, flint, smoke, and loads of spices that linger in its exceedingly long finish. Anticipated maturity: now–2005. Of the two *cuvées* of 1997 Meursault Narvaux, I tasted the Mise Spéciale. Behind a touch of reduction, dense nuts and minerals could be discerned in this wine's nose. On the palate it is layered, crammed with sweet white fruit, medium- to full-bodied, and intensely rich yet balanced. It is a highly impressive offering that finishes strongly with impressions of spiced and baked pears. Anticipated maturity: now–2006.

According to Patrick Javillier, 1999 was "a classic vintage," and 2000 is "more elegant and refined. It is a hypothetical blend of two-thirds 1992 and one-third 1986." He is of the opinion that "it has excellent acidity, though less than 1996, and will give lots of pleasure both in its youth and in its old age." When asked why yields were so high in 2000, Javillier answered, "The vines never suffered from drought. We constantly alternated between rain and sun. However, even though yields were quite large, the maturity the grapes attained was excellent. While 1999 was a vintage of minerality because the fruit flavors were dissipated by rain, 2000 is packed with fruit."

Javillier's 2000 Meursault Cuvée Tête de Murger "Mise Spéciale" exhibits herbal tea, spiced pear, and fruit salad aromas. On the palate, this harmonious wine has an outstanding underlying minerality whose flavors last throughout its long and pure finish. Drink it over the next 7–8 years. Loads of spiced white fruits can be found in the aromatics of the 2000 Meursault Charmes "Mise Spéciale." This refined wine is medium-bodied, pure, and satin-textured. It exhibits a lovely panoply of apples, pears, apricots, and a faint hint of lychee nuts, all lingering in its long, supple finish. Drink it over the next 8–9 years.

Other recommended wines: 1997 Bourgogne Blanc Cuvée des Forgets "Mise Spéciale" (87–89), 2000 Bourgogne Blanc Cuvée des Forgets "Mise Spéciale" (87–89), 1997 Bourgogne Blanc Cuvée Oligocéne "Mise Spéciale" (88–90+), 2000 Bourgogne Blanc Cuvée Oligocéne "Mise Spéciale" (87–89), 1999 Corton-Charlemagne "Mise Spéciale" (88), 2000

Corton-Charlemagne "Mise Spéciale" (87–89+), 1997 Meursault Les Clous (89), 1997 Meursault Clos du Cromin (88), 2000 Meursault Clos du Cromin (88), 1998 Meursault Cuvée Tête de Murger (88), 1998 Meursault Cuvée Tête de Murger "Mise Spéciale" (88–89+), 1999 Meursault Cuvée Tête de Murger "Mise Spéciale" (88–90), 1999 Meursault Narvaux (88), 2000 Meursault Narvaux (88), 1997 Meursault Les Tillets (88), 1997 Meursault Les Tillets "Mise Spéciale" (88–90), 1999 Meursault Les Tillets "Mise Spéciale" (89+), 1997 Puligny-Montrachet Le Levron (88), 2000 Puligny-Montrachet Le Levron "Mise Spéciale" (88–90), 1997 Savigny-les-Beaune Les Serpentières (red) (88)

DOMAINE JAYER-GILLES (MAGNY-LES-VILLERS)

1999 Echézeaux	EEE	(90–92)
1997 Echézeaux	EEE	92+
1997 Nuits-St.-Georges Les Damodes	EE	92

Gilles Jayer says that his yields ran from a high of 37 h/h on the Bourgognes Hautes Côtes de Beaune to a low of 28 h/h on both Nuits-St.-Georges Les Hauts Poirets and Echézeaux. The wines were left on their lees without undergoing any rackings until having been bottled unfined and unfiltered. Jayer stated that none of his offerings had been acidified. "The freshness in my wines comes from the CO_2 they absorbed while sitting on the lees."

The 1997 Nuits-St.-Georges Les Damodes has this estate's trademark tobacco, burned leaf, and cassis-scented nose. On the palate, it is tangy, crammed with blackberries, licorice, and hints of violets. This medium- to full-bodied wine has gorgeous purity of fruit, a velvety texture, and loads of sweet, supple tannins. It will be at its best if consumed over the next 7–8 years. The slightly darker-colored 1997 Echézeaux offers an expressive nose of fresh, spicy red fruits amid notes of cedar and cigar smoke. Layers of blackberries, road tar, licorice, and cherries can be found in this supple yet structured, medium- to full-bodied wine. It is impressively ripe, powerful, muscular, and intense. It exhibits the vintage's trademark *sur-maturité* fruit, yet is surprisingly vibrant and well-structured. Anticipated maturity: now–2010.

In 1999, Jayer began to harvest his reds on September 22, starting with the Echézeaux and his Nuits-St.-Georges. By the 23rd and 24th he and his teams were hard at work picking his Côtes de Nuits-Villages parcels, and he harvested his Hautes Côtes parcels from the 25th to the 30th. These last vineyards typically produce powerful, flavorful wines, but the rains that began on the 23rd affected them in 1999. Jayer's yields averaged 48 h/h in the Côte de Nuits after a 10% *saignée* and 55 h/h in the Hautes Côtes after a 15% *saignée*. The 1999 Echézeaux, harvested at 40 h/h, displays dark fruit, Asian spice, and sweet oak aromas. It has outstanding depth of red and black fruits (mostly cherries and blackberries) as well as Asian spices in its pure, dense personality. This medium- to full-bodied wine is fresh, harmonious, and boisterous. It reveals loads of ripe tannin and sweet oak in its long finish. Drink it between 2004–2012.

Other recommended wines: 1998 Bourgogne Hautes Côtes de Beaune (white) (88), 1997 Bourgogne Hautes Côtes de Nuits (red) (89), 1997 Bourgogne Hautes Côtes de Nuits (white) (88+), 1998 Bourgogne Hautes Côtes de Nuits (white) (89+), 1999 Bourgogne Hautes Côtes de Nuits (white) (88), 1997 Côte de Nuits-Villages (89), 1999 Côte de Nuits-Villages (87–89), 1999 Nuits-St.-Georges Les Damodes (88–90), 1997 Nuits-St.-Georges Les Hauts Poirets (89+?), 1999 Nuits-St.-Georges Les Hauts Poirets (87–89)

DOMAINE FRANÇOIS JOBARD (MEURSAULT)

1997 Meursault Charmes	EE	(89–92+)
1997 Meursault Genevrières	E	(89–91)
1997 Meursault Poruzots	E	(89–91+)

Candied apples awash in liquid minerals are displayed by the 1997 Meursault Poruzots's nose. How Jobard was able to craft an elegant wine with such overripe characteristics as pear compote and hazelnut cream pastries is admirable! This is a super Poruzots, medium- to full-bodied, opulent, focused, somewhat austere in the finish, but, oh so good. Anticipated maturity: now–2004. Jobard's 1997 Meursault Genevrières has rich, toasty ripe pears in its aromas, and it possesses a sweet, layered, medium- to full-bodied character. This wine, crammed with candied nuts and mocha, has all the components for a higher rating (density, ripeness, power, fruit, complexity, concentration), except elegance, focus, and a long, seamless finish. Nevertheless, this offering's fabulous attributes should ultimately earn it an outstanding score. Drink it between now–2006. Produced from 34-year-old vines, the 1997 Meursault Charmes is first-rate, with a nose redolent of apples, white raisins, and red currants. This expansive, broad, and impressively persistent wine shares flavors of earth, apricots, and minerals. Without overlooking this wine's austerity and its somewhat warm (alcoholic) finish, it should merit an outstanding rating after bottling. Drink it between now–2006.

Other recommended wines: 1997 Meursault en la Barre (87–89), 1999 Meursault Charmes (87–89), 2000 Meursault Charmes (88–90), 1996 Meursault Genevrières (92+), 1998 Meursault Genevrières (87–90), 1998 Meursault Poruzots (87–89), 2000 Meursault Poruzots (88–90)

DOMAINE RÉMI JOBARD (MEURSAULT)

2000 **Meursault Charmes**	EE	(90–92+)
1997 **Meursault Charmes**	EE	94
1997 **Meursault Chevalière**	E	(89–90+)
1997 **Meursault En Luraule**	E	90
1997 **Meursault Les Genevrières**	EE	92+
1999 **Meursault Poruzots-Dessus**	E	(89–91)
1997 **Meursault Poruzots-Dessus**	E	(90–92)

Rémi Jobard, the young, intelligent, and dedicated director of this estate, has added a new dimension to his already impressive commitment to quality winemaking (he uses no chemical fertilizers in his vineyards, plows their soils, has modest yields, and harvests as late as feasible). Jobard decided to bottle his 1997s without filtering. Eschewing filters is now commonplace at Burgundy's finest red wine–producing estates. It remains a process that is utilized on the majority of white wines, because producers fear that consumers will reject whites that do not have a polished brilliance. In effect, most wine-makers believe that the public is willing to sacrifice flavor and quality in exchange for a perfectly clear white wine. I did not find any problems with clarity in the five unfiltered 1997s Jobard served me. What matters most is a wine's quality, and Rémi Jobard's 1997s sing!

The 1997 Meursault En Luraule has a beguiling nose of gravel and lemony white fruits. Its personality is broad, complex, bright, and extremely well delineated. Flavors of ripe white peaches and buttered toast linger in this beauty's long finish. Anticipated maturity: now–2005. Surprisingly, the 1997 Meursault Chevalière's sautéed porcini–scented nose is more reminiscent of a red than white wine. Its ample character is redolent in layers of minerals, citrus, and white fruits. This is a 1997 Côte de Beaune that is truly elegant. That being said, this wine also has its vintage's telltale plumpness, huge ripeness, and thick fruit. It should be at its best between now–2006. The 1997 Meursault Poruzots-Dessus exhibits awesome aromas of spiced apples and red berry fruit. This medium- to full-bodied, intense, massive, yet highly defined offering is powerful as well as elegant. As if that were not enough, its mouthwatering caramelized apple flavors are carried through in its exceedingly long finish. Anticipated maturity: now–2005.

Rémi Jobard crafted a spectacular 1997 Meursault Genevrières. Its buttery, cream pastry, spicy, and toast scents lead to an explosive and opulent character. This medium- to full-bodied wine is crammed with anise, cinnamon, superripe pears, and loads of sweet butter. It is a wine made for hedonists, velvety-textured, pleasure-inducing, immensely broad, and intensely flavorful. Drink it over the next 6 years. Unusually low yields (particularly for Chardonnay), a warm growing season, and a notoriously late harvest all combined to fashion an unbelievably dense, ultraripe, and massive 1997 Meursault Charmes. Not for the fainthearted, or those who crave elegance and delineation, this butterscotch, tropical fruit, and spice-scented offering is pure unadulterated decadence. Presently its flavor profile, packed with richly textured layers of pureed quince, apricots, peaches, honeysuckle, and minerals, has a candied lime element that brings some freshness to this otherwise mouthcoating gem. Is this Meursault's version of Helen Turley's Marcassin Chardonnay? My inclination is to believe that this example of awe-inspiring ripeness will not sustain extended cellaring, but who cares? Anticipated maturity: now–2004.

Rémi Jobard likes the 1999s. "They are very round, nothing sticks out, there are no angles, and the longer it goes the more I think they will be ageworthy." Like many white Burgundy producers in 1999, Jobard had exceedingly slow alcoholic and malolactic fermentations. This posed a serious problem as he doesn't have room to store two vintages in his cellars. Instead of forcing the wines through their fermentations by adding artificial yeasts or bacteria, Jobard purchased state-of-the-art stainless steel tanks and installed them in an abandoned barn near his home. It was in this barn that the 1999s were tasted, as Jobard shoved whatever he could find to serve as insulation into the holes in the walls.

The 1999 Meursault Poruzots-Dessus has a rich, yellow fruit–scented nose. Medium- to full-bodied, opulent, lush, and concentrated, this is a wine that has outstanding plumpness as well as grip and depth. Pears, apples, and hints of apricots can be found in its supple, flavorful personality. Drink it over the next 7–8 years. The intense 2000 Meursault Charmes reveals acacia blossom and mineral aromas. This wine is hugely expressive, coating the palate with tangy white fruits, quartz, minerals, and spices. It is bright, concentrated, and possesses a wonderfully long, fresh finish. Drink it over the next 10–12 years.

Other recommended wines: 1998 Meursault Les Charmes (87–89+), 1999 Meursault Chevalières (87–89), 2000 Meursault Les Genevrières (88–90), 2000 Meursault En Luraule (87–89), 1998 Meursault Poruzots-Dessus (88), 2000 Meursault Poruzots-Dessus (88–90), 1997 Meursault Sous la Velle (88–89), 2000 Meursault Sous la Velle (88–90), 1997 Volnay Santenots (89)

DOMAINE JOBLOT (GIVRY)

1999 Givry Bois Chavaux	C	90
1999 Givry Clos du Cellier aux Moines	D	93+
1997 Givry Clos du Cellier aux Moines	D	(89–92)
1997 Givry Clos de la Servoisine (red)	D	93+
1997 Givry Clos de la Servoisine (red)	D	(88–90+)
1999 Givry Pied de Chaume	C	90

Jean-Marc Joblot, one of the world's great Pinot Noir producers, harvested extremely early in 1997, in order to "maintain adequate levels of natural acidity." Since Joblot's work in the vineyard always ensures moderate yields (the 1997 Clos du Cellier aux Moines was harvested at 28 h/h), his grapes achieve physiological ripeness earlier than most, providing him with the luxury of setting early harvest dates. The 1997 Givry Clos de la Servoisine (red) reveals Joblot's typical dark ruby color, as well as a beautifully ripe, black fruit–laden nose. On the palate, this expansive, well-extracted, deep, black cherry–packed wine boasts flavors that last 25 seconds. Anticipated maturity: now–2007+. The dark purple-colored 1997 Givry Clos du Cellier aux Moines has cassis-like aromas, and a mouthcoating character crammed with blackberries, stones, and hints of oak. This is a masculine, powerful, structured wine that exhibits tar and licorice-like nuances in its long, supple finish. As previous vintages of this Côte Chalonnaise benchmark have amply demonstrated, this is a wine that will age and evolve magnificently with cellaring. Anticipated maturity: now–2010.

While the 1999 vintage was outstanding in certain areas, good in others, and difficult in some, in Givry, it was stunning if the vineyards were trained to ripen early, as were Domaine Joblot's. "I have never before seen a vintage like this, and I may never again," said the understated Jean-Marc Joblot. "It is unquestionably a great year, with virtually perfect ripeness, sanitary conditions, and balance." Readers of *The Wine Advocate* have seen Robert Parker and me heap praises on Joblot's wines for years, yet if there was ever a not-to-be missed vintage from this supertalented winemaker, 1999 is the one. These wines have unheard-of purity of fruit, opulence, power and elegance, at prices to kill for. These are Pinots to buy by the carload.

The medium to dark ruby-colored 1999 Givry Pied de Chaume was aged entirely in first-year oak barrels. Hazelnuts and blackberries can be found in its expressive aromas. This medium-bodied, sweet, broad wine coats the mouth with its seemingly unending layers of cherries and candied raspberries. It is prodigiously balanced, impressively long in the finish, and has perfectly ripened, supple tannin. Anticipated maturity: now–2010. The slightly lighter-colored 1999 Givry Bois Chavaux bursts from the glass with cassis, leather, and blackberry aromas. Medium-bodied and satin-textured, it is fresh, seamless, and harmonious. Its incredibly well balanced personality is loaded with red fruits, mostly candied cherries, whose flavors are carried through its seemingly unending finish. Drink it over the next 10 years.

The medium to dark ruby-colored 1999 Givry Clos de la Servoisine (red) puts many Côtes de Nuits grands crus to shame. Its piercing aromas of cassis, blackberry, fresh cherry, and flowers lead to a superb medium-bodied character. Loads of dark berries, spices, and candied blackberries are intermingled with toasted oak as well as a myriad of spices in this profound, magnificently focused wine. It has admirable purity and a stunning finish. Drink it between 2004–2012+. The similarly colored 1999 Givry Cellier aux Moines has candied red and black cherry aromas. Medium-bodied and chewy-textured, it is opulent, lush, and awesomely structured. Copious quantities of perfumed blackberries, cassis, blueberries, cherries, and oaky spices can be found in its penetrating character. It is more structured than the Servoisine, yet its tannin is prodigiously well ripened. Anticipated maturity: 2005–2015. These Burgundies are *splendid bargains!* Kudos to the Joblot family!

DOMAINE MICHEL LAFARGE (VOLNAY)

1997	Pommard Pézerolles	EE	(89–91)
1997	Volnay Clos des Chênes	EE	(89–92)
1999	Volnay Clos du Château des Ducs	EE	(89–92)
1997	Volnay Clos du Château des Ducs	EE	(90–92)

Frédéric Lafarge and his father, Michel, crafted delicious wines in the 1997 vintage, which will come as no surprise to readers of *The Wine Advocate*. From the estate's Bourgogne Passe-Touts-Grains to its premier cru Volnays, every wine can be recommended. The Lafarges said that this vintage was fashioned by the dry, hot summer that promoted rapid ripeness. Their opinion is that the key to success was to harvest as soon as the grapes attained physiological ripeness and to cool down the grapes immediately. They stated that they did not acidify their wines, as they felt that sufficient acid was present, yet melted "in the wine's forward fruit." Malolactic fermentations took place relatively early (in January and February), and the wines thereafter were slightly reduced, requiring a racking in April. The Lafarges both like 1997. "The fruit is wonderful, and the *terroir* differences come through marvelously well." Only a few wines were chaptalized, and much less new oak was used in 1997 than usual, resulting in lighter-colored wines than usual at this estate.

The light to medium ruby-colored Volnay Clos du Château des Ducs has a fabulous nose of candied cherries and red and black fruit syrups. On the palate, it exhibits marvelous breadth, medium to full body, sublime elegance, structure, and a floral, black cherry–dominated flavor profile. It is extremely flavorful, soft, and immensely enjoyable. Drink it over the next 6–8 years. The similarly colored 1997 Volnay Clos des Chênes reveals cassis and violet aromas. This is a wine of purity and structure. Foursquare and medium- to full-bodied, it is crammed with stones, blackberries, and brambleberries. This broad-shouldered, muscular wine will require a year or two of cellaring and should evolve extremely well over the coming 7–8 years. Lafarge's ruby-colored 1997 Pommard Pézerolles possesses an opulent, mouthwatering nose that boasts highly expressive candied red cherry aromas. This medium- to full-bodied, seductive, well-structured wine is ample and decadently crammed with black raspberries. Masculine, powerful, and extroverted, it combines its vintage's characteristic superripe qualities with admirable freshness and backbone. Anticipated maturity: now–2007.

The medium to dark ruby-colored 1999 Volnay Clos du Château des Ducs has a tangy Bing cherry and earthy nose. It is a medium- to full-bodied wine filled with lush, dark fruits, including plums, grapes, blackberries, and cherries. This plump, rich, concentrated wine possesses loads of well-ripened tannins. Drink it between 2003–2010.

Other recommended wines: 1997 Beaune Grèves (87–89), 1999 Pommard Pézerolles (87–89), 1997 Volnay (87–89), 1999 Volnay Clos des Chênes (88–90+), 1997 Volnay Premier Cru (88–90), 1997 Volnay Vendanges Sélectionées (88–90)

DOMAINE DES COMTES LAFON (MEURSAULT)

2000	Meursault Charmes	E	(92–94)
1999	Meursault Charmes	E	(90–92)
1998	Meursault Charmes	E	(89–92)
1997	Meursault Charmes	E	(91–93)
2000	Meursault Clos de la Barre	E	(89–91)
1997	Meursault Clos de la Barre	E	(90–92)
1997	Meursault Désirée	E	(89–91)
2000	Meursault Genevrières	E	(92–94)
1997	Meursault Genevrières	E	(93–95)
2000	Meursault La Goutte d'Or	E	(90–92)
1999	Meursault La Goutte d'Or	E	(89–91)
1997	Meursault La Goutte d'Or	E	(90–92)
2000	Meursault Perrières	E	(93–96)
1998	Meursault Perrières	E	(88–91)
1997	Meursault Perrières	EE	(93–95)
2000	Montrachet	EEE	(93–95)
1999	Montrachet	EEE	(93–95)
1998	Montrachet	EEE	(91–94+)
1997	Montrachet	EEE	(95–97+)
2000	Puligny-Montrachet Champs-Gains	EE	(89–91)
1997	Puligny-Montrachet Champs-Gains	EE	(91–93)
1999	Volnay Champans	E	90+
1998	Volnay Clos des Chênes	E	(88–91)
1997	Volnay Clos des Chênes	E	(89–92)
1999	Volnay Santenots du Milieu	E	92
1998	Volnay Santenots du Milieu	E	(89–91)
1997	Volnay Santenots du Milieu	E	(91–93)

Dominique Lafon has been a heralded wine-maker for years, yet he appears to improve with each passing vintage. Unlike many others in his profession, Lafon does not settle on a recipe or formula to use again every year. He ponders his actions each time, questions what the vintage's strengths and weaknesses are, and adapts. In 1997, Lafon hit the nail on the head with both his whites and reds. Lafon, whose wines are increasingly difficult to purchase (only 15–18% of his production is sold in the U.S.), is red-hot. I have always enjoyed his wines, particularly in their youth, but sense that Lafon has raised his winemaking to new heights. Whereas I used to believe that he was striving to merit his reputation, now I feel he is surpassing it.

In contrast to 1996, where Lafon tried to lengthen the fermentations of his whites, he did the opposite in 1997. "The key to success in 1997 was to have short fermentations, very little *bâtonnage* [lees stirring], and retain as much CO_2 [a natural by-product of fermentation] as possible during the *élevage*." The 1997 Meursault Désirée is opulent and has a long finish. It displays apricot, acacia blossom, and grilled wood scents as well as a seductively rich character. White peaches, currants, and minerals can be found in its forward, rich, yet structured, medium- to full-bodied personality. Anticipated maturity: now–2006. Harvested at 13.3% natural potential alcohol, the 1997 Meursault Clos de la Barre reveals sweet aromas of candied pears, apples, and honeysuckle. This vibrant, medium- to full-bodied, deeply rich wine is crammed with peaches, minerals, and clay. It is velvety-textured, thick, exquisitely dense, and possesses an admirably long finish. Drink it between now–2007.

I was immensely impressed with Lafon's extremely spicy, toasty, white/yellow fruit–scented 1997 Puligny-Montrachet Champs-Gains. This boisterous, medium- to full-bodied, opulently textured yet gorgeously refined wine is broad, rich, and impressively concentrated. Its harmonious, complex, layered flavor profile reveals white peaches, flowers, stones, and hints of tropical fruits. It will be at its best between now–2007. The delightful 1997 Meursault La Goutte d'Or, harvested at a whopping 13.5% natural potential alcohol, has a nose composed of minerals, honeysuckle blossoms, stones, and citrus fruits. This creamy-textured, masculine, dense wine explodes on the palate with a dizzying array of tropical fruits, hazelnut butter, candied lemons, and spicy oak. It is full-bodied, hedonistic, and powerful. It would have merited a more glowing review if its finish had not betrayed its high level of alcohol. Drink it between now–2006.

The 1997 Meursault Genevrières is spectacular! As he poured it, Lafon enthusiastically said, "It is the best wine of my life, I'm very proud of it." Sweet almond cookies intermingled with juicy citrus fruits can be found in this beauty's aromas. It explodes on the palate with richly textured, expansive flavors reminiscent of spiced apples, earth, minerals, and mangoes. This is a medium- to full-bodied, intensely flavored, opulent wine that is amazingly refined. Its exceptionally long finish lasted at least 40 seconds. Impressive! Anticipated maturity: now–2008+.

The 1997 Meursault Charmes offers an extraordinarily elegant nose of earth, minerals, nuts, and flowers. This vivacious, medium- to full-bodied harmonious wine has sweet mineral, chalk, citrus, and floral flavors. It is rich, gorgeously refined, and velvety-textured. Drink it between now–2008. The magnificent 1997 Meursault Perrières displays profound aromas of stones, limes, flowers, and crisp pears. This thick, dense, and satin-textured wine offers loads of caramel covered apples, fresh butter, minerals, and oak spices in its explosive yet elegant personality. It is full-bodied, fat, impeccably balanced, and possesses a stupendously long finish. Anticipated maturity: now–2009+. The 1997 Montrachet is a candidate for the wine of the vintage. Lafon believes it is one of the two best (1992 being the other) he has ever crafted. I prefer the 1996, but at this level of quality it is splitting hairs. It exhibits deep aromas of stones, minerals, honeysuckle blossoms, candied hazelnuts, and sweet oak spices. It is extraordinary, expansive, pure, richly textured, and superbly delineated. Akin to liquid silk, it has enormously ripe yet fresh flavors of red currants, raspberries, minerals, peaches, apricots, and poached pears that persist in the finish. It is a levitating experience to taste, one I have not yet forgotten. Anticipated maturity: 2005–2014+.

All four of Lafon's 1997 red offerings could potentially merit outstanding scores, even the

Monthélie Les Duresses, a wine that he has struggled with for years. Aged in 33% new oak barrels, the medium to dark ruby-colored 1997 Volnay Clos des Chênes offers red and black cherry aromas. This velvety-textured, elegant, beautifully fashioned wine is replete with sweet cherries and oak spices. Reminiscent of the 1995, it offers liquid satin with syrupy fresh fruit. A delight to drink today, it should easily hold for 6–7 years. The similarly colored 1997 Volnay Champans reveals luscious black cherry, porcini mushroom, and blackberry aromas. With absolutely no hard edges to be found, this is a velvety-textured, broad, seductive, and black fruit–flavored wine. More structured than the Clos des Chênes, it should be capable of slightly longer cellaring. Anticipated maturity: now–2007+. The bright, dark ruby-colored 1997 Volnay Santenots du Milieu came from yield of only 25 h/h and was harvested at a whopping 13.5% natural potential alcohol. It offers intense aromas of plummy cherries. Its awesome aromatics reveal the *sur-maturité* levels of Lafon's harvest. This is a mouthcoating, medium- to full-bodied, broad, velvety wine that abounds with layers and layers of sweet black fruits. Its candied, almost confectionary finish is extremely long and reveals supple, ripe tannins. Anticipated maturity: now–2007.

"What can I tell you about the 1998 vintage?" said Lafon. "After the cold, the hail, the rain, the disease, the drought, the heat, nature provided us with a short harvest period, no more than five days to get it all done. Then, on the last day, massive thunderstorms came crashing down on us." Lafon characterized 1998 as "the hardest vintage of my life. We all worked like dogs for nothing," he said as he pointed to a cellar containing only 120 barrels of wine (this estate normally produces a minimum of 200). As the alcoholic fermentations ended, Lafon witnessed what virtually every other vigneron of the Côte discovered. The 1998 white Burgundies, particularly those produced from vineyards that were struck by the April frost, were extremely oxidative. As the first dose of sulfur (added to curtail the potentially disastrous effects of oxidation) proved insufficient, Lafon realized he had a considerable problem. Unlike the overwhelming majority of his colleagues, who responded by following the oenologists' incessant call for more sulfur (this resulted in all too many 1998s losing the little fruit the vintage naturally provided), Lafon searched elsewhere and found his solution in carbon dioxide. He proceeded to pump 200 milligrams of CO_2 into each and every barrel in his cellar, then sealed them shut and waited. This technique protected his wines from the deleterious effects of oxygen, and maintained a high level of freshness and purity.

Lafon's parcel of Meursault Les Charmes is located just below the Meursault Perrières vineyard on the Puligny-Montrachet border. The 1998 exhibits mouthwatering almond, hazelnut, and white flower scents. Medium-bodied, silky-textured, and possessing superb refinement and focus, this is a mineral, pear, and apple-flavored wine. Its character is harmoniously sustained from the attack through the mid-palate. Moreover, the finish is long, focused, and flavorful. There are no hard edges or angles in this complete 1998. Anticipated maturity: now–2008. Delicate floral aromas are found in the nose of the 1998 Meursault Perrières. Beautifully intense and focused, this silky-textured, medium-bodied wine is complex, harmonious, and has a long, flavorful finish. Minerals, cedar, acacia blossoms, and hazelnuts can be found in its broad, pure flavor profile. Anticipated maturity: now–2008.

Dominique Lafon's parcel of Montrachet produced his highest yields (30 h/h) in 1998. Four and a half barrels of this magnificent nectar were made. Harvested at 14% natural potential alcohol, it reveals pears, peaches, apricots, and flowers in its intense aromatic profile. Medium- to full-bodied, expansive, and palate-coating, this elegant, classy, rich wine is crammed with spices, white fruits, and minerals. It has outstanding presence, detail, and focus. It is not a muscular wine, yet possesses extraordinary underlying power in its precise character. This tour de force has an extraordinarily long, delineated, and mineral-laden finish. Anticipated maturity: now–2012+.

Harvested at 12.5–12.8% natural potential alcohol, the ruby-colored 1998 Monthélie Les Duresses (it was to be bottled immediately after my visit) reveals a sweet, red cherry–filled nose. This medium-bodied wine is silky-textured and displays an appealingly soft finish. Loads of wild red berry fruit can be found in its fresh, juicy personality. Drink it over the next 4–5 years. Produced from microscopic (18 h/h) yields, the ruby-colored 1998 Volnay Clos des Chênes has a nose of candied plums and cherries. This medium-bodied, well-detailed, refined wine displays a mouth of cherries, raspberries, and blueberries. It has an outstanding breadth of fruit that envelops its ripe yet copious tannins. Anticipated maturity: now–2006. The similarly colored 1998 Volnay Santenots is intensely aromatic and flavorful. Spicy black cherry scents lead to a medium-bodied character that coats the palate with stones and fresh black fruits. This silky-textured yet reasonably structured wine should be consumed over the next 7 years.

The 1999 Meursault La Goutte d'Or bursts from the glass with intense white peach, poached pear, and apricot aromas. Medium-bodied and possessing outstanding depth and concentration, this is a fat, plump, pear- and peach-flavored wine. Its sexy personality lasts throughout its harmonious, long, plush finish. Drink it over the next 7 years. Talcum powder, perfume, and flowers can be discerned in the aromatics of the 1999 Meursault Les Charmes. Medium-bodied and silky, it offers toast, mineral, white currant, and crisp pear flavors. It is tangy, flavorful, extremely well balanced, and graceful. This wine also boasts an admirably long, smooth finish. Drink it over the next 7–9 years.

Lafon's 1999 Montrachet is one of the vintage's few blockbusters. Boisterous flowers, minerals, and pears can be discerned in its explosive aromatics. Medium-bodied and impeccably delineated as well as nuanced, this rich, broad, and opulent wine is exceptionally refined. Satin-textured and loaded with stones, pears, apples, toast, and hints of crème brûlée and vanilla bean, this is a powerful, harmonious, elegant, and complete wine. Its majestic finish displays buttered toast as well as a myriad of spices. Anticipated maturity: 2004–2012.

Dominique Lafon is enamored of his 1999 Pinot Noirs, stating that it is his best vintage in red wines. While his Pinots have averaged 20–25 h/h over the past 10 years, in 1999 he harvested 40 h/h. The medium to dark ruby-colored 1999 Volnay Champans offers highly expressive and pure red cherry, earth, and blackberry aromas. On the palate, it is medium- to full-bodied and has excellent density to its cherry, blackberry, stone, and cassis-flavored personality. This is a chunky, firm, concentrated, structured wine that should be at its best between 2004–2012. The outstanding dark ruby-colored 1999 Volnay Santenots du Milieu has plum, licorice, cherry, currant, and jammy black raspberry aromas. Medium- to full-bodied and packed with loads of red and black fruits, it is a zesty, immensely concentrated, tangy, blackberry, cherry, raspberry, and red currant–flavored wine. This wine possesses enormous depth as well as structure, and will therefore require cellaring. Anticipated maturity: 2006–2012.

To Dominique Lafon, 2000 is "a vintage I enjoy a great deal. And even though I loved the 99s, I believe this one is a hair better." The 2000 Meursault Clos de la Barre bursts from the glass with aromas reminiscent of ripe pears and sweet white peaches. It is soft, medium-bodied, loaded with apple compote, minerals, and spices. This well-structured wine should be consumed over the next 7–8 years. The fresh apple-scented 2000 Puligny-Montrachet Champs-Gain is a feminine, medium- to full-bodied wine. Angle free and lush, it reveals toast, raspberries, candied pears, and apples in its layered character. Anticipated maturity: now–2010. The 2000 Meursault La Goutte d'Or explodes from the glass with buttered spices, smoky pears, and toasted apples. Medium- to full-bodied and velvety-textured, this is a soft, juicy, plump wine. Copious quantities of superripe white fruits can be found throughout its expressive character as well as in its admirably long, pure finish. Anticipated maturity: now–2010.

The gorgeous 2000 Meursault Genevrières reveals juniper berries, spices, and anise in its aromatics. Rich, fat, and vinous, this is a spice fruit bomb with a sexy, fruit-forward character and a long, persistent finish. It is concentrated, deep, and dense. Drink this highly expressive wine over the course of the next 10–11 years. The mineral, apple, and pear-scented 2000 Meursault Charmes combines both power and finesse. It explodes on the palate with candied pear, butter, anise, and spiced apple flavors that, while highly expressive, seem delicate and lacelike. It is medium-bodied, precise, and exceptionally long in the finish. Drink it over the next 10 years. The 2000 Meursault Perrières exhibits intense smoke and mineral scents, and has great aromatic depth. Medium- to full-bodied and vinous, this seamless stone and mineral-laden wine is rich, well balanced, and very long in the finish. Anticipated maturity: now–2012.

The spice- and anise-scented 2000 Montrachet is a lush, medium-bodied wine. Soft layers of creamed minerals and spices can be found in its broad, soft character. It is expansive and reveals loads of underlying minerals in its persistent finish. Anticipated maturity: now–2014. *Other recommended wines:* 1997 Meursault (88–90), 2000 Meursault (88–90), 1999 Meursault Clos de la Barre (88–90), 1999 Meursault Désirée (87–89), 2000 Meursault Désirée (87–89), 1999 Meursault Genevrières (88–90), 1999 Meursault Perrières (88–89), 1997 Monthélie Les Duresses (88–90), 1999 Puligny-Montrachet Champs-Gains (88–89), 1999 Volnay (88), 1997 Volnay Champans (88–90+), 1999 Volnay Clos des Chênes (89+)

DOMAINE DES LAMBRAYS (MOREY-ST.-DENIS)

1999 Clos des Lambrays	EE (89–91)
1997 Clos des Lambrays	EE 91

The 1997 Clos des Lambrays is a medium to dark ruby-colored wine with aromas reminiscent of blood oranges, cumin, spices, and black cherries. It offers an expansive, soft, easygoing, velvety-textured personality, with a massively spicy, tobacco, cedar, and blackberry-flavored core. This deep yet soft wine will require early drinking. Anticipated maturity: now–2005.

The medium to dark ruby-colored 1999 Clos des Lambrays exhibits blackberry, cassis, blood orange, and spice aromas. It is medium-bodied, with a well-made candle wax, blackberry, cassis, and hoisin sauce–flavored personality. This spicy, extroverted wine is velvety-textured and appealing. Drink this wine over the course of the next 10–12 years. *Other recommended wine:* 1997 Morey-St.-Denis Premier Cru (88+)

DOMAINE LAROCHE (CHABLIS)

1997 Chablis Blanchots	EE	(89–91)
1997 Chablis Blanchots Réserve de l'Obédiencerie	EEE	(92–95)
1997 Chablis Les Clos	EE	(90–93)

Michel Laroche adores the 1997 vintage, which he says has the same richness as 1996, but 30% less acidity. Furthermore, Laroche says, "It is fundamental to have high maturity at harvest to make great wines." Oak barrels, even new oak (a rarity in Chablis) are present in his cellars. "One only learns by trying new things," he said. A lover of rich, dense, and flavorful wines, Laroche asserts that he has never acidified, and never will.

The 1997 Chablis Blanchots offers a nose with fabulous ripeness of fruit, and its palate is velvety-textured, dense, and thick. Minerals, hazelnuts, white flowers, and hints of peanut oil are found in this intensely flavored and persistent wine. Anticipated maturity: now–2006.

The 1997 Chablis Les Clos is fabulous. It boasts a profound nose of marzipan, minerals, stones, earth, and toasted hazelnuts. This wine, produced entirely in oak barrels, coats the taster's mouth with liquid minerals, poached pears, apple-flavored candies, and hints of vanilla. It is extremely well balanced, medium- to full-bodied, chewy, broad, dense, and possesses an impressively long and suave finish. Anticipated maturity: now–2007.

Laroche's expensive yet superb 1997 Chablis Blanchots Réserve de l'Obédiencerie is a blockbuster. Fresh white flowers, toasted spices, and pears can be found in its complex aromatics. It is a feminine wine, impeccably crafted, ethereal, and sublimely elegant. Layers of precise flint, mineral, honeysuckle, and candied apple flavors dominate its medium to full body as well as its exceedingly long finish. Wow! Drink this stunner between now–2008.

Other recommended wine: 1997 Chablis Les Fourchaumes Vieilles Vignes (88–90)

DOMAINE ROGER LASSARAT (VERGISSON)

2000 Pouilly-Fuissé Clos de France Très Vieilles Vignes Cuvée Unique	D	92
1999 Pouilly-Fuissé Clos de France Très Vieilles Vignes Cuvée Unique	D	91
2000 Pouilly-Fuissé La Côte Très Vieilles Vignes Cuvée Unique	D	90
1999 Pouilly-Fuissé La Côte Très Vieilles Vignes Cuvée Unique	D	90
1998 Pouilly-Fuissé Très Vieilles Vignes Réserve	D	93
1997 Pouilly-Fuissé Très Vieilles Vignes Réserve	D	90
2000 St.-Véran Les Châtaigniers Vieilles Vignes Cuvée Unique	D	90
2000 St.-Véran Les Cras Vieilles Vignes Cuvée Unique	D	92

Note: These "Réserve" and "Cuvée Unique" bottlings are special *cuvées* crafted with and for David Hinkle and Peter Vezan for the U.S. market.

Roger Lassarat's old-vine *cuvée*, produced from vines over 100 years old, is consistently one of the finest wines made in the Mâconnais. The 1997 has a concentrated nose of deeply rich spices and minerals. This superb Pouilly-Fuissé is dense, medium- to full-bodied, and fabulously focused, offering seemingly unending layers of liquid stones, nuts, and flowers. The power and refinement of this wine need to be tasted to be believed! Anticipated maturity: now–2007.

Assiduous readers who have made it this far in the text will have noticed that the vast majority of wines produced from the Côte de Beaune's most hallowed (and, yes, expensive) vineyards did not earn scores as high as Roger Lassarat's 1998 Pouilly-Fuissé Très Vieilles Vignes Réserve. It possesses amazing aromatic intensity, revealing spices, minerals, stones, flowers, and assorted ripe white fruits. This noble, medium- to full-bodied, powerful wine has magnificent breadth to its stunningly long character. Spiced apples, poached pears, assorted spices, and a muscular minerality can be found throughout this breathtaking Pouilly-Fuissé's core. Drinkable now, it will easily hold for 12 or more years.

The 1999 Pouilly-Fuissé La Côte Très Vieilles Vignes Cuvée Unique has demure floral and mineral aromas. It is medium-bodied and has admirable depth, concentration, intensity, and a long, pure, supple finish. Minerals, flowers, and hints of dried honey can be found throughout its flavorful personality. Drink it over the next 6–7 years. The 1999 Pouilly-Fuissé Clos de France Très Vieilles Vignes Cuvée Unique is even better. Stones, rocks, toast, and sweet oak notes can be discerned in its aromas. On the palate, crème fraîche, gravel, minerals, and poached pears can be found in its medium-bodied, well-delineated, and balanced character. This outstanding wine is harmonious, fresh, and complete. Anticipated maturity: now–2007.

The mineral-scented 2000 St.-Véran Les Châtaigniers Vieilles Vignes Cuvée Unique is an outstanding wine. This chewy, satin-textured beauty is medium-bodied, precise, and delineated. Loads of minerals and poached pears can be found in its flavorful and persistent personality. Anticipated maturity: now–2010. The superb 2000 Pouilly-Fuissé Clos de France Très Vieilles Vignes Cuvée Unique is a deep, intense, powerful wine. Medium-bodied, it is concentrated, pure, and exceedingly well focused. Copious quantities of minerals and spices can be discerned throughout this profound wine's character. Anticipated maturity: now–2012. The spice, stone, flint, and mineral-scented 2000 Pouilly-Fuissé La Côte Très Vieilles Vignes Cuvée Unique is medium- to full-bodied and crammed with copious quantities of forward pear, apple, and anise-laden fruit. It is flavorful and highly expressive. Anticipated maturity: 2003–2011. The 2000 St.-Véran Les Cras Vieilles Vignes Cuvée Unique has mineral, floral, metallic shaving, and chalk scents. Medium- to full-bodied and intense, it is loaded with cream, minerals, lime syrup, quinine, and candied lemons. This highly defined and muscular wine additionally reveals an exceptionally long, flavorful finish. Drink it between 2003–2013.

Other recommended wines: 1998 Mâcon-Vergisson La Roche Réserve (88), 2000 Mâcon-Vergisson La Roche Cuvée Unique (88), 1999 Pouilly-Fuissé Clos de la Grange Murgets Vieilles Vignes Cuvée Unique (88), 1999 Pouilly-Fuissé La Roche Vieilles Vignes Cuvée Unique (89), 1999 St.-Véran Les Châtaigniers Vieilles Vignes Cuvée Unique (88), 1999 St.-Véran Les Cras Vieilles Vignes Cuvée Unique (89+), 2000 St.-Véran Les Fournaise Vieilles Vignes Cuvée Unique (88), 1999 St.-Véran Les Mûres Vieilles Vignes Cuvée Unique (88), 2000 St.-Véran Les Mûres Vieilles Vignes Cuvée Unique (89), 1998 St.-Véran La Rôtie Vieilles Vignes Réserve (89+), 1999 St.-Véran La Rôtie Vieilles Vignes Cuvée Unique (88+), 2000 St.-Véran La Rôtie Vieilles Vignes Cuvée Unique (88)

MAISON LOUIS LATOUR (BEAUNE)

2000	Bâtard-Montrachet	EEE	(90–92)
1999	Bâtard-Montrachet	EEE	(91–92)
1997	Bâtard-Montrachet	EEE	(92–93)
1997	Beaune Vignes Franches	D	90
1998	Bienvenue-Bâtard-Montrachet	EEE	(89–92)
1997	Chambertin	EEE	90+
1999	Charmes-Chambertin	EE	92+
1997	Chevalier-Montrachet	EEE	(92–94)
1999	Corton-Charlemagne	EE	(90–91)
1997	Corton-Charlemagne	EE	(91–93+)
1999	Corton Clos du Roi	E	91+
1999	Corton Clos de la Vigne au Saint	E	90
2000	Criots-Bâtard-Montrachet	EEE	(90–92)
1997	Criots-Bâtard-Montrachet	EEE	(91–93)
2000	Montrachet	EEE	(90–92)
1999	Montrachet	EEE	(90–92)
1998	Montrachet	EEE	(90–93)
1997	Montrachet	EEE	(92–94)
1997	Romanée-St.-Vivant	EEE	90
1999	Volnay Clos des Chênes	E	91

Jean-Pierre Jobard, this firm's talented and ever-smiling wine-maker, has been with Maison Louis Latour for 35 years now. While his brothers François and Charles created their own domaines (Charles has recently transferred the estate to his son Rémi), Jean-Pierre has quietly been crafting fabulous white Burgundies for this famous *négociant* firm.

When I asked if the 1997s had been acidified, Maison Latour's young director, Louis-Fabrice Latour, said, "We are not obsessed with acidity at Latour, it is ripeness we search for. We have never acidified, and we never will. If we feel we need better acidity in our grapes, we leave them on the vine longer so they can obtain it naturally through concentration." Jobard did not perform a *débourbage* in 1997, nor did he do any *bâtonnage*. As per the firm's tradition, the whites were transferred to barrels only after their fermentations had begun (the norm in Burgundy is for the entire fermentation to take place in wood).

Latour's Corton-Charlemagne is this *négociant*'s flagship wine. The 1997's nose was rather unyielding on my visit to the firm's Château Grancey (in Aloxe-Corton) cellars. With aeration, it revealed huge ripeness in its poached white fruit and hazelnut aromatics. On the palate, it is broad, creamy, luscious, and hedonistic. This medium- to full-bodied Corton's flavor profile is composed of sweet pears, candied/spiced apples, sugarcoated nuts, and hints of new oak. Moreover, it possesses a long, dense, and flavorful finish. Anticipated maturity:

now–2007. Aromatically, the 1997 Criots-Bâtard-Montrachet is austere and scented with salty minerals. It is exceedingly well focused for a 1997, medium- to full-bodied, and crammed with gravel, chalk, sun-baked rocks, and dried earth–like flavors. This wine, like many Criots, doesn't quite fulfill the taster's hedonistic needs, yet is complex, defined, and intellectual. It should be at its best between now–2008. I got immense enjoyment from Latour's 1997 Bâtard-Montrachet. It is the absolute opposite of the Criots, delivering corporeal pleasure in a bold, assertive, flashy manner. Sweet white fruits, hazelnut purée, honeysuckle, and roses can be discerned in its blatant aromatics. This massive, broad-shouldered, full-bodied wine is not for the weak. Thick, fabulously ripe layers of candied apples, spiced pears, toasty oak, and hints of tropical fruits are found in its ample character. It is not made for extended cellaring, yet will deliver enormous pleasure over the next 5–6 years.

The 1997 Chevalier-Montrachet is more refined and focused and better balanced. Minerals, toast, and floral scents are followed by a rich, full-bodied, detailed personality. Flavors reminiscent of seashells, stones, grilled oak, and flint are found in this oily-textured, dense, complex wine. While it reflects the vintage's richness, weight, and fat, it also offers delineation and precision and is slightly less evolved. Anticipated maturity: now–2008. My efforts to become acquainted with the 1997 Montrachet's aromatics were unsuccessful, as it was completely closed. With its elegant, expansive, and medium- to full-bodied personality, it offers superbly focused layers of minerals, sweet nuts, white flowers, and spiced pears. A highly refined and well-crafted wine, it is marvelously ample, focused, concentrated, and complex. A prodigious 1997, it combines the vintage's richness with structure, outstanding balance, and an impressively long, detailed finish. Anticipated maturity: now–2009+.

Latour is primarily known in the U.S. for high-quality white wines. Yet, according to its director, Louis-Fabrice Latour, they sell more grand cru red Burgundies in the U. S. each year than any other firm. While Latour's reds are often lean and tannic, in years of high physiological ripeness, they are capable of producing Pinots that admirably marry sweet fruit, elegance, and complexity.

The 1997 Beaune Vignes Franches is medium to dark ruby-colored and has a lovely nose filled with deeply ripe red and black fruits. This is a huge, rich, fat, deep wine with plum syrup–covered, cookie dough flavors, and hints of candied orange rinds. Medium- to full-bodied, silky-textured, and with evidence of *sur-maturité*, it is a wine that provides enormous hedonistic pleasure. Anticipated maturity: now–2004. The medium to dark ruby colored 1997 Romanée-St.-Vivant reveals floral, mocha-covered red and black fruit aromas. This medium- to full-bodied, thickly textured wine is dense, feminine, and packed with chocolate as well as red cherries. It is soft, refined, opulent, and possesses a long, somewhat chalky finish (this characteristic lowered its score). Drink it over the next 7 years. The dark ruby-colored 1997 Chambertin has spicy, blackberry, and cinnamon-laced aromas. It is dense, concentrated, well extracted, masculine, and broad-shouldered. This medium- to full-bodied, thick, chocolate, mocha, and cassis-crammed wine is backward when compared to most wines of this generous vintage, yet has the intensity of fruit and structure for moderate cellaring. Anticipated maturity: now–2008.

Latour's medium- to full-bodied 1998 Bienvenue-Bâtard-Montrachet's aromatic and flavor intensity leaves little doubt to its quality. Brandishing scents of well-ripened yellow fruits and minerals, this deep, powerful wine is silky-textured, rich, and possesses an extraordinarily long finish. Well concentrated and highly expressive, it should be at its best over the next 5–6 years. Minerals, white flowers, and toasted oak are found in the 1998 Montrachet's nose. This medium- to full-bodied, deep, dense, creamy wine is crammed with layers and layers of minerals, pears, and stones. It is complex, harmonious, compelling, and reveals an extremely long, flavorful, focused finish. Anticipated maturity: now–2010.

Jobard and Latour described the white 1999s as a cross between 1989 and 1990. They both feel it is a "very commercial" vintage with abundant quantities of pleasing, easily accessible white Burgundies. The 1999 Corton-Charlemagne offers mineral and stone aromas. Medium-bodied, fat, and wide, yet elegant, it is a well-balanced, austere wine. Minerals, white fruits, and toasty oak can be discerned in this wine's character as well as throughout its impressively long finish. Anticipated maturity: 2003–2009. The toasted oak–scented 1999 Bâtard-Montrachet bursts on the palate with loads of power and density. This medium-bodied, expansive wine is chewy-textured, deep, and loaded with spicy white fruits. It is well balanced, lush, and possesses an admirably long, flavorful finish. Anticipated maturity: now–2008. Spices, anise, red berries, and pears are found in the nose of the 1999 Montrachet. This medium-bodied wine has outstanding breadth, concentration, and length. Toasted oak, spices, candied apples, and hints of minerals can be discerned in its satin-textured personality. Anticipated maturity: now–2009.

Louis-Fabrice Latour loves the reds he and winemaker Jean-Pierre Jobard fashioned in both 1999 and 1997. "These are some of the finest wines we've made in the last 50 years," he said. The 1999 vintage was particularly successful in two areas, Volnay premiers crus and Charmes-Chambertin. Latour's ruby-colored 1999 Volnay Clos des Chênes boasts dark fruit aromas and a dense, lush personality. It is crammed with blackberries, plums, cherries, and spices. Its fat, velvety-textured, medium-bodied personality reveals an admirably long finish studded with prodigiously ripened tannin. Anticipated maturity: 2003–2010.

The enthralling aromatics of the ruby-colored 1999 Corton Clos de la Vigne au Saint offer blackberries, raspberries, violets, and spices. This is a deep, intense, medium-bodied wine stuffed with copious quantities of coffee-drenched red and black fruits. It is fresh, possesses loads of supple tannin, and has a long, zesty finish. Drink it between 2003–2010. Even better, the slightly darker-colored 1999 Corton Clos du Roi reveals a candied raspberry–scented nose and a rich, layered personality. This is a medium-bodied, silky-textured wine with gorgeous depth, waves of sweet cherry fruit, and an intensely long and candied finish. Anticipated maturity: 2004–2012. The medium to dark ruby-colored 1999 Charmes-Chambertin is the finest young red I've tasted from Louis Latour. It bursts from the glass with dark cherry syrup and toasted oak scents. Medium- to full-bodied and luscious, it exhibits untold quantities of candied red and black fruits in its sexy, complex, persistent character. Drink it over the next 10 years.

Louis-Fabrice Latour believes that the 2000 white Burgundies "lack power, but are refined." He added, however, that they will be less expensive than previous vintages, because prices at the bulk level are dropping. They paid about 15% less for the 2000s, so they should appear on the U.S. market 10–15% cheaper than the 1999s. To demonstrate his point, Latour mentioned that wine he had purchased in 1992 at 6,500 FF per barrel had hit an all-time high of 20,000 FF in 1998. By 1999, those same wines were at 17,500 FF, and by 2000, 15,500 FF. "This fluctuation in pricing can be attributed to Japan's exuberance for our wines, and our exuberance for the Japanese market. As the Japanese were buying more and more Burgundy, at one point being our largest export market in both value and quantity, many négociants tried to get market share in Japan by producing more. Therefore, they had to buy additional wines, and this increased demand drove prices through the roof by 1998. However, the Japanese are not buying as they once did, and are now Burgundy's fifth- or sixth-largest export market."

Applesauce and red berries can be discerned in the aromatics of the 2000 Criots-Bâtard-Montrachet. Medium- to full-bodied, rich, ripe, and round, this plush, plump, sexy wine is silky-textured and sensuous. Loads of spicy white/yellow fruits can be found in this fruit-dominated offering's character. Drink it over the next 12 years. The boisterous 2000 Bâtard-Montrachet is rich, vinous, tangy, and focused. It displays spiced minerals and toast in its aromatics as well as in its flavor profile. Loaded with fruit, this broad, full-flavored wine has outstanding depth, a vivacious character, and an admirably long and flavorful finish. Drink it over the next 12 years. The cinnamon, ginger, and vanilla-scented 2000 Montrachet has loads of spices and minerals in its medium-bodied personality. Broad, ample, and expressive, it bastes the palate with its buttery flavors. This concentrated and well-balanced wine will be at its peak of maturity between 2004–2012.

Other recommended wines: 1997 Aloxe-Corton Les Chaillots (88), 2000 Bienvenue-Bâtard-Montrachet (87–89), 1999 Chassagne-Montrachet Les Caillerets (87–89), 2000 Chassagne-Montrachet Les Chenevottes (88–89), 1997 Chassagne-Montrachet Morgeot (red) (87–89), 1999 Chevalier-Montrachet (88–89?), 2000 Chevalier-Montrachet (89–90), 1998 Corton-Charlemagne (87–89+), 1997 Corton-Grancey (88), 1999 Criots-Bâtard-Montrachet (88–89), 1997 Meursault La Goutte d'Or (88–90), 2000 Meursault La Goutte d'Or (88–89), 1997 Puligny-Montrachet Les Folatières (88–90+), 1999 Puligny-Montrachet Les Folatières (88–89), 1997 Puligny-Montrachet La Garenne (87–89), 1997 Puligny-Montrachet Les Referts (87–89), 1999 Romanée-St.-Vivant (88?).

DOMAINE LATOUR-GIRAUD (MEURSAULT)

2000 Meursault Charmes	E	(90–91)
2000 Meursault Genevrières	E	(89–91)
2000 Meursault Genevrières Cuvée des Pierre	EE	(91–93)
1999 Meursault Genevrières Cuvée des Pierre	EE	(89–91)
1997 Meursault Genevrières Cuvée des Pierre	EE	(90–92)

Jean-Pierre Latour used his new, state-of-of-the-art press for the first time in 1997. Even though he felt compelled to "rectify" the acidity on a few of his whites, he credits this new press with having allowed him to draw as much natural acidity as possible from the grapes. Latour's 1997s are excellent, and his luxury *cuvée* of Meursault Genevrières outstanding. They all beautifully display the vintage's telltale ripe and dense fruit. The 1997 Meursault Genevrières Cuvée des Pierres (only 75 cases were produced) reveals intensely ripe white fruit and candied orange rind aromas that lead to an awesomely sweet, dense wine. This full-bodied, concentrated, and complex offering is crammed with caramelized apples, spiced and poached pears, and traces of grilled oak. It has admirable balance for a wine of this richness. With its long, mouthcoating finish, this opulent beauty should be drunk between now–2006.

"The 1999 whites are good, honest wines," said Jean-Pierre Latour, this estate's owner and wine-maker, "but certainly not in the league of the decade's three best vintages, 1996, 1992, and 1995. However, I would say the contrary for the 1999 reds. They can be wonderful if yields were kept within reason. To me 1999 is the third best vintage for reds of the 1990s, after 1990 and 1996." When discussing the high yields Burgundy had in both 1999 and 2000, Latour said, "what many growers don't understand is that the extra 10–20% they produce simply pollutes their wines. Whether they hide it from the authorities or send it off to the distillery, the result is the same, the quality of their wines suffer." Rich yellow fruits make up the nose of the 1999 Meursault Genevrières Cuvée des Pierre. Apricots, peaches, minerals and toast are found in its layered, velvety-textured, medium-bodied character. This smooth, flavorful wine also boasts a long, sensuous finish. Drink it over the next 7–8 years.

To Jean-Pierre Latour, 2000 will be a vintage to drink in its youth, whereas 1999s should be cellared. "I really loved the 2000s. It is a very pretty vintage. It has exceptional richness and fat, much more than 1999," he said. The floral and apricot-scented 2000 Meursault Charmes is a concentrated, vinous, medium- to full-bodied wine. Satin-textured, it coats the palate with ripe pears and apples whose flavors last throughout its long finish. Anticipated maturity: now–2009. The superexpressive 2000 Meursault Genevrières is bursting at the seams with spice and liquid mineral aromas. This delightfully broad wine is medium- to full-bodied, crammed with butter, spices, juicy apples, and pears. It is layered, muscular, plush, and fruit-forward. Enjoy it over the next 10 years.

Latour-Giraud's 2000 Meursault Genevrières Cuvée des Pierre sports a boisterous spice- and mineral-laden nose. Medium-bodied and gorgeously expressive, it butters the palate with red/white berries, spices, minerals, and poached pears. Satin-textured, concentrated, and focused, this is an admirably persistent wine. Anticipated maturity: now–2012.

Other recommended wines: 2000 Meursault Bouchères (88–90), 2000 Meursault Cuvée Charles Maxime (87–89), 1999 Meursault Charmes (88–89), 1997 Meursault Genevrières (87–89), 1999 Meursault Genevrières (88–89), 2000 Meursault Le Limozin (88–89), 1997 Meursault Narvaux (87–89), 2000 Meursault Narvaux (88–90), 1997 Meursault Perrières (88–90), 1999 Meursault Perrières (88–89), 2000 Meursault Perrières (88–90), 2000 Meursault Poruzots (89–90), 1999 Pommard Refène Cuvée Sélectionnée (87–89), 1999 Puligny-Montrachet Champs-Canet (88–90), 2000 Puligny-Montrachet Champs-Canet (88–90), 1997 Volnay Caillerets Cuvée Sélectionnée (87–89), 1997 Volnay Clos des Chênes Cuvée Sélectionnée (87–89), 1999 Volnay Clos des Chênes Cuvée Sélectionnée (87–89)

DOMAINE PHILIPPE ET VINCENT LÉCHENEAUT
(NUITS-ST.-GEORGES)

1997 Chambolle-Musigny Premier Cru	E	(89–91)
1997 Clos de la Roche	EE	(92–94)
1999 Nuits-St.-Georges Les Cailles	E	(90–93)
1997 Nuits-St.-Georges Les Cailles	E	(91–93)
1999 Nuits-St.-Georges Les Pruliers	E	(90–93)

The Lécheneaut brothers were "extremely satisfied" with their 1997s. "We've worked hard to regulate our yields. Our approach is to make sure that each vine produces the same amount of fruit. This is much more important than the overall yields." In 1997, the Lécheneauts harvested between 24–35 h/h, obtaining grapes of "great health and ripeness." None of the wines was acidified, a slight chaptalization was performed, and they were left on their lees without racking throughout their *élevage*. The medium to dark ruby-colored 1997 Chambolle-Musigny Premier Cru displays delightfully fresh aromas of ripe cherries. This is a medium- to full-bodied, elegantly styled, forward wine. It is feminine, pure, and deep. Its finish reveals a structured backbone that would benefit from 2–3 years of cellaring. Anticipated maturity: now–2007. The dark ruby-colored 1997 Nuits-St.-Georges Les Cailles has a fabulous nose of deeply sweet black fruits, perfume, and talcum powder. This opulent, oily-textured, creamy offering is crammed with powerful, yet supple and feminine, red berries. It is seductive, sensual, immensely expressive, and, simply put, delicious! Drink this beauty over the next 6+ years.

The hyperripe, nearly black 1997 Clos de la Roche displays a nose of tar, blackberry liqueur, and sweet oak spices. Almonds, flowers, red berries, and licorice can be found in this muscular yet elegant, medium- to full-bodied wine. This is a powerhouse, yet it possesses the elegance that has made Burgundy's great Pinot Noirs famous the world over. Its immensely long and flavor-packed finish reveals copious quantities of supple, round tannins. Drink this beauty over the next 10 years.

According to Philippe and Vincent Lécheneaut, after loads of work aimed at reducing yields in 1999, they still had to sort out the biggest bunches (10% of the harvest) and bleed another 10% of the juice to reach 45–50 h/h. As is often the case, their barrel samples always taste tighter and harder than the finished product, largely because of their belief in reductive (oxygen-free) winemaking. Produced from a 0.5-hectare parcel of 25-year-old vines the Lécheneaut brothers purchased from the Château de Bligny, the 1999 Nuits-St.-Georges Les Pruliers is a medium to dark ruby-colored wine with fresh sweet cherry and black fruit aromas. This dense, broad, profound wine is medium- to full-bodied and silky-textured. Loads of candied red and black fruits are found in this lush, opulent, and exceptionally long finishing beauty. Anticipated maturity: 2004–2012. The dark ruby, almost black 1999 Nuits-St.-Georges Les Cailles has stony black fruit aromas. Medium- to full-bodied and spicy, this is a harmonious, powerful, muscular wine crammed with spices, blackberries, black cherries, cassis, and candied raspberries. Violets and Asian spices can be found in its admirably long, pure finish. Anticipated maturity: 2004–2012.

Other recommended wines: 1997 Nuits-St.-Georges (87–89), 1999 Nuits-St.-Georges (87–89), 1997 Vosne-Romanée (87–89)

DOMAINE RENÉ LECLERC (GEVREY-CHAMBERTIN)

1997 Gevrey-Chambertin Combe aux Moines	E	(91–92+)
1997 Gevrey-Chambertin Lavaux St.-Jacques	E	(89–92)
1997 Griotte-Chambertin	EE	(91–93)

"I've had to adapt to the tastes of others," dejectedly responded Renée Leclerc when asked to comment on all the new barrels in his cellar (33% new oak is employed for the Gevreys). While he may be unhappy about the changes he has instituted, this taster believes the estate's wines have never been better. The medium to dark ruby-colored 1997 Gevrey-Chambertin Lavaux St.-Jacques's reticent nose only reveals hints of red fruit aromas. However, its impressive medium- to full-bodied personality regales the taster with loads soft, spicy, and fresh red/black fruits. This is an oily-textured, seductive wine with an impressive, ageworthy structure. Anticipated maturity: now–2008. Similarly colored, the 1997 Gevrey-Chambertin Combe aux Moines reveals spiced corn and candied cherry aromas. On the palate, this waxy, superrich, powerful, dense wine is replete with blackberries, cherries, and licorice-like tones. Well crafted and admirably long, this beauty will be at its best if drunk between now–2008. Spice cake, cumin, cinnamon, and smoked bacon can be discerned in the 1997 Griotte-Chambertin's aromatics. A refined yet muscular effort, it is crammed with red cherries verging on *sur-maturité*. It is satin-textured, supple, sweet, and luscious. Anticipated maturity: now–2009.

Other recommended wines: 1997 Gevrey-Chambertin (87–89), 1997 Gevrey-Chambertin Clos Prieur (87–90)

MAISON OLIVIER LEFLAIVE (PULIGNY-MONTRACHET)

2000 Bâtard-Montrachet	EEE	(88–91)
1997 Bâtard-Montrachet	EEE	(89–91)
1997 Chevalier-Montrachet	EEE	(89–91)
2000 Criots-Bâtard-Montrachet	EEE	(92–94)
1998 Criots-Bâtard-Montrachet	EEE	(88–91)
2000 Montrachet	EEE	(93–95)
1999 Montrachet	EEE	(91–93)
1998 Montrachet	EEE	(89–92+)
1997 Montrachet	EEE	(90–92)
2000 Puligny-Montrachet Champs-Gain	EE	(89–91)
1999 Puligny-Montrachet Les Pucelles	EE	(89–91)

This Puligny-based *négociant* is run by Olivier Leflaive, the cousin of Anne-Claude Leflaive (of Domaine Vincent Leflaive). Located just down the street from the domaine, 32 of its shareholders are also part of the 36-person consortium that owns the Domaine Vincent Leflaive. The gregarious Olivier Leflaive, whose handsome features and dapper clothing bring to mind Hollywood's characterization of the archetypical romantic Frenchman, is first and foremost a businessman. With the assistance of his now-deceased uncle Vincent, Leflaive set up this firm with the plan to sell all of its wines as futures. Today, 70% of its production is sold in this manner, with the balance sold prior to the *élevage* being completed. The U.S. and England, the firm's largest markets, each purchase 15,000 cases of the 70,000 cases total production.

Started in 1984, the firm's first wine-maker was Jean-Marc Boillot, who left in 1989 to manage his own estate. The talented Franck Grux, who previously ran Domaine Guy Roulot in Meursault, has since been at the reins, and is crafting a delicious array of offerings from 65 different appellations. For quality control, Olivier Leflaive insists on purchasing only grapes or must (98% of the 1997s were acquired this way). Stylistically, Leflaive's goal is to produce elegant wines, reminiscent of those crafted at the Domaine. While I found that this philosophy did not work wonders in the 1996 vintage, it did quite well with the fat and dense 1997s.

Franck Grux believes that the 1997 vintage "will not be fascinating for collectors and professionals, but it is certainly a very good year." He went on to explain that the weather, not the producers, "directed" the vintage. A good flowering was followed by an extremely hot and dry summer. The maturation of the grapes was blocked by the drought conditions, and when the *ban de vendange* (the first day growers can legally harvest) was announced, Grux realized many vineyards were not mature. Acids were low, and Grux "saved" about 20% of the firm's production by acidifying them. "I was not looking to attain a specific pH the way they teach in school, all I wanted was for the wine to have enough acidity to survive."

Maison Olivier Leflaive's wines are not powerhouses. They are well crafted, sometimes understated, and often refined. As Grux said, "We want elegance, not richness or power." The toasty pear–scented 1997 Bâtard-Montrachet is fun, extravagant, and will offer lots of satisfaction to hedonists. This plump, smile-inducing, opulent wine is medium- to full-bodied with intense flavors of ripe white fruits, spices, and anise. Anticipated maturity: now–2005. The 1997 Chevalier-Montrachet reveals red currant and violet aromas. This fresh, concentrated, thick wine is medium-bodied and velvety-textured. Its flavor profile, filled with minerals and pears, offers excellent grip and flavor intensity. Drink it between now–2005.

Maison Leflaive purchased three barrels of 1997 Montrachet as grape must. The day of my tasting it was in an oxidative state, displaying some gold in its color. It exhibits a rich, spicy, butterscotch, and mineral-laden nose as well as an intense and densely packed personality. Flavors of almond cookies, stones, clay, and baked apples can be found in this sensual and thick offering. Franck Grux was planning to add sulfur to the barrels after my tasting to take the Montrachet out of its oxidative condition. Anticipated maturity: now–2006.

Produced from a grand cru vineyard that performed well in this difficult vintage, Olivier Leflaive's 1998 Criots-Bâtard-Montrachet reveals searing mineral aromas. This creamy, rich, medium- to full-bodied wine impressively combines power, richness, and concentration with elegance. Buttered toast, anise, a myriad of spices, as well as sweet lemons and ripe pears can be discerned in this expressive, persistent, intense wine. Anticipated maturity: now–2006+. Leflaive's admirable 1998 Montrachet exhibits complex mineral and white fruit aromas. This medium- to full-bodied, deep, fat, rich wine is velvety-textured, concentrated, and elegant. Ripe pears, stones, and hints of grilled oak can be found throughout its symmetrical personality and long, lush finish. Anticipated maturity: now–2007+.

Franck Grux, characterized the 1999 whites as "fun and pleasant, but not great. The harvest was simply too big and the August drought prevented the skins from ripening." Furthermore, his comments on the 2000 vintage may prove illuminating. "The yields are massive and the ripeness uneven. The whites look very good but let's not talk too much about the reds."

Leflaive produced five barrels (125 cases) of the 1999 Puligny-Montrachet Les Pucelles. It reveals mineral and earth aromas and an outstanding, deep, focused, concentrated personality. Liquid minerals, quartz, and pears are found in this crystalline, pure, elegant wine, which possesses a long, crisp, smooth finish. Anticipated maturity: now–2009. The outstanding 1999 Montrachet reveals toast, stone, and white flower aromas. This medium-bodied wine expands on the palate to display copious quantities of minerals, fresh pears, apples, and spices. It is extremely focused, almost laserlike, and penetrating. It coats the palate with its flavors and has an exceptionally long finish. Anticipated maturity: 2004–2012.

The lovely 2000 Puligny-Montrachet Champs-Gain offers spice, apricot, buttered toast, and white peach aromas. This broad, creamy-textured wine is medium-bodied and lush, yet reveals outstanding focus. Its velvety waves of pears and apples coat the taster's palate. Anticipated maturity: now–2010. The plump, sexy 2000 Bâtard-Montrachet exhibits poached pear aromas. Medium-bodied and possessing outstanding depth and intensity, this wine has flavors of spiced apple, candied pear, and butter. It tightens somewhat in the mid-palate, but then expands to reveal a fruit-filled finish. Anticipated maturity: 2003–2012.

The outstanding 2000 Criots-Bâtard-Monrachet bursts from the glass with minerals, stones, and spices. Medium- to full-bodied, fat, and lush, this is a silky-textured wine of exceptional ripeness. Layers of oily pears, juniper berries, and spice-coated apples permeate the palate, lingering for an exceptionally long time. This superb 2000 should be at its best between 2004–2014. The 2000 Montrachet displays toasted minerals and spiced butter aromas. Medium-bodied, this vinous, plump wine is rich and opulent. Its sexy personality bastes the mouth with buttery pears, apple compote, and spice cake flavors. Its finish is as persistent and flavorful as the Criots's. Anticipated maturity: 2004–2015.

Other recommended wines: 1998 Bâtard-Montrachet (87–89), 1999 Bâtard-Montrachet (88–90), 1997 Bienvenue-Bâtard-Montrachet (88–90), 1998 Bienvenue-Bâtard-Montrachet (87–90), 2000 Chablis Fourchaume (88+), 2000 Chablis Valmur (88–90), 2000 Chassagne-Montrachet Abbaye de Morgeot (87–89), 1997 Chassagne-Montrachet Chaumées (87–89), 1997 Chassagne-Montrachet Ruchottes (87–89), 1997 Chassagne-Montrachet Vergers (87–89), 1997 Corton-Charlemagne (88–89), 1999 Corton-Charlemagne (88–89+), 1997 Criots-Bâtard-Montrachet (89–90), 1997 Meursault Charmes (87–89), 2000 Meursault Charmes (88–89), 1997 Meursault Perrières (88–89), 2000 Meursault Perrières (87–89), 1999 Pommard Charmots (87–89), 1997 Puligny-Montrachet Champs-Gain (88–89), 1999 Puligny-Montrachet Les Folatières (88–89), 2000 St.-Aubin En Remilly (89)

DOMAINE VINCENT LEFLAIVE (PULIGNY-MONTRACHET)

2000 Bâtard-Montrachet	EEE	(90–92)
1999 Bâtard-Montrachet	EEE	(90–91)
1997 Bâtard-Montrachet	EEE	(91–93)
2000 Bienvenue-Bâtard-Montrachet	EEE	(92–93+)
1999 Bienvenue-Bâtard-Montrachet	EEE	(89–91)
1997 Bienvenue-Bâtard-Montrachet	EEE	(91–92+)
2000 Chevalier-Montrachet	EEE	(91–93)
1999 Chevalier-Montrachet	EEE	(90–92)
1997 Chevalier-Montrachet	EEE	(92–94)
2000 Montrachet	EEE	(92–94)
1999 Montrachet	EEE	(91–93)
2000 Puligny-Montrachet Clavoillon	EE	(89–91)
2000 Puligny-Montrachet Les Combettes	EEE	(90–92)
2000 Puligny-Montrachet Les Folatières	EEE	(89–91)
2000 Puligny-Montrachet Les Pucelles	EEE	(91–93)
1997 Puligny-Montrachet Les Pucelles	EEE	(90–92)

Both Anne Claude Leflaive (the estate's director) and Pierre Morey (its wine-maker) are pleased with the 1997s. "It was an easy vintage to vinify, with the malolactic fermentations going smoothly, in contrast to the 1996s," said Morey. They are "very satisfied" with the equilibrium in their 1997s, attributing it to their biodynamic viticultural methods. Morey was ecstatic about the vintage's sanitary conditions and the ideal weather at harvest. "With the benefit of hindsight, it is possible that maybe we should have waited to harvest a little bit longer," he said. "However, if we had pushed the harvesting date back it may very well be that we would not have the balancing acidity in our 1997s." Morey mentioned that the alcoholic fermentations were "quite rapid" and that the estate's then existing cooling systems were not powerful enough to slow them down. Natural potential alcohol levels were

12.2–13% for the 1997s (in comparison, some 1996s attained 14%!). The yields were in the domaine's normal range. I was surprised to learn, however, that the estate's yields in 1996 were 5–8 h/h below average.

Morey believes the 1997 vintage produced "lots of wines that will provide pleasure in the short to mid-term, yet many will last 10 to 15 years." When asked how he would rank the vintages of the 1990s, from best to worst, he listed them as 1996, 1995, 1992, 1990, 1997, 1993, 1994, and 1991. Mme Leflaive had a slightly different answer: she listed them as 1995, 1996, 1997, 1993, 1994, 1992, with 1991 and 1990 tied for last place. Overall, I believe the Domaine Leflaive's 1997s are an extremely successful effort for the vintage. While they reflect 1997's gorgeous ripeness, they are better balanced and focused than many of their peers.

Once again, Domaine Leflaive has crafted a superb Puligny-Montrachet Les Pucelles. The 1997 exhibits bright aromatics of lemon juice, stones, and white flowers, as well as a highly expressive, medium- to full-bodied character. This wine's velvety-textured flavor profile is resplendent, serving up layers of nuts, toasty oak, and a fabulous minerality. It has crystalline purity, a rarity in this vintage, and a long, fresh, and defined finish. Anticipated maturity: now–2008. The 1997 Bienvenue-Bâtard-Montrachet possesses a much more austere nose than the les Pucelles. With coaxing, it reluctantly displays white flowers, almonds, and citrus fruits. This broad, medium- to full-bodied, undeniably rich wine boasts a delicious array of minerals, clay, toast, stones, and pears. It is silky-textured, well focused, concentrated, and combines impressive ripeness with balance. Anticipated maturity: now–2008+.

Leflaive's fabulous 1997 Bâtard-Montrachet offers superripe aromas of candied apples intermingled with minerals, chalk, sea salt, and racy lemons. This concentrated wine has awesome density, medium to full body, and layers of mouthcoating grilled almonds, citrus fruits, crisp pears, and toasted oak. Unlike most of the other 1997 Bâtards, it has exceptional balance, delineation, and class. It should be at its peak between now–2010. I adored the precision, purity, and vibrancy of the lemon-soaked minerals found in the 1997 Chevalier-Montrachet's aromatics. It is a magnificent wine, combining refinement with power, as well as precision with richness. This medium- to full-bodied, silky-textured, compelling offering regales the palate with grilled pears, chalk, and an expansive minerality. It has the density and ripeness characteristic of the 1997 vintage, yet the focus and brightness of 1996—a rare achievement. Anticipated maturity: now–2010+.

According to Wilson-Daniels, Domaine Leflaive's American importer, the U.S.'s allocation of 1997 Montrachet is only 36 bottles. This wine is certainly one of the finest 1997s produced in the Côte de Beaune. It offers fresh yet immensely ripe aromas of pears, apples, red berries, and candied almonds. On the palate, it reveals massive breadth, spectacular refinement, as well as huge concentration and complexity. Toasted white fruits, minerals, lemons, currants, hazelnuts, salt, and minerals can be found in its highly defined and extracted personality. This is quintessential Montrachet, combining the density, ripeness, and richness of a Bâtard, with the elegance, precision, and purity of a top-flight Chevalier. It is an unfortunate fact of life that only a handful of millionaires have the resources to locate and acquire this wine. C'est la vie! Anticipated maturity: 2003–2012.

Only a few of the estate's 1998s are recommended (see below), as they were found to be ungenerous and hard, and appeared to be high in sulfur.

Morey informed me that the weather in 1999 had been tailor-made for producing high yields. "The flowering was extremely early and quick, with an extraordinary number of blossoms. From that point on the vines were never stressed and enjoyed great health. The rains that fell during harvest were saturated but I do not believe they caused any dilution. In order to dry the grapes before sending out the pickers we had helicopters hover over the vineyards."

Rich almond aromas emerge from the 1999 Bienvenue-Bâtard-Montrachet. Medium-bodied and oily-textured, it is ample, plump, and has excellent grip. Its flavor profile, composed of white and yellow fruits intermingled with nuts, lasts throughout the finish. Anticipated maturity: now–2009. The 1999 Bâtard-Montrachet reveals intense, sweet, mineral and white fruit aromas. Medium-bodied, well structured, and tightly wound, it is rich, concentrated, and fresh. This mineral, apple, and pear-flavored wine should be at its peak of maturity between now–2010. Pure and nuanced mineral aromas make up the nose of the 1999 Chevalier-Montrachet. Expansive, broad, and deep, this spicy, mineral, and pear-flavored wine is harmonious and well balanced. It has a long, crisp, crystalline, and softly textured finish. Drink it over the next 10 years.

Leflaive's Montrachet, like many 1999s from this famed vineyard, is first-rate. It offers a gorgeously defined, mineral and spice cake–scented nose. On the palate, it is medium-bodied, powerful, deep, broad, and harmonious. It coats the palate with layers of lush and supple white/yellow fruits, spices, and cream. Anticipated maturity: 2003–2012.

The ripe apple and acacia blossom–scented 2000 Puligny-Montrachet Clavoillon is medium-bodied and softly textured. It delights the palate with a panoply of sweet white fruits, toast, and underlying minerals. This satiny wine has outstanding concentration and a highly delineated, precise character. Anticipated maturity: now–2008. The spice- and mineral-scented 2000 Puligny-Montrachet Les Folatières is medium-bodied, broad, and silky. Minerals, gravel, and flowers can be found in this detailed wine's personality. It is ample, loaded with fruit, and has a long, pure finish. Anticipated maturity: now–2009. The 2000 Puligny-Montrachet Les Combettes's nose is composed of candied pears and apples. Medium-bodied and vinous, this is a well-balanced, harmonious, and broad wine. It is feminine, crammed with minerals, flowers, pears, as well as butter, and has an extensive finish. Anticipated maturity: 2003–2014. Toasted minerals are found in the nose of the 2000 Puligny-Montrachet Les Pucelles. Light- to medium-bodied and highly defined, this wine has outstanding depth to its silky, lush personality. Minerals and pears are found in this concentrated wine's character as well as in its supple, fresh, and exceptionally long finish. Drink it over the next 13 years.

Produced from 45-year-old vines (the oldest of the estate), the 2000 Bienvenue-Bâtard-Montrachet sports a sexy, tropical fruit–scented nose. This is an extravagant wine with a broad, hugely intense flavor profile, packed with spices, minerals, and toasted oak. It is exuberant, crammed with fruit, and long. Anticipated maturity: now–2010. The mineral- and toast-scented 2000 Bâtard-Montrachet is broad, silky, and light- to medium-bodied. A myriad of spices, minerals, and toasted white fruits can be discerned in this detailed wine's personality. Anticipated maturity: 2003–2011.

The aromatically intense 2000 Chevalier-Montrachet boasts toasted mineral scents. This medium-bodied wine is vinous, deep, and packed with floral, mineral flavors. Anticipated maturity: 2003–2013. Anise, minerals, butter, and toast can be found in the nose of Leflaive's 2000 Montrachet. An intense wine, it is medium-bodied, juicy, crammed with French toast, mineral, and acacia blossom flavors. It is highly expressive, concentrated, and profound. Anticipated maturity: 2003–2014.

Other recommended wines: 1996 Bienvenue-Bâtard-Montrachet (95), 1998 Bâtard-Montrachet (88), 1998 Bienvenue-Bâtard-Montrachet (88), 2000 Bourgogne Blanc (88–89), 1996 Chevalier-Montrachet (96), 1996 Puligny-Montrachet (94–96), 1997 Montrachet (94–96), 2000 Puligny-Montrachet (88–89), 1996 Puligny-Montrachet Clavoillon (91+), 1997 Puligny-Montrachet Clavoillon (87–89), 1999 Puligny-Montrachet Clavoillon (87–89), 1996 Puligny-Montrachet Les Combettes (92+), 1997 Puligny-Montrachet Les Combettes (88–90+), 1999 Puligny-Montrachet Les Combettes (88–89), 1996 Puligny-Montrachet Les Folatières (93+), 1997 Puligny-Montrachet Les Folatières (88–89+), 1999 Puligny-Montrachet Les Folatières (88–89), 1996 Puligny-Montrachet Les Pucelles (95), 1999 Puligny-Montrachet Les Pucelles (89–90)

DOMAINE LEROY (VOSNE-ROMANÉE)

1999	Chambertin	EEE	95
1998	Chambertin	EEE	94+?
1997	Chambertin	EEE	97+
1999	Chambolle-Musigny Les Charmes	EEE	92+
1997	Chambolle-Musigny Les Charmes	EEE	93
1998	Chambolle-Musigny Les Fremières	EEE	90
1997	Chambolle-Musigny Les Fremières	EEE	92
1999	Clos de la Roche	EEE	96+
1998	Clos de la Roche	EEE	96?
1997	Clos de la Roche	EEE	98
1999	Clos de Vougeot	EEE	93+
1998	Clos de Vougeot	EEE	92?
1997	Clos de Vougeot	EEE	96
1999	Corton-Charlemagne	EEE	90+
1997	Corton-Charlemagne	EEE	93
1999	Corton-Renardes	EEE	97+
1998	Corton-Renardes	EEE	95
1997	Corton-Renardes	EEE	96
1999	Gevrey-Chambertin Les Combottes	EEE	92
1998	Gevrey-Chambertin Les Combottes	EEE	92
1997	Gevrey-Chambertin Les Combottes	EEE	94
1999	Latricières-Chambertin	EEE	94
1998	Latricières-Chambertin	EEE	95
1997	Latricières-Chambertin	EEE	93+
1999	Musigny	EEE	94+
1998	Musigny	EEE	96?
1997	Musigny	EEE	95+
1999	Nuits-St.-Georges Aux Allots	EE	90+
1997	Nuits-St.-Georges Aux Allots	EE	90
1999	Nuits-St.-Georges Les Boudots	EEE	94+
1998	Nuits-St.-Georges Les Boudots	EEE	92
1997	Nuits-St.-Georges Les Boudots	EEE	93
1997	Nuits-St.-Georges Aux Lavières	EE	90
1999	Nuits-St.-Georges Les Vignesrondes	EEE	91?
1997	Nuits-St.-Georges Les Vignesrondes	EEE	91+
1998	Pommard Les Vignots	EE	90+
1997	Pommard Les Vignots	EE	90
1999	Richebourg	EEE	95
1998	Richebourg	EEE	95
1997	Richebourg	EEE	98
1998	Romanée-St.-Vivant	EEE	93
1997	Romanée-St.-Vivant	EEE	95+
1999	Savigny-les-Beaune Les Narbantons	EE	93
1997	Savigny-les-Beaune Les Narbantons	EE	92
1999	Volnay Santenots	EEE	93
1997	Volnay Santenots	EEE	94
1999	Vosne-Romanée Les Beaux Monts	EEE	93
1997	Vosne-Romanée Les Beaux Monts	EEE	94
1997	Vosne-Romanée Aux Brûlées	EEE	93+
1999	Vosne-Romanée Les Genevrières	EE	90

1998 Vosne-Romanée Les Genevrières	EE	90
1997 Vosne-Romanée Les Genevrières	EE	91+

This estate, owned by a consortium that includes Madame Lalou Bize-Leroy and Japanese investors, is responsible for the finest Burgundies of the last decade. Domaine Leroy's sole white, the 1997 Corton-Charlemagne, reveals magnificently ripe aromas of poached pears, apples, smoke, anise, earth, and grilled oak. This sweet, rich, tangy, lively, medium- to full-bodied wine offers a flavor profile composed of candied lemons, minerals, and nuts. It is extremely well balanced, concentrated, and possesses a long, toasty finish. Drink it over the next 10–12 years. Bravo!

The medium to dark ruby-colored 1997 Pommard Les Vignots reveals sweet dark cherry aromas intermingled with fresh herbs. This medium- to full-bodied wine bursts on the palate with licorice-imbued red/black fruit flavors. Its copious (yet supple) tannins and oak-dominated finish should be absorbed into this offering's impressively dense fruit within one or two years. Anticipated maturity: now–2008. The slightly lighter-colored 1997 Nuits-St.-Georges Aux Allots offers a nose reminiscent of mocha cream–covered cherries. This explosive effort's structured personality is crammed with blackberries and stones that give way to new oak flavors in its persistent finish. It had excellent grip and Nuits-St.-Georges's trademark foursquare character, and is wonderfully flavorful. Drink it between now–2007. Medium to dark ruby-colored, the 1997 Nuits-St.-Georges Aux Lavières's nose exhibits perfume, blueberries, and blackberries. It is medium- to full-bodied, meaty, fresh, and chewy. This dense wine's flavor profile offers stones, minerals, and black fruits. Its finish is presently heavily marked by oak, but this should dissipate with cellaring. Anticipated maturity: now–2008.

The medium to dark ruby-colored 1997 Vosne-Romanée Les Genevrières reveals violets, roses, and red berries in its aromatics. Silky-textured, medium- to full-bodied, and intense, this concentrated wine saturates the palate with candied red cherries, blueberries, and Asian spices. Its outstanding depth of fruit and seamless structure portend a bright future. Anticipated maturity: now–2010. Similarly colored, the 1997 Chambolle-Musigny Les Fremières has a floral, mocha, and red/blue fruit–scented nose. Mouth-coating layers of cherries and asphalt are found in this medium- to full-bodied, concentrated, seductive wine. Well structured and admirably persistent, it is already delicious, yet can be held for a decade or more. The medium to dark ruby-colored 1997 Savigny-les-Beaune Les Narbantons possesses a dense, backward, *sur-maturité* fruit-laden nose. On the palate, it is stuffed with baked blackberries, freshly laid road tar, and stones. This highly concentrated, intense, powerful, and firm wine also possesses a long, warm (slightly alcoholic), embracing finish. Anticipated maturity: now–2008.

Leroy's 1997 Volnay Santenots is virtually black in color. Boasting a licorice- and blackberry syrup–scented nose, this unbelievably massive, dense, backward wine represents the essence of Pinot Noir. This hugely chewy, almost viscous, full-bodied offering is crammed with dates, figs, and jellied black fruits, and sports a strong tannic structure. Readers who believe that Pinot Noirs are all about finesse will be blown away by the flavor intensity found in this blockbuster. Anticipated maturity: now–2010+.

The ruby-colored 1997 Nuits-St.-Georges Les Vignesrondes displays sweet red cherry and violet-laden aromas. Medium- to full-bodied and powerful, this tightly wound, foursquare offering is filled with road tar, stone, and blackberry flavors. It is impressively structured, muscular, and intense. Anticipated maturity: now–2010+. Fresh coffee beans can be found in the medium to dark ruby-colored 1997 Nuits-St.-Georges Les Boudots's aromatics. This muscular, medium- to full-bodied, dense offering is highly concentrated, firm, and velvety-textured. Layer upon layer of fresh, herb-tinged, dark fruits are found in this highly expressive yet foursquare offering. Drink it between now–2010.

The ruby/purple 1997 Vosne-Romanée Les Brûlées reveals a richly spicy nose, filled with red and black cherries. This plump, glycerin-imbued, oily-textured, broad wine offers super-ripe, spiced red fruit characteristics. Thick, harmonious, elegant, and extremely persistent, this complete wine should be at its best between now–2010. The 1997 Vosne-Romanée Beaux Monts exhibits red fruits, roses, and candied orange wines in its profound aromas. This tannic, backward, and hyperconcentrated wine is just as powerful and intense as the Les Brûlées, yet more elegant and precise. Anticipated maturity: 2005–2010+.

The medium to dark ruby-colored 1997 Chambolle-Musigny Les Charmes has a sublimely feminine and elegant nose of violets and roses. Gorgeously silky, dense, powerful, and intense, it is crammed with fresh, lively black fruits and red cherries. Long, refined, extremely flavorful, and well structured, this wine should be at its peak between now–2010. The slightly darker-colored 1997 Gevrey-Chambertin Les Combottes reveals overripe red fruits and spices in its richly aromatic nose. Loads of glycerin can be found in this broad, feminine, immensely flavorful, and awesomely persistent wine. Tar, licorice, black cherries, and black-berries make up this full-bodied offering's flavor profile. It combines the superripe qualities of a New World wine with the elegance generally associated with the Côte d'Or. Anticipated maturity: now–2011. The saturated purple/black 1997 Corton-Renardes offers profoundly spicy red fruit aromas. This rich, broad, intense wine has fabulous blackberry flavors. Full-bodied, expansive, and possessing impeccably ripe tannins in its firm structure, it should have the capacity to age remarkably well. Anticipated maturity: now–2012. The medium to dark ruby-colored 1997 Richebourg possesses a reticent nose that reveals sweet candle wax only with aeration. It is ample, full-bodied, powerful, and muscular. This broad-shouldered, tightly wound, and tannic offering regales the palate with wave after wave of juicy black fruits, cherries, spices, fresh herbs, and hoisin. Anticipated maturity: now–2014. Flowers, spices, perfume, and hints of coffee can be found in the aromatics of the 1997 Romanée-St.-Vivant. It is a richer and broader wine than I generally associate with this vineyard. However, it possesses its trademark precision, elegance, and definition. Tangy currants and cherries make up this thick, complex, and medium- to full-bodied wine's immensely pleasurable character. Anticipated maturity: now–2013.

The 1997 Clos de Vougeot has a medium to dark ruby color and overripe mixed fruit aromas. Oily-textured, unbelievably dense, broad, sweet, and full-bodied, this cherry- and blackberry-flavored blockbuster has untold intensity and power. Almost candied and jellied, it saturates the palate with jammy fruit. Drink this hedonistic wine over the next 8–10 years. The similarly colored 1997 Musigny reveals gorgeous aromas of flowers, blackberries, mocha, and cherries. It is an intense, velvety-textured, full-bodied, and powerful wine that, given the vintage's characteristics, is surprisingly fresh, elegant, and pure. This broad, ample wine possesses a long, well-delineated, and spice-laden finish. Anticipated maturity: now–2012. The slightly darker-colored 1997 Clos de la Roche offers figs, baked blackberries, smoked bacon, and Asian spices in its captivating aromatics. Highly structured, full-bodied, and fresh, this muscular wine offers flavors reminiscent of cedar, overripe apples, minerals, and stones. Anticipated maturity: 2003–2012.

Medium to dark ruby-colored, the 1997 Latricières-Chambertin possesses sweet red and black fruit aromas. Masculine, superstructured, foursquare, and tight, this is a licorice- and cassis-flavored wine. Immensely powerful, dense, and backward, it will require cellaring patience. Anticipated maturity: 2004–2012+. Lalou Bize-Leroy's 1997 Chambertin must be included in any list of this vintage's superstars. Medium to dark ruby, and sporting a jammy blackberry, licorice, and cherry-scented nose, this is a broad, fresh, complex offering. Its blueberry and cherry jam, tar, earth, and tangy currant-flavored mouth is immensely concentrated, ripe, and thick, yet possesses superb purity and precision. This profound blockbuster should be cellared until 2004, and should evolve marvelously well through 2012+.

Lalou Bize-Leroy's yields averaged 18 h/h in the 1998 vintage (compared to 24 h/h in 1999). "I like them, yet they have another style than the 1997s. Overall, 1998 is a very harmonious vintage. The Côtes de Nuits were more successful than the 1997s, but the 1997s may have been stronger in the Côte de Beaune." Mme Bize-Leroy bottled her 1998s in December 1999 and January 2000. The ruby-colored 1998 Pommard Les Vignots has exceptional depth to its blackberry and black cherry aromatics. Medium- to full-bodied and concentrated, this velvety-textured wine has loads of red and black fruits in its personality. Drink it over the next 7–8 years.

The light to medium ruby-colored 1998 Nuits-St.-Georges Au Bas de Combe offers strawberries, red currants, and cherries in the nose. Light- to medium-bodied, elegant, and nicely detailed, the wine's flavor profile offers red fruits and toasty oak. Anticipated maturity: now–2005. The darker-colored 1988 Vosne-Romanée Les Genevrières has a floral and red berry–scented nose. Medium- to full-bodied and silky-textured, it exhibits a cherry syrup and baked black fruit–flavored character. Anticipated maturity: now–2007.

The ruby-colored 1998 Chambolle-Musigny Les Fremières displays scents reminiscent of black cherries, violets, and roses. This well-structured wine is medium- to full-bodied, feminine, and satin-textured. Its long finish reveals notes of sweet, charred oak. Drink it over the next 7 years. The similarly colored 1998 Nuits-St.-Georges Les Boudots boasts café au lait, mocha, and creamed cherry aromas. Medium- to full-bodied and structured, it has outstanding focus, depth, and length. Hints of mint can be discerned in its red berry–dominated core of fruit. Anticipated maturity: now–2007. The 1998 Gevrey-Chambertin Les Combottes is ruby-colored and reveals delightful aromas of red and dark fruits. Sweet black cherry syrup and oak spices are found in this medium- to full-bodied wine's elegant character. It is etched, feminine, and possesses a long, pure finish. Anticipated maturity: now–2008.

In this mediocre vintage, Mme Bize-Leroy's medium to dark ruby-colored 1998 Corton-Renardes is awesome. Its profound dark cherry aromas lead to a medium- to full-bodied, broad, complex core of red cherries, spices, plums, and vanilla-infused oak. This expansive wine is deep, well balanced, and velvety-textured, and has a long, flavor-packed finish. Anticipated maturity: now–2012. Red berries, raspberries, and cherries are found in the nose of the ruby-colored 1998 Romanée-St.-Vivant. Medium- to full-bodied and elegantly styled, this strawberry jam and fresh raspberry–filled wine is intricate, well defined, and concentrated. Drink this feminine offering over the next 8–9 years. The saturated medium to dark ruby-colored 1998 Clos de Vougeot has superb talcum powder, rose, spice, and juicy blackberry aromatics. On the palate it has huge sweetness in the attack, with black pit fruits and cassis flavors. It then slams shut on rugged, hard tannins that will most likely never soften. Anticipated maturity: now–2009. The similarly colored 1998 Richebourg reveals demure aromas of spices and sweet dark cherries. Medium- to full-bodied and powerful, it is a broadly built, muscular wine. Firmly structured yet fruit-dominated, it is packed with loads of cassis, red cherries, spices, and plums. While it possesses the vintage's strong tannins, they are, at present, buried in thick, expressive fruit. Drink it over the next 8–9 years. The medium to dark ruby-colored 1998 Latricières-Chambertin displays a mouthwatering nose of spicy blackberries, cinnamon, and blueberries. Medium- to full-bodied and ample, it is velvety-textured and muscular, and has an impressively long finish. This powerful wine is firmly structured yet appears to have the requisite density of fruit to sustain its tannin over the short to medium term. Anticipated maturity: now–2008.

The medium to dark ruby-colored 1998 Chambertin is one of Mme Leroy's 1998s that left me wondering: Will this wine blossom or dry out? It exhibits a nose of dark fruits and fresh herbs that gives way to a broad, medium- to full-bodied character. This wine has massive layers of tarry black fruit, yet also possesses the woody, scraping tannins that may spell future doom for many wines from this vintage. Either drink it in the very near term with a dish containing lots of tannin-hiding fat, or wait 10+ years and pray. The medium to dark ruby-colored 1998 Musigny has gorgeous aromas of red and black fruits as well as a magnificent array of spices and flowers. While it has extraordinary quantities of fruit (including raspberries, blackberries, and flower-imbued cherries), it is also extremely tannic and hard. This expressive, well-ripened wine poses a quandary for a wine critic. Its fruit is mightily impressive, and its tannin is equally scary. Drink it over the next 7 years. When the medium to dark ruby-colored 1998 Clos de la Roche drops its seductive baby fat, the verdict on its future will be determined. It has huge quantities of sweet cherry, blackberry, and violet-infused blueberries, a huge velvety-textured character, and full body. However, like its brethren from this difficult vintage, it is also astonishingly tannic and firm. While this wine may have the requisite power and depth to sustain significant cellaring, will it outlast its rugged tannins?

Lalou Bize-Leroy, the reigning queen of Burgundy, told me that 1999 registered the second highest yields in Domaine Leroy's brief but illustrious history—24 h/h compared with 1996's 24.4. The flower- and anise-scented 1999 Corton-Charlemagne is medium-bodied, powerful, and tightly wound. This is an austere wine with outstanding richness to its gravel, mineral, and stone flavors. Its depth, concentration, and length indicate that this youthful offering has a long life ahead of it. Anticipated maturity: 2004–2014+.

The medium to dark ruby-colored 1999 Nuits-St.-Georges Aux Allots has a tight, muted nose. This is a medium-bodied, rich, powerful offering that coats the mouth with concentrated layers of black fruits and fresh herbs whose flavors last throughout its outstandingly long and ripe finish. Anticipated maturity: 2003–2010. Medium to dark ruby-colored, the 1999 Vosne-Romanée Les Genevrières offers a beguiling nose of violets, assorted flowers, and fresh fruits. Medium-bodied, plummy, and dense, this is a fat, feminine, lovely wine. It is packed with layers of sweet, ripe fruit that lasts throughout its admirably long finish. Anticipated maturity: now–2010. The 1999 Savigny-les-Beaune Les Narbantons is an outstanding wine. It displays intricate aromas of roasted blackberries, superripe plums, and candied cherries. It has awesome depth and a profound, concentrated, muscular personality. Copious quantities of blackberries, metals, stones, and cassislike flavors can be found in this magnificent wine's personality and lush finish. Anticipated maturity: 2004–2015.

Harvested at 14.7% natural potential alcohol, the 1999 Volnay Santenots has a saturated medium to dark ruby color and reveals rose, violet, and cherry aromas. This is a medium- to full-bodied, powerful wine that reveals huge waves of blackberries, cassis, and plums that inundate the taster's palate. It is extremely structured and possesses a firm backbone, yet has the requisite depth of fruit for mid- to long-term cellaring. Anticipated maturity: 2005–2015. The similarly colored, medium- to full-bodied 1999 Nuits-St.-Georges Les Vignesrondes reveals blackberry aromas and possesses outstanding depth of fruit, yet is so structured and tannic that I am not convinced the fruit will ever overtake the tannin. Oak, licorice, and blackberries can be discerned in this masculine, muscular wine's powerful character. If its fruit outlasts its tannin, it will certainly be an outstanding wine. If not, my rating will appear exceptionally generous. Anticipated maturity: 2006–2015?

The dark-colored 1999 Nuits-St.-Georges Les Boudots reveals refined aromas of roses, violets, blueberries, and blackberries. This is a profound, highly concentrated, intense, elegant wine. Loads of cherries, blackberries, blueberries, and spices can be found in this awesomely fruit-dominated, harmonious offering. It is admirably long in the finish and reveals an outstanding structure. Anticipated maturity: 2005–2015. The similarly colored 1999 Vosne-Romanée Les Beaux Monts reveals a complex nose of violets, roses, and Bing cherries. This medium- to full-bodied wine has remarkable depth of dark cherries, blackberries, and cassislike fruit that lasts throughout the long, harmonious finish. It reveals copious quantities of ripe, supple tannin. It is a velvety-textured, extroverted, elegant, and boisterous wine for drinking between 2005–2015.

The saturated, medium to dark ruby-colored 1999 Chambolle-Musigny Les Charmes has a fresh cherry- and earth-scented nose. Medium- to full-bodied, satin-textured, and round, it exhibits loads of sweet cherries in its feminine, gorgeous personality. This is an expansive wine that appears to gain power and strength as it comes in contact with air. Additionally, it possesses a seamless, extremely long finish. Anticipated maturity: 2004–2015+. The similarly colored 1999 Gevrey-Chambertin Les Combottes has a dark roasted berry–scented nose. This glycerin-packed, medium- to full-bodied wine is crammed with blueberry, vanilla, oak, and blackberry flavors. It has an awesome, oily-textured mouth-feel, and a powerfully flavored and structured character. Anticipated maturity: 2005–2015+. The dark ruby-colored 1999 Corton-Renardes was harvested at 14.9% natural potential alcohol. ("I almost made port," said Mme Bize-Leroy.) A prodigious effort, it exhibits a nose of candied cherries, jammy strawberries, and blueberry jelly. On the palate, this magnificent wine is indescribably intense and powerful yet majestically harmonious and elegant. Loads of cherries and other assorted red fruits are intermingled with spices, fresh herbs, and hints of new oak in its velvety-textured, full-bodied character. This gem also possesses a stupendously long, pure, and supple finish. Anticipated maturity: 2006–2018.

The medium to dark ruby-colored 1999 Richebourg has a demure nose that leads to a broad-shouldered, powerful, concentrated personality. This muscular, masculine wine is packed with huge waves of black cherries, plums, and blueberries. Velvety-textured and dense, this marvelous offering should be at its peak of maturity between 2005–2018. The slightly darker-colored 1999 Clos de Vougeot reveals provocative toast and vanilla bean aromas. This medium- to full-bodied wine is densely packed with cherries, spices, licorice, and candied blueberries. It is velvety-textured, intense, and possesses an amazingly long, supple finish. This harmonious and extremely well balanced wine should be at its peak of maturity between 2005–2018. The demure aromatics of the 1999 Musigny reveal spices, violets, cherries, and hints of veal *demi-glace*. Medium- to full-bodied and satin-textured, it is a lovely, detailed, feminine wine with loads of depth to its red fruit, spice, and flower-flavored personality. This seamless, elegant wine also possesses an exceptionally long, pure, supple finish. When tasted in January 2000 out of barrel, I believed this was potentially perfect wine, but shortly after bottling, it appears to be an exceptional wine with the potential to become even better with cellaring. Anticipated maturity: 2006–2018.

The medium to dark ruby-colored 1999 Clos de la Roche has sweet black cherry, earth, and plumlike aromas. This powerful, intense, meaty wine is filled with plums, blackberries, gelatinous veal stock, and Asian spices. It is pure, muscular, dense, and profound. Anticipated maturity: 2006–2018. The demure blackberry aromas of the medium to dark ruby-colored 1999 Latricières-Chambertin lead to a masculine, highly structured, and firm personality. This wine is intense, loaded with stony blackberry fruits and roasted black currants. This dense, powerful, chewy wine should be at its peak of maturity between 2006–2018. Mme Bize-Leroy's medium to dark ruby-colored 1999 Chambertin reveals a nose of fresh herbs, spices, blackberries, and violets. Medium- to full-bodied, intense, and powerful, this wine is loaded with dark fruits and toast flavors. It is a structured, stony wine that has an outstanding, muscular, masculine personality. Anticipated maturity: 2006–2018.

Other recommended wines: 1999 Chambolle-Musigny Les Fremières (89+), 1998 Nuits-St.-Georges Au Bas de Combe (88), 1999 Nuits-St.-Georges Au Bas de Combe (89), 1999 Nuits-St.-Georges Aux Lavières (89), 1999 Vosne-Romanée Les Brûlées (88?)

Past Glories: 1996 Chambertin (96+), 1995 Chambertin (93+), 1994 Chambertin (91?), 1993 Chambertin (91?), 1992 Chambertin (93), 1991 Chambertin (92+?), 1990 Chambertin (94), 1989 Chambertin (89), 1996 Clos de la Roche (99), 1995 Clos de la Roche (94+?), 1994 Clos de la Roche (92), 1993 Clos de la Roche (98), 1992 Clos de la Roche (93), 1991 Clos de la Roche (92), 1990 Clos de la Roche (98+), 1989 Clos de la Roche (94), 1996 Clos de Vougeot (95+), 1995 Clos de Vougeot (93+), 1994 Clos de Vougeot (92+), 1993 Clos de Vougeot (93?),

1992 Clos de Vougeot (89), 1991 Clos de Vougeot (92+), 1990 Clos de Vougeot (96), 1989 Clos de Vougeot (88), 1996 Corton-Renardes (94+), 1995 Corton-Renardes (93+), 1994 Corton-Renardes (92), 1993 Corton-Renardes (94), 1992 Corton Renardes (90), 1991 Corton-Renardes (91), 1990 Corton-Renardes (92+), 1989 Corton Renardes (88), 1996 Latricières-Chambertin (97+), 1995 Latricières-Chambertin (95+?), 1994 Latricières-Chambertin (88?), 1993 Latriciéres-Chambertin (89+?), 1991 Latricières-Chambertin (100), 1990 Latriciéres-Chambertin (95), 1989 Latricières-Chambertin (91), 1996 Musigny (96+), 1995 Musigny (93+), 1994 Musigny (90), 1993 Musigny (92?), 1992 Musigny (89), 1989 Musigny (90), 1996 Richebourg (97+), 1995 Richebourg (96+), 1994 Richebourg (92), 1993 Richebourg (96+), 1992 Richebourg (91), 1991 Richebourg (90+?), 1990 Richebourg (96+), 1989 Richebourg (93+), 1996 Romanée-St.-Vivant (97), 1995 Romanée-St.-Vivant (95+?), 1994 Romanée-St.-Vivant (91), 1993 Romanée-St.-Vivant (99), 1992 Romanée-St.-Vivant (88), 1991 Romanée-St.-Vivant (95+), 1990 Romanée-St.-Vivant (93), 1989 Romanée-St.-Vivant (89)

DOMAINE HUBERT LIGNIER (MOREY-ST.-DENIS)

1997	Chambolle-Musigny Les Baudes	EE	90
1999	Charmes-Chambertin	EEE	(92–94)
1997	Charmes-Chambertin	EEE	(91–93)
1999	Clos de la Roche	EEE	(94–96)
1997	Clos de la Roche	EEE	95
1999	Gevrey-Chambertin Les Combottes	EE	(92–94)
1997	Gevrey-Chambertin Les Combottes	EE	(91–93)
1999	Morey-St.-Denis Premier Cru Vieilles Vignes	EE	(91–93)
1997	Morey-St.-Denis Premier Cru Vieilles Vignes	E	93
1999	Morey-St.-Denis La Riotte	EE	(89–92)
1997	Morey-St.-Denis La Riotte	E	(88–91)

Regardless of the fact that this estate has not historically enjoyed much praise from the world's wine critics (with the exception of *The Wine Advocate*), its wines are lauded by Burgundy lovers for their combination of elegance and power, as well as purity and complexity. The estate's success story is far from over. The sometimes difficult transition from father to son was performed flawlessly with Hubert Lignier handing the reins to his honorable, intelligent, energetic, conscientious, and supertalented son Romain. Under the guidance of young Romain Lignier, this estate continues to fashion some of the finest wines produced in the Côte d'Or. In fact, they may be even better than the superb offerings his father crafted.

An avid traveler who enjoys tasting the finest wines from the world over, Romain Lignier is a man of the vineyards. His true love (with the obvious exception of his American bride) are his parcels of vines, and he spends untold hours toiling in them. The estate's crowning jewel, its parcel in Morey-St.-Denis's Clos de la Roche grand cru vineyard, was recently enlarged by the purchase of a 0.2 hectare plot, rounding out its parcel to an even hectare (2.471 acres).

The ruby-colored 1997 Morey-St.-Denis La Riotte offers herbal red berry aromas as well as a beautifully ripe medium-bodied character. It is a silky-textured, sultry wine with dense and concentrated red/black fruit flavors. This seamless, well-crafted effort should be consumed over the next 6 years. The medium to dark ruby-colored 1997 Morey-St. Denis Premier Cru Vieilles Vignes displays spicy aromas of smoked bacon immersed in cassis and blackberry juice. This is a velvety-textured, medium-bodied, powerful wine that is expansive on the palate, precise, refined, and extremely well balanced. It boasts copious quantities of Asian spice–laden, dark fruits that linger throughout its impressively long and soft finish. Drink this beauty over the next 7–8 years.

Tasted twice, once out of barrel and again shortly after bottling, the ruby-colored 1997

Chambolle-Musigny Les Baudes was remarkably consistent. Aromatically, it reveals raspberries and pungent roses. On the palate, this medium-bodied wine is soft, lush, velvety-textured, and intensely flavored. Its harmonious core of fruit exhibits candied blackberry flavors intermingled with rosemary and hoisin. Anticipated maturity: now–2006.

Regrettably, only one barrel (25 cases) of the delicious 1997 Charmes-Chambertin was crafted. Aromatically, it offers sweet red fruits, spices, and toasty oak. This broad, creamy, fresh, sultry wine is medium-bodied, complex, and delicious. Opulent layers of syrupy red cherries and other assorted fruits coat the palate. Anticipated maturity: now–2007. The slightly darker-colored 1997 Gevrey-Chambertin Les Combottes displays a floral, blackberry, spice, and oak-infused nose. It has outstanding density of fruit, power, complexity, and depth. This medium-bodied wine has intense flavors of meat and blackberries. Typical of a Lignier-crafted offering, all its component parts have meshed together in a harmonious and well-balanced manner. Anticipated maturity: now–2007.

Violets, roses, earth, dark fruits, and Asian spices are found in the beguiling aromas of the medium to dark ruby-colored 1997 Clos de la Roche. Certainly one of the stars of the vintage, this wine offers huge ripeness of fruit, exquisite definition, opulence, and the required structure for cellaring. Immensely sweet black fruits, chocolate, cumin, and cinnamon seemingly expand on the palate, saturating the mouth and lingering for up to 45 seconds. It is silky-textured, crammed with loads of supple tannins, and is a wine of exceptional purity and precision. It has the powerful punch of a heavyweight, the opulence of a showgirl, and the elegance of a dancer. Anticipated maturity: now–2010.

"The 1999 vintage is a great year for Burgundy," said Romain Lignier. "It has magnificent purity and quality of tannin." Lignier's yields averaged 50 h/h for his "village" wines and 40 h/h for his premiers and grands crus. Sweet cherries and candied raspberries can be found in the aromatics of the ruby-colored 1999 Morey-St.-Denis La Riotte. This wine has outstanding purity of fruit to its candied raspberry, cherry, toasted oak, and juicy blueberry flavors. It is lively, immensely flavorful, and possesses an admirably long, well-delineated finish. Drink it over the next 8–9 years. The bright, medium to dark ruby-colored 1999 Morey-St.-Denis Premier Cru Vieilles Vignes reveals loads of jammy red and black fruits in its aromatics. This opulently textured, medium- to full-bodied wine has outstanding breadth to its thick-textured character. Cherries, blackberries, strawberries, raspberries, and hints of licorice can be found in its sweet, pure, highly extroverted character. Drink it over the next 10 years.

The ruby-colored 1999 Gevrey-Chambertin Les Combottes has a beguiling black cherry, candied blackberry, and Asian spice–scented nose. Medium-bodied and ample, it is a refined, exceptionally well balanced wine. Loads of sweet cherries, blueberries, and stones can be found in its gorgeously defined, candied character. This wonderful wine should be consumed by 2012. The slightly darker-colored 1999 Charmes-Chambertin has aromas of red cherry preserves. This feminine, medium-bodied wine is a sexy fruit bomb. Its character is packed with lush layers of jammy cherries, candied raspberries, and sugarcoated strawberries whose flavors last throughout its exceptionally long, seamless finish. Anticipated maturity: now–2009. The 1999 Clos de la Roche is the darkest of Lignier's offerings, verging on dark ruby. It exhibits a black cherry, blackberry, licorice, and violet-scented nose that leads to its explosive, immensely flavorful character. Medium- to full-bodied and pure, this fresh, sweet wine is packed to the gills with cherries, raspberries, blueberries, and blackberries. Ample yet highly delineated, it has a magnificently long, fruit-filled finish.

Other recommended wines: 1997 Chambolle-Musigny (87–89), 1999 Chambolle-Musigny (87–89), 1999 Chambolle-Musigny Les Baudes (89–90), 1997 Morey-St.-Denis (88–90), 1997 Morey-St.-Denis Les Chaffots (87–90), 1999 Morey-St.-Denis Les Chaffots (88–89)

Past Glories: 1992 Clos de la Roche (92), 1991 Clos de la Roche (94+), 1990 Clos de la Roche (95), 1989 Clos de la Roche (89), 1988 Clos de la Roche (94), 1986 Clos de la Roche (89), 1983 Clos de la Roche (88), 1980 Clos de la Roche (96), 1978 Clos de la Roche (95)

DOMAINE PHILIPPE LIVERA (GEVREY-CHAMBERTIN)

1999 Chapelle-Chambertin Vieilles Vignes Réserve	EE	91

The outstanding medium to dark ruby-colored 1999 Chapelle-Chambertin Vieilles Vignes Réserve has intense black cherry and blackberry aromas. Medium-bodied and explosive, it coats the palate with juicy layers of cherries and raspberries. This lovely, well-focused, seamless wine also possesses an impressively long, pure finish. Anticipated maturity: now–2010.

Other recommended wine: 1999 Gevrey-Chambertin En Vosne Vieilles Vignes Réserve (88)

MAISON FRÉDÉRIC MAGNIEN (MOREY-ST.-DENIS)

1999 Bonnes Mares	EEE	95+
1998 Bonnes Mares Réserve	EEE	92+
1997 Bonnes Mares Réserve	EEE	92
1999 Chambertin Clos de Bèze	EEE	93
1998 Chambertin Clos de Bèze Réserve	EEE	92
1997 Chambertin Clos de Bèze Réserve	EEE	93
1999 Chambolle-Musigny Les Amoureuses	EEE	94
1998 Chambolle-Musigny Les Amoureuses Réserve	EE	91
1997 Chambolle-Musigny Les Hauts Doix Réserve	E	90
1999 Chapelle-Chambertin	EEE	90
1999 Charmes-Chambertin	EE	92
1997 Charmes-Chambertin Réserve	EE	91
1999 Gevrey-Chambertin Les Cazetiers	EE	90
1997 Gevrey-Chambertin Les Cazetiers Réserve	E	90
1999 Morey-St.-Denis Les Blanchards	E	91
1999 Morey-St.-Denis Clos Baulet	E	92
1999 Morey-St.-Denis Les Ruchots	E	90
1997 Morey-St.-Denis Les Ruchots Réserve	E	91
1999 Vosne-Romanée Les Suchots	EE	91

The French term *négociant* is an all-encompassing word. It includes such diverse operations as (1) companies that purchase from domaine wines that are already bottled, (2) companies that acquire finished wines immediately prior to bottling, (3) companies that buy wines immediately after the alcoholic fermentations and then perform the *élevage*, (4) companies that purchase grapes and vinify the wines themselves, (5) companies that select specific parcels and ask that yields be kept down before purchasing the fruit—therefore being involved in the process from an extremely early stage. All of these companies are called *négociants*.

In order to have complete control over the potential quality of the wines he fashions, Frédéric Magnien and his new Morey-St.-Denis-based *négociant* firm enters into agreements with vineyard owners that allow him to do all the vineyard work for the parcels of vines from which he pledges to purchase the fruit. The results speak for themselves.

The medium to dark ruby/purple-colored 1997 Morey-St.-Denis Les Ruchots Réserve offers aromas of black cherries, bittersweet chocolate, tarragon, and juniper berries. This is a wine of massive richness, depth, and hedonism. Layer upon layer of sweet red fruits capture the palate in this medium- to full-bodied, persistent, and highly expressive wine. Drink it over the next 6–7 years. The similarly colored 1997 Gevrey-Chambertin Les Cazetiers Réserve offers elegant aromas reminiscent of plums, roses, and ripe red fruits. It is more structured than the Les Ruchots and possesses a medium- to full-bodied, chewy, and refined character. Strawberries, cherries, and raspberries can be found in this complex yet seductive and forward effort. Anticipated maturity: now–2006. The purple 1997 Chambolle-Musigny Les Hauts Doix Réserve exhibits a nose of mocha-covered black cherries, minerals, and Asian spices. Medium- to full-bodied, hugely expressive, and broad, its personality is fruit-driven yet structured. Were it not for a slightly warm (alcohol) finish, this blueberry and blackberry liqueur–flavored wine would have been a candidate for a higher score. Drink it between now–2006. The herb, spice, and dark fruit–scented, medium to dark ruby-colored 1997 Charmes-Chambertin is medium- to full-bodied, powerful, chewy, and thickly textured. This is a broad, opulent, berry- and cedar-flavored wine with outstanding grip, length, and focus. Anticipated maturity: now–2006+.

All of Maison Frédéric Magnien's wines are bottled unfined and unfiltered, and from time to time, they can be slightly cloudy, as is the medium to dark ruby-colored 1997 Bonnes Mares. Aromatically, wild berries, game, leather, and blackberries can be discerned. This is a massive, masculine, muscular wine, with a huge breadth of black fruit, stones, earth, tar, licorice, and oak flavors. Firm, well-structured, medium- to full-bodied, and powerful, this is a wine that will require some cellaring patience. Anticipated maturity: now–2008+. The purple/ruby 1997 Chambertin Clos de Bèze reveals overripe plum and cherry aromas. This huge, velvety textured, powerful, intense, chewy wine is massively concentrated. Loads of chocolate-covered licorice, sur-maturité-laced red and black fruits, and assorted spices, such as clove, juniper, and cumin, can be found in its complex, expressive core. Medium- to full-bodied and exuberant, this complete wine should be at its best between now–2010.

The young, hardworking, highly talented Frédéric Magnien intelligently bottled all of his 1998s early (in December 1999). The vanilla- and creamed cherry–scented 1998 Chambolle-Musigny Les Amoureuses Réserve is fresh, medium- to full-bodied, and broad. Sweet red fruits, earth, oak, and white pepper can be found in its delicious, well-balanced, concentrated flavor profile. Drink it over the next 5–6 years. The medium to dark ruby-colored 1998 Bonnes Mares Réserve offers aromas reminiscent of coffee and black cherry. Full-bodied, chewy-textured, and intense, this is a roasted black fruit, mocha, and kirsch-flavored wine. It is dense, broad-shouldered, and exceptionally long in the finish. This outstanding wine should be consumed between now–2009. The similarly colored 1998 Chambertin Clos de Bèze Réserve reveals baked yet bright fruit aromas. Masculine, extremely concentrated, and powerful, it possesses a highly expressive blackberry, licorice, and kirsch-flavored personality. This muscular wine should be at its best between now–2009.

According to Magnien, "1999 was a consistently good year; you didn't need to be a genius to make good wines, as there were no problems to overcome." In order to ensure that the grapes he was purchasing came from acceptable yields, Magnien performed the green harvests himself in the vineyards of the growers he has contracts. He bled out 5–10% of the juice and performed at least one stirring of the lees on all his red 1999s. The outstanding, dark ruby-colored 1999 Morey-St.-Denis Clos Baulet has an awesome nose of sweet cherries, candied raspberries, juicy blackberries, and thyme. Medium- to full-bodied and intense, it is a dense, plump, ample wine. This concentrated, rich, sexy fruit bomb is crammed with impressive layers of cherries and raspberries whose flavors last throughout its well-focused, plush finish. Drink it over the next 7–8 years. The similarly colored 1999 Morey-St.-Denis Les Ruchots has demure blackberry aromas. On the palate, this medium-bodied, refined, well-focused wine displays dense waves of candied black cherries, blueberries, blackberries, and red currant liqueur. It has an outstanding, sweet tannin-filled structure. Drink it over the next 8 years.

Produced from over 50-year-old vines, the saturated dark ruby-colored 1999 Vosne-Romanée Les Suchots reveals dark roasted cherry aromas. This is an ample, medium- to full-bodied wine with broad, dense, chewy flavors. It is pure, extremely well focused, and displays velvety red and black fruit that is intermingled with toasty oak throughout its flavor profile, plus it boasts a prodigiously ripe, tannin-filled finish. Anticipated maturity: 2003–2010. The similarly colored 1999 Gevrey-Chambertin Les Cazetiers has a nose reminiscent of sweet, juicy raspberries and cherries. Medium-bodied and firm, this is a wine that is packed with candied blackberry and licorice flavors. It possess copious amounts of tannin, yet they are ripe and supple. Drink it between 2004–2010.

The medium to dark ruby-colored 1999 Morey-St.-Denis Les Blanchards has candied blackberry aromas and a sweet, dense, medium- to full-bodied personality. Loads of cherries can be found throughout its highly expressive, concentrated flavor profile. It reveals a long, supple, softly textured finish. Drink it over the next 8–9 years. The oak-scented, medium to dark ruby-colored 1999 Chapelle-Chambertin is a soft, intense, medium-bodied wine. Blackberries, cassis, and toasted oak are present in its dense, well-ripened character. This is a concentrated and seamless wine for drinking over the next 8–9 years.

The dark ruby-colored 1999 Charmes-Chambertin has mouthwatering, red cherry syrup aromas. Medium-bodied and pure, it is polished, seamless, and highly concentrated. This profound, candied wine is decadent and opulently styled. Drink it over the next 8–9 years. The medium- to full-bodied, dark ruby-colored 1999 Chambolle-Musigny Les Amoureuses is exceptional. It reveals a nose reminiscent of cookie dough immersed in blackberry syrup. Broad layers of velvety blackberries, cassis, and black cherries coat the mouth. It is rich, thick, and a hedonist's dream. There are no edges in this prodigiously ripened wine's character. It is feminine, harmonious, and the vinous equivalent of liquid satin. Drink it over the next 9 years. The similarly colored 1999 Chambertin Clos de Bèze has intense black cherry aromas. Chewy-textured and masculine, this is a dense, powerful, blackberry- and cassis-flavored wine. It is fresh and loaded with superripe tannin and possesses an extraordinarily long, supple, sweet finish. Drink it over the next 12 years. The magnificent dark ruby-colored 1999 Bonnes Mares has blackberry syrup and cassis aromas. Medium- to full-bodied and crammed with freshly laid asphalt, blackberries, Asian spices, licorice, and cassis, it is a huge, chewy-textured wine whose flavors are seemingly unending. This supple, powerful, thick wine has all the components to insure wonderful cellaring potential. Anticipated maturity: 2004–2015. Bravo!

Other recommended wines: 1999 Chambolle-Musigny Les Grands-Mûres (88+), 1999 Chambolle-Musigny Les Hauts-Doix (88+), 1997 Chambolle-Musigny Les Sentiers Réserve (89+), 1997 Chambolle-Musigny Vieilles Vignes Réserve (88), 1998 Charmes Chambertin Réserve (88), 1999 Chassagne-Montrachet La Maltroie (white) Cuvée Unique (89–90), 2000 Chassagne-Montrachet La Maltroie (white) (87–89), 1999 Corton-Charlemagne Cuvée Unique (89–90), 2000 Corton-Charlemagne (88–89), 1999 Gevrey-Chambertin La Perrière (88), 1997 Gevrey-Chambertin Les Seuvrées Réserve (88), 1997 Morey-St.-Denis Les Herbuottes (red) Vieilles Vignes Réserve (88), 1999 Morey-St.-Denis Les Herbuottes (red) (88), 1999 Morey-St.-Denis Les Larrets (white) Cuvée Unique (87–89), 1998 Morey-St.-Denis Les Ruchots Réserve (89), 1999 Morey-St.-Denis Clos Sorbè (88), 1997 Morey-St.-Denis Les Sorbès Réserve (88), 1999 Vosne-Romanée Les Beaux Monts (89)

DOMAINE MICHEL MAGNIEN ET FILS (MOREY-ST.-DENIS)

1999	Chambolle-Musigny Les Fremières	D	90
1999	Charmes-Chambertin	EE	95
1999	Clos de la Roche	EEE	93
1999	Clos St.-Denis	EEE	96
1999	Gevrey-Chambertin Les Cazetiers	EE	92
1999	Gevrey-Chambertin Aux Echézeaux	D	90
1999	Gevrey-Chambertin Vieilles Vignes	D	90
1999	Morey-St.-Denis Les Chaffots	E	92+
1999	Morey-St.-Denis Les Millandes	E	92+

Domaine Michel Magnien et Fils did not put any wines from either 1997 or 1998 on the market. When I met with Frédéric Magnien, who runs this estate as well as his own *négociant* house, to taste his 1997 Burgundies a few years ago, I found that every single one of his wines tasted corked, as did the second set of samples he hurriedly fetched in a desperate hope that his entire production had not been tainted. It turns out that the new winery Frédéric and Michel Magnien had constructed contained bacteria that infected their entire production of 1997s and 1998s. Two and a half years later, that winery was still sealed off and quarantined while the different parties involved battled in the courts to find out who was ultimately responsible. Thanks to the generosity and graciousness of Jacques Seysses of Domaine Dujac, who provided space to the Magniens, these magnificent 1999s were produced in a healthy, taint-free environment. At present, the Magniens are building a new cellar. The Magniens should be highly commended for the way they dealt with this disaster. Instead of selling their 1997s and 1998s, something many wineries would have done, they bought back the 1997s that had already been released, sacrificing any income from wine sales for two and a half years. To inaugurate the 1999 vintage, a rebirth of sorts for Domaine Michel Magnien et Fils, new labels were designed.

The ruby-colored 1999 Chambolle-Musigny Les Fremières has tangy blueberry and cherry aromas. Medium-bodied and delicious, it displays copious quantities of chewy-textured candied cherries and fresh blueberries. This sweet, supple, and long-finishing wine will be at its best if drunk over the next 5–6 years. The ruby-colored 1999 Gevrey-Chambertin Aux Echézeaux has fresh dark fruit aromas. Medium-bodied and silky-textured, it is loaded with sweet cherries that coat the palate. This opulent wine has an immensely appealing mouth-feel. It is detailed yet plush, with prodigiously well-ripened tannin. Anticipated maturity: now–2008. Copious quantities of Asian spices and black cherries can be found in the aromatics of the 1999 Gevrey-Chambertin Vieilles Vignes. Medium-bodied and supple, it is a dense, candied black raspberry–flavored offering. Its fruit immerses loads of soft tannins in its long, velvety finish. Drink it over the next 7 years.

The outstanding medium to dark ruby-colored 1999 Morey-St.-Denis Les Millandes has a magnificent nose of cassis and blackberry syrup. Medium- to full-bodied and velvety-textured, this is a chewy, intensely spicy wine. Cherries, plums, black raspberries, and chocolate can be found throughout its explosive character and exceptionally long, sweet finish. This concentrated, seamless, decadent wine should be drunk over the next 9 years. The similarly colored 1999 Morey-St.-Denis Les Chaffots has mocha, violet, and rose aromas. Medium- to full-bodied and hugely dense, this is a superripe, cherry-flavored wine. It is pure, powerful, and opulently textured. This outstanding Morey will be at its best if consumed over the next 8 years. The medium to dark ruby-colored 1999 Gevrey-Chambertin Les Cazetiers has beguiling floral and sweet red/black cherry aromas. It is pure, fresh, medium-bodied, and thickly textured. This supremely elegant, highly delineated, yet rich wine also possesses an impressively long, soft finish. Anticipated maturity: now–2010.

The dark ruby-colored, smoked bacon and spice-scented 1999 Clos de la Roche is a sexy medium- to full-bodied wine. Loads of spices, candied cherries, stones, juniper berries, and plums can be found in its deep, satin-textured character. It is exceptionally long and possesses loads of prodigiously ripened tannin. Anticipated maturity: now–2014.

The similarly colored 1999 Charmes-Chambertin boasts a magnificent nose of Asian spices, cherries, blackberries, and flowers. Medium-bodied, even kinky, this is a seamless, pure, harmonious wine. Its seemingly incessant waves of candied fruits are highly expressive and flavorful. Though not made for extended cellaring, it delivers awesome amounts of concentrated fruit and is guaranteed to put a smile on any wine lover's face. Drink it over the next 8 years. The stunning 1999 Clos St.-Denis has a dark ruby, almost black, saturated color. Leather, licorice, and blackberry syrup can be found in its boisterous aromatics. This full-bodied, chewy wine has a magnificent breadth of black fruits, cherries, blueberries, and spices in its dense character. It is satin-textured, thick, powerful, and seamless. This exceptional wine should be consumed between 2004–2012.

Other recommended wines: 1999 Morey-St.-Denis Les Monts Luisants (88), 1999 Morey-St.-Denis Les Très Girard (89)

DOMAINE JOSEPH/PIERRE/THIERRY MATROT (MEURSAULT)

2000 Meursault Charmes	E	(89–91)
1998 Meursault Charmes	E	91
2000 Meursault Perrières	E	(88–91)
1999 Meursault Perrières	E	91
1997 Meursault Perrières	E	90
2000 Puligny-Montrachet Les Chalumeaux	E	(91–92)
2000 Puligny-Montrachet Les Combettes	E	(91–92)
1998 Puligny-Montrachet Les Combettes	E	90

Thierry Matrot is the gregarious director and wine-maker of the Joseph/Pierre/Thierry Matrot Estates. (These three legally separate entities will be combined into one estate, Thierry et Pascal Matrot, in 2004.) Matrot was extremely happy with his 1998 whites when I visited him to taste his 1997s. "When all is said and done," he told me, "the 1998s may be as good as the 1996s." This led me to ask him a question I posed to many Burgundians over the course of my visits—qualify the vintages of the 1990s from best to worst. While Matrot is exceedingly straightforward and would have given me an honest assessment of the 1997 vintage, most of his colleagues have the habit of always touting the vintage they have to sell. This question forced them to put their thoughts, likes, and dislikes on record. Matrot's preferred white Burgundy vintage of the 1990s (it is also his favorite for reds) is 1996. After the 1996s, he listed 1990, 1992, 1995 (he says the 1995 whites are so concentrated and alcoholic that they need to be consumed over the next 7–8 years), 1993 ("they will last forever"), 1997, 1994 ("too heavy and too much *sur-maturite*"), and, lastly 1991 ("a bitter and vegetal vintage").

Matrot asked for and received permission to harvest his 1997s prior to the *ban de vendange.* "My grapes were fully ripe (he did not chaptalize any whites in 1997) and my acidities were dropping, yet the *ban* was not announced. Since I have never, and will never acidify a white, I needed to harvest quickly," he said. The pear- and gravel-scented Meursault Perrières is Thierry Matrot's classiest, most complex, and most complete 1997. This silky, medium-bodied wine is crammed with intricate layers of citrus fruits, apricots, crisp pears, honeysuckle blossoms, and gravel. Well balanced, this offering's exceedingly long finish serves up white flowers and toasted hazelnuts.

Thierry Matrot is the affable, intelligent, fun-loving president of Meursault's syndicate of *vignerons.* According to Matrot, his recent harvests have averaged 14% natural potential alcohol, a whoppingly high figure for Burgundy. The 1998 Meursault Charmes, the product of 25 h/h yields, was described by Matrot as "the finest Charmes I have ever made." Its spicy, mineral aromatics lead to a broad, intense, and powerful, medium-bodied character. Assorted flowers, honeysuckle, and acacia blossoms are intermingled with lemons and crisp pears in this superbly focused, elegant, and nuanced wine. Concentrated, possessing outstanding depth of fruit, and an admirably long, citrus finish, this is undoubtedly one of the finest premiers crus fashioned in the 1998 vintage. Anticipated maturity: now–2007. The outstanding 1998 Puligny Montrachet Combettes offers demure nut and mineral aromas. Sweet toasted hazelnuts, pears, herbal tea, and flowers can be found in this well-fashioned, medium-bodied wine. Produced from low yields, it has outstanding depth of fruit, and a long, lemon-lime-filled finish. Drink it over the course of the next 7 years.

The 1999 Meursault Perrières, though muted, is medium-bodied and possesses outstanding concentration. Dense, superripe layers of liquid minerals, white fruits, and spices are found in this gorgeously focused, complex wine. It is deep, harmonious, and pure. Anticipated maturity: now–2009.

Matrot feels that the 2000 vintage is "extremely interesting. It began with a marvelous flowering and, like 1999, was exceedingly abundant. The vines were never thirsty, and the weather was perfect for high yields. Unlike 1999, which was a vintage of minerality, 2000 reflects nuances of flowers." The aromatically intense 2000 Meursault Charmes bursts from the glass with mineral scents. Rich, broad, and fat, it is a boisterous wine with admirable depth and concentration. Loads of minerals and ripe fruits can be found in this persistent wine's character. Anticipated maturity: 2003–2009.

The 2000 Puligny-Montrachet Les Chalumeaux has a nose crammed with spices, poached pears, candied apples, and flowers. It is rich, ripe, and medium- to full-bodied. Candied lemons are interspersed with soft, sweet pears in this refined offering's personality. It is broad, plush, highly expressive, and impressively combines sensuality and brightness. Anticipated maturity: 2003–2010. Flowers and almonds can be found in the aromatics of the 2000 Puligny-Montrachet Les Combettes. This vinous, layered wine is powerful, concentrated, and crammed with rich waves of minerals, nuts, lemons, and white fruits. A highly successful 2000, it should be at its best if consumed between 2004–2011. Lively spiced lemons are found in the aromatics of the 2000 Meursault Perrières. A rich wine, it is tight, but with coaxing displays a rich underlying minerality in its concentrated character. Medium-bodied, this impressively balanced wine will require cellaring. Anticipated maturity: 2005–2012.

Other recommended wines: 1997 Meursault Blagny (88), 1999 Meursault Blagny (88), 2000 Meursault Blagny (87–89), 1997 Meursault Charmes (88), 1999 Meursault Charmes (88+), 1997 Puligny-Montrachet Les Chalumeaux (88), 1999 Puligny-Montrachet Les Chalumeaux (89), 1997 Puligny-Montrachet Les Combettes (89+), 1999 Puligny-Montrachet Les Combettes (89+)

DOMAINE MÉO-CAMUZET (VOSNE-ROMANÉE)

1997	Clos Vougeot	EE	(89–91)
1999	Corton	EEE	(93–95)
1997	Corton	EE	(90–93)
1999	Echézeaux	EEE	(90–91)
1999	Richebourg	EEE	(91–93)
1997	Richebourg	EEE	(91–93)
1997	Vosne-Romanée Les Brûlées	EEE	(90–93)
1999	Vosne-Romanée Cros Parentoux	EEE	(90–93)

Jean-Nicolas Méo, this estate's owner and wine-maker, described the emotional roller coaster that he went through in 1997. He was "slightly worried and anxious" prior to experiencing a "euphoria" at harvest. Very little work was required at the sorting table in 1997, according to Méo. While he was forced to cull out some unripe grapes in 1996, and found himself discarding 15–20% of his harvest in 1998, only 3–4% of the grapes from the 1997 vintage had to be disposed. As vinification began, Méo says that he became worried that his acid levels were exceedingly low. "I felt deceived, because I expected so much better, having seen the harvest." His fears of having over-ripe, flabby wines, lacking in color density, were assuaged as the *élevage* progressed, and the wines gained density and richness. "It reminds me a little bit of the 1992s. However, in that vintage, the *élevage* was detrimental to the wines, whereas in 1997 it helped greatly." He went on to state that, in his opinion, 1997 was a vintage for early drinking, not one whose bottles should be forgotten in a cellar.

Méo's 1997s were extremely impressive, boasting the vintage's gorgeous ripeness, yet possessing good focus and precision. For whatever reason, this is the second consecutive vintage where the Vosne-Romanée Cros Parentoux has been disappointing (given its pedigree and price). It appears to lack the depth, power, and structure that have made its vineyard so famous the world over. Méo concedes this fact and is perplexed as to its cause.

The medium to dark ruby-colored 1997 Clos Vougeot exhibits huge ripeness in its otherwise tight aromatics. This is a big, broad, *sur-maturité*-laced wine, with flavors reminiscent of a compote of red and black fruits. Suave, medium- to full-bodied, possessing lovely intensity and a spice-laden finish, this wine should be consumed over the next 6–7 years. Harvested at a whopping 13.9% natural potential alcohol, the dark purple 1997 Corton Clos Rognet offers sweet wax scents. It is an explosive wine, crammed with creamed red fruit and stonelike flavors. Fresh, medium- to full-bodied, expansive, and powerful, it successfully marries the vintage's hallmark ripeness with focus and delineation. Anticipated maturity: now–2007.

The black/purple 1997 Vosne-Romanée Les Brûlées displays plum and sweet grape aromas, intermingled with smoky spices. This is a lovely wine with admirable complexity, expansiveness, and intensity. Medium- to full-bodied, elegant, well focused, and balanced, it is replete with cassis, blackberries, and Asian spices. Anticipated maturity: now–2007. The ruby/purple 1997 Richebourg has enthralling aromas of perfume, flowers, cherries, and blueberries. On the palate, it bursts with scrumptious layers of cherries, blackberries, and oak spices. A medium-bodied wine of outstanding breadth, detail, and refinement, it delivers enormous intellectual gratification. Anticipated maturity: now–2007+.

Jean-Nicolas Méo feels that the finest vintages of the 1990s are 1990, 1993, 1996, and 1999. "They are all great years," he said. This famed estate's yields averaged over 40 hectoliters per hectare in 1999. Readers will be interested to learn that Méo has started a *négociant* business, the Maison Méo-Camuzet, that will "concentrate on smaller appellations."

The medium to dark ruby-colored 1999 Echézeaux has demure, sweet blackberry aromas. Medium- to full-bodied, broad, and expansive, it is packed with red and black cherries and blackberries. Its long finish possesses loads of soft, well-ripened tannins. Anticipated maturity: 2003–2011. The medium to dark ruby-colored 1999 Corton is outstanding. Its rose, violet, perfume, spice, and candied raspberry–scented nose leads to an unctuous, medium- to full-bodied personality. Cherry syrup, sugarcoated blackberries, a myriad of spices, and vanilla-imbued oak can be found in this plush, hedonistic, powerful wine. Its admirably long finish reveals loads of superripe, sweet tannin that will allow this wine to age remarkably well. Anticipated maturity: 2005–2015.

The medium to dark ruby-colored 1999 Vosne-Romanée Cros Parentoux has a gorgeous nose of intensely sweet cherries. Medium- to full-bodied, it reveals a wonderful breadth of lush red and black cherry fruit in its exuberantly spicy personality. Toasted oak and copious quantities of marvelously ripe tannin characterize its impressively long finish. Anticipated maturity: 2004–2012. The darker-colored 1999 Richebourg has a blackberry, spice, and oak-scented nose. Medium-bodied and expansive, it displays black cherries, candied raspberries, and blackberries in its velvet texture. It has outstanding depth and concentration as well as a long, pure finish. Anticipated maturity: 2005–2015.

Other recommended wines: 1999 Clos Vougeot (88–90), 1999 Nuits-St.-Georges (87–89), 1997 Nuits-St.-Georges Les Murgers (89), 1999 Nuits-St.-Georges Les Murgers (88–90), 1999 Vosne-Romanée Les Brûlées (88–90), 1997 Vosne-Romanée Les Chaumes (88+), 1999 Vosne-Romanée Les Chaumes (88–90)

MAISON/DOMAINE OLIVIER MERLIN (LA ROCHE VINEUSE)
1998 Pouilly-Fuissé Terroir de Vergisson   **D   90**

Olivier Merlin is an honest, intelligent, funny, dedicated, and thoughtful man from the Charolais region of Burgundy who decided to move to the Mâconnais to make wine (his first vintage was 1987). He works as both a domaine and a *négociant* (in 2000, 65% of his wines are from estate-grown fruit, for example) and strives to produce "wines of harmony and equilibrium." He bemoans the fact that the Mâconnais's vineyards are now planted (60–70% by his assumption) with high-yielding clones of Chardonnay, and that his neighbors have almost all turned to machine harvesters (Merlin harvests his parcels entirely by hand). Instead of constructing a modern winery with loads of stainless steel tanks as have his neighbors, Merlin opted to buy an ancient building in La Roche Vineuse (this village was known as St.-Sorlin prior to the anti-clerical days of the French Revolution). In its vaulted cellars he found stone racks for cradling barrels, which he gladly points to each time his fellow vignerons claim that doing *élevage* in wood is atypical for the Mâconnais.

Apples, pears, hints of citrus fruits and oak can be discerned in the lively aromas of the 1998 Pouilly-Fuissé Terroir de Vergisson. This focused, candied lemon and mineral-flavored wine has outstanding concentration and depth. It is rich, elegant, and has a formidable, pure finish. Anticipated maturity: now–2006+.

Other recommended wines: 1999 Mâcon-la Roche Vineuse Les Cras (89–90), 1999 Mâcon-la Roche Vineuse Vieilles Vignes (88–89), 1998 Pouilly-Fuissé Terroir de Fuissé (88+), 1999 Pouilly-Fuissé Terroir de Vergisson (87–89), 1999 St.-Véran Grande Bussière (88–89), 1999 Viré-Clessé (88)

DOMAINE LOUIS MICHEL (CHABLIS)

1997 Chablis Les Clos	E	90
1997 Chablis Les Grenouilles	E	90

Fans of Domaine Louis Michel's wines should note that the estate has changed its labels, starting with the 1997 vintage. The new design emphasizes each vineyard's name, and the domaine's nomenclature is now printed in tiny lettering at the bottom of the label. Jean-Loup Michel describes the 1997 vintage as "rich, healthy, and ripe but without the breadth of the 1996s." Like many of his vigneron colleagues, Michel said he was "scared early that the 1997s would be lacking in acidity, but after the malolactics I feel they have turned out quite nicely. Since they are delicious to drink now they will serve to protect the 1996s that require patience." Michel's wines undergo multiple bottlings but since they are kept in airtight stainless steel tanks there are only minimal differences between them. All of Domaine Louis Michel's wines are machine-harvested, then vinified and aged in tanks.

The 1997 Chablis Les Clos offers floral, red/white currant, and candied pear aromas. It has superb richness and complex flavors reminiscent of gun flint, fruit pits, and smoke. This medium- to full-bodied wine has outstanding grip as well as a long, bone dry finish. Anticipated maturity: now–2007. The chalk, mineral, and flint-scented 1997 Chablis Les Grenouilles exhibits superb richness, breadth, and concentration in its medium to full body. It is an oily-textured offering packed with earth, stone, and honeysuckle-like flavors that last throughout its persistent finish. Anticipated maturity: now–2007.

Other recommended wines: 1995 Chablis Les Grenouilles (92), 1997 Chablis Montée de Tonnerre (88), 1997 Chablis Vaudésir (88+)

DOMAINE FRANÇOIS MIKULSKI (MEURSAULT)

2000 Meursault Charmes	E	(88–91)
1997 Meursault Charmes	E	(88–91+)
2000 Meursault Genevrières	E	(89–92)
1997 Meursault Genevrières	E	(90–91)

François Mikulski fashioned delightfully ripe and rich 1997s. When asked what his pH levels were like he responded that he never had pH tests performed on his wines and was not a fan of oenologists. He added that in 1997 he neither acidified nor chaptalized any wines. The 1997 Meursault Genevrières's nose is crammed with superripe aromas of red berries, mangoes, and passion fruit. On the palate red currants, spiced/candied apples, poached pears, and vanilla-infused oak can be found. It is a chewy, viscous, medium- to- full-bodied wine, well focused and immensely flavorful. Anticipated maturity: now–2005. Two-thirds of Mikulski's parcel of Meursault Charmes was planted in 1930, the rest in 1913. The 1997 reveals fresh green apple scents and a concentrated, delineated, medium-bodied, and extremely well balanced core. This wine has superb grip and a flower, nut, and mineral-flavored character.

As with the Poruzots, this wine's finish is slightly dry and chalky. How Mikulski copes with this prior to bottling will determine its ultimate score in the indicated range. Drink it between now–2007.

To the forthright Mikulski, "2000 is the only good vintage we've had for whites since 1995. It has depth, balance, and good acidity." Produced from vines planted in 1930 and 1913, the 2000 Meursault Charmes has delightful spiced hazelnut and floral aromas. Medium-bodied and revealing gorgeous breadth, it is an intense, fresh mineral, talcum powder, spice, and lemon zest–flavored wine. Anticipated maturity: now–2009. The 2000 Meursault Gene-vrières exhibits poached pear, spice, baby powder, white flower, and apple aromas. Medium-bodied and fat, this floral and mineral-flavored wine is broad, lush, and bright. Drink from 2003–2008.

Other recommended wines: 2000 Meursault (87–89), 1997 Meursault Poruzots (87–89), 2000 Meursault Poruzots (88–89+), 1997 Volnay Santenots du Milieu (89+), 1998 Volnay San-tenots du Milieu (88)

MAISON LUCIEN LE MOINE (BEAUNE)

1999	Bonnes Mares	EEE	92
1999	Chambolle-Musigny Les Amoureuses	EE	93
1999	Charmes-Chambertin	EE	90
1999	Chassagne-Montrachet Morgeot (white)	E	90
1999	Clos de la Roche	EE	93
1999	Echézeaux	EE	93
1999	Montrachet	EEE	93
1999	Nuits-St.-Georges Les St.-Georges	E	90
1999	Pommard Les Rugiens	E	90+
2000	Puligny-Montrachet Les Folatières	EE	(90–92)
1999	Puligny-Montrachet Les Folatières	EE	92
1999	Volnay Caillerets	E	91

This brand-new Beaune-based *négociant* firm was founded by Mounir Saouma, a Lebanese immigrant, and his Israeli girlfriend. Saouma moved from war-torn Lebanon to a Cistercian monastery in Israel at the invitation of an uncle who was a monk. During his six years at the monastery he worked in its winery, was bitten by the wine bug, and left to study oenology at France's University of Montpellier. Saouma works as wine-maker for a large Beaune firm (Maison Picard), but now runs his own operation during his free time. The name of the firm comes from the fact that the French translation of Mounir is Lucien and that Saouma is called *le moine* (the monk) by his friends because of his years as a monastery's resident.

Saouma only works with small lots (there are no more than three barrels, or 75 cases, of each wine, and a total production of 32 barrels in 1999, 45 in 2000) and wishes to have his wines come from no more than two sources. They are all purchased as wine, aged in 100% new oak (Séguin-Moreau) barrels, have their lees stirred regularly (even the reds in 1999), and are bottled with neither fining nor filtration.

The outstanding 1999 Chassagne-Montrachet Morgeot is medium- to full-bodied, rich, and plump. Tangy lemons, anise, spices, and poached pears can be found in this boisterous, fat wine. Though it is thick, velvety-textured, and creamy, it remains fresh, pure, and focused. Anticipated maturity: now–2006. The 1999 Puligny-Montrachet Les Folatières is a stunner. This lush, medium- to-full-bodied wine is seamless, concentrated, and powerful. Its beauti-fully refined personality is satin-textured, loaded with candied white fruits, and has out-standing focus, richness, and length. Anticipated maturity: now–2009. The 1999 Montrachet reveals demure mineral and sweet perfume aromas. On the palate, it is feminine, lacelike, and gorgeously pure. Its toasted pear, ripe apple, stone, and spice flavors last throughout its extensive and exemplary finish. Drink it over the next 12 years.

Each of the following 1999 reds was purchased as wine from growers (no more than two sources per cru), aged in 100% new oak (Séguin-Moreau) barrels. Additionally, Saouma repeatedly stired the lees on his red 1999s because "in my opinion this vintage needs the fat and density that lees stirring brings. I also find that the more I do *bâtonnage* the less the oak can be detected in the wines." The ruby-colored 1999 Volnay Caillerets has demure blueberry and cherry aromas. Medium- to full-bodied, lush, and juicy, it is packed with fresh and candied blackberry flavors. This is a sweet, supple, tannin-filled fruit bomb of a wine. It is satin-textured, nuanced, and immensely pleasing. Anticipated maturity: now–2009. The slightly darker-colored 1999 Pommard Les Rugiens has a blackberry and spicy oak-scented nose. Medium- to full-bodied and jammy, it is crammed with blackberries and cassis. It is more firmly structured than the Volnay, yet its tannin is ripe and supple. Anticipated maturity: 2003–2009.

The medium to dark ruby-colored 1999 Nuits-St.-Georges Les St.-Georges has a mouthwatering, Asian spice, and jammy grape-scented nose. This big, chewy, medium- to full-bodied wine is loaded with black cherry flavors. It is highly structured, yet its tannins are extremely ripe and supple. Anticipated maturity: 2004–2009. The slightly darker-colored 1999 Clos de la Roche boasts dark cherry and black raspberry aromas. Medium- to full-bodied, rich, and opulent, this is a plush, satin-textured, penetrating wine. Its layers of candied black cherries and raspberries penetrate the palate. This is a lively, extraordinarily long, well-balanced, and seamless offering. It should be at its best if drunk between 2004–2012.

The black cherry–scented, medium to dark ruby-colored 1999 Chambolle-Musigny Les Amoureuses is medium- to full-bodied and opulent. It inundates the palate with loads of sweet cherries, candied raspberries, and juicy blackberries. It is a highly expressive wine with a decadently sweet, velvety character whose flavors last throughout its extraordinarily long finish. Anticipated maturity: now–2010. The aromatically demure, medium to dark ruby-colored 1999 Charmes-Chambertin is a gorgeously dense wine. Medium- to full-bodied and loaded with smoky bacon, jammy cherries, and lively blackberries, this firmly structured wine has loads of fine, supple tannin. Drink it over the next 10 years.

The outstanding medium to dark ruby-colored 1999 Echézeaux has mouthwatering black raspberry, sweet oak, cherry, and jammy blackberry aromas. It coats the palate with untold quantities of jellied red and black fruits and a myriad of spices. Medium- to full-bodied, focused, and fresh, it also reveals a stunningly long and delineated finish. The slightly darker-colored 1999 Bonnes Mares was produced from three barrels purchased from two different sources. It has a jammy blackberry-scented nose and a gorgeously plump, medium- to full-bodied personality. This dense, thick, velvety wine is packed with dark fruit flavors as well as hints of freshly laid road tar and licorice. It is powerful, masculine, expansive, and possesses a firm, tannin-filled finish. Drink it between 2005–2012.

The outstanding 2000 Puligny-Montrachet Les Folatières, from vines nearing 100 years of age, exhibits gorgeous aromatics of rich, floral, apple, and spice. Medium- to full-bodied and robust, this is an ample, vinous wine with lots of stuffing. Toasted white fruits, butter, anise, and cardamom can be found in its beautifully delineated character. Drink it over the next 9 years.

Other recommended wines: 2000 Corton-Charlemagne (87–89), 2000 Meursault Perrières (87–89), 2000 Montrachet (90–92). 1999 Gevrey-Chambertin Les Cazetiers (88)

DOMAINE MONGEARD MUGNERET (VOSNE-ROMANÉE)

1997	Clos de Vougeot	E	90
1997	Echézeaux Vieilles Vignes	E	(89–91)
1997	Grands-Echézeaux	EE	(89–92)
1997	Richebourg	EEE	(90–92+?)
1997	Vosne-Romanée Les Suchots	E	(88–91)

Vincent Mongeard, who now runs this famous estate, is extremely happy with his 1997s. "When I compare my wines to those of my colleagues, I am comforted in what I was able to achieve. Even though it is not the vintage of the century, it is certainly extremely good." Tasted immediately prior to its bottling, the ruby-colored 1997 Vosne-Romanée Les Suchots reveals red cherry, raspberry, and violet scents. This medium- to full-bodied wine bursts on the palate with thick layers of black fruits. It is dense, powerful, expressive, silky, and admirably persistent in the finish. Anticipated maturity: now–2006. Crafted from vines planted in 1929 and 1931 (the latter were grubbed prior to the 1998 vintage), the ruby-colored 1997 Echézeaux Vieilles Vignes has perfume, pit fruits, and black cherries in its aromas. This iodine, blackberry, licorice, and tar-flavored offering is full-bodied, muscular, and thick. Its velvety-textured personality is masculine and highly structured. Anticipated maturity: now–2008.

Sweet red cherries and spices can be found in the aromatics of the ruby-colored 1997 Clos de Vougeot. This soft, silky-textured, jammy wine has a medium to full body and a plump flavor profile that reveals creamed cherry flavors. Opulent, forward, and slightly warm (alcoholic), this offering does not have the structure required for aging and should be consumed over the next 4–5 years. The similarly colored 1997 Grands-Echézeaux reveals black fruit aromas intermingled with notes of tobacco and cedar. This is a powerful, full-bodied, supple wine with flavors reminiscent of stones, earth, minerals, cigar smoke, and mixed berries. Well structured and extremely flavorful, it should be at its best over the next 6 years. The slightly darker-colored 1997 Richebourg exhibits aromas reminiscent of a compote of red and black fruits, figs, and violets. On the palate, this medium- to full-bodied wine is complex, expansive, broad, and offers briary blackberries, white pepper, and earthlike flavors. Its finish appeared to be compressed and somewhat hot (hence the question mark), yet if Mongeard is capable of overcoming this during *élevage*, it has the making of a first-rate wine. Anticipated maturity: now–2010.

DOMAINE DE MONTILLE (VOLNAY)

1999 Puligny-Montrachet Les Caillerets	EE	(89–91)
1998 Puligny-Montrachet Les Caillerets	EE	92

This Volnay estate, known for its reds, also owns a parcel of premier cru Puligny-Montrachet whose wine have been made in recent years by Meursault's Jean-Marc Roulot (of Domaine Guy Roulot). They have consistently been excellent or outstanding. Starting with the 2000 vintage, Etienne de Montille will begin vinifying this wine himself, with the assistance of Roulot, his former brother-in-law.

The 1999 Puligny-Montrachet Les Caillerets offers white flower, stone, and hints of dried honey in its aromas. This rich, medium-bodied, broad, beautifully elegant wine is packed with honeyed, stone flavors as well as a myriad of spices. It is well concentrated, elegant, and begged to be consumed right from the cask. Anticipated maturity: now–2006.

The 1998 Puligny-Montrachet Les Caillerets is one of the top successes of the vintage. It offers a gorgeous, exotic nose of spices and toasted almonds. Medium-bodied, subtle, and satin-textured, it is lush, beautifully balanced, and packed with magnificent layers of minerals, pears, and toast. This forward, expressive, yet refined wine should be consumed over the next 5–6 years.

DOMAINE ALICE ET OLIVIER DE MOOR (COURGIS)

1998 Sauvignon de St.-Bris Réserve	C	90

Having consumed more than my share of lean, green, unpalatable Sauvignons de St.-Bris—the overwhelming majority are more reminiscent of battery acid than wine—I was pleasantly shocked to witness the heights achieved in 1998 by Alice et Olivier de Moor. Its expressive nose bursts from the glass with boisterous gooseberry and grapefruit aromas. This big, broad, rich, in-your-face Sauvignon is very reminiscent of some of New Zealand's finest. Medium- to full-bodied, displaying floral, citrus, freshly mown grass, and red raspberry flavors throughout its personality and extensive finish, it is unequivocally the finest Sauvignon de St.-Bris I have ever put to my nose or mouth. Bravo! Drink it over the next 2–3 years.

DOMAINE MOREAU-NAUDET (CHABLIS)

1999 Chablis Valmur	D	91
1997 Chablis Valmur	D	90+

This little-known 15-hectare (37-acre) estate produced delicious 1997s. The domaine's intelligent young director told me he wanted to extend his wines' *élevages* in order to abandon filtration (he already eschews cold stabilization, a detrimental practice employed by the majority of his neighbors). He still needs to consider additional steps to take his estate to the next level (a reduction of the number of finings, bottling his wines himself, and barrel aging, to name three), yet I believe this is a producer whose wines deserve consumer attention.

Moreau-Naudet owns 0.6 hectares (1.48 acres) of Chablis Valmur. Their 1997 is a wonderful wine, revealing a complex nose of minerals, nuts, berries, honeysuckle, and acacia blossoms. This medium- to full-bodied, mouth-filling, deeply concentrated wine is packed with sea shells, flint, smoke, and white fruits. It is bone-dry, yet very rich and ripe. Additionally, it possesses a long and intricate finish. Anticipated maturity: now–2006. The white flower and mineral-scented 1999 Chablis Valmur is medium-bodied, rich, and oily-textured. This broad, glycerin-packed wine is loaded with salty citrus fruit flavors and hints of quinine. It is pure, fresh, powerful, and flavorful. Drink this outstanding Chablis over the next 6–7 years.

Other recommended wines: 1997 Chablis Montée De Tonnerre (89+), 1999 Chablis Montée De Tonnerre (89), 1996 Chablis Montmain (88), 1997 Chablis Montmain (89), 1999 Chablis Montmain (89), 1997 Chablis Vaillons (88), 1999 Chablis Vaillons (88), 1996 Chablis Valmur (91)

MAISON BERNARD MOREY ET FILS (CHASSAGNE-MONTRACHET)

2000 Bâtard-Montrachet	EEE	90+
1999 Bâtard-Montrachet	EEE	90+
1998 Bâtard-Montrachet	EEE	92
1997 Bâtard-Montrachet	EEE	92
2000 Chassagne-Montrachet Les Caillerets	E	93
1999 Chassagne-Montrachet Les Caillerets	E	91
1998 Chassagne-Montrachet Les Caillerets	E	90
1997 Chassagne-Montrachet Les Caillerets	E	93
2000 Chassagne-Montrachet Les Embrazées	E	92
1997 Chassagne-Montrachet Les Embrazées	D	91
2000 Chassagne-Montrachet Les Macherelles	E	90
2000 Chassagne-Montrachet La Maltroie	E	91
2000 Chassagne-Montrachet Morgeot (white)	E	90
1998 Chassagne-Montrachet Morgeot (white)	D	90
1997 Chassagne-Montrachet Morgeot (white)	D	91+
2000 Chassagne-Montrachet Vide Bourse	E	92
1997 Chassagne-Montrachet Vide Bourse	E	92
2000 Puligny-Montrachet La Truffière	E	92
1999 Puligny-Montrachet La Truffière	E	92
1998 Puligny-Montrachet La Truffière	E	92
1997 Puligny-Montrachet La Truffière	E	90+
1997 Santenay Grand Clos Rousseau (red)	D	90

I was extremely impressed with Bernard Morey's 1997 white Burgundies. He was able to harness the vintage's telltale ripeness and density while maintaining lovely equilibrium and precision. Additionally, Morey's 1997s appear to have the potential to improve with cellaring, a rarity in this vintage. The 1997 Chassagne-Montrachet Les Embrazées exhibits aromas reminiscent of minerals and earth awash in sweet lemons. Its fabulously oily-textured core of pear, apples, berries, and intense spiciness is medium- to full-bodied, thick, and mouthcoating. In addition, this plump yet fresh and balanced wine offers an enticing, long and pure finish. Anticipated maturity: now–2006. The 1997 Chassagne-Montrachet Morgeot reveals a nose of flowers, white currants, and almonds. It is a powerful, hyperexpressive wine crammed with loads of toasty pears and honeysuckle. This concentrated, nicely etched offering is medium- to full-bodied, intense, deep, and mouthcoating. It is already delicious to drink, yet may improve with cellaring. Anticipated maturity: now–2007.

As the score suggests, I adored Morey's 1997 Chassagne-Montrachet Les Caillerets. Its kinky nose of wet wool, earth, rocks, and minerals is followed by a superb medium- to full-bodied personality. Pure lemon, stone, toast, and clay flavors are found in this profound, broad, expansive, and admirably persistent wine. It is exceedingly well balanced, refined, muscular, and ageworthy. Anticipated maturity: now–2007. Produced from 70-year-old vines, the 1997 Chassagne-Montrachet Vide Bourse has intense aromas of minerals and stones. It is a broad, rich, medium- to full-bodied wine with complex and detailed layers of white fruits, gravel, and flowers in its flavor profile. This etched, deep, concentrated, elegant, and gorgeously flavorful offering should be at its peak between now–2007.

The 1997 Puligny-Montrachet La Truffière possesses a wonderful nose reminiscent of baby powder, chalk, and earth. It is a refined wine, with a highly detailed core of white fruits, lemons, limes, and minerals and a medium to full body. I have tasted it on four occasions since its September 1998 bottling, and it appears to be taking on more density and richness with age. Anticipated maturity: now–2006. The 1997 Bâtard-Montrachet, crafted from grape must purchased from vines located in the heart of this grand cru, has an immensely ripe nose of tropical fruits, sweet minerals, and poached pears. It is balanced, delineated, and well defined, yet superrich and opulent. Loads of candied white fruits, mangoes, and spicy oak are found in this medium- to full-bodied, exceedingly long, superb Bâtard. Drink it over the next 7 years.

Tasting through Morey's opulent, fruit-driven 1997 reds was a joy. His medium- to dark ruby-colored 1997 Santenay Grand Clos Rousseau displays aromas reminiscent of perfumed cherry jam dusted with baby powder. It is a medium- to full-bodied, immensely ripe, powerful, and expansive fruit bomb. This opulent, sultry offering is crammed with black cherries whose flavors linger for up to 30 seconds in the finish. Drink this beauty over the next 4–5 years.

The famed Bernard Morey, one of Burgundy's finest vignerons (as well as a man who truly enjoys a great meal and a good laugh), adapted admirably well to this difficult vintage's characteristics. "After alcoholic fermentation all my wines went into a hugely oxidative state. I added sulfur yet within a week noticed that the oxidative tendencies were returning." While oenologists witnessing the same phenomenon in many Burgundian cellars recommended the repeated addition of sulfur, Morey was worried about the loss of fruit that sulfur treatments cause. He and his sons proceeded to perform weekly bâtonnages (stirring of the lees) to ensure that the sulfur that had been originally added was redistributed throughout the wine. The result? Many of Morey's wines have more depth of fruit, richness, and body than those crafted by his neighbors.

Stones and white fruits are found in the aromatics of the 1998 Chassagne-Montrachet Morgeot. This medium- to full-bodied, satin-textured, intense wine reveals admirable concentration, depth, and power. Pears, apples, and fresh earthlike flavors make up this expressive, broad-shouldered wine's character. Drink it over the next 5 years. The 1998 Chassagne-Montrachet Les Caillerets possesses a bright stone, mineral, and lemon-scented nose. Medium-bodied, rich, plump, and admirably concentrated, this deep, citrus-dominated effort has the requisite fruit and balance to stand the test of time. Anticipated maturity: now–2007+.

The enthralling 1998 Puligny-Montrachet La Truffière has a creamy, floral, and spicy nose. Rich, broad, and expansive, this medium- to full-bodied wine impressively combines power and elegance in its velvety-textured personality. Anticipated maturity: now–2007. Morey's 1998 Bâtard-Montrachet is a huge success for the vintage. Its dense, stony aromatics are followed by a clean, substantial personality. Medium- to full-bodied, bright, thick (for a 1998), this lemon, pear, and spice-flavored wine possesses an admirable minerality. This rich, focused, and exceedingly long Bâtard will be at its best if consumed between now–2008.

The 1999 Chassagne-Montrachet Les Caillerets reveals demure mineral aromas. It has outstanding breadth, concentration, power, and medium body. This refined, well-defined offering has lovely smoke, stone, mineral, and pear flavors in its harmonious and exceptionally long personality. Anticipated maturity: now–2009. Refined aromas of flowers and talcum powder can be discerned in the nose of the 1999 Puligny-Montrachet La Truffière. This medium-bodied wine reveals a gorgeously expressive personality of minerals, stones, pears, and anise. It is broad yet detailed and elegant, with outstanding depth and an exemplary finish. Anticipated maturity: 2003–2010. Smoked bacon and toasted bread can be found in the aromatics of the 1999 Bâtard-Montrachet. This outstanding, medium-bodied wine expands on the palate with mouthcoating layers of toast, minerals, and white fruits. It is plump and rich, and has impressive grip. It will merit a better review if it resolves the warmth (alcohol) revealed in the finish. Anticipated maturity: 2003–2010.

To Morey, 2000 is a great vintage. "These wines have loads of fruit, outstanding balance, and come from an extremely healthy harvest," he said. The 2000 Chassagne-Montrachet Les Macherelles exhibits mouthwatering aromas of fresh earth, sweet butter, and rich pears. Medium-bodied and opulent, it is lush, deep, and fat. A white wine crafted for red wine lovers, it is concentrated, highly expressive, and velvety-textured. Anticipated maturity: now–2008. The mineral- and earth-scented 2000 Chassagne-Montrachet La Maltroie is medium-bodied and satin-textured. Tangy apples, spiced pears, and toast can be found in its broad, concentrated personality. This flavorful, seamless wine also reveals an admirably long finish. Drink it over the next 9 years.

The outstanding 2000 Chassagne-Montrachet Les Embrazées (Morey declassifies all of the vines in his vineyard that have not yet celebrated their sweet 16) explodes with vanilla, almond, anise, and spice aromatics as well as flavors. It is rich, opulent, and medium- to full-bodied. This layered, deep wine displays exceptional amplitude and an impressively long, supple finish. Drink it over the next 10 years. The 2000 Chassagne-Montrachet Morgeot has a white flower, vanilla, anise, and spice-scented nose. It is broad, medium-bodied, and reveals loads of earthy minerals, toast, and candied lemons in its fresh as well as persistent character. Anticipated maturity: now–2010.

Produced from 75-year-old vines, the 2000 Chassagne-Montrachet Vide Bourse has a white flower, black currant, and yogurt-scented nose. It is concentrated, intense, ample, and medium- to full-bodied. Layers of creamed pears and spice cake can be found intermingled with minerals in its vinous personality. Anticipated maturity: 2004–2012. The aromatically rich 2000 Chassagne-Montrachet Les Caillerets displays buttered hazelnut scents. It is broad-shouldered, spicy, and fat. Medium- to full-bodied, this offering exhibits candied lemon, pear compote, spiced apples, and cinnamonlike flavors whose attributes linger in its exquisite finish. Anticipated maturity: now–2012+.

The fresh earth, mineral, and flower-scented 2000 Puligny-Montrachet La Truffière is medium-bodied and satin-textured. Its broad, stone, mineral, spice, and pear-flavored personality is feminine yet muscular. Anticipated maturity: now–2012. Morey's 2000 Bâtard-Montrachet has an intensely spicy nose composed of vanilla, cinnamon, anise, and cardamom. On the palate, it is medium-bodied with an ample pear and spice-dominated core of fruit. This highly detailed yet plump, satin-textured wine should be at its best between 2003–2013.

Other recommended wines: 1997 Chassagne-Montrachet Les Baudines (88), 1999 Chassagne-Montrachet Les Baudines (89), 2000 Chassagne-Montrachet Les Baudines (89), 1999 Chassagne-Montrachet Clos St.-Jean (89), 2000 Chassagne-Montrachet Clos St.-Jean (89), 1999 Chassagne-Montrachet Les Embrazées (89), 1999 Chassagne-Montrachet Les Macharelles (88), 1997 Chassagne-Montrachet La Maltroie (white) (89), 1998 Chassagne-Montrachet La Maltroie (white) (88), 1999 Chassagne-Montrachet La Maltroie (white) (89), 1999 Chassagne-Montrachet Morgeot (white) (89+), 1998 Chassagne-Montrachet Vide Bourse (89), 1999 Chassagne-Montrachet Vide Bourse (89+), 1997 Chassagne-Montrachet Vieilles Vignes (red) (88+), 1999 Chassagne-Montrachet Vieilles Vignes (red) (87–89), 1997 Maranges (88), 2000 Meursault (88), 1997 Puligny-Montrachet (88), 1999 Santenay Grand Clos Rousseau (red) (87–89)

MAISON/DOMAINE MARC MOREY (CHASSAGNE-MONTRACHET)

1998 Bâtard-Montrachet	EEE	91
1997 Bâtard-Montrachet	EEE	92
1999 Chevalier-Montrachet	EEE	90
1998 Chassagne-Montrachet Morgeot	E	90
1997 Chassagne-Montrachet Les Virondots	E	90

Bernard Mollard, this estate/firm's director and wine-maker, is an engaging and friendly man. He says he feels that 1997 was "a very good vintage, but I prefer the 1996s. However, the '97s are more flattering and will be ready earlier." When I asked him to rank the vintages of the nineties for white Burgundies from best to worst he listed 1996 and 1990 as tied for first place, followed by 1995, 1992, 1997, 1994, 1993, and 1991.

I loved the 1997 Chassagne-Montrachet Les Virondots each time I tasted it (I've tried it on at least six occasions to date). It has a fresh, earthy, white/red fruit, and gravel-scented nose. On the palate, creamy pears, apples, and a gorgeously pure minerality can be found. It is medium- to full-bodied, tangy, silky, fresh, rich, and possesses a well-delineated and complex finish. Anticipated maturity: now–2007. Mollard's Bâtard-Montrachet, one of my favorites from the 1997 vintage, exhibits aromas of sweet pears, talcum powder, spices, creamed hazelnuts, and buttered toast. This is a full-bodied wine of considerable richness, ripeness, and depth. It coats the mouth with oily layers of earth, minerals, vanilla beans, and crème brûlée that linger throughout its impressively persistent and pure finish. It is already fabulous to drink, yet at a tasting, it sat in my glass for an hour with no evidence of oxidation. Anticipated maturity: now–2008.

Intense herbal tea and stone aromas can be found in the 1998 Chassagne-Montrachet Morgeot's nose. It displays excellent concentration, depth, power, and a plump, deep, white fruit-filled personality. This harmonious, flavorful, and persistent wine will be at its best if drunk over the next 7 years. Mollard harvested his 1998 Bâtard-Montrachet at 13.4% natural potential alcohol. It is gorgeously ripe, exhibiting red berry, fresh earth, and mineral aromas. This broad, intense, powerful wine is medium- to full-bodied, plump, fresh, and vibrant. Grilled buttered toast, minerals, and yellow fruits can be found throughout its expressive character and persistent finish. Anticipated maturity: now–2008.

The 1999 Chevalier-Montrachet offers aromas reminiscent of a vanilla-infused crème brûlée. It has excellent depth to its light- to medium-bodied, mineral- and poached pear–flavored core. This fresh, beautifully balanced, pure wine would have merited an outstanding review if it had had more depth of fruit. Drink it over the next 6–7 years.

Other recommended wines: 1999 Bâtard-Montrachet (89), 1998 Chassagne-Montrachet (88), 1997 Chassagne-Montrachet Les Caillerets (88), 1997 Chassagne-Montrachet Morgeot (89+), 1997 Chassagne-Montrachet Vergers (88+), 1999 Chassagne-Montrachet Vergers (89), 1998 Chassagne-Montrachet Virondots (88), 1998 Chassagne-Montrachet Virondots (89), 1997 Puligny-Montrachet Les Pucelles (88), 1998 Puligny-Montrachet Les Pucelles (88+)

DOMAINE PIERRE MOREY (MEURSAULT)

2000	Bâtard-Montrachet	EEE	(90–92)
1999	Bâtard-Montrachet	EEE	(89–91)
1997	Bâtard-Montrachet	EEE	(90–93)
1997	Meursault Perrières	EE	(89–91)

Pierre Morey runs this estate, a *négociant* firm that bears his and his wife's names (Maison Morey-Blanc), and is also Domaine Leflaive's wine-maker. The 1997 Meursault Perrières has extremely refined aromas of citrus fruits and minerals. This is a medium- to full-bodied, broad, complex, vibrant wine. It has first-rate balance, definition, and a flavorful personality packed with gravel, limes, and apples. Anticipated maturity: now–2006. The 1997 Bâtard-Montrachet has superb aromatics of white fruits and candied nuts. This fresh, focused, expressive, broad wine is medium- to full-bodied and powerful. It coats the palate with its great minerality, pears, and spiced apples. It is concentrated, well balanced, has outstanding delineation of flavors, and a long, detailed finish. Drink it between now–2008+.

The pear, apple, and mineral-scented 1999 Bâtard-Montrachet is medium-bodied, gorgeously focused, and packed with minerals, white/yellow fruits, and stones. It is deep, broad, delineated, and has a long, crystalline finish. Drink it over the next 8 years. White peaches and other assorted yellow fruits are found in the aromatics of the 2000 Bâtard-Montrachet. This rich, opulent, and layered wine is soft and broad as well as persistent. Loads of ripe pears can be discerned in its complex character. Anticipated maturity: 2004–2012.

Other recommended wines: 2000 Meursault Perrières (87–89), 1997 Meursault Les Tessons (88–89), 1997 Pommard Epenots (87–89)

MAISON MOREY-BLANC (MEURSAULT)

1997	Meursault Les Genevrières	EE	(89–91)
1997	Montrachet	EEE	(91–94)

Superripe fruit aromas are interspersed with toasty minerals and smoke in the 1997 Meursault Les Genevrières's nose. Extremely rich, thick, and broad, it manages to retain both vibrancy and refinement while displaying overripe flavors of candied apples, poached pears, and apricots. It should be consumed over the next 5–6 years.

Morey-Blanc's 1997 Montrachet is a first-rate wine. It exhibits elegant yet superripe aromas of peaches and apricots intermingled with minerals. This oily-textured, thick, expansive offering has stones, gravel, pears, and mineral flavors in its medium to full body and throughout its impressively long and detailed finish. Anticipated maturity: 2001–2008.

Other recommended wines: 1998 Corton-Charlemagne (88), 1997 Meursault Les Bouchères (88–90), 1997 Meursault Charmes (88–90), 1999 Meursault Charmes (87–89), 1999 Meursault Genevrières (88–90), 2000 Meursault Les Genevrières (88–90), 1997 Meursault Les Narvaux (88–90), 2000 Meursault Les Narvaux (87–89)

DOMAINE ALBERT MOROT (BEAUNE)

1997	Beaune Bressandes	D	(89–92)
1997	Beaune Marconnets	D	(88–91)
1997	Beaune Teurons	D	(90–92)
1997	Beaune Toussaints	D	(88–91)

Mademoiselle Choppin has every reason to be proud of her delicious 1997s. Yields were quite moderate, overall averaging 28 hectoliters per hectare, and none of the 1997s were chaptalized. After the 1999 harvest, Mlle Choppin passed the reins of the estate to her nephew, Geoffroy Choppin de Janvry.

The medium to dark ruby-colored 1997 Beaune Toussaints has excellent depth to its superripe black fruit aromas. Its *sur-maturité*-laced flavor profile is composed of candied blackberries spiced with hints of toasty oak. In addition, this medium-bodied wine offers a long, pure, lush finish. Already immensely pleasurable to drink, it will easily last 6 years. The lighter-colored 1997 Beaune Marconnets is a fruit lover's dream. Hyperripe red/black fruits are intermingled with tangy candied orange rinds and metal shavings in this surprisingly fresh, medium-bodied offering. This palate-saturating, silky smooth, and persistent wine should be consumed over the next 6 years.

The medium to dark ruby-colored 1997 Beaune Bressandes has excellent depth to its smoky, waxy, licorice-like aromas. On the palate, it combines the creamy texture and opulent, forward flavors of superripe baked red and black fruits with a structured, firm personality. This medium-bodied and expressive wine has a long, complex finish that reveals copious quantities of soft tannins. Delicious today, it can be cellared for up to 7 years. The 1997 Beaune Teurons reveals spicy blackberry scents and offers a mouthful of highly expressive *sur-maturité*-laced blackberries and cassis. This explosive, fruit-packed, medium- to full-bodied wine has excellent purity and precision, yet is dense, thick, and powerfully flavored. Anticipated maturity: now–2007.

Other recommended wines: 1997 Beaune Cent Vignes (88–90), 1999 Beaune Cent Vignes (87–89), 1999 Beaune Toussaints (88–90), 1997 Savigny-les-Beaune La Bataillière (87–89)

DOMAINE DENIS MORTET (GEVREY-CHAMBERTIN)

1997 Chambertin	EEE	(92–95)
1997 Chambolle-Musigny Les Beaux Bruns	E	(90–93)
1997 Clos Vougeot	EE	(90–93)
1997 Gevrey-Chambertin Les Champeaux	E	(90–92)
1997 Gevrey-Chambertin En Champs	E	(88–91)
1997 Gevrey-Chambertin Lavaux St.-Jacques	E	(90–92)

Denis Mortet is now to be considered as one of Burgundy's finest producers. He is extremely pleased with his 1997s, three-quarters of which didn't require chaptalization. "Not a gram of rot could be found on this magnificent harvest. The grapes were tiny, black in color. I had never seen more visually attractive grapes," said Mortet. He then winked, smiled, and said, "But the 1998s will be great." Mortet's harvest started quite early, on September 15, yet his natural potential alcohols were very high, including a Gevrey-Chambertin En Champs that came in at 13.9% potential alcohol, and the first Chambertin in the history of the estate that did not require chaptalization. Mortet echoed the sentiments expressed by many Côte d'Or vignerons when he said that he was fearful of the quality at first. "The wines disappeared for the first three months, but they then enriched themselves enormously." He attributes this gain in richness to the fact that he put the wines in barrels with as many lees as possible 24 hours after having pressed them.

Mortet's saturated black/purple 1997 Gevrey-Chambertin En Champs offers dense black fruit aromas. Extraordinarily sweet (from ripeness, not sugar) and expressive, this chewy, structured effort reveals flavors of asphalt, licorice, cherry syrup, and cassis. It is an exuberant wine, bursting at the seams with loads of fruit whose flavors admirably linger in its extensive finish. However, its somewhat firm backbone will require cellaring patience. Anticipated maturity: now–2007. Though crafted from relatively young vines (planted in 1984), the 1997 Chambolle-Musigny Les Beaux Bruns is consistently one of the finest wines produced at this estate. The 1997, harvested at a whopping 13.9% natural potential alcohol, displays a gorgeous nose of rose petals, violets, and blueberries. This satin-textured, medium- to full-bodied, soft, and expansive wine is crammed with flavors reminiscent of blackberries, candied cherries, and bacon. It is fresh, bright, well structured, refined, and has a finish that broadens like a peacock's tail and intensifies with time. This luscious and seductive offering should be drunk over the next 7 years. Medium to dark ruby-colored, the 1997 Gevrey-Chambertin Les Champeaux exhibits complex cinnamon, earth, and blackberry aromas. This tangy red fruit, briar, and brambleberry-flavored wine has huge density of fruit as well as copious quantities of ripe tannins—a combination that suggests the potential for a long life. It is medium- to full-bodied, concentrated, and powerful. Anticipated maturity: 2003–2010+.

Due to the *combe* (a break in the hillside) that funnels cool wind from the west onto its vines, Mortet had never before seen the level of ripeness that his parcel of Gevrey-Chambertin Lavaux St.-Jacques was able to attain in 1997. It is a dark ruby-colored wine with stony, black fruit aromas, as well as a firm, refined, fresh character crammed with blueberry jam, black fruits, and metal-like flavors. This masculine, enormously expressive, and well-delineated wine will be at its best over the next 7–8 years. Similarly colored, the 1997 Clos de Vougeot reveals spicy and earthy blackberry scents. This is a big, broad, dense wine, packed with intensely ripe fruit. Tar, licorice, and eucalyptus are intermingled with briary blackberries in this medium- to full-bodied, structured, and impressively long-finishing offering. Anticipated maturity: now–2008.

The 1997 vintage was particularly successful in the Chambertin vineyards. Mortet says this was his best ever. It has a dark ruby color and a magnificently ripe, expressive nose that boisterously offers blackberry jam, fresh herbs, and Asian spices. This awesome wine explodes on the palate with velvety waves of chocolate-covered cherries, blueberry pie, cinnamon, and briarlike flavors. It is full-bodied, expansive, hugely powerful, massive, and impressively structured. Its stunning palate presence extends up to 40 seconds throughout its supple and sweet finish. This superb Chambertin will be at its best between now–2010+.
Other recommended wines: 1997 Gevrey-Chambertin (87–89), 1997 Gevrey-Chambertin Combe du Dessus (87–89), 1997 Gevrey-Chambertin En Motrot (88–90), 1997 Gevrey-Chambertin au Vellé (88–90)

DOMAINE GEORGES MUGNERET/MUGNERET-GIBOURG
(VOSNE-ROMANÉE)

1997	**Chambolle-Musigny Les Feusselottes**	E	(89–92)
1997	**Clos de Vougeot**	EE	93
1997	**Echézeaux**	EE	(88–91)
1997	**Ruchottes-Chambertin**	EE	(90–93)

The two daughters of Mme Georges Mugneret, Marie-Christine and Marie-Andrée, informed me that their yields had been quite low in 1997. While they did notice some frost damage in the springtime, they attribute the small yields to "nature achieving balance after the high yields of 1996." Yields ranged from 18 h/h on the Ruchottes-Chambertin to a high of 35–38 h/h on the Vosne-Romanée. Even the Bourgogne regional appellation wine was harvested at a paltry 22 h/h. Marie-Andrée said, "Everything was small—the grapes, the bunches, and the yields." As with many other estates, a number of Domaine Georges Mugneret/Mugneret-Gibourg's 1997s were not chaptalized. The alcoholic fermentations were tumultuous, and Marie-Andrée said she had to be extremely vigilant during the vinification to prevent the onset of volatile acidity. Malolactic fermentations were quite early, and the bottling (unfined and unfiltered) was planned for an earlier date than normal.

Medium to dark ruby-colored, the 1997 Chambolle-Musigny Les Feusselottes displays profound aromas of red/black fruits and Asian spices. It is a broad, expansive, masculine wine with complex blueberry, cumin, stone, boysenberry, and black currant flavors. Medium-to full-bodied, well structured, and admirably persistent, this broad-shouldered, expressive effort blows away the theory that Chambolles are delicate, feminine Burgundies. Anticipated maturity: now–2006+. The ruby-colored 1997 Echézeaux possesses an orange rind, perfume, and talcum powder–scented nose. A gorgeously ripe (nonchaptalized) wine, it is broad, rich, packed with red berries, and has excellent structure. If its somewhat clipped finish fleshes out prior to bottling it will merit an outstanding score. Drink it between now–2007.

The medium to dark ruby-colored 1997 Ruchottes-Chambertin reveals deeply spicy aromatics reminiscent of rosewater, red berries, and perfume. It bursts on the palate with flavors of sweet cherries, smoke, black raspberries, and plums. Its seductive, velvety texture and medium- to full-bodied personality lead to a somewhat firm and structured, yet not tannic, finish. This complex, harmonious wine will be at its best between now–2008. The similarly colored 1997 Clos de Vougeot displays dense aromas of jellied cherries. On the palate, this medium- to full-bodied, beautifully structured, fresh offering is crammed with red and black candied berry fruit, Asian spices, and toasty oak. It beautifully combines the vintage's characteristic *sur-maturité*-laced flavors with outstanding grip and structure. Anticipated maturity: now–2009.

Other recommended wine: 1997 Nuits-St.-Georges Chaignots (88–90)

DOMAINE JACQUES-FRÉDÉRIC MUGNIER (CHAMBOLLE-MUSIGNY)

1998	Bonnes Mares	EE	(88–92)
1999	Chambolle-Musigny Les Amoureuses	EEE	(91–93+)
1999	Chambolle-Musigny Les Fuées	EE	(89–90+)
1999	Musigny	EEE	(90–93)
1997	Musigny	EEE	93

Jacques-Frédéric Mugnier no longer works part-time as an airline pilot, and is now in Burgundy year-round as a full-time vigneron. Like many Burgundians, Mugnier feels that the 1997 vintage produced wines for near-term drinking, yet is perplexed as to why these rich yet seemingly fragile wines show no signs of oxidation after hours of aeration. Deep, sweet, plummy fruits are found in the delightful aromatics of the 1997 Musigny. Candied cherries, jammy plums, and a thick, velvety texture make up this wine's personality. Satiny-textured yet well structured, it also proposes a long, well-wrought finish that reveals layers of chocolate and sweet candied fruits. This bottle had been opened for four and a half hours when it was tasted, driving home the point that 1997s are much more ageworthy than many people believe, including M. Mugnier. Anticipated maturity: now–2012+.

The ruby-colored 1998 Bonnes Mares offers intense, wild berry aromas. Medium- to full-bodied and satiny-textured, it has outstanding depth of fruit, power, and detail. Loads of red and black cherries enrobe its ripe but firm tannins. Anticipated maturity: now–2006.

Of the 1999s, Jacques-Frédéric Mugnier said, "I've never had more barrels in my cellar." He went on to add, "I'm pleased by these wines, and surprised at how full they taste given our yields. I did a *saignée* of 15–20% and still ended up having to send some wines to the distillery." (Any wine above the allowable yields, including the PLC, must be sent to state-run distilleries.) Produced from 50-year-old vines that border Bonnes Mares, the medium to dark ruby-colored 1999 Chambolle-Musigny Les Fuées is a medium-bodied, satin-textured wine. Its broad and concentrated personality offers loads of red and black cherries with a long, ripe, tannin-filled finish. Anticipated maturity: now–2008. Sweet cherries, minerals, and earth can be found in the aromatics of the 1999 Chambolle-Musigny Les Amoureuses. This is a lush, gorgeously sexy, pure, and precise wine. Juicy layers of raspberries, cherries, and spicy strawberries can be found throughout its velvety-textured personality and in its admirably long, supple finish. This delightful wine should be consumed between 2003–2010.

The medium to dark ruby-colored 1999 Musigny has a demure, raspberry, cherry, and gravel-scented nose. It offers layers of black cherry, sweet blackberry, stone, and violet-imbued fruits. Its concentrated personality reveals loads of beautifully ripened tannin as well as an impressively long, delineated finish. Anticipated maturity: 2004–2011.

Other recommended wine: 1997 Chambolle-Musigny (88)

DOMAINE MICHEL NIELLON (CHASSAGNE-MONTRACHET)

2000	Bâtard-Montrachet	EEE	94
1999	Bâtard-Montrachet	EEE	91+
1997	Bâtard-Montrachet	EEE	93
2000	Chassagne-Montrachet Champs-Gains	E	91
1997	Chassagne-Montrachet Champs-Gains	E	90
1999	Chassagne-Montrachet Chaumées	E	90
1997	Chassagne-Montrachet Chenevottes	E	91+
1999	Chassagne-Montrachet Clos St.-Jean	E	90
1999	Chassagne-Montrachet La Maltroie	E	91
2000	Chevalier-Montrachet	EEE	92
1999	Chevalier-Montrachet	EEE	92
1997	Chevalier-Montrachet	EEE	92+

Michel Niellon, like many of his forthright colleagues, described the 1997 whites as "delicious and easy to drink." No hyperbole at this address. In the corner of Niellon's cellar stands a barrel on which he places the bottles he serves visitors. When I arrived for my annual tasting, Niellon did what he always does, he pulled new, unopened ones from the stacks awaiting shipping. To my shock they were painfully closed and reeked of sulfur. After some prodding, Niellon allowed me to taste from the wines that had been opened for a few hours. Readers take note: these comments are from bottled wines that were opened and had benefited from exposure to air (with the exception of the Vergers).

Offering tangy lemon and mineral aromas, the 1997 Chassagne-Montrachet Les Champs-Gains is well balanced and medium- to full-bodied. This wine is beautifully delineated, with precise clay, earth, stone, and anise flavors and a velvety-textured personality. It is rich and dense, yet Niellon somehow maintained its outstanding balance. Anticipated maturity: now–2005. The 1997 Chassagne-Montrachet Les Chenevottes has floral red berry aromas and a deeply rich yet balanced personality. This offering is filled with delightful waves of minerals, flint, chalk, lemons, and crisp pears. Its medium body is beautifully delineated and concentrated, and has admirable persistence. Anticipated maturity: now–2006+.

Both of Niellon's 1997 grands crus are outstanding. The Chevalier-Montrachet reveals superb ripeness in its expressive mineral- and chalk-packed nose. This fabulous offering is medium-bodied, rich, concentrated, beautifully focused, and has mouthwatering mineral flavors that last throughout its extended and bone-dry finish. Anticipated maturity: now–2009. Sadly, Niellon plans to rip out his parcel of 1997 Bâtard-Montrachet after the 2000 harvest. Planted in 1928, these old vines have produced numerous stunning wines. The 1997 is certainly one of the finest Bâtards of the vintage. It offers hyperripe pear and apple aromas as well as a highly concentrated and extracted core of fruit. This is an extremely profound wine, with intense honeyed fruit cake flavors and an opulent, viscous, and almost flabby texture. If it had better balance there is no telling how high my score could have gone. Drink it over the next 5–6 years.

When asked whether he liked the 1999 vintage, Niellon, a man of few words, said, "Some things about it yes, and some things no." I failed at getting him to flesh out his words. Because the malolactic fermentations had finished so late, Niellon was compelled to sulfur his wines in one shot (wines have an easier time resolving SO_2 additions if it is done in small, consecutive doses). Hence, the bottles he opened were extremely difficult to judge, so we also tasted from bottles opened 24 hours earlier. Longtime fans of Michel Niellon's wines should know that he recently grubbed the old vines in his extraordinary Chassagne-Montrachet Les Vergers parcel. "They were sick and simply no longer productive," he said. However, because he ripped out Vergers, he has postponed his plans to do the same to his 74-year-old Bâtard-Montrachet parcel.

Rich mineral, stone, and earth aromas characterize the nose of the 1999 Chassagne-Montrachet Clos St.-Jean. Medium-bodied, broad, deep, and silky-textured, it is an extremely well balanced and pure wine. Assorted white fruits, minerals, quartz, and spices can be found throughout its personality and its long, lush finish. Anticipated maturity: 2003–2010. Two bottles of the 1999 Chassagne-Montrachet Les Chaumées displayed the negative effects of sulfur. The first bottle had a completely muted nose. On the palate, it was pure, focused, and light- to medium-bodied. It revealed minerals, lemons, and a long, crisp finish. The second bottle, having had the benefit of 24 hours of aeration, revealed pear, apple, spice, and mineral aromas. It was medium-bodied, broad, pure, concentrated, and fat, with loads of white fruits and minerals in its deep personality. Anticipated maturity: 2003–2010. The mineral-scented 1999 Chassagne-Montrachet La Maltroie is medium-bodied and superbly focused. This deep, concentrated, precise wine is loaded with quartz, citrus fruits, and pears. It is a satin-textured wine that has a long, supple finish. Anticipated maturity: 2003–2010.

Niellon's 1999 Chevalier-Montrachet reveals gorgeously pure mineral aromas. Medium-bodied, refined, and highly delineated, this satin-textured wine offers stone, crisp pear, and apple flavors in its deep personality. It also has a long finish. Anticipated maturity: 2004–2012. With coaxing, the aromatically muted, tightly wound 1999 Bâtard-Montrachet reveals a broad, concentrated, and deep personality. Fresh, zesty, and tangy flavors of crisp pears and apples come to the fore with considerable air. Anticipated maturity: 2005–2011+.

To Michel Niellon, 2000 is "a good vintage with which to give oneself pleasure." He went on to add, "From the start, it appeared equal or superior to 1999, and I don't believe we will be let down by its quality. It should be better than 1999 ever could be." As we discussed the 2000s and white Burgundies in general, Niellon stated, "Sure, the 2000s should be drunk in their first decade, but then, so should most white Burgundies. My philosophy is that our region's wines should be consumed within the first six to eight years, while they are drinking well. Why should people wait and risk death?" He went on to add that due to his style of *élevage*, which protects the wine from contact with air, he believes that decanting his wines a half hour to forty-five minutes before they are served "brings them to life."

The gorgeous 2000 Chassagne-Montrachet Les Champs-Gain bursts from the glass with superripe apple aromas. Fresh, rich, and opulent, it coats the palate with a panoply of spices, minerals, white fruits, and buttered toast. With air, its flavor profile gained intensity as well as focus. Anticipated maturity: now–2011. The 2000 Bâtard-Montrachet explodes from the glass with spiced pear aromas. This superb wine bastes the palate with tropical fruits, spices, candied apples, buttered toast, and hints of raspberries. It is powerful, medium- to full-bodied, and boasts an exceptionally long finish. This superb Bâtard should be consumed over the next 11 years. The 2000 Chevalier-Montrachet has a toasty, spicy nose. Well delineated, this medium-bodied wine has loads of gravel, mineral, stone, and apple flavors. It is tighter than the Bâtard, yet is intense, concentrated, and has a long, admirably pure finish. Anticipated maturity: 2003–2013.

Other recommended wines: 1999 Chassagne-Montrachet Les Champs-Gains (89), 2000 Chassagne-Montrachet Chaumées (89), 1997 Chassagne-Montrachet Clos de la Maltroie (89), 2000 Chassagne-Montrachet Clos de la Maltroie (89), 2000 Chassagne-Montrachet Clos St.-Jean (89), 1997 Chassagne-Montrachet Les Vergers (88+?)

DOMAINE DES PERDRIX (NUITS-ST.-GEORGES)

1997 Echézeaux	EE	92+
1997 Nuits-St.-Georges Aux Perdrix	E	92

This *monopole* estate, owned by Maison Antonin Rodet, is producing sumptuous wines that merit serious consumer attention. None of its 1997s was chaptalized, acidified, fined, or filtered. Moreover, they are the results of one of the latest harvests on the Côte d'Or. Produced from grapes harvested at over 14% natural potential alcohol, the 1997 Nuits-St.-Georges Aux Perdrix is dark ruby-colored and reveals a gorgeously ripe cherry- and spice-laden nose. This is an opulent, luscious wine with a penetrating flavor profile crammed with red and black candied cherries. Medium- to full-bodied and sexy, it has loads of sweet, supple tannins in its lengthy finish. Anticipated maturity: now–2008+. The lighter-colored 1997 Echézeaux has ethereal floral aromas. A feminine, silky-textured, well-defined, and elegant wine, its smile-inducing personality is sublimely flavored with violets and red berries. It has outstanding grip, balance, and structure. Anticipated maturity: now–2008.

Other recommended wines: 1997 Nuits-St.-Georges (89), 1997 Vosne-Romanée (89+)

DOMAINE HENRI PERROT-MINOT (MOREY-ST.-DENIS)

1999 Chambertin	EE	(88–92?)
1999 Chambolle-Musigny La Combe d'Orveaux Vieilles Vignes	EE	(89–91)
1997 Chambolle-Musigny La Combe d'Orveaux Vieilles Vignes	EE	(91–93)
1999 Chambolle-Musigny Les Fuées	E	(89–91)
1997 Chambolle-Musigny Les Fuées	EE	(90–93)
1999 Charmes-Chambertin Vieilles Vignes	EE	92+
1997 Charmes-Chambertin Vieilles Vignes	EE	(91–93)
1999 Mazoyères-Chambertin Vieilles Vignes	EE	(90–92+)
1997 Mazoyères-Chambertin Vieilles Vignes	EE	93
1997 Morey-St.-Denis La Riotte	E	(89–92)

Christophe Perrot-Minot has established himself as one of Morey-St.-Denis's top four or five producers, as well as one of Burgundy's finest wine-makers. In February 2000, Perrot (with the help of outside investors) purchased Domaine Pernin-Rossin, thereby increasing his holdings to 14 hectares. Early on in the 1997 growing season he noted uneven flowering, which leads to uneven ripening. He therefore went into the vineyards (which had low yields, 28 h/h Chambolle-Musigny La Combe d'Orveaux, for example), and performed a green harvest (dropping Orveaux to 22 h/h) in order to have all of his grapes at the same high level of ripeness. On average, his yields in 1997 are 60% less than in 1996. He performed 10–13 day cold macerations prior to fermentation and used extremely small levels of SO_2 (5–7 centiliters). Perrot-Minot loves to experiment, and in the 1997 vintage, both of his grands crus had the majority of their alcoholic fermentation in new oak barrels, as opposed to the traditional vats (*cuves*). None of the wines was ever racked prior to the prebottling assemblage.

The medium to dark ruby-colored 1997 Morey-St.-Denis La Riotte reveals lovely black fruit and spiced oak aromas. Medium- to full-bodied, it is soft, lush, concentrated, and loaded with black cherries and mint chocolates. Additionally, this deep, complex, sultry wine offers a long, pure, supple finish. Drink it over the next 6–7 years. Only 62 cases of the medium to dark ruby-colored 1997 Chambolle-Musigny Les Fuées were produced (and only 37 in 1998!) This wine (as well as the next three) was fashioned in 100% new oak barrels. It offers smoked bacon and grilled oak aromas, as well as a fat, dense, fruit-packed, concentrated character. Licorice, stones, and blackberry liqueur saturate the palate in this masculine, powerful, structured, medium- to full-bodied wine. Beautifully layered and velvety-textured, it is an intense, immensely flavorful, and complete offering that should be consumed over the next 7 years. The dark ruby-colored 1997 Chambolle-Musigny La Combe d'Orveaux (produced entirely in brand-new Rémond barrels) displays candied cherry and cassis scents. It is a big, full-bodied, tarry, rich, and chewy wine. Flavors of leather, baked blackberries, rocks, and toasty oak can be discerned in this concentrated and muscular wine. Its exuberant character lasts throughout its strongly flavored and supple, tannin-filled finish. Anticipated maturity: now–2006. The medium to dark ruby-colored 1997 Mazoyères-Chambertin exhibits aromas reminiscent of sugarcoated cherries. This is a wine of outstanding concentration, density, freshness, and focus. Medium- to full-bodied, highly expressive, and crammed with candied red fruits, Asian spices, and sweet, toasty oak, this is a well-structured yet opulent red Burgundy. Anticipated maturity: now–2007.

The most hedonistic and sensual of Perrot-Minot's 1997s is his medium to dark ruby-colored Charmes-Chambertin. Raspberry jam, violets, roses, and spices can be found in its luxuriant nose. Its boisterous personality is broad, complex, concentrated, and lusciously sweet, crammed with hyperripe red fruits, and hints of stones. This prodigiously long, well-wrought, harmonious offering will be at its best if consumed over the next 8 years.

Perrot-Minot believes 1999 is "a great, ripe vintage, for those that controlled yields." His "villages" vineyards produced 45 h/h, and the premier and grand crus between 35 and 37 h/h. I loved his extraordinary 1996s, but his desire for power led him to increase extract with each vintage. The marriage of purity and elegance with power and ripeness in 1996 has given way to a highly extracted character.

The dark ruby-colored 1999 Chambolle-Musigny Les Fuées reveals aromas of dark fruits and fresh herbs. Its roasted coffee, blackberry, and red cherry–flavored character reveals outstanding depth of fruit, a fresh personality, and a long, defined, and elegant finish. This well-balanced, medium-bodied wine should be at its peak of maturity between 2004–2010.

The dark ruby-colored 1999 Chambolle-Musigny La Combe d'Orveaux Vieilles Vignes has a superripe black fruit–scented nose. Medium-bodied and highly extracted, this is a muscular, sweet, blackberry, plum, and blueberry-packed wine. It reveals outstanding ripeness to its tannin and powerful tar and licorice-like flavors that are also found in its long, supple finish. Anticipated maturity: 2003–2010+. The sweet red cherry and rose-scented 1999 Charmes-Chambertin Vieilles Vignes is a broad, superripe, lush, mouthcoating wine. Abundant candied cherries and blackberries can be found in this soft, supple, exquisitely long and pure offering. In its highly detailed finish, notes of strawberries and violets can also be discerned. Drink it over the next 12–15 years.

The oak- and blackberry-scented 1999 Mazoyères-Chambertin Vieilles Vignes is a highly structured, masculine wine. Blackberries, licorice, tar, and herbs characterize its powerful, medium-bodied character. This extracted wine has excellent density of fruit and firm yet well-ripened tannins that are revealed in its long finish. Drink it between 2005–2015.

Perrot-Minot's 1999 Chambertin is produced from five rows of vines owned by a friend. This medium to dark ruby-colored wine has a sexy, plummy, sweet, perfumed nose. On the attack and mid-palate, it is forward, soft, and opulent, revealing loads of dark, plummy fruits. However, this medium-bodied wine has a firm, highly structured, and tannic finish. Which personality will win out—the extroverted, lush, and forward one or the tannic, backward and tight one? Time will tell. Anticipated maturity: now–2008+?

Other recommended wines: 1997 Chambolle-Musigny (88–90), 1999 Chambolle-Musigny Vieilles Vignes (87–89), 1997 Gevrey-Chambertin (87–89), 1997 Morey-St.-Denis La Riotte Vieilles Vignes (89–92), 1999 Morey-St.-Denis La Riotte Vieilles Vignes (88–90), 1997 Morey-St.-Denis en la Rue Vergy (87–89), 1999 Morey-St.-Denis en la Rue Vergy (88)

MAISON NICOLAS POTEL (NUITS-ST.-GEORGES)

1999	Bonnes Mares	EE	(91–93)
1998	Bonnes Mares	EE	(89–91)
1999	Charmes-Chambertin	EE	(91–93)
1999	Clos St.-Denis	EE	(92–93)

1997 Clos St.-Denis	**EE**	**(90–93)**
1997 Clos de la Roche	**EE**	**(89–91)**
1997 Clos de Vougeot	**EE**	**(90–92)**
1997 Echézeaux	**EE**	**(88–91)**
1999 Grands-Echézeaux	**EE**	**(89–91)**
1997 Pommard Rugiens	**E**	**(91–93)**
1997 Volnay Champans	**E**	**(89–91)**
1999 Volnay Chevret	**D**	**(90–92)**
1999 Volnay Mitans	**D**	**(90–91)**
1997 Volnay Pitures	**E**	**(89–92)**
1997 Volnay Santenots	**E**	**(90–93)**
1999 Vosne-Romanée Les Suchots	**E**	**(90–92)**

Nicolas Potel, the son of the late Gérard Potel of Volnay's Domaine de la Pousse d'Or fame, has created a new *négociant* firm. Well liked and respected throughout the Côte d'Or, Nicolas Potel is able to purchase grapes, musts, and wines from some of Burgundy's great stars. Armed with excellent contacts among the Côte d'Or's vignerons, his extensive knowledge of Burgundy's vineyards, as well as the experience gleaned from years of working with his father, Potel's goal is to acquire grapes from well-placed vineyards with vines over 30 years of age. He is firmly against the fining of Pinot Noirs and is not a believer in new oak. He notes that he "will only filter if I absolutely have to. None of my 96s went through that process." Furthermore, none of his wines was acidified or chaptalized in the 1997 vintage.

Produced from grapes purchased from a grower who subscribes to biodynamic viticultural techniques, the saturated ruby-colored 1997 Volnay Pitures displays tobacco and blackberry aromas. It is a refined, medium- to full-bodied wine with outstanding power, grip, delineation, and balance. Silky-textured and chewy, this masculine effort offers layers of red/black fruits and cedarlike flavors. Drink it over the next 6 years. The darker-colored 1997 Volnay Champans boasts a grapy, oaky, and floral nose. Reminiscent of a young, oak-aged Châteauneuf-du-Pape (La Nerthe Cuvée des Cadettes, for example), it offers superripe cassis and Provençal herb flavors significantly marked by sweet, toasty oak. What this medium- to full-bodied wine lacks in elegance and sophistication it makes up for with sheer power and brawn. Anticipated maturity: now–2006+.

As might be expected, given Potel's superb contacts in the Côte de Beaune, his 1997 Volnay Santenots is absolutely first-rate. Medium to dark ruby-colored and revealing deeply sweet fruit aromas, this is a wine of outstanding depth, power, and backbone. Medium- to full-bodied, crammed with explosive black fruit, floral, and candied flavors, it is fresh, wonderfully concentrated, and admirably long. Anticipated maturity: now–2008. The highly impressive medium to dark ruby-colored 1997 Pommard Rugiens offers sugarcoated cherry and blueberry aromas. This chewy, broad, expansive, muscular, and masculine freight/train of a wine coats the palate with waves of dense blackberries. Tangy, expansive, and immensely gratifying, this first-rate Pommard is one of the finest wines crafted from this famous village in 1997. Anticipated maturity: now–2008. Fashioned from purchased wine, the medium to dark ruby-colored 1997 Echézeaux reveals smoky black fruit scents. It is medium- to full-bodied, huge, deep, powerful, and loaded with cherries, bacon, blackberries, and cassis. Were it not for a somewhat dry and clipped finish, it would have merited a higher score. Anticipated maturity: now–2007.

Crafted from old vines located in the middle of Clos St.-Denis, Potel's 1997 is ruby/purple-colored. Its restrained yet superripe aromatics lead to a profound personality packed with jammy cherries. Medium- to full-bodied, and offering outstanding grip, elegance, and power, this harmonious and well-structured wine should of capable of mid-term cellaring. Drink it between now–2009. Potel's saturated ruby-colored 1997 Clos de la Roche displays floral, cassis, and rose-scented aromatics. Currants, black cherries, and metal-like flavors are found in this medium- to full-bodied wine. Highly expressive, bright, and well structured, this effort also possesses a firm, tannic backbone that will require patience. Anticipated maturity: 2003–2008. Verging on overripe, the dark ruby-colored 1997 Clos de Vougeot reveals mocha and grapy aromas. Cherries, Asian spices, figs, dates, and plums are found in this boisterous, broad, medium- to full-bodied offering. Though its somewhat tannic finish prevented it from meriting an even more exalted review, this is assuredly an outstanding wine. Anticipated maturity: now–2010.

The young, bright, and ever-smiling Potel put it bluntly: "1998 is not a great vintage, simply because we didn't have sufficient ripeness." The 1998 Bonnes Mares is medium to dark ruby-colored, and offers a grapy, plummy nose. Medium-bodied, dense, concentrated, and masculine, this is a deep, intense, harmonious wine. Loads of sweet black fruits can be found throughout its character and long, pure finish. Drink it over the next 7–8 years.

The medium to dark ruby-colored 1999 Volnay Mitans has jammy plum and blackberry aromas. It is a masculine, muscular, medium-bodied wine with a focused, fruit-packed personality. It coats the palate with loads of jammy black fruits and candied cherries. Its finish reveals copious quantities of impeccably ripe tannin. Drink it over the next 10 years. The outstanding medium to dark ruby-colored 1999 Volnay Chevret has earthy, stony dark berry aromas. Medium-bodied and loaded with sweet blackberries and licorice, this is a dense, round, satin-textured wine. Its lush, superripe personality engulfs its copious, supple tannin. Drink it over the next 10–12 years.

Superripe cherries, plums, and candied raspberries are found in the mouthwatering aromas of the medium to dark ruby-colored 1999 Vosne-Romanée Les Suchots. This is an intensely sweet, blackberry, blueberry, cherry, and Asian spice–flavored wine. Medium-bodied and pure, it offers a lush, opulent character that drowns its present yet supple tannins. Anticipated maturity: 2004–2010. The similarly colored 1999 Grands-Echézeaux has sweet raspberry and toasted oak aromas. It is an expansive wine with lush layers of black cherries, raspberries, and strawberries that lead to a firm yet long and somewhat satiny finish. Anticipated maturity: now–2009.

The dark berry and toasted oak–scented 1999 Bonnes Mares has a medium- to full-bodied, intense, and concentrated personality. Black cherries, bacon, and candied raspberries can be found in this chewy-textured, firm, and long-finishing offering. It is fresh and pure. Anticipated maturity: 2004–2012. The slightly darker-colored 1999 Clos St.-Denis has beguiling licorice and violet aromas. This fat, round, medium- to full-bodied wine has outstanding density and concentration. It is crammed with lush layers of blueberries, cherries, blackberries, and a myriad of spices, all of whose flavors last throughout its impressively pure and long finish. Drink it between 2003–2012. The tangy morello cherry–scented 1999 Charmes-Chambertin is medium to dark ruby-colored. This zesty, fresh, and highly delineated wine is crammed with raspberries, cherries, tangy currants, and juicy blueberries. It has outstanding purity and an extraordinarily long, suave finish. Drink it over the next 8–10 years.

Other recommended wines: 1997 Beaune Boucherottes (87–89), 1999 Beaune Epenottes (87–89), 1999 Bourgogne Vieilles Vignes (88), 1997 Pommard Arvelets (87–89), 1999 Pommard Epenots (87–89), 1997 Santenay Les Gravières (88–89+), 1997 Savigny-Lès-Beaune La Dominode (88–90), 1997 Volnay (87–89+), 1997 Volnay Mitans (87–89+), 1999 Volnay Santenots (88–89+)

DOMAINE JACQUES PRIEUR (MEURSAULT)

1997	Chambertin	EEE	94+
2000	Chevalier-Montrachet	EEE	(91–93)
1999	Chevalier-Montrachet	EEE	(89–91)
1998	Chevalier-Montrachet	EEE	(89–92)
1997	Chevalier-Montrachet	EEE	(90–93)

1997	Clos Vougeot	EE	91
1999	Corton-Bressandes	EE	(91–93)
1997	Corton-Bressandes	E	91+
1999	Corton-Charlemagne	EE	(89–91)
1998	Corton-Charlemagne	EE	(88–91)
1997	Corton-Charlemagne	EE	(91–93)
1997	Echézeaux	EEE	(89–91)
1998	Meursault Perrières	EE	(88–91)
1997	Meursault Perrières	EE	(90–92)
2000	Montrachet	EEE	(93–94)
1999	Montrachet	EEE	(92–94)
1998	Montrachet	EEE	(90–94)
1997	Montrachet	EEE	(93–95)
1999	Musigny	EEE	(91–93)
1997	Musigny	EEE	(93–95)
2000	Puligny-Montrachet Les Combettes	E	(89–91)
1997	Puligny-Montrachet Les Combettes	EE	(88–91)
1999	Volnay Champans	E	(91–92+)
1999	Volnay Clos des Santenots	E	(89–92)
1997	Volnay Clos des Santenots	E	(91–93)

Under the guidance of Martin Prieur and with the assistance of Maison Rodet's highly talented wine-maker, Nadine Gublin, Domaine Jacques Prieur crafted fabulous wines from the 1997 vintage. The estate's yields averaged 28 h/h. None of its wines has a natural potential alcohol below 12.5%, and not a single offering was chaptalized or acidified, according to Prieur and Gublin. The 1997 Puligny-Montrachet Les Combettes offers appealing, complex, and elegant aromas of minerals, honeysuckle, and apricots. This is a dense wine with silky layers of white fruits, flower blossoms, and tangy lemons in its medium- to full-bodied flavor profile and in its long and focused finish. Anticipated maturity: now–2005+. Prieur's 1997 Meursault Perrières exhibits fresh cream scents and an expansive, mouthcoating (yet refined) personality. This outstanding wine is broad, thick, medium- to full-bodied, and crammed with nuts, minerals, stones, and ripe pears. Its long, detailed finish displays flavors reminiscent of sea shells and sun-baked rocks. Anticipated maturity: now–2005. Only two barrels of the aromatically muted 1997 Chevalier-Montrachet were produced. On the palate it displays magnificent power, intensity, and concentration. This is a dense, oily, and medium- to full-bodied offering packed with pears, apples, and minerality. Furthermore, it possesses an impressive finish. Though its nose was muted, this wine has all the attributes of a grand vin. Anticipated maturity: now–2008.

Fourteen months after being harvested at 14.5% natural potential alcohol, the 1997 Montrachet was still slowly fermenting (it still had 3 grams of sugar). Neither Prieur or Gublin appeared concerned about the abnormal length of time the conversion of the sugars to alcohol was taking. On the contrary, they were ecstatic about the complexity and depth this glacially paced fermentation would impart to their Montrachet. This is a spectacular wine, with dense aromatics of flower blossoms, minerals, anise, spices, apples, and apricots. The palate revealed some CO_2 (quite normal during fermentation and extended lees contact), yet its sheer power, complexity, concentration, and expansiveness were mind-boggling. Its explosive personality, loaded with tropical fruits, buttered toast, allspice, poached pears, and currants, is surprisingly fresh and structured given its corpulence. It is a full-bodied, mouthcoating, elegant, and formidably long wine. Wow! Anticipated Maturity: 2003–2014.

The 1997 Corton-Charlemagne was also completing fermentation (it had less than 3 grams of residual sugar), having been harvested (on October 10) with a potential alcohol of 14%. Its immensely rich and ripe nose reveals pears and toast aromas that are followed by a slightly warm personality filled with raspberries, apples, anise, and spices. This medium- to full-bodied wine is thickly textured, broad, and decadently constituted. Its lavish quantities of superripe fruit, toasty oak flavors, and concentrated fruit persist throughout its impressive finish. Anticipated maturity: now–2011.

Crafted from unbelievably low yields of 6 h/h, the stunning medium to dark ruby-colored 1997 Volnay Clos des Santenots reveals superb aromatics of flowers, creamed cherries, and spices. This medium- to full-bodied, complex, fresh, and magnificently concentrated wine is crammed with superripe black fruits and roses. It is intensely flavorful, velvety-textured, and possesses an admirably long, fresh, and pure finish. Anticipated maturity: now–2012. The similarly colored 1997 Corton Bressandes (bottled unfined and unfiltered, like most of Domaine Jacques Prieur's offerings) displays a *sur-maturité*-laced cherry- and licorice-scented nose. This is an expansive, beautifully rendered, elegant, and powerful wine. Medium- to full-bodied, intricate, opulent, and sweet, its flavor profile is composed of blackberries and tar. Anticipated maturity: now–2009.

Harvested at 14–14.5% natural potential alcohol, the ruby-colored 1997 Clos de Vougeot offers aromas of figs and prunes. This hyperripe, massive, fat, and obscenely opulent wine explodes on the palate with flavors of cherry jam and licorice. Medium- to full-bodied and tantalizingly sexy, this is not for those searching out elegance, class, or breed in a Burgundy. Rather, it is a wine for those seeking immediate corporeal satisfaction. Drink it over the next 4 years. The darker-colored 1997 Echézeaux offers spiced corn, talcum powder, and toast aromas. Stylistically, this is the complete opposite of the previous one. Refined, elegant, detail-oriented, it offers broad yet delicate cherry flavors in its medium- to full-bodied core. This well-balanced, satin-textured offering should be consumed over the next 7+ years.

Prieur's 1997 Musigny, tasted just before bottling, displays deep black cherry, violet, and mocha aromas. It is broad, refined, well delineated, and full-bodied, replete with overripe blackberry and chocolate flavors. This well-wrought, harmonious, and elegant wine appears to expand and gain in strength from the attack all the way through its impressively long and detailed finish. One of the vintage's most impressive wines, it should be at its best between now–2010+. The slightly darker colored 1997 Chambertin was harvested at a whopping 14.5% natural alcohol. It reveals an exuberant nose of roses and massively ripe red and black fruit. In their youth, Chambertins are generally rather backward and ungiving, yet this powerhouse explodes on the palate with untold layers of sweet cherries and blueberries. Velvety-textured, medium- to full-bodied, broad, muscular, yet refined and noble, it is stunning to drink today, and yet should evolve magnificently over the next dozen or so years.

The toasty white fruit and stone-scented 1998 Meursault Perrières is a refined, medium-bodied wine. Its lemon- and mineral-filled flavor profile is detail oriented, well delineated, and persistent in the finish. If this wine gathers richness and body as it completes its *élevage*, it will merit a score in the upper end of the range provided. Anticipated maturity: now–2005.

Prieur's medium-bodied 1998 Corton-Charlemagne offers soft mineral and earth aromas. This austere, structured, and tightly wound wine is presently dominated by spicy citrus fruit flavors. It is well balanced, harmonious, and possesses a long, detailed finish. Anticipated maturity: now–2008. Minerals immersed in white chocolate are found in the aromatics of the 1998 Chevalier-Montrachet. Medium-bodied, powerful, and intensely focused, this complex, silky-textured wine has outstanding grip to its fresh, clean personality. White flowers, stones, gravel, and touches of pear can be found in its flavor profile and throughout its long finish. Anticipated maturity: now–2009. The highly impressive 1998 Montrachet has a nose composed of white fruits, toasted oak, and minerals. Medium-bodied, muscular, and thick, this is a dense, spicy wine, filled with ripe apples, red berries, and anise. Extremely well balanced and harmonious, it has an extraordinarily long finish that reveals loads of warm (alcoholic) fruit that should integrate as the *élevage* progresses. Anticipated maturity: now–2010.

The 1999 Corton-Charlemagne has a mouthwatering nose of almonds, cream, and spices.

Medium-bodied and rich, yet austere, and pure, this lime, mineral, and stone-flavored wine is silky-textured and admirably long in the finish. Concentrated and deep, it may merit a more positive review if it opens. Anticipated maturity: 2003–2011. The 1999 Chevalier-Montrachet exhibits floral, mineral, and pear aromas. Medium-bodied, deep, and round, this white fruit and acacia blossom–flavored wine is plump, rich, and lush. It is well concentrated, extremely well balanced, and has a long, crystalline finish. Anticipated maturity: now–2010. The outstanding 1999 Montrachet reveals toasty pears, apple, and minerals in its nuanced aromas. Medium-bodied and complex, this is a rich, deep, dense, intense wine. Plump waves of white fruits, spices (including cinnamon and nutmeg), and honey-coated minerals can be found throughout this gem's personality and in its admirably long, pure, and smooth finish. Anticipated maturity: 2003–2012.

Produced from 38 h/h, the 1999 Volnay Clos des Santenots displays sweet, plummy, blackberry fruit aromas. Medium-bodied and broad, this is a candied, tangy wine crammed with concentrated layers of blueberries, blackberries, and cherries. It is fresh, zesty, and possesses a long, supple, ripe, tannin-filled finish. Anticipated maturity: 2005–2012. The 1999 Volnay Champans has a boisterous nose of baked plums and blackberries. Medium- to full-bodied, lush, and opulent, this is a massive, velvety-textured wine. It is jam-packed with cherries, blackberries, blueberries, and candied raspberries whose flavors last throughout its exquisitely pure and long finish. Drink this beauty between 2004–2012.

The medium to dark ruby-colored 1999 Corton-Bressandes has a perfumed violet and red cherry–scented nose. This is a medium- to full-bodied, powerful, massive wine with layer upon layer of cherries, plums, and blackberries in its chewy, satin-textured character. It possesses loads of superbly ripened tannin that give it an exemplary structure. This concentrated, muscular wine will be at its best between 2005–2012. The violet and blueberry-scented, medium to dark ruby-colored 1999 Musigny has a medium- to full-bodied personality. It bursts from the glass with massive waves of raspberries, and plums and hints of fig and licorice. This is an opulent, sweet, lush, and softly textured wine that is superripe. Its firm, tannic backbone is encased in loads of *sur-maturité* fruit. Drink it between 2005–2012.

The white fruit–scented 2000 Puligny-Montrachet Les Combettes is a soft, plump, medium-bodied wine. Minerals and stones are intermingled with buttered toast and ripe pears in this chewy-textured, rich, fresh offering. It has outstanding depth of fruit and a beautifully nuanced character. Anticipated maturity: now–2009. The 2000 Chevalier-Montrachet bursts from the glass with boisterous spice aromas. Candied berries, loads of minerals, and stones are found in this rich, ample wine's intense character. It is vinous, concentrated, and has outstanding depth. Anticipated maturity: 2004–2012. The superb 2000 Montrachet has a flower, anise, spice, and mineral-scented nose. Medium- to full-bodied and profound, this rich, concentrated wine offers intense layers of minerals, assorted white fruits, spices, and vanilla. Though it does not possess the overwhelming depth of Prieur's finest Montrachets, this is undoubtedly one of the best wines of the 2000 vintage, combining power with refinement and expressiveness with harmony. Anticipated maturity: 2004–2014.

Other recommended wines: 2000 Corton-Charlemagne (89–90), 1999 Meursault Clos Mazeray (red) (89), 1999 Meursault Perrières (88–89+), 2000 Meursault Perrières (89–90), 1995 Montrachet (97), 1999 Puligny-Montrachet Les Combettes (87–89), 1997 Volnay Champans (89), 1997 Volnay Santenots (89)

CHÂTEAU DE PULIGNY MONTRACHET (PULIGNY-MONTRACHET)

1997	Bâtard-Montrachet	EEE	(88–92)
2000	Chevalier-Montrachet	EEE	(92–94)
1997	Chevalier-Montrachet	EEE	(93–94)
1997	Meursault Perrières	E	(89–91)

2000 Montrachet	EEE	(88–91)
1999 Montrachet	EEE	(90–93)
1998 Montrachet	EEE	(90–93)
1997 Montrachet	EEE	(93–95)
1997 Puligny-Montrachet Les Folatières	E	(89–91)
2000 Puligny-Montrachet La Garenne	EE	(89–91)
1997 Puligny-Montrachet La Garenne	E	(89–91)

Jacques Montagnon, Château de Puligny-Montrachet's highly talented wine-maker, captured the 1997 vintage's best qualities and avoided all of this year's potential weaknesses, joining a select group of wine-makers, including Jadot's Jacques Lardière, Domaine d'Auvenay's Lalou Bize-Leroy, and Dominique Lafon, all of whom admirably succeeded in 1997. Montagnon did not acidify his wines. "Why would I have resorted to that? I knew what the acidity levels were, and was aware that they would not change after the malolactic fermentations," he confidently stated.

The 1997 Meursault Perrières displays enthralling almond butter aromas as well as a fat, creamy character. This dried honey, mineral, and hazelnut extract–flavored offering is bold, deeply ripe, and possesses fine length. An exceptionally well-balanced wine for the vintage, it should evolve well with cellaring. Anticipated maturity: now–2006+.

The 1997 Puligny-Montrachet La Garenne was slightly reduced, yet with air, its profound nose of minerals, lemons, and honeysuckle emerged. A well-concentrated and medium- to full-bodied wine with copious layers of clay, citrus fruits, and toasted oak, it also had a persistent finish. Anticipated maturity: now–2006+. The 1997 Puligny-Montrachet Les Folatières is more elegant. Its aromas exhibit acacia blossoms, grilled nuts, and wood spices. On the palate, this medium- to full-bodied, flavorful wine offers well-defined mineral and hazelnut flavors. Though not as dense as the La Garenne, it appears to be more harmonious. 1997's telltale alcoholic warmth was detectable in its otherwise deliciously oak-imbued finish, lowering my score. Drink it over the next 5–6 years.

The 1997 Chevalier-Montrachet was harvested at 14% natural potential alcohol. It has an extraordinary nose of minerals, cardamom, peanuts, acacia blossoms, and anise. This impeccably focused, precise, and concentrated wine has enormous complexity, a medium to full body, and a magnificently long finish. Its flavor profile is composed of chalk, flint, crisp pears, boisterous minerals, and sweet spicy oak. Anticipated maturity: now–2008+. The 1997 Bâtard-Montrachet displays passion fruit, mangoes, and overripe pear aromas. Reminiscent of Chardonnay jelly, this is a hugely thick, hyperdense, and full-bodied wine revealing an extraordinary panoply of cherries, raspberries, and tropical fruits. Its power, texture, and weight are extremely impressive. Might it be too intense and/or over the top? Drink it over the next 4–6 years. The 1997 Montrachet reveals dusty mineral, peach, and earth aromas. This powerful, medium- to full-bodied, opulent, viscous wine recalls the enormous Bâtard, but it is substantially better balanced and delineated. Buttered toast, stones, chalk, minerals, poached pears, apricots, and red currants can be discerned in its complex, explosive, and highly concentrated personality. Anticipated maturity: now–2009.

The estate's 1998 Montrachet was fashioned in a brand-new half barrel, yet it possesses the requisite depth of fruit and structure to stand up to the woody onslaught. Minerals, acacia blossoms, and toast can be found in its expressive aromas. Full-bodied, chewy-textured, and broad, this dense, mouthcoating, and powerful wine conquers the palate with layers of gorgeously ripe pears, apples, minerals, and spices. This complex, compelling offering is harmonious and well balanced and will prove to be a classic Montrachet. Anticipated maturity: now–2012.

Jacques Montagnon informed me that the estate's yields in 1999 averaged 54 h/h, well below the permissible 63. When asked to list the white Burgundy vintages in the nineties in his order of preference from best to worst, he stated that his favorite was 1992, followed by

1995, 1996, 1998, 1999, 1997, 1994, 1991, and lastly, 1993. The 1999 Montrachet (only 170 liters were produced of this wine) was vinified and aged in a 57-liter barrel, as well as a 114-liter barrel. It reveals sweet, creamy vanilla and spice cake aromas. Medium-bodied, rich, deep, and plump, this velvety-textured wine displays loads of spices and minerals in its personality, as well as in its exceptionally long, pure, smooth finish. Anticipated maturity: now–2010.

The 2000 Puligny-Montrachet La Garenne has floral and stone aromas. Medium-bodied and refined, this is a pure, well-focused, yet broad wine. It exhibits outstanding grip to its spice, mineral, and pear flavors. Anticipated maturity: 2003–2009. The exquisite 2000 Chevalier-Montrachet bursts from the glass with honeysuckle, mineral, and white flower aromas. Medium-bodied and broad, this silky-textured wine offers concentrated waves of spices, minerals, pears, and apples in its deep flavor profile as well as in its exceptionally long finish. It is a beautifully fashioned, elegant wine that is complex and intense. Drink it between 2005–2014. The ripe white fruit–scented 2000 Montrachet has a medium-bodied personality. This wine displays outstanding depth to its tangy citrus fruit and mineral-flavored personality. It suffers from the tightness often found in the vintage, yet has loads of depth and a long, focused finish. If this wine fills out as it finishes its *élevage*, it will ultimately merit a score in the upper end of the range provided. Anticipated maturity: 2003–2015.

Other recommended wines: 1999 Bâtard-Montrachet (88–90?), 1999 Chevalier-Montrachet (88–90), 2000 Meursault Perrières (88–90), 1999 Puligny-Montrachet (88–89), 1997 Puligny-Montrachet Les Chalumeaux (88–90), 2000 Puligny-Montrachet Les Folatières (87–89), 1997 St.-Aubin En Remilly (88–89), 1999 St.-Aubin En Remilly (88–89), 2000 St.-Aubin En Remilly (87–89)

DOMAINE RAMONET (CHASSAGNE-MONTRACHET)

1998	Bâtard-Montrachet	EEE	(89–92)
1997	Bâtard-Montrachet	EEE	(90–93)
1998	Bienvenue-Bâtard-Montrachet	EE	91
1997	Bienvenue-Bâtard-Montrachet	EE	(90–92+)
2000	Chassagne-Montrachet Les Ruchottes	E	(90–92)
1998	Chassagne-Montrachet Les Ruchottes	E	90
2000	Montrachet	EEE	(91–93)
1999	Montrachet	EEE	(90–92?)
1998	Montrachet	EEE	(91–94)
1997	Montrachet	EEE	(92–95)

Noël Ramonet described his 1997s as not for long-term aging but supple and delicious right from the barrel. Unlike many of his less than forthright neighbors, Ramonet was straightforward concerning his need to reacidify. "It was, in 1997, a necessity, not a choice for many wines." Upon subsequent visits to taste the 1999s and 2000s, he announced he had reacidified those vintages as well. Like many of his colleagues in Burgundy, Ramonet prefers to use barrels crafted by a variety of *tonneliers*, the theory being that this eliminates one barrel maker's aromatic and flavor signature dominating the finished wine. I was served Ramonet's 1997 grands crus from a total of six different *tonneliers* and the following notes are based on a hypothetical blend of the barrels.

The 1997 Bienvenue-Bâtard-Montrachet, aged in 35–45% new oak, offers aromas reminiscent of caramel, spices, sweet pears, and toasty oak. It possesses a fat, dense, medium- to full-bodied, broad character filled with layers of superripe peaches, quince, dried honey, and tangy currants. This rich and plump wine has excellent grip, a thick texture, and has a forward, decadent style uncommon for such a youthful Ramonet offering. Anticipated maturity: now–2005. Ramonet's outstanding 1997 Bâtard-Montrachet (tasted from six barrels) has a floral, honeyed, roasted peach, spiced apple, and candied almond–scented nose. On the palate, I found it to be dense, plump, thickly textured, and medium- to full-bodied. A two-year-old barrel from Toutant and a sample taken from one crafted by Berthomieu were bright and tangy, yet the wines I tasted from the Damy barrel, as well as from a new Toutant, were denser, and oilier. Overall, it is an opulent wine, with huge ripeness, and filled with red berries, dried honey, apples, pears, white currant, and buttered toast. Anticipated maturity: now–2007. Two hundred cases of the fabulous 1997 Montrachet were produced. Smoky pears, toasted almonds, and elegant aromas of minerals are found in this wine's expressive nose. It is extremely classy, medium- to full-bodied, well focused, and expansive on the palate. Broad layers of lavishly oaked sweet white fruits, bacon, gravel, roasted peaches, and hazelnuts form this concentrated and complex wine's flavor profile. It has a combination of power, elegance, depth, balance, and ripeness that defines great white Burgundy. Antici-pated maturity: now–2009.

The Ramonet family should be commended for not having raised its prices since 1990. "At the estate, my wines sell at the same price today as they did ten years ago, yet I see they have multiplied many times by the time they get to consumers in your country," lamented Noël Ramonet while quoting prices from a New York retailer's catalogue.

Given that 1998 is qualitatively inferior to 1997, 1996, and 1995, I was surprised to find that Domaine Ramonet produced as good or better wines in this complicated vin-tage than in the three preceding ones. Even though Ramonet's home-base (Chassagne-Montrachet) is responsible for the finest 1998's, they are not typically as concentrated as the '95s, as pure as the '96s, or as rich as the '97s. Yet at this estate "the fruit is more pleasing in 1998 than in 1997," said Ramonet, "and it also has higher natural acidity levels." He felt compelled to acidify only a few 1998 *cuvées*, whereas other recent vintages required more in his opinion.

The 1998 Chassagne-Montrachet Les Ruchottes displays aromas of toasted hazelnuts, minerals, and crisp, ripe apples. This broad, deep, powerful wine is packed with lemons, pears, and gravel-like flavors. Medium-bodied, intense, and admirably long, this well-defined, flavorful wine should have the potential to withstand the test of time. Anticipated maturity: now–2009+. Aromatically, the impressive 1998 Bienvenue-Bâtard-Montrachet of-fers rich, ripe apples and pears. This broad, medium-bodied, thick, and exuberant wine dis-plays flavors reminiscent of minerals, gravel, spices, and assorted white fruits. Well concentrated and deep, it should be consumed between now–2008. Ramonet's citrus, stone, fresh earth, and spice-scented 1998 Bâtard-Montrachet has outstanding depth, power, and balance. Medium-bodied, filled with minerals, white fruits, and lemons, this well-balanced wine also possesses an impressively long, detailed finish. Anticipated maturity: now–2009.

Ramonet's multidimensional 1998 Montrachet is certainly one of the stars of the vintage. Its spice, star anise, toasted oak, and mineral-scented nose gives way to a rich, broad, pow-erful character. Medium- to full-bodied, and exhibiting layers of ripe apples, white pears, and stone-like flavors, this is an intense, concentrated, compelling effort. Anticipated matu-rity: 2003–2010. The explosive nose of the 1999 Montrachet displays toast, yeast, smoke, pears, quince, and minerals. This medium- to full-bodied wine has huge richness, breadth, density, and power. It is plump, has outstanding grip, and would unquestionably have mer-ited an exceptional score if its acidity had not been somewhat sharp and tart. Nevertheless, this wine's density of fruit and concentration lead me to hope it may well overcome this trait with cellaring. Anticipated maturity: 2005–2014.

To Ramonet, 2000 is "a charming, flattering vintage, one for rapid consumption." As is more often than not the case at this estate in recent years, the 2000s were, for the most part, acidified and chaptalized. Some of the wines, however, either sustained the acidification process because they had enough density of fruit, or Ramonet chose not to acidify them. For example, the toasted mineral–scented 2000 Chassagne-Montrachet Les Ruchottes is an out-standing wine. Medium- to full-bodied and broad, it coats the palate with raspberries, smoky pears, apples, and minerals. Broad, satin-textured, and persistent in the finish, this is a gorgeous, lush wine. Drink it over the next 7–9 years. The ripe apple, mineral, and toast-scented 2000 Montrachet is a concentrated, intense, and deep wine. It reveals an appealing vinous quality, loads of spiced pear flavors, and a backward characteristic. It is, at present, youthfully tight, though not to the extent of the Bâtard. This wine's finish is exceptionally long, loaded with flavor, and reveals enormous depth of fruit. Anticipated maturity: 2005–2015.

Other recommended wines: 1999 Bâtard-Montrachet (88–89), 2000 Bâtard-Montrachet (88–90?), 1999 Chassagne-Montrachet Clos de la Boudriotte (red) (88), 1998 Chassagne-Montrachet Les Caillerets (89), 1997 Chassagne-Montrachet Morgeot (white) (88), 1998 Chassagne-Montrachet Morgeot (white) (89), 1997 Chassagne-Montrachet Les Ruchottes (88–90+), 1997 Chassagne-Montrachet Les Vergers (87–89), 1999 Chevalier-Montrachet (88–89), 1997 Puligny-Montrachet Champs-Canet (87–89)

DOMAINE ROLAND RAPET (PERNAND-VERGELESSES)

1997	Corton-Charlemagne	EE	93
1997	Corton-Pougets	D	90+

Rapet's claim to fame is his superb Corton-Charlemagne (the estate owns an impressive 2.5 hectares, or 6.17 acres, of this grand cru). Harvested three weeks after the *ban de vendange,* the 1997 reveals fabulous *sur-maturité,* red fruit, and poached pear aromas. This opulent, oily-textured, and flavorful wine is densely packed with apricots, peach pits, buttered toast, and spiced apples. It possesses wonderful richness, massive ripeness, and a long, detailed finish. This impeccably crafted Corton-Charlemagne can be drunk now or held through 2008.

The saturated ruby/purple 1997 Corton-Pougets has waxy aromas and a medium- to full-bodied character. It displays outstanding ripeness, depth, and density in its black fruit, fresh herb, mocha, and cherry-flavored personality. Broad, expressive, and persistent, it is already delicious and will hold for 7+ years.

DOMAINE JEAN RAPHET ET FILS (MOREY-ST.-DENIS)

1999	Chambertin Clos De Bèze Réserve	EEE	92
1999	Charmes-Chambertin Réserve	EE	91
1997	Charmes-Chambertin Réserve	EE	91+
1999	Clos de la Roche Réserve	EEE	92
1999	Clos de Vougeot Réserve	EE	90
1999	Gevrey-Chambertin Les Combottes Réserve	EE	90
1997	Morey-St.-Denis Les Millandes Réserve	E	90

The bright, medium to dark ruby-colored 1997 Morey-St.-Denis Les Millandes Réserve reveals profound waxy, cherry aromas. This is a big, broad, concentrated, and deep wine, with layer upon layer of sweet red berry fruit, stones, and minerals. Intensely flavored, supple, and velvety-textured, it is a wine that will deliver enormous pleasure over the course of the next 6–7 years. Readers in search of a hedonistic wine to sink their teeth into should look no further. Raphet's dark purple-colored 1997 Charmes-Chambertin Réserve is loaded with dark chocolate and cherry syrup aromas. This is a massively ripe, silky-textured, medium- to full-bodied wine fashioned in a sultry, sexy, opulent style. Candied red fruits, mocha, and kirsch can be detected in its oily character. Anticipated maturity: now–2006+.

The medium ruby-colored 1999 Gevrey-Chambertin Les Combottes Réserve has a delectable nose of spices, candle wax, strawberries, and cherries. Medium- to full-bodied, lush, and dense, it coats the palate with copious quantities of candied cherries and sugarcoated strawberries. This fresh, well-balanced, and harmonious wine would have been awesome if its finish had been longer. Drink it over the next 8 years.

Copious spices, cherries, and blackberries can be discerned in the aromatics and flavors of the 1999 Clos de Vougeot Réserve. Ample, palate-coating, and medium-bodied, it reveals a long, supple finish that is pure and well focused. Drink it over the next 8 years. The outstanding 1999 Clos de La Roche Réserve has a potpourri, blackberry, and cherry-scented nose. Medium- to full-bodied, dense, and velvety-textured, this zesty, tangy wine is packed with black cherries and sugarcoated blueberries. Its long finish reveals loads of exceptionally well-ripened tannin. Anticipated maturity: 2003–2011.

The highly expressive aromatics of the 1999 Charmes-Chambertin Réserve display enormous levels of red and black cherries. This medium-bodied wine is plump, rich, and fat, yet it remains pure and precise. It has outstanding depth to its cherry- and blackberry-dominated flavor profile, and possesses an admirably long, silky finish. Drink it over the next 9 years. The dark ruby-colored 1999 Chambertin Clos de Bèze Réserve has a nose reminiscent of chocolate-covered cherries. Medium-bodied, precise, and pure, this outstanding wine displays creamed mocha, black cherry, and cassis-like fruit. It is fresh, delineated, and highly flavorful.

Other recommended wines: 1999 Bourgogne Les Grands Champs Réserve (88), 1999 Chambolle-Musigny Les Bussières Réserve (89), 1997 Clos Vougeot Réserve (89+), 1999 Gevrey-Chambertin Les Champs Chenys Réserve (89), 1999 Gevrey-Chambertin Lavaux St.-Jacques Réserve (89), 1997 Morey-St.-Denis Vieilles Vignes Réserve (89)

DOMAINE RAVENEAU (CHABLIS)

1997	Chablis Blanchots	EE	(89–91+)
1997	Chablis Les Clos	EE	(93–95)
1997	Chablis Montée de Tonnerre	EE	(89–91+)
1997	Chablis Valmur	EE	(90–93)

In contrast to most proprietors who boast that they were "the last to harvest," Bernard Raveneau proudly told me they had been the first to do so in 1997. As a matter of fact, Domaine Raveneau had completed its harvest when other estates were just beginning. "We had the grapes analyzed and saw that we were gaining very little sugar yet were quickly losing acidity. We responded." Raveneau went on to say that "the 1997s are in the style of 1995, yet not at the level of the 1996s. Hot nights led to a loss of acidity, yet the maturity of the grapes did not surpass 1996 because of drought conditions." Raveneau chaptalized his 1997s only half a degree, proof of their ripeness. The estate's yields, moderate by Chablis standards, were 48 h/h in 1997 and 35h/h in 1996.

Wineries in Chablis have an industrial feel to them. Large gateways lead to modern facilities. Massive warehouse-like rooms contain humongous stainless steel tanks connected to computers with blinking multicolored lights. High-tech equipment, the latest pumps, filters, and temperature control gizmos are found amid the steel catwalks, pipes, and shiny—recently disinfected—floors. The locales are industrial, as are, all too often, the wines . . . except for Chablis's two finest estates, Domaine René et Vincent Dauvissat and Domaine Raveneau. The entrance to the Raveneau cellars is a small door leading directly into the street. The lucky few who taste here must bend in half to clear the doorway, and adjust their eyes to the dark, humid, and cool confines of the *cave*. As in the Côte d'Or, barrels are stacked on top of one another, the floor is dirt, the walls are moist and moldy. This is the domaine of a vigneron, not a winery.

The 1997 Chablis Montée de Tonnerre has magnificent aromatics of sweet white fruits, candied apples, almonds, and red berries. This concentrated and medium-bodied wine offers loads of minerals, chalk, and flint in its mouthcoating personality. It has Raveneau's trademark purity of fruit, grip, and delineation. Anticipated maturity: now–2006. The structured, firm, and masculine 1997 Chablis Blanchots displays a nose of minerals intermingled with lemon zest. Its medium-bodied character is tightly wound, well proportioned, and exhibits flavors reminiscent of rock dust, flint, and sun-baked stones. This Blanchots is fresh, lively, persistent, and crystalline. Drink it between now–2007. The 1997 Chablis Valmur is superb. Fresh aromas of red currants, honeysuckle, and pears give way to an explosive, medium- to full-bodied personality. Its flavor profile, crammed with flint, quartz, stones, and a magnificently pure minerality, is complex and impeccably balanced. Consumers fortunate enough to acquire a few bottles of this wine should exercise cellaring patience. Anticipated maturity: 2003–2009.

Raveneau's 1997 Chablis Les Clos is undoubtedly a grand vin. It offers a plethora of nuanced aromas, including lemons, minerals, flint, clay, and flowers. On the palate, this expansive, powerful, mouthcoating wine exhibits extraordinary purity to its liquid mineral-dominated flavors. While it may not be as rich as the Valmur, it possesses mind-boggling focus and length. Wines from Les Clos, considered by many to be Chablis's finest vineyard, have a tendency to gain power and body with cellaring. I predict that this presently lacelike yet extremely flavorful and expressive effort will blossom into a wine of considerable depth and richness. Drink it between 2003–2009+.

Other recommended wines: 1994 Chablis Montée de Tonnerre (88), 1996 Chablis Montée de Tonnerre (92), 1996 Chablis Valmur (94+)

DOMAINE MICHEL REY (VERGISSON)

2000 Pouilly-Fuissé Les Charmes Vieilles Vignes Cuvée Unique	C	91

Note: These are special "Cuvée Unique" bottlings that are produced with and for David Hinkle and Peter Vezan for the U.S. market.

Produced from vines planted in 1953, the 2000 Pouilly-Fuissé Les Charmes Vieilles Vignes Cuvée Unique bursts from the glass with toasted mineral aromas. Medium-bodied, it reveals outstanding intensity, concentration, and breadth. Stones, gravel, nutmeg, and minerals are found in this refined, rich, yet detailed offering. Anticipated maturity: now–2010.

Other recommended wines: 2000 Pouilly-Fuissé Les Crays Vieilles Vignes Cuvée Unique (88), 2000 St.-Véran Les Champs de Perdrix Cuvée Unique (88)

MAISON JEAN RIJCKAERT (LEYNES)

1999 Arbois En Paradis Vieilles Vignes (Savagnin)	C	90
1999 Arbois Pré Levron Vieilles Vignes (Chardonnay)	C	90
1999 Mâcon-Bissy Les Crays Vers Vaux	C	90
1999 Viré-Clessé Les Vercherres Vieilles Vignes	C	90
1998 Viré-Clessé Les Vercherres Vieilles Vignes	C	90

While the name Jean Rijckaert is largely unknown to Burgundy wine lovers, he was one of the major financial backers and principals of Maison Verget. It was there, while working with Jean-Marie Guffens, that he learned how to make wine. Rijckaert, a Flemish Belgian, left Verget after the 1997 vintage and has been selling off his shares in that firm ever since, reinvesting the money by purchasing vineyard land in the Mâconnais and Jura. Additionally, Rijckaert has built, in the small town of Leynes, a new winery that bears his name. All of Maison Rijckaert's wines are hand-harvested, carried back to the winery in small boxes, and completely vinified in oak. Maison Rijckaert's production is divided into two categories— those that are made from vineyards owned by Rijckaert himself (these have green capsules and lettering) and those from grapes purchased from other growers (brown capsules and lettering). All of this firm's releases are single-estate wines and list the name of the domaine on the label.

The 1998 Viré-Clessé Les Vercherres Vieilles Vignes (Domaine Jean Rijckaert) has a perfumed nose reminiscent of white flowers and earth. Plump, concentrated, and intense, this powerful, medium-bodied, expressive wine has a satiny, rich personality. Its outstanding minerality is infused with citrus fruits and floral notes that last throughout its impressively long and well-focused finish. Drink this wine over the next 6 years.

Rijckaert is pleased with the 1999 vintage as he was able to harvest his vineyards prior to the heavy rains that commenced on Friday, September 21. "Thankfully, due to our insistence on moderating yields, we had high sugars and physiological ripeness early. In fact, for some parcels, we had to get a special permission to harvest before the legal harvesting date, then we had to request a dispensation for those same parcels because our natural sugars were above the maximum limit. In both the Mâconnais and Jura, if people worked in the vineyards to lower yields, their grapes were ripe before the official starting date for harvests."

The 1999 Mâcon-Bissy Les Crays Vers Vaux was produced from 50-year-old vines, harvested at a modest (for 1999) 40–45 h/h. Toasted nuts can be found in this wine's rich aromas (yet no oak was used). It is big, medium to full-bodied, bold, and concentrated. White and yellow fruits are found in this almost syrupy-textured offering's flavor profile. Its extensive finish reveals layers of minerals that coat the palate. Anticipated maturity: now–2005. The outstanding 1999 Viré-Clessé Les Vercherres Vieilles Vignes was harvested at a whopping 14% natural potential alcohol. It has a fresh, vibrant, mineral and lemon-lime-scented nose. On the palate, this crystalline, gorgeously focused offering has exquisite depth, richness, and concentration. Very much like a Chevalier-Montrachet in its mineral- and stone-dominated character, this wine from 50-year-old vines should be at its apogee between now–2006. The 1999 Arbois Pré Levron Vieilles Vignes (Chardonnay) (Domaine D. Horbach) yields beautiful aromas of toasted pears, minerals, and chalk. This plump, concentrated, rich wine has outstanding depth to its layered, mineral-dominated personality. It is fat, yet displays gorgeous precision and a long, supple finish. Drink it over the next 6 years.

The next wine is produced from Savagnin, a little-known varietal common in the Jura. Lively spices, almonds, and toasted hazelnuts can be discerned in the aromatics of the 1998 Arbois En Paradis Vieilles Vignes (Savagnin) (Domaine Pierre Morin). This deep, spice cake, orange rind, and sweet red/white currant–flavored wine is complex, medium-bodied, and plump. It is rich and fat, yet well-balanced, detailed, and possesses an admirably long, supple finish. Drink it over the next 6–7 years.

Jean Rijckaert states that 2000 was an exceptional vintage for the Jura and an excellent one for the Mâconnais. "Even though 2000 has large yields in the Côte d'Or and the Mâconnais, in the Jura yields were normal. Across the board there was lower maturity than in 1999, but better physiological ripeness," said Rijckaert. Like many *négociants*, Rijckaert informed me that an economic catastrophe was taking place in the Beaujolais, with bulk prices having dropped to less than $100 per barrel (25 cases), and that a crisis was well on its way in the Mâconnais. "When the region's top producers are asking you to purchase their wines, you know that the crisis has arrived." None of the estate's 2000s earned outstanding scores and therefore detailed tasting notes are not listed. However, these are excellent wines that are very reasonably priced.

Other recommended wines: 1998 Arbois En Paradis Vieilles Vignes Savagnin (Domaine Pierre Morin) (89), 1999 Arbois En Paradis Vieilles Vignes Savagnin (Domaine Pierre Morin) (90+), 2000 Arbois Pré-Levron Vieilles Vignes (Domaine Dominique Horbach) (88), 2000 Côtes du Jura Les Sarres Chardonnay (Domaine Jean Rijckaert) (87–89), 1999 Côtes du Jura Les Sarres Savagnin (Domaine Jean Rijckaert) (89), 2000 Côtes du Jura Vigne Des Voises Chardonnay (Domaine Jean Rijckaert) (89), 1999 Mâcon-Fuissé Grandes Bruyères Vieilles Vignes (Domaine M. Panay) (87), 1998 Mâcon-Montbellet En Pottes Vieilles Vignes (Domaine Jean Rijckaert) (88), 1999 Mâcon-Montbellet En Pottes Vieilles Vignes (Domaine Jean Rijckaert) (87), 1999 Pouilly-Fuissé Vers Chânes (Domaine Serge Mornand) (89), 1999 St.-Véran En Avonne Vieilles Vignes (Domaine Jean Rijckaert) (89), 1999 St.-Véran En Faux (Domaine J.-P. Voluet) (88), 1999 Viré-Clessé l'Epinet (Domaine Jean Rijckaert) (88)

DOMAINE DANIEL RION (PRÉMEAUX-PRISSEY)

1997	Chambolle-Musigny Les Charmes	EE	90
1997	Nuits-St.-Georges Clos des Argillières	E	90
1997	Vosne-Romanée Les Beauxmonts	E	90

Patrice Rion, this estate's wine-maker (up to and including the 1998 vintage), stated that in 1997, for the first time in his career, he had chaptalized only one wine, his Bourgogne Aligoté. To Rion, the key to a successful 1997 was to harvest late. The grape sugars were high, yet the skins and pits were not physiologically ripe when the *ban de vendanges* was set. He feels as though the vast majority of wines crafted in the 1997 vintage are reminiscent of the 1985s and 1989s, yet the best 1997s remind him of the 1990s.

The medium to dark purple/ruby 1997 Nuits-St.-Georges Clos des Argillières reveals fresh red and black cherry, candied raspberry, and vanilla aromas. It possesses a jellied texture, medium to full body, and opulent layers of fat, dense fruit. This sweet, luxurious, and hedonistic wine will be at its best if drunk over the next 6–7 years. Similarly colored, the 1997 Vosne-Romanée Les Beauxmonts offers a nose of spiced cherries, violets, and creamed mocha. This is a dense, structured, complex wine, with coffee bean, bacon, licorice, and blackberry flavors. Medium- to full-bodied and firm, it will be at its best between now–2007.

The spicy oak scented, saturated ruby/purple 1997 Chambolle-Musigny Les Charmes is a lovely, refined, and well-delineated wine. Medium- to full-bodied, pure, and thickly textured, it reveals superripe chocolate-covered cherry flavors. Rion successfully combines elegance with 1997's characteristic fruit density in this delightful effort. Drink it over the next 7 years. *Other recommended wines:* 1997 Chambolle-Musigny (88+), 1997 Nuits-St.-Georges Les Grandes Vignes (88), 1997 Nuits-St.-Georges Les Lavières (88+), 1997 Nuits-St.-Georges Les Vignes Rondes (89+), 1997 Vosne-Romanée (88), 1997 Vosne-Romanée Les Chaumes (89+)

DOMAINE ROBERT-DENOGENT (POUILLY)

1997 Pouilly-Fuissé Les Carrons Vieilles Vignes	D	94
1997 Pouilly-Fuissé Cuvée Claude Denogent	D	92+
1997 Pouilly-Fuissé Les Reisses Vieilles Vignes	D	91+

Jean-Jacques Robert defined 1997 as "a school vintage," explaining that "the analyses were extraordinary. We had great maturity and magnificent acidity." He feels as though the 1995s are possibly too rich and that the 1996s "are magnificently pure, have high acidity levels and will age exceptionally well." The 1997s will not last as long the 1996s, in his opinion, but have excellent aging potential.

Produced from vines more than 60 years old, the 1997 Pouilly-Fuissé Les Reisses Vieilles Vignes's nose reveals peanuts, hazelnuts, and white flowers. This medium-bodied, complex, and structured wine offers loads of acacia blossoms, chalk, and pears in its tightly wound and concentrated core of fruit. Drink it between now–2006. Like the previous wine, the 1997 Pouilly-Fuissé Cuvée Claude Denogent was vinified in 60% new oak with the balance being one year old. Produced from 77-year-old vines, this fabulous offering displays admirable ripeness in its concentrated aromatics. It has a clenched, intense, and powerful personality with mineral, chalk, and citrus flavors. Traces of oak spices can be discerned in the impressively long and pure finish. Anticipated maturity: now–2007+.

Jean-Jacques Robert describes his 1997 Pouilly-Fuissé Les Carrons as "very Zen-like." Crafted from 82-year-old vines and aged in 100% new oak barrels, this stunning wine reveals a profound nose composed of acacia blossoms, smoke, and sun-drenched gravel. Explosive, jam-packed with flavors that saturate the palate (liquid minerals, chalk, crisp pears, and earth) it also boasts exceptional purity, precision, ripeness, and balance. This massively concentrated and complex wine should age remarkably well. Drink it between 2003–2009. *Other recommended wines:* 1997 Mâcon-Solutré Bertillonnes (88), 1997 Pouilly-Fuissé La Croix Vieilles Vignes (88–89)

MAISON ANTONIN RODET (MERCUREY)

1999 Charmes-Chambertin Cave Privée	EE	(92–94)
1997 Charmes-Chambertin Cave Privée	EE	(89–91)

1999	Clos de Vougeot Cave Privée	EE	(91–93)
1997	Clos de Vougeot Cave Privée	E	(91–93)
1997	Mazis-Chambertin Cave Privée	EE	(92–94)
2000	Meursault Perrières Cave Privée	E	(89–91)
1999	Meursault Perrières Cave Privée	E	(89–91)
1997	Meursault Perrières Cave Privée	E	(89–91)
1999	Nuits-St.-Georges Les Porets Cave Privée	E	(89–91)
1997	Nuits-St.-Georges Les Porets Cave Privée	E	(90–91+)
1999	Nuits-St.-Georges Les St.-Georges Cave Privée	E	(89–91)
1999	Pommard Epenots Cave Privée	E	(89–90+)
1997	Puligny-Montrachet Le Cailleret Cave Privée	EE	(88–91)
1997	Puligny-Montrachet Hameau de Blagny Cave Privée	E	(91–94)
1999	Vosne-Romanée Beaumonts Cave Privée	E	(89–91)

Some of the most successful wines from the 1997 vintage were fashioned by Maison Antonin Rodet's Nadine Gublin. "The key to this vintage was to harvest late, and to be willing to leave the wines on their lees. In short, people had to be willing to take risks to make great wines," said Gublin, Rodet's super-talented wine-maker. When speaking about the estate-owned vineyards, Gublin stated that the Rodet teams had harvested, literally, when all of the vignerons had already finished. Not a single grape, according to her, had a natural potential alcohol under 12.5%. Readers should note that Rodet's Cave Privée offerings are made from grapes, must, or wines purchased form single estates (i.e., the Clos Vougeot was purchased in its entirely from one domaine, the Mazis-Chambertin from another). The wines, therefore, reflect the individual grower's viticulture and, often, their vinification techniques, yet the Gublin *élevage* and noninterventionist (unfined and unfiltered) bottling leave a significant mark.

The 1997 Meursault Perrières Cave Privée was fermented and aged in 100% new oak. This wine's nose is reminiscent of flower blossoms, flint, and rocks. It exhibits mouthcoating richness, a silky texture, and a refined flavor profile composed of minerals, sun-baked stones, and sweet pears. The wine is well concentrated, complex, and possesses a persistent, spicy, and focused finish. Anticipated maturity: now–2006. My favorite Rodet Cave Privée of the 1997 vintage is from the rarely encountered premier cru Puligny-Montrachet Hameau de Blagny (this vineyard is sandwiched between La Garenne and La Truffière). Vinified in 50% new oak with the balance evenly split between first- and second-year barrels, it offers mouthwatering leesy, red berry, and spiced apple aromas. This wine has great density, an expansive personality, boldly assertive flavors, and magnificent richness. Its minerals, candied oranges, and red currants seemingly build both on the palate and in the awesome finish. Impressive! Anticipated maturity: now–2008. The 1997 Puligny-Montrachet Le Cailleret Cave Privée, purchased as grape must, has rich, toasty, creamy, mineral, and salty aromas. This elegant, flinty, and white fruit–filled wine has superb aromas and flavors, yet lacks the punch of the previous wine, and has a shorter, ever-so-slightly dusty finish. While certainly excellent, and potentially outstanding, it does not have the Hameau de Blagny's depth and power. Drink it over the next 6 years.

The 1997 Clos de Vougeot Cave Privée is medium to dark ruby-colored and reveals a nose of cherry jam, roses, and licorice. This broad, expansive, feminine, refined, medium- to full-bodied wine possesses superb precision to its jammy, red berry–flavored character. It is concentrated, immensely pleasing, and persistent in the finish. Drink it over the next 8–9 years. The medium to dark ruby-colored 1997 Charmes-Chambertin Cave Privée reveals profound red and black fruit, rose, and toasty aromas. This spiced cherry and charred oak–flavored wine is expansive, medium- to full-bodied, and offers a supple, luscious character. It would have merited a higher score if its finish had not been slightly dry. Drink from now–2007. Sadly, only 25 cases were produced of the spectacular medium to dark ruby-colored 1997 Mazis-Chambertin Cave Privée. Overripe aromas of figs, dates, and mocha lead to an oily-textured, ample, and deep personality. Medium- to full-bodied, gorgeously pure, and elegant, this powerful and flavorful wine displays layer upon layer of oak-imbued candied cherries. Harmonious, extremely well balanced, and complete, this wine also offers a long, supple, fruit-packed finish. Drink it between now–2010+.

Minerals, stones, and fresh green grapes can be found in the aromas of the 1999 Meursault Perrières. This beauty has gorgeous depth, harmony, and lushness to its medium-bodied character. Loads of white and yellow fruits can be found in its plump, juicy, fresh, opulent personality, as well as throughout its long, supple finish. Drink it over the next 6 years.

The medium to dark ruby-colored 1999 Pommard Epenots Cave Privée has an intensely rich, spice, black cherry, and blackberry-scented nose. This big, bold, muscular, massive wine is medium- to full-bodied and crammed with blackberries, black cherries, and cassis. It is highly impressive, with a muscular, masculine character and a boisterous, highly expressive personality. It is somewhat rustic yet overcomes that trait with its awesome amounts of fruit. Anticipated maturity: 2004–2010. The similarly colored 1999 Vosne-Romanée Beaumonts Cave Privée has a sweet cherry– and new oak-scented nose. This satin-textured wine reveals smoked bacon, roasted oak, and sweet cherry flavors in its fresh, medium- to full-bodied personality, excellent to outstanding depth of fruit, loads of ripe tannins, and a long, seamless finish. Anticipated maturity: 2004–2010.

The medium to dark ruby-colored 1999 Nuits-St.-Georges Les St.-Georges Cave Privée has an oak, bacon, and blackberry jelly–scented nose. Medium-bodied and lively, it is well focused, refreshing, and highly expressive. This firm, black cherry and toasted oak–flavored wine should be at its best between 2004–2010. The similarly colored 1999 Nuits-St.-Georges Les Porets Cave Privée has delectable aromas of talcum powder, candied blackberries, and blueberry juice. Medium-bodied and lively, it exhibits a cassis, blackberry, and blueberry coulis–flavored character. Its finish is firm, yet the tannin appears marvelously ripe and supple. Drink it between 2004–2011.

The dark-colored 1999 Clos de Vougeot Cave Privée has a marvelous nose of sweet blackberries and spices. There is lovely depth to this massive, medium- to full-bodied wine. It combines power with elegance in its zesty, highly expressive, blackberry, black currant, and spicy personality. Additionally, this harmonious, seamless wine possesses a long, supple, sweet finish. Drink it between 2005–2012. The highly impressive, medium to dark ruby-colored 1999 Charmes-Chambertin Cave Privée has gorgeous baked red fruit aromas intermingled with figs, plums, and spices. This lush, opulent, creamy-textured, medium-bodied wine displays coffee, chocolate milk, cherries, and raspberries throughout its sexy character and exceptionally long, pure finish. Anticipated maturity: now–2008.

"When will Burgundians understand that acidity and sugar have nothing to do with ripeness?" Nadine Gublin asked rhetorically. "Skins, pits, and physiological ripeness, that's what matters. Grapes are fruits. You only want to eat them or make wine from them when they are good to put in your mouth!" she exclaimed at the beginning of our tasting of the 2000 whites. According to Gublin, at 2000's *ban de vendange,* no grapes in Burgundy were ripe, and waiting was paramount. The 2000 Meursault Perrières Cave Privée has appealing toasted mineral aromas and a focused, light- to medium-bodied character. Reminiscent of a successful 1996, it is a linear, laserlike wine with an appealing vinous characteristic. Loads of minerals and lemons can be found throughout its personality as well as in its pure, highly defined finish. Drink it over the next 8–9 years.

Other recommended wines: 1997 Beaune Cave Privée (88–89+), 1997 Chablis Côte de Léchet Cave Privée (88–89), 1997 Chambolle-Musigny Cave Privée (88+), 1997 Chassagne-Montrachet Cave Privée (87–89), 1999 Chassagne-Montrachet La Grande Montagne (89–90), 1998 Corton-Charlemagne (87–90), 1998 Meursault-Perrières Cave Privée (87–90), 1997 Nuits-St.-Georges Cave Privée (87–89), 1997 Pouilly-Fuissé Cave Privée (88–90), 1998 Pouilly-Fuissé Cave Privée (88–90+), 2000 Puligny-Montrachet Cave Privée (87–89),

1998 Puligny-Montrachet Hameau de Blagny Cave Privée (87–90), 2000 Viré-Clessé Cave Privée (87–89)

DOMAINE DE LA ROMANÉE-CONTI (VOSNE-ROMANÉE)

1999 Echézeaux	EEE	(91–93)
1999 Grands-Echézeaux	EEE	(90–93)
1997 Grands-Echézeaux	EEE	91
1999 Montrachet	EEE	93
1998 Montrachet	EEE	92
1997 Montrachet	EEE	94+
1996 Montrachet	EEE	96+
1999 Richebourg	EEE	(94–97)
1997 Richebourg	EEE	93
1999 Romanée-Conti	EEE	(95–99)
1997 Romanée-Conti	EEE	95
1999 Romanée-St.-Vivant	EEE	(88–91)
1997 Romanée-St.-Vivant	EEE	90
1999 La Tâche	EEE	(93–96+)
1997 La Tâche	EEE	93+
1999 Vosne-Romanée Premier Cru	EEE	(90–92+)

The Domaine de la Romanée-Conti's light-colored 1996 Montrachet is spectacular. Its profound, rich, embracing nose reveals toasted minerals, white fruits, and hints of lemons. On the palate it displays enormous complexity, a broad, layered core of tropical fruits (mostly mangoes), liquid minerals, and stones. It is terribly refined, bracing, satin textured, medium- to full-bodied, and mind-blowingly long in the finish. Its tightly wound core of fruit will require extended cellaring to blossom and reveal all that this glorious wine has to offer. Anticipated maturity: 2004–2016.

"The 1997 vintage arrived like a child whose qualities are hard to perceive in its youth. With *élevage* it blossomed, as with a child who becomes a lovely adult," said Aubert de Villaine, this famous estate's co-director. In 1997 the domaine's yields were below 25 hectoliters per hectare, extremely low even in this moderate yielding vintage. Readers should note that in the estate's efforts to treat its wines as gently as possible, everything is bottled by hand directly from the barrel. While this practice should be applauded because it eliminates the deleterious effects of pumping, it also leads to bottle variation as each barrel is different.

When de Villaine sent out his teams to harvest the Domaine's Montrachet in 1997, the entire vineyard had already been harvested, save for Domaine Jacques Prieur's parcel. It reveals a straw/goldish color and loads of tropical fruit, mineral, anise, and buttered aromas. This massive, medium- to full-bodied, dense wine displays layers of spice, creamy superripe pears, crème brûlée, and hints of butterscotch in its opulent flavor profile. Velvety-textured and broad, it is forward yet better balanced than originally perceived. Drink it between now–2012.

The ruby-colored 1997 Grands-Echézeaux offers red and black raspberry liqueur aromas. It is a medium- to full-bodied, oily-textured wine that possesses good power and density. Smoked bacon, sweet wax, and spices are found in the fat, plump, seductive offering. Drink it over the next 6–8 years. The blackberry, violet, and rose-scented 1997 Romanée-St.-Vivant is also ruby-colored. This is a medium- to full-bodied wine with outstanding concentration and density. Loads of fresh and lively red fruits are intermingled with spicy, smoky, grilled notes in its personality. It reveals a hint of dryness on the finish that prevented it from meriting a higher rating. Anticipated maturity: now–2007. The similarly colored 1997 Richebourg is substantially bigger and more flavorful. Its rose, violet, talcum powder, and crushed berry–scented nose leads to a boisterous, dense personality. Medium- to full-bodied and loaded with spices, freshly ground black pepper, and blackberries, this is a deeply ripe, expressive wine. Anticipated maturity: now–2009.

Dark in color, the aromatically tight 1997 La Tâche reveals Asian spices, pepper, cherries, and black currants. This is a velvety-textured, expansive, massively ripe wine boasting flavors reminiscent of licorice and blackberry jam. It has superb depth of fruit (particularly for this sometimes "simple" vintage), medium to full body, and admirable length to its supple finish. Anticipated maturity: now–2012. The 1997 Romanée-Conti reveals a saturated dark ruby color as well as a mouthwatering nose of leather, juniper berries, cherries, and spices. On the palate, it marvelously combines the powerful, ripe fruit characteristic of the vintage with magnificent delineation and elegance. This soy sauce, licorice, flower, and blackberry-flavored wine is dense and concentrated, yet lacelike and gloriously precise. As expected given its rarity, price, and reputation, it stands as one of the stars of the vintage. Anticipated maturity: now–2012+.

Notes of *Botrytis cinerea* (noble rot) are evident in the hedonistically appealing, bright gold-colored 1998 Montrachet's nose. Its honeyed spice and vanilla aromas are followed by a decadently sexy personality. This round, hyperrich wine is crammed with overripe fruits, touches of caramel, and French toast soaked in syrup. It is magnificently flavorful and pleasing yet does not have the capacity to gain in complexity with cellaring. Drink this spicy fruit bomb over the next 5–6 years.

"Since 1990 we've adopted a new philosophy at the Domaine concerning the Montrachet," said de Villaine, "We now believe in harvesting as late as possible and bottling as early as possible." The 1999 Montrachet reveals golden hues to its color and a nose of massive ripeness. Powerful spice scents are intermingled with tropical yellow fruits and anise. Medium- to full-bodied, it is fat, plump, oily-textured, and unbelievably rich. Its layers of spices and hyperripe fruits are sensually decadent and linger on the palate for a long while. This is a broad, massively dense Montrachet for drinking over the next 8–10 years.

For reds, "the 1999 vintage is the greatest we have had in a long time, better than 1990," said de Villaine. The Domaine de la Romanée-Conti averaged 32 h/h in 1999 and did not bleed out any juice. The estate sells to *négociants* the wines from its youngest grand cru vines and from all of its premier cru vineyards; wines sold under the DRC label are from parcels averaging between 45 and 55 years of age. The medium ruby-colored 1999 Echézeaux has a demure, dark fruit–scented nose. It bursts on the palate with lush layers of intensely sweet cherries, candied black raspberries, and spices. This lovely wine is forward, feminine, and satin-textured. It is medium- to full-bodied, highly expressive, and possesses prodigiously ripened tannin. Drink it over the next 10–12 years. The darker-colored 1999 Grands-Echézeaux has gorgeous talcum powder, perfume, and candied cherry aromas. This sumptuously sweet, yet elegant, medium-bodied wine is crammed with blackberries and sugarcoated cherries. Oak shows through in this wine's satiny finish. Drink it over the next 12 years.

The medium to dark ruby-colored 1999 Romanée-St.-Vivant has superripe black cherry and violet aromas. Medium-bodied and dense, it is austere, foursquare, and firm. This juicy red and black berry–flavored wine has a tannic oak-imbued finish. Anticipated maturity: 2003–2013. Magnificent, the 1999 Richebourg has a saturated dark ruby color. It explodes from the glass with loads of superripe dark fruits, including blackberries, cassis, plums, and black cherries. This dense, plush, and broad wine has prodigious depth to its roasted red and black fruit–flavored personality. A myriad of spices can be found in its chewy-textured, full-bodied, highly concentrated, powerful character. Its extraordinarily long finish is dominated by fruit, yet copious quantities of sweet and supple tannin can be discerned. Anticipated maturity: 2006–2018.

The medium to dark ruby-colored 1999 La Tâche has sweet, tangy raspberry, black currant, candied cherry, leather, and spice aromas. This medium- to full-bodied wine is harmonious, refined, and powerful. It is expansive, magnificently delineated, and feminine, particularly for La Tâche. Its flavor profile is crammed with an assortment of superripe red and black fruit laced with vanilla beans. It has loads of sweet tannin that can be detected in its admirable finish. Anticipated maturity: 2006–2020. The medium to dark ruby-colored 1999 Romanée-Conti is mind-boggling. It has a hugely expressive nose of superripe black cherries, candied plums, and violets. Full-bodied and possessing a magnificent breadth of sweet, penetrating fruits, this is an unbelievably complex wine. It coats the palate with its velvety sweet cherries, jammy blackberries, and fruit-soaked tannin. Perfectly balanced and seamless, this gem has a remarkably long finish. This is a wine of exemplary precision, de-lineation, and power with undescribable class and refinement. Anticipated maturity: 2006–2020. In 1999, the Domaine de la Romanée-Conti for the first time produced a Vosne-Romanée Premier Cru. This wine was made from a second harvest that took place a few days after the initial harvest in La Tâche. The wine is medium to dark ruby-colored and has a rose, violet, and red cherry–scented nose. Medium-bodied, lush, and expansive, it is fresh, filled with crunchy red and black berries, and has an impressively long, sweet, tannin-filled finish. Anticipated maturity: 2003–2010.

Other wine tasted: 1997 Echézeaux (89)

DOMAINE ROSSIGNOL (VOLNAY)

1999	Pommard Jarollières	D	90+
1997	Volnay Les Caillerets	D	91
1999	Volnay Chevrets	D	90
1999	Volnay Santenots	D	90+
1997	Volnay Santenots	D	91+

Note: This estate is known as Domaine Nicolas Rossignol and Domaine Rossignol-Jenniards in all markets except the United States.

This estate is run by Nicolas Rossignol, who has been responsible for the vinification at this estate for nine years. He and his father own or farm 16 hectares, interspersed between Pommard and Meursault. While Nicolas Rossignol handles the cellar work, his father is re-sponsible for the vineyards. Yields are moderate, 30–38 hectoliters per hectare, according to Rossignol. No defoliants are used in the vineyards, a green harvest (crop-thinning) is per-formed, and the Rossignols hoe the earth around their vines to control vegetation as well as to provide air to the soil.

In the winery, many of the new techniques being employed by Burgundy's younger gener-ation are used. Grapes are entirely destemmed, a cold maceration is employed, and during fermentation, Rossignol separates the juice from the solids, raises its temperature to 40°C, and then dumps the juice back onto the cap. Press wine is kept separate from the free-run juice, and for the bottlings crafted for the estate's U.S. importer, no fining or filtration is per-formed. (Wines meant for other markets are filtered using the Kieselguhr system.) Nicolas Rossignol loves to experiment. In his cellars, there were wines that had been fashioned using different techniques, and therefore, the results were vastly different from one wine to another, allowing importer Kacher the luxury of selecting wine styles that fit his taste. The *Wine Advo-cate*'s readers who reside in other countries should note that this means the wines available in their markets may vary widely in style (for example, the '97 Pommard Noizons was not destemmed and is rather hard whereas the wines selected by Kacher in 1997 were crafted in an opulent, lush style).

Crafted from 12-year-old vines, trained in such a way as to control their yields, the medium to dark ruby-colored 1997 Volnay Les Caillerets was harvested at a pH of 3.55. It of-fers an intensely sweet, blackberry and dark cherry–scented nose, as well as a refined, bacon and cassis-flavored character. It is a plump, velvety-textured, chewy wine with a long and supple, tannin-packed finish. This lip-smackingly good offering will make for outstanding drinking over the next 6 years. The medium to dark ruby-colored 1997 Volnay Santenots is from vines that averaged 30 years of age, in the lower sector of this vineyard. Its black cherry syrup aromas lead to a large, broad-shouldered, and firm personality, filled with red and black fruit flavors, as well as licorice and Asian spices. This medium- to full-bodied wine is powerful, concentrated, and saturates the palate. Delicious today, it has the potential to evolve through 2007. The medium to dark ruby-colored 1999 Volnay Chevrets was also tasted twice. It offers oak-infused dark fruit aromas and an outstanding density of sweet black cherry, blackberry, and licorice flavors. It is medium- to full-bodied, highly extracted, and loaded with copious quantities of ripe tannin. This wine, from vines averaging more than 40 years of age, is fresh, tangy, and powerful. Anticipated maturity: 2003–2010.

The medium to dark ruby-colored 1999 Volnay Santenots offers creamy red cherries and raspberries as well as spices in its aromatics. Medium-bodied, deep, and concentrated, it has an expressive red and black fruit–packed personality. Its long, satiny finish displays the influence of toasty new oak. Drink it over the next 8–9 years. The darker-colored 1999 Pommard Jarollières has an immensely appealing fresh, floral, cherry, blackberry, and spice-scented nose. This big, chewy, medium- to full-bodied wine is broad-shouldered and packed with loads of delicious candied cherries and blackberries. It is lively, highly expressive, concentrated, and should age well in the mid-term. Anticipated maturity: 2003–2010.

Other recommended wines: 1997 Pernand-Vergelesses (88–90), 1997 Volnay Chevret (89), 1999 Volnay Fremiets (88), 1999 Volnay Roncerets (89)

DOMAINE JOSEPH ROTY (GEVREY-CHAMBERTIN)

1999	Charmes-Chambertin Très Vieilles Vignes	EEE	(95–97)
1999	Gevrey-Chambertin Fonteney	EE	(89–91)
1999	Griotte-Chambertin	EEE	(95–98)
1999	Mazis-Chambertin	EEE	(92–94)

The medium to dark ruby-colored 1999 Gevrey-Chambertin Fonteney offers licorice and black cherry aromas. Medium- to full-bodied, concentrated, and powerful, this wine has a baked black fruit and toasted oak-flavored character. It is extremely well made and has a solid structure as well as a long, well-delineated finish. Anticipated maturity: 2004–2013.

The dark-colored and blackberry-scented 1999 Mazis-Chambertin has extraordinary concentration to its ample flavor profile. Stones, black fruits, and freshly laid road tar can be found in its muscular, backward personality. Full-bodied and deep, this is a masculine, somewhat rugged wine that will require patience. Anticipated maturity: 2008–2015+. The sublime, dark ruby-colored 1999 Griotte-Chambertin was aged in 80–90% new oak. Its black cherry– and blackberry-scented nose leads to a full-bodied personality that has magnificent breadth and concentration. This powerful wine coats the palate with layers of jammy blackberries, cassis, licorice, and smoked bacon. Anticipated maturity: 2008–2016.

Produced from extremely old vines, as its name suggests (65% of this parcel dates back to 1881), the 1999 Charmes-Chambertin Très Vieilles Vignes is dark ruby-colored. Bacon, jammy black cherries, and candied blackberries can be found in its aromatics. This huge, medium- to full-bodied wine is extraordinarily concentrated, powerful, and chewy-textured. Its black fruit, licorice, asphalt, and cherry flavors are extremely expressive and last throughout its unbelievably long, thick, and sweet finish. Drink this magnificent wine between 2007–2016+. Sadly, only 50 cases of the Griotte, 75 cases of the Mazis, and 225 cases of the Charmes were produced.

Other recommended wine: 1999 Gevrey-Chambertin Champs-Cheney (87–89)

DOMAINE EMMANUEL ROUGET (FLAGEY-ECHÉZEAUX)

1997	Echézeaux	EE	91+
1997	Vosne-Romanée Les Beauxmonts	EE	91+
1997	Vosne-Romanée Cros Parentoux	EEE	94

Emmanuel Rouget is one of those vignerons who nailed the 1997 vintage. He was able to maintain structure while having his wines express the extraordinary ripeness of this warm and fruit-packed year. Two of his wines, the Bourgogne and the Nuits-St.-Georges, will require drinking in the near term, yet his remaining offerings, including the "village" Vosne-Romanée, have the structure for some cellaring. Saturated ruby/purple-colored, the 1997 Vosne-Romanée Les Beauxmonts displays fresh aromas laced with spicy baked fruits. It is opulent, thick, rich, and sexy. Layers of cherry syrup, mocha, candied blackberries, and hoisin are found in its hedonistic, medium- to full-bodied personality, as well as throughout its immensely impressive finish. Drink this beauty over the next 6–7 years.

The medium to dark ruby-colored 1997 Echézeaux offers a nose packed with dark cherries and notes of grilled oak. This is a large, masculine, structured wine, crammed with blackberries and cassis. It is rich, sweet, complex, medium- to full-bodied, and has an admirably persistent finish. Anticipated maturity: now–2009. Rouget's 1997 Vosne-Romanée Cros Parentoux is an awesome wine. Medium to dark ruby-colored, it exhibits superb aromas of spices, hints of oak, and powerful, fresh red fruit scents. Extremely well balanced, this medium- to full-bodied offering is thick, broad, and well extracted. Moreover, it exhibits a flavor profile loaded with chocolate-covered cherries, red fruit syrups, and copious quantities of vanilla-infused oak that linger through its impressively long finish. This is a wine that combines power with elegance. It will deliver pleasure early yet evolve magnificently with cellaring. Anticipated maturity: now–2008.

Other recommended wine: 1997 Nuits-St.-Georges (89)

DOMAINE GUY ROULOT (MEURSAULT)

2000	Meursault Bouchères	EE	(90–91)
1999	Meursault Bouchères	EE	(89–91)
2000	Meursault Charmes	EE	(91–93)
1999	Meursault Charmes	EE	(89–91)
1997	Meursault Charmes	EE	(89–92)
2000	Meursault Perrières	EE	(91–93)
1997	Meursault Perrières	EE	(92–94)
1997	Meursault Les Tessons	E	(89–90+)
2000	Meursault Les Tillets	D	(89–91)
1997	Meursault Les Tillets	D	(89–90+)

I enormously enjoy the small amount of time I spend with Jean-Marc Roulot each year. In addition to his many other personal attributes, he is also bluntly honest. Virtually every vigneron in Burgundy assured me that the 1997 harvest was almost as sanitary as 1996, but Roulot informed me that he had sorted out 10–15% of his yields due to rot. It speaks volumes about this man's honesty that he was the only Burgundian I spoke with that was so forthcoming with information. Roulot said he was "pleasantly surprised" by 1997. His early concerns about the vintage's low-acid profile and the relatively rapid alcoholic fermentations were tempered by the fact that the malolactic fermentations did not affect the wines' balance and structure.

Produced from a vineyard that performed admirably well in 1997, the Meursault Les Tillets has a pure, crystalline nose of steel, minerals, and anise. This elegant offering reveals slightly toasted white fruits, flowers, and stones. It is stylish, *aérien* (ethereal), and possesses a lacelike yet flavorful medium-bodied personality. Anticipated maturity: 2000–2006. Equally impressive, the 1997 Meursault Les Tessons is stylistically different. While the Tillets will appeal to those seeking refinement, the Tessons is for those who crave hedonistic wines. The Tessons offers thick aromas of sweet yellow and white fruits, as well as a flavor profile verging on *sur-maturité*. Its medium body is crammed with spiced pears, peaches, and hints of chalk. This is Roulot's most opulent 1997 yet is not lacking in freshness, balance, or focus. Drink it over the next 4–5 years. Produced from 65-year-old vines in the lower part of the vineyard (a "bad placing," says Roulot), the 1997 Meursault Charmes displays apples, pears, acacia blossoms, and limes to the nose. It is silky-textured, medium- to full-bodied, thick, and imbued with chocolate, lemon, and oak flavors. This impressive wine possesses loads of well-ripened fruit, and a long, pure finish. Anticipated maturity: now–2006. Roulot owns a tiny parcel (26 ares, equal to 0.64 acres) of Meursault Perrières, from which he fashioned a stunning 1997. Unlike his marvelous 1996, which will require at least five years of cellaring to become approachable, the 1997—though ageworthy—will be delicious relatively young. It exhibits a fresh, steely nose made up of toasty minerals as well as a fully focused, highly delineated character. This medium- to full-bodied, pure, bright, and magnificently refined wine has powerful gravel, stone, and citrus flavors that linger through its long finish. It combines 1997's telltale richness with gorgeous balance, a rare combination in this vintage. Anticipated maturity: now–2008.

Roulot sees 1999 as a "hypothetical blend of 1982 and 1992, I really like this vintage as it is extremely healthy and pleasing to the drinker." The 1999 Meursault Charmes offers ripe pear and white peach aromas. Medium- to full-bodied, ripe, dense, and ample, it is a plump, rich, fat wine but also refined and elegant. Flowers, white and yellow fruits, as well as hints of oak can be found throughout its chewy-textured character and its long, corpulent finish. Anticipated maturity: now–2009. The 1999 Meursault Bouchères has a reticent lemon- and mineral-scented nose. Light- to medium-bodied, gorgeously elegant, and lacelike, this is a detailed, superbly structured wine. Minerals, flowers, and hints of apples can be found in its personality, as well as in its pure, crystalline finish. Anticipated maturity: now–2009.

Roulot is one of the few Burgundians who did not need to use the PLC's (Plafond Limite de Classement, the percentages by which growers can surpass the pre-established maximum allowable yields) in 2000 because the storm of September 12 brought hail to his Meursault *villages* parcels. Roulot believes that 2000 will be a better vintage than 1999 for Meursault's premiers crus, yet not as good for *villages* wines as they lost some of their acidity and maturity in that storm. His sense is that the 2000s are comparable to the 1997s, but slightly better. "These are easy to drink wines with fresh, flavorful characters."

Medium-bodied, the 2000 Meursault Les Tillets has outstanding depth to its ripe, dense, and vinous personality. Liquid minerals and pears can be found in this feminine, seamless wine's flavor profile. Anticipated maturity: now–2010. The outstanding 2000 Meursault Charmes explodes from the glass with poached pear, spiced apple, and mineral aromas. Powerful, broad, and dense, this is a highly expressive wine. Loads of white fruits, assorted spices, and hints of gravel can be discerned in this harmonious, fruit-forward offering. Anticipated maturity: 2003–2012. The gorgeous aromatics of the 2000 Meursault Bouchères exhibit refined floral, spice, and mineral scents. This elegant chalk, stone, and pear-flavored wine is more demure than the Charmes, but has an added note of finesse. It is concentrated, delineated, and reveals beautiful floral touches in its long, soft finish. Mineral and white flowers make up the nose of the outstanding 2000 Meursault Perrières. This wine explodes on the palate with gorgeous breadth of spicy minerals, anise, quinine, quartz, and pears. It is deep and possesses outstanding grip as well as a lush, satin-textured character. Anticipated maturity: 2003–2012.

Other recommended wines: 1998 Meursault Charmes (88), 2000 Meursault Les Luchets (87–89), 2000 Meursault Meix Chavaux (88–90), 1999 Meursault Perrières (88–89), 1995 Meursault Les Tessons (89), 1999 Meursault Les Tessons (88–89+), 2000 Meursault Les Tessons (88–90), 1999 Meursault Les Tillets (88–90), 2000 Meursault Vireuils (88–89)

DOMAINE GEORGES ET CHRISTOPHE ROUMIER
(CHAMBOLLE-MUSIGNY)

1999	Bonnes Mares	EE	(92–94)
1998	Bonnes Mares	EE	90

1997	Bonnes Mares	EE	93+
1999	Chambolle-Musigny Les Amoureuses	EE	(92–94)
1997	Chambolle-Musigny Les Amoureuses	E	92
1997	Charmes-Chambertin	EE	90
1997	Corton-Charlemagne	EE	93
1999	Musigny	EEE	(90–92)
1998	Musigny	EEE	91
1997	Musigny	EEE	92
1997	Ruchottes-Chambertin	EE	92+

The thoughtful, gracious, and intelligent Christophe Roumier bottled all his 1997s early, because "I didn't want these wines affected any more than they already had been by my oak barrels." He finds this to be "a friendly vintage, one that is harmonious, that I will want to drink with people I like. It will last from the premier cru level on up. It reminds me of the 1985s, even though some compare it to 1962." Roumier's 1997s are huge successes for the vintage. However, what separates them from the greatest wines crafted at this famed address is that they are less complex and structured than the estate's past glories.

The medium to dark ruby-colored 1997 Chambolle-Musigny Les Amoureuses reveals a floral nose of violets, black cherries, and spices. It is broad, sweet, easygoing, soft, sensual, and medium- to full-bodied. On the palate, it is expansive, extremely expressive, refined, and gracious. Red and black fruits, flowers, good structure, and a delightfully long finish are found in this harmonious offering. Drink it over the next 7–8 years. The similarly colored 1997 Charmes-Chambertin offers aromas and flavors of black fruit, spice, and fresh herbs. It is firmer and more structured than the Amoureuses. Medium- to full-bodied, possessing outstanding breadth and concentration, it is a wine of excellent balance and grit. Anticipated maturity: now–2005. The slightly darker-colored 1997 Ruchottes-Chambertin is, as Roumier describes it, a "passionate" wine. Spicy red cherries, dense layers of currants, and hints of oak can be discerned in its profound aromatics. It is a sensual, satin-textured, feminine, deep, and marvelously structured, medium- to full-bodied offering. Stony black fruits and red cherries can be found throughout its seductive personality and persistent, harmonious finish. Drink this beauty over the next 7 years.

I preferred Roumier's 1997 Bonnes Mares to his outstanding yet less sensual and intense Musigny, generally this estate's flagship wine. The Bonnes Mares is medium to dark ruby-colored, and offers beguiling aromas of red and black fruits, stones, and earth. It explodes on the palate with superexpressive candied red cherries, as well as licorice and road tar flavors. This rich, dense, gorgeously structured, powerful, and expansive wine is masculine and broad-shouldered yet opulent and hedonistic. Medium- to full-bodied, complex, and harmonious, it should be at its peak of drinkability between now–2010. The ruby-colored 1997 Musigny has an enthralling nose of fresh herbs, flowers, and black cherries. On the palate, it is expressive, yet not as boisterous as the Bonnes Mares. Tobacco, cedar, blackberries, and currants are found in this refined, lacelike, medium-bodied offering. While it pales in comparison to the blockbusters fashioned at this estate in 1995 and 1996, it remains a beautifully elegant, detail-oriented, and complex wine. Drink it over the next 8–10 years.

The 1997 Corton-Charlemagne is a superb wine, harnessing the vintage's superripe qualities while maintaining outstanding freshness, focus, and harmony. Aromatically, it reveals candied white and yellow fruits, grilled toast, and vanilla. This dense, medium- to full-bodied, broad, powerful, mouth-filling wine is crammed with tropical fruits, grilled oak, and hints of minerals. Its impressively long and well-delineated finish exhibits luscious spice cake flavors for additional complexity. Anticipated maturity: now–2009.

The ruby-colored 1998 Chambolle-Musigny has an herbal, spice, and cedar-scented nose. Medium-bodied and chewy-textured, it is an excellent example for those who wish to know what a mature Burgundy tastes like. Hints of cherries can be found among its exotic wood and sweet decaying leaf flavors. This is not a wine to cellar, as it is evolving quickly, yet it is delicious and should be consumed over the next year or two. The chocolate- and earth-scented, medium ruby-colored 1998 Bonnes Mares has a medium-bodied, rich personality. Roasted coffee and baked cherries can be found in its ample, warm, and embracing character. It possesses loads of tannin, yet it is encased in fruit. Additionally, this wine has an exceptionally long and focused finish. Anticipated maturity: now–2007. The violet- and cherry-scented 1998 Musigny is medium ruby-colored. This is a concentrated wine with outstanding depth of fruit. Loads of flowers, cherries, and brambleberries can be found in its precise, lively personality. I do not have faith that its fruit will sustain its dominance of the tannin for long, so would recommend drinking it over the next 4–5 years.

With the exception of his Chambolle-Musigny (52 hectoliters) and Morey-St.-Denis Clos de la Bussière (53 hectoliters), Roumier's yields in 1999 were below 40 h/h due to his assiduous pruning and two green harvests. The outstanding 1999 Chambolle-Musigny Les Amoureuses has a medium to dark ruby color and an intense candied raspberry and sweet cherry–scented nose. Medium- to full-bodied and ample, this wine has impressive concentration and structure. It is loaded with blackberries, cherries, blueberries, and violets. The flavors last throughout its admirably, long, ripe tannin-filled finish. Anticipated maturity: 2004–2012. The medium to dark ruby-colored 1999 Bonnes Mares has a rose- and black cherry–scented nose. Medium- to full-bodied, rich, broad, and expansive, this is a firm, muscular, masculine wine. Its flavor profile, composed of blackberries, assorted flowers, jammy blueberries, and candied cherries, is silky-textured and leads to an admirably long, black pepper–filled finish. Anticipated maturity: 2004–2014. The similarly-colored 1999 Musigny reveals excellent aromatic depth to its blackberry and smoked bacon scents. Medium-bodied and foursquare, this is a firm wine packed with candied cherries and expansive dark fruit flavors. It is broad, fresh, and has an impressively long finish. Anticipated maturity: 2005–2012.

Other recommended wines: 1997 Chambolle-Musigny (88), 1999 Chambolle-Musigny (87–89), 1997 Chambolle-Musigny Les Cras (88+), 1999 Chambolle-Musigny Les Cras (87–89), 1999 Charmes-Chambertin (87–89), 1997 Morey-St.-Denis Clos de la Bussière (88+), 1999 Ruchottes-Chambertin (88–90)

DOMAINE ARMAND ROUSSEAU (GEVREY-CHAMBERTIN)

1999	Chambertin	EEE	(90–93+)
1997	Chambertin	EEE	(91–93+)
1999	Chambertin Clos de Bèze	EEE	(92–95)
1997	Chambertin Clos de Bèze	EEE	(91–94)
1999	Gevrey-Chambertin Clos St.-Jacques	EEE	(90–92)
1997	Gevrey-Chambertin Clos St.-Jacques	EE	(90–93)
1997	Ruchottes-Chambertin Clos des Ruchottes	EE	(89–92)

"There was a little rot in 1997, and those that say there wasn't any are liars," said the unabashedly forthright Charles Rousseau. "It is a good vintage but not a great one like 1995 or 1996. In 1997 and 1998 we have high natural potential alcohol at harvest but low acidity that required adjusting. However, that being said, the wines from those two vintages only needed minimal chaptalization." Rousseau's favorite vintages of the 1990s are, in order, 1995, 1993, 1990, 1999, 1991, 1992, 1998, 1997, and 1994. He is the only vigneron I spoke with who did not place 1990 in the top slot.

The ruby-colored 1997 Ruchottes-Chambertin Clos des Ruchottes displays crushed wild berry aromas and an extremely expressive, feminine, and elegant personality. It is lush, intensely flavorful, densely packed with red cherries, and possesses a long, pure, and satiny finish. Drink it over the next 7 years. The similarly colored 1997 Gevrey-Chambertin Clos St.-Jacques has a floral, black/red berry–scented nose. This silky-textured, medium- to full-bodied, broad, complex, and expansive offering is flavored with jammy berry fruit. Its extremely long finish blossoms with additional layers of fruit in the oft-mentioned but rarely encountered "peacock's tail" effect. Anticipated maturity: now–2008.

The medium to dark ruby-colored 1997 Chambertin Clos de Bèze displays ethereal black fruit aromas. It has jammy fig, tar, licorice, grilled stones, bacon, earth, and spicy oak flavors in its medium- to full-bodied character. This hedonistic, muscular, well-delineated, and intricate wine should be consumed over the next 10 years. Rousseau's 1997 Chambertin is the most powerful, yet the Clos de Bèze is more opulent and the Clos St.-Jacques has a longer finish. This Chambertin's dark berry scents lead to a tar, cinnamon, briar, blackberry, black raspberry, and assorted dried fruit–flavored personality. It is thick, chewy, medium- to full-bodied, and will certainly be the longest-lived 1997 from this property. Anticipated maturity: now–2010+.

Rousseau showed me photographs of his estate's 1999 green harvests, in which he can be seen ankle-deep in lime-colored clusters of grapes. However, he pointed out, "The best time to green harvest is in the early stage of *veraison* [when the grapes start to change color], yet we in France cannot do that because that's when all the workers take vacation. We Burgundians do it too early and allow the vines to compensate by making the clusters we leave get bigger than they should be." Rousseau's yields in 1999 ranged from 50 hectoliters per hectare for his Gevrey-Chambertin, to 45 hectoliters per hectare for the Ruchottes-, Charmes-, and Mazis-Chambertins, 42 for the Gevrey-Chambertin Clos St.-Jacques, 39.5 for the Chambertin Clos de Bèze, and 36.5 hectoliters for the Chambertin. He did not bleed any tanks, yet did remove 10% of the juice's water on two wines using reverse osmosis.

When I arrived at the estate to taste the 1999s, Rousseau's first words to me were, "You will not believe me, but my daughter and I were served bottles of my domaine's 1959s. They were magnificent! I drank all of mine many years ago, in the first years after the vintage. They had no capacity to age since they lacked tannin and acidity. Yet, these bottles were stunning! How do you explain that?" When I explained that Pinot Noir ages on concentrated fruit rather than acidity and tannin, Rousseau wouldn't believe me, citing his opinion that the 1997s should be drunk quickly. It seems that the lesson of his 1959s was lost.

The dark ruby-colored 1999 Gevrey-Chambertin Clos St.-Jacques has exuberant sweet blackberry fruit aromas. This medium- to full-bodied wine has amplitude to its mouth-coating black cherry, oak, and cassis flavors. It is velvety-textured, lively, and boisterous. Drink it over the next 10–11 years. The medium to dark ruby-colored 1999 Chambertin Clos de Bèze has a beguiling perfume of red cherry and violet. It is medium- to full-bodied, elegant, and unctuously textured. This juicy, sweet red cherry, currant, and raspberry-flavored wine has impeccably ripened tannins detectable in its exceptionally long and delineated finish. Anticipated maturity: 2004–2012. Produced from 45-year-old vines, the 1999 Chambertin is medium to dark ruby-colored. It has superripe talcum and blackberry aromas that lead to a medium- to full-bodied wine of outstanding depth. Loads of oak-laced black fruits can be found throughout its zesty, firm character. Anticipated maturity: 2004–2012.

Other recommended wines: 1999 Charmes-Chambertin (87–89), 1997 Clos de la Roche (87–89), 1999 Clos de la Roche (87–89), 1997 Mazis-Chambertin (87–89), 1999 Mazis-Chambertin (88–90), 1999 Ruchottes-Chambertin Clos des Ruchottes (88–90+)

DOMAINE/MAISON ETIENNE SAUZET (PULIGNY-MONTRACHET)

2000	Bâtard-Montrachet	EEE	(93–94)
1999	Bâtard-Montrachet	EEE	93
1998	Bâtard-Montrachet	EEE	92
2000	Bienvenue-Bâtard-Montrachet	EEE	(91–92)
1999	Bienvenue-Bâtard-Montrachet	EEE	92
1998	Bienvenue-Bâtard-Montrachet	EEE	92
2000	Chevalier-Montrachet	EEE	(92–93)

1999 Chevalier-Montrachet	EEE	92+
1998 Chevalier-Montrachet	EEE	92+
2000 Montrachet	EEE	(93–94)
1999 Montrachet	EEE	93+
1998 Montrachet	EEE	94
2000 Puligny-Montrachet Les Champs-Canet	EE	(89–91)
1999 Puligny-Montrachet Les Champs-Canet	EE	92
2000 Puligny-Montrachet Les Combettes	EEE	(92–94)
1999 Puligny-Montrachet Les Combettes	EEE	94
1998 Puligny-Montrachet Les Combettes	EEE	90
1999 Puligny-Montrachet Les Folatières	EEE	90
1999 Puligny-Montrachet Hameau de Blagny	EEE	91
2000 Puligny-Montrachet Les Referts	EE	90

"In 1998, we were at war with the weather until harvest," said Etienne Sauzet's director and wine-maker, the intelligent Gérard Boudot. In order to provide his wines with harmony, Boudot felt compelled to block the malolactic fermentations using sulphur. The majority of his 1998s—in fact, all of those recommended in this report—had their malolactic fermentations interrupted with approximately 20% malic acid remaining. As the scores suggest, Boudot's 1998s are some of the most successful wines made in the vintage.

The apple- and toast-scented 1998 Puligny-Montrachet Les Combettes is a broad, rich, deep, medium- to full-bodied wine. This beautifully crafted mineral- and apple-flavored effort is concentrated, harmonious, and possesses an extremely long, subtly oaky finish. Anticipated maturity: now–2010. Produced from 64-year-old vines, Sauzet's 1998 Bienvenue-Bâtard-Montrachet yielded 30 hectoliters per hectare (three barrels, or 75 cases). French toast, apricots, and spices can be discerned in its mouthwatering aromatics. This medium- to full-bodied, thick, rich, powerful, focused wine is crammed with expressive toasted mineral flavors. It is superb to drink today, and should easily hold for 6–7 years.

The 1998 Chevalier-Montrachet exhibits acacia blossom and spice aromas. Superbly focused, elegant, and medium-bodied, it is a graceful, feminine wine. Hazelnuts, almonds, minerals, and assorted white flowers can be found in its delicate yet extroverted personality. Readers may be interested to learn that Gérard Boudot said he "adored" this wine, and feels it is one of the classiest he has ever produced. Anticipated maturity: now–2009.

This estate makes only 10 barrels, or 250 cases, of Bâtard-Montrachet. The 1998 reveals tropical fruit aromas, intermingled with hints of English toffee. Rich, plum-colored, and thick, this medium- to full-bodied, pear, apple, vanilla, and buttered toast–flavored wine is concentrated, fresh, and intense. Drink this beauty over the next 10 years.

Sauzet's 1998 Montrachet is a superb wine. Lovely anise, almond, hazelnut, and mineral aromas lead to a medium- to full-bodied, compelling character. This supple, soft, extremely flavorful, and harmonious wine is filled with layers and layers of spiced pears, candied apples, minerals, and toast. It is stunning to find such a profound wine made in what can best be described as a difficult vintage. Anticipated maturity: 2003–2012.

Boudot feels that 1999 can best be compared to 1992, 1985, 1982, 1979, and 1973. "Yes, the yields were huge," he said, "but the harvest was magnificently healthy and the grapes had good natural acidity. These were easy wines to produce, with no rot." Boudot explained to me that he had stirred the lees for 9½ months, "with perfect lees what else would you do?" When asked where he would place 1999 in a line-up of his favorite vintages of the nineties, Boudot placed it second, right after 1992. "After that? 1990, 1996, a tie between 1997 and 1993, then 1995, 1998, 1994, and my least favorite, 1991."

Produced from 50-year-old vines, the 1999 Puligny-Montrachet Hameau de Blagny (its entire production is sold in the U.S.) has delightful acacia blossom, orange, pineapple, and spice aromas. Medium-bodied, supple, sexy, and lush, it is dense, fat, and velvety-textured. Minerals, pears, and apples can be found in its lively yet opulent character. Anticipated maturity: now–2008. Loads of white flowers are noticeable in the aromatics of the 1999 Puligny-Montrachet Les Folatières. Medium-bodied, deep, detailed, and elegant, this pure, gravel, stone, mineral, and ripe pear–flavored wine has excellent grip, as well as an admirably long, fleshed-out finish. Anticipated maturity: now–2009. From 40-year-old vines, the 1999 Puligny-Montrachet Les Champs-Canet offers spicy floral and anise aromas. This gorgeously balanced wine has ample richness, breadth, and concentration. It has a forward personality, packed with toasted stones, acacia blossoms, and spices, yet has the depth and structure for aging. Its finish is pure as well as intensely long and flavorful. Anticipated maturity: now–2010.

Gérard Boudot believes his outstanding 1999 Puligny-Montrachet Les Combettes is the finest wine he has produced from this vineyard since 1992. Produced from over 50-year-old vines, it sports a rich, spice-laden nose as well as a hugely-concentrated, medium- to full-bodied character. This profound wine has great richness, superb balance, and loads of depth to its stone, liquid mineral, and spice-flavored core. One of the finest 1999 white Burgundies, it will benefit from 3–4 years of cellaring and will be exceptional through 2014.

There are only 750 bottles of the 1999 Bienvenue-Bâtard-Montrachet (64-year-old vines). It has an aromatically rich nose filled with spices and poached pears. On the palate, this medium- to full-bodied wine displays stones, minerals, and candied apples in its pure, focused, balanced personality. Anticipated maturity: now–2012. The aromatics of the 1999 Chevalier-Montrachet consist of limestone, minerals, talcum powder, and flowers. This deep wine is beautifully refined, revealing layers of gravel, stones, and spice flavors in its personality. It is medium-bodied, rich, and it possesses a precise, pure, and extensive finish. Anticipated maturity: now–2012.

Domaine Etienne Sauzet's 1999 Bâtard-Montrachet has a fabulous nose of candied white fruits, juniper berries, poached pears, and sweet, sexy spices. It is medium- to full-bodied, broad-shouldered, and reveals great concentration in its lush, voluptuous personality. This wine is densely packed with fruits, spices, perfume, and talcumlike flavors that linger throughout its long finish. Drink it over the next 10–12 years. There are 175 cases of Sauzet's mineral, flower, and perfume-scented 1999 Montrachet. It is fresh, with outstanding concentration, power, and refinement. This liquid mineral, assorted white flower, and apple-flavored wine has impressive grip as well as a lovely long finish. Anticipated maturity: now–2012.

According to Gérard Boudot, "I like 2000 a great deal. It is not very different from 1999 at this stage in the game, and I don't believe that there will be much to differentiate them in two or three years, whether in their balance or their aromas." He informed me that his malolactic fermentations were rather rapid in 2000, whereas many other producers stated the contrary. While Boudot's yields were "slightly lower" in his premier and grand cru vineyards, on average, his natural potential alcohols were 0.2% below those attained in 1999.

Produced from vines averaging over 35 years of age, the earth-scented 2000 Puligny-Montrachet Les Referts is an opulent, plump, medium-bodied wine. Anise, pears, and minerals can be found in this deep, sexy offering's character. Anticipated maturity: now–2008.

Loads of white fruits can be discerned in the aromatics of the 2000 Puligny-Montrachet Les Champs-Canet. This is a pretty wine, with highly expressive apple and pear flavors in its deep, bright personality. Anticipated maturity: now–2011. The 2000 Puligny-Montrachet Les Combettes, from some of the estate's oldest vines, was vinified and aged in 40% new oak barrels. It explodes from the glass with sweet minerals and hints of buttered toast. Dense and deep, this is a medium- to full-bodied wine with an ample, white fruit–filled personality and a long, soft finish. It is concentrated, intense, and powerful, yet retains the elegance that has made this village world-renowned. Anticipated maturity: 2004–2014.

Year in and year out, Etienne Sauzet produces two and a half barrels of Bienvenue-Bâtard-Montrachet. The 2000 sports fresh mineral and floral aromas, a medium body, and a concentrated, profound character. It is intense, coating the palate with minerals, and displays loads of delineation and purity. Anticipated maturity: 2003–2012. The candied apple– and spice-scented 2000 Bâtard-Montrachet is immensely aromatic. Medium- to full-bodied, rich, and ample, this velvety-textured wine is plush, reveals untold quantities of peaches and pears, and possesses a layered, fruit-filled finish. It is an outstanding Bâtard with fresh, powerful character. Anticipated maturity: 2003–2013.

The mineral- and toasted pear–scented 2000 Chevalier-Montrachet is a silky-textured, dense, medium-bodied wine. Immensely elegant and profound, this concentrated, white fruit and gravel-flavored offering has the requisite depth for extended cellaring, and also the forward fruit required for providing near-term enjoyment. Drink it over the next 12–14 years. Harvested at 13.4% natural potential alcohol, the earth, stone, mineral, pear, apple, and candied lime–scented 2000 Montrachet is a viscous, medium- to full-bodied wine. Hugely concentrated and oily-textured, this hugely spicy, white fruit–dominated offering is profound, exquisitely balanced, and persistent. Anticipated maturity: 2004–2015.

Other recommended wines and past glories: 1986 Bâtard-Montrachet (96), 2000 Chassagne-Montrachet (88), 1999 Puligny-Montrachet (88), 2000 Puligny-Montrachet (88), 2000 Puligny-Montrachet Les Folatières (89), 1999 Puligny-Montrachet La Garenne (89), 2000 Puligny-Montrachet La Garenne (88+), 1998 Puligny-Montrachet Les Perrières (89), 1999 Puligny-Montrachet Les Perrières (89), 2000 Puligny-Montrachet Les Perrières (89), 1999 Puligny-Montrachet Les Referts (89)

DOMAINE FRANCINE ET OLIVIER SAVARY (MALIGNY-CHABLIS)

2000 Chablis Sélection Vieilles Vignes	D	90

The 2000 Chablis Sélection Vieilles Vignes has a demure, mineral-dominated nose. This medium-bodied wine is ample, plump, and concentrated. Loads of clean, fresh white fruits and minerals can be found in its bright, plump character as well as throughout its impressively long, supple finish. Drink it over the next 5 years.

Other recommended wines: 1997 Chablis (88), 2000 Chablis Fourchaume (88)

DOMAINE CHRISTIAN SERAFIN (GEVREY-CHAMBERTIN)

1999 Chambolle-Musigny Les Baudes	E	90
1997 Chambolle-Musigny Les Baudes	E	(88–91)
1999 Charmes-Chambertin	EE	97+
1997 Charmes-Chambertin	EE	(91–93)
1999 Gevrey-Chambertin Les Cazetiers	E	(90–92+)
1997 Gevrey-Chambertin Les Cazetiers	E	(90–92)
1999 Gevrey-Chambertin Le Fonteny	E	(91–93)
1997 Gevrey-Chambertin Le Fonteny	E	(89–91)
1999 Gevrey-Chambertin Vieilles Vignes	E	91
1999 Morey-St.-Denis Les Millandes	E	90
1997 Morey-St.-Denis Les Millandes	E	(88–91)

The highly talented and straight-shooting Christian Serafin described 1997 as a modern-day 1989. "They are delicious yet will last ten years, no more." He went on to say that the lack of rain, combined with excessive heat lead to an unbalanced vintage. Saturated ruby-colored, the 1997 Gevrey-Chambertin Le Fonteny reveals sweet red currant and cherry aromas. It is medium-bodied, elegant, yet hugely fruit wine packed with red and black cherries as well as Asian spices. Anticipated maturity: now–2005. The 1997 Gevrey-Chambertin Les Cazetiers is medium to dark ruby-colored, and has a demure but exceedingly ripe nose. On the palate, black fruits, licorice, and spicy oak can be found in this intense, plump, medium- to full-bodied, and thickly textured wine. It is chewy, immensely flavorful, and offers a long, supple finish. Anticipated maturity: now–2006.

Serafin has recently added two new wines to his line-up. He purchased parcels of premiers crus from Morey-St.-Denis and Chambolle-Musigny from Domaine Pierre Amiot. In the first two vintages since the acquisition, 1996 and 1997, the viticulture and vinification were performed by Amiot. Starting with the 1998s the transfer will be complete and Serafin will have total control over the vines and the resulting wines. Produced from 22-year-old vines, the medium to dark ruby-colored 1997 Chambolle-Musigny Les Baudes displays aromas and flavors reminiscent of black raspberries, cherries, cookie dough, and blackberries. It is an easygoing, feminine, soft, supple, medium-bodied wine with an appealingly long finish. Drink it over the next 6 years. The similarly colored 1997 Morey-St.-Denis Les Millandes (29-year-old vines) exhibits sweet candied fruit scents intermingled with rosemary and thyme. It is medium-bodied, well-ripened, and refined. It is not as lush or persistent as the Baudes but offers beautiful delineation as well as a delightfully spicy character. Anticipated maturity: now–2005.

Serafin's fabulous, dark ruby-colored 1997 Charmes-Chambertin has sweet candied cherries, Asian spices, and cookie dough aromas. The wine explodes on the palate, with super-sweet red and black fruit flavors, interspersed with fresh herbs, spices, and hints of cinnamon candies. It is an extremely expressive wine, though not as powerful as some of Serafin's other 1997s. However, it regales the palate with its *sur-maturité* fruit, as well as its complexity and refinement. Drink this beauty over the next 8 years.

The medium to dark ruby-colored 1999 Gevrey-Chambertin Vieilles Vignes reveals sweet black cherry aromas. This is a medium-bodied, plush, dark fruit–filled wine. It is rich, beautifully ripe, plump, immensely appealing, and possibly the finest *"village"* Gevreys I have tasted. Drink it over the next 5–6 years. The outstanding medium to dark ruby-colored 1999 Gevrey-Chambertin Le Fonteny has a violet- and sweet black currant–scented nose. Medium- to full-bodied and concentrated, this wine is loaded with blueberries, sweet cherries, and candied raspberries. It is harmonious, seamless, supple, immensely elegant, yet powerful and full-flavored. Its exceptionally long, focused finish reveals copious quantities of exquisitely ripened tannin and hints of vanilla-infused oak. Drink it between 2004–2011. The muscular, broad-shouldered 1999 Gevrey-Chambertin Les Cazetiers is medium to dark ruby-colored. It offers black cherry and Asian spice aromas that lead to its ample, fat, roasted oak, and dark berry–flavored character. It is firm yet has the density and depth of fruit to easily cover its tannin. Anticipated maturity: 2005–2012.

The plum- and candied grape–scented 1999 Chambolle-Musigny Les Baudes has a powerful blackberry- and spice-flavored character. It is medium-bodied, foursquare, and firm. This wine has loads of fruit, yet is structured and austere. Drink it between 2005–2010. The same can be said about the slightly darker-colored 1999 Morey-St.-Denis Les Millandes. It bursts from the glass with plummy dark fruit aromas, yet has a firmly structured, masculine, foursquare personality. Freshly laid road tar, blackberries, and currants can be found in this powerful wine, yet its aggressive tannin restrains the wine's copious fruit. It is excellent, and will provide delicious drinking between 2005–2009.

The spectacular dark ruby-colored 1999 Charmes-Chambertin, from 40 hectoliters per hectare yields, displays mouthwatering violet and sweet berry aromas. This rich, medium- to full-bodied wine is loaded with candied cherries, blueberries, Asian spices, and sugarcoated blackberries. It has a beguiling, sweet, supple, and extraordinarily long finish that reveals copious quantities of fruit and prodigiously ripe tannin. This gem should be at its peak of maturity between 2005–2012+. Kudos to Christian Serafin for his spectacular 1999s!

Other recommended wines: 1997 Gevrey-Chambertin Les Corbeaux (87–89), 1999 Gevrey-Chambertin Les Corbeaux (88–90), 1997 Gevrey-Chambertin Vieilles Vignes (87–89)

DOMAINE DU CLOS DE TART (MOREY-ST.-DENIS)

1999 Clos de Tart	EEE	(93–95)

Sylvain Pithiot, who is responsible (with his father-in-law, Pierre Poupon) for the exceptional topographical maps of Burgundy's vineyards, is also the director and wine-maker at this fine estate. He characterizes 1999 as a "dream year, one I'd have to place along with 1990 and 1996." He went on to explain that the estate's philosophy in recent years has been to have five bunches per vine, which generally translates to 30 h/h. Yet, in 1999, "the weather was so extraordinary, we left six bunches, which resulted in 42 hectoliter per hectare yields. In 2000, we returned to our five bunch per vine practice and harvested 31 hectoliters per hectare." The 1999 Clos de Tart is certainly outstanding and potentially exceptional. It displays a gorgeous nose of rich plums, sweet black cherries, candied blueberries, and loads of spices. Medium- to full-bodied and opulent, this is a lush, deep, and fresh wine. Its velvety-textured flavor profile is crammed with blueberries, red cherries, and blackberries that seem to burst in the mouth, revealing their sweet, refreshing juices, in a way not dissimilar to the finest 1996s. It also displays complex nuances of spices, oak, and hints of orange zest. This marvelous wine should be at its peak of maturity between 2005–2012.

MAISON ERIC TEXIER (CHARNAY)

1999 Noble Rot "Botrytis" Sélection de Grains Nobles	D/375ml	94

Though every Tom, Dick, Pierre, and Marcel make late-harvest sweet Chardonnays, only a handful are outstanding (among them the Mâcon's Jean Thevenet and Austria's Alois Kracher). This being said, Eric Texier has fashioned a stunning 1999 Noble Rot "Botrytis" Sélection de Grains Nobles. Only 900 half bottles of this amber-colored beauty were fashioned. Caramel, sweet herbal teas, spices, and candle wax can be discerned in its intense aromatics. Medium- to full-bodied, huge, and candied, this wine butters the palate with jellied mandarin oranges, raspberries, and spices. It is lush, opulent, highly expressive, fresh, and exquisitely balanced. Drink this gorgeous wine over the next 12–15 years.

Other recommended wine: 1999 Mâcon-Bussières Vieilles Vignes (89)

DOMAINE THIBERT PÈRE ET FILS (FUISSÉ)

1999 Pouilly-Fuissé Vignes de la Côte	D	90+

There are 125 cases of this wine, which was produced from two vineyards, Vignes Blanches and Vers Cras, and aged for 18 months on its lees in one-year-old barrels. It boasts mineral and anise aromas, and a broad, medium-bodied personality. This is a thick, oily-textured wine loaded with glycerin. Pears, spices, and minerals can be found in its vinous, powerful, and intense character. Drink this impressive Pouilly-Fuissé over the next 6–8 years.

DOMAINE TOLLOT-BEAUT (CHOREY-BEAUNE)

1997 Corton	E	(89–91)
1999 Corton-Bressandes	E	(89–91)
1997 Corton-Bressandes	E	(90–92)
1999 Corton-Charlemagne	EE	(89–91)
1998 Corton-Charlemagne	EE	92
1997 Corton-Charlemagne	EE	(91–94)

1997 was another successful vintage for this large (by Burgundy standards) family-run estate. According to Nathalie Tollot, the yields were 20% lower than normal, 30% lower than in 1996. She attributed it to *millerandage* (the small embryonic grapes that result from poor flowering), and the fact that they misjudged the vintage, and dropped too much fruit in the vineyards. Across the board, Tollot-Beaut's 1997s are truly delicious. They are packed with fruit, have creamy textures, and the reds have soft, supple tannins.

The fabulous 1997 Corton-Charlemagne was harvested extremely late. Its complex aromatics reveal peach pits, apricots, minerals, and traces of buttered toast. This extremely well balanced wine is medium- to full-bodied, displays huge ripeness, and is crammed with mouthcoating layers of oily nuts, poached pears, and smoked bacon. As a fan of Tollot-Beaut's generally elegant, highly focused, and often austere (when young) Corton-Charlemagnes, I found the 1997 atypical for this estate. It has excellent delineation and definition yet is opulent, forward, luxuriously fruity and decadent. Drink from now–2006+.

The ruby-colored 1997 Corton has beguiling red cherry and fresh raspberry aromas. On the palate, it offers a medium- to full-bodied, velvety-textured core of red fruits, blackberries, and plums. It has good grip, hints of mocha, and is plump, long in the finish, and was a delight to drink right out of the barrel. Anticipated maturity: now–2007. Even better, the similarly colored 1997 Corton-Bressandes has a candied nose of sweet black cherries and red currants. Verging on confectionary, this medium- to full-bodied, feminine, cherry, and toasty oak–flavored wine is luscious, forward, and giving. It is silky, as well as opulent, and will offer superb drinking over the next 8 years.

The vanilla- and mineral-scented 1998 Corton-Charlemagne is a rich, velvety-textured wine. Medium-bodied, thick, and dense, it is crammed with notes of pears, apples, and assorted spices. Wonderfully harmonious, and giving the impression of having been crafted from well-ripened fruit, it is sweet as well as opulent. Drink it between now–2009.

The 1999 Corton-Charlemagne offers delightful spice and pear aromas. Medium-bodied, detailed, and exceedingly well balanced, this fat, rich, and broad wine has excellent to outstanding concentration. In addition, it possesses a long, supple, flavorful finish. Anticipated maturity: now–2011. The Bing cherry, candied strawberry, and jammy black raspberry–scented 1999 Corton-Bressandes is a fresh, medium- to full-bodied wine. It has loads of depth to its broad-shouldered, highly structured character. Loads of sweet tannin are present, yet this wine appears to have more than enough fruit to sustain it. Anticipated maturity: 2005–2012.

Other recommended wines: 1997 Aloxe-Corton Les Vercots (87–89+), 1999 Savigny-les-Beaune Les Lavières (87–89)

DOMAINE JEAN ET JEAN-LOUIS TRAPET (GEVREY-CHAMBERTIN)

1997 Chambertin	EE	(93–95)
1997 Chapelle-Chambertin	E	(91–94+)
1997 Gevrey-Chambertin Petite Chapelle	D	(89–91+)
1997 Latricières-Chambertin	E	(91–93)

The recent resurgence of Domaine Jean et Jean-Louis Trapet is gratifying, and terrific news for red Burgundy aficionados, as the estate has a bevy of top vineyard sites (and prices have yet to catch up to the quality!). Facing what Jean-Louis Trapet described as a "Mediterranean vintage," due to its heat, dryness, and high natural potential alcohol levels, Trapet opted to cool the grapes immediately after they had been sorted. They were left to do an 8–10 day cold maceration, with daily *pigeages* without *remontage* (pumping over), and then performed a 21–27 day *cuvaison*. The wines were left on their lees throughout their *élevage*, with sulphur being added directly to the lees, using a long syringe. At Domaine Jean et Jean-Louis Trapet, 30–70% new oak is employed.

The medium to dark ruby-colored 1997 Gevrey-Chambertin Petite Chapelle offers blackberry, rosemary, and tarlike aromas. It is a well-extracted, dense, powerful, intense, broad wine. Flavors reminiscent of superripe blackberries and spices can be found in its intricate and flavorful core. Anticipated maturity: now–2008. The bright, medium to dark ruby-colored 1997 Chapelle-Chambertin exhibits rosemary, thyme, blackberries, and roasted stone scents. It bursts forth on the palate with licorice, blackberry jam, iodine, and oak spice flavors. This muscular wine saturates the taster's mouth with its boisterous personality yet maintains a soft, chewy texture. Its impressively long and complex finish reveals, through the suave nature of its tannic backbone, the magnificent ripeness of its grapes. Anticipated maturity: now–2012. The darker-colored 1997 Latricières-Chambertin has profound prune, plum, and licorice flavors. This satin-textured, explosive, deep, masculine wine is more tannic, structured, and powerful than even the Chapelle-Chambertin. Blackberry juice, mint, and plums can be found throughout its deep flavor profile and opulently flavored, persistent finish. It is one of the rare 1997s that will require cellaring patience yet has the potential for mid- to long-term aging. Anticipated maturity: 2003–2012+. Trapet's medium to dark ruby-colored 1997 Chambertin is one of the vintage's superstars. Its fresh, blackberry, Asian spice, and earth-scented nose leads to a stupendously profound, deep, expansive personality. Prunes, earth, leather, blackberries, and juniper berries can be discerned in this chewy, thick, velvety-textured wine. If the color black has a flavor, this wine embodies it. This tour de force in winemaking and vineyard work should be consumed between 2003–2012+.

Other recommended wine: 1997 Gevrey-Chambertin Clos Prieur (88)

DOMAINE VALETTE (VINZELLES)

2000 Pouilly-Fuissé Clos de M. Noly Réserve Vieilles Vignes	E	(92–94)
1997 Pouilly-Fuissé Clos de M. Noly Réserve Vieilles Vignes	E	(92–94)
2000 Pouilly-Fuissé Clos Reyssié Réserve Particulière	E	(91–93)
1997 Pouilly-Fuissé Clos Reyssié Réserve Particulière	E	(90–92)

Gérard Valette, like other top producers in the Mâconnais, is concerned about the possibility of losing the right to appellation-designate his wines. The authorities, democratically governed by the region's vignerons (the vast majority produce mediocre wines), use "typicity" as one of the most important criteria for label approval. Valette's wines, like those of other Mâconnais stars, are significantly better than the norm and are therefore atypical. If this trend continues, the Mâconnais will become like Tuscany, where the most sought-after wines are only permitted to carry the designation of "table wine." Beginning with the 1997 vintage, all of Domaine Valette's wines were bottled at the estate using a new state-of-the-art bottling machine.

The 1997 Pouilly-Fuissé Clos Reyssié Réserve Particulière was vinified in oak barrels, two-thirds of them new. It reveals smoke, pears, apples, honeysuckle, and grilled wood aromas. On the palate, this medium- to full-bodied, dense, powerful wine has admirable purity of fruit (primarily white peaches and apples) and a mouthcoating oily texture with no hard edges. This wine offers pure, unadulterated pleasure. It took considerable self-discipline not to swallow at my tasting. Anticipated maturity: now–2004. Valette's most complete wine is the 1997 Pouilly-Fuissé Clos de Monsieur Noly Réserve Vieilles Vignes. Its super-concentrated aromatics reveal evidence of *sur-maturité* as well as scents reminiscent of almond and acacia flower extracts. Its muscular, powerful, medium- to full-bodied, surprisingly vibrant personality saturates the palate with layers of peach pit, mineral, peanut oil, anise, and poached pear flavors. This hedonistic, thick, unctuously textured gem is particularly stunning because of its brilliant balance and well-delineated finish. Anticipated maturity: now–2008.

Gérard Valette is "quite happy" with the 2000 vintage. "These are pleasing wines, with loads of fruit that will bring joy to our customers in the next few years." The highly expressive 2000 Pouilly-Fuissé Clos Reyssié Réserve Particulière bursts from the glass with minerals, roasted white fruits, and buttered toast. It is medium-bodied, intense, and has lovely definition and an exceptionally long, pure finish. Anticipated maturity: 2004–2012. The fresh pear and apple-scented 2000 Pouilly-Fuissé Clos de M. Noly Réserve Vieilles Vignes is an opulent, medium-bodied wine. It possesses outstanding depth to its superripe, white fruit and mineral-flavored character. Vinous, studded with minerals, and bright, this is a vivacious, lush, highly concentrated wine with an exceptionally long, pure finish. Given Valette's contrarian belief in long *élevages*, it should be bottled sometime in 2003 or 2004. Anticipated maturity: 2004–2012.

Other recommended wines: 1997 Mâcon-Chaintré Vieilles Vignes (88–90), 1998 Mâcon Chaintré Vieilles Vignes (88), 1999 Mâcon-Chaintré Vieilles Vignes (87–89), 2000 Mâcon-Chaintré Vieilles Vignes (88–89), 1998 Pouilly-Fuissé Clos de M. Noly Réserve Vieilles Vignes (92–94), 1999 Pouilly-Fuissé Clos Reyssié Réserve Particulière (89–90), 1997 Pouilly-Fuissé Tradition (88–90), 1998 Pouilly-Fuissé Tradition (89), 1999 Pouilly-Fuissé Tradition (88–89), 2000 Pouilly-Fuissé Tradition (88–90), 1997 Pouilly-Vinzelles (88–89), 2000 Pouilly-Vinzelles (89–90)

MAISON VERGET (SOLOGNY)

2000	Bâtard-Montrachet	EEE	(91–93)
1999	Bâtard-Montrachet	EEE	(90–91)
1998	Bâtard-Montrachet	EEE	91
1997	Bâtard-Montrachet	EEE	(89–91)
1997	Chablis Bougros	EE	(91–93)
2000	Chablis Bougros Côte de Bouquereaud	E	(90–91)
1997	Chablis Fourchaume	D	90
1997	Chablis Fourchaume Vieilles Vignes	E	(90–92)
2000	Chablis Montée de Tonnerre	D	(90–92)
2000	Chablis Terroir de Chablis	C	91
2000	Chablis Vaillons	D	91+
1997	Chablis Vaillons	D	90+
1997	Chablis Valmur	EE	(92–94)
2000	Chassagne-Montrachet Franchemont	E	(91–93)
1999	Chassagne-Montrachet Franchemont	E	(90–92)
1997	Chassagne-Montrachet Morgeot Vieilles Vignes	EE	(91–93+)
1997	Chassagne-Montrachet Remilly	EE	(89–91)
1997	Chassagne-Montrachet La Romanée	EE	(91–93)
1997	Corton-Charlemagne	EEE	(92–94)
2000	Mâcon-Burgy En Chatelaine	D	91
2000	Mâcon-Bussières Vieilles Vignes de Montbrison	C	90
1997	Meursault Les Casses Têtes	E	(88–91)
1997	Meursault Charmes Vieilles Vignes	EE	(92–93+)
1997	Meursault Poruzots	EE	(92–94+)
2000	Meursault Rougeots	E	(90–91)
2000	Meursault Les Tillets	E	(91–93)
1997	Meursault Les Tillets	E	(89–91+)
2000	Pouilly-Fuissé Cuvée des 10 Ans	D	(91–93)
1999	Pouilly-Fuissé Terroirs de Vergisson	D	90+
1997	Pouilly-Fuissé Tête de Cuvée	D	90+
1997	Puligny-Montrachet Les Enseignères	E	(88–91)
1997	Puligny-Montrachet Sous le Puits	EE	(90–93)
2000	St.-Véran Terres Noires	D	90
1999	St.-Véran Terres Noires	D	90
2000	St.-Véran Vigne de Ste.-Claude	D	90+
1999	St.-Véran Vigne de Ste.-Claude	D	90+

My annual visit to Jean-Marie Guffens's *négociant* firm is always one of the year's highlights to the consistently high quality of his wines, Guffens is a forcefully candid man who suffers no fools. In short, a tasting Chez Guffens is an educational experience. Readers who have acquired Maison Verget's wines may be interested in the experience I had following the tasting. Jean-Marie Guffens opened, decanted, and served a few bottles of his older wines. At first they had the characteristics associated with whites that have gone over the hill—dark colors, caramelized or butterscotch-scented noses, and flavor profiles with oxidized notes. With a few minutes of air, the colors became bright, clear, and youthful, and the noses as well as gustative elements that suggested oxidation disappeared. Guffens explained that he bottled his wines in an oxidative state, which allowed them to be long-lived and fresh. Instead of being their nemesis, air and oxygen brought them to life when they were uncorked. While this explanation clashes with my rudimentary knowledge of chemistry, I have to believe what I saw and tasted.

Concerning 1997, Guffens said "some may believe 1997 is a better vintage than 1996. I compared 1996 to an Ingmar Bergman movie. You have to understand it to appreciate it. It can be very intellectual. 1997 is like the movie *Titanic,* much more Hollywood. It is a very good vintage." Guffens believes that 1997 is superior to 1996 in the Mâconnais because yields tended to be lower. One of Guffens's undeniable successes in 1997 is the Pouilly-Fuissé Tête de Cuvée. Produced in equal parts from fruit purchased in the villages of Fuissé and Vergisson, and aged in 30% new oak barrels, it offers aromas of white chocolate–covered pears. It is medium- to full-bodied, packed with white fruits, flint, stones, and flower blossoms. Densely layered, fat, and profoundly ripe, this intense wine has enormous sweetness of fruit in addition to a long, bone-dry finish. My instincts suggest that it may become even better with cellaring. Anticipated maturity: now–2007+.

The immensely impressive 1997 Chablis Vaillons exhibits a crystalline, pure nose of pears, minerals, and chalk. Medium-bodied and hugely flavorful, it is a rich, admirably delineated wine crammed with ripe mineral and fresh water and fresh seawater flavors that linger throughout its exceedingly long finish. Anticipated maturity: now–2007. The 1997 Chablis Fourchaume reveals sweet mineral, sea shell, and spicy oak aromas. A flamboyant, pear, honeysuckle, and acacia blossom–infused wine, it is concentrated, full-flavored, and medium- to full-bodied. In contrast to the Vaillons, it is a larger, more powerful offering that may develop additional complexity with cellaring. Drink it between now–2006.

Displaying mocha, toast, and sweet mineral aromas, the 1997 Chablis Fourchaume Vieilles Vignes is a sweet, intense, powerful wine. Its flavor profile is loaded with liquid minerals, candied pears, steel, and flint. This complex, medium- to-full-bodied, expressive Chablis is the result of exquisitely ripe fruit, evidenced by the wine's unending layers of oily-textured, flavor-packed waves. Anticipated maturity: now–2006+. The salt, mineral, and chalk-scented 1997 Chablis Bougros is fatter, denser, and richer, yet not as intense or full-flavored as the Fourchaume Vieilles Vignes. It is a complex, concentrated, pristine wine with extraordinary balance (particularly for the vintage). Sweet oak spices, stones, and a salty sea breeze can be found in this superb offering's flavor profile and long finish. Anticipated maturity: now–2007. The 1997 Chablis Valmur has toasted hazelnut, eucalyptus, lemon, and stonelike aromas. The biggest and most delineated of Verget's 1997 Chablis, it has a velvety-textured, precise, and complex core of white/red berries intermingled with spiced pears and anise. It lasts longer on the palate than even the Bougros. This blockbuster does not compare in quality with the heroic 1995, yet is an extraordinary wine, offering further evidence of Guffens's brilliant winemaking skills. Drink it between now–2007+.

I adored the velvety-textured 1997 Chassagne-Montrachet Morgeot Vieilles Vignes! Its nose smells like a shovelful of fresh earth and it possesses an enthralling richness. This thick, powerful, immensely ripe wine is jam-packed with minerals, red cherries, poached pears, oak spices, and earth. It is magnificently concentrated, revealing wave upon wave of dense yet expressive fruit. The pure finish is mind-bogglingly long. Anticipated maturity: now–2008. The 1997 Chassagne-Montrachet En Remilly has a spiced oak and toasted almond–scented nose as well as a thick, fat, sweet personality. While it lacks the Morgeot Vieilles Vignes's intensity, it is immensely pleasing because of its forward display of fruit. A pear, peach, and anise-flavored wine, it does not have the equilibrium of Verget's finest 1997s. A broad, ample, dense offering, it will provide super near- to mid-term drinking. Anticipated maturity: now–2005. The 1997 Chassagne-Montrachet La Romanée exhibits fruit-cake, acacia flower, and anise aromas. On the palate, its acidity and fruit appeared to be slightly disjointed, but there was no mistaking this wine's outstanding potential. Its full-bodied, concentrated, complex, oily-textured flavor profile is loaded with hazelnut cream, spices, minerals, and hints of red berries. As it finishes its *élevage,* I am certain that this su-perb wine will integrate all its components. Drink it between now–2008.

The 1997 Puligny-Montrachet Les Enseignères is a sweet white fruit and buttered toast–scented wine that will certainly be excellent. If its medium- to full-bodied, powerful, focused, superripe core of pears and apples is able to integrate its acidity better, it will merit an outstanding rating. Drink it between now–2005. I have no doubts about the compelling 1997 Puligny-Montrachet Sous le Puits. It possesses a magnificent nose of red currants, rocks, and candied apples. On the palate, this complex, magnificently delineated, precise wine is medium- to full-bodied, harmonious, and packed with gorgeously ripe pears and cherries. Its impressively long finish offers an elegant mineral and stone component more reminiscent of a zesty, well-delineated 1996 than the often low-acid, somewhat flabby 1997s. Anticipated maturity: now–2007.

The 1997 Meursault Les Casse Têtes was aromatically reduced but its certain quality showed through on the palate. It is a medium- to full-bodied, gorgeously ripe, dense, beauti-fully balanced wine with a delightful hazelnut and almond-flavored core. Drink it between now–2006. The 1997 Meursault Les Tillets (a *terroir* that performed impressively well for a number of estates) has a beguiling nose reminiscent of a nutty cream sauce. It is fresh, well delineated, and medium- to full-bodied, with a citrus, spiced apple and red currant–laced personality. This penetrating, powerful, elegant, and extremely well crafted offering is a first-rate *village* wine. Readers should note that Les Tillets, a vineyard located high on the hill overlooking Poruzots (a premier cru), produced numerous successes in 1997. This offering should be at its peak between now–2007. In contrast, the magnificent 1997 Meursault Charmes Vieilles Vignes will provide consumers years of pleasure. Its extremely expressive aromatics reveal earthy red fruit scents interspersed with new oak spices. On the palate, this full-bodied, broad, powerful, highly concentrated, magnificently focused wine offers multiple dimensions of minerals, nuts, superripe apples, and grilled oak flavors. This huge yet refined Meursault pleases the intellect with its purity and complexity, yet will also satisfy hedonists with its thick, chewy, sultry depth of fruit. Anticipated maturity: now–2008. Verget's 1997 Meursault Poruzots is a work of art. Its droll-inducing nose of candied hazelnuts and lemons leads to a full-flavored and humongous personality densely packed with tropical fruits and nuts. This wine is amazingly ripe yet has impeccable precision and balance, an anomaly given its oily, almost viscous texture. Many wines tasted at this stage of their *élevage* appear to be holding some of their components in reserve. This offering flaunts everything it has in an unabashedly sexy and voluptuous manner. Anticipated maturity: now–2007.

I tasted Verget's 1997 Bâtard-Montrachet with the greatness of the 1996 still vivid in my memory. While 1996 was truly a Bâtard year, 1997 was not. I don't want to take anything away from this wine—it is excellent and may ultimately merit an outstanding score—how-ever, it lacks the focus, elegance, concentration, and complexity necessary for greatness. It reveals mango, papaya, and candied orange rind aromas that lead to an enormously fat (verg-ing on flabby) core of tropical fruit flavors. Full-bodied and very flavorful, it is hedonistically appealing and will provide enormous pleasure over the next 5–6 years. Displaying fresh but-ter, minerals, and candied lemon scents, the 1997 Corton-Charlemagne has many of the qualities the Bâtard lacks. This profoundly rich yet structured wine is intense, highly con-centrated, powerful, full-bodied, refined, and beautifully delineated. Baked apples, kiwis, stones, and hints of mango are found in this beauty's flavor profile and throughout its impres-sively long finish. While it is a delight to drink now, this is one of those rare 1997s that is likely to be better with a few years of cellaring. Anticipated maturity: now–2008+.

"The 1998 vintage is an average year, qualitatively comparable with 1994 or 1988," asserted Maison Verget's brutally honest and forthright Jean-Marie Guffens. His actions followed his words. Guffens found little to like in the 1998 vintage, so he resold in bulk much of what he was compelled to purchase from vignerons to maintain future allocations. Beaune *négociant* firms, including the most highly regarded for the quality of their wines, purchased what Guffens was dumping in order to satisfy worldwide demand. Maison Verget's 1998 production, described as a "short" vintage, was half what it was in 1997.

When I visited Maison Verget to taste the 1998s, Guffens greeted me with the statement that he had harvested the vintage "like everybody else, before *a* rain." He then proceeded to burst out laughing. He readily admitted that it had rained continually prior to the third week of September 1998, and the skies opened up again on the 26th. Knowing that his colleagues were greeting me with the news that they had picked during a "window of excellent weather," Guffens stated "to have quality in 1998 we needed a large bay window of excellent weather in August and September, not a four day window! Over the next three years everybody in Burgundy will tell you that 1998 is a better vintage than 1994. When they are all sold out of the 1998s they'll admit that it is 1994's equal, no better. I therefore have raised the prices of my remaining 1997s because it would be a criminal act to raise prices on the 1998s. We should all accept 1998 for what it is, but we should not accept these prices. Personally, I would not buy any 1998 white Burgundies at these crazy prices." Guffens, who maintains a first rate private cellar understands the woes of being a consumer in search of the best vinous offerings. Additionally, since Maison Verget does not own any vineyards in Burgundy, he is singularly well placed to discuss the effects of rising retail *and* bulk prices. "I just can't understand these prices, the drinkers must be making loads of money. The Dow Jones and NASDAQ stock options are establishing prices. Show me future Dow and NASDAQ returns and I'll tell your what Burgundy's prices will do," Guffens lamented.

Verget's 1998 Bâtard-Montrachet is outstanding. Aromatically displaying red berries, butter, spices, and fresh herbs, this is a creamy yet bright, medium- to full-bodied wine. Poached pears, peaches, baked apples, and candied lemons compose this lively, persistent effort's racy personality. Anticipated maturity: now–2008.

"I didn't make a single work of art in either 1999 or 2000," said Jean-Marie Guffens when I visited Maison Verget to taste the 1999s. Even though he received enormous flak from importers and *négociants* for his outspoken comments to me a year ago ("Personally, I would not buy any 1998 white Burgundies at these crazy prices"), the brutally honest Guffens has not been silenced. "The wines are not bad, in fact some are good, however they are priced as though they were exceptional. Since you love to use scores, here's an easy way for you to understand the problem we are facing: the 1998 and 1999 vintages, two 14 point [out of 20] years for Côte d'Or whites, are selling at 20 point prices." Guffens believes that wine prices have hit their peak, and that a crisis is imminent. "Crises are announced by large producers, those in Bordeaux, Champagne, and Châteauneuf-du-Pape, for example, not by Burgundians who produce comparatively small quantities. Today there are loads of stocks of Champagnes and Bordeaux throughout Europe, yet the prices haven't slipped . . . but they will, as they must. And when they do they will drag Burgundy down with them. I hope the pendulum will soon swing back towards consumers, *négociants*, and retailers. Today the prices being asked by the estates are not based in reality."

Unlike virtually all of his peers, Guffens does not believe that 1999 or 2000 is better than 1998 for Côte d'Or whites. "I'd score all three vintages 14 out of 20 for the Côte de Beaune, but in the Mâconnais 1999 is an 18 out of 20." He characterizes 1999 as "a vintage marked by rain. Anything harvested after Friday the 21st was soaked. We were therefore faced with a problem as the fruit and acidities of the wines had been diluted. The Côte de Beaune's lack both concentration and fat. The last thing you would ever want to do is acidify a vintage like

1999. What we did was throw out the low acid press wines so we could keep the good acidities of the free run juice. As far as density is concerned, you couldn't stir the lees of the Côte de Beaunes because it is foolish to look for fat when there simply isn't any. For the Mâconnais wines we did do lots of *bâtonnages* because they had more density so stirring the lees could actually help."

Guffens loves to poke fun at the less than honest rationalizations/propaganda of his fellow wine producers, as he did a year ago when virtually every Burgundian had claimed that a "window of good weather" had saved the 1998 vintage ("what we needed was a large bay window of great weather throughout August and September, not a few days during harvest"). Knowing that all Burgundians were claiming their wines had achieved superb ripeness in 1999, he said "of course, here in Burgundy we obtain ripeness through the ground, not through sunlight. Maturity is raised by the rains if you believe those in the Côte d'Or." Guffens knows the difference between high sugar levels and actual ripeness. "I barely had to chaptalize anything in 1999; I'm talking about maturity, not sugar." He then burst out laughing and added, "In the Luberon [where Guffens has an estate, the Château des Tourettes], we don't have the great *terroirs* of the Côte d'Or so we must depend on the sun to ripen our grapes." Still, he maintains that 1999 is a *grand millésime* (great vintage) for the Mâconnais. A year ago he had said, "The 1999 vintage is responsible for the best raw materials I've seen over the past ten years in the Mâconnais. Not so much because the overall quality was gorgeous but rather it is due to the fact that so much was produced that I had the luxury to pick and choose what I wanted to purchase. Many growers who could fill their normal bulk sales by simply using their machine harvested younger vines were willing to hand harvest their older vine parcels (where harvesting machines can't penetrate) later for extra cash. I paid for those grapes at the same prices as others were paying for finished wines. I had the pick of the litter in the Mâconnais in 1999 and took advantage of it." This year he added, "The Mâconnais and the Côte d'Or are like Avis and Hertz . . . and here in the Mâconnais 'we try harder.' "

The 1999 St.-Véran Terres Noires displays gorgeous chalk and limestone aromas. Reminiscent of the Riesling produced by Alsace's famed Mark Kreydenweiss, it is floral, bursting with minerals, and exquisitely elegant. Medium-bodied and velvety-textured, this wine also offers a long and silky finish with a touch of bitterness. Anticipated maturity: now–2005. The 1999 St.-Véran Vigne de St.-Claude, one of the finest St.-Vérans ever tasted, bursts from the glass with flowers, fresh earth, and stone-scented aromas. It has outstanding intensity, focus, and balance to its extravagantly acacia blossom– and stone-flavored character. This beautiful, tangy, long-finishing wine will be at its best drunk over the next 6 years.

Rich white fruits and spices can be found in the aromatics of the 1999 Pouilly-Fuissé Terroirs de Vergisson. This syrup-textured, medium-bodied wine is loaded with minerals, spices, vanilla, and hints of lemons. It is deep, fresh, and powerfully flavored. Anticipated maturity: now–2007. The 1999 Chassagne-Montrachet Franchemont (Guffens's favorite among his offerings this year) reveals lush apple and pear aromas. Medium- to full-bodied, powerful, and concentrated, it explodes in the mid-palate with loads of satiny white fruits, minerals, and hints of fresh earth. This outstanding wine is focused, fat, dense, and opulent. Anticipated maturity: now–2007. Toasted white fruits and minerals characterize the aromatics of the 1999 Bâtard-Montrachet. This concentrated, rich, well-made wine has an impressive streak of dense apples and pears that last from the attack through its long, supple finish. It is flavorful, powerful, yet elegant and detailed. Anticipated maturity: now–2008.

Discussing the 2000s, Guffens said, "They are like the 1999s in the Côte de Beaune, maybe a tiny bit below them in the Mâconnais, and certainly much better in Chablis. Since you and Parker are obsessed with scores, I'd say that the Côte de Beaune 2000s merit 14/20, the Mâconnais 17/20, and the Chablisien a 16.5/20. The finest wines in 2000 come from hillside vineyards, as their slopes allowed the pre-harvest rains to run off." According to Guffens, "The economic crisis has arrived, and it is striking us in Burgundy first in our least expensive wines. It costs approximately 28,000 Francs to make a hectoliter of Beaujolais, and at today's rates the best a producer could expect to earn would be 15,000 Francs. The Mâconnais has also been struck, yet not to the same extent as the Beaujolais." Guffens added, "My biggest problem here at Verget, after the attitudes of the Côte d'Or vignerons, is the quality of corks available on the market. We're moving more and more towards synthetic corks, as it is heartbreaking to see our work ruined by tainted corks."

Expressive liquid mineral and spice aromas can be discerned in the nose of the 2000 Mâcon-Bussières Vieilles Vignes de Montbrison. Hugely concentrated and broad, this ample, medium-bodied wine is filled with well-delineated stone, quartz, and mineral flavors. It is broad, pure, and precise. Drink it over the next 8 years. The expressive, verbena-scented 2000 Mâcon-Burgy En Châtelaine is a powerful, rich, and concentrated wine. Medium-bodied, it is loaded with minerals and white fruits that coat the taster's palate. It is intense, rich, beautifully ripe, and deep. Drink it over the next 10 years.

The beautifully defined 2000 St.-Véran Vignes de St.-Claude reveals candied lemons and minerals in both its aromas and flavor profile. Loaded with fruit and highly detailed, this medium-bodied, vivacious wine should be consumed over the next 7 years. The crystalline 2000 St.-Véran Terres Noires is tightly wound yet displays loads of underlying richness. Clay, lemons, and minerals are found in this beautifully ripened yet bright and lively offering's character. It will benefit from cellaring. Anticipated maturity: 2003–2009.

To celebrate the 10-year anniversary of the Maison Verget, Guffens produced two "birthday" *cuvées*, a Pouilly-Fuissé and a Chablis. The 2000 Pouilly-Fuissé Cuvée des 10 Ans reveals toasted white fruit aromas and a delightful, medium-bodied personality. This wine gorgeously combines breadth and focus in its lemon-lime and mineral flavor profile. It has intense concentration, depth, and exceptional length. Anticipated maturity: 2004–2012. The mouthwatering nose of the 2000 Chablis Terroir de Chablis exhibits earth, gun flint, white flowers, and minerals. It is ample, muscular, and delineated. This is an intense, medium-bodied wine, loaded with apples, pears, and citrus fruits whose flavors last throughout its extensive finish. Drink it over the next 10 years.

The 2000 Chablis Vaillons has a lively nose dominated by citrus fruits, mineral, gravel, and flint. This huge, concentrated wine is pure, loaded with candied lemons, minerals, and herbal tea. It has exceptional delineation, superb length, and purity. This wine was vinified and aged 95% in stainless steel *cuves* and 5% in old barrels. Anticipated maturity: 2003–2011. With a highly expressive, concentrated personality, the mineral- and lemon-scented 2000 Chablis Montée de Tonnerre is a rich, opulent, ample, medium-bodied wine. Sweet lemons and limes can easily be detected in its long and well-defined finish. Drink it between 2004–2010. Ripe white fruits are found in the aromatics of the 2000 Chablis Bougros Côte de Bouquereaud. Medium- to full-bodied and chunky, this is a satin-textured, pear- and apple-flavored wine. Its character is lush, highly expressive, and possesses a long, fruit-filled finish. Anticipated maturity: 2004–2012.

Maison Verget has significantly reduced the number of wines from the Côte de Beaune that it produces, at the same time increasing its portfolio of wines from the Chablisien and Mâconnais. The tangy 2000 Meursault Rougeots is a medium-bodied, plump wine. Pears and apples can be found in both its aromatics and flavor profile. It is concentrated, intense, and offers a long, flavorful finish. Drink it over the next 8–9 years. Loads of spices and pears can be found in the aromatics of the outstanding 2000 Meursault Les Tillets. This rich, opulent, medium-bodied wine is crammed with toasted nuts and tangy candied lemons that coat the taster's palate. Silky-textured and impressively persistent, it is a lush, complete wine. Drink it between 2003–2011.

The superb 2000 Chassagne-Montrachet Franchemont is a deep, broad, concentrated wine. It bursts from the glass with ripe pear and mineral aromas that lead to a broad, medium- to full-bodied character. This intense, delineated wine coats the palate with earthy apples, anise, minerals, toast, and hints of vanilla. It is highly nuanced and rich while being expressive. Furthermore, this gorgeous offering possesses a long, flavorful, supple finish. Drink it over the next 12 years. Creamed white peaches and minerals are found in the aromatics of the 2000 Bâtard-Montrachet. Opulent and sexy, it is a medium- to full-bodied wine, loaded with superripe apples, almonds, and pears. Rich and plump, this wine also retains admirable precision in its powerful and complex personality. Anticipated maturity: 2003–2013. *Other recommended wines:* 2000 Chablis Cuvée des 10 Ans (89+), 1998 Chablis Bougros (89), 1999 Chablis Bougros (88–90), 1999 Chablis Bougros Côte de Bouquereaud (89–90), 2000 Chablis Les Forêts (89), 1998 Chablis Fourchaume Vieilles Vignes (89), 1999 Chablis Fourchaume Vieilles Vignes de Vaulorens (87–89), 2000 Chablis Terroir de Fleys (89), 2000 Chablis Terroir de Poinchy (89), 1998 Chablis Vaillons (89), 1999 Chablis Vaillons Les Minodes (88–90), 1997 Chassagne-Montrachet (88+), 1997 Chassagne-Montrachet Les Chaumées (88–90+), 1998 Corton-Charlemagne (89+), 1999 Corton-Charlemagne (89–90), 1997 Ladoix (88), 1999 Mâcon-Burgy En Chatelaine Cuvée Levroutée (89), 2000 Mâcon-Burgy Les Prusettes (89), 1999 Mâcon-Bussières Vieilles Vignes de Montbrison (89+), 1999 Mâcon-La Roche Vineuse Vieilles Vignes de Somméré (88), 1999 Mâcon-Vergisson La Roche (88), 2000 Mâcon-Vergisson La Roche (89), 1997 Mâcon-Villages Tête de Cuvée (88), 1997 Meursault Charmes (89–90), 1997 Meursault Rougeots (88–89), 1998 Meursault Tête de Cuvée (88), 1999 Meursault Les Tillets (89–90), 1998 Pouilly-Fuissé Tête de Cuvée (89), 1999 Pouilly-Vinzelles Cuvée Levroutée (88), 1999 Pouilly-Vinzelles Les Quarts (88+), 2000 Pouilly-Vinzelles Les Quarts (88), 1998 Puligny-Montrachet Les Enseignères (88), 1999 Puligny-Montrachet Les Enseignères (88–89), 2000 Puligny-Montrachet Les Enseignères (89–90), 2000 Puligny-Montrachet Sous le Puits (89–90), 1999 St.-Véran Terroirs de Davayé (89), 2000 St.-Véran Terroirs de Davayé (88), 1997 St.-Véran Tête de Cuvée (88), 1999 Viré-Clessé Vieilles Vignes de Roally (89)

DOMAINE DU COMTE DE VOGÜÉ (CHAMBOLLE-MUSIGNY)

1997	Bonnes Mares	EEE	(91–93+)
1997	Bourgogne Blanc	D	91
1997	Chambolle-Musigny Les Amoureuses	EEE	(91–93)
1999	Musigny	EEE	(90–92)
1997	Musigny	EEE	(93–95)

The Domaine du Comte de Vogüé is one of the finest wine-producing estates in the world because 1) it has extraordinary vineyard holdings (including 70% of the Musigny grand cru), 2) its wine-maker, François Millet, has limitless talent, and 3) it truly abides by its "quality at any expense" philosophy. Like other quality-minded estates, de Vogüé maintains extremely low yields, yet this estate goes a step further, declassifying wines that it does not believe merit their lofty appellations. For example, Vogüé's "village" Chambolle-Musigny is actually crafted only partially from vines within the appellation vineyards. It also contains the estate's grapes from the premier crus Baudes and Fuées. Moreover, the wines sold under the label Chambolle-Musigny 1er Cru is fashioned entirely from the youngest vines of Musigny. And finally, the estate's Bourgogne Blanc is entitled to the grand cru appellation Musigny. According to Millet and administrative director Jean-Luc Pépin, the Baronne Bertrand de Ladoucette (the domaine's owner) will deny the Musigny label to her white wine until she deems that it merits it.

The estate's 1997s were neither chaptalized nor acidified. Described by Pépin as "suave," and by Millet as "elegant, sensual, balanced, and structured, with extremely refined tannins," they deliver immense pleasure in the present and yet have the capacity to age and evolve well. Millet performed a number of experiments with his 1997s to determine how oxygen and aeration would affect them. His results, echoed at other estates that performed the same tests, indicate that the wines stand up extremely well to air and do not oxidize quickly.

The ruby-colored 1997 Chambolle-Musigny Les Amoureuses has a gorgeously floral nose, packed with violets and roses. On the palate, this thick, satin-textured wine bursts forth with powerful and deeply ripe flavors. It is sweet as jam, yet refined, and crammed with red fruit and stone-like nuances. It is opulent, sensual, complex, rich, precise, and possesses a long and supple finish. This sexy, hedonistic wine should be consumed over the next 7–8 years. The similarly colored 1997 Bonnes Mares has huge aromatic depth to its stone, earth, perfume, and candied blackberry/cherry-scented nose. This is a broad, masculine, muscular, expansive wine, with a wild (*sauvage*) streak in its structured personality. This powerful wine is not as sensual as Les Amoureuses, yet it possesses the required frame to stand up to moderate cellaring. Anticipated maturity: now–2010.

Vogüé's 1997 Musigny is medium to dark ruby-colored and exhibits a breathtaking nose of blueberries, licorice, jammy blackberries, violets, Asian spices, and stones. This magnificent wine is medium- to full-bodied, sublimely refined, and detailed. It is certainly one of this famed estate's greatest Musignys, yet it is in a lighter and more lacelike style than most of the domaine's past glories. Red currants and cherries vie for the taster's attention with spices and fresh clay in its luxurious yet well-defined personality. To top things off, this awesome wine's immensely long finish reveals loads of supple tannins, which will ensure the necessary backbone for cellaring. Anticipated maturity: now–2012+.

The 1997 Bourgogne Blanc (2,000 bottles were produced) reveals smoky, toasty, and minerally aromas, intermingled with candied lemons and fresh white fruits. This is a thick, medium- to full-bodied, broad, and sensual wine, crammed with poached pear, hazelnut, stone, lemon grass, and tropical fruit (some banana) flavors. It is a forward, in-your-face, luxurious wine that will require drinking over the next 5–6 years.

According to Millet the estate dropped half its fruit in green harvests in 1999 to attain a 35 h/h average. "The natural size of this harvest, what Nature herself wanted to produce, was huge, so it was important to drop grapes. Also, the harvest date was extremely important. We began our harvest with the Musigny and Bonnes Mares starting on September 20, and some rain had already fallen but hadn't caused any damage. The rains that appeared on the 24th, and some rain had already fallen but hadn't caused any damage. The rains that appeared on the 24th and stayed with us were problematic for those with grapes still in the vineyards," he said. Overall, Millet sees 1999 as "a very approachable, positive vintage, one that will give a lot of pleasure." The ruby-colored 1999 Musigny has lovely aromas of violets, blueberries, and candied cherries. Medium-bodied and deep, it is filled with red fruits, stones, pomegranates, and strawberries. Loads of supple, ripe tannins can be discerned in its fresh, long, pure finish. Drink it between now–2009.

Other recommended wines: 1998 Bonnes Mares (88), 1999 Bonnes Mares (89–90), 1999 Chambolle-Musigny Les Amoureuses (88–90), 1998 Chambolle-Musigny Premier Cru (88), 1998 Musigny (89)

DOMAINE JOSEPH VOILLOT (VOLNAY)

1999 Volnay Champans	D	90+
1999 Volnay Les Fremiets	D	90+

Jean-Pierre Charlot, a straight-talking bon vivant, has significantly improved the quality of the estate's wines since taking over as wine-maker and director of Domaine Joseph Voillot.

The 1999 Volnay Les Fremiets is medium to dark ruby-colored and has a roasted oak– and blackberry-scented nose. There is massive depth to this chunky wine. It is loaded with spicy, cinnamon-laced blackberries and cassis. This powerful, extracted, and firm wine also has a long, pure finish. Anticipated maturity: 2003–2010. There are two bottlings of the 1999 Volnay Champans. The one for the U.S. market was produced from the estate's oldest vines (40 years old) in its Champans parcel, and was not filtered prior to bottling. It exhibits blackberries, cherries, and stones in its mouthwatering nose. This lush, expansive, medium- to full-bodied wine is crammed with plums, black cherries, blueberries, and floral flavors. It is tangy, juicy, and has a long yet highly structured finish. Anticipated maturity: 2004–2012. *Other recommended wines:* 1997 Pommard Clos Micault (87–89), 1997 Pommard Pézerolles (87–89), 1997 Pommard Rugiens (88–90), 1997 Volnay Les Caillerets (88–90), 1997 Volnay Les Champans (87–89), 1997 Volnay Les Fremiets (88)

Other Estates with Highly Recommended Wines

DOMAINE AMIOT-SERVELLE (CHAMBOLLE-MUSIGNY)
Recommended wine: 1999 Chambolle-Musigny Derrière la Grange (88–90)

DOMAINE CHARLES AUDOIN (MARSANNAY)
Recommended wines: 1997 Gevrey-Chambertin (88), 1997 Marsannay (white) (88), 1998 Marsannay (white) (89), 1997 Marsannay Longeroies (88)

DOMAINE BACHELET-RAMONET (CHASSAGNE-MONTRACHET)
Recommended wines: 1997 Bâtard-Montrachet (88), 1997 Bienvenue-Bâtard-Montrachet (88)

DOMAINE LUCIEN CAMUS-BROCHON (SAVIGNY-LES-BEAUNE)
Recommended wines: 1997 Savigny-les-Beaune Les Lavières (88), 1997 Savigny-les-Beaune Les Narbantons (89)

CHÂTEAU DE CHAMIREY (MERCUREY)
Recommended wine: 1998 Mercurey La Mission (87–89)

MAISON CHAMPY (BEAUNE)
Recommended wines: 1999 Corton-Bressandes (87–89), 1999 Corton-Charlemagne (88–89), 1999 Gevrey-Chambertin Les Cazetiers (88–90), 1999 Nuits-St.-Georges La Richemone (88–90), 1999 Volnay Les Caillerets (87–89), 1999 Vosne-Romanée Les Suchots (87–89)

DOMAINE DE CHASSORNEY (ST.-ROMAIN)
Recommended wine: 1997 Nuits-St.-Georges Clos des Argillières (89+)

DOMAINE CHAVY-CHOUET (MEURSAULT)
Recommended wines: 1999 Meursault Les Casses-Têtes Vielles Vignes (88), 1999 Puligny-Montrachet Hameau de Blagny Vieilles Vignes (89)

DOMAINE CHEVALIER PÈRE ET FILS (LADOIX)
Recommended wines: 2000 Corton-Charlemagne (89–92), 2000 Ladoix Les Gréchons (89–90)

DOMAINE DU CLOS NOLY (MÂCONNAIS)
Recommended wine: 1999 Pouilly-Fuissé Elevé en Fût de Chênes (89)

DOMAINE ALAIN COCHE-BIZOUARD (MEURSAULT)
Recommended wine: 1999 Meursault Charmes (88–89+)

DOMAINE DE LA CONDEMINE (PERRONE)
Recommended wine: 2000 Mâcon-Péronne Cuvée Réserve (89)

DOMAINE EDMOND ET PIERRE CORNU (LADOIX)
Recommended wines: 1997 Aloxe-Corton Les Valozières (89), 1997 Corton-Bressandes (89+)

DOMAINE DE LA CROIX-SENAILLET (DAVAYÉ)
Recommended wine: 2000 St.-Véran (88)

DOMAINE BERNARD DEFAIX (MILLY-CHABLIS)
Recommended wine: 1997 Chablis Côte de Léchet (89)

DOMAINE DESAUNAY-BISSEY (FLAGEY-ECHÉZEAUX)
Recommended wine: 1997 Grands-Echézeaux (88–90)

MAISON DRUID (MOREY-ST.-DENIS)
Recommended wines: 1997 Meursault Le Limozin (88), 1997 Puligny-Montrachet (88)

DOMAINE JEAN-LUC DUBOIS (CHOREY-LES-BEAUNE)
Recommended wines: 1997 Aloxe Corton Les Brunettes Réserve (88), 1997 Beaune Bressandes Réserve (89), 1997 Chorey-les-Beaune Clos du Margot Réserve (88), 1997 Savigny-les-Beaune Les Picotins Réserve (89)

DOMAINE DIDIER ERKER (GIVRY)
Note: These "Réserve" bottlings are special *cuvées* made for David Hinkle and Peter Vezan for the U.S. market.
Recommended wines: 1999 Givry Les Bois Chevaux Réserve (89), 1999 Givry Les Grands Prétans Réserve (89)

DOMAINE DE LA FOLIE (RULLY)
Recommended wine: 1998 Rully Clos St.-Jacques (white) (88)

DOMAINE ANDRÉ FOREST (VERGISSON)
Recommended wines: 1999 Pouilly-Fuissé Les Crays (88), 1999 Pouilly-Fuissé Vieilles Vignes (89+)

DOMAINE DE FUSSIACUS (FUISSÉ)
Recommended wines: 2000 Pouilly-Fuissé Cuvée Vieilles Vignes (89), 2000 Saint-Véran (89)

DOMAINE PAUL GARAUDET (MONTHÉLIE)
Recommended wines: 1997 Monthélie Clos Gauthey (88), 1997 Monthélie Les Duresses (89), 1997 Volnay (88)

DOMAINE DES GERBEAUX (SOLUTRÉ)
Recommended wines: 1999 Mâcon-Solutré Le Clos (88), 1999 Pouilly-Fuissé En Champs Roux (88), 1996 Pouilly-Fuissé Cuvée Prestige Très Vieilles Vignes (90), 1997 Pouilly-Fuissé Cuvée Prestige Très Vieilles Vignes (90), 1999 Pouilly-Fuissé Cuvée Prestige Très Vieilles Vignes (89), 1999 Pouilly-Fuissé Terroirs de Pouilly et Fuissé Vieilles Vignes (88), 1999 Pouilly-Fuissé Terroir de Solutré Vieilles Vignes (2nd bottling) (88)

DOMAINE THIERRY HAMELIN (LIGNORELLES-CHABLIS)
Recommended wines: 1997 Chablis Vieilles Vignes (88), 1999 Chablis Vieilles Vignes (88)

DOMAINE VINCENT ET FRANÇOIS JOUARD (CHASSAGNE-MONTRACHET)
Recommended wine: 1999 Bâtard-Montrachet Vieilles Vignes (88+)

DOMAINE DES HÉRITIERS DU COMTE LAFON (MÂCON-MILLY)
Recommended wine: 2000 Mâcon-Milly Clos du Four (87–89)

DOMAINE LORENZON (MERCUREY)
Recommended wine: 1999 Mercurey Les Champs Martin Vieilles Vignes (89+)

DOMAINE DES MARRONNIERS (PRÉHY)
Recommended wine: 1999 Chablis Montmains (89)

CHÂTEAU DE MONTHÉLIE/ERIC DE SUREMAIN (MONTHÉLIE)
Recommended wine: 1997 Monthélie Sur la Velle (88–90)

DOMAINE BERNARD MOREAU (CHASSAGNE-MONTRACHET)
Recommended wines: 1997 Chassagne-Montrachet Champs-Gains (88), 1997 Chassagne-Montrachet Chenevottes (88), 1997 Chassagne-Montrachet Morgeot (88+), 1997 Chassagne-Montrachet Grandes Ruchottes (89)

DOMAINE LUCIEN MUZARD (SANTENAY)
Recommended wine: 1999 Santenay Clos Faubard (88)

DOMAINE ALAIN NORMAND (LA ROCHE VINEUSE)
Recommended wine: 1999 Mâcon-La Roche Vineuse Vieilles Vignes (88)

DOMAINE CORINNE PERCHAUD (FLEYS)
Recommended wine: 1998 Chablis Vaucoupin (89+)

DOMAINE PERRAUD (FUISSÉ)
Recommended wine: 1997 St.-Véran Les Crays Roses Réserve (89)

DOMAINE HENRI PERRUSSET (FARGUES-LÈS-MÂCON)
Recommended wine: 1999 Mâcon-Farges Sélection de Vieilles Vignes (88)

MAISON JEAN-MARC PILLOT (CHASSAGNE-MONTRACHET)
Recommended wines: 1998 Chassagne-Montrachet Les Caillerets (88), 1997 Puligny-Montrachet Les Caillerets (88+), 1998 Puligny-Montrachet Les Caillerets (88)

DOMAINE DENIS POMMIER (POINCHY-CHABLIS)
Recommended wines: 2000 Chablis (88), 1997 Chablis Beauroy (89), 1999 Chablis Beauroy (88), 1999 Chablis Côte de Léchet (88), 2000 Chablis Côte de Léchet (88)

DOMAINE ROBLET-MONNOT (VOLNAY)
Recommended wine: 1997 Volnay St.-François (89)

DOMAINE DU CHÂTEAU DES RONTETS (FUISSÉ)
Recommended wines: 1997 Pouilly-Fuissé Les Birbettes (88–90), 1997 Pouilly-Fuissé Pierrefolle (87–89)

DOMAINE F. SERVIN (CHABLIS)
Recommended wine: 1998 Chablis Les Clos (88)

DOMAINE J. TRUCHOT-MARTIN (MOREY ST.-DENIS)
Recommended wine: 1999 Clos de la Roche Vieilles Vignes (89)

DOMAINE DE VIEUX MURS (FUISSÉ)
Recommended wine: 2000 Pouilly-Fuissé (88)

DOMAINE CHRISTOPHE VIOLOT-GUILLEMARD (POMMARD)
Recommended wine: 1997 Pommard Epenots (88+)

CHÂTEAU VITALLIS (FUISSÉ)
Recommended wines: 1998 Pouilly-Fuissé Les Rochettes (88), 1998 Pouilly-Fuissé Vieilles Vignes (89+)

Beaujolais

DOMAINE GUY BRETON

2000 Morgon Vieilles Vignes	C	92

This medium to dark ruby/purple-wine has extraordinarily inviting red and black fruit aromas. On the palate, there is unbelievable purity in its unctuous cherry, raspberry, and blueberry personality. It combines power with elegance, precision with massive density of fruit. Medium- to full-bodied and sporting an extraordinarily long, supple finish, this is a show-stopping Morgon. Drink it over the next 5–6 years.

DOMAINE JEAN-MARC BURGAUD

2000 Morgon Vieilles Vignes Côte de Py	B	89

A delightful blackberry- and dark cherry–scented perfume is followed by a medium-bodied red with loads of depth to its grape, cherry, blackberry, and spice-filled character. There is excellent structure, outstanding length, and an expansive personality. As it ameliorated with air, I believe this is a Beaujolais that will repay cellaring. Anticipated maturity: now–2006.

DOMAINE CHIGNARD

2000 Fleurie Les Moriers	C	91

The ruby/purple 2000 Fleurie Les Moriers bursts from the glass with black cherry aromas. Medium-bodied and possessing outstanding depth to its red fruit–packed character, this is a fresh, complex, lip-smacking good wine. It is velvety-textured and has an extraordinarily long currant- and blueberry-filled finish. This is a dreamy Beaujolais that consumers should race to find. Drink it over the next 4 years.

DOMAINE DIOCHON

2000 Moulin-à-Vent Vieilles Vignes	C	89

This ruby-colored 2000 Moulin-à-Vent has appealing red cherry aromas. On the palate, it is medium-bodied and has a layered personality filled with fresh Bing cherries. It is dominated by fruit and has excellent grip, as well as a long, supple finish. It is a delicious wine to drink over the next 2–3 years.

GEORGES DUBŒUF

2000 Brouilly Domaine des Pierreux	B	89
2000 Chiroubles (flower label)	B	89
2000 Chiroubles Château de Javernand	B	88
2000 Fleurie (flower label)	B	(86–88)
2000 Fleurie Château de Bachelard	B	(89–91)
2000 Fleurie Château des Déduits	B	(87–89)
2000 Morgon (flower label)	B	(88–89)
2000 Morgon Jean Descombes	B	(89–91)
2000 Moulin-à-Vent (flower label)	B	(89–91)
2000 Moulin-à-Vent Cuvée Prestige	C	(91–92+)

2000 Moulin-à-Vent Tour de Bief	B	(89–91)
2000 Régnié (flower label)	A	89

Georges Dubœuf believes 2000 is a "glorious" vintage for Beaujolais. "Only 1947 and 1976, the year of the heat wave and drought, were as precocious as 2000. . . . These are the only three vintages in my memory where we harvested in August," said Dubœuf. "Also, unlike in 1999 where the ripeness was achieved in a spurt right before harvest, in 2000 we had a slow, even ripening," he added. The 2000 vintage produced 10% less wine than 1999, with 10% more hours of sunshine. When asked what potential problems existed for winemakers, Dubœuf said that the warm weather at the harvest might have been cause for concern if the estates didn't have refrigeration equipment. "Today, all the self-respecting vignerons of my region have the necessary tools to deal with a warm vintage," he said.

As is always the case, certain appellations outperformed others. Chiroubles, Régnié, Morgon, Fleurie, Moulin-à-Vent, and Brouilly all had banner years, but Chénas, Juliénas, and St. Amour were damaged by successive hailstorms at the end of July. The best 2000s have magnificent colors, with deep ruby and purples hues. They are also supremely aromatic, which was obvious from the get-go as the entire tasting room filled with raspberry and cherry scents when the first two wines were poured. The 2000 Beaujolais vintage from the most successful appellations has highly impressive depth of fruit, virtually perfect acidity for balance, and ripe tannins. Some of the wines are firmly structured and reveal loads of tannins, but they are generally ripe, sweet, and supple. The communes that did not fare too well have astringent finishes and are not recommended in this report. All of the following wines are superb values.

The 2000 Régnié (flower label) has a dense, medium to dark ruby/purple robe. It is a fabulous Régnié, with an explosive candied cherry, talcum powder, blueberry, and raspberry-scented nose. Medium-bodied and sensual, this wine's character overflows with juicy red, blue, and black fruits whose flavors last throughout its wonderfully sweet and supple finish. Anticipated maturity: now–2005.

The similarly colored 2000 Chiroubles Château de Javernand has a more demure nose that exhibits rose and cherry aromas. It has gorgeous amplitude, coating the taster's palate with softly textured, overripe blueberries and cherries intermingled with violets and other assorted flowers. This elegant, well-structured wine is seamless and flavorful. Anticipated maturity: now–2005.

The excellent 2000 Chiroubles (flower label) is bright purple-colored and reveals a fabulous bouquet of freshly cut flowers in its aromatics. This harmonious, medium-bodied wine is packed with candied blackberries, blueberries, black cherries, and violets. It also possesses a long, lush, fruit-filled finish. Drink it over the next 4 years.

The saturated, medium to dark ruby/purple 2000 Brouilly Domaine des Pierreux has beguiling rose and violet aromas. Medium-bodied and structured, this broad, expansive wine is filled with layers of wild blueberries, dark cherries, and flowers. It is highly expressive, and has a firm yet long and flavorful finish. Anticipated maturity: now–2006.

The 2000 Morgon (flower label) has a dark purple color and reveals black and red cherry aromas. This is a foursquare Beaujolais of impressive depth and concentration. Loads of red and dark fruits can be discerned in its presently tightly wound and unyielding character. It is medium- to full-bodied, powerful, and will repay consumers who dedicate cellar space to a Beaujolais. Anticipated maturity: now–2006.

Dubœuf, not a man given to false propaganda concerning his wines, believes that the 2000 Morgon Jean Descombes is the finest he has tasted. It bursts from the glass with pure red/black fruit and stone aromas. On the palate, this medium- to full-bodied wine is gorgeously refined, broad, and beautifully balanced. It offers loads of cherries, sweet blackberries, and plums in its serious yet forward personality. Anticipated maturity: now–2007.

The Fleurie appellation, known as "the Queen of Beaujolais," did particularly well in the 2000 vintage. Displaying a dense ruby/purple color, the 2000 Fleurie (flower label) has a feminine nose of perfume and sweet cherries. Medium-bodied and well structured, it is loaded with black fruits, violets, and sweet, ripe tannin. Anticipated maturity: now–2005.

The 2000 Fleurie Château des Déduits has a stony, blackberry-scented nose. This medium-bodied, foursquare wine has copious quantities of black fruits and candied grapes in its serious, firm character. This concentrated and extracted Fleurie will require cellaring. Anticipated maturity: now–2006.

The outstanding medium to dark ruby/purple 2000 Fleurie Château de Bachelard offers blackberry and black cherry aromas reminiscent of a first-rate premier cru from Beaune. This is a powerful, masculine wine that is rich, broad, and muscular. Medium- to full-bodied and silky-textured, it boasts multiple layers of dark cherries, cassis, and plumlike flavors. Anticipated maturity: now–2006.

The dark-colored 2000 Moulin-à-Vent (flower label) at first revealed some reduction in its aromatics and flavor profile. With air, its nose blossomed to reveal classic Pinot Noir aromas minerals and red cherries, demonstrating that it will shed all traces of reduction with a pre-bottling aeration. It is medium-bodied, fresh, has excellent depth to its ripe cherry-flavored character, and has a fabulously velvety texture. At $13, this wine is a steal! Anticipated maturity: now–2006.

The 2000 Moulin-à-Vent Tour de Bief has a similar color and an intense nose of red fruits. It explodes on the palate with loads of boisterous yet elegant cherry flavors. It is broad, ample, concentrated, and Pinot Noir–like. This juicy, silky-textured wine is powerful, deep, refined, and firm. Drink it between now–2007.

The 2000 is the maiden vintage for a new Dubœuf project. In close collaboration with five of his growers, he has undertaken to craft a Moulin-à-Vent from the "very best *terroirs,* with the finest growers, low yields (no more than 40 hectoliters per hectare), and from old vines. . . . My goal is to re-create magnificent, ageworthy Moulin-à-Vents similar to those I've recently tasted from 1945 and 1947." In order to accomplish this goal, Dubœuf and his team visit the growers' vineyards regularly to ascertain that the required work is being performed, pay the five growers as though they had produced the maximum allowable yields of the appellation, and participate in all the winemaking decisions.

The 2000 Moulin-à-Vent Cuvée Prestige is dark ruby-colored and reveals toasted oak and black cherry aromas. It is big, backward, intense, and powerful. This medium- to full-bodied wine is highly concentrated and extracted. Loads of blackberries, cassis, and dark cherries can be discerned in its highly structured character. Its extensive, fruit-packed finish displays loads of wonderfully ripe tannin. Anticipated maturity: 2005–2012+.

DOMAINE J. FOILLARD
2000 Morgon Côte de Py   C   89+

Red raspberries and roses can be found in the fresh, expressive aromas of this medium-bodied wine. Loads of chewy cherry, strawberry, and raspberry can be found throughout its densely packed, fruit-dominated personality, as well as in its long, supple finish. Drink it over the next 4–5 years.

DOMAINE MARCEL LAPIERRE
2000 Morgon   C   90

Marcel Lapierre's 2000 Morgon bursts from the glass with dark cherries and raspberries. Medium-bodied, fresh, and focused, it is loaded with plums, earth, cherries, and spices. This outstanding Morgon was of fined, filtered, or sulfured. Impeccable storage is imperative for this gorgeous yet fragile wine. Purchasers should be sure to keep this wine in a cool environment, and confirm that their retailer and wholesaler did the same thing. Drink it over the next 5–6 years.

DOMAINE DES NUGUES

2000 Beaujolais-Villages   **B   89**

Produced from 25- to 40-year-old vines, this medium to dark ruby/purple 2000 Beaujolais-Villages bursts from the glass with candied blackberries and black cherries. It is a rich, medium-bodied effort with excellent depth of fruit, and a soft, sensual, opulent personality. It envelops and coats the taster's palate with loads of sweet, juicy red fruits whose flavors last throughout its cotton candy–like finish. This *superb value* should be consumed over the next 2 years.

DOMAINE J.-P. THEVENET

2000 Morgon   **C   91**

The intense 2000 Morgon explodes from the glass with a myriad of red fruits, principally cherries. Medium-bodied and possessing outstanding focus and concentration, this is a layered, seamless wine crammed with raspberries, strawberries, cherries, and blueberries. It is an extraordinary Morgon that should ameliorate with a 1–2 years of cellaring. Anticipated maturity: 2003–2008.

CHÂTEAU DE THIVIN

2000 Côte de Brouilly Cuvée Zaccharie Geoffrey   **D   91**

This medium to dark ruby/purple wine has intense cherry syrup aromas. Medium-bodied and possessing tremendous density of fruit, it is rich, opulent, and chewy-textured. An extraordinary Côte de Brouilly, it contains massive quantities of cherries, raspberries, and candied strawberries. Its smooth-as-silk finish lasts at least 40 seconds. It is the finest wine I have tasted from this appellation. Drink it over the next 4 years.

DOMAINE DU TRACOT

2000 Régnié Cuvée de Montmeron et du Portet   **B   89**

Tracot's excellent 2000 Régnié Cuvée de Montmeron et du Portet is a stunning value and may well merit an outstanding rating after a year of cellaring. It bursts from the glass with lively plum and black raspberry aromas. Medium-bodied and sporting a terrific oily-textured character, this wine is loaded with cherries, blue berries, and sweet plums. It is rich, glycerin-imbued, and fat. Anticipated maturity: now–2004.

DOMAINE DU VISSOUX

2000 Beaujolais Pierre Chermette   **B   88**

2000 Fleurie Les Garants   **C   89**

The ruby-colored 2000 Beaujolais Pierre Chermette exhibits tangy red fruit aromas. It is medium-bodied and loaded with lush red cherries, raspberries, and strawberries. With its supple finish, this fruit-forward, smile-inducing Beaujolais is perfect for quaffing over the next 18 months.

The ruby-colored 2000 Fleurie Les Garants has delectable blueberry and cherry aromatics. It is well structured, filled with Bing cherries, kirsch, wild blueberries, and juicy blackberries. Medium-bodied and suave, it is meant for drinking over the next 3 years.

CHAMPAGNE

Does anyone remember all the doom and gloom stories about widespread shortages of high-quality Champagne because of the millennium celebrations? Of course, none of that materialized. Instead, a sagging worldwide economy, the sobering effects of the terrorist strikes against the United States, and a relatively bullish American dollar that defies gravity have resulted in a buyer's market. That's the good news. The bad news is that there has been no great vintage for Champagne since 1990, and while those wines can still be found at auction, or by those houses that release their wines much later (Salon, for example), vintage dated Champagnes from 1992, 1993, and 1994 are, at best, above average in quality. 1995 is a better vintage, but the wines are not nearly as exciting as the creamy, rich, structured 1990s. 1996 promises to be the finest vintage since 1990, because of high acidity and intense flavor characteristics. Early tastings of the 1996s reveal tightly knit yet promising wines. Nevertheless, consumers are foolish to pay top retail prices for Champagne, as bargains abound.

One of the more positive developments in the Champagne business has been the increase in the number of small Champagne houses now available in the United States market, which has traditionally been dominated by the giant houses. This has added to the competitive marketplace.

All things considered, it is a good time to buy Champagne, and consumers have the leverage to drive a hard bargain.

The Basics

TYPES OF WINE

Only sparkling wine (about 200 million bottles a year) is produced in Champagne, a viticultural area 90 miles northeast of Paris. Champagne is usually made from a blend of three grapes—Chardonnay, Pinot Noir, and Pinot Meunier. A Champagne called Blanc de Blancs must be 100% Chardonnay. Blanc de Noirs means that the wine has been made from red wine grapes, and the term *crémant* signifies that the wine has slightly less effervescence than typical Champagne.

GRAPE VARIETIES

Chardonnay: Surprisingly, only 25% of Champagne's vineyards are planted with Chardonnay.
Pinot Meunier: The most popular grape in Champagne, Pinot Meunier accounts for 40% of the appellation's vineyards.
Pinot Noir: This grape accounts for 35% of the vineyard acreage in Champagne.

FLAVORS

Most people drink Champagne young, often within hours of purchasing it. However, some observers would argue that high-quality, vintage Champagne should not be drunk until it is at least 10 years old. French law requires that nonvintage Champagne be aged at least one year in the bottle before it is released, and vintage Champagne three years. As a general rule, most top producers are just releasing their 1996s in 2002. Good Champagne not only should taste fresh but should also have flavors akin to buttered wheat toast, ripe apples, and fresh biscuits. When Champagne is badly made, it tastes sour, green, and musty. If it has been abused in shipment or storage, it will taste flat and fruitless. A Blanc de Blancs is a more delicate, refined, lighter wine than those Champagnes that have a hefty percentage of Pinot Noir and Pinot Meunier, the two red grapes utilized.

AGING POTENTIAL

Champagne from the most illustrious houses such as Krug, Bollinger, and Pol Roger can age for 25–30 years, losing much of its effervescence and taking on a creamy, lush, buttery richness not too different from a top white Burgundy. Moët & Chandon's Dom Pérignon 1947, 1964, 1969, and 1971 were gorgeous when tasted in 1994. The 1982 and 1985 were superb in late 2001. Also, Krug's 1947, 1961, 1962, 1964, and 1971; and Bollinger's 1966, 1969, and 1975 R.D. were exquisite when drunk in 1994, as were Pol Roger's 1928 and 1929 when drunk in 1992. These were profound examples of how wonderful Champagne can be with age. But readers should realize that each Champagne house has its own style, and the aging potential depends on the style preferred by that producer. Below are some aging estimates for a number of the best-known brands currently available in the market. The starting point for measuring the aging potential is 2002, not the vintage mentioned.

1990 Bollinger Grande Année: now–2015	1995 Louis Roederer Cristal: 2003–2012
1990 Bollinger Vieilles Vignes: now–2020	1990 Louis Roederer Cristal: 2003–2020
1989 Krug: now–2020	1990 Salon: 2004–2020
1985 Krug: now–2020	1985 Salon: now–2010
1993 Dom Pérignon: now–2005	1990 Taittinger Comtes de Champagne
1990 Dom Pérignon: now–2010	Blancs de Blanc: now–2010
1990 Pol Roger Brut Chardonnay:	1990 Veuve Clicquot La Grande Dame:
now–2008	now–2015

OVERALL QUALITY LEVEL

French Champagne is irrefutably the finest sparkling wine in the world. Despite the hoopla and vast sums of money invested in California, there is no competition from any other wine-producing region if quality is the primary consideration. Nevertheless, the extraordinary financial success enjoyed by many of the big Champagne houses has led, I believe, to a lowering of standards. Commercial greed has resulted in most firms' calling nearly every harvest a vintage year. For example, in the 1950s there were four vintage years, 1952, 1953, 1955, and 1959, and in the 1960s there were five, 1961, 1962, 1964, 1966, and 1969. This increased to eight vintage years in the 1970s (only 1972 and 1977 were excluded). In the 1980s, eight vintages were again declared, the exceptions being 1984 and 1987. A number of the top Champagne houses need to toughen their standards when it comes to vintage Champagne.

In addition to too many vintage years, the quality of the nonvintage brut *cuvées* has deteriorated. The wines, which are supposed to be released when they are showing some signs of maturity, have become greener and more acidic, suggesting that producers have lowered quality standards and are releasing their wines as quickly as possible. But there really is no alternative to the complexity and finesse of French Champagne produced and released under the right conditions. There are less expensive alternatives, particularly sparkling Loire Valley wines, some *crémants* from Alsace and Burgundy, and the sparkling wines from California, Spain, and Italy. However, save for a few exceptions, none of these bubblies remotely approaches the quality of French Champagne.

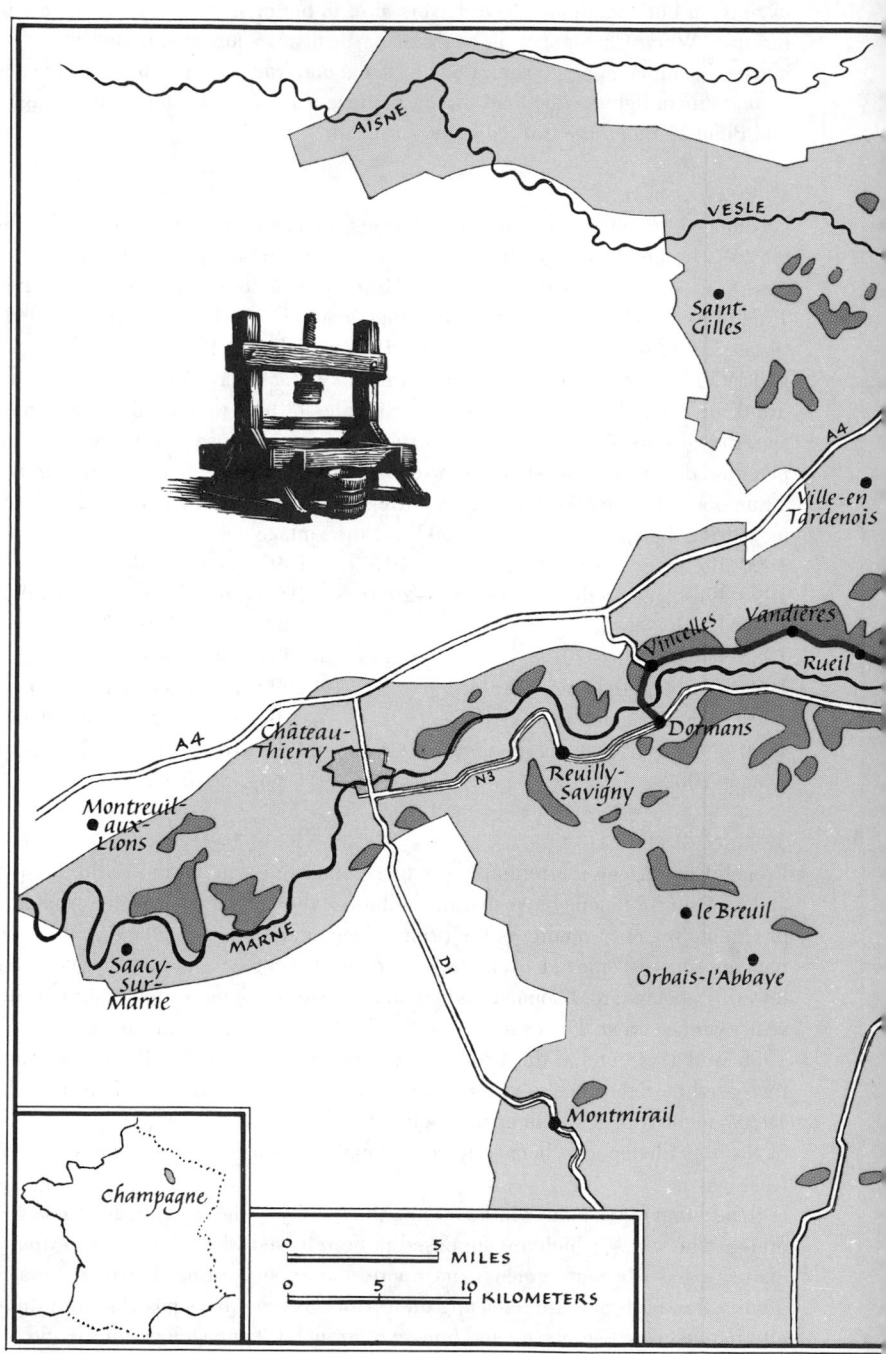

AISNE

VESLE

Saint-
Gilles

A4

Ville-en-
Tardenois

Vincelles

Vandières

Rueil

A4

Château-
Thierry

Dormans

Montreuil-
aux-
Lions

N3

Reuilly-
Savigny

MARNE

le Breuil

Saacy-
sur-
Marne

Orbais-l'Abbaye

D1

Montmirail

Champagne

0   5 MILES

0   5   10 KILOMETERS

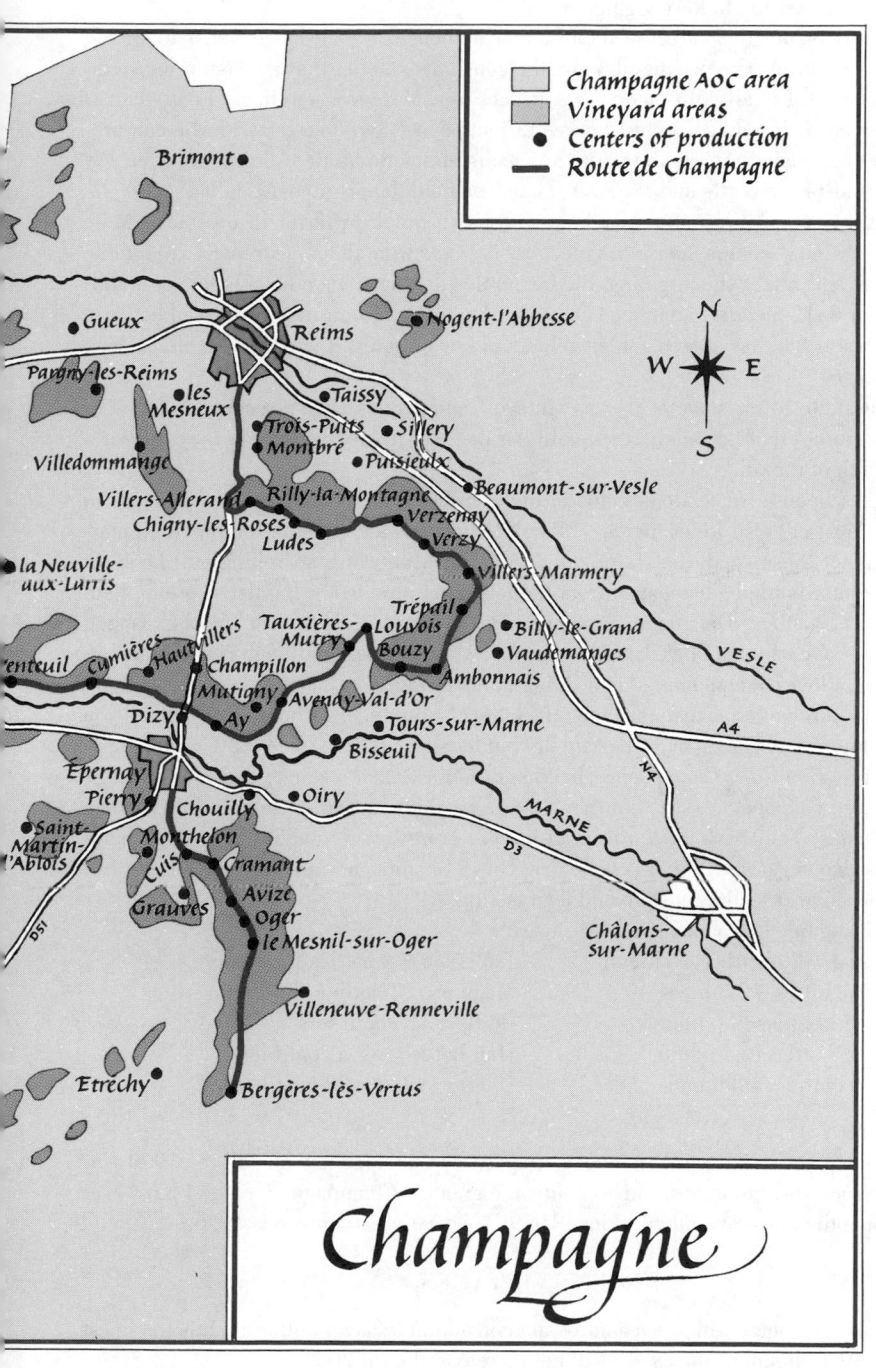

Brimont •

N
W • E
S

Gueux •
• Nogent-l'Abbesse
Reims
Pargny-les-Reims
les
Mesneux •
• Taissy
Trois-Puits • Sillery
Montbré • Puisieulx
Villedommange •
Villers-Allerand • Rilly-la-Montagne •
Chigny-les-Roses • Verzenay
Ludes • Verzy
la Neuville-
aux-Larris •
• Villers-Marmery
Trépail
Tauxières- • Louvois
Mutry Bouzy •
• Billy-le-Grand
• Vaudemanges
Hautvillers
VESLE
Champillon
Ambonnais
Cumières • Mutigny
Venteuil • Avenay-Val-d'Or
Dizy • Ay • Tours-sur-Marne
A4
Bisseuil
Épernay
Pierry • N4
Chouilly • Oiry
Saint-
Martin-
d'Ablois • Monthelon
Cuis Cramant MARNE
Avize
Grauves • Oger
le Mesnil-sur-Oger
D3 Châlons-
sur-Marne
Villeneuve-Renneville
D51
Étrechy •
Bergères-lès-Vertus

Champagne

MOST IMPORTANT INFORMATION TO KNOW

First, you have to do some serious tasting to see which styles of Champagne appeal to you. Additionally, consider the following guidelines:

1. The luxury or prestige *cuvées* of the Champagne houses are always expensive (all sell for $125–300 a bottle). The pricing plays on the consumer's belief that a lavish price signifies a higher level of quality. In many cases it does not. Moreover, too many luxury *cuvées* have become pawns in an ego contest between Champagne's top houses as to who can produce the most expensive wine in the most outrageous, dramatic bottle. Consumers often pay just for the hand-blown bottle and expensive, hand-painted, labor-intensive label.

2. Purchase Champagne from a merchant who has a quick turnover in inventory. More than any other wine, Champagne is a fragile, very delicate wine that is extremely vulnerable to poor storage and bright shop lighting. Buying bottles that have been languishing on retailers' shelves for 6–12 months can indeed be a risky business. If your just-purchased bottle of Champagne tastes flat, has a deep golden color, and few bubbles, it is either too old or dead from bad storage.

3. Don't hesitate to try some of the nonvintage Champagnes I have recommended. The best of them are not that far behind the quality of the best luxury *cuvées,* yet they sell for a quarter to a fifth of the price.

4. There has been a tremendous influx of high-quality Champagnes from small firms in Champagne. Most of these wines may be difficult to find outside of major metropolitan markets, but some of these small houses produce splendid wine worth searching out. Look for some of the estate-bottled Champagne from the following producers: Baptiste-Pertois, Paul Bara, Bonnaire, Cattier, Delamotte, Drappier, Duval-Leroy, Egly-Ouriet, Michel Gonet, Lancelot-Royer, Guy Larmandier, Lassalle, Legras, Mailly, Serge Mathieu, Pierre Moncuit, Joseph Perrier, Ployez-Jacquemart, Alain Robert, and Tarlant.

5. Several technical terms that appear on the label of a producer's Champagne can tell you things about the wine. *Brut* Champagnes are dry but legally can have up to 0.2% sugar added (called *dosage*). *Extra-dry* Champagnes have between 1.2–2% sugar added. Most tasters would call these Champagnes dry, but they tend to be rounder and seemingly fruitier than brut Champagnes. The terms *ultra brut, brut absolu,* or *dosage zéro* signify that the Champagne has had no sugar added and is bone dry. These Champagnes are rarely seen, but can be quite impressive as well as austere and lean tasting.

6. Below is a guide to Champagne bottle sizes:

Nebuchadnezzar = 20 bottles (16 liters)	Jeroboam = 4 bottles (3.2 liters)
Balthazar = 16 bottles (12.8 liters)	Magnum = 2 bottles (1.6 liters)
Salmanazar = 12 bottles (9.6 liters)	Bottle = 75 centiliters
Methuselah = 8 bottles (6.4 liters)	Half bottle = 37.5 centiliters
Rehoboam = 6 bottles (4.8 liters)	Quarter bottle = 20 centiliters

BUYING STRATEGY

I have only one piece of advice for a buying strategy for Champagne—buy all the 1990 vintage Champagnes you can afford. This remains the greatest Champagne vintage I have ever tasted, and it is the finest overall year since 1959. The next great vintage is 1996.

RECENT VINTAGES

1996—A superb vintage with fresh acidity and considerable flavor authority. It is the finest vintage after 1990, but most top *cuvées* will not be released until 2003.

1995—A good to very good vintage, but not exceptional.

1994—Very difficult weather conditions (considerable rain between August 20 and September 14) have resulted in a small crop of average quality. Because of this, pressure to increase prices significantly is likely.

1993—With a large crop of mostly average-quality juice, 1993 is unlikely to be a highly desirable vintage year.

1992—This hugely abundant yet potentially good-quality vintage escaped most of the bad weather that plagued the southern half of France. The quality is above-average and the quantity is enormous. A vintage year, but I don't anticipate many inspiring wines.

1991—1991 is a small, exceptionally difficult vintage that is unlikely to be declared a vintage year except by the greediest producers. It rivals 1987 and 1984 as one of the three worst vintages for Champagne in the last 15 years.

1990—A gigantic crop of splendidly rich, opulently textured, full-bodied, gorgeously proportioned Champagnes were produced. This is unquestionably the finest Champagne vintage I have ever tasted. I have not tasted anything less than an excellent wine, and the Blancs de Blanc *cuvées* have a surreal elegance allied to richness.

1989—Another high-quality, abundant year should produce wines similar to the ripe, rich, creamy style of the 1982 Champagnes, with a very ripe, fat style of fizz.

1988—Not much Champagne was made because of the small harvest, but this is undoubtedly a vintage year. The 1988s are leaner, more austere, and higher in acidity than the flamboyant 1989s and 1990s.

1987—A terrible year, the worst of the decade.

1986—This is a vintage year, producing an abundant quantity of soft, ripe, fruity wines.

1985—Along with 1982 and 1989, 1985 is the finest vintage of the 1980s, thanks to excellent ripeness and a good-sized crop. A superb Champagne vintage!

1984—A lousy year, but there were vintage Champagnes from 1984 in the market. Remember what P. T. Barnum once said?

1983—A gigantic crop of good-quality Champagne was produced. Although the wines may lack the opulence and creamy richness of the 1982s, they are hardly undersized wines. Most 1983s have matured quickly and are delicious now. They should be drunk up.

1982—A great vintage of ripe, rich, creamy, intense wines. If they were to be criticized, it would be for their very forward, lower than normal acids, which suggest they will age quickly, but no one should miss the top Champagnes from 1982; they are marvelously rounded, ripe, generously flavored wines.

1981—The Champagnes from 1981 are rather lean and austere, but that has not prevented many top houses from declaring this a vintage year.

OLDER VINTAGES

The 1980 vintage is mediocre; 1979 is excellent; 1978 is tiring; 1976, once top-notch, is now fading; 1975 is superb, as are well-cellared examples of 1971, 1969, and 1964. When buying Champagne, whether it is 3 years old or 20, pay the utmost care to the manner in which it was treated before you bought it. Champagne is the most fragile wine in the marketplace, and it cannot tolerate poor storage.

RATING CHAMPAGNE'S BEST PRODUCERS

Where a producer has been assigned a range of stars (***/****), the lower rating has been used for placement in this hierarchy.

* * * * * (OUTSTANDING)

Bollinger (full-bodied)	Henriot (full-bodied)
Egly-Ouriet (full-bodied)	Krug (full-bodied)
Gosset (full-bodied)	J. Lassalle (light-bodied)

Laurent-Perrier (medium-bodied)   Salon (medium-bodied)
Alain Robert (full-bodied)   Taittinger (light-bodied)
Louis Roederer (full-bodied)   Veuve Clicquot (full-bodied)
Pol Roger (medium-bodied)

* * * * *(EXCELLENT)*

Baptiste-Pertois (light-bodied)   Guy Larmandier (full-bodied)
Paul Bara (full-bodied)   Lechère (light-bodied)
Billecart-Salmon (light-bodied)   R. & L. Legras (light-bodied)
Bonnaire (light-bodied)   Mailly (medium-bodied)
de Castellane (light-bodied)   Serge Mathieu (medium-bodied)
Cattier (light-bodied)   Moët & Chandon (medium
Charbaut (light-bodied)   bodied)****/*****
Delamotte (medium-bodied)   Pierre Moncuit (medium-bodied)
Diebolt-Vallois (medium-bodied)   Bruno Paillard (light-bodied)
Drappier (medium-bodied), since 1985   Joseph Perrier (medium-bodied)
Alfred Gratien (full-bodied)   Perrier-Jouët (light-bodied)
Grimonnet (medium-bodied)   Ployez-Jacquemart (medium-bodied)
Heidsieck Monopole (medium-bodied)   Dom Ruinart (light-bodied)
Jacquart (medium-bodied)   Jacques Selosse (light-bodied)
Jacquesson (light-bodied)   Taillevent (medium-bodied)
Lancelot-Royer (medium-bodied)   Tarlant (full-bodied)****/*****

* * * *(GOOD)*

Ayala (medium-bodied)   Charles Heidsieck (medium-bodied)
Barancourt (full-bodied)   Lanson (light-bodied)
Bricout (light-bodied)   Launois Père (light-bodied)
Canard Ducheafne (medium-bodied)   Mercier (medium-bodied)
Deutz (medium-bodied)   Mumm (medium-bodied)
Duval-Leroy (medium-bodied)   Philipponnat (medium-bodied)
H. Germain (light-bodied)   Piper Heidsieck (light-bodied)
Michel Gonet (medium-bodied)   Pommery and Greno (light-bodied)
Georges Goulet (medium-bodied)

* * *(AVERAGE)*

Beaumet-Chaurey (light-bodied)   Jestin (light-bodied)
Besserat de Bellefon (light-bodied)   Oudinot (medium-bodied)
Boizel (light-bodied)   Rapeneau (medium-bodied)
Nicolas Feuillatte (light-bodied)   Alfred Rothschild (light-bodied)
Goldschmidt-Rothschild (light-bodied)   Marie Stuart (light-bodied)

THE BEST PRODUCERS OF NONVINTAGE BRUT

Billecart-Salmon   Gosset Grand Réserve
Bollinger Special Cuvée   Alfred Gratien
Cattier   Krug
Charbaut   Larmandier
Delamotte   Lechère Orient Express
Drappier Maurice Chevalier   Pierre Moncuit
Egly-Ouriet   Bruno Paillard Première Cuvée

Perrier-Jouët
Ployez-Jacquemart
Pol Roger

Louis Roederer Brut Premier
Tarlant Cuvée Louis
Veuve Clicquot Yellow Label

THE BEST PRODUCERS OF ROSÉ CHAMPAGNE

Billecart-Salmon NV
Billecart-Salmon Cuvée Elizabeth Salmon
 1990, 1995
Bollinger Grande Année 1985, 1988, 1990
Nicolas Feuillatte 1995
Gosset 1990
Heidsieck Monopole Diamant Bleu 1990,
 1995
Krug NV
Laurent-Perrier Grand Siècle Cuvée
 Alexandra 1990
Moët & Chandon Brut Imperial 1988,
 1989, 1990

Moët & Chandon Dom Pérignon 1986,
 1990
Perrier-Jouët Blason de France NV
Perrier-Jouët Fleur de Champagne 1986,
 1988, 1990
Louis Roederer Cristal Rosé 1995
Pol Roger 1985, 1986, 1988, 1990
Dom Ruinart 1985, 1988
Taittinger Comtes de Champagne 1990,
 1993, 1995
Veuve Clicquot La Grande Dame 1988,
 1990

THE BEST PRODUCERS OF 100% CHARDONNAY BLANC DE BLANCS

Ayala 1988, 1990
Baptiste-Pertois Cuvée Réservée NV
Billecart-Salmon 1990, 1995
Delamotte 1990, 1992
Jacquesson 1990, 1995
Krug Clos de Mesnil 1983, 1985, 1988,
 1989, 1990
Lancelot-Royer
Guy Larmandier Cramant NV
R. & L. Legras
A. R. Lenoble 1995

Jean Milan NV
Moncault NV
Bruno Paillard
Joseph Perrier Cuvée Royale
Alain Robert
Louis Roederer 1995
Pol Roger Brut Chardonnay 1985, 1990,
 1995
Salon 1985, 1988, 1990
Taittinger Comtes de Champagne 1990,
 1995

THE BEST PRODUCERS OF LUXURY CUVÉES

Billecart-Salmon Grande Cuvée 1990,
 1995
Bollinger R.D. 1975, 1982, 1985, 1988
Bollinger Grande Année 1985, 1988, 1990,
 1992
Bollinger Vieilles Vignes 1985, 1990
Cattier Clos du Moulin 1985, 1990
Deutz Cuvée William Deutz 1995
Drappier Grand Sendrée 1985, 1990
Nicolas Feuillatte Cuvée Palmes d'Or
 1990, 1995
Gosset Celebris Brut 1990, 1995
Heidsieck Monopole Diamant Bleu 1985,
 1988, 1990, 1995
Henriot Cuvée des Enchanteleurs 1990

Krug 1982, 1985, 1988, 1989, 1990
Lassalle Cuvée Angeline 1985, 1990
Laurent-Perrier Grand Siècle 1985, 1988,
 1990
Moët & Chandon Dom Pérignon 1982,
 1985, 1988, 1990
Mumm René Lalou 1985, 1990
Joseph Perrier Cuvée Josephine 1985,
 1990
Perrier-Jouët Fleur de Champagne 1990,
 1995
Philipponnat Clos des Goisses 1988,
 1990
Ployez-Jacquemart d'Harbonville 1990
Pommery Cuvée Louise 1989

Alain Robert Le Mesnil Séléction 1979
Louis Roederer Cristal 1985, 1988, 1990
Pol Roger Cuvée Winston Churchill 1985,
    1988, 1990, 1993
Salon Blanc des Blancs 1985, 1988, 1990

Jacques Selosse Origine NV
Taittinger Comtes de Champagne 1985,
    1988, 1990, 1995
Veuve Clicquot La Grande Dame 1985,
    1988, 1990, 1993

THE LOIRE VALLEY

The Basics

The Loire Valley is by far France's largest wine-producing area, stretching 635 miles from the warm foothills of the Massif Central (a short drive west from Lyon and the vineyards of the Rhône Valley) to the windswept shores of the Atlantic Ocean in Brittany. Most wine drinkers can name more historic Loire Valley châteaux than Loire Valley wines. That is a pity, because the Loire Valley wine-producing areas offer France's most remarkable array of wines from a wide range of varietals, the best known being Sauvignon Blanc, Chenin Blanc, Pinot Noir, and Cabernet Franc. Its vineyards are some of the world's oldest, yet Loire Valley wines remain relatively inexpensive. Stylistically, the whites range from the bone dry to the amazingly sweet. Similarly, the Loire's reds can be found in a wide variety of styles, from carbonic maceration (Beaujolais-like) wines meant for immediate consumption to ageworthy, austere, yet serious Cabernets.

Over the last few years consumers have experienced soaring wine prices from the world's best-known regions, with California, Italy, and Bordeaux leading the way. The wines of the Loire Valley, a little-known and underappreciated region, have the combination of quality and value that merits considerable attention from consumers.

WHY ARE THE LOIRE'S WINES SO LITTLE KNOWN?
The vast majority of wine lovers have only a passing knowledge of the Loire's wines. Why? Consider the following:

1. The Loire Valley is confusing. Its ever-growing number of appellations (well over 60), thousands of vignerons, numerous varietals, and countless vineyards of varying quality make grasping Burgundy seem like child's play by comparison.

2. The overall quality of wines is average at best. Consumers who blindly purchase wines from this region have the odds stacked against them, because the majority of the Loire's wines are mediocre (well over 50% of the wines tasted from the excellent 1995, 1996, and 1997 vintages cannot be recommended).

3. Vintage quality is highly erratic, largely because much of the Loire is in northern Europe, where the climate is marginal and unpredictable. In great vintages, this region's offerings combine ripeness with high acidity, resulting in wines as outstanding as any in the world. In vintages characterized by cold, damp summers, the wines have searing acidity and

insufficient fruit. Since 1997, an excellent vintage for the Loire, this region has experienced several difficult years.

4. Finally, the Loire is, in large measure, ignored. Importers, with few exceptions, have approached the Loire as a secondary wine-growing region, spending extremely little time and energy ferreting out good producers or working closely to improve the quality with those they do represent. The efforts of hands-on, quality-driven importers, whose positive influence is felt strongly in Burgundy, the Rhône, and the south of France, do surprisingly little in the Loire. While it is all but impossible to visit Burgundy without tripping over famous American importers, there are numerous quality producers in the Loire that have never sold a bottle in the United States. Furthermore, wine merchants and writers have not done an adequate job teaching consumers about the spectacular gems this region is capable of producing.

TYPES OF WINE

Dry white table wines dominate the production, as do the three major white wine grapes found in the Loire. The Sauvignon Blanc is at its best in Sancerre and Pouilly-Fumé. The Chenin Blanc produces dry, sweet, and sparkling white wines. It reaches its zenith in Vouvray, Savennières, Bonnezeaux, Coteaux du Layon, and Quarts de Chaume. Last, there is the Muscadet grape (its true name is Melon de Bourgogne), from which Muscadet wines are made. There are plenty of light, frank, fruity, herbaceous red wines produced, and a few serious and ageworthy ones, from Gamay, Pinot Noir, Cabernet Franc, and Cabernet Sauvignon grapes in appellations such as Anjou, Anjou-Villages, Bourgueil, Chinon, St.-Nicolas-de-Bourgueil, and Touraine. Rosés, which can be delicious but are frightfully irregular in quality, tend to emerge from Anjou, Sancerre, Chinon, and Reuilly.

GRAPE VARIETIES

Chenin Blanc, Sauvignon Blanc, Muscadet, and Gros Plant are the four dominant white wine grapes, but Chardonnay, especially from Haut-Poitou, is frequently seen. For red wines, Gamay, Grolleau and Pinot Noir are seen in parts of the Loire (Pinot Noir is the varietal used for red Sancerres), but in the top red wine Loire appellations it is virtually all Cabernet Sauvignon and Cabernet Franc.

A QUICK GUIDE TO THE DIVERSITY OF THE LOIRE VALLEY FROM WEST TO EAST

THE WINES OF THE PAYS NANTAIS

The Pays Nantais, which gets its name from the Atlantic port city of Nantes, is the westernmost viticultural region of the Loire River valley. Two grape varietals dominate the area, and the resulting wines are named after their grapes. Regrettably, this region's wines are typically produced from high yields that are machine-harvested. Furthermore, they rarely receive the care and attention during vinification and *élevage* that are lavished on more highly respected wines.

Gros Plant du Pays Nantais   I have unfortunately tasted many wines produced from Gros Plant. As with other varietals, Gros Plant has alternative names in the different viticultural regions it is grown in. Some of my favorites, because I feel they more adequately describe this varietal, include Folle, Fou (both words meaning "crazy" in French), and Enragé ("enraged"). Even its finest producers fashion such acidic wines that I can only recommend purchasing any other wine available—or drinking water!

Muscadet   This vast area is known for making inexpensive, fresh wines that should be consumed within several years of the vintage. There is generic Muscadet, but even better is the

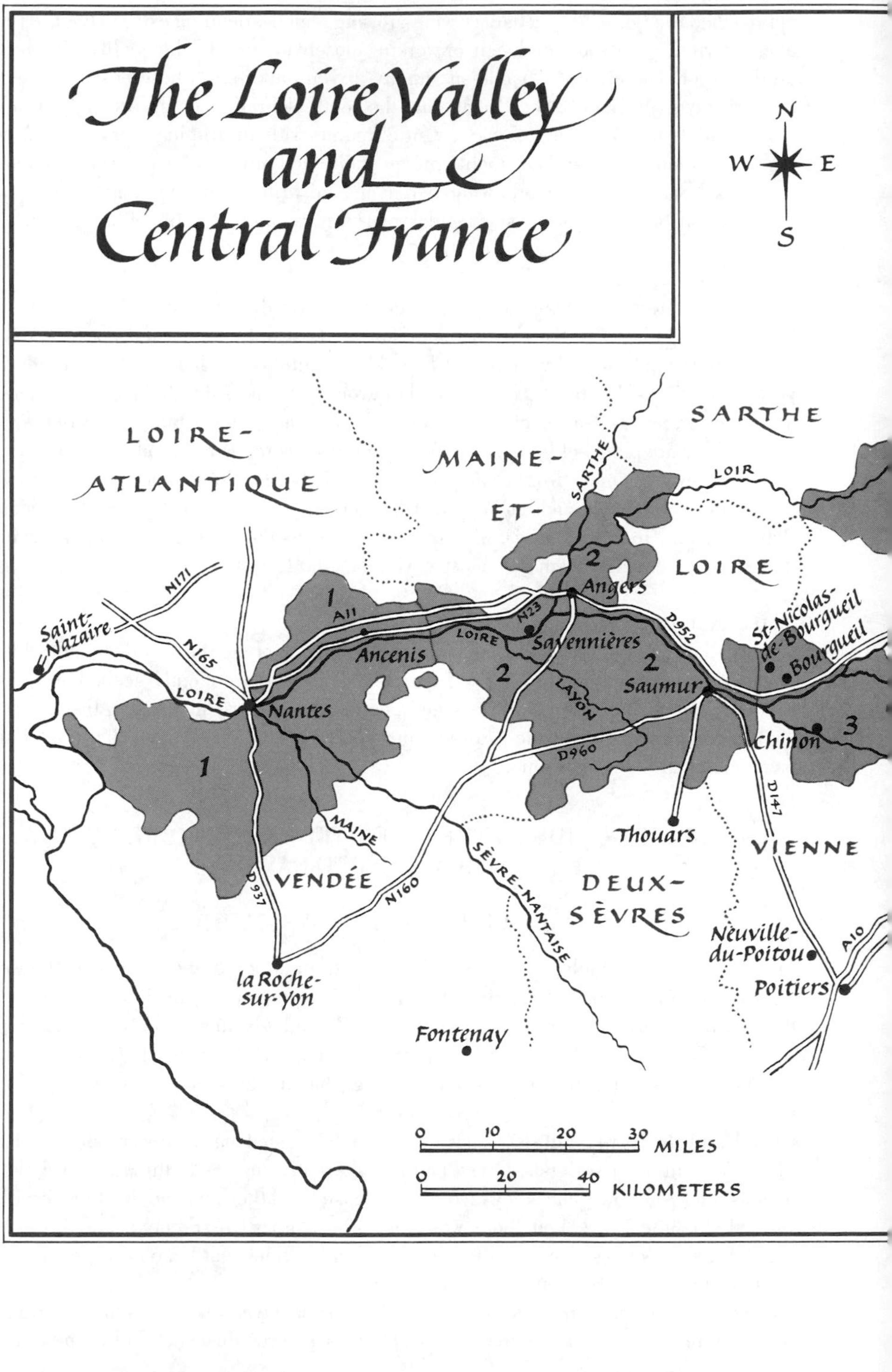

The Loire Valley and Central France

N
W · E
S

LOIRE-
ATLANTIQUE

MAINE-
ET-
LOIRE

SARTHE

LOIR

SARTHE

N171

Saint-
Nazaire

N165

1   A11

Ancenis

LOIRE

N23

Angers   2

Savennières

LOIRE

St-Nicolas-
de-Bourgueil

Bourgueil

D952

LOIRE

Nantes

2

LAYON

Saumur   2

Chinon   3

1

D960

D147

MAINE

D937

VENDÉE

N160

SÈVRE-NANTAISE

Thouars

DEUX-
SÈVRES

VIENNE

A10

Neuville-
du-Poitou

Poitiers

la Roche-
sur-Yon

Fontenay

0   10   20   30   MILES

0   20   40   KILOMETERS

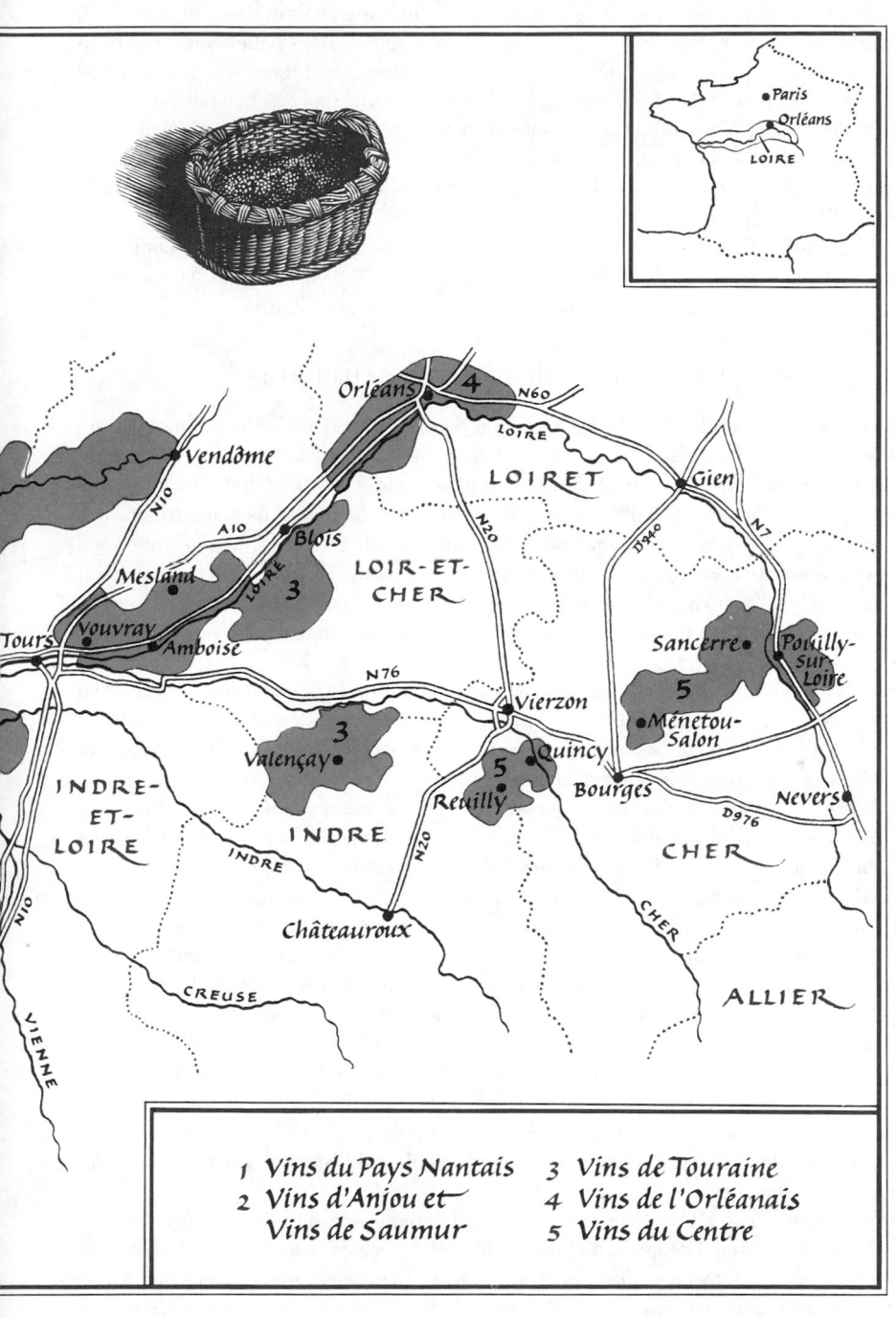

Paris
Orléans
LOIRE

Orléans · 4 N60
LOIRE
LOIRET
Vendôme
Gien
N10
A10
N20
Blois
LOIR-ET-
CHER
Mesland
3
Sancerre · Pouilly-
sur-
Loire
Tours
Vouvray
Amboise
N76
Vierzon
Ménetou-
Salon
Valençay
3
Quincy
5
INDRE-
ET-
LOIRE
5
Reuilly
Bourges
Nevers
D976
INDRE
CHER
INDRE
Châteauroux
CREUSE
ALLIER
VIENNE
CHER

1 Vins du Pays Nantais   3 Vins de Touraine
2 Vins d'Anjou et   4 Vins de l'Orléanais
  Vins de Saumur   5 Vins du Centre

Muscadet de Sèvre et Maine, which is bottled *sur-lie* by the best producers. Muscadet, which possesses an enthralling crispness and freshness, works wonders with fresh shellfish. This vast area offers a tremendous range in quality, from insipid, vapid, hollow wines to wines with considerable personality. Top producers are capable of crafting wines with noteworthy richness, complexity, and character. While I believe these wines are at their best young, when they are expressing considerable freshness and primary fruit, they do not fall apart with aging. Topflight older Muscadets take on some Chenin-like nuances of almonds and herbs with cellaring. The best recent vintages for Muscadet have been 1997 and 1996.

Muscadet's finest producers include Château de Chasseloir, Chêreau-Carré (particularly its Château l'Oiselinière de la Ramée), Domaine des Dorices, Domaine de l'Ecu, Domaine le Fief Dubois (particularly its Le Fief du Breil), Domaine de la Haie Trois Sols, Louis Métaireau, Domaine du Moulin de la Minière (particularly its Cuvée Prestige), Domaine La Quilla, and the Vignerons de la Noëlle (particularly its Les Follies Siffait).

THE WINES OF ANJOU AND THE SAUMUROIS

Angers (the region around it is called Anjou) and Saumur (its region is the Saumurois) are towns located on the Loire River in western France. As the crow flies, Angers is approximately 100 miles from the Atlantic Ocean and Saumur slightly less than 200. The vineyards around Angers and Saumur are all located quite close to the Loire and its many tributaries, which serve to moderate vineyard temperatures. In fact, freezing temperatures in winter and early spring prevent vines from growing just a few miles north of the Loire. The geology of each region differs, with Anjou's being primarily composed of schist, volcanic rocks, sedimentary deposits, sandstone, and slate and the Saumurois's having mostly chalk and sedimentary deposits.

Whites What both regions' whites have in common is their reliance on Chenin Blanc. All the whites produced in the appellations of Anjou and the Saumurois are made either entirely from Chenin Blanc or, in the case of the regional appellations, from a preponderance of Chenin. Whites from these neighboring areas can be either dry, off-dry, or sweet.

Sweet Whites Some of the best-kept secrets in the wine world are the sweet wines produced in Anjou. These are without a doubt the finest values to be found in French sweet wines. Produced from Chenin Blanc, a varietal that, like Riesling, can produce world-class sweet *and* dry wines, many of these offerings have prodigious cellaring capacity. Anyone who has ever tasted a top Quarts de Chaume, Coteaux du Layon, or Bonnezeaux knows the amazing heights that can be attained by these wines in top vintages. Whereas young Sauternes and New World sweet wines can often be heavy (sometimes even flabby) and oak-laden, sweet Anjou Chenin Blancs can be amazingly delicate, lacelike, supremely nuanced wines. In their youth they are often more accessible than German sweet offerings because their acidity, while quite high, is generally more integrated and the fruit more dominant. In time, like all sweet wines, those from Anjou take on an added dimension as their sweetness and fruit melt into their mineral-laden cores. Some of the most extraordinary wines I have ever tasted have been mature Chenins from Anjou (including René Renou's 1947 Bonnezeaux and Baumard's 1945 Quarts de Chaume).

Off-Dry Whites The off-dry wines of Anjou and Saumur, in addition to being virtually unknown, suffer the same fate as most of the world's off-dry wines—they are ignored by consumers who seem to want wines to be either dry *or* sweet. In my view, this is a mistake. Anjou and the Saumurois's off-dry wines can often provide the best of both worlds. They have a trace of residual sugar that excites the palate and matches well with spicy and intensely flavored foods, yet they do not possess the overpowering weight of fully sweet wines.

Dry Whites Dry Chenin Blanc has many faces, best exemplified by the extremely ageworthy, mineral-laden Savennières and the crisp lemon-lime Saumurs, which require immediate consumption. They often possess bracing acidity, providing a lively and refreshing alternative to the thick, and often dry flabby whites routinely encountered on the market.

Red and Rosé Wines   Anjou is (mistakenly) acclaimed for its rosé wines, which can range from dry to medium sweet. In the 1980s, Anjou and Saumur reds produced from Cabernet Franc, Cabernet Sauvignon, Gamay, and Grolleau began to receive considerable attention from bargain hunters looking for inexpensive, light-bodied, fruity red wines. In particular, Gamay has done well in Anjou, producing richly fruity wines. Cabernet Franc and Cabernet Sauvignon have made considerable progress in the 1990s as some producers realized that ripeness matters. Presently, a handful of producers craft wines with intense dark fruit aromatics and rich Cabernet personalities packed with blackberries and fresh herbs. Hard tannins in this northern region continue to be a problem, yet considerable progress has been made. While there is still much work to be done, Anjou, Anjou-Villages, Saumur, and Saumur-Champigny do offer a few delicious (very reasonably priced) alternatives to frightfully expensive Bordeaux for Cabernet lovers.

A FEW NOTEWORTHY APPELLATIONS

Anjou (whites, dry)   Wines from this regional appellation (similar to the generic Bourgogne and Bordeaux appellations) must be produced from a minimum of 80% Chenin Blanc with Chardonnay and Sauvignon Blanc providing the balance. Recent tastings have confirmed that Anjou is making enormous progress in the quality of its wines. Yields are being reduced and innovative vignerons are doing their best to provide consumers with a viable option to the omnipresent Chardonnay. In the past few years, the vignerons of Anjou (and a few other appellations such as Bonnezeaux) have taken steps to ensure this qualitative resurgence. In order to be entitled to appellation status, each grower must now submit his or her vineyards to three inspections during the growing season by experts who check to make sure proper viticultural practices are employed to remain within the legal yield limits.

The finest recent vintages include 1997 (rich) and 1996 (vibrant and lemony). Consumers searching out great values in lemony, minerally whites should consider some offerings from the Domaine de la Bergerie, Château du Breuil, Château de Fesles ("F" de Fesles), Domaine Vincent Ogereau, or Domaine Richou.

Cabernet d'Anjou (sweet rosé)   The name suggests a red wine, but in essence this is a rosé that tends to be herbaceous and sweet. It is a style of wine that does not particularly appeal to me, but in superripe vintages such as 1997 some producers crafted supple, sweet, cherry-flavored rosés that some consumers may enjoy. Domaine Vincent Ogereau and Château de Passavant are Cabernet d'Anjou producers of merit.

Coteaux de l'Aubance (off-dry or sweet)   This appellation is all but unknown in the United States (and even in France!). Its wines are generally off-dry or sweet, delicate, floral, with touches of honeysuckle, almond extract, and flavors reminiscent of cool Earl Grey tea with cream and sugar. They are not as long-lived as some others from the region, and should be drunk in their first 10 years of life. They can easily accompany food, as their sweetness is not overpowering (except in very ripe years such as 1997). Several of my favorite matches are with fish or lightly spiced chicken dishes. I use them when a full-bodied Alsatian Vendanges Tardives would be too much for a dish or meal, or when a dry wine would be overpowered by a food's intense flavors. The finest recent vintages include 1997, 1996, 1995, 1990, and 1989. Some of the better producers to search out include Domaine des Charbotières, Domaine de Montgilet, Moulin des Besneries, and Domaine Richou.

Coteaux du Layon (sweet)   Truly one of the world's most undervalued sweet wines, a Coteaux du Layon can sport the names of seven recognized villages (including Faye, St.-Aubin, St.-Lambert, Rablay, Beaulieu, Rochefort, and Chaume). The local cognoscenti consider Chaume the best (at present, Chaume producers are attempting to have their appellation upgraded to grand cru status). Bonnezeaux and Quarts de Chaume are crus of

Coteaux du Layon. They must be produced from vines in specifically delimited areas and, in addition, must attain certain minimum sugar levels in order to legally be called Bonnezeaux and Quarts de Chaume. If they cannot meet these requirements, they are entitled only to Coteaux du Layon status. The finest recent vintages include 1997, 1996, 1995, 1990, and 1989.

Coteaux du Layons are sweet wines that are not generally as powerful as the Bonnezeaux and Quarts de Chaume but tend to be significantly richer than wines from Coteaux de l'Aubance. The flavors of Coteaux du Layon are very much like those of Coteaux de l'Aubance, but with more density and an added mineral dimension. These are often elegant wines with a refined blend of fruit, sweetness, and acid. In France, wines from Coteaux du Layon, Bonnezeaux, and Quarts de Chaume are often consumed as the ideal apéritif or to accompany foie gras, but I enjoy them as a substitute for dessert. These wines age remarkably well, with bottle age revealing flavors of spiced apples, minerals, traces of honey, caramel, butterscotch, and loads of honeysuckle. Some of the finest Coteaux du Layon producers are Patrick Baudoin, Domaine des Baumards, Domaine de la Bergerie, Château du Breuil, Philippe Delesvaux, Domaine Gaudard, Château de la Genaiserie, Domaine des Grandes Vignes, Château de la Guimonière, Domaine Vincent Ogereau, Domaine du Petit Val, Jo Pithon, Château de Plaisance, Château de la Roulerie, Domaine des Sablonnettes, Domaine Sauveroy, and Château Soucherie.

Some of the finest Bonnezeaux producers include Château de Fesles, Domaine des Grandes Vignes, Domaine du Petit Val, Domaine des Petits Quarts, and Domaine René Renou. Some of the finest Quarts de Chaume producers include Domaine des Baumards, Château de Plaisance, and Château de Suronde.

Coteaux de Saumur (off-dry) These 100% Chenin Blanc–based wines can be delicate, lacelike beauties with superb delineation. Lively herbal tea, mineral, and citrus flavors are softened by small amounts of residual sugar. I recommend drinking them as an apéritif or with cream-based, grilled, or spicy foods. The 1997s are excellent, yet richer than the norm, and the 1996s are bright, lemony, and vibrant. Both vintages are highly recommended. Some of the best producers of Coteaux de Saumur include Domaine des Champs Fleuris and Domaine de Nerleux.

Saumur Reds Lower yields, less manipulation, and good vintages have produced some excellent wines in this historically underachieving appellation. These reasonably priced Cabernet Franc– and Cabernet Sauvignon–dominated wines can be delicious near-term drinking wines from the region's best producers.

Some Coteaux de Saumur producers of merit include Domaine Langlois-Château and Domaine des Raynières.

Saumur Whites (dry) Saumur, a town to the east of Angers on the Loire, is best known for its red wines, yet its refreshing, crisp, lively, and citrus-flavored whites merit attention. As with Anjou whites, this regional appellation's wines must be produced from a minimum of 80% Chenin Blanc (Sauvignon Blanc and Chardonnay can be added to the blend). The finest recent vintages include 1997 (rich) and 1996 (vibrant and lemony). The best producers include Domaine des Nerleux and Domaine de Saint Jean.

Saumur-Champigny (reds) Primarily produced from Cabernet Franc (known as Breton in this region), Saumur-Champignys may also include up to 20% Cabernet Sauvignon or Pineau d'Aunis in their blends (this last varietal is slowly disappearing). Just a few years ago, this appellation's reputation for producing first-rate reds was unjustified. The wines were often hollow, revealing evidence of unripe fruit, and finished on hard, astringent tannins. Recently, however, the efforts of a handful of producers have paid enormous dividends. While topflight Saumur-Champignys are far from inexpensive, they are noteworthy values when compared to Bordeaux's absurdly high prices. Young, the finest Saumur-Champignys display dark ruby colors, cassis, and fresh herb aromas and rich personalities crammed with blackberries and dark cherries. Hard tannins remain a concern in some vintages. With aging, these wines develop considerable complexity, with slate, earth, and mineral notes intertwined with strawberries, raspberries, and black currants. Consumers take note, this appellation has a few producers crafting truly outstanding wines. The finest recent vintages include 1997 (the ripest and most supple), 1996 (bright and in need of cellaring), and 1990 and 1989 (at their peaks).

Saumur-Champigny's finest producers include Domaine des Champs Fleuris, Château de Hureau, Domaine René Noël Legrand (particularly the Les Rogelins), Château de Parnay, Domaine des Roches Neuves (particularly the Cuvée Marginale), Clos Rougeard (the famed Foucault brothers), and Domaine de St.-Just (particularly the Clos Moleton).

Savennières (generally dry, but can be off-dry or sweet)   Located on the northern bank of the Loire, just west of Angers and directly across the river from the vineyards of Coteaux du Layon and Coteaux de l'Aubance, Savennières's vineyards benefit from the moderating climatic influence of the river. These are not lush, oaky wines but rather austere, steely, crisp, highly delineated, and amazingly long-lived whites that exhibit mineral, stone, floral, and earth flavors. Prior to World War I, Savennières were so prized by wine aficionados that a bottle often sold for more than a Montrachet! Today they are largely forgotten, so extraordinary, complex, ageworthy wines can be purchased for little more than a song. These wines are delicious within the first 4 years of their release when they are expressing primary fruit flavors, then shut down and become awkward for 5–6 years. Ten years or so of cellaring reveals wines of considerable complexity and magnificent minerality.

The best producers of Savennières include Domaine des Baumards, Château de Chamboureau, Domaine du Closel, Château d'Epiré, Domaine de la Monnaie, Château Soucherie, and Clos des Varennes.

THE WINES OF TOURAINE

Touraine, as the region around the city of Tours is known, is responsible for some of the Loire's most famous red and white wines. Names such as Vouvray and Chinon are not unknown to the majority of the world's wine lovers. Interestingly, however, while the names are known, the wines themselves are not. This bucolic region stretches from Bourgueil, St.-Nicolas-de-Bourgueil, and Chinon in the west (about a 45-minute drive from Tours), to the regional Touraine appellation vineyards that stretch across vast plains and rolling hills to the east and southeast of Tours. The glorious Chenin Blanc is the predominant varietal (Vouvray, Montlouis, and the whites of Chinon are 100% Chenin) for whites, Cabernet Franc is the driving force behind Chinon, Bourgeuil, and St.-Nicolas-de-Bourgueil, and a host of different grape types is found in the regional appellation wines (Sauvignon Blanc, Gamay, Cabernet Franc, and Cabernet Sauvignon dominate).

Bourgueil   If you ask a Parisian about Bourgueil, chances are it is one of his or her favorites. More popular in France than in America, Bourgueil makes a fruity, raspberry-scented and -flavored wine that should be drunk in its first 5–6 years of life. The problem is that unless the vintage is exceptionally ripe, as it was in 1989, 1990, 1996, and 1997, these wines are strikingly vegetal. The finest producers include Jean-Yves Billet (for his Vieilles Vignes and Cuvée les Bezards), Domaine de la Chanteleuserie (Thierry Boucard), Domaine des Chesnaies, Domaine de la Chevalerie (Pierre Caslot), and all the *cuvées* of the supertalented Pierre-Jacques Druet (including his scrumptious and moderately priced Bourgueil Rosé).

Chinon   This appellation is considered by many to produce the best red wines of the Loire Valley. Made from Cabernet Franc, in exceptionally ripe years such as 1997, 1996, 1990, and 1989 it possesses abundant herb-tinged raspberry fruit. In less ripe years, Chinon wines are intensely acidic and vegetal. Several minimal interventionists turn out handcrafted wines that deserve to be tasted, however the vast majority of Chinons are harvested phenologically unripe, a problem that plagues the Loire's reds. Grape sugars can attain adequate levels (and are invariably boosted via chaptalization), yet if the skins, pits, and stems (for those that don't destem) have not had sufficient time to ripen, the resulting wines have hard, astringent, and rustic finishes. The best recent vintages have been 1997, 1996, 1990, and 1989.

Chinon's finest producers include Philippe Alliet, Bernard Baudry, Couly-Dutheil (particularly the Clos de l'Echo), Pierre-Jacques Druet, Château de la Grille, Charles Joguet, Wilfred Rousse (particularly the Vieilles Vignes), and Gérard Spelty (particularly the Clos de Neuilly).

Jasnières This 47-acre appellation north of Tours produces very dry, often excellent white wines from Chenin Blanc. These powerfully minerally wines are not easy to find, but if you come across any, you are well advised to try them for their delicacy as well as their rarity.

Montlouis Montlouis is often regarded as the stepchild of its more famous northern neighbor, Vouvray. These wines can be dry, medium-sweet, or sweet, and are generally less expensive than those from Vouvray. Given the greatness of Chenin Blanc as a varietal and the excellent *terroirs* at their disposal, it is a travesty that Montlouis's producers do not craft better wines. This appellation's finest producers include Olivier Delétang and François Chidaine.

St.-Nicolas-de-Bourgueil This may well be the most overrated red wine–producing appellation of the Loire. Parisians, enamored of this appellation's name, have led its once reasonable prices to skyrocket. When they are good, they are either light early drinkers with delightful perfumes of raspberry and currant fruit flavors, followed by a soft, round, supple texture, or dark fruit–filled, highly structured, and deserving of cellaring. Regrettably, however, the majority of St.-Nicolas-de-Bourgeuils are harvested unripe, chaptalized to an "acceptable" alcohol level, and have rustic, tannic finishes—perfect for the Parisian bistros that serve them as cold as their whites.

Touraine This general appellation covers considerable acreage, so it is important to know who are the best producers, as generalizations about the wines cannot be made. Certainly the Sauvignon Blanc and Chenin Blanc range from plonk to delicious fruity, vibrant wines. The red wines can also range from disgustingly vegetal to richly fruity, aromatic offerings. One constant is that any Touraine white or red wine should be consumed within 2–3 years of the vintage. The best recent vintages have been 1997 and 1996. The region's finest wine-maker, the Domaine de la Charmoise's Henri Marionet, produces one of France's and the world's greatest Sauvignon Blancs (the M de Marionet) in top vintages. His reds are meticulously crafted and fruit-packed, and offer superb value. Touraine's finest producers include Domaine de la Charmoise and Maurice Barbou's Domaine des Corbillières (Sauvignon Blanc is a perennial "best buy").

Vouvray Vouvray vies with Sancerre for the best-known appellation of the Loire Valley. Unlike in Sancerre, no rosé or red wine is produced in Vouvray. It is all white and all from the Chenin Blanc grape, which can reach spectacular levels of acidity in the limestone and chalky/clay soils of these charming vineyards located a short distance east of Tours. A huge appellation (over 3,800 acres), Vouvray produces tasty, sparkling wines, wonderfully crisp, delicious, bone-dry wines, medium-sweet wines that are superb as an apéritif or with spicy foods, and some of the most spectacularly honeyed sweet wines one will ever taste.

Regrettably, the majority of this appellation's producers live off its reputation in England and France and generally produce diluted, rot-infested, oversulfured wines. Pinot Noir may be the most fragile and fickle grape, but Chenin Blanc is possibly the world's most unforgiving varietal—any and all flaws in these wines appear magnified. From a good producer, Vouvray can be as great as any wine made on earth. From a mediocre or bad producer it is simply awful.

The sweet wines, sometimes indicated by the word *moëlleux* or *liqoureux* on the label (or a proprietary name or a variation of *réserve*), are the result of the noble rot and can last 40–50 or more years. The finest sweet wines produced in the 1997, 1996, 1995, 1990, and 1989 vintages are showstoppers, mind-numbing and awe-inspiring. The 1996 vintage is a particularly great year as it forced even mediocre producers to make stellar wines, while only the best were able to harness the potential greatness of 1995 and 1997. The finest wines from these recent vintages are modern-day equivalents of the 1959s and 1947s (both vintages are still delicious today), and consumers are well advised to stock up.

Following is a list of Vouvray's top producers, but two deserve special mention. Domaine Gaston Huet's Noël Pinguet and Domaine du Clos Naudin's Philippe Foreau are two of the best producers of white wines in the world. Pinguet, a biodynamic farmer, crafted stellar, world-class dry, demi-sec (medium-sweet), and sweet wines in 1989, 1995, and 1997. Foreau, one of the finest tasters I have had the honor to meet, made out-of-this-world wines in 1990 and 1996. Both producers craft sparkling wines (Domaine Huet's Pinguet a *pétillant* and Foreau a *brut traditionel*) that are superb and compete qualitatively with top-notch Champagnes at a fraction of the price. Regrettably, this appellation's two locomotives (Pinguet and Foreau) are pulling very few wagons behind them. Of the 200–300 vignerons and *négociants* who fashion wines from Vouvray's great *terroirs*, only a handful can be recommended. Vouvray's finest producers include Domaine Huet—Noël Pinguet, Domaine du Clos Naudin—Philippe Foreau (both of these are five-star estates), followed (alphabetically) by Domaine des Aubuisières (Bernard Fouquet), Domaine de la Biche (Christophe et Jean-Claude Pichot), Domaine Bourillon-Dorléans, Domaine Champalou, Domaine de la Fontainerie (Catherine Dhoye-Deruet), Château Gaudrelle, Thierry Nérisson, Domaine des Orfeuilles (Bernard Hérivault), Domaine François Pinon, Domaine de la Saboterie, Vigneau-Chevreau, Vignobles Brisebarre, Domaine du Viking.

THE WINES OF THE SANCERROIS

Ménétou-Salon   Ménétou-Salon, a relatively small appellation of 250 acres, produces excellent white wines from Sauvignon Blanc and some herbal, spicy, light-bodied rosé and red wines from Pinot Noir. In my opinion, the wines to buy are the Sauvignons, which exhibit a pungent, herbaceous, earthy, currant nose and crisp, rich, grassy flavors. The best recent vintages have been 1997 and 1996. Ménétou-Salon's finest producer is Henri Pellé.

Pouilly-Fumé   Pouilly is the name of the village; *fumé* means smoke. This appellation, renowned the world over for its richly scented, flinty (some say smoky), earthy, herbaceous, melony white wines that can range from medium-bodied to full and intense, does indeed produce some of the world's most exciting wines from Sauvignon. The best recent vintages include spectacular 1990s that should drink well for another 2–3 years, 1996s that will be excellent over the next 5–7 years, and 1997s that should be drunk over the next 2–3 years. By the way, a food that is heavenly with Pouilly-Fumé is goat cheese.

One producer, Didier Dagueneau, is clearly this appellation's finest. His wines have purity, richness, depth, complexity, concentration, and significant aging potential. Is it any wonder that he is one of the rare vignerons of the appellation to have moderate yields and to eschew machine harvesters? After Didier Dagueneau, the finest producers of Pouilly-Fumé are Francis Blanchet, Domaine A. Cailbourdin, Jean-Claude Châtelain, Domaine La Croix Canat (F. Tinel-Blondelet), Domaine Serge Dagueneau et Filles, Charles Dupuy (particularly the Vieilles Vignes), Domaine des Fines Caillottes (Jean Pabiot), Masson-Blondelet, Château de Nozet/de Ladoucette, Régis Minet, La Moynerie (particularly the Cuvée Majorum), and Hervé Seguin.

Pouilly-sur-Loire   This tiny yet interesting appellation relies on the Chasselas grape, a lowly-regarded varietal that can make fruity, floral, soft wines when yields are restricted. Wines from this appellation should be inexpensive and can be an ideal apéritif if consumed within one year of the vintage. The finest Pouilly-sur-Loires I have tasted have come from Domaine Serge Dagueneau et Filles.

Quincy Another appellation dedicated to Sauvignon Blanc, Quincy, which is near the historic city of Bourges, takes Sauvignon to its most herbaceous, some would say vegetal, limit. This can be an almost appallingly asparagus-scented and -flavored wine in underripe years, but in top years, such as 1997, that character is subdued. Quincy wines are bone dry and, even though their ageworthiness is touted, should be drunk within 4 years of their release.

Sancerre Sancerre and Vouvray are probably the best-known appellations of the vast Loire Valley viticultural region. A highly fashionable wine for more than two decades, white Sancerre's success is based on its crisp acidity allied with rich, zesty Sauvignon fruitiness. A small amount of red and rosé, which are rarely recommendable, is made from Pinot Noir. Sancerre's success with whites is justifiable in view of the number of high-quality producers in this region. The steep slopes of chalk and flint that surround Sancerre's best villages—Bué, Chavignol, and Verdigny—are undoubtedly responsible for the flinty, subtle, earthy character evident in so many of the top wines.

Consumers should note that two of this appellation's finest vignerons, Edmond Vatan and Paul Cotat (whose wines also appear with the names Francis and François Cotat), produce old-style Sancerres, quite different from the norm found today. Cotat's and Vatan's wines are rich, full-flavored, thick, and sometimes not bone dry. They are also some of the finest Sauvignon Blancs I have ever put to my lips.

The finest recent vintages have been 1997, 1996, 1995, and 1990. White Sancerre and the limited quantities of rosés should be drunk within 2–3 years of the vintage, although some can last longer. Red Sancerre can last for 4–5 years.

A small group of standouts clearly produce this appellation's best wines. They are Paul Cotat, Lucien Crochet (Gilles Crochet), André Neveu, Vincent Pinard, and Edmond Vatan. Sancerre has many topflight producers, including Franck et Jean-François Bailly, Henri Bourgeois, Domaine le Colombier (Roger Neveu), Vincent Delaporte, Charles Dupuy (Vieilles Vignes *cuvée*), Comte Lafond, Domaine de Montigny (Henri Natter), Domaine de la Moussière (Alphonse Mellot), Domaine Henri Pellé (from Ménétou-Salon), Hippolyte Reverdy, Etienne Riffault, Domaine Jean-Max Roger, Domaine de la Rossignole (Pierre Cherrier et Fils), Domaine de St.-Pierre (Pierre Prieur et Fils), Domaine de St. Romble (Paul Vattan), and Domaine Lucien Thomas (Jean and Ginette Thomas).

BUYING STRATEGY

If you can still find any of the great 1989s, 1990s, 1995s, 1996s, and 1997s from Vouvray, Savennières, Bonnezeaux, Coteaux de l'Aubance, Coteaux du Layon, and Quarts de Chaume, you should move quickly to purchase them. Recent vintages have suffered from late-season rains, rot, and mildew.

RECENT VINTAGES

2000—A difficult year for the Loire. Incessant rains promoted the outbreak of rot and diluted wines. As with 1999, a number of growers fashioned good wines (but few are better).

1999—Another good vintage for Muscadet but a poor one for the majority of the Loire. Late-season rains and rot posed serious problems for growers.

1998—This will not be remembered as a good vintage, at least for dry whites and reds. However, some sweet-wine producers in Anjou and Vouvray were able to craft excellent if not outstanding wines in this vintage, but they were few and far between.

1997—The heat that plagued Europe during 1997's summer and early fall, combined with untimely rains in certain areas of the Loire, fashioned this vintage. High temperatures are responsible for the ripest, most approachable, and most succulent Loire reds in memory. Thick, supple, fruit-packed reds were produced by the best estates in all of the Loire's red wine appelations. Given the absurdly high prices of the more famous red wine–producing regions, consumers should certainly look to the Loire's 1997s for a reprieve. In general, the Loire's whites, from Sancerre in the east to Muscadet in the west, are ripe, dense, and often plodding wines (for the Loire). Some sweet wine producers, notably Domaine des Baumards' Florent Baumard (Quarts de Chaume), Domaine Gaston Huet's Noël Pinguet (Vouvray), and Domaine René Renou in Bonnezeaux, were able to maintain freshness and vibrancy in this hugely rich and superripe vintage.

1996—Throughout the Loire, 1996 was a superb vintage. A warm and sunny summer was followed by an equally fine late summer and fall (many vignerons commented that they had never seen such a bright autumn, stressing its "luminosity") that saw moderate daytime temperatures and cool evenings in addition to a persistent dry wind from the north. This combination of light (photosynthesis) and relatively cool temperatures promoted the ripening of the grapes without a significant loss of acidity (heat is blamed for reducing acid in grapes), while the north winds dehydrated (concentrated) the grapes. The resulting wines, in both red and white, have exceptional ripeness (including well-ripened tannins in the reds), vibrancy, and exceptional ageworthiness. For the Loire, 1996 is certainly one of the finest vintages of the century.

1995—The 1995 vintage, as in many parts of France, is a year of intense concentration. Warm and dry summer months led to great ripeness in the grape sugars, yet sporadic rains prior to the harvests promoted rot in many of the region's vineyards. Sorting was a necessity. The red wines of the Loire are densely crammed with black fruits (because of the heat) yet all share one thing in common: astringent tannins (because of the rains they were harvested without having attained full phenolic ripeness). From the reds of Anjou through the famous red appellations of Touraine to the reds of Sancerre, all of the Loire's 1995 are impressive for their colors, aromatics, attacks, and mid-palates, yet are aggressive and harsh in the finish. The 1995 vintage in whites, however, was a great success in the Sancerrois, with the top producers of Vouvray (Domaine Huet [Pinguet], Domaine du Clos Naudin [Foreau], and Domaine François Pinon), and with many top vignerons of Anjou (Domaine Baumard, for example).

1994—A stormy, hot summer had most producers hoping for a repeat of 1989 and 1990. September's three weeks of intermittent rain and storms prevented 1994 from being a great vintage. Nevertheless, the top producers have fashioned very good dry white wines, if the rot-tinged grapes were left in the vineyard. Production is smaller than normal for the finest estates that practiced serious selection. Consequently, pressure to raise prices is a strong possibility. Sauvignon Blanc is the most successful varietal in 1994. With respect to the red wine grapes, Gamay was the least affected by the rains. The Chenin Blancs were more mixed.

1993—Another rain-plagued harvest, 1993 has turned out to be a good to very good vintage for the dry whites, an average-quality vintage for the reds, and an irregular vintage for the sweet white wines. The 1993 dry Sauvignons are crisp, lively, medium-bodied wines, with more pleasing aromas than the soft, diffuse 1992s or the lean, high-acid 1991s. All things considered, 1993 is a far more successful vintage than was expected following the miserable, wet, cold month of September.

1992—The Loire Valley escaped most of the horrific downpours that plagued southern France, but the crop size was appallingly large. Reports of excessive yields came in from almost every appellation. Growers had a chance to pick relatively ripe fruit that produced a good vintage, but only those who kept their yields low produced good wines. This is a vintage of pleasant, straightforward, fruity, soft wines that should have been drunk up by 1996. The most successful appellations for white wines are Muscadet, Sancerre, and Pouilly-Fumé. Chinon was the most successful for red wines.

1991—This is a difficult vintage throughout the Loire Valley, with relatively acidic, lean, light-bodied wines that lack ripeness and flavor authority. Successes can be found, but overall, a small crop combined with inadequate ripeness produced ungenerous wines lacking fruit and charm.

1990—This is one of the all-time greatest vintages for just about every region of the Loire Valley, especially the sweet wine appellations and the great dry white wines of Savennières, Pouilly-Fumé, and Sancerre. The levels of richness and intensity of the 1990s are mind-boggling. Consumers lucky enough to be able to find and afford the top *cuvées* of the decadently sweet wines from Bonnezeaux, Coteaux du Layon, Quarts de Chaume, and Vouvray, as well as some of the spectacularly full-bodied, awesomely rich, dry Savennières, will have treasures that will last in their cellars 25–30 or more years.

The red wines are also surprisingly good. Because of the drought and superripeness, they are less herbaceous than usual and offer copious quantities of red and black fruits.

1989—Somewhat similar to 1990, although yields were higher and there was less botrytis in the sweet wine vineyards, 1989 is an excellent, in many cases a superb, vintage for Vouvray, Quarts de Chaume, Coteaux du Layon, and Bonnezeaux. It is also a super vintage for Savennières. All the drier wines from Sancerre, Pouilly-Fumé, Touraine, and Muscadet should have been consumed by now.

1988—A good but unexciting vintage produced pleasant, textbook wines that admirably represent their appellation or region but lack the huge perfumes, richness, and depth of the finest 1989s and 1990s.

1987—A mediocre to poor year.

OLDER VINTAGES

The decadently rich dessert wines of the Coteaux du Layon, Bonnezeaux, Quarts de Chaume, and Vouvray from 1983, 1976, 1971, 1962, 1959, 1949, and 1947 can be spectacular wines. These wines are still modestly priced and are undoubtedly the greatest bargains in rich dessert wines in the world. Though it is not easy to find these older vintages, consumers should put this information to good use by stocking up on the 1989s, 1990s, 1995s, 1996s, and the best 1997s.

Savennières is probably the world's greatest buy in dry, full-bodied white wines. Older Savennières vintages to look for are 1986, 1985, 1978, 1976, 1971, 1969, 1962, and 1959. Occasionally, small quantities of these wines come up for auction. They are well worth the low prices being asked.

Consumers who have the opportunity to travel to the bucolic Loire Valley should be aware of one of the wine world's great secrets: no other viticultural region I know of has better natural cellars than those found in Vouvray. The cold and humid caves, dug deep into the tufa hillsides, offer extraordinary wine storage conditions. Vouvray producers have seemingly always known this, so their caves are stocked with large quantities of older vintages (including wines going back to the 19th century), and many are still for sale.

THE LANGUEDOC-ROUSSILLON

Where the Quality and the Values Are

The Wine Advocate, the bimonthly journal authored by Robert Parker and myself, was among the first publications to tout the Languedoc-Roussillon as one of the undiscovered bastions of delicious, value-priced wines. Its relative importance to consumers continues to increase as wine prices from many of the world's best-known regions have reached absurd levels.

The Basics

The Languedoc-Roussillon is, in fact, two distinct yet bordering provinces located in the south of France. Together, they cover a vast area that encompasses the corridor adjacent to the Mediterranean running north from the Spanish border to the hillsides immediately west of the Rhône river delta. (These two viticultural regions border each other just north of Perpignan, the ancient French capital of Catalonia.)

Though neither region is well known to the consumers of top-end wines, both play, by any measure, an extremely important role in the world of wine, if only because of sheer size. Combined, the Languedoc-Roussillon has more acres under vine than the entire United States—more than 830,000 acres (337,000 hectares), as compared to the United States' 770,000 (310,000 hectares).

Forming a crescent shape on France's Mediterranean coastline, the Languedoc-Roussillon's vineyards are found on flat alluvial plains (Languedoc) as well as on hillsides, some of which can be quite steep, including the foothills of the Pyrenees (Roussillon). There are the sun-baked vineyards that border the Mediterranean (for example, La Clape, Banyuls, and Frontignan), as well as many that are inland (Pic-St.-Loup, Montpeyroux, and Minervois, for example).

Average annual rainfall tends to be meager. 1998 suffered drought conditions (some appellations reported as little as 150 mm—5.9 inches—of rain for the entire year). As a point of reference, that is less than Bordeaux received in both September 1998 and September 1999. Temperatures can often exceed 90° F in the summer, with relief provided by the cool mountain winds known in the Languedoc as the *tramontane*.

Many different grape varieties are planted in the Languedoc and Roussillon. Most common for the reds are Carignan (a high-yielding vine that does not allow the area's dry, hot climate to affect its productivity), Grenache, Cinsault, Mourvèdre, and, increasingly, Merlot, Syrah, and Cabernet Sauvignon. White wine varietals are equally diverse. Muscat, Grenache Blanc, Rolle, Malvoisie, Chardonnay, Viognier, Sauvignon Blanc, Marsanne, and Roussanne can all be found in the Languedoc-Roussillon's vineyards.

Past, Present, and Future

The majority of historians agree that the Languedoc was the site of France's first vineyards, planted by the Romans near the town of Narbonne between 150 and 125 B.C. Following a phylloxera epidemic in the late 19th century, most of the Languedoc-Roussillon was planted with high-yielding, lesser varietals and clones. It soon became the source of nearly half of France's annual wine production, yet quality was secondary to quantity. The Languedoc, and to a lesser degree the Roussillon, were quickly viewed in France as producers of table wine and *gros rouge qui tache* (big red that stains—a derogatory expression). What is more important is that the world's wine enthusiasts took little notice of the region.

Both the Languedoc and Roussillon appear to be regions in search of themselves. Even though they are the site of France's first vineyards, they are less established and confident about their present and future in the wine world than this nation's other large viticultural areas. While regions such as Bordeaux and Burgundy have stuck with certain basic varietals and winemaking styles, the Languedoc-Roussillon has attempted to adapt to market conditions—much to its detriment. Its market strength in the early 1900s—table wines often bolstered with Algerian red wine—died out. Today the region's sweet (mostly fortified—*vin doux naturel*) and cheap table wines have been casualties of fashion. Inexpensive varietal-designated wines (mostly Merlot, Cabernet-Sauvignon, and Chardonnay), the rage in the 1980s and early 1990s, now appear to be losing market share to similarly priced wines from South America and Australia.

The truth is that bad reputations die slowly. Today, even the finest producers in the Languedoc and Roussillon regions find it easier to sell their wines abroad than in France. Fortunately, the English and Americans have not approached the area with the preconceived notions ingrained in the French. Because of this interest, a much-needed infusion of capital has allowed many producers and cooperatives to invest in state-of-the-art production facilities, including temperature-controlled refrigeration, once a rare luxury in this torrid, sun-drenched region.

American importers such as Robert Kacher, Kermit Lynch, Eric Solomon, and Peter Weygandt, as well as France-based brokers such as Jeffrey Davies, Patrick Lesec, and Peter Vezan, have advocated low yields, noninterventionist winemaking, and the abandonment of excessive fining and filtration. This has obviously led to better and better wines from their clients. Robert Kacher has used his influence on the estates he represents to have them adopt such modern techniques as *microbullage* (a system that performs controlled releases of tiny bubbles in wine tanks in an effort to soften the region's often rustic tannins). Thanks in large measure to the work of these importers and brokers, as well as the efforts of Martin Sinkoff, fine wines that qualitatively compete with the best that the world has to offer can now be found in the Languedoc-Roussillon.

With regard to the area's little-known dry white wines, Kermit Lynch has obtained good results by encouraging growers to allow malolactic fermentations to take place. Typically in the Languedoc-Roussillon, where the overwhelming sentiment among the region's cognoscenti is that the whites lack acidity, producers have blocked these secondary fermentations (to maintain the lively malic acids). The results all too often are light-bodied efforts with clipped, compressed finishes. The majority of the whites tasted for this report that received recommended scores had benefited from malolactic fermentation.

The Languedoc has been producing wine for over two millennia, yet continues to search for the finest varietals that are best adapted to its diverse climates and *terroirs*. Most producers appear convinced that its most prolific varietals, Carignan and Cinsault, have no place in their future. In my tastings, two Rhône Valley qualitative giants, Syrah and Roussanne, exhibited the greatest potential. Syrah, a relative newcomer to the area (the oldest vines encountered in the research for this report date back to 1967), was responsible for the finest reds I tasted. Roussanne, another recent addition to the panoply of varietals found in the Languedoc and Roussillon, appears well placed to be the white grape with the finest pedigree in these hot, arid regions.

There is a schizophrenic feel to tastings of reds from these regions. Bordeaux look-alikes are mixed in with New World/internationally styled varietal wines and rustic Langue-doc versions of southern Rhônes. Interspersed among these are cedary, spicy, *garrigue* (the sun-dried herb aromas commonly found in the south of France) and black fruit–filled wines that appear to be representative of the region's potential signature and not dissimilar from fine southern Rhônes. As astronomically high yields are reduced, modern viticultural and winemaking techniques adopted, and excesses (oak and both under- and overextraction) abandoned, the Languedoc-Roussillon's identity may emerge, but in so many places, including vineyards and wineries, everything remains a work in progress. Yet inescapably, the future looks bright for the Languedoc-Roussillon. The international demand for fine wine, combined with the stratospheric prices being charged by the world's best-known viticultural regions, has set the stage for the Languedoc-Roussillon's breakout from obscurity.

RECENT VINTAGES

1999—Another study in contrasts. Unquestionably cooler than 1998, the regions enjoyed a good growing season until mid-August when the rains commenced and lasted through September. In certain areas the impact was cataclysmic, in others barely felt (the domaine Prieuré St.-Jean de Bébian had its Mourvèdre destroyed by hail yet neighboring vineyards were untouched; a September 6 storm northwest of Montpellier devastated vineyards by dumping six inches of rain in one night, yet La Grange des Pères, just a few miles away, remained dry).

Overall, 1999 is not a good vintage for either the Languedoc or the Roussillon. One importer, whose portfolio is dominated by these regions' wines, described it in his "Vintage and Market Report" as "rather poor." Yet there are positive exceptions, unsurprising for regions as vast and diverse as these. In Pic St.-Loup, for example, few good wines could be found, but those protected from approaching storms by the bowl-like hills of the Roque escarpment were favored. In Collioure, where Grenache and Syrah are widely planted, only those wines dominated by Mourvèdre were successful. Areas with excellent drainage were able to perform well, particularly for growers who have repeatedly learned the lesson of maintaining low yields. Therefore, estates like La Grange des Pères (Vin de Pays de l'Hérault) and the Château de la Négly (La Clape) fashioned marvelous wines.

1998—Torrid heat (temperatures in the summer routinely surpassed 105° F) and severe drought characterized the 1998 vintage. A number of the Languedoc-Roussillon's 1998 reds merited outstanding reviews because of their gorgeous depth and intensity of fruit. The finest possessed concentration, power, and long, supple finishes. Producers who were able to harness the vintage's potential crafted some of the finest wines in their abbreviated history. That's the good news.

On the other side of the ledger, a large percentage of wines suffered from the unmistakable effects of astronomically high yields. Overall, 1998 reds are substantially better than the vintage's whites (whose aromatics and balance often appear crushed by their richness). Interestingly, whites from the 1997 vintage, a difficult year for reds, taste more successful than the 1998s.

The region's top estates agreed that the key to a successful harvest was low yields. Those vines stressed by excessive grape bunches and lack of rainfall never attained physiological ripeness. These wines are marked by a lack of flesh and concentration, as well as by bitter and astringent finishes. A number of Languedoc-Roussillon reds from the 1998 vintage were reminiscent of 1976 red Burgundies, with jammy, unfocused personalities and hard tannins. Sadly, in what can be an exciting vintage, too many disappointments exist.

A GLIMPSE AT THE 2000 VINTAGE

2000 is better than 1999 yet also problematic, primarily because of enormous yields. The weather was excellent during the growing season, from flowering to *veraison* (when the grapes change color). This pattern favored huge grape loads. Rains prior and during harvest further increased yields.

Only a few top 2000s are in this chapter because they were still in barrel when the region was visited and will not reach the market for months. However, tastings of the less heralded reds, which are often bottled quickly, as well as barrel tastings of the luxury bottlings, indicate that estates that were conscientious enough to prune for moderate yields were capable of making superb 2000 reds. In contrast, many whites, even from the top producers, appear to lack depth. The Roussillon, which has many superb *terroirs* yet few great winemakers, appears to have enjoyed a slightly better vintage than the Languedoc.

An Overview of the Most Important Zones of the Languedoc-Roussillon

Whereas over a third of France's vines are located in the Languedoc-Roussillon, these regions are responsible for only approximately 15% of the nation's *appellation d'origine contrôlée* (AOC) wine production. Many of these AOCs were created over the last fifteen years, and the largest (Coteaux du Languedoc, for example) contain a number of subappellations. Areas under consideration for AOC status by the Institut National des Appellations d'Origine (also known as the INAO, the French organization responsible for granting and regulating AOCs) can be granted VDQS (Vin Délimité de Qualité Supérieure) status. Wines from outside these areas, those that are made from varietals not accepted by the INAO, and those that are varietal-designated are labeled with the all-encompassing *vin de pays* (VDP) designation. Readers should note that many of the Languedoc-Roussillon's finest wines are VDPs.

Costières de Nîmes The easternmost appellation of the Languedoc-Roussillon, which received *appellation contrôlée* status in 1986, produces white, red, and rosé wines. In the 1980s, it was largely known as the Costières du Gard. The area takes its name from the extraordinary Roman city of Nîmes. The vineyard area consists of a group of pebble-strewn slopes and a plateau region that lie in the Rhône delta. Seventy-five percent of the production is in red wine, 20% in rosé, and the remainder in white. The best estates are, irrefutably, Château de Nages, Château de la Tuilerie, Château de Campuget, Grande Cassagne, Mas des Bressades, Mas Carlot, and Mourgue du Grès. Other interesting domaines include the Domaine St.-Louis-La-Perdrix, Domaine St.-Antoine, Valcombe, and Château Belle-Coste. The red wines are permitted to be made from a maximum of 50% Carignan. Other allowable grape varieties include Cinsault, Counoise, Grenache, Mourvèdre, Syrah, Terret Noir, and two obscure red varietals called Aspiran Noir and Oeillade. White varietals are dominated by Clairette and Grenache Blanc, with small amounts of Picpoul, Roussanne, Terret Blanc, Ugni Blanc, Malvoisie, Marsanne, Maccabeo, and Viognier. The potential vineyard area is 62,000+ acres. Readers who place a high premium on quality and value should take note of Costières de Nîmes.

Coteaux du Languedoc This vast area (given *appellation contrôlée* status in 1985) includes vineyards in three French departments, Aude, Garde, and Hérault. It runs from Nîmes in the north to Narbonne in the south. Consumers will find wines labeled merely with the appellation of Coteaux du Languedoc, as well as those where the individual village names are affixed. Two of the finest villages, St.-Chinian and Faugères, were elevated to their own *subappellation contrôlée* status in 1982. The grape varieties are essentially the same as in the Costières de Nîmes, although the more serious estates use higher percentages of Syrah, Mourvèdre, Grenache, and Counoise in their red wines, generally at the expense of Carignan and Cinsault. The best wines of Faugères have consistently come from Haut-Fabrègues and Gilbert Alquier. Among the best wines of St.-Chinian are those from Domaine des Jougla and Cazal Viel. Perhaps the greatest wine of the entire appellation of Coteaux du Languedoc (as well as the most expensive) is the Prieuré de St.-Jean-de-Bébian. This wine, and the Mas-de-Daumas Gassac, a *vin de pays*, were two of the earliest reference-point red wines of the Languedoc-Roussillon region. Acreage under vine is in excess of 19,000 acres.

Minervois   Granted *appellation contrôlée* status in 1985, Minervois has some of the best long-range potential of any appellation in the Languedoc-Roussillon area. To say that there are still many underachievers would not be unfair. This area of nearly 14,000 acres of vineyards is bounded on the west by the extraordinary fortified fortress city of Carcassonne and on the east by St.-Chinian. Minervois flourished under Roman rule but never recovered from the phylloxera epidemic that devastated France's vineyards in the late 19th century.

The best vineyards tend to be located on gently sloping, south-facing, limestone hillsides sheltered from the cold north winds, and they endure the hottest microclimate of the region. Virtually all of the wine production is red, but there are also microquantities of a surprisingly tasty rosé. White wine makes up less than 2% of the total production. Readers should pay particular attention to the fact that some of the finest wines to date have come from the low-yielding vineyards on the slopes of the south-facing *terroirs* of a region called Cévennes. Some of the best estates represented in America include Château de Paraza, Château de Gourgazaud, Daniel Domergue, Tour-St.-Martin, and Domaine St.-Eulalie.

Corbières   Corbières, located further down the coast, south of Minervois, was recently elevated to *appellation contrôlée* status. It boasts a large production area (over 57,000 acres). Red wine accounts for 90% of production, and the predominant varietal is the omnipresent Carignan, although the more serious estates have begun to employ increasing percentages of Syrah and Mourvèdre. The outstanding estates in Corbières include the brilliant Château Le Palais, Château Mansenoble, Château Etang des Colombes, Domaine St.-Paul, and Domaine de Villemajou.

It is impossible to generalize about soils and microclimates, given the diversity, from inland lofty inland vineyards to those on the coastline. Harvest dates can be as early as September in the warmer *terroirs* and as late as mid-October in the cooler hillside climates.

Faugères   Over 4,000 acres of vineyards are planted in this small but promising red wine appellation, which was formerly part of the Coteaux du Languedoc. Most of the better vineyards sit above sea level on rocky subsoils. Local authorities have moved to replace the omnipresent Carignan with better grapes, such as Syrah, Grenache, and Mourvèdre. Under current policy, no wine can contain more than 40% Carignan, although the better *cuvées* from the likes of Alquier and Léon Barral are wines from extremely old-vine Carignan bolstered by increasing quantities of Syrah, Grenache, and Mourvèdre. White wine is produced in Faugères, but it has shown less promise than the fleshy, rustic reds.

Fitou   Fitou, the oldest of the *appellation contrôlée* regions of the Languedoc-Roussillon area (its *appellation contrôlée* status was bestowed in 1948), represents two separate areas bounded on the north by Corbières. One region, consisting of low-lying vineyards near the coast, is planted on shallow, gravelly soil atop limestone beds. No one I have ever talked with believes that top-quality wines can emerge from this particular sector. On the hillsides farther inland, the best vineyards are planted on sloping, well-drained, mixed soils of sandstone and limestone. The ripest, fattest, fruitiest wines from Fitou generally emanate from this area. The grape varieties for Fitou are the same as for the other regions of Languedoc, with Carignan once again the dominant varietal, but the more serious producers are utilizing more Mourvèdre, Syrah, and Grenache. Acreage under vine: 6,200 acres.

Côtes de Roussillon and Côtes de Roussillon-Villages   The Roussillon vineyards, all of which run from the Mediterranean Sea inland, surrounding Perpignan, France's last urban bastion before the Spanish border, may have produced wines as early as the 7th century B.C. There is immense potential, not only for dry red table wines but also for the sweet, fortified wines that often excel in this windy, sun-drenched region. The best vineyards, which are entitled to the Côtes de Roussillon or Côtes de Roussillon-Villages appellation, stretch out over a semicircle of hills facing the Mediterranean. These hillside vineyards, planted on expanses of limestone and granite, enjoy a phenomenally sunny, hot summer. Virtually all of the rainfall results from thunderstorms. It has always amazed me that these wines are still so reasonably priced, given the amount of labor necessary to cultivate so many of the terraced vineyards of this region. The tiny amount of white wine produced is generally from such obscure varietals as Malvoise de Roussillon and Maccabeo. The red wines are produced from the ubiquitous Carignan, as well as Grenache, Syrah, and Mourvèdre. These are full-bodied, relatively rich wines, with a big, fleshy, peppery character. Despite their softness and easy drinkability when young, several properties make wines that can last for up to a decade. The best estates in the Côtes de Roussillon and Côtes de Roussillon-Villages are Pierre d'Aspres, Cazes Frères, Château de Jau, Domaine Sarda-Malet, Domaine Salvat, and Domaine St.-Luc. There is also a bevy of cooperatives, several of which have received high praise, particularly the cooperative of Maury.

Collioure   This tiny appellation, the smallest in the Languedoc-Roussillon region for dry red wine, is located just to the south of the Côtes de Roussillon on an expanse of terraced hillside vineyards called the Côtes Vermeille. Virtually all of the Collioure vineyards are located on these steeply terraced slopes, and the red wine is produced largely from a blend of Grenache, Carignan, Mourvèdre, Syrah, and Cinsault. Tiny yields are commonplace in Collioure, and as a result the wines tend to be relatively rich and full. They have yet to be discovered by American wine enthusiasts. The best Collioures come from the great Domaine du Mas Blanc of the late Dr. Parcé, also renowned for his fabulous fortified, portlike Banyuls. There are generally two *cuvées* of Collioure, one called Les Piloums and the other, Cosprons Levants. Other interesting producers include Thierry Parcé at the Domaine de la Rectorie and the Celliers des Templiers.

Montpeyroux   This small region within the Coteaux du Languedoc appellation is prized for its potential. Some of the Languedoc-Roussillon's most impressive, concentrated, intense wines have come from the rocky soils of Montpeyroux and its nearby rival, Pic-St.-Loup.

Pic-St.-Loup   Pic-St.-Loup has some of the Languedoc-Roussillon's most avant-garde, highest-quality producers. They have staked out their reputations in the rocky soils of this area north of Montpellier. The quality of the Syrah, Grenache, and Mourvèdre has been impressive, and the finest wines rival some of the top Rhône Valley efforts. Along with Montpeyroux, Pic-St.-Loup is one of the most exciting areas of the Languedoc-Roussillon for the 21st century.

Vins Doux Naturels   Though they remain out of fashion, the Languedoc-Roussillon area abounds with some of the greatest values in sweet and fortified dessert wines in Europe. The most famous are those from Banyuls (located on the coastline south of Perpignan) and Maury (located in the hillsides north of Perpignan). Both appellations require that these decadently rich, fortified wines be made from at least 50% Grenache. In the case of those wines entitled to the Banyuls grand cru designation, they must be composed of at least 75% Grenache.

Other areas producing sweet wines include Muscat de Rivesaltes, Muscat de Lunel, Muscat de Frontignan, and the two smaller appellations of Muscat de Mireval and St.-Jean-de-Minervois. Both the Muscat de Frontignan and Muscat de Mireval are located near Hérault. Muscat de Lunel is produced east of Nîmes in the northern sector of the Languedoc-

Roussillon. The most famous of these wines are the great Banyuls from Dr. Parcé. They have a legendary reputation in France but remain, to my surprise, largely unknown in the United States. Almost all of these wines can handle considerable aging and are remarkable for their value, particularly when compared with the soaring prices of vintage and tawny ports.

RATING THE LANGUEDOC-ROUSSILLON'S BEST PRODUCERS

Where a producer has been assigned a range of stars (***/****), the lower rating has been used for placement in this hierarchy.

* * * * * (OUTSTANDING)

Domaine Clavel
Clos des Truffiers
La Grange des Pères

Domaine du Mas Blanc (Dr. Parcé)
Château de la Négly

* * * * (EXCELLENT)

Domaine de l'Aiguelière
Gilbert Alquier et Fils
Domaine d'Aupilhac
Domaine Les Aurelles****/*****
Domaine Léon Barral
Domaine de Baubiac
Hugues Beaulieu
Domaine Borie de Maurel
Château de Campuget
Domaine Canet-Valette****/*****
La Casenove
Domaine Cazes
Clos de l'Escandil
Clos Marie****/*****
Les Clos des Paulilles****/*****
Col des Vents
Domaine de la Combe Blanche
Domaine Cros
Domaine Ferrer Ribière
Domaine Foulaquier
Domaine Gardiés
Domaine Gauby
Château Grande Cassagne
Château Grès St.-Paul****/*****
Domaine de l'Hortus

Château de Jau (for Muscat and Talon wines)
Château de Lancyre
Château Mansenoble
Domaine Mas Amiel****/***** (for sweet wines)
Mas des Aveylans****/*****
Mas des Bressades****/*****
Mas Cristine
Mas de la Dame
Mas de Gourgonnier
Mas Jullien
Château de Montpezat****/*****
Domaine Mortiès****/*****
Mourgues du Grès
Château Les Palais
Domaine Peyre Rose
Domaine Picquemal
Prieuré de St.-Jean-de-Bébian
Domaine Puech Chaud****/*****
Domaine Richeaume
Château La Roque
Tardieu-Laurent****/*****
Château Tour Boisée

* * * (GOOD)

Domaines des Aires-Hautes
Domaine de l'Arjolle
Château de Belles Eaux
Château de Caladroy
Domaine des Cantarelles
Château de Capitoul***/****
Clos Bagatelle***/****
Domaine La Colombette

Château Coupe Roses
Domaine de la Croix Belle
Guilhem Durand
Domaine de l'Ermitage du Pic-St.-Loup***/****
Domaine Font Caude***/****
Domaine Fontsainte
Domaine La Gauphine

Domaine du Grand Crés
Château Hospitalet La Clape
Domaine Lacroix-Vanel***/****
Domaine Lalande
Château de Landure***/****
Château Lavabre***/****
Societé Vinicole de Lesquerède (for Cuvée
  Georges Pous)
Mas de la Barben***/****
Mas Carlot
Mas de Daumas Gassac***/****
Mas de Guiot***/****
Château Mas Neuf
Domaine Massamier

Château de Nages***/****
Novellum***/****
Château d'Or et de Gueules
Domaine Piccinini***/****
Château Puech-Haut***/****
Domaine Rimbert***/****
Domaine du Roc
Château Russol-Gardey***/****
Domaine de St.-Antoine***/****
Domaine St.-Martin de la Garrigue
Domaine de la Tour Vieille
Val d'Orbieu (for Cuvée Mythique)
Château de Valcombe***/****
Château Valflaunes***/****

* * (AVERAGE)

Abbaye de Valmagne**/***
Clos Fantine
Domaine Fontanel**/***
Domaine Gautier**/***
Château de Jau (for regular *cuvées*)
Les Jamelles
Château Lascaux**/***
Domaine Mas Amiel**/*** (for dry wines)
Mas Champart
Mas de Fournel**/***
Mas Gabinelle**/***
Domaine des Moulines

Domaine la Noble
Domaine de Poujol
Château Prat de Cest**/***
Domaine St.-Sernin**/***
Château St.-Eulalie**/***
Domaine St.-Hilaire**/***
Domaine Salvat**/***
Domaine Sarda-Mallet**/***
Val d'Orbieu
Vignerons d'Octaviana**/***
Château de Villenouvette**/***

DOMAINE DE L'AIGUELIÈRE

1997 Coteaux du Languedoc-Montpeyroux Côte Dorée	D	90
1997 Coteaux du Languedoc-Montpeyroux Côte Rousse	D	90
1999 Coteaux du Languedoc-Montpeyroux Tradition Elevé en Fûts de Chêne	C	88

The 1997 Côte Dorée was aged in Burgundy barrels. It is medium to dark ruby-colored and offers lovely spiced oak and plummy fruit aromas. On the palate, this bacon, blackberry, caramel, and coffee liqueur–flavored wine is extremely well concentrated and extracted. Medium- to full-bodied and velvety-textured, it possesses a long, harmonious, supple finish. It will be at its best if consumed over the next 4 years.

The 1997 Côte Rousse was aged entirely in Bordeaux barrels. Aromatically, it reveals blackberries and hints of toasted oak. Medium- to full-bodied and satin-textured, it is more structured and austere than the preceding wine, yet regales the palate with tangy black currant and spice flavors. This extremely well made and powerful wine should be consumed over the next 5 years.

The medium to dark ruby-colored 1999 Tradition Elevé en Fûts de Chêne reveals cassis and white pepper aromas. Black currants, blackberries, and raspberries can be found in its medium-bodied, silky-textured personality. It is well focused, elegant, and exhibits a long, freshly cracked pepper–filled finish. Drink it over the next 5–6 years.

GILBERT ALQUIER ET FILS

1998 Faugères	B	88

Cherries and blackberries are intermingled with sun-drenched herbs in the aromatic profile of the medium to dark ruby-colored 1998 Faugères. Medium-bodied and well balanced, this is a well-made, satin-textured, tar, *garrigue* (Provençal herbs), and dark fruit–flavored wine. It is masculine, muscular, somewhat foursquare, and should benefit from aging. Anticipated maturity: now–2008.

DOMAINE DE L'ARJOLLE

1998 Côtes de Thongue Lyre de l'Arjolle	C	88
1998 Vin de Pays de Côtes de Thongue Equinoxe de l'Arjolle	B	88

Crafted from 50% Viognier, 40% Sauvignon Blanc, and the balance Muscat, the 1998 Equinoxe de l'Arjolle reveals rich, ripe orange peel, apricot, and smoky aromas. This oily-textured, flavorful, and broad wine is medium-bodied, crammed with yellow fruits, and possesses excellent balance. A superb apéritif, it would also be a good accompaniment to lighter-styled seafood dishes. Drink it over the next 2 years.

The 1998 Côtes de Thongue Lyre de l'Arjolle is a late-harvest Muscat dessert wine. It exhibits lovely orange marmalade and white flower–like aromas. Medium-bodied and jellied, this is a well-balanced wine filled with apricots, orange blossoms, and hints of raspberries. It is an excellent wine that simply lacks the length and complexity required for an outstanding rating. Drink it over the next 5 years.

DOMAINE D'AUPILHAC

1998 Coteaux du Languedoc Le Clos	D	(87–89)
1999 Coteaux du Languedoc-Montpeyroux	C	88+
1998 Coteaux du Languedoc-Montpeyroux	C	88+

The 1998 Coteaux du Languedoc Le Clos, a blend of 40% Mourvèdre, 40% Carignan, and 20% Grenache, aged for 30 months in new and one-year-old oak barrels, offers a saturated black/ruby color. Aromatically intense, it displays superb aromas of blackberries, licorice, and cassis. On the palate, this medium- to full-bodied wine is well structured and crammed with sweet black currant fruit. Intense, powerful, yet refined, it should be at its best between now–2005.

The dark ruby-colored 1998 Coteaux du Languedoc-Montpeyroux has blackberry, roasted coffee bean, and tar aromas. Medium-bodied, chewy-textured, and redolent with chocolaty black fruit flavors, this is a structured, intense, powerful wine. Anticipated maturity: now–2008.

Readers who do not find fault with firmly tannic wines will adore d'Aupilhac's 1999 Coteaux du Languedoc-Montpeyroux. It has an awesome nose of *garrigue* (Provençal herbs), spices, black fruits, and freshly laid asphalt. This is an expansive offering, loaded with blackberries, chocolate, spices, and mocha. Medium-bodied, it has a rustic edge and a firm, foursquare finish. Anticipated maturity: 2005–2009.

DOMAINE LES AURELLES

1998 Coteaux du Languedoc Aurel	D	90
1999 Coteaux du Languedoc Solen	C	89

The medium to dark ruby-colored 1999 Solen was produced with Grenache, Carignan, and Syrah. It has demure dark fruit aromas that lead to a pure, medium-bodied personality crammed with blackberries, road tar, and hints of licorice. This harmonious wine displays loads of superripe tannin in its long and supple finish. Drink it over the next 7–8 years.

The 1998 Aurel contains 50% Syrah with the balance split between Grenache and Carignan. It explodes from the glass with powerful black fruit, spice, and creamy aromas. Medium- to full-bodied and seamless, it is an intense wine, jam-packed with freshly laid asphalt, juicy blackberries, and dark cherries. This highly delineated and expressive wine has admirable persistence in the finish. Anticipated maturity: now–2008.

DOMAINE LÉON BARRAL

1998 Faugères	B	90
1998 Faugères Jadis	C	90
1997 Faugères Jadis	C	88

The dark ruby-colored 1997 Faugères Jadis has perfume and herbal aromas. Medium-bodied and displaying good depth to its floral, dark berry, and ripe tomato character, this firm, structured offering does not possess the 1998's superripe, fruit-dominated character, yet has impressive complexity to its slightly rustic personality. Drink it over the next 4–5 years.

The outstanding, medium to dark ruby-colored 1998 Faugères exhibits waxy, superripe dark cherry aromas. Medium- to full-bodied, velvety-textured, and expansive, this impressive offering reveals loads of chewy cherries, blackberries, and spices in its expressive character. This terrific value is an intense, powerfully flavored wine that possesses a long tannin- and fruit-filled finish. Anticipated maturity: now–2008.

The dark ruby/black-colored 1998 Faugères Jadis boasts extravagant blackberry and cedar aromas. This is a hugely concentrated, tarry, backward wine loaded with chocolate, asphalt, and *garrigue* (Provençal herb)-like flavors. It has outstanding grip to its massive, concentrated, and extracted personality. Anticipated maturity: 2003–2010.

DOMAINE DE BAUBIAC

1998 Coteaux du Languedoc	B	89+
1998 Vin de Pays d'Oc Merlot	A	88

The saturated ruby/purple-colored 1998 Vin de Pays d'Oc Merlot offers aromas of blackberries, olives, and Italian tomatoes. This powerful, dense, intense wine is crammed with tarry black fruit and chocolate flavors. Medium- to full-bodied, chewy, and admirably long in the finish, it should be at its best if consumed over the next 4–5 years.

Produced from 60% Syrah and 40% Mourvèdre, the 1998 Coteaux du Languedoc is medium to dark ruby-colored and offers aromas distinctly reminiscent of roasted thyme and rosemary. Gorgeously ripe and concentrated, this medium- to full-bodied wine coats the palate with blackberry, wild berry, tobacco, cedar, and tarlike flavors. This intense wine comes on full throttle and is not for the weak at heart. Anticipated maturity: now–2006.

HUGUES BEAULIEU

2000 Picpoul de Pinet	A	89

Possibly the finest Picpoul I have ever tasted, the 2000 (the Muscadet of southern France) offers an explosive, citrusy, grapefruit-scented bouquet, an excellent texture, and a dry, fresh finish. Drink it before 2003, as these wines have a short lifeline.

CHÂTEAU DE BELLES EAUX

1997 Coteaux du Languedoc Elevé en Fût de Chêne Cuvée Sylveric	B	89

This estate, under the watchful eye of proprietors Hélène Mir and her brother-in-law, has a bright future ahead of it, as the nine wines I tasted from a variety of vintages (most do not appear as they are no longer available) indicate that they have already mastered one of the hardest tasks for wine-makers: their wines all have gorgeous textures. The 50-hectare

(20.23-acre) domaine produces 350,000 bottles of wine each year and sells 250,000 of it to *négociants*. The estate's luxury *cuvée*, the medium to dark ruby-colored 1997 Coteaux du Languedoc Elevé en Fût de Chêne Cuvée Sylveric, is named after the proprietors' sons (Sylvain and Americ). An assemblage of 70% Syrah, 20% Grenache, and 10% Mourvèdre, this wine reveals superripe aromas of candle wax and jammy blackberries. Its thick, medium- to full-bodied personality is crammed with roasted black fruits and a myriad of spices. Somewhat firm, it will require 1–2 years of cellaring. Drink it between 2004–2008.

DOMAINE BORIE DE MAUREL

1999 Minervois Cuvée Sylla	C	89+
1998 Minervois Cuvée Sylla	C	(89–91)

The impressive 1998 Minervois Cuvée Sylla, fashioned from 100% Syrah, hand-harvested at 30 hectoliters per hectare, possesses a saturated, dark ruby color. Its superripe nose offers loads of candied black raspberry aromas. On the palate, this medium- to full-bodied, mouth-coating, and massively ripe wine represents a terrific expression of tank-fermented Syrah fruit. Hints of chocolate appear in its admirably long and supple finish. Drink this wonderful wine over the next 4–5 years.

The 1999 Minervois Cuvée Sylla is produced from 100% Syrah, vinified and aged entirely in stainless steel tanks. It sports a sexy nose of sweet saddle leather, black raspberries, and blackberries. On the palate, loads of dark fruits as well as tannin coat the taster's mouth. Well made, it is powerful, intense, and medium- to full-bodied. Somewhat rustic in its youth, this wine may ultimately merit an outstanding score if cellaring civilizes its structure. Anticipated maturity: 2003–2008.

CHÂTEAU DE CALADROY

1998 Côtes du Roussillon-Villages La Cuvée du Docteur Bobo	C	89
1998 Côtes du Roussillon-Villages Les Grenats	C	88+

The 1998 Les Grenats offers sweet blackberry and leather aromas. On the palate, this dense, plump, fruit-forward, medium- to full-bodied wine provides a mouthful of gorgeously ripe black fruits, tar, and licorice. Crafted from 10% Grenache, 20% Mourvèdre, and 70% Syrah (unfiltered for the U.S. market), this firm yet fruit-packed offering will make for delicious drinking over the next 4–5 years.

The 1998 La Cuvée du Docteur Bobo is big, broad, and intensely structured. Its dark ruby color and black raspberry aromas lead to huge layers of tar and licorice-imbued black fruits. As this powerful wine ages, it may well merit an even better score if its tannic backbone melts before its fruit dissipates. Anticipated maturity: now–2007.

CHÂTEAU CALISSANNE

1998 Clos Victoire Coteaux d'Aix	C	90

Although this property is situated outside the Languedoc-Roussillon, it deserves to be included in this report since there are so few estates making wines of this quality from the Coteaux d'Aix-en-Provence. The superb 1998 Clos Victoire, made from a 10-acre parcel and composed primarily of Syrah, with the balance Cabernet Sauvignon, boasts a dense purple color and a big, sweet nose of blackberry jam, cedar, licorice, truffles, and pepper. Terrific fruit intensity and purity, full body, and nicely integrated tannin, acidity, and new oak result in an impressive Coteaux d'Aix. Anticipated maturity: now–2012.

CHÂTEAU DE CAMPUGET

2000 Costières de Nîmes (white)	A	89
1998 Costières de Nîmes Cuvée Prestige	B	(89–91)

1998 Vin de Pays du Gard Syrah Cuvée Prestige	C	90
2000 Vin de Pays du Gard Viognier Cuvée Prestige	B	89
1999 Vin de Pays du Gard Viognier Cuvée Prestige	B	88
2000 Vin de Pays d'Oc	A	88

Eighteen thousand cases of Château de Campuget's potentially outstanding 1998 Costières de Nîmes Cuvée Prestige will come to the United States. Crafted from 50% Syrah and 50% Grenache (two-thirds aged in new oak, the balance in first-year barrels), it reveals an elegant floral, red and black fruit–scented nose. Its explosive flavor profile offers cassis, cherries, leather, and spice that regale the palate in mouthcoating ways. Oily-textured and superbly ripe, this long, supple, tannin-filled wine will make for admirable drinking over the course of the next 6–7 years.

The 1998 Syrah Cuvée Prestige has fulfilled the promise it held in barrel. It bears the same label as this estate's regular red wine bottling yet can be easily differentiated because it is in a Burgundy-shaped bottle and has a back label that indicates "Syrah Prestige." Harvested at 30 hectoliters per hectare and aged entirely in new oak barrels and *demi-muids,* this dark ruby-colored wine offers dense black fruit and freshly laid asphalt aromas. Firmly structured, highly extracted, thick, full-bodied, and intense, it is crammed with blackberry, tar, and cassis-like flavors. It is an excellent value. Anticipated maturity: 2003–2008.

A small dose of Muscat (5%) was included in the blend of the 1999 Viognier Cuvée Prestige. Aromatically, fresh white peaches are intermingled with orange rinds in this lovely, characterful offering. Crisp yellow fruits, potpourri, perfume, and apricots are found in its softly textured, medium-bodied character. This excellent value will serve as a first-rate apéritif if consumed by 2003.

The deep ruby/purple-colored 2000 Vin de Pays d'Oc, a tank-fermented and -aged blend of 55% Grenache and 45% Syrah (5,500 cases exported to the U.S.), offers a gorgeous bouquet of berries, pepper, and spice, a lovely texture, abundant quantities of sweet fruit, terrific purity, and a long finish. A serious, dry red wine that can be served slightly chilled, it is totally captivating and delicious. Drink it over the next 2–3 years.

The 2000 Costières de Nîmes, a tank-fermented and -aged blend of 65% Roussanne, 30% Grenache Blanc, and 5% Clairette, offers notes of rose petals, honeysuckle, and bananas. This medium-bodied, richly fruity, dry wine has been impeccably vinified and bottled. It is a delicious Provençal white to enjoy before 2003.

The barrel-fermented 2000 Viognier Cuvée Prestige is as good. It boasts a sumptuous nose of honeysuckle, peach, and orange marmalade with good underlying acidity. Fresh, lively, and exceptionally well made, it, too, should be drunk before 2003.

DOMAINE CANET-VALETTE

1998 St.-Chinian Une et Mille Nuits	B	88
1997 St.-Chinian Le Vin Maghani	C	90
1998 St.-Chinian Le Vin Maghani Réserve	C	90

This organic estate is composed of a single 18-hectare (7.3-acre) parcel surrounded by *garrigue,* the wild herbs of southern France. The 1997 Le Vin Maghani sports a saturated dark ruby/purple color. It bursts from the glass with herb-tinged blackberries and possesses a sexy, medium- to full-bodied personality. Candied fruit can be found in its rich, opulent, expressive personality. This angle-free wine also reveals a long, lush, sweet and slightly warm (alcohol) finish. Drink it over the next 6–8 years.

A fragrant nose of framboise, blueberry pie, and orange Grand Marnier–like aromas emerge from the medium ruby-colored 1998 Une et Mille Nuits. In the mouth, it is spicy and peppery, with dried Provençal herbs and beef blood characteristics added to the blueberry/orange flavors. Dominated by its Grenache component (approximately 60%, with the rest Syrah and Carignan), it is earthy, rich, rustic, and full of personality. Drink this out-standing value over the next 5–7 years.

Red/black fruits are intermingled with spices and licorice in the aromatics of the 1998 Le Vin Maghani Réserve. Medium-bodied, it is loaded with depth, jam-packed with cherries and blackberries. Well balanced, it is a wine of power and concentration. Huge quantities of tannin are found in its extensive finish, yet they are ripe and supple. Anticipated maturity: 2004–2009.

DOMAINE DES CANTARELLES

1998 Vin du Pays du Gard Cabernet Syrah	**B**	**88+**

Domaine des Cantarelles's 1998 Vin du Pays du Gard Cabernet (40%)/Syrah (60%) is fash-ioned from Cabernet Franc, Cabernet Sauvignon, and Syrah (50% of this last varietal was aged in new-oak barrels). Aromatically, it reveals sweet cassis intermingled with spicy oak. On the palate, this is a chewy, youthful, well-balanced wine, crammed with black raspberries and cherries. Deep, structured, and tannic (yet ripe), it should be even better with 1–2 years of cellaring.

CHÂTEAU DE CAPITOUL

2000 Coteaux du Languedoc-La Clape Les Rocailles	**B**	**89**
1998 Vin de Pays d'Oc Les Oubliées Viognier Vendanges Tardives	**C/500ml**	**89**

Medium- to dark ruby-colored and intense, the 2000 Coteaux du Languedoc-La Clape Les Rocailles reveals candied red cherry aromas. This luscious wine, a blend of Grenache, Mourvèdre, and Carignan, is loaded with juicy blueberries, sweet blackberries, and jammy cherries. It is broad, ample, velvety-textured, and possesses a long, lush finish. Drink it over the next 4–5 years.

The lovely 1998 Vin de Pays d'Oc Les Oubliées Viognier Vendanges Tardives (Les Ou-bliées means "the forgotten ones") was harvested at 5 hectoliters per hectare and aged for 36 months in new-oak barrels. Toasted peach and apricots can be discerned in its boisterous aromatics. On the palate, it is well balanced, fresh, and loaded with yellow fruits (mostly peaches) whose flavors linger in its extensive finish. Only 1,500 bottles of this excellent sweet wine were produced. Drink it over the next 5–6 years.

LA CASENOVE

1998 Côtes de Roussillon Cuvée de Commandant Jaubert	**D**	**(90–92)**

Eighty percent of this *cuvée* is low-yielding, ripe Syrah (20–25 hectoliters per hectare). The wine sees moderate amounts of new oak in its upbringing. This has always been one of the stars of the Côtes de Roussillon, and in 1998, given the additional ripeness and power pro-vided by the vintage, it is a wine of exceptional intensity, power, richness, and upside poten-tial. A dark ruby/purple color is followed by a full-bodied, thick, rich, moderately tannic wine in need of 12–18 months of bottle aging. Impressively pure, well balanced, and mouth-staining, this large-scaled effort should drink well between now–2012.

DOMAINE CLAVEL

1998 Coteaux du Languedoc-Terroir La Méjanelle La Copa Santa	**C**	**(91–93)**
1998 Coteaux du Languedoc-Terroir La Méjanelle Les Garrigues	**B**	**(88–91)**

The 1998 Les Garrigues, produced from equal parts Syrah and Grenache, is first-rate. Its black/purple color and sweet, floral, black raspberry liqueur–scented nose lead to its mouth-coating, structured personality. Tangy blackberries, asphalt, and hints of mint can be found in this muscular, medium- to full-bodied, long-finishing offering. It is a full-flavored, full-throttle, in-your-face wine. Anticipated maturity: now–2007.

The outstanding 1998 La Copa Santa, 80% Syrah, 10% Grenache, and 10% Mourvèdre, has a black, saturated color. Aromas of ink and sweet blackberries are followed by a massive, muscular, hugely powerful character. Beef blood, licorice, and road tar–like flavors capture the palate and seemingly refuse to relinquish their control. This full-bodied, expansive, he-man of a wine is highly concentrated and extremely well extracted. Anticipated maturity: 2003–2010.

CLOS BAGATELLE

1998 St.-Chinian La Gloire de Mon Père	C	(87–89)

The medium to dark ruby-colored 1998 St.-Chinian La Gloire de Mon Père possesses floral, superripe, red fruit aromas. Medium- to full-bodied, powerful, and intense, this wine coats the palate with its licorice, tar, and blackberry-like flavors. Its admirably long finish reveals loads of ripe, supple tannins. Anticipated maturity: now–2006.

CLOS MARIE

1998 Coteaux du Languedoc-Pic-St.-Loup Les Glorieuses	E	91
1998 Coteaux du Languedoc-Pic-St.-Loup Les Olivettes	B	89
1998 Coteaux du Languedoc-Pic-St.-Loup Simon	D	90+

Clos Marie, unquestionably one of Pic-St.-Loup's up-and-coming estates, suffered through the 1999 vintage. "It was very difficult. August was a catastrophe," said its owner and wine-maker, yet it produced outstanding 1998s. The dark ruby/purple-colored 1998 Les Olivettes (a blend of 45% Syrah, 45% Grenache, and 10% Mourvèdre fermented and aged in tank) is a delicious, elegant wine with sumptuous quantities of blackberry, licorice-infused fruit, and a touch of pepper. With its low acidity, gorgeous ripeness, and mouthcoating richness and seamlessness, this offering should drink well for 4–5 years. Sadly, only 100 cases were exported to the United States.

The 1998 Simon is a medium to dark ruby-colored wine with cedar and blackberry aromas. This broad, chewy, medium- to full-bodied wine is packed with blackberries, cassis, and hints of cola in its broad-shouldered, slightly rustic character. It is intense, firm, and powerful. Anticipated maturity: 2005–2012.

The 1999 Les Glorieuses, tasted three days after bottling, revealed a violet, blackberry, and blueberry-scented nose. This feminine, medium- to full-bodied wine is highly expressive, satin-textured, and lush. Spices, cinnamon, red cherries, and black raspberries can be found in its juicy, hugely structured personality. It is elegant yet muscular. Anticipated maturity: 2005–2012.

LES CLOS DES PAULILLES

2000 Banyuls Rimage	C/375ml	92
1998 Banyuls Rimage	B/375ml	(87–89)
1993 Banyuls Rimage	B/375ml	88
1998 Banyuls Rimage Mise Tardive	C/500ml	92
1995 Banyuls Rimage Mise Tardive	D	89
1998 Banyuls Cap Béar	D	93
1994 Banyuls Cap Béar	D	90
1999 Collioure	C	91+

Les Clos des Paulilles currently has a number of compelling Banyuls on the market. These fortified sweet reds (fashioned exclusively from Grenache) are one of the rare wines that can be served with chocolate desserts. They are delicious to drink young, yet are also capable of extended cellaring. The dark ruby-colored 1993 Banyuls Rimage displays baked cherry and prune aromas intermingled with hints of caramel. Its medium-bodied personality boasts 105 grams of residual sugar, yet the wine comes across as almost dry. Lovely blackberry liqueur, mocha, and dark chocolate are found in its flavor profile and throughout its supple finish. Anticipated maturity: now–2010+.

The saturated black 1998 Banyuls Rimage has coffee ice cream and jammy red cherry aromas. It is medium- to full-bodied, creamy-textured, and crammed with loads of chocolate, blueberries, and assorted black fruits. This warm, extroverted, flavorful wine is refined and possesses excellent grip. Anticipated maturity: now–2015+.

The 1995 Banyuls Rimage Mise Tardive exhibits scents of creamed blackberries, candle wax, and roasted spices. This velvety-textured wine boasts admirable depth, grip, and focus in its exuberant character. Mocha candies awash in red cherry syrup are found in this offering. Drink it over the next 15–20 years.

The mahogany-colored 1994 Banyuls Cap Béar reveals some orangeish amber on the edge of the glass. It was left outdoors in demijohns for a year and a half before being placed in three-year-old barrels for six months. The resulting wine is outstanding. Mocha, spice cake, tobacco, and sweet cedar aromas are detected in this creamy-textured, medium- to full-bodied wine. Its refined, detailed, yet powerful personality offers a myriad of spice, prune, plum, and baked cherry flavors. Having been subjected to the torrid temperatures common in this region bordering Spain, this complex and well-balanced wine should be capable of extremely long-term cellaring. Anticipated maturity: now–2030+.

While many producers of Collioure struggled in 1999 because the only varietal to ripen fully was Mourvèdre, proprietor Bernard Daure was ecstatic, as that's the varietal he depends on for his Collioure. The saturated, black-colored 1999 Collioure displays tarry dark fruit aromas and a medium- to full-bodied character with loads of depth. A blend of 72% Mourvèdre and 28% Syrah, this is a powerful, intense, manly wine crammed with gorgeous black fruits, violets, freshly laid asphalt, and jammy grapes. Anticipated maturity: 2004–2012.

The dark-colored 2000 Banyuls Rimage has a sumptuous nose of candied blackberries, jammy plums, and mocha. A supple, rich, luscious wine, it regales the palate with opulent waves of cherries, chocolate, and compote of black raspberries. This broad, fresh, velvety-textured wine has exquisite balance and a long, flavorful finish. Drink it over the next 15 years.

Waxy black raspberries can be found in the nose of the dark ruby-colored 1998 Banyuls Rimage Mise Tardive. Medium-bodied, this wine's divine texture is pure satin. Violets, baked cherries, cedar, mocha, candied plums, and jammy black raspberries are found throughout its ample personality as well as in its extensive finish. Anticipated maturity: now–2015.

The mahogany and amber-colored 1998 Banyuls Cap Béar is crafted in a distinctive way. It is left outside in 60-liter demijohns for an entire year, regardless of weather, then transferred to barrels for four months "to bring it back together," said Bernard Daure. Each demijohn loses 5 liters to evaporation over the course of that year, further concentrating the flavors of the wine. It has a highly defined nose of cigar box, cedar, and sweet pipe tobacco that leads to a surprisingly fresh, intensely complex personality. Broad, lush, satin-textured, and medium-bodied, it displays a cacophony of flavors, including cherries, raspberries, cedar, chocolate, plums, blackberries, and tobacco, whose effects linger throughout its extraordinarily long finish. Interestingly, experience suggests that some drinkers adore this style of wine (I would certainly be in that category), while others find its somewhat oxidized character problematic. Drink this gem over the next 20+ years.

CLOS DES TRUFFIERS
1998 Coteaux du Languedoc Hommage à Max	**E (92–95)**

The spectacular 1998 Coteaux du Languedoc Hommage à Max was crafted from the oldest Syrah vines in the Languedoc (planted in 1967) and harvested at a natural potential alcohol of 15.6% from incredibly low yields (11 hectoliters per hectare). This unfined and unfiltered wine has a saturated black/purple color and extraordinary blueberry syrup, cedar, and cookie dough aromas. Its awesome personality is crammed with sweet cherry and raspberry fruit, intermingled with hints of oak. Powerful, refined, and palate-staining, this huge, well-balanced, complex offering is truly extraordinary. Deeply concentrated and extracted, yet seamless, it is a tour de force in winemaking and, simply put, the finest dry 1998 I tasted from the Languedoc and Roussillon provinces. Anticipated maturity: 2003–2012.

COL DES VENTS

1998 Corbières Grand Cuvée Castelmaure	B	90

In essence, this is a cooperative of 20 families who control some of the best vineyard sites in Corbières. The outstanding, limited-production (15,000 bottles) 1998 Corbières Grand Cuvée Castelmaure (45% Grenache, 45% Syrah, and 10% Carignan) spends time in new oak. Dense ruby/purple-colored, with copious quantities of black pepper, sweet black raspberry, and black currant fruit, this deep, supple, rich, full-bodied wine possesses fine glycerin, purity, and a heady, lush finish. Drink it over the next 2–3 years.

DOMAINE DE LA COMBE BLANCHE

1998 Minervois-La Livinière "La Chandelière"	D	88+
1999 Vin de Pays des Côtes de Brian Tempranillo Le Dessous de l'Enfer	D	89

The 1998 Minervois-La Livinière "La Chandelière" was produced from 12- to 15-year-old Syrah (60%) and 60- to 70-year-old Grenache (40%) aged for 16 months in new French oak. Tobacco, cigar box, and cedar aromas can be discerned in its mouthwatering nose. Medium-bodied and extremely spicy, this well-made, structured, complex wine offers loads of silky-textured, dark fruit flavors that linger throughout its long finish. Anticipated maturity: now–2006.

Produced from 50% Viognier and 50% Roussanne, the 2000 Vin de Pays des Côtes de Brian has a ripe floral, pear, and peach-scented nose. This silky-textured, medium-bodied wine has a rich, plump, yet fresh personality filled with assorted white and yellow fruits. Its finish reveals a hint of alcoholic warmth, which kept my score in the "good" range. Drink it over the next 12 months.

CHÂTEAU COUPE ROSES

1999 Minervois Cuvée Orience	C	88
1998 Minervois Cuvée Orience	B	(88–89+)

The 1998 Minervois Orience is medium to dark ruby-colored. A blend of 75% Syrah, 19% Grenache, and 6% Carignan, it reveals black fruits, *garrigue* (Provençal herbs), and oak spice notes. This is a big, broad, ample, medium- to full-bodied wine. Loads of minty black fruits, licorice, and road tar are found in this warm, well-structured, muscular offering. Anticipated maturity: now–2006.

The similarly colored 1999 Minervois Cuvée Orience, produced from 70% Grenache, 20% Carignan (both aged in new first- and second-year barrels), and 10% Grenache (stainless steel tanks), reveals a spicy, toasty, blackberry-scented nose. This concentrated wine is loaded with smoky raspberries, blackberries, cassis, and hints of chocolate. Medium-bodied and bright (this estate's vineyards are located at high altitudes), it is an extremely well balanced, expressive, and flavorful wine. Anticipated maturity: now–2007.

DOMAINE DE LA CROIX BELLE

2000 No. 7 Vin de Pays des Côtes de Thongue (white)	B	88

A kitchen sink assemblage of seven varietals (Viognier, Chardonnay, Grenache Blanc, Sauvignon Blanc, Carignan Blanc, Muscat, and Chasan), which explains its numerical name, the

2000 No. 7 Vin de Pays des Côtes de Thongue has toasted white fruit and spice aromas. Rich, velvety-textured, and medium-bodied, this lovely wine offers a panoply of fruit flavors ranging from apples to apricots, white peaches, and pears. Toasty new oak brings an additional touch of complexity to the finish. Drink it over the next 1–2 years.

DOMAINE CROS

1998 Minervois Vieilles Vignes	B	90

Produced from Carignan planted in 1905, the dark ruby/purple-colored 1998 Minervois Vieilles Vignes offers lovely fruit, forward candied blackberry, and cassis aromatics. Medium- to full-bodied and velvety-textured, it boasts penetrating red/black cherry, blueberry, and licorice flavors in its powerful, jammy personality. This extremely well made wine is a concentrated, supple, fruit-packed mouthful. Drink it over the next 5 years.

GEORGES DUBŒUF

2000 Merlot Domaine de Bordeneuve	A	(88–90)

I was floored by the superexpressive nose of the dark-colored 2000 Merlot Domaine de Bordeneuve. Hyperripe cherries are intermingled with sweet violets and cassis jam in this medium- to full-bodied, intense wine. It is concentrated, well extracted, packed with juicy blackberries, and has a long, luscious, seamless finish. It is a hedonist's delight! Drink it over the next 4 years.

GUILHEM DURAND

2000 Vin de Pays d'Hauterive Merlot	A	88

If made dictator, I pledge that I will force all California Merlot producers to taste what can be purchased from France for a measly $9. This medium to dark ruby-colored 2000 Merlot boasts intensely sweet plum and blackberry aromas, medium body, a velvety texture, and a long, supple finish. Fat, powerful, and expansive, it coats the palate with abundant, concentrated layers of chewy blackberries, cherries, and hints of tar. Drink this superb value over the next 4 years.

DOMAINE DE L'ERMITAGE DU PIC-ST.-LOUP

1998 Coteaux du Languedoc-Pic-St.-Loup Cuvée Ste.-Agnès	C	89
1998 Coteaux du Languedoc-Pic-St.-Loup Guilhem Gaucelm	C	(90–92)

There is no doubting the outstanding quality of the 1998 Guilhem Gaucelm. Produced from 90% Syrah and 10% Grenache and aged in barrels for 18–24 months (40% new oak), it offers an extraordinarily waxy, potpourri-like nose. On the palate, layer after layer of blackberries, toast, and a myriad of spices coat the palate. This is a powerful, seamless, highly expressive, medium- to full-bodied wine. Velvety-textured and intense, it should be at its best between now–2007+.

The medium to dark ruby-colored 1998 Cuvée Ste.-Agnès is built for the long haul. Its deep aromas of spices and roasted black fruits lead to a medium- to full-bodied, oily-textured character, crammed with satiny blueberries and blackberries. It has outstanding depth and structure, as well as an impressively long, ripe, tannin-packed finish. Anticipated maturity: 2004–2012.

DOMAINE FERRER RIBIÈRE

1998 Côtes du Roussillon Cana	C	(88–89+)
1998 Côtes du Roussillon Cuvée Caroline	B	(88–90)
2000 Vin de Pays Catalan Carignan Empreinte du Temps	C	89

The 1998 Côtes du Roussillon Cana is dark ruby-colored and reveals supersweet black raspberry and cherry aromas. This soft, jammy, candied red and black fruit–filled wine is oily-textured and reveals hints of mocha in its somewhat firm (yet ripe) finish. Drink it over the next 4 years.

The dark ruby-colored 1998 Côtes du Roussillon Cuvée Caroline offers roasted black fruit, spice, and chocolate aromas. This is a fruit-forward, velvety-textured wine with powerful red meat, cherry syrup, and chocolate flavors. It is dense, extroverted, and not for the weak at heart. Drink it between now–2005.

Produced from 123-year-old Carignan vines, the medium to dark ruby-colored 1999 Vin de Pays Catalan Carignan Empreinte du Temps boasts a nose of licorice and sweet blackberries. A myriad of dark fruits and spices can be found throughout its silky-textured, medium-bodied character. Its long, fruit-filled finish reveals copious quantities of tannin, yet it is ripe and supple. Drink it over the next 4–5 years.

DOMAINE FONT CAUDE

1998 Coteaux du Languedoc-Montpeyroux "Alain Chabanon"		
Les Boissières	C	88

The sweet red raspberry–scented 1998 "Alain Chabanon" Les Boissières Coteaux du Languedoc-Montpeyroux (note: the estate's name is barely noticeable on the label as "Alain Chabanon" is the dominant text) is medium to dark ruby-colored and has a lush, medium-bodied personality. Loads of soft, velvety fruit can be found in its spicy character. While it is firm in the finish, its tannin is soaked in red/black raspberries. Drink it over the next 4–5 years.

DOMAINE FONTSAINTE

1999 Corbières Réserve de la Demoiselle	A	88+

This ruby-colored 1999 exhibits a freshly cracked pepper and juicy cherry–scented nose. A pretty, elegant, feminine effort, it possesses excellent focus as well as depth of fruit, medium body, and deep layers of peppery red and black berries. This seamless, refined wine is best consumed over the next 5 years.

DOMAINE FOULAQUIER

1999 Coteaux du Languedoc-Pic-St.-Loup l'Orphée	B	90
1999 Coteaux du Languedoc-Pic-St.-Loup Le Rollier	C	89

Domaine Foulaquier, acquired in 1999 by two Swiss gentlemen, one of whom, Pierre Jequier, took early retirement from his career in architecture to pursue his passion for wine, has burst onto the scene with two lovely debut offerings. Both are superb values. A blend of equal proportions of Syrah and Grenache harvested at 14.2% natural potential alcohol, the 1999 Le Rollier exhibits a medium to dark ruby color as well as an intense nose of sweet cherries. Medium-bodied and chewy-textured, with huge breadth, it is filled with Bing cherries, liquid potpourri, and spice. While it possesses a slight rustic edge, it is pure and has a long, fruit-filled finish. Drink it over the next 9 years.

Even better, the medium to dark ruby-colored 1999 l'Orphée was produced from 90% Grenache and 10% Syrah. It bursts from the glass with blackberry and candied red cherry aromatics. Rich and thick, with loads of overripe blackberries, candied cherries, and jammy raspberries, outstanding depth of fruit, superb balance, and a hedonistic personality, this sweet, in-your-face, full-flavored red will drink well over the next 8 years.

DOMAINE GARDIÉS

1999 Côtes du Roussillon-Villages Les Millères	B	88
1999 Tautavel	C	90

Produced from 50% Syrah, 25% Grenache, and 25% Mourvèdre, the 1999 Côtes du Roussillon-Villages Les Millères exhibits a grape- and blackberry-scented bouquet. This rich, expansive, intense, extroverted, powerful effort reveals roasted black fruits, spice, and *garrigue*-like flavors as well as a long, sweet, fruit-filled finish. Drink it over the next 6–7 years.

The 1999 Tautavel is dark ruby-colored. Produced from 40% Syrah, 30% Grenache, and 30% Mourvèdre and aged in 20% new oak, this is a cedar, tobacco, and licorice-scented wine. Medium- to full-bodied and chewy-textured, it is muscular, highly extracted, and crammed with massive layers of black fruits, tar, and spices. It is an intense powerhouse with copious quantities of prodigiously ripened tannin. Anticipated maturity: now–2008.

DOMAINE GAUBY

1998 Côtes du Roussillon La Muntada	D	(88–89+)

The 1998 Côtes du Roussillon La Muntada (this word means "the rise" in Catalan, the local language) was produced with 80% Syrah and 20% 50-year-old Grenache vines. Aromatically, it reveals sweet cassis, spice, and fresh herblike scents. Its mouthcoating, palate-staining personality is chewy, concentrated, and has excellent grip. Blackberries, road tar, and black currants can be found in this thickly textured, fresh, full-throttle wine. Anticipated maturity: 2003–2009.

DOMAINE LA GAUPHINE

1998 St.-Chinian Cuvée Vieilles Vignes	B	88
2000 St.-Chinian Viognier	B	89

A Condrieu look-alike (at one-fourth the price), the 2000 St.-Chinian Viognier is deep, rich, and dry, with superb aromatics of honeysuckle, lemon butter, orange, and peaches. It should be drunk over the next 8–12 months.

The earthy, peppery, raspberry, chocolaty, smoky 1998 St.-Chinian Cuvée Vieilles Vignes is a blend of 70% Syrah, 25% Grenache, and 5% Mourvèdre aged in French and American oak. It displays good flesh, medium to full body, and a soft, earthy personality. Think of it as a larger-scaled Côtes du Rhône. It should drink well for 2–3 years.

DOMAINE DU GRAND CRÉS

1999 Corbières	B	87

Produced from 50% Grenache, 25% Syrah, and 25% Cinsault, this dark ruby-colored 1999 Corbières displays an inky, blackberry-laced perfume as well as intense blackberry, tar, and cassis flavors. Medium-bodied and rustic, it is a highly concentrated offering meant for consumers who love powerful, chewy, roasted wines. Anticipated maturity: now–2005.

CHÂTEAU GRANDE CASSAGNE

2000 Costières de Nîmes (white)	A	88
2000 Costières de Nîmes "GS" La Civette	A	89
1999 Costières de Nîmes "S" Les Ramaux	A	88+

The dark ruby-colored 1999 "S" Les Ramaux was produced from a blend of 90% Syrah and 10% Grenache. Its demure mocha and black fruit aromas are followed by a medium- to full-bodied character packed with fresh black cherries and cassis, whose flavors last throughout its persistent finish. This superb value should be drunk between now–2005.

The 2000 Costières de Nîmes (white), a blend of 60% Roussanne and 40% Grenache Blanc, tastes like Chablis made in Provence. It possesses excellent fruit, good lemony acidity, real zestiness as well as delineation, and a focused, mineral, floral finish. Drink it over the next 12–18 months.

The sensational 2000 "GS" La Civette (equal parts Grenache and Syrah) boasts a deep ruby color as well as a sweet nose of blackberry and cassis fruit intermixed with pepper and licorice. Dense, chewy, and fleshy, with outstanding purity, and wonderful ripeness and palate presence, this captivating wine should be consumed over the next 2–3 years.

LA GRANGE DES PÈRES

1999 Vin de Pays de l'Hérault (white)	E	93
1998 Vin de Pays de l'Hérault (white)	E	91
1996 Vin de Pays de l'Hérault (white)	D	93
1998 Vin de Pays de l'Hérault (red)	D	93
1997 Vin de Pays de l'Hérault (red)	D	(88–91+)

The young Laurent Vaillé has skyrocketed to the forefront of the Languedoc's greatest producers of wine. Not surprisingly, his résumé reads like a *Who's Who* of France's top estates (he has done stints at Domaine Trevallon, Domaine Jean-Louis Chave, and Domaine Coche-Dury). When asked about his favorite wines, he smiled and said, "Rayas is Rayas, the greatest in the south." Vaillé's white wine, predominantly made from Roussanne, is the finest dry white this taster has encountered from the Languedoc-Roussillon. Furthermore, it competes with the Château de Beaucastel's Roussanne Vieilles Vignes for the honor of being the finest and most multidimensional Roussanne produced in France.

The full-bodied 1996 Vin de Pays de l'Hérault white reveals aromas reminiscent of buttered toast dripping with honey and spices. This fresh, velvety-textured, magnificently balanced wine has great breadth of candied minerals, yellow fruits, and pears. Harmonious, nuanced, and deep, this world-class white displays an astonishingly long finish. Anticipated maturity: now–2005+.

Different lots that will be assembled in the 1997 Vin de Pays de l'Hérault red were tasted, and the range of scores given above reflects this hypothetical blend. The dark ruby-colored Cabernet lot (from yields of 14 hectoliters per hectare) offers complex, spicy, blackberry aromas, and elegant, black cherry, spice, herb, and rose flavors. The Mourvèdre (harvested at 16.5% natural potential alcohol) was incredibly Rayas-like in taste. This hedonistic fruit bomb reveals candied cherry and kirsch aromas that give way to a mouthful of mocha-covered red berries. This is a delicious, sultry, creamy wine on its own, and will ultimately be a substantial part of the final blend. The bottled 1997 will most assuredly be an outstanding wine, and certainly one of the finest efforts from this difficult vintage. Anticipated maturity: now–2010.

According to Vaillé, "The 1999 white will be as good as or better than my 1996." He's right. The 1999 Vin de Pays de l'Hérault white has a boisterously rich nose of minerals, dried honey, and buttered toast. It's medium-bodied, intense, and loaded with yellow fruits, minerals, smoke, and spices. A complex wine, it also reveals exemplary focus, balance, and a long, supple finish. Vaillé believes it will close down in its youth before blossoming after a few years of cellaring, something that often happens with Roussanne-based wines. Drink it between 2005–2014.

The 1998 Vin de Pays de l'Hérault white is a rich wine with extroverted dried honey, smoke, apricot, and spice aromas. Medium- to full-bodied and expansive, its broad layers of pears, white peaches, and flowers are ensconced in a fat, superripe character. Anticipated maturity: now–2010.

The saturated, dark ruby-colored 1998 Vin de Pays de l'Hérault red bursts from the glass with candied red and black fruits. It is a powerful, medium- to full-bodied wine with oodles of blackberries, cherries, currants, and spices that conquer the palate and seemingly never dissipate. Superbly pure, detailed, and possessing loads of exquisitely ripened tannin, this is a wine that can be consumed in its youth or cellared for over a decade. Anticipated maturity: now–2015.

CHÂTEAU GRÈS ST.-PAUL

1999 Coteaux du Languedoc Cuvée Antonin	B	90
1998 Coteaux du Languedoc Cuvée Antonin	B	90

The 1998 Cuvée Antonin exhibits copious quantities of jammy black raspberry and cassis fruit, subtle new oak, a viscous texture, and tremendous length and finish. It should drink well for 5–6 years.

What smells like Côte Rotie and tastes like Côte Rotie, yet sells for one-fifth the price? Answer: the 1999 Cuvée Antonin from Château Grès St.-Paul. This 100% Syrah cuvée boasts a big, sweet, bacon fat and black raspberry–scented bouquet with a hint of honeysuckle (suggesting Viognier has been included in the blend, but that is not the case). Pit fruit, wet stones, minerals, and gorgeous layers of fruit fight for attention in the wine's plush texture. It should be drunk over the next 4–5 years.

CHÂTEAU HOSPITALET LA CLAPE

1998 Vin de Pays d'Oc Cuvée Béatrice	B	88+

The 1998 Vin de Pays d'Oc Cuvée Béatrice reveals toast aromas intertwined with black currant and licorice in its black/purple-colored personality. Thick, rich, and full-bodied, with low acidity and moderate tannin, it should drink well between now–2010.

CHÂTEAU DE JAU

2000 Muscat de Rivesaltes	C/375ml	89
1998 Muscat de Rivesaltes	B/375ml	88+
2000 Côtes du Roussillon-Villages Talon Rouge	C	90
1998 Côtes du Roussillon-Villages Talon Rouge	C	89

According to Bernard Daure, this estate's proprietor, "During the reign of Louis XIV the elegant aristocrats at Versailles always wore red heels [*talons rouges* in French], which is where we got the idea for our top wine's name." Purchasers will be interested to know that those eyes on the label that are staring back at you belong to Mr. Daure's daughter Estelle, who handles many of the day-to-day operations at the château. If an entire case is purchased, the owner will have the pleasure of having the entire Daure family's eyes predominantly displayed in his or her cellar. The dark ruby/purple 1998 Côtes du Roussillon-Villages Talon Rouge displays a nose reminiscent of candied blackberries and dark cherries. Medium- to full-bodied and intense, this wine is loaded with dark fruits, licorice, *garrigue*, and raspberries. Made predominantly from Syrah with the addition of Mourvèdre, it was vinified and aged entirely in tank, yet distinctive toasted vanilla notes appear in the finish. Anticipated maturity: 2003–2009.

Daure described 1999 as "a difficult vintage at the estate; the wines appear to be evolving quickly, so we chose not to produce a Talon Rouge from that year." However, 2000 is "the finest vintage we've had to date," in his estimation. The black-colored, aromatically roasted 2000 Côtes du Roussillon-Villages Talon Rouge exhibits layers of sweet black raspberries, cassis, and superripe plums in its medium- to full-bodied personality. Ample and broad, this is an intense, outstanding wine that admirably combines power, refinement, and balance. Anticipated maturity: 2004–2010.

The Château de Jau crafts its Muscat de Rivesaltes (a fortified sweet wine) entirely from Muscat à Petits Grains, the noblest variety of Muscat. The citrus-scented 1998 Muscat de Rivesaltes boasts wonderful focus and ripeness. Layers of candied lemons, white fruits, and red berries are found in this elegantly rendered, flavorful wine. In France this wine would typically be served before dinner, yet it will work wonders with powerful cheeses that destroy most reds (such as Roquefort). Anticipated maturity: now–2005.

The delicately aromatic 2000 Muscat de Rivesaltes offers scents of orange blossoms and raspberries. A delightful apéritif wine, it is light-bodied, floral, loaded with demure mandarin orange flavors, and possesses a lacelike personality sure to please those wanting an elegant sweet wine to serve before or after dinner. Drink it over the next 2 years.

DOMAINE LACROIX-VANEL

1999 Coteaux du Languedoc Clos Mélanie	C	89

The medium to dark ruby-colored 1999 Coteaux du Languedoc Clos Mélanie was produced from 70% Syrah and 30% Grenache. It bursts from the glass with loads of cedar, *garrigue* (Provençal herbs), and black fruit aromas. Medium-bodied and firm, this is a satin-textured wine with juicy, intense road tar, dark fruit, and spice flavors. Its finish is long and loaded with ripe tannin. Anticipated maturity: now–2007.

CHÂTEAU DE LANCYRE

1998 Coteaux du Languedoc-Pic-St.-Loup Grande Cuvée	C	91
1998 Coteaux du Languedoc-Pic-St.-Loup Vieilles Vignes	C	89

The dark-colored 1998 Vieilles Vignes has intense dark berry aromas. It is a large, broad, extroverted wine with delicious layers of blackberries, cassis, plums, and asphalt. Well balanced and focused, this excellent medium-bodied wine should be drunk over the next 4–5 years.

The dark ruby-colored 1998 Grande Cuvée reveals violet, black cherry, cassis, and floral aromas. This extremely well made, medium- to full-bodied, powerful, broad wine offers great depth of fruit in its black pepper, kirsch, black currant, cedar, and asphalt-flavored character. It is gratifying to see that such outstanding wine can still be had for under $25 a bottle. It is an excellent value. Anticipated maturity: now–2008.

CHÂTEAU DE LANDURE

1998 Minervois Cuvée Abbé Frégouse	C	90

This outstanding, dark-colored wine is a blend of 30% Mourvèdre and 30% Syrah, with the balance divided equally between Grenache and Carignan. Its penetrating aromas of candied blackberries and cedar lead to a dense, medium-bodied personality. It has gorgeous depth of fruit, revealing wave after wave of jammy red/black raspberries, cherries, and blackberries. Anticipated maturity: now–2007.

CHÂTEAU LAVABRE

1998 Coteaux du Languedoc-Pic-St.-Loup	B	(88–90+)

The 1998 Coteaux du Languedoc-Pic-St.-Loup is medium to dark ruby-colored and reveals black pepper, leather, and blackberry scents. This cream-textured wine is crammed with candied blackberries, jammy cassis, and hints of leather. It is medium- to full-bodied, mouthcoating, intense, and possesses an extensive, soft, and supple finish. Drink it over the next 6–7 years.

PATRICK LESEC

1998 Vin de Pays d'Oc Merlot Tonneaux	B	(87–90)
1998 Vin de Pays d'Oc Syrah Tonneaux	B	(88–89+)

Note: Paris-based wine broker Patrick Lesec has taken it upon himself to find growers willing to sell their fruit and/or their wines, follow his noninterventionist winemaking guidelines, and bottle them under his labels. None of the following wines was fined or filtered.

The 1998 Merlot Tonneaux is a blend of 80% Merlot and 20% Cabernet, aged 80% in new barrels and 20% in tank. Its cherry, blackberry, and spicy oak-scented nose leads to a medium- to full-bodied, chewy, thickly textured character. This dense wine, flavored with red and black fruit as well as chocolate, is intense, flavorful, and reveals an appealingly long, supple finish. Anticipated maturity: now–2004.

The delicious, dark ruby-colored 1998 Syrah Tonneaux was fashioned from 90% Syrah and 10% 50-year-old Carignan. It displays deeply ripe, waxy, black fruit aromas, as well as an awesomely thick, creamy personality. This is an intense, deep, fruit-packed, medium- to full-bodied wine that will require 2 years of cellaring and could potentially merit an out-standing score.

SOCIÉTÉ VINICOLE DE LESQUERÈDE

1998 Côte de Roussillon-Lesquerède Cuvée Georges Pous	B	88

The Societé Vinicole de Lesquerède, this area's co-op, fashions with its highest-quality grapes a luxury *cuvée* called the Cuvée Georges Pous. The 1998 is medium to dark ruby-colored, and offers cherry and freshly cracked black pepper aromas and flavors. Medium- to full-bodied and satin-textured, it is an admirably ripe wine with excellent depth to its spicy plum, cherry, and black pepper–laden character. It is, at present, firm and somewhat foursquare, yet, given 1–2 years of cellaring, should blossom into a full-flavored, intense, and complex southern French red. This is a superb value. Anticipated maturity: now–2007.

CHÂTEAU MANSENOBLE

1998 Corbières Réserve du Château Mansenoble	B	(89–91+)

The dark ruby/purple 1998 Corbières Réserve du Château Mansenoble has blackberry liqueur, vanilla, and buttered toast aromas. This is a thick, intense, dense, powerful wine crammed with black fruits, licorice, and road tar. This wonderful, palate-conquering offering is massively ripe, embracing, warm, and possesses an admirably long finish. Anticipated maturity: now–2005+.

DOMAINE MAS AMIEL

NV	10 Ans d'Age Cuvée Spéciale	C	89
NV	15 Ans d'Age Prestige	D	90
1980	Millésime	D	94
2000	Muscat Collection Vin Doux Naturel Muscat de Rivesaltes	C	90
2000	Muscat Vin Doux Naturel Muscat de Rivesaltes	B	89
2000	Plénitude Maccabeu Maury	C	90
2000	Plénitude Muscat d'Alexandrie Vin de Table	D/375ml	90
2000	Vintage Maury	C	91
1999	Vintage Maury	C	89
2000	Vintage Blanc Maury	C	89
2000	Vintage Charles Dupuy Maury	D	(91–93)
1999	Vintage Réserve Maury	C	88+

Purchased in July 1999 by the frozen-food magnate Olivier Decelle (Picard), the famed Do-maine Mas Amiel comprised 150 hectares of vines. The estate's vines were planted predom-inantly in Grenache Noir (90%), yet Decelle has chosen to plant Syrah, raising the estate's acreage to 180 hectares (73 acres). While the estate produced mostly sweet wines, Decelle's plan is to ultimately have a balanced production between sweet and dry offerings. In the 2000 vintage, for example, 70% of the estate's production is sweet and 30% dry.

This estate is best known for its Maurys, sweet red wines made in the same manner as Banyuls or port. (They are *vins doux naturels,* which means that alcohol is added to the fer-menting juice, raising the degree of alcohol to the point where the yeast can no longer func-tion, thereby retaining natural, unfermented sugars.) Decelle understands that though Maurys can be extraordinarily complex, the market for this type of wine is not what it once was. So he intends to continue the estate's traditional production of Maury, but he is also pro-ducing a large lineup of dry offerings.

The medium ruby-colored 1999 Vintage Maury, produced entirely from Grenache Noir, sports a complex nose of candied blood oranges and blackberries. This exquisitely balanced wine (15.5% alcohol and 105 grams of residual sugar per liter) delights the palate with sweet plums, black raspberries, dark cherries, and molasses-like flavors. It is broad, full-flavored, and extroverted. Drink it over the next 5–9 years.

The ruby-colored 1999 Vintage Réserve Maury was vinified and aged in oak (none new), whereas the regular bottling was done entirely in tank. Spicy black raspberries can be found in this excellent wine's aromas and flavors. It is deep, pure, fresh, and loaded with fruit. Medium-bodied and powerful, this wine can withstand most intensely flavored desserts, including chocolates. Anticipated maturity: now–2014.

The medium to dark ruby-colored 2000 Vintage Maury has a delectable plum- and molasses-scented nose. Broad, rich, intense, and pure, it is crammed with jammy raspberries, candied cherries, and a myriad of dark fruits as well as spices. A powerful yet elegant wine, it is medium- to full-bodied, fat, and well balanced. Drink it over the next 15 years.

The darker-colored 2000 Vintage Charles Dupuy Maury was vinified and aged entirely in new oak. Its intense aromas reveal copious quantities of black fruits intermingled with spices. Loads of black raspberries, molasses, cherries, and plums can be found in its extroverted, oak-infused personality. Satin-textured and medium- to full-bodied, it is a superb Maury for drinking over the next 15+ years.

The 2000 Vintage Blanc Maury (100% Grenache Gris) sports 114 grams of residual sugar per liter. Its hazelnut-scented nose leads to a fresh, white pear– and apricot-flavored character. Medium-bodied and gorgeously balanced, it is delicate, elegant, and intricate. Drink it over the next 5 years.

The 2000 Plénitude Maccabeu Maury may be the finest wine I have tasted to date from this rarely seen varietal. Decelle explained that in June of 2000, he had his laborers pinch the stems that connected the clusters to the vines, thereby hampering the vine's ability to ripen its grapes (this varietal tends to ripen exceedingly fast), then two weeks later he had the clusters cut from the vines and dropped on the ground, where they dehydrated in the sun for three weeks. Upon pressing the Maccabeu, it was revealed that the grapes had been harvested at 18% natural potential alcohol. (The finished wine contains 15.5% alcohol and 115 grams of residual sugar.) It boasts a fresh, floral, apricot-scented nose and a lively, delicate, focused character. Light- to medium-bodied and filled with white berries, apricots, and peaches, this is a full-flavored wine with a long, expressive finish. Drink it over the next 5–6 years.

The 2000 Muscat Vin Doux Naturel Muscat de Rivesalte (a blend of 80% Muscat à Petits Grains and 20% Muscat d'Alexandrie) has an exquisite nose of oranges and candied tangerines. Fresh citrus blossoms and kumquats can be found in this lacelike, complex, precise wine. It is lively, full-flavored, and extremely well balanced. Drink it over the next 3–4 years.

Harvested at 15 hectoliters per hectare from the estate's finest parcels of Muscat à Petits Grains, the 2000 Muscat Collection Vin Doux Naturel Muscat de Rivesaltes has an expressive orange blossom–scented nose. Well focused, this light-bodied wine has outstanding grip to its orange candy–flavored personality. Drink it over the next 3–4 years.

The 2000 Plénitude Muscat d'Alexandrie had to be labeled as a *vin de table* instead of a more exalted appellation name because it was made naturally, without the addition of alcohol to arrest fermentation. It is exquisite, boasting a tangerine- and orange blossom–scented nose. Intense, fresh, and complex, it exhibits floral, red berry, currant, raspberry, and candied kumquat flavors. This light- to medium-bodied, lacelike wine should be drunk over the next 4 years.

The mahogany-colored 10 Ans d'Age Cuvée Spéciale offers chocolate and coffee aromas. On the palate, sweet cedar, dried molasses, raspberries, cherries, spices, coffee, and almonds can be found in its satin-textured, smooth character. This medium-bodied, extroverted wine can be consumed as an apéritif or in lieu of dessert over the next 10 years.

Interestingly, the 15 Ans d'Age Prestige contains the same amount of residual sugar as its

10-year-old sibling, yet comes across as totally dry. It reveals intense candied nut aromas and flavors reminiscent of sweet cigar tobacco, cedar, and hazelnuts. It is medium-bodied and has outstanding balance as well as a silky-textured personality. Drink it over the next 10 years.

The stunning 1980 Millésime is a compelling wine of magnificent complexity and delicacy. It reveals aromas and flavors of sweet pipe tobacco, cedar, and dried molasses, as well as plums. It is pure, fresh, smooth as silk, and possesses an extraordinarily long, voluptuous finish. This great wine can be consumed over the next 12–15 years.

MAS DES AVEYLANS

1998 Vin de Pays du Gard Syrah	B	90

Mas des Aveylans's 1998 Vin de Pays du Gard Syrah has provided me with enormous pleasure twice—once in France and once with a steak au poivre at a neighborhood restaurant (Washington, D.C.'s Bistro Français). It possesses an extroverted nose of blackberry jam and licorice, as well as a medium- to full-bodied, highly expressive mouth, crammed with sweet cassis and black raspberries. This fruit-packed wine is supple, intensely ripe, sweet, and reveals hints of leather in its long and silky finish. Drink it over the next 3 years.

MAS DE LA BARBEN

1998 Coteaux du Languedoc	B	(88–90)

The 1998 Coteaux du Languedoc is dark ruby-colored and reveals aromas reminiscent of beef jerky amid loads of sweet red fruits and cedar. This palate-staining, huge, muscular, powerful wine is packed with tar and licorice flavors. Full-bodied, expansive, and intense, it will require some cellaring to soften. This 80% Syrah and 20% Grenache blend should be at its best between now–2007.

DOMAINE DU MAS BLANC (DR. PARCÉ)

NV	Banyuls Cuvée du Dr. Andre Parcé	D	91
NV	Banyuls Hors d'Age Vieilli en Solera (tirage 1999)	D	94
2000	Banyuls Blanc	C	89
2000	Banyuls Rimage	D	90
1998	Banyuls Rimage	D	89
1997	Banyuls Rimage	D	90
2000	Banyuls Rimage La Coume	D	94
1998	Banyuls Rimage La Coume	D	94+
1996	Banyuls Rimage La Coume	D	94+
1999	Collioure Clos du Moulin	D	89+
1998	Collioure Clos du Moulin	D	89+
1997	Collioure Clos du Moulin	D	93+
1998	Collioure Cosprons Levants	C	88+
1997	Collioure Cosprons Levants	D	90
1997	Collioure Les Junguets	D	92

Made famous by the recently deceased Dr. André Parcé, the Domaine du Mas Blanc continues to produce some of the very finest wines from Banyuls and Collioure, two French towns located just a few miles from the Spanish border on the Mediterranean. Jean-Michel Parcé, the doctor's son, has been responsible for the estate's winemaking since 1976. While his father made the estate and its wines famous, it was Jean-Michel who crafted them. The winery is situated no more than 100 yards from the quaint little fishing port of Banyuls. Collioure, a picturesque fortified port town just a couple of miles up the coast, is considered by locals (and by this food lover) to be the anchovy capital of the world. Unlike the salty/fishy anchovies we find in the United States, Collioure's are typically marinated in olive oil and are sweet, a magnificent match for the region's garlic-drenched roasted sweet peppers. Wines from Collioure benefit from the warm microclimate and schist-based soils. Its wines are dominated by Mourvèdre and Syrah, yet Grenache, Counoise, and other varietals are generally included as well. The best Collioures can be drunk young and will age for up to 20 years.

Banyuls, one of the rare wines that can accompany chocolate, is a Grenache-based fortified red wine. Alcohol is added to the fermenting juice, raising the alcohol level to the point where fermentation grinds to a halt, leaving residual grape sugars in the wine. They can be made in a number of different manners (as will be seen in the following notes) and are capable of extended (25+ years) cellaring.

The medium to dark ruby-colored 1998 Collioure Cosprons Levants was crafted from 60% Syrah, 30% Mourvèdre, and 10% Counoise. Its plum aromas lead to a medium- to full-bodied personality with loads of black fruits, dark cherries, and hints of freshly laid road tar. Its admirably long finish displays exquisitely ripe and supple tannins. Anticipated maturity: now–2008+. The medium to dark ruby-colored 1998 Collioure Clos du Moulin is a blend of 80% Mourvèdre and 20% Counoise. It possesses a sweet blueberry, cherry, and assorted black fruit–scented nose. On the palate, this foursquare, medium- to full-bodied wine is packed with blackberries, asphalt, and tangy currants. It is well structured and has copious quantities of tannin that are buried in loads of fruit. Anticipated maturity: now–2009+.

While Jean-Michel Parcé prefers the 1998 vintage (saying that it will be more ageworthy), my predilection leans toward his 1997s. The ruby-colored 1997 Collioure Cosprons Levants has a perfumed, sweet, violet-scented nose. This complex, medium-bodied wine has a highly expressive flavor profile composed of wild game, flowers, saddle leather, plums, black olives, salt, and perfume. Drink it over the next 7 years. The darker-colored 1997 Collioure Clos du Moulin has a kinky, red/black fruit and rose-scented nose. Medium- to full-bodied, its embracing character coats the palate with intense layers of roasted dark fruits, sweet black cherries, stones, and a northern Rhône–like leather component. This velvety-textured beauty has loads of soft, ripe, virtually perfect tannins that appear in its exquisitely long finish. Anticipated maturity: now–2010+.

The medium to dark ruby/purple 1997 Collioure Les Junguets has gamey black currant and blackberry aromas. Blueberries, mulberries, and hints of licorice can be found in this exceedingly well balanced, silky-textured wine. Its superb flavor panoply lasts throughout its extensive finish. Anticipated maturity: now–2007+.

Domaine du Mas Blanc's Banyuls Rimage and Banyuls Rimage La Coume wines are produced from a parcel known as La Coume del Mas that is planted with 90% Grenache Noir, 5% Syrah, and 5% Mourvèdre. The dark-colored 1998 Banyuls Rimage offers intense plum aromas intermingled with touches of mocha. Medium- to full-bodied, velvety-textured, rich, and broad, this is a fresh, precise, dark fruit and black pepper–flavored wine. Anticipated maturity: now–2015.

The similarly colored 1997 Banyuls Rimage has creamy plum, sweet blackberry, warm chocolate, and raspberry aromas, all reminiscent of a young port. Medium- to full-bodied, velvety-textured, and hugely intense, this well-balanced, focused, elegant offering is packed with sweet raspberries, licorice, and assorted dark fruits. Anticipated maturity: now–2015.

In selected vintages, Parcé selects his best lots of Rimage to fashion a Banyuls Rimage La Coume. The 1998 exhibits spectacular aromas of kumquats, orange peels, and dark fruits. Broad, silky-textured, and awesomely detailed, this powerful, elegant wine is filled with roses, violets, other assorted flowers, and red/black fruits. It admirably combines refinement with muscle. Drink it over the next 15–20 years.

Almond cake, flowers, marzipan, and linzertorte can be found in the nose of the outstanding 1996 Banyuls Rimage La Coume. Raspberry and cherry jams are intermingled with freshly cracked pepper in this gorgeously elegant, pure, and focused wine. Medium- to full-bodied and oily-textured, its copious quantities of fruit last throughout its unbelievably long finish. Anticipated maturity: now–2020+.

Jean-Michel Parcé has created a new wine (named in honor of his father) in the hopes that it will "guide young wine lovers toward the extraordinary secondary aromas that can be found in slightly oxidized wines." It is made using the solera method of blending multiple vintages under controlled oxidation. The nonvintage Banyuls Cuvée du Dr. André Parcé is the result of a solera assemblage of three vintages of Banyuls Rimage. Medium to dark ruby-colored with touches of gold on the edge, it reveals fresh cedar, mocha, and cigar box aromatics. Medium-bodied, satin-textured, and beautifully vibrant, it is packed with sweet plums and blackberries as well as hints of creamed coffee. This long-finishing, detail-oriented wine has the capacity to age for 20 or more years.

The medium to dark ruby and slightly amber-colored 1985 Banyuls Vieilles Vignes has youthful tobacco box and plum aromas. Medium-bodied, silky-textured, and lively, it is a rich violet, rose, and caramel-flavored wine. This elegant, flavorful, and mature offering can be drunk over the next 10 years. The nonvintage Banyuls Hors d'Age Vieilli en Solera (the sample tasted for this report was from the "Tirage 1999") is from a solera started in 1925 that includes Banyuls from all the different parcels owned by the Domaine du Mas Blanc. Wines are added to the solera each vintage, and every two years some are bottled. This cedar- and amber-colored wine displays chocolate and baked plum aromas. Medium- to full-bodied and silky-textured, its flavor profile is composed of chocolate-covered cherries, almond cake, and raspberry coulis. This compelling wine's intricate character lasts throughout its amazingly long finish. Given the fact that it has already undergone a good deal of measured oxidation, it should be capable of aging for up to 20 years.

Throughout Collioure, growers all had the same refrain: "Yes, 1999 was difficult, but the Mourvèdre-based wines are a success." The 1999 Collioure Clos du Moulin, the estate's Collioure produced with the most Mourvèdre, is proof of this fact. Its freshly laid asphalt and blackberry aromas lead to a medium- to full-bodied personality crammed with a myriad of dark fruits and tarry notes. Well focused, beautifully ripe, and intense, this velvety-textured wine has outstanding concentration, depth, and balance. Its admirably long finish is packed with fruit and loads of ripe tannin. Drink it over the next 8 years.

Produced from Muscat d'Alexandrie, the 2000 Banyuls Blanc reveals a nose of orange blossoms and tangerines. On the palate, red fruits are intermingled with tangy citrus flavors in this opulently ripe and boisterous wine. Parcé feels it may be too ripe, but my opinion is that it delivers exactly what most whites from the Languedoc and Roussillon lack: intense flavor and fruit. Anticipated maturity: now–2004.

The dark-colored 2000 Banyuls Rimage displays a dark fruit and orange peel–scented nose. This hugely concentrated wine is jam-packed with blackberries, molasses, mocha, spices, and blueberries. It is fat yet juicy and exquisitely well balanced. Anticipated maturity: now–2015.

Sadly, Parcé lost half of his 1.25-hectare La Coume parcel to a brush fire in 2000, so only a small amount of the 2000 Banyuls Rimage La Coume was produced (10 hectoliters). As the charred vines will have to be replanted, it will be many years before this magnificent vineyard's production gets back to normal. The 2000 is a magnificent wine, with blackberry, blueberry, plum, and spice aromas. Medium to dark ruby-colored, it is medium-bodied, satin-textured, complex, and sports layers of candied black fruits, molasses, sweet cedar, pipe tobacco, and spices. This is a compelling wine with intricate nuances, sublime balance, and a prodigiously long, velvety finish. Drink it over the next 20 years.

MAS DES BRESSADES

2000 Costières de Nîmes	A	90
2000 Vin du Pays du Gard Cabernet/Syrah	B	90

1998 Vin du Pays du Gard Cabernet Syrah	B	(90–92)
2000 Vin du Pays du Gard Roussanne/Viognier	B	89
2000 Vin du Pays du Gard Syrah/Grenache	A	90

The 1998 Vin du Pays du Gard Syrah is a superb example of what could be achieved in this warm, dry year in the south of France. It possesses a saturated black/purple color and offers jammy, sweet black raspberry aromas. This is an intense, flavorful wine, packed with road tar, licorice, jammy black fruits, spices, and oak flavors. Medium- to full-bodied, silky-textured, and admirably long, this outstanding wine finishes with sweet cassis flavors. Anticipated maturity: now–2006.

These wines are perennial best buys that merit serious purchasing. In a top vintage for southern France such as 2000, one expects Mas des Bressades to hit the peaks. They have done just that with these *cuvées*. The 2000 Vin du Pays du Gard Roussanne/Viognier sees some barrel, yet is all fruit declassified from their holdings in Costières de Nîmes. This sumptuous, quasi-Condrieu look-alike offers notes of rose petals, orange marmalade, apricot liqueur, and assorted white flowers. It reveals superb ripeness, good underlying acidity, and a fleshy, fruity feel. Wood notes are detectable in neither the aromas nor the flavors. Drink it over the next year to take advantage of its exuberance, purity, and up-front fruit.

The 2000 Costières de Nîmes is dominated by Grenache (75%). Its dark ruby color is followed by crisp cherry and berry fruit and a complete, sensual style. There is good freshness to this supple, fleshy 2000. While these wines offer outstanding quality, do not expect them to make old bones; they are best consumed during their first 2–3 years of life.

The 2000 Vin du Pays du Gard Syrah/Grenache (a tank-fermented and -aged 50-50 blend) is, as the French would say, a *vin de plaisir* (a wine of pleasure). Neither pretentious nor complex, it is broad, expansive, fleshy, and loaded with jammy red and black fruit scents as well as flavors. A joy to drink, it requires drinking over the next 12–18 months.

Readers looking for a Provençal offering that tastes like a Médoc should check out Mas des Bressades's 2000 Vin du Pays du Gard Cabernet/Syrah (65% Cabernet, 35% Syrah). Although 45% of this *cuvée* sees new oak, it offers a Pauillac-like nose of cedarwood, tobacco, black currants, and vanilla. The wine is medium- to full-bodied and ripe (the Cabernet achieved 14.3% alcohol naturally), with moderate tannin in the finish. It is a firmer-structured effort than the big fruit bombs represented by the other *cuvées*. While it should age and mature for a decade, I would recommend consumption over the next 3–4 years.

MAS CARLOT

2000 Cuvée Tradition (Marsanne)	A	88
2000 Vin du Pays d'Oc	A	90
2000 Vin de Table (100% Riesling)	A	89

Another stunning discovery from the Costières de Nîmes by importer Robert Kacher, these wines are virtually too good to be true. The 2000 Cuvée Tradition is a tank-fermented and -aged 100% Marsanne revealing abundant quantities of minerals, orange blossom, and citrus presented in a medium-bodied, fresh, lively style. This delicious effort can easily compete with top white Châteauneuf-du-Pape. Drink it over the next 1–2 years.

Made from a 42-year-old vineyard, the 2000 Vin de Table (100% Riesling) may be the only Riesling produced in Provence. Green apples, wet stones, pit fruit notes, and a hint of petroleum can be found in this dry wine. It finishes authoritatively. Drink it over the next 1–2 years. The finest wine among these exceptional bargains is the 2000 Vin du Pays d'Oc (1,800 cases for the U.S.), a blend of 55% Grenache and 45% Syrah that has never seen one day in wood. Made from yields of 46 hectoliters per hectare, this $8 wine tastes like one costing 3–4 times as much. With admirable texture, great purity, and abundant quantities of fat, peppery, spicy, black cherry, plum, and berry fruit, this delicious wine will offer character and complexity over the next 2–3 years.

MAS CHAMPART

1998 St.-Chinian	**C**	**88**

The dark ruby-colored, tar-scented 1998 St.-Chinian proposes chewy blackberry and freshly laid asphalt flavors. Medium- to full-bodied, firm, and tannic, it is an excellent wine, particularly for those searching out dark, brooding, foursquare offerings to accompany grilled and full-flavored foods. Drink it over the next 7–8 years.

MAS CRISTINE

1996 Rivesaltes	**B**	**88**
1997 Rivesaltes	**B**	**89**

This estate is owned by the Daure family, also the proprietors of the Château de Jau and the Domaine du Clos des Paulilles. A small restaurant is located at the Château de Jau for visitors to the estate's cellars and Bernard Daure's world-renowned modern art collection. This restaurant is also known throughout the region for its signature dessert, a scoop of ice cream laden with the Mas Cristine's Rivesaltes. The amber/gold 1996 Rivesaltes was produced entirely from Grenache Blanc aged for two and a half years in wooden casks without any topping off. Thanks to the Mas Cristine's refrigerated cellars (still a rarity in this region), this wine is fresh and vivacious, not oxidized or heavy. Orange blossoms and assorted white flowers are encountered in its lively aromatics. On the palate, this plump, deep, and rich effort boasts 120 grams of residual sugar. Its medium- to full-bodied, thickly textured (verging on syrup) character is packed with white/yellow fruits and candied lemons. It could be served after a meal in place of dessert. Drink it over the next 12+ years.

The golden bronze–colored 1997 Rivesaltes displays jammy apricot, candied orange, flower, and jellied mandarin orange aromas as well as flavors. It is sexy, luscious, and oily-textured, almost a syrup of Grenache Blanc. Drink it over the next 12 years.

MAS DE LA DAME

1998 Les Beaux Coin Caché	**B**	**90**
1998 Les Beaux Cuvée Gourmande	**A**	**88**
1998 Les Beaux Cuvée de la Stèle	**B**	**90**
1998 Les Beaux Réserve du Mas	**B**	**88**

One of the finest and most consistent estates in this area of France, these four *cuvées* are all very different. Readers looking for near-term gratification would be advised to search out the 1998 Cuvée Gourmande or 1998 Réserve du Mas. Made from primarily Grenache, with some Carignan and other local varietals in the blend, the 1998 Cuvée Gourmande is aged in large *cuves* without any exposure to wood. This dark ruby/purple-colored effort possesses a beautiful cherry, spice, pepper, and dried Provençal herb–scented nose. Good black fruits in the mouth, medium body, and pepper add to the spice and richness of this fleshy, straightforward southern French red. It is ideal for drinking over the next several years. The 1998 Réserve du Mas includes 50% Grenache, 30% Syrah, and 20% Cabernet Sauvignon. A small number of small barrels are added to give the wine more backbone and tannin. Not surprisingly, it is a denser example than the Cuvée Gourmande, but it is also less immediately appealing and beguiling. There is good up-front fruit, more tannin, and Syrah's blackberry note makes an appearance. Nevertheless, as in its sibling, the Cuvée Gourmande, there is enough kirsch and cherry fruit to satisfy most hedonists. Drink it over the next 3–4 years.

The tannic, woody 1998 Cuvée de la Stèle is a blend of primarily Cabernet Sauvignon with about 30% Syrah. This wine sees 100% small barrels, of which 20% are new. Although closed and backward when I tasted it, it is unquestionably loaded with potential. The dense ruby/purple color is followed by weedy, black currant fruit intertwined with cassis, tobacco, and spice. Give it 1–2 years of cellaring and drink it over the next decade. The 1998 Coin Caché is a micro *cuvée* of 90% Grenache and 10% Syrah. The wine's wonderful sweetness, rich, jammy fruit, and seamless texture with black raspberry and kirschlike flavors are reminiscent of a good vintage of the famed Châteauneuf-du-Pape, Rayas. An ethereal richness without heaviness gives this wine extra class and complexity. It should drink well for 7–10 years. Jean-Luc Colombo is the consulting oenologist for this estate.

MAS DE DAUMAS GASSAC

2000 Vin de Pays de l'Hérault	D	89

While I was disappointed by this estate's 1999 and 2000 reds, the white 2000 Vin de Pays de l'Hérault is a huge success. It displays huge richness in its pear and orange blossom–laden aromatics as well as in its broad, flavorful character. Spices, tangerines, apricots, pears, apples, and white peaches can be discerned in this medium-bodied offering's personality as well as throughout its lush finish. Drink it over the next 2–3 years.

MAS DE FOURNEL

1999 Coteaux du Languedoc-Pic-St.-Loup Cuvée Classique	B	88

This medium to dark ruby-colored 1999 exhibits fresh herb and black fruit aromas. Medium-bodied, rustic, yet juicy, this is a big, blackberry, cassis, spice, and *garrigue* (Provençal herb)-flavored wine. It possesses excellent depth of fruit as well as a fresh, flavorful character. Enjoy it over the next 6 years.

MAS GABINELE

1998 Faugères	C	88

From tiny yields of 18 hectoliters per hectare, this blend of equal parts Grenache, Syrah, and Mourvèdre reveals impeccable balance, an elegant, delicate style for the region, and delicious raspberry and currant flavors infused with earth and smoke. Drink it over the next 4–5 years.

MAS DE GOURGONNIER

1997 Les Baux de Provence	B	89

This estate consistently produces extraordinary values. Produced from organically grown fruit, the medium to dark ruby-colored 1997 Les Baux de Provence offers sweet black cherry, cookie dough, and spice aromas in its enthralling nose. On the palate, it is medium-bodied, silky-textured, and reveals dark cherries, black fruits, and *garrigue* (Provençal herbs) in its supple yet well-structured character. Its long, drawn-out finish displays loads of well-ripened tannins. Anticipated maturity: now–2005.

MAS DE GUIOT

2000 Vin de Pays du Gard	B	89
1998 Vin de Pays du Gard 60% Cabernet–40% Syrah	B	89

Produced from a blend of new-oak-barrel-aged Cabernet and one-year oak barrel–raised Syrah, Mas de Guiot's 1998 Vin de Pays du Gard 60% Cabernet–40% Syrah exhibits jammy black raspberry and spice aromas. Exceptionally ripe, it is packed with black fruits, leather, and hints of road tar in its medium- to full-bodied, structured core. This wine will be at its best if permitted to age for a year or so for its oak flavors to become better integrated, and for its fruit to expand on the palate. Anticipated maturity: now–2005. The 2000 Vin de Pays du Gard, a tank-fermented and -aged blend of 40% Grenache and 60% Syrah, boasts a dense purple color as well as a sumptuous bouquet reminiscent of Châteauneuf-du-Pape. Notes of kirsch, blackberries, smoke, earth, and leather are followed by a superpure, full-bodied, rich, intense wine with no hard edges. It continues to amaze me that wines such as this can be found for under $12 a bottle. Anticipated maturity: now–2006.

CHÂTEAU MAS NEUF

1999 Costières de Nîmes Cuvée Prestige	B	89
1998 Costières de Nîmes Cuvée Prestige	B	88

I have been praising the wines emerging from Costières de Nîmes for a number of years. Located south of Châteauneuf-du-Pape, Lirac, and Tavel, it is an appellation with tremendous potential. The 1998 Cuvée Prestige, a blend of 85% Syrah, 5% Grenache, and 10% Mourvèdre, aged in old wood and tank, is a dark ruby/purple-colored, smoky, spicy effort displaying dense blackberry and currant fruit, an excellent texture, vibrant acidity, and good length. It should drink well for 3–4 years.

The 1999 Cuvée Prestige is a dense, chewy, deep ruby/purple-colored wine revealing abundant quantities of blackberry and cassis fruit intermixed with licorice. Beefy and big, with a supple texture and admirable finish, it should drink well for 7–8 years.

DOMAINE MASSAMIER

2000 Vin de Pays des Côtes de Peyriac Carignan La Mignarde	C	88

The black-colored 2000 Vin de Pays des Côtes de Peyriac Carignan La Mignarde was produced from 55-year-old Carignan vines. This blackberry-scented, medium-bodied wine is filled with licorice, cassis, chocolate, and spices. It is silky-textured, concentrated, and intense. Anticipated maturity: now–2007.

CHÂTEAU DE MONTPEZAT

1999 Coteaux du Languedoc La Pharaonne	C	92
2000 Vin de Pays d'Oc Cuvée Prestige	C	91+
1999 Vin de Pays d'Oc Cuvée Prestige	B	91

A spectacular offering, this wine has been a bell-ringer in past vintages, and the 1999 is no exception. The Le Pin of the Languedoc, it is a blend of 60% Cabernet Sauvignon and 40% Syrah aged in 50% new-oak barrels. Extremely ripe, with notes of blackberries, crème de cassis, and new oak, it is opulent, rich, viscous, and full-bodied, with gorgeous fruit as well as a long finish. An amazingly serious wine, it will not age like a topflight Bordeaux, but for drinking over the next 4–6 years, it is a marvelous effort.

Aged entirely in French oak, the 2000 Prestige Vin de Pays d'Oc has an enthralling candied raspberry–laden nose. On the palate, this outstanding wine is velvety-textured, medium- to full-bodied, and crammed with black currants, dark cherries, and black raspberries. It is juicy, marvelously balanced, and possesses a long, lush, fruit-filled finish. Drink it over the next 6–7 years.

Regrettably, Château de Montpezat's U.S. importer doesn't purchase the estate's top wine, its luxurious 1999 Coteaux du Languedoc La Pharaonne. Produced almost entirely from Mourvèdre crop-thinned to 3–4 clusters per vine, this is a dark-colored beauty with boisterous black fruit aromas. It is medium- to full-bodied, broad, and displays huge power while maintaining exquisite elegance. Silky blackberries, cassis, leather, and hints of plums can be found in this fresh, dense wine. Its extensive finish reveals loads of admirably ripened tannin. Drinkable now, it will most certainly keep for another decade.

DOMAINE MORTIÈS

1998 Coteaux du Languedoc-Pic-St.-Loup Classique	B	(89–91)
1998 Vin du Pays d'Oc Que Sera Sera	C	(91–92+)

Two of the three 1998s I tasted from Domaine Mortiès were fabulous. A third, the Grande Cuvée, appeared to be overoaked. The 1998 Coteaux du Languedoc-Pic-St.-Loup Classique is dark ruby-colored and offers scrumptious jammy blueberry aromas. This highly concentrated and extracted mouthful of a wine is powerful and gorgeously layered with black fruits.

Medium- to full-bodied, intense, and backward, it will require some patience. Anticipated maturity: now–2007.

The 1998 Vin du Pays d'Oc Que Sera Sera (100% Syrah) is black/purple-colored. Superb leather and tar aromas are found in this magnificent wine's nose. Multiple layers of red cherries, cassis, black raspberries, and chocolate, intermingled with hints of vanilla, coat the palate. This is a powerful, full-bodied, backward, intense, beautifully made wine that demonstrates that Syrah can be compelling in the Languedoc. Anticipated maturity: 2003–2010.

MOURGUES DU GRÈS

1999	Costières de Nîmes Capitelles des Mourgues	B	90
2000	Costières de Nîmes Les Galets	B	89

One of the finest estates in Costières de Nîmes, Mourgues du Grès has fashioned a sensational rosé as well as a delicious, full-bodied red, and both are available for a song. The 2000 Les Galets (a dry rosé made from 60% Syrah and 40% Grenache) exhibits a gorgeous nose of cassis and strawberry liqueur, abundant fruit, medium body, and a loaded palate. It is a serious rosé to consume before 2003.

The 1999 Capitelles des Mourgues is a 100% Syrah selection from the estate's oldest vines (40 years). It is a dense, opaque purple-colored wine with a superb bouquet of blackberry and cherry fruit and spice. Bottled unfiltered, there are abundant fat and chewiness to this purely made 1999. Drink it over the next 5–6 years.

CHÂTEAU DE NAGES

1998	Costières de Nîmes Cuvée Joseph Torres (red)	B	89
1998	Costières de Nîmes Cuvée Joseph Torres (white)	B	88

If the 100% Syrah 1998 Cuvée Joseph Torres (red) had a bit more complexity, it would have earned an outstanding rating. Nevertheless, it is full-bodied, with a dense ruby/purple color as well as a gorgeous nose of blackberries, licorice, spice box, and pepper. Elements of *surmaturité* add to the seductiveness of this lush, succulently styled Syrah. Drink it over the next 5–6 years.

The nearly outstanding 1998 Cuvée Joseph Torres (white) is fashioned from 95% Roussanne and 5% Viognier cropped at 28 hectoliters per hectare. Production was 1,000 cases. It reveals honeyed notes along with acacia flowers, rose petals, and ripe tropical fruits. Full-bodied, with an unctuous texture and a dry, lush finish, it should be consumed over the next 1–2 years.

CHÂTEAU DE LA NÉGLY

1998	Coteaux du Languedoc-La Clape l'Ancely	E	95
2000	Coteaux du Languedoc-La Clape La Côte	A	88
1999	Coteaux du Languedoc-La Clape La Falaise	C	91
1998	Coteaux du Languedoc-La Clape La Falaise	B	(90–92)
1999	Coteaux du Languedoc-La Clape La Porte du Ciel	E	96
1998	Coteaux du Languedoc-La Clape La Porte du Ciel	E	(92–94)

Proprietor Jean Paux-Rosset and his brilliant wine-maker, Claude Gros (a consulting oenologist who deserves worldwide recognition), craft spectacular wines by employing low yields and noninterventionist techniques. Grapes are harvested when they are physiologically ripe, regardless of pH (most are well over 4) or acidity levels. Every penny earned from wine sales is reinvested in the winery, as the gravity-fed tanks being installed during my visit and the refrigerated barrel room (a rarity in the south of France, even though summer temperatures can be extremely warm) made clear. This is a first-class operation, with every member of the team, from the vineyard manager to the oenologist, dedicated to producing France's finest wines.

The Château de la Négly has crafted three spectacular red wines in the 1998 vintage. The La Falaise is medium to dark ruby-colored and offers supersweet cherry, kirsch, and spice aromas. Crafted predominantly from Syrah, with some Grenache and Mourvèdre in the blend, and aged entirely in new-oak barrels, this highly concentrated wine offers an extraordinarily syrupy texture. Inky black fruits and cassis can be found throughout its powerful personality and extensive finish. Anticipated maturity: now–2008.

The spectacular 1998 La Porte du Ciel was fashioned entirely from Syrah harvested at 14 hectoliters per hectare. Each bunch was destemmed by hand and crushed by foot. The wine's alcoholic fermentation lasted 40 days, after which it was placed in new Seguin-Moreau barrels. In short, this wine was produced in an uncompromising manner. Its awesomely elegant and complex nose is composed of cassis and candied red raspberries. On the palate, it is massive, powerful, hugely intense, yet refined. Full-bodied, crammed with *sur-maturité*-laced red and black fruit flavors, this benchmark-setting Languedoc combines the embracing warmth often associated with the wines of this region with the nobility and class generally attributed to more highly touted viticultural areas. Readers who adore Syrah or cherish profound wine should not miss this one. Anticipated maturity: now–2012.

Produced from yields that would make even Burgundy's Lalou Bize-Leroy jealous (10 hectoliters per hectare), the 1998 l'Ancely is a prodigious wine. Regrettably, only 100 cases of this nectar were produced and none of it was purchased by its U.S. importer. Aged in *demi-muids*, it was never racked, filtered, or fined. Cassis dominates this wine's aromas and flavors. Medium- to full-bodied, it is awesomely rich, hugely concentrated, and lush. Layers of candied red and black fruits conquer the taster's palate. It has untold power, yet retains graceful refinement and a sublimely balanced character. In addition, it possesses an exquisitely long, fruit-filled, opulent finish. Drink it over the next 12 years.

The medium to dark ruby-colored 1999 La Falaise is a blend of 60% Syrah and 40% Mourvèdre. It explodes from the glass with blackberry jam and cassis. This intensely rich, medium- to full-bodied wine coats the palate with layer after layer of raspberries, blackberries, blueberries, and plums. It is satin-textured, powerful, intense, and deep. Drink it over the next 10 years.

The unbelievable 1999 La Porte du Ciel stands as testimony to what can be achieved in this often-disregarded region of France. Produced from yields of 11 hectoliters per hectare, with grapes harvested at a pH of 4.3, it explodes from the glass with candied cherry aromas. This exceedingly rich wine embraces the palate with ginger, molasses, spice, jellied blackberry, cassis, and wild blueberry flavors. It is amazingly rich, yet somehow retains freshness and elegance. Its long, sumptuous finish reveals copious quantities of superbly ripened tannin. Drink it over the next 15 years.

Produced from a blend of 70% Carignan and the balance Grenache, the 2000 La Côte has sexy sweat and sweet blackberry aromas. Medium-bodied and rich, it coats the palate with copious quantities of dark fruits and cassis, as well as hints of licorice. Well made and fruit-forward, this is a delicious, velvety-textured wine for drinking over the next 4 years.

NOVELLUM

1998 Côtes du Roussillon	B	(88–90)
1999 Vin de Pays d'Oc Chardonnay	A	88

The 1999 Vin de Pays d'Oc Chardonnay (7,000 cases exported to the U.S.) is a non-malolactic, rich, fruity effort that was aged on the lees of Viognier to give it more honeysuckle aromas. Only a small amount of oak was utilized, and the wine is all the better for it. Sweet, ripe notes of pineapple, peach, and honeysuckle are found in the bouquet as well as the flavors of this medium-bodied, juicy, pure, honeyed Chardonnay. There is a surprising amount of character and flavor for a wine of this price. It will not make old bones, so buy it by the case and drink it with pleasure before 2003.

The medium to dark ruby-colored 1998 Côtes du Roussillon offers mocha-imbued, sweet red raspberry aromas. This thick, dense, jammy, backward wine offers powerful layers of red raspberry and cherry fruit. Intense, powerful, and admirably long, it is best drunk over the next 5 years.

CHÂTEAU D'OR ET DE GUEULES
1998 Costières de Nîmes	A	88?

This 1998 Costières de Nîmes, a blend of Mourvèdre, Syrah, and Carignan, is made in an earthy, mushroomy style, and is not as fruit-driven as some of importer Robert Kacher's other selections from this up-and-coming appellation. A deep ruby color is followed by a spicy, peppery, earthy nose, plenty of tannin, and a style not unlike that of a top-class Bandol. While it may never resolve all its tannin and rusticity, there is plenty going on in this wine. Drink it over the next 4–5 years.

CHÂTEAU LES PALAIS
1998 Corbières Cuvée Randolin Vieilles Vignes	B	(90–91)
1998 Corbières Cuvée Tradition	A	(88–89)

The medium to dark ruby-colored 1998 Corbières Cuvée Tradition offers a lovely nose of cherries, flowers, and fresh perfume. Its penetrating red, blue, and black fruit flavors are intermingled with cedar for added complexity. This attractive, medium- to full-bodied, exquisitely balanced wine also offers a long, supple finish. Drink it over the next 4–5 years.

The saturated, black-colored 1998 Corbières Cuvée Randolin Vieilles Vignes exhibits blackberry and roasted herb aromas. This is a powerful, highly extracted, dense, and concentrated wine, crammed with chocolate and black raspberry fruit. Silky-textured, medium- to full-bodied, and firm, this admirably long wine should be at its peak of maturity between now–2007.

DOMAINE PEYRE ROSE
1998 Coteaux du Languedoc Cistes	D	(88–89)
1996 Coteaux du Languedoc Cistes	D	88
1998 Coteaux du Languedoc Léone	D	(89–90)
1996 Coteaux du Languedoc Léone	D	88

With each year that has gone by, Domaine Peyre Rose has increased its extraction (presently the grapes macerate for 75 days) as well as the length of its *élevage*. When I visited the estate, the 1998s had still not been bottled three years after the harvest. These are wines of power and intensity, with gripping tannins and flavors that can best be described as black. Readers tempted to visit the estate should know that an all-terrain vehicle is a must, as the long, dirt-and-rock access road is filled with ruts and canyons. Located on the top of a hill in an area that looks like a lunar landscape, the Domaine Peyre Rose produces two wines, Cistes (85% Syrah and 15% Grenache) and Léone (90–95% Syrah, with the balance Mourvèdre). The saturated, medium to dark ruby-colored 1996 Cistes has cedary black fruit aromas. This firm and rustic wine is medium-bodied, loaded with tobacco-laced tar and dark fruit flavors, and reveals excellent depth. It is harmonious, well made, and intense. Anticipated maturity: 2003–2010.

The darker-colored 1996 Léone is firm, foursquare, and tannic. Highly extracted black fruit flavors are intermingled with road tar in this slightly jagged yet impressive wine's character. Anticipated maturity: 2004–2012.

The similarly colored 1998 Cistes has intense blackberry and cassis aromas. Licorice and dark fruits are intermingled in this super-concentrated, massively extracted, rustic wine. It is mouthcoating, palate-staining, and intensely powerful. Anticipated maturity: 2006–2012.

The 1998 Léone is the proverbial "black hole." Dried licorice, asphalt, mint, and roasted herbs can be found in its full-bodied personality. This hyperextracted wine will require 5–6 years of cellaring but should blossom into a civilized offering. Drink it between 2007–2015.

DOMAINE PICCININI

1998 Minervois Clos Langely	B	89
1999 Minervois Cuvée Line et Loetitia	B	88
1998 Minervois Cuvée Line et Loetitia	B	90?

Piccinini has turned out three very fine efforts, although the highest-rated wine, the 1998 Cuvée Line et Loetitia, may turn out to be a bit too oaky (I am hoping the oak becomes better integrated, hence the optimistic score). The 1998 Clos Langely exhibits jammy kirsch, blackberries, pepper, and dried Provençal herbs. Rich and medium- to full-bodied, with a Châteauneuf-du-Pape-like character to its fruit flavors, this is a hedonistic, lush wine to drink over the next 2–3 years—in its youthful exuberance.

As mentioned, the 1998 Cuvée Line et Loetitia reveals abundant toasty new oak. It also possesses good length, ripe fruit, and fine density and overall balance. If the oak becomes better integrated, this wine will be outstanding and potentially the longest-lived (5–6 years) of this trio. Give it 3–4 months of bottle age and enjoy it over the following 5 years.

The tobacco- and blackberry-scented 1999 Cuvée Line et Loetitia is medium-bodied, silky-textured, and redolent of cherries and black raspberries. Well balanced, it is bright, loaded with fruit, and has an enormously appealing mouth-feel. Soft and lush, this is a wine for drinking over the next 4–6 years.

DOMAINE DE POUJOL

1999 Vin de Pays de l'Hérault (white)	C	88

The medium-bodied 1999 Vin de Pays de l'Hérault (white) was produced from a blend of 46% Rolle (also known as Vermentino), 43% Carignan Blanc, and the balance Roussanne. Pears and apricots are found in its expressive aromatics. Medium-bodied and rich, this broad, mouthcoating wine is packed with an assortment of lush white fruits, as well as mangoes and peaches. It is an impressive, flavorful, and supple wine, ideal for drinking before 2004.

CHÂTEAU PRAT DE CEST

2000 Corbières	A	88

This medium to dark ruby-colored, expansive, light- to medium-bodied 2000 Corbières offers fresh blackberry and cherry aromas as well as licorice, blackberry, and tarlike flavors. Drink this pretty, seamless 2000 over the next four years.

PRIEURÉ DE ST.-JEAN-DE-BÉBIAN

1999 Coteaux du Languedoc (red)	D	88
1998 Coteaux du Languedoc (red)	D	91+?
2000 Coteaux du Languedoc (white)	D	88
1998 Coteaux du Languedoc (white)	D	88

Philippe Le Brun and Chantal Lacouty, the former head honchos of *La Revue du Vin de France*, France's leading wine publication, run this famed estate. Mme Lacouty, who is responsible for the winemaking, sorts the grapes twice at harvest, once in the vineyard and then later on sorting tables. She has modified the winery to allow for the use of gravity to move her juice and wine, and neither fines nor filters her reds (the whites are filtered for clarity). A bright, engaging woman, Mme Lacouty is constantly tweaking her winemaking techniques to raise this estate's wines to the next level.

The 1998 Coteaux du Languedoc (white) displays rich, toasty, leesy, and smoky aromas. Medium- to full-bodied, velvety-textured, and broad, this lovely pear- and spicy oak–flavored wine should be drunk over the next 3 years.

The 2000 Coteaux du Languedoc (white) offers appealing aromas of spices, pears, and minerals. It is a medium- to full-bodied wine with a rich, broad personality and oodles of fruit. Its finish exhibits some warmth (alcohol) and is somewhat constricting, yet this is a delicious wine for drinking over the next 3–5 years.

The 1999 Coteaux du Languedoc (red), a blend of Syrah, Grenache, and 5% Mourvèdre (in other vintages this wine contains more of this last varietal, but in 1999 the estate's Mourvèdre vines were devastated by hail just prior to harvest), is medium to dark ruby-colored. Blackberries, spices, and currants can be found in its aromas as well as in its flavor profile. It is medium-bodied, thick, has admirable amplitude and a fat, roasted fruit–filled core. Alcohol and rustic tannins appear in the finish, preventing a more exalted review. Anticipated maturity: 2004–2010.

The 1998 Coteaux du Languedoc (red) is impressive due to its powerful, massively dense, black fruit and chocolate-filled personality, yet, having tasted the wine three times, I remain concerned about its hard tannin. If it is capable of shedding some of its rusticity with cellaring, it will be glorious, if not, it will dry out. Anticipated maturity: 2006–2015+?

DOMAINE PUECH CHAUD

1999 Coteaux du Languedoc	D	91

What happens when you take one of Côte Rotie's stars and bring him to the Languedoc? You get a stunning 100% Syrah 1999 Coteaux du Languedoc that is styled like a Côte Rotie, yet with the distinctive richness and depth of this southerly region. René Rostaing, famous for his northern Rhône wines, owns this estate and has produced an extraordinary wine in his debut vintage. Sweet black raspberry aromas lead to a broad, spicy, sweet, red/black raspberry–packed personality. This chewy-textured offering is powerful, huge, concentrated, yet maintains Rostaing's trademark elegance and detail. It is complex, sultry, crammed with fruit, and possesses a splendid, pure, and long finish. Anticipated maturity: now–2012.

CHÂTEAU PUECH-HAUT

1999 Coteaux du Languedoc-Pic-St.-Loup	C	89+
2000 Coteaux du Languedoc-St.-Drézéry Le Blanc Epicurien/ Tête de Cuvée	D	(88)
1999 Coteaux du Languedoc-St.-Drézéry Le Rouge Epicurien/ Tête de Cuvée	C	88+
1997 Coteaux du Languedoc-St.-Drézéry Le Rouge Epicurien/ Tête de Cuvée	C	(87–89)

Note: In the United States, Château Puech-Haut sells its luxury bottlings under the Le Rouge Epicurien and Le Blanc Epicurien labels. In other markets, the Tête de Cuvée moniker is employed.

This estate, owned by Gérard Bru, a highly successful businessman, has 80 hectares of vines planted (out of a total potential of 105 hectares). There are some older vines (for example, 60-year-old Carignan and 25-year-old Syrah and Mourvèdre), but 80% of the domaine is comprised of 20-year-old or younger vines. With the assistance of super oenologist Michel Rolland, Bru's goal is to craft the region's finest wines. The medium to dark ruby-colored 1997 Le Rouge Epicurien/Tête de Cuvée offers red currant, spice, raspberry, and cedar aromas. This medium- to full-bodied wine reveals excellent depth, power, and layers of black fruit flavors. Anticipated maturity: now–2007.

The 2000 Le Blanc Epicurien/Tête de Cuvée, a blend of 60% Roussanne, 30% Marsanne,

5% seven-year-old Viognier, and 5% Grenache Blanc, offers scents reminiscent of smoke and minerals. It is medium-bodied, with rich layers of white peaches, pears, apricots, and apples. A lush white, a rarity in the Languedoc, it has a velvety texture, loads of fruit, and a long, supple finish. Anticipated maturity: now–2005.

The 1999 Le Rouge Epicurien/Tête de Cuvée exhibits aromas of black fruit and *garrigue* (Provençal herbs). It displays a beguiling silky-textured core, particularly impressive considering the firm nature of the vintage, and loads of dark fruit flavors. Some warmth (alcohol) is apparent in the finish. Anticipated maturity: 2003–2007.

The 1999 Coteaux du Languedoc-Pic-St.-Loup has a nose reminiscent of a spicy compote of black fruits. On the palate it is medium- to full-bodied, foursquare, and stuffed with blackberries, cassis, and black raspberries. Loads of tannin appear in the finish, yet it is bathed in fruit. Anticipated maturity: 2004–2008.

DOMAINE RICHEAUME

1998 Côtes de Provence Cuvée Tradition	B	(87–89)
1998 Cuvée Columelle	D	(90–92+)
1998 Vin de Pays d'Oc Cabernet Sauvignon	C	(89–91)

While not part of the Languedoc-Roussillon (Provence is much further east), Domaine Richeaume's wines merit mentioning because they hit the bull's-eye in the 1998 vintage. The Côtes de Provence Cuvée Tradition, a blend of 60% Grenache and 40% Syrah, is medium to dark ruby-colored and reveals aromas reminiscent of a grilled steak covered with freshly ground pepper, immersed in red fruits. On the palate, this delicious, refined, beautifully crafted, medium-bodied wine is crammed with candied red cherries. This silky-textured offering will be at its best if drunk over the course of the next 4–5 years.

The 1998 Cabernet Sauvignon (it has 10% Syrah in the blend) is medium to dark ruby-colored and offers roasted herb, chocolate, and blackberry aromas. This medium- to full-bodied, backward, exquisitely balanced, elegant wine is crammed with flavors reminiscent of licorice, black cherries, and jammy blackberries. It may very well carry the day if served blind against New World Cabs that cost twice as much. Anticipated maturity: now–2006+.

The superb 1998 Cuvée Columelle (fashioned almost entirely from Syrah, with traces of Merlot) is medium to dark ruby-colored and exhibits a gorgeous nose of red cherries, raspberries, and vanilla. This powerful, full-throttle, yet highly detailed and refined wine is crammed with red fruits, asphalt, licorice, roasted herbs, mocha, and new oak spices. It is highly expressive, well structured, and has all the necessary components to age well. Anticipated maturity: now–2009.

DOMAINE RIMBERT

1999 St.-Chinian Le Mas au Schiste	C	89
1999 Vin de Pays d'Oc Le Chant de Marjolaine	B	89

Domaine Rimbert's dark ruby/colored 1999 Le Chant de Marjolaine was produced entirely from old-vine Carignan. Licorice and jammy blackberry aromas are accompanied by a gorgeously intense, medium- to full-bodied wine offering copious quantities of plummy blackberries, cherries, cassis, leather, cedar, and tobacco. This superb value exhibits lovely breadth, a concentrated character, and a firm, slightly rustic finish. Drink it over the next 6–7 years.

The medium to dark ruby-colored 1999 St.-Chinian Le Mas au Schiste has a baked red cherry and spice-laden nose. Its Rayas-like flavor profile is filled with kirsch, cracked pepper, and sweet blackberries. This medium-bodied wine is highly expressive and possesses a slightly rustic, coarse finish that prevented a more exalted review. Drink it over the next 6 years.

DOMAINE DU ROC

2000 Minervois Expression	A	88
2000 Minervois Tradition	B	89

Produced from a blend of 65% Grenache, 30% Carignan, and 5% Syrah, the medium to dark ruby-colored 2000 Expression offers delightful cherry and blackberry aromas. This soft, pure, medium-bodied, satin-textured Minervois is crammed with blackberries, cherries, and blueberries. It is a marvelously expressive offering that delivers loads of fruit in a well-balanced, consumer-friendly style. Consume it over the next 4–5 years. The 2000 Tradition is made entirely from Syrah harvested at 35 hectoliters per hectare. Scrumptious blackberry, violet, and cookie dough aromas are accompanied by an intense, boisterous wine loaded with raspberries, cherries, blueberries, and blackberries. More structured than the Expression *cuvée*, with ripe, supple tannin and an admirably long, fruit-filled finish, it will drink well for 7–8 years. Vinified and aged entirely in tank, both wines express the pure essence of their varietal. Furthermore, neither of these superb values was filtered.

CHÂTEAU LA ROQUE

2000 Coteaux du Languedoc	B	88
2000 Coteaux du Languedoc Cuvée Clos des Bénédictins	B	88
1999 Coteaux du Languedoc Mourvèdre Vieilles Vignes	B	88
1999 Coteaux du Languedoc-Pic-St.-Loup	B	89
1999 Coteaux du Languedoc-Pic-St.-Loup Cupa Numismae	C	91
1998 Coteaux du Languedoc-Pic-St.-Loup Cupa Numismae	B	90
1998 Coteaux du Languedoc-Pic-St.-Loup Vieilles Vignes de Mourvèdre	B	89+

The 1998 Coteaux du Languedoc-Pic-St.-Loup Vieilles Vignes de Mourvèdre is a blend of 95% Mourvèdre (55-year-old vines) and 5% Grenache. Its nose reveals deeply ripe, waxy black fruits, and its personality combines elegance with power. Intense blackberry, licorice, and tar flavors are found in this medium- to full-bodied, muscular, yet refined offering. Its long and supple finish displays loads of exquisitely ripened tannins. Anticipated maturity: now–2010.

Château La Roque's top red is the 1998 Coteaux du Languedoc-Pic-St.-Loup Cupa Numismae. It offers a dark ruby/purple color, as well as a blackberry- and oak-infused nose. In the mouth, waves of cassis, dark berries, black raspberries, and cherries are found in this enticing, fruit-forward, yet well-structured wine. Medium- to full-bodied and muscular, it will require a year or two of cellaring. Anticipated maturity: 2003–2012.

The apple and white peach–scented 2000 Coteaux du Languedoc was produced from Viognier, Rolle, Marsanne, and Grenache Blanc. Medium-bodied, lively, and rich, this smile-inducing white possesses excellent balance to its silky-textured, candied apple, smoke, mineral, and spice flavors. Enjoy this pure, refreshing, well-made 2000 over the next year.

The 2000 Cuvée Clos des Bénédictins is a more concentrated, powerful, and longer-finishing effort. Its lively, white fruit–scented perfume leads to a medium-bodied character revealing hints of the oak used in the wine's vinification. While it lacks the regular *cuvée*'s joie de vivre and zest, it makes up for it in density and lushness. Drink this first-rate southern French white over the next 2–3 years.

The dark ruby-colored 1999 Mourvèdre Vieilles Vignes displays exuberant red cherry and road tar–like aromas. Rustic, powerful, and firm, it is for those who love muscular, tarry offerings. Freshly laid asphalt, blackberry, and Provençal herb (*garrigue*) flavors can be found in this dense, concentrated, intense red. Anticipated maturity: 2003–2009.

The more civilized 1999 Coteaux du Languedoc-Pic-St.-Loup reveals aromas of plums, blackberries, and mocha. Medium- to full-bodied, beautifully layered, and massive, with chewy mocha, cherry, plum, and blackberry flavors, it is more harmonious than the Mourvèdre *cuvée,* yet it is not for those seeking delicacy. This full-flavored powerhouse will be at its best between 2004–2009.

The magnificent dark ruby-colored 1999 Coteaux du Languedoc-Pic-St.-Loup Cupa Numismae has intense blackberry, road tar, and licorice aromas. This powerful, muscle-bound wine offers a flavor profile composed of copious quantities of cherries, blackberries, kirsch, cassis, freshly laid asphalt, and (Provençal herbs) *garrigue.* This wine is not for sissies. It is an in-your-face, powerful, full-flavored beauty. Drink it over the next 12 years.

CHÂTEAU RUSSOL-GARDEY

NV	Elevé en Fût de Chêne	C	88
1999	Minervois Grand Réserve Syrah	C	90
1998	Minervois Grand Réserve Syrah	C	89

Note: This estate labels its wines as either Château Russol-Gardey or Domaine Russol.

The 1998 Minervois Grand Réserve Syrah was aged for 8–9 months in new oak barrels. It is medium to dark ruby-colored and reveals mouthwatering, sweet, black raspberry aromatics. This satin-textured, plump, flavorful wine was neither fined nor filtered. It is rich, has lovely balance, and is crammed with ripe blackberries and freshly ground black pepper flavors. Its extensive finish reveals loads of supple, ripe tannins. Anticipated maturity: now–2005.

Château Russol-Gardey's nonvintage Elevé en Fût de Chêne has a goldish-amber color. It displays sweet orange and kumquat aromas that lead to a medium- to full-bodied, oily-textured personality. Red berries, rich, honeyed yellow fruits, and an enticing freshness make this an excellent wine. Beginning with the 1999 vintage, the estate plans to vintage-date this wine. Drink it over the next 3–4 years.

The dark ruby-colored 1999 Minervois Grande Réserve Syrah has intense spicy, plummy aromas. Its enormously appealing nose is followed by a powerful, light- to medium-bodied, concentrated character. This wine is chewy-textured, with loads of intense plum, licorice, black cherry, and blackberry flavors. It is well balanced, exhibits superb ripeness, and has a long, lush finish. Anticipated maturity: now–2008.

DOMAINE DE ST.-ANTOINE

2000	Vin du Pays du Gard Syrah	A	90

This 2000 Vin du Pays du Gard Syrah is a sensational value. It offers notes of *garrigue* (Provençal herbs), smoke, licorice, and copious quantities of black currant fruit. Ripe, with excellent opulence as well as a long, chewy, pure, surprisingly intense finish, it will drink well for 2–3 years.

CHÂTEAU ST.-MARTIN DE LA GARRIGUE

1999	Coteaux du Languedoc	C	88
1998	Coteaux du Languedoc La Bronzinelle	B	(87–89)
1998	Coteaux du Languedoc Cuvée St. Martin	B	(88–90)

This large estate presently produces 300,000 bottles of wine a year. (This number will soon hit 350,000 when its newly planted vineyards come into production.)

The medium- to dark ruby-colored 1998 La Bronzinelle exhibits spicy, dark, creamy fruit aromas. This fat, velvety-textured, tar and roasted black fruit–flavored offering is medium- to full-bodied and extroverted. Its full-throttled personality delivers an enormous amount of flavor and punch for its price. Anticipated maturity: now–2004. The black/purple 1998 Cuvée St. Martin exhibits spice and cedar aromas in its elegantly nuanced nose. Awesome layers of cherries, blackberries, tar, mint, and cassis are found in its full-bodied, structured character. This impressively endowed wine was fashioned primarily from Mourvèdre (70%, with the balance composed of other traditional regional varietals), yet has none of the rusticity generally associated with that grape. Anticipated maturity: now–2007.

The 1999 Coteaux du Languedoc has a medium to dark ruby color and boasts gorgeous aromatic depth to its cherry fruit–scented nose. Medium-bodied and expressive, this blackberry, talcum powder, cracked pepper, and chocolate-flavored wine has excellent palate presence. Anticipated maturity: now–2007.

DOMAINE ST.-SERNIN

1998 Minervois Le Bois des Merveilles	B	(87–89)

The 1998 Le Bois des Merveilles tasted for this report is a special *cuvée* crafted for the U.S. market. Medium to dark ruby-colored and revealing spicy raspberry aromas, this is an extremely well made, medium- to full-bodied, chewy wine. Red and black fruits, tar, licorice, and roasted herbs are found in this satin-textured, powerful, deeply ripe, persistent wine. Anticipated maturity: now–2004.

TARDIEU-LAURENT

1998 Corbières d'Embres	D	(90–92)
1998 Corbières d'Ornaison	D	(88–90)
1998 Corbières Roquefort	D	(90–93)
1998 Minervois	D	(87–89)
1998 Vin de Pays d'Oc Les Grands Augustins	B	88

These are five amazing *cuveés* from the brilliant Michel Tardieu and Dominique Laurent. All four will be bottled without fining or filtration, as is their policy. Readers looking for superrich, ripe, seamless expressions of Languedoc-Roussillon should check out these spectacular efforts. Although not complex, the 1998 Vin de Pays d'Oc Les Grands Augustins (80% Syrah, 10% Merlot, and 10% Grenache) offers a black ruby color as well as sweet, straightforward, jammy, blackberry/cassis fruit and a full-bodied, fleshy mouth-feel. Drink this supple fruit bomb over the next 1–3 years.

The 1998 Minervois (a blend of 90% Syrah and 10% Grenache) exhibits a Burgundy–like elegance and refinement. Medium-bodied, without the size of the Corbières selections, it offers nicely balanced, supple black cherry and berry flavors, along with sweet oak, earth, and spice. Consume it during its first 2–3 years of life.

The old-vine selections from Corbières include the 1998 Corbières d'Ornaison, a blend of 70% Grenache and 30% Carignan. It reveals abundant black fruits in its herb-tinged, licorice, smoky cassis personality. Dense, full-bodied, rustic, gloriously fruity, and mouthcoating, this fleshy, full-flavored wine should be drunk over the next 2–3 years to take advantage of its youthful exuberance. My favorite of this spectacular group of wines is the 1998 Corbières Roquefort. A blend of nearly equal parts Grenache, Mourvèdre, and Carignan from rocky soils, this saturated black/purple wine exhibits a ripe (nearly overripe) nose reminiscent of a top-notch Turley Cellars Zinfandel from northern California. Thick, juicy, black fruits intertwined with cedar, spice box, fruitcake, pepper, and leather soar from the glass of this unctuously textured, thick wine. With the 14.9% alcohol well hidden, this great example of Corbières should provide sumptuous drinking over the next 7–8 years. Wow!

More classic and less exuberant, but potentially complex and impressive, is the 1998 Corbières d'Embres. Revealing sweet blueberry jam, flower, earth, pepper, and spice aromas, it is a blend of nearly equal parts Carignan, Grenache, and Syrah. This full-bodied mini-Hermitage is impressively constituted, rich, and long. The most backward of these five *cuvées*, it will benefit from another 12 months of bottle age; it should drink well for a decade.

These debut releases from Tardieu-Laurent's Languedoc-Roussillon operation are indicative of this *négociant*'s commitment to quality. As Michel Tardieu said, the key is to get high-quality Mourvèdre, Syrah, and Grenache from good sites, but when dealing with Carignan, to be permitted by the grower to reduce crop yields to 10–15 hectoliters per hectare! This is exactly what was done in 1998.

CHÂTEAU TOUR BOISÉE

1998 Minervois	B	88
1998 Minervois Marie-Claude	B	(88–90+)
1998 Minervois Marielle et Frédérique	C	(89–92)

The 1998 Minervois reveals a dark, saturated color and overripe plum and tar aromas. Medium- to full-bodied and muscular, it is an in-your-face wine. Thick-textured, it coats the mouth with *sur-maturité*-picked plums, juicy blackberries, freshly laid road tar, and *garrigue* (Provençal herbs). This blend of Syrah, Grenache, and old-vine Carignan is firm, structured, and has a rustic finish. Anticipated maturity: now–2006.

The dark ruby-colored 1998 Minervois Marie-Claude reveals super jammy, blackberry, and cassis aromas. This *sur-maturité*-laced, medium- to full-bodied, dense, intense wine is crammed with roasted berries, black fruits, and hints of cedar. Extremely well made, intense, and long, this beauty should be consumed over the next 6 years.

Regrettably, the 1998 Minervois Marielle et Frédérique was not imported to the U.S. It is dark ruby-colored and offers a powerfully spicy, enthralling nose. Huge ripeness, jammy blackberries, tar, and licorice can be found in this huge, muscular, highly impressive Minervois. Obviously crafted from beautifully ripened fruit, it is dense, powerful, and possesses a long, supple, tannin-filled finish. Those readers lucky enough to find some of this wine should consume it between now–2007.

DOMAINE LA TOUR VIEILLE

1997 Banyuls Mise Tardive	C	90
1999 Banyuls Vintage	C/500ml	91
1999 Collioure La Pinède	C	89
1999 Collioure Puig Oriol	C	90

The medium to dark ruby/amber-colored 1997 Banyuls Mise Tardive has profound mocha, waxy, plum, and spice aromas. Sweet, supple, and lush, red fruits, dark plums, violets, roses, and candied cherries can be discerned in this opulent yet structured offering. It is an expansive, well-ripened, intense wine for drinking between now–2014+.

The saturated dark ruby-colored 1999 Collioure La Pinède boasts plummy, grapy, black raspberry aromas. This medium-bodied wine has a chewy texture and gorgeous depth to its mocha and cherry syrup–like personality. It is powerful, layered with loads of fruit, and has admirably ripe tannin. Drink it over the course of the next 10 years. The similarly colored 1999 Collioure Puig Oriol has black raspberry and blackberry aromas. This dark fruit–filled wine is lush, pure, and rich. Intense waves of black raspberry liqueur dominate this wine's personality as well as its long, supple finish. Anticipated maturity: now–2012.

The 1999 Banyuls Vintage has a dark ruby color. Its aromatics, composed of sweet plums, cherries, roses, and violets, are intense and complex. On the palate, this medium-bodied, velvety-textured wine is crammed with molasses, cherries, blackberries, and plums. It is fat yet well focused and sports a sumptuous finish. Drink it over the next 15 years.

CHÂTEAU DE VALCOMBE

1998 Costières de Nîmes Prestige de Valcombe	B	(88–91+)

A blend of Grenache and Syrah, the medium to dark ruby-colored 1998 Prestige de Valcombe reveals herbal, tar, and licorice aromas. This wine's medium- to full-bodied, chewy-textured flavor profile is fabulous. Layer upon layer of red cherries, black fruits, asphalt, and hints of eucalyptus coat the palate. This is a deep, immensely flavorful, intense wine that will be at its best if drunk between now–2006.

CHÂTEAU VALFLAUNES

1998 Coteaux du Languedoc-Pic-St.-Loup Cuvée Favorite	D	91
1998 Coteaux du Languedoc-Pic-St.-Loup Cuvée Hardiesse	C	88

Two impressive offerings from Pic-St.-Loup, these wines are all concentrated, with beautifully pure flavors and excellent textures. The 1998 Cuvée Hardiesse, a barrel-aged blend of 90% Grenache and 10% Syrah, is opaque ruby/purple-colored with a full-bodied, international style (because of the new oak). Copious quantities of glycerin, fruit extract, sweet tannin, lavish new oak, and a chewy, fleshy finish can be found in this beauty. It should drink well for 4–5 years. The limited-production 1998 Cuvée Favorite (100% Syrah aged 16 months in new French oak) has an opaque purple color as well as an explosive nose of black cherry liqueur intermixed with blackberries and cassis. Muscular, deep, and full-bodied, with outstanding extract, purity, and overall harmony, this large-scaled effort should drink well for 7–8 years. Unfortunately, only 4,500 bottles were produced.

VIGNERONS D'OCTAVIANA

1998 Corbières Cuvée Sextant	B	88

The 1998 Corbières Cuvée Sextant (40% Carignan, 20% Grenache, 20% Syrah, and 20% Mourvèdre), a selection culled from this large cooperative by Vintex, a Bordeaux *négociant*, reveals some new oak yet has a deep ruby/purple color with black cherry and currant notes. Spicy and peppery, this medium-bodied wine is rich, well balanced, and ideal for drinking over the next 2–4 years.

CHÂTEAU DE VILLENOUVETTE

1998 Corbières Cuvée Marcel Barsalou	C	(87–89)

The Château de Villenouvette is owned by Yves Barsalou, the affable founder and chairman of the board of the Val d'Orbieu megacooperative (he is also chairman of the board of Crédit Agricole, one of the world's largest banks). Produced from Carignan harvested at 20 hectoliters per hectare, the 1998 Corbières Cuvée Marcel Barsalou reveals a nose composed of sweet, tarry black fruits. Medium- to full-bodied and intense, this excellent wine is crammed with layers of chewy-textured blackberries, roasted spices, as well as hints of mint. Anticipated maturity: now–2007.

PROVENCE

It is easy to regard Provence as just the dramatic playground for the world's rich and famous, and few wine lovers realize that this vast viticultural region in southern France is at least 2,600 years old. For centuries, tourists traveling through Provence have been seduced by the aromatic and flavorful thirst-quenching rosés that complement the distinctive cuisine of the region so well. Today Provence is an exciting and diverse viticultural region turning out not only extremely satisfying rosés but immensely promising red wines and a few encouraging whites. However, it remains largely uncharted territory for wine consumers.

Provence is a mammoth region with seven specifc viticultural areas. The best way to approach the subject is to learn what each of these viticultural areas has to offer, and which properties constitute the leading wine-producing estates. While Provence is blessed with ideal weather for grape growing, not all the vintages are of equal merit. Certainly for the white and rosé wines of Provence, which require consumption in their youth, only 2001 ought to be drunk today. The super vintages for all of Provence are 2000, 1998, and 1995. As a general rule, the top red wines of Provence can handle aging for up to a decade in the aforementioned vintages. Following is a brief synopsis of the seven major wine-producing areas in Provence, along with a list of the top wines from each area that merit trying. While the wines of Provence are not overpriced, the recent collapse of the American dollar against the French franc has made these wines less attractively priced than they were several years ago. Yet when the top wines are compared with wines of similar quality from Burgundy and Bordeaux, their relative value as French wines is obvious.

Bandol   In France, Bandol is often called the most privileged appellation. Certainly, the scenic beauty of this storybook area offers unsurpassed views of the azure Mediterranean, and the vineyards are spread out on the hillsides overlooking the water. Bandol produces red, rosé, and white wines. It is most famous for its rosé wine, which some people consider the best made in France, and its long-lived, intense, tannic red wine, unique in France because it is made from at least 50% of the little-known Mourvèdre grape. If anyone has any doubts about the quality of Mourvèdre, proof can be found in Pradeaux's monumental 1989 and 1990 Mourvèdre Vieilles Vignes. Prices for Bandol have never been cheap, largely because of the never-ending flow of tourists to the area, who buy up most of the wine made by the local producers.

There is consensus among connoisseurs that the best red wines come from such producers as the Domaine Pradeaux, Domaine Tempier, Domaine de Pibarnon, Ott's Château Romassan, Château Vannières, and two properties called Moulin des Coste and Mas des Rouvière. While most of these producers also make a white wine, I cannot recommend it with a great deal of enthusiasm, as it seems to always taste dull and heavy. However, the red wines as well as the fresh, personality-filled rosés from these estates are well worth seeking out and are available in most of the major markets in America. Prices for the rosés now average $15–20 a bottle and the red wines $20–30 a bottle. While I have had the good fortune to taste red wines of Bandol as old as 15–20 years, most of the wines seem to hit their peak after 6–10 years in the bottle. Bandol, one of the most strictly regulated appellations in France, is certainly the leading candidate of all the Provence appellations for producer of the longest-lived and best-known red wines.

Bellet   Like all of the Provence appellations, the tiny appellation of Bellet (tucked in the hillside behind Nice), produces red, white, and rosé wines. The history of Bellet is rich, as its vineyards were originally cultivated by the Phoenician Greeks in 500 B.C. But unless one spends time on the Riviera, one is unlikely ever to know how a fine Bellet tastes. Most of the wine produced in this microappellation of only 100+ acres never makes it outside of France, as the local restaurant demand is insatiable. There are only a handful of producers making wine here, and the very best is the Château de Crémat, owned by the Bagnis family, a splendid estate of 50 acres that produces nearly 6,000 cases of wine. It is imported to the United States, but its high price of $20–25 a bottle has ensured that few consumers know how it really tastes. Château de Crémat is a unique estate in Provence in that the white wine is of extremely high quality, and the local connoisseurs claim the rosé and red wines are the best made in this part of the French Riviera. The best recent vintages have been the 2000 and 1988, but I have tasted the red wines from Château de Crémat back through 1978, and they show no signs of decline. However, the wines of Bellet remain esoteric, enjoyed only by a handful of people, with prices that seem steep for the quality.

Cassis   The tiny village of Cassis, at the western end of France's famous Côte d'Azur, is one

Provence

0 5 10 15 KILOMETERS
0   5   10 MILES

St-Rémy-
de-Provence
Plan d'Orgon
les Baux
1
Eygalières
Arles
2
A7
N7
DURANCE
Salon-de-
Provence
Lambesc
RHÔNE
N113
Meyrargues
N568
2
Rians
2
Vauvenargues
Eguilles
Istres
2
La Fare-les-Oliviers
Aix-
en-Provence
4
N7
BOUCHES-
DU-RHÔNE
ÉTANG DE BERRE
Rognac
Vitrolles
Palette
3
A8
Martiques
A55
A57
4
A52
Trets
St-
Zacharie
Allauch
A52
Marseille
A50
7
4
Cassis
A50
La
Ciotat
Bandol

MEDITERRANEAN

Paris

Provence
Marseille

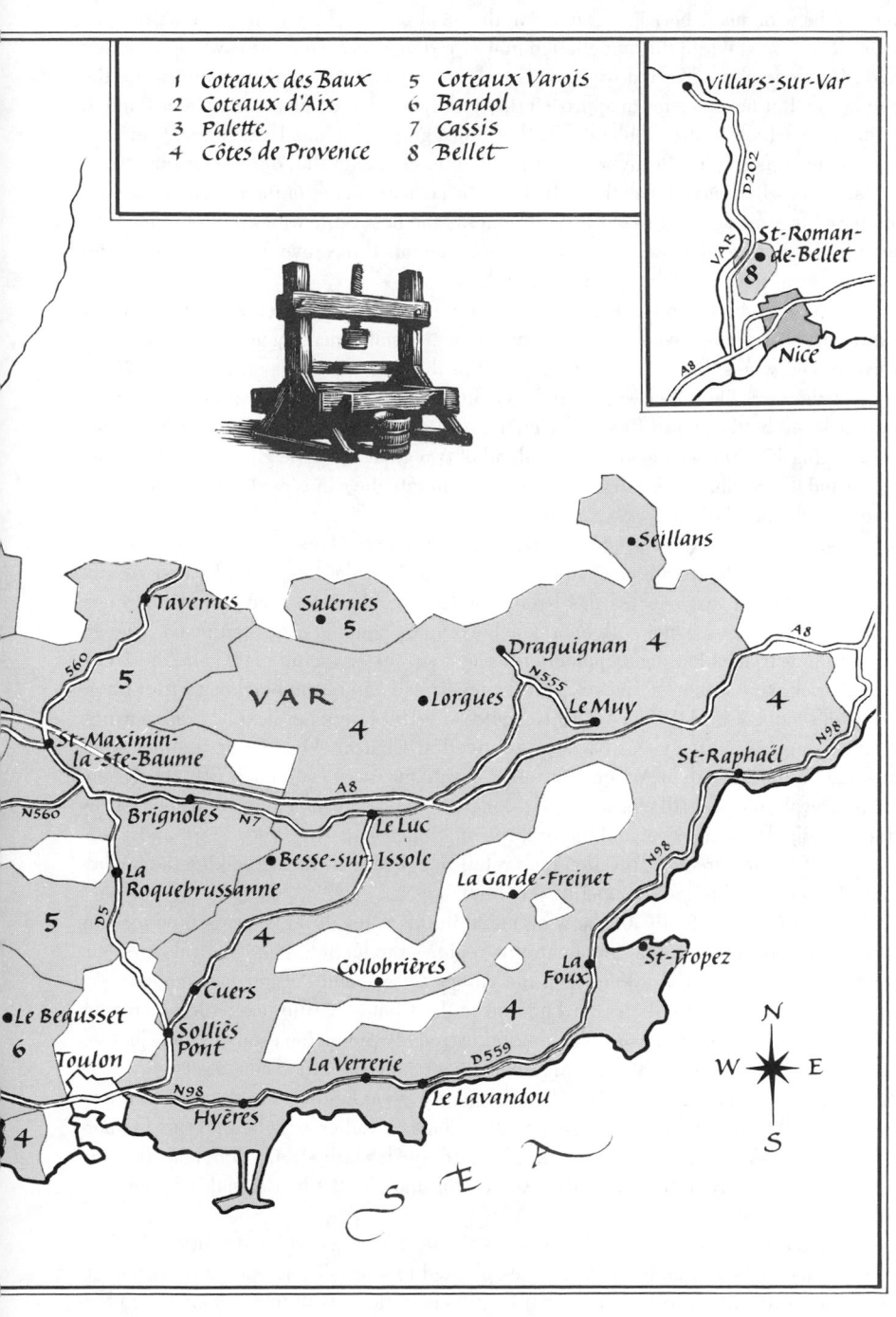

1 Coteaux des Baux
2 Coteaux d'Aix
3 Palette
4 Côtes de Provence
5 Coteaux Varois
6 Bandol
7 Cassis
8 Bellet

Villars-sur-Var

D202

VAR

St-Roman-
de-Bellet

8

A8

Nice

Seillans

Tavernes

Salernes
5

Draguignan   4

A8

VAR

5

Lorgues

N555

Le Muy

4

560

4

St-Maximin-
la-Ste-Baume

St-Raphaël

N98

A8

N560

Brignoles

N7

Le Luc

N98

Besse-sur-Issole

La Garde-Freinet

La
Roquebrussanne

5

D5

4

Collobrières

La
Foux

St-Tropez

N98

Cuers

4

Le Beausset

6

Solliès
Pont

La Verrerie

D559

N

Toulon

W   E

N98

Le Lavandou

4

Hyères

S

S   E   A

4

of the most charming fishing villages on the Riviera, located on a secluded bay and dwarfed by the surrounding steep limestone cliffs. The hordes of tourists that frequent the area ensure that most of the wine made here is consumed at the local bistros along with the area's ubiquitous *soupe de poisson.* While this appellation makes red and rosé wines, it is white wine that has made Cassis famous. The red wine tends to be heavy and uninteresting, and while the rosé can be good, it never seems to approach the quality level of its nearby neighbor Bandol. The white wine, which is often a blend of little-known grapes such as Ugni Blanc, Clairette, and Bourboulenc, is a spicy, fleshy wine with a distinct character that often seems unattractive by itself, but when served with the rich, aromatic seafood dishes of the region, it takes on a character of its own. The estates of Cassis producing the best white wines include Clos Ste.-Magdelaine, La Ferme Blanche, and Domaine du Bagnol. Prices average $20 or more for these white wines, not a good value even in 2002.

Coteaux d'Aix-en-Provence   This gigantic viticultural region, which extends primarily north and west of Aix-en-Provence, has numerous small estates making acceptable but generally overpriced wines that require drinking within the first 7–8 years of their lives. However, two of the very finest red wines produced in Provence are produced here: Domaine Trevallon and the better-known Château Vignelaure. Both producers specialize in red wine, capable of aging 15–20 years, made from a blend of two great red wine grapes, the Cabernet Sauvignon and the Syrah. Other estates have tried to imitate the wines made by Trevallon and Vignelaure, and a handful are worth watching.

The Domaine Trevallon is owned by Eloi Durrbach, who carved his vineyard out of the forbidding and lunarlike landscape near the medieval ghost town of Les Baux. Its first vintage was only in 1978, but that success has been followed by others that have produced compellingly rich and intense wines with enormously complex bouquets and significant concentration, as well as tremendous aging potential. Recent successes include 1995 and the 1990, a fabulously rich wine with a cascade of silky, concentrated cassis and blackberry fruit intermingled with scents of wild thyme. Yet 1997, 1998, and 1999 were perplexingly uninspiring.

Not surprisingly, proprietor Durrbach apprenticed at Château Vignelaure, another well-known estate in the Coteaux d'Aix-en-Provence. Vignelaure's wines, though not as bold and striking as Trevallon's, are still elegant expressions of Provençal winemaking at its best. They are widely available in America, and the best recent vintages are the 1990, 1989, and 1985.

The wines of Vignelaure and Trevallon both retail in the $20–25 range, making them modest values for their quality level and aging potential.

Côtes du Lubéron   Virtually all the wine made in the Côtes du Lubéron is produced by one of the many cooperatives that dominate this region's production. However, this area, located in the northern area of Provence near the villages of Apt and Pertuis, has immense potential. The best estate in the Côtes du Lubéron is the Château Mille, meticulously run by Conrad Pinatel. However, there is also a new and extremely promising estate called Château Val-Joanis, launched in 1978 with an initial investment of $6 million to construct a 494-acre vineyard and château near Pertuis. The Chancel family, great believers in the idea that top-quality wines will ultimately be produced from the Côtes du Lubéron, is behind this extraordinary investment. At present, they are making a good, fresh white wine, a delicious, fragrant rosé, and an increasingly serious red wine. All sell for under $12 a bottle, making them outstanding values.

Côtes de Provence   The Côtes de Provence is the best-known and largest viticultural region of Provence, with just under 50,000 acres planted in vines. This appellation is famous for the oceans of dry, flavorful rosé wine that tourists gulp down with thirst-quenching pleasure. There are many fine producers of Côtes de Provence wines, but the best include the very famous Domaines Ott, which is available on virtually every restaurant wine list in southern France, the Domaine Gavoty, the Domaine Richeaume, and the Domaine St.-André de

Figuière. All these estates, with the exception of the Domaine Richeaume, produce out-standing rosé wine. The Domaine Richeaume specializes in intense, rich, complex red wines that are surpassed only by the wines from the aforementioned Domaine Trevallon and Château Vignelaure. In addition, one of the best white wines produced in Provence is made by the Domaine St.-André de Figuière. All these wines are currently available in most of the major metropolitan markets in the United States, but they are not inexpensive. The Ott wines, no doubt due to their fame in France, sell for fairly hefty prices, but I have never heard any-one complain regarding the quality of their superb rosés and underrated red wines. Certainly, the white wine made by St.-André de Figuière is not overpriced and is an especially fine rep-resentative example of just how good a white wine from Provence can be. St.-André de Figu-ière also makes a delicious, supple red wine that is well worth trying. Should you find a bottle of the Domaine Richeaume's red wine, made by a fanatical German by the name of Henning Hoesch, it is well worth the $20 to taste one of Provence's finest examples of red wine. These serious, densely colored red wines are loaded with heaps of fruit, power, and tannin, and give every indication of being capable of aging for over a decade, as they are usually made from a blend of Cabernet Sauvignon and Syrah with some Grenache added at times.

Palette   Palette is a tiny appellation just to the east of Aix-en-Provence that in actuality consists of only one serious winemaking estate, Château Simone. Run by René Rougier, this tiny estate of 37 acres produces a surprisingly long-lived and complex red wine, a fairly oaky, old-style rosé wine, and a muscular, full-bodied white wine that behaves as if it were from the northern Rhône Valley. Simone's wines are not inexpensive, but they do age extremely well and have always had a loyal following in France.

The Basics

TYPES OF WINE
A huge quantity of bone-dry, fragrant, crisp rosés is made as well as rather neutral but fleshy white wines, and higher and higher quality red wines.

GRAPE VARIETIES
For red wines, the traditional grape varieties have always been Grenache, Carignan, Syrah, Mourvèdre, and Cinsault. Recently, however, a great deal of Cabernet Sauvignon has been planted in the Côtes de Provence and Coteaux d'Aix-en-Provence. The most interesting red wines are generally those with elevated levels of either Syrah, Mourvèdre, or Cabernet Sauvi-gnon. For white wines, Ugni Blanc, Clairette, Marsanne, Bourboulenc, and to a lesser extent Sémillon, Sauvignon Blanc, and Chardonnay are used.

FLAVORS
There is immense variation due to the number of microclimates and different grapes used. Most red wines have vivid red fruit bouquets that are more intense in the Coteaux des Baux than elsewhere. In Bandol the smells of tree bark, leather, and currants dominate. The white wines seem neutral and clumsy when served without food, but when drunk with the spicy Provençal cuisine, they take on life.

AGING POTENTIAL
Rosés: 1–3 years
White wines: 1–3 years, except for that of Château Simone, which can last 5–10 years.
Red wines: 5–12 years, often longer for the red wines of Bandol and specific wines such as Pradaux and Tempier, two Bandol estates with superb track records for long-aged wines.

OVERALL QUALITY LEVEL
The quality level has increased and in general is well above average, but consumers must remember to buy and drink the rosé and white wines only when they are less than 3 years old.

MOST IMPORTANT INFORMATION TO KNOW
Master the types of wine of each appellation of Provence, as well as the names of the top producers.

BUYING STRATEGY
The vintages of choice for the wines of this region are 2000 and 1998 for the reds, and 2001 for the whites and rosés.

RATING PROVENCE'S BEST PRODUCERS

* * * * * (OUTSTANDING)

Domaine des Béates Terra d'Or (Coteaux
    d'Aix-en Provence)
Château Pradeaux (Bandol)
Château Pradeaux Mourvèdre Vieilles
    Vignes (Bandol)

Domaine Tempier Cabasseau (Bandol)
Domaine Tempier La Migoua (Bandol)
Domaine Tempier La Tourtine (Bandol)

* * * * (EXCELLENT)

Antoine Arena (Corsica)
Château de Calissanne (Coteaux d'Aix-en-
    Provence)
Domaine Canorgue (Côtes du Lubéron)
Domaine Champagna (Côtes du Ventoux)
Clos Canaredi (Corsica)
Clos Culomba (Corsica)
Luigi-Clos Nicrosi (Corsica)
Commanderie de Peyrassol (Côtes de
    Provence)
Jean-Pierre Gaussen (Bandol)
Domaines Gavoty (Côtes de Provence)
Domaine Hauvette (Coteaux des Baux)
Domaine de l'Hermitage (Bandol)
Mas de la Dame (Coteaux d'Aix-en-
    Provence-Les Baux)

Mas de Gourgonnier (Coteaux d'Aix-en-
    Provence-Les Baux)
Domaines Ott—all cuvées (Bandol and
    Côtes de Provence)
Domaine de Pibarnon (Bandol)
Domaine Richeaume (Côtes de Provence)
Tardieu-Laurent-Domaine Bastide de
    Rodares (Côtes du Lubéron)
Domaine Tempier Rosé (Bandol)
Domaine Tempier Cuvée Spéciale
Domaine de la Tour de Bon (Bandol)
Domaine de Trevallon (Coteaux d'Aix-en-
    Provence-Les Baux)

* * * (GOOD)

Domaine du Bagnol (Cassis)
Château Barbeyrolles (Côtes de Provence)
Château Bas (Coteaux d'Aix-en-Provence)
La Bastide Blanche (Bandol)
Domaine de Beaupré (Coteaux d'Aix-en-
    Provence)
Domaine La Bernarde (Côtes de
    Provence)
Domaine Caguelouf (Bandol)
Château de Calissanne (Coteaux d'Aix-en-
    Provence)

Castel Roubine (Côtes de Provence)
Cave Cooperative d'Aleria Réserve du
    Président (Corsica)
Chapoutier Matines Beats (Coteaux d'Aix-
    en-Provence)
Clos Catitoro (Corsica)
Clos Ste.-Magdelaine (Cassis)
Château de Crémat (Bellet)
Domaine de Curebreasse (Côtes de
    Provence)
Domaine de Féraud (Côtes de Provence)

Château Ferry-Lacombre (Côtes de
   Provence)
Domaine Fiumicicoli (Corsica)
Château de Fonscolombe (Coteaux d'Aix-
   en-Provence)
Domaine du Fontenille (Côtes du Lubéron)
Domaine Frégate (Bandol)
Domaine Le Gallantin (Bandol)
Domaine de la Garnaude Cuvée Santane
   (Côtes de Provence)
Hervé Goudard (Côtes de Provence)
Château de l'Isolette (Côtes du Lubéron)
Domaine de Lafran-Veyrolles (Bandol)
Domaine La Laidière (Bandol)
Domaine Lecci (Corsica)
Domaine du Loou (Coteaux Varois)
Château Maravenne (Côtes de Provence)
Mas de Cadenet (Côtes de Provence)
Mas de la Rouvière (Bandol)
Mas Ste.-Berthe (Coteaux d'Aix-en-
   Provence)
Château de Mille (Côtes du Lubéron)
Moulin des Costes (Bandol)
Domaine de la Noblesse (Bandol)
Domaine Orenga (Corsica)
Domaine de Paradis (Coteaux d'Aix-en-
   Provence)

Domaine Comte Peraldi (Corsica)
Château de Rasque (Côtes de Provence)
Domaine Ray-Jane (Bandol)
Château Real-Martin (Côtes de
   Provence)
Domaine de Rimauresq (Côtes de
   Provence)
Château St.-Estève (Côtes de Provence)
Château St.-Jean Cuvée Natasha (Côtes de
   Provence)
Domaine St.-Jean de Villecroze (Coteaux
   Varois)
Château Ste.-Anne (Bandol)
Château Ste.-Roseline (Côtes de
   Provence)
Domaine des Salettes (Bandol)
Domaine de la Sanglière (Côtes de
   Provence)
Château Simone (Palette)
Domaine de Terrebrune (Bandol)
Domaine Torraccia (Corsica)
Toussaint Luigi-Muscatella (Corsica)
Domaine de la Vallongue (Coteaux des
   Baux)
La Vieille Ferme (Côtes du Lubéron)
Château Vignelaure (Coteaux d'Aix-en-
   Provence-Les Baux)

THE RHÔNE VALLEY

Grape Varieties

RED WINE VARIETALS

Cinsault   All the growers seem to use a small amount of Cinsault. It ripens very early, gives good yields, and produces wines that offer a great deal of fruit. It seems to offset the high alcohol of the Grenache and the tannins of the Syrah and Mourvèdre. Despite its value, it seems to have lost some appeal in favor of Syrah or Mourvèdre, but it is a valuable asset to the blend of a southern Rhône wine. It is an important component in two of the region's finest Côtes du Rhônes, Fonsalette and Tardieu-Laurent.

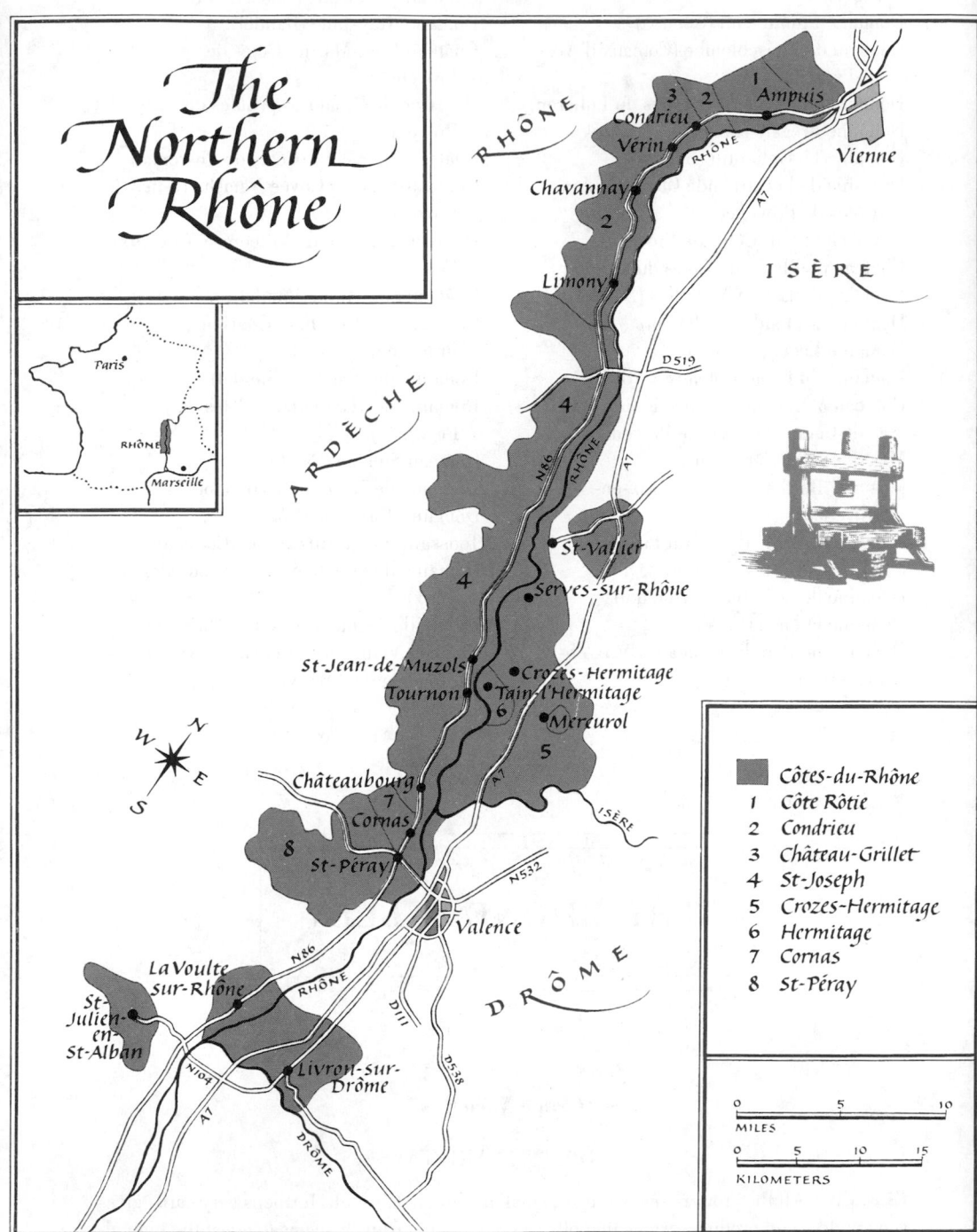

The Northern Rhône

Côtes-du-Rhône
1 Côte Rôtie
2 Condrieu
3 Château-Grillet
4 St-Joseph
5 Crozes-Hermitage
6 Hermitage
7 Cornas
8 St-Péray

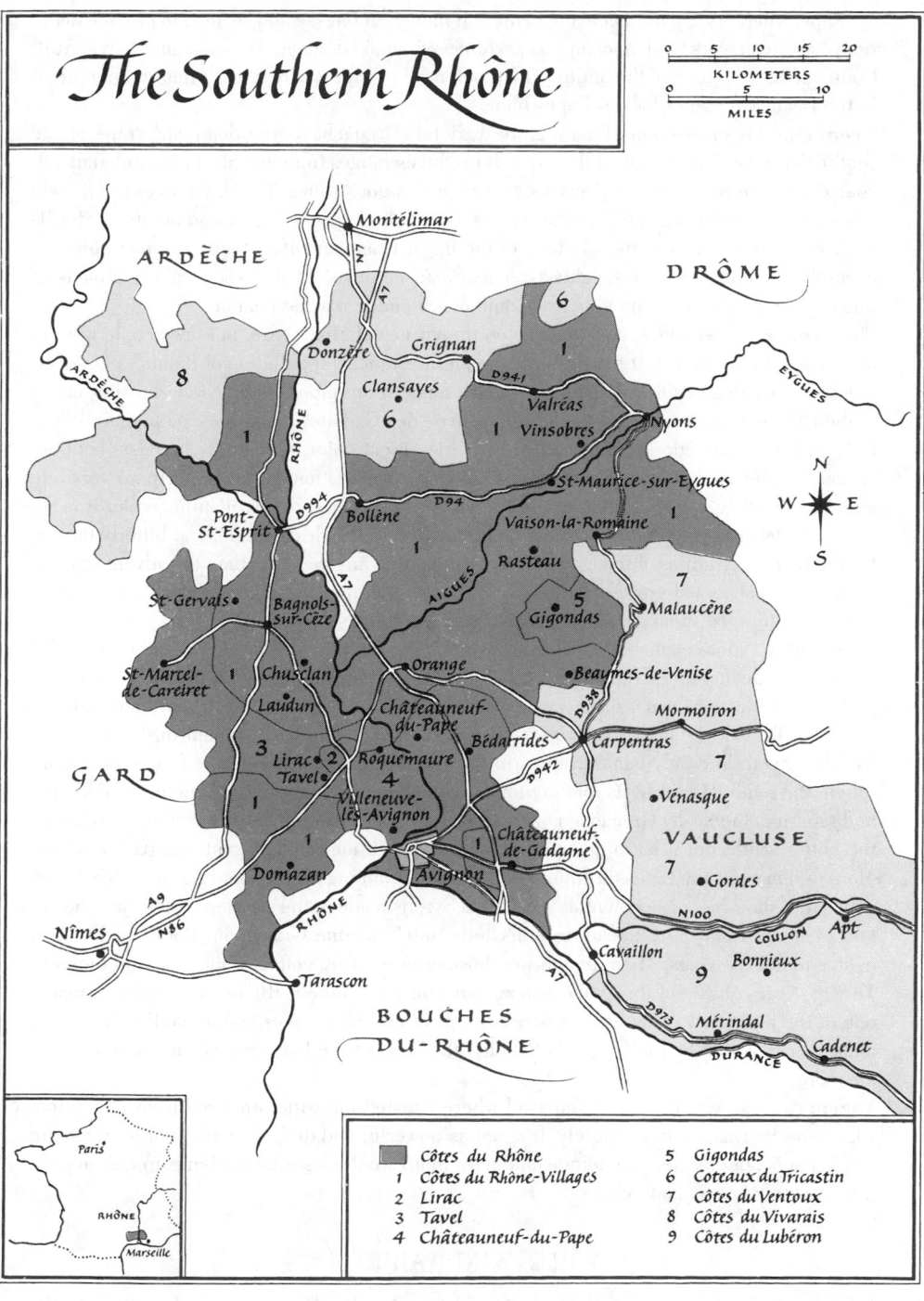

The Southern Rhône

KILOMETERS 0 5 10 15 20

MILES 0 10

ARDÈCHE

DRÔME

Montélimar

Donzère   Grignan

8   Clansayes

1   6   Valréas   Nyons

Vinsobres

St-Maurice-sur-Eygues

Pont-St-Esprit   Bollène   Vaison-la-Romaine

Rasteau

St-Gervais   Bagnols-sur-Cèze   7

Gigondas   5   Malaucène

St-Marcel-de-Careiret   Chusclan   Orange   Beaumes-de-Venise

Laudun   Mormoiron

3   Lirac   2   Châteauneuf-du-Pape   Bédarrides   Carpentras   7

Tavel   Roquemaure

4   Vénasque

Villeneuve-lès-Avignon   VAUCLUSE

GARD   Châteauneuf-de-Gadagne   7

Domazan   Avignon   Gordes

Nîmes   N100   COULON   Apt

Cavaillon   9   Bonnieux

Tarascon   Mérindal   Cadenet

BOUCHES DU-RHÔNE   DURANCE

Paris

RHÔNE

Marseille

	Côtes du Rhône	5	Gigondas
1	Côtes du Rhône-Villages	6	Coteaux du Tricastin
2	Lirac	7	Côtes du Ventoux
3	Tavel	8	Côtes du Vivarais
4	Châteauneuf-du-Pape	9	Côtes du Lubéron

Counoise   Little of this grape exists in the south because of its capricious growing habits. However, I have tasted it separately at Beaucastel and Clos des Papes in Châteauneuf-du-Pape, where its use has been augmented. It had great finesse and seemed to provide deep, richly fruity flavors and a complex perfume of smoked meat, flowers, and berry fruit. Counoise has as much of the antioxidative potential as Mourvèdre, a high-quality ingredient in the Beaucastel and Clos des Papes blends.

Grenache   A classic hot-climate grape varietal, Grenache is the dominant grape of the southern Rhône. The quality of the wines it produces ranges from hot, alcoholic, unbalanced, coarse wines to rich, majestic, very long-lived, sumptuous wines. The differences are largely caused by the yield of juice per vine. Where Grenache is pruned back and not overly fertilized, it can do wondrous things. Many of the finest Châteauneuf-du-Papes remain poignant examples of what majestic heights Grenache can achieve. At its best, it offers aromas of kirsch, black currants, pepper, licorice, and occasionally roasted peanuts.

Mourvèdre   Everyone seems to agree on the virtues of Mourvèdre, but few people want to take the risk and grow it. It flourishes in the Mediterranean appellation of Bandol, but only a handful of Châteauneuf-du-Pape estates have made it an important part (one-third or more) of their blend (Beaucastel and La Nerthe's Cuvée des Cadettes being the exceptions). When fully mature Mourvèdre is harvested, it provides great color, a complex, woodsy, leathery aroma, and superb structure, as well as a resistance to oxidation. However, it ripens very late and, unlike other grape varietals, has little value until it is perfectly mature. When it lacks maturity, the growers say it gives them nothing, for it is colorless, acidic, and bitterly tannic. Given the eccentricities of this grape, it is unlikely that anyone other than the adventurous or passionately obsessed growers will make use of this grape. Its telltale aromas are those of leather, truffles, fresh mushrooms, and tree bark.

Muscardin   More common than Terret Noir, Muscardin provides perfume as well as a solid measure of alcohol and strength. Beaucastel uses Muscardin, but by far the most important plantings of Muscardin at a serious winemaking estate are at Chante Perdrix in Châteauneuf-du-Pape. The Nicolet family uses up to 20% in their excellent Châteauneuf-du-Pape.

Syrah   Syrah, the only game in town in the northern Rhône, is relegated to an accessory role in the south. However, its role in providing needed color saturation, structure, backbone, and tannin to the fleshy Grenache is incontestable. Some growers believe it ripens too fast in the hotter south, but it is, in my opinion, a strong addition to many southern Rhône wines. More and more of the Côtes du Rhône estates are producing special bottlings of 100% Syrah wines that show immense potential. The finest Syrahs made in the southern Rhône are the *cuvées* of Syrah from the Château de Fonsalette and Domaine Gramenon. Both can last and evolve for 15–25 years. Their aromas are those of berry fruit, coffee, smoky tar, and hickory.

Terret Noir   Little of this grape is now found in the southern Rhône, although it remains one of the permitted varieties. It was used to give acidity to wines and to mollify the strong character provided by the Grenache and Syrah. None of the best estates cares to employ it anymore.

Vaccarese   It was again at Beaucastel where I tasted the wine produced from this grape, which the Perrins vinify separately. It is not as powerful and deep as Syrah, nor as alcoholic as Grenache, but has its own unique character that I would describe as giving aromas of pepper, hot tar, tobacco, and licorice.

WHITE WINE VARIETALS

Bourboulenc   This grape offers plenty of body. The local cognoscenti also attribute the scent of roses to Bourboulenc, although I cannot as yet claim the same experience.

Clairette Blanc   Until the advent of cold fermentations and modern equipment to minimize the risk of oxidation, Clairette produced heavy, alcoholic, often deep yellow-colored wines that were thick and ponderous. Given the benefit of state-of-the-art technology, it produces soft, floral, fruity wine that must be drunk young. The excellent white Châteauneuf-du-Pape of Vieux Télégraphe has considerable Clairette in it.

Grenache Blanc   Deeply fruity, highly alcoholic yet low-acid wines are produced from Grenache Blanc. When fermented at cool temperatures and when the malolactic fermentation is blocked, it can be a vibrant, delicious wine capable of providing near-term pleasure. The exquisite white Châteauneuf-du-Pape from Henri Brunier, Vieux Télégraphe, contains 25% Grenache Blanc; that of the Gonnet Brothers' Font de Michelle, 50%. In a few examples such as this, I find the floral scent of paperwhite narcissus and a character vaguely resembling that of Condrieu.

Marsanne   The Marsanne planted in the south produces rather chunky wines that must receive help from other varieties because they cannot stand alone. British author Jancis Robinson often claims it smells "not unpleasantly reminiscent of glue." More often than not, I find it resembles a high-class fino sherry with a nutty character.

Picardin   This grape has fallen out of favor, largely because the growers felt it added nothing to their blends. Apparently its neutral character was its undoing. Yet, the Jaboulets have made several fine white Châteauneuf-du-Papes with high proportions of Picardin.

Picpoul   Frankly, I have no idea what this grape tastes like. I have never seen it isolated or represented in such a hefty percentage as to be identifiable. Today, it is rarely seen in the southern Rhône.

Roussanne   For centuries, this grape was the essence of white Hermitage in the northern Rhône, but its small yields and proclivity to disease saw it largely replaced by Marsanne. Making a comeback in the southern Rhône, it has the most character of any of the white wine varietals—aromas of honey, coffee, flowers, and nuts—and produces a wine that can be very long-lived, an anomaly for a white wine in the southern Rhône. The famous Châteauneuf-du-Pape estate Beaucastel uses 80% Roussanne in their white wine, which, not surprisingly, is the longest-lived white wine of the appellation. Since 1986, they have also produced a 100% old-vine Roussanne that can be profound. Grand Veneur, Janasse, and La Nerthe also utilize considerable Roussanne. Because of its oxidative tendencies, vinification is tricky.

Viognier   Viognier produces a great and unique white wine that is synonymous with Condrieu and Château Grillet, both in the northern Rhône. In the south, especially in the Côtes du Rhône, there are extensive new plantings. The finest example in the southern Rhône is the Domaine Ste.-Anne in the Côtes du Rhône village of Gervais. St.-Estève is another domaine in the Côtes du Rhône that produces a good Viognier. Beaucastel began to utilize it in their white Coudoulet in 1991. Unfortunately, Viognier is not a permitted varietal in Châteauneuf-du-Pape, where it could immensely enhance the neutral character of so many of that village's white wines. It is an increasingly important component of white Côtes du Rhône and in large measure, the most significant reason why these wines have risen in quality.

Appellations

NORTHERN RHÔNE

Condrieu   This exotic, often overwhelmingly fragrant wine is low in acidity and must be drunk young, but it offers hedonistic aromas and flavors of peaches, apricots, and honey, with an unbelievably decadent, opulent finish.

Cornas   The impenetrable black/ruby color, the brutal, even savage tannins in its youth, the massive structure, and the muddy sediment in the bottle are all characteristics of a wine that tastes as if it were made in the 19th century. But Cornas wines are among the most virile, robust wines in the world, with a powerful aroma of cassis and raspberries that develops into chestnuts, truffles, licorice, and black currants as it ages. These wines are among the most underrated red wines of the world, but patience as well as a fondness for rustic wine is essential if they are to be appreciated.

Côte Rôtie   This is an immense, fleshy, rich, fragrant, smoky, medium- to full-bodied, stunning wine with gobs of cassis fruit frequently intertwined with the smells of frying bacon, tapenade, and smoke. It is one of France's greatest wines and can last for up to 25 years when well stored.

Crozes-Hermitage   Despite this appellation's proximity to the more famous appellation of Hermitage, the red wines tend to be soft, spicy, fruity, chunky, vegetal, and rather one-dimensional, instead of distinguished. The white wines vary enormously in quality and can be pleasant, but are often neutral and acidic.

Hermitage   At its best, Hermitage is a rich, almost portlike, viscous, very full-bodied, tannic red wine that can seemingly last forever. It is characterized by intense, even pungent smells of pepper and cassis, intertwined at times with aromas of licorice, melted asphalt, and truffles. The white Hermitage can be neutral, but the finest examples display a bouquet of herbs, minerals, nuts, fino sherry, acacia flowers, peaches, and a stony, wet slate–like component. The rare sweet *vin de paille* offers an intoxicating smell of truffles at 8–10 years of age.

St.-Joseph   This is the northern Rhône's most underrated appellation for red and white wine. The reds and whites are juicy and best drunk young, preferably within 10 years of the vintage. No northern appellation has made as much qualitative progress as St.-Joseph. Moreover, these wines are fairly priced.

St.-Péray   Tiny quantities of still and sparkling white wines are made from this forgotten appellation of the Rhône Valley. Few merit consumer interest, as the wines are often dull, heavy, and diffuse. However, some producers, most notably Clape and Voge of Cornas, are trying to make interesting white wines.

SOUTHERN RHÔNE

Châteauneuf-du-Pape   There is an enormous diversity in the styles of Châteauneuf-du-Pape produced. It can be made to resemble Beaujolais, in which case it offers jammy, soft, fruity flavors and must be drunk quite young. If the wine is vinified in a classic manner, it can be very dense in color, sumptuously rich, and full-bodied, and it can last 15–25 years. It is often characterized by the smell of saddle leather, fennel, licorice, black truffles, pepper, nutmeg, and smoked meats. Wines made by both these methods, and then blended together and dominated by the Grenache grape, often smell of roasted peanuts and overripe Bing cherries. White Châteauneuf-du-Papes are usually neutral and uninteresting, but a few have a floral- and tropical fruit–scented bouquet. However, they must be drunk extremely young.

Côtes du Rhône-Villages   This is another appellation requiring closer study given the increasing number of high-quality estates. The most exciting "villages" include Cairanne, Rasteau, Sablet, Séguret, St.-Gervais, Beaumes de Venise, Lirac, and Tavel (produces France's most famous rosé).

Côtes du Rhône   The best Côtes du Rhônes offer uncomplicated but deliciously succulent, crunchy, peppery, blackberry and raspberry fruit presented in a supple, full-bodied style that is meant to be consumed within 5–6 years of the vintage. A handful can improve for 10–15 years. The finest Côtes du Rhônes and Côtes du Rhônes-Villages offer some of the greatest red wine values in the world.

Gigondas   Gigondas offers up a robust, chewy, full-bodied, rich, generous red wine that has a heady bouquet and supple, rich, spicy flavors. A tiny quantity of a very underrated rosé wine is made often and should be tried by consumers looking for something special.

Muscat de Beaumes de Venise   This sweet, alcoholic, but extraordinarily perfumed, exotic wine offers up smells of peaches, apricots, coconut, and lychee nuts. It must be drunk in its youth to be fully appreciated.

Vacqueyras   Given its own appellation designation in 1990, Vacqueyras is an exciting hotbed of activity. The wines are increasingly sought out by shrewd value-conscious buyers looking for Châteauneuf-du-Pape look-alikes selling for half the price. Overall, the number of top estates in Vacqueyras surpasses its better-known next-door rival, Gigondas.

AGING POTENTIAL

Château Grillet: 5–15 years

Châteauneuf-du-Pape (red): 5–25 years

Châteauneuf-du-Pape (white): 1–2 years, with a few notable exceptions

Condrieu: 2–5 years

Cornas: 5–15 years

Côte Rôtie: 5–25 years

Côtes du Rhône: 4–8 years

Côtes du Rhône-Villages: 4–8 years

Crozes-Hermitage: 3–10 years

Gigondas: 5–15 years

Hermitage (red): 5–30 years

Hermitage (white): 3–25 years

Muscat de Beaumes de Venise: 1–3 years

St.-Joseph: 3–6 years

Tavel: 1–2 years

OVERALL QUALITY LEVEL

In the northern Rhône appellations of Côte Rôtie, Hermitage, Condrieu, and Cornas, the general level of winemaking is excellent. In the other appellations, it is irregular. In the southern Rhône, Châteauneuf-du-Pape has the broadest range in quality, from thrilling, world-class, sumptuous wines to thin, industrial, diluted ones. However, Châteauneuf-du-Pape is one of France's most exciting regions because of the young generation of wine-makers who are fashioning greater and greater wines. Just behind Châteauneuf-du-Pape are Vacqueyras and Gigondas.

NORTHERN RHÔNE

Côte Rôtie at a Glance

Appellation creation:	October 18, 1940
Type of wine produced:	Red wine only
Grape varieties planted:	Syrah and Viognier (up to 20% can be added, but as a rule, few producers utilize more than 5% in their wines; Guigal's famed La Mouline boasts 11% in most vintages)
Acres currently under vine:	497
Quality level:	At least good, the best exceptional, among the finest red wines in the world
Aging potential:	The finest age 5–30 years.
General characteristics:	Fleshy, rich, very fragrant, smoky, full-bodied, stunning wines
Greatest recent vintages:	1999, 1998, 1997, 1995, 1991, 1990, 1989, 1988, 1985, 1983, 1978, 1976, 1969
Price range:	$40–75, except for Guigal's and Chapoutier's single-vineyard and/or luxury *cuvées*, which cost $150 or more
Aromatic profile:	These intensely fragrant wines offer compelling bouquets showcasing scents and flavors of cassis, black raspberries, smoke, bacon fat, violets, olives, and grilled meats. For wines

where a healthy dosage of new-oak casks are employed, add toasty vanilla aromas.

Textural profile: These are elegant yet authoritatively powerful wines that are often chewy and deep. They are usually medium- to full-bodied, with surprisingly good acid levels for such ripeness and power. Tannin levels are generally moderate.

The Côte Rôtie appellation's most profound wines:

P. et C. Bonnefond Les Rochains
Chapoutier La Mordorée
Clusel-Roch Les Grandes Places
Delas Frères La Landonne (since 1997)
Delas Frères Seigneur de Maugiron (since 1997)
Pierre Gaillard Côte Rozier
Pierre Gaillard Le Cret
Pierre Gaillard Les Viallières
J. M. Gérin La Landonne
J. M. Gérin Les Grandes Places

Guigal Château D'Ampuis
Guigal La Landonne
Guigal La Mouline
Guigal La Turque
Jasmin (since 1999)
Domaine Monteillet Les Grandes Places
Michel Ogier (since 1991)
Michel Ogier Belle-Hélène
René Rostaing Côte Blonde
René Rostaing Côte Brune La Landonne
Vidal-Fleury La Chatillonne

RATING THE CÔTE RÔTIE PRODUCERS

* * * * * (OUTSTANDING)

Chapoutier La Mordorée
Clusel-Roch Les Grandes Places
Delas Frères La Landonne
Pierre Gaillard Côte Rozier-La Rose Pourpre
Pierre Gaillard Le Cret
Jean-Michel Gérin Les Grandes Places
Jean-Michel Gérin La Landonne
Guigal Château D'Ampuis

Guigal La Landonne
Guigal La Mouline
Guigal La Turque
Jean-Paul et Jean-Luc Jamet
Michel Ogier
Michel Ogier Belle-Hélène
René Rostaing Côte Blonde
René Rostaing Côte Brune La Landonne
Tardieu-Laurent

* * * * (EXCELLENT)

Patrick et Christophe Bonnefond
Patrick et Christophe Bonnefond Les Rochains
Bernard Burgaud
Domaine Clusel-Roch (other cuvées)
Yves Cuilleron Bassonon
Yves Cuilleron Terres Sombres
Delas Frères Les Seigneurs de Maugiron
Pierre Gaillard
Henri Gallet
Yves Gangloff

Jean-Michel Gérin Champin Seigneur
Guigal Côtes Brune et Blonde
Jasmin
Laffoy et Gasse
Laffoy et Gasse Vieilles Vignes
Domaine de Monteillet Les Grande Places
René Rostaing (regular cuvée)
René Rostaing Côte Brune
Eric Texier
Vidal-Fleury La Chatilhonne
Vidal-Fleury Côtes Brune et Blonde

* * * (GOOD)

Gilles Barge Côte Brune
Gilles Barge Cuvée du Plessy
Guy et Frédéric Bernard
De Boisseyt Côte Blonde

Domaine de Bonserine Côte Brune
Domaine de Bonserine La Garde
Domaine de Bonserine Les Moutonnes
Domaine de Bonserine La Sarrasine

Emile Champet
Joel Champet La Viaillère
Chapoutier (regular *cuvée*)
Domaine Clusel-Roch (regular *cuvée*)
Albert Dervieux-Thaize‡
Edmund et David Duclaux

André François
Mouton Père et Fils
Domaine de Rosiers (Louis Drevon)
J. Michel-Stephan
J. Michel-Stephan Vieilles Vignes en
   Coteaux

Condrieu at a Glance

Appellation creation:	April 27, 1940
Type of wine produced:	White wine only
Grape varieties authorized:	Viognier
Acres currently under vine:	Condrieu: 250, Château Grillet: 7.6
Quality level:	The top wines are exceptional, as this is one of the rarest and most unique wines in the world, but quality is increasingly irregular.
Aging potential:	1–4 years; Château Grillet will keep 4–8 years.
General characteristics:	An exotic, often overwhelming apricot/peach/honeysuckle fragrance is followed by low-acid, very rich wines that are usually short-lived; ironically, the less successful vintages with higher acidity age longer.
Greatest recent vintages:	2001, 1998
Price range:	$45–75
Aromatic profile:	Honeysuckle, peaches, apricots, and candied tropical fruit aromas should soar from a glass of a top Condrieu.
Textural profile:	In ripe vintages, Condrieu tends to be low in acidity, but not flabby. Fleshy, decadent, dry, and gloriously fruity and layered flavors should be intense, but not heavy. In most vintages, a tiny quantity of late-harvested Viognier is produced. It is usually very sweet and somewhat cloying.

The Condrieu appellation's most profound wines:

Yves Cuilleron Les Chaillets Vieilles
   Vignes
Yves Cuilleron Les Eguets Vendange
   Tardive
Delas Frères Clos Boucher
Madame P. Dumazet Coteau de Côte
   Fournet
Madame P. Dumazet Rouelle Midi

Yves Gangloff
Guigal La Doriane
Domaine de Monteillet (Antoine Montez)
André Perret Coteau du Chéry
René Rostaing
Georges Vernay Les Chaillées de l'Enfer
Georges Vernay Coteaux du Vernon
François Villard Deponcins

RATING THE CONDRIEU PRODUCERS

* * * * * *(OUTSTANDING)*

Yves Cuilleron Les Chaillets Vieilles
   Vignes
Yves Cuilleron Les Eguets
Madame P. Dumazet Côte Fournet
Yves Gangloff

Guigal La Doriane
Guigal (*négociant* bottling)
Domaine du Monteillet (Antoine Montez)
André Perret Clos Chanson
André Perret Coteau du Chéry

‡ Dervieux-Thaize, retired since 1991, leases his vineyards to René Rostaing.

* * * * *(EXCELLENT)*

Patrick et Christophe Bonnefond Côte
   Chatillon
Chapoutier
J. L. Chave
Yves Cuilleron (regular *cuvée*)
Delas Frères Clos Boucher

Madame P. Dumazet Rouelle Midi
Philippe et Christophe Pichon
Hervé Richard
René Rostaing
Georges Vernay
François Villard (various *cuvées*)

* * * *(GOOD)*

Gilles Barge
Domaine du Chêne-Marc Rouvière
Domaine Louis Chèze
Delas Frères La Galopine
Domaine Farjon

Philippe Faury
Philippe Faury La Berne
Château Grillet‡
Vidal-Fleury

Hermitage at a Glance

Appellation creation:	March 4, 1937
Type of wine produced:	Red, white, and *vin de paille,* a dessert-styled white wine
Grape varieties planted:	Syrah for the red wine; primarily Marsanne and some Roussanne for the white wine; up to 15% white wine grapes can be blended with the red wine, but as a practical matter, this is widely eschewed.
Acres currently under vine:	321
Quality level:	Prodigious for the finest red wines, good to exceptional for the white wines
Aging potential:	Red wine: 5–40+ years; white wine: 3–25 years
General characteristics:	Rich, viscous, very full-bodied, tannic red wines; full-bodied white wines with a unique scent of herbs, minerals, nuts, peaches, and on occasion, top-rated fino sherry
Greatest recent vintages:	1999, 1998, 1997, 1995, 1991, 1990, 1989, 1979, 1978, 1972, 1970, 1966, 1961, 1959
Price range:	$40–100 will purchase any wine except for single-parcel wines such as Chapoutier's l'Orée and Le Pavillon, or Chave's Cuvée Cathelin, which can cost $250 a bottle, or more.
Aromatic profile:	*Red wine*—Cassis, black pepper, tar, and very ripe red and black fruits characterize a fine young vintage of red Hermitage. With a decade of bottle age, cedar, spice, and cassis can (and often do) resemble a first growth Pauillac. *White wine*—Pineapple aromas intertwine with acacia flowers, peach, and honey scents. With extended age (15 or more years), scents of smoked nuts, fino sherry, and honey can be overpowering.
Textural profile:	*Red wine*—Unusually full-bodied, powerful, and tannic, as well as resistant to oxidation, results in a wine that ages at a glacial pace. *White wine*—Fruity, full-bodied, and fragrant when young, white Hermitage closes down after 4–5 years of

‡ Prior to 1979 *****; since 1979 ***. Château Grillet is entitled to its own appellation—a very unusual situation in France.

bottle age, only to reemerge 15–25 years later as an unctuous, dry, thick white wine.

The Hermitage appellation's most profound wines:

Chapoutier Le Pavillon (red)

Chapoutier Cuvée l'Orée (white)

Chapoutier l'Ermite (red)

Chapoutier Le Méal (red and white)

J. L. Chave (red)

J. L. Chave (white)

J. L. Chave Cuvée Cathelin (red)

Bernard Faurie Le Méal (red)

Delas Frères Les Béssards (red)

Paul Jaboulet-Aîné La Chapelle (red)

Domaine des Remizières Cuvée Emilie (red and white)

Marc Sorrel Gréal (red)

RATING THE RED HERMITAGE PRODUCERS

* * * * * (OUTSTANDING)

Chapoutier l'Ermite

Chapoutier Le Méal

Chapoutier Le Pavillon

J. L. Chave Cuvée Cathelin

J. L. Chave (regular *cuvée*)

Delas Frères Les Bessards (since 1997)

Domaine des Remizières Cuvée Emilie

* * * * (EXCELLENT)

Albert Belle

Chapoutier (La Sizeranne) (since 1989)

Domaine du Colombier

Delas Frères (Les Bessards)

Bernard Faurie (regular *cuvée*)

Bernard Faurie Le Méal

Paul Jaboulet-Aîné La Chapelle (prior to 1996, 5 stars)

Marc Sorrel Cuvée Classique

Marc Sorrel Le Gréal

* * * (GOOD)

Bernard Chave

Delas Frères Marquise de la Tourette

Domaine Fayolle

Ferraton Père et Fils Les Dionnières

Ferraton Père et Fils Le Méal

Alain Graillot

Guigal

Paul Jaboulet-Aîné Pied La Côte

Jean-Michel Sorrel

Vidal-Fleury

RATING THE WHITE HERMITAGE PRODUCERS

* * * * * (OUTSTANDING)

Chapoutier Cuvée de l'Orée

J. L. Chave

Domaine des Remizières Cuvée Emilie

* * * * (EXCELLENT)

J. L. Grippat

Guigal

Paul Jaboulet-Aîné Chevalier de Stérimberg (since 1989)

Marc Sorrel Les Rocoules

Crozes-Hermitage at a Glance

Appellation creation:	March 3, 1937
Type of wine produced:	Red and white wine
Grape varieties planted:	Marsanne and Roussanne for the white wine; Syrah for the red wine, which represents 90% of the appellation's production

Acres currently under vine:	2,550
Quality level:	Mediocre to good, occasionally excellent, a few wines are superb.
Aging potential:	White wine: 1–4 years; red wine: 3–10 years
General characteristics:	Tremendous variability in the red wines; white wines are fleshy, chunky, solid, and rather undistinguished.
Greatest recent vintages:	1999, 1998, 1997, 1995, 1991, 1990, 1989, 1988, 1978
Price range:	$18–35
Aromatic profile:	It is not dissimilar to Hermitage, but less intense, and often with more Provençal herb and olive scents. The Crozes-Hermitage *terroirs* are variable, and the Syrah does not achieve the exceptional ripeness found in Hermitage. The top wines are medium- to full-bodied, with attractive, smoky, peppery, cassis scents and flavors that can resemble a downsized Hermitage.
Textural profile:	In addition to its deep ruby/purple color, this wine generally possesses medium to full body, moderate tannin, and fine depth in the best examples. It rarely rewards cellaring for more than a decade, except in vintages such as 1990, 1989, and 1978.

The Crozes-Hermitage appellation's most profound wines:

Albert Belle Cuvée Louis Belle (red)
Chapoutier Les Varonnières (red)
Laurent Combier Clos des Grives (red)
Delas Frères Clos St.-Georges (red)
Delas Frères Tour d'Albon (red)
Ferraton Le Grand Courtil (red)
Alain Graillot Les Guiraudes (red)

Paul Jaboulet-Aîné Domaine Raymond Roure (red)
Paul Jaboulet-Aîné Thalabert (red)
Domaine du Pavillon Vieilles Vignes (Stephan Cornu)
Remizières Cuvée Christophe (red and white)

RATING THE CROZES-HERMITAGE PRODUCERS

* * * * (EXCELLENT)

Albert Belle Cuvée Louis Belle (red)
Chapoutier Les Varonnières (red)
Domaine du Colombier Cuvée Gaby (red)
Domaine du Combier Clos des Grives (red)
Delas Frères Clos St.-Georges (red)
Delas Frères Tour d'Albon (red)

Alain Graillot Cuvée La Guiraude (red)
Paul Jaboulet-Aîné Domaine de Thalabert (red)
Domaine du Pavillon (G.A.E.C. Cornu) Cuvée Vieilles Vignes (red)
Domaine Remizières Cuvée Christophe (red and white)

* * * (GOOD)

Albert Belle Cuvée Les Pierrelles (red)
Chapoutier Les Meysonnières (red)
Chapoutier Petite Ruche (red)
Bernard Chave (red)
Domaine Collonge (red)
Dard et Ribo/Domaine Blanche Laine (red)
Domaine des Entrefaux Le Dessus des Entrefaux (red)
Domaine Fayolle La Grande Séguine (red)
Domaine Fayolle Les Voussères (red)

Michel Ferraton Le Grand Courtil (red)
Alain Graillot Cuvée Classique (red)
Guigal (red)
Domaines Pochon/Château de Courson (red)
Domaine Jacques et Jean-Louis Pradelle Les Hirondelles (red)
Raymond Roure (acquired by Paul Jaboulet-Aîné in 1996) (red)
Vidal-Fleury (red)

St.-Joseph at a Glance

Appellation creation:	June 15, 1956
Type of wine produced:	Red and white wine
Grape varieties planted:	Marsanne and Roussanne for the white wine; Syrah for the red wine
Acres currently under vine:	1,729
Quality level:	Average to excellent
Aging potential:	White wine: 1–5 years; red wine: 3–8 years
General characteristics:	The red wines are the lightest, fruitiest, and most feminine of the northern Rhône. The white wines are perfumed and fleshy with scents of apricots and pears.
Greatest recent vintages:	1999, 1998, 1997, 1995, 1990, 1989, 1978
Price range:	$18–25; several old vine *cuvées* cost $75 or more.
Aromatic profile:	*White wines:* At the top level, the finest white wines are medium-bodied, refreshing, peach/apricot, sometimes pear-scented wines with good citrusy acidity that are delightful to drink within their first 2–3 years of life. Unfortunately, only a small percentage of dry whites meet these criteria. The majority of white St.-Joseph tend to be neutral, monolithic wines lacking charm and personality. *Red wines:* Syrah can be at its fruitiest, lightest, and most charming in this appellation. A good St.-Joseph red should display a Burgundy-like black cherry, raspberry, and occasionally cassis-scented nose with medium body, light tannin, and zingy acidity. These are the Rhône Valley's lightest reds and are thus best drunk in their first 5–6 years of life.
Textural profile:	*White wines:* Light to medium body is the prevailing rule with not much weight. Good freshness, crisp acidity, and uncomplicated fruit give these wines an appealing lightweight character. *Red wines:* Good fruit presented in a medium-bodied, zesty format is the hallmark of a fine St.-Joseph red. They should not possess tannin for support, but rather crisp acidity.

The St.-Joseph appellation's most profound wines:

F. Boissonnet Cuvée de la Belive (red)
Chapoutier Les Granits (red and white)
J. L. Chave (red)
Domaine du Chêne Anaïs (red)
Domaine Chèze Cuvée des Anges (red)
Domaine Chèze Cuvée Prestige de Caroline (red)
Domaine Courbis Les Royes (red)
Pierre Coursoden La Sensonne (red)
Yves Cuilleron Coteau St.-Pierre (white)
Yves Cuilleron Lyseras (white)
Yves Cuilleron Prestige l'Amarybelle (red)
Yves Cuilleron Prestige Le Lombard (white)
Yves Cuilleron Les Serines (red)
Delas Frères François de Touron (red)

Delas Frères Ste.-Epine (red)
Paul Jaboulet-Ainé Le Grand Pompée (red)
Pierre Gaillard Clos de Cuminaille (red)
J. L. Grippat Vignes de l'Hospice (red)
J. L. Grippat (white)
Domaine du Monteillet (Antoine Montez) Cuvée de Papy (red)
Alain Parent 420 Nuits (red)
Alain Parent Rochecourbe (red)
André Perret (white)
André Perret Les Grisières (red)
Pascal Perrier Domaine de Gachon (red)
Pascal Perrier Cuvée de Collonjon (red)
Tardieu-Laurent Les Ruches (red)
Raymond Trollat (red)

François Villard Les Côtes du Mairlant (red   François Villard Reflet (red)
and white)

RATING THE ST.-JOSEPH PRODUCERS

***** *(OUTSTANDING)*

Chapoutier Les Granits (red)   Domaine Louis Chèze Cuvée Prestige de
Domaine Louis Chèze Cuvée des Anges   Caroline (red)
  (red)   Pascal Perrier Domaine de Gachon (red)

**** *(EXCELLENT)*

Chapoutier Les Granits (white)   Bernard Faurie (red)
J. L. Chave (red)   Alain Graillot (red)
Domaine du Chêne Cuvée Anaïs (red)   Jean-Louis Grippat (white)
Courbis Les Reyes (red)   Paul Jaboulet-Aîné Le Grand Pompée (red)
Coursodon Le Paradis (red)   Domaine du Monteillet (Antoine Montez)
Coursodon St.-Pierre (red)   Cuvée du Papy (red)
Coursodon La Sensonne (red)   André Perret (white)
Yves Cuilleron (white)   André Perret Les Grisières (red)
Yves Cuilleron Cuvée Prestige Le Bois   Pascal Perrier Cuvée de Collonjon (red)
  Lombard (white)   Raymond Trollat (red)

*** *(GOOD)*

Clos de l'Arbalestrier (red)   J. L. Grippat (red)
Roger Blachon (red)   Paul Jaboulet-Aîné (white)
Chapoutier Les Deschants (red and white)   Jean Marsanne (red)
Domaine du Chêne (red)   Domaine du Monteillet (Antoine Montez)
Domaine Louis Chèze (red)   (red)
Domaine Collonge (red)   Alain Paret Chais St.-Pierre l'Arm de Père
Courbis (regular *cuvée*)   (red)
Pierre Coursodon l'Olivaie (red)   Alain Paret Chais St.-Pierre Domaine de la
Yves Cuilleron (red)   Couthiat (red)
Yves Cuilleron Cuvée Prestige (red)   André Perret (red)
Bernard Faurie (white)   St.-Désirat Cave Coopérative (red and
Philippe Faury (red)   white)
Bernard Grippa (red)   Vidal-Fleury (red)
Bernard Grippa Cuvée Le Berceau (white
  and red)

Cornas at a Glance

Appellation creation:	August 5, 1938
Type of wine produced:	Red wine only
Grape varieties planted:	only Syrah
Acres currently under vine:	220
Quality level:	Good to exceptional
Aging potential:	5–20 years
General characteristics:	Black/ruby in color, very tannic, full-bodied, virile, robust wines with powerful aromas and rustic personalities
Greatest recent vintages:	1998, 1997, 1991, 1990, 1989, 1985, 1979, 1978, 1976, 1969

Price range: $30–60
Aromatic profile: Black fruit, earth, minerals, occasionally truffles, smoked
                             herbs, and meats are common.
Textural profile: Massive, tannic, nearly coarse flavors have full body,
                             intensity, length, and grip, but are often too savage and
                             uncivilized for many tasters.

The Cornas appellation's most profound wines:

Auguste Clape   Michel Perraud (Patric Lesec)
Jean-Luc Colombo La Louvée   Tardieu-Laurent Coteaux
Jean-Luc Colombo Les Ruchets   Tardieu-Laurent Vieilles Vignes
Domaine Courbis Cornas Les Eygats   Noel Verset
Domaine Courbis Cornas La Sabarotte   Alain Voge Les Vieilles Fontaines
Paul Jaboulet-Ainé Domaine St.-Pierre   Alain Voge Vieilles Vignes

RATING THE CORNAS PRODUCERS

* * * * * (OUTSTANDING)

Auguste Clape   Tardieu-Laurent Coteaux
Jean-Luc Colombo La Louvée   Alain Voge Les Vieilles Fontaines
Jean-Luc Colombo Les Ruchets   Alain Voge Cuvée Vieilles Vignes

* * * * (EXCELLENT)

Thierry Allemand Cuvée Les Chaillots   Eric et Joel Durand Empreintes
Thierry Allemand Cuvée Reynard   Paul Jaboulet-Ainé Domaine St.-Pierre
L. et D. Courbis-Domaine des Royes   Jacques Lemencier
   Champelrose   Domaine du Tunnel
L. et D. Courbis-Domaine des Royes La   Domaine du Tunnel Cuvée Prestige
   Sabarotte   Noël Verset

* * * (GOOD)

René Balthazar   Domaine de la Fauterie (Sylvain
Cave Coopérative de Tain l'Hermitage   Bernard)
Caves Guy de Barjac   Paul Jaboulet-Ainé (négociant bottling)
Chapoutier   Paul Jaboulet-Ainé Domaine St.-Pierre
Jean-Luc Colombo Terres Brûlées   Marcel Juge (regular cuvée)
L. et D. Courbis (regular cuvée)   Jean Lionnet Cuvée Rochepertuis
Delas Frères Cuvée Chante-Perdrix   Robert Michel Cuvée des Coteaux
Charles Despesse Les Côtes   Robert Michel Cuvée le Pied du Coteau
Cave Dumien-Serette   Robert Michel Le Geynale
Eric et Joel Durand Les Coteaux   J.L. Thiers
Eric et Joel Durand Cuvée Classique   Alain Voge Cuvée Barriques

St.-Péray at a Glance

Appellation creation: December 8, 1936
Type of wine produced: Still and sparkling white wines, the latter representing 60%
                             of the production
Grape varieties planted: Marsanne and Roussanne
Acres currently under vine: 160
Quality level: Below average to average
Aging potential: 2–4 years

General characteristics:	Dull, somewhat odd, uninteresting wines that are heavy and diffuse
Greatest recent vintages:	None
Price range:	$15–20
Aromatic profile:	The acceptable examples—sadly, there are too few—offer a vague lemony/peachlike smell with neutral fruit flavors. The majority of the wines are acidic, heavy, and lacking fruit.
Textural profile:	The sparkling wines are crisp, and at times refreshing, but in a lowbrow sense. The still wines can be flabby, full-bodied, and chewy with no real vibrancy.

RATING THE ST.-PÉRAY SPARKLING WINE PRODUCERS

* * * (GOOD)

Jean-François Chaboud	Jean-Marie Teysseires
Pierre et Guy Darona	Jean-Louis Thiers

RATING THE ST.-PÉRAY STILL WINE PRODUCERS

* * * (GOOD)

Auguste Clape	Domaine du Tunnel
Jean-Louis Thiers	Alain Voge

SOUTHERN RHÔNE

Côtes du Rhône at a Glance

Appellation creation:	November 19, 1937
Type of wine produced:	Red, white, and rosé, although over 95% of the production is red wine
Grape varieties planted:	24 grapes are authorized, 14 designated as primary varietals, and 10 as accessory, but for all practical purposes, the predominant red wine grape is Grenache, followed by Syrah, Mourvèdre, and Cinsault. For the white wines, Grenache Blanc, Clairette, Bourboulenc, and increasingly Viognier and Roussanne are the principal grapes.
Acres currently under vine:	110,495
Quality level:	At the cooperative level, which accounts for 75–80% of the entire generic Côtes du Rhône production, quality ranges from insipid and sterile to very good to excellent; at the estate-bottled level, the quality ranges from below average to exceptional in the case of a half-dozen or so overachievers.
Aging potential:	Over 95% of every bottle of generic Côtes du Rhône, whether red, white, or rosé, should be drunk early; the whites and rosés within 2 years of the vintage, and the reds within 2–4 years of the vintage. However, some of the seriously endowed wines from the top estates can age for 20+ years.
General characteristics:	At the top levels, the white wines have made tremendous progress in quality as a result of modern cold fermentation and the introduction of Viognier and Roussanne in the blend. Even with these improvements, these are wines that are

fresh, lively, and meant to be drunk quickly. The red wines vary enormously. A well-made Côtes du Rhône should be bursting with red and black fruits, have a peppery, Provençal herb–scented nose, a supple, velvety texture, and a heady, lusty, spicy finish.

Greatest recent vintages: 2001, 2000, 1999, 1998, 1995

Price range: $8–25, except for the single-vineyard and old-vine *cuvées* of a handful of estates. The best of these wines (i.e., the four- and five-star producers that follow) irrefutably represent many of the greatest red wine values in the world, particularly in vintages such as 2001, 2000, and 1998.

RATING THE CÔTES DU RHÔNE AND CÔTES DU RHÔNE-VILLAGES PRODUCERS

* * * * *(OUTSTANDING)

Daniel et Denis Alary La Font d'Estevanas Cairanne
Daniel et Denis Alary La Jean de Verde Cairanne
Domaine des Aphillantes Cuvée des Galets
Domaine des Aphillantes Cuvée du Gros
Domaine des Aphillantes Trois Cépages
André Brunel Cuvée Sommelongue
Robert Charavin Coteaux des Travers Cairanne
Charvin
Coudoulet de Beaucastel
Clos du Caillou Bouquet des Garrigues
Clos du Caillou Très Vieilles Vignes
Olivier Cuilleras Visan Vieilles Vignes
Fèraud-Brunel Cairanne
Château de Fonsalette
Château de Fonsalette Cuvée Syrah
Domaine Gramenon Ceps Centenaire

Domaine de la Janasse Les Garrigues
Mordorée-Reine des Bois Lirac
Mourre du Tendre
Domaine de L'Oratoire St.-Martin
Domaine La Réméjeanne Les Eglantiers
Domaine La Réméjeanne Les Genevrières
A. Romero Cuvée Confiance Rasteau (Soumade)
A. Romero Cuvée Prestige Rasteau (Soumade)
A. Romero Fleur de Confiance Rasteau (Soumade)
Ste.-Cosme Les Deux Albion
Tardieu-Laurent Cuvée Guy Louis
Eric Texier Brezeme Vieilles Vignes
Eric Texier Séguret
Eric Texier Vaison-La-Romaine
Les Vins de Vienne Cairanne
Les Vins de Vienne Crannite

* * * *(EXCELLENT)

Daniel et Denis Alary (regular *cuvée*)
Domaine de l'Ameillaud
Domaine di Andezon
Domaine des Anges
Max Aubert Galifay
Max Aubert Velours Rouge
Domaine de la Bécassonne
Bressy-Masson Rasteau
Domaine de la Cabasse
De la Canorgue
Jean-Luc Colombo Les Abeilles
Domaine de Couroulu
Cros de la Mure
Domaine de Ferraud

Domaine de Ferraud Cuvée des Demoiselles
Domaine Gramenon (various *cuvées*)
Château du Grand Moulas
Château du Grand Prébois
Domaine des Grand Devers
Domaine Les Grands Bois Cuvée Eloise Cairanne
Domaine Les Grands Bois Cuvée Gabrielle Carianne
Domaine Les Grands Bois Cuvée Maximilien Cairanne
Domaine Les Grands Bois Cuvée Mireille Cairanne

Domaine de la Guichard
Guigal
Paul Jaboulet-Ainé Parallel 45
Patrick Lesec Aurore
Patrick Lesec Les Beaumes
Patrick Lesec Cairanne Vieilles Vignes
Patrick Lesec Perillière
Patrick Lesec Pierredon
Patrick Lesec Rasteau Vieilles Vignes
Jean-Marie Lombard
Domaine de la Réméjeanne Les Arbousiers
Domaine de la Réméjeanne Les
  Chevrefeuilles
Domaine des Richaud l'Ebrescade
  Cairanne

Domaine des Richaud Les Garrigues
Roharse-Charavin
Domaine St.-Gayan
Château St.-Maurice
Domaine St.-Apollinaire
Domaine Santa Duc
Domaine de la Solitude
Eric Texier St. Gervais Vieilles Vignes
Château des Tours
Domaine des Treilles
Vidal-Fleury
La Vieille Ferme (Perrin Réserve de
  Vieilles Vignes)
Domaine du Vieux Chêne (various
  cuvées)

* * * (GOOD)

Domaine des Aires Vieilles
Daniel Combe
Château de Domazan
Domaine de l'Espigouette
Domaine les Goubert
Domaine du Grand Prieur
Domaine de la Millière
Domaine Mireille et Vincent
Domaine Mitan
Domaine de Mont Redon

Domaine des Moulins
Domaines Mousset
Domaine Pélaquie
Domaine de la Présidente (various
  cuvées)
Domaine de la Renjarde
Château St.-Estève d'Uchaux
Château de Segries
Château de Trignon (various cuvées)
La Vieille Ferme (other cuvées)

Châteauneuf-du-Pape at a Glance

Appellation creation:	May 15, 1936
Type of wine produced:	Red: 93%; white: 7%
Grape varieties planted:	13 (actually 14 if the white clone of Grenache is counted) varieties are permitted; for red wines, Grenache, Syrah, Mourvèdre, Cinsault, Muscardin, Counoise, Vaccarèse, and Terret Noir; for white wines, Grenache Blanc, Clairette, Bourboulenc, Roussanne, Picpoul, and Picardin
Acres currently under vine:	8,100
Quality level:	*Red wine:* at the estate-bottled level, very good to exceptional; at the *négociant* level, mediocre to very good. *White wine:* mediocre to exceptional
Aging potential:	*Red wine:* depending on the style, 5–20 years; *white wine:* 1–3 years, except for Beaucastel and La Nerthe's Beauvenir
General characteristics:	*Red wine:* considerable diversity in stylistic approach can result in full-bodied, generous, rich, round, alcoholic, and long-lived wines, to soft, fruity wines that could be called the Beaujolais of Provence. *White wine:* floral, fruity, straightforward, and fresh if drunk within 2 years of the vintage
Greatest recent vintages:	2001, 2000, 1999, 1998, 1995, 1990, 1989, 1981, 1979, 1978, 1970, 1967, 1961

Price range:	$25–40, with special old-vine and/or single-vineyard *cuvées* costing considerably more; $50–125 is not an unusual price for such rarities.
Aromatic profile:	*Red wine:* Given the enormous diversity of winemaking styles in this appellation, the following is a simplified view: Producers who turn out carbonic maceration wines are aiming for early bottling and easy to understand red/black fruit aromas that are appealingly jammy. Those producers aiming for fuller-bodied, classically made Châteauneuf-du-Pape fashion wines with a vast array of aromatics, ranging from black cherries/currants and blueberries to roasted herbs, the noted Provençal *garrigue* smell (an earthy, *herbes de Provence* aromatic concoction), to overripe peaches and raspberry jam. *White wine:* The great majority of Châteauneuf-du-Pape white wines have their malolactic fermentation blocked and are made in a style that sees no oak and very early bottling (usually within 3–4 months of the vintage). These wines are meant to be consumed within 1–2 years. They offer floral, tropical fruit aromas in a pleasing but uncomplicated bouquet.
Textural profile:	*Red wine:* The lighter-styled red wines that have seen partial or full carbonic vinifications can be full-bodied, but tend to be soft and fruity with the appellation's lusty alcohol present, but not the weight and layered, multidimensional personality. More classical offerings vary from muscular, full-bodied, concentrated wines to some with immense proportions that are chewy and thick with high glycerin and alcohol. They saturate the palate and fall just short of staining the teeth. *White wine:* The modern style, non-malolactic, early bottled whites are surprisingly full-bodied and alcoholic, as well as plump and mouth-filling. Their size suggests longevity, but they are meant to be consumed quickly. The few producers who practice full malolactic fermentation and later bottling produce honeyed, unctuously-textured, thick, juicy wines that can be special if they are bottled without oxidizing.

The Châteauneuf-du-Pape appellation's most profound wines:

WHITE WINES

Château Beaucastel Cuvée Classique
Château Beaucastel Roussanne Vieilles
  Vignes
Les Cailloux
Clos des Papes
Font de Michelle
Grand Veneur La Fontaine

Domaine de la Janasse
Domaine du Marcoux
Domaine de Nalys
Château de la Nerthe Cuvée Beauvenir
Château Rayas
St-Benôit Vieille Vigne de Roussanne
Vieux-Télégraphe

RED WINES

Paul Autard La Côte Ronde
Château Beaucastel Cuvée Classique

Château Beaucastel Jacques Perrin
Domaine de Beaurenard Cuvée Boisrenard

Bois de Boursan Cuvée des Felix
Henri Bonneau Réserve des Céléstins
Bosquet des Papes Cuvée Chantemerle
Du Caillou Réserve Le Clos du Caillou
Du Caillou Cuvée Unique (also called
   Tradition)
Les Cailloux
Les Cailloux Cuvée Centenaire
Chapoutier Barbe Rac
Chapoutier Croix de Bois
Domaine de la Charbonnière Mourre des
   Perdrix
Domaine de la Charbonnière Vieilles
   Vignes
Charvin
Clos du Mont Olivet Cuvée Papet
Clos des Papes
Clos St.-Michel Cuvée Réservée Grand
   Clos
Domaine de Ferrand
Font de Michelle Cuvée Etienne
   Gonnet
Les Galets Blonds (Séléction Patrick
   Lesec)
Château de la Gardine Cuvée des
   Générations
Domaine du Grand Tinel Cuvée Alexis
   Establet
Domaine du Grand Veneur Cuvée Les
   Origines
Domaine de la Janasse Cuvée Chaupin

Domaine de la Janasse Cuvée Vieilles
   Vignes
Domaine de Marcoux Vieilles Vignes
Domaine de la Mordorée Cuvée de la
   Reine des Bois
Château de la Nerthe Cuvée des
   Cadettes
Pierre Paumel
Domaine du Pégaü Cuvée de Capo
Domaine du Pégaü Cuvée Laurence
Domaine du Pégaü Cuvée Réservée
Domaine du Père Pape La Crau de Ma
   Mère
Roger Perrin Réserve des Vieilles Vignes
Château Rayas
Domaine Roger Sabon Cuvée Prestige
Domaine Roger Sabon La Secret des Sabon
Domaine Saint-Benôit Cuvée de Grande
   Garde
Domaine Saint-Benôit Truffière
Tardieu-Laurent Vieilles Vignes
Pierre Usseglio Cuvée de Mon Aïeul
Pierre Usseglio Réserve Deux Frères
Raymond Usseglio Cuvée Impériale
Cuvée du Vatican Réserve Sixtine
Domaine de la Vieille Julienne Cuvée
   Réservée
Domaine de la Vieille Julienne Vieilles
   Vignes
Le Vieux Donjon
Vieux-Télégraphe

RATING THE RED CHÂTEAUNEUF-DU-PAPE PRODUCERS

* * * * * (OUTSTANDING)

Château Beaucastel
Château Beaucastel Hommage à Jacques
   Perrin
Domaine de Beaurenard Cuvée Boisrenard
Bois de Boursan Cuvée Félix
Domaine Henri Bonneau Réserve des
   Céléstins
Le Bosquet des Papes Cuvée Chantemerle
Les Cailloux
Les Cailloux Cuvée Centenaire
Chapoutier Barbe Rac
Chapoutier Croix de Bois
Charbonnières Les Hautes Brusquières
Charbonnières Vieilles Vignes
Gérard Charvin
Clos du Mont Olivet Cuvée Papet

Clos des Papes
Font de Michelle Cuvée Etienne Gonnet
Château de la Gardine Cuvée des
   Générations
Domaine de la Janasse Cuvée Chaupin
Domaine de la Janasse Cuvée Vieilles
   Vignes
Domaine de Marcoux Cuvée Vieilles
   Vignes
Domaine de la Mordorée Cuvée de la
   Reine des Bois
Château du Mourre du Tendre
Château de la Nerthe Cuvée des Cadettes
Domaine du Pégaü Cuvée de Capo
Domaine du Pégaü Cuvée Laurence
Domaine du Pégaü Cuvée Réservée

Domaine Roger Perrin Réserve de Vieilles
  Vignes
Château Rayas
Domaine Roger Sabon Cuvée Prestige
Domaine Roger Sabon la Secret des
  Sabon
Tardieu-Laurent Vieilles Vignes

Pierre Usseglio Mon Aïeul
Pierre Usseglio Réserve des Deux Frères
Raymond Usseglio Cuvée Impériale
Vieille Julienne Cuvée Réservée
Vieille Julienne Vieilles Vignes
Le Vieux Donjon
Domaine du Vieux-Télégraphe

* * * * *(EXCELLENT)*

Pierre André
Paul Autard Cuvée La Côte Ronde
Paul Autard Cuvée Mireille
Lucien Barrot
Domaine de Beaurenard Cuvée Classique
Domaine Bois de Boursan
Henri Bonneau Cuvée Marie Beurrier
Le Bosquet des Papes Cuvée Classique
Château Cabrières Cuvée Prestige
Domaine de Chante-Perdrix
Domaine de la Charbonnière Mourre des
  Tendre
Domaine Les Clefs d'Or
Domaine Clos du Caillou
Clos du Mont Olivet Cuvée Classique
Clos St.-Michel
Domaine de la Côte de l'Ange
Domaine de Cristia
Henriet Crouzet-Féraud
Cuvée de Boisdauphin
Cuvée du Vatican
Domaine de Ferrand
Font du Loup Le Puy Rolland
Font de Michelle Cuvée Classique
Domaine de Fontavin
Château Fortia (since 1994)

Domaine du Galet des Papes
Château de la Gardine
Grand Veneur Les Origines
Domaine Haut des Terres Blanches
Domaine de la Janasse Cuvée Classique
Domaine de Marcoux Cuvée Classique
Mas de Bois Lauzon
Domaine de Montpertuis Cuvée Tradition
Domaine de la Mordorée Cuvée Classique
Moulin-Tacussel
Domaine de Nalys
Château de la Nerthe Cuvée Classique
Père Caboche Cuvée Elisabeth Chambellan
Domaine du Père Pape
Domaine de la Présidente
Domaine de la Roquette
Domaine Roger Sabon Cuvée Réservée
Domaine St.-Benoît Grande Garde
Domaine St.-Benoît La Truffière
Domaine de St.-Siffrein
Tardieu-Laurent Cuvée Classique
Pierre Usseglio Cuvée Classique
Raymond Usseglio Cuvée Classique
Domaine de la Vieille Julienne Cuvée
  Classique
Domaine de Villeneuve

* * * *(GOOD)*

Paul Autard
Jean Avril
Domaine de Bois Dauphin
Domaine des Chanssaud
Domaine Chantadu
Domaine Chante-Cigale
Chapoutier La Bernardine
Clos de l'Oratoire des Papes
Clos St.-Jean
Domaine Durieu
Château des Fines Roches
Lou Fréjau
Domaine du Grand Tinel
Domaine Grand Veneur

Guigal
Domaine Haut des Terres Blanches
Paul Jaboulet-Ainé Les Cèdres
  (***** prior to 1970)
Domaine de la Jaufrette
Domaine Mathieu
Château Maucoil
Château Mongin
Domaine de Mont Redon
Domaine de Montpertuis Cuvée
  Tradition
Domaine de Palestor
Père Anselme
Père Caboche Cuvée Classique

Roger Perrin
Domaine de la Pinède
Domaine Pontifical
Domaine des Relagnes
Domaine Riche
Domaine Roger Sabon Les Olivets
St.-Benoît Cuvée Elise
St.-Benoît Soleil et Festins

Domaine des Sénéchaux
Château Simian
Domaine de la Solitude
Domaine Terre Ferme
Domaine Trintignant
Jean-Pierre Usseglio
Château Vaudieu
Vidal-Fleury

RATING THE WHITE CHÂTEAUNEUF-DU-PAPE PRODUCERS

* * * * * (OUTSTANDING)

Château Beaucastel Roussanne Vieilles
    Vignes
Grand Veneur La Fontaine

Domaine de la Janasse Cuvée Prestige
Domaine de la Nerthe Cuvée Beauvenir

* * * * (EXCELLENT)

Château Beaucastel Cuvée Classique
Domaine de Beaurenard
Domaine du Caillou
Clos des Papes
Font de Michelle
Domaine de la Janasse

Domaine du Marcoux
Domaine de Nalys
Domaine Roger Perrin
Château Rayas
Domaine du Vieux-Télégraphe

* * * (GOOD)

Château de la Gardine
Domaine de Mont Redon
Château de la Nerthe

Domaine du Père Caboche
Domaine de la Roquette
Domaine Trintignant La Reviscoulado

Gigondas at a Glance

Appellation creation:	January 6, 1971
Type of wine produced:	Red: 97%; the only other wine permitted is rosé
Grape varieties planted:	Grenache, Syrah, Mourvèdre, and Cinsault are the dominant varietals.
Acres currently under vine:	2,569
Quality level:	Average to exceptional
Aging potential:	5–15 years
General characteristics:	A robust, chewy, full-bodied, rich, generous red wine; light, vibrant, fresh, underrated rosé
Greatest recent vintages:	2001, 2000, 1999, 1998, 1995, 1990, 1989, 1985, 1979, 1978
Price range:	$20–30, with old-vine/luxury cuvées $35–50
Aromatic profile:	Earth, garrigue (that earthy, Provençal herb mélange), pepper, sweet black cherry, blueberry, and cassis fruit are evident in top examples of Gigondas.
Textural profile:	Light, fruity, soft, commercially styled wines are produced, but classic Gigondas possesses a full-bodied, muscular, unbridled power that is fine-tuned in the best examples, but rustic to the point of being savage in the more uncivilized styles.

The Gigondas appellation's most profound wines:

Domaine des Bosquets
Domaine La Bouissière Cuvée Prestige La
    Font de Tonin
Domaine La Bouissière Cuvée Tradition
Brusset Les Hauts de Montmirail
Domaine de Cayron
Clos du Joncuas
Domaine des Espiers Cuvée des Blanches
Domaine Font Sane Cuvée Futée
Domaine Les Gouberts Cuvée Florence

Moulin de la Gardette Cuvée Spéciale
Château Redortier
Château de Saint-Cosme Cuvée Tradition
Château de Saint-Cosme Cuvée Valbelle
Santa Duc Cuvée des Hautes Garrigues
Santa Duc Cuvée Tradition
Tardieu-Laurent Cuvée Vieilles Vignes
Domaine de la Tourade Font des Aieux
Château du Trignon (since 1995)

RATING THE GIGONDAS PRODUCERS

* * * * * *(OUTSTANDING)*

Les Bouissière La Font de Tonin
Les Hauts Montmirail (Daniel Brusset)
Château de Saint-Cosme Cuvée Valbelle

Domaine Santa Duc Cuvée des Hautes
    Garrigues
Tardieu-Laurent Vieilles Vignes

* * * * *(EXCELLENT)*

Domaine des Bosquets Préférence
Domaine la Bouissière Cuvée Tradition
Clos du Joncuas
Clos du Joncuas Cuvée Esprit de Grenache
Cros de la Mure
Domaine de la Garrigue
Domaine les Goubert
Domaine de Longue-Toque
Montirius

Moulin de la Gardette
Moulin de la Gardette Cuvée Ventabren
Domaine les Pallieroudas (Edmonde Burle)
Domaine de Piauger
Domaine Raspail (Dominique Ay)
Château Redortier
Château de Saint-Cosme
Domaine St.-Gayan
Domaine du Terme

* * *(GOOD)*

La Bastide St.-Vincent
Domaine des Bosquets Cuvée Tradition
Domaine de Cassan
Caves des Vignerons de Gigondas
Domaine le Clos des Cazaux
Domaine des Espiers
Domaine de Font-Sane
Domaine de Font-Sane Cuvée Futée
Domaine du Gour de Chaulé
Domaine Grand-Romane
Domaine du Grapillon d'Or
Guigal
Domaine de la Mavette
Château de Montmirail
Notre Dame Les Pallières

L'Oustau Fouquet
Domaine Les Pallières
Domaine du Pesquier
Château Raspail (Meffre family)
Domaine Romane-Machotte
Domaine Roucas de St.-Pierre
Domaine Ste.-Anne
La Soumade
Domaine Les Teyssonières
Domaine Les Teyssonières Cuvée
    Alexandre
Domaine de la Tourade
Domaine des Tourelles
Château du Trignon
Vidal-Fleury

Muscat de Beaumes de Venise at a Glance

Type of wine produced: The appellation is most famous for its sweet *vins doux
                      naturels,* which are essentially fortified sweet wines made

	from the Muscat grape. But dry red, white, and rosé are also produced, some of it excellent.
Grape varieties planted:	All permitted southern Rhône varietals, as well as the only legal plantations of Muscat à Petits Grains in the Rhône Valley (both the white and black variety).
Acres currently under vine:	1,087
Quality level:	Good to exceptional
Aging potential:	2–4 years
General characteristics:	The Muscat is a sweet, alcoholic, extraordinarily perfumed and exotic, rich, decadent dessert wine. The best examples of red wine are classic Côtes du Rhône-Villages with plenty of red and black cherry fruit, peppery, Provençal herb–scented noses, and gutsy, lusty flavors.
Greatest recent vintages:	2001, 2000
Price range:	Muscat de Beaumes de Venise: $15–30
	Côtes du Rhône-Villages Beaumes de Venise red: $10–16
The village's best-kept secret:	The excellent dry red wines produced by Domaine de Fenouillet, Domaine les Goubert, and Château Redortier

RATING THE MUSCAT DE BEAUMES DE VENISE PRODUCERS

***** (OUTSTANDING)

Domaine de Baumalric   Paul Jaboulet-Ainé
Domaine de Durban

**** (EXCELLENT)

Domaine des Bernardins   Domaine de Fenouillet
Chapoutier   Château St.-Sauveur
Domaine de Coyeux   Vidal-Fleury

*** (GOOD)

Cave des Vignerons de Vacqueyras   Vignerons de Beaumes de Venise

Vacqueyras at a Glance

Appellation creation:	August 9, 1990
Type of wine produced:	Red wine represents 95% of the production, with 4% rosé and 1% white.
Grape varieties planted:	Grenache, Syrah, Mourvèdre, and Cinsault for the red and rosé wines, and Grenache Blanc, Clairette, and Bourboulenc for the white wines
Acres currently under vine:	3,211
Quality level:	Very good, and increasingly an appellation that is beginning to explode in quality
Aging potential:	4–12 years
General characteristics:	Powerful, rustic, full-bodied red wines that increasingly compete favorably with Châteauneuf-du-Pape and appear to be surpassing Gigondas!
Greatest recent vintages:	2001, 2000, 1999, 1998
Price range:	$15–20

Aromatic profile: A classic Provençal/Mediterranean nose of *herbes de Provence, garrigue*, red and black fruits, earth, and olives

Textural profile: Unbridled power along with a fleshy mouth-feel make for a substantial and mouth-filling glass of wine.

RATING THE VACQUEYRAS PRODUCERS

* * * * * *(OUTSTANDING)*

Domaine des Amouriers Les Genestes   Sang des Cailloux Cuvée Doucinello
Domaine Le Couroulu Vieilles Vignes   Sang des Cailloux Cuvée Lopy
Sang des Cailloux   Tardieu-Laurent Vieilles Vignes

* * * * *(EXCELLENT)*

Domaine Bouletin Sélécion Michel   Domaine La Garrigue Cuvée
Domaine de la Charbonnière   Traditionnelle
Domaine le Clos des Cazaux   La Monardière Réserve des Deux
Domaine Le Couroulu Cuvée Classique   Monarchs Vieilles Vignes
Féraud-Brunel   Domaine de la Tourade
La Font de Papier   Château des Tours
Domaine La Fourmone   Vidal-Fleury
Domaine La Garrigue Cuvée de   Les Vins de Troubadour (various *cuvées*)
   l'Hostellerie   Les Vins de Vienne La Sillote

* * * *(GOOD)*

La Bastide St.-Vincent   Domaine des Lambertins
Domaine de Boissan   Château de Montmirail
Domaine Chamfort   Domaine de Montvac
Domaine le Clos des Cazaux   Château des Roques
Paul Jaboulet-Ainé   Domaine de Verquière

Tavel at a Glance

Appellation creation: May 15, 1936

Type of wine produced: Dry rosé only—the sole appellation in France to recognize rosé as the only authorized wine

Grape varieties planted: There are nine authorized varieties: Grenache and Cinsault dominate, followed by Clairette, Syrah, Bourboulenc, Mourvèdre, Picpoul, Carignan, and Calitor

Acres currently under vine: 2,340

Quality level: Average to very good rosé wines

Aging potential: 1–3 years

General characteristics: The finest Tavels are dry, full-bodied, and boldly flavored.

Greatest recent vintages: 2001

Price range: $14–22

Aromatic profile: Strawberries, cherries, and a vague scent of Provençal *garrigue*

Textural profile: Dry, sometimes austere, full-bodied wines can taste surprisingly rugged and shocking to those weaned on semi-sweet, soft, flabby, New World rosés.

RATING THE TAVEL PRODUCERS

* * * (GOOD)

Château d'Acqueria   Guigal
Domaine Canto-Perdrix   Domaine Méjan-Taulier
Domaine de Corne Loup   Domaine de la Mordorée
Domaine de la Forcardière   Domaine de Roc Epine
Domaine de la Genestière   Château de Trinquevedel

Lirac at a Glance

Appellation creation:	October 14, 1947
Type of wine produced:	Red, rosé, and white wines, of which 75% of the production is red, 20% rosé, and 5% white
Grape varieties planted:	*Red:* Grenache Noir, Syrah, Mourvèdre, Cinsault, and Carignan; *White:* Grenache Blanc, Clairette, Bourboulenc, Ugni Blanc, Picpoul, Marsanne, Roussanne, and Viognier
Acres currently under vine:	1,037
Quality level:	Mediocre to good, but improving
Aging potential:	2–8 years
General characteristics:	Soft, very fruity, medium-bodied red wines; neutral white wines; exuberantly fresh, fruity rosés (the frugal consumers' Tavel)
Greatest recent vintages:	2001, 2000, 1999, 1998
Price range:	$15–22
Aromatic profile:	Similar to a Côtes du Rhône, with scents of red fruits, spices, and *herbes de Provence*
Textural profile:	Soft, fruity, generally medium-bodied red wines, and relatively innocuous, one-dimensional white wines. The rosés can be excellent, and are not dissimilar from a top Tavel.

The Lirac appellation's most profound wine: Domaine de la Mordorée

RATING THE LIRAC PRODUCERS

* * * * * (OUTSTANDING)

Domaine de la Mordorée Reine des Bois

* * * * (EXCELLENT)

Domaine de Cantegril   Château St.-Roch
Domaine Roger Sabon   Domaine de Ségriès

* * * (GOOD)

Château Boucarut   Domaine de la Forcardière
Domaine Canto-Perdrix   Domaine des Garrigues
Domaine des Causses et de St.-Eymes   Domaine Jean Marchand
Domaine Les Costes   Domaine de Roc Epine

RECENT VINTAGES

2000—This is a year of considerable contrast between the south and the north. There was no problem with ripeness in either region, but in the north, high yields and the growers inattention to crop thinning resulted in a ripe, but superficially styled vintage. From Côte Rôtie through Cornas the wines are attractive, with saturated colors, low acidity, and sweet fruit. But, as the famous advertisement from a few years ago asked, "Where's the beef?" Although there are a few noteworthy exceptions (i.e., the wines of Gérard and Jean-Louis Chave, and Guigal's single-vineyard Côte Rôties), overall the wines lack fat, concentration, and depth. The year 2000 vintage may be a modern-day clone of the similarly styled northern Rhône 1985 vintage. Except for the bigger wines of Hermitage, the 2000 northern Rhônes will be drinkable early and last for 10–15 years.

In the south, Châteauneuf-du-Pape, Gigondas, Vacqueyras, and the surrounding villages of the Côtes du Rhône enjoyed a splendid vintage of great ripeness and concentration. Unlike their siblings to the north, there is no problem with depth or richness in the finest 2000 southern Rhônes. Stylistically they are similar to 1999, with high alcohol, low acidity, and concentrated, ripe, fleshy, sumptuous personalities. It is the third consecutive impressive vintage for this sector. Readers will love these wines, which although different in style, will rival the prodigious 1998s. Most 2000s will be drinkable upon release in 2002. The top Châteuneuf-du-Papes and the most concentrated old-vine *cuvées* of Côtes du Rhône, Gigondas, and Vacqueyras will age well for 15 years.

1999—In nearly a quarter of a century of professional tasting experience, this is the finest Côte Rôtie vintage I have seen. Admittedly, a young generation of growers is pushing quality higher and higher, and finding disappointing wines is not as easy as it was a decade ago. But for pure opulence, concentration, and extraordinarily high levels of glycerin and extract, the 1999 Côte Rôties are exceptional. They are easily the finest vintage for this region since 1978. Oddly, 1999 offered both abundant yields and spectacular quality. In the other appellations, it is unquestionably a top vintage, but perhaps less consistent than in Côte Rôtie. The 1999 Hermitages possess sweet tannin, great ripeness, and opulent, voluptuous textures with plenty of underlying structure. In Crozes-Hermitage, St.-Joseph, and Cornas, quality is generally high, with St.-Joseph being the most consistent. The most inconsistent are Cornas and Condrieu, where yields were high. The white wines of Condrieu lack the concentration of 1998. While there are some impressive efforts from Cornas, the wines generally reveal less concentration, more acidity, and a frustrating inconsistency.

In the south, 1999 will largely be ignored as the increasing throngs of southern Rhône wine enthusiasts drink up their 1998s and flock to buy the 2000 and 2001 vintages, all undeniably great years for the southern Rhône. This excellent vintage will simply be overshadowed by those that surround it. Fine ripeness was achieved in all varietals, with Mourvèdre and Syrah performing better in 1999 than in 1998. While very good, Grenache was slightly less successful, without the saturated fatness, flesh, and complexity of 1998 and 2000. Nevertheless, this is a very fine vintage in Châteauneuf-du-Pape, Gigondas, Vacqueyras, and the villages of Côtes du Rhône. Occasionally, producers who tend to use higher percentages of Mourvèdre and Syrah made better wines than they did in 1998. Elegance and balance are the operative words to describe the southern Rhône's 1999s, a vintage that will get better and better press as it evolves. For now, however, it is a forgotten year given the hype over the surrounding vintages.

1998—In the northern Rhône, a late spring frost severely curtailed yields, particularly on the Côte Rôtie plateau as well as certain sectors of Condrieu, St.-Joseph, Hermitage, and Crozes-Hermitage. Now that the wines are in the bottle, the vintage is excellent, with all the top domaines producing concentrated, ripe, structured, but tannic and closed wines that come closest in style to 1995. There is plenty of character and high quality at the finest estates, but the bottled wines have shut down, requiring at least 5 years (a decade or more for

Hermitage) of cellaring to reveal their character. The tannin is high, but so is the concentration. This is a vintage for patient connoisseurs who have proper storage facilities. While the 1998 Côte Rôties, Hermitages, Crozes-Hermitages, St.-Josephs, and Cornas are very good, they are less successful than their 1999 counterparts. Condrieu enjoyed a fabulous vintage, but those wines should be consumed before the end of 2002.

In the southern Rhône, 1998 is a great vintage that continues to build in stature and majesty. It is a benchmark vintage for Châteauneuf-du-Pape. When I first reported on these wines in my journal *The Wine Advocate* (twelve months after the vintage), I indicated that it was the finest vintage since 1990. However, it is even better than 1990, producing wines with extraordinary balance. Moreover, the 1998 vintage was produced in part by a younger generation of wine-makers dedicated to producing world-class wines. From young hotshots such as Sophie and Karine Armenier (Domaine de Marcoux's Châteauneuf-du-Pape), Vincent Avril (Clos des Papes' Châteauneuf-du-Pape), Louis Barruol (St.-Cosme's Gigondas), Nicolas Boiron (Bosquet des Papes' Châteauneuf-du-Pape), Philippe Bravay (Domaine de Ferrand's Châteauneuf-du-Pape), André Brunel (Les Cailloux's Châteauneuf-du-Pape), Daniel Brunier (Vieux-Télégraphe's Châteauneuf-du-Pape), Gérard Charvin (Charvin's Châteauneuf-du-Pape), Frédéric and Daniel Coulon (Beaurenard's Châteauneuf-du-Pape), Christopher Délorme (La Mordorée's Châteauneuf-du-Pape and Lirac), Jean-Marc Diffonty (Cuvée de Vatican's Châteauneuf-du-Pape), Laurence Féraud (Pégaü's Châteauneuf-du-Pape), Pierre Perrin (Domaine Perrin's Châteauneuf-du-Pape), Christophe Sabon (La Janasse's Châteauneuf-du-Pape), Michel Tardieu (a *négociant* producing wines from all the southern and northern Rhône appellations), Thierry and Jean-Pierre Usseglio (Pierre Usseglio's Châteauneuf-du-Pape), and Jean-Paul Versino (Bois de Boursan's Châteauneuf-du-Pape) have emerged great wines that did not exist in 1990. Multiple tastings of the 1998 Châteauneuf-du-Papes out of bottle (I bought as much as I could afford) have proven that these wines have gained amazing weight and richness, surpassing even their pre-bottling conditions. This is a profound, possibly once-in-a-lifetime vintage to buy in quantity. Moreover, these wines will drink well young or can be cellared for 15–20+ years. As great a vintage as it was for Châteauneuf-du-Pape, the surrounding areas of Gigondas, Vacqueyras, and Côtes du Rhône produced excellent, often outstanding wines, but there is much more variation in quality.

1997—This vintage is gorgeous in the north, with wines of low acidity, outstanding ripeness, concentrated styles, and considerable accessibility. It is undoubtedly a superior vintage in the north. The 1997s may be slightly more irregular given the difficult harvest conditions, but the wines are ripe, low in acidity, and somewhat diluted. They possess many of the characteristics of the 1996s, being forward, fruity, and charming, but they are not intensely concentrated or capable of significant longevity.

DANIEL ET DENIS ALARY

1999	Côtes du Rhône	A	86
2000	Côtes du Rhône-Villages Cairanne	B	87
1999	Côtes du Rhône-Villages Cairanne	B	88
2000	Côtes du Rhône-Villages Cairanne La Font d'Estevenas	C	90
2000	Côtes du Rhône-Villages Cairanne Le Jean de Verde	C	90
2000	Côtes du Rhône-Villages Cairanne Réserve du Vigneron	D	88
1999	La Grange VDP	A	87

Daniel and Denis Alary are superstars of the sun-drenched, windswept Provençal village of Cairanne, a short 30-minute drive northeast of Châteauneuf-du-Pape. They produce some of the richest, most complex and complete wines in the southern Rhône. Even in the light vintages their wines are meritorious. This is a fine source for Côtes du Rhône as well as a reasonably priced *vin de pays*. Other than the *vin de pays*, the Côtes du Rhône (a blend of Grenache and Syrah) and the Côtes du Rhône-Villages Cairanne (a blend of Syrah and Grenache), aged both in tank and oak *foudre* and bottled unfiltered, the estate fashions three prestige *cuvées*, Réserve du Vigneron, La Font d'Estevenas, and a special *cuvée* called Le Jean de Verde, produced from 100% 60-year-old Grenache vines, all of which were destemmed, the debut vintage of which is 2000.

The 2000 Côtes du Rhône-Villages Cairanne (80% Grenache and 20% Syrah) reveals the telltale Provençal *garrigue* (a mélange of herbs and earth) characteristic in addition to abundant quantities of pure cherry fruit. It is a medium-bodied, elegant Côtes du Rhône to drink during its first several years of life. A blend of 70% Grenache and 30% Mourvèdre, the 2000 Côtes du Rhône-Villages Réserve du Vigneron exhibits a dark ruby color, medium body, and clean, sweet berry fruit mixed with cherries, earth, and licorice. It is a fresh, stylish effort with excellent definition as well as length. Enjoy it over the next 4–5 years. The exceptional 2000 Côtes du Rhône-Villages La Font d'Estevenas is a blend of 60% Syrah and 40% Grenache. It offers ripe Syrah's classic crème de cassis character, surprisingly good acidity for the vintage, a lush mid-palate, fine definition, deep, medium- to full-bodied flavors, and well-integrated tannin, acidity, and alcohol. It should drink well for 5–8 years. Alary's new *cuvée*, the 2000 Côtes du Rhône-Villages Le Jean de Verde (14.5% alcohol; 300 cases), reveals a generous, kirsch-scented bouquet, elegant, sweet fruit on the attack, good underlying acidity, surprising focus as well as zestiness, and a medium-bodied, attractive finish. It should drink well for 4–5 years.

All of Domaine Alary's 1999s averaged slightly higher alcohol than their superb 1998s. The medium ruby-colored 1999 La Grange VDP (a blend of 50% Grenache, 20% Syrah, and 30% Cabernet Sauvignon) offers aromas of *herbes de Provence*, black cherry liqueur, pepper, and spice. Medium-bodied, richly fruity, spicy, and supple, it is meant to be consumed over the next 2–3 years. The 1999 Côtes du Rhône (a blend of 80% Grenache and 20% Syrah) was muted the day I tasted it. While it revealed a dark ruby/purple color as well as fine density and ripeness, it displayed an inexpressive character. It may merit a higher score in the future, but because of its present monolithic state, it was scored conservatively. The 1999 Côtes du Rhône-Villages Cairanne achieved nearly 14% natural alcohol. It offers a peppery, sweet black cherry nose, medium- to full-bodied flavors, a supple texture, and admirable body as well as depth. It should drink well for 5–6 years.

DOMAINE DE L'AMEILLAUD

2000	Côtes du Rhône	B	86
2000	Côtes du Rhône-Villages Cairanne	B	88
1999	Côtes du Rhône-Villages Cairanne	B	87
2000	VDP du Vaucluse	B	85
1999	VDP du Vaucluse	B	86

These wines are available for a song and represent excellent values.

The inexpensive 2000 VDP du Vaucluse (a blend of 60% Grenache, 20% Syrah, and 20% Carignan) reveals a medium ruby color along with a charming berry- and strawberry-scented perfume, medium body, a soft texture, and an easily understood personality. Enjoy it over the next 1–2 years. More rustic is the deep ruby/purple-colored 2000 Côtes du Rhône. It possesses abundant quantities of black cherry fruit intertwined with pepper, earth, and spice. Drink this medium-bodied, well-made 2000 over the next 2–3 years. Produced from a blend of 65% Grenache, 30% Syrah, and the rest Carignan and Mourvèdre, the 2000 Côtes du Rhône-Villages Cairanne boasts a deep ruby/purple color as well as an excellent nose of blackberry and cherry fruit, medium to full body, low acidity, and admirable purity and texture. Drink it over the next 3–4 years.

The delicious, straightforward, dark ruby-colored 1999 VDP du Vaucluse displays the vintage's ripe black cherry fruit in a medium-bodied, silky-textured format. With surprising depth and length, it should drink well for 2 years. Revealing a denser, ruby/purple color, the 1999 Côtes du Rhône-Villages Cairanne exhibits more blackberry, plum, and cherry fruit. It is medium- to full-bodied, sweet, velvety-textured, and capable of lasting 4–5 years.

DOMAINE DES AMOURIERS

1999	Vacqueyras Les Genestes	C	90
1998	Vacqueyras Les Genestes	C	89+
1999	VDP Les Hautes Terrasses	B	(87–88)
1998	VDP Les Hautes Terrasses	B	86

This has long been one of my favorite Vacqueyras properties as well as a reference point for the appellation. I have been remiss in not covering vintages since the mid-1990s, and tasting this estate's wines recently was a treat.

The 100% Syrah 1999 Vin de Pays Les Hautes Terrasses is a rustic effort loaded with black fruit, glycerin, and low tannin. While it will never be complex, it should be long-lived given its intensity and richness. Yet this VDP is best consumed during its exuberant, robust youthfulness. The 1998 Vin de Pays Les Hautes Terrasses displays more rugged tannin in its deep, spicy, chewy personality. Both offer plenty of spicy, peppery, cherry-flavored fruit.

The star at this domaine is the Vacqueyras Les Genestes. The opaque purple/black-colored 1999 Vacqueyras Les Genestes offers a gorgeous bouquet of roasted herbs, grilled meats, blackberries, and smoke. Full-bodied, with supple tannin and loads of concentration, this is a super Vacqueyras. Like the 1998, it is a blend of 50% Grenache, 48% Syrah, and 2% Mourvèdre. Anticipated maturity: now–2012. The 1998 Vacqueyras Les Genestes could turn out to be as fine as the 1999, but it has more tannin, power, and substance on the palate. In addition to the 1999's characteristics, it reveals licorice, fennel, and underbrush among the black fruits, leather, and earth. Both wines are very pure and substantial. Anticipated maturity: now–2012.

DOMAINE D'ANDEZON

2000	Côtes du Rhône Syrah Vieilles Vignes	A	89
1999	Côtes du Rhône Syrah Vieilles Vignes	A	89
1998	Côtes du Rhône Syrah Vieilles Vignes	A	89

A reliable offering in many vintages, this 100% Syrah tank-fermented and aged *cuvée* is selected by the American importer and bottled unfiltered. It is an excellent value that emerges from a well-run cooperative south of Avignon. I just finished my last magnum of 1995, which was still youthful and full of rich blackberry fruit.

The dense ruby/purple-colored 2000 Côtes du Rhône Syrah Vieilles Vignes offers a sweet perfume of jammy cassis and licorice. Supple, fleshy, full-bodied, and loaded with fat and fruit, it will drink well for 3–4 years, although bottles of the 1995 in my cellar are holding up beautifully. The 1999 Côtes du Rhône Syrah Vieilles Vignes possesses gorgeously pure, rich, blackberry and cassis fruit, medium to full body, low acidity, and ripe, sweet tannin. Drink this fruit bomb over the next 3–4 years for its gutsy exuberance.

The sumptuous 1998 Côtes du Rhône Syrah Vieilles Vignes is ripe and surprisingly powerful. It exhibits a dark ruby/purple color as well as copious quantities of cassis fruit and a juicy, fat texture. This hedonistic fruit bomb is a savory, mouth-filling Côtes du Rhône that offers outstanding quality/price rapport. Enjoy it over the next 2 years.

DOMAINE LES APHILLANTHES

2000	Côtes du Rhône-Villages Cuvée du Cros	D	(91–93)
1999	Côtes du Rhône-Villages Cuvée du Cros	D	91
2000	Côtes du Rhône-Villages Cuvée des Galets	D	90

1999	Côtes du Rhône-Villages Cuvée des Galets	D	(91–93)
2000	Côtes du Rhône-Villages Cuvée des Trois Cépages	D	92
1999	Côtes du Rhône-Villages Cuvée des Trois Cépages	D	91
2000	Côtes du Rhône-Villages Cuvée Vieilles Vignes	D	91

This estate in Travaillan is fashioning spectacularly powerful, concentrated Rhônes that will be hugely successful. Quantities are relatively small. All of these wines are bottled without filtration, and they may be the richest Côtes du Rhônes I have tasted. Although they are expensive for wines of this appellation, they still represent great values because they are comparable to the finest Gigondas and Châteauneuf-du-Papes. They are all stunningly concentrated, brilliant examples from owner Daniel Boulle.

For starters, the 2000 Côtes du Rhône-Villages Cuvée des Trois Cépages (equal parts Grenache, Syrah, and Mourvèdre) offers an opaque purple color along with a gorgeous perfume of sweet cassis and blackberry fruit, full body, remarkable purity, and considerable power. Given its concentration, it will easily evolve for a decade or more, but I suspect its low acidity will cause most purchasers to consume it earlier. It is very impressive! The dense purple-colored 2000 Côtes du Rhône-Villages Cuvée des Galets (a blend of 60% Grenache, 20% Syrah, and 20% Mourvèdre from tiny yields) is a blockbuster Côtes du Rhône, revealing sweet, jammy blackberry and cherry fruit, a succulent, open-knit texture, full body, and wonderful opulence. It is capable of evolving for a decade. The black/purple-colored 2000 Côtes du Rhône-Villages Cuvée du Cros (100% Syrah) offers notes of crème de cassis, minerals, licorice, and chocolate. Full-bodied, super-concentrated, and tannic, as well as hugely extracted, this effort is even bigger and richer than Château Rayas's famed Fonsalette Côtes du Rhône Cuvée Syrah. The Cuvée du Cros should be at its prime in 4–5 years and last for 15+. It is an amazing tour de force Syrah from the southern Rhône.

The 2000 Côtes du Rhône-Villages Cuvée Vieilles Vignes's sweet nose of black raspberry liqueur is not dissimilar from certain Châteauneuf-du-Papes. It is medium- to full-bodied, pure, and impeccably balanced. In fact, the longer this wine sat in the glass, the more it resembled a grand cru Musigny. Although lighter than its siblings, it is wonderfully cerebral, pure, fresh, and ideal for drinking over the next 8–10 years.

The 1999 Côtes du Rhône-Villages Cuvée des Trois Cépages (equal parts Grenache, Syrah, and Mourvèdre) is an opaque purple-colored effort with a meaty, licorice, and smoky-scented nose, sweet blackberry and cassis fruit flavors, good acidity, full body, and impressive concentration as well as length. It achieved 14.7% natural alcohol and will easily evolve for 10, perhaps 15, years. The opaque black/purple-colored 1999 Cuvée des Galets (60% Grenache, 20% Syrah, and 20% Mourvèdre from yields of 20–22 hectoliters per hectare) is a softer effort, with black cherry, licorice, smoke, dried herb, and roasted meat aromas presented in a robust, flavorful format. Ideally, it should be given several years of cellaring and is a candidate for 12–20 years of aging. Lastly, the 1999 Cuvée du Cros (100% Syrah from yields of 17–18 hectoliters per hectare) reveals a similar black/purple color, but more roasted herb, chocolate, and espresso notes in its blackberry/kirsch-scented bouquet. Super-extracted, rich, powerful, and full-bodied, this 1999 will be at its peak between 2003–2015. These are very impressive, unfiltered Côtes du Rhône *cuvées* with a style not dissimilar from, but even more concentrated than, some of the blockbuster vintages of Château de Fonsalette. Don't miss these exceptional wines!

DOMAINE MAX AUBERT

| 1999 | Châteauneuf-du-Pape Domaine de la Présidente | D | (85–86) |
| 1998 | Châteauneuf-du-Pape Domaine de la Présidente | D | 85 |

None of these offerings displayed as much concentration or intensity as most of their peers. However, these are not Max Aubert's top *cuvées*, but rather his traditional blends. The 1999 Châteauneuf-du-Pape Domaine de la Présidente exhibits a dark ruby color in addition to spicy, herb-tinged, peppery fruit, medium body, and a soft finish. It should drink well for 4–5 years. The 1998 Châteauneuf-du-Pape Domaine de la Présidente is a solid, competent, medium garnet-colored effort with a soft underbelly, plenty of spice and herbs, but not a great deal of depth or texture. It should be consumed over the next 3–4 years.

PAUL AUTARD

2000	Châteauneuf-du-Pape	C	(88–89)
1999	Châteauneuf-du-Pape	C	87
1998	Châteauneuf-du-Pape	C	89
1997	Châteauneuf-du-Pape	D	85
2000	Châteauneuf-du-Pape Cuvée La Côte Ronde	D	(91–93)
1999	Châteauneuf-du-Pape Cuvée La Côte Ronde	D	90
1998	Châteauneuf-du-Pape Cuvée La Côte Ronde	D	92
1997	Châteauneuf-du-Pape Cuvée La Côte Ronde	D	87

There are two Châteauneuf-du-Pape *cuvées* produced at this excellent estate situated in the northern section of the appellation, not far from Château Beaucastel. The regular *cuvée* is a softer, fruitier wine that is meant to be drunk young. The Cuvée La Côte Ronde, made from a five-acre parcel of 70–95-year-old vines, is given a lengthier fermentation/maceration and aged for 18 months, with 50% of the production kept in new-oak casks for 12 months and then assembled. Autard has produced very fine wines over recent years, their finest in 1998, followed by top-notch performances in both 1999 and 2000.

Full-bodied, with glycerin, sweet blackberry and cherry fruit, smoked herb, meats, and spicy notes, the excellent 2000 Châteauneuf-du-Pape is a dark ruby-colored effort with plenty of flesh and succulence. It should drink well for 8–12 years. The opaque ruby/purple-colored 2000 Châteauneuf-du-Pape Cuvée La Côte Ronde displays an overlay of tannin along with huge quantities of glycerin, licorice-imbued black cherry and cassis fruit, a creamy texture, and a long, 30-second finish. This serious, concentrated, muscular Châteauneuf-du-Pape requires 2–3 years of cellaring, and it should keep for 15–18 years.

The 1999 Châteauneuf-du-Pape is an atypically spicy (allspice, cinnamon), peppery, earthy effort with abundant quantities of black cherries. This easy to drink, medium-bodied, soft, round, Châteauneuf should be consumed over the next 7–8 years. The 1999 Château-neuf-du-Pape Cuvée La Côte Ronde exhibits aromas of smoked Provençal herbs, black cherry and berry fruit, an unctuous texture, and a lush, complex, medium- to full-bodied style with notes of mincemeat. With outstanding concentration and purity as well as an up-front style, it should be drunk over the next 12–14 years.

Some readers will award both 1998s outstanding ratings, and I can understand why. The 1998 Châteauneuf-du-Pape offers a terrific nose of spice box, cherry jam, pepper, and assorted berries. It is medium- to full-bodied, with plenty of glycerin, moderately sweet tannin, a fat mid-palate, and a dense, thick, powerful finish. Already accessible, it promises to last for another 10–15 years. The sensational, opaque plum/garnet-colored 1998 Châteauneuf-du-Pape Cuvée La Côte Ronde displays an expansive nose of tobacco, charcoal, smoke, kirsch, and blackberries. This full-bodied, large-scaled Châteauneuf possesses sweet tannin, low acidity, and a boatload of glycerin. Anticipated maturity: now–2016.

The 1997 Châteauneuf-du-Pape reveals an evolved medium plum color, a sweet, spicy, cherry-scented nose, good fruit, medium body, and a pleasing, pure, elegant, spicy finish. It is ideal for drinking over the next several years. The 1997 Châteauneuf-du-Pape Cuvée La Côte Ronde offers kirsch, cedar, and spice aromas, and sweet black cherry fruit intermixed with coffee and fruitcake smells. A juicy, pure, expansive, medium- to full-bodied wine, it may turn out to be as good as, perhaps better than, the 1996. It should be consumed over the next 5–6+ years.

RENÉ BALTHAZAR

2000	Cornas	D	(88–90)
1999	Cornas	D	81
1998	Cornas	D	87

What a contrast in styles between the 2000 and the 1999! The 2000 Cornas is a huge improvement for what has been an underwhelming source of Cornas over recent vintages. An impressive, dense opaque purple color is accompanied by classic Syrah aromas of new saddle leather, jammy blackberry fruit, licorice, and minerals. It possesses the vintage's hallmark characteristics of low acidity and a corpulent, fat style, but there is more mid-palate and length than in many northern Rhônes. Anticipated maturity: now–2014. The acidic, austere, lean 1999 Cornas lacks fruit, but does have plenty of appellation authenticity. It will last for a decade, but do not expect a great deal of pleasure. Along with the 2000, the 1998 Cornas is undoubtedly one of the finest wines I have tasted from Balthazar. Produced from hillside vineyards, this low acid, black/purple-colored Cornas offers gorgeously silky, cassis, smoke-infused blackberry fruit with underbrush-like notions in the background. Full-bodied and concentrated, with no rusticity or hardness, this is a sumptuous Cornas to drink over the next 10–12 years.

GILLES BARGE

2000	Côte Rôtie Côte Brune	D	(86–88)
1999	Côte Rôtie Côte Brune	D	89
1998	Côte Rôtie Côte Brune	D	87
1997	Côte Rôtie Côte Brune	D	87
2000	Côte Rôtie Cuvée du Plessy	D	(83–85)
1999	Côte Rôtie Cuvée du Plessy	D	85
1998	Côte Rôtie Cuvée du Plessy	D	87
1997	Côte Rôtie Cuvée du Plessy	D	85

Gilles Barge, the president of the Côte Rôtie syndicate, remains a staunch protector of the appellation's traditional winemaking style. His traditionally made Côte Rôties are to be admired. One of the few growers to continue producing wines with all the stems included, he appears to utilize more *barriques* for his Côte Brune bottling as opposed to the lighter Cuvée du Plessy. This latter wine (made primarily from Côte Blonde fruit, with some Viognier in the blend) is unquestionably one of the more elegant, aromatic expressions of the appellation. Barge calls it his *cuvée du plaisir.* Not only do some buyers prefer this style, it is important that Côte Rôtie's vignerons offer a diversity of tastes to the public.

Barge's 2000 Côte Rôtie Côte Brune exhibits smoky, olive, and black fruit characteristics, medium body, soft tannin, low acidity, and a straightforward style. Consume it during its first 8–10 years of life. The soft, fruity, light- to medium-bodied 2000 Côte Rôtie Cuvée du Plessy displays a stemmy, green/vegetal character.

The well-made 1999 Côte Rôtie Côte Brune offers new *barrique* notes as well as aromas of herbs, earth, leather, and aged beef. An herbaceous character reveals evidence of stems. There is decent acidity, medium body, sweet fruit on the attack, and a moderately long finish. Give it 1–2 years of cellaring and drink it over the following decade. The earthy, stemmy 1999 Côte Rôtie Cuvée du Plessy is full of spice and herbs, with little evidence of cassis. Drink it over the next 2–4 years.

The 1998 Côte Rôtie Côte Brune displays the stemmy, earthy herbaceousness that is the result of fermentation with 100% stems, in addition to high acidity for the vintage, sweet blackberry and raspberry fruit, and notes of cured olives. Medium-bodied, with moderate tannin, it should drink well for a decade. The 1998 Côte Rôtie Cuvée du Plessy is a soft, fruity effort made in a straightforward style with notions of dried herbs, black raspberries, and cherries. With medium weight, good sweetness on the attack, and a soft finish, it should be consumed over the next 4–5 years.

The 1997 Côte Rôtie Côte Brune reveals more structure and a deeper ruby color than the special *cuvée*, as well as earthy, black raspberry, licorice, and truffle notes, medium body, and moderate tannin. This very good, possibly excellent Côte Rôtie should be at its finest before 2008. The medium ruby-colored (with some garnet at the edge) 1997 Côte Rôtie Cuvée du Plessy exhibits an herbaceous, peppery nose with notes of bacon fat in a soft, round, perfumed style. This evolved, open-knit, soft Côte Rôtie should be consumed within its first 5–6 years of life.

LUCIEN BARROT

2000 Châteauneuf-du-Pape	C	(87–88)
1999 Châteauneuf-du-Pape	C	87
1998 Châteauneuf-du-Pape	C	89
1997 Châteauneuf-du-Pape	C	(85–87)

I recently drank my last bottle of Barrot's sumptuous 1981 Châteauneuf-du-Pape and thought how remarkably consistent his wines have been, yet he rarely gets the accolades he deserves. Readers unhappy with the ever-increasing high prices of wines would be well advised to check out this source for very good Châteauneuf-du-Pape. However, recent vintages of Barrot have not hit the highlights of earlier efforts.

The surprisingly evolved, dark plum/garnet color of the 2000 Châteauneuf-du-Pape is followed by excellent sweet, jammy black cherry/prune-like aromas. Medium- to full-bodied, open-knit, user-friendly, and plump, it will drink well for 6–8 years.

The 1999 Châteauneuf-du-Pape displays an evolved ruby color with ample pink at the rim. It is a medium-bodied, peppery, spicy Châteauneuf offering notes of spicy, Provençal herbs intermixed with *garrigue* and kirsch. Consume it over the next 5–6 years as it does not possess the stuffing required for extended cellaring.

The complex, earth, plum, herb, cherry, and currant-scented 1998 Châteauneuf-du-Pape is a more complete, richer, layered wine. It reveals considerable structure at present (it was just bottled), with moderate levels of tannin, a spicy, animal-like characteristic, and flavors of black cherry, kirsch, and incense. It has the potential to improve for 5–6 years and drink well for 12–14 years. As for the 1997 Châteauneuf-du-Pape, it is undoubtedly a successful wine for this vintage. The color is medium to dark ruby, and the wine offers up iodine, licorice, roasted herb, and black cherry scents intermixed with hints of Provençal herbs. Spicy, fat, and juicy, with low acidity, an element of *sur-maturité,* and a lusty finish, this smooth, silky-textured Châteauneuf-du-Pape demonstrates what could be achieved if growers did not over-extract in this vintage. It should drink well for 3–4 years.

DOMAINE DE LA BEARDIERE

1999 Côtes du Rhône	A	85
1998 Côtes du Rhône Cuvée de l'An 2000	A	89

The 1999 Côtes du Rhône (a blend of 60% Grenache and 40% Syrah) is made in a soft, light- to medium-bodied style with copious quantities of spicy, peppery, berry fruit. It is a tasty, cleanly made, pleasant Côtes du Rhône that will offer uncritical quaffing over the next 1–2 years. The 1998 Côtes du Rhône Cuvée de l'An 2000 is a stunner. This 400-case lot should be embraced by readers looking for a full-bodied blast of Grenache and Syrah fruit presented in an exuberant, concentrated style with no hard edges. A blend of 70% Grenache and 30% Syrah, it possesses oodles of fat, chewy, black cherry and berry fruit flavors, an opulent texture, a heady alcohol content (14.5% natural), and a lusty finish. It is an expressive, gutsy, hedonistic Côtes du Rhône to drink over the next 2–3 years.

CHÂTEAU DE BEAUCASTEL

2000	Châteauneuf-du-Pape	D	(92–94)
1999	Châteauneuf-du-Pape	D	91+
1998	Châteauneuf-du-Pape	D	95
1997	Châteauneuf-du-Pape	D	(89–91)
2000	Châteauneuf-du-Pape Blanc	D	94
1999	Châteauneuf-du-Pape Blanc	D	95
1998	Châteauneuf-du-Pape Blanc	D	89
1997	Châteauneuf-du-Pape Blanc	D	93
1996	Châteauneuf-du-Pape Blanc	D	89
2000	Châteauneuf-du-Pape Hommage à Jacques Perrin	EEE	(96–100)
1999	Châteauneuf-du-Pape Hommage à Jacques Perrin	EEE	96+
1998	Châteauneuf-du-Pape Hommage à Jacques Perrin	EEE	100
1997	Châteauneuf-du-Pape Roussanne Vieilles Vignes	EE	95
1996	Châteauneuf-du-Pape Roussanne Vieilles Vignes	EE	92
1995	Châteauneuf-du-Pape Roussanne Vieilles Vignes	EE	96
2000	Châteauneuf-du-Pape Roussanne Vieilles Vignes Blanc	EE	96
1999	Châteauneuf-du-Pape Roussanne Vieilles Vignes Blanc	EE	97
1998	Châteauneuf-du-Pape Roussanne Vieilles Vignes Blanc	EE	92
2000	Côtes du Rhône Coudoulet	C	(90–92)
1999	Côtes du Rhône Coudoulet	C	90
1998	Côtes du Rhône Coudoulet	C	90
2000	Côtes du Rhône Coudoulet Blanc	C	88
1999	Côtes du Rhône Coudoulet Blanc	C	87
1998	Côtes du Rhône Coudoulet Blanc	C	88
1998	Côtes du Rhône Perrin Réserve Blanc	B	86

François and Jean-Pierre Perrin continue to produce both white and red reference point wines from Beaucastel's vineyards, located in the northeast quadrant of the Châteauneuf-du-Pape appellation. Following its spectacular success in 1998, Château de Beaucastel has produced fabulous wines in both 1999 and 2000. The 1999s reveal fresher acidity, more delineation, and will undoubtedly close down in the bottle, as most young Beaucastels do. The exception to this rule may be the 2000s, which possess the lowest acidity as well as the ripest, fleshiest, most accessible styles produced at Beaucastel in many years.

A less expensive introduction to this estate's wines is their superb Côtes du Rhône. The 2000 Côtes du Rhône Coudoulet is a luscious, richly fruity offering with considerable fat as well as texture. Revealing a dense purple color along with terrific aromatics of licorice and cassis, this full-bodied, low-acid effort will no doubt be bottled earlier than usual to preserve its fruit and freshness. Although it will not be long-lived, it will provide delicious drinking for a decade. A delicious blend of 30% Viognier, 30% Marsanne, 30% Bourboulenc, and 10% Clairette that sees no new oak, the 2000 Côtes du Rhône Coudoulet Blanc offers exotic ripe apricot and floral scents, fat, low acid, flavors, good freshness, and abundant fruit. Given the powerful, low-acid style of the 2000 whites, it should be consumed over the next 2–3 years. The exceptional, light gold-colored 2000 Châteauneuf-du-Pape Blanc was not put through malolactic fermentation (the first vintage since 1995 where malolactic was not done) because of extremely low acidity. It exhibits a bouquet of crushed currants, quince, honeysuckle, citrus, and butter. Evolved, rich, and full-bodied, with a sensational texture as well as richness, this blend of 80% Roussanne and 20% Grenache Blanc, fermented in *cuves* (80%) and barrels (20%), requires drinking during its first 5–6 years of life given its fragile acid balance. The same can be said for the blockbuster 2000 Châteauneuf-du-Pape Roussanne Vieilles Vignes Blanc. Representing the essence of Roussanne, it is extremely full-bodied, super-concentrated, and unctuously textured. This is Le Montrachet of the southern Rhône Valley. Its honeyed floral, marmalade, and buttery characteristics are somewhat fragile, so consumption over the next 5–6 years is warranted.

Superripe blackberry and cassis fruit dominate the 2000 Châteauneuf-du-Pape aromatics. Reminiscent of the fuller, beefier version of 1985, this low-acid, accessible Beaucastel is likely to be bottled earlier than normal according to François Perrin. A classic blend of 30% Grenache, 30% Mourvèdre, 10% Syrah, 10% Counoise, with the remainder miscellaneous varietals, this deep ruby/purple-colored 2000 possesses a sweet nose dominated by black fruits, loads of glycerin, full body, and superb purity. It will be atypically delicious young, yet will last 15–20 years. Produced from the same blend as the 1999, the spectacular 2000 Châteauneuf-du-Pape Hommage à Jacques Perrin is even more opulent, with unreal levels of glycerin in addition to a staggering bouquet of black fruits, new saddle leather, licorice, underbrush, truffles, roasted herbs, and meats. Fabulously dense, with lower acidity than the 1999, it saturates the palate with sweet fruit, glycerin, and pleasure. A candidate for perfection, the 2000 should be accessible upon release, but keep for 20–25 years. Anticipated maturity: 2004–2025. Both the 1999 and 2000 represent the essence of Châteauneuf-du-Pape as well as Beaucastel.

The 1999 Côtes du Rhône Coudoulet Blanc (a blend of 30% Viognier, 30% Marsanne, 30% Bourboulenc, and 10% Clairette) is a medium-bodied, elegant wine with crisp notes of citrus, orange skin, and white peaches. This stylish white wine will keep for 4–5+ years because of its refreshing acidity. Readers seeking white Beaucastels for long-term aging should check out the 1999 Châteauneuf-du-Pape Blanc. It offers a sensational bouquet, but its acid profile results in more delineation as well as greater potential for longevity. Full, concentrated, and layered, it will drink well for 10–15 years. A singular effort of great concentration, the 1999 Châteauneuf-du-Pape Roussanne Vieilles Vignes Blanc exhibits honeysuckle, marmalade, rose petal, and acacia flower characteristics along with immense body, high glycerin, and good acidity. It can be drunk now, but promises to last for 12–15 years. These wines are idiosyncratic in aging terms, offering gorgeous drinking for a couple of years after bottling, then shutting down and taking on an oxidized, fino sherry–like style, only to reemerge at age 8–10 with fresh, vibrant, even more complex personalities.

The slightly acidic 1999 Côtes du Rhône Coudoulet offers aromas of blackberry/cassis fruit infused with licorice, medium to full body, and more noticeable Mourvèdre (leather, tree bark, and spice notes). This supple 1999 is a candidate of 10–15 years of cellaring. As are most Coudoulet vintages, it is a blend of 30% Mourvèdre, 30% Grenache, 20% Syrah, and 20% Cinsault, all aged in *foudre* prior to being bottled unfiltered.

The prodigious 1999 Châteauneuf-du-Pape boasts aromas of blackberry fruit intermixed with cassis, licorice, roasted meats, leather, and truffles. While it does not possess the fat or precociousness of the 1998 or 2000, it displays more definition and elegance. This full-bodied, concentrated, classic Beaucastel is built along the lines of the 1995 and 1990. Anticipated maturity: 2007–2025.

The 1999 Châteauneuf-du-Pape Hommage à Jacques Perrin, a classic blend of 60% Mourvèdre, 20% Grenache, 10% Syrah, and 10% Counoise, possesses equal potential to the 1998. Aged in *foudre* prior to being bottled without filtration, it represents the essence of Beaucastel's distinctive and atypical Mourvèdre-dominated style of Châteauneuf-du-Pape. Its inky/black/purple color is accompanied by a fabulous perfume of licorice, smoke, truffles, tapenade, blackberries, and cassis. Extremely full-bodied, with masses of extract, high tannin, and a structured, long finish (lasting nearly a minute), this sumptuous effort requires 6–7 years of bottle age. It should keep for 25–35 years. Given its acid profile, this offering is a candidate for closing down sooner rather than later.

The 1998 Côtes du Rhône Perrin Réserve Blanc is dominated by the white clone of Grenache, and also contains 20% Viognier, which is evident in its exotic, honeysuckle/

apricot-scented nose. It is a chunky, husky, dry white to enjoy over the next 1–2 years. The 1998 Côtes du Rhône Coudoulet Blanc (30% Marsanne, 30% Bourboulenc, 30% Viognier, and 10% Clairette) is a rich, honeyed offering with notions of white fruits, excellent purity, medium to full body, and a fleshy finish. It should drink well for 3–4 years, but should evolve for a decade. It is no secret that the finest dry white wines of the southern Rhône are Beaucastel's Châteauneuf-du-Papes. The 1998 Châteauneuf-du-Pape Blanc (80% Roussanne, 15% Grenache, and 5% Picardin) is a rich, full-bodied, powerful white with notes of honeysuckle, rose petal, cinnamon, and oranges. The 1998 is more restrained, and in need of several years of cellaring. These wines possess uncommon longevity (a 1980 tasted at Beaucastel in June was remarkably fresh and vigorous), so do not be surprised to see the 1998 evolve slowly and last for two decades. The Montrachet of the southern Rhône is unquestionably the Perrins' old-vine Roussanne *cuvée*. The 1998 Châteauneuf-du-Pape Roussanne Vieilles Vignes Blanc may not be as ostentatious or concentrated as the 1997, 1996, and 1995, but it is an extremely impressive wine with aromas and flavors of grapefruit, orange marmalade, honey, and white flowers. Full-bodied, dense, and super-concentrated, this is a stunningly pure winemaking tour de force that admirably demonstrates what can be achieved in selected *terroirs* of the southern Rhône. It should age beautifully for 20 years.

The open 1998 Côtes du Rhône Coudoulet is dominated by the warmth and glycerin of the Grenache component. A dark ruby/purple color is followed by a jammy, sweet nose of black fruits, pepper, and spice. In the mouth, cherry jam emerges, along with a chewy, long finish. This 1998 will benefit from another 1–2 years of cellaring, and should keep for 12–15 years.

More accessible is the spectacular 1998 Châteauneuf-du-Pape. This effort includes more Grenache (40%) in the final blend, as well as 20% Mourvèdre, 10% Syrah, 10% Counoise, and the balance from other authorized grape varietals. It is an explosively rich, remarkably flattering Beaucastel, even after bottling. Most Beaucastels have a tendency to shut down completely and not reemerge for 6–10 years. Bottled early in the summer, the 1998 is flamboyant, no doubt because of the larger than normal percentage of Grenache. It boasts explosive richness, thick, juicy blackberry and kirsch, smoke, licorice, roasted meats, and truffles. The acidity seems low (analytically it is the same as 1999), and the wine fat, full-bodied, and intense. It will be hard to stay away from this wine, even though it will evolve for 25–30 years. Could it turn out to be similar to the 1981 rather than the 1989?

The 1998 Châteauneuf-du-Pape Hommage à Jacques Perrin contains an atypically high percentage of Grenache (60%), in addition to 20% Mourvèdre, 10% Syrah, and 10% Counoise. It is one of the most voluptuous, opulently textured Beaucastel offerings I have ever tasted. Unlike previous examples of Jacques Perrin, which all required a decade of cellaring, the 1998 can be drunk in 2–3 years. It possesses huge levels of glycerin, layers of succulent black cherry and berry fruit, gorgeous purity as well as Châteauneuf-du-Pape's quintessential flavors of herbs, saddle leather, coffee, truffles, and black cherry jam. This massive wine will provide awesome drinking in several years and last for 25–30 years.

François Perrin said 1997 was a difficult vintage in the northern sector of Châteauneuf-du-Pape. After damaging spring frosts, there was a major hailstorm, which significantly cut yields. August was exceptionally rainy, and the early ripening varietals (Syrah and Cinsault) were affected by *pourriture*. At Beaucastel, the red varietal harvest was finished by October 15, and in spite of the disappointments with Syrah and Cinsault, they were pleased with their later ripening old-vine Grenache, Mourvèdre, and Counoise.

The 1997 Châteauneuf-du-Pape Blanc is a blend of 80% Roussanne, 15% Grenache Blanc, and 5% diverse white varietals. 1997 was an excellent vintage for Châteauneuf-du-Pape Blanc, and this wine reveals the bold, fleshy, sappy, full-bodied fruit so evident in the vintage. The 1997 exhibits plenty of honeyed citrus and floral (rose) scents, an unctuous texture, good glycerin, and heady alcohol in the long, luscious finish. This impressively endowed Châteauneuf is ideal for drinking over the next decade or more. The 1997

Châteauneuf-du-Pape Roussanne Vieilles Vignes (100% Roussanne from 50-year-old vines) could easily be called the Montrachet or Chevalier-Montrachet of Châteauneuf-du-Pape. This *cuvée* has been remarkable in the past, and the 1997 is spectacular. It reveals more definition than the regular bottling, as well as spectacular concentration, a viscous texture, honeyed floral and citrusy-like flavors, full body, and a finish that goes on for 40–50 seconds. A quintessential Roussanne, it is a great example of the heights this unheralded varietal can achieve. The 1997 should drink well for two decades or more. There is significantly less wine in 1997, which is a shame as it is a forward style of wine for this estate, which tends to produce classic *vin de garde* wines that often require years of bottle age. Yields for the 1997 Châteauneuf-du-Pape were tiny, averaging 22 hectoliters per hectare, and the wine is one of the most seductive and forward young Beaucastels I have tasted since the 1985. The blend was 35% Mourvèdre, 30% Grenache, 10% Counoise, 5% Syrah, 5% Cinsault, and the rest other southern Rhône varietals. The deep ruby color is accompanied by forward, attractive aromatics consisting of black raspberries, cherries, licorice, floral, and herb scents. The wine is fruit-driven, with less structure than usual, but luscious cassis, licorice, and blackberries inundate the palate with no hard edges. A seductive, supple-textured, medium- to full-bodied Beaucastel, this wine should drink well young and last for 15 or more years.

The 1996 *cuvées* of white Châteauneuf-du-Pape contain more noticeable acidity than the 1997s. The 1996 Châteauneuf-du-Pape Blanc (70% Roussanne, 20% Grenache Blanc, and 10% various varietals) offers a citrusy, spicy nose, medium body, tangy acidity (a hallmark of this vintage), and good weight and richness. It has already begun to close down and is in need of 2–3 years of cellaring. It should keep for 15 or more years. The 1996 Châteauneuf-du-Pape Roussanne Vieilles Vignes was extremely closed, but it is loaded with extract. With coaxing, scents of minerals, mint, honey, acacia flowers, and spice emerge. The wine is medium- to full-bodied, long, and powerful, with everything buttressed by zesty acidity. It is extremely backward, especially when tasted alongside the flamboyant, ostentatiously styled 1997. Look for this wine to evolve for two decades.

The 1995 Châteauneuf-du-Pape Roussanne Vieilles Vignes is a wine of extraordinary richness, with profound quantities of rose petals, honey, and smoke, as well as luxuriant richness, unctuous textures, and super density. This blockbuster full-bodied, multidimensional effort is glorious. The jury is still out as to how well it will age, but the debut vintage of this wine, 1986, is still relatively young, and even lighter years are proving to be stunning, even better than many people (including me) initially thought. This *cuvée* is, however, developing much more rapidly than normal, so consumption prior to 2005 is suggested.

Past Glories: Beaucastel red—1990 (95), 1989 (97), 1988 (90), 1985 (92), 1983 (91), 1979 (90), 1978 (91?), 1970 (91?); Hommage à Jacques Perrin—1990 (100), 1989 (100)

CHÂTEAU BEAUCHENE

1998 Châteauneuf-du-Pape Vignobles de la Serrière	C	86
1998 Châteauneuf-du-Pape Vignobles de la Serrière Grande Réserve	D	88

The 1998 Châteauneuf-du-Pape Vignobles de la Serrière offers aromas of tobacco, spice box, olives, and red fruits. It is a modern-bodied, moderately sized effort with decent acidity, copious spice, and a good finish. Consume it over the next 8–9 years. The 1998 Châteauneuf-du-Pape Vignobles de la Serrière Grande Réserve is a richer, full-bodied wine with abundant quantities of peppery spice in addition to black cherry and berry fruit, a denser constitution, and more tannin, body, and extract in the finish. It can be drunk now, but promises to be even better with 2–3 more years of cellaring; it will last for 12+ years.

DOMAINE DE BEAURENARD

2000 Châteauneuf-du-Pape	D	(90–91)
1999 Châteauneuf-du-Pape	D	89

1998 Châteauneuf-du-Pape	D	90
1997 Châteauneuf-du-Pape	D	85
2000 Châteauneuf-du-Pape Cuvée Boisrenard	E	(92–95)
1999 Châteauneuf-du-Pape Cuvée Boisrenard	E	90
1998 Châteauneuf-du-Pape Cuvée Boisrenard	E	94
1997 Châteauneuf-du-Pape Cuvée Boisrenard	E	87

This 75-acre estate continues to be one of the leaders in Châteauneuf-du-Pape, offering both a *cuvée* classique and a luxury *cuvée*, the latter revealing evidence of exposure to new oak casks. There is also a round, generous Côtes du Rhône produced as well as a rustic Rasteau Côtes du Rhône-Villages. The Coulon family continues its successful string of vintages with top-notch ones in 2000, 1999, and 1998.

The sexy, full-bodied, voluptuous 2000 Châteauneuf-du-Pape reveals a deep ruby/purple color as well as jammy, fleshy, black fruit flavors, no evidence of new oak, a boatload of glycerin, and a user-friendly, substantial palate feel. Already hard to resist, it should drink well for 12–14 years. One of the most prodigious efforts of the vintage, the saturated purple-colored 2000 Châteauneuf-du-Pape Cuvée Boisrenard combines elegance with power. While there is a whiff of new oak in the aromatic profile, it is dominated by cassis, blackberry, and licorice scents. Exceptionally pure and multilayered, with superb concentration and a 40-second finish, this topflight effort is one of the stars of the vintage. Anticipated maturity: 2004–2020.

The 1999 Châteauneuf-du-Pape exhibits a dark ruby/purple color along with a sweet nose of crushed cherries, cassis, licorice, and spice. Low in acidity, ripe, opulent, and nicely textured, it will provide gorgeous drinking over the next decade. The saturated ruby/purple-colored 1999 Châteauneuf-du-Pape Cuvée Boisrenard offers a classy nose of black fruits intermixed with cedar and vanilla (a portion of this *cuvée* spends time in new oak), followed by powerful, full-bodied, admirably pure flavors. A modern-styled Châteauneuf, it combines its Provençal soul with a forward-thinking, progressive style. It requires 2–3 years of cellaring and should drink well for 15–16 years. Beaurenard's outstanding dark ruby/purple-colored 1998 Châteauneuf-du-Pape displays a vivid nose of blackberries, cassis, spice box, and truffles. Full-bodied and dense, with superb texture, a dense mid-palate, and long finish, there is tannin present, but it is sweet and well integrated. Anticipated maturity: now–2014. The 1998 Châteauneuf-du-Pape Cuvée Boisrenard is the finest wine the Coulon family has made since 1990. A blend of 85% Grenache, 10% Mourvèdre, and 5% miscellaneous varietals, this staggering offering from 65–90-year-old vines is limited in availability (1,500 cases), but it rivals the incredible 1990. The deep ruby/purple-colored 1998 Boisrenard exhibits an exquisitely pure bouquet of jammy blackberry and cassis, roasted herbs, and vanilla. Made in a quasi-modern style, but with the power and richness one expects of a top Châteauneuf-du-Pape, it is multilayered, with beautifully integrated acidity, tannin, and wood (about 20% new-oak casks are used). The finish lasts for 40+ seconds, and there is tremendous purity and palate presence to this wine. Anticipated maturity: now–2020. Bravo!

The dark plum/garnet-colored 1997 Châteauneuf-du-Pape is an evolved, medium-bodied, richly fruity offering with dried herb, peppery, plum, black cherry, and berry aromas and flavors. This soft, fruit-driven, charming, delicious Châteauneuf should be consumed over the next 3–4 years. The 1997 Châteauneuf-du-Pape Cuvée Boisrenard (made from 70–90-year-old vines and aged 12 months in small casks and *foudres*) is a completely different animal. It displays a dark ruby/purple color, as well as an intense blackberry and raspberry-scented nose with some toast. Dense, rich, and medium- to full-bodied, with a lush texture, good glycerin and alcohol, and a heady finish, this flamboyant, tasty, rich Châteauneuf-du-Pape should drink well for a decade.

Past Glories: Boisrenard 1990 (94)

DOMAINE DE LA BÉCASSONNE

2000	Côtes du Rhône Cuvée Sommelongue	B	90
1999	Côtes du Rhône Cuvée Sommelongue	B	90
1998	Côtes du Rhône Cuvée Sommelongue	B	88

André Brunel, one of Châteauneuf-du-Pape's most erudite and forward-looking proprietors, is the owner of Les Cailloux. It is amazing to see how he keeps pushing the quality level higher and higher. The exceptional Cuvée Sommelongue, a blend of Grenache and Syrah from 35-year-old vines cropped low, does not see any new oak and emerges from a vineyard near the old Roman city of Orange. It is consistently a great value.

Even jammier, thicker, and more hedonistic than the 1999, Brunel's 2000 Côtes du Rhône Cuvée Sommelongue is a blend of 85% Grenache and 15% Syrah. Dense, chewy, full-bodied, and sumptuous, it is a textbook Côtes du Rhône for drinking over the next 2–3 years. The 1999 Côtes du Rhône Cuvée Sommelongue offers gorgeously sweet black cherry fruit intermixed with *garrigue*, pepper, and sandalwood. Full-bodied, lush, and velvety-textured, with a plump, fat finish, it will drink well for 2–3 years. The delicious 1998 Côtes du Rhône Cuvée Sommelongue would be an outstanding choice for restaurants to serve by the glass. It is textbook Côtes du Rhône, exhibiting a medium ruby color and a ripe nose of kirsch intermixed with pepper and spice. This velvety-textured, medium-bodied, deliciously fruity wine can be drunk over the next 2 years.

ALBERT BELLE PÈRE ET FILS

1999	Crozes-Hermitage Blanc	C	87
1999	Crozes-Hermitage Cuvée Louis Belle	D	91
1997	Crozes-Hermitage Cuvée Louis Belle	D	88
1997	Crozes-Hermitage Cuvée Louis Belle Blanc	D	83
1999	Crozes-Hermitage Les Pierrelles	D	90
1996	Hermitage Blanc	E	85
1999	Hermitage Les Murets	E	91+

To my taste, Belle's wines continue to exhibit improvement, taking on more complexity and richness with each high-quality vintage. Given their prices, they represent super bargains.

The 1999 Crozes-Hermitage Blanc (a blend of 70% Marsanne and 30% Roussanne) offers aromas of rose petals and spice box. With ripe fruit, excellent texture, a lush, richly fruity character, and enough acidity for definition, it will provide beautiful drinking over the next 3–4 years.

The 1999 reds are the strongest lineup from Domaine Albert Belle that I have tasted. The 1999 Crozes-Hermitage Les Pierrelles (10% new oak is utilized) is a sumptuous, fleshy, dense ruby/purple-colored effort bursting with Syrah fruit. With medium body, loads of glycerin, low acidity, and copious sweetness as well as character, this fruit bomb will drink well for 8–10 years. The old-vine selection, the 1999 Crozes-Hermitage Cuvée Louis Belle, was aged 12 months in oak barrels, of which 30% were new. It all emerges from the hillside sector known as Larnage. There are nearly 4,000 cases of this spectacular wine, which has more in common with Hermitage than Crozes-Hermitage. A saturated ruby/purple color is followed by fabulous aromas of crème de cassis, licorice, minerals, and spice. Multilayered and full bodied, with superb purity as well as harmony, it can be drunk or cellared for 12–15 years. Another impressive effort is the 1999 Hermitage Les Murets. This section of Hermitage is well known for its white wines, but this serious, highly extracted, rich, full-bodied red Hermitage was aged in cask, of which 50% were new. More backward than its less expensive sibling, the Cuvée Louis Belle, it reveals notes of minerals, blueberries, blackberries, and flowers. Dense, full-bodied, chewy, and in need of 4–5 years of cellaring, it is Albert Belle's most profound Hermitage yet produced. Anticipated maturity: 2007–2020.

The 1997 Crozes-Hermitage Cuvée Louis Belle was picked at high sugars, resulting in nearly 13% natural alcohol. This soft, sexy Crozes offers plenty of strawberry and jammy cherry fruit intermixed with aromas of smoked herbs, meats, and wood spice. There is excellent purity and ripeness, medium to full body, a supple texture, and a chewy finish. It should drink well for 5–7 years. The mineral, citrusy, light- to medium-bodied 1997 Crozes-Hermitage Cuvée Louis Belle Blanc (80% Marsanne and 20% Roussanne) is correct and serviceable. It should be consumed over the next 2–3 years.

The 1996 Hermitage Blanc was closed when I tasted it. A blend of 70% Marsanne and 30% Roussanne, aged half in *barrique* and half in tank before being blended, it is a medium-bodied, fresh, citrusy white Hermitage with floral notes in the nose and crisp, tangy acidity. It should drink well for 4–5 years. I would have enjoyed more flesh and fruit concentration.

GUY ET FRÉDÉRIC BERNARD-GAEC BERNARD

1998 Côte Rôtie	E	87

This estate has most of its vineyards situated in the southern sector of Côte Rôtie, adjoining Condrieu. It offers a very good, spicy, dark ruby-colored 1998 Côte Rôtie that will provide ideal drinking during its first decade of life. The Bernards have a tendency to produce herbaceous wines, but by primarily destemming the fruit, they have avoided any greenness in this *cuvée.* Copious peppery, blackberry, and cassis fruit flavors result in a tasty offering with medium body, good purity, and admirable balance. Anticipated maturity: now–2008.

DOMAINE BERTHET-RAYNE

1999 Châteauneuf-du-Pape	C	(88–90)
1998 Châteauneuf-du-Pape	C	89

One of the strongest showings yet for this domaine's wines, Berthet-Rayne's 1999 Châteauneuf-du-Pape reveals outstanding potential. Made in an impressive quasi-modern style, it exhibits a deep ruby/purple color, evidence of *barrique* aging, full body, and rich, concentrated notes of black cherries and cassis. Not a squeaky clean, innocuous effort, it offers substance, richness, and good balance between the wood, fruit, and structure. Anticipated maturity: now–2015. The 1998 Châteauneuf-du-Pape reveals a less saturated ruby/purple color and a sweet, fragrant bouquet of black cherries infused with smoke and herbs, with a touch of oak noticeable in the aftertaste. Already drinking well, it should age nicely for 10–12 years.

DOMAINE BOIS DE BOURSAN

2000 Châteauneuf-du-Pape	D	(89–90)
1999 Châteauneuf-du-Pape	D	89
1998 Châteauneuf-du-Pape	D	90
1997 Châteauneuf-du-Pape	D	(87–89)
2000 Châteauneuf-du-Pape Cuvée des Felix	E	(92–95)
1999 Châteauneuf-du-Pape Cuvée des Felix	E	94
1998 Châteauneuf-du-Pape Cuvée des Felix	E	97
1997 Châteauneuf-du-Pape Cuvée des Felix	D	88

Under the administration of Jean and Jean-Paul Versino, Bois de Boursan has become one of Châteauneuf-du-Pape's super estates. This is one of many estates where the bottled Châteauneuf-du-Pape is even better than barrel/*foudre* samples.

Not surprisingly, Bois de Boursan's 2000s reveal the ripeness and jammy red and black fruits achieved in this topflight vintage. The dense ruby/purple–colored 2000 Châteauneuf-du-Pape offers up a big, sweet nose of crème de cassis, fleshy, seductive flavors, an unctuous texture, and a ripe, long, concentrated finish dominated by a black fruit character. It should be ready to drink early because of its low acidity. Anticipated maturity: now–2014. If the full-bodied 2000 Châteauneuf-du-Pape Cuvée des Felix builds in the bottle like the 1998

Cuvée des Felix has done, it will turn out to be prodigious. A dense, saturated purple color is followed by aromas of blackberry liqueur, licorice, smoke, dried herbs, and new saddle leather. This wine represents the essence of Châteauneuf-du-Pape, with considerable tannin and structure buried beneath a wealth of fruit, glycerin, and extract. While more accessible than the 1998 was at a similar age, it is a formidable offering that should provide compelling drinking over the next two decades.

The saturated dark ruby-colored 1999 Châteauneuf-du-Pape offers a big, Provençal bouquet of earth, crushed pepper, *garrigue,* and black fruits. Pungent and spicy, with rich, soft, full-bodied flavors, it is ideal for drinking over the next 10–12 years. The superb 1999 Châteauneuf-du-Pape Cuvée des Felix is a profound example of the vintage. An opaque purple color is accompanied by intense aromas of salty sea breezes intermixed with *garrigue,* blackberry and cherry jam, dried herbs, and Asian spices. It is exceptionally powerful as well as super-concentrated, with great purity and overall symmetry. Give it another 2–3 years of cellaring and enjoy it over the following 16–18 years.

The 1998s are both outstanding, with the Cuvée des Felix nearly mind-boggling. The 1998 Châteauneuf-du-Pape is an opulent, sexy effort with silky tannin, a deep, plum/purple color, and notes of cherry liqueur intermixed with smoke, earth, and herbs. The tannin is nearly hidden by the wine's high levels of fruit, glycerin, and extract. Ripe, heady, and hedonistically styled, it will drink well over the next 10–12 years. The 1998 Châteauneuf-du-Pape Cuvée des Felix is an amazing creation that pushes the sensory circuits into overdrive. The color is an impressively saturated ruby/purple. The nose offers up sumptuous aromas of wood spice, scorched earth, and blackberry and cherry liqueur. Extremely thick and unctuously textured, with massive richness, full body, and a multidimensional personality, this exquisite Châteauneuf-du-Pape is exceptionally well balanced, very pure, and possesses a 45-second finish. I would not quibble with those who want to drink it now, but it will be even better with another 1–2 years of cellaring, and should evolve for 12–20 years.

As for the 1997s, the 1997 Châteauneuf-du-Pape exhibits a dense ruby/purple color as well as stunning aromas of overripe blackberry fruit intermixed with cassis, cherries, and a toasty touch. This medium- to full-bodied, topflight Châteauneuf-du-Pape displays terrific fruit intensity, and a layered, pure, concentrated finish. It should be one of the most concentrated and delicious wines of the vintage. Anticipated maturity: 2001–2012. The 1997 Châteauneuf-du-Pape Cuvée des Felix possesses a more international style due to its new oak (*barrique*) influence. The wine's opaque saturated purple color is accompanied by thick, juicy, full-bodied black currant and blackberry flavors with explosive richness and depth. Atypical for a 1997, it is impressively endowed, and it should age nicely for 12 or more years.

DOMAINE DE BOIS DAUPHIN

1998 Châteauneuf-du-Pape	C	86
2000 Châteauneuf-du-Pape Clos des Pontifes	E	(88–90)
1999 Châteauneuf-du-Pape Clos des Pontifes	E	87
1998 Châteauneuf-du-Pape Clos des Pontifes	E	89

Proprietor Jean Marchand turns out distinctively modern-styled Châteauneuf-du-Papes that reveal some evidence of *barrique* as well as less Provençal typicity than many of the appellation's finest wines. Nevertheless, they are deeply fruited, attractive, and ideal for drinking during their first 8–12 years of life. The regular *cuvée* is a typical Châteauneuf-du-Pape, soft and peppery, with the salty, seaweed, iodine, *garrigue,* kirsch components that are so much a part of many of the wines from this Provençal village. The Clos des Pontifes sees some aging in small new oak casks and represents a more concentrated, internationally styled, but still authentic Châteauneuf-du-Pape. It is just bigger, richer, and more influenced by new oak.

Displaying a saturated ruby/purple color, the 2000 Châteauneuf-du-Pape Clos des Pontifes reveals new oak intermixed with blackberry and cassis fruit. It is medium-bodied and elegant with excellent purity, but it lacks Châteauneuf-du-Pape's typicity. The 1999 Châteauneuf-du-Pape Clos des Pontifes exhibits a dark ruby color along with a perfume of sweet black cherries, toast, currants, and licorice. Medium-bodied, fleshy, open-knit, and accessible, it will drink well for 7–8 years.

The 1998 Châteauneuf-du-Pape is a soft, straightforward, commercially styled effort with plenty of cherry fruit intermixed with pepper, Provençal herbs, and spice. Medium-bodied and fruity, it is best consumed over the next 5–6 years. More serious is the 1998 Châteauneuf-du-Pape Clos des Pontifes. A medium ruby-colored 1998, it possesses more flesh, glycerin, concentration, and intensity than its sibling. Notes of herbs, crushed pepper, kirsch, and spice jump from this medium- to full-bodied, expansively-flavored wine. Drink it over the next 7–8 years.

DE BOISSEYT-CHOL

1999 Côte Rôtie Côte Blonde	D	(86–87)
1998 Côte Rôtie Côte Blonde	D	86

In a sense, these are fickle wines from the Côte Blonde—fruity, soft, and round, with little concentration. Stylistically, they are reminiscent of those of the young, new estate-bottler, Jean-François Garon, not surprising since the vineyards are nearly adjacent.

The 1999 Côte Rôtie Côte Blonde reveals better ripeness than the 1998, an elegant, finesse-filled personality with abundant fruit, but no depth, and a certain open-knit style to its appeal. The fruit character is attractive, but more weight and depth would be welcome. Consume this 1999 during its first 7–8 years of life. The dark plum-colored, soft, round 1998 Côte Rôtie Côte Blonde offers moderately intense black raspberry and cherry fruit as well as spice. This low-acid effort is ideal for drinking now and over the next 4–5 years.

FRÉDÉRIC BOISSONNET

1999 Condrieu	D	86
1999 St.-Joseph	C	(85–87)
1998 St.-Joseph	C	86
1999 St.-Joseph Blanc	C	82
1999 St.-Joseph Cuvée de la Bélive	D	(87–89)
1998 St.-Joseph Cuvée de la Bélive	D	87

This northern Rhône estate's rise in quality can be attributed to the 35-year-old owner, Frédéric Boissonnet. Boissonnet's top *cuvée*, Cuvée de la Bélive, is a selection of old vines which aged in one-third new oak casks. The red wines are much stronger efforts than the whites, which are usually lacking in intensity.

The 1999 Condrieu and 1999 St.-Joseph Blanc are both competent examples, although they reveal lighter-styled personalities without the expected intensity.

The pure 1999 St.-Joseph exhibits the liquid mineral characteristic that comes from the granite *terroir* of St.-Joseph's hillside vineyards, as well as ripe blackberry and cherry fruit. It should drink well for 4–5 years. The 1999 St.-Joseph Cuvée de la Bélive's impressive saturated ruby/purple color is followed by rich black currant, cherry, minerals, and toasty, smoky oak aromas. Pure and ripe, this 1999 will provide ideal drinking over the next 10+ years.

The deep ruby/garnet-colored 1998 St.-Joseph offers sweet, spicy, cherry fruit, a round, tangy personality, medium body, decent acidity, and a spicy, straightforward personality. Drink it over the next 3–4 years. The excellent, opaque ruby/purple-colored 1998 St.-Joseph Cuvée de la Bélive displays abundant smoky oak, mineral, black currant, and spice notes. It is rich and medium-bodied, with admirable purity. Anticipated maturity: now–2012.

HENRI BONNEAU

1997 Châteauneuf-du-Pape	D	(87–89)
2000 Châteauneuf-du-Pape (probably Marie Beurrier)	E	(88–91)
1999 Châteauneuf-du-Pape (probably Marie Beurrier)	E	(87–88)
1998 Châteauneuf-du-Pape Cuvée Speciale	E	(90–94)
2000 Châteauneuf-du-Pape (probably Réserve des Célestins)	EEE	(92–95)
1999 Châteauneuf-du-Pape (probably Réserve des Célestins)	EEE	(90–92)
1998 Châteauneuf-du-Pape Réserve des Célestins	EEE	(95–98+)

Henri Bonneau remains one of the most compelling wine personalities on planet Earth. For multiple reasons, my annual visit, one of the most eagerly anticipated sojourns of the tasting year, is always memorable. Of course the wines are prodigious, particularly when the southern Rhône has enjoyed a top-notch vintage. In addition, Bonneau's uplifting personality, with his strong Provençal dialect, nasty sense of humor, and predilection to wax philosophical about his favorite subjects, cuisine and wine, are all part of a visit to the Bonneau cellars. Henri Bonneau must represent the anti-Christ to modern-day oenologists. He continues to make sumptuous wines in a cellar that is cramped, dingy, and filled with mind-boggling quantities of mold. Rarely does a vintage of Réserve des Célestins make it into bottle in less than five years of living through what most modern day oenologists would consider deplorable conditions. But what emerges after 4–5 years of aging, from an assortment of ancient barrels, prehistoric *foudres,* and antique *demi-muids,* are wines of exhilarating complexity, richness, and aging potential. It has been a privilege and honor for me to be able to taste some of Bonneau's old vintages (1981, 1978, 1970, 1967, 1961, 1959, 1949, 1947, and 1935). They were either perfect or close to perfection. Bonneau remains the appellation's most ferocious guardian of traditionally made Châteauneuf-du-Pape, producing, from his tiny 15-acre old-vine domaine in La Crau, wines that defy all logic.

Henri Bonneau claimed 2000 was *trop facile,* meaning too easy a vintage for Châteauneuf-du-Pape. Moreover, he thought the wines were too fruity and behaved like "nice whores" rather than "real" Châteauneuf-du-Pape. Of course, a good vintage to him is usually a great one for me. More than a decade of visits to Chez Bonneau have taught me that even when he turns out something prodigious, it is hard for him to say something other than *"ça c'est correct."* After extended questioning, the only vintage Bonneau will remotely compare 2000 with is 1985, another easy drinking year. His top *cuvée* of 2000 Châteauneuf-du-Pape, which will undoubtedly be the Réserve des Célestins, is a big, juicy, lush, fat effort with fabulous notes of liqueur of cherries, *herbes de Provence,* roasted meats, and licorice. This dense ruby-colored Châteauneuf has huge levels of glycerin as well as a monstrously impressive, long finish. The alcohol content of the component parts ranges from 15–17%, and the wine is fermented totally dry. With any luck, Bonneau might bottle it by 2004. It is a candidate for three decades of aging. The 2000 Châteauneuf-du-Pape that will probably be called Marie Beurrier reveals a boatload of earth, pepper, *garrigue,* and jammy cherries offered in a fat style. While large-scaled with sweet tannin, it is not as spectacular, massive, or multidimensional as its bigger sibling.

Henri Bonneau prefers the vigor, definition, and grip of the 1999s although I did not think they were nearly as powerful as his 2000s or 1998s. Both *cuvées* contain between 14.6–15% alcohol. The 1999 Châteauneuf-du-Pape (probably Marie Beurrier) offers aromas of licorice, smoke, pepper, and animal-infused, kirsch/plum/prune notes. A slightly rough finish should age out before this full-bodied wine is bottled. The 1999 Châteauneuf-du-Pape (probably Réserve des Célestins) reveals a notion of elegance (a word not often applied to Bonneau's wines), full body, excellent density, and moderately high tannin. It will require 4–5 years of cellaring and should last for two decades. The telltale gamey nose of beef blood, smoked meats, herbs, and jammy red and black fruits continues throughout the taste and finish. This wine might turn out similar to his majestic 1986 Célestins. Anticipated maturity: 2006–2025.

The awesome 1998 may be Bonneau's greatest since 1990. Alcohol levels range from 16.2–16.7%. However, Bonneau fells that the 1950s was the greatest for him, claiming that 1959, 1957, 1956, 1955, 1954, and 1953 all produced thrilling wines, whereas in the 1990s, only 1999, 1998, 1995, and 1990 produced superb Châteauneuf-du-Pape. The dense ruby-colored 1998 Châteauneuf-du-Pape Réserve des Célestins is loaded. Bonneau feels the remaining few grams of residual sugar should ferment out over the next year. He will not bottle the wine until 2004–2005, depending on his personal whims. This massive, full-bodied effort offers notes of beef blood, smoke, and alcohol-macerated black cherries, prunes, figs, and plums. Layered, textured, sumptuous, and unctuous, with a finish that lasts for nearly a minute, this is a Châteauneuf-du-Pape with 30–40 years of aging potential. In 1998 there is a Châteauneuf-du-Pape Cuvée Spéciale much like Bonneau produced in 1990. This unctuous, port-like offering possesses a small quantity of residual sugar. It is weird, eccentric, and pruny, but fabulously concentrated and loaded with such Provençal characteristics as dried herbs and charcuterie. My instincts suggest this kinky wine will age for 30–40 years.

There will not be a Réserve des Célestins, and probably no Marie Beurrier, in 1997. As always, this is subject to the proprietor's last-minute decision. The 1997 Châteauneuf-du-Pape is a straightforward, spicy, Pinot Noir–like effort with notes of decaying flowers intermixed with autumnal leaves, kirsch, licorice, and spice.

Past Glories: Réserve des Célestins—1995 (95+), 1992 (93), 1990 (100), 1989 (98+), 1988 (95), 1986 (95), 1985 (96), 1981 (94), 1978 (100), 1970 (98), 1957 (96), 1949 (100); Marie Beurrier—1990 (92), 1989 (93), 1988 (90)

PATRICK ET CHRISTOPHE BONNEFOND

1999 Condrieu Côte Châtillon	E	88
2000 Côte Rôtie	E	(81–83)
1999 Côte Rôtie	E	90
1998 Côte Rôtie	E	86
2000 Côte Rôtie Les Rochains	EE	(87–90)
1999 Côte Rôtie Les Rochains	EE	93
1998 Côte Rôtie Les Rochains	EE	90

Patrick and Christophe Bonnefond are two young wine-makers in Côte Rôtie. The two brothers have taken over the running of this estate from their father, and the results are wines that have risen from mediocre/so-so to very good/outstanding efforts. Their single vineyard *cuvée* Les Rochains comes from a parcel of vines situated next to La Landonne on the Côte Brune. The Bonnefond brothers also fashion a fine Condrieu. The 1999s are the finest Côte Rôties I have ever tasted from this estate. They provide further evidence that this vintage not only succeeds 1991 in quality, but is among the finest Côte Rôtie vintages of the last 25 years.

The innocuous, diluted but pleasant, medium ruby-colored 2000 Côte Rôtie requires consumption during its first 4–6 years of life. The 2000 Côte Rôtie Les Rochains exhibits a deep ruby color with a purple hue. Medium-bodied, with plenty of toasty new oak intermixed with black fruit and vanilla flavors, it is excellent for the vintage, but lacks the depth and majestic richness found in the 1999. Drink this low acid, charming, seductive 2000 during its first 8–9 years of life.

The 1999 Condrieu Côte Châtillon exhibits exotic tropical fruits (mango) along with Condrieu's typical peach, apricot, and tangerine concoction, good depth, a hint of toasty oak, and a medium-bodied, glycerin-imbued, refreshing finish. The deep saturated ruby-colored 1999 Côte Rôtie offers up sweet aromas of plums, cassis, and flowers. Succulent, ripe, and heady, with plenty of fat and a seductive, low-acid, rich style, it should drink well now and over the next 12–14 years. The 1999 Côte Rôtie Les Rochains boasts a saturated opaque purple color in addition to a splendidly complex bouquet of espresso, black cherries, cassis, licorice, new oak, and that elusive floral component reminiscent of paper white narcissus or violets. Medium- to full-bodied, intense, and opulently textured, with low acidity, sweet, well-integrated tannin, and a stunning, 40+-second finish, this is a sumptuous yet structured Côte Rôtie. While accessible, it requires 3–4 more years of cellaring. Anticipated maturity: 2004–2015.

The 1998 Côte Rôtie reveals Syrah's herbaceous side, but is medium weight, well made, and best drunk over the next 4–5 years. More interesting is the 1998 Côte Rôtie Les Rochains. It reveals spicy new oak in the nose along with intense black currant and cassis fruit, good spice, and a supple texture with medium body and moderate tannin. It should drink well for 10–12 years.

DOMAINE DE BONSERINE

2000 Côte Rôtie Côte Brune	E	(85–87?)
1999 Côte Rôtie Côte Brune	E	87+?
1998 Côte Rôtie Côte Brune	E	89
2000 Côte Rôtie La Garde	E	(87–89)
1999 Côte Rôtie La Garde	E	89?
1998 Côte Rôtie La Garde	E	89
2000 Côte Rôtie Les Moutonnes	E	(85–87)
1999 Côte Rôtie Les Moutonnes	E	87+?
1998 Côte Rôtie Les Moutonnes	E	87
2000 Côte Rôtie La Sarcasine	E	(83–85)
1999 Côte Rôtie La Sarcasine	E	86

Domaine de Bonserine's four offerings include one from the Côte Blonde (La Garde) and three from the Côte Brune (Côte Brune, Les Moutonnes, and La Sarcasine). All of these wines generally perform well, although they are made in an oaky, international style, with less typicity than some wines of the appellation.

The 2000s reflect the excessive yields that existed in the Côte Rôtie vineyards. None is very concentrated, and some are surprisingly austere and tannic, particularly the Côte Brune. The others are elegant but oaky examples that will not age beyond a decade.

As for the 1999s, wood addicts will rate them higher than I have. The 1999 Côte Rôtie La Sarcasine is the most forward and evolved, revealing sweet cherry fruit dominated by oak. Medium-bodied, with light tannin and fine depth, it will drink well for 7–8 years. Extremely oaky with harder tannin is the dark ruby/purple-colored 1999 Côte Rôtie Côte Brune. Un-evolved and extremely woody, I am not sure if there is enough fruit to absorb all the new oak. The same can be said for the 1999 Côte Rôtie Les Moutonnes, which possesses an overlay of toasty characteristics with black cherry and smoky cassis fruit notes playing a supporting role. It is medium-bodied, short, and compressed, with aggressive wood tannin in the finish. A better bet is the 1999 Côte Rôtie La Garde. While the oak is dominant, the wine shows more depth, sweeter fruit, and a certain roundness and lushness the other *cuvées* lack. There is good fruit and ripeness on the attack as well as a medium-bodied, spicy finish. It should drink well for a decade.

The vineyard production in 1998 was heavily curtailed because of the late June frost. The international style is most apparent in the dark ruby/purple-colored 1998 Côte Rôtie Les Moutonnes. It offers lavish quantities of toasty new oak as well as attractive black cherry and currant fruit, medium body, sweet tannin, and low acidity. Drink it over the next 7–8 years. The 1998 Côte Rôtie La Garde reveals more cassis and black raspberry notes along with smoke and fried bacon. Spicy oak is present, but it is sweeter and better integrated than in Les Moutonnes. Rich, medium- to full-bodied, and excellent, it will drink well for a decade.

Lastly, the 1998 Côte Rôtie Côte Brune exhibits aromas of olives, black currants, smoke, and minerals in its medium-bodied, moderately oaky personality. It, too, should be consumed over the next decade.

LE BOSQUET DES PAPES

2000 Châteauneuf-du-Pape	D	(90–92)
1999 Châteauneuf-du-Pape	D	90
1998 Châteauneuf-du-Pape	D	90
1997 Châteauneuf-du-Pape	D	(84–86)
2000 Châteauneuf-du-Pape Cuvée Chante Le Merle	D	(90–93)
1999 Châteauneuf-du-Pape Cuvée Chante Le Merle	D	91
1998 Châteauneuf-du-Pape Cuvée Chantemerle	E	93
2000 Châteauneuf-du-Pape Cuvée Grenache	D	(88–90)
1999 Châteauneuf-du-Pape Cuvée Grenache	D	89
1998 Châteauneuf-du-Pape Cuvée Grenache	D	89

This modestly sized estate produces some of the finest Châteauneuf-du-Pape of this sun-drenched appellation. As from 1990, an old-vine (average age of 90 years) *cuvée* called Chantemerle was added to the portfolio, which has been changed to Chante Le Merle starting with the 1999 vintage because of a trademark legal challenge. In 1998, a Cuvée Grenache produced from 60–80-year-old vines was introduced. All three offerings are well worth trying.

The 2000 Châteauneuf-du-Pape displays the most saturated ruby/purple color of the 2000 offerings. Full-bodied, fat, juicy, succulent, and long, it offers sweet black raspberry/currant notes mixed with pepper, Provençal herbs, leather, and mincemeat. Although it is not noticeable, there is no doubt plenty of tannin lurking beneath all the glycerin and fruit. Anticipated maturity: now–2015. The flamboyant, up-front 2000 Châteauneuf-du-Pape Cuvée Grenache offers a boatload of black cherry/strawberry fruit. The dark ruby color is followed by a medium-bodied Châteauneuf displaying dusty tannin in the moderately endowed finish. Drink it during its first decade of life. The 2000 Châteauneuf-du-Pape Cuvée Chante Le Merle's fabulous perfume offers an exotic concoction of Asian spices, roasted herbs, licorice, lavender, mincemeat, and black fruits. It is powerful yet elegant, extremely pure, and medium- to full-bodied, with low acidity, superb concentration, and a Pomerol-like (without any new oak characteristics) plushness as well as density. This provocative, compelling 2000 should easily score in the low to mid-90s. Anticipated maturity: 2004–2018.

The 1999 Châteauneuf-du-Pape reveals a dark ruby color with a pink rim. Its superb aromatics offer notions of roasted herbs, meat juices, sweet cherries, pepper, and spice box. Full-bodied, fleshy, and charming, with no hard edges and plenty of glycerin, it will drink well for a decade. While it reveals the most saturated ruby color of the 1999s, the Châteauneuf-du-Pape Cuvée Grenache is not as expansive, complex, or concentrated as its two siblings. It is a lighter, more fruit-forward effort, with a deep midsection, but neither the length nor complexity of the other two *cuvées*. Nevertheless, there is a lot to like in this undeniably disarming 1999. Its black cherry, raspberry, roasted herb, peanut, and spice-scented bouquet is followed by a medium- to full-bodied, deep, supple wine to enjoy over the next 8–10 years. The more closed, broodingly backward, dark ruby-colored 1999 Châteauneuf-du-Pape Cuvée Chante Le Merle exhibits 15–20 years of aging potential. With airing, it opens to reveal pepper, lavender, Provençal herb, licorice, blackberry, and cherry aromas. Full-bodied and moderately tannic, it requires 2–3 years of cellaring. Anticipated maturity: 2003–2018.

The deep ruby/plum-colored 1998 Châteauneuf-du-Pape is a dense, concentrated, muscular effort with an intense aromatic profile offering dried Provençal herbs, new saddle leather, melted licorice, roasted meats, and copious quantities of black fruits. Full-bodied, powerful, ripe, and dense, it is best cellared for 2–3 years and drunk over the following 15. The 1998

Châteauneuf-du-Pape Cuvée Grenache reveals a more evolved character. Deep ruby-colored with a pink rim, it offers sweet strawberry jam–like notes along with kirsch in its fruit-driven, straightforward, but undeniably beguiling aromas. Fleshy, fat, and dense, with low acidity, it is a Châteauneuf-du-Pape fruit bomb. Drink it over the next 7–8 years. The dense garnet/plum-colored 1998 Châteauneuf-du-Pape Cuvée Chantemerle (500 cases produced) is closed aromatically, but with airing, it begins to reveal some of its explosive personality. Scents of underbrush, smoke, saddle leather, soy, and other assorted Asian spices begin to emerge along with kirsch and black fruit notes. When the wine hits the palate, there is an explosion that is altogether satisfying. This 1998 is spectacularly concentrated, with multiple layers, huge quantities of glycerin, surprisingly strong tannin, and massive concentration and depth. It will be even better with 2–3 years of cellaring, and it should keep for 16–20 years.

Bosquet des Papes produced a peppery, herbal 1997 Châteauneuf-du-Pape with seductive cherry fruit intermixed with notes of licorice, coffee, and cedar. It is a pleasant, open-knit, round, slightly diluted but fruity wine to drink over the next 4–5 years.

Past Glories: Cuvée Chantemerle 1990 (96)

DOMAINE DES BOSQUETS

1999 Gigondas	C	(90–93)
1999 Gigondas Préférence	C	(91–94)

I do not know why Bosquets' proprietor did not show his 1998s, but certainly both 1999s are remarkable. Both were explosive examples of Gigondas, with smashing levels of crème de cassis and blackberry characteristics, as well as flamboyant personalities. The 1999 Gigondas reveals slightly lower acidity than the luxury *cuvée*, Préférence, but amazing body, extract, and richness. The 1999 Gigondas Préférence is reminiscent of dry vintage port being super-concentrated and intense, with multiple dimensions. I have never before tasted wines such as this from Domaine des Bosquets, so I hope this is what turns up in the bottle. Both wines have 15–18 years of aging potential.

DOMAINE LA BOUISSIÈRE

2000 Gigondas	D	(85–87)
1999 Gigondas	D	88
1998 Gigondas	D	89
2000 Gigondas La Font de Tonin	D	(88–90)
1999 Gigondas La Font de Tonin	D	89
1998 Gigondas La Font de Tonin	D	91
1997 Gigondas La Font de Tonin	D	(88–90)

Under Thierry Faravel this estate has emerged as one of the stars of Gigondas. There are two *cuvées* produced, a regular Gigondas (from a 17.3-acre vineyard; a blend of 70% Grenache and 30% Syrah, although in some vintages Mourvèdre is added) and a luxury *cuvée* called La Font de Tonin (from a 45-year-old, 1.2-acre vineyard; a blend of 85% Grenache and 15% Syrah aged in 60% new oak casks). Both wines are bottled without fining or filtration. The 1998s are the finest efforts to date, with the 1999s revealing more austerity and higher acidity. I do not think either the 1999 or 2000 vintage equals the quality produced in 1998.

The sexy, oaky, modern-styled 2000 Gigondas exhibits a deep purple color, medium to full body, low acidity, and chewy fruit. Hedonistically satisfying and long, it will drink well for a decade. Revealing additional layers as well as concentration, the 2000 Gigondas La Font de Tonin possesses more smoky, oaky notes intermixed with blackberry and currant fruit, minerals, pepper, and *garrigue*. Full-bodied, juicy, and succulent, with low acidity, it will drink well for 10–11 years. The saturated purple-colored 1999 Gigondas displays a sweet, pure nose of blueberries and cassis, surprisingly tart acidity, a strong underpinning of minerals, ripe tannin, and a medium-bodied, straightforward finish. Although excellent, it is not as impressive as I had hoped it would be. Anticipated maturity: now–2011. The 1999 Gigondas La Font de Tonin (a blend of 70% Grenache and 30% Mourvèdre) reveals more sweetness and expansiveness as well as a savory, medium- to full-bodied palate with good definition, flesh, and vague notes of wood in the background. It is an impressive effort that falls just short of being brilliant. Anticipated maturity: now–2012.

The 1998s have closed down since bottling, revealing considerable structure. Nevertheless, they are loaded, but readers must be patient. The 1998 Gigondas (70% Grenache and 30% Syrah) exhibits a dense purple color as well as a sweet, unevolved nose of minerals and black fruits. There is good underlying acidity, finesse, sweet cassis, and plenty of density and concentration. It will be long-lived, but it requires 3–5 years of cellaring. Anticipated maturity: 2005–2018. The saturated dark purple/plum-colored 1998 Gigondas La Font de Tonin (70% Grenache and 30% Mourvèdre) offers aromas of new oak, minerals, black cherries, and cassis in addition to surprisingly elegant yet powerfully concentrated flavors, with moderate levels of tannin and intensity. This 1998 Gigondas requires 2–3 years of cellaring and should drink well for two decades. The impressive, black/purple-colored 1997 Gigondas La Font de Tonin exhibits toasty new oak, gobs of cassis, blackberry fruit, and powerful, concentrated, medium- to full-bodied flavors. Its low acidity and plump, forward style suggest it should be drunk during its first 8–10 years of life. Hopefully, it will be bottled without excessive fining and filtration.

DOMAINE BRESSY-MASSON

1999 Côtes du Rhône-Villages Rasteau	C	86
1998 Côtes du Rhône-Villages Rasteau Cuvée Paul-Emile	C	88

These are two impressive efforts from Rasteau, a village that is finally emerging from the shadows with a bevy of young producers all trying to emulate the appellation's unchallenged superstar, André Romero of Domaine La Soumade. Bressy-Masson has fashioned a 1999 Côtes du Rhône-Villages Rasteau with chocolaty, blackberry, and plum-like fruit presented in an earthy, medium- to full-bodied, straightforward, robust style. It is ideal for drinking over the next 2–3 years. Even better is the 1998 Côtes du Rhône-Villages Rasteau Cuvée Paul-Emile (this property's top *cuvée*). Its dense ruby/purple color is accompanied by a sweet nose of black cherry liqueur, smoke, chocolate, and earth. Full-bodied and chewy, it will drink well for 5–6 years.

DANIEL BRUSSET—LES HAUTS DE MONTMIRAIL

2000 Gigondas	D	(88–90)
1999 Gigondas	D	87
1998 Gigondas	D	89
1997 Gigondas	D	(89–92)
2000 Gigondas Les Hauts de Montmirail	E	(89–91)
1999 Gigondas Les Hauts de Montmirail	E	89
1998 Gigondas Les Hauts de Montmirail	E	91

This estate, with 68 parcels of terraced vineyards on the craggy slopes of the Dentelles behind the village of Gigondas, continues to produce one of the appellation's most extraordinary wines. It celebrated its 50th birthday in 1997. Daniel Brusset was one of the first Gigondas producers to use new oak during the aging process of his top *cuvée*, Les Hauts de Montmirail (a blend of 60% Grenache, 25% Mourvèdre, and 15% Syrah that sees 60% new oak and 40% one- and two-year-old barrels). His regular Gigondas, Domaine Le Grand Montmirail, a blend of 75% Grenache, 15% Syrah, and 10% Cinsault, is aged in a combination of *foudre*, tank, and 2–3 year old barrels.

The 2000 Gigondas possesses a more saturated plum/purple color as well as aromas and flavors of plums, blackberries, cherries, earth, truffles, and flowers. It is a soft, succulent, low-acid Gigondas to drink over the next 7–8 years. With more pepper, new oak, and lead pencil characteristics in addition to black cherry, raspberry, and blueberry jam, the 2000 Gigondas Les Hauts de Montmirail exhibits concentrated flavors, medium to full body, and outstanding purity. Anticipated maturity: now–2013. The 1999 Gigondas is a dense ruby/purple-colored, medium-bodied, plum, curranty, and raisiny-scented and -flavored effort with fine ripeness and a round, spicy personality. Enjoy it over the next 5–6 years. The aromatically styled 1999 Gigondas Les Hauts de Montmirail offers scents of new oak, blueberries, black cherries, and minerals. Medium- to full-bodied, ripe, plump, open-knit, and plush, it should drink well for 8–10 years.

The 1998s have shut down a bit since bottling, but they are loaded with potential, and I suspect they may be one to two points better than the above scores. The dense ruby/purple-colored 1998 Gigondas reveals a tight but promising bouquet of black cherries, pepper, *garrigue*, and raspberries. It is medium- to full-bodied, tannic, dense, spicy, and long. Anticipated maturity: now–2012. The 1998 Gigondas Les Hauts de Montmirail boasts a saturated purple color in addition to excellent depth, toasty new oak, and exotic spices intermixed with black raspberries, minerals, kirsch, and blackberries. Intense and moderately tannic, this 1998 requires 2–3 years of cellaring; it should keep for 12–14 years.

Brusset's 1997 is a textbook Gigondas for him—oaky, with huge, jammy aromas of blackberries, cassis, and toast. A highly extracted, formidably endowed Gigondas made in an international style, it should be a stunning wine, even better than the 1996. Additionally, it should drink well young given its low acidity and plump, forward fruit. Anticipated maturity: now–2010.

BERNARD BURGAUD

2000 Côte Rôtie	E	(87–89)
1999 Côte Rôtie	E	91+
1998 Côte Rôtie	D	91
1997 Côte Rôtie	D	87

Burgaud has evolved well as a wine-maker. His Côte Rôties, which I have followed for nearly two decades, were once dominated by rustic tannin, old leather and animal characteristics, and high levels of the yeast known as brett. However, recent vintages reflect less animal notes, as well as greater fruit purity and ripeness, all achieved without sacrificing the power and muscle that are so much of the Burgaud style. His Côte Rôties have always been made in such a concentrated style that they could easily stand up to 15–20 years of cellaring. That fact has not changed, it is just that the wines are more progressive with sweeter, cleaner fruit in evidence.

The 2000 Côte Rôtie is lighter than the 1999 (a general trait of the vintage), but Burgaud appears to have gotten more out of it than many of his peers. It exhibits a deep ruby/purple color as well as a backward, concentrated, moderately tannic style with more depth and chewiness than most 1999 northern Rhônes. Additionally, there are abundant quantities of earthy black fruits intermixed with underbrush and meaty notes. Anticipated maturity: 2003–2014. The 1999 Côte Rôtie will rival the finest Burgaud has produced. An opaque ruby/purple color is followed by a tight but blossoming bouquet of blackberries, hickory smoke, damp earth, underbrush, and licorice. Full-bodied, chewy, thick, but civilized, this inky, powerful, full-throttle 1999 possesses plenty of tannin and enough acidity to provide definition. However, patience will be required. Anticipated maturity: 2004–2016.

The opaque ruby/purple-colored 1998 Côte Rôtie is full-bodied with copious quantities of blackberry and raspberry fruit intertwined with mineral and scorched earth notes. Deep, rich, and moderately tannic with great purity of fruit, the wine cuts a broad, substantial swath across the palate. Anticipated maturity: now–2016.

The 1997 Côte Rôtie is big and dense, but slightly disjointed and out of balance. The wine possesses a dark ruby/purple color, an explosive licorice, incense, black fruit, and earth-scented nose, plenty of power and ripeness, and surprisingly high tannin for the vintage. A blend taken from both *foudre* and barrel, this offering reveals good power and richness, but needs to achieve better integration of its elements. It is one of the few 1997s that will keep for a decade or more.

CHÂTEAU CABRIÈRES

2000	Châteauneuf-du-Pape	D	(87–88)
1999	Châteauneuf-du-Pape	D	87
1998	Châteauneuf-du-Pape	D	88
1997	Châteauneuf-du-Pape	D	85
2000	Châteauneuf-du-Pape Cuvée Prestige	D	(90–91)
1999	Châteauneuf-du-Pape Cuvée Prestige	D	90
1998	Châteauneuf-du-Pape Cuvée Prestige	D	91
1997	Châteauneuf-du-Pape Cuvée Prestige	D	87
2000	Châteauneuf-du-Pape La Lettre à Louis Arnaud	E	(92–95)

The 2000s of Château Cabrières appear to be as fine as the topflight 1998s. The 2000 Châteauneuf-du-Pape is similar to the 1999 in weight, but it possesses less spice and more black fruits. It is sweet on the attack (because of high glycerin/alcohol) with a voluptuous texture, and a fleshy, fat, open-knit, expansive style. Drink this crowd-pleaser during its first 8–9 years of life. The fuller-bodied, more concentrated 2000 Châteauneuf-du-Pape Cuvée Prestige Tête de Cru displays a dense ruby color with purple hues. Loaded with black currant, prune, and kirsch characteristics, it boasts full body, a complex, sensual, opulent mid-palate, and a viscous, low-acid finish. It should drink well for 14–15 years.

The limited production *cuvée* (110 cases) of 2000 Châteauneuf-du-Pape La Lettre à Louis Arnaud was produced by the daughter in memory of her father. It is a fabulous, concentrated effort. If this level of quality could be achieved in the Cuvée Prestige, it would catapult Château Cabrières back to its position of making prodigious Châteauneuf-du-Pape as it did in the late 1950s and early 1960s. This offering boasts a dense plum color as well as a fabulously intense bouquet of smoke, prunes, black cherries, and chocolate. Extremely full-bodied, with an unctuous texture, low acidity, and a wealth of fruit as well as glycerin, this is a blockbuster Châteauneuf-du-Pape that will be approachable young, yet age for two decades.

The 1999 Châteauneuf-du-Pape is an evolved, soft, sexy, medium ruby-colored wine with plenty of spice, pepper, and kirsch notes. Easygoing and ripe, with decent acidity and a medium- to full-bodied palate impact, it should be consumed over the next 6–7 years. The expansively flavored 1999 Châteauneuf-du-Pape Cuvée Prestige Tête de Cru reveals a big nose of cinnamon and smoky black cherries, an opulent, voluptuous style, full body, sweet glycerin, outstanding purity, and a seamless mouth-feel. It is a gorgeous wine to drink over the next 7–10 years.

The dark plum/garnet-colored 1998 Châteauneuf-du-Pape reveals spicy, leathery, cedary aromas with jammy fruit in the background. Lusty and medium- to full-bodied with copious fruit, it is made in an open-knit, expansive style that begs to be drunk during its first decade of life. The 1998 Châteauneuf-du-Pape Cuvée Prestige should turn out to be sensational, and it looks to be the finest Cabrières since their 1961. A dark ruby/purple color is followed by scents of smoked herbs, grilled meats, spice box, licorice, and abundant red and black fruits. It is full-bodied and moderately tannic, with a chewy texture and an impressive finish. It should drink well for two decades.

The dark ruby-colored 1997 Châteauneuf-du-Pape exhibits copious quantities of black cherry and strawberry fruit intermixed with Provençal herbs, smoke, and spice. This medium-bodied, soft wine is ideal for current consumption. Made from a selection of the estate's oldest vines, the 1997 Châteauneuf-du-Pape Cuvée Prestige offers more glycerin, alcohol, fruit, and ripeness. It cuts a broader swath on the palate and possesses more volume, but it remains a forward wine redolent with black cherry fruit intermixed with earth, pepper, and Provençal spices. Drink it over the next 4–5 years.

LES CAILLOUX

2000 Châteauneuf-du-Pape	D	(91–93)
1999 Châteauneuf-du-Pape	D	90
1998 Châteauneuf-du-Pape	D	90
1997 Châteauneuf-du-Pape	D	87
2000 Châteauneuf-du-Pape Cuvée Centenaire	EEE	(94–96)
1998 Châteauneuf-du-Pape Cuvée Centenaire	EEE	100

The Brunel family has run this estate with unassailable ability for more than two decades. Through hard work and an open mind concerning all facets of viticulture and vinification, André Brunel has become one of the stars of Châteauneuf-du-Pape. Remarkably consistent in difficult vintages, he hits the bull's-eye in the great years. In the great vintages of Châteauneuf-du-Pape his wines are ethereal. At Les Cailloux, other than a standard *cuvée*, he produces a luxury *cuvée* called Cuvée Centenaire, made from a 5.6-acre parcel of Grenache vines planted in 1889. Annual production of this wine is 500 cases.

Brunel sees 2000 in the same light as 1998, a year of high ripeness for Grenache with massive extract and considerable power. His 2000 Châteauneuf-du-Pape looks to be a winner, boasting a deep ruby/purple color and a gorgeous perfume of smoke, underbrush, blackberry and cherry jam, pepper, and spice. Unctuously textured, layered, and full-bodied, with sweet tannin and low acidity, it should drink beautifully for 12–16 years. It was reminiscent of Les Cailloux's glorious 1990. The saturated ruby/purple-colored 2000 Châteauneuf-du-Pape Cuvée Centenaire is a wine of exceptional concentration in addition to majestic ripeness and richness, with a multidimensional personality, huge body, sweet tannin, and unobtrusive acidity and alcohol (15%). The finish lasts for nearly a minute. Displaying the essence of blackberry and cherry flavors intermixed with underbrush and pepper, this fascinating effort is a candidate for two decades of cellaring. Bravo!

The famed Cuvée Centenaire (produced from 100-plus-year-old vines) was included in the *cuvée* classique in 1999. Made in an evolved style for proprietor André Brunel, the 1999 Châteauneuf-du-Pape exhibits a dark plum/ruby color as well as a sweet, spicy nose of red and black fruits mixed with *garrigue,* pepper, spice box, and tobacco. Rich, full-bodied, layered, and undeniably captivating, this sumptuous, forward, flavorful, savory Châteauneuf can be drunk now and over the next 12–14 years.

The classic 1998 Châteauneuf-du-Pape represents a blend of traditional and progressive winemaking techniques. A southern Rhône nose of *garrigue* (the Provençal earthy/herb aroma), pepper, wood spice, and gorgeously sweet black cherry and plum-like flavors are intense as well as alluring. Once past the bouquet, this dark ruby/garnet-colored wine offers a full-bodied, powerful, layered impression, with impressive levels of glycerin, ripe fruit, and extract. Tannin is present, but it is sweet. This 1998 will easily drink well for 10–12 years. The special *cuvée* of 100-year-old Grenache vines, the 1998 Châteauneuf-du-Pape Cuvée Centenaire, is awesome. It took over a year to ferment dry, and it is one of numerous candidates for "wine of the vintage" in Châteauneuf-du-Pape. A dark saturated purple color is accompanied by an extraordinarily promising nose of jammy red and black fruits, licorice, espresso, and lavender. On the palate, it is a skyscraper, with multiple levels, high extract, and amazing delineation for a wine of such depth, mass, and intensity. It is a sure candidate to surpass the 1995 and rival the virtually perfect 1990 and 1989. It represents the essence of Grenache as well as Châteauneuf-du-Pape. Anticipated maturity: 2005–2025.

I was not surprised by the high quality of proprietor André Brunel's 1997 Châteauneuf-du-Pape. The dark ruby-colored 1997 Châteauneuf-du-Pape offers a juicy, succulent, fruit-driven personality and a black raspberry/kirsch rich fruitiness with good glycerin in its medium- to full-bodied, lush, low-acid finish. It should drink well for 5–6 years.

Past Glories: Les Cailloux—1990 (94), 1989 (90), 1978 (92); Cuvée Centenaire—1990 (99), 1989 (96+)

CAVE DE CAIRANNE

1998 Côtes du Rhône-Villages Cairanne Cuvée Antique	B	85
1998 Côtes du Rhône-Villages Cairanne Cuvée Temptation	B	86
1998 Côtes du Rhône-Villages Cairanne Réserve des Voconces	B	87

These are all noteworthy values from the cooperative in the Côtes du Rhône village of Cairanne. They are all a selection made and brought to bottling by the renowned northern Rhône oenologist, Jean-Luc Colombo. These wines not only represent good values, they are delicious, pleasure-giving efforts.

The 1998s take advantage of the vintage's ripe, luscious fruit. The 1998 Côtes du Rhône-Villages Cairanne Cuvée Temptation (100% Grenache) reveals a chunky personality to go along with its brash display of kirsch, freshly ground pepper, and vivid cherry fruit. It is a robust, deep, heady Côtes du Rhône to enjoy over the next several years. The 1998 Côtes du Rhône-Villages Cairanne Cuvée Antique was less enthralling, no doubt because some Mourvèdre has been added to the blend, giving the wine more leanness, austerity, and structure. It comes across as a serious Côtes du Rhône, but is less pleasurable. It should drink well for 2–3 years. The finest wine of this trio is the 1998 Côtes du Rhône-Villages Cairanne Réserve des Voconces. Primarily Grenache, with a tiny dosage of Syrah, it sees a touch of barrel. Ruby/purple-colored, with pure, blackberry, cassis, and cherry-like flavors, this fruit-driven, medium-bodied, low-acid Côtes du Rhône is ideal for drinking over the next 5–6 years. It represents an outstanding value!

DOMAINE DE CASSAN

2000 Gigondas	D	(86–88)
1999 Gigondas	D	87
1998 Gigondas	D	89
1997 Gigondas	D	88

The Domaine de Cassan's Gigondas emerge from the limestone terraces of this modestly sized 20-acre vineyard. Made from a blend of 55% Grenache, 40% Syrah, and 5% Mourvèdre, with manual punch-downs, they are aged in both *foudre* and barrel.

The 2000 Gigondas has a saturated ruby/purple color as well as aromas of cherries, raspberries, gravel, and flowers. It is a medium- to full-bodied, lush, bigger, jammier style than the 1999. It should drink well for 7–8 years. The deep ruby/purple-colored 1999 Gigondas is elegant and restrained with good acidity and notes of minerals, pepper, *garrigue*, and black cherry/berry fruit. Medium-bodied and pure, it is best drunk over the next 4–5 years.

One of the most impressive wines yet tasted from Domaine de Cassan, the potentially outstanding 1998 Gigondas exhibits terrific fruit purity and intensity. A dark ruby/purple color is followed by a wine exhibiting the vintage's purity, opulence, and superb concentration. Considerable tannin in the finish suggests this wine may need 2–3 years of cellaring. Gutsy, thick, and highly concentrated, it should be at its finest between 2005–2014.

Another impressive Gigondas, Domaine de Cassan's 1997 offers an opaque ruby/purple color and a big, thick, black cherry and blackberry nose, with pepper and *garrigue* notes. In the mouth, there is pure blackberry fruit, surprising power and tannin, and a full-bodied, lengthy finish. It is one of the biggest wines I tasted from Gigondas in this vintage. Anticipated maturity: now–2012.

DOMAINE CAYRON

2000 Gigondas	D	(88–91)
1999 Gigondas	D	92
1998 Gigondas	D	86
1997 Gigondas	D	(86–88)

After a disappointing 1998 vintage, proprietor Faraud has turned out a classic 1999 Gigondas followed by a solid, meaty effort in 2000. The dense ruby/purple-colored 2000 Gigondas's excellent bouquet displays fewer nuances, being dominated by pure blackberry and cherry fruit mixed with smoke, earth, and licorice. High levels of glycerin and alcohol result in a sweet attack. This nicely textured, low-acid, plump, succulent 2000 will provide considerable pleasure during its first 7–8 years of life. The funky 1999 Gigondas possesses an opaque plum/purple color as well as kinky notes of incense, roasted meats, sausage, herbs, licorice, truffles, and black cherries. It is full-bodied and superrich, with copious glycerin, no hard edges, and a 30+-second finish. This sumptuous, old style Gigondas is filled with personality. Drink it over the next 10–12 years.

For whatever reason, proprietor Faraud's 1998 Gigondas has turned out to be a medium-weight, uninspiring example from one of the appellation's better estates. The dark ruby-colored 1998 exhibits surprisingly high acidity and a sinewy framework, without the levels of intensely ripe fruit normally found. It is an austere but solidly made, competent Gigondas that should be consumed over the next decade.

The 1997 Gigondas's dark plum color is followed by a sweet nose of licorice, tar, incense, and cherry jam. The wine is medium- to full-bodied, with a spicy, rustic style and plenty of weight and richness. The wine's low acidity and plump, chewy, evolved fruit suggest it should be drunk during its first 7–8 years of life.

DOMAINE CHANABAS

2000 Châteauneuf-du-Pape	D	(88–90+)
1999 Châteauneuf-du-Pape	D	88
1998 Châteauneuf-du-Pape	D	90

Robert Champ, whose cellars are in Piolenc, a small town north of Châteauneuf-du-Pape known as the garlic capital of France, produces superb wines that are worthy of attention. The potentially outstanding 2000 Châteauneuf-du-Pape is crammed with black fruits, spice, dried Provençal herbs, and blackberry/cherry fruit. It boasts a multilayered, abundantly rich palate with loads of fruit. If more complexity develops, it will be a candidate for a 90-point rating. Anticipated maturity: 2003–2015. The complex 1999 Châteauneuf-du-Pape reveals notes of earth, seaweed, black cherry jam, and pepper, excellent texture, ripe fruit, medium to full body, and a seductive style with no hard edges. Drink it over the next decade. The muscular, weighty 1998 Châteauneuf-du-Pape reveals a similar bouquet of charcoal, scorched earth, beef blood, and black fruits. In the mouth, it is full bodied and chewy, with powerful, super-concentrated flavors and high tannin. It is not a wine for readers seeking immediate gratification, or for a more modern-styled, supple-textured offering. Anticipated maturity: 2005–2018.

DOMAINE DES CHANSSAUD

1999 Châteauneuf-du-Pape	D	(85–87)
1998 Châteauneuf-du-Pape	D	89

The dark ruby-colored, medium-bodied, fruity, soft 1999 Châteauneuf-du-Pape will be admired for its immediate accessibility. Although not packed with enough stuffing or fruit for the long term, it will provide attractive drinking over the next 6–7 years. While more structured, the 1998 Châteauneuf-du-Pape is made in a seductive style with abundant glycerin, ripe black cherry and cassis fruit, excellent purity, and a sexy bouquet of black fruits and spice. I may be shortchanging it by not giving it one extra point for an outstanding rating. Anticipated maturity: now–2010.

DOMAINE CHANTE PERDRIX

2000	Châteauneuf-du-Pape	D	(87–88)
1999	Châteauneuf-du-Pape	D	89
1998	Châteauneuf-du-Pape	D	89
1997	Châteauneuf-du-Pape	D	86

I have always enjoyed this estate's wines and continue to liquidate what once was a considerable stock of the sumptuous 1989 (by the way, it is drinking fabulously well). The proprietors, the Nicolets, look for overripeness in their wines, thus producing one of the more flamboyant, exotically scented, Provençal-styled Châteauneuf-du-Papes.

The 2000 Châteauneuf-du-Pape exhibits exotic spices in the nose and plenty of plum, prune, and black fruit characteristics. It is medium- to full bodied, opulent, open-knit, and friendly. Low acidity and jammy fruit provide a lush, disarming personality. Enjoy it during its first decade of life. Cut from the same mold as the 2000, the seductive, complex 1999 Châteauneuf-du-Pape is more exotic and offers aromatic fireworks, including notes of *herbes de Provence,* incense, soy, licorice, and blackberry/cherry fruit. Supple and sexy, with layers of fruit and glycerin and a succulent, velvety-textured finish, it will drink well for 7–9 years.

The deep ruby-colored 1998 Châteauneuf-du-Pape is even more expressive, revealing notes of seaweed intermixed with pepper, olives, leather, and black cherry/cassis fruit. It has intense flavors, medium to full body, abundant glycerin, and a soft finish. More depth and a longer finish would have raised the score by a point or two. Anticipated maturity: now–2012.

The 1997 Châteauneuf-du-Pape reveals a textbook olive, peppery, black cherry–scented nose intermixed with *garrigue*/earthy smells. There is plenty of thickness, surprising glycerin for the vintage, deep fruit, and a pruny ripeness and richness. The wine's low acidity and supple, up-front character suggest it will be delicious to drink during its first 5–6 years of life. *Past Glories:* 1989 (93)

CHAPOUTIER

1996	Banyuls	D	92
1995	Banyuls	D	93
1999	Banyuls Terra Vinya	D	(90–92)
1998	Banyuls Terra Vinya	D	93
1996	Banyuls Terra Vinya	D	92
1995	Banyuls Terra Vinya	D	91
2000	Châteauneuf-du-Pape Barbe Rac	EE	(94–96)
1999	Châteauneuf-du-Pape Barbe Rac	EE	92
1998	Châteauneuf-du-Pape Barbe Rac	EE	95
1997	Châteauneuf-du-Pape Barbe Rac	EE	(87–88)
2000	Châteauneuf-du-Pape La Bernardine	D	(90–92)
1999	Châteauneuf-du-Pape La Bernardine	D	89
1998	Châteauneuf-du-Pape La Bernardine	D	89
1997	Châteauneuf-du-Pape La Bernardine	EE	(87–89)
2000	Châteauneuf-du-Pape Croix de Bois	EE	(93–95)
1999	Châteauneuf-du-Pape Croix de Bois	EE	91
1998	Châteauneuf-du-Pape Croix de Bois	EE	94
2000	Condrieu	D	90
2000	Cornas	D	(83–85)
1999	Cornas	D	84

1998	Cornas	D	88
1997	Cornas	D	(83–85)
1997	Côte Rôtie	D	(87–89)
2000	Côte Rôtie Les Bécasses	D	(84–86)
1999	Côte Rôtie Les Bécasses	D	90
1998	Côte Rôtie Les Bécasses	D	88
2000	Côte Rôtie La Mordorée	EEE	(86–88)
1999	Côte Rôtie La Mordorée	EEE	95
1998	Côte Rôtie La Mordorée	EEE	94
1997	Côte Rôtie La Mordorée	EEE	(92–94)
2000	Coteaux d'Aix Domaine des Béates Terra d'Or	E	(92–95)
1999	Coteaux d'Aix Domaine des Béates Terra d'Or	E	93
1998	Coteaux d'Aix Domaine des Béates Terra d'Or	E	94
1997	Coteaux d'Aix Domaine des Béates Terra d'Or	E	(90–93)
2000	Coteaux d'Aix Les Béatines	B	86
1999	Coteaux d'Aix Les Béatines	B	87
1998	Coteaux d'Aix Les Béatines	B	87
2000	Coteaux du Tricastin Château des Estubiers	A	(87–89)
1999	Coteaux du Tricastin Château des Estubiers	A	88
1998	Coteaux du Tricastin Château des Estubiers	A	85
2000	Coteaux du Tricastin La Ciboise	A	(81–84)
2000	Côtes du Rhône Belleruche	A	86
2000	Crozes-Hermitage Les Meysonnièrs	C	(85–86)
1999	Crozes-Hermitage Les Meysonnièrs	C	87
1998	Crozes-Hermitage Les Meysonnièrs	C	87
2000	Crozes-Hermitage Les Meysonnièrs Blanc	C	88
1999	Crozes-Hermitage Les Meysonnièrs Blanc	C	84
2000	Crozes-Hermitage Petite Ruche	C	84
1997	Crozes-Hermitage Petite Ruche	C	86
2000	Crozes-Hermitage Petite Ruche Blanc	C	87
1997	Crozes-Hermitage Petite Ruche Blanc	C	85
2000	Crozes-Hermitage Les Varonnières	E	(90–93)
1999	Crozes-Hermitage Les Varonnières	E	88+
1998	Crozes-Hermitage Les Varonnières	E	91
1997	Crozes-Hermitage Les Varonnières	E	(90–93)
2000	Ermitage l'Ermite	EEE	(91–93)
1999	Ermitage l'Ermite	EEE	96+
1998	Ermitage l'Ermite	EEE	98
1997	Ermitage l'Ermite	EEE	(91–94)
2000	Ermitage l'Ermite Blanc	EEE	(98–100)
1999	Ermitage l'Ermite Blanc	EEE	100
2000	Ermitage Le Méal	EEE	(91–94)
1999	Ermitage Le Méal	EEE	93+
1998	Ermitage Le Méal	EEE	96+
1997	Ermitage Le Méal	EEE	(91–94)
2000	Ermitage Le Méal Blanc	EEE	(96–100)
1999	Ermitage Le Méal Blanc	EEE	95+
1998	Ermitage Le Méal Blanc	EEE	96
1997	Ermitage Le Méal Blanc	EEE	(96–100)
2000	Ermitage De l'Orée	EEE	(94–97+)
1999	Ermitage De l'Orée	EEE	99

1998	Ermitage De l'Orée	EEE	99
1997	Ermitage De l'Orée	EEE	(98–100)
1996	Ermitage De l'Orée	EEE	99
2000	Ermitage Le Pavillon	EEE	(96–98+)
1999	Ermitage Le Pavillon	EEE	96+
1998	Ermitage Le Pavillon	EEE	98+
1997	Ermitage Le Pavillon	EEE	(96–98)
2000	Hermitage Chante-Alouette	D	(92–94)
1999	Hermitage Chante-Alouette	D	91
1998	Hermitage Chante-Alouette	D	91
1997	Hermitage Chante-Alouette	D	90
1995	Hermitage Chante-Alouette	D	93
2000	Hermitage Mûre de Larnage	D	(86–88)
1999	Hermitage Mûre de Larnage	D	88
2000	Hermitage Mûre de Larnage Blanc	D	89
2000	Hermitage La Sizeranne	E	(87–89)
1999	Hermitage La Sizeranne	E	88
1998	Hermitage La Sizeranne	E	91
1997	Hermitage La Sizeranne	E	(87–88+?)
2000	Hermitage Vin de Paille	EEE	(91–96)
1999	Hermitage Vin de Paille	EEE	91
1997	Hermitage Vin de Paille	EEE	(96–99)
1996	Hermitage Vin de Paille	EEE	(96–99)
1995	Hermitage Vin de Paille	EEE	97
2000	Muscat de Beaumes de Venise	C	89
2000	Muscat de Rivesaltes	C	91
1997	Muscat de Rivesaltes	C	90
1997	Muscat Sec VDP Côtes Catalane	A	89
2000	St.-Joseph Deschants	D	(86–88)
1999	St.-Joseph Deschants	D	88
1998	St.-Joseph Deschants	D	86
1997	St.-Joseph Deschants	D	85
2000	St.-Joseph Deschants Blanc	D	87
1999	St.-Joseph Deschants Blanc	D	87
1997	St.-Joseph Deschants Blanc	D	86
2000	St.-Joseph Les Granits	E	(91–94)
1999	St.-Joseph Les Granits	E	91
1998	St.-Joseph Les Granits	E	92
1997	St.-Joseph Les Granits	E	92
2000	St.-Joseph Les Granits Blanc	E	(91–93)
1999	St.-Joseph Les Granits Blanc	E	91
1998	St.-Joseph Les Granits Blanc	E	94
1997	St.-Joseph Les Granits Blanc	E	(90–93)
1996	St.-Joseph Les Granits Blanc	E	93
1995	St.-Joseph Les Granits Blanc	E	94
2000	St.-Péray Blanc	C	89

Michel Chapoutier is one of the most fascinating personalities in the wine world. His extraordinary takeover of his father's firm, totally revolutionizing the winemaking, is well documented. He expanded the firm's interest in southern France, upgraded the level of both their *négociant* and estate-bottled offerings, and introduced an exquisite series of micro-*cuvées* from selected old-vine parcels in multiple appellations. Chapoutier's brash outspokenness as well as his exuberant youthfulness are not always looked upon with favor by some of his winemaking colleagues, but there is no question that he has produced many brilliant wines in less than a decade. His obsession with biodynamic farming is another source of contention with many of his neighbors, but I notice that as Michel Chapoutier matures, he has become less critical of those who do not follow this practice. Chapoutier is evolving as a wine-maker. He has been widely quoted as saying he made "noise" in the late eighties and early nineties, but is now making "music."

Chapoutier continues to invest in both his vineyards and winemaking facilities. A new bottling and storage facility was completed recently. They have also eliminated the problem of multiple *mise en bouteilles,* with the top wines now receiving only one bottling. This is an important distinction that guarantees the world's consumers receive the same wine, as opposed to *négociants* and growers who continue to practice multiple *mises,* thus introducing a frustrating array of bottlings into the marketplace. Regardless of what changes Chapoutier makes (he is beginning to sound a lot like California's Tim Mondavi with his "obsession with subtlety and finesse"), he has given the Rhône Valley, and the world, a great deal to talk about. The quality of his wines is often extraordinary, and his ambitious new projects in southern France, not to mention Australia, result in wines of high quality, and frequently brilliant efforts.

One area of noticeable improvement is the tank-fermented and aged, lighter-styled whites. This is particularly evident in wines such as the 2000 Crozes-Hermitage Petite Ruche, 2000 Crozes-Hermitage Les Meysonnièrs, 2000 St.-Péray, and 2000 St.-Joseph Deschants. All of these *cuvées* are loaded with fruit, with the 2000 Crozes-Hermitage Petite Ruche revealing a charming nose, ripe, mineral/orange-like flavors, good fruit, excellent purity, and a crisp, dry finish. The 2000 Crozes-Hermitage Les Meysonnièrs exhibits more texture, as well as a similar citrusy and mineral-laced style with lively fruit, medium body, and a solid mid-palate as well as length. Both of these whites should drink well for several years. The biggest surprise for me was Chapoutier's 2000 St.-Péray Blanc. It is good to see Chapoutier and a few others attempting to do something with this long forgotten appellation south of Cornas. A blend of Marsanne and Roussanne grown in decomposed limestone, it reveals a Chablis-like character in its minerality and crisp, lemony, zesty personality. Light- to medium-bodied and pure, with laser-like focus, this is a sleeper from Chapoutier's portfolio. Sadly, only 8,000 bottles were produced. The 2000 St.-Joseph Deschants, which emerges from granite soils, exhibits orange, tangerine, and other tropical fruit aromas, excellent concentration, and a long, crisp finish. It's medium-bodied and, like its siblings, loaded with fruit. Readers looking for a surprisingly strong effort as well as the least expensive white Ermitage, should check out the 2000 Hermitage Mûre de Larnage, made from young vines. Aromas and flavors of acacia flowers, fino sherry, and a touch of honey dominate this full-bodied, chewy, fleshy white Hermitage. To produce this wine, Chapoutier dropped his production of Chante-Alouette. It should drink well for a decade.

Michel Chapoutier, who is never at a loss for words, claims 2000 is the finest vintage for white wines that he has produced since he took over the firm in the late 1980s. The strength of the 2000 Hermitage Chante-Alouette would make anyone a believer. This is a sensational, full-bodied *cuvée* with an unctuous texture, gorgeous notes of smoky, leesy fruit, and a ripe nose of quinine, honeysuckle, pineapple, and fino sherry. Loaded as well as long, it should keep for 20–25 years and be delicious for 4–5 years before it closes down. While similarly styled, the 1999 Hermitage Chante-Alouette is less voluminous and expansive. A telltale nose of mineral, chalk, white flowers, and honeyed citrus is followed by a powerful, concentrated wine with good acidity, distinctive liquid minerality, and a full-bodied, powerful finish. As this viscous, concentrated wine sat in the glass, Alsatian Riesling–like petroleum notes made an appearance. The superb 1998 Hermitage Chante-Alouette is showing well. A light gold color is followed by deep, concentrated notes of melted licorice, minerals, pineapple, quinine, and honey. It is a full-bodied, rich, dense offering to drink between now–2005, cellar between 2005–2010, and drink again over the following 10–15 years. The Burgundy-styled 1997 Hermitage Chante-Alouette achieved 13.9% natural alcohol. It offers the telltale acacia flower, white peach, honeyed citrus character commonly found in top white Hermitage. Full-bodied, with good fat and glycerin, it is ideal for drinking over the next 8 years (although it will undoubtedly keep much longer). The powerful 1995 Hermitage Chante-Alouette is a honeyed peach/pear, intensely concentrated wine with terrific fruit, a chewy texture, long luscious flavors, and decent acidity for a wine of such power and intensity. Either drink it early or put it away for 10–15 years.

Chapoutier continues to fashion fine Condrieus. The 2000 Condrieu (a good vintage for this appellation) reveals outstanding ripeness and richness as well as a textured, layered mouth-feel. It possesses Viognier's classic Condrieu characteristics of minerality intermixed with apricot and peach jam. Drink it over the next 1–2 years.

The finest white wine of the St.-Joseph appellation is Chapoutier's 100% Marsanne, Les Granits. The light gold-colored 2000 St.-Joseph Les Granits Blanc displays a peach-like aroma (reminiscent of Viognier) intermixed with notes of apples, marmalade, and tangerines. Layered, full-bodied, extracted as well as rich, with the weight and depth of a grand cru white Burgundy, it should drink well for 7–8 years. The 1999 St.-Joseph Les Granits Blanc offers a stunning perfume of Grand Marnier, liquid minerals, and acacia flowers. Soft, ripe, and full-bodied, it is an amazing accomplishment. Enjoy it over the next 5–6 years. The 1998 St.-Joseph Les Granits Blanc offers an explosive bouquet consisting of orange liqueur intermixed with honeysuckle, peach, and acacia flowers. Full-bodied, with layers of concentration, lively acidity, and a compelling finish, it should drink well for a decade. Slightly alcoholic, the 1997 St.-Joseph Les Granits Blanc offers an apricot/orange liqueur–like note, along with the pronounced mineral characteristic of the granitic soil in which this 80-year-old parcel of vines is planted. The 1996 St.-Joseph Les Granits Blanc was made from incredibly tiny yields of 10–15 hectoliters per hectare. The wine reveals a remarkable liquid mineral/orange marmalade character. This intense, medium- to full-bodied, beautifully pure wine should drink well for a decade. Because of low acidity, look for the 1997 to have a faster evolutionary track than the 1996—about 7–10 years. The 1995 St.-Joseph Les Granits Blanc is rich and full-bodied with loads of glycerin and a distinct minerality combined with the apricot/peach-like fruit. It is a gloriously dense, powerful, yet elegant white St.-Joseph that, along with the 1996, should age for 10–15 years.

I am a huge fan of Chapoutier's white Hermitages, which, for me, along with Chave's, are the finest being made in the appellation. None is more prodigious than the Ermitage De l'Orée, a 600-case lot of 100% old-vine Marsanne. I have been buying as much as I can get of these wines in every vintage since 1991. The Montrachet of Hermitage are full-bodied, with almost endless aging capacities (at least 50 years), as well as extraordinary textures and complex, nuanced personalities. Chapoutier believes his 2000 Ermitage De l'Orée is even better than its 1999 counterpart—which is saying something. Its light medium-gold color is accompanied by gorgeous aromas of flowery fruit, high levels of concentration, abundant muscle as well as structure, but a closed, backward style. Although voluminous and weighty in the mouth (and no doubt a 50-year wine), it is not as easy to see through its transparent expression of *terroir* as the bottled 1999 is. Nevertheless, this is a compelling, full-bodied, massively endowed white that should be even better after bottling. The awesome 1999 Ermitage De l'Orée flirts with perfection. It is full-bodied with an incredible bouquet of liquid minerals, licorice, honeysuckle, citrus, and a hint of tropical fruits. 100% new oak aging has been completely absorbed by the wine's fruit and glycerin. Made from exceedingly low yields of 12–15 hectoliters per hectare (less than one ton of fruit per vine), this is a winemaking tour de force. However, readers should understand that these are often unusual wines to drink because they tend to show exceptionally well for 4–5 years after bottling, then close up until about age 12. They can last for 4–5 decades. Anticipated maturity: now–2006; 2012–2050.

The 1998 Ermitage De l'Orée's explosive bouquet offers a liquid minerality, honeyed tropical fruits, peaches, and acacia flowers. Amazingly, the 100% new oak treatment has been totally absorbed. The wine is extremely full-bodied, fresh, and pure, with an immense palate presence as well as finish. Drink it over the next 4–5 years, or forget about it for a decade. The 1997 Ermitage De l'Orée is also a huge, chewy, multidimensional wine with spectacular concentration and richness. Notes of white flowers, honey, minerals, and peaches are present in astronomical quantities. In short, these wines must be tasted to be believed. The 1996 Ermitage De l'Orée possesses some of the most amazing glycerin levels I have ever seen in a dry white wine. In fact, both wines represent the essence of white Hermitage. They possess extraordinary intensity, full body, the multilayered texture of a great Montrachet, and intense, honeyed, mineral-like fruit flavors that ooze over the palate with remarkable richness, yet no sense of heaviness. Both wines should easily last 40–50 years—assuming excellent storage. Do not open them before 2010.

In 1997, Michel Chapoutier introduced another luxury *cuvée* of white Hermitage called Le Méal. This white Hermitage Le Méal is not as muscle-bound, full-bodied, and unctuous as l'Orée. Nevertheless, it is usually an impressive effort. The amazing 2000 Ermitage Le Méal possesses huge levels of glycerin, intensity, and concentration, the likes of which I have never before tasted in a dry white Hermitage. It is hard to say where this wine is going or how long it will take to get there, but this should be a riveting example for true connoisseurs. Anticipated maturity: 2012–2060+? The brilliance continues with Chapoutier's 1999 Ermitage Le Méal, which is essentially liqueur of white Hermitage. Notes of pear liqueur intertwined with fino sherry, peaches, minerals, nuts, and licorice are offered in an amazingly concentrated, super-extracted style that manages to be delicate as well as precise. Another 40–50-year dry white, it will undoubtedly close down in 3–4 years and reemerge a decade later. The 1998 Ermitage Le Méal offers aromas and flavors of butterscotch and caramel in its full-bodied, thick, juicy personality. It possesses the same liquid minerality, but reveals more oak than the other Hermitage *cuvées*. This is an amazingly layered wine! Anticipated maturity: 2007–2030. The 1997 Ermitage Le Méal Blanc displays, in addition to cherry notes, more of an orange Grand Marnier characteristic to its fruit. It is an immense, full-bodied, fabulously powerful and concentrated dry white with a steely finish. There are approximately 300 cases of this spectacular offering. Look for it to shut down in 3–4 years, and last for 3–4 decades.

Two of the greatest dry white wines I have ever tasted are the 1999 and 2000 Hermitage l'Ermite. The 2000 Ermitage l'Ermite Blanc is virtually identical to its 1999 counterpart, with slightly more weight and oiliness, yet amazing freshness and definition. The 1999 Ermitage l'Ermite Blanc is a liquid mineral, crystalline expression. It is the essence of its grape as well as *terroir*. It may be the greatest expression of *terroir* I have seen outside of a handful of Alsatian Rieslings (Clos Ste. Hune comes to mind). It has that transparent character that *terroirists* talk more about than actually recognize. Drinking it is like consuming a liquefied stony concoction mixed with white flowers, licorice, and honeyed fruits. Frightfully pure, dense, and well-delineated, there is no real fruit character, just glycerin, alcohol, and liquid stones. That's about it, but, wow, what an expression! Anticipated maturity: 2012–2050. These are all enormous efforts for the rare connoisseur.

Michel Chapoutier is making the finest wines from the Coteaux d'Aix en Provence at his Domaine des Béates. The top *cuvée*, which comes from a single vineyard, is called Terra d'Or. Usually a blend of 40% Cabernet Sauvignon, 40% Syrah, and 20% Grenache, aged in 100% new oak and bottled with neither fining nor filtration, it is capable of lasting 20–25 years. The two other *cuvées* are called Les Béatines and Les Matines.

The 2000 Coteaux d'Aix Les Béatines is a sweet, jammy offering with plenty of kirsch notes intermixed with resiny balsam wood characteristics. With fine ripeness in addition to a soft texture, it should last for 2–3 years. The 1999 Coteaux d'Aix Les Béatines is even better, offering a dramatic perfume of Provençal herbs, cherry liqueur, and earth. This spicy, medium-bodied, fresh, Zinfandel-like offering possesses sweet fruit as well as light tannin. Anticipated maturity: now–2005. The 1999 Coteaux d'Aix Domaine des Béates could turn out to be outstanding. It is a powerful, black/ruby–colored effort with copious quantities of sweet black currant and blackberry fruit, a sense of elegance and harmony, medium to full body, low acidity, and sweet tannin. The finish is long and the wine is impressively constituted. It should last for 15 years. Also very good, the dark ruby-colored 1998 Coteaux d'Aix Domaine Les Béatines displays more saddle leather aromas and flavors, intermixed with black cherries, herbs, earth, and spice box, in addition to medium body and light tannin. It will drink well for a decade or more.

The 2000 Coteaux d'Aix Domaine des Béates Terra d'Or's inky purple color is followed by sumptuous aromas of blackberry and cassis intermixed with smoky, roasted coffee, chocolate, licorice, and minerals. Powerful, dense, and splendidly concentrated, this pure, seamless 2000 should drink well for two decades. The exquisite, opaque purple-colored 1999 Coteaux d'Aix Domaine des Béates Terra d'Or offers a gorgeous nose of mineral and licorice-laced black fruits, huge body, fabulous concentration, and a long, sweet finish with noteworthy levels of crème de cassis, blackberries, and toasty oak. This enormous wine displays perfect equilibrium. Anticipated maturity: 2006–2020. The 1998 Coteaux d'Aix Domaine des Béates Terra d'Or is an astonishing effort. Opaque purple-colored, with an explosive nose of blackberry liqueur intermixed with minerals, flowers, and toast, this massive, concentrated effort fills the mouth with layers of ripe black fruits infused with smoke, minerals, and toast. As the wine sits in the glass, notes of licorice also emerge. A wine of exceptional concentration, purity, and equilibrium, the 1998 Terra d'Or will be at its best between 2003–2020. Remarkably, the 1997 Coteaux d'Aix Domaine des Béates Terra d'Or is richer and more concentrated. It may be the finest wine from this region that I have ever tasted. The color is a saturated black/purple. The wine offers jammy aromas of black raspberries, blackberries, incense, smoke, fennel, and toasty new oak. Extremely full-bodied, chewy, and unctuously textured, it is a strikingly concentrated, compelling example of what can be achieved in this area of southern France. Anticipated maturity: 2003–2020. The offerings from Coteaux du Tricastin's Château des Estubiers are also worthwhile. The 2000 Coteaux du Tricastin Château des Estubiers exhibits a saturated ruby/purple color along with glycerin and alcohol. It should drink well for 6–7 years. The 1999 Coteaux du Tricastin Château des Estubiers falls just short of being outstanding. Loads of black cherry and currant fruit jump from the glass of this lush, succulent effort. Medium- to full-bodied and fruit-driven, with plenty of glycerin and enough acidity to provide focus as well as a clean mouth-feel, it is a hedonistic red to consume over the next 3–4 years. The 1998 Coteaux du Tricastin Château des Estubiers is a solidly constructed, rustic, compressed effort offering aromas of dried herbs and cherry fruit.

One of the finest Crozes that Chapoutier has made, the supple, soft, richly fruity 2000 Crozes-Hermitage Petite Ruche is meant to be consumed during its first several years of life. Its Syrah character comes through in the black fruit, herb-tinged elegance.

The soft, low-acid 2000 Crozes-Hermitage Les Meysonnièrs exhibits medium body, pleasant currant- and herb-tinged fruit flavors, and good ripeness. It is a well made, user-friendly effort of no great distinction. The same can be said for the 1999 Crozes-Hermitage Les Meysonnièrs. It possesses a medium ruby color, tart berry fruit, and a fresh finish revealing notes of fennel and licorice. Drink it over the next 3–4 years. The 1998 Crozes-Hermitage Les Meysonnièrs rouge represents a tasty, rich, chewy example of the appellation that is just beginning to close down. It reveals abundant quantities of red and black fruits, plenty of dried herbs, notes of meat and smoke, and a medium-bodied, lightly tannic finish. Drink during its first 5–7 years of life to take advantage of its exuberance and spiciness.

In order to improve the quality of his Hermitage La Sizeranne, Chapoutier is declassifying the young vines into a separate *cuvée* called Ermitage Mûre de Larnage. The 2000 Hermitage

Mûre de Larnage is sweet, ripe, and fruity, but neither as deep nor as long as its 1999 counterpart. It appears to be a candidate for drinking during its first 5–7 years of life. The delicious 1999 Hermitage Mûre de Larnage offers aromas of cassis, smoke, fennel, and earth. This up-front, supple, medium-bodied, sexy, approachable wine will drink well for 7–8 years.

The Hermitage La Sizeranne is consistently a good value. Revealing more tannin as well as a sweeter, fatter, fleshier mid-palate, and significantly more concentration and ripeness than its 1999 counterpart, the 2000 Hermitage La Sizeranne is an elegant, pure offering with very good to excellent depth. Anticipated maturity: 2004–2014. The 1999 Hermitage La Sizeranne is a more elegant, lighter-styled offering. The color is deep ruby, and the wine offers notes of plums, figs, cassis, and that inky aroma that emerges occasionally in Hermitage. Medium- to full-bodied, with moderate tannin and a short finish, it will be at its finest between now–2012. One of the strongest efforts Chapoutier has produced from Hermitage is the 1998 Hermitage La Sizeranne, which is performing even better from bottle than it was from cask. It offers up an earthy, smoky, sweet black currant–scented nose, followed by big, chewy, full-bodied flavors, excellent texture, and an intriguing liquid mineral nuance to the deep, sweet, ripe flavors. This wine was made from small yields of 15 hectoliters per hectare and aged in 50% new-oak casks. The crop size was 40% less than normal. Anticipated maturity: 2004–2025. The 1997 Hermitage La Sizeranne possesses huge amounts of tannin, some of which is vegetal and green. The wine is dry and structured, with a tough finish. Michel Chapoutier feels it is the finest La Sizeranne made since 1990, but my tasting notes are at odds with that position. The color is impressively saturated, but the wine is pinched and compressed, particularly in the finish.

Chapoutier does a particularly fine job with St.-Joseph and his Deschants is consistently one of the finest wines of the portfolio for the money. The 2000 St.-Joseph Deschants offers a soft, round, seductive, Burgundy-like personality filled with big, sweet, black cherry and currant characteristics intertwined with scents of lavender and spice box. This delicious, plump offering will have plenty of mainstream appeal over the next 6–7 years. The dark ruby-colored 1999 St.-Joseph Deschants reveals a telltale liquid granite quality intermixed with floral and black fruit characteristics. With loads of fruit on the attack, it is both accessible and delicious. Enjoy it over the next 5–6 years. The 1998 St.-Joseph Deschants rouge exhibits a dark ruby/purple color, as well as an excellent black cherry and berry-scented bouquet with an underlying mineral component. There is tangy acidity in the clean finish.

Chapoutier purchases his Cornas from one of the better-known producers of that appellation. The light- to medium-bodied 2000 Cornas reveals plum and currant fruit mixed with earth and dusty tannin. Drink it during its first 5–6 years before it becomes more attenuated. For whatever reason, the bottled 1999 Cornas tasted austere, emaciated, and fruitless. Notions of figs, plums, and washed out currant fruit were disappointing. The 1998 Cornas, which was very good last year, seems more rustic and tannic, without as much depth and concentration as I discerned last year. A dark ruby color is accompanied by a peppery, blackberry, dusty bouquet, and moderately-endowed, tannic, compressed flavors. It may dry out, and I am also concerned about a higher acid profile than I remember from last year. The straightforward, *barrique*-aged 1997 Cornas reveals a dark ruby/purple color and ripe blackberry/cassis fruit in the nose. However, the wine narrows out and becomes attenuated in the lean, austere finish.

The 2000 Côte Rôtie Les Bécasses exhibits aromas of berries, olives, and dried herbs, but it lacks the volume, flavor intensity, and overall completeness of the 1999. Drink this lighter-styled effort during its first 7–8 years of life. The 1999 Côte Rôtie Les Bécasses is the finest Côte Rôtie Chapoutier has made at this price level in many years. It offers a classic nose of cassis, smoke, espresso, and tapenade. Spicy, rich, and medium- to full-bodied, this wine is both voluptuous as well as elegant; it should drink well for 12–15 years. The impressive, dark ruby/purple-colored 1998 Côte Rôtie Les Bécasses offers aromas of black olives, smoke, bacon fat, and cassis. This medium-bodied, fresh, tart but concentrated Côte Rôtie can be drunk now as well as over the next 10–12 years.

The 1997 Côte Rôtie is sweet and flattering, with a textbook black olive, bacon fat, black raspberry, and cherry-scented nose, medium body, an accessible, soft style, and good density and ripeness. There is some tannin, but because it is low in acidity, it comes across as user-friendly.

Chapoutier is an excellent source for Châteauneuf-du-Pape even though their cellars are in Tain l'Hermitage, not in the southern Rhône. From their important vineyard holdings in Châteauneuf-du-Pape they fashion three *cuvées*, La Bernardine and two vineyard designated wines, Barbe Rac and Croix de Bois.

The 2000 Châteauneuf-du-Pape La Bernardine reveals a classic Provençal herb–scented bouquet with notions of lavender and kirsch. Expressive, soft, fat, voluptuous, and gorgeously fruited, it is a decadently rich, concentrated 2000 to consume during its first decade of life. The 1999 Châteauneuf-du-Pape La Bernardine offers a sweet perfume of jammy black cherries, cassis, licorice, and minerals, moderate tannin, medium to full body, and excellent ripeness as well as flesh. It will age well for 10–12 years. Chapoutier's 1998 Châteauneuf-du-Pape La Bernardine (100,000 bottles produced) may be outstanding. It is drinking even better from bottle than it did from cask. Chapoutier feels it is his finest since the 1990, which he still rates as superior, followed by 1995. The 1998 exhibits a deep plum/garnet color and a big, smoky nose of dried herbs, black cherry jam, plums, and licorice. There is excellent concentration, considerable quantities of spice box in the flavors, a dense, chewy mid-palate, and a long, moderately tannic finish. It can be drunk now as well as over the next 12–15 years. The 1997 Châteauneuf-du-Pape La Bernardine exhibits a Provençal herb, kirsch, licorice, cherry, and spicy-scented nose. Medium- to full-bodied, soft, and round, with heady alcohol in the supple finish, it will drink well young and keep for 5–7 years.

There are approximately 500 cases of both the Barbe Rac and Croix de Bois. The Barbe Rac emerges from the western side of Châteauneuf-du-Pape from a parcel planted in 1901. The Croix de Bois is from the appellation's eastern side, where clay soils underlie the famed *Les Galets Roulés* (which contains the melon- and football-size boulders that cover much of the appellation). Both wines tend to be ripe, concentrated, and powerful with 15.5% alcohol typical in big vintages such as 2000, 1999, and 1998.

The 2000 Châteauneuf-du-Pape Barbe Rac appears to be one of the greatest yet produced, rivaling the 1998 and 1990. It offers the essence of black cherry fruit intertwined with resiny characteristics, Provençal herbs (especially lavender), roasted meat, and extremely ripe fruit bordering on pruny. With a fabulous, unctuous texture, a voluptuous, full-bodied palate, and a 45-second finish, this is a sumptuous Châteauneuf-du-Pape. Anticipated maturity: now–2020. While the 1999 Châteauneuf-du-Pape Barbe Rac is not as outstanding as the 1998, it is a beautiful, medium dark ruby-colored effort with a gorgeously sweet nose of kirsch, Provençal herbs, licorice, earth, and spice. Cropped at an amazingly low 15 hectoliters per hectare, it possesses full body, super concentration, and a long finish. Anticipated maturity: now–2016. The 1998 Châteauneuf-du-Pape Barbe Rac's dark plum/purple color is accompanied by a smoky, kirsch, roasted meat, and saddle leather–scented bouquet. The wine took a full year to ferment dry. The result is a blockbuster, full-bodied, super-concentrated Châteauneuf-du-Pape with multiple nuances of spice and Christmas fruitcake, as well as a lusty, heady, alcoholic finish nicely balanced by abundant quantities of glycerin and dense, layered fruit. Don't hesitate to drink it now as well as over the next two decades. The deep ruby-colored 1997 Châteauneuf-du-Pape Barbe Rac exhibits plenty of kirsch, smoke, and herbs in its meaty, fragrant bouquet. Full-bodied, dense, rich, and layered, with good volume and persistence (particularly for a 1997), but hard and tough in the finish, it should be consumed over the next 7–8 years.

The dark plum/ruby-colored 2000 Châteauneuf-du-Pape Croix de Bois displays elements of *sur-maturité* (overripeness) in its notion of black cherries macerated in alcohol. Telltale *garrigue* (that Provençal mélange of herbs and earth) notes are abundantly present in this full-bodied, full-throttle, stunning Châteauneuf. This is one of the finest examples of the appellation as well as the vintage; it will be drinkable upon release and over the following 14–15 years. The 1999 Châteauneuf-du-Pape Croix de Bois exhibits a classic Provençal bouquet of rosemary, thyme, earth, and kirsch. Scents of licorice emerge as the wine sits in the glass. Ripe, full-bodied, and sweet, with moderate tannin, copious spice, and a firm structure, it will be at its finest between 2003–2016. The 1998 Châteauneuf-du-Pape Croix de Bois, which emerges from a vineyard situated in the Bédarrides section of the appellation, is a profound effort offering classic Châteauneuf-du-Pape characteristics. The dark plum/ruby/purple color is followed by aromas of new saddle leather, balsam wood, *garrigue* (that mélange of Provençal herbs and earth), pepper, and sweet, nearly overripe black cherries and plums. Full-bodied, rich, and chewy, with low acidity, high glycerin, and moderately high tannin, this sumptuous, mouth-filling Châteauneuf-du-Pape can be drunk now, but promises to age well for two decades.

The tasting notes that follow are for the luxury *cuvées* of single-vineyard wines made by Michel Chapoutier. All of these wines are aged in 100% new oak, given little racking, minimal SO_2 additions, and are bottled with neither fining nor filtration. Many of them are as good as a wine can be from their respective appellations. While producing 500–700 cases of each of these offerings, Chapoutier should be applauded for proving what can be done at the highest level of quality.

It is hard to find a better Crozes-Hermitage than Les Varonnières. This wine is made from a six-acre vineyard of Syrah vines that average 65–70 years in age. From the granite hills behind the Hermitage appellation emerges the luxury *cuvée* of Crozes-Hermitage Les Varonnières. This is the finest wine of the appellation, but, sadly, only 500 or so cases are produced. The sweet, expansive, opulently-textured 2000 Crozes-Hermitage Les Varonnières was obviously harvested at higher sugars given its levels of glycerin, alcohol, and sweet fruit married with ripe, seamless tannin. Big, earthy, peppery, berry fruit notes mix with cassis and licorice in this chewy, full-bodied, approachable 2000. Anticipated maturity: 2003–2015. The 1999 Crozes-Hermitage Les Varonnières is less successful than previous efforts. While it may ultimately merit an outstanding score, it possesses more austerity as well as firm tannin than previous examples. This saturated dark ruby-colored, medium-bodied 1999 offers up aromas of plums, currants, cherries, smoke, and dried herbs. Although firm, with good grip as well as impressive concentration, it requires additional aging. Anticipated maturity: 2004–2012. The 1998 Crozes-Hermitage Les Varonnières is showing much better after bottling than it did from cask. A profound Crozes, it boasts an opaque purple color and an extraordinary nose of spice box, smoke, flowers, licorice, and powdered stones. Extremely expressive, full-bodied, rich, spicy, and supple-textured, it should drink well young yet age for 15+ years. Wow! The 1997 Crozes-Hermitage Les Varonnières is a softer, fatter, less acidic offering. It possesses a saturated dark ruby/purple color, as well as a pronounced cherry liqueur nose with smoke, roasted herbs, and underbrush notes in the background. Full-bodied, dense, chewy, and made in a user-friendly, accessible style, this wine should be delicious when released and age well for 12–15 years.

I do not believe there is a better St.-Joseph produced than the 500+ cases of Chapoutier's Les Granits. Made from a vineyard planted in decomposed granite with full southerly exposure, just above the village of Mauves (the vines average 60–70 years in age), it is an extraordinary offering. Potentially better than the 1999 because it is more supple and accessible is the 2000 St.-Joseph Les Granits. Its blackberry and raspberry flavors border on overripeness. There is a liquid stony character to the fruit, plenty of licorice, and a layered, pure, ripe personality. The fruit and glycerin undoubtedly conceal considerable tannin. Anticipated maturity: 2004–2016. As are many of Chapoutier's 1999s, the superb 1999 St.-

Joseph Les Granits is tightly knit, but there is no doubting its mineral, smoky, black currant and berry fruit intermixed with subtle wood. The dark ruby/purple color and austere attack are followed by a fleshy, super-concentrated wine with plenty of depth, purity, and length. Anticipated maturity: 2004–2015. The opaque purple-colored 1998 St.-Joseph Les Granits rouge exhibits an explosive bouquet of blueberry and blackberry liqueur, minerals, and smoke. A wine of exceptional richness, texture, length, and purity, it is super. Moderate tannin suggests that 2–3 years of cellaring are required, but this 1998 will drink well young and age for 15–18 years. The 1997 St.-Joseph Les Granits is massive and full-bodied, with a floral component to go along with the blackberry/cassis fruit and flinty *terroir* characteristic. Superb ripeness, low acidity, and fleshy, ripe fruit result in an opulent, splendid wine. Anticipated maturity: now–2012.

Chapoutier's La Mordorée *cuvée* is produced from 75–80-year-old Syrah vines planted in both the Côte Blonde and Côte Brune, aged in 100% new oak casks, and bottled with neither fining nor filtration. The lighter, less concentrated 2000 Côte Rôtie La Mordorée exhibits a deep plum color, but lacks substance compared to 1999 or 1998. Notes of tapenade, smoke, and earth are present, but the finish is short, with little grip and depth. Anticipated maturity: 2003–2012. The 1999 Côte Rôtie La Mordorée is the finest Chapoutier has produced since 1991. It has closed down since its pre-bottling tasting. The color is an inky purple, and the wine is dense and powerful, with notes of smoky blackberries, creosote, and espresso. Concentrated flavors reveal high levels of tannin (surprising in view of last year's report), and a rich, long, 45-second finish. This impressive 1999 will take longer to reach its plateau of drinkability than I initially thought. Anticipated maturity: 2009–2023. The 1998 Côte Rôtie La Mordorée exhibits an opaque ruby/purple color in addition to a spectacular nose of grilled toast, cured olives, cassis, fried bacon, and smoke. As it sits in the glass, additional nuances emerge. Deep, full-bodied, powerful, and concentrated, this 1998 is already approachable. The unctuous texture and long, 45-second finish suggest even greater promise for the future. Anticipated maturity: 2004–2020. The 1997 Côte Rôtie La Mordorée is an extremely expressive, open-knit, aromatic, and seductive example. Chapoutier believes it is the finest he has ever made, but I would still give that honor to the 1991. The saturated ruby/purple color is accompanied by telltale aromas of black raspberries, roasted herbs, smoke, and meat. The wine is medium- to full-bodied and moderately tannic, with low acidity, superb concentration, and an intense black cherry, camphor-like, olive component. This wine should be drinkable upon release and last for two decades.

There are three luxury *cuvées* of Hermitage—Méal, from the vineyard of the same name, Pavillon, from the extremely old vines of Les Bessards, and l'Ermite, from the vineyard of the same name situated at the top (or dome) of the Hermitage hill. These represent Hermitage at its greatest, with Pavillon the most concentrated, l'Ermite the most elegant and dominated by minerals, and Méal a synthesis of the two styles.

The 2000 Ermitage Le Méal smells of cassis and ink. It boasts power, concentration, texture, high tannin, and lower acidity than the 1999, with a sweet crème de cassis–filled finish. No doubt its tannin level will reassert itself once the wine is bottled. Anticipated maturity: 2010–2045. The 1999 Ermitage Le Méal will not be ready to drink for at least 15 years. One must admire Michel Chapoutier for fashioning a wine that goes against the modern day predilection for wines of immediate gratification. This effort is reminiscent of Bordeaux's famed Château Ausone. A dense ruby/purple color is accompanied by subtle notions of powdered stone, chalk, violets, cassis, graphite, and pepper. Dense, tough-textured, tight, and tannic, it possesses considerable weight and depth, but it is not revealing the opulence it did last year. Anticipated maturity: 2015–2050. The 1998 Ermitage Le Méal rouge represents the essence of Hermitage—a wine of elegance, power, symmetry, and extraordinary purity. Aromas and flavors of black and red fruits as well as liquid granite emerge in this superb, multilayered wine of fabulous intensity and length. The finish lasts for nearly a minute. The tannin is high, and a decade of cellaring is warranted. This 1998 will last for half a century. The 1997 Ermitage Le Méal displays more fat, plumpness, and richness, without losing the floral minerality so obvious in the 1996. It is a finesse-styled Hermitage with more concentrated black fruits and a high-toned, structured, well-delineated personality. Because of low acidity and a plump, plush texture, this wine will be approachable at an earlier age. Anticipated maturity: 2005–2035.

The saturated black/purple-colored 2000 Ermitage Le Pavillon reveals telltale aromas of crème de cassis, more succulence, and smoke, licorice, and inkiness, but lower acidity, brutal tannin in the finish, massive concentration and extract, and an uncompromising style that says to any potential buyer, "Don't touch me for at least 12–15 years." This has the potential to be another legend from this vineyard that has consistently produced compelling wines since 1989. Anticipated maturity: 2015–2060. The prodigious 1999 Ermitage Le Pavillon boasts crème de cassis aromatics intermixed with unmistakable aromas of ink. It is pure fruit compared to the minerality of l'Ermite. Full-bodied and fabulously concentrated as well as powerful, with a finish that lasts for 50 seconds, this saturated black/purple-colored 1999 exhibits remarkable symmetry, purity, and overall massive size all juxtaposed with a sense of elegance and restraint. It is a monumental achievement, but ultimately is less successful than the great 2000 or 1998. The 1998 Ermitage Le Pavillon flirts with perfection . . . again. Revealing a striking bouquet of violets, blackberries, smoke, licorice, and minerals, it is luxuriously rich, full-bodied, and layered on the palate. It is another wine with a finish that lasts beyond a minute. Remarkably, yields were a mere 10 hectoliters per hectare. There is plenty of tannin in the finish, but it is ripe and well integrated. Anticipated maturity: 2010–2050. The 1997 Ermitage Le Pavillon displays a similarly saturated purple color and a fabulously intense nose of blackberry liqueur intermixed with floral scents, smoke, licorice, tar, and Chinese black tea. There is wonderful concentration, massive body, and a monster finish in this decadently rich Hermitage. It possesses lower acidity than the 1996, but every bit as much concentration, extract, and length. Anticipated maturity: 2008–2035.

Chapoutier's Ermitage l'Ermite possesses a transparent character that almost allows the taster to see through the wine's multiple levels. It is made from a small parcel of vines, believed to be over 100 years old, located close to the tiny white chapel owned by the Jaboulets on the highest part of the Hermitage Hill. Yields are a minuscule 9–15 hectoliters per hectare. The 2000 Ermitage l'Ermite is behaving the way the 1999 did at the same stage, revealing austerity, tightness, high levels of tannin, and more mineral and liquid granite characteristics than fruit. That will undoubtedly emerge with time as there is abundant evidence of cherries and black currants. While full-bodied and weighty, it is dominated by its structure and minerality. It appears to be a candidate for 15+ years of cellaring. Anticipated maturity: 2016–2060. A wine that borders on perfection compared to its backward performance from barrel is the 1999 Ermitage l'Ermite. From bottle, the 1999 l'Ermite reveals an old-style Lafleur character in its kirsch intermixed with raspberries, blackberries, and striking minerality. It has put on considerable weight since last year, but is essentially an elegant, ethereal effort with incredible intensity as well as amazing lightness. It is a phenomenal expression of *terroir*. However, be forewarned, anyone expecting to derive a lot of pleasure from this before another 15 years elapse will be disappointed. Anticipated maturity: 2015–2060.

The elegant 1998 Ermitage l'Ermite rouge is lighter than either Le Méal or Pavillon, but exquisitely balanced, with subtle notes of smoke and black currants. The flavors unfold gently and gracefully, with nothing overstated. The power is restrained, the tannin is well integrated, and the acidity is barely noticeable. However, the wine is fresh and beautifully delineated. Anticipated maturity: 2010–2040. The fabulous 1997 Ermitage l'Ermite possesses the ripeness and exotic characteristics of a great Pomerol, but the structure, smoky minerality, and power of Hermitage. The color is a saturated black/ruby. The wine is rich, chewy, thick, and impeccably well balanced. This wine will be more approachable in its youth than the 1996 l'Ermite, but it is capable of lasting 30–40 years.

For those with a sweet tooth, the 2000 Muscat de Rivesaltes (rated 91) is a light gold-colored offering with considerable floral and honeyed apricot fruit characteristics. Extremely sweet, it is meant to be drunk at the end of the meal. It will age for 1–3 years. The 2000 Muscat de Beaumes de Venise (rated 89) is a selection made from the cooperative in that village. Aromas of orange marmalade intermixed with tropical fruit cocktail–like scents are followed by a medium- to full-bodied, moderately sweet, somewhat obvious wine. Drink it over the next year. The 1999 Banyuls Terra Vinya also exhibits a big, smoky nose, but it is unevolved and less nuanced and detailed compared to the 1998. The 1999 is a big, chewy, rich effort with moderate sweetness as well as a roasted chocolate/blackberry-laced personality. It should become more delineated with cellar aging, and should come close to equaling what was produced in 1998. The exquisite 1998 Banyuls Terra Vinya was produced from 90-year-old Carignan vines with a touch of Grenache included. Yields were a minuscule 10 hecto-liters per hectare. It offers a big, smoky, chocolaty, black cherry and berry-scented nose, marvelous intensity and purity, a luxurious texture, and a moderately sweet, long, pure finish balanced by decent acidity and sweet tannin. It will drink well for 15+ years. As most read-ers know, this is France's quasi-answer to vintage port. The 1996 Banyuls, 1996 Banyuls Terra Vinya, and 1995 Banyuls Terra Vinya are rich, chocolaty wines that smell like cappuc-cinos infused with cherry liqueur. Rich and pure, they are not the least bit heavy. The 1995 Banyuls is a fruity, non-oxidized style of Banyuls with tons of chocolaty black cherry fruit, moderate sweetness, medium to full body, outstanding purity, and real vibrancy and fresh-ness, something not usually associated with Banyuls. This wine will drink impeccably with chocolate desserts. It should last for a decade or more.

There are limited *cuvées* of Chapoutier's sweet, oily, viscous *vin de paille*. While obviously great stuff, the 2000 Hermitage Vin de Paille was still fermenting when tasted in August 2001, and thus was exceptionally rich and sugary. Made from grapes harvested in late October/early November, and kept on straw mats for two months prior to being crushed and vinified, these wines can last 100+ years. The amber-colored 1999 Hermitage Vin de Paille reveals more new oak than expected, but it had just finished fermentation and perhaps is not as seamless as it will be in several years. The 1997 and 1996 Hermitage Vin de Paille are both huge, thick, unctuously-textured, sweet wines that will last for 50 or more years. What I found striking about the 1996 Vin de Paille was that the nose was identical to white truffles. Chapoutier's 1995 Hermitage Vin de Paille is also an extraordinary, nectar-like wine. It ex-hibits an orange marmalade, honeyed corn, and super-sweet richness that is almost too in-tense to have with dessert. While the 1996 possesses slightly better acidity, the 1995 is a heavier, fatter wine. This wine will last 50+ years.

Past Glories: Châteauneuf-du-Pape Barbe Rac—1994 (92), 1993 (92), 1992 (90), 1990 (96), 1989 (93); Ermitage De l'Orée—1994 (97), 1993 (92), 1992 (96), 1991 (94+); Ermitage Le Pavillon—1994 (95), 1993 (92), 1992 (94), 1991 (100), 1990 (100), 1989 (100); Côte Rôtie La Mordorée—1994 (92), 1993 (90), 1992 (90), 1991 (100), 1990 (93)

DOMAINE DE LA CHARBONNIÈRE

2000	Châteauneuf-du-Pape	D	(87–89)
1999	Châteauneuf-du-Pape	D	87
1998	Châteauneuf-du-Pape	D	88
1997	Châteauneuf-du-Pape	D	78
2000	Châteauneuf-du-Pape Les Hautes Brusquières	E	(91–93)
1999	Châteauneuf-du-Pape Les Hautes Brusquières	E	89
1998	Châteauneuf-du-Pape Les Hautes Brusquières	E	91

1997	Châteauneuf-du-Pape Les Hautes Brusquières	E	87
2000	Châteauneuf-du-Pape Mourre des Perdrix	E	(90–93)
1999	Châteauneuf-du-Pape Mourre des Perdrix	E	90
1998	Châteauneuf-du-Pape Mourre des Perdrix	E	90
1997	Châteauneuf-du-Pape Mourre des Perdrix	E	86
2000	Châteauneuf-du-Pape Vieilles Vignes	E	(91–93)
1999	Châteauneuf-du-Pape Vieilles Vignes	E	90+
1998	Châteauneuf-du-Pape Vieilles Vignes	E	89+
1999	Vacqueyras	C	89
1998	Vacqueyras	C	89

Rhône wine enthusiasts need to jump on the bandwagon before Domaine de la Charbonnière becomes better known. Proprietor Michel Maret is doing everything right, producing wines with terrific individual character from low yields and, over several years, bottling without filtration. It is one of the most serious Châteauneuf-du-Pape estates, and, fortunately, has good representation in the United States. Domaine de la Charbonnière is also a very good source of Vacqueyras. By the way, I consistently underrated this property's 1998 Châteauneufs by one to three points. I hope I have not done that with the 2000s and 1999s, two top-class vintages. The 1997s and 1996s are generally well made wines that take advantage of the forward, easygoing nature of these vintages. As for Domaine de la Charbonnière's 1995s, they have a more saturated color than the 1996s, cut a deeper, fuller impression on the palate, and possess more character and aromatics. Readers should also note that Michel Maret is fashioning competent white Châteauneuf-du-Papes (generally an innocuous category). He uses approximately 40% Roussanne in the blend. These wines are very good, but require consumption during their first 2 years of life.

Michel Maret's 2000s reveal sweeter glycerin levels as well as additional ripeness, fat, and fruit, although there is plenty of underlying structure and tannin. It is another top vintage for Maret, who has not missed a beat over the last three years. The dark ruby/plum-colored 2000 Châteauneuf-du-Pape displays a classic Provençal nose of dried herbs, saddle leather, pepper, and plum/black cherry fruit. Medium-bodied, lush, and easy to drink because of the high glycerin and ripeness, it will provide considerable enjoyment over the next decade. Also dark ruby/plum-colored, the rich, full-bodied 2000 Châteauneuf-du-Pape Mourre des Perdrix offers aromas of flowers, plums, cherries, currants, and lavender. It is an impressive example of power combined with elegance. The finish is long and moderately tannic. Anticipated maturity: now–2016. The 2000 Châteauneuf-du-Pape Les Hautes Brusquières Cuvée Spéciale is reminiscent of its 1998 counterpart, offering explosive levels of ripeness and glycerin and a seamless, fat, voluptuous mid-palate as well as finish. It is a full-bodied, large-scaled, rich, in-your-face style of Châteauneuf-du-Pape possessing glorious levels of black cherry/kirsch fruit. At present, the structure and tannin are concealed by its luxurious richness. Anticipated maturity: now–2017. The most backward of this quartet is the large-scaled but closed 2000 Châteauneuf-du-Pape Vieilles Vignes. A more cerebral offering, it possesses plenty of tannin and structure as well as abundant quantities of blueberry and black cherry fruit. This long, pure, full-bodied 2000 needs 4–5 years of cellaring. Anticipated maturity: 2005–2018.

The 1999s are the most forward efforts produced by Maret over the last three vintages, with the exception of the Mourre des Perdrix and Vieilles Vignes, which both require time in bottle. The medium plum/ruby-colored 1999 Châteauneuf-du-Pape exhibits a big, spicy nose of balsam, berries, and cherry fruit. It is a medium-bodied, easygoing Châteauneuf to drink over the next 4–5 years. The deep ruby-colored 1999 Châteauneuf-du-Pape Mourre des Perdrix is a blend of 70% Grenache, 15% Syrah, and 15% Mourvèdre from vines averaging 30–50 years of age. Atypically for the vintage, it requires 1–3 years of cellaring. It offers glorious notes of blackberry and new saddle leather aromas. Medium- to full-bodied, impressively concentrated, and pure with moderate tannin, this is a beautifully knit, well-balanced effort. Anticipated maturity: now–2015. Readers seeking more openness should check out the 1999 Châteauneuf-du-Pape Les Hautes Brusquières Cuvée Spéciale (an unusual blend of 60% Grenache and 40% Syrah). While not as big as the blockbuster 1998 (a 93–94 point wine), it is hedonistic and full-bodied, offering sumptuous aromas and flavors of jammy black fruits and cherries galore. Lush, succulent, and a thrill to drink, this sexy Châteauneuf-du-Pape can be consumed over the next decade. Revealing a less saturated color than the Mourre des Perdrix, the 1999 Châteauneuf-du-Pape Vieilles Vignes reveals a mineral-laced, black cherry, and plum-scented perfume. Full-bodied, with exceptional purity as well as abundant tannin in the finish, it is a layered, serious *vin de garde,* especially for the vintage. Anticipated maturity: 2004–2017.

Maret's finest value is his Vacqueyras, and the 1999 is another top-notch effort. Its dark plum color is accompanied by copious amounts of black cherry and berry fruit intermixed with earth, smoke, and spice. Chewy, low in acidity, and ripe, it is ideal for drinking over the next 3–4 years. Readers will find the 1998 Châteauneuf-du-Pape to be a reasonably good value. It is a long, rich, fat effort with plenty of Provençal spice intermixed with cherry liqueur, pepper, and olives. Long and pure, with medium to full body, low acidity, and a succulent texture, it is a hedonistic Châteauneuf-du-Pape to drink over the next decade. The 1998 Châteauneuf-du-Pape Mourre des Perdrix is a firmer, more tannic effort offering scents of pine trees, balsam wood, resin, and black cherry and berry fruit. Earthy and firm, with moderate tannin, it will benefit from 2–3 years of cellaring and should keep for 14+ years. This may be a case where the 1999 turns out to be the better wine, but it is still too close to call. I was surprised by the restrained, elegant, mineral, spice, and red/black fruit character- istics of the 1998 Châteauneuf-du-Pape Vieilles Vignes. Its medium ruby/garnet color re- veals more evolution than expected. Although excellent, this 1998 lacks that extra dimension of richness, concentration, and depth necessary to justify a 90-point score. However, it will drink well for 10–12 years. It is obvious when tasting these wines in sequence that the 1998 Châteauneuf-du-Pape Les Hautes Brusquières Cuvée Spéciale is the most layered, concen- trated, and complete, with more viscosity than its siblings, as well as an outstanding combi- nation of Provençal spice/herbs and intense yet pure kirsch notes. Full-bodied and powerful, it has not lost the telltale elegance and moderate restraint that Maret builds into his wines. On the palate, this 1998 reveals impressive texture, richness, and length. Anticipated matu- rity: now–2018.

As usual, the Vacqueyras is a sleeper in the portfolio. Generally as good as the Châteauneuf-du-Papes, it is made in the telltale elegant yet concentrated, medium-bodied style Maret prefers. The 1998's aromas of strawberries, black cherry jam, mineral, and spice create an inviting as well as complex aromatic impression. In the mouth, the wine is medium- bodied, with lovely purity, superb equilibrium, and a long finish with abundant quantities of fruit, glycerin, and sweet tannin. Drink it over the next 7–8 years.

While the 1997 Châteauneuf-du-Pape Cuvée Tradition was austere, tart, and straightfor- ward, the 1997 Châteauneuf-du-Pape Mourre des Perdrix was an elegant, stylish wine with Burgundy-like black cherry fruit mixed with floral scents, pepper, and earth. With good depth, nice softness, some structure, but a forward and appealing, layered texture and rich- ness, it should drink well for 7–8 years. The 1997 Châteauneuf-du-Pape Les Hautes Brusquières Cuvée Spéciale exhibits more glycerin, with a forward, lusty, up-front personal- ity. It should be consumed over the next 5–7 years.

G.A.E.C. CHARVIN

2000 Châteauneuf-du-Pape	D	(94–96)
1999 Châteauneuf-du-Pape	D	92
1998 Châteauneuf-du-Pape	D	93

1997 Châteauneuf-du-Pape	D	87
2000 Côtes du Rhône	A	(89–92)
1999 Côtes du Rhône	A	86

This gem of an estate, tucked away in the section of Châteauneuf-du-Pape known as Grès, remains largely unknown among Rhône wine enthusiasts. Until 1990, all of their grapes were sold to various *négociants*, but beginning with the 1990 vintage, a small portion was estate-bottled. Today, most of Charvin's harvest is bottled on the premises. The young Laurent Charvin continues to increase quality from the estate's extremely old vines (which resemble small trees) by practicing traditional, natural, and uncompromising winemaking. His Châteauneufs represent the quintessential expressions of their vineyard as well as vintage. Often similar to Rayas because of their pure black raspberry/kirsch-scented nose and flavors, they also offer an impressive, expansive, chewy texture. The estate is also a good source of value-priced Côtes du Rhône, produced from a 35-year-old vineyard planted with 85% Grenache, 10% Syrah, and 5% Carignan. There are 2,000 cases of Charvin's Châteauneuf-du-Pape and a bit more of the Côtes du Rhône.

Readers looking for a wonderful introduction to Charvin's style should check out the 2000 Côtes du Rhône, the finest Laurent Charvin has made in the last decade. It is a sensual, sexy, dense ruby/purple-colored effort revealing a creamy texture, gorgeous levels of licorice, black cherry/blackberry fruit, loads of glycerin (it achieved 14% natural alcohol), and an authentic taste. Enjoy this sumptuous Côtes du Rhône over the next 3–4 years, although it will undoubtedly keep longer. The explosive 2000 Châteauneuf-du-Pape has the potential to eclipse Charvin's great 1998 and 1990. It achieved 14.5% natural alcohol. No wood was used in its upbringing, and there was no bleeding of the tanks to increase concentration. Made from extremely old vines, it is a fabulous effort boasting an opaque purple color along with a gorgeously sweet nose of candied licorice, blackberry liqueur, underbrush, pepper, and kirsch. It is superbly concentrated, multilayered, voluptuously textured, and exceptionally long (45 seconds). Like its predecessors, it is a traditional blend of 82% Grenache, 8% Syrah, 5% Mourvèdre, and 5% Vacqueyras. It should hit its prime in 4–6 years, peak at around age 10–15, and last for 20+ years. It is an awesome performance from one of Châteauneuf-du-Pape's emerging stars.

Also a brilliant effort, the 1999 Châteauneuf-du-Pape (14% natural alcohol) exhibits a big, spicy nose of balsam, juicy, fat, black cherry and berry flavors, full body, a creamy texture, superb purity, and a long finish. It will provide abundant pleasure over the next 12–15 years. The 1999 Côtes du Rhône exhibits spicy, peppery, *garrigue* aromas in addition to cherry fruit. Drink this medium-bodied, soft, fruity 1999 over the next 1–2 years.

In bottle, the 1998 Châteauneuf-du-Pape is living up to all the promise it exhibited from *foudre*. A blend of 82% Grenache, 8% Syrah, 5% Mourvèdre, and 5% Vaccarèse, it is a bigger, more tannic, currently less appealing effort than the 1999. However, it is loaded, offering abundant quantities of dried herbs, smoke, blackberry, cherry, and plum-like fruit, a sensational mid-palate, as well as a blockbuster finish. A traditional Châteauneuf-du-Pape, made purely, expressively, and impressively, it will be at its peak between 2004–2019.

The 1997 Châteauneuf-du-Pape possesses dark ruby colors, a distinctive raspberry/framboise fruitiness, medium body, good ripeness, excellent purity, and a fruit-driven, open-knit, forward personality. It should be consumed over the next 5–7 years.

J. L. CHAVE

1998 Ermitage Cuvée Cathelin	EEE	98
2000 Hermitage	EE	(95–99)
1999 Hermitage	EE	96
1998 Hermitage	EE	93+
1997 Hermitage	EE	92

2000 Hermitage Blanc	EE	(91–94)
1999 Hermitage Blanc	EE	94
1998 Hermitage Blanc	EE	92+
1997 Hermitage Blanc	EE	94
1996 Hermitage Blanc	E	93
1995 Hermitage Blanc	E	94
1997 Hermitage Vin de Paille	EEE	(96–98+)
1996 Hermitage Vin de Paille	EEE	99
2000 St.-Joseph	C	(87–89)
1999 St.-Joseph	C	88
1997 St.-Joseph	D	86
1999 St.-Joseph Offerus	C	88

This is the model estate for a family-owned vineyard—a great family, a great domaine, a great *terroir*, and great wines. While the father and son, as well as the other 500 years or so of Chaves who have made wines from the hallowed hills of Hermitage, may be world-class tasters, superb chefs, and gifted storytellers, the fact remains that Gérard Chave and, increasingly, his talented young son, Jean-Louis, are among the staunchest guardians of *terroir* and artisanal/artistic winemaking in France. The humility with which they go about their business (mere custodians of privileged spots on planet Earth is how they look at it) is refreshing, particularly in a world dominated by greed, and an industrial wine culture.

Only Michel Chapoutier's luxury *cuvée* of l'Orée captures the same magic as Chave's white Hermitage. Tasting Chave's white Hermitage (just more than 1,000 cases produced), a blend of 80% Marsanne and 20% Roussanne, is a wonderful tour of the different *terroirs* from which he obtains grapes, Les Rocoules, Maison Blanche, l'Ermite, and Péleat.

Since son Jean-Louis Chave joined father Gérard, there have been subtle refinements in the winemaking program. The white wine always went through full malolactic, but now there is *bâtonnage* (stirring the lees), as well as more barrel fermentation and a greater percentage of new oak. I have always loved Chave's white Hermitage, and have been buying it consistently since the 1978 vintage. However, I must say that if the 1994 signaled a new level of quality, the vintages that follow continue the trend, producing blockbuster white Hermitages that possess the texture of a great white Burgundy, in addition to extraordinary intensity and richness. White Hermitage drinks beautifully for 4–5 years after its release, and then closes down, seemingly losing its fruit, becoming monolithic, neutral, and occasionally oxidized, only to magically reemerge 10–15 years after the vintage. With such additional age, it exhibits a roasted hazelnut, buttery, honeyed, full-bodied, powerful, exceptionally complex style. Americans have never taken a liking to white Hermitage, but it ages as well as the red, and if you do not drink it during the first 2–3 years after the vintage, it is best to wait for two decades to consume it as it goes through a long, stubborn, dumb period.

The 2000 Hermitage Blanc had not been assembled at the time of my tasting, but every component part, from l'Ermite through Rocoules and Péleat, easily merited 92–95 points. Extremely powerful, opulent, and concentrated, it appears to be another superlative vintage for this estate. The Chaves recognized that the key to success in 2000 (a year where Mother Nature was overly generous) was a draconian crop thinning, not just once, but multiple times. Yields at Chave were the lowest in the northern Rhône. That is reflected in the concentration achieved. The 2000 white Hermitage should drink well in its youth, close up in 6–7 years, and reemerge and drink well for 10–25+ years.

The 1999 Hermitage Blanc is another glorious effort. Like the 2000, it is a 1,000-case blend of 80% Marsanne and 20% Roussanne, all from Les Rocoules, Maison Blanche, l'Ermite, and Péleat. It is an oily, unctuously textured wine with low acidity and fabulously concentrated honeysuckle, citrus, liquid mineral, and acacia flower-like flavors. The finish lasts for nearly 45 seconds. It will be gorgeous young, but evolve for two decades or more. A retasting of the 1998 Hermitage Blanc confirmed its brilliant quality. An elegant, floral-scented, structured white Hermitage, it boasts fabulous concentration, but is less flattering and precocious than either the 1999 or 2000. If the latter two wines lean toward a flamboyant style, the 1998 should prove to be one of the more muscular, long-lived, backward efforts requiring patience. The brilliant 1997 Hermitage Blanc is an unctuously textured effort with aromas and flavors of honeysuckle, peach, white currants, and quince. Rich, with low acidity and a forward, low-acid, super-concentrated character, it is unbelievably delicious and should remain so for another 1–2 years before it closes down. What reemerges at age 10 or 12 should be fascinating, but seems less of a sure bet for long-term aging than the 1998 and 1999. The 1996 Hermitage Blanc is sensational. While it is not as fat as the 1997, it is a powerful, heady, alcoholic, deep, chewy, superb white Hermitage offering notes of grilled nuts, fino sherry–like scents, thick, juicy, honeyed citrus, and a touch of peach and roses. Structured and powerful, it should have 10–15 or more years of longevity. The 1995 Hermitage Blanc is low in acidity, but fabulously rich, with an extraordinary floral, honeysuckle, peach-like fruit character. With awesome intensity and an unctuous texture, this may be the finest white Hermitage Chave has ever produced. It is powerful and extremely showy at present. Given its equilibrium and overall density, this wine should last 20+ years. Chave said the yields were a minuscule 20 hectoliters per hectare in 1995, versus 30 h/h in 1996 (about one-half the yield of most top white Burgundy producers' Chardonnay vineyards).

Tasting through Chave's red wines is always immensely educational. It is fascinating to see the differences between each parcel of vines. While Les Dionnières and l'Hermite are generally the least impressive, they do exhibit good raspberry/cassis fruit, although Les Dionnières seem to be mostly pepper and tough, hard tannin. The superb *cuvées* included Le Méal (pure cassis, full body, and gobs of fruit), Beaumes (explosive richness, very Burgundian, with black raspberry, earth, truffle, and spice), Péleat (extremely ripe, fleshy, voluptuously textured, low-acid, yet dynamite crème de cassis richness), and the monster, full-bodied, profound Les Bessards (huge, chewy, thick, blackberry/cassis, roasted herb, and an iron-like mineral character that gives the wine great complexity). Les Bessards, which represents one-third of the blend, is usually the finest *cuvée*, although Péleat, Beaumes, and Le Méal are all exceptional, and l'Hermite provides elegance. In the best vintages, the Chaves produces a luxury-priced *cuvée* called Cuvée Cathelin, the production of which rarely exceeds 200 cases.

Chave's 2000 Hermitage is a strong candidate for the wine of the vintage. The brutal crop thinning as well as selection process in the cellars has resulted in a wine that transcends the vintage's character. Most 2000 northern Rhônes reveal flavor superficiality because of excessive yields, which caused a lack of depth as well as concentration (in spite of the fact that they are charming, ripe, and low in acidity). Chave's 2000 Hermitage is a tour de force. Tasting through the component parts is a lesson in the differences in Hermitage's *terroirs*. Moreover, the blend is always better than its individual parts. This profound Hermitage boasts a saturated blue/black/purple color as well as gorgeous aromas of liquid minerality intermixed with crème de cassis and graphite. Full-bodied, with low acidity, high tannin, and sensational extract and length, it is a fabulous Hermitage that combines extraordinary power, flesh, and succulence with remarkable freshness and delineation. Anticipated maturity: 2005–2040.

In 1999, the Chaves felt every *cuvée* was so stunning there was no justification for doing a special Cuvée Cathelin, which they did produce in 1998, 1995, 1991, and 1990. A brilliant effort, the dense saturated purple-colored 1999 Hermitage exhibits fabulous texture, purity, and sweetness as well as a finish that lasts for nearly a minute. There is high tannin, remarkably rich, concentrated extract, and telltale Hermitage fruit characteristics (blackberries, cassis), minerals, and spice. Representing the essence of Syrah, it is the greatest vintage Chave has produced since 1990. While it requires 7–10 years of cellaring, it will last for 4–5 decades.

In the topflight 1998 vintage (reminiscent of 1995 and 1989) there are two *cuvées*, both of which were bottled without filtration. The 1998 Hermitage rouge is a tannic, backward, large-scaled, dense ruby/purple-colored wine with high tannin, sensational extract, and formidable power and length. It needs 5–10 years of cellaring. Anticipated maturity: 2007–2030. The opaque black/purple-colored 1998 Ermitage Cuvée Cathelin (200 cases) offers a huge nose of smoked licorice, blackberry, cassis, new saddle leather, and vanilla. Tasting like liqueur of Syrah, it is extremely full-bodied and awesomely concentrated, with formidable tannin as well as mind-blowing levels of extract and density. The tannin is sweet, and the wine seamless for a young Chave Hermitage.

The 1997 Hermitage rouge is unusual in its fruit-forward, user-friendly style. The color is a dense ruby/purple. The gorgeous, evolved bouquet of cassis, minerals, herbs, underbrush, and licorice is intense. Creamy-textured, full-bodied, and opulent, this low-acid, gloriously ripe, layered 1997 can be drunk now, but promises to be even better with another 5–6 years of cellaring; it will last for 20–25 years.

Jean-Louis Chave has started a *négociant* business to take advantage of the family's contacts with some of the better growers in the appellation of St.-Joseph. The wine being produced is called Offerus (named after the man who is believed to have planted the first Syrah vines in the Rhône). Chave's goal is to make a limited quantity of high-quality St.-Joseph from purchased grapes. The wine is vinified at a new installation built several blocks from the family's cellars. From a superb vintage in terms of raw materials, the delicious 1999 St.-Joseph Offerus boasts a deep ruby/purple color as well as a big, peppery, bouquet of black currants, minerals, licorice, and earth. Sweet, fleshy, and ripe, this hedonistic offering should be consumed over the next 4–5 years.

The Chaves have also planted five acres on the St.-Joseph hillsides, behind their home village of Mauves. Their St.-Joseph is quickly becoming one of the most delicious wines of the appellation. The 2000 St.-Joseph is an elegant, mineral- and berry-scented effort with medium body as well as a Burgundy-like, floral/black cherry character with a hint of cassis. Fruit-driven, with adequate acidity and good length, it is best drunk during its first 5–7 years of life. The deep ruby/purple-colored 1999 St.-Joseph offers vivacious, crunchy, black raspberry and cassis aromas with flinty mineral notes in the flavors and finish. It will be delicious young, but should keep for a decade or more. The 1997 St.-Joseph is an excellent example of a lush, richly fruity, berry/cherry, elegant style. This fruity St.-Joseph will provide delicious drinking for the next 5–7 years.

Gérard and Jean-Louis Chave produced a Vin de Paille in both 1997 and 1996. Previously, the *cuvée* was only made in 1990, 1989, and 1986. Both the 1997 and 1996 are spectacular, extremely unctuous offerings with awesome flavors, massive sweetness, glycerin, and extract, as well as amazing honeyed, earthy, spicy, jammy aromatics. After spitting the 1997, orange marmalade, apricot jam, and white truffle–like flavors continued to linger on the palate, even though there was no wine left in my mouth. These legendary wines will have 50–100 years of longevity.

Past Glories: Hermitage (red)—1991 (90), 1990 (100), 1989 (95), 1988 (94), 1985 (92), 1983 (91?), 1982 (92), 1978 (92); Ermitage Cuvée Cathelin—1991 (93), 1990 (100)

DOMAINE DU CHÊNE

1999 Condrieu	E	89
1998 St.-Joseph	D	87
1998 St.-Joseph Anaïs	E	90
1999 St.-Joseph Blanc	D	87

The Rouvier family continues to turn out fine wines from this estate that have not yet received the accolades they merit. Readers should take note, as prices remain reasonable. The white wines have gone from strength to strength over recent vintages. The 1999 St.-Joseph Blanc exhibits a smoky, mineral, white peach–scented nose, crisp, medium-bodied flavors, good acidity, and an attractive, moderately long finish. Drink it over the next 3–4 years. The 1999 Condrieu displays a combination of finesse and power. It reveals some of the subtle restraint that is a characteristic of some 1999 Condrieus, as well as admirable richness, medium to full body, and fine length. Although muted at present, it possesses excellent purity and depth. Drink it over the next 2–3 years.

The 1998 St.-Joseph offers a tangy, blackberry, and cassis-scented nose, medium to full body, and abundant fruit, glycerin, and ripeness. It is a moderately weighty, fruit-driven effort with some tannin in the finish. Consume this 1998 over the next 5–6 years. Revealing more concentration as well as aging potential is the 1998 St.-Joseph Anaïs. This wine, which sees plenty of new oak judging by its toasty-scented nose, offers a dark ruby/purple color, sweet black cherry and black raspberry fruit, well integrated acidity and tannin, and a rich, full-bodied finish. It is an impressive St.-Joseph that has obviously been *barrique* aged. Anticipated maturity: now–2012.

LOUIS CHÈZE

1999	Condrieu	D	89
1999	Condrieu Coteau de Brèze	D	89
2000	St.-Joseph Cuvée des Anges	D	(85–86)
1999	St.-Joseph Cuvée des Anges	D	91
1998	St.-Joseph Cuvée des Anges	D	89+
1997	St.-Joseph Cuvée des Anges	D	(88–90)
2000	St.-Joseph Cuvée Prestige Caroline	D	(84–86)
1999	St.-Joseph Cuvée Prestige Caroline	D	88
1998	St.-Joseph Cuvée Prestige Caroline	D	90
1997	St.-Joseph Cuvée Prestige Caroline	D	(86–87)
2000	St.-Joseph Cuvée Ro Rée	D	(85–86)
1999	St.-Joseph Cuvée Ro Rée	D	88
1998	St.-Joseph Cuvée Ro Rée	D	87
1997	St.-Joseph Cuvée Ro Rée	D	(85–86)
1999	St.-Joseph Cuvée Ro Rée Blanc	D	87

This is a northern Rhône estate to watch carefully. Chèze, who appears to be in his late thirties, has already made considerable progress with the quality of both his red and white wines. Moreover, he seems poised to soar enormously in quality over the next 4–5 years. The investments made in the vineyards and cellars, as well as Chèze's philosophical commitment to producing special wines, are evident. All of these wines represent excellent values.

The red wines are very good, with a couple of *cuvées* meriting outstanding ratings. The 2000 St.-Joseph Cuvée Prestige Caroline is a lighter, more diluted version of the 1999, with a limited aging potential of 3–5 years. While the 2000 St.-Joseph Cuvée Ro Rée possesses more depth than the 2000 Caroline, it remains a soft, superficial, fruity, straightforward effort with sweet tannin. It should drink well for 4–5 years. The 2000 St.-Joseph Cuvée des Anges reveals more oak, because the fruit concentration is not sufficient to support 100% new wood. This dark ruby/purple-colored, medium-bodied wine is fruity, soft, and nicely textured, but one-dimensional. Drink it over the next 4–5 years.

The three 1999 whites are all strong efforts in what is a more challenging vintage for whites than reds. The 1999 St.-Joseph Cuvée Ro Rée Blanc is a blend of 75% Marsanne and 25% Roussanne, aged in 100% used barrels. It exhibits ripe peach, apricot, and orange marmalade notes, good integrated acidity and wood, and a deep, concentrated, medium- to full-bodied palate. It is a delicious dry white to drink over the next 2–3 years. Condrieu is a mixed bag in 1999, but those who got it right have produced topflight wines, although they do not possess the concentration levels of the glorious 1998s. A very good effort, Chèze's 1999

Condrieu exhibits a ripe apricot and honeysuckle-scented nose, an opulent, sexy texture, and open-knit, fleshy fruit and glycerin. Drink it over the next 12–24 months. From a hillside vineyard, the 1999 Condrieu Coteau de Brèze displays a similar weight, but more delineation as well as that liquid mineral characteristic found in top-notch Condrieu. It is less opulent, but finer and more poised, with restrained notes of apricot jam, orange marmalade, and honeysuckle. It should be consumed over the next several years.

The dark ruby/purple-colored 1999 St.-Joseph Cuvée Prestige Caroline reveals considerable ripeness along with great fruit on the attack, toasty oak, medium to full body, and a plump, fleshy finish. The similarly styled 1999 St.-Joseph Cuvée Ro Rée offers notes of dried herbs, chocolate, and black cherry liqueur in addition to a sweet, medium- to full-bodied, pure personality. It reveals a subtle influence of toasty oak (40% new) along with multiple layers and excellent depth. Drink it over the next 6–7 years. The brilliant 1999 St.-Joseph Cuvée des Anges (100% new oak) is a dense, opaque purple-colored effort displaying an exceptional nose of blackberries and currants mixed with smoke, minerals, licorice, and espresso. It possesses well-integrated acidity, tannin, and alcohol as well as a layered, medium- to full-bodied personality, and an impressive palate impact without any heaviness. It should drink well for 10–12 years.

The 1998 St.-Joseph Cuvée des Anges was also produced from Chèze's finest Syrah parcels, and again aged in 100% new oak. Although closed down and tannic, it is superrich, with a saturated plum/purple color, large volume and thickness, and characteristic new oak, mineral, blackberry and cassis notes. While impressively built, this 1998 requires 2–4 years of cellaring; it will keep for 15 years. An outstanding effort, the 1998 St.-Joseph Prestige Caroline will provide delicious drinking over the next 10–12 years. The bouquet offers spicy new oak, jammy black fruits, crushed stone, and melted asphalt aromas. The wine is ripe, sumptuously textured, fat, fleshy, and altogether captivating. Anticipated maturity: now–2012. The 1998 St.-Joseph Cuvée Ro Rée, a forward-styled effort with full body, displays notes of chocolate, plums, black cherries, and herbs. While spicy, with loads of fruit, it does not possess the volume, density, extract, or structure of the other *cuvées*. It should drink well for 7–8 years.

This estate turned out very good 1997s possessing saturated purple colors, low acidity, accessible rich, concentrated fruit, medium body, and forward styles. The amount of new oak increases with each *cuvée*, from little oak in the Cuvée Ro Rée, more noticeable oak in the Cuvée Prestige Caroline, and 100% new-oak casks for the Cuvée des Anges. The 1997 St.-Joseph Cuvée des Anges is a rich, chewy, full-bodied, impressively endowed wine that should drink well for a decade.

AUGUSTE CLAPE

2000	Cornas	D	(90–93)
1999	Cornas	D	91
1998	Cornas	D	90+
1997	Cornas	D	88
1999	Cornas Renaissance	D	88
1998	Cornas Renaissance	D	86
2000	Côtes du Rhône	B	87
1999	Côtes du Rhône	B	86
2000	VDP Le Vin des Amis	A	85
1999	VDP Le Vin des Amis	A	86

The classic name for Cornas, Auguste Clape, and his son, Pierre-Marie, produce rugged, age-worthy, often profound Cornas from their holdings on the hillsides above this one-horse village. They have introduced a new Cornas *cuvée* from younger vines, called Renaissance, and continue to produce fine values for readers looking for under-$15 Syrah-based wines, such as their Côtes du Rhône and VDP Le Vin des Amis, with the former made from Syrah planted in St.-Péray with a touch of Cornas, and the latter from the flat ground between the village of Cornas and the Rhône River.

The rustic, tannic, dark purple-colored 2000 VDP Le Vin des Amis possesses plenty of up-front fruit, but a touch of coarseness and astringency. While it will not develop into anything special, it offers unbridled Syrah fruit in a muscular format. Better is the 2000 Côtes du Rhône, a 100% Syrah *cuvée* made just outside the Cornas appellation. I would not be surprised if there were some declassified Cornas from younger vines included in the blend (most of the fruit is Syrah planted within the appellation of St.-Péray, which is only allowed to produce white wine). The Côtes du Rhône's dark ruby/purple color is followed by delicious blackberry and cassis fruit with earth, asphalt, and mineral characteristics in the background. Heady, powerful, and mouth-filling, it should be consumed over the next 4–5 years.

The dark ruby/purple-colored 1999 VDP Le Vin des Amis (from 25-year-old Syrah vines) is a fruit-driven, solidly constructed effort with a monolithic personality, but it is gutsy and exuberant . . . the ideal bistro wine. Drink it over the next several years. The 1999 Côtes du Rhône exhibits a dense ruby/purple color, good fat, a notion of blackberries and minerals, and a medium-bodied finish. It should drink well for 2–4 years.

Clape's 2000 Cornas stands out as one of the appellation's finest efforts. It boasts an opaque purple color as well as a strikingly pure bouquet of blackberry liqueur with notions of oak (from its aging in ancient *barriques* and *foudres*), full body, sweet tannin, low acidity, and concentrated, layered flavors. Unlike many northern Rhône producers, Clape has achieved a serious mid-palate in his 2000. This effort is reminiscent of the 1985 (which was still drinking terrifically in summer 2001). Anticipated maturity: now–2016.

The saturated dark purple-colored 1999 Cornas Renaissance displays a thick, juicy nose of cassis and blackberry fruit presented in a style similar to the 2000 Côtes du Rhône. There is more acidity, earthy austerity, and tannin in the Renaissance, which should easily age for 10–12 years. The 1999 Cornas does not possess the fat or precociousness of the 2000, but it is a brilliant effort in a Cornas vintage that produced an atypically high percentage of dogs. The 1999 displays soft tannin, but good underlying acidity, terrific blackberry and cassis–like fruit, a saturated black/purple color, and aromas of roasted meats, jammy black fruits, hickory smoke, and licorice. Fine purity, sweet tannin, and well-integrated acidity and alcohol result in a seamless impact. This full-bodied, large-scaled offering will be at its finest between 2005–2016. The 1998 Cornas Renaissance is a creamy, medium-weight wine with bright, jammy, black cherry and blackberry fruit, good purity, low acidity, and light tannin in the finish. Drink it over the next 7–8 years. The big, classic 1998 Cornas reveals hard tannin, medium to full body, a dense ruby/purple color, and a muscular, back-strapping, husky style that requires 5–6 years of cellaring. It will last for 16–18 years, but it does not have the fat, glycerin, and sweetness of the 1999.

The 1997s are excellent. Clape's 1997 Cornas flirts with an outstanding rating. The wine boasts a saturated purple color, as well as a sweet, blackberry-scented nose with violets, tar, and truffle-like aromas. Medium- to full-bodied, with low acidity, excellent purity, and light to moderate tannin, this is an atypically soft, expansive, forward Cornas that should drink well when released and keep for a decade or more.

Past Glories: Cornas—1995 (92), 1991 (90), 1990 (90), 1985 (90), 1983 (90?), 1978 (91), 1976 (90)

LES CLEFS D'OR

2000 Châteauneuf-du-Pape	D	(87–88)
1999 Châteauneuf-du-Pape	D	87
1998 Châteauneuf-du-Pape	D	88

With more stuffing and concentration (from lower yields and/or a stricter selection in the cellar), these wines could easily merit outstanding ratings as this estate owns fine vineyards. Nevertheless, there is plenty to enjoy in these straightforward, open-knit, user-friendly Châteauneuf-du-Papes. It is an unfortunate truth that wines that are too friendly and ready to drink, with limited aging potential, are probably not given enough value in scoring to those that have the greatest potential for longevity and are more concentrated. I realize many readers just want a good wine for immediate drinking, and Les Clefs d'Or certainly fills that need.

The 2000 Châteauneuf-du-Pape exhibits jammier fruit, potentially more stuffing, sweet tannin, and a medium- to full-bodied, plummy/cherry finish. It should be drunk during its first decade of life. The dark ruby-colored 1999 Châteauneuf-du-Pape reveals a Provençal nose of roasted herbs, ground pepper, plums, and cherries. Medium-bodied and soft, it is best consumed over the next 6–7 years. The dark ruby-colored 1998 Châteauneuf-du-Pape is dense, with mineral, pepper, and *garrigue* notes, but seemed muted when I tasted it. It displayed all the characteristics of a wine that had just been bottled, so I suspect there is more to it. The wine offered a *garrigue*/spicy-scented nose, medium to full body, obvious notes of kirsch intermixed with crushed stones and a pleasant earthiness, admirable layers of flavor, and moderate tannin. It requires several years of cellaring before consumption. Anticipated maturity: now–2012.

DOMAINE CLOS DU CAILLOU

2000	Châteauneuf-du-Pape	D	(91–92)
1999	Châteauneuf-du-Pape	D	90
1998	Châteauneuf-du-Pape	D	90
2000	Châteauneuf-du-Pape Les Quartz	E	(92–94)
1999	Châteauneuf-du-Pape Les Quartz	E	93
2000	Châteauneuf-du-Pape Réserve Le Clos du Caillou	E	(97–99+)
1999	Châteauneuf-du-Pape Réserve Le Clos du Caillou	E	94
1998	Châteauneuf-du-Pape Réserve Le Clos du Caillou	E	96
1998	Châteauneuf-du-Pape Cuvée Unique	E	90
2000	Côtes du Rhône Bouquet des Garrigues	C	90
1999	Côtes du Rhône Bouquet des Garrigues	C	90
1999	Côtes du Rhône Très Vieilles Vignes	C	91
2000	Côtes du Rhône-Villages Clos du Caillou	C	90+

The Vacheron family (from the Loire Valley) has been fashioning extraordinary wines at this estate situated in Châteauneuf-du-Pape's northeast sector. All three Châteauneuf-du-Pape *cuvées* are fabulous, ranking among the finest of the appellation. The 1999s in particular are strong, and the 2000s are equal to the 1998s. Bottling is done without fining or filtration. This is an incredible source for great Côtes du Rhône. Sadly, in March 2002, Jean Denis Vacheron, the architect behind these wines, was tragically killed in an accident.

The inky/purple–colored 2000 Châteauneuf-du-Pape offers spectacular aromatics, stunning ripeness, and a long, multilayered finish revealing low acidity, ripe fruit, and full body. If the renowned Pomerol, Château Lafleur, were on steroids, it might resemble some of Domaine Clos du Caillou's *cuvées*. Anticipated maturity: now–2015. The amazing 2000 Châteauneuf-du-Pape Les Quartz is a jammy, crème de cassis, black raspberry/cherry-filled effort with notions of liquid minerals and flowers in the background. There is superrichness, spectacular purity and delineation, and a full-bodied, massive finish that is every bit as long as the 1999's. The tannin is nearly concealed by the wealth of fruit. Anticipated maturity: now–2018. The prodigious 2000 Châteauneuf-du-Pape Réserve Le Clos du Caillou is a legend in the making. Representing the essence of Châteauneuf-du-Pape, this inky/purple-colored wine's concentration is akin to a dry vintage port. It boasts astonishing layers of licorice, blackberries, black cherries, and cassis. Essentially, it tastes like liqueur of Châteauneuf-du-Pape, with phenomenal purity, perfect equilibrium, and a 50-second finish (one of the longest I have ever tasted in a dry red wine). The style being produced at Domaine Clos du Caillou is a synthesis between the modern approach to winemaking and that which adheres to traditions of the past. This 2000 displays the typicity of Châteauneuf-du-Pape, but has ratcheted up the levels of concentration and richness to unbelievable heights. Anticipated maturity: 2005–2025.

The 1999 Châteauneuf-du-Pape is a sweet, plump, voluptuous, sexy offering with copious quantities of blackberry and dense cherry fruit. It is extraordinarily pure, full-bodied, and unctuously textured, with low acidity as well as splendid freshness and delineation. Drink it over the next 12–14 years. In 1999, the Vacheron/Pouzin families introduced a new offering called Les Quartz (named for this *terroir*'s soils). The 1999 Châteauneuf-du-Pape Les Quartz has lived up to its pre-bottling character. A star of the vintage, it is richer and more complex and layered than most 1999 Châteauneufs. Scents of *garrigue*, spicy mincemeat, black currants, minerals, and hot gravel emerge from the provocative bouquet. It is full-bodied and multidimensional, with supple, sweet tannin, immense concentration, and a long finish of nearly 45 seconds. Anticipated maturity: now–2018. Domaine Clos du Caillou's flagship offering, Clos du Caillou, was virtually perfect in 1998 (rated 99–100 in three separate tastings after bottling), and the 1999 Châteauneuf-du-Pape Réserve Le Clos du Caillou is unquestionably one of the top half-dozen wines of the vintage. Normally a blend of 45% Grenache, 40% Mourvèdre, and the balance Syrah and other miscellaneous grapes, the opaque purple-colored 1999 boasts a spectacularly nuanced perfume of blackberries, crème de cassis, licorice, *garrigue,* and spice. Massive yet opulent and unctuously textured, with exceptional purity plus a sexy, voluptuous finish, it is drinking fabulously and, given its richness and overall harmony, will continue to do so for 15–16 years. This is a splendid achievement in 1999!

The 1998 Châteauneuf-du-Pape (80% Grenache, 10% Syrah, and 10% Mourvèdre) offers a beautifully sweet nose of black raspberries, kirsch, and liquid minerals. It possesses high glycerin, layers of concentration, exquisite purity, and a full-bodied finish. Like many of the Domaine Clos du Caillou offerings, it is a brilliant example of purity, finesse, and power. Anticipated maturity: now–2015. The 1998 Châteauneuf-du-Pape Cuvée Unique (an exclusivity for the American market) tastes nearly identical, but appears to possess greater color saturation as well as a deeper, richer mid-palate. Anticipated maturity: now–2017. The monumental 1998 Châteauneuf-du-Pape Réserve Le Clos du Caillou (50% Grenache, 40% Mourvèdre, and 10% Syrah) is awesome. It is a great, concentrated Châteauneuf-du-Pape that manages to retain its purity, balance, and remarkable equilibrium. The first word I wrote in my notebook was "Geez!" This inky purple-colored 1998 is tight and unevolved, with plenty of firm tannin, unreal levels of richness, and a compelling finish that lasts nearly a minute. It represents the essence of this appellation, being a synthesis in style between the more modern approach to winemaking with the character of a traditionally produced Provençal red. This is a prodigious Châteauneuf-du-Pape, but patience is required. Anticipated maturity: 2004–2020.

This estate's terrific Côtes du Rhônes are made in a style similar to their profound Châteauneuf-du-Papes. The opaque ruby/purple-colored 2000 Côtes du Rhône Bouquet des Garrigues is a gorgeously fat, broadly flavored, layered effort with sumptuous fruit, a full-bodied texture, and low acidity. It should drink well for 4–6 years, if purchasers can resist it for that long. Potentially better is the more serious, structured, and muscular 2000 Côtes du Rhône-Villages Clos du Caillou. This opaque purple-colored offering is better than many Châteauneuf-du-Papes and Gigondas. Sweet, rich, and pure, with gobs of crème de cassis, liquid mineral, pepper, and spice characteristics, it is not as charming (at least at the moment) as the Bouquet des Garrigues, but it should drink well in another year and last for a decade. Both sumptuous 1999 Côtes du Rhônes are amazing wines for their price. Textured, full, rich, and pure, they are meant to be drunk during the next 4–6 years. While the 1999 Côtes du Rhône Bouquet des Garrigues is dominated by Grenache, it includes more Syrah and Mourvèdre in the blend. In contrast, the 1999 Côtes du Rhône Très Vieilles Vignes is principally made from 70–85-year-old Grenache with only a touch of Syrah and Mourvèdre. Buy these by the case!

CLOS DU CAVEAU

2000 Vacqueyras	C	(85–86)
2000 Vacqueyras Cuvée Lao Muse	D	(90–92)
2000 Vacqueyras Cuvée Prestige	D	(86–87)

Based on these 2000 *cuvées*, Clos du Caveau appears to be an emerging star of Vacqueyras. The easygoing, mainstream 2000 Vacqueyras possesses copious quantities of black cherry fruit, *garrigue*, pepper, and spice. Enjoy this delicious offering during its first 3–4 years of life. Similarly styled, the soft, expansive 2000 Vacqueyras Cuvée Prestige exhibits additional concentration as well as flavors, along with plenty of Provençal typicity. It should drink well for 5–6 years. The blockbuster 2000 Vacqueyras Cuvée Lao Muse is great stuff . . . assuming it makes it into the bottle with minimal fining and filtration. Its deep purple color is accompanied by a concentrated bouquet of blackberry liqueur, cherries, licorice, pepper, and truffles. With superrichness, an opulent, voluptuous texture, and a pure, ripe, layered finish, it can easily compete with the appellation's finest estate wine, Sang de Cailloux. Anticipated maturity: now–2010.

CLOS DU JONCUAS

1998 Gigondas	C	88
1997 Gigondas	C	87

This estate continues to turn out impressively made, concentrated, opulent Gigondas. The spectacular 1995 has been followed by two noteworthy efforts in the more difficult 1996 and 1997 vintages. The 1998 is also excellent. The wine is generally composed of 80% Grenache and 20% Mourvèdre and comes from a largely homogeneous vineyard of limestone soils.

The 1998 is a saturated black/purple-colored Gigondas with sweet kirsch/cassis fruit, medium body, a rich mid-palate, and the vintage's sweet tannin. The alcohol is modest, particularly for the vintage. This wine should evolve for a decade or more. The saturated black/ruby/purple-colored 1997 Gigondas exhibits sweet, pure, jammy black raspberries and cassis in its spicy nose, opulently textured, fat, low-acid, velvety flavors, and a heady glycerin/alcoholic finish. This hedonistic, plump Gigondas should drink well for 7–8 years.

CLOS DU MONT OLIVET

2000 Châteauneuf-du-Pape	D	(89–91)
1999 Châteauneuf-du-Pape	D	89
1998 Châteauneuf-du-Pape	D	89
1997 Châteauneuf-du-Pape	D	84
2000 Châteauneuf-du-Pape La Cuvée du Papet	D	(91–93)
1998 Châteauneuf-du-Pape La Cuvée du Papet	D	92+

One of the largest and most important families of Châteauneuf-du-Pape, the Sabons, produce the traditionally made, ageworthy Clos du Mont Olivet. Readers who happen across any of the great old vintages (1990, 1989, 1985, 1978, 1970, and 1957) should not hesitate to purchase them. In top vintages, a luxury *cuvée* called Cuvée du Papet is also produced. The 1990 and 1989 Cuvée du Papet are celestial.

The 2000 Châteauneuf-du-Pape exhibits a saturated dark ruby/garnet color along with a less evolved bouquet of sweet berry fruit intermixed with kirsch, pepper, and spice box. It is full-bodied and chewy with admirable depth as well as jammy fruit infused with glycerin. While forward (2000 is a low-acid, ripe vintage), it will benefit from 1–2 years of cellaring and keep for 15. The old-vine Grenache offering, the 2000 Châteauneuf-du-Pape La Cuvée du Papet (only made in 1998, 1990, and 1989), exhibits the essence of cherry fruit in its strikingly intense fragrance. Full-bodied and expansive, with plenty of power, structure, and muscle, it offers the whole spectrum of Provençal herbs in its provocative, rich, concentrated, heady personality. Look for it to gain stature after bottling and drink well for two decades. Anticipated maturity: 2004–2020.

Readers seeking immediate gratification should check out Clos du Mont Olivet's 1999 Châteauneuf-du-Pape. Displaying a complex nose of mincemeat, dried Provençal herbs, balsam wood, pepper, and sweet cherry fruit, it is round, broad, and medium- to full-bodied, with no hard edges. The color is an evolved garnet with plenty of pink at the edge. Clos du Mont Olivet's offerings have an uncanny ability to age well given their overall balance. Anticipated maturity: now–2013.

The 1998 Châteauneuf-du-Pape is a bigger effort, displaying more spice, pepper, and tannin. Its dense ruby/plum/purple color is followed by a full-bodied wine with the telltale kirsch flavors, and nicely layered fat and texture. Although not the blockbuster I thought it might turn out to be, it is an impressive Châteauneuf-du-Pape with more firmness and spice than the fruit-driven 1999. Anticipated maturity: now–2015. The 1998 Châteauneuf-du-Pape La Cuvée du Papet, made from extremely old vines, may not be the heavyweight blockbuster that the 1990 and 1989 are, but it is a beautifully made, old-style Châteauneuf-du-Pape that is more evolved than the 1990 and 1989 were at a similar age. The deep saturated ruby/garnet color is accompanied by notes of *garrigue* (that Provençal mélange of earth and herbs), pepper, cherry jam, and resiny balsam. Enormously thick and viscous (notice the tears on the side of the glass), this full-bodied classic has oodles of kirsch-like fruit, is dense, moderately tannic, and in need of 2–3 years of cellaring. Anticipated maturity: now–2020.

The 1997 Châteauneuf-du-Pape is a very good, yet forward, tasty effort from Clos du Mont Olivet. It exhibits a spicy, peppery, cherry-scented nose, a forward, evolved style, a plump, tasty mid-palate, and good jammy fruit. Drink this evolved (note the ruby/garnet color), low-acid, elegant Châteauneuf over the next 4–5 years.

CLOS DE L'ORATOIRE DES PAPES

2000 Châteauneuf-du-Pape	C	(88–90)
1999 Châteauneuf-du-Pape	C	89
1998 Châteauneuf-du-Pape	C	88

One of the first Châteauneuf-du-Pape domaines to estate bottle, Clos de l'Oratoire des Papes had a record of producing sumptuous wines 30–40 years ago. But the modern era brought a new vinification, resulting in light, fruity, delicious yet essentially one-dimensional Châteauneuf-du-Papes. That appears to have changed over recent years, with the 2000 and 1999 being the finest back-to-back years for Clos de l'Oratoire in decades. This is great news as this estate owns excellent vineyards.

Exhibiting marvelous potential, the 2000 Châteauneuf-du-Pape displays a saturated plum/purple color in addition to a sweet, jammy nose of black fruits, smoke, incense, and minerals. Opulent, full, and layered, it has dry tannin in the powerful finish. Both vintages are admirable departures from the light, Beaujolais-styled wines made during the 1980s and 1990s. Anticipated maturity: 2004–2016. The 1999 Châteauneuf-du-Pape boasts a saturated dark ruby/purple color as well as dense, impressive aromatics consisting of spice box, pepper, dried herbs, and black cherry/currant fruit. Powerful for a 1999, with a multilayered texture and moderate tannin in the finish, it may merit an outstanding rating if it develops more complexity. Anticipated maturity: now–2015. Made in an elegant style, the 1998 Châteauneuf-du-Pape offers copious quantities of black cherry and berry fruit intermixed with pepper and spice. Sexy, lush, and forward, with low acidity and a hedonistic personality, it will drink well for 8–10 years.

CLOS DES PAPES

2000 Châteauneuf-du-Pape	D	(91–93)
1999 Châteauneuf-du-Pape	D	91
1998 Châteauneuf-du-Pape	D	89
1997 Châteauneuf-du-Pape	D	87
2000 Châteauneuf-du-Pape Blanc	D	90
1999 Châteauneuf-du-Pape Blanc	D	88

This extraordinary estate is enjoying an even higher level of quality now that proprietor Paul Avril has the full-time assistance of his son, Vincent. Most Clos des Papes require some aging as there has been a tendency over the last decade to increase the percentage of Mourvèdre (now about 20%) in the final blend.

The 2000 Châteauneuf-du-Pape (14.3% alcohol) was produced from relatively abundant yields (for this estate) of 30 hectoliters per hectare. Its dense ruby/purple color is followed by an elegant bouquet of black raspberries mixed with cherries, minerals, tree bark, and spice. There is abundant power and elegance as well as a pure style and surprising finesse for a Châteauneuf-du-Pape. Like most big vintages of Clos des Papes, the 2000 requires 3–4 years of cellaring. Anticipated maturity: 2005–2020. The 1999 Châteauneuf-du-Pape was made from yields of 27 hectoliters per hectare, about one-half of the Bordeaux average and one-third of what many Burgundy vineyards achieve. Reminiscent of a grand cru Corton, it offers abundant quantities of sweet cherry fruit intertwined with flowers and minerals. There is a certain earthy *terroir* character as well as copious amounts of red and black fruits, full body, good spice, and moderate tannin in the long, firm finish. This is a beautifully knit Châteauneuf-du-Pape that convincingly eclipses Clos des Papes' 1998. The 1999 needs 3–4 years of cellaring and should keep for two decades. Very impressive!

The 1998 Châteauneuf-du-Pape lacks the power and concentration generally found in this estate's wines. Although excellent, it is lighter in the mid-palate than such great vintages as the 1995, 1990, and 1989. Vincent Avril thinks the wine is better than I do; time will prove who is right. The wine's dark ruby color reveals purple nuances. Sweet black cherry and currant aromas are intertwined with pepper, fruitcake, and spice box. Medium-bodied, moderately tannic, with good depth, but not the fat, concentration, and power of the more flattering 1999, it will be at its best from now–2015.

The estate performed well in the lighter-styled 1997 vintage. It's a sexy example with significantly more density and richness than the majority of the Châteauneuf-du-Papes from this vintage. The 1997 Châteauneuf-du-Pape's deep ruby color is followed by aromas of cherry jam intermixed with pepper, pine, and earth. In the mouth, cassis/blackberry fruit (no doubt from the Mourvèdre and Syrah components) makes an appearance. This soft, low-acid, medium-bodied, seductive offering should drink well for 5–8 years.

Other wines worth noting include Avril's gorgeous 2000 Châteauneuf-du-Pape Blanc. A blend of Roussanne, Grenache Blanc, Clairette, Bourboulenc, Picardin, and Picpoul, its terrific bouquet of melted wax, honeysuckle, and pear is followed by full-bodied, fresh, lively flavors. It should drink well for 5–6 years. Sadly, there are only 1,000 cases. In the past, I have been critical of most white Châteauneuf-du-Papes, but over the last several years quality has improved dramatically. Clos des Papes also produced one of the finest white Châteauneuf-du-Papes of the vintage in 1999. The color is a more saturated dense ruby/purple. The ripeness in the nose is more extravagant and intense than in 1998, and on the palate, the 1999 is a full-bodied effort that cuts a larger, more impressive swath. Rich and chewy, as well as elegant and moderately tannic, it should last for 15–20 years.

Another wine thrifty tasters should seek out is the *vin de table* produced by the Avrils called Le Petit d'Avril. This is a nonvintage blend of numerous grapes, including Cabernet Sauvignon, Syrah, Grenache, Mourvèdre, and Merlot. The latest release from the 2000 vintage is a light-bodied, richly fruity, smooth, bistro-styled red that merits 85 points. It is generally priced under $10, and needs to be consumed during its first 12–18 months of life. *Past Glories:* Châteauneuf-du-Pape—1995 (94), 1990 (95), 1981 (92), 1978 (94)

CLOS SAINT-MICHEL

2000 Châteauneuf-du-Pape	C	(87–89)
1999 Châteauneuf-du-Pape	C	89
1998 Châteauneuf-du-Pape	C	86
2000 Châteauneuf-du-Pape Cuvée Réservée	D	(91–93)
1999 Châteauneuf-du-Pape Cuvée Réservée	D	90
1998 Châteauneuf-du-Pape Cuvée Réservée	D	90
1999 Châteauneuf-du-Pape Cuvée Réservée Grand Clos	E	90
1998 Châteauneuf-du-Pape Cuvée Réservée Grand Clos	E	91+

This up-and-coming estate deserves attention given the efforts being expended by Franck Mousset. In 1998, this young producer introduced a new offering (packaged in a very heavy bottle) called the Cuvée Réservée Grand Clos.

Surprisingly, the 2000 Châteauneuf-du-Pape reveals more tannin and firmness, but the same weight and depth as the 1999, an atypical performance given the overall style of both vintages. Anticipated maturity: now–2012. The highly extracted, dense 2000 Châteauneuf-du-Pape Cuvée Réservée reveals notes of Provençal herbs, copious pepper, and intense cherry and black currant flavors. With a boatload of glycerin, low acidity, and a hedonistic, chewy finish, this seamless Châteauneuf will be at its best before 2016.

The dark ruby-colored 1999 Châteauneuf-du-Pape exhibits an earthy, peppery, herb, and underbrush-scented bouquet, medium to full body, dense, glycerin-packed fruit flavors, and low acidity. Drink it over the next decade. The superb, deep ruby/purple-colored 1999 Châteauneuf-du-Pape Cuvée Réservée is a powerful, full-bodied effort, particularly for the vintage. It possesses aromas of *garrigue* intermixed with pepper, blackberries, and cherry fruit. Spicy, muscular, rich, and long, with excellent definition as well as length, it will be at its finest between now–2016. The 1999 Châteauneuf-du-Pape Cuvée Réservée Grand Clos boasts a perfumed nose of pepper, Provençal herbs, mincemeat, cherry liqueur, and currants. Big, full-bodied, voluptuously textured, and pure, this hedonistic, classic Châteauneuf-du-Pape should be drunk over the next 12+ years.

The 1998s include an attractive, spicy, peppery, medium-bodied Châteauneuf-du-Pape that should be consumed over the next 7–8 years. The level of concentration, potential longevity, and pleasure climb considerably with the 1998 Châteauneuf-du-Pape Cuvée Réservée. Powerful, tannic, and in need of 3–4 years of cellaring, it emphasizes traditional characteristics of black cherry jam, spice, dried herbs, and meat. This muscular offering should be at its best between now–2018. Ratcheting up the level of power, concentration, tannin, and body is the 1998 Châteauneuf-du-Pape Cuvée Réservée Grand Clos. It boasts concentrated notes of *garrigue* (that medley of Provençal herbs and earth), plenty of pepper, high tannin levels, and muscular, powerful, deep, intense flavors. This 1998 needs 4–5 years of cellaring and should age for two decades.

CLUSEL-ROCH

2000 Côte Rôtie	E	(88–89)
1999 Côte Rôtie	E	92
1998 Côte Rôtie	E	87
2000 Côte Rôtie Les Grandes Places	E	(90–92)
1998 Côte Rôtie Les Grandes Places	E	90

Clusel-Roch is located at the northern end of Côte Rôtie in the hamlet called Verenay. Almost all of their vineyards are in the northern Côte Brune, with their most important holdings in Viaillière and Les Grandes Places. The special *cuvée* Les Grands Places is a 100% Syrah wine aged in barrel, with 50% new oak.

The deep ruby/purple-colored, medium-bodied 2000 Côte Rôtie exhibits aromas of new saddle leather, cherry liqueur, a touch of honeysuckle (from Viognier), olives, cassis, smoke, earth, and minerals. Low acidity and an open-knit style suggest it is best consumed during its first decade of life. The limited micro *cuvée*, the 2000 Côte Rôtie Les Grandes Places reveals notes of sweet toasty new oak intermixed with blackberry, cassis, smoke, and minerals. This rich, layered, medium- to full-bodied yet elegant wine is one of the most concentrated of the vintage. Anticipated maturity: now–2014.

I cannot imagine how profound the 1999 Côte Rôtie Les Grandes Places might be, but only one barrel (just under 25 cases) was produced, so there is little likelihood readers will come across a bottle. When I tasted it from barrel, the wine was stupendous. The profound 1999 Côte Rôtie boasts a dense ruby/purple color as well as an explosive bouquet of peach jam, crème de cassis, smoke, minerals, and licorice. It is full-bodied, opulent, and a total hedonistic turn-on. No doubt there is some tannin underlying the wealth of fruit and flesh, but this gorgeous offering is impossible to resist. It should drink well for 12–15 years. Bravo!

The dense ruby/purple-colored 1998 Côte Rôtie, which does not contain any fruit from Les Grandes Places, offers notes of roasted meats, black fruits, and smoke, plus good acidity. Classy, rich, medium-bodied, and solidly constituted, it will evolve for 10 years. The 1998 Côte Rôtie Les Grandes Places is a backward, dense, full-bodied effort with copious quantities of black currant and smoky raspberry fruit interwoven with toasty new oak, spice box, and earth. Deep, tannic, and muscular, this impressive wine should be at its best before 2016.

JEAN-LUC COLOMBO
(All Estate Wines Except for Les Mejeans)

2000	Cornas La Louvée	D	(90–92)
1999	Cornas La Louvée	D	93+
1998	Cornas La Louvée	D	92
1997	Cornas La Louvée	D	90
2000	Cornas Les Méjeans	D	(86–88)
1999	Cornas Les Méjeans	D	90
1997	Cornas Les Méjeans	D	(86–88)
2000	Cornas Les Ruchets	D	(88–90)
1999	Cornas Les Ruchets	D	91
1998	Cornas Les Ruchets	D	92
1997	Cornas Les Ruchets	D	88
1999	Cornas Terres Brûlées	D	88
1998	Cornas Terres Brûlées	D	90
1997	Cornas Terres Brûlées	D	(88–90)

Jean-Luc Colombo has become one of the stars of Cornas. Well-known as an oenologist for dozens of Rhône Valley clients, Colombo has had a positive influence in the Rhône, undoubtedly improving the quality of many estate's wines. He is making some of the finest Cornas produced. His wines, made in a completely different style than those of such superstars as Auguste Clape, are an intelligent blend of *barrique* and concentrated Syrah from this appellation's sun-baked hillsides. There are four *cuvées* offered, all packaged in a distinctive Bordeaux bottle (the only wines of the appellation not put in a Burgundy-shaped bottle). Les Ruchets comes from 80–100-year-old vines, La Louvée from 70-year-old vines, and Terres Brûlées from younger vines. The Cornas Les Méjeans is produced from purchased wines. The biggest, richest wines made by Jean-Luc Colombo are from his Les Ruchets and La Louvée vineyards. These hillside parcels tend to produce structured, concentrated wines that admirably soak up their oak cask aging. The La Louvée *cuvée* was formerly known as *cuvée* JLC. Colombo has fashioned his two finest back to back Cornas vintages in 1999 and 1998. The 1999 Cornas are atypically concentrated with softer acidity than most wines from the appellation. Rather restrained and light-weight, the 2000 Cornas Les Méjeans offers good fruit and a soft, up-front style, but lacks the depth and expansiveness of the 1999. The opaque purple-colored 2000 Cornas Les Ruchets has less tannin and body, but displays gorgeous fruit in a soft, supple, seductive style. With low acidity and ripe fruit, this is not a potentially long-lived classic, but it is well-built, intensely concentrated, and impressively made. Anticipated maturity: now–2012. The 2000 Cornas La Louvée boasts an inky black/purple color as well as an opulent personality displaying flamboyant notes of black fruits, melted licorice, asphalt, and minerals. There is some spicy new oak, but the wine's low-acid, sweet, tannic personality makes for a sumptuous glass of Cornas that is destined to be drunk young. Nevertheless, it has the concentration and overall balance to age well for 12–15 years.

The outstanding 1999 Cornas Les Méjeans (2,000 cases) boasts a black/purple color as well as a sweet nose of licorice, cassis, and creosote. Medium- to full-bodied, deep, ripe, loaded with fruit, glycerin, and sweet tannin, with enough acidity for definition, it will be at its finest between 2004–2015. The 1999 Cornas Terres Brûlées offers both red and black currant aromas intertwined with mineral and smoke characteristics. New oak makes an appearance, but it is subtle. The wine is elegant and medium-bodied with a hint of tannin in the finish. Anticipated maturity: now–2014. The 1999 Cornas Les Ruchets reveals toasty new oak in the nose, raising the specter of an internationally styled Cornas. However, once past the oak, this dense purple-colored effort exhibits notes of minerals, pepper, blackberries, and cassis without the uncivilized, rustic tannin Cornas often possesses. This full-bodied 1999 reveals a multilayered palate, considerable glycerin, outstanding fruit purity, and a long, impressive finish (20–25 seconds). Anticipated maturity: 2004–2015. The opaque purple-colored 1999 Cornas La Louvée is Cornas at its most intense and concentrated, with a nod to the modern technique of *barrique* aging. It possesses superb aromas of crème de cassis intermixed with liquid minerals. Full-bodied with huge extract and enough acidity to provide delineation to its large-scaled personality, it requires 3–5 years of cellaring to absorb all the oak and drop some tannin.

The 1998s are impressive from bottle. The dense purple-colored 1998 Cornas Terres Brûlées offers an earthy, roasted concoction of black fruits, minerals, spicy oak, and flowers. Rich and fleshy, with abundant quantities of minerals and spice, it is already drinkable because of its low acidity and sweet tannin, and it should age well for a decade. This is the only Colombo Cornas that emerges from the appellation's lower hillsides. The 1998 Cornas La Louvée is a prodigious effort. A black/purple color is accompanied by a sweet nose of minerals, roasted nuts, scorched earth, black currants, and berry fruit. This full-bodied, fleshy, impressively endowed effort offers sweet tannin as well as low acidity. Anticipated maturity: now–2016. The dense plum/purple-colored 1998 Cornas Les Ruchets offers notes of jammy cassis, smoke, earth, and minerals. The wine is velvety textured, full-bodied, with relatively low acidity and moderate tannin. Already accessible because of its fleshy mid-palate and sumptuous texture, it can be consumed now and over the next 15 years.

The 1997 Cornas Les Méjeans is a forward, low-acid, plush wine with uncommon accessibility. The wine exhibits a dark ruby color, a sweet nose of grilled meats, roasted herbs, and black fruits, excellent richness, and a sweet, round, surprisingly elegant palate-feel. It should be drunk over the next 7–8 years. The saturated ruby/purple-colored 1997 Cornas Terres Brûlées reveals more blackberry fruit in the aromas and flavors, medium to full body, supple tannin, low acid, and a deeper, fuller, longer finish. It will keep for 10–12 years. The 1997 Cornas Les Ruchets possesses a deep opaque ruby/purple color and a reserved, but impressively built, personality with telltale cassis intermixed with licorice, minerals, and smoke. Dense and full-bodied, with outstanding purity and length, the 1997 is more forward than most vintages and will keep for 12–15 years. The 1997 Cornas La Louvée is similarly styled, but fuller-bodied, with more mineral characteristics, as well as a heavier, weightier feel in the mouth. Dense, concentrated, and powerful, with outstanding purity, it is accessible (because of the vintage's low acidity), but still a backward, formidably endowed Cornas that will keep for 15 years or more.

JEAN-LUC COLOMBO
(*Négociant* Wines)

1999	Châteauneuf-du-Pape Les Bartavelles	D	90
1998	Châteauneuf-du-Pape Les Bartavelles	D	89
1999	Condrieu Amour Dieu	D	90
1999	Côtes du Rhône Les Abeilles	A	87
2000	Côtes du Rhône Les Abeilles Blanc	A	87
1999	Côtes du Rhône Les Figuières Blanc	A	87
1998	Côtes du Rhône Les Figuières Blanc	A	87
2000	Côtes du Rhône Les Forot Vieilles Vignes	A	86
1999	Côtes du Rhône Les Forot Vieilles Vignes	A	85
2000	Crozes-Hermitage La Tuilière	C	(85–87)
1999	Crozes-Hermitage La Tuilière	C	85
1999	Crozes-Hermitage La Tuilière Blanc	C	87
1999	Hermitage Le Rouet	E	90
1999	Hermitage Le Rouet Blanc	E	90
1997	Hermitage Le Rouet Blanc	E	90
2000	St.-Joseph Les Lauves	C	(86–87)
1999	St.-Joseph Les Lauves	C	86
1998	St.-Joseph Les Lauves	C	86
2000	St.-Joseph Le Prieuré	C	(84–86)
1999	St.-Joseph Le Prieuré	C	85
1999	St.-Péray La Belle de Mai Blanc	B	86

While the quantity of his estate's wines remains small, Jean-Luc Colombo has begun a large *négociant* business that will eventually produce 60,000 cases of wine. Early on, some of these *cuvées* were lackluster and indifferent, but he now appears to be accessing better fruit and getting it into the bottle with freshness and character. Colombo's *négociant* offerings continue to improve. These wines are definitely worth seeking out. In the fiercely independent Rhône Valley, Colombo is the most influential oenologist.

Among the white *négociant* wines are the 2000 Côtes du Rhône Les Abeilles and 1999 Côtes du Rhône Les Figuières, which are classy offerings. The 2000 Côtes du Rhône Les Abeilles Blanc is a blend of Viognier, Clairette, and Grenache Blanc. It possesses delicious peach, honeysuckle, and citrusy fruit, light to medium body, excellent purity, and a clean, dry finish. Slightly better is the 1999 Côtes du Rhône Les Figuières Blanc, a blend of 60% Viognier and 40% Roussanne. Abundant floral and honey notes are presented in a medium-bodied, fresh, lively, exuberant style. It should drink well for 12–14 months. The 1999 Hermitage Le Rouet Blanc offers an intriguing perfume of peaches, rose petals, and honeysuckle. Broad, expansive, and full-bodied, with impressive concentration, it experienced 100% malolactic in barrel, and spent 18 months on its lees prior to being bottled. A blend of 80% Marsanne and 20% Roussanne, it should age well for a decade. By the way, if readers can find any, they should also check out Colombo's finest white, the 1997 Hermitage Le Rouet Blanc, a brilliant, character-filled white offering notes of hazelnuts, smoke, flowers, and honeysuckle. The outstanding 1999 Condrieu Amour Dieu exhibits copious quantities of lychee nut, peach, and honeyed fruit presented in a full-bodied, chewy, unctuous style. With outstanding purity in addition to a plump, fleshy mouth-feel, it will not make old bones, but will provide beautiful drinking over the next year.

The very good 1999 Crozes-Hermitage La Tuilière Blanc, a blend of 80% Marsanne and 20% Roussanne that spent eight months in wood, offers an attractive bouquet of apricot jam, medium body, and plenty of fruit and glycerin. Enjoy it over the next 2–3 years. A blend of equal parts Roussanne and Marsanne, the 1999 St.-Péray La Belle de Mai Blanc is a citrus/grapefruit-dominated wine with medium body and fine freshness. Another very good dry white is the 1998 Côtes du Rhône Les Figuières Blanc. A blend of 70% Viognier (from the northern Rhône) and 30% Roussanne (from St.-Péray), it possesses admirable texture in addition to dried apricot, tropical fruit, and honeysuckle aromas and flavors.

With respect to the red wine *cuvées*, the Côtes du Rhône Les Forot Vieilles Vignes is a 100% Syrah. The deep ruby/purple-colored 2000 Côtes du Rhône Les Forot Vieilles Vignes reveals surprising acidity for the vintage as well as smoky, black currant flavors and medium body. It requires consumption during its first 2–3 years of life. The 1999 Côtes du Rhône Les Forot Vieilles Vignes reveals a briery, wild berry character not dissimilar from Zinfandel. With high acidity, a monolithic personality, clean fruit, and fine ripeness, this attractive 1999 will drink well for 2–3 years.

Among the northern Rhône *négociant* offerings, both the 2000 and 1999 Crozes-Hermitage La Tuilière possess good spice, pepper, herb, and red fruit characteristics. While not inspiring, they are correct examples of their appellation. Consume them during their first 5 years of life. Surprisingly, in view of the vintage character, the 2000 St.-Joseph Le Prieuré displays considerable acidity. Spicy with good fruit, this straightforward 2000 will drink well for 3–4 years. The 1999 St.-Joseph Le Prieuré exhibits more acidity now that it is in bottle, but it offers good, ripe, crunchy, tangy blackberry and cherry fruit mixed with an underlying minerality.

Made from hillside vineyards behind the village of Mauves, the 2000 St.-Joseph Les Lauves possesses sweet cassis fruit, mineral characteristics, and a deep, fleshy style. It should drink well for 7–8 years. The deep ruby/purple-colored 1999 St.-Joseph Les Lauves offers good acidity, some tannin, and a tart character, but lovely ripe strawberry and cherry fruit. It should drink well for 5–6 years. The excellent, dark ruby-colored 1998 St.-Joseph Les Lauves possesses black cherry fruit, an elegant, soft, medium-bodied palate impression, and a clean finish. This wine is sourced from vineyards behind the town of Tournon.

Colombo's brilliant Hermitage Le Rouet includes 5% Roussanne in the blend, and it is aged in *barriques*, of which 70% are new. The 1999 is an impressive, well-made, backward but chewy effort with rich cassis fruit, impressive purity, and a long finish. Anticipated maturity: 2005–2020. The 1999 Côtes du Rhône Les Abeilles is a blend of 40% Grenache, 30% Mourvèdre, and 30% Syrah primarily from vineyard sources in Vacqueyras and Rasteau. It possesses a deep purple color, refreshing acidity (a characteristic of some 1999s), and plenty of red and black currant fruit intermixed with smoke and gamey notes. Drink it over the next several years. The finest of Colombo's southern Rhône *négociant* offerings is the 1999 Châteauneuf-du-Pape Les Bartavelles. A blend of Grenache (from the Gonnet brothers at Font de Michelle) and Syrah (from Château Fortia), it exhibits an excellent deep ruby/purple color, high alcohol (14.5%), a sweet, nicely textured, fleshy palate, and a long, concentrated finish. Drink this pure, rich, full-bodied Châteauneuf-du-Pape between now–2015. Impressive! The 1998 Châteauneuf-du-Pape Les Bartavelles (a blend of 50% Grenache, 30% Syrah, and 20% Mourvèdre) reveals kirsch, floral, lavender, and black currant aromas and flavors as well as admirable structure, full body, excellent purity, and an authentic Châteauneuf-du-Pape style. It should drink well for a decade.

DOMAINE COMBIER

1999	Crozes-Hermitage	C	87
1999	Crozes-Hermitage Blanc	C	86
1999	Crozes-Hermitage Clos des Grives	D	(88–90)
1998	Crozes-Hermitage Clos des Grives	D	88
1999	Crozes-Hermitage Clos des Grives Blanc	D	88
1998	Crozes-Hermitage Clos des Grives Blanc	D	88

This is another example of a young (35+ years) producer, in this case Laurent Combier, taking an estate and pushing it to higher quality levels. A biodynamically farmed vineyard, à la Michel Chapoutier, Domaine Combier produces two *cuvées* of both red and white Crozes-Hermitage. The 1999 Crozes-Hermitage Blanc exhibits the telltale Marsanne characteristic of lemon honey, citrus, grapefruit, and notes of white flowers (the cognoscenti say acacia). Fresh, with good texture, ripeness, and a medium-bodied, dry finish, it will drink well for 2–3 years. The more seriously endowed, *barrique*-aged 1999 Crozes-Hermitage Clos des Grives Blanc is a blend of 50% Roussane and 50% Marsanne. A bigger, richer, more textured, honeyed wine with smoky new oak as well as gobs of fruit and additional glycerin and thickness, it should drink well for 4–5 years.

Combier's 1999 Crozes-Hermitage rouge reveals an herbaceous, smoky, black cherry, and spice-scented bouquet, medium body, good fruit, and a soft, forward character. Consume it over the next 4–5 years. The 100% barrel-aged *cuvée* (half new and half one-year-old), the 1999 Crozes-Hermitage Clos des Grives rouge, exhibits a deep ruby/purple color as well as a dense nose of black cherry liqueur, smoke, toast, minerals, and tapenade. Medium- to full-bodied, with admirable acidity and excellent concentration, it should drink well during its first decade of life.

The serious 1998 Crozes-Hermitage Clos des Grives Blanc is one of the finest dry whites produced in this diverse appellation. Ripe honeyed lemon, peach, and grapefruit aromas and flavors easily soak up the wood from new oak aging. The acidity is well integrated, and the wine is muscular and concentrated. It should drink well for 4–5 years. The dark plum/purple-colored 1998 Crozes-Hermitage Clos des Grives rouge reveals less acidity along with spicy new oak, rich, concentrated cassis and cherry notes, and a subtle Provençal herbaceousness. Well-made, nicely-textured, and mouth-filling, it should drink well for a decade.

DOMAINE DE LA CÔTE DE L'ANGE

2000	Châteauneuf-du-Pape	D	(86–87)
1999	Châteauneuf-du-Pape	D	86
1998	Châteauneuf-du-Pape	D	89
2000	Châteauneuf-du-Pape Cuvée Vieilles Vignes	D	(87–90)
1999	Châteauneuf-du-Pape Cuvée Vieilles Vignes	D	87

Côte de l'Ange fashions rustic, spicy, meaty Châteauneuf-du-Papes that tend to be short on sweet fruit. However, they are distinctive, and readers who like the southern Rhône's roasted herb, leather, and sausage-like, rather gamey characteristics will prefer them more than me.

The 2000 *cuvées* display good color saturation. The 2000 Châteauneuf-du-Pape begins well, offering sweet cherry fruit intertwined with spice box, pepper, and Provençal herb notes, but it is short in the mouth. The superb 2000 Châteauneuf-du-Pape Cuvée Vieilles Vignes offers spicy, earthy, sweet kirsch, seaweed, and pepper aromas as well as flavors, good length, ripeness, and density, and dusty tannin in the finish. An impressive, old-style Châteauneuf, it should last for 12–14 years.

The plum/ruby-colored 1999 Châteauneuf-du-Pape exhibits an outrageously peppery, spicy nose, medium body, and flavors of soy, seaweed, and earth. Short and superficial, it should be consumed over the next 3–5 years. Slightly deeper, the 1999 Châteauneuf-du-

Pape Cuvée Vieilles Vignes reveals a note of Italian sausage intermixed with dried herbs, lavender, spice box, and dried cherry fruit. The finish is angular, with moderate tannin.

Fairly masculine, with rustic tannin, the 1998 Châteauneuf-du-Pape offers a muscular, full-bodied palate feel, with notes of *herbes de Provence*, damp earth, and black cherry and plum-like fruit. Still firm and structured, it will hold until 2018.

DOMAINE DES COTEAUX DES TRAVERS

1999 Côtes du Rhône-Villages Cairanne	B	89

The 1999 Côtes du Rhône-Villages Cairanne is a superb blend of 60% Grenache, 30% Mourvèdre, and 10% Syrah. A top-notch value, this nearly outstanding wine reveals a saturated dark ruby color as well as sweet aromas of pepper, black fruit, kirsch, and spice box. Rich, textured, and medium- to full-bodied, with sweet tannin and unobtrusive alcohol as well as acidity, it will drink well for 4–5 years.

DOMAINE COURBIS

1999 Cornas Champelrose	D	(86–87)
1998 Cornas Champelrose	D	89
1997 Cornas Champelrose	D	83
1999 Cornas Les Eygats	D	(88–90)
1998 Cornas Les Eygats	D	90
1997 Cornas Les Eygats	D	87
1999 Cornas La Sabarotte	D	(88–90+)
1998 Cornas La Sabarotte	D	91
1997 Cornas La Sabarotte	D	88
1999 St.-Joseph	D	88
1999 St.-Joseph Blanc	D	85
1999 St.-Joseph Les Royes	D	90
1998 St.-Joseph Les Royes	D	87

Brothers Laurent and Dominique Courbis are turning out modern-styled Cornas that emerge from three different sectors of the appellation. The Champelrose is aged in 2–3-year-old *barriques*, Les Eygats in 20% new and 80% old *barriques*, and La Sabarotte in 50% new oak and 50% one-year-old barrels. All the Syrah is destemmed, and the wines are bottled with minimal clarification. The estate also fashions St.-Josephs that are very good, but less impressive than the Cornas. Domaine Courbis is moving forward quickly, as the following tasting notes illustrate.

The 1999 Cornas Champelrose exhibits a dark purple color, medium body, tangy acidity, and a refreshing, moderately weighty style offering up cassis and blackberry fruit. This is an easygoing, lightly tannic effort to drink over the next 6–8 years. The 1999 Cornas Les Eygats, which comes from a vineyard planted higher up the slopes than the Champelrose, reveals more smoky, blackberry, and mineral characteristics, better ripeness, full body, excellent density, moderate tannin, and an inky black color. The vines are only 10 years old, but this is a potentially outstanding *cuvée*. Anticipated maturity: now–2015. The older vine *cuvée* from the mid-slope is the 1999 Cornas La Sabarotte. More new oak as well as noticeable acidity result in a more internationally styled wine. Ripe and medium- to full-bodied, but closed and impenetrable, what is discernable is impressive. Anticipated maturity: 2005–2016. A *vin de garde* for sure.

The 1999 St.-Joseph Blanc (aged in 50% tank and 50% barrel) is a crisp, elegant, modern-styled dry white with notes of tropical fruits (primarily pineapple). Drink it within 2 years.

The two 1999 red St.-Josephs are both revealing more character in bottle than they did during their *élevage*. The 1999 St.-Joseph is a seriously concentrated offering displaying a deep ruby/purple color as well as a sweet nose of currants, plums, figs, minerals, and cherries. Ripe, delicious, hedonistic, and pure, with no hard edges, it will drink well for 6–7 years. The 1999 St.-Joseph Les Royes comes from a vineyard planted on limestone hillsides near the village of Châteaubourg. An exceptional, opaque purple-colored effort, it possesses a fabulous perfume of black currant fruit intermixed with cherry liqueur, licorice, smoke, and minerals. The new oak is totally integrated, and the wine is textured, full-bodied, and impressive. This opulent St.-Joseph should drink well for a decade or more. Bravo!

The 1998s are better than their 1999 counterparts, revealing less acidity, more depth and power, sweeter tannin, and a more expansive texture (no doubt because of the lower acids). The dark ruby/purple-colored 1998 Cornas Champelrose offers an elegant, sweet, gamey, smoky, cassis-scented nose, good texture on the palate, low acidity, and a fleshy character. Drink it now and over the next 10–12 years. The 1998 Cornas Les Eygats's opaque purple color is followed by peppery, charcoal, earth, and truffle aromas with abundant quantities of blackberry and cassis fruit. It tastes more like a Côte Rôtie than a Cornas, but the oak is well integrated, the acidity low, and the tannin noticeable, but also well integrated. Rich and complex, this 1998 should evolve nicely for 12–15 years. The saturated black/purple-colored 1998 Cornas La Sabarotte offers aromas of pure crème de cassis, blackberries, and toasty smoky oak. With sweet tannin, superb texture, and impressive concentration and density, it should be drinkable in 2–3 years, and last for 18 years. Very impressive! The substantial, medium- to full-bodied 1998 St.-Joseph Les Royes offers black cherry and cranberry fruit in addition to a vibrant, oaky style. This fruit-driven, low-acid 1998 is meant to be consumed over the next 5–7 years.

While the 1997 Cornas Champelrose possesses a dark ruby color, it is neither extracted nor rich. Medium-bodied, with tar and black currant fruit, this spicy, straightforward, monolithic Cornas should be drunk during its first 5–6 years of life. The 1997 Cornas Les Eygats is a more serious effort. This ruby/purple-colored wine exhibits superb ripeness, medium to full body, excellent extraction of fruit, and copious quantities of mouth-searing tannin. Surprisingly, this wine has more acidity than I expected given the vintage. It will be at its finest between now–2012. The top wine of this trio of 1997s is the 1997 Cornas La Sabarotte. It boasts an old-vine intensity and mid-palate, as well as gobs of sweet plum, black raspberry, and currant fruit, with notes of toasty new oak. I suspect this *cuvée* sees more new barrels than its two siblings. The wine is medium- to full-bodied, pure, moderately tannic, and impressively long. Anticipated maturity: now–2014.

DOMAINE LE COUROULU

2000 Vacqueyras	C	(87–89)
1999 Vacqueyras	C	87
2000 Vacqueyras Vieilles Vignes	C	(88–90)
1999 Vacqueyras Vieilles Vignes	C	90

This estate also produces delicious Côtes du Rhône. Based on prior successes, readers are advised to check them out. The Vacqueyras are also top-notch. The two *cuvées* of Vacqueyras are close in quality.

The ripe, succulent 2000 Vacqueyras *cuvées* are impressive, offering loads of glycerin as well as concentrated fruit along with more fat than the 1999s. The 2000 Vacqueyras Vieilles Vignes reveals more body as well as blackberry characteristics than its sibling. Both 2000s should be consumed during their first 5–8 years of life. The dark ruby-colored 1999 Vacqueyras offers a big, sweet, charming nose of black fruits (primarily earthy black cherries), plenty of spice, low acidity, and a sexy, lush, captivating personality. Consume this medium- to full-bodied 1999 over the next 5–6 years. The 1999 Vacqueyras Vieilles Vignes reveals a more saturated ruby/purple color along with expansive aromas of plum liqueur, kirsch, earth, and pepper. Full-bodied and fat, it will drink well for 7–8 years . . . absolutely delicious!

DOMAINE COURSODON

1999 St.-Joseph	C	87
2000 St.-Joseph Blanc	C	85
1999 St.-Joseph l'Olivare	C	88
1999 St.-Joseph La Paradis St.-Pierre	D	89+
2000 St.-Joseph La Paradis St.-Pierre Blanc	C	86
1999 St.-Joseph La Sensonne	D	88+

The committed young grower who runs this estate has fashioned pleasant, fruity whites over recent vintages. The 2000 St.-Joseph Blanc offers aromas and flavors of peaches and apricots in a straightforward, plump style. The 2000 St.-Joseph La Paradis St.-Pierre Blanc exhibits more minerality (it emerges from granite soils) as well as additional complexity, but less fruit. Both 2000s should be consumed over the next 1–2 years.

The stars in this portfolio are the red wine *cuvées,* which have improved dramatically over the last several years. Aged in old *foudres* and barrels, the 1999 St.-Joseph (30,000 bottles) displays a dense ruby/purple color as well as a big, sweet nose of cherries, plums, figs, and currants. Medium-bodied, with excellent ripeness as well as a soft, plump style, it will drink well for 5–7 years. The 1999 St.-Joseph l'Olivare (10,000 bottles) is produced from 60-year-old Syrah vines. Richer and more complex, with better structure, definition, and a thicker, richer mid-palate, it offers earthy black fruits mixed with creosote and plum notes. It has a layered texture, good acidity, and a pure, refreshing personality. It should drink well for 7–8 years. My favorite of this quartet is the 3,000 bottle *cuvée* from 85-year-old Syrah vines planted on granite hillsides called St.-Joseph La Paradis St.-Pierre. The 1999 reveals a pronounced bouquet of liquid minerals, cassis, and flowers with a touch of blackberries. Ripe and full-bodied, with good tannin, grip, purity, and length, it may merit an outstanding score with another 1–3 years of cellaring. Anticipated maturity: now–2015. There are 4,000 bottles of the more internationally styled 1999 St.-Joseph La Sensonne, which sees 80% new oak. While it lacks some St.-Joseph typicity, it offers a boatload of cassis fruit, an unctuous texture, plenty of toasty notes, and a long, layered finish. Intellectuals may prefer La Paradis St.-Pierre, but hedonists will go ga-ga over La Sensonne.

DOMAINE DE CRISTIA

2000 Châteauneuf-du-Pape	C	(87–88)
1999 Châteauneuf-du-Pape	C	85
2000 Châteauneuf-du-Pape Cuvée Renaissance	D	(90–93+)

This is an estate to take particular note of beginning with 2000. The young, energetic Baptiste Grangeon has full control and is doing creative things, as evidenced by his 2000 *cuvées.* Both the 2000 and 1999 standard Châteauneufs are blends of 70% Grenache, 20% Syrah, and 10% Mourvèdre. The Châteauneuf-du-Pape Cuvée Renaissance emerges from 10 acres of old vines (80–100 years) that border the Rayas vineyard.

The 2000 Châteauneuf-du-Pape is obviously concentrated. This deep ruby-colored 2000 exhibits a moderately intense bouquet of blackberries, cherries, and spice. Medium- to full-bodied, open-knit, and accessible, with light to moderate tannin in the finish, it will be at its best between now–2012. The sensational 2000 Châteauneuf-du-Pape Cuvée Renaissance's opaque ruby/purple color is accompanied by a super nose of blackberry, kirsch, spice box, and mineral scents. Thick and full-bodied, with tremendous purity, a sense of elegance, and a layered, multidimensional finish, it is a breakthrough effort for Domaine de Cristia. Anticipated maturity: now–2018.

The medium-bodied, pretty, soft 1999 Châteauneuf-du-Pape offers notes of cherries and currants along with good spice and purity. It is an elegant, moderately weighty effort to enjoy during its first 7–8 years of life.

Readers should also take note of the 2000 Côtes du Rhône and 2000 Côtes du Rhône-Villages. They score in the mid-80s and are attractively priced.

OLIVIER CUILLERAS

2000 Côtes du Rhône Domaine La Guintrandry	A	87
2000 Côtes du Rhône Cuvée Louise	A	(86–88?)
2000 Côtes du Rhône-Villages Visan Vieilles Vignes	A	90

Olivier Cuilleras' Côtes du Rhônes emerge from the village of Visan located in the northern area of the southern Rhône. The Visan and Domaine La Guintrandry are aged completely in tank prior to being bottled without filtration. The Cuvée Louise spends eight months in *barrique*, a small percentage of which is new. When I tasted the 2000 Côtes du Rhône Cuvée Louise (a blend of 80% Grenache and 20% Syrah), the wood gave it a more international style and less typicity. Nevertheless, it possesses loads of fruit and flesh along with a full-bodied style that saturates the palate. My instincts suggest the wood will become better integrated in another six months. The less expensive 2000 Côtes du Rhône Domaine La Guintrandry is a deep ruby/purple-colored, elegant, sweet offering made from 70% Grenache, 20% Carignan, and 10% Syrah. It possesses copious quantities of black currant and cherry fruit, medium body, and excellent purity. Enjoy it over the next 1–2 years. Even better is the 2000 Côtes du Rhône-Villages Visan Vieilles Vignes. A 90% Grenache/10% Syrah *cuvée*, it exhibits good acidity (typical for wines from the northern tier of the southern Rhône), superb freshness, and gobs of black cherry and currant fruit with a touch of licorice and minerals. This lively 2000 should age nicely for 4–5 years. Olivier Cuilleras appears to be a serious wine-maker capable of doing fine work.

YVES CUILLERON

2000 Condrieu Les Chaillets Vieilles Vignes	E	87
1999 Condrieu Les Chaillets Vieilles Vignes	E	90
1999 Condrieu Essence d'Automne	EE	93
2000 Condrieu La Petite Côte	E	89
1999 Condrieu La Petite Côte	E	89
1999 Côte Rôtie Coteau de Bassenon	E	89
1998 Côte Rôtie Coteau de Bassenon	E	86
2000 Côte Rôtie Terres Sombres	D	(87–89)
1999 Côte Rôtie Terres Sombres	D	87?
1999 St.-Joseph l'Amarybelle	D	89
1998 St.-Joseph l'Amarybelle	D	87
2000 St.-Joseph Le Bois Lombard	D	89
1999 St.-Joseph Le Bois Lombard	D	87
2000 St.-Joseph Coteau St.-Pierre	D	88
1999 St.-Joseph Coteau St.-Pierre	D	89
2000 St.-Joseph Izeras	D	86
1999 St.-Joseph Izeras	D	86
2000 St.-Joseph Les Serines	D	(87–88)
1999 St.-Joseph Les Serines	D	90
1998 St.-Joseph Les Serines	D	85?

Yves Cuilleron, one of the northern Rhône's most brilliant makers of white wines, seems to be capturing some of his white wine magic with his newest red wine *cuvées*, particularly those from St.-Joseph. His gorgeous whites from St.-Joseph are essentially from the Marsanne grape, although the Coteau St.-Pierre *cuvée* is 100% Roussanne! However, the Côte Rôtie still lags behind the quality of the other wines.

Although the 2000 whites are lighter and less intense than usual, they remain tasty. Among the three St.-Josephs, the 2000 St.-Joseph Izeras (75% Marsanne and 25% Roussanne, all barrel-fermented) exhibits crisp citrus/grapefruit notes with a hint of honey. It is a pleasant, medium-bodied, elegant offering to enjoy over the next year. The finest of this trio, the 2000 St.-Joseph Le Bois Lombard (100% old-vine Marsanne), reveals a complex bouquet of honeyed citrus and exotic flowers, medium body, lovely fruit and lushness as well as impressive focus. It should be drunk over the next 2–3 years given this vintage's low-acid characteristic. The 100% Roussanne cuvée, the 2000 St.-Joseph Coteau St.-Pierre, exhibits a telltale perfume of rose water intermixed with honey, roasted nuts, and a touch of caramel. Fat, medium-bodied, and expansive, it will drink well for 2–3 years.

Cuilleron's Condrieu cuvées reveal the vintage's high yields. The 2000 Condrieu La Petite Côte is an elegant, floral, mineral-dominated effort with excellent fruit, medium body, and an up-front, precocious style. It should drink well for two decades. The 2000 Condrieu Les Chaillets Vieilles Vignes enjoys 40% new French oak (in contrast to La Petite Côte, which is aged in old barrels). Les Chaillets possesses a flamboyant bouquet of tropical fruits, peaches, and spice. Unusually crisp and tart, with noticeable acidity, it is leaner and more austere than the fatter La Petite Côte.

The 100% Marsanne 1999 St.-Joseph Izeras is aged in old oak prior to blending. It is a citrusy, light- to medium-bodied, clean effort that is best consumed over the next 2 years. The very good 1999 St.-Joseph Le Bois Lombard is a blend of 80% Marsanne and 20% Roussanne, aged in 50% new and 50% used barrels. It reveals a honeyed, wood smoke, pear, and grapefruit-scented bouquet, medium body, good acidity, and an elegant, clean finish. It should drink well for 2–3 years. The 100% Roussanne cuvée aged in 100% new oak, the 1999 St.-Joseph Coteau St.-Pierre, exhibits a light gold color, exotic, honeyed, tropical fruit aromas and flavors, and admirable fat and intensity. Drink it over the next 2–3 years.

Condrieu was a mixed bag in 1999 because yields were significantly higher than 1998. While some wines reveal dilution, others lack balance. Cuilleron has unquestionably produced some of the finest 1999 Condrieu. There are two dry and two sweet cuvées. The 1999 Condrieu La Petite Côte is a finesse-filled, elegant, medium-bodied, beautifully balanced Condrieu with notes of white peaches, apricot jam, and a touch of minerals. The 1999 Condrieu Les Chaillets Vieilles Vignes reveals more liquid mineral in addition to dried apricots, peach jam, acacia flower–like notes, and a richly textured, medium- to full-bodied finish with lively acidity. This superb Condrieu should drink well for 2–3 years. Lastly, there are only minuscule quantities of the 1999 Condrieu Essence d'Automne. This wine reveals a sensationally sweet, nectar-like personality. With 9% alcohol and 300 grams of residual sugar, this serious, full-bodied, opulent Condrieu exhibits a botrytised, honeyed character, amazing viscosity, and surprising lightness for such thickness and sweetness. It should age well for 10–20 years, perhaps longer; it is hard to determine given my lack of experience with this style of wine. Nevertheless, it is showing far better out of bottle than it did from cask.

Yves Cuilleron has augmented the quality of his reds lately. The black/ruby-colored 2000 St.-Joseph Les Serines offers attractive, asphalt-laden, black currant/cherry fruit, medium body, and more depth than many wines from this vintage. Drink it during its first decade of life. On my recent visit, I only tasted one cuvée of 2000 Côte Rôtie, the 2000 Côte Rôtie Terres Sombres. It exhibits a deep purple color, excellent concentration, sweet cassis fruit intermixed with notions of olives and new oak in addition to some tannin. Anticipated maturity: 2004–2012.

The dense purple-colored 1999 St.-Joseph l'Amarybelle displays intense aromas of black fruits, minerals, oak, and graphite. With medium to full body, gorgeously sweet fruit on the attack, and a long, layered finish, it will drink well for 5–8 years. Even better is the 1999 St.-Joseph Les Serines. Its dense plum/purple color is followed by aromas and flavors of cassis, flowers, and minerals. Medium- to full-bodied, with a serious, concentrated style, plenty of muscle, and moderate tannin, it needs 2–3 years of cellaring and should last for 15. Approximately 9% Viognier is included in the 1999 Côte Rôtie Coteau de Bassenon, which is performing better out of bottle than it did last year. It possesses a classic bacon fat, cassis, and tapenade-scented perfume with notions of oak in the background. Medium-bodied and elegant, with considerable aromatic complexity, sweet fruit on the attack, excellent purity, and a moderately long finish, it will drink well for a dozen years. The 1999 Côte Rôtie Terres Sombres is more internationally styled, largely because of 100% new oak utilized. That component currently dominates the wine's aromatics. An austere finish is also cause for concern. However, this 1999 has plenty of mid-palate, richness, and density. It should be long-lived, but will it ever fully come together? Anticipated maturity: 2005–2016.

The 1998 St.-Joseph l'Amarybelle reveals an herbaceousness, but sweet black cherries intermixed with smoke, pepper, and minerals. It is a soft, seductive wine to drink over the next 6–7 years. The 1998 Côte Rôtie Coteau de Bassenon, for which I had such high hopes, appears to have absorbed too much oak, and it tastes far more tannic than it did last year. *C'est la vie* (of a wine critic).

CUVÉE DU VATICAN

2000	Châteauneuf-du-Pape	D	(90–91+)
1999	Châteauneuf-du-Pape	D	90
1998	Châteauneuf-du-Pape	D	89
1995	Châteauneuf-du-Pape	D	90
2000	Châteauneuf-du-Pape Réserve Sixtine	E	(91–94)
1999	Châteauneuf-du-Pape Réserve Sixtine	E	91
1998	Châteauneuf-du-Pape Réserve Sixtine	E	91+
2000	Côtes du Rhône-Villages	A	85

This estate has been invigorated under the youthful, committed direction of Jean-Marc Diffonty, one of many young Rhône Valley proprietors who are part of the youthful revolution taking place. Cuvée du Vatican made impressive 1998s, but their 1999s are even better and the 2000s are the finest efforts I have ever tasted from this estate. In 1998, Jean-Marc Diffonty introduced his 20,000 bottle *cuvée* called Réserve Sixtine, a blend of approximately 50% Grenache, 30% Syrah, and 20% Mourvèdre aged in equal parts barrel and *foudre*. Additionally, the estate offers a fine Côtes du Rhône.

The 2000 Châteauneuf-du-Pape is a powerful, highly extracted, moderately tannic example that requires 1–2 years of cellaring. Its dense purple color is accompanied by high levels of glycerin and tannin. Anticipated maturity: 2004–2018. The opaque purple-colored 2000 Châteauneuf-du-Pape Réserve Sixtine boasts an impressive, concentrated, muscular, old-fashioned personality with plenty of ripe tannin, admirable depth, and the potential for 20 years of longevity. Anticipated maturity: 2006–2025.

The 1999 Châteauneuf-du-Pape, a strong, powerful offering, requires some cellaring, unusual for this vintage. A blend of 70% Grenache and equal proportions of Syrah, Cinsault, and Mourvèdre, it exhibits a healthy ruby/plum/purple color as well as a big, sweet nose of black fruits intertwined with resin, seaweed, and earth. There is marvelous concentration, a firm, tannic underpinning, a seriously extracted style, and a tight but long, powerful finish. Anticipated maturity: now–2015.

The deep ruby/purple-colored 1999 Châteauneuf-du-Pape Réserve Sixtine displays a broodingly backward personality. Extremely rich and full-bodied, with notes of blueberries, new saddle leather, crushed minerals, and spice, it has put on additional weight since last year and looks set to have a long life of 20+ years. Anticipated maturity: 2005–2020.

The 1998 Châteauneuf-du-Pape offers a complex nose of cherry liqueur intermixed with smoke, pepper, and spice. It is medium- to full-bodied, with excellent power and harmony among its diverse elements. Although closed, there is a sense of weight and intensity in the mouth. Quasi-traditional in style, the fruit is fresher and the wine sweeter and more delin-eated than older vintages of Cuvée du Vatican. Anticipated maturity: now–2016. The excep-tional 1998 Châteauneuf-du-Pape Réserve Sixtine boasts abundant quantities of jammy black cherry fruit as well as subtle notes of wood, smoke, herbs, and earth. As the wine sits in the glass, notions of plum liqueur and allspice emerge. It is thick, structured, and tannic, so patience is required. Full-bodied, deep, and layered, this blend of equal parts Grenache, Mourvèdre, and Syrah that was aged both in *barrique* and *foudre,* needs a few years of cellar-ing. Anticipated maturity: 2006–2020.

I am impressed by how well the 1995 Châteauneuf-du-Pape has turned out. It may be the finest wine Jean-Marc Diffonty has produced in several decades, and my score may turn out to be conservative. This is a big, old-styled, classic, blockbuster Châteauneuf-du-Pape with a saturated garnet/plum color, a gorgeous display of roasted *herbes de Provence,* licorice, kirsch, truffles, and earth. Explosive on the palate, with full body, mouthcoating glycerin, and copious quantities of jammy fruit that cascade down the gullet with no hard edges, this is a luscious, flamboyant wine with a terrific personality. Anticipated maturity: now–2012.

Readers looking for an elegant, restrained Côtes du Rhône-Villages should check out Cuvée du Vatican's 2000. It offers aromas of sour cherries, balsam, and pepper in an elegant, medium-bodied, accessible style. Enjoy it over the next 2 years.

DELAS FRÈRES

1999	Châteauneuf-du-Pape Calcernier	C	(85–86)
1998	Châteauneuf-du-Pape Calcernier	C	86
1999	Châteauneuf-du-Pape Hautes Pierres	C	88
2000	Condrieu Clos Boucher	E	92
2000	Condrieu La Galopine	D	90
2000	Cornas Chante-Perdrix	D	(85–87)
1999	Cornas Chante-Perdrix	D	(81–83)
1998	Cornas Chante-Perdrix	D	91
2000	Côte Rôtie La Landonne	EE	(87–89)
1999	Côte Rôtie La Landonne	EE	96
1998	Côte Rôtie La Landonne	EE	95+
2000	Côte Rôtie Seigneur de Maugiron	E	(82–85)
1999	Côte Rôtie Seigneur de Maugiron	E	92
1998	Côte Rôtie Seigneur de Maugiron	E	91
2000	Crozes-Hermitage Le Clos	D	(87–89)
1999	Crozes-Hermitage Le Clos	D	90
1998	Crozes-Hermitage Clos St.-Georges	E	90
2000	Crozes-Hermitage Les Launes	C	(82–85)
1999	Crozes-Hermitage Les Launes	C	86
2000	Crozes-Hermitage Les Launes Blanc	C	85
2000	Crozes-Hermitage Cuvée Tour d'Albon	C	(84–86)
1999	Crozes-Hermitage Cuvée Tour d'Albon	C	89
1998	Crozes-Hermitage Cuvée Tour d'Albon	C	88
1999	Gigondas	C	(90–92)
1998	Gigondas	C	86
1999	Gigondas Les Reinayes	C	88
2000	Hermitage Les Bessards	EE	(90–92)
1999	Hermitage Les Bessards	EE	95+
1998	Hermitage Les Bessards	EE	96+
2000	Hermitage Marquise de la Tourette	E	(86–88?)
1999	Hermitage Marquise de la Tourette	E	90+

1998	Hermitage Marquise de la Tourette	E	92+
2000	Hermitage Marquise de la Tourette Blanc	E	(90–92)
1999	Hermitage Marquise de la Tourette Blanc	E	90
2000	St.-Joseph Les Challeys	C	(84–86)
1999	St.-Joseph Les Challeys	C	87
1998	St.-Joseph Les Challeys	C	87
2000	St.-Joseph Les Challeys Blanc	C	85
2000	St.-Joseph Cuvée François de Tournon	D	(85–87)
1999	St.-Joseph Cuvée François de Tournon	D	89
1998	St.-Joseph Cuvée François de Tournon	D	90
2000	St.-Joseph Sainte-Epine	D	(87–88)
1999	St.-Joseph Sainte-Epine	D	91
1998	St.-Joseph Sainte-Epine	D	93
2000	St.-Joseph Sainte-Epine Blanc	D	87
2000	St.-Péray Blanc	B	87
1999	Vacqueyras	B	(84–86)
1998	Vacqueyras	B	86
2000	VDP Viognier	A	86

The firm of Delas has joined the ranks of the finest Rhône Valley producers. The impetus for the change is Jacques Grange, a Burgundian who worked with Michel Chapoutier before joining Delas. He has revolutionized the winemaking at this estate with techniques such as (1) utilizing more new oak, (2) 100% destemmed fruit, (3) cold pre-fermentations, (4) minimal rackings, (5) reducing the sulphur levels, (6) extensive lees aging, and (7) bottling the top *cuvées* without fining or filtration. The results are extraordinary, with the finest northern Rhône offerings being as majestic as Côte Rôtie, Hermitage, St.-Joseph, and Crozes-Hermitage can be. The wines have been spectacular since 1997. The offerings from the southern Rhône Valley still need work, but they are improving with each vintage. While they are not as exciting as the northern Rhône efforts, good values exist.

With respect to the white wines, the 2000 VDP Viognier (5,000 cases) is a good buy. It is a straightforward effort offering a peach, apricot, and honeysuckle-scented perfume. Consume it over the next year. The same can be said for the 2000 Crozes-Hermitage Les Launes Blanc. This 100% Marsanne is tasty in a straightforward, monolithic style. This must be the coming-out vintage for white St.-Péray as there are a number of good examples. Most interesting is the 2000 St.-Péray Blanc, a blend of 60% Marsanne and 40% Roussanne. An excellent effort, with lovely fruit, it is a good value. The other whites I tasted included good commercial examples of the 2000 St.-Joseph Les Challeys Blanc and 2000 St.-Joseph Sainte-Epine Blanc. More impressive is the 2000 Hermitage Marquise de la Tourette Blanc. Made from 90% Marsanne and 10% Roussanne and aged 100% in barrel, it exhibits deep flavors, an unctuous texture, and a long, concentrated finish. The 1999 Hermitage Marquise de la Tourette Blanc is also outstanding. It boasts 14% natural alcohol, abundant glycerin, and notes of honeysuckle mixed with fino sherry, pineapples, minerals, and a hint of acacia flowers. I tasted two exceptional efforts from Condrieu. The 2000 Condrieu La Galopine reveals plenty of heady, intoxicating honeysuckle and jammy peach-like fruit. Medium- to full-bodied and intense, it is ideal for drinking over the next year. More serious as well as concentrated, the exotic, full-bodied, luxuriously fruited 2000 Condrieu Clos Boucher is one of the four or five finest efforts of the appellation. A barrel-fermented Condrieu, with 70% spending time in *barriques*, it is significantly better than the 1999. Drink it over the next 2–3 years.

The deep ruby/purple-colored, medium-bodied 2000 Crozes-Hermitage Les Launes displays surprisingly good acidity as well as fine fruit on the attack, but there is not much behind it. Drink it over the next 2–3 years. The deep ruby-colored 1999 Crozes-Hermitage Les

Launes exhibits sweeter fruit with similar body and weight, but more depth and layers. It is best drunk over the next 2–4 years.

The Crozes-Hermitage Cuvée Tour d'Albon is a serious wine, which has its malolactic fermentation done in barrel. There are approximately 20,000 bottles produced. The 2000 Crozes-Hermitage Cuvée Tour d'Albon's dark ruby/purple color is followed by aromas of sweet cassis, herbs, and pepper. It is a well-made, medium-bodied, straightforward effort to enjoy during its first 3–4 years of life. A totally different animal, the 1999 Crozes-Hermitage Cuvée Tour d'Albon is powerful, fat, and fleshy, with sweeter fruit in addition to impressive aromatic fireworks. It is a gorgeous Crozes that combines elegance, power, length, and harmony. Its delicious primary fruit characteristics will serve it well over the next 4–6 years. Already complex, the 1998 Crozes-Hermitage Cuvée Tour d'Albon reveals aromas of jammy black fruits, licorice, and flowers. It is a dense ruby/purple-colored, medium- to full-bodied 1998 with plenty of weight, depth, and intensity. Anticipated maturity: now–2015.

There are 7,000 bottles of the Crozes-Hermitage Le Clos, an 11.5-acre vineyard located near the Rhône River in the area known as Les Chassis. Only the finest grapes from Clos St.-Georges are included in this *cuvée*, an extraordinary Crozes-Hermitage. The wine is 100% barrel-aged. As of 1999 the words "St.-Georges" have been dropped from the label because of a legal issue. The top *cuvée* of Crozes-Hermitage, the 2000 Le Clos possesses the most depth, ripeness, and minerality of the 2000s. Its dark ruby/purple color is accompanied by a blacker fruit flavor spectrum in addition to a deeper, more penetrating mouth-feel. With fine elegance as well as purity, it should drink well for 5–6 years. The exceptional 1999 Crozes-Hermitage Le Clos exhibits a saturated ruby/purple color, sweet black currant, black raspberry, and cherry flavors, with hints of licorice, smoke, and minerals. There is beautiful purity, considerable finesse, and impeccable balance. This 1999 is best cellared for another 1–3 years. Anticipated maturity: now–2012. The outstanding, deep ruby/purple-colored 1998 Crozes-Hermitage Clos St.-Georges possesses power allied to elegance. An intense bouquet of cassis, minerals, licorice, and smoke is followed by a wine with superb concentration, a layered mid-palate, medium to full body, and exquisite purity. Not a blockbuster, it is a beautifully etched 1998 that should be at its best before 2015.

The basic *cuvée* of St.-Joseph is called Les Challeys, and it tends to be a fruit-driven wine. 60% is aged in new barrels and 40% in used wood. The 2000 St.-Joseph Les Challeys displays a dark ruby color along with a straightforward perfume of currants, cherries, earth, and herbs. It is medium-bodied and pleasant, but one-dimensional. The 1999 St.-Joseph Les Challeys possesses a similar saturated dark ruby color as well as a more complex nose of cherry, raspberry, and mineral aromas. Fresh, with tangy acidity, excellent ripeness on the attack, good follow-through on the mid-palate, and a layered, pure finish, it will drink well for 5–6 years. The dark plum/purple-colored 1998 St.-Joseph Les Challeys reveals a sweet nose of candied cherries and minerals, as well as a medium-bodied, dry, moderately tannic finish. It needs 1–2 years of cellaring, and it should keep for a decade or more.

The impressive François de Tournon *cuvée* is at the top of the St.-Joseph qualitative hierarchy. This wine emerges from three vineyard sources—one behind the town of Tournon, one behind the village of Mauves, and one near the Delas headquarters in St.-Jean de Muzols. There are 16,000 bottles produced annually.

Revealing surprising acidity, the 2000 St.-Joseph Cuvée François de Tournon is an elegant, finesse-styled, straightforward effort with ripe berry fruit as well as a touch of oak. As Jacques Granges said, "2000 produced too large a crop to achieve impressive levels of concentration." Drink this wine over the next 3–4 years. The beautiful 1999 St.-Joseph Cuvée François de Tournon is performing even better from bottle. The dense ruby color is accompanied by a crunchy nose of black raspberries intertwined with cherry liqueur. Sweet, ripe, and seductive, this hedonistic, medium- to full-bodied 1999 possesses gorgeous ripeness, outstanding concentration, and good underlying acidity, which provides uplift, definition, and a refreshing character. It should drink well for 12–15 years. The exceptional 1998 St.-Joseph Cuvée François de Tournon boasts an opaque purple color as well as a gorgeously sweet nose of jammy black fruits intermixed with underbrush, minerals, and smoke. On the attack and mid-palate, the wine is superbly concentrated and elegant. The tannin, acidity, alcohol, and limited new oak (about 5%) are well-integrated. Like many 1998s, it possesses firm tannin. Anticipated maturity: now–2018.

One of the great St.-Josephs now being produced is the Delas St.-Joseph Sainte-Epine. Made from a vineyard planted directly behind the winery and aged 100% in barrel, of which 50% is new, it is only produced in very small quantities. Along with the luxury *cuvée* produced by Chapoutier, the St.-Joseph Les Granits, this is a reference point for what can be achieved in this diverse appellation. These wines possess a minerality and elegance characteristic of St.-Joseph, but the concentration and intensity of a profound Hermitage.

The dark ruby-colored, medium-bodied 2000 St.-Joseph Sainte-Epine offers aromas of black fruits, minerals, and graphite. The vintage's high yields have resulted in a weaker mid-section than normal. Drink this 2000 during its first 5–6 years of life. The exceptional 1999 St.-Joseph Sainte-Epine admirably demonstrates the characteristics of a great vintage. A saturated ruby/purple color is followed by aromas of crème de cassis, liquid minerals, smoke, and flowers. Medium-bodied, with a seamless personality, gorgeous levels of fruit, and a long, 30-second finish, this terrific St.-Joseph rivals the superb Les Granits produced by Michel Chapoutier. Anticipated maturity: now–2016.

After bottling, the 1998 St.-Joseph Sainte-Epine is even more remarkable than it was from barrel. An explosive offering, with amazing persistence on its multilayered mid-palate, this wine displays a riveting concoction of minerals, crème de cassis, and flowers. Anticipated maturity: now–2016.

As for the Cornas, the 2000 Cornas Chante-Perdrix reveals attractive characteristics in a sweet style, but the mid-palate is deficient and the finish is all muscle and tannin with only a hint of licorice and black currants. An egregious screw-up on my part, I was excited by the 1999 Cornas Chante-Perdrix when tasted from cask, but from the bottle, this wine, like too many 1999 Cornas, is dried out and hard, with a lean, astringent, tough personality and an austerity that only a Puritan could admire. Who knows what happened, or what I was tasting, but I'll take the blame. The 1998 Cornas Chante-Perdrix reveals black/purple colors in addition to a concentrated, powerful, muscular format and is meant to withstand 15+ years of cellaring. It will not begin to strut its stuff for 5–6 years, but it should last for two decades.

As for the Côte Rôties, they are 100% Syrah and spend nearly two years in small oak casks (half new and half one-year-old). The wine is a blend of fruit from the Côte Blonde (30%) and Côte Brune (70%). The dominance of the Côte Brune can be seen in the wine's dense black/purple color, and full-bodied, chewy, robust, concentrated, meaty personality. While the 2000 Côte Rôtie Seigneur de Maugiron is a disappointing, austere, rigid, tannic effort with no flesh, mid-section, or finish, the 1999 Côte Rôtie Seigneur de Maugiron is brilliant. It boasts a black/purple color as well as sumptuous aromas of espresso, graphite, violets, and blackberry/cassis fruit. This is underlined by abundant power, good acidity for definition as well as freshness, and a superb, pure finish. This exceptional Côte Rôtie requires 4–5 years of cellaring. Anticipated maturity: 2005–2018. The 1998 Côte Rôtie Seigneur de Maugiron (15,000 bottles) boasts a black/purple color, aromas and flavors of tapenade, licorice, bacon fat, black raspberry and blackberry liqueur, and formidable levels of tannin present in a structured, hyper-concentrated style. This 1998 requires 6–7 years of cellaring, and it is a candidate for 15–16 years of aging. Stylistically, it is reminiscent of Chapoutier's Côte Rôtie La Mordorée. Appearing undernourished next to its 1999 sibling, the 2000 Côte Rôtie La Landonne possesses a deep ruby/purple color in addition to complex aromatics of earth, flowers, black currant fruit, and new oak. Some of the vintage's hollowness emerges in the mid-palate, but the finish is well balanced with sweet tannin, ripe fruit, and low acidity. However, this is not the type of vintage where the wines eventually fill out as yields were too high. Anticipated maturity: 2004–2014. The 1999 Côte Rôtie La Landonne is prodigious. Readers lucky enough to track down a bottle or two will own a legend in the making. However, 8–9 years of cellaring are required before this wine rounds into drinkable form. An opaque black/purple color is accompanied by sublime aromas of licorice, espresso, scorched earth, tapenade, bacon fat, and blackberry/cassis liqueur. A wine of great intensity, explosive richness, and brutally high tannin, this compelling, majestic Côte Rôtie should be at its finest between 2008–2025. The opaque black/purple-colored 1998 Côte Rôtie La Landonne offers vanilla, espresso bean, licorice, blackberry, and cassis scents and flavors with scorched earth and olive notes in the background. Extremely full-bodied, tannic, and monstrous on the palate, it possesses huge ripeness and extraction, as well as mouth-searing levels of tannin. This wine will need 8–10 years of bottle age; it should drink well for 3–4 decades. These are profound Côte Rôties!

The *cuvées* of Hermitage are powerful, rich wines that, like the Côte Rôties, are aged in 50% new oak and 50% one-year-old barrels. They are bottled with neither fining nor filtration. The dramatic differences between 2000 and 1999 carry over into Hermitage. The dense purple-colored 2000 Hermitage Marquise de la Tourette exhibits an austere personality and sweet black cherry and cassis fruit intermixed with mineral/dusty notes. The compressed, attenuated finish may prove problematic after 5–6 years of cellaring. The deep ruby/purple-colored, velvety-textured, full-bodied, accessible 1999 Hermitage Marquise de la Tourette offers an open-knit nose of pepper, cassis, minerals, and cedar. With sweet tannin, medium to full body, and a supple-textured yet delineated style, it will be at its finest between 2004–2016. In contrast, the 1998 Hermitage Marquise de la Tourette exhibits a remarkably huge, chewy mid-palate as well as formidable persistence, but it is very tannic and backward. Readers who are not willing to invest 8–10 years of cellaring should forget about this wine. Some toasty new oak is present, but the primary characteristic is the layer of black fruits intertwined with minerals.

The titan of Delas's portfolio is their luxury *cuvée*, Hermitage Les Bessards. There are 500 cases of this offering, made from 70-year-old Syrah vines in the famed Les Bessards vineyard (the dominant component of Chave's great Hermitages). The 2000 Hermitage Les Bessards should prove to be outstanding. The color is a deep blue/purple, and the nose offers classic aromas of crème de cassis, melted licorice, and creosote. Sweet yet unevolved, this medium- to full-bodied effort does not have the affliction of many 2000 northern Rhônes . . . a hole in the middle. Ripe, fleshy, and rich, with moderately high tannin, it will last for 20–25 years. Anticipated maturity: 2008–2025. The compelling 1999 Hermitage Les Bessards exhibits an opaque purple color along with an extraordinary bouquet of blackberry fruit, crème de cassis, creosote, and minerals. Full-bodied, with great purity as well as palate presence, this super-extracted, rich yet backward 1999 spent 23 months in barrel prior to being bottled without fining or filtration. Readers should be forewarned, this wine is only for those with considerable patience. It is revealing even more structure and muscle than it did last year. Anticipated maturity: 2005–2030. The 1998 Hermitage Les Bessards reveals more licorice, coffee, cassis, minerals, smoke, and meat scents, full body, great depth, teeth-coating tannin, and a persistent, sweet, well-delineated, 45-second finish. One of the great Hermitages of the vintage (which was stunning in that appellation), it will be at its peak between 2007–2035.

From the southern Rhône, the exceptional, deep purple-colored 1999 Gigondas boasts admirable fatness, an impressive texture, medium to full body, sweet tannin, and a long, concentrated, black cherry-flavored finish. The 1998 Gigondas is more rustic, with drier fruit as well as peppery herb and cherry notes. The medium- to full-bodied 1999 Gigondas Les

Reinayes was aged in both *foudre* and tank before being bottled without filtration. Its dark ruby color is accompanied by a muscular, concentrated wine with notes of black cherry and berry fruit mixed with dried herbs and pepper. Consume it over the next 5–8 years.

The medium-bodied, restrained, lighter-styled 1999 Châteauneuf-du-Pape Calcernier is pleasant, but unexciting. The 1998 Châteauneuf-du-Pape Calcernier reveals a medium-dark ruby color, a peppery, spicy, leathery-scented bouquet, but little depth or intensity. The surprisingly elegant 1999 Châteauneuf-du-Pape Hautes Pierres is a soft, round, supple-textured red without the muscle and breadth of flavor that many of this appellation's finest wines possess. It exhibits sweet black cherry fruit, fine intensity, and excellent purity. Drink it over the next 6–7 years.

The dark ruby-colored, fruit-dominated 1999 Vacqueyras (a blend of Grenache and Carignan) reveals good freshness, medium weight, and notes of herbs, black cherries, and leather. Delas's Gigondas is made from one of that appellation's top domaines (I was asked to not mention the name). It is a blend of 95% Grenache and 5% Syrah. Exhibiting a denser color than its 1999 counterpart, the 1998 Vacqueyras obviously benefited from the fact that 1998 was a better vintage for Grenache than 1999. Deeper and more expansive on the palate, it can be drunk over the next 3–4 years.

LOUIS DREVON

2000 Côte Rôtie Domaine des Rosières	D	(84–86)
1999 Côte Rôtie Domaine des Rosières	D	87
1998 Côte Rôtie Domaine des Rosières	D	87

Drevon has never emerged as a Côte Rôtie leader, but his style has progressed considerably, from rustic, dried out, *foudre*-aged winemaking, to a synthesis between modern and more artisanal efforts. He still ages his wines primarily in *foudre* and *cuvée*, although a few *barriques* have made their way into the cellars. Drevon has begun to totally destem his grapes, thus eliminating the tart acid and vegetal stem characteristics. Although Drevon's 2000 Côte Rôtie Domaine des Rosières possesses a forward style as well as charm, it lacks richness and length (as do many wines from this vintage). It displays a medium ruby color, soft style, peppery/herbal notes, low acid, and a ripe, moderately concentrated style. Drink it over the next 5–6 years. Also forward, but with more stuffing, the 1999 Côte Rôtie Domaine des Rosières reveals a deep ruby color as well as sweet berry fruit intermixed with herbs and earth. Jammy, richly fruity, round, and blatantly commercial, it will provide delicious drinking over the next 4–8 years. The garnet/plum-colored 1998 Côte Rôtie Domaine des Rosières is a surprisingly plump, tasty effort with attractive sweet black cherry fruit, earth, and dried herb notes. Medium-bodied and soft, it is best drunk over the next 6–7 years.

DOMAINE DUCLAUX

2000 Châteauneuf-du-Pape	D	(89–91)
1999 Châteauneuf-du-Pape	D	88
1998 Châteauneuf-du-Pape	D	89

This estate, owned by Jérôme Quiot, is on the rise. Potentially outstanding, the 2000 Châteauneuf-du-Pape is a big, chewy, unctuously textured offering with explosive levels of fruit, beautiful purity, fine ripeness, low acidity, and mouth-filling extract. There is not a hard edge to this seamless, somewhat modern-styled effort. Drink it over the next 10–12 years. Their excellent 1999 Châteauneuf-du-Pape offers up aromas of Provençal herbs, ground pepper, mincement, black currants, and cherries. Round, spicy, and open-knit, it is best consumed over the next 7–8 years. The 1998 Châteauneuf-du-Pape is a deep, full-bodied, open-knit, fragrant offering with low acidity and abundant fruit, glycerin, and extract. It is hard to resist given its fleshy, ripe, jammy style. It will drink nicely for 10–12 years.

EDMUND & DAVID DUCLAUX

2000	Côte Rôtie	D	(87–88)
1999	Côte Rôtie	D	90
1998	Côte Rôtie	D	87

Edmund's son, David, has taken over the winemaking at this estate, whose vineyards are all located in the southern half of the appellation. The style has changed—there is 100% destemming, with more barrels plus some new oak being utilized. These are supple Côte Rôties with sweet fruit and forward personalities. David is pushing this small estate into a higher-quality echelon, as evidenced by the 1999, the finest Duclaux Côte Rôtie I have tasted.

The dark ruby-colored, medium-bodied, elegant 2000 Côte Rôtie exhibits good fruit and ripeness for this vintage. The bouquet offers notes of sweet toasty oak (from aging in 50% new oak *barriques*), black currants, smoke, and minerals. Anticipated maturity: now–2012. The exceptional 1999 Côte Rôtie is a hedonistic fruit bomb possessing a dark ruby color, a creamy texture, and a sweet, evolved perfume of black fruits mixed with smoke, dried herbs, bacon fat, and spice. Rich, round, and seductive, it will drink well for 12+ years. The dark plum/garnet-colored 1998 Côte Rôtie's ripe black cherry and blackberry, mineral, and spice box aromas are followed by a medium-bodied, dense, concentrated, sweet, ripe palate. It should evolve easily for a decade.

MADAME P. DUMAZET

2000	Condrieu Coteau Fournet	E	90
2000	Condrieu Cuvée de la Myriade Coteau Fournet	E	88
2000	Condrieu Rouelle Midi	E	91

Some of the finest 2000 Condrieus I tasted were made by Madame Dumazet. The 2000 Condrieu Coteau Fournet reveals a green hue to its medium straw color. It offers an intoxicating, precise combination of finesse with fat, full body, good underlying acidity, and remarkable delineation. It should drink well for 3–4 years. The exotic, mineral-laden 2000 Condrieu Rouelle Midi reveals more tropical fruit notes along with telltale peach and apricot characteristics. Intriguing liquid stone-like notions add a complex element. It should drink well for 2–3 years. I am generally not a fan of super-sweet, late harvest Condrieus, but the 2000 Condrieu Cuvée de la Myriade Coteau Fournet is well made, slightly heavy, but ripe and sweet. Drink it over the next 3–5 years.

DUMIEN-SERETTE

2000	Cornas Vieilles Vignes	D	(87–89)
1999	Cornas Vieilles Vignes	D	87

The 2000 Cornas Vieilles Vignes exhibits a more saturated blackberry color as well as soft acids (atypical of the appellation, but reflective of the vintage character), abundant quantities of liquid minerals and cassis fruit, a savory mid-palate, medium to full body, and a tannic finish. It is a more exuberant, robust effort that should drink well for a decade. The 1999 Cornas Vieilles Vignes is an elegant, sweet, civilized effort with a restrained, measured style. Aromas and flavors of cherries, black fruits, and minerals dominate this spicy, medium-bodied 1999. It is almost too polished and refined to suggest Cornas. Drink it during its first 10–12 years of life.

ERIC ET JOEL DURAND

2000	Cornas	D	(87–88)
1999	Cornas	D	86
1998	Cornas	D	(87–88?)
1997	Cornas	D	(87–88)

2000	Cornas Empreintes	D	(88–90)
1999	Cornas Empreintes	D	90
2000	Cornas Les Coteaux	D	(87–88)
1999	Cornas Les Coteaux	D	85?
1998	St.-Joseph Les Coteaux	C	(87–88)

The dark ruby/purple-colored 2000 Cornas Les Coteaux exhibits a lower acid/sweeter fruit character (typical of the vintage) and cassis fruit intermixed with smoke, earth, and mineral notions. This medium-bodied 2000 is best consumed during its first 5–6 years of life.

The friendly, modern-styled 2000 Cornas *cuvée* classique possesses a deep purple color, medium body, and a short finish, but plenty of charming fruit on the attack and in the mid-palate. Enjoy it during its first 5–6 years of life. The star of this portfolio is the Cornas Empreintes. The seriously endowed 2000 boasts a saturated dense purple color and a big, fat, jammy personality with loads of smoke, minerals, licorice, and blackberry/cassis fruit. It reveals the vintage's low acidity along with a juicy midsection, and a pure, ripe finish with well-integrated tannin. Anticipated maturity: now–2014.

I had hoped that Durand's 1999 Cornas Les Coteaux would turn out to be an upper-80-point wine. From the bottle, it reveals underripe, cool climate, red currant, and sour cherry notes, an austere mid-palate, and an acidic, harsh finish. It does display an attractive perfume and, hopefully, will soften with a few years of cellaring. Nevertheless, it is far less successful than my former barrel tastings suggested. Unlike Les Coteaux, the bottled 1999 Cornas *cuvée* classique was as good as it was from barrel, so perhaps Les Coteaux was just off-form the day I saw it. The 1999 *cuvée* classique offers copious quantities of red currants, plums, herbs, earth, leather, and licorice. Round and sweet, with ripe tannin as well as decent acidity, it will drink well for 5–8 years. Rather elegant, the 1999 Cornas Empreintes offers pure black fruits intermixed with smoke, mineral, graphite, and new *barrique* aromas. Sweet cassis, saddle leather, earth, and spice characteristics cascade over the palate in a rich, full-bodied style with just enough acidity for grip and definition. Drink this beauty over the next 12–14 years.

I was surprised by the tart acidity of the 1998 Cornas, but there is no doubting its concentration. Although made in a savage, unevolved, tannic manner, it reveals an admirable black fruit character and ripe Syrah style. Anticipated maturity: now–2012.

On the other hand, the Durands' 1998 St.-Joseph Les Coteaux is much rounder, with a dense ruby/purple color, and up-front, intense, jammy black cherry notes with red and black currant overtones. This fruit-driven St.-Joseph reveals excellent concentration, a touch of rocky, mineral notes, and a medium- to full-bodied, voluptuous, concentrated finish. Drink this delicious offering over the next 3–4 years. The 1997 Cornas displays a dark ruby/purple color, an excellent floral, tar, and blackberry-scented nose, rich, medium- to full-bodied flavors, with low acidity and sweet tannin. This will be a Cornas to drink early, but it has the necessary richness to keep 4–5 years.

DOMAINE DURBAN

2000	Côtes du Rhône-Villages Beaumes-de-Venise Cuvée Prestige	B	88
1999	Côtes du Rhône-Villages Beaumes-de-Venise Cuvée Prestige	B	88
1999	Muscat de Beaumes-de-Venise	C	91

This estate, renowned for its sweet Muscats, has fashioned a beautiful dark ruby/purple-colored 2000 Côtes du Rhône-Villages Beaumes-de-Venise Cuvée Prestige with no hard edges. Sweet, creamy blackberry and currant fruit dominate this medium- to full-bodied, velvety-textured, lush effort. Although it will not make old bones, it is a hedonistic Côtes du Rhône-Villages fruit bomb to drink over the next 3–4 years. The big, thick 1999 Côtes du Rhône-Villages Beaumes-de-Venise Cuvée Prestige offers copious quantities of herb-tinged, black cherry and plum-like fruit intermixed with pepper, licorice, and earth. Drink this dense, full-bodied, seamless, mouth-filling, gloriously juicy Beaumes-de-Venise over the next 2–3 years.

As for the sweet 1999 Muscat de Beaumes-de-Venise, it is hard to find a better effort than Domaine Durban's. The color is a light straw with hints of amber and copper. The spectacular aromatics offer candied apricots and peaches, with orange marmalade thrown in for additional allure. The wine is unctuously textured, with enough underlying acidity to support the glycerin and sweetness. It is an ideal wine to sip while sitting under the Provençal sun (or imagining that you are). Drink it over the next 2 years.

DOMAINE DURIEU

2000	Châteauneuf-du-Pape	C	(87–88)
1999	Châteauneuf-du-Pape	C	87
1999	Châteauneuf-du-Pape Réserve Lucile Avril	D	89

It has been several years since I have tasted Durieu's Châteauneuf-du-Papes, but I have always enjoyed his wines. Magnums of the earthy 1986 in my cellar still provide considerable enjoyment.

The deep ruby/purple-colored 2000 Châteauneuf-du-Pape offers ripe, jammy black cherry and berry fruit, full body, a soft, fleshy attack mid-palate, and abundant glycerin and alcohol in the finish. Drink this forward Châteauneuf during its first 10–12 years of life.

The 1999 Châteauneuf-du-Pape exhibits that classic, peppery, Provençal mélange of earth and herbs known as *garrigue,* along with abundant black cherry fruit, medium body, moderate weight, excellent concentration, and fine overall balance. It is an evolved, forward effort to drink over the next 6–7 years. Revealing a more saturated ruby/garnet color as well as more tannin and weight, the 1999 Châteauneuf-du-Pape Réserve Lucile Avril is a big wine with excellent concentration and moderate tannin. Notes of saddle leather, dried herbs, blackberry and cherry fruit, smoke, and mincemeat provide a provocative aromatic as well as flavor profile. It will benefit from 2 years of cellaring and should last for 12–15.

DOMAINE DES FILLES DURMA

2000	Côtes du Rhône	A	85
1999	Côtes du Rhône	A	86
2000	Côtes du Rhône La Galance	A	87

A newly emerging estate in Vinsobres run by two sisters, Domaine des Filles Durma's first vintage was 1999. Similar to its 1999 counterpart, the 2000 Côtes du Rhône reveals lower acidity and sweeter fruit, with the 1999 revealing more definition. Both are Grenache-based wines to drink over the next 1–2 years. The 2000 Côtes du Rhône La Galance (a blend of equal parts Syrah and Grenache) is an earthy, peppery offering with abundant quantities of black cherry and currant fruit intertwined with notes of herbs. Medium-bodied and well made, it should drink well for 3–4 years. The 1999 Côtes du Rhône is a straightforward, solidly made, medium-bodied effort with fleshy, black currant and cherry fruit and fine depth.

DOMAINE DES ESPIERS

1999	Gigondas Cuvée des Blanches	C	(90–91)
1998	Gigondas Cuvée des Blanches	C	92

Although unevolved, the 1999 Gigondas Cuvée des Blanches is loaded from an extract point of view. Opaque purple-colored, full-bodied, with layers of concentration, sweet tannin, adequate acidity, and a mouth-filling style, this intense Gigondas requires 4–5 years of cellaring, and it should keep for 18+ years. The superb 1998 Gigondas Cuvée des Blanches is the finest wine I have tasted from this small producer. A black/purple color is accompanied by a sumptuous bouquet of blackberries, licorice, smoke, and scorched earth. This tannic, full-bodied, serious effort requires 3–4 years of cellaring and should keep for 16–20 years. It is a blockbuster in the making.

BERNARD FAURIE

2000 Hermitage	E	(87–89)
1999 Hermitage	E	89

Bernard Faurie is a serious producer who has made some great wines in the past. The finest Faurie wine I have ever tasted is his 1990 (which I still have in my cellar), which remains a young, powerful, blockbuster Hermitage years away from its zenith.

Typical of many 2000 northern Rhônes, Faurie's 2000 Hermitage is a fat, succulent, ripe, low-acid effort with plenty of fruit, but a lack of definition, grip, and intensity. It offers beautiful black currant fruit intermixed with mineral and melted asphalt notes. However, there is an absence of definition and depth. Anticipated maturity: now–2012. More complete, with additional fullness, the opaque purple-colored 1999 Hermitage reveals aromas of cassis, licorice, spice, and pepper. Medium- to full-bodied, thick, and rich, it is an excellent, possibly outstanding Hermitage to drink between 2006–2018.

PHILIPPE FAURY

2000 Condrieu	D	86
1999 Condrieu	D	89
2000 Condrieu La Berne	D	87
1999 Condrieu La Berne	D	89

Philippe Faury, now the president of the syndicate of Condrieu growers, is fashioning better and better wines. Faury's wines are made half in tank and half in barrel, of which 10% is new.

The 2000 Condrieu is fresh and pretty, but essentially monochromatic. Offering notes of underripe peaches and citrus, it is a light, fresh, but innocuous effort to consume over the next year. The older vine *cuvée* of 2000 Condrieu La Berne exhibits good acidity, better ripeness, and notes of honeyed fruit. It should age nicely for 3–4 years.

The 1999 Condrieu is an elegant, tropical fruit–scented effort with subtle, spicy oak, good structure, and an impressive mid-palate as well as length. It should drink well for 1–2 years. Made from a 25-year-old hillside vineyard, the 1999 Condrieu La Berne sees 25% new oak barrels and the rest older oak. It is a subtle, restrained effort with impressive elegance, notes of white fruits, honeysuckle, apricots, and lychee, medium to full body, a liquid minerality, and a pure finish.

EDDIE FÉRAUD

2000 Châteauneuf-du-Pape	D	(87–89)
1999 Châteauneuf-du-Pape	D	85
1998 Châteauneuf-du-Pape	D	88

Far better than its 1999 counterpart is the 2000 Châteauneuf-du-Pape, an intense, smoky, earthy offering with copious quantities of peppery black currant and cherry fruit intermixed with that Provençal mélange of herbs and earth called *garrigue*. Rich, medium- to full-bodied, and spicy, with a significantly longer finish than its older sibling, it will age well for a decade. Anticipated maturity: now–2014. The dark plum/ruby-colored 1999 Châteauneuf-du-Pape reveals considerable pink at the rim. There is good fruit on the attack in addition to medium body, adequate flesh, notes of *garrigue*, pepper, and cherries, but a short, uninspiring finish. Drink it over the next 5–6 years. The dense ruby-colored 1998 Châteauneuf-du-Pape offers notes of crushed pepper, sweaty saddle leather, cherry jam, cassis, and Provençal herbs, and it has excellent texture, good stuffing, and a longer, richer finish, with more glycerin and extract. Anticipated maturity: now–2012.

FÉRAUD-BRUNEL

1999	Châteauneuf-du-Pape	C	89
2000	Côtes du Rhône-Villages Cairanne	B	87
2000	Gigondas	C	(88–90)
1999	Gigondas	C	89
2000	Vacqueyras	B	90

This is a joint effort between two of Châteauneuf-du-Pape's finest wine producers, André Brunel of Les Cailloux and Laurence Féraud of Domaine de Pégaü. They have fashioned the following wines from purchases made in the southern Rhône. There are approximately 1,700 cases of Côtes du Rhône and Châteauneuf-du-Pape, 500 cases of Vacqueyras, and 900 cases of Gigondas. All are excellent offerings that should be available for realistic prices.

A blend of 70% Grenache, 10% Carignan, and 20% Syrah, the 2000 Côtes du Rhône-Villages Cairanne exhibits the appellation's rustic side, with moderate tannin, plenty of earthy, leathery, black fruits, and medium body. It should drink well for 3–4 years. The superb 2000 Vacqueyras boasts a deep saturated ruby color as well as a bombastic bouquet of kirsch, earth, herbs, and leather. Dense, full-bodied, and chewy, it offers a sumptuous mouthful of primarily old-vine Grenache. Drink it over the next 4–5 years. A blend of 90% Grenache and 10% Mourvèdre aged in *foudre*, the excellent, deep ruby/purple-colored 2000 Gigondas reveals aromas of liquefied minerals, blueberries, and raspberries.

A blend of 70% Grenache and 30% Syrah, the 1999 Gigondas offers up notes of framboise, chocolate, minerals, and kirsch. Full-bodied, concentrated, and pure, it ranks as one of the better wines from this appellation. Lastly, the 1999 Châteauneuf-du-Pape is a dark purple-colored effort exhibiting ripe aromas of black fruits intermixed with licorice and resiny notes. It possesses serious concentration, full body, powerful, concentrated flavors, and a strong finish with noticeable tannin, suggesting that 2–3 years of cellaring is warranted. Anticipated maturity: now–2015.

DOMAINE DE FERRAND

2000	Châteauneuf-du-Pape	D	(91–93)
1999	Châteauneuf-du-Pape	D	90
1998	Châteauneuf-du-Pape	D	92
1998	Côtes du Rhône	B	88
2000	Côtes du Rhône Cuvée Antique Vieilles Vignes	C	(87–88)
2000	Côtes du Rhône Cuvée des Demoiselles	C	(81–83)

Domaine de Ferrand may be an estate worth watching. The young vigneron, Philippe Bravay, has begun to estate bottle the production from this 5-hectare (12+ acres) estate located in the northern sector of Châteauneuf-du-Pape, in what is known as the Quartier de Grès. Previously, the wines were sold to the *négociant* Bernard. The 1996 vintage is the first harvest to be controlled completely by the estate. Domaine de Ferrand is also a good source of value-priced Côtes du Rhône.

The 2000 Châteauneuf-du-Pape will equal, perhaps surpass, Bravay's sensational 1998. With a character reminiscent of dry vintage Port, it is an uncompromising Provençal blend of wildflowers, herbs, smoke, sausage, black cherries, and berries. Moderately tannic, layered, full-bodied, and pure, it will require patience. Anticipated maturity: 2005–2020.

Given the excellence of Bravay's Châteauneuf-du-Papes, I was surprised the 2000 Côtes du Rhône Cuvée des Demoiselles did not reveal more fruit. Perhaps I tasted it during an angular stage. While it possesses aromas of pepper, spice, and *garrigue*, the flavors revealed high tannin and a compressed finish. Far better is the 2000 Côtes du Rhône Cuvée Antique Vieilles Vignes. Its dark ruby color is followed by aromas of sweet cherry liqueur and fleshy, leathery, earthy, rich flavors that coat the palate. Drink this attractive, muscular Côtes du Rhône over the next 5–6 years.

The 1999 Châteauneuf-du-Pape offers up aromas of iodine, sweet candied licorice, pepper, seaweed, black cherry and plum fruit, and spice box. This singular, distinctive, full-bodied Châteauneuf possesses a firm, moderately tannic finish, yet is accessible with outstanding depth, ripeness, and succulence. It should drink well over the next 14–15 years.

The 1998 Châteauneuf-du-Pape is better from bottle than it was from cask. Bravay's wines are extremely artisanal and come to life in the bottle, whereas they may be a bit funky prior to bottling. The 1998 exhibits an impressively saturated ruby/purple color plus a gorgeous bouquet of black fruits mixed with licorice, walnuts, Provençal herbs, and roasted meats. In the mouth, it is thick, unctuously textured, juicy, and full-bodied with considerable tannin and oodles of concentrated black fruits. Young and accessible, although unevolved, it requires 2–3 years of cellaring and should drink well over the following two decades. The 1998 Côtes du Rhône, made from 80% Grenache, 15% Syrah, and 5% Cinsault, from vines planted between 1933–1946, is a beautiful example of how much flavor, character, and complexity can be packed into a Côtes du Rhône. A deep ruby/purple color is accompanied by a sweet nose of black fruits, pepper, licorice, seaweed, and spice. Ripe, with dense, jammy black cherry fruit, smoke, earth, and herbs, it is a rich, medium- to full-bodied, deep effort. Tannin in the finish suggests this is a Côtes du Rhône that will hold up for 8–10 years. Very impressive!

FERRATON

2000	Châteauneuf-du-Pape Les Parvis	D	89
1998	Châteauneuf-du-Pape Les Parvis	D	86
2000	Côtes du Rhône Samorens	A	86
1999	Côtes du Rhône Samorens	A	82
2000	Crozes-Hermitage Le Grand Courtil Estate	B	(86–88)
1999	Crozes-Hermitage Le Grand Courtil Estate	B	90
1998	Crozes-Hermitage Le Grand Courtil Estate	C	87
2000	Crozes-Hermitage La Matinière	B	85
1999	Crozes-Hermitage La Matinière	B	(84–83)
1998	Crozes-Hermitage La Matinière	B	87
2000	Crozes-Hermitage La Matinière Blanc	B	87
1999	Crozes-Hermitage La Matinière Blanc	B	86
2000	Hermitage Les Dionnières Estate	E	(88–90)
1998	Hermitage Les Dionnières Estate	E	90
2000	Hermitage Le Méal Estate	EE	(90–92)
1999	Hermitage Le Méal Estate	EE	88+
1998	Hermitage Le Méal Estate	EE	89+
1999	Hermitage Le Méal Estate Blanc	E	86
1998	Hermitage Le Méal Estate Blanc	E	86
2000	Hermitage Les Miaux	D	(85–86)
2000	Hermitage Les Miaux Blanc	D	90
2000	Hermitage Le Reverdy Estate	E	90
1999	Hermitage Le Reverdy Estate	E	89+
1998	Hermitage Le Reverdy Estate	E	87+
2000	St.-Joseph Les Oliviers Estate	D	88
1999	St.-Joseph Les Oliviers Estate	D	89
1998	St.-Joseph Les Oliviers Estate	D	88
2000	St.-Joseph La Source	C	86
1998	St.-Joseph La Source	C	84
2000	St.-Joseph La Source Blanc	C	87

Ferraton's portfolio has grown significantly under the parenting of the Chapoutier firm. Starting in 1997, Michel Chapoutier, along with his talented oenologist, Albéric Mazoyer, took over the winemaking at this estate. They introduced a *négociant* line of wines that should be considered separately from the wines marked Domaine. The latter wines come from the estate's own vineyards. Ferraton's white wines emphasize a crisp, tangy style, and the reds, while rustic, are now being made in a more fresh, fruity manner.

The *négociant* white wine offerings include a crisp, citrusy, full-flavored, medium-bodied, soft 2000 Crozes-Hermitage La Matinière Blanc, and the mineral-dominated, ripe, lush 2000 St.-Joseph La Source Blanc. Both are best drunk during their first 1–2 years of life. A serious effort, the 2000 Hermitage Les Miaux Blanc offers honeyed notes intermixed with licorice and acacia flowers in its full-bodied, rich, chewy, dry personality. It should drink well for 4–5 years then close down, only to reemerge after 10–12 years.

The 1999 Crozes-Hermitage La Matinière Blanc, which includes a touch of Roussanne, went through full malolactic fermentation. Even so, it is high in acidity, with medium body in addition to aromas and flavors of orange rind, roasted nuts, and citrus. The medium- to full-bodied 1998 Hermitage Le Méal Estate Blanc exhibits evolved caramel characteristics, along with orange marmalade and fino sherry notes. Behind all this is tangy, tart acidity. This wine should be consumed over the next 1–2 years.

A blend of Grenache and Syrah, the dark ruby/plum-colored 2000 Côtes du Rhône Samorens exhibits sweet blackberry and kirsch fruit, medium body, adequate acidity, and copious fruit. It is ideal for drinking over the next several years. The straightforward, light-bodied, pleasant, cherry-scented and -flavored, clean 1999 Côtes du Rhône Samorens requires consumption over the near term. The 2000 Châteauneuf-du-Pape Les Parvis is dominated by Grenache (80% of the blend). This dark ruby-colored Châteauneuf exhibits a classic bouquet of violets, kirsch, and licorice, good underlying acidity, full body, and deep, concentrated flavors. It is an excellent Châteauneuf-du-Pape to drink over the next 7–10 years. More substantial is the attractive 1998 Châteauneuf-du-Pape Les Parvis. Its plum color is followed by an intense kirsch-scented bouquet with notions of leather, earth, meat, and pepper in the background. Although not a big Châteauneuf, it is flavorful, medium-bodied, and ideal for drinking over the next 2–3 years. Among the red *négociant* offerings, the 2000 Crozes-Hermitage La Matinière exhibits a smoky, tapenade-scented, herbaceous nose and medium-bodied, currant/cherry flavors. This spicy, lightweight, but fruity red will drink well for 2–3 years. The 1999 Crozes-Hermitage La Matinière rouge exhibits tangy acidity, moderate tannin, and a ripe, blackberry, cherry, and herb-tinged component. It is pure, medium-bodied, and ideal for drinking over the next 5–6 years. The 1998 Crozes-Hermitage La Matinière rouge is even better, exhibiting a deep ruby/purple color, more fat, and abundant cassis and blackberry fruit. The acidity is softer in the 1998, and thus the wine has more texture and plushness.

More peppery, with sweet currants as well as a certain grapiness is the medium-bodied, ripe, fruity, straightforward 2000 St.-Joseph La Source. It should drink well for 4–5 years. The dark ruby-colored 1998 St.-Joseph La Source exhibits high acidity, mineral scents, and a robust, tannic, austere finish. It was one of my least favorite offerings in the *négociant* lineup. Readers looking for more tannin, structure, and austerity should check out the earthy, spicy, peppery, floral, and black currant–scented and –flavored 2000 Hermitage Les Miaux. If it were not for a pinched, compressed finish, this medium-bodied effort would have merited a higher rating. The domaine wines are all more interesting than the *négociant* line.

The 2000 St.-Joseph Les Oliviers Estate reveals more oak, alcohol, glycerin, and concentration. It offers an intoxicating mouthful of fruit in a lusty, forward style. It should be drunk during its first 3–4 years of life. The impressive 1999 St.-Joseph Les Oliviers Estate is a dry, full-bodied white exhibiting scents of smoke, orange marmalade, and rose water. Heady and fruity, with considerable glycerin as well as length, it should be consumed over the next 2–3 years. The impressive, fat, honeyed, intense 1998 St.-Joseph Les Oliviers Estate blanc offers a liquid minerality as well as a long, concentrated finish. It should drink well for 4–5 years.

The Hermitage Le Reverdy, a blend of equal parts Marsanne and Roussanne, emerges from the two Hermitage vineyards of Les Beaumes and Dionnières. The light medium gold-colored 2000 Hermitage Le Reverdy Estate exhibits aromas of pears, peaches, and smoke in a nearly overripe style. Full-bodied, textured, and juicy, with surprising precociousness, it should be drinkable sooner than its 1999 counterpart and evolve much faster. The 1999 Hermitage Le Reverdy Estate is a 100% Marsanne *cuvée* displaying notes of fino sherry, nuts, white flowers, and minerals. Smoky and deep, with plenty of body and a formidably structured personality, it should drink well for a decade.

The 1998 Hermitage Le Reverdy Estate blanc was closed compared to the 1999, but did reveal dense, chewy, mineral, roasted nut, rhubarb, and cherry flavors as well as good acidity and a firm structure. Anticipated maturity: now–2010.

The Crozes-Hermitage Le Grand Courtil Estate is also very good. The 2000 Crozes-Hermitage Le Grand Courtil Estate offers straightforward, peppery black currant notes with hints of herbs in the background. It is low in acidity but high in tannin, and somewhat tough-textured and disjointed. It does not reveal the charm and depth offered by the 1999. The outstanding 1999 Crozes-Hermitage Le Grand Courtil Estate is showing even better in bottle than it was last year. Dominated by tangy red and black currant fruit, it is well defined, spicy, beautifully textured, and, like all these single-vineyard reds, bottled with neither fining nor filtration. It should drink well for a decade. The 1998 Crozes-Hermitage Le Grand Courtil Estate rouge represents a vivid expression of gamey, herb-tinged, blackberry- and cassis-flavored Syrah. It possesses tangy acidity, good finesse, excellent density, and a ripe, medium-bodied finish. Drink it over the next 5–6 years.

Under the Domaine Ferraton label there are now two *cuvées* of red Hermitage, Le Méal and Les Dionnières. The 2000 Hermitage Le Méal Estate exhibits a more saturated dense purple color as well as a big, sweet nose of jammy cassis intermixed with mineral, smoke, and a hint of new wood. More opulent, with sweeter tannin than the 1999 and a flamboyant personality, it will be drinkable between 2004–2018. While disappointing prior to bottling, the 1999 Hermitage Le Méal Estate is close to outstanding. Although closed, with coaxing it displays a saturated ruby color as well as a striking perfume of crème de cassis intermixed with minerals. With excellent concentration and moderately high tannin, it is significantly better than my notes last year suggested. However, patience will be essential. Anticipated maturity: 2006–2015. The 1998 Hermitage Le Méal Estate rouge exhibits aromas of melted asphalt, smoke, minerals, and meat as well as a rustic, medium- to full-bodied, muscular format. While big and rich, it is also stubbornly tannic and backward. Give it 4–5 years of cellaring, and consume it over the following 15–20 years.

The 2000 Hermitage Les Dionnières Estate reveals the most tannin of any Ferraton red. Its dense ruby/purple color is accompanied by a sweet nose of blackberries, currants, earth, truffles, and minerals. Deep and chewy, but extremely tannic, it is a *vin de garde* for serious connoisseurs who have the requisite cellaring conditions to store it properly. Anticipated maturity: 2007–2020+. An outstanding *cuvée*, the 1998 Hermitage Les Dionnières Estate rouge, comes from the southern sector of the Hermitage appellation. It boasts a dense ruby/black color as well as an intense bouquet of smoked herbs, framboise, violets, and blackberries. Pure and rich, with admirable finesse, full body, and a sweet, concentrated, moderately tannic finish, this 1998 requires 2–3 years of cellaring and should keep for two decades.

DOMAINE DE FONDRÈCHE

2000	Côtes du Ventoux	A	88
2000	Côtes du Ventoux Cuvée Nadal	B	(90–91)
1999	Côtes du Ventoux Cuvée Nadal	B	90

2000	Côtes du Ventoux Cuvée Persia	B	(90–92)
1999	Côtes du Ventoux Cuvée Persia	B	90
2000	Côtes du Ventoux Cuvée Persia Blanc	B	89

Domaine de Fondrèche has become a reference point for high-quality wines from the Côtes du Ventoux. Moreover, they do an amazing job with both white and red varietals. All of these wines are sensational values. The serious 2000 Côtes du Ventoux Cuvée Persia Blanc, a 100% Roussanne *cuvée* aged one year in wood on its lees, is bottled with minimal clarification. Unquestionably the finest white made in Ventoux, it offers up a citrusy, honeysuckle-scented perfume with notions of rose petals. Medium-bodied and lively, with a hint of spicy oak in the background, this fresh, nicely textured, dry white should be drunk over the next 2 years.

The 2000 Côtes du Ventoux (60% Grenache, 30% Syrah, and 10% Carignan aged in stainless steel) exhibits a dense purple color as well as a sexy, ripe personality crammed with currants, blackberries, and cherries with a hint of smoke (although no wood is utilized). This corpulent red is best drunk during its first 2–3 years of life. The *barrique*-aged, blockbuster 2000 Côtes du Ventoux Cuvée Nadal (55% Grenache and 45% Syrah that sees some new oak) possesses an amazing 15.5% alcohol. Full-bodied and unctuously textured, with compelling levels of fruit (blackberries and cherries), ripeness, and purity, this crowd-pleaser will drink well for 7–8 years. The 2000 Côtes du Ventoux Cuvée Persia is a blend of 80% Syrah and 20% Grenache aged in *barrique*, of which 50% is new. Fondrèche's smallest production at 550 cases, the 2000 represents the essence of crème de cassis. A black/purple-colored wine with an unctuous texture, great purity, and sensational extract as well as richness, it is hard to believe this is a Côtes du Ventoux. It should drink well for 7–8 years.

Readers lucky enough to find any of Fondrèche's 1999 reds should not hesitate to buy them. The outstanding 1999 Côtes du Ventoux Cuvée Nadal (equal parts Grenache and Syrah) is full-bodied, with big, chewy, ripe flavors, excellent purity, and a long finish. Drink it over the next 2–3 years. The 1999 Côtes du Ventoux Cuvée Persia reveals more tannin than detected in its 2000 counterpart. Nevertheless, it is a full-bodied effort dominated by blackberry and crème de cassis fruit. Dense, layered, and immensely impressive, it should drink well for 8–10 years. My aging curve on these wines may be conservative. Why? No Ventoux estate has ever before produced wines this concentrated and balanced.

CHÂTEAU LA FONT DU LOUP

2000	Châteauneuf-du-Pape	C	(87–89)
1999	Châteauneuf-du-Pape	C	85
1998	Châteauneuf-du-Pape	C	86
1999	Châteauneuf-du-Pape Le Château	C	87
2000	Châteauneuf-du-Pape La Comtesse	C	(88–90)
2000	Châteauneuf-du-Pape Les Demoiselles	C	(78–82?)
2000	Châteauneuf-du-Pape Les Fondateurs	C	(85–86?)
2000	Châteauneuf-du-Pape Le Puy Rolland	D	(87–89)
1999	Châteauneuf-du-Pape Le Puy Rolland	D	88
1998	Châteauneuf-du-Pape Le Puy Rolland	D	87

Proprietor Charles Mélia continues to increase the number of *cuvées* produced at his estate. They are all relatively elegant, medium-weight Châteauneuf-du-Papes revealing bright fruit as well as a progressive, modern day winemaking style. While meant for early consumption, the 2000 Châteauneuf-du-Pape Les Demoiselles is inconsequential. It offers strawberry fruit, but the dry tannin mars an otherwise delicate, restrained effort. The 2000 Châteauneuf-du-Pape exhibits aromas of sweet black cherries mixed with damp earth, vanilla, and pepper. Tightly structured and concentrated, with medium to full body and a long, pure, impressive finish, it will drink well between now–2012. Moderately intense aromas of plums, cherries, balsam, and spice are found in the dark ruby-colored 2000 Châteauneuf-du-Pape La Comtesse. Medium- to full-bodied, with noticeable tannin, a sweet mid-palate, and an angular, dry finish, it should be drunk between now–2014. The less saturated, medium ruby-colored 2000 Châteauneuf-du-Pape Les Fondateurs reveals more noticeable tannin as well as spice and a dry, lean finish. If it develops more expansiveness and a less compressed texture, it will merit a higher score. Lastly, the 2000 Châteauneuf-du-Pape Le Puy Rolland is a dark ruby-colored, medium-bodied effort revealing abundant quantities of sweet cherry and raspberry fruit interlaced with minerality. Clean, measured, and restrained, it should drink well for 12–13 years.

The 1999 Châteauneuf-du-Pape is a light, straightforward effort with sweet cherry fruit, medium body, no hard edges, and a style that requires consumption over the next 3 years. Deeper, with more structure, the 1999 Châteauneuf-du-Pape Le Château exhibits a dark plum/ruby color and sweet kirsch aromas, medium to full body, moderate tannin, and a slightly austere finish not dissimilar from a Bordeaux. Anticipated maturity: now–2011. The medium-bodied 1999 Châteauneuf-du-Pape Le Puy Rolland reveals a striking bouquet of red currants, raspberry fruit, and minerals. Made in a more Burgundy than Provençal style, its moderate tannin suggests 2–3 years of cellaring is warranted. Anticipated maturity: now–2012.

The surprisingly evolved medium ruby/garnet-colored 1998 Châteauneuf-du-Pape offers moderate levels of black cherry fruit infused with spice, smoke, and Provençal herbs. In the mouth, it is pleasant and easygoing, but lacks substance and length. Drink it over the next 6–7 years. The 1998 Châteauneuf-du-Pape Le Puy Rolland exhibits more glycerin, sweetness, and concentration, a moderately weighty style with supple tannin, low acidity, and very good fruit and texture. It should drink well for a decade.

DOMAINE FONT DE MICHELLE

2000	Châteauneuf-du-Pape	C	(87–89)
1999	Châteauneuf-du-Pape	C	88
1998	Châteauneuf-du-Pape	C	90
2000	Châteauneuf-du-Pape Cuvée Etienne Gonnet	E	(90–92)
1999	Châteauneuf-du-Pape Cuvée Etienne Gonnet	E	90
1998	Châteauneuf-du-Pape Cuvée Etienne Gonnet	E	94

This is one of the best-run estates in Châteauneuf-du-Pape, making topflight modern-styled, concentrated, character-filled wines. However, I don't think anyone will confuse the elegant, lighter-weight 1999s with the sensational 1998s produced by the amiable Gonnet brothers.

Exhibiting a more saturated color, the soft, succulent, hedonistic 2000 Châteauneuf-du-Pape offers up notes of herbs, smoke, earth, lavender, and pepper. With medium to full body, copious glycerin, and no hard edges, this sumptuous fruit bomb should be enjoyed over the next decade. The deep purple-colored 2000 Châteauneuf-du-Pape Cuvée Etienne Gonnet reveals a firmer underpinning of tannin and structure than its 1999 counterpart. Sweet licorice-infused blackberry fruit, cherry, smoke, and dried herb aromas and flavors are found in this deep, chewy, fleshy, atypically spicy effort. It possesses high glycerin levels, low acidity, and terrific ripeness as well as purity. All things considered, it is a slightly more complete wine than the 1999. Anticipated maturity: now–2014. The 1999 Châteauneuf-du-Pape offers a medium ruby/purple color as well as a big, forceful, perfumed bouquet of licorice, crushed pepper, Provençal herbs, blackberries, and cherries. The aromatic fireworks are followed by a soft, easygoing, medium- to full-bodied wine that the French would call a *vin de plaisir*. The complex nose, evolved palate, luscious fruit, abundant glycerin, and velvety texture have resulted in a charming, forward Châteauneuf to enjoy over the next 6–8 years. The 1,000 case *cuvée* of 1999 Châteauneuf-du-Pape Cuvée Etienne Gonnet (a blend of 65% Grenache, 15%

Cinsault, 10% Syrah, and 10% Mourvèdre) is a more saturated dark ruby/garnet color. The nose reveals intense aromas of blackberry jam intertwined with cherries, *garrigue,* pepper, and smoke. It is an outstanding effort made in a modern style, but with plenty of the region's typicity. This sexy, full-bodied, layered wine can be drunk now–12+ years.

The 1998 Châteauneuf-du-Pape has turned out to be a seductive, gorgeously classy example of the appellation. Notes of cured olives, *herbes de Provence,* leather, soy, smoked meats, and black cherries soar from the glass of this complex, evolved wine. In the mouth, there is a combination of strength, elegance, full body, and purity. It is a sexy, complete, generously endowed, plump effort to drink over the next 12–14 years. The extraordinary 1998 Châteauneuf-du-Pape Cuvée Etienne Gonnet (I have already consumed two bottles from my stash) is one of the vintage's blockbusters. The saturated ruby/purple color is accompanied by aromas of crème de cassis, licorice, lavender, truffles, and spice. The wine is unctuously textured, with great richness, huge levels of glycerin, extraordinary purity, and a finish that lasts nearly 40 seconds. This is a sexy, disarmingly enjoyable Châteauneuf-du-Pape that will get even better over the next decade and last for 15–18 years. It is hard to resist because of its ultra ripeness and intensity, but those with discipline should hold on to a few bottles for 1–2 years and drink them over the following 10–15.

DOMAINE DE FONT SANE

1998 Gigondas	C	89
1998 Gigondas Cuvée Futée	C	90

Two excellent, possibly outstanding Gigondas, Font Sane's 1998 Gigondas possesses a dense ruby/purple color as well as low-acid, supple, concentrated, black cherry and berry flavors, with licorice, smoke, and minerals in the background. A blend of 70% Grenache, 25% Syrah, 3% Cinsault, and 2% Mourvèdre, this powerful effort should drink well for 10–12 years. The 1998 Gigondas Cuvée Futée (a *barrique*-aged wine with some new oak) reveals a fuller-bodied, more tightly knit style with gobs of black cherry and blackberry fruit, toasty vanilla, and mineral characteristics. Dense, concentrated, and moderately tannic, it will be at its best between now–2015.

DOMAINE DE FONTAVIN

2000 Châteauneuf-du-Pape	C	(88–90)
1999 Châteauneuf-du-Pape	C	89
1998 Châteauneuf-du-Pape	C	88
1998 Gigondas	C	(86–88)

Domaine de Fontavin is a sleeper estate emerging as a source for high-quality Châteauneuf-du-Pape. Proprietors Michel and Martine Chouvet turn in very good efforts every year, even in lighter vintages.

The 2000 Châteauneuf-du-Pape is jammy, with superb purity, a seamless, medium- to full-bodied personality, and abundant black cherry, black currant, pepper, and *garrigue* flavors. Drink this impressively endowed 2000 before 2014. The dense ruby/purple-colored 1999 Châteauneuf-du-Pape offers a big, sweet bouquet and flavors of plums, black cherries, pepper, *herbes de Provence,* and earth. Concentrated, full-bodied, and layered, with considerable volume, density, and silky tannin, it will drink well for 5–6 years. The lighter-styled, lush, cleanly made, medium-bodied, dark ruby-colored 1998 Gigondas is evolved for the vintage. It displays sweet black fruits in addition to a velvety textured, attractively long finish. It should drink well during its first decade of life. Proprietor Chouvet has produced a typical 1998 Châteauneuf-du-Pape, a dark ruby/purple-colored, fruit-driven wine with an unctuous texture, superb purity and ripeness, an element of jamminess, low acidity, and a fleshy, succulent, full-bodied richness and texture. It should drink well young yet keep for 10–12 years.

CHÂTEAU FORTIA

2000 Châteauneuf-du-Pape	D	(85–86)
1999 Châteauneuf-du-Pape	D	87
1998 Châteauneuf-du-Pape	D	88

While this estate has benefited from the young Baron Leroy paying more attention to details, it has not yet returned to its 1970s form, a decade when it often produced one of the top half-dozen Châteauneuf-du-Papes of each vintage. Having just drunk bottles of 1978 and 1970 Château Fortia (both majestic wines), it is obvious that this estate can do a considerably better job. The surprisingly light-colored (medium ruby with considerable pink at the edges) 2000 Châteauneuf-du-Pape exhibits medium body, a short finish, and little weight, richness, or depth. Perhaps more will emerge with barrel aging, but it appears to be a loosely knit, moderately weighted Châteauneuf-du-Pape to drink between now–2008.

Tasting lighter than it did during its *élevage,* the 1999 Châteauneuf-du-Pape is a medium-bodied effort lacking punch, substance, and length. It offers sweet black currant fruit intertwined with spice and floral notes. Easygoing and consumer-friendly, but essentially superficial, it should be drunk over the next 6–7 years.

Château Fortia's 1998 is one of the latest-bottled Châteauneuf-du-Papes. The wine's deep ruby color is followed by moderately intense aromas of dried herbs, pepper, cassis and blackberry fruit, a silky texture, good freshness, medium to full body, and a corpulent, rich, long finish. It will be drinkable upon release, and it should age well for 10 years.
Past Glories: 1978 (94), 1970 (92)

DOMAINE LA FOURMONE L'OUSTEAU-FAUQUET

2000 Gigondas	C	(87–88)
1999 Gigondas	C	89

The jammy, expansive, open-knit, fat, fleshy 2000 Gigondas possesses a saturated ruby/purple color, gobs of fruit, little acidity, and a plump style. Although it lacks definition, there is no doubting its hedonistic appeal. Drink it over the next 5–7 years. Another impressive offering, the 1999 Gigondas exhibits a dense ruby color along with a sweet perfume of black fruits intermixed with spicy oak, medium to full body, loads of fruit as well as glycerin, and a ripe, pure finish with good definition. Drink it over the next decade.

DOMAINE DE GACHON (PASCAL PERRIER)

1997 St.-Joseph	D	(89–91)
1996 St.-Joseph	D	90

Readers looking for spectacularly rich, brilliantly made wines from one of the less expensive northern Rhône appellations should check out the work Pascal Perrier is doing. These *cuvées* were put together by the American importer, so the tasting notes that follow relate only to those wines sold in the U.S. The 1997 St.-Joseph has the potential to be even more explosive given its lower acidity and lusher, more flamboyant personality. 50% of this *cuvée* is aged in new-oak casks and is then blended with the balance, which has been aged in *cuve.* It boasts a saturated ruby/purple color, as well as a sumptuous nose of Asian spices, black currants, blackberries, and toasty vanilla. Explosively rich, full-bodied, and savory with low acidity, this chewy, tasty, intense St.-Joseph can be drunk now as well as over the next 7–8 years. Excellent value. The 1996 St.-Joseph exhibits an opaque ruby/purple color, and a knockout nose of nearly overripe prunes, black raspberries, and cherries. Made from 20-year-old vines and modest yields of 30 hectoliters per hectare, this wine is rich and full bodied, with tons of cassis fruit intermixed with pepper and an almost vinous, sappy, refreshing yet not intrusive acidity. Drink this chewy, full-bodied Syrah now and over the next 3–4 years.

PIERRE GAILLARD

2000 Condrieu Fleurs d'Automne	E	89
2000 Côte Rôtie Côte Rozier Réserve	EE	(85–88)
1999 Côte Rôtie Côte Rozier Réserve	EE	92+
1998 Côte Rôtie Côte Rozier Réserve	EE	91+
1999 Côte Rôtie Côte Rozier La Rose Pourpre	EE	94+
2000 Côte Rôtie Le Cret Réserve Côte Blonde	EE	(87–88)
1999 Côte Rôtie Le Cret Réserve Côte Blonde	EE	95
1998 Côte Rôtie Le Cret Réserve Côte Blonde	EE	89+
2000 Côte Rôtie La Viaillère Réserve	EE	(87–88?)
1999 Côte Rôtie La Viaillère Réserve	EE	94
1998 Côte Rôtie La Viaillère Réserve	EE	93+
2000 Côtes du Rhône	B	86
1999 Côtes du Rhône	B	88
2000 St.-Joseph	C	(85–87)
2000 St.-Joseph Blanc	C	86
1999 St.-Joseph Les Pierres Réserve Clos de Cuminaille	D	90
1998 St.-Joseph Les Pierres Réserve Clos de Cuminaille	D	87
1999 VDP Roussanne	B	86
1999 VDP Viognier	B	88

Pierre Gaillard has always been a vigneron with considerable promise. I visited him a decade ago when he was among the youngest of the new generation of northern Rhône Valley producers. For a number of years, Gaillard's wines were mixed in quality. Good wines would be followed by irregular, uninteresting offerings. However, over the last 4–5 years, Gaillard has begun to fulfill his potential. The 1999s and 1998s are the finest wines he has produced, reflecting not only the superlative quality of the vintage, but his progression as a wine-maker.

The 2000 whites are light, but fruity, precocious, and charming. The light green/gold-colored 2000 St.-Joseph Blanc (100% barrel-fermented Roussanne that was kept *sur-lie*) exhibits a lovely honeyed citrus character, medium body, and good underlying acidity. The elegant, medium-bodied 2000 Côtes du Rhône (100% Viognier planted in the appellation of St.-Joseph) offers aromas of fresh citrus intermixed with minerals. Tasty and straightforward, it is best drunk over the next 1–2 years. More interesting, the 2000 Condrieu Fleurs d'Automne reveals a certain minerality along with more honeyed apricot/peach flavors presented in a medium-bodied, fresh, pure format. Readers looking for intensely flavored whites should check out the 1999 Roussanne and 1999 Viognier. The excellent, light to medium straw-colored 1999 VDP Roussanne (100% Roussanne primarily aged in old wood, with about 10% in new) exhibits a honeyed, meaty nose, and rich, chewy flavors with good underlying acidity. There is plenty of depth and ripeness in addition to the honeysuckle-like fruit of the Roussanne grape. Drink it over the next 1–2 years. The VDP 1999 Viognier (50% of this *cuvée* is declassified Condrieu) reveals the elegant side of this varietal. Scents of white peaches and apricots emerge from the stylish, pure aromatics. In the mouth, it is medium-bodied, well delineated, and pure, with rich fruit and an attractive, clean finish with no wood influence (thankfully). Drink it over the next year. The 1999 Côtes du Rhône is a Viognier-based effort produced from the area around St.-Joseph. It is a sexy, seductive wine with a ripe, honeyed nose, excellent fruit, medium to full body, and a long, dry, crisp finish. Drink it over the next 1–2 years.

Of the 2000 Côte Rôties I tasted, Le Cret Réserve Côte Blonde, Rozier Réserve, and La Viaillère Réserve, as well as the 2000 St.-Joseph, are good wines, but lack the depth and concentration achieved in 1999. La Viaillère is more austere and tannic, and Le Cret Réserve Côte Blonde is a softer, medium-weight effort without the dimensions or nuances of the 1999s. Nevertheless, they are well-made, above-average-quality wines destined to be consumed during their first 8–10 years of life.

As for the 1999 Côte Rôties, they are simply awesome. The 1999 Côte Rôtie Le Cret Réserve Côte Blonde is my favorite, largely because the 10% Viognier added to the blend gives it an astonishingly complex bouquet as well as more supple flavors. Its black/purple color is accompanied by a knockout nose of honeysuckle, peach, cassis, and fried bacon scents. Concentrated, succulent, opulently textured, full-bodied, rich, and pure, it will be drinkable between now–2016. The 1999 Côte Rôtie La Viaillière Réserve (20% Viognier included) offers up a potent perfume of violets, spring flowers, sausage, black fruits, and vanilla. It is more tannic as well as full-bodied, dense, backward, and long. Less approachable and civilized than Le Cret, it will be drinkable between 2005–2016. The monster 1999 Côte Rôtie Côte Rozier La Rose Pourpre is tannic and backward, but the tannin is sweeter and the fruit dominated by smoky black currant/cassis. Notes of incense, minerals, oak, and earth as well as a hint of melted road tar are present in this full-bodied, massive Côte Rôtie. It requires five years of cellaring. Anticipated maturity: 2006–2020.

One of the best buys in this portfolio is the 1999 St.-Joseph Les Pierres Réserve Clos de Cuminaille. It boasts a deep ruby/purple color along with sweet blackberry fruit intermixed with graphite, new oak, and spice. Long, rich, and supple-textured, this beauty will drink well for a decade.

The 1998 red wines reveal the vintage's more rugged tannin and structured, backward style. The deep ruby-colored 1998 St.-Joseph Les Pierres Réserve Clos de Cuminaille exhibits a big, blackberry- and cassis-scented nose with hints of cherry jam in the background. Ripe and long with moderate tannin, it should drink well for 7–8 years. The dark ruby-colored 1998 Côte Rôtie Le Cret Réserve Côte Blonde is a tight, tannic, harder wine with plenty of depth, excellent richness on the palate, but formidable tannin and a closed, tightly knit style. There is good weight and sweetness, but the tannin is high and the wine needs 3–4 years of cellaring. Anticipated maturity: now–2018. Readers seeking notes of animal fur and steak tartare intermixed with olives, blackberry, and cassis fruit should check out the fragrant, earthy, muscular 1998 Côte Rôtie La Viaillière Réserve. An opaque purple color is followed by an exceptionally dense wine with more supple tannin than Le Cret, yet additional concentration, depth, and potential. Give it 3–5 years of cellaring and drink it over the following 15–18 years. The opaque purple-colored, somewhat monolithic but powerful, concentrated, backward 1998 Côte Rôtie Côte Rozier Réserve possesses aromas of black cherry and cassis fruit, earth, spice, olives, new oak, and a distinctive iron, vitamin-like nuance. Full-bodied, deep, chewy, and muscular, with moderate tannin in the finish, it requires 2–4 years of cellaring and should drink well for 15–18 years.

DOMAINE DU GALET DES PAPES

2000	Châteauneuf-du-Pape	D	(86–87)
1999	Châteauneuf-du-Pape	D	85
1998	Châteauneuf-du-Pape	D	88
2000	Châteauneuf-du-Pape Vieilles Vignes	E	(89–90)
1999	Châteauneuf-du-Pape Vieilles Vignes	E	87
1998	Châteauneuf-du-Pape Vieilles Vignes	E	90

Jean-Luc Mayard runs one of the finest estates in Châteauneuf-du-Pape. A modestly sized property of just over 31 acres, the wines are a synthesis in style between the old, traditionally made examples, and the more modern fruit-driven Châteauneufs.

The 2000 Châteauneuf-du-Pape's dark plum color is followed by a sweet, medium-bodied, fleshy offering displaying notes of *garrigue*, smoke, balsam, and currant/cherry fruit. Drink this low-acid Châteauneuf over the next 6–8 years. The exceptional, dark plum-colored 2000

Châteauneuf-du-Pape Vieilles Vignes offers a terrific nose of smoked herbs, plum liqueur, cassis, cherries, underbrush, and licorice. Once past the provocative aromatics, this full-bodied 2000 reveals layers of fruit and glycerin and a sweet midsection as well as finish. It should drink well for 10–15 years. The soft, evolved 1999 Châteauneuf-du-Pape exhibits a medium garnet color with a pink rim. Notes of *herbes de Provence*, soy, earth, and smoke combine with cherry fruit to provide a straightforward, medium-bodied, lush, light but attractive offering. It is best consumed over the next 3–4 years. The dark garnet-colored 1999 Châteauneuf-du-Pape Vieilles Vignes reveals an earthy, cherry, and ripe peach–scented bouquet. Good depth, medium body, and plenty of spice and leather notes are accompanied by dry tannin and an attenuated finish. This is an austere, but well-made wine for drinking now and over the next 5–6 years.

The 1998s possess more punch, muscle, concentration, and aging potential than their 1999 counterparts. The medium ruby/garnet-colored 1998 Châteauneuf-du-Pape reveals a complex bouquet of cigar smoke, minerals, kirsch, and pepper. There is an elegance to this medium- to full-bodied effort, with fine texture, low acidity, and impressive ripeness. Drink it over the next 10 years. The 1998 Châteauneuf-du-Pape Vieilles Vignes ratchets up the level of intensity, offering more notes of *garrigue*, crushed black pepper, kirsch, and spice box. Full-bodied and intense, with impressive glycerin, low acidity, and ripe tannin, this dense, long, fat Châteauneuf-du-Pape can be drunk now or cellared for 10 years.

HENRI ET PHILIPPE GALLET

2000 Côte Rôtie	E	(87–88)
1999 Côte Rôtie	E	89+
1998 Côte Rôtie	E	89
1997 Côte Rôtie	E	86

The Gallet estate, located on the plateau region of Côte Rôtie overlooking the Côte Brune et Blonde, is now a whopping 8.7 acres. 5% Viognier is added to the wine. Son Philippe is now in charge of the winemaking, and in 1998 he instituted complete destemming of the fruit. Gallet's wines are aged in a combination of old barrels and larger *demi-muids*, and they are bottled unfiltered. About 5–10% new oak appears to be utilized.

The 2000 Côte Rôtie, sampled from an assortment of barrels, is a soft, ripe, easygoing effort offering notes of black fruits, cherries, and herbs. As the wine sits in the glass, a hint of Viognier-like peach jam makes an appearance. Although not significantly concentrated, it is succulent, with low acidity and a charming personality. It should drink well for 5–10 years. Gallet's 1999 Côte Rôtie is this small vigneron's finest vintage since 1991 and 1990. It possesses a dark ruby/purple color, medium body, and a sweet nose of violets, black currants, cassis, and earth. There is some tannin, but the fruit's up-front fleshiness dominates the palate. One to two years of cellaring will be beneficial, but this beautifully balanced wine is already accessible. It should drink well for 12–15 years.

I tasted the third bottling of the 1998 Côte Rôtie (there are three separate *mises,* which raises the specter of different aromas and flavors, although the estate tries to make sure the blend is equal for each bottling). The wine I tasted exhibited a dark plum color as well as a sweet bouquet of dried herbs, new saddle leather, black raspberries, and currants. It is tighter and more compressed in the finish than the 1999, with medium to full body, noticeable tannin, and a spicy, mineral characteristic in the fruit. Although excellent, the tannin may be slightly elevated for the amount of extraction and richness. Drink it over the following 12–15 years. The last wine to include 100% stems during fermentation, the 1997 Côte Rôtie reveals more herbaceous, vegetal characteristics in the cedary, spicy nose. While ripe, round, and seductive in the mouth, readers should recognize that this wine does have more stemmy characteristics, with some of the veggie notes that some tasters find objectionable. A forward effort, it is best drunk over the next 7 years.

CHÂTEAU DE LA GARDINE

2000	Châteauneuf-du-Pape	D	(87–88)
1999	Châteauneuf-du-Pape	D	(88–90)
1998	Châteauneuf-du-Pape	D	90
1997	Châteauneuf-du-Pape	D	(85–86)
2000	Châteauneuf-du-Pape Cuvée des Générations	E	(91–92)
1999	Châteauneuf-du-Pape Cuvée des Générations	E	(90–93)
1998	Châteauneuf-du-Pape Cuvée des Générations	E	93+
1996	Châteauneuf-du-Pape Cuvée des Générations	E	88+
1995	Châteauneuf-du-Pape Cuvée des Générations	E	92
2000	Châteauneuf-du-Pape Cuvée l'Immortelle	EE	(90–92)
1999	Châteauneuf-du-Pape Cuvée l'Immortelle	EE	(91–92+)

The Brunel family has over 140 acres dedicated to red wine production, most of it in the northwestern sector of Châteauneuf-du-Pape. In 1999, they introduced a third *cuvée* that is called l'Immortelle. The Cuvée des Générations continues to be produced only in the finest vintages. I am not overstating it by saying that for the last decade or so, the proprietors have been making superlative wines. Some critics carp about the Cuvée des Générations being too international in style (it does spend 9–18 months in 100% new-oak barrels), but vintages I have purchased seem to develop the typicity of Châteauneuf-du-Pape after about a decade of cellaring. It is a long-lived wine, with the potential in years such as 1998, 1990, and 1989 to age for a minimum of 20–25 years.

There are three *cuvées* in 2000, including the Châteauneuf-du-Pape Cuvée l'Immortelle, which is packaged in a heavy, Burgundy-shaped bottle. It is a succulent, complex, hedonistic effort displaying a sexy concoction of pepper, dried Provençal herbs, black cherry jam, and smoky espresso. Seductive, fleshy, and opulent, with layers of concentration, this full, luscious 2000 will be at its peak between now–2014. The dense ruby/purple-colored 2000 Châteauneuf-du-Pape is a medium- to full-bodied offering with a sweet, black cherry/currant, licorice, vanilla, and spice-scented bouquet. Long, jammy, and impressively concentrated, it should be consumed between now–2015. As for the famed Châteauneuf-du-Pape Cuvée des Générations, the 2000 is extremely young and unevolved. It exhibits an opaque dense purple color as well as a big, thick nose of blackberry liqueur intermixed with espresso, vanilla, and toast. Full-bodied and powerful, this modern-styled Châteauneuf-du-Pape possesses enough tannin to warrant 1–2 years of cellaring. It will evolve for 20–25 years. This wine moves toward being internationally styled, but it has plenty of Châteauneuf-du-Pape Provençal character. Anticipated maturity: 2005–2025. The dark ruby/purple-colored 1999 Châteauneuf-du-Pape displays an impressive constitution, with full body, considerable structure, and admirable delineation. Spice box, vanilla, and black fruits show through, but the wine is big, backward, and needs 2–3 years of cellaring, somewhat atypical for a 1999. It should last for 15+ years. The inky purple-colored 1999 Châteauneuf-du-Pape Cuvée des Générations reveals toasty new oak in the nose along with minerals, cassis, licorice, and roasted nuts. Full-bodied, highly extracted, dense, and unevolved, it will require patience, but should turn out to be one of the longest lived 1999s. Anticipated maturity: 2005–2020. Revealing evidence of *sur-maturité*, the 1999 Châteauneuf-du-Pape Cuvée l'Immortelle has the extract of a vintage port. Although thick and revealing evidence of new barrels, it has not lost the typicity of Châteauneuf-du-Pape. However, it is a powerhouse . . . very tannic, concentrated, and inky purple in color. This wine will need at least 5 years of cellaring and will keep for 25+ years.

The 1998s are both top-notch, and may equal what La Gardine produced in its last prodigious vintage, 1990. The 1998 Châteauneuf-du-Pape boasts a dense, saturated purple color, as well as an enticing, sweet nose of black fruits, licorice, and violets. Full-bodied, moderately tannic, and impressively concentrated, with a long finish, it will be at its finest between

now–2016. The inky purple-colored 1998 Châteauneuf-du-Pape Cuvée des Générations offers a big, smoky, licorice, blackberry, and cassis-scented nose with obvious toasty new oak.
The wine is unevolved and youthful, with superb purity, immense extract levels, high tannin,
and gorgeous amounts of fruit and glycerin. It is a powerful, muscular effort that requires 5
years of cellaring. It is a candidate for 20–30 years of aging.

The 1997 Châteauneuf-du-Pape is a dark ruby-colored wine with medium body and attractive cassis fruit, revealing earth, cherry, and peppery fruit. It is a soft, fruity wine meant
for near-term consumption—over the next 3 years.

Past Glories: Châteauneuf-du-Pape Cuvée Générations—1990 (94+)

DOMAINE DE LA GARRIGUE

1998 Gigondas	C	89
1999 Vacqueyras	C	90
1999 Vacqueyras Cuvée l'Hostellerie	C	90

These Gigondas and Vacqueyras are produced by the proprietor of Les Florets, the beautiful
country restaurant on the hillside above the village of Gigondas. By the way, it is a restaurant
that I enthusiastically recommend, with excellent cooking and a wine list of Gigondas offerings that may be the best in the world. To my knowledge, their wines, which can be purchased for a song at the restaurant, are not exported to the United States.

Both 1999s are exceptional efforts. They offer terrific bouquets of Provençal herbs, earth,
and pepper as well as copious quantities of sweet kirsch and other black fruits. Both are full-
bodied, textured, rich, plump wines to drink over the next 4–5 years.

The 1998 Gigondas is a well-made, fruit-driven, full-bodied, exuberant effort loaded with
smoky black cherry fruit. It also possesses more power and density because of the high quality of the vintage. Anticipated maturity: now–2012.

VINCENT GASSE

2000 Côte Rôtie	E	(86–88)
1999 Côte Rôtie	E	88+
2000 Côte Rôtie Vieilles Vignes	E	(88–89)
1999 Côte Rôtie Vieilles Vignes	E	90

About half of the grape bunches are destemmed for these traditionally made Côte Rôties.
After fermentation, the wine is moved to old, small barrels where they remain for 22 months.
They are bottled without filtration. The dark ruby-colored 2000 Côte Rôtie offers sweet aromas of berry fruit, earth, pepper, and dried herbs. Ripe, with low acidity and medium body, it
is more evolved and precocious than the 1999. Enjoy it during its first decade of life. In
2000, Gasse decided to utilize 100% of the stems for the Côte Rôtie Vieilles Vignes. While
there is not substantial depth, the wine is layered, sweet, and medium-bodied, with good purity. Notes of ground pepper, black fruits, smoke, leather, and herbs dominate the complex
aromatics. In the mouth, there is good sweetness, medium body, and excellent density as well
as ripeness. Anticipated maturity: now–2013. The 1999 Côte Rôtie displays surprisingly tart
acidity for a wine from this vintage as well as tangy, black cherry/currant fruit, smoke, and
olive characteristics. Medium-bodied and spicy, with moderate tannin and a closed personality, it will be at its finest between 2004–2016. The outstanding 1999 Côte Rôtie Vieilles
Vignes exhibits a deep ruby/purple color as well as a smoky, earthy bouquet with scents of
flowers, blackberries, raspberries, cherries, and underbrush. Concentrated, rich, medium-
bodied, tightly knit, and pure, it is an elegant, unevolved 1999 that will benefit from 3–4
years of cellaring. Anticipated maturity: 2004–2016.

JEAN-MICHEL GÉRIN

2000 Côte Rôtie Champin Le Seigneur	D	(88–90)
1999 Côte Rôtie Champin Le Seigneur	D	90

1998	Côte Rôtie Champin Le Seigneur	D	90
1997	Côte Rôtie Champin Le Seigneur	D	89
2000	Côte Rôtie Les Grandes Places	EE	(89–91)
1999	Côte Rôtie Les Grandes Places	EE	95
1998	Côte Rôtie Les Grandes Places	EE	91
1997	Côte Rôtie Les Grandes Places	EE	91
2000	Côte Rôtie La Landonne	EE	(90–92)
1999	Côte Rôtie La Landonne	EE	94+
1998	Côte Rôtie La Landonne	EE	91
1997	Côte Rôtie La Landonne	EE	90

Jean-Michel Gérin, one of the most serious wine-makers in Côte Rôtie as well as one of the most powerful forces among the appellation's younger generation, employs a terrific wine-making philosophy. He is critical of under-performers and is thrilled by the number of young Côte Rôtie vignerons who are making better and better wines. A relative youngster himself, Gérin has adopted many of the methods that made Guigal's three crus (La Mouline, La Turque, and La Landonne) so famous worldwide. This includes minimal use of SO_2 during the aging process, very little racking prior to bottling, and bottling with no fining or filtration. Over the last vintages, his wines have been topflight.

The excellent 2000 Côte Rôtie Champin Le Seigneur is the result of a severe crop thinning implemented to reduce excessive yields. It offers a deep ruby/purple color as well as a sweet perfume of toast, black fruits, and espresso. A medium-bodied effort with solid tannin and a sweet finish, it should drink well for 10–12 years. The dark ruby/purple-colored 2000 Côte Rôtie Les Grandes Places reveals a classic smoky bacon fat, tapenade, and currant-scented nose in addition to dense, oaky, medium- to full-bodied flavors with good sweetness, low acidity, and plenty of flesh. If it continues to expand, it will be an outstanding effort. Anticipated maturity: 2003–2015. The opaque purple-colored 2000 Côte Rôtie La Landonne exhibits scents of minerals, licorice, cassis, roasted meats, and black fruits. Chewy, muscular, and moderately tannic, it will be at its peak between 2004–2016.

The most forward wine, the 1999 Côte Rôtie Champin Le Seigneur, offers a dense purple color, copious quantities of sweet, spicy oak, and an opulent, fleshy, medium- to full-bodied texture with loads of fruit and glycerin. Low acidity and exceptional ripeness suggest drinking it now and over the next 10–12 years. Sadly, there are only 175 cases of the 1999 Côte Rôtie La Landonne. A marvelous example of the vintage, it boasts a roasted, meaty, smoky-scented nose with notions of minerals, blackberries, and underbrush. Full-bodied, thick, and muscular with superb extraction, this inky/purple-colored wine needs 4–6 years of cellaring. Anticipated maturity: 2005–2020. The sumptuous, profound 1999 Côte Rôtie Les Grandes Places (625 cases) is great stuff in an outrageously ripe, concentrated vintage. A Syrah masterpiece, this opaque purple-colored offering beautifully juxtaposes its muscle, power, and depth with considerable elegance and precision. The tannin is sweet, the acidity adequate, and the wine layered, majestically rich, full-bodied, and moderately tannic. It can be drunk now, but 3–4 years of cellaring will be beneficial. Anticipated maturity: 2004–2020.

The 1998 Côte Rôtie Champin Le Seigneur exhibits a deep ruby/purple color as well as a sweet bouquet of roasted earth, black fruits, licorice, coffee, and toast. Fleshy and medium- to full-bodied, with excellent texture, this impressive Côte Rôtie can be drunk now, or cellared for a decade. Although more tannic, the 1998 Côte Rôtie Les Grandes Places is loaded with flavor and potential. A dense ruby/purple color is accompanied by aromas of blackberries, raspberries, cherries, licorice, and charcoal. Dense and full-bodied with high tannin, it should keep for 15+ years. The 1998 Côte Rôtie La Landonne displays an earthy, roasted meat, smoky component reminiscent of baked minerals. Thrilling levels of blackberry and prune–like fruit are found in the bouquet and flavors. Deep, full-bodied, and opulently textured, with the glycerin and concentration concealing lofty tannin, this wine should be at its best between now–2018.

Gérin produced super 1997s. Even the 1997 Côte Rôtie Champin Le Seigneur may merit an outstanding score. It is a low-acid, sexy, voluptuously textured wine with tons of smoky new oak, gobs of sweet black cherry and blackberry fruit, a sweet, rich, chewy attack, and a full-bodied mouth-feel. The display of fruit and wood is almost garish in this immensely enjoyable, hedonistic Côte Rôtie. Anticipated maturity: now–2007. The 1997 Côte Rôtie La Landonne boasts a saturated black/purple color, as well as seductive, sweet oak in the aroma that, with airing, becomes increasingly intermixed with plums, blackberries, licorice, and bacon fat. Surprisingly silky and more seductive than I would have expected from this Côte Brune vineyard, this rich, low-acid, concentrated Côte Rôtie should prove to be a head-turner. Anticipated maturity: now–2012. The splendid 1997 Côte Rôtie Les Grandes Places reveals an impressively saturated opaque purple color. The nose offers up gorgeous quantities of superripe black raspberries, blackberries, toasty oak, and smoke. Expansive and full-bodied, with fabulous concentration, outstanding purity, and low acidity, this is a hedonistic, lush, heady, decadently styled Côte Rôtie to consume over the next 10+ years.

DOMAINE GIRAUD

2000	Châteauneuf-du-Pape	C	(85–86)
1999	Châteauneuf-du-Pape	C	85
1998	Châteauneuf-du-Pape	C	86
2000	Châteauneuf-du-Pape Les Gallimardes	D	(86–88)
1999	Châteauneuf-du-Pape Les Gallimardes	D	88
1998	Châteauneuf-du-Pape Les Gallimardes	D	88

Former rugby player Pierre Giraud is slowly improving this estate's quality. His well-placed vineyards (some near Rayas and others close to Vieux-Télégraphe, Les Crau, and Le Nerthe) have turned out very good, but uninspiring efforts over recent vintages.

Giraud's 2000 Châteauneuf-du-Pape is a soft, commercial, straightforward effort with a dark ruby color, low acidity, and jammy berry fruit. There is not a lot to it, but it is grapy, easygoing, and quaffable. It should drink well for 5–7 years. The dark ruby/purple-colored 2000 Châteauneuf-du-Pape Les Gallimardes is a more serious, spicy effort revealing aromas and flavors of earth, licorice, pepper, cherries, and black fruits. This medium- to full-bodied, well-made 2000 reveals moderate tannin in the finish, suggesting 2–3 years of aging is warranted. Enjoy it over the following 10–12 years.

The medium plum/garnet-colored 1999 Châteauneuf-du-Pape offers a peppery, spicy nose with notes of black fruits and autumnal, leafy, foresty characteristics. Lush, round, and pleasant, it should be consumed over the next 4–5 years. More serious, richer, concentrated, and revealing a notion of *barrique* is the 1999 Châteauneuf-du-Pape Les Gallimardes. Its dark plum/garnet color is accompanied by moderately intense aromas of pepper, spice, kirsch, and earth. Medium- to full-bodied, rich, and luscious, it will provide enjoyment over the next decade.

The 1998 Châteauneuf-du-Pape reveals the telltale Provençal aromatic concoction of herbs, soy, licorice, earth, and pepper. Intermixed with these seasonings is straightforward black cherry fruit. While spicy, well made, and ripe, this 1998 is not especially deep or long. Drink it over the next 5–6 years. The 1998 Châteauneuf-du-Pape Les Gallimardes is a full-bodied, dense offering with abundant tannin, a deep ruby color, concentrated earthy/black cherry fruit flavors, and an exuberant yet rustic finish. It should keep for 10–12 years.

DOMAINE LES GOUBERT

2000	Gigondas	C	(85–86)
1999	Gigondas	C	85

1998 Gigondas	C	87
2000 Gigondas Cuvée Florence	D	(87–89)
1999 Gigondas Cuvée Florence	D	89
1998 Gigondas Cuvée Florence	D	91

Jean-Pierre Cartier, who did so much to bring attention to the high-quality wines of Gigondas in the 1980s, seemed to slump at the end of that decade and the beginning of the 1990s, but he has made a strong comeback with his current releases. Cartier produces more wines than just Gigondas, turning out one of the finest Viogniers of the southern Rhône, in addition to making very good wines in Beaumes de Venise and Sablet. His top wine is the Gigondas Cuvée Florence, a wine made from a selection of the best lots and named after his fiery-haired daughter. This estate is a perennial choice for good Gigondas, although neither the 1999s or 2000s appear to be as strong as their *cuvées* of 1998.

The plum-colored 2000 Gigondas offers expansive, open-knit, fleshy fruit, but little depth and follow-through. It needs to be consumed during its first 3–4 years of life. Not surprisingly, the 2000 Gigondas Cuvée Florence, while showing more of an international style with new oak notes, exhibits plenty of earthy, blackberry and cherry fruit, graphite, pepper, and minerals. Not a blockbuster, it is an easy to drink Gigondas that should mature gracefully for 7–8 years. The 1999 Gigondas is a medium-bodied, soft effort with blueberry and cherry fruit as well as notions of minerals and pepper. It is best consumed over the next 3–4 years. More impressive is the 1999 Gigondas Cuvée Florence. Its dark plum/ruby color is accompanied by big, sweet, smoky, black currant aromatics with notions of new oak. Medium- to full-bodied, soft, and round, it will provide excellent drinking over the next decade

The 1998 Gigondas is a solidly made, dense, muscular effort with a ruby/plum color, notes of currants and cherries, and a medium- to full-bodied, velvety-textured, mineral-laced style. It is drinkable now, but promises to be even better in 5–6 years. The 1998 Gigondas Cuvée Florence is a quasi-blockbuster. It sees some new oak, but has evolved into a classic Gigondas more than some soulless, internationally styled wine. Plum/purple-colored, medium- to full-bodied, with copious quantities of glycerin, this opulent, rich Gigondas should drink well for 10 years.

ALAIN GRAILLOT

2000 Crozes-Hermitage	D	(85–86)
1999 Crozes-Hermitage	D	89
1998 Crozes-Hermitage	D	89
1997 Crozes-Hermitage	D	88
1999 Crozes-Hermitage La Guiraude	E	90
1998 Crozes-Hermitage La Guiraude	E	90
1999 Hermitage	E	87
1998 Hermitage	E	(88–90)
1997 Hermitage	E	87
2000 St.-Joseph	C	(84–86)
1999 St.-Joseph	C	87
1998 St.-Joseph	C	88
1997 St.-Joseph	C	86

Alain Graillot consistently produces one of the classic examples of Crozes-Hermitage, at least those made from the sector known as Les Chassis. His top *cuvée*, La Guiraude, is culled from his production around 15 months after harvest.

Both of Graillot's 2000s reveal herbaceous, peppery characteristics as well as medium body and good red and black fruits, but a certain austerity and lack of succulence, particularly when compared to his brilliant 1999s. Although the 2000s are good, they lack depth.

The dense ruby/purple-colored 1999 Crozes-Hermitage is Graillot's finest *cuvée* since

1990. It offers a striking perfume of smoke, earth, Provençal herbs, bacon fat, and black currants. Excellent purity and medium body are displayed in a concentrated, structured, well-focused style. Give this 1999 another 1–2 years of cellaring and enjoy it over the following 12 years. The exceptional, backward 1999 Crozes-Hermitage La Guiraude is a tour de force. The bouquet is dominated by blackberry and cassis intermixed with licorice, lavender, fennel, and a touch of new oak. Full-bodied, ripe, moderately tannic, and concentrated, it will be at its finest between 2003–2015. The 1998 Crozes-Hermitage reveals more peppery, gamey notes along with the classic blackberry, cassis, and tapenade characteristics. Subtle notes of vanilla from oak barrels are noticeable in this medium- to full-bodied, moderately tannic, well-endowed Crozes. Anticipated maturity: 2003–2015. The exceptional, black/purple-colored 1998 Crozes-Hermitage La Guiraude (about 900 cases produced) offers impressive harmony in addition to gorgeous aromas and flavors of scorched earth, dried Provençal herbs, blackberries, olive, and cassis. Exhibiting beautiful integration of wood, acidity, and tannin, it will be drinkable young yet last for 12 years. The open-knit, atypically forward and luscious 1997 Crozes-Hermitage exhibits a deep ruby/purple color as well as abundant quantities of black cherry jam, smoke, licorice, and dried herb aromas and flavors. Its low acidity and sexy, up-front appeal suggest it will be at its best over the next 4–5 years.

The 1999 St.-Joseph exhibits sweet black cherry fruit intermixed with stony notions. Ripe, medium-bodied, and elegant, it will drink well for 5–6 years. The attractive 1998 St.-Joseph reveals a slightly herbal, ripe black cherry and cassis-scented nose, medium-bodied, concentrated flavors, low acidity, and moderate tannin. However, the wine is open and impressive, so consumption over the next 7–8 years is recommended. The dark ruby-colored, medium-bodied 1997 St.-Joseph reveals good fruit, a floral- and cassis-scented nose, and an easygoing personality that suggests consumption over the next 1–2 years is warranted.

Graillot's Hermitage is usually his least impressive offering. While it has the most prestigious pedigree, it comes from a parcel of Les Greffieux that appears incapable of producing wines of much depth or weight. The elegant, medium-bodied, stylish 1999 Hermitage, from one of that appellation's least favored sectors, exhibits scents of minerals mixed with red and black currants. It lacks the substance and majesty of the appellation's top wines. It possesses admirable character, but less concentration than the Crozes-Hermitage La Guiraude as well as the *cuvée* classique. Anticipated maturity: now–2014. Graillot has done a fine job with his 1998 Hermitage, as he did *pigéage* and completely destemmed the fruit. It offers a dense purple color, plenty of black fruit character, and a sweet mid-palate and length. The tannin is supple, and the wine is elegant yet rich. Look for it to drink well young, and keep for 10–15 years. The medium-bodied 1997 Hermitage offers up jammy cherry aromas intermixed with tomato skin, pepper, minerals, and smoke. Drink this soft wine during its first 5–6 years of life. Interestingly, I thought the St.-Joseph possessed more depth than the Hermitage. How can that be?

DOMAINE GRAMENON

1998	Côtes du Rhône Ceps Centenaire	C	90
1998	Côtes du Rhône Cuvée Pascal	C	90
1998	Côtes du Rhône Le Gramenon	C	86
1998	Côtes du Rhône Les Laurentides	C	89
1998	Côtes du Rhône La Sagesse	C	87
1998	Côtes du Rhône La Sierra du Sud	C	86

These are the finest wines this estate has produced since the blockbuster vintage of 1990. By the way, the 1990 Ceps Centenaire is still a gloriously rich, exotic, powerful Côtes du Rhône the likes of which are hard to find. All of the following wines are noteworthy Côtes du Rhônes that are reasonably priced for such high quality. Among the most natural wines made in France, they are bottled with neither fining nor filtration and possess high levels of CO_2 because the SO_2 levels are extremely low. As the sign on the winery says, they are "*vin du raisin*," and are uncommonly natural, which is Gramenon's guiding philosophy.

The 1998 Côtes du Rhône Le Gramenon is a tasty, medium-bodied, fresh, juicy, black cherry and spice-scented offering. Exhibiting no hard edges, it is destined to provide delicious, uncomplicated drinking for 2 years. The 1998 Côtes du Rhône La Sierra du Sud (100% Syrah) is vinified completely in wood *cuves* and then moved to old wood barrels. A low-acid, ripe, fleshy Syrah, it displays copious cassis fruit, a touch of tar, and unreleased CO_2 giving it freshness and liveliness. Although not the most complex or concentrated of the Gramenon *cuvées*, it is a vibrant, pure, tasty, delicious wine. Drink it over the next 3–4 years.

A blend of 80% Grenache and 20% Syrah, the 1998 Côtes du Rhône Les Laurentides is potentially outstanding. A dark ruby/purple color is followed by sumptuous aromas of dried herbs, cherry liqueur, and pepper, superb purity, vibrant, chewy, crunchy red and black fruits, fine glycerin, and a touch of toasty oak (about 20% of the Grenache is aged in new casks). This complex, expansive wine is a gorgeous value that should drink well for 4–5 years. The 1998 Côtes du Rhône La Sagesse (90% Grenache and 10% Syrah) reveals a more floral, Burgundy-like bouquet with notions of black fruits, tar, and pepper. There is more natural acidity in this *cuvée*, resulting in a tangy personality. Deep, backward, and unevolved, it possesses this winery's omnipresent elevated levels of carbon dioxide. It is important to mention the CO_2, which gives the wine a slight spritz early in life but protects the fruit and allows the producer to use low levels of SO_2, something that can dry out a wine and exaggerate its astringency. Readers who do not like a recently bottled wine with elevated CO_2 gas should decant the wine 10–15 minutes prior to serving. This will disperse the CO_2.

The fabulous 1998 Côtes du Rhône Ceps Centenaire (20 barrels, or just under 500 cases) is the essence of old-vine Grenache. Made from a parcel of 100-year-old, head-pruned Grenache vines, this dense effort is akin to drinking the blood of Grenache. Unlike the 1990, the viscous, thick, juicy 1998 reveals more acidity and vibrancy to its fruit flavors. This is a powerful yet gorgeously knit, symmetrical wine with great purity and presence in both its aromatics and flavors. A tour de force for a Côtes du Rhône, it will keep for 8 years or longer. Made from Grenache harvested in late October, there are just under 475 cases of the 1998 Côtes du Rhône Cuvée Pascal. This wine is the Côtes du Rhône equivalent of a late-harvest Zinfandel, but more complex, vibrant, and concentrated. It avoids the heaviness that wines with residual sugar and this kind of weight, alcohol, headiness, and thickness frequently exhibit. Pure, with gobs of jammy black fruits intermixed with tangy acidity and a slight notion of residual sugar, it is sweet, fat, rich, and best drunk with flavorful bistro dishes or full-flavored cheese. It should last easily for 8 years or more.

DOMAINE DU GRAND TINEL

2000	Châteauneuf-du-Pape	D	(88–90)
1999	Châteauneuf-du-Pape	D	88
1998	Châteauneuf-du-Pape	D	90
2000	Châteauneuf-du-Pape Cuvée Alexis Establet	D	(90–92)
1999	Châteauneuf-du-Pape Cuvée Alexis Establet	D	89+
1998	Châteauneuf-du-Pape Cuvée Alexis Establet	D	91

This large estate (136 acres) produces classic Châteauneuf-du-Pape that is consistently successful. Given the good availability of Grand Tinel's wines, it is not surprising that this is a crowd-pleasing Châteauneuf. It never quite hits the lofty heights, but it is an immensely enjoyable wine. In 1997, the estate introduced an old vine *cuvée* called Alexis Establet.

Sweet jammy fruit intertwined with crushed pepper, dried herbs, and new saddle leather are evident in the layered, fat, fleshy, low-acid 2000 Châteauneuf-du-Pape. The color is a deep ruby, and the wine is pure, sensual, and impossible to resist. Drink it during its first 10–12 years of life. Fuller-bodied and more expansive, revealing abundant black cherry fruit infused with spice box, pepper, and herbs, is the well-endowed, nicely layered, plump 2000 Châteauneuf-du-Pape Cuvée Alexis Establet. It possesses larger quantities of everything found in the regular *cuvée*, without additional tannin. This wine should hit its prime in 2–3 years and last for 15. The evolved medium ruby/plum-colored 1999 Châteauneuf-du-Pape exhibits a classic bouquet of earth, spice box, red fruits, and herbs. This ripe, medium- to full-bodied, lush, textbook 1999 Châteauneuf will drink well over the next 8–9 years. The old-vine *cuvée* of 1999 Châteauneuf-du-Pape Cuvée Alexis Establet exhibits a darker plum color as well as more muscle, depth, and tannin. However, at the moment, there is less charm and accessibility. It is full-bodied and spicy, with notes of smoke, herbs, plum and cherry fruit, and earth. This seriously endowed wine may justify an outstanding score after another 2–3 years of bottle age. Anticipated maturity: 2004–2015.

The dark ruby/garnet-colored 1998 Châteauneuf-du-Pape offers up a sexy nose of fruitcake, spice box, plums, and kirsch. It is immensely seductive and voluptuously textured, with loads of alcohol, glycerin, and fruit. This luxuriously rich, decadently styled Châteauneuf-du-Pape is hard to resist. Drink it over the next 8 years. The deep plum/garnet-colored 1998 Châteauneuf-du-Pape Cuvée Alexis Establet is a broader, more expansive effort with silky yet noticeable tannin. The wine is deep and full-bodied, with great purity of kirsch/cherry fruit intermixed with this vintage's sweet, concentrated fullness, a deep, chewy mid-palate, and a long, low-acid finish. It is a classic, very rich, lusty, full-throttle Châteauneuf-du-Pape. Anticipated maturity: now–2016.

Readers should note that this estate bottles the wine as it is sold, so there can be multiple *mise en bouteille*, with some wines not being bottled for a number of years. The later the wine is bottled, the less fruity and fresh it will be. I believe that earlier bottlings of Grand Tinel offer the most potential for the wine to develop.

DOMAINE DU GRAND VENEUR

2000 Châteauneuf-du-Pape	C	(90–92)
1999 Châteauneuf-du-Pape	C	89
1998 Châteauneuf-du-Pape	C	89
1999 Châteauneuf-du-Pape Cuvée La Fontaine	E	90
1998 Châteauneuf-du-Pape Cuvée La Fontaine	E	93
2000 Châteauneuf-du-Pape Cuvée Les Origines	D	(91–93)
1999 Châteauneuf-du-Pape Cuvée Les Origines	D	91
1998 Châteauneuf-du-Pape Cuvée Les Origines	D	93
1998 Côtes du Rhône	A	88

Alain Jaume, who also produces one of the finest white Châteauneuf-du-Papes (try his 100% Roussanne *cuvée*, La Fontaine), has significantly elevated the level of his red wines. With excellent 2000s, 1999s, and 1998s, he has enjoyed three superlative vintages in succession. In 1998, he introduced the luxury *cuvée* Châteauneuf-du-Pape Cuvée Les Origines, a blend of 35% Grenache, 35% Syrah, and 30% Mourvèdre aged in Allier oak casks. The estate also produces topflight Côtes du Rhônes. Prices continue to be astoundingly reasonable for wines of such quality.

The superb, deep opaque ruby-colored 2000 Châteauneuf-du-Pape is the finest regular *cuvée* Jaume has produced in my experience. Sexy and opulent, with gorgeous sweet cassis and black cherry liqueur notes, exuberant, full-bodied flavors, dazzling purity, and a layered palate impression, this 2000 is meant to be consumed during its first 10–12 years of life. The finest wine I have ever tasted from Alain Jaume is the 2000 Châteauneuf-du-Pape Cuvée Les Origines, which has the potential to eclipse the fabulous 1998 Les Origines. Opaque ruby/ purple-colored, with a knockout nose of cherry liqueur intermixed with crème de cassis, licorice, spice box, and earth, this expansively flavored, multilayered, textured, fat, opulent 2000 boasts exciting ripeness, purity, and delineation, a difficult accomplishment in wines of such obvious fruit maturity. Consume it over the next 12–15 years. It should be a stunner! The 1999 Châteauneuf-du-Pape exhibits a sweet, complex perfume of roasted herbs, mincemeat, black cherry liqueur, pepper, and spice box. It is captivating and ripe, with abundant glycerin and medium to full body. Most of its seductive power is on a superficial level, and it probably will not last more than a decade, but this medium- to full-bodied, pure, delicious 1999 was singing beautifully in 2001. The 1999 Châteauneuf-du-Pape Cuvée Les Origines displays that wonderful autumnal nose of clean foresty aromas intermixed with dried Provençal herbs, roasted meats, pepper, black cherries, and leather. This dark ruby/garnet-colored 1999 is exceptionally seductive, layered, and expansive as well as elegant and pure. Rich, full, and long, it is meant to be drunk during its first 12–14 years of life.

The 1998 Châteauneuf-du-Pape is a bigger, fuller-bodied offering with kirsch, pepper, spice, black raspberry, and earthy *garrigue* (that mélange of Provençal herbs and soil overtones) aromas. Medium- to full-bodied and soft, with light tannin in the finish, it should drink well for a decade. The 1998 Châteauneuf-du-Pape Cuvée Les Origines' dark ruby color is accompanied by an elegant, classy nose of new saddle leather, black plums, raspberries, and kirsch. With a multilayered texture, it boasts wonderful ripeness and intensity as well as full body and moderate tannin. This beauty should age for 10–15 years. The 1998 Côtes du Rhône (an 80% Grenache and 20% Syrah blend) is a juicy effort as well as a super value. Dark ruby-colored with kirsch aromas, abundant quantities of sweet cherry fruit on the palate, and a medium-bodied, soft, succulent texture, this 1998 will provide enormous hedonistic appeal. Drink it over the next several years.

Along with Beaucastel's famous *cuvée* of old vine Roussanne, no other Châteauneuf-du-Pape estate makes as dazzling a white wine as Grand Veneur. While the 1999 Châteauneuf-du-Pape Cuvée La Fontaine does not appear to be as rich as the 1998, it is a gorgeous, honeyed, fruit-driven effort with considerable personality and character. The spectacular 1998 Châteauneuf-du-Pape Cuvée La Fontaine is an amazing tour de force in white winemaking, especially from the southern Rhône. A soaring aromatic impression composed of orange marmalade, honeyed nuts, spice, and rose petals is followed by a full-bodied, concentrated, viscous wine. It is hard to say how long it will age, but I would opt for drinking it over the next 3–4 years.

DOMAINE LES GRANDS BOIS

2000 Côtes du Rhône	A	85
1999 Côtes du Rhône	A	87
2000 Côtes du Rhône-Villages Cuvée Gabrielle	B	86
1999 Côtes du Rhône-Villages Cuvée Gabrielle	B	89
1998 Côtes du Rhône-Villages Cuvée Gabrielle	B	87
2000 Côtes du Rhône-Villages Cairanne Cuvée Maximilien	B	88
1999 Côtes du Rhône-Villages Cairanne Cuvée Maximilien	B	90
2000 Côtes du Rhône-Villages Cairanne Cuvée Mireille	B	89

An excellent source for value, this winery has produced a rugged, monolithic, spicy, peppery 2000 Côtes du Rhône with medium body, plenty of cherry fruit, and an up-front style. Drink it over the next year. The 2000 Côtes du Rhône-Villages Cuvée Gabrielle (unfiltered) displays a more saturated ruby color in addition to a sweet nose of cassis and cherry liqueur. The finish possesses plenty of tannin, some rusticity, medium body, and excellent depth. It should drink well for 3–4 years.

Offerings from Cairanne include the Cuvée Maximilien and Cuvée Mireille. The saturated purple-colored 2000 Côtes du Rhône-Villages Cairanne Cuvée Maximilien offers an intense perfume of blackberry/cherry fruit, sweet tannin, medium body, and excellent purity as well as length. Consume this impressive Côtes du Rhône-Villages over the next 5–6 years. The 2000 Côtes du Rhône-Villages Cairanne Cuvée Mireille reveals an equally saturated deep ruby/purple color. The bouquet offers aromas of violets, blackberries, and ripe cherries. Succulent, with sweet tannin, medium to full body, and layers of black fruits, minerals, and licorice, it is a long, ripe, supple-textured effort to enjoy over the next 6–7 years.

Many knowledgeable observers feel that in such Côtes du Rhône-Villages as Gigondas, Rasteau, Cairanne, Vacqueyras, and Sablet, 1999 is a better vintage than 1998. As good as Domaine les Grands Bois' 1998s were, the 1999s are even better. Marc Besnardeau's 1999s reveal deeper colors and slightly higher alcohols. These are unquestionably some of the best values in the marketplace, and Rhône wine enthusiasts should snap them up by the case. The exceptional 1999 Côtes du Rhône-Villages Cairanne Cuvée Maximilien (a blend of 55% Grenache, 25% Mourvèdre, and 20% Syrah) achieved an unprecedented 14.4% natural alcohol. It was aged in *barrique* before being bottled unfiltered. A sensational value, it offers a dense purple color as well as a sweet nose of kirsch, black raspberries, spice box, herbs, and licorice. Ripe, full-bodied, and super-concentrated, with excellent freshness and harmony, this intense, gorgeously succulent Cairanne should drink well for 7–8 years, although my instincts suggest it may live even longer.

The 1999 Côtes du Rhône (70% Grenache, with the balance Syrah and Carignan) is a special, unfiltered selection of 2,000 cases produced for the American importer. An excellent effort, it offers aromas of black cherries, pepper, and plums. Ripe, robust, medium- to full-bodied, and delicious, it should be consumed over the next 2–3 years. Slightly richer, more complex, and aromatic, the 1999 Côtes du Rhône-Villages Cuvée Gabrielle (50% Grenache, 25% Syrah, and the balance equal parts Mourvèdre and Carignan) achieved 13.7% natural alcohol. With a deeper, denser ruby/purple color, as well as a gorgeously sweet bouquet of blackberries, framboise, pepper, and cherry liqueur, it is opulent, lush, full-bodied, big, and chewy, with outstanding purity and a nicely textured mid-palate and finish. It should drink well for 5–6 years.

Marc Besnardeau has turned out a delicious, unfiltered 1998 Côtes du Rhône-Villages Cuvée Gabrielle produced from a blend of two-thirds Grenache and one-third Syrah. I have already consumed six bottles of this wine, all of which were immensely enjoyable. Notes of raspberry liqueur, cherries, and *fraises des bois* jump from the fruit-driven aromatics of this dark ruby-colored 1998. Luscious, round, seductive, sexy, and fruity, there is not a hard edge to be found in this delicious, disarming Côtes du Rhône. It should drink well for 2–3 years, but why wait?

GUIGAL

1999 Châteauneuf-du-Pape	D	(89–91)
1998 Châteauneuf-du-Pape	D	91
2000 Condrieu	D	91
1999 Condrieu	D	90
2000 Condrieu La Doriane	E	93
1999 Condrieu La Doriane	E	94
1999 Condrieu Luminescence	E	92
2000 Côte Rôtie Brune et Blonde	D	(87–89)
1999 Côte Rôtie Brune et Blonde	D	(91–93)
1998 Côte Rôtie Brune et Blonde	D	90
2000 Côte Rôtie Château d'Ampuis	EE	(88–91)
1999 Côte Rôtie Château d'Ampuis	EE	(95–97)
1998 Côte Rôtie Château d'Ampuis	EE	(92–95)
1997 Côte Rôtie Château d'Ampuis	EE	91+
2000 Côte Rôtie La Landonne	EEE	(91–95)
1999 Côte Rôtie La Landonne	EEE	100
1998 Côte Rôtie La Landonne	EEE	99

1997	Côte Rôtie La Landonne	EEE	98
2000	Côte Rôtie La Mouline	EEE	(90–93)
1999	Côte Rôtie La Mouline	EEE	100
1998	Côte Rôtie La Mouline	EEE	97
1997	Côte Rôtie La Mouline	EEE	96
2000	Côte Rôtie La Turque	EEE	(91–93)
1999	Côte Rôtie La Turque	EEE	100
1998	Côte Rôtie La Turque	EEE	98+
1997	Côte Rôtie La Turque	EEE	96
2000	Côtes du Rhône	A	(87–89)
1999	Côtes du Rhône	A	87
1998	Côtes du Rhône	A	87
2000	Côtes du Rhône Blanc	A	87
1999	Côtes du Rhône Blanc	A	86
2000	Côtes du Rhône Rosé	A	87
2000	Crozes-Hermitage	C	(86–88+)
1999	Crozes-Hermitage	C	87
1999	Gigondas	C	(88–89)
1998	Gigondas	C	89
1999	Hermitage	E	(91–94)
1998	Hermitage	E	90
1997	Hermitage	E	89
2000	Hermitage Blanc	E	(90–92)
1999	Hermitage Blanc	E	(89–91)
1998	Hermitage Blanc	E	89
2000	St.-Joseph	C	(87–88)
1999	St.-Joseph	C	(88–89)
2000	St.-Joseph Vigne de l'Hospice	D	(91–93)
1999	St.-Joseph Vigne de l'Hospice	D	(90–91)
2000	Tavel	B	89

As difficult as it may be to find the limited production (400–800 cases each) of Côte Rôtie La Mouline, La Turque, and La Landonne, readers should have no problem securing Guigal's very good Côtes du Rhône and sumptuous Condrieu. I remember when this was just a tiny *négociant* firm, but today it seems like the entire underside of the village of Ampuis is a maze of Guigal cellars. Over 100,000 cases of red Côtes du Rhône are produced, and the white wine production has also grown. In addition, Guigal is the most significant producer of Condrieu, as well as the largest producer of Côte Rôtie. As I have stated many times over the last 20 years, Marcel Guigal is not only a brilliant wine-maker, but perhaps even more of a genius *éléveur*. The practice of upbringing wines, knowing when to sulphur and when to rack, was learned from his father, who Marcel claims was the real genius behind this lost art. Who in their right mind would keep a wine for over 40 months in 100% new-oak casks? Marcel Guigal routinely does that with his single-vineyard Côte Rôties. Having followed them for over two decades, I can unequivocally say that their overt oakiness is completely absorbed by the wines within their first 5–7 years of life.

The quality of Guigal's rosés is also impressive. The excellent, fresh, medium-bodied 2000 Côtes du Rhône Rosé offers a medium strawberry color as well as a delicious perfume of framboise and cherries. Consume this fun rosé now. Even better is the deeper-colored, fuller-bodied 2000 Tavel. Loaded with glycerin, flavor, and notes of framboise and Provençal herbs, this beautiful Tavel is as good as any estate-bottled efforts in the appellation.

The 2000 Côtes du Rhône Blanc (50% Viognier and the rest Marsanne, Roussanne, and other white wine varietals) is an excellent, fleshy, surprisingly character-filled, dry white that should be consumed over the next 12–18 months. It possesses freshness and depth as well as considerable character. The 1999 Côtes du Rhône Blanc reveals his increased emphasis on blending with large quantities of Viognier (40%). It is a medium-bodied, dry, tasty offering with a straightforward but alluring nose of honeysuckle and peach as well as excellent purity. Consume it over the next 1–2 years.

Guigal is consistently one of the two or three finest producers of Condrieu. He claims to make about one-third of this small appellation's total production, while some of his colleagues claim it is closer to 50%. Whichever is correct, we should be grateful. His 1998 Condrieus (a great vintage for the appellation, superior to 1999) are still holding up despite their age, my basic rule being to drink these wines within three years of the vintage. However, the extra levels of concentration achieved from the tiny 1998 crop has kept the top wines alive. Nevertheless, I would not push my luck more than another year. The 2000 Condrieu offers up an excellent perfume of peach and apricot jam, a fat personality, low acidity, superb ripeness, and an unctuous texture. Enjoy it during its first several years of life. The single-vineyard 2000 Condrieu La Doriane exhibits more smoke, spice, and minerality in addition to telltale jammy apricot/peach/honeysuckle notes. While more backward as well as more structured than the regular *cuvée*, it is profoundly concentrated, exotic, and rich. It should drink well for 2–4 years. The classic 1999 Condrieu reveals higher acidity and not the fat of the 1998, but it is an elegant, perfumed, medium-bodied effort with aromas and flavors of bananas, peaches, and apricots. It will be more flexible with food than the fatter 1998. Look for it to drink well for 1–3 years. Two-thirds of this wine is tank-fermented and aged, and the rest is barrel-fermented. The 1999 Condrieu La Doriane emerges from Guigal's own vineyard, which he crop-thinned twice to lower yields. A stunning Condrieu, it offers intense aromas of peaches, apricots, and bananas, as well as a long, multilayered, rich, full-bodied palate with exquisite purity and intensity.

Guigal's excellent Côtes du Rhône is consistently a very good value. Production of this *cuvée* is gigantic, with speculation that there are close to a half million cases made. Remarkably, Guigal maintains an exceptionally high level of quality as well as consistency from bottle to bottle, despite the fact that there are generally five to six separate bottlings. Tasting through the 2000 Côtes du Rhône's component parts revealed that it may be even better than the 1998. The Syrah component exhibits full body along with crème de cassis–like flavors. The Grenache component offers sweet kirsch notes. This should be a delicious, velvety-textured, full-flavored, knockout value to enjoy during its first 2–4 years of life. Made from a slightly different blend of 55% Syrah, 40% Grenache, and 5% Mourvèdre, the delicious, deep ruby/purple-colored 1999 Côtes du Rhône offers abundant fruit, some tannin, a higher acid profile than the 1998, medium body, and excellent purity.

The deep ruby/purple-colored 1998 Côtes du Rhône rouge (50% Syrah, 30% Grenache, and 20% miscellaneous varietals) offers a moderately intense bouquet of cassis, licorice, and flowers. An amazing effort, with moderate tannin, excellent concentration, and the potential to improve for several years and last for 6–8, this is a wine to purchase by the case.

Among Guigal's most notable *négociant* wines (for which he buys wines to blend) is his Hermitage. It is no secret that he has been seeking to purchase a top domaine from this hallowed appellation. At present he purchases wine from several small producers. These wines are rotated between tank, *foudre*, and small barrels. Better white Hermitages are produced by such wine-makers as Chave and Chapoutier, but Guigal consistently fashions full-bodied, concentrated wines that drink well for 4–5 years, then close down and reopen at age 10–12. The fat, dense, chewy, low-acid 2000 Hermitage Blanc displays aromas and flavors of pineapples, apricots, and acacia flowers in addition to a smoky, leesy character. This flamboyant offering should drink well young and age for a decade. More backward and austere with additional structure, the 1999 Hermitage Blanc requires cellaring. It will last for 15 years. The powerful, structured, dense 1998 Hermitage Blanc offers up aromas of white flowers, minerals, oranges, and pineapple. A big-bodied effort needing time in the bottle, it should prove to be the longest-lived of this trio. Anticipated maturity: 2005–2016. This large-scaled, backward effort will ultimately be better than either the 1997 or 1996.

The 2000 Crozes-Hermitage, which includes fruit from De Vallouit's vineyards in the blend, is more difficult to evaluate. It possesses aromas of grilled meats, smoked herbs, red as well as black fruits, and a soft, open-knit, smoky character. It did not reveal the grip or concentration of the 1999, but these may emerge after the Guigal *élevage* (cellar upbringing). The debut vintage of Guigal's Crozes-Hermitage, the 1999 is dense ruby-colored. It exhibits a terrific perfume of pepper, dried Provençal herbs, cassis, and spice. Long, round, and sexy, this luscious wine should be consumed during its first 7–8 years of life.

In 2000, there will be two *cuvées* of St.-Joseph under the Guigal label, probably with some acknowledgment that they were once part of the Jean-Louis Grippat domaine. There is a regular *cuvée* of St.-Joseph as well as the spectacular Vignes des Hospices. While Guigal controlled the vinification in 2001, Grippat produced the 2000 and 1999. However, the 1999s are stunning. The 2000 St.-Josephs are fatter and fleshier than many wines from the vintage. The soft, low-acid 2000 St.-Joseph is made in a flattering, up-front, ripe, fat style with abundant black currant fruit. It should be consumed during its first 3–4 years of life. The 2000 St.-Joseph Vigne de l'Hospice is a sexy, fruit-forward effort offering aromas as well as flavors of black fruits, smoke, licorice, and minerals. Although it does not possess the density or definition of the 1999, it displays copious fat and flesh, low acidity, and an accessible, easygoing style. It should drink well for 7–8 years. The 1999 St.-Joseph is a Burgundy-styled effort offering copious quantities of black cherry fruit, currants, licorice, pepper, and spice. Soft and delicious, it is best consumed during its first 5–7 years of life. The spectacular 1999 St.-Joseph Vigne de l'Hospice continues to add weight, revealing a dense ruby/purple color as well as a gorgeous bouquet of powerful, macerated blackberry and cassis fruit along with an unmistakable liquid minerality. It is a terrific example of great hillside St.-Joseph that should drink splendidly for at least a decade. Readers looking for a reasonably priced northern Rhône should check out this 1999.

The red Hermitage primarily comes from Hermitage Hill's two top vineyards, Le Méal and Les Bessards, with some fruit from Les Dionnières. Readers will notice a significant increase in the quality of Guigal's Hermitage beginning with 1999, largely because of the fruit from Grippat and De Vallouit (particularly the latter's Les Greffières). The 1999 Hermitage looks like a candidate for a score between 91–94. It appears to be the best red Hermitage Guigal has made, and the addition of the new components has improved the wine. In fact, I would not be surprised to see Guigal ultimately cull out the best lots of red Hermitage and introduce a new luxury *cuvée* spéciale. The 1999 Hermitage is great stuff, with a saturated ruby/purple color and a striking nose of crème de cassis, a layered texture, sweet tannin, and a sumptuous mouth-feel. This should prove to be a stunningly outrageous Hermitage to drink between 2006–2020. The powerful, backward 1998 Hermitage was produced from wine purchased from such vineyards as Les Bessards, Les Baumes, Le Méal, and Les Dionnières. It is powerful, tannic, slightly austere, but is long in the mouth with copious quantities of cassis fruit. Anticipated maturity: 2007–2020. The excellent, seductive 1997 Hermitage rouge possesses a dense ruby color, abundant cassis fruit, excellent texture, sweet tannin, and a low-acid, long finish. It is a wine to drink over the next 10–12 years.

Guigal's other *négociant* wines emerge from two of his favorite southern Rhône appellations, Gigondas and Châteauneuf-du-Pape. The Châteauneuf-du-Papes are made primarily from Grenache, although he has begun to add about 20% Mourvèdre to the blend to give the wines more structure and ageability.

The Châteauneuf-du-Pape is fashioned from purchased wine which Guigal then blends and ages in large wood *foudres*. The potentially outstanding 1999 is a blend from 25 different Châteauneuf-du-Pape growers. It exhibits a deep ruby color as well as a sweet nose of pepper, black cherries, and earth. A spicy, fleshy, Provençal-styled wine with considerable glycerin and depth, it should drink well for a decade. Even better is the 1998 Châteauneuf-du-Pape, the finest Châteauneuf produced by any Rhône Valley *négociant* from purchased juice. Remarkably, there are 200,000 bottles of the 1998. It is full-bodied, dense, rich, and chewy, with an opulent texture as well as a classic nose of Provençal herbs mixed with kirsch, pepper, and balsam. Drink it over the next 15 years.

Like the Côtes du Rhône, Guigal's Gigondas is kept in *cuve*, seeing no oak whatsoever. The 1999 Gigondas exhibits a dense, saturated ruby/purple color along with a black currant and berry-scented nose infused with pepper, spice, and a floral note. It should be delicious upon release and drink well for a decade. The dark ruby-colored 1998 Gigondas offers a sweet perfume of mineral-laced black cherries backed up by pepper. Medium-bodied, elegant, and savory, it is ideal for drinking over the next 7–8 years.

Guigal admits to producing in excess of 20,000 cases of Côte Rôtie Brune et Blonde. I suspect the amount is even higher given the fact that there is one master blend for each vintage and 3–5 different *mis en bouteilles*. Having frequently conducted tastings of all his Côte Rôtie Brune et Blonde from different *mise* within the same vintage, there are subtle differences, but in general it is the same wine. Some may be more fragrant, but the level of richness and quality is uniform. Marcel Guigal purchased the only château in Ampuis, the Château d'Ampuis, and is in the process of renovating this huge edifice. In 1995 he launched his *cuvée* of Côte Rôtie, which is made in limited quantities of approximately 28,000 bottles. It is a blend of some of Côte Rôtie's finest hillside vineyards, i.e., La Garde, Le Clos, La Grande Plantée, La Pommière, Le Pavillon Rouge, and La Moulin. The strength of this *négociant* also lies in its worldwide famous luxury-priced Côte Rôties La Mouline, La Turque, and La Landonne, which are aged a whopping 42 months in new oak, and manage to perfectly soak up the wood as they are always so concentrated, rich, and powerful, with phenomenal extraction.

The lighter 2000 Côte Rôtie Brune et Blonde possesses less heftiness, concentration, and structure, but offers sweet black currant fruit infused with bacon and smoke. Although toasty, spicy, and seductive, it lacks depth as well as length. It will be best consumed during its first 8–9 years of life. I found fairly important variation in the six component parts of the 2000 Côte Rôtie Château d'Ampuis. The scores ranged from the high 80s to low 90s, but make no mistake about it, this wine will put on weight. However, it is not in the same league as the 1999, 1998, 1997, or 1995. A lighter-styled, medium-bodied effort, it possesses sweet jammy fruit and bacon fat characteristics, but is already easy to drink, without the structure, weight, and depth of other vintages. Nevertheless, it will have its place given the charm, purity, and up-front, easygoing character. Anticipated maturity: 2004–2014. Even the 2000 vintage, which certainly produced less promising raw materials than 1999, 1998, or 1997, has turned out well for these *cuvées*. Keep in mind, as I have reiterated time and time again, Guigal's wines put on extraordinary weight during their *élevages*, as tastings from bottle so frequently attest. While the 2000 Côte Rôtie La Mouline is a lighter wine than the three previous vintages, it is outstanding. Possessing sweet fruit, medium body, and La Mouline's characteristics displayed in a more precocious, compact style, it will probably be built along the lines of the 1987 or 1982. Also lighter than the previous three vintages, the 2000 Côte Rôtie La Turque offers sweet black cherry fruit intermixed with smoke, asphalt, and truffles. It exhibits good denseness as well as richness. While seemingly bigger and chewier than La Mouline, it does not possess the size or dimension of its predecessors, the 1999, 1998, and 1997. Like La Mouline, it will be best drunk during its first 12–15 years of life. Lastly, the 2000 Côte Rôtie La Landonne appears to be the finest of these 2000s. It offers smoky, earthy, asphalt, and truffle-like aromas mixed with jammy blackberries and creosote. With medium to full body and admirable tannin as well as weight, it will require 3–4 years of cellaring after its release, yet last for 15–18 years.

According to Marcel Guigal, "1999 is the greatest vintage in my lifetime for Côte Rôtie."

His 1999 Côte Rôtie Brune et Blonde has the finest potential of any Brune et Blonde I have tasted in nearly 20 years. Its deep ruby/purple color is accompanied by a gorgeous, fat, exotic nose of bacon fat, honeysuckle, cassis, and tapenade. A touch of new saddle leather also makes an appearance in this opulent, fleshy, full-bodied 1999. It will be seductive upon release and drink well for 15+ years. The 1999 Côte Rôtie Château d'Ampuis has put on additional weight, and it is the most awesome effort Guigal has produced under this brand name. All of the component parts were tasted, several of which bordered on perfection, particularly La Pommière, Pavillon Rouge, and Le Moulin. The sumptuous 1999 boasts a spectacularly sweet perfume of jammy blackberry and cassis fruit intertwined with smoke, tapenade, and new saddle leather notes. Unctuously textured, explosively rich, and amazingly well delineated for a wine of such size and richness, this is an exquisite Côte Rôtie that should drink well young, yet age nicely for two decades. All three 1999 La La's are perfect. It is undoubtedly the greatest vintage for Guigal since 1978. Take all the characteristics I describe for the wines in 1998 and 1997, then add an ethereal lightness of character, surreal aromatics, and a seamlessness that is uncanny given the massive richness and layers of flavors these wines possess. The explosive aromatics tend to be more exaggerated in 1999. In terms of Côte Rôtie, they represent the essence of these crus. All three are more evolved and seductive than the 1998s, but their aging potential should not be underestimated. La Mouline and La Turque have at least two decades of life, and La Landonne 30–40 years. In short, Guigal has performed a classic hat trick in 1999 with his La La's.

The 1998 Côte Rôtie Brune et Blonde exhibits some of the vintage's hard tannin, as well as complex aromatics of roasted olives, black currants, creamy oak, sweet cherries, and dried herbs. Medium- to full-bodied and structured, with a sweet attack, it will benefit from another 2 years of cellaring, and last for 15 years. The extraordinary 1998 Côte Rôtie Château d'Ampuis is more structured, powerful, and concentrated. My ratings for the component parts ranged from a low of 90–92 for La Grande Plantée, to a high of 94–96 for La Pommière and Pavillon Rouge. All revealed huge colors, earthy, smoky noses with bacon fat and black currants, and various degrees of tannin. This is unquestionably a vintage for patient connoisseurs as it requires cellaring. Dense, chewy, and muscular, it will be at its finest between 2007–2020. The awesome 1998 Côte Rôtie La Mouline is a seamless, full-bodied classic with many of the previously described characteristics, but more structure, tannin, and muscle. It will need 2 years of cellaring and will last for 20 years. Stylistically, it is reminiscent of the 1988. The 1998 Côte Rôtie La Turque may end up being a perfect wine. Smoky black fruits intermixed with licorice, roasted meats, cassis, and flowers create an explosive, exotic perfume. The wine reveals considerable tannin, immense structure, and potentially legendary depth as well as intensity. Anticipated maturity: 2005–2022. The 1998 Côte Rôtie La Landonne is a perfect wine . . . at least for my palate. Its saturated black/purple color is accompanied by an extraordinary nose of smoke, incense, tapenade, creosote, blackberry, and currant aromas. Densely packed with blackberry, truffle, chocolate, and leather-like flavors, it possesses high tannin but perfect harmony, impeccable balance, and gorgeous integration of acidity, alcohol, and tannin. It is a tour de force in winemaking. Anticipated maturity: 2007–2025.

The 1997 Côte Rôtie Château d'Ampuis is now in the marketplace. Its dense ruby color is followed by gorgeous aromas of sweet truffles intermixed with road tar, cassis, smoke, and coffee. Low in acidity, but ripe and concentrated with a voluptuous texture, this stunning Côte Rôtie is more developed and forward than the 1998, 1996, or 1995. Anticipated maturity: 2004–2018. The spectacular, dense ruby/purple-colored 1997 Côte Rôtie La Mouline boasts a complex nose of violets, peaches, and cassis. Soft, voluptuous, medium- to full-bodied, and incredibly seductive, it is reminiscent of the 1991 and 1987. Anticipated maturity: now–2015. The dense purple-colored, profound 1997 Côte Rôtie La Turque (5–7% Viognier added to the blend) offers more crème de cassis, licorice, and espresso aromas as well as notions of melted asphalt. Compared to La Mouline, it has additional layers as well as structure, sweet tannin, and exhilarating levels of opulence and ripe fruit. Anticipated maturity: now–2018. The nearly perfect 1997 Côte Rôtie La Landonne is an amazing achievement for the vintage. An astonishing saturated purple color is followed by scents of licorice, roasted meats, coffee, toasty oak, plums, and blackberries. Extremely smoky, earthy, and more *terroir*-driven, this 1997 offers exceptional expansiveness on the palate, sweet tannin, low acidity, and a ripe, robust finish. 1–3 years of cellaring is warranted, but it is capable of lasting for two decades.

A new offering from Guigal is a sweet dessert wine made in the style of Condrieus of the last century. A total of 10,200 375-ml bottles of the 1999 Condrieu Luminescence were produced. A ripe, concentrated Condrieu, it possesses 37 grams of residual sugar per liter, and 15% alcohol. It was aged half in new oak and half in old, and malolactic fermentation was blocked (a first in the Guigal cellars). The result is a honeyed wine that can be served as either an aperitif or with fresh fruit desserts. It possesses unctuous, honeyed orange marmalade and pear liqueur aromas and flavors. This pure, impressive sweet dessert offering is best drunk over the next 2–5 years.

Past Glories: Côte Rôtie La Landonne—1995 (99+), 1994 (92), 1991 (99), 1990 (98), 1989 (98), 1988 (100), 1987 (96), 1985 (100), 1983 (100), 1982 (95), 1980 (94), 1978 (100); Côte Rôtie La Mouline—1995 (99), 1994 (94), 1991 (100), 1990 (99), 1989 (98), 1988 (100), 1987 (95), 1985 (100), 1983 (100), 1982 (96), 1980 (95), 1978 (100), 1976 (100), 1969 (100); Côte Rôtie La Turque—1995 (100), 1994 (92), 1991 (99), 1990 (98), 1989 (99), 1988 (100), 1987 (96), 1985 (100)

DOMAINE LES HAUTES CANCES

1999	Côtes du Rhône-Villages Cairanne Clos du Débat	C	86
1999	Côtes du Rhône-Villages Cairanne Cuvée Tradition	C	89
1999	Côtes du Rhône-Villages Cairanne Vieilles Vignes	C	89

Readers looking for powerful, concentrated, muscular reds that sell for a song should check out Domaine Les Hautes Cances' offerings. These unfiltered, unfined Cairannes possess abundant quantities of earthy, muscular fruit, rustic tannin, and nearly savage personalities. If these impressive efforts soften, they will be even better than my scores suggest. The 1999 Côtes du Rhône-Villages Cairanne Cuvée Tradition, a blend dominated by Grenache (42%) and equal parts Syrah, Cinsault, Mourvèdre, and Carignan, exhibits a saturated dense plum color, full body, and deep, broodingly backward mushroom and cherry flavors with notes of underbrush, pepper, and meat. Big, mouth-filling, and tannic, it should evolve for 5–6 years. Potentially too tannic for its own good is the 1999 Côtes du Rhône-Villages Cairanne Clos du Débat. Its excellent aromatics (earth, minerals, *jus de viande,* dried herbs) are followed by concentrated, intense fruit as well as huge tannin. A blend of 64% Grenache, 19% Carignan, 13% Syrah, and 4% Counoise, it will drink well for 6–7 years. Lastly, the 1999 Côtes du Rhône-Villages Cairanne Vieilles Vignes (70% Grenache, 15% Syrah, and 15% Mourvèdre) reveals superb ripeness and purity along with a boatload of kirsch intermixed with black currants. Despite all the fruit, glycerin, and extract, it must contend with seriously high tannin which may or may not melt away. It could turn out to be a sleeper, or a tannic, hard wine. There is a lot to like about this estate, which is pushing extract levels to the maximum.

PAUL JABOULET-AINÉ

2000	Châteauneuf-du-Pape	D	87
2000	Condrieu	D	89
1999	Condrieu	D	85
2000	Cornas	D	(78–82)
1999	Cornas	D	77

1998	Cornas	D	86
2000	Cornas Domaine St.-Pierre	D	(85–86)
1999	Cornas Domaine St.-Pierre	D	84
1998	Cornas Domaine St.-Pierre	D	91
2000	Côte Rôtie Les Jumelles	E	(77–80)
1999	Côte Rôtie Les Jumelles	E	85
1998	Côte Rôtie Les Jumelles	E	87*
2000	Côtes du Rhône Parallèle 45	A	87
1999	Côtes du Rhône Parallèle 45	A	85
1998	Côtes du Rhône Parallèle 45	A	85
2000	Côtes du Rhône-Villages	B	87
1999	Côtes du Rhône-Villages	B	(79–82)
1998	Côtes du Rhône-Villages	B	85
2000	Côtes du Ventoux	A	85
2000	Crozes-Hermitage Les Jalets	C	(83–85)
1999	Crozes-Hermitage Les Jalets	C	85
1998	Crozes-Hermitage Les Jalets	C	78
1999	Crozes-Hermitage La Mule Blanche	C	87
1998	Crozes-Hermitage La Mule Blanche	C	87
2000	Crozes-Hermitage Raymond Roure	D	(88–90)
1999	Crozes-Hermitage Raymond Roure	D	85
1998	Crozes-Hermitage Raymond Roure	D	86
2000	Crozes-Hermitage Raymond Roure Blanc	D	86
1999	Crozes-Hermitage Raymond Roure Blanc	D	87
1998	Crozes-Hermitage Raymond Roure Blanc	D	86
1997	Crozes-Hermitage Raymond Roure Blanc	D	87
2000	Crozes-Hermitage Thalabert	C	(87–89)
1999	Crozes-Hermitage Thalabert	C	88
1998	Crozes-Hermitage Thalabert	C	86
2000	Gigondas Pierre Aiguille	D	(86–88)
1998	Gigondas Pierre Aiguille	D	88
2000	Hermitage La Chapelle	EE	(87–89)
1999	Hermitage La Chapelle	EE	87?
1998	Hermitage La Chapelle	EE	90?
1997	Hermitage La Chapelle	EE	(95–98+)
2000	Hermitage Chevalier de Stérimberg	EE	90
1999	Hermitage Chevalier de Stérimberg	EE	90
1998	Hermitage Chevalier de Stérimberg	EE	92
1997	Hermitage Chevalier de Stérimberg	EE	92
1996	Hermitage Chevalier de Stérimberg	EE	91
2000	Hermitage Pied de la Côte	E	(85–87)
1999	Hermitage Pied de la Côte	D	84
1998	Hermitage Pied de la Côte	D	78
2000	Muscat de Beaumes-de-Venise	C	88
1999	Muscat de Beaumes-de-Venise	C	90
1999	Muscat de Beaumes-de-Venise Réserve Spéciale	C	91
2000	St.-Joseph Le Grand Pompée	C	(84–86)
1999	St.-Joseph Le Grand Pompée	C	87
1998	St.-Joseph Le Grand Pompée	C	85
1999	St.-Joseph Le Grand Pompée Blanc	C	85
1998	St.-Joseph Le Grand Pompée Blanc	C	86

2000 Vacqueyras	B	88
1998 Vacqueyras	B	87

My last tasting at Jaboulet was the most disappointing I've ever had, largely because of a frustrating lack of consistency. It is hard to say what is going on, but it is a huge family, and perhaps the death of Gérard Jaboulet several years ago has left this renowned house with too many chefs. There is no doubt that immense talent exists with the likes of Jacques Jaboulet and a younger generation of Jaboulets coming into their own. The fact is that by and large, many of the Jaboulet wines are not as impressive as they were in the past. Moreover, many bottled wines taste less impressive, making me wonder whether there is too much fining and filtering, thus depriving the wines of texture as well as aromatic and flavor intensity. As a wine enthusiast, with a cellar crammed with multiple vintages of Hermitage La Chapelle, many vintages of Crozes-Hermitage Thalabert, and a handful of bottles left of their extraordinary Châteauneuf-du-Pape Le Cèdres 1967, there is no doubt that this has always been one of my reference points for many Rhône Valley appellations. Based on what was accomplished in 2000, 1999, and 1998, Jaboulet has fallen behind such rivals as Guigal, Delas, and Chapoutier.

For starters, the 2000 Côtes du Ventoux is a Grenache-based *cuvée* with little Syrah included as the Jaboulets were not happy with the southern Rhône's 2000 Syrah crop. It exhibits good ripeness, fatness, and a straightforward, medium-bodied style. It should drink well for 2–3 years. According to Jacques Jaboulet, the 2000 Côtes du Rhône Parallèle 45 (85% Grenache and 15% Syrah) is the "best since 1970." A sexy, full-bodied effort, it is significantly better than the light, innocuous 1999. The deeply colored 2000 offers sweet black fruits intermixed with scents of kirsch, pepper, and spice. Drink this rich, fleshy Côtes du Rhône over the next 2–3 years. The 1999 Côtes du Rhône Parallèle 45 includes 65% Syrah and 35% Grenache. It exhibits a dense purple color, medium weight, a cassis-scented bouquet, and a monolithic, fresh, lively, impressive amount of fruit for a wine in this price range. It will drink well for 3–5 years. Containing slightly less Syrah, the 1998 Côtes du Rhône Parallèle 45 exhibits sweet cherries in its ripe, peppery style, but the wine is essentially one-dimensional. Nevertheless, it is a competent effort that should drink well for 3–4 years. Another densely colored effort is the 2000 Côtes du Rhône-Villages. Copious aromas of road tar, truffles, black fruits, pepper, and *garrigue* are followed by a fleshy, friendly styled wine with low acidity as well as abundant fruit. The 1999 and 1998 Côtes du Rhône-Villages are firmer, more tannic, and not as enjoyable, although the 1998 has more stuffing than the 1999.

Jaboulet did not produce a 1999 Vacqueyras, but 2000 is a top-notch vintage for this southern Rhône village. The 2000 Vacqueyras exhibits classic Provençal characteristics of lavender, thyme, and rosemary intertwined with kirsch and currants. Fat, opulent, medium-to full-bodied, and peppery, this gorgeous Vacqueyras may merit an outstanding score. Drink it over the next 4–5 years. The sensual 1998 Vacqueyras possesses admirable quantities of black cherry and kirsch-like fruit, medium to full body, nicely integrated tannin, and sweet glycerin on the mid-palate.

While it does not have the power and muscle of the 2000 Vacqueyras, the 2000 Gigondas Pierre Aiguille reveals more minerality, a balanced mouth-feel, and a sense of elegance. Significantly richer and more concentrated than the 1999 (which merited a score in the low 80s), it will drink well for 5–10 years. The dark plum-colored 1998 Gigondas Pierre Aiguille reveals a sweet entry on the palate, good flesh, medium to full body, and overall is more typical of what Gigondas represents. It should drink well for 6–7 years.

In a vintage that produced many sumptuous Châteauneufs of great richness and purity, the Jaboulet's 2000 Châteauneuf-du-Pape is merely a pleasant, light- to medium-bodied wine that lacks depth as well as richness. It will be hard-pressed to merit an 80-point score when bottled. The Jaboulets did not produce a 1999 Châteauneuf-du-Pape because they did not like the quality. The 1998 Châteauneuf-du-Pape (a blend of 80% Grenache and the rest

Syrah and Cinsault) exhibits an evolved dark plum/garnet color, soft, ripe berry and kirsch notes, good pepper and spice, medium to full body, and a straightforward, easygoing finish. It should drink well for 7–8 years.

The least expensive Crozes-Hermitage red and the lightest Crozes-Hermitage *cuvée* is Les Jalets. The 2000 is a smoky, easygoing effort revealing scents of crushed cherries, pepper, and herbs. It is best drunk over its first 2–3 years of life. The 1999 Crozes-Hermitage Les Jalets exhibits good cherry and currant fruit along with a peppery herbaceousness. Although fruity and attractive, it is essentially superficial. Drink it over the next 4–5 years. Jaboulet's Crozes-Hermitage Thalabert used to be the finest wine of the appellation, but that is no longer the case. Anyone who has tasted some of the great vintages of this wine (1990, 1978) knows it can provide sumptuous drinking for 15+ years. The 1998 Crozes-Hermitage Les Jalets is a vegetal, undernourished effort that requires drinking over the next 2–4 years.

The soft, low-acid, innocuous 2000 St.-Joseph Le Grand Pompée is pleasant in a superficial manner. It is best drunk over the next 3–4 years. The slightly more acidic, delineated, and deeper 1999 St.-Joseph Le Grand Pompée exhibits aromas of cherries, plums, and liquid minerals. With a good, spicy, peppery nose, excellent freshness, and a medium-bodied finish, it should drink well for 7–8 years. The dark ruby-colored 1998 St.-Joseph Le Grand Pompée offers mineral, black cherry, and berry fruit notes, low acidity, and a creamy texture. Drink this medium-bodied, refreshing St.-Joseph over the next 4–5 years.

Shrewd purchasers have no doubt long found the Crozes-Hermitage Thalabert to be one of the finest Jaboulet offerings in terms of its quality/price rapport. I have been buying the better vintages of this wine for 20 years, and it is always a solidly made, mini-Hermitage that drinks exceptionally well for 10–15 years. The 2000 Crozes-Hermitage Thalabert is one of the better wines I tasted at Jaboulet, and it appears to be just as good as their flagship offering, Hermitage La Chapelle. That doesn't make sense, but taste is everything. The Thalabert offers a deep ruby/purple color as well as round, opulent flavors, low acidity, and a seductive, up-front style that begs to be drunk during its first 8–10 years of life. It is sexy, with plenty of black fruits intermixed with pepper, herbs, and incense. Also excellent, the 1999 Crozes-Hermitage Thalabert is a complex, perfumed effort with less fat than the 2000, but good spice and ripeness, medium body, and firm, underlying acidity. It needs another 1–2 years of cellaring and should last for 10–14 years. The 1998 Crozes-Hermitage Thalabert has closed down, revealing austere, herbal notes.

Another impressive offering from Crozes-Hermitage is Jaboulet's Crozes-Hermitage Raymond Roure. 1,000 cases were produced of this fabulous wine, which was aged nearly 2 years in wood. Jacques Jaboulet claims the 2000 Crozes-Hermitage Raymond Roure is the best he has ever made. Potentially outstanding, it is one of the finest 2000s I tasted from this appellation. Its deep ruby/purple color is followed by explosive aromas of jammy black fruits, licorice, truffles, *herbes de Provence,* and minerals. Lush, round, and layered, with surprising depth and intensity, it will drink well for 10–12 years. For whatever reason, the 1999 Crozes-Hermitage Raymond Roure is good, but uninspiring. Herbaceous notes along with notions of old saddle leather and vague cherry/currant fruit are found in this soft, medium-bodied effort. It lacks the depth and ripeness expected from this potentially stunning vintage. Consume it during its first 5–7 years of life. From barrel, the 1998 Crozes-Hermitage Raymond Roure was impressive. Now that it is in bottle, it appears tough-textured, lean, tannic, closed, and uninteresting. I either blundered with my first tasting from barrel, or this wine is in complete hiding at present.

Cornas has never been one of Jaboulet's strong points, but they now produce two *cuvées,* the regular Cornas and Cornas Domaine St.-Pierre. The unimpressive 2000 Cornas is a superficial, hollow effort with no mid-palate, tart acidity, and dry, abrasive tannin in the finish. The 1999 Cornas is even worse. Again, it looked impressive prior to bottling, but has turned out mediocre, with high acidity, little ripeness, and a washed out, eviscerated mid-palate as well as finish. What happened? The 1998 Cornas does not reveal the herbaceousness I noted during its *élevage*. However, it possesses more acidity as well as a monolithic, dull character in addition to a hard finish.

The 2000 Cornas Domaine St.-Pierre is quite good. Its dark ruby color is followed by a generous attack, but leanness dominates. There is good purity and elegance, but surprisingly high acidity, particularly for this low-acid vintage. Drink it during its first 8–10 years of life. Another outstanding effort prior to bottling, the 1999 Cornas Domaine St.-Pierre is lean, medium-bodied, and closed, with little stuffing, density, or muscle. It is an emaciated example that has not survived the *mise en bouteilles*. Although it will last for 10–12 years, it will not provide much pleasure. The saturated dark purple-colored 1998 Cornas Domaine St.-Pierre offers sweet black fruits, earth, minerals, smoke, and new saddle leather in its aromas and flavors. Softer than the 1999, with full body, outstanding concentration, and fine overall balance, it should drink well for 15 years.

I have never been a great fan of Jaboulet's Côte Rôtie Les Jumelles. It can be very good, sometimes outstanding (1961 and 1959), but is generally a solid effort with high acidity. One of the major disappointments at this estate continues to be their Côte Rôtie Les Jumelles. The 2000 is unacceptable. It is a hollow, thin, acidic offering with a medium dark ruby color, underripe characteristics, and an attenuated, lean, austere finish. Even more disappointing is the 1999 Côte Rôtie Les Jumelles, which exhibited outstanding potential prior to bottling. Out of bottle, the dark ruby color remains, but there is a leanness with a sense of dilution, faint cherry and currant flavors, a distinct, overt herbaceousness, and astringent tannin. The wine's finish is virtually non-existent. This is a perplexing and distressing wine in what is a great vintage for Côte Rôtie. While good, the 1998 Côte Rôtie Les Jumelles*, which winemaker Jacques Jaboulet calls "completely Burgundian," is problematic because it was bottled at two different times. I rated the first bottling 87, but the second bottling was far more herbaceous and dried out.

For a number of years, the Jaboulets have been bottling their younger vines and lighter *cuvées* of Hermitage under the label Hermitage Pied de la Côte. This wine generally has more in common with a Crozes-Hermitage than a serious Hermitage. Both the 2000 and 1999 Hermitage Pied de la Côte are open-knit, herbaceous, medium-bodied, and superficially attractive. While they reveal some Hermitage character, they are essentially soft and fluid. The 2000 possesses round, easygoing, user-friendly flavors, but minimal depth. The same can be said for the 1999, which has a distinct herbaceous note running through the aromatics and flavors. Both wines are best consumed during their first 7–8 years of life. The 1998 Hermitage Pied de la Côte is acidic, tannic, hollow, and herbal.

The performance of recent vintages of Jaboulet's Hermitage La Chapelle has been a major disappointment. I have been increasingly disappointed with the performance of the 1998 from bottle (I rated it 90? during its *élevage*, but in two recent tastings it performed in the mid-80s). The 1999 Hermitage La Chapelle, which seems to have far less to it in bottle than it did previously, and the uninspiring 2000 are next in line. The 1997 and 1996 La Chapelles are topflight, although totally contrasting styles. However, the last profound La Chapelles are 1990 and 1989. The 2000 Hermitage La Chapelle, which the Jaboulets compare to 1988 and 1982, is an open, soft, fragrant effort, but relatively light (and this is before bottling). It offers sweet, jammy currant and cherry notes intermixed with spice, pepper, and minerals. Soft, with a superficial style, it begs the question . . . where are the multiple layers, texture, and intensity of flavor on the mid-palate and finish? Drink it during its first 12–14 years of life. As for the 1999 Hermitage La Chapelle, this is a mid-weight, elegant, dark ruby-colored effort that lacks color saturation. It exhibits moderately intense cassis flavors intermixed with minerals, a touch of pepper, and herbs. The finish is decidedly watery as well as light. It needs 2–3 years of cellaring and should last for 12–15, but given the fact that Jaboulet's Hermitage La Chapelle has a 50-year track record as one of the world's greatest wines, this is a disappointment. The outstanding, elegant 1998 Hermitage La Chapelle's dark plum/purple color is followed by scents of new saddle leather, black currants, blackberries, and underbrush. In the mouth, the wine reveals sweet tannin, medium to full body, excellent depth, and an intriguing smokiness. It displays slightly lower acidity than the 1999. While not one of the great La Chapelles, it represents a modern day example of the 1991 or 1988. The 1997 Hermitage La Chapelle competes with the monumental wines made in 1990, 1978, and 1961. The harvest was completed on October 14, with some *cuvées* achieving 14.5% natural alcohol (the alcohol level in the final blend is 13.5%). The wine looks impressive, with a viscosity and unctuous richness. There is amazing fat and chewiness, as well as spectacular aromatics of overripe black currants and blackberries intermingled with barbecue spices, soy, and jammy black fruits. The tannin seems lost in the wine's full-bodied, silky-textured, voluptuously rich, staggeringly concentrated style. The mid-palate explodes with sweetness, glycerin, and extract. The finish lasts for 40+ seconds. The 1997 should be remarkably approachable given its opulence, although, like the 1990, it will firm up and close down. The wine was scheduled to be bottled without filtration in February 1998, and released in late 1999. It is undoubtedly a mind-blowing Hermitage La Chapelle. Anticipated maturity: 2004–2035.

The Jaboulet white wines have increased significantly in quality over the last decade. The 2000 white wine *cuvées* are soft, fruity, agreeable offerings. The 2000 Crozes-Hermitage Raymond Roure Blanc is a citrusy, mineral-laden, medium-bodied effort displaying notes of glue and fino sherry. Drink it over the next 2–3 years. The 1999 and 1998 Crozes-Hermitage Raymond Roure Blanc (100% Marsanne) are both chewy, straightforward, fruity, medium-bodied efforts. Both the 1999 and 1998 St.-Joseph Le Grand Pompée Blanc offer notes of citrus, pear, and minerals, with the 1999 revealing slightly more weight. The 1999 and 1998 Crozes-Hermitage La Mule Blanche (blends of equal parts Roussanne and Marsanne) are two of the better values in the Jaboulet portfolio. The elegant 1999 offers good honeyed citrus fruit, whereas the 1998 is richer and deeper, with plenty of candied citrus, medium body, and good freshness. The good, elegant 2000 Condrieu offers a classic combination of honeysuckle and apricot/peach-like fruit. It is best drunk over the next year. The straightforward 1999 Condrieu is lighter, with adequate concentration and purity, but little length. Both Condrieus require drinking over the next year.

The most interesting and ageworthy of these whites is the Hermitage Chevalier de Stérimberg, a blend of 50% Roussanne and 50% Marsanne, that is encouraged to go through malolactic fermentation. The finest of the 2000 whites is the 2000 Hermitage Chevalier de Stérimberg, a barrel-fermented blend of 66% Marsanne and 34% Roussanne. With great texture, super ripeness, a light gold color, and abundant power, concentration, and depth, it is one of the most profound wines Jaboulet has produced over recent vintages. It will easily equal the 1998. Needless to say, the gregarious Jacques Jaboulet claims it is "the best since 1964." The 1999 Hermitage Chevalier de Stérimberg reveals notes of tropical fruits, honey, spice, and nuts. Although tight, it is medium- to full-bodied, dense, and impressive. It should last for 12–15 years. The fatter 1998 Hermitage Chevalier de Stérimberg reveals terrific texture, a big, full-bodied, powerhouse style, and exceptional purity and concentration. The wine is drinkable at present, but it will undoubtedly close down in 3–4 years, not to reemerge for a decade. Made in the same style as the 1996, the 1997 Hermitage Chevalier de Stérimberg is a bigger, richer, fuller wine with massive honeyed characteristics, a white Burgundy–like texture, and an impressive 14% natural alcohol. Nevertheless, there is enough acidity to provide clarity and freshness in this superbly rendered, full-bodied, unctuously thick wine. The spectacular 1996 Hermitage Chevalier de Stérimberg (33% Roussanne and 67% Marsanne) has been 100% barrel-fermented, put through 100% malolactic fermentation, and aged in 100% new oak. However, the oak is completely submerged beneath the wine's extraordinary rose petal, apricot, nutty, and peach-like richness. The wine displays huge quantities of glycerin, a sensational texture, and terrific purity and depth. This spectacular offering is capable of lasting for 10–20+ years.

Much like Vidal Fleury in the village of Ampuis, the Jaboulets have long produced one of the top *cuvées* of Beaumes-de-Venise. The rich, fat, honeyed, fragrant (apricot and peach) 2000 Muscat de Beaumes-de-Venise is an impressive offering that requires consumption during its first year of life. In 1999, they produced two *cuvées*. The beautiful 1999 Muscat de Beaumes-de-Venise offers abundant quantities of tangerine, buttery apricot and honeyed fruit, full body, an unctuous texture, and moderate sweetness. It should be consumed over the next several years. More complex and multidimensional, the 1999 Muscat de Beaumes-de-Venise Réserve Spéciale is less syrupy, with more floral, mineral-like notes, exquisite perfume, and a rich, full-bodied palate. It should drink well for 1–2 years.

Everyone goes through slumps, and given this firm's incredible track record, I am sure they will pull out of it. For everyone who loves Rhône wines and has been an admirer of Jaboulet, let's hope it comes quickly.

Past Glories: Hermitage La Chapelle—1996 (92), 1991 (91), 1990 (100), 1989 (96), 1985 (90), 1983 (90?), 1982 (91), 1979 (92), 1978 (100), 1972 (93), 1971 (96), 1970 (95), 1966 (94), 1961 (100), 1959 (98)

JEAN-PAUL ET JEAN-LUC JAMET

2000 Côte Rôtie	E	(90–91)
1999 Côte Rôtie	E	96
1998 Côte Rôtie	E	92+
1997 Côte Rôtie	E	(91–94)

This estate has been one of the most consistent small producers of Côte Rôtie over the last decade. Aside from a disappointing 1993, the Jamets have fashioned super wines in 1997, 1996, 1995, 1991, 1989, and 1988. Aged for nearly two years in a combination of small barrels and larger *foudres*, the wines are bottled without fining or filtration. I asked Jean-Luc Jamet when the best time to drink their wines was, and he surprised me by saying, "Between 8–12 years of age." I have found Jamet's dense, powerful vintages to only begin to evolve and open at age 10 (i.e., the 1988 and probably the 1991 as well).

One of the finest efforts of the vintage, the 2000 Côte Rôtie exhibits surprising power and fullness. A deep ruby/purple color is followed by notes of cassis, blackberries, smoke, underbrush, herbs, and tar. It is deep, chewy, and atypically refined for a young Jamet Côte Rôtie. With its low acidity and fine ripeness, this 2000 will be delicious upon release and drink well for 10–12 years. The profound 1999 Côte Rôtie is the finest I have ever tasted from Jamet. It is even better from bottle than it was from cask. There are 25,000 bottles of this saturated ruby/purple-colored effort. It possesses a striking perfume of roasted meats, violets, graphite, blackberries, raspberries, and cherry liqueur. Smoky, intense, full-bodied, muscular, concentrated, layered, and dominated by ripe fruit, with the tannin well hidden by the wealth of extract, glycerin, and fruit, it will be at its finest between 2004–2020.

The 1998 Côte Rôtie, a modern day clone of his brilliant, powerful 1988, exhibits a deep, opaque plum/garnet color and a smoky, fried meat, blackberry/cassis-scented bouquet with notions of earth and licorice. A classically proportioned effort, with full body, superb ripeness, high tannin, and layers of concentration and extract, this is not a Côte Rôtie for those unable to defer their gratification. It needs time in the bottle. Anticipated maturity: 2005–2018.

In 1997, the Jamets were the last to finish harvesting; a fact that shows in the 1997 Côte Rôtie, which possesses elements of *sur-maturité* and phenomenal ripeness. The color is an opaque saturated purple (one of the most intensely colored wines of the vintage). The spectacular aromatics consist of framboise, bacon fat, leather, coffee, pepper, and Asian spices. Full-bodied, with massive fruit saturation, this monster Côte Rôtie is one of the most concentrated and richest wines of 1997. Its low acidity and explosive, flamboyant style argue in favor of early maturity, but it will unquestionably keep for 10–12+ years.

Past Glories: 1995 (92+), 1991 (94), 1989 (92), 1988 (95), 1985 (90)

DOMAINE DE LA JANASSE

2000	Châteauneuf-du-Pape Cuvée Chaupin	D	(92–94)
1999	Châteauneuf-du-Pape Cuvée Chaupin	D	91
1998	Châteauneuf-du-Pape Cuvée Chaupin	D	93
1997	Châteauneuf-du-Pape Cuvée Chaupin	D	88
2000	Châteauneuf-du-Pape Cuvée Classique	D	(90–91)
1999	Châteauneuf-du-Pape Cuvée Classique	D	89
1998	Châteauneuf-du-Pape Cuvée Classique	D	89
1997	Châteauneuf-du-Pape Cuvée Classique	D	87
2000	Châteauneuf-du-Pape Cuvée Vieilles Vignes	E	(92–95)
1999	Châteauneuf-du-Pape Cuvée Vieilles Vignes	E	92+
1998	Châteauneuf-du-Pape Cuvée Vieilles Vignes	E	95+
1997	Châteauneuf-du-Pape Cuvée Vieilles Vignes	E	89
2000	Côtes du Rhône	A	(87–89)
2000	Côtes du Rhône Les Garrigues	A	(87–89)
1998	Côtes du Rhône Les Garrigues	A	89
2000	Côtes du Rhône-Villages	A	(90–91)
1998	Côtes du Rhône-Villages	A	88
1999	VDP d'Orange (Merlot/Syrah)	A	87

This is a dynamically run property with a young wine-maker, Christophe Sabon, turning out sumptuous Châteauneuf-du-Papes, delicious, value-priced Côtes du Rhônes, and a delicious *vin de pays* from a blend of Syrah and Merlot. Sabon is only in his early thirties, which suggests he has another 30+ years of winemaking in him—great news for wine consumers. In past years I have touted his remarkable blend of equal parts Merlot and Syrah, and his VDP d'Orange is generally a fruit-driven, gorgeous effort that can be purchased for a song.

The 2000 Châteauneuf-du-Papes, which can rival Sabon's finest wines to date, the 1998s, possess extraordinary ripeness, voluptuous textures, and seamless, long finishes. The 2000 Châteauneuf-du-Pape Cuvée Classique exhibits a layered, succulent personality, gobs of fruit, admirable purity, and a knockout finish. It would be hard to find another $25 wine this ageworthy, complex, and satisfying. Drink it over the next 12–15 years. The sensual 2000 Châteauneuf-du-Pape Cuvée Chaupin boasts a black raspberry/kirsch-scented perfume, a marvelous texture, fine sweetness (because of high glycerin), low acidity, and a flawless, 40+-second finish. This big wine is light on its feet and super-concentrated. It should drink well for 15+ years. Lastly, the opaque purple-colored 2000 Châteauneuf-du-Pape Cuvée Vieilles Vignes is a southern Rhône masterpiece. While not as accessible as its siblings, it displays uncanny purity, remarkable delineation for a wine of such mass and density, and a multidimensional personality. There are abundant quantities of black fruits as well as more definition, minerality, and notions of licorice and flowers. Because of its formidable concentration of power and tannin, patience will be required. Anticipated maturity: 2005–2020.

The 1999s are also delicious, so readers can't go wrong with recent vintages from this talented producer. The beautifully made 1999 Châteauneuf-du-Pape Cuvée Classique exhibits an opaque ruby/purple color as well as a sweet nose of black cherries, a layered texture, supple tannin, and a ripe, long, full-bodied finish with outstanding purity. Drink it over the next 10–12 years. The 1999 Châteauneuf-du-Pape Cuvée Chaupin's dense ruby/purple color is accompanied by a big, sweet bouquet of blackberries, cassis, and a hint of kirsch. This sexy, full-bodied, opulent 1999 combines fat and flesh with a sense of elegance, purity, and delineation. Already delicious, it will last for 12–15 years. The floral-scented, structured, backward, powerful 1999 Châteauneuf-du-Pape Cuvée Vieilles Vignes boasts a dense purple color. Gorgeously rich flavors on the attack are followed by a powerful, muscular, long wine requiring 2–3 years of cellaring; it should age for two decades. The bottled 1998s confirm the greatness of this vintage for Christophe Sabon.

The 1998 Châteauneuf-du-Pape Cuvée Classique is an excellent wine, but in the company of its siblings, it gets blown away. However, it is not to be ignored. It possesses a dark ruby/plum color as well as a rich, sweet nose of black fruits, roasted meat, spice, and pepper. There is more grip, fat, and tannin than in its 1999 counterpart, but it can be drunk now and over the next 10–12 years. It is an excellent, possibly outstanding Châteauneuf-du-Pape. The 1998 Châteauneuf-du-Pape Cuvée Chaupin (14.5% alcohol) is a voluptuous, opulently textured, blockbuster with terrific fruit purity and gorgeous aromas of roasted herbs, kirsch, blackberries, and Asian spices. The palate impression is one of sweetness because of the wine's high glycerin and ripe, jammy fruit. The chewy, long finish lasts for 40+ seconds. It can be drunk now, but readers should save a bottle for drinking in about a decade. Anticipated maturity: now–2018. The 1998 Châteauneuf-du-Pape Cuvée Vieilles Vignes is another exquisite effort that rivals some of the finest Châteauneuf-du-Papes made in the last decade. It boasts fabulous intensity, explosive aromatics and depth, more tannin and structure than its siblings, and a seemingly more impenetrable mid-palate. However, the wine has huge weight, superb concentration, and much of the character of the Cuvée Chaupin, yet it is simply bigger, thicker, denser, and more tannic. It requires 4–5 years of cellaring and should keep well for two decades or more.

A late spring freeze as well as hail significantly reduced Domaine de la Janasse's 1997 production. The saturated dark ruby-colored 1997 Châteauneuf-du-Pape Cuvée Classique exhibits the telltale cherry, kirsch, and peppery-scented nose, full body, admirable ripeness and purity, and a low-acid, heady, precocious style. It should drink well for 5 years. The 1997 Châteauneuf-du-Pape Cuvée Chaupin possesses greater color saturation (dark ruby/purple), as well as a heady, black raspberry and cherry jam–scented nose with pepper, allspice, and fruitcake-like aromas and flavors. Voluptuously textured and lush, with a marvelous combination of red and black fruits intermixed with Provençal herbs, this tasty, nicely layered, supple Châteauneuf-du-Pape should continue to drink well for 5 years. The outstanding 1997 Châteauneuf-du-Pape Cuvée Vieilles Vignes displays an impressively saturated dark ruby/purple color. The wine is more reserved aromatically, with scents of incense, licorice, fennel, olives, and black raspberry liqueur. Notes of cherries and blackberries make an appearance in the mouth. This offering possesses the highest levels of extract and glycerin, the fullest body, and the most power, muscle, and tannin. Nevertheless, it is precociously styled, and thus best consumed in its vigorous youth—over the next 7–8 years.

The estate is also a reliable source of value-priced Côtes du Rhône. The three 2000 Côtes du Rhônes all exhibit dense ruby/purple colors as well as gorgeous, hedonistic bouquets of cassis, raspberries, and cherry liqueur, supple textures, and abundant glycerin. There is little difference between the 2000 Côtes du Rhône and the 2000 Côtes du Rhône Les Garrigues except that the latter reveals more of the Provençal rosemary/thyme herb concoction in its aromatics. The outrageously sumptuous 2000 Côtes du Rhône-Villages is a splendid value. A full-bodied, superrich offering boasting copious cherry and blackberry fruit, it will provide immediate gratification and drink well for 3–5 years.

The 1999 VDP d'Orange is another fruit-driven, gorgeous effort that can be purchased for a song. It offers notes of orange rind, blackberry fruit, chocolate, and smoke in an uncomplicated but gorgeously plump, fat, juicy style. It will not make old bones, but who can resist drinking it over the next 2–3 years?

The nearly outstanding, rich 1998 Côtes du Rhône Les Garrigues possesses black cherry fruit flavors, medium body, excellent purity, and a long, nicely textured finish. The 1998 Côtes du Rhône-Villages is almost as good, similar in style, but not quite in fragrance.

PATRICK JASMIN

2000 Côte Rôtie	E	(87–88)
1999 Côte Rôtie	E	90
1998 Côte Rôtie	E	90

Regrettably, Robert Jasmin passed away recently, and his son Patrick has taken the estate in his hands. However, he was already involved in the winemaking over recent vintages as it is he who convinced his father to destem both in 1999 and 1998. Also, for the benefit of consumers, Patrick now does only two bottlings, as opposed to the multiple bottlings his father practiced. The elegant, lighter-styled 2000 Côte Rôtie reveals low acidity along with sweet, ripe, cherry, raspberry, and currant fruit intermixed with mineral and floral notes, soft tannin, medium body, and a flowery, lacy style. Drink this well-made 2000 over the next 7–8 years. The 1999 Côte Rôtie offers pretty flavors redolent with scents of black cherries, raspberries, plums, and cherries, with smoke, mineral, and paper white Narcissus notes in the background. It is medium-bodied, pure, supple-textured, and delicious. If it builds in the bottle, it will merit an even higher score. This is undoubtedly the finest Jasmin Côte Rôtie produced in over a decade. Anticipated maturity: now–2016.

The late Robert Jasmin's 1998 Côte Rôtie offers both finesse and concentration. In 1998, about one-third of the crop was lost due to a frost in late June, which has resulted in a finesse-filled, concentrated wine with Burgundy-like complexity and nuances. Aromas of black cherries, raspberries, and flowers emerge from this dark ruby-colored wine. In the mouth, it tastes like a grand cru from the Côtes de Beaune, exhibiting abundant quantities of black fruits, an underlying minerality, exceptional elegance, and good acidity. The oak is not obtrusive, and the fruit and delicacy dominate. Aged in both barrels and *demi-muids,* it should last for 10–15 years.

Past Glories: 1978 (95), 1976 (92)

LAFFOY ET GASSE

1997 Côte Rôtie	D	(84–86)
1997 Côte Rôtie Vieilles Vignes	E	(86–88+)

The wines from this estate, owned by Vincent Gasse and Marie-Claude Laffoy, are cultivated under the strict biological requirements of organic farming. The 1997 Côte Rôtie exhibits a dark ruby color, followed by sweet cherry/berry fruit in the nose, medium body, and surprisingly good acidity for the vintage. However, it comes across as one-dimensional and four-square, at least at this stage of its development. Drink it over the next 2–4 years. The 1997 Côte Rôtie Vieilles Vignes possesses more flavor dimension and aromatic complexity than its sibling. Its deep ruby color is accompanied by an herb-tinged nose with blackberry fruit intermixed with allspice, cranberries, cherries, cassis, and earth. Good ripeness, excellent definition, and a medium-bodied, nicely textured mouth-feel make for a very good to excellent Côte Rôtie. Anticipated maturity: now–2008.

JACQUES LEMENICIER

1999 Cornas	D	(84–86)
1998 Cornas	D	88

Two contrasting styles, Lemenicier's 1999 Cornas reveals this vintage's variableness in this appellation. High in acidity and lacking depth and concentration, this medium-bodied, compressed 1999 is best drunk during its first 7–8 years of life. In 1998, Lemenicier, who uses no new oak and destems 100% of his fruit, produced a more significant effort. The 1998 Cornas's complex bouquet of earth, truffles, cassis, and underbrush is followed by a sweet, medium- to full-bodied wine with low acidity, ripe tannin, and a complex, concentrated, velvety-textured finish. It should drink well for 8 years.

PATRICK LESEC RHÔNE VALLEY SELECTIONS

2000	Châteauneuf-du-Pape Aurore	E	(86–88)
1999	Châteauneuf-du-Pape Aurore	E	(87–88)
2000	Châteauneuf-du-Pape Les Galets Blonds	E	(91–93)
1999	Châteauneuf-du-Pape Les Galets Blonds	E	91
1998	Châteauneuf-du-Pape Les Galets Blonds	E	92
2000	Châteauneuf-du-Pape Les Galets Blonds-Tonneaux	E	(88–91)
2000	Châteauneuf-du-Pape Marquis	D	(89–91)
2000	Cornas Cuvée Sarah	E	(87–89)
1999	Cornas Cuvée Sarah	E	88
2000	Cornas Le Vignon	E	(90–91)
1999	Cornas Le Vignon	E	90
2000	Côtes du Rhône Aurore	B	89+
1999	Côtes du Rhône Aurore	B	89
2000	Côtes du Rhône Les Beaumes	B	(87–89)
2000	Côtes du Rhône Domaine de Pierredon	A	87
2000	Côtes du Rhône Pierrot	A	(84–86)
1999	Côtes du Rhône-Villages Cairanne Vieilles Vignes	B	87
1998	Côtes du Rhône-Villages Cairanne Vieilles Vignes	B	87
2000	Côtes du Rhône-Villages Perillière Vieilles Vignes	A	89
1999	Côtes du Rhône-Villages Perillière Vieilles Vignes	A	88
1999	Côtes du Rhône-Villages Rasteau Beaumistral Vieilles Vignes	B	(87–88)
1998	Côtes du Rhône-Villages Rasteau Beaumistral Vieilles Vignes	B	86
2000	Côtes du Rhône-Villages Rasteau Vieilles Vignes	B	(88–89+)
1999	Côtes du Rhône-Villages Rasteau Vieilles Vignes	B	85?
2000	Gigondas Les Blanches	C	(86–87)
2000	Gigondas Les Espalines-Les Tendrelles	C	(88–90)
1999	Gigondas Les Espalines-Les Tendrelles	C	(90–92)
1998	Gigondas Les Espalines-Les Tendrelles	C	89

The following wines are selections of French wine broker Patrick Lesec. He sources top-quality estates (sometimes a cooperative also) with extremely old vines, and hand-selects a blend that is then given a cutting edge treatment for making unmanipulated, natural wines. That includes low levels of SO_2, minimal or no racking until bottling, and neither fining nor filtration. Quantities of these *cuvées* range from about 200 cases to nearly 1,000. Although Lesec has only been doing this for a few years, quality is impeccably high and these wines are well worth searching out as authentic examples of their southern Rhône appellations. Everything in Lesec's portfolio is, at the minimum, above average.

The least expensive offerings are Lesec's selections from a cooperative south of Avignon. They are all tank-fermented and -aged efforts that emphasize ripe, concentrated fruit.

The excellent 2000 Côtes du Rhône Domaine de Pierredon (the largest *cuvée* at 6,500 cases) is a blend of equal parts Grenache, Mourvèdre, and Syrah. The dense ruby/purple color is followed by abundant amounts of unencumbered blackberry and cherry fruit. Drink this delicious, pure, exceptional value over the next 12–18 months. A blend of equal parts Grenache and Syrah, the dark ruby/purple-colored 2000 Côtes du Rhône-Villages Perillière Vieilles Vignes is dominated by black fruits. Succulent, ripe, and impressive, this medium- to full-bodied, low-acid wine is a total turn-on. Enjoy this fruit bomb over the next 2 years. Another promising, value-priced offering, the 2000 Côtes du Rhône Les Beaumes (a blend of 70% Grenache and 30% Syrah) was about to be bottled when I saw the wine. It possesses a deep ruby/purple color, a sexy, layered texture, and notes of pepper, kirsch, framboise, and *garrigue* (that earthy, Provençal herb combination). A bigger wine than its two siblings, it will drink well for 2–3 years. The 2000 Côtes du Rhône Pierrot, a blend of 60% Grenache and the rest Carignan, Mourvèdre, and Syrah, had not been bottled at the time of my visit, and it appeared rustic and hard. If the fruit becomes more dominating, and the tannin less intrusive, it should develop into a mid-80-point or higher wine. A more expensive Côtes du Rhône is the 2000 Aurore (1,500 cases produced). Made primarily from old-vine Grenache (95%), from a vineyard abutting Châteauneuf-du-Pape, this exceptional effort is further evidence of the amazing bargains that exist in this section of France. It could easily pass for a Châteauneuf-du-Pape. Aromas of kirsch, *garrigue*, meat, and licorice are followed by a seriously endowed, supple-textured Côtes du Rhône with a surprisingly long finish. Consume it over the next 5–6 years.

Patrick Lesec has begun to offer high-quality selections culled from such well-known Côtes du Rhône-Villages as Cairanne and Rasteau as well as the appellation of Vacqueyras. Lesec's ability to search out fine Châteauneuf-du-Pape is particularly impressive. A good effort, the 2000 Côtes du Rhône-Villages Rasteau Vieilles Vignes benefited from the vintage's lower acidity, sweeter tannin, and jammy fruit. Its saturated ruby/purple color is followed by a perfume of licorice, chocolate, and blackberries, and a jammy, lusty mouth-feel. It should age handsomely for 5–6 years. The 2000 Châteauneuf-du-Pape Les Galets Blonds-Tonneaux (a micro *cuvée* of 1,000 bottles) reveals more rigidity as well as *barrique* influence. Because of that, it tastes slightly less typical. Otherwise, it is similar to the non-barrel-aged Les Galets Blonds. Anticipated maturity: now–2012. Patrick Lesec's newest *cuvée*, the 2000 Châteauneuf-du-Pape Marquis is a 3,000-case blend of 90% Grenache and 10% Syrah. Its medium dark ruby color is followed by a jammy bouquet of strawberries, black cherries, pepper, and resin aromas. Full-bodied and richly fruity, with admirable sweetness (from glycerin), it will drink well for 7–8 years. Strong herbaceous characteristics in the 2000 Châteauneuf-du-Pape Aurore kept my score down. Otherwise, this 400-case exhibits classic aromas of kirsch, pepper, and *garrigue*. Medium- to full-bodied, with moderate tannin and a powerful finish, it should drink well for 8–10 years. The 1999 Châteauneuf-du-Pape Aurore comes from the same estate where Lesec is making the Côtes du Rhône Aurore. Essentially all Grenache, this is a soft, open-knit, medium- to full-bodied Châteauneuf with oodles of black cherry fruit, a forward, precocious texture, and a silky finish. It is meant to be drunk during its first 7–8 years of life. Formerly, the Cornas offerings were listed under the name Michel Perraud, but that is the brand name created by Patrick Lesec. Now he is putting his name on the label so there can be no confusion. Whatever the name, they are gorgeous efforts. Made in a Burgundy-like fashion, they experience a five-day cold soak, low sulphur levels, no rackings, and bottling with neither fining nor filtration. From an appellation with numerous underachievers, it is remarkable that an outsider (from Paris by way of Santa Barbara) can produce Cornas with such richness, complexity, and appellation authenticity.

In 2000, the Cornas wines have less stuffing than their 1999 counterparts, but are certainly successful. The 2000 Cornas Cuvée Sarah exhibits a deep saturated ruby/purple color as well as aromas of sweet black fruits, licorice, asphalt, minerals, and smoke. Medium-bodied, with sweet tannin and lower acidity than the 1999, it will drink well during its first decade of life. Once again the 2000 Cornas Le Vignon displays more liquid minerality along with a dry vintage portlike character and plenty of overripe plum, blackberry, fig, and black currant fruit intermixed with leather and smoke. Although not as rich as the 1999 Le Vignon, it is an impressive effort with superb ripeness, a multilayered texture, and well-integrated acidity and tannin. It should drink well for 12–15 years.

The 1999 Cornas Cuvée Sarah comes from 80-year-old vines from the sector called Les Chaillets. Its plum/purple color is followed by a big, thick, juicy nose offering scents of asphalt, blackberries, and cassis. Relatively civilized and refined for Cornas, with ripe tannin, 80% new oak was used for this *cuvée* and it was aged with no racking, *sur-lie*, for 15 months prior to bottling. Anticipated maturity: now–2012. The prodigious 1999 Cornas Le Vignon is one of the finest wines of the vintage. Made from 80-year-old vines, it exhibits more minerality in its superb blackberry and cassis-scented bouquet. There are also hints of violets, new saddle leather, and truffles. Remarkably, 79% stems were used in fermentation, something that is not detectable in the aromatics or flavors, but contributes considerably to the wine's definition and grip. This large-scaled, massive Cornas captures a style between the traditional behemoths of the past and the more polished, *barrique*-aged Cornas of the future. Anticipated maturity: now–2016.

Lesec produces some excellent *cuvées* from the southern Rhône's most famous red wine appellations, Gigondas and Châteauneuf-du-Pape. The 2000 Gigondas Les Blanches (90% Grenache and 10% Mourvèdre which sees no oak) possesses a deep ruby color, a bouquet of autumnal leaves and damp forest scents, rough tannin, and cherry/black currant fruit. It is a traditional, rustic effort with tough tannin. A better offering is the 2000 Gigondas Les Espalines-Les Tendrelles, a blend of 70% Grenache and 30% Mourvèdre which sees approximately 30% new oak. This attractive Gigondas exhibits full-bodied, attractive flavors dominated by black cherry fruit. Although not complex, it will provide a pleasant mouthful of wine over the next decade. The 1999 Gigondas Les Espalines-Les Tendrelles (750 cases) appears to be even better, with silkier tannin, riper, more concentrated, jammy fruit, elevated glycerin, and a full-bodied, dense, silky finish. It should drink well for 10–12 years. The 1998 Gigondas Les Espalines-Les Tendrelles (500 cases) offers a dark purple color as well as a dense constitution with aromas and flavors of new oak, plums, cherries, and tree bark. Full-bodied, deep, and moderately tannic, it will be at its best between now–2012.

The deep ruby-colored 1999 Côtes du Rhône-Villages Cairanne Vieilles Vignes (60% Grenache and the rest Syrah, Carignan, and Mourvèdre) reveals notes of lavender, pepper, and cherries, as well as rustic tannin in the austere finish. Drink it over the next 3–4 years. The 1999 Côtes du Rhône-Villages Rasteau Beaumistral Vieilles Vignes tasted closed, but it did reveal rude tannin, chocolaty, cherry-infused fruit, and medium body. I am not convinced the tannin will ever age out. The 1999 Côtes du Rhône Domaine de Pierredon (a blend of equal parts Grenache, Syrah, and Mourvèdre) reveals notes of underbrush, black cherries, and cassis, a soft, plump texture with astonishing richness for a wine of this price range, decent acidity, and a nicely textured, ripe, heady finish. It was vinified and aged with virtually no SO$_2$ adjustments. Drink it over the next 2–3 years. The 1999 Côtes du Rhône-Villages Perillière Vieilles Vignes (an equal blend of Grenache and Syrah) is fat, with abundant quantities of sweet, low-acid, blackberry fruit, high glycerin, and a chewy, fruity impact on the palate. It fills the mouth, offering a plump, hedonistic impression. Drink it over the next 2–3 years. The 1999 Côtes du Rhône Aurore, from 80-year-old Grenache vines (95%) and Syrah (5%), all kept in tank and bottled without fining or filtration, is a terrific expression of Grenache. A dark ruby color is followed by a wine reminiscent of a big, lusty, full-bodied Châteauneuf-du-Pape. Intense, pure notes of kirsch, spice, and pepper are followed by a surprisingly rich wine exhibiting raspberry flavors on the palate. The wine's low acidity, high glycerin levels, and decadent personality suggest drinking it over the next 2–3 years, but I would not be surprised to see it last even longer. This is a wine to buy by the case!

Patrick Lesec is also working with Domaine Beau Mistral in Rasteau (Kermit Lynch is there as well). The 1999 Côtes du Rhône-Villages Rasteau Beaumistral Vieilles Vignes exhibits better integration of tannin as well as the same scorched earth, chocolate, black cherry, and plum aromas, medium to full body, and impressive color saturation and length. It should drink well for 7–8 years.

The 1998 Côtes du Rhône-Villages Rasteau Beaumistral Vieilles Vignes (a blend of 60% Grenache, 25% Syrah, and 15% Mourvèdre) is a rustic effort, offering chunky, chocolaty, scorched earth flavors, black cherry and plum notes, and high tannin in the finish. While it possesses an uncivilized character, it is big, substantial, and mouth-filling. Drink it over the next 3–5 years. Another fine offering is the 1998 Côtes du Rhône-Villages Cairanne Vieilles Vignes, a blend of 70% Grenache, 10% Counoise, 10% Syrah, and 10% Mourvèdre aged in tank. It offers more structure than some of its siblings, with an underlying resiny, balsam wood character to the fat, chewy, kirsch- and herb-tinged fruit. Rich, medium- to full-bodied, and exuberant/robust, it will drink well for 5–6 years.

The finest Châteauneuf-du-Pape is Les Galets Blonds, an old-vine *cuvée* produced from 93% Grenache and 7% Syrah from the famed La Crau sector of Châteauneuf-du-Pape. The 2000 Châteauneuf-du-Pape Les Galets Blonds possesses a mere 15% alcohol. It is a big, sweet, jammy offering with a saturated ruby/purple color, voluptuous flavors, full body, fabulous concentration of black fruits intermixed with dried herbs and scorched rocks, and an impressive glycerin level that gives the wine plenty of sweetness. This succulent, seamless, mouth-filling Châteauneuf will drink well during its first 12–14 years of life. Aged in both tank and old wood *foudre*, there are 600 cases of the exceptional 1999 Châteauneuf-du-Pape Les Galets Blonds, an impressive effort tipping the scales at a whopping 15.7% alcohol (none of which is detectable in either the aromatics or flavors). Its deep ruby/purple color is followed by a sweet nose of jammy black fruits intermixed with mineral, fruitcake, balsam, and herb scents. This dense, unctuously textured, layered Châteauneuf can be drunk now as well as over the next 12–15 years. The 1998 Châteauneuf-du-Pape Les Galets Blonds is fashioned from extremely old Grenache vines in La Crau, the sector of eastern Châteauneuf-du-Pape where some of the finest wines of the appellation emerge (Bonneau's Réserve des Célestins, Vieux-Télégraphe, and Font du Michelle for example). It is even more sensational from bottle than it was from *foudre*. Classic notes of new leather, dried Provençal herbs, kirsch, and smoke are intense and persistent. On the palate, the wine is full-bodied, with layers of glycerin and extract. The finish lasts for over 30 seconds. There is some tannin to shed, but the overall impression is of a large-scaled, concentrated, traditionally made Châteauneuf-du-Pape. Sadly, there are only 8,600 bottles of this blockbuster. Anticipated maturity: now–2020.

DOMAINE DE LONGUE TOQUE

2000 Gigondas	C	(90–92)
1999 Gigondas	C	90

This estate, which changed hands several years ago, had an impressive résumé based on the wines it produced in the late 1970s and 1980s, after which it went through a period of decline. These two offerings are undoubtedly the finest wines to emerge from Longue Toque in over a decade. My first tasting note on the 2000 Gigondas reads "yummy." An opaque ruby/purple color is accompanied by sweet, crème de cassis, jammy fruit–like notes, low acidity, and a fat, opulent, succulent style with terrific levels of glycerin as well as extract. This will be a hedonistic head-turner when released next year. Consume it during its first 10–12 years of life. The deep ruby/purple-colored 1999 Gigondas' intriguing perfume of violets, red currants, blackberries, and minerals is followed by excellent, sexy, medium- to full-bodied flavors redolent with floral-infused red and black fruits. This elegant, classy, complex, well-defined Gigondas can be enjoyed between now–2009.

DOMAINE DE MARCOUX

2000 Châteauneuf-du-Pape	D	(90–93)
1999 Châteauneuf-du-Pape	D	90
1998 Châteauneuf-du-Pape	D	90
2000 Châteauneuf-du-Pape Vieilles Vignes	EE	(93–95)
1999 Châteauneuf-du-Pape Vieilles Vignes	EE	91
1998 Châteauneuf-du-Pape Vieilles Vignes	EE	98

This bio-dynamically farmed vineyard has produced its three finest consecutive vintages in 2000, 1999, and 1998. Domaine de Marcoux's superb 1998s have been followed by strong 1999s and profound 2000s. The 2000 Châteauneuf-du-Pape boasts a fabulous floral-scented nose with the telltale blackberry liqueur notes typically found in this estate's wines. Full-bodied and jammy, with low acidity, a voluptuous texture, multiple layers of flavor, and a plump, fat, fleshy finish, it will drink well for 14–15 years. The compelling, plum/purple-colored 2000 Châteauneuf-du-Pape Vieilles Vignes possesses additional concentration and glycerin, as well as exceptional purity and distinctive blackberry, licorice, and floral components in both its aromas and flavors. It is akin to drinking liqueur of Châteauneuf-du-Pape. Anticipated maturity: now–2020.

The dark ruby-colored 1999 Châteauneuf-du-Pape offers a gorgeous perfume of licorice, cherry jam, spring flowers, and blackberries. Relatively evolved (typical for Châteauneuf from this vintage), with sweet fruit, multiple layers of flavor, and a long, seamless finish, this captivating, opulent 1999 can be enjoyed now and over the next 12–14 years. Even better is the 1999 Châteauneuf-du-Pape Vieilles Vignes. Its dark ruby color with notions of pink at the rim is followed by a striking bouquet of violets mixed with blackberry jam, licorice, and tapenade. This full-bodied, expansive, concentrated, spicy wine may not be as profound as the 1998, 1995, or 1990, but it is dazzling stuff. Anticipated maturity: now–2016.

The 1998s are unquestionably the finest wines produced by this domaine since 1990 and 1989. The 1998 Châteauneuf-du-Pape's peppery, plum, cherry liqueur, and cassis-scented nose is followed by opulent, long, open-knit flavors crammed with glycerin and alcohol. The high levels of richness and glycerin obscure much of the wine's structure and tannin. This sexy, voluptuously textured, creamy 1998 should drink gorgeously for 10–12+ years. The profound, dense ruby/purple-colored 1998 Châteauneuf-du-Pape Vieilles Vignes is all of the above, and more. The telltale blackberry liqueur aromas and flavors are present, as well as a formidable level of glycerine, admirable richness, and a soaring bouquet of black fruits, minerals, lavender, and exotic spices. The finish lasts 50+ seconds, and the wine's purity and multiple dimensions are staggering. This is a dazzling, full-throttle Châteauneuf-du-Pape that is unbelievably concentrated, unctuous, well balanced, and silky-textured. There is not a rough edge to be found. Anticipated maturity: now–2020.

Past Glories: Châteauneuf-du-Pape Vieilles Vignes—1995 (95), 1992 (93), 1990 (100), 1989 (100)

MAS DE BOIS LAUZON

2000	**Châteauneuf-du-Pape**	D	**(89–91)**
1999	**Châteauneuf-du-Pape**	D	**88**
1998	**Châteauneuf-du-Pape**	D	**90**
2000	**Châteauneuf-du-Pape Cuvée du Quet**	E	**(90–93)**
2000	**Côtes du Rhône-Villages**	A	**(86–87)**
1999	**Côtes du Rhône-Villages**	A	**86**

This reliable Châteauneuf-du-Pape producer fashions elegant yet substantially flavorful wines possessing both a seamlessness and immediate accessibility. The 2000 Châteauneuf-du-Pape is a hedonist's dream. Velvety textured, ripe, and explosively fruity, with loads of glycerin, a sweet kirsch-scented perfume, and a long, lusty finish, it will not make old bones given its low acidity as well as forward style, but for drinking over the next 10–12 years, it will be a crowd-pleaser. In 2000, proprietor Chaussy introduced a special *cuvée*. The 2000 Châteauneuf-du-Pape Cuvée du Quet is a broodingly backward, less open and charming effort than the regular *cuvée*. Its deeper, more powerful, concentrated black fruit, underbrush, pepper, and kirsch/blackberry characters are accompanied by more structure along with less accessibility. Abundant quantities of sweet tannin suggest 2–3 years of cellaring is warranted. Anticipated maturity: now–2018. A fine introduction to this estate's style, as well as a good value, the 2000 Côtes du Rhône-Villages is a crowd-pleasing, fruity offering dominated by pepper/cherry aromas as well as flavors. Medium-bodied and supple, it is best consumed over the next 1–3 years.

Revealing classic Provençal aromas of crushed pepper, dried herbs, new saddle leather, and black cherry liqueur, the supple 1999 Châteauneuf-du-Pape possesses excellent texture, medium to full body, and fine purity. Enjoy it during its first decade of life. Mas de Boislauzon's 1999 Côtes du Rhône-Villages is an exuberant, robust effort with plenty of peppery, dried herb, and black cherry fruit. Drink it over the next 2 years.

Daniel and Monique Chaussy's sexy 1998 Châteauneuf-du-Pape exhibits a deep ruby/purple color and a superbly pure nose of black cherry liqueur intermixed with raspberries, minerals, and spice. In the mouth, it is medium- to full-bodied, with an elegant, finesse-filled personality. Disarming, fleshy, with gorgeously pure fruit and beautiful symmetry, this well-endowed Châteauneuf-du-Pape will seduce tasters, yet it has excellent structure as well as sufficient tannin to evolve for 12 years.

MAS DE GOURGONNIER

1999 Les Baux	C	91
1999 Réserve du Mas Les Baux	C	91

The 1999 Les Baux (a blend of 50% Cabernet Sauvignon, 25% Grenache, and 25% Syrah, Mourvèdre, and Carignan) boasts an opaque black/purple color as well as gorgeous aromas of plum liqueur, licorice, truffles, roasted herbs, and graphite. Deep and full-bodied, with superb purity, a voluptuous texture, and abundant fruit and glycerin, this 5,000-case *cuvée* was bottled unfined and unfiltered. Consume it over the next 7–8 years. The 1999 Réserve du Mas Les Baux (8,000 cases from a blend of equal parts Syrah, Cabernet Sauvignon, and Grenache) sees some new oak, but it is completely hidden by the wine's explosive blackberry and cassis fruit. Incredibly decadent, rich, and luxuriously constructed, it exhibits full body plus fabulous concentration and purity. Offering the essence of black fruits intermixed with dried Provençal herbs and licorice, it is a sumptuous, full-throttle, super-endowed, seamless, mouth-filling wine that should drink well for 10–12 years. These are awesome examples of great wine selling at very fair prices. Do as I did . . . buy these by the caseload.

DOMAINE MATHIEU

1999 Châteauneuf-du-Pape	C	86
1998 Châteauneuf-du-Pape	C	87
1999 Châteauneuf-du-Pape Marquis Anselme Mathieu	D	87
1998 Châteauneuf-du-Pape Marquis Anselme Mathieu	D	90

The two 1998s are the two most impressive offerings I have yet tasted from Domaine Mathieu, another up-and-coming Châteauneuf-du-Pape producer. The 1999s are both lighter than their 1998 counterparts, not surprising given the differences in vintage character (1998 is a great year, 1999 a very good one).

The medium ruby-colored 1999 Châteauneuf-du-Pape reveals considerable pink at the rim. It is a charming, light- to medium-bodied effort with sweet cherry fruit infused with notions of balsam and spice. Drink it over the next 4–5 years. More textured, richer, and fruitier with additional stuffing, the 1999 Châteauneuf-du-Pape Marquis Anselme Mathieu is a mid-weight Châteauneuf with sweet tannin as well as a seamless texture. It requires consumption over the next 5–7 years.

The 1998 Châteauneuf-du-Pape's uninspiring medium ruby color is deceptive given the fact that this is a sexy, open-knit, ripe, hedonistic, expansive, full-bodied, jammy offering. Abundant levels of cherry and currant fruit compete with spice, pepper, and herbs to provide a seductive, pure, well-balanced wine. Drink this delicious 1998 now and over the next 7 years. The 1998 also exhibits an unimpressive medium ruby color, but the wine offers a gorgeous bouquet of black cherry liqueur and spice. In the mouth, it is voluptuous, with sumptuous glycerin levels, high extraction of black and red fruits, a soft, fat mid-section, and a long, juicy, succulent finish. It will not make old bones, but it will provide a user-friendly mouthful of Grenache-based fruit over the next 10 years.

CHÂTEAU MAUCOIL

2000 Châteauneuf-du-Pape	C	(87–88)
1999 Châteauneuf-du-Pape	C	87
1998 Châteauneuf-du-Pape	C	87
2000 Châteauneuf-du-Pape Privilège	D	(88–90)
1999 Châteauneuf-du-Pape Privilège	D	88
1998 Châteauneuf-du-Pape Privilège	D	90
2000 Côtes du Rhône	A	86

A good value, the bottled 2000 Côtes du Rhône exhibits copious quantities of sweet cherry fruit and peppery notes presented in an uncomplicated, quaffable, fleshy style. With admirable levels of glycerin as well as alcohol, it should be consumed over the next 1–2 years.

There is more fruit, glycerin, alcohol, and fat in the 2000 *cuvées* than in the 1999s because the vintage is better. The dark ruby-colored 2000 Châteauneuf-du-Pape displays an intense bouquet of sweet black cherry fruit, plums, leather, and pepper. It is medium-bodied and spicy, with low acidity, attractive levels of glycerin, and silky tannin. Consume it over the next 8–9 years. The 2000 Châteauneuf-du-Pape Privilège may merit an outstanding score. It offers sweet black currant and cherry liqueur characteristics in its fruit-dominated personality. Full-bodied, with impressive glycerin, supple tannin, and a plump, voluminous mouthfeel, it will drink well for 8–10 years.

Maucoil's medium ruby-colored 1999 Châteauneuf-du-Pape is a fully mature, fruity offering with notes of plums, pepper, and cherries, medium body, and a round, pleasant, mainstream style. Drink this user-friendly Châteauneuf over the next 3–5 years. There is more to the 1999 Châteauneuf-du-Pape Privilège, including aromas of orange rind, cherry liqueur, pepper, and plums. While medium- to full-bodied and fleshy, there is not much depth behind the overall appealing superficiality. Drink it over the next 6–7 years.

The 1998 Châteauneuf-du-Pape is a ripe, fleshy, black cherry–dominated effort with full body, superb ripeness, and copious quantities of spicy, chewy fruit. It should drink well during its first 7–8 years of life. The 1998 Châteauneuf-du-Pape Cuvée Privilège sees some new oak, but all of its gorgeous flavors, glycerin, richness, and aromatic nuances will stay intact as it will not be subjected to the fining and filtration other *cuvées* must endure. This example of old-vine Grenache offers a deep ruby/purple color in addition to a sweet nose of Asian spices, licorice, pepper, and jammy black fruits. Full-bodied, ripe, and chewy, with high alcohol, impressive extract, and a touch of new oak, this should drink well upon release and last for 12+ years.

LA MONARDIÈRE

2000 Vacqueyras Réserve des Deux Monarques	C	(87–89)
1999 Vacqueyras Réserve des Deux Monarques	C	87
2000 Vacqueyras Vieilles Vignes	D	(88–90)
1999 Vacqueyras Vieilles Vignes	D	89

The 2000 *cuvées* possess more saturated ruby/purple colors and jammier fruit, with the Vieilles Vignes *cuvée* revealing a touch of new oak. However, the 1999s are serious performers. The 2000 Vacqueyras Vieilles Vignes is full-bodied and evolved, with thick, muscular flavors and loads of black fruits intermixed with licorice, dried herbs, and vanilla. Drink it over the next 7–8 years. The deep ruby/purple-colored 2000 Vacqueyras Réserve des Deux Monarques boasts a big, sweet nose of blackberries, currants, and kirsch intermixed with earth and spice. Expansive and corpulent, it is best consumed during its exuberant youth, over the next 4–5 years. La Monardière's 1999 Vacqueyras Réserve des Deux Monarques is a big, spicy, surprisingly elegant effort with plenty of grapy, curranty fruit intermixed with a touch of cherries. Medium-bodied, round, and well balanced, it should drink well for 3–4 years. More expansive and fuller-bodied, with sweeter, jammier fruit as well as higher extract, the 1999 Vacqueyras Vieilles Vignes exhibits this region's telltale notes of kirsch, pepper, and dried herbs. It should drink well for 5–6 years.

DOMAINE MONPERTUIS

1999 Châteauneuf-du-Pape	D	89

Somehow I missed tasting this domaine's 1998, which should have been outstanding. Monpertuis's talented owner, Paul Jeune, is known for producing long-lived wines. His 1999 Châteauneuf-du-Pape exhibits a dark plum/ruby color in addition to a serious nose of ripe fruit, *garrigue*, pepper, minerals, and earth. Full-bodied, with excellent depth, purity, and a layered finish, it is a complex, surprisingly approachable (undoubtedly part of the vintage character) offering to drink now and over the next dozen or so years.

DOMAINE DE MONTEILLET

2000 Condrieu	E	89
1999 Condrieu	E	90
1998 Condrieu	E	92
2000 Condrieu Les Grandes Chailles	D	87
1998 Côte Rôtie Les Grandes Places	EE	90+
1997 Côte Rôtie Les Grandes Places	EE	92
2000 St.-Joseph	C	(85–86)
1999 St.-Joseph	C	(85–87)
1997 St.-Joseph	C	90
1999 St.-Joseph Blanc	C	86
2000 St.-Joseph Cuvée du Papy	D	(86–88)
1999 St.-Joseph Cuvée du Papy	D	(88–90)
1997 St.-Joseph Cuvée du Papy	D	90+
1999 St.-Joseph Fortior	C	88

Proprietor Stephan Montez is part of the youth movement in the Rhône Valley. He has done work at Joseph Phelps in California, as well as at Brown Brothers in Australia, and has a wise man's perspective that France cannot rest on its famous hierarchy of *terroirs* in order to stay on top of the world's platform of quality wines. Readers should note that this producer fashions wines under two labels. His estate wines are labeled Domaine de Monteillet, and the others are Vignobles de Monteillet. I did not have an opportunity to retaste his 1999s from bottle, but they are impressive from barrel, particularly the 1999 St.-Joseph Cuvée du Papy.

As for the Domaine de Monteillet offerings, the 1999 St.-Joseph Blanc (mostly Marsanne with a touch of Roussanne) is aged one-third in tank and two-thirds in old wood. It offers a fresh, mineral, citrusy, lemon, and orange blossom–scented nose, elegant, medium-bodied flavors, good, clean, ripe fruit, and a zesty finish. Drink it over the next 2 years.

The 2000 Condrieu is a serious effort produced from 35 hectoliters per hectare (modest by this vintage's overabundance). This excellent, apricot-scented wine exhibits plenty of tropical fruit in addition to an intriguing minerality. Medium- to full-bodied, with good underlying definition as well as purity, it will drink well for 1–2 years. The 1999 Condrieu (which sees about one-third new-oak casks) is exceptional. One of the appellation's finest wines, from a good rather than exceptional vintage for this area, this wine comes primarily from the Côteau Chanson. It exhibits an exotic fruit character consisting of pineapple, tangerine, and orange marmalade notes, along with Viognier's honeysuckle qualities. Medium- to full-bodied, dry but unctuous, rich, and impressive, it is a gorgeous effort, although slightly less concentrated than the blockbuster 1998. The sumptuous 1998 Condrieu, one of the most striking Condrieus I have tasted over recent years, was made from a minuscule 17 h/h. This 100% barrel-fermented (25% new oak) offering achieved 14% natural alcohol (easy in California, but much more difficult in the northern Rhône Valley). It offers a striking nose of peach jam intertwined with apricots, spring flowers, and honeysuckle. Full-bodied, dense, and lively, with explosive ripeness and gorgeous purity, this is a dazzling wine to enjoy over the next 2 years.

The Montez St.-Josephs are outstanding, with the *barrique,* new oak–aged Cuvée du Papy more closed and needing time, but ultimately, the better of the two wines. The two *cuvées* of 1999 red wines are more elegant, and slightly less dense and classic than the 1998s. Furthermore, their acidity levels are more tangy, the tannin less noticeable, and the fruit more vibrant and vivid. However, the wines are not as concentrated as their 1998 counterparts.

The 2000 St.-Joseph (from vineyards surrounding the village of Chavannay) exhibits a medium-bodied, soft, ripe style, good cherry and currant fruit, low acidity, and attractive ripeness. It was aged in both *demi-muids* and old barrels. Enjoy it over the next 4–5 years. There are 7,000 bottles of 2000 St.-Joseph Cuvée du Papy, the estate's top offering that is culled from old vines and is aged in 100% new oak. Not surprisingly, it reveals a more saturated ruby/purple color along with a pure nose of black fruits, licorice, and toast. Medium-bodied and elegant, it requires consumption during its first 7–8 years of life.

The dark ruby-colored 1999 St.-Joseph offers a fruity, strawberry and cherry-scented bouquet with notions of granite and minerals in the background. Tart acidity gives the wine good definition and tanginess. Drink it over the next 4–5 years. This effort is aged only in old *demi-muids.* There are only 5,000 bottles of the deep ruby-colored 1999 St.-Joseph Cuvée du Papy (made from 35-year-old vines and aged in 66% new oak). It exhibits a moderately intense nose of black raspberry jam mixed with toasty cherries and minerals. This 1999 is rich, ripe, and lively, with vibrant acidity, medium body, and excellent, nearly outstanding concentration. The 1997 St.-Joseph (13% natural alcohol; produced from yields of 32 hectoliters per hectare, and no new oak) is a ripe, dense purple-colored wine with abundant quantities of jammy black fruits, a seductive, lush, concentrated palate, admirable fruit purity, and plenty of glycerin and layers of flavor. Aged only in *demi-muids,* like all of Montez's reds, it is bottled unfiltered. The 1997 St.-Joseph Cuvée du Papy (a selection of the estate's oldest vines, aged in 50% new oak) reveals toasty notes in addition to blackberry and cherry liqueur–like fruit. Although closed when tasted, there was significant weight and richness on the palate as well as moderate tannin and exceptional purity in the finish. While the regular St.-Joseph can be drunk over the next 8 years, the Cuvée du Papy should last for 14–15 years.

The Montez family purchased a tiny (just over one acre) parcel of Côte Rôtie Les Grandes Places in 1997. From the decomposed granite soils of this parcel, 150 cases of wine are produced annually. This Côte Rôtie is aged in 100% new oak for 30 months and is bottled unfined and unfiltered. Like Marcel Guigal (as well as increasing numbers of young vignerons), Montez believes in little racking of the wine, or use of SO_2, thus the wine is put in barrel, kept on its side, and often not racked for 12–18 months.

The 1998 Côte Rôtie Les Grandes Places, which spent 32 months in new oak barrels, is not displaying the succulence or lush opulence of the thrilling 1997 Les Grandes Places. Like many 1998 northern Rhônes, it is presently closed. Nevertheless, it exhibits an opaque ruby/purple color as well as a backward but promising nose of black fruits intermixed with spring flowers, vanilla, and graphite. Tannic, medium-bodied, muscular, and deep, it needs 3–4 years of cellaring. Anticipated maturity: 2005–2016. The 1997 Côte Rôtie Les Grandes Places is a spectacular Côte Rôtie! Readers may have forgotten that 1997 was a highly successful year for the northern Rhône, where the reds are low in acidity, but ripe, concentrated, and jammy. It is a seductive, somewhat underrated vintage that has been largely forgotten because of the hype concerning the 1998 vintage. Made from 100% Syrah, the 1997 Côte Rôtie Les Grandes Places exhibits a dense purple color, as well as a glorious bouquet of blackberries, cassis, licorice, and toast. Full-bodied and seamless, with beautifully integrated acidity, tannin, and alcohol, this voluptuous effort is undeniably thrilling to drink . . . already. Look for this grand Côte Rôtie to drink well for 12–15+ years. Bravo!

Under the Vignobles de Monteillet label, the lighter-styled 2000 Condrieu Les Grandes Chailles offers notions of honeysuckle and apricots in its medium-bodied, fresh, fruit-driven personality. It is best drunk over the next year. The 1999 St.-Joseph Fortior reveals excellent richness as well as sweet plum/cherry fruit presented in an uncomplicated, medium-bodied, lush style with nicely integrated wood, acidity, and tannin. It is meant to be consumed during its first 3–4 years of life.

DOMAINE DE LA MORDORÉE

2000	Châteauneuf-du-Pape Cuvée de la Reine des Bois	E	(96–98)
1999	Châteauneuf-du-Pape Cuvée de la Reine des Bois	E	94
1998	Châteauneuf-du-Pape Cuvée de la Reine des Bois	E	99+
1999	Côtes du Rhône	A	88
1999	Lirac Cuvée de la Reine des Bois	C	89+
1998	Lirac Cuvée de la Reine des Bois	C	91
1999	Lirac Cuvée de la Reine des Bois Blanc	C	89

Domaine de la Mordorée, the property of Christophe Delorme, has become one of the superstar estates of the southern Rhône, turning out exquisite Châteauneuf-du-Pape, as well as high class Lirac, Côtes du Rhône, and Tavel rosé. Not all of the wines qualify as "best buys," but readers who adore these Provençal wines would be foolish not to try the wines from this impeccably run estate. There are generally two *cuvées* of top wines from Lirac and Châteauneuf-du-Pape, a regular *cuvée* and the Cuvée de la Reine des Bois, the latter being produced from the estate's oldest vines and most concentrated juice. Domaine de la Mordorée is at the top of its game, producing some of the finest wines in the southern Rhône.

Among the finest being produced in the southern Rhône, the white wines are surprisingly powerful and rich. The 1999 Lirac Cuvée de la Reine des Bois Blanc (this is the Reserve designation for the estate) is made of equal parts white Grenache, Roussanne, Viognier, Bourboulenc, and Picpoul. This fruit-driven 1999 exhibits copious quantities of dried apricots and peaches, medium body, impressive ripeness, and a creamy-textured mid-palate and finish with just enough acidity to provide definition. It is a worthy successor to the equally impressive 1998. Drink it over the next 2–3 years.

The 2000 Châteauneuf-du-Pape Cuvée de la Reine des Bois is akin to the virtually perfect 1998. It possesses a level of richness found in only a handful of the world's greatest wines. The dense purple color is followed by a wine with multiple dimensions as well as massive concentration and thickness. It is reminiscent of a dry vintage Port, without the weight. The knockout nose of framboise, blackberry liqueur, cassis, licorice, and lead pencil shavings is followed by layers of flavor, remarkable purity, and a finish that lasts nearly a minute. This is a sumptuous, profound wine. Anticipated maturity: 2004–2020. A candidate for wine of the vintage, the 1999 Châteauneuf-du-Pape Cuvée de la Reine des Bois boasts a saturated black/ruby color as well as amazing concentration of fruit extract (blackberries and cherries) intermixed with graphite and crème de cassis. Spectacularly concentrated, full-bodied, extremely pure, well delineated, and opulent, this superb wine is more forward/accessible than the similarly styled 1998, which has even more muscle and structure. Anticipated maturity: now–2018.

I have tasted the 1998 Châteauneuf-du-Pape Cuvée de la Reine des Bois three times, and it is astonishing. It boasts an opaque black/purple color plus an extraordinary nose of pepper, blackberry liqueur, cherries, smoke, scorched earth, and *garrigue*. As the wine sits in the glass, licorice and crème de cassis notes also become apparent. Awesomely concentrated, with immense body, massive fruit, sweet tannin, and fabulous symmetry, this is one of the most remarkable Châteauneuf-du-Papes I have ever tasted. Anticipated maturity: 2004–2022.

With respect to the red wines, besides their top of the line Châteauneuf-du-Pape Cuvée de la Reine des Bois, Mordorée produces delicious Côtes du Rhônes as well as impressive Liracs. The 1999 Côtes du Rhône (a blend of 50% Grenache, 20% Syrah, 10% Mourvèdre, 10% Carignan, and 10% Counoise) is a serious effort with a dense ruby/purple color and excellent richness. Notes of pepper and sweet, jammy black cherries soar from the glass of this tasty, succulent Côtes du Rhône. Ripe, rich, pure, and well balanced, it can be enjoyed over the next 3–4 years. Even more serious, with slightly more tannin, is the black/purple-colored 1999 Lirac Cuvée de la Reine des Bois. The 1999 southern Rhônes tend to be softer and more fruit-driven than the more structured, muscular, powerful 1998s. This offering reveals intense fruit, abundant quantities of black raspberry and blackberry aromas and flavors, in addition to licorice and pepper. It is a beautifully made, soft, low-acid effort that should drink well for 4–5 years. I previously reviewed the 1998 Lirac Cuvée de la Reine des Bois prior to bottling, and it is living up to my expectations. It exhibits a dark ruby/purple color as well as a moderately intense nose of black fruits, licorice, spice, pepper, and smoke. Displaying moderate tannin with exceptional concentration, it is one of those rare Liracs that will age for 10–15 years.

MOULIN DE LA GARDETTE

1999	Gigondas	D	(87–88+)
1998	Gigondas	D	91
1999	Gigondas Cuvée Ventabren	D	(88–90)
1998	Gigondas Cuvée Ventabren	D	90+

Proprietor Jean-Baptiste Meunier is fashioning impressive wines from this small 17.4-acre estate. Other than a standard Gigondas, aged 18 months primarily in vat with about 10% in old barrels, he produces a luxury *cuvée* called Ventabren emerging from 70-year-old vines and aged in 100% oak barrels, of which one-third are new. These two wines are bottled with neither fining nor filtration.

If the 1999s improve as much in one year as their 1998 counterparts did, their scores will look conservative. The dark ruby/purple-colored 1999 Gigondas exhibits minerals, black raspberries, and cherry fruit, medium body, and moderate tannin. The impressive 1999 Gigondas Cuvée Ventabren possesses a more saturated purple color as well as sweet, pure, black fruits intermixed with smoke, licorice, and minerals. It is medium- to full-bodied and moderately tannic. Both 1999s suggest they will be drinkable when released and should last for a decade or more. I was pleasantly surprised by how strongly Gardette's 1998s performed from bottle. They have improved immensely with their *élevage* and I clearly underestimated them when they were in cask. The 1998 Gigondas (a blend of 80% Grenache, 10% Mourvèdre, and 10% Cinsault) is an impressive, succulent, opaque purple-colored wine with hedonistic levels of blackberry, cherry, truffle, licorice, and Asian spice notes. Full-bodied and sweet, with low acidity and thrilling levels of extract, it will be at its finest before 2015. The 1998 Gigondas Cuvée Ventabren (a 70% Grenache, 20% Syrah, 10% Cinsault blend) is more backward, with spicy new oak in the nose, along with a blackberry/kirsch note. In the mouth, a creamy texture, powerful, sweet, pure flavors, adequate acidity, and sweet tannin suggest this wine should hit its stride in about 3 years and evolve for 12 years.

MOULIN-TACUSSEL

2000	Châteauneuf-du-Pape	C	(88–89)
1999	Châteauneuf-du-Pape	C	87
1998	Châteauneuf-du-Pape	C	87

One of the many gentlemen of Châteauneuf-du-Pape is Monsieur Moulin, a gentle, enthusiastic man who fashions lighter-styled wines filled with character. The similarly styled, medium- to full-bodied, pure 2000 Châteauneuf-du-Pape offers aromas of cedar, tobacco, spice box, currants, and kirsch. It should drink well for 10–12 years. The dark ruby-colored 1999 Châteauneuf-du-Pape exhibits a big, sweet nose of ripe cherries mixed with mincemeat, pepper, and balsam wood. Medium-bodied, soft, and richly fruity with excellent purity, it will drink well for 7–8 years. The medium plum/garnet-colored 1998 Châteauneuf-du-Pape offers a complex nose of pepper, dried Provençal herbs, allspice, and cherry liqueur. Round and medium- to full-bodied, with very good to excellent fruit intensity, it is already drinking well and should keep for 5 years.

DOMAINE DE MOURCHON

2000	Côtes du Rhône-Villages Séguret	C	(85–87)
1999	Côtes du Rhône-Villages Séguret	C	85
1998	Côtes du Rhône-Villages Séguret	C	87
2000	Côtes du Rhône-Villages Séguret Grande Réserve	C	(86–87)
1999	Côtes du Rhône-Villages Séguret Grande Réserve	C	(86–87)
1998	Côtes du Rhône-Villages Séguret Grande Réserve	C	87

This new estate is the creation of transplanted Englishman W. McKinley, and his debut vintage, 1998, is a good beginning. The traditional *cuvée* is a blend of 60% Grenache, 25% Syrah, 10% Cinsault, and 5% Carignan aged in tank. The Grande Réserve includes 35% Syrah (aged in *barrique*) and 65% Grenache. All of these offerings exhibit excellent dark ruby/purple colors, sweet black cherry/cassis fruit, medium to full body, outstanding purity, and high-quality winemaking. The Grande Réserves possess more structure and muscle, but no more charm than their siblings. A serious newcomer to the southern Rhône Valley, Domaine de Mourchon should offer fine value. The 2000s and 1998s possess more stuffing as well as aging potential. All of these vintages should drink well for 3–5 years, with the best kept examples lasting for 7–10 years.

CHÂTEAU DU MOURRE DU TENDRE

2000	Châteauneuf-du-Pape	E	(94–96)
1999	Châteauneuf-du-Pape	E	(92–93+)
1998	Châteauneuf-du-Pape	E	(92–94)
1999	Côtes du Rhône	B	(86–87)
2000	Côtes du Rhône-Villages Vieilles Vignes	C	(89–91)

The seriously endowed, full-bodied, blockbuster 2000 Côtes du Rhône-Villages Vieilles Vignes could easily pass for a Châteauneuf-du-Pape. Its dense plum color is accompanied by a knockout nose of Provençal herbs, roasted meats, balsam, cherry liqueur, and *jus de viande*. It appears that the soft, ready to drink 1999 Côtes du Rhône should be bottled as well as consumed.

Once the 2000 Châteauneuf-du-Pape is released, Châteauneuf-du-Pape lovers will agree it was worth the wait. This opaque plum-colored, gargantuan-styled offering exhibits full body, immense extract, mouth-searing levels of tannin, and a heavy, full-throttle style. A blockbuster that requires patience, it will easily last for 2–3 decades. Anticipated maturity: 2007–2030. The 1999 Châteauneuf-du-Pape is one of the most powerful wines of the vintage. A dense plum/garnet color is followed by aromas of roasted meats, earth, truffles, dried black fruits, pepper, and spice box. Massively concentrated, it is reminiscent of an old-vine Cornas *cuvée* from the northern Rhône. In addition to copious tannin, it possesses fabulous extract as well as a tremendous sweetness that only comes from low yields and/or old vines. Anticipated maturity: 2007–2020.

The 1998 Châteauneuf-du-Pape is an awesome wine that achieved 15% natural alcohol from yields of less than 1.5 tons of fruit per acre. It boasts a dense, opaque ruby/plum color, and an extremely sweet, thick, juicy nose of black fruits intermixed with spice box, kirsch, dried herbs, and animal characteristics. Terrific on the palate, with layers of concentration, it has some rustic tannin to shed, but more than enough glycerin, extract, and richness to balance out the wine's structural component. As it finishes, it is almost like candy flowing across the palate, but ripe, concentrated, and possessing all the good things that turn wine lovers on. Anticipated maturity: 2005–2025. Readers who love mouthcoating, thick, old, traditionally styled Châteauneuf-du-Pape will get a blast from these offerings.

MOUTON PÈRE ET FILS

2000 Côte Rôtie	E	(85–86)
1999 Côte Rôtie	E	88

The light, delicate, straightforward 2000 Côte Rôtie displays notions of minerals, herbs, smoke, earth, and berry fruit. Although cleanly made, there is not much to it. Consume it during its first 7–8 years of life. The more interesting, sensual, attractive, dark ruby-colored 1999 Côte Rôtie is meant to be enjoyed immediately as there is not much substance, depth, or structure. It is a disarmingly charming, ripe effort offering sweet berry fruit, smoke, and dried herb characteristics. Enjoy this flattering 1999 over the next 5–7 years.

DOMAINE DE NALYS

2000 Châteauneuf-du-Pape	D	86
1999 Châteauneuf-du-Pape	D	87
1998 Châteauneuf-du-Pape	D	88
1999 Châteauneuf-du-Pape Cuvée Châtaignier	E	(88–90)

Domaine de Nalys' medium-bodied 2000 Châteauneuf-du-Pape exhibits a jammy fruit as well as a very good texture. It is an open-knit 2000 with copious quantities of currants/cherries, a plush fatness, and a hedonistic, seductive style. Drink it during its first 10–12 years of life. Made in a similar style, the 1999 Châteauneuf-du-Pape performed better from bottle than it did from barrel. Offering classic strawberry liqueur notes intermixed with pepper and spice, it is a mid-weight, charming, seductive effort dominated by fruit. Open-knit, round, generously endowed, and seamless, it should be drunk over the next 7–10 years. The top *cuvée*, the 1999 Châteauneuf-du-Pape Cuvée Châtaignier, which I was unable to retaste after bottling, reveals a denser ruby/purple color in addition to a complex bouquet of *garrigue* (a blend of Provençal herbs and earth), and peppery, black cherry and plum-like fruit, a deep, rich, concentrated, medium- to full-bodied style with excellent purity. It will provide delicious drinking for a decade. I did not retaste the 1998 Châteauneuf-du-Pape Cuvée Châtaignier (I gave it a potential rating of 88–90+ when it was in barrel), but the 1998 Châteauneuf-du-Pape is excellent. One of the finest traditional *cuvées* Nalys has produced over recent vintages, it exhibits a dark ruby/plum color, as well as an impressive bouquet of sweet, candied strawberry and cherry fruit intermixed with pepper, dried herbs, and leather. The wine is sweet, rich, and fat, with kirsch, medium to full body, a nicely layered texture, well-integrated tannin, and a silky finish. My notes read, "cherry liqueur galore." Anticipated maturity: now–2010.

CHÂTEAU DE LA NERTHE

2000 Châteauneuf-du-Pape	D	(88–91)
1999 Châteauneuf-du-Pape	D	88
1998 Châteauneuf-du-Pape	D	90
1997 Châteauneuf-du-Pape	D	(87–90)
2000 Châteauneuf-du-Pape Blanc	D	89
1999 Châteauneuf-du-Pape Blanc	D	88
1999 Châteauneuf-du-Pape Clos de Beauvenir	E	91

1998 Châteauneuf-du-Pape Clos de Beauvenir	E	89
1997 Châteauneuf-du-Pape Clos de Beauvenir	E	88
1995 Châteauneuf-du-Pape Clos de Beauvenir	E	89
2000 Châteauneuf-du-Pape Cuvée des Cadettes	EE	(91–94)
1999 Châteauneuf-du-Pape Cuvée des Cadettes	EE	91
1998 Châteauneuf-du-Pape Cuvée des Cadettes	EE	93
1997 Châteauneuf-du-Pape Cuvée des Cadettes	EE	(90–91)

Under the meticulous administration of Alain Dugas, this estate is beginning to exploit its considerable potential. The wines have consistently been very good to excellent, but I get the impression they are pushing the envelope of quality even higher. In most vintages there are two *cuvées* of both red and white Châteauneuf-du-Pape, the *cuvée* classique and the limited production, old-vine Mourvèdre-based Cuvée des Cadettes. For the whites, there is the *cuvée* classique and a Roussanne-dominated Châteauneuf-du-Pape Clos de Beauvenir.

The 2000 Châteauneuf-du-Pape, a blend of 47% Grenache, 25% Syrah, 18% Mourvèdre, and the remainder Cinsault and other varietals, is a sexy, soft, plump effort displaying notes of licorice, blackberries, cassis, and cherries. Densely colored, spicy, full-bodied, and opulent, it will provide sensual drinking for 12–14 years. The opaque purple-colored 2000 Châteauneuf-du-Pape Cuvée des Cadettes (40% Grenache, 29% Mourvèdre, and 31% Syrah) offers a combination of power and elegance in its sweet blackberry liqueur and toasty notes. With high levels of glycerin and extract, this layered, complex, rich, sweet, low-acid 2000 should be drinkable at an early age yet last for two decades. It has the potential to be just as good as the 1998 (the finest Cuvée des Cadettes produced since 1978).

The 1999 Châteauneuf-du-Pape reveals the vintage's higher acidity, a finesse-filled personality, a dark ruby color, and a spicy, herbaceous, leather-scented bouquet. This medium-bodied, fine-tuned Châteauneuf offers copious quantities of berry/cherry fruit as well as fine freshness. While not as big as the 2000 or 1998, it should drink well for 10–12 years. The luxury *cuvée* of 1999 Châteauneuf-du-Pape Cuvée des Cadettes (a 1,000-case blend of 39% Grenache, 36% Syrah, and 25% Mourvèdre, aged in small barrels, of which 50% are new) does not possess the fat or volume of either the 2000 or 1998. Nevertheless, it is a top-class wine offering an attractive, moderately intense nose of spice box, blackberries, vanilla, and minerals. Medium- to full-bodied and layered, with superb ripeness and purity, a sweet attack, and moderate tannin in the finish, it is accessible, but will be even better in 2–3 years. It will keep for 15–18 years.

Produced from 49% Grenache, 15% Mourvèdre, 22% Syrah, 8% Cinsault, and the remainder miscellaneous varietals, the 1998 Châteauneuf-du-Pape (25,000 cases) reveals more plum, licorice, meat, herb, and pepper characteristics, along with telltale black cherry and berry fruit in the aromas and flavors. It also possesses a fatter, juicier texture, more weight and mass, but, like its younger sibling, sweet tannin, low acidity, and an accessible, fleshy personality. It should drink well for 12–14 years. The 1998 Châteauneuf-du-Pape Cuvée des Cadettes was made from a blend of 39% Grenache, 37% Mourvèdre, and 24% Syrah. Full-bodied, powerful, and fat, with layers of concentration, this modern-styled Châteauneuf-du-Pape exhibits new oak, loads of glycerin, extract, and richness, and a complex nose of black fruits, minerals, toast, and spice. Bigger and weightier than the 1999, but less elegant, it should drink well for two decades.

The 1997 Châteauneuf-du-Pape (44% Grenache, 24% Syrah, 20% Mourvèdre, 7% Cinsault, and the balance tiny portions of other varietals) is a richer, more successful offering. The color is a deeper, more saturated ruby with purple nuances. The wine offers sweet, jammy plum/black cherry and raspberry aromas, deep, rich, full-bodied, fat flavors, some of the telltale pepper and spice, and a finish with substantial fruit and glycerin. This wine, which will be the first *cuvée* classique to be bottled without fining or filtration, appears to have the potential to drink well for a decade. The outstanding 1997 Châteauneuf-du-Pape

Cuvée des Cadettes (36% Grenache, 32% Mourvèdre, and 32% Syrah; 11,000 bottles produced) is unquestionably one of the stars of this vintage. The color is a saturated ruby/purple. The nose offers up copious quantities of cassis, kirsch, new saddle leather, Asian spices, and earth. Rich and full-bodied, with a creamy texture, low acidity, and a luscious, massive finish for the vintage, this is a superb example from a light year. It should drink well for 10–15 years.

Some of the finest white Châteauneuf-du-Papes emerge from Château de La Nerthe. The 2000 Châteauneuf-du-Pape Blanc (a 30,000 bottle *cuvée* made from 39% Grenache Blanc, 15% Bourboulenc, 21% Clairette, and 25% Roussanne) exhibits a light straw color in addition to a rich, perfumed bouquet of pears, white flowers, and citrus. With excellent body, fruit, and texture, it should drink well for 3–4 years. The 1999 Châteauneuf-du-Pape Blanc is a perfumed, fruit-driven effort that will provide delicious drinking over the next several years. The luxury *cuvée* of white Châteauneuf-du-Pape, the 1999 Clos de Beauvenir, is a blend of 62% Roussanne, 29% Clairette, 4% Bourboulenc, and 5% Grenache Blanc. Sadly, there are only 500 cases of this barrel-fermented offering. It possesses an exciting nose of honeyed citrus mixed with white flowers, honeysuckle, and a hint of wax. Dense, full-bodied, nicely textured, fresh, and lively, it is a substantial dry white that should age well for 5–6 years. Both of these whites had their malolactic fermentation blocked, which, based on my experience tasting 15–20-year-old white Châteauneuf-du-Papes, means they tend to show extremely well young, fall into a dull, dumb, oxidized stage, only to reemerge after a decade. The 1998 Châteauneuf-du-Pape Clos de Beauvenir (a blend of 28% Roussanne, 54% Clairette, 15% Grenache Blanc, and 3% Bourboulenc), exhibits excellent freshness, as well as honeysuckle and buttery fruit in its medium-bodied, toasty personality. It cuts a large swath on the palate. Drink it over the next 5–6 years. The 1997 Châteauneuf-du-Pape Clos de Beauvenir (53% Roussanne, 47% Clairette) was made in limited quantities of just over 400 cases. This 100% barrel-fermented wine has its malolactic fermentation blocked, resulting in a rich, full-bodied, spicy, oaky style. It is more Burgundian in orientation, with the oak influence more noticeable than in the *cuvée* classique. The Clos de Beauvenir should age nicely for 3–4 years.

The 1995 Châteauneuf-du-Pape Clos de Beauvenir (59% Roussanne and 41% Clairette) reveals some of the toasty scents that are the result of barrel fermentation, good, ripe, honeysuckle and tropical fruit flavors, medium body, fine richness, average acidity, and a spicy, long finish. It is a classy, nearly outstanding example of white Châteauneuf-du-Pape that is intended to rival the splendid *cuvée* of old-vine Roussanne produced by Beaucastel.

ROBERT NIERO

1999 Condrieu	E	88
1998 Condrieu	E	90
1999 Condrieu Coteau du Chéry	E	93
1998 Condrieu Coteau du Chéry	E	92

Niero has produced two very fine *cuvées* in what was a tricky vintage with difficult fermentations and relatively high yields. The 1999 Condrieu exhibits dense, exotic, clean, concentrated fruits, medium to full body, fine glycerin, and lofty alcohol. 20% new oak is utilized for this *cuvée*. The exceptional 1999 Condrieu Coteau du Chéry uses slightly more new oak. It is a rich, honeyed apricot/peach jam–scented wine with full body, superb concentration, and an explosive, glorious, hedonistic, fruity personality. This dry Condrieu should last for 2–3 years. The 1998 Condrieu (aged in 1–2-year-old barrels) reveals the vintage's terrific fruit along with an extra dimension of concentration due to low yields (much of the appellation suffered frost damage in the spring so the crop size was dramatically reduced). Full-bodied, pure, and clean, with a mélange of tropical fruits, this luscious wine should be consumed over the next several years. The more powerful 1998 Condrieu Coteau du Chéry is a wonder-fully structured effort with elegance, power, and definition. In addition to Condrieu's textbook flavors, this thick wine reveals an interesting texture with gobs of fruit. Its barrel aging (25% new oak) gives it more delineation than its sibling. It should drink well for several years.

MICHEL OGIER

2000	Côte Rôtie	E	(88–90)
1999	Côte Rôtie	E	95
1998	Côte Rôtie	E	90+
1997	Côte Rôtie	E	89
2000	Côte Rôtie Cuvée Belle Hélène	EE	(90–92)
1999	Côte Rôtie Cuvée Belle Hélène	EE	100
1998	Côte Rôtie Cuvée Belle Hélène	EE	95
1997	Côte Rôtie Cuvée Belle Hélène	EE	94
2000	VDP La Rosine Syrah	C	86
1999	VDP La Rosine Syrah	C	88

Michel Ogier, who is capably assisted by his rugged, tall, handsome 23-year-old son Stéphane, remains an unheralded source of profound Côte Rôtie. He currently estate bottles the entire production of Côte Rôtie, as well as 8,000 bottles of a 100% Syrah made from 12-year-old vines planted just outside the southern borders of Côte Rôtie where the Côte Blonde ends, called La Rosine. Ogier's regular *cuvée* of Côte Rôtie sees about 25–30% new oak. It spends 18 months in barrel, and over 70% of the grapes emerge from their holdings on the Côte Blonde. Like all of Ogier's Côte Rôties, this wine is bottled with no filtration, although the press wine is fined.

In addition to making one of the finest values in Côte Rôtie and one of the village's most el-egant, stylish wines, primarily from Côte Blonde fruit, this producer also fashions a *cuvée* dedicated to his wife, Hélène. It is an impressive 100% new-oak offering (125 cases in 1997) from 45-year-old vines on the Côte Rozier, next to La Landonne. The wine spends 30 months in barrel before it is bottled unfiltered. The debut offering was 1997.

The 2000 Côte Rôtie (a blend of three parcels) was made from 80% destemmed grapes. On my annual visit, Ogier told me that he may decide to back-blend the Cuvée Belle Hélène, de-pending on how this wine evolves. It appears to have outstanding potential, but it is no sure thing at this point. A deep ruby color is followed by aromas of tapenade, black fruits, earth, meat, and herbs. It offers a sweet attack, low acidity, fine ripeness, medium body, and a round, generous finish. In contrast, the more substantial 2000 Côte Rôtie Cuvée Belle Hélène (which comes from a northern hillside known as Rozier) exhibits a sweet blackberry, earthy, graphite character with plenty of new oak. While concentrated, ripe, and round, with considerable expansiveness, readers should keep in mind that this outstanding 125-case *cuvée* may ultimately be blended into the regular Côte Rôtie, depending on the evolution of the latter wine. If not, it will spend 30 months in 100% new French oak with little racking. Those who love Guigal's single-vineyard La Mouline, La Turque, and La Landonne wines will find more than a passing similarity with Ogier's brilliant Belle Hélène. If the 2000 is bottled, it will last for 15 years.

The finest Côte Rôties Ogier has made (and he agrees) are the 1999s. The fabulous, opaque purple-colored 1999 Côte Rôtie, which spent two years in wood (30% new), reveals a glorious bouquet of bacon fat, crème de cassis, licorice, violets, and spice box. It is full-bodied, with sweet tannin, great presence in the mouth, and a knockout finish. Although it will be approachable in its youth, 3–4 more years of cellaring will be beneficial. Anticipated maturity: 2004–2018. The perfect 1999 Côte Rôtie Cuvée Belle Hélène is a seamless, ma-jestic classic with the kind of concentration found only in Guigal's top *cuvées*. It boasts gorgeously sweet tannin, enormous levels of both extract and concentration, and is not only a tour de force in winemaking, but a huge Côte Rôtie Syrah fruit bomb with massive glycerin, layers of extract, and plenty of toasty new oak, which is marvelously integrated given the fact that it spent 30 months in 100% new-wood barrels prior to being bottled without filtration. This outstanding effort requires 5–6 years of cellaring. Anticipated maturity: 2008–2030.

The 1998 Côte Rôtie exhibits scents and flavors of charred earth, smoke, minerals, and cassis. The wine is full-bodied, rich, and dense, with abundant tannin in the finish. The French might call it a true *vin de garde*. It needs 4–5 years of cellaring, and it will keep for 15–18+ years. The 1998 Côte Rôtie Cuvée Belle Hélène boasts an opaque black/purple color as well as a tight but promising nose of new saddle leather, roasted meats, dried herbs, black fruits, and minerals. It is extremely full-bodied, super-concentrated, ferociously backward and tannic, and possesses sufficient extract, fruit, and depth to balance out the wine's structure. This classic, gorgeously proportioned Côte Rôtie will last for a generation. Anticipated maturity: 2006–2025.

The 1997 Côte Rôtie Cuvée Belle Hélène is a spectacular offering, revealing a saturated ruby/purple color as well as a knockout nose of toasty new oak intermixed with cassis, blackberries, and roasted spices. Full-bodied, with the wood well absorbed, this masculine, massive Côte Rôtie possesses spectacular intensity and purity, but has lost neither its typicity nor elegance because of the extensive new oak treatment. It should drink well upon release and last for 10–12+ years. The 1997 Côte Rôtie may also turn out to be outstanding. It displays a deep purple color, a sweet nose of smoke, pine needles, blackberry/cassis fruit, and a floral note. The wine has medium body, outstanding purity, a low-acid, opulent texture, and admirable depth and length. Although some tannin is present, this beauty will drink well young and last for 12 years.

The 2000 VDP La Rosine Syrah was produced from 85% destemmed grapes and went through a five-day cold maceration to emphasize the Syrah fruit. It possesses a deep color, copious quantities of licorice and black currant fruit, medium body, and low acidity. This soft 2000 is ideal for consuming over the next 2–3 years. The super 1999 VDP La Rosine Syrah exhibits a deep ruby/purple color as well as abundant black raspberry and cassis fruit, and an attractive, plump finish. Stéphane Ogier, the owner's son, calls it *trés gourmand* (very hedonistic). It will drink well for 3–4 years. As with all Ogier wines, it was bottled with neither fining nor filtration.

LES PALLIÈRES

2000 Gigondas	D	(90–93)
1999 Gigondas	D	90
1998 Gigondas	D	85

The enthusiasm shown by most Rhône wine lovers when this estate was purchased by importer Kermit Lynch and the well-known proprietor of Vieux-Télégraphe, Daniel Brunier, was put to the test given the lackluster performance of Les Pallières' 1998. However, Brunier and his team did not control the viticulture or the vinification until 1999. The results in 2000 and 1999 recall this estate's great offerings of the early 1980s and late 1970s. Readers familiar with Les Pallières' *terroir* know this is a cool-climate Gigondas vineyard with poor soil. Daniel Brunier calls it the "Château Rayas of Gigondas."

Even more impressive than the superb 1999, with additional layers, glycerin, extract, and richness, is the 2000 Gigondas. Over half of the *cuvée* achieved 15% natural alcohol. Boasting a deep ruby/purple color, a gorgeous perfume of blackberry and cherry fruit, minerals, and subtle *garrigue* scents, low acidity, full body, and exceptional purity, the 2000 is the finest wine produced at this estate since 1981 and 1979. It will drink well for 10–15 years.

Made from 80% Grenache, 15% Syrah, and 5% Mourvèdre kept in *foudre* (14.3% alcohol achieved naturally), the 1999 Gigondas is an elegant, perfumed, dark ruby-colored effort with full body, sweet tannin, and a layered, velvety texture. Notes of smoked herbs, black cherries, kirsch, and minerals are found in the beautiful wine, one of the finest of the vintage. It should drink well for 10–12 years. Bravo!

The new owners did not control the viticulture in 1998, which may explain the 1998 Gigondas's straightforward performance. It possesses a medium ruby color in addition to spice, sour cherries, and *garrigue* aromas. Medium-bodied, with average concentration and dry, astringent tannin in the finish, it is a mid-weight, austere Gigondas that requires consumption over the next 2–3 years.

DOMAINE DE PANISSE

2000 Châteauneuf-du-Pape	C	(87–89)
2000 Châteauneuf-du-Pape Cuvée Spéciale	D	(90–93)

From another estate producing better and better wines, Panisse's 2000 Châteauneuf-du-Pape is nearly outstanding. Its dense ruby/purple color is followed by aromas of sweet fruit, licorice, smoke, and dried herbs. Medium- to full-bodied, modern-styled, pure, and filled with character, it will provide pleasure over the next 7–8 years. The dense saturated ruby/purple-colored 2000 Châteauneuf-du-Pape Cuvée Spéciale offers a gorgeous nose of crème de cassis intertwined with kirsch, licorice, smoke, and a hint of graphite. It possesses superb purity, full body, and impressive concentration, texture, and length. Anticipated maturity: 2004–2016.

ALAIN PARET

2000 Condrieu Les Ceps du Nébadon	E	90
2000 Condrieu Lys du Volan	E	92
1999 St.-Joseph Les Larmes du Père	D	87
2000 St.-Joseph Rochecourbe	D	(87–89)
1999 St.-Joseph Rochecourbe	D	89
1999 St.-Joseph 420 Nuits	D	88
1997 St.-Joseph 420 Nuits	D	(89–91)

Alain Paret has fashioned two of the finest Condrieus of the 2000 vintage. His secret is low yields, ripe fruit, an upbringing *sur-lie*, with lees stirring (*bâtonnage*), and no new oak for Les Ceps du Nébadon, but 100% for the luxury *cuvée*, Lys du Volan. Yields never exceed 25 hectoliters per hectare, even in a super-abundant year such as 2000. The 2000 Condrieu Les Ceps du Nébadon reveals a telltale peach/apricot-scented perfume, delicious, nicely textured, fleshy flavors, excellent purity, and oodles of fruit. This classic Condrieu fruit bomb requires consumption during its first 1–2 years of life. The 2000 Condrieu Lys du Volan reveals no evidence of its 100% new-oak aging. Produced from tiny yields of a hillside vineyard planted in schist, it possesses wonderful aromatics, a concentrated, liquid minerality, and restrained notes of peach and apricot jam intermixed with honeysuckle. This glorious, textured, layered, well-balanced 2000 Condrieu will keep for 3–4 years. It is a worthy rival to the appellation's finest wine, Guigal's Condrieu La Doriane.

Alain Paret's brilliant winemaking techniques also extend to his reasonably priced St.-Joseph *cuvées*. I only tasted one 2000, the St.-Joseph Rochecourbe, which is aged in both small barrels and larger *demi-muids*. Its dense purple color is accompanied by tender tannin, thick, juicy fruit, and surprising concentration as well as depth. It will be approachable after bottling, and drink well for 7–8 years.

There are three *cuvées* of 1999 St.-Joseph. The 1999 St.-Joseph Les Larmes du Père (tears of the father) is a soft effort that sees little new oak (less than 5%). It exhibits herbaceous, black cherry and currant flavors, medium body, and an easygoing finish. Drink it over the next 4–5 years. The serious, more tannic, denser, and muscular 1999 St.-Joseph Rochecourbe reveals a dense purple color in addition to abundant power, purity, ripeness, and tannin. An underlying liquid minerality is reminiscent of a lead pencil/graphite character. This seriously extracted 1999 needs time in bottle. Anticipated maturity: now–2014. The more substantial 1999 St.-Joseph 420 Nuits offers a dark ruby/purple color as well as tangy cassis aromas with notes of Provençal herbs (particularly lavender). This medium-bodied, nicely textured, well-built St.-Joseph requires 1–2 years of cellaring; it will keep for a decade. Readers looking for a terrific, massive 100% Syrah should check out Alain Paret's 1997 St.-Joseph 420 Nuits. Made from 15-year-old Syrah vines and aged in 100% new *demi-muids*, it is sensationally extracted and rich, with super-intense aromas of wood smoke, cassis, pepper, and a touch of dried tomatoes. Full-bodied and beautifully pure and rich, with the oak playing a subtle role, this large-scaled St.-Joseph should provide gorgeous drinking early (because of its low acidity and evolved style), but keep for 8 years.

DOMAINE PAVILLON-MERCUROL (STEPHAN CORNU)

1999 Crozes-Hermitage		C	88

A disappointingly vegetal barrel sample of the 2000 Crozes-Hermitage was tasted, but I am sure this high-quality producer can do better than what I saw. There is no doubting the quality of the 1999 Crozes-Hermitage, which was aged in 25% new-oak barrels. It is a big, juicy, fleshy, medium- to full-bodied effort offering abundant quantities of black currant and cherry fruit intermixed with licorice, a subtle notion of herbs, and spice. Soft, round, and generous, it will drink for 5–7 years.

DOMAINE DU PÉGAÜ

2000	Châteauneuf-du-Pape Cuvée da Capo	EEE	(96–98+)
1998	Châteauneuf-du-Pape Cuvée da Capo	EEE	100
1998	Châteauneuf-du-Pape Cuvée Laurence	D	91
2000	Châteauneuf-du-Pape Cuvée Réservée	D	(93–96)
1999	Châteauneuf-du-Pape Cuvée Réservée	D	92
1998	Châteauneuf-du-Pape Cuvée Réservée	D	93
1997	Châteauneuf-du-Pape Cuvée Réservée	D	87

Since most readers will never have access to a bottle of Henri Bonneau's phenomenal Châteauneuf-du-Pape, the Réserve des Céléstins, they should try a bottle of the wine that comes closest to that style. Paul Féraud produces blockbuster, chewy, old-style Châteauneuf-du-Pape in much the same manner as his mentor, Henri Bonneau. Féraud's offerings are uncompromising, high-alcohol, massive wines that hit the heights in the great vintages, yet do surprisingly well in lighter years. No doubt due to the influence of Laurence, Féraud's daughter, the bottling happens much earlier than Bonneau, who often does not bottle a Céléstins until it has had at least five years of *élevage* in the dark, cramped cellars under his house. At Domaine du Pégaü, bottling is done within two years, except for the limited production Cuvée Laurence, which is bottled after 5–6 years of barrel aging. Laurence also introduced the blockbuster Cuvée da Capo in 1998.

Producing traditionally made Châteauneuf-du-Papes, Domaine du Pégaü has had an impressive track record for nearly 20 years. During the month of December 1998 (what I affectionately call the season of swallowing rather than spitting), I amused myself as well as my wife with a mini-vertical of Pégaü, tasting the 1990, 1989, 1985, 1983, 1981, and 1979. I was pleased that all of these vintages were living up to my high expectations. However, owners of the 1983, 1981, and 1979 should make plans to consume them over the next few years (the 1981 is a phenomenal Châteauneuf-du-Pape). There is a tendency to call these wines rustic, but that is a pejorative I find objectionable. These are full-bodied, concentrated wines containing all the Provençal as well as Châteauneuf-du-Pape flavors and aromas. The wines are based on ripe, low yielding, old-vine Grenache. The wines are now bottled earlier, which is to their benefit, but these boldly styled, powerful Châteauneuf-du-Papes can handle plenty of aging in the estate's old *foudres*.

In another exceptional vintage for Châteauneuf-du-Pape, the 2000 Pégaü offerings are among the stars of the appellation. The 2000 Châteauneuf-du-Pape Cuvée Réservée (a blend of 75% Grenache, 20% Syrah, and 5% miscellaneous varietals) exhibits an opaque ruby/purple color as well as a fabulous nose of black fruits intermixed with roasted meats, licorice, pepper, and a touch of *garrigue*. It is super-charged with extract, has high levels of glycerin, extremely full body, sweet tannin, and a long finish of nearly 40 seconds. It may surpass the 1998, turning out to be the greatest Cuvée Réservée since 1990, 1989, and 1981. Anticipated maturity: 2004–2025. The debut vintage of the Châteauneuf-du-Pape Cuvée da Capo, 1998 (which I would currently rate a perfect 100 after five separate tastings from bottle), has been followed by another black beauty in 2000. The 2000 Châteauneuf-du-Pape Cuvée da Capo exhibits an extreme thickness and intensity of flavor, high tannin, blockbuster richness, and all the characteristics of the Cuvée Réservée exaggerated to the maximum. This wine, which emerges from an old vineyard in the famed sector of Châteauneuf-du-Pape called La Crau, is made from all 13 permitted varietals, although over 90% is Grenache. Look for the 2000 to be slightly more accessible and forward than the 1998, and drink well for 30+ years. It is another prodigious effort that should age into an historic Châteauneuf-du-Pape. Anticipated maturity: 2007–2035.

One of the more powerful, concentrated 1999 Châteauneuf-du-Papes was produced at Château Pégaü. The dense ruby/purple-colored 1999 Châteauneuf-du-Pape Cuvée Réservée boasts a powerful bouquet of pepper, *garrigue*, black fruits, and earth. Full-bodied and expansive, with sweet tannin giving it a more open-knit, accessible style than most young vintages of Pégaü, this is a wine to drink while waiting for the 1998 to become fully mature. Like all of this estate's red wines, it was bottled with neither fining nor filtration.

The 1998 Châteauneuf-du-Pape Cuvée Réservée was bottled one month before my visit, and it has turned out even better than I had hoped. The most powerful effort Pégaü has made since 1990 and 1989, it exhibits the classic Châteauneuf-du-Pape trilogy of ground pepper, *garrigue*, and kirsch. Full-bodied, super-concentrated, and multilayered with a viscous texture, this is blockbuster Châteauneuf, with abundant quantities of meat, flesh, and alcohol. Anticipated maturity: 2004–2020.

In 1998, a new *cuvée* has also been introduced. The 1998 Châteauneuf-du-Pape Cuvée da Capo is a blend of the appellation's 13 authorized varietals (the French word is *cépage*) that achieved a whopping 16.6% alcohol and finished dry. It is an exquisite, multidimensional, compelling blockbuster that comes closest in style to the Réserve des Céléstins made by Henri Bonneau. The color is a dense purple. The floral-scented bouquet reveals thick, kirsch notes intermixed with blackberries, smoked meats, and spice. On the palate, the wine is enormous, unctuously textured, with a finish that lasts nearly a minute. This majestic Châteauneuf-du-Pape will age effortlessly for nearly three decades. Anticipated maturity: 2005–2030. If you can find it, be sure to buy it!

A 1998 Châteauneuf-du-Pape Cuvée Laurence will be released after spending two years in *foudres* followed by one year in small barrels (the only Pégaü wine to be aged in smaller *barriques*). The rich 1998 exhibits abundant wood along with a briery, spicy character, and full body, but not as much typicity as the Cuvée da Capo and Cuvée Réservée exhibit (which represent the essence of Châteauneuf-du-Pape). Nevertheless, it is a big, powerful, more modern-styled effort that should drink well young and age nicely for 10–15 years. My experience with previous vintages of Cuvée Laurence (particularly 1990 and 1989) demonstrates that the longer wood aging dries them out and they do not age as well as the Cuvée Réservée . . . for what it's worth.

The 1997 Châteauneuf-du-Pape Cuvée Réservée is made in a firm, tannic style, with good black cherry fruit and a dry, allspice, peppery character. In the mouth, the wine is spice-driven, with medium body, a slight austerity, and a moderately long finish. Although it is not a star of the vintage, it is a very good 1997 Châteauneuf-du-Pape, but firmer and more backward than most wines of the vintage.

DOMAINE DU PÈRE CABOCHE

2000	Châteauneuf-du-Pape	C	(87–88)
1999	Châteauneuf-du-Pape	C	88
1998	Châteauneuf-du-Pape	C	87
1997	Châteauneuf-du-Pape	C	85
2000	Châteauneuf-du-Pape Cuvée Elisabeth Chambellan	D	(88–89)
1999	Châteauneuf-du-Pape Cuvée Elisabeth Chambellan	D	90
1998	Châteauneuf-du-Pape Cuvée Elisabeth Chambellan	D	90
1997	Châteauneuf-du-Pape Cuvée Elisabeth Chambellan	D	(86–88)

Jean-Pierre Boisson, the mayor of Châteauneuf-du-Pape, tends to bottle these wines early to preserve their fruit and charm. His wines are richly fruity, easily accessible, modern-styled classics. In the bigger, more muscular, structured, and concentrated vintages they possess extra dimensions of depth, but there is no denying the crowd-pleasing appeal of the two *cuvées*, the standard Châteauneuf and the *cuvée* Elisabeth Chambellan.

The easygoing, consumer-friendly, lush 2000 Châteauneuf-du-Pape is loaded with spicy black cherry fruit presented in a medium-bodied, supple, fleshy style. Drink it over the next 6–7 years. The 2000 Châteauneuf-du-Pape Cuvée Elisabeth Chambellan reveals a similar medium ruby color, but more structure as well as fat. It offers notes of spice box, black raspberries, cherries, and pepper, medium body, excellent purity, and a fleshy, velvety texture. Consume it during its first 7–8 years of life.

The dark ruby-colored 1999 Châteauneuf-du-Pape offers a big, thick, fruit-filled bouquet with scents of black cherries, spice, and flowers. Soft and medium- to full-bodied, with a succulent texture and low acidity in the fleshy, well-proportioned finish, it will drink well for 6–8 years. The 1999 Châteauneuf-du-Pape Cuvée Elisabeth Chambellan is a broader effort, with more glycerin, alcohol, and depth of black cherry and kirsch-flavored fruit. There are also notes of raspberries, licorice, and spice, as well as beautiful harmony and purity in this sexy Châteauneuf-du-Pape. Drink this full-bodied wine over the next decade.

If readers missed Père Caboche's 1998s, they are also topflight, with more tannin and structure, but similar weight and character as the 1999s. The sexy, fruity 1998 Châteauneuf-du-Pape is soft, heady, medium- to full-bodied, and pure. Cherries, pepper, and spice are present in addition to copious glycerin and fat. Drink this delicious Châteauneuf over the next 7–8 years. The 1998 Cuvée Elisabeth Chambellan offers a sumptuous glass of silky-textured, rich, fruit-driven, modern-styled Châteauneuf-du-Pape. A dark plum color and explosive bouquet of pepper and black cherries are followed by a rich, opulent, pure, full-bodied wine with a seamless texture. Anticipated maturity: now–2012.

The 1997 Châteauneuf-du-Pape's medium ruby color is followed by an expansive, sweet nose of black cherry candy with a touch of *sur-maturité* (orange/apricot scents). The tropical fruit character continues on the soft, round, medium-bodied palate. Drink this expansive, delicious, up-front Châteauneuf over the next 3 years. Made from older vines, the more expansive 1997 Châteauneuf-du-Pape Cuvée Elisabeth Chambellan possesses layers of fruit, with more glycerin and alcohol. There is virtually no tannin in this hedonistic, richly fruity, round, spicy, fruit-driven wine. Drink it over the next 3 years.

DOMAINE DU PÈRE PAPE

2000	Châteauneuf-du-Pape	C	(87–89)
1999	Châteauneuf-du-Pape	C	88
2000	Châteauneuf-du-Pape Clos du Calvaire	D	(88–89)

1999	Châteauneuf-du-Pape Clos du Calvaire	D	89
1998	Châteauneuf-du-Pape Domaine du Grand Coulet	D	85
2000	Châteauneuf-du-Pape La Crau de la Mère	D	(88–90)
1999	Châteauneuf-du-Pape La Crau de la Mère	D	89
1998	Châteauneuf-du-Pape La Crau de la Mère	D	90

Domaine du Père Pape's wines are modern, richly fruity, concentrated, and meant to be consumed during their first 10 years of life. As the following scores and tasting notes indicate, they are consistently fine efforts. The estate fashions four *cuvées*. Undoubtedly the finest offering from Domaine du Père Pape is the Châteauneuf-du-Pape La Crau de la Mère, which emerges from the *lieu-dit* La Crau, the warmest, most precocious *terroir* in the appellation. A large sector of this area is owned by Vieux-Télégraphe. Wine made from La Crau forms the backbone, if not the entire blend for Henri Bonneau's famed Réserve des Célestins. Amazingly, the Grenache grapes grown in La Crau reach full maturity 10–14 days earlier than those grown less than a mile away.

Cut from the same cloth, with slightly higher alcohol and more noticeable blackberry and cherry fruit, the 2000 Châteauneuf-du-Pape reveals high glycerin, low acidity, and a chewy texture. Exhibiting a more saturated ruby/purple color, the 2000 Châteauneuf-du-Pape Clos du Calvaire offers jammy notes of blackberry, kirsch, licorice, and pepper. Fat and pure, with a hedonistic mid-palate as well as a long, fruit-dominated finish, it will require consumption during its first decade of life. The 2000 Châteauneuf-du-Pape La Crau de la Mère exhibits a denser ruby/purple color as well as sweet, fat, jammy fruit, a creamy texture, a sexy, plump midsection, low acidity, and a gutsy, hedonistic finish. Undeniably appealing in an unctuous, obvious style, it tips the scales at 14.5% alcohol. Anticipated maturity: now–2010.

The 1999 Châteauneuf-du-Pape possesses big fruit, a complex, layered, full-bodied style offering glycerin, succulence, alcohol, fruit, and a friendly personality. Drink it over the next 6–7 years. The single-vineyard 1999 Châteauneuf-du-Pape Clos du Calvaire's dark ruby color is accompanied by aromas of plums, cherries, and earth presented in a layered, opulently textured, sexy, richly fruity style. This beautifully made 1999 can be drunk now and over the next 12 years. The 1999 Châteauneuf-du-Pape La Crau de la Mère is a Provençal-styled Châteauneuf that exhibits the famed *garrigue* (that mélange of earth tones, thyme, rosemary, and lavender) character, crushed pepper, spices, plum, and kirsch notes. This excellent, complex, savory, full-bodied, fleshy wine should be consumed over the next 7–8 years.

The 1998 Châteauneuf-du-Pape La Crau de la Mère exhibits a noteworthy Provençal herb/earthy and black cherry–scented nose. This well-made wine is expansive and silky-textured, with jammy black fruits, plenty of heady alcohol, and succulent levels of glycerin. If it develops slightly more complexity, it should merit an outstanding score. Anticipated maturity: now–2012. More straightforward, the 1998 Châteauneuf-du-Pape Domaine du Grand Coulet exhibits good fruit, but little complexity. It should be drunk over the next 3 years.

MICHEL PERRAUD

1998	Cornas Cuvée Sarah	D	88
1997	Cornas Cuvée Sarah	D	91
1998	Cornas Le Vignon	D	91
1997	Cornas Le Vignon	D	90
1997	St.-Joseph Cuvée Sensonne	D	(92–94)

These special *cuvées* made for the American market by French wine broker Patrick Lesec are aged in 100% new oak and bottled with neither fining nor filtration. The wines spend significant time in contact with their lees, are not racked until bottling, and include 100% stems in the winemaking process. The Cuvée Sarah is produced from 50-year-old Syrah vines planted in the middle of the Cornas hillside. Le Vignon is made from 80-year-old vines planted on the upper slopes of the hills. The deep ruby/purple-colored 1998 Cornas Cuvée Sarah offers aromas of spicy new oak and smoky, black fruits, rustic tannin, a big, chewy, robust constitution, and a moderately long finish. Consume it over the next 7–8 years although it may never fully resolve all of its tannin. The exceptional 1998 Cornas Le Vignon is a terrific example of this appellation. The use of 100% stems is not noticeable although I suspect it has given the wine more complexity and structure. The dense ruby/black color is followed by licorice, scorched earth, blackberry liqueur, and toasty oak. Quite powerful and tannic, this wine will evolve for 10–18 years. Both 1999s are slightly more saturated black/purple in color, potentially fatter, as well as more unctuously textured offerings with 10–16 years of aging potential. These are modern-styled, impressive efforts from Cornas.

The 1997 Cornas Cuvée Sarah possesses more sweetness and richness in the mouth than its older sibling. The color is an impressively saturated black/ruby/purple. The nose offers up aromas of cassis, minerals, mint, and licorice, and the wine is rich, full-bodied, dense, powerful, and muscular. The finish is moderately tannic. Anticipated maturity: now–2015. The classically styled 1997 Cornas Le Vignon is almost uncivilized with its powerful display of rustic tannin, full body, and large quantities of tar-flavored black currant fruit. This earthy, *sauvage*-styled Cornas should be at its finest before 2015.

Lastly, 3,000 bottles of the sensational 1997 St.-Joseph Cuvée Sensonne were produced. This wine can compete with the luxury single-vineyard St.-Joseph Les Granits from Michel Chapoutier. Made from 60-year-old Syrah vines planted on the appellation's northern hillsides, it possesses an opaque black/purple color and a super nose of jammy cassis and minerals. In the mouth, toasty new oak makes an appearance along with abundant quantities of black fruits. This full-bodied wine offers copious glycerin, low acidity, admirable power, and a terrifically long finish. It should drink well for 10+ years.

ANDRÉ PERRET

2000	Condrieu Clos Chanson	E	88
1999	Condrieu Clos Chanson	E	92
2000	Condrieu Coteau du Chéry	E	89
1999	Condrieu Coteau du Chéry	E	95
2000	St.-Joseph	C	(85–86)
1999	St.-Joseph	C	(86–88)
1998	St.-Joseph	C	86
1999	St.-Joseph Blanc	D	(87–89)
2000	St.-Joseph Les Grisières	D	(85–87)
1999	St.-Joseph Les Grisières	D	90
1998	St.-Joseph Les Grisières	D	90

As a long-time fan of Perret's white wines, which are among the finest of the northern Rhône, it is good to see his red wines continue to increase in quality. His 1999 and 1998 *cuvées* of St.-Joseph are the best he has yet produced. However, the 2000 red wine *cuvées* also seem superficial, offering dense colors and good ripeness, but little fat, depth, or palate persistence.

The 2000 St.-Joseph reveals dry tannin in the finish. The 2000 St.-Joseph Les Grisières exhibits more ripeness, but is a light effort, especially compared to the superb 1999 St.-Joseph Les Grisières. As for the latter wine, it is Burgundy-like in its gorgeously delineated, black cherry, floral-like aromas and flavors. It reveals moderate tannin, outstanding depth, purity, and ripeness, and an unmistakable sense of elegance. It should drink well for a decade. The 1999 St.-Joseph exhibits the vintage's dense opaque ruby/purple color as well as an elegant nose of blueberries, blackberries, and minerals, sweet tannin, medium body, well-integrated acidity, and a seductive, lush style. It should drink well for 5–7 years.

The 1998s reveal more tannin as well as seemingly lower acidity and graceful, concentrated personalities. The 1998 St.-Joseph is an earthy, herbal offering with plentiful cherry and black fruits yet a slightly austere finish. Consume it over the next 3–5 years. The 1998 St.-Joseph Les Grisières offers black cherries, blueberries, and cassis, in addition to more noticeable tannin than its 1999 counterpart. There is outstanding purity, a graceful, stylish mouth-feel with copious quantities of sweet fruit, and impressive glycerin and symmetry. Give it 2–3 years of cellaring, and enjoy it over the following decade.

Perret's white wine offerings are consistently brilliant, regardless of vintage conditions. They always achieve complex aromas and layered textures rarely found in other white Rhônes. Perret's 2000 Condrieus are significantly lighter and less concentrated than his 1999s and 1998s, raising the specter of high yields, even for this meticulous, quality conscious grower/wine-maker. The 2000 Condrieu Coteau du Chéry exhibits good ripeness, body, and flavor, but it requires drinking over the next year to take advantage of its moderately intense nose of apricot and honeysuckle. Although medium-bodied and very good, the 2000 is not as profound as past vintages. More superficial, but fruity and lush is the 2000 Condrieu Clos Chanson. It does not possess the minerality of the Coteau du Chéry, but it is a very good effort. As do many 2000 northern Rhônes, it lacks depth. Drink it over the next year.

The 1999 St.-Joseph Blanc exhibits an elegant, floral, apricot, and peach-scented bouquet with excellent freshness. Displaying finesse married to considerable concentrated fruit and intensity, it should drink well over the next several years. Perret is one of the masters of Condrieu; 1999 did not produce wines with the concentration and complexity of 1998, but you would never know that from Perret's offerings. The 1999 Condrieu Clos Chanson is a dense, full-bodied, honeyed effort with excellent ripeness, a big, thick, juicy texture, and a complex, leesy, honeysuckle, and exotic fruit-scented nose. Drink it over the next 2 years. Perret's brilliant Condrieu Coteau du Chéry is, along with Guigal's La Doriane and Vernay's Coteau Vernon, the finest Condrieu produced. The 1999 is one of the candidates for Condrieu of the vintage, integrating its acidity and alcohol with fabulous lychee nut, apricot, orange marmalade, and honeyed pear characteristics, massive body, and unbelievable elegance and purity for a wine of such intensity. However, do not expect it to age well; it requires consumption over the next 2–3 years.

PERRIN

2000 **Châteauneuf-du-Pape Les Sinards**	D	(88–90)
1999 **Châteauneuf-du-Pape Les Sinards**	D	(88–89)
2000 **Côtes du Rhône Réserve**	A	87
1999 **Côtes du Rhône Réserve**	A	89
2000 **Côtes du Rhône Réserve Blanc**	A	86
2000 **Côtes du Rhône-Villages Rasteau**	A	88
2000 **Côtes du Rhône-Villages Vinsobres**	B	85
2000 **Côtes du Ventoux La Vieilles Ferme**	A	86
2000 **Gigondas**	B	86
1999 **Gigondas**	B	(87–88)
1998 **Gigondas**	B	86
2000 **Vacqueyras**	B	87
1999 **Vacqueyras**	B	88
1998 **Vacqueyras**	B	86

These value-priced, tank-aged wines, offered under the *négociant* label of Jean-Pierre Perrin and his son, Pierre, are bottled early to preserve their fruit. The least expensive are the La Vieilles Ferme efforts. The 2000 Côtes du Rhône Réserve Blanc is a blend of 65% Grenache Blanc, 20% Viognier, and 15% Roussanne. Viognier's floral, honeysuckle, and peach characteristics are obvious in this light- to medium-bodied wine's bouquet. Fruity and clean, it is best consumed over the next year. The Grenache-dominated 2000 Côtes du Ventoux La

Vieilles Ferme (150,000 cases) offers a deep ruby color, copious quantities of cherry fruit, a pleasant, open-knit texture, and soft tannin. It is the type of delicious red often found in the southern Rhône, but nowhere else in the world at this quality level and price. The impressive, deep ruby-colored 2000 Côtes du Rhône Réserve possesses loads of black cherry and currant fruit, medium body, and admirable structure. Enjoy it over the next 2–3 years.

The Perrins have branched out to offer many wines from the Côtes du Rhône-Villages. They are all noteworthy efforts that retain their village characters. The 2000 Côtes du Rhône-Villages Vinsobres (60% Grenache and 40% Syrah) exhibits an earthy, peppery bouquet, dry tannin, and abundant quantities of black fruit presented in an austere style. It should drink well for 3–4 years. Readers looking for more chocolate along with deeper, concentrated black fruits as well as fuller body should check out the 2000 Côtes du Rhône-Villages Rasteau. A blend of 80% Grenache and 20% Syrah, it is a big, beefy, palate-coating red capable of lasting 4–5 years. Another serious effort with considerable hedonistic appeal is the 2000 Vacqueyras (a blend of 85% Grenache and 15% Syrah). Produced from that appellation's Sarrians sector, which is all so-called *garrigue* land, it boasts a deep ruby/purple color along with a sweet nose of kirsch, pepper, and earth. Drink this round, soft, fleshy, medium- to full-bodied 2000 over the next 4–5 years. About 20% of the 2000 Gigondas will spend a small period in wood. It exhibits red and black fruits interspersed with mineral, earth, and spice, high acidity and rustic tannin in the finish. Although solidly made, it lacks the charm and seductiveness of the Vacqueyras as well as the power, glycerin, and fruit of the Rasteau. It should drink well for 7–8 years. The dark ruby-colored 2000 Châteauneuf-du-Pape Les Sinards is dominated by Grenache (80%). Full-bodied, with abundant glycerin and fruit, a sweet berry character, low acidity, and a plump, fleshy, long finish, it will be drinkable upon release, but age well for 15 years.

The 1999 offerings are led by the fleshy 1999 Côtes du Rhône Réserve and 1999 Vacqueyras. Both are excellent, dense ruby-colored efforts displaying copious quantities of cherries, earth, and pepper in their medium- to full-bodied personalities—fruit bombs to enjoy over the next 3–4 years. Very good efforts, they are capable of lasting a decade. If the rustic Vacqueyras represents power and exuberance, the 1999 Gigondas displays the southern Rhône's more elegant side. With sweet berry and cherry fruit, it is less massive than the Vacqueyras and more finesse-styled. It also shares a dark ruby/purple color and a precocious personality that suggests drinking it over the next 7–8 years. The closed 1998 Gigondas and 1998 Vacqueyras possess more dry tannin, but are pure and well made. Lastly, the excellent, nearly outstanding 1999 Châteauneuf-du-Pape Les Sinards is a blend from a friend's vineyard near the village of Grès, not far from Beaucastel, as well as declassified wine from Beaucastel. A deep purple color is followed by sweet black cherry fruit infused with smoke, leather, and roasted meat. The wine is medium- to full-bodied, with good underlying acidity and a delineated finish. Its purity and freshness are admirable. Enjoy it over the next 10–12 years.

DOMAINE ROGER PERRIN

2000	Châteauneuf-du-Pape	C	(88–90)
1999	Châteauneuf-du-Pape	C	(87–88)
1998	Châteauneuf-du-Pape	C	89
2000	Châteauneuf-du-Pape Réserve des Vieilles Vignes	D	(93–95)
1998	Châteauneuf-du-Pape Réserve des Vieilles Vignes	D	94
2000	Côtes du Rhône	A	(86–88)
2000	Côtes du Rhône Réserve des Vieilles Vignes	B	(88–90)

Roger Perrin is another up-and-coming star of Châteauneuf-du-Pape. He produced terrific 1998s, with his Réserve des Vieilles Vignes (originally rated 90+, but now rated 93+ . . . at the minimum) a potential superstar in the making. His 2000s and 1999s are impressive. This modest estate of just under 30 acres is clearly on the rebound. Value seekers should consider Perrin's Côtes du Rhône *cuvées*. The delicious 2000 Côtes du Rhône is a creamy-textured, herbaceous, peppery, cherry-dominated offering with a degree of elegance. Enjoy it over the next 2–3 years. The 2000 Côtes du Rhône Réserve des Vieilles Vignes is a lusty, fat, hedonistic offering bursting at the seams with black fruits, abundant glycerin, and a layered, concentrated style that shames many of the commercial Châteauneuf-du-Papes made with no respect for the appellation or their *terroirs*. Drink it over the next 3 years. This is an estate clearly on the rise!

The big, dense, fruity, dark ruby/purple-colored 2000 Châteauneuf-du-Pape offers copious quantities of black cherry liqueur notes presented in a seductive, full-bodied, fleshy style. This consumer-friendly, powerful, concentrated, jammy effort will become more delineated and drink well for 10–15 years. The blockbuster 2000 Châteauneuf-du-Pape Réserve des Vieilles Vignes (15% natural alcohol) is a broodingly backward giant with immense body, huge purity, and a style not dissimilar from André Brunel's famed Les Cailloux Cuvée Centenaire. It is spectacularly rich, with a dense ruby/purple color followed by gobs of blackberry and cherry fruit intermixed with balsam wood, pepper, and dried herb characteristics. Unctuously textured, extremely pure and layered, this potentially prodigious Châteauneuf-du-Pape should be drinkable in 2–3 years and last for more than two decades.

Perrin's 1999 Châteauneuf-du-Pape reveals the vintage's soft, elegant, fruit-driven character as well as overall balance and finesse. It offers loads of cherry and berry fruit, good glycerin, medium to full body, and a seductive, disarming style. It should drink well for 7–8 years. The 1998 Châteauneuf-du-Pape possesses more structure and tannin plus fine accessibility. An evolved dark plum/garnet color is followed by an intriguing nose of roasted herbs, meat juices, cherry liqueur, and plums. Medium- to full-bodied, with an excellent mid-palate, a nicely layered texture, and a succulent, fleshy finish, it will drink well for 12–14 years. Perrin's debut vintage of a limited production, top of the line, old-vine *cuvée* is the 1998 Châteauneuf-du-Pape Réserve des Vieilles Vignes, which has been bottled without filtration. Extremely concentrated, powerful, and muscular, it boasts a dense ruby/purple color in addition to thick aromas of cured olives, dried herbs, blackberries, cherries, and thyme. This full-bodied, moderately tannic effort needs 2–3 years of cellaring, and should last for 16–20 years. Impressive!

DOMAINE DU PESQUIER

1999 Gigondas	D	(87–89)
1998 Gigondas	D	88

Two *cuvées* of 1999 Gigondas were tasted. Both revealed an excellent dark plum/purple color, soft acids, plenty of peppery, *garrigue*, cherry, and blackberry fruit, admirable glycerin, fine opulence, a supple, sexy texture, and medium to full body. This 1999 should last for 10 years. Pesquier's dark plum/ruby-colored 1998 Gigondas exhibits Provençal herbs, licorice, and black cherry jam characteristics. Well made, up-front, soft, fleshy, and appealing, it will drink well for 10 years.

DOMAINE DE PIAUGER

1998 Côtes du Rhône Montmartel	B	86
1998 Côtes du Rhône Réserve Alphonse Latour	B	87
1998 Côtes du Rhône Réserve de Maude	B	85
1998 Côtes du Rhône Tenebi	B	78

Readers looking for a light style of Côtes du Rhône to be consumed over the next 2–3 years should seek out these 1998s. They are earthy, peppery, Provençal-styled offerings, but not terribly concentrated or ageworthy, with one exception, the 1998 Réserve Alphonse Latour. The finest of the group, it is more complete and very supple, with deep black cherry fruit intermixed with licorice and smoke. It has 5 years of aging potential, as does the 1998 Réserve de Maude, which was the only *cuvée* to reveal new oak notes from *barrique* aging. The disappointing herbal, thin 1998 Tenebi is easily forgotten, but the rest of the wines are correct, pleasant offerings, with decent textures. They will drink well over the next several years.

DOMAINE PONTIFICAL

2000 Châteauneuf-du-Pape	C	(87–89)
1999 Châteauneuf-du-Pape	C	89

Pontifical's 2000 Châteauneuf-du-Pape is the qualitative equivalent of the 1999. Medium- to full-bodied and spicy, with slightly riper, jammier fruit as well as more glycerin and fat, it is a pure, excellent Châteauneuf that falls just short of being outstanding. Anticipated maturity: now–2012. The attractive, dark ruby-colored 1999 Châteauneuf-du-Pape is already revealing pink and amber at the edge. A spicy perfume of dried herbs, cedar, pepper, and red and black fruits is followed by a medium- to full-bodied, dense, supple-textured wine that is easy to understand as well as consume. Complex, fleshy, and all that a Châteauneuf-du-Pape should be, it will drink well for a decade.

RABASSE-CHARAVIN

2000 Côtes du Rhône-Villages Cairanne	B	87

Proprietor Corinne Coutourier has fashioned a sexy blend of 75% Grenache, 15% Syrah, and 10% Cinsault. A dark ruby color is accompanied by an open-knit nose of crushed black cherries, pepper, and minerals. This well-made, elegant, flavorful, medium- to full-bodied 2000 reveals copious fruit and no hard edges. Drink it over the next 2–3 years.

DOMAINE RASPAIL-AY

1999 Gigondas	C	(87–88)
1998 Gigondas	C	89
1997 Gigondas	C	86

The dark ruby-colored 1999 Gigondas is a seductive, mid-weight, open-knit effort with abundant quantities of kirsch, pepper, herb, and leathery notes. Plump, evolved, and accessible, I would opt for drinking it during its first decade of life. In contrast, the 1998 Gigondas has closed down completely since bottling. It offers a healthy dense ruby/purple color as well as a structured, powerful personality with moderately intense cherry and blackberry fruit intermixed with smoke, minerals, and truffles. Elegant, dense, moderately high in tannin, and well delineated, it will be at its best between now–2015. The 1997 Gigondas possesses a deep ruby/purple color, a sweet cassis/cherry-scented nose, and an opulent, soft, open-knit personality with low acidity and fine plumpness. Hopefully, it will be bottled early to preserve its fruit as it requires drinking over the next 4–5 years.

CHÂTEAU RAYAS

2000 Châteauneuf-du-Pape	EEE	(91–94)
1999 Châteauneuf-du-Pape	EEE	92
1998 Châteauneuf-du-Pape	EEE	94
1997 Châteauneuf-du-Pape	EEE	88
2000 Châteauneuf-du-Pape Blanc	D	89
1999 Châteauneuf-du-Pape Blanc	D	89
1997 Châteauneuf-du-Pape Blanc	D	87
2000 Châteauneuf-du-Pape Pignan	E	(86–88)
1999 Châteauneuf-du-Pape Pignan	E	89
1997 Châteauneuf-du-Pape Pignan	E	87
2000 Côtes du Rhône Fonsalette	E	(89–91)

1999 Côtes du Rhône Fonsalette	E	89
1998 Côtes du Rhône Fonsalette	E	90
1997 Côtes du Rhône Fonsalette	D	(86–87)
2000 Côtes du Rhône Fonsalette Blanc	D	88
1999 Côtes du Rhône Fonsalette Blanc	D	87
1997 Côtes du Rhône Fonsalette Blanc	D	84
2000 Côtes du Rhône Fonsalette Cuvée Syrah	E	(89–91+)
1999 Côtes du Rhône Fonsalette Cuvée Syrah	E	91
1998 Côtes du Rhône Fonsalette Cuvée Syrah	E	91
1997 Côtes du Rhône Fonsalette Cuvée Syrah	E	88
1999 Côtes du Rhône Pialade	B	85
1998 Côtes du Rhône Pialade	B	86

Françoise Reynaud has been in charge of Rayas since the death of her brother in 1997 (Jacques Reynaud conducted the harvest and winemaking of the 1996s, but died before they were assembled and bottled). She is capably assisted by her nephew, Emmanuel Reynaud.

It is increasingly fashionable in wine (whine) circles to complain, "What's wrong with Rayas?" The passing of Jacques Reynaud in January 1997 was unquestionably an unsettling event, but Françoise and Emmanuel had been apprenticing under the idiosyncratic Reynaud. Ten years ago there were only 7–8 profound Châteauneuf-du-Papes being produced, whereas today there are 40–50. Other producers have ratcheted up their performances, and Rayas has basically stayed the same. Additionally, Rayas may have lost some concentration because one-third of the vineyard was replanted in 1992, and those young vines have to be factored into the final blend. Nevertheless, after tasting the superb 2000 (which reveals all the earmarks of an exceptional vintage), 1999 (which is actually better out of bottle), and 1998, much of the criticism appears overblown. However, I do recognize that wineries cannot rest on their laurels, but this is an eccentric wine made from a very unusual *terroir* (a cold microclimate in a hot zone), yet recent vintages produced under the administration of Françoise and Emmanuel Reynaud have all the same characteristics as those produced by the late Jacques Reynaud.

As it was elsewhere in Châteauneuf-du-Pape, the 2000 vintage at Rayas was extremely sweet and jammy. The 2000 Côtes du Rhône Fonsalette, a blend of 60% Grenache, 25% Cinsault, and 15% Syrah, exhibits a dark ruby color as well as copious aromas of black fruits, balsam, and earth. Medium- to full-bodied and rich with sweet tannin, it should be a top-notch vintage for Fonsalette. The Cinsault came in at a whopping 16.5% natural alcohol and the Grenache at 15%, so there is no lack of power or glycerin in this *cuvée*. The opaque bluish/purple-colored 2000 Côtes du Rhône Fonsalette Cuvée Syrah reveals power along with monster tannin. If this wine is to merit an outstanding score, some of its astringency needs to melt away, but it is packed. It is a surprisingly brooding, backward effort for this accessible vintage.

The 2000 Châteauneuf-du-Pape Pignan appears lighter than other top vintages, but often the wines from these cellars taste considerably better after bottling. Moreover, the nature of Grenache at both Fonsalette and Rayas is that it needs time in bottle. These wines actually put on weight and deepen in color, something its critics should recognize. The medium ruby-colored 2000 Pignan offers sweet, dusty, black cherry flavors, elegance, and an abbreviated finish. It looks to be very good to excellent rather than exceptional. I was very impressed with the 2000 Châteauneuf-du-Pape. It totally conceals the 15.5% alcohol and was produced from a tiny crop, much like the 1999. One-third of the *cuvée* had just finished fermenting dry, which gives you an idea of its power and richness. It is a sexy, aromatic style of Rayas with a deceptively light medium ruby color (much like 1998) as well as sweet, candied, black cherry fruit intermixed with black raspberries and spice. Opulent, with a boatload of glycerin, full body, a velvety texture, and fine length, it should turn out to be a sweeter, jammier version of the 1998, and possibly even better, but it is still early in the game. Anticipated maturity: 2004–2018.

There is more irregularity with the white wines. The medium- to full-bodied 2000 Côtes du Rhône Fonsalette Blanc (a blend of Grenache Blanc, Clairette, and Marsanne) exhibits an excellent citrusy bouquet as well as a fat texture. As the wine sat in the glass, aromas of white flowers and a touch of honey emerged. It should age for 5–7 years. The 2000 Châteauneuf-du-Pape Blanc (equal parts Clairette and Grenache Blanc) reveals big, juicy, buttery honeysuckle-like aromas and flavors, excellent concentration, a chewy palate, and a long finish. It should drink well for a decade or more, as this *cuvée* has an uncanny ability to pull itself together and surprise anyone trying to predict what it is going to do.

The 1999 Rayas production was extremely small, resulting in very fine 1999s, a vintage that generally produced lighter wines. The medium dark ruby-colored 1999 Côtes du Rhône Fonsalette reveals an intriguing perfume of peppery black cherries, earth, and underbrush, medium body, excellent purity as well as light tannin in the finish. If it puts on weight it will merit another point or two. Anticipated maturity: now–2014. The sensational, 250-case *cuvée* of black/purple-colored 1999 Côtes du Rhône Fonsalette Cuvée Syrah should be gobbled up by fans of this offering. This cool-climate vineyard planted on north-facing slopes consistently produces fabulous wines that age for 2–3 decades (the debut 1978 vintage is still an infant). The sweet, rich, full-bodied 1999 reveals ripe tannin along with notes of roasted meats, blackberries, truffles, and licorice. Cellar this monster for 4–8 years, and enjoy the magic over the next 10–12 years. Anticipated maturity: 2007–2020. The 1999 Châteauneuf-du-Pape Pignan displays a light to medium ruby color in addition to a gorgeous nose of sweet kirsch, tobacco, and floral scents. Medium- to full-bodied, lush, and accessible, with light tannin in the finish, it should be at its finest between now–2014. The dark ruby-colored 1999 Châteauneuf-du-Pape admirably conceals its 15% alcohol. With more serious structure and tannin, but not the fat of the 1998 Rayas, this medium- to full-bodied, closed 1999 offers beautiful, sweet kirsch notes in the aromatics and on the attack, but it tightens in the finish. It could turn out to be a modern-day version of the 1979.

The remaining juice left over after Rayas, Fonsalette, and Pignan are bottled is assembled into a *cuvée* called Pialade. The 1999 Côtes du Rhône Pialade (1,000 cases) possesses a light ruby color along with notions of the Rayas/Pignan style, but finishes quickly. It is a pleasant, elegant, cherry fruit–dominated wine to drink over the next 3–4 years.

While the 1999 white wine *cuvées* are not as fat or unctuous as the 2000 whites, they are ripe, distinctive efforts completely dissimilar from most southern Rhône Valley whites (which tend to be innocuous and bland). The floral-scented, fat 1999 Côtes du Rhône Fonsalette Blanc is one-dimensional, but concentrated. The 1999 Châteauneuf-du-Pape Blanc is even more concentrated, with loads of glycerin as well as a citrusy/pineapple characteristic. When I asked Françoise Reynaud what she likes to eat with these wines, she said, "I prefer them as an apéritif." Maybe that's their true calling in life.

The *cuvées* of red Fonsalette include the dark ruby/purple-tinged, tannic 1998 Côtes du Rhône Fonsalette. The attack and mid-palate reveal rich, concentrated, peppery, earthy fruit. Most readers would probably assume the Côtes du Rhône will be ready to drink at an earlier age than Rayas, but this full-bodied, dense, structured 1998 requires 3–4 years of cellaring and should last longer than the 1998 Rayas. Anticipated maturity: 2004–2020. The 1998 Côtes du Rhône Fonsalette Cuvée Syrah exhibits a typical black/purple color as well as a knockout nose of animal fur, licorice, crème de cassis, truffles, and damp earth. This dense, huge, concentrated, formidably-endowed wine is a superb expression of southern Rhône Syrah. It is for serious collectors only. Anticipated maturity: 2006–2020. Every year the least impressive offering is their Pialade. The 1998 Côtes du Rhône Pialade is a nice wine for drinking over the next 2–4 years. Its light to medium ruby color is accompanied by strawberry and cherry fruit, medium body, and peppery spice. It just lacks depth and dimension.

The 1998s do not possess the color saturation of the 1995s, 1990s, or 1989s, but there is no doubting the extraordinary depth and layers of flavor the 1998 Châteauneuf-du-Pape contains. The color is medium to deep ruby and the bouquet offers aromas of ripe strawberry and cherry candy, with kirsch thrown in for additional interest. On the palate, the wine is full-bodied and fat, with high levels of sweet fruit, a velvety texture, multiple dimensions, and an explosive finish. It is an undeniably sexy, compelling Rayas that is already performing exceptionally well. The crop size was 30% bigger than 1999, which means there are several thousand additional bottles available for the world's market. My best guess is that this voluptuous, sexy Rayas should drink well young, yet age easily for 15–16 years. Do not be surprised to see it put on considerable weight over the next few years.

The two white 1997s, which were put through 100% malolactic fermentation, are soft, round, fruity wines, with the 1997 Côtes-du-Rhône Fonsalette Blanc crisp and fresh, with white peach–like fruit. It is a medium-bodied wine to consume over the next several years. The 1997 Châteauneuf-du-Pape Blanc exhibits some of the same peach-like character, but there are more apricot liqueur notes in addition to sherry-like aspects. The wine possesses good fruit flavors, medium body, and a slightly eccentric personality.

It appears the 1997 Côtes du Rhône Fonsalette red will be open-knit and attractive. All the *cuvées* taste in the 86–89 point range. The wine is medium ruby-colored, with cherry and raspberry fruit, a degree of elegance, and a richly fruity, round, generous style that should be pleasing. The 1997 Châteauneuf-du-Pape Pignan, made from 100% Grenache, reveals a deceptively unimpressive medium ruby color, but intense, sweet, raspberry and cherry fruit mixed with kirsch. Spicy, with pepper, roasted peanut, and fine ripeness, it will drink well early and last for 7–10 years. The 1997 Châteauneuf-du-Pape is a medium ruby-colored, moderately weighted wine with plenty of sweet raspberry and cherry fruit, excellent to outstanding aromatics, but neither the depth nor the concentration found in a great vintage. There is plenty of heady alcohol, and the wine reveals an unmistakable cherry liqueur component. Dry tannin can be detected in the wine's finish. Look for it to drink beautifully young and keep for 10–12 years. It reminds me of a better, fruitier version of the 1986. The 1997 Côtes du Rhône Fonsalette Cuvée Syrah exhibits an opaque black/purple color and a sweet blackberry and animal-scented nose. Although the wine is rich on the attack, it narrows out to reveal considerable tannin and a tough, rustic personality. If this wine fleshes out in the finish, it will merit a score in the upper 80s. If it doesn't, expect an impressive-looking wine, but one that is angular and coarse in the mouth. Undoubtedly it will last 10–20 years.

Past Glories: Rayas (red)—1994 (90), 1990 (100), 1989 (97), 1988 (93), 1985 (94), 1983 (95), 1981 (96), 1979 (94?), 1978 (96?); Fonsalette—1994 (90), 1990 (92), 1989 (93); Fonsalette Cuvée Syrah—1995 (94+), 1994 (94), 1991 (92+), 1990 (95), 1989 (93), 1988 (92), 1985 (92), 1978 (93); Pignan—1990 (96)

CHÂTEAU REDORTIER

1999 Gigondas	D	(88–90)
1998 Gigondas	D	90
1997 Gigondas	D	84

This is one of the excellent, sometimes outstanding Gigondas estates, producing just under 2,000 cases from a small vineyard holding of 12.4 acres. The wines, which are all aged in vats, are bottled without filtration.

The opulent, sexy, forward 1999 Gigondas exhibits a deep ruby/purple color, as well as sweet aromas of spice box, herbs, and black cherry jam. Dense, full-bodied, and chewy, with sweeter tannin than its older sibling, the 1999 will last for 10–12 years. Made in a serious *vin de garde* style, the dense ruby/purple-colored 1998 Gigondas is delineated, intense, and smoky, with plenty of meaty black fruit flavors intermixed with spice box and dried herbs. It has put on considerable weight during its *élevage*. Anticipated maturity: now–2014.

The 1997 Gigondas is a sweet, open-knit, attractive, straightforward, mainstream wine lacking the power and richness of a great vintage, but offering plenty of charm and hedonistic appeal, assuming it is consumed within its first 4–6 years of life. The 1997 displays medium body, a peppery, cherry, *garrigue*-scented nose, and a soft, easygoing, low-acid finish.

DOMAINE DES RELAGNES

2000	Châteauneuf-du-Pape	C	(87–88)
1999	Châteauneuf-du-Pape	C	82
1998	Châteauneuf-du-Pape	C	88
1997	Châteauneuf-du-Pape	C	83
2000	Châteauneuf-du-Pape Cuvée Vigneronne	D	(90–91)
1999	Châteauneuf-du-Pape Cuvée Vigneronne	D	89
1998	Châteauneuf-du-Pape Cuvée Vigneronne	D	90
1997	Châteauneuf-du-Pape Cuvée Vigneronne	D	87

Both 2000s are sexy, up-front, jammy efforts, with good fruit, glycerin, and fat. The 2000 Châteauneuf-du-Pape exhibits a medium ruby color along with copious quantities of black cherry fruit presented in a sexy, opulent format. Medium- to full-bodied with low acidity, this user-friendly wine will drink well for 7–8 years. Revealing a more saturated ruby color as well as additional stuffing and concentration is the 2000 Châteauneuf-du-Pape Cuvée Vigneronne. It possesses plenty of pepper and earthy notes in its jammy nose plus structure, medium to full body, and a dense, surprisingly long finish. This is an expansively flavored, seductive Châteauneuf that will drink well young yet last for 12–15 years.

Both 1999 *cuvées* are fruit-forward efforts that need to be consumed over the near term, 4–5 years for the traditional *cuvée* and 7–10 years in the case of the Cuvée Vigneronne. The 1999 Châteauneuf-du-Pape possesses a medium ruby color as well as soft, berry fruit mixed with dried herb, pepper, and spice notes. Round, seamless, velvety-textured, and easy to understand, it is a consumer-friendly, mainstream effort that lacks the concentration needed to be great. The 1999 Châteauneuf-du-Pape Cuvée Vigneronne's medium dark ruby color is accompanied by a big, spicy nose of cherry jam, pepper, *garrigue*, and fruitcake. While some tannin is noticeable, this wine is dominated by its fruit. It is round and medium-bodied with excellent purity.

The 1998s are similarly styled. The dark ruby-colored 1998 Châteauneuf-du-Pape offers up a big, sweet nose of smoke, cherries, plums, and *garrigue*, a plush texture, medium to full body, and slightly more tannin than its 1999 counterpart. Although accessible, it should last for a decade. The exceptional 1998 Châteauneuf-du-Pape Cuvée Vigneronne boasts a deep ruby color as well as flamboyant aromas of black cherry jam, smoke, and underbrush. It is opulent and sexy, with low acidity, impressive levels of glycerin, high alcohol, and a chewy, user-friendly, undeniably rich, long finish with no hard edges. Drink this seamless flesh-pot over the next 12 years.

The 1997 Châteauneuf-du-Pape offers a medium deep-ruby color and a textbook nose of Provençal herbs intermixed with plum, brandy, and cherry notes. The wine reveals sweet fruit, medium body, and some dilution, but it is ripe and seductive. Drink it over the next 2 years. The 1997 Châteauneuf-du-Pape Cuvée Vigneronne is denser, with a deep ruby color, plenty of jammy black cherry fruit in the nose, nice glycerin, light tannin in the finish, and a medium-bodied, nicely-concentrated and textured style. While not a blockbuster, this seductive Châteauneuf is ideal for drinking over the next 4 years.

DOMAINE DE LA RÉMÉJEANNE

2000	Côtes du Rhône Les Arbousiers	B	86
1999	Côtes du Rhône Les Arbousiers	B	87
2000	Côtes du Rhône Les Chèvrefeuilles	B	87

2000 Côtes du Rhône Les Eglantiers	B	90
1999 Côtes du Rhône Les Eglantiers	B	90
1998 Côtes du Rhône Les Eglantiers	B	88
2000 Côtes du Rhône-Villages Les Genévrières	B	90
1999 Côtes du Rhône-Villages Les Genévrières	B	88
1998 Côtes du Rhône-Villages Les Genévrières	B	87

This is a consistently top-notch source for impeccably well made wines that sell for a song. Réméjeanne has been on a qualitative hot streak since the mid-1990s, and their 2000s may be the finest offerings yet produced. The dark ruby-colored 2000 Côtes du Rhône Les Chèvrefeuilles is a blend of 40% Syrah, 40% Grenache, and 20% Cinsault. It possesses a soft bouquet of ripe berry fruit mixed with spice and earth. Round, jammy, and medium-bodied, it will drink well for 2 years. Similarly styled, but displaying more structure along with notes of Provençal herbs and pepper, the 2000 Côtes du Rhône Les Arbousiers is a blend of 70% Grenache and 30% Syrah. There is more noticeable tannin accompanying its deep ruby color and spicy, medium-bodied finish. It should drink well for 2–3 years.

Two exceptional *cuvées* include the 100% Syrah 2000 Côtes du Rhône Les Eglantiers, an opaque purple-colored effort with an extraordinary bouquet of pure cassis, blackberry liqueur, and a touch of chocolate. Full-bodied and rich, with low acidity as well as a layered texture, it is accessible now (because of the vintage's jamminess and low acidity), but should age well for 4–5 years. It is more internationally styled than the 2000 Côtes du Rhône-Villages Les Genévrières (a blend of 65% Grenache, 20% Syrah, and the rest Cinsault and Mourvèdre). The latter wine reveals typical southern Rhône characteristics of leather, *garrigue*, kirsch, spice box, and pepper. Fleshy and fat, it easily competes with top wines from such renowned appellations as Châteauneuf-du-Pape. Drink it over the next 3–5 years.

The 1999s all possess deep ruby/purple colors as well as copious quantities of fruit. The 1999 Côtes du Rhône Les Arbousiers displays more spice, pepper, and Provençal herbs in its blackberry and cherry flavors. The amazing 1999 Côtes du Rhône Les Eglantiers (100% Syrah from a 30-year-old vineyard) offers a blackberry liqueur–scented nose, full body, low acidity, and an opulent texture. It is gorgeous to drink now as well as over the next 7–8 years. The 1999 Côtes du Rhône-Villages Les Genévrières is the most elegant and refined of these *cuvées*. Although not as weighty or concentrated as its siblings, it offers attractive strawberry/blueberry aromas and a medium-bodied, harmonious texture and finish. All of these 1999s have been bottled and can be drunk now. Les Arbousiers and Les Genévrières will drink well for 3–4 years.

I tasted two 1998s. The 1998 Côtes du Rhône Les Eglantiers reveals more tannin and earth, as well as a firmer structure than the 1999. While less charming, it is an impressive effort with abundant cassis fruit intermixed with licorice and smoke. It should drink well for 4–5 years. The 1998 Côtes du Rhône-Villages Les Genévrières offers complex aromas and flavors of *herbes de Provence*, black cherries, plums, berries, and cherries presented in a medium-bodied, supple format. It should drink well for 2–3 years.

DOMAINE DE REMIZIÈRES

2000 Crozes-Hermitage Cuvée Christophe	D	(88–90)
1999 Crozes-Hermitage Cuvée Christophe	D	91
1998 Crozes-Hermitage Cuvée Christophe	D	90
1997 Crozes-Hermitage Cuvée Christophe	D	90
2000 Crozes-Hermitage Cuvée Christophe Blanc	D	(87–89)
1999 Crozes-Hermitage Cuvée Christophe Blanc	D	88
1998 Crozes-Hermitage Cuvée Christophe Blanc	D	88
2000 Hermitage Cuvée Emilie	E	(91–93)
1999 Hermitage Cuvée Emilie	E	96

1998 Hermitage Cuvée Emilie	E	93+
1997 Hermitage Cuvée Emilie	E	89
2000 Hermitage Cuvée Emilie Blanc	E	(88–90)
1999 Hermitage Cuvée Emilie Blanc	E	90
1998 Hermitage Cuvée Emilie Blanc	E	93
1997 Hermitage Cuvée Emilie Blanc	E	90
1996 Hermitage Cuvée Emilie Blanc	E	88

Philippe Desmeures fashions these *cuvées* in consultation with French wine broker Patrick Lesec. Consequently, they are different *cuvées* than sold elsewhere. Lesec's name appears on the strip label along with his importer information. They are made in mostly new oak, with minimal racking and limited sulphur, and they are bottled without fining or filtration. They are superb efforts, and it would be terrific if Desmeures would decide to treat all the wine in his cellars in this manner, as this estate appears to have unlimited potential.

With respect to the white wines, the 1999s are lighter than their 1998 counterparts, but still impressive. There is more similarity between the 2000 and 1999 whites than I expected. Both are low-acid vintages, but the 1999s have more fat and flesh. I had a slight preference for the 2000 Crozes-Hermitage Cuvée Christophe Blanc over the 1999. Both vintages of the Crozes-Hermitage Cuvée Christophe are best consumed during their first 6–7 years of life. The 1998 Crozes-Hermitage Cuvée Christophe Blanc (90% Marsanne and 10% Roussanne) exhibits a honeyed, spicy, woodsy nose with copious quantities of tropical fruit. Full-bodied, thick, and rich, with a style similar to an Alsatian Vendange Tardive Tokay-Pinot Gris (although it is totally dry), it should be drunk over the next 5–7 years.

Domaine de Remizières Hermitage Cuvée Emilie Blanc is produced in 4,000-bottle lots. With respect to the Hermitage Cuvée Emilie Blanc, the 2000 and 1999 are nearly identical in quality, although slightly different in style, with the 1999 having greater aging potential. These are full-bodied, thick, juicy wines, with the Crozes having plenty of unctuosity and richness and the Hermitage more minerality and backbone. Both reveal moderately intense aromas of rose petals, minerals, honeyed grapefruit, and a hint of fino sherry. Look for the 1999 Hermitage Cuvée Emilie Blanc to drink well for up to 20 years. The 2000 is best drunk during its first 10–12 years. The 1998 Hermitage Cuvée Emilie Blanc (all Marsanne with only a tiny dollop of Roussanne) is superb. I often wonder if readers understand these wines as they can be a paradox. They are often delicious to drink during their first 3–5 years of life, after which they go into an oxidized, closed state, only to become even more splendid when they reemerge at age 10–12. Drink them early or late, but not in between. The 1998 Cuvée Emilie Blanc is an unctuously textured, full-bodied, powerful, concentrated effort with notes of toasty new oak, liquid minerals, rose petals, and honeyed grapefruit and pear. Fabulously ripe, thick, and juicy, it will evolve for 15+ years. The disjointed 1997 Hermitage Cuvée Emilie Blanc is revealing copious quantities of new oak. It is a more leesy, buttery, honeyed style of Hermitage with greater richness, more texture, and better length. This large-scaled offering should drink well young, yet last for a decade. The 1996 Hermitage Cuvée Emilie Blanc (almost all of it comes from Les Rocoules *lieux-dit*) displays classy, refined fruit in its grapefruit/pineapple-scented nose. Mineral notes appear in the mouth. The wine is medium-bodied and well made with crisp, tangy acidity. It should last for 5–6 years.

From a challenging vintage (only because crop sizes were too large), the 2000 Crozes-Hermitage Cuvée Christophe rouge possesses surprising weight, fat, and ripeness. Neither diluted nor superficial (as are many 2000 reds), it exhibits a dark purple color, deep, sweet, cassis flavors, and plenty of earth, licorice, pepper, and spice. Although it does not display the extreme depth of the awesome 1999, it should provide lovely drinking for 7–10 years. The profound 1999 Crozes-Hermitage Cuvée Christophe rouge (1,000 cases) is a sumptuous effort offering an opaque purple color as well as an unreal nose of smoky espresso intermixed with crème de cassis, graphite, and licorice. Full-bodied, opulent, and loaded with concentration, it could easily be mistaken in a blind tasting for a topflight Hermitage. Its low acidity, superripeness, and great purity as well as overall balance suggest it will be at its peak between now–2015. The 1998 Crozes-Hermitage Cuvée Christophe rouge exhibits an opaque inky, plum/black color as well as aromas of prunes, cassis, and blackberries in its intense bouquet, low-acid, rich, superbly concentrated flavors coat the palate, and there is a long, opulent finish. It is an outstanding choice for drinking over the next decade. The terrific 1997 Crozes-Hermitage Cuvée Christophe is one of the finest examples of Crozes I have tasted. The wine's saturated black/purple color is accompanied by superb aromatics of roasted coffee, blackberries, cassis, toast, and smoke. Rich, with superb definition, full body, copious quantities of fruit and glycerin, and a long finish, this is about as good as Crozes-Hermitage can be. Anticipated maturity: now–2015.

The 2000 Hermitage Cuvée Emilie rouge is, along with Gérard and Jean-Louis Chave's Hermitage and several of Chapoutier's single-vineyard *cuvées*, one of the finest wines of the vintage. It enjoyed a 30-day *cuvaison* with *pigéage* (punching down the cap) twice a day. Once past the aromatics and impressive attack, there is sweet tannin, exceptional ripeness, and substantial concentration as well as depth. Pure black and blue fruits mix with graphite and toast aromas in this dense, full-flavored offering. While it is a brilliant wine for the vintage, it is not up to the majesty of the 1999. The 2000 will be drinkable in 2–5 years and last for 15+ years. Philippe Desmeures's 1999 Hermitage Cuvée Emilie rouge (1,000 cases) is a candidate for the Hermitage of the vintage. About 70% of the grapes for this *cuvée* emerge from old vines located in l'Hermite (on the crown of the great dome of Hermitage) and the remainder from Les Rocoules. This extraordinarily intense offering boasts an opaque black/purple color (reminiscent of a cult Cabernet Sauvignon from Napa) as well as a sumptuous nose of sweet blackberry liqueur intermixed with espresso, licorice, tobacco, minerals, and toast. There is massive flavor concentration, multiple layers, full body, admirable purity, and beautifully integrated acidity and tannin. A compelling Hermitage, it should evolve for three decades. The saturated black/purple-colored 1998 Hermitage Cuvée Emilie rouge (30% of this offering emerges from Les Rocoules and 70% from l'Ermite) is an ultrarich offering, with wonderfully sweet, jammy, blackberry liqueur, tobacco, licorice, and gravelly scents. Massive in the mouth, with layers of concentrated black fruit flavors, huge glycerin, low acidity, and a blockbuster finish, this wine should enjoy 20–30 years of evolution. In addition to its sweet, jammy fruit characteristics, it reveals noticeable tannin. Anticipated maturity: 2005–2025. The fabulous 1997 Hermitage Cuvée Emilie is an explosive example of Syrah from selected Hermitage vineyards. The opaque black color is followed by a flamboyant nose of bacon fat, smoky licorice, and cassis. Full-bodied, super-concentrated, and massive in the finish, this low-acid, formidably endowed Hermitage should age effortlessly for two decades, but it will be approachable in its youth.

DOMAINE DE LA RENJARDE

1999 Côtes du Rhône	A	(85–86)
2000 Côtes du Rhône-Villages	A	87
2000 Côtes du Rhône-Villages Réserve de Cassagne	B	88
1999 Côtes du Rhône-Villages Réserve de Cassagne	B	87

Readers seeking excellent values are confronted with a treasure trove of wines such as this from recent vintages in the southern Côtes du Rhônes appellations. These offerings are produced by the owners of Château La Nerthe. Renjarde's 2000 Côtes du Rhône-Villages (a blend of 55% Grenache, 25% Syrah, 10% Cinsault, and 10% Carignan, aged completely in tank) is a fat, deliciously fruity, obvious but lush, hedonistic effort with copious quantities of black cherry fruit. Although not complex, it fills the mouth, has a seamless texture, and will provide fine drinking for 2–3 years. The more limited *cuvée* of 2000 Côtes du Rhône-Villages Réserve de Cassagne (a blend of 50% Grenache, 45% Mourvèdre, and 5% Carignan aged in *foudre*) is meant to be consumed over the next 4–5 years. It possesses copious quantities of black fruits, underlying notes of minerals, leather, and tree bark, a sweet attack, and excellent purity as well as definition. This classy, complex, medium- to full-bodied southern Rhône should hold nicely for 5 years. The elegant 1999 Côtes du Rhône-Villages Réserve de Cassagne reveals less body and volume, but could easily pass as a Burgundy premier cru in a blind tasting. It offers sweet red berry fruits intermixed with black currants and blackberries. Medium-bodied, with a supple texture, this cleanly made 1999 should drink well for 2–3 years. The 1999 Côtes du Rhône (25,000 cases) is a textbook effort exhibiting lovely elegance because of the vintage's fresh, lively black cherry and berry fruit. Medium-bodied and soft, it is ideal for drinking over the next 2–3 years.

DOMAINE DE LA ROQUETTE

2000	Châteauneuf-du-Pape	C	(87–89)
1999	Châteauneuf-du-Pape	C	87
1998	Châteauneuf-du-Pape	C	90

These wines are made by Daniel and Frederic Brunier, whose family acquired this estate in 1986. Although the wines were good in the past, quality under the Bruniers has improved immensely. Revealing a saturated ruby/purple color along with sweet black cherry and berry fruit intertwined with a strawberry liqueur note, the 2000 Châteauneuf-du-Pape is plump, fat, and juicy with moderate tannin in the finish. Exhibiting the vintage's hallmark ripeness, low acidity, and sweetness (from high alcohol and glycerin), it can be enjoyed over the next 10–12 years, though it will undoubtedly last longer. The dark ruby-colored 1999 Châteauneuf-du-Pape, a standard blend of 70% Grenache, 20% Syrah, and 10% Mourvèdre, is an elegant, light, Burgundy-like effort with soft cherry fruit, and a consumer-friendly style. The 1998 Châteauneuf-du-Pape is one of the finest la Roquettes I have ever tasted. It boasts a dense dark ruby/purple color, as well as a powerful bouquet of black cherry jam, kirsch, pepper, and Provençal spices, with abundant glycerin, low acidity, and a fleshy, full-bodied finish. Tannin and structure are present, but they play second fiddle to the forward fruit, glycerin, and power. Anticipated maturity: now–2012.

RENÉ ROSTAING

2000	Condrieu La Bonette	EE	90
2000	Côte Rôtie	EE	(88–90)
1999	Côte Rôtie	EE	92
1998	Côte Rôtie	EE	89
1997	Côte Rôtie	EE	87
2000	Côte Rôtie Côte Blonde	EE	(90–92)
1999	Côte Rôtie Côte Blonde	EE	100
1998	Côte Rôtie Côte Blonde	EE	98
1997	Côte Rôtie Côte Blonde	EE	(90–91)
2000	Côte Rôtie La Landonne	EE	(88–90+)
1999	Côte Rôtie La Landonne	EE	98
1998	Côte Rôtie La Landonne	EE	93
1997	Côte Rôtie La Landonne	EE	(88–91)
1997	Côte Rôtie La Viaillère	EE	87?

René Rostaing continues to exhibit considerable winemaking skills, displaying more confidence with each vintage. He has benefited from observing the winemaking of his father-in-law, Albert Dervieux, as well as his uncle, Marius Gentaz. Both men were traditional wine-makers from Côte Rôtie and possessed some of the finest vines, with parcels of La Fongent (La Garde) and La Viaillère. Rostaing decided that beginning in 1998 he would no longer make a separate Viaillère, but would include it as part of the blend of his Cuvée

Classique. Yields usually average 30 hectoliters per hectare, which is quite low by modern-day standards. The wines are bottled unfiltered after spending 16–18 months in a combination of barrels and larger *demi-muids*. Depending on the vintage, this producer does not use more than 10–20% new oak, a slight decrease over recent vintages from 30% in the early 1990s. The 1999s and 1998s are superb, the 2000s very good, and the 1997s are wonderfully soft.

The 2000 Côte Rôtie Cuvée Classique exhibits a dark ruby/purple color in addition to an elegant nose of cassis fruit, dried herbs, and spice. The wine, which was resting in *demi-muids*, reveals low acidity, a soft, elegant style, and medium body. This pretty, precocious Côte Rôtie should drink well during its first 10–12 years of life. The more tannic, muscular, austerely styled 2000 Côte Rôtie La Landonne (about 50% of the stems were used during vinification) had just been racked and probably was not showing its best during my visit. It appears to need 2–3 years of cellaring and should last for 15 years. The color is a dense ruby with purple nuances. Notes of earth, truffles, and licorice are intermixed with this *cuvée*'s typical cassis/smokiness. 50% of the stems were also used during vinification of my favorite offering, the 2000 Côte Rôtie Côte Blonde. It is a velvety textured Côte Rôtie fruit bomb. Even in a lighter vintage such as 2000, this *cuvée* reveals compelling sweetness as well as a rich berry character with notes of honeysuckle. Ripe, fleshy, and low in acidity, it is a hedonistic turn-on. Nevertheless, there is good structure behind all the fluff. Anticipated maturity: now–2014.

René Rostaing was nearly apologetic for his 1999s, undoubtedly the greatest vintage he has ever produced. He was quick to point out that they are "atypical and too rich." Excuse me! These are Côte Rôties at their most concentrated and seductive. Two of them are legends in the making. The 1999 Côte Rôtie Cuvée Classique (14,000 bottles produced) is a brilliant example that should age well for 15+ years. Its sexy concoction of jammy black fruits intermixed with violets, acacia flowers, cherry liqueur, and crème de cassis jumps from the glass. Exotic and nearly portlike, with sweet levels of glycerin coating the mouth, low acidity, and fabulous concentration as well as purity, it is impossible to resist, but it will last for two decades. The profound 1999 Côte Rôtie La Landonne boasts a saturated black purple color as well as scents of graphite, truffles, smoke, bacon, blackberry, and earth. This full-bodied, muscular, powerful effort displays surprisingly sweet tannin for a wine from this *terroir*, awesome concentration, and a finish that lasts for 40+ seconds. Give it 2–3 years of cellaring, and enjoy it over the next 25 years. What can I say about the 1999 Côte Rôtie Côte Blonde? A dry vintage portlike Côte Rôtie, it possesses extraordinary intensity, brilliant harmony, and a staggering bouquet of violets laced with other flowers (paperwhite narcissus come to mind), blackberries, cassis, vanilla, and a touch of honey. Unctuously textured yet remarkably well defined, with elegance married to intense concentration as well as an extremely long finish, this is one of the most profound and seductive Côte Rôties I have ever tasted. There are 500 cases of this nectar. Anticipated maturity: now–2018.

The 1998 Côte Rôtie Cuvée Classique (100% Syrah) exhibits a dark ruby/purple color as well as scents of spice, roasted meats, animal fur, and cassis. Medium-bodied and elegant for a Côte Rôtie, with flavors of violets and black raspberries intertwined with spice and earth, it is a supple, already accessible effort. Drink it during its first 10–12 years of life. Sadly, there are only 7,700 bottles of the 1998 Côte Rôtie La Landonne. This spectacular offering boasts a deep purple color in addition to a dense nose that the French would call a *confiture* of black fruits, particularly plums, blackberries, and black currants. Superb aromatics jump from the glass of this young, unevolved 1998. On the palate, it is deep and dense, with a multilayered texture and terrific purity and concentration. It possesses a sweet, concentrated mid-palate, well-integrated tannin, and a long finish. This wine needs a few years of cellaring, but it is thrilling to taste at present. It will drink well young, but will last for 15–20 years. It is no secret that Rostaing's finest *cuvée* is the 500+ cases of Côte Rôtie Côte Blonde. The 1998 (all from La Garde) is made from vines planted in 1934 and 1970/71. It includes about 4% Viognier (the only Rostaing *cuvée* to contain this varietal), and 50% stems are utilized during fermentation. The exquisite, dense ruby/purple-colored 1998 offers up soaring aromas of peach and blackberry jam. The wine is velvety textured and full, with layers of glycerin, extract, and concentrated fruit, superb richness, impressive purity, and a finish that lasts 40+ seconds. Anticipated maturity: now–2015.

The softness of the 1997s is apparent across the board. For example, the dark ruby-colored 1997 Côte Rôtie Cuvée Classique is an evolved, forward, fat wine with cassis and raspberry fruit flavors, medium body, and an easygoing, succulent, luscious, straightforward appeal. Drink it over the next 7–8 years. The 1997 Côte Rôtie La Viaillère reveals a similar dark ruby color, plenty of pepper, herbs, and ripe black fruits in the nose, vanilla and toasty oak, and a medium-bodied, rich, layered finish. Look for this last vintage of La Viaillère to drink well for 7–8 years after the vintage. The intensely peppery, more animal, leathery, roasted herb and black currant–scented 1997 Côte Rôtie La Landonne is already enticing and exotic. Flattering and rich in the mouth despite its Côte Brune origins, this elegant, rich, concentrated, spicy, flamboyant Côte Rôtie should drink well upon release, yet last for a decade. Year in and year out, the finest offering from Rostaing is his limited production (usually 4,000+ bottles) Côte Rôtie Côte Blonde (which often includes 3–4% Viognier in the blend). The 1997 exhibits a dark ruby color, followed by a sexy apricot, blackberry, raspberry, bacon fat, and toasty nose, and luscious, medium- to full-bodied, open-knit flavors that caress the palate with glycerin and fruit. The wine's low acidity, fleshy texture, and forward, evolved style are appealing. It should drink well for 5–7 years to come.

Lastly, the 2000 Condrieu La Bonette, while not as complete as the 1999, offers aromas of orange peel, apricots, and flowers. Medium- to full-bodied and well defined, it is ideal for drinking now and over the next 2 years.

DOMAINE ROGER SABON

2000	Châteauneuf-du-Pape Cuvée Réservée	D	(87–89)
1999	Châteauneuf-du-Pape Cuvée Réservée	D	88
1998	Châteauneuf-du-Pape Cuvée Réservée	D	90
2000	Châteauneuf-du-Pape Cuvée Prestige	D	(90–93)
1999	Châteauneuf-du-Pape Cuvée Prestige	D	90
1998	Châteauneuf-du-Pape Cuvée Prestige	D	95
2000	Châteauneuf-du-Pape Les Olivets	C	(87–88)
1999	Châteauneuf-du-Pape Les Olivets	C	87
1998	Châteauneuf-du-Pape Les Olivets	C	86
2000	Châteauneuf-du-Pape Le Secret de Sabon	EE	(94–96)
1999	Châteauneuf-du-Pape Le Secret de Sabon	EE	96
1998	Châteauneuf-du-Pape Le Secret de Sabon	EE	99

Roger Sabon, the former mayor of Châteauneuf-du-Pape, continues to turn out a very impressive portfolio of Châteauneuf-du-Pape. His wines are usually charming, richly fruity, expansive wines that are easy to drink and understand. Other than the Cuvée Les Olivets and the Cuvée Réservée, the portfolio comprises a luxury Cuvée Prestige, which is the top wine in most vintages, as well as a micro *cuvée* called Le Secret de Sabon, whose debut vintage was 1996. This wine, which is only produced in the best years, comes from a small parcel of exceptionally old vines (over 70 years of age) and is produced in tiny quantities (1,000 cases). The blend is generally 70% Grenache, 10% Syrah, 10% Mourvèdre, and 10% diverse varietals. One might criticize Roger Sabon for producing four *cuvées* in each of these vintages, but there is a distinctive difference in weight, richness, and concentration between them.

The 2000 Châteauneuf-du-Pape Les Olivets exhibits a similar style, but more jammy fruit, lower acidity, and plenty of roasted herb, smoke, and pepper notes. This soft 2000 will last for 7–8 years. Displaying more glycerin along with a captivating, seductive, fat, fleshy style with jammy black cherry and berry fruit presented in a lush, medium- to full-bodied format, the captivating 2000 Châteauneuf-du-Pape Cuvée Réservée requires consumption over the next 7–10 years. With more glycerin and alcohol, the "sexy, sexy, sexy" (as my tasting notes said) 2000 Châteauneuf-du-Pape Cuvée Prestige is a voluptuously textured effort representing the essence of plum, cherry, currant, fig, and prune-like fruit. It possesses huge quantities of glycerin, an unctuous texture, and a full-bodied, layered finish. Drink this forward 2000 during its first 15 years of life. The awesome, hedonistic, corpulent 2000 Châteauneuf-du-Pape Le Secret de Sabon boasts dazzling aromatics, supple flavor purity, and a long finish. Both of these wines linger on the palate for nearly a minute, which gives readers an idea of just how deep and thick they are. Both are tours de force in winemaking. What a shame so little is produced. Anticipated maturity: now–2016.

The least concentrated of the 1999s is the big, soft, sexy, open-knit, traditionally made Châteauneuf-du-Pape Les Olivets. The 1999 is a well-made, richly fruity effort displaying aromas of herbs and spice. Drink this medium-weight Châteauneuf over the next 7–8 years. The dark ruby/garnet-colored 1999 Châteauneuf-du-Pape Cuvée Réservée exhibits a peppery, dried Provençal herb–scented perfume (particularly rosemary and thyme) as well as sweet kirsch notes, medium to full body, and a soft finish. Anticipated maturity: now–2009.

The 1999 Châteauneuf-du-Pape Cuvée Prestige (14.5% alcohol) reveals a dark plum/garnet color as well as a gorgeously complex nose of licorice, pepper, black cherries, and cassis. As the wine sits in the glass, additional nuances develop. While not as structured as the blockbuster 1998, the 1999 is a seductive, open-knit, layered, succulent, fleshy effort to enjoy now and over the next 12–15 years.

If the 1998 Châteauneuf-du-Pape Le Secret de Sabon is a perfect wine (and I'm convinced it is), the 2000 and 1999 are not far behind. Both *cuvées* represent the essence of low yielding, old-vine Grenache. The 1999 Châteauneuf-du-Pape Le Secret de Sabon offers a blockbuster bouquet of roasted meats, truffles, smoked herbs, prunes, and black cherry jam. Akin to drinking dry vintage port, it tastes like a Châteauneuf-du-Pape on steroids. The alcohol level must be 15% plus, but it is buried beneath the wealth of fruit and flesh. The 1999 appears more evolved and forward than the 1998 did at a similar age, so drinking it over the next 10–12 years is advised.

The 1998 Châteauneuf-du-Pape Les Olivets offers a spicy, herb, leather, and cherry-scented bouquet, medium-bodied, attractive, fruit-driven flavors, and more tannin and grip than the 1999. However, I would still opt for drinking it over the next 7–8 years. The outstanding, saturated dark plum–colored 1998 Châteauneuf-du-Pape Cuvée Réservée possesses notes of scorched earth, roasted herbs, smoked duck, and a boatload of kirsch fruitiness. Full-bodied, with moderate tannin and impressive purity and concentration, this wine should be drunk over the following 12 years. The 1998 Châteauneuf-du-Pape Cuvée Prestige is profound. It boasts a dense saturated ruby/purple color. With airing, the bouquet's earthy concoction becomes increasingly dominated by scents of kirsch and blackberries. This fragrant, immensely concentrated wine has sweet tannin, tastes of smoked duck, and is extremely complex, rich in glycerin, and long. The finish lasts nearly 45 seconds. There is still tannin to shed, so purchasers should defer their gratification for 1–2 years and drink it over the following two decades. Lastly, the 1998 Châteauneuf-du-Pape Le Secret de Sabon is virtually perfect. One of the greatest Châteauneuf-du-Papes I have ever tasted, this wine is reminiscent of the 1990 Henri Bonneau Cuvée des Céléstins. It has a melted black truffle, blackberry, and blood-scented nose with notes of coffee, smoked herbs, and roasted meats. Thick and even more unctuously textured than the Cuvée Prestige, this wine is more akin to dry vintage port than Châteauneuf-du-Pape. It is massive, intense, and a candidate for 20–30 years of evolution. Sadly, it is extremely limited in availability (approximately 100 cases) . . . isn't that always the problem!

DOMAINE SAINT-BENOÎT

2000	Châteauneuf-du-Pape Grande Garde	D	(89–91)
1999	Châteauneuf-du-Pape Grande Garde	D	(89–90)
1998	Châteauneuf-du-Pape Grande Garde	D	90+
2000	Châteauneuf-du-Pape Laureline	D	(86–88?)
2000	Châteauneuf-du-Pape La Truffière	D	(88–90)
1999	Châteauneuf-du-Pape La Truffière	D	(88–89)
1998	Châteauneuf-du-Pape La Truffière	D	89+
2000	Châteauneuf-du-Pape Soleil et Festins	D	(85–87)
1999	Châteauneuf-du-Pape Soleil et Festins	D	(85–86)
1998	Châteauneuf-du-Pape Soleil et Festins	D	86

This estate offers three *cuvées*, the lightest, most straightforward being Soleil et Festins, and the most concentrated, ageworthy effort the Grande Garde. This new estate, created in 1989, continues to turn out interesting, high-quality Châteauneuf-du-Pape from nearly four dozen vineyard parcels spread throughout the appellation.

The easygoing, fruit-forward, medium-weight, dark ruby-colored 2000 Châteauneuf-du-Pape Soleil et Festins is a straightforward effort to enjoy over the next 5–6 years. A new offering in Domaine Saint-Benoît's portfolio is the 2000 Châteauneuf-du-Pape Laureline, an internationally styled wine revealing new-oak characteristics along with black currant and cherry fruit. Although a well-made wine with excellent purity, it is somewhat soulless because of the *barrique* influence. It should drink well for 10–12 years.

Far more interesting are the 2000 La Truffière and 2000 Grande Garde. Classic aromas of black fruits intermixed with tapenade, Provençal herbs, and cherry liqueur are well displayed in the plum-colored 2000 Châteauneuf-du-Pape La Truffière. It is medium- to full-bodied, with excellent purity, rich, earthy flavors, and a long finish. Perceptible tannin should be resolved with 2–3 years of cellaring. Anticipated maturity: now–2015. The seriously concentrated 2000 Châteauneuf-du-Pape Grande Garde offers classic aromas of crushed pepper, balsam wood, *garrigue*, cherry liqueur, and plums. It is the most voluptuous of this quartet, with considerable glycerin as well as sweetness. Moderate tannin suggests cellaring is warranted. Anticipated maturity: 2004–2018.

The 1999s are all successful efforts. The 1999 Châteauneuf-du-Pape Soleil et Festins, a medium-bodied, fruit-driven effort revealing some spice, is essentially a one-dimensional, slightly superficial offering meant to be consumed during its first 5–6 years of life. Far better is the 1999 Châteauneuf-du-Pape La Truffière, a deep ruby-colored wine with notes of black raspberries, cherry liqueur, spice box, and pepper, excellent texture, medium to full body, low acidity, and sweet tannin. Anticipated maturity: now–2012. The 1999 Châteauneuf-du-Pape Grande Garde offers a deep ruby color as well as an impressive bouquet of crushed pepper, Provençal spices, olives, and kirsch. Medium- to full-bodied, with more density, a fatter mid-palate, and a longer finish than La Truffière, it is potentially outstanding and should age well for 15+ years. Anticipated maturity: now–2016.

The most elegant of the three well-made 1998s from Domaine Saint-Benoît is the 1998 Châteauneuf-du-Pape Soleil et Festins. The dark ruby color is followed by abundant amounts of floral/black cherry fruit, earth, cedar, and spice box characteristics. With low acidity, attractive levels of glycerin, and good concentration, it will be at its peak between now–2008. The saturated plum/purple-colored 1998 Châteauneuf-du-Pape La Truffière is more tannic, offering larger volume and a bigger, more muscular presence on the palate. Tightly knit, with black cherry fruit intermixed with pepper, spice, and herbs, this rich, well-structured and -endowed wine requires 3–4 years of cellaring. Anticipated maturity: 2004–2015. The 1998 Châteauneuf-du-Pape Grande Garde is a more earthy wine with notes of minerals, crushed sea shells, and telltale red and black fruits, spice, and pepper. Sweet and expansive on the attack (from extract and ripeness, not residual sugar), this deep, full-bodied offering is more open-knit than its sibling, La Truffière. Both wines are potentially outstanding, with 15+ years of longevity.

SAINT-COSME

2000 Château Saint-Cosme Gigondas	D	(90–92)
1999 Château Saint-Cosme Gigondas	D	89
1998 Château Saint-Cosme Gigondas	D	89
1997 Château Saint-Cosme Gigondas	D	91
1998 Château Saint-Cosme Gigondas Cuvée Valbelle	D	92
2000 Saint-Cosme Condrieu	E	(90–92)
1999 Saint-Cosme Condrieu	E	90
2000 Saint-Cosme Côte Rôtie	E	(89–91)
1999 Saint-Cosme Côte Rôtie	E	95
2000 Saint-Cosme Côtes du Rhône	A	88
1999 Saint-Cosme Côtes du Rhône	A	89
2000 Saint-Cosme Côtes du Rhône Les Deux Albion	A	89
1999 Saint-Cosme Côtes du Rhône Les Deux Albion	A	90
1997 Saint-Cosme Côte Rôtie Montsalier	E	90
NV Saint-Cosme Little James Basket Press	A	85

One of the up-and-coming superstars of the southern Rhône, the young, intensely committed Louis Barruol has turned around the fortunes of this well-placed Gigondas domaine. He has begun producing a small line of impressive *négociant* wines (the Côte Rôtie Montsalier is a splendid example), but most important, he is making blockbuster Gigondas that rivals the finest wines of the appellation. Among the estate wines, there is also a very good nonvintage wine produced from wines that are not deemed old enough to make the Gigondas.

This nonvintage *vin de table* (all from the 2000 vintage) called Little James Basket Press, produced from young-vine Grenache, lacks body, but is a pretty, elegant, fruity wine revealing abundant kirsch notes. It is an inexpensive offering to consume over the next year.

The estate *cuvées* of Gigondas come from the property's well placed 37 acres surrounding the village. In top years, two *cuvées* are produced, the *cuvée* classique and a *cuvée* aged in *barrique* called Valbelle. The prestige *cuvée* made from 100+-year-old vines planted just after the phylloxera epidemic is aged 50% in new oak casks and 50% in one-year-old casks. These wines are kept in contact with their lees for extensive periods and there are very few rackings. All Saint-Cosme's offerings are bottled unfined and unfiltered, with extremely low levels (under 20 parts ppm) of SO_2.

In 2000 and 1999, Saint-Cosme declassified their top Cuvée Valbelle into their regular Gigondas. The 2000 Château Saint-Cosme Gigondas is a low-acid, fat, plump offering made from a blend of 75% Grenache, 20% Syrah, and 5% Cinsault. Natural alcohol was 14.4% and, as Louis Barruol says, this is *très gourmand*. I couldn't agree more. It is a luscious, fleshy, up-front, fruit-forward Gigondas with oodles of blackberry and cherry fruit, considerable glycerin, and admirable purity. Drink it over the next 8–10 years. The 1999 Château Saint-Cosme Gigondas exhibits a deep ruby color along with an earthy nose with notes of smoke, minerals, licorice, black fruits, and pepper. It does not have the power or depth of the 1998, but it is more elegant, medium- to full-bodied, with sweet ripeness and light to moderate tannin. It should drink well for a dozen years.

The 1998 Château Saint-Cosme Gigondas (60% aged in tank and 40% in used barrels) offers a sweet cherry and blackberry-scented nose with notions of smoke and minerals. Fat, chewy, medium- to full-bodied, and delicious, it can be enjoyed over the next decade. The 1998 Château Saint-Cosme Gigondas Cuvée Valbelle (1,350 cases) macerated for 40 days, and was aged one year in barrel, of which 20% was new. It was bottled without fining or filtration, the standard operating procedure at Saint-Cosme. A sensational effort, it boasts sumptuous aromas of smoke, blackberries, cherry liqueur, and licorice presented in a full-bodied, opulently textured, concentrated style. Revealing moderate tannin, excellent concentration, intensity, purity, and balance, this young wine requires 2–3 years of cellaring and should last for 15–16 years. It has absorbed all of the new oak utilized during its upbringing. Anticipated maturity: now–2016. There is no Valbelle in 1997, but the 1997 Château Saint-Cosme Gigondas *cuvée* classique is remarkable. The dark saturated purple/black color is followed by aromas of sweet blackberry liqueur mixed with pepper, floral scents, truffles, and Asian spices. Full-bodied, with spectacular concentration, low acidity, and a blockbuster finish, this powerful yet beautifully harmonious wine should drink well for 8 years.

Among the *négociant* wines emerging from the southern Rhône, there are two Côtes du Rhône *cuvées* that consistently represent good values. The deep ruby/purple-colored 2000 Saint-Cosme Côtes du Rhône (100% Syrah) is a fat, juicy, succulent effort offering smoky blackberry fruit, low acidity, and considerable corpulence. Drink it over the next 1–2 years. Even better is the 2000 Saint-Cosme Côtes du Rhône Les Deux Albion. There are just over 2,000 cases of this sumptuous wine that could be called a "Little La Mouline" because of the white grape Clairette in the blend. Dark ruby-colored, with a dazzling bouquet of honeyed white and black fruits, medium to full body, outstanding ripeness, and a long, plump finish, it will drink well for 3–4 years.

The 1999 Saint-Cosme Côtes du Rhône (7,000 cases), produced from old Syrah vines planted in the Rhône Valley's northern sector, remained in tank prior to being bottled unfiltered. Its opaque purple color is accompanied by a gorgeously sweet bouquet of blackberries, licorice, and a touch of smoke. Medium- to full-bodied and silky-textured, with good freshness and remarkable levels of fruit and intensity, this 1999 Côtes du Rhône may deserve an outstanding rating if it develops more complexity. Enjoy it over the next 4–5 years. The spectacular 1999 Saint-Cosme Côtes du Rhône Les Deux Albion is a blend of 50% Syrah, 40% Grenache, and 10% Clairette blanc, fermented together. It is a sexy, opulent, full-bodied effort that emerges from sources in Cairanne and Rasteau. Sadly, there are only about 525 cases, all of which were aged in tank prior to being bottled without filtration. The Clairette gives this Côtes du Rhône a honeysuckle/Viognier-like character in its blackberry and sweet cherry fruit. Jammy and viscous, this expressive, flamboyant, hedonistic fruit bomb will turn heads. Drink it over the next 5–6 years.

A blend of purchased wine from such well-known hillside vineyards as Les Roziers, Les Grandes Places, Viaillère, and Champin, the lighter-styled 2000 Saint-Cosme Côte Rôtie exhibits peppery, *herbes de Provence*, and olive scents mixed with roasted meat and black currant fruit. Ripe, fleshy, and soft, this medium-weight offering is best consumed during its first 10 years of life. The 1999 Saint-Cosme Côte Rôtie offers a classic perfume of bacon fat, licorice, smoked herbs, tapenade, blackberries, and crème de cassis. With an unctuous texture as well as fabulous ripeness, adequate acidity, and sweet, unobtrusive tannin, this 1999 should drink well for 15+ years. It is a brilliant Côte Rôtie!

The 1997 Saint-Cosme Côte Rôtie Montsalier is compelling. As often as I asked, Barruol would not reveal the source for this extraordinary wine. It emerged from three separate Côte Rôtie *terroirs* and was aged in 100% new casks. Sadly, only 2,400 bottles of this outstanding wine were produced, so the following tasting note is mainly of academic interest. This black-colored wine, a syrup of Syrah, boasts a terrific cassis, bacon fat, and smoky-scented nose with grilled meat notes in the background. Rich and full-bodied, with low acidity, spectacular concentration, and a finish that lasts for nearly a minute, this classic Côte Rôtie could compete with some of Marcel Guigal's great single-vineyard offerings. It should drink well for 10 or more years.

The 2000 Saint-Cosme Condrieu is powerful, rich, and concentrated. It possesses sweet fruit, an unctuous texture, and plenty of mineral, honeysuckle, flower, and peach/apricot characteristics. Enjoy it over the next 1–2 years. The 1999 Saint-Cosme Condrieu is performing well. With excellent ripeness in addition to a floral, honeysuckle, and apricot-scented nose, full body, and mineral characteristics, it is a brilliant Condrieu. While still youthful, I would not hold it longer than 18 months. Both of these wines have 25% of the *cuvée* aged in tank, 25% aged in old *barriques*, and 50% aged in new oak.

DOMAINE DE SAINT-SIFFREIN

1999 Châteauneuf-du-Pape	C	89
1998 Châteauneuf-du-Pape	C	88

This moderately sized estate of 42 acres, owned by the Chastan family, produces textbook, reliable Châteauneuf-du-Pape. A sleeper pick, Domaine de Saint-Siffrein's 1999 Châteauneuf-du-Pape exhibits a fragrant, peppery, spicy perfume with notions of prunes, plums, and black fruits. Medium- to full-bodied, with excellent concentration, impressive balance, and sweet, well-integrated tannin, this ripe, delicious 1999 should be at its best before 2012. The 1998 Châteauneuf-du-Pape is a more substantial wine, with additional glycerin, as well as a sexy, fragrant bouquet of pure cherry jam. Round, opulent, and full-bodied, with black cherry flavors, it is not the most complex style of Châteauneuf, but it is undeniably disarming. It should drink well for 10–12 years.

SANG DES CAILLOUX

2000 Vacqueyras	C	(90–92)
1999 Vacqueyras	C	90
1998 Vacqueyras	C	90
2000 Vacqueyras Cuvée Lopy	D	(92–93)
1999 Vacqueyras Cuvée Lopy	D	93
1998 Vacqueyras Cuvée Lopy	D	93

Over the last several years, this estate has emerged as a superstar in Vacqueyras. These offerings perform well above the relatively high-quality level already achieved by this appellation, just down the road from Gigondas. Sang des Cailloux can compete with the finest Gigondas and Châteauneuf-du-Pape at one-third the price. In short, these are exceptional wine values. None of them sees any filtration. Unlike the majority of Rhône Valley estates, Sang des Cailloux performed better in 1999 than in 1998. The 2000s are also superb.

The opaque purple-colored 2000 Vacqueyras appears to be every bit as spectacular as the 1999, with low acidity, superripe fruit, and layers of concentration. These are Vacqueyras on steroids, with extraordinary richness, from their firework aromatics to sumptuous flavors. Yet there is not a component out of place. The 2000 should easily last for 10 years, but who will be able to resist the compelling charms that already exist? The 2000 Vacqueyras Cuvée Lopy is amazing. I tasted it blind in a Vacqueyras syndicate tasting, and my first impression was "What is this?" Black/purple in color, with creamy blackberry/blueberry liqueur aromas, this opulent, full-bodied 2000 admirably displays the vintage's jammy ripeness as well as low acidity and a viscous style. Similar to the 1999, with slightly jammier fruit, it is a striking example of Vacqueyras that will be delicious young yet last for a decade. The hedonistic, dense ruby/purple-colored 1999 Vacqueyras offers exceptional, concentrated, ripe black cherry and berry fruit, full body, terrific texture, and gorgeous purity. This loaded, seamless 1999 is a total turn-on. Enjoy it over the next 7–8 years. The blockbuster 1999 Vacqueyras Cuvée Lopy (a blend of 70% Grenache and 30% Syrah, half aged in *foudres* and half in old *barriques*) boasts an opaque purple color as well as a bouquet of roasted meats, blackberry and cherry fruit, licorice, and earth. This full-bodied, exuberant Vacqueyras reveals tremendous richness in addition to a long, voluptuous finish with no hard edges. It ratchets up the level of richness from the regular *cuvée*, but both are stunning efforts.

The 1998 Vacqueyras, a blend of 60% Grenache, 30% Syrah, and 10% Mourvèdre, is one of the appellation's stars. It boasts a superripe bouquet of blackberry and cherry liqueur mixed with pepper, roasted herbs, and earth. Full-bodied, with sweet tannin plus a succulent, multilayered texture, this is a hedonistic, complex, southern Rhône fruit bomb that will drink beautifully for a decade. The similarly styled 1998 Vacqueyras Cuvée Lopy is a more structured, heavier, denser effort, with nearly perfect balance. These wines should drink well for 6–10 years. Both should be purchased by the case given their reasonable prices.

Other than the superb *négociant* Tardieu-Laurent (in the beautiful medieval village of Lourmarin), I cannot think of anyone else producing Vacqueyras of such rarity and intensity as Sang des Cailloux. Buy these by the trunkful!

DOMAINE SANTA DUC

2000	Domaine Santa Duc Côtes du Rhône Les Quatre Terres	A	88
2000	Domaine Santa Duc Gigondas	D	(89–91)
1999	Domaine Santa Duc Gigondas	D	89
1998	Domaine Santa Duc Gigondas	D	90
1997	Domaine Santa Duc Gigondas	D	86
2000	Domaine Santa Duc Gigondas Les Hautes Garrigues	E	(91–94)
1999	Domaine Santa Duc Gigondas Les Hautes Garrigues	E	92
1998	Domaine Santa Duc Gigondas Les Hautes Garrigues	E	93
2000	Domaine Santa Duc VDP du Vaucluse	A	87
1999	Santa Duc Selections Côtes du Rhône Vieilles Vignes*	A	87
1999	Santa Duc Selections Côtes du Rhône-Villages Cairanne Les Buissens*	A	87
2000	Santa Duc Selections Côtes du Rhône-Villages Rasteau Vieilles Vignes Les Blovac	A	87

Probably the leading estate in Gigondas, Yves Gras's Santa Duc continues to turn out some of the most complete, concentrated, and potentially complex wines of the southern Rhône. Other than his standard Gigondas, he also produces a Cuvée Les Hautes Garrigues. Made from a 50-year-old parcel of hillside vineyards planted with 70% Grenache, 15% Syrah, and 15% Mourvèdre, yields are as low as a half ton of fruit per acre. Bottled without filtration, this remarkable wine represents the essence of Gigondas. Yves Gras also offers a line of *négociant* wines under the label Santa Duc Selections. (These are marked with an asterisk.)

From the Domaine Santa Duc, the medium ruby-colored 2000 VDP Vaucluse is loaded with cherry fruit as well as a hint of resin and spice. Drink this lush, lively 2000 over the next year to take advantage of its freshness. Gras has fashioned a super 2000 Côtes du Rhône Les Quatre Terres (14.3% alcohol) from a blend of 70% Grenache, 22% Syrah, and 8% Cinsault, Carignan, and Mourvèdre. A plump fruit bomb, it reveals abundant glycerin, excellent fat, and a texture as well as a character not dissimilar from a very good Châteauneuf-du-Pape.

The fat, jammy, full-bodied 2000 Gigondas (14.9% natural alcohol) offers aromas of minerals, blueberries, black raspberries, and cherries. While pure and fruit-driven, I am sure there is more tannin and structure underneath the wealth of fruit and glycerin. Anticipated maturity: now–2012. The prodigious 2000 Gigondas Les Hautes Garrigues is akin to liqueur of Gigondas. The color is a saturated purple. The bouquet of pepper and blackberry as well as blueberry liqueur is followed by immense body, fabulous concentration, excellent purity, and moderate tannin. This mouth-filling 2000 appears to be equivalent to the fabulous 1998 Les Hautes Garrigues Cuvée Prestige. Anticipated maturity: now–2015. The regular *cuvée* of 1999 Gigondas (75% Grenache, 10% Mourvèdre, 10% Syrah, and 5% miscellaneous grapes) was aged in equal parts barrel and *foudre.* Its dark ruby/purple color is followed by elegant mineral and cherry flavors intertwined with licorice notes. An austere finish kept my score low, but this medium-bodied Gigondas possesses excellent purity, loads of fruit, and a layered texture. Drink it over the next 8–10 years. The stunning 1999 Gigondas Les Hautes Garrigues spent 23 months in *barriques,* of which 40% was new. Made from 80% Grenache and 20% Mourvèdre that achieved 15.5% natural alcohol, it boasts a saturated purple color as well as immense body, a layered texture, and pure cassis, kirsch, and blackberry flavors along with a subtle note of wood. The finish lasts for 30–35 seconds. There are 1,500 cases of this 1999, which appears to be the wine of the vintage. Anticipated maturity: now–2016.

The 1998 Gigondas (which achieved a whopping 15.3% alcohol) is a terrific, powerful, multidimensional effort with glorious levels of glycerin as well as black cherry and cassis fruit. Expressive and flamboyant, yet fresh, full-bodied, and lively, it will last for a decade or more. However, it will be hard to resist young. The 1998 Gigondas Les Hautes Garrigues achieved 15.64% alcohol, but the 1998 Mourvèdre battered all records as it came in at a whopping 15.8% natural alcohol. Of course, this wine would not merit its high score if it did not completely hide the lusty alcohol. One of the advantages of low yielding, concentrated Grenache is that it easily hides high alcohol. This full-bodied black beauty offers a terrific bouquet of licorice, blackberry, cassis, and a smoky, subtle dose of wood in the background. In the mouth, it is enormously endowed, very full-bodied and textured, exceptionally pure, with a creamy mid-palate, silky tannin, and a profound finish. Anticipated maturity: now–2018. As for the 1997s, they are soft, forward, open-knit, low-acid wines with good ripeness, but a touch of dilution. The 1997 Gigondas possesses a slightly more saturated color, as well as more pepper and a larger frame in the mouth. Both 1997s are easygoing, forward, bistro-styled reds to drink over the next 3–5 years.

All three Santa Duc Selections *cuvées* are excellent bargains. The 1999 Côtes du Rhône Vieilles Vignes emerges from the famed, flat, windswept vineyards of northeast Châteauneuf-du-Pape called Le Plan de Dieu. There are 7,000 cases of this Grenache-based offering. Displaying scents of berries, spice, and chocolate, it is a medium-bodied, straightforward, chunky, richly fruity Côtes du Rhône to enjoy over the next 1–2 years. The 1,000 case *cuvée* of 1999 Côtes du Rhône-Villages Cairanne Les Buissens is a more earthy-styled red offering aromas of damp forest, medium body, and abundant cherry fruit. While the tannin is more elevated, it is sweet, and the wine is open-knit and best drunk over the next 1–2 years. The 2000 Côtes du Rhône-Villages Rasteau Vieilles Vignes Les Blovac is the biggest and most rustic of this trio. A blend of 70% Grenache, 15% Mourvèdre, and 15% Syrah grown on Rasteau's steep hillsides, it reveals exuberant black cherry and blackberry fruit with a hint of espresso and chocolate. With more tannin and muscle than the other *cuvées,* it will benefit from six more months of cellaring and keep for a minimum of 2–3 years.

CHÂTEAU DE SÉGRIES

1999 Côtes du Rhône	A	86
1998 Côtes du Rhône	A	85
1999 Lirac Cuvée Réservée	B	88
1998 Lirac Cuvée Réservée	B	88

The proprietor, Henri de Lanzac, has made significant improvements to this well-known but often underachieving estate. With the help of his cousin, Christian Delorme, of the superbly run Domaine de la Mordorée (which produces top-notch Châteauneuf-du-Pape and Lirac), Lanzac continues to produce better, cleaner, more complete and concentrated wines and has made Château de Ségries a property to follow. In particular, the Lirac and regular Côtes du Rhône offerings represent excellent values, with the Côtes du Rhône Clos de l'Hermitage controversial because of its high level of tannin. The 1999 Côtes du Rhône exhibits aromas of grilled herbs intermixed with meaty, black cherry fruit presented in a medium-bodied, round, supple format. It is a fruit-driven effort that promises good things to come from the 1999 southern Rhône vintage. Drink it over the next 2–3 years. The 1999 Lirac Cuvée Réservée (check out the terrific neck label) displays a dense dark ruby color in addition to gobs of Provençal herb–infused, black cherry fruit, and kirsch notes. It also has a creamy, juicy, succulent texture, and a spicy, ripe, medium-bodied finish. There are no hard edges to this richly fruity, complex wine. Drink it over the next 5–6 years. The dark ruby-colored, medium-bodied, peppery, juicy 1998 Côtes du Rhône is a supple-textured, delicious, open-knit wine that will have many admirers. It should drink well for 2 years. Even better is the 1998 Lirac Cuvée Réservée. Made from 60% Grenache and 40% Syrah, this is a full-bodied, dense, juicy, ruby/purple-colored wine with layers of concentrated fruit and a jammy kirsch and blackberry-scented nose. Although young, it should develop more complexity and last for 3–4 years.

DOMAINE DES SÉNÉCHAUX

2000 Châteauneuf-du-Pape	D	(88–90)
1999 Châteauneuf-du-Pape	D	89
1998 Châteauneuf-du-Pape	D	89

The 2000 Châteauneuf-du-Pape exhibits a deeper ruby/purple color as well as a more textured, layered feel, higher levels of glycerin and ripeness, presumably higher alcohol, and a fleshy, seductive, sexy, voluptuous style. It should be consumed over the next 10–12 years.

The creamy-textured, dark plum-colored 1999 Châteauneuf-du-Pape offers sweet aromas of pepper, fruitcake, spice, and ripe cherries. As the wine sits in the glass, scents of plum and earth emerge. Savory, supple-textured, and complex, with medium to full body, adequate acidity, and a layered finish, it will drink well for 10–12 years.

One of the finest examples produced by this estate, the 1998 Châteauneuf-du-Pape displays a plum/purple color in addition to an evolved nose of black fruits, fruitcake, resin, and pepper. Dense, opulent, and unctuously textured, this deep, pure, concentrated wine has the potential to be outstanding. Anticipated maturity: now–2012.

CHÂTEAU SIMIAN

2000 Châteauneuf-du-Pape	D	(87–89)
1999 Châteauneuf-du-Pape	D	87
1998 Châteauneuf-du-Pape	D	87
2000 Côtes du Rhône	A	86

This small 10-acre estate is well situated on Châteauneuf-du-Pape's plateau, behind the ruins of the Papal Palace. The cellars are farther north in the village of Piolenc, the "Garlic Capital" of France. This estate deserves more attention, but the tiny production of only 1,700 cases of red wine ensures that most of it is sold to private clients. Other than the Châteauneuf-du-Pape, it offers good Côtes du Rhône that consistently represents a good value. The grapy, simple but delicious, round, lush 2000 Côtes du Rhône is a charmer to enjoy over the next 1–2 years. Even jammier, sweeter, and fleshier, the dark ruby/purple-colored 2000 Châteauneuf-du-Pape reveals aromas and flavors of plums, cherry cough syrup, and pepper. Medium- to full-bodied and ripe, with moderate tannin, it should drink well for 10–14 years. There is no known American importer. The light- to medium-weight, elegant 1999 Châteauneuf-du-Pape exhibits pure cherry, raspberry, and plum flavors. Notes of underbrush and pepper emerge along with tannin in the finish, but overall it is an attractive, plummy, fleshy 1999 to drink over the next 7–8 years. The dark plum-colored 1998 Châteauneuf-du-Pape reveals more mineral, pepper, plum, and kirsch aromas, heavier body, more grip and tannin, as well as additional length and a deeper mid-palate. It will keep for 8–10 years.

DOMAINE DE LA SOLITUDE

2000 Châteauneuf-du-Pape	D	(89–90)
1999 Châteauneuf-du-Pape	D	90
1998 Châteauneuf-du-Pape	D	88

2000 Châteauneuf-du-Pape Cuvée		**D**	**(90–92)**
1999 Châteauneuf-du-Pape Cuvée		**D**	**90**

It has been a long time since I tasted such impressive offerings from this estate, once one of the leaders of Châteauneuf-du-Pape. I have drunk many bottles of Domaine de la Solitude's sumptuous 1967, but that is the only wine that stands out as truly topflight, and it has been tired for a number of years. Of late, there has been a major change in the winemaking style and quality at Solitude, as these *cuvées* evidence.

The 2000 Châteauneuf-du-Pape reveals a dense plum/purple color as well as a lovely nose of sweet pepper intermixed with *garrigue,* cherries, and berries. Full-bodied and ripe, with low acidity, admirable purity, and impressive length, it will be at its finest between now–2014. The 2000 Châteauneuf-du-Pape Cuvée appears to be the finest wine produced by Domaine de la Solitude since the aforementioned legendary 1967. There is no evidence of oak (only 15% was utilized as opposed to 100% for the 1999 Cuvée). The opaque inky/ purple color is followed by a wine with tremendous density, a sumptuous, full-bodied palate, explosive ripeness, a long, textured finish, and total harmony between the alcohol, tannin, and extract. Although still somewhat grapy, it should have a tremendous upside. Anticipated maturity: 2004–2020.

The 1999 Châteauneuf-du-Pape is a deep ruby/purple-colored classic with tremendous concentration, an opulent texture, hedonistic levels of glycerin, superb purity, gobs of fruit, and a mouth-filling, rich style. Its low acidity as well as the vintage's precocious nature suggest drinking over the next 12–15 years is warranted. New wood generally does not work well with Châteauneuf-du-Pape, but even though the 1999 Châteauneuf-du-Pape Cuvée was aged in 100% new oak, it exhibits classic southern Rhône characteristics with only subtle notions of wood in both the aromatics and flavors . . . much to my surprise. A saturated opaque purple color is followed by thick, juicy, blackberry and cassis flavors mixed with *garrigue* and pepper notes. Long, layered, powerful, and rich, it may last even longer than the regular *cuvée* because of the introduction of wood tannin.

The 1998 is undeniably a modern-styled, fruity Châteauneuf-du-Pape, but it has plenty of earthy, sweet black fruits, an open-knit, plush, supple texture, excellent purity, a hint of spicy wood, and very good length. I would opt for drinking it over the next 8 years.

MARC SORREL

2000 Crozes-Hermitage		B	(84–85)
1999 Crozes-Hermitage		B	85
2000 Crozes-Hermitage Blanc		B	85
1999 Crozes-Hermitage Blanc		B	87
2000 Hermitage		E	(87–88)
1999 Hermitage		E	88
1998 Hermitage		E	87+
1997 Hermitage		E	(86–88)
2000 Hermitage Blanc		E	(87–88)
1999 Hermitage Blanc		E	90
1998 Hermitage Blanc		E	87
1997 Hermitage Blanc		E	(85–87)
1996 Hermitage Blanc		E	86
1995 Hermitage Blanc		E	85
2000 Hermitage Le Gréal		EE	(89–92)
1999 Hermitage Le Gréal		EE	90
1998 Hermitage Le Gréal		EE	95+
1997 Hermitage Le Gréal		EE	(90–92)

2000 Hermitage Les Rocoules	EE	(88–90)
1999 Hermitage Les Rocoules	EE	93
1998 Hermitage Les Rocoules	EE	90+
1997 Hermitage Les Rocoules	EE	(88–90)
1996 Hermitage Les Rocoules	EE	90
1995 Hermitage Les Rocoules	EE	87

This small estate, making artisanal-styled wines, usually hits the high notes with their single-vineyard offerings of Hermitage Les Rocoules blanc and Hermitage Le Gréal red (actually a blend of Méal and Greffieux). Marc Sorrel has also been increasing his production of both red and white Crozes-Hermitage, wines that are meant for easy and quick consumption.

The 2000 Crozes-Hermitage Blanc was barrel-fermented with full malolactic in wood. This 100% Marsanne *cuvée* exhibits an evolved, honeyed/mineral style, medium body, and a short finish. Drink it over the next several years. The 1999 Crozes-Hermitage Blanc is very fruity, along with honeyed citrus notes, a straightforward personality, a rich, nicely textured, medium-bodied palate, and a pure finish. It needs to be consumed over the near-term.

The 2000 Hermitage Blanc exhibits telltale characteristics of fino sherry, acacia flowers, honeyed citrus, and a hint of pineapple. Drink this medium-bodied, low-acid, pleasant, light effort during its first 5–6 years of life. The tiny production of 2000 Hermitage Les Rocoules (200 cases) is a blend of 90% Marsanne and 10% Roussanne aged 15 months in old wood. It is fined but not filtered prior to bottling. Always the richest white in Sorrel's cellar, I have purchased many vintages (particularly 1990, 1989, 1988), all of which are just now reemerging following a period of dormancy. (Thomas Jefferson thought it was France's single greatest dry white wine.) The medium- to full-bodied, long 2000 is more forward than usual, and thus is best consumed during its first decade of life. It offers a rich honeysuckle, citrus, earth, mineral, and hazelnut-scented and -flavored personality. The 1999s are both serious white Hermitages that will be enjoyed by the handful of enthusiasts who appreciate these under-rated dry offerings.

The 1999 Hermitage Blanc (most of which comes from Les Greffieux) possesses superb concentration, long, honeysuckle-like flavors, plenty of opulence, a boatload of glycerin, and a chewy, luscious, honeyed white fruit/floral-flavored palate. One of the finest regular *cuvées* of white Hermitage Sorrel has produced, its forwardness suggests it should be drunk over the next decade. Sporting extraordinary levels of glycerin, the 1999 Hermitage Les Rocoules merits a serious wow! The natural alcohol is 14.8% and the wine (93% Marsanne and 7% Roussanne) is unctuously textured with a terrific nose of rose petals, liquid minerals, honeyed pineapple, and hints of sherry. It boasts explosive ripeness, a viscous texture, and tremendous purity as well as length. It will undoubtedly close down in a few years, reemerge after a decade, and last for 25 years. Anticipated maturity: now–2006; 2012–2025. In 1998, the Hermitage Blanc achieved 13.2% natural alcohol. The wine is dense and rich, with a liquid granite–like nose, medium to full body, and low acidity. It is meant to be consumed over the next 7–8 years. The 1998 Hermitage Les Rocoules (14.7% natural alcohol) should be drunk 2–3 years after bottling or be laid away for a decade. This offering, which includes 7–8% Roussanne, is quite structured, with copious quantities of honeyed citrus, roasted nut, and liquid mineral characteristics. This style of wine (as well as white Hermitage in general) is not for everybody, but these wines are loaded with character. However, they must be drunk either very young or cellared for a decade, as they generally go into a dormant stage around age 5, where they remain for 5–6 years. The 1998 Les Rocoules possesses a boatload of glycerin, but I still think it will close down in a few years.

As for the 1997 Hermitage Blanc, it is surprisingly forward, and much lighter than this wine normally tends to be. It achieved 12.4% alcohol and is refreshing with notions of white peach–like aromas intermixed with minerals. However, it lacks the body and power normally found in this *cuvée*. The 1997 Hermitage Les Rocoules exhibits a California-like, tropical fruit–scented nose with a surprising apricot/honeyed note reminiscent of Condrieu. This medium-bodied offering is atypical for Sorrel in its evolved style. Precocious and up-front, it will provide ideal drinking over the next 2–3 years.

The 1996 Hermitage Blanc is elegant, stylish, and well made, with citrusy fruit but not much power or depth. It is made from 100% Marsanne, primarily from Les Greffiers vineyard on Hermitage Hill. The 1996 Hermitage Les Rocoules (13.5% alcohol) includes 10–15% Roussanne in the blend. A more honeyed, richer, fuller-bodied white Hermitage, it is more typical of what Sorrel routinely does with this *cuvée*. Notes of white flowers are apparent in this offering, which possesses decent acidity, but not the obtrusive acidity noticeable in some 1996 wines. The 1995 Hermitage Blanc exhibits crisp acidity, a straightforward nose of white fruits, minerals, spice, and medium body. It is ideal for drinking over the next 3–4 years. The 1995 Hermitage Les Rocoules displays an evolved light golden color, good power, low acidity, and a tendency toward flabbiness, with cherry, almond, and rubber cement–like scents and flavors. This is a spicy, disjointed, and awkward wine. I would opt for drinking it earlier rather than later.

Sorrel made an important decision to destem the Syrah from his Crozes-Hermitage vineyard in Larnage. This has reduced the overt herbaceousness of these wines, although they remain slightly vegetal. The 2000 Crozes-Hermitage is extremely light. Although it is 100% destemmed, it reveals a green pepper character in its cherry fruit. Drink it over the next several years. From a soft, easygoing, user-friendly vintage for red Hermitage, the 2000 Hermitage is a lighter-styled, friendly, elegant effort with pretty black cherry fruit intermixed with licorice, dried herbs, and earth. It is best consumed during its first 7–8 years of life. More serious, the deep ruby-colored, full-bodied 2000 Hermitage Le Gréal offers copious quantities of earthy, smoky, black currants and cherries. With sweet tannin and outstanding concentration, it is unquestionably a success for the vintage. Sadly, there are only 225 cases. Anticipated maturity: 2004–2015.

The 1999 Hermitage reveals a soft, curranty character with surprisingly tart acidity. While it is an elegant, medium-bodied, pure offering, it is more austere and lacks the density and power of his 1998, or 1997 for that matter. It will need to be drunk early in life as it will become more attenuated with aging. The light-colored 1999 Crozes-Hermitage is a pleasant, cherry-scented example with a fragrant nose of strawberries, cherries, pepper, and spice. Enjoy this fruity 1999 over the next several years. The closed, backward 1999 Hermitage Le Gréal seemed to have more potential when I tasted it during its *élevage*. It is medium-bodied, with tart acidity and a sweet nose of strawberry and black cherry fruit intermixed with earth, licorice, and a touch of pepper. A herbaceous character emerges as the wine sits in the glass. In the mouth, refreshing acidity gives uplift, but the weight, substance, and fat of a top Hermitage are lacking. This is a rare case where a northern Rhône 2000 is better than its 1999 counterpart.

The 1998 Hermitages have begun to close down, yet they reflect Marc Sorrel's confidence in having the potential to be his finest, particularly the top *cuvée* of Gréal. The 1998 Hermitage, which emerges primarily from such vineyard sites as Greffieux, Vignon, and Béssards, was totally closed when tasted. It displayed a dense ruby/purple color, a hint of blackberry fruit, and a boatload of tannin. However, it finished with a Bordeaux-like austere character. When sampled in barrel, I predicted this 1998 would be outstanding, but I am backing off. It requires a minimum of 4–5 years of cellaring, but the tough tannin is cause for concern. It should keep for 15–20 years. The 1998 Hermitage Le Gréal is undoubtedly the finest Sorrel has made during his helmsmanship at this estate. His father fashioned two wines of this caliber (1979 and 1978). With a natural alcohol level of 13.7%, this is no wimpish wine, but whoever said Hermitage was? It boasts an opaque black/purple color in addition to a superb bouquet of blackberries, cedar, liquid minerals, spice box, and earth. The concentration and multilayered texture are both fabulous in this thick, viscous, tannic monster. As the 1998 Hermitage Le Gréal sat in the glass, it took on the character of a first growth Pauillac or super second St.-Julien such as Léoville-Barton. It will unquestionably require patience. Anticipated maturity: 2010–2035. By the way, 50% of the grapes for this *cuvée* were destemmed, the first time Sorrel had implemented that practice.

The delicious, sexy, lush, fruity 1997 Hermitage is a dark ruby-colored offering with low acidity that will drink well over the next 5–9 years. The opaque purple-colored 1997 Hermitage Le Gréal is more evolved and flamboyant than the more reserved and elegant 1996. Sexy and rich, with copious quantities of crème de cassis fruit, medium body, and good spicy meaty richness on the mid-palate, it is a showy Hermitage that should drink well young and last for a decade or more.

DOMAINE LA SOUMADE

2000	Cabernet Sauvignon	B	(88–91)
1999	Cabernet Sauvignon Cuvée Prestige VDP d'Orange	B	89
2000	Côtes du Rhône Les Violettes	B	(89–92)
1999	Côtes du Rhône Les Violettes	B	90
2000	Merlot	B	(88–91)
2000	Rasteau Cuvée Confiance	D	(92–94)
1999	Rasteau Cuvée Confiance	D	92
2000	Rasteau Cuvée Prestige	E	(90–92)
1999	Rasteau Cuvée Prestige	E	90
2000	Rasteau Fleur de Confiance	E	(92–95)
1999	Rasteau Fleur de Confiance	E	94
2000	Vin doux Rasteau	C	88

Domaine la Soumade's proprietor, André Romero, is a legend in this somewhat forgotten southern Rhône hillside village. Rasteau has as many old vines planted on its steep hillsides as any village in the region, yet other than Romero, the village has not received the recognition it deserves. There are several up-and-coming Rasteau producers intent on challenging Romero for the leadership position (i.e., Helen Durand of Domaine Trapadis and Jerôme Bressy of Domaine Court-Mauten), but at the moment, he remains the uncontested star of Rasteau, producing wines of ravishing richness as well as aging potential. My visits with Romero, a diminutive, whimsical man with a large head, beaming eyes, and an irreverence that is reminiscent of Châteauneuf-du-Pape's well-known Henri Bonneau, are usually one of the highlights of my trip. Most consumers do not recognize how good these wines can be.

Among the surprises at this estate are the Merlot (planted in the mid-1980s) and Cabernet Sauvignon (from five- and eight-year-old vines) made just outside the appellation and thus entitled to the *vin de pays* d'Orange designation. The over-sized, almost bigger-than-life Rasteau *cuvées* always include a Cuvée Prestige and Cuvée Confiance, but the famed Fleur de Confiance (from an ancient hillside vineyard not far from Romero's cellars) is only produced in the greatest vintages. These are not wines for consumers seeking delicacy or restraint as they represent Côtes du Rhône at its most exuberant and powerful. Romero, who is proud to say he was the first Rhône Valley producer to practice *pigéage*, obtains amazing color as well as intensity. His 2000s are superb, and his 1999s are even better than his 1998s.

André Romero's 2000s possess fabulous fruit, high glycerin, and the vintage's jammy, overripe character. Tannin is present, but it is sweeter and more integrated than in 1999. If the noteworthy 2000 Merlot (a 1,000-case *cuvée* from 15-year-old vines) develops more complexity, look out Bordeaux! It is a dense purple-colored effort with glorious levels of fruit, amazing glycerin, impressive concentration, and sweet tannin. The question is, will it develop complexity? Anticipated maturity: now–2010. The black/purple-colored 2000 Cabernet Sauvignon (a blend of 95% Cabernet Sauvignon and 5% Petit Verdot) exhibits a peppery, cedary, spicy-scented bouquet as well as abundant cassis fruit. While not as succulent as the

Merlot, it offers authentic Cabernet flavors. It should drink well for 10–12 years. The 2000 Rasteau *cuvées* achieved 15% alcohol naturally, and are more accessible, fatter, even plumper efforts than the 1999s and 1998s were at a similar age. The 2000 Rasteau Cuvée Prestige reveals a dense purple color along with a gorgeous nose of blackberry fruit, vanilla, licorice, and spice. Lush and fat, without the structure of the 1999, its gorgeous accessibility and user-friendly style will please readers looking for a wine to coat their palates. It should drink well for 14–15 years. The 2000 Rasteau Cuvée Confiance is comparable to a *confit* of jam. Its dense purple color is followed by spectacular aromas of blueberries/blackberries. With a boatload of glycerin, massive body, and noteworthy purity, symmetry, and length, it will drink well for 12–15 years. The 2000 Côtes du Rhône Les Violettes (a blend of 80% Syrah, 10% Viognier, and 10% Roussanne) reveals a wickedly kinky, exotic nose of flowers, honeysuckle, and black fruits. Full-bodied, unctuously textured, and made in a southern Côte Rôtie–like style, it is a singular effort for this sector of the Rhône. Enjoy it over the next decade. Lastly, the 2000 Rasteau Fleur de Confiance (15.5% natural alcohol) is monumental. Black/purple in color, dense, full-bodied, and loaded with extract, and possessing high levels of cassis, blackberries, glycerin as well as tannin (well-hidden), this fat, chewy, enormously endowed 2000 will drink well for 15+ years. Sadly, there are only 7,000 bottles.

The Rasteau appellation is renowned for its sweet wines, and Domaine la Soumade produces one of the finest. The 2000 Vin Doux Rasteau offers notes of fudge, cocoa, jammy strawberry and cherry fruit, full body, and light to moderate sweetness. These wines need to be drunk as aperitifs or with certain desserts (particularly chocolate). Although the 2000 Vin Doux Rasteau is not as sensational as Romero's other offerings, it is a fine effort.

The *barrique*-aged 1999 Cabernet Sauvignon Cuvée Prestige VDP d'Orange was produced from destemmed grapes that received the Burgundian *pigéage* treatment (punching down of the cap during fermentation), and bottled with no fining after a negligible filtration by gravity. This opaque ruby/purple-colored Cabernet offers boisterous black currant fruit and a thick, full-bodied texture. While lack of complexity may be a shortcoming, the mouthcoating levels of extract and richness are impressive. I tasted a 5-year-old *cuvée* of this wine, which was displaying Cabernet Sauvignon's cedar, spice box, and licorice notes. Sadly, there are only 7,000 bottles of the 1999, a blend of 80% Cabernet Sauvignon, 15% Merlot, and 5% Petit Verdot. Drink it over the next decade.

The 1999s are better than their 1998 counterparts, which is saying something. The big, serious, full-bodied 1999 Rasteau Cuvée Prestige (a tank-aged blend of 80% Grenache, 10% Syrah, and 10% Mourvèdre) exhibits notes of crème de cassis, tar, chocolate, licorice, and spice. Full-bodied and moderately tannic, it requires 2 more years of cellaring and should age well for 15 years. The black/purple-colored 1999 Rasteau Cuvée Confiance (80% Grenache with the balance Syrah and Mourvèdre, all from 50-year-old vines, aged in both tank and small barrels) is terrific. Although it tips the scales at 14.5% alcohol, it is well hidden. This 18,000-bottle *cuvée* possesses a fabulously sweet perfume of blackberries, cassis, minerals, hot stones, and a touch of cocoa. With thick, full-bodied, tannic flavors, this is a big wine, even by New World standards. The finish lasts for 35–40 seconds. Anticipated maturity: now–2015. A curiosity (300 cases produced) is Romero's Côtes du Rhône called Les Violettes. A Côte Rôtie–like blend of 80% Syrah and 20% Viognier, the 1999 offers an exotic nose of orange peel, honeysuckle, crème de cassis, and spicy wood. Full-bodied, juicy, succulent, pure, and concentrated, it should evolve easily for a decade. A 100% old-vine Grenache, the 1999 Rasteau Fleur de Confiance (made from microscopic yields of 12–15 hectoliters per hectare and aged in a combination of small barrels and tank) took a year to ferment dry, and easily hides its 15.8% alcohol. An extravagant nose of black raspberry liqueur intermixed with blackberry, floral, and licorice notes charges from the glass. This full-bodied blockbuster possesses a tannic underpinning in addition to huge concentration and depth. As with the other wines, Romero does little racking and considerable lees contact.

Levels of sulphur utilized in his cellars are extremely small. This *cuvée*, which is, atypically, packaged in a heavy Bordeaux-shaped bottle, should age well for two decades.

JEAN-MICHEL STEPHAN

2000	Côte Rôtie	D	(82–86)
1999	Côte Rôtie	D	88
1998	Côte Rôtie	D	87
2000	Côte Rôtie Coteau de Tupin	D	(87–89)
2000	Côte Rôtie Vieilles Vignes en Coteau	E	(88–89+)
1999	Côte Rôtie Vieilles Vignes en Coteau	E	89
1998	Côte Rôtie Vieilles Vignes en Coteau	E	89

A young grower who has quickly emerged as someone to watch, Jean-Michel Stephan utilizes all *barriques*, of which approximately 50% are new. Moreover, he completely destems the grapes. His wines are all produced from fruit grown in the southern half of Côte Rôtie, primarily from the Côte Blonde. The 2000 Côte Rôtie Coteau de Tupin is a soft, creamy-styled offering with medium body, sweet oak, and red as well as black fruit characteristics. This ripe, low-acid, evolved 2000 will require consumption during its first 5–7 years of life. The 2000 Côte Rôtie is more herbaceous and vegetal. Many wines from this appellation display notes of black olives (sometimes referred to as tapenade), but this effort goes almost too far in the green olive direction. It is a pleasant but essentially superficial, light effort to drink during its first 5–6 years of life. Not surprisingly, Stephan's top *cuvée* is the 2000 Côte Rôtie Vieilles Vignes en Coteau. It exhibits cassis, violet, earth, and sweet new-oak aromas as well as flavors. Dark ruby-colored, with medium body, good ripeness, low acidity, and moderate concentration, it should drink well for a decade.

The 1999 Côte Rôtie offers the appellation's peppery, earthy, roasted characteristics along with excellent sweetness and a pure black currant and crushed black olive–scented bouquet. Medium-bodied and round, it is best consumed during its first 7–8 years of life. The soft 1999 Côte Rôtie Vieilles Vignes en Coteau exhibits more spice as well as grilled herbs, smoky oak, black currants, flowers, and sweet cherry fruit. Made in the style of the *cuvée* classique, it will drink well for 7–8 years. The 1998 Côte Rôtie offers a spicy, coffee, and black currant–scented bouquet with notes of dried herbs and wood in the background. It exhibits excellent concentration, elegance, and more depth than other wines made in this style. Consume this 1998 over the next 6–8 years. The 1998 Côte Rôtie Vieilles Vignes en Coteau reveals the same elegant style, but backs it up with more black raspberry and smoky, cherry fruit notions, in addition to a hint of violets. The wine is ripe and medium-bodied, with sweet, well-integrated tannin, low acidity, and good weight. It should drink well for 10–12 years.

TARDIEU-LAURENT

2000	Châteauneuf-du-Pape	E	(90–92)
1999	Châteauneuf-du-Pape	E	(91–94)
1997	Châteauneuf-du-Pape	E	90
2000	Châteauneuf-du-Pape Vieilles Vignes	E	(93–96)
1999	Châteauneuf-du-Pape Vieilles Vignes	E	(92–94+)
1998	Châteauneuf-du-Pape Vieilles Vignes	E	94
2000	Cornas Coteaux	E	(89–91?)
1999	Cornas Coteaux	E	(90–92)
1998	Cornas Coteaux	E	87
1997	Cornas Coteaux	E	90
2000	Cornas Vieilles Vignes	E	(91–93)
1999	Cornas Vieilles Vignes	E	(91–93+)
1998	Cornas Vieilles Vignes	E	98

1997	Cornas Vieilles Vignes	E	91
2000	Costières de Nîmes	C	(88–90)
1999	Costières de Nîmes	C	(90–92)
1998	Costières de Nîmes	C	(90–92)
2000	Côte Rôtie	EE	(87–90)
1999	Côte Rôtie	EE	95
1998	Côte Rôtie	EE	93
1997	Côte Rôtie	EE	94
1999	Côte Rôtie Cuvée Spéciale Vieilles Vignes	EE	98
2000	Côtes du Lubéron Bastide de Rhodares	B	(88–90)
1998	Côtes du Lubéron Bastide de Rhodares	B	(90–91)
2000	Côtes du Rhône Les Becs Fins	B	91
2000	Côtes du Rhône Guy Louis	B	(91–93)
1998	Côtes du Rhône Guy Louis	B	(88–90)
1997	Côtes du Rhône Guy Louis	B	(89–91)
2000	Côtes du Rhône-Villages Rasteau Vieilles Vignes	D	(91–93)
1999	Côtes du Rhône-Villages Rasteau Vieilles Vignes	D	(87–89)
1998	Côtes du Rhône-Villages Rasteau Vieilles Vignes	D	(91–92)
2000	Crozes-Hermitage Cuvée Coteaux	D	(88–89)
1999	Crozes-Hermitage Cuvée Coteaux	D	(88–91)
2000	Gigondas	D	(89–91)
1998	Gigondas	D	(87–89)
1997	Gigondas	D	89
1999	Gigondas Vieilles Vignes	E	(90–92)
1998	Gigondas Vieilles Vignes	E	92
2000	Hermitage	EE	(90–92)
1999	Hermitage	EE	(95–98)
1998	Hermitage	EE	91+
1997	Hermitage	EE	92+
1998	Hermitage Blanc	EE	(87–88)
1997	Hermitage Eremites	EE	(91–92)
1998	St.-Joseph Les Roches	D	(87–89)
2000	St.-Joseph Les Roches Vieilles Vignes	D	(90–92)
1999	St.-Joseph Les Roches Vieilles Vignes	D	(91–93)
2000	Vacqueyras Vieilles Vignes	D	(93–96)
1999	Vacqueyras Vieilles Vignes	D	(91–92)
1998	Vacqueyras Vieilles Vignes	D	92
1997	Vacqueyras Vieilles Vignes	D	88
1999	VDP d'Oc Les Grands Augustins	A	89

Michel Tardieu and Dominique Laurent are fashioning some of the most intriguing and compelling wines of the Rhône Valley. The following southern and northern Rhône selections are fabulous efforts. Tardieu, whose cellars are located in the beautiful village of Lourmarin, is the quintessential minimal interventionist. After buying finished wine from growers who only have old vines and small yields, most of the wines are transferred to oak barrels made to Dominique Laurent's specifications, where they spend two years untouched. Sulphur additions are minimal, there is no racking, and the bottling is completed with neither fining nor filtration. These brilliant efforts capture the essence of their particular appellations and have fabulous aging potential. I have been a huge fan of Tardieu-Laurent since the operation was begun in the mid-1990s. In a mere five years this *négociant* firm has garnered incredible respect from some of the southern Rhône's finest growers.

The extraordinary 2000 Côtes du Rhône Les Becs Fins (3,200 cases) is a tank-aged blend of old-vine Carignan (50%) and equal parts Grenache and Syrah. This spectacular offering (which was already bottled when I visited) is a fabulous introduction to Tardieu-Laurent's style. Its opaque ruby/purple color is followed by a flamboyant bouquet of blackberry and black raspberry jam. Fruit-dominated, with high levels of glycerin, medium to full body, and pure flavors, this is a great Côtes du Rhône as well as an astonishing bargain. My instincts suggest consuming it during its exuberant, powerful youth (over the next 2–3 years), but I suspect it will last for 4–5. The impressive, opulent, deep purple-colored 2000 Côtes du Lubéron Bastide de Rhodares possesses sweet fruit, toasty oak (one-third new barrels are used), and a juicy, succulent, long finish. It reveals more structure than Les Becs Fins, but not the charm and flattering style. It should drink well for a decade. Possibly the finest Côtes du Rhône Michel Tardieu has made to date, the opaque black/purple-colored 2000 Guy Louis is a blend of 50% Grenache (from 80-year-old vines) and 50% Carignan (from 20–60-year-old vines) from growers located in Rasteau, Gigondas, Valréas, and St.-Joseph. Its 100% new-oak aging is hard to believe given the fact that there is no noticeable wood in the flavors. This multilayered, full-bodied wine bursts with blackberry and cassis fruit. It will provide sumptuous drinking over the next 10–12 years.

I will be cellaring both the Côtes du Rhône-Villages Rasteau Vieilles Vignes and Vacqueyras Vieilles Vignes. The rustic, masculine 2000 Côtes du Rhône-Villages Rasteau Vieilles Vignes (500 cases) is a blend of 75% Grenache, 10% Syrah, and 15% Carignan from 50-year-old hillside vineyards. This black/purple-colored Rasteau carries its 14.5% alcohol impeccably. It offers amazing concentration, plenty of power, and notes of licorice, blackberries, cassis, and truffles. Extremely ripe and corpulent, with an astonishingly long finish, it rivals some of the appellation's finest wines produced by the likes of André Romero. Perhaps the finest Vacqueyras I have tasted, the opaque black/purple-colored 2000 Vacqueyras Vieilles Vignes boasts a stunning bouquet of black fruits, smoke, and earth. Concentrated, viscous, and chewy, with 14% alcohol buried beneath the wealth of fruit and glycerin, this awesome Vacqueyras easily out-performs many Châteauneuf-du-Papes and Gigondas. The finish lasts for 45 seconds, and the wine possesses a level of extract and richness that must be tasted to be believed. Anticipated maturity: now–2017. A legend in the making!

Compared to the Vacqueyras and Rasteau offerings, the 2000 Gigondas is a restrained, elegant, medium-bodied effort with an impressively saturated black/purple color and good acidity, but a leaner, more measured personality. Long and ripe, with copious quantities of mineral-laced black fruits, it should drink well for 10–12 years.

Tardieu is a huge fan of Châteauneuf-du-Pape, and he purchases much of his juice from three of that appellation's finest producers. The dense purple-colored 2000 Châteauneuf-du-Pape (500 cases) possesses loads of jammy black cherry and currant fruit with a hint of licorice and spice box. A fat, jammy, open-knit Châteauneuf with its structure well concealed by the glycerin and fruit, it should be delicious when released and age well for 15 years. The profound 2000 Châteauneuf-du-Pape Vieilles Vignes (425 cases) emerges from a 60-year-old vineyard. This sumptuous, black/purple-colored offering exhibits a fabulously concentrated nose of jammy black fruits backed up by huge levels of glycerin, licorice, and a hint of truffles. The wine goes on and on, unfolding magically on the palate. This prodigious Châteauneuf-du-Pape is a tour de force. Anticipated maturity: 2005–2025.

The 2000 Costières de Nîmes (a blend of 90% Syrah and 10% Grenache) exhibits an impressively saturated opaque purple color and a leaner, more elegant style with medium to full body as well as excellent black fruit characteristics intermixed with notes of wood, earth, and mineral. It should be consumed during its first 7–8 years of life.

The 2000 Crozes-Hermitage Cuvée Coteaux reveals notes of tapenade, black cherries, and plums in its forward, low-acid, spicy personality. Medium-bodied and soft, it will provide delicious drinking during its first 6–8 years of life. More serious, the 2000 St.-Joseph Les Roches Vieilles Vignes offers blackberry and cassis flavors intertwined with liquid mineral notes. This supple, medium- to full-bodied, elegant St.-Joseph possesses superb depth, purity, and balance. The tannin is sweet, the acid low, and there is abundant fruit and glycerin. Drink it during its first 10–12 years of life.

There are two Cornas *cuvées*. The Cuvée Coteaux comes from 20–40-year-old vines, and the Vieilles Vignes from 100-year-old vines. The black/purple-colored, masculine 2000 Cornas Coteaux reveals good richness on the attack, but ferocious tannin in the finish. It should gain texture during its *élevage*. The level of sulphur is extremely low (approximately 15 ppm). This wine has good length, but the high tannin is a concern . . . at least for now. More promising, the saturated black/purple-colored 2000 Cornas Vieilles Vignes boasts a superb nose of blackberry fruit intermixed with graphite, earth, and minerals. Spicy, with moderately high tannin, sweet fruit, and abundant glycerin as well as extract, it will be at its peak between 2006–2016.

After the potentially perfect 1999 Côte Rôtie, it is not surprising that the 2000 Côte Rôtie (100% Syrah from 20–60-year-old vines) seems merely mortal. While it lacks the fatness and majestic depth of the 1999, the 2000 reveals adequate tannin, an earthy, olive, and black currant–scented nose, a good, but uninspiring mid-palate, and a dry finish. If the prolonged *élevage sur-lie* works as well as Tardieu hopes, the mid-palate should fill out. Anticipated maturity: 2004–2016. There are 250 cases of the 2000 Hermitage, a more elegant, finesse-styled effort compared to the blockbuster 1999 and 1998. Concentrated for the vintage, it offers a deep purple color followed by notions of licorice and crème de cassis, sweet tannin, low acidity, and a forward, plump, concentrated style. This well-balanced Hermitage will be drinkable at a younger age than the 1999. Anticipated maturity: 2004–2016.

The dense purple-colored 1999 Crozes-Hermitage Cuvée Coteaux exhibits a wild, almost *sauvage* bouquet of dried herbs, cassis, raspberries, pepper, and licorice. Dense, medium- to full-bodied, and moderately tannic, with tangy underlying acidity providing freshness, it will drink well for 10–12 years. Readers should be aware that some of the potentially greatest yet unexploited vineyard sites in the northern Rhône are the hillside vineyards of St.-Joseph. It is a diverse appellation with many mediocre vineyards as well as a small, but growing number of terrific sites now being exploited by people such as Jacques Granges (the wine-maker at Delas), Michel Chapoutier, Gérard and Jean-Louis Chave, and Michel Tardieu. The 1999 St.-Joseph Les Roches Vieilles Vignes comes from a hillside vineyard near the village of Châteaubourg. A sensational effort, it is one of the finest I have tasted, rivaling the aforementioned. Smoky, licorice-infused, blackberry, and cassis fruit include a liquid mineral characteristic. With excellent texture, full body, brilliant purity, and overall symmetry, it is a fabulous, celestial St.-Joseph to enjoy over the next 15 years.

In a year when Cornas yields were extremely high and the overall quality variable, Michel Tardieu has turned out two of the better wines of the appellation. The black/purple-colored 1999 Cornas Coteaux exhibits powerful, smoky, earthy, concentrated flavors of black fruits, scorched earth, and melted asphalt. Full-bodied, powerful, and muscular, this 1999 will be at its finest between 2005–2015. The stunning 1999 Cornas Vieilles Vignes displays an inky black/purple color in addition to a gorgeous bouquet of blackberry liqueur, melted tar, truffles, and scorched earth. Dense, with an unctuous texture, adequate acidity, and a 30+-second finish, this is a potentially sublime Cornas. Anticipated maturity: 2005–2020.

Three wines that flirt with perfection include the 1999 Côte Rôtie, 1999 Côte Rôtie Cuvée Spéciale Vieilles Vignes, and 1999 Hermitage. Côte Rôtie enjoyed one of its greatest vintages of the twentieth century, which is obvious in both of Tardieu-Laurent's *cuvées*. There are a whopping 30 barrels (approximately 750 cases) of the 1999 Côte Rôtie. It boasts a saturated black/purple color as well as a glorious nose of overripe blackberries, cassis, violets, and vanilla. Unctuously textured, unbelievably fat and dense, with a texture and richness not dissimilar from some of the profound 1947 Pomerols, this low-acid wine is almost over the top, but so rich, concentrated, and pure it should provide head-turning levels of pleasure and joy for 20–25 years. The limited production (about 125 cases) 1999 Côte Rôtie Cuvée Spéciale Vieilles Vignes emerges from such vineyards as Les Roziers, La Landonne, and Les Grandes Places. A prodigious Côte Rôtie produced from 100% Syrah, aged in 100% new oak, it achieved 13.5% alcohol naturally. It expresses the Côte Brune side of Syrah in an amazing fashion. The intense perfume of violets, melted licorice, espresso, cassis, and blackberry is unreal. On the palate, this full-bodied effort is huge, but not heavy. Massively endowed, with a viscous texture, thrilling levels of glycerin, and a compelling finish that lasts nearly a minute, this wine's tannin is barely noticeable given the staggering concentration and glycerin levels. Anticipated maturity: 2007–2030. Nearly as spectacular is the astonishing 1999 Hermitage, another black beauty with outstanding richness, layers of extract and glycerin, and more structure and tannin than evident in the two Côte Rôties. This monster wine (crammed with crème de cassis, licorice, liquid minerals, and smoke) will need 8–10 years of cellaring and will keep for 35 years.

There are just under 7,000 cases of the remarkable 1999 VDP d'Oc Les Grands Augustins. This wine, a blend of Grenache, Syrah, and Carignan, exhibits a black/purple color in addition to a straightforward bouquet of crème de cassis, licorice, and minerals. With a long, full-bodied, gorgeously textured mid-palate and finish, it should drink well for 5–7 years. Michel Tardieu has produced an amazing 1999 Costières de Nîmes (a blend of Syrah, Carignan, and Grenache). This black/purple-colored effort has soaked up its 100% new-oak aging, saturating the palate with exceptional ripeness, richness, and unctuosity. It is an amazing effort that should develop for a decade, although its low acidity and high levels of glycerin and succulence suggest it will drink well young. Readers looking for full throttle, value-priced Côtes du Rhône have never had it so good, with both the 1999 and 1998 vintages producing a plethora of excellent wines.

The rustic 1999 Côtes du Rhône-Villages Rasteau Vieilles Vignes exhibits high tannin and saturated black cherry/berry flavors intermixed with roasted herbs, burnt earth, and coffee characteristics. This robust wine needs to tame down a bit as it is currently uncivilized. Anticipated maturity: 2004–2010. A better bet is the sumptuous 1999 Vacqueyras Vieilles Vignes, a blend of 90% Grenache and 10% Syrah that achieved 14% alcohol naturally. This spectacular, full-bodied, lavishly concentrated, dense 1999 promises to last for 8–15 years. Another knockout effort that is more elegant and finesse-styled is the 1999 Gigondas Vieilles Vignes. The juice for this wine comes from two of the appellation's finest growers (I was asked not to reveal their names). It exhibits sweet blackberry and floral notes intermixed with licorice, truffles, and spice. Medium- to full-bodied and graceful, it is a stylish Gigondas that should drink well for 10–12 years.

There are two *cuvées* of Châteauneuf-du-Pape. The 1999 Châteauneuf-du-Pape, which comes from the northwestern sector known as Grès, is a succulent, hedonistic fruit bomb made primarily from Grenache with a bit of Syrah included. Full-bodied, with low acidity, a thick, unctuous texture, high alcohol, and a blast of kirsch and spice, this multilayered Châteauneuf should drink well when released and last for 15 years. The more tannic, closed, mammothly-endowed 1999 Châteauneuf-du-Pape Vieilles Vignes is a blend of 95% Grenache and 5% Syrah and Counoise. Its opaque dense purple color is followed by a reticent nose of earth, minerals, black fruits, and licorice, with a massive body, blistering tannin levels, and a firm, enormously endowed finish. It has the potential to be great, coming across structurally more like a young Beaucastel than a typical Grenache-based Châteauneuf-du-Pape. Anticipated maturity: 2006–2020.

The 1998 Hermitage Blanc (95% Marsanne and 5% Roussanne) is a restrained, elegant white Hermitage with medium body, subtle toasty oak, and good ripeness. It will not win any awards for flamboyance, but one has to respect its delicacy. Anticipated maturity: now–2006. More concentrated and impressive, the 1998 St.-Joseph Les Roches was produced from yields of 20 hectoliters per hectare. It exhibits a dark ruby/purple color, high tannin, and mineral-infused, flinty, black cherry and cassis fruit. This medium- to full-bodied, backward St.-Joseph requires 2–3 years of cellaring, and will keep for 15 years. There are two *cuvées* of Cornas. The black/purple-colored 1998 Cornas Coteaux possesses noteworthy crème de cassis aromas meshed with smoke and toasty wood. Obviously made from low yields, it is a rustic, tannic, backward wine that will benefit from 3–4 years of cellaring. It will keep for 12–15 years. If the tannin becomes better integrated, it will come close to meriting an outstanding rating. There is no need to worry about the harmony among the diverse elements in the spectacularly black/purple-colored 1998 Cornas Vieilles Vignes (125 cases produced). It boasts an extraordinary bouquet of violets, truffles, black raspberries, cassis, and blackberries. Superrich and extremely full-bodied (it achieved 13% natural alcohol), this profound Cornas needs 5–6 years of cellaring and will keep for 20–25 years. An amazing effort!

Another amazing effort is the 1998 Côte Rôtie, which comes from three hillside vineyards—La Landonne, Les Grandes Places, and Côte Rozier. The wine's dark purple color is followed by an explosive, exotic bouquet of bacon fat, cherry liqueur, black olives, roasted meats, and toasty wood. This expressive, voluptuously textured, full-bodied, powerful, concentrated Côte Rôtie reveals some tannin in the finish. Anticipated maturity: now–2020. The superb 1998 Hermitage reveals a saturated purple color in addition to classic, pure, cassis aromas intermixed with smoke and licorice. Full-bodied and pure, with nicely integrated acidity and tannin, this corpulent, super-concentrated Hermitage requires 3–7 years of cellaring, and will keep for 20–25 years.

The blackest wine in Tardieu-Laurent's entire 1998 portfolio is the 1998 Costières de Nîmes. Made from 60% Syrah, 20% extremely old-vine Grenache, and 20% Carignan (that yielded only 15 hectoliters per hectare), this effort achieved 13.5% alcohol naturally. There are approximately 300 cases of this spectacular offering from one of the world's finest sources for high-quality wines at reasonable prices. Some readers may find the immense tannin level off-putting, but it possesses hugely concentrated flavors of blackberries, cassis, smoke, dried herbs, and licorice. Amazingly opulent, thick, and succulent, it will always have an uncivilized side, but this is one of the all-time great wine values ever produced. Moreover, it will evolve and become more civilized after 10–12 years of bottle age. Amazing! Another astonishing value is the 1998 Côtes du Lubéron Bastide de Rhodares. There are approximately 650 cases of this blend of 60% Grenache (from 40-year-old vines that achieved 14.9% alcohol naturally) and 40% Syrah. The saturated blue/purple color is followed by spectacularly jammy notes of black fruits, smoke, mineral, and spice. Dense, medium- to full-bodied, with thrilling purity, this layered, concentrated, immense Côtes du Lubéron must be tasted to be believed. Its opulence will serve it well in its youth, but do not be surprised to see this wine improve over the next 5–6 years; it should last for a decade or more.

The 1998 Côtes du Rhône Guy Louis rouge (a blend of equal parts Syrah and Grenache) exhibits a saturated ruby/plum/purple color as well as an elegant, clearly defined bouquet of black currants and minerals, with a touch of road tar. Medium-bodied, pure, and fruit-driven, it is a terrific Côtes du Rhône, with perhaps less alcohol than previous renditions, but impressive and beautifully knit. It should drink well for 5–6 years.

From the southern Rhône villages of Rasteau and Vacqueyras, Michel Tardieu and Dominique Laurent have fashioned two unreal *cuvées*. The 1998 Côtes du Rhône-Villages Rasteau Vieilles Vignes rivals those produced by that village's finest wine-maker, André Romero. A blend of 80% Grenache and 20% Carignan that achieved 14.5% alcohol naturally, this dense purple-colored wine is bursting with black fruits, kirsch, licorice, and smoky scents. Ripe, full-bodied, with impressive sweetness and harmony, as well as a superrich midpalate, this staggering wine can be bought for a song. Anticipated maturity: now–2012. There are 150 cases of black/ruby-colored 1998 Vacqueyras Vieilles Vignes (100% Grenache that achieved 14.8% alcohol). Made entirely from what the locals call the *plateau de garrigues,* this explosively hedonistic fruit bomb coats the palate with luxurious levels of fruit and glycerin.

While it will evolve for 10–15 years, few will be able to resist its hedonistic charms and sumptuous personality. It is a spectacular effort! Anticipated maturity: now–2015.

There are two *cuvées* of Gigondas. The dark ruby/purple-colored 1998 Gigondas is a very good, spicy, elegant, restrained offering with abundant berry fruit intermixed with soil and spicy wood scents. Medium-bodied, beautifully concentrated, ripe, and well balanced, it should drink well for a decade. The tasting notes on the 1998 Gigondas Vieilles Vignes are short since there are only 50 cases. Aged in 100% new oak, this 80% Grenache/20% Syrah blend is a blockbuster, but it will be impossible to find. Moreover, there are many other spectacular 1998 Gigondas for readers to try.

Lastly, the 1998 Châteauneuf-du-Pape Vieilles Vignes (125 cases) is a powerful yet remarkably elegant, Burgundy-styled wine with a floral and black cherry–scented nose, full body, beautifully concentrated flavors, and a sense of freshness and equilibrium. Remarkably, its 14.6% alcohol is completely hidden by the wine's fruit, concentration, and overall symmetry. This beautifully knit Châteauneuf was given the so-called 200% new-oak treatment. In spite of that, the oak plays only a subtle background role to the exuberant fruit and freshness. This beauty should provide gorgeous drinking for 10–15 years.

The 1997 Vacqueyras Vieilles Vignes is a potentially superb wine with an opaque purple color and sumptuous aromas of black cherries and raspberries intertwined with pepper and soil scents. Dense, full-bodied, and remarkable for a Vacqueyras, it should drink well for 7–8 years. The 1997 Côtes du Rhône Guy Louis, a blend of equal parts Syrah and Grenache, is one of the most opulently textured, richest Côtes du Rhônes I have ever tasted. The wine's black ruby color is followed by gorgeously sweet aromas of black cherries and blackberries intermixed with raspberries and licorice. Meaty, with elements of *sur-maturité* and low acidity, this well-proportioned Côtes du Rhône will be delicious young, yet keep for a decade or more. The outstanding 1997 Gigondas possesses notes of *sur-maturité*, jammy blackberry liqueur–like notes in both its aromatics and flavors, a superb, full-bodied texture, spectacular concentration, and no evidence of wood from its *barrique* aging. This wine is sensationally long, luscious, and hedonistic. Speaking of decadently rich, full-throttle southern Rhône wines, the 1997 Châteauneuf-du-Pape satisfies those criteria. A star of the vintage for the appellation, it is a shapely, full-bodied, voluptuously textured wine bursting with black raspberry fruit intermixed with kirsch, pepper, cedar, and roasted herb scents and flavors. There is tremendous viscosity and length, as well as low acidity in this full-flavored, expansive, super-concentrated Châteauneuf. It should drink well for 10–15 years.

I tasted six wines from the northern Rhône 1997s, all of them potentially outstanding . . . and then some. The 1997 Crozes-Hermitage Vieilles Vignes comes from a well-known producer in l'Arnage. Michel Tardieu requested that I not reveal his sources for fear that other *négociants* would seek him out. The 1997 Crozes-Hermitage Vieilles Vignes boasts a dazzlingly thick black/purple color, and sweet, bacon fat, leathery, and cassis flavors. This full-bodied, beautifully rich Crozes-Hermitage reached 13.4–13.6% alcohol naturally. It should drink well for a decade.

I have long admired the efforts Michel Tardieu has turned out in Cornas, Côte Rôtie, and Hermitage, and in 1997 he has produced fabulous wines. There are two *cuvées* of Cornas. The 1997 Cornas Coteaux exhibits a saturated black color, as well as a fabulous nose of melted licorice, acacia flowers, jammy cassis, minerals, and smoke. In the mouth, roasted meat and *jus de viande* characteristics, as well as lush tannins, emerge in this superb, full-bodied, succulent Cornas. The *barrique* aging undoubtedly helps tame some of the rustic, coarse tannin frequently found in the wines from this appellation. Look for this Cornas to age nicely for 10–15+ years. One of the greatest Cornas I have ever tasted is Tardieu-Laurent's 1997 Cornas Vieilles Vignes. This wine takes concentration, power, and body to an extreme limit, but it possesses remarkable balance and well-integrated acidity, tannin, and alcohol. Black colored, with Cornas' telltale blackberry, cassis, and tar aromas, fabulous concentration, and a long, intense finish, this fabulous effort is more backward than the Cornas Coteaux and should be at its finest between now–2020. An amazing accomplishment!

My two favorite wines from this estate in 1997 are the Côte Rôtie Côte Brune and Hermitage. The 1997 Côte Rôtie emerges from such topflight vineyards as Rozier, La Landonne, and Les Grandes Places. It offers a spectacular, complex bouquet of roasted coffee, grilled meats, *jus de viande*, bacon fat, and gobs of black raspberry and cassis fruit. It also possesses the telltale roasted characteristic that gives Côte Rôtie its name. Full-bodied, with modest alcohol (13.3%) for such a weighty, rich wine, it also has remarkable elegance and complexity for a wine so massive. A tour de force in winemaking, it can compete with even the single-vineyard efforts from Marcel Guigal. It will drink well when released (because of low acidity) and last for 15–20 years. The 1997 Hermitage (13.7% alcohol) is a blend from such vineyards as Le Méal, Les Greffieux, Les Dionnières, and Beaumes. It is a candidate for the finest Hermitage of the vintage, possibly rivaling those of Jaboulet and Chapoutier. The color is a saturated black/purple. The wine reveals a Richebourg-like floral, violet complexity intermixed with jammy cassis, blackberries, and cherries. Dense, exceptionally full-bodied, massive, unctuous, and pure, this is a huge Hermitage with a blockbuster finish. Any evidence of tannin and new *barriques* are submerged behind the wine's texture and extraordinary fruit extraction. Amazing! Anticipated maturity: now–2020. The 1997 Hermitage Eremites is an impressively endowed dark ruby/purple-colored wine with copious quantities of sweet black currant fruit intermixed with notes of coffee, tar, and earth. Although dense, full-bodied, and outstanding in all aspects, this wine is simply overwhelmed when tasted alongside the profound/compelling 1997 Côte Rôtie and 1997 Hermitage. Look for the 1997 Hermitage Eremites to age well for two decades.

DOMAINE DE TERRE FERME

2000	Châteauneuf-du-Pape	D	(88–90)
1999	Châteauneuf-du-Pape	D	88
1998	Châteauneuf-du-Pape	D	90

This is a relatively small estate since many of the old Terre Ferme vineyards were sold to Château La Nerthe and Max Aubert. However, the remaining vineyards have produced outstanding wines over recent vintages. Terre Ferme's dark ruby/purple-colored 1999 Châteauneuf-du-Pape displays plenty of licorice, fennel, blackberries, cherries, incense, and spice. Ripe, soft, and loaded with both fruit and glycerin, it will drink well for 8–10 years. Very close in style to the 1999, but with a more saturated black/ruby/purple color, jammier blackberry and cherry flavors, less spice, and more fruit, the full-bodied 2000 Châteauneuf-du-Pape is potentially outstanding. It exhibits good purity as well as a hefty fruit and glycerin-driven mouth-feel. Anticipated maturity: now–2014. The 1998 Châteauneuf-du-Pape is reminiscent of the wines made at Font du Michelle, a neighboring estate. Domaine de Terre Ferme's 1998 is a saturated deep ruby/purple-colored, powerful, concentrated, dense effort with full body, abundant glycerin, an unctuous texture, and layers of ripe fruit presented in a thick, robust, exuberant style. Some tannin is present, but this wine is ripe and rich, and thus accessible. Anticipated maturity: now–2016.

ERIC TEXIER

2000	Châteauneuf-du-Pape	E	87
1999	Châteauneuf-du-Pape	E	89
1999	Côte Rôtie Vieilles Vignes	EE	90+
2000	Côtes du Rhône Blanc	B	86
2000	Côtes du Rhône Brezème	C	87
1999	Côtes du Rhône Brezème	C	82?
2000	Côtes du Rhône Brezème Vieilles Vignes	C	(88–90)

2000 Côtes du Rhône-Villages Chusclan	**C**	**86**
2000 Côtes du Rhône-Villages St.-Gervais Vieilles Vignes	**C**	**89**
2000 Côtes du Rhône-Villages Séguret	**C**	**90**
2000 Côtes du Rhône-Villages Vaison-la-Romaine	**C**	**89**

Eric Texier gave up his work in nuclear technology to pursue his love of wine. Working out of an extremely cold cellar in Beaujolais, he does his own vinification and upbringing, bottling his wines with neither fining nor filtration. Overall, his portfolio is impressive, although there were problems with excessively high acidity in his whites and in a few of his reds (particularly the 1999 Côtes du Rhône Brezème). As he told me, perhaps his "Burgundian" background is the reason for the high-acid profiles in some of these offerings. Nevertheless, this is a serious producer working with old vines, transporting the grapes as well as finished wine by refrigerated container and following a philosophy of minimal intervention.

The only northern Rhône wine I tasted from Texier is the 1999 Côte Rôtie Vieilles Vignes. Very backward, it requires significant aeration in the glass or decanter in order to reveal its personality. A deep ruby/purple color is followed by a big, sweet, toasty oak-scented nose that, with air, reveals cassis, black raspberry, olive, bacon, and mineral notes. Medium-bodied, with a sweet mid-palate, but closed as well as austere in the finish, it will need to be decanted for hours in advance of drinking. In lieu thereof, wait 3–4 years for the magic to begin. Anticipated maturity: 2005–2015.

The straightforward 2000 Côtes du Rhône Blanc (100% Viognier) exhibits fresh, lively, apricot and peach fruit, fine acidity, and excellent definition. A clipped finish has resulted in a good rather than exciting wine. Anticipated maturity: now–2004.

The glories from Texier are his village Côtes du Rhônes. The 2000 Côtes du Rhône-Villages Vaison-la-Romaine is primarily from 80-year-old Grenache blended with Syrah. There are 500 cases of this tank-aged red. Its dense purple color is accompanied by gorgeous blackberry and raspberry fruit aromas as well as flavors, terrific texture, and admirable succulence and flesh. It should drink well for 4–5 years. The 2000 Côtes du Rhône-Villages St.-Gervais Vieilles Vignes offers more mineral notes in its dense blueberry and kirsch-filled personality. This full-bodied, beautifully made 2000 should drink well for 5–6 years. The sensational 2000 Côtes du Rhône-Villages Séguret is a 10,000 bottle, 95% Grenache *cuvée* that achieved 14.5% alcohol naturally. It could easily pass for a top-notch Châteauneuf-du-Pape. With enviable stuffing as well as a big, sweet blackberry, black cherry, licorice, pepper, and spice-scented nose, this opulent, full-bodied Séguret is exciting to drink. Moreover, it should age nicely for 5–6 years. More angular, with cooler climate aromas and flavors, the 2000 Côtes du Rhône-Villages Chusclan offers good spice, noticeable new oak (about 25% new-wood barrels are utilized), and an elegant, restrained personality. It can be drunk now and over the next 4–5 years.

Both of Texier's Châteauneuf-du-Papes are *barrique*-aged blends of 75% Grenache and 25% Mourvèdre. Although more restrained, the 2000 Châteauneuf-du-Pape is sweet, ripe, medium-bodied, and understated for a wine from this appellation known for its full-flavored reds. It should drink well for a decade. The potentially stronger 1999 Châteauneuf-du-Pape reveals elements of *garrigue*, seaweed, black cherries, licorice, and earth, big, full-bodied, powerful flavors, light to moderate tannin, and a sense of elegance, power, and rich fruit. It should drink well for 10–12 years.

While the 1999 Côtes du Rhône Brezème is too high in acidity for my palate, the 2000 Côtes du Rhône Brezème and 2000 Côtes du Rhône Brezème Vieilles Vignes are excellent. These are all 100% Syrah from a cool southern Rhône appellation. The Vieilles Vignes experiences some new oak, but only old *barriques* are used for the 800-case *cuvée* of regular Brezème. The 2000 Côtes du Rhône Brezème exhibits aromas of espresso, smoke, and blackberries, medium body, excellent purity, decent acidity, and fine definition. Enjoy this attractive red over the next 5–6 years. There are 175 cases of the 2000 Côtes du Rhône Brezème

Vieilles Vignes (100% old-vine Syrah). Akin to a poor man's Côte Rôtie, it offers wonderful aromas of bacon fat, crème de cassis, tapenade, and spice in addition to dense, full-bodied, concentrated flavors, and a long texture. It is a tour de force in winemaking from this backwater appellation that has received little attention from anyone other than Eric Texier.

CHÂTEAU DES TOURS

1999	Côtes du Rhône	A	87
1998	Côtes du Rhône	A	87
2000	Vacqueyras	C	(88–90)
1999	Vacqueyras	C	89
1998	Vacqueyras	C	90
1998	Vin de Pays	A	87

Proprietor Emmanuel Reynaud, who also makes the wines at Château Rayas and Fonsalette, refuses to use Syrah in his Vacqueyras. For his top *cuvées*, he relies on old-vine Grenache picked extremely ripe. His delicious 2000 Vacqueyras (15.5% natural alcohol) reveals a deceptively light ruby color along with tremendous levels of glycerin and flavors of pure *confiture* of strawberry fruit intermixed with cherries. It is low in acidity, fleshy, and best consumed during its first 5–7 years of life. Although similarly styled, the 1999 Vacqueyras is not as big a blockbuster as the 2000 or 1998. It possesses a light ruby color, this varietal's telltale cherries macerated in an alcohol-like bouquet, and a fragrant, soft personality. Consume it over the next 5–6 years. On my recent visit, Reynaud surprised me by saying wines such as this actually taste better three or four days after they have been opened. I'm not sure I agree, but readers may want to check it out.

The 1999 Côtes du Rhône, a blend of 75% Grenache, 20% Cinsault, and 5% Syrah, possesses a light color by modern day standards, as well as plenty of black cherry fruit intermixed with notes of resin, pepper, and spice. It should drink well for 3–4 years.

An excellent bargain, the 1998 Vin de Pays rouge includes a dollop of Cinsault as well as a touch of Syrah (3%) in the blend. It reveals a deceptively light ruby color as well as a sweet nose of kirsch and strawberries. A big, sexy entry on the palate is accompanied by low acidity, fine ripeness, and a straightforward, lush finish. Drink it over the next 2–3 years. The 1998 Côtes du Rhône rouge (a blend of 70% Grenache, 20% Cinsault, and 10% Syrah) exhibits more flavor intensity and texture than its light ruby color suggests. It offers abundant quantities of jammy cherry fruit in a medium- to full-bodied, plump, corpulent style. It, too, should be consumed over the next 2–3 years.

The 1998 Vacqueyras is similar to the famed Rayas Châteauneuf-du-Pape. Amazingly, it also demonstrates what can go wrong with France's appellation system. The local syndicate, which grants label approval after tasting the appellation's wines, decided this wine was "not typical," and refused to give it the right to the Vacqueyras appellation. Thus in France it is called "Cuvée du Grand Réserve Côtes du Rhône." In the United States, it bears the Vacqueyras label. This is an absurd decision, aimed at denying young producers, who are attempting to make great wines, the freedom to pursue excellence. The only excuse given to Emmanuel Reynaud by the tasting committee (the most influential taster was a local oenologist) was that the wine was "oxidized." Of course it is not oxidized, but it does not contain any Syrah (most Vacqueyras do), and has more glycerin, flavor, alcohol, and flamboyance than the local authorities deem acceptable for "typical" Vacqueyras. No doubt jealousy and fear have played into this decision, but as any wine lover who tastes this wine will find out, it represents an exceptional expression of old-vine, low yielding Grenache. Tasted blind, many will mistake this wine for a Rayas from a vintage such as 1997 or 1996. The color is a deceptively light to medium ruby. The flamboyant bouquet offers a fabulous expression of Grenache harvested at *sur-maturité* that has not been compromised by aging in new oak. The flavors are all fruit, glycerin, and kirsch. Made from 100% Grenache, the wine exhibits a layered texture, low acidity, and 14–15% natural alcohol. This is a superb example of Vacqueyras that should drink well for 5–8 years. Frankly, the decision of the local bureaucrats is shameful! *P.S.:* I bought two cases.

CHÂTEAU DU TRIGNON

1999	Côtes du Rhône	B	87
1998	Côtes du Rhône	B	85
1999	Côtes du Rhône-Villages Rasteau	B	87
1998	Côtes du Rhône-Villages Rasteau	B	87
1998	Côtes du Rhône-Villages Sablet	B	87
1999	Gigondas	C	89
1998	Gigondas	C	90

The elegant, Burgundy-like 1999 Gigondas possesses floral-infused black cherry fruit, attractive purity, a sweet, round attack, medium body, and measured flavors with excellent delineation. It is a model of purity and restraint. Drink it over the next 7–8 years.

Trignon's 1998 Gigondas is already showing well, in what can be a closed, backward vintage for this appellation. A dark ruby/purple color is followed by sweet blackberry, cherry, kirsch, licorice, and damp earth aromas. This rich, medium- to full-bodied, pure, nicely textured, surprisingly elegant 1998 is capable of drinking well for a dozen or more years.

As for the lower-priced Côtes du Rhône offerings, there are some delicious, tempting bargains. The inexpensive, tasty 1999 Côtes du Rhône is a delicious, round effort dominated by cherry fruit and spicy, peppery characteristics. Consume it over the next 2 years. The excellent 1999 Côtes du Rhône-Villages Rasteau offers a medium-bodied, peppery, black cherry, dusty nose, good spice, flesh, and purity, admirable glycerin, and a soft, plump finish. Drink it over the next 3–4 years. The 1998 Côtes du Rhône exhibits a medium ruby color, as well as a Grenache-based nose of kirsch, abundant glycerin, and a medium-bodied, soft, straightforward, disarming style. Drink it over the next 2–3 years. The 1998 Côtes du Rhône-Villages Sablet (a 70% Grenache/30% Syrah tank-aged blend) reveals a deep ruby color, more density, attractive black cherry and berry fruits, medium to full body, low acidity, and a plump, hedonistic style. It should drink well for 4–5 years. The 1998 Côtes du Rhône-Villages Rasteau (70% Grenache and 30% Mourvèdre) offers more chocolate along with rustic tannin, and a stemmy, tree bark characteristic that undoubtedly comes from the Mourvèdre component. Dense, with good fatness and ripeness, it is a more structured, rustic, earthier style of Côtes du Rhône that should drink well for 5–6 years.

DOMAINE DU TUNNEL (STÉPHANE ROBERT)

2000	Cornas	C	(88–90)
1999	Cornas	C	87
1998	Cornas	C	88
1999	Cornas Cuvée Prestige	D	90
1998	Cornas Cuvée Prestige	D	90

A young producer fashioning an elegantly styled Cornas in a quasi-modern style, Stéphane Robert believes in complete destemming as well as barrel aging. The 2000 Cornas exhibits a big, smoky, cassis, fig, and plum-scented bouquet with toasty oak in the background. This medium- to full-bodied, civilized Cornas is typical of the vintage with its low acidity and ripe fruit. It should drink well for 10–12 years. The elegant, stylish, dense ruby/purple-colored 1999 Cornas offers mineral, blackberry, and leathery fruit notes with underlying subtle wood. Good acidity provides grip and definition. Abundant fruit as well as moderate tannin in the finish suggest 2–3 years of cellaring and consumption over the following 12–14 years. The exceptional 1999 Cornas Cuvée Prestige reveals a subtle influence of new oak along with plenty of Cornas typicity. This effort balances the power and rusticity of Cornas with refinement. Medium- to full-bodied, with notes of blackberries, plums, figs, minerals, and licorice, this rich, textured, dense, muscular 1999 will benefit from 2–3 years of cellaring, and age well for 12–14 years. The 1998 Cornas reveals smoky, ketchup-like, and cassis aromas and flavors with intriguing bacon fat, spicy oak, and minerals in the background. It is soft, rich, and medium-bodied, with excellent intensity and tannin that suggests 2–3 years of cellaring is warranted; it will age well for 12–15 years. The 1998 Cornas Cuvée Prestige displays a saturated ruby/purple color as well as a sumptuous bouquet of jammy black fruits, liquid minerals, and scorched earth. It is moderately tannic, but impressively well endowed and full-bodied. Anticipated maturity: now–2016.

PIERRE USSEGLIO

2000	Châteauneuf-du-Pape	D	(88–91)
1999	Châteauneuf-du-Pape	D	90
1998	Châteauneuf-du-Pape	D	90
1997	Châteauneuf-du-Pape	C	(87–88)
2000	Châteauneuf-du-Pape Cuvée de Mon Aïeul	E	(94–96)
1999	Châteauneuf-du-Pape Cuvée de Mon Aïeul	E	91+
1998	Châteauneuf-du-Pape Cuvée de Mon Aïeul	E	95
1999	Châteauneuf-du-Pape Cuvée du Cinquantenaire	EE	96
2000	Châteauneuf-du-Pape Réserve des Deux Frères	EE	(94–97)

This estate has emerged as a legitimate superstar in Châteauneuf-du-Pape largely because of the efforts of two young brothers, Thierry and Jean-Pierre Usseglio, who have taken charge over the last several years. This is an old family from Piedmont's Barolo region, and, as anyone who has visited Châteauneuf-du-Pape knows, there are plenty of Usseglios, Raymond and Jean-Pierre being the other famous wine producers. Recent changes at this estate include lower yields, riper harvests, and the introduction in 1998 of the Mon Aïeul *cuvée* and in 1999 the Cinquantenaire (to celebrate the estate's 50th anniversary). In 2000, the Cuvée du Cinquantenaire became the Réserve des Deux Frères. These offerings are among the most concentrated of the village, yet are still steeped in the traditions of the region.

The spectacular 2000s may be even better than the great 1998s produced at this estate. The 2000 Châteauneuf-du-Pape (14.5% alcohol) is a blend of 85% Grenache, 10% Mourvèdre, and 5% Syrah aged primarily in *foudre* with a tiny quantity spending time in oak. It offers abundant quantities of black raspberry and cherry fruit along with notes of spice, pepper, and minerals. Full-bodied and sweet, with low acidity and high but ripe, well-integrated tannin, this concentrated 2000 should drink well upon release. Anticipated maturity: now–2018. The spectacular, full-bodied (15.2% alcohol) 2000 Châteauneuf-du-Pape Cuvée de Mon Aïeul (a blend of 95% Grenache and 5% Cinsault from 80-year-old vines cropped at a microscopic 15–20 hectoliters per hectare) is breathtaking. A black/purple color is followed by an extraordinary nose of blueberry/blackberry liqueur intermixed with kirsch, minerals, and flower aromas. Extremely full-bodied, with a 45-second finish, this stunning, full-throttle Châteauneuf-du-Pape should age for 20–25 years. Lastly, the 2000 Châteauneuf-du-Pape Réserve des Deux Frères replaces the onetime offering of the 1999 Cuvée du Cinquantenaire. The blend for this wine will change from vintage to vintage, with the 2000 made up of equal parts Grenache and Syrah. There are approximately 5,000 bottles of this effort, the only one to see significant quantities of new oak (about 40% is aged in barrel and the rest in tank and *foudre*). An enormous Châteauneuf (it achieved 16% alcohol naturally), it is extremely full-bodied and strikingly pure with copious quantities of blackberry and cherry liqueur mixed with spice, and subtle toast. Enormously endowed, with multiple flavor dimensions, this voluptuous, prodigious effort should be at its best between 2006–2030. It possesses even more tannin than its siblings. Subscribers need to wake up to what is going on as this is certainly one of the most exciting estates in Châteauneuf-du-Pape.

The classic, deep ruby/purple-colored 1999 Châteauneuf-du-Pape offers scents of *garrigue* (that Provençal mélange of herbs and earth), pepper, black cherries, and kirsch. With admirable structure, it is an authoritative expression of a Mediterranean-styled red with an unmistakable Provençal character. Rich, layered, and full-bodied, it will provide ideal drinking over the next 14–15 years. The 1999 Châteauneuf-du-Pape Cuvée de Mon Aïeul (10,000 bottles produced) has closed down since bottling. It is a dense purple-colored, concentrated effort made from incredibly low yields of 15–20 hectoliters per hectare from 80-year-old vines. A blend of 95% Grenache and 5% Cinsault, this tannic, backward, blockbuster *vin de garde* should open in 4–5 years and last for two decades. It is an extracted, dense, atypically powerful 1999. The prodigious, saturated, opaque ruby/purple-colored 1999 Châteauneuf-du-Pape Cuvée du Cinquantenaire (200 cases) is a candidate for the wine of the vintage. A 100% Grenache *cuvée* aged in older *demi-muids*, it is exceptionally full-bodied with a fabulous perfume of blackberry liqueur, cassis, minerals, spice, and flowers. The texture is sumptuous and the wine accessible, although readers lucky enough to latch on to a few bottles should cellar it for 2–3 years, and watch the magic unfold over the following two decades. Awesome stuff!

From bottle, the 1998s are stunning. The 1998 Châteauneuf-du-Pape exhibits a roasted herb, concentrated style with notes of scorched earth, licorice, cherry liqueur, and pepper. Full-bodied and intense, it is representative of a traditional Châteauneuf-du-Pape made from primarily Grenache. Anticipated maturity: now–2015. The spectacular, black/purple-colored 1998 Châteauneuf-du-Pape Cuvée de Mon Aïeul (from a vineyard called Grande Serres, and composed of 80% 85-year-old Grenache, 10% Syrah, and 10% Cinsault) is one of the most complete and profound wines of the vintage. The fruit is still subdued following bottling, but notes of smoke, minerals, roasted meats, blackberries, and kirsch are present in both the aromas and flavors. In the mouth, the wine is enormously extracted and exceptionally pure, with multiple flavor dimensions and a voluptuous finish. There is plenty of tannin in this tight 1998, which needs 2–4 years of cellaring. It should last for two decades. It is an impressive debut for this *cuvée*.

The 1997 Châteauneuf-du-Pape exhibits admirable depth for the vintage, as well as the year's easy to drink personality. There are cherries galore in this spicy, peppery, fragrant, expansively flavored, medium- to full-bodied wine. While it is an ideal Châteauneuf for beginners, it will satisfy even die-hard fans of the appellation. Enjoy it over the next 3–4 years.

RAYMOND USSEGLIO

2000	Châteauneuf-du-Pape Cuvée Girard Non Filtré	EE	(90–92)
1999	Châteauneuf-du-Pape Cuvée Girard Non Filtré	EE	90
1998	Châteauneuf-du-Pape Cuvée Girard Non Filtré	EE	92
2000	Châteauneuf-du-Pape Cuvée Impériale	EE	(91–93)
1999	Châteauneuf-du-Pape Cuvée Impériale	E	92

Note: Usseglio's Châteauneuf-du-Pape Cuvée Girard is a 400-case lot selected by importer Peter Weygandt and bottled unfiltered. It is distinguished by the fact that it has the words "Cuvée Girard" in the upper part of the label.

Raymond Usseglio has followed his highly regarded 1998s with strong performances in both 2000 and 1999. This producer is at the top of his game, and consumers should be pursuing his splendid wines. A winner, the dense ruby/purple-colored 2000 Châteauneuf-du-Pape Cuvée Girard Non Filtré is made in a hedonistic, exotic, full-bodied style with notes of jammy blackberries and cherries intermixed with kirsch, spice box, and licorice. In the mouth, it is layered, succulent, and ripe; consume during its first 12–15 years of life. Like its 1999 sibling, it is a blend of 70% Grenache, 20% Syrah, and 10% Mourvèdre. The 2000 Châteauneuf-du-Pape Cuvée Impériale is stuffed with glycerin, concentrated fruit, and abundant notions of spice, earth, pepper, and smoke. Full-bodied, thick, unctuously textured, and rich, it possesses enough tannin to warrant 2–3 years of cellaring, but it is already hard to resist. Enjoy it over the next 15–20 years. The 1999 Châteauneuf-du-Pape Cuvée Girard Non Filtré is one of the vintage's finest examples. Its dense ruby/purple color is accompanied by classic aromas of pepper, earth, herbs, meat, and black cherry/berry fruit. Creamy texture, full body, and outstanding purity as well as depth are found in this generous effort. Drink this seamless, mouthcoating 1999 over the next 12–14 years. The top *cuvée* of old vines, the 1999 Châteauneuf-du-Pape Cuvée Impériale reveals a similar color, along with more complexity in the nose (seaweed, balsam, ripe black cherries, and earth). Expansive and fuller-bodied, with more noticeable tannin in the fabulous finish, this sumptuous, powerful 1999 is impressive, particularly in view of the vintage. Anticipated maturity: now–2018.

This *cuvée* of 1998 Châteauneuf-du-Pape Cuvée Girard Non Filtré (70% Grenache, 20% Syrah, and 10% Mourvèdre) exhibits a dense ruby/purple color in addition to a terrific bouquet of black fruits, earth, pepper, licorice, and kirsch. Full-bodied, structured, and tannic, this dense, multilayered wine, produced from extremely small yields of 28 hectoliters per hectare, achieved 14.2% natural alcohol. As indicated, it was bottled without filtration, and also without fining. It requires 2–3 years of cellaring, and should last for two decades.

CHÂTEAU VALCOMBE

1999 Côtes du Ventoux Les Cerisaies	C	88
1999 Côtes du Ventoux Les Genevrières	C	87
1999 Côtes du Ventoux La Sereine	C	90

Château Valcombe is a serious estate in an area I predict will be producing more and more wines of significant quality. The 1999 Côtes du Ventoux Les Cerisaies is a supple, exuberantly fruity, cleanly made effort with abundant black cherry and currant flavors presented in an uncomplicated, medium- to full-bodied, fleshy style. Enjoy it over the next 3–4 years. Similarly styled, with more wild berry notes as well as a briery character, is the dark ruby/purple-colored 1999 Côtes du Ventoux Les Genevrières. As do its siblings, it reveals excellent purity, medium body, and a velvety texture. It should drink well for 5–6 years. The top-flight 1999 Côtes du Ventoux La Sereine is a large-scaled effort (15% alcohol as opposed to 14% for the other two *cuvées*) with an opaque purple color as well as a terrific nose of espresso-infused blackberry and cassis fruit, a layered, voluptuous texture, impressive concentration, sweet tannin, and a long (20–25 seconds) finish. It will benefit from another 1–2 years of cellaring, and it should age for a decade. No known American importer.

CHÂTEAU VAUDIEU

2000 Châteauneuf-du-Pape	C	(86–87)
1998 Châteauneuf-du-Pape	C	87
1998 Châteauneuf-du-Pape Préférence Syrah	D	90
2000 Châteauneuf-du-Pape Le Velours	D	(87–89)

This large estate, southeast of Rayas, produces nearly 23,000 cases of red wine from a blend of 80% Grenache, 10% Syrah, 5% Mourvèdre, and 5% Cinsault. There is an unwarranted tendency to criticize Château Vaudieu because it is owned by the omnipresent Meffre family, who has major holdings throughout the Rhône Valley. Although made in a modern, risk-free style, the wine is richly fruity, medium- to full-bodied, and certainly good. It will never be outstanding, but the wine is consistent and predictable. Château Vaudieu did not present their 1999s, but their 1998s include an impressive 100% Syrah *cuvée* called Préférence. In 2000, there is a 100% Grenache *cuvée* called Le Velours.

The 2000 Châteauneuf-du-Pape Le Velours is a sexy, opulent, flashy effort. Currently it does not reveal much complexity, but it does possess a boatload of glycerin, sweet strawberry and cherry liqueur–like flavors, medium to full body, and a soft texture. Drink this sexy fruit bomb over the next decade. The 2000 Châteauneuf-du-Pape is an open-knit, luscious, mainstream offering with delicious black cherry fruit mixed with lavender, pepper, and *garrigue*. Medium- to full-bodied and supple, it will require consumption over the next 5–8 years.

The dark ruby-colored 1998 Châteauneuf-du-Pape offers a big, seductive, open-knit nose of Provençal herbs, blackberries, and cherries. Velvety textured, round, and loaded with fruit, it should drink well for a decade. The top *cuvée*, the 1998 Châteauneuf-du-Pape Préférence Syrah reveals a saturated dense ruby/purple color as well as a thick, jammy bouquet of blackberries, licorice, and smoke. Already attractive, with abundant glycerin, full body, and a low-acid, corpulent finish, it should develop even more nuances with bottle age. Anticipated maturity: now–2014.

GEORGES VERNAY

1999 Condrieu Les Chaillées de l'Enfer	E	88
1998 Condrieu Les Chaillées de l'Enfer	E	90
1999 Condrieu Coteaux du Vernon	EE	98
1998 Condrieu Coteaux du Vernon	EE	94
2000 Condrieu Les Terrasses de l'Empire	E	90
1999 Condrieu Les Terrasses de l'Empire	E	89
1999 Côte Rôtie	D	87
1998 Côte Rôtie Maison Rouge	E	86+
2000 VDP Viognier Grand *Terroir*	A	85

The lovely Christine Vernay is in charge of the estate made famous by her father, Georges. There are now four *cuvées* of Viognier produced, three of which are Condrieu.

Readers seeking a decent bargain should check out the 2000 VDP Viognier Grand *Terroir*. Made from 100% Viognier, it offers a pretty style, medium body, and sweet fruit on the attack in addition to a narrow finish. The outstanding 2000 Condrieu Les Terrasses de l'Empire offers up aromas of flowers, minerals, honeysuckle, peaches, and tropical fruit. It is a dry, medium- to full-bodied, impressive effort.

The Condrieu Les Chaillées de l'Enfer can be brilliant (i.e., 1998), but the 1999 is acidic, emaciated, and malnourished. While it has excellent perfume as well as good length, it lacks texture and a mid-palate. That is not a problem with the 1999 Condrieu Coteaux du Vernon, a candidate for one of the top wines of the vintage. Sadly, there are only 320 cases of this wine, which consistently exhibits grand cru Burgundy-like richness, a fabulous texture, an intense liquid minerality, and classic Condrieu aromas and flavors of peaches, apricots, honeysuckle, and flowers. Drink this enormously endowed 1999 over the next 2–3 years. The basic *cuvée* of Condrieu, the 1999 Condrieu Les Terrasses de l'Empire is a bit lighter than the superb 1998, revealing a floral, mineral-infused nose, with exotic tropical fruits in the background. Rich, medium- to full-bodied, dry, and pure, it should drink well for 1–2 years. The top *cuvées* of Condrieu are Les Chaillées de l'Enfer and Coteaux du Vernon.

The 1998 Condrieu Les Chaillées de l'Enfer is a honeyed, orange marmalade/apricot jam–scented effort with full body, outstanding ripeness, and plenty of depth and richness. Dry, intense, and symmetrical, it is best drunk over the next 1–2 years. The flagship Condrieu of the Vernay estate is their four-acre parcel of Coteaux du Vernon. This wine comes from 40-year-old vines and is aged for 15–18 months in oak barrels, of which 10% are new. In both 1999 and 1998 this offering is sensational, having achieved 14% alcohol naturally. This *cuvée*, represented by 500 cases, is one of the few Condrieus that is not put through full malolactic fermentation because of the ultra ripeness at which the grapes are picked. According to Christine Vernay, it depends on the vintage, with some vintages being put through 100% malolactic, and others less. The spectacular 1998 Condrieu Coteaux du Vernon exhibits Montrachet-like richness and intensity. However, it does not have Montrachet-like aging ability, as these wines need to be drunk within 3 or so years of the vintage as they lose their aromatic interest after 4 years, although they do not oxidize for 7–8 years.

There are two *cuvées* of Côte Rôtie, the *cuvée* classique and the luxury offering called Maison Rouge. The elegant, herb-tinged 1999 Côte Rôtie exhibits a saturated ruby color and a straightforward, medium-bodied style with black fruits, olives, and herbs. It is a big improvement over previous vintages. The luxury *cuvée* of 1998 Côte Rôtie Maison Rouge displayed hard tannin and a certain greenness. Firm with good grip, it lacked charm and sweetness. It has been difficult for me to muster much enthusiasm for these efforts, but Christine Vernay appears to be upgrading the quality of the red wines with each new vintage.

NOËL VERSET

2000	Cornas	D	(87–88?)
1999	Cornas	D	?
1998	Cornas	D	88
1997	Cornas	D	?

The 2000 Cornas exhibits the essence of black raspberry fruit, but, again, has extremely jagged tannin. There are more mineral notes as well as surprisingly good acidity. A severe finish raises questions about its future performance from bottle, much like the 1999. The 1999 Cornas, which showed good potential from barrel, has an intriguing blueberry/floral/leather-scented nose. But it has a problem. Its chalky, astringent, hard tannin mars an otherwise interesting wine. Tannin in Cornas rarely melts away completely, and this 1999 starts off with excessive tannin. Moreover, once the fruit begins to fade in 5–6 years, the tannin will be even more brutal. The 1998 Cornas possesses more depth as well as attractive ripeness, medium to full body, and aromas and flavors of damp earth, leather, blackberries, and minerals. It should last for 14–15 years. The 1997 Cornas was tasted twice, and I still cannot believe how badly it performed. It was untastable given the bizarre, woody, musty aromas.

J. VIDAL-FLEURY

1998	Châteauneuf-du-Pape	C	87
2000	Condrieu	C	89
1998	Côte Rôtie	D	89
1999	Côte Rôtie La Chatillonne	E	(92–94)
1998	Côte Rôtie La Chatillonne	E	91
1997	Côte Rôtie La Chatillonne	E	92
2000	Côtes du Rhône	A	86
2000	Côtes du Rhône Blanc	A	86
1999	Côtes du Rhône-Villages	A	86
1999	Côtes du Rhône-Villages Cairanne	A	87
1999	Côtes du Ventoux	A	85
2000	Crozes-Hermitage	B	85
2000	Muscat de Beaumes-de-Venise	C	89
1999	St.-Joseph	B	88
1999	Vacqueyras	B	87
1998	Vacqueyras	B	87

Vidal-Fleury tends to release wines into the marketplace much later than other producers. Its current group of offerings are the finest I have tasted recently, and I suspect they will continue to improve given the major investments proprietor Marcel Guigal intends to make.

Produced from nearly 100% Viognier, the 2000 Côtes du Rhône blanc is an elegant, tasty white offering notes of apricots and honeyed peaches. Light- to medium-bodied with excellent purity, it is a 4,000-case *cuvée* to enjoy over the next year. The excellent 2000 Condrieu is a ripe, attractive, tank-fermented offering with a touch of oak aging. It reveals Condrieu's honeysuckle, peach, and apricot-like characteristics. Enjoy it over the next 1–2 years.

The 2000 Crozes-Hermitage is a ready-to-drink, ripe effort displaying juicy currant fruit, a sweet attack, and dry tannin in the finish. Although uninspiring, it is well made. Far better is the 1999 St.-Joseph. An excellent value, it offers a deep ruby/purple color as well as a sweet nose of crunchy cassis fruit intermixed with underbrush, licorice, and dried herbs. Fat, dense, and chewy with low acidity, it will drink well for 5–6 years.

The 1999 Côtes du Ventoux (a blend of 65% Grenache and 35% Syrah) is a dense ruby-colored effort with excellent black fruit and kirschlike aromas. This straightforward, mid-weight, seamless 1999 will provide enjoyable quaffing over the next year. Similar in style but different in character is the 2000 Côtes du Rhône, a blend of 60% Grenache and 40% Syrah. It possesses a medium-bodied, cassis-dominated personality, loads of fruit, low acidity, and an open-knit, accessible, easy to understand personality. Consume it over the next 2 years. The dark ruby-colored, smoky, herb- and cherry-scented 1999 Côtes du Rhône-Villages exhibits classic Provençal characteristics, medium body, and admirable fruit, dried herbs, and spice notes. Consumption over the next 1–2 years is recommended.

The 1999 Vacqueyras (an appellation producing better and better wines) offers a big, spicy, peppery, black fruit, licorice, and damp earth–scented bouquet. Low in acidity, with fine ripeness, an excellent texture, and abundant quantities of smoky, berry fruit, this medium-bodied, delicious Vacqueyras should be enjoyed over the next 2–3 years. More rustic, but still extremely flavorful with excellent purity is the 1999 Côtes du Rhône-Villages Cairanne. Smoky, earth-infused black cherry flavors reveal notions of pepper, spice, and minerals. Consume this plump, medium-bodied Côtes du Rhône over the next 2–3 years.

I was disappointed in the lean, hard, austere 1998 Gigondas, but the 1998 Châteauneuf-du-Pape is a well-made, generous offering with cedar, spice box, balsam wood, pepper, and cherry fruit aromas as well as flavors. It will last for 4–5 years, but it is hardly an inspirational effort for what is a superb vintage for this appellation.

I have generally liked the source for Vidal-Fleury's 1998 Vacqueyras, and again, this is an expansive, herb, spice box–scented effort with good depth and more body with additional concentration than evidenced in the previous wines. It will drink well for 4–5 years.

This estate's Côte Rôties can be very fine. The 1998 Côte Rôtie includes 1–2% Viognier in the blend. While it reveals the vintage's dry tannin and austerity, there is no doubting its bacon fat, honeysuckle, and black currant–scented nose. As the wine sat in the glass, floral, raspberry, and peppery notes emerged. Cellar this 1998 for another year or two and drink it over the following 12–15. As for the 1999 Côte Rôtie La Chatillonne, this is a classic Côte Rôtie revealing notes of violets, black fruits, olives, and spice box. Dense and full-bodied, it has an unctuous texture with splendid length. Like many wines of this vintage, it will drink well young, but age. Anticipated maturity: now–2016. The exquisite 1998 Côte Rôtie La Chatillonne (12% Viognier in the blend) boasts a complex bouquet of honeysuckle, cassis, violets, and cherry liqueur. Medium- to full-bodied and elegant, with wonderful sweetness, considerable finesse, a nicely layered texture, outstanding purity, and ripe, well-integrated tannin, it will drink well over the next 12–13 years. The 1997 Côte Rôtie La Chatillonne is exceptional. Its beautiful deep ruby/purple color is followed by a gorgeous bouquet of melted asphalt, black raspberries, cherries, and cassis, a superb, multilayered texture, medium to full body, soft tannin, and an undeniably seductive personality. It should drink well for 12–15 years.

Lastly, J. Vidal-Fleury is renowned for their outstanding Muscat de Beaumes-de-Venise. The 2000 is the vintage of choice given its powerful flavors of orange marmalade, honeysuckle, and candied tropical fruit. Full-bodied, moderately sweet, and exceptionally pure, it is akin to drinking a liquid fruit cocktail with 14% alcohol. Enjoy it over the next 1–2 years. What surprised me when I visited Vidal-Fleury was that I have always thought (and for the most part still believe) that these wines need to be drunk during their first 2–3 years of life to take advantage of the exuberant fruit and fragile aromatics. However, I was served the 1990

Beaumes-de-Venise, which remains fresh, lively, and aromatic, with little evidence of oxidation. I would still drink them young, but some vintages may prove exceptions.

DOMAINE DE LA VIEILLE JULIENNE

2000 Châteauneuf-du-Pape	D	(92–94)
1999 Châteauneuf-du-Pape	D	90
1998 Châteauneuf-du-Pape	D	88
1997 Châteauneuf-du-Pape	D	82
2000 Châteauneuf-du-Pape Cuvée Réservée	E	(98–100)
1999 Châteauneuf-du-Pape Cuvée Réservée	E	95
1998 Châteauneuf-du-Pape Cuvée Réservée	E	93
2000 Châteauneuf-du-Pape Vieilles Vignes	EE	(96–99)
1998 Châteauneuf-du-Pape Vieilles Vignes	EE	93+

Over the past few years, Jean-Paul Daumen has taken this estate into the stratosphere and has begun to produce serious Châteauneuf-du-Pape from his vineyards, primarily located in the northern sector of Châteauneuf-du-Pape. As he says, all he does is "let the *terroir* speak." Daumen has cut yields, harvests only ripe fruit, and doesn't muck around with the wine in terms of fining and filtering prior to bottling. There are three Châteauneuf-du-Pape *cuvées*, with the Cuvée Réservée representing a selection from 70–100-year-old vines (this wine is made only in top vintages) as well as a Vieilles Vignes *cuvée* (the only recent vintages of the latter have been 2000 and 1998). Readers looking for a good value should seek out the Côtes du Rhône Vieilles Vignes. It is a well-made, fruit-driven, medium-bodied, soft, easy to understand wine with excellent Grenache character (roasted peanuts, kirsch, and *garrigue*).

Remarkably, Jean-Paul Daumen's 2000s are better than his 1998s. The 2000 Châteauneuf-du-Pape (2,000 cases) is a superb, dense purple-colored offering with fabulously ripe black raspberry and cherry fruit (a Rayas-like essence of black fruit character) intermixed with a floral note. Succulent, full-bodied, and seamless, with a sensational mid-palate as well as a 45-second finish, it will drink well young (because of low acidity and incredibly ripe fruit), but last for 15–18 years. The potentially perfect 2000 Châteauneuf-du-Pape Cuvée Réservée is reminiscent of Roger Sabon's 1998 Châteauneuf-du-Pape Le Secret de Sabon, the 1990 Rayas Châteauneuf-du-Pape, and the extraordinary Paul Jaboulet-Ainé 1967 Châteauneuf-du-Pape Les Cédres (which was made from La Nerthe's Cuvée des Cadettes). Vieille Julienne's 2000 Réservée boasts a dense ruby/purple color as well as a phenomenal bouquet of blackberry and blueberry jam combined with pepper, a hint of *garrigue*, and minerals. This massively constituted, full-bodied effort possesses huge amounts of glycerin in addition to a staggeringly concentrated, multilayered attack and mid-palate. The sumptuous finish lasts for nearly a minute. The purity, seamlessness, and overall symmetry are spectacular in this wine, which, in spite of its 15% alcohol, is relatively light on its feet. A riveting Châteauneuf-du-Pape, it is a candidate for wine of the vintage. Anticipated maturity: 2005–2025. The opaque purple-colored 2000 Châteauneuf-du-Pape Vieilles Vignes offers the essence of kirsch intermixed with licorice, smoke, and minerals. It possesses a striking bouquet, but the wine tastes more closed than its sibling, the 2000 Réservée. There is great precision, stunning purity, concentration, and length in this spectacularly constructed Châteauneuf-du-Pape, which should prove to be a future legend. Anticipated maturity: 2006–2025. Credit is due the young, zealous, highly committed wine-maker/proprietor, Jean-Paul Daumen, for creating these masterpieces.

The 1999s are showing even better out of bottle than they did in cask. A stunningly beautiful effort, the 1999 Châteauneuf-du-Pape offers a dense, saturated ruby color as well as a gorgeous nose of cedar, spice box, cherries, kirsch, and pepper. Expansive, full-bodied, lush, and seductive/sexy, this voluptuously textured, long Châteauneuf reveals a seamlessness typical of the vintage's finest efforts. Drink it over the next 10–15 years. One of the undeniable stars of the vintage, the 1999 Châteauneuf-du-Pape Cuvée Réservée is a blockbuster in a year that did not generally produce wines of such power and richness (of course, it includes the declassified Vieilles Vignes *cuvée* in the blend). A deep purple color is followed by aromas of cassis, kirsch, flowers, plums, and blackberries. Full-bodied, multilayered, and fabulously extracted, with low acidity, sweet tannin, and magnificent purity, this is a sumptuous, prodigious Châteauneuf-du-Pape that should drink well for 15–20 years. It is hard to believe that something this special could have been produced in 1999, but there are a half dozen or so at this level.

The softest 1998 *cuvée*, the fruit-driven, elegant, seductive, open-knit 1998 Châteauneuf-du-Pape offers aromas of spicy black cherries, plum liqueur, smoke, and herbs. There is plenty of glycerin, flesh, and body in this concentrated yet supple wine. Drink it over the next decade. The 1998 Châteauneuf-du-Pape Cuvée Réservée (14.5% alcohol) is a deep, full-bodied effort with a terrific multilayered texture, thrilling levels of blackberry and cherry liqueur–flavored fruit, superb length, admirable purity, and huge weight, ripeness, and balance. There is some moderate tannin to shed, so 3–4 years of cellaring is recommended. It should keep for two decades. Even more backward, but also more concentrated is the 1998 Châteauneuf-du-Pape Vieilles Vignes. It also tips the scales at a whopping 14.5% alcohol, but as with its sibling, the alcohol is buried beneath layers of black fruits. Notes of cassis, blackberries, cherries, minerals, earth, and spice are present in abundance. The wine cuts a huge swath across the palate, with mouth-blasting levels of tannin as well as tremendous depth and extract. Anticipated maturity: 2006–2022.

The 1997 Châteauneuf-du-Pape reflects the vintage's character in its soft, open-knit, ripe strawberry/cherry-scented and flavored style. There is good ripeness, medium body, low acidity, and an evolved personality. I would opt for drinking it over the next 2–3 years.

LE VIEUX DONJON

2000 Châteauneuf-du-Pape	D	(90–93)
1999 Châteauneuf-du-Pape	D	91
1998 Châteauneuf-du-Pape	D	93
1997 Châteauneuf-du-Pape	C	86

Traditional wines made with no compromises are produced by the Michel family that owns and farms Le Vieux Donjon (one of my favorite Châteauneuf-du-Pape estates since I first reviewed the wines nearly 20 years ago). The 2000 and 1999 Châteauneuf-du-Papes nearly rival their superb 1998. Like most Châteauneufs, these wines see no new oak and are generally backward upon release, needing (particularly in the most concentrated years) 5–6 years of cellaring. The two component parts of the 2000 Châteauneuf-du-Pape were tasted. The first reveals fabulous concentration, large-scaled, blockbuster power, and notes of pepper, leather, tapenade, and blackberry/cherry fruit. The other *cuvée* was more opulent, but just as full-bodied, emphasizing pure black fruits and less spice/roasted notes. The 2000 will come close to rivaling the 1998 and eclipsing the 1999. Anticipated maturity: 2005–2018.

One of the stars of the vintage, Le Vieux Donjon's 1999 Châteauneuf-du-Pape offers soaring aromas of barbecue spice, licorice, herbs, tar, black cherries, and blackberries. This powerful, rich, full-bodied effort is more up-front and accessible than most vintages, but there is no compromise in the richness and mouth-filling characteristics consistently offered by this estate. Drink this sexy, compelling 1999 between 2004–2020.

The 1998 Châteauneuf-du-Pape is a synthesis in style between the compelling 1990 and exceptional 1989. A dense purple color is followed by a tight but promising nose of ripe blackberries and cherries intermixed with smoke, mineral, licorice, tapenade, and earth scents. On the palate, the wine is enormously endowed and full-bodied, with high tannin levels and low acidity. It cuts a broad swath, is very pure, and a true connoisseur's Châteauneuf-du-Pape in addition to being a *vin de garde*. Anticipated maturity: 2006–2020. The 1997 Châteauneuf-du-Pape offers a big, peppery, iodine, iron, cherry/kirsch-scented nose that jumps from the glass. In the mouth, the wine is medium-bodied, soft, round, and seductive, but it lacks the concentration and intensity of this estate's finest vintages (i.e., 1995, 1990, 1989, and 1988). It should be consumed over the next 4–5 years as it is atypically evolved and forward for Le Vieux Donjon. It is a fine choice for restaurants.

Past Glories: 1995 (91+), 1994 (90), 1990 (96), 1989 (90+), 1988 (90), 1981 (92)

DOMAINE DU VIEUX LAZARET

2000 Châteauneuf-du-Pape	C	(87–88)
1999 Châteauneuf-du-Pape	C	86
1998 Châteauneuf-du-Pape	C	89
2000 Châteauneuf-du-Pape Cuvée Exceptionnelle	D	(90–93)
1999 Châteauneuf-du-Pape Cuvée Exceptionnelle	D	90
1998 Châteauneuf-du-Pape Cuvée Exceptionnelle	D	88

Proprietor Jérôme Quiot has produced his finest wines yet in 2000 and 1999. The 2000 Châteauneuf-du-Pape offers a delicious concoction of black fruits, pepper, and spice. Fleshy, succulent, and jammy with low acidity, this delicious 2000 should drink well for 7–10 years. The tasty, easy to understand and drink 1999 Châteauneuf-du-Pape exhibits a dark ruby color as well as a textbook bouquet of Provençal herbs intermixed with pepper and kirsch. Soft, friendly, round, and generous, it should be consumed over the next 6–7 years.

The dark ruby/purple-colored 1998 Châteauneuf-du-Pape offers a big, heady nose of spice box, tobacco, black fruits, and earth. It provides a hedonistic mouthful of full-bodied, chewy, nicely textured fruit that coats the palate without heaviness or alcoholic hotness. This beautifully pure effort falls just short of being outstanding.

It is good to see Quiot push quality to the maximum with the new luxury offering, the Cuvée Exceptionnelle. Moreover, as indicated by the words *non-filtré* on the label, filtration is no longer being practiced. Even more enjoyable than its 1999 counterpart is the 2000 Châteauneuf-du-Pape Cuvée Exceptionnelle. Its deep ruby/purple color is followed by a spectacular nose of blackberry liqueur, cassis, and kirsch. Full-bodied and fruit-driven, it possesses loads of glycerin, a layered texture, exceptional purity, and a long finish. The dark plum/garnet-colored 1999 Châteauneuf-du-Pape Cuvée Exceptionnelle offers a superb nose of jammy black raspberry and cherry fruit intertwined with scents of new saddle leather, pepper, spice box, and herbs. Fleshy, full-bodied, expansive, and succulent, it should drink well for 10–12 years.

The 1998 Châteauneuf-du-Pape Cuvée Exceptionnelle's dense saturated garnet/plum color is followed by aromas of smoked herbs, soy, pepper, kirsch, and assorted berry fruits. Full-bodied and spicy, with multiple levels that caress the palate with a sweet, glycerin-imbued texture, it is well made, fat, and concentrated. Enjoy it over the next 12–15 years. Anticipated maturity: now–2014.

VIEUX TÉLÉGRAPHE

2000 Châteauneuf-du-Pape	E	(91–93)
1999 Châteauneuf-du-Pape	E	88
1998 Châteauneuf-du-Pape	E	93
1997 Châteauneuf-du-Pape	D	(87–89)

The 2000 Vieux Télégraphe Châteauneuf-du-Pape exhibits a deep ruby/purple color as well as a big, jammy, black fruit–scented nose with notions of pepper, cherry liqueur, and minerals. While fat and unctuously textured with abundant jamminess, high tannin in the finish gives the wine structure and grip. The 2000 may behave like the 1998, shutting down quickly after bottling. Anticipated maturity: 2005–2025. I still think 1998 is the finest

Châteauneuf-du-Pape produced at Vieux Télégraphe since their blockbuster 1978 (drunk most recently in mid-August with extraordinary pleasure . . . 95 on the Parker sensory scale of pleasure). The elegant, restrained 1999 Vieux Télégraphe Châteauneuf-du-Pape may not possess the power, majesty, or aging potential of the 2000 or 1998, but it is a stylish effort. Dark ruby-colored, with a bouquet of sweet black fruit intertwined with mineral, licorice, and resin, it is layered, long, and deep, with bright acidity as well as firm tannin in the finish. Cellar it for several years and drink it over the following 12–15. Sandwiched between the full-throttle 2000 and 1998, Vieux Télégraphe's 1999 will be overlooked.

The powerful, dark ruby/purple-colored 1998 Châteauneuf-du-Pape had totally shut down after bottling. As it sits in the glass telltale notes of seaweed, pepper, cherry liqueur, licorice, and assorted black fruits emerge. It is a full-bodied, muscular 1998 with high extract and tannin, as well as a formidably endowed personality. I thought it would be more accessible based on its performance in cask. It can be drunk now, but ideally it needs 4–5 more years of cellar age. It will evolve and last for two decades. It has all the trappings of a profound Vieux Télégraphe and looks to be this estate's finest wine since their colossal 1978. Anticipated maturity: 2005–2020.

The 1997 Châteauneuf-du-Pape is an evolved, forward, richly fruity wine with medium body and plenty of smoke, pepper, allspice, black cherry, and Provençal herb aromas. It is seductive, round, charming, and sexy, revealing peppery, spicy aromas. Because of its fragility, Daniel Brunier bottled the 1997 early to preserve its attractive level of fruit. It won't make old bones, but will still offer delicious drinking for 3–4 years to come.

Past Glories: 1995 (93), 1994 (92), 1990 (91), 1989 (91), 1988 (90), 1981 (90), 1978 (96)

FRANÇOIS VILLARD

1999	Condrieu Coteaux de Poncins	E	90
1999	Condrieu Le Grand Vallon	E	87
1999	Condrieu Les Terrasses du Palat	E	89
1999	Côte Rôtie La Brocarde	E	90+?
1999	St.-Joseph Les Côtes du Mairlant	D	89
1999	St.-Joseph Reflet	D	88
1997	St.-Joseph Reflet	D	(88–89)

One of the most talented young producers to emerge from the northern Rhône during the decade of the 1990s, François Villard has quickly developed a reputation for very fine Condrieu and increasingly good reds from both St.-Joseph and Côte Rôtie. The three 1999 Condrieus (450 cases of each) exhibit distinctive personalities. The 1999 Condrieu Les Terrasses du Palat offers intense scents of marmalade intermixed with peaches and tangerines. It exhibits rich fruit, medium body, and a hint of wood. Drink it over the next 1–2 years. Crisp and light, with notes of melon, citrus, and minerals, the 1999 Condrieu Le Grand Vallon possesses good ripeness, a fresh, lively, tangy style, and moderate acidity. It should drink well for 1–2 years. The most impressive *cuvée* of this trio is the 1999 Condrieu Coteaux de Poncins. From a vineyard planted in decomposed granite soil, it is a well-built, muscular effort that should age for 3–4 years. Delineated and rich, with a liquid minerality intertwined with honeyed orange, peach, and apricot characteristics, it is a full-bodied, powerful effort.

I was impressed with the 1999 St.-Joseph Les Côtes de Mairlant, a blend of equal parts Marsanne and Roussanne brought up in 30% new French oak. It reveals exotic, honeyed Roussanne characteristics (rose petals, caramel, nuts), some minerality, plenty of glycerin, fine depth, and a rich, chewy finish. It should be consumed during its first 1–3 years of life.

Villard's red wine *cuvées* continue to improve. Recent vintages experienced 80% destemming, a three-week *cuvaison*, two *pigéages* per day, and nearly 20 months in new oak with only one racking. The wines are bottled without filtration. The 1999 St.-Joseph Reflet's dense black/purple color is followed by an internationally styled nose offering copious quantities of new oak, a Bordeaux-like mouth-feel, and notes of vanilla, black currants, and smoke. It is impressive for its ripeness, purity, and overall balance. Anticipated maturity: now–2010.

The opaque purple-colored 1997 St.-Joseph Reflet displays medium to full body, and plenty of toasty new oak nicely complemented by ripe cassis fruit. Although monolithic, this excellent wine offers good purity, richness, and palate appeal.

Villard also demonstrates a steady hand with Côte Rôtie, although I can't say these wines are significantly better than his exquisite St.-Joseph. The dense ruby/purple-colored 1999 Côte Rôtie La Brocarde includes 10% Viognier (all from the Côte Brune) in the blend. With noticeable but sweet tannin, medium body, and an austere finish revealing plenty of new wood, this 1999 is disjointed and awkward, largely because of the wood and high tannin. However, there are impressive levels of extract.

VILLENEUVE

2000	Châteauneuf-du-Pape Cuvée des Bien Aimés	D	(88–89?)
2000	Châteauneuf-du-Pape Vieilles Vignes	D	(90–91)
1999	Châteauneuf-du-Pape Vieilles Vignes	D	89

The 2000 Châteauneuf-du-Pape Cuvée des Bien Aimés possesses a deeper, saturated purple color, but the presence of intense, spicy new oak gives it an international style. Although full-bodied, powerful, and dense, it does not exhibit the Provençal character one expects in a Châteauneuf-du-Pape. Nevertheless, it is well made, and if the wood becomes better integrated (which is possible given the wine's impressive extract), it will merit a score in the upper 80s. Anticipated maturity: now–2016. For the moment, I prefer the 2000 Châteauneuf-du-Pape Vieilles Vignes. There is no noticeable oak in this layered, opulent, full-bodied, multidimensional effort. It reveals superb blackberry and cherry fruit intertwined with earth, pepper, and spice. Rich, opulent, and long, with its tannin well concealed by the wealth of fruit, this 2000 will be at its finest between now–2015. The medium plum/ruby-colored 1999 Châteauneuf-du-Pape Vieilles Vignes exhibits an evolved bouquet of smoked herbs, cherry liqueur, currants, spice box, and pepper. Dense, with sweet fruit, a forward, plush, attractively textured palate, serious stuffing, full body, and a supple finish, it will drink well over the next decade.

LES VINS DE VIENNE

1999	Châteauneuf-du-Pape Les Oteliées	E	87
2000	Condrieu La Chambée	E	88
1999	Condrieu La Chambée	E	90
2000	Cornas Les Barcillants	E	(88–90)
1999	Cornas Les Barcillants	E	86
2000	Côte Rôtie Les Essartailles	E	(86–87)
1999	Côte Rôtie Les Essartailles	E	89
2000	Côtes du Rhône Cranille	C	89
2000	Côtes du Rhône Les Vionniers	C	87
2000	Côtes du Rhône-Villages Cairanne La Perdendaille	C	(89–90)
1999	Côtes du Rhône-Villages Cairanne La Perdendaille	C	89
2000	Gigondas La Pimpignole	D	(87–89)
1999	Gigondas La Pimpignole	D	85
1999	Hermitage Les Chirats	D	88
2000	St.-Joseph l'Arzelle	D	(86–87)
1999	St.-Joseph l'Arzelle	D	85
2000	Sotanum	D	(88–90)
1999	Sotanum	D	89

2000 Taburnum (Viognier)	D	89
2000 Vacqueyras La Sillote	D	(86–88)
1999 Vacqueyras La Sillote	D	87

A trio of young northern Rhône producers, Yves Cuilleron, François Villard, and Pierre Gaillard, have set up this *négociant* firm in the hillsides north of Vienne to produce wines from a newly planted vineyard on the slopes north of Côte Rôtie. They also have a burgeoning *négociant* business where they buy both fruit and finished wine to fashion their various *cuvées* throughout both the northern and southern Rhône. The estate wines are called Sotanum (100% Syrah) and Taburnum (100% Viognier). There are approximately 450 cases of each *négociant* offering, which includes nearly every Rhône appellation. Most of the white wines are made from purchased grapes, particularly those from the northern appellations. The reds are made from purchased wine which are brought up in wood barrels in a warehouse situated north of Vienne. This business is a work in progress, but it is worth keeping an eye on. The estate-bottled wines are impressive, and I expect even better things from the 27 acres of hillside vineyards planted with a full southerly exposition. With respect to the *négociant* wines, they are at least good, with some *cuvées* excellent. However, with the increasingly depressed wine market, they may have better opportunities for buying top-quality grapes or finished wines. It is obvious there is no shortage of talent among this trio of young producers.

The 2000 Côtes du Rhône Les Vionniers blanc is a Viognier-based offering revealing plenty of tropical fruit and apricots along with a fresh, lively, medium-bodied style with good texture. It is meant to be drunk during its first year of life. The 2000 Taburnum (100% Viognier) reveals a liquid minerality in its opulent orange and peach-like fruit. This medium-bodied, pure white should be consumed during its first 1–2 years of life. Nearly as good is the elegant, lighter-styled 2000 Condrieu La Chambée. This wine exhibits fine freshness, medium body, and a forward, peach/apricot-filled personality. Enjoy it over the next year. The outstanding, richer, more complete 1999 Condrieu La Chambée possesses medium to full body as well as more noticeable minerality in addition to its tropical fruit notes.

There are 10,000 bottles of the 2000 Côtes du Rhône Cranille, a blend of equal parts Syrah and Grenache. It exhibits a dense purple color as well as sweet, concentrated, blackberry, kirsch, licorice, and vanilla-scented perfume. Drink this full-bodied, supple-textured 2000 over the next 5–6 years. The hedonistic 2000 Côtes du Rhône-Villages Cairanne La Perdendaille is a blend of 70% Syrah and 30% Mourvèdre, Carignan, and Syrah. It is what the French call *trés gourmand,* meaning fat, tasty, and succulent. The 1999 Côtes du Rhône-Villages Cairanne La Perdendaille is more elegant, measured, and focused. Both are powerful, concentrated, medium- to full-bodied efforts with an abundance of black and red fruits. These are among the finest wines produced by the village's estate bottlers. Both should drink well for 5–7 years.

Notions of blackberries, earth, and creosote, as well as surprisingly civilized tannin, are present in the medium- to full-bodied, concentrated 2000 Cornas Les Barcillants. It should drink well for 10–12 years. The 1999 Cornas Les Barcillants reveals rustic tannin, plenty of muscle, and a coarse finish. Typical of the vintage, the 2000 St.-Joseph l'Arzelle and 2000 Côte Rôtie Les Essartailles are pleasant, ripe, and richly fruity on the attack, but essentially superficial. Not surprisingly, one of the finest 1999s is the Côte Rôtie Les Essartailles. Its deep ruby/purple color is followed by aromas of sweet, smoky black fruits intermixed with notions of olives and new oak. Medium-bodied and rich, with adequate acidity as well as a long finish, it will drink well for 10–12 years. Although made from five-year-old vines, the 2000 Sotanum exhibits an opaque purple color as well as gorgeously sweet blackberry fruit intermixed with cassis and minerals. Medium-bodied, with low acidity and outstanding purity, it will require consumption during its first decade of life. The brilliantly made 1999 Sotanum boasts a black/purple color in addition to a sumptuously sweet bouquet of blackberry and currant fruit intertwined with asphalt, pepper, licorice, and vanilla. Possessing great fruit, medium to full body, impressive ripeness, and well-integrated wood, acidity, and alcohol, it should drink well for 12–15 years.

The dense ruby/purple-colored 2000 Vacqueyras La Sillote reveals big, tannic, full-bodied, rustic flavors. Patience will be required. Anticipated maturity: now–2010. The very good 1999 Vacqueyras La Sillote exhibits a dark plum/ruby color as well as a certain dryness and austerity in the mouth, but excellent fruit, noticeable new oak, and a plum/cherry/curranty flavor profile. The blackberry, blueberry, and mineral-scented 2000 Gigondas La Pimpignole possesses a sweet, medium-bodied, elegant style with a good finish. The 1999 Gigondas La Pimpignole is a leaner, more austere offering without the sweetness of the 2000. Angular, with notes of minerals and red fruits, it is similar to the majority of Gigondas produced in 1999, an average to above-average quality vintage for that appellation.

The medium-bodied, austere 1999 St.-Joseph l'Arzelle is good, but uninspiring. Anticipated maturity: now–2010. Also good, the elegant 1999 Hermitage Les Chirats offers sweet cassis fruit, earth, pepper, and spice characteristics, medium to full body, and moderate tannin. Anticipated maturity: 2004–2012.

Lastly, the dark ruby/purple-colored 1999 Châteauneuf-du-Pape Les Oteliées is made in an international style, revealing sweet new oak in the nose, medium body, and ripe fruit. However, it is somewhat soulless compared to the top Châteauneuf-du-Pape offerings.

ALAIN VOGE

1998 Cornas Vieilles Fontaines	D	92
1999 Cornas Vieilles Vignes	D	(90–91)

The 1999 Cornas Vieilles Vignes is, along with Clape and some of the modern-styled *cuvées* from Colombo, as well as the limited *cuvées* from Michel Tardieu and Patrick Lesec, a star of the vintage. It is a black/purple-colored, dense, full-bodied offering with gobs of smoky blackberry fruit and scorched earth notes. It should be drinkable young, yet keep for 15+ years. Even better is the flamboyant, complex, velvety textured 1998 Cornas Vieilles Fontaines. It is the finest Fontaines produced since the glorious 1991. Potentially the wine of the vintage, this dark ruby/purple-colored Cornas boasts knockout aromas of smoke, black fruits, earth, and minerals. Sweet, voluptuously textured, heady, and sexy, this is a decadently rich, lavishly concentrated Cornas to drink now and over the next 14–15 years.

BERGERAC AND
THE SOUTHWEST

The Basics

TYPES OF WINE

This remote corner of France, though close to Bordeaux, remains an unexplored territory when it comes to wine. Some appellations have recognizable names such as Madiran, Bergerac, Cahors, and Monbazillac, but how many consumers can name one producer, good or bad, from the Côtes du Frontonnais, Gaillac, Pacherenc du Vic Bilh, Côtes de Duras, or Pécharmant? The best wines are serious, broodingly deep red wines from Madiran, Pécharmant, and Cahors; lighter, effusively fruity reds from Bergerac and the Côtes du Frontonnais; and some fine sweet white wines from Monbazillac and Jurançon. Remarkable dry white wine values are plentiful in the Côtes de Gascogne.

GRAPE VARIETIES

In addition to the well-known varieties such as Cabernet Sauvignon, Merlot, and Syrah, this vast area is home to a number of grape varieties that are little known and mysterious to the average consumer. In Madiran, there is the Tannat; in the Côtes du Frontonnais, the Mauzac and Negrette. For the white wines of Pacherenc du Vic Bilh and Jurançon, rare varieties such as the Gros Manseng, Petit Manseng, Courbu, and Arrufiac are planted.

FLAVORS

The red wines of Bergerac are light and fruity; those of Madiran and Cahors are dense, dark, rich, and often quite tannic. The red wines from the Côtes de Buzet, Côtes de Duras, and Côtes du Frontonnais, often vinified by carbonic maceration, are light, soft, and fruity. The best dry white wines are crisp, light, and zesty. Some surprisingly rich, sweet wines that resemble fine Sauternes can emerge from Monbazillac and Jurançon.

AGING POTENTIAL

Except for the top red wines of Madiran, Pécharmant, and Cahors, all of the wines from France's southwest corner must be drunk within 5 years.

Bergerac: 2–5 years   Jurançon: 3–8 years
Cahors: 4–12 years   Madiran: 6–15 years
Côtes de Buzet: 1–5 years   Monbazillac: 3–8 years
Côtes de Duras: 1–4 years   Pécharmant: 3–10 years
Gaillac: 1–4 years

OVERALL QUALITY LEVEL

The overall quality level is extremely irregular. Improvements have been made, but most wines are sold for very low prices, so many producers have little incentive (or resources) to increase quality. For the top estates listed below, the quality is good to excellent.

FRANCE'S GREATEST WHITE WINE VALUE?

Just about every shrewd importer has been making a trek to the area of Armagnac in search of crisp, fruity, deliciously light, dry white wines from the Côtes de Gascogne, a region not entitled to either appellation or VDQS status. Grapes such as Ugni Blanc, Colombard, Gros Manseng, and Sauvignon produce dry wines with crisp acidity, fragrant, lemony, fruity bouquets, zesty, lively flavors, and light- to medium-bodied, crisp finishes. Almost all sell for under $6 a bottle. They have proven exceptionally successful in the American marketplace. These are wines to buy by the case and drink within 12 months of the vintage. For example, the 2001s (released in spring 2002) should be consumed by spring 2003. If you are not already gulping these light, fruity wines, you are missing one of the most unlikely success stories in the wine world. The most palate- and purse-pleasing dry white wines are those from Domaine de Pouy, Domaine de Pomès, Domaine de Tariquet, Domaine de Rieux, Domaine de Tuilerie, Domaine Varet, Domaine Lasalle, Domaine de Joy, Domaine de Puits, and Domaine de Puts.

FRANCE'S LEAST-KNOWN AND RAREST SWEET WINE?

Adventurous readers looking for a fascinating sweet wine that is an insider's secret should check out the remarkable offerings of Domaine Cauhaupé, Domaine Guirouilh, Clos Uroulat, and Cru Lamouroux. These sweet white wines age for 15–20 years in top vintages, with flavors not dissimilar to a top Barsac/Sauternes, only with a more roasted nut character. Prices are moderate for wines of such quality.

MOST IMPORTANT INFORMATION TO KNOW
Learn the top two or three estates for each of the better-known appellations and their styles of wine.

BUYING STRATEGY
The finest recent vintages have been 1995, 1996, 1998, and 2000 in Madiran, and 1998 and 2000 in Cahors and the Jurançon. Most of these wines remain undervalued.

RATING BERGERAC AND THE SOUTHWEST'S BEST PRODUCERS

Where a producer has been assigned a range of stars (***/****), the lower rating has been used for placement in this hierarchy.

Dry Red Wines
* * * * * (OUTSTANDING)

Château de Cedre Le Cedre (Cahors)
Château Montus Cuvée Prestige (Madiran)

Moulin des Dames (Bergerac)
Pigonnier (Lagrezette) (Cahors)

* * * * (EXCELLENT)

Château d'Aydie-Laplace (Madiran)
Domaine de Barréjat (Madiran)
Domaine Bibian (Madiran)
Domaine Bouscassé (Madiran)
Château de Cedre Le Prestige (Cahors)
Clos de Gamot (Cahors)

Clos de Triguedina Prince Phobus (Cahors)
Château de Lagrezette (Cahors)
Château Montus (Madiran)
Domaine Pichard (Madiran)
Domaine Pichard Cuvée Vigneau (Madiran)
Tour des Gendres (Bergerac)

* * * (GOOD)

Domaine de l'Antenet (Cahors)
Château de Belingard (Bergerac)
Château Calabre (Bergerac)
Château de Cayrou (Cahors)
Château de Chambert (Cahors)
Château Champerel (Pécharmant)
Clos La Coutale (Cahors)
Clos de Triguedina (Cahors)
Château Court-les-Mûts (Bergerac)
Domaine Jean Cros (Gaillac)
Domaine de Durand (Côtes de Duras)
Domaine du Haut-Pécharmant
  (Pécharmant)
Domaine de Haute-Serre (Cahors)
Château de la Jaubertie (Bergerac)

Château Michel de Montague (Bergerac)
Château de Padère (Buzet)
Château de Panisseau (Bergerac)
Château Le Payssel (Cahors)
Château Pech de Jammes (Cahors)
Château du Perron (Madiran)
Château de Peyros (Cahors)
Château Pineraie (Cahors)
Château Poulvère (Bergerac)
Château St.-Didier Parnac (Cahors)
Domaine des Savarines (Cahors)***/****
Château Thénac (Cahors)
Domaine Theulet et Marsalet (Bergerac)
Château de Tiregand (Pécharmant)

** *(AVERAGE)*

Domaine de Boliva (Cahors)
Château La Borderie (Bergerac)
Château Le Caillou (Bergerac)
Domaine Constant (Bergerac)**/***
Les Côtes d'Oit (Cahors)

Duron (Cahors)
Château Le Fagé (Bergerac)
Domaine de Paillas (Cahors)
Château Peyrat (Cahors)
Domaine de Quattre (Cahors)

Dry White Wines
*** * *(EXCELLENT)*

Château de Bachen (Tursan)
Château Calabre (Bergerac)
Château Court-les-Mûts (Bergerac)
Château Grinou (Bergerac)
Domaine de la Jaubertie (Bergerac)

Moulin des Dames (Bergerac)
Château de Panisseau (Bergerac)
Château Tiregard-Les Galinux (Bergerac)
Tour des Gendres Cuvée des Doges
   (Bergerac)

*** *(GOOD)*

Château Belingard (Bergerac)
Château Haut-Peygonthier (Bergerac)
Domaine de Joy (Côtes de Gascogne)
Domaine Lasalle (Côtes de Gascogne)
Domaine de Pomès (Côtes de Gascogne)
Domaine de Pouy (Côtes de Gascogne)

Domaine de Puits (Côtes de Gascogne)
Domaine de Rieux (Côtes de Gascogne)
Domaine de St.-Lannes (Côtes de Gascogne)
Domaine Tariquet (Côtes de Gascogne)
Domaine de Tuilerie (Côtes de Gascogne)
Domaine Varet (Côtes de Gascogne)

Sweet White Wines
*** * * *(OUTSTANDING)*

Domaine Cauhaupe Cuvée
   Quintessence (Jurançon)
Grande Maison Cuvée Madame
   (Monbazillac)

Tirecul La Gravière Cuvée Madame
   (Monbazillac)

*** * *(EXCELLENT)*

Domaine Cauhaupe (Jurançon)
Clos Uroulat (Jurançon)
Cru Lamouroux (Jurançon)
Grande Maison Cuvée Monsieur
   (Monbazillac)

Domaine Guirouilh Cuvée Petit Cuyalaa
   (Jurançon)
Tirecul La Gravière (Monbazillac)

*** *(GOOD)*

Domaine Bellegarde Sélection de Petit
   Marseng (Jurançon)
Château Le Fage (Monbazillac)

Château du Treuil-de-Nailhac
   (Monbazillac)

** *(AVERAGE)*

Domaine Bru-Baché (Jurançon)
Henri Burgue (Jurançon)

Clos Lapeyre (Jurançon)
Château Rousse (Jurançon)

2. ITALY

PIEDMONT

The Basics

TYPES OF WINE

The glories of Piedmont (aside from the scenery and white truffles) are the robust, rich, multidimensional red wines made from the Nebbiolo grape. The top wines made from the Nebbiolo—Barbaresco and Barolo and, to a much lesser extent, Gattinara and Spanna—are at their best between 6 and 15 years of age but can last up to 25 years. At the opposite extreme are the wines called Dolcetto, which are wonderfully supple, rich, and fruity but are meant to be drunk within their first 4–5 years of life. Then there is Barbera. It has historically been too acidic for non-Italian palates, but a new generation of wine-makers has begun to turn out delicious examples that are splendidly ripe, opulent, and frequently barrel-fermented and expensive. Lastly, there are Cabernet Sauvignon and a host of insipid, usually inferior red wines that are less likely to be seen in the international marketplace. I am referring to Freisa, Grignolino, and Brachetto. Piedmont's white wine production is growing, and while most of the wines remain over-priced and bland, some potential is evident with the indigenous Arneis grape and Cortese di Gavi. Chardonnay is making its ubiquitous presence felt; Erbaluce di Caluso is underrated; and Moscato, the low-alcohol, fizzy, slightly sweet wine, is perhaps Piedmont's finest value in white wine. Lastly, there is the ocean of sweet, industrially produced Asti Spumante.

GRAPE VARIETIES

Nebbiolo, Barbera, and Dolcetto are the top red wine grapes in Piedmont, producing the finest wines. For the white wines, the Muscat, Arneis, Cortese di Gavi, and Erbaluce di Caluso are the most successful. Of course, there are many other grapes, but the wines made from these varietals are generally of little interest.

Flavors

RED WINES

Barolo   Barolo is one of the world's most stern, tannic, austere, yet full-flavored wines; the aromas of road tar, leather, cherries, tobacco, and dried herbs dominate. It is a massive yet intensely fragrant wine with 10–30 years of aging potential.

Northern Italy

0 — 100 KILOMETERS
0 — 60 MILES

WINE REGIONS

1 Valle d'Aosta
2 Piedmont
3 Liguria
4 Lombardy
5 Veneto
6 Trentino-Alto Adige
7 Friuli-Venezia Giulia
8 Emilia-Romagna

Aosta · Gattinara · Como · Bergamo · Sondrio · Trento · Bolzano · Udine · Gorizia · Treviso · Trieste
Novara · Vercelli · Milano · Brescia · Verona · Vincenza · Venezia
Torino · Asti · Piacenza · Cremona · Soave
Alessandria · Mantua
Alba · Parma · Reggio nell'Emilia · Modena · Ferrara · Bologna · Ravenna
Cuneo · Savona · Genova · La Spezia · Forlì · SAN MARINO

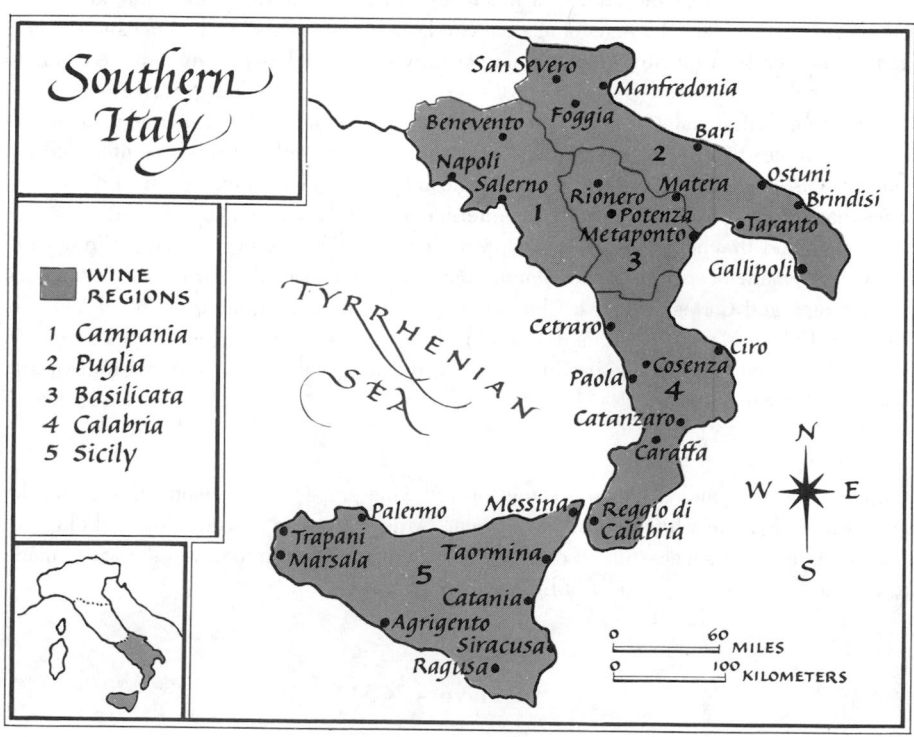

Southern Italy

WINE REGIONS

1 Campania
2 Puglia
3 Basilicata
4 Calabria
5 Sicily

San Severo · Manfredonia · Benevento · Foggia · Bari · Napoli · Salerno · Matera · Ostuni · Brindisi
Rionero · Potenza · Taranto · Metaponto · Gallipoli
TYRRHENIAN SEA
Cetraro · Ciro · Paola · Cosenza · Catanzaro · Caraffa
Palermo · Messina · Reggio di Calabria
Trapani · Marsala · Taormina · Catania · Agrigento · Siracusa · Ragusa

0 — 60 MILES
0 — 100 KILOMETERS

Central Italy

MILES
0 — 60

KILOMETERS
0 — 50 — 100

ADRIATIC SEA

LIGURIAN SEA

•Lucca
•Pisa •Firenze
•Livorno Arrezo•
Siena•
1

•Pesaro
Ancona•
2 •Macerata

3
Perugia•
•Spoleto
Terni•

Ascoli Piceno•

•L'Aquila •Pescara
•Chieti

CORSICA

•Grosseto

Viterbo•

5

•Roma

4

Isernia•
6

TYRRHENIAN SEA

•Latina

Olbia•
•Sassari
•Alghero
Nuoro•
•Bosa 7
Tortoli•
•Oristano

Cagliari•

N
W•E
S

WINE REGIONS

1 Tuscany   5 Lazio
2 Marche   6 Molise
3 Umbria   7 Sardinia
4 Abruzzo   8 San Marino

Barbaresco   Often better balanced as well as lighter than Barolo (less tannin, more fruit), with the same aromas and flavors, Barbaresco frequently has more intense jammy fruit, and sometimes more cedar and chocolate; like Barolo, it can be sublime.

Dolcetto   Purple in color and not at all sweet, as the name incorrectly implies, this dry, exuberant, effusively fruity and grapy wine tastes of blackberries, almonds, chocolate, and spices, and is very soft and supple. It is a joyful wine, which, in top vintages such as 1999 and 2000, is a hedonist's delight.

Barbera   In the old days it was too acidic, harsh, and oxidized—and was dirt cheap. The new-style Barberas, often aged in 100% new French oak, exhibit saturated purple color, great fruit, and superrichness that serve to balance out their naturally high acidity. The best Barberas will set consumers back $25–75, so their potential market is microscopic. But a taste of the finest 1998s, 1999s, and 2000s will make a lasting impression. But be forewarned: for the most part, these wines need to be consumed within 4–8 years of the vintage, regardless of how rich they taste.

Gattinara/Spanna   These wines come from Nebbiolo grown in the hills north of Barolo and Barbaresco. Intense tar and earthy aromas dominate, and there is a pronounced Asian spice box character to the bouquet. Frightfully irregular in quality, with no "superstars" to be found, these wines tend to be softer and fruitier than Barolo but also distressingly mediocre.

Carema   The lightest of the Nebbiolo-based wines, Carema, made in a marginal mountainous climate near Valle d'Aosta, can be quite smooth, fruity, and elegant, but significant ripeness is often a problem.

A CLOSER LOOK AT THE BAROLO AND BARBARESCO REGIONS

The Barolo region consists of more than 3,000 acres of vineyards, most of them situated on the hillsides surrounding five villages—La Morra, Serralunga d'Alba, Monforte d'Alba, Barolo, and Castiglione Falletto.

Barolo   This old village is located south of La Morra. Barolo is said to combine the velvety, supple, easygoing, more feminine side of Nebbiolo with considerable structure and concentration. The word "classic" is frequently used to describe the wines of Barolo by the local cognoscenti. Barolo ranks fourth in importance among the five most significant winemaking communes of Barolo. Barolo has 375 acres of vineyards shared by 139 growers. By analogy to Bordeaux, Barolo might be considered the Margaux or St.-Julien of this viticultural zone.

Highly Regarded Barolo Vineyards: Bricco delle Viole, Brunate (this vineyard is shared with La Morra), Cannubi (often considered the most historic and among the finest of the Barolo vineyards), Cannubi Boschis, Castellero, Cerequio (also shared with La Morra), Coste delle Rose, Sarmassa, and La Villa.

Castiglione Falletto   The smallest of the five principal Barolo communes in terms of acreage and growers, Castiglione Falletto is a picture-postcard-perfect hilltop village situated between Barolo and Serralunga d'Alba. The vineyards are all on steep hillsides ringing the village. Allowing for different styles of wines, Castiglione Falletto's reputation is for wines of boldness, richness, full body, power, and concentration—in brief, it is the Pauillac of Barolo. There are 255 acres of vines owned by 93 growers.

Highly Regarded Castiglione Falletto Vineyards: Bricco Boschis, Fiasc, Monprivato, Montanello, Rocche, and Villero.

Monforte d'Alba   The hilltop town of Monforte d'Alba is the third largest vineyard area in Barolo, consisting of 486 acres farmed by 185 growers. In this most southern of the Barolo zones, all the vineyards are situated on steep hillsides. Monforte d'Alba appears to be the St.-Estèphe of Barolo. The locals claim that Barolo's longest-lived, most concentrated, firmest wines are produced from the hillsides of this small town.

Highly Regarded Monforte d'Alba Vineyards: Bussia (there is a bevy of subvineyards within Bussia, such as Bricco Colonello, Bricotto, Cicala, Dardi, Gran Bussia, and Soprana) and Ginestra (another vineyard noted for its numerous subplots, such as Casa Maté, Ciabot, Le Coste, Mentin, Pernot, Pian della Polvere, Sorì Ginestra, and Vigne del Gris).

La Morra   La Morra, another picture-postcard-pretty hilltop village, is believed to produce the most supple, seductive Barolos. Keeping in mind that individual winemaking styles can easily transcend the historic generalities attributed to a particular area, La Morra's Barolos are believed to be the most velvety-textured and easiest to drink when young. La Morra is to Barolo what the appellation of Pomerol is to Bordeaux. Of the five winemaking zones, La Morra is the largest, with 955 acres under vine and 372 registered producers.

Highly Regarded La Morra Vineyards: Arborina, Brunate, Cerequio, Fossati, Giachini, Marcenasco, Monfalletto, Rocche, Rocchette, La Serra, and Tettimorra.

Serralunga d'Alba   With just under 500 acres, this is the second largest zone in the Barolo area. There is more limestone to be found in Serralunga d'Alba's hillside vineyards than elsewhere. Interestingly, it was in this zone that Angelo Gaja purchased a 70-acre parcel to launch his Barolo estate, and it is in this commune that Bruno Giacosa makes his famed Rionda vineyard Barolo, considered among Barolo's most classic wines. The wines of Serralunga d'Alba are among the richest and fullest-bodied, with great staying power. Continuing the comparison with appellations of Bordeaux, these wines might well be considered a synthesis in style of Pauillac/St.-Estèphe, but of course with a Nebbiolo personality.

Highly Regarded Serralunga d'Alba Vineyards: Arione, Brea, Cerreta, Delizia, Falletto, Francia, Gabutti, Lazzarito, Ornato, Parafada, Rionda, and Sperss.

Barbaresco   There are only three major production zones in the Barbaresco region— Neive (around the village of the same name), Barbaresco (around the picturesque old village), and Treiso (around the town of the same name). All of Barbaresco's vineyards are on hillsides.

Highly Regarded Barbaresco Vineyards: Barbaresco—Asili, Costa Russi, Montefico, Montestefano, Porra, Rabajà, Rio Sordo, Sorì San Lorenzo, and Sorì Tildin; Neive—Albesani, Basarin, and Gallina; Treiso—Marcarini and Pajoré.

SOME THOUGHTS ON THE MODERN VERSUS TRADITIONAL STYLES OF
BAROLO AND BARBARESCO

Today it is fashionable among wine journalists to argue about whether Barbaresco and Barolo are made in the so-called modern style or by "traditionalists" with a healthy respect for the customs of the past. The modernists are said to believe in producing supple wines from riper fruit and aging the wines in small new-oak casks. Since they are produced from riper fruit, the wines tend to be lower in acidity and possess a more creamy-textured personality with sweeter tannin. Many of these wines are stunning and have deservedly won plaudits from wine critics throughout the world. The old- or traditional-style wine-makers of Barolo (Giovanni Conterno, Aldo Conterno, and Bruno Giacosa being the most revered) usually eschew aging in new-oak casks, preferring to age the wines in large, old *foudres.* They make little concession to modern-day taste, which demands up-front, forward wines. These wines can also be profound. The traditionally made Barolos and Barbarescos often taste more tannic. But when they are rich and concentrated (as many are), wines made by the modern style are compelling, since they rely entirely on the intensity of their fruit to express the personality of the vineyard. It is irrefutable that great wines emerge from both schools. In fact, the finest Barolos or Barbarescos, whether made by a modernist or a traditionalist, share more common characteristics than differences. Both schools of thought believe in harvesting physiologically mature fruit. Both schools adhere to the belief that low yields and nonmanipulative winemaking result in wines that best express their *terroirs*. Both schools avoid the excessive use of clarification techniques such as fining and filtration. Barolo and Barbaresco are produced in what must be one of the most pure, unspoiled, virgin countrysides of Europe. All of the finest vineyards are situated on steep hillsides. The locals all possess firmly held opinions as to the quality that emerges from the vineyards throughout these two zones.

WHITE WINES

Arneis   The ancient wine of Piedmont, Arneis is a rich, gloriously fruity, mouth-filling wine that is soft and sexy. This may seem to imply a certain heaviness, but the best examples are light and a joy to drink.

Gavi or Cortese di Gavi   Often outrageously overpriced and frightfully bland, this supposedly prestigious wine is high in acidity, has a lemony, flinty, stony character, and, in the best examples, has good body.

Moscato d'Alba   One of the world's most seductive wines to smell and drink, Moscato d'Alba, when well made and drunk within 12 months of the vintage, is a gorgeously fragrant, apricot- and floral-scented, slightly sweet, crisp, vibrant wine that is ideal as an aperitif. It should not be confused with the cloyingly sweet Asti Spumanti.

AGING POTENTIAL

Barbera: 5–15 years	Gattinara/Spanna: 8–20 years
Barbaresco: 8–25 years	Arneis: 2–3 years
Barolo: 8–25 years	Gavi: 2–4 years
Carema: 6–12 years	Moscato: 12–18 months
Dolcetto: 3–5 years	

OVERALL QUALITY LEVEL

The best Piedmont wines are impeccably made, brilliant wines. Producers such as Bruno Giacosa, Angelo Gaja, Elio Altare, and Luciano Sandrone, to name just a few, fashion wines of great individuality and uncompromising quality. But despite the number of compelling Barolos, Barbarescos, and some *barrique*-aged Barberas, a considerable quantity of wine made in Piedmont is still technically defective, with shrill levels of acidity and a flawed, musty taste. Some of this is the result of inferior grapes still being utilized, but most of it is due to indifferent, as well as careless and primitive, winemaking methods. In short, Piedmont offers both the best and the worst in wine quality. To shop with confidence, you must know who are the finest producers.

MOST IMPORTANT INFORMATION TO KNOW

Learning the top producers of Barbaresco, Barolo, Nebbiolo, Barbera, and Dolcetto is of utmost importance. However, since the early 1980s, more and more of the best producers have begun to make single-vineyard wines, so some understanding of the finest vineyards and who is successfully exploiting them is essential to maximize your purchasing dollars. Below is a list of the major Piedmontese vineyards that consistently stand out in my tastings, and the producers making the finest wine from these vineyards.

PIEDMONT'S BEST RED WINES

VINEYARD	WINE	BEST PRODUCER(S)
Alfiera	Barbera d'Asti	Marchesi Alfieri
Annunziata	Barolo	Lorenzo Accomasso, Silvio Grasso, the late Renato Ratti

VINEYARD	WINE	BEST PRODUCER(S)
Arborina	Barolo, Nebbiolo	Elio Altare
Arionda or Rionda	Barolo	Bruno Giacosa
Asili	Barbaresco	Ceretto, Produttori del Barbaresco, Bruno Giacosa
Baroco	Barbaresco	Roagna
Basarin	Barbaresco	Castello di Neive, Moccagatta
Batasiolo	Barolo	F.lli Dogliani
Bernadotti	Barbaresco	Giuseppe Mascarello & Figlio
Bianca	Barolo	Fontanafredda
Big	Barolo	Podere Rocche dei Manzoni
Bofani	Barolo	Batasiolo
Boscareto	Barolo	F.lli Dogliani, Scarpa, Batasiolo
Briacca	Barolo	Vietti
Bric Balin	Barbaresco	Moccagatta
Bric del Fiasc	Barolo	Paolo Scavino, Azelia
Bric in Pugnane	Barolo	Giuseppe Mascarello & Figlio
Bricco Asili	Barbaresco	Ceretto
Bricco Asili Faset	Barbaresco	Ceretto
Bricco Boschis	Barolo	Cavallotto
Bricco Cicala	Barolo	Aldo Conterno
Bricco Colonello	Barolo	Aldo Conterno
Bricco del Drago Vigna Le Mace	Dolcetto	Cascina Drago
Bricco Faset	Barbaresco	La Spinona
Bricco Fiasco	Barolo	Azelia
Bricco della Figotta	Barbera d'Asti	Giacomo Bologna
Bricco Marun	Barbera d'Alba	Matteo Correggia
Bricco Punta	Barolo	Azelia
Bricco Rocche	Barolo	Ceretto
Bricco dell'Uccellone	Barbera	Giacomo Bologna
Bricco delle Viole	Barolo, Barbera d'Alba	G. D. Vajra
Bricco Visette	Barolo	Altilio Ghisolfi
Briccolina	Barolo	Batasiolo
Brich Ronchi	Barbaresco	Albino Rocca
Brunate	Barolo	Giuseppe Rinaldi, Elvio Cogno, Ceretto, Luigi Coppo & Figli, Roberto Voerzio, Vietti, Mauro Sebaste, Michele Chiarlo, Marcarini, Enzo Boglietti
Bussia	Barolo	Bruno Giacosa, Domenico Clerico, Giacomo Fenocchio, Giuseppe Mascarello & Figlio, Michele Chiarlo, Mauro Sebaste, Prunotto, Armando Parusso
Camp Gros	Barbaresco	Marchesi di Gresy
Campo Quadro	Barbaresco	Punset
Cannubi	Barolo	Luciano Sandrone, Francesco Rinaldi, Bartolo Mascarello, Marchesi di Barolo, Paolo Scavino, Enrico Scavino, E. Pira,

VINEYARD	WINE	BEST PRODUCER(S)
		Carretta, Giacomo Brezza & Figli, Prunotto
Cannubi Boschis	Barolo	Luciano Sandrone, Francesco Rinaldi
Casa Maté	Barolo	Elio Grasso
Cascina Alberta	Barbaresco	Contratto
Cascina Francia	Barolo, Dolcetto, Barbera	Giacomo Conterno
Cascina Nuova	Barolo	Elio Altare
Cascina Palazzo	Barolo	Francesco Rinaldi
Cascina Rocca	Barbaresco	Riccardo Cortese
Castelle	Gattinara	Antoniolo
Cerequio	Barolo	Michele Chiarlo, Marcarini, F.lli Oddero, Roberto Voerzio, Mario Marengo
Ciabot Berton	Barolo	Luigi Oberto
Ciabot Mentin Ginestra	Barolo	Domenico Clerico
Clara	Barbera d'Alba	Eraldo Viberti
Codana	Barolo	Paolo Scavino, Vietti
Cole	Barbaresco	Moccagatta
Collina della Vedova	Barbera d'Asti	Alfiero Boffa
Conca	Barolo	Renato Ratti
Conca Tre Pile	Barbera d'Alba	Aldo Conterno
Costa Russi	Barbaresco	Angelo Gaja
Crichet Pajé	Barbaresco	Roagna
Il Crottino	Barbera d'Asti	Giorgio Carnevale
Cua Longa	Barbera d'Asti	Alfiero Boffa
Darmagi	Cabernet Sauvignon	Angelo Gaja
Delizia	Barolo	Fontanafredda
D'la Roul	Barolo	Podere Rocche dei Manzoni
Il Falé	Barbera d'Asti	Viarengo & Figlio
Falletto	Barolo	Bruno Giacosa
Faset	Barbaresco	F.lli Oddero, Luigi Bianco, Ceretto
Francia	Barolo	Giacomo Conterno
Gaiun	Barbaresco	Marchesi di Gresy
Gallina	Barbaresco	Bruno Giacosa, La Spinetta di Giuseppe Rivetti
La Ghiga	Barbaresco	La Spinona
Giachini	Barolo	Corino
Giada	Barbera d'Alba	Andrea Oberto
Sorì Ginestra	Barolo	Domenico Clerico, Prunotto, F.lli Seghesio, Conterno Fantino
Gramolere	Barolo	Giovanni Manzone
Gran Bussia	Barolo	Aldo Conterno
Gris	Barolo	Conterno Fantino
Larigi	Barbera	Elio Altare
Lazzarito	Barolo	Fontanafredda, Vietti
Marcenasco	Barolo	Renato Ratti
Margaria	Barolo	Michele Chiarlo
Margheria	Barolo	Vigna Rionda di Massolino, Luigi Pira

VINEYARD	WINE	BEST PRODUCER(S)
Maria di Brun	Barbaresco	Ca' Romè
Mariondino	Barolo	Armando Parusso
Martinenga	Barbaresco	Marchesi di Gresy
Masseria	Barbaresco	Vietti
Messoirano	Barbaresco, Barbera, Dolcetto	Castello di Neive
Moccagatta	Barbaresco	Produttori del Barbaresco
Monfalletto	Barolo	Cordero di Montezemolo
Monfortino	Barolo	Giacomo Conterno
Monprivato	Barolo	Giuseppe Mascarello & Figlio, F.lli Brovia
Montanello	Barolo	Montanello
Montefico	Barbaresco	Produttori del Barbaresco
Montestefano	Barbaresco	Produttori del Barbaresco, Prunotto
Montetusa	Barbera	Bertelli
La Mora	Barolo	Corino
Mugiot	Barbera d'Alba	Piazzo
Ornato	Nebbiolo, Barbera, Barolo	Pio Cesare
Osso San Grato	Gattinara	Antoniolo
Otinasso	Barolo	F.lli Brovia
Otin Fiorin Collina Gabutti	Barolo	Giuseppe Cappellano
Ovello	Barbaresco	Produttori del Barbaresco
Pajana	Barolo	Domenico Clerico
Panirole	Barbera d'Alba	Giuseppe Mascarello & Figlio
Pian della Polvere	Barolo	Giacomo Fenocchio
Pian Romualdo	Barbera d'Alba	Prunotto
Pomorosso	Barbera d'Asti	Luigi Coppo & Figli
Pora	Barbaresco	Produttori del Barbaresco
Pozzo	Barbera	Corino
Prapò	Barolo	Ceretto
Rabajà	Barbaresco	Produttori del Barbaresco, Giuseppe Cortese, Bruno Rocca
Rapet	Barolo	Ca' Romè
Ravera	Barolo	G. D. Vajra, Giuseppe Rinaldi
Rio Sordo	Barbaresco	F.lli Brovia, Produttori del Barbaresco
Rionda (same as Arionda)	Barolo	Bruno Giacosa, Michele Chiarlo, Giuseppe Mascarello, Vigna Rionda di Massolino, Luigi Pira
Rocche	Barolo	F.lli Brovia, Corino, Andrea Oberto, Armando Parusso, Aurelio Settimo, Vietti
Rocche di Bussia	Barolo	F.lli Oddero, Armando Parusso
Rocche di Castiglione	Barolo	Vietti
Rocche di Castiglione Falletto	Barolo	Bruno Giacosa, Vietti, Armando Parusso
Rocche di La Morra	Barolo, Barbera	Rocche Costamagna
La Rosa	Barolo	Fontanafredda
Rosignolo	Barbera d'Alba	Cantine Sant'Evasio

VINEYARD	WINE	BEST PRODUCER(S)
San Pietro	Barolo	Fontanafredda
San Rocco	Barolo	Virginia Ferrero, Azelia
Santo Stefano	Barbaresco	Bruno Giacosa, Castello di Neive
La Serra	Barolo	Marcarini, Roberto Voerzio
Serraboella	Barbaresco	F.lli Cigliuti
Sorì Paitin	Barbaresco	Elia Pasquero
Sorì San Lorenzo	Barbaresco	Angelo Gaja
Sorì Tildin	Barbaresco	Angelo Gaja
Sorì Valgrande	Barbaresco	F.lli Grasso Cascina Valgrande
Sperss	Barolo	Angelo Gaja
Terlo Ravera	Barolo	Marziano & Enrico Abbona
La Val dei Preti	Nebbiolo	Matteo Correggia
Vecchie Vigne	Barbera d'Asti	Cantina Sociale di Serra, Vinchio e Vaglio
Vignabajla	Dolcetto d'Alba	Angelo Gaja
Vignarey	Barbera d'Alba	Angelo Gaja
Vignasse	Barbera d'Alba	Roberto Voerzio
Le Vigne	Barolo	Luciano Sandrone
La Villa	Nebbiolo d'Alba, Barbera d'Alba	Elio Altare, F.lli Seghesio
Villero	Barolo	Giuseppe Mascarello & Figlio, Bruno Giacosa, Cordero di Montezemolo
La Volta	Barolo	Bartolomeo di Cabutto
Zonchera	Barolo	Ceretto

PIEDMONT'S BEST WHITE WINES

Americans have always had a fondness for the slightly sweet, sparkling Asti Spumantis of Italy. While "serious" wine enthusiasts have an attitude problem with Asti drinkers, the fact is that there is Asti Spumante in the market, even from such industrial-sized producers as Cinzano, Martini e Rossi, and on a smaller scale, Fontanafredda, that is fresh, clean, and—yes—delicious!

However, the real jewel among these slightly sweet, sparkling wines from northern Italy is not Asti Spumante, but rather Moscato d'Asti. While most Asti Spumantis possess an alcohol level similar to most of the world's dry wines (around 12%), Moscato d'Asti rarely has an alcohol level in excess of 5.5%. Although these sparkling wines are usually bottled with a regular cork rather than a champagne-style cork, they are effervescent, bubbly wines. Their low alcohol content, combined with their extraordinary fragrant, perfumed character, makes them the most underrated delicious aperitif or dessert wines produced in Europe. Most Moscato d'Asti is vintage-dated, and readers should be purchasing nothing older than 2001 in late 2002. These wines are meant to be drunk within 7–8 months of release. They are among the most thrillingly light, exuberant, fresh, perfumed wines in the world. Their lack of aggressive bubbles, in addition to their low alcohol level, accentuates the freshness and liveliness of these wines. They are the perfect summer wine!

The following Moscato d'Asti producers make wines that have consistently stood out for their freshness, elegance, and wonderfully perfumed peach, apricot, and floral bouquets. Most Moscato d'Asti is attractively priced between $12 and $18 a bottle.

MOSCATO D'ASTI'S BEST PRODUCERS

Note: Buy only the freshest vintage.

Giuseppe Barbero Bricco Riella

Gianni Luigi Bera

Giorgio Carnevale

Cascina Fonda

La Caudrina

La Caudrina La Galeisa

Tenuta del Fant Il Falchetto

Marchesi di Gresy La Serra

Sergio Grimaldi

Icardi La Rosa Selvatica

La Morandina

Elio Perrone Clarté

Elio Perrone Sourgal

La Spinetta di Giuseppe Rivetti (various
   cuvées)

Paolo Saracco

Paolo Saracco Moscato d'Autunno

Gianni Voerzio Vigna Sergente

OTHER FINE WHITE WINES FROM PIEDMONT

For what one gets in the bottle, the top white wines of Piedmont are vastly overpriced (Gavi prices have fallen, but this neutral-tasting wine continues to be a rip-off). The exceptions are the aforementioned lovely flower blossom and apricot-scented Moscato and the dry version of Erbaluce. Arneis, a perfumed dry white wine with loads of character, is my favorite white from Piedmont. However, at prices of $18–30, it is expensive. Chardonnay and Sauvignon have arrived in Piedmont; Angelo Gaja produces the finest, but also the most expensive.

The best Piedmont white wines are listed below. Anything older than 1999 should be approached with considerable caution.

WINE	PRODUCER(S)
Arneis	Bruno Giacosa, Ceretto
Brut Spumante	Bruno Giacosa
Chardonnay Gaia & Rey	Angelo Gaja
Chardonnay Giarone	Bertelli
Cortese di Gavi	Pio Cesare, Albino Rocca
Erbaluce di Caluso	Carretta, Boratto, Luigi Ferrando & Figlio
Gavi	La Scolca, La Chiara
Sauvignon	Angelo Gaja
Traminer	Bertelli

BUYING STRATEGY

The marketplace is awash in top vintages of Piedmontese wines. Starting in 1996 and running through 2000, there has been an unprecedented succession of remarkable years for Piedmont. While most of the top 1996s and 1997s have been sold and are squirreled away in the cellars of Italian wine enthusiasts, the 1998s are present in abundant quantities. All things considered, with the relatively strong dollar, there is an embarrassment of riches from Piedmont.

RECENT VINTAGES

2000—This is an exceptional vintage that has produced ripe, concentrated wines with dense colors, sweet fruit, ripe tannin, and sumptuous aromatics—a synthesis in style between the exotic, eccentric, overripe 1997s and the classically styled, fragrant, supple 1998s.

1999—Slightly below the quality (at least for Nebbiolo) of the 2000, 1998, 1997, and 1996, the 1999 is an excellent year, but overall less impressive than the aforementioned vintages. However, it is an undeniably spectacular year for Dolcetto and Barbera.

1998—While the 1998s can appear less concentrated and exotic than the 1997s, less powerful and tannic than the 1996s, and less showy than the 2000s, they are remarkably elegant, symmetrically balanced wines with more depth than the 1995s. They have gained opulence and voluptuousness as they have aged in the cellar as well as bottle. For readers who love Nebbiolo's aromatic fireworks, this vintage may be the most strikingly perfumed year since 1996. With sweet tannin and impeccable balance, this is a classy, highly regarded vintage that can be drunk in its youth, yet has the overall harmony in the finest wines, to be cellared for 15–20 years. In terms of production, 1998 was a slightly more abundant vintage than 1997.

1997—A relatively small crop of overripe, low-acid, high-alcohol, unctuously textured Nebbiolos and Barberas that are off the charts in terms of the hedonistic pleasures they deliver. There is nothing "classic" or "typical" about the vintage, but the wines, while often over the top, are among the most extraordinary Barolos, Barbarescos, and Barberas I have ever tasted. This is the type of vintage that comes along only every 30–40 years. The only comparisons that could be made are with 1947, a year when the alcohol was also extremely high and the acidity very low. Skeptics claim that in the Barolo villages of Barolo and Monforte d'Alba a number of growers harvested too soon, fearing a complete loss of grape acidity. However, this was not borne out in my tastings, although these are low-acid wines. Undoubtedly villages such as La Morra and to a lesser extent Castiglione Falletto hit the bull's-eye. These wines are superexpensive. Contrary to my belief that the Barolos and Barbarescos would be magnificent young, from bottle tastings, these wines have consistently exhibited more definition and firmness than expected. In fact, most of the big wines require 3–5 years of cellaring. Ironically, it is the 1998s that frequently reveal more charm and precociousness than their more exotic siblings.

1996—A great classic vintage made in a style similar to 1978 and 1971, the 1996s are tannic, concentrated, structured, muscular wines that require time in the bottle. It was a cool year with little sunshine, but the saving grace for this fabulous vintage was nearly two months of abnormally dry and warm weather in September and October. The finest wines were made by the producers who waited to harvest until mid-October. All of the big wines require considerable patience—8–10 years.

1995—Called by everybody a very good to excellent vintage, the reality is that it is an irregular vintage with some highlights, as well as a bevy of uninspiring wines. The wines are evolved, forward, and not always well concentrated. Quality varies, so select with care.

OLDER VINTAGES

The early 1990s were a disastrous time for Piedmont, with 1991 and 1992 poor years and 1993 and 1994 average years—despite hype to the contrary. The last great Piedmontese vintages were 1989 and 1990, with 1998 a close third. Prior to that, 1985 and 1982 have turned out to be good rather than exceptional years. 1978 is a fabulous year with very long lived wines that are just reaching their peak of maturity. Before that, the great classics are 1971 and 1964.

RATING PIEDMONT'S BEST PRODUCERS

Where a producer has been assigned a range of stars (***/****), the lower rating has been used for placement in this hierarchy.

* * * * * (OUTSTANDING)

Gianfranco Alessandria Barolo San Giovanni
Elio Altare Barolo Brunate
Elio Altare Barolo Vigneto Arborina
Azelia Barolo Bricco Fiasco
Azelia Barolo San Rocco

Braida Barbera d'Asti Ai Suma
Braida Barbera d'Asti Bricco dell'Uccellone
Cavallotto Barolo Bricco Boschis Vigna
  San Giuseppe
Ceretto Barbaresco Bricco Asili

Ceretto Barolo Bricco Rocche
Domenico Clerico Barolo Ciabot Mentin
  Ginestra
Domenico Clerico Barolo Mosconi
  Percristina Riserva
Domenico Clerico Barolo Pajana
Aldo Conterno Barolo Bussia Soprana
Aldo Conterno Barolo Gran Bussia Riserva
Aldo Conterno Barolo Cicala
Aldo Conterno Barolo Colonnello
Giacomo Conterno Barolo Cascina Francia
  Riserva
Giacomo Conterno Barolo Monfortino
Angelo Gaja Barbaresco
Angelo Gaja Conteisa
Angelo Gaja Costa Russi
Angelo Gaja Sorì San Lorenzo
Angelo Gaja Sorì Tildin
Angelo Gaja Sperss
Bruno Giacosa Barbaresco Asili
Bruno Giacosa Barbaresco Rabajà
Bruno Giacosa Barbaresco Santo Stefano
Bruno Giacosa Barolo Falletto dei
  Serralunga
Bruno Giacosa Barolo Collina Rionda
Bruno Giacosa Barolo Rocche di Falletto
Icardi Barbera d'Alba Surì di Mù
Icardi Barolo Parej
Insieme (seven different proprietary wines
  produced by such top producers as
  Alessandria, Altare, Corino, Grasso,
  Molino, Revello, and Veglio)
Bartolo Mascarello Barolo
Giuseppe Mascarello & Figlio Barolo
  Monprivato

Armando Parusso Barolo Bussia Vigna
  Rocche
E. Pira Barolo Cannubi
Luigi Pira Barolo Marenca
Luigi Pira Barolo Margheria
Luigi Pira Barolo Vigna Rionda
Prunotto Barbaresco Bric Turot
Prunotto Barolo Bussia
F.lli Revello Barolo Vigna Rocche
  dell'Annunziata
La Spinetta di Giuseppe Rivetti Barbaresco
  Valeirano
La Spinetta di Giuseppe Rivetti Barbaresco
  Vigneto Gallina
La Spinetta di Giuseppe Rivetti Barbaresco
  Vigneto Starderi
Albino Rocca Barbaresco Vigneto Brich
  Ronchi
Albino Rocca Barbaresco Vigneto Loreto
Sandrone Barolo Cannubi Boschis
Sandrone Barolo Le Vigne
Paolo Scavino Barolo Bric del Fiasc
Paolo Scavino Barolo Cannubi
Paolo Scavino Barolo Rocche
  dell'Annunziata
F.lli Seghesio Barolo Vigneto La Villa
G. D. Vajra Barolo Bricco delle Viole
Vietti Barolo Brunate
Vietti Barolo Rocche
Roberto Voerzio Barbera d'Alba Vigneto
  Pozzo dell'Annunziata
Roberto Voerzio Barolo Brunate
Roberto Voerzio Barolo Capalot delle
  Brunate Riserva
Roberto Voerzio Barolo Cerequio

* * * * *(EXCELLENT)*

Marziano & Enrico Abbona Barbaresco
Marziano & Enrico Abbona Barbera d'Alba
Marziano & Enrico Abbona Barolo
Giovanni Abrigo Barbera d'Alba
  Marminela
Marchesi Alfieri Barbera d'Asti
Elio Altare Barbera Vigna Larigi
Elio Altare Barolo
Elio Altare Dolcetto d'Alba
Elio Altare Langhe La Villa
Azelia Dolcetto d'Alba Bricco Oriolo
Azelia Dolcetto d'Alba Vigneto Azelia
Batasiolo Barolo Bofani
Enzo Boglietti Barolo Brunate

Enzo Boglietti Barolo Case Nere
Enzo Boglietti Barolo Fossati
Alessandro Brero Barolo Poderi Roset
F.lli Brovia Barolo Ca' Mia
F.lli Brovia Barolo Monprivato
F.lli Brovia Barolo Rocche dei Brovia
F.lli Brovia Barolo Villero
Bussia Soprano Barolo Mosconi
Cantina Sociale di Vinchio e Vaglio Serra
  Barbera d'Asti Superiore Vigne Vecchie
Carretta Barolo Vigneta Cannubi
Cascina Drago Bricco del Drago
Cascina Drago Dolcetto d'Alba
Cascina Drago Nebbiolo

Cascina Luisin Barbera d'Alba Asili
Cascina Luisin Barbera d'Alba Maggiur
Cavallotto Barolo Vignolo
Ceretto Barolo Brunate
Ceretto Barolo Prapò
Ceretto Barolo Zonchera
Sergio Cerutti Barbera d'Alba Ca' du
  Ciuvin
Pio Cesare Barbaresco
Pio Cesare Barolo Ornato
Quinto Chionetti & Figlio Dolcetto di
  Dogliani Briccolero
Quinto Chionetti & Figlio Dolcetto di
  Dogliani San Luigi
F.lli Cigliuti Barbaresco Serraboella
Domenico Clerico Langhe Arte
Domenico Clerico Barolo Bricotto Bussia
Domenico Clerico Dolcetto d'Alba
Elvio Cogno Barbera d'Alba Bricco dei
  Merli
Elvio Cogno Dolcetto d'Alba
Elvio Cogno Langhe Rosso Montegrilli
Aldo Conterno Barbera d'Alba Conca Tre
  Pile
Paolo Conterno Barbera d'Alba Ginestra
Conterno Fantino Barolo Sorì Ginestra
Conterno Fantino Barolo Vigna del Gris
Luigi Coppo & Figli Barbera d'Asti Camp
  du Rouss
Luigi Coppo & Figli Barbera d'Asti
  Pomorosso
Codero di Montezemolo Barolo Bricco
  Gattera
Codero di Montezemolo Barolo Monfalletto
Codero di Montezemolo Barolo Vigna
  Enrico VI
Corino Barbera Vigna Pozzo
Corino Barolo
Corino Barolo Arborina
Corino Barolo Vigna Giachini
Corino Barolo La Morra
Corino Barolo Vigneto Rocche
Corino Dolcetto d'Alba
Matteo Correggia Barbera d'Alba Bricco
  Marun
Matteo Correggia Nebbiolo d'Alba La Val
  dei Preti
Giuseppe Cortese Barbaresco Rabajà
Gianpaolo Destefanis Dolcetto d'Alba
Gianpaolo Destefanis Dolcetto d'Alba
  Vigna Monia Bassa

Luigi Einaudi Barolo
Luigi Einaudi Barolo Cannubi
Luigi Einaudi Barolo Costa Grimaldi
Luigi Einaudi Dolcetto d'Alba Vigna
  Tecc
Luigi Einaudi Dolcetto d'Alba I Filari
Stefano Farina Barbaresco
Stefano Farina Barolo
Giacomo Fenocchio Barolo Bussia
Giacomo Fenocchio Barolo Villero
F.lli Ferrero Barolo Annunziata
Fontanafredda Barolo Coste Rubin
Fontanafredda Barolo La Delizia
Fontanafredda Barolo Vigna Lazzarito
Fontanafredda Barolo Vigna La Rosa
Fontanafredda Barolo di Serralunga
Gianni Gagliardo Barolo Preve
Angelo Gaja Barbaresco
Angelo Gaja Barbera d'Alba Vignarey
Angelo Gaja Cabernet Sauvignon
  Darmagi
Attilio Ghisolfi Barolo Bricco Visette
Bruno Giacosa Barbaresco Gallina
Bruno Giacosa Barolo Villero
Silvio Grasso Barolo Bricco Luciani
Silvio Grasso Barolo Ciabot Manzoni
Marchesi di Gresy Barbaresco Martinenga
Marchesi di Gresy Barbaresco Camp Gros
  Martinenga
Marchesi di Gresy Barbaresco Gaiun
  Martinenga
Marchesi di Gresy Dolcetto Monte
  Aribaldo
Giovanni Manzone Barbera d'Alba
Marcarini Barolo Brunate
Marcarini Barolo La Serra
Mario Marengo Barolo Bricco delle Viole
Mario Marengo Barolo Brunate
Giuseppe Mascarello & Figli Barbera
  d'Alba Panirole
Mauro Molino Barolo Vigna Conca
Mauro Molino Barolo Vigna Gancia
F.lli Mossio Dolcetto d'Alba Bricco
  Caramelli
Andrea Oberto Barbera d'Alba Giada
Andrea Oberto Barolo Vigneto Rocche
Luigi Oberto Barolo Ciabot Berton
Palladino Barolo Serralunga
Palladino Barolo Vigna Broglio
Palladino Barolo Vigna San Bernardo
Armando Parusso Barolo

Armando Parusso Dolcetto d'Alba
Mariondino
Elia Pasquero Barbaresco Sorì Paitin
F.lli Pecchenino Langhe La Castella
F.lli Pecchenino Dolcetto di Dogliani
Bricco Botti
F.lli Pecchenino Dolcetto di Dogliani Sirì
d'Jermu
Luigi Pelissero Barbaresco Vanotu
Vignaioli Elvio Pertinace Barbaresco
Castellizzano
Vignaioli Elvio Pertinace Barbaresco
Marcarini
Vignaioli Elvio Pertinace Barbaresco
Nervo
Luigi Pira Barolo
Produttori del Barbaresco Barbaresco Asili
Produttori del Barbaresco Barbaresco
Moccagatta
Produttori del Barbaresco Barbaresco
Montestefano
Produttori del Barbaresco Barbaresco
Ovello
Produttori del Barbaresco Barbaresco
Rabajà
Prunotto Barbaresco Montestefano
Prunotto Barbera d'Alba Pian Romualdo
Prunotto Barolo Cannubi
Quorum Barbera d'Asti
Renato Ratti Barolo Marcenasco
Renato Ratti Barolo Marcenasco Conca
Renato Ratti Barolo Marcenasco Rocche
F.lli Revello Barolo
F.lli Revello Barolo Vigna Conca
F.lli Revello Barolo Vigna Giachini
Francesco Rinaldi Barolo
Giuseppe Rinaldi Barolo
Giuseppe Rinaldi Barolo Brunate Riserva
La Spinetta di Giuseppe Rivetti Monferrato
Rosso Pin
Roagna Barbaresco
Roagna Barbaresco Baroco
Bruno Rocca Barbaresco Coparossa
Bruno Rocca Barbaresco Rabajà
Rocche Costamagna Barolo Rocche di La
Morra
Rocche Costamagna Barolo Rocche Vigna
Francesco
Podere Rocche dei Manzoni Barolo Riserva
Podere Rocche dei Manzoni Barolo Riserva
Vigna D'la Roul

Podere Rocche dei Manzoni Barolo Riserva
Vigna Big
Luciano Sandrone Dolcetto d'Alba
Giancarlo Scaglione Le Grive
Paolo Scavino Barbera d'Alba Affinato in
Carati
Paolo Scavino Barolo
Mauro Sebaste Barolo Monvigliero
Mauro Sebaste Barolo Prapò
Mauro Sebaste Barolo La Serra
Aurelio Settimo Barolo Rocche
Sottimano Barbaresco Cottà Vigna Brichet
****/*****
Sottimano Barbaresco Currà Vigna
Masué ****/*****
Sottimano Barbaresco Gaia Principe Vigna
del Salto ****/*****
Sottimano Barbaresco Pajoré Vigna
Lunetta ****/*****
Tenuta La Tenaglia Emozioni Vino da
Tavola
Tenuta La Tenaglia Giorgio Tenaglia Vino
da Tavola
Terra da Vino Barbera d'Asti La Luna e I
Falò
Giuseppe Traversa Barbaresco Sorì
Ciabot
Giuseppe Traversa Barbaresco Sorì
Starderi
G. D. Vajra Barbera d'Alba Riserva Bricco
delle Viole
Mauro Veglio Barolo Arborina
Mauro Veglio Barolo Castelletto
Mauro Veglio Barolo Gattera
Mauro Veglio Barolo Rocche
Viarengo & Figlio Barbera d'Asti Il Falé
Superiore
Eraldo Viberti Barbera d'Alba Vigna
Clara
Eraldo Viberti Barolo
Vietti Barbaresco Masseria
Vietti Barolo Castiglione
Vietti Barolo Lazzarito
Vietti Barolo Villero
Gianni Voerzio Barolo La Serra
Roberto Voerzio Barbera d'Alba Vignasse
Roberto Voerzio Barolo La Serra
Roberto Voerzio Dolcetto d'Alba Privino
Roberto Voerzio Vignaserra Vino da
Tavola
Attilio Zunino Barolo Sorì di Baudana

*** *(GOOD)*

Renato Anselma Barolo
Antoniolo Gattinara
Antoniolo Gattinara Osso San Grato
Antoniolo Gattinara San Francesco
Antoniolo Gattinara Vigneto Castelle
Azelia Barolo Bricco Punta ***/****
F.lli Barale Barbaresco Rabajà
F.lli Barale Barolo Castellero
Marchesi di Barolo Barbaresco
Marchesi di Barolo Barolo di Barolo
Marchesi di Barolo Barolo Cannubi
Marchesi di Barolo Barolo Sarmassa
Batasiolo Barbaresco
Batasiolo Barolo
Batasiolo Barolo Cru Boscareto
Batasiolo Barolo Cru Briccolina
Batasiolo Dolcetto d'Alba
Batasiolo Moscato d'Asti
Pietro Berruti Barbaresco La Spinona
Bersano Barbera d'Asti Cascina Cremosina
Bertelli Barbera d'Asti Giarone
Bertelli Barbera d'Asti Montetusa
Bertelli Cabernet Sauvignon I Fossaretti
Boasso Barolo Gabutti
Alfiero Boffa Barbera d'Asti Collina della
   Vedova
Alfiero Boffa Barbera d'Asti Vigna Cua
   Longa
Alfiero Boffa Barbera d'Asti Vigna More
F.lli Serio & Battista Borgogno Barolo
   Cannubi
Giacomo Brezza & Figli Barbera d'Alba
   Cannubi
Giacomo Brezza & Figli Barolo Bricco
   Sarmassa
Giacomo Brezza & Figli Barolo Cannubi
Ca' del Baio Barbaresco Asili
Ca' dei Gancia Barolo Cannubi
Ca' Romè Barbaresco
Ca' Romè Barbaresco Maria di Brun
Ca' Romè Barolo Vigneto Carpegna
Ca' Romè Barolo Rapet
Ca' Romè Barolo Vigna Rionda
Bartolomeo Di Cabutto Barbera d'Alba
   Bricco delle Viole
Bartolomeo Di Cabutto Barolo Vigna La
   Volta
Giuseppe Cappellano Barolo
Giuseppe Cappellano Barolo Otin Fiorin
   Collina Gabutti

Giorgio Carnevale Barbera d'Asti Il
   Crottino
Carretta Barbaresco
Carretta Barbera Bric Quercia
Carretta Nebbiolo d'Alba Bric Paradiso
Carretta Nebbiolo d'Alba Bric Tavoleto
Casa Vinicola Conte Vaselli Santa Giulia
   Rosso
F.lli Casetta Barbaresco Vigna Ausario
F.lli Casetta Barbera d'Alba Vigna
   Lazaretto
Cascina Castlèt Barbera d'Asti
Cascina Castlèt Barbera d'Asti Superiore
Castello di Neive Barbaresco Santo Stefano
Castello di Neive Dolcetto d'Alba Basarin
Castello di Neive Dolcetto d'Alba
   Messoriano
Cavallotto Barolo Bricco Boschis
Ceretto Barbaresco Asij
Ceretto Barbaresco Bricco Asili Faset
Ceretto Barbera d'Alba Piana
Ceretto Dolcetto d'Alba Rossana
Ceretto Nebbiolo d'Alba Lantasco
Pio Cesare Barbera d'Alba
Pio Cesare Barolo
Pio Cesare Dolcetto d'Alba
Michele Chiarlo Barbera d'Asti
Michele Chiarlo Barbera d'Asti Valle del
   Sole
Michele Chiarlo Barilot
Michele Chiarlo Barolo Brunate
Michele Chiarlo Barolo Vigna Rionda
Michele Chiarlo Countacc!
F.lli Cigliuti Barbera d'Alba Serraboella
Aldo Conterno Il Favot
Giacomo Conterno Barbera d'Alba Cascina
   Francia
Conterno-Fantino Barbera d'Alba Vignato
Cordero di Montezemolo Barbera d'Alba
Cordero di Montezemolo Barolo Enrico VI
Cordero di Montezemolo Dolcetto d'Alba
   Monfalletto
Giuseppe Cortese Dolcetto d'Alba
Luigi Dessilani & Figlio Gattinara
Luigi Dessilani & Figlio Ghemme
Luigi Dessilani & Figlio Spanna
Dosio Barolo Vigna Fossati
Cascina Drago Bricco del Drago Vigna Le
   Mace
Poderi Luigi Einaudi Dolcetto di Dogliani

F.lli Ferrero Barolo Manzoni
Fontanafredda Barbera d'Alba Vigna
   Raimondo
Fontanafredda Barolo
Gianni Gagliardo Barolo La Serra
Angelo Gaja Dolcetto d'Alba Vignaveja
Angelo Gaja Nebbiolo d'Alba Vignaveja
Attilio Ghisolfi Barolo Bricco Visette
F.lli Giacosa Barbaresco Rio Sordo
F.lli Giacosa Barolo Pira
F.lli Grasso Barbaresco Bricco Spessa
F.lli Grasso Barbaresco Riserva
Silvio Grasso Barbera d'Alba Fontanile
Icardi Barbera d'Alba Vigna dei Gelsi
Icardi Nebbiolo delle Langhe
Eredi Lodali Barbaresco Rocche dei Sette
   Fratelli
Giovanni Manzone Barolo Le Gramolere
Giovanni Manzone Barolo Le Gramolere
   Bricat
Giovanni Manzone Barolo Santo Stefano di
   Perno
Giovanni Manzone Dolcetto d'Alba
Giovanni Manzone Nebbiolo
Mario Marengo Barbaresco Le Terre Forti
Mario Marengo Barbera Le Terre Forti
Bartolo Mascarello Dolcetto d'Alba
Giuseppe Mascarello & Figlio Barbera
   d'Alba Fasana
Giuseppe Mascarello & Figlio Barolo Dardi
Giuseppe Mascarello & Figlio Dolcetto
   d'Alba Gagliassi
Il Milin di Michelino Rovero Barbera
   d'Asti
Il Milin di Michelino Rovero Barbera
   d'Asti Vigneto Gustin
Luigi Minuto Barbaresco Cascina Luisin
   Rabajà
Luigi Minuto Barbaresco Sorì Paolin
Moccagatta Barbaresco Basarin
Moccagatta Barbaresco Cole
Moccagatta Barbera Basarin
Mauro Molino Barolo
Luigi Oberto Barbera d'Alba Ciabot Berton
Ochetti Barbera d'Asti Superiore
F.lli Oddero Barbaresco
F.lli Oddero Barolo Mondoca di Bussia
   Soprana
F.lli Oddero Barolo Rocche di Rivera di
   Castiglione
F.lli Oddero Barolo Vigna Rionda

Armando Parusso Barbera Pugnane
Agostino Pavia e Figli Barbera d'Asti
   Bricco Blina
Elio Perrone Barbera delle Langhe Vigna
   Grivò
Piazzo Barbaresco Riserva
Piazzo Barbaresco Sorì Fratin
Piazzo Barbera d'Alba Mugiot
Piazzo Barolo Poderi di Mugiot
Produttori del Barbaresco Barbaresco
Produttori del Barbaresco Barbaresco
   Pora
Prunotto Barbaresco
Prunotto Barbera d'Alba
Prunotto Barbera d'Alba Fiulot
Punset Barbaresco Campo Quadro
Bruno Rocca Nebbiolo d'Alba
Rocche Costamagna Barbera d'Alba
   Rocche di La Morra
Rocche Costamagna Rocche della Rocche
Gigi Rosso Barbaresco Viglino
Gigi Rosso Barolo Arione
Scarpa Barbaresco
Scarpa Barbaresco Payore Barberis di
   Treiso
Scarpa Barolo Boscaretti di Serralunga
   d'Alba
Scarpa Barolo I Tetti di Neive
Scarpa Rouchet Vino da Tavola
Enrico Scavino Dolcetto d'Alba
Mauro Sebaste Barolo Le Coste
F.lli Seghesio Barbera
F.lli Seghesio Dolcetto d'Alba
Sigilla dell'Abate Barolo Riserva
Tenuta dei Fiori Barbera d'Asti
Renato Trinchero Barbera d'Asti La
   Barslina
Mauro Veglio Barolo Arborina
Mauro Veglio Barolo Castillero
Mauro Veglio Barolo Gattera
Mauro Veglio Barolo Rocche
Viarengo & Figlio Barbera d'Asti Il Falé
Viarengo & Figlio Barbera d'Asti Bricco
   Morra
Eraldo Viberti Barolo
Vietti Barbera d'Alba Pian Romualdo
Vietti Barbera d'Alba Scarrone
Vigna Rionda di Massolino Barolo
   Parafada
Vigna Rionda di Massolino Barolo Sorì
   Vigna Rionda

Vigna Rionda di Massolino Barolo Sorì   Vigna Rionda di Massolino Barolo Vigna
   Vigneto Margheria   Rionda

GIOVANNI ABRIGO

1999 Barbera d'Alba Marminela	C	89
1998 Barbera d'Alba Marminela	C	88
2000 Dolcetto Diano d'Alba Garabei	C	88
1999 Dolcetto Diano d'Alba Garabei	C	90
2000 Dolcetto Diano d'Alba Söri Crava	C	89
1999 Dolcetto Diano d'Alba Söri Crava	C	88
1998 Nebbiolo d'Alba	C	89

All of Abrigo's unfined/unfiltered red offerings represent attractive values, particularly in today's wine marketplace. They are tank-fermented and -aged, and production is 300–500 cases annually.

The 2000 Dolcetto d'Alba Garabei displays surprising structure for this varietal, as well as abundant notions of chocolate and violet-tinged berry fruit, medium body, and a soft personality. Consume it over the next 2–3 years. An explosively fruity, smoky, ripe, black cherry/chocolate-styled Dolcetto that saw no *barrique* aging, this luscious, opulent 2000 Dolcetto Diano d'Alba Söri Crava offers gobs of fruit as well as a fleshy, pure finish. Drink it over the next 3 years. Two top-notch Dolcettos, the 1999 Dolcetto Diano d'Alba Söri Crava exhibits explosive fruit aromas of black cherries, blackberries, and violets. The flavors are pure cherry and blackberry jam. This excellent effort will drink well for 2–3 years. Even better is the 1999 Dolcetto Diano d'Alba Garabei. This opaque purple-colored Dolcetto boasts intense aromas and flavors of black cherry/blackberry liqueur, chocolate, and flowers. There is enough acidity to provide vibrancy and delineation. Drink this hedonistic fruit bomb over the next 2 years.

The 1999 Barbera emerges from an old-vine vineyard called Marminela. It is tank-fermented and aged in French barrels, of which one-third are new. Ruby/purple in color, it is sweet and fat on the palate, medium-bodied, and fruit-driven, and should be enjoyed before 2003. Readers seeking more complexity and an intensely fragrant style should check out the 1998 Nebbiolo d'Alba. Exhibiting classic characteristics of rose petals, melted road tar, tobacco, and sweet cherry fruit, it could easily pass for a Barolo in a blind tasting. However, the price is about one-third the going rate for most entry-level Barolos. Drink it over the next 5–6 years.

ORLANDO ABRIGO

1997 Barbaresco Vigna Montersino	E	87
1997 Barbaresco Vigna Rongallo	E	88

This producer from the village of Treiso has fashioned a very good, dark ruby-colored 1997 Barbaresco Vigna Montersino. Its aromatic profile consists of new saddle leather, berry fruit, and spice box presented in a medium- to full-bodied, graceful style. With abundant sweetness from its glycerin and alcohol, this 1997 is best drunk over the next 2 years. Deeper and longer, the 1997 Barbaresco Vigna Rongallo exhibits telltale aromas of plums, cherries, prunes, spice box, licorice, and smoke. Medium- to full-bodied and richer than its sibling, it should be consumed over the next 2–3 years.

CLAUDIO ALARIO

1998 Barolo Vigneto Riva	E	89
1997 Barolo Vigneto Riva	E	88

1996 Barolo Vigneto Riva	E	91
1995 Barolo Vigneto Riva	E	87

A new estate from the village of Verduno, Claudio Alario produces small quantities of hedonistic, sumptuous Barolos that are fermented in open-top fermenters and aged in 60–80% new French oak casks.

Alario's 1998 Barolo Vigneta Riva has turned out slightly better than his 1997. It offers a classic concoction of balsam wood, coffee, tar, cherries, and spice box, a sweet entry, medium body, and soft but noticeable tannin in the finish. Drink it over the next 8 years.

Not quite as good from bottle as it was from barrel, the dark ruby-colored, elegant 1997 Barolo Vigneto Riva exhibits restrained, subtle black cherry aromas and flavors mixed with road tar, tobacco, smoke, and earth. It is of an atypical medium weight for a 1997, without the vintage's flamboyant side in evidence. Anticipated maturity: 2003–2015. The saturated ruby/purple 1996 Barolo Vigneto Riva reveals an intense cherry, coffee, cedar, and smoky-scented nose. There are great richness, full body, terrific purity, surprisingly low acidity for a 1996, and a lush, multidimensional personality. While tannin is present in the finish, this is a large-scaled, gorgeously made Barolo that should be at its best before 2015. The 1995 Barolo Vigneto Riva exhibits copious quantities of cedar, smoke, and cherry fruit in its evolved aromatics. With good fat and medium to full body, it is a hedonistic, evolved, lush Barolo to enjoy over the next 2–3 years.

PODERI ALASIA

1999 Barbera d'Asti Rive	C	89
1998 Barbera d'Asti Rive	C	92

The dense, opaque purple-colored 1999 Barbera d'Asti Rive offers a big, sweet nose of black fruits, underbrush, tar, and spice. Medium- to full-bodied, with excellent concentration, admirable purity, and a long finish, this fleshy, mouth-filling Barbera can be enjoyed over the next 2–3 years. The exquisite, opaque ruby/purple-colored 1998 Barbera d'Asti Rive possesses huge body, massive fruit concentration, and copious quantities of toasty new oak. A blockbuster Barbera made in a modern, international style, it offers seductive fruit, glycerin, and new wood. Enjoy it over the next 4–5 years.

GIANFRANCO ALESSANDRIA

1997 Barolo	E	89
1996 Barolo	E	88
1995 Barolo	E	87
1998 Barolo San Giovanni	E	90+
1997 Barolo San Giovanni	E	92+
1996 Barolo San Giovanni	E	90
1995 Barolo San Giovanni	E	88

From Monforte d'Alba, this producer believes in using small open-top fermenters and punching down as opposed to many of his colleagues, who use rotary fermenters. The generic Barolo is aged in *foudres* (large wooden vessels), and the single-vineyard San Giovanni, which emerges from a vineyard facing Bussia, stays in *foudres* and *barriques* (approximately 30% new). These classic Barolos exhibit rose petal, tobacco leaf, and tar-like fragrances with additional nuances. They are generally less seductive and plush, but more powerful and dense, than their counterparts from La Morra.

I did not taste the regular 1998 Barolo. However, I did enjoy the special *cuvée*. Just a notch below the brilliant 1997, Alessandria's 1998 Barolo San Giovanni boasts an opaque ruby/garnet color in addition to an intriguing nose of melted chocolate, cedar and balsam wood, rose petals, and cherry liqueur. The opulent fatness on the attack is followed by plenty of power, structure, and tannin in the long finish. Anticipated maturity: 2005–2020.

The 1997 Barolo is a structured, garnet-colored effort with pink/amber at the edge. Aromas of melted caramel, Chinese black tea, kirsch, tobacco, and licorice emerge from this dense, full-bodied, fleshy, powerful 1997. It is a moderately tannic wine, to be consumed before 2012. The impressively endowed, dark plum-colored 1997 Barolo San Giovanni is a blockbuster. It boasts terrific concentration as well as a sweet bouquet of chocolate, blackberries, cherries, tobacco, asphalt, and smoke. Structured and powerful, with muscle to spare, this massive wine needs 1–2 years of cellaring (despite its low acidity). Anticipated maturity: 2004–2020.

The 1996s are richer and possess more formidable personalities than the 1995s. For example, the 1996 Barolo exhibits Nebbiolo's telltale tobacco, damp earth, black cherry, and melted road tar aromas and flavors. The wine is dense, rich, and full-bodied, with considerable muscle, outstanding purity, and a deep, concentrated, moderately tannic finish. Anticipated maturity: now–2014. The textbook 1996 Barolo San Giovanni offers a classic tar and rose petal–scented bouquet with hints of cherry liqueur, smoke, and dried herbs. This dark ruby-colored wine is full-bodied, dense, and layered, with outstanding concentration and purity. There is moderate tannin plus superb depth and muscle. Anticipated maturity: now–2015.

The traditionally styled 1995 Barolo possesses structure, tannin, and a masculine, austere personality. Although not as fruit-driven as some offerings, it is well made and enjoyable. Drink it over the next 8 years. The dark ruby-colored 1995 Barolo San Giovanni offers a big, sweet nose of soy, seaweed, black cherry liqueur, and pepper. This wine is exotic, medium- to full-bodied, and moderately tannic. It will be at its finest until 2012.

GIOVANNI ALMONDO

1998 Barbera d'Alba Bianchera	C	85?
1998 Roero Bric Valdiana	C	88

The charming 1998 Roero Bric Valdiana reveals a classic Nebbiolo bouquet of floral rose water, sweet cherries, tobacco, and tar. Round and supple with a sweet attack, this delicious 1998 will drink well for 2–3 years. Denser and less charming, but more concentrated as well as structured, with chalky roughness in the finish, is the 1998 Barbera d'Alba Bianchera. There is more size to this 1998 Barbera but less character and sexiness. It, too, should be drunk over the next 2–3 years.

ELIO ALTARE

1996 Barolo	E	89+
1995 Barolo	E	89
1998 Barolo Brunate	E	(92–94)
1996 Barolo Brunate	E	90?
1995 Barolo Brunate	E	90
1998 Barolo Vigneto Arborina	E	(91–93)
1996 Barolo Vigneto Arborina	E	92
1995 Barolo Vigneto Arborina	E	91

Elio Altare, a brilliant La Morra producer, uses rotary fermenters, large oak *foudres* for his regular Barolo, and small *barriques* for his two single-vineyard wines (50% new oak for the Arborina and 75% for the Brunate). Malolactic is done in barrel, and there is no filtration at bottling. These are among the most feminine, gloriously perfumed offerings from Piedmont. They represent beautiful examples of symmetry, complexity, and rich, ripe fruit.

Elio Altare has fashioned two elegant, perfumed, concentrated, immensely satisfying 1998s. The 1998 Barolo Vigneto Arborina boasts a glorious perfume of overripe black cherries intertwined with Asian spices, new oak, and flowers. Layered, gorgeously concentrated, superbly balanced, and seamless, with fabulous fruit, good underlying tannin, and a long, 40+-second finish, it can be drunk now and over the next 15 years. The dark ruby/plum-colored 1998 Barolo Brunate exhibits a smoky, mineral, jammy strawberry, and black cherry–scented nose with notions of leather, toast, and spice box. The wine has fabulously well integrated wood, tannin, and acidity in addition to a complex, layered mid-palate and finish. The outstanding balance, purity, and seamlessness are immensely admirable. Enjoy this 1998 Barolo over the next 12–15 years. The story of Altare's 1997s is worth mentioning. These wines looked spectacular when they were tasted prior to bottling, but they were re-called in a qualitative move that is largely unprecedented in the wine world. In fact, Elio Altare discovered that 40% or more of his 1997s were corked with a batch of tainted corks. Most producers who realize that they have a problem with contaminated corks let the con-sumer assume the risk. But Altare, because of his extraordinary morality and honesty, could not stomach the thought of having his fans have a 40% or better chance of tasting one of his wines tainted to some degree by a moldy cork. Hence, all of his 1997 Barolos were recalled and will not be available in the market. Obviously this is a huge financial loss, but even more so, a spiritual one. Altare deserves admiration by all consumers for making this decision, for being a man of great morality, and for putting the interests of the consumer ahead of his own. Readers should note that the wines that will never be released include all his 1997 Barolos, including the single-vineyard Arborina (rated 93–96), Brunate (92–94), and generic Barolo (90–91), as well as his 1999 Vigneto Arborina and Vigna Langhe Larigi.

The 1996s are superb. The 1996 Barolo exhibits a saturated, evolved dark ruby color. It reveals notes of *sur-maturité* in its ripe, fruity style. Not as sexy and forward as the 1995, the 1996 is less evolved, spicy, rich, and highly extracted. Anticipated maturity: now–2010. Altare's 1996 Barolo Vigneto Arborina is reminiscent of a terrific grand cru from Burgundy's Côte d'Or. Intensely aromatic, with copious quantities of black cherry jam, earth, toast, and floral scents, this saturated dark ruby-colored offering reveals superb ripeness, substantial richness, a full-bodied, layered personality, adequate acidity, and sweet tannin in the finish. It is a stunning Barolo to drink now and over the next 12 years. The 1996 Barolo Brunate is the proverbial "iron fist in a velvet glove." It possesses a dark ruby color, closed personality, powerful, muscular flavors of cherries, incense, smoke, and dried herbs, and a tannic finish. Enjoy it over the following 15–18 years.

Altare has turned out a gorgeous 1995 Barolo with a medium ruby color and a sweet nose of high-quality tobacco intermixed with jammy cherry fruit. It is lush, with spice and oak in the background, a nicely layered, exotic mouth-feel, and no hard edges. This evolved Barolo requires consumption over the next 2 years. The two crus are also stunning efforts. The lush, voluptuously textured 1995 Barolo Vigneto Arborina exhibits one of the most saturated dark ruby/garnet colors of this vintage. Full-bodied, with great purity, the layered complexity that comes from low yields and ripe fruit, and a bouquet of Asian spices, tobacco, smoke, and black cherries, this is a sweet, rich, forward, but hedonistically styled Barolo. Anticipated maturity: now–2008. In contrast, the outstanding 1995 Barolo Brunate is more muscular and backward, although it possesses good density, superb ripeness, and more tannin and body. Consume it over the next 8 years.

ANSELMA

1998 Barolo Adasi	D	87
1997 Barolo Adasi	D	86

An evolved, forward Barolo despite the presence of moderate tannin levels, the medium garnet-colored 1998 Barolo Adasi possesses aromas of fudge, damp earth, cedar, cigar box, and dried red fruits. Although medium-bodied and complex, it lacks the necessary substance as well as length to be considered superb. Anticipated maturity: 2003–2013.

The traditionally made, dark ruby/garnet-colored 1997 Barolo Adasi exhibits notes of soy, dried herbs, earth, and leather. Good density on the attack is followed by abundant tannin, giving the wine a compressed, astringent finish. Drink it over the next 10 years.

GIACOMO ASCHERI

1997 Barolo Sorano	D	(76–78?)
1996 Barolo Sorano	D	87+
1995 Barolo Sorano	D	88

This small producer has turned out a 1995 and 1996 that are much more impressive than the herbaceous, slightly diluted, unusual 1997.

The 1997 Barolo Sorano is unimpressive, with hard, dry tannin, an element of dilution, and a vegetal character to the meager fruitiness. It did reveal such classic Nebbiolo characteristics as melted tar and a floral component, but it was compressed and lean.

The tannic, well-structured, muscular 1996 Barolo Sorano offers an intriguing nose as well as flavors of melted asphalt, tomato skin, and jammy strawberry and cherry fruit. It exhibits some tannin, more muscle than the 1995, an understated, restrained style, and a longer finish than its older sibling. Drink it over the next 8–10 years.

Less structured and less tannic than the 1996, the 1995 Barolo Sorano exhibits a rose petal–scented fragrance. This medium-bodied, elegant, finesse-styled, racy wine offers a graceful combination of cherry fruit intermixed with cedar, leather, and dried herbs. This lovely, forward Barolo can be drunk now and over the next 8 years.

AZELIA

1997 Barolo	D	90
1998 Barolo Bricco Fiasco	E	(92–93)
1997 Barolo Bricco Fiasco	E	93
1996 Barolo Bricco Fiasco	E	(91–93+?)
1995 Barolo Bricco Fiasco	E	90+
1998 Barolo San Rocco	E	(91–93)
1997 Barolo San Rocco	E	94
1996 Barolo San Rocco	E	(91–93)
1995 Barolo San Rocco	E	90

A believer in the use of rotary fermenters, short maceration periods, and 40% new French oak for aging his single-vineyard Barolos, Azelia has been on fire over recent vintages. He produced great 1996s and excellent 1995s, as well as stunning 1997s and 1998s. All the wines emerge from his Castiglione Falletto vineyards except for the San Rocco, which comes from the adjacent commune of Serralunga. They are all topflight.

Two superb efforts, the 1998s are virtually equivalent (although more classic) to Azelia's brilliant 1997s. The 1998 Barolo San Rocco's dark plum/garnet color is followed by a gorgeously fragrant perfume of dried Provençal herbs, smoke, tar, black cherry liqueur, cedar, and soy. Ripe, opulently textured, full-bodied flavors caress the palate with no hard edges. This hedonistic Nebbiolo fruit bomb possesses plenty of complexity. The 1998 Barolo Bricco Fiasco exhibits additional notes of Asian spices, new saddle leather, earth, soy, and nori (the seaweed wrap for sushi). It displays phenomenal sweetness on the attack and mid-palate, full body, no hard edges, and a plush, generously rich finish revealing copious quantities of fruit as well as glycerin. Drink both 1998s over the next 12–15 years.

The generic 1997 Barolo is a delicious, forward, round, supple, approachable effort to consume over the next 5–6 years. Revealing amber and pink at the edge of its color, it is an expansive, sweet, sexy example with overripe cherry, cedar wood, licorice, smoke, and tar characteristics. Dark garnet-colored with an amber edge, the 1997 Barolo San Rocco possesses a phenomenal perfume of tobacco, leather, cedar, fruitcake, and cherry liqueur. Tar and rose petals (classic scents of ripe Nebbiolo) also emerge. Once past the terrific aromatics, the wine is full-bodied, rich, and supple, with an expansive texture, sweet tannin, low acidity, and gobs of fat as well as extract. This alluring Barolo is best drunk over the next 10–12 years. More structured yet also opulent, the dark ruby/garnet-colored, unctuous 1997 Barolo Bricco Fiasco reveals abundant quantities of smoke, tobacco, leather, licorice, and kirsch aromas and flavors. Full-bodied, lusty, and intense, it can be drunk now and should keep for nearly two decades.

Azelia produced two compelling 1996s. The 1996 Barolo San Rocco possesses a spicy, cedar box, fruitcake, and cherry liqueur–scented nose, a sweet, full-bodied personality with loads of glycerin, evidence of charred wood, oak, and a rich, multilayered, low-acid, structured/delineated finish. It is a big, mouth-filling Barolo with considerable complexity. Anticipated maturity: now–2020. The 1996 Barolo Bricco Fiasco explodes with tobacco, balsam wood, cedar, tar, and the telltale cherry fruit. In the mouth, toasty oak makes an appearance. Full-bodied, tannic, deep, and powerful, with a huge impact and density, this modern-styled wine has the body and force of a more traditionally made Barolo. Anticipated maturity: 2004–2020.

The 1995 Barolo San Rocco displays classic rose petal/melted tar aromas combined with exotic scents of soy and roasted meat–like smells. Intense, with full body, toasty oak, and black cherry fruit, this large-scaled, concentrated wine is on a fast evolutionary track, already exhibiting compelling complexity and richness. Anticipated maturity: now–2008. The 1995 Barolo Bricco Fiasco offers a pronounced bouquet of tobacco smoke intermixed with melted asphalt/tar, truffles, and kirsch/cherry liqueur. This fragrant, dense, concentrated, full-bodied Barolo is powerful and long, but more backward than the San Rocco. Anticipated maturity: now–2016.

F.LLI BARALE

1998 Barolo Castellero	D	85

Aromas of apple skins, cherry fruit, earth, and pepper are reminiscent of a straightforward Pommard from Burgundy. While medium-bodied and ripe, this soft 1998 Barolo Castellero lacks depth. Drink it over the next 2 years.

MARCHESI DI BAROLO

1998 Barolo Vigna Cannubi	E	(90–92)
1997 Barolo Vigna Cannubi	E	90
1998 Barolo Vigna Sarmassa	E	(90–92)
1997 Barolo Vigna Sarmassa	E	92

The two 1998s are impressive. The 1998 Barolo Vigna Cannubi exhibits a dark plum/purple color as well as a soft, modern style displaying notes of lavender, rose petals, ripe black fruits, and a touch of toasty oak. A sweet attack is followed by a rich, medium- to full-bodied, long Barolo with tannin as well as outstanding balance. Anticipated maturity: 2005–2015. Even fleshier and more opulent, the 1998 Barolo Vigna Sarmassa is made in a voluptuous, contemporary style with full body, abundant glycerin, and copious amounts of black cherry fruit infused with licorice, espresso, and melted road tar. Layered, pure, and impressive, it will be at its finest between 2004–2016.

The dark ruby-colored, internationally styled 1997 Barolo Vigna Cannubi shows plenty of new oak, but it does not overwhelm the wine's rich black raspberry, currant, and cherry fruit. Sweet, dense, and full-bodied, with low acidity and firm tannin, this pure, clean Barolo will drink well young, yet age for 15–20 years. More extracted, fleshy, powerful, and tannic is the 1997 Barolo Vigna Sarmassa. A dark ruby/purple color is accompanied by copious quantities of ripe, concentrated, black raspberry fruit, licorice, smoke, and mineral aromas and flavors. Dense and powerful, this 1997 is best cellared for 2–3 years and drunk over the following 15+.

A. S. BIAGIO

| 1997 Barolo | D | (88–90) |
| 1996 Barolo | D | (87–89) |

The 1997 Barolo exhibits that overripe fruit characteristic that the French refer to positively as *sur-maturité*. Its dark ruby color is followed by aromas of cherry and blackberry fruit and *garrigue* (that Provençal mélange of earth and herbs). Full-bodied, fat, succulent flavors, low acidity, and a chewy, high-alcohol finish further characterize this wine. This full-throttle Barolo, while not complex, is impressive in a hedonistic sense. Anticipated maturity: now–2015. The 1996 Barolo is an opulent, dark ruby-colored effort with gobs of cherry fruit, earth, olive, Provençal herbs, and cedar. Rich, with good ripeness, and a medium-bodied, firm, but fleshy finish, it should be at its finest before 2014.

FRANCO BOASSO

1998 Barolo Gabutti	D	87
1997 Barolo Gabutti	D	89
1996 Barolo Gabutti	D	(88–91+?)
1995 Barolo Gabutti	D	90

This producer from Serralunga d'Alba uses open-top fermenters with no new oak, preferring to age the wines in small *foudres*. His Barolos emerge from a vineyard with a southern exposure. This light-styled, forward, medium ruby/garnet-colored 1998 Barolo Gabutti offers plump cherry fruit, a velvety texture, and good roundness. Enjoy it over the next 4 years. The 1997 Barolo Gabutti is dark garnet-colored with an amber edge. Aromas of smoke, tobacco, Provençal herbs, kirsch, and dried cherries are followed by a medium- to full-bodied, dense, concentrated, powerful wine with excellent ripeness, a lush texture, and firm tannin in the finish. It gives conflicting indications of whether it will evolve quickly or become more structured and enjoy 18 or more years of longevity. In any event, it is an excellent wine that falls just short of being outstanding. Anticipated maturity: 2003–2016. The dark plum/ruby-colored 1996 Barolo Gabutti offers a nose of overripe black cherries, incense, licorice, smoke, and earth. It is monolithic, dense, and concentrated but slightly disjointed. Hence the question mark. There is huge potential, but this wine has not yet pulled itself together. Anticipated maturity: 2005–2015. The 1995 Barolo Gabutti reveals a Châteauneuf-du-Pape-like, kirschy, peppery nose with licorice and dried herbs. I had expected a more muscular, old style Barolo, but this is a fruit bomb with extraordinary ripeness and glycerin and a sexy, lush style. Anticipated maturity: now–2012.

ENZO BOGLIETTI

1998 Barbera d'Alba Vigna dei Romani	C	90
1998 Barolo Vigna delle Brunate	E	(88–89)
1997 Barolo Vigna delle Brunate	E	90+
1996 Barolo Vigna delle Brunate	E	(87–89)
1998 Barolo Vigna Case Nere	E	(90–91)
1997 Barolo Vigna Case Nere	E	91
1996 Barolo Vigna Case Nere	E	(87–88)
1995 Barolo Vigna Case Nere	E	85
1998 Barolo Vigna dei Fossati	E	(89–91)
1997 Barolo Vigna dei Fossati	E	91
1996 Barolo Vigna dei Fossati	E	(87–90)
1999 Dolcetto d'Alba Tigli Neri	C	90
1998 Langhe Rosso Buio	C	87

This up-and-coming La Morra producer, who fashions attractive wines, deserves significant attention. Based on recent vintages, Boglietti, who produces new-wave, *barrique*-aged Barolos, appears to be racheting up his performance level. His 1998s are fine successes. The superb 1997s all possess saturated purple colors and display copious levels of glycerin and extract. Each appears to have more of the black fruit, cassis/black raspberry character than the more red fruit–dominated 1996s and 1995. These wines are also lower in acidity and more open-knit than their older siblings.

Readers looking for an amazing Dolcetto should check out the 1999 Dolcetto d'Alba Tigli Neri. This astonishing, black/purple-colored, opulent, full-bodied, exquisitely fruited effort displays copious black fruits intermixed with notes of violets and chocolate. Unctuously textured yet not heavy, this beauty should be drunk within 2 years.

Also outstanding, the 1998 Barbera d'Alba Vigna dei Romani reveals plenty of spicy toast characteristics from its *barrique* aging. It is a full-bodied, modern-styled, deep ruby/purple-colored Barbera boasting an explosive bouquet of jammy tomato confit intertwined with black cherries and plums. Dense, chewy, yet soft, it can be drunk now and over the next 2–3 years. The more elegant, earthy, slightly acidic 1998 Langhe Rosso Buio is a blend of declassified young-vine Nebbiolo and Barbera. Exhibiting smoky, cherry notes, plenty of spice, medium body, and some tartness, it should drink well for 2 years. The 1998 Barolo Case Nere is a full-bodied, opaque purple-colored, modern-styled effort. A heady perfume of black fruits intermixed with new oak is followed by a wine with sweet tannin, a layered texture, outstanding richness, and a long finish. The dark plum/purple-colored 1998 Barolo Brunate is a medium-bodied, more elegantly styled effort displaying less obvious new oak influence in its round, sweet flavors but a less impressive finish than the Case Nere. Consume it during its first decade of life. The plum/purple-colored, spicy, smoky, opulent, full-bodied 1998 Barolo Fossati exhibits abundant quantities of black cherry and berry fruit, new oak, sweet tannin, and a long, chewy, lush finish. There are no hard edges to this 1998 Barolo. While it currently reveals the least typicity of these three offerings, it is impossible to hide a good *terroir* no matter how the wine is treated as long as the yields are low and the fruit is ripe. I suspect its Barolo/Nebbiolo character will emerge with another 1–2 years of cellaring. Anticipated maturity: 2003–2016.

The 1997 Barolo Case Nere displays an intriguing perfume of hickory/barbecue smoke intermixed with tar, rose water, black cherries, toffee, and maple syrup. Full-bodied, with large volume, a plush, multilayered texture, low acidity, and a boatload of glycerin, it is a thick, succulent Barolo to consume now and over the next 12+ years. The dark plum/garnet-colored 1997 Barolo Brunate exhibits a strikingly pure nose of melted licorice, kirsch, tobacco, spice box, and toasty oak. Deep, massive, full-bodied, and layered, with huge extract, this is a structured, powerful effort without the charm of its siblings. Nevertheless, it is an immensely impressive 1997 and may be the longest-lived of this trio. Anticipated maturity: 2003–2020. The saturated ruby/garnet-colored 1997 Barolo Fossati possesses thick, blackberry, raspberry, and cherry flavors intermixed with new oak, licorice, and smoke. Pure, opulent, and succulent, this intense, low-acid wine displays the vintage's exoticism as well as copious alcohol and glycerin. Anticipated maturity: now–2015.

The dark ruby-colored 1996 Barolo Case Nere is dense (denser than the 1995, in fact), with licorice, fennel, cedar, and black cherry aromas. Medium- to full-bodied, with moderate tannin and excellent purity, this traditionally made Barolo will be at its finest before 2012. The 1996 Barolo Brunate offers a classic nose of melted tar, cherry and black raspberry fruit, weedy tobacco, herb, and leather scents. Rich, with medium body, moderate tannin, and a dusty, rustic finish, it will keep for 8–10 years. The 1996 Barolo Fossati's bouquet reveals the influence of new oak, along with cherry liqueur, spice, and licorice. Broad and expansive in the mouth, with full body and moderate tannin, it should prove to be Boglietti's longest-lived 1996. Anticipated maturity: now–2018.

The only 1995 I tasted was the Barolo Case Nere, a medium ruby-colored, elegant wine with a smoked herb, cedar, tar, and cherry-scented nose. Spicy, with good ripeness, medium body, and an open-knit, evolved character, it can be drunk now and over the next 1–2 years.

BONGIOVANNI

1998	Barolo	D	(85–86)
1997	Barolo	D	87
1996	Barolo	D	87
1998	Barolo Pernanno	D	(86–87)
1997	Barolo Pernanno	D	87
1996	Barolo Pernanno	E	90
1999	Dolcetto d'Alba	C	89
1998	Langhe Rosso Falletto	D	87
1997	Langhe Rosso Falletto	D	91+

This Castiglione Falletto producer is not one that I know well. However, these are impressive offerings. The 1999 Dolcetto d'Alba is a dense ruby/purple-colored fruit bomb, with a supple texture, thick, juicy flavors, little complexity, but impressive mouth-filling levels of fruit and extract. Drink it over the next 2 years. The 1998 Langhe Rosso Falletto (a 50% Barbera, 25% Cabernet Sauvignon, and 25% Nebbiolo blend aged in *barrique*) is too internationally styled for me, but the wine's quality is unquestionably good. Elegant black currant and cherry notes are combined with abundant quantities of toasty new oak, resulting in a medium-bodied, well-made wine to drink over the next decade.

The following two 1998s are good but uninspiring. Bongiovanni's 1998 Barolo displays a soft, spicy perfume of cola, coffee, chocolate, and red fruits. This easygoing, quaffable (unusual for Barolo), supple 1998 has a moderate finish. Drink it over the next 3–4 years. The darker plum-colored 1998 Barolo Pernanno exhibits more toasty new oak in the aromatics along with notions of caramel, black cherries, and vanilla. Round, generous, and ripe, but not complex, it will drink well for 5–6 years.

As for the 1997s, they are modern, forward-styled Barolos exhibiting evidence of *barrique* aging. Neither will make old bones, but for drinking over the next 5–6 years, they represent an attractive, commercial style with some character. The 1997 Barolo offers a deep ruby color and a fat, low-acid, plush style with low acidity as well as copious cherry fruit. While similarly styled, the 1997 Barolo Pernanno reveals more chocolate in its open-knit, fleshy, medium-weight personality. It, too, should be drunk over the next 5–6 years. The 1997 Langhe Rosso Falletto is an awesome wine! This black/purple-colored blend of 50% Barbera, 25% Cabernet Sauvignon, and 25% Nebbiolo, all aged in new French oak, is hugely extracted and extremely full-bodied. It boasts layer upon layer of jammy, concentrated cassis-dominated fruit with notes of cherry liqueur, spice box, licorice, and cedar. As the wine sits in the glass, some of Nebbiolo's telltale melted asphalt and rose petal perfume emerges. Exceptionally rich, pure and velvet-textured, with a tannic finish, this is another sumptuous wine from the extraordinary, albeit atypical 1997 vintage. Anticipated maturity: now–2015.

The fairly light, medium-weight, round 1996 Barolo exhibits coffee, tobacco, cherry, and herb aromas and flavors, good concentration, fine ripeness, and sweet tannin. It is meant to be drunk over the next 7–8 years. The 1996 Barolo Pernanno reveals spicy new oak (from *barrique* aging), melted tar, rose petal, and black cherry fruit aromas and flavors. Ripe, medium- to full-bodied, concentrated, and supple, it can be drunk over the next 8 years.

BRAIDA

1998	Barbera d'Asti Ai Suma	E	96
1997	Barbera d'Asti Ai Suma	E	95
1998	Barbera d'Asti Bricco dell'Uccellone	E	94
1997	Barbera d'Asti Bricco dell'Uccellone	E	90
1999	Monferrato Rosso Il Bacialé	D	90

One of the original producers of super, "Whopper"-sized, *barrique*-aged Barbera, Braida continues to set the standard, although there are increasing numbers of challengers to these over-the-top, amazingly concentrated, prodigious wines that are nearly impossible to believe are made from Barbera. Braida's top two *cuvées*, which are aged 15 months in French oak prior to bottling, represent the essence of Barbera in a modern but thrillingly concentrated, layered style. Although these wines do not improve significantly in the bottle, they provide sumptuous drinking during their first 5–7 years of life. Their acidity and extract level ensure that they will hold up for two decades or more, but will they taste any better at age 10 than they did at age 5? I don't think so. However, for hedonistic levels of fruit, extract, glycerin, and complex aromatics, in their youth these wines are amazing.

The less expensive 1999 Monferrato Rosso Il Bacialé (a blend of 80% Barbera and 20% Pinot Noir) offers sexy, complex aromas of herb-tinged red and black fruits intermixed with earth and spicy oak. Ripe, round, and succulent, with a supple finish, it can be enjoyed over the next 2 years.

The opaque purple-colored 1998 Barbera d'Asti Bricco dell'Uccellone offers a seductive nose of spicy toast characteristics infused with espresso, roasted meats, black cherries, and raspberries. Dense and full-bodied, with a luxurious texture, this is a superintense, plush Barbera to enjoy over the next 5–6 years, although it will last longer. Even more remarkable is the 1998 Barbera d'Asti Ai Suma. This is the quintessential expression of super-concentrated, *barrique*-aged Barbera that other producers attempt to emulate (successfully so in the case of Roberto Voerzio). Braida's inky black/purple-colored 1998 boasts an explosive bouquet of blackberry and cherry jam mixed with graphite, vanilla, roasted meats, and spice. A sensual, full-bodied, voluptuously textured offering with extraordinary purity, this is a monumental Barbera. Whether it will improve beyond 5–7 years is open to conjecture, but who can resist its provocative charms?

Unquestionably one of the most massive Barberas ever made, the blockbuster 1997 Barbera d'Asti Ai Suma (800 cases) reveals off-the-chart density as well as a terrific bouquet of smoke, blackberries, cherry liqueur, licorice, and violets. With exquisite richness and amazing harmony for such a gargantuan wine, this full-bodied giant should drink well for 10–12 years. However, its low acidity and almost over-the-top richness, so typical of many 1997s, give it immediate appeal. It is a very sexy effort! The dense ruby/purple-colored, explosive 1997 Barbera d'Asti Bricco dell'Uccellone is overwhelmed by its sibling. It boasts aromas of concentrated strawberry jam intermixed with cherries, blackberries, smoky toasty oak, and glycerin. Minimal acidity and a lusty personality result in an already delicious wine, but it should last for 8 years. These are two very impressive Barberas!

ALESSANDRO BRERO

1998 Barbera d'Alba Poderi Roset	C	92
1998 Barolo Poderi Roset	E	88
1997 Barolo Poderi Roset	E	90
1996 Barolo Poderi Roset	E	92+
1995 Barolo Poderi Roset	E	89
2000 Dolcetto d'Alba Poderi Roset	C	88
1999 Dolcetto d'Alba Poderi Roset	C	90

With extremely low yields, ripe fruit, and no filtration at bottling, it is not surprising that Brero's wines are loaded. The 600-case, dense purple *cuvée* of fat, chewy, fruit-driven 2000 Dolcetto d'Alba Poderi Roset possesses loads of berry fruit, a notion of coffee and chocolate, and a full-bodied, compact finish. Although not complex, it has excellent purity as well as a mouth-filling style. Enjoy it over the next 3 years.

Brero's 1999 Dolcetto d'Alba Poderi Roset was fermented and aged in tank. Its saturated ruby/purple color is accompanied by a huge, blackberry, cherry, and chocolate-scented nose, exuberant fruit, and low acidity. This soft, ripe Dolcetto is captivating and delicious. It should drink well for 2 years. Another dazzling effort is the 1998 Barbera d'Alba Poderi

Roset. Aged in both small barrels and larger Slavonian oak *foudres*, it exhibits a dark ruby/ purple color, a superb herbaceous, smoky, toasty, and black cherry liqueur–scented nose, terrific texture, full body, and layers of Barbera fruit. The acidity is low, the purity superb, and the wine chewy and intense. Drink it over the next 5 years.

The soft, supple, Burgundy-styled 1998 Barolo Poderi Roset exhibits a dark ruby color in addition to scents of smoke, chocolate, and black cherries. Medium-bodied and seductive, it can be drunk now as well as over the next decade. While not as exotic or concentrated as the 1997, it is beautifully balanced, pure, and harmonious.

The highly extracted, flavorful, quasi-modern-styled 1997 Barolo Poderi Roset possesses the power, tannin, and force of old-style Barolos but the color, sweet fruit, and ripe tannin of the modernists. Dense chocolate, blackberry, and cherry flavors are thick, heady, and per- sistent. Surprisingly youthful and unevolved, it is nicely textured as well as extremely long. Anticipated maturity: 2003–2016. The impressive 1996 Barolo Poderi Roset requires some additional bottle aging. Aged entirely in large Slavonian oak *foudres* and bottled unfiltered, it boasts a deep ruby color with an amber edge. Spectacular aromatics of sweet black Chinese tea, rose petals, tar, and gobs of strawberry and black cherry fruit explode from the glass. Al- though still an infant, this wine is rich and full-bodied, with loads of flavor, abundant glyc- erin, and enough concentration and extract to cover the framework and tannin. Anticipated maturity: now–2020. The traditionally styled 1995 Barolo Poderi Roset exhibits an evolved deep garnet color with amber at the edge. It offers a spicy, dried herb, earthy, foresty nose with hints of cherry cough syrup, smoke, and leather. Medium- to full-bodied and expansive, it is soft enough to be drunk now and over the next 4–5 years.

GIACOMO BREZZA & FIGLI

1998 Barolo Sarmassa	D	88
1997 Barolo Sarmassa	D	89

While I was disappointed with Brezza's 1999, I enjoyed his 1998 and 1997. This excellent, fat, juicy, silky-textured 1998 Barolo Sarmassa is unusually evolved and forward. It exhibits a dark garnet color as well as copious quantities of smoky, weedy, cherry fruit intermixed with tobacco and damp earth. Chewy, plump, and surprisingly opulent, it will drink well over the next 8 years. The 1997 Barolo Sarmassa is a big, full-bodied, thick, unctuously textured effort with considerable amber at the edge. Notes of dried red fruits, flowers, toffee, choco- late, plums, and cherries are found in this concentrated wine, best consumed over the next 10 years.

F.LLI BROVIA

1997 Barbaresco Riosordo	E	(83–85)
1996 Barbaresco Riosordo	E	86
1995 Barbaresco Riosordo	E	86+
1998 Barolo Ca' Mia	E	(85–87)
1997 Barolo Ca' Mia	E	90+
1996 Barolo Ca' Mia	E	(86–87+?)
1995 Barolo Ca' Mia	E	88
1998 Barolo Rocche dei Brovia	E	(87–89+?)
1997 Barolo Rocche dei Brovia	E	91
1996 Barolo Rocche dei Brovia	E	(88–90)
1995 Barolo Rocche dei Brovia	E	86
1998 Barolo Villero	E	(88–89+)
1997 Barolo Villero	E	(86–88)
1996 Barolo Villero	E	(90–91+)
1995 Barolo Villero	E	89

Brovia, whose cellars are in Castiglione Falletto, produced sound 1995s, very good 1996s, and less impressive 1997s, which nevertheless performed better than their 1998 counterparts. It must be remembered, however, that Nebbiolo, much like Pinot Noir, is an extremely challenging grape to taste and assess at a young age. The 1997s reveal less color saturation and concentration than the 1996s, which adds to the minority school of thought that 1997 was not as consistently superb a vintage as believed. And Brovia's 1996s are far denser, more complete wines, as well as more tannic than the 1995s.

The 1998 Barolo Ca' Mia's dark plum/garnet color is followed by sweet aromas of chocolate, cherries, smoke, and dried herbs. It is a medium- to full-bodied, monolithic effort displaying tough tannin in the finish. If it sweetens and expands in texture, it will merit a higher score. Anticipated maturity: 2005–2015. The dark garnet-colored 1998 Barolo Villero reveals more softness as well as complexity in its spice box, molasses, and cherry-scented nose. There are excellent concentration, sweeter tannin, a more layered personality, and a seamless finish with excellent concentration of fruit (primarily cherries dosed with earth and spice). Anticipated maturity: 2004–2014. Lastly, the plum/garnet-colored 1998 Barolo Rocche dei Brovia is superficially appealing. Its smooth texture is accompanied by complex notes of caramel, cedar, cherry jam, smoke, and flowers. However, in the mouth, the wine shuts down, revealing little texture or depth. It may have been going through an awkward stage when I tasted it. There is plenty up front, but there is a lack of follow-through, depth, and what appears to be concentration in the finish. It will need to be retasted in order to pinpoint its potential quality. Anticipated maturity: 2005–2016.

The complex, supple 1997s do not compromise the power and muscle Brovia's wines routinely achieve. The dark garnet-colored 1997 Barolo Ca' Mia displays a complex bouquet of soy, tobacco, cedar, licorice, and smoke. Expansive, full-bodied, and intensely concentrated, this is an atypically backward 1997 with tightly packed flavors. Anticipated maturity: 2005–2018. The dark plum/garnet-colored 1997 Barolo Rocche dei Brovia begins slowly but grows incrementally until it totally coats the palate. Thick and powerful, it exhibits sexy aromatics of prunes, cherries, and plums. In the mouth, dried fig notes also make an appearance in this intensely flavored, concentrated, muscular wine. Despite its precociousness, there is plenty of tannin lurking beneath the viscosity. Anticipated maturity: now–2018. The 1997 Barbaresco Riosordo tastes similar to a light- to medium-bodied Pinot Noir. Its framboise and cherry flavors are alluring, but the wine is smoky and light. Drink it over the next 3 years. The 1997 Barolo Villero offers spice, cinnamon, and cherry fruit in its moderately endowed nose. Elegant, medium- to full-bodied and lush, it does not reveal any of the vintage's hallmark glycerin, high alcohol, and sweet fruit. Anticipated maturity: now–2012.

The 1996 Barbaresco Riosordo is the most forward. Displaying a ruby color with purple nuances, it offers fresh, tangy black currant flavors with dried herbs in the background. It possesses good concentration but a compressed, narrowly constructed finish. Anticipated maturity: now–2007. The 1996 Barolo Rocche dei Brovia's opaque ruby color with purple nuances is followed by dense black cherry fruit intermixed with raspberry liqueur, spice, and earth. This is a fuller-bodied, rich, potentially outstanding wine with moderate tannin and 15 years' longevity. Anticipated maturity: 2005–2018. The dark ruby-colored 1996 Barolo Ca' Mia is severe and austere, with high levels of tannin and sweet fruit that tastes like cherry cough syrup mixed with cedar and spice box notes. The tannin level is worrisome, thus the question mark. Anticipated maturity: 2004–2015. The outstanding, ruby/purple-colored 1996 Barolo Villero displays a nose of melted road tar, chocolate, earth, black cherries, dried herbs, and coffee. Rich, full-bodied, and nearly massive, this is a classic Barolo that will last for 20–22 years. Anticipated maturity: 2007–2030.

The 1995 Barbaresco Riosordo is a light- to medium-bodied effort for drinking over the next 1–2 years. Forward and evolved, with a medium garnet color already exhibiting considerable amber at the edge, it offers weedy tobacco, smoke, earth, and dried fruit aromas and flavors. Although soft, elegant, and medium-bodied, it lacks depth. Anticipated maturity: now–2005. The 1995 Barolo Rocche dei Brovia is a darker plum-colored wine with cherries, cranberries, and red currants in its slightly spicy nose. Made in a light- to medium-bodied, elegant style, it is soft and easy to drink. Anticipated maturity: now–2007. The more serious 1995 Barolo Ca' Mia exhibits a darker garnet color in addition to more black raspberry and currant fruit in the nose along with new saddle leather and cigar smoke. It possesses good purity, medium to full body, excellent richness, and a moderately long finish. Anticipated maturity: now–2009. The dark ruby/garnet-colored 1995 Barolo Villero is the most backward, youthful, concentrated, and complete of the 1995s. While closed, it does offer aromas of roasted herbs, minerals, tobacco, and leather. In the mouth, sweet black cherry fruit makes an appearance. Anticipated maturity: now–2012.

COMMENDATOR G. B. BURLOTTO

1998 Barolo Vigneto Cannubi	D	(87–88)
1997 Barolo Vigneto Cannubi	D	86

This Verduno producer has fashioned a flavorful, medium-weight, elegantly styled 1998 Barolo Vigneto Cannubi with good softness, finesse, and no hard edges. There is not a great deal of concentration, but the wine is well balanced and ideal for drinking over the next 4–5 years. The medium-bodied, earthy, powerful, tannic, rustic 1997 Barolo exhibits a dark ruby color, good licorice and cherry fruit notes, but a certain toughness as well as compression to its texture. Anticipated maturity: 2003–2012.

BUSSIA SOPRANA

1998 Barolo Mosconi	D	(90–92)
1997 Barolo Mosconi	D	89
1997 Barolo Vigna Colonnello	D	90

A sleeper producer from Monforte d'Alba that I discovered through his 1997s, Bussia Soprana turns out a Barolo Mosconi and a Barolo Vigna Colonnello that are nearly outstanding. Both wines are traditionally made but are bottled early to preserve their rich, concentrated fruit. There is little evidence of new oak, although subtle smoke and vanilla notes are present. I enjoyed the two 1997s immensely, but I tasted only one 1998 cuvée from this producer. The full-bodied, traditionally made 1998 Barolo Mosconi is a sleeper of the vintage. A dark plum/garnet color is accompanied by aromas of espresso, smoke, kirsch, dried herbs, and tobacco. Dense and chewy, with sweet tannin as well as ripe fruit, its harmony and overall balance suggest 10–12 years of longevity.

The creamy-textured, fat (because of the vintage's high glycerin) 1997 Barolo Mosconi reveals excellent concentration as well as a complex bouquet of rose water, licorice, smoke, minerals, and black cherries. In the mouth, the wine is full, rich, and ready to drink. Anticipated maturity: now–2014. The dark plum/garnet-colored 1997 Barolo Vigna Colonnello offers a fragrant, intense perfume of wood smoke, licorice, kirsch, Provençal herbs, and tobacco. Full-bodied, powerful, and dense, it reveals no hard edges, a seamless texture, and a 30-second finish. Drink it now and over the next 12 years.

PIERO BUSSO

1996 Barbaresco	D	86
1998 Barbera d'Alba Vigna Majano	C	91

The 1998 Barbera d'Alba Vigna Majano exhibits spicy new oak, concentrated, opulently-textured flavors redolent with cherry and strawberry jam as well as new oak. Ripe, full-bodied, and super-concentrated, this is another surprisingly voluptuous Barbera to drink over the next 5–6 years. It is a very good value given the wine's quality. Less impressive but competently made is the dark plum/ruby-colored 1996 Barbaresco, which offers an attractive bouquet of leather, wood smoke, sweet and sour cherries, medium body, moderate tannin, and an elegant, restrained style. It should be drunk over the next 4–5 years.

CA' DEL BAIO

1998 Barbaresco Asili	D	(84–85)
1998 Barbaresco Valgrande	D	(83–86)

Both 1998s are light to medium-bodied, pleasant, fruity, superficial Barbarescos meant to be consumed during their first 4–5 years of life. Although cleanly made, they lack substance.

CA' ROMÈ

1997 Barbaresco	D	87
1997 Barbaresco Maria di Brun	E	85
1997 Barolo Rapet	E	90
1996 Barolo Rapet	E	88
1997 Barolo Vigna Cerretta	E	89
1996 Barolo Vigna Cerretta	E	87

This is the producer that I have the most trouble understanding. Many of Ca' Romè's wines seem to lack intensity and are too angular and astringent for my taste (1998 Barbera d'Alba La Gamberaja; 1997 Da Pruvé, a Barbera/Nebbiolo blend; 1997 Barbaresco; and 1997 Barbaresco Maria di Brun). However, I enjoyed the upcoming Barolo releases.

The generic 1997 Barbaresco exhibits a dark plum color in addition to a moderately intense bouquet of sweet cherries, cedar, spice box, licorice, and herbs. With excellent richness and purity as well as a supple texture, it should be consumed over the next 4–5 years. The 1997 Barbaresco Maria di Brun displays an evolved garnet color with considerable amber at the edge. Offering Chinese black tea, cedar, and cherry characteristics, this soft wine appears to be drying out. Drink it over the next 2–3 years.

The opulent 1997 Barolo Rapet exhibits a deep ruby color, sweet, concentrated fruit (cherries, smoke, cedar, and licorice), layers of texture, and a spicy, intense finish. Drink it over the next 12+ years. The 1996 Barolo Rapet reveals an excellent dark ruby color in addition to abundant aromas of cedar wood, spice box, rose petals, and cherries in its medium-bodied, moderately tannic personality. It should drink well for 5–6 years. The 1996 and 1997 Barolo Vigna Cerretta differ only in that the 1997 has less tannin, more sweetness of fruit and glycerin, and the vintage's telltale opulence. The 1997 possesses more volume, ripeness, richness, and intensity. Both wines are best drunk during their first 10–12 years of life. The 1996 exhibits notes of soy and tobacco in its medium- to full-bodied, tannic, cedary, spicy, black cherry–dominated personality.

GIUSEPPE CAPPELLANO

1998 Barolo Franco	E	90
1997 Barolo Franco	E	90
1998 Barolo Gabutti	E	88
1997 Barolo Gabutti	E	83

Both of these offerings are produced from the Gabutti vineyard, but the Franco *cuvée* comes from ancient, ungrafted Nebbiolo vines that are believed to be more than 100 years of age. The 1998 Barolo Franco's medium garnet color is accompanied by a sweet, attractive bouquet of jammy strawberry and cherry fruit, rose petals, licorice, and autumn leaves. There are good fatness, an opulent texture, a fleshy mid-palate, and a lush finish with well-concealed tannin and acidity. Anticipated maturity: 2004–2015. The dark ruby-colored, similarly styled 1998 Barolo Gabutti's aromatics are not as complex, but it offers scents of cherry cough syrup, licorice, tobacco, leather, and spice. Sweet, ripe, medium- to full-bodied, and seductive, it will drink well until 2015.

The finer of the two 1997s, the dark garnet-colored 1997 Barolo Franco reveals an explosive, decadent aroma of mushrooms, jammy red and black fruits, coffee, caramel, smoke, and dried herbs. Thick, fat, plush, and chewy, it tastes like candy. Consume it over the next 8 years. On the other hand, the 1997 Barolo Gabutti is a lighter, straightforward, medium-bodied effort displaying cherry fruit but not a great deal of complexity, texture, or length. Drink it over the next 3 years.

CARRETTA

1997	Barbaresco Cascina Bordino	E	88
1996	Barbaresco Cascina Bordino	E	87
1995	Barbaresco Cascina Bordino	E	86
1998	Barolo Vigneta Cannubi	E	(90–91)
1997	Barolo Vigneta Cannubi	E	90
1996	Barolo Vigneta Cannubi	E	(87–88)
1995	Barolo Vigneta Cannubi	E	86
1997	Bric Quercia	E	88

Carretta's offerings tend to be firmly structured, masculine wines with considerable body and tannin.

A powerful old-style Barolo, Carretta's 1998 Vigneta Cannubi offers up scents of new saddle leather, underbrush, earth, truffles, vitamins, black cherry fruit, rose petals, and tar. Abundant tannin, serious concentration, high extract, and a structured, formidable personality suggest an atypical style in 1998, but one that will repay cellaring. Anticipated maturity: 2008–2020. Contrary to the general style of the estate, the 1997 Barolo Vigneta Cannubi is approachable, although it ideally needs 1–2 more years of cellaring. Notes of camphor intermingle with ripe berry fruit, earth, soy, tobacco, and leather in this full-bodied, powerful, traditionally made Barolo. Anticipated maturity: 2004–2020. In contrast to the tannic, powerful Barolo, the sexy, lush, open-knit 1997 Barbaresco Cascina Bordino is more charming as well as accessible. Offering aromas and flavors of red/black fruits, spice box, and fruitcake, this soft, round wine is best drunk over the next 6–7 years.

The opulently textured and flamboyant 1997 Barbaresco Cascina Bordino is dark ruby/purple-colored. It offers copious quantities of sweet black raspberry and cherry fruit meshed with earth, loamy soil scents, weedy tobacco, and spice. A medium-bodied example, with more glycerin, alcohol, and lower acidity than its siblings, it should drink well young and last for 6 years. The outstanding, powerful 1997 Barolo Vigneta Cannubi exhibits a dense ruby/purple color, in addition to intense aromas of jammy black fruits, spice, cedar, and dried herbs. Powerful and rich, with outstanding ripeness, it will drink well between 2005–2020. The 1997 Bric Quercia *vino da tavola* (a blend of Barbera and Bonarda) was aged in barrel and bottled unfiltered. It is an exotic, opaque purple wine with a beautiful nose of sweet cherry jam and kirsch intertwined with toasty, smoky oak and floral scents. Opulently textured, fat, and chewy (a characteristic of this vintage), this low-acid, hedonistic wine should drink well for 4–5 years.

The 1996 Barbaresco Cascina Bordino exhibits a dark ruby color, as well as attractive scents and flavors of jammy strawberries and cherries, roasted nuts, cedar, and spice box scents. Long, rich, and medium-bodied with moderate tannin, it will be at its finest before 2012. The 1996 Barolo Vigneta Cannubi is a powerful, masculine wine with good tannin and dusty, earthy aromas intertwined with sour cherries. Tobacco and asphalt scents also make an appearance. This structured, muscular wine will be at its finest before 2012.

The 1995 Barbaresco Cascina Bordino is surprisingly soft for a wine from this estate. Exhibiting a plum/garnet color, smoky, soy, gamey, spicy, earthy, fruit flavors, and damp foresty scents, it is medium-bodied and round, and will provide ideal drinking over the next 2 years.

The 1995 Barolo Vigneta Cannubi is totally different from its younger sibling, the 1996.

More open-knit, with good power for the vintage, it is destined to be drunk over the next 3 years. It possesses attractive licorice and tar scents, medium body, and some tannin, but not enough depth to encourage further aging.

CAVALIER BARTOLOMEO DI BORGOGNO DARIO

1998 Barolo Vigneti Solanotto	D	(88–90)
1997 Barolo Vigneti Solanotto	D	88

This Castiglione Falletto producer has turned out an excellent, medium ruby/garnet-colored 1998 Barolo Vigneti Solanotto with a big, spicy, sweet, black cherry–scented nose with hints of soy and balsam wood. There are fine fruit density, medium to full body, and moderate tannin in the admirable finish. Consume it over the next 10 years. An old-style, nicely textured, rich, spicy offering, the 1997 Barolo Vigneti Solanotto reveals aromas of black fruits, ripe cherries, cedar, earth, and seaweed. Medium- to full-bodied, pure, and nicely textured, it can be drunk now and over the next 8–10 years.

CAVALLOTTO

1997 Barolo	D	90
1998 Barolo Bricco Boschis Vigna San Giuseppe	E	(92–93+)
1997 Barolo Bricco Boschis Vigna San Giuseppe	E	93
1998 Barolo Vignolo	E	(91–93)
1997 Barolo Vignolo	E	91

Cavallotto's well-situated vineyards are on the hillsides surrounding the village of Castiglione Falletto. He owns one of the region's great monopole sites, the Bricco Boschis. Older vintages of these wines have tended to be good but never inspiring. However, after tasting through the 1997s, 1998s, and 1999s, it is apparent that something has changed as they are stunning Barolos. They represent a synthesis in style between the old-guard traditionalists and the new wave of rotary fermented, *barrique*-aged wines. The estate produces one standard *cuvée* and two special *cuvées*, the Bricco Boschis and the Vignolo, the latter emerging from a Castiglione Falletto vineyard situated just west of Bricco Boschis and northwest of the famed Monprivato vineyard. The deep ruby/purple-colored 1998 Barolo Vignolo exhibits a gorgeously sweet, textbook bouquet of rose petals, melted road tar, cherry liqueur, spice box, and minerals. Full-bodied, concentrated, seamless, and harmonious, it is reminiscent of a grand cru red Burgundy from Musigny or Flagey-Echèzeaux. Anticipated maturity: 2003–2018. Cavallotto's monopole vineyard, the famed Bricco Boschis Vigna San Giuseppe, produces a singularly styled Barolo with incredible fruit, a layered texture, moderately high tannin, and an enormous follow-through on the palate. It brilliantly marries finesse/elegance with unbridled power and concentration. Although it requires 2–3 years of cellaring to drop some tannin and develop more fully, it should be a spectacular 1998 that will rival the more ostentatious 1997. Anticipated maturity: 2006–2020.

The 1997 Barolo is an impressive generic effort whose fruit all came from the Bricco Boschis. A dense dark ruby/purple color is accompanied by a surprisingly high-toned, well-delineated wine without the over-the-top style evident in many 1997s. Notes of black cherries and blackberries are intertwined with minerals, wet stones, rose petals, and spice. Rich and full-bodied, with fine acidity, this classic, potentially long-lived Barolo should be at its finest between 2003–2018. The 1997 Barolo Vignolo is an elegant old-style offering. The color is a dark plum/ruby. The bouquet offers sweet aromas of melted asphalt, kirsch, leather, dried herbs, truffles, and smoke. It is a pure, full-bodied, moderately tannic effort with classic breeding, terrific purity as well as balance, and a long finish. Anticipated maturity: 2004–2017. The outrageously delicious 1997 Barolo Bricco Boschis Vigna San Giuseppe offers a spectacularly gorgeous nose of ripe fruits, herbs, leather, scorched earth, coffee, and cherry liqueur. A singular style of wine with wonderful spice, full body, and tremendous delineation as well as class, this large-scaled Barolo offers a classic rose petal fragrance as it sits in the glass. It is a quintessential Barolo. Anticipated maturity: 2003–2025.

CEREQUIO

1997 Barolo	D	84

This is an internationally styled, monolithic, straightforward 1997 Barolo without much typicity or depth. It possesses new oak and ripe fruit but little character or soul. Drink it over the next 3–4 years.

CERETTO

1998 Barbaresco Asij	EE	92
1997 Barbaresco Asij	EE	89
1998 Barbaresco Bricco Asili Bernadotte	EE	88
1997 Barbaresco Bricco Asili Bernadotte	EE	90
1998 Barbaresco Bricco Asili Bricco Asili	EE	89+
1997 Barbaresco Bricco Asili Bricco Asili	EE	91
1996 Barbaresco Bricco Asili Bricco Asili	EE	(91–93)
1995 Barbaresco Bricco Asili Bricco Asili	EE	89
1998 Barbaresco Bricco Asili Faset	EE	89+
1997 Barbaresco Bricco Asili Faset	EE	89+
1996 Barbaresco Bricco Asili Faset	EE	(89–91)
1995 Barbaresco Bricco Asili Faset	E	87
1998 Barolo Bricco Rocche	EEE	92
1997 Barolo Bricco Rocche	EEE	96
1996 Barolo Bricco Rocche	EEE	(92–96)
1995 Barolo Bricco Rocche	EE	90
1998 Barolo Brunate	EE	87
1997 Barolo Brunate	EE	94
1996 Barolo Brunate	EE	(91–93)
1995 Barolo Brunate	E	88+
1998 Barolo Prapò	EE	91
1997 Barolo Prapò	EE	95
1996 Barolo Prapò	EE	(92–94)
1995 Barolo Prapò	EE	89
1998 Barolo Zonchera	EE	90
1997 Barolo Zonchera	EE	91

The Ceretto brothers have long produced some of Piedmont's most elegantly styled, complex, flavorful wines from their vineyards in and around the village of Castiglione Falletto. They offer an impressive portfolio of 1995s, 1996s, 1997s and 1998s. Their 1998s are nearly as sensational as their 1997s. While these wines are all relatively well developed, they admirably display the vintage's intense perfume along with wonderful balance as well as harmony. True to the vintage, the 1997s possess more glycerin and lower acidity than the 1996s as well as a forward, unreal, atypical lushness and opulence. The 1996s, which exhibit a more saturated ruby color than the 1995s, are also richer, with more extract, tannin, and body. Of all four vintages, the 1995s are the most evolved, with garnet colors revealing amber at their edges. They are delicious wines that should drink well for another 6–7 years.

The glorious, dark plum/garnet-colored 1998 Barbaresco Asij offers a complex nose of earth, truffles, cherry liqueur, licorice, spice, and tobacco. Sweet and supple with nearly perfect symmetry as well as abundant glycerin and length, it will drink well for 5–6 years. The softer, lighter 1998 Barbaresco Bricco Asili Bernadotte offers notes of leather, balsam wood, underbrush, and cherries. Supple-textured, extremely fragrant, elegant, and light- to medium-bodied, it will drink well for 5–6 years. Similarly styled, but with a harder finish, the 1998 Barbaresco Bricco Asili Faset exhibits a plum/garnet color in addition to intense aromas of cherry liqueur, licorice, and leather. It is medium-bodied, with more concentration than the Bernadotte, but hard tannin in the finish suggests that a few supplementary months of cellaring are required. This wine may become slightly austere. The aromatically complex, medium- to full-bodied, dark garnet-colored 1998 Barbaresco Bricco Asili Bricco Asili offers intense aromas of soy, black cherries, tobacco, spice box, licorice, and incense. With ripe but noticeable tannin and excellent length, this potentially outstanding Barolo needs several more years of cellaring. Anticipated maturity: now–2014.

The dark plum/garnet-colored 1998 Barolo Zonchera is an elegant, spicy, medium-bodied effort revealing the vintage's telltale perfume as well as excellent concentration and purity. Drink it over the next 10–12 years. The concentrated, dark plum/garnet-colored, rich 1998 Barolo Prapò displays a smoky, earthy, black cherry, and new saddle leather–scented bouquet infused with licorice and espresso. Although tight, it is crammed with extract. Dense, full-bodied and long, with moderate tannin, it will be at its best until 2016. Notes of dried herbs, soy, underbrush, tobacco, and red cherries characterize the narrowly constructed, leaner, more austere 1998 Barolo Brunate. This is one example where the 1998 is clearly overshadowed by its spectacular, exotic, compelling 1997 counterpart. Anticipated maturity: now–2016. Ceretto's finest Barolo of the vintage appears to be the 1998 Barolo Bricco Rocche. An incredibly complex perfume of creosote, minerals, smoke, soy, black cherries, and incense is accompanied by a full-bodied, sweet, layered, powerful wine with outstanding balance. Long as well as elegant, this beauty will be at its finest before 2017.

I tasted four 1997 Barbaresco offerings. The most evolved, the 1997 Barbaresco Asij reveals a garnet color with considerable amber already apparent. It exhibits aromas of soy, cedar, ripe fruit, dried herbs, licorice, and rose water as well as a fleshy, open-knit, expansive personality and a medium- to full-bodied, soft finish. It will provide delicious drinking over the next 4–5 years. More tannic, with a firm edge and additional structure, is the dark ruby/purple-colored, amber-edged 1997 Barbaresco Bricco Asili Bernadotte. This medium- to full-bodied, backward, ripe effort possesses aromas of new saddle leather, dried herbs, brandied cherries, and licorice. Consume it over the next 10–12 years. The 1997 Barbaresco Bricco Asili Faset's exquisite perfume offers aromas of ginger, cedar, cigar box, and cherry liqueur. Excellent concentration, medium to full body, undeniable elegance, soft tannin, and copious glycerin result in a seductive wine to enjoy over the next 12 years. The superlative 1997 Barbaresco Bricco Asili Bricco Asili boasts a dark garnet color with amber at the edge as well as smoke, vanilla, leather, cherry liqueur, licorice, dried herb, and subtle oak aromas and flavors. The most complex of Ceretto's Barbarescos, this rich, medium- to full-bodied, suave, seductive 1997 can be drunk now and over the next 12 years.

The evolved, mature ruby/amber color of the 1997 Barolo Zonchera is perplexing since the wine tastes young and vigorous. An exotic offering, it exhibits aromas of smoke, coffee, vanilla, maple syrup, brown sugar, and overripe cherries. This is a full-bodied, luxuriously rich, decadent, young Barolo that should be drunk now and over the next 8 years. Reminiscent of a right bank Pomerol from the late 1940s, the dark garnet/amber-edged 1997 Barolo Prapò possesses aromas and flavors of singed leather, espresso, melted caramel, black cherries, smoke, and fruitcake. Atypical for a young Nebbiolo, it is succulent, fleshy, and undeniably compelling, rich, seamless, and concentrated. Drink it over the next 12 years. The 1997 Barolo Brunate displays a similar evolved dark garnet color with an amber edge. However, in the mouth, it is dense, full-bodied, moderately tannic, structured, and backward with plenty of power, concentration, and youthfulness. Despite the evolved color, this wine should age well for 15+ years. The ostentatious, staggering 1997 Barolo Bricco Rocche also possesses a dark garnet color with amber at the edge. The explosive bouquet of coffee liqueur, licorice, spice box, black cherries, kirsch, raspberries, and cedar is to die for. The wine reveals nu-

merous dimensions and nuances as well as a boatload of glycerin. Full-bodied, massively
concentrated, and exceptionally thick and juicy, with a sweetness due to the high glycerin
and ripeness, this is Barolo on steroids. Anticipated maturity: now–2018.

The seductive, dark ruby-colored 1996 Barbaresco Bricco Asili offers a classic bouquet of
road tar, cherry liqueur, tobacco, and dried herbs. Medium- to full-bodied and surprisingly
supple for the vintage, it exhibits firm tannin in the finish. Anticipated maturity: now–2014.
The 1996 Barbaresco Faset is not as aromatically complex as the Bricco Asili. It reveals
more oak, in addition to a raspberry/black cherry fruit component. Rich, medium-bodied,
and potentially outstanding, it will be at its finest before 2014.

The opaque ruby/purple-colored 1996 Barolo Prapò offers a moderately intense nose of
scorched earth, dried herbs, and sweet black fruits. It is medium- to full-bodied, with an exciting level of fruit extract, superb purity, and a multidimensional, layered personality. This
terrific Barolo will be best before 2018. The 1996 Barolo Brunate's dark ruby color is followed by aromas of Chinese black tea, pepper, earth, and cherries. Ripe, full-bodied, and
structured, with excellent depth, a sweet mid-palate and a firm finish, this wine should be
consumed before 2016. Ceretto's opaque ruby/purple-colored 1996 Barolo Bricco Rocche is
sensational stuff. The richest of these offerings, it combines explosive levels of fruit, glycerin,
and extract with an uncanny sense of elegance and finesse. There are copious quantities of
black cherry fruit intermixed with raspberries, cedar, spicy oak, licorice, and tar. This terrific, complex, multidimensional Barolo should be at its finest before 2018.

The 1995 Barbaresco Bricco Asili exhibits a beautifully etched nose of cherry jam,
vanilla, and dried herbs. Elegantly styled, with medium body, sweet, smoke-tinged fruit, and
soft tannin, this is a sexy, complex, easygoing Barbaresco to enjoy over the next 5–7 years.
The 1995 Barbaresco Faset is less complex, with a dark ruby/garnet color, lushness, medium
body, a spicy, cedary, cigar box–scented nose, ripe fruit, and a supple finish. Drink it over the
next 2–3 years. The 1995 Barolo Prapò offers a dried herb, cedar, tomato, and red currant–
scented nose. Cherries as well as plums make an appearance along with smoked herb and
toasty oak. Medium-bodied, graceful, and layered, it can be drunk over the next 4–5 years.
The 1995 Barolo Brunate is more of a fruit-driven wine, with gobs of cherry liqueur as well as
sandalwood, cedar, and flowers. Firmer, with more tannin, and an earthier personality than
the more open-knit Prapò, it is drinkable but may improve with a few years of bottle age. Anticipated maturity: now–2010. The most concentrated and massive of the Ceretto Barolos is
the 1995 Barolo Bricco Rocche. It offers a classic nose of melted tar, Asian spice, incense,
and cedar, as well as gobs of black fruits, a whiff of high-quality tobacco, full body, and a layered, moderately tannic finish. Anticipated maturity: now–2015.

PIO CESARE

1998	Barbaresco	E	87
1996	Barbaresco	E	(90–91)
1995	Barbaresco	E	88
1998	Barbaresco Bricco	E	(88–90)
1997	Barbaresco Bricco	E	90+
1998	Barolo	E	(86–87+)
1997	Barolo	E	(90–92)
1996	Barolo	E	(89–92)
1995	Barolo	E	(88–89)
1998	Barolo Ornato	E	(90–92)
1997	Barolo Ornato	E	(91–93)

One of the oldest firms in Piedmont (founded in 1881) and one of the few to operate out of the
village of Alba, Pio Cesare is the most recent in an unending string of traditional Piedmontese wine-makers. The house is going through a transitional stage, trying to fashion a middle

ground between the traditionally styled wines of the past and the new-wave modernists. It continues to make subtle winemaking refinements that enhance the wines' fruit character without compromising their full-bodied, ageworthy style. I still have bottles of 1969 and 1970 Pio Cesare Barolos that are drinking beautifully at nearly 30 years of age. Proprietor Pio Boffa feels that 1998 is qualitatively behind 1996, 1997, and 1999, but, as the following tasting notes demonstrate, there is plenty to admire. Interestingly, he also claims that his 1996s are clearly more successful than his 1997s. He believes that 1996, not 1997, will be considered the great classic vintage for the villages of Barolo and Monforte d'Alba. The 1995s are soundly made.

The elegant, medium ruby-colored 1998 Barbaresco (from the vineyards in Treiso) is a more austere version of the 1997. Aromas of dried herbs, balsam wood, flowers, and cherries are followed by a medium-bodied Barbaresco with good density but a slightly angular, austere finish. Anticipated maturity: 2004–2012. The single-vineyard 1998 Barbaresco Bricco (750 cases produced) boasts a deep ruby color as well as a tight but promising nose of spicy new oak, black cherries, and blackberries. It is powerful, full-bodied, and high in tannin. Anticipated maturity: 2006–2015.

The dark ruby-colored 1998 Barolo is a tough-textured, backward effort showing a certain austerity along with notes of minerals, earth, pepper, and truffles. Red fruit notes emerge as the wine sits in the glass, but this is a decidedly stern, backward, atypical 1998. Anticipated maturity: 2006–2018. Cesare's single-vineyard 1998 Barolo Ornato (from a Serralunga vineyard) offers a more explosive perfume of sweet black cherries intermixed with blackberries, new saddle leather, smoke, and vanilla. It possesses outstanding purity, full body, fine density, and a boatload of tannin. However, the glycerin, extract, and concentration are more than adequate to balance out the wine's muscle. Anticipated maturity: 2007–2025.

Pio Cesare's 1997 Barbaresco Bricco is a dense, rich, full-bodied, powerful effort with evidence of *barrique* but wonderfully sweet black cherry and raspberry fruit with notes of spice box, fruitcake, soy, and licorice. Give it 1–2 years of cellaring and drink it over the following 12–15 years. The 1997 Barolo was performing well prior to bottling. Broad, sweet, fat flavors with considerable glycerin and alcohol are present in this full-bodied, structured, powerful, muscular Barolo. Anticipated maturity: 2003–2020. The spectacular 1997 Barolo Ornato (1,000 cases, produced only in the finest vintages), from a Serralunga vineyard planted next to Bruno Giacosa's famous parcel of Falletto di Serralunga, offers a terrific fragrance of raspberries, cherries, smoke, leather, and toasty oak. There are huge quantities of glycerin, a stupendous finish, and gorgeous purity as well as overall symmetry. This 1997 will require 1–2 years of cellaring but will keep for 2–3 decades.

The 1996 Barbaresco is more tannic, with a firmer, more muscular style, but not the charm of the 1995. The wine is concentrated, with dense fruit, and plenty of black cherries, leather, smoke, and tobacco nuances. Anticipated maturity: now–2016. The classic 1996 Barolo is potentially outstanding. Its dark ruby color is accompanied by a smoky, black cherry–scented nose with roasted herb, nuts, and mineral nuances. Full-bodied, spicy, long, and needing 1–2 years of cellaring, this should prove uncommonly long-lived. Anticipated maturity: 2004–2022. The excellent 1995 Barbaresco is one of the vintage's most delicious wines. A smoky, black cherry, and leathery-scented nose is followed by excellent ripeness, medium to full body, moderate tannin, an excellent texture, and a long, spicy finish. Anticipated maturity: now–2011. The dark ruby/garnet-colored 1995 Barolo exhibits a spicy, aromatic nose with scents of earth, dried herbs, leather, and sweet black fruits. In the mouth, it is powerful, with excellent richness, moderate tannin, and a rustic but impressively endowed finish.

MICHELE CHIARLO

1997 Barolo Cannubi   E   87

This internationally styled, dark ruby/purple-colored Barolo displays noticeable new oak along with an elegant, stylish, medium-bodied personality without a great deal of regional typicity. However, it is well made, with sweet tannin, excellent concentration, and plenty of black fruits intermixed with wood, smoke, and spice. The wine's tannin as well as firmness suggest that 1–2 years of cellaring will be beneficial. Anticipated maturity: 2004–2015.

QUINTO CHIONETTI & FIGLIO

1999 Dolcetto di Dogliani Briccolero	C	90
1999 Dolcetto di Dogliani San Luigi	C	89

This Dolcetto specialist never disappoints, as evidenced by these beautifully made 1999s. Chionetti's 1999 Dolcetto di Dogliani San Luigi's dark ruby/purple color is accompanied by a sexy, sweet perfume of espresso, chocolate, almonds, and copious quantities of berry fruit. Lush, layered, fat, and voluptuous, it is all that a Dolcetto should be. Savor it over the next 2–3 years as these wines do not improve in the bottle. Even better, the 1999 Dolcetto di Dogliani Briccolero is a 4,000-case *cuvée* offering a saturated ruby/purple color, medium to full body, and compelling levels of chocolate-tinged black cherry fruit. It is a big, chewy, fleshy, pure effort with admirable vibrancy. When are American consumers going to discover Dolcetto's appeal, particularly when drunk in its first 2–3 years of life?

F.LLI CIGLIUTI

1998 Barbaresco Serraboella	D	90
1997 Barbaresco Serraboella	D	89
1996 Barbaresco Serraboella	D	?
1998 Barbera d'Alba Serraboella	C	88

A complex bouquet of mushrooms, balsa wood, dried red and black fruits, cedar, and black cherries jumps from the glass of the medium to dark plum-colored 1998 Barbaresco Serraboella. Sexy, aromatic, and rich, with a lush, concentrated, tannic finish, it should be drunk over the next 5–6 years. It represents a classic example of the fragrant, harmonious, silky-textured 1998 vintage. The 1998 Barbera d'Alba Serraboella exhibits a dark ruby/purple color as well as a sweet nose of blackberry, raspberry, and toasty oak aromas. Medium-bodied, plump, and fleshy, with enough tangy acidity to provide definition and vibrancy, it can be drunk over the next 2–3 years. Cigliuti's 1997 Barbaresco Serraboella reveals a lighter, medium ruby color, excellent rose petal, cedar, black cherry, and raspberry-scented aromatics, opulent, medium-bodied flavors, moderate tannin, and good acidity. Still young, it is capable of 8 years of evolution.

I had trouble with the only sample I tasted of the 1996 Barbaresco Serraboella, which seemed to possess vegetal tannin and a hard, tough texture. The color is a healthy dark ruby/purple. While the wine exhibits sweet fruit on the attack, it becomes narrow, with greenness and astringency dominating its personality. Given the high quality of this producer, I look forward to tasting another bottle.

DOMENICO CLERICO

1998 Barbera d'Alba Trevigne	C	90
1998 Barolo Ciabot Mentin Ginestra	E	93+
1997 Barolo Ciabot Mentin Ginestra	E	94
1996 Barolo Ciabot Mentin Ginestra	E	90
1995 Barolo Ciabot Mentin Ginestra	E	91
1998 Barolo Mosconi Percristina Riserva	E	(92–93+)
1997 Barolo Mosconi Percristina Riserva	E	93+
1996 Barolo Mosconi Percristina Riserva	E	95
1995 Barolo Mosconi Percristina Riserva	E	92

1998 Barolo Pajana	E	92+
1997 Barolo Pajana	E	93
1996 Barolo Pajana	E	94
1995 Barolo Pajana	E	90+
1998 Langhe Arte	E	89

For almost two decades, Domenico Clerico has been turning out some of Piedmont's most compelling wines. Another modernist who utilizes rotary fermenters, short macerations, and various percentages of new oak, ranging from a minimum of 20% for his Ginestra to 100% for his Mosconi Percristina Riserva (a *cuvée* named after his daughter, who, tragically, died at the age of seven), Clerico's wines could be called the Pauillac premier crus of Monforte d'Alba. They are structured, large-scaled, concentrated Barolos with plenty of muscle and tannin. Moreover, they will handsomely repay two decades of cellaring. I am just finishing my still beautiful 1982s, a very good but less concentrated and lighter vintage than any of Piedmont's recent vintages (1996, 1997, 1998, and 1999). Clerico's wines possess enough character to be accessible young but still require cellaring. These are wines of extraordinary richness, amazing aromatics, and sensual personalities that satiate both the hedonistic and intellectual senses. In general, the 1995s are the most forward and evolved, the 1996s the most muscular and structured, and the 1997s off the chart in terms of their thickness, exoticism, and sumptuousness. While less fragrant than some of their peers, Clerico's 1998s are classic, backward, well-structured wines with superb depth, purity, and overall balance.

Clerico's proprietary offering, the 1998 Langhe Arte, is a blend of 90% Nebbiolo, 5% Barbera, and 5% Cabernet Sauvignon aged for 20 months in 100% new French oak. Internationally styled, it reveals abundant aromas of toasty new oak, red currant as well as cherry fruit, leather, cedar, and spice box. Medium-bodied and elegant, it is best drunk during its first 5–7 years of life. More sumptuous, the dazzling 1998 Barbera d'Alba Trevigne boasts explosive fruit, full body, power, and super-concentration, as well as finesse, elegance, and overall balance. This is a gorgeously rendered Barbera to enjoy over the next 3–4 years. The dense ruby/purple-colored 1998 Barolo Pajana reveals copious new oak along with lead pencil, black cherry, blackberry, licorice, and earth aromas. This structured, powerful, full-bodied, chewy wine requires 1–2 years of cellaring. Anticipated maturity: 2003–2016. The superextracted, blockbuster 1998 Barolo Ciabot Mentin Ginestra assaults the palate with a blast of broodingly tannic, super-concentrated black cherry and raspberry fruit infused with minerals, new oak, licorice, and truffles. With a huge mid-palate as well as an astonishingly long finish, it is not yet ready to drink. Anticipated maturity: 2006–2020. The 1998 Barolo Mosconi Percristina Riserva reveals aromas of sweet black fruit intermixed with new oak, blueberry, flowers, and an underlying minerality. Full-bodied, powerful, deep, and chewy, this youthful, backward 1998 rivals the spectacular efforts produced in 1996 and 1997. Anticipated maturity: 2003–2018.

Clerico's saturated purple-colored 1997 Barolo Pajana offers a classic bouquet (reminiscent of a cross between Mouton and Lafite Rothschild) of cedar wood, cassis, licorice, lead pencil, and mineral scents. The wine possesses abundant quantities of black fruit, tar, truffle, and cigar box flavors. A huge, monstrous Barolo, it is not one of the most forward 1997s, so 1–2 years of cellaring are recommended. Anticipated maturity: 2004–2020. The 1997 Barolo Ciabot Mentin Ginestra is a fearsomely powerful, tannic, ultraconcentrated, explosively rich wine with a mid-palate in which one could get lost. A saturated ruby/purple color is accompanied by scents of lead pencil, cedar, black fruits, smoke, earth, and vanilla. Massive richness, monster extract, sweet tannin, and a blockbuster finish characterize this dazzling, 20–25-year wine. Anticipated maturity: 2005–2025. Clerico's 1997 Barolo Mosconi Percristina Riserva is the most tannic and backward of this group of unevolved, massive 1997s. A dense ruby/purple color is followed by aromas of new saddle leather, licorice, black cherries, and the telltale rose petals. More closed aromatically than its siblings, with huge flavors, copious glycerin, as well as abundant tannin, this full-bodied, loaded 1997 requires an addi-tional 3–4 years of cellaring . . . unusual for the exotic, over-the-top style of many 1997s. An-ticipated maturity: 2007–2030.

The 1996s are spectacularly powerful, rich, concentrated wines. The 1996 Barolo Ciabot Mentin Ginestra possesses a deep, dark purple color, and a nose of overripe plums, cherries, and cassis. Rich and full-bodied, with admirable glycerin, subtle oak, and licorice/floral nuances, it is a large-scaled yet beautifully balanced Barolo to drink between 2004–2018. The striking resemblance of the 1996 Barolo Pajana to a top-class Pomerol is unmistakable. This massive wine possesses fabulous purity of fruit and toast that complements the wine's highly concentrated black cherry/chocolaty personality. Dense and layered, with consider-able viscosity, low acidity, and moderate tannin in the impressive, long finish, it will be at its best between 2006–2020. The profound 1996 Barolo Mosconi Percristina Riserva ex-hibits a black raspberry liqueur–like nose. As it sits in the glass, notes of cherries, cassis, toast, and smoke emerge. Massive, powerful, chewy, unctuously textured, and long, with sub-tle oak and immense fruit concentration, this spectacular Barolo should age effortlessly for 15–16 years.

The 1995 Barolo Ciabot Mentin Ginestra offers a knockout nose of tobacco, mint, dried red fruits, balsa wood, and cherry liqueur. There are tons of glycerin, low acidity, medium to full body, and striking richness and lushness. It is about as sexy a 1995 Barolo as readers will find. I would opt for drinking it over the next 4–5 years as it is already irresistible. The 1995 Barolo Pajana is a synthesis in style between a grand cru Burgundy and a first growth Bor-deaux. It is slightly less aromatic than the 1995 Ciabot Mentin Ginestra, with a saturated ruby/purple color, lush black raspberry and cherry fruit, and a touch of black currants. The medium- to full-bodied, fruit-driven, low-acid 1995 Pajana should be consumed over the next 8 years. The amazing 1995 Barolo Mosconi Percristina Riserva is the richest, most complete of these offerings. This debut vintage offers up kirsch, Chinese black tea, flowers, licorice, and subtle spicy new oak. Amazingly rich and full-bodied, with terrific purity, sym-metry, and length, it can be drunk now but should be even better with 1–2 years of cellaring; it will keep for 10 years.

ELVIO COGNO

1999	Barbera d'Alba Bricco dei Merli	C	89
1998	Barbera d'Alba Bricco dei Merli	C	90
1996	Barolo Ravera	E	90
2000	Dolcetto d'Alba	B	89
1999	Dolcetto d'Alba	B	90
1999	Langhe Rosso Montegrilli	D	90
1998	Langhe Rosso Montegrilli	D	86

A topflight Barolo producer, Cogno also makes excellent Dolcetto and Barbera, as well as a superb proprietary *barrique*-aged blend of Barbera and Nebbiolo called Langhe Rosso Mon-tegrilli. The black/purple-colored 2000 Dolcetto d'Alba possesses extremely powerful, con-centrated, monolithic, chunky, dense, full-blast flavors. If a few additional nuances emerge from behind the mass of fruit and body, this wine will merit an outstanding score. However, readers need to keep in mind that these wines rarely improve, so even this offering requires consumption during its first 3–5 years of life. Cogno's 1999 Dolcetto d'Alba is an excellent example of this tasty varietal. An opaque purple color is accompanied by chewy, berry fla-vors, excellent purity, not much complexity, but mouth-staining levels of richness and inten-sity. It is a fruit-dominated blockbuster to drink over the next 3–4 years. The spicy, fragrant, medium-bodied 1999 Barbera d'Alba Bricco dei Merli exhibits black cherry fruit mixed with strawberry jam, earth, and spicy oak. Pure and fleshy, with a ripe, opulent finish, it will be at its finest before 2007. The most serious, sexiest, and complex of the 1999s is the Langhe

Rosso Montegrilli. This smoky, medium- to full-bodied wine offers scents and flavors of toast, plums, cherry jam, and tobacco. Round, velvety-textured, and seamless, it is a hedonistic turn-on. Enjoy it over the next 3–4 years.

The dark ruby/purple-colored 1998 Barbera d'Alba Bricco dei Merli is made in a sexy, opulent, forward style, with sweet, jammy strawberry and blackberry flavors, good underlying acidity, fat, and density, and a chunky, spicy finish. It should drink well for 4–5 years. Readers seeking a more internationally styled wine will enjoy the 1998 Langhe Rosso Montegrilli. It offers abundant quantities of spicy new oak, sweet, currant/cherry flavors, and toast. Medium-bodied, with good density and purity, it does not reveal the Piedmontese soul of Cogno's other offerings, but it is a well-made effort. Serious connoisseurs will be turned on by the complexity, austerity, and nobility of the 1996 Barolo Ravera. Its dark plum color is accompanied by a sweet nose of smoked herbs, black cherries, minerals, spice, and tobacco. Complex and full-bodied, with outstanding richness and moderately high tannin, this 1996 is approachable but promises to be even better with an additional 1–2 years of cellaring. Anticipated maturity: 2004–2020.

PODERI COLLA

1997 Barbaresco Tenuta Roncaglia	D	89
1996 Barolo Bussia	D	88

This winery has produced forward efforts in both 1996 and 1997. The 1997 Barbaresco Tenuta Roncaglia exhibits a medium ruby color with garnet at the edge. A classic nose of rose petals, strawberry jam, tobacco, and spice emerges gracefully from the glass. Rich, savory, and fleshy, with sweet tannin, well-integrated acidity, and a moderately long finish, this 1997 should drink well for 10 years. The 1996 Barolo Bussia reveals telltale aromas of cedar wood, tobacco, and dried herbs, along with earthy black cherry fruit notes. A supple texture, admirable concentration, medium body, and noticeable tannin in the finish result in an overall impression of a sweet, precocious, up-front Barolo to enjoy over the next 10 years.

ALDO CONTERNO

1998 Barolo Bussia Soprana	E	(90–92)
1997 Barolo Bussia Soprana	E	91+
1996 Barolo Bussia Soprana	E	92
1995 Barolo Bussia Soprana	E	88
1998 Barolo Cicala	EE	(87–89)
1997 Barolo Cicala	EE	91+
1996 Barolo Cicala	EE	94+
1995 Barolo Cicala	EE	87
1998 Barolo Vigna Colonnello	EE	(90–92)
1997 Barolo Vigna Colonnello	EE	91+
1996 Barolo Vigna Colonnello	EE	92+
1995 Barolo Gran Bussia Riserva	EEE	93
1999 Dolcetto d'Alba	B	88
1998 Langhe Rosso Quartetto	D	89

The quintessential gentleman, 70+-year-old Aldo Conterno, the brother of Giovanni Conterno, is one of Piedmont's unapologetic traditionalists. His portfolio includes three single-vineyard Barolos as well as a proprietary red, Langhe Rosso Quartetto, that is a blend of Nebbiolo, Merlot, Cabernet Sauvignon, and Barbera. In great vintages, a limited-production Barolo Gran Bussia Riserva is also produced. The classic and long-lived Barolos represent an enlightened traditional style, often needing 5–6 years to reveal their full character. Conterno, although successful in 1995, produced brilliant wines in 1996, 1997, and 1998. I feel that all of Conterno's 1996s possess greater density, concentration, and overall potential compared to his 1997s, which are nonetheless superb. Moreover, his 1998s appear to be great classics.

Conterno's glorious red wine offerings include the 1999 Dolcetto d'Alba. Aromas of black fruits and violets jump from the glass of this deep, richly fruity yet elegant, round wine. It will provide delicious drinking over the next several years.

The dark ruby/purple-colored 1998 Langhe Rosso Quartetto offers an intense bouquet of black cherry jam, currants, oak, earth, and spice. Dense, medium- to full-bodied, round, and richly fruity, it is meant to be consumed over the next 5–6 years. The dark ruby/garnet color 1998 Barolo Cicala possesses the highest acidity, least weight, and most elegance of the three Barolos. Notes of soy, Asian spices, red cherries, minerals, and herbs are found in this spicy, medium-bodied, stylish, moderately tannic 1998. Anticipated maturity: 2003–2014. The most textured, powerful, and concentrated of this trio is the 1998 Barolo Vigna Colonnello. Offering aromas and flavors of roasted coffee, new saddle leather, black cherry jam, underbrush, earth, and spice box, this tightly structured, full-bodied, dense, impressively extracted wine needs cellaring. Anticipated maturity: 2006–2020. Similarly styled, the 1998 Barolo Bussia Soprana exhibits moderately intense aromas of cedar, spice box, licorice, tar, and cherry jam. This full-bodied, powerful, concentrated 1998 possesses good acidity, excellent cleanliness, and a moderately tannic finish. Anticipated maturity: 2005–2020.

The dense ruby/garnet-colored, tightly knit 1997 Barolo Bussia Soprana offers notions of earth, cherries, and balsa wood. Full-bodied, with good acidity (particularly for the vintage), moderately high tannin, and a firm finish, it possesses plenty of power, although not as much as 1996. Consume this outstanding effort between 2006–2020. The full-bodied, dark garnet-colored 1997 Barolo Vigna Colonnello displays licorice, spice box, and kirsch characteristics as well as more noticeable acidity. As the wine sits in the glass, aromas of soy, herbs, and incense emerge. It is a tightly framed, full-bodied, powerful yet close-to-the-vest offering. Anticipated maturity: 2006–2018. The 1997 Barolo Cicala (from a parcel of vines further up the slope from Colonnello) offers a distinctive bouquet of soy, fresh sardines, earth, cedar, and tar. In the mouth, leather notes are added to this mix. It was my least favorite of the trio, perhaps because the tannin dominates the wine's back end, giving it a more compressed character. Aldo Conterno explained that this wine always takes longer to come around than his other crus and frequently possesses a mineral/steely framework compared to the Colonnello or the Barolo from Bussia Soprana. Anticipated maturity: 2005–2020.

I tasted the three single-vineyard Barolos in 1996. The 1996 Barolo Vigna Colonnello is very aromatic, offering scents of melted asphalt, cedar, tobacco, spice box, and assorted red and black fruits. Following a soft entry, the immense richness and fleshy, full-bodied power of this wine became apparent. The finish offers considerable tannic clout and power. Anticipated maturity: 2005–2022. The dense ruby/plum-colored 1996 Barolo Bussia Soprana exhibits a promising, classic Nebbiolo/Barolo bouquet of tobacco, cigar box, rose petals, melted tar, and copious quantities of sweet black cherry fruit. Although impressively full-bodied, powerful, tannic, and dense, it is oh, so young and backward. Patience . . . please! Anticipated maturity: 2010–2025. The stunning aromatics of the 1996 Barolo Cicala offer everything found in the Bussia Soprana, but even more intensity and fireworks. Full-bodied and muscular, it possesses high tannin as well as extract and a mouth-searing acidity that gives the wine both great precision as well as a frightfully backward character. A superdense, extracted, and rich Barolo, it will not be ready to drink for a decade. Discipline in the form of cellaring is definitely required for this fabulous Barolo. Anticipated maturity: 2012–2030.

The dark ruby-colored 1995 Barolo Cicala possesses a muted but promising nose of spice box, cedar, tobacco, and cherry fruit. It exhibits good ripeness, medium body, high tannin, and noticeable yet subtle oak. This very good 1995 can be drunk now as well as over the next 4–5 years. The denser 1995 Barolo Bussia Soprana displays a more saturated ruby color. The rich, cedary, smoky, tobacco, and tar-scented nose is classic Nebbiolo. Excellent, with a layered texture, and a rich, spicy, austere, moderately tannic finish, it is accessible enough to be drunk now but should evolve nicely for 3–4 years.

The limited-production Gran Bussia was made only in 1970, 1971, 1974, 1978, 1982, 1985, 1988, 1989, 1990, and 1995. In all likelihood, it will be made in 1996, 1997, 1998, and 1999. Seventy percent of this wine comes from the Romirasco vineyard and the rest from Cicala and Colonnello. It is aged for three years in *foudres* and two years in bottle prior to being released. The dense garnet/ruby-colored 1995 Barolo Gran Bussia offers classic scents of rose petals, melted asphalt, kirsch, and dried herbs. Sweet, full-bodied, and rich, it is a terrific effort for the vintage, ranking alongside the fabulous 1995 Monfortino produced by Giacomo Conterno. The Gran Bussia possesses ripe tannin as well as a huge finish. Anticipated maturity: now–2020.

GIACOMO CONTERNO

1996 Barolo Cascina Francia	EE	88+?
1995 Barolo Cascina Francia	EE	92
1994 Barolo Cascina Francia	EE	90
1993 Barolo Cascina Francia	EE	91
1998 Barolo Monfortino	EEE	(93–95+)
1997 Barolo Monfortino	EEE	(91–94)
1996 Barolo Monfortino	EEE	(89–91)
1995 Barolo Monfortino	EEE	(94–95)
1993 Barolo Monfortino	EEE	92
1998 Dolcetto d'Alba Cascina Francia	B	87

Visiting Giovanni Conterno, a stern, initially humorless man who warms up the longer one spends in the cellars, and his son Roberto offers a fascinating view of the traditional school of Piedmontese winemaking. Seventy-three-year-old Giovanni has five children, and it is his youngest, Roberto, who now does most of the work in the cellars. His two Barolo *cuvées*, Cascina Francia and Monfortino, come from hillside vineyards in Serralunga d'Alba. The regular Barolo *cuvée*, the Cascina Francia, is actually the same wine as the Monfortino, at least in theory. However, there are differences in the way in which they are vinified, and they are segregated in the cellars at an early age. As a general rule, Monfortino spends more time on the skins and appears to be a selection of particular lots. It is also bottled much later than the Cascina Francia, which tends to be bottled within four years of the vintage, the Monfortino being bottled between 7–10 years of the vintage. For example, the 1993 Barolo Monfortino was bottled in 2000. These wines are often hard to understand in their youth since they do not have the color saturation of most modern-day reds and seem unyielding, austere, tannic, and hard. Take it from someone who knows better. I have been buying these wines since the late sixties and still have a few bottles of the majestic 1964 and 1967 that are just beginning to tire. The 1970 and 1971 remain relatively young wines, with the 1971 Monfortino one of the most prodigious Barolos anyone could pour over the palate. Surprisingly, this estate does not always produce the finest wines in what are considered to be Barolo's top vintages. In my tastings, the 1995 Barolo Monfortino appeared to be one of their great efforts and significantly richer and more complex than the 1996 or 1997. The 1998, which will not be released for 8–10 years, is another profound vintage for Conterno, but both Roberto and Giovanni think 2000 is their finest vintage in ten years.

The 1998 Dolcetto d'Alba Cascina Francia, a rustic, full-bodied, powerful example with a deep ruby color as well as considerable berry fruit intermixed with minerals, smoke, dried herbs, and fresh almonds. Drink it over the next 2–3 years.

Probably because of its recent bottling, the 1996 Barolo Cascina Francia was subdued, but it does not appear to have the depth of a great vintage for this estate. The color is medium ruby with pink at the edge. Notes of balsa wood, spice box, tar, and rosewood reluctantly emerge from the aromatics. In the mouth, flavors of spice and leather compete with dusty cherry fruit in a tannic, austere, closed, steely style. I do not find enough sweetness, glycerin, or extract to make this profound, but it is very good to excellent. Anticipated maturity: 2008–2025. The youngest and densest of the current Barolo releases is the 1995 Barolo Cascina Francia. It possesses classic Nebbiolo traits of melted asphalt, cedar wood, sweet cherries, rose petals, and truffles. Full-bodied, deep, and chewy, with an intriguing earthy smokiness, this tannic, impressively concentrated, and well-endowed Barolo can be drunk now but will be even better with an additional 2–4 years of cellaring; it will last for 15+ years. The 1994 Barolo Cascina Francia reveals more amber in its ruby/garnet color. Scents of Chinese black tea, cedar wood, smoked duck, soy, licorice, and tobacco jump from the glass of this aromatic Barolo. It is more forward than the 1993, with sweet, round, old-style flavors, dusty tannin, and wonderful glycerin and concentration. It should drink well for 12–15 years.

The 1993 Barolo Cascina Francia exhibits a dark ruby color with purple nuances, in addition to aromas of roasted herbs, tobacco, tar, kirsch, and dried cherries as well as some volatile acidity. In the mouth, it is dense, medium- to full-bodied, with good concentration and dusty tannin in the finish. This 1993 Barolo can be drunk now but promises to evolve for another 15–20 years. The light garnet/ruby-colored 1993 Barolo Monfortino is undoubtedly the wine of the vintage for this challenging year. Like all Conterno wines, it was bottled without fining or filtration, thus preserving its full *terroir* and varietal characteristics. It boasts a knockout aromatic profile of rose petals, tar, new saddle leather, sweet, jammy black cherries, licorice, and raspberries, decent acidity, sweet tannin, copious alcohol, wonderful density, a fleshy texture, and beautiful harmony as well as elegance. It can be drunk now and over the next 15 years. Look for this effort to be one of the great sleeper wines of Piedmont given the fact that most 1993 Barolos are austere and hard-edged.

One of the great Barolo Monfortinos is the 1995, which I hope will be bottled and released before 2005. This was the finest wine I tasted in Conterno's cellars (everything between current releases and 2000). Significantly more concentrated than their 1996 Monfortino, it represents a tiny crop because of hail damage. The wine reveals the essence of licorice, kirsch, smoke, red currant, and cherries, as well as the telltale rose petal and licorice notes. It is ripe and full-bodied, with sweet fruit, copious glycerin, and a seamless finish that lasts for nearly 45 seconds. As the wine sat in the glass, it became even more floral and concentrated. There is abundant tannin, and the wine will undoubtedly taste more structured when it is released. Anticipated maturity: 2010–2040. To reiterate, the 1996 Barolo Monfortino is not as concentrated as the 1995, nor as rich or complex as the 1993. Nevertheless, it is an elegant, stylish, medium-weight effort with less flesh and more austerity than the other offerings. I know that does not make sense given the vintage conditions, but it is what has been produced by Giovanni and Roberto Conterno. The 1997 Barolo Monfortino appears to be a sexy, atypically forward wine for this estate. Dense and sexy, with abundant glycerin, and lush, seamless, black cherry, kirsch, smoke, tar, and meat-like flavors presented in a full-bodied, concentrated style. While much denser than the 1996, it is not as complex and concentrated as the 1995. Anticipated maturity: 2007–2022.

I also tasted the 1998 and 1999 Monfortinos, but they are at least 7–10 years away from release. Both look to be fabulous efforts that should easily surpass the 1997 as well as the lighter 1996. Tasted from a gigantic *foudre* (where the entire Monfortino *cuvée* is sitting), the 1998 Barolo Monfortino is a ruby-colored wine with a forward, evolved style (typical of the vintage) and a sweet bouquet of rose water, tar, truffles, minerals, and cherry fruit. Full-bodied but beautifully balanced, it is delicious enough to drink now, although that would be considered heresy in these cellars.

Let's hope the style at this winery never changes as it produces the quintessential traditional Barolo (along with those of Bruno Giacosa and a handful of other Piedmontese producers). In a world where immediate gratification is often the holy grail, the reality is that most consumers will not wait ten years for the wine to be released and another 10 years for it to hit its peak of maturity. For the few who do, the rewards are immeasurable. The wines produced by Giovanni Conterno are monuments to Nebbiolo as well as to the glory of Piedmont.

PAOLO CONTERNO

1998	Barolo Ginestra	E	(88–90)
1997	Barolo Ginestra	E	88+

Another Conterno from Monforte d'Alba (although less renowned than Giovanni and Aldo), Paolo's dark ruby/purple-colored 1998 Barolo Ginestra exhibits aromas and flavors of soy, balsa wood, dried cherries, tobacco, and herbs. Subtle notions of new oak in the aromatics suggest that at least a portion of this *cuvée* saw some *barrique* treatment. Deep, full-bodied, and opulent, with sweet tannin, it should drink well young (atypical for this producer and region). Anticipated maturity: 2003–2015. The dark ruby/purple-colored 1997 Barolo Ginestra is a traditionally made wine with considerable tannin as well as subtle evidence of new oak. Dense, ripe, and surprisingly tannic, it should be drunk between 2005–2015.

CONTERNO FANTINO

1999	Barbera d'Alba Vignota	C	87
1998	Barbera d'Alba Vignota	C	90
1998	Barolo Sorì Ginestra	E	92
1997	Barolo Sorì Ginestra	E	92+
1996	Barolo Sorì Ginestra	E	92
1995	Barolo Sorì Ginestra	E	85?
1998	Barolo Vigna del Gris	E	90
1997	Barolo Vigna del Gris	E	93
1996	Barolo Vigna del Gris	E	90
1995	Barolo Vigna del Gris	E	87?
2000	Dolcetto d'Alba Bricco Bastia	C	87
1999	Dolcetto d'Alba Bricco Bastia	C	89
1998	Monprà	D	90
1997	Monprà	D	90
1996	Monprà	D	89

Usually a reliable producer, Conterno Fantino, located in the village of Monforte d'Alba, has a mixed portfolio in 1995, 1996, 1997, and 1998. While the 1996s and 1998s are successful, both 1995 Barolos are tannic, with austere personalities, and the 1997s are noticeably oaky and made in an international style that submerged some of the Nebbiolo character behind a veneer of heavy toasty wood.

Conterno Fantino's 2000 Dolcetto d'Alba Bricco Bastia is a lovely, fruity, soft wine offering berries, cherries, cola, and earth in its uncomplicated but pleasing aromatics as well as flavors. Medium-bodied, with fine purity, it is best consumed over the next several years. Tangier and lighter-weight, with notes of tomato skins, strawberries, cherries, and a touch of oak, is the well-made 1999 Barbera d'Alba Vignota. Neither a blockbuster nor a big, oaky Piedmontese Barbera, it is a stylish, restrained effort to enjoy over the next 3–4 years. The 1999 Dolcetto Bricco Bastia may deserve an outstanding rating. The charge against Dolcetti, particularly from a top vintage such as 1999, is that they do not possess a great deal of complexity, even though they deliver a boatload of hedonistic fireworks. This opaque purple-colored, dense, chewy, full-bodied Dolcetto cuts a gloriously robust swath across the palate. Powerful and super-concentrated, it is as hedonistic a Dolcetto d'Alba as readers will find. Drink it over the next 3–4 years. A blend of equal parts *barrique*-aged Nebbiolo and Barbera, the outstanding 1998 Monprà exhibits a dark ruby color with purple hues. A sweet perfume of red and black fruits, smoke, licorice, and flowers jumps from the glass. On the palate, it is Burgundy-like in its medium-bodied, plush, round, beautifully pure style with excellent texture. Not a long-distance runner, it should be consumed over the next 3–4 years.

Two outstanding efforts from Conterno Fantino, the 1998 Barolos combine the best of the traditional school with the modern, enlightened approach to making young Barolo somewhat accessible. The 1998 Barolo Vigna del Gris offers a deep ruby/garnet color, medium to full body, and a sweet nose of lead pencil, new oak, black cherries, and rose petals. Elegant, powerful, beautifully harmonious, and well delineated, with a moderately tannic finish, it will be at its finest between 2003–2016. Even better is the compelling 1998 Barolo Sorì Ginestra. A dense, full-bodied, super-extracted, complex, multilayered Barolo, it exhibits aromas and flavors of tar, camphor, black cherry liqueur, smoke, minerals, and subtle new oak. Full and velvety-textured, with a 40-second finish, this large-scaled yet immensely elegant wine will drink beautifully between 2004–2018.

Another fine effort is the complex, medium- to full-bodied 1998 Barbera d'Alba Vignota, which offers superb black cherry fruit tinged with hints of tomato skins, fresh almonds, and chocolate. With extravagant ripeness as well as a complex, Médoc-like scent of lead pencil shavings, this spicy, dense, fruity Barbera can be drunk over the next 5–6 years. An outstanding blend of equal parts Barbera and Nebbiolo, the 1997 Monprà reveals the vintage's opulent personality. Opaque ruby/purple-colored, with a big, smoky, internationally styled bouquet of black fruits and new oak, it possesses admirable intensity, loads of glycerin, low acidity, and a spicy, chewy finish. Drink it over the next decade.

Conterno Fantino's 1997 Barolo Vigna del Gris displays beautifully sweet black fruits in its aromatic profile and huge, concentrated, full-bodied flavors with enormous muscle, amazing glycerin levels, and exceptional purity. This super-concentrated effort is just beginning to reveal the telltale Nebbiolo/Barolo traits of tar, rose petals, and sweet black cherry fruit. It should easily last for two decades, although I doubt it will ever close down. The 1997 Barolo Sorì Ginestra exhibits a deep ruby/purple color in addition to complex aromas of tobacco smoke and gloriously sweet, jammy cherry liqueur. Ripe, opulent, and full-bodied, with huge amounts of glycerin and extract, yet high tannin in the finish, this 1997 needs 2–3 years of cellaring and should keep for 20+ years. These are superimpressive Barolos.

The 1996 vintage is very successful. The ruby/purple-colored, mineral-dominated 1996 Barolo Sorì Ginestra offers spicy oak in the nose, as well as attractive black cherry fruit intertwined with prunes and toasty oak. With moderate levels of glycerin, full body, high tannin, excellent purity as well as superb richness and extract, this layered wine requires cellaring. Anticipated maturity: 2005–2020. The opaque purple-colored 1996 Barolo Vigna del Gris is dense, with considerable evidence of new oak, powerful, muscular, black currant/cherry flavors, as well as less minerality and earth than in the Sorì Ginestra. It is a huge wine of great intensity. Anticipated maturity: 2004–2020. Although the 1996 Monprà *vino da tavola* (equal parts Barbera and Nebbiolo) is tannic, it is an impressively endowed effort with notes of toasty vanilla, cherries, dried herbs, leather, and spice. Dense, huge, and full-bodied but closed, it should drink well for a decade or more.

The 1995 Barolo Sorì Ginestra reveals cedar and plumlike fruit in the nose but is intensely vegetal and hard and lacks length. The darker ruby-colored 1995 Barolo Vigna del Gris is astringently tannic, extremely compressed, and exceptionally earthy. With airing, cedar, dried herbs, spicy oak, and cherries emerge, but this wine is difficult to evaluate. Anticipated maturity: now–2012.

LUIGI COPPO & FIGLI

1997	Alter Ego	D	87
1999	Barbera d'Asti Camp du Rouss	D	88
1998	Barbera d'Asti Camp du Rouss	D	88

1998 Barbera d'Asti Pomorosso	D	92
1997 Barbera d'Asti Pomorosso	D	90

It is unusual for a Piedmontese winery to accept advice from someone outside the region. The renowned Umbrian oenologist Riccardo Cotarella has been a consultant at Coppo & Figli for several years. As a result, the wines are taking on more ripeness, texture, and complexity. The 1999 Barbera d'Asti Camp du Rouss sees 20% new oak and is bottled unfiltered. Sweet black jammy cherry and earthy aromas emerge from this supple, medium- to full-bodied, lush, sexy Barbera. Enjoy it during its first 3–5 years of life.

1998 was a fine vintage in Piedmont, although it does not appear to have the opulence and flamboyant richness found in the 1997s or the classic structure and long-lived potential of the 1996s. Nevertheless, there is a lot to like, as evidenced by Coppo's 1998 Barbera d'Asti Camp du Rouss. A very good value, this deep ruby-colored wine exhibits toasty new oak, sweet, jammy, strawberry and cherry scents, good spice, medium body, and a round, lush texture. Enjoy it over the next 3–4 years. The stunningly complex 1998 Barbera d'Asti Pomorosso (2,500 cases) was aged in French barrels, of which 80% were new, and also bottled unfiltered. This full-bodied, thick, awesomely concentrated Barbera boasts abundant quantities of black fruit, licorice, tomato skin, and spice box scents. Powerful, rich, and concentrated, it has completely soaked up its exposure to new oak, something the better Barberas seem to do with surprising ease. Drink it over the next 4–5 years. The more ambitiously styled 1997 Barbera d'Asti Pomorosso (13,500 bottles produced) is aged in French oak, of which 80% is new. It exhibits more density and oak in addition to gorgeous, full-bodied, concentrated flavors offering up notes of smoked herbs, ripe cherry jam, plums, and spice. This rich, nicely textured, super-concentrated, moderately acidic Barbera should drink well for a decade. Coppo's proprietary red, Alter Ego, is a blend of 65% Cabernet Sauvignon, 30% Barbera, and 5% Freisa. The 1997 Alter Ego possesses red currant and cherry fruit, toasty new oak, medium body, fine ripeness, and a moderately concentrated finish. Although very good, it is not up to the quality of the two Barberas.

CORDERO DI MONTEZEMOLO

1996 Barolo	D	(90–92)
1995 Barolo	D	86
1998 Barolo Bricco Gattera	E	(87–88)
1997 Barolo Bricco Gattera	E	90+?
1998 Barolo Monfalletto	E	(87–88)
1997 Barolo Monfalletto	E	90
1996 Barolo Monfalletto	E	(91–93)
1995 Barolo Monfalletto	E	88
1998 Barolo Vigna Enrico VI	E	?
1997 Barolo Vigna Enrico VI	E	91+

I had a slight preference for this La Morra producer's 1997s over its 1998s. While the latter are attractive wines, at the prices fetched these days by top Barolos, there are more reasonably priced alternatives. The 1996s and 1995s are also fine successes. The wines of this estate are aged in oak. The Barolo Vigna Enrico VI sees 50% new *barriques* rather than the 100% for the Bricco Gattera and 33% for the Monfalletto.

The medium- to full-bodied 1998 Barolo Monfalletto exhibits scents of earth, leather, cherries, and licorice in a nicely textured, expansive style. With elegance as well as harmony, it can be drunk now and over the next 12–15 years. The dark ruby/garnet-colored 1998 Barolo Bricco Gattera is a midweight, soft, finesse-styled effort displaying some influence of *barriques*. It offers good richness on the attack but narrows in the mouth. I would not be surprised to see it close down to reveal more tannin and less early appeal than the Monfalletto (which may be due to the percentage of *barriques* utilized). Anticipated maturity: 2003–2015. I was perplexed by the closed, lean, austere 1998 Barolo Vigna Enrico VI. This *cuvée* can be a blockbuster, but the 1998 was leathery, compressed, and spartan. Judgment reserved until this wine can be retasted. Anticipated maturity: 2005–2015?

Cordero's 1997 Barolo Monfalletto is a soft, structured offering with muscular, earthy, licorice, and black cherry aromas as well as flavors. With airing, notes of chocolate, truffles, meat, and pepper emerge. Muscular and rustic but substantial and rich on the palate, it requires 1–2 years of cellaring. Anticipated maturity: 2004–2016. The dark ruby/purple-colored 1997 Barolo Bricco Gattera possesses good structure, huge tannin, and a long, powerful, rustic, intense finish. It is a difficult wine to evaluate being huge in the mouth, and the rustic, dry, astringent tannin could be troublesome with aging. It has the potential depth to be outstanding, but is the necessary balance present? Anticipated maturity: 2006–2020. The 1997 Barolo Vigna Enrico VI is the most complex and intense of this trio. The wine's dense ruby/purple color is followed by classic aromas of road tar, rose petals, leather, cedar, and black fruits. Full-bodied, dense, chewy, and powerful, with good underlying acidity as well as sweeter tannin than the Bricco Gattera, this classic should age well for two decades. Anticipated maturity: 2006–2020.

The greatness of the 1996 vintage is obvious in the saturated ruby/purple colors of Codero's wines. The knockout 1996 Barolo will require patience. It possesses a black/ruby/purple color as well as superrich blackberry and cherry flavors combined with licorice, fennel, and subtle new-*barrique* aromas. Long and dense, with mouth-searing tannin, it will be at its finest between 2007–2020. The 1996 Barolo Monfalletto reveals more mineral and new saddle leather scents in addition to black raspberries, cherries, tar, and rose petals. Extremely full-bodied, with new oak coming through in the flavors, this powerful, multidimensional, sensational Barolo should offer thrilling drinking after 4–5 years of cellaring. Anticipated maturity: 2008–2025.

The dark ruby-colored, evolved 1995 Barolo exhibits the telltale rose petal and melted road tar fragrance, along with sweet black fruit notes. Round, medium-bodied, and delicious, it can be enjoyed over the next 3–4 years. The classic 1995 Barolo Monfalletto is an old-style *vin de garde*. It reveals a dark ruby/garnet color, and an earthy nose of truffles, black cherries, tar, and dried herbs. Rich and full-bodied, with excellent concentration, it should keep for 12 years. It will be uncommonly long-lived for a 1995.

CORINO

1997	Barolo	D	89
1996	Barolo	D	87
1995	Barolo	D	88
1998	Barolo Arborina	E	92
1997	Barolo Arborina	E	90
1996	Barolo Arborina	E	(88–92)
1995	Barolo Arborina	E	90
1998	Barolo Vigna Giachini	E	91
1997	Barolo Vigna Giachini	E	94
1996	Barolo Vigna Giachini	E	90
1995	Barolo Vigna Giachini	E	89
1998	Barolo Giachini Vecchie Vigne	E	95+
1997	Barolo Giachini Vecchie Vigne	E	95
1998	Barolo Vigneto Rocche	E	90
1997	Barolo Vigneto Rocche	E	91
1996	Barolo Vigneto Rocche	E	(89–92)
1995	Barolo Vigneto Rocche	E	90

Corino is one of the increasing number of Piedmontese producers utilizing rotary fermenters. With respect to wood cooperage, no new oak is utilized for the generic Barolo, and approximately 40% new-oak casks are employed for the single-vineyard wines. 1997 marks the debut vintage for a limited-production, old-vine (40–65-year-old Nebbiolo) *cuvée* from the Giachini vineyard, the Vecchie Vigne, which emerges from a tiny parcel that sits adjacent and to the east of the famed Rocche cru. The estate also produces a Barolo Vigneto Rocche that comes from a larger cru west of Giachini. Corino's offerings tend to be velvety and forward, even in the classic vintages, so readers can imagine the decadent level of richness they reach in the exotic years. Those looking for up-front, sexy Barolos made with a Pomerol-like lushness should check out those from this La Morra producer. Little cellaring is necessary before purchasers can enjoy the immense pleasures provided by Corino's wines.

The 1998 Barolo Arborina is a sexy, in-your-face, dark ruby/garnet-colored offering with a big, sweet perfume of soy, nori (the seaweed wrapped around sushi), ripe black cherry fruit, and smoky oak. Rich, full, fat, opulent, and decadent, it is meant to be drunk now and over the next 8 years. The more structured and delineated 1998 Barolo Vigna Giachini exhibits a dark ruby color in addition to aromas of earth, coffee, black cherries, and smoke. Full-bodied, ripe, moderately tannic, and long, it will drink well for 12–15 years. The beautifully balanced, seamless, dark ruby/garnet-colored 1998 Barolo Vigneto Rocche possesses fine elegance, a terrific texture, superb purity, light to moderate tannin, low acidity, and total integration of acidity, tannin, and wood. Drink it over the next 10 years. The blockbuster 1998 Barolo Giachini Vecchie Vigne is an awesome follow-up to the spectacular 1997. This dark ruby/garnet-colored, expressive 1998 boasts a provocative bouquet of roasted espresso, chocolate, black cherry liqueur, soy, earth, herbs, leather, and cherry cough syrup. Powerful, unctuously textured flavors cascade over the palate, revealing no hard edges. It is a wine of great purity and intensity, as well as an awesome finish. This is truly spectacular Barolo. Anticipated maturity: now–2012.

The 1997 Barolo exhibits a plum/garnet color with a pink rim. Scents of black tea, cherry liqueur, and sandalwood are followed by an opulent, lush, fleshy wine with copious spice, glycerin, and alcohol as well as low acidity. It is a voluptuous, disarming Barolo to enjoy over the next 6–7 years.

As for the 1997 single-vineyard crus, the dark plum/garnet-colored 1997 Barolo Vigne Giachini offers a luxurious bouquet of black fruits, espresso, roasted herbs, and cherry liqueur. Full-bodied and lush, with layers of glycerin, multidimensional flavors, and great persistence on the palate, this is a fabulously concentrated, compelling offering to drink now and over the next 15 years. The explosive 1997 Barolo Giachini Vecchie Vigne is similarly styled, with additional levels of glycerin and flavor. The plum/garnet color is accompanied by an awesomely layered texture, great purity, abundant quantities of fruit, and complex aromatics as well as flavors. It should drink well over the next 12–15 years. Corino's 1997 Barolo Vigneto Rocche exhibits a deep garnet color in addition to a hedonistic, explosive nose of soy, resin, black cherry liqueur, balsa wood, leather, olives, and roasted meats. Stunningly concentrated, fleshy, and flamboyant, with huge glycerin levels in its low-acid, full-bodied personality, it is impossible to resist yet promises to age for 12–15 years. From a tiny yet renowned hillside vineyard, the 1997 Barolo Arborina displays the most evolved garnet color with considerable amber at the edge. Spice box, licorice, cedar wood, cherries, currants, rose petals, and framboise aromas jump from the glass of this textured, full-bodied, fat, lush wine. This is a sexy, hedonistic, seamless, herb-tinged Barolo for drinking over the next decade.

The 1996s, true to the vintage character, possess more color saturation, tannin, structure, and depth than the 1995s, but they are less evolved. The 1996 Barolo is supple and velvety but not very complex aromatically. Perhaps additional nuances will emerge with further bottle age. Spicy, ripe, and attractive, it can be consumed now and over the next 5–6 years. The dark ruby-colored 1996 Barolo Vigna Giachini offers a big, smoky, Asian spice, seaweed, and cherry liqueur–scented nose. Medium- to full-bodied, lush, and sexy, with some tannin, this delicious wine should be at its finest before 2012. The 1996 Barolo Arborina is a dense, severe, muscular effort with intriguing peppery, seaweedlike scents (or is it *garrigue*?) in the bouquet as well as rich, concentrated, black cherry fruit with subtle oak in the background. This powerful, structured, macho-styled Barolo should be drunk before 2015. The 1996 Barolo Vigneto Rocche also reveals a dried Provençal herb, peppery, smoky character reminiscent of some wines from southern France. The wine has plenty of tannin and sweet black cherry fruit intermixed with charcoal scents. Medium- to full-bodied, moderately tannic, and complex, it will be at its best before 2012.

The surprisingly evolved 1995 Barolo displays a ruby/garnet color with amber at the edge. It offers abundant black cherries in the perfumed, woodsy aromatics. Succulent, round, and gentle, this is a delicious Barolo to enjoy over the next 1–2 years. Corino's 1995 single-vineyard offerings are complex, aromatic, developed, and forward wines. The medium ruby-colored 1995 Barolo Vigna Giachini exhibits a knockout nose of sweet cinnamon, allspice, coffee, black fruits, and toast. An expansive, ripe, medium- to full-bodied, seductive effort, it is not huge but complex and disarming. Consume it over the next 2–3 years. The 1995 Barolo Arborina reveals a more deeply saturated ruby color in addition to an attractive nose of sweet black cherry liqueur, dried herbs, tobacco, and cedar scents. Lush and sexy, with medium to full body, an alluring texture, low acidity, and an evolved, complex style, it can be savored over the next 3–4 years. The 1995 Barolo Vigneto Rocche possesses a dark ruby color, medium to full body, and spicy roasted herb, tobacco, and cherry fruit aromas. As the wine sits in the glass, more of Nebbiolo's road tar and rose petal nuances emerge. Deep and rich, this outstanding 1995 can be drunk over the next 5–6 years.

MATTEO CORREGGIA

1998 Barbera d'Alba Bricco Marun	C	90
1998 Nebbiolo d'Alba La Val dei Preti	C	88
1998 Roero Ròche d'Ampsej	C	90
1997 Roero Ròche d'Ampsej	C	91

Correggia, who died in late 2001, was undoubtedly a star of Piedmont's up-and-coming Roero area. Hillside vineyards, low yields, and meticulous attention to detail resulted in outstanding wines. The 1998 Nebbiolo d'Alba La Val dei Preti offers gorgeous aromas of cherries, tobacco, and spice box, a sweet entry on the palate, abundant glycerin, medium to full body, and a silky finish. It should drink well for 2–3 years. Readers looking for a blockbuster, thick, juicy, fruit-dominated red should check out Correggia's 1998 Barbera d'Alba Bricco Marun. Its black/purple color is followed by aromas of sweet fruit (cherries and blackberries), smoke, new oak, and a lush, succulent finish. Drink it over the next 4–5 years for its exuberance and intensity. Both the 1997 and 1998 Roero Ròche d'Ampsej are outstanding examples of 100% old-vine (50–60 years) Nebbiolo. The 1997 exhibits more succulence, glycerin, and fat, but both are deeply concentrated, dense efforts revealing oodles of black cherry fruit, perfumed personalities, sweet tannin, and medium to full body. The 1998 is more elegant and symmetrical, whereas the 1997 is more exotic and thick. While they are impossible to resist, both should drink well for a decade.

GIUSEPPE CORTESE

1998 Barbaresco Rabajà	D	89
1997 Barbaresco Rabajà	D	92
1996 Barbaresco Rabajà	D	86
1995 Barbaresco Rabajà	D	76

These traditionally made Piedmontese Barbarescos are aged completely in old *foudres*. This delicious, sexy, open-knit 1998 Barbaresco Rabajà reveals a medium ruby color with amber already appearing at the edge. Stunning aromatics of melted licorice, cherry jam, spice box, balsam wood, and herbs leap from the glass of this fleshy, medium- to full-bodied, ripe offering. Drink this seductive 1998 over the next 4–5 years. The 1997 Rabajà is the finest Cortese Barbaresco I have tasted in more than a decade. This wine, which exhibits notes of root vegetables, raspberry and cherry jam, cedar and balsa wood, smoke, and minerals, is full-bodied, powerful yet elegant, supple-textured, and surprisingly deep as well as delineated. Drink this hedonistic as well as intellectually satisfying Barbaresco over the next 10 years. The 1996 Barbaresco Rabajà displays a saturated ruby color and a spicy, tobacco, licorice, and cherry-scented nose. A traditionally styled Barbaresco, with dry tannin, medium body, and very good extract, it should keep for 10 years. Cortese's 1995 Barbaresco Rabajà is disappointing, even in this irregular vintage. Spicy tobacco and dried tomato scents dominate the nose. The wine is medium-bodied, compressed, austere, and lean, with hard tannin in the finish. It will become increasingly attenuated as it ages. Drink it up.

GIANPAOLO DESTEFANIS

2000	Dolcetto d'Alba	C	86
1999	Dolcetto d'Alba	C	87
2000	Dolcetto d'Alba Vigna Monia Bassa	C	89
1999	Dolcetto d'Alba Vigna Monia Bassa	C	90
1998	Dolcetto d'Alba Vigna Monia Bassa	C	90

A new discovery for me, this estate produces only Dolcetto and Barbera, never filters, and, based on these five efforts, makes extremely ripe, explosively fruity wines. Both 1999s possess denser, riper fruit than their 2000 counterparts, with gobs of berries, a touch of chocolate, and medium- to full-bodied personalities. The 1999 Dolcetto d'Alba Vigna Monia Bassa in particular fills the mouth with gorgeous fruit. Just a step behind are the 2000s, which are tangier but loaded with purity, ripeness, and character. Dolcetto remains a great bargain in the wine world, but it must be consumed during its first 2–4 years of life, before the fruit fades. A huge fruit bomb, the tank-fermented and -aged 1998 Dolcetto is produced from 50–60-year-old vines. It offers explosive blackberry and cherry fruit with a hint of violets in the background. As the wine sat in the glass, aromas of roasted coffee also emerged. While it may not get any better, it will drink well for 2–3 years.

LUIGI EINAUDI

1999	Barbera d'Alba	C	89
1998	Barbera d'Alba	C	87
1998	Barolo	D	(90–92)
1997	Barolo	D	90
1996	Barolo	D	90
1995	Barolo	D	86
1998	Barolo Cannubi	E	(91–94)
1997	Barolo Cannubi	E	90+
1996	Barolo Cannubi	E	92+
1995	Barolo Cannubi	E	89+?
1998	Barolo Costa Grimaldi	E	(92–93)
1997	Barolo Costa Grimaldi	E	92
1996	Barolo Costa Grimaldi	E	90+
1995	Barolo Costa Grimaldi	E	87+
1999	Dolcetto d'Alba I Filari	C	90
1998	Dolcetto d'Alba I Filari	C	90
1999	Dolcetto d'Alba Vigna Tecc	C	89
1998	Langhe Rosso	D	90

1997 Langhe Rosso	D	88
1996 Langhe Rosso	D	90

This traditional producer has an excellent portfolio and, at the top level, some undeniably exciting wines. It produces three *cuvées* of Barolo and a proprietary blend composed of equal parts Cabernet Sauvignon, Merlot, Barbera, and Nebbiolo, aged 18 months in French oak. The 1998s appear to be just as impressive as the stunning 1997s. Even in this latter vintage, characterized by low acidity, overripe fruit, and an over-the-top style, Einaudi produced classic, backward, chewy, blockbuster Barolos that will require nearly as much cellaring as its 1996s. Though good, the 1995s are less successful than the other vintages reviewed here. The early-released 1999s are delicious wines, to be drunk within the next several years.

The impressive 1999 Dolcetto d'Alba Vigna Tecc exhibits a saturated dense purple color as well as an uncomplicated yet explosive bouquet of black fruits, excellent texture, big, chewy, thick flavors, abundant glycerin, and good intensity. Tasters should not expect a great deal of nuance now or in the future, but for a robust, large-scaled, well-balanced wine to gulp down with antipasto or steak, this hits all the sweet spots. Drink it over the next 3 years. Sadly, there are only 100 cases of the amazing, super-concentrated, old-vine *cuvée* of 1999 Dolcetto d'Alba I Filari. It boasts dazzling levels of berry fruit, full body, incredible length, and astonishing concentration, extract, and overall balance. There is not a hard edge to be found in this succulent, prodigious Dolcetto. Although it will last for a decade, it will not get any better, so enjoy its blast of fruit and uncomplicated joys over the next 4 years. New oak makes an appearance in the 1999 Barbera d'Alba, a dense, chewy, modern-styled offering with plenty of smoky toasty scents intermixed with strawberry and cherry jam. Medium- to full-bodied and lush, it is best consumed during its exuberant youth . . . over the next 4 years.

At 14.5% alcohol, the sensational 1998 Dolcetto I Filari is no shy wine. A huge, massive, opaque purple Dolcetto, it boasts super-concentrated, raisiny fruit, a massive mid-section, and no hard edges. Drink this mouth-filling, teeth-staining effort over the next 5 years, although I suspect it will last much longer. The 1998 Barbera d'Alba reveals a surprisingly soft personality for this traditional producer. The deep ruby color is accompanied by round, sweet cherry/strawberry fruit flavors, good fat in the mid-section, and a clean, pure finish. Drink it over the next 3–4 years. More complex but equally supple is the 1998 Langhe Rosso. This full-bodied 1998 offers complex notes of tobacco, black currants, and toast. Glycerin and extract coat the palate in this deep, chewy offering that borders on being internationally styled yet retains plenty of Piedmontese typicity. Drink it over the next 4–5 years, although I suspect it will last longer. The 1998 Barolo exhibits a saturated plum/ruby color as well as a classic Nebbiolo perfume of melted road tar, rose petals, tobacco, and sweet cherry jam. Dense, moderately tannic, and balanced, it possesses great fruit on the attack, mid-palate, and finish. Compared to the 1997, the 1998 appears less powerful but just as concentrated, with sweeter tannin and more fragrance. Anticipated maturity: 2004–2018. The dark-colored, well-structured, elegant 1998 Barolo Costa Grimaldi offers purity and harmony allied with power, density, and extract. While relatively seamless for such a young Einaudi Barolo, there is plenty of tannin underneath the glycerin and fruit. I suspect it is only a matter of time before the tannin asserts itself and closes the wine down. Rich and impressive, with no hard edges, it is built for the long haul. Anticipated maturity: 2004–2022. The enormously concentrated, dense ruby-colored 1998 Barolo Cannubi possesses stunningly concentrated black cherry fruit intermixed with truffles, graphite, asphalt, and smoke. Extremely full-bodied, superpowerful, and palate-staining in its richness and dense flavors, it is the most obviously tannic offering of this trio, as well as the most concentrated. It is only for those with patience. Anticipated maturity: 2006–2025.

All three of Einaudi's 1997 Barolos are stunning efforts from this freakish but compelling vintage. The dense ruby-colored 1997 Barolo exhibits a complex bouquet of rose petals, melted tar, cherry liqueur, and Parmesan cheese. Full-bodied, ripe, dense, and chewy, with adequate acidity, ripe, mature tannin, and a 30–40-second finish, this big, old-style, robust Barolo will continue to develop for 10–12 years. The 1997 Barolo Costa Grimaldi exhibits a more saturated dense ruby/purple color as well as aromas of sweet black cherries and plums, licorice, smoke, and minerals. Full-bodied, with impressive fruit, richness, extract, mouth-filling levels of ripe, chewy tannin, and a huge, sweet, concentrated, explosive finish, this 1997 is just beginning to develop secondary nuances. It should age effortlessly for two decades. The most controversial of this trio, the gigantic, austere, tannic 1997 Barolo Cannubi is more raisiny, tasting like brandy-macerated juice from Amarone-styled Nebbiolo grapes. Extremely full-bodied, with high tannin, deep, chewy, formidable flavors, and a backward, chunky personality, this wine could develop spectacularly—if everything goes right. Anticipated maturity: 2004–2025. The 1997 Langhe Rosso is a full-bodied effort with huge levels of fruit and extract, but not much complexity. The new oak is largely hidden by the wine's wealth of jammy red and black fruits. If more complexity emerges, look for the score to rise a few points, but for now, it is a big, thick, monolithic fruit bomb made in an international style. It should drink well for 10 years.

I am not generally a fan of Piedmontese proprietary reds, but the terrific raw materials available in the 1996 vintage have given the 1996 Langhe Rosso a multidimensional, slightly international style with exhilarating levels of black cherry and cassis fruit, spicy new oak, dried herbs, and a long, dense, velvety-textured finish. Luscious and complex, it is ideal for drinking now and over the next 10 years. The backward 1996 Barolo offers a classic bouquet of licorice, tar, and black cherries. It is extremely powerful, large-scaled and full-bodied yet austere, seriously endowed, and aggressively tannic. Cellaring should smooth it out, but it is an old-style powerhouse. Anticipated maturity: 2004–2015. I have no reservation about the outstanding scores given both the 1996 Barolo Costa Grimaldi and 1996 Barolo Cannubi. Both are terrific, old-style, impressively endowed efforts. The saturated ruby-colored 1996 Barolo Costa Grimaldi is a full-bodied, husky, hefty wine with gorgeous aromas of roasted nuts, cherries, dried herbs, licorice, and flowers. This ripe, rich, huge Barolo will require 4–5 years of cellaring. Anticipated maturity: 2008–2020. The opaque ruby/purple-colored 1996 Barolo Cannubi is a powerfully built, uncompromising wine with huge extract, brawny earthy, cherry, licorice, and tobacco flavors, and high levels of tannin. It is a traditionally made Barolo that requires 5–6 years of cellaring. Everything is present for future brilliance, but patience will be essential. Anticipated maturity: 2010–2025.

The medium garnet/ruby-colored 1995 Barolo exhibits a soft, elegant style, as well as herb-tinged berry fruit meshed with foresty, truffle, and dried herb/smoky notes. Round and moderately endowed, it should be consumed over the next 4–5 years. The complex 1995 Barolo Costa Grimaldi is a stylish, graceful, easy to understand and drink wine from this open-knit vintage. Medium-bodied, with smoked herb, cherry, earth, and cedar aromas, it possesses sweet fruit, and a spicy, moderately tannic, lovely finish. Anticipated maturity: now–2012. The dark ruby/garnet-colored 1995 Barolo Cannubi offers aromas of cedar, tobacco, new saddle leather, cherries, and melted road tar. In the mouth, the tannin is astringent and the wine austere. With airing, hints of sweet cherry jam, fennel, and earth emerge. Impressive, but does it possess the fat and concentration to support its structure? Anticipated maturity: now–2014.

ALESSANDRO E GIAN NATALE FANTINO

1998 Barolo Vigna dei Dardi	D	(88–90)
1997 Barolo Vigna dei Dardi	D	88

Fantino appears to be doing a fine job making wines in the modern style. It produces elegant, flavorful, midweight wines that reveal a judicious use of *barriques*.

The 1998 Barolo Vigna dei Dardi is a soft, sexy, dark ruby/purple-colored, well-textured, impressively rich effort offering copious quantities of sweet black cherry fruit mixed with toasty new oak. Clean, ripe, and concentrated, with both depth and personality, it will drink well for a decade. The internationally styled 1997 Barolo Vigna dei Dardi possesses aromas and flavors of ripe cherries and spicy new oak, a creamy texture, and enough Nebbiolo character to provide spice, licorice, leather, and cherry fruit. Drink it over the next 5–6 years.

STEFANO FARINA

1997	Barbaresco	D	89
1996	Barbaresco	D	89
1995	Barbaresco	D	87
1997	Barolo	D	91
1996	Barolo	D	90
1995	Barolo	D	89

While unfamiliar with this La Morra producer, I was impressed by what he has achieved with these six wines. They are well balanced, with nicely integrated acidity, alcohol, and tannin. As a general rule, the Barolos offer more complex aromas and intense, rich, chewy flavors. If new oak was utilized, it has been better integrated than with the Barbarescos.

The 1997 Barbaresco exhibits an opaque purple color, and overripe, cherry, blackberry, smoky, oaky aromas. The wine is fleshy, with excellent richness and a low-acid, succulently textured finish. Anticipated maturity: now–2010. The most gigantic wine of this series is the 1997 Barolo. It displays telltale aromas of roasted herbs, jammy cherries and blackberries, spice, and tar. Thick and viscous, with outstanding ripeness, the vintage's low acid, fleshy/accessible personality, and a heady, high alcohol finish, it will become more civilized as it ages. Anticipated maturity: now–2016.

The opaque purple 1996 Barbaresco would have merited an outstanding score were it not for its slight lack of complexity. There is spicy new oak intertwined with black fruits in this modern-styled effort, as well as good flesh, texture, and purity. The acidity provides vibrancy, and buttresses the wine's weightiness. Drink it over the next 8 years. The superb 1996 Barolo exhibits purple nuances in its plum/ruby color. It possesses an opulent texture, superrichness, copious sweet red fruits and glycerin in the mid-palate, and a long, nicely nuanced, layered finish. Still youthful but impressively endowed, it will be at its peak before 2014.

The saturated ruby/purple 1995 Barbaresco offers a sweet, jammy nose of herb-tinged cherry liqueur intermixed with a touch of toasty new oak. The wine is evolved, fleshy, round, and made with a hedonist's mentality. Drink it over the next 3 years. The evolved plum/ruby-colored 1995 Barolo offers a sweet, fragrant bouquet of roses, black and red fruits, spice, and tar. It is a classic Barolo with medium to full body, fine depth, and an intriguing earthiness in the smooth finish. Anticipated maturity: now–2012.

GIACOMO FENOCCHIO

1997	Barolo Bussia	D	86
1996	Barolo Bussia	D	(85–87)
1995	Barolo Bussia	D	84
1997	Barolo Villero	D	83
1996	Barolo Villero	D	(85–87)
1995	Barolo Villero	D	85

These traditionally made, old-style Barolos are aged in big old Slovenian oak casks. Fenocchio, whose cellars are in Monforte d'Alba, has turned out a competent but largely uninspiring group of wines from 1995 and 1996. His 1997s are relatively light for the vintage.

Fenocchio's 1997 Barolo Bussia exhibits a dark ruby color with amber at the edge. Aromas of minerals, smoke, coffee, raspberries, and earth are present in this medium-bodied, slightly acidic offering. Anticipated maturity: 2003–2016. Even lighter as well as more austere, the 1997 Barolo Villero is a surprisingly mediocre effort for the vintage. It displays plenty of earthiness as well as excessive tannin. Avoid it.

The 1996 Barolo Bussia displays a more saturated color with amber at the edge. It is an elegant, lighter-styled effort with attractive floral/berry fruit combined with herbs, leather, and spice. It should be consumed during the next 2–3 years.

The 1996 Barolo Villero reveals textbook rose petal, melted tar, and cherry fruit flavors, but not much depth or length. I was surprised by its softness as well as by its lack of intensity, although the wine is good to very good. It should be drunk over the next 2 years.

The evolved 1995 Barolo Bussia exhibits an earthy, dried herb, smoky, *garrigue*-scented nose. Drink this soft Barolo over the next 1–2 years. The 1995 Barolo Villero is reminiscent of its 1996 counterpart with its classic aromas of rose petal, melted tar, and cherry fruit flavors. Just as its older sibling, it lacks depth and length but is more structured and intense than the 1996. Drink it over the next 2–3 years.

F.LLI FERRERO

1998 Barolo Manzoni	D	(88–90)
1997 Barolo Manzoni	D	90
1996 Barolo Manzoni	D	(88–90)
1995 Barolo Manzoni	D	86

All four wines from this sleeper La Morra producer are at least very good, with the 1996, 1997, and 1998 potentially outstanding.

Ferrero's excellent dark ruby-colored 1998 Barolo Manzoni reveals sweet, plum, cherry, licorice, espresso, and cedary aromas as well as flavors, supple tannin, medium to full body, and a velvety, layered finish. The overall impression is of sweet fruit presented in a well-endowed format with no hard edges. It should drink well for 10 years although it could prove to be even longer-lived given its impeccable balance. The dark plum/purple-colored 1997 Barolo Manzoni offers a rich, complex perfume of cedar, espresso, licorice, raspberry, and cherry fruit. This full-bodied, concentrated, outstanding Barolo is long, purely made, and impeccably balanced. Anticipated maturity: now–2016. The 1996 Barolo Manzoni is powerful, full-bodied, tannic, and intense. This traditionally made offering reveals earthy, leather, and dried herb–scented cherry fruit in both its bouquet and flavors, as well as dusty, astringent tannin in the finish, suggesting that a couple more years of cellaring is recommended. Anticipated maturity: 2004–2013. Lighter-bodied and less intense than the 1996, the dark ruby-colored 1995 Barolo Manzoni offers up a textbook nose of tar, roses, cherry fruit, and spice. The attack is sweet and the wine medium-bodied, cleanly made, and soft. It lacks concentration and length but will provide attractive drinking over the next 1–2 years.

VIRGINIA FERRERO

1998 Barolo San Rocco	D	(86–87)
1997 Barolo San Rocco	D	86

I have fond memories of Ferrero's Barolos from the 1960s, but recent vintages have possessed less stuffing as well as limited longevity.

A supple, elegantly styled effort without the stuffing of the vintage's most prominent wines, the evolved, medium ruby/garnet-colored 1998 Barolo San Rocco offers notes of balsa wood, smoke, dried herbs, tobacco, and cherries. Soft and moderately endowed, it is best drunk during its first decade of life. Although the 1997 Barolo San Rocco exhibits an evolved medium garnet color with amber at the edge, it has excellent aromatics of caramel, toffee, cherries, licorice, and tobacco. Soft and supple on the entry, with medium body, it does not display the finish expected from a top producer. Drink it over the next 5–6 years.

FRANCO FIORINA

1997 Barbaresco	D	(87–88)
1997 Barolo	D	(88–91)

These 1997s from *négociant* Franco Fiorina are the most impressive I have tasted. The dense ruby-colored 1997 Barbaresco exhibits copious quantities of licorice, cedar, and spice box aromas, medium to full body, a silky texture, and a long finish. It should drink well for 4–5 years. The powerful, super-concentrated, rich, chocolaty, dense, massive 1997 Barolo offers notes of charcoal, hickory smoke, licorice, leather, and cedar. What a blockbuster!

FONTANABIANCA

1998 Barbaresco Sorì Burdin	D	(88–89)
1997 Barbaresco Sorì Burdin	D	89

A sleeper selection from this Neive producer, Fontanabianca's dark garnet-colored 1998 Barbaresco Sorì Burdin reveals classic Nebbiolo aromas of cherry cough syrup mixed with licorice, asphalt, and dried Provençal herbs. Medium- to full-bodied, dense, supple-textured, and loaded with fruit as well as glycerin, it will drink well for 5–6 years. The well-made 1997 Barbaresco Sorì Burdin exhibits an evolved garnet color as well as spicy, dried herb, licorice, tobacco, and red berry aromas. Drink this medium-bodied effort over the next 3–4 years.

FONTANAFREDDA

1998 Barbaresco Coste Rubin	E	(88–90)
1997 Barbaresco Coste Rubin	E	88
1998 Barolo Vigna Lazzarito	E	(89–91+?)
1997 Barolo Vigna Lazzarito	E	91
1998 Barolo Vigna La Rosa	E	(91–93)
1997 Barolo Vigna La Rosa	E	93+
1998 Barolo di Serralunga	E	(90–93)
1997 Barolo di Serralunga	E	92+

One of the great names of Piedmontese winemaking, this estate has had a history of mixed performances. I began purchasing Fontanafredda's wines in the late 1960s, and have enjoyed several stunning bottles of its 1971 Barolo. In the late 1970s and early 1980s, the wines began an irregular period that continued into the 1990s. However, this magnificent estate appears to have rebounded brilliantly with its 1997s, 1998s, and 1999s . . . super news for aficionados of Piedmontese wines.

The dark ruby/purple-colored, impressively extracted, full-bodied, yet monolithic 1998 Barbaresco Coste Rubin should be outstanding after another 1–2 years of cellaring. Anticipated maturity: 2003–2015. The exquisite, well-balanced, sweet 1998 Barolo di Serralunga displays a Graves-like character in its full-bodied, concentrated style. With abundant tannin in the finish, it will require additional cellaring. Anticipated maturity: 2005–2018. Even more powerful and backward, with a hugely sweet, dense mid-palate, is the fat, voluptuous, yet broodingly backward, superextracted 1998 Barolo Vigna La Rosa. It is one of the vintage's most concentrated as well as longest-lived efforts. Anticipated maturity: 2005–2020. More monolithic and muted is the saturated deep purple 1998 Barolo Vigna Lazzarito. Dense, chewy, full-bodied, and tannic, it does not reveal the complexity, sweetness, or overall style of Fontanafredda's other Barolo offerings. Although impressively endowed, this ruggedly muscular 1998 needs 4–5 years of cellaring. Anticipated maturity: 2006–2018.

The dark ruby-colored 1997 Barbaresco Coste Rubin offers an intriguing perfume of roasted peanuts, vanilla, cherries, tar, and spice box. The most internationally styled of Fontanafredda's 1997s, it possesses excellent fruit and a medium- to full-bodied personality. It should drink well for 10 years. The 1997 Barolo di Serralunga exhibits a saturated purple/ garnet color in addition to a stunning bouquet of underbrush, kirsch, lead pencil, licorice, and toasty new oak. Full-bodied and exotic (but not over the top), this is a structured, muscular, concentrated Barolo that will benefit from 2–3 years of cellaring and keep for 2–3 decades. It is an impressive, classic effort that threads the needle between the traditional and modern styles. The opaque plum-colored 1997 Barolo Vigna La Rosa reveals the influence of toasty new oak in its fabulously pure, concentrated nose, which represents the essence of melted licorice, blackberries, and assorted black fruits. As the wine sits in the glass, scents of toast, smoke, leather, tar, and fennel emerge. Full-bodied, massively concentrated, powerful, and dense, it requires 3–5 years of cellaring. Anticipated maturity: 2005–2022. Lastly, the opaque plum/garnet 1997 Barolo Vigna Lazzarito possesses full-bodied notes of dried herbs, leather, tar, black fruits, and truffles presented in a powerful, monolithic style. There is a lot going on in this marvelously endowed, moderately tannic Barolo, but it is not as potentially complex or nuanced as the Serralunga or La Rosa. Nevertheless, it is an outstanding effort and may just have been more muted the day I tasted it. Anticipated maturity: 2003–2016.

GIANNI GAGLIARDO

1997	Barolo Preve	D	(87–89)
1996	Barolo Preve	D	(88–89)

These are two excellent offerings from Gagliardo. The 1996 Barolo Preve is a full-bodied, classically textured and flavored wine with savory cedar, cigar box, and black cherries intertwined with melted road tar. Rich, fleshy, and purely made, it should drink well for 10–12 years. The 1997 Barolo Preve is a fatter, more layered wine with low acidity and powerful cherry liqueur, spice box, fruitcake as well as dried herb aromas and flavors. There is good purity in addition to a rich, fleshy mouth feel. Anticipated maturity: now–2018.

ANGELO GAJA

1998	Barbaresco	EEE	91
1997	Barbaresco	EEE	94
1996	Barbaresco	EE	91
1995	Barbaresco	EE	90
1995	Barbaresco Costa Russi	EEE	90
1995	Barbaresco Sorì San Lorenzo	EEE	91+
1995	Barbaresco Sorì Tildin	EEE	91+
1997	Cabernet Sauvignon Darmagi	EEE	90+
1996	Cabernet Sauvignon Darmagi	EEE	90
1995	Cabernet Sauvignon Darmagi	EEE	88
1998	Conteisa	EEE	92
1997	Conteisa	EEE	98
1996	Conteisa	EEE	95+
1998	Costa Russi	EEE	92
1997	Costa Russi	EEE	96
1996	Costa Russi	EEE	93
1998	Sorì San Lorenzo	EEE	96
1997	Sorì San Lorenzo	EEE	98
1996	Sorì San Lorenzo	EEE	96
1998	Sorì Tildin	EEE	95
1997	Sorì Tildin	EEE	99+
1996	Sorì Tildin	EEE	96+
1998	Langhe Sperss	EEE	94
1997	Langhe Sperss	EEE	99
1996	Langhe Sperss	EEE	(94–96)

It may seem cavalier if not ridiculous to suggest that Angelo Gaja may have produced some of the finest wines in his renowned career over the last vintages, but certainly the 1995s, 1996s, 1997s, and 1998s are astonishing efforts. Readers should note that beginning in 1996, Gaja dropped the appellation names of Barbaresco and Barolo from his single-vineyard wines. At this stage, the 1997s look to be the finest wines he has ever made. My enthusiasm is obviously due in part to the stylistic preference I have for more opulently textured wines with lower acidity and thus a broader window of drinkability. However, the 1998s nearly rival the superexotic, concentrated 1997s and monumental 1996s. Stylistically, the latter vintages are more classic and elegant than the exaggerated but compelling 1997s, but they do not lack intensity. Gaja's wines generally see 40–45% new oak (50% French and 50% from Austria as well as Poland) and spend 24 months in wood, half of that time in small barrels and half in larger wood uprights.

A persuasive argument can be made that Angelo Gaja has long been Piedmont's spiritual and qualitative leader. His recent controversial move to drop the Barbaresco and Barolo appellations from his three Barbaresco crus and two Barolo crus has had an unsettling impact on the local cognoscenti. His rationale for this move is that he wants to pick his Nebbiolo superripe (to obtain what the French call *sur-maturité*) and then blend in some higher-acid Barbera (in 1997, 1998, and 1999, approximately 5% Barbera was used in the Barbaresco crus, 6% in Sperss, and 8% in Conteisa). Gaja believes this gives the wines more freshness as well as focus. Whatever his rationalizations, it seems to me that he would not make this decision unless it improved the wines. And in any case, the results are spectacular.

The dark ruby/purple-colored, supple-textured 1998 Costa Russi possesses sweet, jammy raspberry and cherry fruit, medium to full body, gorgeous glycerin, low acidity, and a lightly tannic finish. Although large-sized, it has good finesse as well as beautifully pure fruit. Anticipated maturity: 2003–2020. More chocolate, coffee, smoke, licorice, and tobacco characteristics are found in the complex, deep purple 1998 Sorì Tildin. Surprisingly seductive for such a young wine, it exhibits abundant aromatic fireworks, fabulous fruit concentration, a layered opulence, more intensity, glycerin, and depth than the Costa Russi, and a spectacularly long finish. Anticipated maturity: now–2025. The multifaceted 1998 Sorì San Lorenzo offers up notes of lead pencil, smoke, tobacco, tar, rose petals, black fruits, and espresso. Already incredibly expressive, soft, sexy, and voluptuous, jammy fruits infused with toasty oak cascade over the palate. This easily understood, seamless, pure, classic 1998 should drink well for 20–25 years.

From the Barolo appellation, the 1998 Conteisa displays a distinctive bouquet of black cherry jam mixed with vitamins, smoke, iron, minerals, and spicy oak. In the mouth, earth, truffle, lead pencil, and espresso-infused cherry flavors make an appearance. Deep, rich, and full-bodied, with moderate tannin and power, this impressive offering requires 2–3 years of cellaring and should age well for two decades. More perfumed, with additional richness, the 1998 Sperss reveals a perfume of black fruits, truffles, earth, and spice box. Dense, massive, yet seamless, this beautifully integrated wine possesses low acidity as well as a terrific finish. Although well evolved and delicious for such a youthful Barolo, it will age well for 20–25 years. While the 1998 Barbaresco may not equal the extraordinary 1997, it is a beautiful effort displaying fleshy, oaky, deep black cherry, raspberry, tar, and truffle scents with subtle new oak in the background. Dense, voluptuously textured, and full-bodied, with gorgeous overall symmetry and beautifully integrated tannin, acidity, alcohol, and wood, it will drink well for 15 or more years.

Gaja's 1997 Barbaresco is undoubtedly the finest he has made. An exquisite effort, it boasts a dense ruby/purple color in addition to an extraordinary nose of black cherry liqueur, smoke, licorice, mineral, and floral aromas. The wine is full-bodied, opulent, and loaded with fruit. Despite its precocious nature, there is abundant tannin, and thus 3–4 years of cellaring is required. It should age effortlessly for 25 years. The opaque ruby/purple-colored 1997

Costa Russi displays a striking bouquet of blackberry and cherry fruit intermixed with espresso and wood scents. Typically the most internationally styled Gaja offering, the 1997 comes across as a Nebbiolo on steroids. Full-bodied, gorgeously pure and symmetrical, it should be at its best between now–2025. The awesome 1997 Sorì Tildin is a candidate for perfection. The saturated purple color is followed by a dense, full-bodied wine possessing extraordinary vibrancy for such a heavyweight, muscular Nebbiolo. It offers a supersweet entry, a boatload of glycerin, notes of earth, licorice, cedar, blackberry and cherry liqueur, and a touch of blueberries. Extremely full, gorgeously pure, with a seamless texture, this spectacular 1997 will enjoy three decades of cellaring. Equally profound, the 1997 Sorì San Lorenzo is, as usual, the most elegant, nuanced, and complex Gaja offering. It exhibits a striking perfume of lead pencil, roasted nuts, black fruits, spice box, leather, cedar, and Chinese black tea. Forward yet enormously well constituted and rich, with an ethereal elegance underpinning its personality, the Sorì San Lorenzo displays a classic combination of power and finesse. As this wine sat in the glass, notes of Japanese soy sauce made an appearance. Anticipated maturity: now–2030.

The 1997 Conteisa offers classic aromas of licorice, melted tar, black cherries, wet stones, and tobacco. It is a full-bodied, unctuously textured wine of remarkable density and thickness. The tannin is high but sweet. This brawny offering cuts an immense swath across the palate, but there are no hard edges and all the component parts are pure as well as well integrated. There are 15,000 bottles of this spectacular wine. Anticipated maturity: 2003–2030. Another virtually perfect effort is the 1997 Sperss, which represents the essence of truffles, earth, and black cherries in its striking aromatics and multidimensional, opulent, full-bodied palate. The acidity seems low because of the huge glycerin levels and prodigious concentration of fruit, but I suspect it is normal in the scheme of oenological measurement. This profound wine requires 2–3 years of cellaring and should age well for 30–35 years.

The exceptional black/purple 1997 Cabernet Sauvignon Darmagi (3–4% Cabernet Franc was added to the blend) is redolent with abundant quantities of smoky, concentrated fruit as well as tannin. It exhibits the vintage's low-acid, thick, glycerin-imbued character and a layered, full-bodied finish. It should develop nicely for two decades.

One of the great wines of the vintage, the spectacular 1996 Barolo Sperss boasts an opaque ruby/purple color plus enormously ripe black cherries, tar, flowers, and white truffles. Extremely full-bodied, with compelling intensity and purity, this is a large-scaled, massive Barolo with plenty of tannin and 2–3 decades of ageability. Anticipated maturity: 2005–2030.

Angelo Gaja likes his 1996 Barbarescos every bit as much as his 1995s. I tend to think the 1996s are more powerful and concentrated. Perhaps it is just a question of Gaja preferring the finesse and elegance of the 1995s to the structure, muscle, and potential of the more massive 1996s. The 1996 Barbaresco exhibits a dense ruby color as well as a forward nose of cherry liqueur, earth, truffle, mineral, and spicy scents. Rich, full-bodied, and seductive, with its moderate tannin largely concealed by the wine's wealth of fruit and extract, this gorgeously pure offering gets my nod as the finest Barbaresco produced by Gaja since 1990. Anticipated maturity: now–2016.

The dense opaque purple 1996 Sorì San Lorenzo possesses the most complex aromatics, consisting of classic Nebbiolo scents of rose petals, dried herbs, spice box, cedar, and abundant jammy black cherry and berry fruit. It is impressively powerful and muscular, with moderate tannin, a sweet, unctuous texture, and a 40+-second finish. Although the aromatics are stunning, this 1996 remains youthful and backward. Anticipated maturity: 2005–2025. It is hard to argue with those who claim that the finest of these single-vineyard offerings is always the Sorì Tildin. The 1996 Sorì Tildin reveals a more pigmented/saturated ruby/purple color in addition to a tighter nose, with aromas of blackberries, cherry liqueur, smoke, licorice, incense, and spice box. Enormous on the palate, with multiple layers of fruit, soft tannin, huge body, and a knockout finish, this is the most backward and brawniest of the single-vineyard 1996s. Anticipated maturity: 2005–2030. Lastly, the 1996 Costa Russi reminds me of how a great Zinfandel or a great red Burgundy would taste if made by Angelo Gaja. A seductive nose of black raspberries, violets, licorice, and toast is followed by a rich wine with pure black fruit flavors intertwined with sweet, smoky oak. Full-bodied, with ripe tannin, this internationally styled, stunningly proportioned, big, compelling 1996 will be at its peak between 2003–2023. The opaque purple 1996 Barolo Conteisa reveals a sweeter, riper nose with an element of *sur-maturité* given its overripe cassis, melted road tar, licorice, and spice-scented bouquet. More accessible than the Sperss, it exhibits a voluptuous texture, layers of concentrated fruit, and full body. Its tannin is largely concealed by the wine's glycerin, alcohol, and extract. Anticipated maturity: now–2020.

The outstanding 1996 Cabernet Sauvignon Darmagi is a structured, dense, black/purple-colored wine with excellent cassis fruit and an unevolved but promising personality. There are copious quantities of tannin, a massive mid-palate, and a sweet, long finish. However, it will require considerable patience. Anticipated maturity: 2008–2025.

1995 tends to be a good rather than great vintage in Piedmont, but Gaja's sensational 1995s are among the stars of the vintage. All of the following wines possess extremely saturated dark ruby/purple colors, almost atypical for Nebbiolo. The 1995 Barbaresco offers a superb nose of licorice, cherry fruit, strawberries, flowers, and toasty scents. Ripe, dense, and lush, with an alluring, sexy personality, it is one of the more forward, generic Barbarescos Gaja has produced. Anticipated maturity: now–2011. The three single-vineyard wines are qualitatively similar but represent different expressions of Nebbiolo. The 1995 Barbaresco Sorì San Lorenzo offers telltale cigar tobacco, spice box, and cedar with black currant and cherry fruit in the background. The new oak plays a subtle role. Structured and more noticeably tannic than the regular *cuvée*, this is a dense wine with surprising levels of glycerin, a saturated plum color, and intriguing flavors of black fruits, soy, and cedar. Although accessible, it needs more bottle age. Anticipated maturity: now–2016. The 1995 Barbaresco Costa Russi reveals the most saturated purple color of any of Gaja's 1995 Barbarescos. A full-bodied, more fruit-driven, and powerful wine, it possesses copious quantities of black raspberry and cherry fruit, as well as toasty new oak. There is even an element of *sur-maturité* in this large-scaled, expansively flavored effort. I would not be surprised to see it age for 20 years. Anticipated maturity: 2004–2020+. The 1995 Barbaresco Sorì Tildin reveals a liqueurlike viscosity to its richness. It offers spicy, black raspberry fruit in addition to melted asphalt, smoke, truffle, and toast. This complex, expansive Barbaresco does not possess the saturated purple/plum color of the Costa Russi, but it is deeply colored for the vintage, with superb richness, full body, and beautifully integrated acidity, tannin, and alcohol. Anticipated maturity: 2004–2020+. The 1995 Cabernet Sauvignon Darmagi is an elegant wine with medium body, classic weedy tobacco and cassis flavors, sweet, supple tannin, and excellent equilibrium. Anticipated maturity: 2003–2018.

GASTALDI

1995 Barbaresco	**D**	**87**

It is hard to define these wines as from either the new *barrique*-aged winemaking school or the classical/traditional persuasion, but they may demonstrate a bit more allegiance to the latter. The 1995 Barbaresco's dark garnet color is followed by a classic bouquet of cherry cough syrup, coffee, rose petals, tar, and cedar. Spicy and medium-bodied, with fine density, a supple texture, and light tannin in the finish, it should drink well for 4–5 years.

ATTILIO GHISOLFI

1998 Barolo Bricco Visette	**D**	**(87–88)**
1997 Barolo Bricco Visette	**D**	**85**

1996 Barolo Bricco Visette	D	(86–87)
1995 Barolo Bricco Visette	D	86

This small producer in Monforte d'Alba has fashioned a fine 1998 Barolo Bricco Visette. This wine is made in a moderately endowed, forward style with sweet black cherry fruit, medium to full body, and ripe tannin. Admirable extract and richness as well as an atypically precocious, up-front personality suggest drinking this 1998 between 2003–2012.

Not nearly as dense and rich as it was from the barrel, the light, commercially styled 1997 Barolo Bricco Visette possesses pleasant fruit but little stuffing or intensity. This medium-weight wine is best drunk over the next 3–4 years. The dense, saturated ruby-colored 1996 Barolo Bricco Visette is full-bodied and extracted, with weedy tobacco intermixed with dried herbs, cherry liqueur, and copious new saddle leather. The wine starts off impressively, but it becomes more compressed and shorter in the finish, which kept my score low. Anticipated maturity: now–2012. The 1995 Barolo Bricco Visette is soft, evolved and mature. The color is already revealing amber and orange at the edge. This Barolo offers the hallmark tar, rose petal, and spicy nose. Medium-bodied and not terribly concentrated, it is ideal for drinking over the next 4 years.

BRUNO GIACOSA

1998 Barbaresco Asili	EE	93
1997 Barbaresco Asili	EE	94
1996 Barbaresco Asili (Red Label Riserva)	EE	98+
1995 Barbaresco Asili	E	90
1998 Barbaresco Rabajà	EE	95
1997 Barbaresco Rabajà	EE	96
1996 Barbaresco Rabajà	EE	93
1998 Barbaresco Santo Stefano	E	92
1997 Barbaresco Santo Stefano	C	93
1996 Barbaresco Santo Stefano	E	94+
1995 Barbaresco Santo Stefano	E	91
1998 Barolo Falletto di Serralunga	EEE	(94–96)
1997 Barolo Falletto di Serralunga	EEE	93
1996 Barolo Falletto di Serralunga (Red Label Riserva)	EEE	98+
1995 Barolo Falletto di Serralunga	EE	90+
1998 Barolo Rocche di Falletto	EEE	(96–98)
1997 Barolo Rocche di Falletto	EEE	96+
1996 Barolo Villero	EE	93
1998 Nebbiolo d'Alba Valmaggiore	C	89
1997 Nebbiolo d'Alba Valmaggiore	C	88

It is always thrilling to visit Bruno Giacosa, Piedmont's undeniable guardian of the traditional school of winemaking. His Barolos and Barbarescos (i.e., memories of his 1978s, 1971s, and 1964s) are among the most exhilarating wines of the world.

This producer acquired some choice vineyard parcels several years ago, from which he is producing the finest wines ever to emerge from these sites. He now owns Barbaresco vineyards in the crus of Rabajà (where the début vintage was 1996) and Asili (first wine produced in 1995), as well as Barolo vineyards in Falletto, from which he makes two *cuvées*. Since 1997, four blocks of the Falletto vineyard have been used for the virtually perfect Rocche di Falletto. These plots possess a southeastern exposure, which accounts for the better maturity of the grapes that emerge from them. None of Giacosa's wines sees any *barrique* treatment, and they are bottled "when they are ready." His humility, unassuming character, dignity, extraordinary pride, and remarkable integrity are reflected in his wines, which, for me, are the benchmarks for great Nebbiolo. Much as I get turned on by some of the modernists' wines, the Giacosa treasures that exist in my cellar are unprecedented in their complexity and richness. I rarely open a bottle of his Barbarescos or Barolos before their tenth birthday and find that most of them do not hit their stride until age 15–18. However, impatient readers should be warned: these wines are frequently uninspiring immediately after bottling and arrival to these shores, but after 10 years of cellaring, their magic always emerges. I have seen this happen in Giacosa's greatest vintages (1964, 1971, 1978, 1982, 1985, and 1988) as well as in lesser years (1980 and 1986). Given my twenty-five years of glorious experience with Bruno Giacosa's wines, I know that cellaring them is not a leap of faith. They have never disappointed, assuming I wait the 8–10 years they require in great vintages (his 1978s are still emerging from a long period of dormancy). To put it another way, Giacosa's Barolos and Barbarescos are among the few wines I will purchase without having tasted first. Bruno Giacosa considers that both 1996 and 1998 are far better vintages than 1997 (according to him, a difficult year—too hot and dry, with raisined grapes, low acidity, and excessive sugars and alcohol). He was not the only producer to express such an opinion (shared by Pio Boffa of Pio Cesare). However, as critical as Bruno Giacosa was of his 1997s, I thought the wines were all potentially outstanding, but I still think that the 1996s are even more spectacular (because of a disastrous flowering in 1996, the crop size was 50% smaller than normal!) and the 1998s are practically on a par with them. That being said, readers should not forget what this producer achieved in 1995, though this vintage does not offer any red label Riserva. The estate's standard *cuvées* bear white labels.

The spice box, tobacco, cherry liqueur, and smoke-scented 1998 Nebbiolo d'Alba Valmaggiore is reminiscent of Giacosa's bigger-styled Barbarescos. It is extremely complex, intense, spicy, and long in the mouth. Consume it over the next 4–5 years. Giacosa's 1998 Barbaresco Asili needs 4–5 years of cellaring. It exhibits a dark ruby color along with a big, sweet nose of dried herbs, cedar, tobacco, tar, and red fruits. Opulent on the attack, with moderately high tannin as well as good underlying acidity, this is a fragrant effort for Giacosa, without the flamboyant size of the 1997 or the massive structure and density of the 1996. Anticipated maturity: 2006–2020. In 1998, the renowned Barbaresco Santo Stefano is the most forward offering, with its medium ruby color already displaying amber at the edge. Aromas of new saddle leather, fennel, smoke, tobacco, kirsch, and licorice soar from the glass of this ripe, opulent, medium- to full-bodied Barbaresco. I hesitate to say it can be drunk young, given the tendency of these wines to shut down, but readers who purchase it (that includes me) should let it settle down for a year or two and drink it over the following 15+ years. Another terrific Barbaresco is the 1998 Rabajà. Complex notes of soy, earth, candied cherry fruit, and cigar box emerge from this concentrated yet intellectually challenging effort. Full-bodied, with a soft attack as well as a tannic finish, it will be drinkable between 2007–2020.

The fabulous 1998 Barolo Falletto di Serralunga appears to be superior to the 1997. When the two are tasted side by side, the 1998 reveals more intensity and volume, although that's splitting hairs. A dark plum color is accompanied by a classic Nebbiolo perfume of rose water, melted tar, truffles, and cherry jam. As the wine sits in the glass, aromas of spice box and cigar smoke also emerge. Full-bodied, dense, and powerfully tannic yet extremely harmonious, it will be at its finest between 2008–2030. Lastly, the limited *cuvée* made from four blocks of the Falletto vineyard called Rocche, the 1998 Barolo Rocche di Falletto borders on perfection. I thought it performed better than the 1997, but in the lofty point scores above 95, that's a matter of personal taste. In any event, this wine is spectacular. A dark plum color reveals lightening at the edge. Stunning aromatics offer up scents of crushed stones intermixed with cherry jam and sweet tobacco. There are loads of glycerin, moderately high tannin, and an amazingly long finish of nearly 50 seconds. As staggering as it is now, I am sure it will close down and require 5–6 years of cellaring. Anticipated maturity: 2008–2035.

The 1997 Nebbiolo d'Alba Valmaggiore is a robust, big-styled Nebbiolo with aggressive tannin, copious quantities of tar, black cherry, cigar box, and spice notes, medium to full body, excellent concentration, and a fine finish. It should drink well for 5–6 years.

The 1997 Barbaresco Asili has developed stunningly since it was first tasted from barrel, a typical characteristic of Giacosa's wines. Surprisingly precocious and well evolved for a wine from this estate, it possesses a dark ruby color with an amber edge, and abundant quantities of tobacco, cherry liqueur, incense, spice box, and licorice in its flamboyant nose. It is like candy, fleshy, full-bodied, unctuous, and silky. This seamless classic should drink well young and last for 10–12 years. The classic 1997 Barbaresco Santo Stefano is more evolved and flamboyant than its more backward 1996 counterpart. A medium ruby/garnet color with an amber edge is followed by a sweet perfume of black cherries, tobacco, leather, spice box, licorice, and tar. Full-bodied, with a creamy texture, superb concentration, and an exquisite finish, it can be drunk now or cellared for 15+ years. Giacosa's second release from the Rabajà vineyard, the 1997 Barbaresco Rabajà, may be better than his debut vintage, the 1996. The 1997 boasts a fabulous nose of caramel, soy, herbs, black cherries, plums, and kirsch. Dense and full-bodied, with a spectacular, silky texture, gobs of glycerin, and a layered, multidimensional palate, it is immensely satisfying from both hedonistic and intellectual perspectives. Anticipated maturity: now–2020.

Giacosa's 1997 Barolo Falletto di Serralunga is an exquisite Barolo offering superb notes of tar, earth, truffles, licorice, minerals, and cherry/raspberry fruit. There is plenty of acidity as well as high tannin, but concentrated, chewy flavors. The wine is tight, dense, impressive, and surprisingly well structured for a 1997. However, it is going to be more accessible than most young Giacosa Barolos. Anticipated maturity: 2003–2025. As mentioned above, the debut vintage of Bruno Giacosa's Barolo Rocche di Falletto, the 1997, emerges from four blocks of his Falletto vineyard with a southeastern exposure; thus the fruit is slightly riper. The amazing, deep plum/garnet-colored 1997 possesses huge body as well as a sweet, sexy, fleshy mid-palate and finish. Classic aromas of rose petals, melted tar, and cherry liqueur not only soar aromatically but saturate the palate and coat the taster's teeth. Profoundly complex and multilayered, with an exquisite texture and overall harmony, for a Giacosa Barolo it is uncommonly precocious, making me think it will provide profound drinking in 1–2 years and last for three decades.

The stunning series of 1996 includes a 1996 Barbaresco Santo Stefano red label that is simply spectacular. Giacosa continues to believe this is the greatest wine he has produced since his legendary 1971 (which is still a prodigious Barbaresco, although clearly near the end of its life). The tight, youthful 1996 requires 3–4 more years of bottle age. The color is a dark ruby/garnet. The bouquet is just beginning to open, revealing scents of dried Provençal herbs, cherry liqueur, tobacco, spice box, and white truffles. In the mouth, the wine is stunningly concentrated, extremely full-bodied, with high tannin, and fabulously pure, sweet, cherry cough syrup–like, licorice, smoke, and dried herb flavors. The finish lasts for more than 45 seconds, although this 1996 is still young and tight. It should enjoy a glorious evolution. Anticipated maturity: 2006–2030. The 1996 Barbaresco Rabajà (Giacosa's debut vintage from this noted vineyard) displays an intriguing nose of soy, dried Provençal herbs, new saddle leather, and red/black fruits. Tannic and full-bodied, with an enormous impact on the palate, it is extremely concentrated, yet the fruit, alcohol, tannin, and acidity are all marvelously well integrated. Anticipated maturity: 2006–2025. The utterly perfect, dense ruby/purple-colored 1996 Barbaresco Bricco Asili (Red Label Riserva) is a heroic offering brilliantly displaying both power and elegance. The bouquet develops incrementally, offering up aromas of black raspberries, cherries, cigar box, licorice, and leather. The wine impresses with its nuances as well as its extraordinarily rich, dense mid-palate and a finish that lasts nearly a minute. There is huge tannin but equally massive concentration, extract, and overall harmony. This is the finest Giacosa Barbaresco since his two greatest classics, the 1990 and 1971 Barbaresco Santo Stefano (Red Label). Anticipated maturity: 2006–2025.

There are two Red Label Riserva Barolos in 1996. The 1996 Barolo Villero should be used to teach a course in what great Barolo smells like. It possesses a classic, rose petal, melted tar, and cherry liqueur–scented nose that soars from the glass. In the mouth, it exhibits licorice, black cherry fruit, fruitcake, spice box, and other assorted nuances in its profoundly complex personality. Full-bodied and marvelously concentrated, with exquisite harmony, this appears to be a fabulously young Barolo that will age effortlessly for three decades. Anticipated maturity: 2010–2035. The 1996 Barolo Falletto di Serralunga (Red Label Riserva) possesses extraordinary presence and stature. Dark garnet/ruby-colored, it offers a tight but promising nose of road tar, scorched earth, truffles, blackberries, cherries, and espresso. This muscular, massive wine gave me chills. It is an exquisite, virtually perfect Barolo that requires a decade of cellaring and should last for 30–40 years. I remember wishing I were twenty years younger when I tasted it prior to bottling . . . I still feel the same way. Awesome! Anticipated maturity: 2010–2040.

The gorgeously elegant 1995 Barbaresco Bricco Asili emerges from a renowned Asili vineyard in Barbaresco. The color is a deceptively light ruby with some amber at the edge. The nose offers aromas redolent of kirsch, dried Provençal herbs, new saddle leather, and smoke. In the mouth, Asian spice and soy make an appearance in the rich, jammy cherry flavors that also offer an intriguing tomato-like characteristic. This lush, open-knit, full-bodied Barbaresco will drink well before 2014. The 1995 Barbaresco Santo Stefano reveals an intensely fragrant nose of coffee, soy, tobacco, dried herbs, and cherry cough syrup. Full-bodied, with moderate tannin in the finish, this is an expressive, rich, expansively flavored Barbaresco that can be drunk now as well as over the next 10–12 years. I also enjoyed the outstanding 1995 Barolo Falletto. It possesses a medium dark ruby color with some lightening at the edge. The intense nose of cedar, spice box, soy, tar, rose petals, and black fruits is followed by a wine with a sweet attack, full body, and dense, layered, concentrated, spicy flavors. As this muscular, tannic wine sat in the glass, allspice and dried herbs became increasingly apparent. Cellar it for 2–3 years, and consume over the following 12 years.

F.LLI GRASSO

1998 Barbaresco	D	87
1997 Barbaresco	D	89
1998 Barbaresco Bricco Spessa	D	90
1997 Barbaresco Bricco Spessa	D	88
1998 Barbaresco Sorì Valgrande	D	89+
1997 Barbaresco Sorì Valgrande	D	88+

This producer, based in the village of Treiso, completely renovated his cellars in 2000, and thus it is believed the quality will rise to an even more admirable level. He performed slightly better in 1998 than in 1997.

One of the 1998 vintage's hallmarks, gorgeous aromatics, appears in all three *cuvées*. The 1998 Barbaresco exhibits an unimpressive, medium ruby color, but it offers sweet, tobacco and herb-tinged cherry fruit presented in an elegant, slender yet beautifully balanced, restrained format. Enjoy it over the next 5–6 years. The gorgeous, exceptionally fragrant 1998 Barbaresco Bricco Spessa possesses an evolved nose of cigar tobacco, cedar wood, cherry jam, petroleum, and rose petals. A wine of finesse as well as lush, rich, concentrated fruit, this medium-bodied 1998 is a classic Barbaresco to drink now and over the next decade. Similarly styled, with more structure, the dark garnet-colored 1998 Barbaresco Sorì Valgrande offers intense, complex aromas of tobacco, cedar, spicy tomato skins, cherry liqueur, and coffee. The finish is more structured and leaner than the more expressive Bricco Spessa, hence the slightly lower score. Nevertheless, it is a flavorful Barbaresco that admirably displays Nebbiolo's extraordinarily complex perfume. Consume it over the next 10 years.

Grasso's 1997 Barbaresco reveals an evolved color with amber at the edge as well as a rich, exotic bouquet of superripe cherries, coffee, herbs, and spice box. Fleshy and seductive, with low acidity, medium body, and a sexy, up-front style, it should be consumed over the next 4–5 years. The dark garnet-colored, medium- to full-bodied 1997 Barbaresco Bricco Spessa is more tightly knit than its generic sibling but offers similar aromas of dried herbs, black cherries, tobacco, and leather, as well as more noticeable tannin. Drink it over the next 8 years. The most structured and tannic of this trio, the 1997 Barbaresco Sorì Valgrande, exhibits a dark garnet color, aromas and flavors of earth, tar, cherries, smoke, and spice, and good density, structure, and depth. Although it is the least appealing at present, it will ultimately be the longest-lived. Anticipated maturity: now–2014.

SILVIO GRASSO

1998	Barolo	D	88
1997	Barolo	D	89
1996	Barolo	D	88
1995	Barolo	D	87
1998	Barolo Bricco Luciani	E	(90–92)
1997	Barolo Bricco Luciani	E	92
1996	Barolo Bricco Luciani	E	92
1995	Barolo Bricco Luciani	E	88
1998	Barolo Ciabot Manzoni	E	(90–91)
1997	Barolo Ciabot Manzoni	E	90
1996	Barolo Ciabot Manzoni	E	91
1995	Barolo Ciabot Manzoni	E	87

Silvio Grasso does not employ any new oak for his standard Barolo and about 20% for his single-vineyard wines from the La Morra hillsides. Grasso has produced a bevy of sensational efforts in recent vintages.

This La Morra producer's 1998 Barolo exhibits abundant quantities of licorice and cherry fruit in a medium-bodied, elegant style with plenty of glycerin but not a great deal of weight. This soft, finesse-styled effort is meant to be drunk over the next 3–4 years. The dark ruby-colored 1998 Barolo Ciabot Manzoni offers a beautiful bouquet of sweet black cherry fruit intermixed with rose petals, tar, and new oak. It possesses fine ripeness, a fresh, lively, high-toned style, and lovely flavors. With sweet tannin, decent acidity, and a seamless style, it can be consumed now and over the next 10–12 years. More earthy and chewy, with cedary, spice box, and black cherry scents and flavors, the full-bodied, moderately tannic 1998 Barolo Bricco Luciani displays the vintage's notable fragrance, outstanding purity, and beautiful symmetry among its component parts. Anticipated maturity: 2003–2015.

The excellent 1997 Barolo is a forward, silky-textured effort exhibiting sweet jammy fruit, a roasted herb/spice box character, medium to full body, excellent weight, fat, and plushness, low acidity, and a chewy, expansive palate. Drink it over the next 8 years. Grasso's 1997 Barolo Ciabot Manzoni's dark ruby color reveals some amber at the edge. It possesses a forward, medium- to full-bodied character with plenty of leather and brandied cherry notes, high glycerin levels, and a velvety texture. The finish is tannic. Anticipated maturity: now–2016. The superintense, powerful, weighty, multidimensional, full-bodied, sweet, sexy 1997 Barolo Bricco Luciani exhibits a more forward character than it did prior to bottling. There are layers of fruit, glycerin, and extract, and the wine reveals abundant quantities of black cherry and berry fruit intermixed with spice box, leather, licorice, and Chinese black tea notes. As it sits in the glass, scents of melted asphalt, rose petals, and tobacco emerge. This is a superb, hedonistic, yet powerful, concentrated Barolo to drink between 2003–2020.

The classic character of the 1996 vintage is well displayed in Silvio Grasso's two single-vineyard crus. The fuller-bodied, lush 1996 Barolo offers a sexy display of glycerin and intense cherry and spice aromatics. It will drink well over the next 8 years. The 1996 Barolo Ciabot Manzoni offers a saturated ruby/purple color in addition to a sumptuous bouquet of truffles, saddle leather, black cherries, and floral scents. This expansive, full-bodied, chewy blockbuster is soft enough to be drunk early but should age nicely for 15 years. Even better is the 1996 Barolo Bricco Luciani. The classic Nebbiolo aromas of rose petals and melted road tar are intermixed with toast, cherry liqueur, tobacco, and spice. With explosive richness, high levels of glycerin, and a powerful, muscular, concentrated finish, this superb example possesses high levels of tannin and extract. Anticipated maturity: now–2016.

The 1995 Barolo exhibits a medium ruby/garnet color, in addition to a textbook nose of cherries, spice, balsa wood, and a touch of tar. Elegant, soft, and medium-bodied, it will provide ideal drinking over the next 4–5 years. The dark ruby-colored 1995 Barolo Ciabot Manzoni exhibits a big, toasty nose with scents of ripe cherries, saddle leather, cedar, and tobacco. This medium-bodied, evolved Barolo requires consumption over the next 4–5 years. The 1995 Barolo Bricco Luciani displays a more saturated ruby/garnet color with no amber at the edge. It possesses spicy oak, a fresh, medium- to full-bodied feel, moderate tannin, and an excellent cherry-dominated nose as well as flavors with hints of Asian spices, leather, and tar. Anticipated maturity: now–2010.

MARCHESI DI GRESY

1998 Barbaresco Martinenga	E	87
1997 Barbaresco Martinenga	E	86
1996 Barbaresco Martinenga	E	87
1995 Barbaresco Martinenga	E	87
1996 Barbaresco Camp Gros Martinenga	E	89
1995 Barbaresco Camp Gros Martinenga	E	87
1996 Barbaresco Gaiun Martinenga	E	90
1995 Barbaresco Gaiun Martinenga	E	86

One of my favorite producers of high-class Barbaresco, Marchesi di Gresy's style is one of exceptional refinement and gracious elegance, without the weight of the region's biggest wines but with considerable flavor authority. The 1995s are very good, and the 1996s are at least excellent. Unfortunately, I was able to taste only one *cuvée* in each of 1997 and 1998 that were sound.

The 1998 Barbaresco Martinenga's evolved dark plum/garnet color reveals considerable amber at the edge. The bouquet offers up spicy new oak, dried fruits (particularly cherries), and floral/rose petal aromas. The finish is slightly tannic as well as short. Drink it over the next 5–6 years. The 1997 Barbaresco Martinenga exhibits a garnet color with pink/amber at the edge. It is a soft wine with notes of lead pencil, cherry, strawberry, and espresso. While it reveals little mid-palate, extract, or length, it is charming and elegant in a spicy, medium-bodied, fruity manner. Consume it over the next 8 years. The 1996 Barbaresco Camp Gros Martinenga offers more black cherry and black raspberry notes with strawberry jam in the mouth. A fuller wine, with more fruit, extract, and structure, this potentially outstanding Barbaresco can be drunk now and before 2012. The superb 1996 Barbaresco Gaiun Martinenga boasts a dark ruby/purple color as well as a gorgeous, Musigny-like nose of flowers, minerals, and black fruits. It is impeccably made, with great elegance, medium body, terrific fruit intensity, and no sense of heaviness. Drink this stylish, harmonious Barbaresco over the next 10 years. For whatever reason, the 1996 Barbaresco Martinenga was backward, lean, austere, and impossible to evaluate. I am sure it has the same level of potential as the other single-vineyard offerings, but it was impossible to penetrate. I will wait until it has had another year of evolution to retaste it.

The 1995 Barbaresco Camp Gros Martinenga reveals a Burgundian nose of black cherries, flowers, spice, and subtle toasty oak. In the mouth, notes of tobacco emerge in this graceful, medium-bodied, refined, supple-textured, lush wine. Drink it over the next 5–6 years. Similarly styled, the 1995 Barbaresco Gaiun Martinenga displays more tannin as well as a more structured personality. The 1995 Barbaresco Martinenga possesses the finest delineation, undeniable finesse, and copious quantities of beautifully etched black cherry fruit interspersed with scents of new oak, minerals, flowers, and spice. It is an attractively rendered, medium-bodied Barbaresco to consume over the next 5–6 years.

GIACOMO GRIMALDI

1998 Barolo Le Coste	E	90+
1997 Barolo Le Coste	E	92
1996 Barolo Le Coste	E	87

This producer, a former policeman from the village of Barolo, whose debut vintage was 1996, produced impressive efforts in both 1996, 1997, and 1998.

Potentially as good as if not better than the 1997, the 1998 Barolo Le Coste exhibits a dark garnet color as well as a classic Barolo bouquet of melted road tar, rose petals, cherry syrup, tobacco, and spice box. Deep-textured and full-bodied, with sweet kirschlike flavors infused with creosote/tar and a moderately tannic finish, this old-style, intense effort will drink well between 2003–2018. A muscular, dark plum-colored Barolo, Grimaldi's 1997 Le Coste offers classic aromatics of melted road tar, rose petals, new saddle leather, beef blood, and kirsch. Impressively endowed, with moderately high tannin, this powerful, thick, juicy effort is a definitive Barolo that needs 2–3 years of cellaring and should keep for two decades. His 1996 Barolo Le Coste revealed a reduced character, and I did not have the opportunity to taste a second sample. Certainly there is a lot to like. This classic old-style Barolo exhibits aromas of melted road tar, rose petals, and petroleum. Although hard to evaluate, it is full-bodied and at least excellent. I look forward to tasting it again. It appears to be a wine that will last for 10–12 years.

ICARDI

1999 Barbera d'Alba Surì di Mù	D	92
1998 Barbera d'Alba Surì di Mù	D	89
1999 Barbera d'Asti Tabarin	D	89
1996 Barolo	D	87
1995 Barolo	D	86
1998 Barolo Parej	E	(90–92)
1997 Barolo Parej	E	92
1998 Langhe Nebbiolo Suris Jvan	D	88
1999 Monferrato Rosso Bricco del Sole	D	88

An impressive, modern-styled producer, Icardi has been doing some top-notch work, as evidenced by these offerings.

Readers looking for a dazzling value should check out the 1999 Barbera d'Alba Surì di Mù. Aged one year in *barrique,* this 3,000-case *cuvée* is dynamite. Opaque purple-colored and full-bodied, with a gorgeous perfume of strawberry, cherry, and blackberry jam aromas mixed with charcoal, graphite, and new oak, this is a succulent, hedonistic, Barbera fruit bomb to drink over the next 3–4 years. The 1999 Barbera d'Asti Tabarin is also a terrific value. Explosive aromas of smoke, cherry fruit, and strawberries jump from the glass of this medium ruby-colored wine. Rich and fleshy, with abundant fruit, it is a seductive Barbera for drinking over the next 5–6 years. More restrained and revealing a more international style, largely because the oak is more noticeable, is the 1999 Monferrato Rosso Bricco del Sole, a blend of Barbera, Nebbiolo, and Cabernet Sauvignon aged 15 months in new French oak. A fine effort, it reveals less typicity and character than the less expensive Barbera d'Alba Surì di Mù. It should mature for easily 10 years. The more classic 1998 Langhe Nebbiolo Suris Jvan displays that varietal's black tea, tobacco, rose petal, and asphalt aromas in its moderately intense perfume. There is lovely ripeness, a supple texture, and a rich, round finish. Tasted blind, it could easily be mistaken for a Barolo if not a Barbaresco. Drink it over the next 5–6 years. The 1998 Barbera d'Alba Surì di Mù is better balanced, with a dark ruby color, a luscious, black cherry and strawberry jam–scented nose, ripe, supple flavors, medium to full body, and enough acidity for delineation and balance. It should drink well for 4–5 years.

These modern-styled Barolos are forward and fruit-driven. Another sleeper of the vintage, Icardi's 1998 Barolo Parej, boasts an opaque purple color as well as a sweet nose of blackberry and cherry liqueur intertwined with aromas of *barriques,* smoke, and graphite. Dense, muscular, and rich, with terrific ripeness and opulence in addition to a layered, moderately tannic finish, it will be at its finest between 2006–2018. One of the sleeper Barolos of the vintage, Icardi's explosive, full-bodied, exotic, dense purple-colored 1997 Barolo Parej boasts a jammy blackberry/cherry bouquet with notions of toasty new oak (clearly from the modern school of Piedmontese winemaking). There are terrific density, purity, and symmetry, as well as an unctuous, long finish with copious quantities of sweet tannin and glycerin. Drink this Nebbiolo fruit bomb over the next 15 years. The 1996 Barolo Parej exhibits a more briery, raspberry, Zinfandel-like personality, with pepper and dried herbs in the background. There are excellent extract, medium to full body, and moderate tannin. The slightly austere, astringent finish suggests that 1–2 years of cellaring will be beneficial. It should keep for 10 years. The 1995 Barolo Parej possesses a dark plum color, plenty of glycerin, a rich, precocious, fleshy appeal, low acidity, and a mélange of tobacco, spice, dried herbs, and jammy cherry fruit. Drink this medium-bodied offering over the next 2–3 years.

INSIEME

1998	Alessandria	E	92
1997	Alessandria	E	92
1998	Altare	E	94
1997	Altare	E	96
1997	Corino	E	92
1997	Grasso	E	90
1997	Molino	E	89
1998	Revello	E	93
1997	Revello	E	91
1998	Veglio	E	92
1997	Veglio	E	94

Originated by Elio Altare to raise charitable contributions to help repair historical Piedmontese buildings, this association was formed by the above-mentioned La Morra producers. Fifteen percent of the proceeds go to charity. All of the wines are aged in *barrique,* ranging from 10% new oak for Revello to 100% new oak for Grasso and Veglio. Altare and Corino utilize 80% new oak and Molino 60%. The blends are as follows: Grasso: 44% Nebbiolo, 16% Barbera, 20% Cabernet Sauvignon, and 20% Merlot; Molino: 40% Nebbiolo, 20% Barbera, 20% Cabernet Sauvignon, and 20% Merlot; Corino: 50% Nebbiolo and 50% Barbera, with a touch of Cabernet Sauvignon and Merlot; Alessandria: 40% Nebbiolo, 20% Barbera, and 40% Cabernet Sauvignon; Revello: 40% Nebbiolo, 30% Barbera, and 30% Cabernet Sauvignon; Veglio: 40% Nebbiolo, 30% Barbera, and 30% Cabernet Sauvignon; Altare: 50% Cabernet Sauvignon, 20% Nebbiolo, and 20% Barbera (only 90%). The wines are all bottled unfiltered, and there are approximately 3,000 bottles of each producer's Insieme. As the scores suggest, they are all gorgeous wines, with terrific levels of perfume and intensity. Given the tiny quantities available, I have provided brief tasting notes only for the 1998s, but readers lucky enough to find either vintage should not hesitate to purchase them. At about $58, they are realistically priced for such high quality.

Veglio's 1998 Insieme is a spectacular effort offering notes of red and black fruits, vanilla, smoke, and tobacco. Made in a full-bodied, opulent style, it should be drunk over the next 7–8 years, although I suspect it will last longer. Revello's 1998 Insieme is a fragrant, lavishly rich, exotic, concentrated wine also best drunk during its first 7–8 years of life. The complex Altare 1998 Insieme is great stuff. It is a Piedmontese wine made in a modern style with the influence of *barrique*. Notes of tobacco, licorice, black cherries, currants, spice box, and cedar are present as well as blackberry jam and cassis. The wine possesses an unctuous texture, huge body, and gorgeous fruit, sweetness, and length. It should drink well for a decade, although who will have the self-discipline to wait? Alessandria's 1998 Insieme is a fabulous, extremely full-bodied effort offering aromas and flavors of blackberries, cassis, cedar, leather, and vanilla. This thick, viscous, chewy, seamless, gorgeously harmonious wine will drink well for 7–8 years.

LA LICENZIANA DI SILVIO GIAMELLO

1998 Barbaresco	D	85
1998 Barbaresco Licenziana	D	87

These are straightforward efforts, with the plum/garnet-colored 1998 Barbaresco revealing moderate levels of cherry, tobacco, and herb-tinged fruit, good spice, Chinese tea, and light to moderate tannin. Consume this easy to understand Barbaresco over the next 2–3 years. More concentrated and deeper is the 1998 Barbaresco Licenziana. It exhibits excellent tobacco, berry, cherry, spice box, and licorice aromas as well as flavors, medium body, good fruit, sweet tannin, and admirable structure. It should evolve nicely for 3–4 years.

GIOVANNI MANZONE

1998 Barolo Le Gramolere	D	86
1997 Barolo Le Gramolere	D	87
1996 Barolo Le Gramolere	D	88
1995 Barolo Le Gramolere	D	91
1998 Barolo Bricat Gramolere	D	86
1997 Barolo Bricat Gramolere	D	87
1996 Barolo Bricat Gramolere	D	86
1995 Barolo Bricat Gramolere	D	89+
1997 Barolo Santo Stefano di Perno	D	88
1996 Barolo Santo Stefano di Perno	D	87
1995 Barolo Santo Stefano di Perno	D	90
1997 Langhe Rosso Tris	D	88

Manzone, whose cellars are located in the village of Monforte d'Alba, owns some of the highest elevated vineyards of this area, and hence the wines he produces tend to have cool-climate characteristics. They are made in a rather herbaceous style, with red rather than black fruit characteristics, fairly high acidity, and a certain leanness. Readers who prefer such a style to more fleshy, opulent, powerful wines will rate these offerings higher. This producer follows a quasi-modern school of winemaking. He utilizes open-top fermenters and believes in pumping over, and uses 20% new-oak casks for the *élevage*, with the rest of the wine being aged in *foudre* prior to bottling, accomplished without filtration. The 1995s are successful and may be as good as what Manzone produced in 1996 and 1997. However, the 1998s leave me asking for more as they tend to be lean, herbaceous, and short.

The austerity and high tannin of the dry, attenuated 1998 Barolo Le Gramolere is a perfect example of this default, even though it possesses attractive underlying cherry, strawberry, and mineral notes. The same can be said for the 1998 Barolo Bricat Gramolere, a delicate Burgundy-style wine with sweet cherry fruit intermixed with earth, wet stones, and flowers. Both of these wines require consumption over the next 5–6 years.

Manzone produced potentially outstanding 1997s. They display the vintage's equilibrium, velvety texture, and an expansive, open-knit richness that conceals moderately high tannin. The 1997 Barolo Le Gramolere possesses a medium ruby color with pink at the edge. An elegant, lighter-styled 1997 with spicy tobacco/herbaceous notes intermixed with cranberries, cherries, and red currants, this vibrant wine, with better acidity than most 1997s, should be drunk over its first 10 years of life. The more sinewy, intellectual 1997 Barolo Bricat Gramolere is less hedonistic than many of its peers. Medium-bodied and tasty, with notions of cherries, coffee, and herbs, it is made in an austere, subdued style. Drink it over the next 8 years. Cut from the same mold but slightly richer, the 1997 Barolo Santo Stefano di Perno emerges from a vineyard on the lower slopes, where more sun exposure results in riper fruit. It offers aromas and flavors of road tar, rose water, minerals, and cherry liqueur. Medium-bodied, pure, stylish, and elegant, it will be drinkable between 2002–2015. Manzone has also turned out an interesting blend of equal parts Dolcetto, Barbera, and Nebbiolo called Langhe Rosso Tris. The 1997 is a sexy, round, dark ruby-colored wine with abundant fruit but not the volume or explosiveness of his Dolcetto. It is a more elegant, restrained offering to consume over the next 2–3 years.

Manzone's 1996s were tannic, austere examples that may have been going through a stubborn phase of their evolution. The ruby/purple-colored 1996 Barolo Santo Stefano di Perno displays an intriguing nose of licorice, cherry liqueur, oak, and earth. There is sweet fruit on the attack, but the tannin and structure take over, compressing the mid-palate and finish. This Barolo has the potential for an outstanding rating . . . if the tannin becomes more integrated. I will be anxious to retaste it after bottling. Anticipated maturity: 2004–2015. The 1996 Barolo Le Gramolere is a dark ruby-colored, earthy, structured, medium- to full-bodied wine with a great deal of muscle and intensity. It displays an herbaceous, tobacco, smoky, dried fruit–scented nose and an old-style, traditional, astringent finish. This wine could turn out to be a classic, but it could also be slightly rustic and tannic. Time will tell. Anticipated maturity: 2005–2016. Even more tannic is the 1996 Barolo Bricat Gramolere. An impressive, powerful example, with cherry cough syrup notes meshed with dried herbs, roasted scents, a touch of tar and earth, this backward Barolo requires 5–6 years of cellaring. Anticipated maturity: 2006–2015.

The 1995 Barolo Santo Stefano di Perno exhibits a deceptively light medium ruby color, as well as knockout aromas of sweet berry fruit intermixed with spice box, floral scents, and subtle toast. Sweet, rich, and fruit driven, with a supple, lush texture, medium to full body, and gorgeous balance, this wine can be drunk now or over the next 10 years. The 1995 Barolo Le Gramolere reveals a candied cassis character, as well as black raspberry and cherry fruit on the palate. The sumptuous aromas and silky texture are reminiscent of a top-class, opulently styled grand cru red Burgundy. Delicious and forward, it will provide ideal drinking over the next decade. The 1995 Barolo Bricat Gramolere, from his parcel of Nebbiolo planted at the top of this hillside vineyard, is more structured and backward, without the expressive characteristics of the other *cuvées*. Anticipated maturity: now–2014.

MARCARINI

1997	Barolo Brunate	E	89
1996	Barolo Brunate	E	89+
1998	Barbera Ciabot	D	86
1997	Barolo La Serra	E	88
1996	Barolo La Serra	E	90
1999	Dolcetto d'Alba Boschi di Berri	C	89

Made from 150-year-old prephylloxera vines (believed to be Italy's oldest Dolcetto plantings in existence), Marcarini's renowned 1999 Dolcetto d'Alba Boschi di Berri boasts an opaque purple color as well as thick, juicy berry fruit, almond extract, and underbrush aromas. Rich but not complex, this mouth-filling, palate-staining Dolcetto can be drunk now or cellared for 5+ years. The dark ruby/purple-colored 1998 Barbera Ciabot exhibits a rougher edge as well as an excellent attack, jagged acidity, and good, ripe fruit. Made in a more rustic style, it will drink well for 4–5 years.

The 1997 Barolo La Serra and 1997 Barolo Brunate are both closed at present, so they may ultimately merit an even higher rating. The 1997 Barolo La Serra exhibits a dark ruby color in addition to Barolo's telltale bouquet of rose petals, black cherries, and balsam wood with hints of underbrush/tobacco. There is good ripeness, medium to full body, moderately high tannin, and a firm but traditionally styled finish with no evidence of new oak. Anticipated maturity: 2004–2014. Sweeter and more elegant, as well as potentially more complex, the dark ruby-colored 1997 Barolo Brunate reveals aromas of cigar box and cherry jam as well as a sweet attack with notes of minerals, subtle spicy wood, firm tannin, and medium to full body. Anticipated maturity: 2004–2015. The first thing that came to mind when I smelled the 1996 Barolo La Serra was brandy-macerated cherries. The wine's medium ruby color is deceptive in view of its concentration. This showy 1996 Barolo offers abundant quantities of sweet black cherry fruit intermixed with high-octane, concentrated, spice box characteristics, medium to full body, fine opulence, and a long, lush, powerful finish that undoubtedly conceals more tannin than exhibited. It should drink well for 10–12 years. In contrast, the 1996 Barolo Brunate reveals a more saturated dark ruby color in addition to a complex bouquet of dried herbs, smoke, minerals, and black fruits. Dense, chewy, and powerful, this big yet backward 1996 requires discipline. Anticipated maturity: 2004–2018.

ALDO MARENCO

1999 Barbera Pirona	D	85
1999 Barbera Pirona Barrique	D	87
1999 Dolcetto di Dogliani Bric	C	86
1999 Dolcetto di Dogliani Parlapà	C	89
1999 Dolcetto di Dogliani Surì	C	88

The straightforward, non–wood-aged 1999 Barbera Pirona offers a medium dark ruby color and good spiciness, but it is essentially foursquare and monolithic. It will provide uncritical quaffing over the next 1–2 years. New oak works well with Barbera, and Marenco's 1999 Pirona Barrique reveals more character in its sweet black cherry, earthy, licorice, and toasty-scented nose. There is also a deeper, more saturated ruby/purple color, medium body, and a soft finish. Enjoy it over the next 1–2 years. Marenco's straightforward, medium-bodied 1999 Dolcetto di Dogliani Bric exhibits soft, mocha, chocolate, and berry fruit flavors along with good ripeness and purity. Consume it over the next 12–18 months. Riper, sweeter, and obviously produced from lower yields and/or older vines, the 1999 Dolcetto di Dogliani Surì possesses Dolcetto's rich, jammy berry fruit mixed with mocha and coffee. Well made, with sweet fruit, excellent length, and a succulent, hedonistic personality, it should be drunk over the next 1–2 years. Lastly, made from the estate's oldest vines, the 1999 Dolcetto di Dogliani Parlapà tips the scales at a lofty 14% alcohol, which is well hidden by the glycerin, fruit, and smoky, berry, fleshy character. Drink it over the next 2 years.

MARIO MARENGO

1998 Barolo Brunate	E	(87–89)
1997 Barolo Bricco delle Viole	E	88
1997 Barolo Brunate	E	89
1996 Barolo Brunate	E	91
1995 Barolo Brunate	E	91

This La Morra producer utilizes open-top vats as opposed to the rotary fermenters so popular with many of the newer-styled Piedmontese wine-makers, and uses approximately 25% new oak casks for aging his Barolos.

An intriguing nose of allspice, cinnamon, and cloves intertwined with cherry cough syrup and smoke is followed by a medium-bodied, complex, yet understated 1998 Barolo Brunate. Drink it over the next 10 years. In 1997, Marengo produced two Barolos. The excellent, soft, lush, exotic 1997 Barolo Bricco delle Viole displays distinctive strawberry liqueur inter-mixed with smoky oak, leafy tobacco, and dried herbs. Open, lush, and medium- to full-bodied, without much structure, this wine should drink well young and last for 10 years. An elegant, Burgundy-styled effort, Marengo's 1997 Barolo Brunate is a spicy, black cherry, and floral-scented, medium- to full-bodied wine with beautiful purity, moderate tannin and struc-ture, and a midweight character that is less ostentatious than many of its peers. The subtle finish reveals well-integrated tannin, acidity, and alcohol. It can be enjoyed now or cellared for 15+ years. It is slightly less impressive from bottle than it was from *barrique*. The velvety-textured 1996 Barolo Brunate offers up a textbook bouquet of rose petals, cherry liqueur, and tobacco leaf scents. Melted tar also emerges with swirling. On the palate, there are gorgeous levels of black cherry and truffle flavors. Dense and full-bodied, with lofty but not excessive alcohol (14%), this sensational Barolo has moderate tannin underlying the layers of glycerin-imbued, rich, chewy fruit. Anticipated maturity: now–2016. The 1995 Barolo Brunate is a beauty for the vintage. It is a wine of tenderness, voluptuous, silky fruit, medium body, and lovely cherry, strawberry, and tobacco flavors with toasty, smoky notes in the subtle finish. Rich, fleshy, and medium- to full-bodied, this offering will drink well for a decade.

GIAN PIERO MARRONE

1997 Barolo	D	87

A modern, internationally styled 1997, Marrone's deep ruby-colored Barolo lacks typicity but is a full-bodied, powerful, mouth-filling, delicious red. Anticipated maturity: now–2010.

FRANCO M. MARTINETTI

1997 Montruc	D	91
1997 Sul Bric	D	89

A terrific example of Barbera is the 1997 Montruc (775 cases). Aging in new French oak gives this wine an international style initially, but with airing, sweet cherry liqueur and spicy notes emerge from this dark plum-colored offering. Voluptuously textured for a Barbera, this fat, ripe, full-bodied 1997 demonstrates how sexy wines from this vintage can be. Loaded with fruit and explosive on the palate, it offers a hedonistic wine-drinking experience. Enjoy it over the next 4–5 years. The elegant 1997 Sul Bric (a blend of equal parts Barbera and Cabernet Sauvignon, aged for one year in French oak) does not possess the power and explosiveness of the Montruc. The Sul Bric exhibits black currant fruit intertwined with toasty new oak, lead pencil, and dried herbs. In the mouth, there are excellent density, purity, and overall balance. While there is noticeable tannin in the finish, the wine is fat and sweet. Drink it over the next 8 years.

BARTOLO MASCARELLO

1998 Barolo	E	(90–93)
1997 Barolo	E	94
1996 Barolo	E	(87–88+)
1995 Barolo	E	86

One of my favorite traditional producers and a quintessential traditionalist, Bartolo Mas-carello appears to have been less successful than some of his peers in 1995 and 1996, but his 1997 and 1998 are topflight.

The 1998 Barolo reveals a deceivingly unimpressive plum/garnet/ruby color. However, the aromatics explode from the glass offering scents of Chinese black tea, licorice, black cherries, tar, and truffles. In the mouth, it is sweet, fleshy, powerful, and heady, with exquisite purity as well as symmetry. This wine's aromas and flavors will convince readers that Nebbiolo is the Pinot Noir of Italy. It will undoubtedly tighten after bottling, reemerge in 2–3 years and age well for nearly two decades.

I underestimated the 1997 Barolo from barrel, but now that it is in bottle, it is an impressive, old-style, heavyweight effort that will age for three decades. A dark plum/garnet color is accompanied by a striking bouquet of cinnamon, balsa wood, roses, tar, minerals, and cherry liqueur. There is good acidity for a 1997, a broad, full-bodied, super-concentrated palate, and telltale truffle, leather, and dried herb notes. Powerful and long, but not as exotic as many 1997s, this well-delineated, gorgeously pure, structured Barolo is a classic from the old school of Piedmontese winemaking. Anticipated maturity: 2005–2030.

The 1996 Barolo reveals surprisingly high acidity in its relatively backward, tannic profile. It was closed and tough-textured when I saw it, with sour cherry, dried nut, and kirsch notes. The wine did not develop in the glass, remaining austere and compressed. Anticipated maturity: 2003–2014. The 1995 Barolo displays a moderate cranberry color with a pink edge leading to amber. It is light- to medium-bodied, with intriguing spice box aromas intermixed with strawberry and cherry fruit. Moderate tannin in the finish suggests this wine will have a limited longevity of 7–10 years. It is a light effort, even considering the vintage.

GIUSEPPE MASCARELLO & FIGLIO

1998 Barolo Monprivato	E	(89–91)
1997 Barolo Monprivato	E	92
1996 Barolo Monprivato	E	(87–89)
1995 Barolo Monprivato	E	87

Mascarello's Barolos rank among Piedmont's perennial stars, particularly in top vintages. A silky, full-bodied, opulent effort, the 1998 Barolo Monprivato reveals good intensity as well as a fleshy, up-front bouquet of licorice, tobacco, sweet cherries, melted asphalt, and rose petals. A classic Nebbiolo, this surprisingly soft, silky-textured Barolo can be drunk now as well as cellared for 15 years. While not as exotic or explosive as the 1997, the 1998 is still top-class. The 1997 Barolo Monprivato exhibits a dense ruby/garnet color as well as a sweet nose of cedar, black fruits, earth, tar, and rose petals. The explosive perfume is followed by a rich, seamless, full-bodied, unctuously textured wine. One of the most precocious and accessible Monprivatos I have ever tasted, the 1997 is the finest since the glorious 1990. Anticipated maturity: now–2015. The 1996 Barolo Monprivato is more structured and muscular, but not as concentrated or powerful as I expected given this producer's track record. It exhibits a dark plum color with amber at the edge. The smoky, dried herb, cedary, tobacco leaf elements compete with cherries, leather, and licorice. Medium- to full-bodied, with a soft attack and moderate tannin in the finish, this is a very good to excellent Barolo that falls short of being outstanding. Anticipated maturity: 2003–2012. This traditional producer has turned out a 1995 Barolo Monprivato with earthy, truffle, licorice, and dusty black cherry fruit. Medium- to full-bodied, with good ripeness, excellent purity, and a nicely extracted, rustic, generous style, it is already accessible, yet promises to last for 10 years.

CASCINA LUISIN DI LUIGI MINUTO

1997 Barbaresco Cascina Luisin Rabajà	D	90
1996 Barbaresco Cascina Luisin Rabajà	D	88
1995 Barbaresco Cascina Luisin Rabajà	D	87
1997 Barbaresco Sorì Paolin	D	86
1996 Barbaresco Sorì Paolin	D	81?
1995 Barbaresco Sorì Paolin	D	86

The standard *cuvées* are very good efforts, but Minuto's Barbarescos from the Cascina Luisin Rabajà vineyard are distinctly superior to his offerings from the Sorì Paolin vineyard. The velvety, supple, impressively extracted 1997 Barbaresco Sorì Paolin's opaque ruby/purple color is followed by gobs of blackberry and cherry fruit aromas, a sweet mid-palate, the vintage's telltale high glycerin and low acidity, and a thick, juicy finish. Drink it over the next 10 years. The outstanding dark ruby/purple-colored 1997 Barbaresco Cascina Luisin Rabajà offers an intense nose of licorice, black cherry fruit, dried herbs, and wood. In addition, it displays a velvety texture, full body, and an opulent, lush, low-acid finish. Already accessible, it should be delicious when released next year. Anticipated maturity: now–2010.

The more closed 1996 Barbaresco Sorì Paolin possesses medium body, high acidity, more tannin, and a colder feel in the mouth than the more generous 1995. It is a bigger, more muscular wine with plenty of structure and excellent fruit and purity, but it is closed, firmly knit and austere. Anticipated maturity: now–2010. The 1996 Barbaresco Cascina Luisin Rabajà is nearly outstanding. It possesses a distinctive cigar tobacco–scented nose with aromas of kirsch, spice, and earth. Medium- to full-bodied, with excellent richness and good spice and length, it displays more tannin than the 1995 but should be drunk over the next 5–6 years. The 1995 Barbaresco Sorì Paolin reveals a dark ruby color, as well as sweet, attractive cherry fruit blended with cedar, cigar box, and leather. Medium-bodied and supple, with decent acidity, this is a stylish, delicious Barbaresco to enjoy over the next 4–5 years. The 1995 Barbaresco Cascina Luisin Rabajà reveals an open-knit, intensely spicy, cedar box and black fruit–scented nose. It is fleshy, expansive, fully mature, and ideal for drinking over the next 3–4 years.

MOCCAGATTA

1998	Barbaresco Bric Balin	D	89
1997	Barbaresco Bric Balin	D	90
1996	Barbaresco Bric Balin	D	90
1998	Barbaresco Vigneto Basarin	D	84?
1997	Barbaresco Vigneto Basarin	D	90
1996	Barbaresco Vigneto Basarin	D	89
1998	Barbaresco Vigneto Cole	D	90+
1997	Barbaresco Vigneto Cole	D	90
1996	Barbaresco Vigneto Cole	D	90+
1998	Barbera d'Alba Vigneto Basarin	C	90

The opaque purple, thick, juicy 1998 Barbera d'Alba Vigneto Basarin oozes with black cherry fruit intermixed with cedar, strawberries, and toasty wood. It exhibits a supple texture, a tremendous palate impression, and a long, lush finish. Enjoy it over the next 2–3 years.

The 1998 Barbaresco Vigneto Basarin is an elegant, lighter-styled effort with an amber edge already noticeable in its medium ruby color. Scents of tobacco as well as ripe strawberry and cherry fruit are present, but the finish is attenuated and lean, without the depth or body expected in a top Barbaresco cru. The aromatically compelling 1998 Barbaresco Bric Balin exhibits aromas of new saddle leather intermixed with tobacco, cedar wood, black cherry liqueur, and smoke. Its dark ruby color also reveals some amber at the rim. Medium-bodied, soft, and well balanced, it is meant to be consumed over the next 4–5 years. The most massive, backward, concentrated, and complex of the 1998s is the 1998 Barbaresco Vigneto Cole. A dense dark garnet color is followed by high-toned, fragrant aromas of menthol, leather, spice box, cherries, and wood. Deep, rich, and medium- to full-bodied, with moderate tannin in the long finish, it will keep for a decade or more.

The 1997s are simply outstanding. While they all merit a 90-point rating, they represent different styles, with the Basarin the most evolved, the Balin the most subtle, and the Cole the most massive, backward, and exotic. They all possess 8–10 years of aging potential. The delicious 1997 Barbaresco Vigneto Basarin is the most forward of this trio, with a deep garnet color and a sweet nose of black cherry fruit, spice box, licorice, smoke, and earth. Full-bodied, silky-textured, seductive, and lush, it is hard to resist. Less aromatic as well as more tannic and firmer-structured is the 1997 Barbaresco Bric Balin. It exhibits a deep ruby color, copious quantities of glycerin, black fruits, herbs, cedar, tar, and spicy oak, medium to full body, admirable delineation, and firm tannin in the finish. Anticipated maturity: now–2013. The 1997 Barbaresco Vigneto Cole's dark plum/garnet color reveals some amber at the edge. The bouquet offers scents of mushrooms, soy, smoked meats, jammy black fruits, root vegetables, and more oak than the other *cuvées*. Complex, juicy, succulent, and full-bodied, with serious tannin in the finish, it should last for 10–12 years.

The terrific 1996s, while not huge, are beautifully knit with fruit-driven personalities and considerable complexity. The dark ruby-colored 1996 Barbaresco Vigneto Basarin offers a sexy bouquet of black cherry jam intermixed with spice and wood. The wine is dense and fat, with abundant glycerin and a hedonistic, up-front appeal. Drink it over the next 10 years. The sensational 1996 Barbaresco Bric Balin displays a saturated ruby color, and a provocative nose of black cherry liqueur, melted road tar, vanilla, and floral scents. Full-bodied, with layers of glycerin and fruit, this is a mouthcoating, rich, surprisingly silky-textured Barbaresco to drink over the next 10–12 years. The 1996 Barbaresco Vigneto Cole reveals more evidence of new oak in its smoky, toasty nose. There are also more extract, concentration, and tannin, as well as good purity and a 40-second finish. Full-bodied and in need of 1–2 years of cellaring, it should keep for 12–15 years.

MAURO MOLINO

1998	Barolo	D	88
1997	Barolo	D	88
1996	Barolo	D	(84–86)
1998	Barolo Vigna Conca	E	(90–92+)
1997	Barolo Vigna Conca	E	91+
1996	Barolo Vigna Conca	E	92+
1995	Barolo Vigna Conca	E	90
1998	Barolo Vigna Gancia	E	(88–90)
1997	Barolo Vigna Gancia	E	89
1996	Barolo Vigna Gancia	E	92
1995	Barolo Vigna Gancia	E	87

Molino continues to raise the quality level of his Barolos, with his 1998s performing as well as his 1997s. The 1998s are elegant and harmonious, with even more enticing aromatics, and the 1997s are very fine indeed.

The dark ruby-colored 1998 Barolo exhibits a classic bouquet of licorice, rose petals, tar, and sweet black cherry fruit. Medium- to full-bodied, delicate, and flavorful in a layered, harmonious style, it will drink well for 5–6 years. The opaque garnet-colored 1998 Barolo Vigna Gancia is made in a firmer style, with abundant nuances as well as muscle but not the expressive personality displayed by its two siblings. It offers excellent to outstanding depth, medium to full body, and moderate tannin in the finish. Give it 1–2 years of cellaring, and enjoy it over the following 10–12 years. The superb, saturated ruby/purple-colored 1998 Barolo Vigna Conca may not possess the opulence of its 1997 counterpart, but it exhibits impressive balance, terrific purity, and fragrant black fruit notes intermixed with smoke, new wood, licorice, and spice box. Given the moderate tannin in the finish, I would cellar it for 1–2 years and consume it over the following 10–15 years.

The generic 1997 Barolo reveals pink at the rim of its ruby/garnet color. A perfume of roasted peanuts, dried Provençal herbs, sweet currants, and cherries is more reminiscent of a classy St.-Emilion than Nebbiolo. However, in the mouth, the wine's opulence, fleshiness, and soft, forward character reflect this vintage's Piedmont style. Enjoy it over the next 4–5 years. Offering a more complex bouquet, the dark garnet-colored 1997 Barolo Vigna Gancia reveals scents of balsam wood, herbs, licorice, cherry liqueur, and soy. Additionally, it possesses firm tannin, good density and ripeness, and a rich, medium- to full-bodied, plush, yet delineated personality. Give it 1–2 more years of cellaring, and consume it over the following 10–12 years. The superb 1997 Barolo Vigna Conca is the most backward, powerful, and concentrated of these offerings. The color is a dark garnet, and the nose offers up aromas of smoke, meat, dried herbs, black fruits, earth, and spices. Dense, full-bodied, concentrated, powerful, and structured, it will be at its best between 2003–2016.

In 1996, Molino produced a generic Barolo in addition to his two single-vineyard *cuvées*. The 1996 Barolo is a pleasant, straightforward, soft, medium ruby-colored wine that needs to be drunk over the next 4–5 years. In contrast, the superb, saturated ruby/purple-colored 1996 Barolo Vigna Conca is a massive effort with oodles of black cherry fruit intertwined with licorice, smoke, and spicy elements. Full-bodied and super-concentrated, with copious quantities of glycerin, it is soft and voluptuous. Enjoy it now and over the next 10 years. The opaque dark ruby/purple-colored 1996 Barolo Vigna Gancia offers a nose of *surmaturité*. This unevolved, backward wine possesses chewy plum/cherry fruit, terrific extraction, fine purity, and a full-bodied, moderately tannic, youthful finish. Anticipated maturity: now–2016.

The 1995 Barolo Vigna Gancia is attractive, evolved, open-knit, and medium-bodied, with fine ripeness and a spice box/cherry-dominated personality. Although not a blockbuster, it is elegant, soft, and ideal for drinking over the next 3–4 years. The richer 1995 Barolo Vigna Conca possesses more depth than its medium ruby color suggests. Additionally, it is pure, well delineated, and made in an elegant, suave, savory style with abundant sweet red fruits, cigar box spices, and a touch of new saddle leather. It should drink well for 7–8 years.

MONTI

1998 Barbera d'Alba	C	89
1997 Barbera d'Alba	C	90+

These two Barberas are produced from exceptionally ripe fruit and low yields and are aged in new French oak. Sadly, there are only 100 cases of the dark ruby/purple-colored, flamboyant 1998 Barbera d'Alba. This wine offers aromas of exotic sweet new oak intermixed with jammy black fruits, coconuts, and dried herbs. Full-bodied and loaded with concentrated fruit, it lacks complexity but delivers plenty of hedonism in its plush personality. Drink it over the next 3–4 years. The internationally styled, blockbuster 1997 Barbera d'Alba is a monster-sized wine that boasts an opaque black/purple color, as well as sumptuous aromas of overripe cherries, strawberries, licorice, and toast. Thick, huge, massive, and layered, with a finish that lasts more than 30 seconds, this low-acid, impressive wine can be drunk now or aged for a decade.

F.LLI MOSSIO

1999 Dolcetto d'Alba	B	87
1999 Dolcetto d'Alba Bricco Caramelli	B	90
1999 Dolcetto d'Alba Piano delli Perdoni	B	86

These wines are evidence that 1999 is a strong vintage for Dolcetto and Barbera. The 1999 Dolcetto d'Alba and 1999 Dolcetto d'Alba Piano delli Perdoni are dark ruby/purple-colored, medium-bodied, sweet wines with plenty of chocolaty, cherry fruit. The Perdoni is tangier, with slightly higher acidity. The blockbuster of this trio is the 1999 Dolcetto d'Alba Bricco Caramelli. It possesses an opaque ruby/purple color as well as a knockout nose of chocolate, espresso, and berries. With copious glycerin, a fleshy, fat texture, and wonderful ripeness and purity, it will drink well for 2–3 years, as these wines rarely improve.

ANDREA OBERTO

1996	Barolo Vigneto Albarella	E	88+
1997	Barolo Vigneto Rocche	E	92
1996	Barolo Vigneto Rocche	E	91+
1995	Barolo Vigneto Rocche	E	86

From a consistently fine producer, the following examples are all fine for their respective vintages. These wines, that merit interest, are quasi-modern-styled wines that combine the best of the traditional and modern schools of winemaking.

The 1997 Barolo Vigneto Rocche boasts huge quantities of glycerin, which, combined with high alcohol, low acidity, and jammy black cherry and blackberry fruit, makes for an opulent texture and viscous mouth-feel. It is a freak as far as classic Barolo goes, but a delicious one. Layered, thick, and almost over the top, it is a knockout, dramatic effort that will be immensely popular. Anticipated maturity: 2003–2020.

The 1996 Barolo Vigneto Albarella's dark plum/ruby color is followed by sweet aromatics consisting of cedar wood, cherries, black raspberries, coffee, chocolate, and spice box. Dry tannin in the finish is typical of the 1996 vintage. Rich and full-bodied, it requires cellaring. Anticipated maturity: 2005–2020. The opaque plum/ruby/purple-colored 1996 Barolo Vigneto Rocche is a full-bodied, powerful, tannic effort with notes of rose petals, asphalt, cedar, black fruits, minerals, licorice, and fruitcake. Complex, layered, thick, and rich, it is best cellared for 3–4 years and drunk over the following 20–25 years.

The dark ruby-colored 1995 Barolo Vigneto Rocche exhibits a rich, modern style, as well as a textbook nose of roses, tar, spicy black cherry fruit, and a touch of *barrique* and foresty aromas. Rich and medium-bodied, with a short finish but excellent ripeness, this moderately sized Barolo can be drunk now as well as over the next 10 years.

F.LLI ODDERO

1997	Barbaresco	D	(85–87)
1996	Barbaresco	D	85
1997	Barolo Mondoca di Bussia Soprana	D	87
1996	Barolo Mondoca di Bussia Soprana	D	87?
1995	Barolo Mondoca di Bussia Soprana	D	88
1997	Barolo Vigna Rionda	D	86
1995	Barolo Vigna Rionda	D	87
1997	Barolo Rocche dei Rivera di Castiglione	D	88
1996	Barolo Rocche dei Rivera di Castiglione	D	87
1997	Furesté	D	89

Another producer from the village of La Morra, Oddero's 1997s exhibit the vintage's attractive levels of glycerin, fat, low acidity, and overripe style. All of them possess Nebbiolo's textbook aromas of cherry jam, dried herbs, tar, and spice. The 1997 Barbaresco displays a dark ruby color as well as chewy, exuberant, cherry liqueur fruit flavors intertwined with dried herb and spice. It is a luscious Barbaresco to enjoy over the next decade. The 1997 Barolo Vigna Rionda (a great vineyard in Serralunga) exhibits a dark garnet color as well as a sweet nose of cedar, spice box, licorice, toffee, and tobacco. In the mouth, it is creamy, round, medium-bodied, and easy to drink. Consume within 4–5 years. The dark ruby/purple-colored 1997 Barolo Rocche dei Rivera di Castiglione is full-bodied, fat, monolithic, and lacking complexity, but chewy and weighty. It is a husky Barolo to drink between now–2015. Even sweeter and riper is the medium- to full-bodied 1997 Barolo Mondoca di Bussia Soprana. It offers an excellent smoke, herb, licorice, and kirsch-scented bouquet. Soy and incense also make an appearance in the flavors. The wine is spicy, with low acidity and noticeable glycerin. Drink over the next 4–5 years. The dense 1997 Furesté (100% Cabernet Sauvignon) possesses cassis fruit, toasty new oak, and an opulent texture, but it is not yet totally formed or delineated. Given its concentration levels and intensity, it should merit an outstanding score after some more bottle age. Anticipated maturity: 2003–2012. Oddero's medium-bodied, garnet-colored 1996 Barolo Rocche dei Rivera di Castiglione exhibits aromas of leather, sour cherries, and ripe fruit. Well made, spicy, open-knit, and attractive, it can be consumed over the next decade.

The 1996 Barbaresco is a good, elegant offering with spicy tobacco-tinged cherry fruit, medium body, and a lightly tannic finish. It is ideal for drinking over the next 7–8 years. Oddero's 1996 Barolo Mondoca di Bussia Soprana possesses a dark color, considerable concentration, huge body, and brutal tannin levels (thus the question mark). The wine is leathery, chunky, and rustic. If the tannin melts away without a proportional loss of fruit, this could be close to outstanding, but the astringency of the tannin is cause for concern. Anticipated maturity: 2003–2015.

Oddero's two 1995s are similar in quality, although the Vigna Rionda is more tannic. The 1995 Barolo Mondoca di Bussia Soprana exhibits a smoky ashtray-like nose with notes of cedar, leather, and dried herbs and fruits. As the wine sat in the glass, the classic tar and rose petal concoction emerged. This is an old-style, rustic Barolo with an evolved plum/garnet color, hard tannin, and a lot of character and spice. It should drink well for 10 years. The herb- and smoke-infused 1995 Barolo Vigna Rionda possesses more rustic tannin, as well as good concentration, and an old-style, tough, chewy character that may not appeal to readers who enjoy modern, supple-styled wines. Nevertheless, it is a fine wine that can be drunk now or cellared for 10–12 years.

PALLADINO

1998 Barolo Serralunga	D	89
1997 Barolo Serralunga	D	89+
1998 Barolo Vigna Broglio	D	88
1997 Barolo Vigna Broglio	D	90
1998 Barolo Vigna San Bernardo	D	89
1997 Barolo Vigna San Bernardo	D	92

A sleeper Serralunga producer whom I discovered a couple of years ago, Palladino has vineyards in the village of Serralunga d'Alba. Its 1997s as well as its 1998s performed extremely well in my Piedmont tastings. These wines appear to be traditionally made with no evidence of *barrique* aging, although they do not display the backwardness or tannin found in most traditionalists' Barbarescos and Barolos.

The 1998s are stylish, elegant, evolved wines that should all drink well during their first 10 years of life. The 1998 Barolo Vigna Broglio exhibits a dark garnet color along with a sweet nose of spice, coffee, black cherry jam, medium to full body, adequate acidity, and a plush style. More evolved, the 1998 Barolo Serralunga displays a dark garnet color with amber hues. Moderately intense aromas of brown sugar, molasses, ripe cherries, soy, and earth are followed by a ripe, sweet, expansive, medium-bodied wine. It's a marginal call, but the garnet-colored 1998 Barolo Vigna San Bernardo may possess slightly more expansiveness and volume than its two siblings. Medium-bodied, long, and purely made, it displays a compelling sweetness in its ripe notes of tobacco, cherry fruit, and earth.

The generic 1997 Barolo Serralunga is a strong effort. Revealing notes of melted caramel, brown sugar, smoke, kirsch, and dried herbs, it tastes like a right bank Pomerol from an extremely ripe vintage. Unctuous, thick, and juicy but without the complexity of its two siblings, this delicious 1997 would merit an even higher score if numbers were given for pure hedonism. Anticipated maturity: now–2015. The outstanding, opaque garnet-colored 1997

Barolo Vigna Broglio is a powerful, impressively endowed effort with copious aromas of black cherry fruit, cedar, fruitcake, dried herbs, licorice, and hints of new oak. Impressive purity, symmetry, and overall winemaking make this an exceptional effort. Tannin in the finish suggests that several years of cellaring is warranted. Anticipated maturity: now–2016. Lastly, Palladino's opaque ruby/purple-colored 1997 Barolo Vigna San Bernardo exhibits a moderate style with new oak in the nose, fabulously concentrated black raspberry and cherry fruit, and subtle notions of minerals, maple syrup, and vanilla in the background. Full-bodied and exceptionally concentrated, with beautiful purity and well-integrated acidity as well as tannin, this terrific Barolo is a sleeper of the vintage. Anticipated maturity: now–2020.

ARMANDO PARUSSO

1999	Barbera d'Alba Ornati	D	91
1997	Barolo	D	(89–91)
1996	Barolo	D	88
1996	Barolo Bussia Vigna Fiurin	E	91
1998	Barolo Bussia Vigna Munie	E	(91–93)
1997	Barolo Bussia Vigna Munie	E	91+
1996	Barolo Bussia Vigna Munie	E	92
1995	Barolo Bussia Vigna Munie	E	90
1998	Barolo Bussia Vigna Rocche	E	(90–92)
1997	Barolo Bussia Vigna Rocche	E	92
1996	Barolo Bussia Vigna Rocche	E	92
1995	Barolo Bussia Vigna Rocche	E	90
1998	Barolo Mariondino	E	(87–88)
1997	Barolo Mariondino	E	90
1996	Barolo Mariondino	E	(90–92)
1995	Barolo Mariondino	E	87
1998	Barolo Piccole Vigne	E	(88–89)
1997	Barolo Piccole Vigne	E	90
1998	Langhe Rosso Bricco Rovella	D	89

Young Marco Parusso, who has completely modernized his cellars on the slopes of Monforte d'Alba, has come of age with his 1995s, 1996s, and 1997s. Moreover, those three vintages have been followed by impressive wines in both 1998 and 1999. As expected from such a youthful producer, Parusso is from the modernist school of winemaking. He believes in the use of rotary fermenters, short macerations, and 25–75% new oak for his finest crus.

The 1999 Barbera d'Alba Ornati is a *barrique*-aged Barbera revealing abundant quantities of strawberry jam intermixed with blackberries, cherries, and toasty, smoky oak. Deep, opulent, and voluptuous, with great purity and presence, it is a fabulous buy, but consume it over the next 3–4 years. The 500+ cases of the 1998 Langhe Rosso Bricco Rovella, a blend of 60% Nebbiolo, 30% Barbera, and 10% Cabernet Sauvignon aged 18 months in new French oak, offer plenty of smoky, toasty oak intertwined with black fruits, smoke, cedar, and cigar box notes. It is medium-bodied and surprisingly elegant for a wine of this modern, international style. Drink it over the next 3–4 years.

Parusso has turned out a deep ruby-colored 1998 Barolo Piccole Vigne with a spicy nose of balsam wood and black cherries. In the mouth, there is plenty of glycerin as well as an attractive open-knit style. Drink this 1998 over the next 5–6 years. More minty, peppery, and oaky, the medium-weight 1998 Barolo Mariondino exhibits plenty of wood and black cherry characteristics in its distinctive personality. It will age well for a decade.

The most powerful wine of this quartet is the 1998 Barolo Bussia Vigna Rocche. Structured, tannic, super-concentrated, well delineated, dense, full-bodied, and broodingly backward, this impressive effort reveals the 1998 vintage's telltale fragrance as well as the power and glycerin of 1997. Anticipated maturity: 2003–2015. The more graceful, delicate, smoky, leathery, earthy, dark ruby/garnet-colored 1998 Barolo Bussia Vigna Munie possesses medium to full body, terrific purity and ripeness, and a more delicate, lacelike style. It can be drunk over the next 10–12 years.

The 1997s reveal this terrific vintage's jammy, low-acid, exotic, flamboyant character. They all possess considerable tannin, but their ostentatious personalities are overwhelming. For example, sipping the dark ruby-colored, low-acid 1997 Barolo is akin to drinking strawberry jam. Ripe, fat, exotic, and hedonistic, this fruit bomb will be drinkable upon release and last until 2010.

Parusso's softest, most forward 1997 is the 1997 Barolo Piccole Vigne. Dark plum-colored with a hint of amber at the edge, it exhibits sexy, herbaceous, kirsch-scented aromas, a fleshy, full-bodied palate, and an evolved personality. Consume it over the next 10 years. The 1997 Barolo Mariondino, from a vineyard in Castiglione Falletto, possesses a dense ruby/purple color, more tannin and structure than Parusso's other offerings, notes of earth, black cherry jam, smoke, coffee, licorice, and soy, outstanding concentration, and a spicy, long finish. The fat and glycerin found in many 1997s are present but are buttressed by obvious tannin. Anticipated maturity: 2003–2020. The explosive, dense ruby/purple-colored 1997 Barolo Bussia Vigna Rocche possesses a dramatic, concentrated personality as well as an exceptional bouquet of minerals, black fruits, tar, tobacco, and subtle new oak. This massive, concentrated Barolo exhibits terrific glycerin and fruit, in addition to a fleshy, nicely structured, well-delineated finish. Anticipated maturity: 2003–2020. Similar in size, the dark ruby-colored 1997 Barolo Bussia Vigna Munie displays a Châteauneuf-du-Pape–like character in its combination of kirsch and roasted Provençal herbs. While not as powerful as the Bussia Vigna Rocche, it is an expansive, chewy, structured effort with wonderful intensity as well as the vintage's telltale overripeness and excessive exoticism. Anticipated maturity: now–2017.

The 1996 Barolo exhibits the most new oak. Sexy, forward, and made in a lush, medium- to full-bodied style with gobs of red and black fruits, lavish wood, sweet tannin, and a concentrated, fleshy mouth-feel, it will be drinkable between now–2012. The dark ruby-colored 1996 Barolo Mariondino displays a distinctive almond, cherry liqueur, licorice, and smoky oak–scented nose. Medium- to full-bodied, expansive, and pure, this classic, nicely structured, layered Barolo should be accessible young, yet keep for 10–12 years. The terrific 1996 Barolo Bussia Vigna Munie is more exotic, with sweet scents of melted road tar, cherries, tobacco, and cigar box. Medium- to full-bodied, dense, and full of fruit, this intense wine will also be accessible young but will keep for 12 or more years. Even better is the 1996 Barolo Bussia Vigna Rocche. In addition to the tar, smoke, dried herbs, leather, and cherry fruit aromas, it reveals a distinctive mineral/powdered rock character. A full-bodied, powerful Barolo that possesses superb richness, a multidimensional personality, and a boatload of tannin, this is Parusso's biggest, most concentrated 1996. There is moderate tannin in the finish, but the fruit and *terroir* characteristics dominate. Anticipated maturity: 2003–2020. While the full-bodied 1996 Barolo Bussia Vigna Fiurin is backward, tannic, and closed, it exhibits impressive potential. There are good spice, smoke, and intense fruit concentration in addition to high levels of tannin. This 1996 will require patience. Anticipated maturity: 2005–2020.

The 1995 Barolo Mariondino's medium ruby color is followed by a fragrant nose of dried herbs, tobacco, spice box, and cherry cola. Ripe, with subtle oak, medium to full body, and an expansive, fleshy, open-knit personality, this Barolo can be enjoyed over the next 5–6 years. The 1995 Barolo Bussia Vigna Munie is more opulent but just as evolved and tasty. It offers intriguing floral elements intertwined with melted tar and berry fruit. Exhibiting toasty oak and light tannin in the long finish, this lush, expansive wine can be drunk over the next decade. The 1995 Barolo Bussia Vigna Rocche is the fullest bodied, most powerful and tannic of the 1995s. In addition to the telltale dried herbs, cherry liqueur, leather, and floral scents, it offers layered, concentrated flavors, outstanding purity, admirable muscle and glycerin, and moderate tannin in the impressively endowed finish. Anticipated maturity: now–2012.

ELIA PASQUERO

1998 Barbaresco Sorì Paitin	D	90
1997 Barbaresco Sorì Paitin	D	89
1996 Barbaresco Sorì Paitin	D	92

A classic Barbaresco as well as a textbook expression of Nebbiolo, this exceptionally complex, dark ruby/garnet-colored 1998 Barbaresco Sorì Paitin offers gorgeous aromatics of cedarwood, Chinese black tea, cherries, smoke, and a whiff of creosote. Dense, fleshy, and voluptuous, yet structured and brilliantly well delineated, it will drink beautifully over the next 4–5 years. Pasquero's structured 1997 Barbaresco Sorì Paitin reveals more tannin and austerity than expected for this vintage. When tasted side by side, his 1998 and 1999 both seemed significantly richer and fleshier. Nevertheless, the 1997 is an excellent effort. It offers notes of tobacco, spice box, licorice, and cherries as well as a touch of herbaceousness. Medium-bodied and firmly structured, it should age for a decade or more. The 1996 Barbaresco Sorì Paitin exhibits terrific fruit intensity, along with toast in the flamboyant aromatics. In addition to oak, there are plenty of tobacco leaf, jammy cherries, and dried herbs. Full-bodied, round, luscious, and accessible, this Barbaresco should drink well for a decade.

F.LLI PECCHENINO

1998 Dolcetto di Dogliani Bricco Botti	C	92
1997 Dolcetto di Dogliani Bricco Botti	C	91
1999 Dolcetto di Dogliani Sirì d'Jermu	C	91
1998 Langhe La Castella	C	90
1997 Langhe La Castella	C	92

These wines' richness and concentration blew me away. All are aged in large wood *foudres* prior to being bottled with minimal intervention.The Bricco Botti is among the finest Dolcetti I have ever tasted. The fabulous 1999 Dolcetto di Dogliani Sirì d'Jermu exhibits an opaque inky/purple color as well as a striking bouquet of blackberry and cherry fruit intermixed with almond extract and chocolate. Full-bodied, with layers of fruit, glycerin, and intensity, it will not become any more complex, but it is a mouth-staining, palate-pleasing, sumptuous Dolcetto to enjoy over the next 3–4 years. As hard as it is to believe, the 1998 Dolcetto di Dogliani Bricco Botti is even more powerful, concentrated, and explosive. It also possesses surprising structure, a characteristic not found in most Dolcettos. This opaque purple-colored, massive (but not heavy) effort is vibrant, opulent, and chewy because of its intense fruit and glycerin. It represents Dolcetto at its most extreme and intense. If the famed Veneto producer of Valpolicella and Amarone, Dal Forno, made Dolcetto, it might taste like this!

The outstanding 1998 Langhe La Castella is a blend of 45% Nebbiolo, 50% Barbera, and 5% Cabernet Sauvignon. Opaque ruby/purple-colored, with a structured personality, it reveals less charm and massive fruit than the Dolcetti, but more perfume and nuances. It is medium-bodied and ripe, with a sweet attack offering notes of strawberries, cherries, tobacco, rose petals, and licorice. The finish reveals some tannin as well as acidity, but it is well integrated. Anticipated maturity: now–2012.

The explosive 1997 Dolcetto di Dogliani Bricco Botti is one of the greatest Dolcettos I have ever tasted. It boasts a black/purple color, awesome extract levels, a massive, chewy, full-bodied palate, with gorgeous sweetness and ripeness, as well as a 30+-second finish. These wines rarely develop much complexity, being fruit- and texture-driven, but this 1997 delivers the goods. Enjoy it over the next 4–5 years. It is an immensely impressive effort. Lastly, the blend of Barbera and Nebbiolo, with a touch of Cabernet Sauvignon, the 1997 Langhe La Castella reveals an opaque black/inky color, super high extraction, full body, high tannin, abundant toasty oak, amazing density and length, and a tightly knit yet opulent/voluptuous personality. Enjoy it over the next 10–12 years.

LUIGI PELISSERO

1998	Barbaresco	D	87
1998	Barbaresco Vanotu	D	91
1997	Barbaresco Vanotu	D	(86–88)
1996	Barbaresco Vanotu	D	86?
1995	Barbaresco Vanotu	D	85

These mainstream Barbarescos are competent, well-made efforts, with the 1998s faring much better than the three previous vintages. The estate produces a standard *cuvée*, as well as a special Barbaresco Vanotu, aged in French oak for two years, the annual production of which averages 575 cases.

The delicious, open-knit, spicy, cedary, herb, tobacco, and red fruit–scented and –flavored, medium-bodied 1998 Barbaresco can be enjoyed now and over the next 3–4 years. The dazzling 1998 Barbaresco Vanotu is sensational. A dark plum color is accompanied by sumptuous aromas of soy, tobacco smoke, Chinese black tea, kirsch, and spice box. Full-bodied and layered, with a multidimensional personality, sweet tannin, and adequate acidity, this exquisite Barbaresco will drink well for 10 years. The finest of this trio is the 1997 Barbaresco Vanotu, a deep ruby-colored wine with ripe black cherry and cassis fruit, a cedary, spicy component, very good ripeness, and a moderately long finish. It should be drunk during its first 5–6 years of life. The 1996 Barbaresco Vanotu reveals a more stemmy, vegetal character, in addition to a lean, tannic, hard finish. I have reservations about its ever achieving full harmony. In both its aromas and its flavors, the elegant 1995 Barbaresco Vanotu exhibits dusty cherry fruit, spice, earth, and medium body. Drink it over the next 2–3 years.

VIGNAIOLI ELVIO PERTINACE

1998	Barbaresco	E	89
1997	Barbaresco	E	87
1998	Barbaresco Castellizzano	E	91
1998	Barbaresco Marcarini	E	90
1997	Barbaresco Marcarini	E	90
1998	Barbaresco Nervo	E	88
1997	Barbaresco Nervo	E	92
1996	Pertinace	D	89

This cooperative (twelve wineries that pool their resources) produces fairly priced wines of impeccably high quality. The 1998s are the finest wines I have tasted from Vignaioli Elvio Pertinace, which seem to be ratcheting up its quality level. They reveal the vintage's open, forward characteristic but are balanced and concentrated enough to last for 12–15 years, particularly the three single-vineyard offerings. The 1997s are also of high quality.

The medium ruby-colored 1998 Barbaresco's sweet nose of cedar, black cherries, and spice box is followed by medium-bodied, ripe, concentrated, pure flavors. Drink it over the next 5–7 years. All three crus possess similar colors, ranging from medium ruby to saturated ruby. Production is moderate, with approximately 750 cases of each. The 1998 Barbaresco Marcarini exhibits a big, juicy, complex perfume of tobacco, cherry cough syrup, balsa wood, herbs, and rose petals. Deep, with a terrific texture, real elegance, an opulent, fleshy mid-palate, and sweet tannin in the finish, it should drink well for 10–12 years. The more angular but similarly styled, attractive 1998 Barbaresco Nervo reveals more licorice in its aromatics and flavors. It, too, will drink well for 10–12 years. The most concentrated and dense offering is the 1998 Barbaresco Castellizzano. It boasts a deep plum/ruby color in addition to intense aromas consisting of cherry jam infused with smoky tobacco, Provençal herbs, licorice, and truffles. Full-bodied, opulent, dense, and accessible, it will drink well for 12 years.

The medium ruby/garnet-colored 1997 Barbaresco offers a fragrant bouquet of cedar, tobacco, plums, raspberries, and cherries, medium to full body, a sweet mid-palate, and a spicy, lightly tannic finish. Consume it over the next 3–4 years. The 1997 Barbaresco Marcarini reveals a classic Nebbiolo bouquet of tar and rose petals intermixed with sour cherries, leather, and earth. It possesses exceptional complexity, full body, exquisite density, and a long, impressive finish. Already approachable, it should continue to drink well for 12 years. Even better is the spectacular 1997 Barbaresco Nervo. An explosive nose of cigar tobacco, cherry liqueur, rose petals, and tar is followed by a full-bodied, gorgeously fruit-driven, dark ruby-colored wine with an expansive, chewy texture, as well as excellent purity and depth. As with its sibling, the Barbaresco Marcarini, the finish lasts for more than 30 seconds. It, too, will drink well for 12 years. Lastly, there are 700 cases of the 1996 Pertinace, a blend of 70% Nebbiolo and 30% Cabernet Sauvignon. This internationally styled, well-made effort possesses an opaque ruby/purple color in addition to a chocolaty, black cherry, tobacco, and spice box–scented nose, a full-bodied, rich, concentrated mid-palate, and a deep structured finish. Anticipated maturity: now–2012.

E. PIRA

1998 Barolo Cannubi	E	(90–91)
1997 Barolo Cannubi	E	91
1996 Barolo Cannubi	E	95

This estate has undergone a complete transformation under the inspired proprietress, Chiara Boschis. The wines' vinification and upbringing were changed beginning with the 1994 vintage, but the first truly great vintage was 1996.

The elegant, sweet, pure, medium ruby-colored 1998 Barolo Cannubi exhibits aromas of tar, rose petals, and cherry jam. These are followed by a medium-bodied offering with a firm tannic underpinning, excellent purity, and spicy, subtle new oak. This wine is a candidate for an outstanding rating after another 1–2 years of cellaring. Anticipated maturity: 2003–2016.

The 1997 Barolo Cannubi is another gorgeous wine, but unfortunately very little was produced. Aged in 100% new *barriques* and bottled with neither fining nor filtration, it is a full-bodied, rich, structured, garnet/ruby-colored effort offering an emerging bouquet of rose petals, cherries, leather, spice box, and tobacco. Powerful, concentrated, pure, dense, and moderately tannic, it is not as flashy and precocious as many of its peers, but is unquestionably a classic. Anticipated maturity: 2005–2020.

A compelling Barolo, as well as a classic example of the more traditional school of winemaking, the 1996 Barolo Cannubi exhibits an unimpressive medium ruby color. However, that is followed by an explosive nose of cherry jam infused with smoke, rose water, tobacco, and spice. With an amazing texture, evidenced by a fabulous concentration of fruit, full body, a boatload of glycerin, and moderately high tannin, this huge, complex, profound Barolo can be drunk now but promises to age effortlessly for two decades.

LUIGI PIRA

1997 Barolo	D	91
1996 Barolo	D	91
1995 Barolo	D	86
1998 Barolo Marenca	E	(94–96)
1997 Barolo Marenca	E	95
1996 Barolo Marenca	E	92
1995 Barolo Marenca	E	91+
1998 Barolo Margheria	E	(91–94+)

1997 Barolo Margheria	E	92+
1996 Barolo Margheria	E	90
1995 Barolo Margheria	E	91
1998 Barolo Vigna Rionda	E	(93–96)
1997 Barolo Vigna Rionda	E	97

Pira has quickly emerged as a fabulous talent, producing wines from vineyards surrounding his hometown village of Serralunga d'Alba. There are so many exceptional wine-makers in Barolo and Barbaresco that it is unfair to single out Luigi Pira as a star, but certainly his performances in 1995, 1996, 1997, and 1998 are remarkable. These wines, which qualify this estate as one of the leaders in Piedmont, are of extraordinary complexity and breathtaking richness. Each *cuvée* is given a different *élevage*, although malolactic is done in either *foudre* or *barrique*. This cellar also employs rotary fermenters. While the regular Barolo is aged completely in large wood *foudres,* the crus are aged in a combination of *foudre* and small casks, ranging from 20% new oak for Margheria to 100% for Rionda. Luigi Pira should not be confused with E. Pira from the village of Barolo, who has also been making spectacular wines, particularly since the 1996 vintage.

The 1998s are nearly as provocative and spectacular as the otherworldly 1997s. The great 1998 Barolo Marenca offers the essence of Nebbiolo in its sweet bouquet of roasted espresso, cedar, Chinese black tea, soy, and black cherry/plum-like fruit. Dense, full-bodied, and viscous, this exceptional Barolo's purity and essence of Nebbiolo-like character make it a compelling wine to drink now and over the next 12–15 years. The dark plum-colored 1998 Barolo Margheria exhibits more structure as well as a more backward character. While not as expressive as the Marenca, it is full-bodied with outstanding concentration, offering notes of chocolate, black cherry liqueur, spice box, and earth. There are plenty of glycerin, moderate tannin, and a long, 40-second finish in this tightly knit effort. It will drink well for 10–14 years. The dense, opulent, flamboyant 1998 Barolo Vigna Rionda possesses soaring aromas of plum and kirsch, smoke, balsa wood, black tea, licorice, and tobacco. Opulent, full-bodied, and gorgeously pure, it has enough glycerin, fruit, and tannin to fill and stain the mouth. This blockbuster Barolo requires 1–2 years of cellaring; it will drink beautifully between 2004–2018.

Luigi Pira's 1997 Barolo is a decadent, luxuriously rich effort offering an opulent texture and gorgeous jammy currant, cherry, licorice, smoke, and cured olive characteristics. It possesses a superb texture, a sexy, forward, low-acid style, and copious quantities of glycerin, fruit, and extract. It is a terrific wine to drink now and over the next 10 years. The profound, dense garnet/ruby-colored 1997 Barolo Marenca displays a spectacular bouquet of roasted espresso, kirsch, blackberries, tobacco, sardines, cedar, and leather. Sumptuous in the mouth, full-bodied, with an exotic overripe character, this dense, thick Barolo tastes sweet because of the high glycerin levels. As it was in cask, this 1997 Barolo remains dominated by its baby fat. Anticipated maturity: now–2015. Luigi Pira, who has the most massive hands I have ever encountered on a vigneron, has fashioned a more structured effort with his 1997 Barolo Margheria. This wine has become more delineated and civilized after spending time in cask and *foudre.* Telltale notes of kirsch, dried flowers, rose petals, licorice, soy, leather, and tobacco combine with scents of seaweed, chocolate, and red/black fruits. The Margheria possesses firmer tannin and more muscle, and is less open-knit and expansive than the Marenca. Nevertheless, it is a sensationally concentrated, full-bodied, powerful Barolo in need of 1–2 years of cellaring. It should drink well between 2004–2020. One of the greatest young Barolos I have ever tasted is Pira's 1997 Barolo Vigna Rionda. The total, minuscule production was aged in a new 600-liter *foudre.* A dense ruby/garnet color is followed by an explosive yet restrained bouquet of tobacco, black cherries, truffles, dried herbs, and new saddle leather, which intensifies as it sits in the glass. On the palate, it offers extraordinary opulence, luxurious richness, a viscous texture, exceptional purity, beautifully integrated acidity, tannin, alcohol, and wood, and a finish that lasts for nearly a minute. Like so many 1997s, it possesses unreal levels of glycerin, resulting in a texture comparable to a fine sauce as opposed to a beverage, yet it is impeccably well balanced. This is a sensational Barolo that magically combines both exoticism and classicism. Anticipated maturity: 2004–2020.

In 1996, Pira appears to have hit all the sweet spots. His 1996 Barolo should prove to be an uncommon value for a sensational generic Barolo. It offers road tar, rose petal, tobacco, woodsy spices, and cherry fruit aromas that jump from the glass of this evolved, gorgeously proportioned, full-bodied effort. The dark ruby color is followed by a sweet, expansive, hedonistic wine that offers a lot of pleasure. Complex and mouth-filling, it is ready to drink. Anticipated maturity: now–2012. The 1996 Barolo Margheria combines the best of the traditional style of Barolo with the more progressive modern winemaking style. The color is a saturated plum. Overripe aromas of black fruits are accompanied by scents of soy, coffee, smoke, licorice, and dried herbs. Dense and full-bodied, with terrific fruit intensity, this multidimensional, layered wine is exceptionally rich, yet sweet and forward. Anticipated maturity: now–2015. The 1996 Barolo Marenca is even more profound, with a dark ruby color and a sumptuous nose of jammy plum liqueur and black cherries. It is a sensual, full-bodied wine with an opulent texture, fabulous extract, and an explosive, 50-second finish. It coats the palate, is unbelievably rich in fruit, glycerin, and extract and should prove to be a modern-day classic. Anticipated maturity: 2005–2020.

The classic 1995s are among the superstars of that good vintage. The 1995 Barolo exhibits an evolved ruby color with some amber at the edge. It offers tobacco, licorice, and cherry fruit aromas, but the wine dries out a bit in the mouth. Fully mature, with a lean finish, it is ideal for drinking over the next 3–4 years. The 1995 Barolo Margheria reveals stunning aromas of smoky wood, truffles, cherry liqueur, cedar, and dried herbs. Evolved, with a soft, opulently textured mouth-feel, full body, and outstanding ripeness as well as purity, its forward, accessible style suggests that it should be drunk over the next 10 years. The 1995 Barolo Marenca displays classic rose petal scents in addition to melted asphalt, truffles, new saddle leather, and cherries. It is a layered wine with tea/coffee flavors that add nuances to the copious glycerin, rich black cherry fruit, and full-bodied, velvety texture. Anticipated maturity: now–2014.

GUIDO PORRO

1998 Barolo Vigna Santa Caterina	D	(88–89)
1997 Barolo Vigna Santa Caterina	D	88
1998 Barolo Vigna Lazzairasco	D	(87–88)
1997 Barolo Vigna Lazzairasco	D	88

This producer from the village of Serralunga has fashioned two excellent, elegant, forward 1998 Barolos. His 1997s performed much better from bottle than they did during their *élevage*.

The 1998 Barolo Vigna Lazzairasco is a soft, supple effort displaying copious quantities of smoky cherry fruit mixed with licorice, tobacco, and weedy notes. It is rich on the attack, medium- to full-bodied, and supple. The saturated ruby-colored 1998 Barolo Vigna Santa Caterina possesses more intensity and depth as well as high levels of volatile acidity (which should not be a problem if it does not become any more elevated). Its complex nose offers aromas of sweet black fruits, smoke, licorice, and incense. Medium- to full-bodied, with low acidity and ripe tannin, it will drink well for 5–6 years.

Both 1997s are evolved and meant to be drunk during their first 5–6 years of life. Offering considerable appeal, the fat, round, low-acid 1997 Barolo Vigna Lazzairasco exhibits a smoky, layered personality with notes of coffee, cherries, herbs, and tobacco. The medium- to full-bodied 1997 Barolo Vigna Santa Caterina reveals an evolved color with amber at the edge. It possesses dusty tannin, plump cherry fruit, and notes of dried roses, melted asphalt, camphor, and licorice.

FERDINANDO PRINCIPIANO

1998 Barbera d'Alba La Romualda	D	90
1997 Barbera d'Alba La Romualda	D	90

Isn't it amazing how many top-notch Barberas are emerging from Piedmont? An outstanding performance for this producer, Principiano's 1998 Barbera d'Alba La Romualda is a deep ruby/purple-colored, layered effort revealing aromas of spicy new oak, copious quantities of red and black fruits, and underlying notes of smoke, underbrush, and licorice. Consume it over the next 4–5 years. Readers looking for sweet, jammy strawberry and cherry flavors with toasty oak, plenty of glycerin, and a forceful, fleshy, full-bodied palate will love this enticing, disarming, thick, juicy 1997 Barbera d'Alba La Romualda. Enjoy it over the next 5–7 years.

PRODUTTORI DEL BARBARESCO

1996 Barbaresco Asili	E	91
1996 Barbaresco Moccagatta Riserva	E	90
1996 Barbaresco Montestefano Riserva	E	88
1996 Barbaresco Ovello Riserva	E	88+
1996 Barbaresco Pora	E	89
1996 Barbaresco Rabajà	E	90+
1996 Barbaresco Rio Sordo Riserva	E	90

The Produttori del Barbaresco, one of Piedmont's top cooperatives, offers these late-released 1996 Barbarescos. I began purchasing these single-vineyard Riservas in 1978 and have continued to do so in most of the top vintages. They are incredibly popular, as well as fairly priced, and hence they disappear rapidly from the marketplace. All of these 1996s had just been bottled and were about to be shipped to the United States when I saw them in 2001, so I suspect that with additional bottle age and rest, they will be even better. From the traditional school of winemaking, they are aged 3–4 years in old wood prior to bottling. While each reflects its vineyard, they are all full-bodied efforts offering complex tobacco, sweet cherry, licorice, smoke, and herb notes. The Ovello and Rio Sordo are the most evolved and elegant. The sweetest, most seductive include the Pora, Montestefano, and Moccagatta. The most profound are the Asili and Rabajà. Production ranges from a minimum of 10,000 bottles for the Asili to a maximum of just under 19,000 bottles for the other single vineyards. All are purely made and merit considerable attention. They all require an additional two years of cellaring, even the more forward Ovello and Rio Sordo. The aging potential of the Ovello, Rio Sordo, Moccagatta, and Pora is approximately 15 years, and 15–20 years for the Montestefano, Asili, and Rabajà.

PRUNOTTO

1998 Barbaresco	D	87
1996 Barbaresco	D	87
1995 Barbaresco	D	78
1998 Barbaresco Bric Turot	E	91
1998 Barbera d'Alba Pian Romualdo	C	90
1998 Barbera d'Asti Costamiole	D	91
1998 Barolo	D	90
1997 Barolo	D	87
1996 Barolo	D	89+
1995 Barolo	D	88

1998 Barolo Bussia	**E**	**(91–93)**
1997 Barolo Bussia	**E**	**94**

This famous estate was acquired by the Marchesi Antinori firm, which continues to upgrade the winery, vineyards, and quality of the wines. Given how well Prunotto's wines performed in difficult vintages such as 1993 and 1994, I expected more from the following years, but some of its Barbarescos (1995 and 1996) have been foursquare, monolithic, and lacking the character I have come to expect from Prunotto's wines, while the Barolos of the same year were sound. The 1997s show a clear improvement, confirmed by excellent 1998s.

From a strong vintage for Prunotto, the 1998 Barbaresco is the lightest offering, but it possesses stylish, attractive, sweet raspberry and cherry fruit mixed with dried herb and spice box characteristics. Although neither concentrated nor deep, it is round, luscious, well balanced, richly fruity, and harmonious. Enjoy it over the next 4–5 years. The *barrique*-aged, blockbuster 1998 Barbera d'Alba Pian Romualdo exhibits a saturated plum/purple color as well as a gorgeously explosive bouquet of sweet toasty new oak intermixed with chocolate, spice box, black fruits, and licorice. Superrich, medium-bodied, and crammed with fruit, it will drink well for 3–4 years, as these wines rarely improve. The complex 1998 Barbera d'Asti Costamiole reveals earthy, toasty notes intermixed with plums, cola, flowers, and roasted herbs. A boatload of fruit and glycerin hit the palate in this full-bodied, fat, fleshy Barbera. Fermented and aged in new oak for 12 months prior to being bottled unfiltered, it will drink well for 5–6 years. The stunning, dark plum/ruby-colored, deep, full-bodied 1998 Barbaresco Bric Turot is layered with smoky black fruit, graphite, new saddle leather, and vanilla aromas. Rich and concentrated, with sweet tannin, it will be at its finest between 2003–2015.

The 1998 Barolo is a full-bodied, fleshy effort revealing telltale notes of licorice, rose petals, melted asphalt, and dried red and black fruits. It is sweet and opulently textured, with surprising harmony for such a young Barolo. Both the tannin and acidity are well integrated in this fleshy, upfront offering. Consume it during its first 10–12 years of life. The dense ruby-colored 1998 Barolo Bussia displays a heady, intoxicating perfume of maple syrup mixed with kirsch, cigar smoke, dried herbs, and cedar. Voluptuously textured, beautifully concentrated, pure, rich, and long (the finish lasts for 35 seconds), it is soft enough to be drunk, but I suspect the tannin will soon reemerge and the wine will shut down. Anticipated maturity: 2005–2018.

Prunotto's generic 1997 Barolo offers an attractive dark ruby/garnet color, low acidity, and soft, fat flavors of smoke-infused cherry fruit, cedar, and toast. Ripe and medium-bodied, it is best drunk over the next 4–5 years. The profound 1997 Barolo Bussia boasts intense aromas of molasses, cherry liqueur, melted tar, licorice, and toast. Dense and full-bodied, with enormous quantities of glycerin and fat, this hedonistic, thick, viscous Barolo can be drunk now and over the next 12–15 years.

The dark ruby-colored 1996 Barbaresco exhibits attractive cherry fruit in the nose along with cedar, roasted almonds, and herbs. Well made, pure, and medium-bodied, with moderate tannin in the angular finish, it should be at its finest before 2008. The 1996 Barolo exhibits more minerality, along with black cherries and melted road tar. Medium- to full-bodied, spicy, rich, and potentially very good, it is foursquare and simple. Perhaps more complexity will emerge with bottle age. Anticipated maturity: 2003–2014.

The 1995 Barbaresco reveals soft, tobacco-tinged cherry fruit, moderate concentration, and a lean, compressed, diluted, austere finish. Drink it over the next 2–3 years. The 1995 Barolo is an elegant, lighter-styled example with attractive smoke-tinged, herbaceous cherry fruit, medium body, and an earth-driven personality. Moderate tannin in the finish suggests that aging is necessary, but this wine does not have the stuffing for extended cellaring. Drink it over the next 3–4 years.

QUORUM

1999 Barbera d'Asti	E	95
1998 Barbera d'Asti	E	96

This cooperative effort from a group of Piedmontese producers displays the spectacular quality that can be achieved with Barbera. The brilliant oenologist Riccardo Cotarella is the magic behind these wines, which are made from modest yields of 35 hectoliters per hectare, experience malolactic in barrel, with pump-overs and punch-downs, and are bottled without filtration after spending 10 months in 100% new French oak.

A spectacular achievement for this varietal, the 1999 Barbera d'Asti may not have the nobility to age longer than 6–8 years, but for drinking over the next 5–6 years, there is no doubting its explosive qualities as well as its extraordinary ripeness and richness. Its opaque purple color is followed by a sumptuous bouquet of black fruits, coffee, vanilla, chocolate, and licorice. This super-endowed, full-bodied, rich, intensely concentrated, opulent Barbera is prodigious. Anticipated maturity: now–2010.

The 1998 Barbera d'Asti has a whopping 13.7% alcohol as well as a reasonably high (for Barbera) pH of 3.6. In short . . . it's a dazzling Barbera. An intense, deep opaque plum/purple color is followed by super-concentrated blackberry, strawberry, and cherry aromas, an opulent, fat, luscious texture, and explosive fruit, purity, and richness. The wine's heady, luxuriously rich finish lasts 30+ seconds. It would be hard to make better Barbera than this! Drink it over the next 4–5 years.

RENATO RATTI

1998 Barolo Marcenasco	E	89
1997 Barolo Marcenasco	E	91
1998 Barolo Conca Marcenasco	E	87+?
1998 Barolo Rocche Marcenasco	E	87
1997 Barolo Rocche Marcenasco	E	92+
1996 Barolo Rocche Marcenasco	E	90
1995 Barolo Rocche Marcenasco	E	88

Ratti's wines tend to be made in a modern style, although they taste as if one foot were still firmly planted in the past—not a bad combination. All of the 1998 Barolos are midweight, fragrant, earthy efforts that are best drunk during their first decade of life. I tasted two 1997s, both of which outperformed the 1998s, and the excellent 1996 surpasses the soundly made 1995. The medium-bodied 1998 Barolo Marcenasco displays the most sweetness and fragrance in its aromas and flavors (leather, cherries, spice box, and tobacco). Although it does not possess much depth, it is charming and well made. Slightly lighter, with less concentration, is the 1998 Barolo Rocche Marcenasco. I may have caught it during a less expressive stage, but it appeared straightforward, with less volume and depth than its siblings. Consumption during its first 8–10 years of life is recommended. The most tannic of this trio is the 1998 Barolo Conca Marcenasco. While it reveals leanness, austerity, and tannin, it also possesses abundant spice in its backward, reserved personality. Ideally, I would wait 1–2 years before pulling the cork. This effort falls midway between the archconservative traditionalists (represented by Giacomo Conterno and Bruno Giacosa) and the vanguard of modernists (i.e., Elio Altare). Anticipated maturity: 2005–2015.

The fragrant, open-knit, sexy 1997 Barolo Marcenasco exhibits glorious sweetness, an expansive, full-bodied palate, a creamy texture, and overripe notes of black cherries, raspberries, currants, and a touch of maple syrup. Fleshy, powerful, and well delineated, it can be drunk now and over the next 12 years. The terrific 1997 Barolo Rocche Marcenasco offers complex aromatics of soy, earth, root vegetables, sardines, and smoky black cherry/berry fruit. This full-bodied Barolo displays more structure and tannin than its sibling as well as a denser, longer finish. Anticipated maturity: 2003–2018.

The 1996 Barolo Rocche Marcenasco exhibits a more impressively endowed ruby/purple color and an aggressive nose of roasted herbs, spices, and black cherry and berry fruit. Full-bodied, with subtle oak in the background, this dense, concentrated, highly extracted wine is a classic. Anticipated maturity: 2004–2018. The 1995 Barolo Rocche Marcenasco is a very good wine for the vintage, offering aromas of tobacco smoke, cedar, spice, and lively, sweet jammy cherries. There are excellent richness, an open-knit, round personality, a sweet mid-palate, and ripe tannin in the moderately long, medium- to full-bodied finish. Drinkable already, this Barolo promises to evolve for 8 years.

F.LLI REVELLO

1998 Barbera d'Alba Ciabot du Re	C	92
1997 Barolo	D	89
1996 Barolo	D	88
1995 Barolo	D	90
1998 Barolo Vigna Conca	E	(92–94)
1997 Barolo Vigna Conca	E	93
1998 Barolo Vigna Giachini	E	(90–91)
1997 Barolo Vigna Giachini	E	93
1996 Barolo Vigna Giachini	E	90
1995 Barolo Vigna Giachini	E	89+
1998 Barolo Vigna Rocche dell'Annunziata	E	(88–90)
1997 Barolo Vigna Rocche dell'Annunziata	E	91
1996 Barolo Vigna Rocche dell'Annunziata	E	91+

Another high-quality La Morra producer who has been making better and better wines, Revello makes 1998s that are all elegant, aromatic, beautifully flavored offerings. Its single-vineyard crus in both 1996 and 1997 are exceptional. Readers who prefer more structure, muscle, and tannin will like the 1996s better; those who are fond of flamboyant, spectacularly rich, nearly overripe, jammy wines with huge quantities of glycerin and extract will enjoy the 1997s.

Readers looking for a *barrique*-aged Barbera with spectacular concentration, density, and perfume should check out Revello's 1998 Barbera d'Alba Ciabot du Re. It possesses a dark ruby/purple color, great intensity, phenomenal aromas of smoke, chocolate, strawberries, cherries, and blackberries, a thick, fat, chewy texture, and a lush, smoky finish. Enjoy it over the next 2–3 years. The 1998 Barolo Vigna Giachini exhibits a dark ruby/garnet color as well as an intensely fragrant perfume of rose petals, herbs, new oak, plums, and black cherries. It reveals a classic structure, moderate tannin, good firmness and purity, and a long, well-delineated, medium- to full-bodied finish. Anticipated maturity: 2003–2015. The dark ruby/garnet-colored 1998 Barolo Vigna Conca offers up an explosive nose of creosote, cherry liqueur, cedar, new saddle leather, soy, and Provençal herbs. Dense, full-bodied, and super-rich, with a 45-second finish, this layered, multidimensional, well-balanced, stunning 1998 will drink well between now–2016. The symmetrical, restrained, delicately styled, dark ruby-colored 1998 Barolo Vigna Rocche dell'Annunziata possesses fine overall balance but not the depth, weight, or palate texture/volume of its two siblings. Nevertheless, there is a lot to like in this wine. Anticipated maturity: now–2012.

Revello's 1997 Barolo exhibits an earthy, root vegetable, herbaceous, black fruit–scented nose, medium to full body, plenty of glycerin, and the texture, fat, and succulence typical of this vintage in Piedmont. Already delicious, it will be best consumed over the next 5 years. The stunning perfume (meat, sausage, and spice) of the dark plum/garnet-colored 1997 Barolo Vigna Giachini is reminiscent of a French charcuterie. Full-bodied, opulent, fat, and rich, with notes of sausage, herbs, pepper, spice box, soy, and new oak, this lush, creamy-textured offering can be drunk now and over the next 15 years. The 1997 Barolo Vigna Conca

(100 cases produced) reveals a maple syrup/brown sugar–like aroma intermixed with scents of cherry liqueur, rose petals, tobacco, and spice. A corpulent, highly extracted, low-acid, plummy wine with a boatload of glycerin as well as flavors, it is one of the most hedonistic Barolos from this luxurious, decadently styled vintage. Drink it over the next 12 years. Based on cask tastings, I had higher hopes for the 1997 Barolo Vigna Rocche dell'Annunziata. While outstanding, my barrel-tasting notes suggested it might turn out to be profound. It possesses an evolved dark plum/garnet color, more structure than its siblings, copious tobacco, herb, pepper, and kirsch aromas, superrichness, and a sweet, full-bodied palate, but not the mass and overall structure I anticipated. Nevertheless, it is a stunning Barolo for drinking during its first 12–15 years of life.

The 1996 Barolo offers a tangy, black cherry–scented nose with hints of smoke, earth, and leather. Spicy, medium-bodied, and moderately tannic, it is more structured and muscular than its more evolved 1995 sibling. Anticipated maturity: now–2008. The 1996 Barolo Vigna Giachini reveals a deep ruby color as well as a muscular, powerfully scented nose of cherry fruit, cedar, fruitcake, dried herbs, and licorice. In the mouth, tobacco flavors make an appearance. This wine is layered, full-bodied, opulent, and dense, with most of the tannin concealed by high extraction and concentration. It is a wine of strength and symmetry with a superb inner core of fruit. Anticipated maturity: now–2020. The 1996 Barolo Vigna Rocche dell'Annunziata is extremely fragrant, offering dried herb, jammy cherry fruit, smoke, Asian spices, and new saddle leather aromas. In the mouth, there are superb purity, full body, and huge amounts of tannin. This backward, dense, monster-sized Barolo will be at its finest between 2005–2020.

Like the other generic Barolos from Revello, the 1995 Barolo was aged in 2–3-year-old oak casks. A successful wine for the vintage, it exhibits a sexy, explosive, Bing cherry–scented nose with chocolate, black tea, and spicy oak. Lush and round, it is not dissimilar from some of the idiosyncratic, opulent 1997s. This evolved 1995 should be consumed over the next 3–4 years. The medium-bodied 1995 Barolo Vigna Giachini is a more tannic, restrained example, with a moderate ruby color revealing amber at the edge. The moderately scented bouquet reveals tobacco, dried herbs, and cherry fruit. This closed Barolo needs another 1–2 years of bottle age. It should drink well for 10 years.

FRANCESCO RINALDI

1998 Barolo Cannubio	D	87
1997 Barolo Cannubio	D	88

The dark plum/garnet-colored, lighter-styled 1998 Barolo Cannubio displays classic Nebbiolo aromas of melted road tar, rose petals, and cherry fruit. Soft, ripe, and medium-bodied, this traditionally made 1998 reveals no evidence of new oak. Enjoy it over the next 4–5 years. The dark plum-colored 1997 Barolo Cannubio is revealing pink hues at the edge. Medium-weight, with rosewater, cherry, leather, and tar notes, this soft, round, gentle, yet flavorful Barolo can be enjoyed now and over the next 10 years.

GIUSEPPE RINALDI

1998 Barolo Brunate Le Coste	D	86?
1997 Barolo Brunate Le Coste	D	90+

Extremely high acidity and astringent tannin make the 1998 Barolo Brunate Le Coste hard to evaluate. The color is a dark plum with amber at the edge. The closed nose reveals hints of tar, rose petal, cherries, and tobacco. The attack is elegant, but the high acidity and tannin combine to compress the mid-palate and finish. There may be more behind the acidity and tannin than I was able to determine, but this closed 1998 needs 2–3 years of cellaring to display its full potential. An austere style for sure, I am not sure the fruit will ever be able to overcome the wine's structural components. An old-style Barolo, Rinaldi's 1997 Brunate Le

Coste exhibits a dense, saturated plum/garnet color in addition to aromas of flowers, cinnamon, allspice, dried herbs, earth, licorice, and mineral-infused black cherries. Layered and powerful, with astringent tannin as well as a huge concentration of fruit, this classic, tough-textured Barolo will be admired by traditionalists. The magic will emerge after 2–3 years of cellaring, although do not expect this wine to have the suppleness or sexy, new-oak style of a modernist's Barolo. Anticipated maturity: 2005–2018.

VIGNA RIONDA DI MASSOLINO

1999 Barbera d'Alba Gisep	C	91
1998 Barolo	D	(82–85)
1997 Barolo	D	82
1998 Barolo Vigna Margheria	D	(83–87)
1997 Barolo Vigna Margheria	E	87
1996 Barolo Vigna Margheria	E	89+
1998 Barolo Vigna Parafada	E	(88–89)
1997 Barolo Vigna Parafada	E	90
1996 Barolo Vigna Parafada	E	90
1998 Barolo Vigna Rionda	E	(87–88)
1997 Barolo Vigna Rionda	E	90
2000 Dolcetto d'Alba Vigna Barilot	B	87
1999 Langhe Rosso Piria	D	88
1997 Langhe Rosso Piria	D	89

Massolino, an important landholder in Serralunga d'Alba, owns some superb vineyards. This traditional wine-maker ages all his *cuvées* in *foudre* except for his Parafada, which sees about 50% *barrique*. His proprietary blend, Piria, is composed of equal parts Nebbiolo and Barbera fermented and aged in French oak casks. He has been fashioning better and better wines over recent vintages. That being said, I did not think the 1998s fared as consistently well as the superb 1997s, but the early-released 1999s and 2000 represent fine values.

The 2000 Dolcetto d'Alba Vigna Barilot is a modern-styled, ripe, richly fruity offering revealing good depth, a supple texture, and fine purity. It is an uncomplicated, quaffable wine to enjoy over the next 2–3 years.

The spectacular, modern-styled 1999 Barbera d'Alba Gisep is aged in 100% new French oak, and its fruit has totally absorbed the wood's toast and vanilla notes. A black/purple color is accompanied by a glorious perfume of licorice, blackberries, cherries, cola, and mocha. The finish is long, textured, full-bodied, and supple. Superripe Barbera seems to love new oak and absorbs it as well as any wine in the world. Drink this beauty over the next 4–5 years. These wines, while super-concentrated and youthful, rarely age well past a half-dozen years. Massolino's proprietary red, the 1999 Langhe Rosso Piria, exhibits a complex bouquet of tobacco, strawberries, and cherries with licorice and spice box in the background. While rich, medium-bodied, and complex, it lacks the exuberance, mass, and thickness of the astonishing Barbera. Readers looking for more subtlety and nuances should check out the 1999 Piria.

The straightforward, light, elegant, medium-bodied 1998 Barolo possesses good roundness and softness, but lacks depth and substance. Moreover, its evolved color is revealing considerable amber at the edge. This Barolo is best consumed over the next 4–5 years. The 1998 Barolo Vigna Parafada exhibits a complex aromatic profile of dried herbs and that autumnal, leafy character often found in traditionally styled Barolos. In the mouth, it is spicy and ripe, with excellent concentration, and a touch of vanilla from *barriques*. Good sweetness, abundant black cherry fruit, and ripe tannin suggest it will be drinkable between 2004–2015. Another soft, light, marginal effort is Massolino's 1998 Barolo Vigna Margheria, which reveals medium body, suppleness, and a short finish lacking depth and length. It requires consumption over the next 4–5 years. Lastly, the medium garnet-colored, silky-textured 1998 Barolo Vigna Rionda offers complex aromatics of cherry cough syrup mixed with Provençal herbs, spice box, and tar. Dense, with excellent fruit concentration, good sweetness on the attack and mid-palate, and ripe tannin, it will be at its peak between 2004–2014.

Exhibiting a dark ruby/garnet color with amber at the edge, the 1997 Langhe Rosso Piria reveals complex cedar, dried herb, cherry, and wood smoke in its fragrant bouquet. Round, ripe, spicy, medium-bodied, and supple-textured, it can be drunk over the next 5–6 years. Revealing surprisingly good acidity for the vintage as well as an evolved garnet color with an amber edge, the medium-bodied 1997 Barolo is a pleasant, traditionally made effort to consume over the next 4–5 years. The outstanding 1997 Barolo Vigna Parafada is a full-bodied, dense ruby/garnet-colored wine with a layered tactile impression and copious quantities of licorice, rose petal, tar, and kirsch aromatics as well as flavors. Deep, with moderate tannin and the vintage's unctuosity and sweetness, it will be at its best between now–2016. Also displaying an evolved appearance with considerable amber at the edge, the 1997 Barolo Vigna Margheria exhibits notes of dried flowers, figs, tobacco, old oak, mushrooms, and cherries in its aromatics as well as flavors. Medium-bodied and spicy, it should drink well for 10 years. The sexy, layered, evolved 1997 Barolo Vigna Rionda was obviously produced from extremely ripe fruit, as evidenced by the dark garnet/amber color and the sweet perfume of smoke, caramel, toffee, and espresso infused with black cherries, plums, and prunes. This multilayered, full-bodied offering exhibits a seamless personality with no hard edges. It should drink well for 15 years.

The outstanding dark ruby/garnet-colored 1996 Barolo Vigna Parafada offers aromas of cigar box, cherry liqueur, licorice, and spice, dense, intense, old-style, concentrated, sour cherry flavors with glycerin and extract. Rich and approachable, it will evolve nicely for 12 years. In contrast, the dark ruby/garnet-colored 1996 Barolo Vigna Margheria is more backward, with spicy, licorice, truffle, strawberry, and black cherry fruit notes, full body, moderately high tannin, sweetness, glycerin, and a dusty, concentrated, layered finish. Anticipated maturity: 2004–2018.

ROAGNA

1998 Barbaresco Pajé	E	(91–94)
1997 Barbaresco Pajé	E	90
1998 Barolo Rocche La Pira	E	(86–87)
1997 Barolo Rocche La Pira	E	87

As with Roagna's 1997s, the 1998s reveal a huge difference in richness and density. The more tannic and backward 1998 Barolo Rocche La Pira offers only hints of tobacco, cherry cough syrup, and dried herbs. With airing, tar and additional fruit notes emerge. However, the overall impression is one of austerity, leanness, and high tannin, atypical for this vintage. Anticipated maturity: 2006–2014? In total contrast, the saturated opaque purple-colored 1998 Barbaresco Pajé combines awesome extract levels with extraordinary precision. Medium- to full-bodied, it offers aromas and flavors of liquid minerals infused with black cherry and raspberry jam. As the wine sat in the glass, blackberry scents also emerged. Aging in small *barriques* has been totally absorbed by the wine's concentration and density. This terrific Barbaresco has an uncanny resemblance to a great grand cru Burgundy (Comtes de Vogüé's Musigny Vieilles Vignes?). Anticipated maturity: 2004–2016.

Although somewhat closed, Roagna's ruby/garnet-colored 1997 Barolo Rocche La Pira offers notes of tobacco, spice box, cherries, and dried herbs. Made in a medium-bodied, elegant style, it is not as complete or concentrated as the Barbaresco Pajé. The 1997 Barbaresco Pajé's evolved garnet color with an amber edge is followed by notes of sweet caramel, coffee, jammy cherry fruit, licorice, and smoke. Elegant, medium- to full-bodied, with wonderful lushness and an expansive, low-acid finish, this 1997 Barbaresco is meant to be drunk now and over the next 5–7 years. Readers should keep an eye out for Roagna's spectacular 1998 Pajé, which was the best of the three most recent vintages I tasted.

ALBINO ROCCA

1998 Barbaresco Vigneto Brich Ronchi	E	90+
1997 Barbaresco Vigneto Brich Ronchi	E	97
1996 Barbaresco Vigneto Brich Ronchi	E	93
1995 Barbaresco Vigneto Brich Ronchi	E	87
1998 Barbaresco Vigneto Loreto	E	91
1997 Barbaresco Vigneto Loreto	E	95
1996 Barbaresco Vigneto Loreto	E	91
1995 Barbaresco Vigneto Loreto	E	89

Albino Rocca, one of my favorite Piedmontese producers, produced very good 1995s and thrilling 1996s, but he hit the bull's-eye in 1997, as well as in 1998. His 1997s rank among the most spectacular Barbarescos I have ever tasted. They are awesomely thick, rich, and textured, with unreal opulence as well as glycerin levels that define the vintage, and while I thought it would be hard to improve on those spectacular, astonishing Barbarescos, this producer has come close to them in 1998.

Made in a more restrained, elegant style, the 1998 Barbaresco Vigneto Loreto exhibits a dark ruby color as well as an elegant, smoky, cherry, oak-scented bouquet. This quintessentially elegant, medium-bodied, supple, delicious Barbaresco will drink well for 6–7 years. The dark ruby/garnet-colored 1998 Barbaresco Vigneto Brich Ronchi reveals abundant aromas of new saddle leather mixed with spice box, kirsch, beetroot, and oak. In the mouth, it is richer as well as more tannic than its sibling. This pure, ripe, long Barbaresco is best cellared for another year and consumed over the following decade.

The 1997 Barbaresco Vigneto Loreto is a luxuriously fruited, nearly over-the-top effort. Extremely full-bodied and loaded with exotic, overripe glycerin, smoke, cedar, and cherry flavors, it is a thick, unctuously textured slut of a Barbaresco. It may not make old bones, but who cares given the extraordinary hedonistic pleasures to be found now and over the next 5 years. Even more awesome, the 1997 Barbaresco Vigneto Brich Ronchi is a tour de force in winemaking. Its dark plum/ruby color is accompanied by explosive blackberry/cherry fruit aromas. In the mouth, its viscous texture, low acidity, and overripe Nebbiolo characteristics provide remarkable intensity, and extraordinary flavor richness with notes of blackberries, cherries, coffee, smoke, licorice, and earth. The finish lasts for nearly 45 seconds. Drink this spectacular Barbaresco over the next 5–6 years.

In contrast to the 100% *barrique*-aged Brich Ronchi, the 1996 Barbaresco Vigneto Loreto is aged in moderately large *foudres*. This dazzling, sexy offering possesses an opaque ruby/ purple color, terrific fruit and purity, and enough glycerin and concentrated flavors to conceal moderate levels of tannin. The black cherry characteristic combined with smoke, cedar, and fruitcake aromas is to die for. This full-bodied, intense Barbaresco will get even better over the next several years and will age for 12 years. The large-scaled as well as compelling 1996 Barbaresco Vigneto Brich Ronchi reveals spectacular aromas of intense chocolate-covered cherry candy intermixed with smoky new wood. It is dense and full-bodied, with layers of concentration and glycerin. This superb, mouth-filling Barbaresco can be drunk now or cellared for 10–12 years.

The 1995 Barbaresco Vigneto Loreto is a dark ruby/purple-colored offering with a sweet nose of cedar, Provençal herbs, chocolate, smoky, jammy black cherry fruit, and new oak. The wine is full-bodied, rich, round, and ideal for drinking now and over the next 7–8 years. The 1995 Barbaresco Vigneto Brich Ronchi is a more structured and noticeably tannic wine with a moderately intense nose of cedar, black cherries, and dried herbs. It has a long after-taste but seems closed and is less seductive than the Vigneto Loreto. This is one 1995 that should keep for a dozen years.

BRUNO ROCCA

1998 Barbaresco Coparossa	E	(90–92)
1997 Barbaresco Coparossa	E	90+
1996 Barbaresco Coparossa	E	90
1995 Barbaresco Coparossa	E	89
1998 Barbaresco Rabajà	E	(89–91)
1997 Barbaresco Rabajà	E	92+
1996 Barbaresco Rabajà	E	87
1995 Barbaresco Rabajà	E	88

Barrique aging clearly puts Bruno Rocca in the modern school of Piedmontese winemaking. This outstanding producer has followed his superb 1997s with two impressive 1998s. The 1996s were also excellent, although more tannic, structured, and less exotic than the 1997s.

The 1998 Barbaresco Rabajà exhibits an exotic perfume of overripe black cherry fruit mixed with blackberries, smoky espresso, and a touch of balsam wood as well as chocolate. Full-bodied, powerful, deep, and super-concentrated, this impressive wine should age nicely for 10 years. Although less complex, the saturated ruby/purple-colored 1998 Barbaresco Coparossa possesses sweet, concentrated aromas of new oak, black currants, and berries, abundant glycerin, and excellent concentration. However, it is more straightforward and less nuanced/layered than the Rabajà. Nevertheless, it will provide outstanding drinking over the next decade.

The large-scaled 1997 Barbaresco Rabajà requires some cellaring, unusual for the vintage. An opaque ruby/purple color is accompanied by aromas of chocolate, coffee, blackberry and cherry fruit, as well as noticeable new oak. This immense, powerful, rich, moderately tannic Barbaresco will be at its finest between 2003–2016. More opulent and accessible, the 1997 Barbaresco Coparossa exhibits abundant quantities of cedary black cherry fruit, a viscous texture, fine power, and a dense finish with sweeter tannin than the Rabajà. This full-bodied, gorgeous, ripe offering can be drunk now and over the next 12+ years.

The 1996 Barbaresco Coparossa is slightly higher in alcohol and more muscular, and, while not as sexy or forward as the 1995, is potentially a better wine. Full-bodied, with cherry cough syrup, tobacco, earth, and hints of white truffle aromas, this nicely layered wine possesses a muscular mouth-feel, no hard edges, and moderately sweet tannin in the long finish. Anticipated maturity: now–2012. The 1996 Barbaresco Rabajà exhibits toasty new oak, jammy cherries, dried herbs, and spice scents. Ripe and tightly structured, with medium body and a muscular, astringent, well-delineated finish, it should drink well between now–2012. The 1995 Barbaresco Coparossa is a sexy, opulently styled wine with elements of *garrigue* (an earthy/herb mélange), cedar, coffee, smoke, and jammy fruit. Round and opulently styled, with a lush texture, a forward, evolved personality, and fine glycerin and depth, this alluring Barbaresco can be drunk now and over the next 3–4 years. Because the oak was more obvious and the wine less exotic and accessible than its sibling, the 1995 Coparossa, the 1995 Barbaresco Rabajà was more subdued. It offered interesting balsam wood, cherry, toast, and spice notes, as well as medium body, attractive sweet fruit, good purity, and a well-endowed but tightly knit finish. Anticipated maturity: now–2009.

PODERE ROCCHE DEI MANZONI

1997 Barolo Vigna Big	E	91
1997 Barolo Cappella di Santo Stefano	E	90
1997 Barolo Vigna d'la Roul	E	90

This Monforte d'Alba producer, a modernist, believes in *barrique* aging for these fragrant, full-bodied, elegant, single-vineyard Barolos. Despite their 100% *barrique* aging, they are not particularly oaky. The dark plum-colored 1997 Barolo Cappella di Santo Stefano offers a gorgeous bouquet of cedar, spice box, maple syrup/brown sugar, and cherries. Sweet, sexy, and seductive, this medium- to full-bodied, low-acid, glycerin-imbued wine will be accessible upon release and should drink well for 12 years. The 1997 Barolo Vigna d'la Roul reveals more espresso characteristics, intermixed with chocolate, caramel, leather, and black cherry/berry fruit. Full-bodied and smoky, with a supple texture as well as hedonistic, luxuriously fat, fleshy appeal, it can be consumed now and over the next 12 years. Displaying the most color saturation, the dark plum/purple 1997 Barolo Vigna Big is a flavorful, dense effort with plenty of spice box, kirsch, pepper, chocolate, and coffee aromas and flavors. The wine possesses decent acidity, firm tannin, an expansive, concentrated, full-bodied palate, and more noticeable tannin as well as structure. Anticipated maturity: now–2018.

GIGI ROSSO

1997 Barolo Arione	D	90+

The 1997 Barolo Arione is significantly better in bottle than when tasted prior to bottling. An explosive, large-scaled effort with high levels of tannin and extract, this dark garnet-colored Barolo offers sweet licorice intermixed with leather, roasted herbs, black cherries, and sardines (I know that does not sound appealing, but believe me, it is). Rich and layered, it requires 1–2 years of cellaring to resolve the high tannin in the finish. There is a boatload of extract, so don't worry about the overall balance. Anticipated maturity: 2004–2020.

LUCIANO SANDRONE

1999 Barbera d'Alba	C	90
1998 Barbera d'Alba	C	90
1998 Barolo Cannubi Boschis	EE	(94–96)
1997 Barolo Cannubi Boschis	EE	96
1996 Barolo Cannubi Boschis	EE	96
1995 Barolo Cannubi Boschis	EE	89
1998 Barolo Le Vigne	EE	95
1997 Barolo Le Vigne	EE	94
1996 Barolo Le Vigne	EE	92
1995 Barolo Le Vigne	EE	90
1998 Nebbiolo d'Alba Valmaggiore	C	87

Brothers Luca and Luciano Sandrone have just finished constructing a fabulous new winery just outside the village of Monforte d'Alba. While everyone raves about their Barolos, they also produce spectacular Nebbiolo d'Alba and Dolcetto d'Alba. Readers who come across any of these wines should grab them, as they are terrific. The Dolcetti should be consumed within their first 2–3 years of life and the Nebbiolos within the first 5–6. I have been purchasing these wines since the 1982 vintage, and while it is tempting to say that Sandrone is part of Piedmont's modernist generation, the wines are really a synthesis in style between the traditional and *barrique*-aged, new school of winemaking. *Barriques* are used, but restraint is exercised when it comes to the aromas and flavors of toasty oak. For the wines' upbringing, the estate utilizes about 10% new oak, with the balance aged in *foudres*. It is not a member of the group that uses rotary fermenters, preferring open-top vats and doing considerable pumping over as well as punching down to extract flavor and color (the Burgundian method). More new barrels are utilized for the Barolos than the other offerings. To my surprise, in two of the three vintages (1995 and 1997) I enjoyed the Barolo Le Vigne as much as the renowned Cannubi Boschis.

One of Sandrone's least heralded yet consistently gorgeous efforts is his Barbera d'Alba.

Both the 1999 and 1998 were aged in old *foudres*, and are beautiful, supple, soft, fruit-driven offerings with fine elegance, loads of strawberry and cherry fruit, earth, and spice. The 1998 is more elegant and the 1999 fatter and deeper-colored. Both are best drunk during their first 4–5 years of life. As for the other 1998s, they are just as extraordinary as the 1997s as well as 1996s. The medium dark garnet-colored 1998 Nebbiolo d'Alba Valmaggiore (a 200-case lot of 100% Nebbiolo) offers complex aromas of tobacco, dried herbs, jammy cherries, and smoke. Round and generous, as well as graceful and well balanced, it will drink well for 3–4 years. The magnificent Barolos exhibit both power and elegance. The multidimensional 1998 Barolo Le Vigne may be even better than its 1997 counterpart. It possesses huge layers of black cherry fruit infused with rose petals, tar, balsa wood, mineral, and subtle new oak notes. Full-bodied, awesomely concentrated, and extraordinarily pure, this exquisite, youthful Barolo will be at its prime between 2004–2020. The deep ruby/purple-colored 1998 Barolo Cannubi Boschis boasts a spectacular bouquet of mineral-infused black cherry liqueur, new saddle leather, and toast. This powerful, ripe 1998 offers full-bodied flavors, silky tannin, low acidity, gorgeous levels of glycerin, and a creamy mouthful of complex, layered, superbly pure Nebbiolo fruit. While it will undoubtedly firm up and reveal more tannin, it is presently more approachable than the Barolo Le Vigne. Can I be accurate? Anticipated maturity: 2006–2020.

The dark ruby-colored 1997 Barolo Le Vigne reveals amber at the edge. It offers stunning aromatics consisting of flowers, black fruits, lead pencil, spice box, and minerals. As is typical of Sandrone's offerings, there are extraordinary purity as well as intensity to the blackberry and cherry fruit flavors. As the wine sits in the glass, mineral and tar notes become more apparent. This is a stunning, gorgeously pure, Château Margaux–like Barolo to consume between now–2018. The prodigious 1997 Barolo Cannubi Boschis, which was on an equal footing with Le Vigne from cask, has moved ahead. The color is a dark, saturated garnet. The sweet nose of black fruits, minerals, scorched earth, smoke, dried herbs, and wet stones is stunning. Amazingly concentrated, with tremendous unctuosity yet superb delineation, this large-scaled as well as elegant Barolo possesses fabulous extract as well as a multidimensional mid-palate and finish. More forward than the 1996 or 1990 were at a similar period, the 1997 will last for 20 years. It is an amazing effort! Anticipated maturity: 2003–2020.

The dark ruby/purple-colored 1996 Barolo Le Vigne is an elegant, large-scaled Barolo with everything in balance. There are sweet tannin and a measured yet powerful, rich style with copious amounts of black fruits intermixed with minerals, spice, and dried herbs. The wine is tight and in need of 3–4 years of cellaring. Anticipated maturity: 2004–2018. The spectacular 1996 Barolo Cannubi Boschis offers aromas of cassis, cherry liqueur, and flowers. It is dense, superb, and full-bodied, with fabulous intensity as well as layers of extract. Muscular, concentrated, broad, and powerful, it demands 3–4 years of cellaring. Anticipated maturity: 2006–2020.

In 1995, I actually had a slight preference for the Barolo Le Vigne. The classic 1995 Barolo Le Vigne offers telltale aromas of tar, rose petals, and cherry liqueur. It provides medium to full body, a silky, open, accessible style, sweet, expansive flavors, a gorgeous texture, and a classic finish with no hard edges. This beautifully made Barolo can be drunk now or cellared for 10–12 years. The 1995 Barolo Cannubi Boschis is more backward but may turn out to be just as exciting, if not more so. Although full-bodied, it was extremely closed and difficult to penetrate. It possesses a dark ruby color in addition to plenty of dried herb, balsa wood, and black cherry aromas and flavors. While it is unquestionably excellent, possibly outstanding, it needs 2–3 years of cellaring; it should keep for 15 or more years.

PAOLO SCAVINO

1997 Barolo	E	92
1996 Barolo	E	89

1995 Barolo	E	90
1998 Barolo Bric del Fiasc	E	(92–94)
1997 Barolo Bric del Fiasc	E	95
1996 Barolo Bric del Fiasc	E	93
1995 Barolo Bric del Fiasc	E	91+
1998 Barolo Cannubi	E	(91–93)
1997 Barolo Cannubi	E	95+
1996 Barolo Cannubi	E	92
1995 Barolo Cannubi	E	91
1998 Barolo Caro Bric	E	(88–90)
1997 Barolo Caro Bric	E	93
1998 Barolo Rocche dell'Annunziata	E	(92–95)
1997 Barolo Rocche dell'Annunziata	E	97
1996 Barolo Rocche dell'Annunziata	E	95
1995 Barolo Rocche dell'Annunziata	E	92
1997 Langhe Rosso Corale	E	91

Paolo Scavino, his wife, and his two daughters run this 8-hectare (20-acre) estate, situated in the commune of Castiglione Falletto. They have been producing extraordinary Barolos throughout the decade of the nineties. At this modern-styled domaine, Scavino employs rotary fermenters with paddles, temperature-controlled fermentation, and malolactic in *barrique*. All the top Barolos are aged with approximately 30% new oak and are bottled without filtration. If readers have not yet discovered Scavino's Barolos, they should, as they are fabulous wines. Their otherworldly 1997s have been followed by slightly lighter but more perfumed and accessible 1998s. The 1996s and 1995s are also excellent.

The 1998 Barolo Caro Bric is an elegant, stylish offering without the flamboyance of its 1997 counterpart. Aromas of black cherry liqueur, smoke, minerals, and new saddle leather are followed by a medium-bodied wine with a distinctive, restrained style. The full-bodied, seamless 1998 Barolo Cannubi offers the essence of black cherry jam/liqueur along with earth, mineral, new saddle leather, coffee, licorice, tobacco, and new wood. It saturates the mouth without any sense of heaviness. Drink this full-throttle, elegant, pure, classic Barolo over the next 12 years. Another dramatic, provocative effort is the 1998 Barolo Bric del Fiasc. It possesses awesome levels of concentration, considerable power, immense body, and a fabulously pure, concentrated style. With impressive quantities of black fruits, licorice, minerals, asphalt, earth, and truffles, this Barolo is notable for its purity, high extract levels, and seamlessness. Anticipated maturity: 2004–2016. The 1998 Barolo Rocche dell'Annunziata will be an undeniable showstopper. An exquisite combination of black fruits, coffee, smoke, new oak, licorice, and incense is found in this medium- to full-bodied, ripe, elegant, pure Barolo. Explosive aromatics are followed by equally riveting flavors as well as a 50-second finish. The tannin is sweet and beautifully integrated. Anticipated maturity: 2005–2018.

Scavino calls his 1997 Barolos "big and fat." He is one of many Piedmontese producers who has had a hard time understanding these wines, which are aberrations in terms of their sumptuous richness, viscous personalities, and high-alcohol, low-acid styles. Readers looking for an amazing generic Barolo should check out Scavino's saturated garnet-colored 1997 Barolo. It offers a marvelous bouquet of Chinese black tea, vanilla, kirsch, and jammy currants. Full-bodied, powerful, unctuously textured, and admirably concentrated, it is a remarkable achievement for a generic Barolo. Do not overlook it in your rush to purchase Scavino's single-vineyard wines. Anticipated maturity: now–2012. A new offering, the 1997 Barolo Caro Bric, is an elegant, stylish example when compared to the other Scavino wines. It reveals the telltale saturated garnet color with amber at the edge, in addition to intense aromas of coffee, smoke, kirsch, herbs, leather, and fruitcake. While full-bodied, with expansive, saturated layers of fruit and abundant stuffing as well as richness, it does not reveal the nuances of Scavino's greatest crus. Nevertheless, it is an exceptional Barolo to enjoy between now–2016. The surreal 1997 Barolo Cannubi boasts a saturated ruby/purple color and an exquisite bouquet of black fruits, lead pencil, minerals, smoke, and licorice. Full-bodied and opulent, with more obvious tannin than many 1997s, this structured, muscular, viscous, formidably concentrated effort will be at its best between 2004–2020. From a well-known Castiglione Falletto vineyard, the 1997 Barolo Bric del Fiasc reveals the essence of cherry jam in its massive constitution. It is a powerful, full-bodied effort displaying pronounced black cherry liqueur–like aromas and flavors, huge extract and glycerin, and 14.5–15% alcohol. Remarkably pure, delineated, and balanced for a wine of such massiveness, it is more forward than the Cannubi but still needs another 1–2 years of cellaring. Anticipated maturity: 2003–2020. The virtually perfect 1997 Barolo Rocche dell'Annunziata offers an amazing perfume of roasted nuts, cedar, Provençal herbs, black cherry jam, rose petals, vanilla, and meat. Fabulously concentrated, with multiple flavor dimensions and a texture that swells in the mouth, this full-bodied, seamless, compelling Barolo is destined to be a legend. Approachable now, it promises to age for two decades. The 1997 Langhe Rosso Corale is a *barrique*-aged (50% new oak) blend of 35% Nebbiolo, 35% Barbera, 20% Cabernet Sauvignon, and 10% Merlot. There are 250 cases of this wine, which should not go unnoticed by fans of Piedmontese winemaking. An opaque ruby/purple color is accompanied by a full-bodied, deep, chewy, Bordeaux-like offering. It reveals cassis, black cherry, leather, cedar, and spice box aromas, medium to full body, superb definition and intensity, and a long, ripe, opulent finish. It should drink well for 7–8 years.

Scavino produced one of the great wines of the classic year of 1996, the Barolo Rocche dell'Annunziata. The color is a healthy dark ruby. The nose offers scents of smoky charcoal, licorice, toast, black cherries, incense, tobacco, and leather. Full-bodied and massive, with superb balance, nicely integrated acidity and tannin, and a finish that goes on for nearly a minute, it is a profound Barolo to drink now and over the next two decades. Nearly as spectacular is the 1996 Barolo Bric del Fiasc. It displays a saturated plum color, a smoky, black cherry–scented nose, explosive, fleshy flavors with plenty of glycerin, a more evolved and seductive character than the larger-scaled Annunziata, extraordinary intensity, and impeccable balance. Exotic Asian spice and fruitcake aromas add to its complexity. Anticipated maturity: now–2018. The dark plum/ruby-colored 1996 Barolo Cannubi reveals cherries galore intermixed with smoke, tobacco, and new saddle leather scents. This full-bodied, suppletextured, glorious Barolo possesses exceptional extract and can be drunk now or cellared for 15–16 years. With more of a fruit-driven personality, the generic 1996 Barolo is also outstanding. Sexy and forward, it does not possess the complexity and stature of the three single-vineyard offerings, but it is a wonderful introduction to the Scavino style. It should age nicely for 10 years.

The medium ruby-colored 1995 Barolo is an expansive, evolved, aromatic offering with cedar and balsam wood, sweet cherry jam, and rose petals. The light color is deceptive given its intense bouquet and expansive, lush, concentrated style. It will not be long-lived, but for drinking over the next 5–6 years, this is a seductive, hedonistically styled Barolo. The 1995 Barolo Cannubi is very sexy. The dark ruby color is accompanied by a sumptuous nose of tobacco smoke, coffee, black fruits, and toast. The wine is dense, velvety-textured, full-bodied, and silky, with no hard edges. This is a voluptuous wine to enjoy over the next decade. The 1995 Barolo Bric del Fiasc is backward, with scents of smoke, tar, soy, jammy black cherry and blackberry fruit, and toast. Full-bodied, concentrated, expansive, soft, and seductive, with 13.5% alcohol and moderate tannin in the finish, it should be drunk over the next 10 years. The intensely fragrant (wood smoke, allspice, black fruits, and tobacco) 1995 Barolo Rocche dell'Annunziata boasts a dark ruby color, as well as terrific extract, full body, and copious quantities of glycerin. While it possesses the velvety, evolved personality of the other 1995s, there are more stuffing and richness but fewer nuances. Drink it over the next 12–14 years. Already complex and approachable, the 1995 Scavino Barolos are all sensual, fragrant, Burgundy-like, forward wines with fine balance.

MAURO SEBASTE

1998	Barbera d'Alba Santa Rosalia	D	88
1997	Barbera d'Alba Santa Rosalia	D	91
1997	Barolo Monvigliero	E	89
1996	Barolo Monvigliero	D	89+
1995	Barolo Monvigliero	D	87
1997	Barolo Prapò	E	90
1996	Barolo Prapò	D	89+
1995	Barolo Prapò	D	89
1997	Barolo La Serra	E	(88–91)
1998	Centobricchi	C	86
1997	Centobricchi	D	91

Sebaste tends to produce wines that reflect the finest aspects of both the traditional and more modern school of winemaking. The estate's total production is about 1,200 cases. Sebaste's Barolos from the Prapò vineyard are fuller-bodied, bigger-structured, and more muscular offerings. The 1998 Barbera d'Alba Santa Rosalia is less expansive and flamboyant than the 1997 but altogether an excellent wine with many of the same characteristics. It should drink well for 3–4 years. The 1998 Centobricchi, a blend of 90% Barbera and 10% Nebbiolo aged in 1- and 2-year-old French barrels, displays attractive strawberry, cherry, and currant aromas and flavors, medium body, good purity, spicy new oak, and a supple, fleshy finish. Drink it over the next 5–6 years.

An outstanding effort, the 1997 Centobricchi reveals an explosive bouquet of cedary, spice box, tobacco, blackberry and cherry aromas, a long, lush, multilayered, concentrated palate, with gorgeous spice and jammy fruit. Rich, unctuously textured, and thick, it is ideal for drinking now and over the next decade. The vintage's opulence is well displayed in the perfumed 1997 Barolo Monvigliero. The color is a dark ruby, and the wine is exotically rich, ripe, and obviously a creation of its vintage's conditions more than its *terroir*. The creamy, fat, succulent texture, gorgeously ripe fruit, and long, glycerin-imbued finish are admirable. It is a candidate for an outstanding rating after bottling. Anticipated maturity: now–2012. The licorice, smoky cassis, overripe style of the 1997 Barolo Prapò defines this exotic, flamboyant vintage. Dark ruby/purple-colored, it possesses abundant levels of glycerin, high alcohol, and low acidity. It should be delicious young yet keep for 15 years. The 1997 Barolo La Serra is the debut vintage of this sexy, lush, ostentatiously styled wine. The color is a dark ruby, and the wine is viscous and open-knit with gobs of fruit, glycerin, alcohol, and extract. This heady, chewy Barolo needs more delineation, but it displays considerable promise. Readers will undoubtedly enjoy the classic fragrance of jammy cherries, smoke, tar, and spice. Anticipated maturity: now–2016.

The two 1996 Barolos are backward. The medium dark ruby-colored 1996 Barolo Monvigliero exhibits a spicy, tobacco, strawberry, and kirsch-scented nose with dried herbs in the background. Dense, rich, and medium- to full-bodied, with high tannin, this wine is still an infant. Give it 1–2 years of cellaring and drink it through 2015. Even more dense, tannic, and muscular is the 1996 Barolo Prapò. A dark ruby color is followed by aromas of spice box, cherry liqueur, cedarwood, rose petals, and tar. This full-bodied, dry, muscular effort needs at least two years of cellaring. It is impressively built and dense and may merit an outstanding rating with additional bottle age. Anticipated maturity: 2005–2018.

The 1995 Barolo Monvigliero reveals an evolved garnet color with a pink/amber edge, in addition to expansive aromas of meats, dried herbs, spice, cedar, and cherries. There are excellent fruit in the mouth, medium to full body, a supple texture, and a fine finish. Drink this accessible Barolo over the next 4–5 years. The 1995 Barolo Prapò offers Nebbiolo's classic bouquet of melted road tar, rose petal, and cherry liqueur–like scents. Medium- to full-bodied, with a distinctive licorice/cherry fruitiness as well as excellent richness and purity, it is an open-knit Barolo to enjoy over the next 12 years.

F.LLI SEGHESIO

1998 Barolo Vigneto La Villa	E	94
1997 Barolo Vigneto La Villa	E	93
1996 Barolo Vigneto La Villa	E	91
1995 Barolo Vigneto La Villa	E	90

This Monforte d'Alba producer utilizes open-top fermenters and about 20% new oak, which is blended with the balance of the wine, which has been aged in *foudres*.

The fabulous 1998 Barolo Vigneta La Villa is even better than the 1997. Its saturated dense plum/garnet color is accompanied by a stunningly ostentatious, brilliantly aromatic nose of smoky tobacco, cedar wood, plums, cherry liqueur, coffee, and dried herbs. A rich, full-bodied, opulent wine, it possesses fabulous spice and fruit as well as a fresh, high-toned character. Powerful, full, and beautifully delineated, it can be consumed over the next 10–12 years. A dense plum/garnet color and exquisite bouquet of cigar box, smoke, licorice, black cherry/berry fruit, and subtle oak are found in the exotic, flamboyant 1997 Barolo Vigneto La Villa. Full-bodied, with a viscous texture and plenty of power, yet impeccable balance as well as harmony between the alcohol, acidity, tannin, and wood, this fleshy, super-concentrated, seamless effort can be drunk now and over the next 15 years. The explosive 1996 Barolo Vigneto La Villa offers redolent aromatics of kirsch, blackberries, soy, toasty new oak, licorice, and dried herbs. The wine is full-bodied, with huge quantities of glycerin, and fabulous concentration as well as richness. There are plenty of tannin and muscle in the finish, so it will benefit from 3–4 years of cellaring. Anticipated maturity: 2004–2018. The deep ruby 1995 Barolo Vigneto La Villa is a Burgundy-styled wine with a nose of cherry liqueur, dried herbs, smoke, toasty oak, and seaweed scents. There are low acidity and a medium- to full-bodied, plush texture. I would opt for drinking it over the next 4–5 years.

ENRICO SERAFINO

1998 Barolo	D	(87–88)
1997 Barolo	D	89

This producer from the village of Canale d'Alba has fashioned an attractive, well-made, smoky, black cherry–scented 1998 Barolo with considerable complexity in the evolved aromatics. It exhibits good density, medium body, moderate tannin, charming sweetness, and clean winemaking. Consume it over the next 12 years. The supple-textured, dark garnet-colored 1997 Barolo possesses full body, a fleshy, plush texture, low acidity, excellent concentration, and admirable length. It should drink well for a decade. I also liked Serafino's lighter, more elegant, fresher, less opulent 1999. A sleeper choice?

AURELIO SETTIMO

1997 Barolo Rocche	E	90
1996 Barolo Rocche	E	90
1995 Barolo Rocche	E	87

These are fine efforts from this small producer in La Morra. The vintage's sweet glycerin, low acidity, and lofty alcohol are well displayed in the 1997 Barolo Rocche. It possesses a boatload of black cherry and berry fruit, as well as a voluptuous texture and a powerful, long, concentrated finish. This impressive old-style Barolo will be ready to drink upon release and should keep for 12 years. The traditionally made, impressively endowed 1996 Barolo Rocche exhibits a fragrant bouquet of chocolate, melted asphalt, soy, smoke, and white truffles. It is powerful, massive, moderately tannic, dense, and chewy, with considerable intensity. There are a few hard edges, and fans of the more modern-style Barolos will feel it is rustic, but it is loaded with flavor and personality. I adored it. Anticipated maturity: now–2015. Settimo's 1995 Barolo Rocche is a complex, evolved effort with scents of soy, roasted meats, dried herbs, and earthy fruits. The color is dark garnet with amber/orange at the edge. Complex, savory, fleshy, and ready to drink, this medium- to full-bodied Barolo should be at its best now and over the next 8 years.

SOTTIMANO

1996	Barbaresco Gaia Principe Vigna del Salto	D	89
1998	Barbaresco Cottà Vigna Brichet	D	90+
1997	Barbaresco Cottà Vigna Brichet	D	92
1996	Barbaresco Cottà Vigna Brichet	D	89+
1998	Barbaresco Pajoré Vigna Lunetta	D	90
1997	Barbaresco Pajoré Vigna Lunetta	D	89
1998	Barbaresco Currà Vigna Masué	D	90
1997	Barbaresco Currà Vigna Masué	D	91
1996	Barbaresco Currà Vigna Masué	D	(91–92)
1998	Barbaresco Fausoni Vigna del Salto	D	90
1997	Barbaresco Fausoni Vigna del Salto	D	90+
1997	Barbera d'Alba Pairolero	C	90
1998	Dolcetto d'Alba Cottà	B	89

Sottimano is based in Neive, where the Barbarescos tend to be larger-framed, deeper-colored, and more tannic and structured than the more elegant offerings from vineyards surrounding the village of Barbaresco or the cooler sites surrounding Treiso. All of the 1998 Barbarescos are complex, expressive offerings with dramatic bouquets as well as gorgeously ripe, multilayered flavors. The only difference is that some are more precocious than their siblings. The 1997s are freaks of Mother Nature, with opulence and levels of glycerin, alcohol, and fruit that are largely unprecedented in Piedmont. The 1996s look classic in the style of 1989 and 1971. I would not be surprised if all the 1996 Sottimano Barbarescos easily achieved 14% alcohol, and I am sure the 1997s are even higher, although it is completely hidden by the wines' wealth of fruit, glycerin, and concentration.

Sottimano's dense purple-colored 1998 Dolcetto d'Alba Cottà is not the soft style of Dolcetto usually produced. This example possesses more structure than most (unusual for Dolcetto), but it is crammed with fruit, extract, and richness. Massive for a Dolcetto, with excellent purity, it will last for 4–5 years. An earthy concoction of herbs, leather, cedar, spice box, and black cherry/plum-like fruit offers an enticing introduction to the 1998 Barbaresco Pajoré Vigna Lunetta. Supple-textured and seemingly low in acidity, with admirable density, excellent purity, and a fleshy finish, it will drink well for a decade. A similar earthiness, with the addition of vegetable root, plum, and cherry characteristics, is found in the 1998 Barbaresco Currà Vigna Masué. Its soft, velvety-textured, black fruit flavors reveal a distinctive spicy earthiness along with notes of leather. Drink this outstanding effort over the next 8 years. A leather component accompanies notes of cigar tobacco, spice box, cedar, herbs, and cherry cough syrup in the deep, full-bodied, richly fruity, dense, layered 1998 Barbaresco Fausoni Vigna del Salto. Again, this wine is delicious to drink, but it displays more tannin in the finish than its two predecessors. Unquestionably, the most backward of Sottimano's Barbarescos is the 1998 Barbaresco Cottà Vigna Brichet. Its dark ruby color is followed by tightly knit but promising aromatics of cherry liqueur, rose petals, melted asphalt, oak, and earth. Structured, powerful, broodingly backward, and extremely well made, with moderate tannin, this impressive effort requires 1–2 years of cellaring. Anticipated maturity: 2004–2020.

The superb 1997 Barbera d'Alba Pairolero offers a saturated black/ruby/purple color, glorious levels of blackberry and cherry liqueur–like fruit, low acidity, a voluptuous, thick, viscous texture, and an intense finish. Drink this superb, pure Barbera over the next 4–5 years. The dark garnet-colored 1997 Barbaresco Pajoré Vigna Lunetta offers sweet, ripe, exotic notes presented in an open-knit style. Fleshy and spicy, with aromas and flavors of tar, dried herbs, and cherry liqueur, it is medium- to full-bodied, lush, and best drunk over the next 4–5 years. For whatever reason, as good as it is (and I would be happy to drink it anytime) it is the least profound of this quartet. The dark garnet-colored 1997 Barbaresco Currà Vigna Masué exhibits aromas of soy, smoke, asphalt, black cherries, and incense, unreal opulence, huge levels of glycerin, plenty of power, a sweet, expansive palate impression, gorgeous purity, and loads of fruit, glycerin, and alcohol. Buried beneath all that is some serious tannin, but it is not causing the wine to shut down or taste astringent. It should firm up in the bottle and drink well for 12 years. The complex 1997 Barbaresco Fausoni Vigna del Salto displays an Asian spice profile to its explosive aromatics. A dark plum color is followed by elegant, full-bodied notes of coffee, cherries, soy, and star anise, in addition to a sweet, fleshy, low acid palate impression. Not as massive as the Currà Vigna Masué, it is a fleshy effort to enjoy over the next 12 years. Sottimano's garnet/plum-colored 1997 Barbaresco Cottà Vigna Brichet is the most structured of this quartet, yet it possesses extraordinary density, concentration, and intensity. The bouquet offers aromas of Asian spices, soy, dried cherries, tobacco, incense, and smoke. Full-bodied, thick, chewy, highly concentrated, and moderately tannic, this 1997 needs another 1–2 years of cellaring; it should drink well for 12 years.

The 1996 Barbaresco Gaia Principe Vigna del Salto is a wine of both richness and structure. Its dark ruby color is accompanied by an intriguing nose of spice box, tobacco smoke, cedar, and cherry liqueur. The wine is dense, medium- to full-bodied, and structured, with moderate tannin. It requires several years of bottle age. Anticipated maturity: now–2015. The 1996 Barbaresco Cottà Vigna Brichet is similarly styled, with more smoke and cherry liqueur components intermixed with attractive scents of new saddle leather and spice. The wine is ripe and full-bodied, with moderate tannin and outstanding purity. Anticipated maturity: now–2015. The 1996 Barbaresco Currà Vigne Masué is the most expansive, full-bodied, and concentrated of the three 1996s. The wine displays a dark ruby color, as well as an explosive nose of cherry liqueur, incense, dried herbs, smoke, cedar, and soy. Dense and powerful, with fabulous concentration and a sweet, layered mid-palate and finish, this large-scaled, mouthcoating Barbaresco will be at its finest between now–2016.

LA SPINETTA DI GIUSEPPE RIVETTI

1995	Barbaresco La Spinetta	E	87
1998	Barbaresco Vigneto Valeirano	E	92
1997	Barbaresco Vigneto Valeirano	E	91
1998	Barbaresco Vigneto Gallina	E	92
1997	Barbaresco Vigneto Gallina	E	96
1996	Barbaresco Vigneto Gallina	E	90
1998	Barbaresco Vigneto Starderi	E	90+
1997	Barbaresco Vigneto Starderi	E	92+
1996	Barbaresco Vigneto Starderi	E	90
1999	Barbera d'Alba Vigneto Gallina	E	96
1998	Barbera d'Alba Vigneto Gallina	E	95
1997	Barbera d'Alba Vigneto Gallina	E	95
1996	Barbera d'Alba Vigneto Gallina	E	92
1999	Barbera d'Asti	E	94
1998	Barbera d'Asti	E	93
1999	Monferrato Rosso Pin	E	95

1998 Monferrato Rosso Pin	E	91
1997 Monferrato Rosso Pin	E	90
1996 Monferrato Rosso Pin	E	89+

Giorgio Rivetti, who has received immensely favorable publicity in the Italian press, appears to have everything going his way. He displays a masterful touch whether he is making Barbera, Barbaresco, or his proprietary red wine, Pin. His most renowned offerings are his extraordinary, slightly sweet, sparkling Moscatos, which are not reviewed here since they must be drunk within a year of their release. His beautiful 1998 Barbarescos are just a notch below his flamboyant, superexotic, almost over-the-top 1997s, which all performed significantly better from bottle than they did from cask. All his vineyards are planted on hillsides surrounding the village of Treiso. Rivetti has recently purchased a vineyard in Barolo, from which small quantities will emerge beginning with the 2000 vintage. The Barbarescos are aged in an assortment of wood, with about 18% being new French oak.

Rivetti's blend of Cabernet Sauvignon and Nebbiolo, the 1999 Monferrato Rosso Pin, is an exotic, ripe, luxuriously intense effort displaying extravagant flavors that border on excess. It is voluptuously textured with terrific aromas of red and black fruits, smoke, and new oak. While there is a tendency to think of this as an internationally styled offering, Nebbiolo gives the wine a finesse and complexity not found in most new-breed wines. Its texture, richness, and thickness are a total turn-on. Who knows how it will age, but certainly it is impossible to resist at present. My instincts suggest drinking it over the next 5–6 years, but it may be uncommonly long-lived.

The 1999 Barbera d'Alba Vigneta Gallina is awesome! I am not sure it will get any better since Barbera is not one of the most noble varietals in terms of complexity and intensity. It does, however, offer glorious levels of concentration as well as a huge nose of smoked meats, blackberry, cherry, and strawberry jam intertwined with licorice, new oak, and barbecue spice. Viscous, remarkably dense, and sexy, it is impossible to resist. For drinking now and over the next 4–5 years, this is as profound a dry red wine as readers will find. More restrained (although that's hardly the appropriate word), the black/purple-colored 1999 Barbera d'Asti offers wonderful sweetness, jammy plum and currant characteristics, and toasty new oak from its new-*barrique* aging. It is viscous, thick, and jammy with oodles of fruit, glycerin, and extract. Extraordinarily pure, mouthcoating, and fascinating, this 1999 should be consumed over the next 3–4 years to take advantage of its exuberance and extraordinary fruit.

The complex, elegant 1998 Barbaresco Vigneto Gallina exhibits aromas and flavors of pepper, cedar, black cherries, plums, soy, earth, and new oak. Full-bodied, pure, seamless, and well balanced, with low acidity, this expressive, beautifully made wine should drink well for 10 years. The ravishingly complex 1998 Barbaresco Vigneto Valeirano possesses a distinctive bouquet of licorice, root beer, earth, cherry liqueur, rose petals, and truffles. Drink this complex, dense, opulently textured, hedonistic offering over the next decade. The 1998 Barbaresco Vigneto Starderi is less expressive than its two siblings, revealing more tannin and structure, as well as a restrained, backward bouquet. Dark ruby-colored, round, and full-bodied, with notes of licorice, new oak, and black cherries, it should drink well over the following 10–12 years.

The opaque purple-colored 1998 Barbera d'Alba Vigneto Gallina (a terrific Barbaresco vineyard outside Neive) was aged in 100% new oak. It offers a glorious perfume of chocolate, cedar, blackberries, cherry liqueur, and smoke. This massive yet well-balanced, layered wine is explosive. Drink it over the next 4–5 years. Of equal size, explosiveness, power, and richness is the 1998 Barbera d'Asti. Even more fruit-driven, with less spice and complexity but equal weight, mass, and intensity, it offers a dynamic mouthful of Barbera.

The 1998 Monferrato Rosso Pin, is a blend of 50% Nebbiolo, 30% Barbera, and 20% Cabernet Sauvignon that spent 20 months in 100% new French oak. The 1998 is terrific. It boasts a dense ruby/purple color as well as complex, Bordeaux-like aromas of cedar and black currants, full body, moderate tannin, and excellent overall balance. It will evolve nicely for a decade.

The magnificent 1997 Barbaresco Vigneto Gallina comes from a steep hillside vineyard just outside the village of Neive, even though it is part of the Treiso commune. A deep plum color is accompanied by a huge, complex, leather, soy, allspice, cherry liqueur, and smoky-scented bouquet. This full-bodied, impressively endowed, layered, ravishing Barbaresco can be drunk now or cellared for 15 years. Equally sensational but more structured is the 1997 Barbaresco Vigneto Valeirano. This wine exhibits more licorice, glycerin, and berry fruit, along with exotic spices, leather, smoke, and herbs. Spicy and full-bodied, with more obvious tannin, structure, and muscle than the more seductive Gallina, it should keep for 15–20 years. The 1997 Barbaresco Vigneto Starderi is the least penetrable and ostentatious of this trio. It boasts a dark plum/purple color in addition to full body, great fruit, concentration, and power, but it is firm and closed compared to its siblings. There is plenty of potential, but this wine needs 2–3 years of cellaring. It should keep for two decades.

The 1997 Barbera d'Alba Gallina may be one of the finest Barberas ever produced in Italy. Opaque purple-colored, with soaring aromatics, huge density and richness, a voluptuous texture and a finish that lasts for nearly a minute, this mind-boggling effort should age gloriously for a decade or more. A proprietary red wine made from a blend of equal parts Nebbiolo, Cabernet Sauvignon, and Barbera, the 1997 Monferrato Rosso Pin *vino da tavola* presents an outstanding combination of concentrated red and black fruits, spicy vanilla, and huge, thick, juicy flavors. Since the new oak is more apparent, the wine should be cellared for 1–2 years and drunk over the following decade.

The classic structure and power of the vintage is well displayed in both of Rivetti's 1996 Barbarescos. The 1996 Barbaresco Vigneto Starderi's deep ruby color is followed by an explosive nose of sweet cherry liqueur, vanilla, and wood smoke. This full-bodied, highly extracted, intense, sexy, moderately tannic wine is powerful yet well balanced. Despite its ability to improve for 10–12 years, it is easy to drink at present. The terrifically fruity, more flattering 1996 Barbaresco Vigneto Gallina is full-bodied, with outstanding concentration, plenty of earthy, plum/cherry, smoky, spice scents, low acidity, and moderate tannin in the layered finish. It should drink well for a dozen or more years. The terrific, formidably endowed, gorgeously pure, full-bodied 1996 Barbera d'Alba Vigneto Gallina has soaked up its new oak beautifully. It possesses such phenomenal layers of concentrated black fruits, full body, and amazing glycerin and depth that it must be tasted to be believed.

Another Rivetti wine that is worth seeking is the 1996 Monferrato Rosso Pin, a proprietary red wine blend of 50% Nebbiolo, 25% Cabernet Sauvignon, and 25% Barbera. The color is a saturated black/purple and the wine tannic and backward, made in a Médoc-like style. Although rich, it was closed and revealed too much oak to merit an outstanding score (it was brought up in 100% new oak casks).

Rivetti's medium garnet/ruby-colored 1995 Barbaresco La Spinetta exhibits a sweet, evolved nose of spicy oak, cherry liqueur, tobacco, and vanilla. Expansive (13.5% alcohol), ripe, and long, with copious quantities of fruit, this medium- to full-bodied Barbaresco should drink well now and over the next 8 years.

LA SPINONA

1997	Barbaresco	D	87
1996	Barbaresco	D	82
1997	Barolo	D	(87–90)

The more interesting 1997 Barbaresco exhibits a layered texture, riper, sweeter black cherry fruit with dried herbs and spice in the background, and medium to full body. It is ideal for drinking over the next decade. The dark ruby-colored 1997 Barolo reveals the vintage's jammy overripeness in its aromatics. Full-bodied, low in acidity, and thick but not complex, it will merit the higher score if more complexity emerges. Anticipated maturity: now–2014. The lean, straightforward, medium-bodied 1996 Barbaresco offers attractive fruit, but it falls away in the mouth. Consume it over the next 3–4 years.

STROPPIANA

1997 Barolo	D	89

Recent vintages of this La Morra producer's wines have all performed well. While made in a solid, muscular, tannic, monolithic style, they possess excellent depth, exuberance, and rustic tannin in the finish. More finesse would be beneficial, but there is a lot to like in this traditionally made Barolo. The dark plum/purple-colored 1997 Barolo reveals a boatload of tannin as well as big, thick flavors with abundant muscle, depth, and breadth. Give it 1–2 years of cellaring and consume it over the following 12–15.

GIANOLIO TOMASO

1998 Barbaresco	D	85
2000 Barbera d'Alba	C	87
1997 Barolo	D	90
1999 Nebbiolo d'Alba	C	88
1998 Nebbiolo d'Alba	C	85
1997 Nebbiolo d'Alba	C	89

The 2000 Barbera d'Alba exhibits more strawberry and cherry fruit as well as acidity, in addition to admirable ripeness, medium body, excellent texture, and a fine finish. Drink it over the next 2–3 years.

The three Nebbiolos d'Alba admirably reflect their vintages. The 1999 Nebbiolo d'Alba appears to be a blend of the exotic 1997 and elegant, streamlined 1998. It offers sweet aromas of strawberries, cherries, leather, and tobacco. It is best consumed over the next 4–5 years. The most elegant, the 1998 Nebbiolo d'Alba, is more measured and restrained and less exotic than the sweeter, voluptuous, deep, chewy 1997 Nebbiolo d'Alba. Both wines are meant to be drunk over the next 2–3 years.

Tomaso's 1998 Barbaresco reveals notes of spice box, leather, soy, tobacco, and cherry fruit, medium body, and a short finish. Far superior is the 1997 Barolo, a sweet, exotic, concentrated offering exhibiting aromas and flavors of espresso, cherry liqueur, soy, and wood in the background. Medium- to full-bodied, with excellent purity, it is best drunk now and over the next 7–8 years.

GIUSEPPE TRAVERSA

1998 Barbaresco Sorì Ciabot	E	90+
1997 Barbaresco Sorì Ciabot	E	89
1996 Barbaresco Sorì Ciabot	E	91
1995 Barbaresco Sorì Ciabot	E	90
1997 Barbaresco Sorì Starderi	E	87
1996 Barbaresco Sorì Starderi	E	(90–91)
1999 Barbera d'Alba La Burdinota del Ciabot	D	88
1997 Barbera d'Alba La Burdinota del Ciabot	D	90

This producer's outstanding, modern-styled Barbarescos are *barrique*-aged and bottled in heavy, thick antique bottles. Traversa also fashions superb Barberas.

The medium-bodied 1999 Barbera d'Alba La Burdinota del Ciabot offers tangy, sweet strawberry and cherry fruit infused with toasty French oak. Plump and fleshy as well as elegant and pure, it will drink well for 2 years.

The *barrique*-aged, dark plum/purple-colored 1998 Barbaresco Sorì Ciabot reveals ripe cherry and blackberry fruit intertwined with toast, smoke, and espresso characteristics. Rich, full-bodied, and powerful, with moderately high tannin, it is one of the few 1998 Barbarescos that requires cellaring. Anticipated maturity: 2003–2014.

As the spicy, complex 1997 Barbaresco Sorì Starderi sat in the glass, tobacco, new saddle leather, fennel, and sweet and sour cherry aromas emerged. Medium- to full-bodied, complex, and already drinkable, it should keep for a decade or more. The medium ruby-colored 1997 Barbaresco Sorì Ciabot already reveals amber at the edge. Notes of rose petals, tar, cedar, spice box, and copious quantities of red and black fruits are classic characteristics of ripe Nebbiolo. Medium- to full-bodied, with enough acidity for delineation and freshness, good spice and richness, and a long finish, it should be drunk over the next 10 years. The serious 1997 Barbera d'Alba La Burdinota del Ciabot boasts a dense ruby/purple color, and terrific fat, jammy blackberry and cherry fruit intermixed with licorice and spice. Medium- to full-bodied and intense, with good underlying acidity, this is a gorgeously pure, nicely textured Barbera to drink over the next 5–6 years.

The 1996 Barbaresco Sorì Ciabot is even richer and fuller-bodied, with huge extract and a terrific black cherry and raspberry fruitiness intermixed with toast, smoke, new saddle leather, and jam. Massive yet impeccably well balanced, this superb Barbaresco can be drunk now as well as over the next 10 years. The 1996 Barbaresco Sorì Starderi is an impressively endowed, modern-styled effort with copious quantities of black cherry and cassis fruit intermixed with new oak, weedy tobacco, and cigar box notes. All are presented in a silky-textured format. Anticipated maturity: now–2012. The 1995 Barbaresco Sorì Ciabot possesses a deep ruby/plum color as well as stunning aromatics consisting of dried herbs, smoke, tobacco, red and black fruits, cedar, and soy sauce. The wine is fleshy, rich, and full-bodied, with subtle new oak, terrific extract, and a succulent texture. It will not be long-lived but should drink well for 4–5 years.

G. D. VAJRA

1998 Barolo	E	(88–90)
1997 Barolo	E	91

Vajra's wines are well made, full-bodied, and powerful. The dense plum-colored 1998 Barolo exhibits a sexy, sweet, open-knit perfume offering aromas of melted licorice, smoke, plums, and cherries. While it does not possess the thickness or exotic, over-the-top character of his blockbuster 1997, the 1998 is supple, full-bodied, layered, forward, concentrated, and impressively rich. It is surprisingly fragrant for such a young Barolo (a consistent characteristic of most 1998 Barolos and Barbarescos). Harmony is the operative word for this young but promising effort. Anticipated maturity: 2005–2016. The dark plum-colored 1997 Barolo exhibits a big, thick, chocolaty, licorice, cherry liqueur, smoke, camphor, and truffle-scented bouquet. This complex, opulently textured wine possesses low acidity, superb ripeness, and a soft, unevolved personality. However, most tasters will not be able to resist its viscous style. Anticipated maturity: now–2016.

MAURO VEGLIO

1998 Barolo Arborina	E	(91–93)
1997 Barolo Arborina	E	90
1996 Barolo Arborina	E	90
1995 Barolo Arborina	E	89
1998 Barolo Castelletto	E	(90–93)
1997 Barolo Castelletto	E	91
1996 Barolo Castelletto	E	91
1998 Barolo Gattera	E	(90–92)
1997 Barolo Gattera	E	89

1996 **Barolo Gattera**	E	87
1995 **Barolo Gattera**	E	?
1998 **Barolo Rocche**	E	(89–91)
1997 **Barolo Rocche**	E	91
1996 **Barolo Rocche**	E	91
1995 **Barolo Rocche**	E	86

This producer has come of age after mixed performances in the mid-1990s. One of Marc de Grazia's "Barolo Boys," Veglio practices modern winemaking techniques. His first great vintage was 1996. He has turned out successful 1998s that are, qualitatively, as interesting as his brilliant 1997s. All of these wines share the vintage's characteristics: intense perfumes as well as harmonious, forward, softly tannic, approachable personalities.

The 1998 Barolo Gattera exhibits a dark plum color in addition to a sweet bouquet of black cherry and plum fruit, spice box, roasted meats, and smoked herbs, a beautiful texture, good softness, and a long (30+-second) finish. With exposure to air, this classic Barolo appears to grow in the glass. Drink it over the next 15 years. More layered as well as fuller-bodied, the 1998 Barolo Arborina boasts a sweet attack and an intense perfume of licorice, tobacco, black fruits, smoked herbs, and toasty oak. This dark garnet-colored, pure, seductive, rich Barolo is nearly exotic in a 1997 sense. Anticipated maturity: 2003–2015.

Although Veglio is from La Morra, his 1998 Barolo Castelletto comes from a vineyard in Monforte d'Alba. The least evolved of these single-vineyard offerings, it displays an opaque ruby/purple color and notes of cinnamon, minerals, earth, meat, and black fruits. In the mouth, the wine is medium-bodied and austere with more tannin and less seductiveness. However, it is loaded with glycerin and extract. Anticipated maturity: 2005–2017. The feminine, delicate 1998 Barolo Rocche is filled with finesse and elegance, without the weight, richness, or concentration of the other three crus. A moderately intense perfume of black cherries, damp earth, truffles, and Provençal herbs is followed by a measured, restrained, sweet, well-balanced wine with ripe tannin and a long finish. Anticipated maturity: now–2012.

The 1997 Barolo Gattera offers an intriguing bouquet of peat moss, licorice, fennel, dried herbs, root vegetables, and black cherry fruit. It possesses a luscious texture, medium to full body, and an up-front, forward ripeness. Look for this wine to drink well during its first decade of life. More tightly knit, with additional structure, the 1997 Barolo Arborina displays a dense plum color with pink/amber at the edge. Full-bodied and tannic, it is a reserved but concentrated effort exhibiting aromas and flavors of strawberry and cherry liqueur intertwined with smoke, earth, and spice. Anticipated maturity: now–2015.

Veglio's 1997 Barolo Castelletto has stunning aromatics of spice box, tobacco, kirsch, licorice, rose petals, and cedar. Corpulent, full-bodied, exotic, and richly layered, with the vintage's telltale glycerin and low-acid, fleshy, higher-than-normal alcohol levels well displayed, it is a nearly over-the-top, exotic Barolo to drink over the next decade. The dark garnet/amber-edged 1997 Barolo Rocche reveals notions of melted caramel, black cherry jam, licorice, fennel, and road tar in its evolved bouquet. Medium- to full-bodied with high glycerin levels, it provides a hedonistic, fat, chewy mouthful of wine that is performing far better from bottle than it did from *foudre/barrique*. Consume this exceptional Barolo over its first 12–14 years of life.

Three of the four Veglio 1996s appear to have outstanding potential. The 1996 Barolo Gattera is a more interesting example than the 1995. Medium-bodied and soft, with an elegant, kirsch-scented and -flavored personality, it is ideal for consuming over the next 5–6 years. Full-bodied and powerful, the 1996 Barolo Rocche possesses copious quantities of cherry liqueur intermixed with leafy tobacco, roasted nuts, smoke, and spice. This moderately tannic, classic Barolo should be at its finest between now–2014. The 1996 Barolo Arborina reveals the telltale rose petal, melted road tar, and jammy cherry–scented nose with tobacco in the background. Made in a soft, forward style, it is medium- to full-bodied, with dazzling fruit intensity, outstanding purity, sweet tannin, and a soft, lush finish. Anticipated maturity: now–2015. The 1996 Barolo Castelletto smells like an herb garden planted next to a roaring charcoal fire. There are copious amounts of cherry fruit, new saddle leather, and animal-like aromas. This is a more *sauvage* Barolo, with impeccable density, medium to full body, and gobs of spicy, cherry fruit flavors. It should drink well for 10–12 years.

I did not understand the lemony, grassy, vegetal 1995 Barolo Gattera. It tastes more like a white wine than a red and is completely at odds with the other Veglio offerings. The 1995 Barolo Rocche is a middleweight, elegant, finesse-styled Barolo with good spice, some tannin, medium body, and attractive cherry fruit. Drink it over the next 5–6 years. The epitome of finesse, the medium ruby-colored 1995 Barolo Arborina is already revealing amber at the edge. Evolved and stylish, with sweet cherry fruit, medium body, and a heady finish, it will drink well for 3–4 years.

ERALDO VIBERTI

1998	Barolo	E	88
1997	Barolo	E	90
1996	Barolo	E	(86–88)
1995	Barolo	E	87

These four attractive Barolos represent a synthesis in style between modern techniques and respect for tradition. A big, smoky, spicy perfume of licorice, truffles, cedar, tobacco, and black fruits jumps from the glass of this forward, dark plum/ruby-colored 1998 Barolo. The complex aromatics are followed by a medium-bodied, elegant, soft, succulent Barolo to enjoy over the next decade. The 1997 Barolo's complex bouquet of soy, earth, truffles, black fruits, iron, and a touch of vitamins is followed by a medium- to full-bodied, beautifully textured, spicy, lush, layered wine. Low acidity and high glycerin levels, in addition to fruit and alcohol, provide a hedonistic yet intellectually satisfying Barolo. Anticipated maturity: now–2015. The saturated ruby/garnet-colored 1996 Barolo possesses a classic, structured, broodingly backward personality with plenty of dried herbs, leather, and cherrylike fruit. The wine is medium- to full-bodied and compressed in the finish, but if the tannin melts away without significant loss of fruit, it will merit a score in the upper 80s. Anticipated maturity: 2003–2015. The 1995 Barolo reveals a healthy, modern dark ruby/purple color, toast notes in the nose, sweet fruit, medium to full body, moderate tannin, and a lush, accessible style. Drink it over the next 5–6 years.

VIETTI

1997	Barbaresco	E	89
1996	Barbaresco	E	85
1995	Barbaresco	E	86
1997	Barbaresco Masseria	E	93
1995	Barbaresco Masseria	E	88
1996	Barolo	E	85
1995	Barolo	E	83
1998	Barolo Brunate	E	(88–90+)
1996	Barolo Brunate	E	89+
1997	Barolo Brunate	E	92
1995	Barolo Brunate	E	86+
1998	Barolo Lazzarito	E	(88–89+)
1997	Barolo Lazzarito	E	93
1995	Barolo Lazzarito	E	85

1998 Barolo Rocche	E	(90–91+)
1997 Barolo Rocche	E	90
1996 Barolo Rocche	E	90
1995 Barolo Rocche	E	85?
1996 Barolo Villero Riserva	E	91

In spite of the modern-style labels that have been used for nearly three decades by the Vietti firm, these wines remain entrenched in a traditional school of winemaking. I have been purchasing Vietti wines since the 1971 vintage, and they have never disappointed in terms of their ability to age well. In top vintages, these big-styled Barolos easily last three decades or more. They often show significantly better after cellaring than they do early in life (much like those of Giacomo Conterno, Aldo Conterno, and Bruno Giacosa).

The saturated ruby-colored 1998 Barolo Lazzarito exhibits an elegant, sweet style with surprising suppleness for a young Vietti offering. Earthy black cherry fruit, dried herbs, and licorice are found in this medium-bodied 1998. It should be drinkable between 2003–2015. The 1998 Barolo Rocche reveals more muscle, volume, and power in its full-bodied, backward, yet well-balanced personality. Deep and chewy, with a saturated ruby color and broad flavors with mouthcoating tannin, it will be at its best between 2006–2020. Lastly, the 1998 Barolo Brunate is soft and forward for a Vietti wine. That could be due to the vintage's elegant, harmonious style, which tends to be less extroverted and more classical than 1997, and more evolved and accessible than either 1997 or 1996. This 1998's plum/ruby/purple color is followed by sweet black cherry fruit and balsa wood characteristics. Full-bodied and muscular, with sweet tannin and a supple style, it should drink well between 2004–2020.

The 1997s are the finest Vietti offerings in twenty years. For starters, the 1997 Barbaresco Masseria is a fabulous example from this appellation. A saturated dark plum/garnet color is followed by a broad, luxurious, sweet nose of cedar, plums, cherries, leather, herbs, earth, and spice. Deep, expansive, and full-bodied, with no hard edges, this mouthcoating, well-balanced effort will drink well now and over the next 15 years. The dark ruby/garnet-colored 1997 Barolo Lazzarito reveals a certain forwardness, no doubt because of the vintage's exotic, opulent, low-acid character. There are plenty of stuffing, full body, and notes of balsam wood, spice box, fruitcake, and cherries. Viscous, chewy, and deep, this precocious wine can be drunk upon release or cellared for 15–20 years. A classic licorice, dried tobacco, rose petal, cherry, and tar-scented bouquet is found in the dark plum-colored 1997 Barolo Rocche. Although broad and rich with noticeable tannin, it is also expansive and chewy. With more length than the Lazzarito, the Rocche will be approachable young and keep for 15–20 years. The exquisite 1997 Barolo Brunate is the most backward of these offerings. Dark ruby-colored with a purple hue, it offers a compelling nose of barbecued pork, cherry syrup, roasted coffee, rose water, and licorice. Full-bodied, muscular, and powerful, with a load of tannin as well as huge richness and thickness, it requires cellaring for 1–2 years and should drink well for 20–25 years.

In 1996 I tasted four Barolos, all significantly better than Vietti's 1995s. The 1996 Barolo exhibits good sweetness, in addition to a distinctive cedary, herb, and spice box aromatic profile. It is medium-bodied, with good concentration and moderate levels of astringent tannin. Anticipated maturity: now–2012. The 1996 Barolo Villero Riserva reveals spicy oak intermixed with copious quantities of jammy cherries, *garrigue*, smoke, and earth. Sweet, deep, and full-bodied, with classic rose petal and tar-like flavors, this bold, masculine, powerful Barolo possesses plenty of tannin. It should age easily for two decades. Anticipated maturity: 2006–2020. Exhibiting a more saturated color, the 1996 Barolo Brunate came across as more closed, but powerful, rich, and potentially outstanding. The wine has good depth but is broodingly backward and unevolved. Anticipated maturity: 2007–2020. The most saturated color and the sweetest, richest red/black fruits are found in the 1996 Barolo Rocche. It is extremely full-bodied and tannic, a bit hard, but impressively endowed. If the tannin becomes better meshed, it will be an outstanding wine, but it will require patience from prospective purchasers. Anticipated maturity: 2007–2015.

The 1995 Barbaresco exhibits an evolved garnet color in addition to a spicy, tobacco-tinged nose with scents of cherry jam and cigar smoke. It is an easygoing, round, fruit/spice-driven wine to drink over the next 3–4 years. More substantial is the 1995 Barbaresco Masseria. The nose offers dried Provençal herbs intermixed with seaweed, smoke, earth, and kirsch. Weighty, expansive, and lush, this medium- to full-bodied offering reveals some of the Nebbiolo's telltale tar characteristics with airing. Drink this beauty over the next 8 years. The dark ruby-colored 1996 Barbaresco reveals a spicy, cedary, sweet nose, excellent fruit, smoky oak, grilled herbs, and meat elements. The finish is short, but it should open with time. This will not be a blockbuster Barbaresco, but it is elegant and well made. Anticipated maturity: now–2010. The dark ruby-colored, fat, soft 1997 Barbaresco exhibits the vintage's succulence as well as gobs of tannin and black cherry fruit intertwined with smoke and damp foresty smells. With high glycerin and low acidity, it is an ideal candidate for consuming over the next 10 years.

I tasted four 1995 Barolos from Vietti. The regular 1995 Barolo's evolved garnet color is followed by a round, soft, fruity nose of dried herbs, red fruits, cedar, and spice box. The finish is slightly pinched, compressed, and austere. This fully mature Barolo is best consumed over the next 3 years. Frankly, I expected more. I was not impressed by the three single-vineyard Barolos, although they are all good wines. The 1995 Barolo Lazzarito exhibits a moderately intense nose of cranberries, cherries, dried herbs, smoke, and earth. It is compressed in the mouth, displaying high levels of astringent tannin. Although it will drink well for 5–6 years, the wine lacks the concentration to stand up to its structure. The well-made 1995 Barolo Brunate offers a low-key, weedy, cedary, herb, and smoky personality with moderate levels of sweet cherry fruit and a short, tannic finish. Anticipated maturity: now–2007. The 1995 Barolo Rocche possesses the most saturated color of all the Vietti 1995s, but it is evolved, with high levels of tannin that scorch the back of the palate. This gives the wine an attenuated, compressed, tough-textured finish. I am not sure it has the proper balance to age gracefully.

VILLA GIADA

1998 Barbera d'Asti La Quercia	D	90
1998 Barbera d'Asti Riserva Bricco Dani	D	90
2000 Barbera d'Asti Vigna d'Arturo	D	89

These are barrique-aged, modern-styled Barberas, which, despite their marvelous intensity and richness, require consumption during their first 4–5 years of life. The 2000 Barbera d'Asti Vigna d'Arturo reveals evidence of barrique aging. Medium- to full-bodied, with notes of toast, black cherry jam, tomato skin, and spice, gorgeous levels of fruit, and a long, uncomplicated, but delicious finish, it should drink well for 3–4 years. The dense purple-colored 1998 Barbera d'Asti La Quercia exhibits an intense nose of black cherry liqueur intertwined with new wood smells. As it is creamy-textured, intense, ripe, and loaded, with no hard edges, early consumption is mandatory. Even more opaque-colored (it resembles ink), the 1998 Barbera d'Asti Riserva Bricco Dani reveals a thicker, more unctuous personality, as well as additional amounts of toasty new oak in its aromas. Another year of bottle age may result in more nuances. This 1998 should be drunk over the next 3–4 years.

VILLA LANATRA

1998 Barolo	D	90
1997 Barolo	D	88

Even better than the excellent 1997, Villa Lanatra's 1998 Barolo is a well-textured, deep, full-bodied, opaque ruby/purple-colored effort revealing loads of black currant and blackberry fruit as well as evidence of *barrique* aging. Chewy and fleshy, with considerable substance, it is a product of the modern school of Piedmontese winemaking, but there is no shortage of Nebbiolo/Barolo typicity. Anticipated maturity: 2004–2018.

A modern-styled effort with good harmony, finesse, and graceful red currant/cherry flavors backed by subtle toasty oak, the full-bodied, deep, long 1997 Barolo is made in an international style. Anticipated maturity: now–2012.

GIANNI VOERZIO

1999	Barbera d'Alba Ciabot della Luna	C	87
1998	Barbera d'Alba Ciabot della Luna	C	88
1998	Barolo La Serra	E	89
1997	Barolo La Serra	E	88
1996	Barolo La Serra	E	(90–92)
1995	Barolo La Serra	E	90
2000	Dolcetto d'Alba Rocchettevino	C	90
1998	Langhe Rosso Serrapiù	C	88

Gianni Voerzio (Roberto's brother) follows the new school of winemaking, utilizing a high percentage of *barriques* for aging his wine. However, these are not internationally styled Nebbiolos as they all display the varietal's textbook characteristics. This small La Morra producer also fashions excellent Barbera, Dolcetto, and Nebbiolo from the Ciabot della Luna vineyard.

Voerzio's 2000 Dolcetto d'Alba Rocchettevino is an explosive offering loaded with chocolaty black cherry fruit. There are adequate acidity for balance, superb purity, and a plump, fleshy style that invites consumption over the next 2 years. Also very good, the 1999 Barbera d'Alba Ciabot della Luna reveals less color saturation but more complex berry, licorice, and herbal characteristics, a fleshy palate with noticeable new oak, and a smoky, spicy finish. It should drink well for 3 years. Not too exuberant but intense, with a spicy, strawberry, black cherry, licorice, and chocolate-scented bouquet, is the 1998 Barbera d'Alba Ciabot della Luna. There is evidence of toasty oak, but the fruit characteristics dominate. Drink it over the next 3–4 years. The 1998 Langhe Rosso Serrapiù (a blend of equal parts Nebbiolo and Barbera, aged in *barrique*) is an earthy, leathery offering with dried herbs, plums, cherry liqueur, and spice box aromas and flavors. Complex in the nose and rich, medium-bodied in the mouth, with good underlying acidity in addition to a nicely layered structure, it should be consumed over the next 4–5 years.

The elegant, medium-bodied, soft 1998 Barolo La Serra possesses aromas of cherry liqueur, tobacco, and smoke and an autumnal leafy characteristic. It is dense and rich, with its structure and tannin nicely concealed by the fruit and overall harmony. This well-balanced, elegant, stylish 1998 is best consumed over the next 12 years. The 1997 Barolo La Serra does not appear to possess the intensity of either the superb 1998 or the 1999. It is a medium-bodied, low-acid, spicy, round, soft, seductive effort with plenty of caramel, tobacco, cherry, and tar aromas as well as flavors. Drink it over the next 8 years. The 1996 Barolo La Serra exhibits a deeper, more saturated ruby color, as well as dried herb, tobacco, spice box, cherry liqueur and coffee aromas, superb density, huge extract, and a long, full-bodied, moderately tannic finish. This classic Barolo possesses super purity and considerable glycerin. Anticipated maturity: 2004–2024. The 1995 Barolo La Serra is unquestionably one of the vintage's most successful wines. Initially appealing spicy oak gets lost in a blast of black cherry fruit, tar, rose petals, dried herbs, and spices. Rich, full-bodied, open-knit, and chewy, with a noteworthy succulence and lushness, this beautifully knit, evolved, precociously styled, mouth-filling Barolo is ideal for drinking over the next 8 years.

ROBERTO VOERZIO

1999	Barbera d'Alba Vigneto Pozzo dell'Annunziata Riserva	E	(92–94)
1998	Barbera d'Alba Vigneto Pozzo dell'Annunziata Riserva	E	96
1997	Barbera Vigneto Pozzo dell'Annunciata Riserva	E	97
1998	Barolo Brunate	E	(91–92)
1997	Barolo Brunate	E	92+
1996	Barolo Brunate	E	93
1998	Barolo Capalot delle Brunate Riserva	EEE	(93–95)
1997	Barolo Capalot delle Brunate Riserva	EEE	98+
1996	Barolo Capalot Riserva	EEE	93
1995	Barolo Capalot Riserva	EEE	91
1998	Barolo Cerequio	E	(90–91+)
1997	Barolo Cerequio	E	92+
1996	Barolo Cerequio	E	90
1995	Barolo Cerequio	E	86
1998	Barolo Sarmassa di Barolo	E	(91–93+)
1998	Barolo La Serra	E	(90–91)
1997	Barolo La Serra	E	92
1996	Barolo La Serra	E	92
1995	Barolo La Serra	E	87
1999	Dolcetto d'Alba Priavino	C	89
1998	Langhe Rosso Vignaserra	E	87
1997	Langhe Rosso Vignaserra	E	90

While Roberto Voerzio's estate is just under 30 acres, he has quickly emerged as one of Piedmont's superstars. Qualitatively, he is on fire, producing one of the region's most profound Barberas as well as some of the most majestic, complex Barolos. He is a fanatical crop thinner, believes in organic growing, and often thins his vineyard by as much as 50% prior to the harvest. This results in 4–5 bunches of grapes per vine (compared with 30–50 bunches per vine in many Napa vineyards). Voerzio is a modernist, fermenting his wines with indigenous yeasts and putting them into a combination of Taransaud and Vicard French new oak. After a light fining, they are bottled without filtration. The Barolos spend 28 months in oak, with malolactic done in barrel. The SO_2 levels, not surprisingly for such a minimalist, are among the lowest in Piedmont. Over the last decade, Voerzio has produced some of Italy's most stunningly complete, complex wines. In fact, an argument can be made that no one makes better Barbera than his fabulous effort from the Vigneto Pozzo dell'Annunziata. In addition to a tiny parcel of Sarmassa di Barolo he purchased in 1998, he owns three vineyards from which emerge the Cerequio (350–400 cases), the Serra (400 cases), and the Brunate (300 cases) *cuvées*. The single-vineyard Capalot Riserva is made from a plot of the oldest vines in the Brunate vineyard. This wine, bottled only in magnums (approximately 1,000), is produced in only the top vintages. In 2000 Voerzio added an additional cru, the famed Pozzo dell'Annunziata, to his portfolio. Consequently, beginning in 2000, there will be six crus, as compared to four in 1997 and former vintages.

The dark ruby/purple-colored 1999 Dolcetto d'Alba Priavino exhibits toasty new oak along with mocha, blackberry, cherry, and herb-like aromas. Enjoy this fruit-driven Dolcetto over the next 3 years. I generally do not like *barrique*-aged Dolcetto, but the subtle influence of oak works well with this *cuvée*. The 1999 Barbera d'Alba Vigneto Pozzo dell'Annunziata Riserva may not hit the lofty peaks of the 1997 and 1998, but it is still a remarkable effort. An opaque blue/purple color is followed by thick, juicy aromas and flavors of chocolate, espresso, cherry and strawberry liqueur, smoke, and toast. Made from extremely low yields of 25–28 hectoliters per hectare, this unctuous 1999 offers an amazing mouthful of wine.

Voerzio does not believe 1998 is up to the level of 1997. Although the grapes were loaded with raw material, he felt that overall the wines were more elegant, without the high levels of extract found in the 1997s. The 1998 Langhe Rosso Vignaserra (a blend of Cabernet Sauvignon, Barbera, and Nebbiolo from La Serra vineyard) offers classic Piedmontese characteristics of licorice, tobacco, black cherry liqueur, and dried herbs, as well as a medium-bodied, elegant, stylish, moderately weighty palate impression. It is meant to be drunk during its first 5–7 years of life. The 1998 Barolo La Serra is the most finesse-styled of these offerings, exhibiting a deep ruby color in addition to a sexy nose of sweet black cherries, fennel, vanilla, and spice. Velvety texture, full body, and overall harmony suggest it will drink well young as well as over the next 10–12 years. Slightly denser, more masculine, and muscular, the 1998 Barolo Brunate displays abundant quantities of blackberry and cherry liqueur aromas intertwined with vanilla, licorice, tobacco, and rose petals. The new oak is brilliantly absorbed by this medium- to full-bodied, sweet, expansively flavored Barolo. Anticipated maturity: 2003–2016. The dark ruby/purple-colored 1998 Barolo Cerequio is the most structured and backward of this quintet. It emerges from a south-facing vineyard from which Angelo Gaja produces his Conteisa. This tannic, structured, rigidly styled Barolo is loaded with black cherry fruit, rose petal, and tar notes. It will be the least pleasing to drink initially but will emerge from its tannic cloak in 4 years and will evolve for two decades. Anticipated maturity: 2006–2020.

The debut vintage of Voerzio's Barolo Sarmassa di Barolo, the 1998, emerges from a vineyard parcel with a full southern exposure. It boasts an opaque black/purple color as well as a gorgeous bouquet of blackberry liqueur, blueberry, and flower aromas. As the wine sits in the glass, a liquid mineral quality develops. This wine could be mistaken for a 1990 grand cru from Burgundy's Côte de Nuits. Backward, dense, and potentially complex and concentrated, it may be even better than my notes suggest. It is an impressive first offering from this vineyard. Anticipated maturity: 2008–2025. From Voerzio's oldest vines (50 years), 1,200 magnums were produced of the 1998 Barolo Capalot delle Brunate Riserva. This effort ratchets up the intensity level, offering more volume, power, density, and flavor extraction. It is his biggest wine of the vintage and potentially the longest-lived. While the 1998 may not equal the nearly perfect 1997, it is an incredible achievement. Its dense ruby/purple color is accompanied by a big, thick nose of black cherries, cherry syrup, espresso, toast, and roasted meats. This massive, huge, tannic 1998 requires 6–7 years of cellaring; it should last for three decades.

The dense opaque purple-colored 1998 Barbera d'Alba Vigneto Pozzo dell'Annunziata Riserva resembles vintage port in its color, texture, and flavor saturation. Opulent, with extreme richness, this full-bodied, superintense, compelling, flamboyant Barbera (less than 1,400 magnums produced) possesses more freshness than the 1997, yet nearly as much exoticism. It boasts unctuous black cherry, chocolate, espresso, licorice, and strawberry liqueur aromas as well as flavors, immense body, major levels of glycerin, and gorgeously integrated sweet new oak (from 100% malolactic in new wood). While it is impossible to predict how such a wine will age, given its size and strength it will certainly drink well for a decade. I recommend consuming it at a young age to take advantage of its exuberance.

The 1997 Barolo La Serra is a sexy, dense ruby/purple-colored effort offering notes of currants, black cherries, and licorice, a huge, chewy texture, plenty of glycerin, and a creamy, supple, velvety finish. Although impossible to resist, it will develop even more nuances over the next 4–5 years and should last for two decades. Anticipated maturity: 2004–2023. The biggest wine of this trio, the dense opaque ruby/purple-colored, tannic 1997 Barolo Brunate, exhibits copious aromas of cassis, black cherry, kirsch, licorice, smoke, truffles, and new oak. Notes of coffee and chocolate emerge as the wine sits in the glass. It possesses amazing density, a lot of muscle, and a roasted character to its fruity personality. This back-strapping, full-bodied Barolo requires 2–3 years of cellaring and should keep for 25. The paradoxical 1997 Barolo Cerequio possesses exquisite purity as well as an open-knit bouquet, but restrained, tannic, forceful, backward flavors. Dense and rich, with the vintage's thickness well displayed but more tannin than its siblings, it will be at its best between 2005–2020. The formidable 1997 Barolo Capalot della Brunate Riserva is a candidate for Barolo of the vintage. A massive wine, it exhibits aromas and flavors of vitamins, coffee, chocolate, black cherry liqueur, licorice, and toast, a terrific palate entry with oodles of glycerin as well as extract, multiple flavor layers, and sweet tannin in the 60-second finish. There is plenty of tannin lurking beneath the surface, so ideally it needs to be aged for 4–5 years. It will age for three decades. This is a tour de force in winemaking!

The compelling 1997 Barbera Vigneto Pozzo dell'Annunciata Riserva (only 1,350 magnums produced) may be the greatest Barbera I have ever tasted. A prodigious effort, it displays the flamboyant opulence of the 1997 vintage in addition to extraordinary unctuosity, unbelievable layers of fruit, and an amazing finish that lasts for nearly 45 seconds. With gobs of black cherry fruit intermixed with chocolate, cedar wood, strawberries, licorice, and a touch of mint in the background, this spectacular wine—a prodigious effort—will age for at least a decade. Lastly, the 1997 Langhe Rosso Vignaserra (a blend of Nebbiolo, Barbera, and Cabernet Sauvignon, aged in 100% new oak and bottled unfiltered) exhibits a bouquet of wildflowers (particularly lavender) and blackberry and cherry fruit. There are fine suppleness, density, and spiciness, as well as a complex, elegant, rich, nicely layered palate and finish. It should drink well for 6 years.

The superb 1996 Barolo La Serra's opaque ruby/purple color is followed by aromas of black fruits (blackberry, cherry, and a hint of raspberry), superb purity, highly extracted, powerful, monster-sized flavors, mouth-searing levels of tannin, and an impressively endowed, 40+-second finish. This backward, pure, intensely concentrated Barolo will require patience. Anticipated maturity: 2008–2025. The opaque ruby/purple-colored 1996 Barolo Cerequio possesses extremely high tannin and extract, but it is very backward and even more closed and firm than the Barolo La Serra. Full-bodied, powerful, and rich but broodingly backward and stubborn, it possesses all the correct component parts, but patience will be required by potential purchasers. Anticipated maturity: 2010–2025. The black/purple-colored 1996 Barolo Brunate is the most gigantic of all the Voerzio Barolos I tasted. Monstrously sized, with huge alcohol content, high tannin, and spectacular extract, this layered, chewy wine is sensationally promising. Although stubbornly backward, it possesses wonderful ripeness, but it is so huge it needs 3–4 years to evolve. Anticipated maturity: 2006–2030. The profound 1996 Barolo Capalot Riserva boasts a dense, ruby/purple color and a pure nose of black cherries, raspberries, and blackberries. Layered and multidimensional, with a sweet mid-palate and a blockbuster finish, this is an immense, full-throttle Barolo that should age effortlessly for 15–20 years. Impressive!

The 1995 Barolo La Serra exhibits a textbook nose of melted road tar, rose petals, and cigar box aromas, moderate tannin, ripe fruit, medium body, and a dry, austere finish. It is a very good, classic Barolo, but the slight austerity kept my score more conservative. Drink it over the next decade. I was surprised that Voerzio's 1995 Barolo Cerequio displayed such an evolved color. The amber, rusty edge suggested a wine that was far older than four years. The nose of tea, dried herbs, and cedar aromas makes this a spice- rather than fruit-driven wine. It is medium-bodied, evolved, and fully mature. The finish is slightly compressed, but the wine possesses the textbook spice, melted road tar, and dried cherry–like flavors of an old-style Barolo. Drink it over the next 3–4 years. The 1995 Barolo Capalot Riserva is a thick, chewy offering with a stunning display of aromatics (cigar smoke, Chinese black tea, new oak, cherry liqueur, and dried Provençal herbs). Extremely full-bodied and rich, and surprisingly huge for a 1995, this Barolo possesses amazing extract as well as a finish that lasts for nearly a minute. Extremely rich and powerful, but accessible, it can be drunk now as well as over the next 12 years.

ATTILIO ZUNINO

1997 Barolo Sorì di Baudana	D	(88–89)
1996 Barolo Sorì di Baudana	D	(88–90)
1995 Barolo Sorì di Baudana	D	88

This small producer from the village of Serralunga has fashioned three very fine wines. The potentially outstanding 1997 Barolo Sorì di Baudana is the sweetest of these offerings, with the most viscosity and fullest body. It reveals low acidity as well as impressively chewy red and black fruit flavors intertwined with earth, soy, asphalt, and spice box characteristics. There is moderate tannin in the luscious, jammy finish. Anticipated maturity: now–2018. Although very close in style to the 1995, the backward 1996 Barolo Sorì di Baudana is fuller-bodied, with more muscle and chewy tannin. Anticipated maturity: 2003–2017. The excellent 1995 Barolo Sorì di Baudana offers up textbook Barolo aromas and flavors of tar, rose petals, cedar, and sour cherries. There are admirable concentration, a powerful structure, good sweetness in the mid-palate, and a fine finish. It is made in a dense, traditional style. Anticipated maturity: now–2012.

TUSCANY

The Basics

TYPES OF WINE

Beautiful Tuscany is the home of Italy's most famous wine, Chianti, and one of Italy's most celebrated wines, Brunello di Montalcino. Both wines can be either horrendous or splendid. Quality is shockingly irregular. Yet it was in Tuscany where Italy's qualitative wine revolution began, with adventurous and innovative producers cavalierly turning their backs on the archaic regulations that govern wine production. They are making wines, often based on Cabernet Sauvignon, Merlot, and Sangiovese, aged in small French oak casks, filled with flavor and personality, and put in designer bottles. I disagree completely with those critics who have called them French look-alikes, and, though not entitled to "appellation status," they represent some of the most exciting red wines made in the world. The same cannot be said for Tuscany's white wines. Except for the light, tasty whites called Vernaccia from the medieval hill fortress of San Gimignano, Tuscan whites are ultraneutral, boring wines. Shame on those producers who package these wines in lavish-looking bottles that are appallingly overpriced.

GRAPE VARIETIES

The principal and greatest red wine grape of Tuscany is Sangiovese. The highest-yielding, most insipid wine from Sangiovese comes from the most widely planted clone, called Sangiovese Romano. The better producers are using Sangiovese with local names such as Sangioveto, Prugnolo, and Brunello. These all produce a richer, deeper, more complex wine. Of course, Cabernet Sauvignon, Merlot, Cabernet Franc, and even Pinot Noir and Syrah are making their presence felt in Tuscany.

As for the white wines, there is the sharp, uninteresting Trebbiano, produced in ocean-sized quantities. Trebbiano is an inferior grape, and the results are distressingly innocuous wines. Vernaccia has potential, and of course there are such international bluebloods as Chardonnay and Sauvignon Blanc. Tuscany, in my mind, means red, not white, wine, but if you are inclined to try a white wine, then take a look at my list of recommended producers of Vernaccia di San Gimignano.

FLAVORS

Chianti Classico   It is virtually impossible to provide specific information given the extraordinary range in quality—from musty, poorly vinified, washed-out wines to ones with soft, supple raspberry, chestnut, and tobacco flavors, crisp acidity, medium body, and a fine finish. Stick to only the recommended producers listed below. Remember, at least 50% of wines called Chianti, despite tighter regulations governing quality, are thin, acidic, and unpleasant.
Brunello di Montalcino   This should be rich, powerful, tannic, superbly concentrated, and heady, with a huge, spicy bouquet of smoky tobacco, meat, and dried red fruits. Only a few are. Most close encounters offer an alarming degree of tannin and musty old oak, to the detriment of fruit. Selection is critical. Rosso di Montalcino is red wine made from the Brunello clone of Sangiovese that is not aged long enough to qualify as Brunello di Montalcino. It is often much less expensive and considerably fresher.
Carmignano   This is an underrated viticultural area wherein the wines show good fruit, balance, and character. The best of them behave like Chiantis with more character and structure. Not surprisingly, Carmignano is made from Sangiovese with 10–15% Cabernet added.
Vernaccia di San Gimignano   Tuscany's best dry white table wine, this nutty, zesty, dry, fruity white is meant to be drunk within 2–3 years of the vintage. It is a satisfying rather than thrilling wine.
Vino Nobile di Montepulciano   A neighbor of Chianti with identical characteristics (the grape is the same), Vino Nobile di Montepulciano costs more but rarely provides more flavor or pleasure.
Morellino di Scansano   This is an emerging viticultural region south of Siena. I have tasted the wines from only a few estates, but it appears that this is an area that requires more attention. Made from Sangiovese, Morellino di Scansano may be the frugal consumer's alternative to Brunello di Montalcino. The wines are rich, expansive, and, for now, undervalued!
Other Tuscan Whites   The names Bianco di Pitigliano, Bianco Vergine della Valdichiana, Galestro, Montecarlo, Pomino, and any Tuscan producer's name plus the word "bianco" translate into wines that taste wretchedly neutral and bland and provide no more flavor than a glass of water. Sadly, most of them cost $20–35, so the operative words are *caveat emptor!*
Vini da Tavola   The most thrilling red wines of Tuscany are the designer show wines that are being made by Tuscany's most innovative growers. They can be 100% Cabernet Sauvignon, 100% Sangiovese, or a blend of these two grapes plus Cabernet Franc. Even some Merlot, Syrah, and Pinot Noir can now be found. They are usually aged in mostly new French oak casks. Top Tuscan vintages, such as 1997, 1999, and 2000, can have sensational aromatic dimension and remarkable flavor breadth.

ITALY'S GREATEST IGTS (INDICAZIONI GEOGRAFICHE TIPICHE) *AND VDTS* (VINI DA TAVOLA)

PRODUCER	WINE	GRAPE(S)	REGION
L. Antinori	Ornellaia Masseto	Merlot	Tuscany
Argiano	Solengo	Cabernet Sauvignon, Merlot, Syrah, Sangiovese	Tuscany

PRODUCER	WINE	GRAPE(S)	REGION
Il Borro		Merlot, Cabernet Sauvignon	Tuscany
Casa Emma	Soloio	Merlot	Tuscany
Castello di Ambra	L'Apparita	Merlot	Tuscany
Castello di Farnetella	Poggio Granoni	Sangiovese, Merlot, Cabernet Sauvignon	Tuscany
Castello dei Rampolla	Sammarco	Cabernet Sauvignon, Sangiovese	Tuscany
Castello dei Rampolla	Vigna d'Alceo	Cabernet Sauvignon, Sangiovese, Syrah, Petit Verdot	Tuscany
Ciacci Piccolomini d'Aragona	Alteo	Sangiovese, Cabernet Sauvignon	Tuscany
Ciacci Piccolomini d'Aragona	Sant'Antimo Favus	Syrah	Tuscany
Collosorbo	Laurus	Sangiovese, Cabernet Sauvignon	Tuscany
Andrea Costanti	Culbello Ardingo	Merlot, Cabernet Sauvignon	Tuscany
Dei	Santa Catharina	Cabernet Sauvignon, Syrah, Sangiovese	Tuscany
Del Cerro	Manero	Sangiovese	Tuscany
Del Cerro	Poggio Golo	Merlot	Tuscany
Falesco	Montiano	Merlot	Umbria/Lazio
Fattoria di Felsina	Fontalloro	Sangioveto	Tuscany
La Fiorita–Lamborghini	Campoleone	Merlot, Cabernet Sauvignon, Sangiovese	Umbria
Fattoria Le Fonti	Vito Arturo	Sangiovese	Tuscany
Fontodi	Flaccianello	Sangiovese	Tuscany
Gagliole	Pecchia	Sangiovese	Tuscany
Galardi	Terra di Lavoro	Aglianico, Piedirosso	Campania
I Giusti & Zanza	Belcore	Sangiovese, Merlot	Tuscany
I Giusti & Zanza	Dulcamara	Cabernet Sauvignon, Cabernet Franc	Tuscany
Guado Al Tasso		Cabernet Sauvignon, Merlot, Syrah	Tuscany
Le Macchiole	Messorio	Merlot	Tuscany
Le Macchiole	Paleo Rosso	Sangiovese, Cabernet Sauvignon	Tuscany
Le Macchiole	Rosso	Sangiovese, Merlot	Tuscany
Le Macchiole	Scrio	Syrah	Tuscany
Marchesi Antinori	Solaia	Cabernet Sauvignon, Sangiovese, Cabernet Franc	Tuscany
Marchesi Antinori	Tignanello	Sangiovese	Tuscany
Monte Bernardi	Saetta	Sangiovese	Tuscany
Montepeloso	Gabbro	Cabernet Sauvignon	Tuscany

PRODUCER	WINE	GRAPE(S)	REGION
Montepeloso	Nardo	Sangiovese, Cabernet Sauvignon	Tuscany
Montevetrano		Cabernet Sauvignon, Merlot, Aglianico	Campania
Nozzole	Il Pareto	Cabernet Sauvignon	Tuscany
Fattoria Paradiso	Saxa Calida	Merlot, Cabernet Sauvignon	Tuscany
Fattoria Petrolo	Galatrona	Sangiovese, Merlot	Tuscany
Fattoria Petrolo	Il Torrione	Sangiovese	Tuscany
Poggiopiano	Rosso di Sera	Sangiovese, Colorino	Tuscany
Querciabella	Camartina	Sangiovese, Cabernet Sauvignon	Tuscany
Riseccoli	Saeculum	Sangiovese, Cabernet Sauvignon, Merlot	Tuscany
San Giusto a Rentennano	Percarlo	Sangiovese	Tuscany
San Giusto a Rentennano	Ricolma	Merlot	Tuscany
San Guido	Sassicaia	Cabernet Sauvignon, Cabernet Franc, Merlot	Tuscany
Sportoletti	Villa Fidelia	Merlot, Cabernet Sauvignon, Cabernet Franc	Umbria
Fattoria Terrabianca	Ceppate	Cabernet Sauvignon, Merlot	Tuscany
Terriccio	Lupicaia	Cabernet Sauvignon, Merlot	Tuscany
Terriccio	Tassinaia	Cabernet Sauvignon, Sangiovese, Merlot	Tuscany
Tenuta di Trinoro	Trinoro	Cabernet Franc, Merlot, Petit Verdot	Tuscany
Tenuta di Trinoro	Palazzi	Cabernet Franc, Merlot	Tuscany
Tua Rita	Giusto dei Notri	Cabernet Sauvignon, Merlot	Tuscany
Tua Rita	Redigaffi	Merlot	Tuscany
Fattoria Valtellina	Il Duca	Merlot	Tuscany
Villa Cafaggio	Cortaccio	Cabernet Sauvignon	Tuscany
Villa Cafaggio	San Martino	Sangiovese	Tuscany
Villa La Selva	Selvamaggio	Cabernet Sauvignon, Sangiovese	Tuscany

AGING POTENTIAL

Brunello di Montalcino: 8–25 years
Carmignano: 5–8 years
Chianti Classico: 3–15 years*
Rosso di Montalcino: 5–8 years

Tuscan whites: 1–2 years
Vino Nobile di Montepulciano: 5–10 years
VDTs and IGTs (red wine blends): 5–20 years
* Only a handful of Chianti producers make wines that age and last this long.

OVERALL QUALITY LEVEL

For one of the world's most famous wine regions, the quality, while on the upswing, is depressingly variable. Some famous estates in Brunello continue to live off their historic reputations while making poor wine, and there is an ocean of mediocre Chianti producers. The exciting new-breed Sangiovese/Cabernet, Cabernet Franc, and Merlot wines can be superb, but they are produced in limited quantities and are expensive. As for the white wines, the situation is intolerable, and the Tuscans need to wake up to the fact that high-tech, computerized, stainless-steel tanks, centrifuges, sterile bottling, and obsessive reliance on micropore filter machines (that result in denuded, characterless wine) are a fail-safe policy for making an insipid beverage.

MOST IMPORTANT INFORMATION TO KNOW

Forget the Italian wine regulations that are supposed to promote a better product. There are many disgustingly poor wines that carry the government's highest guarantee of quality, the DOCG, or Denominazione di Origine Controllata e Garantita. Many of the *vini da tavola* are vastly superior wines, and this title is supposedly left for Italy's lowest level, the generic wines. The operative rule is, who are the top producers? Then and only then will you be able to make your way through the perilous selection process for Italian wines.

BUYING STRATEGY

A fundamental rule with respect to Tuscan wines is to buy all the 1997s and 1999s you can afford. Both are extraordinary vintages of ripeness and richness that should surpass the finest wines produced in such great years as 1990 and 1985. Both are consistently superb throughout Tuscany's viticultural regions.

RECENT VINTAGES

2000—An exceptionally hot, dry year created exciting potential, but also problems from drought and vineyard stress. There will be more irregularity than the wine trade has suggested, but the producers who were able to avoid dehydrated vineyards and handle the ripe fruit impeccably should produce spectacularly ripe, voluptuous, concentrated wines with high tannin as well as intense flavors. This vintage will be more irregular than 1999, but the wines are potentially as great, if somewhat more roasted.

1999—A year that rivals 1997 as one of Tuscany's greatest vintages. Consistency is the operative word, from the humble Chiantis to the majestic proprietary red wine blends and Brunello di Montalcinos. The wines are extremely ripe, with low acidity as well as a freshness and delineation atypical for wines of such size and richness. Readers who love Italian wines, particularly those from Tuscany, should be stockpiling the 1999s.

1998—An irregular vintage of austere, dry, tannic wines with the exception of the wines from Tuscany's coastal regions of Bolgheri, Suvereto, and Val di Cornia. It is a vintage to approach with caution as many wines lack ripeness, fruit, and intensity.

1997—A spectacular vintage of exceptionally high quality, especially for Brunello di Montalcino and central Tuscany. The coastal regions are more irregular, mixing great successes with some uninspiring efforts (particularly Sassicaia).

1996—An average year that produced austere, dry, hard wines that will dry out before they ever provide much pleasure.

1995—A very good vintage that has not lived up to expectations and is now dwarfed by the potential of 1997, 1999, and 2000.

1994—A below-average quality vintage of diluted fruit lacking ripeness because of heavy rains before and during the harvest. There are some fine wines, but this inconsistent vintage needs to be approached with considerable caution.

1993—A below-average year.

1992—A horrendous vintage with few successful wines.

1991—A bad vintage with few interesting wines.

1990—This is the best year for Tuscany since the fabulous 1985 vintage, but not up to the level of 1985 and surpassed by what was achieved in 1997, 1999, and probably 2000. It is very good, but not the great vintage it was felt to be a decade ago.

RATING TUSCANY'S BEST PRODUCERS

Note: Most producers make both a Chianti Classico and a Chianti Classico Riserva. In the following chart, for purposes of simplification, the star rating shown for each producer's Chianti Classico also pertains to its Chianti Classico Riserva, unless otherwise noted. I have treated Brunello di Montalcino and Brunello di Montalcino Riserva in the same manner. Single-vineyard Chiantis are treated as a separate qualitative item, as are the vast number of *vini da tavola*. Production of the single vineyards, VDTs *(vini da tavola)*, and IGTs *(indicazioni geografiche tipiche)* is generally extremely small, often not more than 500–1,000 cases. Thus, as with so many great wines of the world, availability is poor outside a handful of the top Italian wine specialist shops.

* * * * * (OUTSTANDING)

Altesino Brunello di Montalcino Montosoli
Fattoria Ambra l'Apparita
Fattoria Ambra Carmignano Riserva Vigna Alta
L. Antinori Ornellaia
L. Antinori Ornellaia Masseto
Marchesi Antinori Solaia
Marchesi Antinori Tignanello
Argiano Solengo
Il Borro
Casa Emma Soloio
Castello di Farnetella Poggio Granoni
Castello dei Rampolla Sammarco
Castello dei Rampolla Vigna d'Alceo
Ciacci Piccolomini d'Aragona Alteo
Ciacci Piccolomini d'Aragona Brunello di Montalcino
Ciacci Piccolomini d'Aragona Sant'Antimo Favus
Collosorbo Laurus
Andrea Costanti Calbello Ardingo
Dei Santa Catharina
Del Cerro Manero
Del Cerro Poggio Golo
Falesco Montiano

Fattoria di Felsina Chianti Classico Riserva Rancia Berardenga
Fattoria di Felsina Fontalloro
La Fiorita–Lamborghini Campoleone
Fattoria Le Fonti Vito Arturo
Fontodi Flaccianello
Gagliole Pecchia
Galardi Terra di Lavoro
I Giusti & Zanza Belcore
I Giusti & Zanza Dulcamara
Guado Al Tasso
Le Macchiole Messorio
Le Macchiole Paleo Rosso
Le Macchiole Rosso
Le Macchiole Scrio
Monte Bernardi Saetta
Montepeloso Gabbro
Montepeloso Nardo
Montevetrano
Nozzole Il Pareto
Fattoria Paradiso Saxa Calida
Fattoria Petrolo Galatrona
Fattoria Petrolo Il Torrione
Poggiopiano Rosso di Sera
Querciabella Camartina
Riseccoli Saeculum

San Giusto a Rentennano Percarlo
San Giusto a Rentennano Ricolma
San Guido Sassicaia
Livio Sassetti & Figli Brunello di
 Montalcino
Soldera Case Basse Brunello di Montalcino
Soldera Intistieti Brunello di
 Montalcino
Sportoletti Villa Fidelia
Fattoria Terrabianca Ceppate

Terriccio Lupicaia
Terriccio Tassinaia
Trinoro
Trinoro Palazzi
Tua Rita Giusto di Notri
Tua Rita Redigaffi
Fattoria Valtellina Il Duca
Villa Cafaggio Cortaccio
Villa Cafaggio San Martino
Villa La Selva Selvamaggio

* * * * (EXCELLENT)

Altesino Alte d'Altesi
Altesino Brunello di Montalcino
Altesino Palazzo Altesi
Fattoria Ambra Carmignano
Marchesi Antinori Chianti Classico Il
 Pèppoli
Marchesi Antinori Chianti Classico Riserva
 Badia a Passignano
Marchesi Antinori Chianti Classico Riserva
 Marchese
Marchesi Antinori Secentenario
Avignonesi Vino Nobile di Montepulciano
Fattoria Baggiolino Poggio Brandi
Fattoria dei Barbi Brunello di Montalcino
 Vigna del Fiore
Poderi Boscarelli Boscarelli
Poderi Boscarelli Vino Nobile di
 Montepulciano
La Braccesca Vino Nobile di Montepulciano
Caparzo Brunello di Montalcino La Casa
Caparzo Ca' del Pazzo
Federico Carletti Vino Nobile di
 Montepulciano
Castelgiocondo Brunello di Montalcino
 Riserva
Castell'in Villa Chianti Classico
Castell'in Villa Chianti Classico Riserva
Castell'in Villa Santacroce
Castello di Lilliano Anagallis
Castello della Paneretta Chianti Classico
 Vigneto Torre a Destra
Castello della Paneretta Quattrocentenario
Castello di Gabbiano R & R
Castello di Querceto Chianti Classico
Castello di Querceto Chianti Classico
 Riserva
Castello di Querceto Cignale
Castello di Querceto La Corte
Castello di Querceto Il Querciolaia

Castello dei Rampolla Chianti Classico
 Riserva
Castello di Volpaia Balifico
Castello di Volpaia Chianti Classico
 Riserva
Castello di Volpaia Coltassala
Cerbaiona Brunello di Montalcino
Ciacci Piccolomini d'Aragona Rosso di
 Montalcino
Corelli Brunello di Montalcino
Corrina I Cipressi
Andrea Costanti Brunello di Montalcino
Andrea Costanti Rosso di Montalcino
Dei Vino Nobile di Montepulciano
Dei Vino Nobile di Montepulciano Riserva
Farneta Bentivoglio
Fattoria di Felsina Chianti Classico
 Berardenga
Fattoria di Felsina Fontalloro Berardenga
Fontodi Syrah Case Via
Fontodi Chianti Classico
Fontodi Chianti Classico Riserva
Fontodi Chianti Classico Vigna del Sorbo
 Riserva
Geografico Agricoltori del Geografico
Gracciano Vino Nobile di Montepulciano
Isole e Olena Collezione di Marchi l'Ermo
Lisini Brunello di Montalcino
Luce Luce
Monsanto Chianti Classico Il Poggio
Monsanto Nemo
Monsanto Sangioveto Grosso
Monsanto Tinscvil
Monte Antico Rosso
Fattoria di Montevertine Le Pergole Torte
Fattoria di Montevertine Montevertine
 Riserva
Moris Farms Morellino di Scansano
Nozzole Chianti Classico Riserva

Podere Il Palazzino Chianti Classico
Podere Il Palazzino Chianti Classico
  Riserva
Podere Il Palazzino Grosso Sanese
Pieve di Santa Restituta Brunello di
  Montalcino Rennina
Pieve di Santa Restituta Brunello di
  Montalcino Sugarille
Poggio Antico Altero
Podere Poggio Scalette
Il Poggione Brunello di Montalcino
Le Pupille Saffredi
Ricasoli-Firidolfi Chianti Classico
Ricasoli-Firidolfi Chianti Classico Riserva
Ricasoli-Firidolfi Chianti Classico Riserva
  Rocca di Montegrossi
Ricasoli-Firidolfi Rocca di Montegrossi
  Geremia
Ruffino Chianti Classico Riserva Ducale
  (gold label)

Ruffino Chianti Classico Riserva Ducale
  (tan label)
San Felice Brunello di Montalcino
  Campogiovanni
San Giusto a Rentennano Chianti
  Classico
Sant'Anna Vigna Il Vallone
Livio Sassetti & Figlio Rosso di
  Montalcino
Guicciardini Strozzi Sodole
Fattoria Terrabianca Campaccio
Fattoria Terrabianca Campaccio Riserva
Fattoria Terrabianca Chianti Riserva Croce
Fattoria Terrabianca Chianti Scassino
Fattoria Terrabianca Cipresso
La Torre (Luigi Anania) Brunello di
  Montalcino
Villa Cafaggio Chianti Classico
Villa Cafaggio San Martino
Villa Cafaggio Solatio Basilica

* * * *(GOOD)*

Altesino Rosso di Altesino
Altesino Rosso di Montalcino
Avignonesi Cabernet Sauvignon
Avignonesi Grifi
Badia a Coltibuono Chianti Cetamura
Badia a Coltibuono Chianti Classico
Badia a Coltibuono Coltibuono Rosso
Badia a Coltibuono Sangioveto di
  Coltibuono
Erik Banti Morellino di Scansano
Fattoria dei Barbi Brunello di Montalcino
Fattoria dei Barbi Brunello di Montalcino
  Riserva
Poderi Boscarelli Chianti Colli Senesi
Caparzo Brunello di Montalcino
Carpineto Chianti Classico Riserva
Castelgiocondo Merlot
Castellare di Castellina Chianti Classico
Castellare di Castellina I Sodi di San
  Niccolò
Castello di Ama Chianti Classico
Castello di Ama Chianti Classico single-
  vineyard *cuvées*
Castello di Brolio Chianti Classico
  Riserva
Castello di Farnetella Chianti Colli Senesi
Castello di Fonterutoli Brancaia
Castello di Fonterutoli Chianti Classico
Castello di Fonterutoli Chianti Ser Lapo

Castello di Fonterutoli Concerto
Castello di Gabbiano Ania
Castello di Gabbiano Chianti Classico
  Riserva
Castello La Leccia Chianti Classico
Castello di Lilliano Chianti Classico
Castello di Lilliano Chianti Classico
  Riserva Eleanora
Castello della Paneretta Chianti Classico
Castello di Volpaia Chianti Classico
Castruccio
Cennatoio Chianti Classico
Cennatoio Etrusco
Cennatoio Mammolo
Colognole Chianti Ruffina
Fattoria di Dievole Chianti Classico
  Novecento
Fattoria di Dievole Chianti Classico
  Riserva
Fattoria di Dievole Chianti Classico Vigna
  Dieulele
Fattoria di Dievole Chianti Classico Vigna
  Sessina
Fossi Chianti
Marchesi de' Frescobaldi Montesodi Chanti
  Ruffina
Marchesi de' Frescobaldi Mormoreto
Cantina Gattavecchi Chianti Colli
  Senesi

Cantina Gattavecchi Vino Nobile di
  Montepulciano
Geografico Brunello di Montalcino
Geografico Chianti Classico
Geografico Chianti Classico Castello di
  Fagnano
Geografico Chianti Classico Contessa di
  Radda
Geografico Sorbaiano Montescudaio
Isole e Olena Boro Cepparello
Isole e Olena Chianti Classico
Podere Lanciola II Chianti Colli Fiorentini
Podere Lanciola II Chianti Le Masse di
  Greve
Le Masse di San Leolino Chianti Classico
Le Masse di San Leolino Chianti Classico
  Riserva
Monsanto Chianti Classico Riserva
Fattoria di Montevertine Il Sodaccio
Fattoria di Petroio Chianti Classico
  Montetondo
Poggio Antico Brunello di Montalcino
Poggio Antico Rosso di Montalcino

Poggio Bonelli Chianti Classico Riserva
Poggio Galiga Chianti Rufina
Roccadoro Chianti Classico
Rodano Chianti Classico
Ruffino Cabreo Il Borgo
Ruffino Chianti Classico
Ruffino Chianti Classico Aziano
Ruffino Chianti Classico Nozzole
San Felice Vigorello
San Quirico Chianti
Sant'Anna Rosso di Santa Anna
Talosa Chianti
Talosa Rosso di Montalcino
Talosa Vino Nobile di Montepulciano
La Torre Rosso di Montalcino
Toscolo Chianti Classico
Toscolo Chianti Classico Riserva
Trerose Vino Nobile di Montepulciano
  Riserva
Val di Suga Brunello di Montalcino
Val di Suga Brunello di Montalcino Vigna
  Spuntali
Villa di Geggiano Chianti Classico Riserva

RATING THE BEST OF THE REST OF ITALY

Following are wines and/or producers not to be missed from other viticultural regions of Italy.

***** (OUTSTANDING)

Tommaso Bussola Amarone TB (Veneto)
Tommaso Bussola Valpolicella TB (Veneto)
Dal Forno Romano Amarone della
  Valpolicella (Veneto)
Dal Forno Romano Recioto (Veneto)
Dal Forno Romano Valpolicella (Veneto)
Damijan (Friuli–Venezia Giulia)
Falesco Montiano (Lazio)

Maculan Acininobili (sweet) (Veneto)
Maculan Breganze Torcolato (sweet)
  (Veneto)
Montevetrano (Campania)
La Palazzola Rubino (Umbria)
Quintarelli Alzero Cabernet Franc (Veneto)
Schiopetto (Friulia–Venezia Giulia)
Terra di Lavoro (Campania)

**** (EXCELLENT)

Abbazia di Novacella—white wine *cuvées*
  (Trentino–Alto Adige)
Abbazia di Rosazzo—white wine *cuvées*
  (Friuli–Venezia Giulia)
Allegrini La Poja (Veneto)
Allegrini Valpolicella La Grola (Veneto)
Allegrini Valpolicella Palazzo della Torre
  (Veneto)
Roberto Anselmi Capitel Croce (Veneto)
Roberto Anselmi Capitel Foscarino
  (Veneto)
Arano Amarone (Veneto)

Antonio Argiolas Costera (Sardinia)
Antonio Agriolas Turriga (Sardinia)
Bellavista sparkling wine *cuvées*
  (Lombardy)
Boccadigabbia Akronte (Marche)
Boccadigabbia Saltapicchio (Marche)
La Cadalora—white wine *cuvées* (Trentino)
La Carraia Fobiano (Umbria)
Cataldi Madonna Montepulciano di
  Abruzzo (Abruzzo)
Ceuso (Sicily)
Coffele—Soave *cuvées* (Veneto)

Cooperativa San Patrignano Sangiovese
   (Emilia-Romagna)
Di Majo Norante Don Luigi (Molise)
Diesel Farm (Friuli–Venezia Giulia)
Girolamo Dorigo (Friuli–Venezia Giulia)
Feudi di San Gregorio (Campania)
Walter Filiputti (Friuli–Venezia Giulia)
Foradori Pinot Bianco Sgarzon
   (Trentino–Alto Adige)
Foradori Teroldego Sgarzon (Trentino–Alto
   Adige)
Gini—Soave cuvées (Veneto)
Giorgio Grai—white wine cuvées
   (Trentino–Alto Adige)
Francesco Gravner—white wine cuvées
   (Friuli–Venezia Giulia)
Il Carpino (Friuli-Venezia Giulia)
Librandi Cirò Rosso Duca Sanfelice
   Riserva (Calabria)
Librandi Gravello (Calabria)
Roberto Mazzi Amarone (Veneto)
Roberto Mazzi Valpolicella (Veneto)
Salvatore Molettieri Aglianico (Campania)
Monti Montepulciano d'Abruzzo (Abruzzo)

Morgante Don Antonio (Sicily)
Murgo Cabernet Sauvignon (Sicily)
Cantina del Notaio Aglianico del Vulture
   (Basilicata)
La Palazza—red wine cuvées (Emilia-
   Romagna)
La Palazza Massa di Vecchiazzano (Emilia-
   Romagna)
Planeta—red wine cuvées (Sicily)
F.lli Pra Soave (Veneto)
Regaleali Cabernet Sauvignon (Sicily)
Ronchi di Manzano—red and white cuvées
   (Friuli–Venezia Giulia)
Sant'Elena (Friuli–Venezia Giulia)
Santa Lucia (Puglia)
Schiopetto—white wine cuvées (Collio)
Fattoria Le Terrazze (Marche)
Tormaresca (Puglia)
Valori Montepulciano d'Abruzzo
   (Abruzzo)
Vie di Romans—white wine cuvées
   (Friuli–Venezia Giulia)
Zenato Amarone (Veneto)
Zenato Valpolicella (Veneto)

* * * (GOOD)

Bellavista Solesine (Lombardy)
Bellavista Chardonnay Annunciata
   (Lombardy)
Bellavista Chardonnay Storica (Lombardy)

Bellavista Chardonnay Uccellanda
   (Lombardy)
Regaleali Chardonnay (Sicily)

PROSECCO (ITALY'S GREAT VALUE IN SPARKLING WINE)

Readers in search of terrific values in light-bodied, crisp, refreshing sparkling wines should check out the delectable Proseccos from a viticultural region less than fifty miles north of Venice. Some of my favorite producers include the following (all of which sell for less than $16 a bottle): Cartizze, La Cincie, Nino Franco, Zardetto. One caveat: these wines must be consumed within 12–18 months of their release, as freshness and youth are essential.

ALTESINO

1998 Alte d'Altesi	D	89
1997 Borgo d'Altesi	D	91
1998 Palazzo Altesi	D	90
1998 Quarto d'Altesi IGT	D	88
1997 Quarto d'Altesi IGT	D	88
1999 Rosso di Altesino IGT	B	88

One of the leading estates in Brunello di Montalcino, Altesino has been owned by the same proprietor, Giulio Consonno, since 1970. The wines have always been of high quality, but the last decade has consistently revealed a superlative level of performance. A 100% Sangiovese cuvée aged in one-third new French oak (it's all raised in cask), the 1998 Palazzo Altesi reveals terrific aromatics, including violets, cigar box, smoke, black currants, and kirsch. It is dense, rich, and ripe, with moderate tannin as well as a long, full-bodied finish that offers hints of mocha and chocolate. This is a complex wine to drink over the next 7–8 years, although it may last longer. The 1998 Alte d'Altesi, a *barrique*-aged blend of 70% Sangiovese and 30% Cabernet Sauvignon, boasts a deep ruby color along with a big, sweet nose of chocolate, espresso, and berry fruit. It also reveals some of Cabernet's weedy tobacco character, excellent ripeness, and a medium- to full-bodied, long, textured finish. Drink it over the next 5–7 years.

Altesino has fashioned a high-quality, tank-fermented and -aged blend of 95% Sangiovese and 5% Cabernet Sauvignon. The 1999 Rosso di Altesino IGT offers a wonderful concoction of espresso beans, smoky black currant and cherry fruit, excellent texture, medium body, and a lush, heady finish. It is meant to be enjoyed in its exuberant youth—over the next 3–4 years.

The 1998 Quarto d'Altesi IGT, a Merlot-dominated blend with Sangiovese and Cabernet Sauvignon included, spends 15 months in new French oak prior to bottling. While it is not as complex aromatically as Altesino's other wines, it possesses good depth, flesh, and succulence, with abundant quantities of roasted herbs and chocolaty black fruits. If it develops more aromatic nuances, it may merit a higher score. It should drink well for 7–8 years.

The 1997 Borgo d'Altesi (100% Cabernet Sauvignon, just under 1,000 cases produced, aged in French barrels) is California-like with its thick, jammy, black currant fruit, low acidity, opulent texture, and succulent, fat, round finish. Given its up-front appeal, it should be consumed over the next decade. Slightly less successful but still attractive is the 1997 Quarto d'Altesi IGT (a blend of Merlot and Sangiovese aged in French oak). It offers notes of roasted mocha, coffee, and berry fruit, a monolithic attack, but a fine finish. Drink it over the next 6–7 years.

FATTORIA AMBRA

1998 Carmignano Elzana Riserva	D	88
1997 Carmignano Elzana Riserva	D	92
1998 Carmignano Le Vigne Alte Riserva	D	88
1997 Carmignano Le Vigne Alte Riserva	D	90+
2000 Carmignano Vigna di Santa Cristina in Pilli	B	89

One of my favorite Tuscan wineries (the prices are usually fair as well), Ambra's 2000 Carmignano Vigna di Santa Cristina in Pilli is a knockout bargain. A dark ruby/garnet color is accompanied by sweet aromas of smoke, leather, cherry jam, and roasted nuts. Spicy, medium-bodied, long, and generous, it will drink well for 5 years.

The two single-vineyard 1998 Riservas reveal some of the vintage's austerity and dusty tannin. Displaying more new oak as well as excellent berry fruit, Provençal herbs, black fruits, and spice, the 1998 Carmignano Le Vigne Alte Riserva's earthy complexity will be enjoyed by many. Readers who prefer their wines slightly austere will enjoy it even more than I did. The well-made, similarly styled 1998 Carmignano Elzana Riserva exhibits plenty of tannin, a restrained, leaner personality, a more compressed palate, and attractive red and black fruits mixed with smoke, earth, spice, and peppery herbs. Both of these 1998s should evolve nicely for 5–7 years.

These are two terrific 1997s from Carmignano, an undervalued region of Tuscany. The flamboyant, gorgeously rich, dark ruby/purple-colored 1997 Carmignano Elzana Riserva offers exotic aromas of smoke, nuts, new saddle leather, and blackberry/cherry fruit, medium to full body, and a succulent texture and finish. This fully mature, ostentatious Carmignano will age for 5–6 years. In contrast, the 1997 Carmignano Le Vigne Alte Riserva is a less sexy, opulently textured effort that emphasizes structure, tannin, and ageability. Dense, with an impressively saturated ruby/garnet/purple color as well as notes of smoke, roasted herbs, and leather in the aromatics, it is tight and muscular, with broodingly backward, concentrated flavors. Give it 2–3 years of cellaring and drink it over the following decade.

MARCHESI ANTINORI

1996 Brunello di Montalcino	E	90
1999 Chianti Classico Il Pèppoli	C	(87–88)
1998 Chianti Classico Il Pèppoli	C	89
1998 Chianti Classico Riserva Badia a Passignano	D	91
1997 Chianti Classico Riserva Badia a Passignano	D	92
1998 Merlot IGT	E	90
1997 Merlot IGT	E	93
1998 Solaia IGT	EEE	93+
1997 Solaia IGT	E	96
1997 Tenute Marchese Antinori Chianti Classico Riserva	D	92
1998 Tignanello IGT	E	91
1997 Tignanello IGT	D	93
1998 Villa Antinori Chianti Classico Riserva	D	90
1997 Villa Antinori Chianti Classico Riserva	C	90
1997 Vino Nobile del Montepulciano	C	89

Consistently two of Italy's finest *vini da tavola*, Piero Antinori's Tignanello and Solaia have been reference point wines for Tuscany. Both have been produced for more than 20 years, but it would be hard to find a past vintage that surpasses what was achieved in 1997. The 1997 Tignanello is a blend of 80% Sangiovese, 15% Cabernet Sauvignon, and 5% Cabernet Franc, aged in small French oak casks for 12 months and bottled with no filtration. It possesses a dense, ruby/purple color and an expansive nose of black currants, cherry compote, vanilla, and earth. Sweet, jammy, and opulently textured, this expansive, concentrated, low-acid wine is flashy and gorgeously proportioned. It should drink well for 10–15 years, although who can ignore it now? There are 30,000 cases of the 1998 Tignanello, a blend of 80% Sangiovese, 15% Cabernet Sauvignon, and 5% Cabernet Franc. It offers a classic bouquet of berry fruit, new saddle leather, underbrush, earth, and toast from its new-*barrique* aging. Medium- to full-bodied, with more tannin than the plusher, more opulent 1997, good delineation, and a firm, classic style, it requires 2–3 years of cellaring and should drink well for 15–16.

Solaia has been one of Italy's most brilliant wines since the early 1980s. Made in a Bordeaux-like style, it will age for two decades or more. The 1998, a blend of 75% Cabernet Sauvignon, 20% Sangiovese, and 5% Cabernet Franc (8,000 cases), was aged for 14 months in new and one-year-old French oak casks prior to being bottled without filtration. Yields were a low 30 hectoliters per hectare. While less flamboyant, exotic, and voluptuous than the 1997, the 1998 is a classically structured, youthful, well-balanced wine designed for cellaring. Its opaque ruby/purple color is accompanied by a classic bouquet of black currants, vanilla, earth, tobacco, and a touch of mint. Full-bodied, moderately tannic, dense, and concentrated, this backward 1998 needs 3–4 years of cellaring. Anticipated maturity: 2005–2020. The unfiltered 1997 Solaia (75% Cabernet Sauvignon, 20% Sangiovese, and 5% Cabernet Franc from a single 25-acre vineyard) is aged slightly longer than the Tignanello in 100% new French oak. There are 8,000 cases of the 1997. Perhaps the greatest Solaia yet made, it rivals the outstanding 1985. The sensational, opaque blue/purple-colored 1997 exhibits a complex nose of cedar, spice box, cassis, and subtle oak. With yields of only 30 h/h and malolactic fermentation in barrel (à la Tignanello), this wine reveals extraordinary concentration and a thick, viscous texture, yet no sense of heaviness or ponderousness. It is a thrilling Solaia to consume over the next two decades. If a first growth Pauillac were made in Tuscany, this would be it!

The 1998 Villa Antinori Chianti Classico Riserva, a superb blend of 90% Sangiovese and 10% Canaiolo, was aged 14 months in *barrique* and 12 months in bottle prior to release. Its dense plum/garnet color is followed by a sweet nose of black fruits, underbrush, earth, leather, and spice. Sweet on the attack, with medium to full body, good underlying acidity, and a rich, authoritative, concentrated finish, it should age well for a decade or longer. The 1997 Villa Antinori Chianti Classico Riserva (90% Sangiovese and 10% Canaiolo, aged in large French oak casks) reveals the vintage's superripeness as well as abundant quantities of black currant fruit mixed with cherry liqueur, tobacco, saddle leather, and spice aromas. Sweet because of high glycerin and low acidity, this dark ruby-colored, beautifully made, plump, lush Chianti should be drunk over the next 5–7 years. Even better is the 1997 Tenute Marchese Antinori Chianti Classico Riserva. Aged 14 months in small oak *barriques* and one year in bottle, it reveals *sur-maturité* (overripeness) in its strawberry/cassis-scented nose. Full-bodied, with low acidity, superb concentration of black fruit, spice box, cedar, earth, and smoke, it is a wine of exceptional extract and marvelous balance that reflects the vintage's low-acid, opulent/voluptuous personality. It should drink well for 10–15 years. Bravo!

This 123-acre Badia Chianti estate, planted with 100% Sangiovese, is one of the treasures of the Marchesi di Antinori empire. Made from 100% Sangiovese aged 14 months in both barrels and *foudres*, the outstanding 1998 is a smoky, earthy, Tuscan-styled offering with notes of underbrush, black cherries, strawberries, licorice, and herbs. Notes of tobacco and minerals also make an appearance. The wine possesses a supple texture, medium to full body, and excellent length as well as concentration. It will benefit from 1–2 more years of cellaring and should last for 15–16. The dense ruby/purple-colored 1997 Badia Chianti Classico Riserva is the finest wine I have tasted from this relatively new estate (the average age of the vines is a lowly 12 years). The bouquet offers sweet black cherry, strawberry, and plum aromas. Medium- to full-bodied and concentrated, with low acidity and ripe tannin, it is a voluptuous, pure, super-concentrated yet accessible wine. Enjoy it over the next 7–8 years.

The 1997 Vino Nobile del Montepulciano is a lovely, rich, fruity effort revealing excellent ripeness, admirable purity, and a medium-bodied, attractive texture. It should age nicely for 5–6 years.

In 1996, a 100% Merlot *cuvée* was added to the portfolio. The 1,000-case *cuvée* of 1997 Merlot *vino da tavola* is a real blockbuster. Aged 14 months in 100% new French oak, it offers overripe aromas of black cherries, Asian spices, cedar, chocolate, and mocha. Full-bodied, with rustic tannin, it comes across like a huge California Merlot with its thick, unctuous texture, and powerful, concentrated finish. I was surprised to learn that the alcohol is only 13.4%, given the wine's size and intensity. It should drink well for 10–12 years. The intriguing 1998 Merlot was also aged 14 months in new French oak. It offers textbook Merlot aromas of earth, mocha, coffee, chocolate, and black cherry/berry fruit with dried herbs in the background. Full-bodied and thick, with low acidity, it is best drunk over the next 7–8 years. It is an impressive Merlot from Tuscany's Montepulciano area.

Il Pèppoli's vineyards (136 acres) are planted primarily with Sangiovese in addition to tiny quantities of Merlot and Canaiolo. The east/northeast-facing vineyards are unusual for Tuscany. There are approximately 30,000 cases of this Chianti Classico made from a blend of 90% Sangiovese and 10% Merlot. The dark ruby-colored 1998 exhibits a smoky, cherry, earthy, leather-scented nose, excellent fruit purity, and fine elegance as well as focus. It is best drunk over the next 5–6 years. In contrast, once past the sweet cherry fruit, the 1999 is medium-bodied, shorter, and less complex.

The Antinori firm purchased a Brunello estate in July 1995, and although 1995 is generally a superior vintage for Brunello than 1996, they feel their work in the vineyard and stricter selection in 1996 produced a better wine. Most 1996 Brunellos I have tasted are austere and tannic, although there are some gorgeous exceptions. This is certainly one of them. Pian delle Vigne's 1996 Brunello di Montalcino offers a complex bouquet of new saddle leather, spice box, soy, and earthy/plum/cherry fruit. Its deep ruby/garnet color is accompanied by a sweet attack as well as a ripe, medium-bodied, slightly austere finish. It should drink well for 10 years.

ARGIANO

1999 Rosso di Montalcino	C	88
1998 Rosso di Montalcino	C	91
1999 Solengo IGT	E	94
1998 Solengo IGT	E	91
1997 Solengo IGT	E	94+

An impressive producer, Argiano continues to turn out some of Tuscany's finest red wines. This 100-acre estate is owned by the Countess Cinzano and managed by Sebastiano Rosa, who spent six years at the University of California at Davis and also worked at both Lafite-Rothschild and Sassicaia—not a bad résumé.

The soft, fragrant, medium ruby-colored 1999 Rosso di Montalcino exhibits a sexy aromatic profile offering scents of herbs, leather, cherries, and underbrush. Round and richly fruity, with good glycerin as well as a lush follow-through, it will drink well for 5–6 years. Not surprisingly, one of Argiano's finest offerings is the 1999 Solengo, a blend of equal parts Cabernet Sauvignon, Merlot, Sangiovese, and Syrah. This opaque purple-colored offering exhibits gorgeously ripe blackberry and cassis fruit mixed with scents of leather, charcoal, earth, and wood. Dense, opulent, and full-bodied, with sweet tannin in the finish, it is still youthful and unevolved but promises to drink splendidly between 2004–2015.

The profound 1997 Solengo *vino da tavola* (a blend of Sangiovese and Cabernet Sauvignon with a tiny dosage of Syrah) is spectacular. Opaque purple-colored, it displays a fabulously sweet nose of crème de cassis, new saddle leather, toasty new oak, licorice, and flowers. This wine boasts amazing richness, a huge, full-bodied impact on the palate (yet no sense of heaviness), low acidity, gorgeous ripeness, and a finish that lasts for 35+ seconds. I predict a brilliant future for this compelling proprietary red wine.

While not as sumptuous as the 1997, the 1998 Solengo is a terrific offering. An intriguing blend aged in 100% new French oak for 16 months prior to bottling, it boasts an opaque ruby/purple color, as well as a classic black currant and blackberry-scented bouquet infused with high quality, toasty oak, and elements of roasted espresso. Intense, medium- to full-bodied, chewy, and rich, with a multilayered mid-palate and sweet tannin, this mouth-filling, dry red can be drunk now as well as over the next 10–15 years. Impressive!

A terrific value, the 1998 Rosso di Montalcino possesses supersweet, smoke-infused, black cherry fruit, and spice. Round, medium- to full-bodied, velvety-textured, hedonistic, and seductive, it can be consumed over the next 6–7 years.

BADIA A COLTIBUONO

1998 Chianti Classico	C	89
1997 Chianti Classico Riserva	D	91
1997 Coltibuono Chianti Classico Roberto Stucchi	C	90
1997 Sangioveto	E	93

One of Tuscany's historic estates (its origins can be traced back to the third century B.C.), this property, owned by the Stucchi Prinettis, produces a range of wines that offer consumers terrific values at the lower end and world-class wines at the upper end.

A serious wine, the 1998 Chianti Classico was produced from a blend of 90% Sangiovese and 10% Canaiolo. It offers distinctive strawberry jam scents intermixed with dried herbs and earth. Sexy, with a round, voluptuous texture, an elegant, sweet, richly fruity mid-palate, and a medium-bodied, supple finish, it will drink well for 3–4 years. I was knocked out by the exceptional quality of the 1997 Chianti Classico Riserva. Also made from 90% Sangiovese and 10% Canaiolo, it spends part of its 24-month cask aging in once-used French oak casks. The wine reminded me of what Chianti might taste like if it were made in Pomerol. The vintage has a lot to do with the fruit's opulent, succulent character, but this wine shows plenty of complex vanilla, herb, and black cherry fruit, with a noteworthy suggestion of roasted meat juices. Dense and full-bodied, with terrific fruit, high glycerin levels, and a chewy, plush texture, this is about as hedonistic and sumptuous a Chianti as one is likely to find. Drink it over the next 7–10 years.

Coltibuono's 1997 Chianti Classico Roberto Stucchi is an outstanding, remarkably silky-textured wine with the velvety tannin and voluptuous texture that most great vintages in Italy, France, or elsewhere tend to possess. Jammy black cherry and berry notes soar from the glass of this medium-bodied, thick, juicy, succulently styled Chianti. Tannin and acidity lurk just beneath the surface of this hedonistic, full-flavored wine. It should drink well for 7–10 years.

Another thrilling wine is the 1997 Sangioveto. Aged in 25% new French casks, it boasts a splendid bouquet of overripe blackberry/strawberry fruit, smoke, licorice, and spice box aromas. Dark plum-colored, with an explosive mid-palate and finish, this full-bodied, dense, concentrated wine (made from a highly regarded clone of Sangiovese) should continue to drink well (because of its low acidity and superripe fruit) for a decade or more. Impressive!

FATTORIA DI BASCIANO

1999 Il Corto	C	89+

A modern-styled effort from Fattoria di Basciano, the 1999 Il Corto is a blend of 90% Sangiovese and 10% Cabernet Sauvignon. This wine reveals complex aromas of leather, dried herbs, black cherries, charcoal, and earth. Ripe, with a subtle notion of toasty new oak, excellent sweet red and black fruits, and a nicely textured, medium-bodied finish, it should drink well for 7–12 years.

TENUTA DI BIBBIANO

1997 Chianti Classico Montornello	C	88

It could be said that Bibbiano is making Pomerol-styled Chianti. Silky-textured, hedonistic efforts have emerged from both the good 1996 vintage and the splendid 1997. Sultry, sexy, and lush, with gobs of fruit and low acidity, the plump, heady 1997 Chianti Classico Montornello will have huge crowd appeal. Drink it over the next 2 years.

BORGO SALCETINO

1998 Chianti Classico	B	88
1998 Chianti Classico Riserva Lucarello	D	88
1997 Chianti Classico Riserva Lucarello	D	90
1999 Rossole IGT	D	90
1998 Rossole IGT	D	90

The exceptional 1999 Rossole (a proprietary blend of 70% Cabernet Sauvignon and 30% Merlot aged in French oak for 12 months) is a fat, jammy, seductive, deep ruby/purple-colored wine with plenty of sweet oak as well as copious fruit, considerable glycerin, and a low-acid, thick, juicy finish. It should develop more definition in the bottle and age nicely for 12–15 years. The dark ruby-colored 1998 Chianti Classico Riserva Lucarello (aged 24 months in French oak) is an impressive, stylish, but restrained offering. It exhibits aromas of sweet jammy cherries intertwined with licorice, herbs, tobacco, and earth. Medium-bodied, with excellent texture and fine ripeness as well as lushness (atypical for the austerely styled 1998 Chiantis), it will drink well for 5–7 years.

The 1998 Chianti Classico is one of the finest examples I have tasted from this vintage, which appears to be superior to 1996 but less flamboyant and opulent than 1997 or 1999. This 1998 exhibits a dark ruby/purple color as well as beautifully pure, nicely textured, ripe, smoky, black cherry and currant aromas and flavors intermixed with high-class new leather and Provençal herbs. It is medium- to full-bodied, with excellent depth in addition to impressive balance and length. Like all of the wines from proprietor Tonino Livon, it was bottled without filtration. The deep ruby/purple-colored 1997 Chianti Classico Riserva

Lucarello reveals a more international personality, with copious quantities of spicy new oak, black currants, strawberries, and cherries, dense, ripe, medium- to full-bodied flavors, adequate acidity, and a plush, nicely layered, sweetly tannic finish. It should drink well for 7–8 years. The 1998 Rossole, a *barrique*-aged blend of 65% Sangiovese and 35% Merlot, combines power with elegance and finesse with considerable flavor authority. A dark ruby/purple color is accompanied by sweet, jammy, black fruit with the oak better meshed and more subtle than in the 1997 Lucarello. Lovely ripe berry fruit is present in the medium- to full-bodied palate, which shows considerable harmony and refinement. This wine is soft enough to be drunk now or cellared for another decade.

IL BORRO

1999 Il Borro	E	92

A Bordeaux-inspired blend of 50% Merlot, 40% Cabernet Sauvignon, and small quantities of Syrah, Petit Verdot, and Sangiovese, this *barrique*-aged 1999 produced from 5-year-old vines is an impressive debut release. A dead ringer for a top-class Médoc, it offers a deep purple color in addition to a complex bouquet of chocolate, earth, black currants, and toast. It possesses a full-bodied, concentrated, layered, harmonious personality, sweet fruit, abundant glycerin, and exceptional purity. The finish lasts for 25–30 seconds. Consume it now and over the next 12–15 years.

PODERI BOSCARELLI

1997 Boscarelli IGT	D	88
1998 Vino Nobile di Montepulciano	D	90
1997 Vino Nobile di Montepulciano	D	89
1997 Vino Nobile di Montepulciano Riserva del Nocio	D	91

The stars of proprietor Paola De Ferrari's estate are the Vini Nobili di Montepulciano. A sensational effort, the 1998 Vino Nobile di Montepulciano is a blend of 90% Sangiovese, 7% Merlot, and 3% Cabernet Sauvignon aged in various-sized wood *barriques*. A dark plum/purple color is accompanied by an exotic, ripe, earthy, spicy, flowery, sweet perfume, gorgeous fruit on the attack, excellent texture, medium body, and an elegant, pure, balanced finish. With all its component parts in perfect harmony, this 1998 can be enjoyed now, or cellared for a decade. The 1997 Vino Nobile di Montepulciano's dark ruby/purple color is accompanied by aromas of singed dried herbs, saddle leather, and sweet and sour cherry fruit. It possesses an attractive lushness as well as a seductive, sexy style with admirable finesse and flavor. Drink it over the next 7–8 years. A blend of 85% Sangiovese, 7% Mammolo, and 8% Merlot, aged in small oak casks, the terrific 1997 Vino Nobile di Montepulciano Riserva del Nocio exhibits a saturated ruby/purple color in addition to aromas of lead pencil, jammy blackberry and cherry fruit intermixed with smoke and high-quality new oak. There is remarkable sweetness on the palate, a lush, concentrated, fleshy texture, low acidity, and a long, spicy finish with a note of roasted nuts. Dense, ripe, and intense, it can be drunk now or cellared for 10–15 years. Lastly, the 1997 Boscarelli (a *barrique*-aged blend of 93% Sangiovese and 7% Cabernet Sauvignon) offers up aromas of tobacco as well as spicy cherry, strawberry, and red currant fruit. Long, elegant, and sweet, with firm tannin and an overall sense of restraint and balance, it should be consumed over the next 7–8 years.

CA' DEL VISPO

2000 Rovai IGT	C	89

The internationally styled yet seriously concentrated, ambitious 2000 Rovai exhibits an opaque ruby color as well as a sweet nose of black currants, blackberries, licorice, and spice. A fleshy, opulently textured, medium-bodied wine with excellent extract in addition to impeccable balance and purity, it is a sexy, up-front effort to enjoy over the next 5–6 years.

LE CALCINAIE

2000	Chianti Colli Senesi Gimignano	B	88
1999	Teodoro	D	90
1998	Teodoro	D	92

This trio includes an excellent bargain from proprietor Simone Santini. The 2000 Chianti Colli Senesi Gimignano (a 90% Sangiovese and 10% Merlot blend) is a fine value. An excellent, fat, chewy Chianti, it provides further evidence that this will be an exciting vintage for Tuscany. A deeply colored effort, it possesses plenty of glycerin as well as a heady, medium-bodied finish. Enjoy it over the next 3–4 years.

Undoubtedly the finest red wine I have tasted from Tuscany's San Gimignano region, the super-concentrated 1998 Teodoro (a blend of *barrique*-aged Cabernet Sauvignon, Sangiovese, and Merlot) boasts a deep, thick, black/purple color, chewy, full-bodied, opulently textured flavors, admirable purity, and a long, velvety, seamless finish. Drink this loaded 1998 over the next 7–8 years to take advantage of its exuberant youth. The 1999 Teodoro is a *barrique*-aged blend of Sangiovese and Merlot. This dense, chewy, internationally styled 1999 reveals plenty of espresso, toast, chocolate, and black cherry fruit aromas as well as flavors. Drink it over the next 10–12 years.

LE CALVANE

1997	Borro del Boscone	D	92+
1997	Chianti Classico Riserva Il Trecione	B	89

My first experience with the wines of Le Calvane was promising. Its superb 100% Cabernet Sauvignon, the 1997 Borro del Boscone, boasts an opaque purple color, super-concentrated cassis aromas and flavors, moderate tannin, and a full, thick, unctuous style. Dense and chewy, with superb ripeness, it needs 2–3 years of cellaring and should age well for 15–16 years. The 1997 Chianti Classico Riserva Il Trecione (an 800-case blend dominated by Sangiovese) exhibits a dark ruby/garnet color and a classic bouquet of earth, cedar, tobacco, black cherries, and dried herb aromas. Medium- to full-bodied, sweet, concentrated, supple, and fleshy, it is a hedonistic turn-on. Enjoy it over the next 4–5 years.

LA CAMPANA

1999	Rosso di Montalcino	D	89

The seductive, sexy, soft, plum/cherry fruit characteristics of the 1999 Rosso di Montalcino will make it a big hit with consumers. It exhibits abundant fruit and glycerin, as well as a succulent texture. It will provide considerable pleasure over the next 4–5 years.

CAPANNELLE

NV	Capannelle 2000 IGT	EEE (1.5 liters)	91+
1997	Capannelle & Avignonesi 50 & 50	EE	90+
1997	Chianti Classico Riserva	D	91

It has been almost a decade since I tasted these wines, which at that time were imported into the Washington, D.C., market by the now-defunct Mayflower Wine & Spirits. While they have always been impressive, they were made in extremely limited quantities and were outrageously expensive. The company's ownership has changed, but there does not appear to have been any philosophical shift in pricing. The proprietor, American James Sherwood, owns many famous luxury commodities (the Hotel Splendido in Portofino, Cipriano in Venice, and the world-renowned Orient Express). Only minute quantities of Capannelle's new releases are available, but there is no doubting that this state-of-the-art winery spares no expense in turning out world-class wines, all aged in French oak prior to bottling.

Available only in magnums, the sensationally packaged nonvintage Capannelle 2000 is an intriguing 80% Sangiovese/20% Cabernet Sauvignon blend of six vintages, 1990, 1991,

1992, 1993, 1994, and 1995 (obviously the year 2000 relates to the release date, not the vintage). It is a serious, concentrated, medium- to full-bodied, dark plum/ruby-colored effort with an excellent perfume of balsam wood, black fruits, tobacco, spice box, and smoke. It is rich, youthful, exuberant, and full-bodied. Although it may be expensive, it is an exceptional, rare offering. Anticipated maturity: now–2012.

The least expensive effort (and to my palate the finest) is the 1997 Chianti Classico Riserva, a *barrique*-aged blend of 90% Sangiovese and 10% Cabernet Franc and Malvasia Nero. It is beautifully textured, dense, chewy, rich wine, with a glorious bouquet of spring flowers, red and black fruits, tobacco, spice box, leather, and earth. The sweet tannin, acidity, and oak are all well integrated in this medium- to full-bodied, beautifully harmonious 1997. It will be at its apogee between 2003–2018. Bravo!

Lastly, the joint effort between Capannelle and Avignonesi, 1997 50 & 50, is a blend of equal parts Sangiovese from Capannelle and Merlot from Avignonesi's vineyard. It is sold only as a future, but I was told by the importer that there are about 25 cases available for the United States. A seriously endowed, dense ruby/purple-colored effort with plenty of new oak, it is somewhat internationally styled, with loads of extract, tannin, and richness. Wines such as this can be found at lower prices, but they will not have the names Capannelle and Avignonesi on them. Anticipated maturity: 2003–2016.

PODERE LA CAPPELLA

1997 Corbezzolo IGT	D	91

A gorgeous, sweet perfume of black cherry liqueur, high-quality French oak, and black raspberries soars from the glass of this dark ruby/purple-colored, supple-textured, rich, layered, and multidimensional wine. Despite its size and richness, it is extremely elegant and well balanced. Drink it now and over the next 10–15 years. Very impressive!

CASA EMMA

1997 Chianti Classico	C	88
1998 Soloio IGT	D	90+
1997 Soloio IGT	D	90

Casa Emma's 1997 Chianti Classico displays all the hallmarks of this fascinating vintage. The dark ruby color, silky texture, round, opulent, fruit flavors, and easy accessibility make it a reasonably good value that should drink well for 5–6 years. The outstanding, dark ruby/purple-colored, dense, rich 1997 Soloio reveals intense aromas of roasted herbs intermixed with chocolate, mocha, and black fruits. Long, chewy, and fleshy, with outstanding richness and purity, this impressive Merlot was aged for 15 months in 100% new French oak. Production was 500 cases. Drink it over the next 10–12 years.

One 1998 that has developed beautifully is Casa Emma's 1998 Soloio (a 500-case *cuvée* of 100% Merlot aged in French oak for 15 months). Its opaque ruby/purple color is accompanied by a sweet perfume of berry jam mixed with smoke, espresso, and chocolate. There are superb concentration, terrific purity, and a layered, opulent, nearly exotic character. The vintage's structure is noticeable, but it does not overwhelm the wine's personality. Anticipated maturity: 2003–2016.

FATTORIA CASALOSTE

1997 Chianti Classico Riserva	D	90
1997 Chianti Classico Riserva Don Vincenzo	EE	91

The ambitious, complex, full-bodied, *barrique*-aged 1997 Chianti Classico Riserva Don Vincenzo exhibits a dense ruby color as well as a superb nose of black fruits, tobacco, spice box, and vanilla. Chewy, layered, and intense, it can be drunk now and over the next 8–9 years. Nearly as good, the 1997 Chianti Classico Riserva (100% Sangiovese) is a seriously endowed effort revealing evidence of *barrique* aging as well as copious quantities of strawberry and black cherry fruit, new saddle leather, tobacco, and spice box. Rich and full-bodied, it is best drunk over the next decade.

CASANOVA DI NERI

1999 Rosso di Montalcino	C	88

A big, sweet Rosso di Montalcino offering up aromas of overripe cherries, new saddle leather, incense, and spice, this medium-bodied, plush 1999 is meant to be drunk now and over the next 3–4 years.

FATTORIA I CASCIANI

2000 Chianti di Montespertoli	B	88
1999 Villa Gaia	C	91

A 50–50 blend of Merlot and Cabernet Sauvignon aged 12 months in French oak, the 1999 Villa Gaia is an impressive, unfiltered offering from a vineyard farmed biodynamically. It boasts a dense dark ruby/purple color in addition to a sweet bouquet of blackberry and cassis fruit intertwined with toasty new oak. Initially I thought it was too international, but with airing, Tuscany's earthy, underbrush, leather, truffle, spice box, and dried red/black fruit characteristics emerged. Impressive purity, texture, and length suggest it will age well for 10–15 years. The boldly styled, tank-fermented and -aged 2000 Chianti (primarily Sangiovese) boasts a youthful dark ruby color, excellent texture, fine flesh, and loads of black cherry and currant fruit intertwined with subtle herb and cedar components. Enjoy this robust, exuberant Chianti over the next 2–3 years.

CASTELLO DI AMA

1998 L'Apparita IGT	EEE	(91–93)
1997 L'Apparita IGT	EEE	92+
1997 Chianti Classico	D	89
1997 Chianti Classico Bellavista	EEE	91
1997 Chianti Classico La Casuccia	EEE	92

With 500 acres, 200 of which are in vine, Castello di Ama is one of Tuscany's most significant high-altitude vineyards. My first experience with a Castello di Ama offering was the 1985 L'Apparita tasted in Brussels more than a decade ago. After a period of experimentation, when multiple single-vineyard offerings were produced, Ama has focused on producing a Chardonnay, rosé, Merlot, a terrific regular Chianti, and, in top vintages, two single-vineyard Chiantis. Recent releases are all impressive.

Readers seeking fine Chianti Classico should check out Castello di Ama's 1997 Chianti Classico. Made from a blend of 80% Sangiovese, 12% Merlot, and 8% Caniolo whose yields were 2.4 tons of fruit per acre, this dark ruby-colored Chianti possesses a pure style, outstanding ripeness, and spicy, cedary aromas and flavors intertwined with black raspberries, cigar box, and vanilla. Dense, medium-bodied, soft, and opulent, it will drink well for 7–8 years. The dark ruby-colored 1997 Chianti Classico Bellavista (8,000 bottles produced) is filled with finesse and elegance. Intense black cherry aromas intertwined with berry fruit, tobacco, and spice box are followed by good denseness and richness, medium to full body, sweet tannin, and impeccable symmetry and balance. This youthful Chianti is approachable and should drink well for a decade. The dense purple-colored 1997 Chianti Classico La Casuccia (another microproduction of 8,000 bottles) is fuller-bodied, more powerful and opulent, with the most flamboyant personality of Castello di Ama's Chiantis. Long, with more tannin as well as richness and structure, it will benefit from 1–3 years of cellaring and will keep for 15+ years.

The impressive L'Apparita (a 100% Merlot *cuvée* of approximately 8,000 bottles) is aged completely in French oak casks. At a recent mini—vertical tasting, it was hard to find an unimpressive effort, with the 1993 rated at 87 points, the 1992 at 90 points, and the 1990 at 88 points. The stunning 1997 L'Apparita may be the finest L'Apparita since the 1985. It exhibits a deep ruby/purple color in addition to a distinctive nose of mocha, espresso bean, cherry liqueur, and blackberries. Full-bodied, dry, and rich, with good sweetness and fatness on the mid-palate, this long, dense, still youthful wine requires an additional 3–5 years of cellaring; it should keep for two decades. New oak (about 70% new French wood is utilized) plays a secondary role in the wine's aromatic and flavor profiles. Also impressive, although less flamboyant, the opaque purple-colored 1998 L'Apparita reveals aromas and flavors of new saddle leather, spicy oak, and blackberry/cherry fruit. Powerful, muscular, and tannic, without the sweet, silky, sumptuousness of the 1997, it needs 4–5 years of cellaring and should keep for 15+ years.

CASTELLO DI BROLIO

1998 Chianti Classico Castello di Brolio	D	88

This opaque purple-colored, tannic effort is somewhat internationally styled but chewy, well made, and reminiscent of a midlevel Bordeaux. Aged in *barrique*, of which 65% was new French oak, it easily carries its 13.7% alcohol but requires another year or two of cellaring given its big, backward style. It should age well for 12–15 years.

CASTELLO DI CACCHIANO

1997 Chianti Classico Millennio Riserva	D	90
1999 Rosso Toscano IGT	B	89

A terrific buy, the 1999 Rosso Toscano IGT is a delicious, opulently textured blend of 85% Sangiovese and 15% Merlot. It boasts a dark ruby color as well as sweet, jammy aromas of strawberries, cherries, and currants backed up with earth, old wood, and leather. Medium- to full-bodied, lush, and fleshy, it provides a balanced, chewy mouth-feel. Drink it over the next 3–4 years. The outstanding, saturated ruby/garnet-colored 1997 Chianti Classico Millennio Riserva boasts an opulent nose of ripe plums, black cherries, licorice, earth, and cedar. Fleshy and full-bodied, this exotic, rich, concentrated, low-acid Chianti possesses this vintage's flamboyant personality. Enjoy it over the next 10–12 years.

CASTELLO DI FARNETELLA

1999 Chianti Colli Sensi	B	90
1999 Lucilla IGT	C	91
1998 Lucilla IGT	C	90

Wow! Castello di Farnetella's explosive 1999 Chianti Colli Sensi boasts a deep saturated ruby color as well as superripe black cherry jam characteristics intermixed with blackberries, graphite, and spice. Succulent, medium- to full-bodied, opulent, fleshy, and rich, it exhibits considerable depth in addition to burgeoning complexity. For the amount of richness and complexity, it is about as fine a Chianti as money can buy. Moreover, it can be drunk now or cellared for 7–8 years.

Farnetella's 1999 Lucilla is a stunning value. A blend of 90% Sangiovese and 10% Merlot aged for 10 months in French *barriques*, it boasts an explosive nose of smoke, blackberry, plum, and cassis fruit, leather, and pencil shavings. Dense, full-bodied, and voluptuously textured, it is a hedonistic turn-on that also satisfies the taster's intellectual cravings. Drink it over the next 5–7 years. Yummy! The 1998 Lucilla, which spent 12 months in French oak, is also a reasonably good value. Its opulent, dark ruby color, Pomerol-like lushness, and emphasis on black cherry liqueur infused with coffee and smoky notes are impressive. The wine exhibits gorgeous ripeness, admirable richness, and a long, low-acid, fleshy finish. It should drink well for 5–7 years.

CASTELLO DI FONTERUTOLI

1999 Brancaia IGT	E	88
1999 Chianti Classico	C	89
1998 Chianti Classico Riserva	D	88
1997 Poggio alla Badiola IGT	B	88
1999 Siepi IGT	EE	90

Another splendidly ripe, sweet, layered, exuberantly fruity Chianti Classico from the 1999 vintage, Fonterutoli has turned out a dark ruby/purple-colored effort with plenty of density, abundant mineral-infused black cherry fruit, and good spice as well as earthy overtones. It is supple, yet dense and structured enough to last for a decade. From a more austere vintage, the 1998 Chianti Classico Riserva exhibits a deep ruby/purple color as well as copious extract, more muscle and tannin, but neither the charm nor seductiveness of its younger sibling. It should age well for 12–15 years.

The 1999 Siepi, an outstanding blend of equal parts Sangiovese and Merlot aged for 16 months in French oak, boasts a dense ruby/purple color along with sumptuous aromas of new oak, black currants, blackberries, and new saddle leather. It is dense, powerful yet harmonious, with sweet tannin and plenty of structure. Give it 1–2 years of cellaring and enjoy it over the following decade. Along with a less saturated dark ruby color, the 1999 Brancaia reveals an interesting perfume of licorice, dried herbs, black fruits, and a hint of animal scents. On the palate, it is leaner and more compressed than the Siepi, with more noticeable tannin as well as more structure. Anticipated maturity: 2003–2012.

Another excellent value is the 1997 Poggio alla Badiola, a super Tuscan Sangiovese with a touch of Merlot and Cabernet Sauvignon in the blend. This dark ruby/purple-colored, fruit-dominated wine exhibits a sweet midsection, excellent purity, and a long, ripe, luscious finish. It can be drunk now and over the next 4–5 years.

CASTELLO DI MELETO

1998 Fiore IGT	D	89
1997 Fiore IGT	D	89

Castello di Meleto's 1998 Fiore (95% Sangiovese and 5% Merlot) is a sweet, oaky, ripe, opulent effort with sweet tannin, plenty of berry fruit, and notes of coffee. It is a round, generous red to consume over the next 5–6 years. For a 1998, it possesses an atypical forward, plump personality. Also primarily Sangiovese with a tiny dollop of Merlot added, the dark ruby-colored, medium- to full-bodied 1997 Fiore exhibits sweet jammy black cherry and currant fruit, smoke, and espresso aromas and flavors. Fleshy and soft, it is ideal for drinking over the next decade.

CASTELLO DELLA PANERETTA

1999 Chianti Classico	C	88
1998 Chianti Classico	C	88
1997 Chianti Classico Riserva	C	91
1997 Chianti Classico Vigneto Torre a Destra Riserva	D	90
1998 Quattrocentenario 1596–1996 IGT	E	90
1997 Quattrocentenario IGT	E	91
1998 Le Terrine IGT	D	88
1997 Le Terrine IGT	D	89

These are purely made efforts from an estate located in the Monsanto region of Tuscany. This small, 2,000-case winery has a 404-year winemaking history. The Castello della Paneretta's offerings are all bottled unfiltered and represent classic, pure expressions of Tuscany. The best buy is the deliciously fat, fruity, dark ruby-colored 1999 Chianti Classico. Revealing a vibrant nose of black cherries and subtle earth, as well as low acidity (for a Tuscan wine), this fleshy, ripe Chianti should drink well for 3–4 years.

The dark ruby-colored 1998 Le Terrine, an unusual blend of equal parts Sangiovese and Canaiolo, spent 12 months in French oak prior to bottling. The complex bouquet reveals scents of black fruits, flowers, and subtle minerals. Complex, supple-textured, and lush, this intriguing, character-filled, mid-weight Italian red will drink well for 5–6 years. Made from 100% old-vine Sangiovese, the 1998 Quattrocentenario 1596–1996 (celebrating the winery's 400th anniversary) boasts a dark ruby color in addition to a stunning nose of blackberries, cherries, spice, and earth. Sweet, rich, fleshy, and complex, it can be drunk now as well as over the next 7–8 years.

It is hard to find a better 1998 Chianti Classico than Paneretta's. It possesses a deep ruby color in addition to smoky, herb-infused, meaty aromas with abundant berry fruit, and excellent flavor concentration. A sense of finesse, elegance, and intensity, with medium body, sweet tannin, and fine acidity further characterize this wine. It should drink well for 4–5 years. Given the fact there is no oak influence, it should be remarkably flexible with an assortment of cuisines. The dark plum/ruby-colored 1997 Chianti Classico Riserva offers an opulent, sweet, jammy nose of black fruits, earth, and spice. Supple-textured, dense, and chewy, it reveals the vintage's gorgeous ripeness in addition to an exquisite balance between alcohol, acidity, and tannin. Ripe, rich, youthful, and exuberant, it should age effortlessly for 7–10 years. The 100% Sangiovese, single-vineyard, dark ruby-colored 1997 Chianti Classico Vigneto Torre a Destra Riserva exhibits melted tar and asphalt notes along with charcoal, cherry jam, and spice. It possesses more acidity and tannin than the 1997 Riserva, but the vintage's creamy texture and opulence are well displayed. Ripe, dense, and impressive, it should be consumed over the next decade. More monolithic, and, as the French would say, *sauvage* (wild or uncivilized, but not in a pejorative sense), the 1997 Le Terrine, a blend of equal parts Sangiovese and old-vine Canaiolo, exhibits more black fruits and foresty, earthy notes, as well as a foursquare personality. It possesses abundant concentration, body, and density but does not display the charm, complexity, or soul of the other offerings. It may improve with another year or so of bottle age.

In the finest vintages, a *cuvée* called Quattrocentenario is produced. The 1997 (celebrating the winery's first 400 years) was made from 100% Sangiovese aged in French *barriques*. Approximately 200 cases were produced. Not surprisingly, it is the most concentrated of these offerings, but only marginally more than the Chianti Classico Riserva and the Torre a Destra Riserva. It exhibits a dense ruby/purple color as well as abundant aromas of sweet black cherry fruit intermixed with minerals, smoke, iron, and meat. Chewy and full-bodied, with new saddle leather and black cherry–flavored fruit, it is powerful yet elegant, rich yet balanced. Sweet tannin and well-integrated acidity give it immediate accessibility, but the wine is capable of lasting for 10–15 years.

CASTELLO DI QUERCETO

1997 Cignale IGT	E	91+

An impressive, French *barrique*–aged blend of 90% Cabernet Sauvignon and 10% Merlot from the Greve region of Tuscany, this deep ruby/purple-colored 1997 boasts a provocative perfume of black currants, cherries, balsa wood, cedar, tobacco, and smoke. Although backward, it possesses powerful, concentrated flavors, moderately high tannin levels, good acidity, and a style built for the long haul. Readers seeking immediate gratification should pass it by. Those with patience and cool cellars will be rewarded with a splendid wine in 4–6 years. Anticipated maturity: 2004–2025.

CASTELLO DEI RAMPOLLA

1997 Chianti Classico Riserva	D	89
1998 Sammarco IGT	EE	90

1999 Vigna d'Alceo IGT	EEE	99
1998 Vigna d'Alceo IGT	EEE	92

For 25 years this has been one of my favorite Tuscan producers. Amazingly, this 90-acre estate has been in the Di Napoli family for 300 years. Elegance, balance, and restraint are the operative words when it comes to understanding the wines of Castello dei Rampolla.

For more than two decades one of the greatest Tuscan proprietary red wines has been Castello dei Rampolla's Cabernet Sauvignon/Sangiovese blend called Sammarco. What has always made this wine exceptional, especially in the top vintages, is its complexity and elegance. It is closer to a great Graves than any other wine I have ever tasted outside France. The 1998 Sammarco, a blend of 85% Cabernet Sauvignon and 15% Sangiovese, reveals more structure and tannin than is present in the 1997 or, I suspect, the 1999. Additionally, it possesses formidable underlying concentration and depth, along with that multilayered mid-palate that always seems to separate exceptional wines from good ones. The 1998 Sammarco's deep, saturated ruby color is followed by a complex bouquet of charcoal, roasted herbs, smoke, hot gravel, black currants, and cherries. It is medium-bodied and deep, with high but sweet tannin and extraordinary purity as well as delineation. Anticipated maturity: 2003–2016. The monumental 1999 Vigna d'Alceo is a 20,000-bottle *cuvée* of 85% Cabernet Sauvignon and 15% Sangiovese aged in oak. It tastes like the Sammarco on steroids. The essence of both varietals, it boasts an exceptionally provocative nose of liquid minerals, graphite, plums, crème de cassis, and cherry liqueur. It is fabulously concentrated yet remarkably light on its feet, with medium to full body, sweet tannin, and layer upon layer of flavor nuances. There is plenty of glycerin in this rich but neither heavy nor overbearing effort. This is a thrilling tour de force! However, it requires cellaring. Anticipated maturity: 2005–2025. Bravo!

The dark ruby-colored 1997 Chianti Classico Riserva (90% Sangiovese and 10% Cabernet Sauvignon) offers aromas of toasty oak, tobacco, wood smoke, cherries, herbs, and new saddle leather. Medium- to full-bodied, concentrated, dense, and ripe, with moderate tannin, this fleshy, youthful Chianti is just reaching full maturity, where it should remain for 10–12 years. An even finer offering is the 1998 Vigna d'Alceo. An opaque purple-colored blend of Cabernet Sauvignon, Sangiovese, and small quantities of Syrah and Petit Verdot, it is a large-scale wine with exceptional elegance and complexity as well as more power and richness than the Sammarco. A sweet entry on the palate is followed by abundant quantities of smoky, complex, black currant fruit intermixed with lead pencil and vanilla flavors. Medium-bodied, beautifully knit, and suave, it possesses sweeter tannin than the Chianti Classico Riserva. Anticipated maturity: now–2017.

CASTIGLION DEL BOSCO

1997 Bernaia IGT	EE	90
1998 Rosso di Montalcino	C	89

Value seekers should search out the delicious, supple-textured, complex 1998 Rosso di Montalcino. A dark ruby color is accompanied by abundant aromas of spice box, sweet berry fruit, and grilled meat. With an accessible personality as well as fine concentration, it is close to full maturity, although it will keep for 4–5 years. The luxury-priced 1997 Bernaia (70% Sangiovese and 30% Cabernet Sauvignon) exhibits a Pomerol-like style. It offers notes of coffee, mocha, and chocolate in addition to black cherry and currant fruit. Toasty oak also makes an appearance as the wine sits in the glass. It is a medium- to full-bodied, perfumed effort with outstanding richness and purity. Sadly, only 500 cases were produced.

CENSIO

1999 Erte	B	89

The 1999 Erte, a proprietary blend of equal parts Sangiovese and Cabernet Sauvignon, sees no new oak but is *barrique*-aged. A fine value, it boasts a deep ruby/purple color as well as intense aromatics consisting of saddle leather, cherry jam, black currants, licorice, and cigar box. Medium-bodied with light tannin, this polished, elegant effort possesses power, richness, and finesse. Enjoy this classy Italian red over the next 2–3 years.

CERBAIONA

1997 Cerbaiona IGT	D	88

Cerbaiona's proprietary red wine, the 1997 Cerbaiona, is a blend of 60% Sangiovese and 40% Cabernet Sauvignon, Merlot, and Syrah. Its dark ruby/purple color is followed by a sweet nose of new saddle leather, soy, cherries, damp earth, and toasty oak. Round and ripe, this 1997 is ideal for consuming over the next 7–8 years.

FATTORIA DEL CERRO

1999 Manero	D	92
1998 Merlot Poggio Golo	D	91
1998 Vino Nobile di Montepulciano Vigneto Antica Chiusina	E	89+
1997 Vino Nobile di Montepulciano Vigneto Antica Chiusina	D	90

The 1998 Vino Nobile di Montepulciano Antica Chiusina could turn out to be an outstanding wine with another 1–2 years of cellaring. Concentrated and powerful (particularly for this vintage), it exhibits a dense plum/garnet color, and sweet, earthy, leathery, berry aromas mixed with underbrush, licorice, and cherry jam. Full-bodied and highly extracted, with noteworthy structure as well as moderately high tannin, it should be at its best between 2003–2016. The brilliant 100% Sangiovese *cuvée* aged in *barrique*, the 1999 Manero is internationally styled, but it is hard to resist its compelling cherry liqueur, espresso, toast, and spice box aromas and flavors. Dense, opulent, full-bodied, and thick, this brilliantly made, flamboyant, succulent 1999 will drink well for 7–8 years.

In a previous tasting, Cerro's stars were the 1998 Merlot Poggio Golo and 1997 Vino Nobile di Montepulciano Vigneto Antica Chiusina. The latter wine boasts an opaque ruby/purple color as well as a big, smoky, sweet nose of black cherries, blueberries, and cedar. Ripe and full-bodied with an opulent texture, and luscious, fat, concentrated flavors, it is a blend of 90% Prugnolo and 10% Colorino aged 18 months in French oak casks. It will drink well for a decade or more. Even more flashy/flamboyant is the opaque purple-colored 1998 Merlot Poggio Golo. This dense, chewy, voluptuously textured 100% Merlot is huge in the mouth, exhibiting gobs of chocolate/mocha-infused jammy black cherry fruit, a boatload of glycerin, low acidity, and sweet tannin. Thick and fleshy, it will have enormous appeal if drunk over the next 7–8 years.

VINCENZO CESANI

1997 Rosso di Pancole Luenzo	C	90

A terrific wine made from Sangiovese grown near the historic village of San Gimignano, this special *cuvée* made for American importer Eric Solomon of European Cellars is full-bodied, with a knockout nose of roasted hazelnuts, cappuccino, black currants, and toasty new oak. The wine is huge, with impressive structure, great purity, and a 30+-second finish. It can be drunk now or cellared for a decade.

CIACCI PICCOLOMINI D'ARAGONA

1998 Ateo IGT	D	93
1997 Brunello di Montalcino	EE	96

1999 Rosso di Montalcino Vigna della Fonte	C	89
1998 Rosso di Montalcino Vigna della Fonte	C	88
1999 Sant'Antimo Rosso Favius	D	94
1998 Sant'Antimo Rosso Favius	D	92

From one of my favorite Tuscan producers, Ciacci Piccolomini d'Aragona's 1999 Rosso di Montalcino Vigna della Fonte is another fine example from this vintage. Burgundy-like in its sweet strawberry, cherry, and mineral-infused flavors, this medium- to full-bodied, plump, complex, soft, lush *rosso* is best consumed over the next 3–4 years. Ciacci's 1998 Rosso di Montalcino Vigna della Fonte is a charming, seductive, ripe effort with sweet fruit but not a great deal of complexity. Richly fruity and sexy, it will provide enjoyment over the next 4–5 years. The terrific 1997 Brunello di Montalcino boasts a staggering aromatic profile of soy sauce, roasted meats, dried herbs, jammy black and red fruits, and Asian spices. This full-bodied, superbly concentrated, layered, multidimensional Brunello is the kind of wine one expects from such a renowned region but so rarely receives. This beauty should drink well young yet evolve effortlessly for 15+ years.

The 1998 Ateo (a blend of 60% Sangiovese and 40% Cabernet Sauvignon) is a gloriously ripe, full-bodied, velvety-textured effort with a dark ruby/purple color, plenty of smoky, earthy, blackberry, cherry, and currant fruit, a touch of graphite, decent acidity, and a seamless, opulent, voluptuous finish. This compelling wine is meant to be drunk over the next 10–12 years. There are only 15 barrels (approximately 375 cases) of the 100% Syrah 1998 Sant'Antimo Rosso Favius, which may be the finest Italian Syrah I have tasted. An opaque purple color is followed by a classic bouquet of bacon fat, blackberry liqueur, and cassis. This monstrous fruit bomb is unctuous, thick, and unbelievably concentrated. The wine's new-oak aging has been absorbed by its formidable concentration of fruit. Drink this exuberant, in-your-face offering over the next 5–7 years. Even more fabulous is the 1999 Sant'Antimo Rosso Favius (500 cases). A huge black/purple-colored effort, it boasts notes of roasted espresso, blackberries, asphalt, truffles, and pepper. Explosive, rich, unctuously textured, and full-bodied, with low acidity, it is stunning at present, yet unformed and primary. Anticipated maturity: 2003–2015. Bravo!

LE CINCIOLE

1997 Chianti Classico Riserva Petresco	D	90

The superb, deep ruby-colored 1997 Chianti Classico Riserva Petresco boasts a sweet bouquet of raspberries, strawberries, leather, dried herbs, and cedar. An elegant wine, it combines power and flesh with a stylish, graceful entry on the palate. Medium- to full-bodied and pure, it will provide delicious drinking over the next decade.

CISPIANO

1997 Chianti Classico	B	88

What a sexy, opulently textured, delicious wine! Its dark purple color is followed by gorgeously rich blackberry, raspberry, and cherry fruit aromas intermixed with a touch of earth and wood. Low in acidity, fat, and juicy, with a succulent finish, this is a mouth-filling, dazzling Chianti to enjoy over the next 5–7 years. An excellent value.

COLLE SANTA MUSTIOLA

1997 Poggio ai Chiari IGT	D	90

This complex, dark ruby/purple-colored, 100% Sangiovese reveals the vintage's telltale opulence, low acidity, and ripe, jammy fruit. Aromas of wood smoke, new saddle leather, black cherry and strawberry jam, intermixed with toast emerge from this deep, concentrated, dense, medium- to full-bodied, velvety-textured 1997. Drink it over the next 10–12 years.

COLLELUNGO

1999 Chianti Classico	C	89
1998 Chianti Classico Riserva	E	89
1997 Chianti Classico Riserva	D	93
1999 Chianti Classico Roveto	E	91
1997 Chianti Classico Roveto	D	91

This impressive new estate (its first vintage was 1997) is turning out expensive but brilliant offerings (bottled without fining or filtration) from the Castellina region of Chianti. The 1999 Chianti Classico and its sibling, the 1999 Chianti Classico Roveto, are dense ruby/purple-colored efforts possessing loads of blackberry and cherry fruit, subtle dosages of wood, and multitextured personalities displaying considerable flesh and ripeness. The only difference is that the regular bottling is soft and best consumed over the next 3–4 years; the Roveto exhibits more structure, although it is dominated by its fruit, glycerin, and concentration. Both represent modern, sumptuously styled Chiantis that are meant to be accessible in their youth. No Roveto was produced in 1998, but the modern-styled 1998 Chianti Classico Riserva is a 500-case *cuvée* exhibiting toasty new oak as well as copious quantities of black currant and cherry fruit intermixed with new saddle leather and tea notes. Tannin is present, but this 1998 is much sweeter than many of its peers, with good texture and length. It is an excellent Chianti to drink over the next 10–12 years.

The outstanding 1997 Chianti Classico Roveto exhibits superb ripeness, richness, and density, low acidity, and glorious levels of black cherry/raspberry fruit as well as spice box and toast characteristics. It should drink well for 7–8 years. It is unusual to compare a Chianti Classico with Burgundy, but there is no question that Collelungo's 1997 Chianti Classico Riserva could easily pass for a fine premier cru Volnay. Bottled unfined and unfiltered and made from 100% Sangiovese aged in new French oak, it boasts a glorious ruby/purple color in addition to fabulous aromatics, including flowers, black raspberries, and kirsch. As the wine sits in the glass, mineral and spicy new-oak scents emerge. Extraordinarily well delineated, full-bodied, and layered, with a sensationally deep mid-palate and a gorgeously proportioned finish, this dazzling Chianti can be drunk now or cellared for 10–12 years. Impressive!

COLLOSORBO

1997 Brunello di Montalcino	EE	90
1999 Laurus IGT	D	92
1999 Rosso di Montalcino	C	90
1998 Rosso di Montalcino	C	90

This impressive portfolio includes an outstanding 1999 Rosso di Montalcino. A deep ruby/purple color is accompanied by powerful, full-bodied, deep, chewy flavors, wonderful sweetness, good purity, and a whopping finish crammed with glycerin, black cherries, spice box, and currants. Enjoy this superb Rosso over the next 5–7 years. The 1999 Laurus, an intriguing, explosively scented and flavored blend of equal parts Sangiovese and Cabernet Sauvignon aged in new oak, is a Tuscan fruit bomb. It possesses a deep purple color, dazzling levels of plum, black cherry, and currant fruit, and a voluptuous, opulent, thick, rich personality. Drink it during its first 6–7 years to take advantage of its exuberance and lavishly fruited qualities.

Collosorbo's 1998 Rosso di Montalcino could easily be mistaken for a serious Brunello di Montalcino. There are sweet tannin and plenty of softness, as well as big, rustic, powerful, earthy, meaty, herb aromas and flavors. Complex, spicy, and medium- to full-bodied, it is ideal for drinking over the next 4–5 years. The dark ruby/garnet-colored 1997 Brunello di Montalcino boasts an intoxicating perfume of new saddle leather, cherry jam, dried

Provençal herbs, and spice box. This complex, medium- to full-bodied, supple-textured 1997 can be drunk early because of its fat and glycerin, but it promises to age well for 10–12 years.

COLOGNOLE

1997 Chianti Rufina Riserva del Don	**C**	**88**

I know it sounds unappealing, but occasionally (more frequently in Nebbiolo than in Sangiovese) an unmistakable scent of fresh sardines emerges along with aromas of cherries, earth, leather, underbrush, etc. I found that characteristic in this lean but impressively constituted, dark plum-colored 1997 Chianti Rufina Riserva del Don. It possesses complex aromatics, excellent texture, and a medium-bodied, ruggedly constructed finish. I am not sure it will ever resolve its rusticity, but it will provide a big mouthful of Chianti over the next 7–10 years.

COLOMBAIO DI CENCIO

1997 Chianti Classico Riserva	**D**	**89**
1997 Il Futuro IGT	**D**	**90**

Two impressive, modern-styled Italian reds, the dense ruby/purple-colored 1997 Chianti Classico Riserva exhibits aromas of black fruits, licorice, spice, and a touch of wood. Medium- to full-bodied and pure, with layers of flavor, this is a superb example of the renowned 1997 vintage. Consume it over the next decade. The 1997 Il Futuro is a well-endowed, *barrique*-aged effort with plenty of color, oak, and flavor. Revealing a saturated ruby/purple color, it boasts a superripe nose of blackberry liqueur mixed with crème de cassis and subtle oak. This layered, rich, concentrated offering should drink well for 10–12 years.

CONSTANTIA

1999 Morellino di Scansano Malfatti	**D**	**90**

A limited-production *cuvée* of Morellino di Scansano (a promising, up-and-coming subregion of Tuscany), this 1999 is a seriously endowed, opaque ruby/purple-colored offering boasting a dazzling aromatic display of violets, blueberries, black currants, minerals, and new oak. Rich, round, medium- to full-bodied, exceptionally pure, and beautifully textured, this stylish, classic red should drink well during its first decade of life.

CORRINA

1997 Chianti Rufina	**B**	**89**
1997 I Cipressi IGT	**C**	**89**
1997 Vigna Spartigalla IGT	**C**	**90**

This excellent winery practices a fair pricing policy that makes these offerings essentially steals, given today's inflated wine prices. The dark ruby/purple-colored 1997 Chianti Rufina (93% Sangiovese) offers a sweet nose of strawberries and cherries. Lovely glycerin gives the wine a creamy texture, and the finish is pure, ripe, and authoritative, with no hard edges or bumps. Drink this dense Chianti over the next 5–6 years. It is a terrific value. A steal in today's surreal wine market is the 1997 Vigna Spartigalla *vino da tavola*. A blend of 90% Sangiovese and 10% Cabernet Sauvignon aged in 75% new French oak, it borders on an international style, and mineral and lead pencil notes kick in to add complexity to the toasty wood. There are copious quantities of black currants and cherries, tangy acidity, and outstanding purity as well as harmony in this full-bodied wine. Delicious now, it will improve for 7–8 years and last for 12–15. Another excellent value is the dense ruby/purple-colored 1997 I Cipressi, a blend of equal parts Sangiovese and Cabernet Sauvignon. Medium-bodied and structured, with elegant, smoky, blackberry and cassis fruit intertwined with toast and leather, it will benefit from another 6–12 months of bottle age and last for a decade. These are all excellent values.

ANDREA COSTANTI

1999 Calbello Ardingo IGT	D	90
1998 Calbello Ardingo IGT	D	93

Costanti is a traditional winery consistently turning out classic offerings. Serious, stern, austere wines that age brilliantly are produced by Andrea Costanti. Bottled by Costanti under the Calbello label and produced from a vineyard in Montosoli, the terrific 1998 Calbello Ardingo (a *barrique*-aged blend of 75% Merlot and 25% Cabernet Sauvignon) is another example of the stunning quality Merlot can achieve in Tuscany (in my view, unequaled anywhere in the world except Pomerol). This opaque purple-colored 1998 boasts a knockout nose of espresso-infused cherry jam as well as dense, full-bodied, unctuously textured flavors that ooze across the palate. The new-oak characteristics from *barrique* aging are completely concealed by the wine's wealth of fruit and extract. This intense, chewy, internationally styled effort is in total contrast to the austere Brunellos di Montalcino produced by Costanti. It should drink well for a decade or more. The closest thing to a modern-styled red is the 1999 Calbello Ardingo, a dark plum/purple-colored, sexy effort revealing aromas of espresso, chocolate, and sweet, plum/black cherry fruit. Full-bodied and succulent, with sweet tannin as well as exceptional ripeness, it will drink well for 5–6 years.

DEI

1997 Santa Catharina IGT	D	92
1997 Vino Nobile di Montepulciano	C	90
1997 Vino Nobile di Montepulciano Riserva	D	90

The opulence of the 1997 vintage is well displayed in the dark ruby/garnet-colored 1997 Vino Nobile di Montepulciano Riserva. It exhibits jammy black fruits intermixed with underbrush, leather, tobacco, and caramel, plump, fleshy fruit, medium- to full-bodied, low-acid but impressively textured flavors. Drink it over the next 5–7 years. The spectacular, opaque purple-colored 1997 Santa Catharina (equal parts Cabernet Sauvignon, Syrah, and Sangiovese) boasts a rich, full-bodied, chewy personality with copious quantities of blackberry and cassis fruit intermixed with smoky wood. Thick, corpulent, dense, and moderately tannic, this enormously endowed yet harmonious wine can be drunk now and over the next 12+ years. Another gorgeously delicious 1997 from Tuscany, the dark ruby-colored 1997 Vino Nobile di Montepulciano offers up sweet, jammy, black cherry fruit intertwined with scents of new saddle leather. Aged in large *foudres* prior to bottling, it exhibits notes of over-ripeness, explosive fruit, and a boatload of glycerin. This medium-bodied, seductive wine should be drunk over the next 5–6 years.

ELISABETTA

1998 Le Marze	C	89

Elisabetta's 1998 Le Marze, a blend of 45% Merlot, 45% Cabernet Sauvignon, and 10% Cabernet Franc, is reminiscent of a midlevel St.-Emilion. It offers up scents of cedar, tobacco, licorice, dried herbs, red and black currants, but no evidence of new oak. Ripe, medium-bodied, complex, and supple, it should be consumed over the next 5–6 years.

FANTI

1999 Rosso di Montalcino	C	90
2000 Sant'Antimo	C	89

One of Italy's most brilliant winemaking consultants, Stefano Chioccioli, has been assisting this estate over the last several years. The 2000 Sant'Antimo (from a vineyard close to the appellation of Montalcino) is a 3,000-case *cuvée* of 100% Sangiovese aged in barrel. It is a full-bodied offering with an opulent, fleshy texture and copious quantities of red and black fruits intermixed with licorice and smoke. It is best drunk during its first 4–6 years of life. The superb 1999 Rosso di Montalcino flaunts sumptuous aromas of strawberry liqueur, cherries, grilled herbs, and meaty notes. Dense, rich, full-bodied, and succulent, with soft tannin, low acidity, and admirable plushness, this fruit bomb should be consumed over the next 3–5 years. Don't miss it!

FATTORIA DI FELSINA

1999 Chianti Classico	C	91
1997 Chianti Classico Riserva	D	90+
1998 Chianti Classico Rancia Riserva	D	90
1997 Chianti Classico Rancia Riserva	D	92+
1997 Fontalloro	E	92
1997 Maestro Raro	E	88

One of my favorite Tuscan producers, Felsina's estate vineyards are situated in a cooler microclimate not far from Siena. Felsina offers two Chianti Classico Riservas, its top-notch regular *cuvée* and its spectacular single-vineyard Rancia Riserva. The serious 1997 Chianti Classico Riserva (4,000 cases of 100% Sangiovese) is structured, dense, concentrated, and ageworthy. It is one of the few 1997s that requires 1–2 years of cellaring. A deep ruby/garnet color is followed by aromas of dried herbs, roasted beef, black cherries, plums, cedar, and leather. On the palate, blackberry fruit makes an appearance. Sweet, pure, long, ripe, and moderately tannic, it will be at its finest between now–2015. The dark ruby-colored 1997 Chianti Classico Rancia Riserva (3,000 cases) is aged two years in large wood as well as small *barriques*. With its chewy, powerful, meaty aromas, this wine begs to be drunk with steak. Notes of licorice, smoke, spice box, cedar, and black cherry jam can be found in this ripe, concentrated, muscular wine. Lay this one away for 2–3 years, and consume it over the following 17–18 years.

The 1998 Chianti Classico Rancia Riserva exhibits plenty of promise for a less highly regarded vintage. A deep ruby/purple color is accompanied by a sumptuous bouquet of sweet licorice intertwined with soy, herbs, leather, spice, black cherries, and plums. Ripe and medium-bodied, with good muscle and structure, it will be drinkable early but will not have the aging potential, volume, or concentration of the 1997.

A dazzling example of a fabulous vintage for Chianti, the full-throttle, opulently textured, explosively ripe, fruity 1999 Chianti Classico possesses a deep ruby color as well as glorious levels of black cherry and berry fruit mixed with tobacco and new saddle leather. It reveals superb purity, a generous mouth-feel with no heaviness, and enough acidity to provide delineation. This ripe, mouth-filling, impeccably balanced Chianti will drink well for 7–8 years, but who can resist its current charms?

Felsina produces two proprietary red wines, one made from 100% Sangioveto, called Fontalloro, and a Cabernet Sauvignon called Maestro Raro. The 1997 Fontalloro may be the finest made from this single vineyard (and I have tasted them back through the early 1980s). There are 3,000 cases of this spectacular wine, aged two years in French oak. Dense ruby/purple-colored, with a chocolate espresso–scented nose infused with cherry liqueur, it is a full-bodied, sweet wine with wonderful fatness, terrific ripeness, plenty of glycerin, and a chewy, long, spicy finish. There is some tannin in this youthful offering, but its appealing flamboyance is attention-getting. It should last for 12–15+ years. Last, the 1997 Maestro Raro (400 cases of 100% Cabernet Sauvignon) is still unformed. A ripe, plum/purple color is accompanied by straightforward cassis fruit, toasty oak, and a rich, chewy, but monolithic personality. It needs more time to firm up and reveal its complexity and delineation. Anticipated maturity: now–2014.

FATTORIA LA FIORITA

1997 Brunello di Montalcino	EE	90

Complex characteristics of leather, plums, prunes, Asian spices, licorice, and dried herbs jump from the glass of this full-bodied, rich, well-endowed Brunello. Its deep garnet/ruby color is accompanied by impressive sweetness, moderate levels of ripe tannin, and a long finish. Based on this effort, among the finest Brunellos I have tasted from this vintage, 1997 promises reasonably forward and accessible wines. Anticipated maturity: 2003–2016.

FONTALEONI

1999 Rosso di San Gimignano	B	88

The 1999 Rosso di San Gimignano represents a superb wine bargain. Its dark ruby/purple color is accompanied by a gorgeous perfume of berry fruit, spice, pepper, and minerals, a sweet entry, good fatness, and a lush, hedonistic finish. It is a wine to purchase by the case and consume over the next 2–3 years.

FATTORIA LE FONTI

1997 Chianti Classico Riserva	D	90
1998 Vito Arturo IGT	D	88
1997 Vito Arturo IGT	D	92

Readers seeking Chiantis with distinctive lushness as well as sweet, espresso-infused, black chocolate, and in-your-face black cherry and berry fruit should check out these offerings from Le Fonti. They reveal a sexy, Pomerol-like seamlessness as well as considerable fat and ripeness. The 1997 Chianti Classico Riserva (100% Sangiovese) reveals smoky notes, great concentration, a voluptuous personality, and gobs of sweet, jammy black fruits intermixed with smoke, chocolate, and espresso. With tremendous purity and ripeness, it is a total turn-on. Drink it over the next 5–7 years. Made in the same style, with more fat as well as additional layers of lush, plump fruit, is the 1997 Vito Arturo (100% Sangiovese Grosso, primarily aged in new French oak). This seamless effort tastes like a chocolate mocha/black cherry infusion. A dense ruby/purple color is accompanied by a creamy-textured, dense, concentrated, medium- to full-bodied, seductive wine. It should drink well for 7–10 years. Made from 100% Sangiovese Grosso, the 1998 Vito Arturo reveals an international style (it was obviously aged in French oak), as well as abundant character in its earthy, black currant, licorice, leathery nose and flavors. Medium-bodied, with ripe tannin and a lot of class, this modern-styled Sangiovese can be consumed now and over the next 7–8 years.

FONTODI

1999 Chianti Classico	D	91
1998 Chianti Classico	C	88
1998 Chianti Classico Vigna del Sorbo Riserva	D	89
1997 Chianti Classico Vigna del Sorbo Riserva	D	90
1998 Flaccianello della Pieve IGT	E	89
1997 Flaccianello della Pieve IGT	E	93
1998 Syrah Case Via IGT	D	90?
1997 Syrah Case Via IGT	D	90

One of Tuscany's finest producers, Fontodi is a name readers can rely on for high-quality wines, particularly in the finest vintages. In particular, its single-vineyard Chianti Classico

Vigna del Sorbo and proprietary Sangiovese, Flaccianello della Pieve, are among the best of their types. The knockout 1999 Chianti Classico (100% Sangiovese) provides more evidence of just how terrific this vintage is in Tuscany, particularly for Chianti. Complex aromas of new saddle leather, jammy black cherry liqueur, and other black fruits jump from the glass of this dense ruby-colored wine. There are layers of fruit and extraction, full body, no hard edges, and an explosive, long finish that lasts for nearly 30 seconds. Enjoy it now and over the next decade. The quality of the 1999 vintage is even more apparent when one tastes the 1998 Chianti Classico Vigna del Sorbo Riserva. This can be a stunning *cuvée*, but in the more austere, tannic 1998 vintage, the Riserva is not as good as the less expensive 1999 regular bottling. However, it is still a fine effort. The 1998's dark ruby/purple color is followed by a big nose of licorice, liquefied minerals, tar, underbrush, and plum/berry fruit. Spicy, dense, medium-bodied, and moderately tannic, 1–2 years of cellaring is recommended, although the tannin will never completely melt away. Anticipated maturity: 2003–2012.

The dark ruby-colored, soft, earthy, smoky, berry fruit–laden 1998 Chianti Classico possesses beautiful purity, sweet fruit, and adequate acidity. It is meant to be drunk over the next several years. The outstanding 1997 Chianti Classico Vigna del Sorbo Riserva (a 2,000-case blend of 85% Sangiovese and 15% Cabernet Sauvignon) exhibits a dense ruby color, as well as Chianti's quintessential blend of elegance and power. Deep, rich, and concentrated, with notes of sweet new saddle leather, black cherries, balsa wood, spice box, and smoke, it has terrific fruit intensity and purity, together with balance and finesse. This compelling Chianti should drink well for a decade.

The proprietary 100% Sangiovese *cuvée*, the 1998 Flaccianello della Pieve, was aged 12 months in French oak. Unlike the more opulent 1997 Flaccianello, the 1998 reveals dry, hard tannin in the finish. A deep ruby/purple color is followed by abundant scents of toasty new oak, black cherries, minerals, and spice box. Dry, long, and well made for the vintage, it will be at its finest between 2003–2012. The 1998 Syrah Case Via (100% Syrah aged one year in French oak) exhibits a classic bacon fat, blackberry, crème de cassis character, full-bodied, smoky flavors, rustic tannin, and gorgeous levels of fruit, extract, and ripeness. The only flaw in this impressive, somewhat internationally styled offering is the slightly elevated tannin. Drink it over the next 10–12 years.

There are 3,500 cases of the 1997 Flaccianello della Pieve, a 100% Sangiovese aged in new French oak for 18 months. The 1997 is one of the finest Flaccianellos yet produced. A dark ruby/purple color is followed by a strikingly fragrant nose of saddle leather, cedar, licorice, vanilla, and black cherry/blackberry fruit. The wine possesses medium to full body, gorgeous delineation, fine ripeness, and a sweet, glycerin-imbued, long finish. Given the vintage's glycerin level and opulence, it can be drunk now, but it promises to last for 15 or more years. One of Tuscany's breakthrough Syrah efforts is Fontodi's 1997 Syrah Case Via (1,000 cases). It offers textbook peppery, blackberry notes, low acidity (particularly for an Italian wine), deep, chewy, unctuously textured fruit, full body, and a chunky, husky finish. It should drink well for 8–10 years.

FRIGGIALI

1999 Rosso di Montalcino	C	90

Another gorgeous 1999 Rosso di Montalcino, Friggiali's offering exhibits a dark plum color along with a gorgeous bouquet of currants, cherry jam, underbrush, spice, and balsa wood. Extremely spicy, with tremendous fruit, a supple, fleshy texture, and medium to full body, it is meant to be consumed over the next 5–6 years.

LA FUGA

1999 Rosso di Montalcino	D	89

The delicious, sweet, fleshy, freakishly ripe, deep ruby-colored 1999 Rosso di Montalcino reveals copious quantities of glycerin as well as strawberry and black cherry fruit. This fruity Rosso should be enjoyed over the next 3–4 years for its exuberance and fruit.

EREDI FULIGNI

1997 Rosso di Montalcino Sanjacopo	D	90

The 1997 Rosso di Montalcino Sanjacopo is a gorgeously rich, ripe, low-acid offering made of 80% Sangiovese Grosso and 20% Merlot. It exhibits sweet strawberry jam–like notes intermixed with Asian spices, underbrush, and incense. Dense and rich, with a voluptuous texture, low acidity, and outstanding ripeness and fruit, it should be consumed over the next 3–4 years.

GAGLIOLE

1999 Pecchia IGT	E	92
1999 Rosso IGT	E	89
1998 Rosso IGT	E	90
1997 Rosso IGT	E	92

There are 1,200 cases of the 1999 Rosso and 250 cases of the 1999 Pecchia. More important, Gagliole's consulting oenologist is the brilliant Luca d'Attoma, the man responsible for some of the most exciting wines emerging from Tuscany. The 1999 Rosso is a blend of 90% Sangiovese and 10% Cabernet Sauvignon, aged 18 months in French oak prior to being bottled unfiltered. Its dense ruby/purple color is followed by smoky, ripe scents of black currants, cherries, and vanilla. Layered, with a plush midsection, an enticing texture, and a firm, elegant, pure finish, this stylized wine can be drunk now or cellared for a decade. The sensational, opaque ruby/purple-colored 1999 Pecchia (100% Sangiovese) displays how unusually ripe and concentrated the 1999 vintage was in Tuscany. It boasts an opaque purple color as well as a glorious bouquet of black fruits, lead pencil, vanilla, smoke, and flowers. Dense and full-bodied, with abundant structure, outstanding purity, harmony, and overall depth, this is a powerful (14.5% alcohol) effort with extraordinary finesse. Anticipated maturity: 2003–2020.

This relatively young (the debut vintage was 1994) operation fashioned two beautiful blends of 90% Sangiovese and 10% Cabernet Sauvignon in 1997 and 1998. Yields are kept extremely low (less than 30 hectoliters per hectare), and production prior to 1999 was approximately 1,300 cases of each vintage. The impressive 1997 Rosso boasts a dense purple color as well as a ripe nose of blackberries, smoke, tobacco, chocolate, and toast. Complex aromatics lead to a medium- to full-bodied wine with a gorgeously sweet, opulently textured attack and mid-palate. With beautiful purity, freshness, and overall harmony, it will drink well for a decade. Although less opulent, the 1998 Rosso is a medium- to full-bodied, ripe, evolved, tobacco-tinged, cedary, spice box, and red cherry/black currant–scented and –flavored wine with mature tannin, a fat, chewy mid-palate, and good acidity for freshness and delineation. It should drink well for 7–8 years.

LA GERLA

1997 Birba IGT	D	88

The deep ruby-colored 1997 Birba reveals a big, spicy, internationally styled nose of new oak, red and black currants, and smoke. Medium-bodied, clean, and supple, this 1997 red is best drunk over the next 3–4 years.

I GIUSTI E ZANZA

1999 Belcore	D	91
1998 Belcore	C	90

1998 Dulcamara	E	91+
1997 Dulcamara	E	93

A new limited-production winery (1996 was its first vintage), I Giusti e Zanza produces a 90% Sangiovese/10% Merlot blend called Belcore and an 80% Cabernet Sauvignon/20% Cabernet Franc and Merlot blend called Dulcamara. Both of these wines are aged in French oak and bottled following a light filtration. From one of Tuscany's warmest microclimates, these wines are fashioned by one of Italy's up-and-coming brilliant consultants, Stefano Chioccioli. The 1999 Belcore is a 3,000-plus-case *cuvée* of 90% Sangiovese and 10% Merlot aged in large, 300-liter barrels. Its dense purple color is followed by a sexy, open-knit nose offering explosive aromas of toast, blackberry, and cherry liqueur intermixed with currants. Spicy, fleshy, full-bodied, ripe, and seductive, it will drink well for 5–6 years. A blend of 80% Cabernet Sauvignon and 20% Cabernet Franc/Merlot, the 1998 Dulcamara was produced in only 580 cases. Opaque purple-colored, with a heavy overlay of graphite and smoky oak mixed with jammy cassis, it comes across like a top-quality Bordeaux with its cedar, mineral, and black fruit characteristics. Dense, full-bodied, long, ripe, and concentrated, with impressive delineation as well as extract, sweet tannin, and low acidity, it will be at its finest between 2003–2017.

The 1998 Belcore (17,000 bottles) is typical of the newer-styled, high-quality Italian reds, being low in acidity, dense, and opulent, with explosive ripeness (some might say over-ripeness) and rich black cherry and blackberry fruit infused with toasty oak, spice box, and cedar notes. There are gorgeous layers of concentration. Since there is no history on this wine, it is probably best consumed during its first 7–8 years of life. The opaque ruby/purple-colored 1997 Dulcamara (500 cases) exhibits a knockout nose of cigar tobacco, cedar wood, blackberry liqueur, cassis, and vanilla. Exciting on the palate, it offers a combination of power and glycerin in addition to a multilayered texture. The finish of this full-throttle, concentrated wine is equally impressive. It should drink well for a decade.

GORELLI

1997 Brunello di Montalcino Le Potazzine	E	96
1999 Rosso di Montalcino Le Potazzine	C	89

Another tasty Rosso di Montalcino from the superb 1999 vintage, the high-altitude vineyard of Le Potazzine produced a deep ruby/purple-colored effort with a sweet nose of black raspberry and cherry fruit, medium body, no hard edges, and excellent purity as well as liveliness. Drink it over the next 3–5 years. Gorelli's 1997 Brunello di Montalcino Le Potazzine is reminiscent of the famed Spanish wine called Pingus from Ribera del Duero. Its opaque garnet color is followed by an extraordinarily provocative perfume of black fruits, espresso, roasted meats, and plum/prune elements. New saddle leather and Asian spice aromas also make an appearance. Viscous, huge, and oozing with concentration, this remarkable effort is pure, thick, and surprisingly approachable for such a young, massive Brunello. Anticipated maturity: now–2016. This is a tour de force in winemaking!

PODERE LANCIOLA II

1997 Terricci IGT	D	89

One of Italy's young, talented wine consultants, Stefano Chioccioli, is behind Lanciola's rise in quality. The proprietary red wine offering, the 1997 Terricci, is a blend of 80% Sangiovese, 10% Cabernet Sauvignon, and equal parts Cabernet Franc and Merlot. It is a compressed, complex, plum/purple-colored effort with plenty of chewy currant/cherry fruit, saddle leather, animal fur, earth, and graphite. Although approximately 70% new French *barriques* were utilized, the oak characteristic is subdued in the wine's aromas and flavors. The finish is moderately tannic. Cellar this 1997 for another 1–2 years, and enjoy it over the following 12–14 years.

LISINI

1999 Rosso di Montalcino	C	90

With the consultation of Franco Bernabei, Lisini has been producing fine wines after a slump in quality during the late 1970s and early 1980s. Lisini has produced a stunning 1999 Rosso di Montalcino. Its deep ruby color is accompanied by terrific sweet black cherry and strawberry fruit notes intermixed with new saddle leather, balsa wood, spice box, and cedar. Sweet, with loads of glycerin, medium body, ripe tannin, and abundant spice, this wine will provide provocative, compelling drinking over the next 8–10 years.

FATTORIA DI LUCIGNANO

1999 Chianti Classico Colli Fiorentini	A	88

There are 8,000 cases of Lucignano's 1999 Chianti Classico Colli Fiorentini, consistently one of the finest values from Chianti. It is a richly fruity, delicious, strawberry and cherry fruit bomb with supple texture, abundant spice, medium body, and good glycerin. Enjoy it over the next 2–3 years.

LE MACCHIOLE

1999 Macchiole Rosso	D	90
1998 Macchiole Rosso	C	91
1998 Messorio	EEE	96+
1997 Messorio	EE	98
1997 Paleo Rosso	E	92
1999 Scrio	EEE	95
1997 Scrio	E	90

This 42-acre estate situated along the Tuscan coast is owned by Eugenio Campolmi, who had the foresight to bring in one of the region's most brilliant wine-makers, Luca d'Attoma. Production ranges from 2,000+ cases of the Macchiole Rosso to 2,500 cases of the Paleo Rosso and a minuscule 250 cases or less each of the Messorio (100% Merlot) and Scrio (100% Syrah). Among the most compelling wines being produced in Italy, they are extraordinary examples of an owner's uncompromising commitment to producing world-class wines.

The 1999 Macchiole Rosso is a blend of 95% Sangiovese and 5% Cabernet Sauvignon aged in French *barriques* before being bottled without fining or filtration. Its complex bouquet offers scents of cedar, new saddle leather, dried herbs, espresso beans, chocolate, and black fruits (plums and currants). Supple, complete, concentrated, and lush, it will drink well for 7–8 years. Even more promising is the 1997 Paleo Rosso, an unfined, unfiltered, *barrique*-aged blend of 80% Cabernet Sauvignon, 10% Sangiovese, and 10% Cabernet Franc. Its opaque ruby/purple color is followed by a sweet nose of licorice, smoke, graphite, blackberries, and cassis. Full-bodied, with a roasted meat character to its flavors, extraordinary purity and concentration, and beautifully integrated acidity as well as tannin, this blockbuster is a candidate for drinking now or cellaring for 15–17 years.

There are only microscopic quantities available of the following two wines, so I will keep my tasting notes somewhat streamlined, even though both wines merit near-perfect scores. Le Macchiole's Scrio is the most profound Syrah being made in Italy. Unfined, unfiltered, and produced from incredibly tiny yields, the black/purple-colored 1999 offers scents of licorice, melted tar, truffles, and blackberry liqueur. Full-bodied and opulent, with high tannin but compelling sweetness and a multilayered palate, it requires 3–4 years of cellaring but should age for two decades. It could easily compete with some of the Rhône Valley's great Hermitages. The 1998 Messorio (100% Merlot) rivals some of the finest Merlots being produced anywhere in the world. Mind-blowing in its richness and intensity, it can compete with the finest wines being made on the Pomerol plateau. Representing the essence of Merlot in its concentrated jammy blackberry and cherry notes, it is a well-defined, beautifully poised effort revealing both power and elegance. Full-bodied, dense, and super-concentrated, with an incredibly long 50-second finish, it is a tour de force in winemaking that must be tasted to be believed. Anticipated maturity: 2004–2016. These are prodigious wines. It's a shame that the quantities are so limited.

There are approximately 2,000 cases of the 1998 Macchiole Rosso, a wine aged in barrel prior to being bottled with neither fining nor filtering. Aromas of blackberry/cassis fruit intertwined with smoke and licorice jump from the glass of this fragrant wine. Intense and opulently styled, with low acidity, medium to full body, and nicely integrated toasty oak, this blend of 95% Sangiovese and 5% Cabernet Sauvignon will offer compelling drinking over the next 7–8 years.

Quantities of the Merlot from the Messorio vineyard are limited (approximately 40–50 cases in 1997), but production is expected to increase slightly in future vintages. The purpose of writing about a wine of such limited availability is that *Wine Advocate* subscribers can get a head start, as this will certainly become one of the great new wines of Italy. The awesome 1997 Merlot Messorio is truly prodigious. Black/purple-colored, it boasts an astonishingly rich nose of black raspberries, smoky new oak, dried herbs, and cedar. Chocolate, new saddle leather, and exhilarating levels of black fruits give this wine a luxurious, voluptuous texture. The finish lasts for nearly a minute! A winemaking tour de force that is already accessible given its expansive, open-knit texture, it should last for 12–15+ years.

The rustic 1997 Syrah Scrio is a dense, chewy, muscular wine with rough tannin, yet impressive concentration and purity. It should become more civilized with another 1–2 years of bottle age and will last for 10–12 years. Bravo!

LE MACIOCHE

1997 Brunello di Montalcino	E	88+

An attractive coconut-like aroma (reminiscent of American oak) rises from the glass of this medium-bodied, elegant, stylish, plum/garnet-colored 1997 Brunello di Montalcino. The coconut scents are accompanied by abundant quantities of currant fruit, smoke, and toast. While not the most flamboyant or concentrated of the soon-to-be-released 1997 Brunellos, it is exotic and distinctive. Drink it over the next 8 years.

FATTORIA LA MAGIA

1999 Rosso di Montalcino	C	89

1999 Rossos di Montalcino are high on my list of realistically priced wines to purchase in 2002. They offer loads of sweet fruit, plenty of glycerin, and a rich, concentrated, velvety style. Fattoria La Magia's 1999 (3,000 cases) is a chewy effort displaying gorgeous levels of sweet cherry fruit intermixed with a kirschlike note. Fresh, ripe, medium-bodied, and supple, it will drink well for 3–5 years. It was bottled unfiltered by the estate's oenologist, Roberto Cipresso.

LA MASSA

1999 Chianti Classico	D	88
1998 Chianti Classico Giorgio Primo	E	89+?
1997 Chianti Classico Giorgio Primo	E	90

Of these three attractive offerings, the less expensive 1999 Chianti Classico is further proof of how wonderful this vintage was throughout Tuscany. For a low-level wine, it delivers plenty of pleasure in its dark ruby color and a bouquet of sweet currant and black cherries intermixed with oak and spice. Fleshy and succulent, it should be consumed over the next 2–3 years to take advantage of its youthful charm. The single-vineyard Giorgio Primo *cuvée* is successful in both the more austere 1998 and more exotic, ripe 1997 vintages. The dark ruby-colored 1998 Chianti Classico Giorgio Primo offers dense currant and cherry aromas mixed with scents of new French oak. Structured, rich, and concentrated, it possesses abundant tannin but adequate sweetness for balance. Drink it over the next 12–14 years. The fleshier, more open-knit 1997 Chianti Classico Giorgio Primo exhibits that vintage's higher glycerin and more expansive nature. Beautiful notes of black cherries, currants, new oak, and spice are found in this dark ruby/purple-colored offering. Long, dense, youthful, and vibrant, it is best consumed during its first 10–15 years of life.

MONTE BERNARDI

1997	Chianti Classico	C	90
1999	Chianti Classico Paris	D	90
1999	Sa'etta IGT	E	91+
1997	Sa'etta IGT	E	90+
1999	Tzingana IGT	EE	90
1997	Tzingana IGT	E	92

These artisanal wines come at a high price, but they are interestingly packaged and, most important, impressive. The dazzling, dark ruby/purple-colored 1999 Chianti Classico Paris offers a fabulous aromatic profile of sweet black raspberry and currant fruit, new oak, and saddle leather. Ripe, textured, and intense, with super purity and a long, medium- to full-bodied, symmetrical finish, it is accessible but promises to be even better with another 1–2 years of cellaring. It will last for 12–15 years. The *barrique*-aged *cuvée* of 100% Sangiovese, the 1999 Sa'etta, boasts an opaque purple color in addition to a sweet nose of black currants, blackberries, smoke, and vanilla. The wine is full-bodied and ripe, with melted tannin, exceptional concentration, and a long finish. Initially, I thought it was internationally styled, but Sangiovese's distinctive character emerges as the wine sits in the glass. Anticipated maturity: now–2014. The superexpensive, internationally styled 1999 Tzingana (a Bordeaux-like blend of Merlot, Cabernet Franc, Cabernet Sauvignon, and Petit Verdot) is impeccably well made. There are copious quantities of new oak in its blackberry, currant, licorice, and smoke-scented bouquet, medium- to full-bodied flavors, and moderate tannin in the long finish. No trace of Tuscan typicity can be found in this exceptional offering. Drink it over the next 10–14 years.

It will be hard, even in the top-notch vintage of 1997, to find a better Chianti than Monte Bernardi's 1997 Chianti Classico. Dense ruby-colored, with fabulous fruit, it unwinds on the palate to reveal expansive, sweet black cherry and berry flavors intertwined with tobacco, spice box, and dried herbs. With abundant glycerin and an opulent texture, this *barrique*-aged Chianti is terrific. Drink it over the next 5–6 years. The proprietary red, the 1997 Sa'etta *vino da tavola*, is a *barrique*-aged 100% Sangiovese. The dense ruby/purple color is followed by a voluptuously textured, medium- to full-bodied, low-acid wine with stunning quantities of red and black fruits. It should drink well for 7–8 years. The Cabernet Sauvignon, Merlot, and Cabernet Franc *vino da tavola* from Monte Bernardi is called Tzingana. The 1997 Tzingana is undeniably sexy, revealing a dense purple color in addition to a gorgeous display of blackberries, plums, licorice, and toasty new oak. Sweet (because of high glycerin and alcohol), with low acidity and layers of concentrated fruit, this terrific proprietary red should drink well for a decade.

FATTORIA DI MONTELLORI

1997	Salamartano	D 89

Montellori's proprietary red wine, the 1997 Salamartano (equal parts Cabernet Sauvignon and Merlot), is noticeably tannic and backward, as well as internationally styled. The dark ruby/purple color is followed by moderately intense aromas of black currants, sweet cherries, and spicy new oak. Structured and tannic, it requires 1–2 years of cellaring and should age well for 10–12 years.

MONTEPELOSO

1999 Gabbro IGT	EE	94
1998 Gabbro IGT	EE	93
1999 Nardo IGT	EE	94
1998 Nardo IGT	E	90
1997 Nardo IGT	E	89
1999 Rosso Val di Cornia	D	92

This estate is located in Suvereto, a subregion of Tuscany that is becoming famous for the extraordinary quality of its wines. (The impressive estate of Tua Rita is nearby.) Montepeloso's wines are made by the highly esteemed consultant Luca d'Attoma. All three of the 1999s were produced from incredibly low yields (24 hectoliters per hectare for the Rosso and 8 hectoliters per hectare for the Gabbro and Nardo), aged in *barrique* (1–2 years old for the Rosso and 100% new for the Gabbro and Nardo), and bottled without filtration. The dazzling 1999 Rosso Val di Cornia combines power, luxurious fruit, and elegance. Its dense saturated ruby/purple color is followed by a sweet nose of ripe black fruits, licorice, smoke, and graphite. Opulent, rich, and full-bodied, with layers of fruit, no hard edges, amazing delineation, and admirable concentration, this pure, symmetrical effort should drink well for 8–10 years. The limited-production 1999 Nardo, a blend of 90% Sangiovese and 10% Cabernet Sauvignon, takes concentration to its limits. It exhibits toasty new oak and the essence of black cherry liqueur in its perfumed bouquet. A full-bodied as well as layered palate impression, combined with fabulous purity and depth, are hallmarks of this wine. The 14.5% alcohol content is high by Tuscan standards, but it is beautifully integrated and not the least bit hot. This tour de force in winemaking should age for 12–15 years.

Produced from 100% Cabernet Sauvignon and aged in 100% new French oak, the 1999 Gabbro boasts an inky, opaque purple color as well as a backward but promising bouquet of lead pencil, crème de cassis, toast, and melted licorice. Full-bodied, powerful, and profoundly concentrated, this dramatic wine could easily be inserted into a blind tasting with barrel samples of the 2000 Médocs. The finish lasts for 30–35 seconds. The evolution of this wine should be fascinating to follow.

The debut vintage of the 100% Cabernet Sauvignon *cuvée*, the 1998 Gabbro, is a terrific example of what can be produced in this area adjacent to the Mediterranean. Keep in mind that the famous Sassicaia is close by, as are the hillside vineyards of the cult wine Tua Rita. The saturated black/purple-colored 1998 Gabbro boasts sumptuous aromatics of cherry liqueur, cassis, toasty new oak, minerals, spice box, and tobacco. There are extravagant intensity, an opulent texture, and a large-scaled, rich, concentrated finish. It should be cellared for 2–3 years and drunk over the following 12–15.

The 1997 Nardo has an elegant, dark ruby/purple color followed by abundant quantities of sweet blackberry and currant fruit and a rich, spicy, concentrated, medium- to full-bodied palate with good underlying acidity. Gritty tannin kept my score low. This wine should age nicely for a decade. Better balanced is the 1998 Nardo. In this area of Tuscany, known as Bolgheri, many growers consider 1998 an even better vintage than 1997. That is certainly borne out by the 1998 Montepeloso Nardo. It exhibits a deeper, more saturated ruby/purple color in addition to gorgeously jammy blackberry and cassis flavors infused with smoke, minerals, licorice, and toast. There are terrific intensity as well as a long, medium- to full-bodied finish with well-integrated acidity, tannin, and wood. It should drink well for 10–15 years.

GIACOMO MORI

2000 Chianti	B	90
1999 Chianti Castelrotto	C	91
1998 Chianti Castelrotto	C	88

Since Marc De Grazia began working with this estate, quality has risen. For $13.50 it will be hard to find a better Tuscan offering than Mori's 2000 Chianti. An opaque purple color is accompanied by powerful aromas of black cherry jam, blackberries, licorice, minerals, and earth, considerable stuffing, a succulent, full-bodied, supple style, and loads of fruit as well as extract. A layered finish adds to the overall appeal of this dynamite Chianti. Drink it over the next 4–5 years, although I suspect it will last longer. Aged 100% in *barrique*, the single-vineyard 1999 Chianti Castelrotto is a full-bodied, dense purple-colored effort with extraordinary opulence, a more complex perfume than its less expensive sibling, and more volume/length. With higher tannin as well as extract, it will benefit from another 1–2 years of cellaring. It will age for 10–12 years. Giacomo Mori's 1998 Chianti Castelrotto reveals spicy oak along with leather, mineral, licorice, and cherry flavors. With medium body, some tannin, but unobtrusive structure, it is best consumed over the next 3–5 years.

I MORI

1999 Chianti Colli Fiorentini	B	88
1998 Moresco IGT	C	92

The 1998 Moresco, a *barrique*-aged blend of 70% Sangiovese and 30% Cabernet Sauvignon, boasts an opaque purple color as well as a bouquet of earth, vanilla, black currants, and espresso. Full-bodied, powerful, concentrated, and moderately tannic, with a long, intense, pure finish, this youthful, unevolved IGT requires 2–3 years of cellaring. It should evolve for 12–15 years. Bravo! The 1999 Chianti Colli Fiorentini (100% Sangiovese) is a serious effort, revealing cherries, strawberries, and new saddle leather joined by earth, dried herb, and tobacco characteristics. The wine is long and structured, with excellent fruit as well as depth. Drink it over the next 4–5 years.

MORIS FARMS

1999 Avvoltore IGT	D	90
1998 Avvoltore IGT	D	88+
1997 Avvoltore IGT	D	92
1999 Morellino di Scansano	B	88
1997 Morellino di Scansano Riserva	C	91

The two Morellinos di Scansano represent sensational bargains. They might be called the "poor person's Brunello di Montalcino," but they are qualitatively better than that suggests. The 1999 Morellino di Scansano smells like a chocolate espresso. Moreover, there are 2,500 cases exported to the United States. It exhibits lush, black cherry fruit, explosive ripeness, a supple texture, low acidity, and copious quantities of black fruit. Consume it now and over the next 4–5 years. The 1997 Morellino di Scansano Riserva boasts a dense ruby color as well as the telltale opulence of the 1997 vintage. Five hundred cases made it to U.S. shores. Creamy, coffee, blackberry, and cherry notes jump from the glass of this full-bodied, dense, supple-textured, voluptuous wine. A hedonist's dream, it is a fruit bomb with complexity, balance, and richness. Drink it over the next 6–7 years.

The 1999 Avvoltore from the single vineyard called Poggio alla Mozza is made from 75% Sangiovese, 20% Cabernet Sauvignon, and 5% Syrah aged for 18 months in French *barriques*. Yields were a lowly 24 hectoliters per hectare. The wine is deep, backward, medium-to full-bodied, powerful yet elegant, with sweet black currant and cherry fruit intermixed with lead pencil, vanilla, and spice. Displaying superb purity, a beautiful mid-palate, good fleshiness, and a long, pure finish, it is young and unevolved but accessible. Drink it over the next 10–15 years. Moris Farms' 1998 Avvoltore was closed the day I saw it, revealing a dense, dark ruby color, and notes of Provençal herbs mixed with black cherries, earth, and oak. Although medium- to full-bodied, with plenty of power, it was muted and not exhibiting nearly as much character, charm, or hedonistic appeal as its two less expensive siblings. Anticipated maturity: now–2014.

The 1997 Avvoltore, a blend of 20% Cabernet Sauvignon, 75% Sangiovese, and 5% Syrah, was aged for 12 months in French oak casks. Sadly, there were only 200 cases produced, but readers lucky enough to latch onto a bottle or two are in for a spectacular drinking experience. The wine's opaque purple color is followed by a sweet nose of minerals, white truffles, black raspberries, and cherry jam. Massively flavored, with full body, a silky texture, and a touch of spice and tar in the long, convincing finish, it should drink well for at least a decade.

LE MURELLE

1998 Niffo IGT	C	90

One hundred fifty cases of this opaque purple-colored blend of 90% Sangiovese and 10% Cabernet Sauvignon were produced. It exhibits aromas of blackberry and cassis fruit mixed with allspice, cinnamon, and vanilla. Deep and heady, with gorgeous fruit purity, full body, and low acidity, this superrich, lush, concentrated wine should drink well for 7–8 years.

NOTTOLA

1998 Vino Nobile di Montepulciano Vigna del Fattore	C	90
1997 Vino Nobile di Montepulciano Vigna del Fattore	C	92

The 1998 has a beautifully complex, elegant bouquet of cedar, spice box, tobacco, strawberries, and black cherry jam followed by medium body and supple texture, with luscious fruit, superb harmony, and ripe tannin. Nothing is out of balance in this seductive 1998. Drink it over the next 4–7 years. One of the finest Vini Nobili I have ever tasted, the dark ruby/plum-colored 1997 offers a sweet, explosive nose of melted chocolate, cedar, saddle leather, jammy blackberry/cherry fruit, and flowers. The wine offers tremendously dense, concentrated richness, a velvety texture, and low acidity, as well as this historic vintage's telltale high glycerin, opulence, and fruit. Drink this beauty over the next 12–15 years. Given the score vis à vis the cost, this is an exceptional value. Not surprisingly, Riccardo Cotarella is Nottola's oenologist.

OLIVETO

1999 Rosso di Montalcino Il Roccolo	C	90

An outstanding offering, Oliveto's 1999 Rosso di Montalcino Il Roccolo (100% Sangiovese Grosso aged 12 months in a combination of new and one-year-old French oak) exhibits a deep ruby color in addition to a provocative bouquet of sweet blueberry and black currant fruit, lovely ripeness, a balanced, medium-bodied personality, and a long, fruity, ripe, tannic finish. It should drink well for 5–7 years. Oliveto's oenologist is Roberto Cipresso.

PODERE IL PALAZZINO

1999 Chianti Classico Argenina	C	89
1998 Chianti Classico Grosso Sanese	D	91
1999 Chianti Classico La Pieve	C	91
1997 Grosso Sanese	D	88

The hallmark of these wines has always been concentrated intensity married to exceptional elegance in a delineated style. Il Palazzino's new offerings performed remarkably well, and the fact that I rated the 1998 Grosso Sanese higher than the 1997 makes me think that I seriously underrated the 1997 (a better vintage than 1998).

The two 1999 releases are both topflight. The deep ruby-colored 1999 Chianti Classico Argenina reveals an elegant style not dissimilar from that of a top-notch Burgundian Volnay from a producer such as d'Angerville. Sweet floral-infused black cherry/framboise-like aromas are accompanied by rich, medium-bodied flavors, a beautiful texture, considerable finesse, and stunning elegance as well as purity. It should drink well for a decade. The sensational 1999 Chianti Classico La Pieve represents a fabulous bargain for such a complex and multidimensional effort. It offers a gorgeous display of strawberry jam intermixed with nearly overripe cherries, subtle vanilla, and abundant mineral/floral notes. Extraordinary ripeness, tremendous fat and glycerin, and uncanny delineation/focus have resulted in a prodigious Chianti Classico to drink over the next decade. The opaque ruby/purple-colored 1998 Chianti Classico Grosso Sanese does not suffer from the excessively austere, tannic style revealed by many 1998 central Tuscan efforts. It is rich and multilayered, with copious quantities of blackberry and cassis fruit mixed with cherries, licorice, toast, and spice. This dense Chianti will benefit from 1–2 years of cellaring and last for 14–15 years. Bravo!

I expected the 1997 Grosso Sanese to possess more opulence and richness given the vintage, but it comes across like a mid-weight Burgundy with its raspberry and cherry fruit and floral character. New oak makes an appearance in this dark ruby/purple-colored, stylish, graceful, subtle effort. It should drink well for 7–8 years.

FATTORIA PARADISO

1998 Eterno II IGT	D	90
1997 Paterno II IGT	D	91
1999 Saxa Calida IGT	D	92
1997 Saxa Calida IGT	D	93

An impressive quartet from proprietor Paolo Caciorgna, these gorgeous, heavy-duty fruit bombs are atypical for Tuscany. Produced from 100% Sangiovese, the 1998 Eterno II exhibits a striking nose of black fruits, cedar, and spice box aromas. Full-bodied, sexy, and silky-textured, this luscious Italian red deftly balances power and precision with a sense of freshness. Drink this hedonistic 1998 over the next 5–6 years. The inky/black/purple-colored 1999 Saxa Calida, a blend of Cabernet Sauvignon and Merlot, reveals a textbook bouquet of black currants, licorice, melted tar, and new-*barrique* aromas. Extremely full-bodied, low in acidity, and nearly viscous, this chewy, thick, modern-styled red is hard to resist. Importer David Hinkle claims that his clients refer to this wine as "hot sex." Ummm! Enjoy it over the next 7–8 years.

Made from 100% Sangiovese aged in French oak, the 1997 Paterno II exhibits a dense ruby/purple color, flamboyant, smoky, chocolate, espresso, and cherry-driven aromas and flavors, a voluptuous, beautifully rendered texture, fine purity, superb, jammy ripeness, and a dense, chewy, full-bodied finish that lasts for nearly 30 seconds. It is an outstanding wine that should drink well for 7–8 years. Even better is the single-vineyard 1997 Saxa Calida (Latin for "hot stones"). There are 300 cases of this Merlot/Cabernet Sauvignon blend aged in French oak. It boasts a dense ruby/purple color as well as big, thick, chewy, mocha, black currant, and kirschlike aromas and flavors, fabulous purity, well-integrated, smoky wood, an unctuous texture, low acidity, and an explosive finish. Already delicious, it promises to evolve for a decade. These are impressive offerings from the historic village of San Gimignano.

FATTORIA DI PETROIO

1999 Chianti Classico	C	90
1998 Chianti Classico Riserva	D	88?

I have enjoyed tasting the 1999 Tuscan wines, including the early-released, big, fruity Rossos di Montalcino and the first Chiantis to hit these shores. There are 4,000 cases of the 1999 Chianti Classico, an elegant, dark ruby/purple-colored Chianti with excellent sweet raspberry and cherry fruit presented in a pure style. Saddle leather, underbrush, and Provençal herb characteristics are present, but this wine is dominated by its fruit, purity, and symmetry. Medium-bodied and luscious, it will drink well for 2–3 years. The 1998 vintage produced more austere wines, except for the coastal areas, particularly Bolgheri. The densely-colored 1998 Chianti Classico Riserva possesses earthy, smoky, charcoal, meat, and truffle-like notes along with dark red fruits. Medium-bodied, well balanced, serious, tannic, and broodingly backward, this wine has tannins that will never fully melt away. Consume it over the next 7–10 years.

FATTORIA PETROLO

1999 Galatrona IGT	E	95
1997 Galatrona IGT	D	94
1999 Terre di Galatrona IGT	C	88
1998 Torrione IGT	D	89
1997 Torrione IGT	D	91

This 77-acre estate has turned out five interesting red wines. The 100% Sangiovese, *barrique*-aged 1998 Torrione avoids some of the vintage's austerity as well as its tough tannin. Unlike many 1998s, it is soft with sweet cherry, saddle leather, and damp soil aromas. Stylish, elegant, rich, and seamless, it will drink well for 6–7 years. The extremely concentrated, massive, full-bodied 1999 Galatrona takes Merlot to the limits of ripeness and intensity. This is "extreme" Merlot, but wow, what an impressive wine! Made from 100% Merlot aged in 100% new French oak, this opaque purple-colored 1999 exhibits phenomenally ripe notes of jammy blackberry and cherry fruit intermixed with roasted coffee and toast. Unctuously textured and thick, with moderate tannin, this huge, viscous wine needs to settle down, but there is unbelievable upside potential to the raw materials present in the bottle. Anticipated maturity: 2005–2020.

A blend of 70% Sangiovese and 30% Merlot, the dark ruby-colored 1999 Terre di Galatrona offers copious quantities of red and black fruits intermixed with spicy wood, new saddle leather, and earth. It possesses surprising complexity for its price, in addition to medium body, a harmonious palate, and nicely integrated acidity and tannin. It should drink well for 3–4 years. The stunning, opaque purple-colored 1997 Torrione (100% Sangiovese, aged 12–18 months in French barrels) offers a supersweet nose of cherry and strawberry jam intertwined with new saddle leather, spicy oak, tobacco, and cigar box aromas. Full-bodied, rich, and multilayered, with a sweet mid-palate and inner core of concentration, this sumptuous, low-acid, fat Sangiovese will provide opulent drinking for a decade. Absolutely awesome is the 100% Merlot *cuvée*, the 1997 Galatrona. Aged in 100% new oak, it offers additional evidence that outside Pomerol, the world's finest Merlot is produced in Tuscany. An opaque purple color is followed by an explosively rich bouquet of jammy blackberries, chocolate, mocha, and espresso. This full-bodied, thick, unctuously textured effort possesses superb purity, great concentration, and overall symmetry, as well as a finish that lasts for 35+ seconds. The acidity is low, with the wine's tannin largely concealed by the high extract level. Anticipated maturity: now–2015. Very impressive!

PIAGGIA

1997 Carmignano Riserva	D	93
1998 Piaggia Riserva	D	90+

A prodigious Carmignano, this 1997 is made primarily from Sangiovese, with 22% Cabernet Sauvignon and 10% Merlot. It offers spectacular aromatics consisting of cherry jam, chocolate, cedar, spice, and earth. The color is an opaque ruby/purple, and the wine possesses great purity, terrific texture, a rich, fleshy, medium- to full-bodied mouth-feel, and a seamless finish. Drink this opulent effort over the next 5–7 years.

A serious, slightly internationally styled offering, the 1998 Piaggia Riserva exhibits an opaque inky purple color in addition to a sweet blackberry/cassis-scented perfume with hints of new oak and espresso. Layered, massively rich, and full-bodied, with sweet tannin, it possesses considerable potential but needs another 2–3 years to settle down as it still tastes like a barrel sample. It is a very impressive effort from Tuscany's 1998 vintage! Anticipated maturity: 2003–2018.

FATTORIA DI PIAZZANO

1998 Chianti Classico Riserva Rio Camarata	B	89

The 1998 Chianti Classico Riserva Rio Camarata reveals more density along with smoky, leathery notes intermixed with black cherries, earth, and graphite. Medium- to full-bodied and harmonious, it is best consumed over the next 5–7 years.

SALADINI PILASTRI

1997 Rosso Piceno Vigna Monteprandone IGT	C	88+
1997 Rosso Piceno Vigna Piediprato IGT	B	89

The 1997 Rosso Piceno Vigna Piediprato *vino da tavola* (a 50–50 blend of Montepulciano and Sangiovese) exhibits an attractive dark purple color in addition to dense, rich, sweet, supple fruit flavors reminiscent of blackberries, cherry jam, and cassis. Low in acidity, with evidence of toasty oak, this is a fat, hedonistically styled wine to drink over the next 2–4 years. The 1997 Rosso Piceno Vigna Monteprandone *vino da tavola* (100% Montepulciano) sees more new oak, but I am not sure it is better for it. It gives the wine more serious ambitions, but it comes across as monolithic, with imposing tannin. It does have delicious fruit, so perhaps another 6 months or so of aging will give the wine as much character as its sibling. It should drink well for 4–5 years. The consultant for these wines is Roberto Cipresso.

PODERUCCIO

1997 Camigliano IGT	C	88

This unfiltered blend of 40% Cabernet Sauvignon, 50% Sangiovese, and 10% Merlot was aged in a combination of small French *barriques* and larger Slavonian *foudres*. The dark ruby/purple-colored 1997 Camigliano offers sweet chocolate, berry fruit, nicely integrated wood, and notes of underbrush. Soft, round, and velvety-textured, with excellent ripeness and overall balance, it should be drunk over the next 5–7 years.

POGGIO LUNGO

1998 Morellino Riserva	D	90

The debut vintage for a new producer from the up-and-coming appellation of Morellino di Scansano, this deep ruby/purple-colored 1998 exhibits abundant quantities of toasty new oak in addition to impressively ripe red and black currant fruit intermixed with cherry jam. Sweet, rich, and medium- to full-bodied, with a supple texture, it is a delicious offering with a hint of mineral and leather in the background. Drink it over the next 5–6 years.

PODERE POGGIO SCALETTE

1998 Il Carbonaione	E	91
1997 Il Carbonaione	D	91

One of my favorite new wines from Tuscany, this 30-acre estate, owned by Vittorio Fiore and Adriana Assjè, produces wines from a type of Sangiovese called Lamole. The wine is aged in small 350-liter *foudres* for 18 months prior to bottling. Yields are extremely low, averaging approximately 1.2 tons of fruit per acre (about 20 hectoliters per hectare). Every vintage to date has been impressive, and the 1997 Il Carbonaione is a spectacular effort. It may even improve further in the bottle. It is incredibly opulent and expansive, with copious quantities of fruit and glycerin as well as long, concentrated, blackberry and jammy cherry flavors. The tannin is beautifully integrated, the acidity is adequate but low, and the wine is fleshy and hedonistic. It should drink well for a decade.

A brilliant 100% Sangiovese *cuvée* aged in both French and American oak for six months, the 1998 Il Carbonaione (3,300 cases) boasts a deep ruby color in addition to a sweet nose of black cherries, vanilla, minerals, and tobacco. Medium-bodied, fleshy, and well balanced, with superb purity as well as overall harmony, this classy, concentrated red marries finesse with power. Drink it over the next 5–7 years.

FATTORIA DI POGGIOPIANO

1999 Rosso di Sera IGT	E	92
1998 Rosso di Sera IGT	E	89+
1997 Rosso di Sera IGT	D	93

Poggiopiano's Rosso di Sera (800 cases produced) spends 18 months in wood, of which 50% is new. It is made from extremely low yields of 20 hectoliters per hectare and is bottled unfiltered. Tuscany's well-known consultant Luca d'Attoma assists in the winemaking. The sumptuous 1997 Rosso di Sera is an explosive, full-bodied, magnificently concentrated wine with fabulous intensity. The saturated ruby/purple color is followed by aromas of jammy blackberries, currants, new saddle leather, chocolate, Provençal herbs, and smoky new oak. Ripe, voluptuously textured, and low in acidity, it should drink well for 10–15 years. The 1998 Rosso di Sera reveals leather, chocolate, and ripe berry fruit but possesses less opulence, more structure as well as a backward personality. Unlike the flamboyant 1997, the 1998 should be cellared for another year or two and drunk over the following decade.

The stunning 1999 Rosso di Sera is an unfiltered blend of 90% Sangiovese and 10% Colorino aged 12 months in French oak, of which 50% was new. A serious, opaque purple-colored, backward effort, it exhibits superb purity as well as copious quantities of black fruits intermixed with spice box, tobacco, and leather. Full-bodied, powerful, and structured, it is meant for serious cellaring. While promising, it is not yet ready for prime-time drinking. Anticipated maturity: 2003–2018.

POLIZIANO

1998 Vino Nobile di Montepulciano Vigna dell'Asinone	D	90

Poliziano's ambitious 1998 Vino Nobile di Montepulciano Vigna dell'Asinone is a medium-bodied, stylish effort revealing evidence of *barrique* aging, gorgeous coffee-infused black cherry and berry fruit, a lush, layered texture, sweet tannin (atypical for the vintage), and a spicy, ripe, succulent finish. Enjoy it over the next 7–8 years.

PRATESI

1999 Carmignano	D	92
1997 Carmignano Riserva	D	93
1999 Locorosso IGT	C	89
1998 Locorosso IGT	C	90

This small, 12-acre estate discovered by Italian wine importer Leonardo LoCascio has four impressive offerings, including one of the finest Carmignanos I have ever tasted. The 1998 Locorosso (100% Sangiovese) possesses a dense ruby color in addition to an explosive nose of roasted espresso beans, chocolate, cherry jam, and spice. In the mouth, it is rich, chewy, sexy, and opulently textured. It is a hedonistic mouthful of juicy red selling for a song. Enjoy it over the next 3–4 years. The profound, opaque purple-colored 1997 Carmignano Riserva is a multidimensional, opulently textured, voluptuously rich wine. A blend of 80% Sangiovese and 20% Cabernet Sauvignon, it possesses thrilling levels of extract, a seamless texture, extraordinary purity, and explosive aromatics and flavors. It can be drunk now and over the next decade. Wow!

This impressive quartet also includes the 1999 Locorosso, a 2,000-case *cuvée* of 100% Sangiovese aged in small oak *foudres*. Its dense ruby/purple color is accompanied by a sweet nose of black cherries, strawberry jam, leather, and tobacco. With excellent texture, fleshy, ripe, sweet, chewy flavors, fine purity, and a plump, precocious style, it will drink well for 5–6 years. The stunning, dense purple-colored 1999 Carmignano (a blend of 80% Sangiovese and 20% Cabernet Sauvignon, also aged in small *foudres*) exhibits fabulously ripe blackberry fruit intermixed with licorice, new saddle leather, and spice box. It possesses a layered, succulent texture, a full-bodied, multilayered mid-palate, and a finish that lasts for more than 30 seconds. Outstanding purity, ripeness, concentration, and overall harmony characterize this 1999 made by the brilliant winemaking consultant Stefano Chioccioli.

LE PUPILLE

1997 Morellino di Scansano Poggio Valente	D	90
1997 Saffredi IGT	E	96

One of the best-run estates of Tuscany, proprietor Elisabetta Geppetti, along with wine-maker/oenologist Riccardo Cotarella, has turned out two juicy, impressively concentrated, hedonistic wines. The single-vineyard 1997 Morellino di Scansano Poggio Valente spends time in barrel and is bottled without fining or filtration. This offering could be called a Tuscan Pomerol. Dense, opaque, and purple-colored, this 100% Sangiovese (made from extremely low yields of 2.3 tons of fruit per acre) is medium- to full-bodied with no hard edges. Succulent and velvety-textured, with copious amounts of fruit (black cherries, plums, and cassis), this gorgeously styled, hedonistic, plump wine will provide thrilling drinking. It should evolve nicely for 6–7 years.

Readers may remember the profound review given the 1990 Saffredi *vino da tavola* (it is still in terrific condition). The 1997 Saffredi appears to be equal, if not superior, to the 1990. Made from a blend of 70% Cabernet Sauvignon and the rest Merlot, with a touch of Alicante, it was aged for 18 months in 100% new French oak. It boasts an exquisite toasty, smoky, cassis, floral, and licorice-scented nose that is reminiscent of a hypothetical blend of Châteaux Mouton-Rothschild and Margaux. With fabulous richness, multiple dimensions, and outstanding symmetry, purity, and length, it is a compelling example of what can be achieved from tiny yields (2.2 tons of fruit per acre) as well as impeccable winemaking. Anticipated maturity: now–2020.

QUERCIABELLA

1997 Camartina IGT	E	92
1997 Chianti Classico Riserva	D	89

I have been pleased with this estate's wines in the past (particularly the 1995s), so I was not surprised to see how well these 1997s performed. The medium garnet-colored 1997 Chianti Classico Riserva exhibits a complex nose of smoke, dried berry fruit, truffles, cedar, and smoke. Sweet black cherry fruit intermixed with herb and spice notes are presented in a nicely layered, soft, well-structured format. There are some tannin, adequate acidity, and excellent delineation. Drink it over the next 6–7 years. A superb blend of Sangiovese and Cabernet Sauvignon, the stunning, *barrique*-aged 1997 Camartina offers toasty, smoky new-oak scents as well as a black cherry liqueur–infused aroma. Full-bodied, with low acidity, considerable glycerin, and a multilayered, concentrated, fat, opulent finish, this hedonistic, seductive effort is capable of lasting for a decade.

LA RAMPA DI FUGNANO

1999 Bombereto IGT	D	90
1998 Bombereto IGT	C	89

1997 Bombereto IGT	C	90+
1999 Chianti Colli Senesi Via dei Franchi	B	88
1999 Gisèle IGT	D	94
1998 Gisèle IGT	D	88
1997 Gisèle IGT	D	94

Run by a Swiss couple and situated a few kilometers west of the historic walled village of San Gimignano, La Rampa di Fugnano is quickly propelling itself into Tuscany's top echelon. The interesting red wines are fairly priced for their quality.

Two exceptional efforts from La Rampa di Fugnano include the 1999 Bombereto, a *barrique*-aged 100% Sangiovese, and the extraordinary 1999 Gisèle Merlot. The dense ruby/purple-colored 1999 Bombereto is a seriously endowed offering with abundant quantities of strawberry and black cherry fruit. Half of this *cuvée* is aged in French barrels, of which one-third are new, and the rest in larger *foudres*. This gives the wine good structure but no noticeable toasty notes. This ripe, layered, concentrated, impressive Italian red should drink well for 10–12 years. The blockbuster 1999 Gisèle is an exotic, over-the-top style of Merlot that is reminiscent of the provocative Pomerols produced by Le Pin and Clinet (especially those from the late 1980s). This opaque purple-colored, full-bodied, multilayered, unctuously textured, fabulous wine boasts a fascinating nose of espresso, blackberries, mocha, smoke, and minerals. New oak is noticeable, but this component will ultimately be absorbed by the luxurious wealth of fruit and glycerin. This wine offers profound evidence of my belief that the only place in the world other than Bordeaux where phenomenal Merlot can consistently be grown is Tuscany. Anticipated maturity: 2003–2015.

The 1999 Chianti Colli Senesi Via dei Franchi is a soft, tasty effort with aromas of cherry fruit, leather, and spice. This delicious, gorgeously ripe fruit bomb is the result of extremely ripe Sangiovese. It is 100% tank-aged and bottled early to preserve its freshness and lively fruit character. An outstanding value, it should be consumed over the next 1–2 years. The 1998 Bombereto may not be as spectacular as the 1997, but this single-vineyard, 100% Sangiovese aged in French *barriques* exhibits complex, earthy, strawberry, red currant, and leather characteristics. Elegant for a 1998, with good depth, spicy wood, and a moderately endowed, slightly tannic finish, it should evolve for 10–12 years. The 1998 Gisèle (100% Merlot) is a dark ruby/purple-colored offering made in an international style. While it possesses highly extracted fruit, toasty new oak, smoke, and coffee-tinged berry and cherry fruit, it does not display the personality of the Bombereto or, for that matter, the Chianti Colli Senesi Via dei Franchi. The 1998 Gisèles should drink well for a decade.

The outstanding 1997 Bombereto *vino da tavola* is a 100% Sangiovese that was picked ripe and bottled unfiltered. One-third of it spent time in new French oak. It is more structured and surprisingly tighter than the 1996, even though the vintage produced wines with more significant ripeness and lower acidity. The fruit, glycerin, and richness detonate on the palate. With undeniable promise and massive structure, it has the feel of a Cabernet-based wine. Cellar it for 2–3 years, and consume it over the following 10–12 years. Lastly, the fabulous 1997 Gisèle (100% Merlot aged in new French oak and bottled unfiltered) boasts an opaque purple color as well as a dense, jammy, enormous nose of blackberry liqueur, vanilla, and licorice. Its low acidity and almost over-the-top, hugely extracted, full-bodied style result in a behemoth impression in the mouth. Nevertheless, everything is in alignment, and the wine is exceptionally well balanced for its size and highly extracted style. This terrific Merlot should age effortlessly for 15+ years. Wow!

LA RASINA

1998 Rosso di Montalcino	C	89

A small, low-key estate run by farmers as opposed to aristocrats or millionaires, La Rasina has produced a delicious, dark ruby-colored, fruit-dominated 1998 Rosso di Montalcino. It possesses a jammy, sweet, black cherry and strawberry-scented bouquet. Seductive, round, and delicious, it should be consumed over the next 2–3 years.

E. REICHENBERG

1997 Villa Monte Rico IGT	C	89

Dark plum/ruby-colored, with an intriguing nose of brandy-macerated black cherries, earth, and dried herbs, this opulent, dense, heady, succulently textured wine is delicious. Made from 100% Sangiovese, it is best drunk over the next 5–6 years.

RIECINE

1997 Chianti Classico Riserva	D	88
1997 La Gioia IGT	E	90

I often find the wines from this estate austere and tannic, but the 1997 vintage's exceptional ripeness and sweet, jammy style have given these offerings more charm and early flesh. For example, the dark ruby-colored 1997 Chianti Classico Riserva exhibits abundant quantities of sweet berry and cherry fruit, cedar, balsa wood, and spice scents. Flavorful, with moderate tannin, medium to full body, and excellent to outstanding purity and length, this substantial Chianti can be drunk now or cellared for 10–12 years. The dark ruby/purple-hued 1997 La Gioia (100% Sangiovese) offers intriguing smoky, toasty aromas mixed with jammy red and black fruits. Plump and fat, with low acidity and exceptional richness and symmetry, this large wine offers plenty of muscle, glycerin, and concentration. Approachable already, it promises to evolve and improve for 4–5 years and last for 12–15 years.

RISECCOLI

1999 Saeculum IGT	D	93
1997 Saeculum IGT	D	92

Riseccoli's opaque, purple-colored 1999 Saeculum (a proprietary blend of 60% Sangiovese, 30% Cabernet Sauvignon, and 10% Merlot aged in 100% new French oak) offers spectacular aromas of jammy cherries, strawberry cream, and toasty oak. It is a full-bodied, layered, super-endowed offering with significant potential. There is plenty of glycerin, sweet tannin, and a 45-second finish in this terrific Tuscan red. Drink it over the next 10–15 years.

The 1997 Saeculum is superb. Opaque purple-colored, with a thick, viscous texture, this full-bodied, explosively rich, massive 1997 exhibits huge aromas of black fruits, smoke, charcoal, truffles, and toasty oak. It possesses sweet tannin, fabulous fruit extraction, an immense finish, and tremendous overall balance and purity. Give this spectacular effort 2–3 years to become more delineated, and drink it over the following two decades. Very impressive!

ROCCA DI MONTEGROSSI

1999 Chianti Classico	C	89
1997 Chianti Classico Riserva Vigneto San Marcellino	D	90
1998 Geremia IGT	D	88
1997 Geremia IGT	D	88+

The nearly outstanding, deep garnet/ruby-colored 1999 Chianti Classico boasts a fragrant perfume of leather, soy, strawberry jam, raspberries, and spice. Minerals make an appearance in this attractive, fresh, vibrant, medium-bodied wine. Drink this fruit bomb over the next 3–4 years. The proprietary red, the 1998 Geremia, exhibits a deep ruby/purple color in addition to a dry, medium-weight, tannic style with good texture but a certain toughness and rusticity. Although it reveals some new oak, it is primarily characterized by its black cherry and currant fruit intermixed with leather and earth. Anticipated maturity: 2003–2012.

The outstanding 1997 Chianti Classico Riserva Vigneto San Marcellino displays the vintage's superripe, glycerin-imbued, highly concentrated fruit flavors. Thick, candied, jammy, and hedonistic, it can be drunk over the next 5–7 years. Closed and tannic, yet promising is the 1997 Geremia (a blend of 95% Sangiovese and 5% Merlot). Not a blockbuster like the San Marcellino, it exhibits fine complexity in addition to an elegant mineral, dried herb, cherry, and toast-scented nose as well as flavors. Medium-bodied, moderately tannic, firmly structured, and backward, it requires 2–3 years of cellaring and should age for 10–12 years.

RUFFINO

1997 Cabreo Il Borgo IGT	D	90
1997 Romitorio di Santedame IGT	E	90
1997 Terzo Millennio	E (magnums only)	89

This historic Tuscan estate has fashioned some interesting wines. An outstanding effort, the 1997 Romitorio di Santedame is a blend of Prugnolo Gentile and Colorino aged in French *barriques*. It is a full-bodied, expansive, powerful wine with gorgeous levels of black cherry and cassis fruit, lead pencil, toast, and smoky scents. It reveals the vintage's telltale, lush, opulent texture, excellent purity, and oodles of fruit and glycerin. Drink it over the next 7–10 years. Another limited-production offering is the 1997 Terzo Millennio (20,000 magnums produced). It is a velvety-textured, deep ruby/purple-colored 1997 exhibiting flamboyant characteristics of flashy new oak, black fruits, dried herbs, smoke, and cedar. The wine's low acidity and plush, succulent texture suggest that it can be drunk now as well as over the next decade. The proprietary 1997 Cabreo Il Borgo (an 8,000-case blend of 70% Sangiovese and 30% Cabernet Sauvignon aged 16 months in new French oak) displays the vintage's voluptuous style. A single-vineyard offering first produced in 1982, the high-altitude vineyard results in an elegant personality. The vintage's richness is well displayed in this silky, low-acid, intense, medium- to full-bodied 1997 with copious quantities of red and black fruits infused with abundant quantities of smoky new oak. It can be drunk now, or cellared for a decade. I did a mini-vertical of this wine, and following are my scores: 1996 (78), 1995 (84), 1993 (87), 1988 (87), 1987 (86), 1985 (89).

PODERE SALICUTTI

1999 Rosso di Montalcino	D	88
1997 Rosso di Montalcino	C	91

A sweet cherry-scented effort with spice and tobacco notes in the background, the 1999 Rosso di Montalcino possesses medium body and good fruit as well as spice. Drink it over the next 3–4 years. Given the abundance of excellent, reasonably priced Rossos di Montalcino from the 1999 vintage, this offering appears pricy.

What an amazing 1997 Rosso di Montalcino! The 1997 vintage produced wines of exceptional ripeness and richness, both of which are hallmarks of this prodigious young wine. It is deep ruby/purple-colored, with a stunning nose of blackberries, tar, and truffles. An amazing glycerin content gives the wine a voluptuous texture to go along with its super purity and jammy, ripe flavors. Adequate acidity and tannin provide the framework. Drink it over the next decade.

SAN BIAGIO

1999 Bellaria IGT	C	88
1999 Cabernet Sauvignon Sant'Antimo IGT	C	89+

Two internationally styled offerings, the 1999 Cabernet Sauvignon Sant'Antimo (100% Cabernet Sauvignon) and 1999 Bellaria (a blend of Sangiovese and Cabernet Sauvignon) are muscular, concentrated, *barrique*-aged efforts revealing abundant quantities of new oak, deep ruby/purple colors, medium to full body, moderate tannin, excellent purity, and fine overall balance. The 1999 Bellaria is more muscular and rustic than the 1999 Cabernet Sauvignon, which exhibits that varietal's classic black currant/tobacco combination. Both wines are more sculptured and less Tuscan than San Biagio's other offerings. Nevertheless, they are well worth a look, particularly in view of their reasonable prices. Both wines should drink well for 12–14+ years.

FATTORIA SAN FABIANO

1997 Armaiolo IGT	D	89+

The 1997 Armaiolo, a proprietary blend of equal parts Sangiovese and Cabernet Sauvignon, exhibits an opaque ruby/purple color, as well as aromas of spice box, sweet leather, cigar smoke, and cherry jam. Ripe, full-bodied, moderately tannic, and powerful, this 1997 requires 2–3 more years of cellaring; it should keep for 15 years.

SAN GIUSTO A RENTENNANO

1999 Chianti Classico	C	90
1998 Chianti Classico Riserva	D	88
1997 Chianti Classico Riserva	D	92
1998 Percarlo IGT	D	91+?
1997 Percarlo IGT	E	98
1998 La Ricolma IGT	E	91+
1997 La Ricolma IGT	EE	96

This has been one of my favorite Tuscan producers since I first tasted its wines in the early eighties. In 1999 I had my last bottle of the 1985 Percarlo (100% Sangiovese aged in *barrique*), which remains one of the most sumptuous Tuscany offerings I have ever tasted, with years of life still left. One of Tuscany's blue-chip properties, this estate has an impressive track record of turning out top-notch wines for more than 20 years. In addition to its splendid Chiantis, its proprietary Percarlo (a luxury *cuvée* of 100% Sangiovese) and the new *bambino*, the 100% Merlot *cuvée* called La Ricolma, are cult wines. The newest releases include a sensational bargain, the 1999 Chianti Classico. This vintage has produced superripe, opulently textured, thick, juicy, sexy wines that will prove sensationally popular with consumers. A deep ruby color is followed by a sumptuous effort loaded with jammy black fruit, smoke, earth, and leather aromas as well as flavors. Enjoy this compelling Chianti over the next 4–5 years. I preferred it to the more expensive 1998 Chianti Classico Riserva. The vintage's austerity and high tannin are evident in this complex, herbaceous, medium-bodied Chianti. With notes of saddle leather, black cherry fruit, and asphalt, it reveals excellent texture and a slight austerity in the finish. Drink this well-made 1998 over the next 6–7 years.

The 1998 Percarlo IGT exhibits characteristics of overripe black cherry fruit, toasty new oak, and a touch of volatile acidity. Flamboyant, rich, chewy, and unctuously textured, it possesses abundant quantities of fruit as well as moderate tannin. Give it another 2 years of cellaring and enjoy it over the following 14–15. The limited production, superripe 1998 La Ricolma IGT (100% Merlot aged in 100% new French oak) exhibits huge tannin (not surprising given the vintage) along with equally massive concentration of fruit and extract. It is powerful, dense, and palate-staining. The sweet French oak is well displayed in the aromas of espresso, black cherries, caramel, and smoke. This 1998 needs 2–3 years of cellaring and should last for two decades. My only concern is that the tannin may never be fully absorbed, but only time will tell. Anticipated maturity: 2004–2020.

The spectacular, saturated ruby/purple-colored 1997 Chianti Classico Riserva reveals intense aromas of smoked meats as well as jammy black cherries, raspberries, and overripe plums. Opulent and full-bodied, with extraordinary power, richness, and concentration, this is a decadently intense, rich, voluptuous Chianti that must be tasted to be believed. Drink it over the next 10–15 years.

Is the dense ruby/purple-colored 1997 Percarlo as compelling as the 1985? It may be even more massive than I remember the 1985 tasting in the late 1980s. Enormous in aromas, flavors, and persistence on the palate, it exhibits profound levels of concentration as well as unbelievably dense black currant and blackberry liqueur notes infused with new saddle leather, licorice, truffles, and toasty oak. Enormously thick and viscous, with low acidity and mouthcoating levels of extract, this wine's tannin level is high but largely obscured by the wealth of fruit, glycerin, and extract. It is an amazing accomplishment! Anticipated maturity: now–2020. Another mammoth offering is the black/purple-colored 1997 La Ricolma (100% Merlot aged in 100% new French oak and bottled with virtually no clarification). It is unctuously textured, phenomenally concentrated, and extraordinarily intense, with surreal levels of extract, glycerin, and richness. Its olfactory bombardment begins with scents of melted chocolate, roasted espresso, and oodles of black cherry and blackberry fruit. It is reminiscent of La Mondotte, the ultraconcentrated St.-Emilion, in its thickness and phenomenal richness. However, despite its monstrous size, weight, and constitution, this wine is well delineated and remarkably refreshing to drink, although knocking off a bottle between two people might prove challenging. This sensational effort is a tour de force in winemaking. Anticipated maturity: 2003–2025.

FATTORIA SANTA MARIA DI AMBRA

1997	Casamurli IGT	D	88
1998	Chianti Riserva La Bigattiera	C	88
1997	Gavignano IGT	D	89

A delicious offering, the deep plum/garnet-colored, nicely textured 1998 Chianti Riserva La Bigattiera reveals spicy new oak along with sweet cherry/berry/currant flavors. Dense, chewy, and dry, with well-integrated tannin, wood, and acidity, it will drink well for 5–7 years.

Both of the proprietary reds are excellent but tightly knit wines begging for a few more years of cellaring, particularly the 1997 Gavignano. This *barrique*-aged blend of 60% Sangiovese and 40% Cabernet Sauvignon exhibits a deep ruby/purple color as well as a sweet nose of lead pencil, new saddle leather, black currants, and cherry liqueur. Deep, rich, medium- to full-bodied, well structured, and moderately tannic, it will be at its finest between 2004–2012. The 1997 Casamurli (a blend of Sangiovese and Malavasia Nera with a touch of Merlot) is structured, rich, backward, pure, and in need of another 1–2 years of cellaring. It should evolve nicely for 12–15 years.

LIVIO SASSETTI & FIGLI

1997	Brunello di Montalcino	E	96
1998	Fili di Seta IGT	D	90
1997	Fili di Seta IGT	D	90
1999	Rosso di Montalcino	C	90
1998	Rosso di Montalcino	C	90

I have been purchasing better vintages of Livio Sassetti's wines since 1982, and it remains a favorite. The new efforts are impressive. The 1999 Rosso di Montalcino's incredible perfume soars from the glass, offering up scents of raspberry liqueur, sweet new leather, flowers, earth, and minerals. A glorious, hedonistic turn-on, the wine is elegant, supply textured, and complex. It is one of the finest *rossi* this small artisan producer has made. Enjoy it over the next 5–6 years.

Readers should note that with the 1997 Brunello di Montalcino, the label changed to emphasize the proprietor's name, Livio Sassetti, rather than the estate name, Pertimali. These Brunellos have always been top-notch, but the 1997 is staggering in its aromatic fireworks and concentrated, long, intense flavors. Sumptuous aromas of dried Provençal herbs, roasted meats, soy, spice box, asphalt, truffles, and black fruits linger in the air. Flavors of new saddle leather are added to jammy black fruit characteristics. Opulently textured, full-bodied, and gorgeously pure, this wine creates an olfactory overload. Its low acidity, high glycerin, and huge fruit reserves suggest drinking it now and over the next 12–18 years. *Mamma mia!*

The 1998 Fili di Seta (a *barrique*-aged blend of 60% Sangiovese and 40% Cabernet Sauvignon) is a dark ruby/purple-colored, full-bodied, sweet, luscious offering. Rich and dense, it boasts abundant quantities of spicy new oak as well as fruit, earth, leather, black currants, and tobacco. Despite the addition of Cabernet Sauvignon, it has not lost any of its Tuscan typicity. Consume it over the next 10–15 years.

A gorgeously opulent, sweet, sexy, low-acid Rosso di Montalcino, Sassetti's ripe, fruit-driven 1998 will have many converts. Drink this beauty over the next 4–6 years. The 1997 Fili di Seta *vino da tavola* (75% Sangiovese and 25% Cabernet Sauvignon) offers a flamboyant nose of cedar wood, melted chocolate, underbrush, smoke, and red/black fruits. Medium-bodied, with gorgeous levels of dense, concentrated fruit nicely complemented by subtle new oak, this long, rich, opulently textured wine should be drunk over the next 6–7 years.

SASSOTONDO

1999 San Lorenzo Rosso di Sovana	D	89

This stylish *cuvée* is produced from an indigenous varietal called Ciliegiolo. It offers sweet black cherries and berries in its moderately intense nose, fine purity, medium body, admirable finesse, a supple texture, and a hint of spicy new oak in the finish. Drink it over the next 7–8 years.

MICHELE SATTA

1998 Piastraia IGT	E	90
1997 Piastraia IGT	D	93
1998 Vigna al Cavaliere IGT	E	92
1997 Vigna al Cavaliere IGT	D	91

Satta's two impressive 1998 offerings emerge from Tuscany's coastal area, which enjoyed a greater 1998 vintage than did the interior. The 1998 Piastraia (a blend of equal parts Merlot, Cabernet Sauvignon, Syrah, and Sangiovese aged one year in French oak) exhibits a complex, internationally styled bouquet of black currants, vanilla, smoke, and graphite. Medium-to full-bodied and dense, with supple tannin and a nicely layered mouth-feel, it should drink well for 7–10 years. More complex and distinctive is the 1998 Vigna al Cavaliere, a 100% Sangiovese *cuvée* also aged one year in French oak. A deep ruby/purple color is accompanied by sumptuous aromas of espresso infused with blackberries, licorice, soy, and truffles. This long, layered, multidimensional Tuscan wine is extremely impressive. Why can't California come remotely close to producing Sangiovese of this quality? This beautiful 1998 can be drunk now or cellared for 10–12 years.

This is another up-and-coming Tuscan star, with vineyards planted on the coastline near Bolgheri. Concentrated and made in an opulent, Pomerol-like style is the 1997 Vigna al Cavaliere. About 1,150 cases were produced of this 100% Sangiovese. A dark ruby color is accompanied by a fragrant bouquet of black fruits, smoke, toasty oak, and spice box. The wine is fleshy, luscious, low in acidity, and fat. With tremendous reserves of fruit, and a full-bodied, voluptuous texture, this plump, succulent 1997 lingers on the palate for more than 30 seconds. Drink it over the next 7–10 years. Even better is the riveting 1997 Piastraia, a blend of equal parts Merlot, Sangiovese, Syrah, and Cabernet Sauvignon aged in French oak for 14 months. It possesses a thick, dark ruby color, in addition to an explosive nose of red and black fruits, pepper, vanilla, and smoke. Full-bodied and opulent, with even more concentration and flavor dimensions than the 1997 Cavaliere, this is a wine of fabulous fruit intensity, complexity, and overall symmetry. It should drink well for 10–12 years. Bravo!

SCOPETONE

1999 Rosso di Montalcino	C	89

Sign me up for these 1999 Rossos di Montalcino, a great value from Tuscany in what looks to be an extraordinary vintage for Brunello di Montalcino. Scopetone's 1999 Rosso di Montalcino exhibits a Bordeaux-like bouquet of sweet black currants, saddle leather, dried herbs, earth, and spice. Complex and ripe, with gorgeous fruit, elegance, and symmetry, it will drink well for 4–5 years.

FATTORIA SELVAPIANA

1997 Chianti Rufina Riserva	D	90

One of the finest wines I have ever tasted from this producer, this powerful, dark ruby/purple-colored Chianti exhibits copious quantities of smoky, toasty scents intermixed with a Pomerol-like, mocha-infused, black cherry liqueur character. Rich and full-bodied, with a layered texture, decent acidity, superb purity, and a finish that lasts for 30–35 seconds, it should provide handsome drinking for 10–12+ years.

SEMIFONTE

1998 Chianti Classico Riserva	D	88
1998 Di Semifonte IGT	D	90
1997 Di Semifonte IGT	D	90

Semifonte is the property of the same Latini family that owns one of Florence's most famous *trattorie*/steak houses, Il Latini. The impressive 1998 Chianti Classico Riserva (85% Sangiovese and 15% Cabernet Sauvignon) displays more sweetness and depth than some of its harder peers. Offering aromas and flavors of lead pencil, dried herbs, black fruits, new saddle leather, spice, berry fruit, and subtle oak, it is a medium-bodied, smoky, earthy, tannic effort that should drink well for 5–7 years. The supple, elegant 1998 Di Semifonte (a blend of equal parts Sangiovese, Merlot, and Cabernet Sauvignon aged 16 months in French *barriques*) possesses sweet black and red fruits as well as new oak, tobacco, and spice box aromas. Dense, rich, medium- to full-bodied, and long, with attractive levels of glycerin as well as sweet tannin, it will drink well for a decade. These are two well-made offerings.

The 1997 Di Semifonte, a *barrique*-aged blend of 30% Sangiovese, 30% Merlot, and 40% Cabernet Sauvignon aged 15 months in French oak, is outstanding. It possesses impressive intensity, fine opulence, and a fat, chewy, black currant and cherry-flavored mid-palate with admirable purity, a layered texture, and an explosive finish revealing copious quantities of glycerin, fruit, and extract. It is a beautifully made, flashy effort to enjoy over the next decade. It would undoubtedly drink well with one of Il Latini's Florentine steaks.

FATTORIA LE SORGENTI

1998 Scirus IGT	D	88

This *barrique*-aged blend of 70% Cabernet Sauvignon and 30% Merlot exhibits an opaque bluish/purple color, a sweet bouquet of black currants, cherry jam, cedar wood, dried herbs, spice box, and vanilla, medium to full body, excellent flavor density, good purity and harmony, and nicely integrated acidity and tannin. It should drink well for 10–12 years.

TENUTA DEL TERRICCIO

1998 Lupicaia	EE	90
1998 Tassinaia	E	88

The dark ruby-colored 1998 Tassinaia is a blend of Cabernet Sauvignon, Sangiovese, and Merlot aged in French oak for 12 months prior to bottling. Copious quantities of black currant and cherry fruit are followed by medium body, sweet tannin, and plenty of spicy oak. Drink it over the next decade. A blend of Cabernet Sauvignon and Merlot, the 1998 Lupicaia reveals a darker, more saturated ruby/purple color along with a sweet nose of black currants, espresso, and chocolate. Dense, rich, and muscular, it needs an additional 1–3 years of cellaring and should drink well for 12–15 years.

TENUTA DI TRINORO

1999 Palazzi IGT	EE	93
1998 Palazzi IGT	EE	93
1997 Palazzi IGT	E	90?
1998 Tenuta di Trinoro IGT	EE	92
1997 Tenuta di Trinoro IGT	E	91
1999 Trinoro IGT	EE	92+

I continue to be amazed by the high-quality wines produced by proprietor Andrea Franchetti. Self-trained but a good friend of Jean-Luc Thunevin (of Château Valandraud and others) and Peter Sissick (of Pingus), Franchetti has been producing Cabernet Franc–based, Cheval Blanc–like efforts. Prices are steep, but the quality is in the bottle. In 2000, there will be a number of changes as 1999 is the last vintage for his *cuvée* of Palazzi. As a side note, barrel samples of the 2000 Trinoro IGT and his less expensive 2000 Trinoro Cupole di Trinoro were astonishing and clearly the finest wines he has yet produced. If they continue to evolve, they will be mid-90-point efforts when released in July 2002. Readers should keep in mind that these are prodigious offerings that will sell out quickly.

The 1999 Palazzi (800 cases of a blend of 50% Cabernet Franc and 50% Merlot) boasts a dense ruby/purple color in addition to a complex nose of currants, cigar box, plums, and cherry liqueur with a hint of toasty oak in the background. Full-bodied, elegant, and complex, with a savory mid-palate and sweet tannin, it will drink beautifully for 12–14 years. Even better are the 1,300 cases of the 1999 Trinoro, a blend of 70% Cabernet Franc, 20% Merlot, 6% Cabernet Sauvignon, and 4% Petit Verdot. Cropped at yields of 26 hectoliters per hectare, this profound, dark purple-colored offering reveals noteworthy aromas of mocha, black fruits, spice box, and toast. It possesses multiple layers, astounding richness, gorgeous purity, definition, and elegance, medium to full body, and a beautiful texture. Anticipated maturity: now–2015. These wines, in the style of Franchetti's friends Sissick and Thunevin, were not fined, filtered, or stabilized and essentially represent the most honest/authentic essence of their vineyard. They are the wines of a genius.

No expense has been spared in the replanting of this ancient vineyard (dating from 1892) or on the lavish attention given to the wine. Made from extremely low yields of 20 hectoliters per hectare, aged 14 months in 100% new French oak, and bottled without fining or filtration, these wines benefit from a process known as *microbullage*, which aerates the lees without having to rack the wines, thus minimizing damage to the wine's freshness. To date, these have been spectacular efforts with fabulous potential. The Tenuta di Trinoro is a blend of 80% Cabernet Franc, 10% Merlot, and 10% Petit Verdot. The Palazzi is a blend of 50% Cabernet Franc and 50% Merlot (reminiscent of St.-Emilion's famed Cheval Blanc). The 1998 Palazzi (1,000 cases) exhibits an exotic, sweet nose of blackberries and spices, an opulently textured, jammy, ripe style with wonderful sweetness on the attack, copious quantities of glycerin, supple tannin, and a blockbuster, rich finish with tremendous complexity. It should age effortlessly for 10–15 years. Also remarkably complex, the 1998 Tenuta di Trinoro reveals notes of coconut, Asian spices, and generous quantities of black cherry, blackberry, and smoke-infused fruit flavors. The wine is jammy, full-bodied, viscous, and voluptuously textured with extraordinary purity and overall balance. In both wines, the tannin is obscured by the luxurious fruit and high glycerin. The 1998 Tenuta di Trinoro will also drink well for 10–15 years.

The question mark concerning the 1997 Palazzi is because the bottle I tasted, while possessing a saturated purple color and gobs of sweet black cherry and berry fruit backed up by toasty new oak, also had a level of volatile acidity that was at the limit of my tolerance. Volatile acidity can add complexity, and it is certainly one of the hallmarks of some of this century's greatest wines (i.e., the 1947 Pétrus and 1947 Cheval Blanc), but it is surprising to find this much volatile acidity in such a young wine. The 1997 Palazzi possesses loads of glycerin, a thick, chewy texture, and superb fruit. It should evolve nicely for 12–15 years. If the volatile acidity does not become any more exaggerated, this wine will be controversial and thought-provoking, yet undeniably delicious. Less concentrated, the purple-colored 1997 Tenuta di Trinoro *vino da tavola* is cleaner, with pure blackberry and cherry notes nicely complemented by spicy oak. Medium- to full-bodied, with attractive oak, this sweetheart wine should drink well for 10–12 years.

TENUTA DI VALGIANO

1997 Scasso dei Cesari	C	88

This is primarily a Sangiovese-based wine with some Syrah in the blend. It offers an impressively saturated opaque purple color, and attractive black currant, berry, and cherry fruit flavors. Medium- to full-bodied, with the fruit dominating, this excellent, hedonistic wine should be drunk over the next 2–3 years. The consultant for these wines is Roberto Cipresso.

FATTORIA TERRABIANCA

1997 Campaccio IGT	D	91
1997 Campaccio Riserva IGT	E	92
1998 Ceppate IGT	E	93
1997 Ceppate IGT	E	90
1997 Chianti Classico Vigna della Croce Riserva	C	88
1999 Chianti Classico Scassino	C	88
1997 Piano del Cipresso IGT	D	89
1997 Scassino IGT	B	88

This excellent producer has fashioned his finest wines since 1990. All of the above-mentioned offerings merit serious interest. The largest production is the 7,000-case *cuvée* of 1999 Chianti Classico Scassino. This excellent, reasonably priced Chianti was aged in Slovenian oak for 8–9 months prior to bottling. Its dark ruby color is accompanied by aromas of sweet cherry fruit, herbs, earth, and spice. There is a nicely layered mouth-feel, adequate acidity, and a fleshy, concentrated palate. Drink it over the next 5–7 years.

The 100% Sangiovese *cuvée*, the 1997 Piano del Cipresso (3,700 cases) was aged 12 months in French oak. Its dark ruby color is followed by a big, leafy, earthy, underbrush-scented nose with sweet cherry and currant fruit in the background. Medium-bodied, moderately tannic, open-knit, and supple, it is meant to be drunk over the next 4–7 years. One of Terrabianca's finest *cuvées* is Campaccio. The 1997 (a 6,000-case blend of 70% Sangiovese and 30% Cabernet Sauvignon aged one year in primarily French oak) is a complex, deep ruby-colored wine displaying scents of saddle leather, dried Provençal herbs, and subtle toasty oak. It is medium- to full-bodied, with excellent depth, superb purity, and an open-knit, complex, structured personality. Delicious now, it promises to evolve for 7–8 years. The 1997 Campaccio Riserva (a 1,000-case blend of 65% Sangiovese and 35% Cabernet Sauvignon aged 2 years in primarily French oak) ratchets up the concentration level a notch or two, revealing a more expansive, layered palate, a deep ruby/purple color, more noticeable new oak, thicker, juicier flavors, plenty of power, yet admirable elegance, purity, and overall harmony. The tannin is well integrated in this large-scale, concentrated, complex red. Anticipated maturity: now–2015.

The 1998 Ceppate (a blend of 50% Cabernet Sauvignon from the Chianti Classico region and equal parts Cabernet Sauvignon and Merlot from the coastal Maremma region) is terrific, no doubt because the Tuscan coastline enjoyed a far better vintage in 1998 than the inland viticultural regions. The color is a healthy dark ruby/purple, and the bouquet exhibits super fruit (primarily crème de cassis and new oak). Aged 12 months in 100% new oak, of which 70% was French, this youthful wine (1,800 six-packs produced) is full-bodied, ripe, textured, rich, and promising. It should drink well for 12–15 years.

The dark ruby-colored 1997 Chianti Classico Vigna della Croce Riserva is a fruit-driven offering with abundant quantities of sweet strawberry, cherry, and currant fruit mixed with floral, spice, mineral, and wood notes. Round, ripe, and medium- to full-bodied, this delicious Chianti should be consumed over the next 5–7 years. The fat, hedonistic, intense, lavishly wooded 1997 Ceppate (a blend of 75% Cabernet Sauvignon and 25% Merlot aged in both French and American oak) exhibits a dense ruby/purple color, an exotic, flamboyant personality, gorgeous ripeness and richness, and a layered, full-bodied palate impression. The oak is a bit intrusive, but it should become better meshed given the extraction of fruit. This wine will benefit from another year of cellaring and should age well for 10–15 years. The excellent dark ruby/purple-colored 1997 Scassino *vino da tavola* (100% Sangiovese) is less expensive than the previous wines. It should be sought out by readers looking for a very good value. The wine offers a spicy, open-knit aromatic profile with notes of new saddle leather, cherry jam, dried herbs, and smoke. Rich, deep, medium-bodied, and spicy, this is delicious, low-acid Sangiovese without hard tannins. Drink it over the next 7–8 years.

TUA RITA

1999	Giusto di Notri IGT	E	96
1998	Giusto di Notri IGT	E	93
1997	Giusto di Notri IGT	E	90
1999	Perlato del Bosco	D	91
1999	Redigaffi IGT	EE	99
1998	Redigaffi IGT	EE	96
1997	Redigaffi IGT	EE	94

Many of the greatest wines made in central Italy emerge from one of three winemaking consultants, Riccardo Cotarella, Luca d'Attoma, or Stefano Chioccioli, the wine-maker for Tua Rita, a superstar of the coastal Tuscan region known as Bolgheri. As longtime readers know, these wines have received lavish praise in the past, and that continues with the 1999 releases. A new star in Tua Rita's galaxy is the 1999 Perlato del Bosco (1,000+ cases produced), a 100% Sangiovese aged in *barrique* and bottled with neither fining nor filtration. A friend of mine described it best—as a "sex machine." Supercharged, complex notes of espresso, chocolate, and black fruits emerge from the aromatics. Full-bodied, opulent, and voluptuous, this hedonistic turn-on will not make old bones, but for drinking over the next 5–6 years, it will provide an undeniable blast of fun. It is among the most explosively complex, succulent Sangioveses I have ever tasted. Amazing! The more brawny, serious, opaque purple-colored 1999 Giusto di Notri is a *barrique*-aged, unfined, unfiltered blend of 65% Cabernet Sauvignon and 35% Merlot. Its opaque purple color is accompanied by awesome aromas of weedy tobacco, espresso, smoke, chocolate, black currants, and blackberries. Dense, full-bodied, thick, viscous, rich, and pure, it requires another 2–3 years of cellaring and should last for 15+. Sadly, production was a measly 800 cases. The 250-case *cuvée* of 100% Merlot, the 1999 Redigaffi, has an astonishing 36 grams per liter of dry extract, which exceeds most top Pomerols in a great vintage! Unfined and unfiltered, it is as close to perfection as a wine can get. The color is a deep saturated blue/purple. The powerful, pure nose offers smoke, licorice, black cherry, and blackberries. The most structured of this trio, it boasts awesome concentration, a fabulously dense, viscous mid-section, and a finish that lasts for nearly a minute. I'm tempted to say this is the Pétrus of Tuscany, but the only recent vintages of Pétrus that have scored this high have been 1989, 1990, and 1998! This is riveting juice. Anticipated maturity: now–2015.

The spectacular 1998 Giusto di Notri is a 60% Cabernet Sauvignon/40% Merlot blend aged in French oak, of which 50% was new, and bottled unfined and unfiltered. A dense, murky ruby/purple color is followed by aromas of melted Valrhona chocolate, blackberries, smoke, and toast. Rich and full-bodied, with superb concentration, a seamless texture, low acidity, and a 40+-second finish, this huge wine should drink well for a decade.

The 1998 Redigaffi (2,000+ bottles produced) is profound. I do not normally quote dry extract numbers, because taste is more important than numbers. However, I could not help but notice one of the highest measured dry extract numbers I have ever seen in a wine in the 1998 Redigaffi—39 grams per liter! Made from 100% Merlot, aged in 100% new Allier and Troncais French barrels, it is bottled without fining or filtration. An opaque purple-colored, powerful, enormously endowed effort, it offers gorgeous black currant, plum, and blackberry fruit characteristics infused with spice box, chocolate, and vanilla. This harmonious wine oozes with extract and glycerin. Extraordinarily pure and impressive, with copious tannin nearly hidden beneath the wine's superb richness, this beauty should be at its apogee between 2004–2020.

The outstanding 1997 Giusto di Notri (a 60% Cabernet Sauvignon and 40% Merlot blend aged in French oak and bottled with neither fining nor filtration) exhibits a dark ruby/purple color, and excellent aromatics consisting of toasty new oak, lead pencil, black currants, chocolate, and smoke. Layered and rich but backward and unevolved, with copious tannin in the finish, this wine should improve with further cellaring. The low acidity and sweet fruit give it immediate accessibility, but the wine has not yet developed its secondary aromatics. Anticipated maturity: now–2012. The spectacular black/purple-colored 1997 Redigaffi boasts huge, chocolaty, blackberry, smoky nose and flavors, a full-bodied personality oozing with extract and ripe, juicy fruit, sensational length (45+ seconds), and brilliant purity and symmetry. Anticipated maturity: now–2012.

FATTORIA DELL'UCCELLIERA

1997	Brunello di Montalcino	E	94
1998	Rapace IGT	D	90
1999	Rosso di Montalcino	C	88
1998	Rosso di Montalcino	C	88

Fattoria dell'Uccelliera's 1999 Rosso di Montalcino is a herbaceous, creamy-textured, powerful effort displaying user-friendly, soft, lush fruit flavors, low acidity, and surprising levels of glycerin as well as ripeness. It is an excellent, modern-styled *rosso* for drinking over the next 3–4 years. Readers seeking a fruity Rosso di Montalcino should check out Uccelliera's 1998. Although not complex, it is velvety-textured, fleshy, and loaded with ripe, herb-tinged, berry fruit. It should be consumed over the next 2–4 years.

The 1998 Rapace (a blend of 60% Sangiovese, 30% Merlot, and 10% Cabernet Sauvignon) offers an opaque dense ruby/purple color and a gorgeous nose of roasted herbs, black fruits, chocolate, licorice, and espresso. Deep and full-bodied, with power and grace, this is a super-concentrated, velvety-textured effort to consume during its first decade of life.

The spectacular 1997 Brunello di Montalcino is a thrilling, seamless example of Brunello that I hope is indicative of how special this vintage will be. A deep opaque ruby/purple color is atypical for Brunello, but the nose of dried herbs, spice box, fruitcake, red and black fruits, minerals, and earth is stunningly complex. It is full-bodied, with supple tannin, a velvety texture, and a tremendously long finish. It can be drunk now or cellared for 14–15+ years.

VALDICAVA

1999 Rosso di Montalcino	D	90

A strong argument can be made that Valdicava is among the top three or four Brunello di Montalcino producers. I can't wait to taste the 1997s. Certainly the 1999 Rosso di Montalcino is a splendid example of what can be expected from this vintage. Its dark ruby/purple color is accompanied by a black cherry, spicy, tobacco, mineral, earth, and underbrush-scented nose and glycerin-imbued, sweet, jammy, fleshy fruit. Drink this dense, fat, luscious wine over the next 5–8 years. Has anyone made less than a delicious 1999 Rosso di Montalcino?

FATTORIA VALTELLINA

1997 Chianti Classico	C	89
1997 Chianti Classico Riserva	D	90
1997 Convivio IGT	E	91
1997 Merlot Il Duca	EE	92

These impressive offerings from proprietor Christoph Schneider come at a lofty price, but readers looking for dense, powerful, concentrated, muscular reds with considerable upside will appreciate this quartet. The extremely concentrated, dark ruby/purple-colored 1997 Chianti Classico Riserva possesses huge body along with gobs of black cherry fruit infused with licorice, truffle, leather, and earth notes. Dense, mouth-filling, and powerful, this wine has a tannic finish suggesting that 1–2 years of cellaring would be beneficial. This formidable Chianti will age well for 10–15 years. The opaque purple-colored 1997 Convivio (a *barrique*-aged blend of 75% Sangiovese and 25% Cabernet Sauvignon) exhibits abundant quantities of black currant and cherry jam, bay leaf, and toasty new-oak scents in its aromatic fireworks. Layered and massive, with moderately high tannin, this full-bodied, chewy 1997 requires additional time in the cellar. Anticipated maturity: 2003–2016.

The dense purple-colored 1997 Merlot Il Duca (100% Merlot, *barrique*-aged) is succulent, opulent, and explosive, both aromatically and flavor-wise. The vintage's overripeness, high levels of glycerin and alcohol are present in this full-throttle, multidimensional 1997. It already provides considerable pleasure and promises to age well for 15 years. Admittedly, this offering is priced for the rich and famous, but it delivers a boatload of flavor.

The 100% Sangiovese 1997 Chianti Classico offers a dense ruby/purple color as well as a sweet nose of black fruits, licorice, dried herbs, and damp soil. There is superb concentration, terrific fruit purity, and admirable density and opulence, all characteristics of this marvelous vintage. Drink it over the next decade.

VARRAMISTA

1998 Varramista IGT	E	90
1997 Varramista IGT	E	88

I would have rated the 1998 Varramista even higher had it not been for the aggressive new oak. Otherwise, this is an exotic, smoky, blackberry, and bacon fat–scented effort with sweet tannin, complex, full-bodied flavors, and an unctuous style. A blend of 90% Syrah, 5% Sangiovese, and 5% Merlot, its forward, precocious style suggests that consumption over the next 5–6 years is warranted. Made from 95% Syrah and 5% Sangiovese, the supple, smoky, toasty, black currant–scented and –flavored 1997 lacks the profound concentration of France or California's greatest Syrahs, but it possesses a delicious, superficial sweetness, ripeness, and heady perfume. Although not offering the tremendous finish of a great Syrah, it does possess plenty of charm as well as an open-knit, up-front appeal. Drink it over the next 5–6 years.

CARLA BENINI VENTIMIGLIA

1997 Sassotondo San Lorenzo Riserva Sovana	C	90

The outstanding black/purple-colored 1997 Sassotondo San Lorenzo Riserva Sovana was produced from old-vine Ciliegiolo and aged in 100% new oak. It possesses layers of black cherry and blackberry jam–like fruit. Full-bodied and rich, with superb purity, this terrific wine is a result of low yields and old vines. Drink it over the next decade.

IL VESCOVINO

1997 Il Merlotto	D	90

This small estate (just under 10 acres) is located in one of Tuscany's coolest microclimates. Its nearby neighbors include Castello dei Rampolla and Villa Cafaggio. My favorite effort from Il Vescovino is the 1997 Il Merlotto, a blend of 90% Sangiovese and 10% Cabernet Sauvignon aged in two-year-old French barrels. Its opaque ruby/purple color is followed by a sumptuously ripe nose of blackberries, cherry liqueur, and toast. Deep, full-bodied, and rich, with a layered, low-acid, chewy texture and an intense, lightly tannic finish, it can be drunk over the next 10–12 years.

VILLA ARCENO

1998 Arguzzio IGT	D	88
1997 Chianti Classico Riserva	D	89

These wines emerge from the Tuscan estate owned by California's incomparable Jess Jackson. Not surprisingly, both are of high quality. The 1997 Chianti Classico Riserva offers a dark ruby/purple color in addition to a sweet nose of black cherry and *barrique* smells. Nicely textured, medium-bodied, with supple tannin and vibrant acidity, this well-focused, pure, delicious Chianti should drink well for 7–8 years. The luxury-priced 1998 Arguzzio's deep ruby/purple color is followed by sweet aromas of new oak, blackberries, and cherries. The wine is spicy, slightly austere, and complex, displaying notes of saddle leather and black fruits. Consume it over the next 7–8 years.

VILLA CAFAGGIO

1997 Cortaccio IGT	E	96
1997 San Martino IGT	E	90

I have always admired the elegance and sweet raspberry/cherry flavors this producer tends to obtain. I was underwhelmed by its 1997 Chianti Classico Riserva, but there are no problems with the performances of the 100% Sangiovese 1997 San Martino or the 100% Cabernet Sauvignon 1997 Cortaccio. Both are stunning proprietary red wine offerings from the spectacular 1997 vintage. The plum-colored 1997 San Martino exhibits gorgeously thick, juicy aromas of black fruits, cherries, earth, smoke, and dried Provençal herbs. High in glycerin and husky, with ripe fruit, low acidity, sweet tannin, and a long, 35–40-second finish, its precocious, opulent texture and up-front fruit suggest that it will evolve effortlessly for 10–12 years. Impressive! Even more powerful, concentrated, and well endowed is the dark ruby/purple-colored 1997 Cortaccio. Aromas of *sur-maturité* (overripeness, but in a positive sense) emerge from this wine. It also offers notes of espresso beans, chocolate, and jammy cassis/blackberry fruit. It is extraordinarily fat and juicy, with oodles of glycerin and concentrated fruit, full body, silky tannin, and a finish that lasts for 40+ seconds. This is a terrific example of Cortaccio. Drink it over the next 10–15 years.

FATTORIA VILLA LA SELVA

1997 Felciaia IGT	C	89
1997 Selvamaggio IGT	C	91

Fattoria Villa La Selva's wines are fashioned under the guidance of the well-known consulting oenologist Stefano Chioccioli. The 1997 Felciaia (100% Sangiovese aged in an assortment of French and American oak) exhibits a smoky, oaky, earth-scented bouquet with a distinctive international style. Complex in the mouth, revealing elegant black currant and herbaceous flavors, it is a stylish, restrained, soft (no doubt because of the vintage's ripeness) effort to be drunk over the next 7–8 years. The Selvamaggio is a blend of 70% Cabernet Sauvignon and 30% Sangiovese made from extremely low yields and aged in five separate types of oak. The 1997 Selvamaggio boasts a deep ruby/purple color as well as a sweet, ostentatious bouquet of smoked herbs, burning wood fires, jammy black currant and cherry fruit, an opulent texture, terrific fruit purity, and admirable intensity. For its quality, complexity, richness, and aging potential of 10–15 years, it is also a reasonably fine value.

OTHER SIGNIFICANT RED WINES OF ITALY

ABBAZIA DI ROSAZZO (FRIULI–VENEZIA GIULIA)

1995 Pignolo	E	89

This winery is best known for its expressive, light- to medium-bodied, fruit-driven whites that are meant to be drunk within 18 months of the vintage. However, it also produces a very fine red from Pignolo, one of Friuli's indigenous varietals.

The 1995 Pignolo is tannic, but it possesses a wonderful chocolate-covered cherry–scented bouquet, dense, spicy, black fruit characteristics, medium body, and a structured, concentrated personality. It should age nicely for 10 years.

ALLEGRINI (VENETO)

1997 Amarone Classico	E	95
1996 Amarone Classico	C	95
1998 La Grola	B	90
1997 La Grola	C	90
1998 Palazzo della Torre IGT	B	88
1997 Palazzo della Torre IGT	B	90
1996 Palazzo della Torre IGT	B	87
1997 La Poja IGT	E	90
1996 La Poja IGT	E	91
1995 La Poja IGT	E	89
2000 Valpolicella Classico	A	87
1999 Valpolicella Classico	A	86

This estate, which has been on a hot streak for several years, offers three excellent bargain-priced wines—the Valpolicella Classico, Palazzo della Torre, and La Grola—as well as two more expensive luxury *cuvées* (La Poja and the Amarone Classico), which still represent good values in view of their quality. Frustrated with the relaxation of quality controls in Veneto,

Allegrini is another wine-maker who has left the appellation system to redefine local standards. As a consequence, La Grola and La Poja no longer carry Valpolicella designations.

A delicious, fruity, exuberant, zesty Valpolicella Classico, the 2000 offers notes of black cherries intermixed with crushed almonds and dried herbs. It possesses an excellent texture as well as elegant, medium-bodied flavors crammed with fruit and character. No wood is noticeable, the tannin is sweet, and the acidity is unobtrusive. Drink it over the next 1–2 years.

A good value, the 1999 Valpolicella Classico exhibits good berry fruit, notes of almonds, medium body, and light tannin. A delicious lighter-styled red with good purity, it can be drunk with simple pasta dishes or as an apéritif over the next 1–2 years.

The name Valpolicella has been dropped from Allegrini's stunning 1998 La Grola. Made from 70% Corvina, 15% Rondinella, 10% Syrah, and 5% Sangiovese, this 12,000+-case *cuvée* is aged in large wood *foudres* and endures a light filtration prior to bottling. It exhibits a full-bodied, dense, layered character with gobs of berry fruit intertwined with almonds and flowers. Opulent, sexy, and seductive, with low acidity in addition to abundant fat and flesh, this ripe, ostentatiously styled red can be drunk now and over the next 5–7 years. The outstanding dark ruby/purple-colored 1997 La Grola is a fuller-bodied, serious effort. It combines concentration with elegance, a supple texture, impressive levels of black cherry and currant fruit, sweet, subtle wood, and an intriguing underlying mineral note. Supple and rich, it should drink well for 3–5 years.

The Palazzo della Torre is aged in large 2,000- and 8,000-liter Slavonian wood *foudres*. The excellent 1998 Palazzo della Torre is a straightforward, earthy, Pomerol-inspired effort. It displays copious cola and black cherry fruit notes, medium body, low acidity, good lushness, and a fleshy, straightforward finish. Consume it over the next 5–6 years. The outstanding 1997 Palazzo della Torre is a dark ruby/purple-colored wine that is full-bodied, dense, with Rhône-like beef blood and *garrigue* (that blend of earth and dried Provençal herbs) scents intertwined with copious quantities of black cherry and currant fruit. Rich, chewy, and impressive, it should be drunk over the next 8 years. The 1996 Palazzo della Torre displays plenty of cherry and tar flavors with notes of chocolate and grilled herbs in the background. A dark ruby-colored wine with a good texture, medium to full body, and excellent purity and length, this robust Valpolicella should drink well for 2–3 years.

Readers should keep in mind that the grapes for the Amarones are dried for four months prior to being crushed and fermented. The spectacular, opaque purple-colored 1997 Amarone Classico (15.4% alcohol) is from an exceptional vintage for this appellation. It possesses a gorgeous bouquet of graphite, blackberries, plums, cherries, and truffles. Although it reveals some of Amarone's pruny, raisiny, nearly over-the-top characteristics, it is full-bodied, superrich, and concentrated, with striking purity as well as a fabulous perfume. A touch of volatile acidity gives it even more complexity and aromatic uplift. Full, voluptuous, and deep, with huge extract hiding impressive tannin levels, this winemaking tour de force will drink well for 20+ years. The outstanding, dark purple-colored 1996 Amarone Classico offers a knockout nose of wood charcoal intermixed with black truffles, melted asphalt, blackberries, and roast beef. Amazingly rich and full-bodied but not heavy, this chewy, thick, exceptionally pure, harmonious offering should drink well for 10–12+ years. Its low acidity and gorgeously ripe fruit provide immediate accessibility.

La Poja *vino da tavola*, a wine that emerges from the tenderloin hilltop of Allegrini's finest vineyard, displays the winery's belief that great wines can be produced from the indigenous Corvina Veronese grape. Made entirely from this varietal and aged in 100% Taransaud French barrels, La Poja is generally outstanding. The brilliant, young, still undeveloped 1,000-case *cuvée* of 1997 La Poja is derived from a six-acre vineyard situated at a high elevation. Combining power and finesse in a rich, concentrated style, it offers aromas and flavors of minerals, graphite, black currants, cherries, and subtle wood. This dense ruby/purple-colored effort unfolds by increments on the palate, always remaining noble, measured, and stylish. It will benefit from another 1–2 years of cellaring and last for 14–15 years. Built along the lines of the 1990 and 1993 (two superb vintages), the 1996 La Poja is an admirable effort. This dense purple-colored wine is rich and complex, with strong mineral undertones to its blackberry and currant fruit, medium to full body, and plenty of spice. It should continue to evolve for 10–12 years. Very impressive, it is unquestionably one of the finest dry reds I have ever tasted from Veneto. The 1995 La Poja boasts an opaque purple color and full-bodied, concentrated flavors with black raspberry and cherry notes. Powerful and rich, with a velvety texture, good underlying acidity, and moderate tannin, this serious, concentrated, intriguing wine should drink well for 4–7 years.

DE ANGELIS (CAMPANIA)

2000 Lacryma Christi del Vesuvio	B	86

This is a delicious, simple, dry red to drink with prosciutto or salami. Spicy, herb, cherry, currant, and pepper flavors are found in this medium-bodied, easygoing 2000. Consume it over the next 1–2 years.

APOLLONIO (PUGLIA)

2000 Copertino	A	88
1997 Copertino Riserva Divoto	B	89
1998 Primitivo Terragnolo	B	90
1998 Salice Salentino	A	85
1998 Valle Cupa	A	87

Apollonio is typical of the higher-quality producers emerging from southern Italy. Whereas once the wines were thin, astringent, rustic, and fruitless, they are now revolutionary in the sense of their ripeness, purity, supple textures, and concentration. All of them are bottled without filtration. Moreover, they represent very fine values. Apollonio's offerings should definitely be checked out by shrewd consumers.

The 2000 Copertino is a big, robust, full-bodied (14% alcohol), deep ruby/purple-colored effort displaying sweet aromas of jammy black fruits, melted licorice, and asphalt. There is no hint of oak in this fruit-driven, glycerin-filled, fleshy red. Drink it over the next 1–2 years for its exuberance as well as purity. Impressive!

The 1998 Salice Salentino is a modern-styled Salice exhibiting excellent fruit (black raspberries and berries) as well as scorched earth and melted tar. Chewy, rustic, dense, and mouth-filling, with good purity, it should drink well over the next 12 months. The 1998 Valle Cupa, which spends six months in old oak, comes across as more internationally styled, with abundant quantities of blackberry and cherry fruit intermixed with smoke and fennel scents. Full-bodied, ripe, and chewy, this forthright but savory 1998 will drink well for 3–4 years. Apollonio's top effort is the 1998 Primitivo Terragnolo. This opaque purple-colored wine offers up abundant quantities of jammy black cherry and blackberry fruit, truffles, tar, and spice. A full-bodied, luxuriously fruity 1998 with good glycerin, purity, and overall balance, it cuts a broad, rich, concentrated swath across the palate, with no hard edges. Drink it over the next 4–5 years. Interestingly, this wine spent 4–6 months in new oak, which is not discernible because of the wealth of fruit and concentration. Bravo!

The 1997 Copertino Riserva Divoto reveals more finesse and elegance along with sweet black cherry fruit, cedar wood, and spice box characteristics. There are good lushness, a velvety-textured palate, and fine ripeness, purity, and length. Drink it over the next 6–7 years.

ARANO (VENETO)

1997 Amarone	E	91
1997 Valpolicella	C	87

My first taste of this producer's offerings revealed a delicious, expansive, sweet 1997 Valpolicella with good fruit, medium body, and good depth presented in a round, elegant, supple format. Drink this wine over the next several years. The seriously endowed, full-throttle 1997 Amarone (15% alcohol) offers a dark plum/ruby color in addition to a big, earthy nose of asphalt, chocolate, roasted herbs, and black fruits. It saturates the mouth and possesses sweet tannin, gorgeously pure fruit, and none of the raisiny, oxidized characteristics found in old-style Amarones. This 1997 should drink well for two decades.

ANTONIO ARGIOLAS (SARDINIA)

1999 Costera	B	90
1998 Costera	A	89
1999 Korem	D	88+?
1998 Korem	D	88
1997 Korem	C	90
1999 Perdera	A	89
1998 Perdera	A	87
1997 Turriga	D	90
1995 Turriga	D	87
1994 Turriga	D	91

This large winery (494 acres) is fashioning splendid wine values from the island of Sardinia. It did particularly well in 1999, producing a Perdera and a Costera that rank among its finest successes to date. Argiolas also produces two luxury *cuvées*, Turriga and Korem (the debut vintage of which was 1997). They struck me as slightly more internationally styled and possibly not as character-filled as their less expensive siblings.

It is hard to find a better bargain than the Perdera, a blend dominated by the indigenous varietal called Monica. This wine is generally rustic and Rhône-styled. The 1999 Perdera reveals a dark plum color as well as a big, smoky nose of earth, barbecue spices, black cherries, and a touch of white chocolate. It possesses terrific fruit intensity, big, full-bodied flavors, and a supple texture. Drink it over the next 1–2 years. The 1998 Perdera exhibits a deep ruby color that is followed by peppery, kirsch, and berry scents and flavors. Supple, fleshy, and deep, with excellent purity and good spice, this gutsy, Côtes du Rhône–like red tastes of sunshine and ripe fruit. Enjoy it over the next 12 months.

The quality level increases with the Costera—also an excellent value—which is primarily made from the Cannonau grape (believed to be a kissing cousin of Grenache) and aged with a touch of new French oak. The 1999 Costera is dense, chewy, full-bodied, layered, and seamless with sweet kirsch notes intermixed with licorice and vanilla. Drink it over the next 1–2 years. Nearly outstanding, the 1998 Costera is deep ruby-colored, with medium to full body, robust, peppery, black cherry, and raspberry flavors, high glycerin, a sweet, chewy mid-palate, and a dense, dry, powerful finish. This substantial, mouth-filling red can be drunk over the next 2–3 years.

Korem is a proprietary blend of Merlot, Syrah, Carignan, and two local varietals, Cannonau and Bovale Sardo. Aged 12 months in both tank and *barrique* before being bottled unfiltered, it was first produced in 1997. The 1999 Korem is a full-bodied, rich, spicy, layered effort that impacts the palate with high levels of tannin. There are noticeable wood and earth notes in the long finish. It is ambitious, dense, and chewy, but whether it will ever develop the charm found in Argiolas's less expensive wines remains to be seen. The 1998 Korem exhibits earthy, black cherry fruit, roasted herbs, good spice, medium to full body, and fine density. To my taste, it reveals less individuality than the other 1998s of this excellent winery. Drink it over the next 2–3 years. The 1997 Korem is a knockout, opaque ruby/purple-colored wine which possesses a rich, chocolaty, blackberry-scented nose and flavors, fabulous intensity, smoky, hickory, barbecue-like spice notes, low acidity, and a plump, flashy, luscious, full-bodied finish. It should drink well for 4–5 years.

This estate's flagship wine, the Turriga, is a blend of 85% Cannonau and 15% Malvasia Nera, with tiny dollops of Carignano and Bovale Sardo. It is a *barrique*-aged, unfiltered, gorgeous red that is more generally evolved than the Korem, but complex and attractive. In fact, this wine can be outstanding. The 1997 Turriga is aged in 100% new French oak. A serious effort, it boasts a dense ruby/purple color followed by scents of blackberries, cherry liqueur, and toast in its internationally styled bouquet. There are notes of new saddle leather, full body, a concentrated, powerful style, and copious tannin, depth, and structure. Still an infant, it should drink well for 10–12 years. The 1995 Turriga, which does not quite attain the level of previous vintages, is nevertheless very good. It exhibits abundant quantities of toasty, new French oak in its lavishly wooded nose. Competing with the oak are black cherry and berry notes. In the mouth, the wine is medium- to full-bodied, ripe, and internationally styled, with a compressed, dry, tannic finish. Drink it over the next 2–3 years. The 1994 Turriga's dark ruby color is accompanied by a textbook, internationally styled nose of spicy new oak, cedar, chocolate, and black currants. Dense, long, and rich, it has pure fruit and attractive fat, cedary, grilled meat–like flavors. This is an outstanding wine with considerable complexity plus a nicely layered texture and finish. Close to full maturity, it will continue to age for 4–5 years.

BASILISCO (BASILICATA)

1999 Aglianico del Vulture	D	88
1998 Aglianico del Vulture	D	89
1997 Basilisco	D	89

The intriguing, opaque purple-colored 1997 Basilisco possesses a bouquet of lavender, spring flowers, blueberries, and melted asphalt. As it sits in the glass, cigar box aromas emerge. Rich, dense, and full-bodied, with 14.5% alcohol, it may be controversial given its eccentric yet intriguing aromatics.

The two modern-styled Italian reds are produced from Aglianico, a grape that should begin receiving more attention given the level of quality evident in my tastings over the last few years. A serious varietal, it may not provide the complexity of such great international grapes as Pinot Noir, Syrah, Cabernet Sauvignon, Merlot, Cabernet Franc, Tempranillo, and Nebbiolo, but it is comparable to the quality of Sangiovese, Mourvèdre, and Zinfandel. Basilisco's Aglianicos are aged for 12 months in new oak, resulting in serious, dense purple-colored efforts with telltale notes of melted asphalt intermixed with earthy black cherry and currant fruit. While both vintages are similar in style, the 1998 appears to have more texture and volume than the 1999. The aging potential of these two wines is unknown, but I would recommend drinking them during their exuberant youth, over the next 5–6 years.

BOCCADIGABBIA (MARCHE)

1998 Cabernet Sauvignon Akronte	D	88
1997 Cabernet Sauvignon Akronte	D	90
1998 Rosso Piceno Saltapicchio	C	87
1997 Rosso Piceno Saltapicchio	C	88

Among the finest wines I have tasted from this region, these modern-styled, proprietary reds are exceptionally well made.

What the internationally styled 1998 Akronte lacks in soul and regional typicity, it makes up for in its blast of black currant fruit intermixed with toasty new oak. Made in a pure, fleshy, concentrated style, it is meant to be consumed over the next 5–6 years. The opaque ruby/purple-colored 1997 Akronte reveals classic Cabernet Sauvignon aromas of cedar and black currants presented in a rich, full-bodied, Bordeaux-like style. It displays low acidity, excellent purity, and the influence of new oak. Drink it over the next decade.

The medium-bodied 1998 Saltapicchio exhibits elegant, smoky, oaky black cherry and currant flavors presented in a moderately endowed, supple style. Tannin as well as intriguing espresso notes are present in the finish. Drink it over the next 2 years. The 1997 Saltapicchio (100% Sangiovese) offers an elegant, cherry, strawberry, and leathery-scented nose, medium body, good spice and ripeness, and a round, open-knit texture. It is meant to be drunk over the next 2–3 years.

BRIGALDARA (VENETO)

1997 Amarone	E	90
1995 Amarone	D	91
1998 Valpolicella Classico	A	86

The light ruby-colored 1998 Valpolicella Classico exhibits scents of sweet strawberry and berry fruit intertwined with smoke and almond extract. Fruity and round, it is ideal for drinking over the next 12 months. A smoky, full-bodied, earthy effort, the dark ruby-colored 1997 Amarone offers up scents of animal fur, melted tar, and ripe plum, prune, and black cherries. Drink this dense, chewy, heady Amarone over the next 10–15 years. More serious is the big, bold, southern Rhône–like 1995 Amarone. Full-bodied, dense, and chewy, with notes of melted asphalt and earthy, animal-tinged blackberry and cherry fruit, this is a concentrated, lusty effort. There are no hard edges in this impressively built, smoky, earthy Amarone. Drink it over the next 10 years.

TOMMASO BUSSOLA (VENETO)

1997 Amarone TB	E	92
1997 Amarone Vigneto Alto TB	EE	96
1995 Amarone Vigneto Alto TB	E	92
1997 Recioto della Valpolicella TB	E	98
1997 Valpolicella Classico TB	C	91
1995 Valpolicella Classico TB	C	88

The young, self-taught Tommaso Bussola, unquestionably one of the region's up-and-coming superstars, continues to fashion some of the finest wines of Veneto, a region enjoying the same kind of renaissance that occurred in Tuscany and Piedmont a decade ago. This young producer is making an effort to compete with some of Veneto's most serious wine-makers (i.e., Giuseppe Quintarelli and Dal Forno Romano). Bussola's wines are beautifully intense, with gorgeous purity and powerful ripe fruit flavors, yet a freshness and harmony that make them stand out. Readers should note that Tommaso Bussolo has two quality levels of wine. His introductory-level offerings have the letters "BG" on the label. I did not taste any of those wines. His top selections all have the letters "TB."

Forgetting the remarkable wines from Dal Forno Romano, it would be hard to find a better Valpolicella than Bussola's 1997 Valpolicella Classico TB. It puts to shame most of the industrial swill that dominates the marketplace. Bussola's 1997 exhibits terrific concentration, a gorgeously voluptuous texture, and plenty of sweet berry fruits intermixed with a touch of marzipan and spice. This seductive, luscious, richly fruity Valpolicella is best consumed over the next 3–4 years. The 1995 Valpolicella Classico TB is in stark contrast to the vast quantities of wine that emerge from this appellation. This is a medium ruby-colored, deliciously ripe, fat offering with gobs of herb-tinged, spicy, black cherry fruit with a touch of balsa wood, tar, and roasted nuts. Drink this medium-bodied, fleshy Valpolicella over the next 1–2 years.

The 1997 Amarone TB is a broad, expansive, muscular, dense, full-bodied, pure effort offering aromas and flavors of melted asphalt, black plums, cherries, and earth. This concentrated Amarone cuts a large swath across the palate. Drink it over the next 10–15 years.

The prodigious 1997 Amarone Vigneto Alto TB is reminiscent of Henri Bonneau's 1990 Châteauneuf-du-Pape Réserve des Céléstins. The lofty 16% alcohol level is barely noticeable. Yields were a minuscule 20 hectoliters per hectare. Sadly, there are only 300 cases of this extraordinary Amarone. It boasts notes of smoke, truffle oil, blackberries, plums, and earthy, concentrated black currant jam. Layered, thick, full-bodied, and dry, with extraordinary purity as well as definition, it is an amazing achievement. While not for everybody, this is a singular, impeccably balanced wine. Anticipated maturity: now–2020. The profound 1995 Amarone Vigneto Alto TB exhibits a dense plum color as well as superb aromatics of melted chocolate, asphalt, and cherry liqueur intermixed with grilled steak and Provençal herb notes. Powerful, thick, full-bodied, muscular, and dry, this intense, layered, superb Amarone is ideal for drinking over the next 10–12 years. It should be paired with appropriately rich dishes or a cheese course.

Lastly, the 1997 Recioto della Valpolicella TB is a fabulously layered, slightly sweet offering with huge levels of glycerin, extract, and fruit. I am not a big fan of Recioto della Valpolicella as it is usually too sweet and heavy, but this example is riveting. Concentrated and pure yet neither overwhelmingly heavy nor cloyingly sweet, it is great stuff. Moreover, it will last for three decades or more.

CA' DEI FRATI (LOMBARDY)

1998 Ronchedone IGT	C	89

The 1998 Ronchedone is a blend of Cabernet Sauvignon, Merlot, Barbera, Sangiovese, Groppello, and Marzemino. Notes of spice, smoke, cedar, and red fruits are presented in an elegant, pure format. There are good density on the palate, a sweet attack, abundant spice and red fruits, and light tannin in the finish. Drink it over the next 3–4 years.

LA CADALORA (TRENTINO–ALTO ADIGE)

1998 Majere IGT	C	88
1997 Majere IGT	C	89
2000 San Valentino	B	85
1999 San Valentino	B	86
1998 San Valentino	B	87
1998 Vignalet Pinot Nero	C	87

This is a fine group of wines emerging from La Cadalora, whose vineyards are located in the lower section of Trentino known as Vallagarina.

The three San Valentinos, which are good bargains, are essentially made of an indigenous grape called Marzemino. These tank-fermented and -aged wines reminiscent of a Beaujolais are meant to be consumed over the near term, within the next 2–3 years. The 2000 San Valentino exhibits tangy cherry fruit, good acidity, and a simple, straightforward style. The 1999 San Valentino boasts an opaque purple color in addition to scents of herbs, earth, and black fruits. Although not complex, it is a fat, mouth-filling, cleanly made red. The 1998 San Valentino is a Beaujolais-styled Italian red with plenty of dried herb, spicy, round, berry/cherry fruit as well as roasted espresso notes. With good fat in addition to a chewy, nicely textured mid-palate and finish, it lacks complexity but offers good flavor density.

The smoky, herb, and cherry-scented 1998 Vignalet Pinot Nero is medium-bodied, pleasant, and best drunk over the next 2–3 years.

With good body, structure, and delineation as well as evidence of *barrique* aging, the 1998 Majere reveals copious quantities of spicy oak, blackberries, and cherry fruit. A blend of 70% Casetta (a local varietal) and 30% Cabernet Sauvignon, it should drink well for 4–5 years. The tightly knit, but impressively endowed, nearly outstanding, opaque ruby/purple-colored 1997 Majere (70% Casetta and 30% Cabernet Sauvignon) is a dense, medium- to full-bodied, concentrated effort with moderate tannin as well as a youthful vigor and exuberance. It does not reveal many secondary nuances, but it should age well for 7–8 years.

ANTONIO CAGGIANO (CAMPANIA)

1999	Salae Domini	D	89
1998	Salae Domini	D	90
1997	Salae Domini	D	90
2000	Taurì	D	88
1998	Taurasi	D	89
1997	Taurasi	D	87

The attractive, medium-weight 2000 Taurì (100% Aglianico) does not reveal the roasted, eccentric characteristics often found in wines from Campania. Its deep ruby color is followed by copious quantities of berry fruit, melted asphalt, spice, and meat. Drink it over the next 2–3 years.

The 100% Aglianico 1998 Taurasi exhibits that varietal's telltale melted asphalt/soil notes along with saddle leather and black fruits. This perfumed, medium-bodied 1998 possesses supple tannin as well as considerable complexity. It should drink well for 5–6 years. The 1997 Taurasi reveals notes of melted road tar, black cherries, chocolate, leather, and spice box. Medium-bodied and husky, with some rusticity, it will drink well for 3–4 years.

An outstanding wine produced from 100% Aglianico, aged in small French oak casks, the Salae Domini usually reveals an international style in its youth, but its southern Italian heritage emerges with some further aging. Notes of earth, leather, pepper, mushrooms, and wood emerge from the 1999 Salae Domini. Dense, medium- to full-bodied, and rustic, it is made in the modern school yet retains some of the region's uncivilized aspects. Drink it over the next 5–6 years. The striking 1998 Salae Domini is a *barrique*-aged 100% Aglianico. Kirsch intermixed with chocolate, pepper, leather, spice, and earth are all present in this multilayered, rich wine produced from extremely young vines. This terrific effort is a reasonably fine value in today's inflated wine market. Drink it over the next 7–8 years. Deep ruby/purple-colored, with medium to full body, the ripe, concentrated 1997 Salae Domini offers abundant quantities of sweet toasty oak intermixed with black fruits and licorice. Deep, ripe, and nicely layered, with low acidity and a fine mid-section and length, it can be drunk now and over the next 4–5 years.

CANTINA DELL'ABBAZIA DI NOVACELLA (TRENTINO–ALTO ADIGE)

1999	Lagrein	D	85
1997	Praepositus Rosso Riserva	D	89

This winery, founded in 1142, boasts that it is the oldest in the world. It produces both whites and reds, the former being meant for near-term consumption—they are best drunk within 12–18 months after the vintage. The soft, round, dark ruby-colored 1999 Lagrein offers copious quantities of berry fruit, earth, and spice. Acidity and tannin are present but unobtrusive. Fresh, lively, and spicy, it is meant to be drunk over the near term. The more serious 1997 Praepositus Rosso Riserva (100% Lagrein) spent time in new oak. It offers toasty vanilla scents intermixed with jammy, ripe blackberry and cherry fruit. Thick, rich, and full-bodied, with admirable depth, this surprising effort is capable of lasting 5–6 years.

CANTINE DEL NOTAIO (BASILICATA)

1999	Aglianico del Vulture La Firma	D	90
1998	Aglianico del Vulture La Firma	D	92
1999	Aglianico del Vulture Il Repertorio	C	86

The blockbuster, super-concentrated, dense ruby/purple-colored 1998 Aglianico del Vulture La Firma is one of the finest Aglianicos I have ever tasted. It admirably displays the potential of this area of southern Italy. Impressively dense and concentrated, with competing aromas of blackberries, cherries, roasted herbs, meats, licorice, and high-quality toasty French oak, this thick, juicy, well-balanced, mouthcoating wine should age nicely for a decade.

The 1999 Aglianico del Vulture Il Repertorio is a soft, fleshy, straightforward, chunky effort with robust, earthy, peppery characteristics, red and black fruits, and dusty tannin. Consume it over the next 3–4 years for its primitive charm. The superior 1999 Aglianico del Vulture La Firma was aged in 50% new oak. It is a modern-styled red that has not lost the typicity of this region of southern Italy. It offers flamboyant aromas of pepper, earth, black fruits, sausage, and vanilla. Ripe, chewy, forceful, and dense, it should drink well for 7–8 years.

IL CARPINO (FRIULI–VENEZIA GIULIA)

1999 Rubrum	C	91

This is the debut release from Il Carpino, which had the foresight to bring in renowned oenologist Roberto Cipresso. It is an immensely impressive effort made from extremely small yields of 12 hectoliters per hectare, which contribute significantly to its intense flavors. After undergoing malolactics and 18 months aging in 100% new French oak, it is bottled unfiltered. The 1999 Rubrum may be the finest Merlot I have tasted from Friuli. This explosive effort must be tasted to be believed. A black/purple color is accompanied by sweet, toasty, black cherry liqueur, mocha, cola, and currant fruit aromas. Full-bodied, moderately tannic, and youthful, it resembles a barrel sample as opposed to a finished wine. A revelation for the appellation, this fabulous Merlot should evolve for 10–15+ years. Bravo!

LA CARRAIA (UMBRIA)

1999 Fobiano IGT	D	90
1998 Fobiano IGT	C	90
1997 Fobiano IGT	C	92
2000 Sangiovese IGT	B	88
1999 Sangiovese IGT	B	87

One of Riccardo Cotarella's Umbrian estates, La Carraia is a source of value-priced Sangiovese. Moreover, the quantities produced ensure large availability as there are about 250,000 bottles of this unfiltered/unfined, 100% Sangiovese, which embarrasses virtually all California Sangioveses selling for two to four times the price. The estate also fashions a Merlot-based wine called Fobiano, which, although it is more expensive than the Sangiovese, is a very fine value.

The 2000 Sangiovese IGT is a richly fruity wine with excellent texture, fine purity, and lively, tart flavors. This deep ruby-colored, medium-bodied offering is meant to be drunk during its first 2–3 years of life. La Carraia's 1999 Sangiovese IGT is dark ruby-colored, with an enticing bouquet of smoke, blackberries, strawberries, and spice, this elegant, soft wine has an attractive, supple-textured mid-palate, and sweet tannin. This medium-bodied, fruit-driven effort possesses complexity, charm, and suppleness. Drink it over the next 1–2 years.

The Fobiano, a blend of Merlot and Cabernet Sauvignon (the proportions varying with each vintage), is aged in new French oak casks and bottled without fining or filtration. Unfortunately, the production is extremely small and rarely exceeds 2,500 cases annually. The exceptional 1999 Fobiano (70% Merlot and 30% Cabernet Sauvignon) exhibits a dense ruby/purple color as well as an intensely perfumed nose of black cherries, mocha, smoke, and earth, deep, medium- to full-bodied flavors, and a nicely layered personality. This beauty should drink well for 7–8 years. The outstanding 1998 Fobiano (70% Merlot and 30% Cabernet Sauvignon) exhibits dense opaque purple color that is accompanied by notes of new saddle leather, blackberry liqueur, smoke, and licorice. An opulently textured wine with medium to full body, a chewy, lush mid-palate, and outstanding purity and ripeness, it can be drunk now as well as over the next 7–8 years. The Fobiano 1997 (90% Merlot and 10% Cabernet Sauvignon) reflects the great ripeness and richness achieved in 1997. The wine's black/purple color is followed by a stunning nose of licorice, smoke, black fruits, and minerals. Amazingly rich, with no hard edges, this sumptuous, silky-textured, full-bodied offering coats the mouth but is neither heavy nor out of balance. Its 40+-second finish is dazzling. Anticipated maturity: now–2015.

CASALE DEL GIGLIO (LAZIO)

1998	Cabernet Sauvignon	D	89
1997	Mater Matuta	D	89
1996	Mater Matuta	D	90
1995	Mater Matuta	D	88
1999	Merlot	C	88
1997	Merlot	C	87
1999	Petit Verdot	C	87

These are all exceptionally well made offerings from a region in central Italy, not far from Rome's international airport. All are *barrique*-aged, 12 months in the case of the Merlot and Petit Verdot and 15–18 months for the Cabernet Sauvignon and Mater Matuta (a blend of 85% Syrah and 15% Petit Verdot). All the wines are technically impressive, possessing dense ruby/purple colors as well as plenty of toasty new oak and sweet tannin. That being said, there is a certain international style to them. Tasting them blind, I would not have the slightest idea whether they were from Italy, Australia, France, or America. Nevertheless, there is a lot to like.

The plum/purple-colored 1999 Petit Verdot offers aromas of cedar, tobacco, underbrush, and new oak. Forceful and concentrated, with moderate levels of tannin, it will undoubtedly become increasingly cedary and herbaceous with age. Consume it over the next 5–8 years.

Readers looking for reasonably good Merlot that won't break the bank should check out Casale del Giglio's Merlots. The 1999 Merlot exhibits a deep ruby color in addition to dense, sweet notes of mocha, berry fruit, and espresso in its soft, fleshy, forward, jammy style. Enjoy it over the next 5–6 years. Dried herbs, mocha, coffee, and berry notes emerge from the dark ruby-colored 1997 Merlot. Soft, with supple tannin, fine richness, and a compact, fruity personality, it should be consumed over the next 12 months.

The opaque purple-colored, smoky, oaky, crème de cassis–scented and –flavored, seriously endowed 1998 Cabernet Sauvignon offers good density, soft tannin, and plenty of appeal. It is a fairly priced Cabernet to enjoy over the next decade.

The intriguing Mater Matuta is a blend of 60% Syrah and 40% Petit Verdot aged 18 months in French oak prior to bottling. The noteworthy, dense purple-colored 1997 Mater Matuta offers blackberries mixed with smoke (from its Syrah component) along with new oak characteristics, which give it an international feel. Overall, it is an excellent red with abundant ripeness, authentic varietal character, and a nicely textured, long, supple finish. Drink this appealing effort over the next 7–8 years. The deep ruby/purple-colored 1996 Mater Matuta reveals more density and complexity as well as medium to full body, fine opulence, and rich, peppery blackberry and cassis fruit intermixed with smoky wood. Not a blockbuster, it is an elegant, complex effort that should drink well for 7–8 years. The dark plum/purple-colored 1995 Mater Matuta exhibits a surprisingly complex, Bordeaux-like nose of cedar wood, black currants, licorice, and tobacco. Rich, spicy, and medium-bodied, it is ideal for drinking over the next 5–6 years.

I CASTEI (VENETO)

1997	Amarone della Valpolicella Campo Casalin	D	(87–89)
1995	Amarone della Valpolicella Campo Casalin	D	91
1997	Rosso Veronese	D	(88–90)
1997	Valpolicella Classico	B	85
1995	Valpolicella Classico Ripassa	C	88

The fresh, lively fruit found in these offerings stood out in my tastings. The 1997 Valpolicella Classico is a straightforward, ruby/plum-colored effort with attractive nut-infused cherry and strawberry fruit. It should be consumed over the next 12 months. The 1997 Rosso Veronese appears to be excellent, possibly outstanding. A dark ruby color is accompanied by copious quantities of smoky blackberry and cherry fruit. This medium- to full-bodied wine reveals evidence of cask aging but is dominated by its earthy, foresty, animal components. That being said, the fruit is extremely fresh, lively, and pure.

The Amarone della Valpolicella Campo Casalin is a single-vineyard selection, aged in both *foudres* and small French casks. The 1997 Amarone della Valpolicella Campo Casalin reveals sweet, ripe, nearly overripe blackberry and cherry fruit with a kirsch characteristic. Notes of truffles, damp forest, asphalt, and rose petals also emerge. Full-bodied, layered, and rich, this example should come close to being outstanding. The 1995 Amarone della Valpolicella Campo Casalin is a powerful, concentrated example of these robust, high-alcohol, heavyweight wines. It possesses a dark ruby/purple color, tremendous intensity, and gorgeous levels of chocolate-infused, truffle-scented black cherry and plum fruit. Full-bodied, heavy, and thick, it is a wine to drink with robust cheese or winter-weight dishes. It should age well for 10–12 years. The 1995 Valpolicella Classico Ripassa (made with the Ripassa technique, where the wine is passed over the pressed grape skins that are used to make Valpolicella's Amarones and Reciotos) is a leathery, dense, complex wine with notes of melted chocolate, creosote, and dense, dried cherry, medium-bodied flavors. It is a robust Valpolicella to drink over the next 1–2 years.

CATALDI MADONNA (ABRUZZO)

1999	Montepulciano d'Abruzzo	B	87
1999	Malandrino	C	88
1998	Malandrino	C	88
1997	Malandrino	C	88
1998	Tonì IGT	D	90
1997	Tonì IGT	D	90
1995	Tonì IGT	D	89

From one of my favorite Montepulciano d'Abruzzo producers, these delicious wines are robust, exuberant, and concentrated, and many readers will find them even better than my ratings suggest. Although not complex, they are loaded with fun and fruit, extremely pure (because of clean, healthy vinification), and well balanced, with fruit-dominated personalities. I highly recommend them, even though my scoring system does not do justice to wines such as these that represent 100% pleasure, yet may not be that complex.

The dark ruby-colored 1999 Montepulciano d'Abruzzo offers telltale aromas of cocoa, red and black currants, with a touch of herbs and cinnamon for additional complexity. In the mouth, it is sexy, ripe, opulent, and fleshy with plenty of fruit as well as a hint of almonds. Consume this pure, fat effort over the next year.

The Malandrinos are blends of Cabernet Sauvignon and the indigenous grape, Montepulciano. The 1999 Malandrino offers luscious red and black currant fruit intermixed with Bing cherry characteristics, a sweet attack, plenty of succulence, medium body, no evidence of wood, and a ripe, luscious finish. Enjoy it over the next 4–5 years. The 1998 Malandrino offers the same delicious, exuberant, fruity characteristics of its peers but is denser, with more ripeness and some of the structure afforded by Cabernet Sauvignon. A deep ruby color is followed by knockout aromatics (particularly if you are a fruit fanatic), excellent purity, and a supple, medium-bodied, lusty finish. Drink it over the next 1–2 years. The opaque ruby/purple-colored 1997 Malandrino reveals thick, juicy, roasted herb, earth, blackberry, and cherry flavors. Dusty tannin is present, but this wine is mouth-filling as well as substantial in weight and size. It should drink well for 1–2 years, but do not expect a great deal of finesse from this concentrated, earthy, full-bodied spice bomb.

The exceptional 1998 Tonì boasts a ruby purple color as well as a gorgeously expressive nose of black fruits, balsa wood, dried herbs, and soil notes. With superb purity, ripe fruit, a lush, layered texture, and a long, seamless finish, it will drink well for 5–6 years. The opaque purple-colored 1997 Tonì is a serious wine. It boasts great fruit, terrific ripeness, a black cherry/blackberry jammy character, medium to full body, wonderful density, but no hardness, angular acidity, or rough tannin. A fruit bomb from central Italy, it can be enjoyed over the next 2–3 years. The 1995 Tonì is a full-bodied, super-concentrated, earthy, tarry, chocolaty, blackberry-scented and -flavored wine with considerable concentration and force. Dense, thick, and juicy, with plenty of personality and soul, it should drink well for 2–3 years.

CEUSO (SICILY)

1998 Vigna Custera	**D**	**90**

An impressive effort from Sicily, this blend of 50% Nero d'Avola, 20% Merlot, and 30% Cabernet Sauvignon boasts a dark ruby/purple color along with a knockout nose of black fruits intermixed with smoke, minerals, and graphite. Displaying only a hint of its 12 months of aging in new French oak, there are no hard edges to this textured, rich, ripe, distinctive 1998. Consume it over the next 7–8 years.

COCCI GRIFONI (MARCHE)

1997 Rosso Piceno Il Grifoni	**D**	**89**
1997 Rosso Piceno Vigna Messieri	**B**	**86**

An excellent value from one of Italy's backwater regions, Cocci Grifoni's 1997 Rosso Piceno Vigna Messieri (a blend of Montepulciano and Sangiovese) offers copious quantities of fruit presented in an elegant, round, medium-bodied, soft, cherry-dominated format. Drink it over the next 1–2 years. The 1997 Rosso Piceno Il Grifoni (a blend of Montepulciano, Sangiovese, and Cabernet Sauvignon) may be outstanding. It offers an opaque ruby/purple color as well as a gorgeously sweet bouquet of black currants, cherry liqueur, fresh almonds, and minerals. Medium- to full-bodied and well made, with sweet tannin, spicy, ripe, concentrated fruit, excellent purity, and a long finish, it should drink well for 5–6 years.

COLLE PICCHIONI (LAZIO)

1998 Vigna del Vassallo	**D**	**90**
1996 Villa del Vassallo	**D**	**92**

The wines of Colle Picchioni taste amazingly similar to topflight St.-Emilions. Produced from a vineyard situated ten miles from Rome, they are blends of Cabernet Franc, Cabernet Sauvignon, and Merlot—could they be the Cheval Blancs of the Adriatic coast?—aged in French oak. The 1998 Vigna del Vassallo boasts a complex bouquet of black currants, toast, licorice, spice box, and tobacco. Rich, full-bodied, and chewy, with superb concentration, great individuality, and undeniable complexity, this is a stunning effort. Drink it over the next 12–15 years. The 1996 Villa del Vassallo, an intriguing blend of 50% Cabernet Franc and the remainder Merlot and Cabernet Sauvignon, is a saturated purple-colored, gloriously fragrant wine with a complex nose of saddle leather, flowers, black currants, and coconuts. It boasts a rich, medium-bodied, superintense attack, as well as a glorious mid-palate and a finish loaded with copious quantities of sweet tannin. Notes of licorice emerge on the palate. This brilliant wine was aged for 24 months in French wood before being bottled following a light filtration. Drink it over the next 7–8 years. Bravo!

COLLI AMERINI (UMBRIA)

1999 Carbio IGT	C	89
1998 Carbio IGT	C	87
1997 Carbio IGT	C	89
1998 Torraccio	C	90
1997 Torraccio	C	90

Winemaking genius Riccardo Cotarella is the guiding force behind this estate's substantial, flavor-filled, reasonably priced reds. Carbio is generally a blend of Sangiovese, Barbera, Merlot, Montepulciano, Canaiolo, and Ciliegiolo that ages seven months in 100% new French oak before being bottled unfined and unfiltered. It is a good value given today's inflated wine pricing. The estate also produces a fine unfined/unfiltered 100% Sangiovese Torraccio, a top-notch choice for readers seeking a quality Sangiovese with complexity as well as depth of flavor.

The 1999 Carbio is a complex, black cherry and berry-scented offering with a style not dissimilar from that of a topflight California Zinfandel. It displays excellent purity, medium body, and a subtle dosage of oak. As the wine sits in the glass, it displays a Burgundy-like character. Drink this lush, serious, plump 1999 during its exuberant youth—over the next 3–4 years. The 1998 Carbio is a dark ruby-colored effort that exhibits a noteworthy bouquet of strawberry jam intermixed with cherries, dried herbs, leather, and toast. Spicy and medium-bodied, with a lush personality, this nicely concentrated, supple-textured wine should drink well for 3–4 years. The highly extracted, well-balanced, soft, leathery 1997 Carbio possesses a dark ruby color and sweet plum, cherry, and black currant notes intermixed with scents of cedar and new saddle leather. Velvety-textured, rich, and exuberant, this tasty wine should be drunk over the next 2–3 years.

The 1998 Torraccio tastes like a premier cru Côtes de Beaune with its emphasis on black cherry and strawberry fruit mixed with floral, new saddle leather, and spicy new-oak notes. Supple, medium- to full-bodied, ripe, and harmonious, this is a beautifully made wine to enjoy over the next 6–7 years. The outstanding 1997 Torraccio boasts a dark ruby color as well as a terrific floral-scented nose with aromas of new saddle leather, strawberry jam, cherries, and spice box. Rich and medium-bodied, with a silky mid-palate and fine length, this is a beautifully knit, elegant red to enjoy over the next 2–3 years.

COOPERATIVA SAN PATRIGNANO TERRE DEL CEDRO
(EMILIA-ROMAGNA)

1999 Sangiovese Avi Riserva	D	91
1998 Sangiovese Avi Riserva	D	87
1997 Sangiovese Avi Riserva	D	88

The story behind Terre del Cedro is a touching one. The proprietor, Vincenzo Muccioli, has dedicated this estate to trying to salvage the lives of drug addicts. There is a 100% Sangiovese vineyard of 112 acres worked by the young men and women who enter this program. They are required to give up drugs and work exclusively for the production of high-quality wine. While Chardonnay, Merlot, and Cabernet Sauvignon have been planted, the wines made under the guidance of consulting oenologist Riccardo Cotarella (who also feels a strong sense of commitment to this operation) are currently made from 100% Sangiovese, aged for 12 months in French oak casks and bottled without fining or filtration. Within this community, Vincenzo Muccioli has established a private vineyard known as San Patrignano, from which he produces a luxury *cuvée* Avi. Unfortunately, availability does not exceed 200 cases, with yields being as low as 15 hectoliters per hectare (i.e., one bottle per three vines).

The 1999 Avi is the finest yet produced. Its dry extract number of 38.5 grams per liter is one of the highest I have seen. My tasting notes said, "the Bryant Family Vineyard of Sangiovese." That probably says it all for anyone who has tasted Bryant Family's marvelous Napa Valley Cabernet Sauvignon. This large-scaled, superdense, concentrated Sangiovese should be tasted by California producers so they can understand just what heights this grape can achieve and how far they are from producing remotely legitimate Sangioveses. Long, concentrated, and filled with notes of grilled herbs intermixed with blackberry and kirschy fruit and a touch of spicy new oak, this opulent, voluptuous offering is a thrill to drink. Anticipated maturity: now–2010. I also enjoyed the 1998 and 1997 Avis. The deep ruby-colored 1998 Avi reveals aromas of black cherry fruit, dried herbs, earth, and spice. Medium-bodied, chewy, and spicy, with a Mediterranean-like personality, it should be consumed over the next 1–2 years. The smoky, meaty, low-acid, dark ruby/purple-colored 1997 Avi possesses more opulence in addition to a heady, ripe, rich, black cherry/plum fruitiness. Like its younger sibling, it is fruit-driven and ideal for near-term consumption—over the next 1–2 years.

COPPO-JULI (PIEDMONT)

1999 Barbera di Monferrato	D	90

Roberto Cipresso is the oenologist responsible for this offering. This big, thick, full-bodied Barbera from Coppo-Juli was produced from extremely low yields of 20 hectoliters per hectare, aged 18 months in new French oak, and bottled unfiltered. It exhibits hints of oak as well as vibrant mineral, strawberry, and cherry aromas in its explosive, ostentatious aromatics and high levels of glycerin and concentration. The wine hits the palate with a dense, concentrated, muscular feel, but the acidity gives uplift as well as delineation. Drink this impressive Barbera over the next 4–5 years.

DAL FORNO ROMANO (VENETO)

1996 Amarone della Valpolicella	EEE	99
1995 Amarone della Valpolicella	EEE	98
1994 Amarone della Valpolicella	EEE	97
1997 Valpolicella	D	93
1996 Valpolicella	EE	94
1995 Valpolicella	EE	91

The Dal Forno family is unquestionably the leading Veneto producer of Valpolicella and Amarone. It is remarkable what proprietors Luigi and Romano Dal Forno have accomplished, given the fact that they took over this estate in 1983 and built a new winery in 1990. In terms of European winemaking experience, they have a short résumé. Their wines, which go from strength to strength, have established new benchmarks for Valpolicella and Amarone, redefining this category—in both price and quality. Regrettably, they are both hard to find and priced in the stratosphere. However, anyone who has tasted a Dal Forno Romano offering realizes that this is the reference point for prodigious Valpolicella and Amarone. They possess off-the-chart levels of complexity, richness, and aging potential, and reveal a style totally unlike anything else produced in the region. If California's famed winemaking/viticultural husband-and-wife team of Helen Turley and John Wetlaufer were to make Valpolicella or Amarone, it would taste like Dal Forno Romano's. Sadly, there are only about 18,000 bottles of the Valpolicella and even less Amarone. Decent quantities are exported, although most stays in Italy to be drunk by the local cognoscenti and in the country's finest restaurants.

For example, the 1997 Valpolicella is the greatest Valpolicella I have ever tasted. An opaque purple color is accompanied by a thick, glycerin-imbued texture with immense concentration, fabulous purity, and copious quantities of smoky, earth-infused blackberry and cherry fruit. This awesome effort must be tasted to be believed. It should drink well for 10 years. The 1996 Valpolicella is amazing. Readers will have to redefine their definition of Valpolicella to understand this blockbuster. The color is a dense purple. The bouquet offers glorious levels of blackberry and cherry fruit intertwined with vanilla, minerals, lead pencil shavings, and spice. The wine is full-bodied and voluptuously textured, with sweet tannin and a seamless finish. It is an enormous yet incredibly symmetrical Valpolicella to drink over the next 2–5 years; it will last for 15–18 years. Though slightly less rich than the 1997, the 1995 Valpolicella is an amazing effort, with an opaque dark ruby color as well as an explosive nose of smoke, earth, jammy berry and blackberry fruit, great richness and purity, full body, and abundant glycerin and intensity. Remarkably, there is little evidence of new oak, even though the wine spent 36 months in barrel before being bottled without filtration. It tips the scales at a whopping 14.5% alcohol, high for Valpolicella. It should drink well for 10 years.

Amarone is an acquired taste, given its size as well as its earthy, tarry characteristics. Certainly Dal Forno Romano's Amarones reach new levels of extract and richness yet are dry, well balanced, and, because of their extravagant richness, able to hide the whopping 16–17% alcohol they routinely possess. The three following wines are the products of a true genius. The virtually perfect 1996 is undoubtedly the finest Amarone della Valpolicella I have ever tasted. Its inky black/purple color is accompanied by extraordinarily pure, graphite-infused, blackberry, plum, mineral, licorice, and espresso flavors. Despite its monumental intensity and richness, this wine is not heavy, somehow managing to conceal its 17.5% alcohol! As compelling an Italian wine as I have ever tasted, it should prove to be unbelievably long-lived. Anticipated maturity: 2004–2030. The opaque purple-colored 1995 Amarone della Valpolicella is nearly perfect. It is reminiscent of super-concentrated blackberry liqueur infused with incense, smoke, and minerals. Full-bodied, dense, and chewy, this huge offering possesses remarkable purity and liveliness for its size and intensity. The spectacular 1994 Amarone della Valpolicella exhibits amazing freshness for a wine of such mass, size, and concentration. It oozes across the palate but never comes close to being heavy. There are amazing quantities of truffles, smoke, black fruits, and licorice present in this exquisite wine. These two last wines should drink well for a minimum of 15–18 years.

DI MAJO NORANTE (MOLISE)

1997	Aglianico Vigneto Contato	A	87
1999	Don Luigi	B	91
1998	Ramitello Rosso	A	86
1997	Ramitello Rosso	A	87
1996	Ramitello Rosso	C	87
2000	San Giorgio	A	88
1999	San Giorgio	A	86

All of these offerings from Di Majo Norante are excellent values, especially since oenologist Riccardo Cotarella has been brought in as a consultant. He has changed the trellising system and lowered vineyard yields, in addition to modifying vinification techniques.

Di Majo Norante's San Giorgio (100% Sangiovese) may be the finest value in pure Sangiovese in the marketplace. There are 15,000 cases of this offering. A great buy, it is an embarrassment to 90% of the California Sangioveses that sell for three to five times the price—and are inferior wines. The deep ruby-colored 2000 San Giorgio offers an expressive perfume of sweet black cherries, new saddle leather, and spice. This fleshy, fruit-driven Sangiovese is a total treat to drink. It will not make old bones, but for consuming over the next 12–18 months, it delivers the goods. The 1999 San Giorgio exhibits a medium ruby color followed by a sweet nose of berry and currant fruit, earth, and dried herbs. This soft, tasty, richly fruity wine can be consumed over the next 12–18 months.

A superb breakthrough for Di Majo Norante, the 1999 Don Luigi is a barrel-fermented and -aged blend of 80% Montepulciano and 20% Tintiua. A monster, opaque purple-colored effort, it reveals a sexy, seductive nose of jammy black fruits combined with smoke, graphite, licorice, and new wood. It is voluptuous, full-bodied, chewy, and loaded with concentrated black fruits. Possessing adequate acidity, ripe tannin, and a multidimensional personality, it represents an amazing achievement for these two varietals. Drink it over the next 7–8 years.

The three following vintages of Ramitello Rosso are blends of Aglianico and Prugnolo, a type of Sangiovese, and are aged in large oak *foudres*. The 1998 Ramitello Rosso reveals some of the rusticity these wines possessed prior to the hiring of Riccardo Cotarella. It possesses chunky, dusty, berry fruit, medium body, and notions of leather and old wood. Drink it over the next year. The dark ruby-colored 1997 Ramitello Rosso offers notes of dried cherries and ripe plums in addition to a fat, lush, concentrated palate. Although not complicated, it displays quantities of fennel and black fruit characteristics, low acidity, and a fleshy texture. Drink this hedonistic effort over the next 12 months, preferably with meat dishes. The medium-bodied 1996 Ramitello Rosso reveals aromas and flavors of cedar, smoked almonds, chocolate, and cherries, a touch of fennel/anise, and a fine finish.

The dark ruby-colored, elegant 1997 Aglianico Vigneto Contato exhibits a supple texture in addition to smoke-infused black cherry and currant fruit intermixed with herb and earth notes. Round and concentrated, with a smooth finish, it should drink well for 1–2 years.

DIESEL FARM (VENETO)

1999 Rosso di Rosso IGT	D	89+

An oddly named Italian winery, Diesel Farm has turned out a fine 1999 Rosso di Rosso (a blend of 70% Merlot and 30% Cabernet Sauvignon). This is a backward, dense, powerful red exhibiting blackberry, cherry, and currant fruit with a touch of new oak. This chewy effort requires 3–4 years of cellaring and should last for 12–15. The highly talented Tuscan oenologist Roberto Cipresso is responsible for this wine.

GIROLAMO DORIGO (FRIULI–VENEZIA GIULIA)

1999 Montsclapade	EE	87
1999 Pignolo di Buttrio	EE	87?
1999 Refosco	E	92+

Not surprisingly, Dorigo's oenologist is the renowned Roberto Cipresso. The undisputed superstar in this trio is among the finest Refoscos I have ever tasted. Dorigo's opaque purple-colored 1999 Refosco smells like 1998 Lafite Rothschild but tastes like a barrel sample of 2000 Mouton-Rothschild—and that's no bull. It offers a gorgeous bouquet of graphite, black currants, plums, smoke, and licorice. This full-bodied effort exhibits more rusticity than a Bordeaux, as well as remarkable palate presence, huge flavors, and a massive, long finish. Everything is present for a splendid evolution—if you can resist its current exuberant, robust charms. There are 500 cases of this superb wine. It was produced from extremely small yields of 15 hectoliters per hectare, enjoyed malolactic in new French oak, and spent 18 months in new barrels before being bottled unfiltered.

Produced from an indigenous grape, the 1999 Pignolo di Buttrio (125 cases) may be Italy's answer to southwest France's brawny, muscular, oversized, excessively tannic Madirans. It boasts an opaque black/purple color as well as enormous concentration (yields were 15 hectoliters per hectare), but the wine is ferociously tannic, backward, and intimidating on the palate. Optimists and those with youth on their side might gamble on this 1999 as it is pure, intense, concentrated, and impressive. However, much of my fondness for it is due to its purity and size as opposed to its ultimate balance and/or drinkability. Nevertheless, it is a terrific effort for this varietal. Lastly, the internationally styled, dense ruby/purple-colored 1999 Montsclapade is a blend of Cabernet Sauvignon, Cabernet Franc, and Merlot aged 18 months in new French oak and bottled unfiltered. This rustic, monolithic offering is too international in style to merit a higher score. Nevertheless, it is well made and better balanced than the Pignolo. Drink it over the next decade.

LE DUE TERRE (FRIULI–VENEZIA GIULIA)

1997 Sacrisassi Rosso IGT	D	90
1996 Sacrisassi Rosso IGT	D	87

These two red wines are blends of Schioppettino and Refosco. Both are highly extracted, *barrique*-aged wines revealing the influence of toasty vanilla/spicy wood from new Taransaud barrels. The dark ruby/purple-colored 1996 Sacrisassi Rosso offers a distinctive nose of chocolate, new oak, and black cherry fruit. The wine possesses good underlying acidity, but the smoky, chocolaty flavors dominate. Drink it over the next 1–2 years. The opaque purple 1997 Sacrisassi Rosso exhibits the vintage's greater ripeness and richness. It saturates the mouth with juicy, nearly unctuously textured black cherry flavors intertwined with smoke and toast. Drink this fat, opulently textured wine over the next 3–4 years. The consultant for these wines is Roberto Cipresso.

FALESCO (UMBRIA/LAZIO)

2000 Merlot	B	90
1999 Merlot	B	92
1998 Merlot	A	90
1999 Montiano	E	95
1998 Montiano	E	94
1997 Montiano	E	95
2000 Vitiano	A	91

Located only fifty miles from Rome is the 360-acre home vineyard of Riccardo Cotarella. His vineyards, which straddle the Umbria/Lazio border, produce some of Italy's finest wines, particularly his spectacular Montiano and his fabulous value-priced wines, Vitiano and Merlot dell'Umbria. No one makes better Merlot (not even France's Michel Rolland) in Italy than Riccardo Cotarella and his Vitiano, which is generally a blend of equal parts of Merlot, Cabernet Sauvignon, and Sangiovese and consistently qualifies as one of the greatest dry red wine bargains in the world. It is aged four months in new French oak and bottled with neither fining nor filtration. Production averages 45,000 cases annually, which ensures a fairly large availability. Also, there is only one bottling, so it is not a situation where various lots appear at different times. Vitiano is really a wine to buy by the case. Drink it before the end of 2003.

The spectacular 2000 Vitiano offers up a sweet nose of blackberries, cassis, licorice, and subtle toast scents. Amazingly concentrated, full-bodied, seamless, and beautifully pure, this spectacular wine will drink well for 3–4 years. Mouth-filling and harmonious, it is a fabulous achievement that must be tasted to be believed. Bravo!

Another remarkable achievement, and also one of the world's greatest red wine values, is the estate's 100% Merlot. This unfined/unfiltered effort aged in barrel is, unfortunately, less widely available than the Vitiano, production being 15,000–25,000 cases annually. The opaque purple-colored 2000 Merlot possesses an opaque purple color as well as a big, thick perfume of chocolate, mocha, blackberries, and cherry liqueur. Medium- to full-bodied and ripe, with low acidity and sweet tannin, this unfined, unfiltered, classy, concentrated red will drink beautifully over the next 4–5 years. The 1999 Merlot boasts an opaque purple color as well as a sumptuous nose redolent of blackberry liqueur, espresso beans, mocha, and smoke. Dense, full-bodied, chewy, and low in acidity, it provides a sumptuous drinking experience.

This remarkably intense, concentrated wine can be drunk now or cellared for 5–6 years. It is one of the greatest wine values I have ever tasted! The 1998 Merlot exhibits an impressively saturated ruby/purple color in addition to rich blackberry/cherry notes interspersed with vanilla, tobacco, and spice. It is medium- to full-bodied and dense, with great fruit purity and a layered texture. Most New World Merlots of this quality level sell for $50 or more a bottle. Drink it over the next 2–3 years.

Lastly, Cotarella's flagship wine, his 100% Merlot called Montiano, is aged in 100% new-oak casks for 12 months and bottled with neither fining nor filtration. In most vintages, this wine could be inserted into a blind tasting with the finest California Merlots and French Pomerols/St.-Emilions without suffering. Annual production averages 2,000 cases. The 1997 was spectacular and probably more opulent and voluptuous than the brilliant 1998 (but that is splitting hairs), while the 1999 is close to perfection. The profound, dense ruby/purple-colored 1999 Montiano offers a smorgasbord of aromas, including melted chocolate, espresso, blackberries, cherries, currants, and smoke. Full-bodied, with terrific purity, a multilayered texture, and surprising freshness for a wine of such depth, it can be drunk young or cellared for 10–15 years. For technicians who care about such things, it has a whopping 37 grams per liter of dry extract! The terrific opaque purple-colored 1998 Montiano exhibits a spectacular bouquet of black cherry liqueur, licorice, and toasty vanilla. The wine explodes on the palate, offering copious quantities of glycerin, cassis, black cherries, and blackberries. As it sits in the glass, aromas and flavors of melted chocolate and toasty oak emerge. The finish lasts for 40+ seconds. This 1998 should drink well for 10–12 years. Bravo! The 1997 Montiano is fabulous. It displays multiple layers that build in the mouth, exploding at the back of the palate. From its opaque purple color, the huge sweet notes of chocolate, smoke, black fruits, and toast satiate the olfactory senses, yet please the mind's intellectual yearnings. Pure and powerful, yet brilliantly knit together with no hard edges and no sense of high alcohol level or heaviness, this sensational wine is one of the finest Merlots made in Italy. Anticipated maturity: now–2014.

FEUDI DI SAN GREGORIO (CAMPANIA)

1999	Pàtrimo	D	90
1998	Rubrato	B	87
1997	Rubrato	B	87
1999	Serpico IGT	D	91
1996	Serpico IGT	D	89
1996	Taurasi	D	85
1995	Taurasi	D	86
1995	Taurasi Montevergine	D	89

This winery has made considerable qualitative progress, and these offerings are the finest I have yet tasted from Feudi di San Gregorio.

Readers should keep an eye out for the 1999 Pàtrimo (1,100 cases). Made from 100% Merlot and cropped at a low 22 hectoliters per hectare, this spectacular wine had not been bottled when I tasted it, but I was assured there would be no filtration prior to bottling. It did not surprise me to learn that the famed Umbrian oenologist Riccardo Cotarella had been brought in as a consultant for this wine. It reveals his signature in its opaque purple color, stunning notes of ripe blackberries, cherries, and full-bodied personality with super extract, high glycerin, sweet tannin, and beautifully integrated, toasty new French oak. This looks to be a terrific example of Merlot from southern Italy. It should drink well for 7–8 years.

The spectacular 1999 Serpico (a blend of 70% Aglianico and 30% Merlot, with a touch of Syrah and Piedirosso) is aged in French oak prior to being bottled without filtration. It is a blockbuster, opaque purple-colored effort offering a sumptuous bouquet of blackberry liqueur intermixed with truffle, licorice, and smoke. Full-bodied, with fabulous concentration, sweet tannin, a sumptuous mid-palate, and a knockout finish, this dazzling 1999 has an unbelievable statistic supporting its level of concentration. Numbers can sometimes add up to nothing, but this wine's level of dry extract measures 40 grams per liter, among the highest I have ever seen in a dry red. Give it another 1–2 years of bottle age, and enjoy it over the following 15–16 years. Bravo! The 1996 Serpico (a blend of 60% Aglianico, 30% Piedirosso, and 10% Sangiovese) displays an opaque ruby color with purple nuances. It is full-bodied and rich, with copious quantities of pepper, chocolate, and cherry jam. If not for the presence of gritty tannin in the finish, this wine may have merited an outstanding score. Perhaps that will dissipate with age as this offering is capable of evolving for 6–7 more years.

Among the red wines, the Rubrato (100% Aglianico) is aged in both steel tanks and large wood *foudres*. The 1998 Rubrato possesses black cherry/blackberry fruit with earth, licorice, and smoke in the background. Rich, medium- to full-bodied, and pure, with a nicely textured mid-palate and finish, it should drink well for 2–3 years. The dark ruby-colored Rubrato 1997 reveals a moderately intense nose of chocolate, black cherries, and spice. It possesses good stuffing, a robust, richly fruity personality, medium body as well as a peppery, spicy finish.

I was not much impressed by the rustic, peppery, raspberry, and tar-scented and -flavored, medium-bodied 1996 Taurasi. While good, it is angular and lacks concentration and harmony. The competent 1995 Taurasi, which was aged in French oak, possesses a dark ruby color, a monolithic personality, medium to full body, and plenty of pepper, spice, berries, and new oak. It should drink well for 1–2 years. One of my favorite reds from Feudi di San Gregorio is the 1995 Taurasi Montevergine. This deep, flavorful wine boasts a dense ruby/purple color as well as a noteworthy bouquet of wood, new saddle leather, vanilla, and blackberry fruit. Peppery, spicy components emerge in the mouth. This full-bodied, dense, rich, forward yet concentrated wine can be drunk over the next 4–5 years, although it will last longer.

LA FIORITA–LAMBORGHINI (UMBRIA)

1999 Campoleone	E	96
1998 Campoleone	E	91
1997 Campoleone	E	97
1999 Trescone	B	87
1998 Trescone	B	84

As you may have guessed, this 79-acre estate is owned by a member of the luxury car manufacturer, and the two *cuvées* it offers are made with the assistance of the famed Umbrian oenologist Riccardo Cotarella. The flagship wine, the Campoleone, is emerging as one of the finest wines of central Italy. It is a blend of Merlot, Cabernet Sauvignon, and Sangiovese produced from a 20-acre plot. Picked at high sugars, vinified dry, and aged 12 months in new French oak, it is bottled with neither fining nor filtration. Production is just under 1,500 cases. Lately, the Lamborghini family has also added a lower-priced offering, Trescone, to its portfolio. This wine is a blend of Sangiovese, Merlot, and Ciliegiolo, and is bottled without filtration. Lamborghini's 1999 Trescone is a richly fruity, soft, seductive red meant to be consumed during its first 3–4 years of life. It exhibits abundant quantities of berry fruit, medium to full body, and an uncomplicated, disarming style. A straightforward blend of Sangiovese, Merlot, and Ciliegiolo, the 1998 Trescone is light-bodied and round, with pleasant raspberry and cherry fruit. Enjoy it over the next several years.

The compelling 1999 Campoleone may be as complex and majestic as the phenomenal 1997. A dense opaque purple color is accompanied by scents of new saddle leather, blackberry and cassis fruit, licorice, roasted meats, and graphite. Full-bodied and sweet, with a fabulous texture, ripe tannin, adequate acidity, and brilliant definition, this is a tour de force in winemaking. It should drink well for 10–15 years. While the 1998 Campoleone (50% Merlot, 30% Cabernet Sauvignon, 20% Sangiovese) is not as perfect as the 1997 (that is due to the vintage more than to a change in winemaking or commitment to quality), it is an impressive, exceptional effort. An opaque purple color is accompanied by knockout aromas of new saddle leather, roasted espresso, chocolate, blackberries, and grilled steak. This rich, multilayered, full-bodied, moderately tannic wine is deep and serious. Cellar it for 1–2 years and consume it over the following 12–15. The 1997 Campoleone (a blend of roughly equal portions of Merlot, Cabernet Sauvignon, and Sangiovese) shows unbelievable concentration combined with uncanny balance and symmetry, as well as a staggering bouquet, flavor depth, and length, making for one of the most extraordinary wine-tasting experiences. The color is a saturated purple. Bursting with black fruits, spice, minerals, and character, this is a prodigious, fabulously intense wine that must be tasted to be believed. Anticipated maturity: now–2020.

FORADORI (TRENTINO)

1999 Granato	E	90+
1998 Granato	E	87
1997 Granato	E	90+
2000 Teroldego Rotaliano	C	87

One of the finest productions of Trentino, Foradori's dense ruby/purple-colored 2000 Teroldego Rotaliano is not complex, but it reveals sweet, earthy, black cherry and currant fruit, a rustic texture, generous roundness, and a chunky, muscular mouth-feel. It is a good country wine to enjoy over the next 5–6 years.

There are 2,500 cases of Granato, which spends 18 months in French oak. This wine possesses more polish and finesse as well as additional concentration and intensity than the Teroldego. The 1999 Granato's opaque purple color is followed by a chewy, black currant, cherry, saddle leather, earth, pepper, and underbrush-scented perfume. This full-bodied, complex, rich, highly extracted Bordeaux-style wine possesses abundant quantities of sweet tannin. Anticipated maturity: 2005–2016. Though it does not have the power, impact, or volume of its older sibling, the 1998 Granato is an intense wine, with a dark ruby/purple color, chocolaty, earthy, black cherry, and herb-tinged aromas and flavors, medium to full body, excellent ripeness, and plenty of guts. It should drink well for 10–12 years. The spectacular 1997 Granato is an enormously concentrated, massive, full-bodied, rustic, huge, chewy offering with abundant quantities of tarry black fruits drenched in toasty oak. Although far from drinkable, it is a highly promising blockbuster. Give it 1–2 years of cellaring; it should keep for 15–18 years.

GALARDI (CAMPANIA)

1999 Terra di Lavoro	E	96
1998 Terra di Lavoro	E	96
1997 Terra di Lavoro	D	95

Sadly, there are only 200+ cases of wine produced from the 5-acre Terra di Lavoro vineyard. Some past vintages have been too rustic (no doubt due to the indigenous grapes used in the blend), but recent vintages show sweet tannin as well as an extraordinary earthy, graphite character that undoubtedly is due to the vineyard's decomposed volcanic soils. If the Aglianico grape is to achieve world fame, it will be with a wine such as this. A blend of 80% Aglianico and 20% Piedirosso, it is aged for 12 months in new French oak and bottled with neither fining nor filtering. Not surprisingly, the winemaking genius behind this operation is Riccardo Cotarella.

The color of the 1999 Terra di Lavoro is an opaque black/purple. The bouquet offers up scents of concentrated black cherries and blackberries intermixed with leather, licorice, lead pencil shavings, and new oak. An unfined, unfiltered effort aged for 12 months in new French oak, this spectacular 1999 is the most harmonious and complete Terra di Lavoro to date. This is compelling juice! Anticipated maturity: now–2018. The profoundly complex, black/purple-colored 1998 Terra di Lavoro boasts wild blackberry/blueberry and mineral scents intertwined with smoke, tobacco, and licorice aromas. The flavors mirror the bouquet. Displaying a wealth of fruit, glycerin, concentration, and body, it is a massive, huge effort with sweet tannin, low acidity, and a spectacular 45+-second finish. This amazing offering is more civilized and less funky than some previous vintages, which have been stunning but clearly individualistic and rustic. Look for the 1998 to drink well for 15+ years. The 1997 Terra di Lavoro is a monster, with extraordinary intensity and richness. It is black/purple in color, and its knockout aromas of tar, jammy black raspberries, licorice, truffles, and smoke are simply intoxicating. It is fabulously concentrated, with terrific glycerin, multiple layers of flavor, and a blockbuster, pure finish that lasts more than 40 seconds. For the lucky few who are able to find a bottle, it will be absolutely amazing! Anticipated maturity: 2003–2020.

MACULAN (VENETO)

1998 Acininobili	EE	95
1997 Acininobili	EE	92
1998 Brentino	A	87
2000 Dindarello	B	87
1999 Dindarello	B	91
1999 Fratta	E	90
1998 Fratta	EE	88
1997 Fratta	EE	89
1999 Torcolato	C	90
1998 Torcolato	C	90

This producer consistently fashions some of Italy's most refreshing, light, zinging, dry whites in addition to that country's most profound sweet wines. The whites are not reviewed here as they must be consumed within a year or so of the vintage. The reds have historically tasted too herbaceous and vegetal, but that problem appears to have been rectified in recent vintages. A blend of 66% Cabernet Sauvignon and 34% Merlot, Maculan's outstanding 1999 Fratta is a dead ringer for a top-class Bordeaux. Made from extremely low yields of 1.5 tons of fruit per acre, it offers copious new oak notes, superb concentration, and high alcohol (14.5%). This boldly styled, full-bodied, concentrated, tannic blockbuster requires 3–5 years of cellaring and should age nicely for 15–16 years. Neither the 1997 nor 1998 Fratta (69% Cabernet Sauvignon and 31% Merlot, aged in new French oak) reveal any of the herbaceous, vegetal characteristics that plagued efforts in the past. Both vintages are similar in quality, although I suspect the 1997 has more opulence. The 1998 has more structure, depth, and complexity. Both are dense ruby/purple-colored, with ripe berry fruit drenched in chocolate and toasty new oak, in addition to fine balance, density, and weight. They are capable of drinking well for 5–6 years.

The 1998 Brentino (a blend of 85% Merlot, 10% Cabernet Sauvignon, and 5% Cabernet Franc, aged in small barrels) offers a spice box, cedar, and tobacco-scented bouquet, a soft, juicy, black and red currant–flavored palate, medium body, light, sweet tannin, and a clean finish. Drink it over the next 2–3 years.

Maculan's real glories remain its splendid sweet wines. At the introductory level, the Dindarellos are made from Moscato grapes that are dried until the January following the harvest and then vinified. The 2000 Dindarello is a richly fruity, straightforward, somewhat simple but delicious offering with moderate sweetness. It should be consumed during its first 1–2 years of life. Readers with a sweet tooth will get a blast from the hedonistic 1999 Dindarello. It is full-bodied, with gorgeous aromas of orange marmalade and tangerine blossoms, superb fruit purity, notes of honey and flowers, glorious levels of fruit, and a long, chewy, moderately sweet finish. This is unquestionably a dessert wine.

The Torcolatos are blends of Vespaiola, Tocai, and Garganega that are aged in one-third new French oak. The 1999 Torcolato is at once complex, intense, and complete. Its light gold color is accompanied by a sweet nose of honeysuckle, orange marmalade, caramel, and new oak. Full-bodied and rich, revealing evidence of botrytis, it should drink well for 7–8 years. The 1998 Torcolato exhibits crème brûlée, honeyed caramel, and apricots in both its aromatics and flavors. Medium- to full-bodied, with admirable zesty acidity, and a moderately sweet, rich finish, it will drink well for 5–8 years.

The top *cuvée* of botrytis-infected sweet wine is Acininobili. One of the greatest sweet wines made in Italy, it can compete with the finest Barsacs and Sauternes. The compelling 1998 Acininobili (made from 85% Vespaiola, 10% Tocai, and 5% Garganega) is an opulent, unctuously textured wine with notes of honeyed grapefruit, Mandarin oranges, overripe pears, and crème caramel presented in a full-bodied, concentrated style. The new oak has been totally absorbed by the wine's concentration and extract. It should drink well for 12–15 years. The 1997 Acininobili boasts enormous honeyed notes as well as underlying mineral characteristics in the sweet, rich, buttery pineapple and caramel aromas and flavors. Acininobili's intensity, richness, and overall refreshing personality make it one of the finest dessert wines produced in Italy. It will drink well for 10–12 years—at the minimum.

MARTILDE (LOMBARDY)

1997 Oltrepò Pavese Barbera La Strega, la Gazza e il Pioppo	D	92
1997 Oltrepò Pavese Bonarda Ghiro Rosso d'Inverno	D	87+
1996 Oltrepò Pavese Bonarda Ghiro Rosso d'Inverno	D	88+
1993 Oltrepò Pavese Pindaro Riserva	C	87

This winery is a source of very good to excellent values in today's overheated wine marketplace. A sensational wine, the black/purple-colored 1997 Oltrepò Pavese Barbera La Strega, la Gazza e il Pioppo is aged for six months in French oak. It is an explosive, huge, amazingly concentrated Barbera that may be over the top for some tasters. The natural alcohol level is 15%, and the wine is extraordinarily thick, unctuously textured, and dense. It is impressive, but most people will require assistance to finish a bottle. Nevertheless, it is a showstopping conversational work of vinous art. Drink it over the next 10–12 years, although it may last even longer.

The Oltrepò Pavese Bonarda Ghiro Rosso d'Inverno is made from extremely old, low-yielding vines. It is generally the best of this estate's portfolio, and certain vintages rank among the biggest and most massive efforts I have tasted from this varietal. The opaque purple 1997 Oltrepò Pavese Rosso d'Inverno Bonarda Ghiro is unevolved and rustic but immense, full-bodied, and chewy, with massive fruit and extract as well as huge levels of tannin and power. It requires 1–2 years of cellaring but should keep for a decade or more. It is probably the finest red wine I tasted from Martilde. The 1996 Oltrepò Pavese Bonarda Ghiro Rosso d'Inverno is the biggest, most massive, powerful wine I have ever tasted from this varietal. The wine has noticeable acidity, high tannin, an opaque purple color, and huge quantities of extract and richness. How complex it will turn out to be is uncertain, but it is a mouth-filling, rustic, gutsy, full-blast country red from Italy that is very distinctive and no doubt capable of lasting for another 6–7 years.

A field blend of 45% Bonarda, 45% Barbera, and 10% Uva Rara, the ruby-colored 1993 Oltrepò Pavese Pindaro Riserva exhibits concentrated, sweet/sour cherry fruit intertwined with almonds, spice, earth, and wood. The wine is round and tasty, but underneath the fruit and extract is sound acidity. Drink it over the next 1–2 years.

ROBERTO MAZZI (VENETO)

1997 Amarone Punta di Villa	D	90
1996 Amarone Punta di Villa	D	92

| 1998 Valpolicella Classico Vigneto Poiega | C | 88 |
| 1997 Valpolicella Classico Vigneto Poiega | B | 89 |

This brilliant Veneto producer has fashioned a delicious, slightly herbaceous sweet cherry, strawberry, and currant-flavored, medium-bodied, zesty 1998 Valpolicella Classico Vigneto Poiega. Reminiscent of a midweight Burgundy, it is ideal for drinking over the next 3–4 years. The terrific 1997 Valpolicella Classico Vigneto Poiega is an excellent value. Dark ruby-colored, with an intense, sweet, strawberry liqueur, new saddle leather, and tobacco-scented bouquet, this medium-bodied, fruit-driven, velvety-textured red possesses enough acidity to provide delineation. Drink it over the next 12–18 months.

The dry, chocolaty, dense, leathery 1997 Amarone Vigneto Punta di Villa is a full-bodied, powerful effort displaying notes of tar, prunes, raisins, and black fruits in its big, earthy aromas and robust, exuberant flavors. This mouth-filling Amarone should age well for 10–15 years. Readers seeking a robust, muscular, powerful wine should check out the dry 1996 Amarone Punta di Villa. A dense plum/garnet color is followed by oversized aromatics offering intense smells of licorice, tar, plums, tobacco, damp earth, and herb-lathered grilled steak notes. Rich, dense, and muscular, with abundant quantities of ripe fruit and a crushed seashell character, this dry, full-bodied wine should be served with intensely flavored dishes or sipped at the end of a meal. It is not sweet, but it has at least 15% alcohol. Drink it over the next 10–12 years.

MIANI (FRIULI–VENEZIA GIULIA)

1997 Merlot	E	92
1997 Ronco Calvari	E	94
1996 Ronco Calvari	D	91
1995 Ronco Calvari	D	87

Kudos to both Miani and consulting oenologist Roberto Cipresso for these extraordinary offerings. The wines of this estate are produced from unbelievably low yields.

The blockbuster 1997 Merlot (aged in 100% new oak) is an astonishing example, but coming from Friuli, it is even more noteworthy. The color is a saturated dark purple. The nose offers an amazing array of jammy black cherry fruit, smoke, berries, and sweet toast. Thick and full-bodied, with a long, nuanced finish, this exuberant, youthful Merlot should be at its peak in 1–2 years and last until 2010.

Miani's 100% Rufosco is called Ronco Calvari. All three following vintages were macerated for nearly a month, and in 1996 and 1997, the wines achieved natural alcohol levels of 14.5%. In essence, they taste more like Syrah than Rufosco. The unctuously thick, black/purple-colored 1997 Ronco Calvari is the most astonishing wine of the trio. It displays the most Syrah-like characteristics (crème de cassis, blackberries, and melted road tar), as well as a thick, unctuous texture and a blockbuster finish. This remarkable effort will be at its finest between now–2020. The spectacular 1996 Ronco Calvari is a massive, thick, full-bodied effort with great symmetry and balance. Sumptuous aromas of blackberries, creosote, and flowers jump from the glass. Although still unevolved, it exhibits considerable potential. Anticipated maturity: now–2012. The 1995 Ronco Calvari, a poor vintage for this area, is a very good wine, with more noticeable tannin than its two siblings but with ripe blackberry fruit intermixed with cherries, dusty earth, and spicy wood aromas. It should be drunk over the next 1–2 years.

SALVATORE MOLETTIERI (CAMPANIA)

1999 Aglianico Irpinia	B	90
1998 Taurasi Vigna Cinque Querce	C	86
1997 Taurasi Vigna Cinque Querce	D	90

The dense ruby/purple-colored 1999 Aglianico Irpinia reveals a distinctive licorice, floral, and black fruit–scented nose with truffles, earth, and spice in the background. Medium- to full-bodied and loaded with character, it is one of a new wave of wines from Campania that showcase how special the Aglianico grape can be. Drink it over the next 5–7 years.

The 1998 Taurasi Vigna Cinque Querce is stern, structured, and foursquare. It reveals an earthy/peppery note in addition to its lovely red and black fruit character. Consume it over the next 2–3 years. The finest Taurasi I have tasted since the 1968 Mastroberardino, the stunning 1997 Taurasi Vigna Cinque Querce offers a dense ruby/purple color in addition to aromas of cherry liqueur intermixed with melted asphalt, truffles, and spice. A touch of earthiness is dominated by the wine's high glycerin level, ripe, concentrated fruit, and full-bodied, unctuous texture. Drink this serious Taurasi over the next 8 years.

MONTEVETRANO (CAMPANIA)

1999 Montevetrano	E	94
1998 Montevetrano	E	92
1997 Montevetrano	E	96

Proprietor Silvia Imparato and her oenologist, Riccardo Cotarella, continue to fashion one of southern Italy's most distinctive wines. Since the debut vintage in 1994, this offering has been a testament to the conservative viticulture of the proprietor as well as the extraordinary winemaking skills of Cotarella. Sadly, this small vineyard of 10 acres produces only 500 cases of a blend of 60% Cabernet Sauvignon, 30% Merlot, and 10% Aglianico. The wines are bottled unfined and unfiltered after spending 12 months in 100% new French oak, and amazingly, the new oak is completely absorbed by the fruit. I love these wines' individualistic style. Each year, regardless of vintage conditions, they offer up compelling amounts of blueberry, blackberry, and black raspberry fruit presented in a distinctive medium- to full-bodied, fruit-driven, complex personality. They also exhibit a touch of minerals and marvelous purity and symmetry, as well as the potential for 10–20 years of evolution. Stylistically, they are reminiscent of an Italian version of the Colgin or Bryant Family Vineyard Cabernet Sauvignon and are generally staggering in their complexity and richness.

The elegant yet singular 1999 Montevetrano boasts a deep ruby/purple color as well as a sweet nose of blueberry pie, cassis, minerals, and violets. Dense, medium- to full-bodied, and harmonious, with a fabulous underlying liquid minerality, it is a distinctive, pure wine to drink now and over the next 15 years. The 1998 Montevetrano is another outstanding success, with elegance allied to power and intensity. Montevetrano's hallmark blackberry and black raspberry component is present, as well as beautiful purity/symmetry and a long, medium- to full-bodied, highly concentrated finish. The 1998 should drink well for 10–12 years. The mild blackberry/vivid blueberry, fabulously fragrant, floral-scented nose of the 1997 Montevetrano jumps from the glass. Opaque purple-colored, with a layered, naturally textured feel, this full-bodied, spectacularly concentrated, multidimensional wine must be tasted to be believed. A prodigious effort, it may be the finest Montevetrano yet made—which is saying something, given how spectacular other vintages have been. Anticipated maturity: 2004–2020.

MONTI (ABRUZZO)

2000 Montepulciano d'Abruzzo Pignotto	C	94

Undeniably the greatest Montepulciano d'Abruzzo I have ever tasted, this spectacular 15,000-bottle *cuvée* made by famed Umbrian oenologist Riccardo Cotarella must be tasted to be believed. It is a superb value and a revelation for the region. Cotarella's magic touch has produced a wine from extremely low yields with amazingly high concentration levels (37 grams per liter of dry extract!). It was bottled unfiltered after aging in barrel. The wine hides its 15.1% alcohol level with grace as there is no hotness given its super wealth of fruit and extract. Full-bodied and explosive, with terrific richness as well as a knockout nose of licorice, flowers, blackberries, and cassis, this pure, beautifully textured 2000 is a tour de force in winemaking. Don't miss it! This wine is best drunk during its exuberant youth, so early consumption (7–8 years) is recommended.

MORGANTE (SICILY)

1999 Don Antonio	C	92
1998 Don Antonio	C	89
1999 Nero d'Avola	A	88
1998 Nero d'Avola	C	86

This winery is making a breakthrough with Sicily's indigenous Nero d'Avola grape. Not surprisingly, their consultant for recent vintages has been the renowned Umbrian oenologist Riccardo Cotarella. His Midas touch has introduced more texture, fat, and flesh into the wines, as well as sweeter tannin.

The 1999 Nero d'Avola's deep purple color is accompanied by a sweet nose of blackberry and licorice-infused fruit, with plenty of fat and supple tannin in the lush, concentrated finish. It represents a super value in big, mouth-filling, robust dry reds. Drink it over the next 1–2 years. The 1998 Nero d'Avola reveals a Burgundy-like softness in addition to plenty of spicy, sour cherry notes in its elegant bouquet, medium body, and round, attractive, subtle flavors. It should be drunk over the next 12–18 months.

The Don Antonio *cuvées* are entirely made from Nero d'Avola. They undergo malolactics and age in 100% new French oak, and are bottled without filtration. They are more expensive than the standard *cuvées*. The finest wine I have ever tasted from the Nero d'Avola grape is Morgante's 1999 Don Antonio. This exquisite effort boasts an opaque purple/blue color as well as an extraordinary bouquet of creamy new oak intertwined with blackberry liqueur, flowers, and cassis. This ripe, full-bodied beauty possesses great intensity, explosive richness, and a finish that lasts for more than 35 seconds. This is a revolutionary example of a varietal indigenous to Sicily. Moreover, it should drink well for a decade or more. The more expensive opaque purple-colored 1998 Don Antonio boasts a gorgeous nose of blueberry and raspberry jam intermixed with smoke, licorice, and minerals. There is impressive fruit intensity as well as an undeniable elegance and overall symmetry/balance. The wine was aged in various sized wood vessels, and bottled unfiltered. It should drink well for 4–5 years.

ALESSANDRO MORODER (MARCHE)

1997 Rosso Conero Dorico IGT	C	88

Made from Sangiovese grapes aged in French barrels for two months, the dark ruby/purple-colored 1997 Rosso Conero Dorico displays abundant quantities of ripe, earthy, black cherry, and currant fruit, impressive density, rustic tannin, noticeable new oak, and a spicy, muscular finish. It should drink well for 4–5 years.

DAVIDE MOSCHIONI (FRIULI–VENEZIA GIULIA)

1999 Celtico Rosso	E	94
1999 Pignolo	EE	95
1999 Refosco	D	89+?
1999 Schioppettino	EE	90

I have never before tasted Refosco or Pignolo of this quality. These limited-production *cuvées* (200 cases) are obviously made from extraordinarily low yields and ripe fruit. All are aged in French oak for 12–15 months and bottled without filtration. These are compelling examples of dry reds from Friuli, and they set new standards in terms of what can be achieved in this

region—at a high price. Nevertheless, readers with deep pockets should check out these astonishing efforts.

The 1999 Refosco offers a compelling bouquet of English walnuts (reminiscent of that of
Château Latour), flowers, blackberries, licorice, and graphite. Highly extracted and full-
bodied, with sweet tannin and well-integrated wood and acidity, this blockbuster will drink
well for 10–15 years. Produced from 100% Ribolla Nera, the 1999 Schioppettino displays a
distinctive character of blueberries, blackberries, liquid minerals, and licorice. Full-bodied,
spicy, ripe, and extremely concentrated, with sweet tannin as well as adequate acidity, it
should drink well for a decade or more (although I have no prior experience with this varietal's ageability).

The most prodigious offerings of the series include the 1999 Celtico Rosso (a blend of 60%
Cabernet Sauvignon and 40% Merlot) and the 1999 Pignolo (100% Pignolo). They may be
expensive, but they are blockbuster efforts of extraordinary richness and intensity. The 1999
Celtico Rosso, which spent 15 months in French oak before being bottled unfiltered, came in
at an amazing 15% alcohol level, all of which is hidden by layers of concentrated blackberry
and crème de cassis fruit. Smoky graphite, floral, and toasty notes emerge from the bouquet.
The wine possesses a terrific entry, a multidimensional mid-palate, and a finish that lasts for
nearly 40 seconds. This corpulent, concentrated, yet incredibly well balanced heavyweight
should drink well for 15+ years. It is a tour de force. Lastly, the otherworldly 1999 Pignolo
(also aged 15 months in new French oak and bottled without filtration) boasts an explosive
nose of black fruits, violets, minerals, and tar. Full-bodied, super-extracted, immense, yet remarkably symmetrical as well as vibrant, it possesses amazing delineation for a wine of such
mass and concentration. It is unquestionably the most astonishing Pignolo I have ever tasted.
Since nothing like this has ever been produced from this grape (as far as I know), its aging
potential is unknown. These are the wines of an eccentric genius who is pushing the envelope
of quality to the maximum. Kudos to Moschioni!

LA PALAZZOLA (UMBRIA)

1999 Merlot	D	92
1998 Merlot	D	90
1997 Merlot	D	88
1999 Rubino	D	93
1998 Rubino	D	90
1997 Rubino	D	93

This 52-acre estate has fashioned a number of stunning wines in recent vintages. Proprietor
Stefano Grilli works with Umbrian oenologist Riccardo Cotarella to produce two impressive
reds, a Merlot and a Rubino. The average production of the Merlot, which emerges from a
tiny 6.17-acre vineyard, is around 1,000 cases. The Rubino, a proprietary blend of 80%
Cabernet Sauvignon and 20% Merlot, is more widely available (2,000 cases annually). The
wines spend 12 months in 100% new French oak, and are bottled unfined and unfiltered.

The 1999 Merlot is stunning. It boasts a dense purple color along with a sweet perfume of
espresso, blackberry and cherry fruit, licorice, cigar box, and vanilla. A fabulous texture,
beautiful harmony, and admirable purity combine in this full-bodied, dense, concentrated offering. With adequate acidity, sweet tannin, and a long finish, it should drink well for 10–15
years. The 1998 Merlot exhibits an opaque purple color in addition to dense, chewy, full-
bodied, succulent, fat flavors loaded with black cherry and blackberry fruit intertwined with
mocha and chocolate notes. Full, concentrated, and thick, this effort is simply amazing.
Drink it over the next 7–8 years. The 1997 Merlot is medium- to full-bodied, dense, monolithic, with an opaque purple color, as well as gobs of fruit, glycerin, and texture. As yet, it
does not reveal the necessary complexity to merit an outstanding score. It can be drunk now
or cellared for 10–12 years.

The prodigious 1999 Rubino is seductive. It exhibits a smoky, chocolaty bouquet with hints of cassis, tobacco, and toasty new oak. With superb definition, moderate tannin, excellent structure, and exceptional concentration as well as overall purity, this full-bodied, blockbuster effort can be drunk now or cellared for 10–12 years. The black/ruby-colored 1998 Rubino offers a complex bouquet of cedarwood, cigar box, black currants, and vanilla. While more linear and less fat than the Merlot, it is full-bodied, powerful, structured, and intense. It should last for 10–12 years. The staggeringly rich, complex 1997 Rubino exhibits a dense ruby/purple color in addition to a sumptuous nose of blackberries, raspberries, and cassis intertwined with toasty new oak, minerals, and licorice. Full-bodied, ostentatious, and flashy, with loads of glycerin and a 35+-second finish, it can be drunk now and over the next 12 years. Bravo!

PIEVE DEL VESCOVO (UMBRIA)

1998 Lucciaio IGT	C	87
1997 Lucciaio IGT	C	91
1998 Piovano	C	87

Riccardo Cotarella oversees the winemaking at this Umbrian estate, which offers two outstanding blends of Sangiovese, Gamay, Cannaiolo, and other miscellaneous indigenous varietals. The medium dark ruby-colored, fruit-dominated 1998 Piovano offers a sweet, fragrant nose of jammy blackberries and cherries. Round, with low acidity and a plump, fleshy, corpulent personality, this chunky wine makes an ideal trattoria red to consume over the next 12–18 months.

The 1998 Lucciaio reveals the influence of French *barrique* aging in its spicy, vanilla, toasty-scented nose, complemented nicely by currant and berry fruit. This offering is more structured and international in style, with medium body. Drink it over the next 2–3 years. A beauty, the 1997 Lucciaio boasts an opaque purple color, and dense, blackberry and currant flavors intermixed with subtle oak. The wine displays a natural texture (it was bottled unfiltered), outstanding purity, multiple dimensions, and an explosive finish. This terrific offering should age well for 10 years.

PLANETA (SICILY)

1999 Burdese	D	90
1998 Cabernet Sauvignon	D	90
1997 Cabernet Sauvignon	D	87
1999 Merlot	D	90
1998 Merlot	D	89
1997 Merlot	D	88
2000 Rosso La Segreta	B	87
1999 Rosso La Segreta	B	86
1999 Santa Cecilia IGT	D	89
1998 Santa Cecilia IGT	D	89
1997 Santa Cecilia IGT	D	86
1999 Syrah	D	88

This winery—now one of the most fashionable in Sicily—has won numerous accolades from the Italian wine press. It is encouraging to see wines of such quality emerging from this region. Except for Rosso La Segreta, which generally qualifies as a good value, Planeta's red wines are relatively expensive (in particular the Syrah/Nero d'Avola blend called Santa Cecilia as well as the Merlot and the Cabernet Sauvignon) but interesting. These three *cuvées* present an international style, no doubt due to their 12 months' aging in 100% new oak. These modern-styled, concentrated, complex wines merit significant attention. Prices are high but not out of control—yet.

The inexpensive, internationally styled 2000 Rosso La Segreta (a blend of 45% Nero d'Avola, 45% Merlot, and 10% Cabernet Sauvignon) offers sweet black cherry, mocha, and spice characteristics. Fat, fleshy, pure, and chewy, with 14% alcohol providing plenty of glycerin and texture, it will provide pleasure for 1–2 years. The 1999 Rosso La Segreta is also produced from Nero d'Avola, Merlot, and Cabernet Sauvignon. A dark ruby color is followed by loads of cherry and currant fruit. This fresh, crisp, tangy red is an ideal bistro/trattoria offering that will be flexible with an assortment of culinary dishes. Drink it over the next 12–18 months.

The supple, soft, California-style 1999 Syrah lacks the complexity of the finest Rhône Valley Syrahs and the old-vine Shiraz *cuvées* from Australia's Barossa and McLaren Vale regions. Nevertheless, it exhibits a good, creamy vanilla oakiness to its blackberry fruit characteristics, soft, fleshy flavors, medium body, and plenty of mainstream appeal. Drink it over the next 5–7 years.

The indigenous Nero d'Avola grape makes a brilliant appearance in the 1999 Santa Cecilia. It reveals a deep ruby/purple color along with a dense, chocolaty, black fruit–scented nose with telltale toasty new oak. Although not as complex as its siblings, it possesses plenty of suppleness and richness as well as a layered mouth-feel presented in a quasi-international style. Drink it over the next 6–7 years. The impressive, dark ruby/purple-colored 1998 Santa Cecilia (85% Nero d'Avola and 15% Syrah) offers abundant quantities of peppery blackberry fruit intermixed with cassis. Supple, with low acidity, fine density, and a chewy constitution, it can be drunk over the next 4–5 years. The dark ruby/purple-colored 1997 Santa Cecilia displays aromas of roasted nuts, black cherries, cassis, and licorice, medium body, sweet tannin, and excellent ripeness. While not complex, it is well made and mouth-filling. Drink it over the next 2–3 years.

I was knocked out by the remarkable 1999 Merlot, a multilayered, explosively ripe effort exhibiting aromas and flavors of espresso, black cherry jam, chocolate, and mocha. It is rich, full-bodied, and seamless with obvious toasty oak as well as admirable length and individuality. Consume it over the next 10–12 years. The sexy 1998 Merlot offers sweet, mocha-tinged, coffee, and black cherry notes with plenty of chocolate and toast. Medium-bodied, with good density and ripeness as well as a long finish, it will drink well for 4–5 years. The dark purple-colored 1997 Merlot, made in an international style, exhibits excellent purity, good fatness, and copious quantities of blackberry and cherry fruit intermixed with toasty oak and spice. A low acid, plump Merlot, it will offer pleasant drinking over the next 2–3 years.

Another exceptional effort, the 1999 Burdese (Cabernet Sauvignon) reveals Cabernet's complexity in its tobacco, cedar, herb-tinged, black currant, and toasty new oak–scented bouquet. There is more structure in the mouth, along with moderately high tannin, medium to full body, and sweet fatness in the mid-palate. This complex Cabernet Sauvignon will benefit from 2–3 years of cellaring and keep for 12–15 years. The Cabernet Sauvignon is the most complex of the three 1998s of the portfolio. It boasts textbook cedarwood, tobacco-tinged soy, and black currant flavors, an opulent texture, low acidity, full body, and outstanding ripeness, purity, and richness. It should drink well for 7–8 years. The dark purple-colored 1997 Cabernet Sauvignon exhibits a classic bouquet of cigar box, cedar, and black currant aromas nicely supported by subtle toasty oak. Made in an international style, without any characteristics that speak specifically of Italy or Sicily, it is chewy and rich, with good jammy fruit, decent acidity, and low tannin. It should drink well for 6–7 years.

PROMESSA (PUGLIA)

2000	A-Mano Primitivo	A	87
1999	A-Mano Primitivo	A	87
1999	Negroamaro	A	85
1999	Prima-Mano Primitivo	B	90

2000 Rosso Salento	A	87
1999 Sangiovese	A	86

These offerings are produced by a young American, Mark Shannon, who has decided that the isolated, rural lifestyle of southern Italy suits him fine. All the wines of his portfolio are excellent values. They share ripe fruit, little winemaking intervention, aging in stainless steel, and early bottling to protect their fruit and charm. Shrewd readers seeking bargains, as well as restaurants looking for wines to sell by the glass, would be well served to check out these fruity, cleanly made, value-priced Italian reds.

The 2000 Rosso Salento (a blend of 85% Negroamaro and 15% Primitivo aged three months in oak) is deep and complex. A deep ruby color is followed by a medium- to full-bodied red with a sweet nose of briery fruit intermixed with cherries, tar, and earth. Possessing excellent texture as well as purity, it is best consumed in its exuberant youth—over the next several years.

The 1999 Negroamaro exhibits a medium ruby color and a sweet bouquet of berries and melted asphalt that is reminiscent of a medium-weight Zinfandel. It reveals good ripeness, straightforward fruit, and a smooth personality. Drink it now. Slightly better is the dark ruby-colored 1999 Sangiovese. Earthy, peppery, herb notes as well as ripe fruit suggest plenty of sunshine. Exhibiting a Côtes du Rhône–like character, this 1999 possesses good ripeness, an attractive, round texture, fine purity, and a jammy berry character. Like the Negroamaro, it should be consumed now.

A notch up the ladder of concentration and seriousness is A-Mano Primitivo. This well-made 100% Primitivo *cuvée* is a noteworthy value. It is aged five months in a combination of French, American, and Slovenian oak. However, the wood is barely noticeable, given the wine's fruity character and fat. The 2000 A-Mano Primitivo offers a deep ruby color as well as a sweet, candied nose of berry fruit, earth, oak, and tar. There are loads of glycerin, sweet, succulent fruit on the attack and mid-palate, and a velvety-textured, seamless finish. Although not complex, it will provide delicious, uncomplicated drinking over the next year. The 1999 A-Mano Primitivo exhales a big, sweet, juicy, fruity nose with smoky, dried herbs, saddle leather, and soil overtones. A fruit-driven, fat, ripe, chewy effort with admirable density as well as appeal, it should drink well for 12–18 months.

Mark Shannon has decided that in great Puglia vintages he will offer a limited-production (1,000+ cases) *cuvée* from a single vineyard of old-vine Primitivo. The Prima-Mano Primitivo 1999 is aged in 100% new American oak, and bottled with neither fining nor filtration. It is an outstanding, modern-styled wine. A saturated deep ruby color is accompanied by aromas of sweet blackberry and cherry liqueur, vanilla, and smoke. Full-bodied, opulently textured, chewy, pure, and loaded with fruit, it will drink beautifully over the next 3–4 years.

RONCHI DI MANZANO (FRIULI–VENEZIA GIULIA)

1999 Merlot Ronc di Subule	C	89
1998 Merlot Ronc di Subule	C	87
1997 Merlot Ronc di Subule	C	90
1998 Refosco	B	86
1999 Rosazzo Rosso Ronc di Rosazzo	C	88
1998 Rosazzo Rosso Ronc di Rosazzo	C	88
1997 Rosazzo Rosso Ronc di Rosazzo	C	89
1998 Le Zuccole	C	87
1997 Le Zuccole	C	88+
1996 Le Zuccole	C	88

From one of Friuli's finest wineries, these offerings go from strength to strength with each new vintage. The proprietors continue to reduce yields, resulting in wines with distinctive personalities, exceptional purity, and vibrant freshness allied with considerable richness.

Readers should definitely take a look at these serious efforts being produced by Ronchi di Manzano.

The dense ruby-colored 1999 Merlot Ronc di Subule offers up scents of roasted coffee, dried herbs, and black cherries. Medium-bodied, with a restrained, elegant style, it should drink well for 7–8 years. The 1998 Merlot Ronc di Subule offers delicious black cherry fruit with a mocha fudge–like characteristic as well as subtle wood in the background and medium body, as well as an attractive texture and finish. It should drink well for 2–3 years. One of a handful of Friuli Merlots I have given an outstanding rating, Manzano's 1997 Merlot Ronc di Subule possesses sumptuous aromas of roasted coffee, blackberry, and cherry fruit. Dense, chewy, and lush, with decent acidity, this gloriously fruit-driven Merlot can be consumed over the next 3–4 years.

The Rosazzo Rosso Ronc di Rosazzo is a blend of equal parts Refosco, Merlot, and Cabernet Sauvignon aged in 100% new French oak. Although the 1999 Rosazzo Rosso Ronc di Rosazzo was closed the day I tasted it, what I could see was impressive. Notes of smoke, melted asphalt, graphite, and black currants/cherries were present. The wine was tight but spicy and pure, with a certain leanness. Give it 1–2 years of cellaring, and enjoy it over the following 10–12 years. It is a noteworthy choice for readers seeking subtlety and delicacy. The 1998 Rosazzo Rosso Ronc di Rosazzo offers a noteworthy berry fruitiness in addition to a melted chocolate flavor in its medium-bodied, lush, concentrated personality. Very close in style to the 1998, the 1997 Rosazzo Rosso Ronc di Rosazzo possesses a deep ruby/purple color and smoked ham–like aromas along with chocolate, berry flavors. It is medium-bodied, richly fruity, and ideal for drinking over the next 3–4 years.

I enjoyed the robust, gutsy, blackberry, and cherry-scented and -flavored 1998 Refosco. Displaying good ripeness, sweetness, and medium body, it can be drunk over the next 1–2 years.

Le Zuccole is a blend of equal parts Merlot and Cabernet Sauvignon from Manzano's finest vineyards. While 75% new oak is utilized in this wine's aging (the same as for the Merlot Ronc di Subule), the wood is kept in check. Like all reds from this estate, it is bottled without filtration. A stylish, measured effort, the evolved 1998 Le Zuccole reveals notes of cedar, spice box, herbs, red and black currants, and a touch of vanilla. Drink this medium-weight Italian red over the next 4–5 years. In a blind tasting, it could easily be mistaken for a mid-level Médoc. The 1997 Le Zuccole offers spicy, toasty new oak, an unevolved, ripe, black currant, and dense cherry style with notes of cedar and chocolate, moderate tannin, and plenty of depth and richness. It should improve over the next 1–2 years and last for a decade or more. The 1996 Le Zuccole reveals elements of overripeness, along with good acidity (particularly when compared to the low-acid 1997s), a complex, cedary, spice box, tobacco, and currant-scented nose, medium body, and light to moderate tannin. It should continue to drink well for 3–5 years.

F.LLI SPERI (VENETO)

1997 Recioto della Valpolicella	B	91
1998 Valpolicella La Roverina	A	86
1997 Valpolicella Sant'Urbano	C	90

It is amazing how much progress has taken place in Veneto. Speri is one of the estates of this region where the wines have greatly improved, and it now offers tasty and reasonably priced Valpolicellas. The elegant, dark ruby-colored 1998 Valpolicella La Roverina offers aromas of fresh almonds and sour cherries as well as a tangy, medium-bodied personality. It is soft and light enough to be drunk slightly chilled, if readers so desire. It is an excellent value. Consume it over the next 12–18 months.

The outstanding dark ruby/purple-colored 1997 Valpolicella Sant'Urbano exhibits tremendous density and richness, medium to full body, and notes of black truffles intermixed with cherry jam, spice, and minerals. It boasts super purity, wonderful, refreshing, lively, vivacious fruit, and a rich, concentrated, textured finish. Drink this beautiful Valpolicella over the next 3–4 years. Readers looking for robust, mouth-filling, earthy, meaty, full-throttle, sweeter reds should check out the 1997 Recioto della Valpolicella. Dense and full-bodied, with chewy, unctuously textured flavors of roasted meats, dried herbs, melted asphalt, and black fruits, it will provide a wonderful accompaniment to any hard cheese at the end of a meal. Drink it over the next 10 years.

F.LLI SPORTOLETTI (UMBRIA)

2000 Assisi Rosso	B	86
1999 Villa Fidelia Rosso	E	96
1998 Villa Fidelia Rosso	D	94

This 50-acre estate located between the towns of Assisi and Perugia produces 1,000 cases of Villa Fidelia each year. This is a prodigious 70% Merlot, 20% Cabernet Sauvignon, 10% Cabernet Franc blend made from modest yields of 35–38 hectoliters per hectare. The wine spends 12 months in French oak casks and is bottled with neither fining nor filtration. The estate also offers a *cuvée* called Assisi Rosso that is made of equal parts Sangiovese and Merlot and aged in large *foudres*. Both wines are made with the assistance of Riccardo Cotarella.

The 2000 Assisi Rosso is soft, ripe, stylish, and graceful. It displays Burgundy-like cherry and floral notes. Drink it over the next 1–2 years.

Sportoletti's compelling, unfiltered 1999 Villa Fidelia Rosso is undoubtedly the superstar of this area. Its dense ruby/purple color is accompanied by gorgeous aromas of blackberries, cassis, espresso, chocolate, and a touch of smoke. There are fabulous concentration, full body, great precision as well as purity, and a long, 45-second finish. Displaying an overall sense of elegance and gracefulness despite its depth and richness, this prodigious effort can be drunk now and over the next 14 years. The 1998 Villa Fidelia Rosso is an explosively rich, opulently textured, full-bodied red that offers aromas of chocolate, roasted espresso, blackberries, cherries, and currants. A smoky, thick, chewy wine with terrific flavor extraction, great harmony/symmetry, and a multilayered, sumptuous finish, it can be drunk now or cellared for 10–12 years. Wow!

TASCA D'ALMERITA (SICILY)

1998 Regaleali Cabernet Sauvignon	D	87
1997 Regaleali Cabernet Sauvignon	D	86+?
1999 Regaleali Rosso del Conte	D	88
1998 Regaleali Rosso del Conte	D	86
1999 Regaleali Rosso IGT	A	87

Perhaps the most important winery on the island of Sicily (in terms of quality), Tasca d'Almerita owns 600 acres of vineyards, produces more than 200,000 cases of wine, and has one of the most modern winemaking facilities in Italy. The estate fashions an array of wines, many of which are realistically priced. Moreover, the quality level appears to be increasing. Interestingly, the current releases seem less powerful than previous vintages (no doubt a result of vintage conditions).

The Regaleali Rosso is a blend dominated by a local varietal called Nero d'Avola that sees some aging in old wood. Although this wine spends time in oak, there is no evidence of wood in the aromas or flavors. The 1999 Regaleali Rosso exhibits notes of cherries, balsam, and pepper, which are followed by a soft, medium-bodied, flavorful wine to enjoy over the next 1–2 years.

Tasca d'Almerita has turned out some blockbuster Cabernet Sauvignons, but the 1998 Regaleali Cabernet Sauvignon is a more elegant, less weighty effort than previous vintages. A deep ruby/purple color is followed by sweet black currant/cassis fruit, and licorice aromas and flavors. This elegant, tasty, well-made Cabernet can be enjoyed young because of its low acidity, yet it possesses the capacity to age well for 7–8 years. While the 1997 Regaleali Cabernet Sauvignon is good, it is not equal to its older siblings. It displays more herbaceousness in addition to a distinctive note of briny olives intermixed with black currants. A sweet, heavy-handed, full-bodied wine with plenty of fat and fruit, its herbaceousness and cumbersome feel in the mouth kept my score down, particularly when compared to vintages where the wine had more concentration without as much heaviness. The 1997 should drink well for 6–7 years.

Lastly, the 1999 Regaleali Rosso del Conte is a *barrique*-aged offering made primarily from Nero d'Avola. The influence of new French oak is apparent in the toast, spicy bouquet, but the fruit comes through strongly on the palate. This medium- to full-bodied, rustic yet concentrated red is loaded with blackberries and cherries intertwined with tar, earth, and pepper and has plenty of depth and a mouth-filling finish. It should drink well for 4–8 years. The 1998 Rosso del Conte (90% Nero d'Avola and 10% Perricone) exhibits a complex, spicy, berry, cigar box, and smoke-scented nose with excellent fruit. Medium-bodied, soft, and round, it is ideal for grilled meats or barbecued dishes. Enjoy it over the next 1–2 years.

COSIMO TAURINO (PUGLIA)

1995	Notarpanaro	B	89
1994	Notarpanaro	B	87
1994	Patriglione	D	87?
1998	Salice Salentino	A	86
1997	Salice Salentino Riserva	A	84

Sadly, Cosimo Taurino, someone who has done much for this area of Italy, has passed away, but his son Francesco continues in his father's footsteps. He has built a state-of-the-art winery that was first used for the 2001 harvest. Under his auspices, this estate remains a perennial source of rustic, earthy southern Italian reds. It has made many friends in the international marketplace for its combination of quality and value.

The 1998 Salice Salentino's complex bouquet of damp earth, spice box, sausage, and dried herbs is followed by medium-bodied, flavorful, rustic flavors. It should drink well for 2–3 years. The amber/ruby/garnet-colored 1997 Salice Salentino Riserva, an old-style Italian red, offers scents of roasted herbs, sweaty saddle leather, dried cherries, medium body, and a slightly astringent finish. There is plenty of personality in this 1997, but it is not representative of the new, fruit-driven style of modern-day Italian reds. Drink it with spicy cuisine over the next 12–18 months.

The two following vintages of Notarpanaro are blends of Negroamaro and Malvasia Nera. These wines have spent some time in oak barrels, of which one-third were new. The 1995 Notarpanaro is a dense, rich, full-bodied wine displaying licorice, dried fruit, pepper, truffle, and spice characteristics. Filled with personality, it possesses rustic tannin but plenty of depth as well as a chewy, muscular, robust finish. It should drink well for 3–4 years. The dark garnet color of the 1994 Notarpanaro is followed by an earthy concoction of dried herbs, black cherry fruit, underbrush, truffles, and smoke. Ripe, chewy, and full-bodied, with abundant quantities of concentrated fruit, this gamey, robust, southern Italian red is the perfect foil for a cheese course or with grilled meats. Drink it over the next 2–3 years.

Made in a late-harvest, Amarone-like style, Taurino's 1994 Patriglione offers scents and flavors of melted asphalt, old saddle leather, licorice, and earth with sweet cherry fruit in the background. Although broad and dense, it is not as interesting, fresh, or lively as the Notarpanaro. It takes a cultivated palate to fully appreciate this 1994; hence, readers weaned on modern-styled wines should take heed. It should drink well for 3–4 years.

VIE DI ROMANS (FRIULI–VENEZIA GIULIA)

1997 Voos dai Ciamps	D	92

This 100% new-oak-aged luxury *cuvée*—a blend of 95% Merlot and 5% Cabernet Sauvignon—is fashioned only in the finest vintages, such as 1987, 1990, 1991, and 1997. Production averages 600 cases. An explosively rich and powerful as well as impressive effort, the 1997 Voos dai Ciamps ranks among the most astonishing red wines I have tasted from Friuli. It reveals copious quantities of toasty, smoky notes complemented by sweet, unctuously textured, full-bodied, black cherry, blackberry, caramel, and licorice aromas and flavors with terrific fruit intensity and purity. This superb, opulent wine can be drunk over the next 10 years. Impressive!

VILLA MATILDE (CAMPANIA)

1999 Falerno del Massico Rosso	B	87
1998 Vigna Camarato	D	90+?

Villa Matilde is an estate where the dominant red grape utilized is Aglianico. The potentially superb 1998 Vigna Camarato (100% Aglianico aged in 100% new French barrels and bottled without filtration) reveals a complex, blackberry and floral-scented perfume with a hint of licorice and new oak. Dense and full-bodied, as well as brutally tannic, it appears to possess the constitution, robustness, and depth of fruit to support such high tannin, but this is not certain, hence the question mark. Nevertheless, there is a lot going on in this individualistic, intense 1998. Anticipated maturity: 2004–2018. The attractively priced 1999 Falerno del Massico Rosso exhibits a deep ruby color as well as a big, sweet nose of chocolate-covered black cherries, plums, spice, and dried herbs. Drink this medium-bodied red over the next 1–2 years.

ZENATO (VENETO)

1997 Amarone	E	88
1995 Amarone	E	91
1997 Merlot delle Venezie	A	86
1998 Valpolicella Classico	A	86
1997 Valpolicella Classico	A	88
1998 Valpolicella Classico Ripassa	B	88
1997 Valpolicella Classico Ripassa	B	90

These wines are all super bargains.

The 1998 Valpolicella Classico offers light berry/cherry fruit in a lush, unstructured, round, tasty style. Drink it over the next year.

Readers seeking a fruit-driven, delicious Merlot that won't cost a fortune should check out Zenato's 1997 Merlot delle Venezie. Made from 90% Merlot and 10% Cabernet Sauvignon, it exhibits a dark ruby color, abundant fruit, low acidity, and a round finish. It will not make old bones, but for drinking over the next 12–18 months, it is a fine value.

The Valpolicellas Ripassa exhibit more substance and richness than most wines from this area in Veneto. The word "Ripassa" on the label indicates that it is made like Amarone, by passing the wine over the dry pomace during vinification, resulting in more complexity, body, and depth. The dense 1998 Valpolicella Classico Ripassa exhibits a Rhône-like, earthy, robust, peppery, spicy personality. Passing the grape must over the pomace left over from the Amarone adds concentration, complexity, and earthiness to Valpolicella's typically light style. This excellent, medium- to full-bodied, stuffed 1998 reveals notes of asphalt, black cherries, and berries. Drink it over the next 5–6 years. The 1997 Valpolicella Classico Ripassa is a full-bodied, plum/garnet-colored effort with dense, earthy, tar, and black fruit characteristics. Heady, ripe, pure, and well balanced, it should drink well for 2–3 years.

The standard Valpolicellas are made in steel tanks and aged in large Slavonian wood *foudres.* They make a joke of the industrial swill parading under the Valpolicella label. The medium dark ruby-colored 1997 Valpolicella Classico, which is lighter-bodied than the 1997 Ripassa, offers a gorgeous nose of chocolate-covered cherries, berries, and almonds, excellent suppleness, delicious fruit, and a medium-bodied, fruit-driven finish with considerable character. Drink it over the next 12–18 months.

The 1997 Amarone, a great vintage for this small appellation, possesses a deep plum/garnet color in addition to a sweet perfume of roasted herbs, melted road tar, dried black fruits, smoke, and truffles. Dense and chewy, this wine has pruny/raisiny characteristics. It will drink well for 10–15 years. Lastly, the outstanding 1995 Amarone reveals abundant charcoal wood notes in its melted asphalt, blackberry, meaty, roasted bouquet. Full-bodied, muscular, big, chewy, and thick, this pure wine cuts a heavy swath across the palate and offers a long, impressive finish. Drink it over the next 10–12 years.

FATTORIA ZERBINA (EMILIA-ROMAGNA)

1997	Marzieno Ravenna Rosso	D	89
1997	Sangiovese di Romagna Torre di Ceparano	B	86
1998	Sangiovese di Romagna Ceregio	B	87
1997	Sangiovese di Romagna Ceregio Vigna Querce	B	87
1997	Sangiovese di Romagna Pietramora	D	88

This well-run winery offers an attractive portfolio of wines. The 1998 Sangiovese di Romagna Ceregio and the 1997 Sangiovese di Romagna Ceregio Vigna Querce both exhibit dark ruby colors as well as attractive ripe strawberry and cherry jam aromas intertwined with new saddle leather and spice. Soft, medium-bodied, round Sangioveses, they possess excellent fruit and textures. The 1998 reveals a smokier character. Drink over the next several years.

Although not as seductive as the 1998 Sangiovese Ceregio and 1997 Sangiovese Ceregio Vigna Querce, the dense, chewy, mouth-filling, gutsy, rustic 1997 Sangiovese di Romagna Torre di Ceparano is ideal for drinking over the next several years.

Zerbina's two finest offerings are the 1997 Marzieno Ravenna Rosso and the 1997 Sangiovese di Romagna Pietramora. The dark ruby/purple-colored 1997 Marzieno Ravenna Rosso (a 62% Sangiovese/38% Cabernet Sauvignon blend) is a ripe, wonderfully textured effort with low acidity, a plush, Pomerol-like texture, toasty new oak in the nose, and abundant black fruits. This dense, medium- to full-bodied blend can be drunk now as well as over the next 7–8 years. The 1997 Sangiovese di Romagna Pietramora's (100% Sangiovese) dark ruby color is accompanied by abundant quantities of sweet black cherry, strawberry, earth, toast, and creosote aromas and flavors. With excellent richness, medium to full body, and a supple texture, it should drink well for 5–6 years.

3. GERMANY AND AUSTRIA

GERMANY

The Basics

TYPES OF WINE

Germany's wine kingdom is controlled by the 1971 law that divided German wines into seven grades, based on ascending levels of ripeness and sweetness, as well as price. These seven levels are:

1. Tafelwein
2. Qualitätswein (QbA)
3. Kabinett
4. Spätlese
5. Auslese
6. Beerenauslese
7. Trockenbeerenauslese

In addition to these there are other categories of German wines. The Trocken and Halb-trocken wines are the two generic types of dry German wine. The Trockens tend to be drier, but also boring, thin wines with little body or flavor. Halbtrockens also taste dry but are permitted to have slightly more residual sugar and are marginally more interesting. I rarely recommend either because they are not very good; they are commercial creations made to take advantage of the public's demand for "dry" wine. A third type of wine is called Eiswein, Germany's rarest and most expensive wine. It is made from frozen grapes, generally picked in December or January, or even February. It is quite rare and a very, very sweet wine, but has remarkably high acidity and can last and improve in the bottle for decades. It does have great character, but one must usually pay unbelievably steep prices to experience it.

There are also the sparkling wines of Germany called Deutscher Sekt, which should be drunk only by certified masochists, as they are a ghastly lot of overly sulfured wines. Lastly, there is the German wine that everyone knows about, the ubiquitous Liebfraumilch. This sugary, grapy drink is to quality German wine what California wine coolers are to that state's serious wines.

GRAPE VARIETIES

Müller-Thurgau   Representing 25% of Germany's vineyards, Müller-Thurgau has become the most widely planted grape because it can give prolific yields of juice (90–100 hectoliters per hectare is not uncommon). Ignore all of the self-serving promotion from German wine importers about Müller-Thurgau, because it is not a great wine grape and the Germans have planted it for quantity, not quality.

Riesling Riesling accounts for only 20% of the vineyards in Germany, but it produces about 95% of that country's finest wines. If the bottle does not say Riesling on it, then chances are you are not getting Germany's best wine. Riesling produces some of the world's most complex whites, and it achieves its greatest pinnacles of success in Germany, whether it be a dry, crisp, tangy Kabinett or a decadently sweet, nectarlike Trockenbeerenauslese.

Sylvaner This unimpressive grape accounts for 10% of Germany's vineyards and rarely results in anything interesting. Most Sylvaners either have a nasty vegetal streak to them or are simply dull and flat.

Other Grape Varieties Much of Germany's problem today is that a large proportion of its vineyards are planted with mediocre grape varieties. The remaining 45% of the vineyards generally consist of grapes that have little personality and names such as Kerner, Gutedel, Morio-Muskat, Bacchus, Faberrebe, Huxelrebe, Optima, and Ebling. The only other grapes that can do something special are Gewürztraminer, Rulander (Pinot Gris), Scheurebe, and Germany's answer to Pinot Noir, Spätburgunder.

FLAVORS

Müller-Thurgau At its best it resembles a can of fruit salad, obvious but pleasant in an open-knit, uncomplicated manner. At its worst, it tastes washed out, acidic, green, and reminiscent of a watered-down, mediocre Riesling.

Riesling The most exciting flavors in German wines come from Riesling. In the drier and slightly sweet versions there is a lovely concoction of apple, lime, wet stone, and citric flavors and scents. As the Riesling becomes sweeter, the flavors move in the direction of tropical fruits such as mangoes and pineapples, as well as honeyed apples, peaches, and apricots. Behind all the flavor (in the top Rieslings) is a steely, zesty, vibrant natural fruit acidity that gives those wines an exceptional degree of clarity and focus.

Rulander From some of the best vineyards in Baden and the Rheinpfalz, this grape produces oily, rich, honeyed, intense wines that are probably the most underrated great white wines of Germany.

Scheurebe Discovered by Dr. G. Scheu, Scheurebe is a clone achieved by crossing Sylvaner and Riesling. Once scoffed at for its neutral character, this varietal has become increasingly popular with consumers. Top producers of Scheurebe, such as Müller-Catoir, H. & R. Lingenfelder, and Kruger-Rumpf, have performed wonders with this grape, producing deeply flavored wines that feature flowery, curranty fruit and rich, complex personalities.

Spätburgunder This is the German Pinot Noir, a grotesque and ghastly wine that tastes akin to a defective, sweet, faded, diluted red Burgundy from an incompetent producer. Need I say more?

Sylvaner On occasion, Sylvaner from selected vineyards in Franken and the Rheinhessen can be a rich, muscular, deep wine, but more often it is vegetal, thin, and dull.

AGING POTENTIAL

Auslese: 3–18 years	Qualitätswein (QbA): 2–4 years
Beerenauslese: 10–40+ years	Spätlese: 3–12 years
Kabinett: 3–6 years	Tafelwein: 8–16 months
Liebfraumilch: 8–16 months	Trockenbeerenauslese: 10–40+ years

OVERALL QUALITY LEVEL

The top level of quality is impeccably high, dominated by small estates that usually produce Riesling. However, the German government has been inexcusably remiss over recent decades in allowing too many high-yielding, low-quality grapes to be planted (the 1987 average yield per hectare was an incredible 97 hectoliters), and this has caused consumers to become increasingly skeptical about the seriousness of German wine quality. For example, in the me-

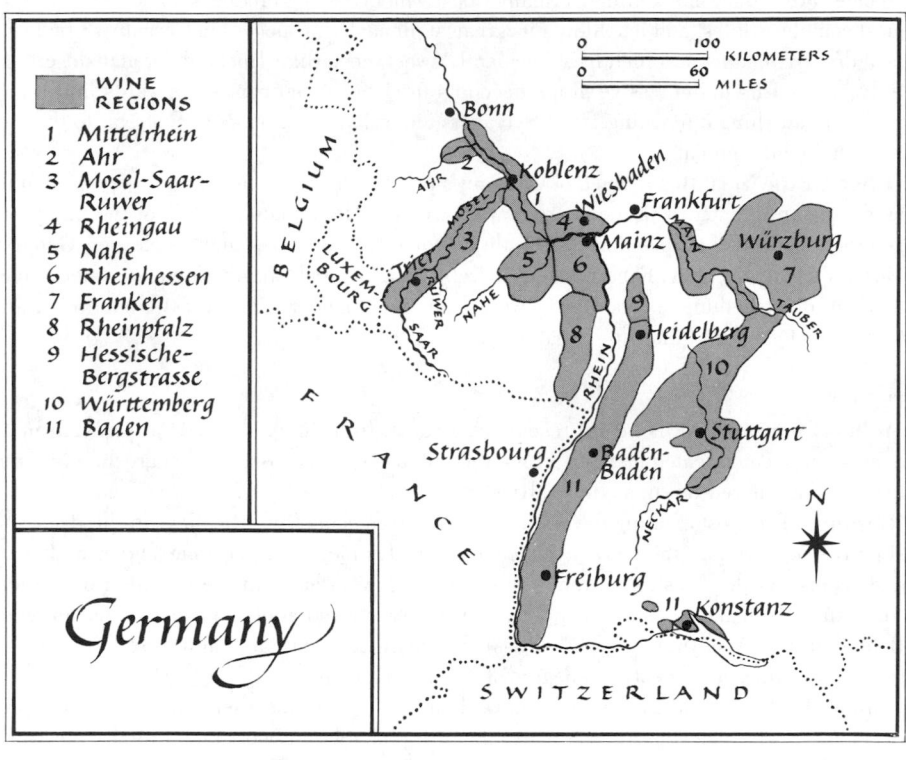

WINE
REGIONS

1 Mittelrhein
2 Ahr
3 Mosel-Saar-
   Ruwer
4 Rheingau
5 Nahe
6 Rheinhessen
7 Franken
8 Rheinpfalz
9 Hessische-
   Bergstrasse
10 Württemberg
11 Baden

Germany

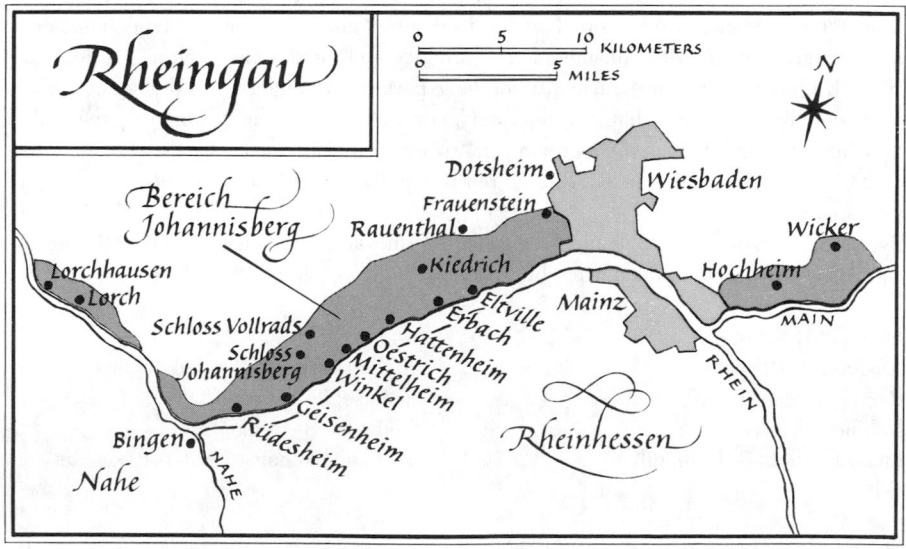

Rheingau

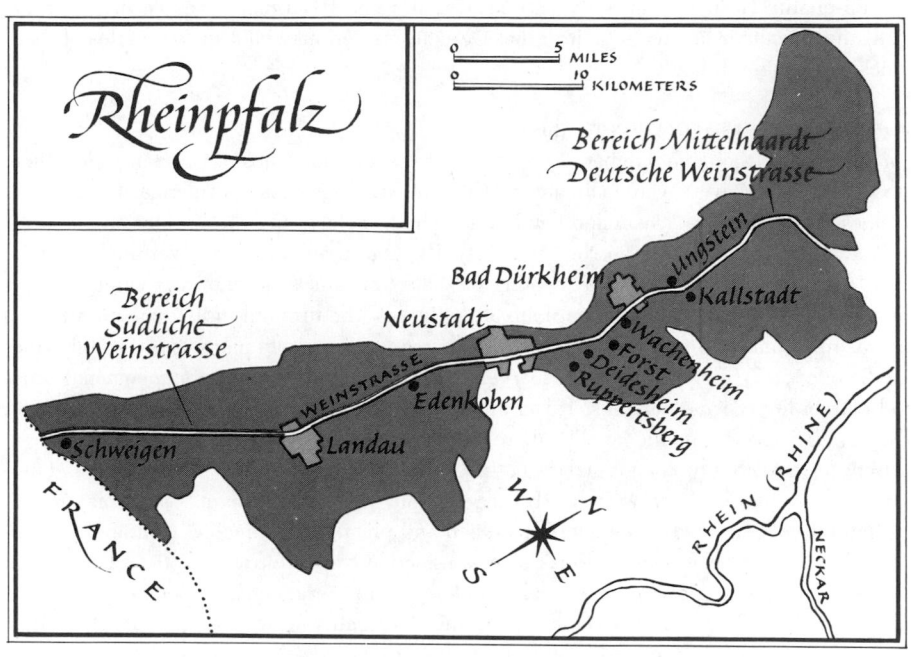

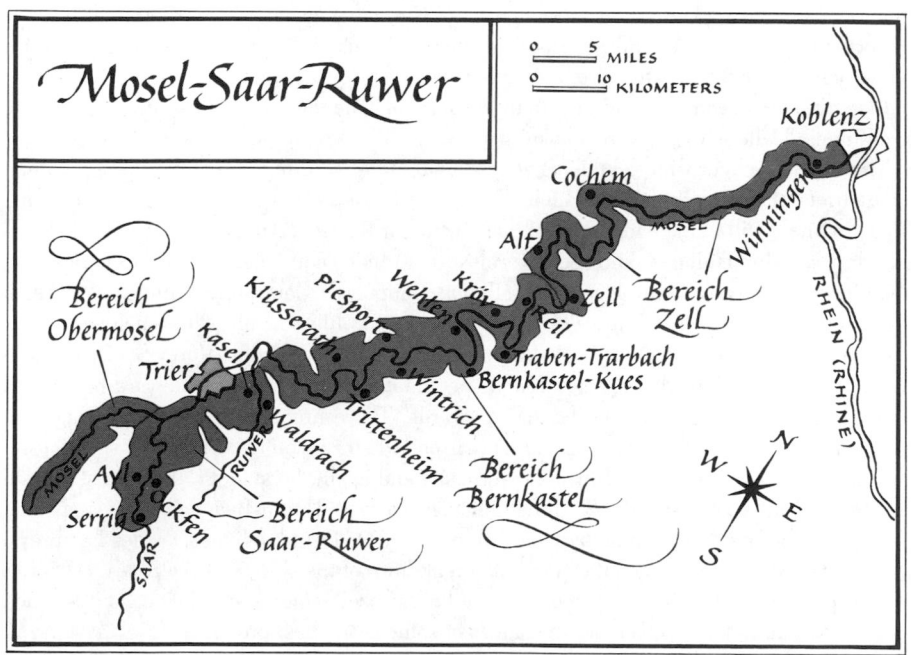

diocre year of 1987, 77% of the wine produced was allowed to be called QbA and only 2% was declassified as simple table wine (Tafelwein). That's ridiculous. A campaign to promote the top-quality German estates that are making the finest German wines is long overdue. Until the consumer begins to believe that Germany is serious about quality, sales of these wines will remain difficult.

MOST IMPORTANT INFORMATION TO KNOW

For Americans, though a number of importers have small portfolios of German wines, there are three major players who dominate the German wine business in America. From a consumer's perspective, the most important is Terry Theise Selections, whose wines are imported by Michael Skurnik Imports in New York City. By ignoring many of the overrated, more famous German wine names and by beating the back roads of less-renowned viticultural regions, Theise has put together a portfolio of producers who turn out individualistic wines of astonishing quality, often at modest prices. Theise keeps his profit margins low so the wines can be effectively represented in the marketplace. The result is a bevy of phenomenal wines and extraordinary wine bargains. If you are going to buy German wines seriously, look for *Terry Theise Selection* on the label. You are unlikely to be disappointed.

Between the other two major players in the German wine market, the most visible and promotion-conscious is Rudy Weist of ILNA Selections in Santa Barbara, California. Weist's portfolio is concentrated on the more renowned and prestigious domaines that are all members of an elite association of winemaking estates collectively referred to as the VDP. Each of these estates sports a neck or back label that identifies its more than 200 members. In theory, all of them are dedicated to producing the highest-quality wines, usually from Riesling. There are a number of fabulous producers in this group, as well as an appalling number of underachievers who charge exceptionally high prices because their wines are produced from renowned vineyards. The third major importer of German wines is Chapin Cellars/Billington Imports in Springfield, Virginia. Formerly owned by Romaine "Bob" Rice, this importer has numerous excellent wines that are reasonably priced.

In addition to becoming familiar with these German wine importers, there are other facts to keep in mind when buying German wines:

• There are 11 major wine-producing zones in Germany. Within these zones there are three subdistricts, the most general of which is called a Bereich. This is used to describe a wine from anywhere within the boundaries of that particular Bereich. An analogy that may help facilitate this distinction would be the closest French equivalent, a wine entitled to appellation Bordeaux Contrôlée or Appellation Bourgogne Contrôlée. Within the Bereich there are more specific boundaries called Grosslagen, to which the closest French equivalent would be the generic Appellation St.-Julien Contrôlée or Appellation Morey St.-Denis Contrôlée. These are wines that are not from a specific château or specific vineyard but from a specific region or collection of sites for vineyards. There are 152 different Grosslagen in Germany. The most specific zone in Germany is called an Einzellage, which is a specific site or vineyard. There are 2,600 of them in Germany, and again, by analogy, the closest French equivalent would be a specific St.-Julien château such as Ducru-Beaucaillou or a specific premier cru or grand cru Burgundy vineyard in Morey St.-Denis such as Clos des Lambrays. Perhaps this will help one to understand the breakdown of the German wine zones. However, few people have the patience to memorize the best Einzellagen or Grosslagen, so it is much more important to try to remember the names of some of the best producers.

• The majority of the best producers in Germany are located in the following nine wine zones.

OVERALL CHARACTERISTICS OF THE NINE MAJOR GERMAN WINE ZONES

Middle Mosel For German wine lovers, as well as tourists to Germany's wine regions, the Middle Mosel is the most beloved and scenic. The frightfully steep, slate-based slopes are so forbidding it seems impossible that vineyards could be planted on them. With its plethora of high-profile producers, such as J. J. Prüm, Willi Haag, Ernest Loosen, and Dr. Thanisch, this region has no shortage of admirers and potential buyers. The fact is that while Riesling grown on these slopes has unlimited potential, this is also an area filled with overpriced, underachieving producers who have long lived off their reputations. Nevertheless, anybody who has tasted a great Wehlener Sonnenuhr, Brauneberger Juffer, Erdener Treppchen, Zeltinger Sonnenuhr, or Graacher Himmelreich knows that this area's soils can produce magical Rieslings. The Middle Mosel is to Germany what Puligny-Montrachet is to Burgundy. There are a number of great producers, but prices are high, and the quality is frightfully irregular.

Lower Mosel   This obscure vineyard area with supersteep slopes is located at the junction of the Mosel and the Rhine. The wines from the Lower Mosel are underestimated, a fact that consumers should put to good use. Try some recent vintages from two of this area's most spectacular producers, von Schleinitz and von Heddesdorff, and experience the high quality available at reasonable prices. Although the vineyard sites are not considered to be as ideal as those in the Middle Mosel, the best Lower Mosel producers can produce wines equal in quality to those from the Middle Mosel.

Saar   Also referred to as the Upper Mosel, this cool region is able to maintain the steely, razor blade sharpness of the Riesling grape. Many authorities consider the Saar vineyards among the greatest in Germany, but, as in the Middle Mosel, fame has its price. Some fabulous producers are located in this area. However, some well-known Saar producers have a tendency to overcrop, making relatively hollow, flabby wines that lack definition. Superlative producers include Egon Müller, Dr. Wagner, von Kesselstatt, and, from time to time, Zilliken.

Ruwer   Trier is the spiritual and commercial center for the Ruwer wines. Textbook, quintessential Rieslings emerge from this area from producers such as Friedrich-Wilhelm-Gymnasium, Geltz Zilliken, Karthäuserhof, von Kesselstatt, Karlsmuhle, and von Schubert's Maximin Grunhaus.

Rheingau   Many of the most famous producers of German wine are located in this highly renowned region. However, it is not unusual for many of the unknown overachievers to outperform their more celebrated neighbors. Three of the most prominent underachievers are Schloss Groenesteyn, Schloss Vollrads, and Schloss Johannisberg. If you want to taste what many consider to be some of the finest Rieslings made in Germany, check out producers such as H. H. Eser, Freiherr zu Knyphausen, Deinhard's Konigin Victoria Berg, Dr. Heinrich Nagler, and the best *cuvées* of Schloss Schonborn.

Rheinhessen   All of the German wine zones offer considerable diversity in quality, but none more than the Rheinhessen, which has Nierstein as its commercial center. Müller-Thurgau and Sylvaner are the two most popular grape varieties of this region. In addition, odd grapes such as Scheurebe, Huxelrebe, and Kerner have found an enthusiastic reception among this region's producers. This is also the region where most of Germany's Liebfraumilch is produced. Consumers often make major errors in buying wines from this region. Over recent years, some of the best producers have included Freiherr Heyl zu Herrnsheim, J.U.H.A. Strub, and Merz.

Rheinpfalz   The Rheinpfalz is the warmest of the major German wine zones. Although Müller-Thurgau is widely planted, it is Riesling, Rulander, and Scheurebe that produce the most stunning wines. If you think German wines are too understated, light, and wimpy, check out the powerful, meaty, fleshy, supergenerous wines from the Rheinpfalz. The quality level appears to be hitting new heights with every vintage. This is the home of the producer Müller-Catoir, who is making some of the most riveting wines of Germany. It is also the base for supertalented producers such as H. & R. Lingenfelder, Kurt Darting, Klaus Neckerauer, Koehler-Ruprecht, Kimich, Werleaa, and perhaps one of the best-known Rheinpfalz estates, Dr. Burklin-Wolf.

Nahe   This is another underrated source of high-class Riesling, as well as a wine zone with a competitive group of producers who, for now, lack the one superstar needed to draw world-wide attention to this region's virtues. A Nahe wine is considered to possess some of the character of a Saar wine and the spice, meatiness, and flesh of a Rheingau. The curranty, smoky aromas of a Nahe are reminiscent of those found in a red wine, making it among the most distinctive of all German wines. None of the Nahe producers is well known, so prices tend to be low, except for those producers who are members of the prestigious VDP group (e.g., Hans Crusius). Top producers include von Plettenberg, Hehner-Kiltz, Kruger-Rumpf, Adolph Lotzbeyer, and perhaps the finest, Helmuth Donnhoff and Prince zu Salm.

Franken   With the wonderful city of Würzburg as its commercial center, the wines of Franken have developed a considerable cult following. Although these wines fetch high prices and are put in unattractive squat bottles that are impossible to bin, Franken wines can be bold, dramatic, and heady. Moreover, they enjoy remarkable loyalty from their admirers. This is one region where the Sylvaner grape hits heights that exist nowhere else on earth. The two best estates are Burgerspital and Hans Wirsching. I have also been increasingly impressed (especially by the 1990s) with wines from Schloss Sommerhausen. Once past the quality of these superlative producers, caveat emptor.

MOST IMPORTANT INFORMATION TO KNOW (CONTINUED)
• The best German wines are those produced at the Kabinett, Spätlese, Auslese, Beerenauslese, and Trockenbeerenauslese levels of ripeness and sweetness. Most consumers tasting a Kabinett would not find it particularly sweet, although there is residual sugar in the wine. Because of a high natural acidity found in German wines, a Kabinett generally tastes fresh, fruity, but not sweet to most palates. However, most tasters will detect a small amount of sweetness in a Spätlese, and even more in an Auslese. All three of these types of wines are ideal as an apéritif or with food, whereas the wines entitled to Beerenauslese and Trockenbeerenauslese designations are clearly dessert wines, very rich and quite sweet. One should keep in mind that the alcohol level in most German wines averages between 7–9%, so one can drink much more of this wine without feeling its effects. One of the naive criticisms of German wines is that they do not go well with food. However, anyone who has tried a fine Kabinett, Spätlese, or Auslese with Asian cuisine, with roast pork, or even with certain types of fowl such as pheasant or turkey can tell you that these wines work particularly well, especially Spätlese and Auslese.
• The best German wines age like fine Bordeaux. In great vintages, such as 1990 or 1971, one can expect a Kabinett, Spätlese, or Auslese from a top producer to evolve and improve in bottle for 3–20 years. Beerenauslese and Trockenbeerenauslese have the ability in a great vintage to improve for two to four decades. This is a fact, not a myth, to which those who have recently tasted some of the great Auslesens from 1959 can easily attest. German wines at the top levels, from the top producers, do indeed improve remarkably in the bottle, although the trend among consumers is to drink them when they are young, fresh, and crisp.

RECENT VINTAGES

2000—The 2000 vintage in Germany is the third in a row that suffered from late-season rains. A warm, humid, muggy year led to huge yields and major outbreaks of rot in the vineyards. A mediocre vintage at best, 2000 suffers from the debilitating effects of high yields and excessive rains. The mildew and rot that were rampant in the vineyards can be found in all too many of the 2000s.

1999—Stylistically, the 1999 vintage is reminiscent of 1997 in that the wines are soft, fruit-forward, and easily appreciated by those who do not usually like German wine. Those searching out the vibrancy and complexity that only Riesling can attain will not be enamored with this vintage. A warm growing season led to high yields throughout Germany. Rains in September and October were soaked up by the vines, resulting in many wines exhibiting signs of dilution. The finest 1999s, generally those at the Kabinett level from conscientious producers, should be consumed in the near term.

1998—The last excellent year of the millennium, 1998 succeeded despite nature. A scorching sun in August led to sunburn on a significant percentage of grapes, and constant rains began in mid-September and didn't stop until late October. The following three weeks were dry and windy, concentrating the grapes and preventing the onset of rot. The finest wines (mostly at the Auslese level and above) have appealing levels of acidity, loads of intensity, and vibrant personalities. This is a vintage that, unlike 1997, 1999, and 2000, reflects *terroir*. In addition, the finest 1998s will be excellent candidates for cellaring.

1997—After the tooth-shattering acidity of the 1996s, Mother Nature reversed gears for the 1997 vintage. As opposed to the 1996s, the 1997s are forward, lush, low-acid offerings for near-term drinking. In this vintage consumers should concentrate on wines from the Spätlese level and below; the Auslesen rarely have the complexity to match their higher prices, nor do they have the balance for extended cellaring. This is an excellent vintage for consumers who want to discover German wines, as there are multitudes of delicious Kabinetts at reasonable prices.

1996—This is an atypical vintage. High levels of maturity are combined with exceedingly high levels of acidity. In fact, the 1996 Germans may be the most acidic wines I have ever tasted. At the Spätlese level and above (Auslese and above for those fearing searing acidity) a multitude of incredibly pure wines were fashioned. These efforts will require patience for their richness to cover some of the acid. Below the Spätlese level the vast majority of wines are to be avoided; they simply don't have the stuffing to face the record acidity levels. Consumers searching for extraordinary wines at the Auslese level and above for extended cellaring are well advised to search out 1996s crafted by Germany's finest producers.

1995—The 1995 vintage is extremely uneven, with some concentrated, profound, and exceptionally balanced wines having been produced, as well as many that are plagued by the negative characteristics of rot (as opposed to the positive effects of botrytis). The Mosel fared best, and the Rheinpfalz suffered immensely (even outstanding producers such as Lingenfelder were unable to escape the vintage's rot in the Pfalz).

1994—Superb weather in October resulted in an abundant crop of sweeter-styled wines. Quality is uneven, but some outstanding wines were produced. In complete contrast to the stylish, elegant, high-acid 1993s, the 1994s are relatively powerful, rich, and made for near-term drinking.

1993—Delicate, crisp, light-bodied wines were produced in bountiful quantities. The vintage favors Kabinett, Spätlese, and Auslese producers.

1992—This is a good vintage with some superlative, drier-style wines coming from the Ruwer and Middle Mosel. Most estates reported it was very difficult to produce sweet wines in these areas. Therefore, this is a vintage of mostly Kabinetts and Spätleses—a good sign for consumers looking for wines from the drier end of the German wine spectrum. All things considered, 1992 is a good to very fine year throughout the Mosel, Saar, and Ruwer regions, with fewer superrich dessert wines than in years such as 1990 and 1989. In the Rheingau, Rheinpfalz, and Rheinhessen, the vintage looks to be very good to excellent, with plenty of rich wines as well as sweet late-harvest wines, particularly in the Rheinhessen.

1991—This has turned out to be a surprisingly good vintage, far better than many of the doom-and-gloom reports suggested. Although not of the level of 1990 or 1989 in terms of rich, intense, sweet Spätlese and Auslese wines, it is a very appealing vintage, particularly for the top estates in the drier Kabinett styles. The downside of the 1991 vintage is that some wines have shrill levels of acidity, raising questions as to whether their fruit will hold up. Most German-wine specialists suggest this was a year of the wine-maker rather than of Mother Nature, and those producers who were able to keep yields down and who picked physiologically ripe fruit made wines with crisp acidity and good depth and character. Those who didn't made hollow, high-acid wines that merit little attention.

1990—An outstanding, perhaps even great vintage. The wines have fabulous ripeness, surprisingly crisp acidity, and an intense perfume and mid-palate. In addition to many outstanding Kabinetts and Spätleses, this is another vintage, much like 1989, where there were spectacular sweet Ausleses and even more decadently rich Beerenauslese and Trockenbeerenauslese wines produced. If you are a German-wine enthusiast, this vintage is a must buy.

1989—This is another top-notch vintage that has been compared with 1976, 1971, and 1959. The late harvest and the extraordinary amount of sweet wine made at the Auslese, Beerenauslese, and Trockenbeerenauslese levels have garnered considerable enthusiasm. Unlike in 1990, where every wine zone enjoyed success, or 1991, where it was a question of the wine-maker's ability, in 1989 the Saar, Rheinpfalz, Ruwer, and Rheinhessen produced top wines. This was not a rain-free harvest, production yields were high, and acidity levels in many cases remain suspiciously low, suggesting that most consumers would be well advised to drink up the wines below the Auslese level. One area of good but somewhat disappointing wines in the context of the vintage is the Middle Mosel, where a number of the most famous domaines overcropped and produced somewhat fluid, loosely knit, fragile wines.

1988—The strength of this vintage is the Middle Mosel. Based on my tastings, the drier Kabinetts and Spätlese offerings look to be the best wines made. This vintage has now been largely forgotten in the hype over 1989 and 1990.

1987—A mediocre vintage followed an unusual growing season that was characterized by a poor, wet, cold summer but a glorious September and mixed-bag weather in October. The quality is expected to be better than in either 1980 or 1984, and many growers reported harvests close in size to those in 1986. The average production was a whopping 96 hectoliters per hectare, which is excessive. Interestingly, this appears to be a good year for the rare nectarlike Eisweins. All 1987s should have been drunk by 1998.

1986—A copious crop resulted in pleasant, agreeable, soft, fruity wines that had broad commercial appeal. Because of the crop size, prices dropped after the smaller-than-normal crop in 1985. This vintage will be regarded by the trade as a useful, practical year of good rather than great wines. Wines below the Auslese level should already be drunk up.

1985—The German wine trade has touted this year rather highly, but except for a handful of areas, it is not comparable to the outstanding 1983 vintage. Nevertheless, it is a very good year with a moderate production of wines with good acidity and more typical textures and characteristics than the opulent, richly fruity 1983s. As in 1983, the dryness during the summer and fall prevented the formation of *Botrytis cinerea*. The Rieslings in many cases can be very good but will be firmer and slower to evolve and less open than the more precocious, overt, fruity 1983s. Overall, the 1985s should be past their prime. The top successes are in the Middle Mosel, with potentially great wines from villages such as Urzig and Erden. Wines below the Auslese level should already have been drunk and the Auslesen are at their peak.

1984—Fresh, light, very pleasant, straightforward wines that are neither green nor too acidic were produced in this vintage of average quality and below-average quantity. The Mosel estate of Dr. F. Weins-Prüm Erben made excellent wines in 1984, as did Monchhof. All 1984s should have been drunk by 1998.

1983—This vintage received the most publicity between the 1976 and 1990 vintages. Most growers seemed to feel that it was certainly the best since the 1976. It was a very large crop throughout all viticultural areas of Germany, but it was especially large and exceptional in quality in the Mosel-Saar-Ruwer region. The wines have excellent concentration, very fine levels of tartaric rather than green malic acidity, and a degree of precocious ripeness and harmonious roundness that gives the wines wonderful appeal now. However, because of their depth and overall balance, Ausleses remain delicious but should be drunk by 2004. The vintage seemed strongest at the Spätlese level, as there were very little Auslese, Beerenauslese, and Trockenbeerenauslese wines produced. This was also a great year for Eiswein, where, as a result of an early freeze, above-normal quantities of this nectarlike, opulent wine were produced. However, despite larger quantities than normal, the prices are outrageously high for the Eisweins but very realistic and reasonable for the rest of the wines.

OLDER VINTAGES

The great sweet wine vintage that can sometimes still be found in the marketplace is 1976, a vintage that, by German standards, produced incredibly ripe, intense, opulent wines, with a significant amount of wine produced at the Auslese and Beerenauslese levels. The top wines should continue to last another 2–12 years. Some critics have disputed the greatness of this vintage, saying that the 1976s are low in acidity, but that is a minority point of view. The wines remain reasonably priced at the Auslese level, but the Beerenausleses and Trockenbeerenausleses from this vintage are absurdly expensive. The 1977 vintage should be avoided, and 1978, unlike in France, was not a particularly successful year in Germany. Well-kept 1975s can provide great enjoyment, as can the 1971s, another great vintage. I would avoid the wines from 1972, and the once good 1973s are now in serious decline.

RATING GERMANY'S BEST PRODUCERS

Where a producer has been assigned a range of stars (***/****), the lower rating has been used for placement in this hierarchy.

* * * * * *(OUTSTANDING)*

J. J. Christoffel (Mosel)
Kurt Darting (Rheinpfalz)
Hermann Dönnhoff (Nahe)
Fritz Haag (Mosel)
Heribert Kerpen (Mosel)
J. F. Kimich (Rheinpfalz)
H. & R. Lingenfelder (Rheinpfalz)

Egon Müller (Saar)
Müller-Catoir (Rheinpfalz)
Klaus Neckerauer (Rheinpfalz)
J. J. Prüm (Mosel)
Willi Schaefer (Mosel)
von Schubert-Maximin Grünhaus (Ruwer)
Selbach-Oster (Mosel)

* * * * *(EXCELLENT)*

Christian-Wilhelm Bernard (Rheinhessen)
Josef Biffar (Rheinpfalz)
von Bretano (Rheingau)
Burgerspital (Franken)
Dr. Burklin-Wolf (Rheinpfalz)
Schlossgut Diel (Nahe)
August Eser (Rheingau)
H. H. Eser-Johannishof (Rheingau)
F. W. Gymnasium (Mosel)
Willi Haag (Mosel)
Freiherr von Heddesdorff (Mosel)
Hehner-Kiltz (Nahe)
Weingut-Weinhaus Henninger (Rheinpfalz)
Freiherr Heyl zu Herrensheim
   (Rheinhessen)
von Hoauvel (Saar)
Immich-Batterieberg (Mosel)

E. Jakoby-Mathy (Mosel)
Weingut Karlsmühle (Mosel-Ruwer)
Christian Karp-Schreiber (Mosel)
Karthauserhof (Christophe Tyrell) (Ruwer)
von Kesselstatt (Mosel-Saar)
Freiherr zu Knyphausen (Rheingau)
Koehler-Ruprecht (Rheinpfalz)
Königin Victoria Berg-Deinhard
   (Rheingau)
Kruger-Rumpf (Nahe)
Kuhling-Gillot (Rheinhessen)
Franz (Günter) Künstler (Rheingau)
Dr. Loosen-St.-Johannishof (Mosel)
Alfred Merkelbach (Mosel)
Meulenhof/Erben Justen/Erlen (Mosel)
Monchhof (Mosel)
Nahe Staatsdomaine (Nahe)

Pfeffingen (Rheinpfalz)
von Plettenberg (Nahe)
Jochen Ratzenberger (Mittelrhein)
Jakob Schneider (Nahe)

von Simmern (Rheingau)****/*****
J.U.H.A. Strub (Rheinhessen)
Dr. Heinz Wagner (Saar)

* * *(GOOD)

Paul Anheuser (Nahe)
Basserman-Jordan (Rheinpfalz)
Erich Bender (Rheinpfalz)
Bischoflisch Weinguter (Mosel)
Bruder Dr. Becker (Rheinhessen)
Christoffel-Berres (Mosel)
Conrad-Bartz (Mosel)
Hans Crusius (Nahe)
Josef Deinhart (Mosel-Saar)
Epenschild (Rheinhessen)
Dr. Fischer (Saar)
Four Seasons Co-op (Rheinpfalz)
Hans Ganz (Nahe)
Gebrüder Grimm (Rheingau)
Gernot Gysler (Rheinhessen)
Grans-Fassian (Mosel)
Gunderloch-Usinger (Rheinhessen)
J. Hart (Mosel)
Dr. Heger (Baden)
von Hoauvel (Mosel)
Toni Jost (Mittelrhein)***/****
Klaus Klemmer (Mittelrhein)
Johann Koch (Mosel)
Gebrüder Kramp (Mosel)
Lehnert-Matteus (Mosel)
Josef Leitz (Rheingau)
Licht-Bergweiler (Mosel)
Lieschied-Rollauer (Mittelrhein)
Schloss Lieser (Mosel)
Weingut Benedict Loosen Erben (Mosel)
Adolf Lotzbeyer (Nahe)
Mathern (Nahe)***/****
Weingut Merz (Rheinhessen)
Herbert Messmer (Rheinpfalz)
Theo Minges (Rheinpfalz)
Eugen Müller (Rheinpfalz)

Dr. Heinrich Nagler (Rheingau)
Peter Nicolay (Mosel)
von Ohler'sches (Rheinhessen)
Dr. Pauly Bergweiler (Mosel)
Petri-Essling (Nahe)
Ökonomierat Piedmont (Mosel-Saar-
   Ruwer)
S. A. Prüm (Mosel)
S. A. Prüm-Erben (Mosel)
Erich Wilhelm Rapp (Nahe)
Reuscher-Haart (Mosel)
Max Ferdinand Richter (Mosel)
Salm (Nahe)
Prinz zu Salm (Nahe)
Peter Scherf (Ruwer)
von Schleinitz (Mosel)
Georg Albrecht Schneider (Rheinhessen)
Schloss Schönborn (Rheingau)
Schumann-Nagler (Rheingau)
Wolfgang Schwaab (Mosel)
Seidel-Dudenhofer (Rheinhessen)
Bert Simon (Saar)
Schloss Sommerhausen (Franken)
Sturm (Rheinhessen)
Dr. Thanisch (Mosel)
Unckrich (Rheinpfalz)
Christophe Vereinigte Hospitien (Mosel)
Wegeler-Deinhard (Mosel, Rheinpfalz,
   Rheingau)
Adolf Weingart (Mittelrhein)
Dr. F. Weins-Prüm (Mosel)
Domdechant Werner (Rheingau)
Winzer Vier Jahreszeiten (Pfalz)
Günter Wittman (Rheinhessen)
Wolff-Metternich (Rheinhessen)
G. Zilliken (Mosel)

* * (AVERAGE)

Baumann (Rheinhessen)
Bollig-Lehnert (Mosel)
von Buhl (Rheinpfalz)
Stephan Ehlen (Mosel)
Alexandre Freimuth (Rheingau)
Le Gallais (Mosel)
Siegfried Gerhard (Rheingau)

Martin Gobel (Franken)
Schloss Groenestegn (Rheingau)
Louis Guntrum (Rheinhessen)
Schloss Johannishoff (Rheingau)
Burgermeister Carl Koch (Rheinhessen)
Lucashof (Rheinpfalz)
Milz-Laurentiushof (Mosel)

Claus Odernheimer/Abteihof St.-Nicolaus
  (Rheingau)
Geh. Rat Aschrott'sche (Rheingau)
J. Peter Reinert (Mosel-Saar)
Schloss Reinhartshausen (Rheingau)
Schloss Saarstein (Saar)

Schmidt-Wagner (Mosel)
Henrich Seebrich (Rheinhessen)
Staatsweingüter Eltville (Rheingau)
Studert-Prüm/Maximinhof (Mosel)
Schloss Vollrads (Rheingau)

AUSTRIA

The Basics

Thanks to the enormous talents of some of its wine-makers as well as the dedication and hard work of two high-quality U.S. importers (Terry Theise and Vin Divino), Austria is bursting onto the American scene as a source of superb white wines. Since the 1985 scandal (when it was discovered that many Austrian wineries were adulterating their wines with diethylene glycol to give them the appearance of more body and sweetness), Austria has made great strides to improve the quality of its wines. Presently, Austria's average yields are less than half of Germany's (where industrial winemaking still dominates the market), and it has a number of super-high-quality producers that consistently fashion world-class white wines.

While many varietals can be found in Austria, Grüner Veltliner and Riesling dominate its fine dry wine production. Grüner vines make up more than one third of the nation's plantings. It is a pepper, spice, pear, and citrus-flavored white wine that sometimes reveals characteristics reminiscent of rhubarb and green beans. As cutting-edge sommeliers have discovered, it is extremely versatile when paired with food as well as delicious to drink immediately after bottling. While they are capable of aging, my inclination is to consume Grüner Veltliners young, generally within their first 3–6 years of life.

The finest Austrian Rieslings are as mind-boggling as any dry Rieslings produced in the world. They tend to have the expressive nature and harmony reminiscent of Alsatian wines, yet often have the focus and balance of Rieslings from Germany (but not as searing). They are less floral and candied (and generally drier) than their Alsatian counterparts but more fruit-driven than those from Germany. Like Alsatian Rieslings, those from Austria successfully complement a wide variety of foods. While ageworthy, they are generally best consumed within 10 years of the vintage (unlike a number of German and Alsatian Rieslings, which require aging).

Austria's most famous (and deservedly so) dry wine–producing region is the Wachau. As with all of this nation's top wine regions, it is located in eastern Austria. This small area (only 3,500 acres of vines), is situated to the west of Vienna (in fact, it is the westernmost of eastern Austria's wine-producing regions) on the Danube River. Its terraced vineyards are located on steep hillsides and enjoy the full benefit of the area's warm days and cool nights. The Wachau has instituted strict labeling rules to allow consumers to know the natural potential alcohol of the grapes at harvest (Steinfeders are from grapes with 9.5% to 10.7%

natural alcohol, Federspiels with 10.7% to 12%, and the finest, richest wines—over 12% natural potential alcohol—are Smaragds). Other high-quality, dry wine–producing regions include Kremstal, Kamptal, Styria, and Wien. Austria's finest sweet wines come from an area adjacent to the Neusiedlersee area of Burgenland. The Neusiedlersee is a large, shallow lake that separates Austria from Hungary. This humid area regularly benefits from outbreaks of *Botrytis cinerea* (noble rot), essential for the production of complex sweet wines.

Austria's red-wine producers have made efforts in recent years to improve the quality of their wines. However, with a few notable exceptions, they are generally lean, metallic, vegetal, and hard.

A MINI GLOSSARY

The following are a few words that readers will find in the accompanying notes as well as on the labels of other Austrian wines. Familiarizing yourself with these words should assist you in making your initial forays into the vinous treasures of Austria less intimidating.

-er: Words ending in "er" indicate what village or small area the wine comes from, and it is generally followed by the name of the actual vineyard. Thus, a label that reads "Dürnsteiner Freiheit" means it comes from the Freiheit vineyard in the town of Dürnstein.

Alte Reben: The Austrian term for old vines, or *vieilles vignes*.

Ausbruch: Sweet wines made near the town of Rust. To earn the right to include this term on a label, a wine had to have a must weight of at least 139° Oeschle (this German term relates to the must weight of a wine. 139° is extremely high and indicates that Ausbruchs are very sweet).

Beerenauslese: Sweet wine made from must with at least 127° Oeschle. The grapes may have been affected by noble rot (*Botrytis cinerea*).

Ried: Often found on labels preceding another word, this simply means vineyard or cru. For example, in California, Araujo's famous Cabernet Sauvignon would be referred to as Ried Eisele by Austrians. Not every single-vineyard wine has this term on its label.

Smaragd: This term is earned by Wachau's top dry wines. To merit this designation, the wine's grapes had to be harvested with more than 12% natural potential alcohol, and they cannot have been chaptalized or sweetened with *süssreserve* (unfermented grape juice).

Spätlese: Wines with this term on the label must have been harvested with more than 12% natural potential alcohol (94° Oeschle) and cannot be chaptalized or sweetened by using a *süssreserve* (this technique of adding unfermented grape juice is allowed and commonly employed in Germany).

Trockenbeerenauslese: Sweet wine made from must with at least 156° Oeschle. The grapes must have been affected by noble rot (*Botrytis cinerea*).

RATING AUSTRIA'S BEST PRODUCERS

Where a producer has been assigned a range of stars (***/****), the lower rating has been used for placement in this hierarchy.

*****(OUTSTANDING)*

Franz Hirtzberger	F. X. Pichler
Emmerich Knoll	Prager
Alois Kracher	

****(EXCELLENT)*

Willi Bründlmayer****/*****	Hirsch
Feiler-Artinger****/*****	Nikolaihof
Hiedler	Nigl****/*****

Rudi Pichler

Erich & Walter Polz

Heidi Schröck

Tement

*** *(GOOD)*

Leo Alzinger

Gross***/****

Josef Jamek

Dinstlgut Loiben

Fred Loimer***/****

Erich Salomon

Ernst Triebaumer

Freie Weingärtner

Fritz Wieninger

WILLI BRUNDLMAYER (KAMPTAL)

1999 Grüner Veltliner Ried Lamm	D	88
1999 Riesling Zöbinger Heilingenstein	D	88

The 1999 Grüner Veltliner Ried Lamm offers intense mineral and spice aromatics. It is plump, medium- to full-bodied, velvety-textured, and deep. This large, expressive offering has butterscotch and spices intermingled with its mineral backbone. It reveals its high alcohol in the finish and lacks the balance necessary for aging (and for a better review), yet is an excellent, full-flavored Grüner for near-term drinking. Anticipated maturity: now–2003.

The 1999 Riesling Zöbinger Heilingenstein has a demure, mineral-scented nose. On the palate, this medium-bodied, silky-textured offering has powerful stone, gravel, flower, and citrus flavors. It is delineated, expressive, and reveals a long, precise finish. Anticipated maturity: now–2007.

FEILER-ARTINGER (NEUSIEDLERSEE)

1997 Weißburgunder Ruster Ausbruch Essenz "Kurt"	375ml/D	95
1997 Welschriesling Ruster Ausbruch Essenz "Sabine"	375ml/E	92+

The superb 1997 Weißburgunder Ruster Ausbruch Essenz "Kurt" is an apricot jam, honey, and papaya-scented wine. Its full-bodied, viscous, and tangy character is decadently unctuous. Loads of apricots and tropical fruits, as well as bananas, can be found in this intensely sweet, forward offering. While it obviously has good acidity, it is doubtful that it is high enough to face its monstrously powerful fruit, and therefore this wine should be drunk in the near term. Anticipated maturity: now–2005. The 1997 Welschriesling Ruster Ausbruch Essenz "Sabine" is a more civilized, oily-textured, medium- to full-bodied wine. Apricots and peaches can be discerned in its boisterous aromatics. On the palate, this wine has better balance than the "Kurt" yet remains a thick, sweet, plump wine. It is supple, pure, and immensely flavorful. Anticipated maturity: now–2010.

GROSS (STYRIA)

1999 Sauvignon Blanc Ratscher Nussberg	D	89
1999 Sauvignon Blanc Sulz	D	89

Lively gooseberries and white flowers can be discerned in the aromatics of the 1999 Sauvignon Blanc Sulz. This fresh, intense, juicy, silky-textured, medium-bodied wine is loaded with zesty white fruits and gravel-like notes. Well made and balanced, it also possesses an appealingly long, soft finish. The 1999 Sauvignon Blanc Ratscher Nussberg displays white berries, spices, and citrus fruits in its aromas. Medium-bodied, complex, and rich, it is a focused pear, apple, smoke, and spice-flavored wine. Interestingly, its favor profile would lead me to guess that it was aged in oak barrels for at least a few months, yet Seth Allen of Vin Divino (this estate's American importer) assures me that it is oak free. Drink both of these excellent Sauvignon Blancs over the next 2–3 years.

HIEDLER (KAMPTAL)

| 1999 Grüner Veltliner Thal-Novemberlese | D | 88 |

The fresh white fruit and hazelnut purée–scented 1999 Grüner Veltliner Thal-Novemberlese is a rich, medium-bodied wine. Its red and white fruit–flavored character is plump, satin-textured, and powerful. This harmonious wine should be consumed over the next 4–5 years.

HIRSCH (KAMPTAL)

| 1999 Riesling Zöbinger Heilingenstein | D | 88+ |

Hirsch's 1999 Riesling Zöbinger Heiligenstein displays delightful perfume, white fruit, and floral aromas. It is medium-bodied, rich, fat, and reveals layers of well-delineated pear, mineral, and gravel flavors. This excellent wine has the potential to improve with a year or two of cellaring. Anticipated maturity: now–2008.

FRANZ HIRTZBERGER (WACHAU)

1999 Grauburgunder Smaragd Pluris	D	88
1999 Grüner Veltliner Smaragd Axpoint	D	89
1999 Grüner Veltliner Smaragd Honivogl	E	92
1999 Grüner Veltliner Smaragd Rotes-Tor	D	90+
1999 Riesling Smaragd Hochrain	E	91
1999 Riesling Smaragd Singerriedel	EE	95+

The mineral-dominated nose of Franz Hirtzberger's 1999 Grauburgunder Smaragd Pluris leads to a medium-bodied and oily-textured character. Tangy citrus fruits and stones can be found in this well-balanced, appealingly intense, concentrated offering. Drink it over the next 4–5 years. The 1999 Grüner Veltliner Smaragd Axpoint displays spicy white fruit aromas. Medium-bodied, fat, and voluptuous, it offers a complex flavor profile made up of green beans, white pepper, and pears. This wine has excellent depth and concentration. It should be consumed over the next 7 years.

The 1999 Grüner Veltliner Smaragd Rotes-Tor exhibits white flower and mineral aromas. Medium-bodied and satin-textured, it offers gravelly white fruit, stone, and mineral flavors in its highly expressive, concentrated, admirably persistent personality. This outstanding wine can be drunk now or over the next 7–9 years. Honeysuckle, acacia blossoms, and stones can be discerned in the aromatics of the 1999 Grüner Veltliner Smaragd Honivogl. This tobacco, cedar, and mineral-flavored wine has gorgeous definition, precision, and focus. It is medium-bodied, silky-textured, and possesses a long, flavorful finish. Anticipated maturity: now–2008.

The Earl Grey tea–scented 1999 Riesling Smaragd Hochrain is medium-bodied, tangy, and silky-textured. Minerals, quinine, zesty citrus fruits, and candied white berries are found in this well-delineated and persistent wine. Anticipated maturity: now–2008.

The 1999 Riesling Smaragd Singerriedel is a legitimate candidate for Austria's dry white wine of the vintage. It displays candied lemon, mineral, honeysuckle, spice, and herb tea aromas. Medium-bodied, rich, and oily-textured, this is a highly concentrated and complex wine with exquisite balance. Minerals, tangy citrus fruits, gravel, pear, apples, and cherries can be found in its superbly rich and focused character. If that were not enough, it also possesses an exceptionally long, wild strawberry–laden finish. Readers taken aback by its high price should consider that its cost is approximately equivalent to that of premier cru white Burgundy or one-third the price of Haut-Brion blanc. Anticipated maturity: now–2015.

JOSEF JAMEK (WACHAU)

| 1999 Riesling Smaragd Ried Klaus | D | 89 |

The 1999 Riesling Smaragd Ried Klaus reveals fresh mineral, chalk, and flower aromas. Medium-bodied and silky-textured, this is an expansive, complex, and elegant wine with spice-laden mineral and citrus flavors. Anticipated maturity: now–2008.

KNOLL (WACHAU)

1999 Grüner Veltliner Smaragd Ried Loibner Loibenberg	D	90
1999 Riesling Smaragd Loibner Loibenberg	D	89
1999 Riesling Smaragd Ried Dürnsteiner Schütt	D	93

While many of Knoll's colleagues in the Wachau produce wines that are excellent to drink in their youth, Knoll's tend to require patience. Readers who have never seen Knoll's labels should make a special effort to do so, as Knoll's wines sport some of the world's most distinctive labels within the small community of the world's finest producers.

The stone- and mineral-scented 1999 Grüner Veltliner Smaragd Ried Loibner Loibenberg is tightly wound, complex, and light- to medium-bodied. This deep gravel- and mineral-flavored wine is intense and powerful. Anticipated maturity: now–2010.

The 1999 Riesling Smaragd Loibner Loibenberg offers powerful petrol and herbal tea aromas. Medium-bodied, broad, expansive, and exquisitely balanced, this is a backward, mineral- and quinine-dominated wine. It is extremely well made and tangy and should, with cellaring, blossom into an outstanding wine. Anticipated maturity: 2003–2012.

The 1999 Riesling Smaragd Ried Dürnsteiner Schütt displays intense petrol aromas. This medium-bodied, muscular, oily-textured wine has extraordinary focus, depth, and strength. It is extremely backward, revealing only hints of its mineral and candied citrus fruit–dominated personality, yet its thick, dense, and deep flavor profile promises a long, outstanding future. Anticipated maturity: 2004–2012+.

ALOIS KRACHER (NEUSIEDLERSEE)

1997 Bouvier Beerenauslese Number 2 (ZDS)	375ml/E	91
1997 Chardonnay Beerenauslese Number 6 (NV)	375ml/E	91
1998 Chardonnay Trockenbeerenauslese Number 2 (NV)	E/375ml	93
1998 Chardonnay Trockenbeerenauslese Number 9 (NV)	E/375ml	96
1998 Chardonnay Trockenbeerenauslese Number 13 (NV)	EE/375ml	98
1998 Chardonnay/Welschriesling Trockenbeerenauslese Number 7 (NV)	E/375ml	94
1998 Grande Cuvée Trockenbeerenauslese Number 10 (NV)	E/375ml	94
1997 Muskat Ottonel Beerenauslese Number 1 (ZDS)	375ml/E	92
1997 Muskat Ottonel Beerenauslese Number 5 (ZDS)	375ml/E	94
1998 Muskat Ottonel Trockenbeerenauslese Number 5 (ZDS)	E/375ml	96
1997 Scheurebe Beerenauslese Number 3 (ZDS)	375ml/E	92+
1998 Scheurebe Trockenbeerenauslese Number 3 (ZDS)	E/375ml	95
1998 Scheurebe Trockenbeerenauslese Number 12 (ZDS)	EE/375ml	93
1998 Traminer Trockenbeerenauslese Number 8 (NV)	E/375ml	93
1998 Welschriesling Trockenbeerenauslese Number 4 (NV)	E/375ml	95
1998 Welschriesling Trockenbeerenauslese Number 6 (ZDS)	E/375ml	92
1997 Welschriesling Trockenbeerenauslese Number 7 (ZDS)	375ml/EE	94+
1998 Welschriesling Trockenbeerenauslese Number 11 (ZDS)	EE/375ml	96
1997 Zweigelt Rosé Beerenauslese Number 4 (NV)	375ml/E	91
1998 Zweigelt Rosé Trockenbeerenauslese Number 1 (NV)	E/375ml	92

As always with Alois Kracher, he has labeled his sweet wines either "Nouvelle Vague" or "Zwischen den Seen." The Nouvelle Vague (listed as NV above) were vinified and aged in new-oak barrels, whereas the Zwischen den Seen (ZDS) were produced using the area's traditional oakless methods. Nouvelle Vague means "new wave" in French, and Zwischen den Seen means "between the lakes" in German. Kracher also numbers his wines based on concentration, with the least concentrated receiving the lower numbers.

The 1997 Muskat Ottonel Beerenauslese Number 1 (ZDS) reveals sweet orange blossom aromas. On the palate, loads of candied kumquats can be found in this pungent, extroverted, satin-textured wine. Medium-bodied and well balanced, its forward flavors last at least a minute and a half in its seemingly unending finish. Drink this powerful, concentrated wine over the next 10 years. The 1997 Bouvier Beerenauslese Number 2 (ZDS) has a smoke- and apricot-laden nose. Medium- to full-bodied and thickly textured, this peach- and apricot-flavored, decadently strewn wine is plump, fat, and supple. Drink this extroverted beauty over the next 6–7 years.

The fresh orange- and apricot-scented 1997 Scheurebe Beerenauslese Number 3 (ZDS) offers a broad red berry, spice, citrus, and yellow fruit–packed character. This well-balanced, lush, thick-textured wine is concentrated, powerful, and exceptionally long. Drink this outstanding wine over the next 12 years. The dark sherry-colored 1997 Zweigelt Rosé Beerenauslese Number 4 (NV) displays nut, dark roasted berry, spice, and stone aromas. It is thick, oily-textured, medium- to full-bodied, and loaded with mulling spice flavors. This concentrated, flavorful wine should be consumed between now–2009.

The 1997 Muskat Ottonel Beerenauslese Number 5 (ZDS) displays superb orange blossom, candied kumquat, spice, and apricot aromas. This hugely complex, deep, and concentrated wine is crammed with red, yellow, and tropical fruits. Spices, flowers, and oranges are intermingled throughout this medium- to full-bodied, decadent effort. Anticipated maturity: now–2010. Oak spices and yellow fruits can be discerned in the aromatics of the 1997 Chardonnay Beerenauslese Number 6 (NV). Its medium- to full-bodied and satin-textured core of apricots, spiced pears, and tropical fruits also reveals Kracher's use of new oak barrels. It is plump, forward, and reminiscent of an over-the-top California Chardonnay. Because of its loads of sweet fruits and oak, drink it over the next 6–7 years. The thick, almost impenetrable nose of the 1997 Welschriesling Trockenbeerenauslese Number 7 (ZDS) offers spicy red and white fruit flavors. On the palate, this extraordinarily concentrated, thick, viscous, decadent, backward wine is densely packed with untold quantities of red, yellow, and white fruits. It coats the palate with layers of honey-dripping fruit flavors that linger for two minutes or more. Drink this gorgeous sweet wine over the next 12+ years.

According to Alois Kracher, 1998 is the first of a three-year string of outstanding vintages for sweet wines from Austria's Burgenland/Neusiedlersee region. "We have never before had three successive vintages of such high quality," he said. It is a vintage of massive ripeness and huge amounts of *Botrytis cinerea*, the noble rot that concentrates and provides additional complexity to the world's finest sweet wines. These are some of the finest sweet wines produced on earth, and they are less expensive than many of their qualitative equals from Germany and Sauternes/Barsac.

The 1998 Zweigelt Rosé Trockenbeerenauslese Nouvelle Vague Number 1 has a deep goldish amber color (in previous vintages this wine has had a redish pink color, but Kracher says that "botrytis steals color"). Aromatically, it reveals rich, spicy caramel scents. This is a medium- to full-bodied, velvety-textured wine with boisterous botrytis, spice, candied kumquat, caramel, and butterscotch flavors. It has excellent focus and freshness, yet is extremely concentrated (and this is the least concentrated of Kracher's thirteen 1998 Trockenbeerenausleses!). Its extensive finish reveals the drying effect of wines dominated by botrytis. Anticipated maturity: now–2012.

The pale yellow-colored 1998 Chardonnay Trockenbeerenauslese Number 2 (NV) displays aromas of jammy peaches and apricots dusted with botrytis. Medium- to full-bodied and thick, this is a sweet red raspberry, jellied apricot, candied peach, and spice-flavored wine. It is dense and oily-textured, yet pure and fresh. Anticipated maturity: now–2020. The orange/yellow 1998 Scheurebe Trockenbeerenauslese Number 3 (ZDS) explodes from the glass with spices, lychee nuts, roses, and candied white raisins. It is gorgeously focused, fresh, medium-bodied, and packed with smoky minerals as well as loads of jammy yellow fruits. This exceptionally long wine reveals a firm tannic backbone, a rarity for a white wine but typical of its varietal. It has an immensely impressive combination of power, concentration, balance, and elegance. Anticipated maturity: now–2020+.

The 1998 Welschriesling Trockenbeerenauslese (NV) Number 4's color reveals hints of gold. This medium- to full-bodied wine offers candied white raisin and caramel aromas. It is fat, thick, and dense on the palate. Loads of jellied fruits, spices, botrytis flavors, and overripe apricots conquer the palate (my notes say "Wow! Rolling thunder!") and refuse to relinquish their grip for what seems like minutes. Remarkably, given this wine's intensity and thickness, it appears fresh, well balanced, and precise. Drink it over the next 25+ years. The similarly colored 1998 Muskat Ottonel Trockenbeerenauslese Number 5 (ZDS) displays kumquat and candied apricot aromas. Fat jellied oranges explode on the palate and appear to transform themselves into elegant orange blossoms, red berries, and cherries. This is a refined wine with exemplary focus, precision, and purity to go along with its massive concentration as well as power. It is medium- to full-bodied, muscular, and graceful. Drink it over the next 20+ years.

The 1998 Welschriesling Trockenbeerenauslese Number 6 (ZDS) has a musty (it wasn't corked) nose (from its massive levels of botrytis) that also reveals loads of sweet white and yellow fruits. It is crammed with overripe fruit flavors, as well as the distinctive effects of spicy botrytis. This superbly focused wine has bountiful levels of acidity to cope with its lush, opulently thick character. Drink this refined liquid botrytis over the next 20+ years. The yellow/orange 1998 Chardonnay/Welschriesling Trockenbeerenauslese Number 7 (NV) exhibits aromas reminiscent of poached pears, flowers, and candied berries. It is medium- to full-bodied, ample, velvety-textured, and crammed with fresh pears, apples, oranges, white flowers, and jammy apricots. It is rich, broad, lively, and has exceptional acidity and an impressively long finish. Anticipated maturity: now–2025+.

The 1998 Traminer Trockenbeerenauslese Number 8 (NV) is a scrumptious gold-colored wine with an intensely spicy nose, packed with white peaches, freshly cracked pepper, apricots, herbs, and botrytis flavors. It is seamless, harmonious, and has the distinctive tannic mark of its varietal in its botrytis-laced finish. Anticipated maturity: now–2025. The oak, vanilla, toast, acacia blossom, and crème brûlée–scented 1998 Chardonnay Trockenbeerenauslese Number 9 (NV) is an intensely sweet, fat, and candied wine. Full-bodied and powerful, this is a dense (yet harmonious) offering jam-packed with sugarcoated oranges, candied apples, and honey. Its seemingly unending finish reveals additional layers of luxurious jellied fruits. Drink this exceptional wine over the next 25–30 years.

Produced from 50% Chardonnay and 50% Welschriesling, Kracher's 1998 Grande Cuvée Trockenbeerenauslese Number 10 (NV) reveals hints of sweet oak in its otherwise jammy yellow fruit–dominated aromatics. This medium- to full-bodied wine has abundant candied white grapes and apples intermingled with poached pears in its peppery character. It is thick, spicy, oily-textured, and possesses an amazingly long, apricot-flavored finish. Anticipated maturity: now–2030. The 1998 Welschriesling Trockenbeerenauslese Number 11 (ZDS) has a yellow color with golden hues. It exhibits white peach, apricot, smoke, botrytis, and freshly cracked white pepper aromas. Medium- to full-bodied and elegant, this wine is stuffed with candied kumquats, jellied peaches, spices, and fresh apricots. It has an exceptional combination of refinement, power, and concentration. This decadently textured wine is intense, pure, and immensely long. Anticipated maturity: now–2030+.

The gold-colored 1998 Scheurebe Trockenbeerenauslese Number 12 (ZDS) has a chemical-scented nose that also displays white pepper and graham cracker aromas. Medium- to full-bodied and lush, this wine offers copious layers of jellied yellow fruits in its fat, plump, yet wonderfully fresh personality. As its nose sheds its chemical notes with air, this wine offers a compotelike character that reveals caramel and butterscotch flavors. Readers who wish to drink this wine while it displays fruit should consume it over the next 5–8 years. Those who prefer aged, dark-colored, heavily botrytized wines dominated by burnt sugar flavors can drink it between 2007–2030+. The 1998 Chardonnay Trockenbeerenauslese Number 13 (NV) is Kracher's most concentrated wine from this vintage. Cedar, spices, apricots, and overripe peaches are displayed by this full-bodied, muscular offering. It is hugely dense, almost syrupy, with loads of jammy and jellied fruits in its round, sexy personality. This Rubenesque wine has untold quantities of fruit (mostly apricots), spices, and botrytis in its expressive, seamless flavor profile. This harmonious, muscular, and graceful wine will retain its fruit for at least 15 years and will potentially live longer than anyone reading this book.

DINSTLGUT LOIBEN (WACHAU)

1999 Riesling Loibner Loibenberg "L"	C	88

The herbal tea and sweet spice–scented 1999 Riesling Loibner Loibenberg "L" has a medium-bodied and satin-textured character. It is a brazen hussy wine, a forward Riesling loaded with potpourri, perfume, and white raisin flavors. This expressive wine should be consumed over the next 3–5 years.

LOIMER (KAMPTAL)

1999 Grüner Veltliner Spiegel Alte Reben	D	89

The sweet spring onion–scented 1999 Grüner Veltliner Spiegel Alte Reben is medium- to full-bodied, rich, and plump. Broad layers of minerals, white fruits, freshly cracked white pepper, and garbanzo beans can be discerned in this excellent wine's complex personality. Drink it over the next 4–5 years.

FAMILIE NIGL (KREMSTAL)

1999 Grüner Veltliner Alte Reben	D	88
1999 Riesling Senftenberg Piri Privat	E	89+
1999 Sauvignon Blanc	D	89

The 1999 Grüner Veltliner Alte Reben offers lovely mineral aromas. It displays excellent depth to its quinine, pear, and citrus fruit–flavored personality. This medium-bodied, well-made, seamless wine also possesses a long, tangy finish. Anticipated maturity: now–2006.

Nigl's 1999 Sauvignon Blanc is a strange yet compelling wine. Consumers who dislike Sauvignons with vegetal aromas and flavors are advised to steer clear of Nigl's 1999. However, readers searching for wines that are distinctively unusual will love this controversial wine. It offers bell pepper and roasted peanut scents as well as a complex, medium-bodied personality. Spices are intermingled with sautéed green beans in this detailed and silky-textured effort's character. Unlike the vast majority of wines with distinct vegetable aromas and flavors, this one is ripe and rich. Drink it over the next 2–3 years. Pears and apples can be discerned in the aromatics of the 1999 Riesling Senftenberg Piri Privat. Light to medium-bodied and satin-textured, it has a flavor profile composed of white fruits, red berries, flowers, minerals and lemons. Refined, this flavorful wine has impressive depth as well as a finish that appears to roar back to life after 30 seconds or so. Anticipated maturity: now–2008.

NIKOLAIHOF (WACHAU)

1999 Grüner Veltliner Smaragd im Weingebirge	D	88
1999 Riesling Jungfernweim im Weingebirge	E	89
1999 Riesling Spätlese Steiner Hund	E	91+

The white pepper and flower-scented 1999 Grüner Veltliner Smaragd im Weingebirge is a medium-bodied, satin-textured wine. This explosively rich, layered Grüner is filled with expressive pear, apple, and spice flavors that linger throughout its long finish. Anticipated maturity: now–2005. The Nikolaihof winery, a biodynamically farmed estate, produced a superb 1999 Riesling Spätlese Steiner Hund. Its gorgeous aromas of perfume, flowers, and spices lead to a highly expressive core of voluptuous red and white berries that nearly obscure this outstanding wine's underlying minerality. Well balanced and delineated, it is a rich, refined Riesling that can be drunk over the next 10–12 years. The 1999 Riesling Jungfernwein im Weingebirge is an excellent wine for near-term drinking. It displays creamed spice aromas and a plump, medium-bodied, velvety-textured character. This offering has impressive depth to its cherry, raspberry, and spice-flavored personality. Anticipated maturity: now–2005.

F. X. PICHLER (WACHAU)

1999 Grüner Veltliner Smaragd Dürnsteiner Kellerberg	E	91
1999 Grüner Veltliner Smaragd M	D	90
1999 Grüner Veltliner Smaragd von den Terrassen	D	90
1999 Riesling Smaragd Dürnsteiner Kellerberg	EE	93
1999 Riesling Smaragd Loibner Berg	EE	92

The 1999 Grüner Veltliner Smaragd von den Terrassen boasts an explosive nose of spices and deep white fruits. Medium-bodied and hugely expressive, this is a precise, satin-textured wine. Loads of pepper, pears, apples, and spices can be discerned in its boisterous flavor profile. Drink this wine over the next 7–8 years. The quinine- and mineral-scented 1999 Grüner Veltliner Smaragd Dürnsteiner Kellerberg is medium-bodied and silky-textured. Red and white berries as well as minerals can be found in this highly detailed, concentrated, complex wine. It is extremely well balanced and possesses a long, supple finish. Anticipated maturity: now–2008. The 1999 Grüner Veltliner Smaragd M has rather subdued aromas and a light- to medium-bodied character. Silky-textured, tight, and powerful, this is a bell pepper and freshly cracked white pepper–flavored wine, highly defined yet rich, with an admirably long, lush finish. Anticipated maturity: now–2007.

The extroverted nose of the 1999 Riesling Smaragd Loibner Berg offers red/white berries and flowers. This deep, hugely concentrated, medium-bodied, intricate wine is packed with a myriad of spices as well as pears, apples, white peaches, apricots, and minerals. This outstanding Riesling can be enjoyed over the next 12 years. The superb 1999 Riesling Smaragd Dürnsteiner Kellerberg offers searing mineral, candied lemon, flower, and spiced pear aromas. Medium-bodied, magnificently elegant, and complex, this is a cherry, wild strawberry, and tropical fruit–flavored wine whose flavors seamlessly last throughout its exceptionally long finish. Rich, deep, yet highly detailed and refined, it is a wine that is forward and drinkable young yet has all the requisites for a long, fruitful life. Drink this beauty over the next 15 years.

RUDI PICHLER (WACHAU)

1999 Grüner Veltliner Smaragd Wösendorfer Hochrain	D	89
1999 Grüner Veltliner Smaragd Wösendorfer Kollmutz	D	88
1999 Riesling Smaragd Weissenkirchner Achleiten	D	90
1999 Riesling Smaragd Wösendorfer Kirchweg	D	89

Pure, racy minerals can be found in the aromatics of the 1999 Grüner Veltliner Smaragd Wösendorfer Kollmutz. Medium-bodied, rich, and dense, it reveals minerals, white pepper, and pearlike flavors in its silky-textured character. Anticipated maturity: now–2006. The herbal tea and mineral-scented 1999 Grüner Veltliner Smaragd Wösendorfer Hochrain is light- to medium-bodied, broad, and plump. Grapefruit and assorted other citrus fruits are intermingled with spices and pepper in this complex, silky-textured wine. Anticipated maturity: now–2007.

The 1999 Riesling Smaragd Wösendorfer Kirchweg has tangy berry and freshly cracked black pepper aromas. Medium-bodied, zesty, and broad, it reveals pear, apple, mineral, and stone flavors in its long, focused character. Drink it over the next 7–8 years. Expressive lemon and white flower aromas are found in the nose of the 1999 Riesling Smaragd Weissenkirchner Achleiten. This medium-bodied, expansive, admirably focused wine is spicy and filled with minerals, quinine, and red/white berries. Satin-textured and intricate, it is full-flavored, elegant, and admirably persistent. Drink this wine over the next 8–10 years.

ERICH & WALTER POLZ (SUDSTEIERMARK)

1999 Sauvignon Blanc Hochgrassnitzberg	D	89

Lively lemons and gooseberries can be found in the aromatics of the 1999 Sauvignon Blanc Hochgrassnitzberg. This medium-bodied, rich, concentrated Sauvignon displays a wonderful velvety-textured character. Its powerful personality is filled with an assortment of white and citrus fruits, as well as a complex underlying minerality. Anticipated maturity: now–2003.

PRAGER (WACHAU)

1999 Riesling Smaragd Dürnstein Hollerin	D	89+
1999 Riesling Smaragd Dürnstein Kaiserberg	D	92
1999 Riesling Smaragd Weissenkirchen Achleiten	E	92
1999 Riesling Smaragd Weissenkirchen Klaus	E	92+
1999 Riesling Smaragd Weissenkirchen Steinriegl	C	90
1999 Riesling Smaragd Weissenkirchen Wachstum Bodenstein	E	94

The 1999 Riesling Smaragd Dürnstein Hollerin displays chalk, mineral, and herbal tea aromas. This vivacious, medium-bodied, highly focused (almost searingly so) wine is packed with stones, white fruits, and minerals. Anticipated maturity: now–2008. Pears, apples, and expressive mineral aromas are found in the nose of the 1999 Riesling Smaragd Dürnstein Kaiserberg. Medium- to full-bodied, rich, broad, and massively concentrated, this gravel-flavored beauty has extraordinary precision and an exceptionally long, flavorful, and delineated finish. Drink it over the next 8–10 years.

The 1999 Riesling Smaragd Weissenkirchen Steinriegl has a mineral-dominated nose. This medium-bodied, silky-textured, and tangy wine is redolent with lemony minerals, quinine, and flowers. This admirably balanced wine should be consumed over the next 7–9 years. The stone- and mineral-scented 1999 Riesling Smaragd Weissenkirchen Achleiten is medium-bodied, powerful, and tightly wound. This citrus, mineral, and white fruit–dominated wine has outstanding intensity and complexity to its persistent personality. Drink it over the next 8 years.

The 1999 Riesling Smaragd Weissenkirchen Klaus offers mineral, lemon, and pear aromas. Medium-bodied and silky-textured, it has outstanding depth, intensity, and focus. White flowers, gravel, minerals, and quinine (slightly reminiscent of a gin and tonic) can be found throughout its tangy flavor profile as well as in its impressively long finish. Drink it over the next 8–10 years. The superb 1999 Riesling Smaragd Weissenkirchen Wachstum Bodenstein has a nose of citrus fruits, flowers, white pepper, honeysuckle blossoms, and minerals. Medium-bodied and explosive, this powerful, gorgeously detailed, and intense wine coats the taster's palate with deep layers of liquid minerals and white fruits. It has exquisite balance, an expressive yet elegant personality, and a seemingly unending finish. Drink this wine over the next 10–12 years.

ERICH SALOMON (KREMSTAL)

1999 Riesling Kögl Reserve	D	89

The acacia blossom–scented 1999 Riesling Kögl Reserve is light- to medium-bodied and well delineated. It possesses a complex white fruit, gravel, spice, and mineral-filled character as well as an impressively long, flavorful finish. This extremely well made and highly detailed wine should be consumed over the next 6–8 years.

TEMENT (STYRIA)

1999 Sauvignon Blanc Zieregg   **D   88**

The 1999 Sauvignon Blanc Zieregg was aged four months in new-oak barrels. It displays sweet white fruits intermingled with spicy oak notes in its aromatics. On the palate, this buttery-textured, medium-bodied wine is redolent with ripe pears, gooseberries, and spices. Drink it between now–2003.

ERNST "ET" TRIEBAUMER (NEUSIEDLERSEE)

1997 Blaufrankisch Ried Mariental   **EE   88**

The medium to dark ruby-colored 1997 Blaufrankisch Ried Mariental displays a lovely nose of spices and deep red fruits. Medium-bodied, chewy-textured, and well structured, this is an intense, stony black fruit–flavored wine. Drink it over the next 4–5 years.

WEINGARTNER (WACHAU)

1999 Riesling Smaragd Loibner Loibenberg   **C   89**

1999 Riesling Smaragd Weissenkirchner Achleiten   **D   88+**

The 1999 Riesling Smaragd Weissenkirchner Achleiten displays a powerful, spice-laden nose. Medium-bodied, juicy, and fat, it is well balanced and offers a deep stone- and mineral-laden character. Anticipated maturity: now–2007. The 1999 Riesling Smaragd Loibner Loibenberg has aromas of bergamot (the zesty citrus fruit used to flavor Earl Grey tea) and stone. It is medium-bodied, rich, and loaded with white and red berries, as well as notes of spicy herbal teas. This detailed, flavorful, complex wine should be consumed over the next 6 years.

WIENINGER (VIENNA)

1999 Grüner Veltliner Nussberg   **C   88**

1999 Nussberg Alte Reben   **C   88**

The smoke, spice, and fresh earth–scented 1999 Grüner Veltliner Nussberg is medium-bodied and silky-textured. This juicy, rich, well-balanced wine reveals pear, spice, and white pepper flavors in its focused character. Anticipated maturity: now–2005. The 1999 Nussberg Alte Reben is the result of a field blend (when the different commingled grape varietals within a specific vineyard or *terroir* are harvested and vinified together). Its subdued aromatics are followed by a rich, complex, medium-bodied personality. Spices, pepper, apples, and pears can be found throughout its silky-textured character, as well as in its long, lush finish. Anticipated maturity: now–2005.

4. SPAIN AND PORTUGAL

SPAIN

The Basics

TYPES OF WINE

Aside from the glories of sherry, which is synonymous with Spain, this beautiful sun-drenched country is best known as a treasure trove for red wine values. The majority of white wines, which in the past tasted musty and oxidized, are now, thanks to high technology, usually innocuous, with sterile personalities and no real flavor. There are exceptions, such as the fragrant, crisp, tasty whites made from the Albarino grape. Other refreshing, inexpensive white wines have emerged, but they are in the minority. And while the booming Spanish sparkling wine business stays in the headlines, few makers of sparkling wine actually produce exceptional wine; most of it is reliably pleasant, relatively innocuous, and very cheap—under $15—hence the appeal.

Red wine is king in Spain, but regrettably this country is still one of largely unrealized potential. The best red wines all come from northern Spain. The two areas best known for quality are Rioja and Penedès. Yet these traditional bastions of Spanish wine are being rivaled and occasionally surpassed by upstart regions. The Ribera del Duero, Priorato, Navarra, and Toro are today's overachievers, and Jumilla is beginning to attract attention.

To understand Spanish red wines one must first realize that the Spanish want their red wines supple, with an aged taste of maturity, as well as a healthy (many would say excessive) dosage of oak, usually the blatant American variety. Once you realize this, you will understand why many Spanish wineries, called *bodegas,* age their wines in huge oak or concrete vats for seven or eight years before they are released. While tastes are changing, the Spanish are not fond of grapy, tannic, young wines, and historically have expected the wineries to mature the wines for the Spanish consumer. Consequently, traditionally styled Spanish wines have an advanced garnet color, and are smooth and supple with the sweet vanilla taste of strong oak well displayed. Many wineries actually hold back their best lots for a decade or more before releasing them, enabling the consumer to purchase a mature, fully drinkable wine. However, the international demand for big, dark wines with intense flavors is causing a revolution in winemaking, led by the aforementioned regions.

GRAPE VARIETIES

RED WINES

Cabernet Sauvignon   An important part of Vega Sicilia, Spain's most expensive and prestigious red wine, Cabernet Sauvignon has flourished in Spain.

Carinena This workhorse grape (Carignan in English) has muscles like Arnold Schwarzenegger. Big and brawny, the tannic, densely colored wine made from this grape varietal is frequently used as a blending agent, particularly with Grenache.

Garnacha Garnacha (Grenache) is widely planted in Spain. There are three types of Garnacha utilized. Garnacha Blanc, which produces white wines, is relatively limited, although it is especially noticeable in Tarragona. Garnacha Tinto, similar to the Grenache known in France, is one of the most widely planted red wine grapes in Spain. There is also the Garnacha Tintorera, which is actually Alicante, the grape that produces black-colored, tannic, dense wines, and is primarily used for blending.

Merlot This relatively new varietal for Spain has performed competently.

Monastrell This varietal (Mourvèdre) primarily produces surprisingly rich, alcoholic wines. Although widely planted, it is most frequently found in hotter microclimates. Some producers from the backwater viticultural region of Jumilla have done interesting work with Monastrell.

Tempranillo The finest indigenous red wine grape of Spain, and a noble one, Tempranillo travels under a number of names. In Penedès it is called Ull de Llebre and Tinto in the Ribera del Duero. It provides rich, well-structured wines with good acidity and plenty of tannin and color. The bouquet often exhibits an intense berry/black raspberry character with a floral note. It makes an ideal blending mate with Garnacha, but it is easily complex enough to stand on its own. Tempranillo is also called Tinta del Pais, Tinta del Toro, Tinto de la Rioja, and Tinto Madrid.

WHITE WINES

The white wine grapes parade under names such as Albarino, Chardonnay, Macallo, Malvasia, Palomina (utilized for sherry), Parellada (the principle component of most sparkling wines), Pedro-Ximenez, Riesling, Sauvignon, Torrontés, Verdejo, Xarello, and Moscatel. Few of these varietals have proven to be capable of making anything more than neutral-tasting wines, but several appear to have potential, as yields have been kept low and the wines have been impeccably vinified, not eviscerated by processing. The best is the Albarino, which, when produced by a top winery in Galicia, has a stunning perfume similar to that of a French Condrieu. However, in the mouth the wine is much lighter, with less body and intensity. At its finest, it is light, refreshing, fragrant, and an ideal apéritif or seafood wine.

Other white wines that have shown potential include some of the Chardonnays, and Torrontes, which, when made in Galicia, has a perfumed personality, lovely fruit salad–like flavors, and a pleasant finish.

FLAVORS

Penedès The dominant winery here is Torres, which produces a bevy of red wines from the typical Spanish varietals. But the top wine is the 100% Cabernet Sauvignon Black Label Gran Coronas, which has a rich, open-knit bouquet of plums, sweet oak, and often licorice and violets. Its chief rival is the Cabernet Sauvignon from Jean Leon, another concentrated, blackberry-scented and -flavored, full-throttle wine with a whopping influence from sweet, toasty oak. The best recent vintages are 1998, 1996, 1995, and 1994.

Ribera del Duero Three of Spain's greatest red wines are produced in this broad river valley: Pesquera, which comes primarily from the Tempranillo grape, Vega Sicilia, primarily a Cabernet Sauvignon/Merlot/Malbec blend, and Tempranillo-based Pingus. These are world-class wines of considerable majesty. What is noticeable about them is the remarkable purity of berry fruit that can be found in the top vintages. Take superripe fruit and combine it with a minimum of three years (in the case of Vega Sicilia, 8–12 years) in oak casks, and you have powerfully heady, supple, explosively rich wines that offer a great deal of spicy, sweet,

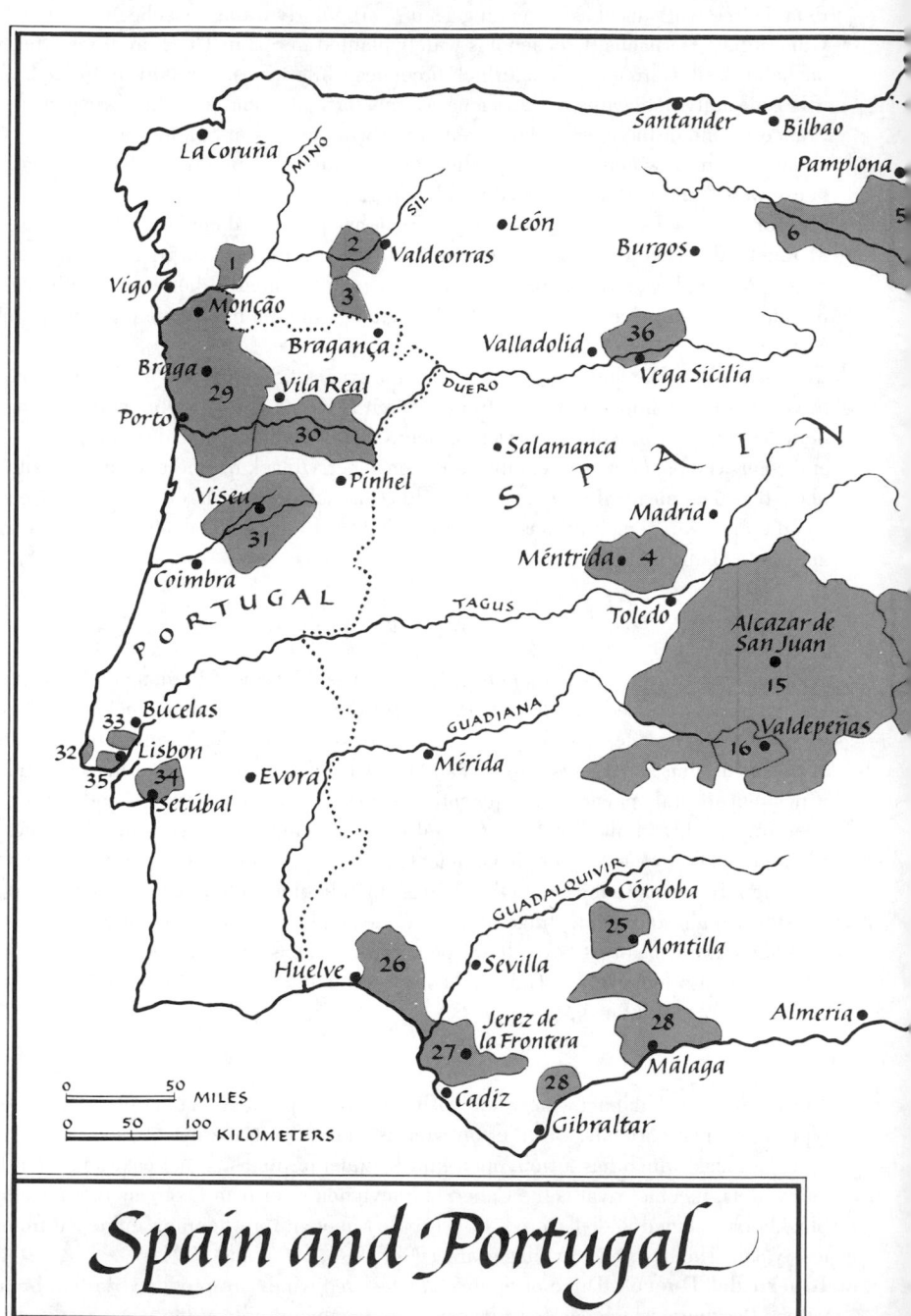

Spain and Portugal

La Coruña
MINO
SIL
Santander • Bilbao
Pamplona •
5
León •
Burgos •
6
Valdeorras
2
Vigo •
Monção •
1
3
Braga •
Vila Real •
29
Porto •
30
Pinhel
Viseu •
31
Coimbra •
PORTUGAL
Valladolid •
36
Vega Sicilia
DUERO
Salamanca •
S P A I N
Madrid •
Méntrida • 4
TAGUS
Toledo •
Alcazar de
San Juan
15
Bucelas
33
GUADIANA
Mérida •
Valdepeñas
16
32
Lisbon •
35
34
Setúbal
Evora •
GUADALQUIVIR
Córdoba •
25
Montilla
Huelve •
26
Sevilla •
Jerez de
la Frontera
28
Almería •
27
28
Málaga
Cadiz
Gibraltar

0   50   MILES
0   50   100 KILOMETERS

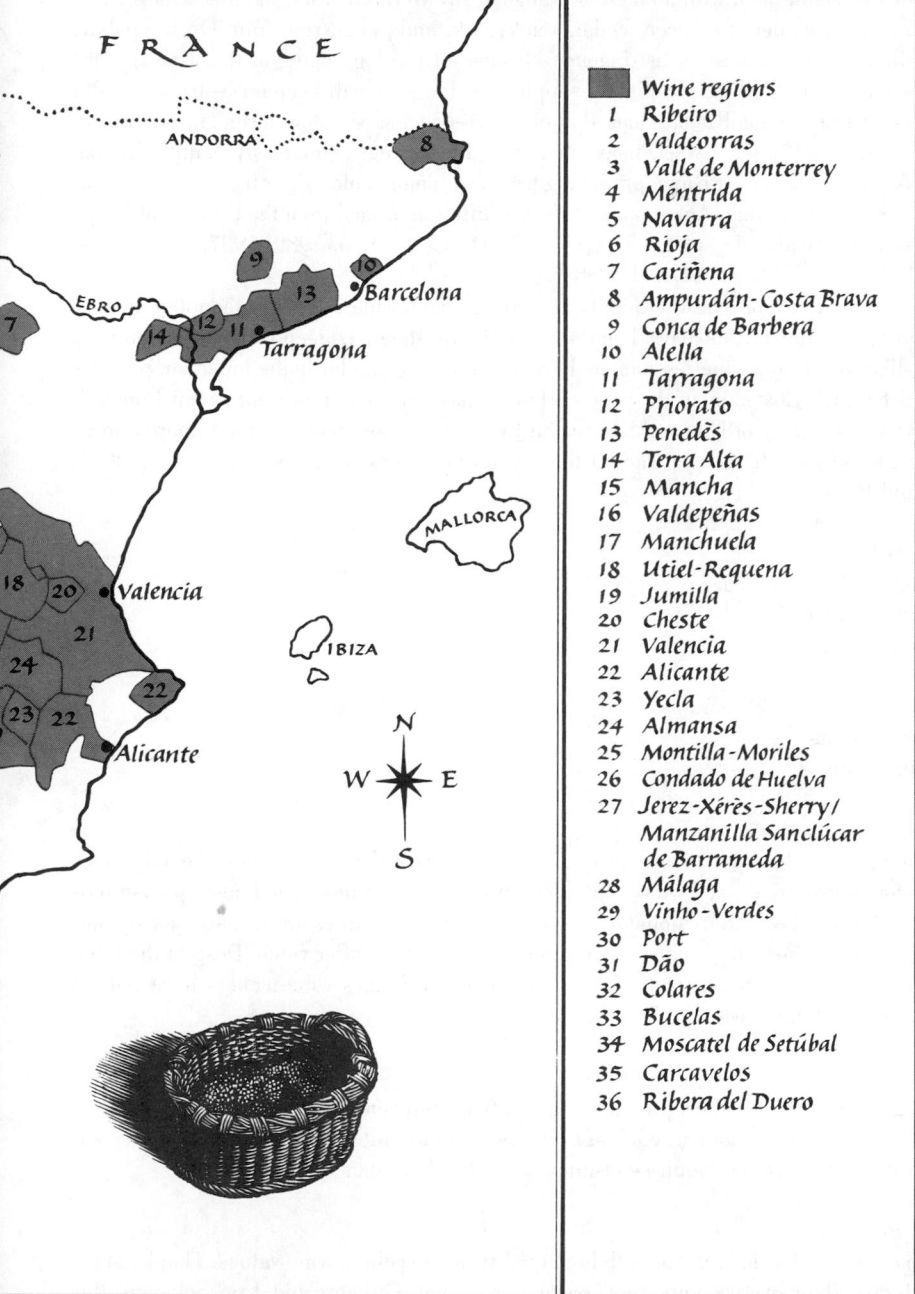

FRANCE

ANDORRA

EBRO

Barcelona

Tarragona

MALLORCA

Valencia

IBIZA

Alicante

N
W ⬥ E
S

Wine regions
1   Ribeiro
2   Valdeorras
3   Valle de Monterrey
4   Méntrida
5   Navarra
6   Rioja
7   Cariñena
8   Ampurdán- Costa Brava
9   Conca de Barbera
10 Alella
11 Tarragona
12 Priorato
13 Penedès
14 Terra Alta
15 Mancha
16 Valdepeñas
17 Manchuela
18 Utiel-Requena
19 Jumilla
20 Cheste
21 Valencia
22 Alicante
23 Yecla
24 Almansa
25 Montilla-Moriles
26 Condado de Huelva
27 Jerez-Xérès-Sherry/
    Manzanilla Sanclúcar
    de Barrameda
28 Málaga
29 Vinho-Verdes
30 Port
31 Dão
32 Colares
33 Bucelas
34 Moscatel de Setúbal
35 Carcavelos
36 Ribera del Duero

toasty, vanilla-scented oak. The best vintages have been 2001, 2000, 1999, 1996, 1995, 1994, 1991, 1990, 1989, 1986, 1983, 1982, 1976, 1975, 1968, and 1962.

Rioja   When made by the finest traditional producers, Rioja is a mature wine having a medium-ruby color, often with a touch of orange or brown (normal for an older wine), and a huge, fragrant bouquet of tobacco, cedar, smoky oak, and sweet, ripe fruit. On the palate, there will be no coarseness or astringence because of the long aging of the wine in cask and/or tank prior to bottling. Despite its suppleness, the wine will keep for 5–10 years after its release. Even a young Rioja, released after just 3–4 years, will show a ripe, fat, rich, supple fruitiness, and a soft, sweet, oaky character. Increasingly, progressive antitraditional winemaking has taken over Rioja, producing wines with more color, riper fruit, and the influence of French rather than American oak. It is a different animal from the traditional Rioja. The best vintages include 2001, 1996, 1995, 1994, 1991, 1990, 1989, 1987, 1982, 1981, 1978, 1973, 1970, 1968, 1964, and 1958.

Toro   Once known for overwhelmingly alcoholic, heavy wines, Toro has adopted modern technology, and the results have been some rich, full-bodied, deeply flavored, southern Rhône–like wines from wineries such as Farina. They taste similar to the big, lush, peppery wines of France's Châteauneuf-du-Pape and Gigondas, and they represent astonishing values. The luxury cuvée of Numanthia, created by cutting-edge Spanish wine importer Jorge Ordoñez, showcases the great potential this region possesses. The best vintages are 2001, 1999, and 1998.

AGING POTENTIAL
Albarino (whites): 1–2 years
Navarra: 5–7 years
Penedès: 6–15 years
Priorato: 6–25 years
Ribera del Duero: 6–30 years
Rioja: 6–25 years
Sparkling white wines: 1–4 years

OVERALL QUALITY LEVEL
While it may be fashionable to tout the quality and value of all Spanish wines, the only wines with serious merit are the red wines and a handful of the Albarinos. The finest Spanish reds can hold up to the best international competition. Most of the whites are still atrociously boring, and while the sparkling wines are inexpensive, only a few offer value. Despite the fabulous climate and high percentage of old vines, most of Spain's wine-makers have not yet realized their potential, which is formidable.

MOST IMPORTANT INFORMATION TO KNOW
Knowing the names of the best producers, and a few top recent vintages (1994, 1995, 1996, and 1999) will get you a long way if you avoid most of the white wines from this country, except for the Albarinos that require consumption within 1–2 years of the vintage.

BUYING STRATEGY
Spain has become fashionable for both high quality and excellent wine values. Thanks to the work of several innovative importers, particularly Jorge Ordoñez and Eric Solomon, this country is securing a bigger and bigger share of the fine-wine market, as well as continuing to provide many exceptional bargains. The slow transformation of the Spanish mentality from a cooperative-based, industrial winemaking philosophy to one based on quality, individuality, and *terroir* has resulted in better and better wines. There are some storm clouds on the

horizon due to the fact that much of Spain had less than stellar vintages in 1997 as well as 1998. Combine that with increasingly high prices for many wines with no established track record, and consumer resistance is inevitable. However, there are abundant quantities of high-quality 1994s, 1995s, and 1996s in the marketplace, as well as others scheduled to be released over the next several years. Given the terrific climate, multitude of fabulous *terroirs*, and the requisite financial incentive to produce world-class wine, look for more and more unknown names to become overnight stars, assuming prices do not get out of touch with the realities of the marketplace.

RECENT VINTAGES

2000—A huge harvest throughout Spain, especially in Rioja, Ribera del Duero, and Navarra, this will be an irregular year with some superb wines. Rioja will be more irregular than Ribera del Duero.

1999—It was a sensational harvest in Ribera del Duero, although rain was a problem in some areas. Rioja is at best average because of uneven ripening and a rainy harvest. Overall, it is a good vintage in Ribera del Duero, mediocre in Rioja, and average to above average in such regions as Navarra and Penedès.

1998—This is a relatively tannic vintage for most Spanish wine regions, with a good-sized crop. The Ribera del Dueros are less successful than in 1999, but the Riojas are better. Priorato enjoyed an excellent vintage, nearly as fine as the great 1994.

1997—A difficult vintage throughout Spain, the quality in 1997 is significantly below the levels achieved in 1994, 1995, and 1996, and in subsequent years such as 1999 and 2000.

1996—A spectacular vintage in Ribera del Duero, good to very good in Rioja, and mediocre in Priorato.

1995—In many areas of Spain, this vintage has turned out to be as stunning as 1994. Everyone from Rioja, Ribera del Duero, and Priorato was thrilled with the ripeness and richness. It appears to be a great vintage for Spain's top producers.

1994—Spanish wine producers have pronounced 1994 as Spain's vintage of the century. It was one of the hottest years on record and, unlike France, Spain was not troubled by September rain. From bottle, the top wines are indeed impressive, especially those from Priorato, Rioja, and Ribera del Duero.

RATING SPAIN'S BEST DRY RED TABLE WINES

* * * * * *(OUTSTANDING)*

Abadia Retuerta Cuvée El Campanario
   (Sardon del Duero)
Abadia Retuerta Pago Negralato (Sardon
   del Duero)
Abadia Retuerta Valdebon (Sardon del
   Duero)
Bodegas Ismael Arroyo Valsotillo Reserva
   (Ribera del Duero)
Artadi Rioja Grandes Anadas Reserva
   Especial (Rioja)
Artadi Rioja Viña El Pison Reserva
   (Rioja)
Cims de Porrera (Priorato)
Clos Erasmus (Priorato)

Clos Mogador (Priorato)
l'Ermita (Priorato)
Mauro Vendimia Seleccionada (Ribera del
   Duero)
Muga Prado Enea Reserva (Rioja)
Muga Torre Muga (Rioja)
Marqués de Murrieta Castillo Ygay Gran
   Reserva (Rioja)
Marqués de Murrieta Dalmau Reserva
   (Rioja)
Numanthia (Toro)
Pesquera Ribera del Duero (Castilla-
   León)
Pingus (Ribera del Duero)

Fernando Remirez de Ganuza Rioja Old Vines Unfiltered (Rioja)

Rotllan Torra Tirant (Priorato)

Sierra Cantabria Rioja Coleccion Privada (Rioja)

Vega Sicilia NV Gran Reserva Especial (Ribera del Duero)

Vega Sicilia Unico Reserva (Castilla-León)

* * * * (EXCELLENT)

Abadia Retuerta (Sardon del Duero)

Abadia Retuerta Cuvée El Palomar (Sardon del Duero)

Abadia Retuerta Rivola (Sardon del Duero)

Albet I Noya Sat (Penedès)

Finca Allende (Rioja)

Bodegas Ismael Arroyo Valsotillo (Ribera del Duero)

Artadi Rioja Pagos Viejos Reserva (Rioja)

Artadi Rioja Viña de Gain Crianza (Rioja)

Bodegas Arzuaga Reserva (Ribera del Duero)

René Barbier (Cataluna)

Can Rafols dels Caus Penedès (Cataluna)

Capcanes (Tarragona)

Capcanes Garnacha Especial (Tarragona)

Casa Castillo (Jumilla)

Castano (Yecla)

Bodegas Julian Chivite 125 Anniversario Reserva (Navarra)

Clos Dofi (Priorato)

Oliver Conti (Costa Brava)

Costers del Siurdana—Clos de l'Obac (Priorato)

CVNE Contino (Rioja)

CVNE Imperial (Rioja)

CVNE Viña Real (Rioja)

J. M. Fuentes Gran Clos (Priorato)

Fra Fulco (Priorato)

Grandes Bodegas Marqués de Velilla Reserva (Ribera del Duero)

Marqués de Griñon (Ribera del Duero)

Marqués de Griñon (Rioja)

Iberus (Terra Alta)

Leda (Castilla-León)

Jean Léon Penedès (Cataluna)

Martinez Bujanda Conde de Valdemar (Rioja)

Martinez Bujanda Conde de Valdemar Gran Reserva (Rioja)

Mas Igneus (Priorato)

Bodegas Mauro (Ribera del Duero)

Bodegas Moro (Ribera del Duero)

Bodegas Muga (Rioja)

Marqués de Murrieta Coleccion 2100 (Rioja)

Olivares Monastrell (Tarragona)

Pago de Carraovejas (Ribera del Duero)

Remelluri (Rioja)

Castell de Remei (Costers del Segre)

Bodegas Reyes Teofilo Reyes (Ribera del Duero)

La Rioja Alta Reserva 890 (Rioja)

La Rioja Alta Reserva 904 (Rioja)

Bodegas Roda (Rioja)

Telmo Rodriguez (Ribera del Duero)

San Vicente (Rioja)

Hermanos Sastre (Ribera del Duero)

Sierra Cantabria (Rioja)

Bodegas Valcona (Rioja)

Val Llach (Priorato)

Vega Sicilia Valbuena Ribera del Duero (Castilla-León)

Villa Creces (Ribera del Duero)

* * * (GOOD)

Agricola de Borja (Campo de Borja)

Señorío de Almansa (Castillo-La Mancha)

Amezola de la Mora (Rioja)

Arboles de Castillejo (La Mancha)

Palacio de Arganza Bierzo (Castilla-León)

Bodegas Ismael Arroyo (Ribera del Duero)

Pablo Barrigon Tovar (Castilla-León)

Pablo Barrigon Tovar San Pablo (Castilla-León)

Pablo Barrigon Tovar Viña Cigalena Reserva (Castilla-León)

Pablo Barrigon Tovar Viña Solona (Castilla-León)

Masia Barril Priorato (Cataluna)

Bilbainas Viña Pomal (Rioja)

Marqués de Cáceres (Rioja)

Marqués de Cáceres Reserva (Rioja)

Campo Viejo (Rioja)

Julian Chivite Gran Feudo (Navarra)

Martin Codax Albarino white wine
(Galicia)
CVNE Cune (Rioja)
Domecq-Marqués de Arienzo Reserva
(Rioja)
Enate Crianza (Somontano)
Estola (Castillo-La Mancha)
Farina Colegiata Toro (Castilla-León)
Farina Gran Colegiata Toro (Castilla-
León)
Faustino Martinez Faustino (Rioja)
Franco Españolas Bordon (Rioja)
Marqués de Griñon Cabernet Sauvignon
(Dominio de Valdepusa)
Inviosa Lar de Barros (Extremadura)
Baron de Ley El Coto (Rioja)
Lan Viña Lanciano Reserva (Rioja)
Los Llanos Valdepeñas (Castillo-La
Mancha)
Lopez de Heredia Bosconia Reserva
(Rioja)
Lopez de Heredia Tondonia Reserva
(Rioja)
Bodegas Magana (Navarra)
Martinez Bujanda Conde Valdemar Viño
Tinto (Rioja)
Mauro Ribera del Duero (Castilla-León)
Montecillo Viña Monty Reserva (Rioja)
Bodegas Hermanos Morales (La Mancha)
De Muller Tarragona (Cataluna)
Marqués de Murrieta Reserva (Rioja)
Bodegas Nekeas Vega Sindoa El Chaparral
Old Vine (Navarra)
Ochoa Reserva (Navarra)
Baron de Ona Rioja Reserva (Rioja)
Parxet Alella white wine (Cataluna)
Perez Pascuas Viña Pedrosa Ribera del
Duero (Castilla-León)
Pazo de Señorans Rias Baixas white wine
(Galicia)
Piqueras Castilla de Almansa (Castillo-La
Mancha)
Salvador Poveda (Alicante)

Raimat Costers del Segre (Cataluna)
La Rioja Alta Viña Alberdi (Rioja)
La Rioja Alta Arana (Rioja)
La Rioja Alta Ardanza (Rioja)
Rioja Santiago Gran Condal (Rioja)
Riojanas Monte Real Reserva (Rioja)
Marqués de Riscal Baron de Chirel
(Rioja)
Bodegas Rodero S.L. Val Ribeno Crianza
(Ribera del Duero)
Santiago Ruiz Rias Baixas Albarino white
wine (Galicia)
Bodegas de Sarria Gran Viño del Señorío
Reserva (Navarra)
Bodegas de Sarria Viña del Perdon
(Navarra)
Scala dei Priorato Cartoixa Priorat
(Cataluna)
Scala dei Priorato Clos Mogador (Cataluna)
Scala dei Priorato Negre (Cataluna)
Miguel Torres Coronas Penedès
(Cataluna)
Miguel Torres Gran Coronas Penedès
(Cataluna)
Miguel Torres Gran Coronas Black Label
Penedès (Cataluna); since 1981, for
vintages prior to and including
1981*****
Miguel Torres Gran Sangre de Toro
Penedès (Cataluna)
Miguel Torres Gran Viña Sol Green Label
Penedès (Cataluna)
Miguel Torres Viña Sol Penedès
(Cataluna)
Vega Sauco Reserva (Toro)
Bodegas de Vilarino-Cambados (Rias
Baixas)
Viñas del Vero Compania Somontano
(Aragon)
Castilla de Vinicole Grand Verdad
(Castillo-La Mancha)
Castilla de Vinicole Señorío de Duadianeja
(Castillo-La Mancha)

RATING SPAIN'S BEST SPARKLING WINES

* * * * * (OUTSTANDING)

None

* * * * (EXCELLENT)

None

*** *(GOOD)*

Albet I Noya Cava Brut	Juvé y Champs Gran Cru
Bilbainas	Juvé y Champs Gran Reserva
Cadiz	Juvé y Champs Reserva de la Familia
Cava Avinyo	Mont Marcal Brut
Cavas Ferret	Josep-Maria Raventos Blanc Brut
Chandon	Segura Viudas Aria
Gran Cordornieu Brut	Segura Viudas Brut Vintage
Freixenet Cuvée DS	Segura Viudas Reserva
Freixenet Reserva Real	

SPAIN'S GREATEST WINE BARGAINS

Abadia Retuerta Primicia (Sardon de Duero)	Finca Luzon Merlot (Jumilla)
Abadia Retuerta Rivola (Sardon de Duero)	Castillo de Maluenda Viña Alarba (Calatayud)
Agricola de Borja Viña Borgia (Campo de Borja)	Martinez Bujanda Conde Valdemar Viño Tinto (Rioja)
Agricola de Borja Borsao (Campo de Borja)	Montecillo Rioja (Rioja)
Albet I Noya Cava Brut (Penedès)	Bodegas Nekeas—various *cuvées* (Navarra)
Señorío de Almansa (Castillo-La Mancha)	Osborne Solaz (Spain)
Capcanes Mas Donis (Tarragona Zona Falset)	Real Sitio de Ventosilla (Ribera del Duero)
Casa Castillo (Jumilla)	Castell de Remei (Costers del Segre)
Castano Hecula (Yecla)	Thelmo Rodriguez Dehesa Gago (Ribera del Duero)
Castano Solana (Yecla)	
Martin Codax Albarino (Rias Baixas)	Bodegas Sierra Cantabria Rioja (Rioja)
Dominico de Egueren (Manchuela)	Solar de Urbezo (Carinena)
El Cep Marquis de Gelida (Penedès)	Tresantos (Zamora)
Los Llanos Valdepeñas (Castillo-La Mancha)	

ABADIA RETUERTA (SARDON DEL DUERO)

1999	Abadia Retuerta	C	92+
1998	Abadia Retuerta	C	90
1997	Cuvée El Campanario	D	90
1997	Cuvée Lapsus	EEE	92
1997	Cuvée El Palomar	D	89
2000	Primicia	A	88
1999	Rivola	B	90
1998	Rivola	B	89

This multimillion-dollar showcase winery is best known for its classic, potentially long-lived reds that sell for moderately high prices. However, it is also a bargain hunter's dream, as there are 10,000 cases of value-priced Primicia. The 2000 Primicia is a blend of 60% Tempranillo, 20% Cabernet Sauvignon, and 20% Merlot. This fruit bomb offers pure flavors of black cherries and berries intermixed with spice box and minerals. It offers good sweetness, exceptional purity, and a boatload of fruit. Enjoy it over the next 2–3 years.

The U.S. received 6,000 cases of the 1999 Rivola, a blend of 60% Tempranillo and 40% Cabernet Sauvignon aged eight months in both French and American oak before being bottled unfiltered. Another fabulous value, it reveals all the characteristics of a great vintage—

superripeness, terrific purity, a multidimensional, textured feel on the palate, and copious quantities of black cherry and currant fruit nicely dosed with spicy, toasty oak. Drink it over the next 4–5 years. Kudos to wine-maker Angel Anociba for not only making great wines but also for providing consumers with needed relief at this level. The 1999 Abadia Retuerta also reveals an opaque purple color as well as a classy, complex bouquet of flowers, black currants, raspberries, cherries, and vanilla. Full-bodied and elegant yet concentrated and powerful, with impressive overall harmony, this nicely textured, rich 1999 can be drunk now or cellared for 10–15 years.

The 1998 Rivola is one of the finest that Abadia Retuerta has made. A blend of 60% Tempranillo and 40% Cabernet Sauvignon from their estate vineyards, many readers may award this wine an outstanding score. The opaque ruby/purple color is accompanied by a knockout nose of tobacco, cedar, spice box, black currants, and a Zinfandel-like briary fruitiness. The wine is medium- to full-bodied and opulently textured, with outstanding purity, extract, and balance. There are no hard edges, and the finish lasts over 20 seconds. This is a remarkable value! Moreover, it will drink well for 2–4 years, perhaps longer. The unfiltered, opaque purple-colored 1998 Abadia Retuerta (65% Tempranillo, 30% Cabernet Sauvignon, and 5% Merlot) was aged 16 months in both French and American oak (50% new). Although closed and tannic, it offers a promising nose of minerals, vanilla, and black currants. Powerful and full-bodied, with moderately high tannin as well as an austere finish, it requires 2–3 years of cellaring. Anticipated maturity: 2004–2020.

The 1997 Cuvée El Palomar (equal parts Cabernet Sauvignon and Tempranillo from a chalky, hillside vineyard) is Bordeaux-like with its notes of dried Provençal herbs intermixed with smoke, cedar, and red and black currants. After spending 16 months in French oak barrels, it was bottled unfiltered. The wine reveals good softness, plenty of spice, attractive red and black fruits, medium body, and excellent symmetry and harmony between all of its elements. Drink it over the next 5–8 years. The 1997 Cuvée El Campanario (100% Tempranillo) reveals greater intensity, ripeness, and richness. Made from some of this huge estate's finest Tempranillo parcels, its dark ruby color is followed by sweet, jammy, black raspberry fruit aromas with notes of licorice and toasty oak. Soft and voluptuously textured, with meaty notes in the mouth, this wine reveals good ripeness, well-integrated acidity and tannin, and a long, 20–25-second finish. Drink it over the next 10–15 years.

Abadia Retuerta introduced a new *cuvée* in 1997, the Cuvée Lapsus. Made from equal parts Merlot, Syrah, and Petit Verdot, this unfiltered wine was made from extremely low yields of 18 hectoliters per hectare. Only 150 cases were produced, approximately one-third of which will make it to America's shores. The grapes were vinified together, and the resulting wine is one of considerable intensity, concentration, and color. Notions of blackberries, chocolate, melted asphalt, and flowers jump from the glass of this medium- to full-bodied, opulently textured, gorgeously proportioned offering. The acidity is present but low, and the wine is concentrated, fleshy, and seamless. Interestingly, malolactic fermentation was done completely in new French oak. Enjoy this beauty over the next 10–15 years.

ALBET I NOYA (PENEDÈS)

1999 Tempranillo	C	90
1998 Tempranillo Col-Leccio	B	88

Albet I Noya produces a bevy of wines, many of them compact and austere. I immensely enjoyed the 1998 Tempranillo Col-Leccio, which was aged one year in French and American oak. It offers an opaque purple color as well as a gorgeous nose of black cherries, blackberries, smoke, and toasty oak. Mouth-filling, rich, and supple-textured, with abundant extract and richness, it will drink well for 5–7 years.

The 1999 Tempranillo represents a positive departure from Albet I Noya's typical austere style. It reveals less rugged tannin, a pleasing mid-palate and texture, and less aggressive notes of wood and herbs. This textured, long, full-bodied effort reveals beautiful sweet black cherry fruit mixed with smoke, spice, and lead pencil. Multilayered, rich, open-knit, and supple, it is a seductive, nicely concentrated offering to drink over the next 4–5 years.

FINCA ALLENDE (RIOJA)

1998	Aurus	EE	90
1997	Aurus	EE	88
1996	Aurus	EEE	91+
1999	Calvario	D	91
1997	Cuesta Dulce	C	90+
1996	Rioja	C	90

There is little value to be found from Allende, but the quality of the wines is impressive.

The luxury-priced 1997 Aurus emerges from old vines planted at 1,200–1,500-foot elevations. Made from 85% Tempranillo (60 years old) and 15% Graciano, and low yields of 1.5 tons of fruit per acre, it is bottled unfiltered after undergoing malolactic fermentation as well as aging in new French oak. There are 125 cases of both the 1997 and 1998 imported to America. From a difficult vintage, the dense ruby/purple-colored 1997 Aurus offers an elegant, classy bouquet of red and black fruits, minerals, and smoke. Medium-bodied and deep for a 1997, with moderate tannin, and sweet, earthy black fruits, it will be at its prime between now–2012. The 1998 Aurus exhibits more toasty new oak in the nose, as well as more depth, fruit, glycerin, and body. This Bordeaux-like effort possesses good structure in addition to notes of black cherries, black currants, licorice, and tobacco/spice box. Full-bodied and backward, it requires 1–3 years of cellaring. Anticipated maturity: 2003–2014.

The 1997 Cuesta Dulce (216 cases), made from small-grained Tempranillo, is produced from microscopic yields of 0.8 tons of fruit per acre (or about a pound of fruit per vine). The wine was aged 14 months in new French oak before being bottled unfiltered. An opaque purple color is followed by licorice, blackberry, cherry, and currant fruit, a layered texture, superb extract, enormous weight and richness, and a huge, tannic, muscular finish. It represents a remarkable achievement for the vintage. While it has enormous potential, it requires 3–4 years of cellaring. Anticipated maturity: 2004–2020.

My favorite offering from Finca Allende is the 1999 Calvario, a single-vineyard Rioja produced from vines planted in 1945. Aged completely in new French oak, this wine is layered, rich, and concentrated, with soft tannin, better balance, and more up-front appeal than the two vintages of Aurus. A blend of 90% Tempranillo, 8% Grenache, and 2% Graciano, it is made from small yields of 1.8 tons of fruit per acre. Deep, layered, and impressive, it should drink well for 10–15 years.

The 1996 Aurus, an estate-bottled, unfiltered Rioja made from a blend of 85% Tempranillo and 15% Graciano, is the first release from what the Spanish refer to as a "super Rioja." This opaque purple-colored wine spent 18 months in 100% new French oak casks after a 28–day maceration. Its international style of new French oak combined with intensely concentrated, ripe, black fruits may be criticized, but with aging, this wine should reveal some of its typicity and Rioja character. Call it "traditional winemaking meets international inclinations." Full-bodied, with great purity of fruit, this impressive, limited production (about 450 cases) Rioja should meet with enthusiastic reviews, even if eyebrows are raised at the price. Anticipated maturity: 2003–2018. A modern-styled, exotic Rioja, the dark ruby/purple 1996 Rioja from Finca Allende reveals sumptuous aromas/flavors of roasted coffee and sweet jammy blackberries as well as cassis. Fruit-driven, with sweet French oak in the background, this medium- to full-bodied, intensely concentrated, luscious offering is truly exciting. It can be drunk now or aged for a decade.

JOAN D'ANGUERA (TARRAGONA)

1998 El Bugader	D	89+?

The 1998 El Bugader, a limited-production (333 cases) blend of 70% Syrah, 15% Grenache, and 15% Cabernet Sauvignon, enjoyed malolactic fermentation in wood and spent 18 months in new French oak before being bottled unfiltered. It offers a saturated opaque purple color along with a sweet nose of black fruits, earth, truffles, and chocolate. Full-bodied, rich, dense, and powerful, with moderate tannin, it requires 2–3 years to become more civilized. If it ages as gracefully as I suspect, it will last for 12–15 years.

ANIMA NEGRA (MAJORCA)

1997 Anima Negra	D	88

A rarity from the island of Majorca, this 55% Cabernet Sauvignon/45% Callet blend from a red clay soil vineyard enjoyed a long maceration, and was then aged in a combination of French and—get this—Virginian oak barrels. The nose offers up notes of smoked meats, red and black fruits, and toasty wood. Cassis as well as cherry liqueur make an appearance on the succulent palate. An internationally styled effort with dominant characteristics of new oak and jammy fruit, it is well made, pure, and ideal for enjoying over the next decade. I suspect more regional characteristics (whatever they might be) may emerge with cellaring.

BODEGAS ISMAEL ARROYO (RIBERA DEL DUERO)

1998 Valsotillo	C	89
1996 Valsotillo Reserva	D	91+

The wines from Arroyo tend to be enormously rich, muscular, rustic efforts filled with mouth-staining levels of extract, and sometimes tannin. I have laid away a few vintages hoping that everything will come into balance, but only time will tell. The new releases are all impressive, especially the 1996 and 1994.

The 100% Tinta del Pais (Tempranillo) 1998 Valsotillo emerges from this family's 38.4 acres of hillside vineyards. It is an earthy, tannic effort exhibiting notes of plums, black raspberries, mushrooms, and tree bark. Yields were only 1.25 tons of fruit per acre, and the wine was aged 14 months in American oak casks. Because Arroyo's cellars are extremely cold, these wines are often unevolved upon release. While the 1998 does not have the power, depth, and volume of previous vintages, it is an excellent effort offering earthy, ripe tobacco, cedar, and black cherry flavors, high tannin levels, and underbrush characteristics with toasty oak in the background. This chunky, nearly uncivilized, mouth-filling Spanish red will drink well for 10–12 years. The 1996 Valsotillo Reserva, a selection of the vineyard's finest fruit, is aged for two years in American oak, in a cellar where the temperature never exceeds 52°F. Sadly, only 300 cases of this behemoth have made it to America's shores. A young, muscular heavyweight, it boasts an opaque plum/purple color in addition to aromas and flavors of melted road tar, jammy black fruits, truffles, and roasted meats. Dense, powerful, and full-bodied, with sweeter tannin than the 1998 possesses, this monstrously sized wine is not for everybody, but it has abundant power, weight, richness, and extract. Anticipated maturity: 2005–2022.

ARTADI (RIOJA)

1997 Crianza Viñas de Gain	C	88
1998 Grandes Anadas	EE	96+
1998 Pagos Viejos	E	96
1996 Pagos Viejos	E	93
1998 Viña El Pison	E	95
1996 Viña El Pison	EE	97
1998 Viñas de Gain	B	92

This extraordinary Rioja producer is one of my personal favorites from that famed viticultural area. 1997 was a poor vintage in Rioja, yet Artadi has produced an elegant 1997 Crianza Viñas de Gain with notes of red cherries, peanut butter, and vanilla. It is a beautifully etched, finesse-styled Crianza with sweet fruit, medium body, and fine length. Drink it over the next 3–5 years.

The dark ruby/purple 1996 Pagos Viejos (400 sixpacks available for the U.S.) is a fabulous Rioja boasting a complex bouquet of lead pencil, red and black currants, spice box, cedar, and tobacco. Made from low yields, the wine displays a gorgeous mid-palate, great depth and purity, and a finish that lingers nearly 40 seconds. Drink this spectacular effort over the next 15–25 years. The superb 1998 Pagos Viejos is one of the greatest Riojas I have ever tasted. A dense ruby/purple color is accompanied by a sweet nose of violets, black fruits, minerals, toasty new oak, and smoke. The wine is full-bodied, with gorgeous purity, amazing symmetry for its exceptional size, and an incredibly well delineated finish. In short, it is great stuff! Anticipated maturity: 2005–2025.

At the top of the Artadi hierarchy are the limited-production *cuvées* of El Pison and Grandes Anadas. El Pison is Burgundian in its orientation, whereas Grandes Anadas is a majestic, ageworthy Rioja that may well be the single greatest wine made in that appellation. The 1998 El Pison is made from a Tempranillo vineyard planted in 1945, and aged 18–24 months in new French oak, from yields of only 22 h/h. It offers a deep ruby/purple color and a glorious nose of raspberry jam intermixed with cherries and smoky new oak. As the wine sits in the glass, more complex, floral aromas with a graphite-like character emerge. A sexy, elegant, medium- to full-bodied, beautifully made wine transcends the Rioja appellation with a singular style and character. Drink it over the next 12–15 years. The 1998 Grandes Anadas (100% Tempranillo from 70–100-year-old vines) has only been made twice in the last seven years, 1994 and 1998. It is more tannic and highly extracted, with more body and is a less sexy and seductive effort than either El Pison or Viñas de Gain. However, it is a broodingly backward, formidable wine with amazing concentration, purity, and overall balance. It is more of a Bordeaux style than the Burgundy-like El Pison. Long and concentrated, with a 40–50-second finish, it requires 3–4 years of cellaring and should evolve gracefully for 30 years. These are classic yet singular expressions of Rioja the likes of which can be found nowhere else in that viticultural area. Anticipated maturity: now–2027.

The 1996 Viña El Pison is outrageously rich, complex, and profound. A dense ruby/purple color is followed by aromas of sweet black fruits, vanilla, flowers, and minerals. There are layers of fruit, great flavor extraction, unbelievable finesse, complexity, and elegance. The finish lasts for nearly a minute. Full-bodied and super-concentrated, this compelling Rioja will be at its peak between now–2025. Sadly, only 300 sixpacks were exported to the U.S., but it is well worth seeking out.

Readers should check out the sensational 1998 Viñas de Gain (1,500 cases made it to the U.S.). A selection from three hillside parcels where the vines average 40 years, and bottled after 18 months in French oak (no filtration), it is an elegant, stylish effort with terrific fruit, a sweet, complex nose of black cherries, minerals, lead pencil, spice box, and vanilla. Made from 100% Tempranillo, it possesses an impressive texture, medium to full body, and beautiful balance as well as purity. It is a wine to drink now and over the next 10–12 years. For $18, it is a superb value.

BODEGAS BG (PRIORATO)

1998 Gueta Lupia   **D   90**

An intensely concentrated, fat, full-bodied Priorato, the 1998 Gueta Lupia exhibits notes of new oak, minerals, black raspberry, and cassis. While more fruit-driven than some of its peers, it has plenty of body, mass, and structure underneath all the glycerin and concentrated fruit. Give it 2–3 years to develop more complexity and fragrance, and drink by 2016.

AGRICOLA DE BORJA (CAMPO DE BORJA)

2000 Borsao	A	89
2000 Borsao 3 Picos	B	90

Year after year the wines from the Agricola de Borja have made the pages of *The Wine Advocate* as superb values. Based on the positive mail I have received, they are a huge hit with readers who are into pleasure rather than insufferable elitism or prestige labels. That being said, these are the finest wines Borja has yet produced. Even their new, more expensive selection qualifies as one of the greatest wine values in the marketplace. The 2000 Borsao is a tank-fermented and aged blend of 80% Grenache and 20% Tempranillo. This luxurious, seamless, voluptuous red reveals an array of sweet, jammy red and black fruits, excellent purity, fine texture as well as concentration, multiple dimensions, and a finish normally found in wines costing $20–30 a bottle. However, its low acidity and precocious character suggest it is best drunk during the next 2–3 years. Readers should not have any problem finding this wine as there are 15,000 cases of the Borsao.

There are 2,000 cases of the 100% old-vine *cuvée* called 2000 Borsao 3 Picos. It is an explosive, rich, concentrated, deep ruby-colored wine offering a gorgeous bouquet of black fruits, kirsch, licorice, and minerals. Full-bodied, spicy, and seamless, with low acidity as well as layers of fruit and glycerin, this amazing effort easily competes with good southern Rhônes and premier cru red Burgundies. Put this wine in a blind tasting with the finest red Burgundies and see what happens. Anticipated maturity: now–2003.

CAPCANES (TARRAGONA)

1999 Cabrida	D	90+
1998 Cabrida	D	94
1998 Capcanes Costers del Gravet Les Vinyasses	C	89
1999 Mas Donis Barrica	A	89
1997 Pansal del Calas	C (500 ml)	93
1998 Val del Calas	B	90

A special *cuvée* made for importer Eric Solomon, the 1999 Mas Donis Barrica is a blend of 80% Grenache and 20% Syrah that spent eight months in barrel. A super value, it is a big, rustic, concentrated, dense, dark ruby/purple effort with notes of earth, licorice, black fruits, meat, and spicy wood. Chewy and thick, it admirably displays Grenache's wonderful sweetness. Moreover, there are 5,000 cases. Enjoy it over the next 3–5 years.

Another impressive effort from this Tarragona winery, the 1998 Val del Calas, a blend of Grenache, Cabernet Sauvignon, and Syrah, is an exceptional value. Six hundred cases of this serious Côtes du Rhône look-alike offer up scents of chocolate, smoky, black cherry fruit, and a robust, concentrated, full-bodied palate impression. It is dominated by its purity as well as a wealth of black fruits. Buy this one by the case, and drink it over the next 4–5 years. A Grenache/Cabernet Sauvignon blend aged 14 months in small barrels, the 1998 Les Vinyasses is made in a lighter style. Although more serious and ambitious, it is not as hedonistic and visceral as the Val del Calas. Medium- to full-bodied, with moderate tannin, good purity, and a more international style, it should drink well for a decade.

The limited-production 1998 Cabrida is the product of 100% Grenache from a single nine-acre vineyard. Made only in the finest vintages, from 95–110-year-old vines, it is aged in 100% new French oak casks. A remarkable effort, it has copious quantities of black cherry, chocolate, and vanilla aromas. Full-bodied, concentrated, tight, and muscular, with moderate tannin, this wine will benefit from 1–3 years of cellaring, and will keep for 12–15 years. This is undoubtedly the most impressive offering I have ever tasted from Tarragona. Anticipated maturity: 2003–2016. The 1999 Cabrida is a serious, though closed offering for true connoisseurs. Made from small yields of 17 h/h, it exhibits a deep purple color as well as a muscular, powerful personality with notes of kirsch mixed with blackberries, currants, licorice, truffles, new saddle leather, and roasted meats. As the wine sat in the glass, the essence of cherry liqueur exploded with even more ferocity. Deep, robust, moderately tannic, and in need of several years of cellaring, it will age well for 12–15 years.

Readers should treat Capcanes's 1997 Pansal del Calas as they would a Banyuls from France, or even a young vintage port. Made from 90–110-year-old Grenache vines, it displays moderate sweetness, as well as Grenache's thick, chewy richness, and roasted nut, herb, and kirsch character. This is a full-bodied, high-alcohol, blockbuster effort that is meant to be served after a meal with cheese or by itself. It should last for a decade or more, but I would opt for drinking it in its exuberant, fiery youth.

CASTANO (YECLA)

1998 Coleccion		B	89
1999 Hecula		B	90
1999 Solana		B	92

The Hecula and Solana are strong candidates for the two best values in dry red wine that I have tasted this year. Both come from terraced vineyards at high elevations (for this area), not far from the emerging viticultural region of Jumilla. The 1999 Hecula is a blend of 70% Mourvèdre, 20% Tempranillo, and 10% Merlot aged six months in new American oak prior to being bottled with no filtration. It exhibits an opaque black color and a dense, chewy, muscular personality with copious quantities of licorice-infused blackberry fruit, saddle leather, and roasted meat aromas as well as flavors. This full-bodied, powerful effort should drink well for a decade. While it is not the most refined style of red winemaking, for $10–12, it is an excellent value. The U.S. will receive 2,000 cases of this *cuvée*. Some of the Mourvèdre (Monastrell) component is from 100-year-old vines. Drink it over the next 8–10 years. The 1999 Solana (2,500 cases for the U.S.), primarily old-vine Mourvèdre aged seven months in wood, is a special *cuvée* made for importer Eric Solomon. This spectacular, opaque black/purple, seamless, fabulously concentrated offering is deep and chewy, with glorious quantities of earthy black cherry/blackberry fruit, full body, velvety, sweet tannin, and a mouthcoating, long, concentrated finish with no hard edges. The oak has been totally absorbed by the wine's wealth of fruit. Like its sibling, it is an astonishing value. Consume it over the next decade.

The 1998 Coleccion (90% Mourvèdre and 10% Cabernet Sauvignon that receives a small amount of barrel aging) is elegant and complex, revealing notes of licorice, black raspberries, and plums. It possesses good density, firm tannin, excellent purity and ripeness, and the potential to last 7–8 years. It is a very good value.

CASA CASTILLO (JUMILLA)

1999 Las Gravas		B	90
1998 Las Gravas		B	90+
2000 Jumilla		A	89
1999 Monastrell		A	88

If we begin seeing more wines such as this from Jumilla, this region will take on the importance and prestige now accorded Priorato. The 1999 Monastrell is a blend of 85% Monastrell (Mourvèdre) and 15% Syrah from the estate's vineyards. Much of the Mourvèdre comes from 40-year-old, ungrafted vines. Yields were an absurdly low 1.0 to 1.25 tons of fruit per acre, all hand-harvested. The wine was aged completely in new American oak for four months prior to bottling. It exhibits a dense purple color with expressive aromatics of tree bark, mushrooms, blackberries, and earth. Boasting an elegant yet powerful mid-palate as well as a forceful personality, it reveals high tannin in the chalky finish. This impressively rich, full-bodied 1999 will benefit from several years of cellaring, and keep for a decade.

A remarkable value for $8.50, the 2000 Jumilla, a blend of 85% Mourvèdre and 15% Syrah, exhibits a saturated purple color in addition to a full-bodied, serious, *vin de garde* style, and dense cherry, blackberry, mineral-tinged fruit. Frankly, this impressive red is too big, rich, and structured for a wine in this price category. It enjoyed malolactic fermentation in new French and American oak where it was aged four months prior to bottling. Yields were a minuscule 1.0–1.25 tons of fruit per acre. For power, intensity, and richness, this wine must be tasted to be believed! Drink it over the next 5–6 years.

The 1999 Las Gravas is not as massive as the 1998, but many readers will consider it better balanced. The tannin is sweeter, and the wine reveals less volume but beautiful harmony as well as gorgeous notes of blackberries, cherries, underbrush, sweet oak, minerals, and earth. Luxuriously rich and supple-textured, it is best consumed over the next 12–15 years. For the quality, it is a super value. The 1998 Las Gravas (a blend of 40% Mourvèdre and 60% Cabernet Sauvignon) gets its name from the large stones that overlay the chalky soils of these hillside vineyards. Again, yields were preposterously low, 0.4 tons of fruit per acre for the Mourvèdre and 0.5 tons per acre for the Cabernet Sauvignon. Malolactic fermentation occurred in wood barrels, and the wine was fined, but not filtered. Fifty percent new French and 50% new American wood was utilized. There are 700 cases of this spectacular wine, which sets a new reference point for Jumilla. Opaque black/purple (it looks more like vintage port than wine), it reveals a fabulous nose of crushed stones and black cherry/blackberry liqueur intermixed with smoke and vanilla. Intensely concentrated, full-bodied, and muscular, with sweet tannin, low acidity, and a fabulous, concentrated finish that lasts 40+ seconds, this is an enormously endowed yet well-balanced offering that is not over the top. Because of the wealth of fruit, glycerin, and extract it is accessible, but give it another 2–3 years of cellaring, and drink it over the following 15+ years. Both of these wines are exceptional values, particularly the 1998 Las Gravas.

CERVOLS (COSTERS DEL SEGRE)

1998 Costers del Segre	C	89

This blend of 40% Tempranillo, 30% Cabernet Sauvignon, and 30% Grenache was aged 14 months in new French oak casks prior to being bottled unfiltered. It is made in an international style, with sweet black currant and berry fruit intertwined with toasty new oak. Ripe, dense, and medium- to full-bodied, with excellent purity, it will drink well for 6–7 years.

CIMS DE PORRERA (PRIORATO)

1998	E	91

This blend of 65% Carignan (from 80-year-old vines), 32% Grenache, and the rest Cabernet Sauvignon exhibits a saturated purple color as well as a gorgeous perfume of overripe grapes, blackberries, prunes, licorice, smoke, and earth. Full-bodied, with high alcohol (14.9%), huge unctuosity and density, it is extremely well balanced despite its weight and mass. Drink it over the next two decades.

CLOS ERASMUS (PRIORATO)

1998 Priorato	E	99
1997 Priorato	D	93
1996 Priorato	D	90

Along with l'Ermita, this is the most concentrated, powerful, and ageworthy of the promising wines of Priorato. I was disappointed with most of the 1996s I tasted from Priorato. However, Clos Erasmus made one of the finest wines I have tasted to date. Production of the 1996 Clos Erasmus was only 300 cases. This is a dark ruby/purple wine with a spicy, oak-driven nose intermixed with black cherry and raspberry fruit notes. Spicy and dominated by wood at present, it is full-bodied, rich, and promising. Yields were a mere 18 h/h. This wine requires 2–4 more years of cellaring and should drink well for 10–15 years. The 1997 exhibits a dense ruby/purple color as well as scents of minerals, toasty new oak, blueberry, black raspberry, and currant fruit, and a full-bodied, impressively endowed, highly extracted personality. Gorgeously pure, with adequate underlying acidity, and a well-delineated, structured, muscular, and concentrated finish, this unevolved 1997 is accessible because of its wealth of fruit and suppleness. It should age gracefully for 10–20 years.

The spectacular 1998 flirts with perfection. Its saturated opaque blue/purple color is not dissimilar to ink. Dazzling aromas of ripe, pure blackberries, violets, blueberries, wet stones, and smoky, toasty oak soar from the glass. Powerful, with an unctuous texture, and super-extracted, rich, concentrated flavors, this blockbuster effort boasts extravagant quantities of fruit, glycerin, extract, tannin, and personality. The wine displays a firm, structured edge, but a viscous texture from super-concentration gives it immediate accessibility. This 1998 should hit its plateau of maturity in 7–8 years, and is a strong candidate for 20–30 years of aging. It is a winemaking tour de force.

CLOS MARTINET (PRIORATO)

1997 Priorato	E	90

Far better than the lean, tough, high-acid 1996, Clos Martinet's 1997 reveals a dark ruby/purple/plum color, sweet black raspberry and blackberry fruit, full body, an expansive, rich, heady, alcoholic finish, and nicely integrated wood. It is a concentrated, lusty style of Priorato to consume over the next decade.

CLOS MOGADOR (PRIORATO)

1998 Priorato	D	94
1997 Priorato	D	91

It is a pleasure to see how much better the 1997 Priorato wines are performing than the lean, emaciated 1996s. Clos Mogador's 1997 boasts a saturated ruby/purple color, a fat, dense, concentrated, black currant, mineral-infused character, full body, layers of concentration, sweet tannin, and a 35-second finish. Impressive and pure, with nicely integrated toasty oak, it will drink well for 10–15 years. Perhaps the finest Clos Mogador to date, the inky purple-colored 1998 (40% Grenache, 35% Cabernet Sauvignon, 20% Syrah, and 5% Mourvèdre and Petit Verdot) boasts a huge nose of blueberries, blackberries, minerals, and vanilla. It is a wine of great purity, intensity, and mass, with extraordinary richness, a blockbuster mid-palate, and a whoppingly long finish. This decadent offering requires a few more years to fully develop. Anticipated maturity: 2003–2020.

OLIVER CONTI (AMPURDAN-COSTA BRAVA)

1998	C	90

This new winery, located four kilometers from the Mediterranean Sea, not far from the internationally renowned Spanish restaurant El Bulli, is making a Bordeaux-like blend of 70% Cabernet Sauvignon, 20% Merlot, and 10% Cabernet Franc aged in French oak for six months prior to being moved to large vats. This sleeper effort needs time in the bottle to reveal its full potential. Aromas of black currants, blackberries, olives, cedar, and spicy French oak are followed by a long, impressively built red with a fat midsection and supple tannin in the finish. Concentrated as well as elegant, it should drink well for 10–12 years.

COSTERS DEL SIURANA (PRIORATO)

1999 Clos de l'Obac	D	92
1998 Clos de l'Obac	D	90
1999 Miserere	D	88

Although I was disappointed with this winery's tough-textured, undernourished 1998 Miserere, their 1998 Clos de l'Obac, a blend of Cabernet Sauvignon, Grenache, Syrah, Merlot, and Carignan, is outstanding. While many Prioratos can be superrich, thick-textured efforts, Clos de l'Obac represents a more elegant, restrained effort from this highly promising, relatively new appellation. Bottled unfiltered, and made from meager yields of 0.5 tons of fruit per hectare, the opaque ruby/purple 1998 offers up notes of black raspberries intertwined with strawberry and cherry fruit. As it sits in the glass, mineral and subtle oak aromas emerge. Beautifully textured and pure, with high tannin, it is a wine of undeniable elegance, finesse, and concentration. It requires 3–4 years of cellaring and should keep for 15+ years. This is unquestionably the most stylish, restrained, high-quality wine emerging from Priorato. Anticipated maturity: 2005–2016.

The two 1999 offerings are the finest wines I have tasted from this estate in a number of years. The 1999 Miserere, a blend of Cabernet Sauvignon, Grenache, Tempranillo, Merlot, and Carignan, spent 12 months in French oak before being bottled unfiltered. It is an elegant, mineral-laced, medium-bodied effort with notes of raspberry and cherry fruit, good purity, and a soft, tangy finish. It should drink well for 4–6 years. The only problem is the price. The impressive 1999 Clos de l'Obac is produced from a similar blend, but the Grenache and Carignan vines range in age from 50–100 years, and yields were kept to a microscopic 14 h/h (about one ton of fruit per acre). The wine spent 14 months in new French oak. Sadly, there are only 200 cases for the U.S. Its opaque purple color is accompanied by a sweet nose of raspberry liqueur intermixed with black currants, minerals, and toasty oak. Medium- to full-bodied and rich, with moderate levels of tannin, decent acidity, excellent delineation, and a long, concentrated finish, it is still youthful and unformed. Anticipated maturity: 2005–2018.

DEHESA GAGO (TORO)

2000 Toro	**B**	**89**

Made from 100% Tinta de Toro, this wine, aged in temperature-controlled stainless steel tanks, offers a dense ruby/purple color in addition to a glorious nose of jammy black fruits intermixed with underbrush and pepper. Dense, chewy, and fleshy, it is best consumed over the next 3–4 years. Of all these best buys, this is the most limited *cuvée*, as only 700 cases are exported to America.

CASA DE LA ERMITA (JUMILLA)

2000 Tinto	**B**	**90**

Jumilla, one of Spain's up-and-coming backwater areas, is the origin of this estate-bottled blend of 75% Tempranillo, 15% Cabernet Sauvignon, and 10% Mourvèdre. The wine boasts a dense purple color as well as a big, smoky, volcanic ash–like, chocolate, graphite, and blackberry/cassis-scented nose. Layered, full-bodied, dense, and super-concentrated, it is an amazing offering for the price. Enjoy it over the next 5–6 years.

AGRICOLA FALSET MARCA (TARRAGONA)

1999 Etim	**B**	**90**
1998 Etim	**B**	**88+?**

A blend of 85% Grenache and 15% Cabernet Sauvignon, the sumptuous, thick, juicy 1999 Etim offers knockout aromas of black fruits and earth, outstanding ripeness, impressive purity, and a long, layered finish. Drink it over the next 3–4 years.

The 1998 Etim is a monster wine (a blend of 85% old vine Grenache and 15% Cabernet Sauvignon that was aged in French and American oak) possessing sensational concentration, power, and depth. However, the rustic tannin in the finish may be off-putting to readers looking for a more succulent, velvety-textured style. Nevertheless, there is amazing depth and richness in this clean, blockbuster-sized offering. If the tannin becomes better integrated, the score could increase. For now, think of it as a muscular, full-throttle powerhouse that should be consumed with robustly flavored foods. It should last 5–7 years.

J. M. FUENTES (PRIORATO)
1998 Gran Clos   **D   90**

This internationally styled effort from Priorato is a blend of 70% Grenache, 20% Carignan, and 10% Cabernet Sauvignon. It displays aggressive levels of toasty new oak as well as concentrated black currant and kirsch characteristics. While full-bodied, pure, and rich, the oak needs to become better integrated to justify my rating. Nevertheless, there is plenty of depth, and the fruit quality is impeccable. Cellar this 1998 for 3–4 more years, and enjoy it over the following 15+ years.

FRA FULCO (PRIORATO)
1999 Priorat   **D   91**

Made from 60–100-year-old Carignan vines, and aged in new oak, the exuberant, full-bodied, rustic, but mouth-staining as well as filling 1999 Priorat is loaded with concentrated black fruits intermixed with scents of earth, new saddle leather, and vanilla. Full-bodied, powerful, and rich yet seamless, this terrific wine is best drunk during its first 5–6 years of life to take advantage of its exuberance and purity. Carignan is not a noble varietal, and despite how impressive this wine is, I cannot imagine it developing more complexity. Consume it early for its intensity, richness, and freshness.

LO GIVOT (PRIORATO)
1998 Priorat   **D   90**

This oak-aged, attractive, sweet, concentrated, dense purple 1998 is a blend of 33% 90–100-year-old Grenache, 32% 100-year-old Carignan, and the rest young-vine Cabernet Sauvignon and Syrah. While still tightly knit, it is deep, pure, and rich, offering notes of black fruits, minerals, licorice, and barrique. Anticipated maturity: now–2012.

GRANDES BODEGAS (RIBERA DEL DUERO)
1996 Monte Villalobon   **D   88**

The 1996 Monte Villalobon, made from 90% Tinta del Pais and 10% Cabernet Sauvignon, exhibits a deep saturated purple color in addition to sweet blackberry and cherry fruit intertwined with earth and underbrush notes. Following an excellent entry on the palate, the wine reveals an internationally styled personality. Spicy, ripe, monolithic, the wine should develop over the next 3–4 years and evolve for 12–15.

IBERUS (TERRA ALTA)
1999   **D   91+**

Sadly, there are only 100 six-bottle cases of this wine, which emerges from an area near the Mediterranean coastal appellation of Penedès. A blend of Grenache, Tempranillo, Cabernet Sauvignon, Syrah, and two local varietals, Morenillo and Morselan, this is a powerhouse. Opaque purple-colored, with a thick, jammy bouquet of blackberries, licorice, prunes, and plums, its aroma is reminiscent of Turley Cellars's famed Petite Syrah. Full-bodied and highly extracted, with monstrous levels of flavor balanced by equally high tannin, this massive 1999 requires 5–6 years of cellaring and should keep 20 years. It is an impressive, monolithic wine of considerable power as well as richness.

LEDA (CASTILLA Y LEON)

1998	**E**	**90+**

This 20,000 bottle *cuvée*, made from old-vine Tempranillo fermented and aged in new oak, is essentially a *vin de pays*, even though it is just outside the appellation of Ribera del Duero. It reveals abundant spicy oak, full body, and layers of fruit and richness in its concentrated, powerful personality. Two to three years of cellaring will help it become more civilized, but there is a lot going on in this massive offering.

FINCA LUZON (JUMILLA)

2000 Merlot	**A**	**89**
1999 Merlot	**A**	**89**

A blend of 85% Merlot and 15% Monastrell (Mourvèdre), Finca Luzon's Merlot is produced from a family-owned estate vineyard located a mere 60 miles from the Mediterranean. The Mourvèdre vines are 45 years old, and the Merlot are 18. Unbelievably, yields for the Merlot were 1.6 tons per acre, and for the Mourvèdre, 1.25 tons per acre—lower than yields for most of the great châteaux on the Pomerol plateau (i.e., Pétrus, Lafleur, Vieux Château Certan). The wine boasts a saturated opaque purple color, an amazingly rich, chocolaty, blackberry, and mocha-scented nose of moderate intensity, and explosive, full-bodied, concentrated flavors with chewy extract. The 1999 Merlot may merit an outstanding rating given its purity, richness, and potential to evolve for a decade. The wine's low acidity provides immediate accessibility, but it will keep for 10 or more years. It is an amazing effort from what may be Spain's most promising undiscovered viticultural region.

A sensational value, the 2000 Merlot boasts an opaque ruby/purple color as well as big, thick, dense flavors of black fruits, earth, graphite, and minerals. It possesses soft tannin, outstanding palate richness, and impressive overall purity and balance. More good news— 7,000 cases were exported to the U.S. Buy this one by the case and drink it over the next 4–5 years to take advantage of its exuberant youth.

MAS IGNEUS (PRIORATO)

1998 Costers de Poboleda	**D**	**90**
1998 F.A. 112	**C**	**90**
1998 F.A. 206	**B**	**88**

A noteworthy producer from Priorato, Mas Igneus's 1998 F.A. 206 is a blend of 70% Carignan, 19% Grenache, and 11% Cabernet Sauvignon aged six months in French oak. Soft and round, with earthy, strawberry, and cherry flavors, an elegant personality, and fine purity as well as overall balance, it is meant to be consumed now and over the next 4–5 years. It is an excellent value. The more expensive as well as more compelling 1998 F.A. 112 is a blend of 65% Grenache, 25% Carignan, and 10% Syrah grown in primarily slate-based soils. Yields were a minuscule 0.6 tons of fruit per acre. A deep ruby/purple color is accompanied by sweet, jammy aromas of blackberries and cherries intermixed with minerals and toast. The wine is full-bodied, intense, and pure, with moderate tannin as well as low acidity. It can be drunk now or cellared for 7–8 years. Another outstanding effort is the 1998 Costers de Poboleda. A blend of 80–100-year-old Grenache (65%) and 80-year-old Carignan (35%), aged for one year in 100% new French oak, and bottled unfiltered, it is a full-bodied, powerful effort revealing notes of new saddle leather, kirsch, minerals, and spicy new wood. Intensely concentrated and spicy, with a tannic finish (although the tannin is both sweet and well integrated), it will drink well for 10–15 years.

MAS MARTINET (PRIORATO)

1998 Bru	**C**	**88**
1998 Clos Martinet	**E**	**91**

Mas Martinet's 1998 Bru (a blend of 45% Grenache, 20% Cabernet Sauvignon, 20% Merlot, and the rest Carignan and Syrah) possesses a deep ruby/purple color as well as thick, juicy notes of black cherries and currants intermixed with earth, minerals, and oak. This wine is dominated by its fruit and richness. Additional complexity should emerge after more time in the bottle. Impeccably made, pure, and medium- to full-bodied, with no hard edges, it should be consumed between now–2014. Its bigger sibling, the 1998 Clos Martinet, boasts a dense purple color and a huge nose of liquid minerals, blackberry liqueur, and cassis. Full-bodied and unctuously textured with terrific presence on the palate, this large-scaled effort is never heavy or overbearing. Sweet tannin in the finish suggests 2–3 years of cellaring will be beneficial, but readers can drink it now as well as over the next 12–18 years.

MAURO (RIBERA DEL DUERO)

1998 Terreus	EE	91+
1996 Terreus	EE	91+
1996 Vendimia Seleccionada	E	90

These offerings are produced just outside the appellation of Ribera del Duero from 100% Tempranillo, barrel-fermented, and bottled with minimal clarification. The dense purple-colored 1996 Vendimia Seleccionada exhibits a sweet bouquet of black cherries, toasty new oak, licorice, and smoke. Full-bodied, ripe, and moderately tannic, this internationally styled Tempranillo will be at its peak between now–2015.

The huge, full-bodied 1998 Terreus (a single-vineyard effort) demands 4–5 years of cellaring. Packed with concentrated blackberry and cassis fruit interspersed with notes of licorice, new wood, and melted asphalt, this potent effort possesses high tannin and extract as well as abundant glycerin. Anticipated maturity: 2005–2020. If everything comes together over the next 4–5 years, look for my rating to go even higher. The muscular, broodingly backward 1996 Terreus exhibits a saturated dark purple color, as well as a tight but promising nose of minerals, black raspberries, and blackberries. Spicy new oak makes an appearance in this dense, full-bodied, nearly impenetrable wine. It requires 4–6 years of cellaring, and should last two decades. Everything appears to be well balanced enough to present fascinating potential for the future.

ABEL MENDOZA (RIOJA)

1999 Rioja	D	92
1998 Rioja	D	90+

This micro-estate sold 200 cases of its stylish, individualistic 1998 Rioja to the U.S. Impressive depth but a closed, structured style make the 1998 a wine for connoisseurs rather than those seeking immediate gratification. The saturated plum/purple color is accompanied by aromas of cherry liqueur, black currants, spice box, vanilla, and underbrush. It is dense and rich, with sweet tannin, a notable, layered midsection, and a long, moderately tannic finish. Anticipated maturity: 2003–2016. Even better is the 1999 Rioja (100% Tempranillo aged in new French oak for 12 months). Sadly, there are less than 100 cases for the U.S. From a producer who strives to fashion one of the world's greatest wines, this Rioja is the result of a fanatical selection process. An opaque purple color is accompanied by a fabulous, sweet perfume of blackberry liqueur, licorice, vanilla, and mineral aromas. Thick and rich, with a beautiful texture, superb purity, and supple tannin, this compelling Rioja possesses more depth and overall complexity than the impressive 1998. Consume it over the next 10–15 years.

HACIENDA MONASTERIO (RIBERA DEL DUERO)

1996 Crianza	D	90

This project, from a large estate in Ribera del Duero, has the gifted Danish wine-maker Peter Sisseck (of Pingus fame). Produced from extremely low yields (15–20 hectoliters per hectare), the 1996 Crianza is a blend of Tempranillo, Cabernet Sauvignon, and Merlot. It is unquestionably an outstanding wine. It possesses 14.5% alcohol, and plenty of guts and richness. The color is a saturated plum/purple. The wine reveals copious quantities of sweet toasty new oak intermixed with nearly overripe scents of prunes, blackberries, and cassis. Full-bodied and spicy, with a lush texture and low acidity, this generous wine can be drunk now and over the next decade.

BODEGAS EMILIO MORO (RIBERA DEL DUERO)

1998 Malleolus	C	90+
1999 Moro	C	92
1998 Moro	C	90
1997 Ribera del Duero	C	89

The Moro family has been fashioning wines from Ribera del Duero for over 120 years. These impressive offerings emerge from relatively young vines (12–20 years of age), and modest yields of 1.6–2.1 tons of fruit per acre. The vinification and upbringing are classical, with 25 days of maceration and 12 months of aging in a combination of old and new French and American oak. One thousand cases of each vintage have been exported to the U.S. Given the quality, these are realistically priced wines that merit considerable attention. The difference between the 1999 and 1998 comes down to structure and accessibility. The 1999 Moro, which reveals the vintage's superripeness, is a sexy, full-bodied, opulently styled effort bursting with black fruits, licorice, smoky, toasty oak, and truffle notes. Lush and dense, it is an ideal candidate for drinking over the next 10–12 years. The 1998 Moro exhibits a saturated color, more tannin, structure, and muscle, but not the charm and forward fruit of the 1999. I would not be surprised to see the 1998 catch up in 5–6 years, but for now, they are both outstanding wines, with a slight edge going to the 1999.

The 1998 Malleolus is produced from 25–75-year-old vines and minuscule yields of 0.85–1.0 ton of fruit per acre. Aged completely in French oak, it is a tighter, more structured effort revealing some of the same characteristics of the 1998 Moro, but more underlying depth as well as aging potential. While dense, powerful, and concentrated, it requires 2–3 years of cellaring and should age gracefully for 12–15 years.

The opaque ruby/purple, 100% barrel-fermented 1997 Ribera del Duero (American oak) is an exuberant, exotic-styled offering with copious quantities of blackberry and cherry fruit, chocolate, smoked herbs, and barbecue spices. Delicious, with abundant oak in addition to the jammy fruit, it has not developed much complexity or delineation, but I suspect that will emerge with another 1–2 years of bottle age. It might even merit an outstanding rating. Anticipated maturity: now–2012.

BODEGAS MUGA (RIOJA)

1996 Rioja Reserva	B	91
1995 Rioja Reserva Seleccion Especial	C	88
1994 Rioja Reserva Seleccion Especial	C	92
1996 Torre Muga	D	92

As longtime readers know, this is one of my favorite Spanish producers. The late-released 1994 Rioja Reserva Seleccion Especial (a blend of 70% Tempranillo, 20% Grenache, and 10% Mazuelo and Graciano) is a selection of the finest vineyard sites. After spending six months in large oak vats, and 30 months in small French and American barrels, it was bottled without filtration. A dark garnet color is followed by aromas of roasted coffee, smoke, black as well as red currants, minerals, and scorched earth. Dense and sweet, with notions of lead pencil, plum, and black currant fruit, this spectacular, medium- to full-bodied Rioja possesses gorgeous purity. It is a harmonious effort with intense flavor concentration, a beautiful texture, and subtle wood. Enjoy it now as well as over the next 20 years.

The 1995 Rioja Reserva Seleccion Especial reveals leathery, earthy, leafy notes along with graphite, cherry jam, and minerals. The bouquet is reminiscent of a lighter-styled Lafite-Rothschild. The wine spent 30 months in a combination of both French and American oak before being bottled without filtration. Although elegant and stylish, it lacks the substance as well as depth necessary to merit an outstanding rating. Anticipated maturity: now–2012.

The 1996 Rioja Reserva (a blend of 70% Tempranillo, 20% Grenache, and 10% Mazuelo and Graciano) spent 24 months in French and American oak prior to being bottled without filtration. The color is a dense plum/purple. The wine displays an Haut-Brion–like note of asphalt, roasted earth, lead pencil, smoke, and black cherry jam. Medium- to full-bodied and complex, with moderate tannin, adequate acidity, and a spicy, classy, rich finish, it requires 2–3 more years of cellaring. Anticipated maturity: 2003–2017.

The luxury *cuvée* of 1996 Torre Muga is a blend of 75% Tempranillo, 15% Mazuelo, and 10% Graciano that spent 22 months in large American oak vats, followed by 16 months in French casks prior to being bottled without filtration. An amazing effort, it somehow benefits from such a long wood aging regime. The opaque dense purple color is accompanied by scents of black fruits, minerals, scorched earth, cedar, tobacco, and spice box. Full-bodied, with great concentration, as well as a tightly knit personality, this powerful, muscular wine demands 4–5 years of cellaring. Anticipated maturity: 2005–2025.

BODEGAS DE MURRIETA (RIOJA)

1970	Castillo Ygay Gran Reserva Especial	EE	89
1996	Dalmau Reserva	D	90
1995	Dalmau Reserva	D	90+?

Murrieta's finest wines include a surprisingly youthful, exuberant 1970 Castillo Ygay Gran Reserva Especial. It possesses a remarkably deep ruby color as well as a pronounced nose of fresh mushrooms and toasty new American oak. The wine narrows in the mouth, but it provides cherry, cedary, and leather-infused fruit. It is hard to believe this wine is over 30 years old, as it appears capable of lasting another decade.

The luxury *cuvée* of 1996 Dalmau Reserva offers a dense saturated plum/ruby color followed by aromas of ripe black fruits intermixed with smoked meats, new oak, and game. Full-bodied, moderately tannic, rich, and concentrated, this structured, accessible yet youthful Rioja will benefit from 4–5 years of cellaring. It will last for 15+ years. The dark plum/ruby 1995 Dalmau Reserva appears to be closing down, but it has promise. New oak dominates at present, but notions of lead pencil, black fruits, earth, and smoked game are all present. A creamy attack is followed by copious amounts of tannin. I would cellar this wine for another 3–4 years and drink it over the following 15.

BODEGAS NEKEAS (NAVARRA)

1998	Vega Sindoa El Chaparral	B	88
1999	Vega Sindoa Merlot	A	88
1998	Vega Sindoa Merlot	A	88
1995	Vega Sindoa Izar de Vega	C	88
2000	Vega Sindoa Tempranillo/Merlot	A	88

Readers looking for wine bargains should make Bodegas Nekeas and its wines called Vega Sindoa must purchases. Nekeas owns approximately 550 acres of nonirrigated hillside vineyards in an area that was far more famous in the 15th century under King Phillip II than today. Most of the vineyards were uprooted because yields were too low. Thankfully, this area is enjoying a resurgence, and the following wines (which are priced preposterously low) are amazingly good. They merit interest especially from those who do not believe an $8–10 wine can provide delicious, complex drinking. A new offering from this reliable producer, the

1995 Izar de Vega (a 3,000-case blend of 40% Cabernet Sauvignon, 30% Merlot, and 30% Tempranillo) is Spain's version of a mid-level Pauillac. Notes of cassis, plums, tobacco, and cedar emerge from this dark ruby/purple-colored wine. Rich and medium-bodied, with supple tannin as well as low acidity, it should be consumed over the next 2–3 years.

Consumers know how difficult it is to find good Merlot in the marketplace. There is an ocean of industrial/insipid swill parading under the name Merlot, most of it thin, acidic, vegetal, and uninteresting. The finest Merlot tends to come from Bordeaux or Tuscany, but Bodegas Nekeas's soft, ripe, chunky 1999 Merlot (3,000 cases made from 100% Merlot from 10-year-old vines) is a winner. Aged in both American and French oak, it offers scents of wood, coffee, and berry fruit presented in a medium-bodied, user-friendly format. Drink it over the next 1–2 years. Another serious effort, the 1998 Merlot is also available for a song. Aged in 60% American and 40% French oak, it exhibits a dark ruby/purple color in addition to a classic Merlot bouquet of mocha, coffee, and berry/cherry fruit. The wine possesses low acidity, well-integrated, soft tannin, medium to full body, a fat, plush texture, and a surprisingly long finish. An exceptional value, it should drink well for 2–3 years.

The 1998 El Chaparral, the second vintage of this sensational old-vine Grenache (60–100-year-old vines), is once again a hedonist's dream. This inexpensive, dark ruby-colored offering is loaded with kirsch, pepper, and spice as well as lusty levels of glycerin. Additionally, it has sufficient underlying acidity to give vibrancy and freshness. Think of this fleshy, meaty Grenache as Spain's answer to France's Gigondas. Two thousand cases were imported. Drink it over the next 2 years.

Ten thousand cases of the 2000 Vega Sindoa Tempranillo/Merlot, a Spanish fruit bomb, were exported to the United States. A blend of 80% Tempranillo and 20% Merlot, aged in tank prior to bottling, it exhibits wonderful sweetness, soft, explosive, berry and cherry aromatics as well as flavors, medium to full body, low acidity, and superb purity. It ranks alongside wines costing 2–3 times as much. Anticipated maturity: now–2003.

NUMANTHIA (TORO)

1999 Toro	D	95
1998 Toro	D	95

This sensational wine will prove to be a breakthrough effort for the Toro appellation. Made from old (70–100 years), ungrafted vines planted at an elevation of 2,300 feet, yields were a minuscule 1.5 tons of fruit per acre. The wine was aged 18 months in 100% new French oak, with malolactic in barrel, and was bottled without fining or filtration. This 100% Tinta de Toro (the local name for Tempranillo) comes from a vineyard with sandy, chalky-textured soils overlaying clay. The wine is named after a legendary Spanish city that was destroyed (after 20 years of resistance) by Roman legions in 133 B.C. It is to Spain what the hilltop village of Masada is to Israel, a monument to foreign and national aggression.

The 1998 Numanthia is an explosively rich, super-concentrated wine of riveting intensity. The color is a dense purple, and the wine has soaked up 18 months in new French oak. It offers a smoky, blackberry- and cherry-scented nose of extraordinary purity and precision. Full-bodied, enormously endowed, and unctuously textured, this monstrous wine displays tremendous potential. Because of its low acidity, it can be approached now, but it is best aged for another 2–3 years and drunk over the following two decades. This compelling new offering proves what can be achieved in the appellation of Toro. Bravo! The 1999 Numanthia confirms just how special these wines are. An amazing effort from Toro, it was made from yields of 1.5 tons of fruit per acre, aged 18 months in new French wood, and bottled with neither fining nor filtration. A black/ruby color is followed by an explosive perfume of sweet blackberries, cassis, licorice, minerals, and smoke. With great intensity, fabulously sweet tannin, and high glycerin levels, this wine, likes its sibling, establishes a new benchmark for the Toro appellation. There are 300 cases of the 1999 for the U.S. marketplace.

OLIVARES (TARRAGONA)

1998 Dulce Monastrell	C	91?
1996 Dulce Monastrell	D	88?

Both of these wines may be controversial. They are late-harvest offerings exhibiting notions of prunes, raisins, and moderate levels of residual sugar. They are clearly designed to be drunk with flavorful cheese, or served at the end of the meal as dessert. Neither is overly sweet, and both are thick, heavy, and overripe. They are produced from 128-year-old Mourvèdre vines! The 1996 is more uncertain as it possesses rustic animal-like notes, whereas the purer 1998's blackberry and raisiny fruit is more cleanly displayed. Nevertheless, both wines will be met with "love it or leave it" sentiments. Both should last for at least a decade.

PAGO DE CARRAOVEJAS (RIBERA DEL DUERO)

1998 Tinto	D	90
1998 Tinto Reserva	D	92

The noteworthy 1998 Tinto reveals a dark plum color in addition to sweet aromas of black cherries, earth, and spice. Round and velvety-textured, with ripe, chewy fruit, and a supple, round, generously constituted personality, this seamless, full-bodied offering should be enjoyed over the next 6–7 years. Although similarly styled, the 1998 Tinto Reserva has a deeper color saturation, the use of new American and French casks is more noticeable, and the wine is fleshier, with additional layers of flavor. It is an impressive effort to drink over the next 10–12 years. Both wines are approximately 75% Tempranillo and 25% Cabernet Sauvignon.

ALVARO PALACIOS (PRIORATO)

1998 l'Ermita	EEE	97
1998 Finca Dofi	D	92
1998 Les Terrasses	C	88

An increasingly well known and pricy superstar, Alvaro Palacios has fashioned three fine wines from what appears to be a top-notch Priorato vintage. The soft, opulently styled 1998 Les Terrasses offers a deep dense ruby color as well as abundant quantities of blackberry and cherry fruit, subtle wood, a lush, juicy texture, and low acidity. This is a *négociant* offering from Palacios made to satisfy the immense demand for his wines. Drink it over the next 2–5 years. From his estate-bottled production, the terrific 1998 Finca Dofi boasts an opaque ruby/purple color in addition to a gorgeous bouquet of minerals, black fruits, and vanilla. It offers a full-bodied, concentrated, intense style with great purity, symmetry, and length. Enjoy it over the next 10–12 years.

The blockbuster, opaque purple-colored 1998 l'Ermita (the finest since the 1995 and 1994) exhibits a full-bodied personality with copious quantities of sweet oak, a boatload of glycerin, and superb blackberry, cassis, and cherry fruit that explodes on the mid-palate and in the finish. The elevated quantities of new oak should become better integrated as the wine ages over the next 15–20 years. This is an exceptionally impressive and expressive wine.

PESQUERA (RIBERA DEL DUERO)

1995 Gran Reserva	E	91
1994 Gran Reserva	EE	92
1996 Reserva	D	90

Dense plum/ruby/purple, with a sweet perfume of earth, herbs, jammy black fruits, and oak in the background, the opulently textured, round, fleshy 1994 Gran Reserva possesses full body, moderate tannin, and an accessible yet structured personality. It should drink well for 12–15 years. The dense plum-colored 1996 Reserva exhibits an ostentatious bouquet of smoky oak, earth, tobacco, licorice, and jammy red and black fruits. Full-bodied, thick, rich, and mouth-filling, this opulent wine possesses structure as well as tannin. However, it is delicious already. Anticipated maturity: now–2014.

While the regular 1997 and 1998 Tintos were less inspiring than expected (scoring in the low 80s), the 1995 Gran Reserva possesses a deep ruby/garnet/plum color as well as a sweet nose of earth, licorice, black fruits, underbrush, and spicy new oak. In the mouth, it is medium- to full-bodied, with refreshing acidity, and outstanding depth, ripeness, and complexity. It should drink well for 10–15 years.

Past Glories: 1994 Crianza (95), 1994 Gran Reserva (91), 1990 Gran Reserva (90), 1989 Gran Reserva (92), 1986 Gran Reserva (94), 1994 Janus (97)

PINGUS (RIBERA DEL DUERO)

1999	EEE	98
1998	EEE	90
1997	EEE	89
1999 Flor de Pingus	D	90

This limited-production offering, first created by wine-maker/owner Peter Sisseck in 1995, is one of the most exciting wines emerging from Europe. The 1995 is virtually perfect, the 1996 is also spectacular, and the 1999 is brilliant. A barrel sample of the 2000 looks to be magnificent. There were approximately 2,000 cases of the Flor de Pingus in 1999, and 450 cases of Pingus.

The 1997 Pingus reveals a herbaceous note to its medium-bodied, austere character. Aromas and flavors of cedarwood, olives, spice box, black currants, leather, and smoke emerge from this medium-bodied, rich, concentrated wine. It is best consumed now and over the next decade. Though similarly styled, the 1998 Pingus exhibits more chocolate, espresso, and leather characteristics as well as a more expansive mid-palate, a denser, more opaque ruby/purple color, medium to full body, moderate tannin, and gorgeous purity and sweetness. Although outstanding, it is not one of Sisseck's most prodigious efforts. Anticipated maturity: now–2012.

Readers can look forward to a nearly perfect 1999 Pingus. It boasts an opaque ruby/purple color, sensational extract, gorgeous concentration, and spectacularly intense blackberry and cherry aromas and flavors infused with incense, coffee, chocolate, and toasty new oak. Enormous levels of extract and richness are accompanied by a full-bodied, glycerin-imbued, thick, viscous finish. The tannin is nearly hidden by the wine's wealth of fruit and concentration. Anticipated maturity: now–2025. Pingus's second wine, the outstanding 1999 Flor de Pingus, is as good as the 1998 grand vin and unquestionably better than the 1997 Pingus. Sweet, ripe blackberry and currant notes intermixed with licorice, smoke, coffee, and earth emerge from this full-bodied, opulently textured offering. Already evolved and delicious, it is best consumed during its first decade of life.

Past Glories: 1996 Pingus (96), 1995 Pingus (98)

FINCA LA PLANETA (PRIORATO)

1997 Pasanau	D	89+

Sweet black raspberry aromas intermingle with mineral and new oak in this impressively endowed, well-delineated effort from Priorato. The percentage of new oak is high, but there is plenty of concentration and extract for balance. Young, exuberant, and pure, it will last for a decade—at the minimum.

REAL SITIO DE VENTOSILLA (RIBERA DEL DUERO)

1996 Crianza Prado Rey	C	88

A delicious, soft fruit bomb, this Ribera del Duero can be bought for a reasonable price. A round, well-made 1996 Crianza, it possesses a dark ruby color with purple nuances as well as abundant chocolate, black cherry, and berry fruit flavors. The velvety texture in addition to hedonistic up-front aromas and flavors provide a luscious mouthful of wine. Drink it over the next 5–6 years.

CASTELL DEL REMEI (COSTERS DEL SEGRE)

1998 Cervoles	B	88
1998 Gotim Bru	A	90
1997 Gotim Bru	A	90
1996 Gotim Bru	A	89
1997 Oda	B	88
1998 "1780"	C	92
1996 "1780"	C	91

These are serious efforts produced from different proportions of Tempranillo, Merlot, Cabernet Sauvignon, and Grenache. The elegant, polished, refined 1998 Cervoles is a blend of 40% Tempranillo, 40% Cabernet Sauvignon, and 20% Grenache. Its deep ruby/purple color is accompanied by aromas of spicy new oak, creosote, kirsch, and pepper. Medium-bodied and stylish with a Burgundy-like personality, it will drink well for 6–8 years. Although more expensive, the 1998 "1780" (the year this company was founded) is still an excellent value. A blend of 40% Cabernet Sauvignon, 35% Tempranillo, and 25% Grenache, it boasts a deep purple color as well as a sweet nose of vanilla, toast, black cherries, currants, and leather. It is ripe, medium- to full-bodied, and elegant, with sweet glycerin on the attack, great follow-through, and wonderful purity, depth, and length. Moderate tannin in the finish suggests another 1–3 years of cellaring will be beneficial. It should last for two decades.

Readers seeking a sensational bargain should check out the 4,000 cases imported to the U.S. of the 1998 Gotim Bru, a blend of 50% Tempranillo, 25% Merlot, and 25% Cabernet Sauvignon aged 10 months in French oak. From a viticultural area not far from Priorato, it is a deep ruby/purple offering with a delicious, sweet perfume of black cherries, a smooth, velvety texture, medium to full body, light tannin, and nicely integrated new wood. Fleshy and pure, it is best consumed over the next 5–6 years. Consumers seeking a wine that resembles a dry vintage port for $10 a bottle should check out the 1997 Gotim Bru. There are 3,000 cases of this delicious Tempranillo/Cabernet Sauvignon/Merlot blend. Fat, with thrilling levels of jammy cherry and black currant fruit, chocolate, and spice, this dense, chewy effort is a great bargain. Drink it over the next 2–3 years.

The more expensive as well as monolithic 1997 Oda (a blend of Cabernet Sauvignon and Merlot) is pure, rich, and deep, with an overripe character to its fruit. It should age nicely for 5–7 years, and is undoubtedly a very good bargain. The 1996 Gotim Bru is a robust, earthy, spicy, fruity blend of 50% Cabernet Sauvignon and 50% Tempranillo. Aged 15 months in used American oak casks, the wine exhibits a saturated black/plum color, sweet, chewy fruit, full body, obvious glycerin, and a rich, nicely textured, plump finish. This is a mouth-filling, silky-smooth, robust Spanish red to drink over the next 3–4 years. It merits buying by the case.

Readers also do not want to miss Castell del Remei's 1996 "1780," a blend of 70% Cabernet Sauvignon, 20% Tempranillo, and 10% Grenache aged one year in new American casks. Even though it is twice the price of its less expensive sibling, it is an exotic, ostentatiously styled wine that could be called Spain's answer to California's Caymus Special Selection! It should drink well for a decade or more.

REMELLURI (RIOJA)

1999 Rioja	C	90
1996 Rioja	C	89

Remelluri's 1996 Rioja (80% Tempranillo with small quantities of Grenache, Graciano, and Mazuelo) may not be as compelling as the 1995, but it is a smoky, sweet, oaky, rich, complex,

Pomerol-like Rioja with copious quantities of black cherry fruit highly dosed with sweet vanilla. With a velvety texture, medium to full body, and excellent, possibly outstanding concentration, this soft wine can be drunk now as well as over the next 10–12 years.

The 1999 is significantly better than the disappointing 1998. It boasts sweet black cherry fruit infused with toast, smoke, herbs, and tobacco. Layered, rich, medium-bodied, and elegant yet concentrated, it should drink well for 7–10 years.

BODEGAS FERNANDO REMIREZ DE GANUZA (RIOJA)

1998 Rioja	D	95
1996 Rioja	D	94+

Importer Jorge Ordonez told me of the fanatical attention to detail at this estate, which consists of 72 acres of old vines. Crop yields are kept low, and the estate practices the relatively new technique of cutting not only bunches of grapes, but also the bottom of a bunch off, leaving the shoulder to mature. The wine is a blend of 85% Tempranillo, 10% Graciano, 3% Grenache, and 2% diverse varietals, and is bottled unfined and unfiltered after spending two years in a combination of French and American oak. These (the 1994 and 1995 were previously recommended) are spectacular Riojas, but require patience. The 1995 still needs an additional 4–5 years of cellaring, and the 1996, while capable of 25–30 years of evolution, also needs 4–5 years. There are 500 cases exported to the United States.

The 1996 could be called the Château Latour of Rioja. An opaque black/plum color is followed by aromas of minerals, cigar tobacco, cedar, lead pencil, and sweet black currant, plum, and cherry fruit. One of the greatest young Riojas I have ever tasted, it exhibits full body, a huge, concentrated palate feel, an immense, chewy texture, and high tannin in the finish. The proprietor, who started this bodega in 1989, was not satisfied with anything until 1994, when the first wine was released. This looks to be a prodigious Rioja that should age effortlessly for three decades. Anticipated maturity: 2005–2030. To the proprietor's credit, no 1997 was produced, but the 1998 exhibits a dark plum/purple color along with an extraordinary perfume of liquid minerals, cassis, black cherries, tobacco, spice box, and vanilla. There is fabulous density on the palate, high tannin, admirable concentration, and a structured finish reminiscent of a first or second growth Pauillac from a year such as 1996. This Rioja requires 3–5 years of cellaring, but appears to be the finest *cuvée* yet produced by this estate, eclipsing even the 1994. Anticipated maturity: 2004–2020.

HERENCIA REMONDO (RIOJA)

1996 La Montesa	E	88

The internationally styled 1996 La Montesa (30% Tempranillo, 40% Merlot, and 30% Graciano) is given a longer maceration on its skins, then aged for 8 months in new French oak followed by 5 months in American wood. A dense ruby/purple color is accompanied by notes of caramel, cherry liqueur, plums, and licorice. Although monolithic, it is impressively endowed, rich, supple, and long. The obvious wood should become better integrated as the wine ages. Anticipated maturity: now–2010.

BODEGAS REYES (RIBERA DEL DUERO)

1997 Teofilo Reyes	D	88

This is a sexy, open-knit, low-acid wine exhibiting lusty chocolate and black cherry flavors with foresty/herb scents in the background. Deep, rich, round, opulent, and easy to understand and consume, this forward, in-your-face offering can be drunk now as well as over the next 5–6 years.

LA RIOJA ALTA (RIOJA)

1990 Gran Reserva 904	D	90
1985 Gran Reserva 890	EE	92

La Rioja Alta's classics, the Gran Reserva 904 and Gran Reserva 890, are not released until they are 10 and 15 years of age, respectively. These offerings spend a minimum of 10 years in primarily old American oak (about 5% new). Traditionally styled Riojas, they are wines of great subtlety and complexity with slightly oxidized personalities. They are not for everybody, but readers who enjoy mature wines will be impressed.

The medium garnet-colored 1990 Gran Reserva 904 displays considerable amber at the edges. The fragrant, complex aromatics consist of scorched earth, smoke, lead pencil, spice box, and red and black fruits. In the mouth, the wine is round, with no hard edges, medium body, and graceful subtlety as well as delicacy. Though there is a lot going on, it is extraordinarily restrained, and does not bash the taster over the head as so many modern-day "smashmouth" wines do. Fully mature, it will remain at its peak for another decade. Even more aged, complex, and subtle is the 1985 Gran Reserva 890. A compelling nose of smoke, earth, plums, tobacco, cherries, and vanilla emerges from this light garnet-colored 1985 that also reveals considerable amber at the edges. If it were a Bordeaux, the color would suggest a wine of 30+ years of age. It offers complex, savory flavors of spice, faded flowers, and red fruits. There is suppleness yet vivacity to this medium-weight wine that is all finesse and restraint. Although not for everybody, it is a brilliant example of this style of Rioja. Look for the 1985 to continue to drink well for 7–8 years.

Past Glories: Gran Reserva 890 1978 (93), 1981 (92), 1982 (92)

BODEGAS RODA (RIOJA)

1998 Cirsion	EEE	90
1996 Roda I Reserva	D	88+

The striking 1996 Roda I Reserva is made from 100% Tempranillo. It reveals a saturated ruby color in addition to abundant new oak and smoky, earthy, red and black fruits in the nose. With admirable volume and flesh as well as elegance, this spicy, well-made Rioja should improve for 4–5 years and last for 12–15. The 1998 Cirsion is a bigger, richer effort offering a gorgeous bouquet of ripe black fruits, licorice, oak, and spice. Tobacco, herb, black cherry, and currant fruit intermingle with toast and truffle flavors. Medium- to full-bodied, sweet, and pure, this impressive 1998 is youthful but accessible. It promises to evolve for 15 years.

TELMO RODRIGUEZ (RIBERA DEL DUERO)

1999 Dehesa Gago	B	91
1999 Valderiz	C	90

Made from 100% Tinto de Toro (the local clone of Tempranillo), the 1999 Dehesa Gago was vinified and aged in stainless steel tanks. A majestic fruit bomb, it boasts a dense ruby/purple color as well as an intense nose of melted licorice, crème de cassis, and flowers. Extremely full-bodied and unctuously textured, with superb purity, this rich, gorgeously layered wine is almost too good to be true. The bad news is that only 700 cases were made; the good news is that all of it was shipped to the U.S. Enjoy this beauty over the next 5–8 years, although it may last even longer. Readers should run, not walk, to their favorite wine merchant to grab a few bottles of this nectar. The hedonistic, rich, lush, fat, fruity 1999 Valderiz displays notes of melted chocolate, cherries, and blackberries. Supple, with low acidity, ripe tannin, and jammy fruit, it should be consumed over the next 5–7 years for its unabashed display of joy.

SAN VICENTE (RIOJA)

1999 San Vicente	D	92
1998 San Vicente	D	90
1997 San Vicente	D	89
1996 San Vicente	D	91

This continues to be one of the sexiest, most voluptuously textured, exotic wines to emerge from Rioja. At times, it resembles a flashy Pomerol, and at other times, a hypothetical blend of the best of Spain with the finest of the New World. The dark ruby-colored 1996 (100% Tempranillo from a single vineyard called Peludo) displays a flamboyant nose of vanilla, jammy black cherries, Asian spices, licorice, and roasted meats and herbs. Big in the mouth, with medium to full body, outstanding richness, and plenty of sweet tannin, this opulently textured, hedonistically styled wine can be drunk now as well as over the next 10–12 years. The 1997, from a more difficult vintage than 1996 or 1995, is a sexy, dark ruby/purple-colored effort exhibiting notes of Provençal herbs, smoke, roasted tobacco, jammy black fruits, and cherry liqueur. Lush, with a multilayered, expansive texture, exceptional purity, and a touch of overripe prunes in the finish, this supple, voluptuous, compelling Rioja can be drunk now and over the next 5–6 years.

The dark ruby/purple-colored 1998 reveals a big, splashy nose of toasty oak intermixed with jammy black cherries, berries, vanilla, and espresso. Ripe, rich, medium-bodied, and more structured than the explosive 1999, the 1998 should drink well for 7–8 years. The denser, more hedonistic 1999 boasts loads of fruit and glycerin, as well as additional ripeness, volume, fat, and depth. Displaying the same black currant, jammy cherry fruit, and copious toasty new oak characteristics, it will provide enjoyment during its first decade of life.

HERMANOS SASTRE (RIBERA DEL DUERO)

1999	Pago de Santa Cruz	EEE	(92–94)
1996	Pago de Santa Cruz	EEE	90+
1999	Regina Vides	EEE	(92–94)
1998	Regina Vides	EEE	92

This estate's flagship wine, Pago de Santa Cruz, is made in limited quantities and very little will be exported to the U.S. It is made from 100% destemmed Tempranillo, aged 24 months in new American oak, moved to 100% new French oak for an additional 12 months, and bottled unfiltered. The four vintages tasted were all extremely concentrated, dense wines with a quality not dissimilar from the super-extracted, rich, full-bodied blockbusters of Peter Sisseck's Pingus. All three were seamless, opulent, and concentrated efforts offering notes of chocolate, coffee, blackberry liqueur, and sweet cassis fruit. These wines' smoky richness and broad, expansive thickness are sure to provoke excitement, assuming readers can find any of the 400+ cases produced. The narrowly focused 1996 will last 15+ years. The 1999 is spectacular. According to the importer, yields from 60-year-old Tempranillo vines average 20–25 hectoliters per hectare.

The other superb offering I tasted from Hermanos Sestre is the 1998 Regina Vides, a 100% Tempranillo produced from 80-year-old vines with yields of 20 h/h. It is an impressive, opaque purple, full-bodied, opulently textured effort with abundant quantities of sweet, toasty oak, blackberry and cassis fruit, and a long, concentrated, powerful finish. It will drink well for 10–15 years. The 1999 Regina Vides emerged from a far greater vintage for Ribera del Duero than 1998. Extremely full-bodied, unctuously textured, and supersweet, it boasts blackberry, coffee, chocolate, and cassis aromas as well as flavors. This outstanding Spanish red should age effortlessly for two decades.

BODEGAS SIERRA CANTABRIA (RIOJA)

1999	Rioja	A	88
1999	Rioja Coleccion Privada	C	90
1997	Rioja Crianza	B	89
1996	Rioja Crianza	B	89
1999	Rioja Cuvée Especial	B	89

Another name synonymous with excellent value and extremely well made Rioja, Sierra Cantabria has turned out five attractive offerings. The 1997 Rioja Crianza (100% Tempranillo bottled after 14 months aging in a combination of French and American oak) is an excellent, nearly outstanding effort, no small achievement in 1997. Its deep ruby/purple color is accompanied by a gorgeously sweet nose of strawberry and cherry jam intermixed with dried herbs, smoke, earth, and vanilla. Medium- to full-bodied and opulently textured, with a tannic finish, it requires 1–2 years of cellaring, and should age well for 10–12 years.

The dark ruby-colored 1999 Rioja exhibits a sweet, hedonistic style with plenty of fat, smoky, toasty, black cherry and berry flavors presented in a lush, user-friendly format. Drink it over the next 2–3 years. The 1996 Rioja Crianza is another exceptional wine value. The dark ruby color is followed by copious quantities of sweet, spicy oak along with candied black cherries and dried herbs. Noteworthy, complex lead pencil notes also make an appearance. This *cuvée* (6,000 cases imported) possesses good fruit, medium body, and an elegant yet mouth-filling style with no hard edges. It is a gorgeously proportioned, modern-styled Rioja to enjoy over the next 3–4 years.

The 1998 Rioja Cuvée Especial exhibits scents of lead pencil shavings intermixed with tobacco, black cherries, currants, minerals, roasted herbs, and toasty American oak. Layered, ripe, and impressive, it will drink well for 5–7 years. The 1999 Rioja Coleccion Privada (an unfiltered, 100% Tempranillo wine made from tiny yields of 1.3 tons of fruit per acre) was aged 19 months in both American and French oak. Sadly, there are only 250 cases available for the U.S. The wine grows by increments in the glass, improving dramatically with 15 minutes of airing. A deep ruby color is followed by a spicy, herb, berry, graphite, and licorice-scented bouquet. This rich, medium-bodied, elegant, well-balanced Rioja is not a blockbuster, but expands in flavor and nuances as it crosses the palate. Drink it over the next 7–8 years.

ROTLLAN TORRA (PRIORATO)

1997 Amadis	D	90
1998 Tirant	E	93
1997 Tirant	E	92

These are impressive efforts from Rotllan Torra, a winery founded in 1984. The opaque purple 1997 Amadis (2,000 cases from 100-year-old vines and minuscule yields of 10 h/h) was aged 10 months in 100% new French oak before being bottled unfiltered. A blend of 40% Grenache (from 90–100-year-old vines), 25% Cabernet Sauvignon, 20% Carignan (also 90–100-year-old vines), 10% Syrah, and 5% Merlot, it is a blockbuster Priorato with huge, concentrated black raspberry, cassis, and berry fruit mixed with minerals, smoke, licorice, and toasty oak. This intense wine possesses a seamless, sweet, concentrated mid-palate as well as finish. It is a terrific Spanish red to drink over the next 10–12 years.

Even better are the two limited-production offerings of 1997 and 1998 Tirant. This blend of 30% Grenache, 25% Cabernet Sauvignon, 25% Carignan, 10% Syrah, and 10% Merlot (the Carignan and Grenache come from 90–100-year-old vines) spends a full year in new French oak, enjoys malolactic in barrel, and is bottled unfiltered. The superb, opaque purple 1997 Tirant exhibits sweet, concentrated, jammy fruit intertwined with notions of asphalt, pepper, liquid minerals, and subtle spicy wood. A full-bodied, powerful effort, it requires 2–3 years of cellaring but should last 12–15. The 1998 Tirant is richer, with an even more saturated opaque blue/purple color. Extremely full-bodied, dense, powerful, and layered, it has impressive seamlessness, opulence, and thickness. It should drink well for 15+ years.

TRESANTOS (ZAMORA)

2000 Tresantos	B	90

From a viticultural area just north of Toro, this wine is a thermonuclear fruit bomb. Huge levels of hedonistic black currant, cherry, and blackberry fruit are presented in an uncomplicated, fleshy, succulent style that is a total turn-on. This low-acid, beautifully pure 2000 is a treat to drink. Consume it over the next 2–3 years.

BODEGAS VALCONA (RIOJA)

1998 Partal Crianza	C	90

This blend of 60% Mourvèdre and the balance Tempranillo, Cabernet Sauvignon, Merlot, and Syrah, from a vineyard planted 60 miles from the Mediterranean, was aged in 70% French and 30% American oak. It boasts a dense ruby/purple color and a sweet nose of black cherries, vanilla, and spice. This 1998 Crianza is admirably rich and impressively chewy, with a thick mid-palate and a long, spicy, moderately tannic finish. Though it comes close to being rustic, there is a lot of finesse underneath. Drink it over the next 6–7 years.

VALL LLACH (PRIORATO)

1998	E	92+
1998 Embruix	B	90

Proprietor Louis Llach is a well-known Spanish singer who, according to importer Eric Solomon, has produced over 40 albums and has a huge following in his native country. His love of wine has been sanctified by his high-altitude Priorato vineyards. The least expensive offering, the 1998 Embruix, is a blend of 40% Grenache, 40% Cabernet Sauvignon, and 20% Carignan aged in one- and two-year-old French oak barrels. It is a lovely, ripe effort with aromas of plums, black cherries, vanilla, and minerals. Medium- to full-bodied, pure, well balanced, and long, it offers a sweet attack as well as a tannic finish, suggesting another 1–2 years of cellaring is merited. It should keep for 12–15 years. An impressive debut effort.

The 1998 Vall Llach (800 cases produced) is a blend of 50% Carignan (from 80-year-old vines) and 50% Merlot (5–10-year-old vines), aged one year in new French oak. It is an impressive, powerful (15.1% alcohol) wine revealing a deep purple color in addition to a sweet nose of black raspberries, cherry liqueur, and graphite aromas. Full-bodied, thick, and juicy, with moderately high tannin, superb purity, and a Bordeaux-like structure to its flavors and finish, it will benefit from 4–5 years of cellaring, and age well for two decades.

VEGA SAUCO (TORO)

1999 Tinto	B	88

A terrific value, this wine, produced from 70-year-old Tempranillo vines, offers a deep ruby color in addition to explosive, sweet, fragrant aromas of kirsch, smoke, and earth. Powerful, concentrated, and surprisingly rich (particularly for a wine in this price range), it offers more flavor and character than many wines costing 2–3 times as much. Its low acidity and luscious personality suggest consumption over the next 2–3 years.

Past Glories: Unico 1986 (92+), 1985 (93), 1983 (93), 1982 (95), 1980 (90), 1979 (89), 1976 (93), 1975 (95), 1974 (90), 1970 (96), 1968 (99), 1966 (95), 1964 (94), 1962 (93)

VEGA SICILIA (RIBERA DEL DUERO)

NV Reserva Especiale Lot 017/00	EEE	93+
NV Reserva Especial Unico Lot 25	EEE	93
1990 Unico Reserva Especiale	EE	94
1970 Unico Reserva Especiale (Magnum)	EEE	96
1995 Valbuena	D	89

There are 14,000 bottles of the nonvintage Reserva Especial Unico Lot 25, a blend of 1970, 1985, and 1990, all top-quality vintages for Vega Sicilia. This classic boasts a dark ruby color and sweet, creamy, oaky notions intermixed with jammy black raspberry, cassis, and berry aromas. As the wine sits in the glass, roasted herbs, coffee, and floral scents make an appearance. Dense, full-bodied, and superbly concentrated with velvety tannin, low acidity, and nicely integrated wood, this is a complex, delicious effort that can be drunk now as well as over the next 15–20 years. The reasonably priced 1995 Valbuena offers a plum/ruby color followed by aromas of sweet black fruits intermixed with licorice, earth, and spicy oak. Full-bodied, with excellent concentration, a juicy, layered texture, and fine purity, it is forward, plush, and best consumed within its first 10–12 years of life.

The newest Unico Reserva Especiale is the 1990. For a Unico, it exhibits a relatively unevolved style. A deep opaque plum/garnet color is accompanied by noticeable sweet toasty oak in the nose along with copious quantities of black cherry and cassis fruit. Extremely youthful, vigorous, and full-bodied, with notes of overripeness, low acidity, moderately high tannin, and a layered, concentrated personality, this Unico is less mature upon release than many of its siblings. Give it another 3–4 years of cellaring; it should last for 25 years.

Each year Vega Sicilia releases limited quantities of a nonvintage blend. There are 13,680 bottles of the nonvintage Reserva Especiale Lot 017/00 (this number is on the bottle's label), which is claimed to be a blend of 1985, 1990, and 1994 Unico Reservas. This fabulous, youthful effort exhibits jammy blackberry, cherry, mineral, smoke, cedar, and new-oak aromas as well as flavors. Full-bodied, dense, and concentrated, with great purity in addition to stature, this Reserva Especiale can be drunk now but ideally needs another 2–3 years of cellaring. It should age for 2–3 decades. One of Vega Sicilia's other distinctive practices is to release magnums of great vintages well after the wine's initial release. Magnums of the fabulous 1970 Unico Reserva Especiale (for my taste, 1968 and 1970 are the two finest Vega Sicilias produced in the last 35 years) have just been released. This wine boasts an elegant, complex bouquet of cedarwood, blackberries, cherry liqueur, and vanilla. Opulently textured, with fabulous unctuosity, vivaciousness, and vigor, superb ripeness, a full-bodied, super-concentrated attack as well as a lush mid-palate and finish, this seamless classic can be drunk now or cellared for two decades. This wine was brilliant from the 750-ml format and is equally compelling from magnum.

FINCA VILLA CRECES (RIBERA DEL DUERO)

1999 Crianza	C	90
1998 Crianza	C	89
1999 Nebro	EE	95
1998 Pruno	EE	92

Villa Creces has produced very fine wines over recent vintages. A blend of 75% Tempranillo, 15% Merlot, and 10% Cabernet Sauvignon aged 16 months in French oak, the sexy, deep ruby/purple, Pomerol-like 1999 Crianza exhibits a smoky bouquet with notes of espresso, fudge, and jammy black currants as well as cherries. Supple-textured, medium-bodied, lush, richly fruity, and seamless, it should drink well for a decade. The special *cuvée* of 70-year-old Tempranillo vines located next to one of the oldest Vega Sicilia vineyards, the 1999 Nebro is a spectacular effort. It is a single-vineyard offering aged 16 months in new French oak (Darnajou barrels), and made from yields of 17 h/h. Made in a style reminiscent of Peter Sisseck's 1995 and 1996 Pingus, this glorious wine offers up scents of roasted espresso, vanilla, black cherry liqueur, blackberries, licorice, and spice box. Full-bodied and unctuously textured, with an impressive integration of wood, acidity, and alcohol, it is unformed but accessible. Anticipated maturity: 2003–2025. The bad news . . . only 75 cases were produced.

The 1998 Crianza reveals an impressive dense ruby/purple color as well as a sweet, earthy, blackberry, and charcoal-scented nose with new oak in the background. Medium- to full-bodied, chewy, with low acidity, and abundant fruit, glycerin, and extract, it will drink well for 5–7 years. The super *cuvée* of Villa Creces, the 1998 Pruno (200 bottles produced), is reminiscent of the great Pingus made by Peter Sisseck. The Pruno is powerful, thick, chewy, and unctuously textured, with huge quantities of black cherry, plum, and licorice-infused blackberry fruit. Sadly, because of the limited production, only a handful of readers will ever run across a bottle. Anticipated maturity: now–2020.

VINA ALARBA (CALATAYUD)

2000 Old Vines Grenache A 89

Five thousand cases of this *cuvée* have been exported to the U.S. The 2000 Old Vines Grenache (100% Grenache from vines averaging over 50 years of age, and yields of only one ton of fruit per acre) boasts a deeper ruby/purple color and a nose reminiscent of a Châteauneuf-du-Pape or Gigondas. The bouquet offers aromas of kirsch, dried Provençal herbs, licorice, spice box, and underlying pepper. Dense, chewy, and rich, with gobs of fruit, it is best consumed during its first 2–3 years of life. This is an unreal value priced so low most consumers will never believe it is this good.

BODEGAS Y VINEDOS (RIBERA DEL DUERO)

1996 Alion D 90

This beautifully made Spanish red represents a more modern approach to winemaking. Sweet toasty oak competes with jammy black cherry and berry fruit in this deep, low-acid offering. This wine possesses excellent to outstanding concentration, topflight purity, and overall equilibrium. Drink this impressively endowed Ribera del Duero over the next 10–12 years.

BODEGAS Y VINEDOS MAURO-TORO (CASTILLA Y LEÓN)

1997 San Romain D 90

The former wine-maker from Vega Sicilia is involved with this new project with the Tinta de Toro grape. Five hundred cases have been released for the U.S. Completely aged in 100% new French oak, this wine is a Pomerol-like, lush effort with gobs of black raspberry and cherry fruit meshed with toasty new oak. From its saturated dark ruby/purple color to its gorgeously rich flavors, opulent texture, and low-acid, fleshy finish, this is a pleasure-filled wine to enjoy over the next 5–8 years, although I suspect it will last longer.

BODEGAS Y VINEDOS SOLABAL (RIOJA)

1997 Rioja Crianza B 88

A success for this tricky vintage, the 1997 Rioja Crianza (100% Tempranillo) exhibits a ruby/purple color in addition to aromas of melted fudge, vanilla, smoke, and cherry liqueur. Though not complex, it is an impressive, full-bodied, richly fruity, hedonistic offering with copious amounts of accessible fruit. Consume it over the next 3–4 years.

VINICOLA DEL PRIORAT (PRIORATO)

1998 Onix A 88
1996 Onix 1163 C 88

The finest wine I have ever tasted from this producer (selling for one-fifth the price of most Prioratos), the 1998 Onix is made from old-vine Grenache and Carignan. Although monolithic, it is a chewy, boisterous, muscular, full-bodied red. Purely made, with copious quantities of blackberry and cherry fruit in addition to good underlying minerality and spice, it is a substantial, foursquare, but mouth-filling wine to drink over the next 3–4 years.

A blend of 40% Cabernet Sauvignon, 40% Grenache, and 20% Carignan, the 1996 Onix 1163 reveals a deep, opaque purple color in addition to sweet aromas of ripe black raspberry fruit. Full-bodied, with abundant toasty oak, as well as a touch of licorice and prune, this wine, aged in American and French oak casks, is not complex but is chewy, with excellent concentration and purity, and a round, generous, exuberant personality. Drink it over the next 4–5 years.

PORTUGAL

PORT

Americans have finally begun to realize the great pleasures of a mature vintage port after a meal. For years, this sumptuous and mellow fortified red wine was seriously undervalued, as most of it was drunk in the private homes and clubs of the United Kingdom. Prices, which soared in the early and mid-1980s, collapsed in the early 1990s. Although there is not much vintage port produced (there are rarely more than four declared vintages a decade), the international recession and bloated marketplace have resulted in stable prices. Port's richness and sweetness are largely the result of high quality (and high proof) brandy being added as the port wine ferments. This arrests the fermentation process, leaving unfermented sugars in the wine and thus contributing to port's 20% alcohol content.

WHAT TO BUY

It is widely anticipated that 2000 will be considered a great year for vintage port producers. Powerful, thick vines were produced, and, as of this writing, a "vintage year" had been declared by Graham's Dow, Warre, Taylor, Fonseca, Croft, Delaforce, Quinta do Noval, and Symington's Quinta do Vesuvio. Other major houses are also expected to declare 2000 a vintage port year. These wines will be available for sale in 2002–2003. Other outstanding vintage years still available at retail are 1997, 1994, and 1992. As with many fine wines, prices for the newest vintages are higher than older ports that can be purchased through auction houses. Shrewd consumers should consider buying at auction such vintages as 1995 (where it was declared), 1991, 1987, 1983, and 1980. These are very fine rather than great years, but the top houses have turned in impeccable efforts, and the wines are closer to full maturity.

An obvious trend has been the explosion of single-quinta offerings, most of which are very good to excellent, although not as compelling as the greatest vintage ports. Most of the single-quinta ports are offered in years not declared as vintages.

VARIOUS PORT STYLES

Crusted Port Rarely seen today, crusted port is usually a blend of several vintages that is bottled early and handled in the same manner as a vintage port. Significant sediment will form in the bottle and a crusted port has to be decanted prior to drinking.

Tawny Port One of the least expensive ways of securing a mature port is to buy the best shippers' tawny ports. Tawny ports are a blend of vintages aged in wood by the top houses for 10, 20, 30, 40, or even 50 years. Tawnys can have exceptional complexity and refinement. I highly recommend some of the best tawnys from firms such as Taylor Fladgate, Fonseca, and Graham's.

Ruby and Branded Ports Ruby ports are relatively straightforward, deeply colored, young ports that are cherished for their sweet, grapy aromas and supple, exuberant, yet monolithic taste. Most of these ports are meant to be drunk when released. Each house has its own style. Four of the most popular include Fonseca's Bin No. 27, Taylor's 4XX, Cockburn's Special Reserve, and Graham's Six Grapes. All four of these ruby or branded ports are stylistically different. The richest and fullest is the Fonseca Bin No. 27; the most complex is usu-

ally the Taylor 4XX; the sweetest and fruitiest is the Graham Six Grapes; and the most mature and evolved, as well as least distinguished, is the Cockburn Special Reserve.

White Port   I have never understood the purpose of white port, but the French find it appealing. However, the market for these eccentricities is dead.

Late Bottled Vintage Port (L.B.V.P.)   Certain vintages are held back in cask longer
than 2 years (the time required for vintage port) and bottled 5–7 years following the vintage.
These ports tend to throw less sediment, as much of it has been already deposited in cask. In
general, late bottled ports are ready to drink when released. I often find them less interesting
and complex than the best tawnys and vintage ports.

Single-Quinta Vintage Port   This has become an increasingly important area, especially
since the late 1980s, when a number of vintages, particularly 1987, 1990, 1991, and 1992,
could have been declared vintage years but were not because of the saturated marketplace.
Many of the best single-quintas, or vineyards, have been offered as vintage-dated single
quinta ports. These are vintage ports from a single vineyard. Most port authorities feel it is
the blending from various vineyards that gives vintage port its greatest character. Others will
argue that in a top year, the finest single-quinta ports can be as good as a top vintage port. I
tend to believe that a great vintage port is superior to a single-quinta port, yet the finest
single-quintas from 1987, 1990, 1991, and 1992 are stunning. Star ratings of the different
single-quinta port producers are provided where I have had sufficient tasting experience
(more than two vintages) to offer a qualitative ranking.

SINGLE-QUINTA VINTAGE PORTS

Quinta Agua Alta (Churchill)
Quinta Boa Vista (Offley)
Quinta do Bomfim (Dow)
Quinta do Cachao (Messias)
Quinta da Cavadinha (Warre)
Quinta do Confradeiro (Sandeman)
Quinta da Corte (Delaforce)
Quinta do Crasto (a consortium)
Quinta da Eira Velha (R. Newan)
Quinta Fojo (Churchill)
Quinta do Forte (Delaforee)
Quinta da Foz (Calem)

Quinta Guimaraens (Fonseca)
Quinta do Infantado (Roseira)
Quinta Malvedossd (Graham's)
Quinta da Roeda (Croft)
Quinta de la Rosa (Bergquist)
Quinta do Seixo (Ferreira)
Quinta do Tua (Cockburn)
Quinta de Val da Figueria (Calem)
Quinta de Vargellas (Taylor Fladgate)
Quinta do Vau (Sandeman)
Quinta do Vesuvio (Symington)

Vintage Port   Potentially the finest and most complex, and the subject of most of this
chapter, are the vintage ports. Vintage ports are declared by the port shippers the second
spring after the harvest. 1991 was declared a vintage year by most of the top port shippers.
For example, Graham's, Dow, Quinta do Noval, and Warre had declared it a vintage, but Fonseca and Taylor did not, preferring to declare 1992 instead. Vintage port, a blend of the very
best *cuvées* from various vineyards, is bottled unfiltered two years after the harvest. It can improve and last for 50 or more years. To be a vintage port there must be exceptional ripeness,
a great deal of tannin, and plenty of rich fruit and body. In fact, the quality of a shipper's vintage port is the benchmark by which a shipper is evaluated in the international marketplace.
Each top house has a distinctive style, which I have tried to capture in the tasting notes.

These ports tend to be blends made from various vineyards rather than products of a single
vineyard.

VINTAGE GUIDE

The greatest port vintages in this century have been 1912, 1927, 1931, 1935, 1945, 1948, 1955, 1963, 1970, 1977, 1983, 1985, 1992, 1994, 1997, and 2000.

VINTAGE YEARS FOR MAJOR FIRMS

Cockburn   1947, 1950, 1955, 1960, 1963, 1967, 1970, 1975, 1983, 1985, 1991, 1994, 1997, 2000
Croft   1945, 1950, 1955, 1960, 1963, 1966, 1970, 1975, 1977, 1982, 1985, 1991
Dow   1945, 1947, 1950, 1955, 1960, 1963, 1966, 1970, 1972, 1975, 1977, 1980, 1983, 1985, 1991, 1994, 1997, 2000
Fonseca   1945, 1948, 1955, 1960, 1963, 1966, 1970, 1975, 1977, 1980, 1983, 1985, 1992, 1994, 1997, 2000
Graham's   1945, 1948, 1955, 1960, 1963, 1966, 1970, 1975, 1977, 1980, 1983, 1985, 1991, 1994, 1997, 2000
Quinta do Noval   1945, 1947, 1950, 1955, 1958, 1960, 1963, 1966, 1967, 1970, 1975, 1978, 1982, 1985, 1991, 1994, 1995, 1997, 2000
Quinta do Noval Nacional   1931, 1950, 1960, 1962, 1963, 1964, 1966, 1967, 1970, 1975, 1978, 1980, 1982, 1985, 1987, 1994, 1997, 2000
Sandeman   1945, 1947, 1950, 1955, 1957, 1958, 1960, 1962, 1963, 1966, 1967, 1970, 1975, 1977, 1980, 1982, 1985
Taylor   1945, 1948, 1955, 1960, 1963, 1966, 1970, 1975, 1977, 1980, 1983, 1985, 1992, 1994, 1997, 2000
Warre   1945, 1947, 1950, 1955, 1958, 1960, 1963, 1966, 1970, 1975, 1977, 1980, 1983, 1985, 1991, 1994, 1997, 2000

RATING PORTUGAL'S BEST PRODUCERS OF PORT

* * * * * (OUTSTANDING)

Dow	Quinta do Noval Nacional
Fonseca	Taylor
Graham's	

* * * * (EXCELLENT)

Churchill	Graham's Malvedos
Churchill Quinta Agua Alta	Quinta do Infantado Touriga Nacional
Cockburn	Quinta do Noval
Croft	Symington Quinta do Vesuvio
Dow Quinta do Bomfim	Taylor Quinta de Vargellas
Ferreira Quinta do Seixo	Warre
Fonseca Guimaraens	

* * * (GOOD)

Calem Quinta da Foz	Quarles Harris
Croft Quinta do Roeda	Martinez
Delaforce	Niepoort
Delaforce Quinta do Forte	Offley Forrester
Ferreira	Pocalas Junior
Gould Campbell	Quinta do Crasto

Quinta do Passadouro
Quinta de la Rosa
Quinta do Roriz
Ramos-Pinto

Sandeman
Sandeman Quinta do Vau
Smith-Woodhouse
Warre Quinta da Cavadinha

* * (AVERAGE)

Almeida Barros
Borges & Irmao
J. W. Burmester
C. da Silva
Calem
H. & C. J. Feist
Feuerheerd
Hooper
C. N. Kopke

Messias
Osborne
Pintos dos Santos
Quinta do Panascal
Quinta do Romaneira
Vasconcellos
Wiese & Krohn
Van Zellers

COCKBURN

1994 Vintage Port   **D 91**

An attractive, smoky, tarry, roasted black fruit character dominates this opaque ruby/purple wine's aromatic profile. Low acidity, sweet, rich fruit, and a forward, expansive feel suggest this full-bodied wine will mature quickly, but it will last for at least two decades. Like a few other 1994s, it seems almost too easy to drink at this stage. Anticipated maturity: 2004–2020.

Past Glories: Quinta do Tua 1987 (94); Vintage Port 1991 (88), 1985 (90), 1983 (95), 1955 (92)

CROFT

1994 Vintage Port   **D 90**

The 1994 Croft exhibits an impressive dark ruby/purple color and a developed, forward, more evolved style than expected. It is moderately sweet, full-bodied, expansive, pure, and rich, but made in an up-front, flattering style. Although outstanding, it is not one of the superstars of the vintage. It will keep for 20 years. Anticipated maturity: now–2020.

Past Glories: 1991 (93), 1963 (90)

DOW

1997 Vintage Port   **EE 90**

An evolved, less massive than normal port, the 1997 Dow displays a dark ruby/purple color, attractive licorice, chocolate, and roasted coffee aromas, medium to full body, sweet tannin, and a moderately tannic finish. This excellent vintage port should drink well between 2004–2025.

Past Glories: Quinta do Bomfim 1992 (93), 1990 (95); Vintage Port 1994 (96), 1991 (90), 1983 (93), 1977 (95), 1970 (90), 1966 (91), 1963 (93), 1945 (93)

FERREIRA

1997 Vintage Port   **E 89**

This dark ruby/purple offering exhibits aromas of animal fur, licorice, blackberries, and earth. Rich and full-bodied, although more monolithic than many of its peers, this excellent 1997 vintage port falls short of being exceptional. Anticipated maturity: now–2020.

FONSECA

1997 Vintage Port	EE	93

Somewhat lightweight for Fonseca, but undeniably charming, this dark ruby/purple wine offers a floral, exotic, flamboyant bouquet, a sweet, fleshy style, but not a great deal of weight or massiveness. Heady alcohol, sweet tannin, and a velvety texture make for a gorgeous finish. While I would have preferred to have seen more weight, structure, and intensity, this is an outstanding Fonseca. Anticipated maturity: now–2020.

Past Glories: Guimaraens 1991 (93); Late Bottled Vintage Port 1988 (88); Twenty Year Old Tawny Port (86); Thirty Year Old Tawny Port (91); Vintage Port 1994 (97), 1992 (97), 1985 (96), 1983 (92), 1977 (94), 1970 (97), 1966 (92), 1963 (97), 1955 (96), 1948 (100), 1945 (92)

GRAHAM'S

1997 Vintage Port	EE	93

Blackberries, licorice, and melted asphalt stand out in this full-bodied, beautifully made vintage port's moderately intense bouquet. It is not one of the great Graham's ports and is less sweet than normal, but it is full-bodied, rich, concentrated, and impressive. Anticipated maturity: 2004–2025.

Past Glories: Malvedos Centenary 1990 (92), 1987 (92), 1986 (92), 1976 (90), 1958 (90); Malvedos Vintage Port 1993 (92); Vintage Port 1994 (96), 1991 (94), 1985 (97), 1983 (94), 1980 (90), 1977 (95), 1970 (95), 1966 (92), 1963 (96), 1955 (95), 1948 (99), 1945 (96)

QUINTA DO NOVAL

1997 Vintage Port	E	100
1997 Vintage Port Nacional	EEE	100

The 1997 vintage port is the greatest Quinta do Noval I have ever tasted (excluding their Nacional made from prephylloxera vines). The wine of the vintage, this black/purple port boasts fabulous aromatics (espresso, blackberries, licorice, tar, and flowers), followed by massive concentration and levels of depth and richness that surpass every other port of the vintage save for its limited-production sibling, the Nacional. Gorgeously sweet, stunningly concentrated and full-bodied, this profound vintage port should be legendary. Quinta do Noval's production normally approaches 4,000 cases, but in 1997, only 1,200 cases were produced, so availability will be extremely limited. Anticipated maturity: 2005–2035.

The 1997 Nacional is another legend from this prephylloxera vineyard. The color is a saturated black/purple. The nose reveals more floral scents intermixed with coffee, blackberries, tar, cassis, licorice, and chocolate. Extremely full-bodied, but less massive and more seamless than its sibling, this spectacular Nacional will reach its plateau of maturity quickly, where it will remain for 2–3 decades. Anticipated maturity: 2007–2040.

Past Glories: Nacional 1994 (99+), 1987 (92), 1985 (96), 1970 (96), 1966 (92), 1963 (99+), 1962 (98), 1931 (100); Vintage Port 1994 (95), 1991 (89)

QUINTA DO VALE D. MARIA

1997 Vintage Port	E	90

This elegantly styled, dark ruby/purple 1997 vintage port was produced by Niepoort. Rich and full-bodied, with an evolved style, it does not have the weight of the vintage's blockbusters, but it is well made, pure, rich, and concentrated with copious quantities of blackberry, cassis, and licorice-flavored fruit. The long finish displays sweet tannin.

QUINTA DO VESUVIO

1997 Vintage Port	E	90

A delicious, forward, dark saturated ruby/purple port, this 1997 reveals copious quantities of jammy, grapy, black fruit flavors intermixed with earth and spice, full body, and silky tannin. Like other 1997s, it should drink well soon, but last 20 years.

ROMARIZ
1997 Vintage Port   **D 92**

An exceptional vintage port, this saturated purple/black-colored effort offers up sweet, jammy notes of blackberries, licorice, and spice. Full-bodied, rich, and moderately sweet, with huge amounts of glycerin, ripeness, and well-integrated tannin, this blockbuster port can be drunk young, but should evolve nicely for 15–20 years. A sleeper as well as an excellent value.

SILVAL
1997 Vintage Port   **D   93**

A small quinta owned by Quinta do Noval, the 1997 Silval is a splendid effort as well as a sleeper of the vintage. This full-bodied, saturated purple-colored wine displays abundant quantities of chocolate, licorice, and coffee bean notes intertwined with blackberry and cassis fruit. Massive in the mouth, with sweet tannin and stunning concentration, this knockout 1997 should drink well in 3–4 years, and last 20 years or more. Very impressive!

TAYLOR FLADGATE
1997 Vintage Port   **EE   96**

Saturated black/purple, with stunning aromatics of blueberries, blackberries, licorice, and iron, this spectacular vintage port is one of the stars of the vintage. Extremely full-bodied, with silky tannin, spectacular concentration and purity, multiple flavor levels, and a more evolved, forward personality than other top vintages, this is an exquisite yet precocious 1997 vintage port. Anticipated maturity: 2004–2030.

Past Glories: Late Bottled Vintage Port 1988 (89); Quinta de Vargellas 1991 (95), 1987 (90); Vintage Ports 1994 (97), 1992 (100), 1985 (90), 1983 (94), 1980 (90), 1977 (96), 1970 (96), 1966 (91), 1963 (96), 1955 (96), 1948 (100), 1945 (96); Ten Year Tawny Port (93); Twenty Year Tawny Port (92); Thirty Year Tawny Port (87)

DON'T FORGET THE MADEIRAS

Sadly, most consumers think of this as a cooking wine. Madeira's glory days were the 19th century. Today, the bulk of Madeira is decidedly unnoble fortified wine sold cheaply throughout the world. However, the "real" Madeira is exceedingly rare and very limited in production. Moreover, 80- to 200-year-old Madeiras from reliable producers are indeed remarkable wines, balancing sweetness against high acidity in a distinctive sweet-sour flavor profile, with explosive aromatics. The finest retail source in the U.S. for authentic Madeira is the Rare Wine Company in Sonoma, CA; telephone (707) 996-4484; fax (707) 996-4491.

STYLES OF VINTAGE MADEIRA

Current laws require that all vintage Madeira be aged at least 20 years in cask prior to being bottled.

Bastardo   Some ancient Muscatels from the firm of d'Oliviras are remarkable, as several bottles of 1900 tasted have shown. Essentially, Bastardos are fortified Muscats made in very limited quantities. For unknown reasons, they have fallen out of favor, but these rare offerings are generally less expensive than similarly aged Madeiras.

Bual   Undeniably richer, fuller, and sweeter than Verdelhos or Sercials, Bual Madeira possesses a deep amber color and, like its siblings, reveals plenty of roasted, smoky, nutty characteristics.

Malmsey   This is the sweetest, most unctuously textured Madeira, with caramel, roasted nut, and espresso notes, thick, succulent flavors, and good acidity. The legal limit of residual sugar is 96–135 grams per liter.

Sercial   Sercial is the Portuguese name for the grape. Madeiras that bear this name tend to be among the lightest, driest, and palest in color. Most Sercials emerge from Madeira's cooler climates. They have high acidity levels, and no more than 18–65 grams of residual sugar per liter. Their alcohol content is around 17%.

Tarrantez   Rarely seen in recent years, the expensive Tarrantezs are 80- to 200-year-old, powerful Madeiras with immortal aging potential. It is more of an historical varietal for Madeira than one of current use, although one would suspect, given the auction value of ancient Tarrantez bottlings, more of it would be planted.

Verdelho   An amber-colored Madeira, Verdelho is made in a moderately sweet style with good balancing acidity. The finish is full and sweet as the legal limit for residual sugar is 49–78 grams per liter.

TABLE WINES

One other decadent, sumptuous Portuguese wine is the Muscatel de Setubal made by the J. M. da Fonseca firm. Quality today is not what it used to be, but some of the ancient bottlings I have tasted, particularly the 1900, have been spectacular.

As for Portugal's dry wines, they have more potential than actual quality. Nearly all are produced from indigenous varietals. While some reveal considerable potential, the whites generally tend to be either oxidized or innocuous, and the reds range from light, fruity wines of little character, to powerful, concentrated efforts possessing various degrees of rustic tannin. The chart below provides a simplistic overview of the finest producers. To date, the two best are Luis Pato, who is accomplishing fine things in Bairrada (a well-known Portuguese viticultural region between Lisbon and Porto), and the dynamic oenologist, João Portugal Ramos, from Alentejo. Ramos is the locomotive for this viticultural region located south of Lisbon.

VINTAGE GUIDE

While vintages have considerable significance with respect to the port trade, for white and red Portuguese table wines, it is more a question of who is making them than the actual vintages.

RATING PORTUGAL'S BEST PRODUCERS OF TABLE WINES

*** *(GOOD)*

Quinta do Carmo (Alentejo)

Quinto do Castro (Douro)

Chryseia (Douro)

Quinta do Cotto (Douro)

Ferreira (Douro)

Quinto do Fojo (Douro)

J. M. da Fonseca (Dao Terras Altas)

J. M. da Fonseca (Garrafeira TE)

J. M. da Fonseca (Morgado do Reguengo-Portalegre)

J. M. da Fonseca (Quinta da Camarate)

J. M. da Fonseca (Rosado Fernandes)

Quinta de Foz de Arouce (Beiras)

Quinto da Gaivosa (Douro)

Quinta da Ponte Pedrinha (Dao)

Luis Pato (Bairrada)

João Portugal Ramos Marques de Borba (Alentejo)

João Portugal Ramos Trincadeira (Alentejo)

Quinta de la Rosa (Douro)

Vimompor Quinta du Pedro (Vinho Verde)

THE WINES OF
NORTH
AMERICA

California
Oregon
Washington State
The Mid-Atlantic States

5. CALIFORNIA

The Basics

TYPES OF WINE

Virtually every type of wine seen elsewhere in the wine world is made in California. Fortified port-style wines, decadently sweet, late-harvest Rieslings, sparkling wines, and major red and white dry table wines from such super grapes as Chardonnay and Cabernet Sauvignon—all are to be found in California.

GRAPE VARIETIES

The fine wines of California are dominated by Cabernet Sauvignon and Chardonnay, as much of the attention of that state's wine-makers is directed at these two grapes. However, California makes wonderful red Zinfandel and increasing amounts of world-class Merlot and Syrah, plus some Petite Sirah. Despite improved quality, Pinot Noir is still a questionable wine in the hands of all but several dozen or so California wine producers. Two notable trends started in the late 1980s have proven popular with consumers. These include the proliferation of proprietary red wine blends (usually Cabernet Sauvignon–dominated and superexpensive) and the development of authoritatively flavored, robust, supple red wines made from blends of Syrah, Carignan, Grenache, Mourvèdre, and Alicante, collectively referred to as the "Rhône Rangers." As for the white wines, Sauvignon Blanc and Sémillon, and blends thereof, can be complex and fragrant, but the majority remains nondescript. It is a shame that Chenin Blanc has so little sex appeal among consumers, because it can be a very inexpensive, delicious drink. Colombard and Muscat suffer from the same image problems as Chenin Blanc, but shrewd consumers know the good ones and seek them out. Gewürztraminer and dry Rieslings have been dismal wines, although a handful of wineries have broken through the wall of mediocrity. For years California has made it simple for the consumer, naming its wines after the varietal from which it is made. By law a Chardonnay or Cabernet Sauvignon must contain 75% of that grape in the wine. The recent trend, accompanied by very high prices, has been to produce luxury-priced proprietary wines with awe-inspiring, often silly names such as Dominus, Opus, Rubicon, Trilogy, and Insignia. These wines are supposed to be the winery's very best lots of wine blended together for harmony. Some of them are marvelous. But remember: All of them are expensive and most of them are overpriced.

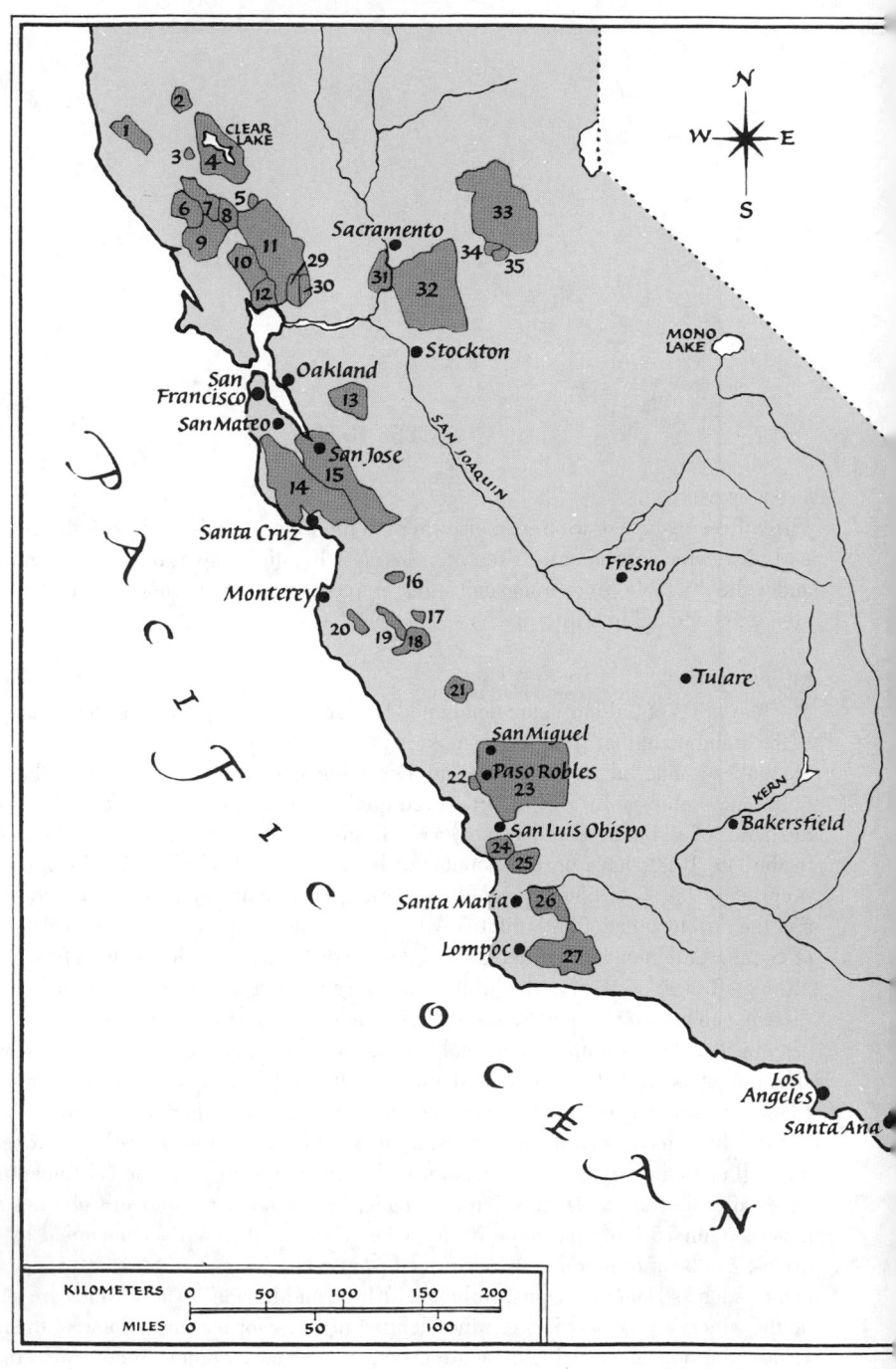

California

NEVADA

Death Valley
Junction

MOJAVE

Barstow

DESERT

San
Bernardino

Palm Springs

28

SALTON
SEA

San
Diego

Flavors

RED WINE VARIETALS

Cabernet Franc   Now being used by more and more wineries to give complexity to a wine's bouquet, Cabernet Franc is a cedary, herbaceous-scented wine that is usually lighter in color and body than either Cabernet Sauvignon or Merlot. It rarely can stand by itself, but used judiciously in a blend, it can provide an extra dimension. Reference-point California wines with significant proportions of Cabernet Franc that have stood the test of time include the 1971 Robert Mondavi Reserve Cabernet, 1977 Joseph Phelps Insignia red wine, La Jota's 1986, 1990, 1991, 1992, 1993, 1994, and 1995 Cabernet Franc, Dalla Valle's 1990, 1992, 1993, 1994, 1995, 1996, and 1997 Maya (an exquisite wine with nearly 50% Cabernet Franc in the blend), the Havens Bourriquot (two-thirds Cabernet Franc), 1997, and Pride Mountain 1996, 1997, and 1998.

Cabernet Sauvignon   The king of California's red wine grapes, Cabernet Sauvignon produces densely colored wine with aromas that can include black currants, chocolate, cedar, leather, ground meat, minerals, herbs, tobacco, and tar. Cabernet Sauvignon reaches its pinnacle of success in Napa, Sonoma, and the Santa Cruz Mountains, although a few excellent examples have emanated, infrequently, from Paso Robles, Santa Ynez, and Monterey. The more vegetal side of Cabernet Sauvignon, with intense smells of asparagus and green beans, is found in wines from Monterey or Santa Barbara, two areas that have generally proven too cool for this varietal.

Merlot   If Cabernet Sauvignon provides the power, tannin, and structure, Merlot provides opulence, fatness, higher alcohol, and a lush, chewy texture when crop yields are not too high. It has grown in importance in California. One strong trend is an increased number of wines that are made predominantly from the Merlot grape. Telltale aromas of a top Merlot include scents of plums, black cherries, toffee, tea, herbs, tomatoes sometimes, and a touch of orange. Merlot wines will never have the color density of a Cabernet Sauvignon because the Merlot grape's skin is thinner, but they are lower in acidity and less tannic. The higher alcohol and ripeness result in a fleshy, chewy wine that offers early drinking. Wines made primarily from Merlot are here to stay. The top examples can challenge the best of France, but the vast majority (about 90%) remains hollow and frightfully acidified, as well as too tannic and vegetal.

Petite Sirah   Unfortunately, this varietal has fallen from grace. Petite Sirah, in actuality the Duriff grape, is unrelated to the true Syrah, yet it produces almost purple-colored, very tannic, intense wines with peppery, cassis-scented bouquets. The wines age surprisingly well, as 15- to 20-year-old examples have shown a consistent ability to hold their fruit. The complexity and bouquet will rarely be that of a Cabernet or Merlot, but these are important wines. The Petite Sirah grape has adapted well to the warmer microclimates of California.

Pinot Noir   The thin-skinned, fickle Pinot Noir is a troublesome grape for everybody. While California continues to produce too many mediocre, washed-out, pruny, vegetal wines from this varietal, no region in the New World has demonstrated more progress with Pinot Noir than California. Major breakthroughs have been made. While good Pinot Noirs are increasingly noticeable from the North Coast areas of Mendocino, Napa, and Sonoma, fine Pinot Noirs also emanate from farther south—the Santa Cruz Mountains, the Monterey area, Arroyo Grande, and Santa Barbara. Yet the areas that have shown the greatest potential are the Sonoma Coast and Santa Barbara's Santa Rita Hills, with their cool maritime climate. A good Pinot Noir will exhibit medium to dark ruby color and an intense explosion of aromatics, including red and black fruits, herbs, earth, and floral aromas. Pinot Noir tends to drop what tannin it possesses quickly, so some acidity is important to give it focus and depth. Most

Pinot Noirs are drinkable when released. Few will evolve and improve beyond 7–8 years in the bottle. Consumers should be particularly apprehensive of any Pinot Noir that tastes too tannic or acidic when young.

Sangiovese   The Italian ancestry of many northern California grape growers and producers is increasingly evident with the number of wineries making Sangiovese. There are significant new plantations of this varietal, which is the most important red wine grape in the pastoral countryside of Tuscany, Italy. It is the predominant grape of most Chiantis and Vino da Tavolas. In California's fertile soils it achieves mind-boggling crop levels—8–12 tons of fruit per acre. Without effective pruning practices or severe crop thinnings, the wines produced are diluted, thin, acidic, and of little interest. However, when the vines are crop-thinned by 50% or more, the result can be fruity, strawberry/cherry/leather-scented and -flavored wines with medium body and penetrating acidity that is ideal for cutting through tomato-based sauces and working with the fusion Mediterranean/Pacific Rim cuisines found in California and elsewhere. To date, impressive Sangiovese has emerged from such wineries as Staglin Family Vineyards, Swanson, Shafer, and Ferrari-Carano. The largest plantations are found in the Atlas Peak Vineyard, whose wines have been disappointing to date. Many producers are beginning to add some Cabernet Sauvignon to the blend in order to give the wine more color, body, and depth, as the higher crop yields tend to produce a lighter wine than desired. Overall, Sangiovese is largely a failure.

Syrah   Syrah is the great red grape varietal of France's northern Rhône Valley. An increasing number of California wineries have begun to bottle 100% Syrah wines, and some have been exquisite. The style ranges from light, fruity, almost Beaujolais-like wines to black/purple-colored, thick, rich, ageworthy, highly extracted wines bursting with potential. A great Syrah will possess a hickory, smoky, tar, and cassis/blackberry-scented nose, rich, full-bodied, occasionally massive flavors, and considerable tannin. Like Cabernet Sauvignon, a Syrah-based wine is a thoroughbred when it comes to aging, easily lasting for 10–20 or more years. Neyers, Alban, Edmunds St. John, Dehlinger, Sine Qua Non, Havens, Martinelli, Ojai, Andrew Murray, and Thackrey have made many of the most compelling examples, but there are a bevy of very good Syrahs at reasonable prices.

Zinfandel   Seemingly against all odds, Zinfandel, the red, full-bodied type, has made a fashion comeback. Its accessibility, combined with its gorgeous, peppery, berry (cherries, blackberries, and raspberries) nose, spicy fruit, and lush, supple texture have helped to boost its image. Additionally, Zinfandel's burgeoning popularity might be explained by a growing, and may I say healthy, trend away from excessively priced glamour wines, particularly the chocolate and vanilla flavors of California's Chardonnay and Cabernet Sauvignon. Zinfandel is grown throughout California, but the best clearly comes from relatively old vines grown on hillside vineyards. Selected vineyards (especially head-pruned old vines) from Napa, the Dry Creek Valley, Sonoma, Sierra Foothills, Paso Robles, and Amador have consistently produced the most interesting Zinfandels. While soil certainly plays an important role (gravelly loam is probably the best), low yields, old vines, and harvesting fully mature, physiologically rather than analytically ripe fruit are even more important. Today, most Zinfandels are made in a medium- to full-bodied, spicy, richly fruity style, somewhat in the image of Cabernet Sauvignon. While there is some backbone and structure, it is usually a wine that consumers can take immediate advantage of for its luscious, rich fruit, and can drink during the first decade of its life. While many Zinfandels can last longer, my experience suggests that the wines rarely improve after 4–6 years and are best drunk within that time. One lamentable trend to monitor is the increasingly high prices demanded for Zinfandels. Most good Zinfandels fetch $25–35 a bottle, with some surpassing $50. This is a dangerous direction.

Carignan   A somewhat lowly regarded grape that deserves more attention, some of California's oldest vineyards are planted with Carignan. As wineries such as Trentadue and Cline have proven, where there are old vines, low yields, and full ripeness, the wines can have surprising intensity and richness in a Rhône-like style. There is a dusty earthiness to most Carignan-based wines that goes along with its big, rich, black fruit and spicy flavors.

Alicante Bouchet   Another grape that has fallen out of favor because of its low prestige, it remains revered by those who know it well. It yields a black/purple-colored wine with considerable body and richness. It needs time in the bottle to shed its hardness, but when treated respectfully, as the two Sonoma wineries Trentadue and Topolos do, this can be an overachieving grape that handsomely repays cellaring. When mature, the wine offers an array of spicy, earthy flavors and significant body and alcohol. Coturri has made some monster wines from this grape.

Mourvèdre/Mataro   This variety is making a comeback. Wineries such as Tablas Creek, Edmunds St. John, Cline Cellars, and Sean Thackrey have turned out fascinating wines from this varietal. Mataro produces a moderately dark-colored wine with a mushroomy, earthy, raspberry-scented nose, surprising acidity and tannin, and considerable aging potential.

WHITE WINE VARIETALS

Chardonnay   The great superstar of the white wines, Chardonnay at its best can produce majestically rich, buttery, honeyed wines with seemingly layers of flavors suggesting tropical fruits (pineapples and tangerines), apples, peaches, and even buttered popcorn when the wine has been barrel-fermented. It flourishes in all of California's viticultural districts, with no area having superiority over another. Great examples can be found from Mendocino, Sonoma, Napa, Carneros, Monterey, Santa Cruz, and Santa Barbara. The problem is that of the 600+ California wineries producing Chardonnay, less than 100 make an interesting wine. Crop yields are too high, the wines are manufactured rather than made, they are too frequently over-oaked, and they are excessively acidified, making them technically flawless, but lacking bouquet, flavor intensity, and character, save for their grotesque oakiness. The results are tart, vapid wines of no interest. Moreover, generally the wines have to be drunk within 12 months of the vintage. Another popular trend has been to intentionally leave sizable amounts of residual sugar in the wine while trying to hide part of it with additions of acidity. This cosmetically gives the wine a superficial feel of more richness and roundness, but these wines also crack up within a year of the vintage. Most Chardonnays are mediocre and overpriced, with very dubious aging potentials. Yet they remain the most popular "dry" white wine produced in California.

Chenin Blanc   This maligned, generally misunderstood grape can produce lovely apéritif wines that are both dry and slightly sweet. Most wineries lean toward a fruity, delicate, perfumed, light- to medium-bodied style that pleases increasing numbers of consumers who are looking for delicious wines at reasonable prices. This varietal deserves more attention from consumers.

French Colombard   Like Chenin Blanc, Colombard is a varietal that is rarely accorded much respect. Its charm is its aromatic character and crisp, light-bodied style.

Gewürztraminer   Anyone who has tasted a fine French Gewurztraminer must be appalled by what is sold under this name in California. A handful of wineries, such as Navarro, Martinelli, and Babcock, have produced some attractive although subdued Gewürztraminers. The bald truth remains that most California Gewürztraminers are made in a slightly sweet, watery, shallow, washed-out style.

Muscat   There are several Muscat grapes used in California. This is an underrated and underappreciated varietal that produces remarkably fragrant and perfumed wines that are loaded with tropical fruit flavors. They are ideal as an apéritif wine or with desserts.

Pinot Blanc   This grape, a staple of Alsace, France, where it is used to produce richly fruity but generally straightforward, satisfying wines, has had mixed success in California.

Some producers have barrel-fermented it, attempting to produce a large-scale, Chardonnay-style wine, with little success. Chalone and Arrowood are two of the few wineries to have succeeded with this style. In my opinion, Pinot Blanc is best vinified in a manner that emphasizes its intense fruity characteristics, which range from honeyed tangerines and oranges to a more floral, applelike fruitiness. Pinot Blancs typically do not age well, but they provide immediate appeal and satisfaction in an exuberant yet uncomplicated manner. Other fine Pinot Blancs have emerged from Murphy-Goode. Most Pinot Blancs should be drunk within 2–3 years of the vintage, the only exception being those made in a full-bodied, structured style such as Chalone.

Sauvignon Blanc   California winemaking has failed miserably to take advantage of this grape. Overcropping, excessive acidification, and a philosophy of manufacturing the wines have resulted in hundreds of neutral, bland, empty wines with no bouquet or flavor. This is unfortunate, because Sauvignon is one of the most food-friendly and flexible wines produced in the world. It can also adapt itself to many different styles of fermentation and upbringing. At its best, the nonoaked examples of this wine possess vivid, perfumed noses of figs, melons, herbs, and minerals, crisp fruit, wonderful zesty flavors, and a dry finish. More ambitious, barrel-fermented styles that often have some Sémillon added can have a honeyed, melony character, and rich, medium- to full-bodied, grassy, melon and figlike flavors that offer considerable authority. Unfortunately, too few examples of either type are found in California. No viticultural region can claim a monopoly on either the successes or the failures.

Sémillon   One of the up-and-coming California varietals, on its own Sémillon produces wines with considerable body and creamy richness. It can often be left on the vine and has a tendency to develop botrytis, which lends itself to making sweet, honeyed, dessert wines. But Sémillon's best use is when it is added to Sauvignon, where the two make the perfect marriage, producing wines with considerable richness and complexity.

White Riesling or Johannisberg Riesling   Occasionally some great late-harvest Rieslings have been made in California, but attempts at making a dry Kabinett- or Trocken-style Riesling as produced in Germany most frequently result in dull, lifeless, empty wines with no personality or flavor. Most Riesling is planted in soils that are too rich and in climates that are too hot. This is a shame. Riesling is another varietal that could prove immensely popular to the masses.

AGING POTENTIAL

Cabernet Franc: 5–15 years

Cabernet Sauvignon: 5–25 years

Chardonnay: 1–6 years

Chenin Blanc: 1–2 years

Colombard: 1–2 years

Gamay: 2–4 years

Merlot: 5–12 years

Muscat: 1–3 years

Petite Sirah: 5–15 years

Pinot Blanc: 1–3 years

Pinot Noir: 4–8 years

Riesling (dry): 1–2 years

Riesling (sweet): 2–8 years

Sauvignon Blanc: 1–3 years

Sémillon: 1–4 years

Sparkling Wines: 2–7 years

Syrah: 5–20 years

Zinfandel: 3–10 years

OVERALL QUALITY LEVEL

The top five or six dozen producers of Cabernet Sauvignon, Merlot, or proprietary red wines, as well as the three dozen or so who produce Chardonnay, make wines that are as fine and as multidimensional as anywhere in the world. However, for well over 20 years, my tastings have consistently revealed too many California wines that are not made but manufactured. Excessively acidified by cautious oenologists and sterile-filtered to the point where there is no perceptible aroma, many wines possess little flavor except for the textural abrasiveness caused by shrill levels of acidity and high alcohol, and in the case of the red wines, excessive levels of green, astringent tannins. Producers have tried to hide their excessive crop yields by leaving residual sugar in the finished wine hoping to give the impression of more body. This practice is only a quick fix, as the white wines tend to fall apart 6–9 months after bottling and the red wines taste cloying.

The time-honored philosophy of California winemaking, which includes the obsession with the vineyard as a manufacturing plant, the industrial winemaking in the cellars, and the preoccupation with monolithic, simplistic, squeaky-clean wines that suffer from such strictly controlled technical parameters, is weakening. It is no secret that the principal objective of most California wineries has been to produce sediment-free, spit-polished, stable wines. The means used to attain this goal too frequently eviscerate the wines of their flavor, aromas, personality, and pleasure-giving qualities. But significant changes (especially noticeable in vintages of the nineties) are underfoot.

Only a fool could ignore the fact that California is now producing many of the greatest wines in the world. While most retailers legitimately carp about the microscopic allocations they receive of the limited-production gems from the most fashionable wineries, it is obvious that California wine quality is surging to greater and greater heights.

Why am I so bullish on California wines? Consider the following:

1. California enjoyed a stunning decade of quality in the nineties. Starting with 1990, every vintage has provided that state's growers with enough high-quality fruit to turn out numerous sensational wines. Only 1998, in reality a good year, offers less excitement than the other vintages.

2. Even more important than the eight out of nine outstanding quality vintages is the shift in mind-set of many top wine producers. I have had little help from my colleagues in attempting to change the industrial/food-processor mentality espoused by the University of California at Davis. For as long as I can remember, this school of thought has resulted in sterile, frightfully acidic, nearly undrinkable harsh and hollow wines that, amazingly, garnered raves from segments of the West Coast wine press. Handcrafted wines that reflected the *terroir*, vintage, and varietal, in addition to providing immense pleasure, have had an enormous influence on others. Two decades ago, it was distressing to see the number of wineries that automatically, without any thought whatsoever, compromised and in many cases destroyed a wine by blind faith in the following techniques: (a) by harvesting grapes based on analytical rather than physiological ripeness; (b) by adding frightfully high levels of tartaric acid to the fermenting juice because it was the "risk-free" thing to do; (c) by processing the youthful grape juice utilizing centrifuges and filters that eviscerated and purified the wine before it had a chance to develop any personality; (d) by prefiltering wine intensely before it was allowed to go to barrel; and (e) by fining and sterile-filtering everything as a rule of thumb so that a wine had no aromatics and nothing but a monolithic personality. The adoption of a less-traumatic and less-interventionalistic wine philosophy, emphasizing the importance of the vineyard's fruit and preserving its characteristics, is increasingly widespread. The results are increasing quantities of compellingly rich, natural-tasting, unprocessed wines that should be causing French wine producers to shudder. And while many wineries continue to fight this trend toward higher-quality, more natural wines, often with considerable support from a gullible wine press, the fact is that you, the wine consumer, are the beneficiary!

3. As financially devastating as the phylloxera epidemic has been for California viticulture, the silver lining is that the replanting of vineyards over the last decade has addressed issues that key industry personnel refused to acknowledge as being important prior to this epidemic. Many new vineyards have been planted with tighter spacing, thus making the vines struggle. The result is deeper root systems and vines that produce lower quantities of higher-quality grapes. Additionally, the problem of varietals planted in the wrong soils and/or microclimates can be rectified by these new plantations. Superior rootstocks and less pro-

ductive clones that produce smaller crops with more individual character are other positive results of the phylloxera epidemic. As time passes, it will become evident that the mistakes made in the forties, fifties, and sixties have been largely corrected, ironically because of phylloxera. If the grapes from these new vineyards are markedly superior, as they should be, it takes no genius to realize that wine quality will also improve.

4. The influence of the French, combined with a new generation of well-traveled, open-minded, revisionist California wine-makers, must also be given credit for the remarkable progress in quality. California wines are as rich as they have ever been, but they no longer possess the heaviness of those great vintages of the sixties and seventies. Do readers realize why the finest French cuisine and French wines are cherished throughout the world as standards of reference? Because France, in both her cooking and her wines, achieves, at the highest level of quality, extraordinary intensity of flavor without weight or heaviness. Call this elegance, harmony, finesse, or whatever, but it is what I now detect in increasing numbers of California's finest wines.

BUYING STRATEGY

Except for the so-so 1998 vintage, California experienced a bevy of terrific vintages in the nineties. There was an unprecedented run of eight consecutive years (1990–1997) where most of the state's producers turned out wines that were made from ripe fruit. Only the top producers who keep crop yields to a minimum and refuse to excessively manipulate and process their wines will turn out the best, but it is clearly a good time to be buying California wines. Yet prices are extremely high, especially for the top-rated wines.

RECENT VINTAGES

2001—A fabulous vintage everywhere, but especially in Napa/Sonoma/Mendecino, where it will be one of the all-time greats.

2000—Overall, a challenging vintage in Napa/Sonoma/Mendecino, but very good in the Central Coast and Santa Barbara regions.

1999—Following 1998, this was another cool year with mountain vineyards and cooler *terroirs* challenged to get their fruit fully ripe. It is an excellent year for thin-skinned varietals such as Chardonnay and Pinot Noir. Syrah has also performed well. As in 1998, mountain vineyards had difficulty obtaining fully ripened Cabernet Sauvignon.

1998—This is the first vintage of the nineties to present irregularities and inconsistencies throughout California's viticultural regions. A cool late spring and abnormally cool summer resulted in one of the latest harvests of the decade. Many Cabernet Sauvignon vineyards on the cooler hillsides were not harvested until late October. Some areas, particularly Santa Barbara and to the north, were touched by some rain. The crop size was moderate, and the quality ranged from exceptional to spotty. Overall, 1998 is the least consistent and compelling year of the nineties.

1997—For California's North Coast, this vintage competes with 1994 and 1991 as one of the decade's finest years for Cabernet Sauvignon, Merlot, and Cabernet Franc. The vintage possesses the characteristics that separate great years from merely excellent ones. The finest wines are seamless, with velvety textures, wonderful purity, sweet tannin, and expressive aromatic profiles. Much to the joy of wine-makers, the abundant crop produced ripe wines with surprisingly high extract and alcohol. Pinot Noir looks exceptional throughout the North Coast, and the Chardonnays are very good to excellent. Consumers need to be careful as yields for many producers were entirely too high to produce quality wines. Hence, 1997, which is undeniably great at the top end, has many deceptions and a frustrating irregularity. In the Santa Cruz Mountains, Central Coast, and Santa Barbara, the vintage becomes trickier, but certainly the potential for high quality exists. My visit to these areas left me with the impression that 1997 is a very good vintage as opposed to a potentially great one. One last caveat—Zinfandel is far less successful because of enormous yields.

1996—If this were a vintage from the eighties, it would stand out as one of the greatest years of that decade. However, sandwiched between 1997, 1994, and 1995, 1996, while having no shortcomings, simply does not match up. A hot drought year with a short growing season, the North Coast wines are powerful, concentrated, and weighty, but some lack the sweet tannin and near perfect equilibrium achieved in 1994, 1995, and 1997. Readers will notice more rustic tannin in many Cabernet Sauvignons and certain Pinot Noirs. Brilliant wines were made, but the tannin level is undeniably more aggressive. There are some stellar North Coast Chardonnays, but the year's heat appears to have muted some of that varietal's aromatics. California is a diverse region, and even within such general appellations as Napa and Sonoma, there are infinite microclimates, soil types, and winemaking philosophies. I do not want to give the impression that there is something wrong with the vintage, because it did produce many exceptional wines. If it were not for 1997, 1995, and 1994, this would be considered a topflight year. For now, it is unquestionably an excellent year. The white wines need to be drunk up by the end of 2002. 1996 does appear to be a great year in the Santa Cruz Mountains, where wines of exceptional ripeness, richness, and balance were achieved. In contrast to the North Coast, 1996 appears superior to 1997. Farther south, the vintage is very good, but the Central Coast and Santa Barbara are more difficult regions to handicap.

1995—Like 1994, 1995 enjoyed a long, cool growing season, and while the wines are not as forward, fragrant, and expressive as many 1994s, a bevy of fabulous wines have emerged from Napa and Sonoma's top wineries. 1995 gets my nod as the finest vintage in the nineties for Chardonnay, but most readers buying high-quality California Chardonnay should have consumed them by 2001. For Cabernet Sauvignon and Pinot Noir, 1995 is an outstanding vintage that comes close to rivaling the greatness of 1994. In fact, some producers may have turned out Cabernet Sauvignons, Merlots, and proprietary reds that surpass what they achieved in 1994. In short, 1995 is another phenomenal vintage in a top-notch decade.

1994—In the last six months I have conducted two blind tastings of the 1994 North Coast Cabernet Sauvignons, Merlots, and proprietary reds. In both settings, the tasters were struck by uniformity and prodigious quality. The wines are approachable, exceptionally aromatic, wonderfully sweet, and rich, but neither heavy nor cumbersome. The top producers have made long-lived classics of remarkable symmetry and opulence. It was also a superb year in the Santa Cruz Mountains.

1993—If the 1993s are not as dramatic as the finest 1994s, 1992s, 1991s, and 1990s, they are by no means inferior. This is another rich, velvety-textured vintage for red wines, and a beautifully balanced year for whites. This vintage has been criticized for reasons I am unable to understand, but there are many great red wines.

1992—An abundant crop was harvested that ranged from very good to superb in quality. When Mother Nature is as generous as she was in most viticultural regions in 1992, the potential high quality can be diluted by excessive crop yields and by harvesting grapes that are not physiologically mature. However, the top producers have turned out fat, rich, opulent, low-acid, dramatic wines. The white wines need to be drunk up. The finest reds are flattering and richly fruity, and will keep for 10–20 years.

1991—A cool, surprisingly long growing season resulted in potentially excessive crop yields. However, those producers who had the patience to wait out the cool weather and harvest fully mature fruit, as well as to keep their yields down, made some superb red wines that will compete with the finest 1997s, 1995s, 1994s, 1993s, 1992s, 1990s, 1987s, 1986s, 1985s, and 1984s. For all the red wine varietals it is a splendid year, with many producers expressing a preference for their 1991s because of the incredibly long hang-time on the vine.

The 1991 vintage produced an enormous crop of good white wines that should have been consumed by the end of 1995.

1990—For Cabernet Sauvignon, Zinfandel, and other major red wine varietals, 1990 was a mild growing season. The crop was moderate in size, particularly when compared with 1991 and 1992. The wines are concentrated, rich, and well made. It was a banner year for California's top red wines. For Chardonnay, it was a super year, but most of these wines should have been consumed by mid-1994.

WHERE TO FIND CALIFORNIA'S BEST WINE VALUES

(Wineries That Can Be Counted On for Value)

Alderbrook (Sauvignon Blanc, Chardonnay)

Arrowood Domaine du Grand Archer (Chardonnay, Cabernet Sauvignon)

Belvedere (Chardonnay *cuvées*)

Beringer (Knights Valley Chardonnay, Sauvignon Blanc, Cabernet Sauvignon)

Bonny Doon (Clos de Gilroy, Ca' Del Solo *cuvées*, Pacific Rim Riesling)

Buehler (Zinfandel)

Carmenet (Colombard)

Cartridge and Browne (Chardonnay, Zinfandel, Cabernet Sauvignon)

Cline (Côtes d'Oakley)

Duxoup (Gamay, Charbono)

Edmunds St.-John (New World and Port o'Call reds, Pinot Grigio and El Niño whites)

Estancia (Chardonnay *cuvées*, Meritage red)

Fetzer (Sundial Chardonnay)

Franciscan (Merlot, Chardonnay)

Guenoc (Petite Sirah)

Hess Collection (Hess Select Chardonnay, Cabernet Sauvignon)

Husch Vineyard (Chenin Blanc, Gewürztraminer, La Ribera Red)

Kendall-Jackson (Vintner's Reserve Chardonnay, Fumé Blanc, Vintner's Reserve Zinfandel)

Kenwood (Sauvignon Blanc)

Konocti (Fumé Blanc)

Marietta Cellars (Old Vine Red, Zinfandel, Cabernet Sauvignon)

Mirassou (white burgundy—Pinot Blanc)

Monterey Vineyard (Classic *cuvées* of Merlot, Cabernet Sauvignon, Chardonnay, Sauvignon Blanc, and Zinfandel, generic Classic White and Classic Red)

Morro Bay Vineyards (Chardonnay)

Mountain View Winery (Sauvignon Blanc, Chardonnay, Pinot Noir, Zinfandel)

Murphy-Goode (Fumé Blanc)

Napa Ridge (Chardonnay, Cabernet Sauvignon, Sauvignon Blanc)

Parducci (Sauvignon Blanc)

J. Pedroncelli (Sauvignon Blanc, Zinfandel, Cabernet Sauvignon)

Joseph Phelps (Vins du Mistral *cuvées*)

R. H. Phillips (Night Harvest *cuvées* of Chardonnay and Sauvignon Blanc)

Preston (Cuvée du Fumé)

Ravenswood (Zinfandel and Merlot Vintner's blends)

Château Souverain (Chardonnay, Merlot, Cabernet Sauvignon, Sauvignon Blanc)

Stratford (the Chardonnay and Canterbury line of wines, particularly Chardonnay and Sauvignon Blanc)

Ivan Tamas (Trebbiano, Fumé Blanc, Chardonnay)

Trentadue (Old Patch Red, Zinfandel, Carignan, Sangiovese, Petite Sirah, Merlot, Salute Proprietary Red Wine)

RATING CALIFORNIA'S BEST PRODUCERS OF CABERNET SAUVIGNON, MERLOT, AND BLENDS THEREOF

* * * * * *(OUTSTANDING)*

Abreu Vineyards Madrona Ranch (Napa)

Araujo Estate Eisele Vineyard (Napa)

Arrowood Reserve Speciale (Sonoma)

Arrowood Reserve Speciale Merlot (Sonoma)

David Arthur Elevation 1147 (Napa)

Behrens and Hitchcock Kenefick Ranch (Napa)

Behrens and Hitchcock Merlot Las Amigas Vineyard (Carneros)

Behrens and Hitchcock TLK Ranch (Napa)

Beringer Chabot Vineyard (Napa)

Beringer Merlot Bancroft Vineyard (Napa)

Beringer Private Reserve (Napa)

Blackjack Ranch Harmonie (Santa Barbara)

Blackjack Ranch Merlot (Santa Barbara)

Blankiet (Napa)

Bryant Family Vineyard (Napa)

Cardinale Proprietary Red Wine (California)

Caymus Special Selection (Napa)

Clark-Claudon (Napa)

Colgin Lamb Vineyard (Napa)

Dalla Valle (Napa)

Dalla Valle Maya Proprietary Red Wine (Napa)

Dominus (Napa)

Dunn (Napa)

Dunn Howell Mountain (Napa)

Fisher Lamb Vineyard (Napa)

Fisher Wedding Vineyard (Sonoma)

Flora Springs Hillside Reserve (Napa)

Grace Family Vineyard (Napa)

Harlan Estate Proprietary Red Wine (Napa)

Hourglass (Napa)

Jones Family Vineyard (Napa)

La Jota Anniversary Cuvée (Napa)

Lokoya Diamond Mountain (Napa)

Lokoya Howell Mountain (Napa)

Lokoya Mount Veeder (Napa)

Lokoya Rutherford (Napa)

Peter Michael Les Pavots Proprietary Red Wine (California)

Robert Mondavi Reserve (Napa)

Robert Mondavi To-Kalon Estate Reserve (Napa)

Château Montelena Estate (Napa)

Pahlmeyer Merlot (Napa)

Pahlmeyer Proprietary Red Wine (Napa)

Joseph Phelps Insignia Proprietary Red Wine (Napa)

Pride Mountain Claret (Napa)

Pride Mountain Reserve (Napa)

Ridge Monte Bello (Santa Cruz Mountain)

Rudd Estate (Napa)

Saddleback Cellars Venge Family Reserve (Napa)

St. Jean Cinq Cépages Proprietary Red Wine (Sonoma)

Screaming Eagle (Napa)

Seavey (Napa)

Shafer Hillside Select (Napa)

Silver Oak (Napa)

Spottswoode (Napa)

Philip Togni (Napa)

Verité (Sonoma/Napa)

* * * * (EXCELLENT)

Anderson's Conn Valley Vineyard (Napa)

Arrowood (Sonoma)

Atalon Beckstoffer Vineyards (Napa)

Atalon Madrona Ranch (Napa)

Atalon Mountain Estates (Napa)

Bacio Divino Proprietary Red Wine (California)

Barnett Spring Mountain Rattlesnake Hill (Napa)

Behrens and Hitchcock Cuvée Lola Proprietary Red Wine (Napa)

Behrens and Hitchcock Merlot (Oakville)

Behrens and Hitchcock Merlot Alder Springs Vineyard (Mendocino)

Beringer St. Helena Vineyard (Napa)

Beringer State Lane Vineyard (Napa)

Beringer Tre Colline Vineyard (Napa)

Cakebread Cellars Benchland Select (Napa)

Cakebread Cellars Three Sisters (Napa)

Carmenet Moon Mountain Estate Reserve Proprietary Red Wine (Sonoma)

Clos Pegase Hommage Proprietary Red Wine (Napa)

Cornerstone Beatty Ranch (Napa)

Cornerstone Black Sears (Napa)

Cornerstone Collage Vineyard (Napa)

Cornerstone Cornerstone Vineyard (Napa)

Robert Craig Affinity Proprietary Red Wine (Napa)

Robert Craig Howell Mountain (Napa)

Robert Craig Mount Veeder (Napa)

Cuvaison ATS Selection (Carneros)

Diamond Creek Gravelly Meadow (Napa)

Diamond Creek Lake (Napa)
Diamond Creek Red Rock Terrace (Napa)
Diamond Creek Volcanic Hill (Napa)
Ferrari-Carano (Sonoma) (since 1991)
Ferrari-Carano Merlot (Sonoma) (since 1991)
Ferrari-Carano Reserve Red Proprietary Wine (Sonoma)
Fisher Coach Insignia (Sonoma) (since 1991)
Flora Springs Cypress Ranch (Pope Valley)
Flora Springs Merlot Windfall Vineyard (Pope Valley)
Robert Foley Claret (Napa)
Forman (Napa)
Forman Merlot (Napa)
Foxen (Santa Barbara)
Franus (Napa)
Frazier (Napa)
Hartwell Stags Leap (Napa)
Havens Bourriquot (Napa)
Havens Merlot Reserve (Napa)
Heitz Martha's Vineyard (Napa) (prior to 1986 a 5-star wine)
Paul Hobbs Black Vineyard Merlot (Napa)
Paul Hobbs Hyde Vineyard (Sonoma)
Judd's Hill (Napa)
Kendall-Jackson Merlot Buckeye Vineyard (Alexander Valley)
Kendall-Jackson Merlot Great Estates (Sonoma)
Kongsgaard Arietta (Napa)
Kunde Drummond Vineyard (Sonoma)
Kunde Estate Reserve (Sonoma)
La Jota (Napa)
La Jota Cabernet Franc (Napa)
Lail Vineyards J. Daniel Cuvée Proprietary Red Wine (Napa)
Lancaster Reserve Proprietary Red Wine (Alexander Valley)
Larkin Cabernet Franc (Napa)
Laurel Glen (Sonoma)
Laurel Glen Terra Rosa (Sonoma)
Lewelling (Napa)
Lewelling Wight Vineyard (Napa)
Marietta (Sonoma)
Matanzas Creek Merlot (Sonoma)
Philip Melka Metisse Proprietary Red Wine (Napa)
Merryvale Profile Proprietary Red Wine (Napa)

Merus (Napa)
Mount Eden Old Vine Reserve (Santa Cruz)
Newton Cabernet Sauvignon (Napa)
Newton Merlot (Napa)
Opus One (Napa)
Paloma Merlot (Spring Mountain)
Paoletti (Napa)
Joseph Phelps Backus Vineyard (Napa)
Plumpjack Reserve (Napa)
Pride Mountain Cabernet Franc (Napa)
Pride Mountain Vineyards (Napa)
Reverie Diamond Mountain (Napa)
Reverie Special Reserve Proprietary Red Wine (Napa)
Saddleback Cellars (Napa)
Saddleback Cellars Venge Family Reserve Merlot (Napa)
St. Francis Reserve (Sonoma)
St. Francis Merlot Reserve (Sonoma)
St. Jean Estate (Sonoma)
St. Jean Merlot Reserve (Sonoma)
Santa Cruz Mountain Merlot (Santa Ynez)
Seavey Merlot (Napa)
Selene Merlot (Napa)
Shafer Merlot (Napa)
Signorello Founder's Reserve (Napa)
Silver Oak (Alexander Valley)
Silverado Limited Reserve (Napa)
Simi Reserve (Sonoma)
Château Souverain Winemaker's Reserve (Sonoma)
Spring Mountain Estate (Napa)
Spring Mountain Mirabelle Alba Chevalier Proprietary Red Wine (Napa)
Spring Mountain La Perla Chevalier Proprietary Red Wine (Napa)
Staglin (Napa)
Stags Leap Cask 23 Proprietary Red Wine (Napa)
Stags Leap Fay Vineyard (Napa)
Stonefly Cabernet Franc (Napa)
Stonestreet Christopher's Vineyard (Sonoma)
Stonestreet Legacy Proprietary Red Wine (Alexander Valley)
Stonestreet Three Block Vineyard (Sonoma)
Viader Proprietary Red Wine (Napa)
Vine Cliff Cellars (Napa)
Vineyard 29 (Napa)

Von Strasser Diamond Mountain (Napa)
Von Strasser Diamond Mountain Reserve
  (Napa)
White Rock Claret Proprietary Red Wine
  (Napa)

Whitehall Lane Leonardi Vineyard
  (Napa)
Whitehall Lane Morisoli (Napa)
Whitehall Lane Reserve (Napa)

* * * (GOOD)

Ahlgren Bates Ranch (Santa Cruz)
Ahlgren Besson Vineyard (Santa Cruz)
Alexander Valley (Sonoma)
Amizetta Vineyards (Napa)
S. Anderson (Napa)
Arrowood Merlot (Sonoma)
Barnett Spring Mountain (Napa)
Beaulieu Cabernet Sauvignon Private
  Reserve (Napa)
Benziger (Glen Ellen)
Benziger Tribute (Glen Ellen)
Beringer Knights Valley (Napa)
Boeger (El Dorado)
Boeger Merlot (El Dorado)
Brutocao Albert Vineyard (Mendocino)
Brutocao Merlot (Mendocino)
Buehler (Napa)***/****
Burgess Cellars Vintage Selection (Napa)
Cain Cellars Cain Five Proprietary Red
  Wine (Napa)
Cain Cellars Merlot (Napa)
Carmenet Proprietary Red Wines (Sonoma)
Caymus (Napa)
Chalk Hill (Sonoma)
Chimney Rock (Napa)
Cinnabar (Santa Cruz)
Clos du Bois (Sonoma)
Clos du Bois Briarcrest (Sonoma)
Clos du Bois Marlstone (Sonoma)
Clos du Bois Merlot (Sonoma)
Clos Pegase (Napa)
Clos Pegase Merlot (Napa)
Clos du Val Merlot (Napa)
Clos du Val Reserve (Napa)
Cloverdale Ranch Estate (Alexander
  Valley)
B. R. Cohn Olive Hill Vineyard (Sonoma)
Corison (Napa)
Cosentino (Napa)
Cuvaison (Napa)
Cuvaison Merlot (Napa)
Dry Creek Meritage (Sonoma)
Duckhorn (Napa)
Duckhorn Merlot (Napa)

Duckhorn Merlot 3 Palms Vineyard (Napa)
Durney Reserve (Monterey)
Eberle (Paso Robles)
Elyse Morisoli Vineyard (Napa)
Estancia (Alexander Valley)
Estancia Meritage Proprietary Red Wine
  (Alexander Valley)
Estancia Merlot (Alexander Valley)
Far Niente (Napa)
Gary Farrell (Sonoma)
Gary Farrell Ladi's Vineyard (Sonoma)
Gary Farrell Merlot Ladi's Vineyard
  (Sonoma)
Franciscan Meritage Oakville Estate
  (Napa)
Franciscan Merlot (Napa)
Franciscan Oakville Estate (Napa)
Frog's Leap (Napa)
Frog's Leap Merlot (Napa)
Gainey Cabernet Franc (Santa Barbara)
Gainey Cabernet Franc Limited Selection
  (Santa Ynez)
Gainey Merlot Limited Selection (Santa
  Barbara)
E. & J. Gallo Estate (Sonoma)
Gallo Frei Ranch (Sonoma)
Geyser Peak Estate Reserve (Sonoma)
Geyser Peak Reserve Alexandre
  Proprietary Red Wine (Sonoma)
Grgich Hills Merlot (Napa)
Groth Merlot (Napa)
Groth Reserve (Napa)
Gundlach-Bundschu Cabernet Franc
  (Sonoma)
Harrison Winery (Napa)
Havens Wine Cellar Merlot (Napa)
Heitz (Napa)
Heitz Bella Oaks (Napa)
Hess Collection (Napa)
Hess Collection Reserve (Napa)
Husch (Mendocino)
Husch Estate La Ribera (Mendocino)
Iron Horse Cabernets Proprietary Red
  Wine (Sonoma)

Johnson-Turnbull (Napa)
Johnson-Turnbull Vineyard Selection 67
    (Napa)
Jordan (Sonoma)
Justin Cabernet Franc (Paso Robles)
Justin Cabernet Sauvignon (Paso Robles)
Justin Isosceles Proprietary Red Wine
    (Paso Robles)
Justin Merlot (Paso Robles)
Kalin Cellars Reserve (Marin)
Robert Keenan (Napa)
Robert Keenan Merlot (Napa)
Kendall-Jackson Grand Reserve
    (California) (since 1991)
Kathryn Kennedy (Santa Clara)
Kenwood (Sonoma)
Kenwood Artists Series (Sonoma)
Kenwood Jack London Vineyard (Sonoma)
Klein Vineyards (Santa Cruz)
Livingston Moffett Vineyard (Napa)
Long (Napa)
Longoria (Santa Ynez)
Longoria Cabernet Franc (Santa Ynez)
Longoria Merlot (Santa Ynez)
Maacama Creek Melim Vineyard (Sonoma)
Madrone (El Dorado)
Madrone Cabernet Franc (El Dorado)
Madrone Quintet Reserve Red Table Wine
    (El Dorado)
Michel-Schlumberger (Dry Creek)
Robert Mondavi Napa (Napa)
Robert Mondavi Oakville Unfiltered (Napa)
Château Montelena Calistoga Cuvée (Napa)
Monticello Cellars Corley Reserve (Napa)
Monticello Cellars Jefferson Cuvée (Napa)
Monticello Cellars Merlot (Napa)
Mount Eden (Santa Clara)
Murphy-Goode Merlot (Sonoma)
Murrieta's Well Vendimia Proprietary Red
    Wine (Livermore)
Napa Ridge (Napa)
Nelson Estate Cabernet Franc (Napa)
Newton Claret (Napa)
Oakville Ranch (Napa)
Page Mill Volker Eisele Vineyard (Napa)
J. Pedroncelli Reserve (Sonoma)
Robert Pepi Vine Hill Ranch (Napa)
Joseph Phelps (Napa)
Joseph Phelps Merlot (Napa)
Pine Ridge Andrus Reserve (Napa)
Pine Ridge Howell Mountain (Napa)

Pine Ridge Merlot (Napa)
Pine Ridge Rutherford Cuvée (Napa)
Pine Ridge Stags Leap District (Napa)
Plumpjack Estate (Napa)
A. Rafanelli (Sonoma)
Rancho Sisquoc Cabernet Franc (Santa
    Barbara)
Rancho Sisquoc Cellar Select Red Estate
    (Santa Maria)
Rancho Sisquoc Estate (Santa Barbara)
Rancho Sisquoc Merlot Estate (Santa
    Barbara)
Ravenswood (Sonoma)
Ravenswood Merlot Sangiacomo (Sonoma)
Ravenswood Merlot Vintner's Blend (North
    Coast)
Ravenswood Pickberry Proprietary Red
    Wine (Sonoma)
Raymond Private Reserve (Napa)
Renaissance (Yuba)
Ridge Santa Cruz (Santa Clara)
Ritchie Creek (Napa)
Rocking Horse (Napa)
Rockland (Napa)
Rubicon Proprietary Red Wine (Napa)
St. Clement (Napa) (since 1991)
St. Clement Oroppas (Napa)
St. Francis Merlot (Sonoma)
Santa Cruz Mountain Bates Ranch (Santa
    Cruz)
Sebastiani single-vineyard *cuvées* (Sonoma)
Signorello Unfined/Unfiltered (Napa)
Silverado (Napa)
Silverado Merlot (Napa)
Simi (Sonoma)
Château Souverain (Sonoma)
Château Souverain Merlot (Sonoma)
Spring Mountain Estate Miravalle Vineyard
    (Napa)
Stags Leap Wine Cellars (Napa)
Stags Leap Wine Cellars Stags Leap
    Vineyard (Napa)
Sterling Diamond Mountain Ranch (Napa)
Stonestreet (Alexander Valley)
Stonestreet Merlot (Alexander Valley)
Swanson (Napa)
Swanson Merlot (Napa)
The Terraces (Napa)
Trefethen Reserve (Napa)
Trentadue (Sonoma)
Trentadue Merlot (Sonoma)

Truchard Merlot (Napa)
Tudal (Napa)
Tulocay Cliff Vineyard (Napa)
Villa Mt. Eden Signature Series
 (Mendocino)

Whitehall Lane (Napa)
Whitehall Lane Merlot Summer's Ranch
 (Alexander Valley)
ZD Estate (Napa)

** *(AVERAGE)*

Alexander Valley Vineyard Merlot
 (Sonoma)**/***
Bargetto (Santa Cruz)
Beaulieu Beau Tour (Napa)
Beaulieu Rutherford (Napa)
Bel Arbors (California)
Bel Arbors Merlot (California)
Belvedere Wine Co. (Sonoma)
Belvedere Wine Co. Merlot (Sonoma)
Benziger Merlot (Glen Ellen)
Brander Bouchet Proprietary Red Wine
 (Santa Ynez)
Buena Vista Carneros (Sonoma)
Buena Vista Private Reserve (Sonoma)
Buttonwood Farm Merlot (Santa Ynez)
Cafaro (Napa)
Cafaro Merlot (Napa)
Chappellet (Napa)
Chappellet Merlot (Napa)
Clos Pegase Merlot (Napa)
Clos du Val (Napa)
B. R. Cohn Merlot (Sonoma)
Conn Creek (Napa)
Coturri Jessandre Vineyard (Sonoma)
Coturri Merlot Feingold Vineyard (Sonoma)
Coturri Remick Ridge Vineyard (Sonoma)
Coturri View's Land Vineyard (Sonoma)
Creston Manor (San Luis Obispo)
Cronin (Santa Cruz)
Cutler Cellar (Sonoma)
De Loach (Sonoma)
De Moor (Napa)
Dry Creek (Sonoma)
Durney (Monterey)
Fetzer Barrel Select (California)
Field Stone Alexander Valley (Sonoma)
Field Stone Reserve (Sonoma)
Firestone (Santa Ynez)
Firestone Merlot (Santa Barbara)
Firestone Reserve (Santa Ynez)
Firestone Vintage Reserve Proprietary Red
 Wine (Santa Ynez)
Folie à Deux (Napa)
Louis Foppiano (Sonoma)

Louis Foppiano Fox Mountain Reserve
 (Sonoma)
Freemark Abbey Bosché (Napa)
Freemark Abbey Sycamore (Napa)
Gainey Merlot (Santa Ynez)
Glen Ellen (Sonoma)
Grand Cru Vineyards (Sonoma)
Greenwood Ridge (Sonoma)
Groth (Napa)
Guenoc Beckstoffer Vineyard (Carneros)
Gundlach-Bundschu (Sonoma)
Gundlach-Bundschu Rhinefarm Vineyard
 (Sonoma)
Hagafen (Napa)
Hanna (Sonoma)
Hanzell (Sonoma)
Haywood (Sonoma)
William Hill Gold Label Reserve (Napa)
Jekel Home Vineyard (Monterey)
Jekel Symmetry Proprietary Red Wine
 (Monterey)
Château Julien (Monterey)
Château Julien Merlot (Monterey)
Kendall-Jackson Vintner's Reserve
 (California)
Konocti (Lake)
Konocti Merlot (Lake)
Charles Krug Vintage Selection (Napa)
Lakespring (Napa)
Lakespring Reserve (Napa)
Leeward (Ventura)
J. Lohr Reserve (Santa Clara)
Markham (Napa)
Markham Merlot (Napa)
Louis Martini (Sonoma)
Mayacamas (Napa)
McDowell Valley Vineyards (California)
Meridian Vineyards (San Luis Obispo)
Mirassou (Santa Clara)
Montevina (Amador)
Morgan Winery (Monterey)
Mount Veeder (Napa)
Mount Veeder Meritage Proprietary Red
 Wine (Napa)

Mountain View Winery (Santa Clara)
Murphy-Goode (Sonoma)
Nalle (Sonoma)
Domaine Napa (Napa)
Nevada City (Nevada County)
Newlan (Napa)
Parducci (Mendocino)
Parducci Merlot (Mendocino)
Peachy Canyon (Paso Robles)
Peachy Canyon Merlot (Paso Robles)
Robert Pecota (Napa)
J. Pedroncelli (Sonoma)
Peju Province (Napa)
R. H. Phillips (Yolo)
Château Potelle (Napa)
Preston Vineyards (Sonoma)
Raymond Napa (Napa)
Raymond Private Reserve (Napa)
Rocking Horse Claret (Napa)
Rombauer (Napa)
Rombauer Merlot (Napa)
Roudon-Smith (Santa Cruz)
Round Hill (Napa)
Round Hill Reserve (Napa)
Rutherford Hill (Napa)
St. Supery (Napa)
Santa Barbara Winery (Santa Barbara)
Santa Ynez Cabernet Sauvignon Port
    (Santa Ynez)
Sarah's Vineyard Merlot (Santa Clara)
V. Sattui (Napa)
Sebastiani regular *cuvées* (Sonoma)
Seghesio (Sonoma)

Sequoia Grove (Napa)
Sequoia Grove Estate (Napa)
Shenandoah Vineyards Amador (Amador)
Sierra Vista (El Dorado)
Silverado (Napa)
Robert Sinsky Claret (Sonoma)
Smith and Hook Merlot (Santa Lucia)
Stags Leap Winery Napa (Napa)
Steltzner (Napa)
Steltzner Merlot (Napa)
Sterling Merlot (Napa)
Sterling Napa (Napa)
Sterling Reserve Proprietary Red Wine
    (Napa)
Stevenot (Calaveras)
Stone Creek (Napa)
Stonegate (Napa)
Stonegate Merlot (Napa)
Stratford (California)
Rodney Strong Alexander's Crown
    (Sonoma)
Sullivan (Napa)
Sullivan Merlot (Napa)
Sutter Home (Napa)
Ivan Tamas (Livermore)
Tobin James (Paso Robles)
Villa Mt. Eden California (Napa)
Villa Mt. Eden Cellar Select (Napa)
Villa Zapu (Napa)
Weinstock Cellars (Sonoma)
Wellington Vineyards (Sonoma)
Wild Horse (San Luis Obispo)
J. Wile and Sons (California)

RATING CALIFORNIA'S BEST PRODUCERS OF CHARDONNAY

* * * * * *(OUTSTANDING)*

Arrowood Reserve Speciale Michel
    Berthoud (Sonoma)
Beringer Private Reserve (Napa)
Beringer Sbragia Select (Napa)
Brewer-Clifton Katherine's Vineyard (Santa
    Maria)
Brewer-Clifton Marcella's Vineyard (Santa
    Maria)
Brewer-Clifton Sweeney Canyon (Santa
    Maria)
Cuvaison ATS Selection (Carneros)
Ferrari-Carano Reserve (Sonoma)
Fisher Whitney's Vineyard (Sonoma)
Kalin Cellars Cuvée LD (Sonoma)

Kalin Cellars Cuvée W (Livermore)
Kendall-Jackson Clark Vineyard
    (Monterey)
Kendall-Jackson Durell (Sonoma)
Kistler Vineyards Camp Meeting Ridge
    (Sonoma)
Kistler Vineyards Cuvée Cathleen
    (Sonoma)
Kistler Vineyards Durell Vineyard
    (Sonoma)
Kistler Vineyards Dutton Ranch (Sonoma)
Kistler Vineyards Hudson Vineyard
    E-Block (Sonoma)
Kistler Vineyards Kistler Estate (Sonoma)

Kistler Vineyards McCrea Vineyard
(Sonoma)
Kistler Vineyards Vine Hill Road (Sonoma)
Kongsgaard (Napa)
Landmark Demaris Reserve (Sonoma)
Landmark Lorenzo Vineyard (Sonoma)
Littorai Mays Canyon (Sonoma)
Littorai Thieriot Vineyard (Sonoma)
Marcassin Marcassin Vineyard (Sonoma)
Marcassin Upper Barn Alexander Valley
Estate (Sonoma)
Martinelli Charles Ranch (Sonoma Coast)
Martinelli Martinelli Road (Sonoma Coast)
Martinelli Woolsey Road (Sonoma Coast)
Peter Michael Belle Côte (Sonoma)
Peter Michael Clos du Ciel (Sonoma)
Peter Michael Cuvée Indigene (Sonoma)
Peter Michael Mon Plaisir (Sonoma)
Peter Michael Point Rouge (Sonoma)
Mount Eden Vineyards Santa Cruz Estate
(Santa Clara)
Newton Unfiltered (Napa)
Neyers El Novillero (Carneros)

Neyers Thieriot (Sonoma Coast)
Ojai Sanford and Benedict Vineyard (Santa
Barbara)
Ojai Talley Reserve (Arroyo Grande)
Pahlmeyer Unfiltered (Napa)
Patz and Hall Alder Springs (Mendocino)
Patz and Hall Carr Vineyard (Napa)
Patz and Hall Hyde Vineyard (Carneros)
Joseph Phelps Ovation (Napa)
Ramey Hudson Vineyard (Carneros)
Ramey Hyde Vineyard (Carneros)
J. Rochioli Allen Vineyard (Sonoma)
J. Rochioli River Block (Sonoma)
J. Rochioli South River (Sonoma)
Shafer Red Shoulder Ranch (Napa)
Silverado Limited Reserve (Napa)
Robert Talbott Estate (Monterey)
Robert Talbott Diamond T Estate
(Monterey)
Talley Vineyards Rincon Vineyard (Arroyo
Grande)
Talley Vineyards Rosemary Vineyard
(Arroyo Grande)

* * * * *(EXCELLENT)*

Anderson's Conn Valley Fournier Vineyard
(Carneros)
Arcadian Bien Nacido (Santa Barbara)
Arcadian Sleepy Hollow (Monterey)
Arrowood (Sonoma)
Artesa (Carneros)
Artesa Reserve (Carneros)
Au Bon Climat Bien Nacido (Santa
Barbara)
Au Bon Climat Sanford & Benedict
Vineyard (Santa Barbara)
Au Bon Climat Talley Vineyard (Santa
Barbara)
Bancroft (Napa)
Bannister Allen Vineyard (Russian River)
Byron Estate (Santa Barbara)
Byron Reserve (Santa Barbara)
Calera Mt. Harlan (San Benito)
Cambria Estate Bench Break (Santa Maria)
Cambria Estate Katherine's Vineyard
(Santa Maria)
Cambria Estate Reserve (Santa Maria)
Chalone Estate (Monterey)
Clos Pégase Misuko's Vineyard Hommage
Reserve (Carneros)
De Loach O.F.S. (Sonoma)

Dumol (Russian River)
Ferrari-Carano (Sonoma)
Fisher Vineyard Coach Insignia
(Sonoma)
Fisher Vineyard Paladini Vineyard
(Carneros)
Forman (Napa)
Foxen (Santa Barbara)
Gainey Limited Selection (Santa Ynez)
Walter Hansel (Sonoma)
Walter Hansel Cuvée Alyce (Sonoma)
Hanzell Vineyards (Sonoma)
Paul Hobbs Cuvée Agustina (Sonoma)
Paul Hobbs Dinner Vineyard (Sonoma)
Paul Hobbs Kunde Vineyard (Sonoma)
Kalin Cellars Cuvée CH (Sonoma)
Kalin Cellars Cuvée DD (Marin)
Kendall-Jackson Camelot Vineyard
(Lake)
Kunde Estate Kinneybrook Vineyard
(Sonoma)
Kunde Estate Reserve (Sonoma)
Kunde Estate Wildwood Vineyard
(Sonoma)
Landmark Overlook (California)
Longoria (Santa Barbara)

Peter McCoy Clos des Pierres Vineyard (Sonoma)

Merryvale Silhouette (Napa)

Robert Mondavi Reserve (Napa)

Château Montelena (Napa)

Mount Eden MacGregor Vineyard (Edna Valley)

Murphy-Goode Reserve Island Block (Alexander Valley)

Newton (Napa)

Neyers (Carneros)

Neyers (Napa)

Fess Parker Marcella's Vineyard (Santa Barbara)

Patz and Hall (Napa)

Patz and Hall Dutton Ranch (Sonoma)

Pine Ridge Dijon Clones (Napa)

Château Potelle VGS Mount Veeder (Napa)

Ramey Hyde Vineyard (Carneros)

Rancho Sisquoc Estate (Santa Barbara)

Kent Rasmussen (Carneros)

Château St. Jean Belle Terre Vineyard (Sonoma)

Château St. Jean Robert Young Vineyard (Alexander Valley)

Château St. Jean Reserve (Sonoma)

Saintsbury Reserve (Carneros)

Sanford Barrel Select (Santa Barbara)

Sanford Sanford & Benedict Vineyard (Santa Barbara)

Shafer (Napa)

Signorello Vineyards (Napa)

Signorello Vineyards Founder's Reserve (Napa)

Sonoma-Loeb Private Reserve (Sonoma)

Château Souverain single-vineyard *cuvées* (Sonoma)

Steele Durell Vineyard (Sonoma)

Steele Goodchild Vineyard (Santa Barbara)

Steele Lolonis Vineyard (Mendocino)

Steele Du Pratt Vineyard (Mendocino)

Steele Sangiacomo Vineyard (Carneros)

Stonestreet Block 66 (Alexander Valley)

Stonestreet Upper Barn (Alexander Valley)

Stony Hill (Napa)

Robert Talbott Logan (Monterey)

Talley Vineyards (Arroyo Grande)

Testarossa (Santa Maria)

Testarossa Pisoni Vineyard (Santa Maria)

Thunder Mountain Bald Mountain (Santa Cruz)

Thunder Mountain Beauregard (Santa Cruz)

Varner Amphitheater Block (Santa Cruz)

Varner Bee Block (Santa Cruz)

Williams-Selyem Allen Vineyard (Sonoma)

* * * *(GOOD)*

Acacia (Napa)

Adler Fels (Sonoma)

Alderbrook (Sonoma)

Alderbrook Reserve (Sonoma)

S. Anderson (Napa)

Arrowood Domaine de Grand Archer (Sonoma)

Au Bon Climat (Santa Barbara)

Babcock (Santa Barbara)

Bargetto Cyprus (Central Coast)

Beaulieu Carneros Reserve (Napa)

Belvedere Wine Company (Sonoma)

Benziger (Sonoma)

Beringer (Napa)

Bernardus (Monterey)

Brutocao (Mendocino)

Burgess Cellars Triere Vineyard (Napa)

Cain Cellars (Napa)

Calera Central Coast (California)

Canepa (Alexander Valley)

Chalk Hill (Sonoma)

Chimère (Santa Barbara)

Christophe (Napa)

Cinnabar (Santa Clara)

Clos du Bois Barrel-Fermented (Sonoma)

Clos du Bois Calcaire (Sonoma)

Clos du Bois Flintwood (Sonoma)

Clos Pegase (Napa)

B. R. Cohn Olive Hill Vineyard (Sonoma)

Cooper-Garrod (Santa Cruz)

Crichton Hall (Napa)

Cronin *cuvées* (San Mateo)

Cuvaison (Napa)

De Loach (Sonoma)

Dehlinger (Russian River)

Dehlinger Selection (Russian River)

Durney Estate (Monterey)

Edmeades (Mendocino)

Edna Valley (San Luis Obispo)

El Molino (Napa)

Far Niente (Napa)
Gary Farrell (Sonoma)
Fetzer Barrel Select (Mendocino)
Fetzer Sundial (California)
Thomas Fogarty (Monterey)
Folie à Deux (Napa)
Franciscan (Napa)
Frog's Leap (Napa)
Gainey (Santa Barbara)
Gallo Estate (Sonoma)
Geyser Peak (Sonoma)
Green and Red Catacula Vineyard (Napa)
Grgich Hills (Napa)
Guenoc Estate (Lake County)
Guenoc Genevieve Magoon Vineyard
   (Guenoc Valley)
Hacienda Clair de Lune (Sonoma)
Handley (Dry Creek)
Hanna (Sonoma)
Harrison (Napa)
Hess Collection (Napa)
Hess Collection Hess Select (Napa)
Hidden Cellars (Mendocino)
Husch Vineyards (Mendocino)
Iron Horse Vineyards (Sonoma)
Jekel Vineyard (Monterey)
Kendall-Jackson Proprietor's Grand
   Reserve (California)
Kendall-Jackson Vintner's Reserve
   (California)
Kenwood Vineyards Beltane Ranch
   (Sonoma)
Kistler (Sonoma)
Konocti (Lake)
Charles Krug Carneros Reserve (Napa)
Kunde Estate (Sonoma)
La Crema (California)
J. Lohr Riverstone (Monterey)
Lolonis (Mendocino)
Long Vineyards (Napa)
MacRostie (Carneros)
Matanzas Creek (Sonoma)
Meridian Vineyards (San Luis Obispo)
Merryvale Reserve (Napa)
Michel-Schlumberger (Dry Creek)
Robert Mondavi (Napa)
Monterey Vineyards Classic Chardonnay
   (Monterey)
Monticello Cellars Corley Reserve (Napa)
Monticello Cellars Jefferson Cuvée (Napa)
Morgan (Monterey)

Morro Bay (Central Coast)
Murphy-Goode (Sonoma)
Murphy-Goode Reserve (Sonoma)
Napa Ridge (Napa)
Napa Ridge Frisinger Vineyard (Napa)
Napa Ridge Reserve (North Coast)
Navarro Vineyards (Mendocino)
Fess Parker (Santa Barbara)
R. H. Phillips Vineyard (Yolo)
Pine Ridge Knollside Cuvée (Napa)
Pine Ridge Stags Leap District (Napa)
Ravenswood Sangiacomo (Sonoma)
Ridge Santa Cruz Mountain (Santa Cruz)
Rombauer (Napa)
St. Francis (Sonoma)
St. Francis Reserve (Sonoma)
Saintsbury (Carneros)
Sanford (Santa Barbara)
Santa Barbara (Santa Ynez)
Santa Barbara Winery Lafond Vineyard
   (Santa Ynez)
Sarah's Estate (Santa Clara)
Sarah's Ventana Vineyard (Santa Clara)
Sausal Winery (Sonoma)
Seavey (Napa)
Sebastiani single-vineyard *cuvées*
   (Sonoma)
Silverado Vineyards (Napa)
Simi Winery (Sonoma)
Simi Winery Reserve (Sonoma)
Robert Sinsky (Sonoma)
Sonoma-Cutrer Cutrer (Sonoma)
Sonoma-Cutrer Les Pierres (Sonoma)
Sonoma-Cutrer Russian River Ranches
   (Sonoma)
Sonoma-Loeb (Sonoma)
Château Souverain (Sonoma) (since 1990)
Stags Leap Wine Cellars Reserve (Napa)
Steele California (Sonoma)
Sterling Diamond Mountain Ranch (Napa)
Sterling Winery Lake (Napa)
Stratford (Napa)
Stratford Partner's Reserve (Napa)
Rodney Strong Chalk Hill (Sonoma)
Swanson (Napa)
Ivan Tamas (Livermore)
Thunder Mountain Ciardella (Santa Cruz)
Thunder Mountain DeRose Vineyard
   (Santa Cruz)
Marimar Torres (Sonoma)
Trefethen (Napa)

Truchard (Carneros/Napa)
Vine Cliff Cellars Proprietress Reserve
  (Napa)
Wente Brothers Reserve (Alameda) (since
  1988)

Wente Brothers Wente Vineyard (Alameda)
  (since 1988)
Whitehall Lane Reserve (Napa)
Wild Horse (Central Coast)
ZD (Napa)

* * (AVERAGE)

Alexander Valley (Sonoma)
Beaulieu Napa Beaufort (Napa)
Bel Arbors (California)
Boeger (El Dorado)
Bonny Doon (Santa Cruz)
Bouchaine (Los Carneros)
Bouchaine (Napa)
David Bruce (Santa Cruz)
Buena Vista Carneros (Sonoma)
Buena Vista Private Reserve (Sonoma)
Davis Bynum (Sonoma)
Cakebread Cellars (Napa)
Calloway Calla-Lees (Temecula)
Chamisal (San Luis Obispo)
Chappellet (Napa)
Chimney Rock (Napa)
Clos du Val (Napa)
Congress Springs (Santa Clara)
Conn Creek (Napa)
Cosentino (Napa)
Cottonwood Canyon (San Luis Obispo)
Creston Manor (San Luis Obispo)
De Moor (Napa)
Dry Creek (Sonoma)
Eberle (Paso Robles)
Fetzer Bonterra (North Coast)
Firestone (Santa Barbara)
Louis Foppiano (Sonoma)
Fox Mountain Reserve (Sonoma)
Freemark Abbey (Napa)
Freemont Creek (California)
Glen Ellen (Sonoma)
Groth Vineyards (Napa)
Gundlach-Bundschu (Sonoma)
Hagafen (Napa)
Hagafen Reserve (Napa)
Havens (Napa)
Haywood Winery (Sonoma)
William Hill Gold Label Reserve (Napa)
William Hill Silver Label (Napa)
Indian Springs (Sierra Foothills)
Jordan Vineyard (Sonoma)
Château Julien Barrel Fermented
  (Monterey)

Robert Keenan (Napa)
Lakespring (Napa)
Leeward (Central Coast)
J. Lohr Cypress (Santa Clara)
Markham Vineyards (Napa)
Louis Martini (Napa)
Mayacamas (Napa)
McDowell Valley Vineyards (Mendocino)
The Meeker Vineyard (Sonoma)
Meridian (San Luis Obispo)
Merryvale Vineyards (Napa)
Mirassou (Monterey)
Morgan Reserve (Monterey)
Mount Veeder (Napa)
Mountain View Winery (Santa Clara)
Napa Creek Winery (Napa)
Newlan (Napa)
Obester Winery Barrel Fermented
  (Mendocino)
Page Mill (Santa Clara)
Parducci (Mendocino)
J. Pedroncelli (Sonoma)
Robert Pepi (Napa)
Château Potelle (Napa)
Quail Ridge (Napa)
Qupé (Santa Barbara)
Raymond (Napa)
Raymond Private Reserve (Napa)
Richardson (Sonoma)
Round Hill (Napa)
Rutherford Hill Jaeger Vineyard
  (Napa)
St. Clement (Napa)
St. Supery (Napa)
Santa Barbara Winery Reserve (Santa
  Ynez)
Schug Cellars Beckstoffer Vineyard
  (Carneros)
Sea Ridge (Sonoma)
Sebastiani regular *cuvées* (Sonoma)
Seghesio Winery (Sonoma)
Sequoia Grove Carneros (Napa)
Sequoia Grove Estate (Napa)
Sierra Vista (El Dorado)

Stags Leap Wine Cellars (Napa)
Sterling (Napa)
Stevenot (Calaveras)
Stone Creek (all *cuvées*) (Napa)
Taft Street Winery (Sonoma)
Tulocay (Napa)
Villa Mt. Eden Grand Reserve (Napa)
Villa Zapu (Napa)

Weinstock Cellars (Sonoma)
Mark West Vineyards (Sonoma)
William Wheeler (Sonoma)
White Oak (Sonoma)
White Oak Limited Reserve (Sonoma)
Whitehall Lane Le Petit (Napa)
Windemere (Sonoma)
Zaca Mesa (Santa Barbara)

RATING CALIFORNIA'S BEST PRODUCERS OF PINOT NOIR

* * * * * (OUTSTANDING)

Brewer-Clifton (Santa Maria Hills)
Brewer-Clifton Clos Pépé (Santa Rita
    Hills)
Brewer-Clifton Julia's (Santa Ynez)
Brewer-Clifton Melville (Santa Rita Hills)
Dehlinger Goldridge Vineyard (Russian
    River)
Dehlinger Octagon Vineyard (Russian
    River)
Dehlinger Reserve (Russian River)
Dumol (Russian River)
Adrian Fog Floodgate Vineyard (Russian
    River)
Hartford Court Arrendel Vineyard (Russian
    River)
Hartford Court Dutton Ranch/Sanchietti
    Vineyard (Russian River)
Hartford Court Marin Vineyard (Marin
    County)
Hartford Court Sevens Bench Vineyard
    (Napa/Carneros)
Hartford Court Velvet Sisters Vineyard
    (Anderson Valley)
Kistler Cuvée Catherine (Sonoma)
Kistler Hirsch Vineyard (Sonoma Coast)
Kistler Kistler Vineyard (Russian River)
Kistler Occidental Vineyard Cuvée
    Elizabeth (Sonoma Coast)

Kistler Vine Hill Vineyard (Sonoma)
Landmark Grand Detour Van der Kamp
    Vineyard (Sonoma Mountain)
Landmark Kastania Vineyard (Sonoma
    Coast)
Marcassin Marcassin Vineyard (Sonoma
    Coast)
Marcassin Three Sisters–Lambing Barn
    Vineyard (Sonoma Coast)
Marcassin Three Sisters–Sea Ridge
    Meadow Vineyard (Sonoma Coast)
Martinelli Blue Slide Ridge (Sonoma
    Coast)
Martinelli Martinelli Vineyard Reserve
    (Russian River)
J. Rochioli Reserve East Block (Russian
    River)
J. Rochioli Reserve Estate West Block
    (Sonoma)
J. Rochioli Reserve Three Corner Vineyard
    (Sonoma)
Saintsbury Reserve (Carneros)
Siduri Pisoni Vineyard (Santa Lucia
    Highlands)
Talley Vineyards Rincon Estate (Arroyo
    Grande)
Talley Vineyards Rosemary's Vineyard
    (Arroyo Grande)

* * * * (EXCELLENT)

Ancien Poplar Vineyard (Russian River)
Ancien Steiner Vineyard (Sonoma
    Mountains)
Arcadian Pisoni (Monterey)
Arcardian Sleepy Hollow (Monterey)
Au Bon Climat (Santa Barbara)
David Bruce Reserve (Santa Cruz)
Calera Jensen Vineyard (San Benito)
Calera Mills Vineyard (San Benito)

Calera Reed Vineyard (San Benito)
Calera Selleck Vineyard (San Benito)
Cambria Estate Bench Break (Santa Maria)
Cambria Estate Julia's Vineyard (Santa
    Maria) (since 1991)
Cambria Estate Rae's (Santa Maria)
Carmel Road (Monterey)
Conn Valley Vineyards Valhalla Vineyard
    (Napa)

Davis Bynum Le Pinot Rochioli Vineyard (Russian River)

L'Ecosse Rochioli Vineyard (Russian River)

El Molino (Napa)

Etude Winery (Carneros)

Etude Winery Adastre Vineyard (Carneros)

Etude Winery Heirloom (Carneros)

Etude Winery Hudson Vineyard (Carneros)

Etude Winery Hyde Vineyard (Carneros)

Gary Farrell Bien Nacido Vineyard (Santa Barbara)

Gary Farrell Howard Allen Vineyard (Sonoma)

Foxen Julia's Vineyard (Santa Maria)

Foxen Sanford & Benedict Vineyard (Santa Barbara)

Franus-Havens Beau Terroir Vineyard (Carneros)

Gainey Sanford & Benedict Vineyard (Santa Barbara)

Handley Reserve (Anderson Valley)

Walter Hansel (Russian River)

Paul Hobbs Cuvée Agustina (Sonoma Mountain)

Iron Horse (Sonoma)

Kalin Cellars Cuvée DD (Sonoma)

Kalin Cellars Cuvée JL (Sonoma)

Kendall-Jackson Arrendell Vineyard Stature (Russian River)

Kistler Camp Meeting Ridge (Sonoma)

Littorai One Acre Vineyard (Anderson Valley)

Littorai Savoy Vineyard (Anderson Valley)

Longoria (Santa Ynez)

Mayo Family Winery Sangiacomo Vineyard (Carneros)

Peter Michael Le Moulin Rouge (Santa Lucia Highlands)

Robert Mondavi Reserve (Napa)

Morgan Winery Reserve (Santa Lucia Highlands)

Mount Eden Vineyards Estate (Santa Cruz)

Mount Eden Vineyards Vieilles Vignes (Santa Cruz)

Robert Mueller Cellars Emily's Cuvée (Russian River)

Robert Mueller Cellars Ranch 23 (Russian River)

Robert Mueller Cellars Summa Vineyard (Sonoma Coast)

Navarro Methode à l'Ancienne (Mendocino)

Ojai Bien Nacido Vineyard (Santa Barbara)

Ojai Pisoni Vineyard (Santa Lucia)

Patz and Hall (Sonoma)

Patz and Hall Hyde Vineyard (Carneros)

Patz and Hall Pisoni Vineyard (Santa Lucia Highlands)

Kent Rasmussen (Carneros)

J. Rochioli Estate (Sonoma)

Château St. Jean Durell Vineyard (Sonoma)

Sanford (Santa Barbara)

Sanford Barrel Select (Santa Barbara)

Sanford Sanford & Benedict Vineyard (Santa Barbara)

Siduri Christian David (Sonoma Coast)

Siduri Garys' Vineyard (Santa Lucia)

Siduri Hirsch Vineyard (Sonoma Coast)

Siduri Muirfield Vineyard (Oregon)

Signorello (Napa)

Skewis Floodgate Vineyard (Anderson Valley)

Skewis Montgomery Vineyard (Russian River)

W. H. Smith Hellenthal Vineyard (Sonoma Coast)

Solitude Sangiacomo Vineyard (Napa)

Stonestreet (Sonoma)

Talley Vineyards (San Luis Obispo)

Lane Tanner Sanford & Benedict Vineyard (Santa Barbara)

Williams-Selyem Allen Vineyard (Sonoma)

Williams-Selyem Cohn Vineyard (Sonoma)

Williams-Selyem Olivet Lane Vineyard (Russian River)

Williams-Selyem Rochioli Vineyard (Sonoma)

* * * (GOOD)

Au Bon Climat La Bauge Au Dessus Bien Nacido Vineyard (Santa Barbara)

Au Bon Climat Sanford & Benedict Vineyard (Santa Barbara)

Au Bon Climat Talley Vineyard (Arroyo Grande)

Bernardus (Santa Barbara)

Byron (Santa Barbara)

Byron Reserve (Santa Barbara)
Chalone Estate (Monterey)
Chamisal Vineyards Domaine Alfred Pinot
    Noir (Edna Valley)
Chimère (Santa Maria)
Coturri Horn Vineyard (Sonoma)
Dehlinger (Sonoma)
Edna Valley Vineyards (San Luis Obispo)
Ferrari-Carano (Napa)
Foxen (Santa Maria)
The Hitching Post (Santa Maria)
The Hitching Post Highliner (Santa
    Barbara)
The Hitching Post Sanford & Benedict
    Vineyard (Santa Barbara)
Kendall-Jackson Grand Reserve
    (California)
Meridian Reserve (Santa Barbara)
Robert Mondavi (Napa)

Monticello Estate (Napa)
Morgan (Monterey)
Navarro (Mendocino)
Page Mill Bien Nacido Vineyard (Santa
    Barbara)
Saintsbury Garnet (Napa)
Santa Barbara (Santa Barbara) (since
    1989)
Santa Barbara Reserve (Santa Barbara)
    (since 1989)
Santa Cruz Mountain (Santa Cruz)
Robert Sinsky (Sonoma)
Steele Carneros (Sonoma)
Steele Sangiacomo Vineyard (Sonoma)
Robert Stemmler (Sonoma)
Lane Tanner (Santa Barbara)
Westwood (El Dorado)
Wild Horse Cheval Sauvage (Santa
    Barbara)

* * (AVERAGE)

Adler Fels (Sonoma)
Alexander Valley (Sonoma)
Austin Cellars Reserve (Santa Barbara)
Beaulieu Carneros Reserve (Napa)
Bon Marché (Napa)
Bouchaine (Napa)
David Bruce (Santa Cruz)
Buena Vista (Sonoma)
Davis Bynum (Sonoma)
Calera (Central Coast)
Clos du Val (Napa)
Cottonwood Canyon (Santa Barbara)
Cronin (Santa Cruz)
Thomas Fogarty (Santa Cruz)
Gainey (Santa Barbara)
Gundlach-Bundschu (Sonoma)
Hacienda (Sonoma)
Hanzell Vineyards (Sonoma)
Husch (Mendocino)
Charles Krug Carneros Reserve (Napa)
Meridian (Santa Barbara)
Mountain View Winery (California)
Parducci (Mendocino)

Pepperwood Springs (Mendocino)
Richardson (Sonoma)
Roudon-Smith (Santa Cruz)
Santa Ynez Rancho Vineda Vineyard
    (Santa Maria)
Schug Cellars Beckstoffer Vineyard
    (Carneros)
Schug Cellars Heinemann Vineyard
    (Napa)
Sterling (Napa)
Rodney Strong River East Vineyard
    (Sonoma)
Joseph Swan (Sonoma)
Truchard (Napa)
Tulocay (Napa)
Tulocay Haynes Vineyard (Napa)
Mark West (Sonoma)
Whitcraft Bien Nacido Vineyard (Santa
    Barbara)
Whitcraft Olivet Lane Vineyard (Russian
    River)
Whitehall Lane (Napa)
ZD (Napa)

RATING CALIFORNIA'S RHÔNE RANGERS

* * * * * (OUTSTANDING)

Alban Vineyard Syrah Lorraine
Alban Vineyard Syrah Pandora's
Alban Vineyard Syrah Reserve

Alban Vineyard Syrah Seymour's
    Vineyard
Araujo Estate Syrah Eisele Vineyard

Behrens and Hitchcock Petite Sirah
  Barcini Vineyard
Behrens and Hitchcock Syrah Alder
  Springs
Calera Viognier Mt. Harlan
Carlisle Syrah
Carlisle Two Acres (blend)
Clos Mimi Syrah Shell Creek
Edmunds St. John Syrah Durell Vineyard
Jade Mountain Syrah Paras Vineyard
Kunin Syrah French Camp Vineyard
Kunin Viognier Stolpman
Lewis Syrah
Martinelli Syrah
Andrew Murray Syrah Hillside Reserve
Ojai Vineyard Bien Nacido
Ojai Vineyard Roll Ranch
Ojai Vineyard Stolpman Vineyard
Ojai Vineyard Thompson Vineyard
Paloma Syrah
Fess Parker Syrah Rodney's Vineyard
  Reserve

Pride Mountain Viognier
Ridge York Creek Petite Sirah
Rockland Petite Sirah
Shafer Vineyards Syrah
Sine Qua Non Grenache/Syrah (the name
  changes with each vintage)
Sine Qua Non Roussanne and Chardonnay
  blends (the name changes with each
  vintage)
Sine Qua Non Syrah (the name changes
  with each vintage)
Tablas Creek Grand Cuvée (blend)
Tablas Creek Reserve Cuvée (blend)
Sean Thackrey Orion (Syrah)
Titus Vineyards
Turley Cellars Petite Syrah Aida
  Vineyard
Turley Cellars Petite Syrah Hayne
  Vineyard
Turley Cellars Petite Syrah Rattlesnake
  Acres

* * * * (EXCELLENT)

Arrowood Syrah Saralee's Vineyard
Arrowood Viognier Saralee's Vineyard
L'Aventure Optima Syrah/Cabernet Blend
Babcock Vineyards Syrah Black Label
  Cuvée
Beckmen Grenache Purisima Mountain
Blackjack Ranch Le Mas Rouge
Blackjack Ranch Syrah Estate
Bonny Doon Côte de Lune (blend)
Bonny Doon Vin Gris de Cigare Rosé
Linne Caludo Bone Rock
  (Syrah/Mourvèdre blend)
Linne Caludo Cherry Red (blend)
Linne Caludo James Berry Vineyard
  (blend)
Linne Caludo Willow Red (blend)
Cambria Syrah Tepusquet Vineyard
Cline Cellars Côtes d'Oakley (blend)
Cline Cellars Mourvèdre
Robert Craig Syrah
Culler Syrah
Culler Syrah Mt. Veeder
Dehlinger Syrah Estate
Dehlinger Syrah Goldridge Vineyard
Dover Canyon Rhône Reserve
Edmeades Sirah Eaglepoint
Edmunds St. John Les Côtes Sauvage

Edmunds St. John Mourvèdre
Edmunds St. John Syrah Grand Heritage
Familla Jordon Syrah Que Syrah Vineyard
Ferrari-Carano Syrah
Foxen Syrah Carhartt
Foxen Syrah Morehouse
Garretson Wine Co. Syrah Alban Vineyard
  The Finne
Garretson Wine Co. Syrah The Aisling
Havens Syrah Hudson Vineyard
Havens Syrah Napa
Hug Cellars Grenache Alban Vineyard
J. C. Cellars Petite Sirah Frediani Vineyard
J. C. Cellars Syrah Rodney's Vineyard
J. C. Cellars Syrah Ventana Vineyard
Jade Mountain Les Jumeaux (blend)
Jade Mountain Marsanne
Jade Mountain Mourvèdre
Jade Mountain La Provençale (blend)
Jade Mountain Syrah
Jaffurs Syrah Bien Nacido Vineyard
Jaffurs Syrah Melville Vineyard
Jaffurs Syrah Stolpman Vineyard
Jaffurs Syrah Thompson Vineyard
Justin Syrah Halter
Justin Syrah MacGillivray
Kahn Cuvée Jacques (blend)

Kahn Syrah
Kendall-Jackson Syrah Durell Vineyard
Kongsgaard Syrah Hudson Vineyard
Kunin Syrah Santa Rita Hills
La Jota Petite Sirah
Lewis Cellars Alec's Blend (blend)
Loxton Syrah Timberline Ranch
MacRostie Syrah Blue Oaks
MacRostie Syrah Wildcat Mountain
Marietta Old Vine Red
Marietta Petite Sirah
Andrew Murray Les Coteaux
Neyers Syrah Hudson Vineyard
Novy Cellars Alder Springs (blend)
Novy Cellars Syrah
Novy Cellars Syrah Garys' Vineyard
Novy Cellars Syrah Page-Nord Vineyard
Ojai Vin du Soleil (blend)
Ravenswood Icon (blend)
Renard Syrah Timbervine Ranch

Ridge Grenache Lytton Estate
Ridge Mataro Bridgehead
Ridge Mataro Evangelo Vineyard
Ridge Syrah Lytton Estate
Rosenblum Cellars Petite Syrah Rockpile
    Vineyard
Rosenblum Cellars Syrah England-Shaw
    Vineyard
St. Francis Petite Sirah Barlolozzi Ranch
Spring Mountain Syrah Estate
Tablas Creek Petit Cuvée (blend)
Terre Rouge Syrah Ascent
Sean Thackrey Sirius (Petite Sirah)
Sean Thackrey Taurus (Mourvèdre)
Trentadue Petit Sirah
Truchard Syrah
Turnbull Wine Cellars Syrah
Turnbull Wine Cellars Viognier
Unti Syrah Estate
Zaca Mesa Syrah Black Bear Block

* * * *(GOOD)*

Benziger
Beringer Viognier Hudson Ranch
Bonny Doon Le Cigare Volant (blend)
Bonny Doon Clos de Gilroy (Grenache)
Bonny Doon Old Telegram (Mourvèdre)
Bonny Doon Le Sophiste (blend)
Bonny Doon Syrah
David Bruce Petite Sirah
Cambria Viognier
Castle Vineyard Cinsault
Castle Vineyard Syrah
Coturri Alicante Bouchet Ubaldi
    Vineyard
Coturri Petite Sirah Ubaldi Vineyard
Edmunds St. John El Niño
Edmunds St. John Port o'Call (blend)
Edmunds St. John Viognier
Elyse Coeur de Val
Elyse Nero Misto Proprietary Red Wine
Fetzer Petite Sirah Reserve
Field Stone Petite Sirah
Field Stone Viogner Staten Family Reserve
Fife L'Attitude (blend)
Fife Carignan Red Heard
Fife Syrah
Fife Syrah Yokayo Rancho
Folie à Deux Syrah
Frey Syrah

Guenoc Petite Sirah
Hop Kiln Petite Sirah
Jepson Syrah
Marietta Cellars Petite Sirah
McDowell Valley Vineyards Les Vieux
    Cépages
Fess Parker Mélange du Rhône
Fess Parker Syrah
Joseph Phelps Syrah
Joseph Phelps Vin du Mistral *cuvées*
R. H. Phillips Mourvèdre EXP
R. H. Phillips Syrah EXP
R. H. Phillips Viognier EXP
Preston Faux Proprietary Red Wine
Preston Marsanne
Preston Syrah
Qupé Los Olivos Cuvée
Qupé Marsanne
Qupé Syrah Bien Nacido Cuvée
Qupé Viognier Ibarra-Young Vineyard
Ritchie Creek Viognier
Santino Satyricon (blend)
Shenandoah Serene (blend)
Sierra Vista Fleur de Montagne (blend)
Sierra Vista Lynelle (blend)
Stags Leap Winery Petite Sirah
Joseph Swan Côtes du Rosa Unfiltered
Joseph Swan Vin du Mystère

Swanson Syrah
Bedford Thompson Grenache
Bedford Thompson Mourvèdre
Bedford Thompson Syrah
Treanna (white and proprietary blend)
Trentadue Carignan
Trentadue Old Patch Red (blend)

Trentadue Salute
Wellington Vineyards Côtes de Sonoma Old
    Vines
Wellington Vineyards Syrah Alegrai
    Vineyards
Zaca Mesa Cuvée Z (blend)
Zaca Mesa Syrah

* * (AVERAGE)

Alderbrook Syrah Shiloh Hill Vineyard
Christopher Creek Petite Sirah
Christopher Creek Syrah
Duxoup Syrah
Louis Foppiano Petite Sirah
Jory (various *cuvées*)
Karly Petite Sirah
Meridian Syrah
J. W. Morris Petite Sirah Bosun Crest
Parducci Bono Syrah

Parducci Petite Sirah
Preston Viognier
Roudon-Smith Petite Sirah
Sierra-Vista Syrah
Domaine de la Terre Rouge
Topolos Alicante Bouschet
Topolos Grand Noir
Topolos Petite Sirah
William Wheeler Quintet (Blend)

RATING CALIFORNIA'S BEST PRODUCERS OF ITALIAN-INSPIRED VARIETALS—SANGIOVESE, BARBERA, NEBBIOLO

* * * * (EXCELLENT)

Flora Springs Sangiovese
Il Podere Dell'Olivos Barbera
Il Podere Dell'Olivos Teroldego
Jessandre Vineyard (Sangiovese/Cabernet)
Luna Canto
Luna Pinot Grigio
Luna Sangiovese Reserve
Palmina Barbera Bien Nacido Vineyard
Palmina Sangiovese Stolpman Vineyard

La Pantera L'Uvaggio di Giacomo (various
    cuvées)
Pride Mountain Vineyards
Saddleback Cellars Venge Family Reserve
    Sangiovese Penny Lane
Shafer Firebreak (Sangiovese/Cabernet)
Staglin Stagliano
Wild Horse Malvasia Bianca Barrel
    Fermented

* * * (GOOD)

Beringer Sangiovese
Edmunds St. John Pallini Rosso
Edmunds St. John Pinot Grigio
Ferrari-Carano Siena
Robert Pepi Colline di Sassi
Kent Rasmussen Dolcetto

Kent Rasmussen Sangiovese
Staglin Family Vineyard Stagliano
    Sangiovese
Swanson Sangiovese
Ivan Tamas Trebbiano
Wildhorse Tocai Fruilano

* * (AVERAGE)

Atlas Peak Sangiovese
Bonny Doon Ca do Solo Il Fiasco
Brindiamo Gioveto
Brindiamo Nebbiolo
Brindiamo Rosso Vecchio
Dalla Valle Pietre Rosso
Konrad Barbera

Robert Mondavi Barbera
Robert Mondavi Malvasia
Robert Mondavi Sangiovese
Mosby Brunello di Santa Barbara Carrari
    Vineyard
Mosby Moscato di Fior
Mosby Primativo

Preston Barbera   Sean Thackrey Pleiades
Sebastiani Barbera   Trentadue Sangiovese
Sterling Pinot Grigio   Westwood Barbera
Sterling Sangiovese

RATING CALIFORNIA'S BEST PRODUCERS OF SAUVIGNON BLANC, SÉMILLON, AND BLENDS THEREOF

* * * * * (OUTSTANDING)

Araujo Estate Eisele Vineyard (Napa)   Peter Michael Sauvignon Blanc l'Apres-
Ferrari-Carano Fumé Blanc Reserve   Midi (California)
  (Sonoma)   J. Rochioli Old Vine Block (Russian
Iron Horse Cuvée Reserve (Alexander   River)
  Valley)   Château St. Jean La Petite Etoile (Sonoma)
Kalin Cellars Sauvignon Blanc Reserve   Selene Sauvignon Blanc (Napa)
  (Potter Valley)   Simi Sendal Proprietary White Wine
Mason Cellars (Napa)   (Sonoma)

* * * * (EXCELLENT)

Babcock Sauvignon Blanc (Santa Barbara) Kunde Estate Winery Sauvignon Blanc
Babcock Sauvignon Blanc 11 Oaks Ranch   Magnolia Lane (Sonoma)
  (Santa Barbara)   Matanzas Creek Sauvignon Blanc
Beringer Alluvium (Knights Valley)   (Sonoma)
Brander Cuvée Nicolas (Santa Ynez)   Robert Mondavi Fumé Blanc (Napa)
Byron Sauvignon Blanc (Santa Barbara)   Robert Mondavi Fumé Blanc Reserve
Cain Cellars Sauvignon Musqué (Napa)   (Napa)
Caymus Conundrum Proprietary White   Robert Mondavi To-Kalon Estate Reserve
  Wine (Napa)   (Napa)
Chalk Hill Sauvignon Blanc (Sonoma)   Murphy-Goode Fumé Blanc Reserve
Chimney Rock Fumé Blanc (Napa)   (Sonoma)
Clos du Bois Sauvignon Blanc (Alexander Navarro Sauvignon Blanc (Mendocino)
  Valley)   Ojai Cuvée Speciale Ste. Helene
Dry Creek Fumé Blanc (Sonoma)   (California)
Ehler's Grove Sauvignon Blanc Reserve   Page Mill Sauvignon Blanc French Camp
  (Napa)   Vineyard (Napa)
Flora Springs Soliloquy (Napa)   Robert Pepi Sauvignon Blanc Reserve
Gainey Sauvignon Blanc Limited Selection   (Napa)
  (Santa Ynez)   Preston Cuvée de Fumé (Sonoma)
Gary Farrell Sauvignon Blanc Rochioli   Rancho Sisquoc Sauvignon Blanc (Santa
  Vineyard (Russian River)   Barbara)
Handley Cellars Sauvignon Blanc (Dry   J. Rochioli Sauvignon Blanc (Russian
  Creek)   River)
Hidden Cellars Alchemy Proprietary White Signorello Sauvignon Blanc (Napa)
  Wine (Mendocino)   Signorello Sémillon Barrel Fermented
Hidden Cellars Sauvignon Blanc   (Napa)
  (Mendocino)   Spottswoode Sauvignon Blanc (Napa)
Karly Sauvignon Blanc (Amador)   Stonestreet Upper Barn Sauvignon Blanc
Kendall-Jackson Sauvignon Blanc Grand   (Alexander Valley)
  Reserve (California)   Rodney Strong Sauvignon Blanc Charlotte's
Kenwood Vineyards Sauvignon Blanc   Home Vineyard (Sonoma)
  (Sonoma)

*** *(GOOD)*

Adler Fels Fumé Blanc (Sonoma)
Ahlgren Sémillon (Santa Cruz)
Alderbrook Sauvignon Blanc (Sonoma)
Babcock Fathom Proprietary White Wine (Santa Barbara)
Beaulieu Fumé Blanc (Napa)
Bel Arbors Sauvignon Blanc (California)
Bellerose Sauvignon Blanc (Sonoma)
Benziger Fumé Blanc (Sonoma)
Beringer Sauvignon Blanc (Napa)
Bernadus Sauvignon Blanc (Monterey)
Brutocao Sauvignon Blanc (Mendocino)
Buena Vista Fumé Blanc (Lake)
Buttonwood Farm Sauvignon Blanc (Santa Ynez)
Carmenet Meritage Proprietary White Wine (Sonoma)
De Loach Fumé Blanc (Sonoma)
De Lorimer Spectrum Estate (Alexander Valley)
Duckhorn Sauvignon Blanc (Napa)
Ferrari-Carano Fumé Blanc (Sonoma)
Fetzer Fumé Blanc (Mendocino)
Fetzer Sauvignon Blanc Barrel Select (Mendocino)
Field Stone Sauvignon Blanc (Sonoma)

Geyser Peak Sauvignon Blanc (Sonoma)
Geyser Peak Semchard (Sonoma)
Grgich Hills Fumé Blanc (Napa)
Guenoc Winery Langtry Meritage (Lake County)
Louis Honig Cellars Sauvignon Blanc (Napa)
Husch Vineyards Sauvignon Blanc (Mendocino)
Konocti Fumé Blanc (Lake County)
Lolonis Fumé Blanc (Mendocino)
Monterey Vineyards Classic Sauvignon Blanc (California)
Morgan Sauvignon Blanc (Monterey)
Murphy-Goode Fumé Blanc (Sonoma)
Napa Ridge Sauvignon Blanc (Napa)
Page Mill Sauvignon Blanc (San Luis Obispo)
R. H. Phillips Sauvignon Blanc (Yolo)
Preston Vineyards Cuvée de Fumé (Dry Creek)
Sanford Sauvignon Blanc (Santa Barbara)
Stags Leap Sauvignon Blanc Rancho Chimiles (Napa)
Ivan Tamas Fumé Blanc (Livermore)
William Wheeler Fumé Blanc (Sonoma)

** *(AVERAGE)*

Davis Bynum Fumé Blanc (Sonoma)
Calloway Fumé Blanc/Sauvignon Blanc (Temecula)
Christophe Sauvignon Blanc (Napa)
Clos Pegase Sauvignon Blanc (Napa)
Clos du Val Sémillon (Napa)
Louis Foppiano Sauvignon Blanc (Sonoma)
E. & J. Gallo Sauvignon Blanc (California)
Glen Ellen Sauvignon Blanc (Sonoma)
Grand Cru Sauvignon Blanc (Sonoma)
Groth Sauvignon Blanc (Napa)
Jekel Scepter Proprietary White Wine (Monterey)
Château Julien Sauvignon Blanc (Monterey)
Lakespring Sauvignon Blanc (Napa)

Louis Martini Sauvignon Blanc (Napa)
Mayacamas Sauvignon Blanc (Napa)
Obester Sauvignon Blanc (Mendocino)
J. Pedroncelli Primavera Mista Proprietary White Wine (California)
Joseph Phelps Sauvignon Blanc (Napa)
Château Potelle Sauvignon Blanc (Napa)
St. Clement Sauvignon Blanc (Napa)
St. Supery Sauvignon Blanc (Napa)
Santa Ynez Sémillon (Santa Ynez)
Seghesio Sauvignon Blanc (Sonoma)
Shenandoah Sauvignon Blanc (Amador)
Silverado Sauvignon Blanc (Napa)
Simi Sémillon (Napa)
Steltzner Sauvignon Blanc (Napa)
Sterling Sauvignon Blanc (Napa)
Weinstock Sauvignon Blanc (Sonoma)

RATING CALIFORNIA'S BEST PRODUCERS OF ZINFANDEL

***** *(OUTSTANDING)*

Behrens and Hitchcock (Napa)
Hartford Court Fanucchi-Wood Road
  (Russian River)
Hartford Court Hartford Vineyard (Russian
  River)
Martinelli Jackass Hill (Russian River)
Martinelli Jackass Vineyard (Russian
  River)
Ridge Geyserville Proprietary Red Wine
  (primarily Zinfandel) (Sonoma)

Ridge Lytton Springs (Sonoma)
Storybook Mountain Reserve (Napa)
Turley Cellars Black-Sears Vineyard
  (Napa)
Turley Cellars Hayne Vineyard (Napa)
Turley Cellars Moore Vineyard (Napa)
Turley Cellars Vineyard 101 (Alexander
  Valley)

**** *(EXCELLENT)*

Accorn Heritage Alegria Vineyard
  (Russian River)
Albini Family Vineyards (Sonoma)
L'Aventure Stephan Vineyard (Paso Robles)
Bannister (Dry Creek)
Robert Bialé Aldo's Vineyard (Napa)
Robert Bialé Monte Rosso (Sonoma)
Robert Bialé Old Crane Ranch (Napa)
Blockheadia Ringnosi (Napa)
De Loach O.F.S. (Russian River)
Edmeades Ciapusci (Mendocino)
Edmeades Zeni (Mendocino)
Franus Brandlin Ranch (Napa)
Franus Pianchon (Contra Costa)
Gallo-Sonoma Chiotti Vineyard (Dry Creek)
Gallo-Sonoma Frei Ranch Vineyard (Dry
  Creek)
Gallo-Sonoma Stefani Vineyard (Dry
  Creek)
Green and Red Chiles Mill Vineyard
  (Napa)
Hartford Court Dina's Vineyard (Russian
  River)
Hartford Court Highwire Vineyard
  (Russian River)
Hop Kiln Winery Primativo (Sonoma)
Howell Mountain Beatty Ranch (Howell
  Mountain)
Howell Mountain Black-Sears (Howell
  Mountain)
Howell Mountain Old Vine (Howell
  Mountain)
Kunde Estate Robusto (Sonoma)
Limerick Lane Cellars (Sonoma)
Loxton Priest Ranch Orion Vineyard
  (Napa)

Loxton Stonestreet Vineyard (Sonoma)
Marietta Cellars (Sonoma)
Marietta Cellars Angeli Cuvée (Alexander
  Valley)
Mayo Family Winery Ricci Vineyard
  (Russian River)
Neyers Vineyard Pato Ranch (Contra
  Costa)
Neyers Vineyard Tofanelli Vineyard (Napa)
Château Potelle Mount Veeder (Napa)
A. Rafanelli (Sonoma)
Ravenswood Belloni–Wood Road Vineyard
  (Sonoma)
Ravenswood Cooke Vineyard (Sonoma)
Ravenswood Monte Rosso Vineyard
  (Sonoma)
Ravenswood Old Hill Vineyard (Sonoma)
Ravenswood Old Vines (Sonoma)
Ridge Pagani Ranch (Sonoma)
Rosenblum Cellars Brandlin Ranch
  (Napa)
Rosenblum Cellars George Hendry
  Vineyard (Napa)
Rosenblum Cellars Marston Vineyard
  (Napa)
Rosenblum Cellars Samsel Vineyard
  (Sonoma)
St. Francis Old Vines (Sonoma)
Saddleback Cellar Old Vines (Napa)
Saucelito Canyon Vineyard (Arroyo
  Grande)
Sausal Winery (Sonoma)
Sausal Winery Private Reserve (Sonoma)
Seghesio Home Ranch (Alexander Valley)
Seghesio Old Vine (Sonoma)
Seghesio San Lorenzo (Alexander Valley)

Sparrow Lane Demostene Vineyard (Sonoma)

Sparrow Lane Howell Mountain (Napa)

Storybook Mountain Eastern Exposure (Napa)

Storybook Mountain Estate (Napa)

Storybook Mountain Howell Mountain (Napa)

Joseph Swan *cuvées* (Sonoma)

The Terraces (Napa)

Turley Cellars Dogtown (California)

Turley Cellars Duerte Vineyard (Contra Costa)

Turley Cellars Tofanelli Vineyard (Napa)

Zoom (Contra Costa)

*** *(GOOD)*

Amador Foothill Grand Père Vineyard (Amador)

Benziger (Sonoma)

Beringer (Napa)

David Bruce (Santa Cruz)

Brutocao Cellars (Mendocino)

Buehler (Napa)

Cakebread Cellars (Napa)

Caldwell Aida Vineyard (Napa)

Caymus (Napa)

Cline (Contra Costa)

Cline Reserve (Contra Costa)

Clos du Bois (Sonoma)

De Loach Estate (Sonoma)

De Loach single-vineyard *cuvées* (Sonoma)

De Moor (Napa)

Deer Park (Napa)

Deux Amis (Sonoma)

Dry Creek (Sonoma)

Edizione Pennino (Niebaum-Coppola— Napa)

Elyse Howell Mountain (Napa)

Elyse Morisoli Vineyard (Napa)

Gary Farrell (Russian River)

Ferrari-Carano (Dry Creek)

Fetzer Barrel Select (Mendocino)

Fetzer Reserve (Mendocino)

Folie à Deux Old Vine Eschen Vineyard (Amador)

Franciscan (Napa)

Frey (Mendocino)

Frick (Santa Cruz)

Fritz (Sonoma)

Frog's Leap Winery (Napa)

Greenwood Ridge Vineyards (Sonoma)

Grgich Hills (Sonoma)

Guenoc (Lake County)

Hidden Cellars (Mendocino)

Hop Kiln (Sonoma)

Jacuzzi Family Vineyard (Contra Costa)

Kendall-Jackson Vintner's Reserve (California)

Kenwood Jack London Vineyard (Sonoma)

Lake Sonoma Old Vine Reserve (Dry Creek)

Montevina (Amador)

Nalle (Sonoma)

Norman (Paso Robles)

Peachy Canyon Reserve (Paso Robles)

Peachy Canyon West Side (Paso Robles)

J. Pedroncelli (Sonoma)

Joseph Phelps (Alexander Valley)

Preston (Sonoma)

Quivira (Sonoma)

Ravenswood Dickerson Vineyard (Napa)

Ravenswood Vintner's Blend (Sonoma)

Renwood (Amador)

Ridge (Paso Robles)

Ridge Dusi Ranch (Paso Robles)

Ridge Howell Mountain (Napa)

Ridge Sonoma (Santa Clara)

Rocking Horse Lamborn Vineyard (Napa)

Rosenblum Cellars (Contra Costa)

Rosenblum Cellars (Paso Robles)

Rosenblum Cellars (Sonoma)

Rosenblum Cellars Richard Sauret Vineyard (Paso Robles)

Eric Ross Occidental Vineyard (Russian River)

Scherrer Old Vines (Alexander Valley)

Scherrer Shale Terrace (Alexander Valley)

Schuetz-Oles-Korte Ranch (Napa)

Seghesio Winery (Sonoma)

Shenandoah Sobon Estate (Amador)

Sierra Vista (El Dorado)

Sky Vineyards (Napa)

Château Souverain (Dry Creek)

Steele various *cuvées* (California)

Rodney Strong Old Vines River West
   Vineyard (Russian River)
Summit Lake (Napa)
Tobin James (Paso Robles)
Trentadue (Sonoma)

Wellington Vineyards Old Vines (Sonoma)
Whaler Vineyard Estate (Mendocino)
Whaler Vineyard Estate Flagship
   (Mendocino)
Wild Horse (San Luis Obispo)

* * (AVERAGE)

Bel Arbors (California)
Boeger (El Dorado)
Burgess Cellars (Napa)
Clos du Val (Napa)
Cosentino The Zin (Sonoma)
Coturri Chauvet Vineyard (Sonoma)
Coturri Philip Coturri Estate (Sonoma)
Duxoup Wineworks (Sonoma)
Eagle Ridge Fiddletown (Amador)
Eberle (Paso Robles)
Louis Foppiano Reserve (Sonoma)
Gundlach-Bundschu (Sonoma)
Gundlach-Bundschu Rhinefarm Vineyard
   (Sonoma)
Haywood Winery (Sonoma)
Karly (Amador)
Charles Krug (Napa)
Lolonis (Mendocino)
Mariah Vineyards (Mendocino)
Louis Martini (Sonoma)
Mazzocco (Sonoma)
Meeker Vineyard (Sonoma)
Robert Mondavi (Napa)
Obester (San Mateo)

Parducci (Mendocino)
Roudon-Smith (Santa Cruz)
Round Hill (Napa)
St. Supery Vineyards (Napa)
Santa Barbara Beaujour (Santa Ynez)
Santino Wines (Amador)
V. Sattui Suzanne's Vineyard (Napa)
Sebastiani (Sonoma)
Shenandoah Special Reserve (Amador)
Sonora TC Vineyard (Amador)
Sterling (Napa)
Stevenot (Calaveras)
Sutter Home (California)
Sutter Home Reserve (Amador)
Teldeschi (Sonoma)
Topolos Rossi Ranch (Sonoma)
Topolos Russian River Valley (Russian
   River)
Topolos Ultimo (Sonoma)
Twin Hills Ranch (Paso Robles)
Villa Mt. Eden Cellar Select (California)
Mark West Robert Rue Vineyard
   (Sonoma)
White Oak (Sonoma)

RATING CALIFORNIA'S BEST SPARKLING WINES

Where a producer has been assigned a range of stars (***/****), the lower rating has been
used for placement in this hierarchy.

* * * * (EXCELLENT)

Domaine Chandon Reserve Brut (Napa)
Congress Springs Equinox (Santa Cruz)
Maison Deutz Blanc de Noir (San Luis
   Obispo)

Iron Horse *cuvées* (Sonoma)
Mumm Blanc de Noir Rosé (Napa)
Roederer L'Ermitage (Anderson Valley)
Roederer Estate (Anderson Valley)

* * * (GOOD)

Domaine Carneros (Napa)
Domaine Chandon Blanc de Noir (Napa)
Domaine Chandon Brut (Napa)
Domaine Chandon Etoile (Napa)
Maison Deutz (San Luis Obispo)
Handley (Mendocino)

Monticello Domaine Montreaux (Napa)
Domaine Mumm Brut Prestige Cuvée
   (Napa)
Domaine Mumm Brut Winery Lake Cuvée
   (Napa)
Schramsberg Vineyards *cuvées* (Napa)

* * (AVERAGE)

S. Anderson *cuvées* (Napa)**/***

Beaulieu Brut (Napa)

Domaine Carneros (Napa)

Culbertson Blanc de Noir (Riverside)

Culbertson Brut (Riverside)

Culbertson Brut Rosé (Riverside)

Richard Cuneo (Sonoma)

Gloria Ferrer *cuvées* (Sonoma)**/***

Jordan J Cuvée (Sonoma)

Mirassou (Monterey)

Piper Sonoma (Sonoma)**/***

Scharffenberger Cellars *cuvées* (Mendocino)

ABREU VINEYARDS (NAPA)

1999 Cabernet Sauvignon Madrona Ranch	Napa	EEE	(94–96)
1997 Cabernet Sauvignon Madrona Ranch	Napa	EEE	100
1996 Cabernet Sauvignon Madrona Ranch	Napa	E	98
1995 Cabernet Sauvignon Madrona Ranch	Napa	E	95
1994 Cabernet Sauvignon Madrona Ranch	Napa	E	94

David Abreu is a blue-chip vineyard developer and manager whose portfolio of clients includes many of Napa's superstars: Araujo, Bryant Family Vineyards, Colgin, Harlan, Spottswoode, and future superstars such as Sloan and Blankiet. He has also worked closely with Helen Turley and John Wetlaufer in their vineyard development on the Sonoma Coast. Abreu produces 500 cases of spectacular Cabernet Sauvignon from the Madrona vineyard in St. Helena. His wines are made from extremely ripe fruit, picked between 26–28° Brix, given a cold soak, and aged in 100% new French Taransaud oak until they are bottled with neither fining nor filtration. All of this wine is sold through a mailing list, although some of the country's better restaurants seem to get a small allocation. The blend is 90% Cabernet Sauvignon, 5% Cabernet Franc, and 5% Merlot.

The 1999 Cabernet Sauvignon Madrona Ranch reveals all the hallmarks of a David Abreu wine—an opaque black/purple color resembling vintage port, an exquisite bouquet of blackberries, crème de cassis, licorice, and vanilla, immense body, opulent texture, spectacular depth, and a wealth of fruit and extract. This is another profound Cabernet Sauvignon that should drink well young, but last for 20–25 years.

Although I found it to be exceptional, David Abreu decided to declassify his 1998 Madrona Ranch Cabernet as he did not feel it met the standards set by the 1994, 1995, 1996, and 1997.

The 1997 Cabernet Sauvignon Madrona Ranch is a perfect Cabernet Sauvignon. It has been in the bottle for over a year, and this wine, like all the others, has easily soaked up its aging in 100% new Taransaud barrels. It is a sumptuous, unctuously textured, fabulously concentrated Cabernet Sauvignon that hits all the sweet spots on the palate and puts the olfactory senses into overdrive. The wine smells and tastes perfect. It is a compelling effort that one day will be considered part of a small group of elite California Cabernets that may be rewriting the definition of greatness in Cabernet Sauvignon. The 1997 boasts an opaque black/purple color as well as a gorgeous bouquet of roasted meats, scorched earth, blackberry, crème de cassis, minerals, and toast. The soaring aromatics are matched by a phenomenally intense, seamless palate, with full-bodied opulence, exquisite purity and symmetry, and a multidimensional finish that lasts for nearly a minute. This wine will be delicious when released next year, and will last for 25–30 years. It is a tour de force in winemaking.

The 1996 Cabernet Sauvignon Madrona Ranch reveals a blueberry/blackberry, crème de cassis character with smoky oak, new saddle leather, licorice, dried herbs, and mineral scents. Expansive, with terrific intensity, purity, and overall symmetry, it is one of the top half-dozen wines of the 1996 vintage, but with more noticeable tannin in the finish than either the 1997 or 1998. Anticipated maturity: 2003–2030.

The 1995 Cabernet Sauvignon Madrona Ranch is a strikingly superb Cabernet Sauvignon. Although it includes 5% Cabernet Franc and 5% Merlot in the blend, I would never have guessed that. Aged in 100% new Taransaud barrels (as are all his wines), the 1995 boasts an opaque purple color, in addition to a fabulous bouquet of blueberries, blackberries, cassis, licorice, minerals, and smoky, toasty oak. The wine's aromatics soar from the glass, and in the mouth, the bouquet's promise is fulfilled. A thick, juicy, black fruit character comes across in cascades of fruit, glycerin, and extract. All of this has been buttressed by sweet tannin and good acidity. A voluptuously textured, blockbuster, yet remarkably harmonious wine, it is one of the finest efforts of the vintage. Anticipated maturity: now–2025.

The impressively rich, dense purple 1994 Cabernet Sauvignon Madrona Vineyard exhibits a blueberry/blackberry/cassis-scented nose, with a touch of violets and subtle new oak. In the mouth, the wine has disguised its tannic clout with extraordinary extraction of fruit, medium to full body, and a silky yet powerful personality. It, too, is a 20–25 year wine that can be drunk now or cellared.

These are riveting wines produced by a former *Wine Advocate* "Hero of the Year." Once again, readers' only chance of ever sampling one of these sumptuous Cabernet Sauvignons is to get on David Abreu's mailing list.

Past Glories: 1993 Cabernet Sauvignon Madrona Ranch (95)

ACACIA (NAPA)

1998 Pinot Noir Beckstoffer–Las Amigas Vineyard	Carneros	D	88
1998 Pinot Noir Lee Vineyard	Carneros	D	(88–90)

Winemaking at Acacia is in a transitional stage as the tart, high-acid style (historically, their wines had been excessively acidified) is changing in favor of a more natural, open-knit texture with less acid adjustments. This is particularly noticeable with the 1998s, which will introduce a new, seductive, fleshy, friendlier Acacia. The 1998s were completely destemmed, given a pre-fermentation cold soak of several days, and racked less from barrel to barrel. Most important, they possess more natural textures because of less acidification. This is obvious in the single-vineyard 1998 Pinot Noirs, including the 1998 Pinot Noir Beckstoffer–Las Amigas Vineyard. It possesses excellent density and richness in addition to an open-knit texture and fine purity. The outstanding 1998 Pinot Noir Lee Vineyard is the finest Pinot yet produced by Acacia. Plums, sweet black cherries, animal and foresty aromas can be found in this potentially delicious, medium- to full-bodied, concentrated Pinot Noir.

ALBAN VINEYARDS (EDNA VALLEY)

2000 Grenache	Edna Valley	D	(91–93)
1999 Grenache	Edna Valley	D	90
1998 Grenache	Edna Valley	D	89+
1997 Grenache	Edna Valley	D	90
2000 Pandora	Edna Valley	EE	(92–95)
1999 Pandora	Edna Valley	EE	91
1998 Pandora	Edna Valley	EE	90
2000 Roussanne	Edna Valley	D	(90–92)
1999 Roussanne	Edna Valley	D	89
2000 Syrah Lorraine	Edna Valley	E	(92–95)
1999 Syrah Lorraine	Edna Valley	E	90+
1998 Syrah Lorraine	Edna Valley	E	93
1997 Syrah Lorraine	Edna Valley	D	91
1996 Syrah Lorraine	Edna Valley	D	88+
1995 Syrah Lorraine	Edna Valley	D	90
2000 Syrah Reva	Edna Valley	D	(91–94)

1999	Syrah Reva	Edna Valley	D	90
1998	Syrah Reva	Edna Valley	D	90
1997	Syrah Reva	Edna Valley	D	92
2000	Syrah Seymour's Vineyard	Edna Valley	EE	(92–96)
1999	Syrah Seymour's Vineyard	Edna Valley	EE	91+
1998	Syrah Seymour's Vineyard	Edna Valley	EE	90
2000	Viognier Estate	Edna Valley	D	90

One of the pioneers among California's Rhône Valley varietal movement, John Alban settled into a beautiful hillside location in Edna Valley in 1989 and began planting his vineyard the following year. From a family of doctors, Alban broke with tradition by becoming a viticulturist/oenologist. His impressive apprenticeship résumé ranges from Beaujolais to the northern Rhône. His 60-acre vineyard (which could be expanded to 120 acres) is planted with Rhône varietals save for a tiny block of Chardonnay. Production is 5,000 cases as he sells fruit to some of the best Rhône varietal producers (Manfred Krankl of Sine Qua Non is his most prominent client). Alban's wines are aged in small barrels, larger *demi-muids*, and *foudres* or tanks, blended together, and bottled with neither fining nor filtration. This estate is a reference point for what Rhône varietals can achieve in California. In short, Alban not only talks the talk but walks the walk. Low yields, ripe fruit, meticulous handling, and a non-interventionalistic policy result in stunning wines that go from strength to strength.

When I tasted the 2000s, they had not yet been bottled, but they revealed incredible potential. This may be Alban's finest vintage to date, though it is a tough call given the number of profound wines produced at this site. The barrel-fermented 2000 Roussanne is put through full malolactic with a bit of *bâtonnage*. It exhibits wonderful tension between its honeysuckle, thick, juicy fruit, and crisp, citrusy acids. The wine is full-bodied, dense, and chewy, with plenty of upside potential. If it behaves like a French Roussanne, look for it to drink splendidly well for 2–3 years after bottling, close down, then reemerge a decade later.

Alban Vineyards produces California's finest Grenache. According to John Alban, the key is to pick extremely ripe fruit, since Grenache tends to need high sugars to produce its acid and show its full spectrum of flavors. Hence, sugar readings for Grenache can go as high as 27° Brix. The stunningly rich 2000 Grenache (harvested at one-half ton of fruit per acre) boasts amazing color saturation, a boatload of blackberry and kirsch fruit intertwined with licorice and graphite, and a full-bodied, unctuous texture. This stunning effort should turn out to be one of the best Grenaches ever made in California.

The three Syrah *cuvées* emerge from the Reva Vineyard (a relatively cool site with a lot of clay subsoil), Lorraine Vineyard (named after John Alban's elegant wife; planted on stonier soil with terrific drainage), and Seymour's Vineyard (named after his father). The latter vineyard has considerable chalk; perhaps that explains its great complexity. These are all rich, powerful, formidable Syrahs meant for long-term cellaring. The opaque purple-colored 2000 Syrah Reva possesses a superb texture, rich, concentrated, blackberry and cassis flavors, low acidity, and a long finish. Anticipated maturity: 2006–2015. Even sweeter, fleshier, and more flamboyant is the 2000 Syrah Lorraine. It reveals more glycerin, terrific concentration, and an underlying mineral component no doubt attributable to the stony subsoils. This may be the finest Lorraine yet produced. Anticipated maturity: 2005–2015. The outrageously rich 2000 Syrah Seymour's Vineyard boasts an opaque black/purple color as well as aromas and flavors of blackberry liqueur, crème de cassis, licorice, asphalt, and earth. This fabulous 2000 should age gracefully for 15+ years.

The 2000 Pandora blend (usually a Syrah/Grenache blend) had not been assembled when I visited. Normally, it is composed of the finest lots in Alban's cellars and should be profound. The 2000 Viognier Estate is a lovely, peach/apricot-scented and -flavored, honeyed effort with medium to full body, surprising complexity, and a light gold color. It is a muscular, sizeable Viognier to consume over the next 2 years.

In the significantly cooler 1999 vintage, John Alban has succeeded in producing wines which, while not as powerful as his 2000s, are loaded with concentration. His controversial 1999 Roussanne exhibits a pungent, earthy, honeysuckle, and smoky nose with hints of new oak, hazelnuts, and charcoal in the background. This disjointed effort is still seeking its personality. Look for it to evolve for 3–4 years, perhaps longer.

All three Syrahs are extremely successful for such a cool year. The opaque purple-colored 1999 Syrah Reva reveals notes of bacon fat, cassis, spicy oak, and a Hermitage-like character. It comes from the coolest section of the vineyard, and perhaps that's why it seems the most French-like. There are 700 cases of this *cuvée*, which should age well for 10–12 years. With a more saturated color as well as higher extraction, the 1999 Syrah Lorraine (250 cases) offers a combination of structure, elegance, power, and concentration with beautifully integrated wood, tannin, and acidity. This backward effort requires several years of cellaring, but should age for 12–15 years. There are 150 cases of the 1999 Syrah Seymour's Vineyard. It reveals an opaque purple color along with a classic Syrah nose of blackberry and cassis intermixed with smoky oak, bacon fat, and vanilla. Full-bodied, layered, rich, dense, and smoky, this impressively constituted wine will be at its finest between 2004–2014.

The 1999 Grenache (200 cases) exhibits sweet kirsch and raspberry fruit. Although it possesses less color saturation than the Syrahs, it is sexier, more opulent, and hedonistic. My tasting notes said, "a Pinot Noir on steroids." Drink it over the next 5–6 years for its blast of fruit and glycerin. The 1999 Pandora (a 200-case Syrah/Grenache blend) is packaged in a designer bottle with an exquisite label. It boasts a huge, complex bouquet of minerals, black fruits, licorice, earth, and graphite. There is great fruit on the attack, abundant tannin, full body, and a layered, impressive finish. It should drink well for 12–15 years.

The 1998 Grenache's dense ruby/purple color is accompanied by aromas of overripe black cherries, currants, and blackberries, pepper, and spice. Medium- to full-bodied and pure, it plays it tight to the vest, with excellent weight, depth, and a 20-second finish. This youthful 1998 promises to unfold for 4–5 years and drink well for 10–12.

A dynamite effort, the saturated opaque, murky, purple-colored 1998 Syrah Lorraine offers up aromas of bacon fat, mocha, licorice, and crème de cassis. This full-bodied, unctuously textured, stunningly rich, exuberant, robust, super-endowed Syrah is a total turn-on. Still youthful, it promises to evolve gracefully for 10–12 years. The 1998 Syrah Seymour's Vineyard plays it more closely to the vest. Its opaque ruby/purple color is followed by a dense, chewy, tannic, more backward wine revealing more new oak. While loaded with concentrated blackberry and cassis flavors with hints of smoke and underbrush, it requires 1–2 years of cellaring, and should last for 12–18. The 1998 Syrah Reva reveals a dense ruby/purple color as well as a classic nose of bacon fat, smoke, blackberries, and licorice. Full-bodied and rich, with a vanilla note added to the black fruit and smoke characteristics, this lush, full-throttle Syrah is accessible, but should age nicely for a decade. It is the most supple of the three 1998 Syrahs.

The proprietary Rhône varietal blend, the 1998 Pandora, smells like a barrel sample. Its saturated purple color is accompanied by wild (as the French say, *sauvage*) notes of animal fur and black fruits. Slightly rustic, with more noticeable acidity as well as aggressive tannin, this medium-bodied effort reminds me of a coarse, full-throttle, just-bottled Rhône wine. Give it a year or so to settle down and enjoy it over the next 6–15 years.

I adore the 1997 Grenache. It boasts a dense, dark ruby/purple color as well as textbook Grenache aromas of black raspberry liqueur, cherries, and spice. Full-bodied, concentrated, and mouth-filling, this expansive, chewy, gorgeously rich Grenache can be drunk now as well as over the next decade. Impressive! The black/ruby/purple-colored 1997 Syrah Lorraine offers blackberry, tar, and licorice notes in its moderately powerful aromatics. Thick, rich, full-bodied, and concentrated, with excellent purity, this offering exhibits power, richness, symmetry, and the potential to improve for 10–12 years. The 1997 Syrah Reva displays a more saturated purple color along with an element of *sur-maturité*, the telltale blackberry/ cassis fruit, and notes of licorice. Full-bodied, superrich, and impeccably pure, this is an exceptional example of Syrah from Edna Valley. Drink it over the next 10–15 years.

The 1996 Syrah Lorraine has bacon fat and blackberry/cassis fruit flavors, medium to full body, and moderately high tannin in the long finish. It is a well-endowed Syrah, with plenty of grip. If the tannin completely melts away, it will merit a higher score. The superb 1995 Syrah Lorraine displays a saturated dark ruby/purple color, and knockout aromatics consisting of hickory smoke, bacon, and cassis fruit. Opulent on the palate, this full-bodied, concentrated, lush, chewy Syrah has low enough acidity and sweet enough fruit to be drunk now, but it promises to develop nicely for 10–15 years. This is an impressive wine from the "first American winery and vineyard established exclusively for Rhône varieties."

ALBINI FAMILY VINEYARDS (RUSSIAN RIVER)

| 1999 Zinfandel | Russian River | D | 90 |

An outstanding effort, this dark ruby/purple-colored 1999 Zinfandel exhibits impeccable winemaking, a subtle touch of wood, and loads of concentrated black fruits intermixed with spice, pepper, and underbrush. Full-bodied and chewy, it is best consumed over the next 3–4 years. Surprisingly, the alcohol is listed at only 13.8%.

ANDERSON'S CONN VALLEY VINEYARD (NAPA)

1999 Cabernet Sauvignon Reserve	Napa	E	(87–88)
1997 Cabernet Sauvignon Reserve	Napa	E	91+
1996 Cabernet Sauvignon Reserve	Napa	D	90
1995 Cabernet Sauvignon Reserve	Napa	D	91+
1994 Cabernet Sauvignon Reserve	Napa	D	90?
1999 Chardonnay Fournier Vineyard	Carneros	E	(90–92)
1999 Eloge Proprietary Red Wine	Napa	E	(88–90)
1998 Eloge Proprietary Red Wine	Napa	EE	90
1997 Eloge Proprietary Red Wine	Napa	EE	93+
1996 Eloge Proprietary Red Wine	Napa	EE	90
1998 Pinot Noir Dutton Ranch	Russian River	D	88
1996 Pinot Noir Dutton Ranch	Russian River	D	88
1998 Pinot Noir Valhalla Vineyard	Napa	D	90
1997 Pinot Noir Valhalla Vineyard	Napa	D	90

This is an unheralded but interesting as well as excellent source for Pinot Noir and Burgundian-inspired, powerful, non-malolactic, distinctive Chardonnays. Of course, the father-and-son team of Gus and Todd Anderson built their reputation on their long-lived Cabernet Sauvignon Reserve. It is one of the least flamboyant and ostentatious Cabernets from Napa, and thus purchasers need to possess patience, as I have found that most vintages need a good 4–5 years before they begin to strut their stuff. The Andersons also produce a complex Proprietary Red wine called Eloge, a wine with terrific aromatic dimensions as well as elegant, complex flavors. Production has leveled off at 7,000–8,000 cases. Lastly, their Pinot Noirs are sleepers.

At a vertical tasting in October 2000 of all the Conn Valley Cabernet Sauvignons, most of them were rated even higher than their original scores, which is always a good indication of how naturally made wines can improve in the bottle. These are substantially less flamboyant and ostentatious than some of their peers, and perhaps because of that they get the short end of the measuring stick . . . at least out of the starting gate. In any event, readers who have some of the old Conn Valley Cabernet Sauvignons will probably be pleased with the following ratings given at the vertical tasting: 1987 (90, and still youthful), 1988 (85, and fully mature, possibly drying out), 1989 (88, and fully mature), 1990 (94, and absolutely sumptuous), 1991

(93, opulent, sexy, Pomerol-styled), 1992 (90, tight, youthful, structured, tannic, but promising), 1993 (90?, young, tannic, backward, a bit austere), 1994 (90?, gorgeously opulent, sweet, jammy cassis richness), and 1995 (91+, tannic, but complex, with cedar, tobacco, black currants, but tight and needing 3–5 years of cellaring). As for the 1996 Cabernet Sauvignon Reserve, this wine was showing better than it did immediately after bottling. It may not be as concentrated as the 1995 and 1994, but it is a beautifully made Cabernet with a dark ruby/purple color, copious quantities of cassis fruit, and clean, foresty and loamy soil scents. A low-acid, elegant, flavorful, medium- to full-bodied wine, it can be drunk in 1–2 years, yet promises to evolve for 15.

The Cabernet Sauvignon Reserves are challenging to taste. There is no doubt Bordeaux is the inspiration, but the Andersons do not make the mistake of compromising flavor and intensity just for the pursuit of some New World notion of Bordeaux-like elegance. The deep ruby/purple-colored 1999 Cabernet Sauvignon Reserve exhibits excellent ripeness, restrained aromatics, medium body, and a long, austere finish. If past examples are any indication (and I think they are), this wine, which is aged in about 40% new oak, will deepen and put on weight over the next 2–4 years. The outstanding 1997 Cabernet Sauvignon Reserve ranks alongside such top vintages as 1990, 1991, 1994, and 1995. This full-bodied effort exhibits a deep plum/purple color, high tannin, and gorgeously rich, concentrated, floral, and black currant fruit flavors intermixed with mineral, wood smoke, and spice box. It is what the French would call a serious *vin de garde*. Give it 4–5 years of cellaring; it should keep for 30 years, as these wines are built to last. Anticipated maturity: 2005–2030.

Readers looking for more up-front fruit and a more precocious character should seek out Anderson's Eloge. A complex, Cabernet Sauvignon–based effort with Merlot and Cabernet Franc included in the blend, this 100% new oak–aged wine is made in limited quantities (1,000 cases). The 1999 Eloge (a blend of 69% Cabernet Sauvignon, 18% Merlot, and 13% Cabernet Franc) exhibits a dark ruby/purple color in addition to a complex bouquet of dried herbs, blackberries, currants, blueberries, and toasty oak. An outstanding, complete effort, with a sweet attack as well as a rich, medium-bodied, elegant style, a seamless texture, and a long, concentrated finish, it will last for 12–20 years. The 1998 Eloge (65% Cabernet Sauvignon, 25% Cabernet Franc, and 10% Merlot) possesses a more evolved, complex nose offering sweet black cherry and currant fruit intermixed with earth, graphite, tobacco leaf, cedar, and spice. Medium-bodied, velvety-textured, harmonious, and concentrated, it should drink well for 15+ years. The finest Eloge to date is the 1997. This wine has put on weight since last tasted (a tendency of all of the Conn Valley wines). It reveals a complex, Cheval Blanc–like nose of black fruits intermixed with chocolate, cedar, licorice, and Asian spices. A classic, it is deep, opulent, and medium- to full-bodied, with admirable balance between power and elegance. Possessing exceptional purity, an alluring texture, and a long, smooth finish, it can be drunk now or cellared for 15 or more years. In both the 1996 and 1997 vintages, the Eloge is essentially 65% Cabernet Sauvignon, 25% Cabernet Franc, and 10% Merlot. There are 100 cases of the 1996 and 1,000 cases of the 1997. Now that it has had some time in the bottle, the 1996 Eloge reveals more character. Made in an elegant Bordeaux style, it offers tobacco, cedar, and black currant scents and aromas. This medium-bodied, stylish effort is supple enough to be drunk now, yet should age well for 10–12 years.

The 1994 Cabernet Sauvignon Reserve exhibits a dark ruby/purple color and a tight but burgeoning nose of black fruits, white flowers, and earth. On the palate, it reveals a sweet, spicy, black currant–flavored attack, medium to full body, and strong tannin in the finish. The middle needs to fill out a bit more. Drink it over the next two decades. The 1995 Cabernet Sauvignon Reserve may turn out to be the finest Conn Valley Cabernet since 1990. The wine is the sweetest and richest of recent vintages, with nicely integrated tannin, a dense, deep, ruby/purple color, velvety texture, and the seamless quality possessed by many 1994s. It should drink well for 20 years.

One of the sleeper wines in a portfolio justifiably dominated by high-quality Cabernet Sauvignon is Gus and Todd Anderson's Pinot Noir. The 1997 Pinot Noir Valhalla is holding its own, performing better in late 2000 than it did a year earlier. Although the medium ruby color reveals amber at the edge, the bouquet offers up fragrant, spicy, earthy, complex berry scents intermixed with truffle, cherries, and raspberries. There is good underlying acidity as well as a long finish. Drink this 1997 over the next 6 years. In 1998, Pinots were produced from both the Dutton Ranch and Valhalla Vineyard sites. The 1998 Pinot Noir Dutton Ranch offers cherry, root beer, and smoky aromas, followed by a ripe, easygoing, soft, supple texture. It is on a fast evolutionary track, and is best drunk over the next 3–4 years, given its light ruby color and superficial charm and richness. More significant is the 1998 Pinot Noir Valhalla Vineyard. This wine reveals a dark ruby color as well as a sexy, up-front nose of jammy strawberries, cherries, and black raspberries intermixed with toasty new oak. Heady and fleshy, with tangy integrated acidity and tannin, it should drink deliciously for 3–4 years. The 1996 Pinot Noir Dutton Ranch exhibits a light to medium ruby color, a complex nose, and a sweet inner-palate of berry fruit/cherry with a slight notion of chocolate, strawberries, and Asian spices. This attractive Pinot is best consumed over the next 1–3 years.

The impressive, distinctive Chardonnay sees no malolactic fermentation, and thus it must be sterile filtered. However, it is a powerful, concentrated effort from the Fournier Vineyard in Carneros. There are 1,200 cases of this wine, which spends 18 months in French oak, 12 of which are spent on its lees. The wine seems to have all the character of a big Corton-Charlemagne and gives every indication of being relatively long-lived as California Chardonnays go—5–6+ years. The dazzling 1999 Chardonnay Fournier Vineyard may be the finest the Andersons have yet made. Revealing a liquid minerality as well as honey, pineapple, pear, citrus oil, and smoke, it is a full-bodied, intense effort with refreshing, lively acidity.

Past Glories: 1993 Cabernet Sauvignon Reserve (90+), 1993 Eloge Proprietary Red Wine (90), 1992 Cabernet Sauvignon Reserve (92), 1991 Cabernet Sauvignon Reserve (93), 1990 Cabernet Sauvignon Reserve (93)

ARAUJO ESTATE WINES (NAPA)

1999 Cabernet Sauvignon Eisele Vineyard	Napa	EEE	(92–95)
1998 Cabernet Sauvignon Eisele Vineyard	Napa	EEE	92
1997 Cabernet Sauvignon Eisele Vineyard	Napa	EEE	92
1996 Cabernet Sauvignon Eisele Vineyard	Napa	EE	94
1995 Cabernet Sauvignon Eisele Vineyard	Napa	EE	98
1994 Cabernet Sauvignon Eisele Vineyard	Napa	E	95
1999 Sauvignon Blanc	Napa	D	89
1999 Syrah Eisele Vineyard	Napa	E	(92–94)
1998 Syrah Eisele Vineyard	Napa	E	89
1996 Syrah Eisele Vineyard	Napa	E	92
1995 Syrah Eisele Vineyard	Napa	E	97
1994 Syrah Eisele Vineyard	Napa	E	98+

This reference point winery is always one of my favorite stops in northern California. I have been an admirer of the Eisele Vineyard Cabernet Sauvignons since I first tasted the 1974 Conn Creek Eisele. It has been inspiring to see how proprietors Daphne and Bart Araujo have taken this superb *terroir* and built it into a world-class winery and vineyard operation, producing not only spectacular Cabernet Sauvignon but fabulous Syrah and excellent Sauvignon Blanc. One of the more newsworthy stories out of Napa Valley is that famed globe-traveling Pomerol oenologist Michel Rolland was brought in to do consulting work with what is already a talented winemaking team at Araujo. The 1997 Cabernet Sauvignon Eisele Vineyard is a beauty. The healthy ruby/purple color is followed by classic, unevolved but promising aromas of minerals, cedar, smoke, and black currants. The wine is medium- to full-bodied, with admirable purity, a sweet, lush mid-palate, and ripe tannin in the finish. The top-notch 1997 is a more classic, restrained effort than the evolved and flamboyant 1996 as well as the nearly perfect 1995. Anticipated maturity: now–2020. The 1998 Cabernet Sauvignon Eisele Vineyard was bottled earlier than usual as this vintage is not as massive or concentrated as its predecessors. To my palate, the 1998 is as good as the 1997, although I am not convinced it will be as long-lived. There are 2,300 cases of this 90% Cabernet Sauvignon, 7% Petit Verdot, and 3% Cabernet Franc blend. It is supple and elegant, with a complex, evolved bouquet of smoke, black currants, spice box, and cedar. In the mouth, the wine is forward with sweet tannin, gorgeously rich, concentrated fruit, and impressively integrated acidity and tannin. Drink this alluring charmer now and over the next 12–15 years. The 1999 Cabernet Sauvignon Eisele Vineyard appears to be the finest produced by Araujo since their 1995 and 1996. An opaque purple color is accompanied by a sweet nose of crème de cassis intertwined with liquid minerals, flowers, and black fruits. With superb richness, velvety tannin, full body, and a nicely layered, well-textured mid-palate and finish, this is a stupendous effort. The brilliant use of oak adds a subtle toasty note to this impressively endowed Cabernet. It appears to be one of the stars of the vintage. Anticipated maturity: 2003–2025+. The saturated purple-colored 1996 Cabernet Sauvignon Eisele Vineyard offers an attractive nose of black fruits intermixed with toast, minerals, subtle tar, and wood smoke. Full-bodied, with impressive purity, a multilayered mid-palate and finish, it is an expressive, pure, more powerful, and larger-boned wine than either the 1997 or 1998. At this stage, the 1996 would appear to be the slowest to evolve.

I believe the 1995 Cabernet Sauvignon Eisele Vineyard is the finest produced under the Araujo regime. It is close to perfection. The wine combines extraordinary power and richness with remarkable complexity and finesse. The saturated purple/black color is followed by aromas of sweet vanilla intermixed with riveting scents of black currants, minerals, exotic spices, coffee, and toast. There is nothing garish about this subtle yet powerful giant of a wine. A Napa Valley classic, it is full-bodied and extremely rich, yet retains its sense of balance and symmetry. This fabulous Cabernet Sauvignon should age effortlessly for 30 or more years. Anticipated maturity: now–2030. The 1994 Cabernet Sauvignon Eisele Vineyard exhibits an impressively saturated dark purple color. Although slightly less powerful than the 1993 and marginally less concentrated than the 1995, the 1994 is still a profoundly rich, silky-textured wine with an uncanny balance between its smooth tannin and layers of cassis and blackberry/mineral-tinged fruit. This wine is particularly impressive if it is first decanted for 45 or so minutes. It will age well for 15–20 years.

Araujo produces approximately 350 cases of Syrah from their estate vineyards. The 1998 Syrah Eisele Vineyard is a soft, supple-textured, opulent, civilized effort that can be drunk now as well as over the next 8–10 years. Not a blockbuster, it is elegantly rendered, pure, and filled with blackberry/cassis fruit as well as a hint of honeysuckle provided by 8% Viognier in the blend. A potentially superb effort, the 1999 Syrah Eisele Vineyard includes 5% Viognier. It reveals a complex, classic pepper, crème de cassis, blackberry, and bacon fat–scented bouquet. Full-bodied, silky-textured, and crammed with fruit, glycerin, and character, this dazzling Syrah should drink beautifully young, but evolve nicely for at least a decade. Interestingly, the Araujos decided to declassify their 1997 Syrah, which had shown well last year. The 1996 Syrah Eisele Vineyard (350 cases) is a full-bodied, brawny wine revealing the telltale peppery, blackberry, and cassis scents that seem so easy to obtain with this varietal in California. It is rich and pure, with sweet tannin and plenty of power harnessed in a symmetrical, large-scaled effort that is not without considerable elegance for its mass and volume. This wine can be drunk now, but should be even better with 2–3 years of cellaring, and should last for 15 or more years.

The spectacular 1995 Syrah Eisele Vineyard is one of the greatest New World Syrahs I have ever tasted. Approximately 300 cases were made, and it is even better out of bottle than it was in barrel. The color is an opaque purple. The bouquet offers explosive notes of wood fire, licorice, jammy blackberries, and cassis, in addition to the unmistakable scent of black truffles/licorice. Full-bodied and rich, with sensational flavor extraction, remarkable harmony, and a 35+-second finish, this is a profoundly great Syrah. While it is approachable, it will not reach full maturity for another 7–8 years; it will keep for three decades. Wow!

The 1994 Syrah Eisele Vineyard (which is blended with 8% Viognier) may be the single greatest Syrah yet produced in California. The wine exhibits an opaque purple color, followed by a fabulous nose of black fruits, pepper, minerals, and a subtle whiff of Viognier's honeysuckle fruit. It is magnificent on the palate, with massive richness yet, remarkably, no heaviness or coarseness. It is a tour de force in winemaking. Drink it from now–2009.

Lastly, readers should not forget the delicious Sauvignon Blanc produced at Araujo. Some Viognier is included in the blend (10% in 1999) and the wine is partially barrel-fermented (20%). The 1999 Sauvignon Blanc is an elegant, distinctive effort with abundant quantities of mango, passion fruit, grapefruit, and honeysuckle in its complex bouquet. Medium-bodied, dry, crisp, and zesty, it will be a terrific foil for Asian cuisine. Drink this beauty over the next year.

At this high level, it will be interesting to see if Michel Rolland is able to ratchet up the quality. Araujo Estate Wines is another estate where readers should try to get on the mailing list, or at least on the waiting list for the mailing list!

Past Glories: 1993 Cabernet Sauvignon Eisele Vineyard (96), 1992 Cabernet Sauvignon Eisele Vineyard (95), 1991 Cabernet Sauvignon Eisele Vineyard (96)

ARMIDA (DRY CREEK)

1999 Zinfandel Poizin	Dry Creek	E	88

A legitimate debate can be raised concerning whether the lavishly packaged (a designer bottle with a red skull and crossbones packaged in a casket-shaped box) 1999 Poizin is worth $32 more than Armida's regular *cuvée*. It is unquestionably creative, as well as a show-stopping conversation piece. The 1999 Zinfandel Poizin (according to the label, a "wine to die for") offers up aromas of crushed black pepper, soil, berries, and black cherries. Rich and medium- to full-bodied, it reveals underlying Côtes du Rhône–like notes of Provençal herbs and earth. Drink this pure, ripe Zinfandel over the next 3–4 years. In all honesty, the price would appear to be more fatal than the wine.

ARROWOOD (SONOMA)

1999	Cabernet Sauvignon	Sonoma	D	(87–88)
1997	Cabernet Sauvignon	Sonoma	D	90
1996	Cabernet Sauvignon	Sonoma	D	89
1995	Cabernet Sauvignon	Sonoma	D	91
1994	Cabernet Sauvignon	Sonoma	D	91
1997	Cabernet Sauvignon Reserve Speciale	Sonoma	EE	97
1996	Cabernet Sauvignon Reserve Speciale	Sonoma	EEE	90
1995	Cabernet Sauvignon Reserve Speciale	Sonoma	E	94
1994	Cabernet Sauvignon Reserve Speciale	Sonoma	E	95
1999	Chardonnay	Sonoma	D	89
1999	Malbec	Sonoma	D	(89–91)
1997	Malbec	Sonoma	D	89
1996	Malbec	Sonoma	D	89
1995	Malbec	Sonoma	D	90
1994	Malbec	Sonoma	D	92
1999	Merlot	Sonoma	D	(86–88)
1997	Merlot	Sonoma	D	88

1995 Merlot	Sonoma	D	89
1994 Merlot	Sonoma	D	90
1997 Merlot Reserve Speciale	Sonoma	E	90+
1995 Merlot Reserve Speciale	Sonoma	E	90
1994 Merlot Reserve Speciale	Sonoma	E	92
1999 Pinot Blanc Saralee's Vineyard	Russian River	C	91
1999 Syrah	Sonoma	D	(88–90)
1999 Syrah Saralee's Vineyard	Russian River	D	(91–93)
1998 Syrah Saralee's Vineyard	Russian River	D	90
1997 Syrah Saralee's Vineyard	Russian River	D	94
1996 Syrah Saralee's Vineyard	Russian River	D	95
1995 Syrah Saralee's Vineyard	Russian River	D	95
1994 Syrah Saralee's Vineyard	Russian River	D	96+
1999 Viognier Estate	Sonoma	D	88
1999 Viognier Saralee's Vineyard	Russian River	D	90
1999 White Riesling Hoot Owl Vineyard Special Select Late Harvest	Alexander Valley	D	93

Dick Arrowood sold his winery to the Robert Mondavi Corporation in 2000, but he still controls grape acquisition as well as winemaking. His secondary label, Domaine du Grand Archer, gets better and better, and recent vintages of that Chardonnay have been among the best values from California.

Under the Arrowood Winery and Vineyards label, the 1999 Chardonnay may prove to be outstanding. It is a fruit-driven, steely effort with notions of minerals, tropical fruits, and subtle smoky oak. Medium- to full-bodied, with gorgeous purity in addition to an excellent finish, it emphasizes fruit, balance, and flavor intensity. Consume it over the next 2–3 years. Along with Chalone's Pinot Blanc, Arrowood's Pinot Blanc Saralee's Vineyard is one of the finest made in California. The opulent 1999 (14% alcohol, 100% barrel-fermented and put through 100% malolactic) boasts honeyed orange marmalade, buttered apple, and candied citrus aromas and flavors. Sadly, there are only 380 cases. Dick Arrowood told me it is a hard wine to sell, which is puzzling given the fact that no Californian coaxes more character or flavor from this grape than Arrowood. Both the 1999 Viognier Estate (47 cases) and 1999 Viognier Saralee's Vineyard (211 cases) reveal this varietal's ripe honeysuckle, apricot, and peach characteristics. Both are full-bodied, fun whites to enjoy over the next 6–12 months to take advantage of their fragrant aromatics. Both came in with less than 14% alcohol, not easy for Viognier, but still reveal powerful, fruit-bomb personalities. The Saralee's Vineyard reveals more definition as well as a complex underlying mineral component.

This estate rates 1999 alongside 1994 as one of the two finest red wine vintages of the decade. The 1999 Merlot (85% Merlot and 15% Cabernet Franc) exhibits a dense ruby/purple color in addition to big, thick, melted fudge, cocoa, and jammy cherry aromas and flavors. It boasts a high extract level, sweet tannin, medium to full body, and abundant character. This 1999 should easily merit a score in the upper 80s or higher. The 1997 Merlot offers aromas of espresso, mocha, and berry/cherry fruit, a round, medium- to full-bodied texture, and a pure, concentrated finish. Like all of Arrowood's red wines, it was bottled with neither fining nor filtration. The debut vintage of a luxury Merlot *cuvée*, the 1997 Merlot Reserve Speciale (490 cases), is produced from 100% Merlot that was aged for 28 months in predominantly French oak. It possesses super ripeness, beautiful structure, full body, and a dense, thick, chewy personality with exquisite purity, balance, and palate presence. It will be a sumptuous wine after another 1–3 years of cellaring and should keep for two decades, atypically long for a California Merlot.

Each year, Arrowood fashions about 425 cases of one of California's finest Malbecs. This grape tends to fall on its face in most areas of France, but it has done well in selected areas of California. Good Malbecs are produced by Clos du Bois and Pahlmeyer, but the finest is Arrowood's. He obtains a gorgeous blueberry, blackberry, creamy black raspberry character as well as impressive color intensity, intense flavor concentration, and medium body. The wine appears to be weightier than it actually is, with high levels of fruit, extract, and freshness. The 1999 Malbec (100% Malbec) exhibits a sexy, blueberry/blackberry character presented in a medium-bodied, vivacious, exuberant style. The 1999 will spend 26 months in French oak before being bottled without fining or filtration. The 1997 Malbec (250 cases) offers an intriguing perfume of black fruits, gorgeously pure ripe fruit on the palate, decent tannin and acidity, and a lively personality. This wine should drink well during its first 7–8 years.

The dark ruby-colored 1999 Cabernet Sauvignon (9,500 cases) exhibits abundant quantities of black currants, licorice, and tobacco in its unformed aromatics. Ripe and medium- to full-bodied, it represents an excellent blend of 90% Cabernet Sauvignon, 8.5% Merlot, and 1.5% Cabernet Franc. It should drink well for 10–15 years. The outstanding 1997 Cabernet Sauvignon (a blend of 82% Cabernet Sauvignon, 6% Merlot, 5% Malbec, 5% Petit Verdot, and 2% Cabernet Franc) was aged for 23 months in predominantly French oak, and bottled unfined and unfiltered. A classic Cabernet, it is medium- to full-bodied and harmonious, with copious quantities of black currants, black cherries, licorice, and *sous-bois* (underbrush). Pure, fleshy, and multilayered, this moderately tannic, accessible effort will benefit from 2–3 years of cellaring; it should age for 15–16 years.

It sounds preposterous, but when I put my nose in the 1997 Cabernet Sauvignon Reserve Speciale, it reminded me of the 1996 Latour. California Cabernets are bigger, weightier efforts than most Bordeaux, so the comparison ends with the aromatics. There are 1,611 cases of this profound Cabernet Sauvignon, which spent 28 months in primarily French oak (a tiny bit of American oak was utilized), and was bottled with neither fining nor filtration. Its dense black/purple color is accompanied by layers of cassis, cedar-tinged fruit, and abundant spice. Muscular, with remarkable intensity, purity, and overall symmetry, this larger-than-life, full-bodied, profound, 100% Cabernet Sauvignon will be at its best between 2003–2030.

Along with his neighbor Tom Dehlinger, Dick Arrowood was one of the first Sonoma producers to prove how good California Syrah can be. His Saralee's Vineyard Syrah is blended with a touch of Viognier. A big, full-bodied, creamy-textured offering, it can be drunk young but promises to age well for a decade. For 1999, there were two Syrahs. The 1999 Syrah (950 cases) does not contain any Viognier. This fruit bomb exhibits a dense black/purple color, copious quantities of licorice, cassis, and pepper, full body, an unctuous texture, and a long finish. Although still unformed, it is impressive. The 1999 Syrah Saralee's Vineyard (an 825-case *cuvée* with 5% Viognier included) boasts an opaque purple color in addition to a gorgeous bouquet of cassis, bacon fat, black fruits, and licorice. Typically flamboyant, open-knit, expansive, and rich, with low acidity, this hedonistic effort should drink well young, yet keep for a decade. I underrated the superb 1998 Syrah Saralee's Vineyard (575 cases of a 98% Syrah/2% Viognier blend), which has put on considerable weight. This seductive Syrah offers a smoky, charcoal, blackberry, and cassis-scented bouquet with hints of honeysuckle. Full-bodied and long, with fabulous fruit purity, an opulent texture, and sweet tannin, it should drink well for a minimum of 8–10 years. The dazzling 1997 Syrah Saralee's Vineyard, a blend of 97% Syrah and 3% Viognier, boasts wicked aromatics consisting of roasted meats, black fruits, cassis, and bacon. This succulent, fleshy, flamboyantly styled Syrah is more open-knit and accessible than several previous vintages, but it is full-bodied, low in acidity, and loaded with fruit. It is a hedonistic Syrah to drink over the next 8–10 years.

The 1996 Syrah Saralee's Vineyard (made from tiny yields of one ton of fruit per acre) offers up a phenomenal blackberry liqueur–scented bouquet, with a touch of apricot/orange marmalade jam thrown in for additional complexity. Some Viognier was obviously fermented with this offering. Bacon fat, smoky oak, melted road tar, and pepper also emerge in this profoundly complex, super-concentrated, full-bodied classic. This wine is revealing more forwardness than it did previously, but wow, what a stunning Syrah! Anticipated maturity: now–2015. The 1995 Syrah Saralee's Vineyard may be even better. It has the advantage of an extra year of bottle age, so the wine's perfume is more evolved, but both of these *cuvées* are extraordinary. A similar blackberry jam/cassis-scented nose is followed by a sweet, unctuous texture and explosive fruit, glycerin, and extract levels. Soft tannin can be found in the silky 30-second finish. Crammed with fruit, this classic Syrah satisfies both the hedonistic and intellectual senses. It should age effortlessly for 10 or more years.

The excellent 1996 Malbec and Cabernet Sauvignon were bottled with neither fining nor filtration. The 1996 Malbec possesses that varietal's distinctive black raspberry/strawberry liqueur–scented nose with undefined floral aromas (there is nothing quite like it). Spicy and rich, revealing more leanness and austerity than it did last year, it is a delicious Malbec for drinking over the next 5–7 years. The 1996 Cabernet Sauvignon offers spice box, cedar, black currants, and a touch of licorice and toasty wood. Medium- to full-bodied, rich, and moderately tannic, it will age well for 7–8 years.

Arrowood made profoundly rich, complex Cabernet Sauvignon Reserve Speciales in both 1995 and 1994. While the 1996 Cabernet Sauvignon Reserve Speciale is outstanding, it is not up to the quality of the two previous vintages. Aged completely in French oak, this dense, chocolaty, black currant–scented wine possesses abundant spice, richness, power, and intensity. Still youthful, but muscular and impressively endowed, this full-bodied Cabernet requires 2–3 years of cellaring and should keep for two decades or more. The Reserve Speciale wines spend just under two years in oak casks and are bottled unfined and unfiltered. These stunning offerings are among the finest of their type. Production is minuscule for the Reserve Speciale Merlot (108 cases) and modest for the Cabernet Sauvignon Reserve Speciale (1,700 cases for the 1995). The 1995 Merlot Reserve Speciale possesses a dense purple color in addition to a big, smoky, toasty, oaky nose with notes of black currant and cherry fruit. The wine exhibits coffee/chocolate notes in the flavors, an unctuous texture, full body, and outstanding purity and length. Already accessible, this 1995 promises to evolve for 15+ years. The spectacular 1995 Cabernet Sauvignon Reserve Speciale is a worthy rival to the monumental 1994. It offers an opaque purple color and a knockout nose of tobacco, jammy cassis, toast, and floral scents. This wine has superb extract and purity, full body, multiple layers of richness, and a ripe, seamless, palate-staining finish. Although approachable, it is not quite as accessible as the glorious 1994. Anticipated maturity: now–2020.

Arrowood's 1995 Merlot exhibits some of the tannic muscle Dick Arrowood ascribes to this vintage. The wine possesses an opaque purple color, a tight but interesting nose of black cherries and currants intermixed with coffee and smoky notes. Sweet, juicy, intensely ripe fruit hits the palate, yet the wine's tannin gives it definition and a more backward personality than the 1996. While this Merlot can be drunk early, it should keep for 12–15 years. The 1994 Merlot's saturated, inky black color is followed by a sweet, jammy nose of black fruits, licorice, vanilla, and smoke. Full-bodied, with a voluptuous palate, as well as a layered texture, this low-acid, plump, fleshy Merlot should drink well for a decade after its release next year. Yummy!

Arrowood's 1995 Malbec has a slight edge over the 1996, perhaps because it happens to be a year older. It appears to possess more body and intensity. There is no doubting this saturated purple-colored wine's knockout nose of black raspberries, jammy strawberries, and crème fraîche. Extremely opulent and lush, with berry fruit gushing across the palate, this wine possesses a palate feel and texture totally unlike Merlot and Cabernet Sauvignon. It reveals the precision of Cabernet, the body of Merlot, and an indescribable but not unbearable "lightness of being." Pure, with light tannin in the finish, this expressive, personality-filled wine should drink well for 10–12 years. The 1994 Malbec exhibits raspberry jam, vanilla ice cream, and cream puff–scented aromas and flavors. A gush of wild black fruits is allied to a silky texture, medium to full body, and superb purity. Arrowood has been intelligent in not over-oaking these Malbecs, building in just enough new oak to provide delineation. All of these Malbecs can be drunk upon release, yet they promise to last for at least 8–10 years.

There are few Sonoma County Cabernet Sauvignons better than those produced by Dick Arrowood. Arrowood's success with Cabernet Sauvignon, so obvious in the decade of the nineties, continues unabated, with a succession of top-quality wines. The outstanding 1995 Cabernet Sauvignon boasts an opaque purple color, followed by a rich, black currant–dominated bouquet with background aromas of new oak, earth, and spice. Extremely full-bodied with admirable fruit purity and a layered, multidimensional personality, this wine is intensely rich, with formidable levels of glycerin and extract. The wine's tannin is largely concealed by the wealth of fruit. While this Cabernet will be drinkable young, it promises to evolve for 15+ years. Another sensational, opulent, rich, extremely aromatic and concentrated red wine from Arrowood, the 1994 Cabernet Sauvignon possesses stunning concentration and intensity, impressive balance and purity, and copious quantities of sweet tannin in the long finish. It should even eclipse the super 1993.

Arrowood's two 1994 Reserve Speciale wines, a 1994 Merlot and 1994 Cabernet Sauvignon, were made in limited quantities, but, wow, what dazzling wines they are! The 1994 Merlot Reserve Speciale (100 cases) includes about 3.7% Cabernet Franc in the blend. With 13.8% alcohol, it is a sexy, rich, full-bodied Merlot with terrific layers of fruit, glycerin, and extract. The wine spent 22 months in oak casks, but reveals little evidence of new wood given its extraordinary concentration, power, and depth. It possesses a knockout nose of ripe berry fruit intertwined with Asian spices, subtle toast, and a whiff of coffee and chocolate. Powerful, yet round and harmonious, this is a blockbuster Merlot that should drink well for 15+ years. Arrowood's 1994 Cabernet Sauvignon Reserve Speciale is an exquisite wine made from a blend of vineyards (Wildwood, Smothers, Balbi, Belle Terre, and others). The largest percentage of fruit is from Sonoma Valley, although a small quantity comes from Alexander Valley and Dry Creek. The wine exhibits an opaque purple color and a spectacular nose of jammy cassis, lead pencil, vanilla, and spice. Thick, unctuously textured flavors ooze over the palate with extraordinary purity, ripeness, and richness. In spite of its size, the wine somehow manages not to taste heavy or overdone. This sensational Cabernet Sauvignon is one of the finest I have tasted from Sonoma. It is a candidate for 25–30 years of cellaring, although it is soft enough to be drunk young. Production was 1,200 cases.

The 1994 Syrah Saralee's Vineyard, made from yields of one ton per acre, is available in extremely limited quantities. It is one of the most riveting Syrahs I have tasted from California or anywhere for that matter. The color is an opaque inky black, and the nose offers up copious quantities of smoky chocolate, cassis, and bacon fat aromas. The wine is unbelievably rich, yet amazingly well delineated on the palate, with full body, layers of super-concentrated, unctuously textured fruit, and a finish that must be tasted to be believed. It is an exquisite Syrah that even such Rhône Valley icons as Marcel Guigal or Michel Chapoutier would be thrilled to taste. Rhône Ranger fans are advised to get in line for a bottle or two of this Syrah nectar. It should drink well for 15+ years.

Lastly, no one in California has a better track record for producing luxuriously rich, sweet Riesling than Dick Arrowood. His 1999 White Riesling Hoot Owl Vineyard Special Select Late Harvest contains 8.4% alcohol and 25.6% residual sugar. Unctuously textured, with vibrant acidity, and a decadently sweet *trockenbeerenauslese* style, it offers flavors of orange marmalade as well as honeyed tropical fruit. Fresh and lively, without being overbearing, it will be at its best during its first 4–5 years of life.

Past Glories: 1993 Cabernet Sauvignon (90), 1993 Merlot (89+)

DAVID ARTHUR (NAPA)

1996 Cabernet Sauvignon Elevation 1147	Napa	EE	91
1995 Meritaggio	Napa	D	90

David Arthur's Cabernet Sauvignon Elevation 1147 is a beautiful Cabernet Sauvignon, but, sadly, only 100 cases were produced. It is a gloriously fragrant, sweet, dark ruby/purple-colored wine with gorgeously well integrated oak, and ripe black currant fruit intermixed with licorice, toast, and spice. The wine is medium-bodied, with no hard edges, good acidity and tannin, a nicely textured mid-palate, and fine length. This beauty can be drunk now or cellared for 10–15 years. The 1995 Meritaggio, a proprietary blend of 75% Cabernet Sauvignon, 8% Cabernet Franc, 7% Merlot, 5% Petit Verdot, and 5% Sangiovese, displays an opaque purple color and a sweet nose of earth, vanilla, and truffle-scented jammy black fruits. Full-bodied, with low acidity, a viscous texture, and impressive purity and length, this is an exceptionally well endowed, accessible wine that can be drunk now as well as cellared for a decade. Impressive!

ATALON (NAPA)

1997	Cabernet Sauvignon Beckstoffer Vineyard	Oakville	EE	92
1997	Cabernet Sauvignon Mountain Estates	Napa	EE	91+
1998	Merlot	Napa	D	89
1997	Merlot Mountain Estates	Napa	E	91

This is another of the new high-quality wineries that has been set up under the Jackson Family Farms umbrella group of exceptional wine estates. Wine-maker Tom Peffer, who worked at Beringer for many years, is responsible for accessing the fruit that has made the following wines. The 1998 Merlot (2,500 cases) exhibits a dense ruby/purple color as well as a big, thick, chocolaty nose with notes of roasted coffee, black cherry liqueur, and smoke. Full-bodied, dense, with soft tannin, low acidity, and a long, hedonistic, almost succulent finish, it should drink well for at least a decade. The terrific 1997 Merlot Mountain Estates (1,200 cases) is primarily from the Howell Mountain vineyard once owned by Liparita. The wine has a small dosage of Cabernet Sauvignon and Cabernet Franc in the blend, but tastes like pure Merlot, and superb Merlot at that. It is full-bodied with a knockout nose of smoke, coffee, black cherries, plums, and toast. Unctuously textured, very chewy, with fabulous purity and gobs of flavor, this is a hedonistic yet potentially long-lived Merlot that should drink well when released and last for 15 or more years. An exceptional wine, the black/purple-colored 1997 Cabernet Sauvignon Mountain Estates (1,800 cases) has gorgeous blackberry and cassis flavors intermixed with licorice, spice box, Asian spice, and vanilla. It is unctuously textured, full-bodied, with moderate tannin in the finish. Ideally, I would give this wine 2–3 years of cellaring, and drink it over the following two decades. It is a topflight wine and an impressive new entry into the Cabernet sweepstakes. Equally superb (but more expensive) is the 1997 Cabernet Sauvignon Beckstoffer Vineyard. This vineyard, adjacent to Mondavi's To-Kalon Vineyard in Oakville, has been the source of some superb offerings. (Behrens and Hitchcock made a fabulous 1999 from this site.) Black currant liqueur notes intermingled with licorice, chocolate, cedar, and tobacco emerge from this full-bodied, opaque purple-colored wine. Very concentrated, thick, with juicy, very expansive mid-palate and sweet tannin, this is a prodigious Cabernet Sauvignon that can be drunk now or cellared for 15–20+ years. What an impressive set of debut performances.

AU BON CLIMAT (SANTA BARBARA)

1997	Pinot Noir Cuvée Isabelle	California	E	88
1995	Pinot Noir Cuvée Isabelle	California	E	89+
1997	Pinot Noir Rosemary's Vineyard	Santa Barbara	E	88
1997	Pinot Noir Talley Vineyard	Arroyo Grande	E	88
1997	Il Podere dell Olivos Barbera	California	C	88

1995 Il Podere dell Olivos Barbera Riserva Bon Natale	Santa Barbara	C	89
1997 Il Podere dell Olivos Refosco	California	C	88
1996 Il Podere dell Olivos Teroldego	Santa Barbara	C	88

Major changes are planned for Jim Clendenen's Au Bon Climat. Clendenen, one of the most colorful wine-makers in California, has purchased 70 acres and begun to plant a tightly spaced Pinot Noir vineyard from Dijon clones. This will ensure that Clendenen is not dependent on purchased fruit. This winery produces a numbing assortment of offerings, both under the Au Bon Climat label and the funky, quasi-Italian designation, Il Podere dell Olivos label. Given his long-standing image as being in the forefront of Pinot Noir and Chardonnay, I was surprised that Clendenen's efforts with Italian varietals seemed to taste more complete than his recent Chardonnay and Pinot Noir efforts.

Jim Clendenen is successful with Italian varietals. The red wines include a black/purple-colored, licorice, blackberry, melted tar–scented and –flavored, rustic 1997 Refosco and an elegant, rich, strawberry and blackberry-scented and -flavored 1997 Barbera. These are two robustly styled efforts with excellent fruit, an absence of intrusive wood, and lively acids. The Refosco also displays copious tannin. Both should age well, but they are best consumed in their vigorous youth—over the next 3–4 years.

Exuberance, richness, and impressive dimensions are found in the 1995 Barbera and 1996 Teroldego (an unbottled sample of the 1997 Teroldego also looked immensely impressive). The Barbera was opaquely colored and revealed spicy oak, rich, concentrated fruit, and tangy acidity that was balanced by considerable extract and richness. The massive, opaque black-colored 1996 Teroldego boasts an outstanding nose of licorice, tar, prune- and plum-like fruit. Dense, full-bodied, and concentrated, this hulking wine fills the mouth. The 1997 Teroldego should be even bigger if the sample I tasted was an accurate indication. It is hard to predict how long any of these quasi-Italian reds will last, but 4–5 years is a conservative guess, with the Teroldego lasting longer.

The 1997 Pinot Noirs I tasted include a dark plum-colored, excellent 1997 Pinot Noir Cuvée Isabelle. Aromas of damp earth, black cherries, sweet candied plums, and herbs are generous as well as persistent. The wine is medium-bodied, with decent acidity, light to moderate tannin, and a fine finish. It should be consumed over the next 3–4 years. Denser and more concentrated, with black fruit, spicy, leathery, and earthy characteristics, the 1997 Pinot Noir Talley Vineyard reveals excellent ripeness, a fine texture, and a firm, positive finish. It should drink well for 5–6 years. Revealing outstanding potential, Au Bon Climat's 1997 Pinot Noir Rosemary's Vineyard possesses a super ruby/purple color, as well as excellent black raspberry and cherry aromatics intermixed with toast. Medium-bodied, extremely pure, and well knit, this Pinot Noir should reach full maturity in 1–2 years and last for 8–10.

The finest wine among Au Bon Climat's releases is the 1995 Pinot Noir Cuvée Isabelle. It possesses a dark ruby color with purple hues. The nose offers up complex, sweet, black-cherry and raspberry fruit intermixed with toasty, smoky oak. The wine is richer than the 1994, with medium to full body, excellent extract and purity, and a long finish. It is the sweetest, richest, and potentially most complex and long-lived of what is undeniably an irregular showing from one of my favorite Pinot Noir producers.

BABCOCK VINEYARDS (SANTA BARBARA)

1998 Pinot Noir Grand Cuvée	Santa Barbara	E	90
1998 Pinot Noir Mt. Carmel Vineyard	Santa Ynez	E	90
1997 Sangiovese Eleven Oaks	Santa Ynez	D	88
1997 Syrah Black Label Cuvée	Santa Barbara	D	91

This was the strongest group of wines tasted from Bryan Babcock, a longtime member of the Santa Barbara wine community. Although I am not an admirer of most California Sangioveses, Babcock's 1997 Sangiovese Eleven Oaks is a noteworthy effort. It exhibits textbook smoky, ripe cherry jam, saddle leather, and strawberry aromas. Ripe, rich, suave, and medium-bodied, with no hard edges, it should drink well for 2–3 years. Yummy!

Two of the finest Babcock Pinot Noirs produced to date are the 1998 Pinot Noir Mt. Carmel Vineyard and the 1998 Pinot Noir Grand Cuvée. More similar than dissimilar, they both exhibit deep ruby/purple colors, dense, concentrated personalities, ripe, jammy black cherry and raspberry fruit, and a judicious use of toasty new oak. The Mt. Carmel Vineyard may be less intense and powerful in the mouth, but both are topflight. They will offer delicious drinking for 5–7 years. The Grand Cuvée will outlive its sibling. The terrific 1997 Syrah Black Label Cuvée emerges from a cool climate vineyard in Lompoc. This opaque purple-colored Syrah exhibits aromas of melted licorice, blackberries, and cassis. Full-bodied, with great fruit purity and intensity, an alluring texture and superb harmony among its acidity, alcohol, and tannin, this superb Syrah is still an infant in terms of its development. Give it another year of bottle age and drink it over the following 12–15 years.

BACIO DIVINO (NAPA)

1997 Proprietary Red Wine	Napa	EE	90
1996 Proprietary Red Wine	Napa	E	92
1995 Proprietary Red Wine	Napa	E	94

The second awesome release from this tiny winery dedicated to producing intriguing wines, the 1995 Bacio Divino (a blend of 66% Cabernet Sauvignon, 22% Sangiovese, and 12% Petite Sirah) is a formidable wine of exceptional richness, layers of flavor, and a multidimensional personality. The color is a deep saturated ruby/purple. The nose offers up juicy/jammy strawberry, black currant, and blackberry notes wrapped with subtle toasty oak. Full-bodied, with outstanding ripeness and purity, a silky texture, and an explosive finish, this is a sumptuous example of what can be done with three grapes rarely blended together in such proportions. By the way, sentimentalists will be moved by the government warning label that reads "contains sulphites and also some of the wine-maker's heart and soul." This wine should continue to drink well for a decade.

Another terrific offering from this producer, the 1996 Bacio Divino (a blend of 66% Cabernet Sauvignon, 17% Sangiovese, 9% Petite Sirah, and 8% Merlot) offers a spicy, oaky nose with notions of jammy cassis, strawberries, and cherries. Full-bodied and complex, with a dominant black fruit element upstaging the new oak nuances, this fleshy, ostentatious, pure, gorgeously seductive wine will drink well for 7–8 years. Kudos to wine-maker/proprietor Claus Janzen. The 1997 Bacio Divino, an intriguing as well as innovative blend of 63% Cabernet Sauvignon, 20% Sangiovese, 8% Petite Sirah, and 9% Merlot, is again an outstanding effort. Already evolved and delicious, the dark ruby/plum color is followed by aromas of new saddle leather, black raspberries, plum liqueur, cherries, and toasty, smoky new oak. Medium- to full-bodied, with sweet tannin, an open-knit, fleshy texture, and low acidity, this California "super Tuscan look-alike" can be drunk now and over the next decade.
Past Glories: 1993 Proprietary Red Wine (93+)

BALLENTINE VINEYARDS (NAPA)

1999 Zinfandel (Map Label)	Napa	C	90

This offering is differentiated from Ballentine's regular Zinfandel bottling by the fact that this more powerful wine (14.5% alcohol) has an attractive map label. The dark purple-colored, impressively fruity 1999 Zinfandel (Map Label) exhibits Rhône-like characteristics of earth, Provençal herbs, pepper, spice box, licorice, plum, currants, and cherries, a sweet, full-bodied, fruit-driven personality, outstanding ripeness, and superb purity. Drink it over the next 5–6 years.

BANNISTER (SONOMA)

1996 Pinot Noir Floodgate Vineyard	Anderson Valley	D	90
1997 Pinot Noir Seghesio Vineyard–Keyhole Ranch	Russian River	D	88
1996 Zinfandel	Dry Creek	C	89

This excellent producer seems to have a knack for finding terrific sources for high-quality fruit, offering wines that are not only immediately accessible, but already complex, and marked by exceptional fruit quality and purity. The 1997 Pinot Noir Seghesio Vineyard–Keyhole Ranch possesses a dark ruby color, as well as an excellent spicy, toasty, sweet, jammy, red and black fruit–scented nose with a touch of herbaceousness. The wine is round and velvety-textured, with excellent succulence and gobs of fruit. Drink it over the next 2–4 years. The 1996 Pinot Noir Floodgate Vineyard is another example of the high potential for complex Pinot that exists in northern California's Anderson Valley. Other top California Pinot Noir specialists (for example, Siduri, Handley, and Littorai) have also exploited this up-and-coming region. Bannister's 1996 Pinot Noir Floodgate exhibits a dark ruby color, as well as a terrific nose of black fruits, earth, spice, and sweet toast. In the mouth, the wine is ripe, with a nicely layered palate, adequate acidity, exceptional purity and ripeness, and a long, silky-textured, opulent finish. This outstanding Pinot Noir is already delicious, yet promises to last for 4–5 years. The delectable 1996 Zinfandel exhibits a dark ruby color, as well as an elegant, berry-scented nose, and lush, low-acid, medium- to full-bodied flavors with no hard edges. This is a full-flavored yet harmonious and well-balanced wine to consume over the next several years. Kudos to Marty Bannister.

BARBOUR VINEYARDS (NAPA)

1998 Cabernet Sauvignon	Napa	EE	(88–90)
1997 Cabernet Sauvignon	Napa	EE	93

There were about 100 cases produced of this limited production Cabernet. The well-known winemaking consultant, Heidi Barrett, makes the wine, the first vintage being 1997. The dense blue/purple-colored 1997 Cabernet Sauvignon offers a terrific nose of plums, cherry liqueur, cassis, and subtle new oak. It is beautifully pure, with gobs of fruit, low but adequate supporting acidity, and plenty of ripe tannin in the finish. Made from 100% Cabernet Sauvignon and aged for just under two years in French oak, this is a beautifully made wine that can be drunk now or cellared for two decades. The 1998 Cabernet Sauvignon (150 cases) displays good density for the vintage, sweet tannin, and ripe plum and black currant fruit. Slightly less concentrated, with a shorter finish, it is a noteworthy achievement in this difficult vintage. Both of these wines are made from the famed Grace clone of Cabernet Sauvignon (from Grace Family Vineyards).

BARNETT VINEYARDS (NAPA)

1996 Cabernet Sauvignon Rattlesnake Hill	Spring Mountain	E	89+
1994 Cabernet Sauvignon Rattlesnake Hill	Spring Mountain	E	93+

I have superb recollections of Barnett Vineyards' 1991 Cabernet Sauvignon and Cabernet Sauvignon Rattlesnake Hill. The 1996 Cabernet Sauvignon Rattlesnake Hill reveals a saturated ruby/purple color and sweet fruit (rich blueberry, cassis, earth, and wild herbs). Full-bodied, with a nicely layered impact and copious tannin in the long, astringent finish, it requires 2–3 years of cellaring and should keep for 15+ years. The 1994 Cabernet Sauvignon Rattlesnake Hill Estate is undeniably the finest Cabernet Barnett Vineyards has produced since their marvelous 1991. The wine has an opaque purple color, as well as an earthy, raspberry liqueur–scented nose that is vibrant and intense. The wild mountain black fruit quality so common in the top wines of Spring Mountain comes across on the palate of this immensely impressive, explosively rich, super-extracted wine. Patience, however, is required as the tannin is high, and most of the wine's character and richness are in the explosive finish as opposed to its attack. This should turn out to be an exquisite Cabernet Sauvignon, but only for the true connoisseur who is willing to invest in 5–7 years of cellaring. Anticipated maturity: 2003–2030. Wow!

Past Glories: 1991 Cabernet Sauvignon (92), 1991 Cabernet Sauvignon Rattlesnake Hill (96)

BEAULIEU (NAPA)

1995 Cabernet Sauvignon Clone Four	Napa	EE	89?
1994 Cabernet Sauvignon Clone Six Signet Collection	Napa	EE	91
1996 Cabernet Sauvignon Georges de Latour Private Reserve	Napa	EE	88
1994 Cabernet Sauvignon Georges de Latour Private Reserve	Napa	E	91
1995 Zinfandel	Napa	C	88

Beaulieu's flagship, the 1996 Cabernet Sauvignon Georges de Latour Private Reserve, exhibits a deep ruby/purple color as well as aggressive toasty new oak, medium body, and firm tannin. The noticeable acidity exacerbates the firmness and tannic structure. Although very good, possibly excellent, it needs 2–4 years of cellaring. It should keep for 15–20 years. This wine needs more mid-palate as well as additional layers of flavor. Less acidification would open up the wine's texture. Beaulieu's dense, saturated ruby-colored 1995 Zinfandel offers up textbook aromas of jammy black fruits, pepper, and spice. Full-bodied and lush, with loads of glycerin and alcohol (14.5%), this medium- to full-bodied, extremely well made Zin is a treat to drink. The wine's low acidity and luscious abundance of ripe berry fruit suggests near-term drinking (over the next 3–4 years). Kudos to BV for this excellent wine.

The dark ruby-colored, admirably concentrated 1995 Cabernet Sauvignon Clone Four reveals many positive attributes—ripe cassis fruit, loamy soil scents, and toasty notes. It is a rich, medium-bodied, structured, pure wine that needs 4–5 years to settle down. It should last 20–25 years. If the tannin becomes meshed with the wine's other elements, it will be outstanding. If not, the score will fall. Anticipated maturity: 2006–2020. The 1994 Cabernet Sauvignon Clone Six, a limited bottling from BV's Signet Collection series of wines (all expensive and made in small quantities), is an immensely impressive offering. The color is a saturated dark ruby/purple. The wine, from an old clone of Cabernet Sauvignon, is a rich, full-bodied, powerful yet harmonious Cabernet with gobs of black currant fruit, a nice touch of oak, and outstanding ripeness and purity. It is also long in the mouth, with a youthful, unevolved personality. This should prove to be an impressive, long-lived Cabernet Sauvignon. Anticipated maturity: now–2015.

The 1994 Cabernet Sauvignon Georges de Latour Private Reserve is one of the finest efforts from Beaulieu in some time. Not since the mid-1980s has BV made a Private Reserve Cabernet with such richness and potential. The wine boasts a dark ruby/purple color, an attractive nose of sweet, toasty new oak, and ripe red and black fruits. In the mouth, there is a layered texture, full-bodied richness, excellent purity, and sweet tannin in the long finish. This wine can be drunk now as well as over the next 15–20 years.

Past Glories: Cabernet Sauvignon Georges de Latour Private Reserve—1990 (88), 1988 (90), 1985 (89), 1984 (91), 1982 (92), 1980 (93), 1976 (94), 1974 (90), 1970 (94), 1969 (90), 1968 (94), 1958 (95), 1951 (94)

BEDFORD-THOMPSON (SANTA BARBARA)

1997 Cabernet Franc	Santa Barbara	C	88
1997 Syrah	Santa Barbara	C	89

There is no doubting the individuality and artisinal feel to the Bedford-Thompson offerings. Little is held back in the winemaking, and they are to be admired for that. It is hard to find a better Cabernet Franc from southern California than Bedford-Thompson's 1997. Notes of saddle leather, cedar, jammy berries, and spice box offer a fragrant, complex bouquet. The wine is intense, with lovely fruit, not much weight, but medium body, and a long, concentrated finish. Drink it over the next 5–6 years. A more controversial offering is the 1997 Syrah. It has a lot going on, including levels of volatile acidity (VA) that might be off-putting to some technocrats. The wine's dark blue/purple color is followed by jammy, sweet aromas of cherries, black raspberries, smoke, and a bit of VA. Dense and full-bodied, with a luscious texture and outstanding richness, this wine comes close to being over the top, but this could pass for a French Côte Rôtie. Drink it over the next 5–8 years.

BEHRENS AND HITCHCOCK (NAPA)

1998 Cabernet Franc	Oakville	D	(87–89)
1999 Cabernet Sauvignon Beckstoffer Vineyard	Oakville	E	(95–98)
1998 Cabernet Sauvignon Beckstoffer Vineyard	Napa	E	(86–88)
1998 Cabernet Sauvignon Cuvée Juanita	Napa	E	(90–91)
1994 Cabernet Sauvignon Cuvée Lola Unfiltered Reserve	Napa Valley	D	93
1994 Cabernet Sauvignon Hyampom Vineyard Lot 2	Trinity County	C	88
1999 Cabernet Sauvignon Ink Grade	Napa	E	(92–95)
1996 Cabernet Sauvignon Ink Grade	Napa	D	92
1995 Cabernet Sauvignon Ink Grade	Napa	D	92+
1994 Cabernet Sauvignon Ink Grade Vineyard Lot 2	Napa Valley	D	91+
1999 Cabernet Sauvignon Kenefick Ranch	Napa	E	(93–96)
1998 Cabernet Sauvignon Kenefick Ranch	Napa	E	(90–92)
1996 Cabernet Sauvignon Kenefick Ranch	Napa	D	93
1994 Cabernet Sauvignon Staglin Vineyard	Napa Valley	D	90+
1995 Cabernet Sauvignon TLK Ranch	Napa	D	96
1999 Cuvée Lola Proprietary Red Wine	Napa	E	(94–96)
1997 Cuvée Lola Proprietary Red Wine	Napa	D	(90–93)
1996 Cuvée Lola Proprietary Red Wine	Napa	D	92
1999 Merlot	Napa	D	(91–93)
1997 Merlot	Napa	D	(89–92)
1999 Merlot	Oakville	E	(90–92)
1998 Merlot	Oakville	E	(87–88)
1997 Merlot	Oakville	D	(90–93)
1996 Merlot	Oakville	D	94
1995 Merlot	Oakville	D	91
1999 Merlot Alder Springs Vineyard	Mendocino	D	(90–93)
1998 Merlot Alder Springs Vineyard	Mendocino	D	(87–89)
1999 Merlot Las Amigas Vineyard	Carneros	E	(92–94)
1998 Merlot Reserve	Napa	E	(88–90)
1997 Ode to Picasso Proprietary Red Wine	Napa	D	(91–93)
1998 Petite Sirah	Napa	D	(88–90)
1997 Petite Sirah	Napa	D	(91–93)
1995 Petite Sirah	Dry Creek Valley	D	92

1999 Petite Sirah Barcini Vineyard	Napa	D	(89–91)
1999 Syrah Alder Springs Vineyard Hommage to Ed Oliveira	Mendocino	E	(90–92)
1997 Zinfandel	Napa	D	(90–92)
1996 Zinfandel	Dry Creek	D	89
1995 Zinfandel	Napa	D	94

Behrens and Hitchcock and their families represent all that is good about winemaking in the United States. Bob Hitchcock, a former accountant, and Les Behrens, a retired restaurant owner, decided to give up their "real" jobs and begin to acquire fruit to make wines "they liked." Starting first out of a garage in the southern Napa Valley, they have now purchased property on top of Spring Mountain. With a shoestring budget, the Hitchcock/Behrens syndicate has thrown up a functional winery, even going so far as to dig a couple of caves for barrel aging. However, the most important thing is the quality. Neither has an oenological degree, and when you taste these wines, you have to wonder, does anyone need one? The results are spectacular, and the owners are refreshingly candid. The remarkable thing is that these wines embarrass many of the multimillion-dollar corporate wineries on Napa's valley floor that could use a wake-up call from artists/artisans such as Les Behrens and Bob Hitchcock. Readers who are not on their mailing list should sign up immediately.

Behrens and Hitchcock were almost apologetic for what was a good line-up of 1998s. However, their 1999s are the best wines they have yet produced. Made from superripe fruit, they offer bold flavors, high alcohol, and gobs of personality. They are satisfying not only on a hedonistic level, but also intellectually. All of these wines go into the bottle with neither fining nor filtration, and of course, this is another winery that simply refuses to muck around with alcohol levels by reducing them through industrial manipulation or adding water to the fermentation must. For starters, the 1999 Merlot Oakville (500 cases of 100% Merlot) is a dense, very chewy Merlot with oodles of smoky blackberry and cherry fruit. The wine is unctuously textured, with plenty of glycerin, and a heady, concentrated finish. It will be delicious when released and age well for at least 10–12 years. The 1999 Merlot Alder Springs Vineyard (350 cases) is also superb, but shows more of a cooler climate, almost jammy, red berry nose, with notes of graphite, toast, and spice. The wine has gorgeous purity, relatively low acidity, and a thick yet superb finish. Not to be outdone, the 1999 Merlot Napa (700 cases of a blend of three separate vineyards, Kenefick, Jaeger, and Alder Springs) is the most structured of the four Merlots I tasted. It reveals a black/purple color, terrific fruit intensity, a big, weighty, blackberry and cherry-scented nose, and plenty of volume and power in the mouth. The smoky oak is beautifully integrated, as this wine seems to have already sucked up its new oak aging. There is more tannin in the finish, but this is a large-scale, blockbuster Merlot that is probably going to need 2–3 years of cellaring and will last for 15–20 years. Don't be surprised if someone stumbles across a bottle in about two decades and thinks it is one of the finest Merlots ever made in California. If that sounds good, there is an even better Merlot from the Behrens and Hitchcock stable in 1999. Are you ready? The 1999 Merlot Las Amigas Vineyard (350 cases of a thick, 15.6% alcohol, voluptuous Merlot fruit bomb) is full-bodied with remarkable intensity, purity, and equilibrium. This vineyard has been the source of some uninspiring wines from another famed Napa Valley winery, but in the hands of Behrens and Hitchcock, it has turned out a prodigious effort. The wine is opaque black/purple, with plenty of smoke, sweet mulberry, blackberry, and cherry fruit, infused with espresso, cocoa, and toast. This full-bodied, super-extracted, yet velvety-textured wine should drink well for 15 or more years.

The Alder Springs Vineyard Syrah (which is well known for not only Merlot but also Pinot Noir) is the first Syrah from this source. There is a small quantity of the 1999 Syrah Hommage to Ed Oliveira. A 100% Syrah aged in new oak, this wine shows plenty of licorice and cassis notes, gorgeous ripeness, full body, low acidity, but moderate tannin in the finish. It looks to be an outstanding Syrah to drink after several years of bottle age. It should keep for 12–15 years. Another tannic beast is the 1999 Petite Sirah Barcini Vineyard. The wine is a dense purple color, with notes of earth, smoke, licorice, and black fruits. Quite sweet on the attack, full-bodied, with rustic tannin in the finish, this wine will require 5–6 years of cellaring and keep for up to two decades.

The three Cabernet Sauvignons I tasted from Behrens and Hitchcock in 1999 are among the superstars of the vintage. This is a rather remarkable achievement, since these are not from estate grapes but from vineyards they have sourced. The 1999 Cabernet Sauvignon Ink Grade (300 cases of 15.1% alcohol) has an opaque purple color, an intense, very fragrant nose of crème de cassis, smoky new oak, mineral, and almost floral-infused blueberry and blackberry notes. The wine is unctuously textured, with the new wood totally absorbed. Acidity and tannin are also beautifully integrated. This wine should be relatively accessible upon release and last for up to two decades. Another incredible effort is the 1999 Cabernet Sauvignon Kenefick Ranch, located in the northern end of Napa Valley, not far from Araujo's Eisele Vineyard. The 1999 exhibits an opaque purple color and a gorgeous nose of blueberry and cassis fruit, intermixed with melted licorice, mineral, and smoke. Sweet and unctuously textured on the attack, with full-bodied, powerful flavors that are remarkably harmonious, this Cabernet possesses a whopping degree of alcohol (about 15.9%) that is totally integrated and balanced. Look for this wine to evolve for 15 or more years. A potentially prodigious wine is the 1999 Cabernet Sauvignon Beckstoffer Vineyard. From a vineyard located next to the famed To-Kalon Vineyard of Robert Mondavi, it boasts an opaque black/purple color as well as an awesome nose of spice box, black fruits, toast, and mineral. The wine is remarkably rich, full-bodied, and pure, with multiple layers of flavor, sweet tannin, low acidity, and a finish that goes on for a good 45+ seconds. There are 325 cases of this wine that was finished at 15.4% alcohol. Many of the vineyards they draw from are frequently cropped at 5–6 tons, but Les Behrens and Bob Hitchcock reduce yields by 50%.

There was no 1998 Cuvée Lola (named after a deceased cat) but the 1999, a blend dominated by Cabernet Franc (about 75%, with small quantities of Petit Verdot, Merlot, and Cabernet Sauvignon added in), is sensational (375 cases; a "modest" 15.3% alcohol). The wine offers an opaque blue/purple color and an exquisite nose of liquid minerals, black fruits, and spice. Dense, huge, and full-bodied, yet at the same time, remarkably elegant and graceful, it is a tour de force in winemaking, representing a brilliant marriage of power and finesse. Because of the slightly firm tannins in the finish, it will need 2–3 years of cellaring, but should keep 20+ years.

Some potentially outstanding wines were produced in 1998. There is no question that the better 1998s, while lacking power, concentration, and ageability, are ripe, charming, and alluring because of their immediate appeal. Most of the Behrens and Hitchcock 1998s fall within that range. The 1998 Petite Sirah emerges from the same Calistoga vineyard that produces fruit for the Rockland Petite Sirah (a limited production gem I have glowingly reviewed in the past). The Behrens and Hitchcock offering exhibits a dark ruby color with purple nuances. Soft and forward, with supple tannin, good blackberry and peppery-scented fruit, and a pure, lush finish, it will be delicious when released and will last for 7–8 years. The dark ruby-colored 1998 Merlot Oakville displays mineral, smoke, black cherry, and spicy oak aromatics. Medium-bodied, round, and easy to drink, it will be a seductive, delicious Merlot to enjoy during its first 5–6 years of life. Much better is the 1998 Merlot Reserve. Richer and sweeter, with more volume, concentration, and intensity in the mouth, it reveals chocolate, black cherry liqueur, and toasty, smoky oak. Drink this seductive, supple-textured effort during its first 8 years of life. The 1998 Merlot Alder Springs was harvested on November 2 (an indication of just how cold the summer of 1998 proved to be). Dark ruby/purple-colored, with sweet mulberry, blackberry, and cherry fruit, this medium-bodied, dense, attractive Merlot has plenty up-front, but not a great deal of glycerin or intensity once past its superficial appeal. It will be very good, perhaps excellent, but the vintage's lack of generosity and power are clearly evident. Drink it over the next 7–10 years.

I will be anxious to see what Les Behrens and Bob Hitchcock do with Cabernet Franc in a top-notch vintage like 1999. Certainly the 1998 Cabernet Franc Oakville is a complex offering, exhibiting sweet floral, spice, and vanilla aromas as well as black raspberry/blueberry-like fruit. It is medium-bodied, elegant, soft, and seductive. There are about 100 cases of the following new Cabernet Sauvignon from Rutherford. The dense ruby/purple-colored 1998 Cabernet Sauvignon Cuvée Juanita exhibits sweet blackberry and cassis aromas and flavors with spice and toast in the background. A fat, fleshy, low-acid Cabernet Sauvignon, it will be delicious when released and age well for 10–12 years. It is unquestionably a success for the vintage. The 1998 Cabernet Sauvignon Beckstoffer Vineyard reveals excellent purity and ripeness, but not much power and richness. Very good, with sweet black currant and berry fruit intertwined with spice box, vanilla, and cedar, it should drink well for 7–8 years. There are 400 cases of the 1998 Cabernet Sauvignon Kenefick Ranch. This has been a star for Behrens and Hitchcock since they first offered it, and the 1998 appears to be one of the vintage's top efforts. Opaque black/purple-colored, with a knockout bouquet of crème de cassis, blackberry liqueur, and smoky new oak, this intense, full-bodied, surprisingly powerful offering, from a vineyard near the Araujo's Eisele parcel, is long and atypically rich and concentrated for a 1998. Anticipated maturity: now–2015. Bravo!

The dark plum-colored 1997 Merlot Oakville, from a parcel of vines close to Dalla Valle, Screaming Eagle, and the new Rudd Cellars, is a jammy offering with gobs of ostentatiously rich black cherry fruit intermixed with smoke and spicy oak. It hits the palate with generous amounts of glycerin, and thick, juicy fruit. This succulently textured wine is a thrill to drink. It should provide Merlot lovers with plenty of excitement. Moreover, it should continue to drink well for a decade. Named after a long-deceased cat, the 1997 Ode to Picasso (a blend of 80% Syrah and 20% Merlot) is far superior to the very good 1996. It reveals the winery's telltale aromas of blackberries, blueberries, and cassis, as well as terrific fruit intensity, a layered texture, and huge flavors. Although built like a fortress, it possesses glorious levels of fruit and plenty of power. Accessible enough to be drunk young, it will keep for 12–15+ years. The 1997 Cuvée Lola (a blend of 75% Cabernet Franc and 25% Cabernet Sauvignon and Merlot) is one of the finest Cabernet Franc–dominated wines I have tasted from northern California, ranking alongside the superb efforts turned in by Dalla Valle, La Jota, and Pride Mountain. The wine exhibits a cedary, cigar box, black currant, and raspberry-scented nose, superb ripeness, rich, fleshy, low-acid flavors, and a rich but not weighty mid-palate and finish. This wine will be drinkable upon release, and keep for 12+ years.

Readers looking for blockbuster-sized, bigger-than-life wines should check out Behrens and Hitchcock's 1997 Petite Sirah. It boasts a thick, purple color, as well as a huge nose of minerals, Asian spices, smoke, and black fruits. Extremely powerful, full-bodied, and ripe, with a jammy yet well-delineated personality, this monster Petite Sirah will benefit from 4–5 years of cellaring and keep for two decades or more.

I have immensely enjoyed the Zinfandels produced by Behrens and Hitchcock. Their fruit comes from a 30-year-old, head-pruned vineyard. The fine 1997 Zinfandel offers copious quantities of black cherry, briery, raspberry, and peppery fruit. The wine displays loads of glycerin, medium to full body, a lush, round, generous mouth-feel, and heady alcohol in the lusty finish. It is a wine to drink over the next 3–4 years.

My notes also indicate I tasted a 1997 Merlot Napa, which was expected to be bottled separately, rather than blended with Oakville Merlot. This example revealed a more chocolaty, coffee, crème brûlée character than the Oakville *cuvée,* in addition to full body, outstanding richness of fruit, and a spicy, dense, concentrated finish. More monolithic than the Oakville, but potentially outstanding, it is another superb offering from this small winery.

The 1996 Cabernet Sauvignon Ink Grade exhibits a saturated purple color, followed by a fragrant nose of exotic black fruits (blueberries and cassis). In the mouth, subtle doses of attractive floral notes, spice, and vanilla emerge. This multilayered wine possesses sweet tannin, a voluptuous texture, and superb concentration and purity. It is a sexy, opulently styled Cabernet Sauvignon to drink when released and over the next 15 years. As the wine sat in the glass, the blueberry/blackberry liqueur aspect became even more pronounced, making this wine totally disarming. The 1996 Cabernet Sauvignon Kenefick Ranch, a dense, black/purple-colored wine, is full-bodied and extremely rich, with a sweet, black fruit–scented nose, intertwined with licorice and floral notes. Concentrated, full-bodied, and powerful, yet beautifully balanced, this 1996 has managed to tame the vintage's rustic tannin, resulting in a wine of uncommon silkiness and equilibrium. Anticipated maturity: now–2015.

What a sumptuous, knockout, gloriously rich, layered, and juicy 1996 Merlot Behrens and Hitchcock produced. The 1996 Merlot Oakville possesses a dark ruby/purple color, dazzling, sweet, black cherry liqueur–like notes in its aromatics, and judicious notes of spicy oak. The wine's purity, and multiple layers of texture that combine thrilling levels of fruit, glycerin, and extract into a seamless, voluptuously endowed wine, are to be both enjoyed and admired. Diaphanous, this wine can be peeled one layer at a time given its thick, rich, high-rise effect on the palate. The fruit is superripe and well balanced with copious sweet tannin and low acidity. This is a full-bodied, sensationally endowed Merlot to drink over the next decade. Nearly as impressive is the 1996 Cuvée Lola, a proprietary red wine made from a Bordeaux-like blend of Cabernet Sauvignon, Merlot, and Cabernet Franc. This wine is characterized by a saturated ruby/purple color, layers of flavor, outstanding purity, and black currant, plum, and cassis flavors. The wine is rich, but avoids any sense of heaviness or roughness. The wine's structural components—tannin, acidity, and alcohol—are all meshed together into a silky format. This offering can be drunk now or cellared for 12–15 years.

Made from 85% Zinfandel, 10% Petite Sirah, and 5% Carignan, the dark ruby-colored, medium- to full-bodied 1996 Dry Creek Zinfandel reveals copious quantities of sweet black cherry fruit intermingled with spice, pepper, and dusty notes. The wine is classy and powerful yet elegant, particularly for a Dry Creek Zinfandel. Purely made and stylish, it is ideal for consuming over the next 3–4 years. The fabulously rich 1995 Zinfandel Napa (a blend of 85% Zinfandel, 12% Petite Sirah, and, low and behold, 3% Viognier) is one of the finest I have tasted. The saturated opaque purple color is followed by a knockout nose of blackberry liqueur intermingled with raspberries, pepper, and spice. The wine is explosively rich, with loads of glycerin, layers of concentrated, jammy fruit, full body, and a knockout, heady finish. This is a hedonistic, gloriously perfumed, and decadently concentrated wine to drink over the next 3–4 years.

The opaque black/purple-colored 1995 Merlot Oakville (100 cases) possesses an expressive blueberry-scented nose that is a perfect match for its sumptuous personality. The wine exhibits superb richness, medium to full body, and a natural texture, with sensual levels of fruit and glycerin. It is a full-bodied, seamlessly styled Merlot that should drink well for a decade. This exquisite wine merits the attention of serious wine drinkers.

Lovers of the underrated Petite Sirah varietal will adore Behrens and Hitchcock's 1995, which is close in quality to the extraordinary Petite Sirahs from Ridge's York Creek and Turley's Hayne Vineyard. Boasting 15.2% alcohol, this dense black/purple-colored wine is very full-bodied and extremely powerful, with low acidity, a blackberry, blueberry, cassis character, some pepper, and extraordinary viscosity and intensity. This huge, mouthcoating style of Petite Sirah is not for everybody, but for fans of this wine, it is a knockout. It should drink well for two decades.

The two formidable Cabernet Sauvignons are among the superstars of the 1995 vintage. I do have one reservation with respect to the 1995 Cabernet Sauvignon Ink Grade—some leesy, mercaptan notes in the nose are at first disconcerting. However, they quickly blow off as the wine is exposed to air. Once past that, the wine's opaque purple color and blueberry and exotic floral notes (orchids) are impressive. Ripe and dense, with fabulous flavor concentration, and a long, multilayered, textured personality that caresses and saturates the palate with copious quantities of fruit, glycerin, and richness, this is a large-scaled but beautifully balanced Cabernet Sauvignon that should be at its best with another 2–3 years of cellaring, and last for 15 or more years. The 1995 Cabernet Sauvignon TLK Ranch is a powerhouse, but exhibits remarkable symmetry for its massive size. The color is saturated purple, and the wine possesses fabulously sweet blackberry, blueberry, and cassis aromas nicely dosed with subtle, toasty oak. Thick, juicy, and full-bodied, with outstanding purity and admirably integrated acidity, tannin, and alcohol, this stunningly proportioned Cabernet Sauvignon possesses sweet tannin and low acidity, giving it up-front appeal. However, all the component parts are present for 15–20 years of cellaring.

Except for the Trinity County Cabernet Sauvignon, the differences between the 1994 Cabernet Sauvignon *cuvées* are negligible. In fact, the wines could be blended together with no loss of character (I actually did such a blending). Nevertheless, I would be happy to own any of these wines. If Behrens and Hitchcock want to continue to offer small quantities of each *cuvée*, so be it . . . they are superb Cabernets. The only non-outstanding example is the excellent 1994 Cabernet Sauvignon Lot 2 Hyampom Vineyard from northern Trinity County, not far from the Oregon border. I do not believe I have ever tasted a Cabernet Sauvignon from this region. The wine possesses a dark purple color, a spicy, sweet, black currant and blueberry-scented nose, medium body, a multiple-layered texture, and a round, generous finish. It should drink well for 12 or more years. The 1994 Cabernet Sauvignon Ink Grade Vineyard Lot 2 offers explosive levels of black fruits. The wine is full-bodied, powerful, and flawlessly made, with sensational concentration and a character not unlike the other Cabernets, but seemingly more evolved aromatically. Anticipated maturity: now–2020. The 1994 Cabernet Sauvignon Cuvée Lola Unfiltered Reserve is singing slightly more loudly than its siblings. The blueberries, cassis, vanilla, toast, high-extract, full body, and silky texture are all present. This *cuvée* possesses even more weight and presence on the palate. If the Cuvée Lola is the most dramatic among this group of impressive wines, the 1994 Cabernet Sauvignon Staglin Vineyard is the most backward. This wine displays all the potential to be superb—natural texture, great ripeness, impeccable purity, full body, and layers of blueberry and cassis fruit. However, the tannin is more pronounced, thus this is a wine to lay away for 5–6 years and drink over the following 10–15.

Did it occur to anyone else that these two seat-of-the-pants wine-makers, along with several dozen other talented producers in California, may well be rewriting the definition of great wine? Think about it. To reiterate, virtually all of these wines are sold by mailing list.

BELLA (SONOMA)

1999 Zinfandel Belle Canyon	Dry Creek	D	91
1999 Zinfandel Big River Ranch	Alexander Valley	D	90
1999 Zinfandel Lilly Hill Estate	Alexander Valley	D	89

This impressive newcomer has fashioned a trio of admirable, well-made Zinfandels that emphasize ripe fruit, a judicious touch of toasty oak, and full-bodied, balanced personalities with high alcohol, but no hotness. The elegant 1999 Zinfandel Lilly Hill Estate exhibits a Burgundy-like character (although it is much fuller-bodied than most Burgundies) in its bouquet of sweet raspberry jam, cherries, and flowers. This full-bodied, firm, pure, powerful offering reveals classy fruit, but delivers plenty of punch on the palate. It should drink well for 5–6 years. The sexy, full-bodied 1999 Zinfandel Big River Ranch boasts an opaque ruby/purple color as well as big, thick aromas of blackberries, cherries, currants, spice box, tobacco, pepper, and smoke. Full-bodied, opulently textured, and succulent, this hedonistic offering will provide outstanding drinking over the next 3–5 years. Lastly, the well-endowed, saturated ruby/purple-colored 1999 Zinfandel Belle Canyon reveals subtle oak notes in its thick, jammy, pure, black cherry fruit, underbrush, and seaweed-scented bouquet. Rich, multidimensional, and layered, with a 20-second finish, it will drink beautifully for 7–8 years. This is a noteworthy newcomer to the Zinfandel sweepstakes.

BELO (NAPA)

1995 Vintage Port Reserve	Napa	D	91

What a surprise! There are 100 cases of this vintage port look-alike produced from the same Portuguese varietals (used for making vintage port) planted in Napa. There is no doubting its complex, licorice, coffee, and sweet jammy blackberry and plum aromas and flavors. Full-bodied, moderately sweet, and a dead-ringer for a top-notch vintage port, this small, artisanal producer has fashioned a gem. Moreover, it is evolved and already drinking beautifully.

BENESSERE (NAPA)

1997 Zinfandel	Napa	C	88
1999 Zinfandel Black Glass Vineyard	Napa	D	90

This winery is dedicated to producing wines from varietals most commonly associated with Italy. Benessere's outstanding, deep ruby/purple-colored 1999 Zinfandel Black Glass Vineyard offers a sweet nose of black fruits intermixed with smoke, dried herbs, and subtle wood. Superrich and explosively ripe with a multilayered texture, this exceptional wine can be drunk now or cellared for 4–5 years. The dark ruby-colored 1997 Zinfandel offers excellent briery fruit woven with pepper and spice. In the mouth, copious quantities of oak make an appearance, but they are nicely complemented by the wine's ripeness, glycerin, and rich, medium-bodied, fruity style. Drink it over the next 1–2 years.

BENZIGER WINERY (SONOMA)

1995 Cabernet Sauvignon Reserve	Sonoma Mountain	D	88+
1995 Imagery Series Cabernet Franc	Alexander Valley	D	90
1994 Imagery Series Cabernet Franc	Alexander Valley	C	88
1995 Imagery Series Malbec Blue Rock Vineyard	Alexander Valley	C	88
1994 Imagery Series Petite Sirah	Paso Robles	C	90
1994 Imagery Series Syrah	Central Coast	C	88
1995 Zinfandel	Sonoma	C	88
1994 Zinfandel	Sonoma	C	88+

This family-owned winery continues to turn out an attractive portfolio of well-made wines. Moreover, given the lofty pricing strategy being employed by many other California wineries, they remain sensibly priced. The 1995 Cabernet Sauvignon Reserve, a blend of 76% Cabernet Sauvignon, 12% Cabernet Franc, and 12% Merlot, is backward, but promising. Rich and fleshy, with copious quantities of black currant and briery fruit, oak, and soil scents, it is medium- to full-bodied and pure, with a textured, layered personality. This large-scaled Cabernet Sauvignon should be at its finest between now–2016.

Produced from grapes grown in the Blue Rock Vineyard in Alexander Valley, Benziger's 1995 Imagery Series Cabernet Franc provides a seductive, silky mouthful of wine. This deep ruby-colored Cabernet Franc offers up an intense, provocative nose of spice, fruitcake, cedar, and black fruits. On the palate, the wine is round, sweet, elegant, and soft. If it's possible for Cabernet Franc to behave as a sumptuous Pinot Noir, this one does. The wine is not likely to make old bones, nor will it please those who like the feel of rough tannin grinding across the palate, but this is a delicious, stylish, complex, silky-smooth Cabernet Franc to drink over the next 3–4 years. The 1995 Imagery Series Malbec, which is also produced from Alexander Valley's Blue Rock Vineyard, will not make California's premier Malbec producer (Dick Arrowood of Arrowood Winery) jealous, but it is a good effort. The nose possesses sweet red currant and raspberry scents, as well as a touch of herbs and earth. This soft, grapy Malbec is a pleasant, plump yet refreshing wine that should drink well for 3–4 years.

An excellent Zinfandel, Benziger's dark ruby/purple-colored 1995 displays textbook aromas of pepper, spice, and black cherries. Deeply etched, full-bodied flavors possess excellent purity and plenty of varietal character. This low-acid, plush, fleshy wine boasts 14.5% alcohol; it can be drunk now and over the next 4–5 years. Benziger's 1994 Zinfandel had not been bottled when I tasted it. It exhibits a dark ruby/purple color, as well as a deep, spicy, lavishly oaked nose. The attack offers gobs of ripe fruit, noticeably American oak notes, and a rich, medium-bodied, spicy style. There is plenty of Zinfandel varietal character displayed in this in-your-face Zin. Drink it over the next 5–6 years.

The 1994 Imagery Series red wine offerings scored well in my peer group tastings. The 1994 Syrah reveals a healthy dark ruby/purple color, plenty of toasty new oak in its peppery nose, and abundant quantities of sweet black currant flavors. This medium- to full-bodied, lush Syrah is ideal for drinking over the next 5–8 years. While I did not detect its presence, the wine includes 4% Viognier in the blend. Benziger's black/purple-colored 1994 Petite Sirah Imagery Series is a monstrous-sized wine displaying huge, roasted herb, smoky black currant fruit with a touch of tar. Full-bodied, moderately tannic, and extremely concentrated, this wine is best aged for 1–3 years and drunk over the subsequent 10–15. Another attractive wine, the 1994 Imagery Series Cabernet Franc, exhibits a dark ruby color, followed by sweet, complex, red and black currant aromas nicely infused with oak and a whiff of menthol. Spicy, medium-bodied, with excellent depth, adequate acidity, but little tannin, this stylish, well-made Cabernet Franc should drink well for the next 5–7 years.

BERINGER (NAPA)

1998	Alluvium Proprietary Red	Knights Valley	D	88
1997	Alluvium Proprietary Red	Knights Valley	D	89
1996	Alluvium Proprietary Red	Knights Valley	D	88+
1995	Alluvium Proprietary Red	Knights Valley	D	89
1994	Alluvium Proprietary Red	Knights Valley	D	89
1999	Alluvium Proprietary White	Knights Valley	C	89
1997	Cabernet Franc	Howell Mountain	C	(87–90)
1996	Cabernet Franc	Howell Mountain	C	89
1995	Cabernet Franc	Howell Mountain	C	90
1995	Cabernet Franc Terre Rouge	Howell Mountain	C	91
1994	Cabernet Franc Terre Rouge	Howell Mountain	C	91
1997	Cabernet Sauvignon	Knights Valley	C	88
1996	Cabernet Sauvignon	Knights Valley	C	88
1994	Cabernet Sauvignon	Knights Valley	C	89
1997	Cabernet Sauvignon Bancroft Ranch	Howell Mountain	E	95
1996	Cabernet Sauvignon Bancroft Ranch	Howell Mountain	E	92+
1995	Cabernet Sauvignon Bancroft Ranch	Howell Mountain	EE	94
1994	Cabernet Sauvignon Bancroft Ranch	Howell Mountain	EE	92
1998	Cabernet Sauvignon Chabot Vineyard	Napa	EE	90
1997	Cabernet Sauvignon Chabot Vineyard	Napa	EE	93
1996	Cabernet Sauvignon Chabot Vineyard	Napa	EE	93+
1995	Cabernet Sauvignon Chabot Vineyard	Napa	E	92+
1994	Cabernet Sauvignon Chabot Vineyard	Napa	E	93+
1997	Cabernet Sauvignon Marston Vineyard	Spring Mountain	E	(89–92)
1996	Cabernet Sauvignon Marston Vineyard	Spring Mountain	E	89
1994	Cabernet Sauvignon Marston Vineyard	Spring Mountain	E	95
1998	Cabernet Sauvignon Private Reserve	Napa	E	89

1997	Cabernet Sauvignon Private Reserve	Napa	E	94
1996	Cabernet Sauvignon Private Reserve	Napa	E	91+
1995	Cabernet Sauvignon Private Reserve	Napa	E	93
1994	Cabernet Sauvignon Private Reserve	Napa	E	94
1998	Cabernet Sauvignon Quarry Vineyard	Napa	E	(86–88)
1997	Cabernet Sauvignon Quarry Vineyard	Napa	E	(86–88)
1998	Cabernet Sauvignon St. Helena Home Vineyard	Napa	E	90
1997	Cabernet Sauvignon St. Helena Home Vineyard	Napa	E	92
1996	Cabernet Sauvignon St. Helena Vineyard	St. Helena	E	88
1995	Cabernet Sauvignon St. Helena Vineyard	St. Helena	E	93
1998	Cabernet Sauvignon State Lane Vineyard	Napa	E	88
1997	Cabernet Sauvignon State Lane Vineyard	Napa	E	90
1996	Cabernet Sauvignon State Lane Vineyard	Napa	E	90
1995	Cabernet Sauvignon State Lane Vineyard	Napa	E	90
1996	Cabernet Sauvignon Terre Rouge	Howell Mountain	E	90
1995	Cabernet Sauvignon Terre Rouge	Howell Mountain	EE	90
1994	Cabernet Sauvignon Terre Rouge	Howell Mountain	EE	88
1997	Cabernet Sauvignon Tre Colline Vineyard	Howell Mountain	EE	93
1996	Cabernet Sauvignon Tre Colline Vineyard	Howell Mountain	EE	88+
1995	Cabernet Sauvignon Tre Colline Vineyard	Howell Mountain	EE	90
1999	Chardonnay Private Reserve	Napa	E	92
1999	Chardonnay Sbragia Limited Release	Napa	E	94
1994	Meritage Red	Knights Valley	D	91
1998	Merlot Bancroft Ranch	Howell Mountain	E	88
1997	Merlot Bancroft Ranch	Howell Mountain	E	92
1996	Merlot Bancroft Ranch	Howell Mountain	E	93
1995	Merlot Bancroft Ranch	Howell Mountain	E	91
1994	Merlot Bancroft Ranch	Howell Mountain	D	92+
1997	Nightingale	Napa	E	91
1998	Petite Sirah Hayne Vineyard	Napa	D	(90–92)
1997	Petite Sirah Hayne Vineyard	Napa	D	91
1996	Petite Sirah Hayne Vineyard	Napa	D	93
1997	Petite Sirah Marston Vineyard	Napa	D	(92–94)
1996	Pinot Noir Stanly Ranch	Napa	D	90+
1995	Pinot Noir Stanly Ranch	Napa	D	90
1998	Syrah Marston Vineyard	Spring Mountain	D	89
1997	Syrah Marston Vineyard	Spring Mountain	D	90+

Beringer's highly respected wine-maker, Ed Sbragia, when asked which he felt were the finest vintages for Cabernet Sauvignon, Merlot, Cabernet Franc, etc., during the decade of the nineties, emphatically stated that 1991, 1997, 1994, and 1990 were the four top years. The largest crops were in 1997 and 1991, and the smallest in 1996 and 1998. The coolest years were 1998 and 1999 (and probably 2000), an interesting succession of three colder than normal years. Beringer has become one of the biggest wine companies in the world, having been acquired by the huge Australian beermeister Foster's. Let's hope they don't change the current formula for success, as Beringer and its sister wineries continue to be staffed by some of the most talented individuals in California winedom.

The 1999 Alluvium Proprietary White is a Bordeaux-inspired blend of 45% Sauvignon Blanc, 45% Sémillon, and the rest Chardonnay and Viognier. It is aged in 50% new oak and put through a complete malolactic fermentation to increase its texture as well as complexity. The result is reminiscent of a white Graves, with notes of passion fruit, a flinty character, spicy oak, and rich, melony, honeysuckle aromas and flavors. This fleshy, potentially outstanding white should age well for 3–4 years. The 1999 Chardonnay Private Reserve (20,000 cases) enjoys about 75% new oak. It is a structured, smoky, buttery, fat effort with oodles of honeyed fruit as well as outstanding ripeness, all wrapped in high-quality wood. Full-bodied and dense, this exceptional wine will drink well for 1–2 years. Beringer has increased the production of their most limited Chardonnay, the Sbragia Limited Release, to 3,500 cases. Made from a selection of the most highly extracted, richest, and densest wines, this Chardonnay can age well for 5–7 years, although it is probably best drunk in its first 3–4. The Sbragia's core component tends to come from Beringer's Gamble Ranch. The 1999 Chardonnay Sbragia Limited Release reveals more structure than previous vintages (due to the cool growing season). Dense and thick, with an unctuous texture as well as fine underlying acidity, smoky oak, rich, leesy, hazelnut married with copious quantities of tropical fruit, and a flamboyant personality, this sensational Chardonnay should drink well for 4–5 years.

Readers should be aware of the serious Petite Sirah and Syrah coming from Beringer. From Spring Mountain, Beringer is producing a Marston Vineyard Syrah. The 1998 exhibits a dense opaque purple color, copious quantities of blackberry, mineral, tar, and licorice aromas and flavors, medium to full body, and sweet tannin in the finish. From this tasting as well as others, it appears Syrah fared better in 1998 than Cabernet Sauvignon. The opaque purple-colored 1997 Syrah Marston Vineyard exhibits a gorgeous nose of blueberry jam, blackberries, minerals, and creosote. Full-bodied, dense, and super-concentrated, this terrific Syrah is backward, and not as open-knit and forward as many California Syrahs. Anticipated maturity: 2003–2020. I thought both the 1997 and 1998 Petite Sirah Hayne Vineyard were exceptional. The black/purple-colored 1997 Petite Sirah Hayne Vineyard reveals a powerful, smoky, black fruit, earth, and mineral-scented bouquet. Closed, but immense in the mouth, with huge tannin as well as gigantic levels of fruit and glycerin, this wine is set for three decades of evolution. It should be cellared for at least 5, possibly 10 years before consumption. Anticipated maturity: 2010–2035. The 1998 Petite Sirah Hayne Vineyard reveals more smoky charcoal notes as well as a more evolved personality. Powerful, dense, and well made, it will age well for 25 years.

The 1998 Cabernet Sauvignon and Merlot-based wines are the lightest produced during the 1990s. They are very good, but readers should not expect wines similar to the blockbuster efforts produced from 1991 through 1996. The 1997s tend to be denser, more concentrated wines. The 1998 Alluvium Proprietary Red is a blend of 75% Merlot, 20% Cabernet Sauvignon, and 5% Petit Verdot, Malbec, and Cabernet Franc from Beringer's holdings in Knights Valley. It offers a classy nose of minerals, lead pencil, plums, raspberries, and cherries. Drink this elegant, medium-bodied offering over the next 5–7 years. From Howell Mountain, an area that produced more compressed, herbaceous 1998s, the 1998 Merlot Bancroft Ranch was performing better with another year of aging. While lighter than most vintages, the 1998 reveals herb-tinged black cherries and plums. Charming, round, and medium-bodied, it is best drunk over the next 5–6 years. A strong effort, the 1998 Cabernet Sauvignon Private Reserve exhibits a dense ruby/purple color as well as a moderately intense bouquet of black currants infused with olive, smoke, licorice, and new oak. Supple, medium-bodied, and surprisingly evolved, with sweet fruit on the mid-palate and in the finish, it is a harmonious, charming offering to enjoy over the next 7–8 years.

Beringer's single-vineyard Cabernet Sauvignons are culled from their top vineyards, many of which are used in the Private Reserve blend. These are usually available in 200-case lots and are largely sold to Beringer's mailing list or directly from the winery. The tasting notes are short because of the wines' limited availability. The 1998 Cabernet Sauvignon State Lane Vineyard (this vineyard was recently sold and will appear in 3–4 years under the name Kapcsandy Estates) exhibits sweet cranberry, tobacco leaf, spice box, and sour cherry notes, medium body, and an elegant, straightforward finish. It should drink well for a decade. One of Beringer's outstanding single-vineyard Cabernets is the 1998 Cabernet Sauvignon Chabot Vineyard. Like all of these single-vineyard wines, it is produced from 100% Cabernet Sauvignon. Aromas of coffee, licorice, plums, blackberries, and currants emerge from the moderately intense bouquet. This opaque ruby-colored, dense, medium-bodied 1998 offers attractive fruit extract as well as concentration. Drink it over the next 10–12 years. The 1998 Cabernet Sauvignon St. Helena Home Vineyard looks to be another successful effort in this challenging year. A dense ruby color is followed by sweet, ripe black currant and cassis fruit. This open-knit, low-acid, evolved, fleshy, opulent Cabernet should drink well for 10–12 years.

As the following notes indicate, all of the 1997s possess denser, more opaque colors, riper fruit, and more body, volume, and expressive personalities than their 1998 counterparts. The 1997 Cabernet Sauvignon Knights Valley is an excellent introduction to Beringer's style. It offers black fruits, a touch of licorice and cedar, a supple texture, medium to full body, and a soft finish. Drink this delicious Cabernet during its first decade of life. There are 15,000 cases of the 1997 Cabernet Sauvignon Private Reserve. Composed of 97% Cabernet Sauvignon and 3% Cabernet Franc, and aged in 100% new French oak for 22–24 months, it is a sensational effort. The opaque plum/purple color is followed by a superb nose of smoked herbs, melted licorice, and black currant jam. Full-bodied, with a silky texture and an opulent personality, this sexy, full-throttle Cabernet Sauvignon will be delicious young, yet last for 18–20 years. The 1997 Cabernet Sauvignon State Lane Vineyard is an elegant, finesse-styled wine with medium to full body, a seamless personality, abundant mineral, red and black currant fruit flavors, as well as a supple texture and finish. Not a big wine (13.8% alcohol), it should drink well for 10–12 years. The 1997 Cabernet Sauvignon St. Helena Home Vineyard offers copious quantities of blackberry/cassis fruit, in addition to more tannin and structure than the Quarry or State Lane offerings. Spicy, with outstanding ripeness, a big, chewy mid-section, and intriguing roasted coffee and black currant flavors, this will be a large-scaled Cabernet to drink during its first 15 years of life. From the cooler climate Spring Mountain vineyard, the 1997 Cabernet Sauvignon Marston Vineyard is a distinctive blackberry and blueberry-scented and -flavored wine, with medium body, moderately high tannin, and a long finish. The provocative 1997 Cabernet Sauvignon Chabot Vineyard is a denser wine with more loamy soil scents intermixed with chocolate, licorice, creosote, and copious blackberry and cassis fruit. Full-bodied and chewy, with superb concentration, symmetry, and purity, as well as moderate tannin in the finish, it will be at its finest between 2004–2022. The beautiful 1997 Cabernet Sauvignon Tre Colline offers sexy, ostentatious notes of licorice, cherry liqueur, black fruits, and spicy oak. On the palate, cigar box flavors add to the mélange of complex characteristics found in the bouquet. Fleshy, juicy, and succulent, with dazzling ripeness, low acidity, and sweet, well-integrated tannin, it will be ready to drink between now–2020. One of the most prodigious 1997 Beringer wines is the 1997 Cabernet Sauvignon Bancroft Ranch. Opaque purple-colored, with an extroverted, floral, blueberry, mineral, and black currant–scented bouquet, this formidably endowed Cabernet possesses dazzling concentration, explosive richness that stains the palate, and finishes with sensational extract and balance. The tannin is high, but sweet and well integrated. This large-scaled, muscular, mountain Cabernet Sauvignon will require 3–5 years of patience. Anticipated maturity: 2005–2025.

The 1997 Merlot Bancroft Ranch (100% new oak) is a dense, full-bodied effort exhibiting black cherry liqueur, chocolate, mineral, and lead pencil aromas and flavors. Fleshy and chewy, it will be undeniably seductive upon release. It should drink well for 15+ years.

To date, Beringer's Alluvium Proprietary Red has been a Merlot-dominated *cuvée*, with small quantities of Cabernet Sauvignon, Cabernet Franc, Petit Verdot, and occasionally Malbec thrown in to provide additional nuances. The 1997 Alluvium Proprietary Red (about 77% Merlot) was showing better in 2000 than it was the previous year. Most of the fruit comes from Beringer's Knights Valley vineyard, and it sees 40% new oak during its upbringing. It is meant to be an elegant wine, and the 1997 offers intense berry and mocha-tinged fruit with background notes of pencil shavings, minerals, and flowers, a lush mid-section, and sweet tannin in the finish. Seamless for such a young wine (a hallmark of the finest 1997s), it should drink well for 10–15 years. A new single-vineyard offering, the medium ruby/purple-colored 1997 Cabernet Sauvignon Quarry Vineyard exhibits a round, supple-textured personality, depth, and, I suspect, early maturity. It should drink well upon release and last for 10–12 years. Lighter and softer, with less persistence and intensity once past the berry/black currant–scented nose, the 1998 Cabernet Sauvignon Quarry Vineyard will be a candidate for early consumption, over the next 7–8 years.

Two wines of compelling concentration and attention-getting power are the 1996 Petite Sirah Hayne Vineyard and 1997 Petite Sirah Marston Vineyard. Both of these wines saw 100% new oak (50% American and 50% French). They are hugely extracted, black/purple-colored, totally unevolved wines. The 1996 Petite Sirah Hayne Vineyard is beginning to reveal secondary aromas of smoke, Asian spices, and cigar box, in addition to classic cassis, blackberry flavors. A monster wine, it needs at least 5–7 years of cellaring; it will keep for 2–3 decades. The 1997 Petite Sirah Marston Vineyard has a small amount of fruit (25%) from the Hayne Vineyard added to the blend. This wine boasts phenomenal intensity, massive body, and a boatload of tannin and glycerin. A huge example, it will not become civilized for another 5–6 years. It should keep for 20–25 years.

The single-vineyard Cabernet Francs from Howell Mountain are aged in 100% new French oak, which has been soaked up nicely. These are charming, softer, less extracted offerings than the single vineyard Merlots or Cabernet Sauvignons. Nevertheless, they are not wimpish wines. The dark ruby/purple-colored 1995 Cabernet Franc Howell Mountain offers a complex nose of herbs, earth, black fruits, and spicy wood. Medium-bodied, round, and velvety-textured, this attractive wine needs to be consumed during its first decade of life. The same finesse, elegance, spice, and fruit character can be found in the medium-bodied 1996 Cabernet Franc Howell Mountain. However, its aromatics include a slight touch of menthol/mint. Drink this stylish wine over the next 7–8 years. The 1997 Cabernet Franc Howell Mountain is cut from the same mold. Spicy, with ripe fruit and intelligently put together, it is not quite as extracted or as flavorful as the 1995 or 1996. However, it should put on more weight after additional cask aging.

I am largely unconvinced by Beringer's Pinot Noirs. Progress has been made, but this is one varietal that appears to be the Achilles' heel in what is otherwise a superb portfolio. There are now two *cuvées*, a Stanly Ranch and a North Coast offering. Beringer occasionally produces merely mortal wines. However, both the 1995 and 1996 Pinot Noir Stanly Ranch are major improvements. The 1995 Pinot Noir Stanly Ranch actually requires a year or two in the bottle. This black/purple-colored wine exhibits a sweet nose of plum and black cherry fruit, followed by subtle spicy, toasty, oaky notes. In the mouth, it is medium-bodied and rich, with plenty of length, and light to moderate tannin. It should age well for 7–8 years. The deep ruby/purple-colored 1996 Pinot Noir Stanly Ranch reveals a blueberry/raspberry-scented nose. The wine is dense and chewy, with excellent purity and light tannin in the finish. Lower in acidity, with softer tannin than the 1995, the 1996 is significantly more concentrated than the 1994 (as is the 1995).

Beringer does a superb job with its production from the Bancroft Ranch on Howell Mountain. About 8,000 cases of their single-vineyard Merlot are produced. This wine spends 20 months in French oak coopered by the well-known house of Seguin-Moreau. The 1995 Merlot Bancroft Ranch exhibits an opaque ruby/purple color, followed by a stunning nose of chocolate, minerals, black cherries, and toast. A serious, mountain-styled Merlot, it displays full body, outstanding concentration and purity, and moderate tannin. It needs to be cellared for another 2–3 years, but will last 15 years. The 1996 Merlot Bancroft Ranch was showing much better when I tasted it in 1998 than it did 11 months earlier. The wine boasts a saturated purple color, as well as an exquisite nose of brandy-infused black cherries intermixed with melted chocolate. Dense and full-bodied, with striking sweetness and purity, this multi-layered Merlot has developed beautifully. Although it will benefit from another 4–5 years of bottle age, it can be drunk now or cellared. It, too, will keep for 15 years. The 1994 Merlot Bancroft Ranch opens quickly in the glass. The dark ruby/purple color is followed by smoky, chocolaty, and black cherry aromas with new oak in the background. In the mouth, this wine is full-bodied, with explosive levels of glycerin and richness on the back of the palate. Dense, concentrated, tannic, and angular, it is capable of lasting 15+ years. In fact, I recommend 3–4 years of cellaring before serious consumption begins.

The following vintages of Beringer's Alluvium Proprietary Red all include a minimum of 75% Merlot, with 10–20% Cabernet Sauvignon. These wines are made in a claret style, with less power and extraction, but more finesse and accessibility. They appear to contain enough tannin for 10–12 years of aging potential. The 1995 Alluvium Proprietary Red reveals a dark ruby color, an elegant, berry, earth, and cherry-scented nose, medium to full body, and admirable complexity and accessibility. When I tasted it in 1997, I thought the wine was outstanding. While I rated it slightly lower after retasting it in 1998, it is nevertheless an excellent offering. I would opt for drinking it over the next 7–10 years. The 1996 Alluvium Proprietary Red is a lusher, riper wine with nicely displayed sweet black currant and cherry fruit. Although there is some tannin at the back of the mouth, the wine's appeal is its savory, fleshy, up-front style and purity of fruit, with an absence of aggressive acidity, tannin, or alcohol. It should drink well for a decade. The 1994 Alluvium is a textbook proprietary wine. It displays a dark ruby color, followed by an attractive black fruit–scented nose with subtle toasty oak intertwined with herbs, earth, and chocolaty notes. In the mouth, black cherry fruit and toast are presented in a medium- to full-bodied, silky-smooth, delicious format. Very accessible, it should continue to drink well for a decade.

Beringer's limited production, single-vineyard Cabernet Sauvignons are part of what Beringer calls their "Vineyard Collection." Produced in 200-case lots, readers expecting to find them sitting on a shelf in their local retail shops will be disappointed, as they are destined to be sold through Beringer's mailing list or directly from the winery. That is not the case with the Knights Valley Cabernet Sauvignon or Private Reserve Cabernet Sauvignon, both of which are made in abundant quantities. One of the safest choices a consumer can make, both have been consistently fine and accurate representations of Cabernet's varietal characteristics. The 1996 Cabernet Sauvignon Knights Valley offers more smokiness intertwined with jammy black currant fruit. The wine's excellent richness, plush, user-friendly style, and fruit-driven personality have resulted in a crowd-pleasing, modestly priced Cabernet Sauvignon that should last for a decade or more. The excellent, nearly outstanding 1994 Cabernet Sauvignon Knights Valley exhibits a dark ruby/purple color and a sweet black currant–scented nose with smoky oak and earthy, chocolaty notes. I thought this medium-bodied, richly fruity, delicious wine was outstanding in 1996, but slightly less prodigious in 1997. It should drink well for a decade, and possibly earn an even higher score.

I cannot recall a disappointing vintage of Beringer's Private Reserve Cabernet Sauvignon.

A production of 10,000–15,000 cases makes the wine's outstanding quality even more enviable. The 1995 Cabernet Sauvignon Private Reserve is a full-bodied, explosively rich, deep purple-colored wine bursting with ripe fruit. It displays smoky oak, gobs of cassis, a touch of cigar box and cedar, and a layered, multidimensional feel. This voluptuous, seductive offering is already drinking well, yet should age effortlessly for 15–20 years. The 1996 Cabernet Sauvignon Private Reserve reveals more concentration as well as higher tannin. I know it is a trade-off, but I suspect this vintage will not be as sexy in its youthfulness as the 1995. The black ruby/purple-colored 1996 offers more licorice, in addition to the obvious levels of toast, jammy black currant fruit, and spice notes. Structured, full-bodied, and powerful, this may be a Private Reserve to cellar for several years and consume over the subsequent 15–18. By the way, statisticians should note that the Private Reserve is always at least 97% Cabernet Sauvignon and aged for 22–24 months in 100% new French oak. One of the common threads I find in the Private Reserve Cabernet Sauvignon is a smoky, chocolaty, licorice character that works well with the lavish quantities of fruit and glycerin these wines possess. The terrific 1994 Cabernet Sauvignon Private Reserve offers an opaque purple color, a gorgeous nose of toasty oak, and a silky, concentrated texture with unobtrusive acidity or tannin. The wine possesses layered richness, remarkable balance, sweet, pure fruit, and a finish that lasts for nearly 30 seconds. These wines are aged in 100% new oak, and tend to possesses at least 97% Cabernet Sauvignon, with the balance Cabernet Franc. Amazingly, the oak is not a pronounced component in the final wine, a testament to excellent winemaking and the concentration these wines possess. Like so many top 1994s from Napa and Sonoma, this wine was accessible when released in early 1998, but will age well for two decades.

The State Lane Vineyard is situated on extremely rocky soil in the Yountville area. Beringer's 1995 Cabernet Sauvignon State Lane Vineyard possess a St.-Emilion-like cherry, tobacco, and sweet currant-scented nose, and soft, round, ripe, berry flavors. A seductively styled, medium- to full-bodied, accessible Cabernet, it is ideal for consuming now and over the next 15 years. The same silky tannins can be found in the 1996 Cabernet Sauvignon State Lane Vineyard. This vintage tended to produce harder, more tannic and rustic wines, but that is not the case with this *cuvée*. The wine possesses plenty of sweet, jammy, plum and black currant fruit, cigar box, and spice aromas, some cedar, and a silky, layered, lush, medium- to full-bodied personality. It can be drunk during its first 15–18 years of life.

The medium- to full-bodied 1996 Cabernet Sauvignon Marston Vineyard reveals more red currant notes than the 1997, but is slightly less concentrated. It is an impressively constructed, rich wine that is not quite as seductive and forward as the State Lane offering. I envision it lasting for two decades. Two hundred cases were produced of the 1994 Cabernet Sauvignon Marston Vineyard. This stunning Cabernet boasts a dense black/purple color, jammy blueberry and cassis aromas, and a fruit-driven style. Despite being aged in 100% new oak, little wood is noticeable in this sexy, voluptuously textured, dazzlingly concentrated, richly fruity wine. Its low acidity and purity make for a compellingly drinkable Cabernet Sauvignon. Anticipated maturity: now–2012.

Beringer's Cabernet Sauvignon Tre Colline from Howell Mountain debuted in 1995. These are tannic, backward, full-bodied wines with considerable punch and depth. The 1995 is a multidimensional, spicy wine with copious quantities of black currant fruit intermixed with cedar and weedy tobacco. Full-bodied, pure, and nicely textured, it should be at its best with another 2–3 years of cellaring, and keep for two decades. The dense purple-colored 1996 Cabernet Sauvignon Tre Colline is backward, tannic, and in need of 5–6 years of bottle age. All the component parts are present, but this wine requires patience.

The St. Helena Vineyard Cabernet Sauvignon series offers another interesting style. The 1995 Cabernet Sauvignon St. Helena Vineyard exhibits a fragrant, smoky nose of loamy soil scents, underbrush, and ripe, brandy-infused black currants and cherries. This rich wine is full-bodied, with superb density and a lush texture. Beautifully made and complex, with a terrific mid-palate and length (always signs of high quality), it can be drunk now or cellared for 15+ years. The 1996 Cabernet Sauvignon St. Helena Vineyard is the antithesis of the 1995—stern, tannic, and backward. While broodingly powerful and brawny, its tannin dominates at present. It was closed when I tasted it, so I am anxious to retaste it prior to release.

Undoubtedly the best-known Beringer single-vineyard Cabernet is from their Chabot Vineyard. Like the other offerings in this series, this is a 100% Cabernet Sauvignon aged in 100% new-oak casks. The accessible 1995 Cabernet Sauvignon Chabot Vineyard reveals medium to full body and a knockout nose of roasted herbs, grilled meats, coffee, cassis, and cherry fruit. In the mouth, it is viscous and full-bodied, with a chewy mid-section and a spicy, long, rich finish. It will last for two decades. The 1996 Cabernet Sauvignon Chabot Vineyard offers aromas and flavors of chocolate liqueur infused with brandy as well as loamy soil intermixed with damp forest, underbrush scents. Full-bodied, with massive power, and chewy, thick, structured, chocolaty fruit flavors, this is a complex yet backward, formidably endowed Cabernet Sauvignon with palate-staining levels of extract and tannin. Give it 3–4 years of bottle age, and consume it over the following two decades. The 1994 Cabernet Sauvignon Chabot Vineyard is a backward, muscular wine that is 5–7 years away from drinkability. With airing, the wine reluctantly gives up scents of pepper, iodine, cassis, mint, and earth. This full-bodied, large-scaled Cabernet begs for more bottle time. This wine should only be purchased by those willing to invest patience, as it will not provide enjoyable drinking when young.

The limited production Cabernet Sauvignon Bancroft Ranch offerings are also outstanding. Previously I had a slight preference for the 1996 over the 1995, but an extra year of bottle age has caused the 1995 to leap-frog over the 1996. For now, the 1995 looks to be slightly more complete and multidimensional than the 1996, but readers should look out for the phenomenal 1997. The 1995 Cabernet Sauvignon Bancroft Ranch exhibits an opaque black/purple color and stunning aromatics consisting of minerals, blueberries, blackberries, and cassis. Terrific in the mouth, it offers full body, a racy, chewy texture, high tannin, but wonderful sweetness and balance. It was impressive and flamboyant when I tasted it in September 1998. Anticipated maturity: now–2025. The 1996 Cabernet Sauvignon Bancroft Ranch may possess an even more saturated, thicker, black/purple color. Some tannin has emerged since I tasted it last year, when it was far more velvety. This is a powerhouse, extremely full-bodied, palate-staining wine. Its enormous extract, richness, and elevated tannin seem to suggest this wine is about ready to settle down for a long period of dormancy. Anticipated maturity: 2005–2025. Also look for the 1994 Cabernet Sauvignon Bancroft Vineyard. This opaque purple-colored wine offers toasty, smoky oak in its nose, as well as the telltale cassis and mineral aromas that emerge from Howell Mountain wines. Rich, powerful, full-bodied flavors, and excellent purity and sweetness of fruit further characterize this broad-shouldered wine. There is also plenty of tannin, suggesting it will require 3–4 years of cellaring after its release. It will keep for two decades.

A Cabernet Sauvignon Terre Rouge was produced in 1994, 1995, and 1996. These are among the more backward, austere, and angular of these single-vineyard wines. The 1994 Cabernet Sauvignon Terre Rouge reveals a dark ruby color, spice, leafy tobacco, and earthy aromas, sweet black cherry and cassis fruit, medium body, and moderate tannin. It will need 2–4 years of cellaring and keep for 15 or more. The 1995 Cabernet Sauvignon Terre Rouge offers a dense, dark purple color, more fatness and fleshiness to its texture, fuller body, and concentrated, rich flavors. More forward than the 1994, with less austerity, it should drink well for 12–15 years. I found the 1996 Cabernet Sauvignon Terre Rouge to be more fruit- than structure-driven. It exhibits copious quantities of red and black fruit in its nose, low acidity, obvious glycerin, a thick, chewy texture, and a spicy, medium- to full-bodied finish. Although the 1996 will not be as backward as the 1994, neither will it be as fleshy as the 1995.

Beringer's 1995 Cabernet Franc Terre Rouge possesses sweet fruit, along with a structured feel. Medium-bodied, with an attractive red and black currant, mineral, spicy-scented nose, this wine displays a moderately intense personality, as well as spice and sweet tannin in the finish. It should drink well young, yet keep for 10–12 years. The 1994 Cabernet Franc Terre Rouge exhibits a dense ruby/purple color, a spicy, fragrant, black fruit, mineral, and chocolaty nose, rich flavors, and a moderately weighty feel on the palate. The wine's tannin and acidity are soft and well integrated. Although it is easy to understand and drink, this Cabernet Franc promises to evolve gracefully for a decade.

Beringer is also turning out some excellent to outstanding Meritage blends, which are mostly Merlot-based wines. The 1994 is composed of 80% Merlot and 20% Cabernet Sauvignon from grapes grown in the Knights Valley. Fat, rich, and ripe, the 1994 Meritage should ensure that Merlot fans have a steady fix of high-quality Merlot for the next several years.

Lastly, there are 400 cases of the 1997 Nightingale, a blend of botrytis-infected Sémillon (70%) and Sauvignon Blanc (30%). A Sauternes look-alike, it boasts a honeyed pineapple, coconut, assorted tropical fruit–scented nose and flavors. Viscous, with good underlying acidity, the wood is subtle, not aggressive. I cannot imagine these wines will age for 30–50 years like a great French Sauternes, but this delicious offering should keep for a decade.

Past Glories: 1993 Alluvium Red (90), 1993 Cabernet Sauvignon (90), 1993 Cabernet Sauvignon Chabot Vineyard (90?), 1993 Meritage Red (90), 1993 Merlot Bancroft Ranch (93+), Cabernet Sauvignon Private Reserve—1994 (95), 1993 (92+), 1991 (95), 1990 (93), 1987 (93), 1986 (91)

ROBERT BIALE VINEYARDS (NAPA)

1999 Zinfandel Aldo's Vineyard	Napa	D	91
1996 Zinfandel Aldo's Vineyard	Napa	D	90
1999 Zinfandel Black Chicken Vineyard	Napa	D	89
1999 Zinfandel Falleri Vineyard	Napa	EE (1.5 ml)	93
1999 Zinfandel Monte Rosso Vineyard	Sonoma	D	91
1996 Zinfandel Monte Rosso Vineyard	Sonoma	D	92
1999 Zinfandel Old Crane Ranch	Napa	D	88
1996 Zinfandel Old Crane Ranch	Napa	D	90
1999 Zinfandel Robert Biale Vineyards	Sonoma	D	90
1999 Zinfandel Spenker Vineyard	Lodi	D	90
1999 Zinfandel Valsecchi Vineyard	Sonoma	D	93

Biale is emerging as one of California's top half-dozen or so Zinfandel producers. His 1999s are consistently brilliant efforts. For starters, the 1999 Zinfandel Spenker Vineyard (14.8% alcohol) is a knockout example of Zinfandel from the unheralded Lodi region. Its dense ruby/purple color is accompanied by copious quantities of sweet, uncomplicated black cherry and berry fruit offered in a spicy, full-bodied, luxuriously rich style. It is delicious to drink now and over the next 3–4 years. Similar in strength (14.9% alcohol), the dense ruby/purple-colored 1999 Zinfandel Old Crane Ranch exhibits a more subdued aromatic profile that, with air, offers up black cherry and berry fruit intertwined with pepper and underbrush scents. More structured and monolithic, with some tannin, it appears to be more ageworthy, but my experience has shown that Zinfandel rarely improves after 5–7 years in the bottle. The 1999 Zinfandel Aldo's Vineyard (14.9% alcohol) reveals a Rhône Valley–like perfume of dried Provençal herbs, pepper, black cherries, and spicy oak. It is voluptuously textured, full-bodied, rich, pure, and harmonious. Consume this sumptuous, large-scaled, dry, friendly Zinfandel over the next 5–6 years. The dark ruby-colored 1999 Zinfandel Robert Biale Vineyards (14.9% alcohol) offers up a sweet, spicy nose of herbs, jammy cherry fruit, pepper, and earth. Medium- to full-bodied, supple, tangy, and spicy, with plenty of flesh and fruit, it will drink well for 2–3 years.

A new vineyard experience for me, the 1999 Zinfandel Valsecchi Vineyard (15.2% alcohol) exhibits an impressively saturated ruby color as well as a sumptuously sweet nose of pure black fruits infused with floral and blueberry characteristics. It possesses a Pomerol-like lushness, berry fruit (cherries, blueberries, and blackberries), full body, and a seamless personality. While it will not make old bones, it will provide compelling drinking over the next 4–6 years. Another Napa offering, the dense ruby-colored 1999 Zinfandel Black Chicken Vineyard (15.3% alcohol) displays a funky bouquet of herbs, oak, and lees, with none of the fruit notes found in its siblings. In the mouth, however, the wine sings. It has a fat, succulent texture, medium to full body, excellent purity, and a long, 20–30-second finish. If the nose develops more nuances, this wine may merit a 90-point score. Consumption over the next 3–4 years is suggested. From a well-known site, the 1999 Zinfandel Monte Rosso Vineyard (15% alcohol) displays strikingly pure aromatics consisting of black fruits, crushed stones, pepper, and earth. Impeccably balanced, full-bodied, with ripe, clean fruit, and a long, thick, rich, smooth finish, it is another terrific effort. The 1999 Zinfandel Falleri Vineyard (15.2% alcohol) is available only in magnums. There were less than 50 cases produced. From a vineyard near Calistoga, it is a dense ruby/purple-colored offering revealing a bouquet reminiscent of a top-class Châteauneuf-du-Pape. Pepper, black cherry jam, and earth aromas are followed by a full-bodied, velvety-textured, ripe, heady Zinfandel with a boatload of fruit, glycerin, and character. It should drink well for 5–7 years. These are all terrific examples of Zinfandel.

Biale's 1996s are all outstanding Zinfandel. The 1996 Zinfandel Aldo's Vineyard (875 cases) is an unfiltered, sexy wine with considerable personality. This dark plum-colored effort offers up earthy, jammy, sweet cranberry and raspberry notes along with pepper, incense, and spice. Generous, with a robust constitution and gobs of glycerin (14.6% alcohol), this supple, full-bodied, concentrated, hedonistic, opulently textured Zinfandel should be consumed over the next 3–4 years. While it is difficult to pick a favorite from this exceptional trio of 1996s, I had a slight preference for the unfiltered 1996 Zinfandel Monte Rosso Vineyard (675 cases produced). It possesses the most saturated plum/purple color and displays its personality in a flamboyant, full-bodied manner. This gorgeous Zin boasts copious quantities of pepper, spice, and rich cherry/black raspberry jam–like notes. The subtle oak influence adds to the creamy texture of this concentrated, dramatically styled wine. Drink this sinfully rich Zinfandel now and over the next 5–6 years. Lastly, the 1996 Zinfandel Old Crane Ranch (800 cases bottled without filtration) is another hedonistic, fat, layered, ostentatious Zinfandel with copious quantities of berry fruit, glycerin, extract, and alcohol (15.4%). The wine's low acidity, lavish richness, and attention-getting style will be immensely pleasing to Zinfandel enthusiasts over the next 4–5 years.

BLACKJACK RANCH (SANTA BARBARA)

1997	Cabernet Sauvignon	Santa Barbara	D	(87–90)
1999	Harmonie Proprietary Red Wine	Santa Barbara	D	92
1997	Harmonie Proprietary Red Wine	Santa Barbara	D	90
1999	Le Mas Rouge	Santa Barbara/ San Luis Obispo	C	88
1999	Merlot Billy Goat Hill Estate	Santa Barbara	D	93
1998	Pinot Noir Laetitia Vineyard	San Luis Obispo	D	88
1999	Syrah Estate	Santa Barbara	D	87
1998	Syrah Estate	Santa Barbara	D	89

This promising new performer, situated outside the village of Los Olives, is run by Roger Wisted, who farms approximately 17 acres. Wisted is attempting to capture as much as possible in the wines of Santa Barbara. His first releases were impressive offerings, and in 1999 a Syrah was also produced. Roger Wisted has turned out some very interesting Rhône Ranger *cuvées*. The dark ruby-colored 1998 Syrah Estate reveals a Pinot Noir–like complexity in its smoky, cassis, and camphor-scented bouquet. Flavors of plums, herbs, and pepper are apparent in this medium-bodied, serious, complex Syrah. Its style is a combination of a Côte d'Or red Burgundy and a southern Rhône Crozes-Hermitage. Drink it over the next 6–7 years. From a cooler year, the 1999 Syrah Estate exhibits more herbaceousness as well as a tighter, more restrained and closed style. However, there is plenty of underlying complexity and fruit. The less expensive 1999 Le Mas Rouge, a blend of Santa Barbara and San Luis Obispo fruit, reveals copious notes of cherries, Provençal herbs, crushed pepper, and a hint of *garrigue*. It is a medium-bodied, fun wine to enjoy during its first 3–4 years of life.

Wisted's breakthrough efforts are the Merlot and Cabernet Sauvignon produced in 1999, a cool year that managed to produce wines of exceptional richness and concentration, at least for Blackjack Ranch. The awesome 1999 Merlot Billy Goat Hill Estate (544 cases) is one of the finest produced in California. The fact that it is from Santa Barbara is a revelation. It reminds me of the 1990 Clinet from Pomerol. A saturated purple color is followed by an extraordinary bouquet of espresso, black fruits, cocoa, and vanilla, an explosive attack, an unctuous texture, admirable freshness, and amazing concentration and thickness. It will drink well for 15 years. If this wine were from Napa Valley, it would be selling for three times the price. Readers take note. Another great achievement is the 1999 Harmonie, a blend of 51% Cabernet Sauvignon, 39% Cabernet Franc, 7% Merlot, and 3% Syrah. An opaque black/purple color is accompanied by scents of blackberry liqueur intertwined with cassis, licorice, graphite, and toast. Full-bodied, with a seamless texture, beautifully integrated acidity and tannin, and a long, layered, concentrated finish, it will live for two decades.

The red wine program includes a fine Pinot Noir. The 1998 Laetitia Vineyard could easily pass for a good premier cru from Vosne-Romanée. It exhibits an earthy, spicy, vanilla, floral, and cherry-scented bouquet, an elegant, medium-bodied personality, sweet fruit, and unmistakable Pinot characteristics. This complex effort should continue to develop for 4–5 years. My notes state that this wine had a 91-point bouquet and 87-point flavors. The impressive 1997 Harmonie Proprietary Red Wine (a blend of 86% Cabernet Sauvignon, 6% Petit Verdot, 4% Cabernet Franc, and 4% Merlot) offers a complex nose of black fruits, roasted coffee, dried herbs, and earth. The wine possesses outstanding ripeness, sweet, rich fruit, firm tannin, a nicely delineated personality, as well as vigor and exuberance. Age this wine for another 3–4 years; it should evolve nicely for 15+.

The 1997 Cabernet Sauvignon (under 500 cases) is made from purchased fruit grown in a 17-year-old vineyard in Los Olives. Aged in equal parts American and French oak, it is still grapy, unevolved, and backward, but reveals outstanding potential. The vegetal character often found in Cabernets from this area is not present in this offering. Made from extremely ripe fruit, Blackjack Ranch's 1997 Cabernet Sauvignon is an opaque black/purple-colored wine with moderately intense aromatics consisting of cassis, blackberries, licorice, and cigar box scents. The oak is well integrated and the tannin high, but the wine possesses a sweet, rich mid-palate, excellent to outstanding texture, and fine length. It should be an impressive debut release for Roger Wisted's Blackjack Ranch. Anticipated maturity: now–2020.

BLOCKHEADIA RINGNOSII (NAPA)

1998	Zinfandel	Napa	C	89
1998	Zinfandel	Russian River	C	88
1999	Zinfandel Lorenza Lake Winery	Napa	C	90

Michael Ouellette, the former manager of the popular Napa Valley bistro Mustard's Grill, is now a full-time wine-maker. His Rhône Valley–inspired, full-throttle 1999 Zinfandel Lorenza Lake offers up scents of pepper, kirsch, dried Provençal herbs, spices, and earth. Fleshy, full-bodied, hedonistic, and chewy, with outstanding concentration, excellent purity, and abundant personality, this is a sumptuous Zinfandel to enjoy over the next 3–4 years.

The delicious, full-throttle 1998 Zinfandel Napa exhibits a dense ruby/purple color and a Gigondas-like bouquet and flavors of pepper, smoke, Provençal herbs, black cherries, and blackberries. Full-bodied and chewy, it reveals more of a Rhône-like personality than Zinfandel. Delicious and fleshy, with abundant depth, and a low-acid, plump, chewy finish, it will drink well for 5–7 years. Another Rhône-like offering is the 1998 Zinfandel Russian River. A dark plum/ruby/purple color is accompanied by a moderately intense nose of pepper, spice, plums, dried raspberries, and cherries. Velvety-textured, sexy, and opulent, with abundant quantities of succulent fruit, this is a hedonistic wine to drink over the next 2–3 years. Its medium-bodied fleshiness will offer considerable appeal, but readers looking for a textbook, briery, tangy, cherry, raspberry Zinfandel without a lot of spice will be less impressed with this wine than I was.

BONNY DOON VINEYARD (SANTA CRUZ)

1999 Le Cigare Volant	California	C	87
2000 Old Telegram (Mourvèdre)	California	D	86

The dark ruby/purple-colored 2000 Old Telegram displays an intensely fragrant nose of jammy black raspberries and spice. In the mouth, it is rich and medium- to full-bodied, with admirable layers of flavor and extract. This is a classy, young, expansively flavored, rather elegant Mourvèdre that should age effortlessly for a decade or more.

The 1999 Le Cigare Volant, a Grenache, Mourvèdre, Cinsault, and Syrah blend, is proprietor Randall Grahm's interpretation of a California-styled Châteauneuf-du-Pape. Surprisingly, the best vintage Grahm made was the first one, 1984. The 1999 is a good effort, exhibiting a deep ruby color, plenty of jammy, raspberry, and cherry fruit, medium body, good spice, fine purity, and a long finish. It is ideal for drinking over the next 4–5 years. Think of it as a Côtes du Rhône/St.-Joseph blend, rather than a Châteauneuf-du-Pape.

BREWER-CLIFTON (SANTA BARBARA)

2000 Chardonnay Katherine's Vineyard	Santa Maria	D	92
1999 Chardonnay Katherine's Vineyard	Santa Maria	D	88
2000 Chardonnay Marcella's Vineyard	Santa Maria	D	93+
1999 Chardonnay Marcella's Vineyard	Santa Maria	D	91
2000 Chardonnay Mount Carmel Vineyard	Santa Ynez	D	90
2000 Chardonnay Sweeney Canyon	Santa Ynez	D	94
1999 Chardonnay Sweeney Canyon	Santa Ynez	D	90
1998 Pinot Noir	Santa Maria	D	91
1997 Pinot Noir	Santa Maria	D	90
2000 Pinot Noir Clos Pepé Vineyard	Santa Ynez	D	90
2000 Pinot Noir Julia's Vineyard	Santa Maria	D	94
1997 Pinot Noir Julia's Vineyard	Santa Barbara	D	88
2000 Pinot Noir Melville Vineyard	Santa Ynez	D	96
2000 Pinot Noir Rozak Ranch	Santa Ynez	D	88
2000 Pinot Noir Santa Maria Hills	Santa Maria	D	91
1999 Pinot Noir Santa Maria Hills	Santa Maria	D	92

Greg Brewer and Steve Clifton represent the extraordinary potential that exists in selected microclimates in Santa Barbara County. In a few short years, this young, energetic twosome have astonished this critic with the breadth and complexity of their Chardonnays and Pinot Noirs. Their 2000 Pinot Noirs are among the finest New World Pinots I have ever tasted. Sadly, the production is small, averaging 100–200 cases of each *cuvée*.

The Pinot Noirs are produced from small yields, fermented in one-and-a-half-ton, open-top fermenters, with 100% whole clusters, aged in one-third new French oak, and bottled with neither fining nor filtration. The 2000 Pinot Noir Clos Pepé comes from one of the new vineyards in the cool Santa Rita hills. Exhibiting a premier cru Côtes de Beaune–like style, it offers a dark ruby color along with a sweet perfume of black cherries and apple skins. It is a sexy, charming, full-bodied, lush, generous Pinot Noir to enjoy over the next 6–7 years. The medium ruby-colored 2000 Pinot Noir Rozak Ranch displays a pronounced earthy, peppery, spicy nose, high acidity, a meaty, chewy mid-palate, and a firm finish. It possesses less aromatic and flavor dimension than its siblings, but has plenty of structure. Firm and closed, it is not dissimilar from a structured, moderately tannic Pommard. Anticipated maturity: 2003–2010. There are approximately 200 cases of the stunning 2000 Pinot Noir Santa Maria Hills. This offering reveals a complex nose of earth, figs, black cherries, spice, and apple skin. In the mouth, it is Volnay-like, with sweet red and black fruits, beautifully integrated acidity and tannin, subtle wood, a supple texture, and a 30–35-second finish. This beauty can be drunk now as well as over the next decade. The blockbuster 2000 Pinot Noir Julia's Vineyard is the best effort I have tasted from this well-known site in Santa Maria Valley. Reminiscent of a great vintage of Ponsot's Clos de la Roche Vieilles Vignes, it boasts a dark plum color as well as a broodingly backward but promising nose of cloves, plums, black cherries, flowers, and minerals. It possesses profound concentration, surprisingly high but well-hidden alcohol (15.3%), and a multilayered, sumptuous finish that lasts for nearly 45 seconds. It is a tour de force in New World Pinot Noir. Drink it over the next 7–10 years. Another compelling example is the 2000 Pinot Noir Melville Vineyard, from a new vineyard planted with Dijon clones #114 and #115. This wine gave me a sense of déja vu (when I first tasted the 1990 Domaine de la Romanée Conti La Tâche). An incredibly complex nose of flowers, red and black fruits, earth, and prunes is followed by a full-bodied, fabulously concentrated wine that is extremely light on its feet. With terrific definition, refreshing underlying acidity, and a staggeringly long finish, this outrageously complex, rich Pinot Noir should drink well for a decade. Remarkably, it is made from young vines.

The evolved, spicy, rich 1999 Pinot Noir Santa Maria Hills is a seductive tease offering plenty of black fruits intermixed with spice, plum, and floral notes. Offering terrific fruit on the attack, mid-palate, and finish, it's the complete package. Drink it over the next 5–7 years.

The 1998 Pinot Noir exhibits a Domaine Dujac–like fragrance and personality. The light to medium ruby color belies the wine's richness and complexity. Notes of kirsch, cherry jam, cinnamon, black tea, and clean foresty aromas (the French say *sous bois*) soar from the glass of this complex Pinot Noir. It is silky-textured, with fine underlying acidity, subtle and nuanced flavors, and a long, medium- to full-bodied finish. Yields were 0.9 tons of fruit per acre, and the production was extremely limited. Hopefully, more wine will be forthcoming in future vintages.

The 1997 Pinot Noir Julia's Vineyard (72 cases) exhibits an attractive, plump, earthy, smoky, Pommard-like nose with notes of apple skins and black cherries. This deep ruby/ colored wine displays ripe fruit, medium body, and a friendly, open-knit texture. The outstanding 1997 Pinot Noir (72 cases) offers dried herbs, smoked meats, and black fruits in its complex aromatics. Rich, medium- to full-bodied, long, ripe, and nicely layered, it should drink well for 4–5 years.

Brewer and Clifton don't miss a beat when they turn their enviable talents to Chardonnay. All their Chardonnays are put through full malolactic and lees stirring, and the percentage of new oak is small (about one-third). The 2000 Chardonnay Katherine's Vineyard displays a light green hue to its medium straw color. It tastes like a young, backward Chevalier-Montrachet given its striking notes of honeyed citrus intertwined with liquid minerality. A rich, full-bodied, well-delineated effort, it will benefit from additional cellaring and last for 6–8 years, possibly longer. Readers looking for a blockbuster Chardonnay with plenty of buttery popcorn notions mixed with minerals, orange marmalade, and honeysuckle should check out the 2000 Chardonnay Sweeney Canyon. It's no shy wine at 15% alcohol, but that is incredibly concealed beneath the wealth of fruit and extract. A Bâtard-Montrachet–like offering, it is flamboyant, rich, and sumptuous. The 2000 Chardonnay Marcella's Vineyard is reminiscent of a Louis Latour Bâtard-Montrachet. It, too, manages to hide its 15% alcohol.

Full-bodied, with amazing texture, great ripeness as well as richness, and a distinctive minerality underpinning the fruit and texture, it is a sensational effort. The 2000 Chardonnay Mount Carmel Vineyard exhibits buttery, caramel, and honeysuckle-like fruit intermixed with subtle wood. Although the least complex of Brewer-Clifton's 2000 Chardonnays, it is well formed, full-bodied, and seriously concentrated. It should drink well for 4–5 years.

The 1999s possess higher acidity, without the wealth of fruit and breadth of flavor found in the 2000s. Nevertheless, they are successful wines. The 1999 Chardonnay Katherine's Vineyard will be a keeper given its high levels of acidity as well as liquid minerality and hint of tropical fruit. The 1999 Chardonnay Sweeney Canyon again comes across as a New World version of Chevalier-Montrachet. Plenty of substance, lively acidity, notes of tangerine and oranges mixed with minerals and citrus are presented in a full-bodied, substantial style. It will benefit from cellaring and should keep for 7–8 years. The best of the 1999s is the block-buster, high-octane 1999 Chardonnay Marcella's Vineyard. Its light gold color is followed by a rich wine with terrific fruit, an unctuous texture, and surprisingly good acidity. It should drink well for 4–5 years.

These are the wines of two up-and-coming California superstars. Don't miss them.

BRYANT FAMILY VINEYARD (NAPA)

1999 Cabernet Sauvignon Pritchard Hill	Napa	EEE	96
1998 Cabernet Sauvignon Pritchard Hill	Napa	EEE	91
1997 Cabernet Sauvignon Pritchard Hill	Napa	EEE	100
1996 Cabernet Sauvignon Pritchard Hill	Napa	EEE	99
1995 Cabernet Sauvignon Pritchard Hill	Napa	EEE	99
1994 Cabernet Sauvignon Pritchard Hill	Napa	EEE	98

This 100% Cabernet Sauvignon, made from the hillsides of eastern Napa Valley, with a gorgeous view of Lake Berryessa, has become one of the world's greatest red wines. Barrel samples of the 2000 appear to be as spectacular as the 1999, 1997, 1996, 1995, and 1994. The 1999 Cabernet Sauvignon Pritchard Hill (800 cases) boasts an opaque black/purple color that resembles vintage port. It reveals tremendously intense blackberry and cassis fruit intermixed with smoke, minerals, and floral (acacia?) scents. The wine possesses awesome intensity, a voluptuous texture, fabulous purity, and sweet tannin. The multidimensions apparent in both the aromatics and flavors are extraordinary. This majestic Cabernet will have 30–40 years of longevity. The 1998 Cabernet Sauvignon Pritchard Hill is one of the finest wines of the vintage. While it does not reveal the weight of previous vintages, it is a dense plum/purple-colored, big, thick, concentrated effort. Evolved aromas of smoke, cedar, tapenade, blackberries, crème de cassis, and creosote are followed by a lush, full-bodied, voluptuously textured 1998 exhibiting superb intensity as well as low-acid, sweet, pure flavors. This is a dazzling example of extremely ripe Cabernet Sauvignon made under less than ideal conditions. It will drink well upon its release and over the following two decades. I have consumed several bottles of the 1997 Cabernet Sauvignon Pritchard Hill. One of the most awesome young reds I have ever tasted, it possesses a black/purple color, a seamless texture, and freakishly high levels of intensity (cassis, blackberries, and blueberries infused with espresso, chocolate, and licorice) that are flawlessly presented in a full-bodied, massive yet elegant wine. Nothing is out of balance in this explosively rich, thick, highly extracted Cabernet. A compelling, historic Cabernet Sauvignon, it will drink well for 30–35 years. It is not too much to suggest that in the future, Bryant's Pritchard Hill might well be one of the wines that redefines greatness in Cabernet Sauvignon. Anticipated maturity: now–2035.

The opaque purple-colored 1996 Cabernet Sauvignon offers a spectacular, exotic bouquet of Peking duck skins, blackberry liqueur and cassis, roasted herbs, and burning charcoal. It is phenomenally intense, with record levels of dry extract and glycerin. This hedonistic blockbuster is crammed with jammy fruits nicely buttressed and framed by adequate acidity and tannin. Drink this marvelous Cabernet Sauvignon now or cellar it for two decades. This is mind-boggling stuff! The 1995 Cabernet Sauvignon is cut from the same mold as the 1996, displaying astonishing levels of black fruits (the usual suspects—blueberries, blackberries, raspberries, and cassis), phenomenal concentration, and virtually perfect balance and equilibrium. Another potentially perfect wine, the 1994 Cabernet Sauvignon boasts a fabulous nose of cassis, cream, blueberries, violets, minerals, and spice. It smells like a hypothetical blend of a great vintage of L'Evangile, Clinet, and Mouton-Rothschild. The opaque purple/black color is followed by a full-bodied wine stacked and packed with fruit, glycerin, and extract. No component part is out of place in this formidably endowed, remarkably well-balanced wine. The purity, richness, sweetness and depth of fruit suggest that the wine's potential is limitless. Much like its cellarmate, the 1994 Colgin Cabernet Sauvignon (also made by Helen Turley), the Bryant Family Vineyard's 1994 should evolve into one of California's legendary Cabernets. It will age effortlessly for 25–30 years.

Don't I wish there were tens of thousands of cases of wine such as this! Believe me, it is frustrating to write about limited production wines with such distinctive characters. I realize that only a handful of readers will be fortunate enough to obtain a bottle. It is also distressing to see these wines fetch museum prices at auctions, bid up to levels that only multimillionaires can afford. Nevertheless, over 20 years of writing has proven time and time again that glowing reviews on these wines motivate other producers to attain a similar level of quality. I wrote an article in *Food & Wine* magazine itemizing the characteristics of a great wine. They are: 1) the ability to please both the palate and the intellect, 2) the ability to hold the taster's interest, 3) the ability to offer intense aromas and flavors without heaviness, 4) the ability to taste better with each sip, 5) the ability to improve with age, and 6) the ability to offer a singular personality. These wines satisfy every one of those requirements. I often wonder if I get too excited about wines such as this. Yet time is on their side. I truly believe that in 20, 40, or 60 years, when the history of what appears to be a golden age for California wines is analyzed, these wines, and the work of their wine-maker, will be even more admired and appreciated by future generations than they are today.

Past Glories: 1993 Cabernet Sauvignon (97)

CAIN CELLARS (NAPA)

1996 Cain Five Proprietary Red Wine	Napa	E	89+
1994 Cain Five Proprietary Red Wine	Napa	E	91

The 1996 proprietary red wine from Cain Cellars is a blend of 63% Cabernet Sauvignon, 18% Merlot, 12% Cabernet Franc, 5% Petit Verdot, and 2% Malbec. A complex nose of cedar, black fruits, tobacco, spice box, and new wood emerges from this dark ruby/purple-colored effort. Rich and moderately tannic, with excellent to outstanding flavor extraction and overall balance, this 1996 should prove to be long-lived and satisfying. The texture is rich, not compressed or clipped, and the acidity, tannin, and alcohol are well integrated. Anticipated maturity: now–2016. The 1994, a blend of 62% Cabernet Sauvignon, 25% Merlot, 6% Cabernet Franc, 4% Malbec, and 3% Petit Verdot, is one of the finest efforts Cain Cellars has yet made. Fortunately, there were 5,500 cases produced. The wine reveals an opaque purple color, followed by a smoky, sweet cassis, subtle vanilla-scented nose, rich, medium- to full-bodied, supple flavors, and beautifully integrated acidity, tannin, alcohol, and wood. This outstanding effort is accessible, but should age effortlessly for 15 years. Shame on me for underrating this wine from cask!

CAKEBREAD CELLARS (NAPA)

1995 Cabernet Sauvignon Benchland Select	Napa	E	89+
1995 Cabernet Sauvignon Three Sisters	Napa	E	90
1994 Zinfandel Howell Mountain	Napa	C	88+

The two 1995 Cabernet Sauvignons are the most impressive I have tasted from Cakebread Cellars. The 1995 Cabernet Sauvignon Three Sisters comes from hillside vineyards planted on the eastern side of Napa Valley. The wine exhibits a saturated dark ruby/purple color, followed by a pure nose of cassis, minerals, and subtle new oak. Rich and expansive in the mouth, with power and concentration nicely allied to finesse and elegance, this wine possesses a soft texture, as well as enough tannin and acidity for delineation. Charming and intense, this is a beautifully rendered Cabernet Sauvignon that can be drunk now or cellared for 10–15 years. Also dark ruby/purple-colored, the 1995 Cabernet Sauvignon Benchland Select offers restrained aromatics, more tannin, and a closed personality. The predominant flavor characteristics are black currants intermixed with tobacco and cedar. The finish is long, with moderate tannin. Anticipated maturity: now–2014.

A tightly knit, more restrained, and firmer-styled Zinfandel, much of the appeal of Cakebread's 1994 Zinfandel Howell Mountain comes at the back of the mouth. There is a mineral and black raspberry–scented nose, rich, dense, black cherry and raspberry flavors, medium to full body, excellent purity, and a spicy, long, structured, stony finish. This classy, potentially complex Zinfandel should be given 6–12 months of bottle age and drunk over the next 7–8 years. Has anyone else noticed that Cakebread is making better and better wines?

OLIVER CALDWELL CELLARS (NAPA)

1997 Zinfandel Aida Vineyard	Napa	D	89

When Zinfandel from this source were made by Turley Cellars, they always possessed a distinctive southern Rhône, Châteauneuf-du-Pape-like character. Now made by Caldwell Cellars, this 1997 Zinfandel Aida Vineyard retains the unmistakable pepper, spice, dried Provençal herb, meaty, *garrigue* (a mélange of earth and herb scents) character that is found in southern Rhône wines. This rich, medium- to full-bodied, spicy, cherry liqueur–flavored offering is hedonistic and luscious. I would opt for drinking it over the next 5–6 years.

CAMBRIA ESTATE (SANTA MARIA)

2000 Chardonnay Bench Break	Santa Maria	D	88
2000 Chardonnay Katherine's Vineyard	Santa Maria	C	90
2000 Chardonnay Rae's	Santa Maria	D	90
1999 Pinot Noir Bench Break	Santa Maria	D	89+
1999 Pinot Noir Julia's Vineyard	Santa Maria	D	89
1999 Pinot Noir Rae's	Santa Maria	E	91

Cambria is now part of Jess Jackson's newly named Jackson Family Farms organization. All of the estates within this organization produce high-quality wines. The following Chardonnays are the best yet from Cambria Estate, and their Pinot Noirs seem to get better with each new vintage. While the Syrah has not yet caught up with the quality of the Pinot Noir and Chardonnay, it shows more and more promise. There are now three *cuvées* of Chardonnay, 1,000 cases of the Bench Break, 500 cases of Rae's, and a whopping 80,000 cases of Katherine's Vineyard. For readers looking for a dazzling, tropical fruit–scented and –flavored Chardonnay that offers tremendous purity, flavor intensity, and character, the 2000 Chardonnay Katherine's Vineyard is one of the best they have made. The vintage's good acidity buttresses the copious quantities of honeyed orange/pineapple fruit infused with citrus oils and gentle, toasty oak. It is a rich, full-bodied, undeniably attractive Chardonnay fruit bomb that should drink well for 2–3 years. The 1,000-case *cuvée* of 2000 Chardonnay Bench Break, which comes from sandy, alluvial soils, reveals considerable mineral characteristics. It is a classic, restrained, yet intensely flavorful Chardonnay that relies on citrus and liquid minerality for much of its character. There is plenty of weight, body, and length as well as a leesy, smoky complexity reminiscent of great white Burgundies. The 2000 Chardonnay Rae's exhibits buttery popcorn notes, rich, full-bodied, powerful flavors, beautiful purity, and the longest finish, with the most intensity and nuances. It is a fabulous Chardonnay capable of lasting 4–5 years. These are all handsomely rendered Chardonnays.

The Pinot Noir program is reaching new heights at Cambria. The current wines are a long way from the old vegetal, tomato (V-8 juice) tasting offerings of the past. The 1999 Pinot Noir Julia's Vineyard sees about 40% new French oak and is made from totally destemmed grapes. It possesses ripe black cherry and cranberry fruit, along with notes of pomegranate, pepper, and spice. Tangy, medium- to full-bodied, and fruit-driven, it should drink nicely for 4–5 years. The dense ruby/plum-colored 1999 Pinot Noir Bench Break exhibits abundant quantities of vibrant berry fruit intermixed with smoke, charcoal, and mineral. The wine was aged in 100% new French oak, and is slightly more structured and denser than the open-knit Julia's Vineyard. This wine will benefit from another 6–8 months of bottle age, and last for up to a decade. My favorite of the three Pinot Noirs is the Volnay-like 1999 Pinot Noir Rae's. It boasts abundant quantities of jammy black cherry fruit, nicely integrated wood smoke, minerals, and vanilla. Its richness of fruit, supple, yet well-delineated personality, beautiful purity, as well as additional layered complexity suggest it will be an impressive Pinot Noir to enjoy over the next decade.

CARDINALE (NAPA)

1999 Proprietary Red Wine	California	EE	93
1998 Proprietary Red Wine	California	EE	90
1997 Proprietary Red Wine	California	EE	95
1996 Proprietary Red Wine	California	EE	94
1995 Proprietary Red Wine	California	EE	91

One of the flagship properties in the Jackson Family Farm empire, Cardinale is made by one of California's most respected young wine-makers, Charles Thomas. The winery seems to go from strength to strength, producing wines of extraordinary power, but also remarkable delineation and elegance. Most of the fruit, which is a blend from Napa as well as Sonoma, tends to come from Jess Jackson's vineyards on Mount Veeder, and the Alexander Valley Mountain Estate, with some additions from the benchlands of Rutherford. There are 3,900 cases of the prodigious 1997 Cardinale, comprised primarily of Cabernet Sauvignon with a tiny dollop of Merlot. The wine has an opaque bluish black/purple color, a knockout nose of black cherry liqueur intermixed with cassis, lead pencil, mineral, and smoky oak. The glorious richness in the mouth is backed up by a full-bodied, opulently textured, super-extracted wine that is neither heavy nor ponderous. Stunning purity, a fabulous multilayered impression, and a finish that goes on for nearly a minute make this the most exciting Cardinale to date. For statisticians, this is a blend of 91% Cabernet Sauvignon and 9% Merlot, of which 79% of the grapes came from Napa and 21% from Sonoma. It spent 22 months in 100% new French oak before being bottled with neither fining nor filtration. It tips the scales at 14.2% alcohol. Anticipated maturity: 2004–2030. The very severe selection because of the difficulties imposed by the 1998 vintage has resulted in only 1,100 cases of the 1998 Cardinale. It has turned out to be a full-bodied, deep, rich wine with plenty of black currant/cherry fruit infused with some cedar, spice box, tobacco, and toasty new oak. While it does not have the depth, volume, and prodigious length of the 1997, it is an outstanding Cabernet Sauvignon–based wine that defies the vintage's so-so reputation for Cabernet and Merlot. Moreover, it should drink well for at least 15+ years. The 1999 Cardinale is 78% Cabernet Sauvignon and 22% Merlot. The wine has an opaque purple color, a huge, broodingly backward personality with fabulous fruit purity, an unctuous texture, sweet tannin, and dazzling length. Already seamless, it may challenge the fabulous 1997 and awesome 1996. Anticipated maturity for the 1999: 2006–2028.

The 1996 Cardinale is a blend of 89% Cabernet Sauvignon and 11% Merlot, of which 62% came from Napa and 38% from Sonoma. Just under 3,000 cases were produced. It is also a top-rank wine and a star of the vintage. A saturated purple color is followed by licorice, cedar, fruitcake, and black currant aromas. Full-bodied, powerful, and concentrated, with low acidity but high tannin, this young, muscular classic should have fabulous aging potential. Anticipated maturity: 2003–2028. The outstanding 1995 (2,800 cases made from a blend of 77% Cabernet Sauvignon and 23% Merlot) is somewhat overwhelmed when tasted next to the extraordinary 1996 and 1997. The wine's opaque purple color is followed by copious quantities of toast, cassis, tobacco, earth, and spice in a full-blown bouquet. Full-bodied, with superb purity and a gorgeous marriage of power and elegance, this classic offering should age effortlessly for 20–25+ years. Kudos to wine-maker Charles Thomas!

CARLISLE WINERY (SONOMA)

1998 Two Acres	Russian River	D	89
1999 Zinfandel	Dry Creek	D	88
1998 Zinfandel	Dry Creek	D	90
1999 Zinfandel	Russian River	D	90
1998 Zinfandel	Russian River	D	88?

This relatively new, impressive estate has fashioned two stylish, yet different 1999 Zinfandel. The elegant, intensely flavored, medium- to full-bodied 1999 Zinfandel Dry Creek is a balanced, harmonious effort with good flesh as well as copious black cherries intermixed with earth and subtle wood. Concentrated and soft, this delicious 1999 can be enjoyed over the next 4–5 years. The sweeter, richer, fuller-bodied, more concentrated, and denser 1999 Zinfandel Russian River displays a deep ruby color with purple nuances, a sweet attack with more glycerin as well as ripeness, and outstanding purity. It is a compelling mouthful.

I believe Carlisle's 1998s were their debut releases. The 1998 Zinfandel Russian River (118 cases; 15.9% alcohol) has a dense ruby/purple color, followed by thick, chocolaty, berry fruit, truffle, licorice, and smoky notes. The dense ruby/purple-colored 1998 Zinfandel Dry Creek (237 cases; 15.8% alcohol) offers terrific aromas of tar, jammy blackberries, cherry liqueur, and smoke. In the mouth, it is rich and full-bodied, with outstanding concentration and depth. Drink this impressive, full tilt Zinfandel over the next 5–7 years. Lastly, the 1998 Two Acres is a limited production (78 cases) proprietary blend of Petite Sirah, Mourvèdre, Refosco, and Alicante as well as other varietals. It reveals abundant quantities of smoky, blackberry, licorice-infused, tarry fruit flavors, full body, admirable muscle and concentration, low acidity, and a sweet mid-palate and finish. Drink it over the next 5–7 years.

CARMENET VINEYARD (SONOMA)

1997 Cabernet Franc	Sonoma	D	89
1997 Dynamite Cabernet Sauvignon	North Coast	C	88
1994 Meritage Moon Mountain Estate	Sonoma	C	90
1996 Merlot Sangiacomo Vineyard	Carneros	D	88
1997 Moon Mountain Cabernet	Sonoma	D	91
1996 Moon Mountain Cabernet	Sonoma	D	89
1995 Moon Mountain Proprietary Red Wine Estate Reserve	Sonoma	D	90
1994 Vin De Garde Moon Mountain Estate	Sonoma	C	91
1999 Zinfandel Evangelo Vineyard	Contra Costa	C	90

A superb offering produced from 109-year-old, head-pruned vineyards planted in the sandy soils of Contra Costa, Carmenet's dense purple-colored 1999 Zinfandel Evangelo Vineyard offers up sweet, fruit-driven aromas of blackberries, cherry liqueur, and underbrush. Dense, full-bodied, and fruity, with an opulent texture as well as a long, lusty finish, this explosively rich Zinfandel will drink beautifully for 3–4 years.

While the Moon Mountain Cabernet has a relatively limited production of 3,000–5,000 cases, there are 45,000 cases of the 1997 Dynamite Cabernet Sauvignon. Given today's ridiculously overpriced wine market, the Dynamite is a terrific bargain. Most of the fruit comes from Pope Valley, a diverse viticultural area that is, inexplicably, part of Napa Valley. However, it has at least one super Cabernet source in the Cypress Vineyard of Flora Springs. Aged in oak barrels (the majority American), the Dynamite's dense ruby/purple color is accompanied by an overripe nose of black currants and jammy cassis. Lush, medium- to full-bodied, and spicy, with low acidity, this is a mouth-filling, pure, textbook Cabernet Sauvignon to drink over the next decade.

Close to outstanding is Carmenet's 1997 Cabernet Franc (600 cases). Made from the estate's vineyards and aged in 100% French oak, of which one-third is new, this 100% Cabernet Franc exhibits a dark ruby/purple color and an attractive nose of black fruits, cedar, spice box, and tobacco. Excellent richness, a lush texture, and real elegance without dilution are the hallmarks of this fine offering crafted by wine-maker Jeff Baker. Drink it over the next 10–12 years. The excellent 1996 Moon Mountain Cabernet (4,815 cases of a blend of Cabernet Sauvignon, Cabernet Franc, and Petit Verdot) was aged in 75% new French oak. Much of the fruit comes from the famed Martini vineyard called Monte Rosso. Dark ruby/purple-colored, with intense aromas of blackberries, minerals, and currants, this elegant, soft, powerful wine is delicious, and promises to evolve nicely for 12–15 years. Even better is the 1997 Moon Mountain Cabernet (4,400 cases made from a blend of 86% Cabernet Sauvignon, 10% Cabernet Franc, and 4% Petit Verdot). A saturated blue/purple color is followed by aromas of minerals, cassis, cigar box, and licorice. Full-bodied, superbly concentrated, pure, and well balanced, this large-scaled, mountain-styled Cabernet Sauvignon–dominated wine will be at its best between now–2020.

The plump, hedonistic 1996 Merlot Sangiacomo Vineyard reveals a dark ruby color and a big, smoky, berry, chocolaty nose. Fleshy and medium-bodied, with excellent richness and depth, it is meant to be drunk over the next 5–7 years.

The substantially endowed 1995 Moon Mountain Estate Reserve reveals a dark ruby/purple color with a textbook cedary, tobacco, weedy, black currant–scented nose. It exhibits good sweetness and ripeness of fruit on the attack, medium body, obvious spicy new oak (almost too much), and a moderately tannic, narrowly focused, spicy finish. This is a very good, potentially excellent wine that should provide restrained yet elegant drinking for 10–14 years.

The 1994 Vin de Garde Moon Mountain Estate exhibits an opaque ruby/purple color, as well as a huge, exotic nose of cassis, herbs, ginger, and coconut. Sweet tannin and an underlying mineral component are present in this fabulously extracted, rich, full-bodied, spicy wine. This large-scaled, structured wine clearly lives up to its name. It will undoubtedly require 5–7 years of cellaring after its release; it displays the potential to last for 20+ years. Lastly, the 1994 Meritage Moon Mountain Estate stood out for its well-focused personality, which exhibited sensational elegance, and, for the vintage, a soft, supple style that came across as less aggressive and extracted than many other 1994s. Deeply colored, with loads of red and black fruits, this will not be one of the biggest wines of the vintage, but it has the potential to be an outstanding effort in a stylish, measured, but authoritatively flavored manner. Because of its softness, it should drink well when released and keep for up to 15 years.

CAYMUS VINEYARD (NAPA)

1994 Cabernet Sauvignon	Napa	E	91
1995 Cabernet Sauvignon Special Selection	Napa	EE	90
1994 Cabernet Sauvignon Special Selection	Napa	EE	95

Caymus is one of a handful of Napa Valley wineries that has enjoyed an enviable success record since the early 1970s. The winery continues to focus on three wines: Sauvignon Blanc, their exotic white proprietary wine called Conundrum (usually a blend of Viognier, Sauvignon Blanc, Chardonnay, and Sémillon), and Cabernet Sauvignon. Chuck Wagner and his father, Charlie, have begun to look south to develop vineyards in Monterey as there is not enough Caymus to fulfill the marketplace's needs. In Monterey, the winery produces a competent but overpriced white and red Rhône varietal blend called Treanna.

Cabernet is king at Caymus. During the nineties, there was a succession of sumptuous, rich, concentrated, lavishly wooded, cassis-flavored Caymus Cabernet Sauvignons. The sumptuous 1994 Cabernet Sauvignon appears to be one of the best Napa Cabernets Caymus has produced. Remarkably, there is plenty to go around—25,000 cases, approximately the same production as Lafite-Rothschild and Margaux. The wine exhibits a dark purple color, and a sweet, jammy black currant–scented nose. The lush, juicy, succulent texture is crammed with glycerin and extract. Surprisingly soft (a hallmark of this vintage), with a smooth texture, this full-bodied, oaky Cabernet should drink well for 10–12+ years. I have followed the Special Selection Cabernet Sauvignon since the debut 1975 vintage, and the 1994 appears to be one of the finest yet made at Caymus. Its saturated purple color is accompanied by an exuberant, sweet, enveloping fragrance of smoky new oak and jammy blackberry and cassis fruit. In the mouth, this lavishly wooded, black fruit–filled Cabernet is extremely full-bodied, with superb levels of fruit, glycerin, and extract. Like many 1994 Cabernet Sauvignons, it possesses extraordinary equilibrium, with the sweet tannin giving the wine considerable accessibility. The finish lasts for nearly 30 seconds. This will be a fun wine to drink young, but do not discount its aging ability as it should last for two decades.

While it is fashionable to criticize this wine because of its price, and the secrecy surrounding the amount produced (who really cares?), the wine is unquestionably outstanding. The 1995 Special Selection boasts a dark ruby/purple color as well as an attractive bouquet with lavish quantities of toasty new oak and black currants. There is moderate tannin, good purity, and an open-knit, sexy style. If the wine had not fallen a bit short on the mid-palate, it would have merited an even higher score. It should drink well for 10–15 years. Based on the fame of this winery and the price of the wine, one would expect this Cabernet to compete with Colgin, Bryant Family Vineyards, Screaming Eagle, Araujo, and Harlan Estate. It does not. Nevertheless, it is an outstanding Cabernet Sauvignon.

Past Glories: Cabernet Sauvignon Special Selection—1992 (91), 1991 (91), 1990 (94), 1986 (94), 1985 (92), 1984 (96), 1980 (91), 1978 (98), 1976 (99), 1975 (98)

CHALONE (GAVILAN)

1999 Chardonnay Estate	Gavilan Mountains	D	90
1999 Chenin Blanc Estate	Gavilan Mountains	C	90
1999 Pinot Blanc Estate	Gavilan Mountains	D	88
1994 Pinot Noir Estate	California	C	88

Chalone's tank-fermented 1999 Chenin Blanc Estate, fashioned from 82-year-old, head-pruned vines, remains one of California's finest expressions of this grape. Fermented dry, it spends 11 months in French oak, of which 20% is new. A wine of extraordinary minerality, intensity, and character, it presents this varietal's fruit cocktail–like characteristic in a steely format. Full-bodied and powerful, as well as a good value, it should drink well for 7–8 years. Chalone also consistently produces one of California's finest Pinot Blancs. Their 1999 Pinot Blanc Estate (4,280 cases) is fermented in both tank and barrel, and aged in French oak, of which 30% is new. About one-half of this *cuvée* comes from 50-year-old vines, and the rest from younger plantings. While tightly knit, it reveals notions of orange blossoms, citrus, and apple skins along with a liquid minerality. This dense, medium- to full-bodied, intense white will age impeccably for a decade or more.

Chalone has dropped its *cuvée* of Reserve Chardonnay, opting to do one master blend. The 1999 Chardonnay Estate (24,300 cases; 14.1% alcohol) represents one of the finest buys for long-lived Chardonnay in the marketplace. About 30% new French oak, with the balance 2–3-year-old barrels, are utilized, and the wine remains on its lees for 12 months. It is not fined, but is filtered. A light gold-colored, intense, full-bodied, muscular effort, it exhibits notes of minerals, pineapples, oranges, and allspice. Chalone's Chardonnays can be extremely long-lived (certain bottles of the 1981, 1980, and 1979 remain extraordinary). While the powerful, structured 1999 may not last that long, it has at least a decade of life ahead of it.

Chalone's 1994 Pinot Noir Estate exhibits a light ruby color, as well as wonderfully sweet, succulent, cherry and berry fruit intermingled with scents of smoke, earth, and wood. Excellent richness, and a long, lush finish make for a glass of sexy Pinot Noir that is far more forward than the old style Chalone Pinots.

In the future, readers can expect some Rhône Ranger blends to emerge from this winery. They have planted 26 acres on a south-facing mountainside consisting of decomposed granite soils. The majority of the plantings are Syrah, but there are small percentages of Viognier, Mourvèdre, and Grenache.

CHAPPELLET (NAPA)

1997 Cabernet Sauvignon	Napa	D	89+

This may be the most impressive Cabernet Sauvignon Chappellet has produced since their great classics in 1969, 1970, and 1973, all made by Philip Togni. The color is a dense ruby purple. The bouquet offers up tight but promising aromas of minerals, smoke, and black currants. A Bordeaux-like austerity greets the taster, but as with Bordeaux, there is plenty of density and concentration in reserve, which is particularly noticeable on the back of the palate. The wine is pure, promising, tannic, medium- to full-bodied, and nicely extracted. Chewy tobacco, spice box, and black fruit characteristics emerge with airing. It is good to see this winery turn out a wine of this quality. It's an ager, however, and patience will be required. Anticipated maturity: 2003–2018.

P.S. By the way, I recently had a bottle of the 1969 Chappellet Cabernet Sauvignon (made by Philip Togni). I would score this wine in the mid-90s. It is a testament to the fact that some California Cabernet Sauvignon can age. The wine reveals a saturated garnet/purple color as well as a striking bouquet of minerals, black fruits, leather, spice box, and cedar. Unbelievably rich, powerful, and muscular, with at least 20 more years of life remaining, it is one of the classics, but many people have probably forgotten how great it was (a friend and I purchased a pristine case of this at auction for $300).

CLARK-CLAUDON VINEYARDS (NAPA)

1997 Cabernet Sauvignon	Napa	EE	92+
1996 Cabernet Sauvignon	Napa	E	93
1995 Cabernet Sauvignon	Napa	D	93+

Another limited production (300 cases) wine made from a vineyard on the eastern side of Howell Mountain, the brilliantly made 1995 Cabernet from Clark-Claudon suggests this winery knows what to do with top-quality fruit. While the 1995 will be hard to find, readers who are interested in profound California Cabernet Sauvignons should seek out future releases. This opaque purple-colored wine boasts knockout aromatics of smoke, charcoal, black currants, lead pencil, minerals, and high-quality French oak. Impressive on the palate, with a classy richness married to well-integrated wood, acidity, and tannin, this is a full-bodied, fabulously rich, expressive, impeccably balanced Cabernet Sauvignon. Anticipated maturity: now–2015.

A brilliant successor to the 1995, Clark Claudon's 1996 Cabernet Sauvignon exhibits a dark purple color, followed by a classic, Bordeaux-like nose of cassis, lead pencil, and smoky new oak. A wine of considerable complexity and elegance, with outstanding purity, richness, and nicely integrated wood and tannin, this is a classic, backward yet promising, symmetrical Cabernet that can be drunk early in life, or cellared for 15+ years. Impressive!

In light of the superb 1996 this winery produced, it is not surprising to see a broodingly backward, promising Cabernet Sauvignon emerge from the 1997 vintage. Neither up-front nor accessible, readers will need a degree of patience, although it would not be infanticide to drink it now. A serious, concentrated, opaque purple-colored effort, it boasts a moderately intense nose of pure cassis, gravel, vanilla, and blackberries. Full-bodied and impressively built, this deep, powerful, concentrated Cabernet begs for cellaring. It is another impressive effort from this newcomer to the high-end Cabernet Sauvignon sweepstakes. Anticipated maturity: 2005–2020. Bravo!

CLOS MIMI (PASO ROBLES)

1997 Syrah Shell Creek Vineyard	Paso Robles	D	90
1996 Syrah Shell Creek Vineyard	Paso Robles	D	92

Produced in minuscule quantities, the immensely impressive, black/purple-colored 1996 Syrah offers a nose of roasted herbs, meat juices, blackberries, cassis, and earth. Peppery, spicy notes emerge from this large-scaled, super-concentrated, impressively endowed, rustic, brilliantly layered, nuanced wine. It will be even better with 3–5 years of cellaring. It should keep for 10–12 years. Brilliant! While not as much of a blockbuster as the phenomenal 1996, Clos Mimi's 1997 is still an outstanding wine. Dense ruby/purple-colored, with the telltale blackberry, peppery aromas, this elegant offering exhibits abundant glycerin, a seductive texture, full body, sweet fruit, and significant length. The 1996 is more powerful and concentrated, but the 1997 is more charming and open-knit. Clos Mimi is an impressive, impeccably made wine. Anticipated maturity: now–2010. These people are serious!

CLOS PEGASE (NAPA)

1997 Cabernet Sauvignon	Carneros/Napa	D	(88–90)
1996 Cabernet Sauvignon	Carneros/Napa	D	88
1998 Cabernet Sauvignon	Napa	D	88
1995 Cabernet Sauvignon	Napa	C	88
1994 Cabernet Sauvignon	Napa	C	91
1998 Cabernet Sauvignon Graveyard Hill	Carneros	E	90
1998 Cabernet Sauvignon Hommage	Napa	EE	(90–91)
1997 Cabernet Sauvignon Hommage Reserve	Napa	E	89
1998 Cabernet Sauvignon Palisades Vineyard	Napa	E	89+
1997 Cabernet Sauvignon Palisades Vineyard	Napa	E	88
1999 Chardonnay Mitsuko's Vineyard Hommage Reserve	Carneros	E	91
1999 Chardonnay Mitsuko's Vineyard Unfiltered	Carneros	C	90
1994 Merlot	Napa	C	90

Under wine-maker Steve Rogstad, the quality at Clos Pegase has gone from appallingly innocuous/mediocre to at least excellent and, in some cases, outstanding. Both *cuvées* of 1999 Chardonnay are the finest Clos Pegase has yet produced. The 1999 Chardonnay Mitsuko's Vineyard Unfiltered is 100% barrel-fermented and most of it was made utilizing indigenous yeasts. It sees about one-third new French oak. The wine exhibits a big, smoky, leesy, roasted hazelnut, buttery, and honeyed pear nose, full body, excellent texture, and fine purity. Drink it over the next 2–3 years. Culled from the same vineyard, the 1999 Chardonnay Mitsuko's Vineyard Hommage Reserve (about 750 cases) is a selection of the finest barrels. Indigenous yeast-fermented and bottled unfiltered, it boasts a terrific nose of honeysuckle, tropical fruit, and smoky, leesy, roasted nut scents. Full-bodied and multilayered, with gorgeous purity and nicely integrated wood, it should drink well for 2–3 years as well.

Quality is clearly on the upswing, as the 1998s, a much more challenging vintage, are better than the 1997s. The 1998 Cabernet Sauvignon exhibits chocolate, cedar, spice box, and black currant characteristics presented in a medium- to full-bodied format. With good depth, ripe tannin, and a long, spicy finish, it can be consumed over the next decade. Clos Pegase produces two single vineyard wines, approximately 100 cases from their Graveyard Hill Vineyard in Carneros and slightly more from their Palisades Vineyard northeast of Calistoga. The 1998 Cabernet Sauvignon Graveyard Hill, which spent 28 months in French oak, was harvested on November 6 (that may give you an idea of just how cool and late the vintage was). It possesses a dark black/purple color, a distinctive nose of scorched earth, and gravel-like notes similar to those found in Bordeaux's famed Haut-Brion. Medium- to full-bodied, with sweet but firm tannin in addition to outstanding concentration, purity, and intensity, it is an impressive 1998 for drinking over the next 10–15 years. The 1998 Cabernet Sauvignon Palisades Vineyard also spent 28 months in French oak. It reveals a dense plum/purple color and an earthy black currant and spice box–scented bouquet with notions of cedar, licorice, and cassis. The wine possesses firm tannin, full body, and a potentially long-lived personality. Cellar it for 3–4 years and consume it over the following 10–15.

The top barrels from the Graveyard Hill and Palisades vineyards are chosen for Hommage. The 1998 (925 cases of 100% Cabernet Sauvignon) came primarily from Graveyard Hill Vineyard with about one-third from the Palisades. A superb 1998, and certainly one of the vintage's most complete wines, it boasts an opaque ruby/purple color in addition to aromas of sweet cherry, cassis, smoke, fudge, and toasty oak. Full-bodied, powerful, and formidably tannic, with excellent balance, it will drink well between 2003–2020.

There are 215 cases of the 1997 Cabernet Sauvignon Palisades Vineyard. Produced from a vineyard near Calistoga, it possesses a black currant, cedar, licorice, and spicy oak–scented nose, low acidity, sweet tannin, and a medium- to full-bodied, nicely concentrated personality. The well-structured 1997 Cabernet Sauvignon Hommage Reserve (mostly Cabernet Sauvignon, with tiny amounts of Petit Verdot and Merlot, of which 65% is from the Graveyard Hill Vineyard and 35% from the Palisades Vineyard) exhibits classy tobacco, cedar, dried herb, licorice, and black currant aromas. Medium- to full-bodied, with moderate tannin and excellent purity, this *cuvée* (1,350 cases) needs 1–3 years of cellaring; it should keep for 15 years.

The 1996 Cabernet Sauvignon reveals a complex, spice box, cedar, olive, and black currant–scented bouquet, medium-bodied flavors, and moderate tannin in the finish. A well-made Cabernet that has not been excessively manipulated or acidified, it should drink well for a decade. Even better is the 1997 Cabernet Sauvignon, which possesses a dark ruby/purple color, and a firm underpinning of tannin, sweet, creamy, black currant flavors intertwined with cedar, Provençal herbs, and new oak. Medium- to full-bodied, with a relatively long finish, it should be an excellent, possibly outstanding wine that will be drinkable young, yet keep for 10–12 years. The 1995 Cabernet Sauvignon is a medium-weight, nicely made wine with a dark ruby/purple color, and sweet plum, jammy cassis, and cherry-like aromas with lavish toasty oak in the background. On the palate, the wine reveals adequate acidity, an attractive, fleshy, corpulent mouth-feel, good glycerin and extract, and an easy to understand, plump, chewy style. It should drink well for a decade.

The 1994 Merlot offers a dark purple color, and a big, chocolaty, black raspberry/cherry-scented nose bordering on overripeness. Dense and chewy, with surprisingly tough tannin in the finish, this is a fleshy, boldly styled Merlot for drinking during the first dozen years after its release. The 1994 Cabernet Sauvignon exhibits gorgeous ripe blueberry and raspberry fruit in its flamboyant nose. Deep and velvety-textured, with impressive extraction, this full-bodied, sweet-tasting (from ripe fruit, not sugar), sexy Cabernet should drink well now and keep for 12–15 years.

COLGIN CELLARS (NAPA)

1999 Cabernet Sauvignon Herb Lamb Vineyard	Napa	EEE	91
1998 Cabernet Sauvignon Herb Lamb Vineyard	Napa	EEE	90

1997 Cabernet Sauvignon Herb Lamb Vineyard	Napa	EEE	99
1996 Cabernet Sauvignon Herb Lamb Vineyard	Napa	EEE	97
1995 Cabernet Sauvignon Herb Lamb Vineyard	Napa	EE	98
1994 Cabernet Sauvignon Herb Lamb Vineyard	Napa	EE	96
1999 Madrona Ranch (not yet officially named)	Napa	EE	(89–90)

Availability of Colgin will increase as Ann Colgin's new vineyard, Tychson Hill, produced a Cabernet in 2000. Additionally, 23 acres that have been planted in the eastern hills of southern Napa should be fruit-bearing in 3–4 years. From cooler years than 1997, 1996, 1995, and 1994, the three newest offerings possess a more Bordeaux-like weight than previous efforts. Much is expected of new wine-maker Mark Aubert, given his predecessor's (Helen Turley) reputation, but there should be no significant changes in Colgin's harvesting, winemaking, or upbringing. Don't forget, Aubert was responsible for many compelling wines at Peter Michael.

The 1999 Cabernet Sauvignon Herb Lamb Vineyard (300 cases) exhibits a black/purple color along with sumptuously pure aromas of black currants, cassis, charcoal, and toast. Surprisingly medium-bodied as well as lighter than expected, it possesses excellent mineral notes, as well as a Bordeaux-like finesse, austerity, and finish. This beautifully styled Cabernet should be ready to drink in 3–4 years and will keep for 15–18. There are 500 cases of the 1999 Madrona Ranch, a proprietary blend of 55% Cabernet Sauvignon, 35% Merlot, 5% Cabernet Franc, and 5% Petit Verdot. It offers a dense ruby color in addition to an elegant, cedary, and black currant–scented bouquet with smoky oak in the background. There is good ripeness, a soft texture, medium to full body, excellent depth, and sweet tannin in the finish. If this effort puts on a bit more weight it may merit an exceptional rating. Anticipated maturity: 2003–2016. From a tougher vintage, the 1998 Cabernet Sauvignon Herb Lamb Vineyard possesses a dense plum/purple color as well as a sweet perfume of minerals, blackberries, and cassis, medium to full body, an excellent texture, ripe tannin, and a more evolved personality than some of the blockbuster wines that preceded it. An undeniable success for the vintage, it should be consumed over the next 12–15 years.

The nearly perfect 1997 Cabernet Sauvignon Herb Lamb Vineyard was bottled in May 1999 and appears to have recovered beautifully from bottle shock. Saturated black/purple-colored with a knockout nose of blackberries, blueberries, lavender, licorice, and toast, this is a profound, full-bodied Cabernet Sauvignon. It displays a seamless, velvety texture, layers of concentrated fruit, and a 45+-second finish. Am I being too conservative in not giving it a 3-digit score? Anticipated maturity: now–2025. The saturated black/purple-colored 1996 Cabernet Sauvignon Herb Lamb Vineyard displays this winery's hallmark—a provocative nose of blueberry jam, orchid flowers, and smoky new oak intertwined with cassis. Additional aromas of licorice and exotic Asian spices emerge as the wine sits in the glass. Extremely full-bodied and rich, with more noticeable tannin than the 1997, this large-scaled yet extraordinarily rich wine is like drinking cassis/blueberry liqueur. Its sweet tannin and remarkable 40+-second finish are amazing. Anticipated maturity: now–2022.

The 1996 and 1995 could be mistaken for identical twins, although close examination reveals that the 1995 has a slightly firmer tannic edge and the 1996 slightly lower acidity. However, both possess Colgin's telltale opaque black/purple color, phenomenal aromatics consisting of blackberries, raspberries, blueberries, cassis, subtle new oak, and a notion of floral scents (is it acacia or lilac?). In the mouth, both wines are full-bodied, remarkably supple, and opulent, with a purity and presence of fruit that must be tasted to be believed. Their finishes last for 45+ seconds. I suspect each of these wines will get even better over the next 5–10 years before reaching their full plateau of maturity, where they should remain for two decades or more. They are the quintessential examples of Cabernet Sauvignons that marry power with elegance. As a friend said after tasting a Colgin Cabernet Sauvignon, "they float like a butterfly, but sting like a bee." I am not sure Muhammad Ali or Ann Colgin would agree with that, but it paints another picture of these extraordinary wines. These wines were made by Helen Turley, the prodigiously talented wine-maker/consultant.

The potentially perfect 1994 Cabernet Sauvignon Herb Lamb Vineyard is a totally dry wine, but the sweetness and taste of this wine's fruit is akin to a savory blend of a chocolate-covered, blueberry/cassis-filled candy bar, and vanilla ice cream melting in the mouth. This full-bodied wine is silky, seductive, opulent, voluptuously textured, and extraordinarily fragrant, expansive, and rich. In spite of this, the wine remains graceful and well balanced, without any sense of heaviness or obtrusive tannin or acidity. I clearly underrated the 1994 from my earliest barrel tastings, but the last two times I have had it, from barrel immediately prior to bottling and in bottle, have persuaded me that this wine is one of the most exciting and remarkable young Cabernet Sauvignons I have tasted! It should drink well for another 25–30 years. Damn, I adore this wine!

Note: the only way in which to purchase these wines is through the winery's mailing list.
Past Glories: 1993 Cabernet Sauvignon Herb Lamb Vineyard (95)

CONSILIENCE (SANTA BARBARA)

1999 Zinfandel Rhodes Vineyard	Redwood Valley	D	89+?

A serious, internationally styled offering, Consilience's opaque purple-colored 1999 Zinfandel Rhodes Vineyard reveals abundant quantities of new oak along with impressively sweet black currant and blackberry fruit with a hint of cherries. If the oak were not so aggressive, it would be a candidate for an outstanding rating. While it may lack some of Zinfandel's gutsiness, it is a full-bodied effort made in a Bordeaux-like style. It will be interesting to monitor this wine's evolution.

CONSTANT (NAPA)

1995 Diamond Mountain Vineyard Proprietary Red	Napa	EEE	90

This 18-acre vineyard, which sits at a lofty elevation on Diamond Mountain, was replanted in 1984. Proprietors Fred and Mary Constant's objective is to produce complex, elegant, Bordeaux-styled wines from a blend of Cabernet Sauvignon, Merlot, and Cabernet Franc. They obviously believe that no track record is necessary in order to charge high prices. The 1995 Diamond Mountain Vineyard is an outstanding effort. Made with the consultation of Philippe Melka, this blend of 73% Cabernet Sauvignon, 18% Merlot, and 9% Cabernet Franc offers scents of melted tar, loamy soil, black currants, and minerals. Well crafted, with moderate tannin, this austere, medium-bodied effort exhibits a sweet mid-palate, excellent overall harmony, and the telltale lead pencil, toasty oak, and black currant fruit indicative of a high-class Cabernet. Although not weighty, the emphasis is on finesse and complexity. It will benefit from 2–3 years of cellaring, and will last for 15–16 years.

CORNERSTONE (HOWELL MOUNTAIN)

1997 Cabernet Sauvignon Beatty Ranch	Howell Mountain	E	90+
1996 Cabernet Sauvignon Beatty Ranch	Howell Mountain	E	88
1997 Cabernet Sauvignon Black-Sears Vineyard	Howell Mountain	E	93
1996 Cabernet Sauvignon Black-Sears Vineyard	Howell Mountain	E	90
1997 Cabernet Sauvignon Collage Vineyard	Howell Mountain	E	92
1997 Cabernet Sauvignon Cornerstone Vineyard	Howell Mountain	E	94
1996 Zinfandel Beatty Ranch	Howell Mountain	D	88

Cornerstone's 1997s are the most successful efforts yet produced by wine-maker/owner Bruce Scotland. Readers seeking full-throttle Cabernet Sauvignons have plenty to choose from. The opaque purple-colored 1997 Cabernet Sauvignon Black-Sears Vineyard offers a sexy, up-front nose of blackberries, cassis, and smoke. Sweet, succulent, and jammy, with explosive ripeness as well as admirable flavor intensity, this low-acid Cabernet has huge reserves of fruit, glycerin, extract, and tannin that have been melded into a seamless, concentrated wine of exceptional potential. Anticipated maturity: now–2016. The most backward of this quartet is the 1997 Cabernet Sauvignon Beatty Ranch. Notes of new saddle leather, tree bark, and red and black currants emerge from this opaque purple-colored wine. Gritty tannin initially causes concern, but as the wine sits in the glass and on the palate, its substantial richness and powerful, full-bodied, concentrated style becomes apparent. Patience is required. Anticipated maturity: 2004–2018.

Another explosive, succulent, disarmingly thick, opulent effort, the dark purple 1997 Cabernet Sauvignon Cornerstone Vineyard is a hedonist's dream. It offers a combination of powerful black cherry and cassis flavors presented in a flamboyant, full-bodied style with extravagant layers of fruit, glycerin, and extract. New-oak aging is noticeable, but its impact is subtle. The tannin is well concealed by a wealth of fruit. Drink this beauty over the next two decades. Lastly, the 1997 Cabernet Sauvignon Collage Vineyard emphasizes finesse and elegance, although there is no shortage of flavor authority. This beautifully pure, sexy offering boasts abundant quantities of fruit in its intense aromatics as well as medium to full body, low acidity, and sweet tannin. Enjoy it over the next 12–15 years.

The 1996 Cabernet Sauvignon Beatty Ranch is not a typical Howell Mountain Cabernet. Although it possesses plenty of tannin, muscle, and power, it is deep and rich, with more sweetness on the attack than expected considering its origin. It is well balanced, ripe, elegant, and supple for a wine from this area. Drink it over the next 7–8 years. The impressive, opaque ruby/purple-colored 1996 Cabernet Sauvignon Black-Sears Vineyard displays rich blackberry and cassis fruit, excellent purity, a nicely layered mid-palate, and fine sweetness in the intense, glycerin-imbued finish. It should drink well for 12–15 years. Lastly, the 1996 Zinfandel Beatty Ranch (a late release) reveals copious quantities of earthy, smoky, toasty new-oak notes along with saddle leather, and a perfumed, mushroomy, blackberry and cherry-scented nose. Drink this briery, perfumed, concentrated Zin over the next 3–4 years.

ROBERT CRAIG (NAPA)

1997 Affinity Proprietary Red Wine	Napa	D	91
1996 Affinity Proprietary Red Wine	Napa	D	90
1995 Affinity Proprietary Red Wine	Napa	D	90
1997 Cabernet Sauvignon Howell Mountain	Napa	D	92
1996 Cabernet Sauvignon Howell Mountain	Napa	D	91
1995 Cabernet Sauvignon Howell Mountain	Napa	D	91
1994 Cabernet Sauvignon Howell Mountain	Napa	D	90+
1997 Cabernet Sauvignon Mt. Veeder	Napa	D	92+
1996 Cabernet Sauvignon Mt. Veeder	Napa	D	92+
1995 Cabernet Sauvignon Mt. Veeder	Napa	D	90
1994 Cabernet Sauvignon Mt. Veeder	Napa	D	88

Robert Craig's three impressive, concentrated 1997 reds reflect a synthesis between the elegant, austere Bordeaux-styled Cabernet Sauvignon, Merlot, and Cabernet Franc, and the extravagant, ripe, jammy characteristics found in wines fashioned from California's warmer microclimates as well as richer soils. Craig has produced wines with exceptional complexity, gorgeous purity, and 15–20 years of aging potential. The opaque purple-colored 1997 Affinity (primarily Cabernet Sauvignon) possesses exceptional finesse and elegance in addition to authoritative flavors. Highly extracted, medium- to full-bodied, with layers of concentration, it offers notes of lead pencil, well-integrated, subtle, smoky oak, black currants, plums, licorice, and flowers. Everything is well balanced in this classy, gracious Cabernet Sauvignon that combines finesse with intensity. Anticipated maturity: now–2020. The 1997 Cabernet Sauvignon Mt. Veeder exhibits an opaque purple color as well as a gorgeously complex bouquet of cassis, vanilla, minerals, and blueberries. Structured, full-bodied, and opulently textured, this thick, rich, youthful 1997 will be even better with another 2–3 years of cellaring; it will age well for two decades. Readers seeking more earthiness, as well as blackberry, blueberry, and floral characteristics, should check out the saturated ruby/purple-colored 1997 Cabernet Sauvignon Howell Mountain. It is a medium- to full-bodied, tannic, impressively endowed, pure effort that, like its siblings, is gorgeously balanced and intense. Its tannin is more powerful, and thus it requires 2–3 years of cellaring.

Robert Craig's opaque purple-colored 1996 Affinity, a blend of Merlot, Cabernet Sauvignon, and Cabernet Franc, displays a noteworthy blueberry jam–scented nose with aromas of high-quality new oak. The wine is elegant, full-bodied, and complex, with its outstanding aromatics backed up by ripe flavors, and a layered, textured feel with well-integrated oak, acidity, and tannin. Anticipated maturity: now–2012. The powerful, dense, backward, highly extracted, formidable 1996 Cabernet Sauvignon Mt. Veeder boasts a black/purple color. Although impressively endowed and muscular with admirable symmetry, this wine requires 3–5 years of bottle age. Anticipated maturity: 2003–2020. Surprisingly, the 1996 Cabernet Sauvignon Howell Mountain is more supple and velvety-textured than the Mt. Veeder (I would have expected the reverse). This wine exhibits lead pencil, mineral, and black currant notes followed by a structured, concentrated, backward style that, while not impenetrable, certainly requires bottle age. The outstanding purity and sweet fruit suggest cellaring of 2–3 years is prudent. Anticipated maturity: now–2020.

All three of the 1995 offerings from Robert Craig are exceptionally symmetrical, well-balanced wines of elegance, finesse, and purity. They are ideal models of what a Bordeaux-styled red from California should taste like. Although not blockbusters, they offer plenty of flavor depth and complexity. A classic wine, the dark ruby/purple-colored 1995 Affinity reveals a lead pencil, black currant, and vanilla-scented nose that could easily pass for a classy Médoc. It displays good richness and purity on the entry, medium to full body, outstanding concentration, and exceptional harmony. This is a beauty. Anticipated maturity: now–2012. The 1995 Cabernet Sauvignon Mt. Veeder is a fuller-bodied wine more dominated by black currant and cherry fruit. Riper, with more weight, it is still a finesse-styled wine by California standards. Its exceptional purity, subtle oak, complexity, and overall balance suggest it will drink well now, as well as over the next 12–15 years. Not surprisingly, the 1995 Cabernet Sauvignon Howell Mountain possesses the most tannin, but also the richest constitution. The wine exhibits a deep ruby/purple color (similar to its two siblings), a classic, mineral, black currant, and toast-scented nose, deep, rich, powerful flavors with outstanding concentration, considerable finesse, well-integrated tannin, and a structured, well-delineated, austere, but impressively long finish. This wine will benefit from 2–3 years of cellaring, and will keep for 15–20 years.

The 1994 Cabernet Sauvignon Mt. Veeder is a full-bodied, dense, ruby/purple-colored, elegant wine with earthy, cassis fruit. It is a well-structured, medium-weight Cabernet with excellent ripeness, a graceful personality, and attractive layers of fruit. Although tight, it is accessible and should drink well for 10–12+ years. Another enticing offering from Craig is the 1994 Cabernet Sauvignon Howell Mountain. The wine, with a saturated dark purple color, offers up attractive, youthful aromas of lead pencil, vanilla, minerals, spice, and black currant fruit. A typical mountain Cabernet with copious quantities of tannin, this medium- to full-bodied, concentrated, impressively endowed wine is well crafted, yet backward and in need of 4–5 years of cellaring. Anticipated maturity: now–2012.

Past Glories: 1993 Cabernet Sauvignon Howell Mountain (91), 1993 Cabernet Sauvignon Mt. Veeder (90)

DALLA VALLE (NAPA)

1999	Cabernet Sauvignon	Oakville/Napa	E	(92–94)
1998	Cabernet Sauvignon	Oakville/Napa	E	94
1997	Cabernet Sauvignon	Oakville/Napa	E	93
1996	Cabernet Sauvignon	Oakville/Napa	E	93
1995	Cabernet Sauvignon	Oakville/Napa	D	93
1994	Cabernet Sauvignon	Oakville/Napa	D	94
1999	Maya Proprietary Red Wine	Oakville/Napa	EEE	(96–99)
1998	Maya Proprietary Red Wine	Oakville/Napa	EEE	96
1997	Maya Proprietary Red Wine	Oakville/Napa	EEE	99
1996	Maya Proprietary Red Wine	Oakville/Napa	EE	96
1995	Maya Proprietary Red Wine	Oakville/Napa	EE	97+
1994	Maya Proprietary Red Wine	Oakville/Napa	EE	99

These wines, from the property of Naoko Dalla Valle, emerge from the eastern slopes of Oakville. They seem to get better and better. Of course, there is not a lot of room to increase quality, but when readers consider what they achieved in 1998, it is remarkable. Both wines are among the candidates for "Wine of the Vintage."

The 1998 Cabernet Sauvignon (2,400 cases, made from a blend of 88% Cabernet Sauvignon and 12% Cabernet Franc) is even better from bottle than it was from barrel. It is a terrific wine with an opaque blue/purple color and a gorgeously sweet nose of black fruits intermixed with licorice, mineral, and spice. Full-bodied, opulently textured, and drinkable at an earlier age than most vintages, it should keep for at least two decades. The astonishing 1998 Maya (500 cases from a blend of 45% Cabernet Franc and 55% Cabernet Sauvignon) may well *be* the "Wine of the Vintage." This is a staggeringly rich effort that tastes like Cheval Blanc on steroids. It boasts a black/purple color as well as a knockout nose of jammy black fruits, spice, currants, minerals, and spice box, dazzling concentration, multiple layers of flavors, and sweet tannin, giving it that seamless texture that has been so much a characteristic of Maya's greatest vintages. The 1998 should drink well for at least 25 years.

As for the 1999s, they are what one would expect from a vintage that was cool yet less problematic than 1998. There are 2,200 cases of the 1999 Cabernet Sauvignon, which has been blended with 15.5% Cabernet Franc. It offers a beautiful perfume of menthol, black fruits, licorice, mineral, and smoke. Powerful with great purity, full body, and multiple layers, this superrich wine should be even better after bottling. The opaque black/purple-colored 1999 Maya (500 cases of a 45% Cabernet Franc/55% Cabernet Sauvignon blend) offers a superb nose of blueberry, blackberry, cassis, and floral notes intermixed with licorice and mineral. This formidable offering is fabulously intense on the palate with high tannin, full body, and glorious levels of extract and glycerin. It will need 4–5 years of cellaring and keep for at least three decades.

Qualitatively, the 1997s should, based on the vintage, tower over what Dalla Valle's 1998s and 1999s, but that is not the case. Profound they are, but it is a tribute to Naoko Dalla Valle and her winemaking consultant, Mia Klein, that such phenomenal efforts were made in 1998 and 1999. The 1997 Cabernet Sauvignon (2,800 cases from a blend of 85% Cabernet Sauvignon and 15% Cabernet Franc) boasts an opaque purple color as well as a gorgeous nose of mineral-infused black currants and spicy oak. Full-bodied, structured, muscular, and multidimensional, it is approachable, but best cellared for 2–4 years and drunk over the following 20–25 years. Close to perfection, the saturated blue/black-colored 1997 Maya exhibits complex aromatics of crème de cassis, smoke, spice box, iron, and espresso. The wine has a viscous texture, huge, concentrated, ripe fruit, remarkable body, and a seamless, multilayered finish. The tannin, acidity, and alcohol are all beautifully integrated. This is profound stuff! Anticipated maturity: 2005–2030.

The powerful, concentrated, dense ruby/purple-colored 1996 Cabernet Sauvignon, full-bodied and muscular, exhibits copious quantities of black currant fruit mixed with black-berries, minerals, cedar, and Chinese black tea–like notes. The tannin is sweet, in a vintage where this component can be slightly coarse. It can be drunk now or aged for 25 years. The 1996 Maya is another extraordinary example of this sensational blend of Cabernet Sauvignon and Cabernet Franc. Vivid, intense aromas of new saddle leather, plums, black currants, un-derbrush, and licorice are followed by a full-bodied, sensationally concentrated wine with sweet tannin, a deep, exceptionally pure and concentrated mid-palate, and an opulently tex-tured finish. It was surprisingly open-knit and delicious when tasted in October, but there is more tannin lurking beneath the surface. Anticipated maturity: now–2025.

The 1995 Cabernet Sauvignon exhibits an opaque blue/black/purple color, followed by sweet cassis aromas intermingled with scents of earth, spice, smoke, and grilled meats. This dense, powerful, muscular, concentrated wine provides an enormous mouth-feel. Wineries need more than luck to produce multidimensional wines with this concentration, ripeness, sweetness of fruit, and overall intensity and complexity. The terrific 1995 Maya is cut from the same mold as all the great Mayas of this decade. Its tannin may be even riper than in the 1994, but the wine is still an unevolved, massive, and unformed giant, although it is obvious that this will be another legendary effort. Do readers ever wonder why wines such as these are never made in 100,000 case lots? The 1994 Cabernet Sauvignon, which I have drunk with great pleasure despite its backwardness, possesses a full-bodied, multilayered person-ality, with plenty of tannin, but sufficient earthy, black currant/plum-like fruit to balance out the wine's structure. With an opaque purple color, a high tannin level, and gorgeous layers of fruit and intensity, it will be at its peak after 4–6 years of cellaring and will last for 20–25 years. The 1994 Maya is prodigious. The color is saturated opaque purple. The wine offers up restrained but gorgeously sweet earth, oak, mineral, and black fruit aromas. Full-bodied, with substantial quantities of glycerin and extract, this wine's large-scaled tannin seems to be well submerged beneath the wine's fabulous layers of fruit. Although more accessible than I would have thought prior to bottling, it is a candidate for 20–30 years of evolution.

I don't think I need to reinforce the fact that these offerings are extremely difficult to find, but isn't that the way it always is with such extraordinary wines?

Past Glories: Maya—1993 (98), 1992 (100), 1991 (99), 1990 (96)

DASHE CELLARS (SONOMA)

1999	Zinfandel	Dry Creek	C	88
1999	Zinfandel Todd Brothers Ranch	Alexander Valley	C	90

These are both impressive efforts from Dashe Cellars. The 1999 Zinfandel Dry Creek (14.5% alcohol) exhibits copious quantities of deep, rich, earthy, spicy, seaweed, pepper, and black currant/cherry fruit. Medium- to full-bodied, pure, and supple, it should be consumed over the next 3–4 years. The opaque purple-colored 1999 Zinfandel Todd Brothers Ranch boasts a superb bouquet of pure, jammy black raspberries, cherries, minerals, and subtle notions of earth and wood. Full-bodied, powerful, big, and thick, this dense, blockbuster Zinfandel can be drunk now and over the next 7–8 years. Bravo!

DEHLINGER (SONOMA)

1996	Cabernet/Merlot Blend	Russian River	D	91
1995	Cabernet/Merlot Blend	Russian River	D	91
1994	Cabernet/Merlot Blend	Russian River	D	91
1998	Cabernet Sauvignon Estate	Russian River	D	(86–88)
1997	Cabernet Sauvignon Estate	Russian River	D	90
1996	Cabernet Sauvignon Estate	Russian River	D	91
1995	Cabernet Sauvignon	Russian River	D	91
1994	Cabernet Sauvignon	Russian River	D	92

1999	Chardonnay Estate	Russian River	D	(87–89)
1999	Pinot Noir Estate	Russian River	D	(87–88)
1998	Pinot Noir Estate	Russian River	D	91
1997	Pinot Noir Estate	Russian River	D	90
1996	Pinot Noir Estate	Russian River	D	91
1995	Pinot Noir Estate	Russian River	D	89
1994	Pinot Noir Estate	Russian River	C	91
1998	Pinot Noir Goldridge Vineyard	Russian River	D	89
1997	Pinot Noir Goldridge Vineyard	Russian River	D	89
1996	Pinot Noir Goldridge Vineyard	Russian River	D	89
1995	Pinot Noir Goldridge Vineyard	Russian River	C	88
1994	Pinot Noir Goldridge Vineyard	Russian River	C	90
1994	Pinot Noir Goldridge Vineyard 20 Year Old Vines	Russian River	D	91
1999	Pinot Noir Hilltop Vineyard	Russian River	D	(90–92)
1999	Pinot Noir Octagon Vineyard	Russian River	D	(88–89)
1998	Pinot Noir Octagon Vineyard	Russian River	D	92
1997	Pinot Noir Octagon Vineyard	Russian River	D	91
1996	Pinot Noir Octagon Vineyard	Russian River	D	90
1995	Pinot Noir Octagon Vineyard	Russian River	D	90
1994	Pinot Noir Octagon Vineyard	Russian River	D	93
1997	Pinot Noir Reserve Estate	Russian River	D	90+
1994	Pinot Noir Reserve Estate	Russian River	D	92+
1998	Syrah Estate	Russian River	D	(89–90)
1997	Syrah Estate	Russian River	D	90
1996	Syrah Estate	Russian River	D	93
1995	Syrah Estate	Russian River	D	93
1994	Syrah Estate	Russian River	C	91
1998	Syrah Estate East Face	Russian River	D	91
1997	Syrah Goldridge Vineyard	Russian River	D	90
1996	Syrah Goldridge Vineyard	Russian River	D	90
1995	Syrah Goldridge Vineyard	Russian River	C	90
1994	Syrah Goldridge Vineyard	Russian River	C	89

Tom Dehlinger's wines remain among the most reasonably priced in California. It has been a great decade for Dehlinger, who has produced some of California's most hedonistic Pinot Noirs and increasingly tasty Syrahs and Chardonnays. Still in barrel, the 1999 Chardonnay Estate reveals a citrusy, liquid minerality, buttery lemon, pear, honeysuckle, smoke, and steely notes. The wine is full-bodied, clean, and ideal for drinking during its first 3–4 years.

Dehlinger still considers 1994 followed by 1997 to be the two finest vintages for Pinot Noir in the nineties, but his top-notch 1998s are even better this year than they were when tasted a year ago. There are just under 1,200 cases of the 1998 Pinot Noir Goldridge Vineyard. It is a delicious, full-bodied (14.2% alcohol) Pinot Noir with abundant quantities of sweet black cherry fruit, notes of smoke and spicy oak, a velvety texture, and an easy to drink and admire personality. It should be consumed over the next 4–5 years. The outstanding 1998 Pinot Noir Estate (1,050 cases) is a full-bodied, powerful wine with plenty of jammy cherry fruit inter-mixed with smoke, chocolate, earth, and allspice. Voluptuously textured, chewy, and pure, this is a delectable Pinot Noir that will not make old bones, but for drinking over the next 4–5 years, it is hard to resist. There is a tiny (210 cases) production of the dark plum/purple-colored 1998 Pinot Noir Octagon Vineyard. It exhibits a floral/rose petal note to its sweet black cherry, dried herb, earthy, complex aromatics. Medium- to full-bodied, long, and sumptuous, it is a broad, expansively flavored wine to drink over the next 5–6 years.

The alcohols in Dehlinger's 1999 Pinot Noirs are relatively high (averaging about 14.5%), and, as in all vintages, Dehlinger uses 35–40% new oak. His extensive use of 500-liter oak puncheons works well. The 1999 Pinot Noir Estate offers sweet, smoky, black cherry and strawberry fruit presented in a crisp, elegant, medium-bodied style. It does not have the textural fatness or richness of the 1998, but that may come with further barrel aging. Certainly the 1999 Pinot Noir Octagon Vineyard and 1999 Pinot Noir Hilltop Vineyard (from 25-year--old vines) reveal more impressive richness, texture, and viscosity in their medium- to full-bodied personalities. They have the telltale robust, richly fruity Dehlinger style with explosive mid-palates, and plenty of glycerin, concentration, and alcohol. These should turn out to be his finest Pinot Noirs in 1999, with 5–7 years of ageability. I am still enjoying my 1994s, which give no indication of losing their sumptuous fruit.

There is no doubting that Dehlinger's 1997s are terrific, hedonistically styled Pinot Noirs loaded with fruit and enticing, fleshy textures. The 1997 Pinot Noir Goldridge Vineyard exhibits a dark ruby color and an attractive, sweet, moderately intense nose of cherry jam, plums, spicy oak, and smoke. Its full-bodied, velvety, heady style is already delicious, and the wine is ideal for drinking over the next 3–5 years. The dark ruby/plum-colored 1997 Pinot Noir Estate (1,330 cases) could pass for a top Beaune premier cru. With sweet, chocolaty, smoky, black cherry fruit intermixed with spicy cinnamon and earthy scents, this sexy, hedonistic Pinot Noir fruit bomb is undeniably delicious and compelling. Too good to resist, it will be better with another 6–12 months of bottle age, and last for 5–7 years. It tips the scales at 14.5% alcohol. The Pinot Noir that comes from the vineyard surrounding the spooky-looking house at the top of the knoll overlooking Dehlinger's winery is called Octagon. The big, boldly styled 1997 exhibits a dark ruby/purple color as well as copious quantities of cherry liqueur, roasted meats, dried herbs, spice, and chocolate. Explosive on the palate, with Dehlinger's impressive glycerin, concentration, and fruit extraction, this is another crowd-pleasing, sumptuous Pinot Noir to enjoy now and over the next 7–8 years. Production was 390 cases. The Reserve Pinot Noir is made in only the finest vintages, and the 1997 (450 cases) is the tightest, most backward of these four Pinots. Like its siblings, it possesses low acidity, outstanding concentration and purity, as well as abundant black cherry, plum, and meaty characteristics. There is exciting fruit and overall symmetry, but this effort needs 1–2 years of bottle age because of its more noticeable structure and higher tannin level. It cuts a bold swath across the palate and has the most substance of these Pinot Noirs, but it needs more time. Anticipated maturity: now–2010.

While some of the new Dijon clones have been planted (particularly Clone 777), Dehlinger's Pinots are all from such old California clones (which originally came from Burgundy) as Martini, Swan, and Pommard. There can be as many as four separate Pinot Noirs if Dehlinger decides to produce a Reserve bottling, as he did in 1994 and 1997. In 1996, there were three efforts, Goldridge Vineyard (1,150 cases), Estate (990 cases), and Octagon Vineyard (140 cases). What is so likable about the Dehlinger Pinot Noirs is that they are made in a richly fruity, chocolaty style with plenty of spice, plush textures, and copious quantities of glycerin and alcohol. They are both user-friendly and faithful to the varietal's trademark. For example, the 1996 Pinot Noir Goldridge Vineyard exhibits an impressive dark ruby/purple color and a superb bouquet of jammy plums/cherries intermixed with earthy underbrush and melted chocolate. With airing, Asian spices enter the mélange. This is a chewy, medium- to full-bodied, plump, hedonistic Pinot (14.5% alcohol) that can be drunk now as well as over the next 5–6 years. The outstanding 1996 Pinot Noir Estate is similar, with more glycerin, a sweeter black cherry/kirsch component, roasted herb characteristics, full body, 14.5% alcohol, superb purity, and a nicely layered, chewy texture. This wine should drink well for 5–7 years. The 1996 Pinot Noir Octagon Vineyard is the most limited in availability. It offers up a fabulous nose of jammy strawberries, cherries, a touch of prunes, roasted meat, and spicy oak. Full-bodied, with considerable glycerin and extract, and a dense, lush, voluptuously textured finish, it should drink well for 5–6 years.

The 1995 Pinot Noirs reveal a more meaty, animal, plant material side to their aromatics and flavors than the flamboyantly fruit-driven 1994s. For example, the 1995 Pinot Noir Goldridge Vineyard is a medium ruby-colored wine with a big, spicy, earthy, cinnamon, smoky-scented nose, rich, jammy, silky-textured fruit, medium body, and a lush finish. It should drink well for 1–3 years. The 1995 Pinot Noir Estate exhibits more intensity, a marginally deeper ruby color, and a satiny texture with plenty of ripe black cherry and berry fruit. Medium-bodied and soft, it is ideal for drinking now. The deepest and richest of these Pinots, the 1995 Pinot Noir Octagon Vineyard boasts a ripe strawberry, cherry, chocolaty, earthy character. Medium- to full-bodied, hedonistic, and lush, it possesses savory, expansive flavors, low acidity, and gorgeous ripeness.

The dark ruby-colored 1994 Pinot Noir Goldridge Vineyard offers a spicy, gamey, smoky, complex set of aromatics, outstanding richness, a long, round, full-bodied palate with a silky texture, and plenty of spice, jammy black cherries, and underbrush-like flavors. The gorgeous, flamboyant 1994 Pinot Noir Estate possesses sweet, ripe, layered flavors, and a knockout nose of spices, red and black fruits, earth, and smoke. At 14.5% alcohol, the wine has gobs of glycerin and a sweet mid-palate (from extract and glycerin, not sugar). Full, rich, and loaded with personality and flavor, it is a classic Russian River Pinot Noir. Drink it over the next 5–6 years. The 1994 Pinot Noir Octagon Vineyard (10% stems are retained in this *cuvée* during the fermentation) is slightly more expensive as only 100 cases were produced from Dehlinger's minuscule hilltop vineyard. The wine reveals the telltale Dehlinger intense fragrance of allspice, sweet black fruits, toast, and smoke. On the palate, a cascade of raspberry, cherry flavors are accompanied by power, full body, a silky texture, and ripe tannin in the finish. This bold, lusty Pinot Noir is already difficult to resist. The 1994 Pinot Noir Reserve (500 cases produced), the most structured and closed of these offerings, had only been in bottle for a month when I tasted it. It appears to be another exceptional ripe, rich, concentrated, dense, complex, and expansively flavored Pinot Noir with a 30–35-second finish, as well as exceptional purity and personality.

Cabernet Sauvignon is not one of Tom Dehlinger's favorite wines, yet he makes an excellent Cabernet that somehow gets lost in the excitement of this producer's other efforts. He harvests about 34 tons of Cabernet Sauvignon, of which he retains one-third. The 1997 Cabernet Sauvignon exhibits a dense purple color, as well as abundant chocolate and cassis fruit intermixed with licorice and tobacco. It is a full-bodied, concentrated Cabernet that is likely to surprise consumers who think the Russian River is only a source for fine Chardonnay, Pinot, and Syrah. It should drink well for 10–12 years. The 1998 Cabernet Sauvignon has turned out well for the vintage, but it does not have the lusty richness or intensity of the 1999. Nevertheless, it is elegant and cleanly made, with no herbaceousness or astringency. Drink it over the next 7–8 years. There are only 390 cases of the outstanding 1996 Cabernet Sauvignon. Its dense purple color is accompanied by a sweet nose of chocolate, dried herbs, smoke, licorice, and copious berry and cassis fruit. Full-bodied, dense, and chewy, with moderate tannin in the finish, it needs 2–3 years of cellaring, and should keep for 15–20 years. The 1995 Cabernet Sauvignon (460 cases) is a pure Cabernet with an opaque purple color and telltale aromas of cassis, asphalt, loamy soil notes, and smoky, toasty oak. The wine is full-bodied and layered, with a chewy texture, and impressive purity and length. There is good tannin in the finish, but this remains a grapy, unevolved Cabernet with considerable potential. Anticipated maturity: now–2020. The 1994 Cabernet Sauvignon is another top-notch effort from this classic vintage. This opaque purple-colored, sexy wine reveals the vintage's precocious, flattering style. It offers up plenty of jammy black fruits intermingled with smoke, spice, licorice, and charcoal. Full-bodied, with low acidity, outstanding ripeness, and a fleshy, multilayered feel, this wine can be drunk now or cellared for 15+ years.

1992 was the first vintage for Syrah at Dehlinger, and he continues to show a capable hand with this varietal, which has adapted so well in so many different areas of California. He takes about 50% of the crop off, yet he still gets high yields. Nevertheless, the wine always possesses richness, concentration, and character, and lasts for at least a decade. The 1997 Syrah Estate (550 cases) offers plenty of licorice, blackberry, cassis, pepper, and smoke. Full-bodied and juicy, with excellent purity, it will drink well over the next decade. The 1998 Syrah Estate shows more bacon fat intermingled with cassis and licorice. Although full-bodied, it comes across as more elegant and lighter than the 1997. A successful effort, it should keep for a decade or more. The 1998 Syrah Estate East Face reveals a distinctive blueberry, violet, and blackberry-scented nose, good acidity, plenty of power and richness, no hard edges, and a succulent, nicely textured mid-palate and finish. This wine should drink well for 10–15 years. The 1997 Syrah Goldridge Vineyard (420 cases) seemed slightly better from bottle than it was from barrel. A dark ruby/purple color is accompanied by smoky cassis fruit, full body, outstanding purity and concentration, and a huge, explosively rich finish. Low acidity and a forward, sexy style suggest drinking it over the next decade. The 1996 Syrah Estate (370 cases) exhibits an opaque purple color as well as a gorgeous nose of blackberry liqueur and pepper. Dense and full-bodied, with wonderful sweetness (from high glycerin), this fleshy, multilayered Syrah possesses a succulence and richness that is hard to resist. The wine should age nicely for 10–15 years. The 1996 Syrah Goldridge Vineyard (230 cases) is a hedonistic, fat, succulently textured Syrah with gobs of crème de cassis, a notion of burning wood fires, and pepper, full body, outstanding purity, and no hard edges. Despite its size, it is a Syrah to consume over the next 15 years.

The 1994 Syrah Estate has shut down in the bottle and will require 4–5 years of cellaring, after which it will age well for 5–10 years. The color is an impressive opaque purple, and the wine reluctantly offers up sweet cassis, pepper, tar, and earthy scents. Full-bodied and chewy, with excellent purity, this is a well-endowed yet moderately tannic Syrah for laying down for a few years. The 1994 Syrah Goldridge Vineyard is a richly fruity, medium-weight Syrah with a dark purple color, gobs of sweet black currants in the nose, round, generous flavors, and some tannin in the finish. The wine should drink well for up to a decade. The 1995 Syrah Goldridge Vineyard (aged in 20% new oak) reveals an attractive peppery, bacony, sweet blackberry-scented nose, and ripe, rich, full-bodied flavors with plenty of sweet fruit. With an impressive chewy texture and excellent purity, it is a candidate for 6–12 years of cellaring, although it can be drunk now if matched with rich foods. My notes for the 1995 Syrah Estate said, "amazing Syrah." The wine possesses an opaque black/purple color, outstanding smoky, tar-like, blackberry flavors, immense body, admirable purity, and a long, deep, explosively rich finish with the tannin nearly concealed by the wine's wealth of fruit, glycerin, and extract. This terrific Syrah should age effortlessly for another 8–10 years.

Dehlinger's modesty is best exemplified by the fact that he calls his proprietary red wine a Cabernet/Merlot Blend. Production for this outstanding wine is limited to 400 cases. The 1996 reveals a saturated opaque purple color, followed by a gorgeous nose of blackberries, vanilla, licorice, and floral notes. Chewy and full-bodied, with a viscous texture, low acidity, sensational fruit extraction, and a mouthcoating finish, this is a large-scaled yet sexy wine that can be drunk now or cellared for 10 or more years. It tips the scales at 14.5% alcohol. The 1994 Cabernet/Merlot Blend contains equal proportions of these varietals. The opaque purple/black color is followed by sweet, powerful aromas of black currants, licorice, chocolate, and sweet vanilla. The wine is full-bodied, dense, powerful, yet seamless and silky. The tannin is gorgeously well integrated, a characteristic of the vintage. This wine can be drunk now or cellared for 10–15 years. The opaque purple-colored 1995 Cabernet/Merlot Blend (70% Cabernet Sauvignon / 30% Merlot) displays a sweet, rich nose of melted road tar, black currants, earth, minerals, and toast. Rich, with great fruit and ripeness, this full-bodied wine will be at its best after 2–4 years of cellaring; it will keep for 10 years.

Past Glories: 1993 Bordeaux Blend Proprietary Red Wine (91), 1993 Cabernet/Merlot Blend (91), 1993 Cabernet Sauvignon (90)

DEL DOTTO (NAPA)

1997	Cabernet Franc	Napa	D	90
1997	Cabernet Sauvignon Estate	Napa	D	(90–92)
1996	Cabernet Sauvignon Estate	Napa	D	88
1995	Cabernet Sauvignon	Napa	D	89+
1998	Giovanni's Tuscan Reserve	Napa	E	88
1997	Giovanni's Tuscan Reserve	Napa	E (500 ml)	90
1995	Giovanni's Tuscan Reserve	Napa	D (500 ml)	88
1997	Merlot	Napa	E	(88–90)

This small seven-acre vineyard just north of St. Helena is primarily planted with Cabernet Sauvignon and a tiny amount of Sangiovese. Production has been limited, as part of the crop was sold to Whitehall Lane, but that changed with the 1997 vintage. Consequently, Del Dotto's production has soared from just under 500 to 4,000 cases. The wines are aged in both American and French oak, and the proprietary red, Giovanni's Tuscan Reserve, is available only in 500 ml bottles. My favorite new release from Del Dotto is the 1998 Giovanni's Tuscan Reserve, a 1,000-case blend of 85% Cabernet Sauvignon and 15% Sangiovese, all from the estate vineyards in Rutherford. This wine has a handsome, dark ruby color, a nose of black currants, cherries, leather, spice, and vanilla. The wine cuts a slightly deeper swath on the palate but is still medium-bodied, moderately endowed, and best drunk over the next 5–7 years.

Pride Mountain and La Jota routinely produce California's finest Cabernet Franc, but Del Dotto is not far behind with its lavishly wooded, ostentatious example. The 1997 Cabernet Franc reveals beautiful, sweet, black currant and raspberry fruit, toasty wood, and a sweet mid-palate and finish. It is a seductive, well-layered wine to enjoy over the next 7–10 years. The terrific 1997 Giovanni's Tuscan Reserve (1,199 cases of a blend of 75% Cabernet Sauvignon and 25% Sangiovese) is dominated by its cherry liqueur, strawberry jam, and leathery characteristics. Ripe, with medium to full body, a sweet, concentrated, juicy mid-palate, and outstanding purity, this seductive red is ready to drink. Consume it over the next 7–8 years. The outstanding 1997 Cabernet Sauvignon Estate is produced from a vineyard situated at the corner of Highway 29 and Zinfandel Lane in Rutherford. It exhibits a dense ruby/purple color in addition to a gorgeous nose of blackberry jam intermixed with cedar and spicy new oak. Full-bodied, dense, and pure, with a layered texture and low acidity, this beefy yet voluptuously textured Cabernet Sauvignon should drink well young and evolve nicely for 15 years. The 1997 Merlot (96% Merlot and 4% Cabernet Franc) is limited in production (249 cases). The wine's dark ruby color with purple nuances is followed by lush, mocha-tinged, berry fruit and cherry aromas and flavors. This low-acid, plump, chewy Merlot should drink well young and last for 7–10 years.

The 1996 Cabernet Sauvignon Estate is an elegant, medium-bodied effort with an oaky, black currant, cherry, and loamy soil-scented nose, and moderate tannin. It is more monolithic and less seamless than its 1997 counterpart. Anticipated maturity: now–2012. The Cabernet Sauvignons (500 cases of both the 1995 and 1996) are aged in 100% new oak, of which 50% is American oak coopered by French barrel makers. The exotic, opaque purple-colored 1995 Cabernet Sauvignon offers exceptionally ripe, jammy black cherry and currant flavors intermixed with lavish quantities of toasty new oak. Full-bodied and obvious, but undeniably appealing in an ostentatious manner, this brassy, big, thick, juicy wine is already drinking well, but promises to evolve for 10–12 years. The delicious 1995 Giovanni's Tuscan Reserve, a blend of 70% Cabernet Sauvignon and 30% Sangiovese, displays a dark plum color, full body, gorgeous, jammy strawberry fruit intermixed with raspberries and cassis with a subtle touch of spicy oak and a fleshy, chewy texture. Drink it over the next 3–4 years.

DOMINUS (NAPA)

1999 Dominus	Napa	EE	90
1998 Dominus	Napa	EE	89
1997 Dominus	Napa	EE	94
1996 Dominus	Napa	EE	95
1995 Dominus	Napa	E	93
1994 Dominus	Napa	E	99
1999 Napanook	Napa	D	85
1998 Napanook	Napa	D	87
1997 Napanook	Napa	D	90
1996 Napanook	Napa	D	90

The 1998 Dominus (a 7,000-case blend of 73% Cabernet Sauvignon, 15% Cabernet Franc, 6% Petit Verdot, and 6% Merlot) is very Bordeaux-like in its weight and its aromatic and flavor profile. From this dark garnet/ruby-colored wine emerges a moderately intense, complex nose of herbs, earth, cedar, coffee, and dried cherries and plum-like fruit. It is relatively evolved, with soft tannin, an elegant, medium-bodied style, and some tannin in the finish. While lighter than most recent vintages, that has more to do with the vintage than any change in winemaking. Drink it over the next 10–12 years. Perhaps the surprise was the showing of the 1999 Dominus, a 7,000-case blend of 75% Cabernet Sauvignon, 13% Cabernet Franc, 9% Merlot, and 3% Petit Verdot. The wine seemed to show some green pepper notes in the nose and tasted austere and tannic. It offers an impressive plum color as well as notes of blackberries, coffee, prunes, cedar, and herbs in the moderately intense aromatics. On the palate, this medium-bodied wine effort displays a harder style, with tough tannin and a slightly attenuated finish. If it fleshes out over the next six months, it should prove to be outstanding, but it is not one of the more prodigious offerings from this high-quality estate.

Readers waiting for another 1991 or 1994 Dominus, the two finest wines yet made at this French outpost of Pomerol's famed Christian Moueix, will have to wait for another vintage. Certainly, the 1997 Dominus is exquisite, but not at the level of the virtually perfect 1994 and 1991. The 1997 Dominus, a blend of 86.5% Cabernet Sauvignon, 9% Cabernet Franc, and 4.5% Merlot, is showing fabulously well. With 14.1% alcohol and a pH that would make many New World oenologists shudder (about 3.95), this wine is a fleshy, silky-textured, opulent wine with a gorgeous nose of roasted herbs, coffee, jammy black cherry, and plum-like fruit. Asian spice, licorice, and blackberry and cherry notes with tobacco spice all add to this complex, very involved, yet gorgeously symmetrical Dominus. The wine is medium- to full-bodied, very concentrated, and silky-textured. It is gorgeous to drink now, but should age easily for 10–15 years. The 1996 Dominus, a blend of 82% Cabernet Sauvignon, 10% Cabernet Franc, 4% Merlot, and 4% Petit Verdot, tips the scales at 14.2% alcohol. Although this offering lacks the power, intensity, and compelling characteristics of the 1991 and 1994, it is not far off the pace of those two monumental wines. A super nose of roasted coffee, chocolate, dried herbs, black fruits, and kirsch is both intense and persuasive. The wine displays terrific richness, medium to full body, low acidity, a succulent, opulent texture, and superb purity. This beautifully made 1996 is one of the few wines that has successfully tamed the vintage's elevated tannin level. It should be relatively drinkable upon its release, yet evolve nicely for two decades. Impressive!

The 1995 Dominus (a 6,000-case blend of 80% Cabernet Sauvignon, 10% Cabernet Franc, 6% Petit Verdot, and 4% Merlot) is ripe, plummy, supple, and expansively flavored with copious quantities of black currant fruit. Full-bodied and low in acidity, it possesses exceptional concentration and purity. Qualitatively, it is built along the lines of the 1992 and 1990. While it is not as powerful or intense as the 1996 or 1994, the 1995 is a large-scaled, rich wine that should provide splendid drinking for two decades. I have had a difficult time keeping the corks in my bottles of 1994 Dominus. Eight thousand cases were produced from a blend of 70% Cabernet Sauvignon, 14% Cabernet Franc, 12% Merlot, and 4% Petit Verdot. In this vintage, 174 days passed between bud break and the harvest, a remarkable period of time for any wine region in the world. The 1994 is a strikingly thick, compellingly rich wine with the texture of a great Pomerol, despite being made primarily from Cabernet Sauvignon. The wine exhibits a dense purple color and an incredibly fragrant nose of jammy black fruits, spice, smoke, and loamy, truffle-like scents. In the mouth, it is full-bodied, with thrilling levels of extract and richness, but no sense of heaviness or harshness. This seamless Dominus possesses no hard edges, as its acidity, tannin, and alcohol are beautifully meshed with copious quantities of ripe fruit. This wine offers early drinking, yet has the potential to last for 30+ years.

This estate's second wine, Napanook, is a reasonably good value at about one-third the price of Dominus. The 1999 Napanook (a 3,800-case blend of 70% Cabernet Sauvignon, 14% Cabernet Franc, 3% Merlot, and 3% Petit Verdot) shows some sweet chocolate, along with notes of dried herbs, cedar, spice box, black cherries, and coffee. The wine is medium-bodied, quite spicy, with slightly more structure and tannin than the 1998. It should drink well for 8–10 years upon release. The dark saturated ruby-colored 1998 Napanook (a 4,000-case blend of 94% Cabernet Sauvignon and 6% Petit Verdot) exhibits a Pomerol-like lushness, openness, and delicious black cherry and berry fruit. The wine begins with an excellent attack, then falls off slightly. Medium-bodied and round, it is ideal for restaurants and consumers looking for an immediately drinkable wine. It will last well for 7–8 years.

The 1997 Napanook (a 7,000-case blend of 61% Cabernet Sauvignon, 22% Cabernet Franc, and 17% Merlot) shows even better from bottle than it did from cask. The color is dark ruby with purple nuances. A sweet, open-knit nose offering aromas of tobacco, cedar, blackberry and cherry jam is followed by an opulently textured, succulent, rich, fleshy, user-friendly, delicious wine. Undeniably hedonistic, it caresses the palate. Already delicious, it will age nicely for a decade. There are 2,000 cases of the 1996 Napanook, a blend of 74% Cabernet Sauvignon, 13% Cabernet Franc, and 13% Petit Verdot. Made in a peppery, spicy, herbaceous, earthy style, it exhibits a dark plum color, an intensely aromatic cassis and pepper-scented nose, a lush entry on the palate, and succulent, low-acid, rich, concentrated flavors with more tannin than the 1997. Already drinkable, the 1996 is appealing for its intense fragrance and rich flavors. It should age well for 10–12 years.

Past Glories: Dominus—1992 (94), 1991 (100), 1990 (96), 1987 (92), 1986 (90), 1985 (90), 1984 (92)

DOWNING FAMILY VINEYARDS (NAPA)

1999 Zinfandel Fly by Night	Napa	D	90

This creatively packaged Zinfandel (check out the bottle) boasts an opaque purple color in addition to a sweet nose of black fruits, high-quality new oak, minerals, and flowers, outstanding concentration, impressive purity, medium to full body, and well-integrated acidity as well as tannin. A classy, elegant, complex offering made in the style of a classified growth Bordeaux, it will drink well for 7–8 years.

DRY CREEK VINEYARD (SONOMA)

1999 Zinfandel Heritage Clone	Dry Creek	B	90
1998 Zinfandel Heritage Clone	Dry Creek	C	(86–88)

1999 Zinfandel Old Vines	Sonoma	C	90
1998 Zinfandel Old Vines	Dry Creek	D	89
1997 Zinfandel Old Vines	Sonoma	C	88
1995 Zinfandel Old Vines 25th Anniversary	Dry Creek	D	88
1999 Zinfandel Reserve	Sonoma	D	89+
1998 Zinfandel Reserve	Dry Creek	D	90

A 90-point rating for a $15 bottle of California wine is about as rare as a $15 classified growth 2000 Bordeaux. Dry Creek's 1999 Heritage Clone Zinfandel must be the "value of the vintage," but even the $20 Old Vines is a sensational buy. Ironically, I preferred those two offerings to the more structured, backward 1999 Reserve. As for the 1999 Zinfandel Heritage Clone, it boasts a dense purple color and a sweet nose of blackberries, licorice, pepper, and minerals. There is a terrific mid-palate, beautiful harmony, and well-integrated acidity, tannin, and oak. Drink this opulently styled, pure, classic Zinfandel over the next 4–5 years. The similarly styled, opaque purple-colored 1999 Zinfandel Old Vines offers gorgeously sweet aromas of black cherries, raspberries, and currants. Multilayered, powerful, and rich, with more muscle and structure than the Heritage Clone *cuvée*, it is a topflight, balanced, concentrated yet harmonious wine to enjoy over the next 4–6 years. More backward and less evolved, the 1999 Zinfandel Reserve displays more new oak—not always a welcome characteristic for Zinfandel. Full-bodied and well structured, it exhibits aromas and flavors of red and black fruits intermixed with new saddle leather, vanilla, and earth. Dense and chewy, it needs another 1–2 years of cellaring to round into shape. While it may age longer than the Old Vines and Heritage Clone *cuvées*, it is questionable whether it will ultimately taste better.

All of the 1998 Zinfandels, hopefully, will be bottled without excessive fining or filtration. The well-made, deep ruby-colored 1998 Zinfandel Old Vines offers a heady perfume of blackberry and cherry fruit. Medium- to full-bodied and plush, with low acidity, as well as abundant glycerin and concentration, this opulent wine will have many admirers. Even denser, the opaque ruby/purple-colored 1998 Zinfandel Reserve reveals gorgeously thick, rich, concentrated black cherry and raspberry aromas and flavors infused with pepper, earth, leather, and subtle spicy wood. The vintage's low acidity as well as modest yields have resulted in a wine of considerable richness, extract, and ripeness, but no sense of heaviness. It should drink beautifully for 6–7 years. Interestingly, as it sat in the glass, notes of licorice and melted asphalt emerged. Slightly less impressive, although very good, is the 1998 Zinfandel Heritage Clone. It possesses more tannin in addition to a robust, chunky, rustic personality. There is plenty of density and spice, but the wine tastes slightly disjointed. Anticipated maturity: now–2008.

An elegant, flavorful, medium-bodied Zinfandel, Dry Creek's 1997 Old Vines exhibits a dark ruby color, attractive raspberry and cherry fruit in the spicy bouquet. With a tasty, peppery, open-knit texture, this wine has enough acidity to provide vibrancy and freshness. Drink it over the next 3–4 years. The excellent 1995 Zinfandel Old Vines 25th Anniversary is one of the most noteworthy efforts from this vintage. It possesses a dense ruby/purple color, followed by a big, fragrant, spicy, pungent nose of pepper, jammy red and black fruits, and earth. Rich, medium- to full-bodied, and harmonious, this wine exhibits a pleasing midsection and fine length. It should drink well for 5–6 years.

DUCKHORN (NAPA)

1998 Paraduxx	Napa	D	88

A proprietary blend of 65% Zinfandel, 30% Cabernet Sauvignon, and 5% Merlot, aged in both American and French oak (primarily new), this deep opaque ruby/purple-colored effort offers a sexy bouquet of chocolate, cassis, berries, and melted road tar. Some oak emerges with airing. Medium- to full-bodied and chewy, the Cabernet Sauvignon component presently dominates this excellent wine's personality. Consume it over the next 6–7 years.

DUNN VINEYARDS (NAPA)

1999	Cabernet Sauvignon	Howell Mountain	E	(90–93)
1998	Cabernet Sauvignon	Howell Mountain	E	89
1997	Cabernet Sauvignon	Howell Mountain	E	95
1996	Cabernet Sauvignon	Howell Mountain	E	96+
1995	Cabernet Sauvignon	Howell Mountain	E	96
1994	Cabernet Sauvignon	Howell Mountain	D	96+
1998	Cabernet Sauvignon	Napa	D	87
1997	Cabernet Sauvignon	Napa	D	92+
1996	Cabernet Sauvignon	Napa	D	94
1995	Cabernet Sauvignon	Napa	D	94
1994	Cabernet Sauvignon	Napa	D	94

If Godzilla drank California Cabernet Sauvignon, would there be any doubt as to what choice it would be? Anyone who has regularly tasted Randy Dunn's Cabernet Sauvignons (first produced in 1979) realizes several things. They all possess the following characteristics: 1) remarkable color and richness, 2) massive personalities with huge tannic structures, and 3) gorgeous purity and unreal aging potential. In 1999, I reported on a tasting where all of Dunn's top wines back through the 1982 vintage were served. Remarkably, they had hardly budged in development, yet they were still exceptionally rich in their pure crème de cassis, black raspberry, and blackberry fruit notes. These are obviously more than 20–25 year wines. It is not far-fetched to suggest that Dunn is producing Cabernet Sauvignons that, in top vintages, will be fresh, lively, and rich in fruit at age 50. Unbelievably, Dunn has barely raised his prices in the two decades he has been making wine. For those with patience, these are among the finest values in long-lived, classic Napa Cabernet Sauvignon.

The Howell Mountain 1998 and 1999 Cabernet Sauvignons were produced from very small crops characterized by extremely cool growing seasons and unusually late harvests. Dunn dropped 40% of his crop in 1998 in order to attain ripeness. Consequently, his 1998 Cabernet Sauvignon Howell Mountain does not possess the herbaceousness or weediness found in many 1998 Howell Mountain Cabernets. The wine reveals plenty of sweet black currant fruit infused with minerals. While lighter than his more powerful vintages, it is a successful effort. It may last only 20–25 years, rather than 50! The 1999 Cabernet Sauvignon Howell Mountain experienced a similar growing season. Dunn dropped 30% of the crop in order to guarantee ripeness in his vineyard. The 1999 displays excellent intensity along with pure black currant/cassis notes intermixed with earth, spice, and smoke. Again, there is no astringent tannin or vegetal characteristic to be found in this full-bodied, powerful Cabernet.

The 1998 Cabernet Sauvignon Napa (a composite blend) is highly extracted for the vintage, but lighter than most Dunn Cabernet Sauvignons. It obviously reflects the challenges presented by this vintage. Dry tannin in the finish might turn out to be cause for concern, but there is still plenty of cassis fruit in this medium- to full-bodied Cabernet, though it is more compressed than usual. Dunn will undoubtedly build more flesh and fruit into it before bottling, but we will have to wait another year to find out.

Randy Dunn's 1997s are superb examples of the vintage. But be forewarned, readers planning their purchases should remember that these wines usually require at least a decade of cellaring. Keep in mind that some of Dunn's finest early vintages (1982 and 1984) are still infants! They are crammed with the telltale characteristics of blackberry and crème de cassis fruit tinged with an earthy minerality. The 1997 Cabernet Sauvignon Napa exhibits an opaque purple color as well as a gorgeous nose of pure cassis and blackberries with flinty notions in the background. Full-bodied, powerful, tannic, pure, and backward, it needs another 8–10 years of cellaring. Anticipated maturity: 2010–2035+. The enormous 1997 Cabernet Sauvignon Howell Mountain is a super-powerful, fabulously concentrated, 50-year wine. Aromas and flavors of blackberry/cassis jam, minerals, and subtle oak are found in this extravagantly rich, gargantuan Cabernet Sauvignon that should age effortlessly for half a century. Anticipated maturity: 2015–2050.

The 1996s have turned out to be stunning. The opaque blue/purple-colored 1996 Cabernet Sauvignon Napa boasts an exceptional nose of crème de cassis, minerals, and spice. It takes at least a decade for wines such as this to begin to reveal more identity and vintage character. The cassis/blackberry liqueur–like fruit are present, as are mouth-searing levels of tannin and impressive extract. This blockbuster should be at its peak between 2010–2040. Take all those elements, add a bit more ink to the black/blue/purple color, give the texture slightly more unctuosity and thickness, and readers have a glimpse of Randy Dunn's 1996 Cabernet Sauvignon Howell Mountain. Greatness is suggested by a wonderfully sweet mid-section, gorgeous purity, and this humongous wine's overall symmetry. It also possesses sumptuous layers of concentration, phenomenal richness, remarkably sweet tannin, low acidity, and a 40+-second finish. Anticipated maturity: 2009–2040.

As for the 1995s, this appears to be a fabulous vintage. I doubt there will be much difference in quality between the 1995s and Dunn's spectacular 1994s. The saturated black/purple-colored 1995 Cabernet Sauvignon Napa possesses a promising yet backward nose of minerals, lead pencil, and blackberries/cassis. This mammoth offering displays extraordinary concentration and purity, as well as a thick, unctuous texture with high tannin levels. It will evolve for 30–50 years. When will it reach its plateau of maturity? My best guess is 10–15 years . . . minimum. The 1995 Cabernet Sauvignon Howell Mountain is similar in all respects to the Napa, but somewhat heavier in the mouth, with an aggressive tannic bite and more length. It possesses mineral-tinged blackberry and cassis fruit, massive body, and extraordinary purity and length. It should not be touched for 12–15 years. Again, it will undoubtedly live through the first half of the 21st century.

Randy Dunn is sensitive to the fact that his wines are so remarkably consistent that it is often difficult to tell vintages apart. I think the vintage character will become more apparent when the wines are 15–20 years of age. Even the most professional palate will be inundated with a furious blast of tannin and concentrated cassis and blackberry fruit when these wines are young. With that in mind, the following notes do sound similar, but I feel 1994 may turn out to be one of Dunn's finest vintages. At present, 1995 looks to be the most tannic, and 1996, similar to but softer than 1994. Given the fact that both of Dunn's debut vintages of 1979 and 1980 are still relative infants in terms of development, in all likelihood, the 1994s, 1995s, and 1996s possess a minimum of 25–30 years of aging potential!

The 1994s might be ready to drink within 10–15 years. It is hard to believe these wines spend 30 months in oak casks before bottling as they are incredibly unevolved and backward when released. The 1994 Cabernet Sauvignon Napa reveals an opaque purple color, followed by a sweet, rich, black currant and crème de cassis–scented nose with no evidence of oak. This fruit bomb displays considerable breadth and expansiveness on the palate, in essence revealing only two dimensions—fruit and tannin. It is slightly softer and more precocious than the 1995 and 1996, so perhaps it will only need 10 rather than 15 years of cellaring. This immensely impressive Cabernet is a candidate for 20–30 years of cellaring. Look out for the behemoth 1994 Cabernet Sauvignon Howell Mountain. This black/purple-colored wine adds a few more nuances (minerals, licorice, and floral scents) to the lavish display of crème de cassis. Full-bodied, with a blockbuster level of extract and density, this is an outstanding Cabernet Sauvignon for readers with patience, good genes for longevity, or the foresight to purchase it for their children. Anticipated maturity: 2006–2030.

As a postscript, I have been buying Randy Dunn's wines since he first began producing them in 1979. I have worried about whether they will ever become drinkable given their massive personalities and huge tannic structures. I am not sure I know the answer, but a blind tasting in late September of 1998 was a revelation. What was so striking was that in the first flight, which included vintages from the early eighties, the wines were thought to be from the early nineties! Undoubtedly, these wines age at a glacial pace. While I have been consistently advising readers that they will last for 25–30 years, they may be 40–50 year wines, possibly needing 25–30 years just to reach their plateau of maturity! No vintage from the eighties or nineties was revealing much age. All the wines were relatively stunning in quality, with some of the lighter years, such as 1983 and 1988, surprisingly impressive, but not as phenomenal as Randy Dunn's greatest vintages (1982, 1984, 1985, 1990, 1991, 1992, 1993, 1994, 1995, and 1996). One of the interesting findings from this vertical tasting is that the fruit levels remain incredibly fresh and concentrated, yet the tannin levels do soften. Because the wines are sterile filtered, I am not sure they will ever develop aromatic complexity, but who really knows? The remarkable aspect is that at 15–18 years of age, Dunn's Cabernet Sauvignons taste as if they are only 3–5 years old. Furthermore, there are no signs of fruit degradation or oxidation, always positive attributes when measuring a wine's ageability.

Past Glories: Dunn Cabernet Sauvignon Howell Mountain—1993 (95), 1992 (97), 1991 (94), 1990 (96), 1987 (94), 1986 (94), 1985 (95), 1984 (95), 1982 (97), 1981 (90), 1979 (90)

EDMEADES ESTATE (MENDOCINO)

1999 Gewürztraminer	Anderson Valley	B	88
1998 Petite Sirah Eaglepoint	Mendocino	D	88
1996 Petite Sirah Eaglepoint	Mendocino	C	89
1998 Pinot Noir	Anderson Valley	C	88
1997 Pinot Noir	Anderson Valley	C	90
1999 Syrah Eaglepoint Vineyard	Mendocino	D	(87–89)
1998 Zinfandel	Mendocino	C	90
1997 Zinfandel	Mendocino	C	88
1998 Zinfandel	Mendocino Ridge	D	89
1997 Zinfandel	Mendocino Ridge	D	89
1997 Zinfandel Ciapusci Vineyard	Mendocino Ridge	C	91
1996 Zinfandel Ciapusci Vineyard	Mendocino	C	88
1998 Zinfandel Eaglepoint Vineyard	Mendocino	D	91
1995 Zinfandel Eaglepoint Vineyard	Mendocino	D	90
1996 Zinfandel Zeni Vineyard	Mendocino	D	90
1998 Zinfandel Zeni Vineyard	Mendocino Ridge	D	88
1997 Zinfandel Zeni Vineyard	Mendocino Ridge	C	88+

An underrated winery for sure, proprietor Jess Jackson and his wine-maker, Van Williamson, are turning out gorgeous wines that seem to go largely unnoticed, probably because they are realistically priced. This is an excellent source of unfined, unfiltered wines, including one of the finest Pinot Noir values in the land. Edmeades also produces a Gewürztraminer and a Chardonnay that sell for a song. The 1999 Gewürztraminer, from a varietal that rarely produces anything of interest, is surprisingly spot-on in terms of its exotic rose petal/lychee nut aromatics. Rich and full-bodied, with some residual sugar, it will drink beautifully over the next year with Asian dishes or sautéed foie gras. There are 2,638 cases of the artisanal 1998 Pinot Noir, a big, rich, earthy, animal-styled Pinot with plenty of black cherry fruit, pepper, and plum aromas as well as flavors. Medium- to full-bodied and fruit-driven, with good glycerin and a silky texture, it requires consumption over the next 2–3 years. The 1998 Petite Sirah Eaglepoint Vineyard is surprisingly soft, round, and forward for a Petite Sirah. The wine has plenty of character, an opaque ruby/purple color, and good peppery, blackberry, and licorice notes. It should drink well for 10–12 years. Another opulently textured wine is the 1999 Syrah Eaglepoint Vineyard. This 100% Syrah aged in both French and American oak exhibits blackberry liqueur aspects along with smoke, creosote, and pepper. It is a full-bodied, luscious Syrah to drink during its first decade of life. A great value when you divide dollars by points is Edmeades' 1997 Pinot Noir. Aged in both American and French oak, this

100% Pinot Noir from an Anderson Valley vineyard called Philo is more limited in availability (just under 2,000 cases). Reminiscent of some of Domaine Parent's old-fashioned Pommards I enjoyed in the early seventies, its medium ruby color is followed by aromas of overripe plums, blackberries, cherries, and toast. Full-bodied (14.5% alcohol), with a nicely layered, plump texture, this low-acid, luxuriously rich, expressive Pinot Noir is one of the sleepers being made in California. Drink it over the next 2–4 years. It is a great value.

Readers looking for muscular, brawny, full-bodied, tannic reds need search no further than Edmeades' 1996 Petite Sirah Eaglepoint. This wine reveals an opaque black/purple color, as well as a boldly styled nose of jammy blackberry fruit intertwined with cassis and earth. It is a broodingly dense, chewy, uncomplex wine with intense flavors, full body, and excellent, nearly outstanding purity and length. Consume it now, or cellar it for 10–15 years.

The bevy of powerful 1998 Zinfandels from Edmeades (ranging from 15.5–17.5% alcohol) includes debut releases from the new Mendocino Ridge appellation, a series of high-altitude, ridge-top vineyards. The dark plum-colored 1998 Zinfandel Mendocino Ridge (15.5% alcohol) offers aromas and flavors of smoke, plums, black raspberries, and black currants. Spicy and round, with a supple texture, and a rich, medium- to full-bodied, luscious texture, this wine can be drunk over the next 4–5 years. The 1998 Zinfandel Mendocino (15.6% alcohol) reveals a slightly more saturated color than its Mendocino Ridge sibling in addition to full, powerful, chewy flavors redolent with blackberries, cherries, incense, spice box, and subtle wood. A heady alcohol content provides glycerin, and the fleshy, full-bodied texture is a hedonist's dream. Enjoy this Zinfandel over the next 6–7 years. Also from the Mendocino Ridge appellation, the 1998 Zinfandel Zeni Vineyard (16.5% alcohol) exhibits a dark ruby color with amber at the edge. The nose is reminiscent of an Asian restaurant, with scents of soy, smoked duck, plums, and assorted black fruits. Ripe and deep, with a slight hotness, this heady wine requires consumption over the next 3–5 years. Again, low acidity gives the wine an extremely forward feel. Lastly, the superb 1998 Zinfandel Eaglepoint Vineyard (16% alcohol) tastes like a fabulous northern Rhône. Blackberry liqueur infused with smoke jumps from the glass of this stupendous Zinfandel. Explosive in the mouth, with huge extract levels, fruit, and glycerin, but no heaviness or heat, this is a full-throttle, opulently textured, hedonistic offering to drink over the next 3-5 years.

All four 1997 Zinfandels are well-made, reasonably priced efforts. My favorite is the 1997 Zinfandel Ciapusci Vineyard. Sadly, there are only 617 cases of this dry, full-bodied, exotic Zinfandel. Fermented with natural yeasts, it achieved 17% alcohol (not to be sipped as a cocktail next to the swimming pool, please). An earthy, gamey, briery, bramble-like perfume jumps from the glass of this medium ruby-colored, luscious, decadently rich effort. Drink it over the next several years. The 1997 Zinfandel Mendocino (10,000 cases; 15.4% alcohol) was aged 10 months in both French and American oak. It is a fat, big, rich, delicious effort bursting with peppery, spicy, cherry fruit with a touch of blackberries. Interestingly, the blend was 78% Zinfandel, 8% Sangiovese, 3% Syrah, and 11% Petite Sirah. Another nearly outstanding effort from wine-maker Van Williamson is the 1997 Zinfandel Mendocino Ridge. Tipping the scales at a whopping 16.3% alcohol, it is a blend from three vineyards—Alden Ranch, Ciapusci, and Zeni. There are just under 600 cases of this big, briery, dense, full-bodied Zinfandel with more noticeable high acidity than some of its siblings. It should drink well for 2–3 years, but it is not quite as lavishly rich and sumptuous as either the Mendocino or Ciapusci Vineyard. The tightest-knit, most backward of this quartet is the 1997 Zinfandel Zeni Vineyard. Also the lowest in alcohol (14.8%), it spent 18 months in both French and American oak. Production for this 100% Zinfandel is 187 cases. It needs another 3–6 months of cellaring, and while it may not improve, it will open up given its fleshy, structured personality. All the Zinfandel varietal characteristics—black cherries, pepper, briery fruit— are present in moderately high levels. This wine should drink well for 4–5 years.

The two fine 1996 Zinfandels include the 1996 Zinfandel Zeni Vineyard, which possesses plenty of this varietal's peppery, briery, raspberry fruit, good freshness, and loads of glycerin and concentration. This lush, supple-textured wine should be consumed over the next several years. The evolved dark plum-colored 1996 Zinfandel Ciapusci Vineyard offers a spicy, peppery, fruity nose, lush, medium-bodied flavors, and good fat and depth. Although not as deep and rich as the Zeni *cuvée*, it is excellent for drinking over the next 1–2 years.

I adored the 1995 Zinfandel Eaglepoint Vineyard. The wine's saturated opaque purple color is accompanied by intense aromas of black raspberries, cherries, minerals, and spice. Opulently textured and rich, with layers of fruit, this wine is atypical of the vintage given its wealth of fruit, surprising level of glycerin, and gorgeously proportioned, layered finish. This is a beautifully made, pure, medium- to full-bodied Zinfandel that has managed to hide its lofty alcohol (15.2%) content. It is fully mature.

Kudos to part hippie, part wild man, wine-maker Van Williamson!

ETUDE (NAPA)

1998	Cabernet Sauvignon	Napa	E	90
1997	Cabernet Sauvignon	Napa	E	96
1996	Cabernet Sauvignon	Napa	E	92
1995	Cabernet Sauvignon	Napa	D	94
1994	Cabernet Sauvignon	Napa	D	95+
1999	Pinot Noir	Carneros	D	90
1998	Pinot Noir	Carneros	D	88
1996	Pinot Noir	Carneros	D	88
1998	Pinot Noir Heirloom	Carneros	D	90
1996	Pinot Noir Heirloom	Carneros	D	91

Wine-maker Tony Soter seems to go from strength to strength, with his 1999s perhaps the most superlative group of wines I have yet tasted from him. There is a bevy of 1999 Pinot Noirs, all of them interesting. Soter's goal is to produce between 6,000–7,000 cases of Pinot Noir under the Etude label, with about 4,000 cases of the core wine from the Carneros blend of Pinot Noir, and the other 2,000–3,000 cases the Heirloom.

The 1998 Pinot Noir (3,400 cases) is an attractive, medium ruby-colored offering with a spicy, cinnamon, root beer, and plum/raspberry-scented nose. This lush, elegant, tasty Pinot offers savory, fleshy flavors exhibiting a judicious touch of oak, and well-integrated soft tannin and acidity. Drink it over the next 3–4 years. The top California *cuvée*, the 1998 Pinot Noir Heirloom Vineyard (380 cases) boasts a dark ruby color as well as a gorgeous bouquet of plums, black cherries, and cola (or is it root beer?), medium to full body, outstanding stuffing and purity, sweet tannin, and integrated acidity. It is a well-delineated, concentrated Pinot for consuming over the next 5–7 years.

Aged in 60% new French oak and bottled without filtration, the deep ruby-colored 1996 Pinot Noir Carneros exhibits a smoky, spicy, intense nose. The wine possesses fine ripeness, plenty of cherry/berry fruit with vague underbrush notes, and silky, round flavors. While this is not a huge Pinot Noir, it is both silky-smooth and complex. The finest Pinot Noir I have yet tasted from Etude is the 1996 Heirloom, a 275-case lot of the best barrels (in this vintage, a selection of 12 separate barrels). Bottled with no fining or filtration, this dark, saturated ruby-colored offering reveals knockout aromatics of smoke, toast, and black fruits. The wine's texture is rich, multilayered, and plush. There is real depth in the mid-palate, and the finish is long, round, and generous. I should note that Tony Soter has a vineyard in Oregon's Willamette Valley, so readers can look forward to what should be some superlative Pinot Noirs starting with the 1998 vintage.

The 1998 Cabernet Sauvignon Napa is one of the most impressive efforts of the vintage. An opaque ruby/purple color is followed by a soft, precocious, evolved, up-front style with gorgeous black fruits, medium to full body, soft tannin, and good fatness allied to elegance and suppleness. While it does not possess the volume or density of the spectacular 1997, or the potential of the 1999, it is a delicious wine to drink over the next decade.

Etude's 1997 Cabernet Sauvignon (1,800 cases) ranks alongside the finest Tony Soter has produced. Don't miss it! Opaque purple-colored, with a gorgeously seamless personality, this unfined/unfiltered wine exhibits classic aromas of cassis, licorice, chocolate, and toast. Rich and full-bodied, with sweet tannin, a multilayered mid-palate, and a terrific finish, it possesses the accessibility and opulence of the finest 1997s, but its balance and overall concentration suggest it will age for two decades or more. Etude's 1996 Cabernet Sauvignon displays an impressively saturated ruby/purple color, and a tight but promising bouquet of licorice, black currants, and toasty oak. There is more tannin than in the 1995 or 1997, but it is not intrusive. Fleshy, with fine purity, medium to full body, and a sweet mid-palate and finish, this wine should be cellared for 3–4 years and consumed over the following 15–20 years. The 1995 Cabernet Sauvignon boasts a saturated black/purple color, as well as a terrific nose of licorice, cassis, and subtle toasty oak. Full-bodied and crammed with extract and rich, ripe black fruits, this dense, symmetrical Cabernet will require several years of cellaring, but it should age effortlessly for 15–20 years. It is every bit as good as the terrific 1994, and may ultimately prove to be better, as well as longer-lived.

The awesomely rich 1994 Cabernet Sauvignon is another spectacular example of this splendid vintage. It possesses an opaque purple color, a wonderful sweetness, full body, and layers of cedary, mineral, and spice-tinged black berry and cassis fruit. Although there is a boatload of tannin, it is sweet and well integrated. The finish lasts for nearly 30 seconds. This dazzling Cabernet Sauvignon is one of the finest Soter has made at Etude.

By the way, I had a chance to do a mini-vertical of the Etude Cabernet Sauvignons, and all of them performed extremely well. Most of them appeared to need additional cellaring, and each of them suggested to me that they have another two decades of life. I rated the 1993, 92+ (needs 2–4 years of cellaring); 1992, 91 (substantial effort, should drink well for 5–7 years), 1991, 95 (an awesome wine); and the 1990, 90 (outstanding, but dwarfed by more recent efforts).

FIFE (NAPA)

1997	Max Cuvée Proprietary Red Wine	Napa	D	88
1995	Max Cuvée Proprietary Red Wine	Napa	C	90
1994	Max Cuvée Proprietary Red Wine	Napa	C	91+
1995	Petite Syrah Redhead Vineyard	Mendocino	C	89
1999	Zinfandel Dalraddy Chiles Valley	Napa	D	90
1997	Zinfandel Redhead Vineyard	Mendocino	C	88
1994	Zinfandel Redhead Vineyard	Mendocino	C	90
1994	Zinfandel Spring Mountain District	Napa	C	90
1998	Zinfandel Uplands	Mendocino	C	88
1994	Zinfandel Les Vieilles Vignes	Napa	C	90
1998	Zinfandel Whaler Vineyard	Mendocino	C	90

A relatively new winery, Fife continues to produce an impressive array of concentrated, well-balanced, ageworthy wines. The 1994 Max Cuvée, a proprietary blend, boasts an inky black/purple color, as well as an exceptionally ripe, pure nose of black fruits, licorice, and spice. Full-bodied, with layers of concentration, a corpulent, thick texture, yet no sense of heaviness, this is an exceptionally rich wine with soft tannin. Although approachable, it will be at its best between now–2015. I am pleased to report that the 1994 Zinfandel Redhead Vineyard (14.6% alcohol) is another textbook Zin from Fife. It offers a dark ruby/purple color, followed by a spicy blast of briery, black raspberry, peppery fruit. This pure, luscious, soft, mouth-filling wine is meant to be drunk over the next 2–3 years. The 1994 Zinfandel Les Vieilles Vignes displays an opulent personality, with a deep ruby/purple color, and a gorgeous display of sweet, toasty, smoky new oak, and jammy, pure, ripe berry fruit. Luscious in the mouth, with low acidity, copious quantities of fruit, chewy glycerin, and heady alcohol, this is a lusty, full-bodied, rich Zin for drinking over the next 5–6 years. The 1994 Spring Mountain District Zinfandel is also a beauty, offering more of a black raspberry–scented nose, exquisite ripeness and purity, and a more elegant, less bulky style than the Vieilles Vignes. The Spring Mountain *cuvée* is all finesse, fruit, and delicacy. These wines are beautifully made Zinfandels.

The 1995 Max Cuvée exhibits an impressively saturated deep purple color and a closed but promising nose of sweet black currant fruit intertwined with high-quality toast and vanilla notes. The wine is dense, closed, tannic, and medium- to full-bodied, as well as impressively pure and rich. Most of the wine's sweetness and intensity are felt at the back of the mouth, indicating this offering needs 4–5 years of cellaring. Anticipated maturity: now–2015. Petite Sirah (at this estate spelled Syrah) lovers will enjoy Fife's 1995 Petite Syrah Redhead Vineyard. The color is a dense ruby/plum. This wine is as ferociously tannic as the Cabernet Sauvignon Reserve, but it manages to integrate the tannin better because of its high extraction of fruit. There is plenty of blackberry, earthy, peppery, sweet fruit in this dense, full-bodied wine. Only masochists will enjoy it at present, but my instincts suggest this wine will be excellent with another 2–5 years of bottle age.

The 1997 Zinfandel Redhead Vineyard possesses the highest alcohol (14.6%) of Fife's 1997 Zinfandels as well as the most saturated dark ruby/purple color. Although less evolved aromatically, it offers aromas of damp forests intermixed with plums and blackberries. Round and rich, with multiple layers in addition to Zinfandel's telltale peppery spice, it should drink well for 4–5 years. The 1997 Max Cuvée exhibits pepper, blackberry, and cassis fruit, along with medium to full body, more structure, and less charm. A denser, ageworthy wine, it will be even better with 1–2 years of cellaring, and should last for a decade.

The 1998 Mendocino offerings from Fife include the 1998 Zinfandel Uplands. The alcohol for these wines ranges between 14.3–14.5%, hardly excessive by Zinfandel standards. This low-acid, plump, opulently textured effort possesses medium body, a sexy, smoky, spicy, blackberry and cherry-scented nose, loads of fruit, good glycerin, and purity, and nicely integrated wood. It is a sexy, up-front style of Zinfandel to enjoy over the next 3–4 years. The gorgeous 1998 Zinfandel Whaler Vineyard (14.5% alcohol) offers classic briery, mineral, spicy Zinfandel aromas. On the palate, the wine is dense, rich, and full-bodied, with copious quantities of glycerin, abundant black cherry/raspberry fruit, low acidity, and a fleshy, succulent finish. It is a gorgeous Zinfandel to drink during its first 5–6 years of life.

Fife's exceptional 1999 Zinfandel Dalraddy Chiles Valley boasts an opaque ruby/purple color as well as powerful, sweet aromas of ripe black cherries, raspberries, and currants, with subtle wood and spice in the background. Layered, full-bodied, dense, and opulent, it is the most concentrated and best balanced of the 1999 Zinfandels released by Fife. Enjoy it over the next 6–7 years.

FISHER VINEYARDS (SONOMA)

1999 Cabernet Sauvignon Coach Insignia	Napa	E	90
1998 Cabernet Sauvignon Coach Insignia	Napa	E	88
1995 Cabernet Sauvignon Coach Insignia	Napa	D	88
1994 Cabernet Sauvignon Coach Insignia	Napa	C	89
1999 Cabernet Sauvignon Lamb Vineyard	Napa	EE	90+

1997 Cabernet Sauvignon Lamb Vineyard	Napa	EE	95
1996 Cabernet Sauvignon Lamb Vineyard	Napa	E	91
1995 Cabernet Sauvignon Lamb Vineyard	Napa	E	88
1994 Cabernet Sauvignon Lamb Vineyard	Napa	D	90
1999 Cabernet Sauvignon Wedding Vineyard	Sonoma	EE	91
1997 Cabernet Sauvignon Wedding Vineyard	Sonoma	EE	99
1996 Cabernet Sauvignon Wedding Vineyard	Sonoma	EE	95
1995 Cabernet Sauvignon Wedding Vineyard	Sonoma	E	92
1994 Cabernet Sauvignon Wedding Vineyard	Sonoma	E	92
1999 Chardonnay Coach Insignia	Sonoma	D	89
1999 Chardonnay Paladini	Carneros/Napa	D	91
1999 Chardonnay Whitney's Vineyard Estate	Sonoma	D	90
1997 Coach Insignia Proprietary Red Wine	Napa	D	90
1996 Coach Insignia Proprietary Red Wine	Napa	D	90
1999 Merlot RCF Vineyard	Napa	D	(88–89)
1998 Merlot RCF Vineyard	Napa	D	88
1997 Merlot RCF Vineyard	Napa	D	89
1996 Merlot RCF Vineyard	Napa	D	88
1994 Merlot RCF Vineyard	Napa	D	89
1997 Unity Proprietary Red Wine	California	EEE	90
		(1.5 liter only)	

Does this winery receive as much praise as it deserves? It is certainly in an obscure location, tucked in the mountains between Santa Rosa on the Sonoma side and Calistoga on the Napa side. Fred Fisher and his wife, Juelle, have added a new Chardonnay to their portfolio of already impressive whites. The 1999 Chardonnay Paladini Vineyard (240 cases) is a fragrant Chardonnay made primarily from one of the old Wente clones of Chardonnay. It sees about 78% new French oak. The wine shows beautiful passion fruit as well as pineapple intermixed with subtle smoke and toast. Full-bodied and rich, it may be Fisher's most impressive 1999 Chardonnay. The 1999 Coach Insignia Chardonnay has more apricot, peach, and tropical fruit notes, full body, excellent purity, and plenty of lively fruit. Lastly, the estate's 1999 Chardonnay Whitney's Vineyard, which is named after the proprietor's daughter, is another full-bodied Chardonnay that has seen full malolactic fermentation, but is different from the others in that it tends to offer more orange/tangerine, citrus oils, and honeysuckle in a full-bodied, concentrated, very graceful style, with good underlying acidity. The 1999 Chardonnays all show beautiful balance and the potential to last for 2–4 years.

Slightly better than I originally thought, the 1998 Merlot RCF Vineyard (a Napa vineyard not far from the famed Araujo Eisele Vineyard) is showing a dark ruby color, plenty of melted fudge, coffee, and berry fruit. The wine is not weighty (very few 1998s are) but shows good harmony and sweet fruit, and is best drunk over the next 5–6 years. The 1999 Merlot RCF

Vineyard is similar to the 1998 (80% Merlot and 20% Cabernet Franc) and has much the same character, but the color seems a bit more saturated purple. There is a bit more depth and fat to the wine, and slightly more weight. It should drink well for at least a decade.

1996 and 1997 were both strong vintages for Fisher Vineyards. The 1997 reds are high in alcohol (most of the wines came in around 14.5%), which is well hidden by the rich fruit and extract. The 1996s are undoubtedly lower in alcoholic power. The Merlot from Fisher's RCF Vineyard in northern Napa Valley is one of California's high-quality Merlots. The 1996 Merlot RCF Vineyard's dark ruby color is followed by a sweet nose of black cherries, cranberries, and a touch of cherry liqueur. There is excellent richness, medium body, tangy acidity, and an elegant, overall impression. This is a flavorful, moderately weighted Merlot to enjoy over the next 10–12 years. The 1997 Merlot RCF Vineyard exhibits abundant black cherry fruit intertwined with minerals, dried herbs, and melted white chocolate. It is a rich, flavorful, fleshy, dense Merlot to consume over the next 10–12 years.

The dark ruby-colored 1994 Merlot RCF offers medium-bodied, elegant, vanilla-tinged, black cherry aromas and flavors. Still tightly knit, this wine will benefit from another year of cellaring; it will drink well for a decade. I initially thought it had the potential to be outstanding, but at present it appears it will fall a point or two short.

The Fishers have gone back to a Cabernet Sauvignon designation for their Coach Insignia. The 1998 Cabernet Sauvignon Coach Insignia benefitted from the fact that both the Lamb and Wedding Vineyard Cabernet Sauvignons were declassified in 1998, and the wine was blended into the Coach Insignia. A blend of 78% Cabernet Sauvignon, 11% Cabernet Franc, and 11% Merlot, aged in 50% new French oak, it possesses a dark ruby color, a big, chocolaty, licorice, and black currant–scented nose, and tannin in the finish. It has certainly sweetened up considerably and is showing better out of bottle than it did from barrel. Look for it to drink well for 10–12 years. The 1999 Cabernet Sauvignon Coach Insignia looks terrific. Thankfully, there are 2,200 cases of this blend of 76% Cabernet Sauvignon, 18% Merlot, and 6% Malbec. It displays impressive extract as well as beautifully pure black currant, mineral, and blackberry flavors nicely dosed with toasty oak. Full-bodied, powerful, rich, and in need of 3–4 years of cellaring, it is a significantly bigger, denser wine than the 1998. Anticipated maturity: 2003–2018. To reiterate, there is no 1998 Lamb Vineyard Cabernet Sauvignon, but the 1999 Cabernet Sauvignon Lamb Vineyard is 100% Cabernet Sauvignon. From a vineyard in the northern part of Napa Valley, it has been aged in 80–90% new Taransaud French oak barrels. Full-bodied, with good underlying acidity, plenty of depth as well as earthy black fruits intermixed with spice box, cedar, and licorice, this impressive effort will be at its best between 2004–2025. From the estate vineyard in the Sonoma hillsides, the 1999 Wedding Vineyard (100% Cabernet Sauvignon) is a wine of great intensity. It has the telltale scorched earth notes, intermixed with blueberry, blackberry, and mineral. The wine is very full-bodied, powerful, dense, and will need a good 4–5 years of cellaring. It should keep for at least two decades or more. The potentially perfect, opaque purple-colored 1997 Cabernet Sauvignon Wedding Vineyard (400 cases of 100% Cabernet Sauvignon) is made from 27-year-old vines and is aged in 100% new French Taransaud barrels. This prodigious Cabernet Sauvignon has only gotten better since my tasting last year. The finest Cabernet I have tasted from Fisher, it represents a California interpretation of La Mission Haut-Brion. The wine offers sweet, tobacco-infused, scorched earth, blackberry, and blueberry notes, with a liquid minerality. The aromatics are matched by the immense, concentrated, seamless, staggeringly rich, powerful palate. This wine will benefit from 4–5 years of cellaring, and keep for 35–40 years. A modern-day California legend, it is one of the most profound California Cabernet Sauvignons ever made on the Sonoma side of California's North Coast viticultural region. Anticipated maturity: 2005–2040.

The 1996 Coach Insignia (1,380 cases) offers classic cassis, coffee, chocolate, and oaky aromas that are followed by deep, concentrated, spicy, rich, berry fruit flavors. A blend of

69% Cabernet Sauvignon, 20% Merlot, and 11% Cabernet Franc, it offers abundant power, purity, and richness. It should drink well for 10–15+ years. The 1997 Coach Insignia (77% Cabernet Sauvignon, with the rest Merlot and Cabernet Franc) is also powerful, with a more seamless personality than the 1996. The wine is moderately tannic and full-bodied, with loads of chocolaty, black cherry, and cassis fruit. Anticipated maturity: now–2014.

The 1994 Cabernet Sauvignon Coach Insignia reveals a medium dark color, a Bordeaux-like, austere, spicy, oaky, earthy, cassis-scented nose, plenty of tannin, medium body, and a firm, closed personality. This wine needs another 1–3 years of cellaring; it will keep for 12–15 years. The 1995 Cabernet Sauvignon Coach Insignia exhibits a deep, rich ruby/purple color, a loamy, red currant–scented, elegant bouquet, medium-bodied, structured, restrained flavors, high acidity, and a grapy, rich finish. This wine continues to close down, and should be cellared for 3–4 years upon its release. It should keep for two decades, but I suspect it will be a more angular, structured, tannic Coach Insignia than other vintages.

The awesome opaque purple-colored 1997 Cabernet Sauvignon Lamb Vineyard exhibits a fabulous nose of lead pencil, coffee, minerals, black currants, and licorice. The wine's massive richness, full body, and super-intense, concentrated fruit make for a spectacular, unctuously textured, backward wine. As it sat in the glass, some of the mountain blueberry notes came forward. This Cabernet requires 4–5 years of cellaring, and should keep for 25–30 years . . . at the minimum. The powerful (14.1% alcohol) 1996 Cabernet Sauvignon Lamb Vineyard has been aged in barrel, of which 50% are new. Like all of Fisher's reds, it is bottled without filtration. The color is an opaque purple, and the wine is closed, offering hints of licorice, blueberries, black currants, and spicy oak. In the mouth, it is long, rich, restrained, with the tannin still making a noticeable impression, with outstanding purity, a full-bodied mouth-feel, and superb potential. This wine requires another 4–5 years of cellaring. Anticipated maturity: 2003–2020.

The 1994 Cabernet Sauvignon Lamb Vineyard exhibits a dark ruby/purple color, and a sweet nose of cassis fruit, lead pencil, and spice. While the wine may have been slightly tired when I saw it a few months after bottling, it still revealed plenty of intensity, sweet berry fruit nicely wrapped in oak, medium to full body, and moderate tannin in the long finish. Sadly, there are only 595 cases of this 100% Cabernet Sauvignon. The 1995 Cabernet Sauvignon Lamb Vineyard is a leaner, tighter, more angular and astringent wine, with a dark purple color, leafy, tobacco, smoky flavors, a backward, unformed personality, and plenty of tannin in the finish. It is certainly excellent, and probably will unfold over the next decade, but the wine still plays it tight to the vest. Anticipated maturity: 2003–2012.

One of California's statuesque Cabernet Sauvignons is from the Wedding Vineyard. The 1995 Cabernet Sauvignon Wedding Vineyard is a massive, full-bodied, black/purple-colored wine with gobs of fruit, as well as high tannin. It offers up mineral, black cherry, spicy, and charcoal-like notes in the nose and flavors. Extremely dense and powerful, yet needing 4–5 years of cellaring, this wine may evolve for two decades or more. Anticipated maturity: 2003–2025. The 1996 Cabernet Sauvignon Wedding Vineyard (produced from one-fourth ton of fruit per acre) continues to remind me of a hypothetical La Mission Haut-Brion made from California's ripe fruit. The roasted tobacco, cedar, scorched earth, and creosote nuances are present, in addition to copious blackberry, blueberry, and cassis flavors. This is a terrific, full-flavored, highly extracted wine with plenty of tannin. However, the tannin is sweet and well integrated, as is the wine's lusty alcohol (14.1%). This is a profound example of Cabernet Sauvignon that should be accessible in 4–5 years and last for 25–30. The 1994 Cabernet Sauvignon Wedding Vineyard (500 cases) displays a knockout Graves-like nose of sweet, medium- to full-bodied, rich, concentrated flavors, good acidity, high tannin, and profound concentration and length. It comes across like a racehorse ready to burst from the starting gate. This wine needs 4–5 years of cellaring and should keep for two or more decades.

The only other wine to note is the 1997 Unity, a proprietary red that is essentially Cabernet Sauvignon (with a tiny bit of Cabernet Franc) made in limited quantities of 250 1.5-liter bottles. It is a dense, classy blend revealing considerable style, as well as intriguing lead pencil, cedary notes, copious black fruits, medium body, and admirable elegance and grace. It should drink well for 15+ years.

Past Glories: 1993 Cabernet Sauvignon Coach Insignia (90+), 1993 Cabernet Sauvignon Lamb Vineyard (95), Cabernet Sauvignon Wedding Vineyard—1993 (93), 1992 (92), 1991 (93+)

FLORA SPRINGS WINE CO. (NAPA)

1995 Cabernet Sauvignon Cypress Ranch	Pope Valley	D	88
1998 Cabernet Sauvignon Eagle Mountain	Pope Valley	D	87
1997 Cabernet Sauvignon Eagle Mountain	Pope Valley	D	90
1994 Cabernet Sauvignon Estate	Napa	C	90
1999 Cabernet Sauvignon Hillside Reserve	Rutherford	EE	91
1997 Cabernet Sauvignon Hillside Reserve	Rutherford	EE	93
1996 Cabernet Sauvignon Hillside Reserve	Rutherford	E	92+
1995 Cabernet Sauvignon Hillside Reserve	Rutherford	E	92
1994 Cabernet Sauvignon Hillside Reserve	Rutherford	E	94+
1996 Cabernet Sauvignon Rutherford Vineyard	Rutherford	D	88
1997 Cabernet Sauvignon 20th Anniversary Reserve	Napa	EEE (magnums only)	96
1999 Cabernet Sauvignon Wild Boar Vineyard	Pope Valley	D	(90–92)
1998 Cabernet Sauvignon Wild Boar Vineyard	Pope Valley	D	(89–91)
1999 Chardonnay Barrel Fermented Reserve	Napa	D	88
1999 Merlot Windfall Vineyard	Napa	E	(90–92)
1998 Merlot Windfall Vineyard	Napa	D	89
1997 Merlot Windfall Vineyard	Napa	D	90
1996 Merlot Windfall Vineyard	Napa	D	91
1995 Merlot Windfall Vineyard	Napa	D	90
1999 Trilogy Proprietary Red	Napa	E	90
1998 Trilogy Proprietary Red	Napa	E	88
1997 Trilogy Proprietary Red	Napa	D	92
1996 Trilogy Proprietary Red	Napa	D	91
1995 Trilogy Proprietary Red	Napa	D	90
1994 Trilogy Proprietary Red	Napa	D	93+

Quietly, confidently, and without a great deal of fanfare or publicity, Flora Springs continues to turn out some of Napa Valley's finest wines that are, for the most part, reasonably priced. Translation: Flora Spring's wines are not priced according to the owner's egos, as so many Napa wines seem to be these days. The 1999 Chardonnay Barrel Fermented Reserve sees some malolactic, but is harvested very late to obtain maximum ripeness. It is a smoky, roasted hazelnut, tropical fruit–scented and –flavored Chardonnay, with medium to full body, and a style not unlike a good premier cru from Chassagne-Montrachet. Fleshy, with good underlying acidity, it should drink well for 2–3 years, if not longer.

The 1998 Trilogy Proprietary Red reveals the vintage's shortcomings. It is a very good, even excellent wine, but the vintage's short, cool growing season has given the wine more austerity than normal. A blend of 45% Cabernet Sauvignon, 43% Merlot, 6% Cabernet Franc, and 6% Malbec, it offers plenty of spicy new oak, mineral, licorice, and damp, foresty aromas and flavors. Elegant and medium-bodied, it is best drunk over the next 10–12 years. The 1999 Trilogy is significantly richer, more textured, and obviously made from riper, more concentrated fruit. A blend of 42% Cabernet Sauvignon, 39% Merlot, and 19% Cabernet Franc that sees about 50% new French oak, it exhibits a dark plum/purple color as well as a sweet nose of minerals, cassis, and smoke. Medium- to full-bodied, moderately tannic, elegant, pure, and well balanced, it should drink well for 15–16 years.

Two impeccably made 100% Merlots emerge from the Windfall Vineyard at the corner of Route 29 and Bella Oaks Lane. Sexy, plump, and fat, they are among the better Merlots being made in Napa. There are about 1,000–1,200 cases produced in each vintage. A success for the vintage, the 1998 Merlot Windfall Vineyard is a seductive red offering aromas of cocoa, melted fudge, and black cherry fruit. This ripe, very silky-textured, plump wine has added weight since I tasted it last year. Anticipated maturity: now–2010. Even better is the dense ruby/purple-colored 1999 Merlot Windfall Vineyard. It displays a big nose of roasted espresso, chocolate, and black cherry scents, low acidity, dense, sexy, opulently textured flavors, and a full-bodied, glycerin-imbued, enticing finish. Drink it over the next 10–12 years.

There was no 1998 Cabernet Sauvignon Hillside Reserve, as the wine was declassified into Trilogy in order to bulk it up. However, the 1999 Cabernet Sauvignon Hillside Reserve offers a dense, opaque purple color, as well as a gorgeous nose of sweet cassis, mixed with leather, vanilla, and spice box. The wine is full-bodied, with moderate tannin, exceptional purity and symmetry, and a layered mid-palate and finish. It should drink well for at least 15 or more years. The sensational 1997 Cabernet Sauvignon Hillside Reserve boasts an opaque ruby/purple color and a jammy black cherry and cassis nose, intermixed with smoke, toast, cedar, and spice box. Voluptuously textured, concentrated, with hints of smoke, coffee, and toast in its powerful, super-extracted, multilayered flavors, this terrific 1997 should be at its best in 2–3 years and keep for at least 20–25 years. Perhaps the finest Cabernet Sauvignon I have tasted from Flora Springs is their 1997 Cabernet Sauvignon 20th Anniversary Reserve. Bottled only in magnums (250 cases), it is a prodigious Napa Cabernet. Aged in 60% new French oak for 24 months before being bottled without filtration, it reveals an opaque plum/purple color plus an explosive, multidimensional nose of coffee, kirsch, crème de cassis, dried herbs, tobacco, and spice. Full-bodied, with fabulous purity, a seamless texture, and a 40-second finish, it represents Cabernet Sauvignon at its most profound. Remarkably, it is soft enough to be drunk now, but promises to age well for 25 or more years.

More than any other winery, Flora Springs is demonstrating the potential for Cabernet Sauvignon in Napa's Pope Valley. Their only problem is deciding what to name the wine. Formerly called Cypress Vineyard, then Eagle Mountain, they seem to have settled on the name Wild Boar Vineyard. The 1998 Cabernet Sauvignon Wild Boar Vineyard is a big, muscular, back-strapping effort with huge blackberry fruit infused with melted asphalt and earth. Aged in 50% new oak, one-half of which is American wood and the rest French, it is powerful, concentrated, and all-American in its blatant oak and lavish fruit, glycerin, and power. A success for the vintage, it should drink well for another 12–15 years. Even better, the 1999 Cabernet Sauvignon Wild Boar displays more concentrated richness on the palate along with an exuberant, flamboyant nose of black fruits, herbs, leather, tobacco, and licorice. Powerful, gutsy, and chewy, this oversized Cabernet Sauvignon may fall short in terms of elegance and finesse, but it more than compensates for that in its blockbuster display of fruit, glycerin, power, and tannin. It should drink well for 15 or more years.

The 1996 Cabernet Sauvignon Rutherford Vineyard is 100% Cabernet Sauvignon, aged in *barrique*, of which 15% was American. The wine reveals gobs of spicy new oak and tobacco-tinged, weedy, black currant fruit intermixed with cedar, dried herbs, and licorice, high tannin, and medium to full body. This chunky, fleshy, robust Cabernet Sauvignon should be at its best with another 2–3 years of bottle age and keep for 14–15 years.

Flora Springs is making a serious jump into the Merlot sweepstakes, and their effort deserves accolades. The 1995 Merlot Windfall Vineyard (300 cases) possesses a dense ruby/purple color, as well as a gaudy nose of toast, melted chocolate, and jammy cherry flavors. Soft, ripe, medium- to full-bodied, chewy, and fat, this is a delicious, decadent style of Merlot that will drink well for a decade. The outstanding 1996 Merlot Windfall Vineyard possesses a dark purple color, as well as a sweet, expressive, smoky, chocolaty nose with coffee and berry fruit in the background. The wine is succulent, fleshy, full-bodied, and hedonistic. This superb, ripe, mouth-filling Merlot can be drunk over the next 10–12+ years. Bravo! While it is cut from the same mold, the 1997 Merlot Windfall Vineyard displays more tangy acidity, but it shares its predecessor's smoky, roasted coffee, chocolaty, black cherry scents and flavors. There is sweet richness in the mouth, soft tannin, plenty of glycerin, and an evolved style. Once again, the 1997 appears to be on a slightly faster evolutionary track than its older sibling and should drink well during its first decade of life.

The outstanding 1997 Trilogy Proprietary Red Wine offers a dark ruby/purple color and super-expressive aromatics consisting of black fruits, licorice, blueberries, and floral scents. With a fine tannic underpinning, this elegant yet impressively rich, well-endowed, balanced effort is already approachable, and promises to evolve effortlessly for 15–18 years. The 1996 Trilogy, a blend of 44% Cabernet Sauvignon, 40% Merlot, and 16% Cabernet Franc, reveals a saturated dark ruby/purple color and a gorgeous nose of violets, black currants, toast, and minerals. Deep and rich, yet remarkably polished, this medium- to full-bodied, beautifully symmetrical wine has everything in the proper place. Although accessible enough to be drunk early in life, its balance suggests a graceful evolution for 15–20 years. It is a distinctive, beautiful wine! With its curranty, cedary, tobacco-like sweetness and ripeness, Trilogy may be the Napa Valley wine that most recalls certain St.-Emilions. Approximately 3,500–4,000 cases of this wine are made in a top vintage. The 1995 Trilogy (44% Merlot, 39% Cabernet Sauvignon, and 17% Cabernet Franc) is a spicy, Médoc-styled wine with medium to full body, excellent spice and richness, as well as an overall sense of elegance and equilibrium. It is a delicious wine to drink now and over the next 15+ years. The 1994 Trilogy (2,000 cases) exhibits rich, ripe fruit, along with some toasty vanilla and sweet, jammy black fruit scents. Fleshy, harmonious, full-bodied flavors reveal admirable extract and cleanliness. Despite its softness, this impressive wine is unformed, so give it 2–3 years of cellaring; it will age for two decades or more.

The dark ruby/purple-colored, stunningly rich 1996 Cabernet Sauvignon Hillside Reserve is still in need of bottle age. The wine reveals a saturated color, as well as a promising but restrained nose of toasty new oak, jammy blackberries, cassis, licorice, and spice. It is extremely rich and spicy in the mouth, with moderate tannin, full body, superb purity of flavor, and outstanding potential. Anticipated maturity: 2003–2022. The 1995 Cabernet Sauvignon Hillside Reserve is a backward, tannic wine with an opaque purple color and copious quantities of sweet black currant fruit, cedar, and spice. Muscular, rich, and full-bodied, with sweet tannin, this is a layered, concentrated, unevolved, and youthful Cabernet that requires 4–5 years of cellaring. All the necessary "goodies" are present in this formidably endowed wine. While it will not provide seductive drinking at an early age, it will last 20 years. Ken

Deiss thinks that the 1994 and 1995 Cabernet Sauvignon vintages have more similarities than differences. This was borne out in my tastings, as both vintages possess that rare quality of producing very concentrated, ripe Cabernets with sweet, well-integrated tannin. Flora Springs' Hillside Reserve Cabernet Sauvignons have soared in quality in the nineties. This 100% Cabernet Sauvignon is aged in 2–3-year-old barrels, then moved to 1-year-old barrels, and then into 60% new-oak casks for no longer than 8–10 months. The 1994 Cabernet Sauvignon Hillside Reserve exhibits an opaque purple color, a classic, cedar, black currant, and earthy-scented nose, and rich, full-bodied flavors that ooze jammy black currants. The wood influence is subtle, although some spicy vanilla can be detected. This wine possesses terrific fruit purity, an opulent texture, and an impressively long, harmonious finish. The 1994 Reserve should be accessible young, yet long lived (20–30 years).

One of the best bargains in the Flora Springs portfolio is the 1994 Cabernet Sauvignon Estate (unfortunately, only 1,600 cases are available). It is bursting with ripe, jammy black fruits. This full-bodied, fleshy, fat, in your face, 100% Cabernet Sauvignon was bottled unfiltered, revealing a chewy, open-knit texture. It exhibits excellent purity, as well as spicy oak. Drink it over the next 7–10 years.

The 1998 Cabernet Sauvignon Eagle Mountain (harvested during the last week of October) exhibits a jammy cassis-scented nose, full-bodied, pure flavors, and more glycerin, richness, and intensity than many 1998s. It should turn out to be a muscular, surprisingly concentrated 1998 that will drink well for 10–12 years. The outstanding 1997 Cabernet Sauvignon Eagle Mountain is a full-throttle, all-American-styled Cabernet Sauvignon. Aged both in French and American oak, this gutsy, macho, powerful effort is short on finesse, but offers mouthfilling levels of sweet, succulent, jammy black currant fruit combined with toasty oak, cedar, dried herbs, and loamy soil scents. Layered, thick, and juicy, it is fun to drink. Moreover, it will improve over the next 7–8 years, and last for 12–15.

Flora Springs produced a 1995 Cabernet Sauvignon Cypress Ranch. There are only 375 cases of this wine, which is aged in 25% new oak. Like Flora Springs' other wines, with the exception of the barrel-fermented Chardonnay, it was bottled without fining or filtration. A textbook, unformed Cabernet Sauvignon, the Cypress Ranch's pronounced spiciness and weedy, tobacco-tinged black currant fruitiness make for a solid first impression. This lusty, muscular Cabernet possesses aggressive tannin, which should melt away after some time in the bottle. It should age well for 12–15 years.

Past Glories: 1993 Cabernet Sauvignon Hillside Reserve (91+), 1993 Trilogy Proprietary Red Wine (91)

FLOWERS (SONOMA COAST)

1997 Pinot Noir Camp Meeting Ridge	**Sonoma Coast**	**D**	**90+**
1997 Pinot Noir Camp Meeting Ridge Moon Select	**Sonoma Coast**	**E**	**90+**
1997 Pinot Noir Hirsch Vineyard	**Sonoma Coast**	**D**	**92**

This enterprise with well-placed Sonoma Coast vineyards (next to the Marcassin Vineyard and Martinelli's Blue Slide Vineyard) displays considerable promise. The three Pinot Noirs are topflight. The medium ruby-colored 1997 Pinot Noir Hirsch offers a terrific nose of sweet black cherries, cinnamon, earth, and spice, sweet fruit, full body, admirable power and glycerin, and sweet, moderate tannin in the finish. It should drink well for 5–7 years. Equally impressive, the dark ruby-colored 1997 Pinot Noir Camp Meeting Ridge displays a floral and black fruit–scented nose with sweet vanilla in the background. More structured than the Hirsch, with outstanding purity and concentration, this tight but full-bodied Pinot Noir will be even better with another 6–12 months of bottle age. It will last for 7–8 years. The 1997 Pinot Noir Camp Meeting Ridge Moon Select is the most ambitious and concentrated of this Pinot Noir trio. Along with the additional level of extract comes elevated tannin and copious toasty new oak. The wine should settle down, but it does not appear to be the same sure bet as the other two Pinots. Although forceful, rich, and concentrated, it is lavishly wooded and extremely tannic. After 1–2 years of bottle age, it can be drunk over the following decade. Look for a higher score if the tannin and wood become better integrated.

FORMAN VINEYARDS (NAPA)

1999 Cabernet Sauvignon	Napa	E	(90–93)
1998 Cabernet Sauvignon	Napa	E	88
1997 Cabernet Sauvignon	Napa	D	90
1996 Cabernet Sauvignon	Napa	D	92
1995 Cabernet Sauvignon	Napa	D	88+
1994 Cabernet Sauvignon	Napa	D	91
1999 Chardonnay	Napa	D	89
1999 Merlot	Napa	D	(90–92)
1998 Merlot	Napa	D	87
1997 Merlot	Napa	D	88+
1996 Merlot	Napa	D	89
1995 Merlot	Napa	D	88
1994 Merlot	Napa	D	89

Ric Forman, who does not like thick, ripe, or super-concentrated wines, seems to be attempting to build more texture into his wines. His Chardonnays, Merlots, and Cabernet Sauvignons are distinctively elegant, Bordeaux-styled wines, unlike those favored by other cutting-edge California producers. There are 2,000 cases of 1999 Chardonnay, which is to be applauded for its crisp pear, citrus oil, steely style. Medium-bodied, with exceptional purity, it is made in a Chablis-like style and is best drunk during its first 2–3 years of life.

Both 1999 reds have more texture and ripeness, as if Forman is picking at slightly higher Brix than he personally prefers. The 1999 Merlot looks to be terrific. There are 500 cases of this ruby/purple-colored wine that has an opulent texture and plenty of pure, sweet, black cherry and berry fruit. The wine is full-bodied, low in acidity, and intense. The flamboyant 1999 Cabernet Sauvignon reveals a cassis jelly character, medium to full body, excellent mineral-infused, black currant fruit, and superb purity. There are 2,000 cases of this Cabernet, which could turn out to be one of the most hedonistic Forman has made in the nineties.

The 1998s are more austere, without the volume, texture, and overall richness offered by the 1999s. The 1998 Cabernet Sauvignon displays complex, Bordeaux-like aromas that recall a top-notch Médoc. In the mouth, the tannin is dry and angular, but the wine shows plenty of attractive black currant fruit presented in a restrained, understated style. It is medium-bodied, elegant, and best consumed during its first 10–12 years of life. Forman's 1998 Merlot should be appealing upon release. Despite its 14.5% alcohol, it displays good accessibility given its coffee bean, blackberry, and cherry characteristics. Seductive and lush, with low acidity, it should drink well for 7–8 years. It may merit an even higher rating.

The dark ruby/purple-colored 1997 Merlot has closed down since bottling. With coaxing, berry fruit notes intermixed with spice and vanilla emerge. This medium-bodied Merlot possesses a ripe attack, good balance, and moderate tannin. Anticipated maturity: now–2012. The 1997 Cabernet Sauvignon is a beauty. One of Ric Forman's classics, it boasts a dark ruby/purple color as well as a gorgeous bouquet of cassis, dried herbs, cedar, blackberries, and minerals. This medium- to full-bodied Cabernet exhibits firm tannin in the finish, in addition to excellent sweet fruit and a subtle, nuanced personality. Cellar it for 3–4 years and drink it over the following two decades.

The 1996 Merlot (80% Merlot and 20% Cabernet Franc) is made in a Bordeaux-like style. The nose offers up aromas of coffee and berry-tinged fruit intermixed with herbaceous, spicy oak. The wine possesses excellent texture, medium body, and an intriguing black tea flavor in the fruit character. A sexy Merlot made in Ric Forman's telltale polished, refined, and graceful manner, it should drink well for 10–15 years. One of the most impressive recent Cabernet Sauvignons from Forman is their 1996. I was amazed how well it was showing despite having been bottled only a month earlier. The saturated ruby/purple color is followed by gorgeous jammy black currant fruit aromas, along with spicy oak and licorice. There is good acidity, but the wine appears to possess more viscosity than most Forman offerings, as well as a chewy fleshiness, enough acidity for delineation, and moderate tannin in the convincingly long finish. This classic Bordeaux-styled wine should be at its finest between now–2020.

The 1995 red wines were revealing a more closed character than they possessed previously. For example, the 1995 Merlot was softer than the Cabernet Sauvignon, with a deep ruby/purple color, and a cherry and raspberry–scented nose with judicious toasty oak in the background. This is a pretty, elegant, attractive style of Merlot with enough acidity for vibrancy, as well as excellent purity and tasty cherry-like flavors. It should drink well for 10–15 years. The tighter, more tannic 1995 Cabernet Sauvignon exhibits a deep ruby/purple color, followed by an elegant cassis-scented nose with graceful, restrained, and measured fruit flavors. Medium- to full-bodied, with moderate tannin and an overall impression of tightness, this is a harmonious, well-made wine that is not nearly as expressive this year as it was in 1996. Ideally, this Cabernet needs 3–4 years of cellaring and should keep for 20 years.

Forman's 1994 Merlot, the debut vintage for this varietal, is a deep ruby-colored, open, seductive wine with berry/mocha fruit in the nose, medium to full body, and round, generous, nicely oaked flavors. This soft, open-knit, rich, excellent, nearly outstanding Merlot should drink well for 7–8 years. The 1994 Cabernet Sauvignon exhibits a dense, ruby/purple color, an unevolved but promising sweet, cedar, black currant, vanilla-scented nose, medium to full body, fine elegance, underlying acidity, ripe tannin, and a Graves-like tobacco component that provides complexity. This wine should be accessible young, but will not hit its stride for 5–6 years; it will last for two decades.

Past Glories: 1993 Cabernet Sauvignon (92)

FOXEN VINEYARDS (SANTA BARBARA)

1996 Cabernet Sauvignon	Santa Barbara	D	88
1997 Pinot Noir Julia's Vineyard	Santa Maria	D	89
1997 Syrah Morehouse Vineyard	Santa Ynez	D	90
1996 Syrah Morehouse Vineyard	Santa Ynez	D	90

An enviable portfolio of wines has been produced by this high-quality Santa Barbara winery. The red wines are impressive. For example, the 1997 Syrah Morehouse Vineyard offers notes of bacon fat, blackberries, pepper, and vanilla. This large-scaled, full-bodied, dense, powerful Syrah will age well for a decade or more. Another impressive offering is the 1996 Syrah Morehouse Vineyard. This dark ruby/purple-colored wine possesses a textbook bacon fat, fried meat, and smoky-scented nose intermixed with superripe black raspberry and cassis fruit, full body, outstanding concentration and purity, and a luscious, silky finish. Drink this seductive, intensely flavored Syrah now and over the next 7–10 years.

Concentrated, with deep color, the 1997 Pinot Noir Julia's Vineyard's aromas of ripe plums, cherry jam, smoke, and herbs are combined in a medium-bodied, ripe, and dense style of Pinot Noir. It can be drunk now or cellared for 5–7 years. Foxen's dark ruby/purple-colored 1996 Cabernet Sauvignon offers up a dense, black cherry, curranty, weedy, tobacco-tinged nose with plenty of smoke and jammy fruit. This medium- to full-bodied, nicely textured, attractive wine displays better balance between its component parts—alcohol, acidity, tannin, and extract. Although accessible, it promises to age nicely for 10–14 years.

FRANUS (NAPA)

1996 Cabernet Sauvignon	Napa	D	88
1997 Mourvèdre Brandlin Ranch	Mt. Veeder	D	91
1995 Zinfandel	Napa	C	89
1999 Zinfandel Brandlin Ranch	Mt. Veeder	D	90
1998 Zinfandel Brandlin Ranch	Mt. Veeder	D	89
1997 Zinfandel Brandlin Ranch	Mt. Veeder	D	90
1996 Zinfandel Brandlin Ranch	Mt. Veeder	C	90
1995 Zinfandel Brandlin Ranch	Mt. Veeder	C	90
1994 Zinfandel Brandlin Ranch	Mt. Veeder	C	91
1994 Zinfandel Hendry Vineyard	Napa	C	91
1999 Zinfandel Planchon Vineyard	Contra Costa	C	90
1998 Zinfandel Planchon Vineyard	Contra Costa	C	88
1997 Zinfandel Planchon Vineyard	Contra Costa	C	90
1996 Zinfandel Planchon Vineyard	Contra Costa	C	88

For the quality of the wines that consistently emerge from Franus, this winery remains un-heralded. The 1999s are typically structured, concentrated, full-bodied Zinfandels with considerable character and aging potential . . . at least for this varietal. The deep ruby/purple-colored, structured, tightly knit 1999 Zinfandel Planchon Vineyard is reminiscent of a Bordeaux in its slightly austere yet deep, dense, intense personality. This full-bodied effort is loaded with dusty, black cherry, currant, and cranberry fruit, but requires another 6–12 months to open. It should age well for 6–8 years. The 1999 Zinfandel Brandlin Vineyard Mt. Veeder boasts a saturated ruby/purple color in addition to a sweet perfume of black fruits, minerals, graphite, and subtle oak. A sweet attack is followed by a closed finish. This big, forceful Zinfandel should be cellared for 1–2 years and enjoyed over the following 7–8. While not the most charming examples, they are loaded with potential.

The 1998 Zinfandel Planchon Vineyard (with vines planted in 1902 in pure sand) exhibits a medium dark ruby color in addition to a spicy, peppery bouquet with scents of resin, balsam wood, and sweet cherry/berry fruit. Medium to full body, low acidity, a ripe, opulent texture, and good fat can be found in this precocious, evolved Zinfandel. It should drink well for 2–3 years. Even more impressive is the dense dark ruby-colored 1998 Zinfandel Brandlin Vineyard. The nose offers up aromas of wild blackberries, minerals, oak, and black currants. Classic, with a nicely structured, medium- to full-bodied, rich entry and mid-palate, this concentrated, pure, well-balanced effort should age nicely for 2–4 years.

Unlike some of his peers, Peter Franus handled the tricky 1997 Zinfandel vintage well. Both are outstanding efforts for this irregular year. The 1997 Zinfandel Planchon Vineyard displays a deep ruby color, and excellent brambleberry, blackberry, and cherry fruit, with none of the earthy, balsam wood notes that often emerge from Contra Costa Zinfandels. Dense and medium- to full-bodied, with lofty alcohol (14.6%), this nicely textured, chewy Zinfandel should drink well for 2–3 years. Also outstanding, the 1997 Zinfandel Brandlin Vineyard is a big, brawny, briery Zin made in a mountain style. Peppery and spicy, with noteworthy licorice, mineral, and blackberry and cherry fruit well displayed in its powerful (14.6% alcohol), full-bodied constitution, it will also drink well for 2–3 years.

With respect to the 1996 Cabernet Sauvignon, this wine reveals a Bordeaux-like, cedary, cigar box, black currant–scented nose. In addition, chocolate notes appear in the mouth. This classic, well-delineated, expansive, medium-bodied wine possesses fine concentration, an attractive perfume, and admirable complexity. Enjoy it over the next 10–15 years. Peter Franus has fashioned a superb 1997 Mourvèdre from the Brandlin Vineyard on Mt. Veeder. It is hard to believe this is a 100% Mourvèdre as this varietal tends to produce frightfully austere, tannic, and backward wines. There is wonderful sweetness to this effort's gorgeous blackberry and black raspberry fruit. Notes of leather, tree bark, and spice are present, but the black fruit characteristics dominate the wine's personality. Even readers who resist Mourvèdre's intensity, ferocity, and tannic clout will find this wine attractive. It should drink well for a decade or longer. The 1996 Zinfandels are all high-quality wines from Peter Franus. Well made with surprising complexity, these Zinfandels will provide lovely drinking for another 1–2 years. The 1996 Zinfandel Planchon Vineyard tips the scales at 14.3% alcohol, yet there is no hint of overripeness or raisiny/pruny notes. The wine offers up a kirsch/plum-scented nose, with pepper and spice. Ripe and medium- to full-bodied, with low acidity, a chewy, fleshy texture, and good glycerin, this plump, hedonistic Zinfandel should drink well for 1–2 years. The intensely spicy, black fruit, and mineral-dominated 1996 Zinfandel Brandlin Ranch emerges from the slopes of Mt. Veeder. It possesses a darker, more saturated ruby color. While medium- to full-bodied, it is structured and possibly more ageworthy (I believe in drinking most Zinfandels during their first 4–7 years of life). This wine reveals some spice, but black fruits and minerals dominate the nose and flavors. It possesses an inner core of rich fruit. Additionally, there is more delineation and structure in the finish, although I would still opt for drinking this wine now.

The 1995 Zinfandel Napa reveals a textbook, briery (the French would call it *sauvage*) nose with aromas of wild berry fruits. The color is an evolved dark garnet, and the wine is dense, medium- to full-bodied, with crisp, tangy acidity, excellent richness, and a spicy, peppery, earthy personality reminiscent of a Rhône. Somewhat tight and structured, it should be consumed over the next 1–2 years. The beautiful, plum-colored 1995 Zinfandel Brandlin Ranch displays a knockout nose of black cherries, raspberries, cola, and peppery fruit. Loads of yummy, glycerin-endowed, chewy fruit hit the palate with medium to full body and excellent purity. Drink this dense, chewy, mouth-filling, savory Zin over the next 1–2 years.

The dark plum/purple-colored 1994 Hendry Vineyard Zinfandel reveals sweet black fruit in the nose. It explodes on the palate, offering full body, layers of rich, creamy fruit, well-hidden, high alcohol (14.2%), and a clean, succulent, fleshy, large-scaled finish. This beautifully made, lush Zinfandel should drink well for 3–4 years. The 1994 Zinfandel Brandlin Ranch displays a similar dark plummy color, a spicy, mineral, peppery nose, sweet, ripe, full-bodied flavors, an inner core of fruit and expansive chewiness, and a long, ripe finish. These wines are pure and rich, with natural, multilayered textures. The Brandlin Ranch will also drink superbly for 3–4 years. This is high-quality winemaking!

FRAZIER (NAPA)

1995 Cabernet Sauvignon	Napa	D	89
1997 Cabernet Sauvignon Lupine Hill Vineyard	Napa	D	88
1995 Merlot Lupine Hill Vineyard	Napa	D	90

Substantial in weight, size, and concentration, the 1997 Cabernet Sauvignon Lupine Hill Vineyard has a dense ruby/purple color followed by aromas of blackberries, cassis, new saddle leather, earth, and spicy oak. A young, unevolved effort with copious tannin in addition to excellent extraction, this dense, medium- to full-bodied Cabernet reveals underlying foresty notes intermixed with black fruits and oak. It will benefit from 2–3 years of cellaring, and will keep for 12–15 years. Frazier's impressive 1995 Merlot Lupine Hill is a textbook, plump, rich Merlot with a dark ruby/purple color, as well as fragrant aromas of white chocolate and cherry jam. Thick, with a soft, unctuously textured, full-bodied personality, this rich, plush, hedonistically satisfying Merlot is a fruit and body-driven wine with a subtle dosage of oak. It should drink well for 7–8 years. The deep, chocolaty, and blackberry-scented, full-bodied, extroverted, fleshy 1995 Cabernet Sauvignon possesses plenty of character. Although it lacks complexity, finesse, and elegance, it offers substantial flavors in a robust, exuberant format. It should drink well for a decade.

GALLO-SONOMA (SONOMA)

1994 Cabernet Sauvignon Frei Ranch	Dry Creek Valley	C	88
1996 Cabernet Sauvignon Stefani Vineyard	Dry Creek Valley	D	88
1997 Zinfandel	Dry Creek	C	87
1997 Zinfandel Barrelli Creek	Alexander Valley	C	90
1995 Zinfandel Barrelli Creek	Alexander Valley	B	89
1997 Zinfandel Chiotti Vineyard	Dry Creek	B	89
1995 Zinfandel Chiotti Vineyard	Dry Creek	C	88
1997 Zinfandel Frei Ranch Vineyard	Dry Creek	C	88
1995 Zinfandel Frei Ranch Vineyard	Dry Creek	B	90
1994 Zinfandel Frei Ranch Vineyard	Dry Creek	C	91
1996 Zinfandel Stefani Vineyard	Dry Creek	C	90
1997 Zinfandel Rancho Zabaco	Dry Creek	C	87

Gallo-Sonoma is a serious producer, a fact that is evidenced by how well all of these wines performed. Readers not yet familiar with the improved quality of the Gallo estate wines should check out these attractive Zinfandels. Unlike many 1997 Zinfandels, there is no shortage of flavor or character in Gallo's 1997s. The 1997 Zinfandel Rancho Zabaco exhibits a dark ruby color as well as sweet black cherry, smoke, licorice, and toasty American oak aromas. Made in a mainstream, soft, plump style, it will drink well for 1–3 years. The 1997 Zinfandel Dry Creek reveals a late harvest character, noticeable tannin, plenty of muscle, and a beefy, robust personality. An exuberant, hefty Zinfandel, it possesses good ripeness, excellent, sweet cherry fruit, and a long finish. It should drink well for 3–4 years. The dark ruby/purple-colored 1997 Zinfandel Frei Ranch displays potentially outstanding raw materials. Notes of chocolate, pepper, dried herbs, and black fruits are followed by a full-bodied, nicely layered, oaky wine with good power. It should drink well for 2–3 years. My favorite of this quartet is the opaque black/purple-colored 1997 Zinfandel Barelli Creek. Super-extracted, intense, and powerful, with good fat, and layers of blackberry and cherry fruit, new oak, dried herbs, and admirable spice and depth, it should drink well for 2–3 years.

The early-released 1997 Zinfandel Chiotti Vineyard possesses explosive fruit, knockout purity, admirable opulence, and a sexy, hedonistic, exotic character. Soft, round, and pure, its gush of black raspberry, smoke-infused, cherry fruit hides the 14.9% alcohol remarkably well. Drink this seductive Zinfandel over the next 1–3 years. As for the 1995s, the saturated ruby/purple-colored 1995 Zinfandel Frei Ranch continues to perform exceptionally well. It is a full-bodied, powerful, concentrated wine with no hard edges, well-integrated acidity, and copious quantities of earthy blackberry and cherry fruit. It is fully mature. Although similar in character, the 1995 Zinfandel Barrelli Creek comes across as more late-harvest in style, with an Amarone/asphalt note in the nose. Also present are aromas and flavors of black cherries, full body, and loads of glycerin. This powerhouse, concentrated, exotic Zinfandel should be consumed over the next 1–2 years.

The 1996 Zinfandel Stefani Vineyard (14.9% alcohol) exhibits a dark ruby/purple color, followed by highly extracted, chewy, viscous, full-bodied flavors, lavish quantities of toasty oak, and a juicy, succulent finish. Along with the other Gallo-Sonoma Zinfandels, this offering reveals a hedonistic, up-front quality. Drink it over the next 2 years. In spite of what appears to be a concentrated, impressively endowed wine, the 1995 Zinfandel Chiotti Vineyard offers leesy, mercaptan aromas that detract from the otherwise impressive components. Two bottles revealed the same defect. In total contrast, the 1994 Zinfandel Frei Ranch Vineyard is a marvelously concentrated, complex, rich, beautifully made wine. Much has been written about Gallo's efforts to compete at the high end of the quality pyramid. This offering is a textbook, full-bodied, gorgeously pure, complex Zinfandel that should drink well for 2–3 years. The big, sweet, smoky nose offers copious quantities of earthy, black cherry fruit with a subtle touch of wood. Rich, full-bodied, and dense, with well-integrated acidity and tannin, this seamlessly styled Zin is sure to please most readers.

The 1996 Cabernet Sauvignon Stefani Vineyard exhibits a dark plum/purple color followed by a jammy, pruny-styled wine with abundant blackberry fruit mixed with licorice, chocolate, and smoky oak. Medium- to full-bodied, moderately tannic, broodingly backward and dense, this well-endowed, chunky Cabernet lacks complexity, but makes up for it in size and richness. Drink it over the next 8–10 years. The saturated dark ruby-colored 1994 Cabernet Sauvignon Frei Ranch displays a moderately intense bouquet of black currants, coffee, crème de cassis, and spice. Pure and rich, this medium- to full-bodied wine possesses well-integrated, unobtrusive acidity and tannin. The finish possesses some dusty tannin, but this spicy, rich Cabernet Sauvignon should continue to evolve and drink well for 7–8 years.

GRACE FAMILY VINEYARD (NAPA)

1995 Cabernet Sauvignon	Napa	EEE	94
1994 Cabernet Sauvignon	Napa	EEE	94+

This wine is only available through the winery's mailing list, and I am sure there are more potential suitors than wine to be sold.

The 1994 Cabernet Sauvignon is the last wine made from the original vineyard plantings. The opaque purple color is accompanied by an explosive bouquet of black currants and cherries, intermingled with toasty, new oak. Full-bodied, with a lead pencil, cedary, cassis-like characteristic not dissimilar from a high-class Pauillac, this tightly knit yet formidably endowed Cabernet should last for 20–25 years. I hope the handful of multimillionaires who latch onto a bottle or two will have enough patience to cellar it for 5–6 years before pulling a cork. The 1995 is a magnificent Cabernet Sauvignon, but, lamentably, only three barrels (425 magnums) were produced as the vineyard is in the process of being replanted. The wine is powerful for a 1995, with an opaque purple color, and intensely ripe black currant aromas intermingled with smoke, toast, licorice, and chocolate. This deep, full-bodied, multilayered wine is the essence of Napa Cabernet Sauvignon. Although it reveals plenty of tannin, it is well meshed in the wine's impressive richness and layered texture. Still youthful and grapy, it will develop well for another 15–20+ years.

Past Glories: 1993 Cabernet Sauvignon (91)

GREEN AND RED VINEYARD (NAPA)

1999 Zinfandel Chiles Mill Vineyard	Napa	C	90
1998 Zinfandel Chiles Mill Vineyard	Napa	C	90
1997 Zinfandel Chiles Mill Vineyard	Napa	C	89
1996 Zinfandel Chiles Mill Vineyard Unfiltered	Napa	C	89
1995 Zinfandel Chiles Mill Vineyard Unfiltered	Napa	C	86
1994 Zinfandel Chiles Mill Vineyard Unfiltered	Napa	C	89
1999 Zinfandel Chiles Valley	Napa	C	89
1997 Zinfandel Chiles Valley	Napa	C	89

One of my favorite Zinfandel producers, Green and Red Vineyard, a model of balance, elegance, and class, has again fashioned elegant, sexy, stylish wines. The 1999 Zinfandel Chiles Valley (14.2% alcohol) is a spicy, medium dark ruby-colored offering with abundant quantities of cherry fruit intermixed with balsam wood and earth. Lush and medium-bodied, it is ideal for drinking over the next 2–3 years. Richer and more textured, the peppery, earthy, spicy, complex 1999 Zinfandel Chiles Mill Vineyard (14.4% alcohol) reveals notes of soy, kirsch, and berry fruit in its aromas as well as flavors. Medium- to full-bodied and pure, with fine underlying acidity, it should be consumed over the next 5–6 years. The outstanding 1998 Zinfandel Chiles Mill Vineyard exhibits a dark ruby/purple color in addition to sweet, pure aromas of pepper, black fruits, kirsch, and vanilla. Measured and elegant, this medium- to full-bodied, restrained yet concentrated wine unfolds on the palate without a hiccup. It is a delicious Zin to enjoy over the next 5–6 years.

The 1997s from Green and Red Vineyard are both Burgundy-styled, elegant, floral and berry-scented, harmonious efforts that offer delicious drinking. The expressive 1997 Zinfandel Chiles Valley (13.9% alcohol) reveals raspberry and black cherry fruit, and soft, medium-bodied, well-knit, elegant flavors. The acidity, tannin, and alcohol are nicely meshed with the fruit. Restrained yet impressive, it will drink well for 3–4 years. The 1997 Zinfandel Chiles Mill Vineyard (13.5% alcohol) exhibits beautiful purity in addition to a fragrant, sweet berry-scented nose with hints of spice and subtle earth. Delicate yet intense, with medium body, impeccable balance, and a long finish, this wine should drink well for 3–4 years.

The most Burgundian of all the 1996 Zinfandels I tasted, the medium ruby-colored 1996 Zinfandel Chiles Mill Vineyard Unfiltered possesses a gorgeously fragrant nose of black cherries, floral scents, minerals, pepper, and spice. It is medium-bodied, lush, and sexy, in the style of a premier cru Beaune or Volnay. There is a nicely textured finish with lively acidity, sweet fruit, and glycerin. This Zin is ready to drink, so readers should take advantage of its considerable charms. The 1995 is a good example of a restrained, subtle Zinfandel that offers enough sweet fruit to give the wine appeal and attractiveness. The medium ruby color is followed by pure, dusty, black cherry aromas that drift from the glass. Dry and elegant, yet concentrated and harmonious, this is a lighter-styled, pretty, delicious Zin that is fully mature. I am not sure I haven't underrated the 1994. It exhibits a dark ruby color, a pure, ripe, cherry/raspberry fruitiness, a seamless, silky texture, medium to full body, and a luscious finish. It is all fruit, beautifully captured without any excesses. Drink this soft, smooth Zinfandel over the next 3–4 years.

HANSEL FAMILY VINEYARD (RUSSIAN RIVER)

1998 Pinot Noir	Russian River	D	89
1996 Pinot Noir	Russian River	D	89

This appears to be a promising newcomer from Russian River. Hansel's wines reveal Burgundy-like personalities with plenty of texture, ripeness, and complexity. Interestingly, the first person to tell me how good these wines were was Tom Rochioli. The 1998 Pinot Noir exhibits an evolved garnet color as well as an attractive bouquet of underbrush, grilled meats, dried herbs, and sweet, cherry, plum, and raspberry-like fruit. Spicy oak complements the ripe, sweet black fruit flavors. This wine cuts a medium- to full-bodied swath across the palate. Good acidity gives uplift and delineation. Drink it over the next 3–4 years.

The 1996 Pinot Noir from this small winery was made with considerable guidance from proprietor Walter Hansel's friend, Tom Rochioli. Readers should note that quantities of the impressive wines from the Hansel Family Vineyard are limited, and the entire production is sold through a mailing list. The complex 1996 Pinot Noir exhibits a Pommard-like earthy/spicy character. Some of Pinot's sweet, apple skin personality comes through in the black cherry flavors. A broad, dense, medium- to full-bodied Pinot Noir with considerable personality and flavor authority, it should drink well for 5–6 years.

HARLAN ESTATE (NAPA)

1999 Proprietary Red Wine	Napa	EEE	92+
1998 Proprietary Red Wine	Napa	EEE	93
1997 Proprietary Red Wine	Napa	EEE	100
1996 Proprietary Red Wine	Napa	EEE	98
1995 Proprietary Red Wine	Napa	EEE	99
1994 Proprietary Red Wine	Napa	EEE	100
1998 The Maiden	Napa	EE	91
1997 The Maiden	Napa	EE	94

1996 The Maiden	Napa	EE	91
1995 The Maiden	Napa	E	90

While Harlan Estate might be the single most distinctive and compelling Cabernet-based wine in northern California, there is more and more competition. It is also becoming increasingly expensive, jumping an average of $25 a year in price. The 1996 came out at $125, the 1997 at $150, and the 1998 at $175. If we run the math, 10 years from now this wine should cost $425 a bottle. Think that is preposterous? Current vintages of Harlan Estate frequently fetch prices in excess of that at wine auctions. Obviously, no expense is spared in producing what might be the most meticulously made wine in the world. The 1998, a candidate for the "Wine of the Vintage," was produced from yields of 0.9 tons per acre. There are only 1,100 cases, and it is the first Harlan Estate to be composed of 100% Cabernet Sauvignon. A spectacular achievement, it boasts an opaque plum/purple color and a sumptuous nose of espresso, mineral, blueberry, blackberry, tobacco, licorice, Asian spice, and roasted meat smells. In the mouth, it is seamless, full-bodied, with an unctuous texture, gorgeously sweet tannin, and layer upon layer of concentration. This is a tour de force in winemaking. It is hard to believe that such a wine has emerged from 1998. Anticipated maturity: 2003–2030. The 1997 Harlan Estate is one of the greatest Cabernet Sauvignon–based wines I have ever tasted. A blend of 80% Cabernet Sauvignon, with the rest Merlot and Cabernet Franc, this enormously endowed, profoundly rich wine must be tasted to be believed. Interestingly, it is the most precocious of the Harlan Estate wines to date, although the 1998 promises to be open-knit, if not as multidimensional. Opaque purple-colored, it boasts spectacular, soaring aromatics of vanilla, minerals, coffee, blackberries, licorice, and cassis. In the mouth, layer after layer unfold powerfully yet gently. Acidity, tannin, and alcohol are well balanced by the wine's unreal richness and singular personality. The finish exceeds one minute. Anticipated maturity: now–2030. Does anyone wonder if wines such as the 1945 Mouton-Rothschild, 1947 Cheval Blanc, and 1961 Latour had similar personalities at two years of age?

Readers should not overlook the dense purple-colored 1997 Maiden, another creamy-textured, full-bodied, unctuously thick, rich wine. Jammy cassis, new oak, smoke, and espresso notes explode from this blockbuster. An amazing effort, it will drink well when released and last for two decades. The 1998 Maiden is also prodigious. I know it is tempting to pooh-pooh second wines, but this is no afterthought from owner Bill Harlan and the winemaking team of American Bob Levy and Frenchman Michel Rolland. The 1998 Maiden (770 cases) possesses a dense purple color and a knockout nose of cocoa, prunes, blackberries, plums, and cassis. Spicy, with moderate tannin, and a viscosity and richness akin to beef blood, it is a gorgeous, concentrated, thick effort. Anticipated maturity: now–2018.

There are only 1,600 cases of the 1996 Harlan Estate and 600 cases of the 1996 Maiden. The opaque purple-colored 1996 Harlan Estate reveals extraordinary intensity, a spicy, black currant, tobacco, cedar, and fruitcake-scented bouquet, full body, a texture oozing with glycerin and concentrated fruit, and moderate tannin in the blockbuster finish. While not as perfect as the 1997 or 1994, it is one of the most concentrated and complete red wines one could hope to taste. Anticipated maturity: 2004–2030. The 1996 Maiden was performing even better this year. The dark saturated plum/purple color is followed by aromas of prunes, coffee, black fruits, and espresso beans. With an opulent personality, low acidity and a plush texture, it is a sexy, well-endowed wine. Anticipated maturity: now–2015.

As for the two cuvées of 1995, the Maiden is an outstanding offering (300 cases made from 100% Cabernet Franc). It possesses a dense, murky ruby/purple color and an expressive, cedary, leathery, spicy nose with plenty of black fruits. Some minerality comes through, but this complex, evolved yet structured, full-bodied wine is an amazing second wine. It should drink well for 10–15 years. The 1995 Proprietary Red Wine is almost as perfect as the 1994. It has gotten even better in the bottle, and remains one of the most remarkable young Cabernet Sauvignons I have tasted. The wine, a blend of 85% Cabernet Sauvignon and 15% Merlot, was aged in 100% new oak, which adds subtle toasty scents. This opaque purple-colored Cabernet offers up a nose of smoke, coffee beans, black and blue fruits, minerals, and roasted herbs. It is extremely full-bodied, with spectacular purity, exquisite equilibrium, and a seamless personality with everything in total harmony. The finish lasts for more than 40 seconds. This extravagantly rich, profoundly complex 1995 will give its 1994 sibling a run for its money. Anticipated maturity: now–2027.

What can I say about the 1994? It satisfied all of my requirements for perfection. The opaque purple color is followed by spectacular aromatics that soar from the glass, offering up celestial levels of black currants, minerals, smoked herbs, cedar wood, coffee, and toast. In the mouth, this seamless legend reveals full body and exquisite layers of phenomenally pure and rich fruit, followed by a 40+-second finish. While accessible, the 1994 begs for another 5–7 years of cellaring. It should easily last for 30+ years. Every possible jagged edge—acidity, alcohol, tannin, and wood—is brilliantly intertwined in what seems like a diaphanous format. What is so extraordinary about this large-scaled wine, with its dazzling display of aromatics and prodigious flavors and depth, is that it offers no hint of heaviness or coarseness. Harlan's 1994 comes close to immortality in the glass.

The 1999 looks to be outstanding, but seemingly not as compelling rich, textured, and nuanced as previous vintages. For the 1999 vintage, Harlan Estate has converted to wood fermenters, much like their nearby neighbor Robert Mondavi. That decision is interesting in view of the fact that many top Bordeaux châteaux discarded their wood fermenters 10–30 years ago in favor of temperature-controlled stainless steel. More controlled fermentation temperatures and increased sanitation were the obvious reasons for the conversion. Wood fermenters still exist in Bordeaux, particularly among some of the St. Emilion *gargistes,* but elsewhere they are primarily on display for tourists. In short, most of Bordeaux's wood fermenters made their way into barbecue pits.

Past Glories: 1993 (95), 1992 (96), 1991 (94), 1990 (90)

HARTFORD COURT (SONOMA)

1999 Pinot Noir Arrendell Vineyard	Russian River	E	92
1997 Pinot Noir Arrendell Vineyard	Green Valley	D	(88–90)
1999 Pinot Noir Dutton Ranch/Sanchietti Vineyard	Russian River	E	89
1999 Pinot Noir Marin Vineyard	Marin County	D	90+
1999 Pinot Noir Sevens Bench Vineyard	Napa/Carneros	D	92
1999 Pinot Noir Velvet Sisters Vineyard	Anderson Valley	D	90
1997 Zinfandel Dina's Vineyard	Russian River	D	90
1997 Zinfandel Hartford Vineyard	Russian River	D	89
1997 Zinfandel High Wire Vineyard	Russian River	D	90
1999 Hartford Zinfandel Dina's Vineyard	Russian River	D	89
1999 Hartford Zinfandel Fanucchi–Wood Road Vineyard	Russian River	D	92
1999 Hartford Zinfandel Hartford Vineyard	Russian River	D	90
1999 Hartford Zinfandel High Wire Vineyard	Russian River	D	92

The 1999 red wine offerings are the finest I have yet tasted from Hartford Court (another of the small, high-quality producers under the umbrella known as the Jackson Family Farms). While Don Hartford sells off some of the production from their 300 acres of vineyards, approximately 9,000 cases are produced under the Hartford Court and Hartford labels. The Hartford Court label includes their Chardonnays and Pinot Noirs, while the Hartford label is used for their Zinfandels. All the 1999s have been bottled, and all represent outstanding examples of their types.

Based on the stunning Pinot Noirs, it appears that Hartford Court has joined the upper echelon of Pinot Noir and Zinfandel producers in northern California. The 1999 Pinot Noir Velvet Sisters Vineyard (175 cases) comes from the cooler northern area of Anderson Valley. Made from such clones as Dijon #115 and Pommard, this dark ruby-colored offering exhibits a sweet, raspberry, brown sugar–like bouquet as well as smoky, attractively integrated toasty scents, medium to full body, decent acidity, and outstanding purity and ripeness. Sixty percent new French oak was utilized during the aging process. While accessible, it promises to drink well for 5–8 years. An outstanding effort, as well as a curiosity, is the 1999 Pinot Noir Marin Vineyard (425 cases). Most Marin County real estate is stratospherically priced, as this county has more than its share of multimillion-dollar homes as well as some of the wealthiest residents of the San Francisco Bay area. Made from a 14-year-old vineyard planted with the Mt. Eden clone, cropped at a meager one ton of fruit per acre, and bottled with no filtration, this earthy, dark ruby-colored Pinot reveals abundant quantities of sweet black fruits, dry tannin, good structure, and notions of melted fudge intermixed with black cherries, plums, and raspberries. Dense, deep, youthful, and unevolved, it will age nicely for a decade. Don Hartford's wine-maker, Mike Sullivan, told me that, like all their Pinot Noirs, it enjoyed a six-day cold soak prior to fermentation. About 70% new French oak was utilized. The 1999 Pinot Noir Sevens Bench Vineyard comes from a vineyard planted largely with French Dijon clones. This seven-year-old vineyard, which was cropped at two tons of fruit per acre, has produced an opaque purple-colored, dense, full-bodied, superbly concentrated Pinot with plenty of creamy black fruits intermixed with smoke, toast, and spice. Rich, with moderate tannin, sweet levels of glycerin, and enough acidity to provide delineation, this opulently styled wine can be drunk now or cellared for 6–8 years. Very impressive! More monolithic and less evolved, but potentially outstanding, the 1999 Pinot Noir Dutton Ranch/ Sanchietti Vineyard was muted the day I tasted it. Nevertheless, it is a plump, full-bodied, tannic effort with force and muscle, but not the charm or aromatics of its siblings. Those characteristics may develop over the next year, but this forceful, moderately tannic, dense 1999 does not lack concentration or intensity. Anticipated maturity: now–2009. Hartford Court's 1999 Pinot Noir Arrendell Vineyard is exquisite. Black raspberries intermingled with blueberries and cherry liqueur are wrapped with toasty oak. This rich, full-bodied, expressive Pinot possesses impressive purity, decent acidity, sweet tannin, and layers of concentrated fruit, yet it is neither heavy nor overblown. This superb effort should drink well during its first 7–9 years of life.

Under the new Hartford label are some powerhouse Zinfandels that recall the quality and stylistic approach favored by Ehren Jordan and Larry Turley at Turley Cellars (to my mind, California's preeminent Zinfandel producer). Hartford's 1999 Zinfandel High Wire Vineyard (570 cases produced from 90-year-old vines) contains 15.8% alcohol, but you would never suspect that from tasting it. Bottled without filtration, this wine offers an opaque purple color as well as explosive aromas of blackberries, pepper, and spice. In the mouth, ripe cherries also make an appearance in this unctuously textured, rich, full-bodied, exuberant, superbly concentrated, well-balanced Zinfandel. These wines are best consumed during their robust, powerful youth—over the next 5–6 years. Another outstanding effort is Hartford's 1999 Zinfandel Hartford Vineyard (350 cases). Produced from 80-year-old head-pruned vines, it exhibits boysenberry and blackberry fruit, along with pepper notes. Not as massive as the High Wire, this soft, velvety-textured, elegant (if that word can be attributed to a wine with 15.7% alcohol) offering possesses zesty underlying acidity, ripe tannin, and a big, fleshy mouth-feel with no hard edges. Drink it over the next 4–5 years. The awesome Hartford 1999 Zinfandel Fanucchi–Wood Road (325 cases with 16.1% alcohol) is a powerful, concentrated, intense effort produced from 90-year-old vines. Don Hartford said a touch of Petite Sirah was added, but that was not noticeable. It offers abundant quantities of blackberry and cherry liqueur-like aromas and flavors, along with pepper, minerals, and spice. Voluptuously textured, intense, fragrant, pure, and decadent, this dazzling Zinfandel should drink well for a decade.

Readers looking for a more understated, restrained effort will enjoy Hartford's 1999 Zinfandel Dina's Vineyard (204 cases). This 90-year-old vineyard produced 204 cases of Zinfandel that finished with a mere 14.5% alcohol. Offering up spicy red and black fruit aromas, medium to full body, excellent harmony, good acidity, and impressive balance, it should drink well for 6–7 years. All of these old-vine 1999 Zinfandels are made from yields averaging under two tons of fruit per acre.

The 1997 Pinot Noir Arrendell Vineyard is a beautifully fruity, dark ruby-colored wine with loads of apple skin, cherry jam, and spice in its aromatics and flavors. There is tangy underlying acidity, fine ripeness, and a fleshy mouth-feel with just enough acidity and tannin to buttress the wine and give it delineation. This effort should age nicely for 5–6 years.

Hartford Court produced fine 1997 Zinfandels. All were aged in 100% French oak and achieved natural alcohol levels between 14.7% and 15.2%. Production ranged from 300 cases for Dina's Vineyard to 700 cases for the High Wire Vineyard. Exhibiting a dark ruby/purple color, the 1997 Zinfandel Hartford Vineyard offers up an attractive nose of jammy, briery, and raspberry fruit, medium to full body, tangy acidity, and a spicy, exuberant personality. This wine should drink well for 4–5 years. The 1997 Zinfandel High Wire Vineyard reveals a saturated dark purple color, as well as more pepper and black raspberries in its moderately intense aromatics. This lovely, rich, medium- to full-bodied wine balances power with finesse. Drink this stylish, flavorful Zinfandel over the next 5–6 years. The outstanding dark ruby/purple-colored 1997 Zinfandel Dina's Vineyard is close in quality to the High Wire. There are abundant quantities of jammy black cherries and raspberries, intermixed with pepper and toasty oak in this medium- to full-bodied yet elegant wine. It should drink well for 5–7 years given its good underlying acidity and extract.

HAVENS WINE CELLARS (NAPA)

1997	Bourriquot Proprietary Red Wine	Napa	D	92
1996	Bourriquot Proprietary Red Wine	Napa	D	91
1995	Bourriquot Proprietary Red Wine	Napa	D	89
1994	Bourriquot Proprietary Red Wine	Napa	D	88+
1997	Merlot	Napa	D	90
1997	Merlot Reserve	Napa	D	91
1996	Merlot Reserve	Napa	D	90
1997	Syrah	Carneros	D	88
1996	Syrah	Carneros	D	89
1994	Syrah	Carneros	D	90

Mike Havens, working out of a warehouse in the city of Napa, appears to have settled into an admirable pattern, producing richer and richer Merlots, complemented by a fine Syrah, and a Cheval Blanc–inspired proprietary red wine called Bourriquot. There is also a small quantity of Sauvignon Blanc. Havens supplements his Carneros vineyard with purchased grapes.

His 1997s make up the strongest quartet of new releases wine-maker Michael Havens has yet produced. The 1997 Merlot (which is nearly as good as the Reserve offering) exhibits a dense ruby/purple color in addition to a superb nose of chocolate, cocoa, cherries, and smoky, earthy notes. The wine is rich and medium- to full-bodied, with low acidity, a sweet, nicely layered palate, and a lush finish. It should drink well for 7–8 years. Slightly more backward and concentrated, the opaque purple-colored 1997 Merlot Reserve possesses fuller body and greater extract and richness, as well as more tannin, volume, and flavor intensity. Although not as beguiling as the regular bottling, it promises to deliver even more goods with another 1–2 years of bottle age. It should keep for 12–15 years. The 1997 Bourriquot (a Cheval Blanc–like blend of approximately two-thirds Cabernet Franc and one-third Merlot) is sensational. My notes start with the words "great stuff." The dark ruby/purple color is accompanied by a sumptuous nose of coconuts, black currants, vanilla, and floral scents.

This medium- to full-bodied wine exhibits exceptional fruit purity and presence, great finesse and elegance, prodigious potential for complexity, and a sexy, opulently textured finish. It can be drunk early, but promises to be even better with 3–4 years of cellaring; it will keep for two decades. The 1997 Syrah displays a crème de cassis–dominated nose intermixed with smoky, earthy scents that emerge with airing. This dark ruby/purple-colored offering possesses full body, low acidity, lush, ripe fruit, a corpulent mouth-feel, and a soft, ripe finish. There is some tannin, but it is mostly buried beneath the cascade of fruit. If additional complexity develops, this Syrah will merit a higher rating. It should drink well for 8–10 years.

The 1996 Merlot Reserve should satisfy Merlot lovers given its deep ruby color, and rich, chocolaty, weedy, intensely smoky and seductive aromatics. Lushly textured, with impressive black cherry, chocolate, and berry flavors, this full-bodied, elegant, stylish Merlot reveals plenty of depth and richness, but no hard edges. Drink it over the next 7–8 years. The 1996 Syrah, while not a blockbuster, is an attractive tar, cassis, bacon, and smoky-scented wine with medium to full body, excellent concentration, soft tannin, and a round, generous, expansive mouth-feel. This delectable, elegantly styled Syrah is ideal for drinking over the next 5–9 years. The 1996 Bourriquot, Napa's answer to Cheval Blanc (each is made from a blend of two-thirds Cabernet Franc and one-third Merlot), offers an exotic, complex, evolved, coffee bean and berry–scented nose. In the mouth, this rich, full-bodied wine exhibits sweet tannin, low acidity, a lush texture, and a moderately long finish. With its gobs of fruit, expansive palate, and distinctive personality, it is more than a good imitation of Cheval Blanc. Drink it over the next 10–15 years.

The 1995 Bourriquot reveals a deep ruby/purple color, followed by big, spicy, mineral, licorice, floral-tinged, black currant aromas, medium body, excellent to outstanding fruit concentration, a soft, layered palate, and a rich, moderately tannic finish. The wine needs 2–3 years of cellaring, but it should keep for 15–18 years, possibly meriting an outstanding rating. The 1994 Bourriquot is also a blend of two-thirds Cabernet Franc and one-third Merlot. It reveals a deep color, some attractive, leafy, curranty-like scents, medium body, plenty of tannin, excellent richness, and a firm, structured finish. Cellar it for 2–3 years and drink it over the subsequent 15 years. The distinctive dark purple-colored 1994 Syrah exhibits an exaggerated, flamboyant set of aromatics (minty, black raspberry, and cassis scents). The wine is soft and medium- to full-bodied, with excellent richness, well-integrated tannin and acidity, and spicy wood. Already delicious, this wine should drink well for another decade. *Past Glories:* 1993 Merlot Reserve (90)

HAYWOOD (SONOMA)

1998 Zinfandel Morning Sun	Sonoma	D	87
1998 Zinfandel Rocky Terrace	Sonoma	D	85

The dense ruby/purple-colored 1998 Zinfandel Rocky Terrace exhibits jammy black cherry/berry flavors intermixed with spice and pepper, low acidity, and toasty new oak, yet the emphasis is on ripe Zin fruit presented in an exuberant, medium- to full-bodied format capable of aging for 5–6 years. Even better is the 1998 Zinfandel Morning Sun. An excellent dark ruby color is followed by aromas of chocolate, smoky barbecue, and briery, black cherry/raspberry fruit. Full-bodied, dense, and chewy, it has low acidity, an excellent texture, and a multilayered finish. This wine has the potential to merit an outstanding score if it is not compromised by too much fining or filtration prior to bottling. Anticipated maturity: now–2008.

HIDDEN CELLARS (MENDOCINO)

1997 Zinfandel Sorcery	Mendocino	C	89
1997 Zinfandel Zaina-Hitzman Vineyard	Mendocino	D	90

These are impressively made, well-constituted Zinfandels. The 1997 Zinfandel Sorcery (75% Zinfandel, 15% Petite Sirah, and 10% Syrah that achieved 15.5% alcohol) is serious stuff. Its opaque ruby/purple color is followed by blackberry, cassis, and spicy aromas. Dense, full-bodied, tannic, and in need of 1–2 years of cellaring, this is a wine to drink between now– 2010. It may develop additional complexity, thus meriting a score close to outstanding. I was thrilled with the 1997 Zinfandel Zaina-Hitzman Vineyard (15.9% alcohol). It is a forceful, full-bodied, fleshy, nicely layered example with tons of ripe blackberry and raspberry fruit, subtle oak, dried herb notes, as well as a monstrous, concentrated, intense finish. With excellent fat, lushness, and equilibrium, it will drink well for 7–8 years.

PAUL HOBBS (SONOMA)

1998	Cabernet Sauvignon	Napa	E	88
1998	Cabernet Sauvignon Hyde Vineyard	Carneros	E	89
1997	Cabernet Sauvignon Hyde Vineyard	Carneros	E	91
1999	Chardonnay	Russian River	D	90
1998	Merlot Black Vineyard	Napa	EE	90
1997	Merlot Black Vineyard	Napa	E	89
1998	Pinot Noir Cuvée Agustina	Sonoma Mountain	E	92
1998	Pinot Noir Hyde Vineyard	Carneros	E	88
1997	Pinot Noir Hyde Vineyard	Carneros	D	88

This is an impressive group of wines from Paul Hobbs, a winery whose production is inching up to 10,000 cases. The 1999 Chardonnay (1,297 cases) sees about 55% new French oak. It enjoys full malolactic, has its lees stirred, and uses indigenous yeasts to ferment the Chardonnay must. Powerful and concentrated, with plenty of fat, leesy, tropical fruit flavors, gorgeous flesh, and notes of honey, toast, smoke, and minerals, it should be consumed over the next 2 years.

Paul Hobbs has displayed a brilliant touch with Pinot Noir. His 1998 Pinot Noir Cuvée Agustina (only 92 cases are made from such Pinot clones as Pommard, Swan, and Calera) is aged in 100% new oak, which has been totally absorbed. This full-bodied Pinot Noir exhibits earthy, black cherry fruit, notes of smoked game and pepper, and meaty, black raspberry flavors. A distinctive, earthy, full-bodied, powerful, accessible Pinot, it should continue to drink well for a decade. There are 630 cases of the 1998 Cabernet Sauvignon, much of which came from the Beckstoffer sector of the To-Kalon Vineyard. Notes of fudge, licorice, earth, and smoke compete with black currants in this medium-bodied wine. The only drawback is some gritty tannin in the finish. Blended with 25% Merlot to give it more texture and plumpness, it is best drunk over the next 7–8 years. The 1998 Cabernet Sauvignon Hyde Vineyard (786 cases) offers an elegant, supple, well-delineated style with notes of vanilla, chocolate, cassis, cedar, and dried Provençal herbs. Medium-bodied and stylish, with a sweet mid-palate, it can be consumed over the next decade. From a three-acre parcel, the 1998 Merlot Black Vineyard (160 cases of 100% Merlot) offers stupendous richness in its cocoa, scorched earth, and black cherry–scented bouquet. Chewy, with earthy, fudge, and berry flavors, it should continue to evolve nicely for a decade.

The dark ruby/purple-colored 1998 Pinot Noir Hyde Vineyard (463 cases) offers sweet plum and black cherry fruit intertwined with underbrush and soil scents. Naturally fermented and bottled without filtration, this medium- to full-bodied Pinot reveals an expansive texture as well as moderate tannin in the finish. The wood is not excessive. The dark ruby-colored 1997 Pinot Noir Hyde Vineyard offers moderately intense aromas of sweet oak intermixed with attractive black raspberry and cherry fruit. Spicy, earthy, underbrush, and foresty flavors are present in this medium-bodied, spicy, soft Pinot. Drink it over the next 2–3 years.

Chocolate, blackberry, mocha, and cherry notes dominate the aromatics and flavors of the impressive 1997 Merlot Black Vineyard (820 cases). Ripe and chewy, with abundant sweet fruit in addition to moderately high tannin, this Merlot can be drunk now, but promises to be even better with another 12 months of aging. It should keep for a decade. Lastly, the classic 1997 Cabernet Sauvignon Hyde Vineyard (1,020 cases) boasts an opaque black/purple color and a gorgeously sweet bouquet of cassis, licorice, and toasty new oak. Full-bodied, with gobs of black fruit, plenty of glycerin, and excellent symmetry, this seamless effort has well-integrated acidity, tannin, and alcohol. It should drink well for 15+ years.

HOWELL MOUNTAIN VINEYARDS (HOWELL MOUNTAIN)

1997 Zinfandel Beatty Ranch	Howell Mountain	D	90+
1996 Zinfandel Beatty Ranch	Howell Mountain	D	90
1997 Zinfandel Black-Sears	Howell Mountain	D	(90–92)
1997 Zinfandel Old Vine	Howell Mountain	D	90
1996 Zinfandel Old Vine	Howell Mountain	C	89+?

Howell Mountain produced three beautiful 1997 Zinfandels, made from extremely old vines. The 1997 Zinfandel Old Vine (from 25- and 80-year-old vines) exhibits a deep ruby/purple color, a fragrant, black cherry, mineral, peppery nose, explosive fruit, low acidity, and a rich, glycerin-endowed, fleshy, hedonistic mouth-feel. It will provide ideal drinking over the next 4–5 years. It tips the scales at 15.5% alcohol, so be forewarned. The 1997 Zinfandel Beatty Ranch (from 80-year-old vines) is more structured and tannic. The nose offers up black raspberry fruit intertwined with dusty soil, pepper, and mineral scents. Medium- to full-bodied, moderately tannic yet gorgeously pure and layered, this Zin may be even better with another 6–12 months of bottle age. It should keep for 7–8 years. Lastly, the 1997 Zinfandel Black-Sears Vineyard (made from 25-year-old vines) is a fat, chewy, full-bodied, beautifully etched offering with gobs of black cherry, raspberry, and blackberry fruit. It reveals more glycerin and a chewier mouth-feel than its two siblings, as well as a plump, hedonistic, opulently textured finish. Consume this brawny (16% alcohol) yet seductive Zin over the next 4–5 years.

These wines are made by Littorai's Ted Lemon. As the numbers attest, they are exceptionally fine Zinfandels. The outstanding 1996 Zinfandel Beatty Ranch received a "wow" in my tasting notes. At 15.5% alcohol, one would expect it to be hot, but this wine is super-concentrated and beautifully balanced. It boasts a deep ruby/purple color, followed by knockout aromatics of black raspberries, minerals, and spice. Deep, full-bodied, and concentrated, with the alcohol well concealed, this large-scaled, intricately detailed, intensely flavored wine can be drunk now or cellared for 7–10 years (atypically long for Zin). Nearly as superb is the 1996 Zinfandel Old Vine. It delivers a similar alcoholic clout (15.5%), but in this case, some heat shows up at the back of the palate. The wine displays a dark plum color, and sweet blackberry, raspberry, and cherry notes dosed with subtle oak and spice. Full-bodied, rich, and slightly hot in the heady, dense finish, it should drink well for 5–6 years.

IRON HORSE (SONOMA)

1997 Benchmark	Alexander Valley	E	90
1997 Cabernet Franc	Alexander Valley	D	89
1999 Cuvée R	Alexander Valley	D	89
1998 Pinot Noir	Sonoma	D	89

The 1999 Cuvée R, an exuberant blend of 80% Sauvignon Blanc and 20% Viognier (an intriguing as well as highly successful idea), offers copious quantities of tropical fruit, honeyed lemons, and spice in a medium- to full-bodied, gorgeously fresh, flavorful, complex format. Loaded with fruit, with good body and a lovely perfume, it should be consumed over the next several years. The 1998 Pinot Noir, which emerges from Sonoma's Green Valley, is an elegant, flavorful, tasty effort to enjoy over the near-term. With 14.6% alcohol, this 1998 is no wimpish wine. In fact, it is the finest Pinot Noir Iron Horse has yet produced. A dark ruby color is accompanied by sweet, jammy plums, black cherries, dried herbs, and meaty animal notes. The wine is plump and medium- to full-bodied, with plenty of glycerin, purity, and ripeness. Flavors of allspice and cinnamon add to the wine's complexity. Firm tannin and good underlying, zesty acidity will provide 7–8 years of drinkability.

The complex 1997 Cabernet Franc (14.6% alcohol) is outstanding for its purity of expression and graceful yet concentrated style. A classic effort, it offers richness as well as finesse, a combination not easily obtained in California, where richness and power are more the norm. A deep ruby color with purple hues is followed by copious black cherry and mulberry fruit nicely dosed with new oak. This medium-bodied wine possesses good sweetness, refreshing acidity, moderate tannin, and excellent depth and richness. It should develop even more perfume over the next 10–12 years. The 1997 Benchmark is a proprietary blend of 76% Cabernet Sauvignon, 12% Merlot, and 12% Cabernet Franc, with 14.6% alcohol. It boasts an opaque saturated ruby/purple color as well as a tight but promising nose of black currants, raspberries, earth, minerals, and tar. Although extremely concentrated, this wine retains its elegance and overall symmetry. As it sits in the mouth, additional layers and nuances develop. Another 1–3 years of cellaring should prove beneficial, and it should age well for 15+ years. For my taste, it is the finest Cabernet-based wine Iron Horse has yet produced. Bravo!

J. C. CELLARS (PASO ROBLES)

1999 Zinfandel Alegria Vineyard	Russian River	D	89
1998 Zinfandel Alegria Vineyard	Russian River	C	88
1999 Zinfandel Bolduc Vineyard	Napa	D	88
1999 Zinfandel Rhodes Vineyard Cuvée Isabel	Redwood Valley	D	89

These wines are made by Jeff Cohen, the wine-maker at Rosenblum Cellars. These three impressive 1999 Zinfandels display plenty of personality as well as considerable fruit. They are big, ruggedly constructed efforts to drink during their first 5–6 years of life. The 1999 Zinfandel Bolduc Vineyard's dense, opaque ruby/purple color is followed by aromas of herbs, leather, blackberries, and spice. While not complex, it offers a big mouthful of spicy, full-bodied Zinfandel. The dark ruby/purple-colored 1999 Zinfandel Alegria Vineyard reveals a more Rhône-like, pepper, earth, *garrigue* (Provençal herb and soil notes), spicy bouquet, full-bodied, intense black cherry and berry flavors, and a large-framed, muscular finish. The 1999 Zinfandel Rhodes Vineyard Cuvée Isabel exhibits copious quantities of sweet black fruits, medium to full body, currants, blackberries, and a grapier, lustier style with less earth and spice. Unfortunately, there are only 85 cases of the 1998 Zinfandel Alegria Vineyard. This dark ruby/purple-colored effort reveals excellent, briery, sweet black cherry and raspberry fruit infused with spicy, toasty wood. The wine is surprisingly unevolved, robust, slightly foursquare, but deeply concentrated. With a positive upside, this wine will be even better with another year of cellaring. It should drink beautifully for 4–6 years.

JADE MOUNTAIN (NAPA)

1997 Côte du Soleil	California	B	88
1994 Les Jumeaux	California	C	88
1998 Merlot Caldwell Vineyard	Napa	D	90
1997 Merlot Paras Vineyard	Napa	D	90
1997 Mourvèdre	California	C	90
1998 La Provençale	California	C	88
1997 La Provençale	California	C	89
1998 Syrah	Napa	D	90
1997 Syrah	Napa	C	90
1997 Syrah Cask P-10	Napa	D	91
1997 Syrah Hudson Vineyard	Napa	D	91

1995 Syrah Mt. Veeder	Napa	D	88+
1997 Syrah Paras Vineyard	Napa	D	91
1996 Syrah Paras Vineyard	Napa	D	90
1999 Viognier Paras Vineyard	Napa	D	91

Under the helmsmanship of Douglas Danielak, Jade Mountain's promotion of Rhône blends has resulted in a bevy of excellent offerings, all of which are realistically priced. One of the finest Viogniers I have tasted, the 1999 Viognier Paras Vineyard (14.9% alcohol) sees some barrel fermentation. It possesses a superb nose of honeysuckle, peaches, apricots, and tropical fruits. Aged in neutral barrels prior to bottling, the wine exhibits a terrific texture, great fruit purity, and a full-bodied, opulent finish. It requires immediate consumption as these wines do not last. Their least expensive offering, the 1998 La Provençale is a blend of 65% Mourvèdre, 24% Syrah, and 11% Grenache that has been aged 12 months in neutral wood. This medium to dark ruby-colored, Côtes du Rhône–styled effort displays delicious black cherry fruit, smoky notes, and an earthy, middle-weight finish. Drink it over the next 2–3 years as you would an excellent Côtes du Rhône. There are 1,235 cases of the outstanding 1998 Merlot Caldwell Vineyard. A blend of 91% Merlot and 9% Cabernet Sauvignon that achieved 14.5% alcohol, it offers a flamboyant perfume of smoked wood and jammy berry fruit. Seductive, rich, and fruity, it is a treat to drink. This wine will have many admirers for its hedonistic display of fruit and spicy wood presented in a low-acid style. Drink it over the next 5–7 years.

The dark ruby/purple-colored 1998 Syrah (3% Viognier is included in the blend) reveals heady alcohol (14.9%) in its expressive aromas and flavors of camphor, honeysuckle, blackberry, and smoke. Aged 22 months in French oak, this delicious wine exhibits soft tannin as well as plush, fat, round, generous flavors. It is another example of how well Syrah fared in the uneven 1998 vintage. Drink it over the next 5–7 years. The limited production (230 cases) 1997 Syrah Cask P-10 emerges from Mt. Veeder's Paras Vineyard. This 100% Syrah is a dense, powerful, muscular-styled effort that will benefit from another 6–12 months of bottle age. Its opaque black/purple color is accompanied by a dazzling bouquet of chocolate, creosote, cassis, and blackberries. Deep, full-bodied, muscular, and rich, with superb balance between its fruit, tannin, acidity, and alcohol, it will drink well for 10–15 years.

Jade Mountain's 1997s may be their most impressive portfolio of wines to date. Readers looking for immediately appealing, complex, supple reds should check out the 1997 Côte du Soleil and 1997 La Provençale (a blend of Mourvèdre, Syrah, and Grenache). The 1997 Côte du Soleil could be called a California-inspired Côtes du Rhône. The healthy dark ruby color is followed by berry, kirsch, peppery, and sweet fruit aromas, a lush, supple texture, good glycerin, and a heady finish. An attractive, powerful (14.5% alcohol) wine, it is meant for hedonists. Drink it over the next 2–3 years. The 1997 La Provençale (also 14.5% alcohol) reveals blackberry and cassis notes in the nose, as well as a more saturated ruby color. Gorgeously pure black fruits, medium to full body, admirable glycerin, and outstanding purity give this offering tremendous appeal. It should drink well for 4–5 years. The 1997 Mourvèdre (from 100-year-old vines planted in Contra Costa's Evangelho Vineyard) is a successful wine for a varietal that can be difficult to grow and vinify. Moderately intense aromas of blackberries, pepper, loamy soil, leather, and a touch of blueberry are enticing. Expansive, rich, fleshy, and complex, this multidimensional, supple-textured wine can be drunk now and over the next 7–8 years.

The following three 1997 Syrahs all tip the scales at 14.5% alcohol. The 1997 Syrah Napa could have a little Viognier blended in given the honeysuckle, peach/apricot nose intermixed with oodles of blackberry/cassis fruit. Fleshy, succulent, open-knit, and delicious, it may not make old bones, but it will be a velvety-textured, plump, fleshy Syrah to enjoy over the next 5–6 years. From a Mt. Veeder vineyard with a 1,200 foot elevation, the 1997 Syrah Paras Vineyard reveals a murky-looking ruby/purple color in addition to more pepper and intense cassis/blackberry fruit. Thicker, jammier, and fuller-bodied, with additional volume and depth, this superb Syrah has low acidity and sweet tannin, but promises to evolve nicely for a decade. There are a number of Syrahs from the famous Lee Hudson Vineyard in Carneros. Jade Mountain's 1997 Syrah Hudson Vineyard is more structured, closed, and tighter-knit than its two siblings. Nevertheless, it reveals deep, weighty black fruit scents and melted asphalt in the bouquet, along with full-bodied, powerful flavors and a hefty finish. Sweet tannin, low acidity, and superb ripeness characterize this full-throttle Syrah. It will benefit from 6–8 months of bottle age and can be drunk over the following 12+ years.

The 1997 Merlot Paras Vineyard presents an ostentatious, exuberant personality with little in reserve. Dark ruby-colored, this flashy wine offers intense smoky, espresso, sweet cherry/berry aromas, medium to full body, and a low-acid, lush personality. The wine is gorgeous to drink now and over the next 4–5 years, but there is not a great deal of depth behind the sexy display of jammy fruit, oak, and smoke. Seductive! The 1996 Syrah Paras Vineyard reveals smoky bacon fat and cassis aromas. The wine is medium- to full-bodied, lush, nicely textured, expansive, and rich with no hard edges. Drink this seductive Syrah over the next 7–8 years. The 1995 Syrah Mt. Veeder is excellent. It possesses a dense, deep ruby/purple color, followed by a provocative nose of sweet black plums, currants, smoke, and licorice. In the mouth, the wine is ripe, tannic, backward, dense, full-bodied, and pure. This is an excellent, possibly outstanding Syrah that requires 3–4 years of bottle age; it should keep for 15 years.

The 1994 Les Jumeaux (a Cabernet Sauvignon/Mourvèdre/Syrah blend) remains one of my favorite wines from Jade Mountain. It offers an intriguing black cherry, cassis, herb, pepper, spicy component, medium to full body, some tannin, good grip, a savory mouth-feel, and a well-delineated, spicy finish. This wine will continue to improve for another 12–18 months and will keep for 7–8+ years.

JAFFURS (SANTA BARBARA)

1997 Syrah Bien Nacido Vineyard	Santa Barbara	D	89+
1997 Syrah Thompson Vineyard	Santa Barbara	D	90

Stolpman Family Vineyard is one of the large new vineyards coming on line (a percentage of the production will be estate-bottled under its name). This has been a source for high-quality Rhône Ranger grapes such as Roussanne and Syrah, as well as other varietals. The 1997 Syrah Thompson Vineyard (a whopping production of 48 cases) offers a stunning nose of black pepper, blackberries, and floral scents. Dense, rich, and full-bodied, with gorgeously pure fruit, sweet tannin, and unobtrusive acidity, this large but elegant, deep ruby/purple-colored Syrah can be drunk now as well as over the next 10–12 years. What a shame there is not more of it! The 1997 Syrah Bien Nacido Vineyard (49 cases) is more reticent in the nose, but does reveal an impressively saturated dark ruby/purple color, jammy blackberry fruit flavors, more acidity than the Thompson Vineyard, moderate tannin, and a medium- to full-bodied, long finish. It is an excellent, nearly outstanding Syrah to enjoy for 10–12 years.

JONES FAMILY VINEYARD (NAPA)

1998 Cabernet Sauvignon	Napa	EE	90
1997 Cabernet Sauvignon	Napa	EE	94
1996 Cabernet Sauvignon	Napa	D	90+

This wine is the product of a small micro-vinification from a five-acre vineyard on the upper eastern hillsides of Napa Valley. David Abreu, the well-known viticulturist, oversees the vineyard, and acclaimed wine consultant Heidi Barrett makes the wine. The impressive debut release, the 1996 Cabernet Sauvignon, has been followed by two promising efforts. The outstanding 1998 Cabernet Sauvignon (aged in one-third new oak) exhibits a dark ruby/purple color, sweet plum, blackberry, and mineral notes in the moderately intense aromatics, sweet tannin, medium body, and pure fruit. The wine is not massive, but elegant, concentrated, and ideal for drinking over the next 15 years. There were 450 cases produced. The sensational 1997 Cabernet Sauvignon (800 cases produced) is the finest effort yet from the Jones Family. The color is a saturated blue/purple. The nose offers up classic mineral, blueberry, crème de cassis, and subtle toasty oak notes. Full-bodied, with stunning purity, a multilayered palate impression, and an explosive finish, this wine requires 2–3 years of cellaring; it will age nicely for 20–25 years. The first release from this seven-acre vineyard, the 1996 (405 cases) exhibits a dense, dark ruby/purple color, as well as a restrained but promising nose of black currants, blackberries, new oak, and minerals. The wine is sweet, elegant, and medium- to full-bodied, with high tannin and an austere finish. The oak is nicely meshed, and the texture is attractive and chewy. If the tannin softens and its bouquet becomes more forthcoming, this 1996 Cabernet Sauvignon may merit a higher score. Anticipated maturity: now–2014. By the way, this wine improved significantly with exposure to air. The tannin became sweeter and better integrated after 60 minutes of aeration.

The Jones Family is a new star to add to the growing family of impressive Cabernet producers. Because of that, it would be wise for readers to get their names on the winery's mailing list. It may be your only chance to obtain any.

JSJ SIGNATURE SERIES (CALIFORNIA)

1996	Cabernet Sauvignon Buckeye Vineyard	Alexander Valley	D	90
1997	Cabernet Sauvignon Veeder Peak Vineyard	Napa	E	(90–91+)
1996	Cabernet Sauvignon Veeder Peak Vineyard	Napa	E	91+
1996	Merlot Alexander Valley Estate	Alexander Valley	D	89
1996	Merlot Buckeye Vineyard	Alexander Valley	D	88+
1997	Merlot Dry Creek Valley	Dry Creek	D	88
1997	Pinot Noir Arrendell Vineyard	Russian River	E	91

Quantities of these selections personally chosen by Kendall-Jackson's owner, Jess Jackson, range between 250–500 cases. They are packaged in heavy, expensive bottles and are meant to represent the pinnacle of quality that can be obtained from the Kendall-Jackson vineyards.

There are 500 cases of the 1998 Merlot Dry Creek Valley. Produced from a hillside vineyard, this highly extracted, forceful wine was totally closed when I tasted it. It seemed atypically big, full, and rich for a 1998. However, high levels of astringent tannin in the finish raise concerns about the wine's overall balance, but it possesses impressive extract. If the tannin melts away and becomes better integrated, it should merit a score in the upper 80s, possibly 90. However, it will require 2–3 years of cellaring before that question can be resolved. Anticipated maturity: 2004–2016. The 1997 Cabernet Sauvignon Veeder Peak (250 cases) exhibits a terrific nose of scorched earth, minerals, cassis, and blueberries. Full-bodied, powerful, and intensely pure, this brawny, muscular, powerful wine requires 4–5 years of cellaring, but its tannin is sweeter and better integrated than in the 1998 Merlot. Anticipated maturity: 2005–2020. The terrific dark ruby-colored 1997 Pinot Noir Arrendell Vineyard reveals notes of spice, jammy plums, and dried cherry fruit intertwined with toasty oak. A concentrated, medium- to full-bodied, complete, savory, delicious Pinot Noir, it promises to evolve nicely for 5–6 years. There are two single-vineyard Merlots in the JSJ Signature Series. The 1996 Merlot Buckeye Vineyard possesses a dark ruby/purple color, as well as a tightly knit, lavishly oaked nose with black cherry fruit, herbs, white chocolate, and spice scents. Medium- to full-bodied, with good flesh and high tannin, it requires 2–3 more years of cellaring, and should keep for 12–15. The dark ruby/purple-colored 1996 Merlot Alexander Valley Estate offers up a moderately intense, restrained nose of cranberry liqueur intermixed with vanilla and spice. It is a rich, medium- to full-bodied, tannic, backward wine in need of 2–4 years of cellaring. It should age well for 15 years or longer. While it is an impressive offering, it was closed when I tasted it in late September of 1999.

The outstanding 1996 Cabernet Sauvignon Buckeye Vineyard is destined to last for two decades. The wine boasts an opaque purple color and a rich nose of minerals, black currants, and spicy oak. A dense, full-bodied powerhouse, with nicely integrated wood, acidity, and tannin, this firm Cabernet is loaded with extract and richness. The blend contains small quantities of Cabernet Franc and Merlot. Anticipated maturity: now–2020. The opaque purple-colored 1996 Cabernet Sauvignon Veeder Peak offers a Margaux-like nose of spring flower garden scents intermixed with black currants, smoky new oak, and spice. Dense and full-bodied, with outstanding purity and richness, this brawny, muscular, concentrated wine should be at its best between 2003–2022.

JUDD'S HILL (NAPA)

1997 Cabernet Sauvignon Estate	Napa	E	90
1996 Cabernet Sauvignon Estate	Napa	D	88
1994 Cabernet Sauvignon Estate	Napa	C	90

This beautiful estate, tucked high on a hillside overlooking Conn Valley, remains an unheralded as well as underrated source for fine Merlot and Cabernet Sauvignon (the only wines produced). Owners Art and Bunny Finkelstein began Judd's Hill in 1989, after selling their previous winery, Whitehall Lane. Judd's Hill encompasses 14 hillside acres, supplemented by purchases from Knights and Pope Valleys. Their aim is to produce drinkable, supple, yet concentrated wines with both an early appeal and the potential to last for 15 or more years.

The 1997 Cabernet Sauvignon Estate (250-case lot) is a blend of 85% Cabernet Sauvignon and the rest Merlot and Cabernet Franc. It offers a deep purple color, superb concentration and purity, and abundant black currant/cassis fruit intermixed with spice box, cedar, and fruitcake scents. Dried herbs, licorice, and loamy soil notes also make an appearance in this full-bodied, moderately tannic offering. Anticipated maturity: 2004–2017. The dark ruby/purple-colored 1996 Cabernet Sauvignon Estate exhibits a smoky, black currant, dried herb, and licorice-scented nose. Dense, full-bodied, and rich, with excellent concentration and purity, it does not possess the creamy texture and sweet inner mid-palate of the 1997, but it is well made. Anticipated maturity: now–2012. Judd's Hill turned out an outstanding 1994 Cabernet Sauvignon. The wine exhibits a saturated dark ruby/purple color, sweet, ripe, black currant fruit, low acidity, mature tannin, and a well-balanced, flamboyant, succulent, opulent texture with layers of rich fruit nicely married with smoky oak. This hedonistic, forward, Pomerol-styled Cabernet can be drunk now as well as over the next 12–15 years.

ROBERT KEENAN (NAPA)

1998 Cabernet Sauvignon	Napa	D	87
1995 Cabernet Sauvignon Hillside Estate	Napa	D	88
1994 Cabernet Sauvignon Hillside Estate	Napa	D	88
1996 Merlot	Napa	D	88
1997 Merlot Mailbox Vineyard Spring Mountain Reserve	Napa	D	89+
1998 Merlot Reserve	Napa	D	89
1997 Merlot Spring Mountain Estate	Napa	D	86

The Keenan wines are starting to take on more flavor and texture, yet remain fairly priced for their quality level. Saddleback Cellars' renowned wine-maker, Nils Venge, has been brought in to build up the wines. Production remains between 6,000–10,000 cases, although they intend to ultimately produce 14,000 cases. Keenan's 1998 Merlot Reserve (about 35% came from their estate) is excellent and possibly exceptional. A dense plum/cherry color is accompanied by a big, smoky, coffee-scented bouquet revealing abundant berry fruit, low acidity, and a seductive, fleshy, medium- to full-bodied style. This soft, opulent 1998 is already showing exceptionally well. Anticipated maturity: now–2010. The Bordeaux-styled 1998 Cabernet Sauvignon is smooth and round, with aromas and flavors of herbs, earth, and black currants. It has nowhere near the mass and weight of the 1997, but is well balanced and made in a forward, attractive style. Readers should know that 1998 has been deemed by many as a bad vintage for North Coast Cabernet Sauvignon and Merlot, yet many attractive wines have been produced. Anticipated maturity: now–2012.

A wine that may ultimately achieve an outstanding rating is the 1997 Merlot Mailbox Vineyard (430 cases). It exhibits plenty of sweet, toasty oak (much in the Venge style) along with medium- to full-bodied, dense, black cherry/berry flavors, good glycerin, admirable texture, excellent purity, and abundant sweet tannin in the finish. Give it 1–2 years of cellaring, and drink it over the next 15–16 years. Another fine 1997 from Keenan is the 1997 Merlot Spring Mountain Estate. Rich and dense, it exhibits structure, volume, and flavor. While not a superstar, it is a very good effort that should drink nicely for a decade or more. The 1996 Merlot is sweet and rich, with smoky, chocolaty, black cherry fruit, good density, and a clean, long, tannic finish. It should drink well for 10 years.

The 1995 Cabernet Sauvignon Hillside Estate displays the winery's softer, more velvety-textured style of wine without the tough overlay of tannin and compact mid-palate. The 1995 possesses a deep ruby/purple color, spicy, ripe fruit, power and intensity, and moderate tannin in the finish. While it may never merit an exceptional rating, the wine should score in the upper 80s after bottling. The 1994 Cabernet Sauvignon Hillside Estate exhibits a dark ruby/purple color, followed by a sweet, black cherry, earthy, mineral-scented nose, and a fleshy mid-palate with depth and ripe fruit. Some rough tannin springs up in the finish. This wine will benefit from 4–5 years of cellaring and keep for up to 15.

KENDALL-JACKSON (CALIFORNIA)

Year	Wine	Region		Score
1997	Cabernet Sauvignon Buckeye Vineyard	Alexander Valley	E	88
1998	Cabernet Sauvignon Buckeye Vineyard Great Estates	Alexander Valley	E	91
1997	Cabernet Sauvignon Great Estates	Alexander Valley	D	90
1998	Cabernet Sauvignon Great Estates	Napa	D	88
1997	Cabernet Sauvignon Great Estates	Napa	D	90
1997	Cabernet Sauvignon Stature	Napa	EE	92
1999	Chardonnay Camelot Vineyard Great Estates	Santa Maria	D	89
1999	Chardonnay Clark Vineyard Great Estates	Monterey	D	90
1999	Chardonnay Durell Vineyard Great Estates	Sonoma	D	91
1999	Chardonnay Grand Reserve	California	C	89
1999	Chardonnay Great Estates	Monterey	D	88
1999	Chardonnay Great Estates	Sonoma Coast	D	88
1999	Chardonnay Stature	Santa Maria	D	89
1998	Merlot Buckeye Vineyard Great Estates	Alexander Valley	D	90
1998	Merlot Great Estates	Sonoma	D	88
1998	Pinot Noir Arrendell Vineyard Stature	Russian River	D	89
1997	Syrah Grand Reserve	California	C	87

There are now five levels to the enormous Kendall-Jackson hierarchy. At the bottom, or least expensive level, are the Collage wines, followed by the Vintner's Reserve offerings. Moving up the ladder in both price and quality are the Grand Reserve wines as well as the two newest levels of the hierarchy, Great Estates and the wines at the pinnacle called Stature. I have reviewed only the wines that merited 88 points or more. Among the single-vineyard offerings, the 1997 Cabernet Sauvignon Buckeye Vineyard (3,410 cases) is excellent. This wine sees 50% new oak and was closed when I tasted it in October 1999. It exhibits a dark ruby/purple color, abundant spicy oak, medium body, and moderate tannin. This Cabernet Sauvignon cuts a structured, rich mouth-feel, with tobacco, cassis, and licorice characteristics. Give it 3–4 years of cellaring; it should last for 15+ years.

At the Grand Reserve level, the 1999 Chardonnay Grand Reserve (62,190 cases) is a substantial wine that is 100% barrel-fermented, mostly in French oak. It possesses good underlying acidity as well as abundant quantities of tangerine, orange marmalade, honeysuckle, and tropical fruit notes. The oak character is more prominent than in the Vintner's Reserve, but this is a medium- to full-bodied, rich Chardonnay to drink over the next several years.

The 1997 Syrah Grand Reserve could turn out to be excellent given its saturated ruby/purple color, attractive, moderately intense crème de cassis and blackberry-scented nose, and fruity, medium-bodied flavors. Soft, with low acidity and spicy, peppery notes in the background, it should age nicely for 4–5 years.

Under the Great Estates moniker, Kendall-Jackson is making appellation-based wines such as the 1999 Chardonnay Great Estates Camelot Vineyard (15,350 cases). It is a fleshy, medium- to full-bodied, well-delineated Chardonnay loaded with tropical fruits infused with subtle, smoky oak. Consume it over the next 2–3 years. The 1999 Chardonnay Great Estates Monterey (4,160 cases aged primarily in French oak) reveals mineral, citrus, and lemon-lime characteristics to its cooler climate fruit profile. Medium-bodied as well as nicely textured, it should drink well for 4–5 years. Even better is the outstanding 1999 Chardonnay Clark Vineyard Great Estates. There are 1,500 cases of this low-acid, fleshy, full-bodied Chardonnay. Offering up notes of passion fruit, apricot, peach, and honeysuckle, it is rich and ostentatious. Drink it over the next 2–3 years. There is also a Sonoma Coast Great Estates Chardonnay, much of which emerges from three sources, Sangiacomo, Three Sisters, and Durell. The 1999 Chardonnay Great Estates Sonoma Coast (3,715 cases) looks to be better. The wine's bouquet exhibits lemon blossom and ripe, tropical fruit scents intermixed with a liquid minerality. It possesses medium to full body, an excellent texture, and a long finish. The superb 1999 Chardonnay Durell Vineyard Great Estates displays more earth and mineral characteristics in its buttered caramel, pineapple, and custard-filled aromas and flavors. Full-bodied and rich, with terrific texture and a long finish, it should drink well for 3–4 years.

Under the Great Estates, there are a Pinot Noir from Monterey, Merlots from Sonoma and Alexander Valley's Buckeye Vineyard, and Cabernet Sauvignons from Napa as well as Alexander Valley's Buckeye Vineyard. All of them are exceptionally well-made wines, with the production ranging from a high of 5,000 cases for the Napa bottling of Cabernet, to a low of 245 cases for the Cabernet Sauvignon Buckeye Vineyard. Potentially outstanding, the dark ruby/purple-colored 1998 Merlot Great Estates Sonoma exhibits abundant quantities of mocha, black cherry, and currant fruit with smoke and fennel in the background. Textured, rich, pure as well as medium- to full-bodied, this wine should drink well for up to a decade. The dense purple-colored 1998 Merlot Great Estates Buckeye Vineyard is superb. From a vineyard planted at 2,500 feet with very poor soils (yields range between 1.5–2.5 tons of fruit per acre), this formidably endowed Merlot possesses aromas and flavors of roasted coffee, black fruits, iron, and smoke. Full-bodied, chewy, and muscular, yet accessible, it should drink well for 10–15 years. Another outstanding effort, the 1997 Cabernet Sauvignon Great Estates Napa (5,000 cases) exhibits copious quantities of pure black currant fruit mixed with cedar, smoke, and spice box. It is full-bodied, opulent, rich, and best drunk over the next 12–15 years. Although made in a lighter, leaner, less concentrated style, the 1998 Cabernet Sauvignon Great Estates Napa offers blueberry, camphor, and black currant fruit, medium body, and Bordeaux-like weight. It should drink well for up to a decade. There are 4,500 cases of the outstanding 1997 Cabernet Sauvignon Great Estates Alexander Valley. With abundant amounts of Asian spices, minerals, black cherries, and cassis as well as admirable structure, this fruit-dominated, full-bodied, large-scaled, opulent wine should drink well for 15+ years. Another superb effort is the 1998 Cabernet Sauvignon Great Estates Buckeye Vineyard. The most tannic and backward of these wines, it exhibits a saturated ruby/purple color as well as tobacco-tinged, cassis fruit mixed with new oak and minerals. It is large-scaled, highly extracted, and while drinkable now, promises to evolve for 12–15 years.

There are currently four wines in the Stature series. Production ranges from a low of 89 cases for the 1998 Pinot Noir Arrendell Vineyard to 3,073 cases for the 1997 Napa Cabernet Sauvignon. The 1999 Chardonnay Stature Santa Maria reveals more acidity and smokiness, without the voluptuous fatness possessed by the 1998. It is certainly fine, with plenty of tropical fruit and nicely integrated wood. Consume it over the next 3–4 years. The dark plum-colored 1998 Pinot Noir Arrendell Vineyard Stature displays smoky tomato and cherry notes in the nose, medium body, tart acidity in mid-palate, but good fruit and depth in the finish. One of the most beautiful wines in the Stature series is the impressive 1997 Cabernet Sauvignon Stature. Sourced from vineyards such as Veeder Peak and Andy Beckstoffer's To-Kalon Vineyard, it offers up crème de cassis aromas intermixed with new saddle leather, vanilla, spice box, and minerals. Full-bodied, rich, and seamless, this voluptuously textured, thick, juicy Cabernet Sauvignon can be drunk now or cellared for up to two decades.

KISTLER VINEYARDS (SONOMA)

1997 Chardonnay Camp Meeting Ridge	Sonoma Coast	E	95
1999 Chardonnay Cuvée Cathleen	Sonoma	E	97
1998 Chardonnay Cuvée Cathleen	Sonoma Coast	E	96
1997 Chardonnay Cuvée Cathleen	Sonoma County	E	(94–96)
1999 Chardonnay Durell Vineyard	Sonoma Valley	E	94
1998 Chardonnay Durell Vineyard	Sonoma Valley	E	91
1997 Chardonnay Durell Vineyard	Sonoma Valley	E	91
1999 Chardonnay Dutton Ranch	Russian River	E	90
1998 Chardonnay Dutton Ranch	Russian River	E	90
1997 Chardonnay Dutton Ranch	Russian River	E	94
1999 Chardonnay Hudson E-Block	Carneros	E	94
1998 Chardonnay Hudson Vineyard	Carneros	E	95
1997 Chardonnay Hudson Vineyard	Carneros	E	95
1999 Chardonnay Hyde Vineyard	Carneros	E	93
1998 Chardonnay Hyde Vineyard	Carneros	E	94
1999 Chardonnay Kistler Vineyard	Sonoma Valley	E	95
1998 Chardonnay Kistler Vineyard	Sonoma Valley	E	95
1997 Chardonnay Kistler Vineyard	Sonoma	E	93
1999 Chardonnay McCrea Vineyard	Sonoma Mountain	E	93
1998 Chardonnay McCrea Vineyard	Sonoma Mountain	E	92
1997 Chardonnay McCrea Vineyard	Sonoma Mountain	E	93
1999 Chardonnay Vine Hill Vineyard	Russian River	E	96
1998 Chardonnay Vine Hill Road Vineyard	Russian River	E	96
1997 Chardonnay Vine Hill Road Vineyard	Russian River	E	91
1998 Pinot Noir Camp Meeting Ridge	Sonoma Coast	E	(92–95)
1997 Pinot Noir Camp Meeting Ridge	Sonoma Coast	E	(91–94)
1996 Pinot Noir Camp Meeting Ridge	Sonoma Coast	E	92
1995 Pinot Noir Camp Meeting Ridge	Sonoma Coast	E	93+
1994 Pinot Noir Camp Meeting Ridge	Sonoma Coast	E	88
1999 Pinot Noir Cuvée Catherine	Russian River	E	(96–98)
1997 Pinot Noir Cuvée Catherine	Russian River	E	(95–97)
1996 Pinot Noir Cuvée Catherine	Russian River	E	96
1995 Pinot Noir Cuvée Catherine	Russian River	E	94
1994 Pinot Noir Cuvée Catherine	Russian River	E	92
1999 Pinot Noir Hirsch Vineyard	Sonoma Coast	E	(94–96)

1998 Pinot Noir Hirsch Vineyard	Sonoma Coast	E	(93–95)
1997 Pinot Noir Hirsch Vineyard	Sonoma Coast	E	(90–93)
1996 Pinot Noir Hirsch Vineyard	Sonoma Coast	E	89
1995 Pinot Noir Hirsch Vineyard	Sonoma Coast	E	92+
1994 Pinot Noir Hirsch Vineyard	Sonoma Coast	E	92
1999 Pinot Noir Kistler Vineyard	Russian River	E	(93–95)
1998 Pinot Noir Kistler Vineyard	Russian River	E	(93–96)
1997 Pinot Noir Kistler Vineyard	Russian River	E	(94–96)
1996 Pinot Noir Kistler Vineyard	Russian River	E	94
1998 Pinot Noir Kistler Cuvée Catherine	Russian River	E	(95–97)
1999 Pinot Noir Occidental Cuvée Elizabeth	Sonoma Coast	E	(98–100)
1998 Pinot Noir Occidental Cuvée Elizabeth	Sonoma Coast	E	(96–98)
1994 Pinot Noir Vine Hill	Sonoma	E	91

I do not know what to add to the accolades I have given over the last decade to Steve Kistler and his assistant, Mark Bixler. Every year the wines are brilliant. Given the breadth of Chardonnays and Pinot Noirs produced by Steve Kistler, he is the undeniable master of these two varietals in California. In short, his Chardonnays and Pinot Noirs are wines of extraordinary intensity, complexity, and richness. Moreover, they should prove to be amazingly ageworthy. I am more and more convinced that Kistler, along with others (notably Helen Turley and her husband, John Wetlaufer, as well as Tom Rochioli), is producing historic Chardonnays and Pinot Noirs that may one day be considered to have rewritten the definition of greatness for these varietals. Steve Kistler believes his 1999s may be the finest wines he has ever made. There have been so many brilliant wines that it is hard to say at this early stage if the 1999s will turn out better. The malolactic fermentations were the slowest he has ever had, and of course the crop was relatively small, much like 1998. Because of the cool growing season, acids were higher than normal, and, combined with the slow malolactics, it does seem the *terroir* characteristics are more vivid in 1999. In any event, these are the wines of a shy genius who obviously prefers to stay out of the limelight. All of the following notes for the 1999s are from tank samples, as the wines have been racked from wood and are in settling tanks prior to being bottled without filtration.

The 1999 Chardonnay McCrea Vineyard (2,000 cases) exhibits an intense liquid minerality, notes of white currants, a full-bodied personality with citrus oils and white flowers, and a remarkably well-delineated finish. Still tightly knit but concentrated and extremely Burgundian, it needs a couple of years of aging and should last for a decade. The softer 1999 Chardonnay Dutton Ranch (2,000 cases) is made in a more typical California style. Orange marmalade, pineapple, and mango aromas and flavors are apparent in this full-bodied, rich, smoky Chardonnay. While exceptional, it lacks the minerality and definition of Kistler's other offerings. It will have 4–6 years of ageability. Perhaps the best Chardonnay I ever tasted from the Durell Vineyard is the 1999. An intensely steely effort, this big, weighty, gorgeously delineated wine displays awesome concentration, fabulous definition, and huge flavors of roasted hazelnuts, lemon blossom, and liquid minerals. As the wine sits in the glass, it comes across as a grand cru Chablis on steroids. Concentrated as well as long, this should be a fascinating Chardonnay to follow as it has the potential to last for up to a decade. Extremely different is the 1999 Chardonnay Hyde Vineyard (1,000 cases). This wine shows the vintage's good, zesty acidity, a white peach, lemon custard, tangerine-flavored palate, full body, and superb purity and length. In a grouping of prodigious Chardonnays, this is exceptional. Look for it to drink well for 5–6 years. Another awesome effort is the 1999 Chardonnay Vine Hill Vineyard. There are 2,000 cases produced from this Russian River vineyard surrounding the Kistler winery. It exhibits telltale minerality as well as a gorgeous nose of white fruits, citrus oils, nuts, minerals, smoke, and butter. With fabulous intensity, purity, and an expansive, multilayered mid-palate, this powerful, impeccably balanced, restrained Chardonnay unfolds on the palate. This will be another 1999 that will have a long and compelling evolution. Back in the big, smoky, tropical fruit, roasted hazelnut, pedal-to-the-metal, in-your-face style is the 1999 Chardonnay Kistler Vineyard (2,000 cases). This wine has terrific tropical fruit flavors infused with smoke and mineral. Again, it is well detailed, pure, concentrated, and long. There are 500 cases of the 1999 Cuvée Cathleen, a selection from the Kistler and Vine Hill Vineyards. It is a prodigious Chardonnay that may merit a perfect rating. The wine has layers of concentrated fruit, but it is neither heavy nor over the top. Aromas and flavors of ripe oranges, passion fruit, and pineapple, infused with hazelnut oil and floral scents (acacia) can be found in this staggering wine; it should evolve effortlessly for 5–10 years. I can't wait to get my hands on (make that my lips around) a bottle of this stuff. The vineyard that Helen Turley made famous, the E-Block of Hudson Vineyard, has produced a flamboyant, ostentatious, full-bodied, dense 1999 Chardonnay (only 250 cases) with exotic notes in its leesy, scorched earth, smoky, tropical fruit characteristics. This 19-year-old vineyard consistently turns out terrific Chardonnay fruit. These Chardonnays justify their differentiation by the winery (something that is often questionable with other wineries that designate the vineyard of many wines). They are fermented with both indigenous and cultured yeasts, given extensive lees stirring and contact, and bottled unfiltered after full malolactic fermentation. The percentage of new French oak varies, usually less than 50%.

The 1998 Chardonnay McCrea Vineyard (made from an old, low-producing Wente clone) exhibits a striking minerality in its lemony, buttery, citrusy style. Full-bodied and complex, it is reminiscent of a grand cru Chassagne-Montrachet. The wine, which becomes more complex in the glass, is powerful, rich, concentrated, and well balanced. It should drink well for 5–7 years. The 1998 Chardonnay Dutton Ranch is smoky, with copious quantities of exotic tropical fruits jumping from the glass. Pineapple, mango, and passion fruits immediately come to mind when tasting this full-bodied, lusty, in-your-face Chardonnay that should drink well for 4–5 years. One of the tightest and most backward offerings in Kistler's portfolio is the 1998 Chardonnay Durell Vineyard. Always the last to be harvested (because of the extremely cool microclimate), the 1998 possesses considerable force and intensity, with a mineral, citrusy, lemon blossom, orange peel component to its full-bodied richness. It reveals good acidity and power, all of which is harnessed and beautifully balanced. Look for this wine to open with another 12 months of cellaring and drink well for 5–7 years. The sensational 1998 Chardonnay Hyde Vineyard emerges from a block of vines that used to be sold to the Mondavis for their reserve Chardonnay. Roasted hazelnut, espresso, zesty tropical fruit, mineral, and buttery aromas and flavors are accompanied by a full-bodied, powerful, gorgeously pure and well-delineated wine. Made from old Chardonnay vines, it should drink well for 5–7 years, possibly longer. Even richer than the wonderful 1997, the 1998 Chardonnay Kistler Vineyard, made from a vineyard planted with the Mt. Eden clone, is extremely full-bodied, with striking purity, and powerful, concentrated, honeyed flavors with nuances of butter, smoke, roasted nuts, and minerals. The creamy texture is buttressed by good acidity. Toast, gravel, and slate-like richness intermixed with fruit make this a compelling, intensely flavored Chardonnay. It should drink well for 5–7 years, perhaps longer. Readers looking for an ostentatious blockbuster should check out Kistler's 1998 Chardonnay Hudson Vineyard. This offering comes from the Hudson E-Block vineyard that was made famous by Helen Turley and John Wetlaufer's Marcassin bottlings. Smoky, roasted hazelnut scents give this a garish, flamboyant, Meursault premier cru–like character. Big and full-bodied, with considerable glycerin, high alcohol, and terrific fruit richness, this thick, juicy, mouth-staining Chardonnay will impress with its power and brash display of fruit, alcohol, and glycerin. It should drink well for 5–6 years.

The last two 1998 Chardonnays represent an evolution in style. They possess all the power and concentration of Steve Kistler's most successful wines, but they also have a certain restraint allied with extraordinary complexity and elegance that a few years ago would have been found only in the finest Burgundy grand crus. The 1998 Chardonnay Cuvée Cathleen is a spectacularly beautiful, well-delineated effort with everything hitting the olfactory senses and palate in measured doses. However, the overall impression is one of stunning concentration, perfect harmony, fabulous density and richness, and that layered, intense mid-palate and length that only great wines possess. It needs a year or more of cellaring and should evolve in an intriguing manner for up to a decade. The 1998 Chardonnay Vine Hill Road Vineyard is profound. While not as boisterous a blockbuster as the Hudson Vineyard or as showy or rich as the Hyde Vineyard, it is a spectacular Chardonnay. Amazingly, a meager 23 tons of fruit emerged from this 15-acre vineyard, and this wine represents the essence of Chardonnay from Vine Hill. The wine has yet to reveal all of its characteristics, but its extraordinary precision, intense mouth-feel, and glorious display of pure fruit that come across in a full-bodied, perfectly balanced fashion make for a riveting drinking experience. It will evolve along the same lines as the Cuvée Cathleen (being tight but obviously loaded with potential) for another year or two, and then explode over the following 2–4 years. It may last for more than a decade, and evolve much like a great grand cru white Burgundy.

The vintage's high yields do not appear to have had an impact on the 1997 Chardonnays' level of concentration and intensity. Moreover, the 1997s possess an atypical level of tangy, underlying acidity, giving the wines a wonderful vibrancy. Additionally, their splendid aromatics are matched only by the 1995's. I tasted eight Chardonnays. While they share a certain similarity, they possess distinctive attributes that justify the winery's decision to differentiate them. All are fermented with both indigenous and commercial yeasts, given extensive stirring during prolonged contact with the lees, and bottled unfiltered after full malolactic fermentation. The percentage of new French oak varies, with higher percentages for the Camp Meeting Ridge, Hudson, and Cuvée Cathleen offerings. The 1997 Chardonnay McCrea Vineyard, made from an old Wente clone, personifies this varietal's lemony, buttery, citrusy, mineral style. It offers medium to full body, splendid concentration, considerable richness and texture on the mid-palate, and gorgeous elegance, purity, and overall balance. Tangy acidity gives the wine admirable freshness. It should age well for 5–7 years. The 1997 Chardonnay Vine Hill Road Vineyard (from both Hyde and Dijon Burgundy clones) is a more restrained wine with noticeably higher acidity. It reveals suggestions of cold steel, wet stones, and that liquid minerality found in certain Chardonnays. Medium- to full-bodied, with excellent depth, and more austerity and backwardness than its siblings, it will benefit from another year of cellaring and keep for 6–7 years. Readers looking for a Chardonnay that offers the tropical fruit spectrum, without completely abandoning the complex mineral character, will be pleased with the 1997 Chardonnay Durell Vineyard. The poor vigor of these rocky soils, combined with such clones as Hyde, has resulted in a wine with zesty acidity, medium to full body, outstanding ripeness and purity, and loads of orange blossom/lemony fruit in addition to hints of peach and pineapple. This 1997 requires 1–2 years of cellaring and should have an unusually long life of 8–10 years. The more flamboyant, Burgundy-styled 1997 Chardonnay Dutton Ranch displays a roasted hazelnut, sweet, rich, tropical fruit–scented nose, full body, and laser-like clarity to its component parts. Rich and intense, it is similar to a tightly knit Burgundian grand cru. With less minerality yet more of the smoky, leesy, roasted nut characteristics, this wine combines abundant tropical fruit and honeyed citrus. It should be delicious upon release, and keep for 5–7 years.

The 1997 Chardonnay Kistler Vineyard (made from the Mt. Eden clone, which is alleged to be a suitcase clone from Burgundy's Corton-Charlemagne vineyard) is a multidimensional wine with a rich, full-bodied, creamy texture, superb buttery, honeyed fruit, subtle toast, gorgeously rich fruit, white flowers, buttered popcorn, and liquid gravel-like notes. Combining power with finesse, it should drink well young and age for 5–7 years. The dazzling 1997

Chardonnay Camp Meeting Ridge Vineyard is the most explosive, viscous, powerful, and mineral-laden of the Kistler Chardonnays. Like its siblings, it surpasses 14% alcohol, but that is well hidden by the wine's outstanding extract and layered personality. A lush, leesy complexity emerges, but this is an extremely rich, highly concentrated, stunning Chardonnay with prodigious fruit extraction in addition to astonishing length. This is the finest Camp Meeting Ridge Chardonnay to date. Another leesy, smoky, Burgundy-styled, exotic offering is the 1997 Chardonnay Hudson Vineyard. Kistler's effort possesses a Meursault-like, buttery character with gobs of tropical fruit and glycerin, yet firm buttressing acidity. My instincts suggest it will be the most forward of these Chardonnays, as well as the shortest-lived (4–5 years). After being blown away by so many sensational Chardonnays, it is difficult to find the adjectives and superlatives to describe the 1997 Chardonnay Cuvée Cathleen. This offering is produced from a selection of barrels that Steve Kistler and Mark Bixler believe to be the richest and most complete. Negligibly better than the other brilliant *cuvées*, it possesses exceptional richness, length, and intensity. Layers of fruit, smoky, buttery popcorn, tropical fruit, and mineral scents soar from the glass, and are exceptionally intense and well balanced. This terrific, full-bodied effort should age for 8–10 years.

Steve Kistler and Mark Bixler are justifiably proud of what they have achieved with Chardonnay, but what really turns them on is their accomplishments with Pinot Noir, which may be the greatest Pinot Noirs being made in the New World. There are 250 cases of the 1999 Pinot Noir Hirsch Vineyard. It possesses a dense ruby/purple color as well as a knockout nose of blackberries infused with smoke, mineral, earth, and floral scents. As the wine sits in the glass, add cherries and pepper to the complex concoction of aromas and flavors. The wine is full-bodied as well as spectacularly concentrated, yet exhibits a youthful vibrancy and good underlying acidity. These wines are all made from destemmed Pinot Noir, and are bottled unfined and unfiltered after 12 months of 100% new-oak aging. Look for the 1999 Hirsch Vineyard to age well for at least a decade. Also profound, the 1999 Pinot Noir Kistler Vineyard exhibits floral, black raspberry, berry, and earth notes. The wine is strikingly rich, with a velvety texture underpinned by good acidity, full body as well as superb density, purity, and equilibrium. This magnificent Pinot Noir should also age for a decade. The 1999 Pinot Noir Cuvée Catherine, a selection of the best barrels from the Kistler Vineyard, displays a bouquet of roasted meats, earth, truffle, blackberry, raspberry, and smoky cherry fruit. Full body, an unctuous texture, and terrific acidity define this large-scaled effort. A monumental Pinot Noir that has to be tasted to be believed, it should hit its prime in about 3–4 years and last for 12–15, if not longer. Lastly, there are 150 cases of the dense purple-colored 1999 Pinot Noir Occidental Vineyard Cuvée Elizabeth. Blueberry and boysenberry liqueur infused with minerals and violets make for dazzling olfactory fireworks. On the palate, the wine is sumptuous yet remarkably fresh and lively. The wine has incredible concentration, purity, and overall equilibrium. Anticipated maturity: now–2012.

The dark ruby/purple-colored 1998 Pinot Noir Hirsch Vineyard (150 cases) has tamed some of the ferocious tannin this offering frequently exhibits. Rich, pure, and deep, with abundant quantities of black cherry fruit, spice, and pepper, this full-bodied Pinot Noir needs 4–5 years of cellaring and should keep for 10–15 years. The dark ruby-colored 1998 Pinot Noir Camp Meeting Ridge Vineyard's (100 cases) smell is akin to a top vintage of Grands-Echezeaux or Richebourg. Notes of black raspberries, blackberries, flowers, and minerals jump from the glass. While it does not have as much power as the Hirsch Vineyard, it reveals a velvety sweetness and unmistakable individuality and distinctiveness. It will be one of Kistler's more showy efforts. Drinkable already, it promises to last for a decade. There are 500 cases of the super-concentrated, full-bodied, fat, luscious, dark purple-colored 1998 Pinot Noir Kistler Vineyard. Made from the Calera clone, it offers a juicy, black cherry, berry, earth, mineral, and spice-scented nose. In the mouth, beef blood and black fruits are present, along with copious fat, glycerin, and moderate tannin. A sumptuous Pinot Noir, it will be fascinating to follow over the next decade or more.

The 250-case lot of 1998 Pinot Noir Kistler Vineyard Cuvée Catherine and 50-case lot of 1998 Pinot Noir Occidental Vineyard Cuvée Elizabeth are, along with the Marcassin Vineyard Pinot Noir, the finest Pinot Noirs I have tasted from California. The dense ruby/purple-colored 1998 Pinot Noir Kistler Vineyard Cuvée Catherine displays a spectacular floral, black raspberry, and cherry-scented nose. Compelling fruit purity offers jammy cherry, strawberry, and smoky aromas with hints of violets (or is it lilacs?). Full body, fine underlying acidity, and sweet tannin make for a sumptuous wine. Anticipated maturity: now–2012. There are only a measly 50 cases of the 1998 Pinot Noir Occidental Vineyard Cuvée Elizabeth, so the tasting notes are brief. It is an exceptional wine that represents the essence of Pinot Noir. If any readers latch onto a bottle or two, let me know.

The opaque black/purple-colored 1997 Pinot Noir Hirsch Vineyard looks more like Syrah than Pinot Noir. However, the nose offers up aromas of blackberries, cherries, and smoke intermixed with toast, roasted herbs, and meat. Medium- to full-bodied, with light to moderate tannin and an exuberant style with firm acidity, this is a classic. Anticipated maturity: now–2014. The 1997 Pinot Noir Camp Meeting Ridge Vineyard exhibits a dark ruby/purple color and a more feminine, less muscular personality with plenty of sweet black raspberry and cherry fruit. A softer, more luscious style of Pinot Noir, it will provide more flattering drinking than the Hirsch. The wine is extremely expansive, with sweet tannin, adequate acidity, and admirable staying power. Anticipated maturity: now–2010.

Two of the most spectacular Pinot Noirs I have ever tasted are Kistler's 1997 Kistler Vineyard and 1997 Cuvée Catherine. The 1997 Pinot Noir Kistler Vineyard (500 cases) is made from the Dijon clone 777 and two California clones, Pommard and Calera. It boasts a dense, saturated dark ruby/purple color, as well as an exceptionally sweet nose of roasted herbs and black cherry jam intermixed with raspberries, truffles, and toasty oak. Sweet and expansive, this full-bodied wine possesses fabulous concentration and purity, a grand cru–like level of potential complexity, and a 30+-second finish. It must be tasted to be believed. Look for this wine to be drinkable upon release, and last for at least a decade. There are approximately 250 cases of the 1997 Pinot Noir Cuvée Catherine. Like its siblings, it has over 14% alcohol, but that is totally obscured by the wine's sensational concentration, extract, and overall equilibrium. A dense ruby/purple-colored, full-bodied Pinot Noir, it offers up aromas of blackberries, raspberries, and cherry liqueur intermixed with licorice, smoke, and meat. Chewy yet not heavy, this wine does reveal some tannin, but it is largely hidden by the wine's fruit, glycerin, and extract. Wow, what an amazing performance!

The two 1996 Pinot Noirs I tasted are remarkable wines. The 1996 Pinot Noir Kistler Vineyard exhibits a Vosne-Romaneé/Richebourg-like violet, black cherry, and smoky-scented nose of considerable intensity. Full-bodied, with superb richness, admirable delineation, a lush, concentrated mid-palate, and black cherry, earthy notes in the spicy finish, this is another impressive, super-concentrated Pinot Noir with both complexity and equilibrium. It should drink well for a decade. The 1996 Pinot Noir Cuvée Catherine, a blend of fruit from the Sonoma Coast and Kistler Vineyard, is another thrilling, sumptuously styled Pinot. The color is a healthy saturated ruby/purple. The wine is spectacularly rich and extremely full-bodied, with floral (violets and lilacs) scents intertwined with cherry jam, over-ripe strawberries, and smoke. With terrific purity and a multilayered texture, this, like the other Kistler Pinot Noirs, is a tour de force! Anticipated maturity: now–2010.

The dense ruby-colored 1996 Pinot Noir Camp Meeting Ridge Vineyard (150 cases) is a fruit bomb, offering copious quantities of lush black fruits intermixed with underbrush, minerals, and spice. Gorgeously proportioned, medium- to full-bodied, with well-integrated tannin and acidity, its vibrancy, purity, and liveliness are commendable. This wine should drink well young and keep for a decade. The 1996 Pinot Noir Hirsch Vineyard (150 cases) requires 3–5 years of cellaring. It is a macho, muscular, tannic wine with meaty, beefy aromas and flavors, and black cherry fruit intertwined with an earthy *terroir* characteristic. However, the tannins are elevated, and the wine in need of cellaring. Because of that, it is more angular and austere than the other *cuvées*.

Kistler's impressive Pinot Noir portfolio was launched with the 1994s. The 1995 Pinot Noirs appear to be as good as the impressive 1994s. The 1995 Pinot Noir Hirsch Vineyard exhibits an opaque ruby color, a beefy, black fruit, spicy, earthy-scented nose, full body, plenty of tannin, and admirable intensity and richness. The wine needs 1–2 years of cellaring, but it promises to keep for a decade. Only 250 cases were produced from this Sonoma Coast vineyard. The 1995 Pinot Noir Camp Meeting Ridge Vineyard (also 250 cases) is a dense, Côte de Nuits–like wine with gobs of sweet black fruits, earth, and underbrush. Full-bodied and powerful, with more tannin and structure than the Hirsch *cuvée*, this is another impressive Sonoma Coast Pinot Noir. The 1995 Pinot Noir Estate Cuvée Catherine is one of the most remarkable Pinot Noirs I have tasted from California. The opaque ruby/purple color and sweet nose of black fruits, smoked meat, and minerals are followed by a wine of exceptional richness, purity, and delineation. It is still backward and closed, but wow, what concentration, intensity, and overall balance.

The 1994 Hirsch Vineyard Pinot Noir boasts a deep ruby/purple color, with a nose of earth, meat, and ripe black fruits. Full-bodied and powerful, this wine could easily be mistaken for a top grand cru from the Côte de Nuits given its richness, aromatic complexity, and flavor dimension. The medium to dark ruby-colored 1994 Camp Meeting Ridge Vineyard Pinot Noir reveals a meaty, cinnamon, cherry-scented bouquet, round, ripe, medium-bodied flavors, and a long, soft, richly fruity finish. The 1994 Pinot Noir Vine Hill Vineyard exhibits a deeper color, a riper, more intense fragrance, superb richness and depth, full body, lovely integrated oak and acidity, and an opulent, silky-textured finish. It could easily pass as a top grand cru from Burgundy's Côte d'Or. It should drink and age well for 5–6 years. The 1994 Pinot Noir Estate Cuvée Catherine exhibits a dense color and gorgeous wild berry aromas ranging from cherries to raspberries. Rich and full-bodied, with layers of creamy fruit and a super texture, this superb Pinot Noir should drink well young yet keep for another 7–8 years.

I am not sure all readers can appreciate it, but these are historic wines, and have been for some time. What is remarkable about Steve Kistler and Mark Bixler is that they just keep pushing the envelope and improving on what is already an enviable record of achievement.

KONGSGAARD (NAPA)

1998	Arietta	Napa	EE	92
1997	Arietta	Napa	EE	91
1999	Arietta Merlot	Napa	EE	92
1998	Arietta Merlot	Napa	EE	90+
1999	Chardonnay	Napa	EE	93
1997	Merlot	Napa	EE	90
1999	Roussanne/Viognier	Napa	EE	93
1999	Syrah Hudson Vineyard	Napa	EE	(92-94+)
1998	Syrah Hudson Vineyard	Napa	EE	92+

John Kongsgaard's philosophy of winemaking is about as natural as practiced anywhere in the world. It involves harvesting fruit from low-yielding vines, picking it ultraripe, and utilizing no yeast, bacteria strain, or enzyme in the winemaking. Obviously everything, both whites and reds, flows into the bottle with neither fining nor filtration. What is a little harder to explain is what Kongsgaard calls his "Death and Resurrection" style of winemaking. In short, he encourages the wines to "die on their lees" before they fight back and resurrect themselves. As he says, there is not much that can be done in the winery, and the last bastion of creativity to produce better wines is "extreme viticulture." Whatever he does, it works, because these are some of the most distinctive and individualistic wines produced in California.

The 1999 Chardonnay, with the core part of the blend coming from his family's Stone Crest Vineyard in Coombsville, is even more intense and concentrated than the 1997. It is obviously made from lower yields, as there are only 600 cases. The wine seems to have everything concentrated, not only fruit and extract but also acidity. It is tightly knit but incredibly intense, and, like a great Montrachet, requires decanting for 30–45 minutes before consuming. A light green-gold color is followed by a huge, intense, liquid minerality intermixed with subtle notes of marmalade, caramel, honeysuckle, citrus oil, and hazelnut. There is remarkable vibrancy to this full-bodied, powerful 1999, and the finish lingers for 40+ seconds. It is an amazing Chardonnay that took more than 12 months to ferment dry. Moreover, it was aged in 100% new oak, yet there is virtually no wood detectable in the wine's aromas or flavors. Don't be surprised to see this wine evolve for at least a decade—it's that special.

A new offering to look for is a remarkable blend of 50% Roussanne and 50% Viognier. Given John Kongsgaard's love of opera, its name undoubtedly will be plucked from the music world. My first descriptor was "explosive." The 1999 was aged in neutral oak and reveals an Alsatian-like, petrol note in the bouquet. Unctuously textured, decadent, and lavishly rich as well as delineated and elegant, it is close to being over the top. Although a contradiction, it is a marvelously complex, intense, dry, full-bodied white that should drink well for 3–4 years.

Readers looking for a California Syrah that has the structure of a Hermitage might do well to consider Kongsgaard's offerings. They are the antithesis of the big, delicious fruit bombs made elsewhere that are best drunk in their first 7–10 years of life. There are about 200 cases of the opaque black/purple-colored 1998 Syrah Hudson Vineyard. As John Kongsgaard said, it was made from "stupidly low yields." The wine is tight in the mouth, but reveals tremendous stuffing along with scents of blackberries, licorice, earth, truffles, pepper, and graphite. Massively tannic, but sweet and rich, this wine should enjoy two decades of life. However, one word of caution—either decant it for 60 or so minutes prior to drinking or wait 2–3 years. The 1999 Syrah Hudson Vineyard is more unctuous, with an opaque black/blue/purple color as well as intensely sweet crème de cassis, blackberry, smoke, and hickory barbecue spice aromas as well as flavors. Huge, rich, full-bodied, and massive, it is on a more rapid evolutionary track than the 1998. Anticipated maturity: 2003-2016.

In partnership with auctioneer Fritz Hatten, Kongsgaard produces about 500 cases of Arietta (a Cabernet Franc/Merlot blend representing this winery's answer to Cheval Blanc). The 1998 is a complete, complex wine that tastes like a synthesis between a top-class St.-Emilion and a Napa Valley red. It possesses the complexity of a top Bordeaux allied to the ripeness and richness of California. Its dense ruby/purple color is accompanied by aromas of black fruits, leather, spice box, and flowers. Medium- to full-bodied and pure, with moderate tannin in the finish, it opens with extended airing. (Blueberries became apparent after about 10 minutes.) This wine should drink well for at least 20 years. In 1997, production of the Arietta was about 450 cases. Beethoven was blaring from speakers situated throughout the winery as I tasted this wine. Kongsgaard says the Arietta may have a Beethoven label, but it is Wagnerian in style. A blend of 85% Cabernet Franc and 15% Merlot, it ranks alongside such famed Cabernet Francs as La Jota, Pride Mountain, and the Maya cuvée from Dalla Valle. Aromatic, with scents of black currants, cherries, flowers, leather, and spice, the stunningly rich, full-bodied wine displays both power and elegance. Its sweet tannin, finesse, and suppleness argue for near-term consumption, but it has the length and inner depth to last for 15+ years.

The 1998 Merlot (400 cases of 95% Merlot and 5% Syrah) makes its debut under the Arietta label. It is a tightly knit, structured Merlot (remember the outstanding Merlots fashioned when John Kongsgaard was the wine-maker at Newton?) revealing expressive aromas and flavors of jammy berry fruit intermixed with chocolate. Full-bodied and rich, yet backward, it requires 2–3 years of cellaring and should keep for 15–18 years. The 1999 Arietta Merlot was blended with 10% Syrah. This bouquet exhibits a blueberry, floral note that quickly transforms to creosote, blackberry, and coffee. Crammed with highly extracted flavors, it is an unevolved, superripe, pure, structured 1999 that will need 2–3 years of cellaring; it should age for two decades.

Kongsgaard's 1997 Merlot includes 25% Syrah in the blend. There are 125 cases of this peppery, leathery, blackberry-flavored Merlot. Medium- to full-bodied, with a fleshy mid-section and an aromatic style, this delicious effort promises to last for a decade.

Everything at Kongsgaard is sold through a mailing list.

CHARLES KRUG (NAPA)

1997 Cabernet Sauvignon Slinsen Vineyard	Napa	D	87
1997 Cabernet Sauvignon Vintage Selection	Napa	D	88
1997 Merlot Reserve	Napa	D	90
1997 Reserve Generations	Napa	D	(87–88)

This large operation (the Mondavi family owns over 800 acres in Napa) has a long history. The original winery was built in 1861, but modern-day history began when Cesare Mondavi purchased the property in 1943. After Robert Mondavi left to start his own winery in 1965, Peter Mondavi took sole control of this estate. Peter was one of the first to utilize cold fermentation for white wines as well as sterile bottling. His two sons, who are now in charge, realized that quality must increase. I was pleasantly surprised by Charles Krug's new vintages. The winemaking is in a transitional period, with wines such as Chenin Blanc, Johannisberg Riesling, Gamay, and white Zinfandel eliminated in favor of the so-called Bordeaux varietals (i.e., Cabernet Sauvignon, Merlot, Sauvignon Blanc). In 1997, wine-maker Jack Cole, formerly of S. Anderson, was brought in to continue the upgrade in quality. Investments have been made, particularly in a bevy of smaller fermentation tanks, a Delta crusher, and new oak barrels to replace the old *foudres* used for aging. Additionally, approximately 200 of the original 800 acres have been replanted with better clonal material. All in all, there is enormous potential at Charles Krug, much of it still unrealized. For bargain hunters, there are some values to be found. Some offerings are still lackluster and unexciting (1997 Merlot, 1997 Cabernet Franc, 1997 Pinot Noir), but quality is on the upswing. Shrewd readers looking for fairly priced Napa Valley wines should put the following information to good use.

Charles Krug's more expensive offerings include their proprietary red wine, the 1997 Generations (a blend of 50% Cabernet Sauvignon, 30% Cabernet Franc, and 20% Merlot). A dark plum color is followed by an elegant, sweet, cranberry, black currant, and spicy-scented nose. Medium-bodied, with fine ripeness and purity, a touch of wood, and an easy-going, fleshy finish, this is a stylish, St.-Emilion look-alike. Drink it over the next 7–10 years. The 1997 Cabernet Sauvignon Slinsen Vineyard (100% Cabernet Sauvignon and made in limited quantities of 250 cases) was tasted from barrel. While the goal at Charles Krug is to cut back on fining and filtration, most of these wines will be bottled with some degree of clarification/processing. The long-range goal is to eliminate filtration for the top *cuvées*. Let's hope wine-maker Jack Cole, with the assistance of Peter and Mark Mondavi, can achieve that. The narrowly constructed 1997 Slinsen Vineyard reveals a bit too much tannin, as well as attractive cedary, spice box, black currant fruit. The tannin may be elevated in the finish, but this is still a work in progress. Anticipated maturity: now–2012. The outstanding 1997 Merlot Reserve (100% Merlot from a Carneros vineyard) is the finest Charles Krug effort I have tasted since some of their single-lot Cabernet Sauvignons from the 1974 vintage. The dark ruby/purple-colored 1997 Merlot Reserve exhibits a textbook nose of roasted coffee, jammy berry fruit, and dried herbs. Medium- to full-bodied, succulent, and rich, this is a noteworthy introduction to the upgrade in quality taking place at Charles Krug. Drink it over the next 7–8 years. The 1997 Cabernet Sauvignon Vintage Selection is meant to be the

winery's finest Cabernet. Although I caught it in a relatively closed stage, it exhibits potential. The color is a dark ruby/purple. The bouquet offers cigar box, black currant, cedar,
spice, and loamy soil scents. This medium- to full-bodied effort displays excellent concentration and moderately high tannin. It should age well for 15–20 years. Anticipated maturity:
2005–2020.

KUNDE (SONOMA)

1997 Cabernet Sauvignon Drummond Vineyard	Sonoma	C	89+
1997 Cabernet Sauvignon Reserve	Sonoma	D	89
1999 Chardonnay	Sonoma	C	88
1999 Chardonnay C. S. Ridge	Sonoma	C	88
1999 Chardonnay Wildwood Vineyard	Sonoma	C	88
1997 Syrah	Sonoma	C	90
1999 Viognier	Sonoma	C	89
1999 Zinfandel	Sonoma	C	(87-88)
1998 Zinfandel Century Vines-Shaw Vineyard	Sonoma	C	90
1997 Zinfandel Century Vines-Shaw Vineyard	Sonoma	C	88
1998 Zinfandel Robusto	Sonoma	D	90
1997 Zinfandel Robusto	Sonoma	D	90

Shrewd wine consumers seeking both quality and value should check out these offerings
from one of Sonoma Valley's oldest farming families. The affable Kundes maintain a down-to-
earth attitude that is mirrored by their likeable as well as talented wine-maker, David Noyes.
As the prices indicate, egos are kept in check. These very good, unfiltered efforts offer consumers authentic aromatic and fruit profiles that are typical of their varietal composition.

Kunde is an outstanding source for rich, fruit-driven, unfiltered Chardonnays that represent excellent values. The 1999 Chardonnay (30,000 cases) is fermented in 60% barrels and
40% tanks. About 30% new oak is utilized. Pure and clean, it offers a ripe peach, pineapple,
and tropical fruit–dominated personality with only a hint of oak. The 1999 Chardonnay C. S.
Ridge (standing for "chicken shit" as this site was used in the 19th century for dumping
turkey manure) is put through 100% malolactic fermentation. Young and unevolved, it reveals abundant quantities of honeysuckle, white peach, and citrus characteristics in its
medium- to full-bodied, concentrated personality. I suspect this wine is even better than it
was when tasted given the fact that David Noyes said it had an extremely slow fermentation
and had not yet begun to settle down. The 1999 Chardonnay Wildwood Vineyard possesses
higher acidity as well as alcohol. A high-toned, austere, mineral-dominated effort, it exhibits
a crisp personality, excellent concentration, and notes of lemon, grapefruit, white peaches,
and wet stones. It should develop into a complex Chardonnay that will age well for 3–4 years.
The 1999 Viognier, one of the finest examples of this varietal being produced in California, is
available for a realistic price. The crop was tiny, and the wine shows the extra level of concentration achieved as well as an exuberant personality revealing abundant quantities of orange marmalade, honeysuckle, and peach jam characteristics. This thick, juicy Viognier
should drink well until 2003.

The opaque black/purple-colored 1997 Cabernet Sauvignon Drummond Vineyard (100
cases produced from a small 3.5 acre parcel of the Wildwood Vineyard) offers a moderately
intense bouquet of cassis, plums, and smoky oak. It spent 20 months in 60% new-oak barrels
before being bottled unfiltered. A plump, rich, concentrated effort made from 100% Cabernet Sauvignon, it will drink well for a decade. Also opaque black/purple-colored, the 1997
Cabernet Sauvignon Reserve (450 cases selected from the finest Dummond barrels) exhibits
aromas and flavors of prunes, licorice, black currants, and creosote. Rich and seamless, with
low acidity, excellent concentration, and fine density, this is a sleeper of the vintage. There
was no Reserve bottling produced in 1998.

Kunde produces three Zinfandels, a Sonoma estate offering, the Century Vines *cuvée* from the Shaw Vineyard, and their Zinfandel-dominated, late-harvested Robusto, also made from the Shaw Vineyard. The 1999 Zinfandel Sonoma (Petite Sirah, Grenache, and Mourvèdre represent 22% of the blend) possesses a tangy, berry-scented nose, lively acidity, a briery personality, and a straightforward finish. Drink this medium-weight Zinfandel over the next 3–4 years. More interesting is the exceptional 1998 Zinfandel Century Vines-Shaw Vineyard, which includes a touch of Petite Sirah and Alicante Bouchet in the blend. It boasts a dark plum color, full body, and a soft, peppery, spicy personality with toasty oak in the background. Dense, rich, and chewy, it can be enjoyed over the next 3–4 years. It represents a very good effort from the 1998 vintage, a year that has been largely dismissed by those who tend to view quality in black-and-white terms. Another outstanding effort is the 1998 Zinfandel Robusto (500 cases). It has more in common with a big, chewy Italian Amarone than a California Zinfandel. The dark plum color is followed by aromas and flavors of charcoal, melted asphalt, roasted herbs, dried black cherries, and leather. Thick, powerful, and dry, with abundant fruit as well as a muscular, expansive palate, this mouth-filling wine should be drunk during its first 5–7 years of life. It sports a head-spinning 16.4% alcohol.

The 1997 Zinfandel Robusto (15.8% alcohol) is a 100% late-harvested Zinfandel that tastes totally dry. It reveals a melted asphalt, creosote, charcoal-like personality (similar to that found in certain Rhône Valley and Italian wines), in addition to loads of black fruit, pepper, and berries. The alcohol gives the wine a sweet, glycerin-imbued tactile impression. Drink it over the next several years. In addition to the telltale black cherry note, raspberries, licorice, fennel, and spicy oak make an appearance in the impressively endowed 1997 Zinfandel Century Vines-Shaw Vineyard. It is a fleshy, full-bodied, richly layered Zinfandel that comes close to being outstanding. Drink this beauty over the next 5–6 years.

Two other fine efforts from Kunde are their 1997 Syrah *cuvées.* Hopefully, the 1,200 case production of the 1997 Syrah (which includes 10% Viognier) will increase in future vintages. A fine value, this sexy, dense purple-colored Syrah offers a gorgeous nose of blackberry liqueur, pepper, and licorice. Fat and succulent, with low acidity and explosive fruit, this is a consumer friendly fruit bomb that deserves to be drunk over the next 5–6 years.

During a period where most consumers are turned off by arrogant, elitist prices designed for multimillionaires, Kunde's attitude is a breath of fresh air, producing high-quality wines that are faithful to their respective varietal profiles. Moreover, the wines are made by good people who respect the consumer.

Past Glories: 1993 Cabernet Sauvignon Estate Reserve (90)

KUNIN WINES (PASO ROBLES)

1998 Zinfandel Dante Dusi Vineyards	Paso Robles	D	89

An excellent effort from Paso Robles, the 1998 Zinfandel Dante Dusi Vineyards is a dark ruby-colored wine with lusciously ripe blackberry, cherry, cola, earth, and spice aromas. Full-bodied, with low acidity, outstanding purity, and a husky, layered mouth-feel, this impressive Zinfandel (15.4% alcohol) should be drunk over the next 4–5 years.

LA JOTA VINEYARD (NAPA)

1994 Cabernet Franc	Napa	D	93
1999 Cabernet Franc Howell Mountain	Napa	D	87
1998 Cabernet Franc Howell Mountain	Napa	D	90
1997 Cabernet Franc Howell Mountain	Napa	D	94
1996 Cabernet Franc Howell Mountain	Napa	D	93
1995 Cabernet Franc Howell Mountain	Napa	D	93
1994 Cabernet Sauvignon Howell Mountain	Napa	C	92
1997 Cabernet Sauvignon Howell Mountain Select	Napa	D	90

1996 Cabernet Sauvignon Howell Mountain Select	Napa	D	92
1995 Cabernet Sauvignon Howell Mountain Select	Napa	D	91
1994 Cabernet Sauvignon Howell Mountain Select	Napa	C	93
1999 Cabernet Sauvignon 18th Anniversary Release	Napa	E	88?
1998 Cabernet Sauvignon 17th Anniversary Release	Napa	EE	88?
1997 Cabernet Sauvignon 16th Anniversary Release	Napa	EE	93+
1996 Cabernet Sauvignon 15th Anniversary Release	Napa	E	96
1995 Cabernet Sauvignon 14th Anniversary Release	Napa	D	94
1994 Cabernet Sauvignon 13th Anniversary Release	Napa	D	96
1998 Petite Sirah Howell Mountain	Napa	D	89
1997 Petite Sirah Howell Mountain	Napa	D	92
1996 Petite Sirah Howell Mountain	Napa	D	94
1995 Petite Sirah Howell Mountain	Napa	D	92
1994 Petite Sirah Howell Mountain	Napa	D	97

In the cool, upper elevations of Howell Mountain, former owners (the winery was sold in 2000) Joan and Bill Smith struggled in 1998 and 1999 to get their fruit as ripe as they did during much of the nineties. This is evident when tasting through their 1998s and 1999s, which possess less volume, mass, and sweetness than their spectacular successes in 1997, 1996, 1995, 1994, 1993, and 1992. They have given up making Viognier, but still turn out a fine Petite Sirah as well as one of my favorite California Cabernet Francs. The 1998 Petite Sirah (25% Viognier in the blend) has turned out well in this difficult vintage. Revealing a Rhône Valley–like character, it offers peppery, earthy, honeysuckle mixed with black fruits and smoke. The wine is medium- to full-bodied, engaging, soft, and best drunk over the next 7–8 years.

The finest wine in La Jota's 1998 portfolio is the 1998 Cabernet Franc (250 cases). It displays a complex, luxurious bouquet of plum liqueur, truffles, saddle leather, roasted espresso, cedar, and black fruits. A rich, concentrated attack and mid-palate are accompanied by some jagged tannin in the finish. The 1999 Cabernet Franc may turn out to be outstanding, although it is more herbaceous than previous vintages. Its dense ruby/purple color is followed by aromas of cedar wood, Provençal herbs, bay leaves, and blackberry/plum-like fruit. The wine is medium- to full-bodied, with a creamy entry and mid-palate, but finishes with astringent tannin. We'll see how it evolves in barrel. Anticipated maturity: now–2012.

The dense purple-colored 1999 Cabernet Sauvignon 18th Anniversary Release offers a sweet nose of cassis, earth, herbs, and minerals. In the mouth, it is muscular and austere, with firm, high tannin in addition to a compressed finish. It will need 3–4 years of cellaring when released, and should easily evolve for 15 years. The 1998 Cabernet Sauvignon 17th Anniversary Release offers a dark ruby color as well as a big, peppery, spicy, black currant, plum, mineral, earth, and dried herb–scented bouquet. Medium- to full-bodied, with a fine texture in addition to a medium weight, Bordeaux-like style, it has firmer tannin than the Cabernet Franc, but not the lushness and complexity of that wine. It requires 2–3 years of cellaring, and should keep for 15–16 years.

The 1997s are some of the strongest wines La Jota produced during the successful decade. The prodigious 1997 Cabernet Franc Howell Mountain offers a knockout bouquet of smoky cedar/cigar box, roast beef, and gorgeous blackberry and cassis fruit. Full-bodied and fat, with compelling sweetness, intense new saddle leather notes, and low acidity, this terrific wine can be consumed now as well as over the next 12–15 years. Sadly, there are only 300 cases of this rich, thick, unctuously textured wine. Patience will be required with the 1997 Cabernet Sauvignon Howell Mountain Select, which was closed, but powerful. The saturated ruby/purple color is accompanied by aromas of minerals, toasty oak, and jammy black currants. A tannic, muscular, full-bodied wine, it has outstanding extract and purity. Anticipated maturity: now–2018. The sensational black/purple-colored 1997 Cabernet Sauvignon 16th

Anniversary Release is also closed, but its emerging aromas of charcoal, blackberries, cassis, and minerals are promising. The wine is intense, ripe, with a layered, expansive richness, and exotic notes of Asian spices, beef blood, and assorted black fruits. Anticipated maturity: 2004–2025. Readers should try to latch onto a bottle or two of the 350-case production of the 1997 Petite Sirah Howell Mountain. With 12% Viognier in the blend, it boasts sumptuous, exotic aromas of pepper, blackberries, peaches, and honeysuckle. This wine has been a terrific success for La Jota since their debut 1991, and the 1997 is unquestionably another low-acid, sensationally rich Petite Sirah that should drink well for 15+ years.

The 1996s are impressive. The 1996 Cabernet Sauvignon Howell Mountain Select is a beautifully rendered wine with an opaque plum color and knockout aromatics of cedarwood, cassis, cigar box, and roasted Provençal herbs. With more structure than the 1997, it is a jammy, rich, concentrated, full-bodied wine that can be drunk now or cellared for two decades. This beauty remains one of the better values in great California Cabernet Sauvignon. The 1996 Cabernet Sauvignon 15th Anniversary Release (1,050 cases produced) boasts an opaque purple color as well as beautiful aromas of smoke, blackberries, Asian spices, charcoal, and subtle truffle-like scents. Huge, massive, and full-bodied, with phenomenal flavor extraction and beautifully integrated tannin and acidity, this flamboyant, exceptionally well-endowed Cabernet Sauvignon continues the succession of titanic wines made under this label. Anticipated maturity: now–2027. The unfined and unfiltered 1996 Cabernet Franc reveals a smoky, meaty, beef blood and black fruit–scented nose with loamy soil scents providing additional aromatic dimension. The wine possesses exceptional richness of fruit, thrilling quantities of glycerin, an impressive mid-palate, and an admirably long finish. Fruit ripeness, texture, and richness are important in any wine, but La Jota manages to cram all of these components into the difficult to grow and make Cabernet Franc varietal. This effort is another benchmark Cabernet Franc that should drink well for 12–15+ years. The 1996 Petite Sirah also stands out as a reference point for its type. It offers a saturated black/purple color, followed by a stunning nose of roasted meats, saddle leather, beef juices, and spicy wood. There is compelling richness, super intensity, and gobs of black fruit in this surprisingly supple, chewy, exciting offering. It should drink well for 20 years.

I am convinced La Jota is making one of California's finest Cabernet Francs. I love this wine, and I am consistently reminded of how well it ages whenever I taste the 1986, superb since its birth. This is not one of the more delicate styles of Cabernet Franc, but it does have compelling complexity, as well as a rich, intense, concentrated character. The 1995 Cabernet Franc is another knockout effort that may be even better than the 1996. It boasts a black/ruby/purple color, as well as more structured aromatics with smoke, beef juices, saddle leather, and black fruits soaring out of the glass. On the palate, the wine reveals earthy, roasted meat, blackberry, and cassis flavors, with good glycerin, more noticeable tannin than the 1996, and a well-delineated, spicy, intense finish. The wine may take more time to round out when it is released, but their Cabernet Franc redefines the quality standards for this varietal. The spectacular 1994 Cabernet Franc offers a pronounced sweet, smoky, earthy, roasted meat, black cherry, and cassis-scented nose. Dense, with fabulous concentration, a chewy texture, and a full-bodied, long, layered finish, this wine is already difficult to resist, but it should keep for 12–15 years.

One of the cult wines of La Jota is Petite Sirah. The grapes come from the old Park-Muscatine Vineyard now owned by Randy Dunn (and from which Ridge used to purchase grapes). This vineyard has produced some exceptional Petite Sirahs over the last few years. These wines look like ink, yet possess surprisingly sweet fruit in spite of their massive size. The 1995 Petite Sirah is a huge, monolithic wine with an opaque blue/black color, huge body, copious amounts of thick, juicy fruit, and a lashing of tannin at the back of the palate. It is a touch more angular and backward than either the 1994 is or the 1996 promises to be, but it has exceptional potential. Anticipated maturity: 2005–2020. La Jota's 1994 Petite Sirah

Howell Mountain (aged in 90% new French oak) is an awesome wine. It exhibits one of the most extraordinary jammy blueberry-scented noses I have ever encountered. Unbelievably rich and full-bodied, yet remarkably soft, this multilayered, fabulously concentrated wine will be approachable young (rare for Petite Sirah), yet age for 20 or more years. Petite Sirah can be the most underrated wine made in California. Put this one on your shopping list!

The two Cabernet Sauvignon *cuvées* are similar in quality. The Howell Mountain Select and Anniversary Release share dense, concentrated, full-bodied personalities with superlative levels of fruit and extract. The Anniversary *cuvée* usually has a bit more depth, ripeness, and overall potential, but that is not always easily discernable when they are young. Each wine will last—at the minimum—20 years. Readers can decide whether they prefer the more open-knit opulence of the 1994, the more austere, jagged tannins of the big 1995, or the forceful power of the 1996. As for the 1994 Cabernet Sauvignon Howell Mountain Select, this wine performed exceptionally well in a large tasting of 1994 California Cabernets I conducted. The wine is full-bodied, with an opaque purple color, as well as potentially sweeter, more up-front fruit than the Anniversary Release. It is opulent, aromatic (black fruits, truffles, earth, and spice galore), and fleshy, but it boasts plenty of tannin. Look for it to close down in another year or two, not to reemerge for 7–8 years. It will last two decades. The formidable 1994 Cabernet Sauvignon 13th Anniversary Release may be the finest Cabernet Sauvignon Joan and Bill Smith have yet made. It boasts an opaque purple color, followed by a smoky, toasty, mineral, and cassis-scented nose, great persistence in the mouth, massive body, and an expansive, chewy, blockbuster finish, without coming across as excessively heavy or overweight. Give it 5–6 years of cellaring, and drink it over the following 20–25 years. It is a Cabernet legend in the making!

The 1995 Cabernet Sauvignon Howell Mountain Select revealed some rough tannin when I tasted it in October of 1997. While none of these wines is filtered, the Smiths did do a light egg white fining in an attempt to produce a more civilized style. The 1995 is deep, muscular, rich, and impressive, but it is in need of 5–6 years of cellaring. I suspect this wine will age effortlessly for another two decades. Also a monster, the tannic 1995 Cabernet Sauvignon 14th Anniversary Release is unquestionably a huge, mountain-styled Cabernet. It exhibits a black/purple color and a reticent but promising nose of minerals, smoke, black currants, and underbrush. Although full-bodied and excruciatingly tannic, there is enough fruit to balance out the wine's structure. It may be as backward as the Cabernet Sauvignon made by Dunn on another Howell Mountain slope; this wine needs 5–8 years of cellaring. The stunning 1994 Cabernet Sauvignon Howell Mountain reveals an opaque black color, gobs of sweet cassis and licorice scents, remarkable fat and opulence, and a chewy, long finish.

Past Glories: 1993 Cabernet Sauvignon Howell Mountain 12th Anniversary Release (96), 1992 11th Anniversary Release (98), 1991 10th Anniversary Release (91)

LA SIRENA (NAPA)

1998 Cabernet Sauvignon	Napa	EE	89
1997 Cabernet Sauvignon	Napa	EE	92
1997 Sangiovese Juliana	Napa	D	88

La Sirena is the house label of Napa Valley's highly respected winemaking consultant Heidi Barrett. The 1997 Sangiovese Juliana (640 cases) is her finest Sangiovese to date. It exhibits more intensity than many of the overcropped, diluted, acidic offerings that routinely emerge from this varietal. La Sirena's medium ruby-colored 1997 offers an excellent nose of sweet black cherries, saddle leather, strawberries, and spice. Soft and fruit-driven with low acidity, this round, medium-bodied Sangiovese can be drunk now and over the next 4–5 years.

There are approximately 375 cases of the Cabernet Sauvignon, which emerges from a vineyard in the hotter area of Calistoga. The 1998 Cabernet Sauvignon is undoubtedly a success for the vintage. Harvested in late October, this opaque ruby/purple-colored wine reveals ripe black currants intermixed with cedar and spice box scents. Aged in French oak (of which one-third is new), this medium-bodied effort displays more persistence, depth, and ripeness than many 1998s. Anticipated maturity: now–2015. Even better, the 1997 Cabernet Sauvignon boasts a saturated, opaque blue/purple color in addition to classic crème de cassis aromas meshed with spice, licorice, and tobacco. Dense, powerful, concentrated, and backward, this large-scaled Cabernet requires 3–4 years of cellaring. It should keep for two decades. Given her talent and diverse experience with many different vineyards, what is Heidi Barrett's ranking of the finest Cabernet Sauvignon/Merlot proprietary blend vintages of the nineties? In her opinion, the three top vintages were 1997, 1994, and 1992, followed by 1995 and 1993. For her, 1996 and 1998 were the most challenging.

LAIL VINEYARDS (NAPA)

1998 J. Daniel Cuvée	Howell Mountain	EE	89
1997 J. Daniel Cuvée	Howell Mountain	EE	93
1996 J. Daniel Cuvée	Howell Mountain	E	91
1995 J. Daniel Cuvée	Napa	E	91

Robin Lail is a veteran Napa Valley resident who was raised in a winemaking family (her father was the legendary John Daniel, who fashioned many of Inglenook's greatest Cabernet Sauvignons). A former partner of Christian Moueix in the Dominus operation, Robin Lail has branched out on her own to produce limited quantities (about 450 cases) of a graceful, elegant, proprietary red wine from vineyards in Yountville, Vine Hill Road, and Howell Mountain. The 1995 J. Daniel Cuvée was the debut release from Lail Vineyards. An outstanding effort, it is a blend of 56% Merlot and 44% Cabernet Sauvignon made by Philippe Melka (the wine-maker at Seavey). The wine is a beautifully rendered, Médoc-like California red with a dense, saturated ruby/purple color, and stylish, complex aromatics consisting of tobacco, black currants, crème de cassis, and subtle toasty oak (approximately 33% new-oak casks are utilized). The wine is medium- to full-bodied, with sweet tannin, a graceful, long mid-palate and finish, and 15 or more years of potential evolution. From the finesse/elegant school of California proprietary reds, this wine is rich and layered, with everything in impeccable balance. Anticipated maturity: now–2015.

There are 600 cases of the 1996 J. Daniel Cuvée, a blend of 73% Cabernet Sauvignon and 27% Merlot. It exhibits a dense ruby color with a purple hue. The classy nose of chocolate, cassis, black cherries, and toast is followed by a medium- to full-bodied offering with outstanding ripeness, sweet tannin, and a layered, multidimensional personality. Delicious, and already revealing considerable complexity, it can be drunk now and over the next 15 years. The most brilliant wine to date is the 1997 J. Daniel Cuvée, a blend of 64% Cabernet Sauvignon and 36% Merlot (1,200 cases produced). The dense ruby/purple-colored 1997 boasts a lavishly pure nose of blackberries, cassis, minerals, licorice, chocolate, and toast. It is expansive, with the vintage's telltale richness, sweet tannin, and outstanding ripeness and concentration. The persistent finish lasts for nearly 40 seconds. This wine possesses an openness and sweetness that gives it the impression of being ready to drink, but I suspect much more will emerge with aging. Anticipated maturity: now–2020. The softest, most charming and elegant of these wines is the 1998 J. Daniel Cuvée (61% Cabernet Sauvignon and 39% Merlot). It does not possess the power or depth of the 1997, but it may turn out to be outstanding, an enviable achievement in this challenging vintage. There is no herbaceousness (frequently a problem with the 1998 mountain Cabernets) in this black cherry, cassis, and mineral-scented effort. A medium-bodied wine, with excellent sweet fruit on the attack and more persistence than many 1998s, this should turn out to be a Cabernet of considerable charm and seductiveness. Interestingly, the 1998 harvest occurred one month later than it did in 1997.

Kudos to John and Robin Lail for the efforts they have produced to date.

LAMBORN FAMILY VINEYARDS (HOWELL MOUNTAIN)

1999 Zinfandel the Solar Factor	Howell Mountain	D	89
1997 Zinfandel the Team Connection	Howell Mountain	C	88+

The complex, earthy 1999 Zinfandel the Solar Factor offers notes of blueberries, black cherries, currants, and minerals. Beautifully textured, sweet, ripe, and medium- to full-bodied, this dark plum/ruby/purple-colored 1999 will provide delicious drinking over the next 4–5 years. The 1997 Zinfandel the Team Connection is from the first vintage to be produced by well-known wine consultant Heidi Barrett. From a mountain vineyard that has a tendency to turn out rustic, tannic examples, this dense ruby/purple-colored wine possesses fine balance. The bouquet reveals notes of new saddle leather, minerals, and black fruits. The wine is full-bodied and tightly knit, with plenty of muscle and a long, deep, toasty oak-flavored finish. This is one of the few 1997 Zinfandels that will improve for several years and last for 7–8.

LANCASTER RESERVE (ALEXANDER VALLEY)

1995 Proprietary Red Estate	Alexander Valley	E	90

Only 8,600 bottles were produced of this proprietary wine (a blend of 82% Cabernet Sauvignon and 18% Cabernet Franc). It is extremely backward and unevolved, with an opaque purple color and a promising nose of blackberries, raspberries, and copious quantities of toasty new oak. This massive, tightly knit, full-bodied, tannic wine exhibits impressive depth and purity, but it requires 3–4 years of cellaring. Patience will be necessary for those who latch onto this limited production gem. Anticipated maturity: now–2018.

LANDMARK VINEYARDS (SONOMA)

1999 Chardonnay Demaris Reserve	Sonoma	E	91
1999 Chardonnay Lorenzo Vineyard	Russian River	E	91+
1999 Chardonnay Overlook	California	D	90
1999 Pinot Noir Grand Detour Van der Kamp	Sonoma Mountain	D	92
1998 Pinot Noir Grand Detour Van der Kamp	Sonoma Mountain	D	91
1997 Pinot Noir Grand Detour Van der Kamp	Sonoma Mountain	D	90
1996 Pinot Noir Grand Detour Van der Kamp	Sonoma Mountain	D	90
1999 Pinot Noir Kastania Vineyard	Sonoma Coast	D	93
1998 Pinot Noir Kastania Vineyard	Sonoma Coast	D	92
1997 Pinot Noir Kastania Vineyard	Sonoma Coast	D	91

This winery remains one of the best-kept secrets for outstanding Chardonnays as well as increasingly sumptuous Pinot Noirs. Prices are rising, but they remain well behind the stratospheric prices asked for wines of similar quality from other California wineries. Proprietors Mary and Mike Colhoun and their talented wine-maker, Eric Stern, offer consumers a reasonably priced, complex, Burgundy-styled Chardonnay called Overlook. Utilizing indigenous yeasts to ferment the wine, which comes from virtually every region of California (Sonoma Valley and Russian River being the biggest contributors), this wine spends nine months *sur-lie*. It goes through complete malolactic, and is not filtered prior to bottling. The good news is that it sells for a song given its quality. Moreover, there are 18,000 cases available! The 1999 Chardonnay Overlook exhibits a smoky, buttery, leesy nose, a subtle yet delicious display of vanilla and toast, and a layered, concentrated style. Given its purity as well as overall depth, it will drink well for 2–3 years. The 1999 Chardonnay Demaris Reserve (2,500 cases) is a blend of six Chardonnay vineyards averaging 20 years of age. Fermented with indigenous yeasts, aged *sur-lie* for 12 months (with considerable stirring), and bottled unfiltered, it is a bolder, richer effort revealing notes of cloves, honeysuckle, and orange rind, as well as a creamy, full-bodied texture and admirable richness. From the vineyard made famous by Helen Turley (although she no longer purchases grapes from it), the 1999 Chardonnay Lorenzo Vineyard was made from 22-year-old vines cropped at 2.55 tons per acre. There are 400 cases of this stunning, complex Chardonnay that spent 14 months in French oak, of which 60% was new. It boasts a honeyed citrus, tangerine, stony mineral-scented bouquet as well as a full-bodied, concentrated style. More high-toned (because of the mineral character) than its two siblings, with subtle oak, this superb wine will drink well for 4–5 years.

The 1998 Pinot Noir Grand Detour Van der Kamp Vineyard (375 cases) was produced from destemmed grapes fermented with indigenous yeasts in open-top fermenters, transferred to French oak barrels (60% new and 40% one year old) for 12 months, and bottled unfined and unfiltered. It is a complex Pinot that could pass for a top-ranked Burgundy, although it possesses lower acidity. The 1998 has taken on smoky, plum, cherry characteristics infused with violets, roasted herbs, and earthy notes. It tastes like a premier cru Vosne-Romanée from a ripe vintage. Rich, with supple tannin, adequate acidity, and an expansive, rich mouth-feel, it is best drunk over the next 6–7 years. The 1998 Pinot Noir Kastania Vineyard (400 cases) is produced from a combination of old California Pinot Noir clones and new French Dijon clones. Its upbringing is essentially the same as the Grand Detour, but the percentage of new oak is slightly lower. The wine reveals aromas of sweet black cherries mixed with overripe apple skin, earth, clove, spice, and Chinese black tea, plus a ripe pomegranate character. Notes of coffee and smoky new oak add to its tremendous complexity. It should drink well for 6–7 years.

The 1999 Pinot Noirs are also potentially superb. The 1999 Pinot Noir Grand Detour Van der Kamp Vineyard (750 cases) possesses terrific fruit intensity as well as sweet aromas of pepper, cherry syrup, smoke, underbrush, strawberry, and dried tangerines. This full-bodied, sweet (from extract and ripeness, not sugar), long Pinot Noir has completely absorbed its new oak. It has a floral quality reminiscent of certain premier and grand crus from the hillsides of Vosne-Romanée. Drink it over the next 5–7 years. The 1999 Pinot Noir Kastania Vineyard reveals a tighter structure along with its graceful, rich, black cherry, Chinese black tea, floral, pomegranate, smoke, mineral, earth, and new-oak aromas and flavors. This complex Pinot Noir will drink beautifully for 7–8 years. Amazingly, both of these efforts reveal French-like aromatic profiles, but riper, richer fruit as well as plusher textures.

The 1996 Pinot Noir Grand Detour Van der Kamp Vineyard (1,000 cases) offers a big, smoky, complex nose filled with aromas of black cherries, *jus de viande*, clove, and allspice. It is a meaty, full-bodied, richly spicy yet supple-textured, expansive, delicious Pinot Noir. The wine's provocative aromatics and earthy, smoky style will serve it well over the next 5–6 years. Scents of barbecue spice and smoke intermixed with cherry liqueur, sweet foresty smells, and yummy new oak are intense in the full-bodied, hedonistic, nicely textured/ layered, and complex 1997 Pinot Noir Grand Detour Van der Kamp Vineyard (950 cases). Already delicious, it promises to drink well for 5–7 years. From a Sonoma Coast hillside vineyard, Landmark has turned out 100 cases of the 1997 Pinot Noir Kastania Vineyard. The dark ruby/purple-colored 1997 is a Burgundy-styled, tannic, complex effort from a cool climate region. It offers a terrific nose of cherry and black raspberry fruit with a touch of cassis. Medium- to full-bodied, the wine boasts a silky attack in addition to good firmness and delineation. This concentrated, powerful, still youthful Pinot Noir will be even better with another 12–18 months of bottle age. It should drink well for a decade.

Kudos for the remarkable improvements evident in all the Landmark offerings over the last 4–5 years. Readers who have not yet tasted Landmark's wines need a wake-up call.

LAUREL GLEN (SONOMA)

1994 Cabernet Sauvignon	Sonoma Mountain	D	92

Laurel Glen is one of California's most admirable operations, and its estate Cabernet Sauvignon is at the top of the qualitative hierarchy. The 1994 reveals an opaque purple color and a tight but promising nose of jammy black fruits, spice, earth, and a whiff of Provençal herbs.

Full-bodied, with layers of chewy, fleshy, ripe fruit, this highly extracted, moderately tannic, blockbuster Cabernet should be cellared for 4–5 years and drunk over the following 15–20. *Past Glories:* 1993 (95), 1992 (94), 1991 (92), 1990 (89), 1987 (91), 1985 (91), 1984 (91)

LEWIS CELLARS (NAPA)

1997 Cabernet Sauvignon Reserve	Napa	E	90

Traditionally, this winery has had a tendency to dump entirely too much acidity into the fermentation vats. Consequently, the wines often lacked a mid-palate and possessed chalky, tart, compressed personalities. Winemaking consultant Paul Hobbs was brought in beginning with the 1997 vintage, and he hopes to halt the excessive additions of acidity in favor of more natural, handcrafted wines. Certainly the 1997 Cabernet Sauvignon Reserve (2,400 cases) reveals progress. The wine exhibits toasty sweet oak, jammy black currant fruit, and a touch of licorice, cedar, fruitcake, and cigar box aromas. It is a complex, smoky, ripe, layered wine that can be drunk young or cellared for 15–18 years.

LITTORAI (NAPA)

1999 Chardonnay Charles Heintz Vineyard	Sonoma Coast	E	90
1999 Chardonnay Mays Canyon	Russian River	E	92
1999 Chardonnay Thieriot Vineyard	Sonoma Coast	E	93
1999 Pinot Noir Hirsch Vineyard	Sonoma Coast	E	90
1998 Pinot Noir Hirsch Vineyard	Sonoma Coast	E	(89–90)
1999 Pinot Noir One Acre Vineyard	Anderson Valley	E	90
1998 Pinot Noir One Acre Vineyard	Anderson Valley	E	(87–88)
1997 Pinot Noir One Acre Vineyard	Anderson Valley	D	(90–94)
1999 Pinot Noir Savoy Vineyard	Anderson Valley	E	88
1998 Pinot Noir Savoy Vineyard	Anderson Valley	E	(87–88)
1997 Pinot Noir Savoy Vineyard	Anderson Valley	D	(88–89+)
1999 Pinot Noir Thieriot Vineyard	Sonoma Coast	E	91+
1998 Pinot Noir Thieriot Vineyard	Sonoma Coast	E	90

Burgundy-trained Ted Lemon can usually be counted on to produce some of California's most elegant, restrained, finesse-filled wines. However, in 1999, he has demonstrated that he can also build in a few extra layers of flavor. In short, these look to be Lemon's most impressive wines to date, no small feat given his already impressive track record. The 1999 Chardonnays exhibit the vintage's zesty acidity as well as intense flavor and ripeness. The 1999 Chardonnay Charles Heintz Vineyard offers aromas of citrus oil, orange, pineapple, and minerals. From a vineyard planted in fertile Gold Ridge soils, in a cool coastal area, emerges this rich, creamy-textured, medium- to full-bodied, beautifully pure as well as long wine. It should open slowly and drink well for 4–5 years. The 1999 Chardonnay Mays Canyon offers more smoky oak in the nose, in addition to honeysuckle, tropical fruit, and nutty, leesy notes. Full-bodied, rich, yet at the same time elegant, pure, and well delineated, it is more flamboyant than the Charles Heintz. Drink it over the next 5–6 years. The stunning 1999 Chardonnay Thieriot Vineyard offers a light greenish/gold-tinged straw color in addition to a superb nose of candied citrus, tropical fruit, minerals, and orange marmalade. The oak provides a subtle smoky, almost camphor-like note. The wine is dense, long, and full-bodied, yet exquisitely well balanced with nicely integrated acidity and wood. This terrific, multitextured Chardonnay should drink well for 5–7 years. Lemon feels that the extra layers of texture and complexity might have been the result of the extremely slow malolactic fermentations that characterized 1999.

Littorai's Pinot Noirs are made from completely destemmed fruit. While the 1999s were in bottle, they required opening the night before my tasting, because they needed air to reveal their personalities. None of them showed a trace of oxidation and performed well, as the following notes attest. The 1999 Pinot Noir Hirsch Vineyard (14.4% alcohol) is made from such Pinot Noir clones as Pommard, Dijon #114, and Mt. Eden. The wine exhibits a dark plum/ruby color along with a sweet, moderately intense nose of red/black fruits, apple skins, black cherry fruit, smoke, and earth. Medium-bodied and soft, with firm tannin in the finish, it should evolve nicely for 7–8 years. Although the medium ruby-colored 1999 Pinot Noir Savoy Vineyard does not possess the size and depth of the other offerings, it represents a premier cru Beaune in its aromatics and flavors. Made completely from Dijon clones of Pinot Noir, particularly #114 and #115, it offers finesse, elegance, light to medium body, and sweet plum, cherry, and cranberry fruit. Subtle and restrained, it is best drunk during its first 5–6 years of life. The exceptional, dark ruby-colored 1999 Pinot Noir One Acre Vineyard is another high-toned, textured, delicious Pinot with an intricate perfume of black cherries, minerals, flowers, and a touch of blackberries. Once past the perfumed aromatics, the wine reveals good sweetness on the attack, medium body, and a beautiful pure, delicate, intense personality. It should drink well for 7–8 years. The most backward and possibly the most concentrated offering is the 1999 Pinot Noir Thieriot Vineyard. This wine boasts a dark ruby color as well as scents of root beer, cola, vegetable roots, black fruits, smoke, and mineral. Exhibiting a firm underpinning of tannin, outstanding concentration, overall equilibrium, and a spicy finish, this aggressive/animal-styled Pinot should drink well for 7–8 years.

The medium ruby-colored 1998 Pinot Noir Savoy Vineyard possesses a Beaune premier cru–like style. A sweet nose of black cherries, spice, and mineral scents is followed by a medium-bodied, pure, firmly structured Pinot Noir. It requires 12–18 months of bottle age and should last for 6–7 years. The more meaty, animal-styled, potentially outstanding 1998 Pinot Noir Hirsch Vineyard exhibits a dark ruby color as well as aromas of grilled steak, ripe apples, and black cherries. One of the softest Hirsch Vineyard offerings from Ted Lemon to date, it possesses fine density, medium to full body, and a sweet, lush finish. Readers looking for jammy cherry/strawberry notes infused with fresh damp earth-like smells should check out the 1998 Pinot Noir One Acre Vineyard. Exhibiting more tannin than either the Savoy or Hirsch offering, it requires a year of bottle age, and should evolve nicely for 5–7 years. The most volume and intensity can be found in the 1998 Pinot Noir Thieriot Vineyard. Sadly, only 68 cases were produced. It boasts a dark ruby color in addition to a gorgeous nose of sweet blackberry and cherry fruit meshed with plums, rose petals, and spicy oak. Medium-bodied, with a juicy mid-section and excellent purity and symmetry, it is a complex, elegant Pinot to consume over the next 7–8 years.

Ted Lemon told me that he did a *saignée* of all his 1997 Pinots because of high yields, and that all of these wines were scheduled to be bottled with neither fining nor filtration. The stylish 1997 Pinot Noir Savoy Vineyard, made from the Dijon clone #115 and the Pommard clone, possesses a medium ruby color, attractive, deeper, richer, black cherry and cassis aromas, excellent ripeness on the attack, medium body, firm tannin, and a pure style with a subtle influence of wood. This wine will benefit from 1–2 years of cellaring and keep for nearly a decade. Many of the Pinot Noirs I have tasted from the Sonoma Coast's Hirsch Vineyard tend to be powerhouse Pinots that push tannin levels to the limit—at least for my palate. That seems to be the case even with the subtle touch of Ted Lemon. There are 200 cases of the spectacular 1997 Pinot Noir One Acre Vineyard from Anderson Valley. This wine could easily pass for a top-notch premier cru from the Côte de Nuits. Made from modest yields, it reveals a deep ruby color with purple nuances. The aromatics include black cherries, cassis, spice, herb, and flower blossoms. Medium- to full-bodied, with terrific fruit purity and a lush, open-knit texture, this complex Pinot Noir possesses sensational potential. The wine will be approachable when released, yet should age nicely for 7–8 years.

Virtually the entire production of Littorai is sold through a mailing list . . . readers take note.

LOKOYA (NAPA)

1998 Cabernet Sauvignon Diamond Mountain	Napa	EE	95
1997 Cabernet Sauvignon Diamond Mountain	Napa	EE	95
1995 Cabernet Sauvignon Diamond Mountain	Napa	EE	93
1997 Cabernet Sauvignon Howell Mountain	Napa	EE	93+
1995 Cabernet Sauvignon Howell Mountain	Napa	EE	90
1998 Cabernet Sauvignon Mount Veeder	Napa	EE	93+
1997 Cabernet Sauvignon Mount Veeder	Napa	EE	93+
1995 Cabernet Sauvignon Mount Veeder	Napa	EE	91
1994 Cabernet Sauvignon Mount Veeder	Napa	D	94
1994 Cabernet Sauvignon Oakville District	Napa	D	89
1998 Cabernet Sauvignon Rutherford	Napa	EE	92
1997 Cabernet Sauvignon Rutherford	Napa	EE	94
1995 Cabernet Sauvignon Rutherford	Napa	EE	94

Another flagship estate in the Kendall-Jackson empire (to be precise, part of the Jackson Family Farms), Lokoya is a small, 3,000-case operation dedicated to four limited-production, ageworthy Cabernet Sauvignons. These wines have quickly built a cult following, for which much of the credit must go to the outstanding skills of wine-maker Marco Di Giulio (who also makes the wines at Pepi). They spend 22 months in 100% new French oak and are normally bottled with neither fining nor filtration, although in 1997, the Howell Mountain *cuvée* was given a light filtration. The opaque purple-colored 1997 Cabernet Sauvignon Mount Veeder (220 cases), from an elevation of 1,500 feet, reveals classic crème de cassis/mineral aromas, a superb mid-palate, and a full-bodied personality with impressive length and purity. It is not for readers desiring immediate gratification as it requires 4–5 years of cellaring. Anticipated maturity: 2005–2025. More mineral, blueberry, plum, and earthy characteristics can be found in the dark purple-colored 1997 Cabernet Sauvignon Howell Mountain (700 cases). Softer in the mouth, but full-bodied, dense, and rich, it is an immensely impressive effort. Anticipated maturity: now–2020. The most opulent, sexy, and immediately charming of this admirable quartet of 1997 Lokoya Cabernets is the 1997 Cabernet Sauvignon Diamond Mountain (1,100 cases). It exhibits a saturated purple color in addition to an explosive nose of licorice, cedar, roasted herbs, and black plums and currants. Full-bodied, with a voluptuous texture, low acidity, and heady alcohol, this offering possesses considerable tannin, but it is beautifully submerged by the wine's depth of extract and high glycerin. Impressive, with a flamboyant personality, it should drink well for 18–20 years. There are 1,000 cases of the 1997 Cabernet Sauvignon Rutherford. It offers a distinctive kirsch, black cherry liqueur, and loamy soil-scented character to its full-bodied richness. Along with the Diamond Mountain, it is the most expansive and charming of these blockbuster 1997 Cabernets. Full-bodied, with admirable depth and purity, it can be drunk now as well as over the next 20 years.

In 1998, wine-maker Marco Di Giulio decided to declassify the Howell Mountain because of the cold climate in these upper-elevation vineyards. However, he is still perfecting what he calls "the art of viticulture down to each single berry." In 1998, there are 400 cases of the Rutherford, 750 cases of the Diamond Mountain, and 132 cases of the Mount Veeder. They have all been bottled, and are certainly among the superstar efforts of the vintage. The one difference with the 1998s is they are all relatively drinkable at present, whereas the 1997s generally require 3–5 years of cellaring. The 1998 Cabernet Sauvignon Rutherford is a classic Rutherford Cabernet with about 9% Merlot in the blend. Opaque purple in color, with low acidity and a gorgeously explosive nose of black and red fruits intermixed with cedar wood, this profoundly concentrated wine is dense, opulent, and remarkably voluptuous and concentrated for a 1998. In a blind tasting, readers would certainly think this emanated from a vintage such as 1997 or 1994, given its super-concentrated, gorgeously harmonious personality. Anticipated maturity: now–2015. The flamboyant 1998 Cabernet Sauvignon Diamond Mountain (750 cases of 100% Cabernet made from Lokoya's south-facing vineyard) has fabulous fruit intensity offering notes of jammy black currants mixed with violets and minerals. A potential "Wine of the Vintage" candidate, this wine has immense body, great concentration, and gorgeous plum liqueur, cassis/fruit notes that cascade over the palate with remarkable glycerin and richness. Quite an achievement! Anticipated maturity: now–2015. The tiny *cuvée* of 1998 Cabernet Sauvignon Mount Veeder (132 cases of Cabernet Sauvignon) actually is the only 1998 that needs another 2–3 years of cellaring. It will probably last 20–25 years, but will it achieve the greatness of the Diamond Mountain or the suppleness of the Rutherford? With a dense purple color, notes of scorched earth, liquid minerals, black fruits, cedar, and licorice, this full-bodied, powerful, muscular wine has some tannin to shed, but it is loaded with extract and richness. These are amazing achievements in 1998.

The 1995 Cabernet Sauvignon Mount Veeder (1,600 cases) reveals an opaque purple color and a sumptuous, Médoc-like nose of lead pencil, minerals, black currants, and smoky oak. It is extremely full-bodied and massive in the mouth, with sweet tannin, a layered, plushly textured mid-palate, and a firm, exceptionally long, pure finish. This classic mountain-styled Cabernet Sauvignon can be drunk now, but it will be even better with 5–7 years of cellaring. It will keep for two decades. The limited production 1995 Cabernet Sauvignon Howell Mountain (25 cases) is dominated by minerals and wet stones intertwined with blackberry and cassis flavors. More structured and tannic, as well as less extroverted than the Mount Veeder, the Howell Mountain *cuvée* is not for readers seeking immediate gratification. Anticipated maturity: 2005–2018. The sensational 1995 Cabernet Sauvignon Diamond Mountain (330 cases) boasts an opaque blue/black color, followed by outstanding aromatics of jammy blackberry and currant fruit intertwined with roasted herbs, cold steel, minerals, and spicy new oak. There is fabulous intensity, terrific levels of glycerin and extract, full body, and sweet tannin in the long, low-acid finish. This superb, dazzling Cabernet Sauvignon reveals tremendous up-side potential. Anticipated maturity: now–2020. The 1995 Cabernet Sauvignon Rutherford (300 cases) possesses the most developed aromatics, consisting of black currants, cherries, loamy soil scents, and toast. It is the most expansive and fullest-bodied, with stunningly concentrated flavors that exhibit no angularity or sharpness. The acidity, tannin, alcohol, and wood are all gorgeously integrated into this fleshy, succulent, voluptuously textured wine. The finish lasts for 40+ seconds. Despite its accessibility, this Cabernet will be even better with another 5 years of cellaring and will keep for 20–25 years.

The 1994 Cabernet Sauvignon Oakville District (800 cases) is made from 100% Cabernet Sauvignon, 90% of which came from the Vine Hill Ranch and 10% from Mount Veeder. The wine was aged for 22 months in small barrels, of which 40% were new. It exhibits an opaque purple color, a sweet, ripe, olive, chocolate, smoky, cassis-scented nose, dense, full-bodied flavors, moderate tannin, potentially exceptional extract, fine purity, and a long, spicy finish. The wine admirably combines the purity and ripeness of California fruit with a slight degree of the austerity and restraint exhibited by a top Bordeaux. Even more impressive is the 1994 Cabernet Sauvignon Mount Veeder (700 cases). This wine is an immense, monster-styled, mountain Cabernet that is vaguely reminiscent of the pre-1976 vintages of Mayacamas, but with more complexity and finesse. Its opaque black/purple color is followed by a tight, backward, but promising nose of licorice, minerals, and black fruits. The inky color suggests a formidably endowed wine, and that is just what this huge, super-concentrated, impressively endowed Cabernet Sauvignon represents. The wine is not just a ponderous heavyweight, as anyone who examines its equilibrium, harmony, and potential for 20–30 years of aging should notice. Remarkably, this wine was kept in 60% new French oak barrels, but the oak has been soaked up by the wine's intense fruit level. Patience will be a virtue required by prospective purchasers of this wine. Anticipated maturity: 2003–2020.

LOXTON (PASO ROBLES)

1999 Zinfandel Priest Ranch Orion Vineyard	Napa	C	89

Soft, supple, and concentrated, the peppery, earthy, opulent, dark ruby-colored 1999 Zinfandel Priest Ranch Orion Vineyard tips the scales at just over 14% alcohol. Drink this richly fruity, layered example over the next 2–3 years.

LUNA VINEYARDS (NAPA)

1997 Canto Proprietary Red Wine	Napa	E	89
1997 Merlot	Napa	D	89
1997 Sangiovese	Napa	C	89
1998 Sangiovese Riserva	Napa	E	89

This winery, a partnership of John Kongsgaard and George Vare, specializes in Italian varietals. Kongsgaard makes no compromises, believes in using indigenous yeasts for fermentation, and lets the wine make itself. None of these offerings is filtered. Representing some of the finest California wines being produced from Italian varietals, they are all remarkably intense (unlike many of their insipid, one-dimensional, overcropped, bare-bones peers).

Tired of overpriced, appallingly dull, thin, acidic (and even worse, tannic) California Sangiovese? Check out Luna's 1997 Sangiovese. There are 6,000 cases of this blend of 75% Sangiovese, 20% Merlot, and 5% Syrah. Medium ruby-colored, with an explosive nose of strawberry jam, cherries, new saddle leather, and spice, this is a delicious, pure, medium- to full-bodied, plush, hedonistic Sangiovese fruit cocktail. The 1998 Sangiovese Riserva (which includes 10% Syrah) reveals more concentrated juice. A floral, blackberry-scented nose is attributable to that small dosage of Syrah. Cherry fruit, strawberry jam, spicy saddle leather, and meaty aromas are also present. This is a full-bodied, potentially outstanding wine that should drink nicely for 5–7 years. Luna's entry into the super-Tuscan look-alike contest is their 1997 Canto Proprietary Red, a blend of equal parts Merlot, Sangiovese, and Cabernet Sauvignon, aged in small *barriques*, of which 50% were new. The wine's deep plum/purple color is accompanied by a cedary, fruitcake-scented nose, medium to full body, a sweet attack, and a long, structured, moderately tannic, impressively endowed finish. It needs another year of bottle age, and should keep for a decade. Luna also produces 3,000 cases of Merlot. Obviously John Kongsgaard has the right touch with Merlot, as evidenced by some of the Newton Merlots he fashioned. Luna's 1997 Merlot, which includes 20% Cabernet Franc, exhibits a dark ruby color, big, espresso bean, mocha, chocolate, and berry scents and flavors, good spice, moderate tannin, and a dense, concentrated mid-palate that is just beginning to unfold. I would not be surprised to see this wine merit a 90-point score with another 6–12 months of bottle age. It came in at a hefty 14.1% alcohol.

MARCASSIN VINEYARD (SONOMA)

1997 Chardonnay Gauer Ranch Upper Barn	Sonoma	EE	96
1997 Chardonnay Hudson Vineyard E Block	Carneros	EE	91
1998 Chardonnay Lorenzo Vineyard	Sonoma Coast	EE	93
1997 Chardonnay Lorenzo Vineyard	Sonoma Coast	EE	95+
1999 Chardonnay Marcassin Vineyard	Sonoma Coast	EE	97+
1998 Chardonnay Marcassin Vineyard	Sonoma Coast	EE	99
1997 Chardonnay Marcassin Vineyard	Sonoma Coast	EE	97
1999 Chardonnay Three Sisters–Sea Ridge Meadow	Sonoma Coast	EE	94
1998 Chardonnay Three Sisters–Sea Ridge Meadow	Sonoma Coast	EE	95
1999 Chardonnay Upper Barn–Alexander Mountain Estate	Sonoma	EE	(93–96)

1998 Chardonnay Upper Barn–Alexander Mountain Estate	Sonoma	EE	92
1999 Pinot Noir Blue Slide Ridge	Sonoma Coast	EE	(98–100)
1998 Pinot Noir Blue Slide Ridge	Sonoma Coast	EE	95
1997 Pinot Noir Blue Slide Vineyard	Sonoma Coast	EE	96
1999 Pinot Noir Marcassin Vineyard	Sonoma Coast	EE	(95–96)
1998 Pinot Noir Marcassin Vineyard	Sonoma Coast	EE	98
1997 Pinot Noir Marcassin Vineyard	Sonoma Coast	EE	95+
1996 Pinot Noir Marcassin Vineyard	Sonoma Coast	EE	95
1995 Pinot Noir Marcassin Vineyard	Sonoma Coast	EE	93
1999 Pinot Noir Three Sisters–Lambing Barn	Sonoma Coast	EE	(93–95)
1999 Pinot Noir Three Sisters–Sea Ridge Meadow	Sonoma Coast	EE	(94–96)

The American wine industry's first couple, John Wetlaufer and Helen Turley (by the way, they have been married for 35 years), continue to eschew the spotlight, preferring to let their brilliant viticultural and winemaking skills serve notice that no one does it better. Quantities remain agonizingly small, so in a given vintage, only one or two thousand wine nuts get a chance to taste these elixirs. While I am not against size (obviously such huge qualitative giants as Beringer, Robert Mondavi, and Joseph Phelps can produce 20,000+ cases of high-quality Cabernet Sauvignon or Chardonnay), it is virtually impossible to produce large quantities of wines such as these Marcassins. It is hard to find more complex Chardonnays and Pinot Noirs than those produced by Turley and Wetlaufer from their own Sonoma Coast vineyard. Moreover, their crop-sharing agreement with the Martinelli family for the Three Sisters and Blue Slide Ridge Vineyards also looks set to produce some prodigious wines.

The 1999 Chardonnay Upper Barn–Alexander Mountain Estate *cuvée* (previously named Gauer Ranch Upper Barn, but renamed by its owner, Jess Jackson) comes from a vineyard being replanted with Burgundian Dijon clones. Marcassin shares the fruit from this vineyard with Stonestreet Winery. The fabulous 1999 boasts a smoky, honeyed pineapple, toasty nose with plenty of tropical fruit, butter, and roasted hazelnut scents in addition to gorgeously ripe, layered flavors. This rich, full-throttle Chardonnay is both concentrated and intense. It should drink well for 7–8 years. Readers will find two Chardonnays from the Three Sisters–Sea Ridge Meadow Vineyard. One, produced with the consultation of Helen Turley, will be sold under the Martinelli label, and the other under the Marcassin label. This Sonoma Coast vineyard was severely crop-thinned. Marcassin's 1999 Chardonnay Three Sisters–Sea Ridge Meadow Vineyard is a brilliant effort that was given extensive lees stirring until the spring following the vintage, and then not racked until it was absolutely essential. The result is a wine of extraordinary complexity, texture, and richness with striking buttery citrus and liquid mineral notes as well as a juicy, heady, lemon/pineapple, steely personality. Although extremely full-bodied, it remains exceptionally elegant and stylish. Like all the Marcassin Chardonnays, it will be bottled with neither fining nor filtration. There will be approximately 225 cases of the 1999 Chardonnay Marcassin Vineyard. This wine, from a vineyard planted on a steep, rocky hillside with shallow topsoil and meter-by-meter spacing, comes closest to a magical synthesis of Michel Niellon's Bâtard-Montrachet and Coche-Dury's Corton-Charlemagne blended with California's extraordinary ripeness and richness from low-yielding Chardonnay fruit. It is an unctuous, full-bodied, gorgeously delineated offering with an extraordinary perfume of liquid minerals interspersed with citrus oils, honey, and a steely smokiness. The compelling aromatics are matched by the attack, mid-palate, and finish. This profound Chardonnay is California's most singular expression of this varietal. Moreover, it will have an effortless evolution of 10–12+ years.

There are four 1998 Chardonnays, including the final release from the Sonoma Coast's

Lorenzo Vineyard. The 1998 Chardonnay Gauer Ranch–Upper Barn (now called Upper Barn–Alexander Mountain Estate) exhibits a surprisingly cloudy, evolved medium gold color. With notes of honeysuckle, buttery tropical fruit, minerals, smoke, and hazelnuts, this dense, full-bodied, rich, chewy 1998 seems unusually mature. Drink it over the next 3–5 years. The more mineral-dominated 1998 Chardonnay Three Sisters–Sea Ridge Meadow Vineyard reveals the essence of soil in its flavors. Additionally, it offers creamy custard, citrus, honey, and butternut notes, huge amounts of fruit, phenomenal texture, and a spectacularly long finish. Drink this prodigious Chardonnay over the next 7–8 years. The 1998 Chardonnay Lorenzo Vineyard reveals the smoky, leesy, honeyed complexity characteristic of Helen Turley's Chardonnays. There is good density, ripeness, and richness, fine underlying acidity, and a multinuanced, full-bodied finish. It should drink well for 5–6 years. The 1998 Chardonnay Marcassin Vineyard is a tour de force in Chardonnay winemaking. It has developed gorgeously since last year, and is one of the most compelling Chardonnays produced in either France or California. It reveals the essence of crushed sea shells in its complex, multidimensional bouquet, which also offers up aromas of lemon liqueur, minerals, honeyed citrus, orange marmalade, and smoke. Still tightly knit, it possesses full body, layers of concentration, and a red wine–like structure, power, and finish. The whopping 14.9% alcohol is well-concealed behind the wine's fruit and extract. The overall impression is of an extraordinarily well-delineated, intense, powerful Chardonnay trying to burst loose from its reins. Still backward, it has the potential to develop for at least a decade.

The 1997 Chardonnay Marcassin Vineyard shares some of the same characteristics (as does the 1996) with the 1998 and 1999. Liquid mineral and crushed sea shell aromas and flavors are present in this full-bodied, mineral-laced, lemon, honey, buttery Chardonnay. It boasts layers of flavor (citrus oils, orange marmalade, and hazelnuts), majestic concentration, and an unreal finish that lasts for over 40 seconds. Approachable upon its release in 2001, it should age beautifully for a decade. There are nearly 250 cases of the 1997 Chardonnay Gauer Ranch Upper Barn. This wine offers a compelling waxy, honeyed citrus, subtle toasty, lusty nose, followed by a full-bodied, fabulously concentrated mouthful of leesy, multilayered Chardonnay exhibiting honeyed grapefruit, citrus, and mineral flavors. A powerful, multidimensional, long (nearly a minute) finish adds to this Chardonnay's prodigious characteristics. It should drink well for 7–8 years. The 1997 Chardonnay Lorenzo Vineyard is also compelling, offering the liquid slate/petroleum-like notes found more strongly in the Marcassin Vineyard. Full-bodied, powerful, and expansive, with laser-like focus, the Lorenzo possesses lemony, peach, apricot, steely flavors crammed into an impressively concentrated personality. It is simply sensational, so excuse the verbose wine speak. Anticipated maturity: now–2007. Marcassin's last offering from Lee Hudson's Carneros vineyard, the 1997 Chardonnay Hudson Vineyard E Block, displays an evolved light gold color as well as an exotic nose of smoked tropical fruit intermixed with orange marmalade and roasted coffee scents. Layered, rich, and boisterous, but not nearly as complex or nuanced as the Gauer Ranch Upper Barn or Lorenzo, this is a full-throttle, exuberant, flamboyant Chardonnay. Drink it over the next 3–4 years.

With respect to the Marcassin Pinot Noir program, there is no doubting that, along with several of the Kistler Pinot Noirs as well as those from Brewer-Clifton in Santa Barbara, they are the most remarkable Pinot Noirs being produced in the New World. If only some of the infamous league of apologists for Burgundy would put these wines in a blind tasting against Burgundy's greatest grand crus. Don't expect that to happen anytime soon. A 1999 Pinot Noir Three Sisters–Sea Ridge Meadow Vineyard appears under both the Marcassin and Martinelli label (the Martinellis own this land and farm the vineyard with Turley and Wetlaufer). Marcassin's 1999 offering is an exquisite Pinot Noir revealing a dark ruby/purple color and a sweet nose of cherry jam infused with smoke, minerals, and flowers. The wine's finesse and elegance in addition to glorious levels of black raspberry and cherry fruit, expansiveness,

and earthy, rich complexity suggest a grand cru from Morey-St.-Denis. The 1999 Pinot Noir
Three Sisters–Lambing Barn Vineyard comes from a small six-acre parcel planted with
tightly spaced Burgundy Dijon clones. It offers an exotic, spicy (cinnamon, allspice), new
saddle leather, and black cherry/raspberry-scented bouquet. Full-bodied, expansive, dense,
and exceptionally complex, it will drink well for 7–8 years. The 1999 Pinot Noir Blue Slide
Ridge is awesome! This vineyard, planted with such clones of Pinot Noir as Pommard, #115,
#667, and #777, has produced an opaque ruby/purple-colored effort with an exquisite nose
of roasted herbs, vanilla, smoke, black fruits, meat, and violets. Aromatically, it is reminiscent of a top vintage of Domaine de la Romanée-Conti's Richebourg or La Tâche. The wine is
extraordinarily complex, layered, and rich, with well-integrated acidity and oak, as well as a
mind-boggling finish. This exquisite Pinot Noir will be magical to drink over the next 7–10
years. The 1999 Pinot Noir Marcassin Vineyard reveals more of a mineral, soy, Asian plum
sauce characteristic, along with notes of black raspberries, scorched earth, steak tartare, and
assorted black fruits. Subtle notions of toasty vanilla from new-oak aging also emerge. With
full body as well as remarkable concentration, length, and presence, this fabulous Pinot is
the youngest, most unevolved of these 1999s. Anticipated maturity: now–2014.

There are only two 1998 Pinot Noirs. The 1998 Pinot Noir Blue Slide Ridge exhibits a sensational nose of plum liqueur intermixed with blueberries, blackberries, smoke, and liquid
stones. Displaying good underlying acidity, full body, and superb concentration and purity, it
should drink well for a decade. The nearly perfect 1998 Pinot Noir Marcassin Vineyard
boasts a deep saturated ruby/purple color in addition to a spectacular bouquet of blackberries, boysenberries, plums, raspberries, and cherries. In the mouth, it represents the essence
of black fruits intermingled with aromas of grilled steak and scorched earth. With a thick,
rich, full-bodied, meaty chewiness in addition to multiple flavor layers and impressive delineation for a wine of such concentration and size, this is a celestial Pinot Noir. Look for the
1998 Pinot Noir to evolve for 10–15 years.

The 1997 Pinot Noir Marcassin Vineyard has closed down since first tasted. One can sense
the enormous weight, fat, ripeness, and richness in both the aromatics and flavors, but the
tannin is obvious and the wine tight and structured. While it is undoubtedly a blockbuster,
this 1997 Pinot needs 2–3 years of additional bottle age. It should keep for 12–15 years. The
mineral characteristics that emerge from both the Marcassin Vineyard Chardonnay and Pinot
Noir appear to become more pronounced as the wines age. The spectacularly complex, opulently textured, lavishly rich 1997 Pinot Noir Blue Slide Ridge displays a saturated plum/
purple color in addition to gorgeous aromas of blueberries, black cherries, lavender, and
smoky oak. Intense and full-bodied, with fabulous concentration, a voluptuous texture, and a
long finish, this is a stunning effort. Sadly, production was minuscule—25 cases.

The 1996 Pinot Noir Marcassin Vineyard (275 cases) is also outstanding. In order to get
a snapshot of what these wines are really about is to recognize that they are reminiscent of
the finest grand crus I have tasted from such sites as Clos de la Roche and Clos St.-Denis.
They share an extraordinary minerality with fabulously concentrated plum, black cherry,
blueberry/blackberry characteristics. They are fuller-bodied, denser, and more concentrated
and alcoholic than any grand cru red Burgundy (although red Burgundies from vintages such
as 1997, 1990, and 1989 routinely achieved 14% alcohol). The 1996 Pinot Noir Marcassin
Vineyard has not yet begun to reveal additional nuances, but it is the kind of Pinot Noir that
suggests that the Sonoma Coast, in 30–50 years, may be one of the world's most fashionable
spots for this varietal.

The 1995 Pinot Noir Marcassin Vineyard (only 25 cases for the world) was the debut vintage for this wine. It possesses one of the most enthralling and exquisite Burgundy-like Pinot
noses I have ever smelled in a young American Pinot Noir. The color is a healthy medium
dark ruby, and the sweet nose of jammy red and black fruits, truffles, smoked duck, and earth
reminded this taster of a grand cru from Flagey-Echezeaux or Vosne-Romanée. The wine re-

veals a delicacy and sweetness on the palate, without the weight one expects from such intense aromas and flavors. A remarkably complex wine, it will be a dazzling, full-bodied, perfumed style of Pinot Noir that should drink well during its first 5–7 years of life. I doubt it will be long-lived, but all the Marcassin wines have held their fruit and character longer than I would have expected.

All these wines are available through the winery's mailing list, although some preferred Napa Valley restaurants, particularly the French Laundry, and a few in New York (Daniel and Le Bernardin) seem to receive noteworthy allocations.

MARIETTA CELLARS (SONOMA)

1996 Cabernet Sauvignon	Sonoma	C	90
1994 Cabernet Sauvignon	Sonoma	C	88
N.V. Old Vine Red Lot 22	California	B	88
N.V. Old Vine Red Lot 15	Sonoma	B	90
N.V. Old Vine Red Lot 18	Sonoma	B	89
1996 Syrah	California	C	88

The 1996 Cabernet Sauvignon and Syrah, and Old Vine Red Lot 22 make up the strongest group of Marietta wines I have tasted in recent vintages. There are some terrific buys, including the 20,000 cases of nonvintage Old Vine Red Lot 22. This wine has become a darling of intelligent consumers, as evidenced by the fact that the entire production is allocated. The Lot 22 offering, primarily from the 1996 and 1997 vintages, is a blend of Zinfandel, Petite Sirah, Carignan, Gamay, and Cabernet Sauvignon, from vineyard sources in Napa, Sonoma, and Mendocino. It is a weighty, seriously endowed wine with a dark purple color, as well as a super nose of cherries, black currants, pepper, spice, and loamy soil notes. Full-bodied and richly extracted, with copious quantities of berry fruit, excellent purity, and an expansive, silky-textured finish, this wine can be drunk now as well as cellared for 2–3 years. Marietta's Old Vine Red is consistently one of the best bargains in exuberant, dry reds.

I suspect one has to go back to the 1990 vintage to find a Marietta Cabernet Sauvignon with as much quality and potential as the 1996. It is a full-bodied, tannic yet promising, opaque purple-colored Cabernet loaded with potential. Some of the rustic tannin should melt away over the next 2–5 years. At present, it is concentrated, with textbook cedary and black currant fruit displayed in a dramatic, rich style. There is good thickness and richness, as well as plenty of lusty alcohol (14.6%) in this large-scaled Cabernet that should age nicely for 10–12 years. In today's inflated marketplace, Cabernet Sauvignons of this quality usually sell for $30+ a bottle. Readers take note. The 1996 Syrah, which emerges from Sonoma and Mendocino vineyards, is a full-bodied, blackberry-scented wine with pepper, sweet licorice, and weedy, underbrush notes. With excellent ripeness, good spice, and a robust, muscular personality, this Syrah offers gutsy, mouth-filling flavors that should continue to develop for 5–7 years.

Proprietor/wine-maker Chris Bilbro should receive an award from consumers for making such tasty wines while maintaining realistic prices. One of the finest values in the wine world is Marietta's Old Vine Red, a recent rendition being Lot 18. This wine, usually a blend of Petite Sirah, Cabernet Sauvignon, Zinfandel, Carignan, and who knows what else, is always a deep ruby/purple-colored wine with copious quantities of peppery black fruits intertwined with scents of earth. A chewy, fleshy, full-bodied, mouth-filling wine, this juicy, burly effort disappears as quickly as Marietta releases the 10,000+ cases produced. While most of the Old Vine Red is consumed within the first 1–2 months of purchase, it gives every indication of lasting for 5 or more years. The Lot 15 is made from 25% Petite Sirah, 20% Cabernet Sauvignon, 5% Carignan, and the rest Zinfandel and other red wine grapes. This opaque purple-colored wine offers up huge quantities of sweet black cherries and cassis, intermixed with scents of pepper, truffles, and spices. Full-bodied, with a kirsch-like flavor, this dense, chewy, fleshy wine is California's answer to a top-notch Châteauneuf-du-Pape. There may be 10,000 cases of this superb wine, but it disappears quickly from the shelves of retailers.

This winery also does a fine job with Cabernet Sauvignon. Although Marietta's 1994 Cabernet Sauvignon is not as brilliant as the 1992, it tastes as good as most Cabernets that cost $10–15 more a bottle. The wine's deep, dense, ruby/purple color is followed by moderately intense aromas of ripe black fruits with toasty wood notes in the background. Full-bodied, tannic, dense, and chewy, this wine will benefit from 1–2 years of cellaring; it should age well for a decade.

MARTINELLI (SONOMA)

1999 Chardonnay Charles Ranch	Sonoma Coast	E	90
1999 Chardonnay Goldridge Vineyard	Russian River	E	90
1999 Chardonnay Martinelli Road	Russian River	D	91
1999 Chardonnay Woolsey Road	Russian River	D	90
1999 Gewurztraminer Martinelli Vineyard	Russian River	E	90
1999 Pinot Noir Blue Slide Ridge	Sonoma Coast	E	91+
1998 Pinot Noir Blue Slide Ridge	Sonoma Coast	E	93
1994 Pinot Noir Estate	Russian River	C	90
1998 Pinot Noir Martinelli Vineyard	Russian River	D	91
1996 Pinot Noir Martinelli Vineyard	Russian River	D	92
1995 Pinot Noir Martinelli Vineyard	Russian River	D	90
1999 Pinot Noir Martinelli Vineyard Reserve	Russian River	D	93
1998 Pinot Noir Martinelli Vineyard Reserve	Russian River	D	93
1997 Pinot Noir Martinelli Vineyard Reserve	Russian River	D	93
1996 Pinot Noir Martinelli Vineyard Reserve	Russian River	D	94
1995 Pinot Noir Martinelli Vineyard Reserve	Russian River	D	92
1999 Pinot Noir Three Colts	Russian River	E	90
1999 Syrah Hop Barn Hill	Russian River	E	97
1999 Zinfandel Guiseppe and Luisa	Russian River	E	95
1998 Zinfandel Guiseppe and Luisa	Russian River	E	94
1999 Zinfandel Jackass Vineyard	Russian River	EE	92
1998 Zinfandel Jackass Vineyard	Russian River	EE	95
1997 Zinfandel Jackass Vineyard	Russian River	EE	95
1996 Zinfandel Jackass Vineyard	Russian River	EE	93
1999 Zinfandel Jackass Hill Vineyard	Russian River	EEE	96
1998 Zinfandel Jackass Hill Vineyard	Russian River	EEE	97
1997 Zinfandel Jackass Hill Vineyard	Russian River	EE	95
1996 Zinfandel Jackass Hill Vineyard	Russian River	EE	96

Readers who have trouble latching onto a bottle of Helen Turley and John Wetlaufer's famed Marcassin Chardonnay or Pinot Noir should try to secure some of the wines from Martinelli. This old Russian River family has seemingly unlimited resources, as well as a bevy of top-notch vineyards. They have also made major investments on the Sonoma Coast. Their vineyard strategist is John Wetlaufer and their consulting wine-maker is his wife, Helen Turley. Since these two people have come aboard, the results have been remarkable, with a bevy of exquisite Chardonnays, Pinot Noirs, and Zinfandels as well as California's finest Gewürztraminer. Their newest offering is microscopic quantities of an unreal Syrah.

The 1999 Chardonnays from Martinelli possess slightly lower alcohol than previous vintages, as well as more steely, mineral-infused characters. The 1999 Chardonnay Woolsey Road (13.4% alcohol) shows attractive, steely, mineral, and orange characteristics, medium to full body, excellent purity, and a Chablis-like character. Elegant and rich, it is destined to last for 4–5 years. The more powerful 1999 Chardonnay Goldridge (14.4% alcohol) displays the most flamboyant character of the 1999s, with notes of honey, butterscotch, mineral, and smoky, leesy characteristics. Freshly baked bread and/or brioche combine with spicy oak and tropical fruit in the most forward of Martinelli's 1999 Chardonnays. Drink it over the next 3–4 years. Honeyed pineapple, orange marmalade, minerals, and butter characterize the full-bodied, surprisingly nuanced, and stylish 1999 Chardonnay Charles Ranch. With only 13.4% alcohol, this wine possesses less power than previous vintages, but there is liquid minerality underneath all the fruit. Citrus oils also make an appearance. This wine should last for 4–5 years. The 1999 Chardonnay Martinelli Road (a Chardonnay vineyard that is essentially the lower slopes of the Jackass and Jackass Hill Zinfandel vineyards) offers steely, waxy, buttery tropical fruits, great ripeness, good underlying acidity, smoky, leesy characteristics, and a full-bodied, fruit-dominated finish. It should drink well for 2–3 years. It offers a slightly more reserved/restrained style than the 1998.

Readers should not overlook Martinelli's limited production, delicious 1999 Gewürztraminer Martinelli Vineyard, the finest Gewürztraminer made in California. Revealing this varietal's classic lychee nut and honeyed grapefruit aromas and flavors, it is a dry, full-bodied, exotic, ostentatious effort that requires consumption over the next 1–2 years in order to take advantage of its intensity and exuberance.

The saturated plum-colored 1999 Pinot Noir Martinelli Vineyard Reserve displays more evolution than found in recent vintages. A black cherry/raspberry-scented nose reveals lavish quantities of toasty oak, sweet black raspberries, *sous bois,* smoke, and soy. Full-bodied and soft, with splendid concentration and enormous depth, it is ideal for drinking over the next 3–4 years. The dense ruby/purple-colored 1999 Pinot Noir Blue Slide Ridge offers gloriously rich blackberry, blueberry, violet, and mineral aromas. Opulently textured, with fabulous fruit, sensational texture, and a full-bodied, long finish, this 1999 California Pinot Noir could easily stand up to many a grand cru from Burgundy's Côte de Nuits. Drink it over the next 7–8 years. Another debut release from the Pinot Noir portfolio is the 1999 Pinot Noir Three Colts. This comes from three young vineyards the Martinellis have planted with 2,000 vines per acre and vertical trellising. It is a powerful Pinot Noir (15.1% alcohol) exhibiting a dark ruby/purple color, sumptuous aromas, and flavors of prunes, plums, root beer, cocoa, and cherry liqueur, and an opulent, lush texture. This is an outstanding, hedonistically styled Pinot Noir to drink over the next 5–6 years.

The three 1998 Pinot Noirs are all exceptional efforts. The 1998 Pinot Noir Martinelli Vineyard (14.5% alcohol) tastes like a premier cru Pommard. It reveals aromas and flavors of pomegranate, apple skins, black cherries, pepper, and earth in addition to a dense, full-bodied, muscular palate, low acidity, copious alcohol, and abundant glycerin. Drink it over the next 5–6 years. The 1998 Pinot Noir Martinelli Vineyard Reserve's bouquet offers scents of earth, seaweed, smoke, black cherry jam, raspberries, and grilled meats. Full-bodied, chewy, and exotic, with an ostentatious/exuberant personality, it possesses adequate acidity, sweet tannin, and subtle notes of new wood. It should drink well for 7–8 years. There are 100 cases of the debut vintage of Martinelli's 1998 Pinot Noir Blue Slide Ridge. An opaque deep ruby/purple color is followed by aromas of sweet plum, black raspberry, and blueberry fruit, fabulous concentration, exquisite purity, medium to full body, and uncanny balance as well as seamlessness. This glorious Pinot Noir can be drunk now and over the next 5–7 years.

The lavishly rich, full-bodied, gloriously perfumed and flavored 1997 Pinot Noir Martinelli Vineyard Reserve is performing terrifically from bottle. In a recent blind tasting with some of America's finest Pinot and three of my favorite Burgundy grand crus from 1990, it was the group's (not my) favorite. It overloads the olfactory senses with kirsch, plum, black cherry fruit, and smoky oak. Heady and lush, it should be drunk over the next 5–8 years.

When I tasted Martinelli's two *cuvées* of 1996 Pinot Noir, they immediately took me back to the late sixties when I was a student living outside Washington, D.C., making frequent buying trips to what was then called plain old Pearson's Liquor Shop. At that time, Pearson's had

an extraordinary collection of 1961, 1962, 1964, and 1966 red Burgundies that could be purchased for a song. I cut my teeth on many a Domaine Parent Pommard Les Grandes
Epenottes and Pommard Les Rugiens from those vintages. They were marvelously full-
bodied, meaty, fragrant Pinots the likes of which I have never tasted again from either Domaine Parent or any other Pommard producer. When I tasted Martinelli's 1996 Pinot Noir
Martinelli Vineyard and 1996 Pinot Noir Martinelli Vineyard Reserve, I was reminded of my
student days of Parent's gloriously decadent, rich Pinots. These are fascinating wines, offering gorgeous levels of smoky, meaty, earthy, black cherry fruit in a full-bodied, glycerin-
imbued, lusty style that is about as hedonistic as Pinot Noir can be. While I was blown away
by the 1996 Pinot Noir Martinelli Vineyard, the Reserve Pinot Noir was even more spectacular and amazingly concentrated. They have it all! Bottled unfined and unfiltered, they represent the essence of the Pinot Noir grape as translated by the Martinellis and their
consultant wine-maker, Helen Turley. Both wines should drink well for 3–4 years, perhaps
longer, but I can't imagine anyone having enough discipline to hold on to these wines as long
as they continue to drink as well as they do today.

Martinelli's 1994 Pinot Noir Estate, also bottled without fining or filtration, is an outstanding example of this varietal. Unfortunately, only 200 cases were produced of this sumptuously styled, meaty, black cherry and smoke-scented wine. It exhibits a dark garnet color,
sweet, chewy, fleshy, Burgundy-like fruit, high alcohol (14.3%), and a soft, gorgeously proportioned, lusty finish. This is what Burgundy should be—pure, expansive, succulent, and
loaded with gobs of fruit—but so rarely is. The 1994 Pinot Noir Estate was the first outstanding Martinelli Pinot Noir. This was followed by two superlative 1995s. The 1995 Pinot Noir
Martinelli Vineyard exhibits a Domaine Dujac–like complexity with its cinnamon, black
cherry, spicy, smoky nose. It offers sweet, gamey, plum and black cherry–like flavors, excellent richness and purity, and a long, lusty finish. Drink this round, generous Pinot Noir over
the next 3–4 years. Remarkably, there is a 1995 Pinot Noir Martinelli Vineyard Reserve, also
a terrific example of this varietal. It possesses a deep ruby color, a big, spicy, smoky, earth,
and black fruit–scented nose, and layers of ripe, jammy flavors buttressed by new oak, acidity, and sweet tannin. The finish is long and authoritative. These Pinot Noirs offer further evidence of just how exciting California Pinot Noir has become. The Reserve was released in
September 1997; it will drink well for 2–4 years, possibly longer.

Martinelli's 1999 Zinfandels are as concentrated and intense as readers might expect from
previous renditions. Production of the 1999 Zinfandel Guiseppe and Luisa (made from the
same clone planted in the Jackass Hill Vineyard) is a whopping 1,600 cases. The dense
plum/purple color is accompanied by a glorious perfume of jammy blackberry and cassis
fruit, an unctuous, opulent texture, high glycerin (17% alcohol), and a dry, long, dense, pure
finish. This is a stunning, flamboyant Zinfandel elixir to drink over the next 6–10 years. The
spectacular 1999 Zinfandel Jackass Vineyard (1,700 cases of 15.9% alcohol) is nearly as
compelling as the Jackass Hill offering. An opaque garnet/purple/plum color is followed by
an exotic bouquet of smoked Peking duck, plum sauce, blackberry and cherry liqueur, and
Asian spices. The wine is exquisitely concentrated, thick, viscous, and rich, but dry and remarkably well balanced, with a blockbuster finish. It should drink well for a decade. Year in
and year out, the following wine gets my nod as one of California's greatest Zinfandels. The
1999 Zinfandel Jackass Hill Vineyard (16.5% alcohol) reveals notes of lavender, jammy
black raspberries and blackberries, smoky oak, soy, *jus de viande*, and a touch of volatile
acidity, all of which explode in the nose and on the palate. Flamboyant, with excellent structure, immense body, and flavors of blackberries and smoky cherries that ooze across the
palate, this is another prodigious wine that should be consumed over the next decade, although its power and force of character will keep it alive for 2–3 decades.

The 1998 Zinfandel Guiseppe and Luisa (15.5% alcohol) is one of the vintage's superstars.

A terrific nose of plum liqueur intermixed with smoke, coffee, Chinese black tea, cherries, plums, raspberries, and spice soars from the glass. Full body, an unctuous texture, and gorgeously pure flavors conceal the wine's high alcohol. With a stupendous texture, finish, and opulence, it can be drunk over the next 4–8 years, although I suspect it will last longer. The murky, plum/purple-colored 1998 Zinfandel Jackass Vineyard is followed by scents of prunes, plum liqueur, licorice, smoke, coffee, and assorted Asian spices. The wine is spectacularly rich, thick, and chewy, with low acidity. Its 16+% alcohol is barely noticeable. The deep purple-colored 1998 Zinfandel Jackass Hill Vineyard (17% alcohol) appears less flamboyant and more tightly knit and structured than the Jackass Vineyard . . . at least initially. After ten minutes of airing, the wine begins to unfold, revealing multiple dimensions in its glorious perfume, richness, and complexity. It is a massive Zinfandel with spectacular aromatics (smoke, prunes, plums, raspberries, coffee, cedar, new saddle leather) as well as viscous, chewy, full-throttle flavors. A wine of enormous force as well as unbelievable symmetry, it should age for a decade. I would not be surprised to see well-stored examples display considerable fruit and complexity at age 20 or 30.

The 1997 Zinfandel Jackass Vineyard may be the finest offering produced under this designation. It tips the scales at over 16% alcohol, but the alcohol is remarkably concealed by the wine's extraordinary wealth of fruit, extract, and layered richness. The dark ruby/purple/garnet color was no doubt intensified by the 3–5 day cold soak the Martinellis and wine-maker Helen Turley give this wine. The nose offers up a plethora of celestial aromas, including plum liqueur, kirsch, spice box, coffee, prunes, and jammy cherries. As the wine sits in the glass, spicy oak, pepper, allspice, and clove scents emerge. Full-bodied, rich, and mouth-filling, this velvety-textured, voluptuous, hedonistic Zinfandel can be drunk now as well as over the next decade. The 1997 Zinfandel Jackass Hill Vineyard is a massive, totally dry wine that came in at 17.5% alcohol and was bottled unfiltered. Dense and full-bodied, it represents Zinfandel in its most concentrated form. Its singular style, unctuous texture, and fabulously concentrated flavors make for an unforgettable tasting experience. While not for everybody, it is the quintessential powerhouse Zinfandel made from tiny yields, a phenomenal vineyard site, and impeccable winemaking. Its characteristics are similar to those of the Jackass Vineyard, only more intense—jammy black cherries, plums, prunes, dried herbs, licorice, chocolate, and coffee. This wine is best drunk in its exuberant youthfulness, but I suspect it will age well beyond a decade.

Martinelli's 1996s are both exceptional Zinfandels. The 1996 Zinfandel Jackass Vineyard (15.6% alcohol) reveals a murky plum/purple color. Outstanding aromatics soar from the glass, offering aromas of licorice, blackberry liqueur, truffles, underbrush, smoke, and meat. The wine's unctuousness, full body, and supple texture result in a decadently rich, lavishly endowed Zinfandel to drink over the next 3–6 years. The 1996 Zinfandel Jackass Hill Vineyard displays a similar plum/purple color. The nose offers a smorgasbord of aromas, including cherry, blackberry, and strawberry liqueur intermingled with smoky, toasty oak, roasted Provençal herbs, Asian spice, and chocolaty, meaty overtones. Exceptionally full-bodied, with gobs of glycerin, remarkable purity, and profound balance for such a large Zinfandel, this is a true work of art. It should drink well for another 7–8+ years. Are the Jackass 1996s better than the 1995s and 1994s? In my estimation, the 1995 and 1994 Jackass and Jackass Hill Zinfandels are among the most amazing wines I have ever tasted. I cannot say the 1996s are superior, but no one who loves Zin should be without them. They are artistic creations.

Lastly, the opaque blue/purple-colored 1999 Syrah Hop Barn Hill is an amazing achievement. Produced from yields of less than one ton of fruit per vine, this wine demonstrates what can be achieved from extremely ripe fruit (picked at 29° Brix) that is fermented dry, and aged in 100% new French oak. A classic Syrah, it possesses aromas and flavors of blackberry liqueur intermixed with cassis, pepper, and bacon fat. With unreal levels of glycerin, richness, and concentration, it is akin to drinking the blood of the grape. There is a viscosity and unctuosity that must be tasted to be believed. It is a thrilling, historic Syrah for California! Sadly, there were less than 50 cases produced. The good news is that the Martinellis have planted several additional acres of Syrah.

More and more wines made from small, high-quality producers such as Martinelli are being sold through a mailing list. Readers wishing to secure a bottle of their most limited production offerings should know what to do. These wines are best drunk young, despite their lofty alcohol levels and extract. I suggest consuming them during their first 5–8 years of life.

THE MAYO FAMILY WINERY (SONOMA)

1999 Zinfandel Ricci Vineyard	Russian River	D	89

This dense plum/purple-colored, blockbuster effort exhibits abundant black cherry, plum, and currant fruit with pepper, incense, and spice notes in the background. Made in a super-concentrated style, with 15.9% alcohol, this blockbuster has layered, viscous, and pure flavors, with copious quantities of glycerin. It will drink well for 4–6 years.

PHILIPPE MELKA (NAPA)

1999 Métisse Proprietary Red Wine	Napa	E	90
1998 Métisse Proprietary Red Wine	Napa	E	91
1997 Métisse Proprietary Red Wine	Napa	E	93
1996 Métisse Proprietary Red Wine	Napa	D	90

Frenchman Philippe Melka is quickly establishing a reputation as one of the finest consultants in Napa Valley. He oversees the winemaking at Lail Vineyards, and has recently added Caldwell Vineyard, Vineyard 29, and Marston Family Vineyard to his portfolio. He is also the person responsible for the fabulous wines emerging from Seavey in Conn Valley. Melka produces approximately 450 cases under his own name.

The 1998 Métisse (a blend of 87% Cabernet Sauvignon, 10% Merlot, and 3% Cabernet Franc) is a gorgeously proportioned, full-bodied, dark purple-colored effort with superb density, soft, sweet tannin, a generous constitution, and copious quantities of blackberry and cassis fruit nicely dosed with subtle new oak. Low in acidity, it is ideal for drinking over the next 12–15 years. It is an exceptional proprietary red from the 1998 vintage. The 1999 Métisse (an assemblage of 80% Cabernet Sauvignon, 17% Merlot, and 3% Cabernet Franc) represents a trial blend, with slightly more Cabernet Sauvignon than the 1998. Approximately 450 cases were produced. Like the 1998, it sees 40–45% new oak, and, if possible, it will be bottled without filtration, although occasionally Melka will fine the wine (as he did in 1998) to soften the tannin. The 1999 exhibits a dense purple color as well as a Pomerol-like bouquet of espresso, blackberries, cherries, and chocolate. Full-bodied and velvety-textured, this promising red should be at its finest between 2004–2020.

The blend of the 1997 Métisse (450 cases made from 53% Cabernet Sauvignon, 27% Merlot, and 20% Cabernet Franc) is similar to that of the famed Château Haut-Brion, but the wine tastes more like a Pomerol. It is deep ruby/purple, with an exuberant, exotic nose of espresso beans lathered in melted chocolate, and jammy cherry/cassis. Full-bodied and velvety-textured, this opulent, hedonistic, gorgeously textured wine is already thrilling to drink. Anticipated maturity: now–2016. The 1996 Métisse (about 240 cases) is a blend of 40% Cabernet Sauvignon, 30% Cabernet Franc, and 30% Merlot. A Bordeaux-styled red (Melka was trained under Christian Moueix), this 1996 is a stylish, complex, elegant wine. It boasts a dark ruby/purple color, followed by attractive aromatics consisting of black currants, lead pencil, cedar, spice box, and toast. Medium-bodied, with graceful, ripe fruit, and nicely integrated tannin and acidity, this is an exceptionally harmonious wine that opens beautifully in the glass. It will not knock tasters over with its power or extract, but there is plenty going on in this stylish, complete wine. Enjoy it now and over the next 12–14 years.

MERRYVALE VINEYARDS (NAPA)

1995	Cabernet Sauvignon Reserve	Napa	D	89
1995	Merlot Beckstoffer IV Vineyard	Napa	D	88
1995	Merlot Reserve	Napa	D	89
1996	Profile Proprietary Red Wine	Napa	E	90
1995	Profile Proprietary Red Wine	Napa	E	90
1994	Profile Proprietary Red Wine	Napa	E	92

Given the quality of Merryvale's wines, I am surprised this winery does not receive more attention. Their Profile Proprietary Red Wine ranks among the top three or four dozen red wines of northern California, and their Silhouette Chardonnay is a brilliant Burgundian-styled wine with extraordinary richness and complexity.

Among the red wines, the 1995 Merlot Reserve may turn out to be an outstanding wine with another 1–2 years of bottle age. The wine reveals a dense purple color and a tight but promising nose of melted chocolate, and jammy blackberry and cherry fruit. It hits the palate with good richness, an attractive spicy, cinnamon component, excellent equilibrium, and a long, lush, concentrated finish. It should drink well over the next 10–12 years. The opaque purple-colored 1995 Merlot Beckstoffer IV Vineyard (250 cases) reveals toasty new oak in the nose, as well as impressive richness, purity, and body, but it was closed and unevolved when I tasted it. My numerical rating may turn out to be somewhat stingy once this wine has a chance to open and expand. This is the type of wine that I wish could have been given 4–5 hours in a decanter to see what is behind its imposing structure. It will last for 12–15+ years.

Another impressive wine that needs time in the cellar is the 1995 Cabernet Sauvignon Reserve. It boasts a dense dark ruby/purple color, as well as a sweet, cedary, vanilla, and black currant–scented nose with hints of weedy tobacco and olives. Full-bodied and highly extracted, but tannic, this wine may merit an outstanding score after 5–6 years of bottle age. It will last for 20+ years.

The exceptional Profile *cuvées* should receive more attention from consumers. The dense plum/purple-colored 1996 Profile Proprietary Red Wine (a blend of Merryvale's finest lots of Cabernet Sauvignon, Merlot, and Cabernet Franc) boasts a persistent sweet, ripe blackberry, prune, and licorice-scented nose. With full body, an opulent texture, a chewy, fleshy personality, and adequate underlying acidity and tannin, it can be drunk now and over the next 12–15 years. The outstanding 1995 Profile (14.5% alcohol) is made from 50% Cabernet Sauvignon, 39% Merlot, and the balance Cabernet Franc. It needs 4–5 years of cellaring, so readers looking for Cabernet-based wines with immediate accessibility should be forewarned. The wine exhibits an opaque purple color, followed by copious amounts of toasty, smoky, high-quality new oak in the nose, along with equally impressive quantities of black currants, plums, and cherries. Deep and full-bodied, with high tannin but outstanding concentration, this is an impressively built, Bordeaux-like wine. Anticipated maturity: now–2020. Even better is the 1994 Profile (a blend of 60% Cabernet Sauvignon, 30% Merlot, and 10% Cabernet Franc). It possesses an opaque purple color, and seems to hit every sweet spot on the palate, offering loads of cassis, roasted herbs, toast, and licorice. This multilayered, rich, concentrated wine also reveals impeccable balance and elegance. There is restraint, power, and concentration—a rare combination in such a big wine. The 1994 is more accessible than the 1995, and thus can be drunk young or cellared for 15–20+ years.

Past Glories: 1993 Profile Proprietary Red Wine (90)

PETER MICHAEL WINERY (SONOMA)

1999	Chardonnay Belle Côte	Knights Valley	EE	90
1998	Chardonnay Belle Côte	Knights Valley	EE	95
1997	Chardonnay Belle Côte	Knights Valley	E	93
1999	Chardonnay La Carrière	Knights Valley	EE	91

1998	Chardonnay La Carrière	Knights Valley	EE	95
1997	Chardonnay La Carrière	Knights Valley	E	94
1999	Chardonnay Crête d'Or	Russian River	EE	93
1999	Chardonnay Cuvée Indigène	Sonoma	EE	93
1998	Chardonnay Cuvée Indigène	Sonoma	EE	96
1997	Chardonnay Cuvée Indigène	Sonoma	EE	95
1999	Chardonnay Mon Plaisir	Sonoma	EE	91
1998	Chardonnay Mon Plaisir	Sonoma	EE	95
1997	Chardonnay Mon Plaisir	Sonoma	EE	94
1999	Chardonnay Point Rouge	Sonoma	EE	94+
1998	Chardonnay Point Rouge	Sonoma	EE	(96–99)
1997	Chardonnay Point Rouge	Sonoma	EE	98
			(750 ml)	
1998	Les Pavots Proprietary	Knights Valley	EE	89+
1997	Les Pavots Proprietary	Knights Valley	EE	96+
1996	Les Pavots Proprietary	Knights Valley	EE	96
			(750 ml)	
1995	Les Pavots Proprietary	Knights Valley	EE	91
1994	Les Pavots Proprietary	Knights Valley	EE	94
1999	Pinot Noir Le Moulin Rouge	Santa Lucia Highlands	EE	92
1997	Pinot Noir Pisoni Ranch	Santa Lucia Highlands	EE	89
1999	Sauvignon Blanc l'Après Midi	Sonoma	E	90
1998	Sauvignon Blanc l'Après Midi	Sonoma	E	88
1997	Sauvignon Blanc l'Après Midi	Sonoma	E	88

As I have written many times in the past, this is one of the world's finest sources of Burgundy-inspired Chardonnay and Pinot Noir, as well as a Bordeaux-styled red, Les Pavots. And don't forget the Sauvignon Blanc called l'Après Midi. Some topflight wine-makers have walked through the doors of Peter Michael, including Helen Turley, Mark Aubert, and Vanessa Wong. The 1999s, from an even colder year than 1998, with an extremely late growing season, possess higher acids, but the small, concentrated crop appears to have compensated for the tendency of the wines to taste too tart. The following offerings continue Peter Michael's amazing progression of brilliant winemaking. Admirers of the crisp, delicious Sauvignon Blanc l'Après Midi will be disappointed that only 214 cases were produced in 1999. The low production was caused by an irregular flowering and poor crop set. This light- to medium-bodied, 100% Sauvignon Blanc reveals notes of grapefruit, melon, tangerine, and assorted citrus. An underlying minerality emerges as the wine sits in the glass. Elegant, with gorgeous levels of fruit as well as a nicely textured mouth-feel, it remains one of California's most nuanced Sauvignon Blancs. Seventy percent of this *cuvée* was fermented with indigenous yeast. Drink it over the next 1–2 years, although I suspect it will last longer.

The fourth vintage for this estate's Belle Côte Chardonnay, the 1999 was produced from three clones of Chardonnay (the Old Wente, Rued, and See). Most of the fermentation was by indigenous yeast, and the wine was aged in 53% new French oak prior to being bottled with neither fining nor filtration. It reveals gorgeous aromas and flavors of tropical fruits, lemon zest, pears, and minerals. This authoritatively rich, complex, elegant Chardonnay is medium-bodied, well delineated, and beautifully concentrated, with exotic floral and spice notes in addition to well-integrated oak. It should drink well for 4–5 years. The 1999 Chardonnay La Carrière emerges from estate vineyards planted at elevations of 1,600–1,800 feet, with a gradient of nearly 40%. This vineyard is planted with both the French Dijon and Californian Hyde clones. The 1999 La Carrière reveals more roasted hazelnut/stony characteristics along with abundant spice, buttered pears, and guava-like fruit. Produced from extremely low yields of 1.7 tons of fruit per acre, it possesses a creamier texture than the Belle Côte, exotic fruit on the mid-palate, and a ripe, rich finish with fine underlying acidity. It is a brilliant Chardonnay that should last for 4–5 years. One of the most flamboyant Peter Michael Chardonnays is their *cuvée* Mon Plaisir. Produced from the Old Wente clone grown in the Alexander Mountain Estate Vineyard owned by Jess Jackson, and aged totally in French oak (50% new), the 1999 Chardonnay Mon Plaisir reveals abundant tropical fruit characteristics in its ostentatious bouquet. Aromas of oranges, ripe honeyed apples, and buttered citrus jump from the glass of this hedonistically styled Chardonnay. The integration of wood provides subtle notes of vanilla and toast, which add to the wine's complex personality. Medium-to full-bodied, pure, long, and concentrated, with enough acidity to provide freshness and focus, it will drink well for 4–5 years. Consistently one of California's finest Chardonnays, the 100% indigenous yeast-fermented Chardonnay Cuvée Indigène also emerges from the Alexander Mountain Estate Vineyard. Typically, the 1999 exhibits distinctive aromas of smoky tropical fruit intermixed with peaches, apricots, and pears. Long, full-bodied, and layered, with terrific texture, gorgeous purity, and loads of fruit, this effort can stand up against the finest Burgundy grand crus (as could its siblings). The Cuvée Indigène possesses more leesy, smoky notes in its rich, concentrated style. It is a young, pure, super-concentrated Chardonnay to enjoy over the next 5–6 years (although it may last nearly a decade). The limited production Chardonnay Point Rouge represents a selection of the finest barrels. In most years, this is essentially the best barrels of Cuvée Indigène, picked for their extra intensity and complex style. This is routinely one of the three or four finest Chardonnays being produced in California, as well as one of the greatest of the world, as tastings against Burgundy's finest Bâtard-Montrachets, Chevalier-Montrachets, and Le Montrachets have consistently proven, much to the chagrin of Burgundians. The 1999 Chardonnay Point Rouge is more steely than previous vintages, as well as more closed and unevolved, but there is no doubting its immense potential. It boasts honeyed citrus, orange, tangerine, liquid mineral, and smoky hazelnut aromas. The liquid minerality evident in the Point Rouge is a prominent characteristic of the better wines from such grand cru Burgundy vineyards as Le Montrachet, Chevalier-Montrachet, and Meursault-Perrières. The finish lasts for more than 40 seconds. This wine is more backward than the other Peter Michael Chardonnays and should have a slow evolution. Anticipated maturity: now–2010. Exquisite!

After working with a Russian River grower for a number of years, overseeing the replanting of a vineyard, the grower sold one crop to Peter Michael, and then signed a long-term contract with another winery. Consequently, the 1999 is the only Chardonnay made by Peter Michael from that vineyard. They have named it Crête d'Or. Made from the Hyde clone, the brilliant 1999 Chardonnay Crête d'Or is a creamy-textured, flamboyant, ostentatiously styled Chardonnay with aromas and flavors of roasted hazelnuts, dried apricots, peaches, and pineapples. A rich, full-bodied effort with good underlying acidity as well as a judicious touch of toasty oak, it should drink well for 5–6 years.

This is one of the world's great sources for Burgundy-styled Chardonnays, and the 1998s are spectacular. All of the following wines are fermented both with commercial and indigenous yeasts, given extensive lees stirring (which promotes complexity and additional textural nuances), and are bottled unfiltered. The 600 cases of 1998 Chardonnay La Carrière, like all these Chardonnays, tip the scales at a hefty 14.1% alcohol. Made from a vineyard planted on a steep, rocky hillside, it exhibits aromas of white peaches, honey, pears, subtle new oak, and citrus. Full-bodied and complex, with good underlying acidity, this wine is reminiscent of a Burgundian Corton-Charlemagne. It should drink well for 5–6 years. The 1998 Chardonnay Belle Côte (1,300 cases) is the finest yet produced from this vineyard situated on the hillsides above La Carrière. Fortunately, the larger production should guarantee some availability. Made from a vineyard planted with the Wente Chardonnay clone, this mouth-filling, full-bodied, impressively pure wine offers a full-throttle bouquet of roasted hazelnuts, honeyed tropical fruits, and exotic passion fruit/mango notes. Rich and full-bodied, with fine underlying acidity, this dazzling Chardonnay is already drinking well, yet promises to last for 5–7 years. There are 1,200 cases of the light gold-colored 1998 Chardonnay Mon Plaisir. This full-bodied, honeyed, heady, powerful, densely concentrated effort includes flamboyant apricot/peach notes in addition to outstanding concentration and more depth and persistence than the superb 1997. It should drink well for 5–6 years. There are 470 cases of the 1998 Chardonnay Cuvée Indigène. The only wine to be completely fermented with 100% indigenous yeast, this Chardonnay is more restrained aromatically than its siblings, but it is terrific on the palate, displaying explosive lemon/butter/honey flavors mixed with tropical fruit, mineral, and smoky, leesy components. Orange/tangerine notes also make an appearance. The aromatics should develop greater dimensions with another 6–12 months of bottle age.

The only 1998 not yet bottled is the Point Rouge. The light gold-colored 1998 Chardonnay Point Rouge displays an emerging nose of honeyed tropical fruits and citrus. It possesses exquisite concentration, admirable singularity, full body, and terrific purity and delineation. Only marginally riper than the other Peter Michael offerings, it tastes longer in the mouth. This 1998 is a candidate for a perfect score. The 1997 Chardonnay Point Rouge (140 cases) exhibits a terrific texture and a sensational buttery, leesy nose with subtle toasty oak. Passion fruit, oranges, and honeyed lemons compete with minerals in this exceptionally rich, concentrated Chardonnay. A spectacular, full-throttle effort with impeccable balance, it should drink well for 4–5+ years.

There are 3,000 cases of the exquisite 1997 Chardonnay Belle Côte, which is made primarily from such old California Chardonnay clones as Wente, fermented with indigenous yeasts, aged in French barrels (50% new), and bottled unfiltered. The light straw/gold color is followed by sumptuous leesy, toasty, and honeyed pineapple scents with a touch of mineral. The wine is medium- to full-bodied, with exquisite texture, a sexy, rich aftertaste, and superb purity—a hallmark of every Peter Michael wine. The light gold-colored 1997 Chardonnay La Carrière (only 125 cases produced) comes from a hillside situated below the Belle Côte Vineyard. It is planted with Dijon Burgundy Chardonnay clones, in addition to the Hyde clone. Aged in 30% new oak, this offering reveals a distinctive mineral character not dissimilar from certain Corton-Charlemagnes. Liquid stone-like flavors are pronounced in the mouth, in addition to citrus and subtle oak notes. This distinctive, high-toned, *terroir*-driven, concentrated wine is more subtle than some of Peter Michael's efforts. It should drink well for 3–4 years. The dazzling 1997 Chardonnay Mon Plaisir (1,200 cases) displays a light to medium straw color and expressive aromatics consisting of tangerine/orange and other tropical fruits. In the mouth, notes of lemon butter make an appearance in this full-bodied, expansive, rich, fleshy Chardonnay that tips the scales at 14.1% alcohol. With fabulous fruit, the Mon Plaisir appears to be the qualitative equal of the more expensive Cuvée Indigène and Point Rouge. It should drink well for 3–4 years. The 1997 Chardonnay Cuvée Indigène (named so because it is fermented completely with indigenous vineyard yeasts) exhibits a light gold color, and a complex nose of smoky, leesy Chardonnay fruit intermixed with smoky, roasted hazelnuts, orange blossoms, and citrus. Full-bodied, with excellent underlying acidity, and more minerality to its flavors than Mon Plaisir, this profoundly concentrated, complex Chardonnay is a prodigious offering. Production was 550 cases, with the alcohol a boisterous 14.1%. Look for this wine to drink well for 5–7 years.

The other white wine from Peter Michael is their delicious, vibrant, fragrant Sauvignon Blanc l'Après Midi. In 1998, the source for this fruit changed from the Liparita Vineyard on Howell Mountain to Peter Michael's own estate vineyards. In 1998, there were 480 cases of this powerful (14.1% alcohol) 100% Sauvignon Blanc made from the Musqué clone. The 1998 Sauvignon Blanc l'Après Midi offers honeyed grapefruit, passion fruit, and lemon zest in its aromatic profile. Tart acidity provides good tanginess, and the wine's medium-bodied, fresh, lively personality is enthralling. It will be very flexible with food. The light straw-colored 1997 Sauvignon Blanc l'Après Midi possesses terrific acidity (much more than usual), as well as wonderfully intense, mineral-laden, melony, citrusy fruit. Crisp and medium-bodied, it is ideal for current consumption.

The finest Pinot Noir yet produced by Peter Michael is the 1999 Pinot Noir Le Moulin Rouge. This wine is made from the well-known Pisoni Vineyard in the Santa Lucia Highlands (a source of high-quality grapes sold to a half-dozen or more wineries). According to the grower, the clone was smuggled into this country from one of the two most famous vineyards in Vosne-Romanée. The dense ruby/purple-colored 1999 Le Moulin Rouge offers up a sweet nose of blackberries, pomegranate, vanilla, and Chinese black tea. Gorgeous fruit is found in this full-bodied, concentrated, expansive, potentially profound Pinot. The wood adds nice spice and smoke. Look for this Pinot Noir to drink well in 1–2 years, and last for a decade. Peter Michael's dark ruby-colored 1997 Pinot Noir Pisoni Ranch reveals purple nuances, as well as the telltale black raspberry and cassis notes with spicy oak in the background. Medium- to full-bodied and expansive, with excellent purity, and a lush, seductive palate, this heady (14.1% alcohol) wine should be consumed over the next 5–6 years.

Peter Michael's Les Pavots continue to go from strength to strength, with the 1997 Les Pavots the finest yet produced. This wine originates from a hillside vineyard overlooking the Knights Valley that has 23 acres planted with Bordeaux varietals. The 1997 blend consists of 79% Cabernet Sauvignon, 12% Merlot, and 9% Cabernet Franc. The wine was aged in French oak (50% new) and bottled without filtration. Fortunately, there are 4,351 cases, as well as 330 cases of magnums. A blue/black/purple color is followed by an extraordinary bouquet of toast, blackberries, crème de cassis, licorice, and cedar. Full-bodied, with silky tannin, low acidity, and layers of concentrated, pure black fruits judiciously wrapped in subtle toasty oak, this wine can be drunk early, but promises to hit its peak in 5–7 years, and last for two or more decades. The 1998 Les Pavots (80% Cabernet Sauvignon, 11% Merlot, and 9% Cabernet Franc) was produced from minuscule yields of 1.3 tons of fruit per acre. It exhibits a dense ruby/purple color in addition to aromas of melted fudge, cocoa, tobacco, and black currant fruit. In the mouth, the wine is medium- to full-bodied, with firm tannin, and a compressed, moderately long finish. Not surprisingly, it does not exhibit either the flavor dimension or length of the 1997 or 1996. 1998 was a more difficult vintage, but Les Pavots has turned out well, revealing more of a Bordeaux-like weight profile than the more enormously endowed, concentrated 1997. Nevertheless, it is a successful effort in a challenging year. Anticipated maturity: 2003–2014.

The powerhouse, opaque purple/blue-colored 1996 Les Pavots is a blend of 74% Cabernet Sauvignon, 20% Merlot, and 6% Cabernet Franc. The nose offers up blackberry, licorice, cassis, and toast aromas. The superb extract, well-defined personality, and smoky, licorice, Asian spice, and blackberry flavors provide a thrilling tasting experience. Like its 1997 sibling, it was bottled with neither fining nor filtration. There are approximately 2,800 cases of this fabulous effort. Anticipated maturity: now–2025. The black/ruby/purple-colored 1995 Les Pavots (a 73% Cabernet Sauvignon, 14% Merlot, and 13% Cabernet Franc blend), which achieved 13.9% alcohol naturally, reveals a sweet, tobacco, lavender, and cassis-scented nose, medium-bodied, tannic, elegant flavors, outstanding purity, ripeness, and length, yet a measured, restrained style. Less forthcoming than either the 1996 or 1994, this rich, nicely proportioned proprietary red is California's answer to a graceful Médoc. Anticipated maturity: now–2020. Since the bottling of the superb 1994 Les Pavots, this deep, saturated purple-colored wine has taken on a gorgeous nose of cassis intermixed with violets, licorice, and attractive spicy oak. Sweet, rich, and surprisingly showy for a Les Pavots, this medium- to full-bodied wine possesses a luscious, multilayered texture, outstanding depth, and attractively integrated tannin and acidity. When I tasted it, it was more evolved and delicious than I had anticipated given its recent bottling.

All of Peter Michael's top wines, including the Chardonnays, are bottled without filtration. Readers should make it a point to visit this winery situated in Knights Valley, not far from the

Napa/Sonoma county line. The quality is extraordinary, and the commitment and talent of the winery staff laudatory. Moreover, the winery strives to achieve even greater quality.
Past Glories: 1993 Les Pavots Proprietary Red Wine (92)

ROBERT MONDAVI (NAPA)

1999	Boomerang	Napa	C	(88–90)
1997	Cabernet Sauvignon	Napa	D	90
1996	Cabernet Sauvignon	Napa	D	88
1995	Cabernet Sauvignon	Napa	C	89
1994	Cabernet Sauvignon	Napa	C	88
1998	Cabernet Sauvignon	Oakville	E	88
1997	Cabernet Sauvignon	Oakville	D	91
1996	Cabernet Sauvignon	Oakville District	D	92
1995	Cabernet Sauvignon	Oakville District	D	91
1994	Cabernet Sauvignon	Oakville District	D	90
1997	Cabernet Sauvignon	Stags Leap	D	91
1996	Cabernet Sauvignon	Stags Leap	D	88
1995	Cabernet Sauvignon	Stags Leap	D	89
1999	Cabernet Sauvignon Marjorie's Sunrise	Oakville	E	(86–88)
1999	Cabernet Sauvignon Marjorie's Twilight	Oakville	E	(90–92)
1998	Cabernet Sauvignon Marjorie's Vineyard	Napa	E	(86–88)
1998	Cabernet Sauvignon Old Vine	Napa	E	89
1999	Cabernet Sauvignon Reserve	Napa	EEE	88
1998	Cabernet Sauvignon Reserve	Napa	EEE	87
1997	Cabernet Sauvignon Reserve	Napa	EEE	92
1996	Cabernet Sauvignon Reserve	Napa	EE	92
1995	Cabernet Sauvignon Reserve	Napa	EE	93
1994	Cabernet Sauvignon Reserve	Napa	EE	98
1996	Cabernet Sauvignon 30th Anniversary Reserve	Napa	EE	95
1999	Cabernet Sauvignon To-Kalon	Napa	EEE	90
1998	Cabernet Sauvignon To-Kalon Reserve	Napa	EEE	89
1997	Cabernet Sauvignon To-Kalon Reserve	Napa	EEE	94+
1999	Fumé Blanc I Block	Napa	E	90
1997	Merlot	Carneros	D	88
1996	Merlot	Carneros	D	87
1997	Merlot	Napa	C	88
1996	Merlot	Napa	C	88
1997	Pinot Noir	Napa	C	90
1997	Pinot Noir	Carneros	D	90
1998	Pinot Noir Huichica Hills	Carneros	E	90
1997	Pinot Noir Reserve	Napa	D	92
1996	Pinot Noir Reserve	Napa	D	89

In 22 years, I have never been more distressed as well as perplexed by evaluations of a particular winery than those that follow. No one in the United States has done more to promote the image of fine wine than Robert Mondavi and his family. They have had a profound, positive impact on American culture, and we all have benefitted from it. While it is not too late, I am still hopeful that some president of the United States will give Robert Mondavi our highest civilian honor for what he has accomplished. That being said, Tim Mondavi, who has made many great wines in his winemaking career, is on an almost obsessive mission to produce wines that are "bright, fresh, with a cleansing quality." His use of the word "nerve" and expressions such as "clarity of focus" are to justify what appears to be increasingly light and, to my way of thinking, less interesting wines that err on the side of intellectual vapidness over the pursuit of wines of heart, soul, and pleasure. I believe he is going against what Mother Nature has given California, the ability to produce wines of exceptional ripeness and gorgeously pure, intense flavors. Once past some alluring aromatics, many 1998s and 1999s were, in essence, collectively superficial, with tart, almost stripped-out personalities with little textural interest and short, clipped finishes. Obviously, some of the Cabernet Sauvignons are less at fault than the Sauvignon Blancs, Chardonnays, Pinot Noirs, Merlots, and Zinfandels. Yet the trend toward Euro-styled delicacy started in small increments four or five years ago. Tim Mondavi has produced many profound Cabernet Sauvignons. The pursuit of elegance and finesse is certainly a laudable goal, but many other wineries seem to be accomplishing it without compromising the hedonistic richness and multilayered textures that California can achieve as easily as any viticultural region in the world, assuming yields are kept low and ripe fruit is harvested. Thankfully, barrel samples of the 2000s revealed much greater ripeness and texture than the 1998s and 1999s, so perhaps I'm overreacting.

All the white wines, both Sauvignons and Chardonnays, are given partial malolactic fermentation in order to preserve their vibrant natural acidity. Of course, the Mondavis promote the fact that they are bottled unfiltered, and that is true. However, several former wine-makers have told me they centrifuge many of their whites, and while that is technically not filtration, it is a relatively traumatic process where solids are removed from the wine under extreme force. I will leave it at that, but here are my notes on the best of the 1999s, which all have extremely tart, light-bodied personalities with very little textural pleasure. Of course, 1999 was a very cool year, and the Fumé Blancs largely received no malolactic fermentation, but some received various portions of barrel fermentation. Mondavi's 1999 Fumé Blanc from their famed I Block is 100% barrel-fermented with about 20% new oak. This is a light- to medium-bodied effort with more intense aromatics of lemon zest, grapefruit, mineral, and a touch of honeysuckle. In the mouth, there are several layers of flavor before it takes on the Mondavi signature of light body and an attenuated finish, with mostly acidity and alcohol.

A wine with an interesting bouquet and flavors is the 1999 Boomerang, a blend of 68% Syrah, 26% Cabernet Sauvignon, and 6% Cabernet Franc. The potentially outstanding 1999 Boomerang is full-bodied, with copious quantities of blackberry fruit, adequate acidity, an opulent texture, and clean black cherry and blackberry, peppery flavors that linger in the mouth. Drink it over the next 5–8 years.

The Cabernet Sauvignons, particularly the Napa bottlings, also seem texturally deficient. With clipped, tough finishes, they are relatively weak efforts—at least if pleasure is your goal. The wines that did perform well include the special single-vineyard offerings, as well as the Reserves. There are two *cuvées* of their Oakville, called Marjorie's Sunrise and Marjorie's Twilight. The 1999 Cabernet Sauvignon Marjorie's Sunrise shows a medium/dark ruby color and an elegant, sweet nose of graphite, black currants, and vanilla. The wine has aggressive tannin in the finish and less intrusive, vibrant acidity. This is a medium-bodied, claret-styled Cabernet to drink over the next 10–15 years. Sweeter, riper, richer, and more elegant is the 1999 Cabernet Sauvignon Marjorie's Twilight. It exhibits a saturated ruby/purple color, in addition to pure cassis fruit intermixed with minerals and toasty oak. The wine is riper, yet restrained. It is made from 35–40-year-old Cabernet vines and should turn out to be outstanding. Anticipated maturity: 2003–2020. Readers looking for a St.-Emilion from Oakville might check out the 1998 Cabernet Sauvignon Oakville. Soft herbal notes intermixed with cherries and earth emerge from this garnet/plum-colored wine. It is medium-bodied, round, and best drunk over the next decade. This is a harmonious, complex effort that would be more comfortable in a Bordeaux tasting.

As for the flagship wines, the 1998 Cabernet Sauvignon Reserve is more evolved, a characteristic of this vintage. A plum/ruby color is followed by aromas of toasty oak, tobacco, black currants, smoke, and spice box. In the mouth, it is medium-bodied, with excellent fruit on the attack, some real charm and roundness, but the finish is filled with astringent tannin. If this wine continues to hold its fruit, it is going to be a Bordeaux-styled, medium-weight Cabernet Sauvignon to drink over the next 12–14 years. However, the tannin will need to be monitored because this particular wine could possibly dry out. The 1999 Cabernet Sauvignon Reserve has a deeper ruby/purple color, notes of black currants, minerals, and toasty oak, and an elegant, restrained, aromatic profile. In the mouth, there is high tannin, medium body, and excellent concentration. There are approximately 1,000 cases of Cabernet Sauvignon from the famed Oakville vineyard called To-Kalon. The 1998 Cabernet Sauvignon To-Kalon (virtually 100% Cabernet Sauvignon) displays a dense ruby/purple color, as well as a sweet nose of black currants intermixed with cedar, licorice, toast, and earth. It has lost much of the fat it exhibited last year, and no longer seems as impressive as it once did. A wine of finesse and elegance, it offers much more pleasure than many 1998s. Drink it over the next 14–15 years. As for the 1999 Cabernet Sauvignon To-Kalon Vineyard, this is 100% Cabernet Sauvignon, as opposed to the 1998, which was 97% Cabernet Sauvignon, 2% Cabernet Franc, and 1% Petit Verdot. This wine boasts an excellent texture, although the finish is austere. Sweet black currant and blackberry fruit are wrapped with subtle oak and a weedy, tobacco herbaceousness. It is deep, dense, full-bodied, and impressively textured as well as concentrated. However, the high tannin profile suggests it should be cellared for 4–5 years; it will last 20–25 years.

Mondavi's Pinot Noir vineyards produced approximately 1.5 tons of fruit per acre in 1998. All were fermented with indigenous yeasts and were bottled without filtration. A new offering in the Mondavi portfolio is the 1998 Pinot Noir Huichica Hills, which is reminiscent of a premier cru from the Côte de Beaune. Sweet black cherry, spice, smoke, mineral, and floral aromas give this dark ruby-colored, medium-bodied Pinot plenty of appeal. It is pure as well as exceptionally well delineated and elegant. Drink it over the next 7–8 years.

At Mondavi, no varietal has been studied as intensely as Pinot Noir. Farming has moved toward organic, and the wines are being made as naturally as possible. Mondavi's 1997 Pinot Noirs, which are the finest they have yet produced, are indicative of such qualitative efforts. Much of the new production of California North Coast Pinot Noir is emerging from Dijon plant material (i.e., clones such as #667, #777, and #115). Robert Mondavi also utilizes such old California clones (which were brought from Burgundy years ago) as Calera and Swan. Readers looking for an easy to find, gorgeous Pinot Noir need search no further than Mondavi's 1997 Pinot Noir Napa. A remarkable 33,000 cases were produced, mostly from their Carneros vineyard. An outstanding example, it exhibits a deep ruby color, in addition to superb aromatics of black cherry fruit intertwined with spicy oak, loamy soil scents, and forest aromas. A beautifully textured, medium- to full-bodied palate is soft, pure, and bursting with black cherry fruit. The alcohol is a lofty 13.8%, which gives the wine plenty of glycerin and flesh. This Pinot should drink easily for 4–5 years. The denser, dark ruby-colored 1997 Pinot Noir Carneros reveals more noticeable new oak in the aromatics, as well as high-strung cherry/raspberry aromas and a creamy texture. The fruit is beautifully pure in this medium-bodied, elegant, vibrant wine. It is a more finesse-styled Pinot, and perhaps less obvious than the crowd-pleasing Napa Valley bottling. Like its siblings, the 1997 Pinot Noir Reserve (which sees 70% new oak) is bottled with neither fining nor filtration. It boasts the deepest ruby/purple color, a terrific texture, and copious quantities of sweet cherry/kirsch fruit intermixed with cassis and raspberries. While the oak is noticeable, the wine's greater concentration, body, and power have soaked most of it up. This is an opulently textured Pinot with superb potential. It should be at its best after another 1–2 years of cellaring, and will keep for a decade. Bravo to the Mondavi winery for these efforts. The 1996 Pinot Noir Napa Reserve displays a dark plum color and moderately intense, herbaceous, animal, black plum, and cherry aromas. Restrained but rich, with crisp acidity and clean winemaking, this medium-bodied, tightly knit Pinot will benefit from another 1–2 years of bottle age and last for 4–8 years.

Robert Mondavi has joined the Merlot sweepstakes, producing some excellent wines, but not yet hitting the bull's-eye with this varietal. As Tim Mondavi says, "What is Merlot?" The problem may be that California has fewer clones to choose from, and there is a tendency to give this wine less attention because it seems to be such an easy sell in spite of the ocean of insipid Merlots that inhabit the marketplace. Mondavi's efforts are unquestionably fine, and come close to being outstanding. The excellent, nearly outstanding 1997 Merlot Napa exhibits copious quantities of berry fruit, a touch of mocha, firm tannin, and a medium-bodied, crunchy, deliciously fruity, soft mid-palate and finish. It should drink well for 10–12 years. Even more delectable is the 1997 Merlot Carneros. This dark ruby/purple-colored wine displays espresso bean, mocha, berry fruit flavors in addition to an attractive, multilayered, broad mid-palate and finish. A blend of 94% Merlot, 4% Malbec, and 2% Cabernet Sauvignon, it possesses the seamless texture and sweetness characteristic of this vintage. It should drink well for 10–12 years, if not longer. The 1996 Merlot Napa exhibits a dark ruby/purple color, as well as berry aromas and flavors intermixed with loamy soil, coffee bean, and spicy oak notes. The wine is medium-bodied, with good richness, yet it has a slightly monolithic personality. A very good effort, it should evolve nicely over the next 7–8 years. The 1996 Merlot Carneros is a better effort. There is more clay in Mondavi's Carneros vineyard. This example reveals a deeper, more saturated ruby/purple color, in addition to a more intriguing fragrance of black cherry jam intermixed with loamy soil and new-oak scents. Beautifully rendered in the mouth, with medium body, excellent intensity, and well-integrated tannin and acidity, this impressively endowed Merlot comes close to meriting an outstanding evaluation. It should drink well for a decade or more.

The 1998 Cabernet Sauvignon To-Kalon Reserve exhibits more blackberry characteristics, along with cassis, licorice, and toasty new oak. Medium- to full-bodied, with excellent purity, outstanding concentration, and a surprisingly long finish, this blend of 97% Cabernet Sauvignon, 2% Cabernet Franc, and 1% Petit Verdot is one of the vintage's most impressive efforts. Anticipated maturity: now–2018. The lighter-styled 1998 Cabernet Sauvignon Marjorie's Vineyard aims for flavor and finesse, but it appears to falter slightly because of the winery's stylistic predilection for restraint and politeness. It was out of place alongside the sweeter, richer, more concentrated To-Kalon Reserve, Napa Reserve, and the 1998 Cabernet Sauvignon Old Vine. The latter wine is a seamless, velvety-textured, opulently rich 1998 with gorgeous black fruits, well-integrated oak, acidity, and tannin, and plenty of glycerin and follow-through on the palate. Another 1998 that will be uncommonly delicious when released, look for it to last for 15 or more years.

The five 1997 Cabernet Sauvignons range from outstanding to exhilarating. The 1997 Cabernet Sauvignon Napa is one of the finest regular Cabernet Sauvignons Mondavi has produced. A blend of 89% Cabernet Sauvignon, 7% Merlot, 3% Cabernet Franc, and 1% Syrah (13.9% alcohol), this dark ruby-colored wine with purple nuances has sweet black currant flavors mixed with spice box, licorice, and toast notes. Fleshy and open-knit, it should drink well for 10–14 years. The more powerful (14.1% alcohol), superb 1997 Cabernet Sauvignon Oakville (84% Cabernet Sauvignon, 9% Merlot, and 7% Cabernet Franc) exhibits a complex, Pauillac-like nose of cedar, fruitcake, black currants, and spicy new oak. There is medium to full body, well-integrated sweet tannin and acidity, an opulent texture, and a layered, long finish. Anticipated maturity: now–2025. Completely different, the Château Margaux–inspired 1997 Cabernet Sauvignon Stags Leap District exhibits a dark ruby/purple color as well as a knockout nose of black raspberries, currants, and floral scents. Exotic and open-knit, without the sheer force of the Oakville *cuvée*, with gloriously sweet fruit and impeccable harmony, this terrific 100% Cabernet Sauvignon will benefit from 2–3 years of cellaring, and last for 15–20 years. Very impressive!

The profound 1997 Cabernet Sauvignon Reserve boasts a saturated ruby/purple color. Production (about 20,000 cases) of this sweet, opulently textured, rich, full-bodied wine should guarantee widespread availability. Aged in 100% new French oak, this blend of 91% Cabernet Sauvignon, 8% Cabernet Franc, and 1% Petit Verdot offers a textbook varietal nose of cedar wood, licorice, crème de cassis, and toast. Full-bodied, with explosive sweetness and fruit on the attack, this gloriously pure, superbly well-delineated wine should be drinkable young and last for three decades. Anticipated maturity: now–2025. One of the most extraordinary Cabernet Sauvignons Robert Mondavi has produced is the 1,000 case production of the 1997 Cabernet Sauvignon To-Kalon Reserve. Made from 100% Cabernet Sauvignon, aromas of cedar, licorice, new saddle leather, walnuts, and cassis tumble from the glass. The wine boasts fabulous richness, a silky, sumptuous texture, a deep, chewy mid-palate, and an admirably pure, multilayered finish that exceeds 45 seconds. It will require 3–5 years of cellaring, and will keep for three decades or more. It is a prodigious Cabernet Sauvignon.

The 1996 Cabernet Sauvignon Napa is an elegant, medium-bodied example with more tannin than most regular bottlings (a characteristic of the vintage). This structured wine offers weedy black currant fruit, subtle oak, and a well-built, concentrated finish. About 8% Cabernet Franc was added to the blend. The 1996 is approachable, but it promises to be even better with several more years of bottle age, and will last 12–15+ years. The 1996 Cabernet Sauvignon Stags Leap possesses the crisp, restrained, lighter-bodied style of wines from that region. Sweet black cherries intermixed with floral scents are present in the wine's aromatics. In the mouth, tar and floral characteristics combine with black fruit to give this Cabernet an enthralling, supple, approachable style. There is some tannin in the finish, and the wine is more austere than the Napa bottling, but it should drink well for 12–15 years. The outstanding 1996 Cabernet Sauvignon Oakville offers an opaque purple color and knockout aromas of crème de cassis, vanilla, and weedy tobacco. Full-bodied, rich, and muscular, as well as complex, this fleshy, deep wine is immensely impressive. As it sits in the glass, blueberry/blackberry aromas emerge, adding to its overall appeal. Anticipated maturity: now–2020. The 1996 Cabernet Sauvignon Reserve may be no better than the Oakville, but it is made in a slightly different style. The color is opaque purple, and the wine reveals more vanilla, a touch of mint, and plenty of black currant fruit in its moderately intense aromatics. Some of the vintage's dry tannin (from this year's stressed vineyard conditions) are present in the wine's finish. A more stylish, restrained, less exuberant example than the 1996 Oakville, it is an outstanding offering that should be consumed between now–2025. None of the above 1996 Cabernet Sauvignons matches the majesty, richness, and breadth of the 1996 Cabernet Sauvignon 30th Anniversary Reserve. This special bottling (about 1,000 cases) is a fabulous wine. From its opaque purple color and stunning aromatics of blackberries, cassis, toast, licorice, and Asian spices to its full-bodied, concentrated, superbly extracted style, this wine possesses virtually everything. Layers of fruit, glycerin, extract, and sweet tannin are presented in a flamboyant format. The tannin level is high, but so is the wine's richness and length. It is a sensational effort. Anticipated maturity: 2005–2030.

In 1995, Mondavi added a number of new regionally labeled Cabernet Sauvignons to their portfolio. In addition to their Oakville *cuvée*, they have a Stags Leap District Cabernet and a single-vineyard wine from their famed To-Kalon plantation. The 1995 Cabernet Sauvignon Napa is a beautifully made wine that comes close to being outstanding. It boasts a textbook cassis and eucalyptus-scented nose with oak in the background. On the palate, the wine is medium- to full-bodied, with excellent ripeness, clean fruit, and a long, spicy finish. It avoids some of the vintage's hard tannins. The debut release of the 1995 Cabernet Sauvignon Stags Leap District is an uncommonly elegant, Margaux-styled wine with medium body, and sweet black currants in the nose with a notion of toasty oak. Good acidity and a soft underbelly make for a pleasant, seductive wine that should drink well young, but keep for 15 years. In 1995, the Cabernet Sauvignon Oakville District is again outstanding. The wine reveals text-book cedar, cassis, and toast notes in the nose, terrific fruit intensity and purity, medium to full body, and excellent harmony among its elements. This has resulted in an authoritatively flavored yet graceful Cabernet Sauvignon that will benefit from 2–5 years of cellaring, and keep for two decades. The 1995 Cabernet Sauvignon Reserve is slightly less impressive than when I tasted it last year, although still an outstanding wine. I may have caught it at a closed stage following bottling. There are 15,000–20,000 cases of Reserve Cabernet made, and in 1995, a quintessentially elegant style has been produced. The wine is less weighty than the 1994, 1991, or 1990. It has great promise and raw materials, with superb fruit and richness, medium body, and subtle lead pencil notes to go along with black currant, mineral, and toast scents and flavors. Based on this tasting, I would lower my overall rating, but it is still an ex-ceptional California Cabernet Sauvignon made in a compellingly elegant, graceful style. An-ticipated maturity: now–2018.

1994 was unquestionably a great vintage for North Coast Cabernet Sauvignon, standing above 1990, 1991, 1992, and 1993—all outstanding vintages with no shortage of heroic per-formances. Remarkably, 1995 may turn out to be as profound as 1994, giving California its two greatest back-to-back vintages of Cabernet Sauvignon . . . ever! The quality of the 1994 vintage is well displayed at Mondavi. The 1994 Cabernet Sauvignon Napa (about 80,000 cases produced) is one of the finest regular Cabernets Mondavi has made. It exhibits a deep ruby color and sweet, rich, black currant aromas intertwined with scents of vanilla and spice. Soft, round, medium- to full-bodied, and harmonious, the wine is accessible, yet capable of lasting for 10–15 years. The youthful 1994 Cabernet Sauvignon Oakville District (6,900 cases) could be mistaken for a Mondavi Reserve Cabernet. The color is a saturated ruby/purple, and the nose offers up attractive, complex scents of lead pencil, vanilla, toast, and ripe cassis fruit. Dense, rich, and medium- to full-bodied, with moderate tannin, this young, impressively endowed Cabernet Sauvignon should be at its best between now–2010.

I have drunk some memorable Reserve Cabernet Sauvignons from Robert Mondavi, in-cluding the gloriously fragrant, elegant 1971, the powerful, dense 1974, the seductive 1978, the mammothly endowed, tannic blockbuster 1987, the silky, opulent, super-concentrated 1990, and the compellingly rich, layered 1991. However, if I were to select the Reserve Cabernet Sauvignon that may turn out to be the greatest Mondavi has yet made, the 1994 might edge out the 1991 and 1987. It may not appear to be the case, but I am often at a loss for words when it comes to writing about truly profound wines. They seem to have their own stature, presence, and character that transcend the significance of mere words. That being said, Mondavi's 1994 Cabernet Sauvignon Reserve is an exquisite wine, as well as a Caber-net that may turn out to be one of the "wines of the vintage." The deep opaque purple color, and tightly wound nose and flavors still reveal enough profound aromas and flavors to mark this as one of Mondavi's most sensational efforts. The nose possesses a Margaux/Mouton-like cassis, lead pencil, floral aroma, backed up by copious quantities of black currant fruit. In the mouth, my notes said, "great stuff." The wine is full-bodied, layered, multidimensional, and astonishingly well balanced, with an inner depth and core of exceptional richness and intensity. All of this has been accomplished without any notion of obtrusive weight, tannin, or alcohol. The finish lasts for 35+ seconds. Because of its luxurious quantity of fruit, this wine will be accessible young, thus much of it will be drunk long before it ever reaches full maturity. However, for those able to buy more than a bottle or two, and who possess the discipline to wait 10–15 years, this wine should prove to be a formidable California Cabernet with a rare complexity, elegance, and richness. It should be at its best between now–2025.

Past Glories: Cabernet Sauvignon Reserve—1993 (91), 1992 (90), 1991 (96), 1990 (93), 1987 (95), 1978 (90), 1971 (94)

CHÂTEAU MONTELENA (NAPA)

1999 Cabernet Sauvignon Calistoga Cuvée	Napa	D	(87–88)
1998 Cabernet Sauvignon Calistoga Cuvée	Napa	D	89
1997 Cabernet Sauvignon Calistoga Cuvée	Napa	E	(87–88)
1999 Cabernet Sauvignon Estate	Napa	EE	(96–98)
1998 Cabernet Sauvignon Estate	Napa	EE	93
1997 Cabernet Sauvignon Estate	Napa	EE	98
1996 Cabernet Sauvignon Estate	Napa	EE	93+
1995 Cabernet Sauvignon Estate	Napa	EE	94
1994 Cabernet Sauvignon Estate	Napa	EE	95
1999 Chardonnay	Napa	D	90
1997 Merlot Estate	Napa	D	88
1999 Riesling Potter Valley	Napa	C	89
1997 St. Vincent (Zinfandel/Primitivo/Sangiovese)	Napa	C	89
1994 Zinfandel Estate	Napa	C	89

There is always something reassuring about visiting Château Montelena. Over the past two decades, wine-maker/owner Bo Barrett and his father, Jim, have never wavered from their goals of producing some of California's finest, longest-lived Cabernet Sauvignon as well as a non-malolactic, flavorful Chardonnay that is high on character and fruit. Château Montelena is also successful with other varietals. For example, one of their best-kept secrets (only sold at the winery) is the excellent Riesling produced from Potter Valley. The 1999 Riesling Potter Valley (13% alcohol) is a dry, Alsatian-styled effort with a touch of honeyed botrytis in the pineapple, orange, and buttery apple-like flavors. Fresh and lively, it will drink brilliantly with an assortment of cuisines. About 10% of Montelena's Chardonnays are now put through malolactic, and, even more revolutionary, about 10% is now being barrel-fermented in new oak. The wine spends six months in neutral, old barrels prior to bottling. While reserved and tight when compared to some of California's more flamboyant Chardonnays, it does merit considerable interest. A virgin expression of Chardonnay, with abundant quantities of crisp, green apple, tangerine, and pear fruit, this wine reveals good acidity, an elegant yet full-bodied personality, surprising depth, and a reserved, austere palate. The 1999 Chardonnay is one of the finest Montelena has made over recent years. Perhaps the introduction of some malolactic as well as barrel fermentation has given the wine more mid-palate and texture, without compromising Montelena's style. The 1999 possesses abundant quantities of lemon, pear, and apple notes, zesty, full-bodied flavors as well as crisp, nicely integrated acidity, 13.8% alcohol, admirable concentration, and more richness and density than the 1998. It should last for 5–6 years.

I do not know of any other California winery that has put together such a blend as Montelena's St. Vincent. This used to be a wine produced to utilize some of their Sangiovese. However, like many wineries, Montelena feels (as do I) that California Sangiovese is generally a failure and cannot compete with Italian Sangiovese. The 1997 St. Vincent (3,000 cases) is an intriguing blend of 60% Zinfandel, 30% Primitivo, and 10% Sangiovese. It reveals a distinctively Italian personality with notes of melted asphalt, new saddle leather, berry fruit, pepper, and spice. With a fat, robust, hearty personality, as well as character and soul, it is meant to be consumed during its first 3–5 years of life.

Quietly and competently (mirroring the proprietors' personalities), Château Montelena's Cabernet Sauvignon Calistoga Cuvée gets better and better. More estate fruit is being added to this blend in order to bulk it up. The 1998 Cabernet Sauvignon Calistoga Cuvée (13.9% alcohol) is better than the 1997, even though I suspect the raw materials were inferior. It exhibits a dark plum/purple color in addition to dense, sweet black currant aromas, soft tannin, and fat, creamy, cassis flavors with hints of tobacco, spice box, and dried herbs. Drink this delicious Cabernet over the next decade. The tighter, more structured 1999 Cabernet Sauvignon Calistoga Cuvée possesses a higher acid profile, but is ripe, rich, and potentially longer-lived than its older sibling. Whether it will be as supple and charming in its youth as the 1998 remains to be seen. Anticipated maturity: now–2012. The 1997 Cabernet Sauvignon Calistoga Cuvée was the first of the "new and improved" Calistoga *cuvées*. It offers a saturated ruby/purple color, and plenty of blackberry and cassis fruit presented in an uncomplicated, medium- to full-bodied, chewy style. Ten percent Cabernet Franc and 10% Merlot have been added to provide softness and aromatic dimension. The wine should drink well for 7–10 years.

There are 10,200 cases of the remarkable 1997 Cabernet Sauvignon Estate. Opaque purple-colored with a dense, chewy, full-bodied personality, it displays abundant cassis, mineral, and earth notes. This brilliantly made, super-concentrated, pure blockbuster possesses sweet tannin as well as a terrific finish. Having added additional weight since last tasted, this sumptuous, multilayered, profoundly concentrated Cabernet contains 14% alcohol. It is a candidate for 25–30 years of longevity. Anticipated maturity: 2003–2030. The decade's most mixed vintage for North Coast Cabernet Sauvignon is 1998. The mountain Cabernets tend to be more herbaceous and compressed than the valley floor offerings, although that is a broad generalization as there are some highly successful mountain Cabernets, as well as some disappointing valley floor efforts (even from some of the more renowned wineries). Montelena's 1998 Cabernet Sauvignon Estate is unquestionably one of the vintage's most successful wines. More evolved than either the 1997 or 1999, it offers an opaque ruby/purple color as well as a fat, complex nose of charcoal, smoke, blackberries, and cassis. Rich, complex, and full-bodied, it is more enjoyable to drink now than the super-sized 1997. Production was significantly less (8,000 cases), and the wine is supple-textured, rich, and better after bottling than it was when tasted from barrel. Bravo to Bo Barrett and his winemaking team for fashioning a wine of such character. While not released until 2002, the 1999 Cabernet Sauvignon Estate appears to be a worthy competitor to the exceptional 1997. It exhibits an opaque, thick black/purple color, spectacular concentration, a multilayered mid-palate, the seamlessness of a great vintage, and a rich, jammy, concentrated finish. The powerful, gorgeously pure black fruits and unctuous texture suggest it will drink well young, yet be capable of 2–3 decades of effortless evolution. It is more of a blockbuster in the style of the 1997 than the more charming, softer 1998. Another behemoth Cabernet is the stern, tannic, concentrated 1996 Cabernet Sauvignon Estate (13.5% alcohol). Full-bodied, but closed, with gorgeously pure black fruits, powerful, loamy, earthy scents along with fruit and extract, this wine also needs 5–6 years of cellaring, and should easily last through the first 2–3 decades of this century. This is another winery where the 1995 Cabernet Sauvignon Estate may be as strong as the 1994. The color is an opaque purple. The wine is full-bodied and powerful, with classic notes of cassis intermixed with loamy soil scents, underbrush, and spice. There is massive body and elevated but sweet tannin that is well integrated with the wine's other components, a blockbuster mid-palate, and a finish that lasts for 30+ seconds. Anticipated maturity: now–2025. The 1994 Cabernet Sauvignon Estate, which has been closed since bottling, has begun to open and display its enormous potential. The saturated black/purple color is followed by aromas of gorgeously pure blackberry and cassis scents. Toasty oak notes are barely discernable given the wine's bombastic display of black fruits, a huge, chewy glycerin level, and sensational finish. It will be exciting to follow the evolution of the 1994 and 1995. Modern-day society seems to always be in search of new stars, but this winery has been a superhero for great California Cabernet Sauvignon for nearly 25 years!

Some Montelena Zinfandels have carried lofty levels of alcohol, but the 1994 Zinfandel Estate possesses a civilized 14%. The wine reveals a medium ruby color, followed by expansive, silky flavors and low acidity. It is fully mature.

The Merlot Estate (500 cases, 100% Merlot) was produced only in 1997. I am generally unimpressed with most California Merlots, but Montelena's 1997 exhibits a deep ruby/garnet color as well as dense, smoky, black cherry flavors, medium to full body, soft tannin, and a plump finish. Although not great, it is unquestionably very good Merlot.

Past Glories: Cabernet Sauvignon Estate—1993 (91+), 1992 (94), 1991 (95), 1990 (96), 1989 (90), 1987 (90), 1986 (94), 1985 (94), 1984 (94), 1982 (93), 1981 (90), 1980 (91), 1979 (90), 1978 (94), 1976 (92), 1975 (90)

MONTEVINA VINEYARDS (AMADOR)

1997 Zinfandel Deaver Old Vines	Amador	C	89
1999 Zinfandel Terra d'Oro	Amador	C	89
1998 Zinfandel Terra d'Oro Deaver Old Vines	Amador	C	(88–90)
1999 Zinfandel Terra d'Oro Home Vineyard	Amador	C	89

Some of the best values in Zinfandel are these 1999s produced by Montevina. The 1999 Zinfandel Terra d'Oro is a superb value. This Zinfandel fruit bomb reveals ripe blackberry and cherry fruit intermixed with smoke, earth, licorice, and tar. Chewy, full-bodied, opulently textured, and pure, with a whopping 15.5% alcohol, this well-balanced effort will drink well for 5–6 years. The similarly styled although more expensive 1999 Zinfandel Terra d'Oro Home Vineyard possesses slightly lower alcohol (15%) as well as oodles of jammy black cherry and currant fruit in its spicy, peppery, full-bodied, opulent style.

The 1998 Zinfandel Terra d'Oro Deaver Old Vines may turn out to be outstanding and one of the finest Montevina Zinfandels produced in nearly two decades. A dark ruby/purple color is accompanied by sweet, jammy blackberry, cherry, briery, pepper, licorice, and incense aromas. Superripe, with terrific fruit, serious richness, full body, and excellent purity and overall harmony, this muscular, large-scaled Zinfandel should be excellent, possibly outstanding. Moreover, it should drink well for 5–6 years. The opaque purple color of the 1997 Zinfandel Deaver Old Vines is followed by aromas of toasty new oak, black cherry liqueur, pepper, and flowers. Velvety-textured, dense, and full-bodied, with rich fruit, this well-endowed Zinfandel can be drunk now or aged for 5–6 years.

MORAGA VINEYARDS (BEL AIR)

1996 Cabernet Sauvignon	Bel Air	E	89
1995 Cabernet Sauvignon	Bel Air	E	89
1994 Cabernet Sauvignon	Bel Air	E	89

One of California's most interesting vineyards, Moraga is a seven-acre parcel located in the wealthy Los Angeles suburb of Bel Air. Think it over—I bet an acre of land in this high-rent district probably sells for as much as an acre of grand cru Chambertin or Montrachet in Burgundy! These wines are intriguing, offering a Bordeaux-like austerity as well as Médoc-like aromatics of weedy tobacco, cedar, and currants. They give every indication of being ageworthy wines with 15–20 years of possible evolution. The vineyard, which I once walked with the proprietor, is made from decomposed fossils, limestone, and sandstone. Recent vintages have been aged in 100% new French oak casks. The 1996 Cabernet Sauvignon displays a dense purple color, a striking toasty, black cherry, and cassis-scented nose, and rich, spicy, medium- to full-bodied flavors with good acidity and moderately high tannin. The wine is tightly knit, and in need of 4–5 years of cellaring. It should keep for 15+ years. The 1995

Cabernet Sauvignon (450 cases produced) is another Bordeaux look-alike, at least aromatically. It exhibits a tobacco leaf, smoky, cedar, and black currant–scented nose, followed by crisp, tart acidity, some austerity, but flavorful, youthful, rich red and black currant fruit. Medium-bodied and spicy, with moderately aggressive tannin in the finish, it needs 4–5 years of cellaring, and should age for two decades. The 1994 Cabernet Sauvignon (545 cases) reveals evolved fruitcake, cedary, tobacco, roasted herb, and cassis aromas, as well as rich, concentrated flavors. It is impressively rich, with an herb-tinged, black currant personality, medium to full body, sweet but noticeable tannin, and excellent purity, all framed by toasty new oak. The wine gives every indication of being ready to drink with another 2–3 years of cellaring. It should last for 15–20 years.

MOUNT EDEN VINEYARDS (SANTA CLARA)

1997	Cabernet Sauvignon Estate	Santa Cruz Mountain	D	88+
1996	Cabernet Sauvignon Estate	Santa Cruz	D	90
1995	Cabernet Sauvignon Estate	Santa Cruz	D	88
1996	Cabernet Sauvignon Old Vine Reserve	Santa Cruz	E	92+
1995	Cabernet Sauvignon Old Vine Reserve	Santa Cruz	E	90+
1997	Pinot Noir Cuvée Vieilles Vignes	Santa Cruz Mountain	E	89
1996	Pinot Noir Estate	Santa Cruz	D	90

Very few vineyard sites can match the extraordinary view from the top of Mount Eden. Overlooking the Santa Clara Valley, this vineyard, at 2,000 feet, was planted by the legendary Martin Ray. In many respects, Mount Eden was the birthplace of the boutique/garage winery. There are five wines produced, two *cuvées* of Cabernet Sauvignon, a Pinot Noir, and two Chardonnays, the estate offering and one from Edna Valley.

Mount Eden's Pinot Noirs are elegant, Côte de Beaune–styled examples, with surprising longevity. I had my last bottle of 1985 this fall and was extremely pleased to see how fresh, lively, and complex it had remained. The 1996 Pinot Noir is reminiscent of a good Beaune or Volnay premier cru. Bright jammy, strawberry, and fruit flavors are intertwined with spicy oak and minerals. Elegant and medium-bodied, with total harmony, this beautifully rendered Pinot Noir should drink well for 5–7 years. The delicious, light ruby-colored 1997 Pinot Noir Cuvée Vieilles Vignes offers aromas of sweet berries/cherries, earth, animal, and spice. Round and generous, with balancing acidity, this complex, evolved Pinot Noir should continue to drink well for 5–7 years. The dark ruby/purple-colored 1997 Cabernet Sauvignon Estate is dense and closed, with abundant black currant fruit, a strong sense of minerality, firm tannin, and earthy notes in the background. Medium-bodied and slightly austere, but well made, it will drink well between 2003–2014.

There have been some legendary Cabernet Sauvignons produced at Mount Eden, with some of the older vintages requiring 2–3 decades of cellaring (i.e., 1974). I asked winemaker/proprietor Jeffrey Patterson what he thought were the top recent vintages of his estate Cabernet Sauvignon. He felt the finest five vintages in the last two decades have been 1994, 1989, 1988, 1987, and 1985. There are two *cuvées* of Cabernet Sauvignon. The 1995 regular *cuvée* of Cabernet Sauvignon, a blend of 75% Cabernet Sauvignon, 22% Merlot, and 3% Cabernet Franc, sees 30% new American oak and 70% used French barrels. The dark ruby/purple-colored 1995 offers a firm, restrained nose of black currants, minerals, earth, and spicy oak. Medium-bodied, moderately tannic, and firmly structured, it requires 2–3 years of cellaring, and should keep for 15+ years. The outstanding 1996 Cabernet Sauvignon possesses greater thickness and richness, medium to full body, fine purity, and a black cherry/cassis component, intermixed with minerals and spice. Although more accessible than the 1995, it promises to be as long-lived.

Mount Eden's flagship Cabernet Sauvignon Old Vine is a 100% Cabernet Sauvignon from two parcels planted in 1955 and 1958. Jeffrey Patterson feels the greatest vintages for this *cuvée* have been 1973, 1974, 1975, 1976, 1986, 1990, 1992, and 1994. I was impressed with both the 1995 and 1996. The 1995 Cabernet Sauvignon Old Vine Reserve was bottled unfiltered, but was given a slight egg white fining. It is a backward, concentrated example in need of a decade of cellaring. Medium- to full-bodied, with a deep ruby/purple color and plenty of ripe cassis in the nose, it displays an unevolved, austere, formidably dense and muscular personality. Anticipated maturity: 2005–2025. The 1996 Cabernet Sauvignon Old Vine Reserve is more highly extracted and full-bodied, with a saturated ruby/purple color, and a restrained but blossoming nose of minerals, licorice, spicy oak, black cherries, and cassis. Pure, rich, dense, and promising, but destined for considerable longevity, this is another wine that should be cellared for 8–10 years. Anticipated maturity: 2007–2035.

MURPHY-GOODE (SONOMA)

1997 Cabernet Sauvignon Reserve Brenda Block	Alexander Valley	D	88
1994 Cabernet Sauvignon Reserve Brenda Block	Alexander Valley	D	89
1997 Cabernet Sauvignon Reserve Sarah Block Swan Song	Alexander Valley	D	89
1994 Merlot Murphy Ranches	Alexander Valley	C	88
1997 Petit Verdot Murphy Ranch	Alexander Valley	D	88
1995 Zinfandel	Sonoma County	C	89
1994 Zinfandel	Sonoma County	C	89
1999 Zinfandel Liar's Dice	Sonoma	C	89
1998 Zinfandel Liar's Dice	Sonoma	C	88

Murphy-Goode's Zinfandels emerge primarily from two vineyard sources, Sonoma's Cuneo and Saini Vineyards. Production is modest, with only 650 cases produced. A large-scaled, succulent fruit bomb, the ripe, jammy, fleshy, medium- to full-bodied 1999 Zinfandel Liar's Dice is a treat to drink. The alcohol came in at 14.5%, and there is a touch of volatile acidity in the complex aromatics. Fleshy and hedonistic, it is best drunk over the next 2–3 years to take advantage of its exuberant youthfulness. The 1998 Zinfandel Liar's Dice is a delicious, opulently textured, sweet, berry, cherry, and strawberry-scented and flavored wine, with medium to full body, low acidity, and good fat and succulence. A hedonistic personality, wonderful purity, and vivid, delicious fruit make for a mainstream, but immensely pleasing Zinfandel that even wine snobs will enjoy. Drink it over the next 2–3 years.

Murphy-Goode's intensely fragrant (jammy blackberries and spices) 1995 Zinfandel offers a deep, saturated ruby/purple color, sweet, spicy oak, plenty of round, soft, rich, berry flavors, admirable opulence, and a lush, silky texture. Drink it up. The fully mature 1994 Zinfandel displays a deep ruby color, followed by Zinfandel's appealing spicy, ripe, pure, peppery, berry fruit character, and a soft, lush, medium- to full-bodied finish.

Petit Verdot can rarely stand on its own, but Murphy-Goode has produced a blend of 78.5% Petit Verdot, 13.5% Cabernet Franc, and 8% Cabernet Sauvignon that is impressive for its ripeness and overall balance and richness. Attractive notes of black fruits (primarily cassis and berries) are intermixed with toasty new oak in the saturated dark ruby/purple-colored 1997 Petit Verdot Murphy Ranch. The wine is rich, medium- to full-bodied, and pure, with attractive spicy oak, low acidity, and sweet tannin. Drink this plush effort over the next 10–12 years. The saturated dense ruby/purple-colored 1997 Cabernet Sauvignon Reserve Brenda Block reveals abundant, toasty vanilla (from 18 months in French oak and 2 months in new American oak) aromas, along with classic tobacco and black currant scents. Moderate tannin, delicious fruit, and nicely integrated acidity as well as new oak frame this medium- to full-bodied, impressively made Cabernet Sauvignon. It will benefit from 1–2 years of bottle age, and will drink well for the following 10–12 years. The 1997 Cabernet Sauvignon Reserve Sarah Block Swan Song exhibits smoky, toasty aromas along with subtle, herb-tinged, ripe, jammy, blackberry and cassis scents. In the mouth, licorice, cedar, and saddle leather flavors add to the wine's complexity. Medium- to full-bodied, and more supple than the oakier, more tannic Brenda Block, with excellent depth, richness, and overall symmetry, it can be drunk now as well as over the next 10–12 years.

The dark ruby-colored 1994 Merlot Murphy Ranches (83% Merlot and 17% Cabernet Sauvignon) offers up a moderately intense nose of coffee beans, smoke, and ripe berry fruit. Although not complicated, it provides plenty of lush, silky, low-acid flavors with good ripeness, fruit, and glycerin. Slightly more complexity and delineation could have elevated this wine to an even higher qualitative category. Drink it over the next 3–5 years. The 1994 Cabernet Sauvignon Reserve Brenda Block (1,700 cases) is a dark garnet/purple-tinged color. The wine exhibits super ripeness, and a jammy, black cherry, cassis character nicely dosed with spicy oak. This vanilla-scented, medium- to full-bodied, dense, layered, low-acid Cabernet Sauvignon possesses plenty of sweet tannin, but the wine's hallmark is its purity and luscious, rich fruit. It should drink well young and age for 10–12 years. It would appear to be one of the finest Cabernet Sauvignons Murphy-Goode has yet produced.

ANDREW MURRAY VINEYARDS (SANTA BARBARA)

2000	Enchanté	Santa Ynez	C	88
1999	Espérance	Santa Barbara	C	87
1998	Espérance	Santa Barbara	C	90
1997	Espérance	Santa Barbara	C	88
1997	Syrah Hillside Reserve	Santa Barbara	D	93+
1996	Syrah Hillside Reserve	Santa Barbara	D	90+
1999	Syrah Les Coteaux	Santa Ynez	C	89
1997	Syrah Les Coteaux	Santa Barbara	C	90
1996	Syrah Les Coteaux	Santa Barbara	C	90
1999	Syrah Roasted Slope Vineyard	Santa Ynez	D	92
1997	Syrah Roasted Slope Vineyard	Santa Barbara	C	92
2000	Syrah Tous les Jours	Central Coast	B	86
2000	Viognier	Santa Ynez	C	90

Andrew Murray Vineyards is one of the shining stars in the Santa Barbara firmament. Extremely low yields (one-half to three-quarters tons of fruit per acre for the Viognier and Roussanne in 1998) and a dedication to hillside vineyards, ripe fruit, and non-interventionalistic winemaking have combined to propel this estate to the top echelon of the Rhône Ranger hierarchy. Production is small (300 cases for the Roussanne, 500 for the Viognier, 600 for Espérance, 600 for Syrah Roasted Slope, and 1000 for the Syrah Les Coteaux), but these wines are well worth seeking out.

Andrew Murray's 2000s and 1999s reveal considerable promise. The 2000 Enchanté, a blend of 80% Viognier, 10% Roussanne, and 10% Marsanne, is a delightful, slightly herbaceous, charming, fruity, medium-bodied, fleshy offering with excellent notes of honeyed citrus intermixed with a floral component. Drink this soft, stylish white Rhône Ranger blend over the next year. The 2000 Viognier is one of the finest produced in California. It exhibits apricot/honeysuckle fruit as well as more definition than most of these fruit-driven wines. Full-bodied, with a serious mid-palate as well as surprising depth, complexity, and underlying minerality, this classy effort should be consumed over the next year. The dark plum/ruby-colored 2000 Syrah Tous les Jours is a peppery, earthy, cherry-scented and flavored Côtes du Rhône–like effort. Drink this medium-bodied, pleasing Syrah during its first several years of life. More serious is the 1999 Espérance, a blend of Syrah, Grenache, and Mourvèdre. It possesses a Crozes-Hermitage–like herbaceous personality with notes of cassis fruit and cigar box. Medium-bodied and moderately weighty, with plenty of spice, fruit, pepper, and herbs, it will drink well for 4–5 years. The 1,000-case *cuvée* of 1999 Syrah Les Coteaux possesses medium body, good bacon-scented and cassis flavors with hints of earth and vanilla. It does not have the depth of some of Murray's finest vintages, but that is probably attributable to 1999's cold growing season. It reveals elegance, sweetness, and a more restrained personality than previous editions. The exceptional 1999 Syrah Roasted Slope (95% Syrah and 5% Viognier) is a top achievement in such a cool year. Its deep ruby/purple color is accompanied by a complex nose of honeysuckle, blackberries, and licorice. Full-bodied, rich, fleshy, well balanced, and pure, it is a super effort for the vintage. Drink it over the next decade.

The 1998 Espérance, a blend of Syrah, Mourvèdre, and Carignan, comes closest in quality to a topflight Crozes-Hermitage. Notes of dried Provençal herbs, leather, licorice, cedar, and cassis intermixed with chocolate and cherries jump from the glass of this open-knit, complex, spicy red wine. Medium-bodied, with excellent concentration, supple tannin, and enough acidity to provide delineation, this is a delicious, complex, Rhône Ranger blend that should drink well for 4–5 years. Andrew Murray's flagship wine is the 1997 Syrah Hillside Reserve, a concentrated, powerful Syrah meant to improve with bottle age. The opaque purple-colored 1997 offers aromas of creosote, licorice, black raspberries, and blackberries. Full-bodied, with explosive fruit, moderately high tannin, low acidity, superb ripeness, and enviable integration of wood, alcohol, and tannin, this powerhouse Syrah will improve for 3–5 years, and last for an additional 10–15. Impressive! According to Andrew Murray, this selection comes from the Durell clone of Syrah grown in Sonoma.

Readers looking for a terrific red wine value should check out Andrew Murray's 1997 Espérance, a blend of Syrah, Grenache, and Mourvèdre. It is a rustic, exuberant, rich, dark ruby/purple-colored wine with full body, plenty of pepper, black fruits, earth, and spice. Although the tannin is slightly elevated, it is well balanced by the gorgeous fruit, mouth-filling texture, and complete personality of this gutsy red wine. Moreover, it will soften and improve over the next 5–8 years. The black/purple-colored 1997 Syrah Les Coteaux is a rich wine with copious extract and tannin, and gorgeously sweet cassis fruit intermixed with pepper, licorice, and floral scents. The tannin level is elevated, but this full-bodied, layered wine will only improve over the next 7–8 years. It should keep for a decade or more. The saturated black/purple-colored 1997 Syrah Roasted Slope Vineyard is a field blend of 95% Syrah and 5% Viognier, both harvested and fermented together. It reveals jammy, syrupy, black raspberry and cherry flavors combined with a floral note and a touch of honey. Full-bodied, expansively textured, and pure, with less aggressive tannin than in Les Coteaux, this sweet (from ripe fruit, not sugar), rich, long wine should drink well for 10–12 years.

The 1996 Syrah Les Coteaux is more rustic, or as the French would say, *sauvage.* Its robust, exuberant, kinky character is hard to ignore. The color is saturated purple. The bouquet offers leesy, peppery, black currant, and berry aromas intermixed with tar and loamy soil scents. This full-bodied wine exhibits explosive fruit, Syrah's telltale smokiness, and a rich, moderately tannic, spicy finish with copious quantities of glycerin. The tannin is not totally integrated, but the wine is impressively large and aromatic. It would provide an ideal accompaniment to grilled steak or game birds. Moreover, it should continue to improve for 5–7 years, and last for 12 or more. The impressive 1996 Syrah Hillside Reserve is more restrained, elegant, tannic, and backward. I admired its saturated purple color, as well as its pure blackberry/cassis aromas intermixed with spicy new oak. There is a touch of minerality and good spice, but it is a more polite, suave, and gracefully constructed wine than its sibling. Nevertheless, it should unleash more of its personality with another 1–2 years of bottle age; it will keep for a decade or more.

At a time when many California wines seem to be priced proportionally to their producers' egos, Andrew Murray's offerings are a breath of fresh air given their exceptionally high quality and realistic prices—readers take note.

P.S. Readers who visit Los Olivos will find the winery has a tasting room in the quaint village center.

NADEAU FAMILY VINTNERS (PASO ROBLES)

1999 Zinfandel Critical Mass	Paso Robles	C	90
1999 Zinfandel Old Vines	Paso Robles	C	88

The star of this attractive duo is the 1999 Zinfandel Critical Mass (15.6% alcohol). While not complex, it is a sexy, explosive Zinfandel fruit bomb offering compelling drinking. Layer upon layer of black cherry, currant, and blackberry fruit tumble over the palate. The oak is kept well in the background. Unctuously textured, fleshy, and fat, it should be drunk over the next 2–3 years. Supple, harmonious, and richly fruity is the 1999 Zinfandel Old Vines. Plenty of black cherry and currant fruit as well as abundant glycerin can be found in this medium- to full-bodied effort. It should drink well for 2–4 years.

NEWLAN VINEYARDS (NAPA)

1999 Zinfandel	Napa	C	88
1998 Zinfandel	Napa	C	88
1997 Zinfandel	Napa	C	88?

The muscular, substantially sized, dark ruby/plum-colored 1999 Zinfandel displays plenty of jammy black cherry and kirsch-like scents in its moderately intense bouquet. Fat and fleshy, with good underlying acidity, it tips the scales at a modest (for Zinfandel) 14.5% alcohol. Consume it over the next 4–5 years. An excellent effort, the full-bodied, deep ruby/purple-colored 1998 Zinfandel exhibits thick, briery flavors in addition to good ripeness, purity, and overall balance. Although not complex, it offers a chunky personality with plenty of flesh and density. Drink it over the next 3–5 years. The 1997 Zinfandel behaved like a barrel sample. An extremely oaky, black/purple-colored effort, it is sure to be controversial because of the lavish display of spicy new wood. Unevolved and full-bodied, with copious quantities of blackberry fruit mixed with vanilla, there is little complexity in this well endowed, pure Zin. It will benefit from 6–8 more months of bottle age and should drink well for 7–8 years.

NEWTON VINEYARDS (NAPA)

1996 Cabernet Sauvignon Unfiltered	Napa	D	93+
1995 Cabernet Sauvignon Unfiltered	Napa	D	92
1997 Merlot Unfiltered	Napa	D	(90–92)
1996 Merlot Unfiltered	Napa	D	90

Newton has one of the most spectacular settings of any winery on California's North Coast. Situated high in the mountains above St. Helena, with gorgeous terraces and flower gardens, this estate has a distinctly French orientation. Much of the winery's staff appears to be French students trying to improve their English skills. Moreover, proprietress Su Hua Newton makes no secret of the fact that she looks for inspiration from France's finest winemakers. Her wines are unquestionably made with this philosophy in place. Not surprisingly, France's talented Michel Rolland is the consulting oenologist. Newton exports 30% of their production, with Switzerland the largest foreign buyer. All of the Newton wines are fermented with natural yeasts in order to obtain more complex aromatics. The malolactic fermentations take place in barrel to promote greater integration of wood and to encourage more textural richness in the wines. All of the wines are bottled without filtration.

Newton was one of the first California wineries to produce high-quality, ageworthy Merlot made in an elegant style, with admirable character, richness, and depth. The 1997 Merlot Unfiltered (produced from a severely thinned crop) possesses a saturated ruby color and a lovely nose of sweet black cherry fruit intermixed with herbs, minerals, and spice. Lush, ripe, and fragrant, this forward Merlot should be accessible when released and last for 12 or more years. The dense ruby/purple-colored 1996 Merlot Unfiltered is a fuller-bodied example, with more of the varietal's chocolate, coffee, roasted herb, and damp foresty characteristics.

The wine is spicy, lightly oaky, tightly knit, rich, pure, and structured. It requires 2–4 more years of cellaring, and should keep for 12–15.

Newton's Cabernet Sauvignons cut a broader, more textured mouth-feel. The 1996 Cabernet Sauvignon Unfiltered exhibits an opaque purple color, as well as a robust, nearly massive constitution, a boatload of tannin, and considerable power, depth, and muscle. Atypically rugged and brawny for a Newton Cabernet Sauvignon, it should age effortlessly for 2–3 decades. Prospective purchasers should be aware that this vintage will require 4–6 years of cellaring for some of the tannin to melt away. Also tannic, but more classically constructed, the 1995 Cabernet Sauvignon Unfiltered offers rich cassis fruit intermixed with loamy soil scents, toast, and floral notes. Long in the mouth, with an expansive texture, impeccable symmetry, and fine overall balance, this wine finishes with a tannic clout, as well as outstanding ripeness and presence in the mouth. Like the 1996, it should be long-lived, but will be ready to drink at an earlier age. Anticipated maturity: now–2020.

Past Glories: Cabernet Sauvignon—1993 (90), 1992 (92), 1991 (94), 1990 (94)

NEYERS VINEYARD (NAPA)

1995	Cabernet Sauvignon	Napa	D	90
1999	Chardonnay	Carneros	D	93
1999	Chardonnay	Napa	D	91
1999	Chardonnay Thieriot Vineyard	Sonoma Coast	E	92+
1999	Merlot Neyers Ranch	Conn Valley	D	89
1997	Merlot Neyers Ranch	Conn Valley	D	89
1999	Syrah Hudson Vineyard	Napa	D	(90–92)
1998	Syrah Hudson Vineyard	Carneros	E	90
1997	Syrah Hudson Vineyard	Napa	D	(91–93)
1996	Syrah Hudson Vineyard	Napa	D	92
1995	Syrah Hudson Vineyard	Napa	D	91
1999	Zinfandel Pato Ranch	Contra Costa	D	90
1999	Zinfandel Tofanelli Vineyard	Napa	D	89

Bruce Neyers, the national sales manager for Kermit Lynch Wine Merchants, has built his portfolio of impressive wines into a 15,000-case operation. The stars have always been his Chardonnays, but some enticing red wines (particularly Syrah and Zinfandel) are also being produced. Hopefully, Neyers will be able to build a bit more flavor into the Grenache, one of my favorite varietals. The 1999 Chardonnays have all been bottled save for the 1999 El Novillero, which was still going through malolactic fermentation when I visited in late October. While promising, it was too unsettled to review. The other Chardonnays appear to be some of the finest Neyers and his talented wine-maker, Ehren Jordan (of Turley Cellars fame), have produced. The full-bodied 1999 Chardonnay Napa exhibits honeyed citrus, tangerine, and other tropical fruit aromas and flavors. Intense and pure, with good underlying acidity as well as a layered, concentrated finish, the 14.5% alcohol is well integrated in this beautifully balanced wine. The 1999 Chardonnay Carneros (14.3% alcohol) reveals a smoky, complex, leesy-scented bouquet with notes of citrus, roasted hazelnuts, and candied apricots. Flavors of brioche, mango, minerals, and clove emerge in the mouth. This full-bodied wine seems fruit-driven, but the longer it sits in the glass, the more nuances become apparent. It is a dazzling Chardonnay to consume over the next 2–3 years. Both of these Chardonnays were aged completely in French oak (one-third was new), enjoyed full malolactic fermentation, and were bottled without filtration. From a cool Sonoma Coast vineyard, the light gold-colored 1999 Chardonnay Thieriot Vineyard displays a deeper color, and is the tightest, most backward of these Chardonnays. With enticing potential, it is loaded with extract and richness, exhibiting notes of ripe oranges, minerals, smoky, overripe lemons, and a clove/hazelnut character in its scents and flavors. Full-bodied, with good underlying acidity, and nicely integrated, toasty oak, it cuts a broad swath across the palate. Young and unevolved, it requires another six months of bottle age, and should drink well for 4–5 years.

The nearly outstanding, dark plum/purple-colored 1999 Merlot Neyers Ranch exhibits scents of toffee, caramel, cherry and berry fruit, and mocha. Soft, fleshy, and plush, it is reminiscent of a chewy, plump, mid-sized Pomerol. Enjoy it during its first 7–8 years of life. The potentially outstanding 1999 Syrah Hudson Vineyard boasts an opaque black/purple color that suggests an unctuous texture. Aromas of pepper, blackberry liqueur, and creosote emerge from this full-bodied, silky-textured, dense, concentrated Syrah. Approximately 40% was aged in new French oak, and the remainder in older wood. While there is firm tannin in the finish, this admirable Syrah possesses a gorgeously viscous texture as well as gobs of fruit and glycerin. Anticipated maturity: now–2014.

Given Ehren Jordan's undeniable skill for turning out lusty Zinfandel at Turley Cellars, it is not surprising that his 1999 Zinfandel Pato Ranch and 1999 Zinfandel Tofanelli Vineyard are potentially top-notch. The 1999 Zinfandel Pato Ranch (produced from a 104-year-old vineyard planted in sandy soils) displays a dense ruby color in addition to a sweet, jammy nose of berries, pepper, and resiny balsam aromas. Full-bodied, exuberant, and robust, with silky tannin as well as low acidity, it is a delicious, hedonistically styled Zinfandel to consume over the next 5–6 years. The dark ruby/purple-colored 1999 Zinfandel Tofanelli Vineyard reveals aromas of English walnuts intermixed with pepper, spice, and cherry liqueur. Long and full-bodied, with superb fruit purity, a viscous texture, and a medium- to full-bodied, heady finish, it is best drunk during its first 5–6 years of life.

The 1997 Merlot Neyers Ranch (from a vineyard in the Conn Valley) exhibits the telltale black chocolate and cherry liqueur fruit components typical of a fine Merlot. The color is a dark plum. In the mouth, this full-bodied, fleshy, seductive Merlot provides gobs of glycerin, a lush texture, and copious fruit. With a bit more complexity, it would have merited an outstanding score. On a purely hedonistic level, this wine may score higher with many readers. Drink it now and over the next 7–8 years.

The Neyers/Jordan team has consistently done stunning work with Syrah from the Hudson Vineyard. The 1997 Syrah, which was bottled without fining or filtration, will benefit from another 1–2 years of bottle age and should keep for 10–15. A knockout Syrah, it offers up huge bacon fat, *jus de viande,* pepper, and smoky notes intermixed with blackberry and cassis fruit. Dense, full-bodied, and powerful, with exceptional richness, outstanding purity, and nicely integrated new oak (50–60% new French oak barrels were utilized), this terrific Syrah is a must purchase for Rhône wine enthusiasts. A sensational Syrah from the Neyers winery, the 1996 Hudson Vineyard has it all. The color is opaque ruby/purple. The nose offers up creamy blackberry and cassis aromas complemented by spicy wood. In the mouth, the wine is full-bodied, tightly knit, and youthful, with expansive, chewy flavors, as well as outstanding purity and length. It will benefit from another 1–2 years of bottle age, and will keep for 10–15 years. Bravo! Neyers' black/purple-colored 1995 Syrah Hudson Vineyard's nose offers up copious quantities of classic pepper and cassis, with a hint of mint in the background. Some attractive new oak frames a well-constituted, full-bodied, rich, pure, smoky, cassis-flavored wine. This wine should drink well through 2010.

I was impressed by the 1995 Cabernet Sauvignon, which combines both power and elegance in a medium- to full-bodied style. The color is a dense, dark ruby/purple. The wine offers up copious quantities of black currant, berry fruit nicely dosed with smoky oak. Purely made, with a flattering texture (a characteristic of the Neyers wines), this luscious, soft, well-endowed Cabernet Sauvignon can be drunk now as well as over the next 7–8 years.

NORMAN VINEYARDS (PASO ROBLES)

1998 Zinfandel Barbara's Vineyard	Paso Robles	C	88
1998 Zinfandel The Monster	Paso Robles	C	88

Some of the finest Zinfandels ever tasted from Norman Vineyards, these are jammy, full-bodied, thick, juicy offerings meant to be consumed for their boisterous, exuberant gutsiness over the next 3–5 years. The intense, full-bodied, heady 1998 Zinfandel The Monster (15.4% alcohol) possesses copious quantities of glycerin, black cherries, and berry fruit. The acidity is low, and some of Paso Robles' loamy soil-like notes make a subtle appearance, but the wine's fruit and glycerin dominate . . . to its credit. The more Amarone-like 1998 Zinfandel Barbara's Vineyard comes close to being too overripe. Jammy, thick, cherry and berry notes are intertwined with soil overtones, dried herbs, and spice. The alcohol is more noticeable, even though it is essentially the same as in The Monster. Drink this big, juicy, in-your-face Zinfandel over the next 3–5 years.

OAKFORD CELLARS (NAPA)

1996 Cabernet Sauvignon	Oakville	E	88+
1995 Cabernet Sauvignon	Oakville	D	90
1994 Cabernet Sauvignon	Oakville	D	91

Oakford Cellars is a tiny Cabernet Sauvignon producer with an eight-acre vineyard strategically located above the Oakville Grade near the Harlan Estate Vineyard and Heitz's Martha's Vineyard. Proprietor Charles Ball first produced a wine in 1987. In 1994 he hired the immensely fashionable, in demand Heidi Barrett, to assist in the winemaking. The wine is aged in 50% French oak casks and 50% American oak casks (one-third of each type is new) for 18–20 months and is bottled with minor clarification. These are tannic, large-scaled, dense, mountain Cabernet Sauvignons that are not flattering in their youth, but possess considerable promise and aging potential. This is another winery where readers are advised to get on the mailing list if they want an opportunity to purchase the wines, as only 1,000 cases are produced. The 1994 Cabernet Sauvignon, somewhat of a sleeper, is a medium- to full-bodied, rich, smoky, mineral, and black currant–laden Cabernet. It reveals a classic structure, but the austerity it once possessed has been shed in favor of a well-structured, undeniably rich, well-delineated, pure Cabernet Sauvignon that should handsomely repay 5–6 years of cellaring; it will keep for 20+ years. Also impressive, the 1995 Cabernet Sauvignon reveals sweeter tannin than the 1994 (an anomaly in comparing these two vintages), rich, ripe, full-bodied fruit, admirable density and extract, fine overall equilibrium, and a long, heady, concentrated finish. Whether it develops as much intensity as the 1994 remains to be seen, but these wines have lived up to, and even surpassed, my earlier reviews.

A brilliant, backward Cabernet Sauvignon, the dark ruby/purple-colored 1996 exhibits blackberry, cassis, and loamy soil scents in the moderately endowed bouquet. The tannin level is high, and the wine slightly austere, but rich, medium- to full-bodied, and concentrated. It will require patience from prospective purchasers. It exhibits good ripeness, admirable purity, and a long finish. Anticipated maturity: 2004–2018.

Past Glories: 1993 Cabernet Sauvignon Estate (91)

OJAI VINEYARD (SANTA BARBARA)

2000 Chardonnay Bien Nacido Vineyard	Santa Barbara	D	89
2000 Chardonnay Clos Pepé Vineyard	Santa Rita Hills	D	91
1999 Chardonnay Clos Pepé Vineyard	Santa Rita Hills	D	89
2000 Chardonnay Talley Vineyard	Arroyo Grande	D	91
1999 Chardonnay Talley Vineyard	Arroyo Grande	D	90
2000 Pinot Noir Bien Nacido Vineyard	Santa Barbara	D	89
1999 Pinot Noir Bien Nacido Vineyard	Santa Barbara	D	93
1998 Pinot Noir Bien Nacido Vineyard	Santa Barbara	D	90
1997 Pinot Noir Bien Nacido Vineyard	Santa Barbara	D	87
1996 Pinot Noir Bien Nacido Vineyard	Santa Barbara	D	90

2000	Pinot Noir Clos Pepé Vineyard	Santa Rita Hills	D	89
2000	Pinot Noir Pisoni Vineyard	Santa Lucia Highlands	D	93
1999	Pinot Noir Pisoni Vineyard	Santa Lucia Highlands	D	93
1998	Pinot Noir Pisoni Vineyard	Santa Lucia Highlands	D	90
1997	Pinot Noir Pisoni Vineyard	Santa Lucia Highlands	D	91
1996	Pinot Noir Pisoni Vineyard	Santa Lucia Highlands	D	93
2000	Sauvignon Blanc	Santa Barbara	C	89
1999	Syrah	California	D	89
1998	Syrah	California	D	88
1997	Syrah	California	C	88
1996	Syrah	California	C	90
1995	Syrah	California	C	88
1994	Syrah	California	C	89
2000	Syrah	Santa Barbara	D	88
1994	Syrah	Santa Barbara	C	93
2000	Syrah Bien Nacido Vineyard	Santa Barbara	D	89
1999	Syrah Bien Nacido Vineyard	Santa Barbara	D	91
1998	Syrah Bien Nacido Vineyard	Santa Barbara	D	91
1997	Syrah Bien Nacido Vineyard	Santa Barbara	D	92
1996	Syrah Bien Nacido Vineyard	Santa Barbara	D	94
1995	Syrah Bien Nacido Vineyard	Santa Barbara	D	92+
1997	Syrah Cuvée Henry Daniel	Santa Barbara	E	95
2000	Syrah Melville Vineyard	Santa Rita Hills	D	92
2000	Syrah Roll Ranch	Santa Ynez	D	92
1999	Syrah Roll Ranch	Santa Ynez	D	92
1998	Syrah Roll Ranch	California	D	92
1997	Syrah Roll Ranch	California	D	92
1996	Syrah Roll Ranch	California	D	95+
1995	Syrah Roll Ranch	Santa Barbara	C	90
1998	Syrah Roll Ranch E.H.	California	E	95
2000	Syrah Stolpman Vineyard	Santa Ynez	D	91
1999	Syrah Stolpman Vineyard	Santa Ynez	D	94
1997	Syrah Stolpman Vineyard	Santa Barbara	D	91
1996	Syrah Stolpman Vineyard	Santa Barbara	D	95
2000	Syrah Thompson Vineyard	Santa Ynez	D	94
1999	Syrah Thompson Vineyard	Santa Ynez	D	96
1998	Syrah Thompson Vineyard	Santa Barbara	D	94
2000	Syrah White Hawk Vineyard	Santa Ynez	D	(90–92)
2000	Vin du Soleil	California	C	90
1999	Vin du Soleil	California	C	90
2000	Vin du Soleil (white)	California	C	90

This winery generally produces 5,000 cases, although production can jump to 7,500 cases in an abundant vintage. As longtime readers know, Ojai, and its owner/wine-maker, Adam Tolmach, get my nod as one of Santa Barbara's great success stories. Almost everything Tolmach touches turns out at least very good. Both the 2000 and 1999 portfolios look extremely strong. The 2000 Chardonnay Bien Nacido Vineyard was produced from a heavy crop and may lack the extra dimension of concentration found in other vintages. It offers notes of minerals and lemony citrus in its smoky, spicy nose, an excellent texture, and medium- to full-bodied flavors. Drink it over the next 2–3 years. The complex 2000 Chardonnay Clos Pepé comes from the cool, sandy soils of the Santa Rita Hills. It offers an intricate, spicy, mineral, and ripe fruit-scented bouquet, underlying minerality, and a structured, complete style reminiscent of a white Burgundy grand cru. Rich yet remarkably restrained, it should drink well for 3–4 years. From the highly regarded Talley Vineyard, the 2000 Chardonnay reveals forward, tropical fruit, a beautiful texture, lower acidity, and abundant quantities of honeysuckle as well as buttery tropical fruits. Enjoy it over the next 1–2 years. The crisp, high-acid, medium- to full-bodied, Chablis-like 1999 Chardonnay Clos Pepé will drink well for 2–3 years. The tropical fruit, buttery-scented and flavored 1999 Chardonnay Talley Vineyard possesses underlying minerality, but not as pronounced as that found in the Clos Pepé. Drink it over the next 1–2 years.

Adam Tolmach continues to produce a tasty, white Graves look-alike Sauvignon Blanc. The 2000, one of the winery's two wines to have its malolactic blocked, comes from a cool, gravelly site. It is crisp, with excellent concentration as well as a striking citrus/mineral character displaying hints of figs and lemon butter. As it sat in the glass, notions of tangerines also emerged. It is an impressive Sauvignon to drink over the next 12–18 months. A new entry in Tolmach's portfolio is the Vin du Soleil, a blend of 75% Roussanne, 20% Viognier, and 5% Chardonnay. The 2000 reveals waxy, mango, and orange marmalade notes in its medium- to full-bodied, ripe, concentrated personality. Like the Sauvignon, it had its malolactic blocked, which is good as it has just enough acidity to balance out its weighty, rich mouth-feel. Made from extremely low yields, this Rhône Ranger blend will prove exciting.

Pinot Noir hits lofty heights at Ojai. Approximately 75% new oak is utilized for these *cuvées*, which are 100% destemmed and aged 12–16 months in French oak before being bottled without fining or filtration. The 2000 Pinot Noir Clos Pepé has a tightly structured, cool-climate feel, medium to full body, deep cherry and currant fruit, and earthy/spicy notes. It is a well-defined, crisp Pinot to enjoy during its first 4–6 years. Displaying more pepper and herbaceousness is the spicy, earthy, dark ruby-colored 2000 Pinot Noir Bien Nacido. Drink this excellent, up-front, precocious 2000 over the next 2–3 years. From a superb vineyard, the 2000 Pinot Noir Pisoni Vineyard exhibits a deep ruby color plus sweet aromas of blackberry and cherry fruit intermixed with licorice, earth, and floral notes. Complex and full-bodied, with a layered texture, this superb Pinot will drink well during its first 7–8 years of life.

The 1999 Pinot Noirs emerged from a colder growing season. The deep ruby/purple-colored 1999 Pinot Noir Bien Nacido Vineyard offers fabulous aromas of smoke, earth, jammy plums, cherries, and dried herbs. With great fruit, medium to full body, and a layered, sweet, rich, mouth-filling personality, it will drink well for 5–6 years. The sensational 1999 Pinot Noir Pisoni Vineyard boasts a saturated ruby/purple color as well as classic Pinot Noir aromatics of smoky black fruits. This *cuvée* always possesses characteristics similar to a grand cru Vosne-Romanée. Floral notes mix with black fruits as well as a distinctive earthiness. This superb, full-bodied Pinot possesses outstanding concentration and a long finish with nicely integrated acidity as well as alcohol. Drink it over the next 7–8 years.

In both 1999 and 2000 Adam Tolmach produced a red Vin du Soleil made from primarily Grenache with some Syrah. Neither *cuvée* saw any new oak. The excellent 2000 Vin du Soleil (80% Grenache and 20% Syrah) possesses abundant quantities of blackberry and cherry fruit presented in a style not unlike a full-bodied, plump, hedonistic Côtes du Rhône. The 1999 Vin du Soleil (90% Grenache and 10% Syrah) is an opulent, hedonistic, decadently rich effort with plenty of body, loads of black fruit, and an easygoing texture. Neither of these wines will make old bones, but for drinking during their first 4–5 years of life, they provide considerable excitement.

Ojai's basic Syrah is a good introduction to this estate's style. It is always approachable, offering plenty of jammy plum, black cherry, and currant fruit. The 2000 Syrah Santa Barbara is a fleshy, medium- to full-bodied, fruit-forward, mainstream, consumer-accessible effort that is ideal for drinking during its first 4–5 years of life. The single-vineyard Syrahs are more serious. For example, the 2000 Syrah Stolpman Vineyard exhibits a saturated black/ruby color as well as crème de cassis and graphite aromas, and elegant, full-bodied, pure flavors that coat the palate. Rich, thick, and low in acidity, it will drink well for 10–12 years. The super-concentrated 2000 Syrah Melville Vineyard offers notes of pepper, crème de cassis, licorice, leather, and earth. With great intensity and full body, it is another example of this promising vineyard in the Santa Rita Hills. Cropped at one ton of fruit per acre, it requires 2–3 years of cellaring and should last for 15 years. Adam Tolmach was not sure if he was going to do a single-vineyard bottling of the 2000 Syrah White Hawk Vineyard. It is a sensationally concentrated effort, but still awkward and disjointed, with earthy, savage characteristics as well as mouth-staining levels of extract and richness. It has enough character to be bottled separately, but it needs to come together and be less disjointed. It is a candidate for 15 or more years of cellaring. The typically elegant, stylish, medium-bodied, dense purple-colored 2000 Syrah Bien Nacido Vineyard possesses rich fruit as well as a peppery characteristic. Reminiscent of a concentrated, top *cuvée* of Crozes-Hermitage, it will drink well for 7–9 years. The most seductive offering is the 2000 Syrah Roll Ranch. This *cuvée* always possesses a voluptuous texture, low acidity, ripe tannin, and undeniable hedonistic appeal. The black/purple-colored 2000 boasts oodles of fruit, glycerin, and extract. This knockout, pure, layered, long Syrah will drink well for a decade. The prodigious 2000 Syrah Thompson Vineyard's stunning aromatics and flavors consist of roasted meats, crème de cassis, new saddle leather, earth, pepper, and asphalt. Fabulously concentrated and extremely rich, with an admirable seamlessness, it will drink well for 12–15 years.

From a cool year, the 1999 Syrah California exhibits aromas and flavors of plums, cassis, figs, smoke, and herbs. Although there is dry tannin in the finish, the wine possesses abundant richness as well as extract in its straightforward, richly fruity personality. The brilliant 1999 Syrah Stolpman Vineyard reveals an opaque purple color along with scents of blackberries, chocolate, espresso, and licorice. Full-bodied, majestically rich and layered, with moderate tannin, this wine requires 2–3 years of cellaring and should drink well for 10–12 years. The blockbuster 1999 Syrah Thompson Vineyard boasts an opaque black/purple color as well as a bouquet that is the essence of smoky Syrah. Frying lard intermixed with cassis, barbecue spice, and blackberry aromas are followed by an unctuously textured, full-bodied, deep, sensationally pure, prodigious Syrah to drink now and over the next 12–15 years. Once again, the 1999 Syrah Roll Ranch proved to be the most flirtatious of the Ojai Syrahs. Displaying a black/purple color and gobs of black fruits intermixed with licorice and a hint of Viognier (2–3% is added to the blend), this voluptuous, seductive offering is a thrill to drink. Low acidity and wealth of fruit make this a compelling Syrah. It should drink well for 10–12 years. The 1999 Syrah Bien Nacido Vineyard comes across as the most French inspired. The complex, nuanced aromatics reveal scents of pepper, dried Provençal herbs, earth, and spice box. Licorice and red as well as black currants make an appearance in the mouth. Although it is less powerful and thick when compared to its siblings, it is a dead ringer for a Rhône Valley Hermitage or topflight Crozes-Hermitage. Consume it over the next 10–12 years.

Lastly, there are 200 cases of the 1998 Syrah Roll Ranch E.H. A special bottling, it tips the scales at a whopping 15% alcohol, and is the only Syrah that Adam Tolmach bottles in a Bordeaux-shaped bottle. This unique offering possesses extraordinary sweetness, an unctuous texture, and high tannin levels. Ripe, with roasted black fruit notes intermixed with asphalt, camphor, meat, and cassis/blackberries, this structured, backward wine requires 2–3 years of cellaring and should last for two decades. Tolmach likes his 1998s even better than his 1997s, saying it was a smaller crop and he was able to wait out the cool weather, so the wines' potential is exciting. Two 1998 Pinot Noirs from Adam Tolmach were outstanding. My favorite is the 1998 Pinot Noir Bien Nacido Vineyard. This dark ruby-colored Pinot offers up copious quantities of pepper, sweet black cherry fruit, smoke, plum jam, and minerals. There is terrific purity, medium to full body, and a vivacious, lively, concentrated feel in the mouth. It should drink well for 4–5 years. It is hard not to be seduced by the Vosne-Romanée-like nose of the 1998 Pinot Noir Pisoni Vineyard. Intertwined with smoke, minerals, and black cherry fruit are notes of allspice, leather, and wood. Pure, soft, and fleshy, with an open-knit, velvety texture, this luscious Pinot Noir should be drunk over the next 3–4 years.

There are five appealing 1998 Syrahs produced at Ojai. The dark ruby/purple-colored 1998 Syrah California (mostly from the Roll Ranch, Stolpman Vineyard, and Bien Nacido Vineyard) exhibits a ripe nose of cassis, licorice, and barbecue spice. A fruit-driven, thick, juicy Syrah, it is ideal for drinking during its first 7–8 years of life. This supple-textured, fleshy effort possesses plenty of stuffing and fruit, but not a great deal of complexity. There are two 1998 Syrahs from the Roll Ranch. One *cuvée* (225 cases) is designated E.H., which denotes that it was made from a specific clone (Estrella) and bottled separately. It may turn out to be the finest Syrah that Adam Tolmach has yet produced. The 1998 Syrah Roll Ranch, from a warm microclimate, reveals an opaque purple color in addition to a deep, sweet nose of black fruits, low acidity, a muscular, full-bodied personality, and impressive levels of extract and concentration. It is soft and voluptuous enough to be drunk early, but should age nicely for more than a decade. The super-concentrated, essence of Syrah 1998 Syrah Roll Ranch E.H. exhibits a thick, viscous-looking purple color and a bouquet of blackberry liqueur. The wine coats the palate with glorious levels of glycerin, jammy fruit, and sweet tannin. Exceptionally full-bodied, with fabulous intensity and length as well as a blockbuster finish, it is remarkably well balanced and harmonious given its enormous size and inky-colored personality. While it will be fun to drink young, 4–5 years of cellaring will bring multiple secondary nuances and subtleties. Look for this wine to evolve nicely for 10–15 years. The dense black/purple-colored 1998 Syrah Thompson Vineyard (300 cases) displays tell-tale notes of creosote, cassis, blackberries, scorched earth, and smoke. Although it exhibits more tannin than its siblings, there is more than enough richness to balance it out. Full-bodied, mouth-filling, and impressive, it should drink well for 12–15 years. Although 1998 can be a high-acid year, there is no tartness. The 1998 Syrah Bien Nacido Vineyard was harvested on November 17, 1998, from one of the coolest Syrah vineyards in Santa Barbara. Aromas of fruitcake, licorice, dried herbs, tar, and black currants jump from the glass of this fragrant, elegant, less weighty Syrah. Medium-bodied, with impressive concentration, but nowhere near the size, length, or muscle of its siblings, it will drink well young and last for 5–7 years.

Tasting the 1997 Syrahs from bottle confirms just how successful this vintage was for Tolmach. He rates 1997 below 1998 and 1996, equating it with 1995 as a good vintage for the region, but not as excellent as 1994 or 1998. The deep ruby/purple-colored 1997 Syrah Bien Nacido Vineyard offers a gorgeous nose of incense, spice, pepper, cedar, and black fruits. Silky-textured, lush, and forward, with outstanding richness, this is a beautiful wine to drink over the next decade. Out of bottle, the 1997 Syrah Stolpman Vineyard reveals less aromatics, but more power, richness, and size. Opaque ruby/purple-colored, with sumptuous aromas of blackberry liqueur, smoke, pepper, and earth, this creamy-textured, full-bodied, luscious Syrah has some tannin to shed, but it is hard to resist its ostentatious personality. It should drink well for 12–15 years. More backward and powerful, and the slowest to reveal its personality, is the 1997 Syrah Roll Ranch. There is no doubting either its saturated purple color or subtle yet impressively ripe nose of cassis, smoke, vanilla, and spice. Deep, with exceptional intensity, this wine requires 2–3 years of bottle age and should be consumed over the following 12–15. The 1997 Syrah Cuvée Henry Daniel (named after one of Tolmach's children) is a prodigious Syrah, 75% emerged from the Bedford Thompson Vineyard and the rest from the Bien Nacido. Opaque purple-colored, with a huge, smoky, blackberry liqueur–scented nose, this fabulously concentrated wine exhibits abundant sweet tannin, an unctuous texture, well-integrated new oak (about 50% new wood was utilized), and a layered, deep finish. It should evolve beautifully for 10–15+ years. This wine is only available in six-packs, as production was limited to just over 300 cases. Even though the 1997s were made from higher yields than the 1996s, they are among the most concentrated and finest wines I tasted from Santa Barbara. The deep ruby/purple-colored 1997 Syrah California (10% Grenache and 10% Mourvèdre have been added to the blend) offers a peppery, leathery, mineral, kirsch, and blackberry-scented nose, good depth, not as much complexity (as the other *cuvées*), but full body, and a luscious, accessible, low-acid profile that will give it considerable charm and seductiveness during its first 7–10 years of life.

Pinot Noir yields were higher in 1997 than in 1996. While neither of the 1997s equal their 1996 counterparts, both are well made and merit attention. Ojai's Pinot Noirs are destemmed, fermented at relatively hot temperatures, and kept in barrel, on their lees, until assembled prior to bottling. As with all the winery's reds, there is no fining or filtration. The 1997 Pinot Noir Bien Nacido Vineyard reveals an attractive ruby/purple color and a sweet nose of cherry/ plum fruit intermixed with a whiff of green pepper, allspice, and toast notes. The wine is rich and fleshy, with good body and an elegant, Côte de Beaune–like finish, with the cherry fruit component dominating its personality. It should drink well for 3–5 years. The 1997 Pinot Noir Pisoni Vineyard may not be as thick or massively extracted as it was in 1996, but it is a beautifully made Pinot with this varietal's black fruit character offering a complete contrast to the Bien Nacido. The wine's saturated ruby/purple color is followed by a seductive nose of black-berries and raspberries. Full-bodied, with rich fruit, more power, viscosity, and body than Bien Nacido, and a long, silky-textured finish, the Pisoni Vineyard Pinot Noir should drink well for 7–10 years.

Adam Tolmach fashioned two exceptional 1996 Pinot Noirs. The deep ruby/purple-colored 1996 Pinot Noir Bien Nacido Vineyard reveals some of the telltale herb (V-8 vegetable juice) character (a hallmark of Santa Barbara Pinot), combined with copious quantities of full-bodied black cherry and berry fruit. The wine is dense, concentrated, exceptionally pure, and creamy-textured. It is a sumptuous, herb-tinged, full-throttle Pinot Noir with no hard edges. It should drink well for at least 2–4 years. I have been impressed by the quality of Pinot Noirs emerging from the Pisoni Vineyard in the Santa Lucia Highlands (readers may recall that Peter Michael produces a Pinot from this vineyard). Ojai's 1996 Pinot Noir Pisoni Vineyard represents the essence of Pinot Noir. It is one of the most concentrated and well-balanced Pinots I have ever tasted. This wine possesses the extract level one expects from a Domaine Leroy Richebourg or Romanée St.-Vivant. Obviously produced from extremely ripe fruit and low yields, this is a mammoth yet unbelievably harmonious Pinot Noir. The opaque ruby purple color is followed by scents of kirsch, jammy cherries, and spice that are unmistakably Pinot, but leaning toward the black fruit side of this varietal (Côte de Nuits). The wine is full-bodied and saturates the palate with layers of glycerin, ripe fruit, and a sumptuous texture. Beautifully balanced, awesomely rich, and dazzlingly pure, this is one of the most extraordinary expressions of New World Pinot Noir I have ever tasted. I would not be surprised to see this wine evolve magnificently for a decade. Moreover, my score may look stingy with another several years of bottle age.

Ojai turned out four exceptional 1996 Syrahs. If I were to invest in vineyard land in California, I would consider three spots—northern California's Anderson Valley and Sonoma Coast for Pinot Noir and Chardonnay, and Santa Barbara for Syrah. The basic offering, the 1996 Syrah California, is an outstanding wine that could easily pass for a dazzling Rhône. It possesses a beautiful ruby/purple color, as well as a terrific nose of cassis and pepper intermingled with a whiff of tar and herbs. Rich, with luscious smoky fruit, this medium- to full-bodied, ripe, low-acid yet gorgeously knit Syrah can be drunk now and over the next 6–7 years. The 1996 Syrah Bien Nacido is a wine of exceptional extraction, richness, and depth. The color is an opaque black/purple, and the wine offers up classic tar, cassis, and bacon fat aromas. Full-bodied, with no hard edges, this profoundly concentrated, mouth-filling, voluptuously textured Syrah possesses all the necessary components to age beautifully for a decade or more. However, the wine's explosive richness and enticing aromatics will ensure that much of it is drunk within hours of purchase. The 1996 Syrah Stolpman Vineyard comes across as a classic Hermitage with less earth, but with the blackberry liqueur/crème de cassis–like trademarks. It boasts an opaque black/purple color, as well as an extraordinary nose of black fruits, blackberries, and cassis, full-bodied, awesomely concentrated flavors, gobs of glycerin, low acidity, and a 40+ second finish. This is a thrilling, thick, juicy, succulent, formidably endowed Syrah that should age effortlessly for 10–15 years. Lastly, the most backward of this quartet is the 1996 Syrah Roll Ranch Vineyard. Cut from the same mold as its siblings, it is a black/purple-colored, full-bodied blockbuster with gobs of cassis and blackberry liqueur–like flavors, but more tannin and earth in the flavors, as well as a more structured, backward feel in the mouth. The wine has huge extract, fabulous purity, and is another tour de force in Syrah winemaking.

Rhône Ranger enthusiasts will go bonkers over the three splendid Syrahs from the 1995 vintage. The ruby/purple-colored, uncomplicated 1995 Syrah possesses striking levels of sweet cassis fruit in the nose, along with a touch of licorice and pepper. This dense, medium-bodied wine offers delicious levels of jammy fruit and plenty of glycerin and punch. It should drink well for another 5–7 years. The 1995 Syrah Roll Ranch is an explosively rich wine with terrific intensity, a black/purple color, super purity, no hard edges, full body, high glycerin, and moderate tannin, the latter component largely concealed behind the wine's impressive fruit extraction. This is a young, grapy Syrah that should evolve beautifully for 10–12 years. The profound 1995 Syrah Bien Nacido Vineyard makes me think that Syrah may do better than Pinot Noir in selected Santa Barbara microclimates. This killer Syrah boasts an opaque black/purple color and an awesome nose of smoke, licorice, Asian spices, and black fruits. Some toasty notes are present, but they play an accessory role to the wine's cassis-like jamminess. Full-bodied, with superb delineation, this layered, textured, thick yet beautifully balanced, dense Syrah should last for 15 years.

The 1994 Syrah exhibits a deep ruby/purple color, a telltale, smoky, bacon fat, and cassis-scented nose, a succulent, soft, opulent texture, great fruit, and a classic, open-knit Syrah character. The wine almost tastes sweet because of the grape ripeness. This is a hedonistic, lush Syrah to drink over the next 4–5 years. The 1994 Syrah Santa Barbara smells like a terrific Hermitage. A huge, dramatic nose of bacon fat, smoke, and jammy black fruits is followed by a dense, full-bodied, layered wine crammed with ripe fruit. Its creamy texture, sumptuous thickness, lushness, and admirable purity combine to give this full-bodied, flamboyant Syrah a compelling character. I suspect there is more tannin than the wine is currently revealing. This is a mouth-filling, gorgeously proportioned, well-endowed Syrah to drink over the next 10–12 years.

OPUS ONE (NAPA)

1997	Proprietary Red Wine	Napa	EE	88
1996	Proprietary Red Wine	Napa	EE	93
1994	Proprietary Red Wine	Napa	EE	92

Now, don't get me wrong, 88 points signifies a very good to excellent wine. But in the context of the vintage, not to mention the context of what the 1997 should be, this is a disappointment. After a stunningly concentrated, opulent, blockbuster effort in 1996, the 1997 tastes as if it were made from yields that were too high. They may tell you it is elegant and complex, but, truthfully, there is not much depth, and the wine will have a relatively short lifeline of 10–12 years. A dark ruby color is accompanied by a complex nose of plums, black cherries, currants, smoke, and leather. The wine reveals more new oak than normal for Opus, as well as medium body, good depth, dry, hard tannins in the finish, and little weight or length. Drink it over the next 8–10 years. The 1996 is one of the finest Opus Ones to date, offering a dark ruby/purple color, as well as a striking, intense bouquet of sweet licorice intermixed with blackberries, cassis, plums, and saddle leather. This seamless, full-bodied wine is more

velvety-textured, opulent, and succulent than past vintages. The mid-palate is expansive and chewy. The long finish is filled with glycerin, ripe fruit, and sweet tannin. Drink this impressive, user-friendly, yet richly concentrated effort over the next 15 years. The 1994 is another impressive effort from Opus One. The wine, a blend of 95% Cabernet Sauvignon, 2% Cabernet Franc, 2% Merlot, and 1% Malbec, possesses a dark ruby/purple color followed by a generous, complex nose of lead pencil, toasty oak, violets, and black currants. In the mouth, there is a beautiful texture, soft, generous, low-acid, full-bodied richness, and a stunningly proportioned, rich, intense finish. The influence of 18 months in new French oak casks gives the wine a subtle oaky note in addition to giving it excellent delineation. Because of the wine's softness and generosity, it can be drunk now and over the next 18–20 years.
Past Glories: 1992 (90), 1991 (91), 1990 (92), 1987 (92)

PAHLMEYER (NAPA)

1999 Chardonnay	Napa	E	90
1996 Malbec	Napa	E	91
1999 Merlot	Napa	EE	91
1998 Merlot	Napa	EE	90
1997 Merlot	Napa	EE	96
1996 Merlot	Napa	E	97
1995 Merlot	Napa	E	94
1994 Merlot	Napa	E	95
1999 Proprietary Red Wine	Napa	EE	90+
1998 Proprietary Red Wine	Napa	EE	91
1997 Proprietary Red Wine	Napa	EE	98
1996 Proprietary Red Wine	Napa	EE	95
1995 Proprietary Red Wine	Napa	E	96
1994 Proprietary Red Wine	Napa	D	96

Helen Turley, who made Pahlmeyer famous with her intense style of winemaking, was replaced in 2000 by her former assistant, Erin Green. It should have been a smooth transition as both women appear to share the same winemaking philosophy. The 1999 Chardonnay (which emerges from several areas, the core component being the Berlenbach Vineyard in Coombsville) is a dense, concentrated effort with higher acidity than usual (the result of a cool growing season). This outstanding Chardonnay reveals medium to full body, excellent viscosity, and abundant tangerine, citrus oil, mineral, and buttery tropical fruit aromas and flavors.

Pahlmeyer's 1997 Merlot may be the finest Merlot ever produced in California. A profound blend of 85% Merlot and 15% Cabernet Sauvignon, it offers gorgeous smoky, black cherry liqueur aromas mixed with melted fudge. The wine is unctuously textured, super-concentrated, low in acidity, rich, and multilayered. This is a spectacular, hedonistic effort to drink over the next 15–20 years. Not surprisingly, the 1998 Merlot is lighter, but it is undoubtedly one of the finest Merlots produced in this irregular vintage. A blend of 95% Merlot and 5% Cabernet Franc (1,750 cases), Jayson Pahlmeyer and wine-maker Erin Green decided to eliminate 38% of the wine. Full-bodied, thick, and juicy, with low acidity as well as melted chocolate, cherry, smoke, and toast aromas and flavors, it is best drunk over the next 5–8 years. The 1999 Merlot (100% Merlot; 1,650 cases) is richer and riper than the 1998, but it is doubtful that it will achieve the mind-boggling proportions of the 1997. The dense ruby/purple-colored 1999 offers smoky, licorice, cherry, and chocolaty aromas, medium to full body, better acidity than either the 1997 or 1998, and a thick, full-bodied finish. Anticipated maturity: now–2012. The 1996 Merlot (3,000 cases) is a worthy rival to the 1997. Bottled unfined and unfiltered, this blend of 93% Merlot and 7% Cabernet Franc tips the scales at a heady 14.6% alcohol. The wine is opaque black/purple-colored, with a knockout nose of plums, black cherries, chocolate, raspberries, licorice, and toasty new oak. Viscous in the mouth, with superb purity, this is a riveting, mind-boggling Merlot that sets a new reference point for this varietal in California. It can be drunk now, but has the potential to last for 15 or more years.

I do not believe it is an exaggeration to say that Pahlmeyer's Merlot is now the finest being produced in California. One might quibble over other styles of Merlot, but no producer achieves more complexity, flavor, and thrills per sip than Pahlmeyer. The 1995 Merlot is an awesomely endowed, full-bodied, pedal-to-the-metal style of Merlot with great richness, in addition to a knockout nose of blackberry, raspberry, mocha, and smoky aromas that soar from the glass. The wine has a sweet attack (from its formidable glycerin and extract level, not sugar), full body, extraordinary layers of concentrated fruit, and a blockbuster finish. Amazingly, the wine, like its 1996 counterpart, possesses gorgeously integrated acidity, tannin, and alcohol. Can California Merlot get any better than this? Both Merlots will drink well when released and last for 15–20 years. The 1994 Merlot reveals a dense purple color, followed by a super fragrant nose of chocolate, mocha, toast, and black cherry fruit. Fullbodied, but not heavy, this expansive, chewy, opulently textured wine should drink well for 15+ years.

There are small quantities of 1996 Malbec. Produced from fruit grown in the Napanook Vineyard owned by Christian Moueix, this exotic, wild wine is not for everybody, but it ranks with the finest California Malbecs. The dark saturated ruby/purple color is accompanied by aromas of vanilla ice cream drenched with raspberry jam. Smoky, toasty notes (from aging in new Taransaud barrels) also make an appearance. In the mouth, the wine's display of fruit is so ostentatious as to be gaudy. It does not possess the body or length of Pahlmeyer's Merlots or Proprietary Reds, but it is an enormously fat, fruity, and undeniably sexy and disarming wine that is surprisingly light on its feet. It should drink well for 10–15 years.

The finest proprietary red produced by Pahlmeyer to date is their 1997 (a blend of 72% Cabernet Sauvignon, 17% Merlot, and the rest Petit Verdot, Cabernet Franc, and Malbec). Production is 3,300 cases, and the wine tips the scales at 14.7% alcohol. A superrich, blockbuster effort, it exhibits an opaque purple color in addition to a fabulous bouquet of black fruits, espresso, cocoa, mocha, and flowers. A prodigious red, with low acidity, spectacular concentration, and fabulous purity as well as overall symmetry, it can be drunk now, but promises to last for 20–25 years. The 1998 Proprietary Red is a blend of 75% Cabernet Sauvignon, 15% Merlot, 4% Cabernet Franc, 1% Petit Verdot, and 1% Malbec. A sexy, up-front, plush wine with a deep purple color, medium to full body, and copious quantities of sweet blackberry, crème de cassis, and meaty notes, it is on a fast evolutionary track, and thus should be consumed over the next 10–12 years. The promising, opaque purple-colored 1999 Proprietary Red is a blend of 71.5% Cabernet Sauvignon, 21.5% Merlot, 4% Petit Verdot, 2% Cabernet Franc, and 1% Malbec. It exhibits blueberry liqueur, roasted coffee, spice, and smoky wood aromas. Broad, dense, and full-bodied, with the acidity giving it a firmer edge than the 1997 or 1998, this chewy effort is best consumed during its first 15–18 years of life. The 1996 Proprietary Red (a blend of 73% Cabernet Sauvignon with the balance Malbec, Petit Verdot, Merlot, and Cabernet Franc) is a less weighty (14.3% alcohol) offering. It has become more delineated with a year of bottle age, offering up classic crème de cassis, smoked meat, coffee, prune, and toasty new-oak scents. Concentrated, with fabulously high extract, sweet tannin, and full body, this wine has a more elegant feel on the palate, but is still a blockbuster. Anticipated maturity: now–2025.

The 1995 Proprietary Red Wine boasts an explosive blackberry/blueberry/cassis-scented nose that has completely soaked up all the new oak in which it has been aged for the last 22 months. Purple/black in color, it exhibits fabulously extracted, layered black fruit flavors that coat the palate, offering a seamless texture and voluptuous impression. The 1994 Proprietary

Red Wine exhibits a similar purple/black color, as well as sweet, integrated tannin, a gorgeous black currant, toast, tar, and licorice-scented nose, fabulous texture, and a 35–45 second finish. The 1994 may be slightly sweeter in the mid-palate than the 1995, but the differences are negligible. The abundant tannin is mostly concealed by the wine's wealth of fruit, glycerin, and alcohol. This wine should drink well for the next 20 years.

If great wine satisfies both the palate and the intellect, these Pahlmeyer offerings are prodigious. Despite the forward drinkability of these reds, all of them will last for 20–25 years. These are mind-boggling efforts. This is another winery where getting on the mailing list is essential to securing a few bottles of these liquid gems.

Past Glories: 1993 Merlot (90), 1993 Proprietary Red Wine (96)

PALOMA (NAPA)

1997 Merlot	Napa	D	92
1996 Merlot	Napa	D	94
1995 Merlot	Napa	D	92+
1994 Merlot	Napa	D	91+
1997 Syrah	Napa	D	91

Both the 1997 Merlot and 1997 Syrah are rich, concentrated, multilayered efforts with considerable purity, texture, and intensity. The 1997 Merlot exhibits a dark purple color as well as attractive, spicy, oaky notes intermixed with smoke and black cherry jam. Full-bodied, with low acidity, outstanding concentration and purity, and moderate tannin in the impressively endowed finish, it should be cellared for 2–4 more years and drunk over the following 15. The stunning, black/purple-colored 1997 Syrah offers extraordinary purity of crème de cassis and peppery-like aromas, and powerful, concentrated, full-bodied flavors, with the fruit and glycerin dominating all other components. There is enough acidity to buttress this large wine's considerable power and intensity. Vague notions of licorice, tar, and spice emerge with coaxing. However, this is a giant fruit bomb that should continue to gain complexity, and become more delineated with bottle age. It should drink well for 12–15 years.

Bob Foley, the wine-maker at Pride Mountain, produces Paloma's Merlot from Spring Mountain fruit. The 1996 is about as concentrated, thick, and promising a Merlot as readers are likely to find from either the New or Old World. The color is an impressive opaque purple. The nose merely hints at what should emerge with another 2–3 years of cellaring. At present, readers will have to be content with toasty notes intermingled with plums, prunes, and black cherry liqueur. Full-bodied, deep, and exceptionally well balanced, with beautifully integrated acidity and tannin, this massive, rich, ageworthy Merlot should be at its best between now–2015. The 1995 Merlot is another fine effort from this small winery owned by Barbara and Jim Richards. A blend of 80% Merlot and 20% Cabernet Sauvignon, the wine was fined with egg whites, but not filtered prior to bottling. Its opaque purple color suggests a wine of extraordinary intensity. The nose is subdued, but swirling brings forth scents of jammy cassis, licorice, toast, and sweet cherry fruit. It possesses an inner core of intense fruit, a lush texture, and flavors of fruit and chocolate, with a subtle overlay of smoky oak. Full-bodied, moderately tannic, and exceptionally intense with a lingering finish, this is a Merlot to cellar for 2–3 years and drink over the following two decades. Very impressive!

Only 625 cases were produced of Paloma's 1994 Merlot, a blockbuster, inky/purple-colored wine. It is obviously the result of talented winemaking, given its purity and wonderful integration of toasty French oak with gobs of black cherry and raspberry fruit. The wine reveals full body, marvelous extraction and richness, terrific equilibrium, and a layered, textured, expansively flavored personality. This impressive wine is drinking well, yet should last for another 10–12 years. This is an exceptionally impressive wine made in a large-scaled, boldly styled, massively endowed format!

PARADIGM WINERY (NAPA)

1995 Cabernet Sauvignon Oakville Estate	Napa	D	90
1994 Merlot Oakville Estate	Napa	D	88
1995 Zinfandel Oakville Estate	Napa	C	88

These wines are made by one of Napa's most talented wine consultants, Heidi Barrett (the wife of Bo Barrett of Château Montelena), who is also the consultant to such Napa blue bloods as Grace Family Vineyards, Screaming Eagle, Vineyard 29, Hartwell, and, until 1996, Dalla Valle. Paradigm's offerings are elegant wines that marry Bordeaux-like restraint with California's ripe fruit flavors. The 1995 Zinfandel Oakville Estate offers peppery, briery fruit, along with a classy sweet raspberry richness. The wine is medium-bodied, with more length and flavor dimension than the 1994, a sweet, soft mid-palate and texture, and a succulent, classy, spicy finish. It should drink well for 4–5 years. The 1994 Merlot Oakville Estate is an excellent, medium-bodied, elegant wine offering attractive berry fruit and spice, as well as a subtle dosage of toasty new oak. It is a wine to drink over the next 5–7 years.

With respect to the Cabernet Sauvignons, this is one winery where the 1995 outclasses the 1994. While the 1994 Cabernet Sauvignon Oakville Estate is certainly very good, the 1995 Cabernet Sauvignon Oakville Estate cuts a deeper impression on the palate, offering up copious quantities of black cherry, currant, and herb-tinged flavors in a medium- to full-bodied, plush style. The wine possesses more layers of flavor, excellent purity, and a spicy, long finish. It should drink well for 10 more years.

FESS PARKER (SANTA BARBARA)

2000 Chardonnay	Santa Barbara	C	89
2000 Chardonnay Marcella's Vineyard	Santa Barbara	D	90
1999 Pinot Noir American Tradition Reserve	Santa Barbara	D	89
1999 Syrah American Tradition Release	Santa Barbara	D	88
1998 Syrah American Tradition Release	Santa Barbara	D	88
1999 Syrah Rodney's Vineyard American Tradition Reserve	Santa Barbara	D	90

Like many people my age, Fess Parker remains a favorite childhood hero because of his Hollywood roles as Davy Crockett and later, Daniel Boone. Some of Santa Barbara's cognoscenti obviously find it difficult to detach the Hollywood superstar image from the man as a vineyard developer and moving force in the local county viticultural association. What surprises me on each visit to Santa Barbara is that Fess Parker is controversial. He has developed a splendid hotel, Fess Parker's Doubletree Resort, fronting the Pacific Ocean in the town of Santa Barbara, and also has one of the exceptional venues for food and lodging in the wine country, his Wine Country Inn in Los Olivos. While his critics look at him as a shrewd land developer, what I see is someone committed to producing quality wine and developing some of the finest hillside vineyard sites in the Santa Barbara region. While I am not sure he would like to be called cunning, he has been shrewd enough to purchase some of the finest potential vineyard land in and around Los Olivos, and has been generous enough to share the fruit with the area's most renowned wine-makers. His objective of turning out world-class wines from Rhône varietals is right on target. Moreover, his own wines have improved significantly, and the portfolio tasted in November 1999 shows the winery's finest efforts to date. Fess Parker's son, Eli, is the wine-maker, and there is no doubt that he has learned plenty from working with consulting wine-maker Jed Steele. The bottom line is simple—this looks to be one of the more serious, up-and-coming players in Santa Barbara. This will probably not sit well with some of Parker's critics, who would still like people to believe he is just another Hollywood actor with wine as a hobby. That is a myth. This is a winery with serious aspirations for quality, and, as always, the truth is in the bottle.

One of Fess Parker's impressive new hillside vineyards is Rodney's Vineyard. The 1999

Syrah Rodney's Vineyard reveals the potential of this site. Opaque purple-colored, with a sweet, blackberry and cassis-scented nose intermixed with notes of subtle wood and licorice, it is a full-bodied, spicy, rich, concentrated wine with no hard edges and impressive levels of extract and richness. The tannin, wood, and acidity are nicely meshed with the wine's fruit. Drink it over the next 7–8 years. Earthy, peppery, black currant, and berry aromas emerge from the dark ruby-colored 1998 Syrah American Tradition Release. An accessible style of Syrah with good spice, it is medium-bodied, soft, and plump. Drink this crowd-pleasing Syrah over the next 4–5 years. The 1999 Syrah American Tradition Release is made in a non-aggressive, supple, medium- to full-bodied style that emphasizes plenty of peppery, black currant, and plum fruit. Spicy and rich, with no hard edges, this plump, savory, deliciously fruity Syrah should drink well over the next 7–9 years.

The superb 2000 Chardonnay Marcella's Vineyard (named after Parker's wife) is a structured yet full-bodied wine offering copious mineral and tropical fruit aromas and flavors. It has more volume and definition than the delicious fruit cocktail–styled 2000 Chardonnay Santa Barbara. Another noteworthy effort is the 1999 Pinot Noir American Tradition Reserve. A plush, textured, juicy Pinot with abundant plum, cherry, and earthy fruit, it is seductive as well as medium- to full-bodied. It should drink well for 5–7 years.

While I did not taste it on my recent visit, according to my mother there is not a better Muscat made than Fess Parker's. Readers with a sweet tooth or who have friends and family that like these fragrant, slightly sweet Muscats would be well advised to give them a try. All of Fess Parker's offerings are fairly priced wines for such quality.

PATZ AND HALL WINE CO. (NAPA)

1999	Chardonnay	Napa	D	90
1999	Chardonnay Alder Springs	Mendocino	E	93
1999	Chardonnay Dutton Ranch	Russian River	D	89
1999	Chardonnay Hyde Vineyard	Carneros	D	90
1999	Chardonnay Woolsey Road	Russian River	D	91
1999	Pinot Noir	Sonoma	D	89
1999	Pinot Noir Alder Springs	Mendocino	E	88
1998	Pinot Noir Alder Springs	Mendocino	E	90
1997	Pinot Noir Alder Springs	Mendocino	E	90
1999	Pinot Noir Hyde Vineyard	Carneros	E	90
1998	Pinot Noir Hyde Vineyard	Carneros	E	88
1999	Pinot Noir Pisoni Vineyard	Santa Lucia Highlands	E	90+
1997	Pinot Noir Pisoni Vineyard	Santa Lucia Highlands	D	90

The talented quartet of wine producers—James Hall and his wife, Anne Moses, in addition to Donald and Heather Patz—continues to reveal sure-handed talent with their multiple bottlings of Chardonnay and Pinot Noir. The 1999 vintage produced a slightly bigger crop than 1998 and, because of that, required more crop thinning. Overall, the 1999s look extremely strong from this high-quality source of complex Chardonnays and Pinot Noirs. For those who might think there is no need for so many separate vineyard designations, it is certainly not borne out when tasting their wines.

There are 1,436 cases of the 1999 Chardonnay Woolsey Road. This wine performed beautifully, displaying considerable concentration in its leesy, smoky flavors as well as uncanny elegance for a wine of such richness and beauty. Full-bodied, with subtle oak, and premier cru Chassagne-Montrachet-like characteristics, it should drink well for 2–3 years. The 1999 Chardonnay Dutton Ranch (2,620 cases) is more typically California in style, given its marmalade, pineapple, and tangerine notes. While medium-bodied and elegant, with subtle wood in the background, it does not possess the flavor, depth, or texture of the Woolsey Road. However, that may well emerge with another 6–12 months of bottle age. It should last for 3+

years. A blend of fruit from the Caldwell, Hyde, Carr, and Atlas Peak Vineyards was fashioned into the 1999 Chardonnay Napa. This is a terrific Chardonnay, powerful, with hazelnuts, caramel, citrus oils, and leesy, Burgundian notes. There are 2,178 cases of this richly extracted, multilayered, full-bodied, delineated, impressively endowed Chardonnay; it should last for 4–5 years. From alluvial soils, the 1999 Chardonnay Hyde Vineyard offers flamboyant aromatics of orange marmalade, pineapple, and honeysuckle. In addition to the perfume, the wine offers superb fruit, excellent purity, and a ripe, medium- to full-bodied, long finish. Like most of these wines, it tips the scales between 14–14.2% alcohol. It should also drink well for 3–4 years. Lastly, the 1999 Chardonnay Alder Springs Vineyard exhibits the terrific complexity and richness that this northern Mendocino vineyard (near the Humboldt County line) often displays. Produced from 100% Dijon clones of Chardonnay, the wine possesses a layered personality exhibiting honeyed pear, passion fruit, tangerine, roasted hazelnuts, and a steely minerality. Full-bodied, with abundant texture and glycerin, as well as a clean, rich finish, this bold yet graceful Chardonnay will drink well for 3 years. Unfortunately, there are only 574 cases.

The 1999 Pinot Noir Sonoma (1,400 cases) is a seductive, smoky Pinot offering jammy strawberry and cherry fruit, a velvety texture, and a medium- to full-bodied personality. Drink it over the next 3–4 years. The dark ruby-colored 1999 Pinot Noir Alder Springs Vineyard displays abundant power, but comes across as delicate and restrained with tangy berry fruit interspersed with notes of earth, minerals, and raspberries. Paradoxically, the wine is both soft and structured, which I know does not make much sense. My instincts suggest the wine is probably better than the way it performed the day I tasted it, but it was the least expressive and concentrated of the Patz and Hall 1999 Pinot Noirs. The 1999 Pinot Noir Hyde Vineyard is another impressive Pinot, with silky tannin, an opulent, viscous mid-palate, and a noteworthy sexpot personality (in plain English, a slut). It reveals knockout aromas of black fruits intermixed with smoke and subtle toasty oak. In the mouth, it is plush, succulent, and a total turn-on. This is Pinot at its most hedonistic and exotic best. It should drink well for 5–6 years. I have consistently admired most of the Pinot Noirs that emerge from the Pisoni Vineyard in Monterey's Santa Lucia Highlands. Patz and Hall's outstanding 1999 Pinot Noir Pisoni Vineyard (410 cases) is significantly richer and fuller than their 1998. It reveals the most structure of the 1999s, as well as formidable depth and richness. Aromas of black raspberries, cherry liqueur, flowers, minerals, and spice are followed by a rich, full-bodied, tightly knit, concentrated, impressively pure and long wine. Drink it over the next 8–10 years.

Patz and Hall's 1997 Pinot Noir Pisoni Vineyard exhibits a deep ruby/purple color, as well as sweet black fruits (currants and raspberries), and complex, rich, medium- to full-bodied flavors with surprising fat, glycerin, and lushness. This is an exceptionally pure, lengthy, concentrated, seductive Pinot Noir for drinking now and over the next 5–6 years. Very impressive! Even more exciting is the 1997 Pinot Noir Alder Springs, which is a breakthrough Pinot Noir for Mendocino. Sadly, there are only two barrels (about 46 cases). The wine boasts a saturated dark ruby/purple color, and a knockout nose of smoky, toasty oak intermixed with brandied cherries, mocha, and black raspberries. Rich, concentrated, and full-bodied, this is a hedonistic, decadently rich Pinot Noir to consume over the next 5–6 years. Kudos to Patz and Hall for a brilliant portfolio of wines in 1997.

The 1998 Pinot Noirs are similarly sized, but with more tangy acidity than Patz and Hall's successful 1997s. The 1998 Pinot Noir Hyde Vineyard (250 cases) is made from several clones, including Joseph Swan and a French clone called 113. Sweet black cherry, raspberry, earth, and floral scents are followed by a fresh, zesty, strawberry and floral-flavored wine with elegance, medium body, and crisp acidity. Consume it over the next 5–6 years. Not surprisingly, my favorite of Patz and Hall's 1998 offerings is the 1998 Pinot Noir Alder Springs

Vineyard (295 cases). Dark plum, black raspberry, and cherry flavors are immediately appealing. Spicy, with a black fruit character well displayed in its fleshy, medium- to full-bodied personality, this is the biggest, richest, and potentially most complex of their 1998s.

PEACHY CANYON WINERY (PASO ROBLES)

1997 Zinfandel Benito Dusi Ranch	Paso Robles	D	88
1997 Zinfandel Lakeview Vineyard	Paso Robles	D	88
1997 Zinfandel Snow Vineyard	Russian River	C	88
1997 Zinfandel Westside	Paso Robles	D	90

Peachy Canyon's 1997 Zinfandels are noteworthy efforts in this irregular vintage. For example, the 1997 Zinfandel Lakeview Vineyard offers a dark ruby/garnet color as well as wonderfully jammy strawberry and cherry fruit in the fragrant aromatics. This is a gloriously fruity, decadent, luxuriously rich, fat, medium- to full-bodied, delicious example. Drink it over the next 2–3 years. The saturated dark purple-colored 1997 Zinfandel Snow Vineyard reveals spicy, black currant and cherry notes that are less jammy and more backward than in the Lakeview Vineyard. The wine comes across as less successful, more intellectual, and more structured, with considerable muscle, excellent concentration, and a long, well-delineated finish. It is not as charming and hedonistically appealing as the Lakeview, but it is a serious Zinfandel that will drink well for 5–6 years. The exotic 1997 Zinfandel Benito Dusi Ranch offers up a striking nose of incense, black cherry liqueur, and spicy oak. This dark ruby/purple-colored Zinfandel possesses some brooding backwardness, yet the sweet, rich, glycerin-endowed, chewy, cherry flavors intermixed with earthy, forest-like aromas are an obvious positive. A spicy wine with complexity and character, it should drink well for 5–6 years. My favorite of this generally impressive group is the 1997 Zinfandel Westside (15.8% alcohol). Some new oak makes an appearance in this wickedly aromatic wine. Explosive fruit flavors with gobs of cherry, strawberry, plum, and cassis are complemented by copious fruit and glycerin, and light tannin in the voluptuous finish. Drinking well, it should continue to evolve deliciously for 5–6 years.

J. PEDRONCELLI WINERY (SONOMA)

1999 Zinfandel Mother Clone	Dry Creek	B	86

Earthy, peppery, strawberry and cherry aromas emerge from this attractive, restrained, measured, dark ruby/purple-colored Zinfandel (14.5% alcohol). Drink this mid-weight offering over the next 3–4 years.

PEZZI KING (DRY CREEK)

1998 Zinfandel	Dry Creek	D	89
1999 Zinfandel Estate	Dry Creek	D	89
1999 Zinfandel Maple Vineyard	Dry Creek	C	90
1999 Zinfandel Old Vines	Dry Creek	C	88

I preferred the 1999 Zinfandel Dry Creek Estate *cuvée* to the Dry Creek Old Vines offering. However, both wines are fine efforts. Tipping the scales at 15% alcohol, the 1999 Zinfandel Old Vines exhibits a peppery, earthy style with plenty of structure as well as notes of balsam wood, leather, spice box, cherries, and dried herbs. Drink this medium- to full-bodied Zinfandel over the next 2–4 years. Fatter and more fruit driven, with extra layers of glycerin as well as concentration, the 1999 Zinfandel Estate Dry Creek possesses even higher alcohol than the Old Vines (15.5%). Deep, chewy, well made, and exuberant, it should drink well for 4–5 years. The finest wine of the trio of 1999s is the 1999 Zinfandel Maple Vineyard. It is a thick, juicy, jammy offering revealing copious quantities of black cherry and berry fruit, smoke, oak, and earth. Textured, powerful, yet supple, this juicy, hedonistic Zinfandel should be consumed over the next 4–5 years. The 1998 Zinfandel offers heady alcohol, full body, less delineation, but plenty of sweet and sour cherry fruit intermixed with raspberry, plum, leather, and earth notes. It should be drunk over the next 3–4 years.

JOSEPH PHELPS VINEYARD (NAPA)

1999 Cabernet Sauvignon	Napa	D	89
1997 Cabernet Sauvignon	Napa	D	88
1996 Cabernet Sauvignon	Napa	D	88+
1995 Cabernet Sauvignon	Napa	D	90
1994 Cabernet Sauvignon	Napa	C	89
1999 Cabernet Sauvignon Backus Vineyard	Napa	EE	92
1997 Cabernet Sauvignon Backus Vineyard	Napa	EE	93
1996 Cabernet Sauvignon Backus Vineyard	Napa	EE	92
1995 Cabernet Sauvignon Backus Vineyard	Napa	EE	93
1994 Cabernet Sauvignon Backus Vineyard	Napa	E	94+
1999 Chardonnay Ovation	Napa	D	(88–90)
1999 Insignia Proprietary Red Wine	Napa	EE	94
1998 Insignia Proprietary Red Wine	Napa	EE	91
1997 Insignia Proprietary Red Wine	Napa	EE	96
1996 Insignia Proprietary Red Wine	Napa	EE	92
1995 Insignia Proprietary Red Wine	Napa	EE	97
1994 Insignia Proprietary Red Wine	Napa	EE	96
1999 Merlot	Napa	D	87
1997 Merlot	Napa	D	90
1995 Merlot	Napa	D	88
1994 Merlot	Napa	C	88
1997 Vin du Mistral Le Mistral	California	D	89
1996 Vin de Mistral Le Mistral	Napa	D	88
1999 Vin du Mistral Syrah	Napa	C	87
1997 Vin du Mistral Syrah	Napa	D	89
1996 Vin de Mistral Syrah	Napa	D	90

The venerable Joseph Phelps Winery continues to plant new acreage in California. At present, there are 350 acres under vine in Napa, with another 100 that are plantable. Phelps has also acquired a 100-acre parcel in the Russian River, which will probably be given a separate domaine name. Furthermore, they have 160 acres in Monterey County, 55 acres of which are allocated to the Phelps wines with the balance sold to Meridian. As one would expect, the 1997s are topflight, the 1998s competent, and the 1999s potentially impressive.

The top-of-the-line white, Phelps's Chardonnay Ovation, is a big, leesy, barrel-fermented, Burgundian-styled wine that is frequently exceptional. Almost all of the fruit for this *cuvée* emerges from Napa's cooler areas, particularly Carneros and Yountville. The 1999 Chardonnay Ovation reveals the vintage's coolness in its steely, nicely textured personality. It exhibits honeyed citrus, toasty oak, and puff pastry–like characteristics. Ripe, rich, and medium- to full-bodied, it should drink well for 3–4 years.

Joseph Phelps has consistently done a good job with their Le Mistral offering, which is aged primarily in used oak. It represents an amalgam of many different grapes, predominately Grenache backed up by Syrah, Mourvèdre, Petite Sirah, Alicante Bouchet, and Carignan. The percentages vary from vintage to vintage. The excellent, dense ruby/purple-colored 1997 Vin du Mistral Le Mistral (43% Grenache, 28% Syrah, 12% Mourvèdre, 8% Petite Sirah, 7% Alicante Bouchet, and 2% Carignan) possesses a big, ripe, peppery, spicy, black cherry, and raspberry-scented bouquet. Full-bodied, dense, chewy, and concentrated, with no hard edges, it represents a California imitation of a southern Rhône. Drink it over the next

5–6 years. Phelps's Syrah, which originates from vineyard holdings in Yountville, is aged primarily in French oak, of which 20% is new. The gorgeous, dense ruby/purple-colored 1997 Vin du Mistral Syrah offers sweet blackberry and cassis flavors with a touch of spice and pepper. Full-bodied, deep, lush, voluptuously textured as well as seductive, it should drink well for 7–8 years. The 1999 Vin du Mistral Syrah should turn out to be as impressive as the 1997. A dense saturated ruby/purple color is followed by a blackberry/cassis-scented bouquet, medium to full body, adequate acidity, and soft tannin. It is a wine to drink during its first 6–7 years of life. The dark ruby-colored 1996 Le Mistral is a gutsy, bistro red with an exotic nose of incense, peppers, red and black fruits, and perfume. While it is not complex and is displaying less fat than when I tasted it in 1997, it remains a fun, delicious wine to enjoy over the next 7–8 years. About 700–800 cases of both the 1996 and 1997 Vin de Mistral Syrah were produced. The 1996 Vin de Mistral Syrah is a sexy, lush, opulently styled wine revealing more precociousness and early charm than I predicted a year ago. Aged in both American and French oak, it possesses a dark ruby/purple color, a spicy, bacon fat, cassis, and blackberry-scented nose, soft, lush flavors, and a heady, concentrated finish. It is best drunk during its first 10–12 years of life.

Phelps's Merlot program is coming of age. Approximately 10% Cabernet Sauvignon is included in the blend, and the wine is aged in primarily French oak with a touch of American. About 30% of the barrels are new. The 1999 Merlot exhibits a saturated ruby/purple color in addition to a gorgeous perfume of sweet, jammy black cherries and spice, and a full-bodied mid-palate and finish with well-integrated acidity and tannin. It is a big, fleshy, rich Merlot that should age handsomely for a decade. The beautiful 1997 Merlot boasts a dense ruby color in addition to an attractive bouquet of berry fruit infused with smoke and mocha. This full-bodied, rich Merlot has a fat, succulent, plush texture, and a chewy, heady finish. It will drink well for a decade. In contrast, the 1995 Merlot is not as fat or ripe as the 1997. It exhibits a saturated dark ruby color, followed by a soft, friendly personality with copious quantities of chocolate, licorice, and smoky, berry fruit intermixed with tobacco and dried herbs. Lush, full-bodied, and chewy, this wine should drink well for another decade. An excellent Merlot, the dark ruby/purple-colored 1994 offers plenty of sweet, jammy, chocolaty, black cherry fruit in its moderately intense aromatics. The wine is medium-bodied, soft, and succulent, with low acidity, copious amounts of fruit, and good ripeness. Drink this delicious, lush Merlot over the next 2–4 years.

When I asked wine-maker Craig Williams about his rating of the succession of fine vintages for California Cabernet Sauvignon in the nineties, he felt 1999 would be among the finest, but it was still too early to rate it. His top vintages were 1997, 1995, 1991, 1994, and 1996. He thought the three most challenging vintages were 1998, 1993, and 1992. As for the 20,000+ cases of Joseph Phelps Cabernet Sauvignon, the 1997 is excellent. While not as open-knit and expressive as their Merlot, it is well made, with attractive cedary, tobacco, and black currant fruit, excellent color saturation, a spicy, sweet mid-palate, and soft tannin in its medium- to full-bodied finish. It can be drunk now or cellared for 12–15 years. The 1999 Cabernet Sauvignon reveals a saturated purple color, exceptional ripeness, and sweet black currant aromas and flavors intermixed with licorice, smoke, and minerals. Medium- to full-bodied, dense, and multilayered, this impressive Cabernet should drink well for 10–15 years. Among the Cabernet Sauvignon vintages, I preferred the 1995. Although the 1996 matches the former wine in terms of intensity, it had just been bottled when I tasted it and seemed muted and closed. The 1997 looks very fine, but more forward and round. The 1994 Cabernet Sauvignon Napa (a blend of 95% Cabernet Sauvignon, 4% Cabernet Franc, and 1% Merlot) is a deep ruby/purple-colored wine with a sweet, ripe, black fruit, vanilla, and underbrush-scented nose, medium to full body, a layered texture, adequate acidity, and sweet tannin in the finish. The wine is mouth-filling, pure, and impressive. The 1995 Cabernet Sauvignon spent 16 months in cask (primarily French oak) and was bottled with minimal filtration. It exhibits a dark ruby/purple color as well as an attractive black cherry, cassis, and dried herb–scented nose with spicy oak. Rich, full-bodied, and concentrated, it offers plenty of cassis fruit and a chewy style. It can be drunk or cellared for 15+ years. More structured, tannic, and dense, the 1996 Cabernet Sauvignon requires patience. Most readers will prefer to drink the 1995 or 1997 than the more backward 1996. The 1996 reveals a saturated ruby/purple color, low acidity, and plenty of tannin and muscle in the brawny finish. Anticipated maturity: now–2015.

From a hillside overlooking the Oakville District, Phelps produces small quantities of their single-vineyard Backus Vineyard Cabernet Sauvignon, which is aged in 100% new French Taransaud oak. The sensational 1997 Cabernet Sauvignon Backus Vineyard is a muscular, highly extracted, full-bodied effort that requires 3–4 years of cellaring. Although less approachable than the 1997 Insignia, it displays great fruit intensity in its huge, thick, viscous flavors redolent with black currants, new saddle leather, spice box, and toasty oak. Long, powerful, and intense, it exhibits both sweet tannin and immense concentration. Anticipated maturity: 2004–2025. Because of the difficulties in 1998, no Backus Vineyard was produced. However, the 1999 Cabernet Sauvignon Backus Vineyard may turn out to be as fabulous as both the 1997 and 1994. It is an astonishingly rich, full-bodied, powerful, super-extracted, unctuously textured endeavor with layers of mineral-infused black cherry and cassis fruit wrapped in toasty new oak. Tannin is present, but it is silky and well integrated. Sound acidity provides admirable delineation to the wine's huge framework. Anticipated maturity: 2005–2025. The dense ruby/purple-colored 1996 Cabernet Sauvignon Backus Vineyard reveals a gorgeous nose of sweet cassis fruit, chocolate, iron, and licorice. Full-bodied, powerful, and weighty, with moderately high tannin, it requires 3–4 years of cellaring. It should last 25+ years. Compared to the 1997, the 1996 Backus is more foursquare and monolithic, without the sweetness and precociousness of the 1997.

The 1995 Cabernet Sauvignon Backus Vineyard is a wine of great intensity. A massive, saturated black/purple-colored example, it offers an intriguing bouquet and flavors of prunes, black currants, roasted herbs, chocolate, and coffee, huge amounts of glycerin and body, and a gigantic, oversized finish with considerable tannin. This is one wine where the extract level matches the tannin's ferocity, but readers looking for something to cuddle up with over the near-term should be advised that it needs 5–6 years of cellaring. Anticipated maturity: 2003–2025. I believe the 1994 Cabernet Sauvignon Backus Vineyard is one of the finest wines this vineyard has yet produced. Phelps's 1994 Backus exhibits an opaque black/purple color and huge, sweet aromatics consisting of jammy black cherry and cassis fruit, minerals, smoke, and a hickory-like barbecue spice. The wine is thick and super-extracted, with huge proportions of fruit, extract, and tannin. A gargantuan Cabernet Sauvignon, it demands 5–6 years of cellaring and should last for 20–25 years.

Joseph Phelps's flagship wine is their fabulous Insignia, a wine with a tremendous track record back to the debut vintage of 1974. It is produced in significant quantities (18,000–20,000 cases) for a wine of such quality. The prodigious 1997 Insignia (83% Cabernet Sauvignon, 14% Merlot, and 3% Petit Verdot) lives up to its pre-bottling promise. Tasted on three separate occasions, every bottle has hit the bull's-eye. The color is a saturated, thick-looking blue/purple. The nose offers up explosive aromas of jammy black fruits, licorice, Asian spices, vanilla, and cedar. Full-bodied as well as exceptionally pure and impressively endowed, this blockbuster yet surprisingly elegant wine cuts a brilliant swath across the palate. A seamless effort with beautifully integrated acidity, sweet tannin, and alcohol, it is still an infant, but can be drunk with considerable pleasure. Anticipated maturity: now–2025. Perhaps an even greater achievement, the 1998 Insignia (78% Cabernet Sauvignon and 22% Merlot) is not up to the level of the 1997, but it is a fabulous wine from what was a far more challenging vintage. Approximately 18,000 cases were made, an amazing quantity in a year that produced far less promising raw materials. More evolved than the 1997, with a saturated ruby/purple color, it possesses a sumptuous bouquet of smoke, cedar, licorice, and cassis. This full-bodied, fat, succulent effort reveals admirable purity and sym- metry, and a soft finish with remarkably deep flavors that caress the palate. It can be drunk now as well as over the next 15–16 years. Another great Insignia in the making is the 1999. An impressive black/purple color is followed by aromas and flavors of melted licorice and crème de cassis, immense body, a voluptuous texture, and an opulent, multilayered palate. This fabulously concentrated, low-acid yet super-endowed wine should rival the compelling 1997. It is a blend of 80% Cabernet Sauvignon, 17% Merlot, and 1% each of Petit Verdot, Malbec, and Cabernet Franc. After its release in 2002, it should age effortlessly for 2–3 de- cades. The 1996 Insignia (83% Cabernet Sauvignon and 17% Merlot) is a notch below the 1995, 1994, and 1997. It exhibits a dark purple color in addition to an elegant nose of cedar wood, fruitcake, coffee, and black currants. Medium- to full-bodied, with a firm underpin- ning of tannin, classic black currant flavors, and a long finish, this effort is impressive, but tighter and more narrowly constructed than the three aforementioned vintages. Anticipated maturity: now–2020.

Perhaps the best back-to-back vintages ever produced of Insignia are the 1994 and 1995, which rival the great Insignias made in 1974 and 1976. The 1994 Insignia (a blend of 88% Cabernet Sauvignon, 10% Merlot, and 2% Cabernet Franc) is spectacular. I have had the wine a half-dozen or more times, and it is unquestionably opulent, sexy, flamboyant, explo- sively rich, concentrated, and a thrill to drink. Already gorgeous, it promises to evolve grace- fully for two decades or more. The color is a healthy saturated dark purple. The spicy nose offers aromas of black currants, allspice, toast, and soy, with scents of a burning wood fire thrown in for additional complexity. This full-bodied, opulent, dazzling wine is exhilarating to drink. Amazingly, the 1995 Insignia may be slightly better—as hard as that is to believe. The final blend is 90% Cabernet Sauvignon, 7% Merlot, and 3% Petit Verdot. The 1995 ex- hibits a character similar to the 1994—cassis, fruitcake, cedar, herbs, coffee, and black fruits intermixed with smoke—but the 1995 is slightly longer in the mouth. It is a wine of ex- traordinary extraction, full body, and marvelously pure fruit. Moreover, it has managed to soak up the 100% new-oak aging, leaving only subtle toasty notes. The tannin may be slightly more noticeable in the 1994, but my instincts suggest the 1995 is even richer and longer than the 1994—as amazing as that sounds. This prodigious Insignia should be at its best over the next 20–25 years.

Past Glories: 1993 Cabernet Sauvignon Backus Vineyard (93), 1993 Insignia Proprietary Red Wine (96)

PINE RIDGE WINERY (NAPA)

1995	Andrus Reserve Proprietary Red Wine	Napa	EE	90
1994	Andrus Reserve Proprietary Red Wine	Napa	EE	90+
1996	Cabernet Franc Trois Cuvées	Napa	D	88
1996	Cabernet Sauvignon	Howell Mountain	D	90
1994	Cabernet Sauvignon	Howell Mountain	D	90
1994	Cabernet Sauvignon	Rutherford	C	88
1997	Cabernet Sauvignon	Stags Leap	E	89
1994	Cabernet Sauvignon	Stags Leap	D	89
1996	Epitome Proprietary Red Wine	Stags Leap	EE	90
1996	Merlot	Napa/Carneros	D	88
1994	Merlot	Carneros	D	88

The dense ruby/purple-colored 1997 Cabernet Sauvignon Stags Leap offers red and black cur- rants intertwined with gravelly, vanilla notes. Elegant, sweet cassis, licorice, and earthy flavors are present in this nicely concentrated, medium-bodied, pure, graceful Cabernet. It should drink well for 10–12 years. Only 305 cases were produced of the 1996 Epitome (a Bordeaux-like blend). Dark ruby with purple nuances, the complex aromatics offer scents of black currants, lead pencil, oak, and flowers. The wine displays pure symmetry between its building blocks of tannin, acidity, alcohol, and extract. Sweet ripeness, a velvety texture, medium body, and outstanding purity and concentration result in a brilliant Bordeaux look-alike from Napa's Stags Leap area. Currently, this offering is only being sold at the winery's tasting room. Anticipated maturity: now–2014. The 1996 Cabernet Franc Trois Cuvées (a blend of three clones of Cabernet Franc) was bottled with neither fining nor filtration. The bouquet offers rich, juicy, red currant, and intriguing floral scents. Well-integrated oak complements the elegant, stylish, rich fruitiness. Finesse, fruit, purity, and symmetry are the hallmarks of this delicious Cabernet Franc that is meant to be drunk over the next 7–8 years. Pine Ridge has turned out a very fine 1996 Merlot, with perhaps more structure and grip than many, but with excellent fruit and purity as well as attractive smoky, black cherry, and chocolaty notes. It possesses good oak, medium body, and excellent length. A blend of 89% Merlot, 8% Malbec, and 3% Cabernet Franc, it can be drunk now or cellared for 12 or more years. The most impressive of the 1996 Cabernet Sauvignon offerings from Pine Ridge is the subtly oaked 1996 Cabernet Sauvignon Howell Mountain. Atypically rich and intense for a Pine Ridge wine, this dark purple-colored mountain Cabernet exhibits copious quantities of mineral, blackberry, and cassis aromas. Medium- to full-bodied and powerful, yet elegant, it possesses an impressive mid-palate, structure, richness, and length. Anticipated maturity: now–2018.

A classic Bordeaux (Médoc)-styled wine, the 1995 Andrus Reserve exhibits a dark ruby/purple color, followed by attractive aromas and flavors of lead pencil, spice, cedar, and black currants. While it is moderately tannic, medium-bodied, with outstanding concentration and purity, the wine remains tight and backward. It requires 3–4 years of cellaring and should keep for at least 15. It is an impressively elegant, finesse-styled proprietary red.

All of the following Pine Ridge Cabernets will benefit from 2–3 years of cellaring. They are made in a medium-weight, somewhat austere Bordeaux style. The excellent 1994 Cabernet Sauvignon Rutherford reveals a classic black currant, toasty nose, medium body, high tannin, wonderful elegance, and a measured, rich fruit character that is pronounced, but never excessive. The wine finishes with a bite of tannin. While accessible, 2–4 years of cellaring will be beneficial. This wine should age well for 15 or more years. The refined 1994 Cabernet Sauvignon Stags Leap District boasts a dark ruby/purple color, followed by a spicy, vanilla, herb, mineral, and black currant–scented nose. In the mouth, there are more red than black currants, as well as rich, pure, long, medium-bodied flavors that exhibit exceptional purity and equilibrium. The tannin should gradually fall away to reveal a quintessentially elegant style of Napa Cabernet Sauvignon. Anticipated maturity: now–2016. Pine Ridge's 1994 Cabernet Sauvignon Howell Mountain needs at least 5–6 years of cellaring. It possesses a saturated purple color and a Bordeaux-like nose of black fruits, licorice, minerals, and cedar. Tannic and reserved, with intense richness and concentration, this is a medium- to full-bodied, large-scaled, unevolved 1994 Cabernet that should prove to be outstanding for those with enough discipline to wait it out. Anticipated maturity: 2003–2020. Cut from a similar cloth, the 1994 Andrus Reserve exhibits a dark saturated plum/purple color, followed by a tight nose of cedar, vanilla, and praline-tinged cassis fruit. Extremely dense and rich, with a more backward and tannic personality than even the Howell Mountain cuvée, this well-delineated, full-bodied wine will need—yes—a full decade of cellaring. It is a 25–30-year wine, but patience is essential. Anticipated maturity: 2006–2030.

Pine Ridge's 1994 Merlot exhibits a good dark ruby color, attractive spicy notes, a monolithic aromatic dimension, and admirable weight, brightness, and purity. My instincts suggest the wine is closed, but I liked its purity of fruit, depth, and ripeness. I would not be surprised to see this Merlot merit a higher score after it receives some bottle age. It should drink well for a decade.

Past Glories: 1993 Cabernet Sauvignon Howell Mountain (92), 1993 Cabernet Sauvignon Stags Leap District (90+)

PLUMPJACK (NAPA)

1998 Cabernet Sauvignon Estate	**Oakville**	**D**	**87**
1997 Cabernet Sauvignon Estate	**Oakville**	**D**	**90**
1995 Cabernet Sauvignon Estate	**Oakville**	**D**	**91**
1998 Cabernet Sauvignon Reserve	**Oakville**	**EE**	**89**
1997 Cabernet Sauvignon Reserve	**Oakville**	**EE**	**90+**
1995 Cabernet Sauvignon Reserve	**Oakville**	**E**	**95+**

Plumpjack, which is well situated on what used to be the Cabernet Sauvignon vineyard of Villa Mt. Eden (remember the glorious wines produced there between 1974 and 1978 by Nils Venge?), has increased its production to 7,500 cases from 50 acres of vineyards. The 1998s look to be successful for this difficult vintage. In 1998 many of the finest wines tended to emerge from Napa's Oakville corridor. Plumpjack's 1998 Cabernet Sauvignon Estate (5,000 cases of an 80% Cabernet Sauvignon, 15% Cabernet Franc, and 5% Merlot blend) exhibits copious quantities of black currant fruit, a charming up-front personality, soft tannin, low acidity, and a plump, savory finish. It will be delicious young, yet capable of lasting for a decade. About 500 cases were culled out for the 1998 Cabernet Sauvignon Reserve (100% Cabernet Sauvignon). An impressive wine for the vintage, it is powerful with terrific extraction, an opaque purple color, pure crème de cassis fruit, and a touch of licorice and toast. Surprisingly unevolved for a 1998, with a fine mid-palate and finish, this Cabernet requires 3–4 years of cellaring; it should keep for 15 years. It will be one of the better, longer-lived 1998 Cabernet Sauvignons.

The 1997 Cabernet Sauvignon Estate (5,300 cases) exhibits copious cassis and soil scents as well as a full-bodied, moderately tannic, muscular, big-framed finish. This is no shy wine, but it demands 4–5 years of cellaring, and should keep for 15+. It was forward and precocious last year, but it has firmed up. The 1997 Cabernet Sauvignon Reserve (260 cases) is also backward. Loaded with concentration, it offers up scents of lavender, black currants, minerals, licorice, and smoky oak. Mouth-searing levels of tannin are present in this big, brawny Cabernet. While it will evolve for two decades, it was impossibly closed. All the component parts suggest an exceptional offering, but patience will be required. Anticipated maturity: 2006–2025.

The 1995 Cabernet Sauvignon Estate, made by wine-maker Tuck Beckstoffer with back-up consulting from nearby neighbor Nils Venge of Saddleback Cellars, is a highly extracted, extremely rich Cabernet that will win many fans. Approximately 1,000 cases were produced of this dense purple-colored wine that reveals a ripe prune and cassis-scented nose with lavish smoky oak. Full-bodied, deep, and chewy, with sweet tannin and plenty of extract and glycerin, this is an impressively endowed, supple style of Cabernet Sauvignon that should drink well for 10–15+ years. The 1995 Cabernet Sauvignon Reserve (approximately 500 cases produced) is an awesome wine that tastes like a synthesis in style of some of the richest, most powerful Cabernets from the Oakville district. It may come closest in style to resembling the profound Cabernets of Harlan Estate. This spectacular Cabernet Sauvignon is a worthy candidate for 20–30 years of cellaring. The opaque black/purple color is followed by intense aromatics offering smoke, coffee, roasted meats, and copious quantities of blackberry and cassis fruit. Extremely dense, full-bodied, and crammed with extract, this persuasively rich, authoritative Cabernet Sauvignon is among the most noteworthy wines of the 1995 vintage. While it can be drunk young, this wine begs for 5–6 years of cellaring. It will be a long-distance runner, although I am not sure how many readers will be able to ignore its lavish display of decadent levels of ripe fruit and toasty oak.

PRIDE MOUNTAIN VINEYARD (NAPA)

1998 Cabernet Franc	Sonoma	D	94
1997 Cabernet Franc	Sonoma	D	93+
1996 Cabernet Franc	Sonoma	D	91
1995 Cabernet Franc	Sonoma	C	92
1998 Cabernet Sauvignon	Napa	D	90
1997 Cabernet Sauvignon	Napa	D	92
1997 Cabernet Sauvignon Reserve	Napa	EE	97+
1996 Cabernet Sauvignon Reserve	Napa	EE	99
1995 Cabernet Sauvignon Reserve	Napa	E	98
1994 Cabernet Sauvignon Reserve	Napa	E	95+
1999 Chardonnay	Napa Valley	D	88
1998 Merlot	Napa/Sonoma	D	88
1997 Merlot	Napa	D	93
1996 Merlot	Napa	C	90+
1997 Reserve Claret	Napa	EE	95
1996 Reserve Claret	Napa	EE	95
1995 Reserve Claret	Napa	E	96
1994 Reserve Claret	Napa	E	95
1998 Sangiovese	Sonoma	D	90
1997 Sangiovese	Sonoma	D (500 ml)	94

Owner Jim Pride and wine-maker Robert Foley have quickly pushed Pride Mountain to the top of California's North Coast qualitative hierarchy. The 1999 Chardonnay exhibits a leesy, toasty, ripe tropical fruit complexity, medium to full body, ripe flavors, and an excellent finish. Drink this very good effort over the next 2–3 years.

While the majority of California Sangiovese is mediocre, Pride Mountain manages to cram abundant flavor and intensity into their offering. The dark ruby-colored 1998 Sangiovese exhibits a big, sweet, strawberry jam and cherry-scented bouquet with subtle notes of leather and toast. With expressive fruit, medium body, deep, concentrated flavors, and a tangy edge, this intense yet supple Sangiovese can be drunk over the next 3–4 years.

I am amazed by how spectacular Pride Mountain's Cabernet Franc continues to be. The fabulous 1998 Cabernet Franc is a noteworthy achievement in this difficult vintage. Its deep purple color is accompanied by a gorgeous bouquet of cedar, spice box, black fruits, smoke, and earth. In the mouth, there is a smorgasbord of sweet black fruits with a hint of dried Provençal herbs. Opulent and full-bodied, with marvelous concentration yet an eerie sense of weightlessness, this rich, complex 1998 can be drunk now as well as over the next decade.

The dark ruby/purple-colored 1998 Merlot (a blend of 64% Napa and 36% Sonoma fruit) exhibits copious quantities of toasty new oak in the bouquet in addition to deep, chewy, blackberry and cherry aromas. There is excellent richness, medium to full body, adequate acidity, and a forward appeal. Drink it over the next 7–8 years. The outstanding 1998 Cabernet Sauvignon boasts a dark ruby/purple color as well as surprising opulence for a wine from this vintage, admirable elegance, abundant black currant fruit, a dense, chewy mid-palate, a fleshy texture, low acidity, and a tannic finish. It is a classic Cabernet with medium weight, as well as outstanding ripeness, richness, and balance. Drink it over the next 12 years.

Available only in 500 ml bottles at the winery, the spectacular 1997 Sangiovese is clearly the equal to some of the super Tuscan wines emerging from the 1997 vintage. Pride Mountain's offering is unbelievably concentrated for a Sangiovese. A fabulous wine, its opaque purple color is followed by an extravagant nose of smoke, licorice, cassis, and toast. This intense, full-bodied, mouth-staining effort is gorgeously pure, with multiple layers to its personality and a whoppingly long finish. It should drink well for 10–12 years.

The 1997 Merlot might be called liquefied Viagra. An incredibly sexy nose of smoke, black fruits, cappuccino, and toasty wood is followed by an expansive, terrifically concentrated wine with a sumptuous texture, no hard edges, beautifully integrated acidity and tannin, and a long, 35-second finish. According to the back label, about 5% Cabernet Sauvignon was added in the blend of this stunningly aromatic, multidimensional wine. It should drink well for 12–15 years. Just as impressive is the extraordinary 1997 Cabernet Franc. A massive, mountain-styled offering (unlike other California Cabernet Francs, with the possible exception of La Jota's), it boasts an opaque purple color as well as a fabulously sweet nose of black currants, cranberry liqueur, new oak, and roasted notes. Chewy, full-bodied, and exceptionally huge, this offering should become even more complex with another 5–6 years of cellaring. It should keep for two decades. This is a tour de force, particularly for Cabernet Franc. Anticipated maturity: now–2020.

The accolades don't stop with Pride Mountain's Merlot and Cabernet Franc. While only microscopic quantities were produced of the 1997 Reserve Claret and 1997 Cabernet Sauvignon Reserve, both are immense wines of extraordinary concentration and depth. The compelling 1997 Reserve Claret offers an opaque purple color in addition to a sumptuous bouquet of sweet blackberries, crème de cassis, and minerals, superb richness, exceptional concentration, and huge body. However, it manages to avoid being overbearing or unmanageable. Purity and delineation are also present in this multidimensional, prodigious wine. Although an infant in terms of development, it is accessible because of the ripe tannin and spectacularly concentrated fruit. Anticipated maturity: now–2025. Even more amazing, the 1997 Cabernet Sauvignon Reserve pushes richness to unreal levels. Despite its intense, ultra-concentrated style, it possesses a sense of balance and definition. The color is a saturated inky purple. The aromatics consist of lead pencil shavings, minerals, blackberries, cassis, and flowers. Extremely full-bodied, with amazing purity, mouthcoating richness, sweet tannin, and low acidity, it offers profound drinking even though it has not yet begun to develop secondary nuances. Anticipated maturity: 2003–2025.

The opaque black/purple-colored 1997 Cabernet Sauvignon (3,472 cases) offers sensational notes of black currants, minerals, smoke, licorice, and new oak. Full-bodied, with fabulous extract and power, the acidity, tannin, and potentially harsh components are well meshed with the wine's personality. This is a large, ripe, impeccably balanced Cabernet Sauvignon that achieved 14.1% alcohol naturally. Anticipated maturity: 2003–2020. The virtually perfect 1996 Cabernet Sauvignon Reserve (330 cases) is 100% Cabernet Sauvignon. Opaque purple-colored, with a profound bouquet of minerals, flowers, black fruits, and spice, this awesomely concentrated, multilayered wine represents the essence of Cabernet Sauvignon. Amazingly, it is neither ponderous nor heavy-handed, with the oak, acidity, and tannin woven into the wine's formidable, concentrated personality. The finish lasts for nearly a minute. Sadly, it is extremely limited in availability, but what a compelling wine it is! Anticipated maturity: 2008–2025. Nearly as spectacular as the 1996 Reserve Cabernet Sauvignon is the 1996 Reserve Claret. A blend of 63% Merlot, 32% Cabernet Sauvignon, and 5% Petite Verdot (230 cases), it is a gorgeously balanced, super-concentrated yet hauntingly symmetrical wine with copious quantities of black fruits, spicy new oak, minerals, licorice, and roasted herbs. Full-bodied, with a cherry liqueur–like richness to its fruit, this wine has loads of glycerin, fabulous extract, and no hard edges. The velvety finish lasts for 40+ seconds. These are spectacular wines that must be tasted to be believed.

The 1996 Cabernet Franc (a blend of 75% Cabernet Franc and 25% Cabernet Sauvignon) has filled out considerably, exhibiting a dense ruby/purple color, followed by a knockout nose of black cherries, herbs, and spice. In the mouth, the wine is rich with layers of flavor. This superb, medium- to full-bodied example is the quintessential Cabernet Franc, offering elegance along with plenty of power and richness. It should drink well for 10–15 years. Another wine that tasted better in mid-July of 1998 than it did at the winery nine months earlier is the 1996 Merlot. A blend of 95% Merlot and 5% Cabernet Sauvignon, it boasts a dense purple color as well as a beautiful nose of black fruits, smoke, herbs, and underbrush. Thick and full-bodied, with terrific fruit, purity, and extraction, this is a deeper, richer, more complete wine than I originally predicted. It should age well for 10–12 years.

The two limited-production offerings from Pride Mountain Vineyards are the 1995 Claret Reserve and 1995 Cabernet Sauvignon Reserve. There are 230 cases of the former, and 330 cases of the latter. The fabulous 1995 Claret Reserve (a blend of 64% Cabernet Sauvignon, 33% Merlot, and 3% Petit Verdot) offers an opaque ruby/purple color, and a classic crème de cassis nose intermixed with toasty new oak and minerals. Full-bodied, with superb texture, dense, massively rich flavors, and a 40+-second finish, this is a gorgeously made, Bordeaux-styled wine with dazzling levels of fruit and extract. Anticipated maturity: now–2015. The 1995 Cabernet Sauvignon Reserve has come of age now that it is in the bottle. This is the essence of North Coast Cabernet Sauvignon, offering port-like thickness and richness, a superb black currant, mineral, cedar, and toast-scented nose, full-bodied flavors of extraordinary intensity and overall balance, and a long, moderately tannic, multidimensional finish. Anticipated maturity: 2003–2025. Shame on me for underestimating these beauties!

Pride Mountain's 1995 Cabernet Franc, a blend of 75% Cabernet Franc and 25% Cabernet Sauvignon (400 cases produced), reminded me of the unblended *cuvée* of Cabernet Franc that usually goes into Dalla Valle's extraordinary proprietary red wine Maya. For a Cabernet Franc, it possesses an uncommonly dense black/purple color and a sweet nose of licorice, underbrush, red as well as black currants, and toast. Amazingly extracted, yet somehow retaining its elegance, this wine offers the essence of black fruits in its long, rich, medium- to full-bodied flavors. There is enough acidity and some tannin, but its extraordinary purity and equilibrium are hallmarks of this smashing effort. Anticipated maturity: now–2016.

Pride Mountain's 1994 Reserve Claret (98 cases produced) possesses an opaque purple color, followed by a nose with underbrush, cassis, smoke, and toasty notes. Full-bodied, super-extracted, with layers of ripe fruit, and well-integrated tannin and acidity, this is an enormously endowed, layered wine that unfolds magnificently in the glass and on the palate. Anticipated maturity: now–2020. The 1994 Cabernet Sauvignon Reserve (the first Reserve Cabernet Sauvignon they made) is produced from 100% Cabernet Sauvignon and aged completely in French oak casks. It is another profound Cabernet from the exceptional 1994 vintage. The wine's opaque purple color and huge, massive richness do not come across as heavy, despite the wine's extraordinary intensity and thickness. There is enough acidity for freshness, and plenty of sweet, well-integrated tannin. This large-scaled, magnificently endowed Cabernet Sauvignon needs 5–6 years of cellaring, but it should keep for 25+ years.

QUINTESSA (NAPA)

1994 Proprietary Red Wine	Rutherford	E	89

A blend of 39% Cabernet Sauvignon, 31% Merlot, and 30% Cabernet Franc, this dark ruby/purple-colored 1994 possesses an elegant, graceful bouquet (sweet cherries and kirsch) that has been subtly influenced by toasty new oak. The medium-bodied, subtle yet rich, red currant/black currant flavors unfold nicely in the mouth. This is an understated, measured, impeccably well made, claret-styled Cabernet Sauvignon that offers beautiful richness and layers of harmonious flavors. Impressive. Drink it over the next 10–14 years.

QUIVIRA VINEYARDS (SONOMA)

1998 Zinfandel	Dry Creek	C	88
1994 Zinfandel	Sonoma	C	88

A delicious, elegant, fruit-driven effort, Quivira's medium-bodied 1998 Zinfandel exhibits nicely integrated acidity and subtle wood. The emphasis is on this varietal's berry/briery fruit. With excellent purity and refreshing vibrancy, it can be enjoyed over the next 3–4 years. A classically styled Zin, Quivira's fully mature 1994 is rich and pure, with plenty of the varietal's briery, peppery, black and red fruit character. There is moderate body, plenty of purity, and a clean, crisp, long finish. It is an attractive, medium-weight Zinfandel that requires consumption.

QUPÉ WINE CELLARS (SANTA BARBARA)

1997 Syrah Bien Nacido Vineyard	Santa Barbara	D	89
1997 Syrah Hillside Estate Bien Nacido Vineyard	Santa Barbara	D	(90–92)
1997 Syrah Reserve Bien Nacido Vineyard	Santa Barbara	D	(87–90)

Qupé, one of the original Rhône Rangers, continues to do a fine job with an assortment of varietals. The 1997 Syrahs are serious efforts. Qupé's 1997 Syrah Bien Nacido Vineyard exhibits a deep ruby/purple color with purple nuances. Noteworthy quantities of blackberry fruit, dried herbs, spice, and floral scents jump from the glass. There is terrific fruit, medium to full body, a supple texture with sweet tannin lurking in the background, and a fine finish. Drinkable now, it should continue to evolve for 5–7 years. The 1997 Syrah Reserve Bien Nacido Vineyard possesses a deep ruby/purple color and plenty of smoky, blackberry fruit intermixed with toast, damp foresty scents, and pepper. The wine exhibits excellent richness, sweet tannin, and a medium- to full-bodied, long finish. It should drink well during its first 7–10 years of life. The most concentrated Syrah in this estate's portfolio is the 1997 Syrah Hillside Estate Bien Nacido Vineyard. It boasts an opaque ruby/purple color, as well as thick, juicy fruit, full body, adequate acidity and tannin, and a powerful, gutsy, earthy finish. Unquestionably the most complete wine among these offerings, this impressively endowed Syrah should hit its stride with 2–3 years of bottle age and last for 10–15.

A. RAFANELLI WINERY (SONOMA)

1997 Zinfandel	Dry Creek	C	90
1995 Zinfandel	Dry Creek	C	92
1994 Zinfandel	Dry Creek	C	89

Once again Rafanelli has fashioned one of the vintage's stars. In a year where too many Zinfandels taste as if the grapes were harvested too early from an overly abundant crop, Rafanelli's 1997 Zinfandel exhibits superb purity, wonderful fruit, and the classic black raspberry/cherry, spicy Zin aromatic and flavor profile. The wine's deep ruby/purple color is followed by a sweet attack, dried, full-bodied flavors, copious quantities of black fruits, and a long, lusty finish. This is what Zinfandel should be! Per the label, there is 14.5% alcohol, which is neither wimpish nor excessive. Enjoy this beauty over the next 5–6 years.

Rafanelli has made so many gorgeous Zinfandels it is hard to say the 1995 Zinfandel Unfiltered is one of their finest, but, wow, I was knocked out by the opaque purple color, as well as the gorgeously pure display of blackberry, raspberry, and cherry fruit. Full-bodied, with no hard edges, a voluptuous texture, and layers of fruit, this is a delicious, full-throttle, impeccably well balanced wine that should drink well for another 6–7 years. Kudos to Rafanelli.

Not the super-concentrated heavyweight I would have expected from this vintage, Rafanelli's 1994 is, however, a textbook, richly fruity, peppery, soft, generous, medium-bodied wine with excellent depth and balance. Plenty of sweet black-cherry/raspberry, vanilla-tinged fruit slides over the palate with no bumps or bruises. Drink it up.

RAVENSWOOD WINERY (SONOMA)

1996	Zinfandel	Lodi	B	88
1995	Zinfandel	Sonoma	C	88
1999	Zinfandel Barricia	Sonoma	D	90
1998	Zinfandel Barricia	Sonoma	D	90
1999	Zinfandel Big River	Alexander Valley	D	91
1998	Zinfandel Big River	Alexander Valley	D	90
1997	Zinfandel Cooke Vineyard	Sonoma	D	89
1996	Zinfandel Cooke Vineyard	Sonoma	C	90
1995	Zinfandel Cooke Vineyard	Sonoma	D	92
1999	Zinfandel Dickerson Vineyard	Napa	D	89
1998	Zinfandel Kunde Vineyard	Sonoma	D	89
1997	Zinfandel Monte Rosso Vineyard	Sonoma	D	90
1996	Zinfandel Monte Rosso Vineyard	Sonoma	D	92
1995	Zinfandel Monte Rosso Vineyard	Sonoma	D	92
1999	Zinfandel Old Hill Ranch	Sonoma	D	92
1997	Zinfandel Old Hill Ranch	Sonoma	D	90
1995	Zinfandel Old Hill Ranch	Sonoma	D	91+
1996	Zinfandel Old Hill Ranch Limited Edition	Sonoma	D	90
1999	Zinfandel Teldeschi Vineyard	Dry Creek	D	90
1998	Zinfandel Teldeschi Vineyard	Dry Creek	D	88
1997	Zinfandel Teldeschi Vineyard	Dry Creek	D	90
1996	Zinfandel Wood Road–Belloni Vineyard	Russian River	D	90
1995	Zinfandel Wood Road–Belloni Vineyard	Russian River	D	90

Ravenswood's glories are their single-vineyard Zinfandels, which are consistently among the finest produced in California. The 1999 Zinfandel Dickerson Vineyard is the best example produced from this Napa vineyard in more than a decade. It exhibits copious quantities of sweet black cherry and blackberry fruit as well as a hint of raspberries in its big, spicy, peppery bouquet. Medium- to full-bodied, elegant, concentrated, and powerful, it should drink well for 7–8 years. The nicely textured, deep purple-colored 1999 Zinfandel Barricia offers a sweet perfume of black cherries, berries, smoke, earth, and tar. Full-bodied, chewy, and multilayered, it cuts a big swath across the palate with no hard edges. Drink it over the next 5–7 years. I loved the spectacular Zinfandel Old Hill Ranch (normally a classic as well as a candidate for the Zinfandel of the vintage). The 1999 boasts a dense ruby/purple color in addition to a gorgeous nose of new saddle leather, balsam wood, spice box, black cherry liqueur, and blackberries. The attack is sweet (from glycerin and extract, not sugar), and the finish is full-bodied, rich, and explosive. This 1999 will drink well for a decade or more. Another spectacular offering is the 1999 Zinfandel Big River. Tasting like a confiture of black raspberries and blackberries, this full-bodied, unctuously textured, impressively pure, ripe wine is thrilling to smell and taste. It will drink well for 7–8 years. The opaque purple-colored 1999 Zinfandel Teldeschi Vineyard exhibits complex aromatics consisting of incense, crushed black pepper, and black cherry/berry fruit. Dense, full-bodied, opulently textured, and powerful, with tannin and acidity for structure, it requires another year of cellaring, and should drink well for a decade. There are approximately 1,000 cases each of these.

The 1998 Zinfandel Teldeschi Vineyard is a structured, sinewy, earthy effort with plenty of allspice and pepper infused with scents of saddle leather and berry fruit presented in a medium-bodied, sweet format. It should drink well for 4–5 years. More fruit-driven is the 1998 Zinfandel Kunde Vineyard. A dark ruby color is followed by a tasty, delicious, hedonistically styled, medium- to full-bodied, flavorful wine offering abundant quantities of ripe berry fruit, glycerin, and alcohol. This crowd-pleasing Zin should be consumed over the next 5–6 years. Two outstanding wines include the 1998 Zinfandel Big River Vineyard and 1998

Zinfandel Barricia Vineyard. The 1998 Zinfandel Big River's saturated ruby/purple color is accompanied by ground pepper, briery fruit, underbrush, and sweet red and black currant aromas. In the mouth, notes of lavender and dried herbs give the wine a Mediterranean-like personality. Dense, chewy, and concentrated, this ripe but balanced Zin should drink well for 5–7 years. The opaque purple-colored 1998 Zinfandel Barricia is muscular and full-bodied, with outstanding concentration, extract, and admirable levels of glycerin in the long finish. Youthful and chunky, this wine reveals structure, muscle, and impressive intensity. Give it another 6 months of bottle age and enjoy it over the following 5–7 years.

As might be expected, wine-maker par excellence Joel Peterson has turned out some of the 1997 vintage's finest wines. One of Ravenswood's stars is always the Zinfandel Old Hill Ranch. The 1997 (110-year-old vines and 14.5% alcohol) boasts an opaque purple color, in addition to full-bodied, exuberant, powerful flavors with gritty tannin in the long, impressively endowed finish. This purely made wine provides copious quantities of black fruits along with dusty spice elements. It is one of the few 1997 Zinfandels that warrant 6–12 months of bottle age. It should keep for 7–8 years. The opaque purple-colored 1997 Zinfandel Cooke Vineyard (14.9% alcohol) also displays tangy acidity, but the extra layers of concentrated fruit neutralize the acid. There is a gorgeous nose of roasted meats, new saddle leather, dried herbs, and black fruits. Ripe, deep, medium- to full-bodied, and buttressed by the aforementioned acidity, the finish is slightly compressed, but impressive. It should drink well for 7–8 years. The gorgeous, dark purple-colored 1997 Zinfandel Teldeschi (15.5% alcohol) offers knockout aromas of smoke, licorice, blackberries, and cherries. There is sound acidity, medium to full body, dry tannin, copious fruit and glycerin, and a nicely layered, mouth-filling finish. It should drink well for 7–8 years. Another outstanding effort from Ravenswood is the 1997 Zinfandel Monte Rosso (15.5% alcohol). This effort exhibits an impressively saturated ruby/purple color and sweet mineral and blackberry flavors intermixed with dried herbs, kirsch, and stone-like scents. The vintage's telltale zingy acidity is present, but is more than compensated for by the concentrated, rich fruit. I suspect this will be one of Ravenswood's longest-lived Zinfandels, lasting until 2006+.

Not surprisingly, Ravenswood turned out a portfolio of powerful, full-throttle 1996 Zinfandels that live up to the winery's motto "No Wimpy Wines." The hedonistic 1996 Zinfandel Lodi (14.3% alcohol) reveals a southern Rhône–like, peppery, *herbes de Provence, garrigue*-scented nose intermixed with iodine and cherry liqueur. This is an immensely satisfying, rich, expansively flavored wine for consuming over the next 1–2 years. It should blend beautifully with grilled foods. The 1996 Zinfandel Old Hill Ranch Limited Edition offers a saturated ruby/purple color, followed by a knockout nose of briery fruit, charcoal, chocolate, and peppery spice. In the mouth, there is some rusticity to the wine's structure, but it provides a full-bodied, exciting combination of blackberry and cherry fruit supported by copious quantities of glycerin and decent acidity. It will offer a compelling mouthful over the next 1–2 years. The 1996 Zinfandel Cooke Vineyard (14.8% alcohol) exhibits a dense, dark ruby/purple color, a big, dusty, pepper-tinged, cherry liqueur–scented nose, and full-bodied, multi-layered flavors with plenty of muscle and length. This viscous wine saturates the palate, and finishes with notes of earth and jammy fruit. Drink it over the next 1–2 years for its exuberance and fiery character. (Note that the 1996 Cooke Vineyard is sold only at the winery's tasting room.) The highly extracted, saturated purple-colored 1996 Zinfandel Wood Road–Belloni Vineyard is a macho Zin in every sense of the word. Not only does it boast nearly 15% alcohol, it possesses explosive richness and layers of grilled meat, blackberry and cherry liqueur–like flavors that have been heavily spiced, not to mention crammed with glycerin and extract. This knockout Zinfandel is almost *sauvage* (as the French would say), but it is oh, so rich and gutsy. It should drink well for 1–2 years. My favorite of this noteworthy group is the 1996 Zinfandel Monte Rosso. Another powerhouse with 15% natural alcohol, this exquisite example offers a dark saturated plum/purple color. Sweet cedar, iodine, pepper, fruitcake, Rhône-like notes soar from the glass of this fleshy, massive Zin. Huge and rich in the mouth, yet neither coarse nor ponderous, it boasts layers of flavor, outstanding purity and harmony, and a whoppingly long finish. Already delicious, it should be consumed.

The 1995 Zinfandel Sonoma (14.5% alcohol) is a broadly flavored, mouth-filling, savory wine with Zinfandel's telltale, earthy, peppery, sweet, jammy black cherry–scented aromas, medium to full body, an expansive, chewy texture, and a lusty, high alcohol finish. Already delicious, it should continue to drink well for 1–2 years. Zinfandel lovers will be pleased to know there were 3,045 cases produced of the 1995 Zinfandel Wood Road–Belloni, a wine produced from four separate Russian River vineyards (Arata, Belloni, Chelli, and Rue). This nearly opaque purple-colored wine is a powerful, tight, full-bodied, well-structured Zinfandel that is loaded with earthy, dark fruits. Its broodingly backward, yet formidably endowed personality offers spice, jammy black fruits, and plenty of glycerin and alcohol (14.9%). This is a classic, rich, ageworthy Zinfandel that should provide marvelous drinking over the next decade. The 1995 Zinfandel Cooke Vineyard from Sonoma Valley is made in much more limited quantities (435 cases). It offers an explosive nose of licorice, pepper, allspice, black plum and cherry fruit. A great Zinfandel with fabulous concentration, the wine's wealth of fruit and glycerin conceal the lofty alcohol level of 15.2%. Totally dry, this super-concentrated wine reveals none of the late-harvest characteristics suggested by its high alcohol and huge size. This is a tour de force in Zinfandel winemaking! Drink it over the next 1–2 years. I also thought the 1995 Zinfandel Old Hill Ranch (865 cases produced from 110-year-old vines) to be an outstanding Zinfandel. Although it is the tightest-knit of the Ravenswood offerings, the opaque ruby/purple color, exquisite briery and wild berry–scented nose, full-bodied, powerful flavors, and exceptional purity, texture, and length all point to a lustrous future for this massive Zin. It is fully mature.

The 1995 Zinfandel Monte Rosso Vineyard, an Arnold Schwarzenegger–like Zinfandel (15.4% alcohol; 1,650 cases), screams from the glass with peppery, loamy, black fruit–like scents. On the palate, the wine is huge, with mouthcoating layers of highly extracted fruit allied with chewy glycerin. This opaque purple-colored wine appears to possess another 6–8 years of aging potential. It is one of the great wines of the vintage. Kudos to proprietor Joel Peterson for producing a bevy of Zinfandels that are particularly brilliant in view of the overall quality level that has emerged from this vintage.

Past Glories: 1993 Merlot Sangiacomo (90), 1993 Pickberry Proprietary Red Wine (93)

RENARD (RUSSIAN RIVER)

1997 Syrah Timbervine Ranch Cuvée El Niño	Russian River	D	91

A new producer for me, Bayard Fox ("fox" is *renard* in French) has fashioned a powerful Syrah. The superb 1997 Syrah Timbervine Ranch Cuvée El Niño reveals multiple layers of crème de cassis in addition to a touch of licorice and floral notes. Huge, fat, ripe, and layered, with full body and sensational concentration and purity, this gorgeous Syrah will drink beautifully over the next 12 years.

RENWOOD WINERY (AMADOR)

1997 Zinfandel D'Agostini Brothers	Shenandoah	D	89
1996 Zinfandel D'Agostini Brothers	Shenandoah	D	88

The intense, dark ruby/purple-colored 1997 Zinfandel D'Agostini Brothers (15.6% alcohol) offers copious quantities of rich, chewy, cherry, briery fruit, and spice, as well as a full-bodied, tannic, ruggedly constructed, macho finish. Drink it over the next 1–2 years. The 1996 Zinfandel D'Agostini Brothers displays peppery, plum, black raspberry, and cherry fruit, full body, sweetness and richness on the palate (although it is a dry wine), and none of the coarseness or excessive muscular characteristics of this winery's other 1996 Zinfandels. It should drink well for 1–2 years.

REVERIE (NAPA)

1995 Cabernet Franc Diamond Mountain	Napa	D	89
1996 Cabernet Sauvignon Diamond Mountain	Napa	D	89
1995 Cabernet Sauvignon Diamond Mountain	Napa	D	88
1996 Special Reserve Diamond Mountain	Napa	E	90
1995 Special Reserve Diamond Mountain	Napa	E	90

This winery is experimenting with Tempranillo (the 1995, 1996, and 1997 were all pleasant, but uninspiring efforts), as well as Barbera (the 1997 may turn out to be surprisingly good, but this varietal's naturally high acidity needs to be tamed). So far, Reverie's finest efforts have been with Cabernet Sauvignon. For example, the 1996 Cabernet Sauvignon Diamond Mountain (75% Cabernet Sauvignon and 25% Cabernet Franc) is a complex, Bordeaux-styled offering with tobacco, spice box, cedar, and black currant fruit. This dark ruby-colored wine displays a layered mid-palate and excellent length. While some tannin is noticeable, the wine's overall style is elegant and pure. Reverie's one outstanding offering is the 1996 Special Reserve proprietary red (87% Cabernet Sauvignon and 13% Cabernet Franc). Only 252 cases of this beauty were produced. Bottled unfiltered, this is a Bordeaux-styled wine with a Médoc-like, mineral, lead pencil, and black currant fruitiness intertwined with weedy tobacco and spice-box scents. Dense, with high tannin as well as beautiful rich, ripe fruit, this stylish, graceful, potentially complex wine would be difficult to pick out as a California Cabernet in a blind tasting. Anticipated maturity: now–2020.

The medium dark ruby-colored 1995 Cabernet Franc possesses a 92-point nose and an 88-point palate. It offers a terrific raspberry, floral, and vanilla-scented nose that leaps from the glass. The wine possesses excellent richness, medium body, and fine purity and equilibrium. It should drink well for a decade or more. The classic, elegant, restrained, and closed, medium-bodied 1995 Cabernet Sauvignon displays fine density, but extremely high tannin. Enough black currant fruit emerges for optimism, but patience is required. Give this wine 3–5 years of cellaring, and consume it over the following 15 years. The outstanding 1995 Special Reserve makes me think that its 1996 sibling will certainly come around with more time in barrel. The 1995 Special Reserve, a blend of 90% Cabernet Sauvignon, 5% Cabernet Franc, and 5% Petit Verdot, possesses a deep ruby/purple color, a spicy, ripe, concentrated character, tight aromatics, but enticing quantities of red and black fruits, minerals, and toasty notes. This elegant wine should repay readers willing to cellar it for 5–6 years. It appears to have all the necessary raw materials to last for two decades or more.

RIDGE VINEYARDS (SANTA CLARA)

1997 Cabernet Sauvignon Monte Bello	Santa Cruz	EE	91+
1996 Cabernet Sauvignon Monte Bello	Santa Cruz	EE	95+
1995 Cabernet Sauvignon Monte Bello	Santa Cruz	EE	91+
1998 Dusi Ranch	Paso Robles	D	89
1999 Geyserville Proprietary Red Wine	Sonoma	D	91
1998 Geyserville Proprietary Red Wine	Sonoma	D	90
1997 Geyserville Proprietary Red Wine	Sonoma	D	91
1996 Geyserville Proprietary Red Wine	Sonoma	D	89
1996 Grenache Lytton Estate	Sonoma	C	88
1999 Lytton Estate Late Harvest Proprietary Red Wine	Sonoma	D	92
1999 Lytton Springs Proprietary Red Wine	Sonoma	D	90
1998 Lytton Springs Proprietary Red Wine	Sonoma	D	90
1997 Lytton Springs Proprietary Red Wine	Sonoma	D	92
1996 Lytton Springs Proprietary Red Wine	Sonoma	D	90
1998 Mazzoni Home Ranch Proprietary	Sonoma	D	90

1997 Mazzoni Home Ranch Proprietary (ATP)	Sonoma	D	90
1998 Pagani Ranch	Sonoma	D	88
1998 Sonoma Station	Sonoma	D	89
1996 Syrah Lytton Springs	Sonoma	C	88
1999 Zinfandel	Paso Robles	C	88
1997 Zinfandel	Paso Robles	D	(90–92)
1996 Zinfandel Dusi Ranch	Paso Robles	D	88
1997 Zinfandel Jimsonare	Santa Cruz	D	90+
1999 Zinfandel Late Picked	Sonoma	D	89
1997 Zinfandel Lytton Springs	Sonoma	C	91
1995 Zinfandel Lytton Springs	Sonoma	C	91
1999 Zinfandel Nervo Late Picked (ATP)	California	D	94
1997 Zinfandel Pagani Ranch	Sonoma	D	90
1996 Zinfandel Pagani Ranch	Sonoma	D	88
1997 Zinfandel Sonoma Station	Sonoma	D	89
1996 Zinfandel Sonoma Station	Sonoma	D	89
1997 Zinfandel York Creek–Spring Mountain	Napa	D	88
1996 Zinfandel York Creek–Spring Mountain	Napa	D	89

Note that those wines with the designation ATP (meaning Advance Tasting Program) are sold only through Ridge's mailing list. The other wines are distributed nationally.

Nestled high in the Santa Cruz Mountains, with a precipitous view of the San Andreas fault, Ridge Vineyards has long been one of the classic reference points for high-quality California wines. While the winery now has a Japanese owner, longtime wine-maker Paul Draper continues to have complete control of vineyard management and winemaking. Production has inched up to 60,000 cases, with the potential for 8,000 cases of the famed Monte Bello Cabernet Sauvignon. However, most vintages tend to produce between 3,000–4,000 cases.

A blend of 90% Zinfandel and the rest Petite Sirah and Carignan, the dark ruby/purple-colored 1999 Zinfandel Paso Robles displays aromas of sandalwood, pepper, and black cherries. In the mouth, it is medium- to full-bodied, straightforward, and monolithic, without a great deal of complexity, but with good weight, fruit, and extract. It should drink well for 4–6 years. An exceptional offering from Ridge's portfolio is the 1999 Lytton Springs Proprietary Red Wine. This superb blend of 70% Zinfandel, 17% Petite Sirah, 10% Carignan, and 3% Mataro boasts a deep ruby/purple color in addition to a big, sweet bouquet of jammy berries, and a hint of raspberries as well as strawberries. Elegant and full-bodied, with layers of flavor, superb purity, a subtle dosage of American oak, and a full, long finish, it should drink well for 7–8 years. Also compelling, the 1999 Lytton Estate Late Harvest Proprietary Red Wine is produced from 100-year-old Zinfandel and Petite Sirah vines (50% of each). It tips the scales at a whopping 17.3% alcohol, but the residual sugar is a lowly 1.2%. The wine does not come across as sweet, nor does it reveal any of the pruny, Amarone-like characteristics displayed by many late-harvest Zinfandels. This exceptional, dense purple-colored 1999 exhibits a gorgeous perfume of blackberry jam intermixed with barbecue spice, meat, hickory, and earth. Dry in the mouth, with huge levels of glycerin, extract, and richness, this full-bodied, ripe Zinfandel will drink well for 10–15 years.

The exceptional 1999 Geyserville Proprietary Red Wine (a blend of 68% Zinfandel, 16% Carignan, and 16% Petite Sirah with 14.8% alcohol) offers aromas of black currants, kirsch, minerals, smoky oak, earth, and spice. It possesses superb concentration, excellent definition, tremendous purity, and mouth-staining extract without heaviness. A long finish further enhances this sensational, Zin-dominated offering. Consume it over the next 7–9 years. Late-harvest offerings include the 1999 Zinfandel Late Picked, a blend of primarily Zinfandel with a touch of Petite Sirah that tips the scales at 16% alcohol with 1.2% residual sugar. Neither raisiny nor sweet, it offers abundant amounts of glycerin, ripeness, and pepper in its full-bodied, fleshy, muscular personality. It should drink well for a decade. Readers looking for a Zinfandel made in the style of Henri Bonneau's famed Châteauneuf-du-Pape Réserve des Célestins should check out Ridge's 1999 Zinfandel Nervo Late Picked (ATP). A blend of 92% Zinfandel and 8% Petite Sirah, with only .2% residual sugar, this dry wine is made in an enormously concentrated, full-bodied style. It offers huge layers of blackberry and black cherry fruit intertwined with meat, earth, smoke, and underbrush. Formidably endowed, with enormous amounts of glycerin, this powerful yet supple, accessible 1999 is a tour de force in winemaking. Readers on Ridge's mailing list who enjoy large-scaled wines should be sure to latch onto a few bottles of this gem. It should drink well for 10–15 years.

Readers should note that Ridge dropped the word "Zinfandel" from their 1998s. Of course, all of them are in essence Zinfandels, with various percentages of that varietal included in the blend. None is less than 71% Zinfandel, with the Dusi Ranch made from 100% Zinfandel. The dark ruby/purple-colored 1998 Mazzoni Home Ranch (71% Zinfandel, 21% Carignan, and 8% Petite Sirah) exhibits fat, sweet aromas of melted road tar, black currants, cherry jam, and licorice. Full-bodied, deep, and expansive, this low-acid, plump, fleshy offering is meant to be drunk now and over the next 5–6 years. One of Ridge's classic efforts, the 1998 Geyserville (74% Zinfandel, 15% Petite Sirah, 10% Carignan, and 1% Matero) possesses Bordeaux-like complexity and elegance. The alcohol is listed as 14.1%. The wine was reticent on the day I tasted it, but as it sat in the glass, sweet aromas of minerals, smoky wood, red/black currants, and dried herbs emerged. This classy, elegant, restrained, yet authoritatively rich Zinfandel should be consumed over the next 5–6 years. The 1998 Dusi Ranch (the only 100% Zinfandel offering tasted from Ridge) exhibits aromas of roasted peanuts and smoky, black cherry and currant fruit. There is good structure and delineation, a dense, rich, medium- to full-bodied palate, and a long, concentrated finish. Interestingly, the back label indicated that this was the first time in over 25 years that the Dusi Ranch was harvested in October because of the extremely cold, wet spring. Another Ridge classic, the deep ruby/purple-colored 1998 Lytton Springs (14.3% alcohol; 77% Zinfandel, 16% Petite Sirah, 4% Matero, 2% Carignan, and 1% Alicante) boasts a sweet nose of briery fruit mixed with red and black currants, minerals, pepper, and smoke. Medium- to full-bodied, with dried Provençal herb characteristics that emerge with airing, this fleshy, beautifully pure, and stunningly proportioned Zin can be drunk now as well as over the next 5–6 years. Perhaps the best value in Ridge's Zinfandel portfolio is the 1998 Sonoma Station. A blend of 75% Zinfandel, 11% Carignan, 9% Alicante, and 5% Petite Sirah that achieved 13.7% alcohol, this peppery, dried herb, red and black currant–scented and flavored wine is medium-bodied, with abundant levels of berry fruit, good purity, and a soft, straightforward, fleshy character similar to an impeccably made Côtes du Rhône. Drink it over the next 3–4 years. A more Amarone-like late-harvest character can be found in the 1998 Pagani Ranch (a blend of 88% Zinfandel, 9% Alicante, and 3% Petite Sirah). A dense ruby color is followed by scents of melted road tar, animal fur, sweet, jammy plums, and smoky cherries. Medium- to full-bodied, not terribly complex, but round and chewy, this wine should be consumed over the next 4–5 years.

The 1997 Zinfandels are all high in alcohol, largely because of vintage conditions. All are slightly more successful than Ridge's very fine 1996s. For example, the 1997 Zinfandel Paso Robles offers overripe prunes, plums, and cherries in the nose, explosive fruit, copious glycerin, and a full-bodied, chewy, seductive character. It should be drunk over the next 1–2 years. The 1997 Geyserville Proprietary Red Wine (74% Zinfandel, 15% Carignan, 10% Petite Sirah, and 1% Mourvèdre, with 14.9% alcohol) offers explosive aromas of jammy berry fruit and flavors redolent with notes of plums, cherries, raspberries, and smoky wood. Open-knit and expansive, with low acidity, this evolved, forward, hedonistic wine will drink well for 1–2 years. The opaque purple-colored 1997 Zinfandel Pagani Ranch (88% Zinfandel, 7% Mataro, 3% Petite Sirah, and 2% Alicante Bouchet that achieved 14.6% alcohol) exhibits what the French call *sur-maturité* (overripeness). A monolithic wine with huge, muscular, concentrated flavors, it had not yet begun to reveal much delineation or evolution, despite the fact it is already in bottle. There are layers of concentrated fruit, plenty of blackberry, plum, jammy notes, and enough acidity and tannin to buttress this enormously endowed wine. It will be even better with another six months of bottle age, and will last for 3–4 years. The 1997 Zinfandel Lytton Springs is an effusively fruity, full-bodied wine emphasizing Zinfandel's black cherry/raspberry character. With loads of glycerin, high alcohol, and outstanding purity and finish, this will be a hedonistic, luscious wine to enjoy through 2003. Interestingly, Paul Draper told me the alcohol levels for all these 1997 Zinfandels were well above 15%.

The opaque ruby/purple 1997 Mazzoni Home Ranch Proprietary Red Wine (ATP) (60% Zinfandel, 35% Carignan, and 5% Petite Sirah that achieved 13.8% alcohol) offers a beautiful black raspberry–scented nose with notes of licorice and spicy oak. It is a medium- to full-bodied, smoothly textured, hedonistic wine that will provide luscious drinking over the next 3–4 years. The dark ruby/purple-colored 1997 Zinfandel Sonoma Station (75% Zinfandel, 13% Carignan, 8% Petite Sirah, and 4% Alicante Bouchet) exhibits a big, briery, peppery, spicy nose, dense, rich, cherry and blackberry flavors, a deep, lush texture, and fine purity and intensity. It, too, should be drunk before 2004. Made from a blend of 80% Zinfandel, 15% Petite Sirah, 2% Carignan, 2% Mataro, and 1% Grenache, the 1997 Lytton Springs Proprietary Red Wine (14.9% alcohol) exhibits a saturated purple color in addition to sumptuous aromas of truffles, licorice, loamy soil, blackberry liqueur, and cherries. There are layers of concentration, sweet glycerin in the mid-palate, and a blockbuster, concentrated, opulently textured finish. It should drink well for 6 years.

One of the greatest old Zinfandels I ever tasted was the 1970 Jimsonare. Ridge rarely bottles this as a single-source wine because the vineyard is at such a high elevation that the grapes never fully ripen. That was not the case in 1997. The saturated opaque black/purple-colored 1997 Zinfandel Jimsonare (100% Zinfandel) achieved 14.8% alcohol. It boasts enormously rich, massive, blackberry and cherry flavors, rustic tannin, and a gigantic, monster finish that lasts for over 30 seconds. The wine also exhibits copious quantities of toasty oak. It is by far the most concentrated and immense of the Ridge offerings, as well as the least evolved. This Zinfandel should age well for 5–6 years. In contrast, the 1997 Zinfandel York Creek (95% Zinfandel and 5% Petite Sirah that weighs in at 15.3% alcohol) is a more spice, earth, and licorice-scented wine with plenty of rustic tannin, a gritty texture, medium to full body, and deep, concentrated, muscular flavors. With an uncivilized tannin level and rusticity, it should be consumed over the next 3–4 years.

The 1997 Cabernet Sauvignon Monte Bello exhibits an opaque purple color, as well as a black currant, mineral, and smoky oak-scented nose. The wine is medium- to full-bodied, tannic, and in need of 10 years of cellaring. Not a blockbuster, this offering is more elegant and finesse-styled than usual. However, as with previous Monte Bellos, it will take a long time to come around, yet it will keep for 2–3 decades. The 1996 Cabernet Sauvignon Monte Bello (80% Cabernet Sauvignon, 11% Merlot, and 9% Petit Verdot that reached 13.4% alcohol) represents a severe selection of only 40% of the vineyard's crop. A powerful, concentrated blockbuster, it possesses an opaque purple color, plenty of spicy oak in the nose (100% American oak has always been used for aging Monte Bello), and a deep, layered, concentrated style. There is plenty of tannin, but it is sweeter than that found in the 1997, and the wine is more concentrated and extracted. There is a touch of oak in the flavors, which are otherwise dominated by minerals and jammy black fruits. This is a terrific Monte Bello that will have 30+ years of life. The 1995 Monte Bello is actually a Proprietary Red Wine as the blend is 69% Cabernet Sauvignon, 18% Merlot, 10% Petit Verdot, and 3% Cabernet Franc. It was made from an extremely severe selection of only 25% of the harvest. Draper feels it is the biggest, brawniest, and most muscular Monte Bello of the 1990s and in need of 10–15 more years of cellaring. This saturated ruby/purple-colored effort is still backward, with a closed nose of minerals, oak, and subtle black fruits. In the mouth, it is large-scaled, tannic, rich, and long, but nearly abrasive because of its high tannin level. This youthful, muscular monster will require significant cellaring. Anticipated maturity: 2010–2035.

Ridge owns the Lytton Springs estate, from which it produced two interesting Rhône Ranger wines in 1996. The 1996 Syrah Lytton Springs was blended with 5% Viognier and tips the scales at 14.2% alcohol. The Viognier was vinified with the Syrah, resulting in a richly fruity (blackberries and currants), lush, round, hedonistically styled wine with low acidity, and a plump, savory character. It should drink well until 2004. Also intriguing is the 1996 Grenache Lytton Springs (made from 92% Grenache, 6% Zinfandel, and 2% Petite Sirah). This wine's deep ruby color is followed by a gorgeous nose of jammy strawberries, kirsch, and dried cherries. Fruity, with good glycerin, medium to full body, and loads of fruit, this textbook, very yummy Grenache should be consumed before 2004.

Ridge produced a fine series of 1996 Zinfandels. They reveal the vintage's rich, high-alcohol personality, and forward, immediately drinkable style. I do not believe the 1996 vintage will hold together beyond 2005, despite the high alcohol. The tiny Zinfandel crop resulted in concentrated wines, but they are not as exceptionally deep as one might have expected given the small yields. Ridge's 1996 Zinfandel Sonoma Station (an 80% Zinfandel, 8% Petite Sirah, 8% Alicante, and 4% Carignan blend that achieved 14.4% alcohol) displays a dark ruby color and a rich, briery, raspberry-scented nose with gobs of spice and pepper. Medium-bodied, with excellent concentration and subtle new oak in the background, this delicious, broadly flavored Zinfandel is best drunk over the next 1–3 years. Ridge has consistently done a fine job with their Zinfandel from the Dusi Ranch in Paso Robles. The 1996 (95% Zinfandel and 5% Petite Sirah with 14.6% alcohol) boasts a deep saturated ruby/purple color (among the darkest of the Ridge offerings) and subtle aromatics (primarily earth intermixed with black raspberries, pepper, and licorice). This medium- to full-bodied, spicy Zinfandel appears to possess a firm structure and ageability, but it does not have the underlying depth to warrant cellaring beyond 1–3 years. The 1996 Geyserville Proprietary Red Wine (a blend of 75% Zinfandel, 17% Carignan, 6% Petite Sirah, and 2% Mataro) tips the scales at 14.9% alcohol. In spite of the hefty alcohol content, it is an exceptionally elegant wine, with sweet, black raspberry and cherry fruit, medium body, and a dry, crisp, lightly tannic finish. This wine could easily pass for a high-class, mid-weight 1995 red Burgundy. As the wine sits in the mouth, its glycerin and multilayered texture are very appealing. It should drink well for 1–3 years. The 1996 Zinfandel York Creek–Spring Mountain (91% Zinfandel and 9% Petite Sirah) reveals a Bordeaux-like austerity to its flavor profile. There is plenty of tannin, but that does not mean this offering can be cellared for any length of time. The blackberry/cherry notes combine with spicy oak, pepper, and minerals for a moderately intense, enticing bouquet. In the mouth, the wine exhibits firmness, some American oak, as well as good spice and sweet fruit. Consume this classy, complex Zin over the next 1–2 years. The 1996 Lytton Springs Proprietary Red Wine (78% Zinfandel, 19% Petite Sirah, 2% Carignan, and 1% Grenache) possesses 14.5% alcohol. It boasts the sweetest, jammiest nose, as well as a healthy dark ruby/purple color, full body, robust, chewy flavors, and the best length of these offerings. This expansively flavored wine should drink well for 2–3 years. Lastly, the dark ruby-colored 1996 Zinfandel Pagani Ranch (82% Zinfandel, 11% Mataro, 4% Petite Sirah, and 3% Alicante) offers up aromas of earth, prunes, and ripe black fruits (almost Amarone in style). In the mouth, the wine is dry, medium- to full-bodied, rustic, less concentrated, and more civilized and restrained than several previous Pagani Ranch Zinfandels, which were blockbusters. This cleanly made wine should drink well for 2–3 years. These 1996s are all excellent, nearly outstanding Zinfandels that share a certain firmness and structured feel (particularly when compared to the 1995s, 1994s, and 1993s). Because of the definition and angularity, it would be natural for readers to think these wines require cellaring. My instincts and experience suggest these need to be drunk in their exuberant youth—over the next 2–3 years.

Past Glories: Cabernet Sauvignon Monte Bello—1993 (93+), 1992 (94), 1991 (95), 1990 (91), 1987 (92), 1985 (90), 1984 (92), 1977 (93), 1974 (96), 1971 (94), 1970 (95)

ROCHIOLI VINEYARD (SONOMA)

1997	Cabernet Sauvignon Neoma's Vineyard	Russian River	D	90
1996	Cabernet Sauvignon Neoma's Vineyard	Russian River	D	93
1999	Chardonnay	Russian River	D	90
1999	Chardonnay Allen Vineyard	Russian River	D	93
1999	Chardonnay River Block Vineyard	Russian River	D	92
1999	Chardonnay South River Vineyard	Russian River	D	94
1999	Pinot Noir East Block	Russian River	EE	95
1998	Pinot Noir East Block	Russian River	E	93
1997	Pinot Noir East Block	Russian River	E	92
1995	Pinot Noir East Block	Russian River	E	91
1999	Pinot Noir Estate	Russian River	D	90
1998	Pinot Noir Estate	Russian River	D	89
1997	Pinot Noir Estate	Russian River	D	88
1996	Pinot Noir Estate	Russian River	D	88
1995	Pinot Noir Estate	Russian River	C	89
1999	Pinot Noir Little Hill Block	Russian River	E	92
1998	Pinot Noir Little Hill Block	Russian River	E	91
1997	Pinot Noir Little Hill Block	Russian River	E	94
1996	Pinot Noir Little Hill Block	Russian River	E	91
1995	Pinot Noir Little Hill Block	Russian River	E	90
1999	Pinot Noir River Block	Russian River	EE	92
1998	Pinot Noir Three Corner Vineyard	Russian River	D	90
1997	Pinot Noir Three Corner Vineyard	Russian River	E	91
1996	Pinot Noir Three Corner Vineyard	Russian River	E	93
1995	Pinot Noir Three Corner Vineyard	Russian River	E	90
1999	Pinot Noir West Block	Russian River	E	95
1998	Pinot Noir West Block	Russian River	E	92
1997	Pinot Noir West Block	Russian River	E	88
1996	Pinot Noir West Block	Russian River	E	93
1995	Pinot Noir West Block	Russian River	E	93
1999	Sauvignon Blanc	Russian River	C	88
1999	Zinfandel Rochioli Vineyard	Russian River	D	90
1998	Zinfandel Rochioli Vineyard	Russian River	D	91
1998	Zinfandel Sodini Vineyard	Russian River	D	90
1996	Zinfandel Sodini Vineyard	Russian River	C	93

Virtually all the producers I visit in California are candid and direct about vintage conditions, and how their wines are made. That being said, there is probably no more of a "straight-shooter" in the wine world than Tom Rochioli. His refreshing honesty and self-deprecating style are hard to resist. In fact, I often wonder if he realizes the superb quality of his wines! About the only way readers will be able to obtain the limited-production, single-vineyard Rochioli wines is to get their names on the winery's mailing list, something I highly recommend. The modest Rochioli continues to ratchet up the level of quality, turning out better and better wines. In short, they are among the finest Chardonnays and Pinot Noirs money can buy. His commitment to quality is evident in his basic *cuvée* of Russian River Chardonnay and Pinot Noir. The 1999s are the best he has yet made. There are 2,525 cases of the 1999 Chardonnay Estate, which was bottled without filtration. It is a terrific buy for the quality it possesses. A complex, Burgundian-styled Chardonnay with leesy, orange marmalade, pineapple, mineral, and roasted hazelnut notes, a steely character, fine underlying minerality, full body, and admirable structure, it should drink well for 3–4 years. Seventy percent of the 1999 Sauvignon Blanc comes from a vineyard planted in 1959 and 30% from a vineyard planted in 1985. The wine exhibits flinty, gravelly notes, ripe grapefruit and passion fruit characteristics, light to medium body, and an expressive personality. It is best drunk over the next 2–3 years.

The single-vineyard Chardonnays are made in limited quantities (300 or so cases of each). They are tightly knit, expressive wines bottled without fining or filtration. I have been buying these wines since Tom Rochioli first vineyard-designated them, and they have a good 5–7 years of life. The 1999s reveal the vintage's higher acidity. The superb 1999 Chardonnay River Block (332 cases), made from the sandy, loamy soils, is tightly knit, with great fruit, an underlying liquid minerality, and plenty of leesy, smoky, tropical fruit intermixed with roasted almonds as well as a steely note. This wine is unevolved, but should drink well for 4–6 years. Even more impressive, the 1999 Chardonnay Allen Vineyard displays high-quality French oak intermixed with tropical fruit aromas and scents. This big, thick, super-concentrated wine possesses enough acidity to buttress its powerful and formidable size. Ideally, it needs another 6–12 months of bottle age, and should keep for 5–6 years. The spectacular 1999 Chardonnay South River Vineyard is made from the Hanzell clone of Chardonnay planted in the alluvial soils of an ancient river bed. The wine boasts a multilayered texture, super purity, and notions of minerals, pineapples, peach, smoke, and butter. Like all of these Chardonnays, the oak regime includes 50% new French; it is subtle and unobtrusive. Anticipated maturity: now–2009.

The 1999 Pinot Noir Estate enjoys about one-third new French oak (all François Frères). The finest regular Pinot Rochioli has yet produced, it exhibits a dense ruby color as well as a gorgeous nose of black cherry jam intermixed with earth, smoke, vanilla, and spice. The grapes were picked very ripe, which is reflected in the wine's sweet black fruit character. Drink this impressive Pinot Noir over the next 4–5 years. There are 300–400 cases of the single-vineyard wines except for the River Block (only 150 cases). Tom Rochioli believes in picking extremely high sugars (25–27° Brix), giving the wines a three-to-five-day cold soak, and fermenting them with indigenous yeasts. Virtually no racking is practiced until they are assembled for bottling unfined and unfiltered. His wines rank alongside the top four or five Pinot Noirs produced in California. The 1999 Pinot Noir Little Hill (a rocky hillside vineyard) is a dark ruby/plum-colored wine with medium to full body as well as a gorgeous nose of rose petals, black cherries, raspberries, minerals, and smoke. Rich and well textured, it should hit its prime in about 1–2 years, and keep for 8–9. The opaque ruby/purple-colored 1999 Pinot Noir West Block (a vineyard planted in 1969 and 1970) boasts a sumptuous nose of allspice, blackberries, cherries, and toast. This multilayered Pinot Noir exhibits uncanny balance and purity, an unctuous texture, and a 40-second finish. It is a dazzling effort that looks to be even better than the 1998. Anticipated maturity: now–2009. The awesome, black ruby-colored 1999 Pinot Noir East Block reveals an extravagant bouquet of black raspberries, cherry liqueur, and vanilla. Picked ripe, but with no sense of pruniness or hotness, this massive, full-bodied, unctuously textured Pinot Noir is fabulously concentrated as well as beautifully balanced. The wine is low in acidity, but well delineated and extremely fresh and lively. It should drink well for at least a decade. The 1999 Pinot Noir River Block, picked at 27° Brix, displays no late-harvest characteristics, but abundant glycerin as well as copious quantities of black cherry liqueur intermixed with floral, smoke, and earth characteristics. The texture is terrific, and the wine pure and well balanced. Sadly, there are only 150 cases. Anticipated maturity: now–2014.

Rochioli's 1998 Pinot Noirs are all highly successful for the vintage. It is too early to say they are better than the 1997s and 1996s, but there is no doubt that Tom Rochioli is producing some of California's finest wines from this fickle grape. Sadly, production in 1998 was off by 25%, so there are even fewer cases of these wines than normal. All are made from destemmed Pinot Noir fruit, given up to five days of cold soaking prior to fermentation, and put in French oak, with no settling, in order to obtain as much of the lees in the wine as possible. There are only two rackings, the final one being the assemblage of the wine in tank prior to bottling. The 1998 Pinot Noir Estate is essentially a *cuvée* culled from the single-vineyard wines and from the youngest vines of the Rochioli estate. It is a beautiful, strawberry/cherry-scented wine with a dark ruby color, lively, vibrant fruit, medium to full body, excellent concentration, sweet tannin, and enough acidity to provide delineation. It could easily pass for a premier cru Beaune. Drink it over the next 4–5 years. The 1998 Pinot Noir Three Corner Vineyard (150 cases) offers a sweet, jammy nose of black cherries, medium to full body, outstanding ripeness, an excellent texture, and fine purity. It should drink well for 5–7 years. The dark ruby-colored 1998 Pinot Noir Little Hill Block (250 cases) reveals richer, deeper, sweeter black cherry and raspberry fruit, medium to full body, and outstanding purity and length. Both the Little Hill Block and Three Corner Vineyard are aged in 50% new French oak and are bottled unfined and unfiltered. Concentration, extract, and perfume increase with the 350-case lot of 1998 Pinot Noir West Block. Also aged in 100% new François Frères oak barrels, it exhibits an alluring bouquet of black raspberries, flowers, and cherry liqueur. Rich and medium- to full-bodied, with gorgeous purity as well as symmetry, this multidimensional Pinot will require 1–2 years of bottle age in order to shed its aggressive tannin. It will last for a decade. Unquestionably, my favorite Rochioli Pinot is the 1998 Pinot Noir East Block. The grapes were harvested at around 26° Brix, hence it tips the scales at nearly 15% alcohol. Aged in 100% new oak, it reveals no pruniness or late-harvest characteristics. Rich, with glorious levels of black cherries, raspberries, cassis, and blackberries, this dense, full-bodied, superbly concentrated Pinot is pure and seductive. Sweet tannin in the finish complements the high level of glycerin and alcohol. This Pinot may turn out to be among the finest produced by Rochioli. It should drink well for a decade.

The dark ruby-colored 1997 Pinot Noir Estate offers an attractive black cherry, earthy, spicy-scented nose, medium to full body, sweet tannin, and excellent cleanliness and overall symmetry. Fleshy, rich, and mouth-filling, this is a robust yet well-balanced Pinot to enjoy over the next 3–4 years. The 1997 Pinot Noir Three Corner Vineyard exhibits a dark ruby/purple color, a sweet plum, black currant, and cherry-scented nose, silky-textured, medium- to full-bodied flavors, and a smoky, toasty finish. The wine presents a seamless style and wonderful sweet fruit, without tasting overbearing or weighty. The alcohol level must be close to 14%, but the taster will never sense that given the wine's concentration and depth. Look for this to evolve nicely for 5–7 years. My favorite 1997 Pinot in the Rochioli stable is the 1997 Pinot Noir Little Hill Block. It boasts a saturated purple color, followed by a spectacular nose that could easily pass for the crème de cassis/black raspberry liqueur found in a top-notch Richebourg. The vineyard, which is planted in extremely rocky soil, achieved sugars that produced a wine with 13.8% alcohol. Aged in 50% new François Frères barrels, with the balance one year old, this wine's silky texture is crammed with glycerin as well as concentrated red and black fruits. Floral scents and smoky, toasty notes add to the wine's appeal and complexity. This full-bodied, gorgeously complete and concentrated Pinot should be drunk over the next 5–6 years. Classic black cherry aromatics intermixed with smoky new oak jump from a glass of the 1997 Pinot Noir West Block. This dark ruby/purple-colored wine, aged in 100% new François Frères oak, is full-bodied and tighter than its predecessors, but nicely layered, with sweet kirsch and black cherry–like flavors, good glycerin, and fine purity. The slightly angular and tannic finish in this compressed example kept my score conservative. Lastly, the 1997 Pinot Noir East Block is made in the mold of the Little Hill *cuvée*. It is a full-throttle effort that, despite its wonderful richness and density, has retained its elegance and lushness. The color is a healthy dark ruby/purple. In the mouth, the wine displays medium to full body, outstanding flavor extraction, and a long, 30-second finish. The wine possesses adequate acidity and moderate tannin, but these components are virtually buried by the precocious fruit and ripeness. This spicy, black fruit–scented and –flavored Pinot should be at its best with another 6–12 months of aging and will evolve nicely for 5–7 years.

The 1996 Pinot Noir Estate exhibits a sweet, smoky, black plum and cherry–scented nose, medium body, excellent ripeness and purity of fruit, enough acidity for definition, and a moderately long, easygoing finish with toasty new-oak notes. It should drink well for 4–5 years. The 1996 Pinot Noir Little Hill Block offers up a knockout nose of raspberries, cherries, smoky, toasty oak, and floral scents. The wine is full-bodied, with intense flavors, a layered, silky texture, and a lush, heady finish. It is a hedonistic and intellectually pleasing Pinot Noir to drink over the next 4–5 years. Remarkably, both the 1996 Pinot Noir Three Corner Vineyard and 1996 Pinot Noir West Block appear to be even more complex and multidimensional. The dense, deep ruby/purple-colored 1996 Pinot Noir Three Corner Vineyard (125 cases) reveals a sweet black raspberry–scented nose with high-quality toasty notes and intriguing Asian spice scents. Sweet and ripe on the attack (from fruit maturity, not sugar), this full-bodied, dense, lushly textured Pinot is an infant in terms of development, but it promises to drink well young and last for 7–8 years. Each year I seem to have a slight preference for the Pinot Noir West Block and the 1996 is again my favorite. Texturally, as well as from a perspective of concentration and length, this wine could easily pass for a great 1990 grand cru red Burgundy. Aromatically, it remains to be seen whether it will offer the same level of complexity, but my instincts suggest this is a profound Pinot that should rival the finest made in America over recent years. The color is a deep ruby/purple. The exotic nose offers a mélange of black fruits intertwined with toast, spice, and meaty nuances. Full-bodied, dense, superbly concentrated, and pure, yet surprisingly fresh and lively, this is a glorious example of the extraordinary progress being made by a handful of U.S. vintners with the fickle Pinot Noir grape. I would not be surprised to see this wine last for a decade.

In 1995 there were five cuvées of Pinot Noir. The 1995 Pinot Noir Estate exhibits a deep ruby color, a sweet, blackberry-scented nose, evidence of smoky wood, and round, generous, medium- to full-bodied flavors. This supple Pinot is ideal for drinking over the next 4–5 years. There are four limited-production, single-vineyard 1995 Pinot Noirs. The 1995 Pinot Noir Little Hill Block displays an open-knit, sweet, jammy, black fruit–scented nose, ripe, medium- to full-bodied flavors, and a forward, soft style with excellent purity and plenty of Pinot Noir's unmistakable perfumed silkiness and character. Drink it over the next 4–5 years. The 1995 Pinot Noir Three Corner Vineyard exhibits a deeper color, copious quantities of up-front, sweet, smoky, black-cherry fruit, medium to full body, outstanding purity, and no hard edges. This wine should drink for 5–6 years. The impressive 1995 Pinot Noir West Block offers a nose of raspberries and black cherries, wonderful sweetness and richness, and that layered, soft, opulently textured feel of serious Pinot. Round, concentrated, and full-bodied, this is a lush, silky wine to drink over the next 5–6 years. The 1995 Pinot Noir East Block is cut from the same mold, perhaps more earthy, but opulent and flashy, with gobs of rich fruit. It is hard to imagine many wineries turning out five Pinots of this quality from one vintage.

Do readers realize that the Rochiolis still sell 60% of the production from their vineyards, holding back only the best lots for their own estate bottled program? They still make Zinfandel from extremely old vines. The 1999 Zinfandel Rochioli Vineyard (100 cases) offers gorgeous plum, prune, black cherry, and raspberry fruit notes intermixed with chocolate, smoke, pepper, and earth. Drink this viscous, thick, juicy wine during its first 7–8 years of life. The outstanding 1998 Zinfandel Sodini Vineyard (325 cases) emerges from a hillside vineyard planted in 1905. Plums, prune, cherry liqueur, and pepper aromas jump from a glass of this full-bodied, unctuously textured Zinfandel. Totally dry, with considerable viscosity, it comes closest in style to some of the hedonistic Zinfandel fruit bombs produced by Ehren Jordan and Larry Turley. It should drink well for 5–7 years. Readers looking for more briery Zinfandel fruit, as well as classic blackberry and cassis, should check out the concentrated, thick 1998 Zinfandel Rochioli Vineyard. Full-bodied, intense, and syrupy, it was aged in 50% new-oak casks. Sadly, there are only 100 cases. It should drink well for a decade. Two limited rarities include the superb 1996 Zinfandel Sodoni Vineyard (from vines planted in 1905). There are 400 cases of this fabulously intense, rich, black/purple-colored Zinfandel that must contain 15% alcohol. This full-bodied, voluptuously textured Zin will provide sensational drinking for 5–7 years. Another noteworthy wine is the 1996 Cabernet Sauvignon Neoma's Vineyard (150 cases). Made from 38-year-old vines with yields of under two tons per acre, this wine exhibits a saturated black/purple color, and textbook jammy cassis aromas intermingled with minerals, tobacco, and licorice scents. Extremely full-bodied, with phenomenal concentration, this wine reveals the telltale characteristics of the finest 1996s—low acidity, ripe tannin, and drop-dead levels of extract and nearly overripe fruit. Anticipated maturity: now–2025.

I know Tom Rochioli does not get the same thrill from making Cabernet Sauvignon as he does from Pinot Noir, Chardonnay, and Sauvignon Blanc, but that is no reason to ignore his outstanding 1997 Cabernet Sauvignon Neoma's Vineyard, a black/purple-colored wine with superb aromatics of new oak, black raspberries, olives, tar, and smoke. Full-bodied, rich, and chewy, with impressive viscosity and extract, this large-scaled, silky-textured wine should evolve nicely for 15–20 years. Production was approximately 225 cases.

ROCKING HORSE WINERY (NAPA)

1997 Cabernet Sauvignon Garvey Family Vineyard	Rutherford	D	89+
1994 Cabernet Sauvignon Garvey Family Vineyard	Rutherford	D	91

The 1997 Cabernet Sauvignon Garvey Family Vineyard from Rocking Horse has a dense ruby/purple color followed by an earthy, dusty nose with hints of new oak and black currants. On the palate, this wine is long, rich, and full-bodied, with outstanding potential. Pure, with moderate tannin and admirable concentration, it promises to be even better in 3–4 years and keep for 12–15+. Eight hundred and fifty cases of the outstanding 1994 Cabernet Sauvignon Garvey Family Vineyard were produced from 100% Cabernet Sauvignon. The wine boasts an opaque purple color, full body, an explosively rich mid-palate, and a 20–25-second finish. It is loaded with black currant, cedar, chocolate-like fruit, has a glorious texture, superb richness and chewiness, and that telltale, earthy, spicy, "Rutherford dust" characteristic. There are gobs of sweet tannin in the finish, but readers should not conclude that this wine is ready to drink. Purchasers of it should be prepared to give it 3–5 years of cellaring as it is a 20-year wine that could turn out to be even better than my numerical rating suggests.
Past Glories: 1993 Cabernet Sauvignon Garvey Family Vineyard (90)

ROSENBLUM CELLARS (ALAMEDA)

1999 Zinfandel Alegria Vineyard	Sonoma	C	88
1998 Zinfandel Alegria Vineyard	Russian River	D	89
1997 Zinfandel Annette's Reserve Rhodes Vineyard	Redwood Valley	D	88
1999 Zinfandel Carla's Vineyards	San Francisco Bay	C	88
1998 Zinfandel Carla's Vineyards	Contra Costa	C	88
1999 Zinfandel Continente Vineyard	San Francisco Bay	C	90
1998 Zinfandel Continente Vineyard	San Francisco Bay	C	89
1998 Zinfandel Cullinane Vineyard	Sonoma	D	90
1997 Zinfandel Cullinane Vineyard	Sonoma	D	87

1999 Zinfandel Eagle Point Vineyard	Mendocino	C	90
1999 Zinfandel George Hendry Vineyard Reserve	Napa	D	88
1999 Zinfandel Harris Kratka Vineyard	Alexander Valley	C	90
1998 Zinfandel Harris Kratka Vineyard	Alexander Valley	D	89
1999 Zinfandel Lyons Vineyard	Napa	D	91
1998 Zinfandel Lyons Vineyard	Napa	D	90
1997 Zinfandel Lyons Vineyard	Napa	D	89
1999 Zinfandel Monte Rosso Vineyard	Sonoma	D	92
1999 Zinfandel Rhodes Vineyard	Redwood Valley	D	87
1998 Zinfandel Richard Sauret Vineyard	Paso Robles	D	90
1999 Zinfandel Rockpile Road Vineyard	Dry Creek	C	89
1998 Zinfandel Rockpile Road Vineyard	Dry Creek	D	89
1997 Zinfandel Rockpile Road Vineyard	Dry Creek	C	89
1999 Zinfandel Samsel Vineyard Maggie's Reserve	Sonoma	D	92
1998 Zinfandel Samsel Vineyard Maggie's Reserve	Sonoma	D	88
1999 Zinfandel St. Peter's Church Vineyard	Sonoma	D	91
1998 Zinfandel St. Peter's Church Vineyard	Sonoma	D	90

One has to admire the quality Rosenblum is able to achieve given his enormous Zinfandel portfolio, all of which are extremely successful in 1999. The opaque ruby/purple-colored 1999 Zinfandel Lyons Vineyard exhibits a gorgeous perfume of blackberry and raspberry fruit, medium to full body, and a sweet mid-palate with good underlying minerality. There is enough acidity and tannin to provide definition. It should drink well for a decade. Lighter, with higher acidity, the well-made, pure, restrained 1999 Zinfandel George Hendry is a medium-bodied, elegant, mineral, blueberry, raspberry, plum, and currant-scented and -flavored effort to enjoy over the next 7–8 years. The opaque purple-colored 1999 Zinfandel Rhodes Vineyard offers crisp, tangy acidity, an earthy note in its raspberry and cherry fruit, medium to full body, and excellent purity, richness, and overall harmony. It should drink well for 5–6 years. Rosenblum's blockbuster 1999 Zinfandel St. Peter's Church Vineyard boasts a saturated purple color as well as scents of blackberries, blueberries, smoke, minerals, new saddle leather, and earth. Dense, powerful, and muscular, with no hard edges, it exhibits super ripeness, beautifully pure fruit, a multidimensional personality (unusual for Zinfandel), and a long, pure finish. Give it 6–8 more months to round into shape, and consume it over the following decade.

I tasted two offerings from the San Francisco Bay region. The 1999 Zinfandel Carla's Vineyards (14.1% alcohol) is a delicious, open-knit, richly fruity wine exhibiting plum and berry fruit with a touch of pepper and spice. Medium- to full-bodied and soft, it is ideal for drinking over the next 2–3 years. The dark plum/ruby-colored 1999 Zinfandel Continente Vineyard (14.6% alcohol) offers distinctive aromatics of sweet cherry jam and balsam wood. In the mouth, it is fleshy, full-bodied, and unctuous, with good thickness, excellent purity, sweet tannin, and low acidity. Drink it over the next 4–5 years.

The 1999 Zinfandel Alegria Vineyard (14.1% alcohol) is a field blend of 78% Zinfandel, 14% Petite Sirah, and 8% Alicante Bouchet. Some of the vines date back to 1892. Flamboyant aromas of black raspberries, cherries, and currants jump from the glass. There is a subtle oak component, as well as plenty of spice, leather, pepper, and sweet fruit in this medium-bodied, elegant, dark ruby/purple-colored Zinfandel. It is best drunk over the next 4–5 years. The 1999 Zinfandel Eagle Point Vineyard (14.3% alcohol) emerges from a higher-altitude source in the cooler Mendocino region. This superb offering reveals gorgeous blackberry, cherry, and currant aromas. Pure, ripe, and concentrated, with medium- to full-bodied, velvety-textured flavors, and well-concealed wood, this beauty will drink well for 4–5 years. The 1999 Zinfandel Rockpile Road Vineyard (14.6% alcohol) boasts abundant levels of spice, earth, licorice, leather, black cherry, and blackberry characteristics in both its aromas and flavors. Although more subdued than other Rosenblum offerings, it possesses intensity, ripeness, and impressive purity. Fleshy and full-bodied, with good glycerin, purity, texture, and overall balance, this delicious Zinfandel will drink well for 4–5 years.

The powerful (14.8% alcohol) 1999 Zinfandel Harris Kratka Vineyard (a blend of 75% Zinfandel and 25% Carignan) offers a distinctive balsam wood, earthy, crushed sandstone/ mineral note in the intriguing nose of black fruits (predominantly cherries). Rich, fleshy, succulent, and hedonistic, with gobs of fruit, abundant glycerin, and a long, seamless, velvety-textured, full-bodied finish, it will drink well for 4–5 years. The dark ruby/purple-colored 1999 Zinfandel Monte Rosso Vineyard (from a vineyard planted 1,400 feet above Sonoma Valley) is a blend of 85% Zinfandel, 8% Petite Sirah, and 7% unidentified field varietals. At 14.6% alcohol, it is no wimpish wine. Provocative notes of road tar, deep, concentrated, ripe black fruits, licorice, and spice are followed by a rich, full-bodied, deep wine with low acidity as well as supple tannin. This multidimensional Zinfandel cascades over the palate with no hard edges. Drink this dazzling 1999 over its first 5–6 years of life, although I suspect it will age well for a decade. The 1999 Zinfandel Samsel Vineyard Maggie's Reserve (a whopping 15.2% alcohol) includes 5% Alicante Bouchet in the blend. Planted in 1901, this vineyard celebrated its 100th birthday in 2001. The dense ruby/purple-colored 1999 offers jammy, sweet kirsch, pepper, spice, and blackberry aromas. The wine's high alcohol provides plenty of glycerin as well as a full-bodied, voluptuous feel in the mouth. There is admirable purity, fine balance, and a multilayered, super-concentrated finish. This is one of the finest Samsel Vineyard Zinfandels Rosenblum has produced. Enjoy it over the next 5–7 years.

An excellent portfolio from the veterinarian turned Zinfandel specialist, Rosenblum's 1998s reveal great color, ripe fruit, thick, juicy textures, and mature flavors. From the San Francisco Bay area, the 1998 Zinfandel Carla's Vineyards reveals the vintage's low acidity as well as attractive, ripe, black cherry and berry fruit, all presented in a medium- to full-bodied, delicious style. It can be drunk over the next 2–3 years. The structured, dark ruby/purple-colored 1998 Zinfandel Alegria Vineyard offers peppery notes in its sweet, herb-tinged, black cherry, and plum-like fruit. Medium- to full-bodied, with a plush texture, low acidity, and fine intensity, it should drink well for 5–6 years. The outstanding, opaque ruby/purple-colored 1998 Zinfandel Lyons Vineyard is an opulent, voluptuously textured offering with copious quantities of superripe blackberry and cherry fruit, spice, a juicy, succulent texture, low acidity, and a terrific, glycerin-imbued, dense finish. It should drink well for 7–8 years. Another winner from Rosenblum, the 1998 Zinfandel Continente Vineyard exhibits a dense, plum/ purple color in addition to aromas of jammy black fruits, earth, and pepper. Thick and juicy, with a fleshy, opulent texture, low acidity, and luxurious levels of plum, cherry, and raspberry fruit, this fat Zinfandel has immense appeal. Drink it over the next 2–3 years for its exuberance and vigor. The 1998 Zinfandel Cullinane Vineyard is potentially outstanding. An opaque purple color is accompanied by a medium- to full-bodied wine displaying aromas of melted road tar and leather, heady, high alcohol, and evidence of ripe fruit. This full-throttle, chewy Zinfandel with late-harvest characteristics is reminiscent of an Italian Amarone. Enjoy this dense, mouth-filling Zinfandel over the next 6–8 years. It may be controversial given its Amarone-like personality. Perhaps the finest (for my palate) of this portfolio is the 1998 Zinfandel St. Peter's Church Vineyard. A dazzling fragrance of minerals, black fruits, and smoky oak soars from the glass of this intense, powerful, concentrated yet beautifully balanced wine. Multilayered, with terrific fruit purity and intensity, exceptional opulence, and a long, juicy finish, it can be consumed over the next 5–7 years. From the Alexander Valley, the 1998 Zinfandel Harris Kratka Vineyard exhibits a peppery, Côtes du Rhône–like nose, with scents of dried Provençal herbs, sour black cherries, and earth. Medium- to full-bodied and spicy, with fine ripeness, this chewy Zin can be drunk now as well as over the next 5–6 years. From Paso Robles, the 1998 Zinfandel Richard Sauret Vineyard (14.7% alcohol) reveals low acidity, big, full-bodied, concentrated flavors, abundant quantities of earthy, black cherry, raspberry, and plum-like fruit, admirable purity, and a low-acid, fleshy finish. Drink it over the next 6–7 years. Made in a more elegant style, Rosenblum's 1998 Zinfandel Rockpile Vineyard tips the scales at 14.2% alcohol. It exhibits attractive berry, mineral-like characteristics, excellent purity, fine ripeness, and sweet, medium-bodied, stylish, clean flavors. Drink it over the next 3–4 years. Lastly, the 1998 Zinfandel Samsel Vineyard Maggie's Reserve is even lower in alcohol at 13.9%. The wine's dark ruby color is followed by attractive briery, strawberry, and black cherry fruit, soft, medium-bodied flavors, some pepper and wood notes, but the emphasis is on the fruit as well as overall balance and suppleness. Drink it over the next 4–5 years. All things considered, this is a highly successful group of wines that display more ripeness, fruit, and pleasure than their 1997 counterparts.

The question that comes to my mind is, is it really necessary to vineyard-designate all of these Zinfandels? While there are subtle differences, do such minor variations on a theme justify such an extensive portfolio? More important is the quality of Rosenblum's 1997s. Overall, they seem to be a notch below other recent vintages, with narrower textures and the vintage's screechingly high acidity all too obvious. Moreover, few are as well endowed with fruit and concentration as previous efforts. Nevertheless, these are a few excellent Zinfandels. I enjoyed the 1997 Zinfandel Annette's Reserve Rhodes Vineyard. It displays a Rhône-like, dried herb, peppery, earthy, dark plum character, fleshy, tasty, medium-bodied flavors, a soft mid-palate, and spicy oak in the finish. It is one of Rosenblum's stars of the vintage. It should be drunk over the next 1–2 years. Among the deepest-colored of the 1997 Zinfandels is the 1997 Zinfandel Cullinane Vineyard. It reveals ripe black cherry fruit mixed with obvious toasty new oak. It is among the densest, medium- to full-bodied, powerful wines with very good ripeness and richness, and attractive rather than intrusive acid levels. It should drink well for 2–3 years. The saturated ruby/purple-colored, exotic 1997 Zinfandel Lyons Vineyard possesses layers of glycerin, black cherry and raspberry fruit, new oak, pepper, and spice. This is probably the richest offering in Rosenblum's 1997 portfolio. Drink it over the next 3–4 years. Nearly outstanding is the 1997 Zinfandel Rockpile Road Vineyard. One of the most alcoholic wines in the Rosenblum portfolio (14.9%), it displays excellent purity, loads of blackberry and cherry fruit, a soft, nicely textured, open-knit, expansive texture, medium to full body, and an excellent finish. It is a beautifully made Zinfandel.

ERIC ROSS (RUSSIAN RIVER)

1998　Zinfandel Occidental Vineyard	Sonoma Coast	D	89
1997　Zinfandel Occidental Vineyard Old Vines	Russian River	D	91

Not yet bottled, the dense ruby/purple-colored 1998 Zinfandel Occidental Vineyard reveals abundant quantities of high-quality, spicy new oak, chewy, exotic, allspice, black raspberry, cherry, blackberry aromas and flavors, full body, outstanding density and purity, and a rich, multilayered, concentrated finish. Super-extracted and built for the long haul (as Zinfandels go), it will benefit from 1–2 years of cellaring and keep for 10–12 years. It is a seriously concentrated, impressively endowed Zinfandel. The Bordeaux-styled 1997 Zinfandel Occidental Vineyard Old Vines spent 18 months in American oak casks. It boasts a black/purple color, sumptuous aromas of black fruits, toast, and spice. Built along the lines of a Cabernet Sauvignon, there is superb richness and concentration in this tightly wound Zin. Full-bodied, gloriously pure. and concentrated, this atypical Zinfandel possesses zesty underlying acidity. Surprisingly, it requires 1–2 years of cellaring and should drink well over the following decade. It may even last longer.

RUDD ESTATE (OAKVILLE)

1999 Jericho Canyon Vineyard Proprietary Red Wine	Napa	EE	95
1998 Jericho Canyon Vineyard Proprietary Red Wine	Napa	EE	93
1998 Rudd Estate	Oakville/Napa	E	89
1998 Rudd Estate Rudd Jericho Canyon	Oakville/Napa	E	90

This winery, formerly known as Girard, was purchased in 1996 by Leslie Rudd, current owner of the Dean & DeLuca chain of luxury grocery stores and wine shops. It has become one of Napa's showcase properties. Lamentably, we are still a year away from the release of several sensational red wines that have aged fabulously well since I first tasted them in 1999.

Stunned by the performances of the 1998 and 1999 Jericho Canyon Vineyard proprietary red wines, I obviously underrated them earlier. The unfiltered/unfined 1998 Jericho Canyon Vineyard (2,850 cases) spent 16 months in French oak. A sensational effort, it is one of the stars of this challenging vintage. The opaque black/plum color is accompanied by aromas and flavors reminiscent of a blend of Cheval Blanc and La Mission-Haut-Brion from an overripe vintage. Notes of plums, cassis, blackberries, espresso, Asian spices, licorice, cedar, and tapenade make an appearance in both the aromas and flavors. Extremely full-bodied, with sweet tannin, an opulent/voluptuous texture, brilliant purity, and low acidity, this wine represents a synthesis in style between an exotic Right Bank Bordeaux and a California Cabernet. Having achieved 14.2% alcohol naturally, it is a blend of 79% Cabernet Sauvignon, 11% Merlot, and 10% Cabernet Franc from a vineyard in northern Napa Valley (the Rudd estate vineyards have not yet come into production). Exhibiting a similar opaque black/purple color, the 1999 Jericho Canyon Vineyard boasts a superb perfume of charcoal, creosote, blackberry liqueur, espresso, dried Provençal herbs, licorice, and minerals. Smoke from the toasty new oak also emerges. A superbly dense, full-bodied, exquisite effort, it is a blockbuster, yet incredibly harmonious. Both of these wines are winemaking tour de forces. One can only imagine when the 45 acres of estate vineyards planted with 50% Cabernet Sauvignon, 40% Merlot, 6% Cabernet Franc, and 4% Petit Verdot come into production what might be achieved, since this vineyard's neighbors include such luminary sites as Phelps's Backus Vineyard, Dalla Valle, Screaming Eagle, Venge Family Reserve, Plumpjack, and Opus One. The dark ruby-colored 1998 Rudd Estate Napa Valley (approximately 80% Cabernet Sauvignon, 10% Cabernet Franc, and 10% Merlot) exhibits smoky cassis aromas, an elegant, sweet attack, moderate tannin, and a rich, nicely textured, stylish, graceful finish. Although not a blockbuster, it is a harmonious effort ideal for drinking during its first 12–15 years of life. There are 3,500 cases of the opaque purple-colored, outstanding 1998 Rudd Estate Rudd Jericho Canyon. It displays a sweet blackberry and cassis-scented nose with nicely integrated toasty oak. As the wine sat in the glass, aromas of licorice, dried herbs, and minerals emerged. Deep and classy, with sweet tannin, medium to full body, and excellent harmony, this is an outstanding effort in a difficult vintage.

SADDLEBACK CELLARS (NAPA)

1998 Cabernet Sauvignon	Napa	D	88
1997 Cabernet Sauvignon	Napa	D	90
1996 Cabernet Sauvignon Estate	Napa	C	89
1995 Cabernet Sauvignon Estate	Napa	C	90
1994 Cabernet Sauvignon Estate	Napa	C	90
1998 Venge Family Reserve Cabernet Sauvignon	Oakville	EE	90
1997 Venge Family Reserve Cabernet Sauvignon	Oakville	EE	97
1996 Venge Family Reserve Cabernet Sauvignon	Oakville	EE	96
1995 Venge Family Reserve Cabernet Sauvignon	Oakville	D	95

1994	Venge Family Reserve Cabernet Sauvignon	Oakville	D	95
1997	Venge Family Reserve Merlot	Oakville	D	90
1996	Venge Family Reserve Merlot	Oakville	D	90
1995	Venge Family Reserve Merlot	Oakville	D	91
1994	Venge Family Reserve Merlot	Oakville	D	90
1996	Venge Family Reserve Sangiovese Penny Lane Vineyard	Oakville	C	90
1998	Venge Family Reserve Scout's Honor	Oakville	D	90
1997	Venge Family Reserve Scout's Honor	Oakville	C	90
1996	Venge Family Reserve Scout's Honor	Oakville	C	89
1999	Zinfandel Old Vines	Napa	D	90
1998	Zinfandel Old Vines	Napa	D	89

At this all-American winery for sure, wine-maker/owner Nils Venge makes bold, in-your-face, 100% pure California-styled wines that make no pretension about being French, Italian, or some innocuous international and/or dull Euro blend. In short, these wines are what they are—full-flavored and, in the case of his topflight Cabernet Sauvignons, remarkably long-lived. Venge has an impressive résumé of turning out some of the finest Napa Cabernets of the last three decades (e.g., 1974, 1976, 1978 Villa Mt. Eden Cabernet Sauvignons, and the 1984 and 1985 Groth Reserve Cabernet Sauvignons).

Saddleback Cellars' 1998 Cabernet Sauvignon (40% new American oak was utilized) is a relatively fleshy wine, with deep black cherry and currant flavors intermixed with creosote, toast, and cherries. Chunky and muscular for a 1998, it will drink well for 7–10 years.

The Saddleback Cellars wines are the first tier of Nils Venge's offerings and represent very good values. His top-of-the-line wines are all designated as Venge Family Reserve. Consistently his finest efforts, they are made in relatively limited quantities of 300–500 cases. These wines all possess bold, ripe flavors, and obvious toasty oak. They symbolize a flamboyant, intense style of winemaking. An outstanding effort in nearly every vintage (particularly impressive in 1988) is the Venge Family Reserve Scout's Honor. There are 450 cases of the 1998, a blend of 85% Zinfandel and 15% Charbono aged in American oak. The color is a dense ruby/purple, and the wine brashly displays new oak, along with blackberry, cherry, and raspberry notes. Smoky, toasty, rich, full-bodied, and supple-textured, it will drink well over the next 4–5 years. One of the most compelling Cabernet Sauvignons Venge has produced (and there have been many over the last 30 years) is his 1997 Venge Family Reserve Cabernet Sauvignon. Sadly, there are only 300 cases of this 100% new oak–aged effort. Tipping the scales at 14+% alcohol, it is a super-extracted, black/purple-colored effort displaying a gorgeous nose of crème de cassis intermixed with licorice, spice box, cedar, and smoke. Huge layers of glycerin, fat, and fruit from this formidable effort caress the palate. The wine has marvelous balance for its size as well as a long, impressive finish. While there is tannin to be shed, it is still primary, so 4–6 years of cellaring is suggested. It will keep for 25–30 years! For the first time, Venge has turned out a 1997 Venge Family Reserve Merlot from Oakville. Like the Cabernet Sauvignon, this wine spends 30 months in primarily new oak (75% in the case of the Merlot). There are 300 cases. Big, robust, intense, sweet vanilla, chocolate, and licorice aromas, along with thick, juicy black cherry and currant flavors are apparent in this full-bodied, powerful, supple wine. It should drink well for 15–16 years, atypically long for Merlot. Lastly, the 1998 Venge Family Reserve Cabernet Sauvignon may merit an outstanding score. While it does not possess the stature, mass, volume, and length of the 1997 or 1996, it is a full-bodied, typically Venge offering with copious quantities of toasty new oak, black currant fruit, spice box, licorice, and vanilla. It should drink well when released and last for 12–15 years.

As massive as Saddleback Cellars' red wines can be, they stand the test of time, as evidenced by some of Venge's classics that still remain in my cellar (the 1974 and 1978 Villa

Mt. Eden, and the 1985 Groth Reserve). The thrilling levels of viscously textured fruit in the 1995 Cabernet Sauvignon Estate will impress most Cabernet fans. Still backward and un-evolved, it offers juicy, jammy black fruits intermixed with toast. A huge, dense, chewy wine, with a plethora of fruit and glycerin, it should be cellared for 3–4 more years and consumed over the following 10–15. The similarly styled 1996 Cabernet Sauvignon Estate is chewy, full-bodied, and thick. Not yet complex, it is super-concentrated, with gobs of toasty oak (about 40% American oak is utilized in the wine's upbringing), and a low-acid, chunky, heavyweight style. If the 1996 develops more complexity, it will merit a score in the low 90s. Anticipated maturity: now–2015. While the 1998 Cabernet Sauvignon appears to be a good, 88-point effort, it is the 1997 Cabernet Sauvignon that will excite readers. There are 2,000 cases of this potentially outstanding effort. Aged in 60% French and 40% American oak, it is a typical Venge Cabernet Sauvignon, exhibiting an opaque ruby/purple color in addition to almost overripe jammy scents of blackberries, cassis, and prominent wood. Low acidity, in addition to terrific fatness and purity, make this a hedonistically styled Cabernet that will im-prove for 5–10 years and last for 15 or more.

The 1994 Cabernet Sauvignon Estate is reminiscent of the Groth Cabernets produced in the mid-1980s. The wine exhibits plenty of chocolaty, cassis fruit, a nice touch of toasty oak, a thick, chewy texture, and mouth-filling extract and richness. The tannin is obscured by the wine's ripe fruit. The 1994 should drink well for 12–15 years.

Nils Venge's glories are his red wines, as he has the Midas touch when it comes to turning out full-flavored, gorgeously textured, seductive reds. The outstanding, deep ruby-colored 1997 Venge Family Reserve Scout's Honor (a blend of 85% Zinfandel and 15% Charbono) possesses power (14.5% alcohol) along with gorgeous, sexy, seductive notions of cherries, strawberries, and briery, peppery fruit. Deep, fleshy, and heady, this is a hedonistic fruit bomb to enjoy over the next 2–3 years.

The 1996 Venge Family Reserve Cabernet Sauvignon (only 280 cases) is a dazzling effort. It possesses over 14% alcohol and is highly extracted as well as wooded, as it was aged in 100% new French oak. Exceptionally dense, it offers formidable quantities of black fruits, smoky oak, and licorice, awesome purity, and layers of extract. The finish exceeds 30 sec-onds. My best guess for this unevolved, backward Cabernet is that it will require 3–5 years of cellaring, but will last for 2–3 decades. It is a remarkably intense, hugely concentrated wine exhibiting the telltale Venge style of viscous cassis/blackberry fruit crammed into a flamboy-antly oaked, powerhouse, ageworthy personality. Another fabulous wine I tasted was the 1994 Venge Family Reserve Cabernet Sauvignon. An exquisite Cabernet aged for 18 months in oak casks (about 70% of which were new), it boasts an opaque black/purple color and a nose of cassis, prunes, smoke, licorice, and earth. Exceptionally full-bodied with jammy fla-vors, low acidity, and awesome levels of glycerin, extract, and fruit, this is a wild, unre-strained, super-concentrated Cabernet that should become increasingly civilized as it ages effortlessly over the next 15–20 years. The superb 1994 Venge Family Reserve Cabernet Sauvignon may well be matched in quality by the spectacular 1995 Venge Family Reserve Cabernet Sauvignon. Its opaque purple color and nose of blackberries, cassis, licorice, cof-fee, and tar scents are outstanding. Concentrated, thick, and unctuous, with outstanding pu-rity and layers of extract, this large-scaled, beautifully made, all-American-styled Cabernet approaches "bigger than life" status. Anticipated maturity: now–2020.

Nils Venge produces two Sangiovese *cuvées*. The 1996 Venge Family Reserve Sangiovese Penny Lane Vineyard (5% Cabernet Sauvignon is added to the blend) is one of California's finest. The fruit is picked very ripe (14% alcohol), and the wine is aged in Burgundy barrels. There is plenty of sweet, jammy strawberry/cherry/raspberry fruit in the nose, thick, juicy fla-vors, and soft tannin. Drink this offering over the next 3–4 years for its gutsy, exuberant style. The 1996 Venge Family Reserve Scout's Honor is a blend of 88% Zinfandel and 12% San-giovese. (Château Montelena produces a similarly styled wine under the St. Vincent label.)

Aged in 100% American oak, this offering is spicy and toasty, with briery, black raspberry, peppery notes in its sweet, jammy fragrance. Full-bodied, hedonistic, and fun to drink, it should continue to offer immense pleasure for 2–4 years.

The outstanding 1996 Venge Family Reserve Merlot is a match for the fabulous 1994. The 1996 was made from Clone 7 and aged in 100% new French oak. By Venge standards the alcohol is relatively modest (13.5%) in this full-bodied, chewy, thick, highly extracted Merlot, which also possesses toasty, chocolaty, cherry-like flavors. Viscous and succulent, it is impossible to resist. This wine should be drinkable upon release and last for 12–15 years. Readers weaned on sterile, insipid, wimpish Merlots will need to have their palates recalibrated after tasting this blockbuster. As a critic of the insipid, vegetal, often appallingly overpriced Merlots that inundate the marketplace, I found it a pleasure to taste the real thing. Venge has produced a number of terrific wines that will please both Merlot and Cabernet Sauvignon lovers. The first Merlot I tasted from Venge was the 1994 Venge Family Reserve Merlot, a wine aged 18 months in 100% new-oak casks. Unfortunately, only 120 cases were made of this lusty, decadent, chewy, intensely flavored Merlot. Gobs of smoke, vanilla-tinged, black cherry, and chocolaty flavors tumble out of a glass of this mouth-filling, creamy-textured wine. Full-bodied, powerful, and dense, it will drink exceptionally well young, but last for 12–15 years. I suspect anyone not on the winery's mailing list will have little chance of tracking down a bottle or two. The 1995 Venge Family Reserve Merlot has also been aged in 100% new oak, but it is so extraordinarily extracted and rich that the oak plays only a minor role in the wine's aromatics and flavors. There are only 200 cases of this thick, black/purple-colored wine. The acidity is low, and the flavor and concentration extraordinarily high. This is a blockbuster, full-bodied, super-concentrated Merlot with a viscous personality and sensational extract. A pure, full-blooded heavyweight, it is even more impressive than the 1994 and will drink well for 15 or more years.

Nils Venge produces Zinfandel with unbridled power and richness. Some critics suggest it is over the top, but I suspect they would have said the same thing about the 1947 Cheval Blanc or 1947 Pétrus if they had tasted those wines at a young age. That being said, readers looking for wimpish, subtle, innocuous wines (this is usually referred to as "elegance") are advised to keep their distance. A classic offering from Venge, Saddleback Cellars' 1999 Zinfandel Old Vines offers explosive aromas of prunes, jammy black fruits, licorice, spice box, and smoky, toasty new oak. Opulent, viscous, and full-bodied, this blockbuster effort is typically over the top, layered, and super-concentrated, but oh so much fun to drink, and isn't that what wine is all about? Anti-elitists should rejoice in this tasty, juicy, succulent, hedonistic Zinfandel. Enjoy it over the next 4–6 years. Venge has fashioned an opaque purple-colored 1998 Zinfandel Old Vines revealing a late-harvest, nearly overripe tar, asphalt, jammy blackberry, prune-like character. Full-bodied, chewy, and viscous, with powerful, concentrated, muscular, black fruit and American oak flavors, this firm yet heavyweight Zin can be drunk now as well as over the next 7–8 years.

Past Glories: 1993 Cabernet Sauvignon Estate (90), 1993 Venge Family Reserve Cabernet Sauvignon (90)

ST. FRANCIS WINERY (SONOMA)

1997 Cabernet Franc Reserve McCoy Vineyard	Sonoma	D	91
1996 Cabernet Franc Reserve McCoy Vineyard	Sonoma	D	89
1998 Cabernet Sauvignon Reserve	Sonoma	E	87
1997 Cabernet Sauvignon Reserve	Sonoma	D	90
1995 Cabernet Sauvignon Reserve	Sonoma	D	89+
1994 Cabernet Sauvignon Reserve	Sonoma	D	91
1998 Cabernet Sauvignon Reserve King's Ridge Vineyard	Sonoma	EE	91

1997 Cabernet Sauvignon Reserve King's Ridge Vineyard	Sonoma	EE	92
1996 Cabernet Sauvignon Reserve King's Ridge Vineyard	Sonoma	EE	91
1994 Cabernet Sauvignon Reserve King's Ridge Vineyard	Sonoma	EE	92
1997 Merlot Reserve	Sonoma	D	89
1994 Merlot Reserve	Sonoma	D	90
1998 Merlot Reserve Nun's Canyon Vineyard	Sonoma	D	88
1997 Merlot Reserve Nun's Canyon Vineyard	Sonoma	D	90
1999 Petite Sirah Bartolozzi Ranch	Sonoma	D	89
1999 Zinfandel Old Vines	Sonoma	D	88
1998 Zinfandel Old Vines	Sonoma	D	88
1994 Zinfandel Old Vines	Sonoma	C	93
1999 Zinfandel Pagani Vineyard	Sonoma	D	89
1998 Zinfandel Pagani Vineyard	Sonoma	D	90
1997 Zinfandel Pagani Vineyard	Sonoma	D	88
1996 Zinfandel Pagani Vineyard	Sonoma	D	89
1995 Zinfandel Pagani Vineyard	Sonoma	C	90
1994 Zinfandel Pagani Vineyard	Sonoma	C	92

St. Francis has grown by five-fold in the last 10 years and is now producing 250,000 cases of wine from their large, high-tech facility south of Santa Rosa. Partially owned by the well-known American importer Kobrand Corporation, it has 550 acres of vineyards. Longtime wine-maker Tom Mackey seems to have everything under control. Five years ago St. Francis served notice to the wine world that they would no longer risk the damaging aromas of moldy corks and began utilizing synthetic corks. The jury is still out on these corks, but they are made with the same material used in artificial heart valves and have proven to be effective in eliminating the moldy aromas that taint approximately 3–5% of bottled wine. How well they will hold up under prolonged cellaring of big, tannic, alcoholic wines remains to be seen.

For the most part, St. Francis's offerings reflect a moderate pricing policy, although they have several *cuvées* priced in triple digits. Most of their wine range from $15–40, which qualifies them as reasonably good values in California's surreal La-La Land of prices. All of St. Francis's red wines are bottled without filtration. They are boldly styled, oaky, rich, concentrated efforts. There are 6,500 cases of the 1997 Merlot Reserve (100% Merlot aged in equal parts French and American oak). It exhibits aromas and flavors of coffee, mocha, cola, black cherry, and currant fruit presented in a sexy, full-bodied, nearly overripe style. This seductive Merlot is best drunk over the next 5–6 years. The Nun's Canyon Vineyard is a steep hillside parcel planted near the Fisher winery. The 1997 Merlot Reserve Nun's Canyon Vineyard is a 100% Merlot aged in French oak. There are only 2,000 cases of this dense, structured, tannic, and more ambitious effort. Full-bodied and rich, with smoky blackberries and cherries intermixed with soil notes, this thick, juicy, well-structured wine will benefit from 2–3 years of cellaring and keep for 12–15. The 1998 Merlot Reserve Nun's Canyon Vineyard displays a Bordeaux-like herbaceousness to its medium-bodied, lightly tannic, modestly endowed flavors. While very good, it is dwarfed by the 1997. Anticipated maturity: now–2009.

There are 400–500 cases of St. Francis's 100% Cabernet Franc, which is picked at high sugars and then fermented in French oak. The dense ruby/purple-colored 1996 Cabernet Franc Reserve McCoy Vineyard offers an excellent bouquet of spice box, cedar, camphor, black cherry, and cassis aromas. While not huge on the palate, it is rich and medium- to full-bodied, with admirable texture as well as sweet, concentrated fruit. Anticipated maturity: now–2012. The superb 1997 Cabernet Franc Reserve McCoy Vineyard was picked extremely ripe (the alcohol level is a well-hidden 15.5%). It reveals aromas and flavors of blueberry liqueur, black currants, smoke, and liquid minerals. Full-bodied, dense, and chewy, as well as elegant and precise, it can be drunk early, but promises to evolve for 15+ years.

With the inflated prices of California wines, readers should be checking out St. Francis's 6,000-case 100% Cabernet Sauvignon aged in equal parts French and American oak. The 1997 Cabernet Sauvignon Reserve (almost totally from the Nun's Canyon Vineyard) is reasonably priced for a wine of such high quality. An opaque purple color is accompanied by a big, bold, spicy, oaky nose infused with licorice, coffee, and abundant quantities of blackberry and cassis fruit. Full-bodied, rich, and impressive, with sweet tannin as well as abundant wood, it will drink well for the next 15 years. The 1998 Cabernet Sauvignon Reserve shows smoky black fruits, less weight and richness, and big tannin, but looks to be successful for the vintage.

St. Francis's most expensive offerings are their King's Ridge Cabernet Sauvignons from the Sonoma Coast. They exploit eight acres of 100% Cabernet Sauvignon usually picked extremely ripe and late, with the harvest sometimes taking place in November. The 1996 Cabernet Sauvignon Reserve King's Ridge Vineyard is aged in 100% new French oak. There are 600 cases of this serious Cabernet. It boasts a dense purple color in addition to aromas and flavors of minerals, crème de cassis, smoke, and toast. Full-bodied and powerful, with moderately high tannin and a long, concentrated finish, it should benefit from 2–3 years of cellaring and last for two decades (assuming the synthetic cork works as well as they say). Even richer, the 1997 Cabernet Sauvignon Reserve King's Ridge Vineyard (900 cases; 14.4% alcohol) boasts a saturated color as well as a gorgeous bouquet of black fruits intermixed with smoke, minerals, licorice, and tobacco. An unctuous texture, huge body, and moderately high tannin suggest this formidably endowed wine has at least 20–25 years of potential cellaring. Because of the sweeter fruit, it is slightly more accessible than the 1996. The 1998 Cabernet Sauvignon Reserve King's Ridge Vineyard is outstanding in this inconsistent vintage. Black/purple-colored, it offers rich, concentrated flavors, full body, a thick texture, and a long, sweet finish. Wine-maker Tom Mackey, who arrived for my tasting on his custom purple Harley-Davidson, said it takes at least a half day, even on his fast bike, to reach the vineyard, which he said might be the westernmost vineyard in the United States.

Warning! The 1995 Cabernet Sauvignon Reserve is exceptionally oaky, so readers who do not want a blatant dosage of toasty smoke in their wines should avoid it. It supports the wood, even though it is lavishly oaked. The color is a dense ruby/purple. In addition to the wood, the wine reveals creamy blackberry and cassis flavors intermixed with smoke and licorice. Thick, rich, and medium- to full-bodied, with low acidity, this garish, ostentatiously styled Cabernet can be drunk now, but promises to be slightly more civilized with more bottle age. Anticipated maturity: now–2014. The 1994 Merlot Estate Reserve exhibits a saturated dark ruby color, followed by intensely smoky, oaky, jammy black cherry and chocolate aromas and flavors. This full-bodied, chewy, fleshy, soft, opulently styled wine should drink well for 7–8 years. Another outstanding effort from St. Francis is the 1994 Cabernet Sauvignon Reserve. It exhibits an opaque purple color, followed by a big, gaudy, ostentatious nose of cedar, Asian spices, jammy black fruits, prunes, and toasty new oak. This intense, ripe, full-bodied wine possesses explosive richness, lavish toasty notes, low acidity, and a heady, lusty, super-long finish. Yes, the new oak is high, but so is the wine's extract and fruit concentration. This is a Cabernet to be drunk with the stereo at high volume. As massive and rich as it is now, it should become more civilized with 3–5 years of cellaring. Anticipated maturity: now–2015. Even more impressive is St. Francis's 1994 Cabernet Sauvignon King's Ridge Vineyard. This wine, with its opaque purple color and strikingly compelling nose of licorice, tobacco leaf, cassis, and smoke, is a full-bodied, heavyweight Cabernet with layers of flavor, a boatload of glycerin and extract, and copious quantities of sweet tannin in the monster finish. It is a dense, super-concentrated wine that should have heads turning in amazement. Anticipated maturity: now–2020.

St. Francis is making monster, pedal-to-the-metal, full-throttle Zinfandels that are likely to score last in terms of subtlety, but who can ignore these opulent, lavishly rich, thrilling wines? I am not sure I could sit down and knock off a bottle of either of these wines, but a glass or two sure is enjoyable. These flamboyant, ostentatious Zinfandels succeed in pushing richness and new oak to the limit. If actors Robin Williams and Jim Carrey were wine-makers, is this the type of Zinfandel they would produce? The 1994 Zinfandel Old Vines screams from the glass, in a reassuring rather than frightening manner. The wine boasts an opaque purple color, followed by a phenomenal nose of overripe black cherries and raspberries doused with high quantities of sweet, toasty, smoky oak, with plenty of licorice and pepper in the background. Superbly rich, smoky, hedonistic, and decadent, this wine is supple and velvety . . . like eating your favorite candy in liquid form (with plenty of alcohol). This spectacular blockbuster will last for 7–8 years, but it is best drunk in its first 4–5 years to take full advantage of its exuberance. The 1994 Zinfandel Pagani Ranch is cut from the same mold, with more structure and alcohol. It, too, is fabulously opulent and rich, with the same unctuous texture, thickness, and density of fruit as the Old Vine *cuvée*. These are amazing Zinfandels. There are other 1994 Zinfandels that are just as rich and full-bodied, but there are none as ostentatious as this duo. Tipping the scales at 15.1% alcohol, it is amazing how well the strength of the 1995 Zinfandel Reserve Pagani Vineyard is hidden behind its layers of chewy, massively extracted, thick Zinfandel fruit. It boasts a saturated black/purple color, and a big, sweet nose of licorice, earth, vanilla, and raisiny black plums. Lush, full-bodied, and huge, with exceptional concentration, this Zin is sure to turn heads. Readers should not consider buying a bottle unless they enjoy mouth-staining, teeth-coating, full-bodied, behemoth Zinfandels. This wine should age well for at least a decade.

The dark ruby/purple-colored 1996 Zinfandel Reserve Pagani Vineyard (from 100-year-old vines) offers plenty of smoky, toasty new-oak aromas along with jammy blackberry and raspberry, tar, licorice, and pepper notes. Although powerful, rich, and full-bodied, it is not as concentrated as preceding vintages. While it is among the most fruit-driven and glycerin-endowed wines of the vintage, it falls just short of being outstanding. Drink it over the next 3–4 years. The relatively heavy-handed 1997 Zinfandel Pagani Vineyard behaves more like a barrel sample than a finished wine. While it possesses high alcohol, this inky wine also displays viscous, oaky, super-extracted flavors. From its opaque purple color, tasters can glean black raspberries, plums, licorice, Asian spice, and toasty notes. It is whoppingly big, chewy, and powerful. Look for this wine to evolve and continue to drink well (perhaps become even more civilized) over the next 5–7 years. As in the past, St. Francis has produced mammoth, super-concentrated, lavishly wooded 1998s. The deep ruby/purple-colored 1998 Zinfandel Old Vines exhibits a big, sweet, toasty oak-scented nose with abundant quantities of black cherry and berry fruit. Muscular, full-bodied, deep, and low in acidity, it is a plump, mouth-filling, chewy Zinfandel for drinking over the next 3–4 years. The outstanding, opaque purple-colored 1998 Zinfandel Pagani Vineyard is once again luxuriously oaked. This super-extracted, intense, unctuously textured Zin is among the most concentrated wines of the vintage. The high level of wood adds an exotic, almost over-the-top aspect to the wine's style. Thick and jammy, with copious quantities of black raspberry, cherry, and blackberry fruit, this huge effort should drink well for 5–6 years.

The 1999 Old Vines and Pagani Vineyard are typical St. Francis Zinfandels . . . dark ruby/purple-colored with tons of toasty American oak as well as jammy ripe blackberry and cherry flavors infused with licorice, herbs, and smoke. Both are full-bodied, low-acid, decadently fruited and wooded wines with unmistakable "made in California" personalities. Both should be drunk in their exuberant, robust youth . . . over the next 3–4 years.

Readers who enjoy muscular, peppery, earthy, black fruit–filled, excruciatingly tannic Petite Sirah should check out the 1999 Petite Sirah Bartolozzi Ranch (400 cases). Although impressive, it needs 5–10 years of cellaring before it becomes civilized, but it will handsomely repay those who have the discipline and intelligence to hide this beast in the cellar.

CHÂTEAU ST. JEAN (SONOMA)

1997	Cabernet Franc St. Jean Estate	Sonoma	D	90
1996	Cabernet Franc St. Jean Estate	Sonoma	D	91
1997	Cabernet Sauvignon Reserve	Sonoma	E	93
1996	Cabernet Sauvignon Reserve	Sonoma	E	94
1995	Cabernet Sauvignon Reserve	Sonoma	E	90
1994	Cabernet Sauvignon Reserve	Sonoma	E	92
1999	Chardonnay	Sonoma	B	88
1998	Cinq Cépages Proprietary Red Wine	Sonoma	D	89
1997	Cinq Cépages Proprietary Red Wine	Sonoma	D	94
1996	Cinq Cépages Proprietary Red Wine	Sonoma	D	92
1995	Cinq Cépages Proprietary Red Wine	Sonoma	D	92
1999	Fumé Blanc	Sonoma	B	88
1999	Fumé Blanc La Petite Etoile	Russian River	C	90
1997	Malbec St. Jean Estate Vineyard	Sonoma	D	92
1997	Merlot	Sonoma	C	88
1997	Merlot Reserve	Sonoma	E	92
1996	Merlot Reserve	Sonoma	E	90
1995	Merlot Reserve	Sonoma	E	90+
1994	Merlot Reserve	Sonoma	E	91
1997	Merlot St. Jean Estate Vineyard	Sonoma	D	91
1999	Pinot Noir	Sonoma	C	88
1998	Pinot Noir	Sonoma	C	88
1998	Pinot Noir Durell Vineyard	Carneros	D	89
1997	Pinot Noir Durell Vineyard	Carneros	D	88?
1996	Pinot Noir Durell Vineyard	Sonoma	D	88

Château St. Jean, one of the picture-postcard photogenic sites in Sonoma Valley, is making the best wines of its history. This winery has made a 180-degree-turn from the highly sculptured, excessively manipulated, industrial mind-set of the seventies and eighties. Today, St. Jean's winemaking is based on a philosophy of nonmanipulation and natural bottling. The results are obvious, with wines that possess more aromatics and creamier textures. Most important, they provide more pleasure. Wine-maker Steve Reeder continues to fine tune an impressive portfolio of character-filled wines. All of these offerings—from the glorious Fumé Blancs, structured, distinctive Chardonnays, increasingly high-quality Pinot Noirs, to their top-of-the-line Merlots, Cabernet Francs, Cabernet Sauvignon Reserves, and proprietary red called Cinq Cépages—are exciting.

A great value, the 1999 Fumé Blanc includes 11% Sémillon in the blend. Approximately 32% is barrel-fermented and the remainder is fermented in stainless steel. The wine does not see any malolactic, but is picked very ripe, which is obvious from the smoky, honeyed melon, passion fruit, and floral-scented bouquet. Medium-bodied, with gorgeous layers of fruit, it is meant to be consumed over the next 1–2 years. Even better is the exceptional 1999 Fumé Blanc La Petite Etoile. All barrel-fermented (50% new oak is used), it spends 10 months in wood prior to bottling and sees no malolactic. Wine-maker Steve Reeder says it smells like "white Gummi Bears." This powerful (15% alcohol) Fumé reveals a liquid minerality, smoky passion fruit, melon, and citrus in its bouquet and flavors. Structured, rich, and concentrated, this wine should be drunk with full-flavored food. It should last for several years.

Château St. Jean's Chardonnay program is also impressive. All of the wines are barrel-fermented, but there is no lees stirring, and the malolactic fermentation is often blocked. One of the best buys in the Chardonnay world is the 150,000 cases of 1999 Chardonnay. Exhibiting floral, tropical fruit, pear, and peach notes, it is a fruit-driven, beautifully balanced, pure white to enjoy during its first several years.

The Burgundian-styled Pinot Noirs emerging from Château St. Jean are somewhat of a secret, with everyone clamoring over the Chardonnays, Fumé Blancs, Cabernets, and Merlot-based wines. The 1999 Pinot Noir Sonoma exhibits an earthy, smoky, plum, and animal-scented bouquet, and good vegetable root notes in the smoke-infused, cherry flavors. Drink it over the next 3–4 years. The dark plum-colored 1998 Pinot Noir Durell Vineyard possesses more weight and density, in addition to full body, and copious quantities of black cherry fruit endowed with notions of roasted meats, herbs, and flowers. Drink this spicy, rich Pinot over the next 5–7 years. The 1998 Pinot Noir Sonoma was made from 100% destemmed fruit, most of which emerged from the Russian River's Westside Vineyard. A medium ruby color is followed by an attractive sweet, cherry, dried herb, and earthy-scented nose with scents of aged beef, spice, and plums. Complex, supple-textured, and easygoing, this wine should be drunk now and over the next 5–6 years. The 1997 Pinot Noir Durell Vineyard is made in a completely different style. Less charming, more tannic, backward, and restrained, it is a big, oaky, concentrated Pinot with plenty of muscle and structure. I liked it less than its sibling (although it does have more to it). Will it resolve all of its tannin? Give it 1–2 years of cellaring to see what emerges. The 1996 Pinot Noir Durell Vineyard reveals complexity and richness. This dark ruby-colored wine offers meaty, plant, and berry fruit aromas in an exotic, lush, medium- to full-bodied style. It possesses adequate acidity and a supple texture. Drink it over the next 3–4 years.

Château St. Jean's red wine program represents reasonably good value. They are producing attractive Merlots, Cabernet Sauvignons, and proprietary red wines. The 1997 Merlot St. Jean Estate Vineyard, which includes 10% Cabernet Franc in the blend, spent 24 months in new oak before bottling. This sensational, limited-production Merlot boasts a dense ruby/purple color in addition to blackberry, charcoal, cherry, melted fudge, and new-oak aromas. Exceptionally ripe, full-bodied, and opulently textured, this is a mouth-filling Merlot to enjoy over the next 10–12 years. The dark garnet/plum-colored 1997 Merlot Reserve (87% Merlot, 9% Cabernet Franc, and 4% Malbec that spent three years in 100% new oak) reveals a dense, chewy, thick, viscous personality as well as enormously concentrated, black cherry, chocolate, vanilla, and berry fruit aromas and flavors. This powerful, full-bodied, spectacular Merlot still has some tannin to shed. Anticipated maturity: 2004–2020. The excellent 1997 Merlot Sonoma includes 6% Cabernet Sauvignon and 6% Cabernet Franc in the blend. It reveals copious quantities of berry fruit, roasted coffee, chocolate, and cherries. Open-knit and round, this dark ruby-colored, low-acid wine is ideal for drinking over the next 5–6 years. The 1996 Merlot Reserve is less easy to taste, but potentially a better Merlot. It offers subtle aromas of creosote, black cherries, dried herbs, and vanilla. In the mouth, toffee notes mix with sweet, creamy wood, chocolate, and berries. Medium- to full-bodied, closed, with moderate tannin in the finish, this Merlot requires 2–3 years of cellaring. It should keep for 12–15 years. The 1994 Merlot Reserve reveals copious quantities of chocolate-flavored, jammy black cherry fruit intertwined with lavish quantities of toasty new oak. It cuts a larger, more expansive feel on the palate and displays impressive length and richness. The 1995 Merlot Reserve exhibits less aromatic and flavor dimension when compared to the 1994, but it is still a superbly concentrated, thick, juicy wine that may end up having slightly more tannin. With more of a monolithic personality, it tastes slightly muted and more backward in its development than the other vintages. These Reserve Merlots are all made in limited quantities of about 400 cases.

Since 1995, the Cinq Cépages has been an outstanding effort. The dark ruby/purple-colored 1996 Cinq Cépages (75% Cabernet Sauvignon, and the balance Cabernet Franc,

Merlot, Malbec, and Petit Verdot) exhibits a moderately intense nose of black cherries, chocolate, smoke, dried herbs, and toasty oak. It appears to be California's version of a big, rich St.-Emilion. Offering elegance and finesse along with copious quantities of fruit, glycerin, and flavor, this medium- to full-bodied wine has evolved nicely, and can be drunk now as well as over the next 12–15 years. The 1995 Cinq Cépages is tasting even better than it was prior to bottling. The wine, which spends two years in 50% new-oak barrels, is dominated by Cabernet Sauvignon (77%), with the other four varietals making up this blend. The 1995 offers a combination of finesse, complexity, richness, and accessibility. It possesses a saturated ruby color and a flamboyant nose of cedar, licorice, tobacco-tinged black currant fruit, and sweet vanilla. Concentrated, full-bodied, and loaded with fruit, this high-quality, impressively endowed wine can be drunk now as well as over the next 15–20 years. The 1997 Cinq Cépages is even better than the 1996. A blend of 75% Cabernet Sauvignon and the balance Merlot, Malbec, Cabernet Franc, and Petit Verdot, it boasts a super-complex bouquet of licorice, dried herbs, black currants, spice box, and cherry liqueur. In the mouth, notes of chocolate, new oak, and red and black fruits caress the palate in a medium- to full-bodied, succulent style. Aged in 50% new and 50% one-year-old French barrels, it is also bottled with no fining or filtration. Fleshy and complex, and drinkable now, it promises to last for 12–15 years. Made in a lighter style, the medium-bodied 1998 Cinq Cépages (75% Cabernet Sauvignon, 16% Merlot, 6% Malbec, 2% Cabernet Franc, and 1% Petit Verdot) exhibits a sweet nose of toast, earth, cedar, licorice, black cherries, and chocolate. There is excellent concentration, but because of the vintage conditions, this wine does not possess the volume, breadth of flavor, or intensity of its two predecessors. Drink the 1998 during its first 10–12 years of life.

One of St. Jean's most spectacular offerings is their 1997 Cabernet Sauvignon Reserve. A blend of 90% Cabernet Sauvignon and 10% Cabernet Franc that spends 36 months in barrel prior to being bottled without fining and filtration, it is a beautifully fashioned, smoky, rich, super-concentrated, thick effort loaded with black cherry, cassis, earthy, smoky, toasty oak aromas and flavors as well as a full-bodied, unctuous finish. This Cabernet requires another 3–4 years of cellaring; it should keep for two decades. The 1996 Cabernet Sauvignon Reserve remains one of the finest wines yet produced by Steve Reeder. This offering, which spent 36 months in barrel prior to bottling, is primarily Cabernet Sauvignon, with a dollop of Merlot or Cabernet Franc added. Production is limited to 500 cases. The terrific 1996 boasts a saturated purple color, as well as a stunning bouquet of coconut, vanilla, black currants, plums, and smoke. Full-bodied, thick, yet nicely buttressed by adequate acidity, this juicy, thrillingly proportioned, large-scaled Cabernet Sauvignon will be at its finest after another year of bottle age; it will keep for two decades.

The 1994 Cabernet Sauvignon Reserve possesses an open-knit, complex aromatic profile consisting of black fruits, cedar, tobacco, fruitcake, and new oak. Full-bodied, with sweeter tannin than the 1993, this multidimensional, large-scaled Cabernet Sauvignon has impeccable balance, as well as a finish that lasts for nearly 35 seconds. Although it is already accessible, 3–4 years of cellaring is recommended; it should keep for two decades. The 1995 Cabernet Sauvignon Reserve exhibits less aromatic and flavor dimension, but superb depth, ripeness, and richness. As with many 1995s, there is a muted character to the wine, but my instincts suggest that all the right stuff is present to develop into an outstanding wine. Patience is required, as this wine will need at least 4–5 years of cellaring. It is another 20-year wine. No, I do not believe it will achieve the complexity and richness of the 1994, and perhaps not even the 1993, but it is an exceptional wine that could turn out to be a sleeper in 5–10 years.

Readers should also check out the 1996 Cabernet Franc St. Jean Estate. Only 300 cases were produced of this 90% Cabernet Franc, 5% Merlot, 5% Malbec blend. It reveals explosive aromas of violets, blueberries, leather, and black fruits. Dense and rich, with great finesse and complexity, this wine, aged in 100% new French oak, reveals gorgeous flavor concentration and authority, but no heaviness or thickness. An ethereal effort, it is a breakthrough Cabernet Franc for Château St. Jean. It will drink well young and evolve nicely for 10–12 years. Reeder's fabulous 1996 Cabernet Franc has been followed by another exquisite effort. The beautifully made 1997 Cabernet Franc St. Jean Estate has been blended with 10% Merlot and 5% Malbec. As with all of this estate's red wines, there was neither fining nor filtration prior to bottling. The 100% new-oak aging has been completely absorbed. Cabernet Franc is a more delicate wine than Merlot or Cabernet Sauvignon, and this effort has somehow handled the new wood. It is a complex, full-bodied, beautifully made effort with intense aromas of leather, black fruits, and flowers. Combining power and richness with finesse and complexity, it is an ethereal effort that should drink well for 15–18 years. It is undoubtedly the finest Cabernet Franc I have tasted from Sonoma. Another impressive offering is the 1997 Malbec St. Jean Estate Vineyard (a blend of 75% Malbec and 25% Cabernet Franc). Dick Arrowood has also produced fine Malbec, but this effort is as good. Notes of black raspberry liqueur intertwined with violet/acacia smells jump from the glass of this floral offering. A dark ruby/purple color is followed by a rich attack, although the wine is lighter in the mouth than the aromas suggest. It combines super fruit with elegance and character. It is hard to predict how a wine like this will age, but it should have no problem lasting for 10–15 years.

Kudos to wine-maker Steve Reeder and Beringer for what they have accomplished at Château St. Jean.

Past Glories: 1993 Cabernet Sauvignon Reserve (91), 1993 Merlot Reserve (90)

SCREAMING EAGLE (NAPA)

1999 Cabernet Sauvignon	Napa	EE	94
1998 Cabernet Sauvignon	Napa	EE	92
1997 Cabernet Sauvignon	Napa	EE	100
1996 Cabernet Sauvignon	Napa	EE	98
1995 Cabernet Sauvignon	Napa	EE	99
1994 Cabernet Sauvignon	Napa	EE	94

There are 500 cases of each vintage. As most readers know, this wine has become the ultimate collector's Cabernet Sauvignon, routinely fetching $800 to as much as $2,000 a bottle at wine auctions. Of course, this makes no sense to me or Screaming Eagle's owner, the amiable Jean Phillips, who sells the wine for $125 a bottle. Unquestionably an exquisite wine, it offers remarkably rich crème de cassis aromas and flavors in an unmanipulated, compelling fashion. The winemaking is assisted by well-known consultant Heidi Barrett. From the red, iron-rich soils of the Oakville district, the wines are aged in 65% new French oak for 18–20 months. I bestowed both the 1992 and 1997 Screaming Eagles perfect 100-point scores, but all the vintages have been as prodigious. The 1998 Cabernet Sauvignon, which was bottled in late June of 2000, has turned out even better than I thought when I tasted it from barrel. It boasts a saturated ruby/purple color in addition to an expressive bouquet of cassis, minerals, and smoke. Full-bodied and dense, it is more evolved than other vintages tasted at a similar age, a characteristic of 1998, which has produced less massive Napa Cabernet Sauvignons, with less volume and concentration. The multitextured, round 1998 Screaming Eagle exhibits sweet, well-integrated tannin, a great mid-palate and finish, as well as spectacular purity and palate presence. Consume it now and over the next 15–20 years. It is a candidate for the "wine of the vintage" in 1998. The 1999 Cabernet Sauvignon (a blend of 88% Cabernet Sauvignon, 10% Merlot, and 2% Cabernet Franc) is another exquisite effort that may fall just short of the otherworldly 1997 and 1992. An opaque blue/purple color is followed by a jammy blackberry and crème de cassis–scented bouquet of extraordinary precision and purity. It possesses awesome intensity, but manages not to taste overblown, overweight, or overdone. Thick and unctuously textured, but impeccably balanced, it displays terrific equilibrium as well as depth. With its hallmark silky texture and fabulously concentrated, flawlessly presented style, it is another potential legend from this microsized enterprise. Anticipated maturity: now–2020.

It doesn't get any better than the 1997 Cabernet Sauvignon, another perfect wine. Representing the essence of cassis intermixed with blackberries, minerals, licorice, and toast, this full-bodied, multidimensional classic is fabulous, with extraordinary purity, symmetry, and a finish that lasts for nearly a minute. It has the overall equilibrium to evolve for nearly two decades, but it will be hard to resist upon release. Anticipated maturity: now–2020. The 1996 Cabernet Sauvignon reveals more structure than the 1997, an opaque purple color, and the hallmark blackberry and cassis-like notes. Silky-textured, fabulously concentrated, and gorgeously balanced, it has every component part—acidity, alcohol, tannin, and extract—flawlessly presented. Anticipated maturity: now–2020. The opaque purple-colored 1995 Cabernet Sauvignon exhibits a sensational purity of black currant fruit, intermixed with a notion of raspberries, violets, and well-disguised sweet vanilla. Full-bodied, with remarkable intensity, exquisite symmetry, and a mid-palate and finish to die for, this is a compelling, astonishingly seductive Cabernet that can be drunk now or cellared for 20–25 years. I may have done this wine a disservice by not giving it the big three-digit score.

The opaque purple-colored 1994 Cabernet Sauvignon's forward, gorgeously scented nose offers up a smorgasbord of black fruits, along with a subtle dosage of toasty oak and minerals. Full-bodied, with a seamless, lush texture, this is a profoundly generous wine with everything going for it. The finish lasts for 35 seconds. As gorgeous as it is, this wine can be drunk young or cellared for 20–25 years.

I keep asking Jean Phillips what she does in order to achieve such purity of fruit. There are no secrets—yields are modest, grapes are harvested at 24° Brix (which is normal), the wine is aged in Seguin-Moreau French barrels (about 60–65% are new) for 18–20 months and bottled with no filtration. Considerable punching down is done at Screaming Eagle, and the small, one-half-ton fermenters may hold the secret to the extraordinary fruit quality Phillips achieves. On the other hand, it may simply be the *terroir* combined with the owner's obsession with brilliant wines. And let's not forget the consulting oenologist, Napa Valley's Heidi Barrett. Getting on the winery's mailing list is the only way to latch onto a bottle, unless you get lucky and find a bottle at one of Napa Valley's wine shops or restaurants.

Past Glories: 1993 Cabernet Sauvignon (97), 1992 Cabernet Sauvignon (98)

SEAVEY (NAPA)

1999 Cabernet Sauvignon	Napa	E	92
1998 Cabernet Sauvignon	Napa	E	90
1997 Cabernet Sauvignon	Napa	E	96
1996 Cabernet Sauvignon	Napa	D	92
1995 Cabernet Sauvignon	Napa	D	94
1994 Cabernet Sauvignon	Napa	D	91
1999 Chardonnay	Napa	D	90
1999 Merlot	Napa	D	89
1998 Merlot	Napa	D	90
1997 Merlot	Napa	D	90
1994 Merlot	Napa	C	89

Proprietors Mary and Bill Seavey, along with their talented wine-maker, Philippe Melka, continue to fashion some of Napa Valley's finest wines. Moreover, they are all fairly priced compared to so many Napa wineries that operate in their unreal world. Readers looking for a non-malolactic, powerful Chardonnay that has been gently touched by oak should check out Seavey's refreshing 1999. Indigenous yeasts are used during fermentation, but there is little lees stirring, and only 25% new oak is utilized in the wine's upbringing. Yet this 1999 Chardonnay possesses plenty of power as well as gorgeously ripe pear and honeyed citrus notes, full body, excellent freshness, and impressive extract and richness. Most non-malolactic Chardonnays lack texture and interest, but that is not the case with Seavey's offering. It will drink well for 3–4 years.

The dense garnet/plum/purple-colored 1998 Merlot offers expressive, fragrant aromatics consisting of chocolate soufflé, smoke, coffee, mocha, and berry fruit. Full-bodied, lush, silky-textured, and made in a Pomerol-like, ripe style, it is on a fast evolutionary track, so owners should consume it over the next 5–6 years. The 1999 Merlot is similarly styled, exhibiting a full-bodied, chocolate and berry fruit–scented nose, low acidity, and fleshy, succulent flavors. Both wines are 100% Merlot aged in 40–45% new French oak. The 1999 should have a slightly longer aging curve of 8–10 years.

There are 300 cases of the 1997 Merlot, an intense, full-bodied, gorgeously pure, 100% Merlot that saw 40% new French oak. It reveals the telltale espresso bean, chocolaty, sweet, jammy berry fruit, an unctuous, thick texture, full body, and excellent purity and length. It is a gorgeous Merlot to drink now and over the next 12–15 years. The 1994 Merlot (350 cases) was aged in 35–45% new-oak casks. The opaque purple color is followed by a wine with an impressively rich nose of black currants and spice. This ripe, rich, sweet, medium- to full-bodied 100% Merlot should last longer than I suggested in my first review of it. It now appears it will evolve effortlessly for another 7–8 years and hold at that plateau for 5–6 years.

This estate can be a sensational source of Cabernet Sauvignon that goes largely unnoticed because Seavey is hidden in the backwater Conn Valley, east of St. Helena. Their 1991 Cabernet Sauvignon remains one of the greatest Cabernets of the decade, but it is amazing how many people have never tasted it. The 1997 Cabernet Sauvignon (1,400 cases) is potentially every bit as good. I originally rated this wine 96, but after an additional year of bottle age, it may be even better. It spent 18 months in 40–45% new French oak, and was bottled after a light fining yet no filtration. A monumental, classic California Cabernet Sauvignon, it boasts an opaque plum/purple color as well as an extraordinary bouquet of jammy cassis, plums, toast, and licorice. With its humongous fruit and glycerin, full body, smoky blackberry and coffee flavors on the mid-palate, as well as a silky, moderately tannic finish that lasts for nearly a minute, this seamless effort is a modern-day Cabernet elixir. A blend of 98% Cabernet Sauvignon and 2% Petit Verdot, it should be at its best between 2004–2025. The outstanding 1998 Cabernet Sauvignon, produced from an extremely small crop, is an example of what the Napa Cabernet Sauvignon producers are jokingly saying is "another fine wine from a bad vintage." A rich, full-bodied, dense effort on a faster evolutionary track than the 1997, the 1998 is loaded with chocolaty, black cherry, and cassis fruit, an open-knit, sexy, expansive texture, outstanding concentration and purity, low acidity, and a fat, chewy finish. It will be drinkable upon release, yet promises to age well for 12–15 years. The 1999 Cabernet Sauvignon reveals an opaque purple color in addition to a sweet, highly extracted bouquet of black fruits, coffee, chocolate, cedar, and plum aromas. Silky yet assertive tannin, full body, exceptional concentration and purity, and a dense, layered finish further characterize this wine. Anticipated maturity: 2005–2020.

The 1996 Cabernet Sauvignon is superb. This opaque purple-colored effort reveals aromas of black currants, creosote, smoke, minerals, and plums. It is full-bodied, with exquisite density and terrific fruit purity and intensity, particularly in the mid-palate and length (always good signs for wines that are meant to improve and last). There is plenty of tannin, but this is a generous, impressively endowed wine that should stand the test of several decades of cellaring. Anticipated maturity: 2003–2025. Seavey's opaque 1995 Cabernet Sauvignon (950 cases) displays a fantastic nose of classic black currants intermixed with cigar box and cedar scents. In the mouth, it is full-bodied and backward, but persuasively rich, layered, and marvelously well balanced. There is a deep, sweet mid-palate and explosive ripeness and richness in the long, heady finish. A sleeper pick in this outstanding vintage, it should evolve effortlessly for 20–30 years. Anticipated maturity: now–2028.

Made from low yields of approximately two tons of fruit per acre, from Seavey's east-facing hillside vineyards in the Conn Valley, the 1994 Cabernet Sauvignon exhibits an opaque purple color, and an exuberant yet still young and unformed nose of spice, black fruits, and cedar. Full-bodied, with layers of dense, ripe fruit, this rich, moderately tannic wine should be at its best in 3–5 years. It will keep for two decades or more.

This is another property where getting on the mailing list makes good sense.

Past Glories: Cabernet Sauvignon—1993 (91), 1992 (92), 1991 (99), 1990 (94)

SEGHESIO WINERY (SONOMA)

1999 Zinfandel	Sonoma	C	88
1998 Zinfandel	Sonoma	B	88
1999 Zinfandel Cortina	Alexander Valley	D	89
1999 Zinfandel Home Ranch	Alexander Valley	D	90
1998 Zinfandel Home Ranch	Alexander Valley	D	90
1999 Zinfandel Old Vines	Sonoma	D	90
1998 Zinfandel Old Vines	Sonoma	D	90
1997 Zinfandel Old Vines	Sonoma	D	90
1999 Zinfandel San Lorenzo	Alexander Valley	D	91
1997 Zinfandel San Lorenzo	Alexander Valley	D	88

Seghesio, which possesses well-located vineyards in both Alexander Valley and Sonoma, has become a respectable source for high-quality Zinfandel. Fortunately, prices have not caught up with some of the other outstanding Zinfandel producers who are cashing in on the insatiable thirst for high-quality wine. Consistently fashioning topflight Zinfandels from their old vineyards, Seghesio's 1999s are among the stars of the vintage. One of the best buys is the 1999 Zinfandel Sonoma (14.5% alcohol). An excellent dark ruby/purple color is followed by tangy, classic briery, berry, and cherry fruit mixed with pepper, spice, and earth. It is a polished yet flavorful wine to enjoy over the next 3–4 years. Even more complex, fuller bodied, and layered is the 1999 Zinfandel Old Vines (15.3% alcohol). Exhibiting earthy, Rhône-like characteristics of crushed pepper and black cherries presented in a lusty, full-bodied format, it will drink well for 4–5 years.

All three single-vineyard 1999 offerings are impressive. The deep ruby/purple-colored 1999 Zinfandel Home Ranch reveals some new oak, vanilla, pepper, and sandalwood, but briery, berry, currant, and cherry fruit dominate. Fleshy, full-bodied, powerful, and well balanced, with sweet tannin as well as tangy acidity for definition, this large-scaled Zinfandel should drink well for 6–7 years. The most concentrated and complex effort is the dense ruby/purple-colored 1999 Zinfandel San Lorenzo (15.4% alcohol). Aromas of seaweed, new saddle leather, coffee, tobacco, soy, and black cherries are reminiscent of a top-class Piedmontese Nebbiolo. Full-bodied, with tangy acidity and a complex, multilayered style, it should drink well for 6–7 years. The grapy, unevolved, one-dimensional 1999 Zinfandel Cortina (14.7% alcohol) possesses gobs of fruit and glycerin, but less aromatic and flavor complexity than its siblings. This rich offering should develop well and drink nicely for 5–7 years.

The 1998 Zinfandel Sonoma (14.1% alcohol) is a textbook example of this varietal. Dark ruby-colored with purple nuances, this fruit-driven wine exhibits black cherry and briery characteristics with subtle pepper and oak in the background. Rich, medium- to full-bodied, pure, and low in acidity, it can be enjoyed over the next 3–4 years. The 1998 Zinfandel Old Vines is not dissimilar from the Sonoma *cuvée;* it just has more of everything. The 14.6% alcohol results in a fuller-bodied feel, with more glycerin and concentration. Earthy, peppery, spice, big black raspberry, and cherry notes dominate the wine's aromatics and flavors. Pure, long, and rich, with low acidity, it should be drunk over the next 5–6 years. Another impressive effort is the 1998 Zinfandel Home Ranch, made from a vineyard first planted in 1895. This opaque ruby-colored effort offers sweet berry and cherry fruit on the attack, a touch of toasty new oak, medium to full body, and roasted herb, sweet strawberry and cherry jam–like flavors. Consume it over the next 4–5 years. These are impressive efforts from a winery that deserves more attention.

The 1997 Zinfandel San Lorenzo (14.6% alcohol) possesses a dense, dark ruby/purple color, noticeable new oak, a heady, ripe, structured style with muscle, moderately aggressive acidity, yet admirable ripeness, extract, and length. Drink it over the next 7–8 years. With 14.2% alcohol, the 1997 Zinfandel Old Vines is not a huge wine by modern-day standards. Its saturated ruby/purple color is followed by superb aromas of black raspberries, minerals, and flowers. There is gorgeously integrated acidity and alcohol, a nice structured yet fruit-driven mid-palate, and a succulent, concentrated finish. It should drink well for 7–8 years.

SELENE (NAPA)

1998 Merlot	Napa	D	87
1997 Merlot	Napa	D	90
1996 Merlot	Napa	D	91+
1995 Merlot	Napa	D	92
1994 Merlot	Napa	D	90
1998 Merlot Hyde Vineyard	Carneros	D	88
1997 Merlot Hyde Vineyard	Carneros	D	88
1996 Merlot Hyde Vineyard	Carneros	D	90
1995 Merlot Hyde Vineyard	Carneros	D	89

Selene's 1998 Merlots are light but well-made efforts in this difficult vintage. The 1998 Merlot Hyde Vineyard exhibits dried tobacco, Provençal herb, chocolate, and berry fruit aromas. Soft and medium-bodied, it will be delicious upon release. The 1997 Merlot Hyde Vineyard reveals tangier acidity as well as an elegant berry fruit and mocha-scented and -flavored personality. With a fine finish, it should drink well for 5–8 years. The Napa Merlots are always richer and more concentrated. Approximately two-thirds of the fruit comes from the well-known Madrona Ranch, made famous primarily by viticulturist David Abreu. The remainder of the fruit comes from the Caldwell Vineyard, which was formerly used as a source of Merlot fruit by Jayson Pahlmeyer. The excellent, dark ruby/purple-colored 1998 Merlot Napa offers up sweet, chocolaty, coffee-like aromas and flavors that exhibit excellent ripeness, plenty of glycerin, and a medium-bodied, pure finish. It should be delicious during its first 7–8 years of life. The structured 1997 Merlot Napa possesses more noticeable acidity and tannin. Well made, with excellent berry and white chocolate aromas and flavors, it is a bigger, more ageworthy effort than the 1998, but it has less charm and sweetness. Anticipated maturity: now–2008. The 1996 Merlot Hyde Vineyard reveals an attractive purple color, a sweet, licorice, and black cherry–scented nose with medium body, a hint of herbs and coffee, and enough acidity to provide balance. Long, rich, and plump, it will age well for 10 years. Even more impressive is the dense black/purple-colored 1996 Merlot Napa, which is a fatter, richer wine with lower acidity (a higher pH style), an expansive, savory texture, and a long, lush, medium- to full-bodied finish. The wine unfolds beautifully in the glass and will be a hedonistic Merlot to consume over its first decade of life.

The 1995 Merlot Hyde Vineyard offers a dense purple color, followed by a bouquet of black cherries, smoke, and chocolate. Expressive and rich, with abundant black cherry fruit, this tasty, medium-bodied, spicy Merlot should drink well for 5–8 years. The 1995 Merlot Napa is a decadent, luxuriously endowed wine. From its opaque purple color to its knockout nose of roasted coffee, smoky black cherry fruit, and chocolate, this rich, superbly concentrated wine possesses terrific intensity and enough acidity and oak to provide a framework.

The silky finish complements the intensely fragrant personality of this gorgeous Merlot. Drink it over the next 7–8 years. With so many stripped, vegetal, herbal tea–scented Merlots, it is reassuring to taste such yummy stuff as Selene's 1994 Merlot. When it is good, Merlot is a wonderfully soft, silky-textured, medium-weight, aromatically expressive wine with plenty of ripe berry fruit, often intermingled with scents of white chocolate, coffee, and spices. This luscious 1994 possesses plenty of those traits, plus the richness and plumpness to go along with its voluptuous texture. It is already drinking splendidly well—so why wait? I would opt for consuming this beauty over the next 5–6 years.

SEVEN LIONS WINERY (SONOMA)

1999 Zinfandel Martinelli and Duckhorn Vineyard	Russian River	E	89

This opaque purple-colored, medium- to full-bodied Zinfandel is produced from some of the Russian River's finest soils/vineyards. Sweet, ripe black currant and cherry characteristics combine with smoky oak, and tangy acidity provides definition, vibrancy, and freshness in this large-scaled, concentrated, dense effort. This excellent 1999 is sure to please Zinfandel enthusiasts, but the price is hard to swallow.

SHAFER VINEYARDS (NAPA)

1999 Cabernet Sauvignon	Napa	D	90
1998 Cabernet Sauvignon	Napa	D	89
1997 Cabernet Sauvignon	Napa	E	90
1996 Cabernet Sauvignon	Napa	E	89
1995 Cabernet Sauvignon	Napa	E	91
1994 Cabernet Sauvignon	Napa	E	90
1999 Cabernet Sauvignon Hillside Select Stags Leap	Napa	EEE	97
1998 Cabernet Sauvignon Hillside Select Stags Leap	Napa	EEE	92
1997 Cabernet Sauvignon Hillside Select Stags Leap	Napa	EEE	99
1996 Cabernet Sauvignon Hillside Select Stags Leap	Napa	EEE	98
1995 Cabernet Sauvignon Hillside Select Stags Leap	Napa	EE	99
1994 Cabernet Sauvignon Hillside Select Stags Leap	Napa	EE	99
1999 Chardonnay Red Shoulder Ranch	Napa/Carneros	D	(90–92)
1997 Firebreak (Sangiovese/Cabernet Sauvignon)	Napa	C	90
1996 Firebreak (Sangiovese/Cabernet Sauvignon)	Napa	D	88
1999 Merlot	Napa	D	87
1998 Merlot	Napa	D	89
1997 Merlot	Napa	D	90
1996 Merlot	Napa	D	88
1995 Merlot	Stags Leap	D	90
1994 Merlot	Stags Leap	D	89
1999 Syrah	Napa	E	92

Located on the Silverado Trail, in the Stags Leap section of Napa Valley, Shafer Vineyards is the undeniable star of the region. Production is approximately 30,000 cases, with 6,000 cases of Chardonnay Red Shoulder Ranch and 2,000 cases of Cabernet Sauvignon Hillside

Select on strict allocation because of popular demand. The 1999 Chardonnay Red Shoulder Ranch exhibits abundant quantities of rich orange, tangerine, and citrus aromas and flavors, full body, a big, smoky, leesy, barrel-fermented style, good underlying acidity, and tremendous weight and intensity. About 50% new oak (primarily French with a touch of American) is utilized, and the wine is not put through malolactic fermentation. It should age well for 3–4 years.

Shafer's 1998 red wines are successful efforts. The 1998 Merlot (a blend of 76% Merlot, 13% Cabernet Franc, and 11% Cabernet Sauvignon with 14.3% alcohol) offers a blueberry, menthol, and berry-scented nose in addition to crisp but fleshy, pure, long, layered, supple flavors gently touched by spicy oak. This wine has turned out even better than expected. The 1999 Merlot (a blend of 81% Merlot, 10% Cabernet Sauvignon, and 9% Cabernet Franc) reveals a cold-growing-season character, ripe cherry fruit, good acidity, notes of tobacco and spice, medium body, light to moderate tannin, and smoky oak in the background. It will require time to flesh out, but does not appear to be as charming as the 1998.

There is good availability (10,000 cases produced) of the outstanding 1997 Merlot (75% Merlot, 15% Cabernet Franc, and 10% Cabernet Sauvignon). It exhibits copious quantities of cedar, coffee, plum, and black cherry/cassis fruit. The texture is fleshy and open-knit, with gobs of ripeness. Drink this medium-bodied, lush, pure Merlot over the next 10–12 years. The medium- to full-bodied 1996 Merlot (77% Merlot, 16% Cabernet Franc, and 7% Cabernet Sauvignon) is more exotic, with some of Merlot's chocolate overtones emerging in the black cherry fruit. While the 1996 may be fuller and heavier than the 1997, it is also an excellent effort. I would opt for consuming it over the next decade. The 1994 Merlot is one of the best Merlots on the market—soft, velvety-textured, with gobs of ripe cherry/cranberry fruit nicely dosed with smoky oak. The wine is medium- to full-bodied, yet elegant and expansive, with no hard edges. Fully mature, it should drink well and gracefully evolve over the next 3–4 years. The 1995 Merlot appears to be the qualitative equivalent, perhaps slightly superior, to the 1994. Certainly the 1995 is more fragrant and aromatic. Jammy black cherries, toast, and subtle herbaceous notes are followed by a wine with gorgeous layers of rich, glycerin-endowed, creamy-textured fruit. Deeper-colored than the 1994, but as structured, the 1995 possesses more extract and length. It should drink well for 6–8 years.

Shafer's Sangiovese-dominated Firebreak (2,500 cases produced) is to be admired. One of the finest Firebreaks tasted is the 1997. Dark ruby-colored, with sumptuous aromas of black cherries, new saddle leather, dried herbs, licorice, and strawberry jam, this rich, medium-bodied, fruit-driven wine possesses uncanny elegance and complexity for a California Sangiovese (with 15% Cabernet Sauvignon). Displaying beautiful harmony and hitting all the palate's sweet spots, it is fully mature. The 1996 Firebreak (80% Sangiovese and 20% Cabernet Sauvignon) exhibits a dark ruby color as well as a textbook Sangiovese nose of strawberries, leather, cherries, and damp forest scents. The wine possesses excellent richness, medium body, and an elegant, more restrained and subdued style than the richer, more fragrant 1997. It should drink well for another 1–2 years.

A new Shafer project that will tantalize wine consumers is their 17-acre Syrah vineyard planted in southern Napa Valley. While production from the first crop, 1999, will be small, this looks to be a fabulous Syrah. Yields were cut by 50%, producing only 1.5 tons of fruit per acre. The wine is being aged in 75% new French oak casks. The result is a sensational, opaque blue/purple-colored Syrah with a dazzling nose of blackberry liqueur intermixed with barbecue spices and licorice. In the mouth, it is full-bodied, voluptuously textured, super-extracted, and rich, with low acidity. It should provide compelling drinking upon release and keep for 15 years.

The sexy, forward 1998 Cabernet Sauvignon may turn out to be exceptional, particularly for this vintage. A blend of 94% Cabernet Sauvignon and 6% Cabernet Franc, this dense ruby/purple-colored, full-bodied, supple-textured, soft, hedonistic, seductive offering is thick and juicy, with low acidity as well as loads of fruit, glycerin, and appeal. Enjoy it over the next 10–12 years. The 1999 Cabernet Sauvignon (a blend of 97% Cabernet Sauvignon, 2% Cabernet Franc, and 1% Merlot) should be superb. A dense ruby/purple color is accompanied by a full-bodied, concentrated palate, a multilayered mid-palate, and sweet black currant fruit intermixed with minerals, lead pencil, and spice. It should drink well for 10–15+ years. The dark ruby/purple-colored 1997 Cabernet Sauvignon is brilliant. Small quantities (7% of each) of Cabernet Franc and Merlot have been added to the blend, giving the wine more aromatic breadth and flavor dimension. Dense and rich, with high extraction, sweet fruit, full body, outstanding purity, and mineral/spicy aromas, the 1997 should drink well for 10–15 years. The excellent 1996 Cabernet Sauvignon (13.5% alcohol, and made from a blend of 94% Cabernet Sauvignon and 6% Cabernet Franc) is more sternly constructed and possesses rougher tannin than the 1997. The wine's saturated ruby color is followed by a big, spicy, black currant, loamy soil, and smoky-scented bouquet. The mid-palate is rich, pure, and well endowed, and there is noticeable tannin in the moderately long finish (a characteristic of many 1996 North Coast reds). This wine will benefit from 1–3 years of cellaring and will keep for 12–15. The 1995 Cabernet Sauvignon is elegant, yet authoritatively flavored, with copious amounts of cassis fruit, spicy, smoky oak, medium body, and an excellent, restrained but well-balanced personality. It is a nicely extracted, fleshy, complex wine for drinking during its first 10–15 years of life. A gorgeous Cabernet Sauvignon, Shafer's 1994 displays a dark purple color, as well as sweet, floral-scented, cassis fruit mixed with subtle new oak and minerals. Medium- to full-bodied, spicy, and exceptionally pure, with a nicely layered texture and outstanding equilibrium and depth, this is a classic, elegant, authoritatively flavored Cabernet that is impeccably made. It is still youthful, but given the penchant for most Americans (this author included) to enjoy the youthfulness of wines such as this, I would opt for drinking it now and over the next 12–15+ years. Very impressive!

Since 1991, Shafer's Hillside Select Cabernet Sauvignon has unquestionably been one of the top dozen or so California Cabernets. Made from 100% Cabernet Sauvignon and aged 32 months in 100% French oak casks (the majority Taransaud), it possesses the elegance and finesse one would expect from the Stags Leap area, but also monumental power, richness, and intensity. Every Hillside Select *cuvée* produced since 1991 has been spectacular, with the 1994, 1995, 1996, 1997, and 1999 all flirting with perfection. I do not think a blind tasting could establish which is the finest vintage . . . they are all that close in quality. Sadly, there are only about 2,200 cases of this prodigious Cabernet. The 1999 Cabernet Sauvignon Hillside Select exhibits the telltale lead pencil, black currant, and mineral-infused fruit with subtle oak in the aromatics and flavors. Seamless, full-bodied, and fabulously concentrated, with a 45-second finish, it comes closest in style to the 1994. A candidate for Cabernet Sauvignon of the vintage, the 1998 Cabernet Sauvignon Hillside Select is not as massive as the 1996, 1997, or 1999, but it is more concentrated and intense than most top Bordeaux, with beautifully integrated wood. Seemingly on a fast evolutionary track, it offers complex tobacco, mineral, cassis, and vanilla scents in the formidable aromatics. On the palate, the wine is full-bodied and rich, with sweet tannin, perfect balance, and a gentle, layered finish exhibiting no hard edges. The balance, harmony, and complexity suggest this 1998 will be drinkable upon release, and will age well for 15+ years.

Is the prodigious 1997 Cabernet Sauvignon Hillside Select a perfect wine? Bottled in June 2000, this effort is about as spectacular as Cabernet can be. The soaring bouquet of sweet, lavishly rich black currants, plums, cherries, toast, minerals, and smoke cascades from the glass. Opaque purple-colored, extraordinarily intense, and full-bodied, yet amazingly well balanced, this flawless wine will be at its peak between now–2030. One of the greatest young Cabernet Sauvignons I have ever tasted, it represents the quintessential Napa Cabernet, combining both elegance and power. The 1996 Cabernet Sauvignon Hillside Select is one of the vintage's superstars. Its opaque purple color is accompanied by super aromatics, immense body, great fruit extraction, superb purity and overall symmetry, as well as a 40+-second finish. Revealing exceptional intensity (but no heaviness) as well as perfectly integrated acidity, tannin, and alcohol, this fabulous Cabernet will drink wonderfully for three decades. The 1995 Cabernet Sauvignon Hillside Select exhibits the same characteristics as the 1996 and 1997, yet possesses more fatness in the mid-palate. There is plenty of tannin in this full-bodied, rich effort. It is remarkable how the finest California Cabernets combine extraordinary power and richness with balance and elegance. A stupendous wine, it is worth a special effort to obtain. Anticipated maturity: 2003–2030.

The 1994 Cabernet Sauvignon Hillside Select is a prodigious Cabernet. I had it at a tasting in Japan, and the Japanese were as enthusiastic about it as my rating suggested they should be. They were crestfallen when informed they probably would not be able to buy multiple cases of the wine! The 1994 combines the vintage's spectacularly ripe, luscious fruit with a rarely seen degree of elegance and finesse. The wine is extremely rich, as well as gorgeously poised and graceful. The saturated ruby/purple color is accompanied by Médoc-like, lead pencil aromas intermixed with cassis, cedar, minerals, and spice. I wrote the word "great" four different times in my most recent tasting note, which mirrored every other tasting note I have. It is full-bodied and seamless, with a silky texture, voluptuous richness, and fabulous purity. The finish lasts for over 40 seconds. Anticipated maturity: now–2025.

By the way, I asked John and Doug Shafer their ratings of the Hillside Select Cabernet Sauvignon for the vintages of the 1990s. They agreed that the three top vintages were (in no particular order) 1991, 1994, and 1997. Close behind were 1992, 1995, and 1996. They equated 1998 with 1993.

Past Glories: Cabernet Sauvignon Hillside Select Stags Leap—1993 (94), 1992 (96), 1991 (96)

SIDURI (CALIFORNIA)

1998 Novy Cellars Syrah Stage Gulch Vineyard	Petaluma/Sonoma	D	88
1999 Pinot Noir	Santa Lucia Highlands	D	88
1999 Pinot Noir	Sonoma	D	88
1998 Pinot Noir Archery Summit	Oregon	D	93
1997 Pinot Noir Archery Summit	Oregon	D	90
1999 Pinot Noir Christian David	Sonoma Coast	E	90+
1998 Pinot Noir Coastlands Vineyard	Sonoma Coast	D	90+
1999 Pinot Noir Garys' Vineyard	Santa Lucia Highlands	D	89
1999 Pinot Noir Hirsch Vineyard	Sonoma Coast	D	91
1998 Pinot Noir Hirsch Vineyard	Sonoma Coast	D	91
1997 Pinot Noir Hirsch Vineyard	Sonoma Coast	D	88+
1999 Pinot Noir Muirfield Vineyard	Oregon	D	89+
1998 Pinot Noir Muirfield Vineyard	Oregon	D	90
1999 Pinot Noir Pisoni Vineyard	Santa Lucia Highlands	D	92
1998 Pinot Noir Pisoni Vineyard	Santa Lucia Highlands	D	90
1997 Pinot Noir Pisoni Vineyard	Santa Lucia Highlands	D	92
1998 Pinot Noir Van der Kamp Vineyard	Sonoma Mountain	D	(87–88)
1997 Pinot Noir Van der Kamp Vineyard Old Vines	Sonoma Mountain	D	88
1999 Pinot Noir Willamette Valley	Oregon	D	88

I have been a fan of Siduri since their debut offerings. They continue to specialize in high-quality Pinot Noir from choice vineyard sites in both California and Oregon. They have also added a Syrah under the Novy Cellars label. This winery produces numerous Pinot Noirs exhibiting subtle differences, thus the argument supporting separate designations. The 1999 Pinot Noir Willamette Valley, which is a blend of Archery Summit and Muirfield Vineyard fruit, reveals a healthy, dark ruby color, in addition to a sweet nose of black cherries, rich, concentrated fruit, medium body, and excellent purity. It is a delicious wine to drink over the next 5–7 years. The 1999 Pinot Noir Muirfield Vineyard comes from both Dijon clones and the well-known Oregon clone called Wadenswil. Yields were only 1.5 tons per acre. The color is a dense ruby/purple. The wine is thick, quite rich, medium- to full-bodied, and impressively pure, with a thick, black cherry component the distinguishing characteristic. There were 180 cases produced. There are eight offerings of California Pinot Noir from some of the state's most renowned vineyards. For starters, the 1999 Pinot Noir Sonoma has a medium ruby color, a straightforward and sweet nose of jammy cherries, very seductive, medium-bodied, supple flavors, and light tannin. The wine is quite pure and ideal for drinking over the next 2–5 years. There are 226 cases of this Sonoma County Pinot Noir. Siduri has also decided to produce three separate Pinot Noirs from the Santa Lucia Highlands. The 1999 Pinot Noir Santa Lucia (14.4% alcohol) is an open-knit, round, generously endowed wine (214 cases) that shows good, ripe, blackberry and cherry fruit, nicely integrated wood, adequate acidity, and a spicy, clean finish. Drink it over the next 4–5 years. The 1999 Pinot Noir Garys' Vineyard offers overripe jammy strawberry/cherry fruit and a touch of smoky, toasty oak. The wine (542 cases) is relatively fat, fleshy, and pure, with plenty of black fruit and a plump personality. Drink it over the next 4–5 years. Lastly, the superb 1999 Pinot Noir Pisoni Vineyard (576 cases produced) was aged in 60% new French oak and bottled, like all these Pinots, without filtration. The color is a dense ruby/purple. The wine offers up sumptuous quantities of black raspberry, blackberry, and cherry fruit, smoky, toasty oak, and black and Chinese tea in the background. The palate is voluptuous, thick, very pure, rich, and medium- to full-bodied. Even some meatiness is apparent as this wine sits in the glass. This is a terrific Pinot that can be drunk now or aged for 7–8 years.

Siduri produces several Sonoma Coast offerings. The 1999 Pinot Noir Hirsch Vineyard (282 cases made from 1.6 tons per acre of fruit) is a dense, ruby-colored wine with a complex nose of violets, red cherries, and spice. In the mouth, it is voluptuously textured, pure, and ripe, with well-integrated tannin and reasonably low acidity. It is a complex, rich, full, Burgundian-styled Pinot Noir to drink over the next 7–8 years. Named after the proprietor's first child, the 1999 Pinot Noir Christian David (68 cases) was made from 100% Pommard clones from the Hirsch Vineyard. Tight, backward, and tannic, this dense ruby/purple-colored Pinot possesses plenty of structure, but also impressive concentration and overall equilibrium. It needs 1–2 years of cellaring and should keep for 12 or more years. Overall, this is an impressive group of excellent to exceptional Pinot Noirs that merit considerable interest.

1998 can be a terrific vintage for Oregon's top Pinot Noir producers. It is unquestionably the finest vintage since 1994. Siduri's 1998 Pinot Noir Muirfield Vineyard was cropped at only 1.3 tons per acre. Revealing an intriguing Vosne-Romanée style, it possesses a dark ruby color as well as a sweet, toasty nose with aromas of black cherry and raspberry fruit, medium body, sweet tannin, high but well-hidden alcohol (13.9%), and an excellent finish. It should be drinkable upon release next year and evolve nicely for 5–6 years. The superb 1998 Pinot Noir Archery Summit Vineyard was made from Oregon's new Dijon clones for Pinot Noir—#115, #113, and #777. Cropped at an unbelievably low .8 tons of fruit per acre, this wine could easily pass for a grand cru such as Grands-Echezeaux or Richebourg. A dark ruby-colored wine with purple nuances, its soaring aromatics jump from the glass, offering up black raspberries, cherries, plums, toast, and flowers. Medium- to full-bodied, with a terrific mid-palate, a creamy texture, and enough acidity to provide focus and balance, this wine's outstanding purity as well as stunning richness and harmony make for a sumptuous glass of Pinot Noir. It may even improve. Anticipated maturity: now–2007. Bravo! Siduri's persuasive skills convinced the owners of the Coastlands Vineyard to sell them some of their Pinot Noir. (This highly regarded Sonoma Coast vineyard was previously available only as one of the Williams-Selyem offerings.) The dark ruby-colored 1998 Pinot Noir Coastlands Vineyard is one of the firmer, more backward wines of the vintage. It exhibits subtle toasty oak, outstanding concentration, a tight personality, medium body, firm tannin, and a mineral-structured, earthy finish. The 14.1% alcohol is remarkably well hidden. Production was a minuscule half-ton per acre. It should be alluring when released next year. Anticipated maturity: now–2007. Another wine from the Sonoma Coast, the 1998 Pinot Noir Hirsch Vineyard emerges from the Mt. Eden and Pommard clones. A hedonistic Pinot fruit cocktail, it is a gloriously perfumed, exquisitely ripe, rich, lusty, fruit effort. Full-bodied, with well-integrated acidity and tannin, plus copious quantities of black cherries, currants, raspberries, smoke, and toast, this rich, silky-textured wine should be drunk during its first 5–6 years of life.

Almost every good Pinot Noir producer who buys grapes in California seems to want to make a wine from the Pisoni Vineyard in Monterey's Santa Lucia Highlands. Siduri's 1998 Pinot Noir Pisoni Vineyard is not quite up to the quality of the stunning 1997, but it is still an outstanding wine. It displays good underlying tangy acidity (more noticeable in this wine than in other offerings), a pronounced sweet Bing cherry fruitiness, medium body, and an emphasis on finesse and elegance. My guess is that the fruit in the 1998 vintage was not nearly as ripe as in 1997 (just the reverse of Oregon). This wine tastes as if it were made from less concentrated juice than the 1997. Drink it over the next 5–6 years. One of the firmer, more angular Pinot Noirs made by Siduri is the 1998 Pinot Noir Van der Kamp Vineyard. Although closed, with coaxing aromas of black raspberries, licorice, pepper, and earth emerge. Dense, with a ruby/purple color and hints that there is more than meets the nose or palate, I would opt for aging this Pinot Noir for a year and drinking it over the following 7–8.

I tasted four impressive 1997 offerings, all of which are bottled with minimal intervention (i.e., no filtration). The medium ruby-colored 1997 Pinot Noir Van der Kamp Vineyard Old Vines offers a moderately intense nose of black raspberries, cherries, and spicy, roasted herbs. The wine is fleshy and open-knit, with nicely integrated toasty new oak, and a lush, heady (14.1% alcohol) finish. This supple, hedonistic example will offer delicious and complex drinking for 3–4 years. The outstanding 1997 Pinot Noir Archery Summit exhibits a darker ruby color and a firmer, more austere personality, but has beautifully pure black raspberry and cassis notes mixed with earthy and vanilla scents. This is a classy, structured, exceptionally pure, backward, medium- to full-bodied Pinot that should be at its best in 12 months and keep for 6–7 years. The 1997 Pinot Noir Hirsch Vineyard is the most Burgundian of this quartet, exhibiting smoky, gamey, meaty notes in the aromatics, as well as sweet black cherry and berry fruit. There is good firmness, a lean, moderately tannic finish, and medium body. Although closed and angular, it is an intriguing Pinot that appears to be more driven by its *terroir* than its siblings. Anticipated maturity: now–2007. It seems like no one can fail with the fruit emerging from the Santa Lucia Highlands' Pisoni Vineyard. Siduri's 1997 Pinot Noir Pisoni Vineyard is a sumptuously rich, dark ruby/purple-colored wine with soaring aromas of blackberry/raspberry and cherry jam. One of the more hedonistic, lushly textured, and sumptuous Pinots I have tasted from Siduri, it will be a huge success with readers lucky enough to latch onto a few bottles. It should drink well for 3–5 years.

Siduri's first Syrah effort appears to be excellent. The dark plum/purple-colored 1998 Novy Cellars Syrah Stage Gulch Vineyard displays a charming nose of blackberries, pepper, cherry liqueur, and spice. It is low in acidity, soft, round, and generous. The spicy richness and evolved, precocious style are typical of the 1998 vintage. This wine should be drunk during its first 6–7 years of life.

SILVER OAK CELLARS (NAPA)

1999 Cabernet Sauvignon	Alexander Valley	E	90
1998 Cabernet Sauvignon	Alexander Valley	E	88
1997 Cabernet Sauvignon	Alexander Valley	E	89
1996 Cabernet Sauvignon	Alexander Valley	E	92
1995 Cabernet Sauvignon	Alexander Valley	E	94
1994 Cabernet Sauvignon	Alexander Valley	E	93
1999 Cabernet Sauvignon	Napa	EE	92
1998 Cabernet Sauvignon	Napa	EE	88
1997 Cabernet Sauvignon	Napa	EE	94
1996 Cabernet Sauvignon	Napa	EE	91
1995 Cabernet Sauvignon	Napa	EE	95
1994 Cabernet Sauvignon	Napa	EE	93

The story of Silver Oak needs little introduction. These highly successful wines are about as California/American as they can be. Aged in 100% new American oak (all from Missouri) for 30 months prior to bottling, they are gaudy, big, spicy oak and fruit bombs that are delicious young, yet seem capable of lasting 12–15 years, and in certain vintages, much longer. Their legion of admirers seems to get larger and larger and, on my tour of Napa and Sonoma, there is rarely a more packed and boisterous tasting room than Silver Oak's, regardless of the time. The 1999 Cabernet Sauvignon Alexander Valley touts an intense olive, smoky, toasty nose intermixed with kirsch and currant fruit. The wine is sweet, dense, with an opaque ruby/purple color, expansive fat mid-palate, and long finish. This certainly should be as good as most of the Alexander Valley Cabernets released this decade. The 1998 Cabernet Sauvignon Alexander Valley is lighter and more overtly herbaceous. The wine is certainly soft and fleshy with good fruit and is undoubtedly very much in the style of the Alexander Valley, but it does not have the weight, density, or thickness of the finest vintages of the nineties. This wine will be ready to drink upon release and is probably best consumed during its first 8–10 years of life. The 1997 Cabernet Sauvignon Alexander Valley is a dense purple color with boisterous, sweet, spicy, new oak, licorice, and olive notes. This flamboyant wine tastes lighter than I would have expected for a 1997. In the mouth, it reveals medium body, sweet jammy cherry fruit, and a soft finish. It needs to be drunk over the next 7–8 years and, frankly, seems no better than the 1998. By the way, the Alexander Valley *cuvées* are always 100% Cabernet Sauvignon. The dark ruby-colored 1996 Cabernet Sauvignon Alexander Valley exhibits a pronounced smoky, espresso bean, and kirsch-scented nose. Round, dense, rich, full-bodied, and open-knit, its low-acid flavors are undeniably appealing. Black olives make an appearance in the wine's aromatics as it sits in the glass. Anticipated maturity: now–2015. The 1995 Cabernet Sauvignon Alexander Valley is performing far better after a year of bottle age. This dark ruby/purple-colored, seductive wine offers blazingly intense aromas of cigar box, smoky oak, and jammy black currants with a hint of Provençal herbs. Ripe and full-bodied, with low acidity and a fleshy, succulent texture, it is a wine to drink over the next 14–15 years. The 1994 Cabernet Sauvignon Alexander Valley reveals a provocative nose of tobacco, black cherries, cloves, fruitcake, and spice. Some plum and raspberry fruit also emerge on the palate. This is a hedonistic, sexy, seductive, full-bodied Cabernet Sauvignon with low acidity and loads of toasty oak. It will be a huge crowd pleaser and should show well for at least 12–15 years.

The Napa offerings from Silver Oak tend to be less herbaceous and more oriented toward Cabernet Sauvignon's black fruit spectrum. They are every bit as exotic and ostentatious as the Alexander Valley *cuvées,* but more classic, tannic, perhaps longer-lived, and slightly less approachable. A blend of 82% Cabernet Sauvignon, 8% Cabernet Franc, 6% Merlot, and the rest Petit Verdot, the terrific 1999 Cabernet Sauvignon Napa boasts a dense ruby/purple color and a concentrated, opulent personality with flashy notes of black currant, kirsch, spice box, cedar, and smoke. Full-bodied, low in acidity, and juicy, this lush, in-your-face Cabernet should be delicious when released and age nicely for 12 or so years. The 1998 Cabernet Sauvignon Napa (93% Cabernet Sauvignon, 4% Cabernet Franc, and 3% Petit Verdot) shows some aggressive, toasty, charred, oaky notes along with melted asphalt. The wine is highly extracted, has plenty of tannin, and notes of smoke, cedar, cherries, and black currants. It is a very good 1998 with moderate tannin. It should drink well for at least 10 years when it is released. The 1997 Cabernet Sauvignon Napa looks to be one of the finest wines made by the winemaking team of proprietor Justin Meyer and wine-maker/viticulturist Daniel Baron. I know Meyer rates 1995 as the top vintage of the nineties for Silver Oak, but the 1997 Napa is an impressive effort. A blend of 93% Cabernet Sauvignon and the rest 5% Cabernet Franc and 2% Petit Verdot, this wine has a flamboyant nose of fruitcake, licorice, Asian spice, black currants, and toasty wood. Deep, opulent, viscous, intense, chewy, and thick, it is a classic Napa Cabernet Sauvignon made in an all-American oak lovers' style. It should drink well for 12–15 years. The 1996 Cabernet Sauvignon Napa (91% Cabernet Sauvignon, 7% Cabernet Franc, .5% Merlot, and 1.5% Petit Verdot) has a dark ruby/plum color and a gorgeous, complex nose of cedar, spice box, cherries, jammy plums, and cassis. The wine is fleshy, medium- to full-bodied, seductive, and filled with glycerin. The finish is all silk. This low-acid, big, spicy, lavishly wooded, chewy wine should drink well for another 10–14 years. The 1994 Cabernet Sauvignon Napa (89% Cabernet Sauvignon and 11% Cabernet Franc) reveals toasty sweet oak in the nose, bombastic levels of black currant fruit and spice along with a hint of mint in the background. Supple and full-bodied, with delirious levels of cedar and unctuously textured fruit, this fleshy, gorgeously made wine should drink well for 14–15 years. A blend of 96% Cabernet Sauvignon and 4% Cabernet Franc, the 1995 Cabernet Sauvignon Napa has turned out even better than the 1994. It possesses a more saturated ruby/purple color, as well as a more flamboyant and exotic bouquet. Moreover, it seems less evolved. Full-bodied and pure, with layer upon layer of concentrated black fruits, smoke, cedar, and toast, it should drink well for 16–17 years.

Past Glories: Cabernet Sauvignon Alexander Valley—1993 (90), 1992 (93), 1991 (92), 1990 (89); Cabernet Sauvignon Napa—1993 (90), 1992 (94), 1991 (95), 1990 (93)

SIMI WINERY (SONOMA)

1995 Cabernet Sauvignon Reserve	Sonoma	D	89
1994 Cabernet Sauvignon Reserve	Sonoma	D	89+

In my barrel tastings, the 1995 Simi Cabernet Sauvignon Reserve was among the more forward, opulently styled 1995s. This attractive wine, which has the potential to be outstanding, exhibits a deep ruby/purple color and a friendly, open-knit, spicy, sweet black currant nose that borders on jamminess. Pure, with a multilayered texture, excellent concentration, sweet, plush, fat fruit, decent acidity, and a long, lusty finish, this Cabernet is reminiscent of a deep, rich, right-bank Bordeaux made primarily from Merlot rather than Cabernet Sauvignon. It is capable of lasting for 10–15+ years. Although closed, the 1994 Cabernet Sauvignon Reserve displays plenty of potential and may merit an outstanding score with another 12–18 months of bottle age. The saturated ruby/purple color is accompanied by a tight but promising nose of black fruits, damp earth, wood, and spice. Impressive in the mouth for its purity, elegance, and balance, this well-structured, medium-weight Cabernet has plenty going for it, but patience is required. Anticipated maturity: now–2015.

Past Glories: Cabernet Sauvignon Reserve—1991 (94), 1990 (95)

SINE QUA NON (SANTA BARBARA)

1996 Against the Wall Syrah	Santa Barbara	D	94
2000 Gewürztraminer Eiswein	California	EEE	(94–96+)

2000	The Good Girl	California	E	(92–94)
2000	Grenache (name not determined)	California	E	(95–98)
2000	The Hussy	California	E	93
1999	Icarus (Grenache/Syrah/Viognier)	California	EE	91+
1999	The Marauder (100% Syrah)	California	E	95+
1999	Mr. K. Sémillon Vin de Paille	California	EEE	(98–100)
1998	Mr. K. Sémillon Vin de Paille	California	EEE	99
1999	Mr. K. Viognier Eiswein	California	EEE	(92–94)
1998	Mr. K. Viognier TBA	California	EEE	96
1995	The Other Hand (Syrah)	California	D	92
1999	Ox (Pinot Noir Shea Vineyard)	California	E	92
2000	Pinot Noir Shea Vineyard (name not determined)	California	E	94
1995	Red Handed	California	E	94
2000	Syrah (name not determined)	California	E	(94–96)
1997	Syrah Imposter McCoy	Santa Barbara	E	96
1998	Syrah E-Raised	California	E	96
1999	Tarantella	California	EE	95
1998	Veiled Pinot Noir Shea Vineyard	Oregon	E	90

Most people tend to think of Ojai, several hours north of Los Angeles, as a resort community with the fabulous Ojai Valley Inn. There is no doubting the tourist appeal of this cute town, but down on the valley floor is commercial Ventura. It is here where the garage winery of Elaine and Manfred Krankl can be found . . . but not without considerable difficulty. Since the first releases, the wines of Sine Qua Non have been exciting. They are thrilling to drink given their richness, multiple dimensions, and intensity, but they are also stunning examples of what low-tech winemaking (from two conscientious people who still do not own a vineyard) can do with high-quality fruit. One of the ironies of tasting through Santa Barbara is that many of the region's finest wines emerge from Ojai's two bonded wineries, Sine Qua Non and Ojai Vineyard. Both the Krankls and the owner of Ojai, Adam Tolmach, tend to make better wines from purchased grapes than those who own the vineyards.

The 2000 lineup looks super-impressive, with perhaps the finest Pinot Noir from the Shea Vineyard and the finest Grenache yet made by Manfred Krankl. As for the whites, the 2000 Good Girl (a blend of 49% Chardonnay and 25.5% Viognier from the Alban Vineyard, and 25.5% Roussanne from the Alban and Stolpman Vineyards) is a blockbuster, full-bodied, honeyed, dry white with 15.2% alcohol. It possesses striking aromatics of buttery citrus, or-anges, and other tropical fruits. This structured, well-delineated 2000 is a total turn-on. The other white wine offering, the 100% Roussanne that emerged from both the Stolpman and Alban Vineyards, is the 2000 Hussy. The name says it all. Its light gold color is accompanied by fabulously decadent levels of fruit, luxurious glycerin, and a dry, full-bodied, amazingly well-delineated finish. The Hussy or The Good Girl 2000 . . . take your pick. They are both sumptuous, dry whites that are among the most creative produced in California. The spectac-ular 2000 Pinot Noir Shea Vineyard would make the great Henri Jayer of Vosne-Romanée happy. It boasts a deep ruby/purple color as well as a striking bouquet of black cherries in-termixed with subtle oak and floral notes. Ripe, creamy textured, gorgeously pure, and seam-less, this spectacular Pinot will drink well for a decade. The unnamed 2000 Syrah (a 725-case blend of 86% Syrah, 10% Grenache, and 4% Viognier) is from an assortment of such vineyard sites as White Hawk, Stolpman, Bien Nacido, and Alban. Its saturated blue/black/purple color is accompanied by a stunning perfume of blackberry liqueur intermixed with camphor, licorice, vanilla, and a hint of bacon. Full-bodied, with great intensity, low acidity, and stupendous ripeness as well as richness, it should drink well for 15+ years. Potentially even better, and possibly the greatest Grenache yet produced in California, is Sine Qua Non's unnamed 2000 Grenache. A blend of 95% Grenache and 5% Syrah that achieved 15.8% natural alcohol, it emerges from the Alban (two-thirds) and Stolpman (one-third) vineyards. A black/ruby/purple-colored, decadently rich effort, it possesses a sweet nose of macerated black fruits, licorice, earth, and spice. It lasts and lasts and lasts in the mouth.

As for the sweet wines, Manfred Krankl, an Austrian by birth, has joined forces with Austria's most famous sweet wine producer, Alois Kracher, to produce limited quantities of stunning Eisweins and Vin de Pailles. My tastings included the unreleased 2000 Gewürztraminer Eiswein, 1999 Mr. K. Viognier Eiswein, and 1999 Mr. K. Sémillon Vin de Paille. The most compelling sweet wines being made in California, they rival the world's finest. Tasting notes do not do them justice. Readers need to taste for themselves to see what the genius of Manfred Krankl and Alois Kracher, along with Krankl's talented wife, Elaine, has concocted. They are all tour de forces in sweet winemaking, with remarkable concentration and intensity as well as striking underlying acidity. The two I tasted that have been released include the 1998 Mr. K. Sémillon Vin de Paille and 1998 Mr. K. Viognier TBA. The 1998 Mr. K. Viognier Trockenbeerenauslese was made from botrytised Viognier from the Alban Vineyard. There are only 1,245 half bottles. Harvested at 37.8% sugar, it retained 14.5% at bottling. The 1998 Mr. K. Sémillon Vin de Paille is a low-alcohol (7.5%) effort whose grapes were pressed when they ranged between 57–59° Brix, almost unheard-of numbers. It was fermented on indigenous yeasts for 15 months, and then bottled. These nectars must be tasted to be believed. Both will last for 100 years.

Krankl's 1999 Tarantella is one of the finest whites he has made. It possesses outstanding underlying acidity, a terrific, citrusy, honeyed perfume that roars from the glass, full body, and brilliant balance. Given past examples of this blend of Roussanne, Viognier, and Chardonnay, the 1999 should age nicely for 7–8 years. The beautiful, dark ruby-colored 1999 Ox (Pinot Noir Shea Vineyard) reveals sweet black cherry fruit intertwined with subtle wood and floral notes. Medium-bodied, with fine underlying acidity, good freshness, and a style not dissimilar from a top-notch premier cru Côte de Beaune, it will drink well for 7–8 years.

The outrageously rich 1999 The Marauder (100% Syrah from the Alban, Stolpman, and Bien Nacido vineyards) is tightly structured but crammed with blackberry and cassis fruit. Full and rich, but not nearly as precocious or seductive in its youth as previous efforts, it is a candidate for 14–15 years of cellaring. Lastly, the 1999 Icarus (a blend of 80% Grenache, 18% Syrah, and 2% Viognier, three-fourths from the Alban Vineyard and one-fourth from the Stolpman) was closed on the two occasions I tasted it. Its deep ruby color is accompanied by sweet black cherry and kirsch-like aromas with an underlying earthiness. Full-bodied and moderately tannic, but more austere and tightly knit than most Sine Qua Non offerings, it, like The Marauder, should be decanted 45 minutes prior to consumption.

Oregon's Shea Vineyard has been the source for many delicious Pinot Noirs from the likes of Ken Wright and others who live and work near the vineyard. One's sense of rational thought might be questioned to think that a winery two hours north of Los Angeles should be leasing a vineyard in Oregon and shipping the fruit to California in refrigerated reefer trucks, but that is just what the Krankls are doing in order to satisfy their masochistic need to produce world-class Pinot Noir from a cool-climate region. While the 1997 (called The Complicator) was a good effort, the 1998 Veiled Pinot Noir Shea Vineyard is outstanding. It reveals the vintage's strengths in its medium ruby color, attractive, sweet, plum, rose petal, black cherry fruit, and smoky-scented nose. Medium-bodied with outstanding concentration and sweetness in the mid-palate, elegance, and balance, this wine should improve nicely over the next 3–4 years and last for 7–8. That being said, the 1999 looked even more impressive in its jammy, sweet, creamy richness, and flamboyant aromatics.

The stars of this minuscule gem of a winery are their Syrah and Grenache. In the near future, a luscious Grenache will be added to the portfolio. The blended Syrah comes from different vineyard sources, primarily the Alban Vineyard in San Luis Obispo, and Bien Nacido and Stolpman Vineyards in Santa Barbara. These wines are always amusingly named (Black and Blue, Against the Wall, Imposter McCoy). The 1998 Syrah E-Raised is great stuff. It is black-colored, jammy, and super-intense with awesome concentration, terrific, chewy, explosive flavors of blackberries, cherries, and cassis interfused with creosote, pepper, and vanilla. As the wine sits in the glass, notes of roasted coffee, licorice, smoke, and barbecue spices emerge, giving it further dimensions of complexity. It is hard to make a prediction at this point, given how sensational previous vintages have been, but it would not surprise me to see the 1998 Syrah turn out to be the finest yet from Sine Qua Non. As for the 1997 Imposter McCoy (529 cases), I have already wolfed down two bottles with equally voracious friends. A thick, juicy, massive Syrah, it gushes copious quantities of licorice-infused blackberry fruit offering smoke, coffee, and meaty notes. The wine is mouth-filling, teeth-staining, and loaded. Its high alcohol (15.3%), glycerin level, and low acidity make it easy to drink, but I suspect it will age easily for 10–20+ years. The 1996 Against the Wall Syrah is cut from the same mold as the 1997. The color is opaque black/purple, and the nose offers a combination of cassis/blackberry jamminess intermixed with tar, pepper, and spice. Thick, massively full, yet wonderfully rich and expansive, with admirable purity and mouth-staining levels of glycerin and extract, this full-bodied, silky-smooth Syrah is deceptively easy to drink, but I suspect it will age effortlessly for 15–20 years. The 1995 The Other Hand is made from 100% Syrah grown in the Alban, Bien Nacido, and Stolpman vineyards, situated respectively in Edna Valley, Santa Maria, and Los Olivos. Aged 18 months in oak, of which 70% is new, this opaque purple-colored blockbuster offers glorious notes of black fruits (primarily blackberry and cassis), subtle smoke, toast, and licorice, and a whiff of plant material and spice. Full-bodied, yet gorgeously layered and nearly seamless in its flamboyant display of fruit, glycerin, and extract, this large-scaled, yet drinkable Syrah will benefit from another 5–6 years in the bottle, but it is already accessible. It is another example of why I think wineries in this region should be ripping out their Pinot Noir vines and re-planting with Syrah! Look for this super Syrah to age effortlessly for another decade.

The limited-production 1995 Red Handed is a blend of 43% Grenache, 40% Syrah, and 17% Mourvèdre blend also aged 18 months in oak, of which 50% was new. This wine wants to be a southern California Châteauneuf-du-Pape, and comes close to duplicating the character of a hedonistic southern Rhône. Sadly, only 80 six-bottle cases were produced. The color is an impressively saturated red/black/purple. The wine offers up aromas of cigar box, fruit-cake, cedar, pepper, Provençal herb, and glorious levels of kirsch and other black fruits. The influence of oak frames the wine rather than adding much to the aromas or flavors. Extremely full-bodied, rich, chewy, and loaded with personality (another wine that reflects its makers), with a multidimensional palate, and beautifully integrated alcohol, acidity, and tannin, this wine has a singular personality and stupendous quality. Anticipated maturity: now–2014.

One of the globe's most creative wineries, Sine Qua Non is turning out world-class wines of extraordinary complexity and individuality.

W. H. SMITH WINES (SONOMA COAST)

1997 Pinot Noir	Sonoma Coast	D	88
1998 Pinot Noir Hellenthal Vineyard	Sonoma Coast	D	91
1997 Pinot Noir Hellenthal Vineyard	Sonoma Coast	D	90

Five hundred cases of the saturated dark ruby-colored 1998 Pinot Noir Hellenthal Vineyard have been produced. Enticing notes of smoke, black cherry jam, minerals, and toast emerge from the glass. Full-bodied, with loamy, earthy, soil scents intermixed with gobs of jammy cherry/strawberry fruit, this may be the finest Pinot Noir made by Joan Smith under the W. H. Smith label. It possesses copious glycerin, a full-bodied texture, and heady alcohol. A hedonistic, sumptuous Pinot Noir, it should be consumed over the next 5–7 years.

The 1997 Pinot Noir Sonoma Coast exhibits a distinctive nose of cinnamon, cloves, plums, *garrigue,* and red fruits. In the mouth, it is lush, with cherry/plum fruit notes, medium body, low acidity, and a sweet, ripe, glycerin-endowed finish. Its color is an evolved ruby/garnet, but the wine is tasty and expansive. It should drink well for 2–3 years. The outstanding medium ruby-colored 1997 Pinot Noir Hellenthal Vineyard offers a provocative nose of cherry liqueur intermixed with Asian spices and toast. It has more body, length, and depth, in addition to the rich, velvety-textured palate also shared by its two less expensive siblings. Harmonious and complex, this wine will not make old bones, but will provide considerable silky-textured pleasure if consumed over the next 3–4 years.

CHÂTEAU SOUVERAIN (SONOMA)

1997	Cabernet Sauvignon	Alexander Valley	C	88
1994	Cabernet Sauvignon	Alexander Valley	C	89
1996	Cabernet Sauvignon Library Reserve	Alexander Valley	D	91
1994	Cabernet Sauvignon Library Reserve	Alexander Valley	D	92
1997	Cabernet Sauvignon Stuhmuller	Alexander Valley	E	91
1997	Cabernet Sauvignon Winemaker's Reserve	Alexander Valley	D	91
1996	Cabernet Sauvignon Winemaker's Reserve	Alexander Valley	D	90
1995	Cabernet Sauvignon Winemaker's Reserve	Alexander Valley	D	91
1994	Cabernet Sauvignon Winemaker's Reserve	Alexander Valley	D	90
1997	Merlot	Alexander Valley	C	87
1995	Merlot	Alexander Valley	C	89
1997	Merlot Winemaker's Reserve	Alexander Valley	D	(89–91)
1996	Rhône Blend	Sonoma	C	88
1998	Zinfandel Reserve	Dry Creek Valley	D	(87–88)

Smart buyers in search of wines with an excellent quality/price rapport have been seeking out Château Souverain's offerings for a number of years. The current and upcoming releases continue to offer "real" wine drinkers tasty choices. The deep ruby-colored 1997 Merlot Alexander Valley is dense and fat, with excellent berry fruit, mocha/coffee notes, and a touch of herbaceousness. Made in a rich, evolved style, with plenty of glycerin and fleshiness, this wine should drink well for 5–7 years. The 1997 Merlot Winemaker's Reserve may prove to be outstanding. Approximately 200 cases were produced. The wine boasts an opaque purple color and a knockout nose of black and red fruits, plus spicy oak and coffee. A deep, exotic, expansively flavored Merlot, it will provide hedonistic drinking for 7–8 years. The 1995 Merlot has a deep ruby/purple color plus a raspberry and blueberry-scented nose. Its concentrated, ripe fruit infused with toasty, smoky, new oak nicely complements the wine's black fruit–dominated personality. Supple and expansive, it is a candidate for 5–7 years of delicious drinking.

Consumers are taking a beating on prices for high-quality California Merlot and Cabernet Sauvignon. Château Souverain continues to offer very good, sometimes outstanding quality for realistic prices. The dark ruby/purple-colored 1997 Cabernet Sauvignon displays an excellent black currant, dried Provençal herb, toasty oak, and sweet black fruit–scented nose. The wine possesses tremendous fruit, medium to full body, low acidity, and a soft, succulent texture. It is a delicious Cabernet to drink over the next 7–10 years. Both the 1997 Cabernet Sauvignon Winemaker's Reserve and 1997 Cabernet Sauvignon Stuhmuller Vineyard (formerly known as the Library Reserve) are outstanding efforts that will be delicious young, yet keep for 14–15 years. The 1997 Cabernet Sauvignon Winemaker's Reserve's saturated ruby/purple color is accompanied by a forward, fragrant bouquet consisting of black fruits, toasty oak, licorice, and spice aromas. Dense and medium to full-bodied, with outstanding purity and overall balance, this is a seductive, precocious Cabernet. The 1997 Cabernet Sauvignon Stuhmuller Vineyard is produced from a hillside vineyard in the hot Alexander Valley. Generous quantities of black fruits, cedar, spice box, and toasty oak jump from the glass. Highly extracted and dense, this beauty possesses terrific fruit purity, a sweet, succulent mid-palate, and ripe tannin.

The 1995 Cabernet Sauvignon Winemaker's Reserve offers a knockout nose of smoked herbs, black currants, and toasty oak. It is medium- to full-bodied, with fruit purity, outstanding richness, and a deep, nicely layered texture. The wine's low acidity and plump, fleshy style suggest drinking now and over the next 12 years. The deep ruby/purple-colored 1996 Cabernet Sauvignon Winemaker's Reserve displays plenty of spice box, fruitcake, and black currant fruit intermixed with allspice, toasty oak, and weedy tobacco. Sweet (from extract, not sugar) on the attack, this full-bodied wine reveals copious quantities of glycerin, fruit, and extract. A beauty, it has managed to avoid the hard tannin exhibited by some 1996s. Drink it over the next decade. In 1996 there is also a limited-production Cabernet Sauvignon Library Reserve. While it is no better than the Winemaker's Reserve, the oak is more noticeable and the wine slightly more powerful. The Library Reserve is unquestionably an outstanding Cabernet, with new oak and slightly higher alcohol. It should drink well upon release and last for 10–12 years.

The Cabernet Sauvignons are all best buys, even the more expensive yet still reasonably priced Winemaker's Reserve. These are excellent wines that recall the glory days of Souverain in the late sixties and early seventies. I recently drank the 1974 Souverain Vintage Selection, a Best Buy pick from *The Wine Advocate,* and had suggested drinking it within 5–7 years of release. That wine is still holding on to all of its fruit, an example of how a wine that was never a blockbuster but was concentrated and impeccably well balanced can age so well. The supple and precocious 1994 Cabernet Sauvignon Winemaker's Reserve is already complex and evolved. It can be drunk now or over the next 12–15 years. The 1994 Cabernet Sauvignon Alexander Valley tastes similar to a Cabernet costing $20–30. This beauty offers a deep ruby/purple color, a spicy, black currant, tobacco, cedar, and toasty-scented nose, lush, low-acid, ripe flavors, the silkiness that is a hallmark of the 1994 vintage, and a clean, ripe finish. It should drink well for 5–7 years, perhaps longer. The 1994 Cabernet Sauvignon Library Reserve (only 200 cases, priced in the $30 range) boasts an opaque ruby/purple color, as well as a sweet, jammy nose of blue and blackberry fruit intertwined with subtle herbs, toast, Asian spices, and licorice. Full-bodied, powerful, and rich, this wine, although loaded with extract, is accessible. Sweet tannin gives the wine a precocious, up-front appeal. It should age gracefully for 12–15+ years.

Souverain's 1996 Rhône Blend (60% Syrah, 30% Mourvèdre, 10% Zinfandel) is an impressive debut offering. Blueberry, floral, peppery, and cassis aromas and flavors are packed into a medium- to full-bodied wine with good length and attractive sweet, ripe fruit and spice. It should provide delicious drinking for 7–8+ years. 1998 is a good rather than exciting year for Zinfandel. The 1998s will require consumption within several years of the vintage (except for the most concentrated efforts). Souverain's Zinfandels include a serious, wood-influenced, peppery, medium-bodied, structured 1998 Zinfandel Reserve. Another six months of bottle age will reveal more about this wine's personality.

SPOTTSWOODE WINERY (NAPA)

1998 Cabernet Sauvignon	Napa	EE	88
1997 Cabernet Sauvignon	Napa	EE	91
1996 Cabernet Sauvignon	Napa	E	90
1995 Cabernet Sauvignon	Napa	D	94
1994 Cabernet Sauvignon	Napa	D	93

These are some of the most elegant, harmonious, stylish Cabernets being made in Napa. Might Spottswoode be the Château Margaux of Napa Valley? The 1998 Cabernet Sauvignon exhibits more blueberry fruit than usual, in addition to an attractive, elegant, medium-bodied style. Although lacking the persistence and length found in Napa's finest vintage, it is a successful wine for the vintage. It should be uncommonly precocious, forward, and delicious when released. Anticipated maturity: now–2014. The deep ruby/purple-colored 1997 Cabernet Sauvignon (4,800 cases) reveals a Bordeaux-like, lead pencil and black currant–scented nose with nuances of spice, cedar, and minerals. Medium-bodied and elegant, with graceful flavors and fine balance, this suave wine should age nicely for 15 or more years. The medium-bodied 1996 Cabernet Sauvignon displays some of the attractive gravelly notes often found in this wine, along with black currant fruit, lavender, subtle oak, sweet tannin for the vintage, and a well-balanced, pure finish. Anticipated maturity: now–2016.

Another outstanding example from this consistently high-quality performer, Spottswoode's 1995 Cabernet Sauvignon stood out in my barrel tasting as one of the strongest efforts of the vintage. Although tightly wound, it exhibits an opaque purple color and a tight but gorgeous nose of black currants, vanilla, minerals, and a touch of smoke and blueberries. Medium- to full-bodied and impeccably well balanced, this wine's structural components (acidity, alcohol, and tannin) are beautifully meshed together with the lavishly rich fruit that is presented in a medium- to full-bodied format. This should turn out to be a textbook, classic Napa Cabernet Sauvignon that admirably balances elegance and power. Anticipated maturity: now–2015. With respect to the 1994 Cabernet Sauvignon, a beautifully scented nose of cassis, lead pencil, high-quality new oak, and spice is followed by a striking richness and balance. This dark ruby/purple-colored wine possesses fabulous concentration, yet it never comes across as heavy or out of sync. A gloriously made, elegant yet powerfully flavored wine, it is accessible, yet capable of lasting for another 12–20 years. This sensational Cabernet exhibits the more complex, elegant side of California winemaking. Bravo!

Past Glories: Cabernet Sauvignon—1993 (92), 1992 (92), 1991 (90), 1990 (90)

SPRING MOUNTAIN VINEYARDS (NAPA)

1995	Miravalle Alba Chevalier Proprietary Red Wine	Spring Mountain	D	90
1994	Miravalle Alba Chevalier Proprietary Red Wine	Spring Mountain	D	88
1996	Miravalle La Perla Chevalier Proprietary Red Wine	Spring Mountain	D	90

This operation, headed by veteran wine-maker Tom Farrell (who assisted in the winemaking of the monumental 1968 Heitz Martha's Vineyard), is one of the most extraordinary vineyard developments in northern Napa. Over 240 acres, spread over the Spring Mountain hillsides, are being developed. Amazingly, there are 130 separate vineyard blocks. The origins of this vineyard site can be traced back to 1882. More recently, such estates as Château Chevalier produced fruit from these hillsides. Tom Farrell and his assistant, Bill Wren, sell about 20% of the production each year. Presently, they are making a proprietary red wine (primarily Cabernet Sauvignon) and a proprietary white wine, as well as some experimental wines. They have produced some Syrah (the 1997 is promising) and have planted Mourvèdre, Pinot Gris, and a small amount of Pinot Noir. The ultimate goal is to produce 20,000 cases of luxury-priced wines. The debut and upcoming releases are all impressive, French-styled wines with considerable character.

The red wines, which are given extended macerations of between 14–45 days, tend to be primarily Cabernet Sauvignon–based wines, aged in 100% new oak. The 1994 Miravalle Alba Chevalier Proprietary Red Wine (for Spring Mountain, a large production of 6,250 cases) is a blend of 93% Cabernet Sauvignon, 3% Merlot, and 4% Cabernet Franc. While it is less tannic than the 1993, more elegant and California-like, it retains a certain austerity, but does unfold nicely on the palate to reveal stylish, rich black currant fruit intermixed with subtle herbaceous notes, minerals, and wood spices. It requires 3–4 more years of cellaring and should keep for a minimum of 10–15 years. The 1995 Miravalle Alba Chevalier Proprietary Red Wine (3,044 cases) is made from 100% Cabernet Sauvignon. This wine was performing impressively at a recent tasting, displaying an opaque purple color and sweet black currant/crème de cassis notes intermixed with lead pencil and toast. Margaux-like in its deep, rich, full-bodied, palate-staining personality, it is loaded with black fruits and silky tannin, and possesses the most length and deepest mid-palate of these Cabernet-dominated proprietary reds. Anticipated maturity: now–2020. The 1996 Miravalle La Perla Chevalier Proprietary Red Wine (4,231 cases, made from a blend of 87% Cabernet Sauvignon, 8% Merlot, and 5% Cabernet Franc) is as good as the 1995. It is a medium- to full-bodied, sweet, rich, chocolaty, black currant–scented and –flavored wine with a slight Médoc-like austerity, but sweet fruit and excellent balance, in addition to purity and depth. Although less massive than the 1995, it is as concentrated and long. Anticipated maturity: now–2020.

Past Glories: 1993 Cabernet Sauvignon Estate Chevalier Vineyard (91)

STAGLIN FAMILY VINEYARDS (NAPA)

1999	Cabernet Sauvignon	Rutherford	EE	92
1998	Cabernet Sauvignon	Rutherford	E	91
1997	Cabernet Sauvignon	Rutherford	E	90
1996	Cabernet Sauvignon	Rutherford	E	90
1995	Cabernet Sauvignon	Rutherford	E	90
1994	Cabernet Sauvignon	Rutherford	D	88
1999	Chardonnay	Rutherford	D	92
1998	Stagliano Sangiovese	Rutherford	D	89

One of the Napa Valley's more gorgeous winery and vineyard sites, the Staglin Family Vineyard (the house and vineyard were used by Walt Disney Pictures for the update of the movie *Parent Trap*) consists of 50 acres situated on the Rutherford Bench in western Napa Valley. Staglin Family Vineyard's wines exhibit additional strength with each new vintage. They are one of the few producers making a non-malolactic Chardonnay that competes with some of the most complex malolactic efforts. Staglin's Chardonnay philosophy is to harvest ripe fruit, preserve the acidity, give it 100% barrel fermentation as well as numerous lees stirrings, filter the wine, and bottle it. There are just under 2,000 cases of this pure Chardonnay. The 1999 Chardonnay appears to be the finest that proprietors Shari and Garon Staglin have yet produced. A light green/gold color is followed by a perfume of ripe pears infused with liquid minerality, spice, and subtle wood. Full-bodied and loaded with fruit, this impeccably made wine unfolds beautifully on the palate. Notes of candied apples, white corn, and citrus also make an appearance in this impressively rich, distinctive Chardonnay. Although it is best consumed during its first 2–3 years of life, this offering has the ability to age longer.

The Stagliano Sangiovese is produced from small yields, which is why it often turns out better than most other California Sangiovese. The deep ruby-colored 1998 Stagliano Sangiovese (150 cases) exhibits a sweet nose of strawberry jam intermixed with cherries, foresty scents, leather, and spice. This soft, ripe, medium-bodied red is ideal for drinking over the next 2–3 years.

There are 4,000 cases of Cabernet Sauvignon from Staglin's Rutherford vineyard. (They are in the process of building caves under the hills adjacent to the vineyard.) All of these Cabernets include a touch of Cabernet Franc in their blends, are aged in 100% French oak, and are quickly becoming classic examples of Rutherford Cabernet. The 1997 Cabernet Sauvignon offers ripe cassis, new oak, tobacco, and spice box aromas and flavors. Rich, structured, moderately tannic, and long, it needs 2–3 years of cellaring, but should keep well for two decades. Even better is the 1998 Cabernet Sauvignon. In contrast to the structured 1997, it is all charm and velvety richness, with plenty of succulence in the mid-palate, as well as a gorgeous evolved bouquet of black fruits, cedar wood, spice, and vanilla. There is enough acidity for delineation in this compelling, rich 1998. Drinkable now, it will evolve nicely for 15+ years. The finest Staglin Cabernet Sauvignon to date may be the 1999. It boasts spectacular aromatics (jammy black currants, tobacco, cedar, vanilla) as well as a seamless, concentrated, full-bodied palate with terrific purity, symmetry, and length. The sweet tannin, wood, and alcohol are all beautifully integrated in this flawless Rutherford Cabernet. Anticipated maturity: 2003–2025. The 1996 Cabernet Sauvignon (2% Cabernet Franc is blended in) has filled out nicely since I first tasted it. Aromas of cedar, chocolate, spice box, and black currants are moderately intense. Medium- to full-bodied, with good spice, in addition to excellent richness, symmetry, and harmony, this is an intense yet stylish Cabernet to drink now and over the next 16+ years. The 1995 Cabernet Sauvignon is richer and more intense in the mid-palate, as well as more backward. The wine is high in tannin, extract, and richness, yet the overall elegance, symmetry, and harmony among its elements are present. This pure, black fruit–dominated wine should be at finest between 2003–2020. The 1994 Cabernet Sauvignon is a graceful, vanilla-scented, medium- to full-bodied wine that emphasizes Cabernet's red fruit character. It is pure and well balanced, with moderate tannin in the attractive, Bordeaux-like finish. Anticipated maturity: now–2016.

STAGS LEAP WINE CELLARS (NAPA)

1994	Cabernet Sauvignon Fay Vineyard	Napa	D	89
1994	Cabernet Sauvignon Stags Leap Vineyard	Napa	D	89
1995	Cask 23 Proprietary Red Wine	Napa	EE	89

Surprisingly, the 1995 Cask 23 Proprietary Red Wine is light, acidic, and excessively polite. The tart acid that is so much an annoying component of these 1995s is present in the Cask 23, giving it a lean, clipped and compact feel on the palate. I do not believe this is what fans of Stags Leap Wine Cellars have come to expect. Nevertheless, the spicy, coffee, herb, cedary, red currant nose offers promise. There is good depth, but much of it is shielded by the wine's tart veneer. It should turn out to be graceful and elegant, but I am concerned about the textural deficiencies. The 1994 Cabernet Sauvignon Fay Vineyard offers up a sweet, tobacco, coffee, spicy, herbal nose, followed by elegant, fruitcake, medium-bodied red currant flavors with a subtle hint of black fruits. The wine is round, with tangy acidity, but not the abrasive levels of tartness found in some of the other reds. The finish reveals good structure, purity, and tannin. This wine should drink well for 10–12 years. The 1994 Cabernet Sauvignon Stags Leap Vineyard is a medium-bodied, mid-weight, sweet, ripe, smoky, vanilla, spicy (allspice?) wine with red and black fruits in the nose. On the palate, it is subtle and flavorful, with good acidity, medium body, and firm tannin. This Cabernet will benefit from several years of cellaring and last for 10–12 years.

Past Glories: 1993 Cabernet Sauvignon Napa (90), 1993 Cask 23 Proprietary Red Wine (91)

STONEFLY VINEYARD (NAPA)

1999	Cabernet Franc	Napa	D	90
1997	Cabernet Franc	Napa	D	91
1996	Cabernet Franc	Napa	D	89

Stonefly's 1996 is the first Cabernet Franc I have tasted from California that resembles a high-quality Loire Valley red from a ripe year (thoughts of Joguet's 1990 Chinons came to mind). The wine exhibits a raspberry and red currant–scented bouquet with faint notes of tobacco and cedar. Rich and smoky, this medium-bodied, intense yet elegant wine saw no new oak, and is better because of it. A beautifully crafted, luscious, Loire-styled Cabernet Franc, it is a breakthrough for this varietal in California. It should drink well for 6–7 years.

The limited-production 1997 is spectacular, particularly for readers seeking a Cabernet Franc made in the style of France's Loire Valley. This is a superrich offering, but without the weight one would expect from a wine gushing with fruit. It offers a leafy, cedary, black currant, and raspberry-scented bouquet, lush richness, low acidity, striking purity, and a fabulously textured, explosively fruity finish. This serious, gorgeously proportioned Cabernet Franc is a noteworthy successor to the 1996. Another outstanding effort is the 1999 Cabernet Franc, an exquisite wine of flavor, elegance, and balance. It has many of the characteristics of the other vintages. Drink it over the next 7–8 years.

STONESTREET (SONOMA)

1997 Cabernet Sauvignon	Alexander Valley	D	89
1996 Cabernet Sauvignon	Alexander Valley	D	88
1995 Cabernet Sauvignon	Alexander Valley	D	89
1994 Cabernet Sauvignon	Alexander Valley	D	92
1996 Cabernet Sauvignon Christopher's Vineyard	Alexander Mountain	D	92
1995 Cabernet Sauvignon Three Block Vineyard	Alexander Mountain	E	92
1999 Chardonnay	Sonoma	D	88
1999 Chardonnay Block 66	Alexander Valley	E	91
1999 Chardonnay Upper Barn	Alexander Valley	E	92
1997 Legacy Proprietary Red Wine	Alexander Valley	EE	91
1996 Legacy Proprietary Red Wine	Alexander Valley	EE	91
1995 Legacy Proprietary Red Wine	Alexander Valley	EE	91
1994 Legacy Proprietary Red Wine	Alexander Valley	EE	91
1998 Merlot	Alexander Valley	D	88
1997 Merlot	Alexander Valley	D	88
1996 Merlot	Alexander Valley	D	89
1995 Merlot	Alexander Valley	D	90
1998 Pinot Noir	Russian River	D	88
1994 Pinot Noir	Russian River	D	88
1999 Sauvignon Blanc Upper Barn	Alexander Valley	C	89

The red wines from Stonestreet have always been boldly oaked, fleshy, and chocolaty with robust personalities. They are designed for huge crowd appeal, but even connoisseurs get a charge out of their ostentatious flavors and character. The white wines get better and better at this winery, as the oak appears to be more judiciously used in addition to better fruit sources. For example, the 1999 Sauvignon Blanc Upper Barn, from a vineyard made famous by Helen Turley's exquisite Chardonnays, is a full-bodied, flinty, fresh Sauvignon with plenty of passion fruit, earth, and melony notes offered in a boldly displayed, ripe, concentrated style. Over the next several years, this big Sauvignon should work exquisitely with shellfish. The 1999 Chardonnay (13,000 cases) reveals a big, sexy, smoky nose not unlike some of the Meursaults fashioned by Burgundy's Michelot. Aromas of bacon fat are intermingled with new oak, creamy pineapple, and buttery fruit. Round and full-bodied with decent underlying acidity, this gutsy Chardonnay will drink well for 3–4 years. There are only a measly 250 cases of the potentially dazzling 1999 Chardonnay Block 66, produced from Jess Jackson's Alexander Mountain estate. This light gold-colored effort exhibits a huge, mineral-infused, butter, pear, citrus, and honeyed fruit–scented bouquet as well as flavors. The wine is strikingly deep, well delineated, and super-concentrated. Look for it to drink well for at least 2–3 years. Another fabulous offering, the 1999 Chardonnay Upper Barn, is still in barrel. It reveals a powerful, smoky, leesy bouquet of buttered tangerines, honeysuckle, mineral, and citrus oils. Authoritative but restrained, with admirable length, it has super potential.

The 1998s reflect the strict selection Stonestreet employed. They usually make about 15,000 cases of Merlot, but in 1998, after the selection process, there were only 6,000 cases available. A blend of 82% Merlot, 14% Cabernet Sauvignon, and 4% Cabernet Franc, this wine is showing much better from bottle than it did last year. It reveals smoky, chocolaty, and black cherry notes with well-integrated oak. Full-bodied, powerful, yet slightly angular, it should drink well for a decade. I enjoyed the garish 1998 Pinot Noir. Medium ruby-colored, this seductive, sexy Pinot offers candied cherry/strawberry flavors infused with smoke and toasty oak. Full, fleshy, and heady (14.2% alcohol), this is another crowd pleasing, exceptionally well-made wine. Sadly, production is only 1,000 cases.

The 1997 Cabernet Sauvignon, tasted in 1999 and released in 2000, is powerful, but the tannin is sweet and the wine ripe, rich, and expansive on the mid-palate. It should last for 15–20 years. The dark ruby/purple-colored 1997 Merlot offers an expressive nose of cocoa, fudge, herb-tinged blackberry and berry fruit. The wine has some tannin to shed, but it is a muscular, full-bodied, robust Merlot to drink over the next 10–12 years. The outstanding 1997 Legacy, a proprietary blend of 56% Cabernet Sauvignon, 27% Merlot, and 17% Cabernet Franc, possesses abundant jammy black currant/cherry fruit intermixed with lead pencil, toasty oak, and vanilla. Full-bodied and pure, with moderate tannin, this large-scaled effort (14.2% alcohol) can be drunk early, but promises to evolve for at least two decades.

The 1996 Legacy, a blend of 57% Cabernet Sauvignon, 26% Merlot, and 17% Cabernet Franc, exhibits an opaque ruby/purple color in addition to a toasty nose, chocolate, black currants, lead pencil, and smoke. Full-bodied, with high tannin, this pure, concentrated wine needs another 2–3 years of cellaring. Anticipated maturity: 2003–2020. The 1996 Merlot (a blend of 76% Merlot, 19% Cabernet Sauvignon, and 5% Cabernet Franc) exhibits a deep plum color, followed by knockout aromatics of roasted coffee, chocolate, and berry/cherry liqueur. Rich, smoky, exotic, and hedonistic, it should drink well for a decade. Like the Merlot, the 1996 Cabernet Sauvignon (a blend of 88% Cabernet Sauvignon and 12% Cabernet Franc) is an unfiltered, richly fruity, smoky, oaky, full-bodied wine with fine depth, an easy, open-knit, expansive chewiness, a supple personality, and sweet tannin in the finish. Accessible now, it promises to be even better over the next 4–12 years.

Stonestreet's proprietary red wine called Legacy has proven to be not only a wine of exceptional quality but one of remarkable consistency. The blend can vary (the 1993 is a blend of 70% Cabernet Sauvignon, 20% Merlot, 10% Cabernet Franc) to one less marked by Cabernet Sauvignon (the 1994 is a blend of 51% Cabernet Sauvignon, 39% Merlot, 9% Cabernet Franc, 1% Petit Verdot). The 1995 is composed of 59% Cabernet Sauvignon, 23% Cabernet Franc, 17% Merlot, and 1% Petit Verdot. All of these wines are aged for 20–23 months in 100% new French oak barrels, and are bottled unfined and unfiltered. I found them to be flamboyant, opulently textured, rich, expressive, and dramatic proprietary reds that are loaded with character. Moreover, they possess 10–20 years of aging potential. The 1994 and 1995 may merit higher scores with more aging. These vintages are similar in character, as both were years with exceptionally long hang times for the grapes (always a positive sign). Both wines possess a chocolaty, smoky, cassis, lavishly wooded character, juicy, succulent, full-bodied personalities, and plenty of length, extract, and fruit. Both are also remarkably seamless wines with immense potential. Because of their low acidity and ostentatious personalities, these wines will be flattering to drink young, but will easily last for 12–15 years. The 1995 Legacy, at 14.2% alcohol, is a boldly styled, fleshy, full-bodied wine that can be drunk or cellared for 15 years.

The 1995 Cabernet Sauvignon Three Block Vineyard from the Alexander Valley is made from 96% Cabernet Sauvignon and 4% Cabernet Franc. It is an unfiltered, dense, full-bodied wine with considerable power and richness. Aged in 50% new French oak, with more than 14% alcohol, it exhibits plenty of tannin, as well as impressively endowed flavors of roasted herbs, black currants, chocolate, and blackberries. Anticipated maturity: now–2020. The 1996 Cabernet Sauvignon Christopher's Vineyard (previously called the Three Block Vineyard) is cut from the same mold. It is a hedonistic, opaque purple-colored wine with gobs of toasty new oak, thrilling levels of extract, rich, chewy, black currant and blackberry fruit, impressive glycerin, sweet tannin, and a knockout finish that must contain over 14% alcohol. More than 80% new French oak was utilized in this wine's upbringing. There are 500 cases of this unfiltered beauty. The opaque plum-colored 1995 Merlot is a thick wine with compelling scents of roasted coffee, chocolate cake, smoky oak, and rich, jammy fruit. A blend of 84% Merlot, 15% Cabernet Sauvignon, and 1% Cabernet Franc, this wine is exceptional, seductive, rich, medium- to full-bodied, and ideal for drinking now and over the next dozen years. The 1995 Cabernet Sauvignon is no shy wine, coming in at 14.2% alcohol. The wine reveals the ripe fruit their Alexander Valley vineyard achieves. The use of heavily toasted Demptos barrels and indigenous yeasts for fermentation give these wines provocative aromatics. The Cabernet is built along the line of the Merlot, offering a hedonistic mouthful of fleshy, rich, briery, dense, berry, smoky, and herb-tinged fruit. Full-bodied, with a lashing of sweet tannin, this lusty, decadently rich, flamboyant wine should drink well for 12–15 years.

The 1994 Cabernet Sauvignon is intense and powerful, with an opaque purple color and gobs of lavishly oaked, smoky, cassis fruit intertwined with aromas of roasted herbs and high-quality toasty oak, revealing plenty of tannin, low acidity, and outstanding concentration and purity. This large-scaled, remarkably well balanced wine should drink well young yet last for two decades. The medium ruby-colored, unfined and unfiltered 1994 Pinot Noir exhibits a lusty, smoky, sweet berry-scented nose that reveals copious quantities of both ripe fruit and oak. This medium-bodied, softly textured, delicious wine is not the most concentrated or profoundly complex, but it offers a sexy glass of Pinot for drinking over the next several years. *Past Glories:* 1993 Cabernet Sauvignon (90), 1993 Legacy Proprietary Red Wine (91), 1993 Merlot (90)

STORYBOOK MOUNTAIN VINEYARDS (NAPA)

1999 Zinfandel Eastern Exposure	Napa	D	90
1998 Zinfandel Eastern Exposure	Napa	D	90
1999 Zinfandel Estate Reserve	Napa	D	91
1998 Zinfandel Estate Reserve	Napa	D	91+
1999 Zinfandel Mayacamas Range	Napa	C	89
1998 Zinfandel Mayacamas Range	Napa	C	91

Longtime followers of the classic, built-to-age Storybook Mountain Zinfandels undoubtedly are aware that over the last several years proprietor Jerry Seps has been moving toward an accessible, riper style with more elevated alcohol. However, these are still among the handful of Zinfandels that can age gracefully for a decade. 1999 appears to be another top vintage for this estate. The deep ruby/purple-colored 1999 Zinfandel Mayacamas Range (14.5% alcohol) reveals impressive aromatics of black cherries, currants, minerals, and underbrush. Sweet fruit on the attack is followed by a nicely textured, medium- to full-bodied finish. It should drink well for 7–8 years. Even more impressive is the 1999 Zinfandel Eastern Exposure. The addition of 4% Viognier no doubt accounts for the more perfumed, intense aromatic profile (although I could not detect any Viognier characteristics). Elegant, powerful, rich, and medium- to full-bodied, with stylish black currant, cherry, and blackberry flavors, an excellent texture, sweet tannin, adequate acidity, and a pure, concentrated finish, this beautifully etched Zinfandel can be drunk now and over the next 10–12 years. Storybook's flagship wine is the 600-case *cuvée* of Zinfandel Estate Reserve. The beautiful 1999 is a concentrated, backward, long, multidimensional effort exhibiting notes of earth, spice box, black currants, blackberries, and minerals. This multilayered, concentrated, textured Zinfandel displays great purity, a brilliant marriage of power with finesse, and a long, rich finish. Give it 1–2 years of cellaring, and drink it over the following 12 years.

1998 is another strong vintage for Storybook Mountain Vineyards. Followers of this winery should note a few refinements in style over recent vintages. First, some Viognier has been added to the Eastern Exposure *cuvée* to achieve a more complex bouquet as well as more supple flavors. Second, the harvest dates have been pushed back in order to achieve lower acidity, more color, and an accessible style. Traditionally, Storybook Mountain has produced many of the longest-lived Zinfandels, with some vintages aging easily for a decade or more, particularly the Reserve bottling. The 1998 Zinfandel Mayacamas Range exhibits an opaque dark purple color as well as a gorgeous bouquet of blueberry, black raspberry, liquid mineral, and well-integrated oaky aromas. Beautifully pure, medium-bodied, and ripe, with a sweet fruit character and long finish, this wine possesses more structure than most 1998s, yet also accessibility. It should drink well for 7–10 years. The dark ruby/purple-colored 1998 Zinfandel Eastern Exposure reveals a sweet, blackberry/briery-scented nose with hints of Viognier (4% added to the blend) in its subtle, peach jam–like note. The wine possesses a plush texture, blue and black fruits, a notion of minerals, medium to full body, low acidity, and excellent length. It should drink well for 7–8 years. The backward, dense, classic 1998 Zinfandel Estate Reserve (14.4% alcohol) exhibits a deep ruby/purple color in addition to a tight nose of loamy soil, spice, black fruit, and mineral scents. Rich and full, but structured, backward, and moderately tannic, this impressive wine is one of the most classic statements of the vintage. It is capable of evolving for 10–12+ years. However, it is one of the few 1998 Zinfandels that requires patience. Anticipated maturity: now–2015.

SUMMERS (NAPA)

1999 Zinfandel Howell Mountain	Napa	D	88

A deep ruby/purple color is accompanied by sweet scents of blackberry and currant jam, underbrush, spice, and oak. This medium-bodied, slightly austere Zinfandel is built more along the lines of a Cabernet Sauvignon. It should drink well for 4–5 years.

JOSEPH SWAN VINEYARDS (SONOMA)

1998 Zinfandel Frati Ranch	Russian River	D	88
1998 Zinfandel Mancini Ranch	Russian River	D	88
1998 Zinfandel Stellwagen Vineyard	Sonoma	D	89
1998 Zinfandel Zeigler Vineyard	Russian River	D	87

These wines have more in common with the late-harvest, dry, distinctive, sometimes controversial Italian Amarones than most California Zinfandels. All are forceful and concentrated, but the notes of aged beef, animal fur, and melted asphalt as well as their heavy, ponderous personalities are not for everybody. Most are best drunk with cheese or sipped alone at the end of a meal. My favorite Joseph Swan offerings include the 1998 Zinfandel Mancini Ranch. A dense ruby/purple color is followed by a well-balanced wine exhibiting notes of tar, new saddle leather, and overripe black fruits. Licorice, cinnamon, dried herbs, and earth add to the powerful impression. It is thick, totally dry, and the best balanced of this group of mouth-staining Zinfandels. Drink it over the next 7–8 years. The dark ruby/purple-colored 1998 Zinfandel Zeigler Vineyard exhibits aromas of shoe polish, roasted meats, dried herbs, licorice, and sweet, briery fruit. While rustic, thick, big, and chewy, it is not in total harmony. The super-extracted 1998 Zinfandel Stellwagen Vineyard reveals briery, earthy, herb-tinged fruit, kinky, leather, meaty, licorice, and tar notes, excellent density, and full body. The finish is slightly sweet, but the wine tastes dry. The powerful 1998 Zinfandel Frati Ranch (15.6% alcohol) offers up scents of melted tar, licorice, dried black fruits, loamy soil, and beef blood. Powerful, thick, and huge, but somewhat disjointed, this robust, macho wine will age well for 6–8 years, if not longer.

SWANSON VINEYARDS (NAPA)

1997 Alexis Proprietary Red Wine	Napa	D	90

This Bordeaux-inspired blend is the finest wine I have tasted from Swanson since they let winemaking consultant Helen Turley depart a few years ago. The dense ruby/purple-colored 1997 Alexis (3,400 cases) offers an attractive nose of blackberry, cherry, loamy soil, licorice, and vanilla scents. With medium to full body, a creamy, fleshy texture, sweet tannin, low acidity, and admirable extraction, it is impressive and ageworthy. Moreover, it has not been excessively acidified. Consume it over the next 10–12 years.

TABLAS CREEK (PASO ROBLES)

2000 Antithesis (Chardonnay)	Paso Robles	D	90
2000 Clos Blanc	Paso Robles	D	88
2000 Grand Cuvée	Paso Robles	E	92+
2000 Petit Cuvée	Paso Robles	C	92
1999 Petit Cuvée	Paso Robles	C	87
2000 Reserve Cuvée	Paso Robles	D	93
1999 Reserve Cuvée	Paso Robles	D	90

This promising hillside vineyard west of Highway 101, six miles from the Pacific Ocean, is jointly owned by importer Robert Haas and the Perrin family of Château Beaucastel in Châteauneuf-du-Pape. There is a total of 180 acres, 80 of which are under vine and 30 leased. Except for a small parcel of Chardonnay, only Rhône varietals are planted. The plantings include Mourvèdre (45%), Syrah, (22%), Grenache (22%), and the rest Counoise. The white varietals include Roussanne (50%), Viognier (25%), Marsanne (10%), Grenache Blanc, and the aforementioned Chardonnay. This is still a work in progress, with the winery having only been built in 1997. While the quality was at first uninspiring, it has become exciting over recent vintages, particularly with the 2000s. Planted in 1992, at elevations between 1,400–1,600 feet, the first crop was the 1994. The white wine offerings include the Chablis-like 2000 Antithesis, a 250-case, European-styled Chardonnay. Minimal amounts of new oak are utilized, and the wine reveals plenty of stony, mineral-laced, citrusy fruit presented in a Burgundy-like style. Elegant and restrained, this charming effort seduces by its nuances rather than power. The 2000 Clos Blanc (a blend of 45% Roussanne, 19% Viognier, 19% Marsanne, and 17% Grenache Blanc) exhibits an excellent citrusy nose, no evidence of oak, and hints of orange marmalade intermixed with citrus, candle wax, and spice. It possesses good acidity, freshness, full body, and excellent fruit. Although this 2000 may last for 4–5 years, I recommend drinking it over its first 2–3 years of life.

In most vintages there are two *cuvées* of red wine, although in top years a microscopic quantity of a third *cuvée*, the Grand Cuvée, is produced. These offerings are aged in a combination of small barrels, *demi-muids*, and larger *foudres*. The terrific 2000 Petit Cuvée (600 cases of a blend of 80% Grenache and 20% Syrah) is available at a fair price. It exhibits copious aromas of kirsch, blackberries, and currants. Rich, full-bodied, and loaded with fruit, it is restrained as well as elegant. Already delicious, it will age for a decade or more. The top *cuvée*, the 2000 Reserve Cuvée, is a blend of 35% Mourvèdre, 26% Syrah, 25% Grenache, and 14% Counoise. This 4,800-case offering does an impressive job of emulating a full-throttle southern Rhône red produced in California. A saturated black/purple color is followed by aromas of licorice, roasted herbs, meats, blackberries, and cassis. It is intense and full-bodied, with sweet tannin and impressive concentration. The Mourvèdre component will undoubtedly cause this wine to tighten up after bottling and will provide 10–15 years of aging potential. It is no shy wine at 15% alcohol, but it is well hidden beneath the wealth of fruit and extract. This is the most impressive wine yet made by Tablas Creek, and a clear sign that they are going to be a serious producer among the band of producers dedicated to the grapes from southern France known as the Rhône Rangers. The 75-case 2000 Grand Cuvée

(55% Mourvèdre, 35% Syrah, and 10% Grenache) is a more structured, tightly knit, backward, austere effort. It is an elegant, French-styled, impressive offering.

The 1999s display the cool weather conditions experienced in the Paso Robles region. The 1999 Petit Cuvée (65% Grenache, 25% Syrah, and 10% Mourvèdre) is a sexy, up-front effort. Although not as complex or fleshy and textured as the 2000, it offers a beautifully ripe attack followed by dry, firm tannin in the austere finish. Its 15.2% alcohol is well hidden. The 1999 Reserve Cuvée is a blend of 40% Mourvèdre, 27% Grenache, 23% Syrah, and 10% Counoise. It exhibits a dense purple color as well as a sweet perfume of blackberries, leather, licorice, earth, and pepper. Elegant, rich, medium- to full-bodied, and ripe, with nicely integrated tannin, it will drink well for a decade or more.

An insider tip: Should readers have access to it, they should check out the delightful rosé made at Tablas Creek. Keep in mind, these wines need to be drunk within their first six months of life.

TALLEY VINEYARDS (SAN LUIS OBISPO)

2000	Chardonnay	Arroyo Grande	C	89
1999	Chardonnay	Arroyo Grande	C	89
2000	Chardonnay Oliver's Vineyard	Edna Valley	E	90
2000	Chardonnay Rincon Vineyard	Arroyo Grande	C	92
1999	Chardonnay Rincon Vineyard	Arroyo Grande	C	90+
2000	Chardonnay Rosemary's Vineyard	Arroyo Grande	C	92
1997	Pinot Noir	Arroyo Grande	D	89
2000	Pinot Noir Rincon Vineyard	Arroyo Grande	E	90
1999	Pinot Noir Rincon Vineyard	Arroyo Grande	E	91
1997	Pinot Noir Rincon Vineyard	Arroyo Grande	D	91
1995	Pinot Noir Rincon Vineyard	Arroyo Grande	D	90
2000	Pinot Noir Rosemary's Vineyard	Arroyo Grande	E	92
1999	Pinot Noir Rosemary's Vineyard	Arroyo Grande	E	92+
1997	Pinot Noir Rosemary's Vineyard	Arroyo Grande	D	93

The Talleys are prominent farmers in Edna Valley with over 1,000 acres, primarily planted with peppers, beans, avocados, and cilantro. However, their most profitable crop must be grapes. From their 150 acres of vineyards they produce 16,000 cases of estate-bottled wine. About 25% of the grape production is sold. In the Central Coast, Talley stands out as the one superstar producer of Chardonnay and Pinot Noir, both of which display the Burgundian-like characteristic of elegance allied with considerable flavor authority. All are restrained yet intense. The 2000 Chardonnay Arroyo Grande offers aromas of pears, honey, and citrus in a medium, full-bodied, complex yet elegant personality. It should drink well for 2–3 years. The 2000 Chardonnay Rincon Vineyard possesses more ripeness plus a layered texture and a smoky nose exhibiting scents of hazelnuts, minerals, and buttery fruit. It tastes extremely Burgundian given its restraint and measured yet intense style. The 2000 Chardonnay Rosemary's Vineyard (the coolest of the Talley vineyards) has higher acidity as well as notes of minerals, tangerines, butter, and subtle wood. It is a full-bodied, rich, multilayered effort that should age well for 5–6 years. The 2000 Chardonnay Oliver's Vineyard displays notes of buttered citrus, honeysuckle, candle wax, and subtle toasty oak. Medium- to full-bodied, refreshing, measured, and deep, this intense effort should drink well for 3–4 years.

The light gold-colored 1999 Chardonnay Arroyo Grande offers gorgeous aromas of roasted hazelnuts, honey, and ripe fruit. Textured, with good underlying acidity and delineation, excellent freshness, and a moderately long finish, this medium-bodied, complex, Burgundian-styled Chardonnay will drink well for 2–4 years. The 1999 Chardonnay Rincon Vineyard (4,960 bottles produced) possesses copious quantities of buttery, honeyed toast-like notes in the complex aromatics. Tighter than its siblings, but full-bodied and ripe, with zesty acidity for definition, this large-scaled, impressive yet elegant effort will drink well for 4–6 years, possibly longer.

The 2000 Pinot Noir Rincon Vineyard offers elegant, sweet, plum, and black cherry fruit in a medium- to full-bodied, concentrated, stylish format. It is Volnay-like in its elegance and overall balance and character. Enjoy it over the next 6–7 years. Even better is the 2000 Pinot Noir Rosemary's Vineyard. Dark ruby/purple-colored, rich, intense, and full-bodied, with great purity of black raspberry and cherry fruit, a potent mid-palate, and beautiful ripeness, it should drink well for 8–10 years. By the way, Talley's wines, especially the Pinot Noirs, have an impressive track record of aging well even though their first vintage was as recent as 1986. Recent bottles of the 1995 Pinot Noir Rincon Vineyard and 1994 Pinot Noir Rosemary's Vineyard were sumptuous when drunk in late 2001. The 1999 Pinot Noirs are concentrated, backward offerings that need time in bottle to round out. Both possess high richness as well as tannin. The 1999 Pinot Noir Rosemary's Vineyard (10,115 bottles produced) boasts an impressively saturated ruby/purple color plus a gorgeous perfume of black cherry and raspberry liqueur mixed with mineral, new-oak, and floral scents. The compelling, youthful aromatics are almost primary in their vividness and intensity. The wine is tight, full-bodied, and moderately tannic, with exceptional concentration and depth. This brilliant Pinot needs another 1–2 years of cellaring and should keep for 10–12 years. The 1999 Pinot Noir Rincon Vineyard (6,582 bottles produced) offers aromas of red and black fruits, earth, and herbs. Made in a softer, more accessible style, it possesses copious quantities of rich fruit in addition to plenty of density, purity, and depth. This mouth-filling 1999 is more approachable than the Rosemary's Vineyard and should mature 1–2 years earlier. Anticipated maturity: now–2012.

The dark ruby-colored 1997 Pinot Noir exhibits classic black cherry, floral, and subtle spicy wood aromatics. Medium- to full-bodied, with sweet tannin, tangy acidity, and excellent purity, this is a beautifully knit, black fruit–dominated Pinot with admirable delineation and structure. It should drink well for 5–7 years. The more limited-production 1997 Pinot Noir Rincon Vineyard (4,541 bottles) offers copious quantities of high-quality French oak mixed with blackberry and cherry fruit. Gorgeous aromas reminiscent of a top growth from Vosne-Romanée (violets and raspberries) also make an appearance. Tightly knit and full-bodied, with sweet tannin and a rich, nicely layered mid-section, this impressively endowed Pinot will be better with another 1–2 years of bottle age and will keep for a decade. Another impressive effort, the deep ruby/purple-colored 1997 Pinot Noir Rosemary's Vineyard (3,236 bottles) reveals elements of moderately intense, sweet, forest notes intermixed with black fruits and vanilla. Rich, concentrated, tight, and unevolved, this stunning Pinot is among the finest being produced in California. Delicious and seductive, it will get even better with 1–3 years of cellaring and will keep for a decade. Another exceptional Pinot Noir from Talley Vineyards, the 1995 Rincon Vineyard (3,879 bottles produced) possesses a dark ruby color and sweet black plum and cherry fruit nicely dosed with high-quality spicy new oak. Medium-bodied, flavorful, and intense, yet not heavy, this beautifully made, elegant, and flavorful Pinot should continue to improve for 3–4 years and last for a decade.

P.S. Readers should also check out the exquisite *beerenauslese*-styled white Riesling made at Talley Vineyards.

TITUS (NAPA)

1999 Zinfandel	Napa	C	90
1999 Zinfandel Old Vines Redwood Valley	Mendocino	C	91

To date I have enjoyed everything that has emerged from this high-quality producer. The 1999 Zinfandel Napa (14.5% alcohol) displays Châteauneuf-du-Pape–like aromas of saddle leather, roasted meats, pepper, earth, black raspberries, and kirsch. Ripe, full-bodied, and supple-textured, it provides a big, lusty mouthful of Zinfandel to drink over the next 3–4 years. Even better, the deep ruby/purple-colored 1999 Zinfandel Old Vines Redwood Valley is a pure, harmonious, full-bodied, exuberant offering bursting with black fruits infused with mineral and oak characteristics. Dense, chewy, and unctuously textured, this succulent, fat Zinfandel needs to be consumed over the next 4–5 years.

PHILIP TOGNI VINEYARDS (NAPA)

1999	Cabernet Sauvignon	Spring Mountain	EE	95
1998	Cabernet Sauvignon	Spring Mountain	EE	90
1997	Cabernet Sauvignon	Spring Mountain	E	94+
1996	Cabernet Sauvignon	Spring Mountain	E	96
1995	Cabernet Sauvignon	Spring Mountain	D	95
1994	Cabernet Sauvignon	Spring Mountain	D	96

Spring Mountain, a thriving source of vineyards in the last century, is becoming increasingly congested, with a bevy of vineyards sprouting up across these mountain slopes. Most of the top wine producers, from Jim Pride and Bob Foley at Pride Mountain Vineyard to Les Behrens and Bob Hitchcock at Behrens and Hitchcock, cite the inspiring wines made by Philip Togni as the reason they believe in this high-altitude viticultural region. Feisty Philip Togni continues to turn out spectacular wines that give all indications, even in lighter, more challenging vintages such as 1998, of lasting 20+ years. His great vintages—and there have been quite a few (1984, 1985, 1986, 1987, 1990, 1991, 1994, 1995, 1996, and 1997)—will last 30 or more years considering how slowly these wines evolve. Production has been relatively small with the short crops and cool growing seasons of 1998, 1999, and 2000. There are about 1,200 cases of the 1998, and 1,800 or so cases of the 1999 and 2000. You would think, after a brilliant career of more than 30 years making some of Napa's finest Cabernet Sauvignons, that Togni could rest on his laurels, but he keeps pushing the proverbial envelope. Practicing more intense viticulture, Togni is doing more shoot positioning and leaf pulling in the vineyard, picking in tiny, six-inch-deep bins, and using a sorting table to select out only the ripest and most healthy fruit. His 1998 Cabernet Sauvignon is the smallest-scaled wine of the nineties, but as I told him, "If this is as bad as you can do, bravo!" The 1998 exhibits a dense ruby/purple color. Made from fruit that was harvested between October 30–November 4 (50% of the crop was cut off to guarantee only ripe fruit), it reveals aromas of tapenade, licorice, black currants, smoked herbs, and earth. The wine offers abundant black fruits, outstanding richness and complexity, but is more evolved than most Togni Cabernets at a similar age. It can be drunk early, but will easily age for 15 or more years. Togni's 1999 Cabernet Sauvignon (picked between October 11–15) is a blend of 82% Cabernet Sauvignon, 15% Merlot, and 3% Cabernet Franc. It could easily rival some of Togni's greatest wines of the nineties. This stupendous effort has a saturated, black/purple color and a gorgeously pure nose of licorice, blackberries, cassis, mineral, and smoke. With an unctuous texture, firm but sweet tannin, exquisite purity, and fine overall symmetry, it is one of the vintage's top successes. Anticipated maturity: 2006–2030.

The glorious 1997 Cabernet Sauvignon (a blend of 82% Cabernet Sauvignon, 15% Merlot, and 3% Cabernet Franc) is the most opulently textured Togni offering since his 1992. It possesses a saturated purple color in addition to a thrilling but still reticent nose of blackberries, cassis, minerals, dried herbs, and smoky oak. Full-bodied, pure, thick, and creamy textured, this wine's superb concentration conceals its lofty but sweet tannin. Togni's wines possess exceptional aging potential, but it will be hard to keep your hands off this one after it has had another 2–4 years of bottle age. Anticipated maturity: 2003–2025+.

In contrast, the opaque purple-colored 1996 Cabernet Sauvignon is a blockbuster monster crammed with phenomenal potential. It offers up a sensational nose of licorice, chocolate, cassis, Provençal herbs, and toast. The wine is succulent and full-bodied, as well as extraordinarily powerful and backward. It should be drinkable within 5–7 years, and age beautifully for three decades. All of Togni's wines are bottled with neither fining nor filtration, and, as he likes to say, "made as Bordeaux was . . . a long, long time ago."

The 1995 Cabernet Sauvignon, a vintage that produced a number of top-notch wines (as well as some with rough tannin and muted personalities), is one of the year's bright shining successes. The wine displays an opaque purple color, as well as a lavishly intense nose of blackberry/blueberry/cassis fruit intermingled with chocolate and olive nuances. Dense and fruit-driven, with awesome levels of glycerin and extract, this formidably endowed, moderately tannic wine should be at its best with another 7–8 years of cellaring. Once again, Togni has produced a wine with 25 or more years of aging potential. The 1994 Cabernet Sauvignon is a remarkably rich, multidimensional wine. Extremely full-bodied, with extraordinary fruit purity, this wine is, aromatically and texturally, compelling stuff. Unfortunately, the 1994 is already sold out, but those lucky enough to have purchased a few bottles own a monumental mountainside Cabernet that should age gracefully for 25–30 years. Incredibly, in an open bottle, this wine held up without oxidation an amazing six days!

Part mountain goat, part man, Philip Togni continues to fight vineyard diseases, such as Pierce's, and frightfully low yields from his formidably steep Spring Mountain vineyards to produce some of California's most exciting wines.
Past Glories: Cabernet Sauvignon—1993 (92), 1992 (96), 1991 (95), 1990 (95), 1987 (90), 1986 (92), 1985 (92), 1984 (93)

TRENTADUE (SONOMA)

1999 Old Patch Red	Dry Creek	C	88
1999 Zinfandel	California	C	88
1999 Zinfandel	Dry Creek	C	90

After being absent from these pages for several years, Trentadue has rebounded strongly with its 1999 portfolio. All three wines are good values, but the 1999 Old Patch Red is a terrific bargain for California. The dark ruby-colored 1999 Zinfandel California (15% alcohol) exhibits a sweet nose of jammy black cherry and berry fruit, earth, and pepper. Full-bodied, spicy, supple-textured, and loaded, it will drink well for 3–4 years. More complex, the 1999 Zinfandel Dry Creek reveals a sweeter attack as well as complex but subtle notes of toasty American oak, and dense, full-bodied flavors redolent with raspberries and cherries. It is a thick, juicy, gorgeous Zinfandel to enjoy over the next 5–6 years. Lastly, the 1999 Old Patch Red (a field blend of Zinfandel, Carignan, and Petite Sirah from 100-year-old vines) is a Côtes du Rhône look-alike from California. It offers notes of pepper, leather, animal, blackberry and cherry fruit, full body, an excellent texture, robust, muscular flavors, and a mouth-filling style. Drink it over the next 2–3 years to take advantage of its unabashed exuberance.

TURLEY CELLARS (NAPA)

1999 Charbono Tofanelli Vineyard	Napa	C	91
1998 Charbono Tofanelli Vineyard	Napa	C	90
1997 Petite Syrah Aida Vineyard	Napa	D	90
1999 Petite Syrah Estate	Napa	D	91+
1999 Petite Syrah Hayne Vineyard	Napa	D	96
1998 Petite Syrah Hayne Vineyard	Napa	D	90
1997 Petite Syrah Hayne Vineyard	Napa	D	95
1999 Petite Syrah Rattlesnake Acres	Napa	D	94
1998 Petite Syrah Rattlesnake Acres	Napa	D	89
1997 Petite Syrah Rattlesnake Acres	Napa	D	91
1997 Zinfandel Aida Vineyard	Napa	D	93
1999 Zinfandel Black-Sears Vineyard	Howell Mountain	D	93

1998	Zinfandel Black-Sears Vineyard	Howell Mountain	D	88
1997	Zinfandel Black-Sears Vineyard	Howell Mountain	D	95
1999	Zinfandel Dogtown Vineyard	Lodi	D	92
1998	Zinfandel Dogtown Vineyard	Lodi	D	90
1997	Zinfandel Dogtown Vineyard	Lodi	D	(89–91)
1999	Zinfandel Duarte Vineyard	Contra Costa	D	91
1998	Zinfandel Duarte Vineyard	Contra Costa	D	93
1997	Zinfandel Duarte Vineyard	Contra Costa	D	(90–92)
1999	Zinfandel Grist Vineyard	Bradford Mountain	D	90
1998	Zinfandel Grist Vineyard	Bradford Mountain	D	90
1997	Zinfandel Grist Vineyard	Bradford Mountain	D	93
1999	Zinfandel Hayne Vineyard	Napa	E	96
1998	Zinfandel Hayne Vineyard	Napa	E	94
1997	Zinfandel Hayne Vineyard	Napa	D	95
1999	Zinfandel Juveniles	California	C	92
1999	Zinfandel Moore (Earthquake)	Napa	D	95
1998	Zinfandel Moore (Earthquake)	Napa	D	92
1997	Zinfandel Moore (Earthquake)	Napa	D	94
1999	Zinfandel Old Vines	California	C	93
1998	Zinfandel Old Vines	California	C	90
1997	Zinfandel Old Vines	California	C	92
1999	Zinfandel Pringle Family Vineyard	Howell Mountain	D	96
1998	Zinfandel Pringle Family Vineyard	Howell Mountain	D	90+
1997	Zinfandel Spenker Vineyard	Lodi	D	87
1999	Zinfandel Tofanelli Vineyard	Napa	D	94
1998	Zinfandel Tofanelli Vineyard	Napa	D	91
1997	Zinfandel Tofanelli Vineyard	Napa	D	92
1999	Zinfandel Turley Estate	Napa	D	94
1999	Zinfandel Vineyard 101	Alexander Valley	D	92
1998	Zinfandel Vineyard 101	Alexander Valley	D	91
1997	Zinfandel Vineyard 101	Alexander Valley	D	90

California's preeminent Zinfandel specialists, proprietor Larry Turley and wine-maker Ehren Jordan, may have produced the finest Zinfandels of their relatively short careers. The majority of their 1999s taste even better from bottle than they did from barrel. These wines are hugely popular because they represent the best that Zinfandel can be. This varietal does not produce long-lived wines, and Turley Cellars does not pretend that their offerings will age like a classified-growth Bordeaux or California Cabernet Sauvignon. However, for drinking during their first decade of life, few wines match these for pure opulence, pleasure, concentration, exuberance, and personality. The good news is that their production of 8,200 cases of Zinfandel (there is a tiny amount of Charbono and Roussanne as well) will expand considerably since they have purchased a large Paso Robles vineyard with extremely old, head-pruned vines called Presenti. The first vintage where they controlled the viticulture and winemaking was 2000. Readers can look for that area to become one of the hotbeds for Zinfandel, as well as some Rhône-like blends made from these ancient vines.

The formula espoused by Turley and Jordan is simple: Locate old, head-pruned vineyards, persuade some of the idiosyncratic growers to let them control the viticulture, maintain low crop levels, pick superripe fruit, give the wines a pre-fermentation cold soak to extract color and greater phenolic complexity, do not acidify, fine, or filter, bring the wines up in a mix of 75% French and 25% American oak (only 25% is new), and bottle them after 14–16 months of barrel aging without any clarification. They have followed these rules since their debut vintage in 1993, and the wines have been consistently distinctive, luxuriously rich, and, lest I forget, hedonistic. Year in and year out, they are among the finest Zinfandels money can buy. While some competitors whine that they possess too much alcohol, etc., tasting these offerings reveals the alcohol is remarkably well integrated, as none of them tastes hot. In short, these are thrilling Zinfandels, as I have proven many times by serving them not only to American enthusiasts but to many of my friends in France, who go ga-ga over them.

What sets the 1999s apart is the fact that they are superrich, exceptionally pure, well-balanced, exuberant, mouth-staining, harmonious wines that will provide immense pleasure for a decade. Some of the Zinfandels will last even longer. Turley's Petite Syrahs are 40–50 year wines. Turley and Jordan both said the 1999 malolactic fermentations were extremely slow, which is often a good sign in terms of complexity as well as textural development. The 1999 Zinfandel Juveniles (previous called Young Vines; 450 cases, 15.2% alcohol) was made from tiny parcels of replanted vines in the Hayne, Moore, and Duarte vineyards. Turley Cellars does not want to blend these younger vines with wine from the older vines. A sensational effort, it exhibits a dense ruby/purple color as well as a knockout nose of blackberries and spice, an opulent texture, and a superb finish. It should drink well for a minimum of 5–7 years. The wine with the least color saturation, the 1999 Zinfandel Grist Vineyard (350 cases, 15.3% alcohol), reveals cherry liqueur and sandalwood notes in addition to a voluptuous texture, admirable fat and succulence, exceptionally ripe fruit, low acidity, and excellent length. A compelling wine has been produced from the tiny, two-acre Vineyard 101. The 1999 Zinfandel Vineyard 101 (78 cases, 15.4% alcohol) is akin to drinking blackberry liqueur with subtle pepper and soil notes in the background. Exceptionally full-bodied and lavishly concentrated, it will drink well for a decade. The remarkable 1999 Zinfandel Turley Estate (225 cases, 15.4% alcohol) was made from four-year-old vines (with tight 3 x 6 spacing) planted adjacent to the well-known Aida Vineyard. Drinking this wine is akin to drinking blackberry and strawberry liqueur mixed with smoke, spice, pepper, and truffles. A touch of volatile acidity adds to the aromatic fireworks. Full-bodied, unctuously textured, and exceptionally rich, with enough glycerin and thickness to please the most demanding hedonists, this is Zin on steroids. Drink it over the next decade. I often notice a resiny/balsam wood character in Turley's Contra Costa offering. The 1999 Zinfandel Duarte Vineyard (560 cases, 15.8% natural alcohol) is produced from 104-year-old vines planted in pure sand. A wonderful expression of purity and sweetness, it is not the most concentrated of the 1999 Zinfandels, but it offers sweet black cherry liqueur, strawberry, pepper, kirsch, raspberry, and spice aromas. I also detected a complex note of volatile acidity. Long, deep, intense, and well textured, it will drink well for 7–8 years. The fabulous, saturated dark ruby/purple-colored 1999 Zinfandel Tofanelli Vineyard (450 cases, 16.1% natural alcohol) is reminiscent of a wine from the southern Rhône. It displays a knockout bouquet of black fruits intertwined with licorice, asphalt, pepper, and spice. Exhibiting outstanding fruit richness, great purity, an unctuous texture, and a 45-second finish, this prodigious Zin should drink well for 7–8 years.

Made from a collection of miscellaneous parcels too small to bottle under their vineyard names, the 1999 Zinfandel Old Vines (1,800 cases, 15.8% alcohol) offers aromas and flavors of black fruits, a muscular, briery, peppery, forceful personality, a seamless texture, copious glycerin, amazing concentration, and a smooth finish. The acidity, tannin, and wood are beautifully integrated in this classic, full-throttle Zinfandel. Drink it over the next 7–8 years. It is even better from bottle than from barrel! Another provocative as well as prodigious effort is the opaque purple-colored 1999 Zinfandel Black-Sears Vineyard (640 cases, 16% alcohol). This is the only 1999 that I was unable to retaste from bottle. Produced from an 81-year-old vineyard inhabited by mountain lions, bobcats, and wild pigs, the grapes for this *cuvée* were harvested in November 1999. It boasts a gorgeously pure bouquet of blackberries, raspberries, flowers, and licorice, a remarkably full-bodied, viscous texture, fabulous fruit purity, and a ripe, layered, extravagantly rich finish. This whopper of a Zinfandel is unbelievably well balanced. It should drink well for a decade, but who can wait that long?

Guess who let the dogs out? The finest effort yet produced from the amusingly named Dogtown Vineyard, the 1999 Zinfandel (600 cases, 16% alcohol) is great stuff. Blackberries, kirsch, spice, and pepper are present in this flamboyant, muscular, smooth fruit bomb. With low acidity, ripe tannin, and well-integrated wood, it should drink well for 7–8 years. Readers may remember the tannic and austere Zinfandels produced under the Lamborn Family Vineyard label. This vineyard is now owned by the Pringle family, and Turley Cellars produces a Pringle Family Vineyard Zinfandel. The awesome 1999, which exhibits a Hermitage-like floral, blackberry liqueur, and raspberry-scented bouquet, is as elegant as a wine with 16.1% alcohol can be. Rich and sweet (from extract and glycerin, not sugar), with awesome presence on the palate as well as underlying notes of liquid minerals, jammy black fruit, and pepper, this finesse-styled Zinfandel can be consumed over the next 6–8 years. This is amazing stuff! The prodigious 1999 Zinfandel Moore (Earthquake) Vineyard (490 cases, 16.4% natural alcohol), like its siblings, possesses an opaque dense ruby/purple color. It offers explosive yet elegant aromas of blackberries, pepper, and black cherries as well as full body, low acidity, and magnificent fruit concentration. A long, intense, smooth, peppery personality will be a crowd-pleaser. A remarkable effort, it will develop even more complexity over the next 7–10 years. Year in and year out one of Turley's superstars is the Zinfandel Hayne Vineyard. The 1999 (560 cases, 16.8% alcohol) is a tour de force in Zinfandel winemaking, rivaling the 1999 Pringle *cuvée* as the Turley "Zin of the vintage." Again, the alcohol is totally concealed behind a wealth of glycerin, fruit, layered extraction, and a rich, plush texture. The wine possesses an opaque purple color, marvelous purity, and a minerality that frames its extravagant blackberry, cherry, and currant-dominated richness. The finish lasts for nearly a minute. An astounding effort, it will age well for a decade.

Virtually all of the Turley 1998 Zinfandels were produced from extremely low 1–1.5 tons of fruit per acre. Turley and Jordan bottled all these 1998s without fining or filtration in December 1999. Since their debut releases in 1993, these Zinfandels have been among the most luxuriously rich, complex, and interesting efforts of their respective vintages. The 1998s are more forward and evolved than such vintages as 1997 and are best drunk over the next 5–6 years. As a group, they are impressively endowed and already showing extremely well. In short, I see no reason to defer gratification, even though they are bigger, more concentrated, and alcoholic wines than most 1998s.

The dark ruby/garnet-colored, full-bodied 1998 Zinfandel Tofanelli Vineyard (15.9% alcohol) exhibits spice box and berry fruit aromas and flavors, a sweet, luscious texture, soft, low acidity, and gorgeous voluptuousness. Drink it over the next 5–7 years. Produced from a blend of various small plots, the 1998 Zinfandel Old Vines displays similar opulence, but reveals a more earthy, peppery, dried herb component to its dense black cherry, plum, and raspberry fruit. A delicious, round wine, it is best drunk over the next 4–5 years. One of Turley's great successes is the terrific 1998 Zinfandel Duarte Vineyard. Made from one of their oldest vineyards (a 104-year-old vineyard planted in pure sand), whose grapes achieved 15.8% alcohol naturally, it is the finest Duarte yet produced. An explosive nose of black cherry jam ascends from the glass. In the mouth, cherry liqueur notes continue in this full-bodied, super-endowed, luxuriously rich, opulent, fat, juicy Zinfandel. It is a hedonistic turn-on for sure. Drink it over the next 4–5 years. Less successful than in previous vintages is the 1998 Zinfandel Black-Sears. As Larry Turley acknowledged, their hottest *terroirs* often did the best in the cool 1998 growing season. Consequently, vineyards such as Duarte excelled, whereas the Black-Sears, among the coolest microclimates of Howell Mountain, was not harvested until November. Nevertheless, there is nothing to be upset about. A dense garnet/ruby color is followed by scents of raspberries, underbrush, loamy soil, plum liqueur, and pepper.

Spicy and ripe, but less expressive and thick compared to previous vintages, it is an excellent Zinfandel for consuming over the next 4–5 years. For statisticians, the alcohol level is 16%, so there is no obvious lack of ripeness, even from this cool, high-altitude vineyard. Readers looking for a Zinfandel with a Rhône-like personality should check out the 1998 Zinfandel Vineyard 101. Offering an explosive nose of dried herbs, ground pepper, new saddle leather, rose petals, black raspberries, and cherries, this fat, dense, full-bodied, luscious wine possesses low acidity, but gobs of fruit. Drink it over the next 4–5 years.

It is hard to believe, but the 1998 Zinfandel Grist Vineyard (16.4% alcohol) possesses an undeniable sense of elegance and symmetry. In a blind tasting, it could be mistaken for a premier cru from Volnay by some of those silly *terroirists* who always like to do a lot more postulating than tasting. This medium-bodied Zinfandel reveals a flamboyant side to its elegance and somehow manages to hide its alcohol. It exhibits delicious berry and cherry fruit with a strawberry liqueur–like after-finish. Drink it over the next 5–6 years. One of the new stars in the Turley portfolio is their 1998 Zinfandel Pringle Family Vineyard (16.1% alcohol). This is among the most firmly structured and backward of the Turley Zinfandels. It offers a dense ruby/purple color as well as earthy, foresty, black raspberry, and black cherry liqueur aromas. The wine is deep and full-bodied, with some tannin, excellent purity, and overall symmetry. It will benefit from another 6–12 months of bottle age and will last for 7–8 years or more. Turley and Jordan told me that their 1998 Zinfandel Dogtown Vineyard (16.5% alcohol) produced a mere two-thirds of a ton of fruit per acre. An intriguing wine, it reveals a Provençal-like, black cherry and *garrigue* aroma with scents of the seaweed wrap called nori used in sushi preparations. Deep, opulent, rich, and expansive, with fabulous fruit and low acidity, it is one of the finest efforts from Lodi I have ever tasted. Drink it over the next 4–5 years. Another wine with Provençal dried herb notes as well as abundant kirsch, black raspberries, blackberries, prunes, and plums is the 1998 Zinfandel Moore (Earthquake) Vineyard. A dense, full-bodied, stunningly proportioned, multidimensional Zin, it appears to be the finest wine in this impressive lineup, boasting a dark ruby color, thick, juicy, succulent flavors, and a low-acid, heady, alcoholic (16%) finish. Drink it over the next 5–7 years. Year in and year out, one of the most concentrated and spectacular Zinfandels produced in California emerges from the old vines of St. Helena's Hayne Vineyard. The 1998 Zinfandel Hayne Vineyard (16.4% alcohol) may not be quite as good as the nearly perfect examples from the past, but it is one of the vintage's superstars. Dense ruby/purple-colored, with a flamboyant nose of blackberries, cherries, kirsch, pepper, spice, and earth, this massive, chewy, full-throttle, hedonistic Zin is exceptionally pure, with a finish that lasts for 35–40+ seconds. The emphasis is on superripe fruit, subtle dosages of new oak, and spectacular texture. It should drink well for at least a decade.

As for the 1997 Zinfandels, Larry Turley said at the time, they "are the best wines we have yet made." The wines are amazingly good, and as the following tasting notes suggest, readers could buy blind here and always end up with a juicy, complex, mouth-filling Zinfandel. For starters, the 1997 Zinfandel Spenker Vineyard (from 105-year-old vines, with 15.1% alcohol) is a full-bodied, berry-scented and -flavored, lush wine with intriguing pepper, tar, and spicy notes. With excellent depth and purity, it is a candidate for 7–8 years of drinkability. The 1997 Zinfandel Dogtown (15.3% alcohol) is from a 65-year-old vineyard situated on the border of Amador. Its dark ruby/purple/garnet color is followed by copious quantities of briery, berry fruit intermixed with loamy soil, underbrush, and spicy notes. Full-bodied and chewy, with excellent ripeness, this tasty, fleshy, full-throttle Zinfandel should drink well for 5–7 years. From tiny parcels of 55- to 104-year-old, head-pruned vineyards, the Turley team put together a blend called Zinfandel Old Vines. The dark ruby/purple-colored 1997 (15.3% alcohol) is the finest example of this *cuvée* they have produced. It offers a stunning nose of blackberry, raspberry and cherry fruit intermixed with Asian spices, pepper, and balsam wood. Explosively rich in the mouth, with high glycerin, and a smooth, concentrated finish, this wine should drink well for 7–8 years. The 1997 Zinfandel Duarte Vineyard (from 102-year-old vines; 15.4% alcohol) is the finest wine I have tasted from this source. Duarte is one of the few remaining California vineyards where the vines are planted on their own roots, rather than being grafted, as the region's sandy soils have proved to be resistant to the phylloxera disease. This wine always seems to have a dusty, balsam wood, Provençal herb, peppery note, but the 1997 reveals more cherry liqueur and black raspberries. Additionally, the color is a saturated dark ruby/purple. Full-bodied and concentrated, with deep layers of flavor that inundate the palate, it should drink well for 5–7 years. The 1997 Zinfandel Tofanelli Vineyard (from a 65-year-old vineyard; 15.8% alcohol) is a broodingly backward, expansive yet undeniably hedonistically oriented Zinfandel. The dark ruby/purple color is accompanied by notes of blackberries, *jus de viande*, pepper, roasted herbs, and truffles. Full-bodied, with dazzling fruit extract, a voluptuous texture, and a spectacular finish, this is a superb Zin to enjoy over the next 5–7 years. Slightly superior is the 1997 Zinfandel Grist Vineyard (16.3% alcohol). This is a perfumed, aromatic wine with a glorious display of cherry fruit. Think of a terrific red Burgundy with an element of *sur-maturité* and an unprecedented alcohol level, and readers may get a sense of what this blockbuster tastes like. The wine exhibits a dense ruby/purple color, fabulous purity, copious amounts of glycerin, and layers of kirsch/cherry fruit. This head-turning, knockout Zinfandel will be especially admired by both lovers of Burgundy and those who admire the famed Châteauneuf-du-Pape, Rayas. It should drink well for 7–8 years. The 1997 Zinfandel Vineyard 101 (from 85-year-old vines; 16% alcohol) is another Burgundy-styled wine, but more alcoholic and viscous. Full-bodied, with surprising elegance for its weight and size, it displays a strong sense of minerality intertwined with notes of barbecue spices. With thrilling levels of black cherry and raspberry fruit, it should drink well now and over the next 7 years.

Some of Turley's old standbys are once again compelling wines. The 1997 Zinfandel Aida Vineyard (from 30-year-old vines; 16.8% alcohol) is once again the Châteauneuf-du-Pape of northern California. This wine boasts an *herbes de Provence, garrigue,* peppery, black raspberry-scented, exotic nose that is eerily similar to a top-class Châteauneuf. The color is a saturated dark ruby/purple, and the wine unleashes its full power with layers of roasted meats, pepper, and jammy fruit flavors. This stunning Zinfandel will overload most tasters' olfactory sensors. Moreover, it should drink well for 7–8 years. The 1997 Zinfandel Black-Sears Vineyard (81-year-old vines; 17% alcohol) is the finest Black-Sears Turley has yet produced. Flirting with perfection, it is one of the most extraordinary Zinfandels I have ever tasted. This vineyard, located high on Howell Mountain, in a wilderness area inhabited by mountain lions, bobcats, and wild pigs, has turned out a saturated black/purple-colored wine with fabulous aromas of crème de cassis, minerals, cold steel, Asian spices, violets, and licorice. The wine possesses unbelievable fruit richness, layers of extract and glycerin, phenomenal purity, and a 40+-second finish. Somehow, some way, the 17% alcohol has been concealed beneath the wine's extraordinary richness. Is it any wonder that so many other Zinfandel producers are jealous of Turley Cellars? This offering should drink beautifully for 7–8 years. The 1997 Zinfandel Moore (Earthquake) Vineyard (from 91-year-old vines; 17.1% alcohol) is also spectacular. From its saturated black purple color to its knockout aromatics of framboise, raspberries, and kirsch (essentially the entire spectrum of red and black fruits seems to be present in this wine), this gorgeous, massively endowed, jammy yet structured Zinfandel easily disguises its 17.1% alcohol under its remarkable concentration and intensity. It should drink well for another decade. My favorite Zinfandel in the Turley portfolio is usually the Hayne Vineyard. Along with Martinelli's Jackass Hill Zinfandel, it has tended to represent the be-all and end-all Zinfandel. The 1997 Zinfandel Hayne Vineyard is unquestionably a remarkable wine, but I am not sure it is better than the Black-Sears or Moore Vineyard. However, it will be the most backward and potentially longest-lived of these 1997s. It was the least evolved when I tasted it in September 1998, displaying an opaque saturated, thick-looking purple color, and unevolved but promising notes of black raspberry liqueur intermixed with minerals, spice, and cherry fruit. Massive yet phenomenally rich, admirably pure, and representing the essence of this varietal, this wine requires 12–18 months of bottle age; it should drink well for 10–15 years. An extraordinary Zin, with 17.2% alcohol, it is the most powerful offering in the Turley portfolio. Anticipated maturity: now–2010.

The dynamic duo of Turley and Jordan also produces California's finest Charbono. If more wineries could be as successful with this varietal, we would see an explosion of California Charbono rather than the insufferably innocuous Sangiovese produced throughout the state. Turley's 1999 Charbono Tofanelli Vineyard (109 cases, 13.5% alcohol) is analogous to a full-throttle Dolcetto. An intense black/purple color is accompanied by blueberry, cranberry liqueur, cherry, and chocolate aromas and flavors. It should drink well for 7–8 years. The 1998 Charbono Tofanelli Vineyard (200 cases, 14.8% alcohol) continues the great success Turley and Jordan have had with this lowly esteemed varietal. Dark ruby/purple-colored, with an earthy, spicy, gorgeously pure nose, this wine offers blueberry and blackberry flavors, copious quantities of earthy richness, and a spicy, long, full-bodied, powerful finish. It should drink well for 10–15 years.

One of my best friends has been cellaring Petite Sirah for over 30 years, and we have had some extraordinary tastings of this underrated varietal. Such Petite Sirahs as the 1974 Freemark Abbey, 1971 Ridge York Creek, as well as a bevy of others, remain prodigious wines even as they approach 30 years of age. Turley Cellars' Petite Syrahs are wines for collectors to purchase and then forget for at least a decade. They are enormously concentrated, brutally tannic, awesomely endowed efforts made (like the Zinfandels) with no compromises. The blue/black/purple-colored 1999 Petite Syrah Estate (125 cases, 14.6% alcohol) exhibits thick, concentrated, pure flavors of licorice, minerals, blackberries, and cassis. Monstrous on the palate, this 1999 requires a decade of cellaring. Even more amazing is the 1999 Petite Syrah Rattlesnake Acres (225 cases, 14.8% alcohol). With an appearance reminiscent of vintage Port, it offers notes of blackberries, smoke, and minerals. This blockbuster, gargantuan wine boasts awesome concentration, exquisite purity, and a palate-saturating style. Anticipated maturity: 2010–2050. Potentially perfect, the 1999 Petite Syrah Hayne Vineyard (475 cases, 15.5% alcohol) is a 50-year wine. If it is showing any age after a decade of cellaring, I will be as surprised as its producers. An opaque black/blue color is followed by an extraordinary perfume of blackberry and crème de cassis blended with spices, minerals, and earth. Frightfully tannic, with unreal concentration, texture, and length, this behemoth is one of the most concentrated wines I have ever tasted. Anticipated maturity: 2012–2050+.

There are 275 cases of the dense, tannic, concentrated, outstanding 1998 Petite Syrah Rattlesnake Acres (14.2% alcohol), and 325 cases of the blockbuster, sensationally rich, hyper-concentrated 1998 Petite Syrah Hayne Vineyard (14.5% alcohol). The latter wine exhibits better ripeness, more impressive concentration, and a blockbuster, gargantuan finish that lasts for 40–45 seconds. Like all the Turley wines, these two efforts possess exquisite purity and fabulously ripe, unmanipulated fruit that cuts a creamy, lush texture on the palate. The Rattlesnake Acres will drink well in 3–4 years and keep for 15 or more. The Hayne Vineyard requires 3–4 years of cellaring and will keep for at least two decades.

Turley's 1997 Petite Syrah Aida Vineyard (from 80-year-old vines) assaults the palate with such an overload of fruit, tannin, and extract that the taster's first impression is that this is something more than table wine. It is a massive, almost uncivilized, wildly out of control Petite Syrah that will require 10–15 years of cellaring and last for 30 or more. I have been conservative in my judgment because the tannin nearly melted the fillings in my teeth, but this is an amazing, astonishing wine that will be fascinating to follow over the next 3–4 decades. Lamentably, it will certainly outlive me. Anticipated maturity: 2008–2040. New in 1997, the 1997 Petite Syrah Rattlesnake Acres is from a 50-year-old plantation of Petite Sirah. The wine's notes suggested I needed to return to my hotel to grab my floss after tasting this wine.

The color is a saturated, thick black/purple. The wine reveals surprising amounts of toasty new oak in the nose (Turley only uses 25–30% new oak). In the mouth, it is "beyond immense, massive, and gargantuan," and should be purchased only by those seeking an adventurous wine experience. Anticipated maturity: 2005–2040. I do not believe I have ever tasted a more concentrated, essence-like wine than Turley's 1997 Petite Syrah Hayne Vineyard. Made from 55-year-old vines that yielded only 9.8 tons of fruit for five acres, this opaque black-colored wine is the biggest, richest, most concentrated, tannic wine I have ever tasted. It will need at least a decade to shed some of its ferocious tannin, and will undoubtedly last for 40–50 years. Even more remarkable is its purity and overall equilibrium. Despite its Godzilla-like size, this is an astonishingly concentrated, gorgeously made wine.

VÉRITÉ (SONOMA)

1999 La Joie	Sonoma/Napa	EEE	95
1998 La Joie	Sonoma/Napa	EEE	92
1999 Merlot	Sonoma/Napa	EEE	94
1998 Merlot	Sonoma/Napa	EEE	92

A new boutique producer under the Jackson Family Farms moniker, Vérité and its sister operation, La Joie, are run by a Bordelais, Pierre Seillan, who has done some miracle working with outstanding fruit sources. His first efforts are brilliant, particularly from the challenging vintage of 1998. His 1999s look . . . simply awesome. These wines, which Seillan calls "wines without compromise," are all aged in 100% new French oak for about 13 months. His 1998 Merlot is an inter-appellation blend of 62% Sonoma and 38% Napa. It is a 2,000-case blend of 90% Merlot and 10% Cabernet Sauvignon. Eighty-five percent of the malolactic was done in barrel, and the wine was bottled without any clarification. It is a blockbuster Merlot, and certainly a formidable achievement for 1998. The wine shows a dense black/purple color, an enormous nose of espresso roast, melted chocolate, blackberries, cherries, and sweet truffle/earthy notes. Very full-bodied, astonishingly concentrated, extremely pure, and well balanced, this is a blockbuster effort that can be drunk now (it has relatively high pH and low acidity) or cellared for 15–20 years. The 1999 Merlot (a similar blend of 90% Merlot and 10% Cabernet Sauvignon, with 84% of the wine coming from Sonoma and 16% from Napa) is extravagantly concentrated, with a layered, expansive mid-palate, and a blockbuster finish. The wine is out-and-out massive, with spectacular levels of fruit and glycerin. The basic characteristics are lavish richness (cassis, coffee, chocolate galore) and a low-acid, multitextured, flamboyant finish. In short, this is an amazing wine. It should be drinkable young, but with an uncommon ageability of 20–25 years.

The La Joie wines are dominated by Cabernet Sauvignon with some Merlot in the blend. Again, these 2,000 cases are intercounty blends of Sonoma and Napa fruit. They are both made from 70% Cabernet Sauvignon and 30% Merlot. The 1998 is 85% Sonoma fruit and 15% Napa. The 1999 is virtually identical, with 89% Sonoma and 11% Napa. The 1998 La Joie is a more backward wine than the 1998 Merlot, which is not surprising given the fact that it is dominated by Cabernet Sauvignon. The wine has an opaque purple color, big, powerful, highly extracted flavors, amazing richness for a wine of this vintage, and a long, muscular, dense finish. It needs a good 3–4 years of cellaring, yet should keep for two decades. The 1999 La Joie is super stuff, a prodigious wine of fabulous concentration, with licorice, coffee, black currant, leather, and truffle notes, huge body, sweet tannin, and a big, tannic finish. It is not a wine for those looking for immediate gratification, as this will require 5–6 years of cellaring and keep for 25+ years.

It is obvious that wine-maker Pierre Seillan and proprietor Jess Jackson have a mission to "make a world-class Merlot as good or better than Pétrus." These will no doubt be hot items when released next year.

VIADER VINEYARDS (NAPA)

1998 Proprietary Red Wine	Napa	E	88
1997 Proprietary Red Wine	Napa	E	92
1996 Proprietary Red Wine	Napa	D	88
1995 Proprietary Red Wine	Napa	D	91
1994 Proprietary Red Wine	Napa	C	92

One of the many gorgeous hillside estates in Napa Valley, Viader, whose vineyards are situated on the lower slopes of Howell Mountain, produces about 5,000 cases of a blend composed of almost equal parts Cabernet Sauvignon and Cabernet Franc. The dark ruby/purple-colored 1998 Proprietary Red (a blend of 60% Cabernet Sauvignon and 40% Cabernet Franc) offers a bouquet of subtle herbs, minerals, and red currants. Spicy, elegant, and restrained, this subtle, poised effort should drink well young, yet last for 14–15 years. The terrific 1997 Proprietary Red is the finest Viader I have tasted. It is a wine of exceptional finesse and elegance, yet undeniable richness and intensity. This blend of 59% Cabernet Sauvignon and 41% Cabernet Franc tastes like a top Graves from Bordeaux. Subtle spicy oak emerges from this dark ruby/purple-colored wine, along with scents of black currants, minerals, and lead pencil. In the mouth, earthy, *terroir* characteristics combine with sweet black fruits in this medium-bodied, rich wine. There is a juicy mid-palate as well as considerable grace and harmony in the finish. The tannin is largely obscured by the wine's outstanding concentration. Anticipated maturity: now–2018. A blend of 59% Cabernet Sauvignon and 41% Cabernet Franc, the 1996 is made in a polished, graceful style. Medium-bodied, with lush, herb-tinged, raspberry and black currant fruit intermixed with mineral and lead pencil notes, this lovely, stylish, restrained offering already provides pleasant drinking, yet should keep for 10–12 years. The similarly styled 1995 reveals an opaque purple color, remarkably sweet tannin for a wine from this vintage, and gorgeous levels of black currant fruit nicely complemented by toast, smoke, and floral scents. This rich, medium- to full-bodied wine fills the mouth without any sense of heaviness or harshness. It is a beautifully knit, lush, complex, elegant red wine that should drink well for 12–15 years. Smoky, sweet, black and red currant aromas jump from the glass of the intriguing, saturated purple-colored 1994. Some new oak is noticeable in the background. The wine's attack exhibits terrific purity of fruit, more acidity than many 1994s, and sweet, ripe tannin, all packed into a tightly wound, medium- to full-bodied wine that only hints at its ultimate potential. This is not a large-scaled 1994, but it is a beautifully etched wine with considerable personality. It will benefit from 4–5 years of cellaring and is unquestionably another 20-year effort from this vintage.

Past Glories: 1993 Proprietary Red Wine (90)

VINEYARD 29 (NAPA)

1998 Cabernet Sauvignon	Napa	EE	88
1997 Cabernet Sauvignon	Napa	EE	94

This vineyard's innovative name and beautiful presentation in a heavy, tall Italian bottle make for a grandiose impression. These wines, produced by wine-making consultant Heidi Barrett, are impressive. There are 400 cases of the 1998 and 600 cases of the 1997, all from a 3.5-acre Cabernet Sauvignon parcel planted with the Grace clone. The 1998 Cabernet Sauvignon is a successful effort in this challenging vintage for Cabernet producers. The vintage's charm, softness, ripe fruit, elegance, and fine balance are well displayed. Black currants and cherries compete with cedar, spice, and subtle new oak. It is a medium-bodied, appealing Cabernet Sauvignon that will be drinkable upon release, and will evolve nicely for 7–8 years. Sweeter, richer, fuller, and more concentrated is the 1997 Cabernet Sauvignon. A deep ruby/purple color is followed by pure black currant fruit intertwined with tobacco, vanilla, and spice. This lush, full-bodied effort displays sweet tannin and cuts a powerful swath across the palate. The finish reveals high extraction and harmony. It will be even better in 1–3 years and should last for two decades.

VON STRASSER (NAPA)

1995 Cabernet Sauvignon Diamond Mountain	Napa	D	90
1994 Cabernet Sauvignon Diamond Mountain	Napa	D	91
1995 Cabernet Sauvignon Diamond Mountain Reserve	Napa	D	92+

This winery is doing many things right, as evidenced by these releases. Both 1995 Cabernet Sauvignons are outstanding. The 1995 Cabernet Sauvignon Diamond Mountain possesses a dense ruby/purple color, followed by a promising nose of cassis intertwined with earth, flowers, and spice. In the mouth, there is good grip and tannin, but the overall impression is one of a medium- to full-bodied wine where the fruit characteristics dominate the *terroir* and oak. Subtle vanilla and spice are present in this pure, black currant–flavored, long, impressive wine. Accessible now, it promises to get even better over the next decade, and last for 15+ years. The 1995 Cabernet Sauvignon Diamond Mountain Reserve is prodigious. The color is nearly opaque purple. The nose offers up intense aromas of blackberries and cassis, intermingled with earth and vanilla. On the palate, the wine is formidably endowed, backward and tannic, but exceptionally dense, layered, and extremely rich. Yet there is no sense of heaviness, and the tannin is sweet rather than overbearing or astringent. This superb Cabernet Sauvignon has a long, promising future. Anticipated maturity: now–2020.

The 1994 is a beautifully made Cabernet Sauvignon. The healthy dark purple color is followed by a forward, sexy, up-front nose of jammy plums, black currants, vanilla ice cream, and cassis. On the palate, this full-bodied Cabernet reveals silky tannin, an opulent texture, and a full-bodied, concentrated finish. It manages to offer intensity without heaviness—something that is not easy to obtain. Drink this seductive Cabernet Sauvignon young as well as old, as I suspect it will have a very large window of drinkability—say 15 or more years. *Past Glories:* 1993 Cabernet Sauvignon Diamond Mountain (91)

WHITEHALL LANE (NAPA)

1997 Cabernet Sauvignon	Napa	D	88
1995 Cabernet Sauvignon	Napa	C	88
1994 Cabernet Sauvignon	Napa	C	88
1996 Cabernet Sauvignon Leonardini Vineyard	Napa	E	89
1995 Cabernet Sauvignon Leonardini Vineyard	Napa	E	90
1994 Cabernet Sauvignon Morisoli Vineyard	Napa	E	92
1996 Cabernet Sauvignon Reserve	Napa	D	88
1995 Cabernet Sauvignon Reserve	Napa	D	91
1994 Cabernet Sauvignon Reserve Morisoli Vineyard	Napa	D	90
1996 Merlot	Napa	C	88
1994 Merlot Leonardini Vineyard	Napa	D	91
1995 Merlot Reserve Leonardini Vineyard	Napa	D	88
1994 Merlot Reserve Leonardini Vineyard	Napa	D	90

The red wine offerings from this excellent winery are well made, with rich personalities and attractive bouquets. The dark ruby-colored 1997 Cabernet Sauvignon Napa possesses cassis fruit intermixed with spicy wood and earth. Medium- to full-bodied, with some grip but a plush texture, this rich, concentrated Cabernet Sauvignon should drink well for a decade. The 1996 Cabernet Sauvignon Reserve reveals more new oak (in addition to black currant fruit) as well as a tighter framework. More closed and not as supple and evolved as the 1997 Napa, this wine displays more length and intensity at the back of the palate. It is a classy, well-made Napa Cabernet Sauvignon that should be better with 1–2 more years of bottle age and last for 10–15 years. The finest of this trio of Cabernets is the 1996 Cabernet Sauvignon Leonardini Vineyard. Sweet new oak and copious quantities of black currant fruit, cedar, dried herbs, and spice make for a full-bodied impression in the mouth. Expansive and rich, with light to moderate tannin, excellent, possibly outstanding concentration and depth, this beautifully made 1996 should drink well for 12–15 years.

Whitehall Lane's 1995 Cabernet Sauvignon Reserve (2,400 cases) dominated a flight that included 14 of its peers. It exhibits a saturated purple color, as well as a youthful yet promising nose of toasty new oak, briery fruit, cassis, and licorice. The wine is concentrated and pure, with sweet tannin, adequate acidity, and medium to full body. A seamless, beautifully proportioned Cabernet Sauvignon, it should be at its peak with another 2–3 years of bottle age, and keep for 15 or more. The 1996 Merlot is a round, user-friendly, plump wine with significantly more character than most Merlots possess. The color is a dark ruby/purple. The wine offers copious amounts of berry fruit intermixed with smoke, herb, and earthy notes. Fruity and succulent, with medium body and a generous, crowd-pleasing, glycerin-imbued finish, it should be consumed over the next 5–6 years.

The opaque-colored 1995 Cabernet Sauvignon Leonardini Vineyard reveals more new oak, extract, richness, and intensity. There are copious quantities of cassis and vanilla flavors that border on overripeness. Rich, with soft tannin, this larger-scaled, more expansive wine can be drunk now as well as over the next 15 years. The ambitiously styled 1995 Merlot Reserve Leonardini Vineyard reveals an opaque ruby/purple color, less expressiveness aromatically (it's more closed), and more toasty new oak. In the mouth, this wine possesses an extra dimension of richness and concentration. It is not as accessible as the regular Merlot, and over the next several years most readers will probably prefer the latter wine. Nevertheless, the Reserve Merlot is an excellent effort that should age well for 7–8 years. The 1994 Merlot Reserve Leonardini Vineyard is a more extracted, richer, earthier, more aggressively oaked wine with full body, admirable intensity, richness, and length, and a long, spicy finish. Although still youthful and unevolved, it promises to provide considerable enjoyment between now–2010. The blockbuster 1994 Merlot Leonardini Vineyard exhibits a black/purple color, fabulously ripe, rich, concentrated fruit, full body, and a great purity and balance. This is an immensely impressive Merlot that should age well for a decade or more.

An excellent, nearly outstanding Cabernet Sauvignon, Whitehall Lane's 1995 possesses a dark ruby/purple color, as well as sweet, jammy, cassis fruit, an appealingly thick texture, and no hard edges. The acidity, tannin, and alcohol are all well integrated in this seamless, opulently styled Cabernet Sauvignon. It should drink well for a decade or more.

The 1994 Cabernet Sauvignon exhibits a deep ruby/purple color followed by attractive spicy, weedy, cassis aromas, backed up by vanilla and oaky scents. Medium- to full-bodied, with excellent concentration, well-integrated tannin and acidity, and a vibrant, lively feel on the palate, this mid-weight Cabernet should drink well for 7–10 years. The outstanding 1994 Cabernet Sauvignon Reserve Morisoli Vineyard is not quite ready for prime-time drinking. It possesses a healthy dark ruby/purple color, enticing, sweet cassis, cedar, and vanilla components, medium to full body, high tannin, and some of the elusive lead pencil aromas often found in St.-Julien and Pauillac offerings. The wine needs another 2–3 years of cellaring, but it should evolve gracefully for 10–15 years. It is a fine example of this impressive vintage.

The terrific 1994 Cabernet Sauvignon Morisoli Vineyard exhibits a black/purple color, fabulous sweetness and ripeness of fruit, full body, layers of extract and richness, and a stunning finish. The tannin is sweet and long. This gorgeous wine appears to be a terrific effort from what looks to be a sensational vintage for North Coast Cabernet Sauvignon.

Past Glories: 1993 Cabernet Sauvignon Morisoli Vineyard (90), 1993 Merlot Reserve Leonardini Vineyard (90)

WILLIAMS-SELYEM (SONOMA)

1997 Pinot Noir	Sonoma Coastlands	E	90
1997 Pinot Noir Allen Vineyard	Russian River	E	89
1996 Pinot Noir Ferrington Vineyard	Anderson Valley	E	91
1997 Pinot Noir Hirsch Vineyard	Sonoma Coast	E	88
1997 Pinot Noir Precious Mountain	Sonoma Coast	E	89

Williams-Selyem has a near mythical reputation for their wines, which are sold exclusively through a mailing list. This winery was sold in 1997, but Burt Williams has been retained as a consultant to train former Hartford Court wine-maker Bob Cabral. When the history of California wines is written, Williams-Selyem will hold an important place. Not only was it one of the first wineries to exploit the potential of the Sonoma Coast and Russian River, particularly with vineyard-designated Pinot Noir and Chardonnay, but this is the ultimate "garage" winery. It will be interesting to see what direction the new owner follows, as production is scheduled to be increased. Hopefully, the quality can be maintained. All of the following offerings revealed high levels of tangy acidity, a style that allows the winery to utilize extremely low levels of sulphur, a worthy objective.

The 1997 Pinot Noirs possess light ruby colors, aggressive acidity, and copious quantities of the red fruit mélange—kirsch, strawberries, cherries, and red currants. The 1997 Pinot Noir Allen Vineyard (planted in 1972) exhibits a light ruby color, followed by an attractive, jammy strawberry and toasty oak-scented nose. Medium-bodied, with zesty acidity, and a crisp, tart finish, it should drink well for 5–6 years. The 1997 Pinot Noir Sonoma Coastlands exhibits sweeter fruit, intermixed with smoke and toast. This wine possesses a lush, Volnay-like personality with considerable seductiveness and intensity. The acidity is noticeable, but not overbearing. Typical of many wines from this area, the well-made 1997 Pinot Noir Hirsch Vineyard displays a forceful structure, and copious spice, earth, and tannin to go along with its black cherry fruit. It is a candidate for several years of cellaring before consumption. It should keep for 7–8 years, but the tannin may be problematic. The medium ruby-colored 1997 Pinot Noir Precious Mountain reveals a sweet, expansive, black cherry nose intermixed with floral notes, smoky, toasty oak, and herbs. Expansive in the mouth, with fine richness, less intrusive acidity than some *cuvées*, and light tannin in the finish, it should drink well for 5–7 years. I was extremely impressed by the 1996 Pinot Noir Ferrington Vineyard. It boasts the most concentration, richness, and intensity of any Williams-Selyem Pinot Noirs, with enough extract and richness to balance out the tart acidity. The wine's dark ruby/purple color is followed by sweet black cherry and raspberry aromas, with nicely integrated smoky oak. Sweet, floral, and rich, with medium to full body, vibrant acidity, and tannin, this beautifully made, hedonistic, rich, fleshy wine will drink well for 5–6 years.

ZACA MESA WINERY (SANTA BARBARA)

1997 Syrah	Santa Barbara	C	90
1994 Syrah	Santa Barbara	C	92
1996 Syrah Black Bear Block	Santa Barbara	D	88

Zaca Mesa's medium-bodied 1997 Syrah (12% Viognier in the blend) offers a candied blackberry nose with scents of pepper and asphalt. Pure and ripe, with low acidity and sexy, voluptuously textured fruit, this tasty, fleshy, succulent Syrah will have many admirers. According to the winery, the 1996 Syrah Black Bear Block is produced from some of the oldest, most stressed Syrah vineyards. A dark purple color is accompanied by dense, thick, sweet blackberry fruit infused with copious quantities of sweet toasty oak. Fleshy and succulent, with low acidity and excellent concentration, this wine can be drunk over the next decade.

Readers are advised to be on the lookout for the 1994 Syrah from Zaca Mesa. Discounters will probably sell it for $12–13 a bottle, making it unquestionably one of the richest, most hedonistic wines per penny spent that I have tasted and reviewed. This Syrah, blended with

10% Viognier, offers an opaque purple color, an exceptional nose of sweet berry fruit (jammy cassis, tropical fruits, and overripe peaches), a full-bodied, viscous, satiny smooth texture, and outstanding flavor extraction. This is a harmonious, gorgeously rich Syrah that may ultimately turn out to be Santa Barbara's answer to Côte Rôtie. Don't dare miss it!

ZD WINERY (NAPA)

1995 Cabernet Sauvignon	Napa	D	88
1994 Cabernet Sauvignon	Napa	D	90

The opaque purple-colored, exotic 1994 Cabernet Sauvignon is generously wooded, with smoky black raspberry and cassis aromas. Medium- to full-bodied, with copious amounts of fruit and soft tannin, this luscious, youthful, grapy Cabernet can be drunk now, but it promises to be better with 2–3 years of cellaring; it should keep for 12–15 years. The "American-styled" 1995 Cabernet Sauvignon has plenty of macho power, lavish quantities of toasty new oak, and straightforward, pleasing, ripe black currant fruit. Attractive, savory, and mouth-filling, the wine is medium- to full-bodied, monolithic, and cleanly made, with 10–15 years of evolution ahead of it.

ZOOM (PASO ROBLES)

1999 Zinfandel	Napa	C	89
1999 Zinfandel	Paso Robles	C	90
1997 Zinfandel	Paso Robles	C	88
1999 Zinfandel	San Francisco Bay	C	89
1999 Zinfandel Ricetti Vineyard	Redwood Valley	C	90

The four noteworthy 1999 Zinfandels from Zoom offer impressive levels of fruit and ripeness presented in an uncomplicated, full-bodied, user-friendly style with enough complexity and nuances to satisfy both neophytes and connoisseurs. The 1999 Zinfandel Ricetti Vineyard (13.8% alcohol) exhibits a dark ruby/purple color in addition to fat, succulent fruit flavors. Bursting with fruit and glycerin, this full-bodied, layered, hedonistic, sexy Zin should be consumed over the next 3–4 years to take advantage of its exuberance and purity. Made from 31-year-old vines, the dense plum/purple-colored 1999 Zinfandel Paso Robles (14.3% alcohol) reveals loads of kirsch, a layered texture, excellent purity, and a long, spicy, succulent, glycerin-filled finish. Nothing is out of place in this hedonistic, juicy Zinfandel. It, too, should be drunk over the next 3–4 years. Produced from 105-year-old vines, the 1999 Zinfandel San Francisco Bay (14.6% alcohol) is another fruit bomb, but does not express the complexity of the Paso Robles or Ricetti *cuvées*. Nevertheless, there is a lot to like in its current-laden, cherry fruit–dominated style. With abundant glycerin, a corpulent mouth-feel, purity, and exuberance, it will be fun to drink for 3–4 years. The 1999 Zinfandel Napa (from 33-year-old vines; 14.8% alcohol) is the most powerful and alcoholic of this quartet. Measured and less exuberant with a more structured finish than its three siblings, it offers attractive black cherries and currants in its polished personality. It will drink well for 4–5 years.

Made from 29-year-old vines and possessing 14.6% alcohol, the attractive 1997 Zinfandel Paso Robles' evolved dark plum/garnet color is followed by a delightfully sweet raspberry- and cherry-scented nose. In the mouth, it reveals rich, flavorful, medium- to full-bodied flavors, layers of fruit, and a spicy, peppery, earthy finish. Drink this well-made, mouth-filling Zinfandel over the next 3–4 years. Sadly, only 283 cases were produced.

6. OREGON

The Basics

TYPES OF WINE

Oregon makes wine from most of the same grapes used in California, although the cooler, more marginal climate in Oregon's best viticultural area, the Willamette Valley, has meant more success with cool-climate varietals such as Pinot Noir than with hotter-climate varietals such as Cabernet Sauvignon, Merlot, Syrah, and Grenache. Chardonnay and Riesling have done well in Oregon, but the "great white hope" here is Pinot Gris, which has shown fine potential and is the perfect partner for the salmon of the Pacific Northwest. Pinot Blanc has made a significant appearance in recent years, but has not produced wines meriting serious consumer attention, most probably due to severe overcropping. High-quality sparkling wines can be found, particularly under the Argyle label. Oregon's wines are distinctive, with a kinship to European wines. The higher natural acidities, lower alcohol content, and more subtle nature of Oregon's wines bode well for this area's future.

GRAPE VARIETIES

Chardonnay Oregon can make some wonderful Chardonnay, but far too many winemakers let it spend too much time in oak and have not chosen the best clones for their vineyards. The Chardonnay grape in Oregon is naturally high in acidity, and that is the principal difference between California's and Oregon's Chardonnay. In California, most Chardonnays must have tartaric acid added to them for balance. In Oregon, the wines must be put through a secondary or malolactic fermentation, à la Burgundy, in order to lower their perceptible acidity. The high quality of Chardonnays produced from recent plantings of Dijon clones indicates that Oregon may have found the answer to its clonal problems with this varietal.

Pinot Gris This is the hardest wine to find, as virtually all of it is snapped up before it has a chance to leave Oregon. Fruitier and more floral than Chardonnay, Pinot Gris, from the world's most underrated great white wine grape, can be a delicious, opulent, smoky wine with every bit as much character and even more aging potential than Chardonnay. Though a specialty of Oregon, much of it is mediocre and diluted due to overcropping.

Pinot Noir As in Burgundy, the soil, yield per acre, choice of fermentation yeasts, competence of the wine-maker, and type of oak barrel in which this wine is aged profoundly influence its taste, style, and character. The top Oregon Pinot Noirs can have a wonderful purity of cherry, loganberry, and raspberry fruit. Furthermore, they can reveal an expansive, seductive, broad, lush palate, as well as crisp acids for balance. Yet far too many are washed out and hollow because of the tendency to harvest less than fully mature fruit and to permit crop yields to exceed 3 tons per acre.

Other Grape Varieties With respect to white wines, Gewürztraminer has generally proven no more successful in Oregon than in California. However, Oregon can make good Riesling, especially in the drier Alsace style. Recent tastings of delicious sparkling wines from Argyle show promise for this style of wine in Oregon. The Cabernet Sauvignon and Merlot have not been special to date, although some made from vineyards in the southern part of the state have resulted in several good though not exciting wines.

FLAVORS

Chardonnay Compared with California Chardonnay, those of Oregon are noticeably higher in acidity, more oaky, and have less of a processed, manipulated taste than their siblings from California. In many cases the oak is excessive.

Pinot Gris A whiff of smoke, the creamy taste of baked apples and nuts, and gobs of fruit characterize this promising white wine.

Pinot Noir Red berry fruits dominate the taste of Oregon Pinot Noirs. Aromas and flavors of cherries, loganberries, blackberries, cola, and sometimes plums, with a streak of spicy, herbaceous scents characterize these medium ruby-colored wines.

AGING POTENTIAL

Chardonnay: 2–5 years

Dry/Off-Dry Rieslings: 2–4 years

Pinot Gris: 1–3 years

Pinot Noir: 3–10 years

Sparkling Wines: 1–4 years

OVERALL QUALITY LEVEL

Oregon has faced a string of difficult vintages (1995, 1996, and 1997), but these have given the state's wine-makers enormous experience, honing theirs skills and driving them to lower yields. Once a region of underfinanced backyard operations where the owner/wine-makers learned as they went along, Oregon is now stocked with highly skilled and knowledgeable wine-makers. Low-quality grape clones, poorly planted vineyards, and some questionable winemaking decisions can still be found, but the number of high-quality wineries is growing. While they are just beginning to realize the potential for Pinot Noir, Chardonnay, and Pinot Gris, their future is bright. Oregon's wines range in quality from poor to outstanding.

MOST IMPORTANT INFORMATION TO KNOW

To purchase good wine, know the finest vintages, the best wineries, and their best wines. Some additional information worth knowing is that the finest Pinot Noirs generally come from a stretch of vineyards in the Willamette Valley, southwest of Portland.

RECENT VINTAGES

1999—The 1999 vintage in Oregon is outstanding, potentially the finest in this region's short history. With the 1999s, Oregon's top wineries are finally fulfilling their promise to consumers that this state can produce impressively delicious Pinot Noirs with abundant fruit and ageworthy structure. Rains at harvest have been the downfall of numerous Oregon vintages, but 1999 enjoyed an exceptional late season and Indian summer. Sunny days and cool evenings lasted into early October, furthering ripeness while maintaining balanced acidity. In fact, the weather remained excellent through the end of the month, allowing many growers to wait until the third week of October to harvest.

Yields in 1999 were a problem for those wineries that are neither conscientious enough to prune adequately nor unwilling to drop fruit (crop-thin). Wineries that make bad, poor, or

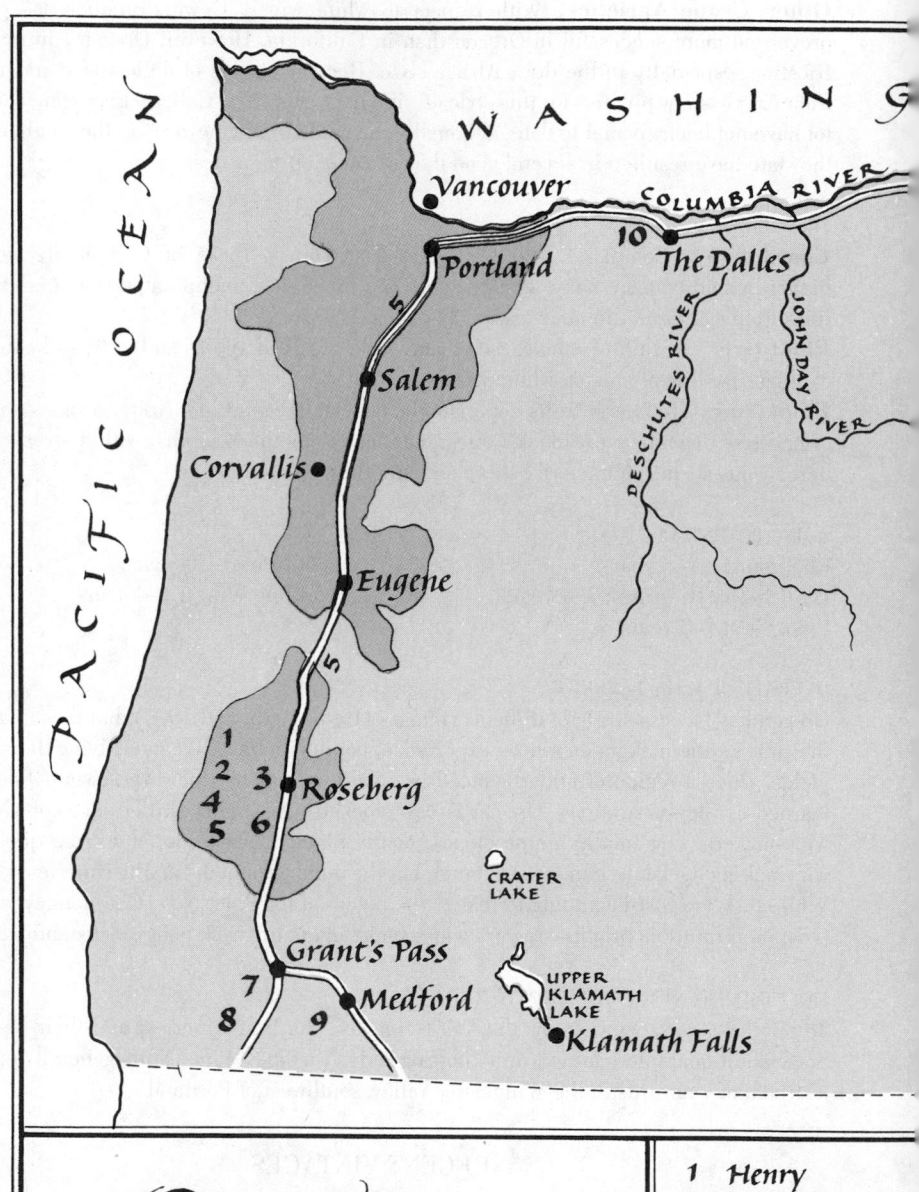

PACIFIC OCEAN

WASHING

Vancouver

COLUMBIA RIVER

Portland

10 The Dalles

DESCHUTES RIVER

JOHN DAY RIVER

Salem

Corvallis

Eugene

1
2 3 Roseberg
4
5 6

CRATER LAKE

Grant's Pass

7
8   9 Medford

UPPER KLAMATH LAKE

Klamath Falls

Oregon

1 Henry
2 Hillcrest
3 Garden Valley
4 Bjelland
5 Giradet

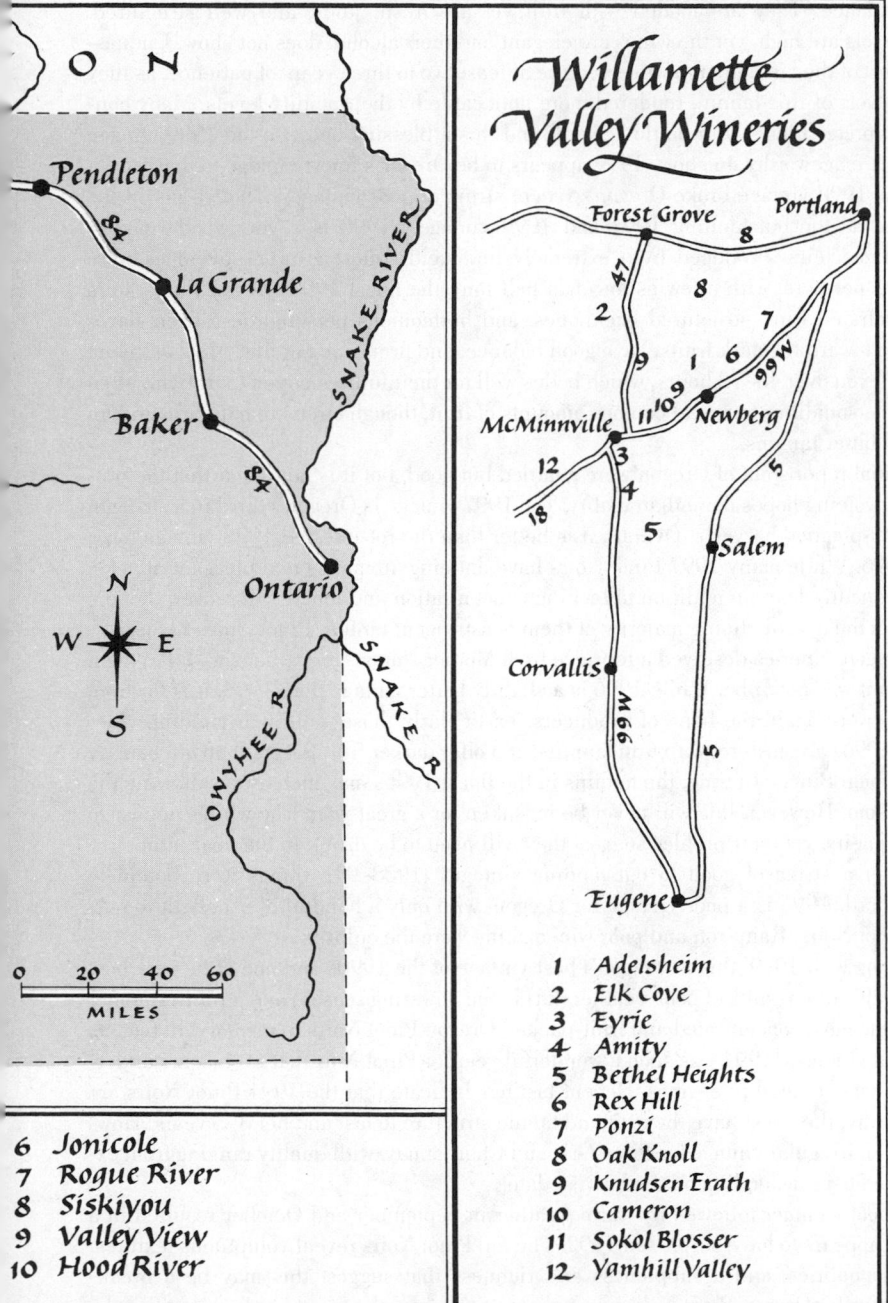

Willamette Valley Wineries

Pendleton

84

La Grande

SNAKE RIVER

Baker

84

N
W E
S

Ontario

OWYHEE R.

SNAKE R.

0 20 40 60
MILES

Forest Grove   Portland
8
47
8
2
7
9   6   99W
1
11 10 9
McMinnville   Newberg
12   3
18   4   5
5
Salem

Corvallis
99W
5

Eugene

1 Adelsheim
2 Elk Cove
3 Eyrie
4 Amity
5 Bethel Heights
6 Rex Hill
7 Ponzi
8 Oak Knoll
9 Knudsen Erath
10 Cameron
11 Sokol Blosser
12 Yamhill Valley

6 Jonicole
7 Rogue River
8 Siskiyou
9 Valley View
10 Hood River

mediocre wine year in and year out also did so in 1999 because they made no effort to control production. So this is an outstanding vintage for the wineries that care about making top-flight wine, and another failure for those that don't. The finest 1999 Oregon Pinot Noirs have exquisite balance. They are loaded with fruit yet are fresh, juicy, and well structured. Ripeness levels are high, yet the wines are elegant and their alcohol does not show. Unquestionably, most of the vintage's top wines require at least two to three years of patience, as they have high levels of ripe tannin, rendered more noticeable by their acidity levels. Many consumers who prefer Pinots with bottle age will find this a blessing because the 1999 Oregon Pinot Noirs are ageworthy. In short, 1999 appears to be Oregon's finest vintage to date.

1998—The 1998 vintage broke Oregon's recent string of poor vintages. Though not in the same league as the outstanding 1994 and 1999 vintages, 1998 is a very good year for Oregon's Pinot Noirs. Produced from extremely low yields (most growers' averages were below 2 tons per acre, with a few as low as a half ton), the finest 1998 Oregon Pinot Noirs have concentrated fruit, structured backbones, and harmonious personalities. Their flavor profiles tend toward the dark fruits, have good balance, and firm, ripe tannins. Many of them, after airing (even over 48–72 hours, which bodes well for their futures), open their tight, often foursquare personalities to reveal copious amounts of fruit, though others remain firm and, in time, reveal bitter tannins.

1997—Initial reports out of Oregon were guarded but good, but it is now clear that the producers were voicing hopes more than reality. The 1997 vintage is Oregon's third in a string of difficult, rain-plagued harvests. Overall, it is better than the rot-infested 1995 vintage, on a par with 1996. While many 1997 Pinot Noirs have enticing aromatics and pleasant attacks, they are frequently lean, in addition to lacking concentration and length. Moreover, the one trait found in the overwhelming majority of them is astringent tannin, Pinot Noir's nemesis.

1996—Oregon wineries deserved a reprieve from Mother Nature after what she did to them in 1995, but it was not to be. While 1996 is a slightly better vintage than 1995, it is far from good. Rains were again the bane of producers, particularly those with high-yielding vineyards. The 1996s are austere, with firm tannins, and offer darker fruit flavors than are usually found in Oregon Pinots. In time, the tannins in the finest 1996s may melt away, allowing the fruit to blossom. However, this will never be mistaken for a great year. The whites appear to be of good quality, yet their profiles suggest they will need to be drunk in the near term.

1995—After a string of good to outstanding vintages (1988–94), things were bound to change. Overall, 1995 is a poor vintage for Oregon, with only a handful of excellent to outstanding Pinot Noirs. Rain, rot, and poor winemaking were the culprits.

1994—Along with 1999, this is Oregon's best vintage of the 1990s and one of its very best ever. Low yields (the results of poor weather during the flowering season) and a warm summer resulted in the most concentrated and fruit-packed Oregon Pinot Noirs in memory. In fact, as with all great vintages, 1994 was such a wonderful year for Pinot Noir that even some under-achieving estates crafted fine wines. Recent tastings indicate that the 1994 Pinot Noirs are quite ageworthy; the finest have the fruit and tannic structure to last another 3–5 years. However, this is an irregular vintage for Pinot Gris and Chardonnay, with quality ranging from excellent to mediocre depending on the harvest date.

1993—A cool summer followed by warm weather in September and October resulted in a vintage that appears to have surpassed 1992. The top Pinot Noirs reveal voluptuous textures, fragrant personalities, and a suppleness and richness that suggest this may be a break-through vintage for Oregon Pinot Noir. Limited quantities from the finest producers will make the top wines hard to find.

1992—This could have been the finest vintage for Oregon Pinot Noirs in decades. The weather was almost too hot and dry, though beneficial rains arrived toward the end of the growing season and alleviated the considerable stress in many of the hillside vineyards. Unfortunately, too many producers, worried about low acidity, used a heavy hand when adding acidity, resulting in many wines with incongruous personalities—very ripe flavors and tart, lean-textured personalities. Nevertheless, some terrific Pinot Noirs and big, dramatic, ostentatious Chardonnays have emerged. The Chardonnays must be drunk up, but the finest Pinot Noirs are at their peak of maturity.

1991—This is a very good, potentially excellent vintage of wines that does not have the power or drama of the 1992s or the intensity of the 1990s. Nevertheless, rain at the end of the harvest caught those growers who had excessive crop yields and were waiting for further maturity. For that reason, this is a tricky vintage to handicap, but certainly the Pinot Noirs look richly fruity, although softer and less structured than the 1992s and less tannic than the 1990s. It has good potential for high-quality wine, both red and white.

1990—A top vintage where yields were kept to a minimum. 1990 had plenty of heat and adequate rain, and the harvest occurred under ideal conditions. In fact, if it were not for 1992, this would be the best Oregon vintage in several decades. From the top producers, the Pinot Noirs are rich and full. If there is a disappointment, it is that many of the Pinot Gris wines lack concentration because yields were too high.

1989—A good vintage for Pinot Noir, Chardonnay, and Pinot Gris, the 1989s should have been drunk by 2000. The wines may not have had the intensity of the 1990s, but they were generally rich, soft, elegant wines. In many respects it was a more typical, classic vintage for Oregon's best producers than 1990 or 1992.

1988—The first of an amazing succession of good years for Oregon wines. Fine weather, an abundant crop, and a trouble-free harvest resulted in a number of excellent Pinot Noirs and Chardonnays.

1987—An excessively hot year resulted in most growers' harvesting too soon because they were afraid of losing acidity in their grapes. However, the stress of the summer's heat caused many vineyards not to reach physiological maturity. As a consequence, many 1987s were lean, too acidic, and disappointing. Six years after the vintage the best wines still had a hard edge; all should have been consumed by 1995. If only the growers had waited!

OLDER VINTAGES

As a general rule, most Oregon Pinot Noirs must be consumed within 7–8 years of the vintage. There are always a few exceptions, as anyone who has tasted the 1975 Eyrie or 1975 Knudsen Erath Pinot Noirs can attest. But in general, aging Oregon Pinot Noir for longer than 7–8 years (10–12 for the absolute finest) is a dangerous gamble.

Oregon's white wines should be drunk within several years of the vintage, even though they tend to have better natural acidity than their California counterparts. Yields are frequently too high, and the extract levels questionable, so whether it is Pinot Gris, Chardonnay, or dry Riesling, if you are not drinking these wines within 3–4 years of the vintage you are more likely to be disappointed than pleasantly surprised.

Note: Robert M. Parker, Jr., has a one-third interest in an Oregon vineyard that was commercially bonded in 1992 and began selling wine in 1993. Because of an obvious conflict of interest, this wine has not been reviewed.

RATING OREGON'S BEST PRODUCERS OF PINOT NOIR

Where a producer has been assigned a range of stars (***/****), the lower rating has been used for placement in this hierarchy.

* * * * *(OUTSTANDING)

Ken Wright Cellars

* * * * (EXCELLENT)

Archery Summit   Panther Creek Cellars
Bethel Heights   Penner-Ash Wine Cellars****/*****
Brick House   St. Innocent****/*****
Cristom****/*****   Domaine Serene****/*****
Hamacher****/*****

* * * (GOOD)

Adelsheim***/****   Elk Cove Cellars
Argyle***/****   Evesham Wood
Brooks   Lemelson
Cameron***/****   Rex Hill***/****
Chehalem***/****   Shea Wine Cellars
J. Christopher   WillaKenzie Estate***/****
Domaine Drouhin***/****

* * (AVERAGE)

ADEA**/***   Granville
Abacela**/***   Griffin Creek
Amity   Hauer of the Dauen
Château Benoit   Henry Estate Winery
Benton Lane   High Pass Winery
La Bête**/***   Hinman Vineyards/Sylvan Ridge
Château Bianca   King Estate
Bridgeview   Lion Valley**/***
Broadley**/***   Medici Vineyards**/***
Callahan Ridge   Montinore Vineyards
Carabella   Oak Knoll**/***
Cooper Mountain Vineyards   Ponzi**/***
Domaine Coteau   Andrew Rich**/***
Duck Pond Cellars   Sokol Blosser**/***
Dundee Springs   Starr
Edgefield   Torii Mor
Erath Vineyards**/***   Tualatin Estate Vineyards**/***
Eugene Wine Cellars   Willamette Valley Vineyards
Firesteed   Winter's Hill
Flynn Vineyards   Witness Tree
Foris**/***   Yamhill Valley Vineyards**/***
Girardet Cellars**/***   Youngberg Hill Vineyards
Golden Valley Vineyards

ADEA

1998 Pinot Noir	D	88
1998 Pinot Noir Reserve	D	89

ADEA, formerly known as Fisher Family Vineyards (renamed to avoid confusion with California's Fisher Winery), was named after the four members of the Fisher family—Anne,
Dean, Erica, and Adam. While the 1999 Pinot Noir appeared too rustic and hard to be recommended, both of this winery's 1998s merit consumer attention. The 1998 Pinot Noir is
medium to dark ruby-colored and exhibits dark fruit aromas. It is a medium-bodied wine
with intense blackberry and cassis-like flavors. This sweet, juicy, fruit-filled wine has some

of this vintage's characteristic firmness yet delivers oodles of fruit in its well-structured character. Anticipated maturity: now–2007.

The slightly darker-colored 1998 Pinot Noir Reserve (100 cases produced) has sweet blackberry aromas. It is medium- to full-bodied, concentrated, and highly expressive. Copious quantities of assorted black fruits can be found in this wine's velvety-textured personality, as well as throughout its long, impressive finish. It should be drunk between 2004–2010.

ADELSHEIM

1999	Chardonnay Stoller Vineyard Clone 76	D	89
1999	Chardonnay Stoller Vineyard Clone 96	D	89
1999	Pinot Gris	B	88
1999	Pinot Noir Bryan Creek Vineyard	D	90+
1999	Pinot Noir Elizabeth's Reserve	D	90+
1999	Pinot Noir Goldschmidt Vineyard	D	90

David Adelsheim is justifiably excited about the work being done by his new wine-maker, Bill Musgnung, and the 1999s are the finest Adelsheim wines I have tasted.

The 1999 Pinot Noir Goldschmidt Vineyard (owned by wine enthusiast Neal Goldschmidt, a former governor of Oregon and President Jimmy Carter's secretary of transportation) is an outstanding ruby-colored wine. Bottled unfined and unfiltered, it exhibits spice and black cherry aromas. On the palate, it is medium- to full-bodied, oily-textured, and crammed with wild cherries, black raspberries, and blueberries. This is an opulent, intense, sweet wine with a lush, pure, extensive finish. Anticipated maturity: 2004–2010. The medium to dark ruby 1999 Pinot Noir Bryan Creek Vineyard offers dark cherry aromas and an oily, glycerin-packed character. It is juicy, hugely ripe, yet well structured. Loads of sweet red and black fruits can be found throughout its personality and its long, supple finish. Drink it between 2004–2010. The dark fruit-scented 1999 Pinot Noir Elizabeth's Reserve offers roasted dark fruit aromas. It is medium- to full-bodied, juicy, fresh, and loaded with black and Bing cherries. This satin-textured wine is highly structured and will require cellaring, yet its personality is dominated by its dense, sweet fruit. Anticipated maturity: 2004–2012.

The fresh, honeysuckle-scented 1999 Pinot Gris has a fat, medium-bodied character. Marzipan, spices, and poached white peaches can be found throughout its highly expressive personality as well as throughout its long finish. It is another excellent value. Drink it over the next 2 years. The pear- and spice-scented 1999 Chardonnay Stoller Vineyard Clone 76 has a medium- to full-bodied, expansive, and rich personality. Its pear and clove flavors coat the palate. It is an excellent wine with exquisite balance, purity, and length. The 1999 Chardonnay Stoller Vineyard Clone 96 has less spice than the previous wine in its aromas, yet boasts loads of pear and apple scents. Medium- to full-bodied and oily-textured, it is broad, rich, imbued with glycerin and loads of fat. This is a more detailed and elegant wine than the Clone 76, yet remains its qualitative equivalent. Both these wines should be at their best if consumed over the next 4–5 years.

ARCHERY SUMMIT

1999	Pinot Noir Archery Summit Estate	EE	94
1998	Pinot Noir Archery Summit Estate	EE	92+
1999	Pinot Noir Arcus Estate	E	90+
1998	Pinot Noir Arcus Estate	E	91
1999	Pinot Noir Louise Vineyard	E	89
1999	Pinot Noir Premiere Cuvée	D	87+
1998	Pinot Noir Premiere Cuvée	D	88
1999	Pinot Noir Red Hills Estate	E	93

1998 Pinot Noir Red Hills Estate	E	88+
1999 Pinot Noir Renegade Ridge Estate	E	90+
2000 Vireton	D	88

The expressive aromatics of the medium to dark ruby-colored 1998 Premiere Cuvée Pinot Noir reveal chocolate-infused, plummy black cherries. This firm, medium-bodied wine's flavor profile is composed of roasted black fruits, cocoa, and hints of cinnamon. At least 2 years of cellaring will be required to soften this offering's tannic backbone and finish. Anticipated maturity: 2003–2008. Produced from yields of .77 tons per acre, the medium to dark ruby-colored 1998 Arcus Estate Pinot Noir displays mouthwatering potpourri, red cherry, sweet plum, and spice aromas. This full-bodied, red fruit–packed wine is intense, immensely flavorful, and exceptionally long in the finish. Concentrated layers of cherries, raspberries, touches of strawberries, and hints of blueberries are found in this gorgeously structured yet opulent Pinot Noir. Anticipated maturity: now–2010.

Blackberries and spices can be found in the aromatics of the 1998 Pinot Noir Red Hills Estate. This firm, tight, and tangy medium- to full-bodied wine offers layers of red currants and blackberries. Somewhat foursquare and in need of cellaring, this wine should ultimately deserve an excellent to outstanding rating. Anticipated maturity: 2003–2010. One of Oregon's first "century" wines ($100 a bottle or more) the 1998 Archery Summit Estate is medium to dark ruby-colored and exhibits blackberry, dark cherry, and vanilla-infused oak scents. Medium- to full-bodied, firm, concentrated, and strict, this highly structured, strawberry and black fruit–packed wine is a masculine, intense, and powerful offering. Though at present closed and foursquare, its formidable layers of fruit, outstanding depth, and highly present yet ripe tannins promise a long, successful life. Anticipated maturity: 2005–2012+.

Gary Andrus, the owner and head wine-maker of Archery Summit, describes 1999 as "a vintage of high ripeness. It is more classical Burgundian with persistent fruit depth than what we've seen before or since." He went on to add that it never rained in the late season, and that his vines enjoyed a very long hang time, 120–131 days. "We had a long hang time in 2000 as well," said Andrus, "yet those wines appear to be more tannic than 1997, 1998, or 1999."

Three thousand cases were produced of the 2000 Vireton. Made from a blend of 80% Pinot Gris, 12% Chardonnay, and 8% Pinot Blanc, it boasts white and yellow fruit aromas with an appealing floral element. Medium-bodied and packed with flavors reminiscent of tangy red currants, orange zests, and juicy pears, this is a well-focused, expansive wine. Its silky-textured character leads to a white peach and apricot-flavored finish. It is a delicious wine, loaded with well-ripened fruit. Drink this highly expressive offering over the next 2 years.

The medium to dark ruby-colored 1999 Pinot Noir Louise Vineyard was harvested at two tons per acre. It has a gorgeous nose of sweet black cherries and violets. On the palate, this medium-bodied wine is opulent, with loads of lush black cherries, blackberries, and roses. It is broad yet elegant and harmonious. Anticipated maturity: 2004–2010. Produced entirely from Dijon clones, the medium to dark ruby-colored 1999 Pinot Noir Renegade Ridge Estate has a wild cherry, earth, and Asian spice–scented nose. Loads of juicy, satiny, dark cherry fruits can be found in this seamless, silky-textured offering. It boasts a concentrated, dense nugget of fruit that envelops its superbly ripened tannin. Anticipated maturity: 2004–2011.

The medium to dark ruby-colored 1999 Pinot Noir Arcus Estate (842 cases produced) has a gorgeously pure nose of red cherries, blackberries, and violets. This intense, medium-bodied wine is crammed with cassis, black cherries, blackberries, loads of spices, and dark raspberries. Its attack and mid-palate are focused, juicy, and highly expressive. Its finish is foursquare, yet it possesses the requisite fruit to dominate its tannin. Anticipated maturity: 2005–2012. The outstanding 1999 Pinot Noir Red Hills Estate is medium to dark ruby-colored and has boisterous wild berry and fresh herb aromas. Medium- to full-bodied and hugely concentrated, this elegant wine combines power with harmony, refinement with muscle. It is juicy, deep, and has loads of powerful blackberry and cassis flavors. Drink this marvelous Pinot between 2005–2015. Only 2,604 bottles of the magnificent medium to dark ruby-colored 1999 Pinot Noir Archery Summit Estate were produced. Its spice, rose, and black cherry–scented nose leads to a full-bodied, hugely concentrated personality. This expansive, cherry, chocolate, plum, and licorice-flavored wine is opulent, possesses loads of depth, and yet remains refined, fresh, and exceedingly well balanced. Its sweet, lush fruit carries through its admirably long, impressive finish. Anticipated maturity: 2006–2017.

ARGYLE

1999	Chardonnay Reserve	C	89
1989	Extended Tirage Brut	D	89
1999	Pinot Noir Clubhouse	D	90+
1999	Pinot Noir Nuthouse	D	89
1999	Pinot Noir Reserve	D	88
1999	Pinot Noir Spirithouse	D	90
1999	Riesling Dry Reserve	B	88
1998	Riesling Dry Reserve	B	88

The 1989 Extended Tirage Brut has been recently disgorged. Grilled toast and anise aromas lead to a rich, complex, graham cracker, toast, yeast, and mineral-flavored personality. It is complex, has excellent to outstanding concentration, and a satiny texture rendered lively with present yet unobtrusive bubbles. Drink it over the next 2–3 years.

The 1999 Chardonnay Reserve has a white flower and toasted oak–scented nose. Medium-bodied and possessing excellent focus, it is a delineated spice, honeysuckle, and anise-flavored wine whose flavors last throughout its pure, extensive finish. Anticipated maturity: now–2006. Produced from vines planted in 1975, the 1998 Riesling Dry Reserve has a hugely expressive, Germanic nose of minerals and flowers. Medium-bodied and well focused, it is a boisterous, sweet herbal tea, candied lemon, stone, and white fruit–flavored wine. This excellent Riesling should be consumed over the next 4–5 years. In comparison, the 1999 Riesling Dry Reserve has a demure, somewhat muted nose of stones and earth. However, on the palate, it is rich, opulent, beautifully delineated, and highly expressive. Candied limes, minerals, and spices can be found in this wine's intense personality as well as throughout its long finish. Anticipated maturity: now–2005. These are both excellent values.

Toasted oak and loads of cherries and black raspberries can be found in the aromatics of the 1999 Pinot Noir Reserve. Medium-bodied and extremely spicy, it is packed with Bing cherries and candied raspberries. This is a broad, juicy, fresh wine that possesses a long, pure, tannin-filled (yet ripe) finish. Drink it between 2004–2009. The toasted oak and black fruit–scented 1999 Pinot Noir Nuthouse is medium to dark ruby-colored. Satin-textured and rich, this plump, sweet, candied wine is exceptionally light and loaded with blackberries and cherries. It is pure, well balanced, and long in the finish. Anticipated maturity: 2004–2010.

The medium to dark ruby-colored 1999 Pinot Noir Spirithouse has demure blackberry aromas. On the palate, this medium- to full-bodied, rich, highly concentrated wine is bright, exceedingly well focused, and loaded with layers of cassis, black cherries, and raspberries. It is an outstanding wine, dominated by its luscious fruit and possessing the requisite structure and balance for aging. Anticipated maturity: 2004–2011. The similarly colored 1999 Pinot Noir Clubhouse (only 120 cases produced) has Asian spice and fruitcake aromas. It is a rich, plump, intensely concentrated wine crammed with black cherries, blackberries, red currants, and strawberries. Medium- to full-bodied, delineated, and pure, it is a seamless, fruit-filled wine with an impressively long, fresh finish. Anticipated maturity: 2005–2011.

BETHEL HEIGHTS

1997	Chardonnay Reserve	C	88
1998	Pinot Noir Estate Grown	D	89

1999 Pinot Noir Flat Block Reserve	D	89
1998 Pinot Noir Lewman Vineyard	D	88
1999 Pinot Noir Nysa Vineyard	D	88
1998 Pinot Noir Nysa Vineyard	D	89
1999 Pinot Noir Southeast Block Reserve	D	92+
1998 Pinot Noir Southeast Block Reserve	D	89
1999 Pinot Noir Wädenswil Block Reserve	D	88
1998 Pinot Noir Wädenswil Block Reserve	D	89

Butterscotch and creamed anise aromas are found in the nose of the 1997 Chardonnay Reserve. This silky, flavorful, delicious wine is packed with mouthwatering creamed hazelnut and toasty, sweet oak spices. Extremely well crafted and harmonious, this wine also possesses a long, supple, fruit-filled finish. Drink it over the next 3–4 years.

As with many 1998 Oregon Pinot Noirs, those produced by Bethel Heights evolve and soften considerably after contact with air. The 1998 Pinot Noir Estate Grown offers a nose of red cherries and dark berries. Loads of tangy currants can be discerned in its medium-bodied character. This firm yet silky-textured wine will require patience in order for it to blossom. Anticipated maturity: 2003–2009+.

The medium-bodied and ruby-colored 1998 Pinot Noir Lewman Vineyard offers metallic red fruit aromas. This well-made, spicy berry and black cherry–flavored offering is intense, masculine, and in need of 3–4 years of cellaring. Anticipated maturity: 2004–2009.

The medium to dark ruby-colored 1998 Pinot Noir Nysa Vineyard reveals aromas reminiscent of mocha, strawberries, blackberries, and hints of oak. Medium- to full-bodied and chewy-textured, it is packed with cherries and dark raspberries, whose flavors linger throughout its firm yet focused and expressive finish. Anticipated maturity: now–2008.

The similarly colored 1998 Southeast Block Reserve benefited enormously from air. At first it was firm, foursquare, and hard, yet in time revealed tangy red cherry aromas and a medium-bodied, raspberry and assorted red fruit–packed character. Readers with patience will admire this wine's considerable density and structure. Anticipated maturity: 2004–2010.

The medium to dark ruby-colored 1998 Pinot Noir Wädenswil Block Reserve displays blackberry and blueberry aromas. It is broad, ample, and filled with sweet dark fruits whose flavors persist throughout its delightfully long finish. Anticipated maturity: 2003–2009.

The ruby-colored 1999 Pinot Noir Nysa Vineyard has toasted oak and blackberry aromas. On the palate, this wine shows excellent breadth to its blackberry and dark cherry flavors. It is juicy, medium-bodied, firm, and well made. Anticipated maturity: 2003–2009. The slightly darker-colored 1999 Pinot Noir Wädenswil Block Reserve has dark berry and currant aromas. Medium-bodied and filled with plummy blackberries and cherries, this is a well-balanced, lively, expressive, yet firm wine. Its finish is admirably long and reveals loads of ripe tannin. Drink it between 2004–2009.

The medium to dark ruby-colored 1999 Pinot Noir Flat Block Reserve has blackberry and dark cherry aromas. It is juicy, expansive on the palate, and medium-bodied. This mouth-coating blackberry- and brambleberry-flavored wine is masculine, muscular, and possesses a long, pure finish. Anticipated maturity: 2004–2010. The medium to dark ruby-colored 1999 Pinot Noir Southeast Block Reserve is the finest wine I have tasted from this excellent winery. Spicy dark fruits can be discerned in its aromatics. On the palate it is broad, ample, and hugely expansive. Copious quantities of red and black cherries are intermingled with candied raspberries and currants in this dense, satin-textured, and deep wine. Its exceptionally long finish reveals loads of prodigiously ripe tannin. Anticipated maturity: 2005–2014.

BRICK HOUSE

1999 Chardonnay	D	89
1998 Chardonnay Cuvée du Tonnelier	D	88

1999 Gamay Noir	C	90
1998 Gamay Noir	C	88
1999 Pinot Noir Cinquante	D	88
1998 Pinot Noir Cuvée du Tonnelier	D	91+
1997 Pinot Noir Cuvée du Tonnelier	D	88+
1999 Pinot Noir Les Dijonnais	D	89+
1998 Pinot Noir Les Dijonnais	D	90

Proprietor Doug Tunnell's 1997 Pinot Noir Cuvée du Tonnelier is a beauty. Asian spices, violets, and red berries are found in its enthralling aromatics. Medium- to full-bodied, beautifully ripe, and luscious, its character is packed with sweet red and black fruits amid hints of licorice. Like most of Oregon's 1997 Pinot Noirs, this wine's finish reveals copious tannin. However, unlike the majority of its brethren, this offering appears to have the requisite depth of fruit to offset them. Anticipated maturity: now–2006. The anise, gingerbread, and orange rind–scented 1998 Chardonnay Cuvée du Tonnelier has medium body and an oily texture. This broad, well-made wine reveals orange blossom and white fruit flavors. It is lovely, full of character, and flavorful. Drink it over the next 1–2 years.

Tunnell crafted a marvelous, medium to dark ruby-colored 1998 Gamay Noir. Aromatically, it reveals leather, black fruit, and white pepper scents. On the palate, this medium-bodied, velvety-textured wine is packed with juicy blackberries, cracked black pepper, and touches of freshly laid asphalt. This fruit-forward wine should be drunk over the next 2 years. The medium to dark ruby-colored 1998 Pinot Noir Les Dijonnais gets its name from the fact that it is produced entirely from Dijon clones of Pinot Noir. Sweet black cherries, cola, and assorted dark fruits are found in this offering's aromatics. Medium- to full-bodied, well structured, and expressive, it exhibits candied red fruits, cookie dough, and hints of clay in its complex flavor profile. It should be consumed over the next 5–6 years. The slightly darker-colored 1998 Pinot Noir Cuvée du Tonnelier was produced from the Pommard clone of Pinot Noir. Fresh black cherry and pit fruit aromatics lead to a cassis, blueberry, grape, and blackberry-flavored character. Medium- to full-bodied, dense, satiny-textured, and backward, this impressive, long-finishing wine will require cellaring. Anticipated maturity: 2003–2010.

As with all of owner Doug Tunnell's estate-made wines, the 1999 Chardonnay is from organically grown grapes. Its highly expressive aromas reveal loads of spices with anise and an underlying hint of almond paste. Medium-bodied, fresh, and softly textured, this well-delineated wine has flavors reminiscent of a spicy fruitcake, candied apples, and poached pears. It is a juicy, tangy wine for drinking over the next 4 years.

Brick House's 1999 Gamay Noir may be the finest example of this varietal I have tasted from the United States. Harvested on October 19 (as Doug Tunnell said, "We almost forgot it") at 25.2 Brix, or 14.2% natural potential alcohol, this is a medium to dark ruby-colored wine with intense black pepper, spice, and dark berry aromas. Medium- to full-bodied and boasting a fabulously oily texture, this sweet blackberry, jammy, cherry, cassis, and spice-flavored wine is supple, juicy, and intense. Its flavors last throughout its juniper berry, clove, and cracked pepper–laced finish. Drink this outstanding wine over the next 5 years.

The ruby-colored 1999 Pinot Noir Cinquante ("fifty" in French, a reference to the 50% whole clusters used in making this wine) has dark, spicy fruit aromas. It is a firm, blackberry, currant, and fresh herb–flavored, medium-bodied wine, slightly fatter and plumper than the Cuvée du Tonnelier. Anticipated maturity: 2004–2010. The medium to dark ruby-colored 1999 Pinot Noir Les Dijonnais (produced entirely from Dijon clones) has a coffee, caramel, and blackberry-scented nose. Medium-bodied, juicy, and packed with dark fruit flavors, this is an intense, concentrated, and well-extracted wine. The fruit dominates its firm structure, yet it will require patience. Anticipated maturity: 2005–2011.

CAMERON

1997 Chardonnay Reserve Abbey Ridge	D	88
1999 Pinot Noir Abbey Ridge	D	(90–92)
1999 Pinot Noir Clos Electrique	D	(89–91)

The 1997 Chardonnay Reserve Abbey Ridge displays a rich anise- and toast-scented nose. This medium- to full-bodied, thick, oily-textured wine is crammed with spices, touches of vanilla, and jammy white fruits in its full-throttle, plump character. Hints of lemons and baking spices come up in its long, buttery finish. Drink it over the next 4 years.

The medium to dark ruby-colored 1999 Pinot Noir Abbey Ridge (from 25-year-old vines) has boisterous black raspberry, dark cherry, and Asian spice aromas. It is a pure, extremely elegant, medium-bodied wine loaded with cherries, coffee, raspberries, and candied strawberries. This charming, satin-textured wine is complex, intense, yet harmonious and seamless. This exceedingly well made wine will be at its best consumed between 2003–2010.

The 1999 Pinot Noir Clos Electrique is medium to dark ruby-colored and boasts pure dark cherry aromas. Produced from 17-year-old vines, this is a medium-bodied, chewy-textured wine with loads of candied cherries, juicy blackberries, and dark raspberries in its character. It has excellent to outstanding depth, a juicy, lively personality, and hints of rusticity in its flavorful finish. If John Paul is able to civilize this wine prior to bottling, it will certainly merit an outstanding rating.

CHEHALEM

1999 Chardonnay Ian's Reserve	D	89
1998 Chardonnay Ian's Reserve	D	89
1997 Chardonnay Ian's Reserve	D	88
2000 Pinot Gris Reserve	C	89
1998 Pinot Noir 3 Vineyard	D	88
1999 Pinot Noir Ridgecrest Vineyard	D	92+
1999 Pinot Noir Rion Reserve	D	93+
1997 Pinot Noir Stoller Vineyards	D	89
2000 Riesling Dry Reserve	C	88
1999 Riesling Reserve Coral Creek Vineyards	C	88

The 1997 Chardonnay Ian's Reserve displays sweet yellow plum and hints of apricots in its aromas. Medium-bodied, oily-textured, and impressively ripe, this thick, extroverted wine is packed with golden fruit and oak spice flavors. It is certainly one of the finest Chardonnays that has been crafted in Oregon. Anticipated maturity: now–2005.

The admirable 1997 Pinot Noir Stoller Vineyards displays cinnamon-laced, dark cherry aromas. Its silky smooth texture leads to a gorgeously ripe character crammed with blackberries and black cherries. Medium- to full-bodied, sweet, and structured, this wine may be one of the rare Oregon 1997 Pinots to improve with time. Drink it over the next 5 years.

The 1998 Pinot Noir 3 Vineyard is medium to dark ruby-colored and offers delightful aromatics of black cherries, flowers, and dark raspberries. Medium-bodied and redolent, with loads of dark fruits, this tight yet silky-textured wine is intense and full-flavored. Anticipated maturity: now–2008. Certainly one of the finest Oregon Chardonnays I have tasted to date, Chehalem's 1998 Ian's Reserve offers aromas of tropical fruits, loads of spices, and hints of vanilla. This plump yet well-balanced, medium-bodied wine is broad, pure, and has excellent amplitude. Superripe pears and apples can be found in its harmonious, well-crafted character. Drink it over the next 3–4 years.

The flower and Earl Grey tea–scented 1999 Riesling Reserve Coral Creek Vineyards is a highly expressive, concentrated, tangy, focused wine. Spices, minerals, and assorted white fruits can be found in its flavorful and persistent personality. Drink it over the next 3–4 years.

The 2000 Riesling Dry Reserve has intense sweet herbal tea aromas. On the palate, this rich, plump, medium-bodied wine has lovely depth to its boisterous white fruit, mineral, and tea-like flavors. It is highly expressive, well balanced, and a delight. Drink it over the next 4–5 years. The 2000 Pinot Gris Reserve bursts from the glass with white peaches, poached pears, and hints of smoke. On the palate it is fresh, pure, rich, and crammed with white and yellow peach flavors. It is a broad, highly expressive wine for drinking over the next 3 years.

Chehalem's Chardonnay Ian's Reserve is one of Oregon's finest Chardonnays. The 1999 exhibits rich white fruit aromas intermingled with intense spices in its aromatic profile. Medium-bodied, fat, and buttery, it offers layers of superripe pears, white peaches, and candied apples in its intense, lush character. Anticipated maturity: now–2005.

The outstanding 1999 Pinot Noir Ridgecrest Vineyard bursts from the glass with sweet blackberry aromas. This medium-bodied, gorgeously concentrated wine explodes on the palate with dramatically intense sweet cherries, raspberries, strawberries, and candied currants, and sports ripened tannin. It is harmonious, seamless, extremely extroverted, and completely dominated by its lush fruit. Anticipated maturity: 2004–2012. The black cherry, rose, and blackberry-scented 1999 Pinot Noir Rion Reserve is produced from a barrel selection of the Ridgecrest Vineyard. Medium- to full-bodied and layered, with candied berries, compotes of cherries, and jammy strawberries, it is a broad, big, muscular wine with an elegant character and an impressively long, supple, fruit-filled finish. Anticipated maturity: 2005–2012.

J. CHRISTOPHER

1999 Pinot Noir Charlie's Vineyard		D	88

The ruby-colored 1999 Pinot Noir Charlie's Vineyard has blackberry and fresh herb aromas. Medium-bodied and tangy, this wine is filled with sweet red and black cherries as well as cassis and blackberry-like flavors. It has a long yet firmly structured finish. Anticipated maturity: 2003–2008.

CRISTOM

1998 Chardonnay Celilo Vineyard		C	89
1999 Pinot Noir Jessie Vineyard		D	91
1999 Pinot Noir Louise Vineyard		D	90+
1999 Pinot Noir Marjorie Vineyard		D	94
1998 Pinot Noir Marjorie Vineyard		D	92
1999 Pinot Noir Mount Jefferson Cuvée		C	88
1999 Pinot Noir Reserve		D	91
1998 Pinot Noir Reserve		D	89+
1998 Pinot Noir Signature Cuvée		EE	93

Cristom's ability to weave elegance into its fruit-dominated wines has made it one of my favorite estates in Oregon. Owned by Paul Gerrie, this winery's vineyards are the responsibility of Paul Feltz, and its winemaking is in the hands of Steve Doerner.

The white peach, lees, toast, and butter-scented 1998 Chardonnay Celilo Vineyard is another highly successful effort from the Cristom Winery. From the finest *terroir* for this varietal in the Northwest, it exhibits the richness of a Meursault and the beautifully elegant balance of a Puligny-Montrachet. This exuberant, tangy, white fruit, vanilla, and spice-flavored wine is velvety-textured and delightfully rendered. Drink it over the next 4 years.

The medium to dark ruby-colored 1998 Pinot Noir Reserve offers toasted oak and blackberry aromas. Juicy black cherries, cookie dough, and raspberries can be found in its harmonious, well-balanced, and focused personality. This exceptionally long-finishing wine is elegant and medium- to full-bodied. Anticipated maturity: 2003–2008. The similarly colored 1998 Pinot Noir Marjorie Vineyard exhibits roasted fruit and grilled oak aromas. This medium- to full-bodied, concentrated, fat, yet precisely defined and expressive wine is crammed with juicy black cherries. While it has a boisterous personality, it also possesses an outstanding structure, complexity, and a long, detailed finish. Anticipated maturity: now–2010.

Cristom is one of the first two Oregon wineries (Archery Summit is the other) to release $100-a-bottle wines. The medium to dark ruby-colored 1998 Pinot Noir Signature Cuvée (the label bears the signatures of Doerner, Feltz, and Gerrie) reveals delicate cherry and raspberry aromas. On the palate, this medium- to full-bodied wine offers superbly intense red and black fruit, chocolate, roasted cherry and blackberry, as well as fresh black raspberry and spiced flavors. It is well structured, complex, powerful, and elegant. This outstanding offering should be at its best between 2003–2012.

As wine-maker Doerner said, "1999 was a fantastic year, but it will require some cellaring. It is a vintage that can be characterized by its exquisite balance due to extremely high levels of ripeness yet excellent levels of acidity that we retained because the evenings were cool." The medium to dark ruby-colored 1999 Pinot Noir Mount Jefferson Cuvée has expressive black cherry aromas. This is a juicy, medium-bodied wine with loads of lush, sweet, red black cherry cherry fruit flavors. Its supple finish is loaded with exceptionally ripe and round tannin. Drink it between 2003–2009. The similarly colored 1999 Pinot Noir Reserve has a nose of black cherries, cloves, and juniper berries. This wine has outstanding depth to its medium-bodied character. Copious quantities of assorted dark fruit, mostly cherries, are intermingled with spices in its structured core. It will require 5 years of cellaring and last at least through 2013.

The 1999 Pinot Noir Jessie Vineyard is this parcel's third crop. Medium to dark ruby-colored, it has an immensely appealing nose of plums, talcum powder, perfume, roses, and violets. Velvety-textured and seamless, this medium- to full-bodied wine is packed with lush cherries, blackberries, spices, and cloves. Its exceptionally long finish displays beautifully ripened tannin. Anticipated maturity: 2005–2010. The similarly colored 1999 Pinot Noir Louise Vineyard has a brooding, black fruit–scented nose. Medium- to full-bodied, foursquare, and tight, it reluctantly reveals juicy blackberry and currant flavors. This exceedingly youthful wine has outstanding levels of fruit plus loads of ripe tannin. Anticipated maturity: 2006–2014.

The star of the show is Cristom's 1999 Pinot Noir Marjorie Vineyard. Medium to dark ruby-colored and boasting a floral, candied black cherry and spice-scented nose, this is an opulent, silky-textured wine. Its sultry yet complex personality exhibits huge amounts of candied fruits and loads of juicy cherries, as well as a myriad of spices whose flavors linger throughout its admirably long and pure finish. Anticipated maturity: 2005–2014.

DOMAINE DROUHIN

1999 Pinot Noir Laurène	D	89+

The 1999 Pinot Noir Laurène displays spices, cherries, and raspberries in its aromatic profile. It is a structured, tightly wound wine that is concentrated and juicy. Black/red cherries and brambleberries are intermingled with currants and Asian spices in its lively yet foursquare personality. This wine may ultimately merit an outstanding score if it fleshes out with bottle aging. Anticipated maturity: 2005–2011.

ELK COVE

1999 Pinot Noir La Bohème	D	91+
1999 Pinot Noir Estate Reserve	E	90?
1999 Pinot Noir Roosevelt	D	90+
1999 Pinot Noir Windhill	D	88

Elk Cove's winemaking team attributes the success of their 1999 Pinot Noirs to the long hang time in 1999. Harvested at 1.8 tons per acre and produced from 25-year-old vines, the 1999

Pinot Noir Windhill is medium to dark ruby-colored and has gorgeous red cherry aromas. This is a medium-bodied, opulent, juicy wine with attractive black cherry fruit ensconced in a well-structured character. Its texture is soft in the attack and on the mid-palate and leads to a somewhat firm finish that should melt away with 2–3 years of cellaring. Anticipated maturity: 2004–2009. The 1999 Pinot Noir La Bohème is slightly darker-colored and was produced from 16-year-old vines. Plumlike aromas lead to a medium to full-bodied, satin-textured personality. This is a sultry wine crammed with loads of blueberries, blackberries, and cherries. Well focused, concentrated, pure, and admirably long in the finish, this is an outstanding, fruit-packed Pinot for drinking between 2005–2010.

Only 360 cases of the 1999 Pinot Noir Roosevelt were produced. This dark ruby-colored wine has blackberry, cassis, and fresh herb aromas. Loads of dark fruits, licorice, and black currants can be found in its dense, highly structured character. It is intense, powerful, and highly expressive. Anticipated maturity: 2005–2011. One hundred cases of the dark ruby-colored, chocolate, licorice, and black fruit–scented 1999 Pinot Noir Estate Reserve were produced. Medium- to full-bodied, concentrated, backward, and muscular, this is a chewy, tight, dense, and intense wine. It has copious quantities of firm tannin that at present offset its admirable fruit. Only time will tell whether this wine will merit an outstanding rating or remain dominated by its tannin. Anticipated maturity: 2005–2012?

EVESHAM WOOD

1998 Chardonnay Mahonia Vineyard	B	88
1999 Pinot Noir Cuvée J	D	90
1999 Pinot Noir Seven Springs Vineyard	D	89+
1999 Pinot Noir Shea Vineyard	D	89

The 1998 Chardonnay Mahonia Vineyard Unfiltered has a floral nose that also reveals hints of talcum powder and citrus fruits. On the palate this medium-bodied and elegant wine is softly textured, focused, and well balanced. Crisp pears, spices, anise, and loads of minerals can be found in its personality and throughout its impressively fresh finish. Drink this excellent value over the next 4 years.

The ruby-colored 1999 Shea Vineyard Pinot Noir Unfiltered has an appealing spice and sweet cherry–scented nose. Medium-bodied and packed with soft candied cherries, this is a sweet, pure, raspberry, strawberry, and assorted red fruit–flavored wine. It is velvety-textured, has excellent depth, and a long, subtle finish. Drink it between 2003–2009.

The 1999 Seven Springs Vineyard Unfiltered Pinot Noir is medium to dark ruby-colored and has an immensely appealing violet as well as red/black cherry–scented nose. At present it is tight but reveals excellent levels of fruit in its medium-bodied character. This wine has excellent depth, a gorgeously detailed personality, and the potential to ultimately merit an outstanding score. Drink it between 2004–2009. Forty percent of the 1999 Cuvée J Pinot Noir Unfiltered comes from the Temperance Hill Vineyard, 5% from Seven Springs, and 55% from the estate's Le Puits Sec Vineyard. It is medium to dark ruby-colored and has a spicy, black cherry–scented nose. This wine has excellent to outstanding breadth of red and black cherries as well as a distinct new oak signature to its character. It has excellent balance, loads of fruit, and a medium- to full-bodied personality. It is lively, fresh, and has a firm finish that will require 5 years of cellaring and should hold through 2014.

HAMACHER

1999 Chardonnay Cuvée Forêts Diverses	D	89
1998 Chardonnay Cuvée Forêts Diverses	D	89+
1999 Pinot Noir	D	93
1998 Pinot Noir	D	92

1997 Pinot Noir	D	89+
1999 Pinot Noir Mantia	D	90+

The medium to dark ruby-colored 1997 Pinot Noir is one of the vintage's success stories. Gorgeous ripeness can be discerned in its chocolate milk and cherry syrup–scented nose. Blackberries, cherries, and strawberries coat the palate in this thick, medium- to full-bodied, supple-textured wine. Expressive yet well structured, it may very well improve with time. Anticipated maturity: now–2005.

Eric Hamacher, the owner and wine-maker of Hamacher Winery, is one of Oregon's finest makers of white wine. The 1998 Chardonnay Cuvée Forêts Diverses (produced in 100% Taransaud barrels, 50% of which are new, from a blend of different forests) has butterscotch, spice, and anise aromas. Medium-bodied and creamy-textured, this mouthcoating wine expands on the palate with loads of candied lemon, spice, and poached pear flavors. It is seamless, harmonious, and lively. Additionally, its expressive flavors last throughout its pure, fresh, and long finish. Anticipated maturity: now–2005. The 1999 Chardonnay Cuvée Forêts Diverses has a hugely rich nose of anise, almonds, and spices. Medium- to full-bodied, it is fat, plump, and loaded with poached pear and marzipan flavors. At present its oak is in the forefront, but this should be remedied with a few months of bottle age, as its luxuriously textured character displays excellent concentration of fruit. Anticipated maturity: now–2006.

Dick Ponzi, one of Oregon's winemaking pioneers, is Eric Hamacher's father-in-law. He said, "Eric loves Pinots with delicacy and makes absolutely gorgeous ones." Claude Dugat, when served Hamacher's 1999, said, *"la texture et la pureté de fruit de ce vin sont splendides."* ("The texture and purity of fruit in this wine are splendid"). They are both right.

The 1998 Pinot Noir is an outstanding wine. It exhibits a medium to dark ruby color and cedar, tobacco, and dark fruit aromas. Medium-bodied and gorgeously expansive, this is a satin-textured wine crammed with dark fruits, black cherries, and loads of spices. Hints of chocolate can be discerned in its fruit-dominated yet well-focused and refined personality. It has the firmness characteristic of the 1998 vintage yet possesses the density of fruit to cope with it. Anticipated maturity: 2004–2010.

Hamacher's ruby-colored 1999 Pinot Noir will not win any contests for power or extract, but once again (both his 1997 and 1998 are stars of their respective vintages) it demonstrates that this young wine-maker has grasped two of the hallmarks of Pinot: 1) this varietal can achieve exceptional purity, and 2) its texture is paramount. Hamacher himself stated, "Pinot Noir *must* have great texture, or else it is nothing." This wine exhibits a nose of extraordinary purity, redolent with fresh red cherries, raspberries, and currants. It is sumptuously textured, bringing to mind liquid silk, and coats the mouth with highly detailed sweet red fruit whose flavors linger throughout its admirably long finish. This wine's tannin is well ripened and barely noticeable. If Hamacher can build more depth and concentration into his wines without losing their sublime purity and texture, he will produce some of the most compelling Pinots on earth. Drink this wine over the next 10 years. The medium to dark ruby-colored 1999 Pinot Noir Mantia, named after this vineyard's owner, Joe Mantia, reveals jammy blackberry and licorice aromas. This is a medium- to full-bodied, concentrated, muscular, meaty wine with loads of power and chewy layers of dark fruits. This is a Cabernet lover's Pinot, built for the long haul. Anticipated maturity: 2005–2012.

LEMELSON

1999 Pinot Noir Jerome Reserve	D	90+
1999 Pinot Noir Stermer Vineyard	D	89
1999 Pinot Noir Thea's Selection	D	88

This brand-new winery has already planted 82 acres of vines and plans to have 110 acres planted by next year. Named after owner Eric Lemelson's mother, the 1999 Pinot Noir Thea's Selection is a medium to dark ruby-colored wine with appealing red fruit aromas. This opulent, medium-bodied, velvety-textured wine offers lush cookie dough, candied red fruit, and cherry syrup–like flavors. It is soft, highly expressive, and what it may lack in complexity, it makes up for with loads of delightful fruit flavors. Drink it over the next 4 years.

The 1999 Pinot Noir Stermer Vineyard is dark ruby-colored and has timid, sweet red fruit aromas. On the palate, this medium-bodied wine is firm yet expansive, coating the mouth with blackberry and fresh herb flavors. Its tannin, at first somewhat firm, softens with aeration, promising a good future. Anticipated maturity: 2004–2010. The similarly colored 1999 Pinot Noir Jerome Reserve has mouthwatering licorice and jammy blackberry aromas. Medium-bodied and chewy-textured, this is an intense, muscular wine with dense layers of black fruits, dark cherries, and Asian spices whose flavors last throughout its impressive finish. Anticipated maturity: 2005–2012.

PANTHER CREEK CELLARS

1998 Pinot Noir Bednarik Vineyard	D	91
1999 Pinot Noir Freedom Hill Vineyard	D	91
1998 Pinot Noir Freedom Hill Vineyard	D	92
1999 Pinot Noir Nysa Vineyard	D	91
1998 Pinot Noir Nysa Vineyard	D	88+
1999 Pinot Noir Red Hills Estate Vineyard	E	91
1999 Pinot Noir Reserve	D	93
1998 Pinot Noir Reserve	D	90+
1999 Pinot Noir Shea Vineyard	D	89
1998 Pinot Noir Shea Vineyard	D	89+

The medium to dark ruby-colored 1998 Pinot Noir Shea Vineyard has fresh, sweet, and candied red/black cherry aromas. Tangy currants, juicy berries, stones, and hints of oak can be found in this medium-bodied, well-made, structured offering. It will certainly merit an outstanding score if it is able to integrate its oak and soften with cellaring. Anticipated maturity: now–2007. The firm, medium to dark ruby-colored 1998 Pinot Noir Nysa Vineyard displays dark berry, spice, cookie dough, and red currant aromas. This tight, tangy fruit-flavored wine may develop to earn an excellent, possibly outstanding score. Anticipated maturity: 2003–2008.

The medium to dark ruby-colored 1998 Pinot Noir Bednarik Vineyard has highly expressive pumpkin pie spice and sweet cherry aromas. It is medium- to full-bodied, round, plump, luscious, and sexy, yet has outstanding structure. Lovely cherry, cinnamon, and juniper berry flavors can be discerned in its harmonious, medium- to full-bodied personality. Drink it over the next 8–9 years. The opulent 1998 Pinot Noir Reserve has a gorgeous spice and red fruit–scented nose. This medium-bodied, broad, decadent wine has highly expressive red cherry and pit fruit flavors. It is delicate yet powerful, detailed yet dense. This wine's long and focused finish reveals supple, ripe tannins. Anticipated maturity: now–2010. The explosive dark cherry aromatics of the medium to dark ruby-colored 1998 Pinot Noir Freedom Hill Vineyard lead to a medium- to full-bodied, velvety-textured, and lush personality. This decadent, chewy, and broad wine bursts on the palate with copious quantities of red cherries. It is well balanced, intensely flavored, and harmonious. Anticipated maturity: 2003–2010+.

The medium to dark ruby-colored 1999 Pinot Noir Shea Vineyard has boisterous black fruit aromas. Medium- to full-bodied and deep, this wine is crammed with highly expressive blackberry, black cherry, and cassis flavors. It is beautifully rendered and harmonious. Drink it over the next 7–8 years. The similarly colored 1999 Pinot Noir Nysa Vineyard bursts from the glass with loads of spices, blackberries, and hints of mint. Medium- to full-bodied, big, broad, and supple-textured, this is a prodigiously ripe elderberry, spice, and jammy black raspberry–flavored wine. It is harmonious and possesses a long, fruit-packed, smooth finish. Drink it between 2003–2010.

I had a love affair with the nose of the 1999 Pinot Noir Red Hills Estate Vineyard. This medium to dark ruby-colored wine bursts from the glass with a myriad of spices, flowers, sweet tea, and red cherries. Medium-bodied and intricate, this black cherry–dominated wine is soft, supple, gorgeously balanced, and elegant. Its lush layers of fruit envelop the palate and last throughout its impressively long finish. Anticipated maturity: 2004–2010.

The medium to dark ruby-colored 1999 Pinot Noir Freedom Hill Vineyard has rose, black-berry, and Asian spice aromas. Medium- to full-bodied, muscular, and highly structured, it is packed with road tar, black cherries, and sweet cassis-like flavors. This is a firm, fruit-dominated wine that will require cellaring. Anticipated maturity: 2005–2011. The 1999 Pinot Noir Reserve is my favorite of Panther Creek's recent releases. It has a mouthwatering nose of violets, perfume, potpourri, and cherries. On the palate, this elegant wine is medium-bodied, expansive, and packed with cherries, raspberries, strawberries, and hints of freshly cracked pepper. It is pure, harmonious, has no hard edges, and possesses a long, sweet, fruit-filled finish. Drink this gorgeous Pinot between 2004–2010.

PENNER-ASH WINE CELLARS

1999 Pinot Noir	D	93
1998 Pinot Noir	D	91

The 1998 Pinot Noir is the inaugural wine from Lynn Penner-Ash's (Rex Hill's wine-maker's) winery. It has a medium to dark ruby color and delightful black raspberry, plum, and black cherry aromas. This sweet, voluptuously textured, medium- to full-bodied wine is packed with gorgeously ripe red cherries and touches of strawberry jam. Well structured, bal-anced, and focused, it is a concentrated, powerful, yet elegant wine. Anticipated maturity: 2003–2008+. The 1999 Pinot Noir has a magnificent nose of cookie dough and cherry syrup. Medium- to full-bodied and broad, it is rich, intense, wonderfully concentrated, and highly expressive. Loads of sweet red and black fruits coat the palate and linger for 30–40 seconds. It is a seamless, harmonious wine with gorgeous balance and purity. Anticipated maturity: 2004–2012.

PHANTOM HILL

1998 Pinot Noir Revelation Cuvée	D	88

Located in Idaho, this winery produces Pinot Noir from grapes purchased in Oregon. The medium to dark ruby-colored 1998 Pinot Noir Revelation Cuvée offers black fruit aromas and a forward, medium-bodied character. Plump black raspberries and plums can be found in this wine's flavor profile. It has a somewhat tight finish that will require a year or two of cel-laring. Anticipated maturity: now–2006.

REX HILL

1999 Pinot Gris Reserve	C	89
1999 Pinot Noir Croft Vineyard	E	88
1999 Pinot Noir Jacob-Hart Vineyard	E	91
1998 Pinot Noir Jacob-Hart Vineyard	E	90+
1999 Pinot Noir Maresh Vineyard	E	90
1999 Pinot Noir Reserve	D	89+
1998 Pinot Noir Reserve	D	89
1999 Pinot Noir Seven Springs Vineyard	E	93
1999 Pinot Noir Weber Vineyard	E	89

The medium to dark ruby-colored 1998 Pinot Noir Reserve reveals intense cherry aromas. This potentially outstanding wine has a concentrated, medium- to full-bodied personality. It is velvety-textured and displays loads of dark fruits in its firm and backward flavor profile. Anticipated maturity: 2003–2008. The 1998 Pinot Noir Jacob-Hart Vineyard is aromatically unyielding. This medium to dark ruby-colored wine is, like the previous offering, backward and ungenerous at present, yet it exhibits all of the qualities required for an outstanding rating. Copious quantities of black cherries, blackberries, cola, spices, and hints of mocha can be found in this intensely flavored effort. Firmly structured and somewhat foursquare, it will require cellaring, but should blossom into a powerful, extroverted, and flavorful Pinot. Drink it between 2003–2008+. The darker-colored 1999 Pinot Noir Weber Vineyard has violet, rose, and dark fruit aromas. Medium-bodied, broad, and immensely appealing, it is filled with spices, candied blackberries, and dark cherries. This satin-textured wine should be consumed over the next 5–6 years.

The medium to dark ruby-colored 1999 Pinot Noir Croft Vineyard has an exuberant nose of potpourri, black raspberries, and toasted oak. Medium-bodied and expansive, it is sweet, lush, pure, and loaded with red/black cherries. Some warmth can be discerned in the finish of this otherwise harmonious wine. Drink it over the next 5–6 years.

Loads of spices and black cherries can be discerned in the aromatics of the 1999 Pinot Noir Reserve. Medium-bodied and boasting a fabulously oily texture, this wine is crammed with Asian spices and candied cherries. It is boisterous, opulent, and loaded with fruit. Drink this well-balanced, highly expressive wine over the next 7–8 years.

The beguiling aromatics of the medium to dark ruby-colored 1999 Pinot Noir Jacob-Hart Vineyard reveal dark cherry and hints of chocolate. Medium-bodied and soft, this is a sweet, velvety-textured wine. Its personality is big, broad, and plush. It has a sexy, velvety mouth-feel and loads of candied red fruits whose flavors last throughout its exceedingly long and pure finish. Anticipated maturity: 2003–2011.

Dark spices, cherries, and toast can be discerned in the aromatics of the ruby-colored 1999 Pinot Noir Maresh Vineyard. Medium-bodied, well structured, and spicy, this is a large, muscular wine loaded with sweet blackberry-like flavors. It possesses more tannin than the previous wines, yet they are ripe and supple. Anticipated maturity: 2005–2011.

The outstanding, medium to dark ruby-colored 1999 Pinot Noir Seven Springs Vineyard has intricately detailed violet, blackberry, and cherry aromas. It coats the palate with loads of candied red and black fruits as well as floral flavors. It is gorgeously delineated, powerful, detailed, and exceptionally long. This magnificent wine combines elegance with muscle and subtlety with extravagance. Anticipated maturity: 2004–2012.

The 1999 Pinot Gris Reserve has spicy, smoky, white peach aromas. Medium-bodied and expansive, it is a rich, flavorful wine filled with white peaches, apricots, poached pears, and stones. It is extremely well balanced and has a long, supple, flavor-packed finish. Kudos to Rex Hill's wine-maker, Lynn Penner-Ash, for her gorgeous lineup of 1999s.

ROCKBLOCK CELLARS

1999 Syrah Seven Hills Vineyard	D	89

This winery is owned by Ken and Grace Evenstad, who also own Domaine Serene, and was created to market their non-Burgundian varietal wines. The 1999 Syrah Seven Hills Vineyard (most of this vineyard is located in Oregon, even though it was made famous by Washington State wineries, particularly Leonetti) has sweet blackberry, jammy black raspberry, and Syrah's distinctive sweat aromas. Medium- to full-bodied and loaded with candied blackberries, black cherries, and elderberries, this lush, extremely well made wine also has a touch of fresh herbs that come out in its long, sweet, and supple finish. This highly expressive wine should be consumed over the next four years.

ST. INNOCENT

1999 Chardonnay Seven Springs Vineyard Dijon Clone	C	90
1998 Chardonnay Seven Springs Vineyard Dijon Clone	C	88
1999 Pinot Gris Shea Vineyard Vendange Tardive	C/375ml	89

1999 Pinot Noir Brick House Vineyard	D	89+
1996 Pinot Noir Brick House Vineyard	D	89+
1999 Pinot Noir Freedom Hill Vineyard	D	91
1998 Pinot Noir Freedom Hill Vineyard	C	90+
1996 Pinot Noir Freedom Hill Vineyard	D	90
1998 Pinot Noir O'Connor Vineyard	C	91
1996 Pinot Noir O'Connor Vineyard	D	88
1999 Pinot Noir Seven Springs Vineyard	D	93+
1998 Pinot Noir Seven Springs Vineyard	D	94
1999 Pinot Noir Shea Vineyard	D	92

None of St. Innocent's 1997 Pinot Noirs tasted for this report could be recommended, yet this estate is responsible for some of Oregon's finest 1996s. The 1996 Pinot Noir O'Connor Vineyard is ruby-colored and reveals red and black cherry aromas. It is harmonious, beautifully pure, and offers kirsch and blackberry flavors in its well-crafted, medium-bodied character. Its finish displays ripe, supple tannins. Anticipated maturity: now–2006. Similarly colored, the 1996 Pinot Noir Brick House Vineyard offers sweet, creamy red fruit aromatics. Medium- to full-bodied, satin-textured, and powerful, this is a luxurious, cherry-dominated wine. Highly detailed, yet plump and flavorful, it also possesses a long, supple, sweet finish. Anticipated maturity: now–2007.

The 1996 Pinot Noir Freedom Hill Vineyard is medium to dark ruby-colored and reveals black currant and Asian spice aromas. The most powerful of St. Innocent's 1996s, this wine's personality is dense, medium- to full-bodied, chewy-textured, and structured. Road tar, black cherries, and cassis can be found in its intense flavor profile. It is certainly one of the stars of its vintage. Anticipated maturity: now–2006.

As at most of Oregon's quality estates that wish to produce Chardonnay, St. Innocent has adopted the use of Dijon clones, which are earlier-ripening than other clones (in the past, all Oregon Chardonnays were produced from clones originally engineered for California's hot, dry climate). Vlossak's eggnog, spice, and creamy anise–scented 1998 Chardonnay Seven Springs Vineyard Dijon Clone is extremely rich and mouthcoating. Butterscotch, loads of spices, and superripe pears can be found in this medium- to full-bodied, highly expressive wine. Drink it over the next 2–3 years.

While many of Oregon's best-known estates appear to be in a horse race to see who will have the state's most expensive Pinot Noirs, St. Innocent has maintained an intelligent, honorable, and consumer-friendly policy of pricing. The 1998 Pinot Noir O'Connor Vineyard (this is the last vintage St. Innocent will produce from this site) is medium to dark ruby-colored and offers hugely expressive and sweet black cherry and raspberry aromas. This velvety-textured, voluptuous, and supple wine is packed with multitudes of dark fruits, hints of spices, and exhibits first-rate, supple, ripe tannins in its extensive finish. Anticipated maturity: now–2009. In a manner typical of Pinot Noirs from the Freedom Hill Vineyard, St. Innocent's 1998 offers a boisterous, red fruit–packed nose. This big, dense, chewy-textured, medium- to full-bodied wine is well structured and crammed with red and black cherries. While presently firm, this wine has copious quantities of fruit as well as well-ripened tannins. Anticipated maturity: 2004–2010+.

Vlossak believes his 1998 Pinot Noir Seven Springs Vineyard is the finest wine he has fashioned to date (readers should remember he was responsible for making Panther Creek's stellar 1994 Freedom Hill Pinot). I agree. Possessing a nose reminiscent of a Romanée-St.-Vivant, this wine expresses complex aromas of perfume, flowers, red berries, and spices. Medium- to full-bodied, satin-textured, and lush, it possesses great focus, refinement, and complexity. Silky layers of cherries, raspberries, and strawberries can be found in this intricate and exceptionally long-finishing wine. Anticipated maturity: now–2010+. Wow!

Aged in 44% new-oak barrels, the white flower, stone, and pear-scented 1999 Chardonnay

Seven Springs Vineyard Dijon Clone has outstanding focus and delineation to its medium-bodied, broad, and crystalline personality. This pure candied lemon, pear, spice, and mineral-flavored wine is juicy, complex, and expressive. Drink it over the next 5–6 years.

Harvested at 1.6 tons per acre, the 1999 Pinot Gris Shea Vineyard Vendange Tardive has mineral, spice, candied berry, and sweet tea aromas. This rich, opulent, dense, and palate-coating wine was aged 80% in tank and 20% in oak barrels. It boasts white peach and hazel-nut flavors in its deep, medium-bodied personality. Unlike most Oregon whites, this one will require cellaring to fully express itself. Anticipated maturity: 2004–2010.

Save for a strange offering from the Temperance Hill Vineyard, Mark Vlossak has pro-duced a stupendous set of 1999 Oregon Pinot Noirs. He should also be commended for keep-ing his prices reasonable. Am I the only consumer who is shocked that there are many inferior Oregon wines at two or three times the cost of these? The 1999 Pinot Noir Shea Vine-yard is medium to dark ruby-colored and displays a darker fruit as well as a more noticeable structure than is generally associated with this vineyard. It bursts from the glass with loads of blackberries, black cherries, and brambleberries. This is a medium- to full-bodied wine with a gorgeously sappy character, copious quantities of fruitcake, blackberry syrup, dark cherry flavors, and a marvelously long finish. Its tannin is ripe yet present, giving it the backbone that many wines from this vineyard have lacked. Anticipated maturity: 2004–2012.

Produced from fruit acquired from Doug Tunnell's organic vineyard, the medium to dark ruby-colored 1999 Pinot Noir Brick House Vineyard offers massive quantities of spices and violets intermingled with grilled oak in its aromatics. Medium- to full-bodied and possessing outstanding depth, this wine's black fruit is dominated by clovelike flavors. It is firm, yet should soften and ameliorate with cellaring. Anticipated maturity: 2004–2010.

The slightly darker-colored 1999 Pinot Noir Freedom Hill Vineyard is a hugely endowed wine. It bursts from the glass with loads of cherries, red flowers, and sweet, earthy spices (Vlossak compares this last scent to clay). On the palate, it reveals powerful boysenberry, blackberry, and cassis fruit flavors in a more delineated and civilized style than is generally found from wines from this vineyard. It has outstanding focus, copious amounts of ripe tan-nin, and an impressively long finish. Drink it between 2005–2012.

I am enthralled with the aromatics of Vlossak's Pinots from the Seven Springs Vineyard. A magnum of the 1991 served at this year's International Pinot Noir Celebration was super. A bottle of the 1992, which I served a week before to a chef visiting from Paris, was equally lovely. In its youth, this wine reveals hints of its complex aromatics and tends to be tight and backward (the 1998, tasted three months ago, remains an exception). With cellaring, Vlossak's Pinot Noirs from Seven Springs typically blossom into some of Oregon's real stars. Aromatically, the medium to dark ruby-colored 1999 displays wildflowers, berries, cinna-mon, and a myriad of spices. It is rich, juicy, and extremely elegant. Loads of candied red fruits, mostly raspberries and cherries, are found in this ample, structured wine. It is fresh, bright, and beautifully concentrated, and has a long, toasted oak and cherry-flavored finish. Anticipated maturity: 2005–2014.

DOMAINE SERENE

1999 Chardonnay Côte Sud Vineyard Dijon Clones	D	88
1999 Pinot Noir Grace Vineyard	E	90
1998 Pinot Noir Grace Vineyard	E	91+
1998 Pinot Noir Guadalupe Vineyard	E	91
1998 Pinot Noir Mark Bradford Vineyard	E	89
1997 Pinot Noir Reserve	C	88

As would be expected from one of Oregon's premier wineries, Domaine Serene crafted a lovely 1997 Pinot Noir Reserve. Light to medium ruby-colored, it offers demure, spicy red cherry aromas. Its opulent, satin textured character is plush, medium-bodied, and pleasure-inducing. Layers of red and black cherries, intermingled with rosemary and hints of cinnamon, can be found throughout its flavor profile and long, oily finish. Drink it between now–2003.

The luscious 1998 Pinot Noir Grace Vineyard is medium ruby-colored and reveals deep sweet cherry and roasted spice aromas. Medium- to full-bodied, opulent, and hedonistically sweet, this red cherry and candied strawberry–flavored wine is sure to be a crowd pleaser. There are no hard edges or angles in this sexy, pleasure-giving wine. Its finish is long, suave, and silky. Drink it over the next 5 years. The medium to dark ruby-colored 1998 Pinot Noir Mark Bradford Vineyard has loads of blackberry and cassis in its aromatic profile. Medium-bodied and concentrated, this wine has excellent depth to its juicy, blackberry-packed personality. It is backward, tight, and has its vintage's characteristically tough tannin, yet it is an excellent wine, with outstanding density of fruit. Anticipated maturity: 2004–2009. Regrettably, only 100 cases of the dark ruby-colored 1998 Pinot Noir Guadalupe Vineyard were produced. Its gorgeous aromas of blackberries, black cherries, and hints of chocolate lead to a plump, rich, medium- to full-bodied personality. This broad, intense, satin-textured wine possesses copious quantities of assorted dark fruits and Asian spices in its seductive personality. Its impressively long finish reveals ripe tannin. Anticipated maturity: 2004–2010.

Produced from 10-year-old vines, the 1999 Chardonnay Côte Sud Vineyard Dijon Clones has beguiling spice, vanilla, and floral scents. It is silky-textured, expansive, and medium-bodied. This well-focused wine has good to excellent depth of toasty, floral, mineral, and white fruit flavors. It is loaded with white peaches, butter, and hints of hazelnuts. Drink it over the next 2–3 years. The black cherry and fresh herb–scented 1999 Pinot Noir Grace Vineyard has an opulent, lush, medium- to full-bodied character. This feminine, silky-textured, seamless wine is loaded with soft, sweet cherries, raspberries, and strawberries, and has outstanding focus, depth of fruit, and harmony. Anticipated maturity: 2004–2012.

SHEA WINE CELLARS

1999 Pinot Noir Shea Vineyard	D	88

The ruby-colored 1999 Pinot Noir Shea Vineyard has an appealing, if demure, dark cherry and black raspberry–scented nose. Medium- to full-bodied and filled with loads of boisterous red and black cherry fruits, this is a well-made, flavorful Pinot. It displays excellent ripeness, a sound structure, and a long, baked dark fruit–filled finish. Drink it over the next 6 years.

TUALATIN ESTATE VINEYARDS

2000 Semi-Sparkling Muscat	B	89

The 2000 Semi-Sparkling Muscat is a clone of an Italian Moscato d'Asti. Its boisterous orange blossom and raspberry aromas lead to a fresh, zesty, medium-bodied personality. This velvety-textured wine has tangy orange, red berry, and floral flavors in its character. Like the Italian Moscatos, it has low alcohol (6.5%) and an off-dry sweetness. It should be drunk over the next 6–8 months as an apéritif or as I like to drink this style of wine, while watching the first football games of the season on warm Sundays. This is an excellent value that should be consumed soon.

WILLAKENZIE ESTATE

1999 Pinot Noir	C	88
1999 Pinot Noir Aliette	D	91+
1998 Pinot Noir Dijon Clones 777	D	89
1999 Pinot Noir Grande Reserve	E	92
1999 Pinot Noir Pierre Léon	D	89

Regrettably, only 50 cases were produced of the excellent and potentially outstanding medium to dark ruby-colored 1998 Pinot Noir Dijon Clones 777. Candied kumquats and black cherries can be found in its mouthwatering nose. This soft, rich, velvety-textured, medium- to full-bodied wine is packed with plump red and black cherries. Deep, complex, and powerful, this is a firm Pinot to cellar for 2–3 years and drink over the next 7–8 years.

The medium to dark ruby-colored 1999 Pinot Noir has gorgeous blackberry and spice aromas. Dark fruits are intermingled with metallic notes in this medium-bodied, silky-textured wine. Intensely ripe, bordering on overripe, it is supple, soft, and juicy. Anticipated maturity: now–2006. The medium to dark ruby-colored 1999 Pinot Noir Pierre Léon (2,000 cases were produced) bursts from the glass with Asian spices, blackberries, and blueberries. This broad, medium- to full-bodied wine is packed with concentrated layers of black fruits and fresh herbs. It is a masculine, muscular wine with loads of structure, yet remains dominated by its dark fruit flavors. Anticipated maturity: 2004–2010.

The outstanding medium to dark ruby-colored 1999 Pinot Noir Aliette's nose is reminiscent of a compote of red and black cherries intermingled with mocha, thyme, and rosemary. Medium- to full-bodied and expansive, this powerful, concentrated wine is densely packed with blackberries, cassis, black cherries, and a myriad of spices. It is juicy, reveals loads of supple tannin and should do marvelously well with cellaring. Anticipated maturity: 2005–2012. The similarly colored 1999 Pinot Noir Grande Reserve has fresh red and black cherry aromas. Medium- to full-bodied and satin-textured, it is highly concentrated yet elegant. Black cherries, blackberries, and cassis are interspersed with juniper, clove, and cinnamon in this detailed yet boisterous offering. Its flavors last throughout its extensive finish. It is a wine of harmony, power, and seamlessness. Anticipated maturity: 2005–2012.

WILLAMETTE VALLEY VINEYARDS

1998 Pinot Noir Joe Dobbes Signature Cuvée	E	88+

The medium to dark ruby-colored 1998 Pinot Noir Joe Dobbes Signature Cuvée was tasted on three separate occasions, with varying amounts of aeration. It proved to be one of the numerous 1998 Oregon Pinot Noirs that benefited immensely from contact with air. Wildflowers, blackberries, and cherries can be discerned in its aromatics. On the palate, dark fruits, cola, and black raspberries are found in this firm, highly structured, yet densely packed, medium- to full-bodied wine. With proper medium-term cellaring, it should continue to improve and could ultimately merit an outstanding rating. Anticipated maturity: 2003–2008+.

KEN WRIGHT CELLARS

1999 Pinot Noir Abbey Ridge Vineyard	D	90
1998 Pinot Noir Abbey Ridge Vineyard	D	89+
1999 Pinot Noir Canary Hill Vineyard	D	91
1998 Pinot Noir Canary Hill Vineyard	D	92
1997 Pinot Noir Canary Hill Vineyard	D	89
1999 Pinot Noir Carter Vineyard	D	93
1998 Pinot Noir Carter Vineyard	D	90
1997 Pinot Noir Carter Vineyard	D	88+
1999 Pinot Noir Elton Vineyard	D	88
1998 Pinot Noir Elton Vineyard	D	93
1999 Pinot Noir Freedom Hill Vineyard	D	93
1999 Pinot Noir Guadalupe Vineyard	D	92
1998 Pinot Noir Guadalupe Vineyard	D	88+
1997 Pinot Noir Guadalupe Vineyard	D	88+
1999 Pinot Noir McCrone Vineyard	D	92+
1998 Pinot Noir McCrone Vineyard	D	90
1997 Pinot Noir McCrone Vineyard	D	88
1999 Pinot Noir Nysa Vineyard	D	88

1998 Pinot Noir Nysa Vineyard	**D**	**88**
1999 Pinot Noir Shea Vineyard	**D**	**92**
1997 Pinot Noir Shea Vineyard	**D**	**88**
1999 Pinot Noir Wahle Vineyard	**D**	**89+**
1998 Pinot Noir Wahle Vineyard	**D**	**90**

The bright, medium ruby-colored 1997 Canary Hill Vineyard displays spicy blueberry and black raspberry aromas. This smooth, supple, medium-bodied wine coats the palate, bringing to mind the delightful Burgundies of Claude Dugat. This sultry, hedonistic offering may lack complexity, but it is one of the most successful of the 1997s tasted for this report. Drink it over the next 3–4 years. The slightly lighter-colored 1997 McCrone Vineyard offers sweet, spicy, candied berry aromas. Although tight, structured, and tannic, it regales the palate with blackberry and cassis flavors. Medium-bodied and well balanced, this boisterous Pinot should be consumed over the next 2 years, while the fruit still dominates its tannin.

The ruby-colored 1997 Guadalupe Vineyard offers talcum powder–dusted red fruit aromas. Less structured than the McCrone, the Guadalupe is packed with sexy red cherry fruit that lasts throughout its long finish. This wine may ultimately merit a higher score if, with cellaring, its tannin melts away before its fruit. Anticipated maturity: now–2003+.

The light to medium ruby-colored 1997 Shea Vineyard exhibits blackberry and Asian spice aromas. Medium-bodied, firm, and structured, it is neither as sexy nor as opulent as Ken Wright's previous vintages from this vineyard. Readers will enjoy the blackberries and black cherries that are intermingled with new oak in this wine's composite of flavors. Anticipated maturity: now–2003. The ruby-colored 1997 Carter Vineyard displays baby powder, strawberries, and cherry fruit aromas. Medium-bodied, this wine's character is filled with red/black cherries, tangy blood oranges, and hints of tar, as well as spicy oak. Long, with loads of sweet, ripe tannins, Wright's Carter Vineyard has the potential to improve with age. Anticipated maturity: now–2004.

Once again, in 1998, Ken Wright fashioned an impressive lineup of Oregon Pinot Noirs. Two of his 1998s tasted for this report were perplexing (the Freedom Hill and Shea), and I am reserving judgment on those wines. The medium to dark ruby-colored 1998 McCrone Vineyard reveals deep aromas of spices and sweet red cherries. Medium- to full-bodied, supple-textured, and harmonious, this dark cherry–flavored wine exhibits Wright's characteristic fruit-enveloped tannins. It is extroverted, opulent, and possesses a long, sweet, cherry-filled finish. Drink it over the next 6 years. The similarly colored 1998 Guadalupe Vineyard has aromas reminiscent of red cherries and candy corn. This sweet, sexy, medium-bodied wine has loads of superripe dark cherries in its character and a finish clipped by the presence of copious tannin. If its admirable fruit is capable of outliving the tannin, this wine will merit an even more exalted review. Drink it over the next 5–6 years.

Complex spices and dark fruits are found in the aromas of the ruby-colored 1998 Abbey Ridge Vineyard. Medium-bodied and satin-textured, it has lovely palate presence, exhibited by loads of dark fruit flavors that coat the mouth. It is firmly structured and will require patience. Anticipated maturity: 2003–2009. The aromatically demure 1998 Nysa Vineyard offers candied orange, blackberries, and dark pit fruit flavors. This medium-bodied, foursquare wine has a muscular, masculine personality that will demand cellaring. Anticipated maturity: 2003–2008.

The medium to dark ruby-colored 1998 Canary Hill Vineyard reveals lovely perfumed, dark cherry aromas. This expressive, pure, harmonious, expansive wine is medium- to full-bodied, velvety-textured, and seamless. Sweet red cherries, candied raspberries, and assorted spices can be found throughout its boisterous character and long, supple finish. It has outstanding depth and an intensely flavorful character. Drink it over the next 8–10 years. The ruby-colored 1998 Wahle Vineyard has juicy red cherry and popcorn aromas. This ample, voluptuous, medium- to full-bodied wine is sensual, sexy, and oily-textured. While it is unquestionably outstanding, it lacks the Canary Hill exquisite finish. Drink it over the next 7–8 years.

Complex black raspberry, oak, and spice aromas are found in the nose of the medium to dark ruby-colored 1998 Carter Vineyard. This firmly structured wine is medium- to full-bodied, satin-textured, and loaded with blackberries, cassis, and assorted dark pit fruits. It is a firm, concentrated Pinot that should be at its best between 2003–2009. The superb medium to dark ruby-colored 1998 Elton Vineyard reveals sexy aromas of sweet cherries immersed in vanilla-infused oak. It is luscious, sexy, expansive, and opulent. This medium- to full-bodied wine coats the palate with viscous waves of cherries, blackberries, and spices. It is harmonious, seamless, and immensely gratifying. Anticipated maturity: now–2010.

The ruby-colored 1999 Abbey Ridge Vineyard has black cherry and white pepper aromas. It is light- to medium-bodied, sexy, and gorgeously opulent. Silky-textured layers of black cherries and black raspberries are found in its harmonious personality, as well as throughout its extensive finish. This wine bears Ken Wright's trademark suppleness and candied fruit. Drink it over the next 7–8 years. The slightly darker-colored 1999 Nysa Vineyard has demure dark fruit aromas. It is medium-bodied, plump, soft, and satin-textured. Black cherries are found in the attack and mid-palate, and are intermingled with a metallic, almost copperlike flavor in the finish. This is a broad, sweet, lush wine for drinking between 2003–2009.

The ruby-colored 1999 Canary Hill Vineyard has sweet, jammy cherry aromas. On the palate, this medium-bodied wine is seamless, has outstanding focus, and a delightful red/black cherry and violet-flavored core. It is juicy, has no hard edges, and possesses a pure, long, sweet finish. Drink it over the next 8–9 years. The slightly darker-colored 1999 Carter Vineyard has a mouthwatering nose of jammy black cherries and roses. Medium-bodied and boasting dazzling breadth of fruit, this wine penetrates the palate with its crystalline cherry, strawberry, and violet-like flavors. It is a wine of impressive purity, delineation, and harmony. This outstanding wine should be consumed between 2004–2010.

The ruby-colored 1999 Elton Vineyard has blackberry and cassis aromas. Light- to medium-bodied and spicy, it offers loads of clove and dark fruit flavors in its fresh, zesty character. Drink it over the next 6 years. Awesome candied red fruit aromas burst from the glass of the 1999 Shea Vineyard. Medium- to full-bodied and chewy-textured, this wine is packed with cherries, raspberries, blueberries, and blackberries. It is a boisterous, in-your-face Pinot that will deliver considerable flavor. Anticipated maturity: 2004–2011.

The medium to dark ruby-colored 1999 Wahle Vineyard exhibits graphite, toasted oak, and sweet red cherry aromas. Medium-bodied and intense, it is a masculine wine with a firm backbone. Blackberries, cassis, and oak can be found throughout its personality and its admirably long finish. This is a tightly wound wine that will require patience. Anticipated maturity: 2005–2012. The similarly colored 1999 McCrone Vineyard has sweet black fruit and earth aromas. This gorgeous wine has outstanding depth, concentration, and balance. Its pure, fresh, black cherry and raspberry flavors are intermingled with a distinctive mineral quality throughout this wine's character and superb finish. This opulently layered yet zesty wine will be at its best if consumed between 2004–2010.

The Bing cherry–scented, medium to dark ruby-colored 1999 Guadalupe Vineyard displays abundant juicy red berries and cherries in its impressive flavor profile. This highly expressive, fruit-packed wine has loads of sweet red fruits that burst from the glass. It is pure, sweet, candied, and immensely impressive. This wine should be consumed over the next 8–10 years. The medium to dark ruby-colored 1999 Freedom Hill Vineyard has luscious toasty Bing cherry aromas. Medium- to full-bodied and magnificently delineated, this is a chewy black fruit, mocha, and cherry-packed wine. Broad, fresh, focused, and exceedingly long in the finish, it is a Pinot of compelling fruit and refinement. Drink this outstanding wine between 2004–2012.

7. WASHINGTON STATE

The Basics

Washington State is primed to become an increasingly important factor in the fine-wine marketplace. Presently, with the absurdly high prices charged by the top California wineries and Bordeaux châteaux, Washington's finest offerings (often of equal or better quality) are downright cheap in comparison. In fact, the state's largest wineries, such as Château Ste. Michelle, offer a bevy of reasonably priced wines for budget-conscious consumers. If Washington State's finest producers had resisted the temptation to raise their prices, they would have undoubtedly gained significant market share in the past half-dozen years.

Washington State produces some extraordinary wines and many poor ones. There is no doubt that Washington can produce wines as compelling, intense, flavorful, and elegant as any viticultural region in the world. The fact that the majority of the state's wines are average, or simply bad, should not detract consumers' attention from the glories crafted by those producers who are fulfilling Washington's enormous potential.

Washington's wines are not well known outside the Northwest. As a former retailer, I know how rare it was to hear a customer say, "Tonight I would love to have something from Washington with dinner, what do you recommend?" Bearing this in mind, I am offering some information aimed at providing readers with a basic understanding of the region's geography, climate, wine-makers, and growers, as well as the multitude of wine styles.

A GEOGRAPHY PRIMER

Admittedly, I had misconceptions about Washington State prior to traveling there after joining *The Wine Advocate* a half-dozen years ago. I had tasted numerous wines from there and knew that it was the home of Microsoft and numerous other high-tech companies, and that rain was plentiful. My trips have shown me that my middle school geography teachers were not completely daft (mountains do stop rain, and microclimates really do exist). To begin to understand Washington State wines, I believe it is important to know a little about its geography.

Virtually all the wines described here are from the Columbia Valley appellation (which includes the Yakima and Walla Walla valleys). Primarily a desert, it is located in southeastern Washington and overlaps into Oregon. As Pacific Ocean depressions approach the Washington coastline, they are often trapped by the coastal Olympic Mountains, dropping much of their precipitation on the rain forests located on the range's western slopes. When a weather front is powerful enough to remain intact after traversing the Olympic Mountains, it then faces the even higher elevations of the Cascade Mountains. Very few depressions are capable of clearing both these ranges, and as a consequence, eastern Washington experiences desert-like conditions (as a matter of fact, the U.S. Army stages desert training in Yakima).

As I flew from Seattle to Walla Walla on my first tasting trip, I was amazed to see the contrast between the lush green western slopes of the Cascades and the barren eastern side. From the tips of the Cascades all the way to Walla Walla, the only signs of vegetation were the trees bordering rivers and irrigated farms. One statistic dramatizes this weather pattern— within the town of Walla Walla, on the eastern edge of the Columbia Valley appellation, an-nual rainfall increases by one inch per mile as one travels eastward. On the parched western edge of Walla Walla, abutting the l'Ecole No. 41 and Woodward Canyon wineries, are dusty asparagus fields. On the eastern edge, where Walla Walla Vintners and Leonetti's new vine-yards are located, the rolling hills are lush and green.

Rain, the bane of wine producers the world over, is rarely a nuisance for Washington's main grape-growing region. Because Washington State vineyards are irrigated, viticultural-ists can control the quantity of water each row of vines gets.

Readers should not assume that because Washington State borders Canada it has a cold climate. Once spring arrives, the Columbia Valley enjoys a grape-growing season that wine-makers the world over would envy. Sun and heat are plentiful, evenings are cool—excellent for maintaining natural acidity levels.

This is not, however, a viticultural paradise. The winters and early springs can be a grape grower's nightmare. Why? The region is prone, on average once every six years, to "killer freezes" (as they are known in these parts), the last of which descended from the Arctic in late January and early February 1996 and devastated the vineyards. Countless vines were destroyed, their trunks exploding because of the Arctic Express's extreme tem-peratures. Most of the vines that survived produced exceedingly little. Interestingly, Merlot and Sémillon were the most susceptible to the freeze, with Cabernet, Chardonnay, and Rhône varietals faring better. Depending on the varietal, yields in 1996 were down between 25% and 80%.

THE WINE-MAKERS AND GRAPE GROWERS

Unlike those in California, Oregon, Bordeaux, and Burgundy, the majority of Washington State wineries do not own vineyards. With the exception of large producers such as Château Ste. Michelle, Columbia Winery, and some others, wine-makers in this state are dependent upon grapes purchased from growers. For the most part, Washington State's producers are converted home wine-makers. Prior to going into wine full-time, Gary Figgins (Leonetti) was a machinist at the local Walla Walla cannery; Alexander Golitzen (Quilceda Creek) was an engineer for Scott Paper; Chris Camarda (Andrew Will) was a waiter, as was Matthew Loso (Matthews Cellars); and so on. It's the same story—they fell in love with wine, decided to try their hand at it, acquired grapes, and the rest is history.

The grape growers, on the other hand, are farmers. Some are incredibly wealthy, others less so. One grower, whose primary business is producing Washington's famed and delicious Fuji apples, told me that he can earn four times as much money per acre with apple trees than with grapevines. So why the financial sacrifice? I asked. Ego gratification, came the reply. When his apples go to market, they are mixed in with everyone else's. He earns his money by producing the most apples possible per acre, using ingenious systems to ensure that the ap-ples will be evenly colored and unscarred. He has no contact with the people who buy them and laments the fact that there is no market for apples that taste good—only for those that are the most aesthetically pleasing. Growing grapes allows him to compete on a different level. Also, when he drinks wines crafted from his grapes or sees someone order a bottle in a restaurant, he feels he has a strong connection to that wine.

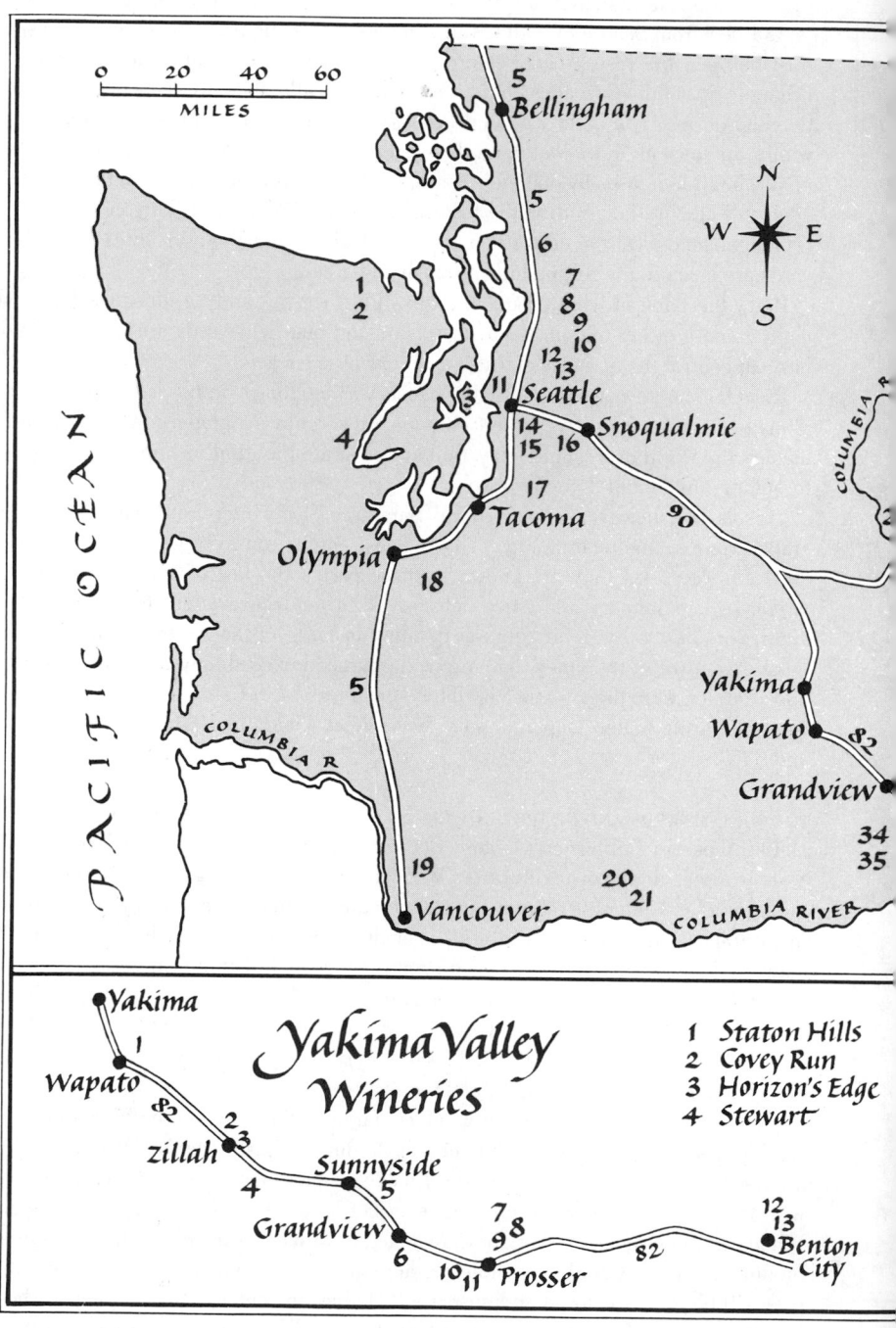

Yakima Valley Wineries

1 Staton Hills
2 Covey Run
3 Horizon's Edge
4 Stewart

Washington

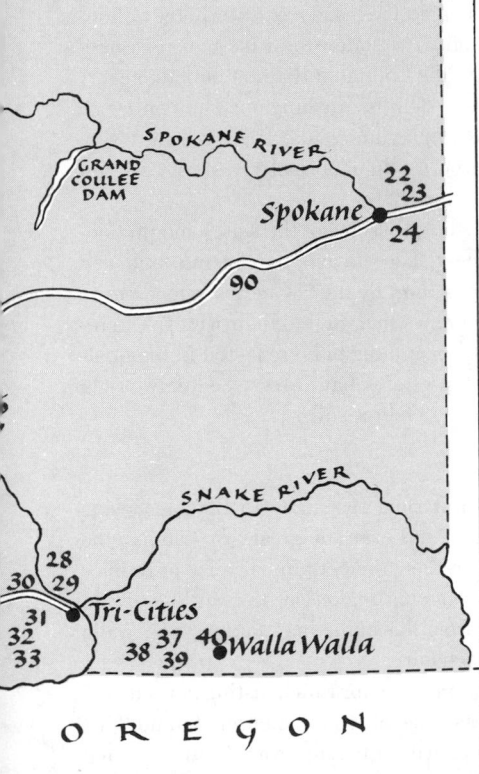

As a wine lover, I respected the answer to my question. His reason for giving up potential earnings leads him to have moderate yields in order to compete qualitatively, and he is immensely respected by wine-makers. Regrettably, however, few growers are as well off as this gentleman and are not prepared to make the same sacrifice. This leads us to one of Washington wine-makers' biggest problems—yields. Farmers are paid by the ton, regardless of the type of crop they grow, and grapes are no different. The more you produce, the more you earn. Numerous wine-makers in Washington fight constant battles with their grape growers (since very few wineries own their own vineyards) to reduce yields, but the incentives are just not there. In California, Burgundy, Oregon, and elsewhere, quality wineries purchase their fruit by the acre, not the ton. The grower, who is paid the same amount whether 2 tons or 10 tons per acre are produced, has a financial incentive to follow the wine-maker's directives. The "killer freezes" that cause severe damage in the Columbia River appellation every six or so years prevent wineries from instituting this system in Washington. They either do not have or do not wish to risk the financial resources. In a vintage like 1996, a winery with this type of arrangement would have had to pay growers their normal rates for very few grapes.

There is, however, a light at the end of the tunnel. Recently some of the state's top producers, including Golitzen, Camarda, Figgins, and others, have begun purchasing land and planting vineyards. They are reinvesting earnings brought in by their wineries' successes to allow them to control the quality and quantity of the grapes that go into their wines. The results from these new, winery-owned vineyards are just beginning to be reflected in the quality of the wines, but it is clear that the state's five top estates have an exceedingly bright future. Now, if we could just get 20 or 30 other wineries to follow suit . . .

WINE STYLES

We all have notions of what a Bordeaux, Burgundy, California, Tuscan, or Piedmontese wine tastes like. Granted, there are exceptions to every rule, and even the greatest palates in the world can easily be tricked in a blind tasting. However, there are certain basic flavor profiles and styles that characterize all of the great wine-producing regions of the world—except Washington State. Having tasted hundreds of wines from the Columbia, Yakima, and Walla Walla Valleys, I was incapable of finding a regional signature.

The vast majority of the wines produced in Washington State (for which tasting notes do *not* appear in the following pages), are disjointed, fruitless, vegetal, and immensely tannic. Furthermore, a large number of Washington wine-makers have yet to learn what California's top 60–75 producers discovered over the past 15 years—excessive acid adjustments make a wine undrinkable! On my trips to Washington I have conducted large tastings as well as numerous estate visits. The group tastings have the enormous benefit of gathering wines from little-known producers, in addition to saving on travel time (Washington's wineries are spread out over hundreds of miles). The number of appallingly acidified wines I've tasted is mind-boggling. More important, they represent out-and-out bad winemaking. Thankfully, the state's leading producers eschew acidification—wine-makers such as Alexander Golitzen (Quilceda Creek), Chris Camarda (Andrew Will), and Gary Figgins (Leonetti) are crafting wines each year that one hopes will serve as a reference point for others in the industry. Though candied, superripe fruit immersed in loads of oak has brought fame and fortune to such wineries as Leonetti, many other producers craft subtle, elegant, and focused wines (DeLille, for example), and still others have achieved an amazing combination of power and finesse (Quilceda Creek) that is reminiscent of Bordeaux at its very best. Their polar opposites—dense, hyperextracted, alcoholic wines—can also be found in Washington.

Washington State as a wine region is still in its infancy, and that's the beauty of it. These converted home wine-makers are defining the future of Washington wines before our eyes—

and palates. There are no traditions and no parameters. Any style is acceptable. Anything goes. It truly is a frontier.

TYPES OF WINE

Virtually all the varietals seen in California are also grown in Washington. However, Washington has added to this mix Lemberger, a fruity red vinifera grape that is capable of being made into a Beaujolais-style, non-oak-aged wine or, more infrequently, into a serious, cellar-worthy wine. A few producers are dabbling with Pinot Noir, and not surprisingly, most have failed. Recently, Rhône Rangers (wines produced from the traditional Rhône varietals) have come into vogue, and a few (particularly those from Glen Fiona and McCrea) show immense promise. However, Washington's wineries are banking on Chardonnay, Cabernet Sauvignon, and especially Merlot to bring them to prominence (Washington is unquestionably one of the three finest regions on earth for Merlot, the other two being Pomerol and Tuscany.) There is also some hope for Sauvignon Blanc and Sémillon. A relatively large percentage of the state's vineyards are planted with Riesling, but this is diminishing as newly planted vineyards rarely include this varietal. Fortunately, Washington's consumers appear to enjoy Riesling, which is usually bargain priced ($8–15), and producers continue to crank it out because it is easy and inexpensive to make—the perfect cash-flow wine. For Riesling aficionados, these wines represent fine values. Washington also produces this country's best Chenin Blancs and Muscats. Their crisp natural acidity, easily obtained due to Washington's northern latitude, makes these wines, finished in an off-dry to slightly sweet style, ideal summer sipping and picnic wines. Sadly, the market for these wines is limited. For better or worse, the state's future rests with the superstar grapes—Cabernet Sauvignon, Merlot, and Chardonnay. The good news is that these are the wines the marketing people claim consumers desire, and Washington State's main rival, California, is pricing itself out of the competition.

RED WINE VARIETALS

Cabernet Sauvignon   This is Washington's most successful grape variety. In capable hands, it renders an almost opaque purple wine. Cabernet Sauvignon usually ripens fully in eastern Washington, resulting in wines with curranty, spicy, plummy, cedary aromas, excellent extract, medium to full body, and good depth and concentration. Overwhelming aromas and flavors of herbs and vegetables are rarely as intrusive in Washington Cabernet Sauvignons as they can be in California.

Merlot   Washington producers are hoping that Merlot will bring the state fame. Some wineries (Leonetti, Andrew Will, Quilceda Creek, and Château Ste. Michelle, for example) are crafting some of the finest Merlots made in the U.S. They have proved that Washington State can compete on the world stage as one of the top three regions for the production of fine wine from this finicky varietal. To no one's surprise, Washington Merlot yields a more supple wine than Cabernet. The acids are lower and the tannins less aggressive. However, due to excessive yields, a number of Merlots continue to exhibit an herbaceous character and frequently lack the depth of flavor and concentration of the state's best Cabernets.

Pinot Noir   Nothing tasted to date remotely resembles what Pinot Noir can achieve in Burgundy or selected California and Oregon vineyards.

Lemberger   Originally grown in Germany, this grape, like Zinfandel, is highly adaptable and can be successfully made in a variety of styles. Only a handful of wineries make Lemberger (vineyard acreage is less than 1% of the total in the state). Sadly, much of the Lemberger produced is dull, hard, and overcropped.

WHITE WINE VARIETALS

Chardonnay   Washington Chardonnay occupies more than 15% of vineyard acreage and can ripen fully while retaining excellent natural acidity. This has caused increasing numbers of producers to barrel-ferment it, and to encourage their Chardonnay to complete malolactic fermentation. Extended lees contact, in vogue in California, is also favored by many Washington producers. A number of wineries have invested heavily in new French oak barrels and are trying to make a wine in the Côte de Beaune style. Others are going after a fruitier style (à la Fetzer's Sundial), and still others are aiming for something in between. In short, there is a wide range of styles, but the potential for making outstanding Washington State Chardonnay exists, although much of it remains unrealized. The state's finest Chardonnays are produced by Château Ste. Michelle and Woodward Canyon.

Chenin Blanc   Washington is capable of making wonderful Chenin Blanc in a slightly sweet style due to the naturally crisp acidity. Yet most wineries seemed surprised that anyone would be interested in tasting this ignored, often maligned varietal. However, at $9 a bottle, Chenin Blanc can be a true delight, especially on a hot summer day.

Gewürztraminer   Fortunately, plantings of this varietal are rapidly decreasing in Washington. It has proven no more successful in Washington than in California.

Sauvignon Blanc   When vinified in Washington, the potentially extroverted, herbal, grassy qualities of this grape are held in check. Many wineries also give the wines some exposure to oak barrels. As in California, most wineries strive for a safe, middle-of-the-road style that too often results in bland, insipid wines. Washington State Sauvignons are, however, priced to sell in the $8–15 range, which makes them attractive to consumers.

Sémillon   This grape has excellent potential in Washington. It yields a wine with plenty of body and richness combined with the lively acidity typically found in Washington grapes.

White (Johannisberg) Riesling   Washington's Rieslings are good but often simple and one-dimensional when compared to the slaty, mineral-scented, aromatic complexity and incredible lightness and zestiness attainable in the best German Rieslings. However, Washington's abundant quantities of Rieslings are practically given away, usually selling for less than $9.

RATING WASHINGTON'S BEST PRODUCERS

Where a producer has been assigned a range of stars (***/****), the lower rating has been used for placement in this hierarchy.

* * * * *(OUTSTANDING)

Andrew Will	Leonetti Cellars
DeLille Cellars	Quilceda Creek

* * * *(EXCELLENT)

Château Ste. Michelle	Northstar****/*****

* * *(GOOD)

Betz***/****	Matthews Cellars
Dunham***/****	McCrea Cellars***/****
l'Ecole No. 41***/****	Reininger***/****
Glen Fiona***/****	Seven Hills
Hedges Cellars	Tamarack
Hightower Cellars	Waterbrook Winery
The Hogue Cellars	Woodward Canyon

* * (AVERAGE)

Apex Cellars**/***

Arbor Crest

Barnard Griffin

Blackwood Canyon

Bookwalter

W. B. Bridgman

Canoe Ridge**/***

Caterina

Columbia Winery**/***

Columbia Crest**/***

Covey Run

Facelli

Gordon Brothers Family Vineyards**/***

Hyatt

Kiona**/***

Latah Creek

Mountain Dome

Patrick M. Paul

Preston

Soos Creek

Stewart

Tagaris

Teft Cellars

Paul Thomas

Tucker

Walla Walla Vintners**/***

Washington Hills

Wilridge Cellars

ANDREW WILL

1999 Cabernet Franc Sheridan	D	90
1999 Cabernet Sauvignon Champoux	D	(93–95+)
1999 Cabernet Sauvignon Ciel du Cheval	D	(92–94)
1998 Cabernet Sauvignon Ciel du Cheval	D	91
1998 Cabernet Sauvignon Klipsun	D	88+
1997 Cabernet Sauvignon Klipsun	D	92
1997 Cabernet Sauvignon Pepper Bridge	D	90+
1997 Cabernet Sauvignon R	D	90+
1996 Cabernet Sauvignon R	D	88+
1998 Cabernet Sauvignon Seven Hills	D	89
1997 Cabernet Sauvignon Seven Hills	D	88
1999 Cabernet Sauvignon Sheridan	D	(90–91)
1999 Merlot Ciel du Cheval	D	90?
1998 Merlot Ciel du Cheval	D	90
1997 Merlot Ciel du Cheval	D	92
1999 Merlot Klipsun	D	88+
1998 Merlot Klipsun	D	91
1997 Merlot Klipsun	D	93
1999 Merlot Pepper Bridge	D	89
1998 Merlot Pepper Bridge	D	91
1997 Merlot Pepper Bridge	D	91
1999 Merlot Seven Hills	D	89+
1998 Merlot Seven Hills	D	89
1997 Merlot Seven Hills	D	89+
1999 Sorella	E	(92–94)
1998 Sorella	E	91+
1997 Sorella	E	92+

Chris Camarda, one of America's finest producers of Merlot, has fashioned an impressive lineup of 1997s. The 1997 Merlot Seven Hills Vineyard is medium to dark ruby-colored and displays an incredibly sweet and spicy, cassis, raspberry, cookie dough, and cherry syrup–scented nose. This beautifully rich, medium-bodied, enticing wine is filled with red cherry and fresh herb flavors. Its slightly warm (alcoholic) finish is long, supple, and sexy. Drink it over the next 5–6 years. The darker-colored 1997 Merlot Pepper Bridge displays candied cherry, cinnamon, and superripe fruit aromas. Complex, oily textured, and structured, this opulent, red and black fruit–crammed wine finishes on loads of firm yet well-ripened tannins. Anticipated maturity: now–2007.

The dark ruby-colored 1997 Merlot Ciel du Cheval exhibits blackberry and candied blood orange aromas. It is explosive, broad, expansive, full-bodied, and intensely ripe. Concentrated layers of jellied red fruits are found in this dense wine and throughout its awesomely long, pure, and soft finish. Anticipated maturity: now–2007+. Camarda's top 1997 Merlot is once again from the Klipsun vineyard (harvested at 3 tons per acre). Its black, saturated color and sweet, jammy, yet fresh red fruit and cookie dough aromas lead to an extravagant, opulent, and elegant character. Coffee ice cream, chocolate-covered cherries, and loads of chewy, intensely ripe red and black fruits are found in this dense, massively intense, full-bodied wine. Its purity of flavors, mind-boggling ripeness, focus, refinement, power, and length impress mightily. Drink it over the next 7–8 years.

Camarda's Cabernet Sauvignons, while not reaching the heights of his Merlots, are certainly some of the finest produced in Washington State. The 1997 Cabernet Sauvignon Seven Hills is medium to dark ruby-colored and reveals oak spice–infused, strawberry aromas. Medium- to full-bodied, it possesses a lovely velvety texture, intense black currant flavors, and a structured, firm character. Anticipated maturity: now–2007. The saturated, medium to dark ruby-colored 1997 Cabernet Sauvignon Pepper Bridge reveals black raspberry and Asian spice aromas. Powerful and medium- to full-bodied, this wine coats the palate with its tarry black fruit flavors. Concentrated, backward, and firm, this wine reveals hints of mint and herbs in its long, tannic finish. Anticipated maturity: now–2008.

The dark ruby-colored 1997 Cabernet Sauvignon Klipsun has candle wax and black fruit aromas. Sweet candied blackberries and cherries are intermingled with vanilla-infused oak flavors in this hugely powerful and concentrated wine. Quite tannic (yet ripe), this muscular, in-your-face Cabernet will require cellaring patience. Anticipated maturity: 2003–2010.

The medium to dark ruby-colored 1996 Cabernet Sauvignon R has ripe Italian tomato and spicy oak aromas. Extracted, firm, tarry black fruits and eucalyptus are found in this tannic, somewhat foursquare Cabernet. If its tannin melts away before its fruit, my score will ultimately appear too conservative. The medium to dark ruby/purple 1997 Cabernet Sauvignon R exhibits blackberry, vanilla, and spice aromatics. Intense, concentrated, and firm, this medium- to full-bodied wine's flavor profile is composed of asphalt, black currants, and notes of toasted oak. It is powerful, muscular, tannic, and firm. Anticipated maturity: now–2008.

The 1997 Sorella (a blend of Cabernet Sauvignon, Cabernet Franc, and Merlot) reveals a saturated medium to dark ruby color. Boisterous aromas of violets and red/blue fruits can be found in this elegant, intense, and harmonious wine's personality. Plums, black currants, chocolate, and spices make up this velvety-textured offering's personality. Camarda's talented hand can be seen in his judicious use of oak; it is present but noticeable only if one searches it out. Anticipated maturity: now–2010+.

The medium to dark ruby-colored 1998 Merlot Ciel du Cheval exhibits sweet Italian tomato and fresh herb aromas, very characteristic of Merlot. This medium- to full-bodied, satin-textured, concentrated, and firmly structured wine will require 2–3 years of cellaring. Anticipated maturity: 2003–2010. The saturated, medium to dark ruby-colored 1998 Merlot Klipsun has overripe dark berry and cherry aromas. On the palate it offers concentrated, powerful layers of beautifully ripened red and black fruits. Velvety-textured and deep, it is muscular, highly concentrated, and well extracted. Anticipated maturity: 2003–2012.

The slightly lighter-colored 1998 Merlot Seven Hills Vineyard reveals rosemary, tomato, and black fruit aromas. This tightly wound, herbal and black fruit–flavored wine is firm, foursquare, and tannic. Anticipated maturity: 2004–2009. The saturated, medium to dark ruby-colored 1998 Merlot Pepper Bridge is full-bodied, thickly textured, and coats the palate with layered black fruit flavors. It is highly extracted, concentrated, and has admirable depth of fruit. This well-structured, powerful, and intense wine should be at its best between 2004–2012.

The dark-colored 1998 Cabernet Sauvignon Ciel du Cheval has a super nose of sweet red fruits, *sur-maturité*-laced blackberries, and copious spices. This medium- to full-bodied wine is crammed with cassis, black cherries, cinnamon, juniper berries, and hints of roasted rosemary. It is powerful, structured, and has a long, ripe tannin-filled finish. Drink it over the next 12–15 years. The medium to dark ruby-colored 1998 Cabernet Sauvignon Seven Hills has a cherry syrup, violet, rose, and perfume-scented nose. Its firm, flavorful character reveals peppery dark berries and tangy black cherries. This well-structured, medium-bodied, ripe wine should be at its peak between now–2008. The medium to dark ruby-colored 1998 Cabernet Sauvignon Klipsun exhibits spicy, sweet cherry aromas. It is medium-bodied, lively, and offers red currants, boysenberries, and brambleberries in its foursquare personality. Anticipated maturity: 2004–2012. The medium to dark ruby-colored 1998 Sorella boasts a sweet, luscious nose of spices, violets, and roses. While it is firmly structured, it is packed with loads of red and black fruits as well as hints of sweet oak spices. This medium- to full-bodied, satin-textured wine should be at its peak between 2004–2015.

The dark ruby-colored 1999 Cabernet Sauvignon Sheridan (it contains 12% Cabernet Franc) bursts from the glass with jammy blackberry, cassis, and Asian spice aromas. It is medium- to full-bodied, silky-textured, and loaded with harmonious layers of blackberries, black cherries, and spices. This seamless, sweet, lush wine is intense, powerful, and harmonious. Anticipated maturity: 2003–2012+. The magnificent dark ruby-colored 1999 Cabernet Sauvignon Champoux contains 20% Cabernet Franc. An extraordinary nose reminiscent of a coulis of cassis leads to a hugely concentrated, broad, candied, medium- to full-bodied personality. It is a satin-textured wine crammed with juicy black fruits whose flavors last 45 seconds or more. An astonishing value given its competition in the $40 range from California, it is exuberant and boisterous, yet deep and refined. A stunning wine loaded with prodigiously ripened tannin. Anticipated maturity: 2004–2015.

Produced entirely from Cabernet Sauvignon, the 1999 Cabernet Sauvignon Ciel du Cheval has a saturated dark ruby color. Its blackberry juice–scented nose leads to a muscular, thick, medium- to full-bodied character. Loads of wild black cherries and blackberries can be found throughout its lively, chewy flavor profile. This superripe, in-your-face Cabernet should be at its best between 2004–2014.

The 1999 Sorella is dark ruby-colored and boasts a floral, black currant, violet-imbued nose. Medium- to full-bodied and refined, it is a wine of gorgeous definition. Silky-textured and crammed with cassis, jammy blackberries, and cherries, this elegant, delineated wine has a magnificently long, pure, flavor-packed finish. Drink it between 2005–2015.

The medium to dark ruby-colored 1999 Cabernet Franc Sheridan reveals violet and sweet red cherry aromas. It is medium-bodied, silky-textured, and loaded with juicy layers of candied red berries, pumpkin, blueberries, and hints of herbs. It is an outstanding, flavorful, and elegant wine for drinking over the next 6–8 years.

The 1999 Merlot Seven Hills Vineyard is medium to dark ruby-colored and offers cherry, blackberry, and vanilla aromas intermingled with hints of candied orange rind. Tangy red and black currants as well as juicy blackberries are found in this medium- to full-bodied wine. It is powerful, concentrated, and has a firm tannic backbone. Anticipated maturity: 2004–2012. The similarly colored 1999 Merlot Pepper Bridge has black fruit and freshly laid asphalt aromas. Its dark, brooding personality reveals loads of blackberries, currants, and hints of grilled herbs. This firm, medium-bodied wine will require cellaring. Drink it between 2005–2012.

The medium-bodied 1999 Merlot Ciel du Cheval has a medium to dark ruby color. It was tasted twice, with vastly different results. The first time it displayed a well-balanced, lively character with cassis, blackberry, black cherry, grilled oak, and tar flavors. It was concentrated, extracted, and had dense layers of fruit as well as a long, highly expressive finish. Additionally, it revealed excellent structure for aging. This bottle earned a 90-point score. The second bottle, tasted two months later with Camarda in Seattle, exhibited aromas of Tallegio, a soft-rind, creamy cheese from Italy, as well as a tight, high-acid personality with an alcoholic streak in the finish. My inclination, given Camarda's outstanding track record, is that the first bottle was the more representative one. However, in the interest of full disclosure, I must report on both. The dark ruby-colored 1999 Merlot Klipsun, often my favorite of Camarda's Merlots, is tightly wound and backward. It offers blackberry jam and hoisin aromas as well as a medium-bodied character. This wine has some rugged tannin, yet it displays impressive amounts of fruit. Blackberries, cassis, charred oak, and hints of Italian tomatoes can be found in its flavor profile. This is a firm wine that has loads of extract and concentration. Its finish reveals abundant quantities of tannin as well as some warmth (from alcohol), which lowered my score. Anticipated maturity: 2005–2012.

BETZ

1998 Cabernet Sauvignon	D	89+
1999 Cabernet Sauvignon Père de Famille	D	(89–91)

The blackberry- and herb-scented, medium to dark ruby-colored 1998 Cabernet Sauvignon is a tight, medium- to full-bodied effort. Delicious layers of intense, powerful blackberries and cassis can be found in its youthfully ungenerous yet muscular personality. This is a bright, well-balanced Cabernet with excellent purity as well as depth. Drink it between 2004–2010. Nine hundred cases of the 1999 Cabernet Sauvignon Père de Famille were produced. It offers sweet black cherry and cassis aromas as well as a broad, medium- to full-bodied character. This intense 1999 is loaded with sweet red and black fruits and a hint of Washington State's trademark fresh herbs. Powerful, highly expressive, and delicious, it will drink well between 2004–2012.

COLUMBIA CREST

1998 Red Wine Reserve	D	88+

The Columbia Crest Winery, part of the larger Stimson Lane corporate structure, which also owns Château Ste. Michelle, produces 1.5 million cases of wine a year, making it all the more remarkable that they are able to achieve the quality of the 1998 Red Wine Reserve (2,000 cases were produced). Medium to dark ruby-colored and boasting a blackberry-scented nose, it is a fat, rich, seamless wine with loads of blackberries and cassis in its juicy character. Its long finish reveals well-ripened tannin and loads of fresh wild herb and black currant flavors. Anticipated maturity: now–2008.

COLUMBIA WINERY

1999 Riesling Cellarmaster's Reserve	A	88

The 1999 Riesling Cellarmaster's Reserve offers delightful candied orange aromas and flavors. This off-dry, medium-bodied wine is silky-textured, well balanced, and immensely flavorful. Drink it over the next 5 years with spicy foods or as an apéritif.

DeLILLE CELLARS

1999 Chaleur Estate (red)	E	(91–92)
1998 Chaleur Estate (red)	D	91+
1997 Chaleur Estate (red)	D	90
1999 Chaleur Estate (white)	D	88
1997 D2	D	88
1998 Doyenne	D	89

1999 **Harrison Hill**	E	(90–91)
1998 **Harrison Hill**	D	90
1997 **Harrison Hill**	D	89

All of DeLille Cellars' wines (including its whites) are aged entirely in new French oak barrels, yet none of their aromas and flavor profiles are dominated by wood influences. In fact, it is difficult to discern the oak in DeLille's reds, a testimony to wine-maker Chris Upchurch's talents. This winery's red wines are crafted from traditional varietals (Cabernet Sauvignon, Merlot, Cabernet Franc) in the style of Bordeaux. Overall, DeLille's 1997s are more backward, less expressive wines than its 1995s and 1996s. The garnet-colored 1997 D2 has a delightful violet, rose, and dark berry–infused nose. This is an elegant, medium-bodied wine with a sultry texture, black cherry, blackberry, and currant fruit. This feminine, well-made wine exhibits exemplary ripeness in its supple, soft, tannin-filled finish. Drink it over the next 6–7 years.

A hint of cedar can be discerned in the floral and dark fruit–scented, garnet-colored 1997 Harrison Hill. Medium- to full-bodied and silky-textured, this spice, exotic wood, cassis, and black cherry–flavored wine is more structured than the forward D2. It reveals excellent concentration and balance in its refined, Bordeaux-like character. Anticipated maturity: now–2008. The 1997 Chaleur Estate is reminiscent of a wine from the Margaux commune in Bordeaux. Dark ruby-colored and boasting a nose of violets, cassis, and blackberries, this is a medium- to full-bodied, powerfully flavored and structured wine. Roses, violets, and assorted other flowers are intermingled with highly expressive cassis, black cherry, and blackberry flavors. Built for the long haul, this is a firmly structured, chewy-textured wine. Anticipated maturity: 2004–2012.

The 1999 Chaleur Estate white, a blend of 70% Sauvignon Blanc and 30% Sémillon from the Red Mountain and Sagemore vineyards, reveals demure aromas of honeydew melon presented in a rich, medium-bodied style. There is excellent fruit depth in its satin-textured, well-balanced personality. Melon and candied citrus flavors last throughout the impressively long finish. This 1999 white should improve with short-term cellaring. Anticipated maturity: now–2007.

The dark-colored 1998 Harrison Hill was produced from vines planted in 1962. Black cherries, blackberries, and spices can be discerned in its aromatic profile. This plump, seamless, refined, light- to medium-bodied, pure 1998 is filled with red and black fruit flavors. There are no hard edges. It is not a powerful wine, but one that delivers oodles of pleasure through its symmetry and detail. Drink it over the next decade.

The medium to dark ruby-colored 1998 Chaleur Estate offers sultry spice, violet, and jammy cherry aromas. This velvety-textured, medium-bodied red reveals loads of muscle to its underlying candied cherry, raspberry, and blueberry character. Another example of Upchurch's elegant, well-detailed offerings, it combines gorgeous layers of sweet, bright, fresh fruit with a delightfully harmonious personality as well as an extensive, pure finish. Enjoy it over the next 10 years. The medium to dark ruby-colored 1998 Doyenne was produced from Syrah acquired from the Boushey and Ciel du Cheval vineyards. It exhibits aromas of smoked bacon, spice, grapes, and blackberries. Medium- to full-bodied and loaded with dark blackberry and black raspberry fruit, this is a silky, deep, pure Syrah with excellent concentration, delineation, and balance. Anticipated maturity: now–2007.

The 1999 Harrison Hill's medium to dark ruby color is followed by aromas of blackberry syrup. On the palate leather, Asian spices, and copious quantities of cherries and blueberries can be found intermingled with prodigiously ripened tannin. Medium- to full-bodied and lush, with an impressively long, pure finish, it will be at its peak between 2004–2012. The similarly colored 1999 Chaleur Estate offers dramatic cassis aromas. It is deep, medium- to full-bodied, and powerful, with outstanding density to its blackberry- and cherry-flavored character. Fresh herbs and black currants can also be discerned throughout this concentrated wine's elegant personality and in its lush finish. Anticipated maturity: 2004–2014.

DUNHAM

1998 Cabernet Sauvignon IV	D	89

The 1998 Cabernet Sauvignon IV is the first wine I have tasted from this Walla Walla–based winery. Dark cherry, herbs, and hints of Scotch whiskey can be found in its aromatics. Velvety-textured and medium- to full-bodied, it is a highly expressive cassis, blackberry, juniper berry, Bing cherry, cigar box, and cedar-flavored wine. This intensely flavored wine has excellent focus and a firm structure. Anticipated maturity: 2003–2010.

L'ECOLE NO. 41

1998 Apogee Pepper Bridge Vineyard	D	89+
1998 Cabernet Sauvignon	D	88
1999 Merlot	D	88
1999 Merlot Seven Hills Vineyard	D	88+
1999 Semillon Fries Vineyard Wahluke Slope	C	88
1998 Semillon Fries Vineyard Wahluke Slope	C	88

The 1998 Semillon Fries Vineyard Wahluke Slope is a fat, rich, ripe wine. Its white peach–laden nose leads to a medium- to full-bodied, ample mouth, crammed with spicy apricots, touches of crème brûlée, and assorted honey-covered berries. This dry, opulent, intense offering should be consumed over the next 3–4 years.

The medium to dark ruby-colored 1999 Merlot displays blackberry aromas and an intense, minty, dark fruit–packed, medium to full body. This is a spicy, licorice-tinged, fruit-filled wine with good structure and loads of ripe tannin. Anticipated maturity: now–2007. The similarly colored 1999 Merlot Seven Hills Vineyard has blackberry and fresh herb aromas. It is medium- to full-bodied and coats the palate with herbal, jammy, dark fruit flavors and highly present yet ripe tannin. This concentrated wine should be at its best between 2003–2008.

The ruby-colored 1998 Cabernet Sauvignon offers minty, dark fruit aromas. It is a juicy, highly structured wine with cassis, fresh earth, mint, and blackberry flavors. This medium-bodied wine is highly expressive, with excellent intensity and loads of firm tannin. Drink it over the next 7–8 years. The 1998 Apogee Pepper Bridge Vineyard is a blend of 60% Merlot, 34% Cabernet Sauvignon, and 6% Cabernet Franc. It is a big, muscular, extracted, and firmly structured wine that offers a rose, violet, and blackberry-scented nose and is crammed with a myriad of black fruits, spices, and touches of red cherries. It has loads of tannins, but they are ripe and should smooth out with aging. Some alcoholic warmth shows through in the finish of this otherwise extremely well crafted Washington State beauty. Anticipated maturity: 2004–2009+.

The 1999 Semillon Fries Vineyard Wahluke Slope is a highly expressive, fascinating wine. Its melon and dried honey aromas lead to a rich, medium-bodied personality filled with yellow fruits and an amazing raspberry bonbon flavor that comes up in the mid-palate and holds throughout its extensive finish. Were it not for the fact that its high alcohol renders the wine somewhat warm, it would have merited even more points. Drink it over the next 3–4 years.

GLEN FIONA

1998 Syrah Basket Press Reserve	E	90
1997 Syrah Basket Press Reserve	D	88+
1999 Syrah Puncheon-Aged	D	88

Berle "Rusty" Figgins, the owner and wine-maker at Glen Fiona (which means "the valley of the vine" in Celtic) is dedicated to making Washington State Syrah. The 1997 Syrah Basket Press Reserve is a blend of 75% Syrah (Morrison Lane Vineyard) and 25% Cinsault (from the

Garton and Coe Farms). Its plum, tar, and black cherry aromas are reminiscent of Syrah-based wines from the Roussillon. Full-bodied and thickly textured, it has American oak spices, dark fruits, and a firm, tight finish. Drink this boisterous wine over the next 5 years.

The 1999 Syrah Puncheon-Aged (1,480 cases were produced) is a blend of 95% Syrah and 5% Viognier. It boasts dark cherry and candied raspberry as well as blackberry aromas. Medium-bodied, fresh, and well made, it is a juicy, black raspberry–dominated, satin-textured wine, full-flavored and harmonious. Drink it over the next 6 years. The 1998 Syrah Basket Press Reserve, a blend of 75% Syrah and 25% Cinsault from 40-year-old vines, has a nose reminiscent of molasses, blackberry, and a silver oak–like spice. Medium-bodied and intense, it is a focused, cassis, juicy blackberry, red cherry, and Asian spice–flavored wine. Additionally, it possesses an immensely impressive, long, delineated finish. This outstanding Washington State Syrah should be consumed over the next 8 years.

HEDGES CELLARS

1997 Three Vineyards	C	88+
2000 Fumé-Chardonnay	A	88

The 2000 Fumé-Chardonnay has apple, grapefruit, and smoke aromas. This expressive, medium-bodied wine reveals crisp pear, lemon, and lime flavors in its zesty, medium-bodied character. A superb value, it is tangy, refreshing, and delicious. Drink this lovely, thirst-quenching wine over the next 2 years. Hedges' ruby-colored 1997 Three Vineyards (a blend of 59% Merlot, 38% Cabernet Sauvignon, and 3% Cabernet Franc) displays lovely red berry and violet-infused aromas. Medium-bodied, this silky-textured offering is packed with cassis and blackberries. Notes of fresh herbs and cedar can be discerned in the well-structured finish. Anticipated maturity: now–2006+.

HIGHTOWER CELLARS

1997 Cabernet Sauvignon	D	89+

The bright ruby-colored 1997 Cabernet Sauvignon is the first wine I have reviewed from Hightower Cellars. A blend of 78% Cabernet Sauvignon, 12% Cabernet Franc, and 10% Merlot from five of the Columbia Valley's better-known vineyards, this is an extremely well made wine with pure red cherry and candied raspberry aromas intermingled with faint touches of vanilla. Medium-bodied and satin-textured, it is refined, red fruit–dominated, and possesses a long, well-furnished finish. Anticipated maturity: now–2006+.

LEONETTI

1999 Cabernet Sauvignon	E	(90–92)
1998 Cabernet Sauvignon	E	93
1996 Cabernet Sauvignon	D	89
1998 Cabernet Sauvignon Reserve	EE	96+
1996 Cabernet Sauvignon Seven Hills Vineyard Reserve	E	90+
1999 Merlot	E	91
1998 Merlot	E	94
1997 Merlot	D	88+
1996 Merlot	D	90
1998 Sangiovese	E	90

No one on earth makes Cabernets and Merlots with quite the same panache as Gary Figgins, Leonetti's owner and wine-maker. In their youth, these are the sweetest, spiciest, most candied wines around. The hedonistic pleasure they dish out is startling. They are sexy, lush, and boisterous. As they age, their opulence wanes and their spiciness/sexiness becomes tamed. This renders them much more civilized yet less distinctive. Do they age? Absolutely, these wines can last for 20–25 years, and maybe longer. However, as they age they seem to lose the characteristics that set them apart from the other thousands of well-made Cabernets and Merlots in the world. My advice is to drink them within their first 5–12 years of life, while they are exotic and totally distinctive. The purple/ruby 1997 Merlot exhibits sweet red cherry and Asian spice aromas. A myriad of wood flavors intermingles with jammy red cherries in this extroverted wine. Figgins's trademark supple personality leads to an atypically firm and structured finish. Anticipated maturity: now–2006.

Because of the killer frost that ravaged Washington State's vineyards, Figgins was compelled to purchase fruit from California's Napa Valley to craft his 1996 Merlot and Cabernet Sauvignon. Sporting the "America" appellation, the 1996 Merlot is medium to dark ruby-colored and reveals a spicy oak and jammy blackberry nose. Medium- to full-bodied, ample, oily-textured, and sexy, this lovely Merlot is crammed with ripe red and black fruits and eucalyptus. This sensual offering's attack and mid-palate lead to a somewhat tannic finish and will be at its peak between now–2006. The medium to dark ruby-colored 1996 Cabernet Sauvignon has a nose composed of blackberries, mint-covered chocolate, and fresh herbs. Intense, mouthcoating layers of red and black fruits are found in this powerful offering. Its sultry personality leads to a tannic, firm finish. Drink this wine between now–2007.

The ruby/purple 1996 Cabernet Sauvignon Seven Hills Vineyard Reserve offers enthralling blackberry, fresh herb, Asian spice, and raspberry aromas. This intense, concentrated, velvety-textured, and medium- to full-bodied wine coats the palate with its blood orange as well as red and black cherry flavors. If its tannic (somewhat bitter) finish softens before the fruit and opulent spices begin to melt away, my score will appear conservative. Anticipated maturity: now–2007+.

Roses, spices, violets, juniper berries, vanilla, candied raspberries, and cherries can be found in the aromatics of the 1999 Merlot. This medium to dark ruby-colored wine has juicy, well-focused layers of spicy cherries, cinnamon, blackberries, and cassis in its well-delineated, concentrated, and long-finishing personality. Anticipated maturity: now–2006.

The 1998 Cabernet Sauvignon's bouquet offers aromas of toasty oak and spice. This mouthcoating, explosive wine is crammed with a myriad of spices, jammy blackberries, sweet cherries, and cherry syrup–drenched fruitcake. This is a hedonist's delight, yet it has loads of tannin that provide a firm, tight, structured finish. Anticipated maturity: now–2011.

I could not help breaking into a smile when I tasted the medium to dark ruby-colored 1998 Cabernet Sauvignon Reserve. Its extraordinarily spicy, cherry syrup–scented nose leads to a flavor profile that explodes on the palate with substantial quantities of cherry syrup, raspberry coulis, and Asian spices. Gary Figgins's Cabernets can be as boisterous as Olivier Humbrecht's Gewurztraminers. The purity and power of the sweet, spicy fruit flavors found in this wine are truly extraordinary. In addition, it possesses an extremely long, candied, sweet tannin–filled finish. This decadent wine should be consumed between 2003–2012.

The outstanding dark ruby-colored 1999 Cabernet Sauvignon exhibits root beer, caramel, black cherry, clove, juniper, and jammy blackberry aromas. This sweet, candied, plump, plush effort is loaded with blackberries, spice, and an assortment of sweet, dark fruits. Sultry, opulent, and highly concentrated, it will drink well for nearly a decade. Potentially the New World's finest Sangiovese producer, Leonetti has fashioned a beautiful 1998 Sangiovese. Its meaty, sweet nose leads to a mouthful of juicy cherries and dark berries. Medium- to full-bodied, spicy, and velvety-textured, this is an in-your-face, fruit-dominated, lush Sangiovese. The dense fruit lingers throughout its long, supple finish. Drink it over the next 5 years.

The medium to dark ruby-colored 1998 Merlot possesses an immensely appealing spice and dark fruit–scented perfume. Though it would be perceived as extroverted, even boisterous from another producer, for Leonetti it is reserved. Medium- to full-bodied and hugely ripe, it is crammed with Asian spices, chocolate, blackberry juice, and a cascade of cherries. This expansive, rich, lively Merlot is unquestionably great stuff! There are no hard edges in its sultry character or exceptionally long, fruit-filled finish. Enjoy it over the next 7–9 years.

McCREA CELLARS

1999 Syrah Boushey Grande Côte Vineyard	D	89
1999 Syrah Ciel du Cheval Vineyard	D	89+
1998 Syrah Ciel du Cheval Vineyard	D	91
1998 Syrah Cuvée Orleans	D	90

The saturated, dark ruby-colored 1998 Syrah Ciel du Cheval Vineyard has a brooding, black cherry, blackberry, and chocolate-scented nose. Medium- to full-bodied and intensely flavored, this is an extremely well made, velvety-textured, highly expressive wine that is sure to please any Syrah lover. Black raspberries, black cherries, cassis, roasted herbs, and touches of leather can be found in its luxuriously layered personality. Drink this winner over the course of the next 6–7 years. The saturated, medium to dark ruby-colored 1998 Syrah Cuvée Orleans displays intense jammy black raspberry aromas. This medium- to full-bodied, velvety-textured wine is plush, lush, sexy, and intense. It coats the palate with oily layers of jammy black raspberries and cassis. Its superripe tannin is barely noticeable in its silky, sweet finish. Drink this immensely appealing fruit bomb over the next 6–7 years.

Dark ruby-colored, the 1999 Syrah Boushey Grande Côte Vineyard is a medium- to full-bodied, highly expressive wine with spicy black cherry scents. On the palate, it is fresh, zesty, and loaded with juicy blackberries, black raspberries, and cherries, with a tight yet ripe finish. Drink this wine over the next 6 years. The black cherry and blackberry syrup–scented 1999 Syrah Ciel du Cheval Vineyard is a tightly wound, medium- to full-bodied wine. It displays loads of sweet, superripe red and black fruit flavors in its velvety-textured personality. A year or two of cellaring will improve its structure. Anticipated maturity: 2003–2008.

NORTHSTAR

1998 Merlot	D	92+

Stimson Lane, which owns Château Ste. Michelle and Columbia Crest as well as a number of other brands, has recently created Northstar Winery, based in Walla Walla, Washington. Northstar's goal is to produce the finest Merlot in Washington State. To reach that end, Northstar's wine-maker has been given the authority to pick and choose among the Merlots from all of the Stimson Lane properties. Just over 1,000 cases were produced of their debut offering, the 1998 Northstar Merlot. Stimson Lane's goal is to raise this figure to 10,000 cases a year. It boasts a saturated dark ruby color and an intense nose of black cherries and cassis. Medium- to full-bodied, broad, big, and juicy, this dense, plump, chewy-textured wine is loaded. Cassis, cherries, blackberries, and hints of licorice can be discerned in this suave, highly concentrated, and expansive wine's character. It is powerful, harmonious, and exhibits an extraordinarily long, fruit-packed, seamless finish. This immensely impressive wine should be at its best between 2003–2012.

QUILCEDA CREEK

2000 Cabernet Sauvignon	E	(93–95)
1999 Cabernet Sauvignon	E	(97–98)
1998 Cabernet Sauvignon	E	95+
1997 Cabernet Sauvignon	E	94+
1996 Cabernet Sauvignon	D	95
1997 Cabernet Sauvignon Champoux Vineyard	E	91
1999 Merlot	E	(91–92)
1998 Merlot	E	(91–93)
1997 Merlot	D	89+

Alexander Golitzen and his son Paul are determined to produce the world's finest Cabernet Sauvignon. Moreover, they are convinced that Washington State is capable of this because of its propitious weather and extensive growing seasons and that it make great wines more regularly than any other Cabernet-producing area in the world. To accomplish this goal, the Golitzens are constantly reinvesting their profits to improve their winery and purchase new equipment. For example, on my last visit to the estate, Alex Golitzen showed me the new system he had designed to punch down the caps (the process of submerging the shell of skins and other solids that rise to the top of vats. "Punching down" increases concentration and structure but can also lead to wines being overextracted if it is done too often or too roughly). An engineer by training, Golitzen uses his inquisitive mind and engineering skills to create new equipment that solves age-old problems.

The Golitzens have also created a second wine (it was not tasted) that is made from the fruit and barrels not deemed good enough for the estate's premiere *cuvées*. Between 36% and 39% of the estate's annual production is relegated to Quilceda Creek's Red Wine.

While Quilceda Creek is dedicated primarily to the production of Cabernet Sauvignon, it also produces small quantities (around 250 cases) of Merlot (which includes 24% Cabernet Sauvignon in the blend). The medium to dark ruby/mahogany 1997 Merlot was made predominantly from fruit purchased from the Klipsun Vineyard. Warm, dark, spicy fruits, fresh herbs, and hints of Italian tomatoes can be discerned in its aromatics. Medium- to full-bodied and velvety-textured, it is an embracing wine, packed with blackberries and cassis. It has excellent concentration, as well as a supple attack in mid-palate. The firm finish suggests cellaring. Anticipated maturity: 2004–2010+. The medium to dark ruby-colored 1998 Merlot boasts a super nose of blackberries, cassis, herbs, and aromatic spices. Medium- to full-bodied and wonderfully elegant, it possesses a flavor profile made up of sweet cassis, lovely black cherries, chocolate, blackberries, and hints of toast. This satin-textured wine is refined and marvelously harmonious. "It's all about pleasure," said Alex Golitzen while serving this beauty. Anticipated maturity: 2003–2012+.

In 1997 the Golitzens purchased a parcel of the Champoux Vineyard. Like the majority of Washington State producers, the Golitzens must purchase fruit from growers, as they have not previously owned any vineyards. The medium to dark ruby-colored 1997 Cabernet Sauvignon Champoux Vineyard displays creamy, sweet, Connecticut white corn and black cherry aromas. Medium- to full-bodied and satin-textured, it is an intense blackberry and dark cherry–flavored wine. This expressive, flavorful offering has outstanding follow-through from its attack to its long, seamless, and focused finish. Anticipated maturity: now–2008. Though it was bottled as a single-vineyard wine to inaugurate the Golitzens' acquisition, they do not plan ever again to produce another single-vineyard bottling.

Strategically placed between Château Margaux and Château Mouton-Rothschild in a blind tasting of the superlative 1996 Bordeaux first growths, the 1996 Cabernet Sauvignon (a blend of 85% Cabernet Sauvignon, 9% Merlot, and 6% Cabernet Franc) not only held its own but was indistinguishable from its Bordeaux brethren. Revealing a saturated dark purple color, its soft, salty, black raspberry jam, licorice, and coconut aromas lead to a medium- to full-bodied character of unbelievable sweetness. Extraordinarily well balanced, this velvety-textured, powerful, elegant wine displays black raspberry flavors that last throughout its exceptionally long, pure finish. Anticipated maturity: 2003–2018. The 1997 Cabernet Sauvignon was fashioned from 89% Cabernet Sauvignon, 9% Merlot, and 2% Cabernet Franc. It offers a boisterous rosemary and black fruit–scented nose. Bigger, broader, and chewier than the 1996, this medium- to full-bodied wine is packed with black fruits, spices, and hints of tar. It is masculine, concentrated, and in need of cellaring. Anticipated maturity: 2005–2020.

The 1998 Cabernet Sauvignon (2,500 cases produced) is the result of a blend of 98% Cabernet Sauvignon and 2% Cabernet Franc. (Sixty percent of this wine is from the estate-owned Champoux Vineyard and 40% from fruit purchased from the Klipsun Vineyard.) Medium to dark ruby-colored, it boasts a compelling perfume of blackberries, cassis, and cherries. It is a huge, intense, medium- to full-bodied effort. This powerhouse expands on the palate to reveal copious quantities of assorted dark fruits and a profusion of spices. Although immensely concentrated and muscular, it manages to retain Quilceda Creek's trademark harmony and elegance. This exceptional offering's dense layers of fruit last throughout its supple, exceptionally long finish. Drink it between 2006–2018.

The medium- to full-bodied, huge 1999 Merlot exhibits a medium to dark ruby color in addition to intensely sweet blackberry aromas. Loaded with juicy black fruits, tar, licorice, and a myriad of spices, it was fashioned from 75% Merlot (from the Klipsun Vineyard) and 25% Cabernet Sauvignon (from the Ciel du Cheval Vineyard). A Cabernet lover's Merlot, this penetrating offering possesses outstanding depth, concentration, and density of fruit, as well as a structured, fresh, chewy-textured character. Anticipated maturity: 2005–2015.

The magnificent dark ruby-colored 1999 Cabernet Sauvignon is a winemaking tour de force. A blend of 97% Cabernet Sauvignon and 3% Merlot, its bouquet can best be described as syrup of Cabernet Sauvignon. Intensely sweet blackberry, cassis, cherry, and blueberry jam aromas burst from the glass. Produced from the Champoux (70%) and Red Mountain (30%) vineyards, it possesses a medium- to full-bodied character as well as extraordinary breadth to its massive personality. Focused layers of black currant jam and blackberry juice surge across the palate, lasting nearly a minute. A wine of unsurpassed power yet prodigious elegance, it is reminiscent of my first taste of the 1990 Château Margaux. Anticipated maturity: 2006–2020. The awesome dark ruby-colored 2000 Cabernet Sauvignon (100% Cabernet Sauvignon, 92.5% from the Champoux vineyard and the remainder from Red Mountain) reveals blackberry and currant aromas as well as a suave, cassis syrup–laden personality. This classy, medium- to full-bodied, powerful, intense effort displays a seamless, harmonious character. Its concentrated fruit and angle-free structure promise a great future. Anticipated maturity: 2007–2020+.

REININGER

1997	Cabernet Sauvignon	D	88
1998	Merlot	D	88

The medium to dark ruby-colored 1998 Merlot, from the Pepper Bridge and Spring Valley vineyards, was produced from a blend of Merlot (92%), Cabernet Franc (6%), and Cabernet Sauvignon (2%). Only 850 cases were produced. It exhibits sweet cherry, violet, and hints of cookie dough in its spicy aromatics. Medium-bodied and silky-textured, this is a concentrated, firmly structured, blackberry- and cassis-flavored wine. Anticipated maturity: now–2006. The fresh herb and roasted eggplant–scented, medium to dark ruby-colored 1997 Cabernet Sauvignon (only 350 cases produced) is fashioned from 91% Cabernet Sauvignon, 5% Merlot, and 4% Cabernet Franc from grapes purchased from the Seven Hills, Pepper Bridge, and Whitney Vineyards. This well-made, black pit fruit–flavored, medium- to full-bodied wine has a satiny texture and loads of intense black fruit flavors. Anticipated maturity: now–2007+.

CHÂTEAU STE. MICHELLE

1998	Cabernet Sauvignon Canoe Ridge Estate	C	89
1996	Cabernet Sauvignon Canoe Ridge Estate Vineyard	C	91
1998	Cabernet Sauvignon Cold Creek Vineyard	D	89
1996	Cabernet Sauvignon Cold Creek Vineyard	C	89
1998	Cabernet Sauvignon Reserve	D	90
1999	Chardonnay Canoe Ridge Estate Vineyard	D	91
1998	Chardonnay Canoe Ridge Estate Vineyard	D	90
1997	Chardonnay Canoe Ridge Estate Vineyard	D	91
1999	Chardonnay Cold Creek Vineyard	D	89

1998	Chardonnay Cold Creek Vineyard	D	89+
1997	Chardonnay Cold Creek Vineyard	C	90
1999	Chardonnay Indian Wells Vineyard	C	88
1997	Chardonnay Reserve	D	88+
2000	Eroica Riesling Dr. Loosen	C	89
1999	Eroica Riesling Dr. Loosen	C	88
1997	Late Harvest White Riesling Reserve	C/375ml	89
1996	Merlot Canoe Ridge Estate Vineyard	C	89
1999	Single Berry Select	EEE/375ml	94

Château Ste. Michelle, one of the cornerstones of the Stimson Lane wine conglomerate, continues to amaze me with its dedication to quality and its reasonable prices. Château Ste. Michelle's highly talented wine-maker, Mike Januik, resigned his duties to start a winery. This is good news for wine lovers: First, Januik's new venture is sure to quickly join the ranks of Washington State's finest wineries, and second, Allen Shoup, the quality-driven former CEO of Stimson Lane (the corporation that owns Château Ste. Michelle), most certainly replaced him with gifted people (Erik Olsen for whites, Ron Bunnell for reds).

Château Ste. Michelle's 1997s and 1996s are pure Januik—Old World structures and styles with New World fruit. They represent some of the finest wines produced to date by this large winery. The 1997 Chardonnay Cold Creek Vineyard offers lovely aromas of yellow fruits, toast, lees, and a hint of orange marmalade. Medium- to full-bodied and well balanced, this Burgundy-styled wine displays flavors of white peaches and ripe pears in its personality as well as stonelike notes in its long, supple finish. Drink it over the next 5+ years. Even better, the 1997 Chardonnay Canoe Ridge Estate Vineyard has a Chablis-like nose and a flavor character reminiscent of Meursault. It exhibits minerally, smoky, leesy scents intermingled with sweet white fruits. This medium- to full-bodied, oily-textured offering is well structured and filled with almonds, hazelnuts, and pears. Anticipated maturity: now–2005+. While the two preceding wines were highly expressive, the 1997 Chardonnay Reserve was much more structured and reserved. Its muted aromatics and unyielding personality permitted only a glimpse of this wine's harmonious white fruit and floral flavor profile. It is extremely well balanced, medium- to full-bodied, glycerin-packed, and in need of cellaring. Ultimately, if prior vintages are any indication, this wine may develop to outshine its two brethren. Anticipated maturity: now–2006+.

The 1996 Merlot Canoe Ridge Estate Vineyard blows away the overwhelming majority of similarly priced California Merlots. This ruby-colored wine's aromatics are dominated by black cherries and roselike scents. This seamless wine has an appealingly soft texture, medium body, and an elegant, structured character. Red and black fruits are found in its tasty flavor profile and throughout its supple finish. Drink it over the next 4–5 years.

Tasting through Washington State's Cabernet Sauvignons is often difficult due to the high levels of acidity (mostly added) and hard, astringent tannins (from unripe fruit, high yields, and excessive extraction). In contrast, Château Ste. Michelle's 1996s were a joy to encounter. They have plenty of structure, yet their tannins are ripe and enveloped in fruit. The ruby-colored 1996 Cabernet Sauvignon Cold Creek Vineyard offers aromas of perfumed blackberries. Its broad character is penetrating, expressive, and filled with black fruits as well as traces of freshly laid road tar. The similarly colored 1996 Cabernet Sauvignon Canoe Ridge Estate Vineyard is more intense, complex, and powerful. Seemingly sporting more alcohol than the Cold Creek (the label lists them both as being 13.5%), this wine has overt blackberry aromas. Lovely layers of cassis, black cherries, and blackberries are found in its velvety-textured, medium- to full-bodied personality. Both of these offerings will be at their peak between now–2007+.

Each year Château Ste. Michelle fashions a delicious and ageworthy Late Harvest White Riesling Reserve. The 1997 may not be as long-lived as most previous vintages of this wine, yet it is more forward and generous. Raspberry jam, flowers, and candied oranges are discernible in its expressive aromatics. Medium-bodied, rich, and broad, this well-balanced wine is crammed with red and yellow fruits as well as flavors reminiscent of fruit punch. It is thick and possesses a long, sweet (yet not cloying) finish. Anticipated maturity: now–2007.

Château Ste. Michelle continues to impress with its single-vineyard Chardonnays. The 1998 Canoe Ridge Estate offers ripe apple, toast, and mineral aromas. It is luscious, opulent, oily-textured, and medium- to full-bodied. On the palate, pears, apples, and grilled hazelnuts can be discerned in this long and fruit-forward effort. Drink it over the next 4 years. The white fruit, flower, and stone-scented 1998 Chardonnay Cold Creek Vineyard shares the same lush texture as the Canoe Ridge but is tighter and more focused. Its pear, mineral, and spice-laden personality is medium- to full-bodied and persistent in the finish. Anticipated maturity: now–2005.

The apricot-scented 1999 Eroica Riesling Dr. Loosen (made in collaboration with the Mosel's famed Ernst Loosen) has a rich, dense, herbal tea– as well as white and yellow fruit–flavored core. Considerable CO_2 is present, providing good freshness to balance out its rich, opulent fruit. Drink it over the next 4–5 years. Produced from a vineyard planted in 1984, the 1999 Chardonnay Indian Wells Vineyard bursts from the glass with superripe apple and pear aromas and flavors. A broad, anise-spiced Chardonnay, it offers a soft texture in addition to an appealingly long finish. This well-made and balanced 1999 should be consumed over the next 5 years. The outstanding 1999 Chardonnay Canoe Ridge Estate Vineyard displays complex aromatics of candied nuts, white fruits, and distinctive smoky scents. It expands on the palate to reveal mouthcoating spiced pears, candied apples, and a myriad of spices. Rich, gorgeously fashioned, and impressively long in the finish, it will drink well for 5 years. Displaying a more demure, lightly fruity bouquet, the medium-bodied, well-focused 1999 Chardonnay Cold Creek Vineyard offers minerals, pears, and stonelike flavors in its broad, ample personality. Drink it over the next 4–5 years.

The 2000 Eroica Riesling Dr. Loosen offers rich pear and apple aromas in a medium- to full-bodied, fat, plump format. This opulent, plush, mineral, tangerine, and sweet tea–flavored Riesling possesses excellent balance and a long, orange rind–flavored finish. Anticipated maturity: now–2012.

It took 600 man-hours to harvest the 1999 Single Berry Select grape by grape from the end of November through December 4. The wine exhibits candied orange, apricot, and botrytis aromas as well as a flavor profile reminiscent of syrup of apricot blended with nectar of mango. Full-bodied, plump, and intense, with a jellied texture and profound personality, it sports 37 grams of residual sugar. Anticipated maturity: now–2020.

The medium- to full-bodied, cassis-scented, excellent 1998 Cabernet Sauvignon Canoe Ridge Estate Vineyard boasts loads of sweet black currant and blackberry fruit in its focused, deep, lively personality. This structured 1998 also possesses a long, fruit-filled finish. Enjoy it between 2003–2010. The medium to dark ruby-colored 1998 Cabernet Sauvignon Cold Creek Vineyard offers aromas of blackberry juice and smoky bacon. Plump, expansive, and medium-bodied, with abundant quantities of dark fruits as well as an elegant yet powerful core, it will drink well between 2004–2010. The intensely aromatic, medium to dark ruby-colored 1998 Cabernet Sauvignon Reserve reveals scents of blackberry and black cherry jam. Medium- to full-bodied and silky-textured, with loads of depth to its dark fruit and fresh herb–flavored character and an impressively long, supple finish, this well-made effort will drink well for years. Anticipated maturity: now–2012.

SEVEN HILLS WINERY

1997 Cabernet Sauvignon Klipsun Vineyard	**D**	**88**

The black-colored 1997 Cabernet Sauvignon Klipsun Vineyard has demure rose and black currant aromas. On the palate, this is a powerful, mouthcoating, highly extracted, black tar and blackberry-flavored wine. Intense and firmly structured, it will require cellaring. Anticipated maturity: 2003–2010+.

TAMARACK CELLARS

1998 Merlot	D	88

The medium ruby-colored 1998 Merlot reveals violet, red cherry, raspberry, and spice aromas. Medium-bodied, velvety-textured, and thick, it exhibits loads of red and dark, well-ripened fruit flavors. Hints of vanilla can be discerned in its firmly structured (loads of tannin) finish. Anticipated maturity: 2003–2008.

WOODWARD CANYON

1999 Chardonnay Celilo Vineyard	D	89
1998 Chardonnay Celilo Vineyard	D	88
1998 Merlot	D	89

The 1998 Chardonnay Celilo Vineyard reveals creamed spices and toasty oak aromas. This satin-textured, medium-bodied, supple wine offers buttered minerals, toast, and apples in its long, silky flavor profile. Drink it over the next 3–4 years. Sweet black cherries and blackberries are found in the aromatics of the medium to dark ruby-colored 1998 Merlot. Medium- to full-bodied and well structured, this is an intensely flavorful cassis, cherry syrup, and boysenberry-flavored wine. Extremely well made and seamless, it is reminiscent of an excellent Pomerol from a warm, ripe year. Anticipated maturity: now–2008+. The spicy anise and poached pear–scented 1999 Chardonnay Celilo Vineyard has an immensely appealing, oily-textured personality. Spiced apples, cardamom, nutmeg, traces of butterscotch, and anise can be found in its expressive, elegant, and well-balanced character. Drink this delicious wine over the next 4–5 years.

8. THE MID-ATLANTIC STATES

From Long Island's North Fork to the Hudson River valley, and from the hillsides of Pennsylvania, Maryland, and Virginia, a few of the Mid-Atlantic's wineries are producing good, very good, and sometimes excellent wines. Overall, it appears that this region's best potential lies in its Cabernet Franc–based wines, as beauties tasted from Long Island and Virginia have proven. For whites, the Mid-Atlantic is a mixed bag, with the exception of New York's Millbrook Winery, nestled in the Hudson River valley, which has consistently surprised me with excellent to outstanding Chardonnays.

Consumers wishing to taste the best of the Mid-Atlantic's wines should search out those produced by the following wineries:

MARYLAND
Basigniani Winery (the state's finest)   Elk Run
Catoctin Winery

NEW YORK
Bedell   Millbrook Winery
Fox Run   Palmer
Gristina Vineyards   Paumanok
Jamesport   Schneider
Lenz   Wolffer
Macari Vineyards

PENNSYLVANIA
Chaddsford Winery

VIRGINIA
Barboursville Vineyards   White Hall Vineyards
Jefferson Vineyards   Willowcroft Farm Vineyards
Rockbridge Vineyards

THE BEST OF THE REST

Australia and New Zealand
Argentina and Chile
South Africa

9. AUSTRALIA AND NEW ZEALAND

AUSTRALIA

TYPES OF WINE

You name it and the Australians no doubt grow it, make it into wine, blend it with something else, and give it an unusual name. The combination of quality and value that many Australian wines offer is the hottest thing in town from London to New York. Australia, like California in America, and Alsace in France, labels its wine after the grape (or grapes) from which it is made. All the major grapes are used here. While great wines are produced from most varietals, Syrah (called Shiraz in Australia) triumphs over all the others. The major viticultural districts (listed alphabetically) are:

Adelaide Hills (South Australia)   Located in southern Australia, this is a high-altitude, cooler-climate region. Petaluma is its most famous winery.

Barossa Valley (South Australia)   In southern Australia, this huge, well-known viticultural area north of Adelaide is the home of some of the quantitative titans of Australia's wine industry (i.e., Penfolds, Henschke, Tollana, Seppelt, Wolf Blass, Orlando, and Yalumba). It is the source for Australia's finest wines, including spectacular old-vine Shiraz *cuvées* produced by Cimicky, Rick Burge, Elderton, Greenock Creek, Rockford, Veritas, Torbreck, and Yalumba. Australia's most renowned wine, Penfold's Grange, is largely a blend from selected Barossa vineyards.

Bendigo (Victoria)   Bendigo is an up-and-coming area, although it has a long history as a wine-producing region. Balgownie, Jasper Hill, and Wild Duck Creek are the finest wineries.

Victoria (Victoria)   The best-known subregions of Victoria are Goulburn Valley, Bendigo, Geelong, Yarra Valley, and Rutherglen, all within a day's drive of Melbourne.

Clare Valley (South Australia)   Located north of Adelaide and the Barossa Valley, this beautiful area is better known for its white than red wines. A number of high-quality wineries call Clare Valley their home, including Clos Clare, Grosset, Pikes, Kilikanoon, Tim Adams, and Knappstein. Some surprisingly fine Riesling emerges from this area.

Coonawarra (South Australia)   Coonawarra is among the most respected red-wine-growing areas of Australia. Situated in South Australia, west of the Goulburn Valley, top wineries such as Penley, Parker, Highbank, Majella, Katnook, and Lindemans (their Limestone Ridge and St. George Vineyards are there) pull their grapes from Coonawarra.

Geelong (Victoria)   Southwest of Melbourne near the coast is the small area of Geelong. The best known wineries are Bannockburn, Clyde Park, and Mount Anakie.

Glenrowan (Victoria)   Located in northeastern Victoria, this hot area is famous for its inky, rich, chewy red wines, especially the full-throttle Shiraz from one of Australia's historic

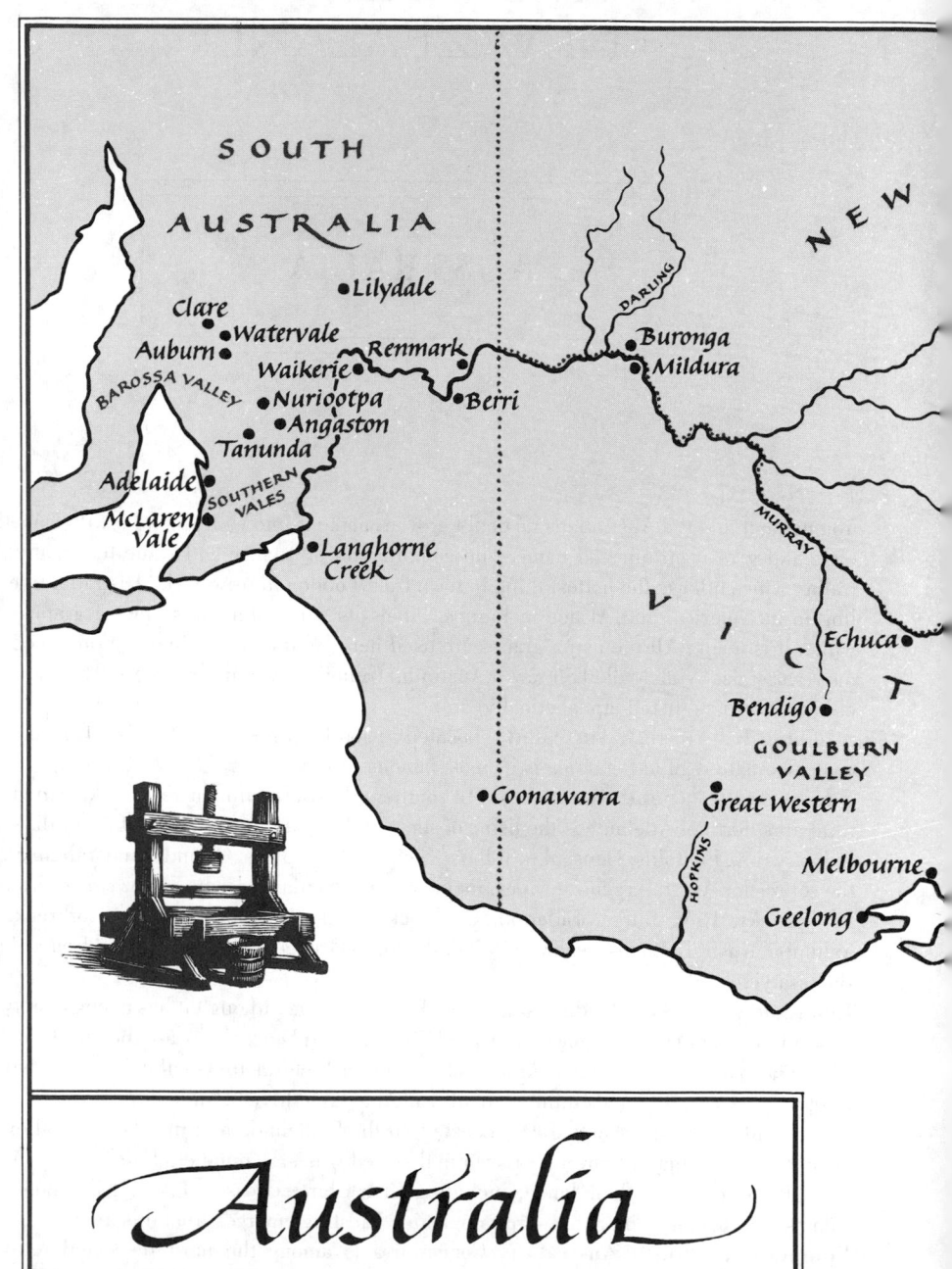

SOUTH

AUSTRALIA

NEW

- Lilydale
Clare
- Watervale
Auburn
- Renmark
Waikerie
BAROSSA VALLEY
- Nuriootpa
Angaston
- Berri
Tanunda
Adelaide
McLaren
Vale
SOUTHERN
VALES
- Langhorne
Creek

DARLING
- Buronga
- Mildura

MURRAY

V
I
C
- Echuca
T
Bendigo
GOULBURN
VALLEY
- Coonawarra
- Great Western
HOPKINS
- Melbourne
- Geelong

Australia

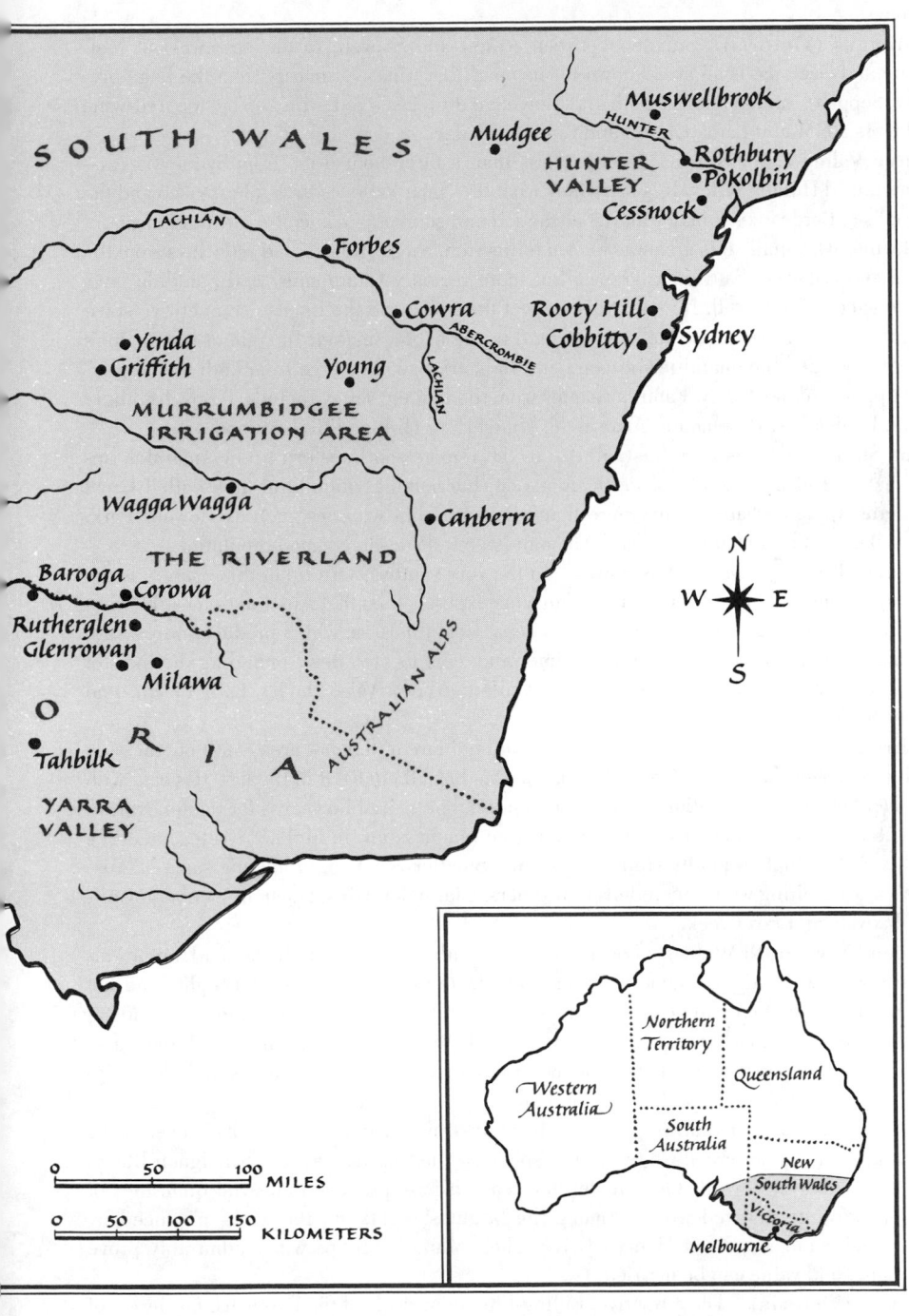

SOUTH WALES

Muswellbrook
Mudgee
HUNTER
HUNTER VALLEY
Rothbury
Pokolbin
Cessnock
LACHLAN
Forbes
Cowra
ABERCROMBIE
Rooty Hill
Cobbitty
Sydney
Yenda
Griffith
Young
LACHLAN
MURRUMBIDGEE
IRRIGATION AREA
Wagga Wagga
Canberra
THE RIVERLAND
Barooga
Corowa
Rutherglen
Glenrowan
Milawa
AUSTRALIAN ALPS
O   R   I   A
Tahbilk
YARRA
VALLEY

N
W   E
S

0   50   100 MILES

0   50   100   150 KILOMETERS

Northern
Territory
Queensland
Western
Australia
South
Australia
New
South Wales
Victoria
Melbourne

producers, Bailey's. A more commercial Cabernet and Shiraz is made by Wynns. At nearby Milawa, Brown Brothers, one of the most successful high-quality Australian wineries, makes its home.

Gramptans (Victoria)   Situated between Ararat and Stawell, to the northwest of Melbourne and Geelong, is an area known for its sparkling wines (primarily from the huge producer Seppelt), and for its smooth, fat, low-acid but tasty red wines. The top red-wine producers are Mount Langi Ghiran and Cathcart Ridge.

Hunter Valley (New South Wales)   Less than a three-hour drive from Sydney is Australia's famed Hunter Valley. It is to Sydney what the Napa Valley is to San Francisco and the Médoc is to Bordeaux—a major tourist attraction and source for some of Australia's most desired wines. Originally this area was known for its rich, exotic, full-bodied red wines from the Shiraz and Cabernet Sauvignon grapes, but more recently Chardonnay and Sémillon have proven successful as well. No doubt because of their size and the intense competitive spirit here, this area's wineries are well represented in the export market. In spite of this region's renown, considerable quantities of mediocre, industrial swill emerge from both the "lower" and "upper" Hunter Valley. Familiar names from the Hunter Valley include Tyrell, Rothbury Estate, Lindemans, Rosemount, Arrowfield, Hungerford Hill, and Brokenwood.

Great Southern (Western Australia)   In the remote southwestern tip of Australia, approximately 150 miles south of Perth, is a vast, burgeoning viticultural area called Great Southern. Apple orchards thrive more than vineyards, but wineries such as Howard Park, Mount Barker, Frankland Estate, and Alkoomi have well-deserved good reputations.

Margaret River (Western Australia)   In the very southwestern tip of this country is the Margaret River viticultural zone. Australian wine experts claim that Australia's most French-like Cabernet Sauvignons and Chardonnays come from this area, which produces wines with higher natural acidities. There are many fine producers located here, including the likes of Vasse Felix, Moss Wood, Leeuwin Estate, Cullen, Abbey Vale, Devil's Lair, Pierro, and Woody Nook.

McLaren Vale (South Australia)   The traditional fare of this hot area south of Adelaide was high-alcohol, thick, rich Grenache wines. This has all changed in the last 10 years with the advent of cold fermentations and the perception that the public yearns for lighter, fruitier wines. Some of the giants of the Australian wine business are in McLaren Vale, including Hardy's and its higher-quality sibling, Reynella. Smaller wineries, producing some of Australia's most exciting wines, include Kay Brothers, Clarendon Hills, Noon, d'Arenberg, Coriole, Maxwell, and Fox Creek.

Mudgee (New South Wales)   Located in New South Wales west of the famed Hunter Valley, Mudgee (an aboriginal name meaning "nest in the hills") with its cool nights and hot days has proven not only to be a fine red wine area but also a consistent source for tropical fruit–scented, luxuriously rich Chardonnays. For whatever reason, the wines of Mudgee also tend to be less expensive than those from other top areas. Reliable producers include Craigmoor, Montrose, Miramar, and Huntington Estate.

Padthaway (South Australia)   This southern Australian viticultural area has developed a following for its value-priced white wines, especially the Chardonnay and Sauvignon Blanc. Sadly, Padthaway vineyards have proven how easy it is to produce industrial quantities of uninspiring white and red wines. Among the brightest lights are the wines produced by Sparky and Sarah Maguis at Henry's Drive. Their Marguis-Philips wines admirably prove that quality and value can be married.

Pyrenees (Victoria)   The attractive, rolling-hill countryside of the Pyrenees, northwest of Melbourne, forms a triangle between Redbank, Moonambel, and Avoca. The top wines are the reds from the Cabernet Sauvignon and Shiraz grapes. Wineries of note include Redbank, Taltarni, Mount Avoca, and Dalwhinnie.

Riverland (South Australia)   Located in South Australia, Riverland is to Australia what the San Joaquin Valley is to California. This vast source of grapes of mediocre quality is dominated by huge cooperatives and producers who turn out Australia's jug wines and bag-in-the-box generic wines. Some big enterprises have their jug wine business centered here, including Penfolds, Kaiserstuhl, Angove, Berri, and Renmano. While most of the wines from this area are decidedly insipid, some good-value, fresh whites at bargain-basement prices can be found.

Rutherglen (Victoria) Rutherglen is synonymous with Australia's fortified sweet wines, many of which are extraordinary. The famous sweet, nectarlike, ageless ports and fortified Muscats and Tokays of William Chambers, Campbells, Stanton and Kileen, and Seppelt are made from Rutherglen grapes.

Swan Valley (Western Australia) This hot, arid area in Western Australia, just northeast of the coastal city of Perth, produces large-framed, muscular red wines and increasingly better white wines. Houghton is the area's most famous winery, but good wines are made by Moondah Brook and Sandalford.

Yarra Valley (Victoria) This is Australia's most fashionable viticultural area, and its proponents (the provincial Australian wine press) argue that the climate and resulting wines come closest in spirit to those of Bordeaux and Burgundy in France. I am not convinced. Located in Victoria, this is a cool-climate area outside Melbourne, and every major red and white glamour varietal is planted, from Cabernet Sauvignon, Merlot, and Pinot Noir to Chardonnay, Riesling, and Gewurztraminer. The best wineries are Lillydale, Yarra Yering, Coldstream Hills, and St. Huberts, but beware, there is much more "sizzle" than substance for most wines from Yarra Valley.

GRAPE VARIETIES

RED WINES

Cabernet Sauvignon This varietal can excel in Australia and generally produces a very fruity, often jammy, intensely curranty, fat wine, sometimes low in acidity, but round, generous, and surprisingly ageworthy in spite of an acid deficiency. Sadly, too many wineries continue to go overboard with acid additions, making a soft yet delicious wine into something akin to an underripe lemon!

Pinot Noir There are those who claim to have made successful wines from this notoriously fickle varietal, but the majority of Australian Pinot Noirs to date have either been raisiny, unusual, and repugnant, or watery, pale, innocuous, and excessively acidified. One prominent exception is Bass Phillip, which produces the country's most profound Pinot Noir from the cool microclimates of South Gippsland in Victoria.

Shiraz Despite the Aussies' present-day infatuation with such international grapes as Cabernet Sauvignon, Merlot, and Pinot Noir, it is Shiraz that produces their greatest wines. The problem is that there is an enormous amount of it, and only a handful of producers treat Shiraz (Syrah) with the respect and care that is accorded Cabernet. It can produce Australia's greatest red wine when left to stand on its own, as Penfolds Grange has convincingly proven for nearly 50 years! Additionally, it can gain dimension and character when blended with Cabernet Sauvignon, as Penfolds and Petaluma have proven time and time again. The greatest examples emerge from only two regions, Barossa and McLaren Vale. Elsewhere, Shiraz usually produces one-dimensional, heavy wines.

WHITE WINES

Chardonnay The shrewd Aussies, taking full advantage of the wine consumer's thirst for Chardonnay wines, have consistently offered plump, fat wines filled with the flavors of apples, pears, oranges, and ripe melons. Although the wines still tend to be overoaked, or worse, artificially oaked as well as excessively acidified, more and more Australian Chardonnays are fresh and exuberant, and bottled early to preserve their youthful grapy qualities. With the advent of centrifuges and micropore filters, many Chardonnays have no bouquet or flavor. The one major disappointment is the aging potential of these naturally low-acid wines, but most consumers are drinking them within several months of purchase, so this is probably a moot issue. One positive trend has been the increasing quantities of delicious "non-oaked" or so-called "virgin" Chardonnays.

Gewurztraminer Contrary to the local salespeople, who hype the quality of Gewurztraminer, this grape produces insipid, pale, watery wines that are a far cry from what Gewurztraminer does in France.

Marsanne Château Tahbilk and Michelton are proponents of this grape, which tends to turn out one-dimensional, bland wines.

Muscat This hot-climate grape excels in Australia and is at its best in the decadently rich, sweet, fortified Muscats that can age for decades. It is also made into a medium-sweet table wine with which Brown Brothers does a particularly admirable job.

Riesling Australia has proven to be the New World's best alternative to German and Alsace, France, Rieslings. This grape has done extremely well with Kabinett and Spatlese-style drier Rieslings in the Barossa Valley, Adelaide Hills, and Clare Valley. Wineries such as Petaluma, Pewsey Vale, Rosemount, Grosset, Leeuwin, and Mount Horrocks have turned out some remarkable wines. Overall, this grape gets good marks.

Sauvignon Blanc The results have been mixed, as the hot climate causes this grape to overripen and to take on a grotesque, vegetal, oily, thick fruitiness. There are some fresh, tasty, dry Sauvignons coming from Australia, but for now, New Zealand consistently beats Australia when it comes to quality Sauvignon-based wines.

Sémillon Sémillon can be delicious, whether it is blended with Chardonnay or Sauvignon, or allowed to stand by itself. It produces big, creamy, rich wines loaded with flavor. Wineries such as Rothbury, Rosemount, Montrose, Peter Lehmann, and Henschke have done better with Sémillon than anyone. Some great sweet wines have been made from Sémillon affected by the botrytis fungus. Look for those from Rothbury, Rosemount, and Peter Lehmann, which are world-class.

FLAVORS

RED WINES

Cabernet Sauvignon These wines can be very ripe, often overripe, with sweet, intense black currant flavors, supple, fat textures, and oodles of fruit. When poorly made or overly acidified, the wines are musty, dirty, and tart.

Pinot Noir Raisiny, pruny fruit flavors with no finesse or complexity represent appallingly bad examples of Pinot Noir.

Shiraz Intense aromas of blackberry liqueur, cassis, leather, licorice, cedar, tar, and pepper are found in wines that have a healthy dosage of Shiraz. Quite full-bodied and rich, with softer tannins than Cabernet Sauvignon, these wines are drinkable young, but usually age better than the more glamorous Cabernet Sauvignons. The finest examples almost always emerge from Barossa and McLaren Vale.

WHITE WINES

Chardonnay Tropical fruit flavors predominate in this creamy-textured, voluptuous wine. Oak is sometimes too noticeable, but better-balanced wines with the fruit in the forefront have been the rule in recent vintages.

Gewurztraminer   Where's the spice and exotic lychee nut character found in the great Gewurztraminers of Alsace? These are generally watery, thin, disappointing wines.

Marsanne   Marsanne can be described as usually neutral or, as Jancis Robinson says, "reminiscent of glue." It usually tastes much better old than young, but because it tastes so uninteresting young, no one ages it.

Muscat   Huge aromas of brown sugar, fruitcake, crème brûlée, buttered and baked apricots, and oranges with honey and nuts give this varietal its appeal.

Riesling   The classic Riesling aromas of spring flowers, green apples, and wet stones are present in the drier versions of this wine. As the wines get sweeter, aromas and flavors of oranges, peaches, apricots, butter, baked apples, and honeyed nuts arise.

Sauvignon Blanc   Unfortunately, these wines seem to be either feeble, bland, and tasteless, or oily, vegetal, and grotesque.

Sémillon   In the drier versions, lemon-lime aromas intertwined with honey and toasty oak are often the most interesting. With the sweet versions, buttery nuts and honey-coated raisin flavors take over.

AGING POTENTIAL

Cabernet Sauvignon:
    5–20 years
Pinot Noir: 4–6 years
Shiraz: 5–30 years
Chardonnay: 1–2 years
Gewurztraminer: 1–2 years
Marsanne: 4–12 years

Muscat (dry): 1–3 years;
    (fortified): 5–50 years
Riesling (dry): 1–4 years;
    (sweet): 4–10 years
Sauvignon Blanc: 1–3 years
Sémillon (dry): 2–8 years;
    (sweet): 4–12 years

OVERALL QUALITY LEVEL

At the top level, wines such as the Penfolds Grange or Bin 707 Cabernet Sauvignon, in addition to some of the old-vine Shiraz *cuvées* from relatively small producers such as Torbreck, Veritas, Greenock Creek, Kay Brothers, and Clarendon Hills, are as fine as any red wine made in the world. Sadly, most of Australia's greatest wines are made in minuscule quantities, but readers lucky enough to latch onto any of the production of my five-star wineries are sure to be impressed. Australia's overall wine quality is average, with oceans of mediocre and poorly made wines. There are, however, plenty of good, agreeable wines at attractive prices, and therein lies the reason for the success of Australia's wines. Australia is the world's leader in offering industrial quantities of tasty, user-friendly wines at low prices. In that area, Australia has little competition.

MOST IMPORTANT INFORMATION TO KNOW

Given the remarkable diversity, the best thing to do is to memorize the names of some of the better producers, and restrict your initial purchases to the surefire successes from that particular winery—usually Chardonnay, Cabernet, and Shiraz. Use the producers' chart for each varietal as a guideline until you have decided which wines and producers you prefer.

BUYING STRATEGY

For 95% of Australia's wines, buy only what you intend to drink over the next 12–16 months. The white wines have a particularly short shelf life, and the great majority of the reds are meant to be consumed within 2–4 years of the vintage. Thus, for dry white wines, only the 2001s, 2000s, and 1999s should be purchased. For inexpensive red wines, readers can safely purchase vintages back to 1996 without worrying about the wine's senility. Australia does produce sensational world-class red wines, but they are often produced in minute quantities, and are just as expensive as a grand cru from France or a California cult wine. Readers should try to buy their Australian wines from some of the most creative American importers, who have done a fabulous job in ferreting out some of the limited-production, spectacularly high-quality estates reviewed on the following pages. In particular, readers should look for Australian wines carrying the import label of Dan Philips, The Grateful Palate, Oxnard, California; John Larchet, The Australian Premium Wine Collection, whose importers at the time of writing were USA Wine West, San Rafael, California, and Chicago Brands, Chicago, Illinois; Peter Weygandt, Weygandt-Metzler, Unionville, Pennsylvania; Ted Schrauth, Old Vines Australia, whose importers are Epic Wines, Santa Cruz, California, and C. Daniele, New York, New York; Benjamin Hammerschlag-Epicurean Wines, Seattle, Washington; and Rob McDonald-Old Bridge Cellars, San Francisco, California. These importers do not have an exclusive on every great wine from Australia, but they are dealing with some of the smaller estates whose approach to winemaking is artisanal and oriented to the true connoisseur. Readers should also remember that Australia produces spectacular late-harvested fortified wines at a fraction of the price one pays for vintage ports and the sweet wines of France and Germany. These decadently rich wines are well worth seeking out.

RECENT VINTAGES

As in California, constant sunny weather virtually guarantees at least good-quality wines in Australia, but each year is different as a result of drought as well as heat or cold waves. However, the extremes in quality that one often sees in Europe do not exist in Australia.

2001—A year of extreme heat as well as drought in southern Australia created problems of dehydration, stress, etc. However, tasting at some of the finest estates in June 2001 revealed that some wines, particularly the old-vine Shiraz and Cabernet Sauvignon *cuvées* from McLaren Vale and Barossa, possess enormous power, concentration, and depth. My instincts suggest it will be an irregular vintage for many varietals, but for the top Shiraz and Cabernet Sauvignons, this is a vintage of extraordinary power, concentration, and longevity.

2000—A light year, the 2000s are good but lack the majesty and multiple dimensions found in southern Australia's finest vintages. In western Australia, quality is more even. Nevertheless, this is not likely to be a top vintage for Australia's most famous regions in Victoria, Hunter Valley, Barossa, and McLaren Vale.

1999—Maligned by the Australian press after the powerful 1998s, 1999 has produced elegant, stylish, well-balanced wines that lack the muscle and power of great vintages. Readers who feel many Australian offerings are over the top in terms of extract, richness, and mouth-staining capacity should check out the 1999s, a more delicate, European-styled vintage.

1998—Most of the top producers claim this may turn out to be the finest vintage in western Australia, South Australia, Victoria, and the Hunter Valley in the 1990s. All the elements came together for a superb year. Full physiological maturity with adequate acidity and an absence of rain has produced potentially great wines in South Australia, Victoria, and possibly Hunter Valley. The only area of concern is Western Australia, where late-summer rains ruined what would have been a great year. Producers who survived the rains and picked later are very pleased with what they have achieved. This is an exciting vintage.

1997—Overall, this vintage does not match the quality of either 1996 or 1998. However, there are pockets of outstanding success. In the Hunter Valley, the red wines should be very good to excellent, but the whites suffered from overripeness. In Victoria, the vintage produced wines of extraordinary ripeness. Producers who kept their yields down made big, forceful, blockbuster wines. The 1997 Victoria offerings could easily rival their 1998 counterparts. In South Australia, rain effected some of the cooler climate areas (i.e., Clare Valley), but producers who waited and harvested ripe grapes in Barossa and McLaren Vale produced excellent, somewhat underrated wines. One varietal that did fantastically well in the cooler areas is Riesling. In Western Australia, the high heat and rainfall before the harvest produced a good rather than great year.

1996—This has turned out to be a great year in Western Australia, producing fabulously concentrated, powerful wines, an excellent to great year in South Australia, with abundant high quality, thick, rich, juicy offerings, and a very good year in Victoria. The latter region experienced more rain, but the grapes were superripe in every area save the Yarre Valley. In the Hunter Valley, 1996 is a very good vintage, although irregular.

1995—A very good to excellent vintage in South Australia and Western Australia. While some of the Coonawarra wines are light, and irregularity surfaced in McLaren Vale, Barossa Valley and Clare Valley both produced excellent wines. The examples from Western Australia possess extraordinary concentration and power. They may turn out to be as good as some of the more highly renowned vintages such as 1998. In Victoria, drought conditions produced tiny berries, as well as stressed fermentations and wines. It is a mixed, irregular vintage. In the Hunter Valley, 1995 is considered close to a disaster. Some of the white wines turned out fine, but the red wines are mixed, revealing the effects of the heavy rain that fell during the harvest.

OLDER VINTAGES

Among the other vintages of the 1990s, 1994 was sensational in South Australia, particularly in the Barossa and Clare Valleys. It was excellent in Coonawarra, terrific in Victoria, and great in Western Australia. 1993 was a generally good year throughout Australia, although it never hit the fabulous peaks of 1994. 1992 was also a sound vintage of very good quality, with the highlight being the Cabernet Sauvignon produced in Western Australia. Both 1991 and 1990 were top vintages throughout Australia. 1991's top wines emerged from the Hunter Valley, Barossa Valley, Coonawarra, Victoria, and Western Australia. The one soft spot in the 1991 vintage was Clare Valley. In 1990, the Hunter Valley was a weak link in an otherwise great vintage, particularly in South Australia. 1990 was excellent in Victoria and Western Australia.

RATING AUSTRALIA'S BEST PRODUCERS OF
CABERNET SAUVIGNON, SHIRAZ, MERLOT, AND GRENACHE

***** *(OUTSTANDING)*

d'Arenberg Cabernet Sauvignon The
Coppermine Road (McLaren Vale)
d'Arenberg The Dead-Arm Shiraz
(McLaren Vale)
d'Arenberg The Laughing Magpie
(Shiraz/Viognier) (McLaren Vale)
Brokenwood Shiraz Graveyard Vineyard
(Hunter Valley)
Brokenwood Shiraz Rayner Vineyard
(McLaren Vale)
Burge Family Grenache Old Vines (Barossa)
Burge Family Shiraz Draycott (Barossa)
Clarendon Hills Astralis (Shiraz)
(Clarendon)
Clarendon Hills Grenache Old Vine
Blewitt Springs Vineyard (McLaren Vale)
Clarendon Hills Grenache Old Vine
Kangarilla Vineyard (McLaren Vale)

Clarendon Hills Grenache Old Vine
Romas Vineyard (McLaren Vale)
Clarendon Hills Merlot (McLaren
Vale)
Clarendon Hills Shiraz Brookman
Vineyard (McLaren Vale)
Clarendon Hills Shiraz Hickinbotham
Vineyard (McLaren Vale)
Clarendon Hills Shiraz Liandra Vineyard
(McLaren Vale)
Clarendon Hills Shiraz Piggott Range
Vineyard (McLaren Vale)
Charles Cimicky Shiraz Signature
(Barossa)
Coriole Lloyd Shiraz (McLaren Vale)
Elderton Shiraz Command (Barossa)
Greenock Creek Shiraz Apricot Block
(Barossa)

Greenock Creek Shiraz Creek Block
(Barossa)
Greenock Creek Shiraz Roennfeldt Road
(Barossa)
Greenock Creek Shiraz Seven Acres
(Barossa)
J. J. Hahn Shiraz Block 1914 (Barossa)
Hardy's Shiraz Eileen Hardy (blend of
regions)
Kay Brothers Shiraz Amery Vineyard
Block 6 (McLaren Vale)
Peter Lehmann Shiraz Eight Songs
(Barossa)
The Magpie Estate Shiraz/Mourvèdre
Black Sock (Barossa)
Noon Cabernet Sauvignon Reserve
(Langhorne Creek)
Noon Eclipse Proprietary Red
(Grenache/Shiraz) (McLaren
Vale/Langhorne Creek)
Noon Shiraz Reserve (Langhorne Creek)
Parker Estate Cabernet Sauvignon Terra
Rossa First Growth (Coonawarra)

Penfolds Cabernet Sauvignon Bin 707
(South Australia)
Penfolds Grange (South Australia)
Penley Estate Cabernet Sauvignon
(Coonawarra)
Penley Estate Cabernet Sauvignon Phoenix
(Coonawarra)
Rosabrook Estate Shiraz Abattoir Block
(Margaret River)
Three Rivers Shiraz (Barossa)
Torbreck Run Rig (Shiraz/Viognier)
(Barossa)
Veritas Shiraz Hanisch (Barossa)
Veritas Shiraz Heysen (Barossa)
Wild Duck Creek Estate Cabernet
Sauvignon Reserve (Heathcote)
Yalumba The Octavius (Old Vine Shiraz)
(Barossa)
Yalumba The Reserve (Cabernet/Shiraz)
(Barossa)
Yarra Yering Dry Red #2
(Shiraz/Viognier/Roussanne) (Yarra
Valley)

* * * * (EXCELLENT)

Tim Adams Shiraz (Clare Valley)
Tim Adams Shiraz The Aberfeldy (Clare
Valley)
Australian Domaine Wines Shiraz The
Hattrick (McLaren Vale)
Australian Domaine Wines Shiraz Valley
Floor (Barossa)
d'Arenberg The Custodian (Grenache)
(McLaren Vale)
d'Arenberg Ironstone Pressings
(Grenache/Shiraz) (McLaren Vale)
Berry's Bridge Shiraz (Victoria)
Brokenwood Shiraz (Hunter
Valley/McLaren Vale)
Brothers in Arms Shiraz (Langhorne
Creek)
Burge Family Grenache Old Vines
(Barossa)
Burge Family Grenache/Shiraz/Mourvèdre
(Barossa)
Canonolas Smith Alchemy (Mount
Canobolas)
Cape d'Estaing Shiraz Admiral's Reserve
(Kangaroo Island)
Charles Cimicky Shiraz Signature (Barossa)
Clarendon Shiraz (Clarendon)

Clarendon Hills Shiraz (McLaren Vale)
Clarendon Hills Shiraz Moritz Vineyard
(McLaren Vale)
Clayfield Shiraz Grampians (Victoria)
Coriole Cabernet Sauvignon (McLaren
Vale)
Coriole Mary Kathleen Proprietary Red
Wine (Cabernet Sauvignon/Merlot)
(McLaren Vale)
Coriole Redstone Cabernet Sauvignon
(McLaren Vale)
Coriole Redstone Proprietary Red Wine
(Shiraz/Grenache/Cabernet
Sauvignon/Merlot) (McLaren Vale)
Coriole Shiraz Lloyd Reserve (McLaren
Vale)
Dromana Estate (Cabernet/Merlot)
(Mornington Peninsula)
Dutsche Oscar Seminler Shiraz (Barossa)
Ebenezer Shiraz (Barossa)
Elderton CSM Proprietary Red (Cabernet
Sauvignon/Shiraz/Merlot) (Barossa)
Elderton Shiraz (Barossa)
Fox Creek Shiraz Reserve (McLaren Vale)
Frankland Estate Olmo's Reward (Cabernet
Franc/Merlot) (Western Australia)

Frankland Estate Shiraz Isolation Ridge (Western Australia)

Galah Shiraz (Clare Valley)

Gemtree Vineyards Shiraz (McLaren Vale)

Gnadenfrei Shiraz St. Michael's (Barossa)

Greenock Creek Cabernet Sauvignon (Barossa)

Grosset Gaia Proprietary Red Wine (Clare Valley)

Chris Hackett Shiraz K-1 (Coonawarra)

Chris Hackett Shiraz The Gatekeeper (McLaren Vale)

Richard Hamilton Cabernet Sauvignon Koonawarra Reserve (McLaren Vale)

Richard Hamilton Old Vine Shiraz Reserve (McLaren Vale)

Henry's Drive Cabernet Sauvignon (Padthaway)

Henry's Drive Shiraz (Padthaway)

Henry's Drive Shiraz Reserve (Padthaway)

Henschke Shiraz Hill of Grace (Barossa)

Henschke Shiraz Mount Edelstone (Barossa)

Howard Park Cabernet Sauvignon/Merlot (Western Australia)

Huntington Estate Cabernet Sauvignon Bin FB (Mudgee)

Irvine Grand Merlot (Eden Valley)

Jasper Hill Shiraz Georgia's Paddock (Victoria)

Stephen John Shiraz (Clare Valley)

Trevor Jones Shiraz Wild Witch (Barossa)

Kaesler Stone House Shiraz Old Bastard (Barossa)

Kaesler Stone House Shiraz Old Vine (Barossa)

Katnook Estate Cabernet Sauvignon Odyssey (Coonawarra)

Kay Brothers Cabernet Sauvignon Amery Vineyard (McLaren Vale)

Kay Brothers Shiraz Amery Vineyard (McLaren Vale)

Kay Brothers Shiraz Amery Vineyard Hillside (McLaren Vale)

Kilikanoon Grenache Prodigal (Clare Valley)

Kilikanoon Shiraz Oracle (Clare Valley)

Killibinbin Shiraz (Langhorne Creek)

Château Leamon Shiraz Reserve (Bendigo)

Leeuwin Estate Cabernet Sauvignon Art Series (Margaret River)

Peter Lehmann Cabernet Sauvignon (Barossa)

Peter Lehmann Shiraz Stonewell (Barossa)

Lengs and Cooter Shiraz Old Vines (Clare Valley)

Lengs and Cooter Shiraz Reserve (Clare Valley)

Liebich Vein Shiraz C. W.'s Block (Barossa)

Limelight Syrah (McLaren Vale)

Lost Wolf Cabernet Sauvignon (Barossa)

The Magpie Estate Grenache The Faker (Barossa)

The Magpie Estate Grenache Gomersol (Barossa)

The Magpie Estate Mourvèdre/Grenache (Barossa)

The Magpie Estate Shiraz The Malcolm (Barossa)

Majella Cabernet Sauvignon (Coonawarra)

Majella Cabernet Sauvignon/Shiraz Maleea (Coonawarra)

Majella Shiraz (Coonawarra)

Mak Cabernet Sauvignon (Coonawarra)

Maxwell Wines Cabernet Sauvignon Lime Cave (McLaren Vale)

Maxwell Wines Merlot Reserve (McLaren Vale)

Maxwell Wines Shiraz Ellen Street (McLaren Vale)

Maxwell Wines Shiraz Reserve (McLaren Vale)

Meerea Park Cabernet/Merlot (Hunter Valley)

Meerea Park Shiraz Alexander Munro (Hunter Valley)

Meerea Park Shiraz The Aunts (Hunter Valley)

Charles Melton Cabernet Sauvignon (Barossa)

Charles Melton Nine Popes (Grenache/Shiraz/Mourvèdre) (Barossa)

Charles Melton Shiraz (Barossa)

Moss Wood Cabernet Sauvignon (Margaret River)

Mount Langi Ghiran Cabernet Sauvignon/Merlot (Victoria)

Mount Langi Ghiran Shiraz (Victoria)

Oliver's Shiraz Taranga (McLaren Vale)

Parker Cabernet Sauvignon Coonawarra First Growth (Terra Rosa)

Parson's Flat Cabernet/Shiraz (Padthaway)

Paxton Shiraz (McLaren Vale)
Penfolds Shiraz Bin 128 (South Australia)
Penfolds Shiraz Magill Estate (South
    Australia)
Penfolds Shiraz/Cabernet Koonunga Hill
    (South Australia)
Penley Estate Shiraz Highland
    (Coonawarra)
Petaluma Cabernet/Merlot (Coonawarra)
Petaluma Shiraz (Adelaide Hills)
Pierro Cabernets (Margaret River)
Pikes Cabernet/Merlot (Clare Valley)
Pikes Shiraz (Clare Valley)
Pikes Shiraz Reserve (Clare Valley)
Primo Estate Cabernet Sauvignon/Merlot
    "Joseph" Moda Amarone (Coonawarra)
Primo Estate Shiraz (Adelaide)
The RBJ Mourvèdre/Grenache
    Theologicum (Barossa)
Redbank Cabernet Sauvignon Long
    Paddock (Victoria)
Redbank Sally's Paddock (Victoria)
Rockford Cabernet Sauvignon (Barossa)
Rosemount Cabernet Sauvignon Show
    Reserve (Coonawarra)
Rosemount GSM
    (Grenache/Shiraz/Mourvèdre) (McLaren
    Vale)
Rosemount Mountain Blue
    (Shiraz/Cabernet Sauvignon) (Mudgee)
Rosemount Syrah Balmoral (McLaren Vale)
Rusden Cabernet Sauvignon Boundaries
    (Barossa)
Rusden Grenache (Barossa)
Rusden Grenache Christine's (Barossa)
Rusden Shiraz Black Guts (Barossa)
St. Hubert's Cabernet Sauvignon (Yarra
    Valley)
Scarpantoni School Block Proprietary Red
    (Shiraz, Cabernet Sauvignon, Merlot)
    (McLaren Vale)
Scarpantoni Shiraz Block 3 (McLaren
    Vale)

Summerfield Shiraz (Pyrenees)
Torbreck The Steading
    (Grenache/Shiraz/Mourvèdre)
    (Barossa)
Turkey Flat Shiraz (Barossa)
Veritas Cabernet/Merlot (Barossa)
Veritas Cabernet Sauvignon (Barossa)
Veritas Grenache/Mourvèdre (Barossa)
Veritas Shiraz/Mourvèdre (Barossa)
Viking Wines Cabernet Sauvignon
    (Barossa)
Viking Wines Grand Shiraz (Barossa)
Viking Wines Shiraz (Barossa)
Virgin Hills Cabernet Sauvignon
    (Victoria)
Waninga Shiraz (Clare Valley)
Waninga Shiraz Reserve (Clare Valley)
Warrenmang Grand Pyrenees (Cabernet
    Sauvignon) (Victoria)
Warrenmang Shiraz Moonambel
    (Victoria)
Wild Duck Creek Estate Cabernet
    Sauvignon Alan's (Heathcote)
Wild Duck Creek Estate Cabernets
    Pressings (Heathcote)
Wild Duck Creek Estate Shiraz Springflat
    (Heathcote)
Wild Duck Creek Estate Shiraz Springflat
    Reserve (Heathcote)
Woodstock Winery Grenache (McLaren
    Vale)
Woody Nook Cabernet Sauvignon
    (Margaret River)
Wynns Cabernet Sauvignon John Riddoch
    (Coonawarra)
Yalumba Grenache (Barossa)
Yalumba Grenache Nursery Vineyard
    (Barossa)
Yalumba The Signature (Cabernet
    Sauvignon/Shiraz) (Barossa)
Yarra Yering Cabernet Sauvignon Dry
    Red No. 1 (Yarra Valley)

* * * *(GOOD)*

Abbey Vale Merlot/Shiraz (Margaret
    River)
Tim Adams Cabernet Sauvignon (Clare
    Valley)
Alkoomie Cabernet Sauvignon (Western
    Australia)

Ashbrook Estate Cabernet Sauvignon
    (Western Australia)
Ashton Hills Oblique Proprietary Red
    (Adelaide Hills)
Ashton Hills Oblique Reserve (Adelaide
    Hills)

Bailey's Cabernet Sauvignon (Glenrowan)
Balgownie Cabernet Sauvignon (Bendigo)
Bannockburn Shiraz (Victoria)
Jim Barry Shiraz McCrae Wood (Clare Valley)
Bowen Estate Cabernet Sauvignon (South Australia)
Brand's Laira Cabernet Sauvignon (Coonawarra)
Brokenwood Cabernet Sauvignon (New South Wales)
Brokenwood Shiraz Coach House (Barossa)
Brown Bros. Cabernet Sauvignon (Victoria)
Capel'Vale Cabernet Sauvignon (Western Australia)
Cullen Cabernet Sauvignon (Margaret River)
Cullen Cabernet Sauvignon/Merlot Reserve (Margaret River)
Deakin Estate Shiraz (Victoria)
Fern Hill Cabernet Sauvignon (McLaren Vale)
Richard Hamilton Burton's Vineyard (McLaren Vale)
Richard Hamilton Merlot Reserve (McLaren Vale)
Geoff Hardy Kuitpo Cabernet (Adelaide Hills)
Hewitson Shiraz l'Oizeau (McLaren Vale)
Hickinbotham Cabernet Sauvignon (Geelong)
Highbank Proprietary Red (Cabernet Sauvignon/Merlot/Cabernet Franc) (Coonawarra)
Katherine Hills Cabernet Sauvignon (South Australia)
Hungerford Hill Cabernet Sauvignon (Hunter Valley)
Jindalee Shiraz (Murrays/Darling)
Katnook Estate Cabernet Sauvignon (Coonawarra)
Kilikanoon Cabernet Sauvignon (Clare Valley)
Tim Knappstein Cabernet Sauvignon (Clare Valley)
Lake Breeze Shiraz/Cabernet Bernoota (Langhorne Creek)
Lake Breeze Shiraz Winemaker Selection (Langhorne Creek)
Château Leamon Cabernets/Merlot (Bendigo)

Château Leamon Shiraz (Bendigo)
Peter Lehmann Shiraz (Barossa)
Lillydale Cabernet Sauvignon (Yarra Valley)
Lindemans Cabernet Sauvignon (Coonawarra)
Lindemans Cabernet Sauvignon St. George (New South Wales)
Lindemans Pyrus Proprietary Red (New South Wales)
Lindemans Shiraz/Cabernet Limestone Ridge (New South Wales)
Geoff Merrill Cabernet Sauvignon (South Australia)
Mildara Cabernet Sauvignon (Coonawarra)
Montrose Cabernet Sauvignon (Mudgee)
Oak Ridge Estate Cabernet Sauvignon (Yarra Valley)
Orlando Cabernet Sauvignon Jacaranda Ridge (Coonawarra)
Orlando RF Cabernet Sauvignon (South Australia)
Passing Clouds Cabernet Sauvignon (Bendigo)
Passing Clouds Cabernet/Shiraz (Bendigo)
Passing Clouds Shiraz/Cabernet (Bendigo)
Penfolds Cabernet/Shiraz Bin 389 (South Australia)
Penfolds Shiraz Kalimna Bin 28 (South Australia)
Penfolds Shiraz St. Henri (South Australia)
Petaluma Cabernet Sauvignon (Coonawarra)
Redman Cabernet Sauvignon (Coonawarra)
Riverside Meritage (Barossa)
Robertson's Well Cabernet Sauvignon (Coonawarra)
Rosemount Cabernet Sauvignon Show Reserve (Coonawarra)
Rothbury Estate Shiraz (Hunter Valley)
Rusden Cabernet Sauvignon (Barossa)
Rymill Merlot/Cabernet Franc/Cabernet Sauvignon (Coonawarra)
Rymill Shiraz (Coonawarra)
Saxonvale Cabernet Sauvignon (Hunter Valley)
Seaview Shiraz Edwards and Chaffey (McLaren Vale)
Seppelt Cabernet Sauvignon (Barossa)

Sevenhill Cellars Cabernet Sauvignon (Clare Valley)

Seville Estate Cabernet Sauvignon (Victoria)

Charles Sturt University Shiraz Reserve (New South Wales)

Summerfield Cabernet Reserve (Pyrenees)

Summerfield Shiraz Reserve (Pyrenees)

Château Tahbilk Cabernet Sauvignon (Goulburn)

Château Tahbilk Shiraz (Goulburn)

Tait Cabernet Sauvignon (Barossa)

Taltarni Cabernet Sauvignon (Victoria)

Taltarni Shiraz (Victoria)

Vasse Felix Cabernet Sauvignon (Western Australia)

Wolf Blass Cabernet Sauvignon President's Selection Black Label (Victoria)

Wolf Blass Cabernet Sauvignon Yellow Label (Victoria)

Wright's Cabernet Sauvignon (Western Australia)

Wyndham Estates Cabernet Sauvignon (South Australia)

Wyndham Estates Shiraz (South Australia)

Wynns Shiraz (Coonawarra)

RATING AUSTRALIA'S BEST PRODUCERS OF CHARDONNAY

* * * * (EXCELLENT)

Bannockburn (Geelong)

Barratt (Adelaide Hills)

Canobolas Smith (Mount Canobolas)

Clyde Park (Geelong)

Cullen (Margaret River)

Dromana Estate Reserve (Mornington Peninsula)

Giaconda (Beechworth)

Grosset Piccadilly (Adelaide Hills)

Howard Park (Western Australia)

Trevor Jones Virgin (South Australia)

Leeuwin Artists Series (Margaret River)

Moorooduc Estate (Mornington Peninsula)

Mountadam (Adelaide Hills)

Nicholson River (Gippsland)

Paringa Estate (Mornington Peninsula)

Petaluma (Piccadilly Valley)

Petaluma Tiers (Piccadilly Valley)

Pierro (Margaret River)

Rosemount Roxburgh (Hunter Valley)

Rosemount Show Reserve (Coonawarra)

Rothbury Estate Broken Back Vineyard (Hunter Valley)

Salitage (Pemberton)

Geoff Weaver (Lenswood)

Wise Vineyards Aquercus Unwooded (Western Australia)

Wise Vineyards (Western Australia)

Wise Vineyards Coat Door (Western Australia)

* * * (GOOD)

Cassegrain (New South Wales)

Cold Stream Hills (Yarra Valley)

Craigmoor (Mudgee)

Dalwhinnie (Victoria)

Katherine Hills (Southeastern Australia)

Hungerford Hill (Hunter Valley)

Jindalee (Murrays/Darling)

Katnook Estate (Coonawarra)

Krondorf (Barossa)

Lake's Folly (New South Wales)

Lindemans Bin 65 (New South Wales)

Maxwell Wines (McLaren Vale)

Michelton (Goulburn)

Miramar (Mudgee)

Moss Wood (Western Australia)

Orlando RF (South Australia)

Penley Estate (Coonawarra)

Petaluma (South Australia)

Reynella (South Australia)

Rothbury Estate Broken Back Vineyard Reserve (Hunter Valley)

Seaview Chardonnay Edwards and Chaffey (McLaren Vale)

Seppelt (Barossa)

Mark Swann (South Australia)

Tarra Warra (Victoria)

Tyrells Vat 47 (New South Wales)

Wynn's (Coonawarra)

Yarra Yering (Yarra Valley)

Yeringsberg (Yarra Valley)

RATING AUSTRALIA'S BEST PRODUCERS OF RIESLING

* * * * (EXCELLENT)

Tim Adams (Clare Valley)
Ashton Hills (Adelaide Hills)
Clos Clare (Clare Valley)
Grosset Polish Hill (Clare Valley)

Kilikanoon Blocks Road (Clare Valley)
Kilikanoon Morts Block (Clare Valley)
Petaluma (South Australia)
Viking Wines (Barossa)

RATING AUSTRALIA'S BEST PRODUCERS OF DRY SAUVIGNON BLANC AND SEMILLON

* * * * (EXCELLENT)

Branson Wines Semillon (Barossa)
Brokenwood Semillon (Hunter Valley)
Burge Family Semillon Olive Hill (Barossa)
Cullen Sauvignon/Semillon (Margaret
River)
Fox Creek Semillon/Sauvignon (McLaren
Vale)
Henschke (Barossa)
Katnook Estate Sauvignon (Coonawarra)
Leeuwin Estate Artists Series (Margaret
River)
Leland Estate Sauvignon Blanc (Lenswood)
Lenswood Vineyards (Knappstein)
Sauvignon Blanc (South Australia)

Maxwell Wines Semillon Old Vines
(McLaren Vale)
Nepenthe Sauvignon (Adelaide Hills)
Nepenthe Semillon (Adelaide Hills)
Nicholson River Semillon (Gippsland)
Pierro Semillon/Sauvignon Blanc
(Margaret River)
Rothbury Estate (Hunter Valley)
Shaw and Smith Sauvignon Blanc
(Adelaide Hills)
Stanley Brothers Semillon Full Sister
(Barossa)
Geoff Weaver Sauvignon Blanc
(Lenswood)

* * * (GOOD)

Berri Estates (South Australia)
Evans and Tate (Margaret River)
Tim Knappstein (Clare Valley)
Krondorf (Barossa)
Peter Lehmann (Barossa)

Lindemans (Padthaway)
Mildara (Coonawarra)
Rosabrook Estate Sauvignon Blanc
(Margaret River)
Rosemount (Hunter Valley)

RATING AUSTRALIA'S BEST PRODUCERS OF FORTIFIED WINES

* * * * * (OUTSTANDING)

d'Arenberg Rare Tawny (McLaren
Vale)
Wm. Chambers Rosewood Tokay and
Muscat (various cuvées) (Rutherglen)
Dutsche Tawny (Barossa)
Ralph Fowler Old and Rare Muscat
(Limestone Coast)
Trevor Jones (various cuvées) (Barossa)

Morris Muscat and Tokay Liquor
(Rutherglen)
Penfold's Grandfather Port (Barossa)
Seppelt Para Port (Barossa)
Seppelt Show Wines (Barossa)
Veritas Tawny (Barossa)
Yalumba Port (Barossa)
Yarra Yarra Portsorts (Yarra Valley)

AUSTRALIA'S GREATEST WINE BARGAINS FOR LESS THAN $12

d'Arenberg The Stump Jump
Grenache/Shiraz

Berri Estates Semillon
Brown Brothers Cabernet Sauvignon

Brown Brothers Chardonnay King Valley
Brown Brothers Muscat Lexia
Buckley's Chardonnay
Buckley's Cabernet/Shiraz
Buckley's Chardonnay-Semillon
Hill of Content Benjamin's Blend
Hill of Content Grenache/Shiraz
Peter Lehmann Cabernet Sauvignon
Peter Lehmann Shiraz
Lindemans Chardonnay Bin 65
Mad Fish Chardonnay
Mad Fish Shiraz
Marguis-Philips (various *cuvées*)
Michelton Semillon/Chardonnay
Montrose Cabernet Sauvignon
Montrose Chardonnay
Montrose Shiraz
Orlando Cabernet Sauvignon Jacob's Creek
Orlando Chardonnay Jacob's Creek
Orlando Sauvignon Blanc Jacob's Creek
Oxford Landing Cabernet Sauvignon
Oxford Landing Chardonnay
Paringa Cabernet Sauvignon
Paringa Merlot
Paringa Shiraz
Penfolds Cabernet/Shiraz Koonunga Hill
Rosemount Cabernet Sauvignon/Shiraz
   Diamond Reserve

Rosemount Diamond Reserve
   Grenache/Shiraz
Rosemount Diamond Reserve Red
Rosemount Diamond Reserve Sauvignon
   Blanc
Rosemount Diamond Reserve
   Semillon/Chardonnay
Rosemount Diamond Reserve Shiraz
Rosemount Diamond Reserve White
Rothbury Estate Chardonnay Broken Back
   Vineyard
Rothbury Estate Shiraz
Seppelt Cabernet Sauvignon Black Label
Seppelt Cabernet Sauvignon Reserve Bin
Seppelt Chardonnay Black Label
Seppelt Chardonnay Reserve Bin
Seppelt Semillon/Chardonnay
Seppelt Shiraz Black Label
Seppelt Shiraz Reserve Bin
Seppelt Tawny Strafford Port
Tyrells Long Flat Red
Wolf Blass Cabernet Sauvignon Yellow
   Label
Wolf Blass Shiraz President's Selection
Wyndham Estates Cabernet Sauvignon Bin
   444
Wyndham Estates Chardonnay Bin 222
Yalumba Clocktower Port

TIM ADAMS (CLARE VALLEY)

1997 Cabernet Sauvignon	D	91
1998 Fergus	D	89
1997 Shiraz	D	89+
1998 Shiraz The Aberfeldy	D	87
1997 Shiraz The Aberfeldy	D	93

Tim Adams, one of the most reliable names from Australia, produces top-notch wines from all varietals. His reds are lusty, intensely flavored, full-bodied offerings with copious fruit and considerable aging potential. The dark ruby-colored 1998 Fergus (a Grenache-dominated blend with small quantities of Cabernet Sauvignon, Cabernet Franc, Shiraz, and Malbec, which sees no new oak) offers a moderately intense nose of blackberries, cherry liqueur, pepper, dried herbs, and earth. Round and dense, this succulent, exuberantly fruity, full-bodied wine is fun. Drink it over the next 2–3 years.

Tim Adams's Shiraz The Aberfeldy comes from an old head-pruned vineyard planted in 1904. The wine spends 12 months in new American oak and another year in one-year-old American casks. The 1998 Shiraz The Aberfeldy's dense plum/purple color is followed by aggressive oak aromas intermixed with mint, black raspberries, and blackberries. This medium- to full-bodied wine is not the blockbuster I expected given the vintage, but it is nicely concentrated, cleanly made, and spicy/peppery. Revealing some tannin and adequate acidity, it can be drunk now as well as over the next 8 years.

The opaque purple-colored 1997 Shiraz The Aberfeldy is an immense, full-bodied, opaque purple-colored Shiraz with gorgeous aromas of licorice, cassis, black cherries, and tar. Massive, with high levels of glycerin that ooze across the palate, this dense, flavorful wine can be drunk now because of its low acidity and sweet tannin, but should become more civilized as well as complex with further cellaring. Impressive! Anticipated maturity: now–2020.

The 1997 Shiraz plays it closer to the vest, possessing a dense ruby/purple color and plenty of black raspberry, earthy, prunelike fruit. Exhibiting excellent sweetness, ripeness, and a nicely textured palate, it should drink well for 6–7 years. The outstanding 1997 Cabernet Sauvignon's dense ruby/purple color is followed by intense cassis, tobacco, cedar, and spice aromas and flavors. Long, full-bodied, and super-concentrated, this large-framed Cabernet Sauvignon should drink well young, yet age effortlessly for 12–15 years.

ANNVERS (LANGHORNE CREEK)

1999 Cabernet Sauvignon	D	90

Annvers is a new winery that started only in 1998. It produces a 100% Cabernet Sauvignon produced from 40-year-old vines. The wine spends 18 months in both French and American oak, of which 60% is new. Impressively made and California-like, with jammy black cherry and currant fruit, and coffee, chocolate, and toasty American oak in the background, the full-bodied, juicy, ripe 1999 Cabernet Sauvignon has low acidity, plenty of alcohol (15%), and a lusty, hedonistic finish. Drink it over the next 8 years.

D'ARENBERG (McLAREN VALE)

1999 d'Arry's Original (Shiraz/Grenache)	B	89
1998 d'Arry's Original (Shiraz/Grenache)	B	91
1997 d'Arry's Original (Shiraz/Grenache)	B	87
1996 d'Arry's Original (Shiraz/Grenache)	B	88
1995 d'Arry's Original (Shiraz/Grenache)	B	87
1998 Cabernet Sauvignon The Coppermine Road	E	95+
1997 Cabernet Sauvignon The Coppermine Road	E	90+
1996 Cabernet Sauvignon The Coppermine Road	E	90+
1999 The Custodian (Grenache)	C	88
1998 The Custodian (Grenache)	C	91
1997 The Custodian (Grenache)	C	89
1996 The Custodian (Grenache)	C	90
1998 The Dead-Arm (Shiraz)	EE	96
1997 The Dead-Arm (Shiraz)	EE	95
1996 The Dead-Arm (Shiraz)	EE	96
1999 The Footbolt Shiraz	C	89
1998 The Footbolt Shiraz	A	90
1997 The Footbolt Old Vine Shiraz	A	87
1996 The Footbolt Old Vine Shiraz	B	86
1999 Cabernet Sauvignon The High Trellis	B	88
1998 Cabernet Sauvignon The High Trellis	B	89
1996 Cabernet Sauvignon The High Trellis	B	85
1998 Ironstone Pressings	D	92
1997 Ironstone Pressings	D	94
2000 The Laughing Magpie (Shiraz/Viognier)	D	94
1998 The Noble Riesling	C	90
1997 The Noble Riesling	C	91
1999 The Noble Semillon	C	94
1999 The Twenty-Eight Road (Mourvèdre)	C	87
1998 The Twenty-Eight Road (Mourvèdre)	C	86

1996	The Twenty-Eight Road (Mourvèdre)	C	90
NV	Rare Tawny	D	95

This winery, founded in 1912, continues to amaze me with their enormous portfolio of extremely high-quality wines. Moreover, except for a few fairly high-priced quasi-luxury *cuvées*, they are remarkably fine bargains. The current wine-maker, Chester Osborn, produces superb dry and fortified reds, as well as sweet white wines, and is equally adept at producing dry whites, which, however, are not reviewed here since they have to be consumed within a few years of the vintage. In short, this historic winery from South Australia offers an enviable selection of wines. D'Arenberg's red wines are aged in American oak, except for their new *cuvée*, The Laughing Magpie Shiraz/Viognier, where French wood is utilized. These offerings are classic examples of their varietal composition, and are not burdened by excessive manipulation or blatant new wood.

Readers seeking a natural, pure Cabernet Sauvignon should check out The High Trellis. This wine emerges from a vineyard planted in the 1920s. It is not head-pruned as are so many Australian vineyards, but is trellised much like those in California. As one would expect from vintage conditions, the 1999 Cabernet Sauvignon The High Trellis reveals more vibrancy, elegance, and charm than the 1998. It is a dark ruby/purple-colored effort with medium to full body, sweet cassis fruit, and not much makeup. It should drink well for 7–8 years. The 1998 Cabernet Sauvignon The High Trellis is a thicker, denser, more muscular wine with a broodingly backward personality. The dense plum-colored 1998 displays a big, sweet, cassis nose, medium to full body, and excellent depth as well as chewiness. Anticipated maturity: 2006–2015. The 1996 Cabernet Sauvignon The High Trellis exhibits pruny, raisiny notes in addition to black currant fruit. This straightforward, medium-bodied, overripe wine needs to be drunk over the next several years.

Another fine value is The Footbolt Shiraz. Again, the contrast between the stylish, graceful, medium-weight 1999 vintage and the blockbuster, thicker, more concentrated 1998 vintage is apparent. The deep ruby/purple-colored 1999 The Footbolt Shiraz offers a sweet perfume of new saddle leather intermixed with blackberries, pepper, graphite, and smoke. Medium-bodied, supple, and lively, it will drink well for 4–5 years. The denser, fuller-bodied, more muscular and concentrated 1998 The Footbolt Shiraz has more to it, as well as more tannin and a less evolved personality. It should ultimately prove to be the better wine, but, will it ever be as charming and seductive as the 1999? Drink it before 2012.

The 1997 The Footbolt Old Vine Shiraz's dark ruby/purple color is followed by blackberry/ cassis fruit and sweet toasty oak. The well-made 1996 The Footbolt Old Vine Shiraz exhibits peppery, blackberry fruit intermixed with damp foresty aromas, pepper, and tar. With good fruit, spice, and a rustic finish, it should drink well for 4–5 years.

Southern Rhône wine enthusiasts will enjoy d'Arenberg's Châteauneuf-du-Pape look-alike called d'Arry's Original. A Shiraz-Grenache blend aged completely in large oak upright tanks, it is generally made in a style that gives it both immediate appeal and the potential to last for a decade. Five vintages were tasted, all of them robust, gutsy, rustic but subtly endowed wines that would be ideal accompaniments to most bistro-inspired dishes. The 1999 d'Arry's Original (52% Shiraz and 48% Grenache) reveals wonderful scents of blackberries, black cherries, cassis, earth, leather, and spice. Medium- to full-bodied, spicy, and supple-textured, it will provide delicious drinking over the next 5–6 years. The terrific, deep ruby/purple-colored 1998 d'Arry's Original (47% Shiraz and 53% Grenache) offers a gorgeous perfume of jammy black fruits intermixed with earth, charcoal, and leather. Spicy, meaty, fleshy, and full-bodied, this palate-staining 1998 should drink well for 8 years.

The dark ruby-colored 1997 d'Arry's Original (53% Shiraz and 47% Grenache) displays a ripe blackberry, spicy, peppery nose, good underlying acidity, and a rich, lusty finish. Anticipated maturity: now–2007. The 1996 d'Arry's Original (58% Shiraz and 42% Grenache) exhibits a similar blackberry/licorice-scented nose with more smoke and cassis in the picture. Medium- to full-bodied and ripe, with moderate tannin and noticeable acidity, this is a ripe, fleshy, attractive wine to consume in its youth and over the next 7–8 years. The opaque ruby/ purple-colored 1995 d'Arry's Original (50% Shiraz and 50% Grenache) offers jammy black cherry fruit infused with earth, pepper, melted asphalt, and dried herbs. Dense, robust, and medium- to full-bodied, this is a gutsy, mouth-filling effort that should drink well for 7–8 years.

D'Arenberg's more tannic, structured, and austere The Twenty-Eight Road (Mourvèdre) emerges from a vineyard planted in the 1920s, and is Australia's version of a French Bandol. The 1999 is sweeter than the more rustic 1998, but both possess considerable tannin levels, earthy, peppery, black cherry and currant notes, and dusty, rustic finishes. They are not for everybody, but they are authentic and well made. Both should drink well for 8 years. In total contrast to the two former vintages, the 1996 The Twenty-Eight Road is outstanding. Dark ruby/purple-colored, with a floral, black raspberry–scented nose, this beautifully ripe, dense, concentrated wine offers up mushroom notes intermixed with tree bark and black fruits. Full-bodied, moderately tannic, and impressively rich, it will keep for 15 years.

I am a sucker for sumptuous Grenache, most of which emerges from the southern Rhône Valley and parts of Spain. Australia has proven that it can also turn out dazzling wines from low-yielding, old, head-pruned Grenache vines. The reference point for Australian Grenache is Clarendon Hills, followed by Greenock Creek. However, d'Arenberg does a noteworthy job with their 100% Grenache cuvée The Custodian. This wine emerges from old head-pruned vineyards and yields of one-third to one ton of fruit per acre. The 1999 The Custodian exhibits copious quantities of kirsch, ripe fruit, medium to full body, excellent purity, and a peppery, spicy, long finish. It is a delicious red to drink over the next 3–4 years. Even more impressive is the exceptional 1998 The Custodian. A larger-scaled effort with more layers and body as well as gobs of black cherry fruit, pepper, and spice, this lusty, multidimensional, impressive 1998 should be consumed over the next 7–8 years. The ruby/purple-colored 1997 The Custo-dian reveals a sweet, peppery, black raspberry and cherry fruit–dominated personality, medium to full body, and a lusty (14.5% alcohol) finish. Drink it over the next 2–3 years. The 1996 The Custodian is deeper and richer, with more black raspberry fruit, a peppery earthi-ness, full body, and a head-spinning level of alcohol (14.9%). Long and fat, it is ideal for drink-ing over the next 4–5 years.

The latest member of d'Arenberg's portfolio, The Laughing Magpie is a blend of 95% Shiraz and 5% Viognier aged completely in French oak. It appears to be an effort to compete with wines such as Torbreck's famed Run Rig. The 2000 is a fabulous debut. I tasted it just after bottling, so it may be even better once it has had a chance to calm down. An opaque purple color is followed by a soaring nose of blackberry and crème de cassis intermixed with honeysuckle, pepper, and high-class French oak. The wine is explosive on the palate, super-rich, full-bodied, voluptuous, and powerful, yet seamless and beautifully balanced with well-integrated tannin, wood, and acidity. It should drink well for 15+ years.

The other d'Arenberg's red wine classics, Ironstone Pressings (a Grenache, Shiraz, and Mourvèdre blend), the renowned Dead-Arm Shiraz (from vines 110+ years old), and their top-of-the-line, staggeringly rich, concentrated Cabernet Sauvignon The Coppermine Road, can rival the luxury-cuvée The Laughing Magpie.

The 1998 Ironstone Pressings (70% Grenache, 20% Shiraz, 10% Mourvèdre) is a power-ful, dense, thick, slightly monolithic effort with copious amounts of blackberry fruit, huge body, and the potential to evolve for two decades. Even though it had been in the bottle for some time when I tasted it, it was still unformed. With silky tannin, explosive richness, and potentially top-flight perfume, it should last for 12 years. A killer wine, the sensational 1997 Ironstone Pressings (70% Grenache, 20% Shiraz, and 10% Mourvèdre) boasts an opaque purple color in addition to a spectacular black raspberry, kirsch, and licorice-scented nose, gorgeously full-bodied, super-concentrated flavors with nicely integrated, toasty oak, and fine acidity. Full-bodied, with high alcohol (15%), this is a blockbuster, New World, Rhône look-alike that can be drunk now or cellared for 10–15 years. Impressive!

Year in and year out, d'Arenberg's finest *cuvée* is their spectacular Shiraz made from head-pruned vines more than 100 years old. The 1998, 1997, and 1996 Dead-Arm Shiraz are ex-quisite, multidimensional wines that are sure to make a formidable impression with readers. This wine is aged in 100% new oak, generally tips the scales at a whopping 14–15% alcohol, yet has glorious levels of fruit and extract. The 1998 Dead-Arm Shiraz is outrageously rich, spectacular stuff, the likes of which only Australia seems capable of making. Whiners may complain that it is too big, too rich, too flavorful, and too damn good, but this opaque purple-colored offering is loaded with blackberry liqueur, smoke, charcoal, pepper, cassis, and licorice. Unctuously textured and full-bodied, but neither heavy nor overbearing, the wine's sweet tannin and low acidity are hidden in the cascade of fruit and glycerin that melt on the palate. This riveting, compelling effort can be drunk now, but promises to age well for two de-cades or more. The 1997 Dead-Arm Shiraz exhibits an opaque purple color as well as a sweet nose of vanilla, blackberries, and licorice. The wood frames this enormously concentrated, rich, chewy wine. Multilayered, with phenomenal concentration and length as well as moder-ately high tannin levels, it will be at its finest after 2–3 years of cellaring and will keep for 20 years. Cut from the same cloth, the full-bodied, portlike 1996 Dead-Arm Shiraz displays scents of black fruits, prunes, licorice, and pepper. Thick, rich, and unctuously textured, this is a dazzling old-vine Shiraz that can be drunk now or cellared for 15–20 years.

Readers looking for sensationally concentrated yet well-balanced Cabernet Sauvignon that can be drunk now or cellared for 20 years should check out the 1998 Cabernet Sauvignon The Coppermine Road. It boasts a dense purple color as well as an exquisitely pure nose of cassis, oak, earth, cedar, and spice box. Full-bodied and powerful, with a seamless personal-ity (because of the melted tannin), this large-scaled, classic southern Australian Cabernet Sauvignon can rival the world's finest Cabernets. Anticipated maturity: now–2025. The dense 1997 Cabernet Sauvignon The Coppermine Road exhibits a youthful opaque purple color, high tannin and acidity, and outstanding concentration, richness, and intensity. It de-velops gorgeous black currant fruit mixed with cedar, tobacco, dried herbs, and earth. This wine should keep for 15+ years. The 1996 Cabernet Sauvignon The Coppermine Road is deep ruby/purple in color and shares the 1997's aromas of cassis, cedar, tobacco, dried herbs, and earth. It also offers additional notes of licorice and prunes in its full-bodied, con-centrated, moderately tannic personality. This 1996 should be at its best before 2015.

The botrytised sweeties from d'Arenberg include a captivating 1999 The Noble Sémillon, a wine I would love to put in a blind tasting of the finest Sauternes and Barsacs. Its evolved color is accompanied by an extraordinary bouquet of caramel, orange marmalade, pineapple, honeysuckle, and earth. It reveals astonishing richness, gorgeous sweetness, fine balance, and admirable purity. Whether it will age as well as a Barsac or Sauternes is questionable, but it will impress tasters for at least a decade. Slightly less impressive but still outstanding is the 1998 The Noble Riesling. Honeyed citrus in an Auslese/Beerenauslese style is at-tractive, but as the wine sat in the glass some of Riesling's less favorable characteristics—paraffin and mothball scents—began to emerge. Drink this 1998 over the next 2–3 years.

The medium amber-colored 1997 The Noble Riesling reveals aromas of peach jam, honey-suckle, and strawberries. Rich and decadent, with enough acidity to provide freshness, this wine should be drunk during its vigorous youthfulness—over the next 5–7 years. Another sensational effort is d'Arenberg's nonvintage Rare Tawny, believed to be 12 years old. The deep amber color is followed by a stunningly rich bouquet offering scents of figs, buttered nuts, smoke, prunes, and sweet dark fruits. It is full-bodied and unctuous, yet remarkably fresh and vibrant. This sensational tawny should continue to drink well for another decade.

ARMSTRONG (VICTORIA)

1998 Shiraz Great Western	EE	89+

From an area renowned as one of the coolest climate regions of this part of Australia, the Médoc-like 1998 Shiraz Great Western exhibits aromas of spice box, mineral, cedar, lead pencil, and black currants. Aged in 100% new French oak, it is a streamlined, linear, interesting product. Tasting more like a stylish Cabernet-based Bordeaux than a Shiraz, it should drink well for 7–10 years given its acid profile.

AUSTRALIAN DOMAINE WINES (BAROSSA)

1998 Cabernet Sauvignon/Merlot Alliance	C	87
1999 Grenache The Alliance	C	85
1999 The Hattrick Proprietary Red	E	89
1998 The Hattrick Proprietary Red	E	95
1999 Shiraz The Alliance	C	88
1998 Shiraz The Alliance	C	91
1999 Shiraz Nova	B	86
1999 Shiraz Sheeraz	C	89+
1998 Shiraz Sheeraz	C	88
1997 Shiraz Valley Floor	E	90

This cooperative alliance among many different wine-makers turns out some tasty offerings. The least expensive wine in the ADW portfolio (around 10 U.S.$) is the Shiraz Nova, which is made from young vines and sees little oak and, in this style, is all the better for it. The 1999 Shiraz Nova shows good briery, spicy, peppery, berry fruit, dark ruby color, supple texture, medium body, and good, clean winemaking. Drink it over the next 2 years.

The Sheeraz is a super value. Annual production is about 2,500 cases. Twenty-five dollars rarely buys such an outstanding wine. The opulently textured 1999 Sheeraz shows a black/purple color, high alcohol, and loads of black fruit in addition to a full-throttle personality with plenty of glycerin, concentration, and power. The wine is ripe, intense, and opulent. It should drink well for 7–8 years. The 1998 Sheeraz is elegant, spicy, straightforward, and French-like in its proportions.

An even better value and slightly superior wine is Shiraz The Alliance. Moreover, there are 4,900 cases of this excellent wine. The 1999 exhibits deep purple color, plenty of spicy, toasty new American oak in the nose, a chewy, fleshy texture, and open-knit, expansive flavors that coat the palate. It is not complex, nor will it be particularly long-lived, but for drinking over the next 7–8 years, there is a lot to like. The dense purple-colored 1998 Shiraz The Alliance reveals a fat, blackberry/cassis-scented and flavored personality, immense body, low acidity, sweet tannin, and subtle integrated wood. This fruit- and glycerin-driven, blockbuster Shiraz should drink well for 10–12 years

The low-key 1999 Grenache The Alliance shows cherry fruit in the nose, some spice, moderate ruby color, medium body, and a straightforward, somewhat one-dimensional character. Nevertheless, there is good fruit. The wine is best drunk over the next 2 years.

The most expensive wine in the portfolio, The Hattrick Proprietary Red, is a 600-case blend of Grenache, Shiraz, and Cabernet Sauvignon. The 1999 shows dense ruby/purple color, excellent, concentrated, smoky black fruits, medium to full body, good sweetness, but then a slight narrowing in the finish that kept it from meriting an outstanding score. Nevertheless, there is a lot to like, and this excellent wine should handsomely repay 5–8 years of cellaring. The blockbuster 1998 The Hattrick is a prodigious effort. Opaque purple-colored, with an explosive nose of melted chocolate, pepper, blackberry jam, and cassis, this chewy, full-throttle, monster red reveals no hard edges. The integration of acidity, alcohol, and tannin have been easily accomplished, but the level of fruit extract is mind-boggling. This wine should drink well for 15–25 years, but who will have the patience to wait?

The Cabernet Sauvignon/Merlot Alliance is a 3,900-case blend of 75% Cabernet Sauvignon and 25% Merlot. It is a reasonably good value given today's excessive prices for Cabernet blends. The 1998 Cabernet Sauvignon/Merlot Alliance is a dark ruby-colored wine with a smoky, sweet, curranty nose, medium body, soft tannin, and a spicy, easygoing finish. Anticipated maturity: now–2008. Another outstanding effort was the 1997 Shiraz Valley Floor. This powerful wine (15% alcohol) has a more earthy, leathery, almost hickory barbecue spice note to the blackberry and cassis fruit. It is sweet, lush, and viscous on the attack, with fine density, full body, and a long finish. Unlike the other wines, where there are reasonable quantities, this is a micro *cuvée* of 70 cases. Anticipated maturity: now–2014.

AUSVETIA (SOUTH AUSTRALIA)

1997	Shiraz	E	87
1996	Shiraz	E	87
1995	Shiraz	E	90+

These wines are a joint venture between Penley Estate and their Swiss importer. They are made in an elegant, European style that avoids the dense, blockbuster style so popular in the States. Made from a blend of 95% Shiraz and 5% Cabernet Sauvignon, they emerge from vineyards in both McLaren and Barossa valleys.

The deep ruby/purple 1997 Shiraz is light-bodied, with excellent fruit, sweet tannin, and admirable purity. It offers an excellent bouquet of sweet blackberries and cassis intermixed with asphalt, licorice, and earth and should be drunk over the next 7–8 years. Similarly styled, the 1996 Shiraz is fuller-bodied, ripe, long, and harmonious. It should drink well for 5–6 years. The 1995 Shiraz is a stunning, flamboyant, black/purple-colored effort with copious quantities of cassis/blackberry fruit and toasty vanilla from new-oak casks. Spicy, dense, rich, full-bodied, and classy, this large-scaled wine will last for 15–17 years.

BALGOWNIE ESTATE (BENDIGO)

1999	Cabernet Sauvignon	C	88
1999	Shiraz	C	90

These are the finest Balgownie offerings I have yet tasted. The deep ruby/purple-colored 1999 Cabernet Sauvignon possesses a smoky, cassis-scented nose, excellent sweet fruit, medium to full body, and an elegant, moderately weighty personality with no hard edges. Drink it over the next 6 years. Even better is the 1999 Shiraz, which includes a touch of Viognier in the blend that gives its aromatics an exotic, decadent note. Aromas and flavors of honeysuckle, blackberries, and cassis are evident in this full-bodied, rich, concentrated wine. Although not a blockbuster, it offers good freshness and delineation, delicious flavors, and plenty of personality. Drink it over the next 5–6 years.

BANNOCKBURN (VICTORIA)

1996	Cabernet Sauvignon/Merlot	D	85
1995	Cabernet Sauvignon/Merlot	D	88
1998	Pinot Noir	E	84
1998	Shiraz	E	89

Bannockburn's 1998 Pinot Noir offers plenty of new oak along with a noteworthy chocolate, burnt cherry character. While not complex, it possesses good fruit, medium to full body, and a soft, ripe style. Drink it over the next 2 years.

My favorite Bannockburn offering is the 1998 Shiraz. It lacks the heft that most Australian Shiraz provide, but this is a cooler-climate wine with a deep ruby/purple color, olive-tinged, black currant flavors, some spice, and wood. It exhibits good sweetness on the attack and a medium-bodied, lightly tannic finish. Drink it over the next 7 years.

The evolved 1996 Cabernet Sauvignon/Merlot reveals a mature, dark garnet color along with cool-climate aromatics of spice box, herbs, violets, and red currants. It is medium-bodied, spicy, but somewhat compressed. It should be drunk over the next 2–3 years.

The tasty 1995 Cabernet Sauvignon/Merlot reveals a herbaceousness and bacon fat/sausage component that is undoubtedly due to the type of wood used for aging the wine, in addition to copious quantities of chocolate and berry fruit. This spicy, woody, obvious but fun blend should be drunk over the next 2–3 years.

BARLETTA BROTHERS (BAROSSA)

1997 Grenache/Shiraz	C	87?
1999 Grenache/Shiraz Barossa Valley	C	89
1999 Grenache/Shiraz Clare Valley	C	88

These wines are all from nonirrigated, old, head-pruned vines in the Barossa, averaging between 30 and 70 years of age. There are 329 cases of the Grenache/Shiraz Barossa Valley and 746 cases of the Grenache/Shiraz Clare Valley. The wines are aged in a combination of both new and old American and French casks. The 1999 Grenache/Shiraz Clare Valley (63% Grenache and 37% Shiraz) shows a smoky, black cherry, and currant nose with some spice and earth. The wine is medium- to full-bodied, supple, and fruit-driven. It is best drunk during its first 4–5 years of life. Somewhat similar in style but a little fuller-bodied, with notes of smoke, wood, earth, and black fruits and a touch of chocolate and animal notes, the fatter, riper, more substantial 1999 Grenache/Shiraz Barossa Valley seems to offer additional volume and length. Drink it during its first 6–8 years of life.

The 1997 Grenache/Shiraz's controversial bouquet of fresh earth, smoke, spice, sweaty saddle leather, and aged beef is followed by a creamy-textured, ripe, delicious wine with copious cherry fruit. The funky bouquet is reminiscent of the old-style Bandols from France's Mediterranean coast. Drink it over the next 2–3 years.

JIM BARRY (CLARE VALLEY)

1997 Cabernet Sauvignon/Malbec McCrae Wood	C	87
1997 Shiraz McCrae Wood	C	87

The 1997 Shiraz McCrae Wood exhibits a big, sweet, woody perfume with scents of jammy blackberry fruit. It is a blatantly fruity/woody effort, with abundant glycerin, low acidity, and a lush, chewy, straightforward appeal. Although not the most complex or ageworthy Shiraz, it will please the masses as well as connoisseurs. Drink it over the next 5 years.

The 1997 Cabernet Sauvignon/Malbec McCrae Wood (60% of the former and 40% of the latter) reveals a more saturated color as well as additional black fruits, earth, licorice, and floral characteristics. Medium-bodied, with sweet fruit, well-integrated wood, and an excellent finish, it should drink well for 5 years.

BASS PHILLIP (WEST GIPPSLAND)

1998 Pinot Noir	E	90
1997 Pinot Noir	E	90
1998 Pinot Noir Premium Vineyard Select	EE	92
1997 Pinot Noir Premium Vineyard Select	EE	91+
1998 Pinot Noir Reserve	EEE	93

Lamentably, Bass Phillip produces only 200 cases of their exquisite Pinot Noirs, among the finest being made in Australia. With a Burgundian character, these wines are made from extremely low yields and are bottled without filtration. They throw a hefty film of sediment at a young age because of their natural winemaking.

All three 1998s exhibit Côte de Nuits–like characteristics in their gorgeously sweet, plum, berry, and cherry fruit flavors infused with cinnamon and allspice. Full-bodied, beautifully concentrated, with superb purity, creamy, big, thick, Burgundian textures (that have not been foolishly acidified), they also develop long, concentrated finishes. Extremely complex, and more forward and evolved than most Burgundies are at a similar age, these are beautifully made wines. There are slight differences (the Premium and Reserve ratchet up the level of concentration), but they are more similar than dissimilar. All three are brilliant efforts. Is the Reserve worth nearly $100 more than the regular bottling? The answer is no, but it is a reference point for what Australian Pinot Noir can achieve in selected microclimates when produced without compromise. Drink all of these 1998s over the next 4–5 years.

The 1997 Pinot Noir's superb aromatic profile consists of black cherries, smoky new oak, and flowers. Lush, with outstanding richness and purity, a multilayered, suave, creamy texture, and terrific fruit, it can be drunk now or cellared for 4–5 years. The opaque ruby-colored 1997 Pinot Noir Premium Vineyard Select offers a huge, concentrated nose of black cherries, bacon fat, dried herbs, and high-quality French oak. Full-bodied, moderately tannic, gorgeously pure and nuanced, this wine will keep for a decade. Impressive!

BERRY'S BRIDGE (PYRENEES, VICTORIA)

1999 Cabernet Sauvignon	D	89
1999 Shiraz	D	93

These top-notch wines are made from ripe fruit and what would appear to be extremely low yields. The blockbuster 1999 Shiraz (14.7% alcohol) has an opaque blue/purple color and an extraordinary nose of blackberries, blueberries, and toast. Full-bodied, ripe, and multilayered with exhilarating levels of glycerin, concentration, and depth, this is a pure, surprisingly supple wine to drink over the next 10 years.

Slightly more structured but not as complex nor as concentrated is the 1999 Cabernet Sauvignon. It has an impressively saturated black/purple color and a sweet nose of blueberry and cassis fruit intermixed with licorice and underbrush. The wine is dense, medium- to full-bodied, and pure, with the fruit holding the upper hand. A bit more complexity and it too would have received an outstanding evaluation. Drink it over the next decade.

BIRCHWOOD (SOUTH AUSTRALIA)

1998 Cabernet Sauvignon Twin Rivers	D	89
1998 Shiraz Decades	D	90

This is a *négociant* operation dedicated to finding good old-vine sources for grapes in South Australia. The 1998 Cabernet Sauvignon Twin Rivers comes from a 40-year-old vineyard. Production is small (250 cases), the wine very good, even excellent, with an elegant black currant, spice box, cedar, and dried herb–scented nose, attractive, medium- to full-bodied flavors, low acidity, sweet tannin, and a clean finish. Drink it over the next 5–6 years.

More interesting is the 1998 Shiraz Decades. Made from vines averaging 30–60 years, this wine was formerly utilized as a component part of the well-known Rosemount Balmoral Shiraz. This dense ruby/purple, full-bodied Shiraz reveals the telltale blackberry liqueur–scented nose with notes of licorice, pepper, and toasty new oak. Dense, powerful, and concentrated, it is a powerhouse to drink over the next 8 years.

BRANSON COACH HOUSE (ASPDEN)

1998 Shiraz Malcolm	EE	97

Limited in availability, this 1998 Shiraz Malcolm entirely made from the "Grange" clone of that varietal, exhibits an opaque black/blue color, a personality similar to a dry vintage port, massive body, phenomenal concentration, and a viscous, huge, juicy, thick underbelly bursting with glycerin, fruit, and extract. The high tannin is nearly concealed by the wine's glycerin and extract level. Tasting more like a barrel sample than a finished wine, this youthful, Goliath-sized Shiraz will handsomely repay 15–20 years of cellaring.

BROKENWOOD (HUNTER VALLEY)

1998 Shiraz	D	86
1998 Shiraz Graveyard Vineyard	EE	90
1997 Shiraz Graveyard Vineyard	EE	92
1998 Shiraz The Mistress Block	E	88+
1997 Shiraz The Mistress Block	E	91
1998 Shiraz Rayner Vineyard	E	90
1997 Shiraz Rayner Vineyard	E	94

Brokenwood has been considered one of the finest practitioners of old-vine Shiraz since their debut vintage in 1970. They are also widely heralded for their interesting whites (Sauvignon Blanc and Sémillon), which are not reviewed here since they have to be consumed within a few years of the vintage. The 1997 Brokenwood Shiraz *cuvées* performed exceptionally well, even though the vintage is considered less successful than the more highly touted 1998. All the impressive, dark ruby/purple 1998s possess admirable levels of fruit and extract and co-pious quantities of toasty wood. The least expensive wine of the portfolio is the Shiraz, a blend from McLaren Vale, King Valley, and Cowra that is aged in American wood for 20 months prior to bottling. The 1998 is a forward, chocolaty/berry-flavored wine with notes of melted tar and hints of tannin and acidity in the finish. This Shiraz is meant to be drunk over the next 2–3 years for its gutsy richness and uncomplicated style.

The Shiraz The Mistress Block emerges from vines averaging 30 years of age and is aged in American oak. The dense purple-colored 1998 offers generous aromas of pepper, spice, blackberries, chocolate, and vanilla. Full-bodied and moderately tannic, with tart acidity, fine intensity, and a generous, robust constitution, this mouth-filling Shiraz will keep for 8–10 years. The dark ruby/purple 1997 Shiraz The Mistress Block possesses exceptional balance. Sexy and lush, with low acidity, a beautiful, American oak–infused, blackberry-scented nose and flavors, it is creamy-textured and full-bodied, with terrific intensity and pu-rity. This ostentatiously styled Shiraz can be drunk now and over the next decade.

The Shiraz Rayner Vineyard emerges from a dry-farmed Shiraz vineyard. The 1998 is the beefiest, most potent of the 1998 Brokenwood offerings at 14.5% alcohol. Licorice, blackber-ries, pepper, earth, and sweet oak are abundantly present in this full-bodied, impressively constituted, rich Shiraz. The finish is long and intense. Tight, with noticeable acidity and high tannin, it will keep until 2014. The voluptuous and seamless 1997 Shiraz Rayner Vine-yard's beautifully integrated acidity, tannin, and alcohol result in a weighty, full-bodied, ex-plosively rich, monster-sized Shiraz with copious quantities of blackberry and blueberry fruit intertwined with melted tar and pepper. Thick, juicy, and disarming, this lusty effort can be drunk now and over the next 10–12 years.

The 1998 Shiraz Graveyard Vineyard is a seriously structured, dense, impressively consti-tuted effort with well-integrated tannin and oodles of blackberry fruit intermixed with new saddle leather, pepper, and asphalt. Full, lush, and delineated, this big wine is accessible and will last for 15+ years. Less weighty than usual, but clearly the flagship wine of Broken-wood, the 1997 Shiraz Graveyard Vineyard is made in an earthy, perfumed style, without the power, concentration, or palate impact of the Rayner Vineyard. Nevertheless, there is plenty to get excited about in this full-bodied, rich, chewy wine with uncanny balance and beautiful overall purity and equilibrium. Drink it over the next 12 years.

BROTHERS IN ARMS (LANGHORNE CREEK)

1998 Shiraz	D	92

This is a reasonably good value for a full-throttle, massive, super-concentrated Shiraz. There are 570 cases of this wine that "modestly" tips the scales at 16% alcohol. It emerges from a vineyard with many vines over 100 years of age, which is said to have been the source for the top *cuvée* of Shiraz for Mildara Blass before the vineyard owners decided to produce their own wine. The 1998 shows a dense purple color and a gorgeous nose of blue- and black-berries intermixed with some cherry liqueur. Full-bodied, opulent, with plenty of spice, creosote, pepper, and subtle wood, this wine is impressive, concentrated, and already delicious. Anticipated maturity: now–2010. It is undoubtedly a sleeper pick at this price. Look for this winery to attract more and more fans.

BURGE FAMILY (BAROSSA VALLEY)

1998 Grenache Old Vines	D	92
1999 Grenache/Shiraz/Mourvèdre Olive Hill	D	90
1999 Shiraz Draycott	D	88
1998 Shiraz Draycott	D	90
1997 Shiraz Draycott	D	89
1999 Shiraz Grateful Reserve	EE	90
1998 Shiraz Grateful Reserve	EE	98

Burge is another of the exceptional wineries of the Barossa that seems to consistently turn out top-flight wines. The red wines are all noteworthy for their brilliant displays of ripe fruit and consistent purity. The 1999 Grenache/Shiraz/Mourvèdre Olive Hill (43% Shiraz, 34% Grenache, and 23% Mourvèdre) is a strong effort from this vintage. The wine shows a dense ruby/purple color, notes of violets, black fruits, licorice, and a powerful leathery and floral note. The wine is full-bodied with a sweet attack, honeyed black fruits, nicely integrated wood (about one-third new French oak was used), and a layered finish.

The 1999 Shiraz Draycott (86% Shiraz and 14% Grenache from 10- to 40-year-old vines) is lighter than its equivalent in 1998. The wine is still very good, with a peppery cassis nose, sweet jammy fruit on the attack, medium body, and a moderately endowed, clean finish. Drink it over the next 6–7 years. The 1998 Shiraz Draycott shows more fat, a broader, more expansive texture, lower acidity, and a sweet, jammy, blackberry, smoky cassis character. The wine is long, pure, and full-bodied (the alcohol is 14.9%). Drink it over the next decade for its exuberant, powerful, in-your-face style. The 1997 Shiraz Draycott is lighter-styled than the colossal 1998. A blend of 70% Shiraz and 30% Grenache, it exhibits a dark ruby color and a pleasant, sweet, blackberry- and cherry-scented nose with pepper and earth undertones. Lush, fruit-driven, and supple, it will drink well for 5–6 years.

Sadly, there are less than 200 cases annually of the Shiraz Grateful Reserve, which is made from a 40-year-old vineyard. The outstanding 1999 shows a smoky, oaky style with medium body, excellent blackberry/cassis fruit, but not nearly the intensity, texture, and layers of flavor found in Burge's 1998s. Anticipated maturity: now–2015.

It would be difficult to find a better Shiraz than the 1998 Shiraz Grateful Reserve. The color is a saturated blue/purple that looks more like vintage port than dry table wine. A spectacular bouquet of melted chocolate, licorice, blackberry jam, blueberries, and cassis is accompanied by an awesomely concentrated, massively proportioned wine that somehow has just enough acidity and tannin to both pull it together and provide some delineation. The wine is gorgeously pure, with massive power and weight, and a finish that lasts nearly a minute. Low acidity, high glycerin, 14.5% alcohol, and thrilling levels of extract/concentration make for a nearly perfect drinking experience. Anticipated maturity: now–2025+.

The ripeness and concentration, volume, and fuller style from the 1998 vintage is also evident in the 1998 Grenache Old Vines. Made from vines ranging in age from 70 to 80 years old, this 100% Grenache *cuvée* (400 cases) shows serious cherry liqueur in the nose, along with some roasted notes, a full-bodied, lavishly rich palate filled with fruit and glycerin, and a fleshy, rather juicy and succulent finish. It is not meant for long-term aging but for drinking over the next 4–5 years. This will score high on the pleasure meter.

CAMPBELLS (RUTHERGLEN)

NV	Isabella Rare Rutherglen Tokay	E	97
NV	Merchant Prince Rare Muscat	E	95
NV	Muscat	D	90
NV	Tokay	D	90

One of the illustrious names in Australian fortified dessert wines, Campbells has been making these gems since 1870. The rare *cuvées*, Isabella and Merchant Prince (blends that average 70 years in age), are superior fortified wines with extraordinary aromatics, unctuous textures, and luxurious levels of sweetness and concentration. However, there is no question that the nonvintage Muscat and Tokay are terrific buys. They may not possess the intensity of their more powerful siblings, but they are loaded with fruit, unctuous, sweet, and already complex, with stunning aromatics. Moreover, they will keep for decades. These sensational offerings are among the treasures of Australia.

CANOBOLAS SMITH (NEW SOUTH WALES)

1996	Alchemy Proprietary Red Wine	D	94
1998	Cabernet Sauvignon/Merlot Wattleview	C	90

A terrific bargain in New World Cabernet Sauvignon/Merlot, the 1998 Cabernet Sauvignon/Merlot Wattleview, a blend of 60% Cabernet and 40% Merlot aged in French oak, shows plum, cherry, and currants in the expressive nose, and hedonistic, lush, medium- to full-bodied flavors that are seamless, low in acidity, and sexy. This is a seductive, reasonably priced wine to drink now and over the next 7 years. Don't miss it!

The prodigious 1996 Alchemy (predominantly Cabernet Sauvignon, with Shiraz and Cabernet Franc) achieved 15% alcohol naturally. Aged in both French and American oak, and bottled unfiltered, it is a wine of extraordinary purity and multiple dimensions. Knockout aromas of blackberry liqueur, cassis, toasty oak, and spice box are followed by a layered wine with sweet tannin and low acidity. It is full-bodied and massive, yet there is no sense of heaviness or hotness. Pure, thick, and viscous, it should drink well for 12 years. Impressive!

CAPE D'ESTAING (KANGAROO ISLAND)

1999	Cabernet Sauvignon	E	89+
1998	Cabernet Sauvignon	E	92+
1999	Shiraz	E	88
1998	Shiraz	E	94
1998	Shiraz Admiral's Reserve	EEE	91+

From an island off the coast of Adelaide renowned for abundant wildlife, Cape d'Estaing seems to be a high quality producer that offers wine made from a somewhat cooler climate than the Barossa Valley to the north. Yields are generally a lowly 1 ton of fruit per acre. The vineyards are young (five years), but the wines, which are aged in French oak, are of spectacular quality. Fortunately, the annual production averages 1,500 cases for each wine.

The 1999 Cabernet Sauvignon shows a full-bodied style with opaque purple color, sweet, classic black currant fruit mixed with spice box and tobacco. The wine is rich, concentrated, and not dissimilar from a high-class Bordeaux. The alcohol is a modest 13.7% (reasonable by Australian standards). This wine shows excellent purity and fine overall balance. Anticipated maturity: now–2012. The 1998 Cabernet Sauvignon (13.4% alcohol) displays a thick-looking, opaque purple color as well as a terrific nose of black currants, cedar, spice box, and minerals. Medium- to full-bodied, with outstanding purity, remarkable symmetry, and potential complexity for a young wine, this beautifully proportioned, intensely concentrated Cabernet should be at its best after another 2 years of cellaring and should last for two decades.

The 1999 Shiraz (100% Shiraz) is medium- to full-bodied, boasts a dark purple color, somewhat monolithic attack, but then unfolds gracefully on the palate, revealing more finesse and restraint than many of the more humongous offerings of Shiraz from warmer mainland microclimates. This wine is pure, stylish, and best drunk during its first 10–12 years of life.

The flashier 1998 Shiraz exhibits terrific blackberry jam–like aromas intermixed with sweet pepper, espresso, and vanilla scents. Super-concentrated, loaded with ripe fruit, and impressively pure and layered, this is a dazzling Shiraz. Despite the fact that it tasted powerful, the alcohol is only 14.1%. Drink this sumptuous Shiraz over the next 10 years.

The 1998 Shiraz Admiral's Reserve is essentially a 125-case batch selected in the cellar from all the barrels of Shiraz. The wine has an opaque purple color and a sweet nose of blackberry liqueur intermixed with road tar, new saddle leather, pepper, and spice. Full-bodied, rich, structured, and backward, this impressive, large-scaled wine admirably marries a degree of finesse with the boldly flavored, bigger style favored by Australians. Anticipated maturity: now–2016.

SERGIO CARLEI (HEATHCOTE)

1999 Shiraz Green Vineyard Forties Old Block	E	88
1998 Shiraz Green Vineyard Forties Old Block	E	89
1998 Tre Rossi	E	87

The 1998 Tre Rossi's blend of 50% Shiraz and 25% each of Egiodola and Marzemino, two varietals that are alien to my palate, has produced a black/purple wine with high levels of rustic tannin and notes of meat, chocolate, plum liqueur, and earth. Although coarse, it is loaded with character. It is hard to know whether this 1998 will age gracefully or become increasingly attenuated and rustic. For now, it is a substantial wine to enjoy with full-flavored dishes. Both the 1998 and 1999 Shiraz Green Vineyard Forties Old Block are aged completely in French oak. The 1999 displays a blackberry, graphite, charcoal, and smoky-scented nose, medium to full body, good complexity, and a moderately weighty feel in the mouth. It is supple enough to be drunk now and over the next decade. The similarly styled 1998 is richer, with more length, power, and extract. To both wines' credit, the French oak is subtle and nicely integrated. The 1998 should drink well for another 10 years.

CASA FRESCHI (LANGHORNE CREEK)

1999 Profondo	E	92
1999 La Signora	E	90

Based on the first wines I have tasted from proprietor/wine-maker David Freschi, this is an up-and-coming star. Both wines are aged in primarily new French oak, are bottled unfined and unfiltered, and combine a power and uncanny elegance which is unusual in Australia.

The 1999 La Signora could easily pass for a St.-Emilion garage wine. It has a somewhat international style, but the opaque purple color offers up notes of coffee, chocolate, and black currants along with cigar box notes. The wine is rich, dense, and ripe, with beautifully integrated acidity, wood, and alcohol. The finish is long and at the same time elegant. It should drink well for at least 10 years. Even more impressive is the Bordeaux look-alike, the 1999 Profondo. Also a blend of Shiraz, Cabernet Sauvignon, and Malbec, it exhibits an impressive saturated, dark ruby/purple color in addition to a gorgeous nose of blueberry liqueur intermixed with cassis, Chinese black tea, vanilla, and licorice. Stunningly rich on the palate, with multiple layers of concentration, this compelling wine is a dead ringer for a top first or second growth Bordeaux. Anticipated maturity: now–2015.

CASTAGNA (VICTORIA)

1999 Syrah Genesis	EE	86

It seems that Julian Castagna, the proprietor of this winery, is a famous film and television director with a wine bug. However, he needs a reality check with respect to his pricing policy.

The 1999 Syrah Genesis has an uncanny resemblance to a midweight Crozes-Hermitage from France's Rhône Valley. Smoky, olive, black currant notes combine with some new oak and pepper to give this moderately weighted wine plenty of appeal, but there must be five or six dozen offerings from the real Crozes-Hermitage that sell for under $25 a bottle that are as good, if not better.

CHAMBERS ROSEWOOD (RUTHERGLEN)

NV	Muscat	E	95
NV	Rare Muscat	EEE	100
NV	Rare Tokay	EEE	100
NV	Special Muscat	EE	98
NV	Special Tokay	EE	99
NV	Tokay	E	96

I have long believed that Australia remains an unheralded but extraordinary treasure trove for fortified Muscat and Tokay. It is amazing how many sensational efforts emerge from this country. With the exception of William Chambers, they have not received the accolades they deserve. Anyone who has ever tasted his fortified Tokay or Muscat realizes that the world's reference point for these wines begins and ends with Chambers. These luxurious offerings possess such extraordinary unctuosity, thickness, complexity, and richness that they must be tasted to be believed. They are not just big, thick sugar balls, because they have sound underlying acidity as well as remarkable complexity and freshness. A spoonful or two of each wine is enough for most nongluttons to appreciate the riveting heights these *cuvées* represent. Obviously the Rare Muscat and Rare Tokay are surreal, but for the price, the $15 *cuvées* of Muscat and Tokay are sensational bargains. One could even argue that the Rare Muscat and Rare Tokay, believed to be 50–70 years old from the solera system (a blend of vintages with a very old base or dominant portion) that Chambers has long maintained, are even spectacular bargains. What do they taste like? The levels of intensity, perfume, and viscosity rise with each tier, from the regular *cuvées* to the special *cuvées* to the rare *cuvées*. All possess notes of smoke, roasted nuts, coffee, brown sugar, maple syrup, prunes, honey, fruitcake, overripe orange/apricots, and remarkable spicy characters. The Muscats tend to be slightly more fruit-driven, with the Tokays more earthy and raisiny. However, these are all riveting examples of fortified dessert wines that I enthusiastically recommend. I use the Rosewoods for many charitable meals/wine tastings I donate, and guests are always gaga about these rarities. In summary, life is too short not to try one of the Muscats or Tokays from Chambers Rosewood, a true Australian treasure.

CHAPEL HILL (McLAREN VALE)

1998 The Vicar (Shiraz/Cabernet Sauvignon)	D	88

A thick, viscous, dense ruby/purple offering, Chapel Hill's 1998 The Vicar exhibits abundant quantities of new oak (primarily American), loads of blackberry and cassis flavors, and a rich, concentrated, blockbuster finish. A blend of 56% Shiraz and 44% Cabernet Sauvignon, this rich, moderately tannic 1998 is best drunk before 2014.

CHERISE (McLAREN VALE)

1997 Sangiovese	C	91

If only California wineries could make Sangiovese such as this! Wine-maker/owner Stephen Hall (formerly of Coriole) has turned out a terrific 1997 Sangiovese with a deep ruby color and a knockout aromatic profile featuring cherry jam galore intertwined with kirsch and sweet leather. Medium- to full-bodied and muscular, with gorgeous levels of fruit, this soft, opulently styled Sangiovese should be enjoyed over the next 2–3 years.

CHARLES CIMICKY (BAROSSA)

1998	Merlot	D	90
1996	Merlot	D	88
1998	The Red Blend	D	90
1997	The Red Blend	D	90
1998	Shiraz Reserve	D	91+
1998	Shiraz Signature	D	92
1997	Shiraz Signature	D	89

Given the bang for the buck, so to speak, Charles Cimicky's wines are excellent values, consistently full-bodied, concentrated, and well structured. His 1998s seem extremely youthful, and tasted more like barrel samples than finished wines, but there is considerable long-term potential for these *cuvées*. The 1998 Merlot exhibits a deep ruby/purple color and a big, sweet nose of blackberry and cherry fruit intermixed with fudge, coffee, and smoky wood. It is full-bodied, ripe, and sexy. Drink it over the next 8 years. The internationally styled 1996 Merlot exhibits black cherry fruit, lavish, high-quality toasty oak, medium to full body, adequate acidity, and a mouth-filling, plump texture. Aromatic and pure, this fleshy Merlot should drink well for 4–5 years.

The dense purple-colored, full-bodied 1998 The Red Blend, a 58% Cabernet Sauvignon, 22% Merlot, and 20% Cabernet Franc blend, reveals explosive fruit, licorice, tobacco, black cherries, currants, and new oak in the nose, and high levels of tannin. It comes across in the mouth like a St.-Emilion on steroids. The wine seems extremely young, and 1–2 years of cellaring may result in an even more multidimensional effort. It should keep well for 14 years.

The 1997 The Red Blend (58% Cabernet Sauvignon, 22% Merlot, and 20% Cabernet Franc) is a thick, rich, full-bodied, fleshy, dry red with abundant quantities of black fruits intermixed with spicy new oak. Concentrated, with low acidity, sweet tannin, and no hard edges, this mouth-filling big red should drink well for 8 years.

The 1998 Shiraz Reserve is a dense purple-colored effort revealing gorgeously pure, vibrant notes of black raspberries, blackberries, mineral, smoke, and creosote. Full-bodied, dense, tightly knit, and explosive, it requires 1–2 years of cellaring. Consume it over the following 12–15 years, although I suspect it will last longer.

Another wine that seems to be bursting at the seams is the profound, black/purple 1998 Shiraz Signature, a 100% old-vine Shiraz. The exquisite aromatics consist of blueberry/blackberry liqueur followed by a sweet, full-bodied, textured mouth-feel, with superb purity, high tannin, but also superb extract. I would drink it over the following 12–15 years.

The 1997 Shiraz Signature is less powerful than the 1998, but more evolved, with sweet black fruit aromas and flavors, full body, low acidity, and an admirably concentrated, nuanced, and lushly textured style. It should drink well for 6 years.

CLARENDON HILLS (CLARENDON)

1999	Astralis	EEE	91+
1998	Astralis	EEE	95+
1999	Cabernet Sauvignon Brookman Vineyard	D	89
1998	Cabernet Sauvignon Brookman Vineyard	D	87
1999	Cabernet Sauvignon Hickinbotham Vineyard	D	90
1998	Cabernet Sauvignon Hickinbotham Vineyard	D	93+
1999	Cabernet Sauvignon Sandown Vineyard	D	88
1998	Cabernet Sauvignon Sandown Vineyard	D	92+
1999	Grenache Old Vines Blewitt Springs Vineyard	D	92
1998	Grenache Old Vines Blewitt Springs Vineyard	D	92
1999	Grenache Old Vines Clarendon Vineyard	D	87
1998	Grenache Old Vines Clarendon Vineyard	D	93

1999	Grenache Old Vines Hickinbotham Vineyard	D	89
1999	Grenache Old Vines Kangarilla Vineyard	D	91
1998	Grenache Old Vines Kangarilla Vineyard	D	90+
1999	Grenache Old Vines Romas Vineyard	E	92
1999	Merlot Brookman Vineyard	D	90
1998	Merlot Brookman Vineyard	D	88
1999	Merlot Hickinbotham Vineyard	D	91+
1999	Pinot Noir Hickinbotham Vineyard	D	87
1998	Pinot Noir Hickinbotham Vineyard	D	89
1999	Shiraz Brookman Vineyard	E	90
1998	Shiraz Brookman Vineyard	D	94
1999	Shiraz Hickinbotham Vineyard	E	90+
1998	Shiraz Hickinbotham Vineyard	D	92
1999	Shiraz Liandra Vineyard	E	92
1998	Shiraz Liandra Vineyard	D	91
1999	Shiraz Moritz Vineyard	E	92
1999	Shiraz Piggott Range Vineyard	E	91+
1998	Shiraz Piggott Range Vineyard	D	92+

I am an unabashed admirer of proprietor/wine-maker Roman Bratasiuk's super-concentrated, muscular, full-throttle red wines, whether they be Cabernet Sauvignon, Merlot, Shiraz, or his undeniable specialty, Grenache. There is no doubt that the red wines pack all the flavor and concentration one would expect from a no-holds-barred "Aussie" style. Yet his wines, as massive and deep as they are, have impeccable balance and purity. I also applaud his judicious use of French rather than American oak. For my taste, Clarendon Hills is today's undisputed superstar of McLaren Vale.

Reminiscent of a good Pinot made in a dense style, the 1999 Pinot Noir Hickinbotham Vineyard reveals a garnet color and a broodingly backward, smoky, earthy nose of root beer, cola, black cherries, raspberries, and prunes. Spicy, medium- to full-bodied, ripe, and well made, it should drink well for 4–5 years. The dark ruby-colored 1998 Pinot Noir Hickinbotham Vineyard offers an intriguing nose of allspice, black fruits, and earth. Ripe, with plenty of stuffing, good underlying acidity, and a robust, chewy style, this is a flavorful, muscular Pinot to drink over the next decade.

In 1999 (a lighter, more elegant, and often less concentrated vintage than 1998 in South Australia) Clarendon Hills has turned out some stylish, flavorful Cabernet. The 1998s are also superb, with the 1998 Cabernet Sauvignon Sandown Vineyard and 1998 Cabernet Sauvignon Hickinbotham Vineyard being more revealing as well as massive, powerful, highly extracted, and broodingly backward. All of these wines are accessible, but the Hickinbotham cuvée, especially the 1998 version, has the best chance of lasting well beyond a decade.

The 1999 Cabernet Sauvignon Brookman Vineyard shows a dark ruby/purple color and a sweet nose of leafy black currants intermixed with earth, spice, and some background wood. The wine is rich, has sweet fruit on the palate, and a supple finish. Drink it over the next 7–8 years. The least impressive and expressive of Cabernet from Clarendon Hills is the 1998 Cabernet Sauvignon Brookman Vineyard. Closed and tannic, with toasty notes in the aromas, it was difficult to penetrate and evaluate. There is size and force to the wine, but it is monolithic. Like its siblings, it is aged in 100% new French oak casks, which is apparent from its toast-scented nose. Anticipated maturity: now–2015. The dark purple-colored 1999 Cabernet Sauvignon Sandown Vineyard possesses chocolate, along with telltale cassis, tobacco, earth, and spice aromas. The wine is very good to excellent, nicely balanced, and best drunk over the first decade of life. The opaque purple-colored 1998 Cabernet Sauvignon Sandown Vineyard displays a dense nose of cassis and jammy cherry fruit intermixed with licorice, tobacco, tar, and dried herbs. Thick, powerful, full-bodied, and moderately tannic, this wine will keep for two decades. The 1999 Cabernet Sauvignon Hickinbotham Vineyard boasts a nice volume and a complex nose of black currants, chocolate, barbecue spice, and toast. The wine is powerful, dense, concentrated, rich, with subtle wood, plenty of fruit, glycerin, and moderate tannin. Anticipated maturity: 2006–2018. The 1998 Cabernet Sauvignon Hickinbotham Vineyard reveals a similar opaque purple color and highly extracted, massive size, with a touch of mint in its black currant/cassis flavors. The acidity is lower as well. This effort possesses a greater degree of ripeness, although all of these wines are ultraripe and concentrated. Huge, chewy, and full-bodied, it should keep for two decades.

The Merlots are outstanding wines. The 1999 Merlot Brookman Vineyard reveals a Starbucks-esque chocolate espresso roasted nose, full body, deep, concentrated flavors, plenty of smokiness, and berry fruit, noteworthy glycerin, low acidity, and a lush, heady texture. This wine will provide hedonistic drinking for at least 8–12 years. The 1998 Merlot Brookman Vineyard is restrained. Its dark ruby color is followed by sweet, ripe aromas of jammy cherries intermixed with herbs and earth. Open-knit and admirably concentrated, with excellent symmetry and purity, this fleshy, fruit/glycerin-dominated Merlot is the finest wine from this varietal being produced in Australia. Drink it over the next 5–7 years. More structured, backward, denser, and delineated is the 1999 Merlot Hickinbotham Vineyard. It reveals similar chocolate, coffee, black cherry, and currant notes, along with more depth, structure, and tannin. Consume it over the following 12–15 years.

I have long been an admirer of the Clarendon Hills Grenaches and have purchased and drunk more than my fair share, always with exceptional pleasure. To my taste, no one makes better old-vine Grenache in Australia than Roman Bratasiuk, and I doubt anyone in California can compete with him. The portfolio comprises five *cuvées*, including the superluxury Grenache called Romas. These are all wines that are gorgeous to drink young, and can probably easily last in a good cellar for 10 years or more. The 1999s are fine efforts that come close to equaling the high-quality *cuvées* of Grenache the proprietor produced in 1998.

The lightest and least impressive of the quintet is the 1999 Grenache Old Vines Clarendon. For a Bratasiuk wine, this has surprisingly modest alcohol (13.5%), an evolved dark garnet color, and notes of Provençal herbs, spice box, cherries, and balsam wood. It tastes like a well-made Côtes du Rhône, with medium to full body and a supple texture. Drink it over the next 3–4 years. More Châteauneuf-du-Pape-like is the 1999 Grenache Old Vines Kangarilla Vineyard (14.5% alcohol). This wine ratchets up the level of volume, depth, and length, offering kirsch, black raspberry, and cherry notes intermixed with roasted herbs and balsam wood notes. The wine is textured, full-bodied, and offers a plum/ruby color. I would opt for drinking this over the next 6–8 years.

Lovers of flamboyant Grenache will get a blast from the exotic, over-the-top 1999 Grenache Old Vines Blewitt Springs Vineyard (14.5% alcohol). This wine has jammy, raspberry notes intermixed with notes of peach/apricot, suggesting ripe fruit. The wine is full-bodied, powerful, super-concentrated, and coats the mouth with enviable levels of glycerin and sweet fruit. It is long, luscious, and a total hedonistic turn-on. Drink it over the next decade. While you are drinking your Blewitt Springs, Clarendon, or Kangarilla, you might still have to wait a few years for the 1999 Grenache Old Vines Hickinbotham to come around (14% alcohol). This is another expression of Grenache, exhibiting more earth, notes of soy sauce, and a sardine-like quality to its herb-tinged, black cherry fruit character. In the mouth, it is tightly structured, with more tannin, mineral, pepper, and spice. The wine is outstanding, but completely different than the other *cuvées*. I would opt for giving it 1–2 years of cellaring and drinking it over the following decade.

The 1999 Grenache Old Vines Romas Vineyard suggests new oak, the only Grenache to exhibit some toasty smells. In addition to that, there is the dense, concentrated, kirsch and raspberry notes intermixed with chewy, ripe, full-bodied, heavy, high alcohol (14.5%) flavors.

Full-bodied, with admirable structure, weight, and volume, it will be even better in another 1–2 years, and last for 10–12 years. The 1998 Grenache Old Vines Clarendon Vineyard reveals characteristics such as kirsch, spicy pepper, a touch of peachlike fruit from its overripeness, and the dried herb, earthy concoction the French call *garrigue*. Full-bodied and ripe, with a fleshy, high-alcohol personality, this voluptuous Châteauneuf-du-Pape look-alike should drink well for 8–10 years.

The 1998 Grenache Old Vines Kangarilla Vineyard exhibits a medium ruby color, a peppery, *garrigue*-scented nose, soft, earthy, medium- to full-bodied flavors, moderate tannin, and a rich, well-concentrated finish. It is not as fleshy, expressive, or explosive as its Clarendon Vineyard sibling. Drink it over the next 10–12 years. The dark ruby-colored 1998 Grenache Old Vines Blewitt Springs Vineyard offers copious quantities of raspberry and cherry jam intermixed with spicy wood, earth, herb, and pepper scents. Heady, high alcohol gives the wine additional levels of glycerin, which coat the palate and teeth. Dense, chewy, and ripe, this large-scaled wine can be drunk now or cellared for 10–12 years.

There are six selections of Shiraz, which are aged in 100% new French oak prior to being bottled with minimum clarification. All of these wines merit outstanding reviews, the 1999s being as superb as the 1998s. The 1999 Shiraz Liandra Vineyard (14.5% alcohol) is a sexy, ripe, multitextured wine with superb fruit, and gorgeous notes of black fruits, saddle leather, and spice. A delicious Shiraz to drink now, it should hold nicely for 10–15 years.

The opaque purple 1999 Shiraz Moritz Vineyard reveals plenty of earth, smoke, and spice in addition to both red and black fruits. The wine is full-bodied, deep, and slightly more fruit-driven, sweeter, with more elevated glycerin than the Liandra. The sweetness (from extract and ripeness, not sugar) is impressive and the wine difficult to resist, even at such a youthful age. Drink it over the next decade.

Readers looking for a more restrained style should check out the lower-key 1999 Shiraz Brookman Vineyard. With 13.5% alcohol, modest for a Clarendon Hills, this dark ruby/purple wine offers a spicy nose of black fruits intermixed with ketchup and vanilla. The wine is excellent, full-bodied, pure, ripe, and impressive. It is more measured and elegant than its two predecessors. Notes of new saddle leather, earth, truffle, smoke, black cherry, and blackberry emerge from the dense purple-colored 1999 Shiraz Hickinbotham Vineyard. It also reveals more new oak in the aromatics. On the palate, it is tannic, closed, and structured. There is a lot going on, but the wine should keep for 12–15 years.

Possibly the most concentrated and unctuously textured of these wines is the 1999 Shiraz Piggott Range Vineyard. A touch of subtle mint emerges along with blackberry liqueur notes intermixed with pepper, melted asphalt, and toast. Viscous, super-concentrated, and moderately tannic, this is a massive Shiraz, particularly in view of the vintage. It came in at 14.5% alcohol and should be cellared for 1–2 years. Anticipated maturity: now–2016.

The dark ruby/purple-colored 1998 Shiraz Liandra Vineyard exhibits beautiful, sweet, blackberry fruit intertwined with pepper, saddle leather, and spice. Rhône-like in its aromatics, this rich, full-bodied, compelling Shiraz displays low acidity as well as a fleshy, succulent mouth-feel. It should drink well for 10–12 years.

The black/purple 1998 Shiraz Hickinbotham Vineyard also reveals extraordinary intensity, but is less precocious and supple than the Liandra. The Hickinbotham exhibits smoky cassis, blackberry, melted asphalt, and toasty oak aromas, purity of fruit, an earthy, peppery character, and massive extract and richness. Drink this blockbuster Shiraz over the next 12 years.

One of the most Hermitage-like wines from Clarendon Hills is the 1998 Shiraz Brookman Vineyard. With a larger-than-life personality, high extraction, opaque purple color, dense, concentrated, peppery, cassis, mineral, and licorice-scented nose, full body, an unctuous texture, and spectacular finish, this superb effort can be drunk now as well as over the next 15–20 years. More closed but exceptionally impressive is the 1998 Shiraz Piggott Range

Vineyard. Exhibiting less revealing aromas than its peers, with coaxing some mint-tinged blackberry fruit emerges. Extremely powerful, with remarkable purity, intensity, and extraction, this Shiraz should keep for 15–20 years.

The limited-production Astralis (450 cases) is entirely made from Shiraz and aged in 100% new French oak. Massive and alcoholic, yet closed, the opaque purple-colored 1999 Astralis reveals abundant quantities of new oak, concentrated blackberry fruit, huge levels of glycerin and concentration, and admirable purity as well as symmetry. It is a gigantic Shiraz that easily competes with the finest wines of Australia. The 1999 requires 3–4 years of patience. Like its predecessors, it should have a prodigious aging potential of 20–30 years.

Closed but enormously constituted, the 1998 Astralis boasts an opaque purple color as well as a sweet mineral, licorice, blackberry- and blueberry-scented nose. This full-bodied, majestic wine is more restrained and subtle than previous efforts. The wine has soaked up the wood beautifully and is dominated by its fruit, glycerin, and high extract. Little complexity has yet emerged, but this is once again a compelling effort that clearly demonstrates what noninterventionalistic winemaking can produce with low-yielding, dry farmed Shiraz vines. Anticipated maturity: 2005–2025.

CLASSIC McLAREN (McLAREN VALE)

1999 Grenache	D	87
1999 Grenache La Testa	E	86?
1998 Grenache La Testa	E	91
1998 Grenache Reserve La Testa	E	85?
1999 La Testa Blend	E	90
1997 Shiraz La Testa	E	98+

The 1999 Grenache, made from 40- to 60-year-old vines, is very good, with plenty of black cherry fruit intermixed with some pepper and roasted notes. The wine shows good texture, purity, and a medium to full body. The Grenache La Testa emerge from 40- to 70-year-old vines that yielded an average of 1.5 tons of fruit per acre. Average production, sadly, is 150 cases annually. The 1999 Grenache La Testa should have been significantly better, but for some reason came across almost too structured and tannic, although there were notes of kirsch along with some pepper and spice. However, the wine's toughness and austerity may be problematic for future aging. Anticipated maturity: now–2010. The dark ruby-colored 1998 Grenache La Testa exhibits a knockout nose of sweet vanilla intermixed with jammy black raspberries and kirsch. Deep, pure, expansive, and fleshy, this is a hedonistic wine to drink over the next decade. The 1998 Grenache Reserve La Testa (only 100 cases produced) tasted tightly knit and muscular, with a dense ruby/purple color, hints of sweet strawberry and kirschlike fruit, but is burdened down by excessive wood and tannin. The 1998 Grenache Reserve and 1999 Grenache La Testa both taste as if they may have spent too long in wood, but perhaps I just caught them in an unflattering period of development.

The one outstanding wine from Classic McLaren is the 1999 La Testa Blend, a typically Australian concoction of 52% Grenache, 41% Shiraz, and 7% Cabernet Sauvignon (70% aged in French oak and the rest in American casks). The wine shows a dense purple color and a big, flamboyant, smoky, black currant, plum, and blackberry-scented nose with noticeable vanilla. Full-bodied, chewy, and full, a multilayered texture, good spice, and an exceptional finish certainly made this the most impressive of the Classic McLaren offerings. Approximately 350 cases were produced. Anticipated maturity: now–2012.

Readers looking for a clone of the famed Clarendon Hills luxury *cuvée* of 100% Shiraz called Astralis can find it in the 1997 Shiraz La Testa. This fabulous effort is one of the great wines from a vintage that has nowhere near the overall quality of 1996 or 1998. Nevertheless, this is a profound, prodigiously rich wine with a saturated black/purple color and knockout aromas of burning charcoal fire, jammy blackberries, cassis, and melted asphalt. Extremely full-bodied, with a viscous texture and high alcohol, this enormously endowed wine will improve for 10–15 years and last three decades.

CLAYFIELD (VICTORIA)

1999 Shiraz Grampians	D	91

Aged in 85% new American oak and 15% one-year French oak and bottled unfiltered, the supple, creamy-textured, ripe, dense 1999 Shiraz Grampians shows plenty of layers of fruit, considerable glycerin, a big, peppery, black fruit–scented nose, and a low-acid, plump, lush finish. Drink it now and over the next 12 years.

CLONAKILLA (SOUTH AUSTRALIA)

1998 Shiraz	D	87
1999 Shiraz/Viognier	D	90
1998 Shiraz/Viognier	D	92

Production of the Shiraz/Viognier blend averages 300 cases annually. This wine, made primarily of Shiraz (95%), also contains a small percentage of Viognier (5%), which is discernible in its aromatics. The elegant, complex, and fragrant 1999 Shiraz/Viognier offers up telltale blackberry and cassis, but also a touch of apricot and white flowers due to its Viognier component. The wine is medium- to full-bodied, with supple texture, silky tannin, and a fleshy, moderately weighty feel. Already delicious, it is best drunk over the next 4 years.

The sexy, ostentatious 1998 Shiraz/Viognier exhibits a dark ruby/purple color, full body, and an explosive bouquet of black fruits and Viognier's apricot/peach component, this dense, structured, pure, concentrated wine is reminiscent of a French Côte Rotie as well as the Australian Shiraz/Viognier blend made by the Torbreck winery. Drink it over the next decade.

The pure 1998 Shiraz reveals a deep ruby/purple color, a straightforward, spicy, berry-scented nose, medium to full body, a soft texture, and pleasant, uninspiring, but satisfying levels of fruit, glycerin, and body. Drink it over the next 3–4 years.

CLOS CLARE (CLARE VALLEY)

1999 Shiraz	C	89

Two renowned Australian wine-makers, Jeffrey Grosset and David Powell, work at Clos Clare, with Grosset turning out a dry Riesling (not reviewed here because it is meant to be drunk within 1–2 years of the vintage) and Powell the Shiraz. The 1999 Shiraz is something of a fruit bomb, with a deep ruby/purple color, low acidity, supple texture, and copious quantities of blackberry and cassis fruit. The wine would have received an outstanding rating, but it is just not all that complex. However, it is a delicious, opulent Shiraz meant to be drunk over the next 5–6 years.

CORIOLE WINES (McLAREN VALE)

1997 Cabernet Sauvignon	D	87
1999 Lalla Rookh Old Vine Grenache	D	88
1998 Lalla Rookh Old Vine Grenache	D	89
1997 Lalla Rookh Old Vine Grenache	D	89
1998 Mary Kathleen	D	94
1997 Mary Kathleen	D	89
1999 Redstone	C	89
1998 Redstone	C	90
1997 Redstone	C	88
1999 Shiraz	D	87
1998 Shiraz	D	90
1997 Shiraz	D	90

1998 Shiraz Lloyd Reserve	E	92
1997 Shiraz Lloyd Reserve	E	90
1996 Shiraz Lloyd Reserve	E	94

Coriole, founded in 1967, has long been known for its Shiraz, but their entire portfolio is extremely well made. The least expensive red of the series is the Redstone blend of Shiraz, Grenache, Cabernet Sauvignon, and Merlot. Given today's wine market, this is a very good value. The dominant varietals are Shiraz and Grenache.

The opaque purple 1999 Redstone displays a sweet nose of blood, meat, leather, pepper, and black cherry and currant liqueur. The wine is medium- to full-bodied, soft, and best drunk over the next 4–5 years. Also opaque purple, the 1998 Redstone is riper and fuller, with more volume and chewiness. Offering abundant quantities of spicy blackberry and cherry fruit with a touch of oak in the background, it will drink well for 7–8 years. The 1997 Redstone reveals a saturated ruby/purple color in addition to a robust, earthy, meaty, gutsy personality, peppery, leathery black fruits, good density and richness, and a ripe finish. Though a little lacking in complexity and softness, it is well made.

The 1999 and 1998 Lalla Rookh Old Vine Grenache, primarily Grenache with small quantities of Shiraz, are impressive efforts. The 1999 is more elegant, with less power but beautifully balanced fruit (sweet black cherries intermixed with pepper). The 1998 reveals a chewier, fuller-bodied, more muscular style with additional depth and structure. Both wines, which possess copious amounts of pepper and sweet cherry fruit, are best drunk during their first 8–10 years of life. I hope I didn't underrate the 1997 Lalla Rookh Old Vine Grenache. Displaying an unmistakable southern Rhône character, it offers scents of crushed black pepper, kirsch, and cherries. The wine boasts a big, full-bodied, expansive palate with abundant earth, smoke, dried herb, and red fruit flavors. The wood is barely noticeable. Produced largely from 75-year-old Grenache vines, it should drink well for 8–9 years.

Fairly light in style, but still delicious is the 1999 Shiraz, an elegant, richly fruity wine to enjoy over the next 5 years. Readers looking for a textbook McLaren Vale Shiraz should check out Coriole's 1998 Shiraz, an opaque black/purple effort offering aromas of blueberries, blackberry liqueur, pepper, graphite, and licorice. Ripe, full-bodied, and fruit-driven, it should drink well for 10 years. The outstanding, opaque purple 1997 Shiraz offers copious quantities of blackberry, pepper, glycerin, and extract complemented by low acidity and a plush, opulent style. Anticipated maturity: now–2010.

The dark garnet/purple 1997 Cabernet Sauvignon's prune, overripe plum, and cassis aromas are followed by a thick, jammy wine that is close to being over the top. However, its softness and accessible style make for a tasty, though perhaps controversial Cabernet. Anticipated maturity: now–2010.

Coriole's flagship wines are their limited-production Mary Kathleen (80% Cabernet Sauvignon, 20% Merlot) and the Lloyd Reserve Shiraz, made from 60-year-old vines and aged in both American and French oak. The 1998 Mary Kathleen is a spectacular, opaque purple effort with tremendous aging potential. It offers a promising nose of cassis, cedar, blackberries, vanilla, and spice. Full-bodied, with fabulous purity and symmetry, and a mouth-filling, palate-staining style without any heaviness or astringency, it should drink well for two decades. Very impressive! Although tightly knit, the 1997 Mary Kathleen is elegant, with a medium deep red/purple color and a spicy, black currant, berry, and tobacco-scented bouquet. The wine possesses full body and outstanding intensity and richness. Drink it over the following 10–15 years. Another superb effort is the 1998 Shiraz Lloyd Reserve. Although big, fat, brawny, and muscular, it reveals polish and refinement for its size. An opaque purple color is accompanied by telltale blackberry liqueur intermixed with spicy oak, low acidity, abundant glycerin, and a chewy, concentrated, long finish. Anticipated maturity: now–2015. Made in a different style, the 1997 Shiraz Lloyd Reserve exhibits a charred-oak nose, a deep ruby/purple color, and notes of soy, black cherries, black currants, earth, and tar. Lighter than the 1998, more developed and evolved, it is best drunk over the next 10 years. The spectacular 1996 Shiraz Lloyd Reserve boasts a thick-looking, dark purple/garnet color as well as lavish quantities of toasty American oak mixed with blackberry liqueur. The wine possesses fabulous concentration, loads of glycerin, full body, low acidity, and a blockbuster 40+-second finish. A huge, chewy, surprisingly harmonious, mouth-filling Syrah, it should drink well for 15+ years.

CRANEFORD (BAROSSA)

1999 Shiraz	D	88

Aged in a combination of French and American oak, the 200 cases of this unfined, unfiltered 1999 Shiraz exhibit deep ruby/plum color and a sweet, fat nose of jammy black fruits inter-mixed with smoke and toasty oak. The wine is a hedonistic, glycerin-imbued fruit bomb. Drink it over the next 4 years.

GARRY CRITTENDEN (KING VALLEY, VICTORIA)

1998 "I" Barbera	C	89
1998 "I" Sangiovese	C	89

Some of California's underachievers with Italian-inspired varietal wines should take a page out of Garry Crittenden's book. He is consistently turning out interesting wines from Italian varietals. The smoky, cherry-scented, ripe, medium-bodied, ripe, and fruity 1998 "I" San-giovese reveals a subtle dosage of wood. Flavorful and cleanly made, it should drink well for 2 years. The exceptional 1998 "I" Barbera could easily pass for a top-notch Piedmontese Barbera, given its strawberry jam, tomato skin, sweet fruit–driven personality, medium to full body, tangy acidity, and nicely layered, pure finish. Drink it over the next 2–3 years.

CULLEN (MARGARET RIVER)

1998 Cabernet Sauvignon/Merlot	D	87
1997 Cabernet Sauvignon/Merlot	D	87
1996 Cabernet Sauvignon/Merlot	D	86
1999 Diana Madeline	E	88

The proprietary red wine blend 1999 Diana Madeline is a blend of 70% Cabernet Sauvignon, 20% Merlot, and 5% Cabernet Franc (95%). Its dark ruby/purple color is followed by sweet aromas of red currants, cedar, plums, earth, and spice. Stylish, elegant, and European in its orientation, it should drink well for a decade. By Australian standards, it is a measured, re-strained red wine. The 1998 Cabernet Sauvignon/Merlot (60% Cabernet Sauvignon, 25% Merlot, and 15% Cabernet Franc) is a fatter, fleshier, more tannic, substantial effort. Youth-ful, with notes of red and black currants, dried herbs, tobacco, and subtle wood, this medium-bodied, elegant 1998 possesses good underlying acidity. It should drink well for 7–8 years.

Both the 1996 and 1997 Cabernet Sauvignon/Merlot blends exhibit elegant, austere per-sonalities, with moderate quantities of black currant fruit. Both are made in a restrained, aus-tere, Bordeaux-like style. Some sweet oak is present (about 80% new oak casks are used), and the wines suggest longevity, although I am not sure the requisite concentration is present for aging beyond 10–12 years. These are well-made, unflashy, polite offerings.

DALWHINNIE (MOONAMBEL)

1997 Shiraz	D	88
1996 Shiraz Eagle Pyrenees	D	90+

Crisp acidity underlies and supports the concentrated cassis and blackberry fruit of the dark ruby/purple 1997 Shiraz. Tightly knit, medium-bodied, dense, and pure, this wine has now emerged from its cloak of tannin and should age nicely for 7–8 years.

Even more impressive is the exquisite 1996 Shiraz Eagle Pyrenees. Aged completely in French oak, this medium- to full-bodied, vibrant, racy Shiraz possesses uncanny elegance and style for this grape, which usually turns out blockbuster heavyweights. Good acidity gives the wine freshness and delineation. Smoky oak is intertwined with blackberry and black currant fruit flavors in this dense, concentrated, backward wine. As it sits in the glass, pepper, cherry liqueur, and roasted herbs emerge. Anticipated maturity: now–2014.

DOG RIDGE (McLAREN VALE)

1999 Shiraz	D	87

There are over 1,000 cases of this 100% Shiraz, aged for 18 months in both new and older French and American wood. The 1999 Shiraz shows a soft yet elegant style with supple black fruits, medium body, good purity, but an ultimately foursquare, somewhat one-dimensional personality. However, the fruit is undeniably charming, making this wine an attractive albeit expensive offering to consume over the next 4–5 years.

DUTSCHKE (BAROSSA)

1998 Shiraz Oscar Semmler	E	90+
1998 Shiraz Saint Jakobi	D	89
NV The Tawny 25-year-old Port	E	96
1998 Willow Bend	D	87

The Dutschke family is the fifth generation in Barossa. Production of these wines ranges from small lots such as 180 cases of the Tawny 25-year-old Port and 1998 Shiraz Oscar Semmler to nearly 800 cases of the Willow Bend and Saint Jakobi Shiraz.

The 1998 Willow Bend has a dark plum/purple color, loads of fruit, glycerin, and ripeness. Not a great deal of complexity, but this is a lush, consumer-friendly styled wine that is a blend of 47% Merlot, 33% Shiraz, and the rest Cabernet Sauvignon. The focus of the wine is its attractively fruity and pleasant personality. Anticipated maturity: now–2009.

For a slightly more peppery and fleshy, larger-sized wine, the dark ruby/purple-colored 1998 Shiraz Saint Jakobi reveals plenty of smoke, earth, and black fruits. A sweet, earthy entry on the palate is followed by full body and a layered finish with low acidity, ripe tannin, and easy accessibility. It should drink well for 8–10 years. The complex, saturated purple-colored 1998 Shiraz Oscar Semmler emanates from 25-year-old vines. Aged 24 months in new French oak, this opulent, full-bodied wine has a distinctive nose of grilled Italian sausage intermixed with blackberry, pepper, vanilla, and smoke. Chewy, powerful, and rich, with moderate tannin and a youthful exuberance, this large-scaled wine (15% alcohol) will be better with 2–3 years of cellaring. It should drink well for 18–20 years.

Readers looking for a prodigious fortified tawny Port should check out the limited quantities of the The Tawny 25-year-old Port. Made from a mysterious blend of different grapes, this stuff is fabulous. With considerable amber at the edge, a spectacular nose of liquefied caramel intermixed with coffee, kirsch, and even floral notes, this full-bodied, moderately sweet, dense, velvety-styled Tawny is spectacular. It is not going to improve, but will certainly keep for at least another decade.

E AND E (BAROSSA)

1996 Shiraz Black Pepper	D	88

Sweet American oak combined with jammy, peppery, blackberry fruit results in an attractive introduction to this medium- to full-bodied 1996 Shiraz Black Pepper. While not a blockbuster, it is a flavorful, concentrated offering to enjoy over the next 4–5 years.

ELDERTON (BAROSSA)

1998 Cabernet Sauvignon	C	90+
1997 Command Shiraz	E	92

1996 **Command Shiraz**	E	93
1997 **CSM Proprietary Red**	C	92
1996 **CSM Proprietary Red**	C	90
1997 **Merlot**	C	92
1998 **Shiraz**	C	93
1997 **Shiraz**	C	93

In the past, Elderton's wines have been love-it-or-leave-it and controversial. Some tasters thought the oak (American and French) was excessive, but an equal number found it compelling. Elderton's latest releases possess far better integrated oak, so some of the complaints leveled by critics may no longer be justified. What these wines have always possessed, and still do, are huge quantities of fruit, glycerin, and personality. With a more subtle integration of the oak, I think Elderton has achieved better wines. The 1998 Cabernet Sauvignon is a super wine that can be drunk now or cellared for 12–15 years. Its saturated black purple color offers up gorgeous notes of sweet, jammy cassis with subtle, smoky wood in the background. The wine exhibits terrific ripeness, an unctuous, full-bodied texture, superb fruit, and a long, lusty finish. This in-your-face, hedonistic, fruit bomb should become more civilized and delineated as it ages. Moreover, the oak is complementary rather than blatant. Bravo!

The superlatives continue with the spectacular 1998 Shiraz. This is another fabulous value. This wine delivers explosive levels of glycerin, and concentrated blackberry and cherry fruit in a sweet, beautifully seamless, ostentatious style of Shiraz, with nicely integrated wood and a huge blockbuster finish. This is teeth-staining, mouthcoating Shiraz, the likes of which can be made nowhere else in the world but from old vines in Barossa. Drink it over the next 10 years. The 1997 Shiraz performed splendidly. This opaque purple wine offers up plenty of sweet blackberry and cassis fruit with a touch of overripe cherries, smoke, and charcoal. This multidimensional, layered, luscious, low-acid, toasty Shiraz is made in an obvious, fat, hedonistic style. Drink it over the next 5–6 years.

The CSMs are blends of 60% Cabernet Sauvignon, 30% Cabernet Franc, and 10% Merlot. My tasting notes for the impressive 1997 CSM started with the words "a whore of a wine." It recalls some of the older Eldertons. While it offers huge amounts of toasty oak in the nose, it is better integrated than young Elderton wines have been in the past. A voluptuous, lusty wine with loads of glycerin, fat, and concentrated fruit as well as decadent levels of pleasure (14.5% alcohol). I doubt there are many Puritans among my readers, but should there be any, they may want to stay clear of this wine. It is so outrageously rich and fruity, it should be a controlled substance. Look for it to drink beautifully young, but age for at least 10–12 years.

Elderton's 1996 CSM Proprietary Red is a glorious, fruit-driven wine with lavish quantities of smoky new oak, dense, thick, juicy, chocolate, blackberry and cherry fruit flavors, low acidity, and a fat, ostentatious, showy midsection and finish. This sumptuous, explosively fruity/oaky wine is not subtle, but it does offer thrilling hedonistic levels of fruit. Drink it over the next 5–6 years. Another blast of fruit, glycerin, smoky oak, though again better integrated and more subtle than in past renditions, is the 1997 Merlot, offering up notes of espresso, coffee, chocolate, and black cherry liqueur in a full-bodied, unctuously textured, lavishly fat, nearly over-the-top style. Its low acidity and sweet tannin suggest it will provide the most pleasure during its first 5–8 years of life.

Elderton's top *cuvée* is their Command Shiraz. These wines see much more French oak and are more structured, with even higher levels of extract as well as tannin. Although not as approachable as the less expensive wines, they are built for 15–20 years of cellaring. The opaque purple 1997 Command Shiraz offers abundant creamy new oak in the nose, gorgeous crème de cassis aromas and flavors, a structured, moderately tannic, full-bodied, powerful, muscular style, and a finish that lasts for 35+ seconds. Anticipated maturity: now–2015. The 1996 Command Shiraz is a bigger, fuller, more powerful offering. While its aromas and flavors are similar to the 1997, there is more to it. A muscular, powerful version of the 1997, it will drink well before 2018.

RALPH FOWLER (LIMESTONE COAST)

NV	Old and Rare Muscat	E	99
1998	Shiraz	E	89
1997	Shiraz	E	89

Ralph Fowler was chosen by Michel Chapoutier to produce that Rhône Valley firm's Australian wines. Fowler has left Chapoutier to start his own label, and these three offerings are the results. Both the 1997 and 1998 Shiraz are mainstream wines with creamy American oak, excellent concentration, and abundant quantities of sweet, peppery, blackberry, and cassis flavors. The textures are supple, and the wines are pure, but both lack complexity and the extra flavor dimensions present in many of the wines from importer Dan Philips. Nevertheless, they are top-notch efforts produced from 30-year-old Shiraz vines cropped at two tons per acre. Anticipated maturity: now–2015. Fowler's nonvintage Old and Rare Muscat is virtually perfect. The material for this wine averages 30 years in age and was kept in small casks until bottling. It exhibits a brown/amber color, the thickness of maple syrup, and unbelievable levels of richness, concentration, and perfume. I cannot imagine any thicker, more concentrated dessert wines than this example except those from William Chambers and Trevor Jones. Fowler's Muscat is almost too rich to drink. A half bottle of this old Muscat will serve 20–30 people! Moreover, it should last for another 40–50 years.

FOX CREEK (McLAREN VALE)

1998	Cabernet Sauvignon Reserve	D	92+
1997	Cabernet Sauvignon Reserve	D	89
1999	Grenache/Shiraz	C	84?
1998	Grenache/Shiraz	D	90
1999	Merlot	D	86
1998	Merlot	D	90
1999	Shiraz Reserve	E	92
1998	Shiraz Reserve	E	98
1999	Shiraz Short Row	D	90
1999	Shiraz/Cabernet JSM	D	89
1998	Shiraz/Cabernet JSM	D	96
NV	Vixen Sparkling Red	C	85?

The largest production of any Fox Creek wine is their 2,500 cases of Shiraz/Cabernet JSM. A blend of Shiraz, Cabernet Franc, and Cabernet Sauvignon, it is aged 12–14 months in one- to three-year-old American oak casks. The 1999 JSM has an opaque ruby/purple color and an intense nose of black cherries and cassis, with noteworthy coffee, vanilla character in the background. In the mouth, this medium- to full-bodied, soft wine introduces some blue- and blackberry fruit to the mix. It is a fruit-driven, up-front style of wine to drink over the next 4–6 years. Readers looking for superintense, ripe wines will be thrilled with the 1998 Shiraz/Cabernet JSM. Opaque purple-colored, with a sumptuous nose of black fruits and spicy new oak, it is explosive on the palate. With an unctuous texture, a full-bodied personality, and intense black cherry/cassis flavors, this is a sensationally layered effort with a 45-second finish. This kind of wine can only be produced in selected areas of California and Australia. It is the antithesis of the polite, restrained, austere style of Bordeaux for which France is so famous. Look for it to drink well young, yet last for 15–20 years.

There are 700 cases of the Merlot, made from young vines, tiny yields of 1.6 tons per acre and aged in new and old French oak. The 1999 Merlot reveals a compact, elegant style typical of the vintage. With pure, ripe, smoky, black cherry fruit, medium body, and an elegant, rather delicate finish, this is a restrained effort for Fox Creek. Drink it over the next 4–5 years. Tannic, but also exhibiting lavish quantities of toasty oak along with equally copious amounts of black cherry and berry fruit, is the 1998 Merlot. This wine is somewhat monolithic, but the terrific intensity, rich fruit, and full-bodied generosity are to be admired. It should last 12+ years.

The 1999 Grenache/Shiraz (65%/35%) tasted austere, lean, and narrowly constructed. The color is dark ruby/purple, but the wine was hard and difficult to penetrate. I don't know whether I caught it in an ungenerous stage, but it seemed mediocre. Anticipated maturity: 2003–2010. The 1998 Grenache/Shiraz (70% and 30% respectively) performed better. Once past its black/ruby/purple color, creamy, oaky notes emerge along with ultraripe cherries and assorted black fruits. This hedonistic, voluptuously textured, spicy, fruit-dominated wine has no hard edges, and fills the mouth with terrific intensity yet good balance and freshness. Drink it over the next 4–6 years.

The 1999 Shiraz Short Row (1,500 cases, aged primarily in new American wood) has a dense black/purple color and a sweet nose of blackberry, tar, pepper, and vanilla. The wine is rich, full-bodied, dense, pure, and chewy. It seems tightly knit at present, but one or more years of cellaring should be beneficial, and the wine should last 10–12 years.

The impressive Shiraz Reserve is a 2,000-case *cuvée* aged 14 months in new American oak. The 1999 is a dense purple color, with a sweet, almost blackberry liqueur nose, and smoke, licorice, and oak in the background. Jammy and rich, with huge body, good purity, adequate acidity, and a long finish, this is an impressive, surprisingly large-scaled 1999. It should age well for 10–16 years. Nearly perfect, the opaque black/purple 1998 Shiraz Reserve plays to the great strength of Australia—powerful, naturally textured, superrich wines that are big and chewy. Exceptionally rich and explosive, with great purity as well as remarkable symmetry and overall balance for such massiveness, this blockbuster can be drunk now or cellared for 12–15 years. Make no doubt about it, this Shiraz will elicit more than a few "wows" in any tasting, blind or otherwise.

Fox Creek produces 1,500 cases of Cabernet Sauvignon Reserve annually. This wine is aged in 100% new French oak. The brilliant 1998 is opaque black/purple-colored, with an explosive nose of licorice, blackberry, cassis, tar, and new oak. This huge, ripe wine is layered, thick, smoky, and concentrated, a true blockbuster from this superb vintage. Anticipated maturity: now–2018. Remarkably civilized, even restrained by the standards of Fox Creek, the 1997 Cabernet Sauvignon Reserve is clearly the product of a lighter vintage. Despite its elegant personality, there is nothing wimpy about this wine. A dark ruby/purple color is followed by an attractive smoky, black currant, and toasty-scented nose. Medium-bodied, with excellent balance, and soft tannin, it should be consumed over the next decade.

Finally, the nonvintage Vixen Sparkling Red is a bubbly blend of 52% Shiraz, 34% Cabernet Franc, and 14% Cabernet Sauvignon. Distinctive but eccentric, it has a deep ruby/purple color and a heavy, leaden style, but it is loaded with fruit. Everyone should try one of these sparkling red wines from Australia, though they seem more appropriate for attention-getting party wines than for matching with food. Anticipated maturity: *now*.

FRANKLAND ESTATE (WESTERN AUSTRALIA)

1997	Cabernet Franc/Merlot Olmo's Reward	C	89
1996	Cabernet Franc/Merlot Olmo's Reward	C	90
1998	Shiraz Isolation Ridge	C	90?

Be forewarned: these distinctive wines are totally different from any other Australian wines I have tasted. What sets them apart is an underlying, singular, graphitelike character that gives them an earthy, *terroir*-driven quality in both the aromatics and flavors of these wines. They are well made, but less fruit-driven than many Australian wines.

I loved the 1998 Shiraz Isolation Ridge. However, it is not for everybody. A dense purple color is followed by a distinctive earthiness, a touch of cow manure, and dense peppery, blackberry, cherry fruit. The wine is full-bodied, dense, chewy, and idiosyncratic but fascinating. This wine should drink well for at least 10–12 years.

One of the most intriguing wines from Frankland Estate is their Bordeaux look-alike, the Cabernet Franc/Merlot blend called Olmo's Reward, which also comprises a touch of Petit Verdot, Malbec, and Cabernet Sauvignon. The classy, graceful 1997 exhibits notes of chocolate, cedarwood, menthol, spice box, and red and black fruits. The attack is savory, the mid-palate medium-bodied and moderately tannic, and the finish complex and long. The wine is accessible but made in a restrained, medium-weight style that is totally unusual for Australia. Drink it over the next decade. The 1996 Cabernet Franc/Merlot Olmo's Reward is an intensely aromatic, spicy, Bordeaux-inspired wine with a dusty, new oak, red and black currant–scented nose. As it sits in the glass, berry and cedar aromas emerge, along with some of the telltale earthiness. Medium-bodied, with decent acidity, moderate tannin, and a stylish, complex personality, this intriguing wine could easily pass for a top-class Bordeaux in a blind tasting. Anticipated maturity: now–2015.

THE GATEKEEPER (McLAREN VALE)

1998 Cabernet Sauvignon Reserve	D	89+
1998 Shiraz Reserve	D	92

Produced by Simon Hackett, the 1998 Gatekeeper Shiraz Reserve (a selection of his best *cuveés*) is aged in 60% American oak and 40% French oak, half of which is new. The vines are claimed to be 50–75 years old. This is superb, full-blooded, brawny, massive Australian Shiraz at its best. The wine is huge, chewy, deep, and thick. There are notes of black fruits, earth, asphalt, smoke, and pepper. Drink it over the next 12–15 years. More tightly knit as well as restrained and elegant, with considerable tannin, is the 1998 Cabernet Sauvignon Reserve. This wine, which comes from a 76-year-old parcel of Cabernet, exhibits good tobacco-tinged, black currant fruit mixed with some spicy wood. The tannin seems high, which may raise cause for concern if it does not become better integrated. Anticipated maturity: now–2016.

GEMTREE VINEYARDS (McLAREN VALE)

1999 Shiraz	D	90
1998 Shiraz	D	87

This is one of the few wineries where I found the 1999 to be a better wine than the 1998. Both wines come from 30-year-old Shiraz vines that are partially used for the famous Balmoral Shiraz made by Rosemount. There are 500 cases of this wine that is aged in American oak, of which 60% is new. The 1999 Shiraz displays notes of melted tar, coffee, and vanilla, beautiful fruit, sweet tannin, and more density and length than the 1998. The 1998 boasts a dark ruby/purple color, a minty cassis nose, full body, good ripeness and flavor, but a one-dimensional personality. While it possesses fruit, depth, and intensity, there is little complexity. Both wines should be drunk in their exuberant youth—over the next 4–5 years.

GENDERS (McLAREN PARK)

1998 Cabernet Sauvignon	E	87
1976 Port	EE	?
1998 Shiraz	E	86?

The 1998 Cabernet Sauvignon is a very good to excellent wine with textbook weedy, black currant flavors intermixed with some spicy wood. The wine shows good purity and a judicious use of new oak. It can be drunk now or cellared for up to a decade.

The 1998 Shiraz is somewhat monolithic and less expressive, but possesses plenty of weight, ripeness, and blackberry fruit infused with smoke and tar. It should drink well for 7–8 years. It is a shame the wine was not more expressive the day I tasted it.

The 1976 Genders Port, a fortified Shiraz/Cabernet Sauvignon blend, is no doubt a controversial wine. The wine has unctuous texture but a pruny, raisiny nose, and somewhat rustic flavors. It is certainly not going to make anyone forget Portuguese vintage ports, nor does it compete with the best from Australia.

GLAETZER (BAROSSA VALLEY)

1997 Cabernet Sauvignon/Malbec	D	89
1997 Shiraz	D	92
1998 Shiraz The Bishop	D	88

A saturated dense ruby/purple color leads to a big, rich, chewy 1998 Shiraz The Bishop with fine balance and overall harmony. It offers abundant quantities of blackberry/cassis flavors, and a touch of pepper and spicy new oak. The wine's texture, purity, and finish are all impressive. Already drinking well, it will age nicely for a decade. A blockbuster, massive wine, the dense ruby/purple-colored 1997 Shiraz tips the scales at 14% alcohol. Full-bodied, with low acidity, terrific intensity, and explosive levels of fruit and glycerin, this multilayered, mouth-staining Shiraz can be drunk now and over the next 12 years.

As for the more civilized, restrained, downsized 1997 Cabernet Sauvignon/Malbec, this intriguing blend offers up an open-knit floral, black raspberry, and currant-scented nose, excellent richness, medium to full body, impressive ripeness and purity, and a long, supple-textured finish. If more complexity emerges, this wine could merit an outstanding review. Anticipated maturity: now–2008.

GNADENFREI (BAROSSA)

1999 Shiraz St. Michael's	D	91
1997 Shiraz St. Michael's	D	92

Tiny yields of one ton of fruit per acre, harvested at 14.5% potential alcohol from nonirrigated old vines, and bottling without filtration after being aged in old wood represents the style of wine-maker Rolf Binder. In 1999, this resulted in a thick, full-bodied, dense, purple-colored Shiraz St. Michael's with notes of Italian sausage, bacon fat, blackberry, and cassis. Full-bodied, unctuously textured, and chewy, it offers a mouthful of blockbuster Australian Shiraz. This is classic Barossa Shiraz at its biggest and boldest. Drink it over the next 10–12 years. I know this does not make any sense, but when smelled and tasted, the 1997 Shiraz St. Michael's brought to mind the 1998 l'Evangile, a wine made from Merlot and Cabernet Franc (Gnadenfrei's 1997 is 100% Shiraz). It is a compelling, lush, Pomerol-styled Shiraz with terrific black raspberry fruit, full body, and soaring aromatics. Low acidity and a lush, concentrated mouth-feel make for a seductive, majestic wine drinking experience. Enjoy this 1997 over the next 10 years. Impressive!

GRALYN (MARGARET RIVER)

1999 Cabernet Sauvignon	E	87+?
1998 Cabernet Sauvignon	E	88

A rustic style of Cabernet Sauvignon, with big, earthy, exuberant tea and currant flavors as well as sharp acidity and tough, nearly uncivilized tannin, the huge, dense, full-bodied 1999 was aged in 100% new French and American oak and bottled unfiltered. The French would call it a *vin de garde*. However, the tannin needs to become better integrated in order for it to merit a higher score. The oak is beautifully absorbed and the wine possesses monstrous levels of concentration and depth. If everything comes together, it will merit an outstanding score. If it doesn't, tasters will get an uncivilized mouthful of Cabernet Sauvignon. Anticipated maturity: 2005–2015. An impressive, dark ruby/purple effort, Gralyn's 1998 Cabernet Sauvignon reveals an earthy, floral, black currant–scented bouquet. Elegant, Bordeaux-like in the mouth, with medium body, sweet fruit, nicely integrated tannin and wood, and a restrained, nicely nuanced personality, it should drink well for a decade.

GREENOCK CREEK (BAROSSA VALLEY)

1998 Cabernet Sauvignon	E	90
1995 Cabernet Sauvignon Roennfeldt Road	EEE	99
1999 Grenache Cornerstone	D	91
1998 Shiraz Apricot Block	E	94+
1998 Shiraz Creek Block	E	98+
1995 Shiraz Roennfeldt Road	EEE	100
1998 Shiraz Seven Acres	E	92

This has quickly become one of my favorite wineries, not only in Australia but in the world. Wine-maker Chris Ringland, assisted by Mike Waugh, continues to turn out brilliant, blockbuster wines that demonstrate the quintessential oversized, flamboyant, in-your-face style that makes Australia's top reds so distinctive.

For starters, the 1998 Cabernet Sauvignon (100% Cabernet Sauvignon from 11-year-old vines, aged in a combination of one-year-old and new French oak) is a fruit-dominated wine with the classic cassis intermixed with a touch of herbs, a slight notion of volatile acidity, and a spicy finish. The wine is full-bodied, ripe, but at the same time elegant, particularly for a Greenock Creek wine. Anticipated maturity: 2005–2015.

Among the finest Grenache wines produced in Australia is Greenock Creek's Grenache Cornerstone, a 100% Grenache from 61-year-old vines, of yields of 2 tons of fruit per acre, and aged in one-year-old French barrels. The 1999 is an explosive wine, much like the 1998. Soft, with luxurious levels of kirsch intermixed with some spice, pepper, and berries, this supple, full-bodied wine has high levels of glycerin, gorgeously concentrated fruit, and a layered finish. It is not going to make old bones, but for drinking over the next 5–7 years, this is hedonism at its best.

The three *cuvées* of Shiraz, from the 10-year-old Seven Acres Vineyard, the 61-year-old Creek Block, and the Apricot Block, are fabulous wines. Made from a so-called difficult vintage, the 1997s are simply superb and taste as if they came from a great vintage, and the 1998s are even better. The Shiraz Creek Block is made from 62-year-old vines and aged in a combination of new and French oak. Sadly, there are only 100 cases of it. The 1998 is a near-perfect wine. This opaque, purple-colored classic shows terrific notes of beef blood, new saddle leather, blackberry liqueur, smoke, and earth. Extremely full-bodied yet seamless, with dazzling levels of extract and ripeness, this is a tour de force in winemaking, but there is too little of it. The Creek Block looks to have the potential to go 20–30 years.

The Shiraz Seven Acres is made from 12-year-old vines and aged in American oak (a combination of new and old). Although by no means a wimpish wine, it is lighter-styled than the Creek Block and has greater availability (500 cases). The 1998 is outstanding but tightly knit. An elegant wine in the context of the normally powerful Greenock Creek style, this wine exhibits dark ruby/purple color and a bouquet of black raspberries intermixed with blackberry, currant, pepper, and spicy wood. The wine is deep, full-bodied, and beautifully knit. Some tannin still needs to be resolved in the finish, but this wine should age well for 10–15 years.

A 100% Shiraz *cuvée*, the Apricot Block is made from relatively young vines (10 years). Perhaps the most backward of the 1998s, this wine shows an opaque garnet/purple color and a sweet nose of melted asphalt, smoke, blackberry, and cassis. Extremely full-bodied with great intensity, tremendous purity, and impeccable overall harmony among its rather large-scale elements (14.3% alcohol), this dense, super-extracted wine should be at its best between 2004–2020.

The 1995 Cabernet Sauvignon Roennfeldt Road is 100% Cabernet Sauvignon from 50-year-old vines. The wine was aged three years in new French oak. It has soaked up the wood beautifully. This is an unctuous, blockbuster, opaque, purple-colored wine with a classic nose of charcoal, black currants, cedar, mineral, and licorice. The wine has phenomenal intensity, great purity, a huge, ripe, yet balanced attack, a multilayered mid-palate with no hard edges, and an awesome finish. This is a terrific classic that can be approached now but ideally needs 1–2 years of cellaring. Anticipated maturity: 2004–2025. The prodigious 1995 Shiraz Roennfeldt Road also spent three years in barrel, but in this case, new American wood. Made from 50-year-old vines, it is another Syrup of Shiraz, with compelling blackberry liqueur intermixed with minerals, smoke, and truffles. Huge in the mouth but not overbearing, this wine has a finish that goes on for nearly a minute. With great purity, massive extraction, and a blockbuster, multidimensional personality, this is one of the greatest Shirazes I have ever tasted, rivaling some of the efforts from Three Rivers. Interestingly, both wines were made by the magician himself, Chris Ringland. Anticipated maturity: 2004–2030. How fun it will be to compare this wine with some of the great Penfolds Grange offerings in about 15 years' time.

GROSSET (CLARE VALLEY)

1998 Gaia Proprietary Red Wine	D	91+
1997 Gaia Proprietary Red Wine	D	92+

Wine-maker/proprietor Jeffrey Grosset is one of the Clare Valley's most talented winemakers, as proven by his array of consistently high-quality wines. Established in 1981, his winery is renowned for its Riesling and Chardonnay (not reviewed here since they have to be consumed within a few months of the vintage), and for its high-class blend of 75% Cabernet Sauvignon, 20% Cabernet Franc, and 5% Merlot called Gaia, aged in French oak. The exceptional 1998 Gaia is a full-bodied, classy Australian red that emulates Bordeaux yet possesses Australia's renowned ripeness, as well as terrific purity, sweet black currant, tobacco, spice box, cedar, and vanilla, beautifully integrated acidity, and a long, promising finish. Anticipated maturity: now–2014. The 1997 Gaia displays a Bordeaux-like red and black currant–scented nose with spice box, cedar, and vanilla. This classy effort represents a perfect marriage of traditional European winemaking with Australia's more modern-day approach. Medium-bodied, with moderate tannin, and well-integrated acidity and wood, this elegant wine should drink well for 12 years.

HAAN (BAROSSA VALLEY)

1998 Merlot Prestige	D	88+
1998 Shiraz	D	89

A former pilot of 747s, James Irvine (of Grand Merlot fame) is the wine-maker at Haan. These wines are aged in a combination of one-, two-, and three-year-old French oak. The 1998 Shiraz, is a graceful, elegant effort atypical for Australia. An imitation of Euro-styled wines, it offers elegance, purity, and balance. Revealing fine ripeness, medium to full body, and blackberry fruit nicely dosed with spicy oak, it should be consumed over the next 7–8 years.

The chocolaty, black cherry–scented and –flavored 1998 Merlot Prestige possesses toasty oak, coffee, and berry fruit, but comes across as more internationally styled than most Australian Merlots. Drink it over the next 4–5 years.

CHRIS HACKETT (COONAWARRA)

1998 Shiraz K-1	D	90

The classy 1998 Shiraz K-1 boasts a saturated ruby/purple color, full body, gorgeously ripe, concentrated fruit (primarily cassis and blackberries), a touch of spice, and nicely integrated new oak. Fleshy and rich, this layered, multidimensional wine saturates the palate. Enjoy it over the next 10 years.

SIMON HACKETT (BAROSSA)

1996 Cabernet Sauvignon Foggo's Road	D	91
1997 Shiraz Anthony's Reserve	D	93

A new discovery, both of these wines are impressive, and priced modestly by today's standards.The 1997 Shiraz Anthony's Reserve, from 106-year-old vines, offers explosive peppery, blackberry, and cassis aromas that segue into raspberry ice cream intermixed with pepper and spice. Thick, viscous, and full-bodied, this luxuriously rich Shiraz should be drunk now and over the next 7–10 years. It provides a quintessential hedonistic drinking experience! The 1996 Cabernet Sauvignon Foggo's Road emerges from a parcel of 75-year-old vines and was aged in both French and American oak. The saturated dense purple color is accompanied by aromas of chocolate, hickory, barbecue spices, and sweet toasty oak. Abundant quantities of black currant and plumlike fruit also jump from the glass. Thick, with chocolate/coffee-infused flavors, this naturally textured, full-bodied, supple Cabernet Sauvignon can be drunk now and over the next 10 years.

J. J. HAHN (BAROSSA VALLEY)

1998 Cabernet Sauvignon Block 79	D	88?
1998 Shiraz Block 1914	D	96

It's happening all over the world—growers who once supplied top-quality grapes to the larger wineries are breaking away to start their own labels. The Hahns were grape growers for large wineries such as Mildara Blass, St. Hallets, and Rockford, but have now launched their own label, and, believe me, wine enthusiasts are better off for it. Their vineyard, which includes some incredible old vine blocks of Shiraz dating back to the early 20th century, used to be the source for some of Australia's better Shiraz and Cabernet Sauvignons. Now the finest blocks of old vines are being selected by the proprietor and are estate-bottled. James Hahn has hired Veritas wine-maker supreme Rolf Binder to make these wines.

The Cabernet Sauvignon Block 79 comes from a 26-year-old vineyard. The 1998 is a dark ruby/purple wine with excellent, sweet, earthy, cassis notes with cedar, tobacco, and spice. This somewhat artisanally styled Cabernet has a few jagged edges but a dense, full-bodied, spicy, and loaded personality. It will drink well for 12 years.

The tour de force in the J. J. Hahn portfolio is the Shiraz Block 1914, made from vines that are over 85 years old. Average production is 440 cases. The 1998 is a sumptuous, opulent, individualistic yet sensational Shiraz. The wine has a peppery nose with hints of blackberry, blueberry, volatile acidity, melted asphalt, Band-Aid, and some subtle wood (all American oak was used, of which approximately one-third was new). In the mouth, it is huge, chewy, distinctive, and a true blockbuster in every sense of the word. This rather large-scaled wine should age easily for 15–20 years and become slightly more civilized with cellaring.

R. HAMILTON (ADELAIDE)

1997 Marion (Shiraz/Grenache)	D	92?
1997 Merlot Reserve	D	86
1997 Old Vine Shiraz Reserve	D	86

The star of this attractive trio of wines from R. Hamilton is the 1997 Marion (58% Shiraz and 42% Grenache). Made from 136-year-old Shiraz vines planted within the Adelaide city limits, it is a full-bodied, velvety-textured, saturated purple-colored wine with extraordinary fruit richness. The question mark reflects concern with a pronounced aroma of fresh manure or stinky cheese intermixed with the extravagant levels of blackberry liqueur–like fruit. Low in acidity, full-bodied, but funky, this massive, concentrated wine tips the scales at a realistic 14.3% alcohol. Drink it over the next 5–6 years.

The 1997 Merlot Reserve displays good underlying, tangy acidity, largely because 1997 was a cooler year than normal. It is an elegantly styled effort, with admirable stuffing as well as noteworthy black cherries in the nose, along with spicy oak and cool, leafy herbaceous scents. Black cherry flavors in the mouth are complemented by the wine's medium body and excellent purity. It, too, should be consumed over the next 5–6 years. The compressed style of the Merlot is also evident in the 1997 Old Vine Shiraz Reserve, a compact wine with aromas and flavors of black currant and berries, is medium-bodied and elegant, with good ripeness and a stylish, nicely-textured finish. It will also drink well for 5–6 years.

HAPPS (MARGARET RIVER)

1999 Shiraz	C	90

The first vintage for this producer has turned out a beautiful 1999 Shiraz with dense ruby/purple color, gorgeous aromas of blueberry/blackberry and currant fruit, and only a subtle hint of new oak. The wine is full-bodied, velvety-textured, and layered with plenty of glycerin as well as a pure, harmonious finish with well-integrated acidity, tannin, and wood. The wine comes across as a graceful yet fruit-dominated wine with considerable layers of flavor. I suspect more complexity will emerge as this wine ages gracefully for at least a decade. Impressive and reasonably priced.

HARDYS (McLAREN VALE)

1994 Cabernet Sauvignon Thomas Hardy	D	88
1996 Shiraz Eileen Hardy	D	90

The outstanding 1996 Shiraz Eileen Hardy reveals a saturated ruby/purple color plus a big, sweet nose of American oak, blackberry jam, tar, and spice. Opulent and viscous, with a full-bodied, layered palate, this cleanly made, chewy, rich Shiraz should be drunk over the next 5–7 years. The dark ruby/purple 1994 Cabernet Sauvignon Thomas Hardy exhibits classic aromas of cassis and oak (primarily American) in its moderately intense bouquet. The wine is full-bodied, supple, and cleanly made, with no hard edges. Drink it over the next 4–5 years.

HARE'S CHASE (BAROSSA VALLEY)

1999 Merlot	E	85
1999 Shiraz	E	92

The rather crisp, elegant, narrowly constructed 1999 Merlot is pleasant but uninspiring, and obviously overpriced. The color is a deep ruby, and the flavors evoke some mocha and cherry fruit, with some spicy wood in the background. It is a competently made wine, but it does not take a genius to find more interesting and less expensive Merlots. Anticipated maturity: now–2009. In complete contrast, the 1999 Shiraz looks to be superb. It has a saturated black/purple color with a knockout nose of smoke, blackberry, and cassis mixed with tar, licorice, and spice box. This rich, opulently textured, full-bodied blockbuster should provide dazzling drinking now and over the next 12–15 years. Thankfully, there are 400 cases of this wine that achieved 14.5% alcohol naturally. As a postscript, proprietor/wine-maker Peter Taylor is the chief red wine–maker at Penfolds.

HASTWELL AND LIGHTFOOT (McLAREN VALE)

1998 Cabernet	D	87
1998 Shiraz	D	89

There are two solid efforts at realistic prices. The 1998 Cabernet reveals a deep ruby/purple color, plenty of earthy, spicy, black currant fruit, soft, supple texture, and notes of American oak in the lusty, straightforward finish. Drink it over the next 4 years. The 1998 Shiraz shows an opaque purple color, plenty of sweet, jammy, black pepper–infused berry fruit, full body, some notes of charcoal, earth, and spice. Drink this opulently textured, user-friendly wine over the next 5 years.

HEATHCOTE (SOUTH AUSTRALIA)

1998 Shiraz Curagée	D	91
1999 Shiraz Mail Coach	C	88

Bottled unfined and unfiltered after being aged all in French oak (40% new), the 1998 Shiraz Curagée has tremendous depth, volume, and expansiveness on the palate. It is a strong effort from a superb vintage in South Australia. The color is a dense purple, and the wine is tight but concentrated and powerful, with outstanding purity and overall balance. Give it 2–3 years of cellaring, and drink it over the following 15+ years.

The 1999 Shiraz Mail Coach, which includes 5.5% Viognier in the blend, is a chunky, robust, full-bodied offering revealing aromas and flavors of blackberries, fudge, cassis, and earth. Although not complex, it is a cleanly made Shiraz that coats the palate. It was aged in a combination of French and American oak, but the wood component is subtle compared to the rich, concentrated fruit. Drink it over the next 5–6 years.

HENRY'S DRIVE (PADTHAWAY)

1999 Cabernet Sauvignon	D	90
1998 Cabernet Sauvignon	D	93
1999 Shiraz	D	91
1998 Shiraz	D	93
1999 Shiraz Reserve	E	92+

These wines from a cool climate area north of Coonawarra are made by Sparky and Sarah Marquis, who did such a fantastic job as wine-makers at Fox Creek. The Shiraz and Cabernet vineyards are young (7 years old), but the quality of these efforts is outrageously rich, ultra-ripe, and filled with extract, not dissimilar from the signature style of Fox Creek. The 1999s of this portfolio are among the strongest I have tasted, a vintage clearly inferior to 1998. Both 1998s are superb. For starters, the 1999 Cabernet Sauvignon is a beautifully stylish, almost European Cabernet with sweet, pure black currant fruit, a moderate dosage of oak (80% French and 20% American wood are utilized), excellent texture, and a fresh, well-balanced, harmonious finish. This wine is user-friendly and meant to be drunk during its first decade of life. Blackberry/cassis lovers can get an easy fix with the 1998 Cabernet Sauvignon. This wine is crammed with fruit, has low acidity, full body, and lusty, concentrated flavors that coat the palate. Already delicious, it should get even better over the next 2 years and last 12–15 years. This is an undeniably sexy style of Cabernet.

The two offerings of 1999 Shiraz are certainly among the stars of that particular vintage. The 1999 Shiraz (100% Shiraz that achieved 14.5% alcohol and was aged in 50% new oak, mostly American) is an opaque ruby/purple wine with classic smoky black fruits in the nose, along with some licorice and pepper. The wine is deep, full-bodied, and admirably concentrated, with a plush texture and serious opulence and length. This thick, juicy fruit bomb can be drunk now and over the next decade. One thousand cases were produced. The even more spectacular, beautifully balanced, saturated black purple-colored 1999 Shiraz Reserve offers a terrific nose of floral notes mixed with melted tar, roasted herbs, black fruits, and smoke. The wine has wonderful sweetness because of the high level of glycerin in the attack, a seamless mid-palate and finish, with beautifully integrated alcohol, tannin, and acidity. It is layered, rich, not huge, but gorgeously proportioned and persuasive. Drink it over the following 14–15 years. Revealing toasty American oak and chewy, blackberry and licorice-infused fruit, the 1998 Shiraz possesses multiple layers of concentration. This super-extracted, rich, low-acid wine displays plenty of smoky oak, pepper, and spice, but the fruit dominates in a big way. Drink it over the next 15 years.

HENSCHKE (BAROSSA)

1996 Cabernet Cyril Henschke	E	86?
1998 Grenache/Mourvèdre/Shiraz Johann's Garden	C	88
1997 Merlot/Cabernet Abbotts Prayer	D	86
1997 Pinot Noir Giles	D	87
1997 Shiraz/Cabernet/Malbec Keyneton Estate	D	87
1995 Shiraz Hill of Grace	EEE	92
1997 Shiraz Mount Edelstone	E	87

This famous winery has a good but (with the exception of the 1995 Shiraz Hill of Grace) largely uninspiring portfolio of wines. Certainly they are all competent efforts, but I wonder if quality couldn't be pushed even higher. The red wines, such as the 1997 Merlot/Cabernet Abbotts Prayer, possess tart, acidic profiles, with cranberry, red currant, and cherry aromas. More reminiscent of Pinot Noir than ripe Cabernet and Merlot, this is a tartly styled offering from what tastes like a cool microclimate. Anticipated maturity: now–2008. The same criticism could be made of the 1996 Cabernet Cyril Henschke. Its high, tart acidity suggests to me that much of it was added, and not with a deft touch. There is good red currant, strawberry, and cherry fruit and medium body but a compressed texture and short finish, no doubt because of the high level of acidity. I do not think this wine is going anywhere, although the acidity will ensure a certain degree of longevity. Anticipated maturity: now–2012.

Only a handful of complex Pinot Noirs emerge from Australia. Henschke's medium ruby-colored, elegant 1997 Pinot Noir Giles displays sweet raspberry fruit, notes of vanilla and toast, and a round, supple, medium-bodied style not dissimilar from a Côte de Beaune. Drink it over the next 3–4 years. Another tart red is the 1997 Shiraz/Cabernet/Malbec Keyneton Estate. A blend of 65% Shiraz, 25% Cabernet Sauvignon, and 10% Malbec, its streamlined personality offers graceful blackberry and currant fruit, leathery notes, medium body, and light tannin. Drink it over the next 4–5 years. Similarly styled but exhibiting more mint/eucalyptus is the compressed, medium-bodied 1997 Shiraz Mount Edelstone. This well-made, pure effort possesses red and black fruits, surprising acidity, and a lighter style than I would have expected from such a famous winery and renowned wine. Drink it over the next 5–8 years.

The two finest red wines are the 1998 Grenache/Mourvèdre/Shiraz Johann's Garden and 1995 Shiraz Hill of Grace. The 1998 Johann's Garden offers sweet blueberry and black raspberry fruit, a silky texture, medium to full body, soft, supple tannin, and a long finish. Though not a blockbuster, it is an elegant, finesse-styled wine with flair and character. Drink it over the next 5–6 years. The opaque ruby/purple-colored 1995 Shiraz Hill of Grace (along with Penfolds Grange, one of the most famous Shirazes of Australia) boasts abundant quantities of toasty American oak, fat, blackberry, tar-infused fruit flavors, a deep, unctuous texture, and a powerful, concentrated, long finish. This renowned Shiraz is indeed all it should be for its lofty price tag. It should drink well for 15–20 years.

HERMITAGE ROAD (LIMESTONE COAST)

1998 Shiraz Reserve	C	89

Licorice, blackberry, and spicy wood aromas emerge from the dense ruby/purple-colored 1998 Shiraz Reserve. It possesses abundant fruit, a fleshy texture, full body, and excellent purity. It would have deserved a better rating, had it not been for its slight lack of complexity. Anticipated maturity: now–2010.

HEWITSON (McLAREN VALE)

1999 Mourvèdre Old Garden	D	90
1997 Mourvèdre Old Garden	D	90
1999 Shiraz Barossa	D	87
1998 Shiraz Barossa	D	86
1998 Shiraz l'Oizeau	D	91
1997 Shiraz l'Oizeau	D	86

Produced from a Mourvèdre vineyard first planted in 1853, the impressive Mourvèdre Old Garden also contains 5% Shiraz. The beautiful blackberry, blueberry, raspberry, leathery, spicy, French oak-scented, elegant 1999 possesses excellent delineation, medium body, and moderate tannin. It is a high-quality Mourvèdre made in a modern-day style. Bravo! Anticipated maturity: now–2010. The 1997 Mourvèdre Old Garden was a surprise. Textbook notes of mushrooms, blueberries, earth, tree bark, and saddle leather jump from the glass of this medium-bodied, racy, stylish yet concentrated Mourvèdre. This type of wine is not for everyone, given Mourvèdre's singular personality and dusty tannin. However, this tastes like the real stuff from France's Bandol appellation. This wine was impressively long, well balanced, and loaded with character. Drink it over the next 5–8 years.

The Shiraz l'Oizeau takes its name from some of the oldest Shiraz vines in McLaren Vale. Elegance along with power can be found in the ruby/purple 1998 with notes of crème de cassis, licorice, and new French wood. Long, deep, and beautifully pure, with an unevolved character, this wine is approachable, but promises to be better in 2–3 years and last two decades. Dark ruby-colored, with subtle oak, blackberry, and black cherry fruit aromas and flavors, the 1997 Shiraz l'Oizeau offers a creamy, medium-bodied personality, excellent purity and ripeness, and a sense of delicacy rather than exuberance. It should drink well for 5 years.

Made in a light style, Hewitson's 1999 Shiraz Barossa is stylistically well defined and fresh, offering creamy oak, but more red than black fruits. It should be drunk over the next 4–5 years. The 1998 Shiraz Barossa exhibits moderate quantities of creamy oak and black fruit in the attractive aromatics. Dark ruby-colored with purple nuances, this medium-bodied, fleshy, stylized effort possesses sweet tannin but not a lot of staying power in the mouth. It is an elegant Australian Shiraz to be drunk over the next 5–6 years.

HIGHBANK (COONAWARRA)

1998 Proprietary Red	D	91

The superb, opaque purple-colored, high-class 1998 Proprietary Red (a blend of 68% Cabernet Sauvignon, 20% Merlot, and 12% Cabernet Franc) has brilliantly absorbed its aging in 100% new French oak. The wine is classy, pure, and, according to my tasting notes, "the Léoville-Las Cases of Australia?" With gorgeous black cherry and black currant flavors intermixed with lead pencil, vanilla, and mineral, medium to full body, high tannin, and superb delineation, it will drink well for 15–16 years. This is another candidate for inserting into a blind tasting of top-class Bordeaux to see how it fares.

HILL OF CONTENT (CLARE VALLEY)

1999 Old Vines Grenache/Shiraz	B	86

The Côtes du Rhône–like 1999 Old Vines Grenache/Shiraz possesses an elegant, medium-weight style with notes of cherries and ripe peaches. It is soft, round, and ideal for drinking over the next 2–3 years.

HOLLICK (COONAWARRA)

1998 Cabernet Sauvignon/Merlot	C	87
1999 Shiraz/Cabernet Sauvignon	C	87
1998 Shiraz Wilgha	D	88

The two *cuvées* of Shiraz include the 1999 Shiraz/Cabernet Sauvignon (93% Shiraz and 7% Cabernet Sauvignon). The wine is soft, ripe, straightforward, yet monochromatic. Nevertheless, it is well made, with the telltale pepper and ripe blackberry characteristics. Drink it over the next 3 years. The 1998 Shiraz Wilgha is slightly deeper. This wine, fermented and aged in new American oak, shows predominant levels of toast in its aromatics, which kept my score from going any higher. That is disappointing, given the wine's dense ruby/purple color, jammy, concentrated, full-bodied fruit, real opulence, and a chewy, long finish. If the wood were better integrated, this wine could flirt with an outstanding rating. It should drink well for 8 years, and hopefully the wood will become better integrated with cellaring.

The 1998 Cabernet Sauvignon/Merlot (85%/15%) possesses Bordeaux-like, curranty, coffee, cedary, and tobacco aromatic and flavor profiles. There is good fruit on the attack, medium body, and an austere, lightly tannic finish. It should drink well for 8 years.

HONGELL (BAROSSA VALLEY)

1998 Grenache	C	86
1999 Grenache Old Vine	C	88
1999 Shiraz	C	90

John Hongell has been a supplier to such famous Barossa producers as Charles Melton, Rockford, and Torbreck. He has now decided, like so many growers, to begin estate-bottling his own wines. His first efforts certainly show promise. The regular *cuvée* of 1998 Grenache (from 56-year-old vines) displays a Côtes du Rhône–like, sweet, kirsch note intermixed with balsam wood and earth. Tasty, well made, and medium-bodied, but straightforward and one-dimensional, it requires consumption over the next 3–4 years.

Far more interesting is the complex, supple-textured, dark ruby-colored 1999 Grenache Old Vine. This wine shows notes of bacon fat, sausage, and jammy red and black fruits in its aromatics. It is sweet, dense, full-bodied, and ripe, and if it had additional length and complexity, would have been outstanding. Nevertheless, it is an excellent wine and ideal for drinking over the next 5–6 years. The best of the three wines from Hongell is the 1999 Shiraz, made from low yields of 1.5 tons per acre, all from 8-year-old Shiraz vines. It is a dense ruby/purple-colored, big, sweet, fat fruit bomb with low acidity, abundant quantities of blackberry fruit, barbecue spice, smoke, and earth, plenty of glycerin, and a hedonistic, user-friendly appeal. Drink it over the next 4 years.

HOWARD PARK (WESTERN AUSTRALIA)

1998 Cabernet Sauvignon/Cabernet Franc/Merlot	D	86
1997 Cabernet Sauvignon/Cabernet Franc/Merlot	D	86
1996 Cabernet Sauvignon/Cabernet Franc/Merlot	D	87
1998 Shiraz Leston	D	89

The impressive 1998 Shiraz Leston reveals generous blackberry fruit as well as a dense, concentrated attack and mid-palate, and sweet tannin in the finish. Rich, medium- to full-bodied, and pure, it can be enjoyed over the next 7–8 years. The Cabernet Sauvignon/Cabernet Franc/Merlot blend spends two years in French oak before bottling. The 1998 (75% Cabernet Sauvignon, 13% Cabernet Franc, and 12% Merlot) is a firmly structured, attractive effort offering aromas of cedar, underbrush, black currants, and spice. Medium-bodied and moderately concentrated with firm tannin, it should drink well now and over the next 7–8 years.

As for the 1997 and 1996 Cabernet Sauvignon/Cabernet Franc/Merlots, the 1997 is more compact, exhibiting a dark ruby/purple color, and an attractive ripe black currant and cherry-scented nose with cedar and spice box in the background. Medium-bodied, with very good concentration, this stylish, elegant wine should drink well for 5–7 years. The 1996 is richer, with more complex aromatics, but is not totally dissimilar from its younger sibling.

Dark ruby-colored, with scents of spice box, cedar, tobacco, and black currants, this medium-bodied, nicely packaged wine exhibits good ripeness and purity as well as an overall sense of grace/balance. Drink it over the next 7 years.

HUTTON VALE (EDEN VALLEY)

1999 Grenache/Mataro	D	91
1998 Grenache/Mataro	D	87+
1995 Shiraz	E	88
1994 Shiraz	E	88?

The Grenache/Mataro blend is a tiny 90-case *cuvée* of old vines. The proportion of the two varietals vary with each vintage. The interesting 1999 Grenache/Mataro (50% of each) is a complex, leathery, spicy, blackberry- and currant-scented and -flavored wine with plenty of depth, good, bright tannin, and a supple, fleshy finish. It should drink well for another 5–7 years. The medium dark ruby-colored, closed, tannic 1998 Grenache/Mataro (60% and 40% respectively) is produced from old vines and tastes as if it came from a cool-climate vineyard. The wine is compressed, but what does pull through the structure is pure cherry and raspberry fruit. The red fruit side of the flavor spectrum dominates this medium-bodied blend. Give it 2 years of cellaring.

I will keep my notes short for both Shirazes, which are only available in small quantities (approximately 30 cases). The 1995 is an earthy, peppery, fully mature wine showing full body, sweet, herb-tinged, cedary, spicy berry fruit. The wine needs to be drunk over the next 4 years. The 1994 reveals intense eucalyptus/minty notes accompanying its blackberry/ currant fruit. There is fine density and medium to full body, but it is a wine for those who crave weediness in the aromatic and flavor profiles. It should drink well for 10 years.

IRVINE (EDEN VALLEY)

1997 Grand Merlot	E	92+?
1999 Merlot	C	88

James Irvine is a famous wine consultant, but he also produces what many consider the finest Merlot in Australia, the Grand Merlot. As for the 1999 Merlot, this blend of Eden Valley and Barossa fruit is a very good value. It possesses a chocolate fudge–like character along with mocha and cherry fruit. Seamless, pure, and ripe, it is best drunk over the next 2 years.

The large-scaled 1997 Grand Merlot is a wine of extraordinary extraction. This exotic, full-bodied, powerful Merlot displays lavish quantities of toasty French oak. Aged for 39 months in what appears to be all new barrels prior to bottling, it is a layered, thick, juicy effort with notes of coffee, chocolate, black cherries, liqueur, spice box, and new oak in addition to enormous quantities of extract, glycerin, and richness. The alcohol is a lofty 15.3%, reflecting Irvine's predilection to pick extremely ripe. It gives every indication of aging for a decade or more, but I must say that a minivertical sponsored by the importer suggested this is a wine that really does not benefit from cellaring. Older vintages such as 1987, 1989, 1992, and 1993 were already drying out and extremely attenuated. However, a handful of old vintages, 1991 in particular, had survived cellaring and were in good shape. Nevertheless, I would opt for drinking these wines in their first 3–5 years of life, despite a style that suggests longevity.

JASPER HILL (HEATHCOTE)

1999 Shiraz Georgia's Paddock	E	89
1998 Shiraz Georgia's Paddock	E	91
1997 Shiraz Georgia's Paddock	E	89+

These three red wine offerings are the finest I have tasted from Jasper Hill. From a lighter vintage, the 1999 Shiraz Georgia's Paddock may merit an outstanding rating. The dense purple color is accompanied by abundant quantities of blackberries, pepper, and melted asphalt in its muscular, full-bodied yet supple-textured personality. Remarkably, the lofty alcohol (15.5%) is well concealed in the rich, fruity, glycerin-filled finish. Drink this 1999 over the next decade. More explosive, thicker, and complex is the dense purple-colored 1998 Shiraz Georgia's Paddock. It exhibits a provocative perfume of smoke, barbecue spice, crème de cassis, and blackberries with pepper and vanilla in the background. Full-bodied, opulent, and voluptuous, this sexy, dense, low-acid wine coats the palate with considerable viscosity and purity. It can be drunk now and over the next 12 years. The opaque purple-colored, concentrated 1997 Shiraz Georgia's Paddock boasts crème de cassis aromas. This sweet-smelling, rich, concentrated, full-bodied, dry red wine exhibits plenty of cassis fruit, good spice, and a heady, moderately tannic finish. Still young, it should keep for a decade or more.

STEPHEN JOHN (CLARE VALLEY)

1998 Shiraz	D	87
1997 Shiraz	D	88
1998 Shiraz Reserve	D	90+

The dark ruby/purple, closed, tightly knit, elegant 1998 Shiraz appears to be very good. It should keep for 12 years. The dark plum/purple-colored, unfiltered 1997 Shiraz exhibits a more evolved, peppery, spice box, black currant, and cherry-scented nose, medium- to full-bodied flavors, well-integrated wood and acidity, and a plush, soft finish. It should drink well for the next 8 years. The unfiltered 1998 Shiraz Reserve is quite backward, but very intense. It displays vibrant acidity along with heady quantities of rich, humongous, chewy blackberry and cassis fruit. Pepper, dried cherries, and spice box aromas also appear in this tannic, large-sized Shiraz. Anticipated maturity: now–2020.

JOHN'S BLEND (LANGHORNE CREEK/McLAREN VALE)

1998 Margarete's Shiraz	D	90

Seventy-year-old Shiraz vines have produced a minty, chocolaty, cassis-scented and -flavored 1998 Margarete's Shiraz with plenty of depth, medium to full body, and rustic, old-style tannins in the finish. The wine was aged 26 months in 100% new American oak, as evidenced by the toasty, spicy wood present in both the aromatics and flavor. Drink it over the next 7–8 years for its exuberant, robust style.

ROBERT JOHNSON (EDEN VALLEY)

1997 Merlot	C	88

An impeccably made, symmetrical, unfiltered Merlot that has been aged in French oak, this 1997 reveals dark berry fruit, medium to full body, adequate acidity, attractive sweetness, and a nicely textured, glycerin-imbued finish. Drink it over the next 5–6 years.

TREVOR JONES (BAROSSA VALLEY)

1998 Boots Grenache	C	88
1998 Cabernet Sauvignon/Merlot	D	87
1996 Cabernet Sauvignon/Merlot	D	88
1995 Cabernet Sauvignon/Merlot	D	90+
NV Old Barossa Muscat	EE	96
NV Old Barossa Tawny Port	EE	98
1998 Shiraz	D	83
1997 Shiraz	D	86
NV Shiraz Liqueur	EE	100
1998 Shiraz Reserve Wild Witch	E	85?

1997 Shiraz Reserve Wild Witch	E	90
1996 Shiraz Reserve Wild Witch	E	92+
NV Tokay Liqueur	EE	100

Trevor Jones's wines are generally impressive. A second label, Boots, a joint project with his American importer, has recently been added to his portfolio, which aims to produce wines of character that are also noteworthy values. The value-priced Boots offerings are in-your-face, fruity wines with surprising character for their modest prices. In addition to his delicious Shiraz and Cabernet/Merlot blends, Jones offers mind-blowing fortified dessert wines. The Muscat and Tawny Port are from base materials at least 30 years old, and the Shiraz and Tokay liqueurs are from base materials at least 50 years old. All four are truly unreal. Coming to the vintages, the three red 1998s are not as good as I hoped, both Shirazes tasting unduly narrow in their textures because of surprisingly high acidity (probably added). However, the 1997s and 1996s are superb. The 1998 Boots Grenache (made from 80-year-old Grenache vines that yielded only 1.5 tons of fruit per acre) is a dead ringer for a top-notch southern Rhône. Medium ruby-colored, with jammy aromas of kirsch, black cherries, and pepper, this spicy, exuberantly fruity, fleshy Grenache tips the scales at 15% alcohol. There is plenty of glycerin as well as a tactile impression of sweetness, even though the wine is totally dry. It is a hedonistic fruit bomb to drink over the next 2–3 years.

The 1998 Shiraz reveals an impressively saturated purple color as well as a sweet perfume of blackberry fruit intermixed with floral and spice notes. In the mouth, it is medium- to full-bodied but becomes compressed because of its copious acidity. Although competent, it lacks excitement and lushness. This wine should last 10–15 years, but how well it will develop remains to be seen. The 1997 Shiraz is a rather elegant, almost claret style of Shiraz with medium body, restrained spice box, red cherry, and currant notes, and a clean, fresh finish. Drink it over the next 5–6 years.

The Shiraz Reserve Wild Witch is produced from extremely old vines (about 40 years of age). Yields are generally a meager one ton of fruit per acre. The 1998 Shiraz Reserve Wild Witch displays generous new oak in its complex bouquet of black fruits, tar, and spice. Rich and full-bodied, with more texture but a narrow finish, it is tightly knit, with surprisingly high acidity. This wine will hold 10–15 years, but how well it will develop remains to be seen. The 1997 Shiraz Reserve Wild Witch is again an elegant, finesse-style Shiraz with notes of cedar wood, red currants, pepper, and a touch of blackberries. It is well made, surprisingly restrained, and subtle for an Australian Shiraz, but distinctive in its individuality and gracefulness. The 1996 Shiraz Reserve Wild Witch's stunning nose reveals scents of freshly ground pepper intermixed with toast, blackberry, and raspberry fruit. With awesome concentration, medium to full body, and zesty underlying tangy acidity, this complex yet firmly structured, backward Shiraz should unfold nicely for at least 15 years. Impressive!

The Cabernet Sauvignon/Merlot blend is composed of 85% Cabernet and 15% Merlot, and emerges from 36-year-old vines. The 1998 exhibits a saturated ruby/purple color in addition to copious quantities of mint, black fruits, and new oak in the nose. Clean and straightforward but monolithic, it will drink well for 7–8 years. The 1996 Cabernet/Merlot is slightly tough-textured, but almost Bordeaux-like in its earthy, black currant style with nicely balanced wood and tannin. The wine is slightly austere but well made and clean. Enjoy it over the following 7–8 years. It is designed for tasters who prefer their reds on the leaner side of the stylistic spectrum. The 1995 Cabernet Sauvignon/Merlot's deep ruby/purple color is followed by a textbook Bordeaux bouquet of black currants, spicy new oak, and cedar. Rich on the attack, with outstanding ripeness, purity, and overall equilibrium, this is a classic example of power allied to elegance. Anticipated maturity: now–2016.

The point scores say it all when it comes to trying to describe the sumptuous, sublime fortified wines produced by Trevor Jones. They all have approximately 18% alcohol, and levels of concentration and perfume that must be experienced to be believed. The nonvintage Old Barossa Muscat offers a medium amber color, fabulous sweetness, great freshness, and layers of concentration. Amazingly, it gets blown away by the other three offerings. The nonvintage Old Barossa Tawny Port, a blend of Shiraz, Grenache, Muscat, and Tokay, boasts awesome aromatics that could fill a large room. Tremendous richness, refreshing underlying acidity, fabulous fruit, and an unctuous texture result in a profound drinking experience. The Shiraz Liqueur and Tokay Liqueur are off the charts. The only thing to compare them to is some of the rare Muscat or Tokay produced by another Australian, William Chambers. They are phenomenally concentrated, amazingly thick and unctuous, yet multidimensional and totally compelling. Why aren't more of these made? The base material for both liqueurs is 50 or more years of age. Production is limited to 30 cases of 375 ml bottles. These are the kind of spectacular fortifieds that are almost worth killing for to get hold of a half bottle or two.

JOSEPH (McLAREN VALE)

1998 Cabernet/Merlot Moda Amarone	E	91

The distinctive 1998 Cabernet/Merlot Moda Amarone, made from dried Cabernet Sauvignon and Merlot fruit, reveals a dense ruby/purple/garnet color, and a big, sweet, toasty nose filled with aromas of melted asphalt, black currants, damp earth, and plums. Rich, full-bodied, and chewy, this is a singularly styled wine which, to my palate, is successful. It is not for everyone, but for serving with full-flavored dishes, or at the end of a meal, it is an intriguing and commendable effort. Moreover, it should drink well for 10+ years.

KAESSLER'S STONE HORSE (BAROSSA VALLEY)

1998 Shiraz	C	89
1998 Shiraz Old Bastard	E	95
1998 Shiraz Old Vine	C	91

These immensely impressive wines are aged in a combination of both old and new American oak. All three *cuvées* emerge from a 38-year-old Shiraz vineyard. An excellent value, the 1998 Shiraz is a rich, full-bodied, robust, typically Australian proportioned wine with plenty of glycerin, alcohol, fruit, and body. Although not complex, it is loaded as well as mouth-staining. Drink it over the next 7–8 years. The exceptional 1998 Shiraz Old Vine, reveals greater extraction, a saturated blue/purple color, and an admirably sweet, blackberry, blueberry, smoky bouquet with oak nuances. Flamboyant, full-bodied, and textured, this powerful, hedonistic, soft wine is ideal for drinking over the next 15–16 years.

Sadly, there are less than 50 cases of the 1998 Shiraz Old Bastard. A selection of barrels from the Shiraz Old Vine *cuvée*, this is a riveting but limited-production offering. It exhibits off-the-chart levels of extract, power, and richness in addition to glorious smoky blackberry and currant fruit. Unctuously textured, enormous, yet symmetrical, this is what Australia does better than anyone. Drink this distinctive/individualistic Shiraz over the next 20 years.

KANGARILLA ROAD (McLAREN VALE)

1999 Cabernet Sauvignon Estate	B	91
1998 Cabernet Sauvignon Estate	B	89
1999 Shiraz Estate	B	90
1997 Shiraz Estate	B	87
1999 Zinfandel	C	86

This relatively new operation has one of the first plantings of Zinfandel in Australia. The wines admirably combine power with a sense of restraint and elegance and possess exuberant personalities and lovely aromatics. Readers looking for exceptional values in outstanding wine should check out Kangarilla Road's Shiraz and Cabernet Sauvignon. The 1999 Zinfandel exhibits briery, cranberry, and peppery notes, medium to full body, and attractive fruit. However, the efforts I have tasted from Australia involving Zinfandel pale in comparison with California's finest, and remain, in large part, uninspiring curiosities. Drink it over the next 2–3 years.

The Shiraz Estate, which was first produced in 1997, is matured in used French and American oak. Availabilities are around 2,000 cases. This one is a great value. The 1999 boasts a dense purple color as well as a gorgeously sweet nose of blackberries, melted licorice, pepper, and caramel. It has admirable purity, layers of fruit and glycerin, full body, a sumptuous mouth-feel, and a long, concentrated finish. It should continue to drink well for another 7–8 years. The 1997 Shiraz Estate, the debut vintage for Kangarilla Road, reveals aromas of pepper, truffle, earth, and black fruits. Medium- to full-bodied, with decent acidity and a forward style, it should be consumed over the next 4–5 years.

Kangarilla's Cabernet Sauvignon is generally impressive, one of the finest Cabernets money can buy for its quality. Composed of 100% Cabernet Sauvignon, it is aged 18 months in American and French oak. The 1999 displays a deep ruby/purple color along with a gorgeous nose of espresso, chocolate fudge, black currants, and cedar. It has sweet tannin, a terrific mouth-feel, medium to full body, and a long, lush finish. Another exceptional value, it will drink well for a decade. The dark ruby/purple-colored 1998 Cabernet Sauvignon Estate offers that varietal's classic hallmarks—cedar, spice box, black currants, and tobacco. This medium-bodied, well-endowed, impressive wine with sweet tannin and adequate acidity should drink well for 10–12 years.

KATNOOK ESTATE (COONAWARRA)

1998 Cabernet Sauvignon	E	87
1996 Cabernet Sauvignon Odyssey	E	89+
1994 Cabernet Sauvignon Odyssey	E	91
1998 Merlot	D	85
1997 Shiraz Jimmy Watson Trophy	E	92

These wines always display a cool-climate character regardless of vintage conditions. Some wines of the portfolio may be disappointing or just pleasant (1998 Shiraz, 1997 Merlot, and 1997 Cabernet Sauvignon), but those reviewed here are very good, if not excellent.

The dense ruby/plum/purple-colored 1998 Cabernet Sauvignon offers aromas of smoke, creosote, cassis, and dried herbs. Medium- to full-bodied, rich, and elegant, this stylish Cabernet can be drunk now and over the next decade. Less saturated in color, the 1998 Merlot offers herb, cedar, black cherry, chocolate, and new oak aromas. It is a medium-weight, moderately endowed offering with a sweet attack, good cleanliness, a distinctive, elegant style, and a narrow finish with tart acidity. Anticipated maturity: 2003–2012.

The nearly opaque purple-colored 1997 Shiraz Jimmy Watson Trophy possesses jammy blackberry and cassis aromas intermixed with scents of melted licorice and pepper. Full-bodied, wild blackberry fruit flavors display abundant glycerin, sweet tannin, and sufficient acidity. As the wine sits in the glass, brandylike, macerated prune aromas and flavors emerge. This superb Shiraz saturates the palate. Drink it over the next 10–12 years.

The luxury *cuvée* Cabernet Sauvignon Odyssey spends 38 months in new French oak barrels before bottling. The 1996's dense plum/purple color is accompanied by distinctive aromas of cedar, spice box, black currants, licorice, and a touch of kirsch and new oak. Full-bodied, highly extracted, and rich, this large-scaled yet balanced wine can be drunk now as well as over the next 15+ years. The black/purple-colored 1994 Cabernet Sauvignon Odyssey offers impressive complexity and richness. The bouquet possesses cedar, black currant, spice box, chocolate, and dried herb scents. Rich, with a thick mid-palate and sweet tannin, it is a powerful yet elegant Cabernet with considerable length and aging potential. Accessible now, it promises to improve over the next 3–4 years and last for 12–15 years.

KAY BROTHERS (McLAREN VALE)

1998	Cabernet Sauvignon Amery Vineyard	D	92?
1998	Merlot Amery Vineyards	D	90
1998	Shiraz Amery Vineyards	D	92
1998	Shiraz Amery Vineyard Hillside	D	94
1996	Shiraz Block 6	D	93
1998	Shiraz Block 6 Amery Vineyards	D	98+

The old-fashioned labels on these wines suggest history, and, in fact, the Kay family's roots in the McLaren Vale go back at least five generations. Their wines are among the most individualistic and impressive wines I have recently tasted from Australia. Possessing undeniable character and individuality, they should be hugely popular in this country. There are just under 850–900 cases of each of these *cuvées*. The 1998 Merlot Amery Vineyards has a dense, opaque purple color, smoky, coffee, black cherry, cough syrup notes, with plenty of toasted new oak. The wine is fat, ripe, pretty, and rather decadent and exotic, with a heavy overlay of new American oak. It is not for everybody, but this is a flamboyant, impressively endowed Merlot from Australia. Drink it over the next 10 years.

The spectacular 1998 Cabernet Sauvignon Amery Vineyard (14.9% alcohol from 25-year-old vines cropped at 2.0–2.5 tons per acre) offers the textbook huge ripeness and burly, muscular style of Australia intertwined with an Italian-like creosote, earthy, rustic, leathery component. The wine has great fruit, a fabulous multilayered texture, massive concentration, and noteworthy levels of glycerin, blackberry, plum, cherry, and cassis fruit. All of this is tied together in a chewy, full-bodied, slightly rustic style. It should continue to evolve for at least two decades. But readers take note—the notions of creosote, bay leaf, anise, and leather are out of the mainstream for Cabernet Sauvignon, and are likely to be controversial.

Shiraz lovers will be electrified by the four offerings from Kay Brothers. The Shiraz Amery Vineyard is made from 15-year-old vines cropped at a meager 1.5–2.5 tons of fruit per acre. It is aged 18 months in American oak barrels, but it is hard to believe there is much new oak based on its aromas and flavors. The 1998, which tips the scales at 14.8% alcohol, is a substantial, full-throttle, somewhat old-style Shiraz with smoky, earthy, leathery, charcoal, and blackberry notes in the nose and flavors. It waddles across the palate with considerable extract, weight, and heaviness. It is deep, chewy, muscular, with the fruit and glycerin largely concealing some tannin. The wood seems to be kept within reason. This wine should evolve for at least another 12–15 years.

The prodigious Shiraz Amery Vineyard Hillside is aged in 100% new American oak from relatively young vines that are the same clone of Shiraz as planted in the Block 6, which still contains 100+-year-old vines. It is vinified in an artisanal way. The 1998 is a full-throttle, powerful, super-concentrated wine with opaque black/purple color, notes of new oak intermixed with licorice, blackberry, cassis, asphalt, and leather. The wine is huge, massive, chewy, and unctuously textured. It is a total turn-on. Drink it over the next 15–20+ years.

Made from 106-year-old head-pruned Shiraz vines, the Shiraz Block 6 is bottled unfiltered after spending 18 months in old American oak upright wood tanks. Annual production averages 900 cases, and the vines are cropped at 1.5–2.0 tons per acre. Both following vintages are nearly perfect. The compelling 1998 is impressively thick-looking, has formidable concentration and gorgeously pure, peppery, crème de cassis notes intermixed with new saddle leather, incense, smoky charcoal, and vanilla. Fabulously concentrated and unctuously textured, with a finish that remained on my palate for 60+ seconds, this large-scaled, classic Australian Shiraz from old, unirrigated, head-pruned vines should age effortlessly for 20–25 years. Anticipated maturity: now–2025.

A sensational blackberry, hickory smoke, and tar-scented and -flavored Shiraz, the 1996 Shiraz Block 6 possesses huge body, fabulous extraction and ripeness, and glorious levels of black fruits, all infused with glycerin and heady alcohol. Fine purity and emerging complexity can be found in this superintense, mouth-filling blockbuster. Anticipated maturity: now–2016. Wow! If you find these wines and can afford them, do not hesitate!

KIES FAMILY WINES (BAROSSA VALLEY)

1999 Shiraz Dedication	D	88

Consulting wine-maker/oenologist James Irvine is the adviser for this wine. The medium- to full-bodied, soft 1999 Dedication Shiraz has more than a passing resemblance to a southern Rhône. Notes of pepper, Provençal herbs, and roasted fruits emerge from the aromatics. Deep, round, and sweet, it is best consumed over the next 5–6 years.

KILIKANOON (CLARE VALLEY)

1999 Cabernet Sauvignon	C	87
1998 Cabernet Sauvignon	D	90
1999 Grenache Prodigal	C	90
1998 Grenache Prodigal	C	88+
1999 Shiraz Oracle	D	94
1998 Shiraz Oracle	D	92

These wines are made at the Torbreck facilities of David Powell. Although I have limited experience with Kilikanoon (I have only tasted three vintages), I have liked everything they have done to date. The Grenache Prodigals are outstanding examples of this varietal, and come close to matching the superb Grenaches made at Clarendon Hills and Greenock Creek. This wine is aged 15 months in old oak prior to being bottled without filtration. The 1999 exhibits a classic Grenache nose of black cherry liqueur mixed with roasted notes and spice. Sweet, exotic, explosive levels of fruit and glycerin cascade seamlessly over the palate. Lush, dense, and impressively hedonistic, it should be drunk over the next 5–6 years. The outstanding 1998 Grenache Prodigal tops the scales at 15% alcohol. Tightly knit for an Australian Grenache, it reveals good structure, tannin, and wood, as well as full-bodied cherry and raspberry flavors. It should drink well for 8 years.

The Cabernet Sauvignons are aged in French oak casks (40% new) and bottled unfiltered. The deep ruby/purple-colored, medium-bodied 1999 is surprisingly graceful. Made in a finesse style that exhibits good, spicy black currant fruit, evidence of new oak, and a round finish, it should drink well for at least a decade. The oustanding 1998 Cabernet Sauvignon boasts a dense purple color, and thick, juicy, cassis, and spicy wood aromas. This wine exhibits good structure and delineation, surprising elegance for an Australian Cabernet, medium to full body, and 12–15 years of aging potential.

The most stunning of this portfolio is the spectacular Shiraz Oracle, made from 40-year-old vines, aged 18 months in 50% new oak, two-thirds American and one-third French, and bottled with no filtration. The 1999 is a serious effort. A dense plum/purple color and stunning aromatics of plum, prune, blackberries, chocolate, and melted road tar are followed by an intense, full-bodied, viscous Shiraz with superb purity, low acidity, and a whoppingly long finish. This mouth-filling wine can be drunk now as well as over the next 10–15 or more years. The 1998 Shiraz Oracle is a full-throttle, opaque purple wine possessing copious quantities of truffle, new saddle leather, pepper, and blackberry fruit aromas. As it sits in the glass, scents of overripe plums, cherries, and spice emerge from this heady, powerful, nicely textured, plush Shiraz. Rich and robust, it should be consumed over the next 8–10 years.

KILLIBINBIN (LANGHORNE CREEK)

1999 Shiraz	D	90
1998 Shiraz	D	96

Killibinbin's amazing 100% Shirazes sell for a song, considering their quality and pleasure-giving characteristics. Annual production averages 500 cases. These wines are unquestionably made from extremely ripe fruit. While the 1999 Shiraz can't measure up to the 1998, it is an outstanding effort. This wine has an opaque purple color and a gorgeous bouquet of sweet cherries, blackberries, and plums mixed with pepper and spice. Fat and fleshy, it offers a chunky mouthful of hedonistic, ripe Shiraz at 14.9% alcohol. The wine shows a subtle influence of wood in its fruit-dominated personality. Drink it over the next 6–8 years.

I was blown away by the 1998 Shiraz. Reminiscent of dry vintage Port, this black/purple behemoth offers aromas of blackberries, cassis, sweet, damp earth, licorice, and chocolate, as well as an explosive, full-bodied entry on the palate. Dry, hugely-concentrated, and clearly a heavyweight, with a whopping 16% alcohol, it is neither hot nor out of balance. An infant in terms of development, this 1998 should continue to evolve for 10–12+ years.

KOPPAMURRA (COONAWARRA)

1998 Cabernet Sauvignon/Merlot/Cabernet Franc	C	89

An excellent value in a high-quality proprietary red (a blend of 46% Cabernet Sauvignon, 27% Merlot, and 27% Cabernet Franc), the 1998 is a smoky, peppery, earthy, black currant–scented effort with good spice, excellent richness, sweet tannin, and a surprisingly well-balanced, long finish. It can be consumed now as well as over the next decade.

LANGMEIL WINERY (BAROSSA VALLEY)

1999 Shiraz	C	86
1998 Shiraz The Freedom	E	88

This winery is reputed to have a plot of the oldest producing Shiraz vines in the world, its vineyards having been planted in 1844. The grapes for The Freedom come from 157-year-old Shiraz vines! Both wines are very good buys. Aged in American oak (50% new), they are bottled with no fining or filtration. The 1998 Shiraz The Freedom exhibits a dark ruby/purple color, a one-dimensional character, but plenty of power, density, richness, and weight. Although foursquare at present, it may develop more nuances/dimensions with another 2–3 years of cellaring. It should age well for 10–12 years. The 1999 Shiraz (2,000 cases) offers a big, peppery, tar, blackberry nose, sweet, ripe, straightforward, fruity flavors, low acidity, and a plump, fleshy finish. Its whopping 16.3% alcohol is surprisingly well concealed beneath the wine's ripe fruit. This is one to drink over the next 2–3 years.

LARRIKIN (SOUTH AUSTRALIA)

1997 Shiraz	D	90

From an 80-year-old Shiraz vineyard, and aged in both French and American oak, the 1997 Shiraz, a "diamond in the rough" (the meaning of the Aboriginal name, Larrikin), is a dense, full-bodied effort offering copious quantities of jammy blackberry fruit and bold, creamy new oak flavors. Spicy, hedonistic, and intense, this low acid, plump, jammy Shiraz will have many fans. Drink it over the next 5–6 years.

LASHMAR (SOUTH AUSTRALIA)

1999 Cabernet	D	87
1999 Shiraz Three Valleys	D	89

The first release from a Cabernet vineyard planted on Kangaroo Island, just off the Adelaide coastline, the 1999 Cabernet (220 cases produced) shows a lighter style than most Australian Cabernets and is a bit narrowly focused, but there is elegance and decent, cool-climate characteristics in its cedary, black and red currant–scented nose. The wine has good density, some sweet tannin, and is well made in a more delicate, restrained style atypical for an Australian wine. Drink it over the next 5–6 years. The 1999 Shiraz Three Valleys shows textbook creosote-infused blackberry liqueur notes. It has medium weight with good ripeness, sweetness, and supple tannin. Drink it over the next 5–6 years.

LEAMON (VICTORIA)

1999 Cabernet Reserve	D	90
1999 Shiraz Reserve	D	88

The 1999 Cabernet Reserve (90% Cabernet Sauvignon and 10% Merlot aged in 100% new French oak and bottled unfiltered) has beautifully absorbed the wood, displaying notes of caramel, black currants, spice box, and earth. It offers an opaque ruby/purple color, deep, full-bodied flavors, good integration of acidity and tannin, and nicely integrated alcohol (listed at 15%). Drink it over the next 10–12 years. The Shiraz Reserve comes from old vines grown in granite soil, is aged in 100% new oak, and is bottled unfiltered. The 1999 is slightly foursquare and monolithic. This wine may be outstanding, but it does not yet exhibit the nuances of the Cabernet. It is full-bodied and loaded with concentrated fruit, spicy new oak, and Syrah's telltale smoky, charred character. Anticipated maturity: 2003–2014.

LEEUWIN ESTATE (MARGARET RIVER)

1995 Cabernet Sauvignon	D	90
1997 Cabernet Sauvignon Art Series	D	91+
1996 Cabernet Sauvignon Art Series	D	91
1998 Cabernet Sauvignon/Merlot Prelude Vineyards	D	88
1997 Cabernet Sauvignon/Merlot Prelude Vineyards	D	90

This estate, better known for its superb whites (not reviewed here since they must be consumed within several months of the vintage), does a great job with respect to the reds. In the past, some of Leeuwin Estate's reds have been slightly herbaceous, but I did not detect that in either their Prelude Vineyards or Art Series offerings.

The 1998 Cabernet Sauvignon/Merlot Prelude Vineyards offers sweet currant, creamy oak, and subtle olive notes in its elegant, medium-bodied, spicy, Provençal-like personality. It is a well-concentrated, excellent Cabernet/Merlot to enjoy over the next 7–8 years. A blend of 83% Cabernet and 17% Merlot, the 1997 Cabernet Sauvignon/Merlot Prelude Vineyards is even better. A Bordeaux-like bouquet of tobacco, cedar, black currants, and new oak is followed by an elegant, austere, but concentrated offering with beautiful purity and flavors, medium to full body, sweet tannin, and a long, nicely textured finish. It should drink well for a decade.

The Art Series Cabernet Sauvignons are powerful efforts (14.5% alcohol) that are meant to evolve for 15+ years. Both the 1996 and 1997 are impressive. Aged in 100% French oak, the dense ruby/plum/purple 1996 offers textbook aromas of tobacco, cedar, cassis, and new oak in addition to deep, full-bodied flavors with good acidity, moderate tannin, and excellent texture. Long, persuasive, rich, and well-balanced, it will be at its finest between now and 2015. The 1997 introduces fudge and cigar smoke to its aromatic combination of cassis, cedar, tobacco, and new oak. It is full-bodied, with super fruit, outstanding purity, and a long, nicely-textured, moderately tannic finish. Anticipated maturity: now–2016.

Another outstanding wine is the 1995 Cabernet Sauvignon. A blend of 75% Cabernet Sauvignon and the rest Merlot and Malbec from their vineyard near the Margaret River, this impressive, highly extracted, dark purple-colored, backward Cabernet requires a little more cellaring. It should keep for two decades. The Bordeaux-like nose of cedarwood, tobacco, red and black currants, and licorice, is followed by a ripe, full-bodied, dense, powerful wine that still plays it close to the vest. Merely hinting at its ultimate potential, this Cabernet Sauvignon should be purchased only by those with the discipline to wait 2–3 years.

PETER LEHMANN (BAROSSA VALLEY)

1999 Cabernet Sauvignon	C	86
1998 Cabernet Sauvignon	C	87
1997 Cabernet Sauvignon	C	89

1999 Clancy's Gold Preference	D	87
1998 Clancy's Gold Preference	D	90
1997 Mentor	E	90
1996 Mentor	E	92
1995 Mentor	E	88
1997 Seven Surveys	C	88
1999 Shiraz	C	87
1998 Shiraz	C	90
1997 Shiraz	C	89
1998 Shiraz Eight Songs	E	93
1997 Shiraz Eight Songs	E	90
1996 Shiraz Eight Songs	E	93
1996 Shiraz Stonewell	E	92+
1994 Shiraz Stonewell	E	95

This is one of the most famous names of Australia's famed Barossa Valley, with a production in excess of 500,000 cases. The consistently reliable wines are made in an exuberant, "Aussie" style. Reasonably good values include the user-friendly, fruit-driven, soft, blackberry- and currant-scented 1999 Shiraz that must be enjoyed over the next 5–6 years. The 1998 Shiraz exhibits a dense ruby/purple color with intense, chocolate-infused, blackberry/cassis aromatics that continue to detonate on the palate with a cascade of jammy, peppery flavors. American oak frames up this full-bodied Shiraz that tips the scales at 14% alcohol. Drink it over the next decade. The deep ruby/purple-colored 1997 Shiraz is a terrific wine value. It offers a big, sweet, peppery, earthy, creosote, blackberry, and cassis-scented bouquet and flavor. Fat and chewy, with low acidity, this plump Shiraz should drink well for a decade.

The Cabernet Sauvignons are also good values. The 1999 is a medium-bodied, spicy offering with plum, cedar, and cherry fruit. This wine requires consumption over the near term. Even better, the 1998 Cabernet Sauvignon is an elegant yet richer version of the 1999, with deep, cedary, currant fruit intermixed with spice box, licorice, and vanilla. It should last 7–8 years. Made in a Pauillac-like style, the dark ruby/purple 1997 Cabernet Sauvignon offers notes of cedar, balsam wood, black currants, fruitcake, and chocolate that emerge from the complex bouquet. On the palate, the wine is full-bodied and concentrated, with low acidity, sweet tannin, and copious glycerin and fat.

A blend of 53% Shiraz, 30% Cabernet Sauvignon, 10% Merlot, and 7% Cabernet Franc, the 1999 Clancy's Gold Preference exhibits an earthy, leathery, meaty bouquet with red and black currants lurking in the background. Some oak is discernible, but this excellent wine is rich, ripe, spicy, and medium- to full-bodied. It should drink well for a decade. The deep ruby/purple-colored 1998 Clancy's Gold Preference, a blend of 54% Shiraz, 22% Cabernet Sauvignon, 12% Merlot, and 12% Cabernet Franc, displays a muted, monolithic nose, but full-bodied, highly concentrated flavors. Another year or two of cellaring will result in more aromatic complexity in this dense, chewy, thick, multilayered wine. It should last for 12+ years.

The 1997 Mentor, a blend of 60% Cabernet Sauvignon, 17% Malbec, 12% Shiraz, and 11% Merlot, is a more tightly knit, less massive effort. It exhibits good aromatics, medium to full body, and pure, sweet red and black currant fruit intermixed with cedarwood and tobacco. Anticipated maturity: now–2015. The seriously endowed 1996 Mentor is a blend of 60% Cabernet Sauvignon, 20% Merlot, 10% Shiraz, and 10% Malbec. An opaque purple color is accompanied by complex aromas of damp earth, cedarwood, mint, plum liqueur, licorice, black currants, and new oak. Full-bodied, deep, and chewy, with moderate tannin and excellent concentration as well as body, it will drink well for 10–15 years. The 1995 Mentor, a blend of 70% Cabernet Sauvignon, 20% Malbec, and 10% Merlot, is rather closed.

It displays few aromas but big, thick, juicy, black raspberry and berry flavors plus weedy tobacco notes. Full-bodied and moderately tannic, it requires some cellaring and should keep for 15+ years.

The excellent 1997 Seven Surveys, a blend of 34% Mourvèdre, 33% Grenache, and 33% Shiraz, offers peppery, cherry jam–like aromas and flavors. Foursquare, spicy, and full-bodied, with austere tannin, it should be drunk in its rustic youth—over the next 4–5 years.

Peter Lehmann's top Shiraz *cuvées* are the Eight Songs and Stonewell. The Shiraz Eight Songs, named for the production of *Eight Songs for a Mad King*, the story of King George III, is aged in 100% French oak and sold only in eight-bottle cases. The Stonewell Shiraz sees 100% American oak. The 1998 Shiraz Eight Songs is a sensational effort. It boasts a black/purple color as well as muscular, full-bodied flavors that make a huge impact on the palate. The abundant black currant and blackberry fruit are intermixed with notes of new oak, minerals, and pepper. Long and layered, with multiple flavor dimensions, it is a powerhouse blockbuster. Anticipated maturity: now–2020. Readers looking for a more laid-back, restrained style that is still robust will enjoy the 1997 Shiraz Eight Songs. It exhibits blackberries, spice box, pepper, and sweet oak in its medium- to full-bodied, more restrained, less massive personality. Deep, harmonious, and concentrated, it will drink well for 10–12 years. The 1996 Shiraz Eight Songs is an exuberant, concentrated effort. A dense opaque purple color is accompanied by flamboyant scents of roasted coffee, cedarwood, cassis, blackberries, and sweet new French oak. In the mouth, flavors of prune liqueur and black currants are backed up by abundant glycerin, extract, and sweet tannin, giving the wine a weighty yet pure, concentrated impression. The French oak provides some restraint in this forward, super-concentrated Shiraz. Consume it now and over the next 10–12 years.

The 1996 Shiraz Stonewell is a big, broodingly backward wine offering aromas and flavors of melted asphalt, black raspberries, smoke, graphite, pepper, and blackberries. Full-bodied and moderately tannic, with good underlying acidity as well as structure, it is still an infant, but should mature over the next two decades, and will be uncommonly long-lived. The thick opaque black/purple-colored 1994 Shiraz Stonewell boasts a sumptuous nose of black raspberries, cassis, toasty American oak, vanilla, spice, and pepper. This monster-sized, chewy, lavishly-endowed Shiraz is soft enough to be drunk now, but promises to age well for 10–15 years.

LENGS AND COOTER (CLARE VALLEY)

1999 Shiraz Old Vines	D	87
1998 Shiraz Old Vines	D	93
1999 Shiraz Reserve	E	89
1998 Shiraz Reserve	E	96
1999 The Victor	B	86

A proprietary blend of 55% Shiraz and 45% Grenache, the 1999 The Victor is a reasonably good value. It is a straightforward, round, ripe, dark ruby/purple-colored wine that is monolithic but pleasant and mouthcoating. Drink it over the next 2–3 years.

Neither the 1999 Shiraz Old Vines nor the 1999 Shiraz Reserve matched the intensity, high volume, and concentration of their 1998 counterparts. Both are more elegant, restrained wines, but are still noteworthy. The Old Vines *cuvée* is made from 25- to 100-year-old vines and aged with 50% new American oak, while the Reserve sees 80% new American oak. There are 450 cases produced of the Old Vines and 140 cases of the Reserve.

The 1999 Shiraz Old Vines is medium weight, has a deep ruby/purple color, a spicy, peppery, black currant nose, and some noticeable American new oak (about 50% is new). Drink it over the next 5–7 years. The opaque purple 1998 Shiraz Old Vines exhibits a stunning, soaring bouquet offering aromas of crème de cassis, smoked herbs, licorice, tar, and creamy new oak. Full-bodied and super-concentrated, with notions of blackberry jam as well as moderate tannin, this dazzling Shiraz can be drunk now or cellared for 10–12 years.

The substantial 1999 Shiraz Reserve shows plenty of toasty notes, but also displays generous licorice, blackberry, and heady fruit. This full-bodied, moderately powerful wine reveals some tannin in the finish and may actually improve with another one to two years of bottle age. However, it seems destined to be best drunk during its first 10–12 years of life.

Even more profound is the 1998 Shiraz Reserve. The telltale bacon fat, pepper, smoke, and blackberry/melted asphalt aromas and flavors can only come from ultraconcentrated, voluptuously textured Shiraz from Australia. Superpowerful, full-bodied, and excitingly pure, this is an unreal wine to drink over the next 15–20 years.

LENSWOOD (ADELAIDE HILLS)
1998 The Palatine   **D   92**

The 1998 The Palatine, a blend of 52% Cabernet Sauvignon, 31% Merlot, and 17% Malbec, is a dense, purple-colored, distinctively styled offering. Twenty percent of the fruit went through the so-called Amarone winemaking technique (an Italian process of running grape must through pomace), and thus there is an earthy, ripe, full-bodied, late-harvest character. The wine shows huge extract, dense, earthy, tar, blackberry, and cassis flavors, superb purity, and good underlying tannin as well as acidity. This rich blend is best drunk with full-flavored meat or earthy dishes. Anticipated maturity: now–2015.

LIEBICH VEIN (BAROSSA VALLEY)
1999 Shiraz C. W.'s Block   **D   93**

With 15% natural alcohol, aging in both older French and American oak and bottled without filtration, this 120-case *cuvée* is sure to sell out quickly. The opaque purple-colored, blockbuster 1999 Shiraz offers notes of melted asphalt, smoke, black fruits, pepper, and animal fur. Full-bodied, thick, and heavy, this massive wine should drink well for 12–15 years.

LIMELIGHT (McLAREN VALE)
1998 Syrah   **D   89**

This is a big, thick, unctuously styled 1998 Syrah with plenty of black fruits intermixed with licorice, tar, pepper, and wood. It spent 18 months in a combination of new and old American oak. Full-bodied, with good structure, plenty of depth, and a chewy mouth-feel, it should be consumed over the next 4–5 years.

LOST WOLF (BAROSSA VALLEY)
1997 Cabernet Sauvignon   **D   88**
1996 Cabernet Sauvignon   **D   91**

I'll keep the tasting notes simple since there are only 50 cases of each of these. The light, graceful 1997 Cabernet Sauvignon offers aromas and flavors of plums, currants, and well-integrated oak, medium body, and sweet tannin. Anticipated maturity: 2004–2015. The 1996 Cabernet Sauvignon is a hedonistic, huge, in-your-face Cabernet with copious quantities of black currant and cherry fruit wrapped in an unctuously textured black fruit and chocolate fruit bomb. Drink this dense, chewy, hedonistic wine over the next decade. A detail worth noting is that these wines were made at David Powell's Torbreck Winery.

MAD FISH (WESTERN AUSTRALIA)
1999 Shiraz   **A   86**

The 1999 Shiraz outperformed many of its peers selling for 3–4 times the price. A healthy dark ruby color is accompanied by peppery, smoky, blackberry, and plum-like fruit. Soft and medium-bodied, it is an ideal choice for uncritical quaffing over the next 2–3 years.

MAGPIE ESTATE (BAROSSA VALLEY)

1999	Grenache Gomersol	E	87?
1999	Mourvèdre/Grenache	C	90
1998	Mourvèdre/Grenache	D	89
1998	Shiraz/Mourvèdre Black Sock	E	95

These wines are made by one of my favorite Australian wine-makers, Rolf Binder. The 1999 Grenache Gomersol (100% Grenache aged in 50% new French and 50% American oak) shows too much creamy wood to merit higher marks. It also has a quasi-international style, moderate tannin, and a structured, almost uncharacteristically tightly knit style for Grenache. The color is a deep ruby/purple, and the wine is cleanly made and pure but lacks the expression and character of other offerings from the Magpie Estate. Drink by 2008.

The Mourvèdre/Grenache blend emerges from 60–80-year-old vines and is composed of equal parts of each varietal. Production is rather small (around 200 cases), but prices remain fair. The outstanding 1999 is a beautiful wine offering a gorgeous nose of pepper, Old Bay spice, black raspberries, and cherries. It is exotic, somewhat kinky, and distinctive, but medium- to full-bodied, with an encroaching note of new saddle leather in the finish. Think of it as an Australian version of Bandol. Anticipated maturity: now–2012. The 1998 Mourvèdre/Grenache's dark plum color is accompanied by a sweet cherry, spice, and dried herb–scented bouquet. It offers lovely, well-balanced, medium-bodied richness, a continuation of the ripe cherry character, low acidity, and a moderately long finish. Drink it over the next 5–6 years.

The Shiraz/Mourvèdre Black Sock emerges from 60–100-year-old vines and is composed of 80% Shiraz and 20% Mourvèdre. It is aged for a whopping 30 months in American wood. Production is small, around 150 cases annually. The prodigious 1998 is a blockbuster. This opaque purple-colored wine offers an almost essence of blackberry and cherry fruit intermixed with earth, leather, charcoal, and new wood. The wine is full-bodied, spectacularly concentrated, with multiple levels to its mid-palate, and a whoppingly powerful, rich finish. I was surprised to learn that the wine has only 13.5% alcohol, given the huge swath it cuts across the palate. Anticipated maturity: now–2018.

MAJELLA (COONAWARRA)

1998	Cabernet Sauvignon	D	91
1997	Cabernet Sauvignon	D	90
1998	Shiraz	D	94
1997	Shiraz	D	88
1998	Shiraz/Cabernet Sauvignon Maleea	E	92
1997	Shiraz/Cabernet Sauvignon Maleea	E	93?

Based on what I have tasted, Majella (owned by Brian and Anthony Lynn) is undoubtedly the finest wine in the Coonawarra. Their current releases all performed admirably and, as readers will note, most of these wines are realistically priced. The most expensive wine of the portfolio, the Shiraz/Cabernet Sauvignon Maleea is worth its price. There are 500 cases of this blend of 55% Cabernet and 45% Shiraz, aged in 100% new French wood. The 1998 is opaque purple in color, with a spectacularly intense and pure nose of melted licorice, cassis, and blackberry. This full-bodied wine is extremely well delineated, has fabulous symmetry and overall harmony, seamless integration of acidity, tannin, and alcohol, and a 35–40-second finish. The wine is still youthful, but promises to evolve nicely for at least 15 or more years. If the lavish quantities of toasty new French oak become better integrated in the 1997 Shiraz/Cabernet Sauvignon Maleea, this wine will easily merit its 93 points. A sensationally rich, impressively structured effort, it possesses a black/purple color, the aforementioned heavy overlay of toasty new oak, gorgeous blueberry, blackberry, and cassis flavors, a ton of toast and vanilla-like scents, full body, and a rich, concentrated finish with impressive levels of sweet fruit. It still tastes like a barrel sample, so give it 1–2 years of cellaring. It should age nicely for two decades.

There are 1,800 cases of the authoritatively flavorful yet stylish 100% Cabernet that is available for a realistic price. The deep ruby/purple-colored 1998 displays notions of American and French oak in its plum, cassis, cedar, and spice box–scented nose. This thick, juicy, full-bodied, opulent, and at the same time well-delineated wine represents a brilliant marriage of power and elegance. Anticipated maturity: now–2015. The 1997 Cabernet Sauvignon exhibits cassis, cedar, smoked herb, prune, and plum liqueur scents. Full-bodied and concentrated, with less noticeable oak, this big Coonawarra Cabernet should be at its finest before 2015.

The 100% Shiraz, which emerges from a cooler climate than the Barossa, is made from 30-year-old vines and aged completely in American oak. There are 1,800 cases of this wine. The 1998 shows dense purple color, a classic cassis, blackberry, leathery, peppery nose, and unctuously textured, full-bodied flavors that are penetrating, brilliantly well defined, and strikingly pure. Again, a long finish, no heaviness, and an almost seamlessness to the wine make it indeed a special offering, and the price makes it a true steal in the marketplace. It can be drunk now and over the next 12–15 years. Abundant quantities of freshly ground pepper and blackberry/cassis fruit jump from the glass of the 1997 Shiraz. It also possesses spicy oak, medium to full body, and a nicely packaged, concentrated style. Although not a blockbuster, it is flavorful, ripe, and well made. Drink it over the next 5–6 years.

MAK (COONAWARRA)

1999 Cabernet Sauvignon/Shiraz Snowy River	B	90
1998 Cabernet Sauvignon/Shiraz Snowy River	B	88

Importer Rob McDonald, of Old Bridge Cellars, has purchased land in Australia and has begun producing his own wine. His first effort, the deep plum/purple 1998 Cabernet Sauvignon/Shiraz Snowy River (which includes tiny dollops of Merlot and Cabernet Franc) is a rustic, tannic, structured effort with plenty of stuffing, muscular, smoky, earthy, blackberry, and cassis flavors offered in a mouth-filling style. It should drink well for 7–8 years.

Even better, the 1999 Cabernet Sauvignon/Shiraz Snowy River (59% Cabernet and 41% Shiraz) is more supple, with a lusher texture. It possesses plenty of power, concentration, and blackberry/cassis fruit intermixed with earth, pepper, smoke, and wood. Consumer-friendly, dense, and chewy, with considerable charm and seductiveness, it will drink well for 5–7 years. Both of these wines are excellent values.

MAXWELL (McLAREN VALE)

1999 Cabernet Sauvignon Lime Cave	D	93
1998 Cabernet Sauvignon Lime Cave	D	94+
1998 Grenache	D	91
1999 Shiraz Ellen Street	D	92
1998 Shiraz Ellen Street	D	91+
1997 Shiraz Ellen Street	D	91

From a winery that consistently turns out fine products, the vines for the Cabernet Sauvignon Lime Cave grow in clay/limestone soils near a cave used for growing mushrooms. This wine is aged in both American and French oak, of which 30% was new, and is bottled unfiltered. The sensational 1999's opaque purple color is followed by an explosive bouquet of black currants, blackberries, and smoke. Full-bodied, with gorgeous density, sweet, concentrated fruit, good purity, and impeccable balance between the tannin, acidity, alcohol, and extract, it will drink well for 12–15 years. The 1998 Cabernet Sauvignon Lime Cave is tightly knit with a beautiful texture. Offering a combination of power and elegance, its Pauillac-like cedary, spice box aromas turn into blackberry liqueur mixed with cassis and other assorted black fruits as it aerates. This spectacular Cabernet requires some cellaring, and should age for 15 years.

The Shiraz Ellen Street is produced from 40-year-old vines. Aged primarily in American oak (and about 20% French oak), it is bottled unfiltered. This wine is consistently an outstanding value in great Australian Shiraz. The 1999 is a dense, fat, thermonuclear Shiraz fruit bomb. Opaque ruby/purple with aromas and flavors of black fruits intermixed with earth, truffles, chocolate, and a hint of coffee, this full-bodied, unctuously textured, pure, large-scaled yet surprisingly well balanced, massive wine can be drunk now and over the next 10–15 years. The promising 1998 Shiraz Ellen Street is quite closed, revealing an opaque black/purple color, sweet, jammy blackberry and cassis fruit, great purity, full body, and multiple layers of fruit. It does not yet display the secondary nuances found in the 1997, but they should emerge after another year of bottle age. It should last 10–15 years. The 1997 Shiraz Ellen Street's black/purple color is followed by an earthy, peppery, spice box, truffle, licorice, and black currant/berry-scented bouquet. Full-bodied and highly extracted, this top-notch, rich, concentrated powerhouse is impressive, even though it has emerged from a less renowned vintage than its younger sibling. Anticipated maturity: now–2016.

The dense purple-colored 1998 Grenache is produced from old vines and bottled unfiltered. This full-bodied Grenache exhibits leathery, earthy, black raspberry, and kirsch flavors, a touch of road tar, and copious glycerin and richness. Drink it over the next 5–6 years.

MEEREA PARK (HUNTER VALLEY)

1999 Cabernet Sauvignon/Merlot	C	88
1998 Shiraz Alexander Munro	D	89
1999 Shiraz The Aunts	C	87

The dark ruby-colored 1999 Cabernet Sauvignon/Merlot reveals aromas of new French oak plus black currants, cherries, and spice box. Although not complex, it is well made, pure, full, deep, ripe, and nicely balanced. As the wine sat in the glass, smoky tobacco characteristics emerged. This Bordeaux-styled good value should drink well for 7–8 years.

The soft, straightforward 1999 Shiraz The Aunts (100% Shiraz) offers chocolaty, blackberry, pepper, earth, and licorice notes. Foursquare but plump and tasty, it will drink well for 4–5 years. The highly extracted, deep purple-colored 1998 Shiraz Alexander Munro was aged in 100% new French and American oak. It is a powerful, moderately tannic, dense wine that remains unevolved and youthful. If it develops more complexity, it will merit an outstanding rating. Large-scaled, muscular, and deep, it offers a classic display of melted tar, blackberries, crème de cassis, and licorice. Drink it over the next 10–12 years.

CHARLES MELTON (BAROSSA VALLEY)

1998 Cabernet Sauvignon	D	86
1998 Grenache	D	90
1998 Nine Popes	D	89
1997 Nine Popes	D	92
1999 Shiraz	D	88
1997 Shiraz	D	88

The Nine Popes, a blend of Grenache, Shiraz, and Mourvèdre, emerges from 80–100-year-old Grenache vines. Beautifully made and fun to drink, this is Australia's version of Châteauneuf-du-Pape. The 1998 Nine Popes boasts a saturated ruby/purple color in addition to abundant quantities of peppery kirsch and earthy notes, and medium to full body, which provide a large, dense, chewy palate impact. Drink it over the next 4–5 years.

The gorgeous 1997 Nine Popes offers aromas of kirsch, cherry jam, raspberries, roasted peanuts, and herbs, terrific fruit intensity, full body, copious glycerin, and a mid-palate that suggests low yields and old vines. Drink it over the next decade.

The big, minty, black currant, and peppery-styled dark ruby/purple 1999 Shiraz offers plenty of spice, excellent concentration plus purity, and a soft finish. Drink it over the next 5–6 years. The 1997 Shiraz seems rather civilized and restrained. It has a dense dark ruby color with purple nuances. Notes of black fruits (particularly berries) emerge from the moderately intense bouquet. Not a blockbuster in the style of many Barossa Valley Shirazes, this is an elegant, well-balanced, concentrated wine exhibiting excellent purity, ripeness, and character. More aromatics will emerge with bottle age. Anticipated maturity: now–2008.

The dense ruby-colored 1998 Grenache exhibits a sweet nose of kirsch, pepper, spice, and earth. Full-bodied, fleshy, and rich, with sweet fruit and copious glycerin, this southern Rhône–like offering can be drunk now and over the next 7–8 years.

The dark ruby/purple 1998 Cabernet Sauvignon offers minty, black currant flavors. Medium- to full-bodied and firm, with moderate tannin, sweet fruit, and a structured, tight finish, it requires 2–3 years of cellaring and should drink well for 10–12 years.

MITCHELL (CLARE VALLEY)

1999 Shiraz Peppertree	C	90

Aged in 100% French oak for 12 months prior to bottling, the impressively endowed 1999 Shiraz Peppertree boasts an opaque ruby/purple color as well as a sweet nose of black fruits, new saddle leather, earth, tar, and licorice—a classic Australian Shiraz aromatic profile. The French oak provides subtlety vis-à-vis some of the more aggressive Shiraz that see American oak. This 1999 possesses supple tannin, full body, outstanding density and purity, and a low-acid, plump finish. It should be drunk over the next decade.

MITCHELTON (VICTORIA)

1997 Cabernet Sauvignon Sidey's	C	87
1999 Shiraz Crescent	C	86
1997 Shiraz Print Label	D	89
1996 Shiraz Print Label	D	88

This Victoria winery offers an array of very good value red and white wines. The whites, which include superb Rieslings, Chardonnays, and a high-quality blend called Airstrip, are not reviewed here since they must be consumed within a few months of the vintage.

The 1999 Shiraz Crescent is a straightforward, ripe, rich, fruity offering with medium to full body, soft tannin, and a peppery, pleasant finish. Anticipated maturity: now–2007.

The 1997 Cabernet Sauvignon Sidey's reveals textbook black currant fruit intermixed with tobacco and coffee. Medium- to full-bodied, with a fruit-driven style, it offers moderate quantities of wood and tannin. It should drink well for 7–8 years. The finest red wine of the portfolio is the dark ruby/purple 1997 Shiraz Print Label. Aromas of plums, blackberries, graphite, smoke, and pepper are followed by a dense, medium- to full-bodied, rich, lightly tannic Shiraz. Anticipated maturity: now–2014.

An opaque ruby/garnet color is followed by heavy, American oak, chocolate, coconut, and black cherry/berry fruit aromas. Full-bodied, soft, obvious, and pleasurable in its blatant combination of fruit and oak, the 1996 Shiraz Print Label should drink well for 5–8 years.

MORAMBRO CREEK (PADTHAWAY)

1999 Cabernet Sauvignon	D	85
1999 Shiraz	D	89

The Bryson family, longtime growers and vineyard owners, is responsible for these wines. Although essentially one-dimensional, the 1999 Cabernet Sauvignon offers a smoky, elegant, black currant nose, medium body, and a cleanly made, pure personality. Anticipated maturity: now–2008. The 1999 Shiraz sports a deep ruby/purple color, a full-bodied, broad, expansive palate, and excellent black fruits intermixed with asphalt, fresh tar, and pepper. There is some oakiness that is not yet integrated. Drink it over the next 10 years.

MOSS WOOD (MARGARET RIVER)

1996 Cabernet Sauvignon	D	93+
1997 Pinot Noir	D	88?

The dark ruby-colored 1997 Pinot Noir does not portray the elegant side of this varietal. It has hefty 14.5% alcohol, and reminds me of well-made Pinot Noirs grown in hot climates. Notes of chocolate, toasty oak, cherry jam, and roasted herbs emerge from this deep, rich, full-bodied offering, which cuts a meaty, earthy profile on the palate. It might be loosely compared to some of the chewier, heavier styles of Pommard from Burgundy's Côte d'Or. In any event, it is a flavorful, intense wine that I enjoyed more because of its flavors and hedonistic qualities than for its depiction of Pinot Noir. Drink it over the next 4–5 years.

Cabernet lovers looking for a compelling example of this varietal should check out the expensive but profound 1996 Cabernet Sauvignon. Opaque purple in color, with a striking bouquet of olives, cassis jam, beef blood, minerals, earth, and new wood, this massive, super-concentrated Cabernet Sauvignon should prove to be a great classic from Down Under. It is oozing with flavor extraction, has high tannin, and cuts a formidable path on the palate. Anticipated maturity: now–2020.

MOUNT HORROCKS (CLARE VALLEY)

1998 Cabernet/Merlot	D	86
1997 Cabernet/Merlot	D	90
2000 Riesling Cordon Cut	D	92
1999 Riesling Cordon Cut	D	92
1998 Shiraz	D	90

The 1998 Cabernet/Merlot is a lean, austere Australian red, with minty, red currant, and cherry characteristics, spice, underlying earthiness, and a moderately long finish. Drink it over the next 5–6 years. The outstanding 1997 Cabernet/Merlot (85% Cabernet and 15% Merlot, aged in 100% French oak) is concentrated, ripe, and backward, exhibiting impressive levels of cassis/blackberry fruit nicely dosed by wood. Deep, classic, and well proportioned, this well-endowed, full-bodied wine will be at its finest until 2015.

The dark ruby/purple 1998 Shiraz is an interesting wine. It offers a sweet, complex, earthy, tar, and jammy red and black fruit–scented bouquet, beautiful purity, medium to full body, and a sense of elegance and overall symmetry. This flavorful, graceful Shiraz can be consumed now and over the next 7–8 years.

The light gold-colored 2000 Riesling Cordon Cut has good acidity, 11% alcohol, and a style somewhere between a sweet Auslese and Beerenauslese from Germany. There are abundant quantities of honeysuckle and jammy tropical fruits in addition to wonderful, refreshing acidity to provide uplift and zest. This pure Riesling is best drunk with fruit desserts over the next 2–4 years. Nectar lovers will be impressed with the Beerenauslese-styled 1999 Riesling Cordon Cut. With 13.5% residual sugar and good underlying acidity, this exceptionally pure wine offers honeyed tropical fruits, an underlying minerality, and a light-bodied, unctuous yet refreshing finish. Drink it over the next 4 years.

MOUNT LANGI GHIRAN (VICTORIA)

1996 Cabernet Sauvignon/Merlot	C	86?
1997 Shiraz	C	91
1997 Shiraz Billi Billi	B	88

Trevor Mast, a longtime proponent of old, head-pruned Shiraz, has produced stunning Shiraz over the last several decades. Readers looking for a reasonably good value in old vine Shiraz should check out the 1997 Shiraz Billi Billi. With its dense ruby/purple color and sweet, jammy, blackberry, pepper, and spicy-scented nose, this full-bodied, supple-textured, luscious, in-your-face wine will have huge commercial appeal. Made from old Shiraz vineyards in both the Barossa and McLaren Vale sectors, it is delicious already, and promises to drink well for 4–5 years. Even more hedonistic and powerful is the black/purple-colored 1997 Shiraz. Exotic, with ripe notes of blackberries, cassis, and spice, this nicely layered wine has considerable tannin, but it is sweet, and hardly noticeable given the wine's low acidity and wealth of rich fruit and copious glycerin. This full-bodied classic should drink well young, yet evolve nicely for 10–12 years.

The 1996 Cabernet Sauvignon/Merlot is less impressive. It has a saturated color, but dry, hard tannin in the finish gives it an attenuated impression. It is medium-bodied, with earthy, black currant fruit and weedy notes on the attack, but then narrows out with severe tannin in the finish. Does it have the requisite depth to balance out the wine's structure?

NEAGLE'S ROCK (CLARE VALLEY)

| 1998 Cabernet Sauvignon | C | 89 |

A touch more complexity and this 1998 Cabernet Sauvignon would have been outstanding. Nevertheless, it is an excellent value. Boldly styled, with an opaque ruby/purple color and explosive black currant fruit intermixed with smoke and earth, this wine shows wonderful richness, sweet tannin, low acidity in the attack, and a corpulent, chewy mouth-feel. Drink it over the next decade.

NEPENTHE (ADELAIDE HILLS)

| 1999 Zinfandel | D | 86 |

Nepenthe, a Greek word meaning "elixir that heals all pain and grief," displays a stronger hand with its whites (Sauvignon Blanc, Chardonnay, and Sémillon) than its red wines. For example, a blend of Cabernet Sauvignon, Merlot, and Cabernet Franc, the 1998 Le Fugue was austere and too dependent on Euro-styled elegance for its appeal. Another wine, the 1999 Pinot Noir, revealed a light style without any real center of flavor. However, the 1999 Zinfandel seems to be a good effort. This wine (only 80 cases available) is a soft, briery, tasty, elegant, medium-bodied wine that somehow magically conceals its whopping 16% alcohol. While it will not make anyone forget the finest California Zinfandels, this Adelaide Hills curiosity is well made. Consume it over the next 2–3 years.

NOON (LANGHORN CREEK)

1999 Cabernet Sauvignon Reserve	E	94
1998 Cabernet Sauvignon Reserve	E	98+
1999 Eclipse	D	94
1998 Eclipse	D	96
1999 Noon V.P.	E	90
1998 Noon V.P.	E	94
1999 Shiraz Reserve	E	96
1998 Shiraz Reserve	E	98

This is one of the brilliant wineries of Australia, offering wines of exceptional purity, symmetry, and individuality. Production ranges from minuscule quantities such as the 85 or so cases of the Noon V.P. to 580 cases of the Shiraz Reserve and nearly 1,000 cases of the Eclipse. This winery made fabulous 1998s and has succeeded admirably in 1999, a lighter year.

The 1999 Eclipse is a blend of 66% Grenache and 34% Shiraz aged in American oak and bottled unfiltered. This wine tips the scales at a hefty 14.9% alcohol. The wine has an opaque purple color as well as a fabulously sweet nose of blackberry and cassis interspersed with licorice, truffle, and vanilla. Full-bodied, heady, layered, ripe, pure, and sumptuous, it is a dazzling 1999 to drink over the next 15–16 years. The 1998 Eclipse (from 35- to 65-year-old Shiraz vines cropped at two tons per acre) possesses a whopping 15.7% alcohol, which is totally concealed by the dense, blackberry liqueur–scented and –flavored fruit. Notes of cassis, toast, pepper, and licorice can also be found in this thick, full-bodied effort. It is a phenomenally rich, super-extracted wine of astonishing intensity. The tannin is sweet, the acidity low, and the wine unreal. Drink it over the next 10–15+ years.

It is a shame there is not more of the Noon V.P. This wine is made from 80-year-old Grenache vines and fortified with alcohol, giving it a dry vintage port character. The alcohol levels are 19.6% for the 1999 and 20.1% for the 1998, yet neither comes across as cloying or sweet. They are, however, dense, viscous, full-bodied, after-dinner cheese course wines with extraordinary levels of black fruits, notes of kirsch, pepper, and spice. It is hard to know how they will age, but I would assume 10–15 years is well within conservative estimates. Their flavors and characteristics are unlike anything I have tasted from the Old or New World. They are undeniably singular expressions that are riveting wines in their own right.

For a more conventional dry table wine still made in a large-scaled style, readers should check out the Shiraz Reserve or Cabernet Sauvignon Reserve.

The 100% Cabernet Sauvignon, whch emerges from 35-year-old vines, is, sadly, not widely available, production averaging 300 cases a year. The 1999 Cabernet Sauvignon Reserve could easily be called a Pauillac from Australia. Dense ruby/purple, a classic Cabernet nose of cedar wood, smoke, cassis, mineral, lead pencil, and new oak soars from the glass. In the mouth, it is full-bodied, with fabulous concentration and multilayered texture, high levels of glycerin, and a seamless, concentrated, long finish with well-integrated tannin, acidity, and alcohol. This is no wimpish wine at 14.6% alcohol. Anticipated maturity: now–2020. It would be interesting to insert the 1998 Cabernet Sauvignon Reserve (15.5% alcohol) in a blind tasting with Cabernet fashioned by Bryant Family Vineyard, Harlan Estate, Colgin, Château Montelena, and Screaming Eagle (a salivating proposition). Nearly perfect, this black/purple-colored Cabernet offers extraordinary sweet black cherry/black currant aromas as well as huge, gorgeously proportioned, voluptuously textured flavors that last 50+ seconds. The wine reveals no hotness from the high alcohol, unbelievable purity, symmetry, and the potential to improve for 10–15 years. It should keep for two decades or more.

The Shiraz Reserve emerges from Shiraz vines that average 35–40 years of age, and is aged in a combination of small and large oak barrels. There are 580 cases of this behemoth. The hugely extracted, massive 1999 Shiraz Reserve tips the scales at 15.2% alcohol. An opaque blue/purple color and a knockout nose of blackberry liqueur intermixed with spice box, pepper, asphalt, and licorice soar from the glass. Opulent and viscous, with tremendous palate presence, beautifully integrated acidity, tannin, and alcohol, this superb, larger-than-life wine is a tour de force for a lighter-weight vintage such as 1999. Anticipated maturity: now–2020. The opaque black/blue-colored 1998 Shiraz Reserve displays a fascinating bouquet of violets, black raspberry and blackberry liqueur, cedar, fruitcake, and pepper. Surreal levels of glycerin and richness are present in this full-bodied, surprisingly supple-textured wine. The finish lasts for several minutes. Anticipated maturity: 2005–2020.

NURIOOTPA HIGH SCHOOL (BAROSSA VALLEY)

1999 Class Shiraz	**E**	**90+**
1998 Class Shiraz	**E**	**94**

This is a winery/school where students get to make wine as part of their education. The expertise and equipment as well as grapes are donated by local wineries. Sadly, the production is extremely small—one barrel, about 30 cases—hence the brief comments. This 100% Shiraz *cuvée*—a limited production blockbuster made from a 31-year-old Koonunga vineyard—is outstanding and certainly a credit to the students of Nuriootpa High School. Neo-prohibitionists and Puritans be warned, high schools in the U.S. may be next in teaching winemaking! Dense, opaque purple-colored with plenty of crème de cassis notes intermixed with some smoke and earth, the full-bodied, slightly rustic, but rich, chewy 1999 Class Shiraz should drink well for at least 10–15 years. The explosive, fabulously concentrated 1998 Class Shiraz is full-bodied and super-concentrated, with abundant quantities of pepper-infused blackberry fruit. Anticipated maturity: now–2017.

ODDFELLOWS (LANGHORNE CREEK)

1998 Shiraz	C	91

A powerful 1998 Shiraz (15.8% alcohol), this chewy, somewhat closed, but dense, muscular Shiraz is crammed with leathery, earthy, blackberry, cassis fruit, has a corpulent personality, sweet tannin, and a lusty, slightly rustic, but powerful finish. I am not sure it is going to gain any finesse, so drink it over the next decade to take full advantage of such exuberance.

OLIVER'S TARANGA (McLAREN VALE)

1999 Shiraz	D	92
1998 Shiraz	D	95
1997 Shiraz	D	90
1996 Shiraz	D	94

For many years, proprietor Don Oliver's family sold fruit to the huge Penfolds operation, where it became one of the primary components of the great Grange. He now produces a 500-case 100% Shiraz from 45-year-old vines cropped at three tons of fruit per acre. These wines appear to be every bit as compelling as recent Granges.

The spectacular 1999 Shiraz (14.5% alcohol) offers a stunning fragrance of black fruits, incense, smoke, pepper, and sausage that soars from the glass in a wickedly exotic yet compelling bouquet. Opaque purple, with full body, awesome concentration, and nicely integrated French and American new wood, this large-scaled, opulent, chewy, super-concentrated wine makes one heck of a hedonistic impression. Anticipated maturity: now–2012.

Potentially the finest effort of this series, the saturated black/purple/blue 1998 Shiraz offers sensational aromas of blueberries, blackberries, and cassis, a huge, super-concentrated palate, fabulous purity, sweet tannin, and well-integrated acidity. While not yet as complex as the 1997 or 1996, the 1998 has more to it, and should prove to be the best wine after some further cellaring. It should age well for two decades.

The lightest wine of this series is the 1997 Shiraz. The most evolved, it provides terrific fruit richness, abundant blackberry, pepper, and sweet earthy notions, an intense, full-bodied palate, low acidity, and a mature, complex finish. The easygoing style and big, rich fruit make it delicious for current consumption. It should continue to drink well for 7–10 years. The 1996 Shiraz reveals mature aromas and flavors of creosote, melted chocolate, and gorgeous blackberry and cassis. Terrific body imbued with lofty glycerin, alcohol, and extract, it is less evolved than the 1997 as well as bigger, richer, and brawnier in the mouth. There is not a hard edge to be found in this accessible Shiraz. It promises to evolve for another 10–15+ years.

PARACOMBE (ADELAIDE HILLS)

1998 Cabernet Franc	C	89
1998 Shiraz	C	88
1997 Shiraz Somerville	E	91

An immensely impressive 100% Cabernet Franc, the 1998, aged 12 months in both American and French oak, exhibits a graceful, stylish, perfumed, raspberry and cherry nose intermixed with flower and subtle wood aromas. Medium-weight, soft, charming, and delicate yet flavorful, it displays hints of underbrush intermixed with floral-infused red and black fruits on the palate. There are no hard edges in this seamless, understated, yet flavorful wine. It is an achievement to produce a wine of such elegance and delicacy that retains plenty of flavor and intensity. Drink it over the next 4–5 years, although it may last longer.

Aged for two years in a combination of French and American barrels, the 1998 Shiraz (14.5% alcohol) possesses a black raspberry, pepper, and earth-scented bouquet, and a soft, layered, fleshy, chunky personality. While it does not have the complexity of the Cabernet Franc, it does offer more depth and fatness. Drink it over the next 4–5 years.

The exceptional 1997 Shiraz Somerville is a limited *cuvée* of 100 cases. I was surprised that the alcohol was listed on the bottle at 15.9%, because it is not apparent in tasting. This full-bodied, ruby/purple Shiraz exhibits a sweet nose of blackberry fruit intermixed with espresso, chocolate, and pepper. Some new wood makes an appearance, but the fruit dominates both the aromas and flavors. Pure, ripe, and long, with plenty of glycerin, it has the potential to drink gorgeously for up to a decade.

PARINGA (SOUTH AUSTRALIA)

2000 Merlot	A	87
2000 Shiraz	A	87
1999 Shiraz	A	88

Importer Dan Philips has hit the jackpot with what looks to be some attractive Australian blends available for a song. The surprises of his portfolio are the Merlot (1,500 cases) and Shiraz (12,000 cases). The 2000 Merlot comes in the door at 14% alcohol. The wine shows jammy, black cherry fruit in a forthright, fat, succulent style. It has deep ruby/purple color and surprising fruit and character. It is ideal to drink over the next 2 years. Plenty of black fruits emerge from the dark ruby color of the full-bodied, dense, chewy, spicy 2000 Shiraz. With undeniable character, this attractive Australian fruit bomb is available for a low price. It should drink well for 2–3 years. The 1999 Shiraz offers a dark purple color, surprising volume and intensity, abundant quantities of cassis fruit, no oak, and plenty of fat and glycerin in its velvety-textured, mouth-filling, friendly style. Drink it over the next 5–6 years.

PARKER COONAWARRA ESTATE (COONAWARRA)

1999 Terra Rosa Cabernet Sauvignon	D	90
1999 Terra Rosa First Growth	E	92+
1998 Terra Rosa First Growth	E	96
1996 Terra Rosa First Growth	E	93

Owner John Parker spares no expense in his attempt to produce Australia's finest Cabernet Sauvignon–based wine. Only 5–10% of any given year's production is used for the Terra Rosa First Growth, and, sadly, there are only 1,500 cases available each year. Parker was not satisfied with the quality of the 1997, 1995, and 1992, so Terra Rosa First Growth was produced, all of it being sold off or bottled under the winery's second label, Terra Rosa Cabernet Sauvignon. Readers weaned on Bordeaux will recognize an affinity to the likes of Mouton-Rothschild or Lynch-Bages, but only in the ripest, most opulently styled vintages. The wines (blends of Cabernet Sauvignon, Merlot, Cabernet Franc, and Petit Verdot) possess tremendous richness and are slightly thicker and juicier than Bordeaux, but they exhibit the telltale lead pencil, chocolate, cedar, spice box, and tobacco characteristics of a terrific Pauillac.

Although outstanding, the 1999 Terra Rosa First Growth is not at the level of the compelling 1998. It offers a ruby/purple color as well as a classic bouquet of black currants, cedar, and high-class French oak. If Jean-Michel Cazes (the proprietor of Lynch-Bages) were making wine in Australia, this is what it would taste like—deep and full-bodied, with attractively integrated acidity, tannin, and alcohol. Anticipated maturity: now–2020.

The second wine, the 1999 Terra Rosa Cabernet Sauvignon, is not to be dismissed. It offers a sweet, cedary, chocolaty, smoky, black currant–scented nose, low acidity, ripe, open-knit

flavors, plenty of concentration, and admirable opulence as well as length. Although outstanding, it is not as majestic as its bigger sibling. Drink it over the next 10–15 years.

The 1998 Terra Rosa First Growth's dense purple color is followed by extraordinarily sweet
fruit, intense glycerin, and a full-bodied, concentrated mouth-feel. The purity, high extract,
and uncanny symmetry are breathtaking. Perhaps the finest Terra Rosa First Growth yet produced, it should drink well for two decades or more. The 1996 Terra Rosa First Growth reveals an opaque purple color, as well as a superb, expressive aromatic profile with the
aforementioned scents, huge, fat, full-bodied flavors that coat the palate, low acidity, sweet
tannin, and a sensationally long finish. This spectacular offering has few Australian rivals for
richness and complexity. It should continue to drink well for 10–15 years.

PARSON'S FLAT (PADTHAWAY)

1999 Cabernet/Shiraz	D	88
1998 Cabernet/Shiraz	D	96

Made by well-known wine-makers Sarah and Sparky Marquis, Parson's Flat Cabernet/Shiraz
is a thrilling blend of 65% Shiraz and 35% Cabernet Sauvignon. The elegant, deep ruby-
colored 1999 exhibits a claretlike delicacy, medium body, and a stylish, supple-textured
finish. Drink it over the next 6–7 years. The opaque purple-colored 1998 Cabernet/Shiraz exhibits layers of concentrated blackberry and cassis fruit intertwined with sausage/charcuterie
scents in its intense, full-bodied, super-concentrated style. A gargantuan wine, it is lush
enough to be drunk now as well as over the next 10–12 years. Impressive!

PAXTON (McLAREN VALE)

1999 Shiraz	D	87
1998 Shiraz	D	90

Proprietor David Paxton, a viticulturalist responsible for a number of vineyards in McLaren
Vale, decided in 1998 to hold back some of the oldest blocks from his own property. The resulting wines were aged in French oak, 60% new. The fairly light and downsized 1999 is elegant, not too alcoholic, and a little lacking in depth and volume. It should drink well for 4–5
years. The 1998 Shiraz (a whopping 14.9% alcohol) has restrained aromatics, but explodes in
the mouth to reveal plenty of depth, full body, cassis, blackberry, and peppery fruit, judiciously integrated oak, and a long spicy finish. Drink it over the next 5–7 years.

PENFOLDS (SOUTH AUSTRALIA)

1998 Cabernet Sauvignon Bin 407	C	87
1998 Cabernet Sauvignon Bin 707	E	90
1998 Cabernet Sauvignon/Shiraz Bin 389	C	89
1996 Grange	EEE	92+
1998 Shiraz	E	87

I was disappointed with several of Penfolds' recent releases, which tasted as if they had been
excessively acidified. Based on a tasting of the current releases, the following five red wines
stood out as the best. The 1998 Cabernet Sauvignon/Shiraz Bin 389's dense saturated purple
color is accompanied by an excellent bouquet of blackberries, licorice, and earth. In the
mouth, it is a plush, fat, luscious, full-bodied effort with considerable appeal. Loaded with
fruit and glycerin, this pure wine should drink well for 7–8 years.

The 1998 Cabernet Sauvignon Bin 407 displays a saturated ruby/purple color as well as
classic aromas of cedar and cassis, medium to full body, considerable fruit, sweet tannin, and
adequate acidity. Drink it over the next 7–8 years. From a terrific vintage for old-vine Barossa Shiraz, Penfolds' 1998 Shiraz offers gorgeously sweet blackberry fruit intermixed with
licorice and pepper. Spicy and medium- to full-bodied, with a velvety texture, this seamless,
straightforward, juicy, succulent Shiraz will drink well for 7–8 years.

The outstanding 1998 Cabernet Sauvignon Bin 707 is a thick, rich, full-bodied Cabernet emphasizing copious quantities of cassis fruit. Pure, with nicely integrated oak, acidity, and tannin, it cuts a broad swath across the palate. While still young and grapy, this 1998 is loaded with potential. Anticipated maturity: now–2015. Lastly, the 1996 Grange is not the blockbuster it can be in the greatest vintages. At one time, this was the most renowned wine produced in Australia. While this remains one of Australia's finest wines, it has plenty of competition. The dense ruby/purple-colored 1996 Grange exhibits aromas of sweet blackberry/cassis, tar, licorice, and spice. Medium- to full-bodied, with sweet tannin, a velvety texture, and surprising elegance, it should age effortlessly for 15–20 years.

PENLEY ESTATE (COONAWARRA)

1998	Cabernet Sauvignon Estate	E	95
1997	Cabernet Sauvignon Estate	E	91
1996	Cabernet Sauvignon Estate	E	89+
1999	Cabernet Sauvignon Phoenix	C	89
1998	Cabernet Sauvignon Phoenix	C	90
1997	Cabernet Sauvignon Phoenix	C	85
1999	Merlot	D	87
1996	Merlot	D	88
1998	Shiraz/Cabernet	D	90
1997	Shiraz/Cabernet	D	89
1999	Shiraz Hyland	C	88
1998	Shiraz Hyland	C	86
1997	Shiraz Hyland	C	84

Penley is another Australian winery that appears to be ratcheting up their level of performance. Good values include the fleshy, velvety-textured, elegant 1999 Shiraz Hyland. Its deep ruby/purple color is followed by aromas and flavors of chocolate, blackberries, and pepper presented in a medium-bodied, supple format. Drink it over the next 4–5 years.

The indifferent 1998 Shiraz Hyland is medium-bodied and muted, while the 1997 Shiraz Hyland is good, but tannic and monolithic. Anticipated maturity: 2004–2012.

The Cabernet Sauvignon Phoenixes are attractively priced. The 1999 and 1998 are very good, and clearly surpass the 1997. Fairly light, approachable, and charming is the supple, medium-bodied, deep ruby/plum-colored 1999 Cabernet Sauvignon Phoenix. It offers sweet aromas of cedar, spice box, and currants, and a supple texture. Enjoy it over the next 4–6 years. The dark purple-colored 1998 Cabernet Sauvignon Phoenix is an excellent buy. Broad, backward, and powerful, it offers plum, black currant, licorice, smoke, and earth aromas as well as flavors. This full-bodied, deeply concentrated, dense 1998 can be drunk now and over the next 10–12 years. The 1997 Cabernet Sauvignon Phoenix is a medium-bodied, fresh, and tangy wine that should be consumed over the next several years.

I was unimpressed with the 1997 and 1998 Merlots (truth be known, there are few top-quality Australian Merlots), but the 1999 Merlot exhibits sweet berry flavors intermixed with red currants, olives, and earth. Drink this medium-bodied effort over the next 3–4 years.

The jammy, dark ruby/purple-colored 1996 Merlot exhibits sweet black cherry fruit intermixed with mocha, toasty oak, and dried herbs. Spicy, rich, and medium- to full-bodied, this tasty, fruit-driven Merlot should be consumed over the next 5–6 years.

Two top-flight offerings from Penley are the 1997 and 1998 Shiraz/Cabernet Sauvignon. These *cuvées* tend to be blends of 60% Shiraz and 40% Cabernet Sauvignon, and are aged in both French and American oak. The smokier, richer, dense purple-colored 1998 possesses more fruit and power than its older sibling. This mouth-filling, beefy, smoky, peppery wine will provide delicious drinking over the next decade. The 1997 is a soft, richly fruity blend with excellent texture, medium body, and good, plump flavors. It should drink well for 4–5 years.

The two finest Penley offerings are the 1997 and 1998 Cabernet Sauvignon Estate. Both are sensational wines that represent a synthesis between an elegant Bordeaux and a full-bodied, opulent, powerful Australian red. The fabulous 1998 is initially less charming than its older sibling, but the wine is stacked and packed in the mouth. Its opaque purple color is accompanied by a sweet, smoky, cedary character revealing notes of cassis, licorice, and olives. Voluptuous, with the tannin largely concealed by its wealth of glycerin, fruit, and concentration, this terrific Cabernet will last for 15 years or more. Impressive! The 1997 Cabernet Sauvignon Estate's notes of vanilla, black currants, cedar, cassis, and spicy new oak are presented in a complex format. It should drink well for 10–15 years. The 1996 Cabernet Sauvignon Estate represents a classy combination of weedy black currant fruit and toasty new oak. Pure, ripe, and medium- to full-bodied, with terrific fruit intensity, good spice, moderately sweet tannin, and a long finish, this Cabernet possesses 5–8 years of upside potential.

PENNA LANE (CLARE VALLEY)

1999 Cabernet Sauvignon	C	88?

With a complex nose of chocolate and cedarwood, the only problem with the medium- to full-bodied 1999 Cabernet Sauvignon might be some chalky tannin in the finish. If that does not resolve itself, this rating will look generous. Anticipated maturity: now–2014.

PENNY'S HILL (McLAREN VALE)

1998 Fortified Shiraz	D	90
1998 Merlot/Cabernet/Shiraz Specialized	D	88+?
1998 Shiraz	D	90
1997 Shiraz	D	90

A fine McLaren Vale estate, Penny's Hill has made a tight but promising, deep, full-bodied 1998 Shiraz. It boasts a saturated ruby/purple color, and elegant, ripe notes of blackberries, chocolate, pepper, and vanilla. Initially restrained, it unfolds and becomes increasingly expansive as the wine sits in the glass. It should drink well in 1–2 years and last 12–15.

A big, rich, succulent, peppery, black fruit–scented and –flavored Shiraz, the lush, low-acid, full-bodied 1997 will saturate the palate. There are gobs of fleshy, concentrated fruit in this soft, tasty wine. It promises to drink well for 4–5 years.

The 1998 Merlot/Cabernet/Shiraz Specialized (a blend of equal parts of these three varietals) shows plenty of toasty oak in the nose as well as internationally styled notes of black currants, vanilla, and spice box. Medium- to full-bodied, with good ripeness on the attack, and moderate tannin in the finish, it will be at its peak before 2012.

Port aficionados may get a blast from the 1998 Fortified Shiraz, a wine offering peppery, blackberry liqueur notes, an unctuous texture, and slight sweetness. This interesting Port look-alike should drink well for a decade, and, hopefully, develop even more perfume.

PIERRO (MARGARET RIVER)

1997 Cabernet	E	89
1998 Proprietary Red Wine	E	87

The dark ruby/purple-colored 1998 Proprietary Red Wine, a blend of Cabernet Sauvignon, Merlot, Petit Verdot, and Malbec, possesses a classy perfume of black currants, cherries, mulberries, and smoky oak. It exhibits an elegant, Bordeaux-like austerity and texture, good purity, nicely integrated wood, and a clean finish. Anticipated maturity: 2005–2016.

Do not be surprised by the Bordeaux-like personality of the 1997 Cabernet. A touch of Merlot, Cabernet Franc, and Petit Verdot were added to the blend of this medium-bodied, spicy, plum-colored wine. Stylish, restrained, and elegant, with black currant flavors nicely dosed with oak, this wine would be impossible to pick out as a New World Cabernet in a blind tasting. Anticipated maturity: now–2012.

PIKES (CLARE VALLEY)

1998	Cabernet Sauvignon	C	86
1999	Merlot	C	87
1998	Premio Sangiovese	C	86
1999	Shiraz	C	88
1998	Shiraz	C	87
1999	Shiraz/Grenache/Mourvèdre	C	88

Almost without exception, Pikes' wines tend to possess aggressive acid profiles (more than I generally like to see). That kind of style works better with the whites than with the reds.

As for the red wines, the Premio Sangiovese seems to be good, but no one in the New World is making anything comparable to what exists in central Italy. The 1998 possesses telltale strawberry fruit infused with notes of saddle leather as well as tangy acidity. While well-made, it is essentially one-dimensional and straightforward. Drink it over the next 2–3 years.

Pikes' Bordeaux varietals include the 1999 Merlot. It exhibits a minty, red currant, cassis, and chocolate-scented bouquet, medium body, tart underlying acidity, and a fleshy finish. Acidity is present, but it is not intrusive. The tartness is more problematic in the dense ruby/purple-colored 1998 Cabernet Sauvignon. It exhibits sweet black currants, but crisp acidity gives the wine a lean, compressed palate. In that sense, it had more in common with a Loire Valley red than an Aussie offering. Pikes' Rhône Valley blend, the 1999 Shiraz/Grenache/Mourvèdre (55% Shiraz, 32% Grenache, and 13% Mourvèdre), reveals telltale eucalyptus notes along with moderate quantities of blackberry and cassis fruit. The wine provides a sweet attack, excellent purity and a bright, well-delineated finish. Interestingly, in 1998 the same *cuvée* tasted muted but also high in acidity, atypical for the vintage.

My favorite of this lean group is the ruby/purple-colored 1999 Shiraz. It exhibits sweet berry fruit, medium body, and well-integrated acidity, tannin, and wood. Consume it over the next 4–6 years. Overall, these wines are cleanly made but generally unexciting. The 1998 Shiraz is well balanced. Attractive aromas of licorice, blackberries, earth, and pepper are present in the moderately endowed bouquet. Acidity is there, but the wine's weight and richness handle it better than its siblings. The finish is short, but the fruit quality is impressive and the wine attractive, medium-bodied, and cleanly made. Drink it over the next 4–5 years.

PUNTERS CORNER SPARTACUS (COONAWARRA)

1998	Shiraz Reserve	D	88

A saturated dark ruby/purple color is followed by scents of smoky wood (both Russian and French casks were utilized), considerable body, a chewy, fleshy texture, and abundant pepper as well as cassis. This 1998 Shiraz Reserve should drink well for a decade.

QUARTETTO (CLARE VALLEY)

1999	Shiraz	D	88

The dark ruby/purple-colored 1999 Shiraz presents a sweet, highly extracted, chewy, cassis fruit mixed with smoke and oak. Ripe and supple-textured, drink it over the next 5–6 years.

RANDALL'S HILL (BAROSSA RANGES)

1995	Shiraz 1910	E	95+

The fruit for this wine comes from the Three Rivers Vineyard owned by Chris Ringland, one of the stars of handcrafted, artisanal, cult, old-vine Shiraz. Made from 90-year-old vines and cropped at two tons of fruit per acre, the 125-case *cuvée* of 1995 Shiraz 1910 exhibits an impressive dark ruby/purple color, and layer upon layer of fruit. Thick, chewy, and full-bodied, this massive Shiraz spent a whopping 32 months in new French oak, but has perfectly absorbed the wood. Majestic flavor breadth, exceptionally pure, and remarkably well balanced, this seamless beauty can be drunk now or cellared for 20–30 years. Bravo!

RBJ (BAROSSA VALLEY)

1998 Theologicum	D	87

Slightly more restrained and less concentrated than several previous vintages, the 1998 Theologicum is still a noteworthy blend of 65% Grenache and 35% Mourvèdre. Aged in old wood, it is reminiscent of an attractive, spicy, cinnamon, cherry, and earthy southern Rhône. The wine is medium-bodied, soft, and best drunk over the next 5–6 years. Approximately 1,000 cases were produced.

RED EDGE (HEATHCOTE)

1998 Cabernet Sauvignon	D	92

This unfined/unfiltered 1998 Cabernet Sauvignon was made from microscopic yields of one ton of fruit per acre. The wine is full-bodied, sensationally concentrated, with fabulous length and purity. Almost over the top, it is beautifully buttressed by decent tannin and low acidity. The purity and density of the cassis fruit is admirable. Anticipated maturity: now–2025.

CHÂTEAU REYNELLA (McLAREN VALE)

1996 Cabernet Sauvignon Basket Press	D	88
1996 Shiraz	C	87
1998 Shiraz Basket Press	D	88

The big, thick, rustic 1998 Shiraz Basket Press exhibits a dense purple color along with scents of smoke, earth, blackberries, asphalt, and pepper. Layered and chewy, with rustic tannin as well as American oak in the background, it should drink well for 10–12 years.

The 1996 Shiraz's deep ruby/purple color is accompanied by smoky, spicy aromas displaying a touch of minerals and pepper. This medium- to full-bodied, well-made Shiraz reveals good purity, noticeable toasty new American oak, and a spicy, supple finish. Drink it over the next 5–6 years. Loads of new oak intermixed with black currants are the hallmarks of the medium- to full-bodied, supple-textured, nicely concentrated, internationally styled 1996 Cabernet Sauvignon Basket Press. The acidity is adequate, and the wine is open-knit, expansive, and ideal for drinking over the next 5–7 years.

ROCKFORD (BAROSSA VALLEY)

NV Black Shiraz	E	?
1997 Cabernet Sauvignon	D	88
1998 Moppa Springs Red	C	87
1998 Shiraz Basket Press	D	90

In spite of Rockford's terrific wine-maker, Chris Ringland, I had a hard time understanding the nonvintage Black Shiraz. For $90, one gets an elegant, tart, fresh but essentially one-dimensional wine with little depth or complexity. I don't know if the bottle I had performed poorly or whether this is typical, but certainly this seems out of character for Rockford and Ringland. The finest offering I tasted was the 1998 Shiraz Basket Press. While not a great value, it is an outstanding effort displaying a dense purple color, a jammy, blackberry fruit bomb character, a supple texture, formidable glycerin, full body, and a lush mid-palate and finish. It should drink well for at least a decade.

The 1998 Moppa Springs Red, a blend of 69% Grenache, 20% Shiraz, and 11% Mataro, aged in larger wood puncheons, reveals a soft, Rhône-ish character with notes of kirsch, pepper, spice, and a sexy, round personality. Drink it over the next 2–4 years.

The 1997 Cabernet Sauvignon is supple-textured, with medium body, excellent cedary, tobacco, and black currant notes, silky tannin, low acidity, and a finish that caresses the palate. It should also be drunk sooner rather than later, over the next 5–6 years.

ROSABROOK (MARGARET RIVER)

1999 Shiraz Abattoir Block	E	92
1998 Shiraz Abattoir Block	E	90+

Two of Australia's most distinctive Shirazes, both the 1998 and 1999 Abattoir Block display Rhône-like, earthy, meaty flavors reminiscent of blood and black fruits. Both are explosive, full-bodied, eccentric efforts made from extremely ripe fruit and aged in 100% French oak before being bottled without filtration. They explode on the palate, offering notes of fruit intermixed with characteristics of meat, sausage, blood, and animal. While not for everybody, they are exquisite expressions of Shiraz made in a different microclimate than those from Barossa or McLaren Vale. The 1998 will keep for 15 or more years, whereas the more seamless, accessible 1999 can be drunk now as well as over the next 12+ years.

ROSEMOUNT (COONAWARRA)

1997 Cabernet Sauvignon Show Reserve	B	89+
2000 Cabernet Sauvignon/Merlot	A	86
1999 Cabernet Sauvignon/Merlot	A	85
1997 GSM	C	89
1996 GSM	C	87
1997 Mountain Blue (Shiraz/Cabernet Sauvignon)	D	87+?
1999 Shiraz	A	86
1999 Shiraz/Cabernet Sauvignon	A	86
1997 Syrah Balmoral	D	89

I tasted nearly three dozen selections from Rosemount, and one-third proved to have considerable merit. The finest Rosemount offerings are terrific values, and some of their upper-end wines are competitive with Australia's finest. Two excellent values are the 1999 and 2000 Cabernet Sauvignon/Merlot. The 2000 is 60% Cabernet Sauvignon and 40% Merlot, and the 1999 is 55% Cabernet Sauvignon and 45% Merlot. Both are fruit-driven efforts revealing the personalities of their blends. The richer, fuller, more forward 2000 reveals no evidence of wood. Soft and lush, with low acidity, it will drink well for 1–2 years. The 1999 is grapy and soft, with plenty of berry fruit, and a silky texture. Anticipated maturity: *now*.

The dark ruby/purple 1999 Shiraz offers copious quantities of black fruits and spice presented in a straightforward, medium-bodied style. Easy to drink as well as understand, it is best consumed over the next 2–3 years to take advantage of its fruit and exuberance.

The dark ruby-colored 1999 Shiraz/Cabernet Sauvignon (65% Shiraz and 35% Cabernet Sauvignon from southeastern Australia) possesses an excellent nose of black fruits and spice. Medium-bodied, soft, silky, and Beaujolais-like, it is a delicious red meant for near-term consumption—over the next 1–2 years.

Among the more prestigious as well as expensive offerings is Rosemount's GSM, a blend of 50% Grenache, 40% Shiraz, and 10% Mourvèdre aged for 18 months in American oak. The 1997's complex bouquet of roasted nuts, flowers, blackberries, smoke, and currants jumps from the glass. This medium- to full-bodied, suave, elegant yet concentrated wine is flavorful. Drink this pure, supple red over the next 5–6 years. The attractive 1996 GSM exhibits a dense, ruby/purple color as well as a big, earthy, leathery, berry-scented nose with abundant oak. Medium- to full-bodied, with sweet fruit on the attack, a good mid-palate, and a compressed finish, this mainstream, attractive blend should be consumed over the next 2–3 years.

The dense ruby/purple-colored 1997 Syrah Balmoral exhibits smoke, blackberry, licorice, and oak aromas, full body, sweet tannin, and a long finish. It is best consumed over the next 7–8 years. The 1997 Cabernet Sauvignon Show Reserve emerges from the red soils of Coonawarra. It was aged for 24 months in a combination of wood barrels. The dense garnet/plum/purple color is accompanied by classic Cabernet aromas of cedar, cassis, and smoky new oak. Thick, rich, and full-bodied, this chewy, structured, well-delineated, still youthful Cabernet will not hit its prime for another 2–3 years and should last 12–15 years.

The 1997 Mountain Blue (a blend of 75% Shiraz and 25% Cabernet Sauvignon aged 24 months in both French and American wood) exhibits a straightforward nose of new oak as well as blueberry and blackberry fruit. Firmly structured, with abundant wood, good tannin, and medium to full body, it is not as expressive as several of its siblings, but it has the potential to age well for 10–12 years.

RUSDEN (BAROSSA VALLEY)

1998	Cabernet Sauvignon Boundary Row	E	92
1997	Cabernet Sauvignon Boundary Row	E	93
1999	Grenache Christine's Vineyard	D	87
1998	Grenache Christine's Vineyard	D	90
1998	Shiraz Black Guts	E	92
1997	Shiraz Black Guts	D	92
1999	Zinfandel Lodestone	E	91

Twenty-two-year-old wine-maker Christian Canute has an impressive résumé, having worked at Rockford and Torbreck. From his family winery, Rusden, he is turning out limited-production gems. Rusden's classic, in a typically Australian oversized sense, is the Cabernet Sauvignon Boundary Row. Sadly, there are only 70 cases of this large, fruit-driven, yet complex effort. Smoky bacon fat, cassis, licorice, and cigar smoke emerge from the dense, plum/purple-colored 1998. In the mouth, it is opulent, full-bodied, and concentrated, with plenty of jammy, low-acid fruit. Drink this between 2005–2014. At first I thought the 1997 Cabernet Sauvignon Boundary Row was controversial, given its pruny, overripe character. However, as the wine sat in the glass, it gathered delineation and its over-the-top personality became more civilized and classic. It is a wine of extreme density, with extraordinary notes of black raspberries, cherries, cassis, prunes, and what the French call *sous-bois* (a clean, foresty/earthy aroma). Low in acidity, thick, and delicious, this Cabernet improved significantly with aeration. Although it will not be long-lived, it will evolve and last for another decade.

The Grenache Christine's Vineyard emerges from 30-year-old Grenache vines. The 1999 is another wine with a barbecue spice, smoky bacon fat–scented, flamboyant nose. Classic Rhône notes of underbrush, pepper, and spice emerge from this medium-bodied, dark plum/ruby-colored wine. Smoky and spicy, it is best drunk over the next 2–3 years.

The 1998 Grenache Christine's Vineyard's dark plum/ruby/garnet color is followed by a sweet nose of kirsch, spice, and earth. Gorgeous fruit and moderately high alcohol (13.7%) provide a sweet, glycerin-dominated impact on the palate. Pure, rich, full-bodied, and delicious, this wine should continue to drink well for 5–6 years. The 1999 Zinfandel Lodestone, a curiosity, is an impressive micro *cuvée* of 56 cases, but only a handful of Americans will ever taste it. Produced from 30-year-old Zinfandel vines and tipping the scales at 15.8% alcohol, it exhibits a Turley Cellars, full-bodied, dry portlike style. Fat, jammy, and full-bodied, with gobs of smoky berry fruit, this is a wine to drink over the next 4–5 years.

Only 115 cases are produced of the Shiraz Black Guts. This wine emerges from 30-year-old vines cropped to two tons per acre. The 1998 is a large-scaled effort. Deep purple in color, with a smoky, creosote/asphalt, blackberry, and cassis-scented bouquet, this ripe, full-bodied Shiraz boasts super fruit, notions of new oak (it was aged for 30 months in a combination of new and old French wood), and plenty of glycerin and length in the long finish. In spite of its size, the wine actually comes across as elegant, particularly for such mass and intensity. It should drink well for up to a decade. The 1997 Shiraz Black Guts tips the scales at a whopping 15.2% alcohol. The high alcohol is barely noticeable, given the wine's wealth of fruit, dense ruby/purple color, and bouquet of rose petals, blackberry liqueur, pepper, and truffles. Deep and full-bodied, with an unctuous texture, superb density, and low acidity, this wine will continue to drink well for 10+ years.

SAINT MICHAEL'S (HEATHCOTE, VICTORIA)

1999 Merlot	E	90

I will keep my notes short since there are only 30 cases of this wine, made at Wild Duck Creek. The dense, textured, opaque purple-colored 1999 Merlot is made in an intense, ripe, over-the-top, full-bodied style with plenty of glycerin, huge amounts of black currant fruit, and a knockout finish. It is hardly subtle, but it is classic, in-your-face Australian Merlot that coats the palate. Drink it over the next 7–8 years.

SCARPANTONI (McLAREN VALE)

1999 Cabernet Sauvignon	C	88
1998 Estate Reserve	C	89
1999 Maslin Beach Blanche Point Proprietary Red	D	87
1999 Merlot	C	85
1999 School Block Proprietary Red	C	88
1999 Shiraz Block 3	C	89
1998 Shiraz Block 3	C	93

One of the more modestly priced wineries in the Grateful Palate portfolio, this family of Italian immigrant origin has produced some interesting wines. One of Scarpantoni's low-keyed efforts, the soft, medium-bodied 1999 Merlot reveals herb-tinged berry fruit. It is acceptable, tasty, soft, and best drunk over the next 3–4 years.

The 1999 School Block Proprietary Red (a blend of 55% Shiraz, 40% Cabernet, and 5% Merlot, 600 cases produced) is a good value. The wine shows excellent blackberry and cassis fruit notes, attractive, supple texture, medium to full body, and gorgeous fruit and length. While it is meant for current drinking, it should hold nicely for another 2–3 years. The 1999 Maslin Beach Blanche Point (named after a nudist beach) reveals abundant spicy American oak in the nose, but pulls back in the mouth to offer concentrated, jammy fruit. With earthiness, spice, and currants plus good overall balance, it will drink well for 4–5 years.

The nearly outstanding 1998 Estate Reserve (a 700-case blend of 75% Shiraz and 25% Cabernet) boasts aggressive sweet oak in addition to jammy black currants, berries, and smoky aromas as well as flavors. With admirable plumpness and fatness, it provides a succulent mouthful of fruit, glycerin, and alcohol (about 14%). Anticipated maturity: now–2011.

Another very good value is the 1999 Cabernet Sauvignon. There are 1,500 cases of this 100% Cabernet Sauvignon made from 28-year-old vines. Offering copious quantities of sweet black currant fruit presented in a fleshy, full-bodied, in-your-face style, this pure, ripe, medium- to full-bodied Cabernet should be consumed over the next 7–8 years. It is hard to find New World Cabernet Sauvignon for under $30 a bottle at this quality level.

The difference between the fabulous 1998 vintage and the good 1999 vintage is sharply displayed in Scarpantoni's two offerings from their 60-year-old Block 3 Shiraz holdings. The 1998 is fabulous, but the restrained 1999, while very good, is no match for its older sibling. The 1998 is a spectacularly full-bodied, black/purple-colored effort with notes of pepper, smoky licorice candy, cassis, blackberries, and earth. It possesses terrific fruit, massive body, sweet tannin, and nicely integrated alcohol as well as wood. At $25, this is one of the great wine bargains in the marketplace today. Moreover, there are 2,500 cases available. This wine can drink well for another 10–15 years. Also a good value, though it does not have the prodigious fat, concentration, and depth of the 1998, the 1999 exhibits a deep ruby/purple color, sweet black currant and berry fruit, an elegant, medium- to full-bodied, spicy personality, and a supple texture. The 1999 is best consumed over the next 6–8 years.

SEVILLE ESTATE (YARRA VALLEY)

1997	Cabernet Sauvignon	C	86

The dark ruby/purple-colored 1997 Cabernet Sauvignon exhibits sweet, ripe black currant fruit infused with subtle French oak. Mint/eucalyptus is also present in this medium-bodied, pure, cassis-flavored, soft, tasty Cabernet. Drink it over the next 3–4 years.

STANTON AND KILLEEN (RUTHERGLEN)

NV	Collector's Muscat	E	90
1997	Durif	C	87
NV	Muscat	D	93
NV	Tokay	D	90

Better known for their fortified dessert wines, Stanton and Killeen's 1997 Durif tips the scales at 14.4% alcohol. Dense ruby/purple, with a peppery, blackberry-scented nose, this full-bodied effort is loaded with fruit. While the finish is rustic, the wine offers plenty of flavor in a straightforward, robust format. Drink it over the next 2–4 years.

The light medium amber-colored nonvintage Tokay is sweet, round, and represents a blend that is approximately 12–15 years of age. Delicious, it is ideal for sipping at the end of a meal. The finest of this trio of fortified dessert wines is the dark amber-colored nonvintage Muscat. It reveals more complexity, richness, and unctuosity than the nonvintage Collector's Muscat. The Muscat is 12–15 years in age, whereas the Collector's Muscat is 25–30 years of age. These powerful, concentrated, impeccably made wines are among Australia's treasures.

THALGARA (HUNTER VALLEY)

1998	Show Shiraz	D	88

In spite of obvious oak, this 1998 Show Shiraz exhibits an opaque ruby/purple color, plenty of fleshy, overripe, blackberry and cassis fruit, a good, chewy, straightforward personality, and a mouth-staining finish. Although not complex, it is an attractive, internationally styled wine for readers looking for immediate gratification. Drink it over the next 2–3 years.

THORN AND CLARKE (BAROSSA VALLEY)

1998	Shiraz	C	86

From a new winery, this dense ruby/purple-colored 1998 Shiraz (300 cases produced) possesses plenty of tannin, an international style, and a foursquare, chunky personality. It is a good wine, but best drunk during its first 3–4 years of life.

THREE RIVERS (BAROSSA VALLEY)

1996	Shiraz	EEE	100
1995	Shiraz	EEE	99

These are colossal efforts and very much in keeping with the style of owner/wine-maker Chris Ringland. The Three Rivers Shiraz (only 100 cases produced) is made from 90-year-old vines. Following malolactic fermentation in cask, it spent 40 months in new oak prior to being bottled unfiltered. This is arguably the greatest Shiraz made in Australia, but, sadly, there is little of it. The viscous, black/purple 1996 Shiraz represents the essence of both wine and Shiraz. With impeccable balance, unreal levels of concentration, yet perfectly integrated tannin, acidity, alcohol, and wood, it is akin to a dry vintage port, but then, so is a 1947 Cheval Blanc, 1947 Pétrus, 1947 Lafleur, and 1947 Latour à Pomerol. Once past the explosive bouquet of crème de cassis, espresso, melted fudge, and graphite, this massive yet seamless wine offers layers of unctuously textured flavors crammed with blackberries, smoke, charcoal, and currants. The finish lasts for 70+ seconds. The wine should prove to be immortal, lasting for 30–50 years, but who is going to wait that long to unleash the magic? This is compelling stuff! Anticipated maturity: 2010–2040. The 1995 Shiraz is a virtually perfect wine of splendid concentration, symmetry, and length (nearly a minute). An opaque black/ purple color is followed by staggering aromas of black fruits, truffles, sweet earth, and wood. With amazing viscosity, density, and concentration that transcend any Shiraz I have ever tasted (except for the 1996), this monumental wine represents an extraordinary achievement. Its low acidity and phenomenal richness should offer early accessibility, but it promises to evolve for two decades or more. Kudos to Ringland for these ultimate Australian blockbuster Shirazes. I just wish there were 10 times the quantity produced!

TORBRECK (BAROSSA VALLEY)

1999	Descendent	E	93
1997	Descendent	E	96
1998	The Factor	E	93
2000	Juveniles	D	90
1999	Juveniles	D	94
1998	Run Rig	EEE	99
1997	Run Rig	EEE	98
1999	The Steading	D	91
1998	The Steading	D	96
1999	Woodcutters	C	90

Wine-maker Dave Powell is quickly establishing himself as one of the geniuses of Rhône Valley–influenced, blockbuster red wines from Australia. I have extolled his previous vintages, but the quality (and prices) continues to soar as these are some of the most exciting wines produced not only in Australia but in the world. Production is somewhat limited, ranging from 240 cases of Juveniles to 1,600 cases of The Steading and 400 cases of Run Rig. These are wines of enormous strength but also riveting individuality and extraordinary purity and symmetry. The reds are all spectacular, even some of the less expensive *cuvées*. Of course, the Run Rig has become one of the most fashionable wines in the world, and it deserves its billing as the Guigal Côte Rôtie La Mouline of Australia. I have recently had both the 1996 and 1997 Run Rig, and I am pleased to say that both of these wines still offer extraordinary combinations of power and complexity in an undeniably sumptuous style.

The most expensive red wine of the portfolio is undoubtedly the Run Rig. However, it is not out of line with what wines of similar quality sell for throughout the world, unfortunately a reality. There are nearly 600 cases annually. The wine is made from vines averaging between 50 and 130 years of age, cropped at 1.25 tons of fruit per acre. It is a blend of 97% Shiraz and 3% Viognier, and is aged completely in French oak for approximately 18 months prior to bottling. The 1998 may well be the most concentrated Run Rig to date. The color is an opaque purple, and the bouquet offers an exotic concoction of tropical fruit, blackberry liqueur, crème de cassis, smoke, and honeysuckle notes. Once past the exhilarating fragrance, the wine is sumptuous and full-bodied, with a skyscraper-like profile of fabulous concentration and length that builds in the mouth. A scenario of black fruits galore unfolds to reveal beautifully integrated wood, acidity, tannin, and alcohol (a mere 14.5%). The balance is virtually perfect, and the finish lasts nearly a minute. This luxurious, compelling gem displays a level of complexity and delineation that is rare in a wine of such size. Anticipated maturity: now–2016. Every bit as spectacular is the 1997 Run Rig. I have been blown away by prior efforts, and this huge, exotic wine, which offers up blueberry liqueur, cassis, flowers, a touch of overripe peaches, and sweet vanilla, is a rich, full-bodied, supple-textured wine. I sent a bottle to my French lawyer for a tasting with several top Médoc proprietors after which I received a fax asking how many cases they could purchase! Two or three bottles a year is most people's allocation. The oak is beautifully integrated. The wine is low in acidity, and the impact on the palate is one of awesome levels of fruit, richness, and complexity. This amazing wine may even merit a perfect rating. It should drink well for 10–12 years.

The second most expensive offering in the Torbreck portfolio is the Descendent, a 100% Shiraz fermented on Viognier pomace emerging from a five-year-old vineyard cropped at a minuscule 1.25 tons per acre. There are 220 cases of this *cuvée*, which spends 18 months in used French barrels prior to bottling. No other wine from Australia remotely resembles it. In truth, the closest wine to which it could be compared is Marcel Guigal's single-vineyard Côte Rôtie La Turque. The 1999's dense purple color is followed by blackberry, crème de cassis, and floral aromas, huge body, terrific fat and glycerin, and a seamless, decadently rich finish. While it will not last as long as the Run Rig, it is a tour de force in pleasure for drinking in its first 7–8 years of life. The 1997 Descendent represents Australia's quintessential example of power and elegance. Though not massive, its level of concentration is extraordinary. This black/purple wine offers a feminine, silky voluptuousness allied to fascinating levels of richness, unbelievably sweet tannin, and layers of flavor. In the glass, the wine develops magnificently. A bottle kept open for 48 hours displayed additional nuances and complexity. Full-bodied, but not heavy, this is a tour de force in winemaking, as well as a thrilling Shiraz to drink. Anticipated maturity: now–2010.

Another stunning effort is 1998's The Factor. This 100% Shiraz *cuvée* (240 cases) is made from 50–130-year-old vines. No new oak is used, although some of the press wine does see new American oak. Supple, with a telltale, ostentatious bouquet of black fruits mixed with smoke, licorice, and melted asphalt, this super-extracted, velvety-textured, sumptuous, pure, rich, impeccably well balanced wine is best consumed during its first decade of life.

Continuing to descend in price but not much in quality is The Steading, a southern Rhône blend of 60% Grenache, 20% Shiraz, and 20% Mourvèdre. Two thousand cases are produced annually of this Châteauneuf-du-Pape look-alike from Australia's Barossa Valley. The 1999 is a terrific, deep purple-colored effort offering a sweet nose of pepper, black fruits, earth, tobacco, and cassis. Sweet on the attack (from ripe fruit, not sugar), this full-bodied, concentrated, powerful wine (14.5% alcohol) builds in the mouth to a creamy-textured, blockbuster finish. Though hard to resist, it will drink well for 7–8 years.

The dense ruby/purple 1998 The Steading boasts a creamy texture in addition to a glorious bouquet of black raspberries, kirsch, cassis, minerals, and licorice. Seductive, voluptuously textured flavors unfold on the palate, and the texture is so plush that it feels like the palate is resting on a waterbed of overripe black fruits. Extremely long (45+ seconds), this sensational wine can be drunk now or cellared for 10–12 years.

If readers want to know what the quintessential Australian fruit bomb tastes like, check out the Juveniles, a tank-fermented blend of 60% Grenache, 20% Shiraz, and 20% Mourvèdre made from tiny yields of 1–2 tons of fruit per acre. It is actually the same wine as The Steading, but it is aged in tank rather than spending 18 months in old French and American wood as The Steading does. Bursting at the seams with juicy blackberry, cherry, and currant fruit, the 2000 offers copious quantities of spicy, peppery characteristics, sexy, seductive glycerin levels, and a creamy texture that defines hedonism. It is not going to make old bones, but for drinking over the next 2–3 years, this is a fabulous, fruit-filled effort from Barossa. Anticipated maturity: now–2005. The 1999 Juveniles is an explosive fruit bomb. It almost has a "nouveau" character, but there are such levels of concentration, body, glycerin, and extract that it transcends that category into something unlike anything tasted previously. Opaque purple-colored, with a celestial perfume of jammy black fruit and floral scents, this dense, monstrous, velvety-textured wine is a total hedonistic turn-on. It is impossible to resist and should continue to drink well for 7–8 years.

Finally, the 1999 Woodcutters red (2,300 cases) is essentially declassified juice that did not make it into The Steading. Produced from the same blend, this is an outstanding, reasonably priced effort from David Powell. Sweet, pure, ripe, full-bodied, rich, decadent, chewy, and fat, it is a thrill to drink. Anticipated maturity: now–2008.

These wines not only make for compelling drinking, they are also a huge amount of fun, and isn't that what it's all about? If I had to give an award to Australia's finest wine-maker in 2001, it would be hard not to consider David Powell.

VASSE FELIX (WESTERN AUSTRALIA)

1998 Heytesbury	D	88

The classy, complex 1998 Heytesbury (a blend of Cabernet Sauvignon, Shiraz, and a touch of Malbec, aged in both French and American oak) exhibits a dense ruby/purple color in addition to an elegant, crème de cassis–scented bouquet with notions of blueberries, wood, and earth. It offers excellent concentration and purity, fine integrated acidity, moderate tannin, and a long finish. Enjoy it now and over the next 10–12 years.

VERITAS (BAROSSA VALLEY)

1999	Cabernet/Merlot	C	89
1998	Cabernet/Merlot	C	91
1998	Clement 1309	E	93
1997	Clement 1309	E	93
1990	Fortified Tokay	B	92
1999	Mourvèdre/Grenache	D	91
1998	Mourvèdre/Grenache	D	90
1998	Shiraz Hanisch	E	99
1997	Shiraz Hanisch	E	97
1998	Shiraz Heysen	E	96
1997	Shiraz Heysen	E	96
1998	Shiraz/Mourvèdre Pressings	D	92
1997	Shiraz/Mourvèdre Pressings	D	92
NV	10-year-old Tawny Fortified Dessert	B	90

One of my favorite Australian wineries, Veritas' offerings are never excessively oaked, but possess extraordinarily ripe, concentrated fruit, great individuality, and the potential, in the top examples, to improve for two decades. The wine-maker/proprietor is Rolf Binder, who already has an impressive résumé. A blend of 70% Cabernet Sauvignon and 30% Merlot from 30-year-old vines, the Cabernet/Merlot blend is aged with only 15% new oak. Annual production averages 900 cases. The 1999 exhibits a dark ruby/purple color and a gorgeously sweet nose of jammy black currants mixed with earth and spice box. The wine is excellent, fresh, and juicy, with sweet tannin and plenty of fat. Readers looking for reasonably priced Cabernet to gulp down over the next 5–7 years should check this beauty out. If you are looking for an over-the-top, jammy, superripe Cabernet Sauvignon/Merlot, you need search no further than Veritas' 1998 Cabernet/Merlot. This is a hedonistic Cabernet bomb with full body, low acidity, and gobs of jammy black fruit flavors. It is a thrill to smell, taste, and drink. Moreover, it will last 15 years, given its flamboyant/ostentatious, fruit-driven style. Complexity has yet to emerge, and there is plenty of tannin lurking beneath the fruit, glycerin, and extract.

In ascending order of quality (yet all three of the following wines are exquisite) are the Mourvèdre/Grenache, Shiraz/Mourvèdre Pressings, and Clement 1309. Rhône Valley enthusiasts will get a blast from all of these exceptionally well made efforts. The Mourvèdre/Grenache blends are made of 65% of the former and 35% of the latter varietals, the vines ranging between 30–100 years of age. This wine sees about 10% new American oak. Sadly, the production is only 250 cases. The 1999 Mourvèdre/Grenache is a dazzling, full-bodied 1999. With notes of new saddle leather, blackberry, currant, and raspberry fruit, superb ripeness, a round, generous mid-palate and finish, and excellent balance, this is a wine to drink over the next 5–7 years. The 1998 Mourvèdre/Grenache's dark ruby color is accompanied by a big, spicy, black raspberry and cherry-scented nose, a creamy texture, full body, gorgeous levels of black and red fruits, a silky texture, and abundant glycerin. Drink it over the next 7–8 years.

The Shiraz/Mourvèdre Pressings (55% Shiraz and 45% Mourvèdre) spends about 22 months in French oak prior to being bottled. Interestingly, the Mourvèdre comes from 100-year-old, nonirrigated vines, among the oldest in Barossa. It may be controversial for some readers, given the fact that it is an Australian version of French Bandol. About 500 cases of this exceptional wine are produced annually. Notes of new saddle leather, earth, sweat, and meaty animal-like characteristics compete with black cherry, blackberry, and currant fruit in the 1998 Shiraz/Mourvèdre Pressings. This wine is explosive in the mouth, full-bodied, deep, and concentrated, with layers of flavor as well as a surprisingly supple finish, given that young Mourvèdre can be dry and tannic. Anticipated maturity: now–2012. Another brilliant effort from Binder is his 1997 Shiraz/Mourvèdre Pressings (with a modest 13.5% alcohol). A dense ruby/purple color is followed by intense black cherry, blackberry, and currant flavors intermixed with spice and tar. Full-bodied, with superb concentration, good delineation, and a rich, layered, accessible finish, this youthful offering displays far more accessibility than its predecessor. Anticipated maturity: now–2015.

The Clement 1309 is a blend of Mourvèdre and Grenache from vines averaging 100 years of age. It is aged a whopping 30 months in French and American oak. Production is extremely tiny (less than 70 cases annually), but readers should approach this wine as they would the ferociously tannic, highly extracted 1990 Pradeaux Mourvèdre Vieilles Vignes from Bandol or a backward, concentrated vintage of Beaucastel Châteauneuf-du-Pape. The brilliant, dark, plum/purple-colored 1998 Clement 1309 (a 50% Mourvèdre/50% Grenache blend) offers a flamboyant nose of black fruits, flowers, earth, leather, and pepper. It is ripe and jammy, with superb concentration, great purity, and a finish that goes on for nearly 50 seconds. The exceptional 1997 Clement 1309 is superintense, with huge body, mouth-searing levels of tannin, and extraordinary concentration and potential complexity. It is not close to prime-time drinking, but who can ignore the blackberry, raspberry, melted road tar, licorice, and truffle notes that emerge from the wine's aromatics? Extremely full-bodied and backward, this offering requires 2–3 years of cellaring and will easily last for two decades.

Two of the consistently great Australian Shirazes made over recent vintages have been the Heysen and the Hanisch. The Shiraz Heysen is a dazzling example of what Australia can do so well. A blend of 95% Shiraz and 5% Cabernet Sauvignon from 26-year-old vines and aged in 40% new oak, its production averages 400 cases. The 1998 Shiraz Heysen is off the charts. An opaque black/purple is accompanied by an ostentatious bouquet of raspberries, blackberries, currants, and cherries. With airing, the bouquet also offers up smoke, pepper, licorice, and earth. In the mouth, the wine is unctuously textured and extremely full-bodied, with great purity and layers of flavor. Anticipated maturity: now–2020. The opaque black/purple-colored 1997 Shiraz Heysen reveals aromas of flowers, licorice, blackberries, and new saddle leather. This full-bodied, fat, succulent, low-acid wine is one of the most concentrated and intense Shiraz drinkers will ever taste. Long, powerful, and concentrated, it can be drunk now, but will age effortlessly for 20 years.

The Shiraz Hanisch series are 100% Shiraz blends from 26-year-old vines that age with 40% new oak (300 cases are produced annually). The virtually perfect 1998 (14.7% alcohol) is a huge but impressively balanced effort. Offering up notes of beef blood, blackberries, and jammy cassis, this viscous, massive, full-bodied, fabulously concentrated but not heavy 1998 has a finish that lasts just under a minute. It represents the essence of Shiraz. It can be drunk now because it is so luxuriously rich, but don't expect secondary nuances to develop for at least another 5–8 years. It should keep for 20–25—at the minimum. The 1997 Shiraz

Hanisch tastes like a dry vintage port. Opaque purple-colored, with a knockout bouquet of blackberries, leather, and foresty scents mixed with licorice and pepper, this intense, super-concentrated, phenomenally extracted Shiraz is beyond massive. Amazingly well balanced and delineated for its gargantuan size, it is accessible and soft enough to be drunk now, but it should evolve past two decades.

A superb value in a tawny port look-alike is the 10-year-old Tawny Fortified Dessert wine. A fortified blend of 70% Shiraz and the rest Mourvèdre, Grenache, and Muscat, this wine has plenty of amber at the edge of its light ruby color. Exhibiting jammy red fruits intermixed with roasted nuts, caramel, and spice, this thick, full-bodied, moderately sweet tawny should drink well for another decade. Veritas consistently produces one of Australia's finest fortified Tokays. The 1990 Fortified Tokay's medium amber color is followed by aromas of sweet honeyed nuts, citrus, and orange marmalade. Full-bodied and sweet, with explosive intensity and richness, this is a terrific value. It should drink well for a decade or more.

VIKING WINES (BAROSSA VALLEY)

1998 Asarna Proprietary Red	E	88
1999 Grand Shiraz	E	91+
1998 Grand Shiraz	E	94

These wines are produced by Thord Soderstrom. The Grand Shiraz is aged all in American oak, with a certain percentage of new oak, and bottled without filtration. The full-bodied, super-concentrated, powerful 1999 Grand Shiraz (aged with 75% new oak) is obviously the product of extremely low yields. It exhibits remarkable density, fine chewiness, and pure, black fruit notes, intermixed with smoke, earth, and underbrush. Powerful, long, and youthful, it should only improve over the next decade, and last for almost 20 years. A bottle opened 24 hours displayed no trace of oxidation. The exceptionally concentrated 1998 Grand Shiraz (15% alcohol; 30% new oak) offers a distinctive nose of lavender, roasted herbs, truffles, and gobs of jammy black raspberries, blueberries, and cassis. With tangy acidity, immense body, explosive richness, and a 60-second finish, this is an exciting, distinctive, individualistic Shiraz that should drink well for 10–12 years.

The 1998 Asarna Proprietary Red is an intriguing blend of two-thirds Pinot Noir and one-third Shiraz. Bottled unfiltered, it possesses 90-point aromatics. Dark dense ruby/purple-colored, with a sweet, floral nose of cherry liqueur and raspberries, the Pinot characteristics are well displayed, and the Shiraz gives the wine spice, pepper, and dense body and volume. Excellent, possibly outstanding, it displays a Burgundy-like texture and weight.

WANINGA (CLARE VALLEY)

1998 Shiraz	D	90
1998 Shiraz Reserve	D	89+

The dark purple-colored 1998 Shiraz exhibits creamy vanilla in its user-friendly, black fruit–scented nose. Intense, supple-textured, full-bodied, and rich, with excellent purity and a nicely layered, mouth-filling style, it can be drunk over the next 7 years.

The closed, dense plum/purple-colored 1998 Shiraz Reserve offers scents of underbrush, earth, chocolate, jammy black fruits, and toasty new oak (100% new wood was utilized). Medium- to full-bodied, pure, and deep, with a chewy, layered texture, this tightly knit Shiraz requires additional bottle age. It will evolve for 12–15 years. Although loaded, it is muted at present, and my score may turn out to be conservative.

WARRENMANG (VICTORIA)

1998 Grand Pyrenées	D	91
1997 Grand Pyrenées	D	88+?
1998 Shiraz	D	94+

The dazzling, compelling 1998 Shiraz is easy to figure out. At 15.5% alcohol, this effort, made from superripe fruit, is one of the more backward Shirazes I tasted. It exhibits an opaque purple color as well as fabulous potential with its glorious display of licorice-infused blackberry and cassis fruit. Dense, with low acidity, high tannin, and a whoppingly thick, stacked and packed mid-palate, this enormous monster needs three years of cellaring; it should age well for 20–25 years.

The 1998 Grand Pyrenées is reminiscent of the classic Heitz Martha's Vineyard Cabernet Sauvignons produced from the late 1960s through the early 1980s. A dense ruby/purple color is accompanied by scents of eucalyptus/mint, ripe black currants, tobacco, and licorice. Full-bodied and pure, with only a hint of oak, it has moderate tannin and impressive balance as well as character. It should drink well for 12–15+ years. The 1997 Grand Pyrenées is a tannic, lean wine with notions of eucalyptus, plums, prunes, and black currants. Well made and clean, but backward and hard to evaluate, this medium- to full-bodied blend has a certain affinity to an austere Bordeaux. Anticipated maturity: now–2016.

WATTLE PARK (SOUTH AUSTRALIA)

1998 Cabernet Sauvignon	D	86

The 1998 Cabernet Sauvignon, a juicy fruit concoction, exhibits little complexity, but emerging from the dark ruby/purple color are oodles of jammy blackberry and cherry fruit with a nice touch of pepper. There is no new oak to be found in this explosively ripe, fruity, uncomplicated, pleasurable wine. Drink it over the next 2 years.

GEOFF WEAVER (LENSWOOD)

1997 Cabernet Sauvignon/Merlot	D	86

The 1997 blend of Cabernet Sauvignon (82%) and Merlot (18%) is good but uninspiring. A Bordeaux-styled blend, it exhibits a medium dark ruby color as well as leather, cassis, spicy oak, and dried herbs in the nose. This medium-bodied, austere, cleanly made wine lacks excitement and density. Drink it over the next decade.

WILD DUCK CREEK (HEATHCOTE, VICTORIA)

1998 Cabernet Pressings	E	90
1999 Cabernet Sauvignon Alan's	E	90
1998 Cabernet Sauvignon Reserve	E	93
1997 Shiraz Duck Muck	E	99
1999 Shiraz Springflat	E	92
1998 Shiraz Springflat	E	91+
NV Sparkling Duck	D	?

These are all interesting, full-throttle wines made by one of Australia's special characters, David Anderson. Yet overpricing seems to be taking on a surreal Hollywood element. For example, the $85 nonvintage Sparkling Duck, a blend of four vintages of Shiraz with some Merlot thrown in that tips the scales at 15.2% alcohol, is an unusual, heavy-handed, dense ruby/purple-colored wine that has plenty of fizz but is bizarre and over the top. A limited production of 65 cases no doubt explains the pricing, but for my palate, this wine is undrinkable.

The dry red wines are all huge, and obviously the lighter style of the 1999 vintage was easily overcome, given what Anderson has done with his 1999 Shiraz Springflat and 1999 Cabernet Sauvignon Alan's. The 1999 Shiraz Springflat has dense, opaque purple color, a real intense, minty, crème de cassis nose, with some spicy new oak. The wine is certainly not shy, at 15.3% alcohol, but the power is well harnessed, and the wine is primarily a big, full-bodied, thick, juicy fruit bomb with plenty of texture, purity, and length. It should drink well for 7–8 years, perhaps longer. With production at 1,200 cases, there is modest availability. A distinctive Shiraz, the black/purple 1998 Springflat's explosive aromatic bouquet is reminiscent of Old Bay spice. The spicy note is accompanied by aromas of blackberries, cassis, licorice, and toasty oak. Rich and backward, with fabulous concentration, it will improve significantly with another 1–2 years of bottle age and should keep for a minimum of 12–15 years. Only 600 cases were produced. The outstanding Cabernet Sauvignon Alan's (100% Cabernet Sauvignon) is aged in French oak, of which 85% is new. Production is 400 cases. The 1999 offers an opaque purple color, and a gorgeously sweet nose of black fruits, licorice, and vanilla. In the mouth, it displays a dry vintage portlike character. It is unctuous, thick, juicy, full-bodied, rich, monolithic, and destined to last for a decade or more.

Two limited-release offerings from Wild Duck include 75 cases of 1998 Cabernet Sauvignon Reserve. Made from 20-year-old 100% Cabernet Sauvignon vines, it exhibits a saturated black purple color plus a gorgeous nose of spice box, licorice, cassis, and classy new French oak. It is deep, full-bodied, and sweet, with supple tannin, and a seamless, concentrated finish that reveals notes of eucalyptus as it cascades over the palate. I was surprised by the sweet tannin as well as overall elegance. Drink this by 2016. Another overpriced offering is the 1998 Cabernet Pressings. Only 150 magnums were produced, and the wine, while not possessing the finish of the Reserve, offers notes of jammy cassis, pepper, creosote, and vanilla. Sweet, rich, and chewy, but rustic, it should drink well for 10–15 years.

Only 70 cases of the terrific 1997 Shiraz Duck Muck (15% alcohol) are available. Made from 1.3 tons of fruit per acre from a relatively young (15 years) vineyard, there is no doubting the extraordinary character and personality Anderson has constructed. My tasting notes begin with the words "great stuff." Opaque black/purple, with a viscosity resembling vintage port, this thick, chewy wine exhibits a panorama of black fruits mixed with licorice, tar, roasted herbs, and sweet oak. The acidity and tannin appear to be missing because of the wine's wealth of fruit, glycerin, and extract. It is a surreal, otherworldly styled Shiraz that needs to be sipped rather than gulped given its power and intensity. Anticipated maturity: now–2025.

WILLOW BEND (BAROSSA VALLEY)

1997 Proprietary Red	D	90?

The intriguing 1997 Proprietary Red (40% Shiraz, 38% Merlot, 19% Cabernet Sauvignon, and 3% Cabernet Franc) reveals a dark ruby/purple color in addition to a big, plummy, fat style with gobs of creamy, oak-infused, black cherry and blackberry fruit. The wood is almost overdone, but there is such a wealth of ripe, chewy fruit that the wine comes across as balanced, if somewhat exotic and aggressive. Drink it over the next 5–6 years.

WIT'S END (McLAREN VALE)

1999 Cabernet Sauvignon	D	90
1998 Shiraz	D	92

The 1999 Cabernet Sauvignon (aged in both French and American oak) offers aromas of toasty sweet vanilla as well as a boatload of crème de cassis–scented and –flavored fruit, full body, a seamless, velvety texture, and a long aftertaste. The 14.5% alcohol is well integrated in this beautifully concentrated, user-friendly, forward 1999. Although hard to ignore, it will drink well for 10–12 years. A stunning 1998 Shiraz, the Wit's End boasts a deep ruby/purple color as well as a sweet nose of blackberry jam intermixed with cassis, blueberries, and flowers. With sweet tannin, subtle vanilla from well-integrated oak, and a full-bodied, layered finish, this seamless effort is best consumed during its first decade of life.

WOODSTOCK (McLAREN VALE)

1998 Grenache	C	89

A blend of 90% Grenache (from 80+-year-old, head-pruned vines) and 10% Shiraz, the dark ruby/purple 1998 Grenache offers scents of kirsch, black pepper, and sweet cassis. A luscious, full-bodied fruit bomb, with low acidity and copious glycerin, it requires consumption over the next 4–5 years. Utterly delicious!

YALUMBA (BAROSSA VALLEY)

1996 Cabernet/Shiraz The Reserve	E	95
1996 Cabernet/Shiraz The Signature	D	91
1995 Cabernet/Shiraz The Signature	D	90
1999 Grenache	B	89
1998 Grenache	B	90
1999 Grenache Nursery Vineyard	D	92
1996 Shiraz Old Vine The Octavius	E	95
1995 Shiraz Old Vine The Octavius	E	90
1998 Shiraz/Viognier	D	90

Yalumba, which traces its origins to 1849, has a strong portfolio of wines, including some sensational values. From their 1,500 acres of vineyards, they produce several levels of quality, starting with their budget-priced Oxford Landing offerings (not reviewed here), and concluding with such flagship efforts as their Signature and Octavius *cuvées*. The estate also produces high-quality whites, which are not reviewed here since they must be consumed within several months of the vintage. Readers looking for fabulous values should check out Yalumba's 1999 and 1998 Grenache *cuvées*. Both wines are made in reasonably large quantities (about 8,000 cases). Neither sees any new oak. They represent Australia's answer to a big, bold, flavorful southern Rhône. The medium- to full-bodied 1999 Grenache reveals pepper and kirsch in its sweet, jammy fruit. Already delicious, it promises to last another 3–4 years.

Even better is the outstanding 1998 Grenache. Like its sibling, it comes from unirrigated, head-pruned vines. A darker ruby-colored effort, it exhibits intense aromas of ground pepper intermixed with strawberry and cherry liqueur, roasted herbs, and spice. Full-bodied, yet silky-textured, and flamboyant, it is a gorgeously fleshy wine to drink over the next 4–5 years.

Readers looking for even more intensity should check out Yalumba's 1999 Grenache Nursery Vineyard. There are 600 cases of this extremely old bush-vine Grenache (some of which date back to 1887). A dense ruby color is accompanied by an explosive nose of black raspberries, intermixed with cherries, pepper, and spice. Full-bodied, unctuous, heady, and a total turn-on to drink, I would love to insert this wine as a ringer in a tasting of sumptuous 1998 Châteauneuf-du-Papes. Drink it over the next 7–10 years.

Yalumba makes 2,000 cases of the 1998 Shiraz/Viognier (15% Viognier, à la Côte Rôtie). The wine sees some American oak, but is characterized by its full-bodied, exotic, jammy, black raspberry and currant fruit. Exotic, complex, fat, low in acidity, and heady, this plush turn-on can be consumed over the next 4–5 years.

One of Yalumba's top *cuvées* is their Cabernet/Shiraz blend called The Signature. Current releases include the 1996 and 1995. Creamy American oak aromas cascade from the dense purple-colored, superb 1996. However, in the mouth, the oak is completely absorbed by the wine's meaty, smoky, blackberry and cassis flavors. As it sits in the glass, notes of melted asphalt, dried Provençal herbs, and additional jammy red and black fruits emerge. Full-bodied and lush, it should drink well for at least 10–12 years. The more austere 1995 The Signature is from a slightly cooler vintage. By the way, for librarians among the readers, the 1990, 1991, and 1992 The Signatures were performing brilliantly, with the 1992 my favorite.

Another premium wine in Yalumba's portfolio is the 600-case *cuvée* of old-vine Shiraz called The Octavius. The current releases are 1995 and 1996. The spectacular 1996 is a basket-pressed Shiraz possessing huge power as well as massive, oozing, cedar- and glycerin-imbued blackberry and cassis aromas and flavors. This superb effort is one of the great old-vine Shiraz *cuvées* available in the marketplace. It should drink well for up to two decades. The similarly styled 1995 Shiraz Old Vine The Octavius, from the same parcel of 70-year-old vines, is aged in American oak. Sweet and oaky, with blackberry/cherry liqueur, high, heady alcohol levels, plenty of glycerin, and a full-bodied, long, spicy finish, it is more evolved than the blockbuster 1996. This is another wine where older vintages have held up gorgeously, including the spectacular 1990 and prodigious 1992. Interestingly, according to the winery, the 1990 and 1992 had 15% Cabernet Sauvignon in the blend. Since 1994, Octavius has been 100% Shiraz.

The other luxury-priced wine from Yalumba is the 300-case *cuvée* of 50% Cabernet Sauvignon and 50% Shiraz called The Reserve. The current release is the 1996. Aged in French oak, it is a compelling, opaque purple-colored wine offering subtle notions of high-class French oak along with enormous quantities of plum liqueur, chocolate fudge, blackberry and cassis fruit, pepper, and smoke. It is enormously concentrated, yet amazingly well balanced and extremely full-bodied, with a seamless personality, and well-integrated acidity, wood, tannin, and alcohol. This classic looks capable of lasting for two decades.

YARRA YERING (YARRA VALLEY)

1998	Dry Red No. 1 (Bordeaux Blend)	E	90
1998	Dry Red No. 2 (Rhône Blend)	E	94
1998	Pinot Noir	E	87
1998	Portsorts	E	92+
1998	Shiraz Underhill	E	91

This historic winery has often left me underwhelmed, but that is not the case with these 1998 efforts, the finest group of Yarra Yering wines I have tasted. They reveal extraordinary authenticity and purity of fruit, giving them each a singular character as well as an unmanipulated, natural style. Packaged in an unconventional light green, Bordeaux-styled bottle, the 1998 Pinot Noir is muted aromatically, but in the mouth textbook flavors of currants, cherries, and cola are present. The texture is supple, the wine builds incrementally, as do all of these dry reds, and follows through with a long, concentrated, noble, elegant finish. It should drink well for 5–7 years. The beautiful texture is also apparent in the 1998 Shiraz Underhill. A dark ruby/purple color is accompanied by a sweet nose of black fruits, minerals, smoke, and spice. This beautifully intense, pure Shiraz displays brilliant flavor definition, medium to full body, and extraordinary intensity without any sense of heaviness or astringent tannin. It is an impressive, stylish, elegant wine to enjoy over the next 10–12 years.

I was blown away by the 1998 Dry Red No. 2. A Rhône blend dominated by Shiraz, with Viognier and Roussanne included, this individualistic, extraordinary effort boasts a dense plum/purple color, as well as a gorgeously complex nose of rose petals, blackberries, cassis, new saddle leather, and truffles. Full-bodied, with a sweet attack, and wonderful harmony among its elements, this exceptionally pure wine can be drunk now, or cellared for 15+ years. It somehow totally conceals its lofty degree of alcohol (14.9%). Sadly, only 50 cases made it to the U.S. The 1998 Dry Red No. 1 is a Bordeaux blend dominated by Cabernet Sauvignon (80–85%) with the rest Merlot, Cabernet Franc, Petit Verdot, and a touch of Malbec. Its finesse, character, complexity, and stature cause it to stand out in a tasting. An individualistic expression of a Cabernet-based wine, it offers notes of red and black currants, minerals, olives, leather, earth, and smoke. This beautifully pure, finely etched, stylish effort requires 2–3 more years of bottle age. It should last nearly two decades.

Made completely from Portuguese varietals used for vintage port (Tourriga Nacional, for example), the 1998 Portsorts is the finest vintage port look-alike I have tasted outside Portugal. It possesses striking complexity, offering notes of licorice, leather, coffee, prunes, blackberries, and cassis. Extremely full-bodied, with beautifully integrated alcohol, this large-scaled, youthful, unevolved wine is a compelling example of what Portuguese varietals can achieve in Australia. This 1998 will drink well for two or more decades.

NEW ZEALAND

An enormous amount of hype is associated with New Zealand's wines. The world's media appears to be enamored of this nation and its vinous products. Having tasted countless wines, it is clear that New Zealand has a number of dedicated producers who craft excellent Sauvignon Blancs and Chardonnays, and a small handful who have made reds capable of competing on the world stage. However, the majority of this nation's wines are overly processed and too expensive for the quality they deliver.

The Sauvignon Blancs elicit the most excitement. They can be surprisingly rich, crammed with juicy gooseberries. However, they can also be mildly herbaceous, or overwhelmingly green. What makes them stand out is that the well-integrated acidity tastes natural, and the best examples possess a stunning mid-palate and length. All you have to do is taste the likes of a Sauvignon Blanc from Cloudy Bay, Goldwater, Grove Mill, Kumeu River, Montana, Morton Estate, Selaks, and Stoneleigh to see that special wines can emerge from this varietal. However, once past these wineries, the Sauvignons are often vegetal and washed out. As for Chardonnay, New Zealanders have learned to handle the cool climate acidity by putting their wines through full malolactic fermentation, giving them less contact, and plenty of exposure to French oak. However, when yields are not kept low, the Chardonnays taste like a two-by-four, with enough oak to turn off a wine-loving lumberjack. The finest Chardonnays, showing balance between oak and fruit, have emerged from Babich's Irongate, Cloudy Bay, Corbins, Delegats, Kumeu River, Matua Valley, Morton Estates Hawke's Bay, Selaks, Te Mata, Vidal Reserve, and the Villa Maria (barrel-fermented).

New Zealand's attempts with Cabernet Sauvignon and Merlot continue to be annoyingly herbaceous and/or atrociously vegetal, with few exceptions. It is unbelievable that anyone can find anything to praise in these offerings. If you like wines that taste like liquefied asparagus, you will find some merit in them. Although recent vintages suggest that New Zealand's wineries are coming closer to purging some of this grotesque character, these wines still possess a nasty vegetal streak. That being said, however, wines produced by Te Mata (Cabernet and Merlot) have demonstrated that New Zealand has potential as a red wine producer if it lowers yields, goes for optimal ripeness, and does not overprocess.

Pinot Noir will most likely prove to be New Zealand's red savior (as Sauvignon Blanc is for its whites). Presently, its vines are too young to predict accurately the potential of the wines, yet it is clear that structurally New Zealand's Pinots are the closest thing to Burgundy any New World region has come. Recently, the high-production, poor-quality clones that made up the vast majority of New Zealand's Pinot vineyards have been replaced with excellent clones from Burgundy. As these vines age, it will be interesting to see if the resulting wines acquire the depth of fruit, complexity, and ageworthiness required to compete with Burgundies. For the other red wines, there are only two words to keep in mind—*caveat emptor*!

Of the vintages currently on the market, 2000 appears better for reds than whites. It was a warm year, optimal for ripening Cabernet and Pinot, yet so hot as to have burned off much of the natural acidity that whites require. In 2001, on the other hand, there was a long, cool season. It fashioned some magnificent Sauvignon Blancs, many of which deliver superb value.

10. ARGENTINA AND CHILE

ARGENTINA

Argentina has broken out of the value category of wines, as has Chile, and now produces wines that can be recommended across the spectrum from below $10 to luxury wines that fetch more than $80. While many wineries have remained faithful to their price points, preferring to fashion large quantities of inexpensive wines, some, like Bodegas Catena Zapata, are presently offering wines that can compete with the finest in the world. Led by Nicolas Catena and others, those wineries wanting to better the quality of their wines have abandoned the Mendoza's highly fertile valley floor for its less productive hillsides.

Delicious and thirst-quenching whites, primarily Chardonnays and Sauvignon Blancs, are produced in Argentina. In recent years, a few outstanding Chardonnays, from the likes of the Catena and Luca wineries, have displayed the depth of fruit, complexity, and concentration found in the world's best examples of this ubiquitous varietal. Malbec, a French varietal that has had limited success in the Old World, can produce magnificent reds in Argentina. Characterized by its spicy dark fruit character, Argentinian Malbecs can be complex, intense, and ageworthy. Cabernet Sauvignon also has the potential to be hugely successful in Argentina, and Merlot can, from time to time, fashion beautiful wines, as well.

Argentina is on the rise. Recent vintages, particularly 1998 and 1999, have been difficult, yet this country's improved viticultural and winemaking practices as well as the arrival on the scene of quality-conscious boutique wineries (such as Luca, Tikal, and Paul Hobbs's Cobos) foreshadow an extremely bright future.

RATING ARGENTINA'S BEST WINES

*****(OUTSTANDING)

Catena Cabernet Sauvignon Agrelo Vineyard

Catena-Alta Cabernet Sauvignon Zapata Vineyard

Catena Chardonnay Agrelo Vineyard

Catena-Alta Chardonnay Adrianna Vineyard

Catena-Alta Malbec Lunlunta Vineyard Yacachuya

****(EXCELLENT)

Alamos

Altos de Madrano Malbec

Luigi Bosca Malbec

Caballero de la Cepa Cabernet Sauvignon

Arnaldo B. Etchart Cafayete

Arnaldo B. Etchart Cabernet Sauvignon

Arnaldo B. Etchart Malbec

Nicolas Fazio Malbec

Fabre Montmayou Grand Vin
Navarro Correas Colección Privada
  Cabernet Sauvignon
Navarro Correas Malbec
Nieto y Sentiner Cadus Malbec
Norton Privada
San Telmo Malbec

Pascual Toso Cabernet Sauvignon
Bodega Weinert Cabernet Sauvignon
Bodega Weinert Carrascal
Bodega Weinert Cavas de Weinert
Bodega Weinert Malbec
Bodega Weinert Merlot

* * * (GOOD)

Bianchi Cabernet Sauvignon Particular
Bianchi Chenin Blanc
Bianchi Malbec
Humberto Canale Cabernet Sauvignon
  Reserva
Humberto Canale Merlot Reserva
Etchart Torrontes
Flichman Cabernet Sauvignon

Nicolas Fazio Cabernet Sauvignon
Château Mendoza Cabernet Sauvignon
Château Mendoza Merlot
Mendoza Peaks Cabernet Sauvignon
San Telmo Cuesta del Madero (Cabernet
  Sauvignon/Malbec)
Trapiche Cabernet Sauvignon Oak Aged
León Unzue Malbec

* * (AVERAGE)

Andean Cabernet Sauvignon
Clos du Moulin Cabernet Sauvignon

Goyenechea (Aberdeen Angus) Cabernet
  Sauvignon
Comte de Valmont Cabernet Sauvignon

CHILE

Like its Andean neighbor, Chile has made enormous progress in recent years. At present, this South American country produces wines that can satisfy any consumer's desires, from cheap quaffing wines to world-class ageworthy reds.

Although some producers (particularly Casa Lapostolle) have fashioned outstanding Chardonnays in the Casa Blanca valley, the country's strengths are centered around its reds, particularly Cabernet Sauvignon and Merlot. Viña Cousiño Macul, Viña Concha y Toro, Casa Lapostolle, and the newly arrived Yacachuya are among the wineries redefining Chile's future.

Having survived the disastrous "El Niño" 1998 vintage, Chile enjoyed an excellent year in 1999 and a good one in 2000.

RATING CHILE'S BEST WINES

* * * * * (OUTSTANDING)

Almaviva (a Cabernet-based wine made by
  the partnership of Mouton-Rothschild
  and Concho y Toro)
Casa Lapostolle Cuvée Alexandre

Casa Lapostolle Merlot Clos Apalta
Concho y Toro Cabernet Sauvignon Don
  Melchor Private Reserve

* * * * *(EXCELLENT)*

Casa Lapostolle Cabernet Sauvignon Cuvée
  Alexandre
Casa Lapostolle Chardonnay Cuvée
  Alexandre
Casa Lapostolle Sauvignon Blanc
Concho y Toro Cabernet Sauvignon
  Marques de Casa Concho

Cousiño Macul Cabernet/Merlot Finis
  Terrae
Cousiño Macul Cabernet Sauvignon
  Antiguas Reserva
Santa Rita Cabernet Sauvignon Casa
  Real
Los Vascos Cabernet Sauvignon Reserva

* * * *(GOOD)*

Concho y Toro Cabernet Sauvignon
  Castillero del Diablo
Concho y Toro Chardonnay Castillero del
  Diablo
Cousiño Macul Cabernet Sauvignon
Errazuriz Panquehue Cabernet Sauvignon
  Don Maximiano

Santa Monica Cabernet Sauvignon
Seña
Los Vascos Cabernet Sauvignon
Los Vascos Sauvignon Blanc
Santa Rita Cabernet Sauvignon Medalla
  Real

* * *(AVERAGE)*

Caliterra Cabernet Sauvignon
Caliterra Chardonnay
Canepa Sauvignon Blanc
Carta Vieja (all *cuvées*)
Cousiño Macul Chardonnay
Cousiño Macul Sauvignon Blanc
Sage Estate (all *cuvées*)
Saint Morillon Cabernet Sauvignon
Santa Carolina Cabernet Sauvignon
Santa Carolina Chardonnay
Santa Carolina Merlot

Santa Rita Cabernet Sauvignon 120
  Estate
Santa Rita Sauvignon Blanc 120 Estate
Tolva Cabernet Sauvignon
Tolva Sauvignon Blanc
Miguel Torres (all *cuvées*)
Traverso Cabernet Sauvignon
Traverso Merlot
Undurraga Cabernet Sauvignon
Undurraga Sauvignon Blanc
Valdivieso Sparkling NV Brut

11. SOUTH AFRICA

The wines of South Africa deserve more attention from consumers, as they presently offer both value and quality. Shortly after the end of apartheid, numerous South African wines appeared on retailers' shelves throughout the United States, but few merited attention (a lovely 1990 Meerlust Merlot was the exception to the rule). Since then, quality has ameliorated due to both viticultural and vinification improvements.

While the country's Chardonnays tend to be overly wooded or green in character, South African Sauvignon Blancs, Sémillons, and Chenin Blancs can be delightfully balanced, pure, and flavorful. For reds, Cabernet Sauvignon is king in South Africa, with estates such as Boekenhoutskloof, Neil Ellis, and Rustenberg regularly producing outstanding wines with the intensity of the New World yet the charm and complexity of the Old World. Even though Meerlust surprised me with its 1990 Merlot, this varietal appears to be as fickle in South Africa as it is elsewhere. Pinot Noir has yet to be successful in South Africa, and Pinotage remains a wine that I have immense trouble appreciating. It is simply too green, rustic, and leathery. Recent releases of Shiraz/Syrah, particularly those from Boekenhoutskloof, indicate that South Africa has outstanding potential with this grape from the northern Rhône. Other Rhône varietals, such as Grenache, Mourvèdre, and Carignan, have shown some potential, particularly with Fairview's line of Goats do Roam wines.

INDEX